OXFORD COMMENTARIES ON
INTERNATIONAL LAW

General Editors: *Professor Philip Alston*, Professor of International Law at New York University, and *Vaughan Lowe QC*, Essex Court Chambers, London and Emeritus Fellow of All Souls College, Oxford.

The 1949 Geneva Conventions
A Commentary

Andrew Clapham (Phd in Law, European University Institute, 1991) is Professor of Public International Law at the Graduate Institute of International and Development Studies, Geneva. Before he joined the Institute in 1997, he was the Representative of Amnesty International to the United Nations in New York. Andrew Clapham was the Director of the Geneva Academy of International Humanitarian Law and Human Rights from 2006 until 2014. He is a member of the International Commission of Jurists. His publications include *The Oxford Handbook of International Law in Armed Conflict* (co-edited with Paola Gaeta) (2014), *Brierly's Law of Nations*, 7th edn (2012), and *Human Rights: A Very Short Introduction*, 2nd edn (2015). He is an academic associate member of Matrix Chambers in London.

Paola Gaeta (PhD in Law, European University Institute, 1997) is Professor of Public International Law at the Graduate Institute of International and Development Studies (Geneva) and Adjunct Professor at the Law Department of Bocconi University, Milan. Before she joined the Institute, she was Professor of International Criminal Law at the University of Geneva. Previously, from 1998 to 2007 Paola Gaeta was consecutively Assistant Professor, Associate Professor and Professor of International Law at the University of Florence. She was the Director of the Geneva Academy of International Humanitarian Law and Human Rights (with Andrew Clapham) from 2010 to 2014, and was the Director of its LLM programmes from 2007 to 2014. Paola Gaeta is currently Member of the Editorial Board of the Journal of International Criminal Justice and previously of the European Journal of International Law. Her publications include *The Oxford Handbook of International Law in Armed Conflict* (co-edited with Andrew Clapham) (2014), the third and updated edition of *Cassese's International Criminal Law* (with Antonio Cassese and others, 2013); *The UN Genocide Convention: A Commentary* (editor, 2009); and *The Statute of the International Criminal Court: A Commentary* (co-editor with A. Cassese and J.R.W.D. Jones, 2001).

Marco Sassòli (PhD in Law, Basel, 1989) is Professor of International Law at the University of Geneva. From 2001–2003, Marco Sassòli was Professor of International Law at the Université du Québec à Montreal, Canada, where he remains Associate Professor. He is member of the International Commission of Jurists. He has worked from 1985–1997 for the International Committee of the Red Cross (ICRC) at the headquarters, inter alia as Deputy Head of its Legal Division, and in conflict areas, in particular the Middle East and the Balkans. He has also served as registrar at the Swiss Supreme Court, and from 2004–2013 as chair of the board of Geneva Call, an NGO engaging non-state armed actors to respect humanitarian rules.

The 1949 Geneva Conventions

A Commentary

Edited by

ANDREW CLAPHAM
PAOLA GAETA
MARCO SASSÒLI

Assistant editors

IRIS VAN DER HEIJDEN
ILYA NUZOV
JULIA GRIGNON
ANNIE HYLTON
TOM HAECK

Geneva Academy of International Humanitarian Law and Human Rights | Geneva Academy
Académie de droit international humanitaire et de droits humains à Genève

OXFORD
UNIVERSITY PRESS

OXFORD
UNIVERSITY PRESS

Great Clarendon Street, Oxford, OX2 6DP,
United Kingdom

Oxford University Press is a department of the University of Oxford.
It furthers the University's objective of excellence in research, scholarship,
and education by publishing worldwide. Oxford is a registered trade mark of
Oxford University Press in the UK and in certain other countries

© The several contributors 2015

The moral rights of the authors have been asserted

First published 2015
First published in paperback 2018
Impression: 1

All rights reserved. No part of this publication may be reproduced, stored in
a retrieval system, or transmitted, in any form or by any means, without the
prior permission in writing of Oxford University Press, or as expressly permitted
by law, by licence, or under terms agreed with the appropriate reprographics
rights organization. Enquiries concerning reproduction outside the scope of the
above should be sent to the Rights Department, Oxford University Press, at the
address above

You must not circulate this work in any other form
and you must impose this same condition on any acquirer

Published in the United States of America by Oxford University Press
198 Madison Avenue, New York, NY 10016, United States of America

British Library Cataloguing in Publication Data
Data available

Library of Congress Cataloging in Publication Data
Data available

ISBN 978–0–19–967544–9 (Hbk.)
ISBN 978–0–19–882567–8 (Pbk.)

Printed and bound by
CPI Group (UK) Ltd, Croydon, CR0 4YY

Links to third-party websites are provided by Oxford in good faith and
for information only. Oxford disclaims any responsibility for the materials
contained in any third-party website referenced in this work.

Preface

As teachers at the Geneva Academy of International Humanitarian Law and Human Rights (a joint centre of the Graduate Institute of International and Development Studies and the Law Faculty of the University of Geneva) we are acutely aware of the universal nature of the Geneva Conventions and their crucial importance not only for people affected by contemporary armed conflicts around the world but also in the context of the prosecution of war crimes. In our day-to-day teaching, research, and practice we found ourselves struggling to find easy access to up-to date explanations as to the meaning of the provisions of the Geneva Conventions. Strangely while the Oxford Commentaries on International Law Series had covered almost all the major universal multilateral treaties, the 1949 Geneva Conventions remained uncommented on in this context. Of course part of the explanation lay in the existence and continuing authority of the Commentaries to the four Geneva Conventions edited by Jean Pictet, and published by the International Committee of the Red Cross (ICRC) as a series of books, the last one on the Second Geneva Convention being published in 1960. These Commentaries trace not only the drafting of the Conventions but also provide suggestions on how the Conventions are to be applied in practice based on the unique experience of the ICRC as a humanitarian organization with a special role with regard to the victims of armed conflict. But fifty years later the Conventions were now universally ratified and had been applied and interpreted by states, armed groups, and in multiple courts and tribunals in hundreds of cases. In addition, the massive development of international human rights law since the 1960s, and international criminal law and criminal justice since the 1990s, has meant that the associated accountability mechanisms for these branches of international law have regularly applied international humanitarian law, and so the Geneva Conventions can today no longer be understood in relative isolation.

We had originally thought that a new Commentary could be jointly authored together with the ICRC. It became apparent, however, that the ICRC preferred to reserve the right to express their own views on the meaning and application of the Conventions. We therefore decided to embark on this Oxford Commentary, which would not seek to represent an institutional or collective point of view, but rather represent the views of the individual scholars who would be asked to contribute to the publication. This Commentary is organized by subject matter, focuses on issues of contemporary relevance and controversy, and systematically takes other branches of international law into account. For each topic dealt with by the Geneva Conventions with regard to international armed conflicts the present Commentary equally discusses how far the same solutions may be applied in non-international armed conflicts, and considers specific routes to bring some accountability for any breaches, including through the mechanisms established under the other branches of international law mentioned above.

Of course, in opting to allow each contributor complete academic freedom we ran the risk of contradictions across chapters and opened ourselves up to the inevitable criticism that the Commentary would lack coherence and contain annoying overlap and repetition. Needless to say, as editors we have sought to avoid these pitfalls. On occasion we have been confronted by diverging opinions, sometimes we have been able to smooth out the rough edges by presenting contributors with alternative ways of seeing things and the contradictions have evaporated. In some instances, however, it became clear that divergent views could not be so simply accommodated and the reader will find cross-references to alternative points of view within this Commentary. We see this as a quality of the eventual publication in that the reader is made aware when the commentator is entering contested territory through multiple footnote references to alternative interpretations. The editors have not sought to tip the scales here, leaving each author complete discretion to conclude how the relevant provisions of the Conventions should be applied today. In such cases, the limit of our intervention has been, from time to time, to request cross-references or footnotes alerting the reader to contrary opinions.

We have also opted not to revisit the Pictet Commentaries through an article-by-article analysis, but rather we have taken a fresh look at the provisions by breaking down the Conventions into a number of cross-cutting and discrete chapter headings. At the same time we have sought to ensure that each Article is properly addressed and readers looking for analysis of a particular provision can of course use the dedicated Table of International Instruments for this purpose. But, as explained, in considering the reasons for a new Commentary we were very much influenced by the need to situate this branch of international law in the realm of international law more generally and particularly with regard to international criminal law and international human rights law.

Since the establishment of the International Criminal Tribunal for the former Yugoslavia (ICTY) (and subsequent international criminal tribunals including the International Criminal Court) a number of key provisions of the Geneva Conventions have been applied by judges from these international tribunals in cases brought against individual defendants indicted for war crimes. In turn judges at the national level are increasingly applying national law which has incorporated the Geneva Conventions (or their provisions through the statutes aimed at ensuring compliance with the International Criminal Court Statute). The ICTY alone has had to deal with around 80 accused, and most cases have involved an application of provisions of the Geneva Conventions. The International Criminal Court is now embarking on its own application of the Conventions. As concerns international human rights law, the developments over the last 60 years have not only led to new interpretations of the terms of the Geneva Conventions, but have also created tensions as these two branches of law have sometimes been seen to pull in different directions. Instead of simply dealing with these issues only in an introductory chapter we sought to have each contributor consider, not only the meaning of their own set of Geneva Convention provisions, but also how the interpretation and application of these provisions have been affected by other humanitarian law treaties, including the Additional Protocols, as well as by other branches of international law (not only international criminal law and international human rights law but other branches such as environmental law and refugee law have also been addressed).

The Commentary is structured as follows:

Part I Cross-Cutting Issues and Common Provisions
    A. Cross-Cutting Issues
    B. Common Provisions
        1. General
        2. Special Rules
        3. Common Article 3
    C. Ensuring Compliance with the Conventions
    D. The Geneva Conventions in Context

Part II Specific Issues and Regimes
    A. Geneva Conventions I and II
    B. Geneva Convention III
    C. Geneva Convention IV
        1. General
        2. Civilians in the Hands of the Enemy: General Protection
        3. Specific Protection
        4. Internment
        5. Occupied Territories

In order to help the reader quickly find answers to particular queries within a chapter, and also to ensure that each author addressed some of the contextual issues that determine the application of these provisions, we insisted that almost all contributors structure their chapters along the following lines.

Select Bibliography
A. Introduction
B. Meaning and Application
C. Relevance in Non-International Armed Conflicts
D. Legal Consequences of a Violation
E. Critical Assessment

    Select Bibliography: each chapter starts with a list of up to a dozen key bibliographical references which represent both the key texts on which authors have relied and a starting point for further research and reading.

    A. Introduction: here one usually finds a historical introduction and the contemporary context in which the relevant provisions of the 1949 Geneva Conventions are applied.

    B. Meaning and Application: here the reader will find an explanation of the interpretation of the terms in the relevant provisions. Contributors have considered the influence of international human rights law, international criminal law, and international refugee law on the interpretation of the relevant provisions of the Geneva Conventions. State practice and case-law, together with resolutions and reports from international organizations, are covered as exhaustively as possible. Doctrine is mentioned to the extent that it sheds light on the interpretation of the provisions and key writings are mentioned.

    C. Relevance in Non-International Armed Conflicts (NIACs): a strict reading of the Geneva Conventions would suggest that only Common Article 3 applies outside situations of international armed conflict; this section explains, sometimes very briefly, whether and how relevant provisions or norms are applicable in NIACs, to what extent they could be applied by analogy, or why they do not apply in NIACs.

D. Legal Consequences of a Violation: this section discusses particular consequences that may flow from the violation of the provisions under examination. This section often has two subheadings: one focusing on criminal responsibility, the other addressing the accountability of states. Although any violation will trigger the consequences that flow from the secondary rules on state responsibility, authors have focused on the particular avenues for accountability that might be available in the context of the provisions under discussion. This often means looking at the extent to which a violation could also come to be considered as a violation of international human rights law or an international crime before a human rights body or criminal court. In some cases, conduct has been considered more generally, irrespective of whether it strictly speaking represents a violation under the Convention, and framed as crimes against humanity or some other breach of international law. One idea is that this section may help practitioners in determining the appropriate forum when considering a complaint involving conduct falling under any of the provisions under scrutiny. Needless to say this section does not include an exhaustive examination of all the legal consequences that may flow from a breach of the provision. The section rather presents examples of how breaches of the Conventions and other related conduct have been dealt with as violations of international law.

E. Critical Assessment: in this last section authors critically consider the adequacy of relevant provisions and in some cases suggest new directions to ensure better protection for the victims of armed conflict.

This Commentary therefore seeks to go beyond a simple explanation of terms, and has the explicit aims of considering, first, how the Conventions have been affected by developments in other branches of international law and, second, how breaches can be better addressed using mechanisms found extraneous to the Geneva Conventions.

Lastly, a word about gender neutral language. The Geneva Conventions often use the masculine personal pronoun 'he' unless specifically referring to the treatment of women. Of course today scholars and those drafting international instruments tend to avoid such exclusionary language, even though the use of the masculine was meant as including the feminine. We have not adjusted the original wording of the Conventions, and we have left each author to deal with this problem as they prefer. Needless to say any remaining uses of he, his, or him should where appropriate also be read as including not only men and boys but also women and girls.

Given the chance would we seek to rewrite the Conventions for the contemporary world? Beyond the question of sexist language, we and our fellow contributors found very little that could be usefully adjusted. The major protections have been now extended as a matter of fact to those caught up in non-international armed conflict; to enshrine this in new international instruments would be fraught with political difficulties, and the contemporary debates over the rules that should apply to counterterrorism would not be easily resolved by adjusting these provisions of the law of armed conflict. What is clearly lacking in many contemporary armed conflicts is sufficient respect for the existing rules; moreover there is an obvious failure to use enforcement measures against those who violate the existing rules. Such failures to respect and ensure respect stem not from the absence of law, but from an absence of political will on the part of the belligerents—states, armed groups, and individuals—and a lack of interest in enforcement from third states and public opinion. Our hope is that this Commentary helps the reader to understand the meaning of the Conventions and how to ensure that they are properly respected. We believe that the vast majority of provisions remains 'fit for purpose', and this Commentary has been prepared as a contribution to ensuring that the provisions of the Geneva Conventions come closer to achieving their aims of protecting the victims of armed conflict and punishing those who commit grave breaches and serious violations of its key provisions.

A. Clapham, P. Gaeta, and M. Sassòli
Geneva, January 2015

Acknowledgements

This project was made possible due to the generosity and support of a number of institutions. First we need to thank the Graduate Institute of International and Development Studies and the Faculty of Law of the University of Geneva. We have received extraordinary support (including financial assistance) from both the Director of the Institute, Professor Philippe Burrin, and the former Dean of the Law Faculty of the University, Professor Christian Bovet. They both saw the significance of this project being undertaken in Geneva and we thank them for helping in multiple ways. In addition we have had unstinting encouragement from the Head of the International Law Department at the Graduate Institute, Professor Andrea Bianchi, and the present Dean of the Law Faculty at the University, Professor Christine Chappuis.

Secondly, the project could not have been completed without the coordination carried out by the Geneva Academy of International Humanitarian Law and Human Rights. As a joint Centre of the Graduate Institute and the Law Faculty of the University of Geneva the Academy carries out research and post-graduate teaching in the field of international law relating to armed conflict. Not only were we able to rely on colleagues, including the new Director, Professor Robert Roth, and the administration to step in and provide the support necessary to complete such a project, but we were also able to meet and hold expert meetings at the Villa Moynier, the home of the Geneva Academy. Apart from being convenient this provided emotional succour as we sat in the former home of Gustave Moynier, one of the founders of what became the International Committee of the Red Cross (ICRC), who must be credited with writing the very first Geneva Convention in 1864.

Thirdly, the Academy received financial and moral support for this project from the Swiss Federal Department of Foreign Affairs and its Directorate of International Law. Ambassadors Paul Seger and Valentin Zellweger were particularly helpful and their support, together with that from the Société Académique de Genève, enabled us to hold an expert meeting with colleagues from the ICRC and other institutions in order to thrash out some of the most controversial questions that arose after the first year. Thanks also go to all the experts and contributors to this book who attended that meeting, and indeed we should like to thank here all the contributors to this Commentary. Their diligence and expertise have led to a rich and penetrating set of chapters that we feel represent a considered view on the contemporary meaning of the Conventions.

We were extremely fortunate to have benefitted from an outstanding team of assistant editors. At the very start of the project Tom Haeck came on board and enthusiastically and knowledgeably helped to shape the questions to be addressed by the authors and the structure of the chapters. He was assisted by several LLM students from the Academy who interned on the project. In a second phase Annie Hylton and Julia Grignon took on much of the editing and logistics of amassing the dozens of contributions that make up this volume. Their hard work and careful scrutiny of the early versions of the chapters improved the coherence of the Commentary and we are extremely grateful to them. In the last phase Iris van der Heijden took over the management of the whole project and with amazing good humour, determination, and tenacity corralled the authors into delivering their final manuscripts. Iris has to be credited with tirelessly working all hours to polish the product and ensure with her gentle reminders that we remained on schedule to the very end. Her commitment was absolutely extraordinary in every sense of the term, and the final product has hugely benefited from her dedication and expertise. Iris, assisted, in particular in the English editing by Ilya Nuzov, liaised between the authors and the copy-editors at Oxford University Press and ensured that every query was satisfactorily resolved, ironing out differences, and continuing with cross-referencing and indexing so that the Commentary now stands, we feel, as a useful reference tool ready for use by multiple constituencies, military lawyers, humanitarian workers, civil society organizations, practising lawyers, and judges.

Lastly, our thanks go to all those at Oxford University Press: John Louth, Merel Alstein, Briony Ryles, Emma Endean, and Jeni Payne. A very special word of thanks is addressed to Catherine Minahan, our key copy-editor, who immersed herself in the detail of the Geneva Conventions and patiently and expertly provided outstanding language editing, adjusting each paragraph so that it became more precise, more lucid, and more accessible to our readers.

Contents

Table of Cases   xvii
Table of Legislation   xxxix
List of Abbreviations   lxxxvii
List of Contributors   xcv

PART I CROSS-CUTTING ISSUES AND COMMON PROVISIONS

A. CROSS-CUTTING ISSUES

1. The Concept of International Armed Conflict (Andrew Clapham)   3
2. The Applicability of the Conventions to 'Transnational' and 'Mixed' Conflicts (Marko Milanovic)   27
3. The Temporal Scope of Application of the Conventions (Gabriella Venturini)   51
4. The Geographical Scope of Application of the Conventions (Katja Schöberl)   67
5. Rights, Powers, and Obligations of Neutral Powers under the Conventions (Yves Sandoz)   85

B. COMMON PROVISIONS

1. GENERAL

6. The Obligation to Respect and to Ensure Respect for the Conventions (Robin Geiß)   111
7. Special Agreements in International Armed Conflicts (Stuart Casey-Maslen)   135
8. Non-Renunciation of the Rights Provided by the Conventions (Pierre d'Argent)   145
9. Final Provisions, Including the Martens Clause (Giovanni Distefano and Etienne Henry)   155

2. SPECIAL RULES

10. The Principle of Non-Discrimination (Gabor Rona and Robert J. McGuire)   191
11. Hospitals (Elżbieta Mikos-Skuza)   207
12. Humanitarian Assistance (Flavia Lattanzi)   231
13. Search for Missing Persons (Anna Petrig)   257
14. The Dead (Daniela Gavshon)   277
15. Taking of Hostages (David Tuck)   297

16. Torture, Cruel, Inhuman, or Degrading Treatment or Punishment
    (Manfred Nowak and Ralph Janik) — 317
17. Rape and Other Sexual Violence
    (Patricia Viseur Sellers and Indira Rosenthal) — 343
18. Protected Areas (Natalino Ronzitti) — 369

3. COMMON ARTICLE 3

19. The Concept of Non-International Armed Conflict (Lindsay Moir) — 391
20. The Addressees of Common Article 3 (Sandesh Sivakumaran) — 415
21. The Beneficiaries of the Rights Stemming from Common Article 3
    (Jann K. Kleffner) — 433
22. Murder in Common Article 3 (Sarah Knuckey) — 449
23. Judicial Guarantees under Common Article 3 (Louise Doswald-Beck) — 469
24. The Right of Initiative of the ICRC and Other Impartial
    Humanitarian Bodies (Nishat Nishat) — 495
25. Applicability of the Conventions by Means of Ad Hoc Agreements
    (Luisa Vierucci) — 509

C. ENSURING COMPLIANCE WITH THE CONVENTIONS

26. The Role of the International Committee of the Red Cross
    (Rotem Giladi and Steven Ratner) — 525
27. Protecting Powers (Robert Kolb) — 549
28. Good Offices, Conciliation, and Enquiry (Théo Boutruche) — 561
29. Prohibition of Reprisals (Jérôme de Hemptinne) — 575
30. Dissemination of the Conventions, Including in Time of Armed
    Conflict (Elżbieta Mikos-Skuza) — 597
31. Grave Breaches of the Geneva Conventions (Paola Gaeta) — 615
32. Domestic Implementation
    (Andreas R. Ziegler and Stefan Wehrenberg) — 647

D. THE GENEVA CONVENTIONS IN CONTEXT

33. The Universality of the Geneva Conventions (Frédéric Mégret) — 669
34. Relationship with Prior and Subsequent Treaties and Conventions
    (Paolo Benvenuti) — 689
35. The Complex Relationship Between the Geneva Conventions and
    International Human Rights Law (Andrew Clapham) — 701
36. The Interplay Between the Geneva Conventions and International
    Criminal Law (Paola Gaeta) — 737

PART II   SPECIFIC ISSUES AND REGIMES

A. GENEVA CONVENTIONS I AND II

37. Who Is Wounded and Sick? (Annyssa Bellal) — 757

38. Who Is Shipwrecked? (Steven Haines)	767
39. The Obligations to Respect, Protect, Collect, and Care for the Wounded, Sick, and Shipwrecked (Gilles Giacca)	781
40. The Status, Rights, and Obligations of Medical and Religious Personnel (Stuart Casey-Maslen)	807
41. Buildings, Material, and Transports (Katja Schöberl)	825
42. Loss of Protection (Tom Haeck)	839
43. The Use of the Emblem (Antoine A. Bouvier)	855

B. GENEVA CONVENTION III

44. Who Is a Prisoner of War? (Sean Watts)	889
45. Status and Treatment of Those Who Do Not Fulfil the Conditions for Status as Prisoners of War (Laura M. Olson)	911
46. Determination of Prisoner of War Status (Marie-Louise Tougas)	939
47. Evacuation and Transfer of Prisoners of War (Keiichiro Okimoto)	957
48. Treatment of Prisoners of War (Silvia Sanna)	977
49. Relations with the Outside World (Sharon Weill)	1013
50. Penal or Disciplinary Proceedings Brought against a Prisoner of War (Peter Rowe)	1025
51. Release, Accommodation in Neutral Countries, and Repatriation of Prisoners of War (Marco Sassòli)	1039

C. GENEVA CONVENTION IV

1. GENERAL

52. The Structure of Geneva Convention IV and the Resulting Gaps in that Convention (Nishat Nishat)	1069
53. Maintenance and Re-establishment of Family Links and Transmission of Information (Heike Spieker)	1089
54. The Derogation Clause (Anne-Laurence Graf-Brugère)	1123

2. CIVILIANS IN THE HANDS OF THE ENEMY: GENERAL PROTECTION

55. Who Is a Protected Civilian? (Elizabeth Salmón)	1135
56. The Prohibition of Collective Punishment (Shane Darcy)	1155
57. The Right to Leave (Pamela Anne Hylton)	1173
58. The Transfer and Deportation of Civilians (Vincent Chetail)	1185
59. Judicial Guarantees (Payam Akhavan)	1215
60. Other Issues Relating to the Treatment of Civilians in Enemy Hands (Iris van der Heijden)	1241

3. SPECIFIC PROTECTION

61. Special Rules on Women (Noëlle Quénivet)	1271
62. Special Rules on Children (Hans-Joachim Heintze and Charlotte Lülf)	1293

63. Special Rules on Refugees
    (Bethany Hastie and François Crépeau) 1313

4. *INTERNMENT*

64. Admissibility of and Procedures for Internment (Laura M. Olson) 1327
65. Treatment of Internees (Bruce Oswald and Lucrezia Iapichino) 1349
66. End of Internment (Bruce Oswald) 1373

5. *OCCUPIED TERRITORIES*

67. The Concept and the Beginning of Occupation (Marco Sassòli) 1389
68. Law-Making and the Judicial Guarantees in Occupied Territories
    (Yutaka Arai-Takahashi) 1421
69. The Administration of Occupied Territory (Michael Bothe) 1455
70. Economic, Social, and Cultural Rights in Occupied Territories
    (Gilles Giacca) 1485
71. Protection of Private Property (Yutaka Arai-Takahashi) 1515
72. Protection of Public Property (Anicée Van Engeland) 1535
73. Prohibition of Settlements (Christian Tomuschat) 1551
74. The Geneva Conventions and the End of Occupation
    (Julia Grignon) 1575

Index 1597

Table of Cases

INTERNATIONAL

African Commission on Human and Peoples' Rights (ACommHPR)

Alhassan Abubakar v Ghana, Com 103/93, 31 October 1996 485
Amnesty International and others v Sudan, Com Nos 48/90, 50/91, 89/93,
    15 November 1999. . . . . 274, 1014
Article 19 v Eritrea, Com 275/2003, 30 May 2007. 485
Avocats Sans Frontières v Burundi, Com 231/99, 6 November 2000 . . . . .479, 1442–3
Centre for Free Speech v Nigeria, Case No 206/97, 15 November 1999 1035
Civil Liberties Organisation and others v Nigeria, No 151/96, Decision,
    15 November 1999. . . . . .1352, 1440
Civil Liberties Organisation, Legal Defence Centre, Legal Defence and Assistance
    Project v Nigeria, Com 218/98, 7 May 2001 477
Commission nationale des droits de l'Homme et des libertés v Chad, Com 74/92,
    11 October 1995 465
Constitutional Rights Project v Nigeria, Com 60/91, 3 November 1994 . . . . .473, 1035
Constitutional Rights Project v Nigeria, Com 153/96, 15 November 1999 486
Democratic Republic of Congo v Burundi, Rwanda and Uganda, Com 277/1999,
    25 May 2006 . . . . 727–8, 731, 1417
Huri-Laws v Nigeria, Com 225/98, 6 November 2000. 799
Malawi African Association and others v Mauritania, Coms 54/91 et al,
    11 May 2000 . . . . .475, 483
Marcel Wetsch o'Konda Koso and others v Democratic Republic of Congo,
    Com 281/2003, 24 November 2008 483
Media Rights Agenda v Nigeria, Com 224/98, 6 November 2000. . . . . 471, 1224, 1440
Mouvement burkinabé des droits de l'homme et des peuples v Burkina Faso,
    Com 204/97, 7 May 2001 465
Rights International v Nigeria, Com 215/98, 15 November 1999. 475
Social and Economic Rights Action Center and the Center for Economic and
    Social Rights v Nigeria, Com 155/96, 27 October 2001. 1490

African Court on Human and Peoples' Rights

African Commission on Human and Peoples' Rights v Great Socialist People's
    Libyan Arab Janiahiriya, App No 00412011, Order for Provisional Measures,
    11 March 2011. 728

Court of Justice of the European Union (ECJ/CJEU)

Apostolides v Orams, Case C-420/07, Judgment, 28 April 2009 1571
Kadi and Al Barakaat v Council of the European Union, Joined
    Cases C-402/05 P and C-415/05 P, [2008] 3 CMLR 41. 1427

Eritrea–Ethiopia Claims Commission (EECC)

Central Front—Eritrea's Claims 2, 4, 6, 7, 8, and 22, Partial Award, 28 April 2004. 1398,
    1408–9, 1459, 1483, 1519

xviii   *Table of Cases*

Central Front—Ethiopia's Claim 2, Partial Award, 28 April 2004 . . . . 1405, 1459, 1483, 1547
Central Front—Ethiopia's Claim 5, Partial Award, 17 December 2004 1186
Civilian Claims—Eritrea's Claims 15, 16, 23 and 27–32, Partial Award, 17 December 2004,
    XXVI *RIAA* (2004) 1130, 1175–6, 1178, 1212, 1245, 1264, 1334, 1439
Civilian Claims—Ethiopia's Claim 5, Partial Award, 17 December 2004 . . . . 1126, 1175, 1177–80
Decision Number 1 64
Eritrea's Damages Claims, Final Award, 17 August 2009 . . . . 64, 975, 982, 1009, 1183
Ethiopia's Damages Claims, Final Award, 17 August 2009 . . . . 64, 975, 1009
Jus ad Bellum—Ethiopia's Claims 1–8, Partial Award, 19 December 2005 64
Prisoners of War—Eritrea's Claim 4, Partial Award, 1 July 2003 . . . . 979, 981, 986, 988–9, 994
Prisoners of War—Eritrea's Claim 17, Partial Award, 1 July 2003, XXVI *RIAA* (2009) 8, 166,
                                                             540, 788, 792, 960–1, 975, 1048–51, 1056, 1058
Prisoners of War—Ethiopia's Claim 4, Partial Award, 1 July 2003 . . . . 55, 534, 540, 959, 961,
                                                                       975, 979, 981, 986–9, 992, 994, 1001–3
Western Front—Aerial Bombardment and Related Claims, Partial Award,
    Eritrea's Claims 1, 3, 4, 5, 9–13, 21, 25 and 26, 19 December 2005 . . . . 1412, 1521

European Commission of Human Rights (ECommHR)

Cyprus v Turkey, Report of the Commission, 10 July 1976 . . . . .715, 1287
Greek Case, Report, 5 November 1969, 12 II *YECHR* (1969), 186 . . . . 1248, 1352
Stewart v United Kingdom, Decision on Admissibility, 10 July 1984 465
X v Germany (1967), App No 3040/67, Decision, 7 April 1967 1053
X v The Netherlands (1965), App No 1983/63, Decision, 13 December 1965 1053

European Court of Human Rights (ECtHR)

A v Norway, Judgment, 9 April 2009 1244
A v United Kingdom, Judgment, 23 September 1998 . . . . 613, 1257
A and others v United Kingdom, Judgment, 19 February 2009 . . . . 477, 480
Abdullah Yilmaz v Turkey, Judgment, 17 June 2008 285
Ahmed v Austria, Judgment, 17 December 1996 1053
Ahmed Özkan and others v Turkey, Judgment, 6 April 2004 799
Akdivar and others v Turkey, App No 21893/93, Judgment, 16 September 1996 . . . . 1169, 1490
Akkum and others v Turkey, Judgment, 24 March 2005 292
Aksoy v Turkey, Judgment, 18 December 1996 487
Al-Jedda v United Kingdom, Judgment, 7 July 2011 . . . . 10, 714, 731, 1342, 1346,
                                                                              1370–1, 1407, 1417, 1427, 1588
Al-Saadoon and Mufdhi v United Kingdom, Admissibility Decision,
    App No 61498/08, 30 June 2009 1142
Al-Saadoon and Mufdhi v United Kingdom, Judgment,
    2 March 2010 . . . . 484–5, 1053, 1057, 1065, 1204
Al-Skeini and others v United Kingdom, Judgment,
    7 July 2011 . . . . 283, 285, 713–14, 733, 1036–7, 1366, 1370, 1411, 1417, 1427, 1471, 1588
Allenet de Ribemont v France, Judgment, 10 February 1995 475
AP, MP, and TP v Switzerland, Judgment, 29 August 1997 302
Arzu Akhmadova and others v Russia, Judgment, 8 January 2009 292
Averill v United Kingdom, Judgment, 6 June 2000 1443
Aydin v Turkey, Judgment, 25 September 1997 . . . . 345, 1275, 1288, 1352
B v United Kingdom, Judgment, 8 July 1987 1093
Banković et al v Belgium et al, Admissibility Decision, App No 52207/99,
    12 December 2001 . . . . .1370, 1471
Bazorkina v Russia, Judgment, 11 December 2006 274

Table of Cases

Belziuk v Poland, Judgment, 25 March 1998 480
Behrami and Behrami v France; Saramati v France, Germany and Norway, Admissibility
    Decision, App Nos 71412/01, 78166/01, 2 May 2007 1370
Borisov v Russia, Judgment, 13 March 2012 1230
Botta v Italy, Judgment, 24 February 1998 1098
Boyle v United Kingdom, Judgment, 8 January 2008 1032
Branningan and McBride v United Kingdom, Judgment, 25 May 1993 .... 486, 1127
Brogan and others v United Kingdom, Judgment, 29 November 1988 476
Campbell v United Kingdom, Judgment, 25 March 1992 478
Campbell and Cosans v United Kingdom, Judgment (Merits), 25 February 1982 1502
Campbell and Fell v United Kingdom, Judgment, 28 June 1984 481
Carbonara and Ventura v Italy, Judgment, 30 May 2000 1527
Chahal v United Kingdom, Judgment, 15 November 1996 .... 1181, 1204
Coëme and others v Belgium, Judgment, 22 June 2000 1221
Colozza v Italy, Judgment, 12 February 1985 .... 482, 1230
Condron v United Kingdom, Judgment, 2 May 2000 482
Cooper v United Kingdom, Judgment, 16 December 2003 1035
Croissant v Germany, Judgment, 25 September 1992 476
Cyprus v Turkey, Judgment, 10 May 2001 .... 259, 274, 282, 1024, 1116, 1224, 1369,
    1400, 1417, 1433, 1459, 1510–11, 1561
Daud v Portugal, Judgment, 21 April 1998 479
Demopoulos and others v Turkey, Decision, App Nos 46113/99, 3843/02,
    13751/02, 13466/03, 10200/04, 14163/04, 19993/04, 21819/04, 1 March 2010 1558,
    1561, 1569, 1572–3
Dogan and others v Turkey, Judgment, 29 June 2004 1490
Ely Ould Dah v France, Admissibility Decision, App No 13113/03, 17 March 2009 ...... 474, 632
Engel v The Netherlands, Judgment, Nos 5100/71; 5101/71; 5102/71; 5354/72;
    5370/72, 8 June 1976 1027
Erdem v Germany, Judgment, 5 July 2001 478
Ergi v Turkey, Judgment, 28 July 1998 .... 283, 465, 712
Fatullayev v Azerbaijan, Judgment, 20 April 2010 1221
Findlay v United Kingdom, Judgment, No 22107/93, 25 February 1997 ...... 473, 1035, 1222
Fox, Campbell and Hartley v United Kingdom, Judgment 475
Grieves v United Kingdom, Judgment, No 57067/00, 16 December 2003 1035
Gurkan v Turkey, Judgment, No 10987/10, 3 July 2012 1035
Gurov v Moldova, Judgment, 11 July 2006 1221
Guzzardi v Italy, Judgment, 6 November 1980 444
Hadjianastassiou v Greece, Judgment, 16 December 1992 483
Hassan v United Kingdom, 16 September 2014 .... 283, 715, 717, 732, 927, 1010, 1036, 1338,
    1341–2, 1346, 1370, 1417, 1471
Helmers v Sweden, Judgment, 29 October 1991 481
Hirst v United Kingdom (No 2), Judgment, 6 October 2005 1128
H.L.R. v France, Judgment, 29 April 1997 1053
Hood v United Kingdom, Judgment, 18 February 1999 1032
I v Finland, Judgment, 17 July 2008 797
Ilaşcu and others v Moldova and Russia, Judgment, 8 July 2004 490
Imakayeva v Russia, Judgment, 9 February 2007 274
Incal v Turkey, Judgment, 9 June 1998 .... 472–3, 1224
Ireland v United Kingdom, Judgment, 18 January 1978 .... 320–1, 327, 338, 1248
Isayeva, Yusupova and Bazayeva v Russia, Judgment, 24 February 2005 .... 284–5, 293, 465, 613,
    712–3, 725
Iskandarov v Russia, Judgment, 23 September 2010 1141
Istratii and others v Moldova, Judgment, 27 March 2007 .... 487, 799

Jabari v Turkey, Judgment, 11 July 2000 1053
Jaloud v The Netherlands, Judgment, 20 November 2014 284
James and others v United Kingdom, Judgment, 21 February 1986 1527
Janowiec and others v Russia, Judgment, 21 October 2013 280
Jaspar v United Kingdom, Judgment, 16 February 2000 480
Johnston and others v Ireland, Judgment, 18 December 1986 1093
Jones v United Kingdom, Judgment, 9 September 2003............................... 1230
Jorvic v Germany, Judgment, 12 July 2007 1227
K.-H.W. v Germany, Judgment, 22 March 2001 1033
Kalashnikov v Russia, Judgment, 15 July 2002 799
Kamasinski v Austria, Judgment, 19 December 1989............................479, 1226, 1444
Keenan v United Kingdom, Judgment, 3 April 2001 1352
Khamzayev and others v Russia, Judgment, 31 May 2011 465
Kokkinakis v Greece, Judgment, 25 May 1993... .474
König v Germany, Judgment, 28 June 1978... 484
Kononov v Latvia, Judgment (Chamber), 24 July 2008 1124
Kononov v Latvia, Judgment (Grand Chamber), 17 May 2010................ 475, 719, 1124
Korbely v Hungary, Judgment, 19 September 2008 .... 394, 720
Kostovski v The Netherlands, Judgment, 20 November 1989........................480, 1231
Kremzow v Austria, Judgment, 21 September 1993 ....479, 482
Kurt v Turkey, Judgment, 25 May 1998..274, 1024, 1369
Lawless v Ireland, Judgment, 1 July 1961 490
Loizidou v Turkey, Judgment (Preliminary Objections), 23 March 1993 1561
Loizidou v Turkey, Judgment, 18 December 1996 .... 1400, 1417, 1459, 1483, 1561, 1568
Lordos and others v Turkey, Judgment, 2 November 2010 1561
Lucà v Italy, Judgment, 27 February 2001 480
MC v Bulgaria, Judgment, 4 December 2003 1256
McCann and others v United Kingdom, Judgment, 27 September 1995 ....465, 851
MK v France, Judgment, 18 April 2013 1098
Mamatkulov and Askarov v Turkey, Judgment, 4 February 2005....................... 1141
Martin v United Kingdom, Judgment, 24 October 2006......................... 1029, 1440
Medvedyev and others v France, Judgment, 29 March 2010........................... 490
Moustaquim v Belgium, Judgment, 18 February 1991................................ 1093
Murray v United Kingdom, Judgment, 8 February 1996 1231
Nuray Sen v Turkey, Judgment, 17 June 2003 487
Öcalan v Turkey, Judgment, 12 May 2005........................... 477–9, 485–6, 1007
Okkali v Turkey, Judgment, 17 October 2006 .... .613
Osman v United Kingdom, Judgment, 28 October 1998............................... .613
Othman v United Kingdom (Abu Qatada), Judgment, 17 January 2012 ......485, 1053, 1204
Palić v Bosnia and Herzegovina, Judgment, 15 February 2011 274
Peek v United Kingdom, Judgment, 28 January 203 1098
Pine Valley Developments Ltd and others v Ireland, Judgment, 29 November 1991.........1527
Pishchalnikov v Russia, Judgment, 24 September 2009..............................476, 482
Poitrimol v France, Judgment, 23 November 1993.................................... 1230
Poltoratskiy v Ukraine, Judgment, 23 April 2003...................................... 799
Pritchard v United Kingdom, App No 1573/11, communicated on
    8 September 2011.. 285
Quaranta v Switzerland, Judgment, 24 May 1991 477
RD v Poland, 18 December 2001.. 1444
Rotaru v Romania, Judgment, 4 May 2000 1098
S and Marper v United Kingdom, Judgment, 4 December 2008 1098
Saadi v Italy, Judgment, 28 February 2008.. 1053, 1141, 1244
Saddam Hussein v Albania et al, Admissibility Decision,
    App No 2327/04, 14 March 2006 1037

Salah Sheekh v The Netherlands, Judgment, 11 January 2007 1053
Salduz v Turkey, Judgment, 27 November 2008 478
Salgueiro da Silva Mouta v Portugal, Judgment, 21 December 1999 205
Sejdovic v Italy, Judgment, 1 March 2006 1229–30
Slivenko v Latvia, Judgment, 9 October 2003 .... 1554, 1573
Soering v United Kingdom, Judgment, 7 July 1989, ... 1053, 1065, 1141, 1203
Solomou et al v Turkey, Judgment, 24 June 2008 1459
Stefanelli v San Marino, Judgment, 8 February 2000 .... 481, 1232–3
Stichting Mothers of Srebrenica and others v Netherlands, Judgment,
    11 June 2013 386
Sufi and Elmi v United Kingdom, Judgment, 28 June 2011 1204
Thorgeir Thorgeirson v Iceland, Judgment, 25 June 1992 473
Timurtaş v Turkey, Judgment, 13 June 2000 .... 274, 1369
Tomasi v France, Judgment, 27 August 1992 1442
Tomic v United Kingdom, 14 October 2003 1204
Toth v Austria, Judgment, 12 December 1991 487
Tyrer v United Kingdom, Judgment, 25 April 1978 .... 322, 1257
Valasinas v Lithuania, Judgment, 27 July 2001 1282
Van Mechelen and others v Netherlands, Judgment, 23 April 1997 481
Varnava and others v Turkey, Judgment, 18 September 2009 .... 274, 280, 282, 294, 713, 799
Vermeire v Belgium, Judgment, 29 November 1991 1093
Vidal v Belgium, Judgment, 22 April 1992 .... 480, 1231
Vilvarajah and others v United Kingdom, Judgment, 30 October 1991 1053
Willis v United Kingdom, Judgment, 11 June 2002 193
X, Y, and Z v United Kingdom, Judgment (Grand Chamber), 22 April 1997 1245
Xenides-Arestis v Turkey, Judgment, 22 December 205 .... 1459, 1561, 1568
Yagci and Sargin v Turkey, Judgment, 8 June 1995 485
Z v Finland, Judgment, 5 February 1997 797
Z and others v United Kingdom, Judgment, 10 May 2001 613
Z and T v United Kingdom, 28 February 2006 1204
Zana v Turkey, Judgment, 25 November 1997 482

Extraordinary Chambers in the Courts of Cambodia (ECCC)

Prosecutors v Kaing Guek Eav (alias 'Duch'), Case No 001/18-07-2007-ECCC-TC,
    Trial Chamber Judgment, 26 July 2010 .... 352, 454, 459, 461–3, 993, 1145
Prosecutors v Kaing Guek Eav (alias 'Duch'), Case No 001/18-07-2007-ECCC-SC,
    Appeals Chamber Judgment, 3 February 2012 .... 352, 1151
Prosecutors v Nuon Chea and Khieu Samphan,
    Case No 002-19-09-2007-ECCC-TC, Judgment, 4 August 2014 1148

Franco-Chilean Arbitral Tribunal

Affaire du Guano (Chili, France), Award, 5 July 1901 1542

Inter-American Commission of Human Rights (IACommHR)

Abella v Argentina, Case No 11.137, Report No 55/97,
    18 November 1997 .... 59, 410–11, 454, 464–6, 483, 722–3, 1366
Aguado Montealegre v Nicaragua, Case No 10.198, Report No 29/89,
    29 September 1989 .... 479, 482
Andrews v United States, Case No 11.139, Report No 57/96, 6 December 1996 473
Avilan et al v Colombia, Case No 11.142, Report No 26/97, 30 September 1997 429

Bronstein and others v Argentina, Case No 11.205, 11.236, 11.238,
 11 March 1997, Report No 2/97, 11 March 1997 .... 475, 487
Case 9466 (Peru), Resolution, 30 June 1987 1369
Case 9786 (Peru), Resolution, 14 September 1988 1369
Case 9844 (El Salvador), Resolution, 13 September 1988 1369
Coard et al v United States, Case No 10.951, Report No 109/99,
 29 September 1999 .... 722, 1084, 1127, 1337–9, 1341, 1346, 1417
Detainees at Guantánamo Bay, Cuba (Decision on Request for Precautionary
 Measures), 12 March 2002 .... 935, 940, 950, 1341
Detainees at Guantánamo Bay, Cuba (Decision to Extend the Scope of
 the Precautionary Measures), 28 October 2005 936
Detainees at Guantánamo Bay, Cuba (Decision to Extend the Scope of
 the Precautionary Measures), 23 July 2013 936
Disabled Peoples' International et al v United States, App No 9213,
 Decision, 22 September 1987 722
Ecuador v Colombia, Case IP-02, Report No 112/10, 21 October 2010 727
Garcia v Peru, Case No 11.006, Report No 1/95, 7 February 1995 472
Hugo Bustios Saavedra v Peru, Case No 10.548, Report No 38/97, 16 October 1997 ... 429
Jorge A. Giménez v Argentina, Case No 11.245, Report No 12/96, 1 March 1996 487
José Miguel Gudiel Álvarez and others ('Diario Militar') v Guatemala,
 Case No 12.590, Report No 116/10, Admissibility and Merits (36.3),
 22 October 2010 709
Lindo et al v Peru, Case No 11.182, Report No 49/00, 13 April 2000 .... 474, 487
Lucio Parada Cea et al v El Salvador, Case No 10.480, Report No 1/99,
 27 January 1999 429
Raquel Martin de Mejía, Case No 10.970 (Peru), Report No 5/96,
 1 March 1996 .... 1275, 1288, 1352
Salinas v Peru, Case No 11.084, Report No 27/94, 30 November 1994 1440
Salas and others v USA, Case No 10.573, Report No 31/93, 14 October 1993 722

Inter-American Court of Human Rights (IACtHR)

Advisory Opinion 11/90, 10 August 1990 477
Anzualdo Castro v Perú, Judgment, 22 September 2009 1151
Bámaca Velásquez v Guatemala, Judgment, 25 November 2000 726
Bámaca-Velásquez v Guatemala, Judgment (Reparations and Costs), 22 February 2002 274
Barrios Altos Case – Chumbipuma Aguirre and others v Peru, Merits, Judgment,
 14 March 2001 180
Blake v Guatemala, Judgment, 24 January 1998 274
Caesar v Trinidad and Tobago, Judgment, 11 March 2005 .... 322, 1258
Cantoral Benavides Case, Judgment 1440
Caso Atala Riffo y Niñas v Chile, 24 February 2012 205
Castillo Petruzzi and others v Peru, Judgment, 30 May 1999 .... 471, 474, 481, 487, 1352
De La Cruz-Flores v Peru, Judgment, 18 November 2004 (Merits, Reparations and
 Costs) 801
Exceptions to the Exhaustion of Domestic Remedies Case, Advisory Opinion,
 OC-11/90, 10 August 1990 1444
Gelman v Uruguay, Judgment, 24 February 2011 1151
Genie Lacayo v Nicaragua, Judgment, 29 January 1997 .... 485, 1442
Gomes Lund et al ('Guerrilha do Araguaia') v Brazil, Judgment (Preliminary
 Objections, Merits, Reparations, and Costs), 24 November 2010 274
Humberto Sanchez v Honduras, Judgment, 7 June 2003 475
Ituango Massacres v Colombia, Judgment, 1 July 2006 .... 465, 726

Judicial Condition and Rights of the Undocumented Migrants, Advisory
  Opinion, 17 September 2003 193–5
'Las Dos Erres' Massacre v Guatemala, 24 November 2009 285
Las Palmeras Case, Judgment on Preliminary Objections, 4 February 2000,
  (Ser C) No 67 (2000) 725–6
Las Palmeras Case, Judgment, 6 December 2001 726
'Mapiripán Massacre' v Colombia, Judgment, 15 September 2005................. 466, 1151
Massacres of El Mozote and Nearby Places v El Salvador, Judgment,
  25 October 2012 .... 453, 465
Mayagna (Sumo) Awas Tingni Community v Nicaragua, Judgment, 3 August 2001 1533
Montero-Aranguran et al (Detention Center of Catia) v Venezuela, Judgment, 5 July 2006 799
Murillo v Costa Rica, Judgment, 28 November 2012................................ 1098
Nadege Dorzema et al v Dominican Republic, Judgment, 24 October 2012 1151
Neira Alegria et al v Peru, Judgment, 19 January 1995 799
Niñas Yean y Bosico v República Dominicana, Judgment, 8 September 2005 1143
Rio Negro Massacres v Guatemala, Judgment, 4 September 2012 1151
Santo Domingo Massacre v Colombia, Judgment, 30 November 2012 465–6
Saramaka People v Suriname, Judgment (Interpretation of the Judgment on
  Preliminary Objections, Merits, Reparations, and Costs), 12 August 2008 1533
Sawhoyamaxa Indigenous Community v Paraguay, Merits, Reparations, and
  Costs, Judgment, 29 March 2006 1533
Suárez Rosero v Ecuador, Judgment, 12 November 1997 .... 475, 486–7
Tibi v Equador, Judgment, 7 September 2004 486
Uzcátegui et al v Venezuela, Judgment, 3 September 2012........................... 1151
Valle Jaramilllo et al v Columbia, Judgment, 27 November 2008 484
Velásquez-Rodriguez v Honduras, Judgment (Merits), 29 July 1988 .... 274, 285, 1352, 1369
Velásquez-Rodríguez v Honduras, Judgment (Compensatory Damages), 21 July 1989 285
Vélez Restrepo and family v Colombia, Judgment, 3 September 2012 1151
Zembrano Velez and others v Ecuador, Judgment, 4 July 2007 474

International Arbitration Awards

Affaire de la délimitation de la frontière maritime entre la Guinée et la
  Guinée-Bissau, Decision, 14 February 1985, *RIAA*, vol XIX, at 165 691
British Claims in the Spanish Zone of Morocco Case, Arbitral Award,
  1 May 1925, *RIAA*, vol II, Section III(II) at 642 339
Case concerning the delimitation of maritime boundary between Guinea-Bissau
  and Senegal, Arbitral Award, 31 July 1989, 20 *RIAA* 119–213, 164
Cessation of Vessels and Tugs for Navigation on the Danube Case (Allied Powers,
  Germany, Austria, Hungary and Bulgaria), Award, 2 August 1921,
  1 *RIAA* (1921) 97 .... 1525, 1538
Responsibility of Germany for acts committed subsequent to 31 July 1914 and before
  Portugal entered the war (Portugal v Germany) ('Cysne Case'),
  30 June 1930, 2 *RIAA* 1035 582
Responsibility of Germany for damage caused in the Portuguese colonies in the South
  of Africa (Portugal v Germany) ('Naulilaa Case') 31 July 1928 *RIAA*, 1011 582

International Court of Justice (ICJ)

Ahmadou Sadio Diallo (Republic of Guinea v Democratic Republic of Congo),
  Judgment, 30 November 2010 1138
Ambatielos case (United Kingdom v Greece) (Preliminary Objection),
  Judgment, 1 July 1952 162

Application of the Convention on the Prevention and Punishment of the
    Crime of Genocide (Bosnia and Herzegovina v Serbia and Montenegro),
    Provisional Measures—Individual Opinion Judge Lauterpacht,
    13 September 1993. . . . . .121, 123
Application of the Convention on the Prevention and Punishment of the
    Crime of Genocide (Bosnia and Herzegovina v Serbia and Montenegro),
    Judgment, 26 February 2007. . . . . 17, 23, 36, 39, 113, 118, 122–3, 126–9,
                                                                        131–2, 164, 166, 638, 1253, 1399
Application of the International Convention on the Elimination of All Forms of Racial
    Discrimination (Georgia v Russian Federation), Order, Request for the Indication of
    Provisional Measures, 15 October 2008. 1491
Application of the International Convention on the Elimination of All Forms of Racial
    Discrimination (Georgia v Russian Federation), Preliminary Objections, Judgment,
    1 April 2011 159
Armed Activities on the Territory of the Congo (Democratic Republic of the Congo v
    Uganda), Judgment, 19 December 2005 . . . . .124–5, 127, 644, 730–1, 1394, 1397,
        1405, 1408, 1417, 1427, 1459, 1477, 1483, 1491–2, 1521–2, 1542–4, 1548, 1565, 1570
Arrest Warrant of 11 April 2000 (Democratic Republic of Congo v Belgium),
    Judgment, 14 February 2002. . . . . 632, 635, 639, 664
Barcelona Traction, Light and Power Company Limited (Belgium v Spain),
    Judgment, 5 February 1970 . . . . 115, 1138, 1260
Certain Criminal Proceedings in France (Republic of the Congo v France) 2003 . . . . 664, 746
Certain Questions of Mutual Assistance in Criminal Matters (Djibouti v France) 2006 664
Colombian–Peruvian Asylum Case, Judgment, 20 November 1950 1566
Continental Shelf Case (Libyan Arab Jamahiriya v Malta), Judgment, 3 June 1985 312
Corfu Channel (United Kingdom v Albania), Judgment, 9 April 1949 . . . . 180, 303, 434,
                                                                                            674, 1254
Elettronica Sicula Case (United States of America v Italy), Judgment, 20 July 1989 136
Fisheries (United Kingdom v Norway), Judgment, 18 December 1951. 1566
Gabčikovo-Nagymaros Project (Hungary/Slovakia), Judgment, 25 September 1997. 582
Interpretation of the Peace Treaties with Bulgaria, Hungary and Romania
    (Second Phase), Advisory Opinion, 18 July 1950 143
Kasikili/Sedudu Island (Botswana v Namibia), 13 December 1999 70
LaGrand (Germany v United States of America), Judgment, 27 June 2001. . . . . .150, 418
Legal Consequences for States of the Continued Presence of South Africa in Namibia
    (South West Africa) Notwithstanding Security Council Resolution 276 (1970),
    Advisory Opinion, 21 June 1971 . . . . 115, 121, 1427
Legal Consequences of the Construction of a Wall in the Occupied Palestinian
    Territory, Advisory Opinion, 9 July 2004. . . . . 6, 59, 113, 120–5, 128, 133, 313,
            685, 711, 729, 731, 753, 1169, 1180, 1183, 1194, 1210, 1218, 1404–5, 1413,
                1417, 1458, 1461, 1465–6, 1470–2, 1475–6, 1482–3, 1488, 1491, 1499,
                        1500, 1505, 1516, 1519, 1523–4, 1548, 1553, 1557, 1560–1, 1563,
                                    1565, 1567, 1569, 1573, 1578–80, 1582–3, 1590
Legality of the Threat or Use of Nuclear Weapons, Advisory Opinion, 8 July 1996 . . . . . . 51–2, 55,
                                        113, 181, 183–5, 320, 465, 671, 674, 685, 689–92,
                                                        700, 721, 729–30, 1136, 1552
Maritime Delimitation and Territorial Questions between Qatar and Bahrain
    (Qatar v Bahrain), Jurisdiction and Admissibility, Judgment, 1 July 1994 136
Military and Paramilitary Activities in and against Nicaragua (Nicaragua v United States of
    America), Judgment, 27 June 1986. . . . . . .19, 36, 39, 45, 47, 77, 113, 115, 122, 130–1, 137, 178,
            187–8, 240, 245, 251, 303, 313, 401, 417, 424, 428, 434–5, 464, 498,
                513, 588, 671–2, 674, 676, 897, 1086, 1216, 1248, 1253, 1399, 1566–7

North Sea Continental Shelf Cases (Federal Republic of Germany/Denmark; Federal
    Republic of Germany/Netherlands), Judgment, 20 February 1969 .... 137, 1567
Nottebohm (Liechtenstein v Guatemala), Judgment, 6 April 1955....................... 1143
Nuclear Tests (New Zealand v France), Judgment, 20 December 1974 .... 138–9, 421
Questions of Interpretation and Application of the 1971 Montreal Convention
    Arising from the Aerial Incident at Lockerbie (Libyan Arab
    Jamahiriya v United States), Order, 14 April 1992 .... 1406, 1427
Questions Relating to the Obligation to Prosecute or Extradite (Belgium v Senegal)
    Judgment, 20 July 2012 .... 126, 338–9, 631, 664
Reparations for Injuries Suffered in the Service of the United Nations,
    Advisory Opinion, 11 April 1949 .... 516, 529
Reservations to the Convention on Genocide, Advisory Opinion, 28 May 1951 .... 173, 185
South West Africa, Second Phase (Liberia and Ethiopia v South Africa),
    Judgment, 18 July 1966 183
Trial of Pakistani Prisoners of War (Pakistan v India) Pleadings of Pakistan 1050
United States Diplomatic and Consular Staff in Tehran (United States
    of America v Iran), Judgment, 24 May 1980............................... 1216, 1254

International Criminal Court (ICC)

Al-Bashir, Decision on the Prosecution's Application for a Warrant of Arrest
    against Omar Hassan Ahmad Al Bashir, ICC-02/05-01/09,
    4 March 2009 .... 423, 664
Al-Bashir, Second Warrant of Arrest for Omar Hassan Ahmad Al Bashir,
    ICC-02/05-01/09, 12 July 2010.. 364, 664
Bemba, Pre-Trial Chamber Decision Pursuant to Article 61(7)(a) and (b)
    of the Rome Statute on the Charges of the Prosecutor against Jean-Pierre
    Bemba Gombo, ICC-01/05-01/08-424, 15 June 2009.................... 459–63, 1152
Harun and Ali Abd-Al-Rahman (Kushayb), Warrant of Arrest,
    27 April 2007... 1289
Katanga and Ngudjolo Chui, Decision on Conformation of Charges,
    ICC-01/04-01/07, 30 September 2008 .... 41, 56, 461, 519, 748, 1142, 1144, 1152
Katanga, Judgment Pursuant to Art 74, ICC-01/04-01/07-3436, 7 March 2014 364
Kony, Warrant of Arrest, ICC-02/04-01/05, 27 September 2005....................... 455
Lubanga, Decision on Conformation of Charges, ICC-01/04-01/06, 29 January 2007 ..... 37, 41,
                                                                413, 461, 519, 626, 1140, 1144
Lubanga, Trial Chamber Judgment Pursuant to Art 74 of the Statute, ICC-01/04-01/06,
    14 March 2012.................................... 356, 394, 397–8, 403, 406–8, 411,
                                                        413, 437, 459, 1144, 1310
Muthaura and Kenyatta, Judgment on the Appeal of the Republic of Kenya against
    the decision of Pre-Trial Chamber II of 30 May 2011, ICC-01/09-02/11,
    2 September 2011.. 364
Muthaura and Kenyatta, Decision on the Confirmation of Charges Pursuant to
    Art 61(7)(a) and (b) of the Rome Statute, ICC-01/09-02/11, 24 May 2012............. 1152
Ntaganda, Pre-Trial Chamber Decision, ICC-01/04-02/06, 13 July 2012................ 456
Ntaganda, Decision Pursuant to Art 61(7)(a) and (b) of the Rome Statute on the Ntaganda,
    Charges of the Prosecutor, ICC-01/04-02/06-309, 9 June 2014 .... 356, 367
Republic of Kenya, Decision Pursuant to Article 15 of the Rome Statute on the
    Authorization of an Investigation into the Situation in the Republic of Kenya,
    ICC-01/09-19-Corr, 31 March 2010 1152
Ruto and others, Decision on the confirmation of Charges Pursuant to Article 61(7)(a)
    and (b) of the Rome Statute, ICC-01/09-01/11, 23 January 2012.................... 1152

International Criminal Tribunal for Rwanda (ICTR)

Akayesu, Trial Chamber Judgment, ICTR-96-4-T, 2 September 1998 .... 65, 324, 345, 352, 394, 404, 421, 423–4, 430, 436, 452, 805, 1275–7
Akayesu, Appeals Chamber Judgment, ICTR-96-4-A, 1 June 2001 430–1
Bagosora, Trial Chamber Judgment, ICTR-98-41-T, 18 December 2008 .... 65, 361, 460
Bagosora and Nsengiyumva, Appeals Chamber Judgment, ICTR-98-41-A,
  14 December 2011 295
Bizimungu et al, Trial Chamber Judgment, ICTR-99-50-T, 30 September 2011 224
Gacumbitsi, Appeals Chamber Judgment, ICTR-2001-64-A, 7 July 2006 352
Hategekimana, Trial Chamber Judgment and Sentence, ICTR-00-55BT,
  6 December 2010 361
Kayishema and Ruzindana, Trial Chamber Judgment, ICTR-95-1-T,
  21 May 1999 .... 332, 457, 1257
Kayishema and Ruzindana, Appeals Chamber Judgment, ICTR-95-1-A,
  1 June 2001 .... 1222, 1231
Muhimana, Trial Chamber Judgment, ICTR-95-1B-T, 28 April 2005 458
Musema, Trial Chamber Judgment and Sentence, ICTR-96-13-T,
  27 January 2000 .... 65, 396, 430, 805
Nahimana, Barayagwiza and Ngeze, Appeals Chamber Judgment,
  ICTR-99-52-A, 28 November 2007 .... 1064, 1222
Ndindiliyimana et al, Trial Chamber Judgment and Sentence,
  ICTR-00-56-T, 17 May 2011 .... 361, 457, 460
Ntagerura et al, Trial Chamber Judgment, ICTR-99-46-T, 25 February 2004 .... 457, 627
Ntagerura et al, Appeals Chamber Judgment, ICTR-99-46-T, 7 July 2006 .... 627, 748
Nyiramasuhuko et al, Trial Chamber Judgment, ICTR-98-42-T, 24 June 2011 .... 224, 227, 460, 1285
Nzabirinda, Sentencing Judgment, ICTR-2000-77-T, 23 February 2007 .... 458, 461
Renzaho, Trial Chamber Judgment, ICTR-97-31-T, 14 July 2009 361
Rutaganda, Trial Chamber Judgment and Sentence, ICTR-96-3-T,
  6 December 1999 .... 65, 76, 394, 396, 411
Rutaganira, Trial Chamber Judgment, ICTR-95-1-C-T, 14 March 2005 749
Rwamakuba, Indictment, ICTR-98-44C-I, 9 June 2005 822
Rwamakuba, Trial Chamber Judgment, ICTR-98-44C-I, 20 September 2006 822
Semanza, Trial Chamber Judgment, ICTR-97-20-T, 15 May 2003 .... 325, 457
Semanza, Appeals Chamber Judgment, ICTR-97-20-A, 20 May 2005 626

International Criminal Tribunal for the former Yugoslavia (ICTY)

Aleksovski, Trial Chamber Judgment, IT-95-14/1-T, 25 June 1999 .... 327, 333–4, 986, 1353, 1355–6, 1367–8
Aleksovski, Appeals Chamber Judgment, IT-95-14/1-A, 24 March 2000 .... 56, 334, 1143–4
Blaškić, Trial Chamber Decision of 4 April 1997 on the Defence Motion to Strike Portions of
  the Amended Indictment Alleging 'Failure to Punish' Liability, IT-95-14-A 166
Blaškić, Trial Chamber Judgment, IT-95-14-T, 3 March 2000 .... 225, 303, 305, 307–9, 315, 330–1, 457, 514, 517, 748, 836, 924, 1064, 1140, 1145–6, 1189, 1399, 1518, 1530–1, 1549
Blaškić, Appeals Chamber Judgment, IT-95-14-A, 29 July 2004 .... 252, 304, 307, 309, 459, 623, 748, 750, 899, 1146, 1151, 1320
Blagojević and Jokić, Trial Chamber Judgment, IT-02-60-T,
  17 January 2005 .... 252–3, 1191–2, 1320
Boškoski and Tarčulovski, Trial Chamber Judgment,
  IT-04-82-T, 10 July 2008 .... 60, 395, 405, 411–13

Table of Cases

Bralo, Appeals Chamber Judgment, IT-95-17-A, 2 April 2007 1151
Brđanin, Trial Chamber Judgment, IT-99-36-T, 1 September 2004 ...... 324, 327, 458–9, 461–2,
　　　　　　　　　　　　　　　　　　　　　　　　　　　　　　　　1140, 1189, 1531
Brđanin, Appeals Chamber Judgment, IT-99-36-A, 3 April 2007 .... 748, 1151
Delalić et al ('Čelebići Camp'), Trial Chamber Judgment, IT-96-21-T,
　　16 November 1998...................... 60, 325, 327–32, 352, 363, 412, 428, 457–9,
　　　　　　461, 743–4, 748, 899, 921–2, 924, 1010, 1126–9, 1132, 1142, 1144, 1176, 1183,
　　　　　　1247–8, 1250, 1264, 1275, 1291, 1331, 1334, 1337, 1345, 1369, 1384, 1514, 1521
Delalić et al ('Čelebići Camp'), Appeals Chamber Judgment, IT-96-21-A,
　　20 February 2001...................... 166, 168, 327, 450, 513, 899, 1132, 1140,
　　　　　　　　　　　　　　　　　　　　　　　　　　　　　　　　1144, 1151, 1345, 1376
Đorđević, Trial Chamber Judgment, IT-05-87/1-T, 23 February 2011.......... 253, 363, 405, 412
Furundžija, Decision on the Defendant's Motion to Dismiss Counts
　　13 and 14 of the Indictment, IT-95-17/1-PT, 29 May 1998 360
Furundžija, Trial Chamber Judgment, IT-95-17/1-T, 10 December 1998....... 60, 186, 323, 325,
　　　　　　　　　　　　　329, 333, 336–7, 352, 360–1, 363, 636, 744, 1064, 1275–7, 1285
Furundžija, Appeals Chamber Judgment, IT-95-17/1-A, 21 July 2000................... 1222
Galić, Trial Chamber Judgment, IT-98-29-T, 5 December 2003 ......253, 385, 455, 517, 520, 744
Galić, Appeals Chamber Judgment, IT-98-29-A, 30 November 2006 .... 219, 227, 385,
　　　　　　　　　　　　　　　　　　　　　　　　　　　　　　　　461, 520, 744, 748, 847
Gotovina et al, Trial Chamber Decision, IT-06-90-PT, 19 March 2007 1320
Gotovina et al, Trial Chamber Judgment, IT-06-90-T, 15 April 2011 1549
Gotovina et al, Appeals Chamber Judgment, IT-06-90-A, 16 November 2012 902
Hadžihasanović et al, Trial Chamber Decision on Joint Challenge to
　　Jurisdiction, IT-01-47-PT, 12 November 2002 408
Hadžihasanović et al, Appeals Chamber Decision on Interlocutory Appeal
　　Challenging Jurisdiction in Relation to Command Responsibility,
　　IT-01-47-AR72, 16 July 2003 .... 186, 407–8, 412, 627, 750
Hadžihasanović et al, Trial Chamber Decision on Motions for Acquittal
　　Pursuant to Rule 98*bis* of the Rules of Procedure and Evidence, IT-01-47-T, 27
　　September 2004.. 458
Hadžihasanović et al, Decision on Joint Defence Interlocutory Appeal of Trial Chamber
　　Decision on Rule 98*bis* Motions for Acquittal, IT-01-47-T, 11 March 2005............ 899
Hadžihasanović et al, Trial Chamber Judgment, IT-01-47-T, 15 May 2006................. 519
Hadžihasanović et al, Appeals Chamber Judgment, IT-01-47-A, 22 April 2008 750
Halilović, Trial Chamber Judgment, IT-01-48-T, 16 November 2005.......... 412, 459–60, 462
Haradinaj, Balaj and Brahimaj, Trial Chamber Judgment, IT-04-84-T,
　　3 April 2008..60–2, 77, 405, 411–13
Jelisić, Trial Chamber Judgment, IT-95-10-T, 14 December 1999 .... 457, 1369
Karadžić and Mladić, Initial Judgment, IT-95-5-1, 24 July 1995 1267
Kordić and Čerkez, Trial Chamber Decision on Joint Defence Motion to Strike all
　　Counts Arising under Article 2 or Article 3 for Failure to Allege a Nexus between the
　　Conduct and an International Armed Conflict, IT-95-14/2, 1 March 1999............. 72
Kordić and Čerkez, Trial Chamber Judgment, IT-95-14/2-T, 26 February 2001 ...... 304–5, 307,
　　　　　　　　　　　　　　　　　　　309–10, 327, 331, 455, 457, 493, 1128–9, 1132, 1144,
　　　　　　　　　　　　　　　　　　　　　　　1331, 1334–5, 1346, 1384, 1528, 1531, 1549
Kordić and Čerkez, Appeals Chamber Judgment, IT-95-14/1-A,
　　17 December 2004................... 300, 304, 411–12, 520, 626, 791, 1151, 1528, 1532
Krnojelac, Trial Chamber Judgment, IT-97-25-T, 15 March 2002................ 327, 329–32,
　　　　　　　　　　　　　　　　　　　　　　　　　　　　　335, 450, 458, 461–2, 953, 1189–90
Krnojelac, Appeals Chamber Judgment, IT-97-25-A, 17 September 2003 ...... 748, 1186–7, 1191
Krstić, Trial Chamber Judgment, IT-98-33-T, 2 August 2001 .... 253, 332, 458, 1189–90,
　　　　　　　　　　　　　　　　　　　　　　　　　　　　　　　　　　　　　1192, 1514

Krstić, Appeals Chamber Judgment, IT-98-33-A, 19 April 2004 385
Kunarac, Kovač and Vuković, Trial Chamber Judgment, IT-96-23-T and
  IT-96-23/1-T, 22 February 2001 . . . . 325–6, 329, 331, 333–5, 354, 361, 430, 805, 1191, 1453
Kunarac, Kovač and Vuković, Appeals Chamber Judgment, IT-96-23 and
  IT-96-23/1-A, 12 June 2002. . . . . .60, 73, 325–6, 352, 363, 404, 1191, 1276, 1281
Kupreškić et al, Trial Chamber Judgment, IT-95-16-T, 14 January 2000 . . . . 132, 180–1,
  186, 276, 451, 579, 587–8, 593–5, 1164, 1369
Kvočka et al, Trial Chamber Judgment, IT-98-30/1-T, 2 November 2001 . . . . . . 325, 327, 329, 363
Kvočka et al, Appeals Chamber Judgment, IT-98-30/1-A, 28 February 2005. . . . . .458, 461–2
Limaj et al, Trial Chamber Judgment, IT-03-66-T, 30 November 2005. . . . . 61, 394–5, 404–5,
  408–9, 411–13, 452, 459, 462
Limaj et al, Appeals Chamber Judgment, IT-03-66-A, 27 September 2007 1228
Martić, Trial Chamber Decision on Review of Indictment Pursuant to Rule 61,
  IT-95-11-R61, 8 March 1996 . . . . .187, 587–8, 593
Martić, Trial Chamber Judgment, IT-95-11-T, 12 June 2007 . . . . 227, 412, 584, 593, 1549
Martić, Appeals Chamber Judgment, IT-95-11-A, 8 October 2008 . . . . 584, 593
Milošević, Trial Chamber Decision for Motion on Judgment of Acquittal,
  IT-02-54-T, 16 June 2004 . . . . .405, 407, 412, 423
Milutinović et al, Trial Chamber Judgment, IT-05-87-T, 26 February 2009 . . . . 356, 364
Mrkšić et al ('Vukovar Hospital Case'), Trial Chamber Judgment,
  IT-95-13/1-T, 27 September 2007 . . . . 227, 359, 459, 462, 519, 804, 821, 975
Mrkšić et al ('Vukovar Hospital Case'), Appeals Chamber Judgment,
  IT-95-13/1-A, 5 May 2009. . . . . 227, 359, 748–9, 974–5, 1007, 1064
Mucić et al ('Čelebići Camp'), Appeals Chamber Judgment, IT-96-21-A,
  20 February 2001. 56
Naletilić and Martinović, Trial Chamber Judgment, IT-98-34-T, 31 March 2003. . . . . . . 519, 744,
  1086, 1140, 1393–4, 1399, 1409, 1411–12, 1459, 1483, 1518, 1531, 1549, 1594
Naletilić and Martinović, Appeals Chamber Judgment, IT-98-34-A, 3 May 2006 . . . . . . .56, 1151
Nikolić, Review of Indictment Pursuant to Rule 61, IT-94-2-R61, 20 October 1995 1189
Ojdanić et al, Appeals Chamber Decision on Dragoljub Ojdanić's Motion
  Challenging Jurisdiction, IT-99-37-AR72, 21 May 2003. 623
Orić, Trial Chamber Judgment, IT-03-68-T, 30 June 2006. 394, 458–62
Orić, Appeals Chamber Judgment, IT-03-68-A, 3 July 2008. 748
Popović, Trial Chamber Judgment, IT-05-88-T, 10 June 2010. 253
Prlić et al, Second Amended Indictment, IT-04-74-T, 11 June 2008 1530
Prlić et al, Decision of the President on Jadranko Prlić's Motion to Disqualify
  Judge Arpad Prandler, IT-04-74-T, 4 October 2010. 1222
Prlić et al, Trial Chamber Judgment, IT-04-74-T, 29 May 2013. 1151
Rajić, Trial Chamber Decision Review of the Indictment Pursuant to Rule 61 of the Rules of
  Procedure and Evidence, IT-95-12-R61, 13 September 1996 . . . . .1140, 1142
Rajić, Trial Chamber Judgment, IT-95-12, 8 May 2006 1151
Simić, Tadić and Zarić, Trial Chamber Decision on the Prosecution Motion under
  Rule 73 for a Ruling Concerning the Testimony of a Witness, IT-95-9, 27 July 1999 544–5
Simić, Tadić and Zarić, Trial Chamber Decision on Application by Stevan Todorovic to
  Reopen the Decision of 27 July 1999 etc, 28 February 2000 545
Simić, Tadić and Zarić, Trial Chamber Judgment, IT-95-9-T,
  17 October 2003 . . . . 329, 331, 744, 954, 1190–2
Simić, Tadić and Zarić, Appeals Chamber Judgment, IT-95-9-A, 28 November 2006. . . . . . . .745, 748
Stakić, Trial Chamber Judgment, IT-97-24-T, 31 July 2003 .356, 458, 1189–90
Stakić, Appeals Chamber Judgment, IT-97-24-A, 22 March 2006. 1189–91
Stanišić and Župljanin, Trial Chamber Judgment, IT-08-91-T, 27 March 2013. 252
Strugar, Trial Chamber Judgment, IT-01-42-T, 31 January 2005 . . . . 60, 253, 455, 459
Strugar, Appeals Chamber Judgment, IT-01-42-A, 17 July 2008. 460

Tadić, Appeals Chamber Decision on the Defence Motion for Interlocutory Appeal on
    Jurisdiction, IT-94-1-AR72, 2 October 1995 .... 16, 30, 41, 43, 45, 48, 50, 55, 57, 60–1,
            64, 71, 76, 78, 143, 254–5, 303, 323, 336, 360, 394–6, 404, 424, 428, 430,
            435, 514, 517, 520, 643, 646, 677, 728, 742, 745, 1142, 1183, 1221, 1288, 1319–20
Tadić, Trial Chamber Judgment, IT-94-I-T, 7 May 1997 .... 295, 362, 410,
            412, 435–6, 455, 460, 514, 1064, 1142, 1258, 1531
Tadić, Appeal Chamber Judgment, IT-94-1-A, 15 July 1999 .... 17, 36–7, 39, 56, 360, 397–8,
            404–5, 408, 413–414, 626–7, 642, 657, 747–8, 897, 922, 926,
            936, 1140, 1143, 1151, 1231, 1253, 1314, 1399
Todorović, Trial Chamber Judgment, IT-95-9/1, 31 July 2001........................1151
Tolimir, Trial Chamber Judgment, IT-05-88/2-T, 12 December 2012..................... 253
Vasiljević, IT-98-32-T, Trial Chamber Judgment, 29 November 2002............... 332, 1064

International Military Tribunal for the Far East

Tokyo Judgment 351, 353–4, 959, 974

International Military Tribunal, Nuremberg

Trial of Major German War Criminals, Judgment and Sentences, 30 September and
    1 October 1946 .... 187, 353, 357, 430, 686, 1156, 1167, 1257, 1532, 1542, 1552

International Tribunal for the Law of the Sea

Responsibilities and Obligations of States Sponsoring Persons and Entities with
    Respect to Activities in the Area, Advisory Opinion, 1 February 2011 158

Permanent Court of International Justice (PCIJ)

Case Concerning Certain German Interests in Polish Upper Silesia
    (Germany v Poland) Judgment, 25 May 1926.................................... 194
Free Zones of Upper Savoy and the District of Gex, Judgment, 7 June 1932................ 163
Jurisdiction of the Courts of Danzig, Advisory Opinion, 26 May 1925 418
Minority Schools in Albania, Advisory Opinion, 6 April 1935......................... 194
S.S. Lotus (France v Turkey), Judgment, 7 September 1927 185

Special Court for Sierra Leone (SCSL)

Brima et al (AFRC Case), Further Amended Consolidated Indictment,
    SCSL-2004-16-PT, 13 May 2004 1166
Brima et al (AFRC Case), Trial Chamber Judgment, SCSL-04-16-T,
    20 June 2007 .... 354, 361, 437, 457, 459, 461–2, 983, 1169
Fofana, Decision on Preliminary Motion on Lack of Jurisdiction: Illegal Delegation
    of Jurisdiction by Sierra Leone, SCSL-2004-14-72(E), 25 May 2004..................515
Fofana, Decision on Preliminary Motion on Lack of Jurisdiction *Materiae*: Illegal Delegation
    of Jurisdiction by the United Nations, SCSL-2004-14-AR72(E), 25 May 2004..........515
Fofana, Decision on Preliminary Motion on Lack of Jurisdiction *Materiae*: Nature of the
    Armed Conflict, SCSL-2004-14-AR72(E), 25 May 2004 515
Fofana and Kondewa, Trial Chamber Judgment, SCSL-04-14-T, 2 August 2007 454
Fofana and Kondewa, Appeals Chamber Judgment, SCSL-04-14-A, 28 May 2008..........1168
Kallon and Kamara, Appeals Chamber Judgment, Decision on Challenge
    to Jurisdiction: Lomé Accord Amnesty, SCSL-2004-15-AR72(E) and
    SCSL-2004-16-AR72(E), 13 March 2004 .... 421, 424, 515

Kallon, Norman and Kamara, Appeals Chamber Decision on Constitutionality and Lack of Jurisdiction, SCSL-2004-14-PT, SCSL-2004-15-PT, and SCSL-2004-16-PT, 13 March 2004.. 1221
Kondewa, Appeals Chamber Decision on Lack of Jurisdiction/Abuse of Process: Amnesty Provided by the Lomé Accord, 25 May 2004........................... 515
Norman, Fofana and Kondewa, Trial Chamber Decision on Motion for Judgment of Acquittal pursuant to Art 98, SCSL-04-14-T, 21 October 2005............ 1169
Norman, Appeals Chamber Decision on Preliminary Motion based on Lack of Jurisdiction, SCSL-2004-14-AR72(E), 31 May 2004........................... 623
Sesay et al ('RUF' Case), Trial Chamber Judgment, SCSL-04-15-T, 2 March 2009 .... 65, 308, 354, 436, 452, 454, 459–61, 463
Taylor, Trial Chamber Judgment, SCSL-03-01-T, 18 May 2012 .... 352, 361, 459–60, 664
Taylor, Appeals Chamber Judgment, SCSL-03-01-A, 26 September 2013............ 664, 1311

Special Panels for Serious Crimes in East Timor

Prosecutor v Jose Cardoso Fereira, Case No 04/2001, 5 April 2003 352

United Nations Committee against Torture (CtteeAT)

Agiza v Sweden, Comm No 233/2003 (2005), CAT/C/34/D/233/2003 1204
Tapia Paez v Sweden, Comm No 39/1996 (1996), CAT/C/18/D/39/1996 1204

United Nations Human Rights Committee (HRCttee)

A v Australia, Com No 560/1993, 30 April 1997 302
Äärelä and Näkkäläjärvi v Finland, Com No 779/1997, 24 October 2001 .... 480, 1442
Acosta v Uruguay, Com No 110/1981, 29 March 1984.................................. 477
Alzery v Sweden, Com No 1416/2005, 25 October 2006........................1053, 1204
AP v Italy, Com No 204/1986, 2 November 1987 1232
Bahamonde v Equatorial Guinea, Com No 468/1991, 20 October 1993 1222
Basso v Uruguay, Com No 1887/2009, 19 October 2010............................... 487
Borisenko v Hungary, Com No 852/1999, 6 December 2002 486
Bousroual v Algeria, Com No 1085/2002, 15 March 2006 273
Campbell v Jamaica, Com No 307/1988, 24 March 1993 479
Coeriel et al v The Netherlands, Com No 453/1991, 31 October 1004 1098
Currie v Jamaica, Com No 377/1989, 29 March 1994 1444
Deidrick v Jamaica, Com No 619/1995, 9 April 1998..........................332, 1352
El Hassy v The Libyan Arab Jamahiriya, Com No 1422/2005, 24 October 2007......... 273
Espinoza de Polay v Peru, Com No 577/19946 November 1997........................1352
Fillastre v Bolivia, Com No 336/1988, 6 November 1991 .... 476, 487
Francis v Jamaica, Com No 320/1988, 24 March 1993 483
Francis v Jamaica, Com No 606/1994, 25 July 1995 302
Gomez de Voituret v Uruguay, 10 April 1984..1352
Gonzalez del Rio v Peru, Com No 263/1987, 28 October 1992 1222
Grant v Jamaica, 597/1994, 22 March 1996.. 475
Gridin v Russia, Com No 770/1997, 20 July 2000.................................... 475
Jansen-Gielen v Netherlands, Com No 846/1999, 3 April 2001........................ 480
Judge v Canada, Com 829/1998, 20 October 2003 484
Karttunen v Finland, Com No 387/1989, 23 October 1992............................ 1222
Kavanagh v Ireland, Com No 819/1998, 26 April 2001 472
Kulomin v Hungary, Com No 521/1992, 22 March 1996 486
Larrañaga v The Philippines, Com No 1421/2005, 14 September 2006.................. 485

Table of Cases

Larrosa Bequio v Uruguay, Com No 88/1981, 29 March 1983 1352
Little v Jamaica, Com No 283/1988, 1 November 1991 1443
Lopez Burgos v Uruguay, Com No 52/1979, 29 July 1981 1411
Lyashkevich v Belarus, Com No 887/1999, 3 April 2003 ....281, 1369
Massiotti and Baritussio v Uruguay, Com No 25/1978, 26 July 1982.....................1352
Marais v Madagascar, Com No 49/1979, 24 March 1983............................1352
Marlem Carranza Alegre v Peru, Com No 1126/2002, 17 November 2005 ....478, 801
Mbenge v Zaire, Com No 16/1977, 8 September 1977..........................1229–30
Mukong v Cameroon, Com No 458/1991, 21 July 1994............................. 302
O.F. v Norway, Com No 158/1983, 26 October 1984 1226
Osborne v Jamaica, Com No 759/1997, 13 April 2000..........................322, 1257
Pennant v Jamaica, Com No 647/1995, 3 December 1998........................... 476
Philip v Trinidad and Tobago, Com No 594/1992, 20 October 1998..................... 479
Quinteros v Uruguay, Com No 107/1981, 21 July 1983 ....273, 1369
Sarma v Sri Lanka, Com No 950/2000, 16 July 2003............................259, 273
Toonen v Australia, Com No 488/1992, 31 March 1994 205
Whyte v Jamaica, Com No 732/1997, 27 July 1998 479
Wolf v Panama, Com No 289/1988, 26 March 1992 480

United Nations Working Group on Arbitrary Detention

Saddam Hussein al-Tikriti v Iraq and United States of America,
    Opinion No 31/2006.. 472

NATIONAL

Argentina

Military Junta Case, Judgment, 9 December 1985, National Court of Appeals 1529

Australia

Trial of Captain Eikichi Kato, 1946, *UNWCC Law Reports*, vol V, Australian
    Military Court, Rabaul 463
Trial of Sergeant-Major Shigeru Ohashi and six others, 1946, *UNWCC Law Reports*,
    vol V, Australian Military Court, Rabaul..................................... 463

Austria

Requisitioned Property (No 2) Case, 20 June 1951, 18 *ILR* 696, Supreme Court 1525

Belgium

Auditeur militaire v Krumkamp, 17 *ILR* (1950) 388, Military Court of Brabant 186–7

Bosnia and Herzegovina

Bogdanović, Verdict and Sentence, Case No S1 1K003336 10 Krl, 29 August 2011,
    Court of Bosnia and Herzegovina, Section I for War Crimes 361
Boudellaa and others v Bosnia and Herzegovina and the Federation of Bosnia and
    Herzegovina, Case Nos CH/02/8679, CH/02/8689, CH/02/8690, CH/02/8691),
    13 BHRC 297 (2002), Human Rights Chamber 1346
Pinčić, Verdict and Sentence, Case No X-KR-08/502, 28 November 2008, Court
    of Bosnia and Herzegovina, Section I for War Crimes 361

Canada

Bil'In (Village Council) v Green Park International Inc, Judgment,
 18 September 2008, Superior Court of the Province of Quebec 1572
R v Semrau [2010] CM 4010; 14 YIHL (2011) 8,
 Court Martial Proceedings 791

China

Trial of Takashi Sakai, 29 August 1946, *UNWCC Law Reports*, vol XIV,
 Chinese War Crimes Military Tribunal, Nanking 351, 462

Colombia

Constitution revision of Additional Protocol II and the Law 171 of 16 December 1994,
 implementing this Protocol, Judgment, Constitutional Case No C-225/95,
 18 May 1995, Constitutional Court 178, 421, 424, 515, 1321
Constitutional Case No C-291/07, Judgment, 25 April 2007, Constitutional
 Court (Plenary Chamber) 450, 464, 850

Croatia

Public Prosecutor v Perišić et al, K. 74/96, Verdict, District Court in
 Zadar, 24 April 1997 379

Democratic Republic of the Congo

Bongi Massaba Case, Judgment on Appeals, 4 November 2006, Military
 Court of the Eastern Province 461

Denmark

Prosecutor v Refik Sarić, Decision, 25 November 1994, Eastern Division
 of the Danish High Court 645

France

Administration des Eaux et Forêts v Falck, Cour de Cassation, Judgment 1927 1544
Javor et al, Decision, 26 March 1996, Cour de Cassation, Chambre criminelle 629
Alois and Anna Bommer and Their Daughters, *UNWCC Law Reports*, vol IX,
 19 February 1947, Permanent Military Tribunal at Metz 187
Gustav Becker, Wilhelm Weber and 18 Others, *UNWCC Law Reports*, vol VII,
 Concluded 17 July 1947, Permanent Military Tribunal at Lyon 187
L'Etat Français v Etablissements Monmousseau, Judgment, 1948, Cour d'appel d'Orléans 1546

Germany

HMHS Llandovery Castle and HMHS Dover Castle, German Supreme Court, Leipzig 226
Serbian Prisoners of War Case, 11 April 2006, Administrative Court of Berlin 1260

India

Monteiro v State of Goa, 26 March 1969, Supreme Court 1139, 1465

Israel

A v State of Israel, Adm Det App 7750/08, 23 November 2008, Supreme Court 929, 1335–6
A Teacher's Housing Cooperative Society v The Military Commander of
    the Judea and Samaria Region et al, HCJ 393/82, Judgment 1982, (1983) 37(4)
    Piskei Din 785; 14 *IsrYBHR* (1984) 301 . . . . 1527, 1550
Abu Aita et al v The Military Commander of the Judea and Samaria Region,
    HCJ 69/81, Judgment, 5 April 1983. 1550
Abu Aita et al v Commander of the Judea and Samaria Region and Officer-in-Charge
    of Customs and Excise, Omar Abdu Kadar Kanzil v Officer-in-Charge of Customs, Gaza
    Strip Region and The Regional Commander of the Gaza Strip,
    HC 69/81–HC 493/81, Judgment, 4 April 1983, Supreme Court. 1463, 1479
Abu Awad v The Military Commander, HCJ 97/79, 12 November 1979, Supreme Court 1188
Abu Rian et al v IDF Commander of Judea and Samaria, HCJ 401/88, 24 July 1988. 1524
Afu v IDF Commander in the West Bank, HCJ 785/87, Supreme Court, 1988 1188
Al-Basyuni and others v Prime Minister and Minister of Defence, HCJ 9132/07,
    30 January 2008, Supreme Court sitting as High Court of Justice 249, 1590, 1593
Al-Nawar v The Minister of Defence et al, HCJ 574/82, Judgment,
    11 August 1985, 16 *IsrYBHR* (1986) 321, High Court 1522, 1538, 1545
Anonymous (Lebanese citizens) v Minister of Defense, FCrA 7048/97,
    12 April 2000, Supreme Court. 1335
Anonymous Persons v Minister of Defense, A.D.A. 10/94, 13 November 1997 1335
Arjov et al v Commander of IDF in the Judea and Samaria Region et al, HCJ 87/85,
    41(1) PD 353, 18 *IsrYBHR* (1988) 255. 1436
Association of Civil Rights in Israel et al v The Minister of Defence et al, HC 5973192 etc,
    47(1) *Piskei Din* 267, 23 *IsrYBHR* (1993) 353, Supreme Court 1196
Ayub v Minister of Defence (Beit El Case), HCJ 606/78, Judgment, 15 March 1979, 9
    IsrYBHR (1979) 337 1571
Beit Sourik Village Council v Government of Israel, HCJ 2056/04, 30 June 2004,
    Supreme Court 1460, 1481, 1519, 1565
Christian Society for the Holy Places v Minister of Defence et al, HCJ 447/71,
    Judgment, 1971, Supreme Court 1543
Daghlas v The Military Commander in the Judea and Samaria Region, HC 698/85,
    40(2) *PD* 42, Supreme Court. 1162
D(u)weikat v Government of Israel (Elon Moreh Case) HCJ 390/79, Judgment,
    22 October 1979, 9 IsrYBHR (1979) 345, Supreme Court 1571
Fawzi Muhammad Mustafa Ayub v State of Israel, 23 Nissan 5768, 2 May 2005. 1335
Flunis v Minsiter of Defense, HCJ 7048/97, *PD* 54(1) 721. 1335
Goha v Military Commander of Judea and Samaria, HCJ 290/89, 43(2) *PD* 116;
    23 *IsrYBHR* (1993) 323 1524
Gtwarawi et al v Minister of Defence et al, HC 454/85, 39(3) *Piskei Din* 401, Supreme
    Court. 1188
Gusin v IDF Commander of the Gaza Strip, HCJ 4219/01, 56(4) *PD* 608; 32 *IsrYBHR*
    (2002) 379. 1519
Iyad v State of Israel, CrimA 6659/06, 11 June 2008, Supreme Court 930, 1336
Jaber Al-Bassiouni Ahmed and others v Prime Minister and Minister of Defence,
    Petition for an Order Nisi and an Urgent Request for Injunction, HCJ 9132/07, 28
    October 2007. 1163
Jaber Al-Bassiouni Ahmed and others v Prime Minister and Minister of Defence,
    30 January 2008, Supreme Court 1279
Jami'at Iscan Al-Ma'almun, Communal Society Registered at the Judea and Samaria Area
    Headquarters v Commander of IDF Forces in the Judea and Samaria Region, HCJ
    393/82, Judgment, 28 December 1983, High Court of Justice. 1543

Kawasme et al v Minister of Defence et al, HC 698/80, 35(1) *Piskei Din* 617,
    11 *IsrYBHR* (1981) 349. 1195
Kipah Mahmad Ahmed Ajuri et al v IDF Commander in the West Bank et al,
    HCJ 7015/02, 3 September 2002, [2002] *Israeli Law Reports* 1,
    Supreme Court 1148, 1152, 1334
Mara'abe et al v Prime Minister of Israel et al (Alfei Menashe Case), HCJ 7957/04,
    Judgment, 15 September 2005, 37 *IsrYBHR* (2007) 345. .... 1519, 1565
Matar v The Military Court in Shechem et al, HCJ 460/86, 40(3) PD 817,
    Supreme Court 1445
Military Prosecutor v Kassem et al 13 April 1969, (1969) 42 *ILR* 470,
    Military Court at Ramallah................ 896, 899, 913, 943, 945, 948, 951, 1030–1
Mustafa Dweikat v Government of Israel et al (Elon Moreh Case),
    HCJ 390/79, Judgment, 22 October 1979 1543
Obeid and Dirani v Defence Minister et al, HCJ 794/98, 23 August 2001................ 534
Physicians for Human Rights v Commander of the IDF in the West Bank,
    The Commander of the IDF Forces in the Gaza, HCJ 2117/02, Judgment,
    28 April 2002, Supreme Court sitting as the High Court of Justice 598
Physicians for Human Rights v Commander of the Israel Defense Forces,
    HCJ 2941/02, HCJ 2936/02, 8 April 2002 795
Physicians for Human Rights v Commander of the IDF Forces in the Gaza
    Strip in 2004, Judgment, 30 May 2004, High Court of Justice 788
Public Committee against Torture in Israel et al v Government of Israel et al
    (Targeted Killings Case), HCJ 769/02, 13 December 2006, Supreme Court 41, 69, 403,
                                                                   453, 924, 930, 1149, 1593
Sheikh Suleiman Abu Hilu et al v State of Israel, HC 302/72, 27(2)
    Piskei Din 69, 5 *IsrYBHR* (1975) 384, Supreme Court 1187
Swarka Case, 1974, Military Court 1030
Tabib et al v Minister of Defence et al, HCJ 202/81, 36(2) PD 622;
    13 *IsrYBHR* (1983) 364 1527
Timraz et al v IDF Commander of the Gaza Strip, HCJ 24/91, 45(2) PD 325;
    23 *IsrYBHR* (1993) 337 1518
Tzemel v Minister of Defence, HCJ 102/82, 13 July 1983, 37(3) PD 365,
    Supreme Court as High Court of Justice 1594

Italy

Bouyahia Maher Ben Abdelaziz et al, Judgment No 1072, 17 January 2007,
    Court of Cassation.. 913
Colorni v Ministry of War, Judgment, 22 March 1950, Corte Suprema di Cassazione 1545
In re Kappler ('Ardeatine Cave Massacre Case'), 20 July 1948, Military
    Tribunal, Rome 583–5, 1158, 1167

Japan

Kamibayashi et al v Japan, 4 April 1989, Tokyo District Court 1006

Netherlands

Enkelstroth, 20 February 1948, Special Court (War Criminals) of Arnhem 463
Esau Case, 21 February 1949, 16 *ILR* (1949) 482, Special Court of Cassation 1525
Hans Albin Rauter, *UNWCC Law Reports*, vol XIV, 4 May 1948, Special
    Court in The Hague; 12 January 1949, Special Court of Cassation 187, 1161, 1167

Judge-Advocate v X et al, Netherlands Temporary Court-Martial in Batavia,
    24 March 1948, Case No 72/1947 (Verdict 231) 351, 353
Mothers of Srebrenica and others v The State of the Netherlands and the United
    Nations, Judgment, 30 March 2010, The Hague Court of Appeal 386
Mothers of Srebrenica and others v The State of the Netherlands and the United
    Nations, Judgment, 23 April 2012, Supreme Court of the Netherlands............... 386
Mothers of Srebrenica v The State of the Netherlands and the United Nations,
    Judgment, 16 July 2014, District Court of The Hague 386
Mr P (Batavia) v Mrs S (Bandoeng), Netherlands East Indies, Court of Appeals,
    Batavia, Annual Digest Case n 118.................................... 1428
Nuhanović (the Case of Srebrenica), Judgment, 5 July 2011, The Hague Court of Appeal 386
Nuhanović (the Case of Srebrenica), Judgment, 6 September 2013, Supreme
    Court of the Netherlands... 386
Pilz, Judgment, 21 December 1949, District Court of The Hague (Special
    Criminal Chamber)... 822
Pilz, 5 July 1950, Special Court of Cassation 760, 822
Shipbuilding Yard 'Gusto', 2 September 1947, Special Criminal Court 1523
Sone Kenitji, 14 August 1946, Netherlands East Indies, Temporary Court Martial,
    Batavia, 13 *ILR* (1994) 299.. .747
Susuki Motosuke, 1948, *UNWCC Law Reports*, vol XIII, Netherlands Temporary
    Court-Martial, Amboina... 449, 463
Washio Awochi, 1946, *UNWCC Law Reports*, vol XIII, Netherlands Temporary
    Court-Martial .... .351

Norway

Trial of Hans Paul Helmuth Latza and Two Others, *UNWCC Law Reports*, vol XIV,
    18 February 1947–3 December 1948, Court of Appeal and Supreme Court........... 187
Trial of Kriminalassisstent Karl-Heinz Hermann Klinge, UNWCC, vol III,
    8 December 1945 and 27 February 1946, Eidsivating Lagmannsrett and
    Supreme Court 187
Trial of Kriminalsekretar Richard Wilhelm Hermann Bruns and Two Others, 1946, *UNWCC
    Law Reports*, vol III, Eidsivating Lagmannsrett and Supreme Court 582, 584

Poland

Marjamoff and others v Włocławek (Command District of), 5 December 1924,
    2 *AD* (1923–4), at 444–5, Supreme Court 1st Division 1527

Singapore

NV de Bataafsche Petroleum Maatschappij and others v The War Damage Commission,
    13 April 1956, 23 *ILR* (1956) 810, Court of Appeal 1525, 1545

Switzerland

A v Ministère public de la Confédération, Decision, 25 July 2012, BB.2011.140,
    Swiss Federal Tribunal... 634
Federal Supreme Court, ATF 124 III 90, Decision, 22 December 1997.................. 658
Federal Supreme Court, ATF 129 II 249, Decision, 17 January 2003..................... 658
Niyonteze Case, Decision, 26 May 2000, Swiss Military Appeals Chamber 1A............. 404
Niyonteze Case, 27 April 2001, Swiss Military Court of Cassation 76, 805

United Kingdom

Al-Skeini v Secretary of State for Defence [2004] EWHC 2911 (Admin) 1366, 1370–1
Al-Skeini and others v Secretary of State for Defence [2007] UKHL 26 1397
Amberger (The Dreierwalde Case), 1946, *UNWCC Law Reports*, vol I,
    British Military Court, Wuppertal 452
General von Mackensen and General Maelzer, 1945, *UNWCC Law Reports*,
    vol VIII, British Military Court, Rome 454, 582, 585
Gerike and Others (The Velpke Children's Home Case), 1946, *UNWCC Law
    Reports*, vol VII, British Military Court, Brunswick 457, 462, 747
Helmuth von Ruchteschell, 21 May 1947, *UNWCC Law Reports*, vol IX,
    British Military Court, Hamburg 747
Heering, *UNWCC Law Reports*, vol I, British Military Court Hanover 961, 965, 975
Heyer and others (Essen Lynching Case), 22 December 1945, [1947]
    1 LRTWC 88; *UNWCC Law Reports*, vol I, 18–19 and 21–22 December 1945,
    British Military Court, Essen 430, 747, 982
Kapitänleutnant Heinz Eck and four others (The Peleus Trial), 1945,
    UNWCC Law Reports, vol I, British Military Court, Hamburg 457, 822
Killinger and others (Dulag Luft Case), 3 December 1945, *UNWCC Law Reports*,
    vol III, British Military Court, Wupperthal 747
Kramer and others (The Belsen Trial), 1945, *UNWCC Law Reports*, vol II,
    British Military Court, Luneburg 454
Kurt Student, 1948, *UNWCC Law Reports*, vol IV, British Military
    Court, Lüneberg 1267
Mackensen, *UNWCC Law Reports*, vol XI, British Military Court,
    Hanover 961–2, 965, 975
Serdar Mohammed v Ministry of Defence [2014] EWHC 1369 (QB) 717, 933–4, 1342–3
Osman Bin Haji Mohamed Ali v Public Prosecutor 29 July 1969, [1969]
    1 AC 430 House of Lords Privy Council 893–4, 914, 945, 1030
Oie Hee Koi and connected appeal [1967] UKPC 21 (4 December 1967) 947, 1030–1, 1033
R v Bartle and the Commissioner of Police for the Metropolis and others,
    ex parte Pinochet [1998] UKHL 41; [1999] UKHL 17 707
R v Gul [2012] EWCA Crim 280 725
R v Zardad (Ruling on the Taking of Hostages Act), Judgment and rulings
    pursuant to second preparatory hearing, Case No T2203 7676; ILDC 264
    (UK 2004), 5 October 2004 .... 314, 708
R (Haidar Ali Hussein) v Secretary of State for Defence [2014] EWCA Civ 1087 729
Rahmatullah v Secretary of State for Foreign and Commonwealth Affairs and
    Secretary for Defence [2011] EWCA Civ 1540 924–5
Rahmatullah ('Rahmatullah II') [2012] EWCA Civ 182 924–5
Rahmatullah ('Rahmatullah III') [2012] UKSC 48 .... 924–5, 1142, 1145, 1386
Sandrock and others (The Almelo Trial), 1945, *UNWCC Law Reports*,
    vol I, British Military Court, Almelo 463
Zyklon B Case [1947] 1 LRTWC 93, 1–8 March 1946, British Military
    Court, Hamburg 430

United States

Al-Adahi v Barack Obama et al, No 09-5333, 13 July 2010, US Court of Appeals DC 68
Al-Bahlul v United States, Case No 11-1324, Doc No 1417123 (DC Cir,
    25 January 2013) 916
Al-Bahlul v United States, Case No 11-1324, Doc No 1502282 (DC Cir,
    14 July 2014) 916–17
Al Marri v Pucciarelli, 534 F 3d 213 (4th Cir 2008) 931

Alfried Felix Alwyn Krupp von Böhlen und Halbach and Eleven Others,
   UNWCC Law Reports, vol X, 17 November 1947–30 June 1948,
      US Military Tribunal, Nuremberg.................... 187, 1426, 1430, 1519, 1523, 1543
Altstötter and others (Justice Trial), 17 February–4 December 1947, *UNWCC
   Law Reports*, vol VI, US Military Tribunal, Nuremberg................ 186–7, 1441, 1520
American Civil Liberties Union v Department of Defense, No 06-3140-cv,
   22 September 2008, US Court of Appeals for the Second Circuit 984
Bauer, Schrameck and Falten, *UNWCC Law Reports*, vol VIII, Dijon 457, 1397
Belkacem Bensayah v Barack Obama et al, No 08-5537, 28 June 2010, US
   Court of Appeals DC... 68
Brandt Case (The Medical Trial), Judgment, 20 August 1947, US Military
   Tribunal, Nuremberg.. 983
Corrie et al v Caterpillar, 403 F Supp 2d 1019 (2005); 503 F 3d 974 (2007)........... 1518, 1534
Cutting Case, 1886 640
Territo (9th Cir) 156 F 2d 142 (1946)... 947
Franz Holstein and others, 1947, *UNWCC Law Reports*, vol VIII, Dijon 450, 454, 457
Flick Trial, *UNWCC Law Reports*, vol IX, US Military Tribunal, Nuremberg 183
General Tomoyuki Yamashita, 1946, *UNWCC Law Reports*, vol IV, US Military
   Commission, Manila.. .351
Griffen, Judgment, 2 July 1968, 39 CMR 586 (1968); pet. rev. den. 18 USCMA 622,
   39 CMR 293 (1968), US Army Board of Review 989
Grisl, Case 5-88, 24 February 1947, US Military Court, Salzburg....................... .747
Guantánamo Bay Cases, Judgment, 31 January 2005, 355 F Supp
   2d 443 (DDC 2005) .... .931, 1230
Guantánamo Bay Detainee Litigation, Misc No 08-442 (TFH)
   (DC Cir 13 March 2009).. .931, 1347
Hadamar Trial, [1947] 1 LRTWC 46, 8–15 October 1945, US Military
   Commission appointed by the Commanding General Western Military
   District, U.S.F.E.T., Wiesbaden, Germany 430–1
Haitian Centers Council Inc, 509 US 155 (1993)................................. 1057
Hamdan v Rumsfeld, 29 June 2006, 548 US 557 (2006), (2006) 126 S Ct 2749,
   US Supreme Court............ 29, 68, 78, 82, 402, 428, 471, 474, 916, 931, 951, 954, 1124,
                                                                    1220, 1229, 1439
Hamdan v United States ('Hamdan II'), 696 F 3d 1238 (DC Cir 2012).................... .916
Hamdi v Rumsfeld, 28 June 2004, 542 US 507 (2004) 930, 950, 1048, 1061, 1129, 1332
Hamlily v Obama, 616 F Supp 2d 63 (DDC 2009) .... .932, 1347
Hartley, 30 June 2011, US Army Court of Criminal Appeals......................... 452
Holder, Attorney General et al v Humanitarian Law Project et al, 561 US 25;
   130 S Ct (2010) 2705, 21 June 2010................................. 427, 503, 685
IG Farben Trial, 14 August 1947–29 July 1948, *UNWCC Law Reports*, vol X,
   US Military Tribunal, Nuremberg... .1530
James W. Duncan, GCMO 153, 8 June 1866..................................... 457
Khan, Stipulation of Fact, Prosecution Exhibit 001 (Khan), 13 February 2012 .... .916
Lindh, 212 F Supp 2d 541 (ED Va 2002)....................................... 659
List and others (The Hostages Trial), Judgment, 19 February 1948, US Military
   Tribunal, Nuremberg....... 132, 185, 187, 299–300, 454, 582, 585, 1070, 1167, 1396, 1401,
                                                              1406, 1457, 1541, 1547, 1594–6
Maqaleh v Gates, US Court of Appeals for the District Court of Columbia,
   21 May 2010, 605 F 3d 1048
Medellín v Texas, 552 US 491 (2008)... 658
Milch, *UNWCC Law Reports*, vol VII, 20 December 1946–17 April 1947,
   US Military Tribunal, Nuremberg... 187
Mukhtar Yahia Naki Al Warafi v Barack Obama et al, No 11-5276, May 2013,
   US Court of Appeals (District of Columbia) 814, 819

Mukhtar Yahia Naki Al Warafi v Barack Obama et al, Petition for a Writ
of Certiorari to the US Court of Appeals for the District of Columbia Circuit,
23 December 2013...815
Mukhtar Yahia Naki Al Warafi v Barack Obama et al, Denial of Petition for
Writ of Certiorari, 13-768, 5 May 2014..815
Noriega, District Court SD Florida, 746 F Supp 1506 (1990); 8 December 1992,
808 F Supp 791 (1992); 694 F Supp 2d 1268 (2007); 695 F Supp
2d 1358 (2007) 659, 943, 948, 970, 973, 1029–30, 1034, 1036–7
Ohlendorf et al (Einsatzgruppen Case), 10 April 1948, Military Tribunal,
Nuremberg 450, 454, 582
Quirin, ex parte, 31 July 1942, 317 US 1 (1942)..................... 913–14, 920, 947, 1124, 1127
Rasul v Bush, 28 June 2004, 542 US 466 (2004)...950, 1129
Roper v Simmons, No 03-633, 1 March 2005, US Supreme Court 483
Sabir, F 3d (2d Cir 4 February 2011), 27... 508
Schmid, 1947, *UNWCC Law Reports*, vol XIII, US General Military
Government Court, Dachau 294
Schultz, 1952 WL 2700 (CMA)... 457
Simpson v Socialist People's Libyan Arab Jamahiriya, 470 F 3d 356, No 05-7048,
21 November 2006, US Court of Appeals, District of Columbia 308
Weizsaecker et al (Ministries Trial) 14 April 1949, 16 *ILR* 344, US Military
Tribunal, Nuremberg..1523
Wilhelm von Leeb et al (High Command Case), Judgment, 27 October 1948,
15 *AD* 376, US Military Tribunal, Nuremberg........................... 965, 1267, 1513
Yamashita, US Supreme Court, 327 US 1, 4 February 1946........................... 627, 640

Table of Legislation

INTERNATIONAL INSTRUMENTS

1648 Westphalian Treaties. 89
1820 Tratado Armisticio between Spain and Colombia
    Art 14 180
1856 Paris Declaration. 768
1863 ICRC Resolutions of the International Conference, Geneva, 26–29 October 526, 858
1863 Lieber Code (General Order No 100, Instructions for the Government of Armies of the United States in the Field) 318, 347, 935, 1226, 1450
    Art 14 . . . . 1495, 1547
    Art 16 323
    Art 22 347
    Art 23 450
    Art 28 580
    Art 31 1546
    Art 34 1546
    Art 35 1546
    Art 37 347
    Art 44 . . . . 347, 434, 1226, 1345, 1536
    Art 47 . . . . 347, 450, 1226, 1345
    Art 49 . . . . 434, 893
    Art 71 . . . . 434, 450
    Art 79 434
    Art 88 1126
    Art 148 450
    Art 155 434
    Art 156 434
1864 Geneva Convention on the Amelioration of the Condition of the Wounded in Armies in the Field 52, 88, 114, 161, 163, 176, 191, 217, 347, 527, 544, 655, 689, 694, 758–60, 770, 782, 808, 825, 840, 858, 879
    Arts 1–7. 782
    Art 1 . . . . 209, 217, 758
    Art 2 758
    Art 6 . . . . 234, 758–9
    Art 7 . . . . 209, 758, 858
    Art 8 114
1868 Additional Articles Relating to the Condition of the Wounded in War
    Arts 6–14. 770
    Art 11 759
1868 St Petersburg Declaration 177, 180, 318, 689, 936, 1136
    Preamble, para 2 1136
1874 Project of an International Declaration Concerning the Laws and Customs of War (Brussels Declaration) 894
    Arts 1–8 1457
    Art 6 1524–5
    Arts 9–11. 912
    Art 13(h) 1516
1899 Hague Convention (II) with Respect to the Laws and Customs of War on Land 52, 177, 180, 234, 318, 563, 599, 657, 689, 695–6, 978
    Preamble 179, 181–2, 318, 673, 926
    Preamble, para 8 179
    Art 1 599
1899 Regulations concerning the Laws and Customs of War on Land, Annexed to Convention (II) with Respect to the Laws and Customs of War on Land (Hague Regulations) 234, 260, 599, 696, 907, 958, 978, 1457, 1523
    Section I, Ch II 696
    Arts 4–20 696
    Art 6(2) 696
    Art 12 696
    Art 14 . . . . 260, 957
    Art 23 . . . . 696, 727
    Arts 32–34 696
    Arts 36–41 696
    Art 42 696
    Art 43 234
    Art 47 785
    Ch II 696
    Section II. 696
    Section III. 696

1899 Hague Convention (III) for the
  Adaptation to Maritime Warfare of the
  Principles of the Geneva Convention of
  1864, 27 July 177, 695, 770
  Arts 1–6 209
  Art 9 771
  Art 11 7
1906 Geneva Convention for the
  Amelioration of the Condition
  of the Wounded and Sick in Armies
  in the Field 52, 114, 161,
    176, 209, 218, 599, 689, 694, 758, 770
  Art 1 . . . . .217, 234, 655, 695, 759, 771
  Art 2 771
  Art 3 260
  Art 4 260
  Art 9 132
  Art 25 114
  Art 26 599
1907 Hague Convention (III) Relative
  to the Opening of Hostilities,
  18 October 5, 54
  Art 1 5
  Art 2 5
1907 Hague Convention (IV) Respecting
  the Laws and Customs of War
  on Land 323, 347, 599, 617, 696, 1536
  Preamble, para 5 1536
  Art 1 599
  Art 3 . . . . 337, 340, 386, 752, 934,
      975, 981, 1252–3, 1307, 1344
1907 Hague Regulations Concerning
  the Laws and Customs of War
  on Land 52, 57, 59, 158, 175–6, 187, 260,
      376, 580, 599, 672, 689, 696–7,
      893–4, 906, 914, 917, 919, 945, 958,
      978, 1070, 1073, 1075, 1078,
      1138–40, 1136–7, 1143, 1153, 1167,
      1169, 1226, 1242–4, 1259, 1262, 1391,
      1393, 1398, 1405, 1408–9, 1412, 1418,
      1423, 1432, 1438, 1457–8, 1460–1,
      1463, 1468–9, 1471, 1476–7, 1479,
      1486, 1500, 1506, 1523, 1530, 1536,
      1538, 1549–50, 1552, 1561, 1593, 1596
  Arts 1–3. 912
  Art 1 . . . . 347, 893, 895, 912, 1138
  Art 2 . . . . .893, 1395, 1397
  Art 3 . . . . 893, 1169, 1252
  Art 4 . . . . .323, 1137
  Art 6(2) 696
  Art 12 696
  Art 14 957
  Art 23 . . . . 696, 1263, 1517
  Art 23(g) 1495, 1516, 1518–20,
      1524, 1529, 1536–7
  Art 23(h) 1431, 1520
  Art 23(2) 1429
  Art 25 . . . . 210, 376, 379, 1136
  Art 27 . . . . 209, 1528, 1532
  Art 28 . . . . 1516, 1520
  Art 29 1126
  Art 30 . . . . .1030, 1131
  Arts 32–34 696
  Arts 36–41 696
  Arts 42–56 1486
  Art 42 . . . . .74, 696, 920, 1074, 1391,
      1393, 1414, 1560, 1593–4
  Art 43 . . . . 175, 1245, 1251, 1299,
      1391, 1397–8, 1401, 1412–13, 1422–3,
      1425–6, 1428, 1432, 1452, 1456, 1461,
      1466, 1469, 1479, 1486, 1488–9,
      1491–3, 1503–4, 1506, 1509,
      1520, 1527, 1552, 1561
  Art 44 . . . . 1256, 1412, 1466, 1469
  Art 45 . . . . 1142, 1461, 1466, 1469
  Arts 46–56 1391
  Art 46 . . . . 323, 347–8, 351, 936,
      1137, 1244, 1246, 1469–70,
      1472, 1474,1476–7, 1520,
      1522,1524, 1552
  Art 46(1) .742, 1522
  Art 46(2) 1522–4, 1527, 1537
  Art 47 . . . . .785, 1521
  Art 48 . . . . 1477, 1479, 1506
  Art 49 . . . . 1477, 1479, 1482, 1506
  Art 50 . . . . 1141, 1156, 1158, 1161,
      1167, 1440
  Art 51 . . . . 1477, 1479, 1506
  Art 52 . . . . .1477, 1482, 1495, 1506,
      1521–5, 1528
  Art 52(1) 1137, 1495, 1523
  Art 52(2) 1137, 1523
  Art 52(3) .1495, 1523
  Art 53 . . . . 1525, 1536–7, 1541, 1544–6
  Art 53(1) 1545
  Art 53(2) 1521–2, 1524, 1526
  Art 55 . . . . 175, 827, 1477, 1536–7,
      1541–2, 1544, 1548
  Art 56 . . . . 222, 1478, 1528, 1532
  Art 56(1) 1528
  Art 56(2) 1528
  Ch II 696
  Section II 71, 696, 1516, 1519
  Section III 696, 1393, 1516, 1519

Table of Legislation

1907 Hague Convention (V) Respecting
the Rights and Duties of Neutral
Powers and Persons in Case of War
on Land 89–90, 1147
  Art 1 89
  Art 2 . . . . .89, 102
  Art 3 89
  Art 4 . . . . .89, 102
  Art 5 102–3
  Arts 6–7 89
  Art 6 102
  Art 9 102
  Art 10 89
  Art 11 . . . . 98, 908
  Art 13 98
  Art 14 101
  Art 14(2) 1045
1907 Hague Convention (IX)
Concerning Bombardment by
Naval Forces in Time of War
  Art 5 . . . . .209, 1528
  Art 7 1520
1907 Hague Convention (X) for the
Adaptation to Maritime Warfare
of the Principles of the Geneva
Convention 114, 161, 175,
                617, 694–5, 770–1
  Arts 1–9. 209
  Art 11 771
  Art 14 771
  Art 16 .785, 1520
  Art 18 177
  Art 19 114
  Art 21(1) 1520
  Art 25 695
1907 Hague Convention (XI) Relative
to Certain Restrictions with Regard
to the Exercise of the Right of Capture
in Naval Warfare
  Art 6 101
1907 Hague Convention (XIII)
Concerning the Rights and Duties
of Neutral Powers in
Naval War 89–90, 222
  Art 5 99
  Art 6 90
  Art 7 89
  Art 8 90
  Art 21 100
  Art 24 99
1909 Declaration Concerning the Laws of
Naval War (London Declaration) 90

  Art 63 771
1912 Draft Convention on the Role
of the Red Cross during
Civil War 79, 234
1919 Covenant of the League of Nations,
  Art 18 171
1919 Versailles Treaty
  Art 227 348
1920 Permanent Court of International
  Justice Statute 181
  Art 38(1)(c) 180
1921 German–Swiss Arbitration
  Treaty 563
1925 Treaty of Arbitration and
Conciliation between France and
Switzerland 563
1926 Slavery, Servitude, Forced
Labour and Similar Institutions and
Practices Convention
  Art 5 1499
1928 Havana Convention on Maritime
Neutrality 91
1929 Geneva Convention for the
Amelioration of the Condition
of the Wounded and Sick in Armies
in the Field (1929 GC I) 7, 52,
         132, 161, 176–7, 209, 300, 569,
           655, 689, 694–5, 758–60,
           770, 784, 862, 876, 879
  Art 1 . . . . .132, 217
  Art 3 785
  Art 3(1) 1520
  Art 4 260
  Art 9 132
  Art 18 830
  Art 25(1) 114, 132
  Art 27 599
  Art 28 876
  Art 30 . . . . 564, 568
  Art 38(3) 177
1929 Geneva Convention Relative
to the Treatment of Prisoners
of War (1929 GC II) 7, 132,
      176–7, 348, 550, 563, 565–6, 580,
      694–5, 790, 890, 906, 957–8, 966,
      975, 978, 980, 1040, 1262, 1350
  Art 1(1) 891
  Art 2(3) 577, 580
  Art 3 . . . . 348–9, 351, 357, 785
  Art 7 . . . . 957, 961, 989
  Art 8(2) 1090
  Art 11(4) 1159

Art 17 1299	Art 1 . . . . .935, 1345
Art 25 957	Art 6(b). 450, 1531–2, 1554
Art 26 957	Art 6(c) 1210
Arts 27–34. 1263	Art 7 634
Art 36(2) 1090	1945 Potsdam Agreement 1553
Art 46(3) 1257	Section VI. 1553
Art 46(4) 1159	Section IX(b). 1553
Art 56 . . . . .957, 972	Section XIII. .1553
Art 77 1090	1945 Statute of the International
Art 79 1113	Court of Justice
Art 82(1) 114	Art 36 1570
Art 83(3) 563	Art 38(1) 136
Art 84 599	Art 38(1)(a) 136
Art 86 550	Art 38(1)(b). 136, 1566–7
Art 87 563	Art 38(1)(c) 181, 186
Art 88 . . . . .242, 250, 533	1945 UN Charter. 4, 10, 14, 19–20, 27,
Art 89 696	86, 91, 129, 158, 171, 174,
Art 96(3) 177	638, 708, 1216, 1386,
1930 ILO Convention concerning	1403, 1484, 1588
Forced or Compulsory Labour	Art 1(3) 194, 1260, 1272
(No 29) 1263	Art 2(3) 4
Art 1 1370	Art 2(4) 4, 128, 1136, 1181, 1559
Art 2(1) 1263, 1499	Art 24 1427
Art 2(2) 1263, 1499	Art 25 1427
Art 2(2)(d). 1263	Art 27(3) 1407
1934 Draft International Convention	Art 39 . . . . 380, 385
on the Condition and Protection	Art 40 380
of Civilians of enemy nationality	Art 41 91
who are on territory belonging to	Art 42 91
or occupied by a belligerent ('Tokyo	Art 43 91
Draft'). 1073, 1140, 1242, 1350, 1516	Art 55 1260
Art 1 1073	Art 56 1260
Art 1(b) 1073	Art 102 171
Art 15 1350	Art 103 . . . . 10, 505, 638, 692, 1342,
Art 16 1350	1406, 1427, 1588
Art 17 1350	Ch VII. 9, 86, 232, 235, 244, 250,
1936 London Submarine Protocol 772	380, 399, 637, 685, 934,
1938 Draft Convention for the Protection	937, 1386, 1414, 1427
of Civilian Populations against	Ch VIII. 380
New Engines of War 1137	1946 Charter of the International
1938 Protection of Civilian Populations	Military Tribunal for the Far East
against Bombing from the Air in	(Tokyo Charter) 1228
Case of War, Resolution of the	Art V(c) 1210
League of Nations Assembly 1137	1946 Draft Convention on the
1944 Chicago Convention on	Protection of Children in the
International Civil Aviation. 1480	Event of International Conflict
1945 London Agreement for the	or Civil War. 1294
Prosecution and Punishment of	1946 UNGA Res 95(I). 1167
the Major War Criminals of the	1947 Chinese Workers' and Peasants'
European Axis, and Establishing	Red Army, Three Main Rules of
the Charter of the International	Discipline and the Eight Points for
Military Tribunal 331, 1167, 1228	Attention. 312

Table of Legislation

1947 Memorandum of Understanding between the United States of America and France on Repatriation and Liberation of Prisoners of War
    para 2(J) 966
1947 Universal Postal Convention 1108
1948 American Declaration of the Rights and Duties of Man. 722, 1339, 1346
    Art I. 1339
    Art XXV 1339
    Art XXV(3) 1339
    Art XXVI 1228
1948 Charter of the Organization of American States. 722
1948 Convention on the Prevention and Punishment of the Crime of Genocide 180, 185, 252, 636–7
    Art I. 121, 129, 131–2
    Art III 623
    Art III, lit e) 131
    Art V 623
    Art VI 637–8
    Art VIII. 129
1948 Universal Declaration of Human Rights 187, 242, 660, 680, 702, 707, 1216, 1244, 1314, 1352–3, 1504
    Art 1 349
    Art 2 194
    Art 4 1499
    Art 5 1248
    Art 6 1353
    Art 7 194
    Art 10 1216
    Art 11 .... 1216, 1225, 1228
    Art 11(2) 719
    Art 12 .... 1093, 1096, 1244
    Art 13 1174
    Art 21(3) 1390
    Art 26(2) 1502
    Art 27 1247
1949 Convention for the Amelioration of the Condition of the Wounded and Sick in Armed Forces in the Field (Geneva Convention I)
    Preamble 694
    Arts 1–12. 58
    Art 1 (Common Article) 9, 104, 107, 111–34, 170, 236, 313, 338, 416, 418, 507, 520, 598, 610, 631, 648, 673, 1139, 1210, 1417–18, 1426

    Art 2 (Common Article) 3–26, 28–41, 45–50, 52–5, 74, 140, 263, 396–400, 402, 519, 897, 906, 1139, 1405
    Art 2(1) 5, 116, 132, 1405
    Art 2(2) 6–7, 74, 1392, 1405, 1413–14, 1576, 1585
    Art 2(3) 7–8, 165
    Art 3 (Common Article) 24, 26, 28–9, 31–50, 53–5, 59–62, 65, 68–9, 75–83, 107, 115, 126, 151–2, 170, 204, 227, 235–6, 249–51, 255, 272, 292–3, 310, 319, 339–40, 344, 362–3, 370, 391–524, 541, 571, 577, 587–90, 600, 610–12, 642–3, 646, 656, 674, 683, 698–700, 708–10, 719–20, 722, 725–6, 744–6, 749, 758, 765, 783, 798–9, 804–5, 819–20, 835, 837, 849, 852, 859, 885, 912, 919, 921, 926–9, 931, 933–4, 951, 973, 1007, 1086–7, 1115, 1131, 1149–50, 1164, 1166, 1168, 1177, 1182, 1186, 1205, 1247–8, 1259, 1265–7, 1285–6, 1306, 1318, 1342, 1367, 1383, 1567
    Art 3(para 1)(1) 192, 201, 436–47, 765, 1266
    Art 3(para 1)(1)(a) 323, 330, 335–7, 359–61, 449–67, 492, 748, 1266, 1285
    Art 3(para 1)(1)(b) 298, 303, 309–13, 315, 1383
    Art 3(para 1)(1)(c) 332–3, 335–7, 349, 359–61, 1248–9, 1267, 1285
    Art 3(para 1)(1)(d) 442, 469–94, 802, 954, 1216, 1217, 1219–24, 1232, 1237–9, 1433, 1438–9, 1450–1, 1452
    Art 3(para 1)(2) 75, 223–4, 249, 445–6, 765, 798, 834, 837
    Art 3(para 2) 250, 255, 495–508, 530, 533–4, 536, 762–3, 765, 798–802, 809, 819–20, 835, 837, 849
    Art 3(para 3) 312, 370, 378–9, 509–21, 973
    Art 3(para 4) 425–426
    Art 4 .... 92, 95, 97, 105, 783, 811
    Art 5 .... 52, 56–7, 70, 1070
    Art 6 .... 135–45, 149, 151, 513–14, 810, 1404
    Art 7 .... 140–1, 145–53, 810
    Art 8 .... 92, 243, 549–60
    Art 9 .... 196, 236, 250, 497–8, 506, 530, 532–3, 811
    Art 10 ..... 92, 137, 530, 533, 550, 552, 557
    Art 11 .... 92, 530, 563, 566
    Arts 12–17. 810

Art 12 . . . . . . 15, 197–8, 201, 232, 236, 299,
    319, 330, 348, 359, 445, 760, 762, 784,
    786, 789, 793–4, 796, 798–799, 801,
    809, 818, 960, 1272–4, 1277, 1285
Art 12(1) 760, 784–5
Art 12(2) 192, 196–7, 323,
    784–5, 790–1, 813
Art 12(3) 197, 790
Art 12(4) 197, 791, 1272–4, 1285
Art 12(5) 655, 793, 960
Art 13 . . . . 213, 236, 643, 757–765,
    773, 1273. See also
    entries for Art 4 GC III.
Art 13(3) 21
Art 14 . . . . 760–1, 783, 789, 793, 960
Art 15 . . . . 137, 269, 278, 280, 286–8,
    655, 744, 785–8, 794, 960
Art 15(1) 279, 787, 1520
Art 15(2) 787
Art 15(3) 787
Art 16 . . . . . 261, 278, 280–1, 289, 785, 789
Art 16(1) 260, 263–4, 280
Art 16(1)(f) 262–3
Art 16(2) 260, 265–7, 278
Art 16(2)(a)–(h) 789
Art 16(3) 260, 263, 266, 278–9,
    280–1, 291, 553
Art 17 288–90
Art 17(1) 263, 278, 280, 286
Art 17(2) 279, 289
Art 17(3) 279, 287, 289, 291
Art 18 . . . . . 210, 655, 784, 793, 795–6, 812
Art 18(2) 192, 197, 796
Art 18(4) 811
Arts 19–25 866
Art 19 . . . . 209–10, 213, 217, 221,
    650, 785, 817, 825–6
Art 19(1) 217, 221, 650, 745, 825
Art 19(2) 213, 650–1
Art 20 . . . . 70, 209, 228, 743, 745
Arts 21–22 841
Art 21 . . . . 209, 816, 825–6, 842, 848
Art 22 . . . . 209, 218–19, 825–6, 841,
    843, 846
Art 22(1) 219, 817, 844
Art 22(1)(2) 219
Art 22(2) 846
Art 22(3) 219, 845
Art 22(4) 219, 846
Art 22(5) 219, 794, 845
Art 23 . . . . 137, 170, 370–1, 373,
    378, 385, 532, 651
Art 23(1) 371
Art 23(2) 371
Art 23(3) 371, 554
Arts 24–32 793
Arts 24–26 241
Art 24 . . . . 97, 101, 132, 745, 785,
    808, 810, 813–15, 840, 866
Art 25 . . . . 810, 818
Arts 26–27 866
Art 26 . . . . 97, 170, 210, 232, 650,
    810–11, 826–7, 869
Art 27 . . . . 97, 210, 232, 811, 815
Arts 28–32 818
Art 28 . . . . 137, 818, 849
Art 28(1) 101
Art 28(2)(c) 818
Art 29 818
Art 30 818
Art 31 . . . . 137, 192, 197, 655, 818
Art 32 . . . . 97, 811
Arts 33–36 225
Art 33 826–8
Art 33(1) 827
Art 33(2) 825, 827–8
Art 33(3) 828, 836
Art 34 . . . . 826, 866
Arts 35–36 866
Art 35 . . . . 826, 829, 1526
Art 35(1) 745, 784, 828–9
Art 35(2) 829
Arts 36–37 841
Art 36 . . . . 137, 826, 829, 838, 860
Art 36(1) 100, 745, 831
Art 36(2) 830
Art 36(3) 830–1
Art 36(4) 830
Art 36(5) 830
Art 37 . . . . 92, 100, 137, 197,
    242, 826, 829–30, 838
Art 37(1) 830
Art 37(2) 100
Art 37(3) 100, 831
Art 38 . . . . 814, 859–61, 864–5, 879
Arts 39–44 866
Art 39 . . . . 860, 871
Art 40 . . . . 814–15, 860, 866
Art 40(2) 262–3
Art 40(3) 262
Art 41 . . . . 815, 860
Arts 42–44 . . . . 650, 866
Art 42 . . . . 212, 650, 860, 882
Art 42(4) 863
Art 43 860
Art 44 . . . . 170, 650, 860, 862–3, 865, 870, 872

Art 44(1) 861, 866–7
Art 44(2) 867, 870
Art 44(3) 868, 870
Art 44(4) 867, 870
Art 45 .... 114, 598, 600, 603, 654
Art 46 .... 218, 577, 580, 785, 1163–4
Arts 47–48 652
Art 47 .... 63, 116, 119–20, 170, 597,
       599, 602, 604–5, 610, 653, 873
Art 48 .... 63, 160, 172, 554, 653
Art 49 .... 63, 103, 119, 251, 339,
       569, 619, 621, 626, 714, 803, 821,
       935, 1216, 1226, 1287, 1345
Art 49(2) 656
Art 49(3) 741, 656, 752
Art 49(4) 656, 1225
Art 50 ...... 225, 275, 299, 330, 339, 385,
       450, 619–20, 656, 714, 739, 758,
       785, 803, 821, 844, 851,
       935, 1286, 1310, 1530
Art 51 .... 632, 934, 1344
Art 52 .... 137, 564, 569
Art 52(1) 569
Art 53 .... 63, 650, 662, 808, 853,
       860–1, 873–5
Art 54 .... 63, 119, 650, 662,
       860, 873–6
Art 55 .... 158, 653
Arts 56–58 160
Art 56 161
Art 57(2) 162, 171
Art 58 162–3
Art 58(2) 169–70
Art 59 .... 176, 694
Art 60 163
Art 61(2) 171
Art 62 .... 165, 170
Art 63 176
Art 63(4) 176–9
Art 64 171
Annex I 370–3
Annex I, Art 2 372
Annex I, Art 3 372
Annex I, Art 11 372
Annex II 262, 814
1949 Convention for the Amelioration of
   the Condition of the Wounded, Sick and
   Shipwrecked Members of Armed Forces at
   Sea (Geneva Convention II)
   Art 1 See Geneva Convention I,
      Art 1 above
   Art 2 See Geneva Convention I,
      Art 2 above

Art 3 See Geneva Convention I, Art 3
   above. For GC II in particular,
   see 445–7 and 798
Art 4 .... 70, 783
Art 4(2) 70
Art 5 .... 92, 95, 97, 105, 783
Art 6 ......135–45, 149, 151, 513–14, 1404
Art 7 .... 140–1, 145–53
Art 8 .... 243, 549–60
Art 9 .... 196, 236, 250, 497–8,
       506, 530, 532–3
Art 10 .... 92, 530, 533, 550, 552, 557
Art 11 .... 92, 530, 563, 566
Arts 12–21 773
Art 12 .... 56, 132, 198, 22, 236,
       299, 319, 330, 348, 359, 445, 760,
       762, 769, 784, 789–90, 794, 796,
       798–9, 1272–4, 1285
Art 12(1) 784
Art 12(2) 192, 197, 323, 789, 791
Art 12(3) 790
Art 12(4) 791, 1272–4, 1285
Art 13 .... 232, 236, 643, 760,
       769–70, 773–4, 777–779, 1273.
       See also entries for Art 4 GC III below.
Art 13(1)–(4) 774
Art 13(3) 21
Art 13(5) 773–4, 776–7, 780
Art 13(6) 774
Art 14 787
Art 15 98
Art 16 .... 70, 760, 769, 777,
       783, 789, 793, 960
Art 17 92
Art 18 .... 269, 280, 744, 786–8, 794
Art 18(1) 278, 286, 787
Art 18(2) 279, 787
Art 19 .... 261, 278, 280–1
Art 19(1) 260, 263–4, 280
Art 19(1)(f) 262–3
Art 19(2) 260, 265, 267, 278, 553
Art 19(2)(a)–(h) 789
Art 19(3) 260, 263, 266, 278–81, 291
Art 20 .... 264, 279, 289
Art 20(1) 263, 278, 280, 286
Art 20(2) 279
Art 21 .... 232, 812
Art 21(2) 795
Art 21(3) 796
Arts 22–35 832
Arts 22–23 .... 209, 866
Art 22 .... 214–16, 221, 232, 557,
       826, 832–3

Art 22(1) 217, 745
Art 22(2) 214
Art 23 . . . . 70, 209, 228, 745, 826
Arts 24–27 826
Arts 24–25 866
Art 24 . . . . 215–16, 833
Art 24(1) 745
Art 25 . . . . 215–16, 811, 833
Arts 26–28 866
Art 26 . . . . 214, 216, 832
Art 27 . . . . 215–16, 832, 834, 866
Art 27(1) 745
Art 27(2) 216
Art 28 . . . . 216, 222, 228, 826, 832
Arts 29–35 826
Art 29 . . . . 221, 228, 833
Art 30 232
Art 30(4) 216
Art 31 . . . . 220–1, 834
Art 31(1) 221
Art 31(4) 220
Art 32 . . . . 92, 833
Art 33 215
Arts 34–37 866
Arts 34–35 841
Art 34 . . . . .220, 833, 842, 848
Art 34(2) 833
Art 34(4) 794
Art 35 . . . . 209, 219–20, 841, 843, 846
Art 35(1) 833, 844
Art 35(3) 845
Art 35(4) 845
Art 36 . . . . 97, 745, 813, 815–16, 840
Art 37 . . . . 97, 816, 819
Art 38 .826, 832, 834
Arts 39–40 841
Art 39 . . . . 826, 829, 841, 866
Art 39(1) 100
Art 39(2) 830
Art 39(3) 830
Art 40 . . . . 92, 100, 197, 826, 829
Art 40(2) 100
Art 40(3) 100
Arts 41–44 866
Art 41 860
Art 42 860
Art 42(2) 262–3
Art 42(3) 262
Arts 43–44 650
Art 43 . . . . .216, 860
Art 43(2) 816
Arts 44–45 .650, 853
Art 44 . . . . .170, 860
Art 45 . . . . .119, 860, 875–6
Art 46 . . . . 114, 598, 600, 603, 654
Art 47 . . . . 218, 577, 580, 785, 1163–4
Arts 48–49 652
Art 48 . . . . 63, 116, 119–20, 170, 598,
            602, 604–5, 653, 873
Art 49 . . . . 63, 160, 172, 554, 653
Art 50 . . . . 63, 103, 119, 251, 330, 339,
            569, 619, 621, 626, 714, 803,
            935, 1216, 1226, 1287, 1345
Art 50(2) 656
Art 50(3) 656, 741, 752
Art 50(4) 656, 1225
Art 51 . . . . 225, 275, 299, 450, 619–20,
            656, 714, 739, 758, 780, 803,
            844, 851, 935, 1286, 1310
Art 52 . . . . 632, 934, 1344
Art 53 . . . . 564, 569
Art 53(1) 569
Art 54 . . . . .158, 653
Arts 55–57 160
Art 55 161
Art 56(2) 162, 171
Art 57 162
Art 57(2) 169–70
Art 58 . . . . .175, 695
Art 59 163
Art 60(2) 171
Art 61 . . . . .165, 170
Art 62 176
Art 62(4) 176–9
Art 63 171
Annex 262

1949 Convention Relative to the
Treatment of Prisoners of War
(Geneva Convention III)
Art 1 *See* Geneva Convention I,
    Art 1 above
Art 2 *See* Geneva Convention I,
    Art 2 above
Art 3 *See* Geneva Convention I,
    Art 3 above
Art 4 . . . . 92, 643, 760–1,
        783, 889–909, 912–17, 919–20, 923,
        929, 933, 940, 943–4, 946–7, 950,
            952, 1031, 1070, 1138, 1343
Art 4(A) 716, 773, 891–908, 912–17
Art 4(A)(1) 18, 893–6, 905, 908, 914
Art 4(A)(2) 18, 26, 397–8, 403,
        893–905, 908–9, 913–14, 918, 922,
            936, 943–6, 968, 1047, 1396
Art 4(A)(2)(a)–(d) 898–905, 913–14
Art 4(A)(2)(a) 898–9, 903

Art 4(A)(2)(b) 899–901, 903
Art 4(A)(2)(c). 901
Art 4(A)(2)(d) 901–3, 946
Art 4(A)(3). 21, 905–6, 908, 944
Art 4(A)(4)–(6) 1028
Art 4(A)(4) 101, 262, 906–9, 946,
                      1026, 1331, 1433
Art 4(A)(5) 101, 907–9, 1026
Art 4(A)(6) 907–8, 1393, 1395
Art 4(B). 891, 908
Art 4(B)(1). 908, 1047, 1393
Art 4(B)(2). 4, 92, 95–8, 908,
                           968, 1045
Art 4(C). 818, 999
Art 5 .... 52, 57, 70, 749, 890, 892,
       895, 913, 939–55, 979, 1029, 1343
Art 5(1) 56, 140, 970, 980, 1029,
              1031, 1049, 1057, 1059–60
Art 5(2) 56, 642, 939–52, 954,
                             980, 1030
Art 6 .... 135–145, 149, 151, 513–14,
          969, 1026, 1044–5, 1054, 1404
Art 6(1) 1042
Art 7 .... 140–1, 145–53, 953,
              1026, 1036, 1044, 1052, 1056
Art 8 .... 243, 549–60, 1035
Art 9 .... 196, 236, 250, 497–8, 506,
                             530, 532–3
Art 10 ....92, 530, 533, 550, 552, 557, 1033
Art 11 .... 92, 530, 563, 566
Arts 12–16. 979
Art 12 .... 485, 715, 749, 925,
              928, 972, 975, 1036–7, 1045,
                      1064–5, 1252, 1385
Art 12(1) 968, 981–2
Art 12(2) 958, 960, 966–9, 971–2,
                      974–6, 1045, 1199
Art 12(3) 958, 960, 967–8,
                      970–2, 976, 1049, 1059
Art 13 .... 15, 286, 295, 299, 319, 333,
              357–8, 749, 791, 798, 959,
              962, 982, 984, 998, 1249
Art 13(1) 330, 790, 983
Art 13(2) 791, 984
Art 13(3) 577, 580, 982, 1050, 1163–4
Art 14 .... 132, 192, 319, 333, 344,
              348–50, 357–9, 1272–5, 1284
Art 14(1) 330, 982
Art 14(2) 198, 357, 987, 1281–2
Art 14(3) 980, 984–5, 1020
Art 15 .... 985, 1003
Art 16 .... 192, 198, 265, 350, 986,
              1032, 1272, 1284, 1297

Arts 17–108. 979
Arts 17–20. 979
Art 17 .... .261, 335, 358, 789,
                         1016, 1030
Art 17(1) 262, 264–5, 963, 992
Art 17(2) 992
Art 17(3) 261–2, 264, 323,
                         326–78, 992
Art 17(4) 319, 992, 1017
Art 17(5) 265
Art 17(6) 264
Art 18 .... 744, 994
Art 18(1) 993, 1520
Art 18(2) 992
Art 18(3) 993
Art 18(4) 994
Art 18(5) 994
Art 18(6) 994
Art 19 .... 534, 787, 957–61,
                             963, 975–6
Art 19(1) 959–61, 988, 990
Art 19(2) 787, 959, 988
Art 19(3) 959, 988
Art 20 .... 787, 798, 958, 960–3,
                             965, 975–6
Art 20(1) 962, 965, 988
Art 20(2) 961, 965–6, 988, 992
Art 20(3) 989
Art 20(4) 962
Arts 21–24. 979
Art 21 .... .310, 716
Art 21(1) 995
Art 21(2) 995
Art 21(3) 995
Art 22 .... 791, 980
Art 22(1) 972, 995–6
Art 22(2) 996
Art 22(3) 986
Art 23 .... 199, 959, 963
Art 23(1) 990
Art 23(2) 991
Art 23(3) 553, 991
Art 23(4) 991
Art 24 .... 199, 962, 990
Arts 25–28 979
Art 25 .... 358–9, 1281
Art 25(1) 996–7
Art 25(2) 996
Art 25(3) 997
Art 25(4) 192, 198, 359, 987
Art 26 791
Art 26(1) 997, 1284
Art 26(3) 997–8

Art 26(4)	997
Art 26(5)	997
Art 26(6)	1156, 1159
Art 27	791, 997
Art 28	997
Art 28(2)	998
Art 28(3)	998
Arts 29–32	979
Art 29	358, 791, 998, 1281
Art 29(1)	1282
Art 29(2)	987, 1282–3
Art 29(3)	1282
Art 30	535, 1003
Art 30(1)	999
Art 30(3)	999
Art 31	999
Art 32	199, 999
Art 33	818, 849, 979, 999
Art 33(1)	1000
Art 33(2)	1000
Arts 34–38	979
Art 34	198, 232, 791, 1000
Art 34(2)	198
Art 35	199, 1000
Art 36	999
Art 37	232, 1000
Art 38	662, 1000, 1300
Arts 39–42	979
Art 39	598, 603, 1032, 1034
Art 39(1)	1001
Art 39(2)	1001
Art 39(3)	265, 1001
Art 40	265, 899, 993
Art 41	598, 603, 653, 1001, 1032
Art 41(1)	160
Art 42	983, 1033
Arts 43–45	979
Art 43	198, 1002
Art 44	265, 1001
Art 45	265, 1001
Arts 46–48	958–9, 963, 972, 979, 990
Art 46	798, 958, 963, 975–6
Art 46(1)	972
Art 46(2)	965
Art 46(3)	965–6
Art 47	957, 975–6
Art 48	957
Art 48(2)	965
Art 48(3)	965
Arts 49–57	979, 1263
Art 49	198, 265, 350, 358, 744, 1032, 1284
Art 49(1)	987, 1002
Art 49(2)	1002
Art 49(3)	1002
Art 50	534, 744, 1003
Art 51	199, 744, 1003
Art 52	199, 744, 1003
Art 53	1003
Art 54	535
Art 54(1)	1004
Art 54(2)	1003
Art 55	1003
Art 56	246, 532
Art 56(3)	553
Art 57(1)	981
Arts 58–68	979
Art 58(1)	994, 1005
Art 58(2)	1005
Art 59	994
Art 60	1004, 1028, 1032
Art 60(3)	1004
Art 60(4)	553
Art 61	1004
Art 62	1004, 1028, 1032
Art 62(1)	554
Art 62(2)	999
Art 63(1)	1004
Art 63(2)	1005
Art 63(3)	554, 1005–6
Art 63(4)	1005
Art 64	1004
Art 65	1005
Art 65(1)	1005
Art 65(2)	554, 1005
Art 66	1005
Art 66(1)	554
Art 68	535
Art 68(1)	554, 1004
Art 68(2)	994
Arts 69–77	979
Art 69	554, 1006, 1014
Art 70	535, 1006, 1014, 1016–18, 1021–2
Art 71	1006, 1014, 1021
Art 71(1)	554
Art 71(2)	1022
Arts 72–75	1006, 1014
Art 72	532, 536, 1023
Art 72(1)	246, 1023
Art 72(2)	246
Art 72(3)	246, 554
Art 72(4)	246
Art 73	246, 532, 536, 1023
Art 73(3)	555
Arts 74–75	1014, 1016

Art 74 535	Art 97(2) 1282
Art 75 . . . . 532, 535–6	Art 97(3) 265
Art 75(1) 555	Art 97(4) 1282–3
Art 76 .1014, 1022–3	Art 98 . . . . .534, 1032
Art 76(1) 1006, 1023	Arts 99–108. . . . . .299, 1217
Art 76(2) 1006	Art 99 . . . . 1033, 1036, 1227,
Art 76(3) 1006, 1022	1230, 1236
Art 77 . . . . 535, 985, 1014, 1020	Art 100 . . . . .983, 1028, 1031, 1033,
Art 77(1) 555	1036, 1216, 1236, 1448
Art 78 . . . . .979, 1002, 1037	Art 100(1) 554
Art 78(2) 555	Art 101 . . . . .554, 983, 1028, 1031,
Art 78(4) 1002	1036, 1236
Arts 79–81 979	Art 102 . . . . .199, 1014, 1019,
Art 79 . . . . 199, 532, 1002, 1014, 1018	1033, 1035–6, 1220, 1236
Art 79(1) 1002	Arts 103–107. .1033
Art 79(2) 265	Art 103 . . . . .1036, 1236
Art 79(3) 265	Art 104 . . . . 1014, 1019, 1031, 1033,
Art 79(4) 553	1035, 1232, 1236, 1442
Art 80 . . . . .1002, 1014	Art 104(1) 554
Art 80(1) 1018	Art 104(4) 1019
Art 81 1002	Arts 105–108 . . . . .641, 1225
Art 81(6) 553	Art 105 . . . . 621, 644, 720, 1029,
Arts 82–108 . . . . .948, 1026–8, 1032, 1038	1035–6, 1220, 1237
Art 82 . . . . .199, 1027, 1029–1031, 1033	Art 105(1) 1225, 1231,
Art 82(2) 1028	1443, 1452
Art 83 . . . . 1028, 1033–4	Art 105(2) 555, 1225
Art 84 . . . . .1028–9, 1034, 1220	Art 105(3) 1226, 1443
Art 84(2) 1441, 1452	Art 105(4) 1224
Art 85 . . . . .620, 641–2, 895, 1029–30	Art 105(5) .555, 1445
Art 86 . . . . 1232, 1434, 1452	Art 106 . . . . 199, 483, 1035–6,
Art 87–90 1032	1234, 1237, 1436, 1445
Art 87 . . . . .199, 323, 335, 1028–9,	Art 107 . . . . 554, 1014, 1019, 1033,
1031–3, 1448	1035, 1237
Art 87(3) 319, 330, 580, 1156, 1159	Art 107(2) 1019
Art 87(4) 265	Art 108 . . . . 199, 319, 335, 358, 534,
Art 88 . . . . 358, 1284	1032–4, 1237, 1282
Art 88(1) 193	Art 108(1) 973
Art 88(2) 1284	Arts 109–119. 1031
Art 88(3) 1284	Arts 109–117. . . . . 924, 960, 1041,
Art 89 . . . . 319, 335, 1028, 1032, 1300	1329, 1343
Art 89(3) 1932	Arts 109–111. 968
Art 89(4) 330	Art 109 . . . . .92, 106, 310, 1041–2
Art 90 1033	Art 109(1) 1042, 1063
Art 91 1033	Art 109(2) 1043–4
Art 92 1034	Art 109(3) 97, 104, 1043–4, 1046, 1063
Art 93 .1027–8, 1034	Art 110 . . . . .95, 98, 100, 1041–2, 1284
Art 94 . . . . 1014, 1017	Art 110(1) 96, 1042, 1064
Art 96 . . . . .1029, 1036, 1224	Art 110(1)(1)–(3) 1041
Art 96(3) 1031	Art 110(1)(2) 1041
Art 96(4) 1231	Art 110(2) 97, 99, 106, 1044
Art 96(5) 555	Art 110(3) 96, 1045, 1063
Art 97 . . . . 358, 957, 1032, 1034, 1281	Art 110(4) 96, 1042
Art 97(1) 972	Art 111 . . . . .92, 1041, 1045

Art 112 . . . . 532, 1041	Arts 127–128. 652
Art 112(2) 1042	Art 127 . . . . 63, 116, 119–20, 170,
Art 113 1041–2	598, 602, 604–5, 653, 873
Art 114 . . . . 97, 1041	Art 127(2) 598
Art 115. 1041	Art 128 . . . . 63, 160, 172, 554, 653
Art 116 . . . . .94, 1041	Arts 129–130. .1019
Art 117 . . . . 1041, 1043–4	Art 129 . . . . 63, 103, 119, 251, 339, 569,
Art 118 . . . . 57, 963, 974, 1041, 1046,	619, 714, 935, 1037, 1216,
1049–52, 1054, 1058, 1065	1226, 1287, 1345
Art 118(1) . . . 95, 310, 1041, 1046–57, 1063	Art 129(2) 656, 1237
Art 118(2) 1049, 1058	Art 129(3) 621, 626, 656, 741,
Art 118(4) 1049, 1058–9	752, 1237
Art 118(4)(b) 1049	Art 129(4) 656, 1225
Art 119 . . . . 63, 261, 963, 1033–4,	Art 130 . . . . . . 148, 275, 299, 330, 339, 450,
1041, 1059	619–20, 622, 656, 714, 739,
Art 119(5) 1041, 1059	747, 844, 851, 935, 971, 975,
Art 119(7) 261, 270, 1059	983, 1003, 1009, 1024, 1026,
Arts 120–122 .1014	1033–4, 1037–8, 1065,
Art 120 . . . . 535, 789	1236, 1286, 1310, 1433
Art 120(1) 278, 554, 1020	Art 131 . . . . 632, 934, 1344
Art 120(2) 266, 278, 280–1, 1019	Art 132 . . . . .564, 1291
Art 120(3) 278, 280, 1019	Art 133 . . . . .158, 653
Art 120(4) 279, 287, 291, 1019	Art 134 . . . . .695, 957
Art 120(5) 279, 286, 289, 1019	Art 135 . . . . .175, 695–6, 893
Art 120(6) 279, 289–90, 1019	Arts 136–138 160
Art 121 . . . . 278, 282, 284–5,	Art 136 161
569, 714, 1019, 1033	Art 137(2) .162, 171
Art 121(1) 569, 1019	Art 138 162
Art 121(3) 1019	Art 138(2) 169–70
Arts 122–124. .1014	Art 139 163
Art 122 . . . . 63, 261, 535,	Art 140(2) 171
649, 789, 964–5, 992,	Art 141 . . . . 165, 170
1014–15, 1017, 1019	Art 142 176
Art 122(1) 260, 266, 281, 1014	Art 142(4) 176–9
Art 122(2)–(7). 263	Art 143 . . . . .171, 890
Art 122(2) 260, 266	Annex I 97, 160, 1041–2, 1284
Art 122(3) 260, 265, 267, 555, 1019	Annex II 160, 532, 1041–2
Art 122(4)–(6). 264	Annex III. 160, 246
Art 122(4) 264, 268, 1017	Annex III, Art 2. 241
Art 122(5) 1017, 1019	Annex IV. 160
Art 122(6) 1017	Annex IV(a). 262
Art 122(7) 261, 269, 1019–20	Annex IV(b) .1016
Art 122(9) 260, 266, 279, 291	Annex IV(c). .1021
Art 123 . . . . 92, 105, 260–1, 281, 532,	Annex IV(d) 280, 1019
535, 789, 1015, 1113	Annex IV(e) 1042
Art 123(2) .268, 1017	Annex V .160, 1005
Art 123(4) 242	1949 Convention Relative to the
Art 124 1016	Protection of Civilian Persons in
Art 125 . . . . 240–1, 246, 536	Time of War (Geneva Convention IV)
Art 125(3) 246	Art 1 *See* Geneva Convention I,
Art 126 . . . . .240, 243, 534, 971	Art 1 above
Art 126(1) 555	Art 2 *See* Geneva Convention I,
Art 126(2) 555	Art 2 above

Art 3 *See* Geneva Convention I,
   Art 3 above
Art 4 .... 56, 102, 305, 373, 643, 774,
         892, 912, 920–3, 1029, 1056, 1060,
         1072, 1075, 1080, 1100, 1123, 1138–50,
         1179, 1256, 1314–16, 1409, 1438–9
Art 4(1) 75, 1073, 1080, 1142–3, 1145,
                                       1315, 1469
Art 4(2) 1073, 1080, 1145, 1147,
                                       1315, 1469
Art 4(3) 1242
Art 4(4) 922, 1138, 1469
Art 5 ...... 301, 912, 920, 923, 926, 1072,
           1123–32, 1141, 1216, 1250, 1344
Art 5(1) .... .923, 1100, 1126, 1128–9
Art 5(2) 923, 1100, 1124, 1126, 1129, 1255
Art 5(3) ...... .923, 1100, 1125–6, 1128–32
Art 6 .... 52, 58–70, 920, 1046, 1060,
           1216, 1377, 1404, 1577–8, 1583–5
Art 6(3) 59, 1060, 1265, 1401,
                                 1461, 1576–96
Art 6(4) 140, 1060, 1264
Art 7 .... .135–45, 149, 151, 513–14,
                                       1265, 1404
Art 7(1) 1427
Art 8 .... 135, 140–1, 145–53, 1265,
                                       1381, 1427
Art 9 .... 243, 375, 549–60, 1495
Art 9(3) 1495
Art 10 .... 196, 236–7, 250, 375,
                         497–8, 506, 530, 532–3
Art 11 .... 92, 530, 533, 550, 552,
                                       557, 1233
Art 11(1) 139
Art 12 .... 92, 530, 563, 566
Art 13 .... 192, 199, 349, 373–4,
                                 1147–8, 1242, 1272
Arts 14–22. 783
Art 14 .... 139, 170, 370, 373–4,
                         376, 378, 385, 532, 651,
                         1278–9, 1295–6, 1501
Art 14(1) 374, 1301
Art 14(3) 373
Arts 15–17. 1301
Art 15 ..... 139, 370, 373–6, 378, 385, 651
Art 15(1) 374
Art 16 .... 280, 761, 784, 791, 793–4, 1278
Art 16(1) .... .761, 785, 1278–9
Art 16(2) 269, 278–9, 286, 786, 1520
Art 17 .... .139, 787, 793–4, 1278, 1280
Art 18 .... .141, 209, 212–13, 217,
                         650, 719, 813, 826, 860, 871–2,
                         1280, 1497, 1526, 1541

Art 18(1) 217, 650, 745
Art 18(2) 211–12
Art 18(3) .... .212, 745, 866
Art 18(5) 213, 650
Art 19 .... 218, 813, 826,
                                 841–3, 848, 860
Art 19(2) 218–19, 794, 845
Art 20 .... 812, 840, 860, 1497
Art 20(1)–(2). 745
Art 20(1) 866
Art 20(2) 262, 866
Art 20(3) 262, 866
Art 21 .... 745, 826, 829, 832,
                                 841, 860, 866, 1280
Art 22 .... 140, 826, 829–31,
                                 841, 860, 866, 1281
Art 22(1) 745
Art 22(2) 745
Arts 23–24 1500
Art 23 .... 140, 237, 248–9, 1279,
                                 1300, 1487, 1493, 1501
Art 23(1) 746
Art 23(2) 248
Art 23(3) 248, 555
Art 23(4) 249
Arts 24–26 1306
Art 24 .... .92, 106, 242, 1296,
                                 1298–300, 1306, 1487, 1501
Art 24(1) 1299, 1301, 1501
Art 24(2) .... .1297, 1301
Art 24(3) .... .1101, 1103–4, 1297
Art 25 ...... .1101, 1110, 1113, 1245, 1298
Art 25(1) 1090, 1097, 1099–100, 1119
Art 25(2) 1103, 1100–1, 1114, 1298
Art 25(3) .... .1101, 1119
Art 26 .... 63, 261, 269, 1090,
                         1101–3, 1110, 1113, 1119–20,
                                 1245, 1298–9
Arts 27–34. 1486
Arts 27–141. 1409
Art 27 .... 58, 132, 192, 200, 295, 299,
           319, 330, 333, 344, 346–50, 353, 357,
           362, 363–4, 360, 728, 744, 791, 798,
           1080–1, 1100, 1177, 1213, 1242–6,
           1249–50, 1256, 1258–61, 1265–7,
           1273–4, 1281, 1363, 1378, 1412, 1468–9
Art 27(1) 346, 348–9, 1104, 1136,
                         1243, 1245, 1247, 1275, 1470, 1476
Art 27(2) 200, 344, 346–51, 353,
                                 355, 361, 363, 1250,
                                 1274–6, 1281, 1285, 1470
Art 27(3) .... .348, 1250, 1272,
                                 1285, 1297, 1470

Art 27(4) 791, 1243, 1246,
 1250, 1256, 1330
Art 28 . . . . 534, 1080, 1242,
 1251–2, 1261, 1265, 1267
Arts 29–34 58
Art 29 . . . . 1242, 1252–3, 1267
Art 30 . . . . 237, 247, 536, 1242,
 1254–5, 1264, 1267
Art 30(1) 555
Art 30(2) 1255
Art 30(3) 1246, 1255
Arts 31–34 1267
Art 31 . . . . 265, 319, 323, 326–8,
 1080, 1230, 1242, 1255–6, 1266
Art 32 . . . . 319, 323, 326, 328,
 330, 335, 790, 1080, 1242, 1247,
 1250, 1256–8, 1266, 1363
Art 33 . . . . 302, 581, 662, 744,
 1080, 1139, 1141, 1156–8,
 1163–4, 1169–70, 1176,
 1226, 1358, 1363,1516
Art 33(1) 580, 1155–64, 1170
Art 33(2) 1416, 1440, 1516–17, 1521,
 1537, 1549
Art 33(3) 577, 580, 1163–4
Art 34 . . . . 298, 300–1, 305–7, 314,
 1080, 1164, 1335
Arts 35–37 1174
Art 35 . . . . 1056, 1074, 1077,
 1174–8, 1181, 1259, 1334
Art 35(1) 1178
Art 35(2) 1178
Art 35(3) 554, 1178
Art 36 . . . . 92, 94, 139, 1174, 1178–9
Art 37 . . . . 798, 1074, 1083, 1105,
 1174, 1177, 1242, 1258–9, 1266–7
Art 37(1) 1259
Art 37(2) 1259
Arts 38–40 . . . . 1242, 1266
Art 38 . . . . 200, 232, 237, 1070,
 1074, 1083, 1212–13, 1237, 1259–62,
 1267, 1279, 1295, 1362, 1500–1
Art 38(1) 247
Art 38(2) 1507
Art 38(3) 1246
Art 38(4) 1252, 1261, 1267
Art 38(5) 1300, 1501, 1507
Art 39 . . . . 200, 1074, 1081, 1245,
 1261–2, 1329
Art 39(2) 1262, 1264
Art 39(3) 555, 1262
Art 40 . . . . 200, 534, 1074, 1245,
 1256, 1263, 1268, 1357

Art 40(1) 1263
Art 40(2) 1263
Art 40(3) 1263
Art 40(4) 1264
Arts 41–43 . . . . 1250, 1258, 1328
Art 41 . . . . 1082, 1213, 1250, 1260,
 1264, 1328, 1331
Art 41(1) 1330
Art 41(2) 1329
Art 42 . . . . 310, 717, 927, 1074,
 1082, 1126–8, 1132, 1176–7, 1250,
 1328–37, 1345, 1376, 1382
Art 42(2) 555, 1330
Art 43 . . . . 104, 716, 924–5, 1082–3,
 1129, 1131–2, 1329, 1331, 1333,
 1336–42, 1345–6
Art 43(1) 1336–7, 1339
Art 43(2) 1096–8, 1104, 1119
Art 44 . . . . 922, 1074, 1141,
 1314, 1316, 1320–1, 1437
Art 45 . . . . . 104, 873, 925, 928, 1054, 1074,
 1083, 1186–7, 1196–1205, 1314,
 1365, 1382, 1385, 1416
Art 45(2) 1385–6
Art 45(3) 485, 1199–1201, 1204
Art 45(4) 485, 1056, 1200–2,
 1204–5, 1314–15, 1317, 1321
Art 45(5) 1198, 1201, 1203
Art 46 . . . . 1083, 1242, 1264,
 1266, 1504
Art 46(2) 1264, 1268
Arts 47–78 1486
Art 47 . . . . 58, 135, 1265–6,
 1402, 1404, 1406, 1413, 1428, 1461,
 1463–6, 1486, 1576–7, 1586–9
Arts 48–50 1578
Art 48 . . . . 1174, 1177, 1179–80, 1413
Art 49 . . . . 58, 106, 728, 925,
 1085–6, 1139, 1148, 1179, 1187–96,
 1205–6, 1208, 1210, 1300–1, 1318,
 1365, 1381, 1412–13, 1416, 1449,
 1466, 1471, 1486, 1504, 1555
Art 49(1)–(5) 1562
Art 49(1) 104, 925, 1056, 1186–90,
 1193, 1196, 1205–6, 1209, 1246, 1315,
 1317, 1334, 1391, 1410, 1562
Art 49(2)–(6) 1317, 1381
Art 49(2) 1187, 1191–2
Art 49(3) 1091, 1104, 1192, 1495
Art 49(4) 554, 1104, 1192
Art 49(5) 1191
Art 49(6) 1186, 1391, 1551–73
Arts 50–61 1468

Table of Legislation

Art 50 . . . . 1245–6, 1295–7, 1299–300,
1306, 1411, 1413, 1465, 1469, 1476,
1486, 1500–1, 1504, 1512, 1583, 1591
Art 50(1) 1299, 1476, 1488, 1500
Art 50(2) 1091, 1104, 1501
Art 50(3) 1246, 1500
Art 50(4) 263, 265, 1110
Art 50(5) 1279, 1298, 1474, 1500
Arts 51–52. 1498
Art 51 . . . . 58, 1263, 1298, 1357, 1461,
1466, 1470, 1486, 1498–9, 1501
Art 51(1) 1413, 1501
Art 51(2)–(4) 1413
Art 51(2) 1296, 1302, 1428–9, 1498–9
Art 51(3) 1498–9
Art 51(4) 1498
Art 52 . . . . 58, 1412–13, 1486, 1499
Art 52(1) 555
Art 53 . . . . .58, 727, 826, 1139, 1250,
1412–13, 1472–4, 1486, 1489,
1516–20, 1526, 1531–2, 1536–7,
1539–41, 1546–50
Arts 54–57 1413
Art 54 . . . . .1413, 1428, 1466, 1468–9
Art 54(1) 1428–30, 1468
Art 54(2) 1428–30, 1468
Arts 55–57. . . . . .1475, 1578
Art 55 . . . . 1170, 1412–13, 1482, 1487,
1494–7, 1506, 1512, 1526, 1583, 1591
Art 55(1) 247, 746, 1474–5,
1488–9, 1493
Art 55(2) 247
Art 55(3) 248, 1495
Art 55(4) 555
Art 56 . . . . .248, 826, 1299, 1412–13, 1465,
1469, 1475, 1487, 1493, 1497,
1500, 1506, 1512, 1583
Art 56(1) 222, 727, 1489, 1495–6
Art 56(2) 1497
Art 56(3) 1497
Art 57 . . . . 209, 222, 783, 826, 1299,
1412–13, 1495, 1497, 1526, 1531
Art 57(1) 222
Art 57(2) 1497
Arts 58–62 1260
Art 58 . . . . 232, 1413, 1470, 1476, 1591
Arts 59–62 . . . . .1412, 1493
Arts 59–61 1413
Art 59 . . . . 58, 249, 532, 536, 1108,
1391, 1413, 1475, 1487, 1493, 1512
Art 59(1) 242, 746, 1495
Art 59(2) 238, 242
Art 59(4) 249, 555

Arts 60–62 1526
Art 60 . . . . 248, 1413, 1475, 1512
Arts 61–63. 58
Art 61 . . . . 532, 536, 1413, 1487
Art 61(1) 241, 247, 555
Art 61(2) 248
Art 62 . . . . 248, 1091, 1108, 1413, 1487
Art 63 . . . . .650, 1413
Art 63(1)(a), (b) 248
Art 63(2) 238
Arts 64–78 720
Arts 64–77 1438
Arts 64–76 1131
Arts 64–75 1413
Arts 64–70 57
Art 64 . . . . 1237, 1245, 1250–1, 1264,
1422–32, 1450, 1452, 1462,
1468, 1504, 1527
Art 64(1) 1413, 1422, 1424,
1429–31, 1434, 1463
Art 64(2) 1424–5, 1435, 1504
Arts 65–77. 1439
Art 65 . . . . 1237, 1440
Arts 66–77 1470
Arts 66–75 1368
Art 66 . . . .471, 1085, 1131, 1219–20, 1223,
1237, 1250, 1413, 1432–6, 1441, 1445
Arts 67–78. 1216
Art 67 . . . . 1227, 1237, 1440, 1448
Art 68 . . . . .1126–7, 1143, 1216, 1237,
1250, 1328, 1331–2, 1374, 1443, 1446,
1448, 1501
Art 68(1) 1329, 1332, 1351, 1447
Art 68(2)–(4). 1446
Art 68(2) 174, 1131, 1447, 1453
Art 68(3) 1448
Art 68(4) 483, 1296, 1302, 1448
Art 69 . . . . .1237, 1328, 1446
Art 70 . . . . .922, 1084–5, 1238, 1314
Art 70(1) 1435, 1438
Art 70(2) 1141, 1314–17, 1321, 1436–7
Arts 71–76. . . . . .299, 1086, 1361
Art 71 . . . . 200, 1219–20, 1223,
1233, 1238, 1441–2
Art 71(1) 141
Art 71(2) 554, 1105, 1224,
1441–2, 1446
Art 71(3) 554, 1442
Art 72 . . . . 1238, 1442–4
Art 72(1) 1226, 1231, 1443–4
Art 72(2) 555, 1226, 1444
Art 72(3) 1226, 1444
Art 73 . . . . .483, 1234, 1238, 1436, 1448

Art 73(1) 1436, 1445
Art 73(2) 1445
Art 74 . . . . 1232–3, 1238, 1442
Art 74(1) 555, 1445–6
Art 74(2) 554, 1105, 1233, 1445–6
Art 75 . . . . 1234, 1238
Art 75(1) 1448
Art 75(2) 554, 1105, 1448
Art 75(3) 1449
Art 76 . . . . 200, 534, 783, 1086, 1177,
 1233, 1368, 1412, 1446, 1449, 1500
Art 76(1) 1434, 1446, 1449
Art 76(2) 1278
Art 76(3) 1246, 1449
Art 76(4) 1281, 1449
Art 76(5) 1449
Art 76(6) 248, 555, 1442, 1446, 1449
Art 76(7) 248
Art 77 . . . . 1014, 1379, 1413, 1449
Art 78 . . . . 104, 310, 716–17, 924–5,
 927, 1084, 1177, 1250, 1327–43,
 1345–6, 1376, 1413, 1443, 1447
Art 78(2) 1329, 1340, 1336–7
Art 78(3) 1329
Arts 79–135. 1482
Arts 79–131. 1351
Art 79 . . . . . 246, 1071, 1250, 1328, 1331–2
Art 80 . . . . 1107, 1353
Art 81 . . . . 783, 1351, 1353
Art 81(3) 1354
Art 82 . . . . 200, 1281, 1302
Art 82(1) 1354
Art 82(2) 1090, 1105
Art 82(3) 1105
Art 83 . . . . 140, 534, 1199, 1354, 1368
Art 83(2) 555
Arts 84–131. 1199
Art 84 1354
Art 85 . . . . . . 349, 791, 1281, 1354, 1367–8
Art 85(1) 1283
Art 85(3) 1283
Art 85(4) 1283
Art 86 . . . . 791, 1246, 1354
Art 87 . . . . 1354, 1368
Art 88 1354
Arts 89–92 1368
Art 89 . . . . 349, 791, 1278, 1296,
 1301, 1354, 1367, 1500–1
Art 89(1) 1284
Art 89(3) 1355
Art 89(5) 1284, 1300
Art 90 . . . . 791, 1354–5, 1367
Art 90(1) 1355
Art 90(2) 1355
Art 90(3) 1355
Art 91 . . . . 200, 349, 783, 1283,
 1301, 1356
Art 91(4) 1114, 1356
Art 92 1356
Art 93 . . . . 791, 1246, 1356, 1367
Art 94 . . . . 1299, 1351, 1357
Art 94(1) 1357
Art 95 . . . . 200, 534, 1263, 1357, 1367
Art 96 . . . . 532, 553, 1357
Art 97 . . . . 349, 1357
Art 97(4) 1281
Art 98 . . . . 200, 1128, 1143, 1358
Art 98(2) 555
Art 98(3) 555
Art 99 . . . . 201, 598, 603, 653, 1358
Art 99(2) 160, 1358
Art 99(3) 1358
Art 100 1358
Art 100(2) 1355
Art 101 . . . . 1358, 1364
Art 101(1) 1358
Art 101(2) 1362
Art 101(4) 1359
Art 102 . . . . 532, 1358
Art 102(1) 553
Art 103 1358
Art 104 . . . . 532, 1358
Arts 105–116. 1100
Art 105 . . . . 554, 1091, 1106, 1143,
 1329, 1360, 1368
Arts 106–116. 1360
Art 106 . . . . 783, 1090, 1098, 1106,
 1109, 1114, 1119, 1360, 1368
Art 107 . . . . 1090, 1106, 1109, 1143,
 1360, 1364, 1368
Art 107(1) 1097, 1106–7
Art 107(2) 1107
Art 107(3) 1108
Arts 108–111. 246
Arts 108–110. 1361
Art 108 . . . . 139, 532, 536, 1091,
 1109, 1367
Art 108(1) 1108
Art 108(2) 1108
Art 109 . . . . 140, 536, 1109
Art 109(3) 555
Art 110 . . . . 1112, 1114
Art 110(1) 1108
Art 110(2) 1108
Art 110(3) 1108
Art 110(4) 1108

Art 110(5) 1091, 1107
Art 111 .... 532, 536, 1360–1
Art 111(1)......... 555, 1091, 1109, 1114
Art 111(2) 1109
Art 111(3) 1109
Art 111(4) 1109
Art 112 ....1091, 1360
Art 112(1) 1097, 1106
Art 112(2) 1097, 1109
Art 112(3) 1107
Art 113 .... 1091, 1109, 1114
Art 113(1) 1107
Art 113(2) 1107
Art 114 ....1107, 1351
Art 115......................1107, 1351
Art 116 ....1090, 1108, 1368
Art 116(1) 1361
Art 116(2) 1361
Arts 117–126....................1361
Art 117 ....201, 1232, 1238, 1361
Art 117(2) 1362
Art 117(3) 1362, 1434, 1452
Art 118 ....330, 335, 1238,
                        1257, 1362, 1448
Art 118(1) 1362
Art 118(3) 1362
Art 118(5) 1362
Arts 119–125....................1362
Art 119 ....330, 1257, 1300, 1362–3
Art 119(1)(3) 1363
Art 119(2) 1363
Art 119(3) 1363
Art 120 1014
Art 120(1) 1364
Art 120(2) 1362, 1364
Art 121 ....1238, 1364
Art 122 1364
Art 122(2) 1363
Art 122(3) 1363
Art 123 .... 1216, 1364–5, 1443
Art 123(2) 1225, 1231, 1441
Art 123(5) 555
Art 124 .... 1281, 1362–4
Art 124(2) 1283
Art 124(3) 1281, 1283
Art 125 .... 534, 1363–4
Art 125(2) 1356
Art 125(3) 1119
Art 125(4) 1107, 1364
Art 126 ....1216, 1220, 1361–2, 1368
Art 127 ....201, 783, 798, 1197, 1284,
                        1301, 1365
Arts 129–131....................1368

Art 129 .... 278, 280, 1115, 1365
Art 129(1) 278
Art 129(2) 278, 280, 1111
Art 129(3) 278, 281, 554, 1111, 1119
Art 130 ....1246, 1365
Art 130(1) 279, 287, 291–2
Art 130(2) 279, 286, 289–91
Art 130(3) 1111
Art 131 ....278, 282, 284–5, 714,
                        1366, 1378
Art 131(1) 1366
Art 131(2) 1366
Art 131(3) 1366–7
Arts 132–135....................1374
Art 132 .... 92, 103–4, 140, 310,
                        569, 783, 924–5, 1061, 1175,
                        1284, 1302, 1329, 1374–6
Art 132(1) 569, 1105, 1118,
                        1374, 1376
Art 132(2) 103, 1105–6, 1301, 1376
Art 133 .... 58, 63, 140, 261, 924–5,
                        1056, 1061, 1329, 1379, 1383
Art 133(1) 270, 1374, 1377, 1380
Art 133(2) 1379
Art 133(3) 261, 270, 1380
Art 134 ....58, 1374–5, 1380–1, 1383
Art 135 .... 140, 1143, 1381, 1383
Art 135(1) 1382
Art 135(3) 1382
Art 135(4) 1382
Arts 136–140....................261
Arts 136–138....................1368
Arts 136–137....................1329
Art 136 .... 281, 535, 649, 1090,
                        1102, 1109, 1112, 1298,
                        1306, 1366, 1441
Art 136(1) 260, 266, 281, 1109
Art 136(2) 260, 263, 265–6,
                        1110–11, 1113, 1115, 1119
Art 137 ....789, 1112–13
Art 137(1) 260–1, 267, 269,
                        555, 1100, 1112, 1441
Art 137(2) 260, 268, 1096,
                        1098–9, 1110–12, 1114
Art 137(3) 1110
Art 138 ....263, 535, 1110
Art 138(1) 265, 268, 1091, 1111
Art 138(2) 265, 1111, 1119
Art 139 .... 260, 266, 279, 291, 1110,
                        1112, 1115
Art 140 .... 92, 105, 260, 268, 1100,
                        1109, 1113, 1298, 1360, 1365, 1441
Art 140(1) 267, 281, 1091, 1112

Art 140(2) 268, 1017, 1090–1, 1096, 1112–14
Art 140(3) 1091, 1114
Art 140(4) 242, 1102
Art 141 . . . . 1107, 1112, 1114
Art 142 . . . . 240, 247, 532, 536, 1103, 1242, 1254–5
Art 142(1) 240, 1255
Art 142(3) 1359
Art 143 . . . . 58, 140, 248, 534, 555, 1233, 1242, 1254–5, 1364, 1442, 1446, 1449,
Art 143(3) 247
Art 143(5) 1359, 1386
Arts 144–145. 652
Art 144 . . . . 63, 116, 119–20, 170, 598, 602, 604–5, 653, 873
Art 144(2) 598
Art 145 . . . . 63, 160, 172, 554, 653
Art 146 . . . . 63, 103, 119, 251, 301, 313–14, 339, 353, 363, 569, 619, 621, 626, 644, 714, 803, 935, 1151, 1226, 1287, 1345, 1432, 1435, 1438
Art 146(2) 105, 284, 656
Art 146(3) 656, 741, 752
Art 146(4) 656, 1216, 1225
Art 147 . . . . 124, 148, 225, 275, 299, 301, 304, 307, 309, 313–14, 328, 330, 339, 361–2, 385, 450, 619–20, 622, 656, 714, 739, 747, 803, 844, 851, 925, 935, 1087, 1132, 1151, 1183, 1190, 1210, 1235–6, 1247, 1249, 1251–2, 1258–9, 1266–7, 1286, 1310, 1334–5, 1345, 1358, 1368, 1376, 1384, 1416, 1435, 1466, 1470, 1495, 1513, 1517, 1530–1, 1536, 1549
Art 148 . . . . 632, 934, 1252, 1344
Art 149 . . . . 140, 564
Art 150 . . . . 158, 653
Arts 151–153 160
Art 152(2) 162, 171
Art 153 162
Art 153(2) 169–70
Art 154 . . . . 175, 696, 1138, 1393
Art 155 163
Art 156(2) 171
Art 157 . . . . 165, 170
Art 158 176
Art 158(4) 176–9
Art 159 171
Annex I 370, 373
Annex I, Art 6 866

Annex II 247, 536, 1361
Annex III. 1106, 1360
1949 World Medical Association International Code of Medical Ethics, October, amended August 1968, October 1983 and October 2006. . . 797, 1497
1950 European Convention for the Protection of Human Rights and Fundamental Freedoms, the Protocols are referenced by relevant year below 10, 280, 285, 302, 319, 473, 712, 714–17, 720, 731, 1010, 1169, 1225, 1244, 1260, 1342, 1352, 1471, 1483, 1558, 1561, 1572
Art 1 . . . . 150, 1417
Art 2 . . . . . . 274, 712–14, 1366, 1370, 1381
Art 2(1) 1193
Art 3 . . . . 274, 320, 322, 712, 729, 1204, 1248
Art 4 1263
Art 4(1) 712
Art 4(2) 1370, 1499
Art 5 . . . . 274, 715–17, 1010, 1036
Art 5(1) 714, 716, 1341–2, 1370
Art 5(2) 716
Art 5(3) 486–7, 1032
Art 5(4) 716
Art 6 . . . . 1027, 1037, 1221, 1230–1
Art 6(1) 481, 484, 1221, 1232–3
Art 6(2) 475, 1228
Art 6(3) 1225
Art 6(3)(a) 475, 1225
Art 6(3)(b) 1226, 1444
Art 6(3)(c) 476–7, 1226, 1229, 1444
Art 6(3)(d) 479–80, 1231, 1364
Art 6(3)(e) 479, 1364, 1444
Art 7 . . . . 712, 719, 1227, 1439
Art 7(2) 623, 660
Art 8 . . . . 1092, 1116, 1244, 1554, 1568
Art 8(1) 1510
Art 8(2) 1510
Art 10(1) 1511
Art 13 294
Art 14 . . . . 193, 205, 1260
Art 15 . . . . 712, 1124, 1127, 1439
Art 15(2) 1227, 1370
1950 Statute of the Office of the United Nations High Commissioner for Refugees (UNHCR) 1259
1951 Convention Relating to the Status of Refugees 365, 381, 1201, 1204, 1259, 1313, 1315–16, 1318, 1321–2, 1375, 1381

Table of Legislation

Art 1(A)(2)................... 1201
Art 1(F)...................... 1201
Art 5 1321
Art 8 1316
Art 9 .... 1202–3, 1321
Art 32 1202
Art 33 .... 1053, 1141, 1202,
                 1204, 1384, 1437
Art 33(1) 1202
Art 33(2) 1203, 1437
1952 Protocol No 1 to the European
   Convention on Human Rights
   Art 1 .... 1511, 1533, 1568–9
   Art 2 1511
1952 UNGA Res 610 (VII) 1054
1954 Hague Convention for the
   Protection of Cultural Property
   in the Event of Armed Conflict ... 587, 700,
                   1246, 1478, 1533
   Art 1 .... 1528–9, 1533
   Art 4 1530
   Art 4(3) 1528, 1533
   Art 4(4) 577, 580, 1164
   Art 5(1) 1478
   Art 5(2) 1478
   Art 7 654
   Art 19 1529
   Art 19(4) 426
   Arts 21–22.................... 556
   Art 22 563
   Art 25 .... 600, 654
   Art 26 653
   Art 28 1226
   Art 29 158
   Annex, Art 6 556
1955 Standard Minimum Rules
   for the Treatment of Prisoners,
   Economic and Social Committee
   (ECOSOC) Res 663 C (XXIV)
   1957 and 2076 (LXII) 1977......... 1352
   Rule 8 1282–3
   Rule 23(1) 1283
   Rule 43, (4) 1358
   Rule 46 1358
   Rule 53 1282
1956 World Medical Association
   Regulations in Times of Armed
   Conflict and Other Situations
   of Violence 790
1957 ILO Convention concerning the
   Abolition of Forced Labour (No 105) ... 1499
   Art 1 1370
   Art 2 1370
1960 Treaty of Guarantee,
   16 August, 382 UNTS 3 1558
1961 European Social Charter
   Art 30 .... 712, 720
1961 Vienna Convention on
   Diplomatic Relations............. 1145
1962 Evian Agreement between
   France and the Provisional
   Government of the Algerian
   Republic 168
1962 UNGA Res 1803 (XVII) 1539
1963 Protocol No 4 to the
   European Convention on
   Human Rights.................. 1510
   Art 3 1194
   Art 4 .... 1194, 1573
1963 Vienna Convention on
   Consular Relations
   Art 36(1) 150
   Art 36(1)(b) 1360
1965 International Convention
   on the Elimination of All Forms
   of Racial Discrimination 196, 1194
   Art 5 1174
   Art 5(d)(i) 1194
   Arts 11–13.................... 567
1966 First Optional Protocol to the
   International Covenant on
   Civil and Political Rights, UNGA
   Res 2200A (XXI) 1483
   Art 1 1359
   Art 2 1359
   Art 3 1359
   Art 5 1359
1966 International Covenant on Civil
   and Political Rights 195, 302, 319, 473,
              483, 703–4, 707, 716, 720–2, 730,
                  1093, 1169, 1180, 1194, 1217,
                  1225, 1235, 1244, 1260, 1352–3,
                  1367, 1417, 1469, 1471, 1569, 1572
   Art 1 1417
   Art 2(1) 150, 193–4, 704, 813, 1272
   Art 2(3) 273
   Art 4 .... 244, 301, 721, 1124,
                     1180, 1219, 1439, 1471
   Art 4(1) 194, 720, 1285, 1353
   Art 4(2) 337, 820, 1131, 1227,
                              1246, 1370
   Art 6 .... 273, 302, 721, 1366,
                             1381, 1472–3
   Art 6(1) 720
   Art 6(2) 483
   Art 6(4) 483

Art 6(5) 483, 1302, 1448	Art 1 1489
Art 7 . . . . 273, 302, 337, 791, 983, 1248, 1258, 1363	Art 1(2) 1539
Art 8(3) 1263, 1370, 1499	Art 2(1) 986, 1490, 1506
Art 9 . . . . 301–2, 721–2, 1194	Art 2(2) 914, 813, 1272, 1489–90
Art 9(1) 301, 721	Art 2(3) 1272
Art 9(3) 486–7, 1442	Art 3 . . . . 194, 1490
Art 9(4) 927, 1337	Art 4 . . . . 1471, 1500
Art 10 . . . . 302, 1351	Art 6 . . . . 1263, 1489, 1499–1500
Art 10(1) 1116	Art 6(2) 1504
Art 12 . . . . 302, 1174, 1180–1, 1183, 1193–4, 1210, 1562	Art 7 . . . . 1489, 1500
Art 12(1) 1193	Art 7(a)(i) 1490
Art 12(3) 1180, 1194	Art 8 1490
Art 12(4) 1194	Art 10 . . . . 1245, 1476, 1500
Art 14 . . . . 302, 470–1, 474, 1217–18, 1230, 1236, 1451, 1471	Art 10(1) 1092, 1095, 1102
Art 14(1) 479, 481, 1027, 1221–2, 1232–3	Art 10(2) 1280
	Art 10(3) 1092, 1102, 1490
Art 14(2) 475, 1228	Art 11 . . . . 1282, 1474, 1489, 1500
Art 14(3) 1225	Art 11(1) 1193, 1494
Art 14(3)(a) 475–6, 1225	Art 11(2) 1494
Art 14(3)(b) 1226, 1444	Art 11(2)(a) 1505
Art 14(3)(c) 484	Art 12 . . . . 791, 799, 1282, 1353–4, 1475, 1489, 1496, 1500
Art 14(3)(d) 476–7, 481, 1229, 1444	
Art 14(3)(e) 479–80, 1231, 1364	Art 12(1) 1354
Art 14(3)(f) 479, 1364, 1444	Art 12(2)(a) 1505
Art 14(3)(g) 482, 1230	Art 12(2)(b) 1505
Art 14(5) 483, 1036, 1235	Art 12(2)(c) 1354
Art 14(7) 484, 1232, 1362	Art 12(2)(d) 1354
Art 15 . . . . 470, 660, 719–20, 1131, 1217, 1227, 1451	Art 13 . . . . 1247, 1476, 1489, 1500, 1502–3
	Art 13(1) 1502
Art 15(2) 623, 660	Art 13(2)(a) 1490
Art 16 1353	Art 13(3) 1490
Art 17 . . . . 1093, 1096, 1244	Art 14 . . . . 1247, 1489, 1500, 1502–3
Art 17(1) 1092, 1102, 1116	Art 15 . . . . 1247, 1489, 1502
Art 17(2) 1092	1967 Protocol relating to the Status of Refugees of 1951 . . . . . . 365, 1259
Art 18 . . . . 820, 1097, 1246, 1476	
Art 18(3) 1357	1967 Treaty on Principles Governing the Activities of States in the Exploration and Use of Outer Space, including the Moon and Other Celestial Bodies (Outer Space Treaty)
Art 19 1097	
Art 20 1246	
Art 23 1476	
Art 23(1) 1092, 1245	Art 2 74
Art 26 . . . . 193–4, 472	Art 3 74
Art 27 1247	1967 United Nations Declaration on Territorial Asylum, UNGA Res 2312 (XXII)
Arts 41–43 567	
Arts 41–42 1359	
1966 International Covenant on Economic, Social and Cultural Rights 703, 731, 986, 1169, 1260, 1288, 1417, 1471, 1486–8, 1490, 1500, 1502, 1504–5, 1511–12, 1569	Art 3(1) 1181
	1968 Convention on Road Signs and Signals
	Preamble 861
	1968 International Conference on Human Rights, Teheran, Resolution XXIII 182
	Preamble, para 9 121
	1968 UNGA Res 2444 (XXIII) 702

1969 American Convention on
  Human Rights 483, 722–6, 801,
    936, 1203, 1244, 1260, 1352, 1417, 1483
  Art 1(1) 193, 709
  Art 2 . . . . 709, 726
  Art 2(a) 1364
  Art 2(f) 1364
  Art 3 709
  Art 4 . . . . 709, 723, 725
  Art 4(2) 483
  Art 4(5) 483, 1302
  Art 4(6) 483
  Art 5 709
  Art 5(1) 274
  Art 5(2) 1248
  Art 5(3) 302, 1160, 1226
  Art 6 1263
  Art 6(2) 1370
  Art 7 709
  Art 7(5) 486
  Art 8 . . . . 471, 709
  Art 8(1) 274, 484, 1221
  Art 8(2) 475, 479, 1225, 1228
  Art 8(2)(a) 479, 1444
  Art 8(2)(b) 475
  Art 8(2)(c) 1226, 1444
  Art 8(2)(d) 476–7, 1226, 1229
  Art 8(2)(e) 1444
  Art 8(2)(f) 480, 1231
  Art 8(2)(g) 1230
  Art 8(2)(h) 483
  Art 8(3) 482
  Art 8(4) 484, 1232, 1362
  Art 8(5) 481, 1232
  Art 9 . . . . 719, 1227
  Art 11 . . . . 709, 1244
  Art 13 . . . . 274, 709
  Art 16 709
  Art 17 709
  Art 17(1) 1092, 1116, 1245
  Art 19 709
  Art 21 . . . . 726, 1533
  Art 22 . . . . 709, 726
  Art 22(1) 1193
  Art 22(5) 1194
  Art 22(8) 928, 1203
  Art 22(9) 1194
  Art 23 709
  Art 24 . . . . 193, 1260
  Art 25 . . . . 274, 709, 723
  Art 27 . . . . 720, 1124, 1439
  Art 27(2) 1227
  Art 29 . . . . 724, 726
  Art 29(a) 159
  Art 29(b) 723
  Art 44 723
1969 Organization of African
  Unity Convention Governing
  the Specific Aspects of the Refugee
  Problem in Africa 1259, 1322
  Art I 1323
  Art II(3) 1053
1969 Vienna Convention on the
  Law of Treaties 70, 73, 139, 157,
    159, 170, 173–6, 419, 648,
    691–2, 1402–3, 1407
  Art 2(1)(a) 136, 139, 517
  Art 2(1)(b) 417
  Art 2(1)(d) 967
  Art 3 517
  Art 4 . . . . 70, 157
  Art 7 . . . . 160, 1403
  Art 7(2) 374
  Art 9 160
  Art 10(a) 161
  Art 11 . . . . 163, 417
  Art 18 161
  Art 18(a) 161–2
  Art 18(b) 161
  Art 24(4) 156
  Art 25 . . . . 165, 170
  Art 25(2) 170
  Art 26 . . . . 117, 417, 693, 943
  Art 27 . . . . 1403, 1426
  Art 28 637
  Art 29 . . . . 70, 73, 83
  Art 30 . . . . 174, 692
  Art 30(2) 174, 692
  Art 30(3) 174, 692
  Art 30(4) 693
  Art 30(5) 693
  Art 31 . . . . 70, 78, 1176
  Art 31(1) 147, 159, 185, 691–2, 1161
  Art 31(2) 691–2
  Art 31(3) 82, 692
  Art 31(3)(b) 121, 716, 1055
  Art 31(3)(c) 235, 443, 716, 727,
    1052, 1180, 1393
  Art 32 . . . . 70, 78, 159, 1081
  Art 33 158
  Art 33(1) 159
  Art 33(3) 159
  Art 33(4) 158–9
  Art 34 . . . . 419, 693
  Art 35 419–20
  Art 36 419–20

Art 39 698
Art 40 690
Art 41 693
Art 41(1) 693
Art 43 .... 178, 185
Art 46 1403
Art 52 1403
Art 53 .... 136, 151, 178, 1406
Arts 54–56 177
Art 54(a) 176
Art 59 .... 174–5, 692, 695
Art 59(1) 692
Art 59(1)(a) 175
Art 59(1)(b) 175
Art 60 .... 579, 693
Art 60(5) 375, 579, 1050, 1141
Art 62 184
Art 64 236
Art 70(2) 176–7
Art 73 157
Art 77 172
Art 77(2) 168
Art 80 171
Art 80(1) 171
1970 Declaration on Principles
 of International Law concerning
 Friendly Relations and Co-operation
 among States in accordance with the
 Charter of the United Nations,
 UNGA Res 2625 (XXV) 20, 708, 1465
1970 Hague Convention for the Suppression
 of Unlawful Seizure of Aircraft
 Art 7 631
1970 UNGA Res 2675 (XXV) 702
1971 OAS Convention to Prevent and
 Punish the Acts of Terrorism taking
 the form of Crimes against Persons
 and Related Extortion that are of
 International Significance 315
 Art 2 315
1971 UNGA Res 2816 (XXVI) 232
1971 UNSC Res 298 (1971) 1556
1971 UNSC Res 307 (1971) 167
1972 UNESCO Convention Concerning
 the Protection of the World Cultural
 and Natural Heritage............ 1478–9
1972 UNGA Res 3032 (XXVII) 610
1973 Convention on the Prevention
 and Punishment of Crimes against
 Internationally Protected Persons,
 Including Diplomatic Agents 315
 Art 2 315
1973 ILO Convention concerning
 Minimum Age for Admission to
 Employment (No 138)............ 1492
1973 Protocol to the Agreement on
 Ending the War and Restoring Peace in
 Vietnam concerning the Return of
 Captured Military Personnel and
 Foreign Civilians and Captured and
 Detained Vietnamese Civilian
 Personnel
 Art 4(b) 1377
 Art 7(b) 1378
 Art 8 1021
1974 Bangladesh–India–Pakistan
 Agreement on the Repatriation
 of POWs and Civilian Internees
 para 10.................... 1377
1974 Charter of Economic Rights and
 Duties of States
 Art 16 1539
1974 Declaration on the Protection of
 Women and Children in Emergency
 and Armed Conflict, UNGA Res
 3318 (XXIX).................... 1167
 para 4 1272
1974 Definition of Aggression, UNGA
 Res 3314 (XXIX)
 Art 3(e) 1405
 Art 5(3) 1465
1974 UNESCO Recommendation
 concerning Education for International
 Understanding, Co-operation and Peace
 and Education relating to Human Rights
 and Fundamental Freedoms 1502
1974 UNGA Res 3220 (XXIX) 1020
1976 Tripoli Agreement between the
 Government of the Republic of the
 Philippines and the Moro National
 Liberation Front 512
1976 UNGA Res 31/106A............ 1556
1977 European Convention on the
 Suppression of Terrorism............ 315
 Art 1 315
1977 Protocol Additional to the
 Geneva Conventions of 12 August 1949,
 and relating to the Protection of Victims
 of International Armed Conflicts
 (Additional Protocol I)
 Preamble, para 3 697
 Art 1 .... 52, 104, 116, 119, 121, 300
 Art 1(1) 132, 338
 Art 1(2) 182, 1160

Art 1(3) 171, 396, 698, 917, 1275	Art 17 784
Art 1(4) 20–1, 39–42, 48, 52, 169, 313, 396, 408, 699, 708, 944, 1057, 1405, 1415	Art 17(1) 796–7, 812
	Art 18 . . . . 119–20, 650, 860, 871–2, 882
Art 2 93	Art 18(1) 866
Art 3 . . . . 52, 59, 1584	Art 18(3) 262, 867
Art 3(b) 53, 1057, 1404, 1576, 1581–4	Art 18(4) 866–7
Art 5 . . . . 530, 550–1	Art 19 95–6
Art 5(1) 552	Art 20 . . . . 577, 581, 785, 1163–4
Art 5(2) 551	Arts 21–31 866
Art 5(3) 552	Art 21 . . . . 829, 1526
Art 5(6) 551	Art 22 . . . . 93, 216
Art 6 . . . . 600, 601, 604	Art 22(1) 216, 832
Art 7 . . . . 128, 172	Art 22(2) 833
Art 8 . . . . 445, 581, 643, 761, 793, 813, 860, 1277–8, 1280	Art 22(2)(b) 215
	Art 22(3) 215, 834
Art 8(a) 95, 444–5, 761, 783	Art 23 . . . . 815, 834, 1526
Art 8(b) 770, 777, 779	Art 23(2) 834
Art 8(c)–(m) 866	Art 25 831–2
Art 8(c)–(d) 867	Art 26 831
Art 8(c) 866–7	Art 27(1) 831
Art 8(d)(i) 813	Art 28(4) 829
Art 8(d)(ii) 813	Art 29 831
Art 8(d)(iv) 813	Art 30(1) 830
Art 8(e) 209, 211, 650, 826, 834, 836, 866	Art 30(2) 830
	Art 30(3) 830
Art 8(g)–(j) 866	Art 30(4) 830
Art 8(g) 100, 828–9, 867	Art 31 . . . . 93, 100
Art 8(i) 834	Art 31(1) 830, 1378
Art 8(l) 861–2	Art 31(2) 100
Art 8(m) 861	Art 31(3) 830–1
Art 9 . . . . 790, 1272	Art 31(4) 100, 831
Art 9(2) 811, 866	Art 31(5) 831
Art 9(2)(b) 866	Arts 32–33 800
Art 10 . . . . 445, 784, 790–1	Art 32 . . . . 105, 258–9, 261, 268, 281, 1090, 1120
Art 10(1) 784	
Art 10(2) 132, 792–3	Art 33 . . . . 261, 269, 281
Art 11 . . . . . . 299, 621, 656, 791, 983, 1258	Art 33(1) 63, 261, 263, 269–70, 1119–20
Art 11(6) 556	Art 33(2) 263
Art 12 . . . . 210, 212–13, 841, 866–7	Art 33(3) 105, 267, 556, 1102, 1119
Art 13 866–7	Art 34 290–1
Art 13(2)(a) 218–19	Art 34(1) 278–9, 291
Art 13(2)(b) 219	Art 34(2) 105, 291–2
Art 13(2)(c) 219	Art 34(3) 291
Art 13(2)(d) 219	Art 36 . . . . 63, 185, 648
Art 14 . . . . 222, 1495, 1526	Art 37 . . . . 93, 853, 874
Art 14(2) 1497	Art 38 . . . . 860, 874
Art 15 . . . . 809, 866	Art 39 93
Art 15(1) 867	Art 40 442–3
Art 16(1) 817	Art 41 . . . . 443, 978
Art 16(2) 817	Art 41(1) 63
Art 16(3) 797, 818	Art 41(2) 442, 444

Art 41(2)(a)	444
Art 41(3)	960, 989
Arts 43–45	979
Arts 43–44	912
Art 43	890, 895, 917, 941, 1138, 1251
Art 43(1)	852, 894, 968
Art 43(2)	725, 1031
Art 44	643, 803, 912, 917–9, 933, 941, 1138, 1343
Art 44(3)–(4)	895
Art 44(3)	174, 900, 917–19
Art 44(4)	918–19, 1030
Art 44(5)	917–18
Art 44(6)	919
Art 44(7)	919
Art 45	643, 803, 940–3, 945, 952–4
Art 45(1)	556, 943, 948
Art 45(2)	948
Art 45(3)	924, 926, 1125, 1129, 1132
Art 46	1030, 1124, 1126
Art 46(3)	1126
Art 47	946
Art 48	1136
Arts 48–56	1160
Art 50	237, 909
Art 51	437, 744
Art 51(1)	132
Art 51(6)	577, 581, 1164
Art 51(7)	1251
Art 52	577, 581, 1517
Art 52(1)	785, 1164
Art 52(2)	213, 1079
Art 53	577, 581, 1528
Art 53(c)	1164
Art 54	244, 577, 581, 1170, 1513, 1526, 1549
Art 54(2)	244, 1526, 1529
Art 54(3)	1529
Art 54(4)	1164
Art 54(5)	1529
Art 55	577, 581
Art 55(2)	1164
Art 56	577, 581
Art 56(1)	1164
Art 56(4)	1164
Art 56(5)	651
Art 57	213
Art 58	213, 650, 1191
Art 58(a)	651, 1251
Art 58(b)	651
Art 58(c)	900
Art 59	370, 376–7, 379
Art 59(2)	377
Art 60	370, 372, 376–9
Art 60(2)	556
Arts 61–67	650
Art 64(1)	243
Art 66(3)	262
Art 67(1)(c)	262
Arts 69–70	1486
Art 69	1475, 1493
Art 69(1)	242, 1493, 1494, 1506
Art 70	242–3, 250, 1278–9, 1493
Art 70(1)	242, 245, 249, 1300
Art 70(2)	249
Art 70(3)(b)	556
Art 70(4)	240
Art 72	301, 512, 926–7, 1218
Art 73	314, 803, 1141, 1259, 1315, 1436, 1438
Art 74	269, 1102, 1120
Art 75	18, 26, 299, 301, 304, 306, 361, 435, 470, 474, 641, 720, 912, 919, 921, 926–8, 942, 951, 1036, 1057, 1086–7, 1125, 1160, 1177, 1217–18, 1220, 1227–8, 1232, 1236–7, 1239, 1246–7, 1259, 1261, 1272, 1341, 1439, 1450–1
Art 75(1)–(3)	926
Art 75(1)	132, 791, 912, 927, 1160, 1217–18
Art 75(2)	349, 1125
Art 75(2)(a)(i)	450
Art 75(2)(a)(iii)	1257
Art 75(2)(b)	347, 349, 355, 360, 1275
Art 75(2)(c)	298, 301
Art 75(2)(d)	580, 1156, 1159–60, 1176, 1334
Art 75(3)	1340
Art 75(4)	474, 631, 926, 1027, 1131, 1217, 1219, 1235, 1433, 1438–9, 1441–3, 1452–3
Art 75(4)(a)	1225, 1441
Art 75(4)(b)	302, 1156, 1159–60, 1226, 1440
Art 75(4)(c)	1440
Art 75(4)(d)	1452
Art 75(4)(e)	1229, 1452
Art 75(4)(f)	1230, 1452
Art 75(4)(g)	480, 1443
Art 75(4)(h)	484, 1434–5
Art 75(4)(i)	481, 1446, 1452
Art 75(4)(j)	1036, 1235, 1445
Art 75(5)	987, 1282

Art 75(8) 927	Art 92 697
Art 76 .... 346–7, 349, 351, 353, 1275, 1301–2	Art 94 .... 163, 697
	Art 96 698
Art 76(1) 355, 359, 1276	Art 96(1) 698
Art 76(3) 483, 1448	Art 96(3) 20, 48, 55, 169, 686, 698
Art 77 .... 359, 1297, 1302–3, 1305, 1311, 1501	Art 97 .... 172, 690
	Art 99 176
Art 77(1) 355–6	Art 102 158
Art 77(2) 1296, 1302, 1306	Annex I 262, 830, 860–1, 864, 885
Art 77(3) 356, 359	
Art 77(4) 359, 1302	Annex I, Ch III 216
Art 77(5) 483, 1302	1977 Protocol Additional to the Geneva Conventions of 12 August 1949, and relating to the Protection of Victims of Non-International Armed Conflicts (Additional Protocol II)
Art 78 .... 106, 1299, 1301	
Art 78(1) 556	
Art 78(2) 1300	
Art 78(3) 1113	
Art 79 512	Preamble 182–3
Art 79(3) 262	Preamble, para 2 1218
Art 80 .... 63, 653, 873	Preamble, para 4 141
Art 81 650	Art 1 .... 60, 77, 293, 311, 440, 491
Art 81(1) 243	Art 1(1) 41, 115, 152, 171, 251, 360, 393, 397, 407–9, 698–9, 1165
Art 81(4) 1255	
Arts 82–83 653	Art 1(2) 409
Art 82 .... 63, 600, 604, 873	Art 2 76
Arts 83–84 652	Art 2(1) 293, 1285
Art 83 .... 119–20, 600, 605–6	Art 2(2) 53, 61, 1508
Art 83(2) 604	Art 2(4) 1285
Art 84 .... 554, 600, 614, 653	Art 4 .... 299, 304, 306, 354–5, 360, 442, 973, 1007, 1165, 1246–7, 1306, 1367, 1383
Art 85 .... 103, 119, 299, 459, 621, 656, 860, 935, 1226	
	Art 4(1) 132, 357, 791, 1165
Art 85(1) 1345	Art 4(1)(c) 1383
Art 85(2) 314, 803, 836	Art 4(2) 357, 588–9
Art 85(3)(d) 385	Art 4(2)(a) 450
Art 85(3)(f) 853, 874	Art 4(2)(b) 580, 1156, 1159, 1164
Art 85(4) 747	Art 4(2)(c) 298, 301, 309, 311
Art 85(4)(a) 1187, 1210–11, 1416, 1555	Art 4(2)(e) 333, 349, 355, 360, 1285
Art 85(4)(b) 1055, 1063	Art 4(2)(g) 1529, 1548
Art 85(4)(c) 201, 1249	Art 4(3) 434, 447, 1306
Art 85(4)(e) 720, 1451	Art 4(3)(a) 1300, 1306
Art 86 .... 627, 1438	Art 4(3)(b) 1115, 1121, 1306
Art 86(2) 749–50	Art 4(3)(c) 356, 1306
Art 87 .... 628, 654, 749–50, 873	Art 4(3)(d) 1306
Art 87(1) 630	Arts 5–6 .... 434, 447
Art 87(2) 600, 603	Art 5 .... 310, 536, 933, 973, 1007, 1131, 1165, 1266, 1342, 1367, 1382, 1383, 1508
Art 87(3) 630	
Art 88 636	
Art 88(2) 656	Art 5(1) 1367
Art 89 .... 125, 129	Art 5(2) 1131
Art 90 .... 128, 313, 564, 570, 630, 1510, 1570	Art 5(2)(a) 434, 447, 1115, 1286
	Art 5(2)(b) 1115, 1119, 1131
Art 90(2)(c)(i) 125	Art 5(2)(c) 973
Art 91 .... 337, 340, 386, 593, 659, 752, 934, 975, 981, 1169, 1253, 1344	Art 5(3) 1259

Art 5(4) 1383	1978 Vienna Convention on Succession
Art 6 . . . . 470, 488, 491, 493,	of States in respect of Treaties 164–5
720, 933, 1164–5, 1217, 1227–8,	Art 2(1)(b) 164
1236, 1239, 1302, 1342, 1451, 1508	Art 2(1)(d) 164
Art 6(2) 472, 474, 1220, 1439, 1450–2	Art 16 166
Art 6(2)(a) 476, 1225	Art 20 174
Art 6(2)(b) 302, 1156, 1159, 1164	Arts 31–33 164
Art 6(2)(c) 474, 1227, 1451	Art 34 . . . . 164, 166
Art 6(2)(d) 1452	1979 Code of Conduct for Law
Art 6(2)(e) 481, 1452	Enforcement Officials,
Art 6(2)(f) 482, 1230, 1452	UNGA Res 34/169 . . . . 465, 606
Art 6(3) 483	Art 2 606
Art 6(4) 434, 447, 483–4, 1306	Art 3 . . . . 606, 983
Art 6(5) 310, 493, 1061, 1367	1979 Convention on the Elimination
Arts 7–12 835	of All Forms of Discrimination
Art 7 . . . . 447, 765, 793, 799, 802, 1286	against Women 345, 365, 1194,
Art 7(1) 445, 784, 799	1272, 1471
Art 7(2) 132, 793, 799	Art 1 345
Art 8 . . . . .272, 278, 286, 292–3,	Art 2 1272
434, 787, 800	Art 10 1476
Art 9 . . . . 434, 447, 819, 850, 866	Art 12 1280
Art 9(1) 819	Art 15(4) 1194
Art 10(1) 802	1979 International Convention Against
Art 10(2) 802	the Taking of Hostages 303, 305,
Art 10(3) 797, 818	307–8, 313–15, 706–8, 1383
Art 10(4) 797	Art 1 . . . . .304, 307–8, 310, 313, 1335
Art 11 . . . . 835, 850, 866	Art 1(1) 1383
Art 11(1) 224, 835	Art 3 314
Art 11(2) 850	Art 6 314
Art 12 . . . . .650, 859–60, 866,	Art 12 . . . . 8, 313–14, 707–8
868, 871–2, 882	1979 Israel–Egypt Peace Treaty,
Art 12(1) 651	18 *ILM* (1979) 362–93 56
Art 12(4) 651	Art 1.1 56
Art 13 .132, 379, 744	1979 UNGA Res 34/37 1459
Art 13(2) 379	1979 UNSC Res 446 (1979)
Art 13(3) 437–8, 1473	para 1 1556
Art 14 . . . . .244, 379, 1529	1979 UNSC Res 452 (1979)
Art 16 .1528, 1530	Preamble, para 3 1556
Art 17 . . . . 434, 447, 1182, 1186,	1980 Convention on Prohibitions or
1205, 1207–8, 1320	Restrictions on the Use of Certain
Art 17(1) 1205–10, 1212	Conventional Weapons which
Art 17(2) 1208–9	may be Deemed to be Excessively
Art 18 . . . . .251, 536, 650	Injurious or to Have Indiscriminate
Art 18(1) 250	Effects 19–21, 699
Art 18(2) 243, 250–1, 434, 447	Art 1 699
Art 19 . . . . . . .426, 600, 610, 652, 654, 873	Art 1(6) 426
Art 20 697	Art 6 600
Art 22 . . . . 163, 697	Art 7(4) 19–20
Art 24 . . . . 173, 690	Art 7(4)(b) 20
Art 25 176	1980 HRComm Res 20 (XXXVI),
Art 25(2) 61	Question of Missing and
Art 28 158	Disappeared Persons 271

1980 Protocol on Prohibitions or
Restrictions on the Use of Mines,
Booby-Traps and Other Devices
(Protocol II) to the Convention
on Certain Conventional Weapons
  Art 3(2) 577
1980 UNSC Res 465 (1980)
  para 5 1556
1980 UNSC Res 467 (1980) 208
1980 UNSC Res 478 (1980) 1465
1981 African Charter on Human
  and Peoples' Rights 727–8, 1194,
                1224, 1260, 1352, 1417
  Art 2 .... 728, 1260
  Art 5 .... 274, 1248
  Art 7 .... 471, 1160
  Art 7(1) 1225, 1228
  Art 7(1)(b) 475
  Art 7(1)(c) 476–7, 1226
  Art 7(1)(d) 484–5, 1221, 1224
  Art 7(2) 302, 719, 1226–7
  Art 12(1) 1193
  Art 12(2) 1194
  Art 12(5) 1194
  Art 14 727
  Art 15 1370
  Art 15(1) 1245
  Art 18(1) 1092, 1116
  Art 18(2) 1092
  Art 26 1221
  Art 60 727
  Art 61 727
1981 Declaration of Malta 91
1982 HRCttee, General Comment 6,
  Article 6 (Right to Life)
  para 3 .... 285, 464
1982 Memorandum of Agreement
  between the United States of
  America and the Republic of
  Korea on the Transfer of Prisoners
  of War/Civilian Internees
  para 1 969–71
  para 2 969–71
1982 Principles of Medical Ethics
  relevant to the Role of Health
  Personnel, particularly Physicians,
  in the Protection of Prisoners and
  Detainees against Torture and
  Other Cruel, Inhuman or
  Degrading Treatment or Punishment,
  UNGA Res 37/194
  Principle 3 1356

1982 United Nations Convention
  on the Law of the Sea 159, 1567
  Art 88 74
  Art 89 74
1983 HRComm Res 1983/5
  para 2 208
1983 HRCttee, General Comment 11,
  Article 20 (Prohibition of Propaganda)
  para 2 1246
1983 Memorandum from the ICRC to the
  States Parties to the Geneva Conventions
  of August 12, 1949 concerning the conflict
  between Islamic Republic of Iran and
  Republic of Iraq, Geneva, 7 May 987, 1023
1983 Protocol No 6 to the European
  Convention on Human Rights . . . 1381, 1453
  Art 2 484
  Art 3 484
1983 UNSC Res 541 (1983) 1558
1984 Cartagena Declaration on
  Refugees 1323
1984 Convention against Torture and
  Other Cruel, Inhuman or Degrading
  Treatment and Punishment 324–5, 340,
                631, 704, 746, 928, 972, 1053,
                1352, 1371, 1375, 1381, 1471
  Art 1 .... 302, 306, 320–1, 323–5, 329,
                341, 1363
  Art 1(1) 324, 328
  Art 2 321
  Art 3 .... 485, 928, 1203–4
  Art 3(1) 1379, 1384
  Art 4 337
  Art 7 635
  Art 7(1) 631
  Art 10 1358
  Art 13 .... 340, 1359
  Art 14 .... 340, 1359
  Art 15 1230
  Art 16 .... 337, 1363
  Art 22 .... 341, 1359
1984 HRCttee, General Comment 13,
  Article 14 (Administration
  of Justice) 1442–3
  para 4 1223
  para 14 1230
1984 Protocol No 7 to the European
  Convention on Human Rights
  Art 2(2) 483
  Art 4 .... 484, 1362
  Art 4(1) 1232, 1435
  Art 4(2) 484

1984 Second Memorandum from the ICRC to the States Parties to the Geneva Conventions of August 12, 1949 concerning the conflict between Islamic Republic of Iran and Republic of Iraq, Geneva, 10 February ... 987, 1021, 1023
1984 UNGA Res 39/119
   para 9 208
1985 Declaration of Basic Principles of Justice for Victims of Crime and Abuse of Power, UNGA Res 40/34 1352
1985 Inter-American Convention to Prevent and Punish Torture 1203, 1352
   Art 1 709
   Art 6 709
   Art 8 709
   Art 13(4) 1203
1985 Nairobi Peace Agreement between the Government of Uganda and the National Resistance Movement 512
1985 UN Basic Principles on the Independence of the Judiciary
   Principle 1 472
   Principle 2 472
   Principle 5 .... 471, 1224
   Principle 7 472
   Principles 11–14 472
   Principles 17–20 472
1985 UNGA Res 40/32 471–2
1985 UNGA Res 40/139
   para 3 208
1985 UNGA Res 40/146 471–2
1985 UN Standard Minimum Rules for the Administration of Juvenile Justice, UNGA Res 40/33
   Rule 4 1295
1986 HRCttee, General Comment 15, The position of aliens under the Covenant
   para 10 1194
1986 ICRC Resolution 14, National Information Bureau, 25th International Conference of the Red Cross 266, 649
1986 Statutes of the International Red Cross and Red Crescent Movement as amended in December 1995 and June 2006 .... 88, 499, 528–9
   Preamble 530
   Preamble, para 2 498
   Art 3 1103
   Art 3(2) 601
   Art 4 .... 165, 241
   Art 4(5) 880
   Art 5 .... 878, 1103
   Art 5(1) 528
   Art 5(2)(c) 878
   Art 5(2)(d)–(3) 533
   Art 5(2)(d) 536
   Art 5(2)(g) 601, 878
   Art 5(2)(h) 528
   Art 5(3) 88, 416, 499, 506
   Art 5(4)(a) 601
1986 UNGA Res 41/157
   para 4 208
1986 Vienna Convention on the Law of Treaties between States and International Organizations or between International Organizations
   Art 2(1)(h) 529
   Art 34 420
1987 European Convention for the Prevention of Torture and Inhuman or Degrading Treatment or Punishment ... 1352
1987 HRComm Res 1987/51
   para 5 208
1987 UNSC Res 598 (1987) 1063
1988 HRCttee, General Comment 16, Article 17 (Right to Privacy)
   para 1 .... 1095, 1116
   para 5 .... 1093, 1245
   para 9 1490
   para 10 1098
1988 UN Body of Principles for the Protection of All Persons under Any Form of Detention or Imprisonment, UNGA Res 43/173 .... 477–8, 1352, 1371, 1443, 1449
   Principle 1 1351
   Principle 10–14 1225
   Principle 12 1369
   Principle 16(1) 1369
   Principle 17 478
   Principle 18 1443
   Principle 18(4) 477
   Principle 21 1230
   Principle 36 1228
1988 UNGA Res 43/131 232
1989 Convention on the Rights of the Child 233, 365, 711, 1235, 1261, 1303–4, 1311, 1352, 1357, 1471, 1476, 1502, 1569
   Preamble, para 9 1294
   Art 1 .... 1295, 1501
   Art 3 1303
   Art 3(1) 1357

Art 9 1102
Art 9(1) 1095, 1116
Art 10 1174
Art 10(1) 1094
Art 16 .... 711, 1500
Art 22 233
Art 24 .... 711, 1500
Art 27 .... 711, 1500
Art 28 .... 711, 1476, 1500, 1503
Art 28(1) 1357
Art 29 .... 1476, 1502–3
Art 34 345
Art 37 483
Art 37(a) 1302
Art 38 .... 345, 367, 434, 447, 711,
                    1303–4, 1311–2
Art 38(1) 113, 711, 719, 1304
Art 38(4) 1304, 1501
Art 40(2)(b)(i) 1228
Art 40(2)(b)(ii) 1225
Art 40(2)(b)(iv) 1230
Art 42 600
Art 45(c) 1303
1989 ILO Convention concerning
  Indigenous and Tribal Peoples in
  Independent Countries (No 169)
  Art 16 1193
1989 Second Optional Protocol to the
  International Covenant on Civil and
  Political Rights 1453
  Art 1 484
  Art 2 484
1990 African Charter on the Rights and
  Welfare of the Child 718, 1295, 1352
  Art 18(1) 1092, 1094, 1116
  Art 19 1102
  Art 19(1) 1116
  Art 19(2) 1095
  Art 19(3) 1095
1990 Basic Principles for the Treatment of
  Prisoners, UNGA Res 45/111 ..... 1352, 1371
  Principle 1 1351
1990 Cairo Declaration on Human
  Rights in Islam
  Art 19(e) 1225
1990 CESCR, General Comment 3:
  The Nature of States Parties
  Obligations (Art 2, para 1)........... 986
  para 2 1490
  para 8 1504
  para 10....................... 1490
1990 HRCttee, General Comment 19,
  Article 23 (The Family)

Protection of the Family, the Right to
  Marriage and Equality of the Spouses
  para 2 1093
  para 5 1116
1990 International Convention on the
  Protection of the Rights of All
  Migrant Workers and Their
  Families....................... 1194
  Art 22(1) 1194
  Art 39 1194
1990 Protocol to the American
  Convention on Human Rights to
  Abolish the Death Penalty...... 1381, 1453
  Art 1 484
  Art 2 484
1990 Turku Declaration of Minimum
  Humanitarian Standards
  Art 14(1) 800
  Art 14(2) 800
1990 UN Basic Principles on the
  Role of Lawyers
  Principle 18 477
1990 UN Basic Principles on the
  Use of Force and Firearms by Law
  Enforcement Officials, A/Conf.144/28/
  Rev.1 606
  Art 9 .... 465, 983
  Art 10 983
1990 UNGA Res 45/6 529
1990 UNGA Res 45/100 232
1990 UNGA Res 45/166 477
1990 UNSC Res 681 (1990)
  para 5 121
1991 Agreement concluded between the
  Yugoslav People's Army, the Croatian
  Government, and a representative of
  the European Community Monitoring
  Mission (Zagreb Agreement)
  18 November................... 519
1991 Agreement on a Comprehensive
  Political Settlement of the Cambodia
  Conflict
  Pt VI, Art 21 .... 1377, 1383, 1386
1991 Arrangement for the Transfer
  of Enemy Prisoners of War and Civilian
  Internees from the Custody of the
  British Forces to the Custody of the
  American Forces, 31 January...... 969–71
1991 ILC Draft Code of Crimes against
  the Peace and Security of Mankind,
  YILC (1991), vol II, Pt II, at 97........ 623
  Art 8(a) 1233
  Art 22(2)(a) 1063, 1167

1991 Inter-American Convention to
 Facilitate Disaster Assistance 235
1991 Memorandum of Understanding
 relating to the conflict between Croatia
 and Yugoslavia, 27 November
 para 13. 612
1991 National Democratic Front of the
 Philippines Declaration of Adherence to
 International Humanitarian Law,
 15 August 421
1991 Peace Accords between the Government
 of Angola and the National Union for the
 Total Independence of Angola
 Art II(3). 512
1991 UN Compensation Commission
 Decision 1, Criteria for Expedited
 Processing of Urgent Claims,
 S/AC.26/1991/1
 para 10. 1183
 para 18(e). 1183
1991 UNGA Res 46/182 . . . . 232, 240
1991 UNSC Res 686 (1991)
 para 2(c). 1377–8, 1386
1991 UNSC Res 687 (1991) 1183
 para 16. 64
 para 18. 64
1991 UNSC Res 688 (1991) 383
1992 Agreement between Croatia
 and the Federal Republic of
 Yugoslavia on the Exchange
 of Prisoners
 Art 1(4) 1383
1992 Agreement between the Parties
 to the Conflict in Bosnia and
 Herzegovina on the Release and
 Transfer of Prisoners
 Art 3(1) 1377
1992 Agreement on the Application of
 International Humanitarian Law
 between the Parties to the
 Conflict in Bosnia-Herzegovina 421,
  426, 510–11, 514, 517–18, 520
 Art 2(1) 225
 Art 2(2) 224
 Art 2(3) 512
 Art 2(6) 512
 Art 3 . . . . 518, 520
 Art 4 612
1992 CEDAW Committee, General
 Recommendation No 19 on
 Violence against Women 364, 1286, 1291
 para 7(c). 345
 para 19. 1280
1992 Code of Conduct of the National
 Resistance in Uganda 312
1992 General Peace Agreement for
 Mozambique 62
 Protocol VI, para 8(III) 1383
 Protocol VI, para 8(III)(1) 1380
1992 HRCttee, General Comment 20,
 Article 7 (Replaces General Comment
 7 concerning Prohibition of Torture,
 or other Cruel, Inhuman or Degrading
 Treatment or Punishment) 320, 983
 para 4 1248
 para 9 . . . . 1053, 1203
 para 12. 1230
1992 Peace Agreement signed by the
 Government of El Salvador and the
 Frente Farabundo Martí, UN Doc
 A/46/863-S/23504
 Annex I 62
1992 UN Declaration on the Protection of
 All Persons from Enforced
 Disappearance, UNGA
 Res 47/133. 1369
1992 UNGA Res 47/37 609
1992 UNSC Res 743 (1992). 383
1992 UNSC Res 762 (1992). 383
1992 UNSC Res 771 (1992) 167
1992 UNSC Res 780 (1992). 430
1992 UNSC Res 794 (1992) 208, 383
1993 Agreement between the ICRC and
 the Swiss Federal Council to
 Determine the Legal Status of the
 Committee in Switzerland, 33
 IRRC 293 (1993) 150
 Art 1 529
 Art 2 530
 Art 22 529
1993 Cotonou Agreement on Liberia
 Art 10 . . . . 1380, 1383
1993 Declaration on the Elimination
 of Violence against Women,
 UNGA Res 48/104 345
 Preamble 1272–3
 Art 4(d) 1287
1993 Final Declaration of the International
 Conference for the Protection of War
 Victims, Geneva
 Pt II, para 11 122
1993 HRComm Resolution 1993/6 589
1993 HRCttee, General Comment 22,
 Article 18 (Freedom of Thought,
 Conscience or Religion)
 para 1 1246

para 3 1246	Art 1 937
para 8 1246	Art 2 937
1993 Statute of the International Criminal Tribunal for the former Yugoslavia 252, 276, 300, 339–40, 354, 363, 593, 629, 1228, 1232, 1249, 1369	Art 2(2) 9
	Art 7 .... 240, 937
	Art 9 251
	Art 20 937
	Art 21 238
Art 2 .... 303, 315, 645–6, 791	1994 HRComm Resolution 1994/84 589
Art 2(b) 339, 1259, 1267	1994 Inter-American Convention on Forced Disappearance of Persons 706, 709, 1352, 1368
Art 2(c) 340, 1267	
Art 2(d) 1532	
Art 2(f) 747	Art I......................... 709
Art 2(g) 935, 1259, 1345	Art XI(2) 272
Art 2(h) 315	Art XV 709
Art 3 .... 143, 252, 303, 315, 339, 359–60, 379, 385, 450, 520, 646, 745, 804, 821, 1267	1994 Inter-American Convention on the Prevention, Punishment and Eradication of Violence against Women 345
Art 3(c) 385	Art 7 709
Art 3(e) 1369, 1521, 1529, 1532	Art 7(f) 1287
Art 4 252	Art 7(g) 1287
Art 5 252	1994 Statute of the International Criminal Tribunal for Rwanda 252, 300, 339, 354, 363, 593, 1171, 1232
Art 5(e) 492	
Art 5(f) 339–40	
Art 5(i) 295, 1369	Art 1 .... 82, 401
Art 7(1) 747, 1227	Art 3 340
Art 7(3) 407	Art 3(e) 492
Art 8(2) 1232	Art 3(f) 339
Art 10 1232	Art 4 .... 355, 360, 401, 430, 450, 805
Art 12 1222	Art 4(a) 339
Art 13 1222	Art 4(b) 1156, 1166
Art 21(2) 1233	Art 4(c) 315
Art 21(3) 1229	Art 4(e) 340
Art 21(4)(a) 1225	Art 4(f) 1369, 1529, 1532
Art 21(4)(b) 1443–4	Art 4(g) 492, 747
Art 21(4)(d) 1230, 1444	Art 6(1) 747, 1227
Art 21(4)(e) 1231	Art 6(3) 407
Art 21(4)(f) 1444	Art 7 401
Art 21(4)(g) 1231	Art 9 1232
Art 24(1) 625	Art 9(2) 1232
1993 UNGA Res 48/52 589	Art 12 1222
1993 UNSC Res 808 (1993) 503	Art 20(2) 1233
para 2 1228	Art 20(3) 1229
1993 UNSC Res 819 (1993) 384	Art 20(4)(a) 1225
1993 UNSC Res 824 (1993) 384	Art 20(4)(b) 1443–4
1993 UNSC Res 836 (1993) 385	Art 20(4)(d) 1230, 1444
1993 UNSC Res 837 (1993) 385	Art 20(4)(e) 1231
1993 UNSC Res 844 (1993) 385	Art 20(4)(f) 1444
1993 Vienna Declaration and Programme of Action, UN Doc A/CONF.157/24	Art 20(4)(g) 1231
	Art 23 625
	1994 Treaty of Peace between the State of Israel and the Hashemite Kingdom of Jordan 56
Part I, para 28 1287	
1994 Convention on the Safety of United Nations and Associated Personnel 9, 16, 238	
	Preamble, para 7 56
	Art 1 56

1994 UNGA Res 49/50 609
1994 UNGA Res 49/207 589
1994 UNSC Res 929 (1994)........... 384
1994 UNSC Res 941 (1994)........... 384
1994 UNSC Res 955 (1994).......... 1166
1994 Universal Postal Convention
　Art 7(3) 1361
1995 Agreement between the International
　Criminal Tribunal for the Former
　Yugoslavia and the ICRC on Procedures
　for Visiting Persons Held on the
　Authority of the Tribunal, 36 *IRRC*
　311 (1996) 238.................. 545
1995 Agreements 'On Ground Rules'
　between the UN Operation Lifeline
　Sudan and the Sudan People's
　Liberation Movement/Army 246
1995 Beijing Declaration and Platform for
　Action, Fourth World Conference on
　Women, A/CONF.177/20 (1995) and
　A/CONF.177.20/Add.1 (1995),
　18 September
　para 33........................ 1287
　para 133....................... 364
　para 135....................... 1273
1995 Commonwealth of Independent
　States Convention on Human Rights
　and Fundamental Freedoms
　Art 25(4) 1194
1995 General Framework Agreement
　for Peace in Bosnia and Herzegovina
　(Dayton Peace Agreement) 271, 1559
　Annex 1A, Art I(2)(a)............. 56
　Annex 1A, Art IX 1058, 1378
　Annex 1A, Art IX(1)(c) 1377, 1381, 1386
　Annex 1A, Art IX(1)(e) 1055
　Annex 1A, Art IX(1)(g) 1380
1995 HRComm Resolution 1995/74 589
1995 Israeli-Palestinian Interim
　Agreement on the West Bank
　and the Gaza Strip............... 1464
　Art XI 1468
　Art XIII....................... 1468
　Art XVII 1468
1995 Protocol on Blinding Laser Weapons
　(Protocol IV) to the Convention on
　Certain Conventional Weapons
　Art 2 600
1995 UNSC Res 999 (1995).......... 1061
1996 Agreement on the Implementation,
　Compliance and Verification Timetable
　for the Peace Agreements and the
　Agreement for a Firm and Lasting
　Peace 29 December 1996 by the Peace
　Commission of the Government of
　Guatemala and the General Command
　of the Unidad Revolucionaria Nacional
　Guatemalteca, UN Doc A/51/796-
　S/1997/114...................... 62
1996 April Cease-Fire Understanding
　between Israel and Hezbollah 572
1996 Council Regulation 1257/96/EC
　concerning Humanitarian Aid
　(modified in 2003 and 2009)......... 235
　Preamble 232
1996 HRComm Resolution 1996/71
　para 12 1058
1996 ILC Draft Code of Crimes
　against the Peace and Security
　of Mankind, *YILC* (1996),
　vol II, pt II, at 53 .... 331, 1189, 1555
　Art 20(c)(i).................... 1555
　Art 20(c)(2) 1063
1996 Protocol on Prohibitions or
　Restrictions on the Use of Mines,
　Booby-Traps and other Devices as
　amended on 3 May 1996 (Protocol II)
　to the Convention on Certain
　Conventional Weapons
　Art 1(6) 426
　Art 3(7) 577, 582
　Art 14 .... 600, 1226
1997 Agreement on the Organization
　of the International Activities of the
　Components of the International Red
　Cross and Red Crescent Movement
　(Seville Agreement) 404
　Art 5.2(b) 410
　Art 5.3.1 1255
　Art 6 536
1997 CESCR, General Comment 7:
　The Right to Adequate Housing
　(Art 11 para 1) (forced evictions)
　para 3 1193
　para 5 1193
　para 12....................... 1193
1997 Convention of the Law of the
　Non-navigational Uses of
　International Watercourses 1478
1997 Council Decision 97/430/EC
　concerning the conclusion of the
　Euro-Mediterranean Interim
　Association Agreement on Trade and
　Cooperation between the European
　Community, of the one part, and the
　Palestine Liberation Organization

(PLO) for the benefit of the Palestinian
Authority of the West Bank and the
Gaza Strip
   Art 73 1481
1997 Kyoto Protocol to the UN
Framework Convention on
Climate Change
   Art 24(1) 163
1997 Ottawa Convention of the
Prohibition of the Use, Stockpiling,
Production and Transfer of
Anti-Personnel Mines and on
   their Destruction 539, 700
   Preamble 182
   Art 9 1226
1997 Sub-Commission Resolution 1997/29
(Freedom of Movement and
Population Transfer),
E/CN.4.Sub.2/1997/23
   Preamble, para 7 1193
   Art 3 .... 1189, 1193
1997 UNGA Res 51/112 1377
1998 Agreement concluded between
the ELN and National Peace
Committee (Acuerdo de la Puerta
   del Cielo) 511
   para 14 223
1998 Comprehensive Agreement on
Respect for Human Rights and
International Humanitarian
Law between the Government
of the Republic of the Philippines
and the National Democratic Front
   of the Philippines 511, 518
   Preamble 612
   Art 4(3) 223
   Art 6 518
   Pt IV, Art 3(1) 312
1998 NATO Standard Agreement 2931 ... 883
1998 Rome Statute of the International
   Criminal Court 24, 60, 142–3,
       149, 201–2, 224, 226, 253–4, 300,
       305, 315, 325, 327, 329, 339, 351–3,
       355, 362, 365–7, 393, 408, 411,
       413–14, 407, 459, 461, 463, 470,
       520, 539, 593–4, 627–8, 634,
       637–8, 657, 661–2, 699–700, 740,
       746, 831, 836, 853, 872, 876, 1063,
       1156, 1166, 1168, 1171, 1193,
       1227–8, 1249, 1261, 1286, 1289,
       1296, 1320, 1367, 1453, 1513, 1530, 1532
   Preamble, para 6 637
   Pt I 746

Art 1 .... 637, 1512
Arts 5–21 851
Arts 5–8 637
Art 5 202
Art 5(1) 520
Art 6 .... 202, 805, 1228
Art 7 .... 202, 324, 805,
              1152, 1228, 1320
Art 7(1) 323
Art 7(1)(b) 1513
Art 7(1)(e) 492, 1370
Art 7(1)(f) 339, 1470
Art 7(1)(g) 1470
Art 7(1)(g)(1) 1276, 1291
Art 7(1)(g)(2) 1277
Art 7(1)(g)(3) 1277
Art 7(1)(g)(6) 1277
Art 7(1)(h) 202, 1291
Art 7(1)(i) 276, 1118–19, 1368
Art 7(1)(k) 254, 332, 340–1, 1228
Art 7(2)(b) 252, 1513
Art 7(2)(d) 1189
Art 7(2)(e) 323, 325, 329–30, 341
Art 7(2)(g) 354
Art 7(2)(h) 202
Art 7(2)(i) 258, 1024, 1118–19
Art 8 .... 24, 202, 225–6,
     357, 363, 656, 745, 748, 805, 1009,
       1118, 1167–8, 1211, 1228, 1310
Art 8(1) 314–15
Art 8(2)(a) 315, 700, 785, 804,
            1132, 1152, 1513
Art 8(2)(a)(i)–(iii) 804
Art 8(2)(a)(i) 748, 851
Art 8(2)(a)(ii) 332, 339, 748, 1065, 1249,
              1259, 1470
Art 8(2)(a)(ii)(2) 1248
Art 8(2)(a)(iii) 340, 1470
Art 8(2)(a)(iv) 836, 851, 1530
Art 8(2)(a)(v) 1466
Art 8(2)(a)(vi) 747, 935, 1037, 1235,
              1433, 1451
Art 8(2)(a)(vii) 935, 1211, 1259, 1345,
              1384, 1416
Art 8(2)(a)(viii) 314, 1267, 1383–4
Art 8(2)(b) 363, 743, 1152
Art 8(2)(b)(i)–(ii) 545
Art 8(2)(b)(i) 385
Art 8(2)(b)(ii) 852
Art 8(2)(b)(iii) 545, 1513
Art 8(2)(b)(v) 385
Art 8(2)(b)(vii) 853, 874
Art 8(2)(b)(viii) 1187, 1211, 1416, 1555

Art 8(2)(b)(ix) 224, 385, 804, 837, 852, 1533
Art 8(2)(b)(x)(1). 1258
Art 8(2)(b)(xi) 853
Art 8(2)(b)(xii). 1530
Art 8(2)(b)(xiii) 748, 837, 1531–2
Art 8(2)(b)(xiv) 1451
Art 8(2)(b)(xvi) 785, 787, 1521, 1532
Art 8(2)(b)(xix) 142
Art 8(2)(b)(xxi) . . . 294, 340, 351, 361, 748, 1249, 1288, 1470
Art 8(2)(b)(xxii). 351, 354, 357, 361, 367, 1470
Art 8(2)(b)(xxii)(1). 1276, 1291
Art 8(2)(b)(xxii)(2). 1277
Art 8(2)(b)(xxii)(3). 1277
Art 8(2)(b)(xxii)(6) 1277
Art 8(2)(b)(xxiii) 853, 991, 1267
Art 8(2)(b)(xxiv) 224, 545, 745, 821, 837, 852, 874
Art 8(2)(b)(xxv) 252–3, 746, 1513
Art 8(2)(b)(xxvi) 437, 1296
Art 8(2)(c)–(f) 395
Art 8(2)(c) 363, 395–6, 430, 700, 746, 798, 820, 837, 1132, 1152
Art 8(2)(c)(i) 332, 339, 450, 492, 804, 837, 1289
Art 8(2)(c)(i)(2) 1258
Art 8(2)(c)(ii) 292, 294, 340, 361, 1289
Art 8(2)(c)(iii) 315, 1383–4
Art 8(2)(c)(iv). 492, 747, 1235, 1451–2
Art 8(2)(d) 395
Art 8(2)(e) 395–6, 743, 837, 852, 1152
Art 8(2)(e)(i) 385
Art 8(2)(e)(ii)–(iv) 545
Art 8(2)(e)(ii) 224, 821, 837, 850, 852, 874
Art 8(2)(e)(iii) 253
Art 8(2)(e)(iv). 224, 385, 804, 837, 850, 852, 1533
Art 8(2)(e)(v) 837, 1521, 1532, 1548
Art 8(2)(e)(vi). 354, 367, 1286, 1289
Art 8(2)(e)(vi)(6) 1277
Art 8(2)(e)(vii) 356, 437, 1296, 1310
Art 8(2)(e)(viii) 1206–7, 1210–11, 1320
Art 8(2)(e)(ix) 853
Art 8(2)(e)(xi) 1258
Art 8(2)(e)(xii) 837, 1529, 1531–2, 1548
Art 8(2)(f) 41, 395, 406
Art 8*bis*(1) 149
Art 10 . . . . .746, 1167
Art 11 1228
Art 12 638
Art 13(b) 1289

Art 17 . . . . .339, 1367, 1435
Art 17(2) 1232
Art 20 . . . . 1232, 1362
Art 21 594
Art 21(1)(b) 594
Art 21(1)(c) 594
Art 21(3) 254, 595
Art 22 1228
Art 24 1228
Art 25 1227
Art 25(2) 520
Art 25(3)(a) 626
Art 25(3)(f) 743
Art 26 1297
Art 27 634
Art 28 . . . . .627, 750, 872, 1227
Art 31 592–3
Art 31(3) 594
Art 33 620
Art 36(2) 571
Art 38 407
Art 40 1222
Art 45 1222
Art 53 631
Art 55(1)(a) 1231
Art 63(1) 1230
Art 66 1229
Art 67 1439
Art 67(1) 1222, 1231
Art 67(1)(a) 1225
Art 67(1)(b) 1443–4
Art 67(1)(d) 1230, 1444
Art 67(1)(f) 1444
Art 67(1)(g) 1231
Art 68 283
Art 75 283
Art 77 625
Art 86 657
1998 UN Guiding Principles on Internal Displacement, E/CN.4/1998/53/Add.2, 10 May 1207, 1381
Principle 6 1193
1998 UNSC Res 1193 (1998) 10
1998 UNSC Res 1208 (1998). 602, 610
1998 UNSC Res 1213 (1998) 10
1998 UNSC Res 1214 (1998) 10
1998 UNSC Res 1216 (1998) 10
1999 CEDAW Committee, General Recommendation No 24 on Women and Health (Art 12)
para 12(a). 1274
para 12(b) 1274

Table of Legislation

 para 12(c). 1274
 para 16. 1280
1999 CESCR, General Comment 12:
 The Right to Adequate Food (Art 11)
 para 6 1494
 para 25. 1494
1999 HRCttee General Comment 27,
 Article 12 (Freedom of Movement)
 para 1 1173
 para 7 1193
 para 8 1180
 para 11. 1181
 para 13 1181
 para 14 . . . . 1181, 1573
 para 15 1181
 para 16 1181
 para 17 1184
 para 18 1180
 para 19 1194
1999 ILO Convention concerning the
 Prohibition and Immediate Action
 for the Elimination of the Worst
 Forms of Child Labour
 (No 182) 1261, 1492
 Art 3 1303
1999 Peace Agreement between the
 Government of Sierra Leone and
 the Revolutionary United Front
 (Lomé Peace Agreement) 62
1999 OAU Convention on the
 Prevention and Combating
 of Terrorism. 315
 Art 1 315
1999 Optional Protocol to the Convention
 on the Elimination of All Forms of
 Discrimination against Women. 365
1999 Second Protocol to the Hague
 Convention of 1954 for the
 Protection of Cultural Property
 in the Event of Armed
 Conflict. 881, 1478
 Art 3 1530
 Art 15 1226
 Art 15(1) 1533
 Art 15(1)(d) 1533
 Art 15(1)(e) 1533
 Art 16(1) 1533
 Art 22(1) 1530
 Art 22(6). 426
 Art 30 600
 Art 34 556
 Art 36 . . . . 556, 567
 Art 37 653–4

1999 UNSC Res 1244 (1999). 1457, 1462
1999 UNSC Res 1251 (1999). 1558
1999 UNSC Res 1261 (1999). 1306
1999 UNSC Res 1265 (1999). 606, 610
1999 UNSC Res 1272 (1999). 1462
1999 UNSC Res 1284 (1999). 1058
2000 Agreement between the
 Government of the State of Eritrea
 and the Government of the
 Federal Democratic Republic
 of Ethiopia 64, 1049
 Art 1 56
 Art 2(2) 1377–8
2000 Agreement on Cessation of
 Hostilities between the Government
 of the Federal Democratic Republic
 of Ethiopia and the Government of the
 State of Eritrea. 1048
2000 Arusha Peace and Reconciliation
 Agreement for Burundi 62
2000 CESCR, General Comment 14:
 The Right to the Highest Attainable
 Standard of Health (Art 12). 1496
 para 12(a). 1496
 para 12(b) 1496
 para 12(c). 1496–7
 para 12(d) 1496
 para 33. . . . . 1243, 1245
 para 50 799
2000 Charter of Fundamental
 Rights of the European Union. 1352
 Art 7 1092
 Art 19(1) 1194
 Art 19(2) 928, 1053, 1203
 Art 21 204
 Art 47 1232
 Art 48(1) 1229
 Art 48(2) 1225
 Art 49 719
 Art 49(2) 660
2000 ICC Elements of Crimes 292, 294,
   303–5, 307–9, 328, 332, 342, 354,
   357, 461, 470, 493, 805, 831, 1168,
   1189–90, 1210–11, 1228, 1235, 1248,
   1258, 1267, 1276–7, 1451, 1521
 Art 7(1)(f) 327
 Art 7(1)(g)-1 352
 Art 8 805
 Art 8(2)(a)(ii). 327, 329
 Art 8(2)(a)(ii)-1 1513
 Art 8(2)(a)(ii)-2 1513
 Art 8(2)(a)(viii) 304, 307–8, 310,
          1335, 1383

Art 8(2)(b)(ix) 224, 226, 1513
Art 8(2)(b)(x)-1 1513
Art 8(2)(b)(x)-2 1513
Art 8(2)(b)(xxi) 334
Art 8(2)(b)(xxii)-1 352
Art 8(2)(b)(xxii)-3 354
Art 8(2)(b)(xxiv) 224, 226
Art 8(2)(b)(xxv) 1513
Art 8(2)(c)(i) 329
Art 8(2)(c)(i)-4 202
Art 8(2)(c)(ii) 334
Art 8(2)(c)(iii) 304, 307–8, 310,
1335, 1383
Art 8(2)(c)(iv) 1222
Art 8(2)(c)(iv)-4 493
Art 8(2)(e)(ii) 224, 226
Art 8(2)(e)(iv) 224, 226, 1513
Art 8(2)(e)(vi)-1 352
Art 8(2)(e)(xi)-1 1513
Art 8(2)(e)(xi)-2 1513
2000 Optional Protocol to the
 Convention on the Rights of the
 Child on the Involvement of
 Children in Armed Conflict 345, 365,
  711, 1261, 1295, 1304–5, 1312, 1501
 Preamble 1304
 Art 2 1304
 Art 3 1305
 Art 3(a)–(d) 1305
 Art 4 . . . . 711, 1226
 Art 4(1) 711, 1304
 Art 4(3) 426
 Art 6 600
2000 Protocol No 12 to the European
 Convention on Human Rights . . . 1260, 1381
 Art 1 193
2000 UNSC Res 1296 (2000) 240, 451,
  602, 605, 609–10
 para 8 244
 para 15 380
2000 UNSC Res 1314 (2000) 1261
2000 UNSC Res 1315 (2000) 1166
2000 UNSC Res 1325 (2000) 364, 1285,
  1287, 1291
 Preamble 1273
 para 8(a) 1377
 para 9 365
 para 10 . . . . 365, 1352
 para 11 1288
2000 UNSC Res 1333 (2000) 489
2000 UN Transitional Administration
 in East Timor, Regulation 2000/15
 on the Establishment of Panels with

Exclusive Jurisdiction over Serious
 Criminal Offences
 s 5 354
 s 6 354
 s 6(1)(a)(vii) 935, 1345
 s 16 407
2001 Committee on the Rights of
 the Child, General Comment 1
 para 11 1257
2001 Council Regulation 44/2001/EC 1571
 Art 36 1572
2001 Declaration of the Conference
 of High Contracting Parties to the
 Fourth Geneva Convention 1417, 1583
 para 4 122
2001 EU Council Common Position
 2001/931/CFSP 427
2001 European Code of Police Ethics,
 Rec(2001)10 606
2001 HRCttee General Comment
 29, Article 4: Derogations during
 a State of Emergency 720, 1369, 1439
 para 3 . . . . .1128, 1218
 para 4 1130
 para 11 . . . . 1131, 1226, 1229, 1440
 para 13 1244
 para 13(d) 1193
 paras 15–16 1131
 para 16 . . . . .474, 1131, 1440
2001 Humanitarian Agreement between
 the Government of Colombia and the
 Revolutionary Armed Forces
 of Colombia–People's Army
 (FARC-EP) 426, 511
2001 ILC Draft Articles on
 Responsibility of States for
 Internationally Wrongful Acts,
 2 *YILC* (2001), Pt 2 . . . . 102, 107, 429,
  644, 1119, 1253, 1307
 Art 1 143
 Art 2 . . . . .143, 1182, 1253
 Arts 4–11 117
 Art 4 . . . . 313, 981, 1182, 1287, 1344
 Art 5 1580
 Art 7 313
 Art 8 .429, 981, 1482
 Art 9 981
 Art 10 429
 Art 14(3) 127
 Art 16 130–1
 Arts 20–27 591
 Art 20 . . . . 136, 1402
 Art 25 136

Art 27 592	2002 Protocol No 13 to the European Convention on Human Rights 484, 1453
Art 28 1451	Art 1 484
Art 30 1451	Art 2 484
Art 31 1451	Art 3 484
Art 34 . . . . 1008, 1573	2002 Statute of the Special Court for Sierra Leone 253, 363, 593, 1168, 1171, 1296–7
Art 40 . . . . 125–6, 338	
Art 40(2) 125	
Art 41 . . . . 125–6, 338	Art 1(1) 1310
Art 42(b)(i) 128	Art 2(g) 354
Art 48 . . . . 126, 507	Art 3 . . . . 355, 360, 430, 1529, 1532
Art 48(1)(b) 338, 1482	Art 3(a) 450
Art 48(2) 1482	Art 3(b) 1156, 1166
Arts 49–54 . . . . 578, 582	Art 3(c) 315
Art 49 . . . . 507, 584	Art 3(e) 354
Art 49(1) 579	Art 3(f) 1369
Art 50 579	Art 3(g) 747
Art 50(1)(b) 594	Art 4 253
Art 50(1)(c) 579, 1050	Art 4(b) 65
Art 52 578	Art 4(c) 437, 1310
Art 54 . . . . 126, 128–9	Art 6 1227
Ch V 136	Art 6(3) 407
2001 UNGA Res 56/83 1573	Art 7 1310
2001 UNGA Res 56/176 489	Art 9 1232
2001 UNSC Res 1373 (2001) 427, 504–5	Art 13 1222
	Art 15(5) 1297
2001 UNSC Res 1379 (2001) 1261	Art 17(2) 1233
2002 ACommHPR Resolution 61 (XXXII) para 20(c) 478	Art 17(3) 1229
	Art 17(4)(a) 1225
	Art 17(4)(b) 1443–4
2002 Agreement between the DRC and Uganda on withdrawal of Ugandan Troops, Cooperation and Normalization of Relations between two countries (Luanda Agreement) para 193 519	Art 17(4)(d) 1230, 1444
	Art 17(4)(e) 1231
	Art 17(4)(f) 1444
	Art 17(4)(g) 1231
	2002 UNGA Res 57/234 489
	2003 ACommHPR Principles and Guidelines on the Right to a Fair Trial and Legal Assistance in Africa
2002 Agreement between the Government of the Republic of Sudan and the Sudan People's Liberation Movement to Protect Non-Combatant Civilians and Civilian Facilities from Military Attack 421, 511, 518	
	Section A, para 2(e) 480
	Section A, para 2(g) 479
	Section A, para 3(a)–(e) 481
Art 1(a) 512	Section A, para 3(f) 481, 1232
Art 1(2) 512	Section G 1443
Art 2(1) 518	Section M, para 3(a) 486–7
Art 4(b) 518	Section M, para 3(b) 486
2002 Agreement between the United Nations and the Government of Sierra Leone pursuant to UNSC Res 1315 (2000) 1166	Section N, para 2 1443
	Section N, para 3(c) 1444
	Section N, para 3(e) 478
	Section N, para 5(b)–(c) 487
2002 ICC Rules of Procedure and Evidence	Section N, para 5(c) 484
Rule 73 545	Section N, para 6(a) 480

Section N, para 6(e)2 475
Section N, para 8 484
Section N, para 10 483
2003 Accord de Cessation des
Hostilités en Ituri 519
2003 Agreement between the United
Nations and the Royal Government
of Cambodia concerning
the Prosecution under
Cambodian Law of Crimes
Committed during the Period of
Democratic Kampuchea
Art 9 . . . . 935, 1345
Art 13 1233
2003 Agreement for the Transfer
of Prisoners of War, Civilian Internees,
and Civilian Detainees between the
Forces of the United States of
America, the United Kingdom of
Great Britain and Northern Ireland,
and Australia 969–71
2003 CESCR, General Comment 15:
The Right to Water
(Arts 11 and 12)
para 29 1282
2003 Coalition Provisional Order No 2:
Dissolution of Entities 1499
2003 Peace Agreement between the
Government of Liberia, the Liberians
United for Reconciliation and
Democracy (LURD), the Movement
for Democracy in Liberia (MODEL)
and the Political Parties
Art IX 1383, 1386
2003 Council Directive 2003/86/EC
on the right to family
reunification 1093, 1095
Recital 10 1095
Recital 13 1095
Art 4 1095
2003 Global Ceasefire Agreement
between the Transitional Government
of Burundi and the National
Council for the Defence of the
Democracy-Forces for the Defence
of Democracy 62
2003 HRComm Resolution
2003/6 1161
2003 HRComm Resolution
2003/53 . . . . 602, 610
2003 Protocol on Amendments to the
Constitutive Act of the African Union
Art 4 380
2003 Protocol to the African Charter on
Human and Peoples' Rights on the
Rights of Women in Africa 367, 718
Art 4 1287
Art 10 1287
Art 11 345
2003 Statutes of the International
Committee of the Red Cross, as
amended in 2013 . . . . 241, 528–9
Art 1 531
Art 2 527
Art 4 531–2
Art 4(1)(d)–(2) 533
Art 4(1)(d) 536
Art 4(h) 528
Art 5(1)(a) 601
Art 7 527
2003 UNESCO Convention for the
Safeguarding of Intangible
Cultural Heritage
Art 2 1247
2003 UNGA Res 58/97
para 3 121
2003 UNGA Res 58/99 1161
2003 UNGA Res 58/122 . . . . 605, 610
2003 UNGA Res ES-10/14
Preamble, para 8 1584
2003 UNSC Res 1460 (2003) 1261
2003 UNSC Res 1471 (2003) 10
2003 UNSC Res 1479 (2003) 10
2003 UNSC Res 1483 (2003) 714, 1457,
1459, 1499
Preamble, para 14 1400
para 4 1467
para 5 57
2003 UNSC Res 1509 (2003) 10
2003 UNSC Res 1511 (2003) 714
para 4 1464
para 13 . . . . 1457, 1464
2004 Agreement on Permanent
Ceasefire and Security Arrangements
Implementation Modalities between
the Government of the Sudan and the
Sudan People's Liberation
Movement/Army during the
pre-interim and interim periods 1383
Art 1(9) 1386
2004 Arab Charter on Human Rights 483
Art 4 720
Art 6 483
Art 7 483
Art 13 471
Art 13(2) 481

Art 14(5) 486–7
Art 15 719
Art 16 475
Art 16(1) 475
Art 16(3) 476, 481
Art 16(4) 477, 479
Art 16(5) 479–80
Art 16(6) 482
Art 16(7) 483
Art 19(1) 484
Art 26(1) 1193
Art 26(2) 1194
Art 27(1) 1207
Art 27(2) 1194
Art 28 1203
2004 Coalition Provisional Authority
  Order No 89, Amendments to
  the Labour Code—Law No 71 of 1987
  Preamble, para 7 1492
2004 Comprehensive Settlement
  of the Cyprus Problem
  ('The Annan Plan')
  Annex III. 1569
  Annex VII 1569
2004 HRComm Resolution
  2004/37. .... 602, 610
2004 HRComm Resolution
  2004/43. 606
2004 HRComm Resolution
  2004/72 606
2004 HRCttee, General Comment 31:
  The Nature of the General Obligation
  Imposed on States 704
  para 8 285
  para 10. 1411
  para 11. 1218
  para 12 1053
  paras 16–18. 492
2004 Law on the Establishment of the
  Extraordinary Chambers in the
  Courts of Cambodia 363, 354
2004 Protocol between the Government
  of the Sudan, the Sudan Liberation
  Movement/Army, and the
  Justice and Equality Movement
  on the Improvement of the
  Humanitarian Situation in
  Darfur 511, 518
2004 Kurdistan Workers' Party
  Rules for the Conduct of Warfare
  Pt B........................... 312
2004 UNGA Res 59/122
  para 3 121
2004 UNGA Res 59/124 1161–2
2004 UNGA Res 59/197 .... 602, 605–6,
                                609–10
2004 UNGA Res 59/211 ...... 602, 605, 610
2004 UNSC Res 1528 (2004) 10
2004 UNSC Res 1539 (2004) 1308
2004 UNSC Res 1546 ...... 1342, 1459, 1588
  para 2 1588
  para 9 1457
2004 UNSC Res 1556 (2004) 384
2004 UNSC Res 1574 (2004) 489
2005 Arrangements for the Transfer of
  Detainees between the Canadian Forces
  and the Ministry of Defence of the Islamic
  Republic of Afghanistan 973
2005 CESCR, General Comment 18:
  The Right to Work (Art 6)
  para 6 1499
2005 Committee on the Rights of
  the Child, General Comment 6
  para 27 1203
2005 Committee on the Rights of the
  Child, General Comment 7
  para 30 1502
2005 Council of Europe, Convention
  on Action against Trafficking in
  Human Beings 1352
2005 Council of Europe, Parliamentary
  Assembly Resolution 1416
  para 1 1458
2005 HRComm Resolution 2005/7 1280
  Preamble..................... 1169
2005 HRComm Resolution
  2005/34. .... 606, 610
2005 HRComm Resolution 2005/39..... 602,
                                606, 609–10
2005 HRComm Resolution
  2005/81..................... 606, 610
2005 Protocol Additional to the
  Geneva Conventions of
  12 August 1949, and relating
  to the Adoption of an Additional
  Distinctive Emblem (Additional
  Protocol III) 113, 115, 158, 160,
                    169, 174, 239, 241, 528,
                    697–9, 808, 859, 862,
                    865, 868, 876, 882
  Preamble, para 4 212
  Art 1 .... 116, 121, 133, 860, 869
  Art 1(2) 171
  Art 2 .... 860, 862, 869
  Art 2(1) 699, 865
  Art 2(2) 699

Art 2(4) 865–6, 882
Art 3 860
Art 3(1)(b) 172
Art 4 860
Art 5 . . . . 860, 869
Art 6 . . . . 119, 860, 872–4
Art 6(1) 662
Art 7 . . . . 119–20, 652, 860, 873
Art 8 697
Art 10 . . . . 163, 697
Art 12 699
Art 13 . . . . 173, 690
Art 14 176
Art 17 158
2005 UN Basic Principles and
    Guidelines on the Right to a
    Remedy and Reparation for
    Victims of Gross Violations of
    International Human Rights
    Law and Serious Violations of
    International Humanitarian
    Law, UNGA Res 60/147 . . . . 492, 569,
                  1287, 1352, 1359
    para 22(b) 492
    para 22(f) 492
    Principle 26 1369
2005 UNGA Res 60/1
    para 116 1291
2005 UNGA Res 60/107 1162
2005 UNGA Res 60/123 . . . . 602, 605
2005 UNSC Res 1612 (2005) . . . 427, 1307–8
    para 2 1512
    section 3 1512
2005 WHO Framework Convention
    on Tobacco Control 1355
    Art 5(2)(b) 1355
    Art 8 1356
2006 Agreement between the International
    Criminal Court and the International
    Committee of the Red Cross on Visits
    to Persons deprived of Liberty Pursuant
    to the Jurisdiction of the International
    Criminal Court 545
2006 Council of Europe Recommendation
    of the Committee of Ministers on the
    European Prison Rules
    para 98 478
2006 ICRC Guidelines on the Use of
    the Red Cross Emblem and the
    Name and Logo of the ICRC for
    Fundraising Purposes 864
2006 ILC Draft Articles on Diplomatic
    Protection 1143
2006 ILC Guiding Principles Applicable
    to Unilateral Declarations of
    States Capable of Creating
    Legal Obligations
    Principle 1 974
    para 7 967
    para 9 967
2006 International Convention for the
    Protection of All Persons from
    Enforced Disappearance 258, 261,
              273, 275, 302, 706, 709, 972, 1119,
                 1352, 1366, 1368–9, 1371, 1385
    Art 1 1117
    Art 1(2) 1119
    Art 2 . . . . 258, 710, 1117
    Art 3 710
    Art 4 1119
    Art 5 . . . . 276, 1118
    Art 6 1118
    Art 7 1118
    Art 7(3)(g) 1366
    Art 16 . . . . 710, 928, 1203
    Art 17(2)(d) 1360–1
    Art 17(3) 272, 1024
    Art 17(3)(g) 1020
    Art 18 1119
    Art 21 1385
    Art 22 275
    Art 24 1359
    Art 24(2) 261, 273, 281
    Art 24(6) 259
    Art 30 . . . . 271, 1359
    Arts 31–32 273
    Art 31 1359
    Art 34 273
    Art 43 . . . . 709, 1361
2006 Protocol adopted by the
    Conference of the Great Lakes
    Region on the Prevention and
    Suppression of Sexual Violence against
    Women and Children 718
2006 Statute of the Special Tribunal
    for Lebanon
    Art 3 1227
    Art 5 1232
    Art 9(1) 1222
    Art 15 . . . . 1225, 1231
    Art 16 1231
    Art 16(3)(a) 1229
    Art 16(4)(a) 1225
    Art 16(4)(e) 1231
    Art 17 1233
    Art 22 1229

2006 UN Convention on the Rights of
  Persons with Disabilities 196, 711, 1194
  Art 10 1151
  Art 11 .... 345, 711, 999
  Art 18(1) 1194
2006 UNGA Res 60/285 1458
2006 UNGA Res 61/30 .... 602, 606, 609–10
2006 UNGA Res 61/34 967
2006 UNGA Res 61/119 1162
2006 UNGA Res 61/173 609
2006 UNSC Res 1674 (2006) 605, 610, 1291
  para 5 .... 244, 1287, 1352
2007 Constitution of the International
  Federation of Red Cross and Red
  Crescent Societies
  Art 5(1)(B)(c) 601
2007 HRCouncil Group of Experts
  on the Situation of Human Rights
  in Darfur Resolution 6/35 1272–3
2007 HRCouncil Resolution 4/8 1272–3
2007 HRCouncil Resolution 5/1
  Annex, para A.2 735
2007 HRCttee, General Comment 32,
  Article 14: Rights to Equality Before
  Courts and Tribunals to a Fair Trial. . . 1440
  para 13 480
  para 19 472
  para 20 472
  para 21 .... 473, 1222
  para 22 .... 471–2, 1224
  paras 28–29 481
  para 28 .... 481, 1232
  para 29 .... 481, 1232–3
  para 30 475
  paras 32–33 1226
  para 32 479
  para 33 479
  para 34 .... 479, 1226
  para 35 484
  para 36 .... 482, 1229
  para 37 476
  para 38 .... 477, 479
  para 39 .... 480, 1231, 1364
  para 40 479
  para 41 482
  para 45 483
  para 48 483
  para 54 484
  para 55 1232
  para 56 484
2007 UN Declaration on the Rights of
  Indigenous Peoples, UNGA Res 61/295
  Art 10 1193

2007 UNGA Res 62/109 1162
2007 UNGA Res 62/149 322
2007 UNSC Res 1746 (2007) 10
2007 UNSC Res 1756 (2007) 605, 609
2007 UNSC Res 1769 (2007) 239
2008 Agreement between the United
  States of America and the Republic
  of Iraq on the Withdrawal of United
  States Forces from Iraq and the
  Organization of their Activities during
  their Temporary Presence in Iraq 1378–9
  Art 22(4) 1378–9
  Art 24 1379
2008 Convention on Cluster
  Munitions 539, 700
  Preamble 182
2008 HRCouncil Resolution 9/11,
  Right to the Truth 281–2
2008 ICRC Model Law Geneva
  Conventions (Consolidation) Act 877
2008 ICRC Model Law on the
  Emblems 871, 877
  Arts 2–5 872
  Art 2 872
  Art 3 871
  Art 4 872
  Art 6 870
  Art 7 871
  Art 9 873
  Art 10 873
  Note 1 877
2008 UNGA Res 62/243 1458
2008 UNGA Res 63/98 1162
2008 UNGA Res 63/125 539
  para 5 600
2008 UNGA Res 63/168 322
2008 UNSC Res 1820 (2008) 364, 1285,
                                    1287
  para 3 1352
  para 4 365
  para 15 1289
2009 African Union Convention for
  the Protection and Assistance
  of Internally Displaced Persons
  in Africa (Kampala Convention) 719
  Art 1(d) 718
  Art 1(k) 718
  Art 1(n) 718
  Art 3(1)(e) 719
  Art 4(1) 719
  Art 4(4) 1193
  Art 4(4)(b) 1207
  Art 4(4)(h) 718–19

Art 7 426
Art 7(1) 718
Art 20(2) 719
Art 22 719
2009 CESCR, General Comment 21:
The Right of Everyone to Take Part
in Cultural Life (Art 15)
para 2 1502
2009 HRCouncil Resolution 9/1,
Preamble, para 9 121
2009 ICRC Model Law on the
Missing 275
Art 2 258
Arts 8–10 259
Art 11 262
Art 11(3) 263
Art 13(1) 266, 272
Art 13(2) 266
Art 24 275
Art 25 275
2009 Terms of Reference of the Civilian
Protection Component of the
International Monitoring Team
between the Government of the
Philippines and the Moro Islamic
Liberation Front 518
2009 UNSC Res 1860 (2009) 249
2009 UNSC Res 1882 (2009) 365,
367, 427, 539, 1308, 1512
para 1 1352
para 16 365
2009 UNSC Res 1888 (2009) 1272
Preamble 1288–9
para 1 1289
para 7 1352
para 7 .... 365, 1288
para 24 1289
2009 UNSC Res 1889 (2009) 364, 1285
para 12 1352
2009 UNSC Res 1890 (2009) 10
2009 UNSC Res 1894 (2009) 380, 426,
451, 605, 610, 1287
para 7 602
para 21 1272
2009 Updated European Union
Guidelines on Promoting Compliance
with International Humanitarian Law,
2009/C 303/06
para 13 733
2010 HR Council Resolution 13/19
para 6 478
2010 Kampala Review Conference of the
Rome Statute Resolution RC/Res.5
on Amendments to Article 8 of the
Rome Statute 1168
2010 OAS General Assembly Resolution
AG/RES 2595 (XL-O/10), Right
to the Truth 281–2
2010 UNGA Res 64/94 1162
2010 UNGA Res 64/292
para 1 1282
2010 UNGA Res 65/206 322
2010 UNSC Res 1960 (2010) 364–5, 427,
1285, 1291, 1352
Preamble 1272
para 3 365
para 6 1289
2010 UNSC Res 1964 (2010) 427
2011 Agreement between the
Government of Sudan and the
Sudan People's Liberation Movement
on Temporary Arrangements for the
Administration and Security of the
Abyei Area 384
2011 Council of Europe Convention on
Preventing and Combating Violence
against Women and Domestic
Violence (Istanbul Convention)
Art 2 345
Art 2(2) 367
Art 3 345
Art 5(2) 1287
Art 30 1287
Art 36 345
2011 Guidelines for the Implementation
of the 1999 Second Protocol to the Hague
Convention of 1954 for the Protection
of Cultural Property in the Event of Armed
Conflict
para 56 881
2011 HRCouncil Resolution16/16 271
2011 ILC Draft Articles on the Effects
of Armed Conflicts on Treaties 16,
707, 730
Art 2 16
2011 ILC Draft Articles on the
Responsibility of International
Organizations
Art 14 131
Art 58 131
2011 UNGA Res 65/105 1162
2011 UNSC Res 1973 (2011) 10
2011 UNSC Res 1991 (2011) 10
2011 UNSC Res 1998 (2011) 1308, 1512
2012 International Small Arms
Control Standards 817

2012 UNGA Res 66/79 1162
    para 3 1170
2012 UNGA Res 67/93
    para 6 600
2012 UNSC Res 2042 (2012) 382
2012 UNSC Res 2043 (2012) 239, 382
2012 UNSC Res 2047 (2012). 166
2012 UNSC Res 2067 (2012). 489
2012 UNSC Res 2068 (2012) 1309
2012 UNSC Res 2071 (2012). 489
2012 WHO Executive Board
    Resolution EB 130.R14 229
2013 Arms Trade Treaty
    Art 6(3) 24, 700
    Art 7(3) 24
2013 CEDAW Committee, General
    Recommendation No 30 on Women
    in Conflict Prevention, Conflict and
    Post-Conflict Situations. 345, 367, 1272
    para 4 345
    para 6 1291
    para 20 1271–2
    para 34 1272
    para 35. 1273
2013 G8 Declaration on Preventing
    Sexual Violence in Conflict 363, 1288
    para 4 366
2013 UNGA Res 68/15 1556
2013 UNGA Res 68/111 967
2013 UNSC Res 2098 (2013). 489
2013 UNSC Res 2106 (2013) ... 364, 1289, 1352
    paras 5–8. 1289
2013 UNSC Res 2113 (2013) 239
2013 UNSC Res 2118 (2013) 382
2013 UNSC Res 2122 (2013). 364,
                                        763, 1352
2014 HRCttee, General Comment 35,
    Article 9 (Liberty and Security of Person)
    para 15. 721
    para 45. 721
    para 64 722
    para 66 721
2014 ILC Draft Articles on The
    Protection of Persons in the Event
    of Disasters 235
2014 Protocol on Amendments to the
    Protocol on the Statute of the
    African Court of Justice and
    Human Rights 719
2014 UNSC Res 2139 (2014) 239, 244,382
    Preamble, para 10 508
    para 6 508
2014 UNSC Res 2165 (2014). 382

NATIONAL INSTRUMENTS

Australia
Crimes (Hostages) Act 1989 (Cth)
    s 7(a) 305
Criminal Code 1995
    Art 101.2 504
Criminal Code Act 1995
    s 268.24. 261
    s 268.70. 261
Geneva Convention Act 1957, as
    amended (2010)
    Pt III, s 10(A). 948
Geneva Conventions Amendment
    Act 1991 658

Belarus
Criminal Code 1999
    Art 135(3) 450

Bosnia and Herzegovina
Law on Missing Persons 2004 275
    Art 2 258
    Art 7 271
    Arts 11–19 259
    Art 25(1) 275
    Art 25(2) 275

Bulgaria
Criminal Code 1968, amended 2010
    Art 108 504

Burundi
Constitution 2005 603

Cambodia
Law on Counter Terrorism 2007
    Art 77 504

Cameroon
Law No 97-2 of 10 January 1997
    on the Protection of the Red Cross
    Emblem and Name 876
    s 12 878
Règlement de discipline générale dans
    les forces de défense 2007/199
    Art 32 450

Canada
Anti-Terrorism Act 2001 427
Code of Conduct for CF Personnel 2005 609
Criminal Code 1985, as amended
    Art 83.18 504
Prisoner-of-War Status Determination
    Regulations 1991, SOR/91-134

| Art 4 948
| Art 10 951
| Art 11 951
| Art 13(g) 952
| Art 16 952
| Art 17 952

Cape Verde
Penal Code 2003
    Art 316 504

Cyprus
Federal Law on Terrorism 2004
    Art 9 504

Democratic Republic of the Congo
Constitution 2005 .... 603, 605

Denmark
Criminal Code 2005
    Para 114b 504

Ethiopia
Criminal Code 2005
    Art 479 504

France
Law no 95-1 of 2 January 1995 629
    Art 1 629
Ordonnance du 28 août 1944 relative à la répression des crimes de guerre, *Journal officiel de la République française*, 30 August 1944 617
    Art 3 618
Penal Code 1810 457

Gambia
Anti-terrorism Act 2002
    Art 6 504

Georgia
Law on Amendments to the Criminal Code 2007
    Art 328 504
Law of Georgia on the Red Cross and Red Crescent Emblems and Names 1997
    Art 9 877

Germany
Act on the German Red Cross and other voluntary aid societies as defined in the Geneva Conventions 2008 1103
Code of Crimes against International Law 2002 661–2
Control Council Law No 10, Punishment of Persons Guilty of War Crimes, Crimes Against Peace and Against Humanity, 20 December 1945 660
    Art II 660
    Art II(1)(b) 450, 1532
    Art II(1)(c) 1210
Criminal Code 1998 661
Joint Services Regulation 15/2 1992 90
Law Introducing the International Crimes Code 2002
    Art 1, § 8(1)(1) 450
Night and Fog Decree 1941 1118
Tracing Services Data Protection Act, 2009
    § 2(1)(4)(a) 1094

Ghana
Anti-Terrorism Bill 2005
    Art 6 504

Grenada
Terrorism Act 2003
    Art 6 504

Iceland
Penal Code 1940, amended 2003
    s 22 504

India
Goa, Daman and Diu (Citizenship Order 1962) 1139
Prevention of Terrorism Act 2002
    Art 21 504

Indonesia
Government Regulation in Lieu of Legislation No 1/2002 on Combating Criminal Acts of Terrorism 2002
    s 16 504

Iraq
Governing Council, Statute of the Iraqi Special Tribunal, 10 December 2003, 'Annex' to CPA Order No 48, 10 December 2003, CPA/ORD/ 9 Dec 2003/48 1435

Islamic Emirate of Afghanistan
Code of Conduct for the Mujahideen, 9 May 2009 612

Israel
Incarceration of Unlawful Combatants Law S762-2002, amended 2008 .... 929–30, 1335–6

s 1 1336
s 2 . . . . .929, 1336
s 7 . . . . .929, 1336

Italy
Penal Code 1930
  Art 270*ter* 504
Wartime Military Penal Code,
  1941, amended 2002
  Art 167 913

Jamaica
Terrorism Prevention Act 2005
  Art 7 504

Jordan
Excise Tax Law. 1479

Kosovo
Law on Missing Persons 2011
  Art 6 259

Malaysia
Penal Code 1997
  s 130J. 504

Mauritius
Prevention of Terrorism Act 2002
  Art 6 504

Namibia
Namibia Red Cross Act 1991 . . . . 652, 663
  s 3 663

Netherlands
Extraordinary Penal Law Decree 1943,
  amended 1947. 618
Military Manual 1993 450

Norway
Law of 13 December 1946 (No 14) on the
  Punishment of Foreign War
  Criminals 617

Palau
Counter-Terrorism Act 2007
  s 2(h)(7). 504

Papua New Guinea
Internal Security Act 1993
  Art 6 504

Philippines
Armed Forces of the Philippines
  Standing Rules of Engagement
  2005 . . . . .608, 611
Anti-Terrorism Act 2005
  s 4 504

Republic of Albania
Criminal Code 1995, consolidated
  version as of 1 December 2004
  Art 109 305

Republic of Korea
ICC Act 2007
  Art 10(1) 450

Republic of Moldova
Criminal Code 2009
  Art 279 504

Republic of Uzbekistan
Criminal Code 1994
  Art 245 305

Russian Federation
Regulations on the Application of
  the Rules of IHL by the Armed
  Forces of the Russian
  Federation 2001 603
  § 81. 450

Saint Kitts and Nevis
Anti-Terrorism Act 2002
  Art 10 504

Saint Vincent and the Grenadines
United Nations (Anti-terrorism Measures)
  Act 2002
  Art 6 504

Slovakia
Criminal Code 2005
  s 297 504

South Africa
Anti-terrorism Bill 2003
  Art 3 504
Promotion of National Unity and
  Reconciliation Act No 34 of 1995 283
  s 3(1)(c) 259, 282

Sri Lanka
Emergency (Prevention and Prohibition
  of Terrorism and Specified Terrorist
  Activities) 2006
  reg 7. 504

Switzerland
2010 Loi fédérale du 18 juin 2010 portant
  modification de lois fédérales en vue de la
  mise en oeuvre du statut de Rome de
  la Cour pénale internationale. 662

Asylum Law, *Recueil systématique du droit fédéral* 142.31, as revised 2012
  Art 3(3) 98
Bases légales du comportement à l'engagement, règlement 51.007/IV (2005) 654
Civil Code
  Arts 60–69 528
Criminal Code
  Art 264j 662
Gesetz und Gebräuche des Krieges (Auszug and Kommentar), Reglement 51.7/IId, 16 January 1987
  Art 152 1398
Military Criminal Code 1927, as amended 657
  Art 109 661

Tanzania
Prevention of Terrorism Act 2002
  Art 18 504

Trinidad and Tobago
Anti-Terrorism Act 2005
  Art 9 504

Turkish Republic of Northern Cyprus
Constitution 1985
  Art 159 1558
Law 67/2005 .... 1569, 1572

Uganda
Anti-terrorism Act 2002
  Art 89 504
Penal Code Act 1950
  Art 26 504

United Kingdom
Air Force Act 1955 658
Army Act 1955 658
  s 30 658
Defence (Emergency) Regulations 1945 1161
Emergency Powers (Collective Punishment) Regulations 1955 1161
Geneva Conventions Act 1957 658
Geneva Conventions (Amendment) Act 1995 658
Human Rights Act 1998 717
Taking of Hostages Act 1982 707
Terrorism Act 2000 427

United States of America
Annual Foreign Operations Appropriations Acts 762
Antiterrorism and Effective Death Penalty Act 1996 503
Authorization for Use of Military Force 2001 .... 1332, 1347
Department of Defense Instruction, DODI2310.08E, 6 June 2006 1356
Military Police: Enemy Prisoner-of-War, Civilian Internees and Other Detainees, US Army Regulation 190-8, 1 October 1997
  § 1-6(c) 948
  § 1-6(e)(5) 951
  § 1-6(e)(8) 951
  § 1-6(e)(9) 952
  § 1-6(e)(10) 952
Executive Order 13567, Periodic Review of Individuals Detained at Guantánamo Bay Naval Station Pursuant to the Authorization for Use of Military Force, 7 March 2011 .... 919, 932, 1347
Federal Tort Claims Act 1948, 28 USC para 2680(j) 1570
Foreign Assistance Act 1961, as amended
  § 104(f) 762
Helms Amendment 1973 762
Intelligence Reform and Terrorism Prevention Act 2004 503
  § 6603 503
Military Assistance Command, Vietnam, Directive No 20-5, Inspections and Investigations: Prisoners of War Determination of Eligibility, 15 March 1968, 768 *AJIL* (1968) 949
  Art 6(e)(1) 949
  Art 6(f)(3) 952
  Art 6(g)(1) 952
  Art 7(a) 951
  Art 7(b) 951
  Art 7(c) 951
  Art 8 951
  Art 10 951
  Art 12 951
  Art 13 952
Military Assistance Command, Vietnam, Directive No 138-46, Military Intelligence: Combined Screening of Detainees, 27 December 1967 949
Military Commissions Act 2006, 10 USC 915–16
  § 821 916
  § 948a(1)(i) 930–1
  § 948a(1)(ii) 930
  § 950v(b)(13) 913

§ 950v(b)(15) 913
Military Commissions Act 2009,
   10 USC 916
   § 948(c) 931–2
   § 950t(13) 913, 915
   § 950t(15) 913, 915
Military Order—Detention, Treatment and Trial of Certain Non-Citizens in the War against Terrorism, 13 November 2001, 66 Fed Reg 57833, 16 November 2001 916
National Defense Authorization Act for Fiscal Year 2012 (PL 112-81)
   §§ 1021–4 1347
   § 1021(b)(1) 932
   § 1021(b)(2) 932
   § 1021(e) 932
   § 1021-4 932
Order Establishing Combatant Status Review Tribunals 2004 930
Uniting and Strengthening America by Providing Appropriate Tools Required to Intercept and Obstruct Terrorism Act 2001 (Patriot Act) 503, 508
   § 805(a)(2)(B) 503

US Code Title 8
   § 1189(a)(1) 503
   § 1189(d)(4) 503
US Code Title 18
   § 2339A(b)(1) 503, 801
   § 2339A(b)(2) 503
   § 2339A(b)(3) 503
   § 2339B 427, 503
   § 2339B(a)(1) 503
   § 2339B(g)(4) 503, 801
   § 2339C(e)(13) 801
US Department of the Army, Regulation 600–20, 20 September 2012
   para 1-5 898
US Restatement of the Law, Third, The Foreign Relations Law of the United States 345

Yemen
Military Criminal Code 1998
   Art 21(1) 450

Zambia
Anti-Terrorism Act 2007
   para 13 504

List of Abbreviations

1929 GC I	Convention for the Amelioration of the Condition of the Wounded and Sick in Armies in the Field, 1929
1929 GC II	Convention Relative to the Treatment of Prisoners of War, 1929
2012 NDAA	National Defense Authorization Act for Fiscal Year 2012
ACHPR	African Charter on Human and Peoples' Rights, 1981
ACHR	American Convention on Human Rights, 1969
ACommHPR	African Commission of Human and Peoples' Rights
AFDI	*Annuaire français de droit international*
AJIL	*American Journal of International Law*
AJPIL	*Austrian Journal of Public and International Law*
ALJ	*Alternative Law Journal*
Annual Digest	Annual Digest of Public International Law Cases
ANSAs	armed non-state actors
AP I	Protocol Additional to the Geneva Conventions of 12 August 1949, and Relating to the Protection of Victims of International Armed Conflicts, 1977
AP II	Protocol Additional to the Geneva Conventions of 12 August 1949, and Relating to the Protection of Victims of Non-International Armed Conflicts, 1977
AP III	Protocol Additional to the Geneva Conventions of 12 August 1949, and Relating to the Adoption of an Additional Distinctive Emblem, 2005
APs	Additional Protocols
AR	Army Regulation
Arab Charter	Arab Charter on Human Rights, 2004
Art(s)	Article(s)
ASEAN	Association of Southeast Asian Nations
ASEAN Human Rights Declaration	Association of Southeast Asian Nations Declaration of Human Rights
ASIL	American Society of International Law
ATT	Arms Trade Treaty, 2013
AU	African Union
AUMF	Authorization for Use of Military Force
AYBIL	*Australian Year Book of International Law*
BiH	Bosnia and Herzegovina
BIICL	British Institute of International and Comparative Law
Bothe/Partsch/Solf	M. Bothe, K.J. Partsch, and W.A. Solf (eds), *New Rules for Victims of Armed Conflicts: Commentary on the Two 1977 Protocols Additional to the Geneva Conventions of 1949* (The Hague: Martinus Nijhoff, 1982)
BYBIL	*British Year Book of International Law*

CA 1	Article 1 Common to the 1949 Geneva Conventions
CA 2	Article 2 Common to the 1949 Geneva Conventions
CA 3	Article 3 Common to the 1949 Geneva Conventions
Can YIL	*Canadian Yearbook of International Law*
CARHRIHL	Comprehensive Agreement on Respect for Human Rights and International Humanitarian Law, 1998
CAT	Convention against Torture and other Cruel, Inhuman or Degrading Treatment and Punishment, 1984
CAT-Commentary	M. Nowak and E. McArthur, *The United Nations Convention against Torture: A Commentary* (Oxford: OUP, 2008)
CCW	Convention on Prohibitions or Restrictions on the Use of Certain Conventional Weapons Which May Be Deemed to be Excessively Injurious or to Have Indiscriminate Effects, 1980
CEDAW	Convention on the Elimination of All Forms of Discrimination against Women, 1979
CERD	Convention on the Elimination of All Forms of Racial Discrimination, 1965
CESCR	Committee on Economic, Social and Cultural Rights
Ch(s)	Chapter(s)
CIDT	cruel, inhuman, or degrading treatment or punishment
CIL	customary international law
Col JIL	*Columbia Journal of International Law*
CPA	Coalition Provisional Authority
CPN-M	Communist Party of Nepal-Maoist
CRC	Convention on the Rights of the Child, 1989
CRC-OPAC	Optional Protocol on the Involvement of Children in Armed Conflict, 2000
CRPD	Convention on the Rights of Persons with Disabilities, 2006
CSRT	Combatant Status Review Tribunals
CTA	Central Tracing Agency
CtteeAT	United Nations Committee against Torture
CtteeED	United Nations Committee on Enforced Disappearances
CUP	Cambridge University Press
DEVAW	United Nations Declaration on the Elimination of Violence against Women, 1993
DPH	direct participation in hostilities
DPH Guidance	ICRC, Interpretive Guidance on the Notion of Direct Participation in Hostilities under International Humanitarian Law (Geneva: ICRC, 2009)
DRC	Democratic Republic of the Congo
ECCC	Extraordinary Chambers in the Courts of Cambodia
ECHR	European Convention for the Protection of Human Rights and Fundamental Freedoms, 1950
ECommHR	European Commission of Human Rights
ECOSOC	Economic and Social Council
ECOWAS	Economic Community of West African States
ECtHR	European Court of Human Rights

EECC	Eritrea–Ethiopia Claims Commission
EHRLR	*European Human Rights Law Review*
EJIL	*European Journal of International Law*
ESC rights	economic, social, and cultural rights
esp	especially
EU	European Union
FARC	Fuerzas Armadas Revolucionarias de Colombia/ Revolutionary Armed Forces of Colombia
Final Record	Final Record of the Diplomatic Conference of Geneva of 1949 (Berne, 1950–51)
FLN	Front national de libération/National Liberation Front
FMLN	Farabundo Martí National Liberation Front
Fordham ILJ	*Fordham International Law Journal*
FRY	Former Republic of Yugoslavia
GC I	Convention for the Amelioration of the Condition of the Wounded and Sick in Armed Forces in the Field, 1949
GC II	Convention for the Amelioration of the Condition of the Wounded, Sick and Shipwrecked Members of Armed Forces at Sea, 1949
GC III	Convention Relative to the Treatment of Prisoners of War, 1949
GC IV	Convention Relative to the Protection of Civilian Persons in Time of War, 1949
GCs	Geneva Conventions
Genocide Convention	Convention on the Prevention and Punishment of the Crime of Genocide, 1948
GPRA	Gouvernement Provisoire de la République Algérienne
GYIL	*German Yearbook of International Law*
Hague Regulations	Regulations concerning the Laws and Customs of War on Land, Annexed to Convention (IV) Respecting the Laws and Customs of War on Land, 1907
Harv HRJ	*Harvard Human Rights Journal*
HCJ	High Court of Justice
HICLR	*Hastings International and Comparative Law Review*
HLR	*Harvard Law Review*
HMSO	Her Majesty's Stationery Office
Hostages Convention	International Convention against the Taking of Hostages, 1979
HPCR	Harvard Program on Humanitarian Policy and Conflict Research
HRComm	United Nations Human Rights Commission
HRCouncil	United Nations Human Rights Council
HRCttee	United Nations Human Rights Committee
HRLJ	*Human Rights Law Journal*
HRQ	*Human Rights Quarterly*
HRW	Human Rights Watch
HVO	Croatian Defence Council

IAC	international armed conflict
IACommHR	Inter-American Commission of Human Rights
IACtHR	Inter-American Court of Human Rights
ICC	International Criminal Court
ICC Elements of Crimes	Elements of Crimes of the International Criminal Court, 2002
ICC Statute	Rome Statute of the International Criminal Court, 1998
ICCPR	International Covenant on Civil and Political Rights, 1966
ICED	International Convention for the Protection of All Persons from Enforced Disappearance, 2006
ICESCR	International Covenant on Economic, Social and Cultural Rights, 1966
ICJ	International Court of Justice
ICJ Statute	Statute of the International Court of Justice, 1945
ICL	international criminal law
ICLQ	*International and Comparative Law Quarterly*
ICRC	International Committee of the Red Cross
ICRC CIHL Database	ICRC, Customary International Humanitarian Law Database, 2. Practice, available at <http://www.icrc.org/customary-ihl/eng/docs/v2_rul>
ICRC CIHL Study	J.-M. Henckaerts and L. Doswald-Beck, *Customary International Humanitarian Law* (Cambridge: CUP, 2005)
ICRC Commentary APs	Y. Sandoz, C. Swinarski, and B. Zimmermann (eds), *Commentary on the Additional Protocols of 8 June 1977 to the Geneva Conventions of 12 August 1949* (Geneva: ICRC, 1987)
ICRMW	International Convention on the Protection of the Rights of All Migrant Workers and Members of Their Families, 1990
ICTR	International Criminal Tribunal for Rwanda
ICTR Statute	Statute of the International Criminal Tribunal for Rwanda, 1994
ICTY	International Criminal Tribunal for the former Yugoslavia
ICTY Statute	Statute of the International Criminal Tribunal for the former Yugoslavia, 1993
IDF	Israel Defense Forces
IDI/IIL	Institut de Droit International/Institute of International Law
IDP	internally displaced person
IFRC	International Federation of the Red Cross and Red Crescent Societies
IHFFC	International Humanitarian Fact-Finding Commission
IHL	international humanitarian law
IHRL	international human rights law
IIFFMCG	Independent International Fact-Finding Mission on the Conflict in Georgia
IIHL	International Institute of Humanitarian Law
IIL/IDI	Institute of International Law
IJRL	*International Journal of Refugee Law*
ILA	International Law Association

ILC	International Law Commission
ILC Articles on State Responsibility	International Law Commission, Draft articles on Responsibility of States for internationally wrongful acts, 2001
ILC Commentary	International Law Commission, 'Draft articles on Responsibility of States for internationally wrongful acts with commentaries', *Yearbook of the International Law Commission* 2001, Vol II, Part I A/CN.4/SER.A/2001/Add.1
ILDC	International Law in Domestic Courts
ILM	International Legal Materials
ILO	International Labour Organization
IMT	International Military Tribunal
IMT Charter	International Military Tribunal Charter, 1945
IMTFE	International Military Tribunal for the Far East
INTERFET	International Force for East Timor
IPC	Immovable Property Commission
IRCM	International Red Cross and Red Crescent Movement
IRCM Statutes of 2006	Statutes of the International Red Cross and Red Crescent Movement
IRL	international refugee law
IRO	International Refugee Organization
IRRC	*International Review of the Red Cross*
IS	Islamic State
ISAF	International Security Assistance Force (Afghanistan)
Isr YBHR	*Israel Yearbook on Human Rights*
ITLOS	International Tribunal for the Law of the Sea
IUCW	International Union for Child Welfare
JEM	Justice and Equality Movement
JIEL	*Journal of International Economic Law*
JICJ	*Journal of International Criminal Justice*
JIL	*Journal of International Law*
JNA	Yugoslav People's Army
Kampala Convention	African Union Convention for the Protection and Assistance of Internally Displaced Persons in Africa, 2009
KLA	Kosovo Liberation Army
Lieber Code	Instructions for the Government of Armies of the United States in the Field, prepared by Francis Lieber, promulgated as General Order No 100 by President Abraham Lincoln, 1863
LJIL	*Leiden Journal of International Law*
LOAC	law of armed conflict
LNTS	League of Nations Treaty Series
LQR	*Law Quarterly Review*
LRA	Lord's Resistance Army
LTTE	Liberation Tigers of Tamil Eelam
MACV	Military Assistance Command, Vietnam
MCA	US Military Commissions Act

Mélanges Pictet	C. Swinarski (ed), *Studies and Essays on International Humanitarian Law and Red Cross Principles in Honour of Jean Pictet* (Geneva/The Hague: ICRC/M. Nijhoff, 1984)
Mich LR	*Michigan Law Review*
MJIL	*Michigan Journal of International Law*
MLR	*Modern Law Review*
MN	margin number
MONUC	United Nations Organization Mission in the Democratic Republic of the Congo
MoU	Memorandum of Understanding
MPEPIL	The Max Planck Encyclopedia of Public International Law, Oxford University Press, Online Edition, available at <http://www.mpepil.com>
MRM	monitoring and reporting mechanism
NATO	North Atlantic Treaty Organization
NDFP	National Democratic Front Philippines
NGO	non-governmental organization
NIAC	non-international armed conflict
NIB	National Information Bureau
NILR	*Netherlands International Law Review*
NJIL	*Nordic Journal of International Law*
NQHR	*Netherlands Quarterly of Human Rights*
NSA	non-state actor
NTC	National Transitional Council
OAS	Organization of American States
OAU	Organization of African Unity
OEF	Operation Enduring Freedom
OHCHR	Office of the United Nations High Commissioner for Human Rights
OIF	Operation Iraqi Freedom
ONUSAL	United Nations Observer Mission in El Salvador
OUP	Oxford University Press
Oxford Manual	Institute of International Law, The Laws of War on Land, 1880
para(s)	paragraph(s)
PCIJ	Permanent Court of International Justice
Pictet Commentary GC I	J. Pictet (ed), *Geneva Convention for the Amelioration of the Condition of the Wounded and Sick in Armed Forces in the Field: Commentary* (Geneva: ICRC, 1952)
Pictet Commentary GC II	J. Pictet (ed), *Geneva Convention for the Amelioration of the Condition of the Wounded, Sick and Shipwrecked Members of Armed Forces at Sea: Commentary* (Geneva: ICRC, 1960)
Pictet Commentary GC III	J. Pictet (ed), *Geneva Convention Relative to the Treatment of Prisoners of War: Commentary* (Geneva: ICRC, 1960)
Pictet Commentary GC IV	J. Pictet (ed), *Geneva Convention Relative to the Protection of Civilian Persons in Time of War: Commentary* (Geneva: ICRC, 1958)

PLO	Palestine Liberation Organization
PMSC	private military security contractor
POW	prisoner of war
PTC	Pre-Trial Chamber
R2P	responsibility to protect
RC Messages	Red Cross/Red Crescent Messages
RCADI	*Recueil des cours de l'Académie de droit international de la Haye*
Refugee Convention	Convention Relating to the Status of Refugees, 1951
Res	Resolution
RFL	restoration of family links
RGDIP	*Revue générale de droit international public*
RIAA	Reports of International Arbitral Awards
RUF	Revolutionary United Front
s (ss)	section(s)
Safety Convention	Convention on the Safety of United Nations and Associated Personnel 1994
SAJHR	*South African Journal on Human Rights*
Sassòli/Bouvier/Quintin	M. Sassòli, A. Bouvier, and A. Quintin, *How Does Law Protect in War?* (3rd edn, Geneva: ICRC, 2011)
SCSL	Special Court for Sierra Leone
SCSL Statute	Statute of the Special Court for Sierra Leone
SFRY	Socialist Federal Republic of Yugoslavia
SLM/A	Sudanese Liberation Movement/Army
SPLM	Sudan People's Liberation Movement
STL	Special Tribunal for Lebanon
subpara(s)	subparagraph(s)
TAC	transnational armed conflict
TO	Territorial Defence [in the former Yugoslavia]
TRNC	Turkish Republic of Northern Cyprus
UCLA JIL & FA	*University of California Los Angeles Journal of International Law and Foreign Affairs*
UDHR	Universal Declaration of Human Rights
UK	United Kingdom
UN	United Nations
UNAMIR	United Nations Assistance Mission for Rwanda
UNCC	United Nations Compensation Commission
UNCIVPOL	United Nations Civilian Police
UNCLOS	United Nations Convention on the Law of the Sea, 1982
UNESCO	United Nations Educational, Scientific and Cultural Organization
UNESCO Convention	UNESCO Convention for the Safeguarding of Intangible Cultural Heritage 2003
UNGA	United Nations General Assembly
UNHCR	United Nations High Commissioner for Refugees
UNICEF	United Nations Children's Fund
UNIFIL	United Nations Interim Force in Lebanon

UNITA	The National Union for the Total Independence of Angola
UNPA	United Nations Protected Areas
UNPROFOR	United Nations Protection Force
UNSG	United Nations Secretary-General
UNSC	United Nations Security Council
UNTAET	United Nations Transitional Administration in East Timor
UNWCC	United Nations War Crimes Commission
UNWGEID	United Nations Working Group on Enforced or Involuntary Disappearances
UPC/FPLC	Union of Congolese Patriots/Forces Patriotiques pour la Libération du Congo
UPLR	*University of Pennsylvania Law Review*
URLR	*University of Richmond Law Review*
US	United States
USC	United States Code
USNS	United States Naval Ship
USSR	Union of Soviet Socialist Republics
UWA	University of Western Australia
Van JTL	*Vanderbilt Journal of Transnational Law*
VCLT	Vienna Convention on the Law of Treaties, 1969
Virg JIL	*Virginia Journal of International Law*
vol	volume
WHO	World Health Organization
WMA	World Medical Association
World Heritage Convention	Convention Concerning the Protection of the World Cultural and Natural Heritage, 1972
Yale HRDLJ	*Yale Human Rights and Development Law Journal*
YECHR	*Yearbook of the European Convention on Human Rights*
YIHL	*Yearbook of International Humanitarian Law*
YILC	*Yearbook of the International Law Commission*
YLJ	*Yale Law Journal*
ZaöRV	*Zeitschrift für ausländisches öffentliches Recht und Völkerrecht*

List of Contributors

Payam Akhavan is a Professor of International Law, McGill University, Montreal, Canada; Fernand Braudel Senior Fellow, European University Institute, Florence, Italy.

Yutaka Arai-Takahashi is a Professor of International Law and International Human Rights Law at University of Kent at Brussels (Belgium) and at Canterbury (UK); and Deputy-Director in Law at University of Kent at Brussels.

Pierre d'Argent is a Professor of International Law at the University of Louvain (UCL) and Guest Professor at the University of Leiden as well as a Member of the Brussels Bar.

Annyssa Bellal was at the time of writing a lecturer at the Irish Centre for Human Rights (National University of Ireland).

Paolo Benvenuti is a Professor of International Law at the University Roma Tre in Italy.

Michael Bothe is Professor Emeritus of Public Law at the J.W. Goethe University in Frankfurt/Main.

Théo Boutruche has a PhD in Law, and is Instructor at Notre-Dame University, Lebanon and Independent Consultant in International Humanitarian and Human Rights Law.

Antoine A. Bouvier is a Legal Adviser at the International Committee of the Red Cross.

Stuart Casey-Maslen is an international lawyer at the University of Pretoria. He was formerly Head of Research at the Geneva Academy of International Humanitarian Law and Human Rights.

Vincent Chetail is a Professor of International Law at the Graduate Institute of International and Development Studies (Geneva) where he is also Director of the Global Migration Centre.

Andrew Clapham is a Professor of International Law at the Graduate Institute of International and Development Studies and former Director of the Geneva Academy of International Humanitarian Law and Human Rights.

François Crépeau is the Hans & Tamar Oppenheimer Professor of Public International Law at McGill University, Montreal, Canada.

Shane Darcy is a lecturer at the Irish Centre for Human Rights, National University of Ireland Galway.

Giovanni Distefano is a Professor of Public International Law at the University of Neuchâtel. He is also Visiting Professor at the Geneva Academy of International Humanitarian Law and Human Rights.

Louise Doswald-Beck is a retired Professor of International Law of the Graduate Institute of International and Development Studies, Geneva.

Anicée Van Engeland is Lecturer in Law (on research leave), SOAS, University of London.

Paola Gaeta is a Professor of International Criminal Law at the Law Faculty of the University of Geneva, Adjunct Professor of International Criminal Law at the Graduate Institute of International and Development Studies and former Director of the Geneva Academy of International Humanitarian Law and Human Rights.

Daniela Gavshon is the Senior Legal Officer for the International Crimes Evidence Project at the Public Interest Advocacy Centre (Sydney, Australia).

Robin Geiß is a Professor of International Law and Security at the University of Glasgow and a former Legal Adviser to the Legal Division of the International Committee of the Red Cross.

Gilles Giacca was at the time of writing Research Fellow and Programme Coordinator at the Law Faculty of Oxford University and currently works as Legal Adviser in the Legal Division of the International Committee of the Red Cross.

Rotem Giladi teaches at Hebrew University Law Faculty, Jerusalem.

Anne-Laurence Graf-Brugère was at the time of writing a researcher at the Chair of International and European Law at the University of Fribourg.

Julia Grignon is a Professor at the Faculty of Law of Laval University (Quebec) and former assistant editor of the Geneva Conventions Commentary.

Tom Haeck is an international lawyer specializing in human rights and international humanitarian law and former assistant editor of the Geneva Conventions Commentary.

Steven Haines is Professor of Public International Law at the University of Greenwich, London, and a retired British naval commander who chaired the Editorial Board of the UK's official *Manual of the Law of Armed Conflict*.

Bethany Hastie is a doctoral candidate at the Institute of Comparative Law, McGill University, Montreal, Canada.

Iris van der Heijden is the assistant editor of the Geneva Conventions Commentary.

Hans-Joachim Heintze is a Professor at the Ruhr-University Bochum and the Institute for International Law of Peace and Armed Conflict.

Jérôme De Hemptinne is a Senior Legal Officer at the Special Tribunal for Lebanon and guest lecturer at the Universities of Louvain-La-Neuve, Strasbourg and the Geneva Academy of International Humanitarian Law and Human Rights.

Etienne Henry is a PhD candidate in International Law and was at the time of writing Teaching and Research Assistant as well as Part-Time Lecturer in Public International Law at the University of Neuchâtel.

Annie Hylton is an international human rights lawyer/advocate and freelance writer. She was previously assistant editor to the Geneva Conventions Commentary and at the time of writing was a PhD candidate in International Law at the School of Oriental and African Studies, University of London.

Lucrezia Iapichino has a PhD in European Law and was at the time of writing a Visiting Scholar at the Melbourne Law School.

Ralph Janik is a lecturer and research assistant in international law at the University of Vienna.

List of Contributors

Jann K. Kleffner is a Professor of International Law and Head of the International Law Centre, Swedish Defence University in Stockholm.

Sarah Knuckey is the Lieff Cabraser Associate Clinical Professor of Law, Director of the Human Rights Clinic, Faculty Co-Director of the Human Rights Institute at Columbia Law School and Special Advisor to the UN Special Rapporteur on Extrajudicial Executions.

Robert Kolb is a Professor of Public International Law at the University of Geneva.

Flavia Lattanzi is a Professor of International Law at LUISS University (Rome), retired Professor of International Law at University Roma Tre and Judge at the International Criminal Tribunal for the former Yugoslavia.

Charlotte Lülf is a research associate at the Institute for International Law of Peace and Armed Conflict (IFHV), Ruhr-University Bochum.

Robert J. McGuire is an associate at Paul, Weiss, Rifkind, Wharton & Garrison LLP. He was formerly an International Legal Fellow at Human Rights First in New York.

Frédéric Mégret is an Associate Professor of Law, and the Canada Research Chair on the Law of Human Rights and Legal Pluralism, at McGill University, Montreal, Canada.

Elżbieta Mikos-Skuza is a Senior Lecturer in International Law at the Faculty of Law and Administration of the University of Warsaw and a Visiting Professor at the College of Europe in Natolin.

Marko Milanovic is Associate Professor at the University of Nottingham School of Law, and Vice-President of the European Society of International Law.

Lindsay Moir is a Professor of International Law at the University of Hull and Deputy Director of the McCoubrey Centre for International Law.

Nishat Nishat was at the time of writing a PhD candidate at the University of Geneva and research assistant at the Geneva Academy of International Humanitarian Law and Human Rights.

Manfred Nowak is a Professor of International Law and Human Rights at the University of Vienna, Austria. He is also Co-Director of the Ludwig Boltzmann Institute of Human Rights in Vienna and he was formerly Swiss Chair of Human Rights at the Geneva Academy.

Keiichiro Okimoto is a Legal Officer, Office of the Legal Counsel, Office of Legal Affairs, Secretariat of the United Nations.

Laura M. Olson is Section Lead, Immigration Section, US Department of Homeland Security's Office for Civil Rights and Civil Liberties. The views expressed in this volume are made in the author's personal capacity and do not represent the position or views of the US Department of Homeland Security or the US Government.

Bruce Oswald is an Associate Professor at Melbourne Law School and Director of the Asia Pacific Centre for Military Law.

Anna Petrig is a post-doctoral researcher at the University of Basel (Switzerland) and a guest researcher at the Max Planck Institute for Comparative Public Law and International Law in Heidelberg (Germany).

Noëlle Quénivet is an Associate Professor of International Law at the Bristol Law School, University of the West of England.

Steven Ratner is the Bruno Simma Collegiate Professor of Law at the University of Michigan Law School.

Gabor Rona is Visiting Professor at Cardozo Law School in New York.

Natalino Ronzitti is an Emeritus Professor of International Law at LUISS University (Rome) and a Member of the Institut de droit international.

Indira Rosenthal is an Independent Consultant in International Humanitarian, Criminal, and Human Rights Law, Women's Human Rights and Gender Mainstreaming.

Peter Rowe is Professor Emeritus at the Law School, University of Lancaster, England.

Elizabeth Salmón is a Professor of International Law at the Pontifical Catholic University of Peru School of Law and Academic Director of the Institute for Democracy and Human Rights of the same university (IDEHPUCP) where she coordinates the Human Rights Master Program.

Silvia Sanna is a Professor of International and European Union Law at the University of Sassari.

Yves Sandoz is a former Professor of International Humanitarian Law at the University of Fribourg and the College of Europe in Bruges and Natolin as well as a former member of the faculty of the Geneva Academy of International Humanitarian Law and Human Rights. He is an honorary member of the International Committee of the Red Cross.

Marco Sassòli is a Professor of International Law as well as Director of the Department of Public International Law and International Organization at the University of Geneva. He teaches international humanitarian law at the Geneva Academy of International Humanitarian Law and Human Rights.

Katja Schöberl is a Legal and Dissemination Advisor at the German Red Cross in Berlin.

Patricia V. Sellers, an international criminal lawyer, is the Special Advisor for Prosecution Strategies in the Office of the Prosecutor of the International Criminal Court and a Visiting Fellow at Kellogg College, Oxford University.

Sandesh Sivakumaran is Professor of Public International Law at the University of Nottingham.

Heike Spieker is the Deputy Director of the International Services and National Relief Division at the German Red Cross—Headquarters and Senior Lecturer at Ruhr-Universität of Bochum, Germany, and Università della Svizzera Italiana, Lugano, Switzerland, as well as Adjunct Lecturer at University College Dublin, Ireland.

Christian Tomuschat is a Professor Emeritus of International and Constitutional Law at Humboldt University Berlin, currently the President of the OSCE Court of

Conciliation and Arbitration. He was a member of the Human Rights Committee under the International Covenant on Civil and Political Rights and a member and chairman of the International Law Commission.

Marie-Louise Tougas is a Legal Adviser at the International Committee of the Red Cross.

David Tuck was at the time of writing with the Geneva Academy of International Humanitarian Law and Human Rights and currently works for the International Committee of the Red Cross.

Gabriella Venturini is a retired Professor of International Law and former Director of the Department of International Studies, University of Milan. She teaches human rights and armed conflict at the Geneva Academy of International Humanitarian Law and Human Rights.

Luisa Vierucci is Assistant Professor of International Law, University of Florence.

Sean Watts is a Professor of Law at Creighton University School of Law. He also serves as an Instructor at the United States Military Academy at West Point in his capacity as a Lieutenant Colonel in the US Army JAG Reserve.

Stefan Wehrenberg is Attorney at Law, Blum & Grob Attorneys at Law Ltd, Zurich and Head of the Legal Advisory Group to the Swiss Military Attorney General.

Sharon Weill is a lecturer and researcher at Sciences-Po Paris as well as at the Geneva Centre for Education and Research in Humanitarian Action.

Andreas R. Ziegler is a Professor at the University of Lausanne and member of the Legal Advisory Group to the Swiss Military Attorney General.

PART I

CROSS-CUTTING ISSUES AND COMMON PROVISIONS

—

A. CROSS-CUTTING ISSUES

Chapter 1. The Concept of International Armed Conflict

	MN
A. Introduction—War and Armed Conflict	1
B. The Applicability of the Geneva Conventions	5
I. The relevance of war and occupation	5
II. The disappearance of the 'general participation clause' (*si omnes* clause)	11
III. Application between a state party and a state which is not a party to the Geneva Conventions	12
IV. International organizations and international armed conflict	16
V. The threshold of violence for an inter-state armed conflict	20
VI. Converting an internal armed conflict into an international armed conflict and the separate issues of state responsibility and armed attack	40
VII. National liberation movements and self-determination struggles	49
VIII. Unrecognized governments and recognized belligerents	55
IX. Cyber warfare	57
C. The Boundary between International and Non-International Armed Conflicts	65
D. Legal Consequences of a Violation	67
E. Critical Assessment	68

Select Bibliography

D'Aspremont, J./De Hemptinne, J., *Droit international humanitaire* (Paris: Pedone, 2012)

Del Mar, K., 'The Requirement of "Belonging" under International Humanitarian Law', 21 *JICJ* (2010) 105

Dinstein, Y., *War, Aggression and Self-Defence* (5th edn, Cambridge: CUP, 2012)

Farer, T., 'Humanitarian Law and Armed Conflicts: Towards the Definition of "International Armed Conflict"', 71 *Columbia Law Review* 1 (1971) 37

Greenwood, C., 'International Humanitarian Law and the *Tadić Case*', 7 *EJIL* (1996) 265

Greenwood, C., 'Protection of Peacekeepers: The Legal Regime', 7 *Duke Journal of Comparative and International Law* (1996) 185

ICRC, 'How Is the Term "Armed Conflict" Defined in International Humanitarian Law?' (2008)

Lauterpacht, H. (ed), *Oppenheim's International Law: A Treatise (Disputes, War and Neutrality)* (7th edn, London: Longmans, 1952) vol II

McNair, A.D./Watts, A.D., *The Legal Effects of War* (Cambridge: CUP, 1966)

Mégret, F., 'War and the Vanishing Battlefield', 9 *Loyola University Chicago International Law Review* (2011–12) 131

Meron, T., 'Classification of Armed Conflict in the Former Yugoslavia: Nicaragua's Fallout', 92 *AJIL* (1998) 236

Nolte, G., 'Intervention by Invitation' in MPEPIL

O'Connell, M.E. (ed), *What Is War?: An Investigation in the Wake of 9/11* (Leiden: Nijhoff, 2012)

Sassòli, M./Olson, L.M., 'The Judgment of the ICTY Appeals Chamber on the Merits in the *Tadić* Case', 82 *IRRC* (2000) 733

Schindler, D., 'The Different Types of Armed Conflicts According to the Geneva Conventions and Protocols', 163 *RCADI* (1979) 117

Schmitt, M. (ed), *The War in Afghanistan: A Legal Analysis* (Newport, RI: Naval War College, 2009) vol 85

Solis, G.D., *The Law of Armed Conflict: International Humanitarian Law in War* (New York: CUP, 2010) 149

Vité, S., 'Typology of Armed Conflicts in International Humanitarian Law: Legal Concepts and Actual Situations', 91 *IRRC* 873 (2009) 69

Wilmshurst, E. (ed), *International Law and the Classification of Conflicts* (Oxford: OUP, 2012)

A. Introduction—War and Armed Conflict

1 Although war used to be considered an appropriate way to settle disputes between states, the United Nations (UN) Charter of 1945 made it clear that all inter-state disputes are now to be settled by peaceful means.[1] While armed force may be used by states in self-defence, or authorized by the UN Security Council, in other circumstances a declaration of war by one state against another state, or the use of armed force by a state against another state, will normally constitute a violation of the UN Charter and customary international law.

2 Hence, as declarations and recognition of war have become less relevant, it has become more usual to refer to the laws of war as the law of armed conflict, or as international humanitarian law (IHL). But the notion of war, and its attendant 'war crimes', 'prisoners of war', and 'war powers', remain omnipresent. References to the global 'war on terror' have reminded us how powerfully the notion of war plays on our emotions and imagination. Claiming to be at war can mobilize support, generate resistance, and shift the paradigm. Evocations of war still suggest to some that 'all's fair in love and war'.

3 On the contrary, as this Commentary will demonstrate, how people are treated in armed conflict is one of the most highly regulated areas of international relations, with international law reaching down to create obligations for multiple actors, including states, organized armed groups, and individuals. Wars and armed conflicts, far from creating lawless zones, trigger multiple binding obligations under international and national law. In some cases, violations of these obligations can result in prosecutions—in the form of war crimes trials.

4 Even if one no longer needs a declaration of war to apply the laws of war, or to claim neutrality,[2] there will be some armed conflicts that are also wars—as that term is understood in law. In some national legal orders, the fact of war, or the declaration of war, will trigger further rights and obligations. This could be related to trading with the enemy, or the simple fact that a contract is said not to apply in times of war. If one reads one's travel

---

[1] Art 2(3) and (4) UN Charter (1945).

[2] For the practice of Switzerland with regard to her neutrality during the 2003 conflict between the US-led coalition and Iraq, see 'Neutrality Under Scrutiny in the Iraq Conflict', Summary of Switzerland's neutrality policy during the Iraq conflict in response to the Reimann Postulate (03.3066) and to the Motion by the SVP Parliamentary Group (03.3050) (2 December 2005); see also P. Seger, 'The Law of Neutrality', in A. Clapham and P. Gaeta (eds), *Oxford Handbook of International Law in Armed Conflict* (Oxford: OUP, 2014) 348; a state which is not a party to an IAC may be considered neutral or non-belligerent for the purposes of the GCs, which, in various circumstances (especially Art 4(B)(2) GC III), provide for a role and obligations for such states; compare Ch 5, MN 20, of this volume.

insurance carefully, it usually excludes war zones. Whether a travel insurance company declares an area a war zone, however, has little to do with whether the Geneva Conventions apply; but a determination that there is a war may have more than rhetorical effect in the contractual world. The term *war* is now used so loosely that one would be very careless to think that because someone calls something a war, the laws of war apply.[3] Nevertheless, there will be situations where an official declaration of war will be technically necessary, not for the application of the Geneva Conventions, but arguably in order to be in compliance with the 1907 Hague Convention III (if these obligations remain relevant),[4] or in order to trigger certain national laws related to relations with the enemy and its nationals.[5]

B. The Applicability of the Geneva Conventions

I. The relevance of war and occupation

The drafters of the Geneva Conventions of 1949 were careful to ensure that the new Conventions, codifying and developing protections for the victims of war, applied to all armed conflicts, even where there is no declaration of war; and it is clear from the Conventions that states cannot avoid their obligations by refusing to recognize a state of war:

> In addition to the provisions which shall be implemented in peacetime, the present Convention shall apply to all cases of declared war or of any other armed conflict which may arise between two or more of the High Contracting Parties, even if the state of war is not recognized by one of them.[6]

Although one could read this last phrase to suggest that where *both* states deny there is a state of war, the Conventions would not apply, such an interpretation finds no support. Christopher Greenwood has simply stated that this phrase 'should be read as if it said: "even if the state of war is not recognized by one *or both* of them"'.[7] The Pictet Commentary captures the essence of the point when it states: 'It must not be forgotten that the Conventions have been drawn up first and foremost to protect individuals, and not to serve State interests.'[8]

---

[3] F. Mégrét, '"War"? Legal Semantics and the Move to Violence', 13 *EJIL* 2 (2002) 361.

[4] Compare Hague Convention III (1907), Art 1: 'The contracting Powers recognize that hostilities between themselves must not commence without previous and explicit warning, in the form either of a declaration of war, giving reasons, or of an ultimatum with conditional declaration of war.' Art 2: 'The existence of a state of war must be notified to the neutral Powers without delay, and shall not take effect in regard to them until after the receipt of a notification, which may, however, be given by telegraph. Neutral Powers, nevertheless, cannot rely on the absence of notification if it is clearly established that they were in fact aware of the existence of a state of war.' See further Y. Dinstein, *War, Aggression and Self-Defence* (5th edn, Cambridge: CUP, 2012), at 3–33. Whether or not a state can claim belligerent rights by declaring war is a topic which is outside the scope of this Commentary; see further C. Greenwood, 'The Concept of War in Modern International Law', 36 *ICLQ* (1987) 283.

[5] A.D. McNair and A.D. Watts, *The Legal Effects of War* (Cambridge: CUP, 1966).

[6] Common Article (CA) 2 para 1.

[7] C. Greenwood, 'Scope of Application of Humanitarian Law', in D. Fleck (ed), *The Handbook of Humanitarian Law in Armed Conflict* (2nd edn, Oxford: OUP, 2007) 45, at 47.

[8] Pictet Commentary GC IV, at 21. See also Pictet Commentary GC I, at 28–9: 'A State does not proclaim the principle of the protection due to wounded and sick combatants in the hope of saving a certain number of its own nationals. It does so out of respect for the human person as such. This being so, it is difficult to admit that this sentiment of respect has any connection with the concrete fact of recognition of a state of war. A wounded soldier is not more deserving, or less deserving, of medical treatment according to whether his Government does, or does not, recognize the existence of a state of war.'

7   As we shall see, international law is fairly clear on the concept of an international armed conflict (IAC) triggering the application of the Geneva Conventions. Nevertheless, there could be a situation where a state declares war on another state, even in the absence of an armed conflict. In such a case, the Geneva Conventions will apply. Even in the absence of fighting or occupation, the Geneva Conventions (especially Geneva Convention (GC) IV) could be relevant to and important for such an inter-state war, for example in the event of internment of enemy aliens.[9]

8   We should also note that Common Article 2 paragraph 2 states that each 'Convention shall also apply to all cases of partial or total occupation of the territory of a High Contracting Party, even if the said occupation meets with no armed resistance'. Unless the occupied state consents to the presence of foreign troops, the Geneva Conventions will apply.

9   The UN Commission of Inquiry on Lebanon applied paragraph 2 in 2006:

> Insofar as it is relevant and having regard to common article 2, paragraph 2, of the Geneva Conventions of 1949, international humanitarian law applies even in a situation, where for example the armed forces of a State party temporarily occupy the territory of another State, without meeting any resistance from the latter. On the same legal basis, it has been stated that the Geneva Conventions apply even where a State temporarily occupies another State without an exchange of fire having taken place or in a situation where the Occupying State encounters no military opposition whatsoever.
>
> The Commission considers that both Lebanon and Israel were parties to the conflict. They remain bound by the Geneva Conventions of 1949, and customary international humanitarian law existing at the time of the conflict.[10]

10 The International Court of Justice (ICJ) has held that although paragraph 2 refers to 'the territory of a High Contracting Party', this does not limit occupation to such territory:[11]

> The object of the second paragraph of Article 2 is not to restrict the scope of application of the Convention, as defined by the first paragraph, by excluding therefrom territories not falling under the sovereignty of one of the contracting parties. It is directed simply to making it clear that, even if occupation effected during the conflict met no armed resistance, the Convention is still applicable.

After referring to the *travaux préparatoires*, the Court recalled that

> [t]he drafters of the second paragraph of Article 2 thus had no intention, when they inserted that paragraph into the Convention, of restricting the latter's scope of application. They were merely seeking to provide for cases of occupation without combat, such as the occupation of Bohemia and Moravia by Germany in 1939.[12]

In short, Common Article 2 means that the Geneva Conventions apply to inter-state armed conflicts, situations where a state has made a declaration of war on another state, and non-consensual occupation.

---

[9] C. Greenwood, 'International Humanitarian Law (Laws of War)', in F. Kalshoven (ed), *The Centennial of the First International Peace Conference* (The Hague: Kluwer Law International, 2000) 161, at 194–5.
[10] See UN Doc A/HRC/3/2, 23 November 2006, paras 59–60 (footnote omitted).
[11] ICJ, *Legal Consequences of the Construction of a Wall in the Occupied Palestinian Territory*, Advisory Opinion, 9 July 2004, para 95. See also ICRC Commentary APs, para 65; Pictet Commentary GC IV, at 21–2.
[12] ICJ, *Wall Advisory Opinion*, above n 11, para 95. For a discussion on the beginning and end of occupation, see Chs 67 and 74 of this volume.

II. The disappearance of the 'general participation clause' (*si omnes* clause)

Some older treaties on the laws of war, such as the 1899 Convention (III) for the Adaptation to Maritime Warfare of the Principles of the Geneva Convention of 22 August 1864, specified that the treaties would not apply if a belligerent who was not a party to the treaty joined the war between two or more states parties to the treaty.[13] This gave rise to the theoretical possibility that the victims of war would lose their protection in the event that a third state, which had not ratified the relevant treaty, joined an ongoing conflict. In practice, states continued to apply the laws of war, even in the event that the treaty, strictly speaking, did not apply. In the context of the war crimes trials in Nuremberg and Tokyo, the International Military Tribunals held that the relevant rules were customary international law, and therefore the question of the applicability of the relevant treaties was not relevant.[14] The Geneva Conventions of 1929 on prisoners of war (POWs) and the sick and wounded, were clear that they would apply between states parties even where a non-party joined the conflict, but in order to clarify the matter for other regimes, all four Geneva Conventions of 1949 now contain a clause which precludes any suggestion that there is a need for general participation in order for the Convention to apply. Common Article 2 paragraph 3 contains the following sentence:

Although one of the Powers in conflict may not be a party to the present Convention, the Powers who are parties thereto shall remain bound by it in their mutual relations.

III. Application between a state party and a state which is not a party to the Geneva Conventions

All four Geneva Conventions contain a common clause which states that parties to the Convention are bound in relation to another belligerent state if that state 'accepts and applies' the provisions of the Convention.[15] This compromise provision sought to retain respect for the idea of reciprocity in the law of treaties, while extending the international protection of the victims of war beyond the logic of inter-state relations. The International Committee of the Red Cross (ICRC) Commentary explained:

The spirit and character of the Conventions lead perforce to the conclusion that the Contracting Power must at least apply their provisions from the moment hostilities break out until such time as the adverse Party has had the time and an opportunity to state his intentions. That may not be a strictly legal interpretation; it does not altogether follow from the text itself; but it is in our opinion the only reasonable solution. It follows from the spirit of the Conventions, and is in accordance with their character. It is also in accordance with the moral interest of the Contracting Power, inasmuch as it invites the latter to honour a signature given before the world. It is finally to its advantage from a more practical point of view, because the fact of its beginning itself to apply the Convention will encourage the non-Contracting Party to declare its acceptance, whereas any postponement of the application of the Convention by the Contracting Party would give the non-Contracting Party a pretext for non-acceptance.[16]

---

[13] Art 11: 'The rules contained in the above articles are binding only on the Contracting Powers, in case of war between two or more of them. The said rules shall cease to be binding from the time when, in a war between the Contracting Powers, one of the belligerents is joined by a non-Contracting Power.'

[14] Discussed in H. Lauterpacht (ed), *Oppenheim's International Law: A Treatise (Disputes, War and Neutrality)* (7th edn, London: Longmans, 1952) vol II, at 234–6; Greenwood suggests that the remaining general participation clauses have become 'largely irrelevant' (above n 9, at 194).

[15] CA 2 para 2.   [16] Pictet Commentary GC III, at 25.

13 Today, this question is largely moot, as nearly every state is a contracting party to the Geneva Conventions. In recent situations where a conflict has broken out between a state party and a non-state party, it has been assumed that the key rules in the Conventions apply to the parties due to their status as rules of customary international law.[17] Nevertheless, the issue of whether the provisions of the treaty apply *stricto sensu* may have to be resolved. For example, other treaties may be excluded where states parties to such treaties are bound by the Geneva Conventions,[18] or issues may arise under the terms of the settlement of an inter-state dispute whereby the dispute settlement mechanism is limited to the application of binding treaty obligations.

14 The issue arose for the Eritrea–Ethiopia Claims Commission, as Eritrea was not a party to the Geneva Conventions from the beginning of hostilities in 1998 until its accession to the Conventions on 14 August 2000. The Commission addressed the application of the clause in Common Article 2 paragraph 3 that binds a state party to the Convention if the other (non-contracting) belligerent state 'accepts and applies' the provisions of the Convention. The Commission found that

> prior to its accession, Eritrea had not accepted the Conventions. This non-acceptance was also demonstrated by Eritrea's refusal to allow the representatives of the ICRC to visit the POWs it held until after its accession to the Conventions.
>
> Consequently, the Commission holds that, with respect to matters prior to August 14, 2000, the law applicable to the armed conflict between Eritrea and Ethiopia is customary international law.[19]

15 The Commission held that one could assume that the Conventions represented customary international law, and determined that a party wishing to challenge the customary nature of a provision would bear the burden of proof:

> [T]he law applicable to this Claim is customary international law, including customary international humanitarian law, as exemplified by the relevant parts of the four Geneva Conventions of 1949. The frequent invocation of provisions of Geneva Convention III by both Parties in support of their claims and defenses is fully consistent with this holding. Whenever either Party asserts that a particular relevant provision of those Conventions should not be considered part of customary international law at the relevant time, the Commission will decide that question, and the burden of proof will be on the asserting Party.[20]

IV. International organizations and international armed conflict

16 A complex set of questions concerns the extent to which the UN, or any other intergovernmental organization, may be considered a party to an IAC. As none of these entities can become parties to the Geneva Conventions, they become bound by the relevant law of IAC to the extent that this law applies to them as a matter of customary international law,[21] or they may be bound by the fundamental rules and principles of humanitarian law

---

[17] See generally ICRC CIHL Study and E. Wilmshurst and S. Breau (eds), *Perspectives on the ICRC Study on Customary International Humanitarian Law* (Cambridge: CUP, 2007).

[18] E.g. International Convention against the Taking of Hostages (1979) Art 12, discussed in Chs 15 and 35 of this volume.

[19] EECC, *Prisoners of War—Eritrea's Claim 17*, paras 37–8, xxvi *Reports of International Arbitral Awards* (2009), at 39; see also Lauterpacht (ed), above n 14, at 236, who points out that although it would seem to be for the state party to determine whether the opposing party in fact applies the provisions, such a determination must 'take place in accordance with the principles of good faith'.

[20] EECC, *Prisoners of War*, above n 19, para 41.

[21] For some of the doctrinal debate concerning whether such conflicts constitute IACs or NIACs, see D. Akande, 'Classification of Armed Conflicts: Relevant Legal Concepts', in E. Wilmshurst (ed), *International*

as a result of their own internal regulations,[22] or through agreements entered into with host states.

The Convention on the Safety of United Nations and Associated Personnel foresees that the UN might become a party to an IAC, at which point that Convention would no longer apply (the context would have to be a UN enforcement operation authorized by the Security Council under Chapter VII).[23] It seems clear that a conflict between the UN and the armed forces of a state would be an IAC and that the relevant rules from the Geneva Conventions should apply. Dapo Akande explains that this is either because

> there is a customary rule that broadens international armed conflicts to include conflicts involving international organizations and States or alternatively it could be said that the conflict is international because the States providing contingents remain bound by the treaties to which they are party since they have an obligation not only to respect them but also to 'ensure respect' for the conventions in circumstances where their troops act, even if for someone else.[24]

Opinion is divided on whether an armed conflict between the UN and a non-state armed group might be considered an IAC, where the UN is acting for neither side in any internal armed conflict yet nevertheless engages in an armed conflict with the non-state party to that conflict.[25] For the present author, it seems that it is not the international character of the UN that determines the classification of the conflict, but rather the non-state character of the opposing forces that means that the conflict is of a non-international character. It seems incongruous that one should begin to suggest that a non-state armed group should have the rights and duties of a state in an IAC when fighting the UN.

Where states are authorized to use force by the Security Council, they remain bound by their obligations under the Geneva Conventions in the event of an armed conflict or

---

Law and the Classification of Conflicts (Oxford: OUP, 2012) 32, at 64–70; B.K. Klappe, 'International Peace Operations', in D. Fleck (ed), *The Handbook of Humanitarian Law in Armed Conflict* (2nd edn, Oxford: OUP, 2007) 635; C. Greenwood, 'International Humanitarian Law and United Nations Military Operations', 1 *YIHL* (1998) 3; L. Condorelli, A.-M. La Rosa, and S. Scherrer (eds), *Les Nations Unies et le droit international humanitaire: Actes du colloque international 19, 20, 21 octobre 1995* (Paris: Pedone, 1996).

[22] See the UN Secretary-General's Bulletin, *Observance by United Nations Forces of International Humanitarian Law*, UN Doc. ST/SGB, 6 August 1999; D. Shraga, 'The Secretary-General's Bulletin on the Observance by United Nations Forces on International Humanitarian Law: A Decade Later', 39 *Isr YBHR* (2009) 357.

[23] Art 2(2): 'This Convention shall not apply to a United Nations operation authorized by the Security Council as an enforcement action under Chr VII of the Charter of the United Nations in which any of the personnel are engaged as combatants against organized armed forces and to which the law of international armed conflict applies.' See M.-C. Bourloyannis-Vrailas, 'The Convention on the Safety of United Nations and Associated Personnel', 44 *ICLQ* (1995) 560. Note that it has been suggested by Bouvier that this provision should be interpreted to cover NIAC; he also suggests that 'the clause implies that in the event of clashes between United Nations forces and organized armed forces, international humanitarian law that relating [*sic*] to international armed conflicts and not to internal conflicts then applies': A. Bouvier, ' "Convention on the Safety of United Nations and Associated Personnel": Presentation and Analysis', 35 *IRRC* 309 (1995) 638, at 662.

[24] See Akande, above n 21, at 69–70. Common Art 1 to the Geneva Conventions provides: 'The High Contracting Parties undertake to respect and to ensure respect for the present Convention in all circumstances.' See further Ch 6 of this volume. On the obligations of troop-contributing states, see further A. Nollkaemper, 'Dual Attribution: Liability of the Netherlands for Conduct of Dutchbat in Srebrenica', 9 *JICJ* (2011) 1143.

[25] See S. Vité, 'Typology of Armed Conflicts in International Humanitarian Law: Legal Concepts and Actual Situations', 91 *IRRC* 873 (2009) 69, at 87–8; E. David, *Principes de droit des conflits armés* (4th edn, Bruylant: Brussels, 2008), at 179–83.

an occupation. It has been suggested that the Security Council may demand a departure from the application of the Geneva Conventions,[26] for example Greenwood suggests the Council adopted 'decisions requiring structural change within occupied territory' (for the situation in Iraq 2003–4).[27] It must be stressed, however, that it ought to be very hard, if not impossible, to show that a state party to the Geneva Conventions is relieved of its obligations, due to a competing obligation arising under Article 103 of the UN Charter. The Article reads:

In the event of a conflict between the obligations of the Members of the United Nations under the present Charter and their obligations under any other international agreement, their obligations under the present Charter shall prevail.

It has been argued that obligations under the Charter include binding decisions contained in Resolutions of the Security Council. The European Court of Human Rights rejected the idea that one can imply that the Security Council intends to impose obligations which run contrary to human rights obligations under the European Convention on Human Rights, and the reasoning would seem to apply *mutatis mutandis* to the protection offered by the Geneva Conventions:

Respect for human rights was one of the paramount principles of the United Nations Charter and if the Security Council had intended to impose an obligation on British forces to act in breach of the United Kingdom's international human rights obligations, it would have used clear and unequivocal language. It followed that the rule of priority under Article 103 of the United Nations Charter did not come into effect.[28]

V. The threshold of violence for an inter-state armed conflict

20 The Conventions make a fundamental distinction between IACs and non-international armed conflicts (NIACs). Once we accept the likelihood that this fundamental distinction is here to stay,[29] we can carefully consider the implications of triggering the law of IAC as opposed to the law of internal armed conflict.[30]

21 Let us first look at the policy implications, which are nevertheless in the background for any 'objective' determination of what constitutes an armed conflict. Here we need to consider briefly the rationale and the consequences of the distinction between IACs

---

[26] As a separate issue, the Security Council may directly or indirectly infer that an armed conflict exists which triggers the application of the Geneva Conventions. E.g., the Security Council in recent years has often called for the parties to respect IHL: for a selection, see Resolutions 1193, 1213, 1214, 1216, 1471, 1479, 1509, 1528, 1746, 1890, 1973, and 1991. On the particular issue of the approach of the Security Council to children in armed conflict, see A. Constantinides, 'Human Rights Obligations and Accountability of Armed Opposition Groups: The Practice of the UN Security Council', 4 *Human Rights and International Legal Discourse* (2010) 89; for a detailed look of the role of the Security Council in this context, see M. Roscini, 'The United Nations Security Council and the Enforcement of International Humanitarian Law', 43 *Israel Law Review* (2010) 330, esp at 342–3.

[27] Greenwood, above n 7, at 53.   [28] ECtHR, *Al-Jedda v UK*, 7 July 2011, para 93.

[29] See further Wilmshurst (ed), above n 21; cf J.T. Stewart, 'Towards a Single Definition of Armed Conflict in International Humanitarian Law: A Critique of Internationalized Armed Conflict', 85 *IRRC* (2003) 313; and T. Farer, 'Humanitarian Law and Armed Conflicts: Towards the Definition of "International Armed Conflict"', 71 *Columbia Law Review* 1 (1971) 37; see also the discussion in Ch 2 of this volume.

[30] For a discussion of transnational, mixed, and NIACs, see Chs 2 and 19 of this volume.

and NIACs (sometimes known as internal armed conflicts or civil wars). In the past, the main concerns were probably that states saw international regulation of civil wars as an interference with their sovereignty, as a hindrance to putting down rebellion, and a sort of implied international recognition of the standing of the rebel forces with whom they were dealing. Today, for some states, these concerns might seem less pressing, and yet the distinction remains.

It is suggested that we need to admit that the distinction is more than a question of the politics of sovereignty. The distinction triggers different regimes, which, in turn, lead to very different rights and obligations for the parties. Simply put, states are not ready to grant combatant immunity to those who take up arms from within. Those who take up arms against their own state are to be detained, tried, and punished, not treated as POWs and released at the end of the conflict. Such fighters are seen by the state authorities as criminals, seditious, treacherous, and sometimes labelled as terrorists. Hence, states see a need to preserve a category of internal (or non-international) armed conflict. On the other hand, when a state's troops venture abroad, that state would not countenance its troops being tried for murder. It would expect its personnel to enjoy a form of sovereign state immunity. The state would expect the members of its armed forces to be treated as POWs if captured by the enemy state, and not be tried for violations of the local law.

In other words, from a state's point of view, it makes sense that there is one rule for an inter-state conflict and another for an internal armed conflict. The international law, which states have agreed to and generated, therefore continues to reflect this distinction, even if in some areas of IHL there has been some convergence in the degree of protection afforded to civilians and detainees.

What does this mean for the design of the thresholds of armed violence required for a conflict to be considered international or non-international? First, if we can see the reason for two separate regimes, we can also admit that there may be good reasons why the threshold is arguably different in each regime. States will be quite keen to ensure that their personnel or civilians are protected in an IAC, even where the level of hostilities is relatively low and the duration of the fighting quite short. This enthusiasm for a low threshold will also be shared by those organizations (such as the ICRC) tasked with guaranteeing the protection of the victims of armed conflict. As we have seen, the wording of the Conventions reflects this, triggering their application even in the absence of resistance to an occupation.

On the other hand, with regard to a rebellion or an insurgency, states may be less keen to see the threshold reached. Even though admitting the existence of an armed conflict would trigger additional international obligations for the organized armed groups they are fighting, the overriding impression will be that attacks on the armed forces of the state and its military objectives will somehow be legitimated if the rebels can claim their acts are in accordance with the laws of war. In turn, humanitarian organizations may be cautious about suggesting that the threshold has been reached, for fear of escalating the violence and implying that those on both sides are entitled to use lethal force against fighters from the other side. There is a fear that one would trigger a sort of a 'licence to kill', even though international law knows no such concept. On the one hand, those who are detained might benefit from some extra guarantees under the law of armed conflict, but on the other hand there is a risk that the IHL regime is said to supplant existing human rights obligations. In short, there may be very good political and 'humanitarian' reasons to refrain from arguing for a low level of violence to trigger the law of NIAC.

26   The ICRC Commentaries, and subsequent publications by the ICRC and its legal advisers, have argued that, for inter-state conflicts, the 'level of intensity required for a conflict to be subject to the law of international armed conflict is very low'.[31]

27   According to Hans-Peter Gasser (at the time Legal Adviser for the ICRC):

> When can an 'armed conflict' be said to obtain? The Conventions themselves are of no help to us here, since they contain no definition of the term. We must therefore look at State practice, according to which any use of armed force by one state against the territory of another triggers the applicability of the Geneva Conventions between the two States. Why force was used is of no consequence to international humanitarian law. It is therefore irrelevant whether there was any justification for taking up weapons, whether the use of arms was intended to restore law and order (in the sense of an international police action) or whether it constituted an act of naked aggression, etc. It is also of no concern whether or not the party attacked resists. From the point of view of international humanitarian law the question of the Conventions' applicability to a situation is easily answered: as soon as the armed forces of one State find themselves with wounded or surrendering members of the armed forces or civilians of another State on their hands, as soon as they detain prisoners or have actual control over a part of the territory of the enemy State, then they must comply with the relevant convention. The number of wounded or prisoners, the size of the territory occupied, are of no account, since the requirement of protection does not depend on quantitative considerations.[32]

28   The use of force or border incursion must be intentional rather than accidental,[33] but there is no longer support for the idea that one needs a belligerent intent to go to war. One cannot avoid the obligations of the Geneva Conventions by claiming that one is engaged in a law enforcement operation in another state rather than admitting an armed conflict with that state. The test should be an objective one. Nevertheless, individual incidents and limited exchanges of fire on the border have not always been treated as IACs.

29   In the wake of the terrorist attacks of 11 September 2001, the subsequent armed conflicts in Afghanistan, and the wider so-called 'war on terror', there was concern that the existing framework of the international law of armed conflict was inadequate. This engendered not only discussion of new types of conflict, but also a new scrutiny of the thresholds. In this context, the aim of certain states has been to assume some of the rights of a belligerent in an armed conflict, while denying Al-Qaeda and others some of the benefits of the law of armed conflict. Others have been concerned that the armed conflict framework is being invoked too liberally, for what should be more properly considered as law-enforcement operations. The result has been increased attention to the threshold used for the application of the law of armed conflict.[34]

30   In 2005, the International Law Association (ILA) mandated a Committee to produce a report on 'the meaning of war or armed conflict in international law'. The final report was published in 2010, and it contains valuable information on how various conflicts

---

[31] Vité, above n 25, at 72; see also ICRC Opinion Paper March 2008, 'How is the Term "Armed Conflict" Defined in International Humanitarian Law?', at 5: 'International armed conflicts exist whenever there is resort to armed force between two or more States.'; Pictet Commentary GC I, at 32–3.

[32] H.-P. Gasser, 'International Humanitarian Law', in H. Haug (ed), *Humanity for All: The International Red Cross and Red Crescent Movement* (Geneva: Henry Dunant Institute, 1993) 491, at 510–11.

[33] See, e.g., A.P.V. Rogers, *Law on the Battlefield* (3rd edn, Manchester: Manchester University Press, 2012), 'an accidental border incursion by a military aircraft caused by navigational error would not amount to armed conflict' (at 3).

[34] For a discussion of how to qualify the conflict with Al-Qaeda, see N. Lubell, 'The War (?) Against Al-Qaeda', in Wilmshurst (ed), above n 21, at 421–54.

have been seen by states. Before looking at their findings, it is important to recall the background. Not only was the Committee addressing the claims by the United States (US) with regard to its operations against Al-Qaeda, but it was additionally interested in the fact that the existence of an armed conflict 'can also have a wide reaching impact on the international legal norms regulating relations between states including asylum obligations, HRL [human rights law], neutrality law, UN operations, and treaty practice'.[35]

The Committee considered that its mandate was to 'report on a general definition of armed conflict', rather than focus on the different categories of armed conflict.[36] Against this background, we should therefore not be surprised that it concluded that all armed conflict involves 'intense fighting among armed groups'. This conclusion is clearly at odds with the ICRC's approach (detailed above), which suggests a low threshold for an inter-state armed conflict. The Committee's conclusion is said to be based on the evidence, and yet one has to consider that if one is searching for a single definition of armed conflict, this leaves little room for finding two separate thresholds. Similarly, if one's concern is to preclude an over-inclusive resort to the law of armed conflict in the 'war on terror', one has to be careful to avoid minimal thresholds.

The Committee's Report suggests that the line is to be drawn between violence and armed conflict, and so 'a distinction is made between [simple violence and] the violence that gives rise to the right of a state to claim the belligerent's privileges to kill without warning, detain without trial, or seize cargo on the high seas'.[37] The present author does not consider that a state is entitled to these rights in an internal armed conflict. It is suggested that the concern related to a state claiming such belligerent rights in the 'war on terror' is better addressed by admitting that such rights apply only in an inter-state conflict, rather than pointing to a higher threshold for an all-encompassing notion of armed conflict.

Nevertheless, the Report is based on the evidence examined by the Committee, and it does contain useful data on which inter-state clashes have been considered as IACs. The following paragraph of the Report lists such conflicts over the first 35-year period:

State practice during [the period 1945–80] indicates that states generally drew a distinction between on the one hand, hostile actions involving the use of force that they treated as 'incidents', 'border clashes' or 'skirmishes' and, on the other hand, situations that they treated as armed conflicts. The following armed conflicts of the period have been classified as 'wars' or invasions: India–Pakistan (1947–48), the Korean War (1950–53), the 1956 Suez Invasion, many wars of national liberation (e.g., Algeria, Indonesia, Tunisia, Morocco, Angola), the Vietnam War (1961–1975), the 1967 Arab–Israeli Conflict, the Biafran War (1967–70), El Salvador-Honduras (the 'Soccer War' 1969), the 1973 Arab–Israeli Conflict (the 'Yom Kippur War'), and the Turkish Invasion of Cyprus (1974).[38]

The Report lists a number of later acknowledged inter-state armed conflicts for the period between 1980 to 2000: the Iran–Iraq War (1980–8); the Falklands (Malvinas) Conflict (1982); the Persian Gulf War (1990–1); Bosnia-Herzegovina (1992–4); Ecuador–Peru (1995). The first decade of the twenty-first century has also seen a number of conflicts that were, generally, acknowledged to be inter-state armed conflicts, including the Afghanistan War (2001–2), the Iraq War (2003–4), the Israel–Lebanon War (2006), and the War between Russia and Georgia (2008). The presence of Russian troops in Ukraine (Crimea)

---

[35] ILA Committee, *Final Report on the Meaning of Armed Conflict in International Law* (2010), at 4.
[36] Ibid, at 3, fn 7.   [37] Ibid, at 2.
[38] Ibid, at 13 (footnotes omitted).

in February 2014 presented a borderline case: as long as no one was shot at or taken prisoner, some saw this as falling short of an armed conflict.[39] The official Russian justification relied on an invitation from the deposed Ukrainian President, therefore precluding the idea of a violation of the UN Charter or occupation. On the other hand, political statements from the US (among others) referred unambiguously to an 'invasion and occupation'.[40] The leaders of the G7 states, joined by the Presidents of the European Council and Commission, condemned a 'clear violation of the sovereignty and territorial integrity of Ukraine' in contravention of the UN Charter.[41] Any theory concerning reliance on an invitation in order to deny an occupation would have to show that the authority issuing the invitation was the effective government of the state concerned.[42]

35   The Report nevertheless highlights those cases which apparently did not qualify as armed conflicts. The extensive excerpts which follow provide a flavour of the sorts of incidents that the Committee considered as evidence that a higher threshold is being applied due to the absence of states' explicitly invoking the laws of war:

By contrast, the following armed clashes during the period involved the engagement of armed forces of two or more sovereign states but on too limited a basis to have been treated as armed conflicts. They are described rather as 'limited uses of force': Saudi–Arabia–Muscat and Oman (1952, 1955), United Kingdom–Yemen (1957), Egypt–Sudan (1958), Afghanistan–Pakistan (1961), and Israel–Uganda (1976) [...]

In one minor incident, namely the 1988 shooting down and capture of a U.S. pilot by Syrian forces over Lebanon, U.S. officials at first said the pilot was entitled to be treated as a prisoner of war under the Third Geneva Convention. President Reagan called that into question when he said, 'I don't know how you have a prisoner of war when there is no declared war between nations. I don't think that makes you eligible for the Geneva Accords'.

Other minor incidents, in terms of duration and casualties, were not classified as armed conflicts even though they involved a clash between forces of two states. For example, in 1981 and 1982 incidents involving Soviet submarines in Swedish waters, including the use of depth charges by the Swedish Navy, were classified by scholars as incidents not armed conflict. Also in 1981, U.S. fighter jets engaged in a fire fight with Libyan aircraft above the Gulf of Sidra, shooting them down. Scholars have classified this case as an incident, not an armed conflict.

In 2002, a 21-minute exchange of fire between North and South Korea resulted in a patrol boat being sunk and four South Korean sailors being killed. It was referred to as an 'incident', 'armed provocation', 'border incursion', 'clash' and the like, but not an armed conflict.

---

[39] A. Riva, 'Russia's Use of Unmarked Troops in Simferopol, Crimea: Shady, But Not Illegal', *International Business Times*, 4 March 2014, quoting G. Solis: '"So far the law of armed conflict does not apply at all, insofar as there hasn't been a shot fired", Solis said. "I assume sooner or later there will be shooting, but as long as the civilians are distinguishable from the combatants the laws of armed conflict are complied with."' See also, on the need for two states to *intend* to engage in an armed conflict, G.D. Solis, *The Law of Armed Conflict: International Humanitarian Law in War* (New York: CUP, 2010), at 149–85.

[40] John Kerry, US Secretary of State, 'The United States condemns the Russian Federation's invasion and occupation of Ukrainian territory, and its violation of Ukrainian sovereignty and territorial integrity in full contravention of Russia's obligations under the UN Charter', Press Statement 1 March 2014, available at <http://www.state.gov/secretary/remarks/2014/03/222720.htm>.

[41] G-7 Leaders Statement, 2 March 2014, available at <http://europa.eu/rapid/press-release_STATEMENT-14-41_en.htm>.

[42] Akande, above n 21, at 63, says that in order to determine whether a new government giving its consent 'is indeed the government, one should look at the degree of effectiveness of its control over the territory of the State and also at whether it has achieved a general international recognition'. See, for more detail, G. Nolte, 'Intervention by Invitation' in MPEPIL; M. Shaw, *International Law* (6th edn, Cambridge: CUP, 2008), at 1151–2; and Ch 67, MN 28–35, of this volume.

In 2007, Iran detained the crew of a small British naval vessel claiming that the vessel was in Iranian waters. The British claimed they were in Iraqi waters. This case, again, involved the intervention of the armed forces of two states. It was not apparently considered an armed conflict. Britain complained when its troops were shown on television, and a spokesperson for the Prime Minister said doing so was a violation of the Third Geneva Convention. The U.K. did not take an official position, however, as to whether the Convention applied. It was certainly consistent with the spokesperson's statement that the U.K. hoped the higher standard regarding protection from public displays found in the Geneva Convention would be honoured (Third Geneva Convention, Article 13) even if Iran were not obligated to apply it. No similar protection appears to exist in peacetime HRL [human rights law]. Iran, however, treated the matter as one of illegal entry and indicated it might put the crew on trial. Iran made no reference to the Geneva Conventions that was reported in the English-language press.

Colombia's 2008 armed incursion into Ecuador was determined by the Organization of American States to have violated the principle of non-intervention and to have posed a threat of armed conflict, without having reached the level of actual armed conflict. Also in 2008, Thailand and Cambodia clashed over a boundary dispute in the vicinity of the Temple of Preah Vihear. Soldiers from the two states exchanged rifle and rocket fire for about an hour leaving two Cambodian soldiers dead and seven Thai soldiers and two Cambodian soldiers wounded. There was a further five minute clash in April 2009, leaving two Thai soldiers dead and ten injured. Two Cambodian soldiers were also injured as well as nine 'others'. Neither state has referred to the clashes as an armed conflict.[43]

The evidence has been taken as suggesting that low intensity engagement is not considered an armed conflict.[44] But perhaps we should return to the ICRC Commentary to the First Geneva Convention on the sick and wounded, for a better appreciation of the dynamics in play:

Any difference arising between two States and leading to the intervention of armed forces is an armed conflict within the meaning of Article 2, even if one of the Parties denies the existence of a state of war. It makes no difference how long the conflict lasts, or how much slaughter takes place. The respect due to human personality is not measured by the number of victims. Nor, incidentally, does the application of the Convention necessarily involve the intervention of cumbrous machinery. It all depends on circumstances. If there is only a single wounded person as a result of the conflict, the Convention will have been applied as soon as he has been collected and tended, the provisions of Article 12 observed in his case, and his identity notified to the Power on which he depends. All that can be done by anyone: it is merely a case of taking the trouble to save a human life![45]

It is suggested that two key points arise. First, there is the notion of a 'difference' between two states. Therefore, where someone accidently strays into enemy territory, even if that person is detained, this does not mean that there is an armed conflict between states. Secondly, the Commentary highlights how the Convention is triggered by a single individual falling into the hands of the enemy as a result of the conflict. It is suggested here that many of the incidents that were not qualified as armed conflicts involved no such situation leading to the application of the rules on the protection of the victims of war.

---

[43] ILA Committee, above n 35, at 14–27.
[44] See, however, M. Asada, 'The Concept of "Armed Conflict" in International Armed Conflict', in M.E. O'Connell (ed), *What Is War?* (Leiden: Brill, 2012) 51, at 66, where he suggests that the existence of such examples where one state claims the application of IAC to conflicts of 'very low intensity (and short duration) means we should hesitate before dismissing the idea that IHL applies to such low intensity conflicts between states'.
[45] Pictet Commentary GC I, at 32–3 (footnote omitted).

Had individuals been shipwrecked, wounded, or interned in the hands of the enemy, there could have been a good case for the application of the Geneva Conventions.

38   Despite the finding of the ILA Committee that *all* armed conflicts require 'intense' fighting, we see no need to depart from the more conventional conclusion that low-level hostilities are sufficient where, in the words of the International Criminal Tribunal for the former Yugoslavia (ICTY), 'there is a resort to armed force between States'.[46] This conclusion seems to be shared by various scholars,[47] and is in line with the definition of 'armed conflict' used by the International Law Commission in the context of its work on the effect of armed conflicts on treaties.[48] For such low-level hostilities between states to trigger the application of the Geneva Conventions, one might take into account factors such as whether the use of force was undertaken by the military and targeted at the other state's military, or is harmful to the state or to those under its jurisdiction, the extent of the damage or casualties, the location of the incident (an attack on the territory of the state carrying particular significance), the level of control exercised over any non-state groups involved in the hostilities, and the significance of any target. This does not represent a scientific formula, but we can see that, for example, a deliberate and attributed attack on a single warship, even with no casualties, could trigger the application of the law of IAC, while a cross-border skirmish involving some over-excited customs officers may not. While the subjective approach of the two states concerned is not determinative, in many situations the admission that the incursion or damage was a mistake may resolve dubious cases. As suggested above, the problem becomes more complex when prisoners are involved: here we can assume that there may be a presumption that the protective regime will apply to those individuals caught up in the conflict. One might even imagine situations where the use of force in another state is deliberate but there is no engagement between the armed forces of the two states. So, for example, a state, reacting to an attack by terrorists on its embassy, may mount a rescue mission involving the use of force but not trigger an armed conflict with the other host state.

39   While the low threshold remains for inter-state conflicts, doubts have been expressed as to whether this is workable where the UN engages in the use of force with a state in the course of a mandate to protect humanitarian assistance or civilians. As we saw above, this question is directly related to the applicability of the Convention for the Protection of UN and Associated Personnel. As Greenwood points out, the drafters of that Convention did

---

[46] ICTY, *The Prosecutor v Duško Tadić*, Appeals Chamber (Decision on the Defence Motion for Interlocutory Appeal on Jurisdiction), IT-94-1-AR72, Decision of 2 October 1995, para 70.

[47] See M.N. Schmitt, 'Classification in Future Conflict', in Wilmshurst (ed), above n 21, 455, at 459–60; R. Kolb and R. Hyde, *An Introduction to the International Law of Armed Conflicts* (Oxford: Hart Publishing, 2008) at 76; Rogers, above n 33, at 3: 'A situation of armed conflict is likely to arise when elements of opposing forces are engaged in military operations against each other, when targets in the territory or territorial waters of another state are attacked or when the troops of one state invade another.' For a detailed examination of this threshold see K. Huszti Orban, *The Concept of Armed Conflict under International Law*, PhD thesis, Graduate Institute of International and Development Studies (2013) and D. Carron, *L'acte déclencheur d'un conflit armé international*, PhD thesis, Université de Genève (2015).

[48] The Draft Articles on the effects of armed conflicts on treaties (2011) include the following definition (for the purposes of the Draft Articles), ' "armed conflict" means a situation in which there is resort to armed force between States or protracted resort to armed force between governmental authorities and organized armed groups'. It is worth noting that the Commentary states that 'it was desirable to include situations involving a state of armed conflict in the absence of armed actions between the parties'. The Commentary goes on to give as examples occupation which meets with no resistance and blockade (paras 6 and 7 of the Commentary to Draft Article 2). Both texts are reproduced in *Yearbook of the International Law Commission*, 2011, II, Part Two (forthcoming).

not intend for UN forces to lose their protection in Bosnia and Herzegovina as a result of the use of force in self-defence.[49] We may have to accept that the threshold and criteria for triggering an IAC may be different when a UN operation engages with the armed forces of a state in the course of such mandated operations. Greenwood predicts that 'A degree of violence which, in the past, would certainly have been regarded as sufficient to constitute an international armed conflict will come to be regarded as something of a lesser nature if it involves UN forces.'[50]

VI. Converting an internal armed conflict into an international armed conflict and the separate issues of state responsibility and armed attack

As we have seen, an IAC usually involves the use of force between two states. However, armed conflicts can be, and often are, fought at arm's length through proxy armed groups. In some circumstances, these conflicts have been considered *international* armed conflicts.

According to the ICTY, where a second state is in 'overall control' of an organized armed group fighting an internal armed conflict against its own government's armed forces, the conflict must nonetheless be considered international. The Geneva Conventions will therefore apply in their entirety.[51]

Although the ICJ has emphasized separate 'complete dependence' and 'effective control' tests for the purposes of attribution of the acts of the armed group to the controlling second state in order to apply the international rules of state responsibility,[52] that Court has neither adopted, nor rejected the 'overall control' test as relevant for the determination of an IAC rather than a NIAC.[53]

If the overall control test is satisfied, the implication is that there is an IAC, and so not only will that specific war crimes regime apply, but the Geneva Conventions should also create rights and obligations for the two states concerned. But complex questions can arise when we consider whether the armed group as such is henceforth bound to apply all the

---

[49] C. Greenwood, 'Protection of Peacekeepers: The Legal Regime', 7 *Duke Journal of Comparative and International Law* (1996) 185, at 202.

[50] Ibid.

[51] '[C]ontrol by a State over subordinate armed forces or militias or paramilitary units may be of an overall character (and must comprise more than the mere provision of financial assistance or military equipment or training). This requirement, however, does not go so far as to include the issuing of specific orders by the State, or its direction of each individual operation. Under international law it is by no means necessary that the controlling authorities should plan all the operations of the units dependent on them, choose their targets, or give specific instructions concerning the conduct of military operations and any alleged violations of international humanitarian law. The control required by international law may be deemed to exist when a State (or, in the context of an armed conflict, the Party to the conflict) has a role in organising, coordinating or planning the military actions of the military group, in addition to financing, training and equipping or providing operational support to that group.' ICTY, *The Prosecutor v Duško Tadić*, Appeals Chamber Judgment (Interlocutory Appeal on Jurisdiction), IT-94-1-A, 15 July 1999, para 137; see also para 84. See further the discussion in Ch 2 of this volume.

[52] ICJ, *Case concerning the Application of the Convention on the Prevention and Punishment of the Crime of Genocide (Bosnia and Herzegovina v Serbia and Montenegro)*, Judgment of 26 February 2007, paras 392–402.

[53] 'Insofar as the "overall control" test is employed to determine whether or not an armed conflict is international, which was the sole question which the Appeals Chamber was called upon to decide, it may well be that the test is applicable and suitable; the Court does not however think it appropriate to take a position on the point in the present case, as there is no need to resolve it for purposes of the present Judgment.' Ibid, para 404; but see the alternatives proposed by Akande, above n 21, at 57 ff. For a discussion of the 'overall control' test in the context of the relationship between Russia and the forces in South Ossetia and Abkhazia, see the *Report of the Independent International Fact-Finding Mission on the Conflict in Georgia* (2009), vol II, at 301–12.

obligations, and acquire all the rights, of a belligerent in an IAC.[54] In practice, the issue may turn on whether the armed group is able to comply with all the obligations stemming from the law of IAC, and on whether the states involved are ready to consider that the members of the armed group are fighting an IAC. It is suggested that the best way to understand this situation is to separate out the classification of the conflict from the status of the individuals concerned.

44   Even if there is an IAC involving armed groups under the overall control of a second state, the fighters from the armed group can enjoy POW status only if they fulfil the criteria set out in Article 4(A)(1) GC III as part of the armed forces of the state, or under Article 4(A)(2) as 'belonging' to the state party to the conflict.[55] In practice, states may baulk at the idea of granting POW status to their own nationals captured in what they may consider an illegal insurrection. At this point everything may turn on whether the second state recognizes that these fighters belong to it. The Pictet Commentary to GC III suggests that no official recognition is necessary and that tacit agreement would be enough. In such cases it will be for the ICRC or other actors in the international community to argue that the captured fighters are entitled to POW status under the Geneva Conventions due to the internationalization of the conflict.

45   An international tribunal concerned with issues either of international criminal responsibility or state responsibility will have to determine first whether or not the relevant conflict was international or non-international, and then under which regime the relevant individual is protected. So, assuming that the tribunal finds convincing evidence of overall control by a state over the armed group, it would then have to determine whether the individual was part of a group which 'belonged' to the controlling state for the purposes of GC III. If the fighters do not so belong, they would seem to be civilians entitled to protection under the customary rules reflected in Article 75 of Additional Protocol (AP) I (but strictly speaking not enjoying protected person status under GC IV where they have the nationality of the detaining state). Furthermore, despite being captured as a fighter in an IAC, those fighters that are not part of the armed forces of the other state would not enjoy combatant immunity, and therefore could be prosecuted for having taken up arms against the state. With such a separation between classification of the conflict and the classification of the individual, the idea of members of an armed group fighting in an IAC can begin to make sense.

46   The two states will be responsible for ensuring that all the laws of IAC are respected. They will also have positive obligations to ensure that these fighters respect the full range of obligations triggered by an inter-state armed conflict. Even where the acts of the fighters are not attributable to the state in question, due to there being no dependency or effective control,[56] the state remains responsible for any failure to prevent violations of the Geneva Conventions which could reasonably have been prevented, as well as for ensuring respect for the Geneva Conventions through the exercise of its overall control over the organized armed group.

47   It should be borne in mind that the fact that a state supports a rebel group fighting another state, is not necessarily enough to show that the supporting state has subjected

---

[54] See Stewart, above n 29.
[55] K. Del Mar, 'The Requirement of "Belonging" under International Humanitarian Law', 21 *JICJ* (2010) 105.
[56] See MN 64 for more detail.

the other state to an 'armed attack', entitling the victim state to act in self-defence under the UN Charter. This support may be considered an illegal use of force or a violation of the sovereignty of another state, but so far the ICJ has held that where such support merely constitutes 'assistance to rebels in the form of the provision of weapons or logistical or other support', this falls short of constituting an armed attack, and so there is no right to self-defence.[57] While these questions are strictly speaking separate from the determination of the existence of an armed conflict, they remain connected because, while an overriding concern has always been to keep war at bay by fixing a high threshold for the right to self-defence, we are equally concerned to keep a low threshold for the application of the laws of war. This seeming contradiction is resolved once we admit that the threshold for triggering an IAC through proxy groups may not be the same as the test for triggering the right to defence in response to an attack by a proxy armed group.

In short, we may have four separate tests: 48

— one for the application of the Geneva Conventions between states (resort to armed force between states requiring only low intensity engagement);
— a second test for the application of the laws of IAC when an armed group fighting a state (overall control of the group by a second state);
— a third test for attributing the acts of an armed group fighting against its own state to a second state (complete dependence or effective control); and
— a separate test requiring that one state actually sends the armed groups abroad to engage in an attack, or be substantially involved in such an attack, in order for the attacked state to claim self-defence as if the state had been attacked by a state acting alone.[58]

VII. National liberation movements and self-determination struggles

Lastly, we should mention a separate type of IAC, wars of national liberation. In theory, 49 the law applicable to IAC will apply where certain armed non-state actors, known as national liberation movements, make a declaration through their authority under the terms of AP I, undertaking to apply the Protocol and the Geneva Conventions to that particular conflict with a state party to that Protocol.[59] Alternatively, the same type of actor may make a declaration under the Convention on Prohibitions or Restrictions on the Use of Certain Conventional Weapons Which May be Deemed to be Excessively Injurious or to Have Indiscriminate Effects (CCW).[60] Such a declaration can bring into force not only the Weapons Convention and its Protocols, but also the 1949 Geneva Conventions, even where the state against which the liberation movement is fighting is not a party to

---

[57] ICJ, *Military and Paramilitary Activities in and against Nicaragua (Nicaragua v USA)*, Judgment, 27 June 1986, para 195.

[58] Ibid, para 195; but see the dissenting opinions on this point by Judges Jennings and Schwebel. It is feasible that overall control could be assimilated to the test for state involvement in a non-state actor armed attack, but so far these two tests have been seen as rather different.

[59] For a detailed discussion, see G. Abi-Saab, 'Wars of National Liberation in the Geneva Conventions and Protocols', 165 *RCADI* IV (1979) 353; H.A. Wilson, *International Law and the Use of Force by National Liberation Movements* (Oxford: OUP, 1988); A. Cassese, 'Wars of National Liberation', in Mélanges Pictet 314.

[60] 10 October 1980; see Art 7(4) CCW, set out in MN 50.

AP I.[61] One such declaration was successfully made under AP I in 2015 by the Polisario Front in the context of Western Sahara.[62]

50   Although these formal procedures have not been applied until recently, they may exert some influence on thinking about the internationalization of internal armed conflicts. One might wonder as to the significance of the relatively recent practice of recognizing armed groups in the armed conflicts in Libya (2011) and Syria (2011–ongoing at the time of writing) as the legitimate representatives of the people of those states. The actual wording of Article 7(4) CCW provides:

> This Convention, and the annexed Protocols by which a High Contracting Party is bound, shall apply with respect to an armed conflict against that High Contracting Party of the type referred to in Article 1, paragraph 4, of Additional Protocol I to the Geneva Conventions of 12 August 1949 for the Protection of War Victims: (a) where the High Contracting Party is also a party to Additional Protocol I and an authority referred to in Article 96, paragraph 3, of that Protocol has undertaken to apply the Geneva Conventions and Additional Protocol I in accordance with Article 96, paragraph 3, of the said Protocol, and undertakes to apply this Convention and the relevant annexed Protocols in relation to that conflict; or (b) where the High Contracting Party is not a party to Additional Protocol I and an authority of the type referred to in subparagraph (a) above accepts and applies the obligations of the Geneva Conventions and of this Convention and the relevant annexed Protocols in relation to that conflict. Such an acceptance and application shall have in relation to that conflict the following effects:
> (i)   the Geneva Conventions and this Convention and its relevant annexed Protocols are brought into force for the parties to the conflict with immediate effect;
> (ii) the said authority assumes the same rights and obligations as those which have been assumed by a High Contracting Party to the Geneva Conventions, this Convention and its relevant annexed Protocols; and
> (iii) the Geneva Conventions, this Convention and its relevant annexed Protocols are equally binding upon all parties to the conflict.

51   The 'authority' referred to here is therefore an authority representing a people engaged in an armed conflict of the type

> in which peoples are fighting against colonial domination and alien occupation and against racist régimes in the exercise of their right of self-determination, as enshrined in the Charter of the United Nations and the Declaration on Principles of International Law concerning Friendly Relations and Co-operation among States in accordance with the Charter of the United Nations.[63]

52   Should such an authority accept and apply the relevant Conventions, the Geneva Conventions will therefore enter into force for the parties to the conflict (assuming that the state involved is a party to the CCW and that there are no valid reservations).[64]

53   The question arises whether self-determination struggles that do not fit the triptych of struggles against colonial domination, alien occupation, or racist regimes (so-called 'CAR conflicts') could qualify for this type of internationalization of their conflicts? It is probably fair to say that when these internationalized national liberation conflicts were being conceived in the 1970s, few states had in mind that they would apply to a group seeking internal self-determination beyond the context of racist regimes in Southern Africa.

---

[61] Art 7(4)(b) CCW.
[62] Although certain other declarations have been sent to the ICRC, the procedure demands a communication with the Swiss Federal authorities. Switzerland circulated the Polisario declaration on 26 June 2015.
[63] Arts 1(4) and 96(3) AP I.
[64] Consider, e.g., the reservations and declarations made by the US, Israel, the UK, and France.

Nevertheless, one could foresee a rebel group claiming to represent a whole people seeking to trigger the full application of the Geneva Conventions. In the face of resistance by the relevant state to the internationalization of such a conflict, the issue would turn on whether such an entity could be considered a national liberation authority.

Akande has reflected on the legal significance of the 2012 recognition of the Syrian Revolutionary and Opposition Forces (NCS) as the 'sole legitimate representative of the Syrian People'. Considering that an argument might be made that military aid may be given to groups struggling for self-determination, he concludes that 'support ought only to be given to those groups that are collectively recognized by the international community as legitimate representatives of peoples fighting for self-determination. Such recognition should ideally be done by the UN General Assembly.'[65] The present author considers that, similarly, for a group to demand that it enjoys all the rights applicable in an IAC under the Geneva Conventions, there needs to be clear international recognition that such a group has achieved the kind of international status envisaged in the CCW and Article 1(4) AP I.[66] Of course there is nothing to prevent any armed group, engaged in a conflict with a state, from taking on any or all of the obligations in the Geneva Conventions that apply in an IAC. This can be done unilaterally or through special agreements.[67]

VIII. Unrecognized governments and recognized belligerents

The Geneva Conventions make special reference to unrecognized governments. A state cannot deny the applicability of the Geneva Conventions in an inter-state conflict by pointing to the fact that it does not recognize the government of the state with which it is in conflict. Geneva Conventions I, II, and III all state that they apply to '[m]embers of regular armed forces who profess allegiance to a Government or an authority not recognized by the Detaining Power'.[68] Recognition of a government changes nothing with regard to the protection afforded to those members of the armed forces who fall into the hands of the detaining state party which has refused to recognize the other state's government.[69]

On the other hand, if a state chooses to recognize the group it is fighting against as a *belligerent* under international law, this will internationalize the conflict and trigger the full application of all the rights and obligations applicable in an IAC. The Geneva Conventions will apply to both parties to the extent that they reflect customary international law. Such

---

[65] <http://www.ejiltalk.org/self-determination-and-the-syrian-conflict-recognition-of-syrian-opposition-as-sole-legitimate-representative-of-the-syrian-people-what-does-this-mean-and-what-implications-does-it-have/> and <http://www.ejiltalk.org/would-it-be-lawful-for-european-or-other-states-to-provide-arms-to-the-syrian-opposition/#more-7410>.

[66] For background see Abi-Saab, above n 59; Cassese, above n 59; Wilson, above n 59.

[67] See Chs 7 and 25 of this volume.

[68] Art 13(3) GC I and GC II; Art 4(A)(3) GC III. With regard to the interpretation of 'regular armed forces' and the debate over the status of Taliban forces engaged against the US in 2001, see Ch 45 MN 9 and 60–70.

[69] A separate question can arise when a state intervenes in an internal armed conflict on the side of the rebels and the intervening state considers that the rebels are the government of a state (albeit a state unrecognized by the state fighting the rebels). If the rebels do indeed represent the government of a state recognized under international law, this will affect the legality of the intervention should that state be acting in self-defence, and it will mean that the rebel forces are in fact the armed forces of a state and their state will indeed be a party to an IAC. The issue nevertheless turns on whether a new state has emerged in international law, rather than the attitude of the two established states. See further J. Crawford, *The Creation of States in International Law* (2nd edn, Oxford: OUP, 2006); Dinstein, above n 4, at 7, suggests that where such a breakaway entity emerges as a state whose existence is contested, 'there may be a transition from a "civil war" to an inter-State war which is hard to pinpoint in time'.

IX. Cyber warfare

57 There seems to be little doubt that a cyber attack by a state on another state, resulting in deaths or damage to property, would trigger the laws of IAC and the Geneva Conventions. The problems start when the cyber attacks have a sort of impact different from that of traditional armed conflicts, and where the source of the attack is not obviously attributable to a state. Let us take each of these issues in turn.

58 Harold Hongju Koh, speaking as the Legal Advisor to the US Department of State, has outlined what would constitute a use of force in the context of cyber activities. To the extent that the resort to force by one state against another triggers an armed conflict, these examples of the use of force would also trigger the application of the law of IAC and the application of the Geneva Conventions.[72]

> In assessing whether an event constituted a use of force in or through cyberspace, we must evaluate factors: including the context of the event, the actor perpetrating the action (recognizing challenging issues of attribution in cyberspace), the target and location, effects and intent, among other possible issues. Commonly cited examples of cyber activity that would constitute a use of force include, for example: (1) operations that trigger a nuclear plant meltdown; (2) operations that open a dam above a populated area causing destruction; or (3) operations that disable air traffic control resulting in airplane crashes. Only a moment's reflection makes you realize that this is common sense: if the physical consequences of a cyber attack work the kind of physical damage that dropping a bomb or firing a missile would, that cyber attack should equally be considered a use of force.[73]

59 Michael Schmitt, having referred to the 'low threshold' needed to trigger the application of the Geneva Conventions in an IAC, considers that if there is a cyber operation attributable to a state that results in 'damage or destruction of object or injury or to death of individuals of another State, an international armed conflict undoubtedly occurs'.[74] He nevertheless highlights that some cyber operations 'may merely cause the target State inconvenience or irritation. Others could involve taking control of its national cyber systems or causing severe disruption to the economy, transportation systems or other critical infrastructure.'[75] He continues, '[o]bviously, not every cyber operation by one State against another should amount to an armed conflict.'[76] But Schmitt seems more worried about under-inclusion than over-inclusion when faced with non-destructive 'computer network exploitation, espionage, denial of service attacks'.[77] He considers that a state

---

[70] See Kolb and Hyde, above n 47, at 65–6 and 81.

[71] See further Akande, above n 21, at 59: states may wish formally to recognize an armed group as insurgents and specify that only a certain number of rules of the law of IAC will apply (in addition to the rules that apply in any event to an internal armed conflict); by contrast, recognition of belligerency triggers the full gamut of the laws of IAC, and the law of internal armed conflict becomes irrelevant.

[72] Issues related to whether the cyber attacks have a nexus to the armed conflict are outside the scope of this chapter; see further and for more detail on cyber warfare, *Tallinn Manual on the International Law Applicable to Cyber Warfare*, M.N. Schmitt (gen ed) (Cambridge: CUP, 2013).

[73] Harold Hongju Koh, 'International Law in Cyberspace', USCYBERCOM Inter-Agency Legal Conference, Ft Meade, MD, 18 September 2012, <http://www.state.gov/s/l/releases/remarks/197924.htm>.

[74] Schmitt, above n 47, at 460. [75] Ibid. [76] Ibid. [77] Ibid.

would probably characterize the attack as the initiation of armed conflict, and concludes that even if a clear threshold for a purely cyber attack has not yet been agreed, it is possible that a new type of armed conflict may emerge, 'which lowers the bar by articulating a standard of significant non-destructive harm to the target State'.[78]

But such concern for under-inclusion runs headlong into competing concerns that we may be lowering the threshold for what constitutes an armed attack, thus entitling states to use force in self-defence. As we saw above (MN 40–48), it is quite possible to construct separate thresholds and keep these two issues separate. But we should admit that it will be difficult for governments to imagine that they are engaged in an armed conflict and obliged to apply the laws of war, yet are unable to respond with force in self-defence. **60**

Of course, any force used in self-defence will need to be necessary and proportionate, be reported to the Security Council, and be used only in conformity with the laws of armed conflict and human rights; but in essence, there is here a danger of weakening the bulwark which prevents self-defence being invoked in response to interventions that fall short of armed attacks.[79] This is all more delicate in light of the cyber warfare dimensions of the problems associated with attribution and overall control. **61**

Attributing the acts of non-state armed groups to states, as we have seen, is a complex question. The case law of the ICJ covers 'complete dependency' or persons acting under the 'effective control' of the third state, or situations where 'instructions were given, in respect of *each operation* in which the alleged violations occurred'.[80] The ICJ explains further that attribution will occur in these last two cases, 'where an organ of the State gave the instructions or provided the direction pursuant to which the perpetrators of the wrongful act acted or where it exercised effective control over the action during which the wrong was committed'.[81] Already, tribunals and fact-finding missions have had difficulty applying this law to the facts. In any one conflict, a non-state armed group may or may not be receiving instructions for a particular operation. A series of cyber attacks is even harder to attribute. The relevant viruses, Trojan horses, or computer worms could be routed through various computers and countries, making the originators and their controllers almost impossible to identify with much certainty. This may be an area where specialized rules emerge to determine not only whether a state is responsible for the acts of non-state actors, including hackers and 'hacktivists', but also the extent to which such activity triggers the law of IAC. **62**

The *Tallinn Manual on the International Law Applicable to Cyber Warfare* takes as its starting point Common Article 2 to the Geneva Conventions as the threshold for the application of the law of IAC. The *Tallinn* commentary then explains how the overall control test might apply to internationalize a cyber attack so that the law of IAC would apply:[82] **63**

Applying the test, if State A exercises overall control over an organized group of computer hackers that penetrate State B's cyber infrastructure and cause significant physical damage, the armed conflict qualifies as 'international' in nature. State A need not have instructed the group to attack

---

[78] Ibid, at 461. See also the *Tallinn Manual*, above n 72.
[79] This issue has divided the experts responsible for the Tallinn Manual, on which see M.N. Schmitt, 'International Law in Cyberspace: The Koh Speech and Tallinn Manual Juxtaposed', 54 *Harvard International Law Journal* (2012) 14 (online version).
[80] ICJ, *Bosnia and Herzegovina v Serbia and Montenegro*, above n 52, para 400 (emphasis added).
[81] Ibid, para 406.   [82] See further the *Tallinn Manual*, above n 72, Rule 22, at 80–1.

particular aspects of the infrastructure, but, instead, only needs to have exerted sufficient control over the group to instruct it to mount a campaign against infrastructure cyber targets.

64 The *Tallinn Manual* is careful to recall that the 'overall control' test, derived from the case law of the ICTY, is only applicable to organized groups and not to individuals. In order to reach the threshold for an IAC, the individuals or 'insufficiently organized group' would have to satisfy the tests for attribution under state responsibility. That means they 'must receive specific instructions (or subsequent public approval) from a State before their conduct can be attributed to that State for the purpose of determining the existence of an international armed conflict'.[83]

C. The Boundary between International and Non-International Armed Conflicts

65 The concept of IAC is bounded on either side by two other concepts: no armed conflict, and NIAC. Although the dividing line between IAC and NIAC will be explored in Chapter 2 of this volume, we can state here that the distinction remains important for the application of the Geneva Conventions, because under treaty law, as opposed to customary international law, only Common Article 3 applies to NIACs. While there may be a trend towards adopting wider protection beyond Common Article 3, most notably through customary IHL and AP II of 1977, the distinction in the 1949 Geneva Conventions remains, and may have concrete consequences as follows.

66 First, some national law will incorporate IHL in accordance with the terms of the 1949 Geneva Conventions rather than by reference to custom or a wider list of applicable obligations in NIAC. In such situations, determining whether one is in the presence of an IAC or a NIAC will dramatically affect the scope of the applicable obligations. Secondly, as will be seen in the discussion in Chapters 31 and 36 of this volume on the relationship with international criminal law, the grave breaches regime of the Geneva Conventions is specifically addressed to IACs rather than NIACs. This dichotomy is reproduced in the Statute of the International Criminal Court (ICC Statute) and elsewhere, so that some courts will have jurisdiction over certain acts only when committed in the context of an IAC rather than a NIAC.[84] The dividing line which separates IACs from NIACs can then become not just a tangle for academics to unpick, but rather the battle-line between a prosecutor and defence counsel seeking to determine whether a prosecution for war crimes may proceed.

D. Legal Consequences of a Violation

67 This chapter has been concerned to delineate a number of separate concepts: intervention, use of force, NIAC, overall control over armed groups, effective control over armed

---

[83] Ibid, at 81–2.
[84] See Chs 31 and 36 of this volume; Art 8 ICC Statute; note also the Arms Trade Treaty (2013), which refers in Art 6(3) to 'grave breaches of the Geneva Conventions of 1949' and 'other war crimes as defined by international agreements to which it is a Party', and in Art 7(3) to 'a serious violation of international humanitarian law'—for further detail, see S. Casey-Maslen et al, *A Commentary to the Arms Trade Treaty* (Oxford: OUP, forthcoming 2016); and see Ch 35 of this volume on the relationship between the GCs and human rights law, which highlights how some human rights treaties may not apply where the law of IAC is applicable under the GCs.

groups, IAC, and armed attack. We have seen that how one classifies a conflict is relevant for the determination of the applicable rights and obligations, not only of states and armed groups, but also of the individual concerned. In several cases—POW status, protected civilian status, combatant immunity, victim of a grave breach, and so on—the associated obligations and enforcement mechanisms that relate to the relevant rules will be dependent on a preliminary finding that there is an IAC as opposed to an internal armed conflict. The distinction between armed conflicts and situations that do not constitute armed conflicts is even more important because war crimes do not exist outside armed conflicts and occupation. In turn this means that the accompanying regimes for penal repression of breaches of the relevant law are obviously part of the context, which determines how and why the concepts are delineated.

E. Critical Assessment

68 The humanitarian imperative pulls us towards adopting a low threshold of violence for ensuring the humanitarian protection of the Geneva Conventions. But there is a risk that this low threshold gets misapplied to determine the existence of a right to use force in self-defence, or the application of the wider law of armed conflict, thus escalating the violence and putting even more people at risk.

69 In addition, even from a humanitarian point of view, it may be preferable to be protected by the law of human rights rather than by the law of armed conflict. This is particularly so when the law of armed conflict is said to permit killings and forms of detention without trial. It is suggested here that one cannot square this circle with a 'one size fits all' definition of armed conflict. The preoccupation has been to bring war criminals within the wider range of offences applicable in IAC. But internationalizing a conflict in this way risks oversimplifying the issues and reducing certain forms of protection (even while it may make prosecution for war crimes easier).

70 Of course, troops on the ground need simple directives and should be clear on which rules they are expected to apply, but the contemporary context is complicated. State forces fighting rebels 'controlled' by another state may be considered by international criminal tribunals to be fighting an IAC, but on the ground the state authorities will be loath to grant such fighters POW status or combatant immunity. Of course we can insist that classification of a conflict is to be separated from the different exercise of determining the status of a captured fighter, but we need to be alert to the temptation of conflating IAC with the mistaken idea of a 'right to fight', or even a 'licence to kill'.

71 Similarly, members of the government armed forces captured by these rebels are unlikely to enjoy the full rights and privileges of POWs, in a prisoner-of-war camp fulfilling all the criteria set out in GC III (due to the incapacity of an armed group to fulfil such state-like obligations and the probable lack of enthusiasm from their controlling state as regards fulfilling them). We could complicate the situation further by recollecting that different factions of the armed group may or may not be controlled by the outside state in various conflict zones. We then have the spectre of an armed group fighting an IAC on a Monday in one town, and an internal armed conflict in the next town on the Tuesday.

72 The better solution seems to be that when states are fighting non-state armed groups who are the proxies of another state, the law of NIAC applies between the state and the non-state armed group; while the law of IAC, including the Geneva Conventions, applies to the conflict between the two states. The fighter from the non-state armed group would

be detained with the guarantees, inter alia, of Common Article 3,[85] while members of the armed forces from the other state would be considered POWs protected by GC III. In short, it is suggested here that in most situations, whether one applies the law of IAC or NIAC depends on whom one is fighting, rather than on the control exercised by outside states. This, however, does not seem to be the conventional way of looking at this.

73   This chapter opened by reminding the reader that the application of the Geneva Conventions is not dependent on a declaration of war, or even on recognition of a state of war. Whether the Geneva Conventions apply remains an objective question, sometimes determined by a tribunal after the fact, but clarity from the outset would go a long way to educating combatants, fighters, and civilians. It is suggested that the best way forward is for states and armed groups to state clearly their commitment to respecting the relevant international law, and to clarify which regime they are applying.

74   Where appropriate, the parties can specify which additional provisions of the Geneva Conventions they are committed to respecting. Here, there need not be a stark choice between the full range of obligations applicable to inter-state conflict and the 'Convention in miniature' found in Common Article 3 applicable to NIACs.[86] The present author sees no reason why one side might not offer more humanitarian protection under the Geneva Conventions than the other side. Reciprocity and equality of application are not ends in themselves. Maximum protection for the victims of war should be an end in itself. The scope of the obligations related to the Geneva Conventions that the parties can take on in this way will be partly determined by their capacities.

75   In conclusion, on the one hand the threshold of violence for triggering the application of the Geneva Conventions in an inter-state armed conflict can be considered relatively low; indeed, we have seen that one does not need any violence at all—a declaration of war or a non-consensual occupation will suffice. The purpose of the Geneva Conventions is that in times of armed conflict, individuals should enjoy protection as soon they fall into the power of the enemy. On the other hand, we have seen that the threshold for an international armed conflict involving control over a proxy group or violence by UN forces is more complex: for this reason it is the subject of further examination in Chapter 2 of this volume, entitled 'The Applicability of the Conventions to "Transnational" and "Mixed" Conflicts'.

ANDREW CLAPHAM

---

[85] Unless of course he or she 'belongs' to the armed forces of the controlling state in accordance with Art 4(A)(2) GC III. One should also mention that the detainees would also enjoy the customary rights reflected in Art 75 AP I.

[86] Pictet Commentary GC I, at 48.

Chapter 2. The Applicability of the Conventions to 'Transnational' and 'Mixed' Conflicts

	MN
A. Introduction: The Conventions' Binary Thresholds of Application	1
B. Terminology and Definitions	5
C. Internalized International Armed Conflict and Internationalized Non-International Armed Conflict	15
I. Internalization	15
II. Internationalization	26
III. Circumstances which do not lead to internationalization	47
D. Cross-Border Non-International Armed Conflict	50
E. Mixed Conflicts	64
F. Critical Assessment	68

Select Bibliography

Akande, D., 'Classification of Armed Conflicts: Relevant Legal Concepts', in E. Wilmshurst (ed), *International Law and the Classification of Conflicts* (Oxford: OUP, 2012) 32

Holland, E., 'The Qualification Framework of International Humanitarian Law: Too Rigid to Accommodate Contemporary Conflicts?', 34 *Suffolk Transnational Law Review* (2011) 145

Kreß, C., 'Some Reflections on the International Legal Framework Governing Transnational Armed Conflicts', 15 *Journal of Conflict and Security Law* (2010) 245

Lubell, N., *Extraterritorial Use of Force against Non-State Actors* (Oxford: OUP, 2010)

Milanovic, M./Hadzi-Vidanovic, V., 'A Taxonomy of Armed Conflict', in N. White and C. Henderson (eds), *Research Handbook on International Conflict and Security Law* (Cheltenham: Edward Elgar Publishing, 2013) 256

Schindler, D., 'The Different Types of Armed Conflicts According to the Geneva Conventions and Protocols', 163 *RCADI* (1979-II) 131

Vité, S., 'Typology of Armed Conflicts in International Humanitarian Law: Legal Concepts and Actual Situations', 91 *IRRC* 873 (2009) 69

A. Introduction: The Conventions' Binary Thresholds of Application

The end of the Second World War brought about a conceptual revolution in the international legal regulation of the use of armed force. The *jus in bello* was separated from the *jus ad bellum*, and the legal concept of 'war', with its many subjective uncertainties, was largely discarded.[1] Together with its separation from the United Nations (UN)

---

[1] For a general overview, see M. Milanovic and V. Hadzi-Vidanovic, 'A Taxonomy of Armed Conflict', in N. White and C. Henderson (eds), *Research Handbook on International Conflict and Security Law* (Cheltenham: Edward Elgar Publishing, 2013) 256, draft available at <http://ssrn.com/abstract=1988915>. The present chapter draws heavily on this previous work.

Charter-based law on the use of force, the introduction of objective, factual criteria for the applicability of international humanitarian law (IHL) was meant to depoliticize IHL and secure its consistent application—always, of course, an aspiration and ideal more than a firm reality.

2   As explained in Chapter 1 of this volume, while very few provisions of the 1949 Geneva Conventions apply in peacetime,[2] the overwhelming majority apply only in situations of international armed conflict (IAC), as set out in Common Article 2 of the Conventions. The concept of IAC was designed as a factual replacement for the concept of 'war', and retained its predecessor's exclusively inter-state nature.[3] As explained in detail in Chapter 19 of this volume, the Conventions also introduced the first systematic regulation of internal conflicts, through the concept of non-international armed conflict (NIAC) under Common Article 3 of the Conventions.

3   At the time of the Conventions' adoption, the NIAC threshold brought about only the application of Common Article 3 itself and its purely humanitarian provisions protecting persons not taking part in hostilities or rendered *hors de combat*. That was the sum total of the law of armed conflict as it applied to NIACs; for example, it contained no rules on the conduct of hostilities analogous to IACs. Over time, however, through the adoption of the 1977 Additional Protocols (APs) and the evolution of customary international law, the law of armed conflict coalesced around the two factual thresholds set out in the 1949 Conventions. International armed conflict under Common Article 2 also became the threshold for application of the 'Hague law' on the conduct of hostilities, not just the Conventions themselves. This was also the case with the Common Article 3 NIAC threshold, whereas the gaps in the regulation of NIACs were filled mainly through custom. The Conventions' thresholds of application thus became the thresholds for the application of IHL more generally.

4   Yet while this process was underway, one fact became more apparent: increasingly, we were faced with situations which did not clearly fit the Conventions' binary IAC/NIAC mould. This chapter will address precisely these unorthodox types of conflicts and how they fit within the Geneva binary. It will begin with definitions and questions of terminology. It will then briefly examine the transformative processes that can lead one type of conflict to mutate into the other, namely, the internationalization of NIACs and the internalization of IACs. It will subsequently look at cross-border NIACs, i.e. NIACs which are not purely internal, and at mixed or hybrid conflicts in which an IAC and a NIAC may exist in parallel. The chapter will conclude with a critical assessment of the current state of the law, including an appraisal of whether the existing IAC/NIAC binary is fit for purpose.

B. Terminology and Definitions

5   Before turning to the typology of armed conflicts, it is necessary to ask ourselves whether there is a *generic* concept of armed conflict. Looking at the text of Common Article 2 and Common Article 3, it seems as if the concept of NIAC is defined *residually* from or

---

[2] See also Ch 3, MN 30 ff, of this volume.   [3] On some exceptions, see MN 42 ff, below.

in opposition to IAC, i.e. a NIAC would be an armed conflict which is *not* an IAC.⁴ The analytical approach to qualifying a particular situation would then be as follows:

— Is it an armed conflict?
— If so, is it an IAC?
— If not, it must be a NIAC.

'Armed conflict' would then be a generic term, the definitional elements of which could logically be met *before* making the further step of qualifying it in kind either as an IAC or a NIAC.⁵

Indeed, not only does this reasoning follow textually from Common Article 2 and Common Article 3, but it is frequently resorted to in practice, if implicitly. A good example is the *Hamdan* case before the United States (US) Supreme Court,⁶ in which the Court found that:

— there was an armed conflict between the US and Al-Qaeda;
— this conflict could not be international in character, since IACs are defined as conflicts between states, and Al-Qaeda was not a state;⁷ and consequently
— the conflict was a NIAC.⁸

The Court was not entirely clear on whether this conflict was a NIAC in *Afghanistan* or in some other locale, or rather was *global* in character.⁹

However, as explained in Chapter 1 of this volume, and as persuasively argued by Dino Kritsiotis elsewhere, this logic is flawed. The elements of the two types of conflicts do not overlap sufficiently to make them subsets of the same set and to be capable of definition by opposition.¹⁰ In particular, the intensity and organization elements of the NIAC threshold serve to protect interests of state sovereignty that do not apply in IACs.¹¹ As well put by Sivakumaran:

I find the descriptor 'non-international' to be somewhat misleading as it unhelpfully defines the category by what it is not. It suggests that there is but one armed conflict and, if it is not international in character, by default it is non-international. However, in practice, an internal/non-international

---

⁴ Cf E. Holland, 'The Qualification Framework of International Humanitarian Law: Too Rigid to Accommodate Contemporary Conflicts?', 34 *Suffolk Transnational Law Review* (2011) 145, at 155; S. Vité, 'Typology of Armed Conflicts in International Humanitarian Law: Legal Concepts and Actual Situations', 91 *IRRC* 873 (2009) 69, at 75–6.

⁵ Perhaps most notably, this was the view of the ILA Use of Force Committee, chaired by M.E. O'Connell, in its *Final Report on the Meaning of Armed Conflict in International Law* (2010). See also Ch 1 of this volume, MN 30 ff.

⁶ *Hamdan v Rumsfeld*, 548 US 557 (2006).

⁷ Ibid, at 630: 'The Court of Appeals thought, and the Government asserts, that Common Article 3 does not apply to Hamdan because the conflict with al Qaeda, being "international in scope," does not qualify as a "conflict not of an international character." 415 F 3d, at 41. That reasoning is erroneous. The term "conflict not of an international character" is used here in contradistinction to a conflict between nations.'

⁸ Ibid: 'The latter kind of conflict [NIAC] is distinguishable from the conflict described in Common Article 2 chiefly because it does not involve a clash between nations (whether signatories or not). In context, then, the phrase "not of an international character" bears its literal meaning.'

⁹ See further M. Milanovic, 'Lessons for Human Rights and Humanitarian Law in the War on Terror: Comparing *Hamdan* and the Israeli *Targeted Killings* Case', 89 *IRRC* 866 (2007) 373; N. Balendra, 'Defining Armed Conflict', 29 *Cardozo Law Review* (2008) 2461, at 2474.

¹⁰ See D. Kritsiotis, 'The Tremors of *Tadić*', 43 *Israel Law Review* (2010) 262.

¹¹ On these elements, see Ch 19 of this volume.

armed conflict is identified in a rather different manner. For example, in order for an internal/non-international armed conflict to exist, the violence must reach a certain level of intensity; yet, for an international armed conflict to exist one dominant view is that there is no such requirement. The category of internal/non-international armed conflict is thus in no way a default category which serves to catch those conflicts which are excluded from the international category. Yet this is what is suggested through the use of the terminology of 'non-international' armed conflict.[12]

8 Rather than being a generic concept, 'armed conflict' is merely shorthand for an IAC or a NIAC and all their descriptive subtypes. If a third category of armed conflict were to develop through treaty or custom, for example transnational armed conflict,[13] then 'armed conflict' would be shorthand for that as well. But one *cannot* first say that a particular situation *clearly* constitutes an armed conflict and then proceed to classify or qualify that conflict. It is precisely as shorthand that the International Criminal Tribunal for the former Yugoslavia (ICTY) Appeals Chamber used the term 'armed conflict' in *Tadić*, when it found that 'that an armed conflict exists whenever there is a resort to armed force between States or protracted armed violence between governmental authorities and organized armed groups or between such groups within a State'[14]—or, in other words, an armed conflict exists whenever there is an IAC or a NIAC, not the other way around.[15]

9 'Armed conflict' is particularly convenient as shorthand when one wants to deliberately *avoid* qualifying the conflict, either because the qualification would be politically or legally difficult,[16] or even because we feel that qualification is unnecessary since the substantive law applicable in both kinds of conflicts is (now) the same.[17] But that this approach is at times appealing does not mean that the identification of an 'armed conflict' is possible *without* qualifying it. It is not, because IACs and NIACs are categorically different rather than defined residually from each other. It is as inappropriate to conceive of NIACs as *non*-IACs as it is for IACs to be seen as *non*-NIACs.

10 In sum, at the heart of the IAC/NIAC binary is the very nature of the state-centric international order: IACs are contests between equal sovereigns, and their participants are at least presumptively privileged belligerents; whereas in NIACs at least one party to the conflict is a non-state actor, normally a rebel group to whom a state cannot accord equal standing. The privilege enjoyed by combatants in IACs means that they have a defence against prosecution for use of lethal force against an adversary as murder under domestic law, except for war crimes, and that upon capture they should be treated as prisoners of war (POWs). In NIACs, on the other hand, no state could existentially tolerate giving non-state groups an *ex ante* licence to rebel and take up arms against it. This is why the

---

[12] S. Sivakumaran, 'Re-envisaging the International Law of Internal Armed Conflict: A Rejoinder to Gabriella Blum', 22 *EJIL* (2011) 273.

[13] See section F of this chapter.

[14] ICTY, *The Prosecutor v Duško Tadić*, IT-94-1, Appeals Chamber, Decision on Jurisdiction, 2 October 1995, para 70.

[15] See Kritsiotis, above n 10, at 267.

[16] For example, the ICRC frequently does not disclose its own qualification of a particular armed conflict publicly (e.g. with respect to the 2006 Israel/Hezbollah/Lebanon conflict), and indeed its internal doctrine, pursuant to which it makes the qualification, remains confidential. See S. Ratner, 'Law Promotion Beyond Law Talk: The Red Cross, Persuasion, and the Laws of War', 22 *EJIL* (2011) 459, at 474–7.

[17] See, e.g., Report of the United Nations Fact-Finding Mission on the Gaza Conflict ('Goldstone Report'), UN Doc A/HRC/12/48, 25 September 2009, paras 281–3, esp para 282 ('as the Government of Israel suggests, the classification of the armed conflict in question as international or non-international, may not be too important').

distinction between IACs and NIACs persists, despite the convergence of the substantive rules regulating the two types of conflict.[18]

This brings us to those situations challenging the IAC/NIAC binary, with the understanding that if a particular situation does not independently qualify as either an IAC or a NIAC, it does not legally constitute an 'armed conflict' and IHL will not apply. It first must be said that while unorthodox conflicts have been the subject of intensive academic inquiry, much of the scholarship has been plagued by confusing and inconsistent terminology and conceptual imprecision, which inevitably causes misunderstanding. I shall thus first set out very clearly what *I mean* by particular words or phrases, with the caveat that this is not necessarily how *others* might use them, even within the confines of this volume. In that regard, all of the categories I shall develop are *descriptive only*, in the sense that they are there to facilitate our understanding of complex questions of classification whose end result can legally and logically only be IAC, NIAC, both, or neither. These categories operate within the binary Geneva framework, not outside it; the question of whether a third category of armed conflict has developed through customary law will be addressed only in the last section of this chapter.

The first definitions I will set out are those of the processes which turn one kind of armed conflict into the other: the internalization of IACs, which is the transformation of an existing or prima facie IAC into a NIAC, and the internationalization of NIACs, i.e. their transformation into IACs. Both processes change the law that is applicable to a given situation. Unlike some authors,[19] I will *not* use the term 'internationalized' conflict as a label for any conflict with some kind of foreign involvement, be it a full-scale military intervention by a third state or the presence of peacekeepers.

Similarly, the phrase 'transnational armed conflict' is frequently used as an umbrella term for conflicts which challenge the IAC/NIAC binary. Beyond the title of this chapter I shall not use it as such, but only as the name for a possible third category of armed conflicts. I will, however, use the term 'cross-border NIAC' for those conflicts which are legally NIACs but are not purely internal, i.e. they are not fought on the territory of a single state.

Lastly, by 'mixed' conflict I mean to denote those situations in which the multiplicity and the different status of the opposing parties mean that an IAC and a NIAC exist in parallel. Even though I specifically discuss mixed conflicts only towards the end of this chapter, we shall see that their exact parameters and incidence are inextricably linked with the other categories.

C. Internalized International Armed Conflict and Internationalized Non-International Armed Conflict

I. Internalization

It may be easy to say that IACs are fought between states. However, statehood may be contested in a given case. Secondly, and more importantly in practice, who gets to *represent* the state may turn out to be a very difficult issue. The state is after all an abstraction that ultimately can act only through human beings—but which ones? Not only is this

---

[18] See also Ch 1, MN 20 ff, of this volume.
[19] See, e.g., R. Geiss and M. Siegrist, 'Has the Armed Conflict in Afghanistan Affected the Rules on the Conduct of Hostilities?', 93 *IRRC* 881 (2011) 11, at 14, fn 8.

16 Consider, first, the invasion of Afghanistan by US-led coalition forces in 2001. The first representational difficulty we encounter in qualifying the conflict is that the Taliban regime was not recognized as the lawful Government of Afghanistan by the states that launched the invasion or by the international community generally. That difficulty is, however, reasonably easy to deal with. It is precisely because, historically, the recognition of states and governments was a way of avoiding the application of the law of war that the position in modern IHL is that it is *de facto* government and not recognition that matters.[20] While they never controlled all of Afghanistan, at the time the Taliban were in effective power in most of the country, including the capital Kabul, and they had established institutions of government. Accordingly, there was an IAC between the US and other coalition states on one side, and the state of Afghanistan, represented *de facto* by the Taliban regime, on the other, while there was also a NIAC running in parallel between the Taliban and the forces of the Northern Alliance.

17 But then the Taliban were defeated; their institutional rule over Afghanistan could not survive the joint coalition-Northern Alliance assault. Today we of course know that the defeat of the Taliban was far from complete, but it is still true to say that they lost the territorial control of the kind that denotes a government rather than simply an armed group. The ensuing governmental vacuum was filled through a long transitional process, lasting from the end of 2001 up until 2003, which was approved by the UN Security Council and ultimately resulted in the establishment of a new Afghan Government. The new Government not only consented to the presence of international forces in Afghanistan, but together with the international forces it continued to fight the growing Taliban insurgency.[21]

18 The key question here is whether, and at what point, the conflict transitioned from a mixed IAC/NIAC to a NIAC pure and simple, i.e. at what point the Taliban lost the capacity to represent the state of Afghanistan, and accordingly lost belligerent rights vis-à-vis third states intervening in Afghanistan.

19 At the heart of this question lies a tension between competing policy considerations. On one hand, we do not want the mere fact of military defeat to allow the intervening states to transform the character of the conflict simply by setting up a quisling administration that could then 'consent' to their presence in the country;[22] think only of the Third Reich's *modus operandi* throughout Europe during the Second World War. At the same time, however, in some cases we want to recognize the changing facts on the ground and enable the situation to move forward, for example by allowing a transition from an authoritarian regime to a more representative one under some level of international supervision. Such introduction of considerations of *legitimacy*, while perhaps inevitable both politically and legally, poses a particular danger for IHL as it smacks of the *jus ad bellum* that we, for good reason, wish to keep IHL insulated from.

---

[20] See D. Schindler, 'The Different Types of Armed Conflicts According to the Geneva Conventions and Protocols', 163 *RCADI* (1979-II) 131, at 128–30. See also Ch 1, MN 55 ff, of this volume.

[21] For a general overview see, e.g., A. Bellal, G. Giacca, and S. Casey-Maslen, 'International Law and Armed Non-State Actors in Afghanistan', 93 *IRRC* 881 (2011) 47; and S. Wills, 'The Legal Characterization of the Armed Conflicts in Afghanistan and Iraq: Implications for Protection', 58 *NILR* (2011) 173.

[22] See, in that vein, D. Turns, 'The International Humanitarian Law Classification of Armed Conflicts in Iraq Since 2003', 86 *US Naval War College International Law Studies* (2010) 97, esp at 113–14.

We can observe the same dynamics at play in the case of Iraq post-2003, where there was initially undoubtedly an IAC which resulted in belligerent occupation; following a transitional process under international supervision, a new Iraqi Government was formed which provided its consent to the presence of coalition forces, thereby terminating the IAC and the occupation; as this process was underway, an insurgency erupted which for a substantial period crossed the threshold of 'protracted armed violence', thereby creating a NIAC.

The most recent examples of such problems of state representation are the conflicts in the Côte d'Ivoire and Libya.[23] As for the former, the story of the disputed Ivorian elections in 2010 and the ensuing crisis is well known. According to international observers, the incumbent President, Laurent Gbagbo, lost the elections to his challenger, Alassane Ouattara, but the results were overturned by a Gbagbo-appointed commission. After a number of unsuccessful attempts at resolving the crisis, Ouattara was formally recognized as the lawful President of the Côte d'Ivoire by the UN, the Economic Community of West African States (ECOWAS), the African Union, and many countries. A conflict erupted between state forces loyal to Gbagbo and various armed groups supporting Ouattara, in which the latter were the ultimate winners. This conflict was at all times undoubtedly a NIAC. But what complicates matters is the intervention near the end of this conflict by UN and French peacekeepers in support of Ouattara.[24] Leaving the involvement of UN forces aside, when the French forces attacked Gbagbo's compound and military assets, was this an IAC between France and the Côte d'Ivoire, or was it rather a NIAC since the French forces acted with the consent of Ouattara, the lawful and legitimate President of the country?

Similarly, in Libya in 2011, the conflict was initially a mixed one: an IAC between Libya and the coalition states, and a NIAC between the Gaddafi regime and the Benghazi rebels. However, as the conflict intensified and the rebels became better organized, forming a National Transitional Council (NTC), a number of states recognized this Council as the legitimate Government of Libya. Together with the crumbling of the Gaddafi regime, did such recognition lead to the transformation of the IAC into a NIAC, with the coalition at some point intervening on behalf of the legitimate Government of the country? As of the time of writing, a similar process is underway in the ongoing conflict in Syria, except that the recognition of the Syrian rebels extended by some states is not couched in terms of recognition of a government, but in terms of their status as the 'legitimate representatives of the Syrian people'.[25]

What is at stake here is a process of internalization, or de-internationalization, of a conflict, i.e. its transformation from an IAC into a NIAC. Looking at the competing policy considerations, we can see what is *not* enough for such internalization to occur. That the incumbent government of a country is defeated cannot by itself transform the conflict, nor can the establishment of a proxy government by the victors, since this would allow them to effectively strip by force the protections granted in IACs to the remaining combatants of the defeated state, turning them into unprivileged belligerents. Similarly, that a

---

[23] See, e.g., C. Henderson, 'International Measures for the Protection of Civilians in Libya and Côte d'Ivoire', 60 *ICLQ* (2011) 767.

[24] See, e.g., 'Strikes by U.N. and France Corner Leader of Ivory Coast', *New York Times*, 4 April 2011, available at <http://www.nytimes.com/2011/04/05/world/africa/05ivory.html?_r=3>.

[25] See generally S. Talmon, 'Recognition of Opposition Groups as the Legitimate Representative of a People', 12 *Chinese JIL* (2013) 219; see also MN 41.

rebel group is recognized as the new legitimate government of the country cannot of itself transform the character of the conflict, as this would again allow the intervening states to unilaterally do what they will.[26] The matter must be one of objective appraisal, rather than of the subjective attitudes of the recognizing or non-recognizing states.

24   When, then, would the transformation of the conflict occur? In my view, both considerations of policy and recent practice support a composite rule consisting of the three elements set out below. The conflict would transform from an IAC into a NIAC only when:

— the old regime has lost control over most of the country, and the likelihood of it regaining such control in the short to medium term is small or none (negative element);
— the new regime has established control over a significant part of the country, and is legitimized in an inclusive process[27] that makes it broadly representative of the people (positive element);
— the new regime achieves broad international recognition (external element).

None of these elements is enough by itself, but jointly they take into account both questions of legitimacy and factual developments on the ground, while providing safeguards against abuse. With regard to both the positive and the negative elements, the degree of control would be looked at holistically, taking into account not just troops on the ground but also direction over state institutions more generally, its economic assets, the media, and the like.

25   Thus, there is at least a strong majority view that the transitional processes in Iraq and Afghanistan at some point led to the transformation of the conflicts from IACs or mixed IACs/NIACs into NIACs pure and simple.[28] Similarly, looking at the Ivorian example, when the Gbagbo regime was effectively reduced to Abidjan, with the forces of the internationally recognized President Ouattara holding the remainder of the country, the intervention by French troops cannot be said to have constituted an IAC. When it comes to Libya, the tipping point probably came with the NTC's takeover of Tripoli, the acceptance of its representatives by the UN General Assembly's credentials committee, and the endorsement of the new Government by the Security Council. Obviously, it is hard to pinpoint the exact moment of internalization in any given case, and thankfully in most cases it may be unnecessary to do so, but it *is* necessary for us to be aware of the relevant elements and their interplay. And while fully acknowledging the fluid nature of these elements, we must also be aware that the internalization of a conflict has as its consequence a possible reduction of various protections under IHL.[29]

II. Internationalization

26   This brings us to the reverse process, that of internationalization, defined as the transformation of a prima facie NIAC into an IAC, thereby applying to this conflict the more

---

[26] See also D. Akande, 'Classification of Armed Conflicts: Relevant Legal Concepts', in E. Wilmshurst (ed), *International Law and the Classification of Conflicts* (Oxford: OUP, 2012) 32, at 62–3.

[27] Not necessarily requiring democratic elections, but certainly favouring them.

[28] See, e.g., Bellal et al, above n 21, at 51–3, and the works cited therein; Geiss and Siegrist, above n 19, at 13–16; Turns, above n 22 (stating that this is the majority view despite disliking it as a matter of policy); J. Pejic, 'The Protective Scope of Common Article 3: More than Meets the Eye', 93 *IRRC* 881 (2011) 189, at 196.

[29] See Wills, above n 21.

comprehensive IAC legal regime. The most important of these legal consequences is the grant, in principle, of privileged belligerency to combatants on both sides of the conflict. As for the mechanism of internationalization, we have seen that under Common Article 2, IACs are defined as differences leading to the use of armed force *between two states*. Accordingly, there are two basic ways of internationalizing a NIAC. First, a prima facie NIAC can be subsumed under the *existing* Common Article 2 definition. In other words, what at first glance looks like a conflict between a state and a non-state actor is, on closer examination, actually a conflict between two states. Secondly, a NIAC can be internationalized through the *redefinition* of IAC in terms of its structure, so that the Common Article 2 definition is exceptionally expanded under a treaty or customary rule so as to potentially include some non-state parties. Internationalization under this heading would require proof of a specific rule to that effect. I shall now deal with both types of internationalization in turn.

27   The first possibility of internationalization under the Common Article 2 definition is if a non-state actor embroiled in a Common Article 3 conflict with a state manages to create a new state in the course of the conflict.[30] Think only of the dissolution of the former Yugoslavia, or the possible emergence of a state of Palestine. Statehood is to be measured by the rules of general international law and not by any special rule of IHL, and from the moment of the new state's creation, any conflict with the other state would become an IAC.

28   The problem, of course, is that the general criteria for statehood can be very unclear, and the issue of statehood is itself highly contested and politicized. Consider Kosovo, which declared independence from Serbia in 2008 but which Serbia still claims as a part of its own territory. If a new conflict were to erupt between them, it would be an IAC only if Kosovo does in fact objectively fulfil the criteria for statehood under international law.[31] Similarly, consider a hypothetical conflict between China and Taiwan, in which the latter formally renounced the authority of Beijing and claimed independence, or indeed the possible resurgence of conflict between Georgia and its separatist territories of Abkhazia and South Ossetia.[32] While the *renvoi* to general international law and its criteria for statehood carries with it its own difficulties and complexities, we can say that it is in principle quite difficult for a secessionist entity to gain statehood on the basis of force alone; while international law does not prescribe a duty of loyalty to one's state nor prohibit secession as such, it does not favour it either.[33]

29   Other than through the process of state creation, internationalization can occur under the Common Article 2 definition in two basic scenarios:

— if state A intervenes on the territory of state B in support of non-state actor C against state B; and
— if state A intervenes on the territory of state B against non-state actor C without B's consent.

In both cases, what at first glance appears to be a NIAC between (1) B and C and (2) A and C, may actually amount to an IAC between A and B.

---

[30] See, e.g., Akande, above n 26, at 43.
[31] At least under the (unlikely) assumption that the international forces deployed in Kosovo took no part in the conflict.
[32] See also MN 72.
[33] See, generally, J. Crawford, *The Creation of States in International Law* (2nd edn, Oxford: OUP, 2006), at 374 ff.

30   In the first scenario, the intervening state must use the non-state actor as a proxy against the territorial state, i.e. A acts through C to attack B, in order for the conflict to be internationalized as a whole, rather than remain a NIAC or a mixed IAC/NIAC. It is generally not disputed in doctrine that internationalization can occur in such circumstances;[34] what is in dispute is the precise nature of the link between the intervening state and the non-state actor that suffices for internationalization.[35] On one view, this link must be that of attribution as a matter of the secondary rules of state responsibility. This, of course, was famously the approach of the ICTY Appeals Chamber in the *Tadić* appeals judgment,[36] where it considered that the acts of the Bosnian Serbs had to be attributable to the Former Republic of Yugoslavia (FRY)/Serbia in order for the conflict to become international in character, and fashioned the 'overall control' test of responsibility in order to do so, thereby rejecting the reasoning of the International Court of Justice (ICJ) on attribution in the *Nicaragua* case.[37]

31   There is an intuitive appeal to the *Tadić* approach. After all, what else could it mean for a non-state actor to be acting on behalf of state than for its acts to be attributable to the state? However, as I argued at length elsewhere,[38] the Appeals Chamber's approach was erroneous for two basic reasons. First, it actually misinterpreted the ICJ's *Nicaragua* judgment as setting out only *one* test of attribution, that of effective control, and thought that this single test was unreasonable and impracticable. Indeed, it would be so, had the ICJ not set out *two* tests of attribution in its judgment: that of complete dependence and control, operating at a general level and seeking to attribute *all* of the acts of a non-state actor to a state, and that of effective control, seeking to attribute *specific* acts controlled by the state.[39] Secondly, and more importantly for our purposes, it is conceptually inappropriate for secondary rules of attribution to determine the scope of application of the primary rules of IHL. Rather, it is for IHL to fashion a test which determines when the relationship between a state and a non-state actor is such that a NIAC is to be internationalized, and that test may well be that of overall control.[40]

32   In its 2007 *Bosnian Genocide* merits judgment,[41] the ICJ rejected the overall control test in the context of attribution, finding that it was too loose to fit that particular purpose. However, the Court left open the possibility that the test is valid for the IHL-specific purposes of qualifying a conflict:

> This is the case of the doctrine laid down in the *Tadić* Judgment. Insofar as the 'overall control' test is employed to determine whether or not an armed conflict is international, which was the sole question which the Appeals Chamber was called upon to decide, it may well be that the test is applicable and suitable; the Court does not however think it appropriate to take a position on the

---

[34] See also Ch 1 of this volume, MN 40 ff.

[35] See, e.g., L. Arimatsu, 'Territory, Boundaries and the Law of Armed Conflict', 12 *YIHL* (2009) 157, at 174–5; N. Lubell, *Extraterritorial Use of Force against Non-State Actors* (Oxford: OUP, 2010), at 97–9; Holland, above n 4, at 162–3; Vité, above n 4, at 90–2; Akande, above n 26, at 60–2.

[36] ICTY, *The Prosecutor v Duško Tadić*, IT-94-1, Appeals Chamber, Judgment, 15 July 1999, paras 88–162, esp para 98.

[37] ICJ, *Military and Paramilitary Activities in and against Nicaragua (Nicaragua v United States)*, Judgment (Merits), 27 June 1986 (hereinafter *Nicaragua*).

[38] See M. Milanovic, 'State Responsibility for Genocide', 17 *EJIL* (2006) 553, at 575 ff.

[39] See also S. Talmon, 'The Responsibility of Outside Powers for Acts of Secessionist Entities', 58 *ICLQ* (2009) 493.

[40] See further Milanovic, above n 38, at 584–5, as well as M. Milanovic, 'State Responsibility for Genocide: A Follow-Up', 18 *EJIL* (2007) 669.

[41] ICJ, *Application of the Convention on the Prevention and Punishment of the Crime of Genocide (Bosnia and Herzegovina v Serbia and Montenegro)*, Judgment, 26 February 2007.

point in the present case, as there is no need to resolve it for purposes of the present Judgment. On the other hand, the ICTY presented the 'overall control' test as equally applicable under the law of State responsibility for the purpose of determining—as the Court is required to do in the present case—when a State is responsible for acts committed by paramilitary units, armed forces which are not among its official organs. In this context, the argument in favour of that test is unpersuasive.

It should first be observed that logic does not require the same test to be adopted in resolving the two issues, which are very different in nature: the degree and nature of a State's involvement in an armed conflict on another State's territory which is required for the conflict to be characterized as international, can very well, and without logical inconsistency, differ from the degree and nature of involvement required to give rise to that State's responsibility for a specific act committed in the course of the conflict.[42]

I submit that the ICJ has the better of this argument.[43] Again, I do not dispute that there is an intuitive appeal to the *Tadić* approach; for example, the ICJ's holding to the contrary was criticized by Marina Spinedi in an excellent article.[44] However, *Tadić* is right only to the extent that, if the acts of the Bosnian Serbs were attributable to Serbia, the conflict would surely have been international in nature, since the Bosnian Serbs would not have been a non-state actor at all but agents of Serbia. In other words, attribution *suffices*, but it need not be *necessary*, for internationalization. As a distinct body of primary rules, IHL can adopt its own solution regarding the link between a state and a non-state actor that would suffice for internationalization of a conflict, and that link need not be attribution as a matter of state responsibility.

In short, the internationalization of a prima facie NIAC in the first scenario set out above—an intervention into a civil conflict by a third state—depends on the nature of the relationship between the intervening state and a non-state actor. That relationship may, but need not be, one of attribution. A relationship of overall control, which does not suffice for attribution, may suffice for internationalization, as the ICJ itself allows.[45] Note that this may lead to IACs in which the conduct of a fighting force is not attributable to a state, even though that state remains a party to the conflict and the enemy in terms of IHL, and even though that state pursues the conflict only through that proxy fighting force.

What then of our second scenario, where state A intervenes on the territory of state B against the non-state actor C? If state B actually *consents* to the intervention, the conflict can only be qualified as a NIAC. For the intervening state or states this is a cross-border NIAC;[46] for the territorial state it is simply internal in nature. Conflicts in Iraq and Afghanistan after the establishment of their new governments, which gave consent to the participation of foreign troops in the conflict, provide good examples. Hence, when it comes to internationalization, the only additional situation is one in which the territorial state does *not* give its consent to the foreign intervention. Consider in that regard the Israel/Hezbollah/Lebanon conflict in 2006—how is it to be qualified?

We can initially treat this second scenario exactly like the first: so long as non-state actor C is under B's overall control or C's acts are attributable to B, there would be an IAC

---

[42] Ibid, paras 404–5. [43] See also Akande, above n 26, at 59–62.
[44] M. Spinedi, 'On the Non-Attribution of the Bosnian Serbs' Conduct to Serbia', 5 *JICJ* (2007) 829.
[45] The *Tadić* overall control test was endorsed for the purposes of conflict qualification by the ICC Pre-Trial Chamber in *Prosecutor v Thomas Lubanga Dyilo*, Decision on the Confirmation of Charges, ICC-01/04-01/06, 29 January 2007, para 211.
[46] See section D of this chapter.

between states A and B. What first looks like a non-state actor is really a state actor, and what first looks like a NIAC is really an IAC. Thus, if the acts of Hezbollah were attributable to the state of Lebanon, for example because Hezbollah acted in the absence or default of official authorities in Southern Lebanon, or because of the participation of Hezbollah in the Lebanese Government, or if regardless of attribution Lebanon exercised overall control over Hezbollah, then the 2006 Israel/Hezbollah/Lebanon conflict would in fact simply have been an IAC between Israel and Lebanon.

37   But what if Hezbollah was not fighting on behalf of Lebanon? How would the conflict be characterized then? One solution would be to say that the conflict was a mixed one: an IAC between Israel and Lebanon, and a cross-border NIAC between Israel and Hezbollah (so long as there was 'protracted armed violence' between the two in Lebanon).

38   Another view would be to say that the territorial state's consent to the foreign intervention, or lack thereof, would have bearing on the matter.[47] Note that there is little doubt that the very fact that state A uses force on the territory of state B without its consent creates an IAC between the two states, at least in addition to any separate conflict with the non-state actor.[48] Israel's invasion of Lebanon initiated a conflict with Lebanon, inter alia by imposing a maritime blockade, not just with Hezbollah. This would have remained the case even if Israel limited itself strictly to attacking Hezbollah targets (which it did not), and Hezbollah fighters could perhaps be classified as civilians taking a direct part in hostilities in the IAC between Lebanon and Israel. Similarly, the 2008 incursions by Colombia into Ecuador in order to attack the Fuerzas Armadas Revolucionarias de Colombia (FARC) rebels could be qualified as an IAC between Colombia and Ecuador in which the FARC were civilians taking a direct part in hostilities, regardless of any institutional link between FARC and Ecuador; all that would matter is that Ecuador did not consent to the deployment of Colombian troops.

39   Relying on consent as an additional criterion for internationalization in our second scenario could greatly simplify the qualification analysis. We would only have a single IAC to deal with. It would not, however, be entirely without its problems. There are cases in which it is hard to say whether the territorial state consented to the foreign intervention or not, because for political reasons that state wishes to maintain an ambiguous position. The best current example is that of the use of drones by the US military against Taliban assets on Pakistani territory. There can also be cases in which consent is given by the territorial state, but the intervening state exceeds the boundaries of that consent.

40   Moreover, the greater the cohesion of the armed group and its organizational independence from the government of the territorial state, the more artificial it would seem to label the conflict as a single IAC, even if the territorial state does not consent.[49] For instance, while the Israeli intervention against Hezbollah in Lebanon significantly affected Lebanon itself, Colombia targeted FARC in the jungle, far away from any assets or the population of Ecuador. One might wonder whether the quality of the territory affected and the potential targets could also play a role in deciding on internationalization. What would be the use of the application of the rules of IAC in the Colombia/FARC/Ecuador scenario, when the only potential addressees of those rules on one side of the conflict would be FARC

---

[47] See, e.g., Arimatsu, above n 35, at 177, 184; Akande, above n 26, at 73–6.
[48] See, e.g., Kritsiotis, above n 10, at 280–1.
[49] See C. Kreß, 'Some Reflections on the International Legal Framework Governing Transnational Armed Conflicts', 15 *Journal of Conflict and Security Law* (2010) 245, at 253–4.

irregulars? The NIAC regime would appear to be more appropriate, and would govern the hostilities between Colombia and FARC, while a parallel IAC between Colombia and Ecuador, while formally in effect, would have very little practical relevance.[50] In the Israel/Hezbollah/Lebanon scenario, however, the exposure of the Lebanese civilian population and infrastructure to the fighting would make internationalization a more viable option; and if not, the conflict would at the very least be a mixed IAC/NIAC.[51] In such circumstances, any hostile acts that did not directly involve Hezbollah—for example, the Israeli bombing of runways at the Beirut airport or the imposition of a naval blockade against Lebanese ports—would be governed by the more comprehensive IAC regime.

In sum, whether consent should be a distinct criterion of internationalization in our second scenario, or whether that scenario should be treated exactly like the first, will be a matter of some controversy. In any event, I would caution against relying exclusively on the secondary rules of attribution in either scenario, as these general rules are not suited for this purpose and do not necessarily take into account IHL-specific policy considerations. Limiting internationalization strictly to those cases where the acts of a non-state actor could be attributed to a state would have a number of adverse consequences. Since the general rules of attribution are strict precisely because they need to be of general application, this would either greatly limit the number of possible cases of internationalized NIACs, or would lead to fragmentationist jurisprudential conflicts on attribution of the *Nicaragua/Tadić/Genocide* variety; it is good both for IHL and for general international law to separate internationalization from attribution.[52]

We have now dealt with internationalization of NIACs under the existing Common Article 2 definition of IACs as conflicts between states. The other broad rubric of internationalization is that of IACs *redefined* as something other than conflicts between states, with the status of a non-state actor upgraded, as it were, so that the same privileges that international law accords to states and their agents are exceptionally extended to some other type of actor. This type of internationalization of necessity requires proof of some additional rule, whether based in treaty or custom; Common Article 2 is not enough. There are several possible candidates for such a rule.

First, the only such rule which exists beyond any doubt is Article 1(4) AP I, on wars of national liberation.[53] The rationale behind this rule is that a people fighting against racist or foreign domination is legitimately entitled to be prospectively treated as a state, even if it has yet to realize external self-determination and create a new state.[54] When AP I was drafted, such conflicts were mostly a historical relic, as decolonization had already largely been completed. The only conflicts that could potentially qualify as such today are the Israeli–Palestinian conflict and that in Western Sahara, although the current spate of recognitions of rebel groups as the legitimate representatives of the people, as in Syria, is invoking the language of self-determination and may open the door to internationalization.[55]

---

[50] Cf Lubell, above n 35, at 110–11. [51] See also Akande, above n 26, at 76.
[52] The same argument can be made for the *jus ad bellum* context. See M. Milanovic, 'State Responsibility for Acts of Non-State Actors: A Comment on Griebel and Plücken', 22 *LJIL* (2009) 307.
[53] See, generally, Schindler, above n 20, at 133 ff. [54] See also Ch 1, MN 49–54, of this volume.
[55] See further D. Akande, 'Self Determination and the Syrian Conflict', *EJIL: Talk!*, 6 December 2012, at <http://www.ejiltalk.org/self-determination-and-the-syrian-conflict-recognition-of-syrian-opposition-as-sole-legitimate-representative-of-the-syrian-people-what-does-this-man-and-what-implications-does-it-have/>.

44   However, this redefinition of IACs in AP I proved to be very controversial and was objected to by a number of states, which for that reason either refused to ratify AP I or did so with reservations.[56] Accordingly, Article 1(4) has not achieved customary status.[57] Internationalization under this rule can occur *only* with respect to prima facie NIACs occurring in the territory of one of AP I's contracting parties which has not made a reservation to this provision.

45   Secondly, despite having fallen into disuse, the recognition of belligerency did not necessarily fall into desuetude and may still have relevance in modern law.[58] Even historically such recognition was rarely explicit, i.e. made as such in a formal declaration, but was made implicitly, for example through the invocation of neutrality by third states. It is possible that such implicit recognition can operate today as well, if the relevant non-state actor is sufficiently state-like in its qualities and exercises institutional control over territory, thereby upgrading a NIAC into an IAC.[59]

46   Thirdly, it is possible that a special customary rule of IHL has evolved that transforms armed conflicts in which international organizations directly participate as parties into IACs when fighting states, even though international organizations are not states themselves and would thus presumably be covered by default by the NIAC regime. This is a difficult and complex question, especially in those situations (rare, if theoretically possible) in which the conduct of the armed forces is attributable *only* to the organization and not also simultaneously to its member states which would independently trigger an IAC. This point will not be developed here any further.[60]

III. Circumstances which do not lead to internationalization

47   Having now defined the circumstances which *do* lead to internationalization, I can briefly dispense with those that do not. Indeed, I have already dealt with all or some of them implicitly in our preceding discussion. First, the mere fact that hostilities cross state borders does not lead to internationalization. In terms of the Common Article 2 definition, it is not the location of the hostilities but the identity of the actors that creates an IAC.[61] Outside of that definition there does not seem to be any practice in support of a rule that a conflict between a state and a non-state actor that crosses a border *ipso facto* becomes internationalized. On the contrary, there is no good reason of policy to grant privileged status to non-state actors merely because of a transnational element and, as we are about to see, the existing framework is perfectly capable of accommodating various kinds of cross-border NIACs.

48   Similarly, the fact that a conflict erupts in an occupied territory between the occupying state and a non-state actor does not mean that this prima facie NIAC becomes internationalized (see for a detailed discussion Chapter 19, MN 14–16, of this volume). It

---

[56] This was, for example, the position of the US government—see President Reagan's Message to the Senate Transmitting a Protocol to the 1949 Geneva Conventions, dated 29 January 1987 and reproduced in 81 *AJIL* (1987) 910.

[57] See, e.g., Akande, above n 26, at 49.

[58] See, in that regard, Y. Lootsteen, 'The Concept of Belligerency in International Law', 166 *Military Law Review* (2000) 109; Akande, above n 26, at 49–50.

[59] See also Ch 1 of this volume, MN 58. One should also bear in mind in that regard the possibility of ad hoc agreements under CA 3, which do not amount to a recognition of belligerency but can bring IAC rules to bear (see Ch 25 of this volume).

[60] See further Ch 1 of this volume, MN 16–19.   [61] See also Holland, above n 4, at 160.

is true that the Israeli Supreme Court, in the *Targeted Killings* case, relying on the opinion of Professor Cassese, held to the contrary,[62] as did the International Criminal Court (ICC) Pre-Trial Chamber in *Lubanga*.[63] However, not only do these decisions not provide adequate reasoning for their holding, but there does not seem to be any relevant practice to support it.[64] Nor is it somehow warranted by logic. The occupation may well outlive the conflict that created it, as it did in the Israeli–Palestinian case. Why should a more or less unrelated outbreak of violence, whose actors are completely different, be treated as an IAC? Unless we follow the controversial logic of Article 1(4) AP I, why should the status of a non-state actor be upgraded to full belligerent rights if the actor is not fighting on behalf of any state? That two legal regimes would apply in parallel is not reason enough. As with cases of mixed or parallel armed conflicts, IHL can allow for the possibility of the simultaneous existence of occupation and of a NIAC in occupied territory.[65]

Lastly, the mere fact that international or foreign forces are deployed in a certain territory does not of itself suffice for the internationalization of the whole conflict.[66] As we have seen, the qualification of such situations depends on the existence, *vel non*, of the consent of the territorial state to the presence of the international forces and of their relationship with the relevant non-state actors.[67] Thus, for instance, the fact that the North Atlantic Treaty Organization (NATO) intervened against Serbia in 1999, which was at the time fighting the Kosovo Liberation Army (KLA) insurgency in Kosovo, does not mean that the whole conflict was internationalized. There was certainly an IAC between the NATO states and Serbia, but the NIAC between Serbia and the KLA would have been internationalized only if the NATO states exerted the necessary degree of control over the non-state actor.

D. Cross-Border Non-International Armed Conflict

All definitions of NIAC are closely bound up with the question of its geographical scope. Common Article 3 refers to conflicts 'occurring in the territory of one of the High Contracting Parties'; Article 1(1) AP II similarly refers to conflicts 'which take place in the territory of a High Contracting Party'; the ICTY in *Tadić* to conflicts 'within a state';[68] and the Statute of the International Criminal Court to conflicts 'that take place in the territory of a State'.[69] The natural interpretation of all these texts would confine the meaning

---

[62] *The Public Committee against Torture in Israel et al v Government of Israel et al*, Supreme Court of Israel sitting as the High Court of Justice, Judgment, 13 December 2006, HCJ 769/02, para 18.

[63] In *Lubanga*, the Chamber seemed to consider that occupation internationalizes any other conflict—see ICC, *The Prosecutor v Lubanga*, above n 45, para 220. In *Katanga*, the Chamber characterized the conflict as international without making explicit the legal basis for doing so; it considered the intervention by Ugandan troops in the Congo to have internationalized the conflict, but it is unclear whether it considered the relevant non-state armed groups to have been under Uganda's overall control, or whether the mere presence of foreign troops led to internationalization. The possibility of parallel conflicts was not discussed. See ICC, *The Prosecutor v Germain Katanga and Mathieu Ngudjolo Chui*, Decision on the Confirmation of Charges, ICC-01/04-01/07, 30 September 2008, para 240.

[64] See further Milanovic, above n 9, at 382–6.

[65] See also Ch 19 of this volume, MN 14–16. See *contra* Akande, above n 26, at 47.

[66] See, e.g., Pejic, above n 28, at 194.

[67] See also J. Stewart, 'Towards a Single Definition of Armed Conflict in International Humanitarian Law: A Critique of Internationalized Armed Conflict', 85 *IRRC* 850 (2003) 313, at 328–35 (discussing relevant ICTY case law).

[68] ICTY, *Tadić*, above n 14, para 70.   [69] Art 8(2)(f) of the ICC Statute.

of NIAC to conflicts which take place within the territory of a single state.[70] In other words, NIAC would equal internal armed conflict.

51   There is little (if any) historical evidence that the drafters of the major IHL instruments had anything other than purely internal conflicts in mind when formulating the relevant provisions. After all, the overwhelming concerns about the possible impact of these instruments on state sovereignty and the freedom of states to deal with their own problems as they see fit, make sense only in the context of internal insurrections and rebellions. Of course, cross-border incursions of armed groups were occurring even prior to the adoption of the Geneva Conventions.[71] While these occurrences did raise significant questions with regard to state responsibility for revolutionary acts and within the *jus ad bellum* framework, they were rarely, if ever, perceived as requiring specific regulation in the *jus in bello*. Even as spillovers of internal conflicts became more frequent, as in the developing world during anti-colonial struggles, the primary concern was legitimization (or not) of national liberation movements, which was the object of Article 1(4) AP I. The sporadic nature and low intensity of cross-border incursions by armed groups meant that the issue was politically hardly one of global concern, and it was largely off the legal radar. For all intents and purposes, NIACs were synonymous with purely internal conflicts, and that was that, for states and scholars alike.[72]

52   Things have since changed. Al-Qaeda's 9/11 attacks and the ensuing US 'war on terror', and conflicts in Iraq and Afghanistan (as well as in Pakistan and Yemen), raised serious issues of conflict qualification and the continuing desirability of the exclusively binary IAC/NIAC mould. And these were not the only such examples. The conflict between Israel and Hezbollah in Lebanon,[73] the situation in the Democratic Republic of the Congo (DRC) and constant spillovers of multiple NIACs occurring there to the territories of neighbouring countries, the incursions of Ogaden militias from Ethiopia and Al-Shabaab militia from lawless Somalia onto Kenyan territory, and the Kurdish fight for independence against Turkey and Iran, all pose serious challenges to the binary framework and NIAC's narrow geographical scope. These conflicts are not IACs as they are not inter-state; nor are they purely internal in character as they cross the borders of several states.

53   What are they, then, and can the text of Common Article 3 accommodate a cross-border dimension? There are two ways in which the Common Article 3 reference to conflicts 'occurring in the territory of one of the High Contracting Parties' can be interpreted. The first, and perhaps more natural, is to say that the territory referred to is that of a state actually taking part in the conflict—in other words, Common Article 3 would inherently be limited to conflicts which are purely internal in scope. The second would be to say that the reference is to the territory of *any* High Contracting Party, not necessarily that of a state actually a party to the conflict.[74] The latter interpretation allows Common Article 3 NIACs to encompass situations which are not confined within the borders of a single state, and should in my view be preferred.[75]

---

[70] See, e.g., Pejic, above n 28, at 199 (citing further commentary to that effect); Lubell, above n 35, at 100.

[71] See, e.g., H. Lauterpacht, 'Revolutionary Activities by Private Persons against Foreign States', 22 *AJIL* (1928) 105; I. Brownlie, 'International Law and Armed Bands', 7 *ICLQ* (1958) 720.

[72] But see D. Jinks, 'September 11 and the Laws of War', 28 *Yale JIL* (2003) 1.

[73] See further Lubell, above n 35, at 250.

[74] In other words, CA 3, just like any other treaty provision, applies *qua* treaty only for the parties to the treaty—see Vité, above n 4, at 88–9; M. Sassòli, 'Transnational Armed Groups and International Humanitarian Law', *HPCR Occasional Paper Series*, Winter 2006, No 6, at 8–9; Pejic, above n 28, at 200–1.

[75] See also Holland, above n 4, at 159–60; Lubell, above n 35, at 101–4; Akande, above n 26, at 71–2.

While NIACs have historically certainly been treated as synonymous with purely internal conflicts, and while such internal conflicts remain the paradigmatic examples of NIACs, NIACs can today also be seen as a somewhat wider category. Interpreted evolutively and in accordance with contemporary practice, the Common Article 3 threshold textually allows for non-internal or cross-border NIAC.[76] I shall distinguish (if not very rigidly) between two major subtypes of cross-border NIACs—spillover and foreign intervention[77]—and then see how the definitions of NIAC, as explained above, would apply to these factual situations.

The first subtype of cross-border or non-internal NIAC, and perhaps the easier to deal with, is the spillover scenario. Initially, an ordinary, internal NIAC is fought on the territory of state A, either between the armed forces of state A and armed group X, or between armed groups X and Y. Then, however, fighting crosses the border and spills over onto the territory of state B (normally, but not necessarily, adjacent to A), which itself may or may not join in the fighting; combat operations on B's territory may be either sporadic, or intense and protracted.

Examples of such spillover conflicts are legion. One of the most recent would be the situation along the Somali border with Kenya. There is an ongoing internal NIAC between Al-Shabaab militants and the Transitional Federal Government of Somalia (TFG) on the territory of Somalia. The Al-Shabaab militants, however, frequently cross onto the territory of Kenya and conduct sporadic attacks there. Kenyan forces respond to these attacks in order to expel the group from Kenyan territory, at times crossing over the Somali border.

How does the law qualify such spillover scenarios? Two basic approaches seem to be appropriate. First, if the spilled-over component of the conflict taking place on the territory of state B by itself satisfies the 'protracted armed violence' intensity and organization threshold,[78] we can speak of two separate NIACs, one in state A and the other in state B. But what if the conflict on the territory of state B never independently reaches the Common Article 3 threshold of NIAC as it is lacking the necessary duration and intensity? In other words, would a *sporadic* spillover scenario that fails to independently reach the NIAC threshold thereby leave those particular instances of violence unregulated by IHL? While human rights law or domestic law could to an extent fill the regulatory gap, in some cases at least such a result would morally be completely arbitrary; a rape by a rebel soldier on one side of the border would constitute a war crime, but not on the other.

Such a gap can largely be avoided. It should be recalled that in its analysis of the geographic scope of NIACs *within* the state, the ICTY Appeals Chamber in *Tadić* held that to subsume these events under the ongoing NIAC, it is sufficient to show that the alleged crimes 'were closely related to the hostilities occurring in other parts of the territories controlled by the parties to the conflict.'[79] In other words, if there is a sufficient nexus between an ongoing NIAC and military operations that are occurring outside the areas in which the conflict and 'protracted armed violence' normally take place, these military operations will nevertheless be understood as part of the overall armed conflict. This reasoning may be extended by analogy to military operations *outside* the state.[80] Thus, IHL would be applicable to sporadic military clashes between Colombian forces and FARC spilling over onto Ecuadorian territory, if a sufficient nexus with the ongoing NIAC between the

---

[76] See also Ch 19 of this volume, MN 22 et seq.   [77] See also Holland, above n 4, at 161.
[78] See Ch 19 of this volume.   [79] ICTY, *Tadić*, above n 14, para 70.
[80] See also Kreß, above n 49, at 265.

two entities in Colombia could be established, i.e. if the component that spilled over was still clearly between the forces of Colombia and FARC that are engaged in the core part of the NIAC, and the hostilities in the two territories were not completely unconnected.[81]

59   Simply put, while NIAC requires 'protracted armed violence' within the territory of a state, it does not necessarily need *all* of that violence to take place within that state, so long as there is an organic or structural link between the sporadic extraterritorial outbreaks of violence and the main body of the conflict. The application of this nexus requirement would of course depend on the facts of each particular case of sporadic spillover. In cases in which the nexus was lacking, and thus the violence could not be tied to an existing NIAC, and the spillover violence failed to independently reach a level of intensity and duration, the spillover violence would not be part of any legally cognizable NIAC and would be unregulated by IHL. The geographical scope of NIACs would accordingly largely resemble the geographical scope of IACs; just as fighting between, say, France and Germany could spill over onto Italian territory, with the IAC not being confined exclusively to French and German sovereign territory, so could a NIAC expand into something more than a purely internal conflict.

60   The second subtype of cross-border NIAC is that of foreign intervention: state A is engaged in internal conflict with armed group X on its own territory, and then invites state B to help it in the conflict against X, which B does on A's territory. The paradigmatic example is of course the US involvement in Afghanistan after the ousting of the Taliban regime, the establishment of a new Afghan Government, and its invitation to the US to assist it in its armed conflict against Al-Qaeda and the Taliban.[82] The ongoing conflict between the Afghan Government and the Taliban is an internal NIAC. As explained above, a foreign intervention on behalf of the country's Government does not *ipso facto* internationalize the NIAC. The US is, therefore, involved in a cross-border NIAC taking place in Afghanistan and not on its own soil.

61   Another variant of a foreign intervention scenario is when state B enters into protracted armed violence against armed group X on the territory of state A, but this time *without* A's invitation, as when Israel intervened in Lebanon against Hezbollah in 2006. Depending on whether the lack of state A's consent is to be given normative relevance in internationalizing the conflict, the conflict could be characterized either as a cross-border NIAC or as an IAC, again as explained above.

62   Not only is a combination of spillover and foreign intervention scenarios possible, but *any* spillover conflict which involves the forces of one state crossing onto the territory of another state is also a case of foreign intervention, with or without the territorial state's consent. Similarly, a foreign intervention may itself spill over, for example if state B intervenes in the conflict between state A and armed group X but that conflict crosses onto the territory of state C, or even onto the territory of more than one state. This is very much the case with the current engagement of the US in Afghanistan and the wider region. In Afghanistan, the US is involved in a NIAC between the Afghan Government and the Taliban. Frequently, however, the US conducts attacks, particularly drone strikes, against Al-Qaeda and Taliban targets on Pakistani territory, with or without the permission of the Pakistani authorities. One such attack was the operation of US special forces which led to the death of Osama bin Laden. For its part, Pakistan also fights its own militants, whose

---

[81] See Ch 4 of this volume.
[82] See, e.g., Vité, above n 4, at 73.

connections with the Afghan Taliban are not always clear, while the US has been using drone strikes against various Al-Qaeda affiliated groups in Yemen and Somalia.

Legally characterizing this politically undeniably connected jumble of conflicts is a difficult exercise. In doing so, it should first be borne in mind that it is entirely possible to have multiple and distinct parallel conflicts even in the same territory. Secondly, if the US engagement with armed groups in Pakistan reaches a level of protracted armed violence, it could be characterized as an independent NIAC, as would any such fighting between Pakistani forces and the armed groups. Alternatively, these operations could be considered as parts of the Afghan NIAC if the nexus criteria outlined above are met.

E. Mixed Conflicts

I have already dealt extensively with parallel or mixed armed conflicts throughout the preceding analysis. In complex conflicts fought between a variety of state and non-state actors, a mixed characterization may be unavoidable, as for example in Bosnia, Afghanistan, or Libya. Internationalizing the whole lot may be an appetizing prospect, as the whole structure—and accordingly the applicable law—is simplified.[83] That, however, may not always be possible, considering the criteria for internationalization that we have just examined. Similarly, as a matter of policy, treating a complex conflict purely as an IAC may risk imposing obligations on non-state actors that were made for and fit states, obligations that those non-state actors may well feel to be over-burdensome and hence simply ignore. Consequently, rather than treating a particular situation as a singular IAC, there may be sound reasons to treat it as a network of separate conflicts or bilateral relationships, whose characterization would depend foremost on the identity of the actors.[84] The downside of this approach is the increased complexity, and hence uncertainty, in the applicable law, where the law of NIACs diverges from that of IACs, mainly with regard to the qualification or status of persons, and consequently targeting and detention.

The possibility of mixed or parallel conflict is generally accepted in the case law, as for instance in *Tadić*. Perhaps the first such example was given by the ICJ in *Nicaragua*, when it stated that:

> The conflict between the *contras*' forces and those of the Government of Nicaragua is an armed conflict which is 'not of an international character'. The acts of the *contras* towards the Nicaraguan Government are therefore governed by the law applicable to conflicts of that character, whereas the actions of the United States in and against Nicaragua fall under the legal rules relating to international conflicts.[85]

Similarly, the 2008 Russia/Georgia conflict was undoubtedly an IAC with regard to the fighting between the forces of the two states. The situation is more complicated when it comes to the fighting between Georgian forces and those of the separatist entities of Abkhazia and South Ossetia, which is a prima facie NIAC. If either one of these entities managed to attain statehood during the conflict, it would have been internationalized and transformed into an IAC, but on the facts this was not the case, as even Russia at the

---

[83] Cf Holland, above n 4, at 177–80.
[84] See Schindler, above n 20, at 150; C. Greenwood, 'International Humanitarian Law and the *Tadić* Case', 7 *EJIL* (1996) 265, at 280; Kreß, above n 49, at 256–7.
[85] ICJ, *Nicaragua*, above n 37, para 219.

time did not recognize the statehood of the entities in question. If, on the other hand, Russia exercised the requisite level of control over the entities, the conflict would again be internationalized, and there would be a single IAC between Russia and Georgia. If it did not, the only option available is a mixed IAC/NIAC, with the two conflicts running in parallel.[86]

67   While acknowledging that it has not been without its opponents,[87] in my view the category of mixed conflicts is so well-established that I will not belabour it any further beyond the analysis already provided. Suffice it to say that mixed or parallel conflicts serve as a fall-back category of sorts in cases in which arguments in favour of internationalization fail. Accordingly, those authors who see the process of internationalization in much broader terms than presented in this chapter will also see the category of mixed conflicts as either misplaced or undesirable, and are at least in part so arguing because of the regulatory complexity of such conflicts. But if the analysis of the current scope of the two main processes of internationalization—under the basic IAC definition or through redefinition—is correct, then the incidence of mixed conflicts will invariably be relatively high.

F. Critical Assessment

68   The preceding discussion has shown that the Conventions' binary IAC/NIAC framework is capable of accommodating various unorthodox types of conflict. Yet the question remains whether that framework is suited to its purpose, and whether the binary mould should be broken rather than refined. The increased political relevance of the activities of transnational armed or terrorist groups, more frequent cross-border interventions of states against such groups, and particularly the controversies regarding the legal characterization of the US 'global war on terror', prompted some authors to contemplate a reform of the IAC/NIAC duopoly of armed conflict by introducing a third category, variously called transnational armed conflict (TAC) or extra-state armed conflict.[88] Different authors offer different reasons for and different conceptions of this third category; some use it only descriptively (which is not problematic in and of itself), others view it as a fully fledged category independent of IAC and NIAC. The purported third category of armed conflict raises two basic questions that I shall try to address briefly. First, *de lege lata*, does this category exist in the modern *jus in bello*? Secondly, *de lege ferenda*, should it exist even if we do not already have it?

69   The first of these questions is easier to answer. Hardly anybody suggests that this new type of conflict already exists as a distinct threshold in positive IHL, independent of IAC

---

[86] This was also the approach of the EU-established Independent International Fact-Finding Mission on the Conflict in Georgia (IIFFMCG), although it declined to make any firm factual conclusions with regard to Russian control over the two entities—see the IIFFMCG Report, September 2009, vol II, available at <http://www.ceiig.ch/pdf/IIFFMCG_Volume_II.pdf>, at 298 ff.

[87] See, e.g., T. Meron, 'Classification of Armed Conflict in the Former Yugoslavia: *Nicaragua*'s Fallout', 92 *AJIL* (1998) 236.

[88] See, e.g., G. Corn, 'Making the Case for Conflict Bifurcation in Afghanistan: Transnational Armed Conflict, Al Qaida, and the Limits of the Associated Militia Concept', 85 *US Naval War College International Law Studies* (2009) 181; G. Corn and E. Talbot, 'Transnational Armed Conflict: A Principled Approach to the Regulation of Counter-Terror Combat Operations', 42 *Israel Law Review* (2009) 46; R. Schöndorf, 'Extra-State Armed Conflicts: Is there a Need for a New Legal Regime?', 37 *New York University Journal of International Law and Politics* (2003) 61; E. Posner, 'Terrorism and the Laws of War', 5 *Chicago JIL* (2005) 421.

and NIAC. It would hardly be reasonably possible to argue differently. A third category cannot be inferred from the treaty rules of IHL. None of the conventions mentions or regulates it. There is no state practice or *opinio juris* which would suggest that such a category of conflicts emerged in customary international law independently of conventional IHL, or that states actually desire the emergence of such a category. This is, of course, not to deny the controversies regarding the qualification of the 'war on terror' or other recent conflicts between states and non-state actors. But as far as states have formally expressed their positions regarding these controversies, they have exclusively limited themselves to arguing about qualification under the existing IAC/NIAC framework, as is well shown by the example of the US, to which we shall turn shortly. One cannot impute to states legal positions that they have themselves not taken.[89] Hence, at least for the time being, any discussion about TAC or some other third category can be had only at the level of *de lege ferenda* policy arguments either in favour or against its emergence.

But even if we do not already have TAC, the question remains whether we need it. This question is clearly far more open to disagreement than the first. There are two related and overlapping reasons, or groups of reasons, for arguing in favour of such a category. First, if the existing regime has gaps in coverage, that is, if there are some situations that for all practical intents and purposes look like armed conflict yet legally are *not* armed conflict because they are neither IAC nor NIAC, this is something that we need to remedy, if nothing else then for humanitarian reasons.[90] Secondly, even if there are no gaps in coverage, the transnational context may warrant the modification of existing substantive rules so as to provide a better fit with reality and/or to remove some of the constraints of the IAC/NIAC binary.

Authors advocating for TAC point out that the responsiveness of IHL to new realities is precisely what has kept this body of law current and relevant.[91] While it is probably true that the drafters of the Conventions and Protocols did not have cross-border armed conflicts between states and non-state armed groups in mind, their novelty is nonetheless exaggerated; their incidence has been growing for at least 30 years.[92] States have had plenty of time to create special treaty or customary rules governing these conflicts if they deemed it necessary. What *is* relatively new is the increasing political relevance of these conflicts, which now have bearing on the interests of the most powerful members of the international community. But even in the past decade states have not shown a particular desire for a third legal category.

In that regard, although the Common Article 3 notion of NIAC was clearly intended to cover situations of internal strife, and it would be ahistorical to claim otherwise, this does not mean that the text of the treaty, its object and purpose, and its customary gloss cannot reasonably apply to cross-border situations.[93] The direction of both state practice and scholarship has indeed been towards such stretching of the idea of NIAC, the

---

[89] ICJ, *Nicaragua*, above n 37, para 207. For discussion, see D. Kritsiotis, 'Arguments of Mass Confusion', 15 *EJIL* (2004) 233, at 238.

[90] See, e.g., Pejic, above n 28, at 203 (discussing the 'gap theory').

[91] See, e.g., Schöndorf, above n 88, at 51; Corn, above n 88, at 184.

[92] For the enumeration of the most prominent examples prior to 9/11, see Schöndorf, above n 88, at 9; H.P. Gasser, 'Internationalized Non-International Armed Conflicts: Case Studies of Afghanistan, Kampuchea and Lebanon', 33 *American University Law Review* 145 (1983), at 155–6; C. Le Mon, 'Unilateral Intervention by Invitation in Civil War: The Effective Control Test Tested', 35 *New York University Journal of International Law and Politics* (2003) 741.

[93] See also Lubell, above n 35, at 122–3.

historical intentions of the drafters notwithstanding. And this *is* new. Admittedly, it is somewhat artificial to call a situation in which the US fights the Taliban in Afghanistan, or Israel fights Hezbollah in Lebanon, a 'non-international armed conflict'. But this does not mean that the category does not do the job, together with the remainder of the IAC/NIAC conceptual apparatus, i.e. internationalized and mixed conflicts.[94] If this apparatus is applied as suggested in this chapter, few, if any, gaps will remain, particularly when it comes to more orthodox or large-scale instances of violence, as in the Israel/Hezbollah/Lebanon and Colombia/FARC/Ecuador examples. But this serves only to better delineate the two lines of inquiry identified above: even accepting all the varieties of cross-border NIAC, will there still be situations which will not be but should be characterized as an armed conflict? And even if not, could TAC introduce new rules that would overcome any substantive deficiencies in treating these situations as NIACs?

73   In order to proceed along these two lines of inquiry, we must first understand some relatively recent shifts in the underlying legal and political dynamics. As originally designed, and through most of its history, IHL was seen by states as a system of *limitations* on their sovereignty and freedom of action, particularly so when it comes to the law of internal armed conflict. In other words, the *baseline* for international regulation from the classical period onwards was that states had the unrestrained freedom to wage war, both against each other and internally, and the law of war evolved precisely to impose such restraints, first and foremost in the inter-state context. States resisted the regulation of internal conflict because of the fear—well founded or not—that it would impose limits on how they could deal with rebels, and confer on these rebels some rights in international law. It is this sovereignty-induced concern of states that explains the IAC/NIAC dichotomy in the modern law and the principal features of NIACs, such as the *Tadić* intensity, organization, and duration criteria, and the distinction between NIACs and mere riots or disturbances. Hence, it was rarely, if ever, in the interest of a state embroiled in internal conflict to recognize the existence of such conflict—it simply *did not want* IHL to apply.[95] This is why, for instance, the UK consistently denied the existence of a NIAC in Northern Ireland, or why it made a reservation to Article 1(4) AP I which explicitly excluded acts of terrorism, whether concerted or in isolation, from the scope of armed conflict.[96]

74   Now, however, human rights have gradually replaced, or are in the process of replacing, the idea of unrestrained freedom of action as the baseline for regulation, as much *culturally* as formally. Instead of IHL being the only set of limitations on states, a more rigid, demanding, and legalistic set of limitations has emerged, particularly in the internal context. States, or at least some states, have accordingly stopped seeing IHL as a constraining body of rules whose application they want to avoid in their engagements with non-state actors.[97] Rather, they have progressively started seeing IHL as an *authorizing* body of rules liberating them or derogating from human rights or other constraints, often on the

---

[94] See also Pejic, above n 28, at 204–5.   [95] See Sassòli, above n 74, at 7–8.

[96] 'It is the understanding of the United Kingdom that the term "armed conflict" of itself and in its context denotes a situation of a kind which is not constituted by the commission of ordinary crimes including acts of terrorism whether concerted or in isolation. The United Kingdom will not, in relation to any situation in which it is itself involved, consider itself bound in consequence of any declaration purporting to be made under paragraph 3 of Article 96 unless the United Kingdom shall have expressly recognised that it has been made by a body which is genuinely an authority representing a people engaged in an armed conflict of the type to which Article 1, paragraph 4, applies.' Reservation of 28 January 1998, available at <http://www.icrc.org/ihl.nsf/NORM/0A9E03F0F2EE757CC1256402003FB6D2?OpenDocument>.

[97] Cf Lubell, above n 35, at 123–4.

dubious basis of the *lex specialis* principle.⁹⁸ For example, while IHL targeting or detention rules evolved as limitations (e.g. you must not deliberately target civilians), they are now seen as permissive rules authorizing departures from human rights (e.g. you may kill an enemy fighter even if he does not pose an imminent threat; you may detain preventively for reasons of security even if human rights law generally prohibits preventive detention).⁹⁹

To see how these dynamics evolved we need only look at US policy post-9/11.¹⁰⁰ The US Government from the outset decided to cast the Al-Qaeda threat and US response as a 'war' for both domestic and international purposes, in order to get the detention and targeting authority that it thought it needed, and thus derogate from any applicable rules of domestic constitutional law as well as international human rights law. The moniker 'global war on terror' denoted a supposed single IHL conflict between the US on one side and Al-Qaeda and its affiliates on the other. Initially, the US characterized this conflict as an IAC, albeit a strange sort of IAC which transcended the Common Article 2 definition since one of its parties was not a state. In the US Government's view, the Common Article 2 definition did not create 'field pre-emption', i.e. was not all-encompassing; put in more traditional international legalese, the notion of IAC was wider under customary law.¹⁰¹ This was a completely ahistorical argument; the notion of IAC was *invented* in Geneva and replaced the equally inter-state notion of war, while there was no evidence that it was redefined either through treaty or through custom in this particular fashion.¹⁰² The Administration also considered that the conflict could not be a NIAC as it transcended the borders of a single state.¹⁰³ In *Hamdan*, the US Supreme Court rejected the Government's arguments and found that the conflict with Al-Qaeda could not be an IAC, and, in an ambiguous holding that we have already examined, applied Common Article 3.¹⁰⁴ The position of both the Bush and Obama Administrations post-*Hamdan* has hence been that the conflict with Al-Qaeda is some sort of *global* NIAC, which is territorially unlimited in scope.

Even under the framework outlined above, which allows for various kinds of cross-border NIACs, the idea of a global NIAC makes sense only as an oxymoron. Any NIAC requires the existence of protracted armed violence which, by definition, has to take place *somewhere*, i.e. has to be localized at least to the territory of one state. As we have seen, that violence can spill over to the territory of another state (which need not necessarily be adjacent to the primary state), but there has to be a *nexus* to the protracted violence in the primary state. Thus, while one can safely speak of a NIAC between the US and the Taliban

---

⁹⁸ See further M. Milanovic, 'Norm Conflicts, International Humanitarian Law and Human Rights Law', in O. Ben-Naftali (ed), *International Humanitarian Law and International Human Rights Law* (Oxford: OUP, 2011) 95.

⁹⁹ See, e.g., J. Bellinger and V. Padmanabhan, 'Detention Operations in Contemporary Conflicts: Four Challenges for the Geneva Conventions and Other Existing Law', 105 *AJIL* (2011) 201 (repeatedly referring to targeting and detention authority under IHL, and identifying gaps of such authority in NIACs, which they feel is needed). See also Kreß, above n 49, at 260 (referring to states 'availing themselves of the wider powers they can derive from the application of the law of non-international armed conflict (compared with international human rights law) than they are concerned by the restraining effect of the ensuing obligations').

¹⁰⁰ In that regard, see esp K. Anderson, 'Targeted Killing and Drone Warfare: How We Came to Debate Whether There Is a "Legal Geography of War"', Hoover Institution (2011), available at <http://ssrn.com/abstract=1824783>.

¹⁰¹ *Hamdan v Rumsfeld*, Government Brief on the Merits, available at <http://www.hamdanvrumsfeld.com/HamdanSGmeritsbrief.pdf>, at 26.

¹⁰² See also Kreß, above n 49, at 255; Sassòli, above n 74, at 4–5; Lubell, above n 35, at 96.

¹⁰³ See Pejic, above n 28, at 195.   ¹⁰⁴ See MN 6.

and other armed groups in Afghanistan, and once in Iraq, and while that conflict can spill over into (say) Pakistan or any other country, the existing legal framework does not seem to allow for a construction as amorphous as a global NIAC,[105] particularly one in which a loose terrorist network such as Al-Qaeda is treated as a single organizational entity and belligerent party.[106]

77 The current IAC/NIAC framework would thus not cover isolated or sporadic instances of use of force. Yet a case could be made that IHL *should* cover even such isolated targeted killings. Especially if the argument that human rights treaties apply extraterritorially is rejected, IHL could provide states not merely with the authorization to use deadly force that they desire, but also with some meaningful humanitarian protection.[107] And it is perhaps precisely the TAC category that could fill this gap, in essence serving the same purpose as the current US construction of a global NIAC while explicitly dispensing with the *Tadić* criteria of intensity and duration. A TAC could thus be defined as any use of force between a state and a non-state actor outside that state's borders.

78 The desirability of such a low threshold of TAC is ultimately a matter of policy and value judgement. I at least remain unpersuaded. To the extent that there are any gaps in need of filling, human rights—applied flexibly—appear to be far better suited to the task,[108] as do other branches of international and municipal law.[109] Similarly, while it is easy to see why a low threshold of TAC would be in the interest of states wishing to use force extraterritorially against non-state actors, it is also hard to see any principled reason why the higher *Tadić* threshold should remain for instances of larger-scale violence, external or internal, and how one could prevent the collapse of any NIAC threshold altogether.[110]

79 In sum, the existing binary framework of IHL is capable of responding to the challenges posed by modern conflicts. I say so without making an appeal to some sort of overly defensive conservatism. While the character of modern armed conflicts has changed significantly, and the political, technological, strategic, and tactical changes may have been great, they do not *ipso facto* require radical changes to the existing legal framework as it has evolved through state practice. Despite some viable policy arguments in favour of recognizing TAC as a third type of conflict, the arguments against it are stronger, even if reasonable people may disagree.

MARKO MILANOVIC

---

[105] See Y. Dinstein, *The Conduct of Hostilities under the Law of International Armed Conflict* (2nd edn, Cambridge: CUP, 2010), at 56, 'from the vantage point of international law […] a non-international armed conflict cannot possibly assume global dimensions'.

[106] See also Kreß, above n 49, at 261; Vité, above n 4, at 92–3; Pejic, above n 28, at 196; Lubell, above n 35, at 114–21.

[107] Cf R. Chesney, 'Who May Be Killed? Anwar al-Awlaki as a Case Study in the International Legal Regulation of Lethal Force', 13 *YIHL* (2010) 3, at 36–8.

[108] See further M. Milanovic, *Extraterritorial Application of Human Rights Treaties: Law, Principles, and Poli* (Oxford: OUP, 2011).

[109] See also Sassòli, above n 74, at 25–7.

[110] See also R. Geiss, 'Asymmetric Conflict Structures', 88 *IRRC* 864 (2006) 757; Lubell, above n 35, at 129–31.

Chapter 3. The Temporal Scope of Application of the Conventions

	MN
A. Introduction	1
B. Meaning and Application	8
I. International armed conflicts	8
a. Beginning of applicability	8
b. End of applicability	14
II. Non-international armed conflicts	20
a. Beginning of applicability	20
b. End of applicability	26
III. Peacekeeping operations	28
IV. Provisions to be implemented in peacetime	30
C. Legal Consequences of a Violation	33
I. International responsibility	33
II. Individual criminal responsibility	34
D. Critical Assessment	36

Select Bibliography

Cullen, A., *The Concept of Non-International Armed Conflict in International Humanitarian Law* (Cambridge: CUP, 2010), at 117–58

Dinstein, Y., *War, Aggression and Self-Defence* (4th edn, Cambridge: CUP, 2005), at 30–59

Dinstein, Y., *The International Law of Belligerent Occupation* (Cambridge: CUP, 2009), at 31–66, 270–85

Greenwood, C., 'Scope of Application of Humanitarian Law', in D. Fleck (ed), *The Handbook of International Humanitarian Law* (2nd edn, Oxford: OUP, 2008) 45

Grignon, J., *L'applicabilité temporelle du droit international humanitaire* (Geneva: Schulthess and LGDJ, 2014)

Koutroulis, V., *Le début et la fin du droit de l'occupation* (Paris: Pedone, 2010)

Moir, L., *The Law of Internal Armed Conflict* (Cambridge: CUP, 2002), at 30–88

Provost, R., *International Human Rights and Humanitarian Law* (Cambridge: CUP, 2002), at 152–81

Siegrist, M., *The Functional Beginning of Belligerent Occupation* (Geneva: The Graduate Institute eCahiers no 7, 2011)

A. Introduction

The words 'peacetime' and 'wartime' have traditionally been used to signify two (suppos- 1 edly) well-delimited conditions of international relations, each one governed by different normative systems, both pertaining to international law: the 'law of peace', and the 'law of war' (i.e., the law of armed conflict, or international humanitarian law: IHL[1]). In order

---

[1] For the purposes of the present chapter these two expressions are used as equivalent. In its *Nuclear Weapons Opinion*, the International Court of Justice (ICJ) distinguished between 'the law applicable in armed conflict' and 'humanitarian law', the former comprising the latter; however, the ICJ recognized 'the intrinsically

to determine their applicability,[2] it is essential to identify the temporal dimension of these two situations. Given that contemporary international law prohibits the use of armed force, 'peacetime' is considered the ordinary condition of the international community, the law of peace applying in its entirety to inter-state relations. If an armed conflict occurs, the law of armed conflict must be applied from the beginning until the end, when the law of peace resumes in full effect.[3] Several types of armed conflict exist (and often intermingle) and are governed by different bodies of rules. Therefore, the beginning and end of applicability of IHL greatly depend on the nature of the armed conflict.

2 Regarding the beginning of applicability, the old 'Geneva law' (Conventions of 22 August 1864, 6 July 1906, and 27 July 1929) did not specify its temporal scope of application. In spite of this, like the 'Hague law' (exemplified by the 1899 and 1907 Conventions respecting the laws and customs of war on land and their annexed Regulations), the Conventions were indisputably deemed to apply in 'wartime', i.e. in the case of inter-state war. At that time, IHL conventions did not cover internal conflicts such as civil wars; they were considered internal matters falling within the domestic jurisdiction of the territorial state.

3 The four Geneva Conventions of 12 August 1949 substantially developed the rules on the temporal scope of application of IHL, with several provisions expressly devoted to the beginning and end of application. Common Article 2 enumerates three situations in which the Geneva Conventions apply, i.e. declared war between states parties, armed conflict between states parties irrespective of the recognition of a state of war, and occupation of territory, even when met with no armed resistance. When an armed conflict occurs between a state party and a non-party state, the Conventions become applicable if the non-party state accepts and applies their provisions.[4] Article 6 of Geneva Convention (GC) IV further provides that applicability of the Convention starts 'from the outset' of any conflict or occupation mentioned in Common Article 2.

4 States which have ratified Additional Protocol I (AP I) are bound to apply the Conventions and the Protocol to a fourth situation, i.e. 'armed conflicts in which peoples are fighting against colonial domination and alien occupation and against racist regimes in the exercise of their right of self-determination' (Article 1(4) AP I).[5] Article 3 AP I further explains that the Conventions and the Protocol shall apply 'from the beginning' of all situations referred to in Common Article 2 and Article 1 AP I.

5 Regarding the end of applicability, both GC I and GC III stipulate that they apply to protected persons who have fallen 'into the hands' (Article 5 GC I) or 'into the power' (Article 5 GC III) of the enemy until their final release or repatriation. Article 6 GC IV establishes two different time limits: the 'general close of military operations' for the

---

humanitarian character [...] which permeates the entire law of armed conflict' (ICJ, *Legality of the Threat or Use of Nuclear Weapons*, Advisory Opinion, 8 July 1996, paras 36, 42, and 75–9).

[2] While applicability envisages the relevance of a regulatory regime to certain facts, application properly refers to the functioning of the substantive rules in a given situation. See R. Kolb and R. Hyde, *An Introduction to the International Law of Armed Conflicts* (Oxford: Hart Publishing, 2008), at 99–100. As a rule, applicability and application coincide temporally. The Geneva Conventions and Protocols use 'application' or 'applicable' but never 'applicability'.

[3] The law of peace and the law of armed conflict, however, are not mutually exclusive. For example, the greater part of international human rights law continues to apply during armed conflict, whilst IHL might provide further protection to victims beyond the end of the armed conflict (see Ch 35 of this volume).

[4] See Ch 1, MN 12–15, of this volume.

[5] For a discussion of Art 1(4) situations related to National Liberation Movements engaged in self-determination struggles, see Ch 1, MN 49–54, of this volume.

territory of states parties to the conflict; and 'one year after the general close of military operations' for occupied territory (see Chapter 74, MN 4–10, of this volume). These stipulations, which depart from customary international law, were based on the view that the application of the Convention for a longer period of time would not be justified in situations like Germany and Japan after the Second World War.[6] However, a number of provisions on the protection of civilians continue to apply as long as the Occupying Power 'exercises the functions of government' in occupied territory. Additional Protocol I also refers to the 'general close of military operations' to determine the end of application of the Conventions and the Protocol (Article 3(b) AP I). Concerning occupation, however, AP I replaces the one-year term with the 'termination of occupation' (see Chapter 74, MN 11–20, of this volume). In addition, both GC IV and AP I prescribe, for the benefit of certain persons, their applicability until the 'final release, repatriation or re-establishment' of protected persons.

One of the main innovations of the Geneva Conventions was Common Article 3, the 'Convention in miniature', dealing with non-international armed conflicts (NIACs). Common Article 3 establishes neither the beginning nor the end of applicability. The beginning must therefore correspond to the start of the conflict, but this means determining what a NIAC is in this context (discussed below, MN 20–25). However, Common Article 3 also stipulates that the parties to the conflict should endeavour to conclude special agreements in order to bring into force the whole, or part, of the provisions of the Geneva Conventions (see Chapter 25 of this volume). Consequently, the conclusion of such an agreement would represent the beginning of applicability of the provisions envisaged. Additional Protocol II (AP II) of 8 June 1977 does not expressly establish the beginning and end of applicability. However, Article 2(2) AP II refers to the 'end of the armed conflict' when it states that persons whose liberty has been restricted must continue to enjoy protection after the conflict. 6

Contemporary practice shows that armed conflicts often assume different characteristics over time, shifting from being non-international to transnational or of a mixed nature (see Chapter 2 of this volume). For instance, the conflict in Afghanistan (2001) shifted from non-international to international and then reverted to non-international; in Iraq (2003), a NIAC persisted after the end of the international armed conflict (IAC).[7] These armed conflicts raise specific problems with respect to the beginning and end of application of different sets of rules. Clearly, fractioning the legal regime applicable to an armed conflict may be a solution *ex post*, but often implies endless controversies and insurmountable practical difficulties in the field. This explains the trend towards the merging of the law of NIAC into the law of IAC, prompted particularly by the International Criminal Tribunal for the former Yugoslavia (ICTY) over the last decades.[8] However, the distinction is still effective on at least one issue, i.e. the recognition of the status of the prisoner of war (POW). Since there are no legitimate combatants in NIACs, it is essential 7

---

[6] See Pictet Commentary GC IV, at 63.

[7] See D. Jinks, 'The Temporal Scope of Application of International Humanitarian Law in Contemporary Conflicts', Background Paper prepared for the Informal High-Level Expert Meeting on the Reaffirmation and Development of International Humanitarian Law, Cambridge, 27–9 January 2003, available at <http://www.gistprobono.org/sitebuildercontent/sitebuilderfiles/scopeofihl.pdf>, at 9; E. David, *Principes du droit des conflits armés* (4th edn, Brussels: Bruylant, 2008), at 129–30.

[8] See C. Greenwood, 'The Development of International Humanitarian Law by the International Criminal Tribunal for the Former Yugoslavia', 2 *Max Planck Yearbook of United Nations Law* (1998) 97, at 130; Kolb and Hyde, above n 2, at 258.

to determine the precise moment when a NIAC becomes international, and vice versa, in order to trigger the application either of Common Article 3, or of the whole contents of the Geneva Conventions.

B. Meaning and Application

I. International armed conflicts

a. Beginning of applicability

8   Traditionally, a 'state of war' began by a formal declaration or an ultimatum announcing a conditional declaration of war, as agreed upon by states parties to Hague Convention III relative to the Opening of Hostilities of 18 October 1907. Such declarations triggered the application of the law of IAC. The provisions of Hague Convention III, however, did not become norms of customary international law. Instead, it was recognized that 'the *jus in bello* is brought into operation as soon as war in the material sense is embarked upon, despite the absence of a technical state of war'.[9] Common Article 2 establishes that the Geneva Conventions apply both to 'declared wars' and to 'any other armed conflict' which may arise between one or more states parties, 'even if the state of war is not recognized by one of them'. Interpreting the wording of this provision literally could lead to an understanding that if both belligerents deny the state of war, the Conventions are not applicable. A well-established interpretation, however, holds that the intention of the belligerent states is entirely immaterial.[10]

9   Contemporary practice confirms that declarations of war are irrelevant for the beginning of applicability of the Geneva Conventions to IACs. For example, during the eight-year Iraq–Iran war, Iran declared war on Iraq only in 1989. In spite of this, both states availed themselves of their belligerent rights from the time of the Iraqi attack on 22 September 1980.[11] Additionally, the initial denial of the state of war between the UK and Argentina by the United Kingdom (UK) Government did not affect the immediate application of the Geneva Conventions at the outbreak of the Falkland/Malvinas conflict.[12]

10   The Geneva Conventions do not specify any threshold for the existence of an IAC. Most authors consider that any use of armed force between states, irrespective of its intensity, duration, or scale, triggers the application of the Conventions.[13] Others stress that states are not always willing to qualify isolated incidents as an armed conflict.[14] Military

---

[9] Y. Dinstein, *War, Aggression and Self-Defence* (4th edn, Cambridge: CUP, 2005), at 10. (For a definition of 'international armed conflict', see Ch 1 of this volume.)

[10] Dinstein, above n 9, at 17. See also Federal Ministry of Defence of the Federal Republic of Germany, *Humanitarian Law in Armed Conflicts—Manual*, VR II, 3 August 1992 (English version of the German triservice manual ZDv 15/2 *Humanitäres Völkerrecht in bewaffneten Konflikten—Handbuch*, issued in August 1992), para 203, available at <http://www.humanitaeres-voelkerrecht.de/ManualZDv15.2.pdf>.

[11] M. Mancini, *Stato di guerra e conflitto armato nel diritto internazionale* (Torino: G. Giappichelli, 2009), at 123.

[12] L.C. Green, *The Contemporary Law of Armed Conflict* (3rd edn, Manchester: Juris Publishing, Manchester University Press, 2008), at 92–3.

[13] See, e.g. Kolb and Hyde, above n 2, at 101; S. Vité, 'Typology of Armed Conflicts in International Humanitarian Law: Legal Concepts and Actual Situations', 91 *IRRC* 873 (2009) 59, at 72; Y. Dinstein, *The Conduct of Hostilities under the Law of International Armed Conflict* (2nd edn, Cambridge: CUP, 2010), at 28–9; Ch 1, MN 20–38, of this volume.

[14] C. Greenwood, 'Scope of Application of Humanitarian Law', in D. Fleck (ed), *The Handbook of International Humanitarian Law* (2nd edn, Oxford: OUP, 2008) 45, at 48; A. Paulus and M. Vashakmadze,

manuals seem to support the first interpretation,[15] as does the ICTY Appeals Chamber in its famous 1995 *Tadić* Decision (Interlocutory Appeal on Jurisdiction), in which it states that 'an armed conflict exists whenever there is a resort to armed force between states'.[16] As soon as a person (whether wounded, sick, shipwrecked, combatant, or civilian) is affected as a result of conflict, the relevant provisions of the Geneva Conventions are applicable.[17] This functional approach to the beginning of applicability of the Geneva Conventions has the merit of gradually bringing the humanitarian machinery into operation in order to ensure the best protection to individuals. Different problems arise with respect to the beginning of the applicability of GC IV in the case of occupation (with or without armed resistance), and the ensuing problems concerning the traditional distinction between invasion and occupation (on these issues, see Chapter 67 of this volume).

i. Ratification, accession, succession, and special agreements

As international treaties, the Geneva Conventions are binding upon their parties. Accordingly, for the Conventions to bind states in conflict, they must have ratified or acceded to them. This may seem immaterial, since the equivalence of the Geneva Conventions to customary international law is widely recognized.[18] The issue, however, becomes relevant in the case of newly formed states. The Eritrea–Ethiopia Claims Commission (EECC), established in 2000 to adjudicate claims resulting from violations of IHL or other violations of international law during the 1998–2000 war between Eritrea and Ethiopia, maintained that since Eritrea had made clear that it did not consider itself bound by the Geneva Conventions as a successor state to Ethiopia, the Conventions became applicable only from the date of Eritrea's accession.[19] 11

As for NIACs, Common Article 3 recommends that parties to a NIAC should endeavour to bring into force all or part of the other provisions of the Geneva Conventions by means of special agreements. Each special agreement will determine the beginning of applicability of the rules agreed upon (see Chapter 25 of this volume). Any non-state armed group may enter into this category of agreement. For example, in 1991 and 1992, all parties to the conflict in the former Yugoslavia entered into a number of special agreements under the auspices of the International Committee of the Red Cross (ICRC), dealing particularly with the exchange and transfer of prisoners.[20] On the other hand, only national liberation movements may make declarations pursuant to Article 96(3) AP I undertaking to apply the Geneva Conventions and the Protocol, which are thus brought into force for that conflict with 'immediate effect'.[21] 12

'Asymmetrical War and the Notion of Armed Conflict—A Tentative Conceptualization', 91 *IRRC* 873 (2009) 95, at 101.

[15] *Humanitarian Law in Armed Conflicts—Manual*, above n 10, para 202; Canada National Defence, *Law of Armed Conflict at the Operational and Tactical Levels*, 2001-08-13, B-GJ-005-104/FP-021 (2004), para 1105.

[16] ICTY, *The Prosecutor v Duško Tadić*, Decision on the Defence Motion for Interlocutory Appeal, IT-94-1-A-R72, 2 October 1995 (hereinafter 1995 *Tadić* Decision), para 70.

[17] See Pictet Commentary GC I, at 32–3.

[18] ICJ, *Legality of the Threat or Use of Nuclear Weapons*, above n 1, para 79.

[19] EECC, *Prisoners of War—Ethiopia's Claim 4*, Partial Award, 1 July 2003, paras 23–8. See David, above n 7, at 203–4.

[20] See Kolb and Hyde, above n 2, at 178; further examples are given by S. Rondeau, 'Participation of Armed Groups in the Development of the Law Applicable to Armed Conflicts', 93 *IRRC* 883 (2011) 649, at 664.

[21] See further Ch 1, MN 49–54, of this volume for national liberation movements.

ii. Beginning of applicability with regard to protected persons

13 Individuals benefit from the protection of the Geneva Conventions as soon as they find themselves in one of the situations envisaged by the Conventions, designated by the expressions 'into the hands of the enemy'[22] or 'into the power of the enemy'.[23] Regarding GC I, GC II, and GC III, this language suggests that the relevant Convention applies to protected persons immediately upon capture by the enemy belligerent.[24] Article 4 GC IV is interpreted in a more general sense, setting out the criteria of nationality for persons protected under the Convention. Any person in the territory belonging to, or under the control of, a belligerent of which he or she is not a national is a protected person, even if that belligerent does not actually exercise its power over him or her.[25] Besides, the ICTY held that in contemporary IACs, the formal requirement of nationality is not entirely adequate to define protected persons, since 'ethnicity may become determinative of national allegiance'. As a consequence, 'allegiance to a Party to a conflict and, correspondingly, control by this Party over persons in a given territory may be regarded as the crucial test'.[26] In later judgments, the Tribunal confirmed and elaborated this assertion,[27] and more recently the Pre-Trial Chamber of the International Criminal Court (ICC) has taken the same view.[28] The particular question of when the rules of GC IV begin to apply on occupied territories is dealt with in Chapter 67 of this volume.

b. End of applicability

14 Traditionally, a state of war was terminated by a treaty of peace between the belligerent states.[29] Given the fact that the issuance of a declaration of war has tended to disappear, current practice offers only a few examples of such treaties, such as the peace treaties concluded by Israel with Egypt in 1979 and with Jordan in 1994.[30] Armistice, formerly a type of suspension of hostilities, became a method for terminating IACs, for example the Arab–Israeli War of 1948 and the Korean War of 1950–3.[31] Currently, even when an IAC is formally terminated by treaty, reference is not made to the end of war but instead to the 'durable cessation' or the 'permanent termination' of hostilities between parties.[32] Various types of cease-fire agreements may also temporarily suspend hostilities, which may or may not last

---

[22] Art 5 GC I and Art 5 para 2 GC III. [23] Art 12 GC II and Art 5 para 1 GC III.

[24] Pictet Commentary GC III, at 74; and R. Provost, *International Human Rights and Humanitarian Law* (Cambridge: CUP, 2002), at 250.

[25] Pictet Commentary GC IV, 47. See, for a definition of 'protected civilian', Ch 55 of this volume.

[26] ICTY, *The Prosecutor v Duško Tadić*, Appeals Chamber Judgment, IT-94-1-A, 15 July 1999, para 166.

[27] ICTY, *The Prosecutor v Zlatko Aleksovski*, Appeals Chamber Judgment, IT-95-14/1-A, 24 March 2000, para 151; *The Prosecutor v Zdravko Mucić et al ('Čelebići Camp')*, Appeals Chamber Judgment, IT-96-21-A, 20 February 2001, para 84; *The Prosecutor v Mladen Naletilić and Vinko Martinović*, Appeals Chamber Judgment, IT-98-34-A, 3 May 2006, para 20.

[28] ICC, *The Prosecutor v Germain Katanga and Mathieu Ngudjolo Chui*, ICC-01/04-01/07, Decision on the confirmation of charges, 30 September 2008, para 292.

[29] See Dinstein, above n 9 at 34–42; Greenwood, above n 14, at 70–1.

[30] 18 *ILM* (1079) 362–93; 34 *ILM* (1995) 43–66. While the treaty between Israel and Egypt expressly refers to the termination of the state of war (Art 1.1), the treaty between Israel and Jordan recalls the (previously declared) termination of the state of belligerency and decides the establishment of peace (preambular para 7 and Art 1). See David, above n 7, at 152.

[31] See Green, above n 12, at 106–8.

[32] See the General Framework Agreement for Peace in Bosnia and Herzegovina of 14 December 1995 (Annex 1A) Art I.2.a, available at <http://www.ohr.int/dpa/default.asp?content_id=380>, and the Agreement Between the Government of the Federal Democratic Republic of Ethiopia and the Government of the State of Eritrea of 12 December 2000 (A./55/686-O/2000/1183, Annex) Art 1. See Mancini, above n 11, at 129–30 and 136.

until an armistice or a peace agreement is reached.³³ However, the end of applicability of the Geneva Conventions does not automatically ensue from the existence of the instruments mentioned above. As the 1995 *Tadić* Decision clearly stated, as far as IACs are concerned, the application of IHL (and therefore also of the Geneva Conventions) 'extends beyond the cessation of hostilities until a general conclusion of peace is reached'.³⁴ Accordingly, a mere cease-fire, an armistice, or even a peace treaty could not suspend or limit the applicability of IHL when hostilities continue or resume.³⁵ After President Bush declared an end to major combat operations in Iraq on 1 May 2003, military activities nevertheless persisted between coalition forces and Iraqi opposition fighters.³⁶ As a consequence, the United Nations Security Council, while recognizing the role of the United States (US) and the UK as Occupying Powers, nevertheless called upon all parties ('all concerned') to 'comply fully with their obligations under international law', mentioning not only the Geneva Conventions, but also 'combat law' as codified in the 1907 Hague Regulations.³⁷

i. End of applicability of Geneva Conventions I–III

The rationale of the Geneva Conventions is to provide a functional termination of applicability, depending on the situation of the protected persons.³⁸ According to Article 5 GC I, the Convention is applicable until the 'final repatriation' of the protected persons. Thus, as long as some wounded and sick are retained by the adverse party (e.g., for medical reasons) after the end of hostilities, they continue to enjoy the protection provided by the Convention.³⁹ Nevertheless, '[w]hile in enemy hands, the wounded and sick—who are also prisoners of war—enjoy protection under both the First and the Third Conventions. Once they have regained their health, only the Third Convention, relative to the treatment of prisoners of war, applies.'⁴⁰

Article 5 GC III establishes that the Convention remains applicable until the 'final release and repatriation' of POWs, who as a rule must be repatriated 'without delay after the cessation of active hostilities' (Article 118 GC III). The related questions, including the relevance of the refusal of POWs to be repatriated, are discussed elsewhere in this Commentary (see Chapter 51 of this volume). Notwithstanding the absolute obligation laid down by GC III, state practice demonstrates that release and repatriation of POWs often takes a long time. Striking examples are the lengthy process of repatriating POWs from the 1980–8 Iran–Iraq war,⁴¹ as well as from the 1990–1 Gulf war,⁴² and (to a lesser extent) from the 1998–2000 Eritrea–Ethiopia war.⁴³ According to one author, 'after the end of the hostilities the Third Geneva Convention can no longer be considered a valid legal framework for the detention of persons who have not been released or imprisoned as a result of criminal process'.⁴⁴ As a consequence, international human rights law (IHRL) and domestic law should regulate their condition. The retention of POW status, however, has important advantages. First, it entails the discharge of all obligations of the Detaining

---

³³ See Dinstein, above n 9, at 50–6.   ³⁴ Above n 16, para 70.
³⁵ See the EU's Independent International Fact-Finding Mission on the Conflict in Georgia, Report, 30 September 2009, vol II, at 299, available at <http://www.ceiig.ch>.
³⁶ See S. Borman, *CRS Report for Congress. Iraq: U.S. Military Operations*, RL31701, 15 July 2007, at 7, available at <http://fas.org/sgp/crs/mideast/RL31701.pdf>.
³⁷ UNSC Res 1483 (2003), 22 May 2003, para 5.
³⁸ R. Kolb, *Ius in bello. Le droit international des conflits armés. Précis* (Brussels: Bruylant, 2003), at 107.
³⁹ See Pictet Commentary GC I, at 65.   ⁴⁰ Ibid.
⁴¹ See ICRC *Annual Report* 2004, at 278.   ⁴² See ICRC *Annual Report* 2011, at 381 and 410.
⁴³ See ICRC *Annual Report* 2002, at 74.
⁴⁴ J. Pejic, 'Terrorist Acts and Groups: A Role for International Law?', 75 *BYBIL* (2004) 71, at 78.

Power under the Convention. Secondly, it enables the ICRC to carry out its visits. Last but not least, it may result in allowances and/or pensions after repatriation. (See Chapter 48, MN 102–109, of this volume.)

ii. End of applicability of Geneva Convention IV on the territory of belligerent states

17 Article 6 GC IV distinguishes between the end of application of the Convention in the territory of belligerent states and the cessation of application in occupied territory (see MN 18–19). The former coincides with the 'general close of military operations'. Although the Convention does not explain the concept, it is currently interpreted to have a wider meaning than the notion of 'active hostilities'. While the end of 'active hostilities' refers to the mere termination of fighting, the 'general close of military operations' entails a 'complete cessation of all military manoeuvres' by all belligerents.[45] A number of provisions of GC IV, however, associate some obligations (like those regarding the cessation of internment and the return of internees to their last place of residence or their repatriation, pursuant to Articles 133 and 134 GC IV) with the actual 'close of hostilities' (see Chapter 66 of this volume). The last sentence of Article 6 ensures that protected persons, whose release, repatriation, or re-establishment takes place later, continue to benefit from the Convention. Like GC III with regard to POW captivity, GC IV seems inadequate to regulate the condition of civilian internees after the end of hostilities.[46] The argument bears more weight in the case of civilian internees, whose protection is better guaranteed by the general framework of IHRL.

iii. End of applicability of Geneva Convention IV in the case of occupation

18 The issue of when an occupation ends is dealt with in detail in Chapter 74 of this volume. Concerning the end of applicability of GC IV during occupation, Article 6 GC IV stipulates that in occupied territory, the Convention ceases to apply one year after the general close of military operations. The drafters of the Convention, however, were concerned about the fate of protected persons throughout the entire period of occupation. As a result, Article 6 provides for the continuing application of a number of provisions of the Convention, i.e.:

— the general provisions laid down in Part I of the Convention;[47]
— those on the status and treatment of protected persons;[48]
— the prohibition of depriving protected persons of the benefits of the Convention;[49]
— the prohibition of forced transfers and forced labour in the armed or auxiliary forces of the occupying state;[50]
— the right of workers to apply to the representatives of the Protecting Powers;[51]
— the prohibition of destruction of real or personal property;[52]
— the duty to supply relief to the population of the occupied territory;[53]
— the operation of the penal laws in the occupied territory;[54] and
— the right of representatives or delegates of the Protecting Powers to visit places of internment, detention, or work of protected persons.[55]

---

[45] See Jinks, above n 7, at 3.
[46] Pejic, above n 44, at 81.   [47] Arts 1–12 GC IV. See Part I.B of this volume.
[48] Arts 27 and 29–34 GC IV. For the substantive application, see Part II.C of this volume.
[49] Art 47 GC IV.   [50] Arts 49 and 51 GC IV.   [51] Art 52 GC IV.   [52] Art 53 GC IV.
[53] Arts 59 and 61–3 GC IV.   [54] Arts 64–70 GC IV.   [55] Art 143 GC IV.

In its *Wall Opinion*, the International Court of Justice (ICJ) accordingly held that '[s]ince the military operations leading to the occupation of the West Bank in 1967 ended a long time ago, only those Articles of the Fourth Geneva Convention referred to in Article 6, paragraph 3, remain applicable in that occupied territory.'[56]

Article 3 AP I supersedes Article 6 GC IV, providing that the Conventions as a whole, as well as the Protocol, remain fully applicable until the termination of occupation. This critical concept is analysed in another chapter of this Commentary.[57] Suffice it to mention here that the rule laid down in AP I corresponds to the customary principle of effectiveness, as embodied in the Hague Regulations, that was derogated from in 1949 for historical and political reasons, as explained above (MN 5). Presently, all states parties to AP I remain bound by GC IV in its entirety (and by the Protocol) as long as an occupation actually continues. The ICJ *Wall Opinion*, mentioned above, suggests that non-party states (Israel, in the case in question) are bound only by those provisions referred to in Article 6 GC IV.[58] However, scholars argue that all substantive rules contained in GC IV apply throughout the entire period of occupation, as indicative of customary international law.[59]

II. Non-international armed conflicts

a. Beginning of applicability

Common Article 3 is silent on the temporal dimension of a NIAC. The sole condition for its applicability is the existence of an armed conflict 'not of an international character occurring in the territory of one of the High Contracting Parties'. As a consequence, the applicability of Common Article 3 coincides with the beginning of a NIAC. But when does such a conflict start? Whereas the beginning of an IAC corresponds to the first shot fired between state armies, such a clear-cut situation does not occur in NIACs for a variety of reasons (see Chapters 1, 19 (in particular MN 34–61), and 20 of this volume). However, for our purposes, suffice it to observe that a NIAC usually results from a progressive series of actions that initially do not amount to armed confrontation. Furthermore, governments are hardly inclined to admit the existence of an armed conflict within their territory. Therefore, elaborating criteria to determine the initial moment of a NIAC has largely been the task of international jurisprudence and legal scholars.

i. The protracted character of the armed violence

In the 1997 *Tablada* case, the Inter-American Commission on Human Rights (IACommHR) established the beginning of applicability of Common Article 3, when, on 23 January 1989, an armed group 'carefully planned, coordinated and executed an armed attack, i.e. a military operation, against a quintessential military objective—a military base'.[60] In 1999, the Review Bench of the Hungarian Supreme Court—referring to the

---

[56] ICJ, *Legal Consequences of the Construction of a Wall in the Occupied Palestinian Territory*, Advisory Opinion, 9 July 2004 (hereinafter ICJ, *Wall Opinion*), para 125. See Y. Dinstein, *The International Law of Belligerent Occupation* (Cambridge: CUP, 2009), at 280–3.

[57] See Ch 74 of this volume.

[58] See MN 18 above.

[59] See R. Kolb and S. Vité, *Le droit de l'occupation militaire: perspectives historiques et enjeux juridiques actuels* (Brussels: Bruylant, 2009), at 164; V. Koutroulis, *Le début et la fin du droit de l'occupation* (Paris: Pedone, 2010), at 181.

[60] IACommHR, *Juan Carlos Abella v Argentina*, Case 11.137, Report No 55/97, 1 November 1997, paras 154–6. See David, above n 7, at 153 and A. Cullen, *The Concept of Non-International Armed Conflict in International Humanitarian Law* (Cambridge: CUP, 2010), at 144–5.

events occurring between 23 October and 4 November 1956 in Hungary—stated that Common Article 3 is applicable every time 'when the population of the state and the armed forces of the state are facing each other'.[61] In neither case did the limited duration of the armed confrontation constitute an obstacle to the applicability of IHL.

22 The 1995 *Tadić* Decision (and subsequently the Statute of the ICC) considered 'protracted armed violence' as being a specific feature of NIACs.[62] In the ICTY jurisprudence, this temporal element is strictly connected, and mostly muddled, with the test of the intensity of the conflict. Within this framework, the Tribunal has often examined incidents of violence to determine the duration of armed conflict, including in cases of terrorist acts.[63] In doing so, however, the Tribunal has paid more attention to the scale and effects of armed activities than to their temporal extent.[64]

23 One scholar argues that the concept of 'protracted armed violence' is more flexible than that of 'sustained' military operations referred to in Article 1 AP II: the requirement that armed violence be 'protracted' does not automatically imply that hostilities must be 'continuous', nor do interruptions in fighting suspend or terminate the obligations of the parties under Common Article 3.[65] In any case, both 'protracted' and 'sustained' present a vexing problem regarding the applicability of Common Article 3 at the beginning of a NIAC. In fact, the moment when armed violence becomes protracted may be determined only *ex post*, while uncertainty prevails in the field, where an authoritative decision is most needed.[66] From a state perspective, this issue must be addressed by enforcement and military instructions, to ensure that the implementation of IHRL gradually gives way to the application of IHL in order to adapt to the situation in the field. Furthermore, special agreements, which bring into force the whole, or part, of the provisions of the Geneva Conventions, may well establish the beginning of applicability of the provisions envisaged, as explained above (MN 12).

ii. The degree of organization of armed groups

24 The requirement that armed groups be structured under a responsible command is set out explicitly in AP II, which also requires dissident armed forces or armed groups to be able to carry out 'concerted' military operations. The *Tadić* wording refers in more general terms to 'organized armed groups', and the ICTY interpreted this condition on the basis of the stability and effectiveness of the organization. In the *Limaj* case, the Tribunal made an extensive analysis of the structure of the Kosovo Liberation Army, demonstrating

---

[61] See T. Hoffmann, 'Individual Criminal Responsibility for Crimes Committed in Non-International Armed Conflicts—The Hungarian Jurisprudence on the 1956 Volley Cases, (February 20, 2009)', in S. Manacorda and A. Nieto Martín (eds), *Criminal Law between War and Peace: Justice and Cooperation in Criminal Matters in International Military Interventions* (Cuenca: Ediciones de la Universidad de Castilla-La Mancha, 2009) 735, at 745, available at <http://ssrn.com/abstract=1531708>.

[62] See ICJ, *Tadić* Decision, above n 16.

[63] ICTY, *The Prosecutor v Anto Furundžija*, Trial Chamber Judgment, IT-95-17/1-T, 10 December 1998, paras 51–7; *The Prosecutor v Zejnil Delalić et al*, Trial Chamber Judgment, IT-96-21-T, 16 November 1998, para 186; *The Prosecutor v Dragoljub Kunarac et al*, Trial Chamber Judgment, IT-96-23-T and IT-96-23/1-T, 22 February 2001, para 186, and Appeals Chamber, IT-96-23 and IT-96-23/1-A, 12 June 2002, para 58; *The Prosecutor v Pavle Strugar*, Trial Chamber Judgment, IT-01-42-T, 31 January 2005, para 217; *The Prosecutor v Ljube Boškoski and Johan Tarčulovski*, Trial Chamber Judgment, IT-04-82-T, 10 July 2008, paras 186–93.

[64] ICTY, *The Prosecutor v Ramush Haradinaj et al*, Trial Chamber Judgment, IT-04-84-T, 3 April 2008, para 49.

[65] See Cullen, above n 60, at 142–3.

[66] See A.J. Carswell, 'Classifying the Conflict: A Soldier's Dilemma', 91 *IRRC* 873 (2009) 143, at 151–3; Vité, above n 13, at 82 and fn 32.

the very strong military and political organization of the group.⁶⁷ Such a high degree of organization should not, however, be deemed essential, since more flexible criteria are better suited to the variety of situations that characterize NIACs. Therefore, Common Article 3 becomes applicable as soon as an armed group possesses the minimum organizational structure to enable its members to respect the provisions on the protection of the wounded, sick, and persons not taking part in the hostilities.⁶⁸

The extent of the organization of opposition forces in the Syrian uprising (ongoing since 2011) has been discussed in relation to the beginning of applicability of Common Article 3. In its Report issued on 12 February 2012, the Commission of Inquiry established by the UN Human Rights Council to investigate the alleged violations of international human rights, was unable to determine the level of organization of the Syrian opposition groups engaged in armed hostilities.⁶⁹ Nevertheless, the subsequent escalation of armed confrontations has led to a widespread acknowledgment of the existence of a NIAC to which Common Article 3 applies; over the years, the ICRC has repeatedly called upon the parties to respect and protect civilians, medical personnel and facilities as well as humanitarian workers.⁷⁰

b. End of applicability

Common Article 3 is silent on the end of its applicability, giving rise to the same problems as encountered when examining the beginning of its applicability. Criteria based on the decreasing intensity of armed clashes and the disbanding of armed groups are grounded on the principle of effectiveness; however, such criteria are difficult to apply in practice. On the personal field of application, Article 2(2) of AP II refers to the 'end of the armed conflict', providing that persons who have been deprived of their liberty or whose liberty has been restricted,⁷¹ during or after the conflict, for causes related to the conflict, continue to benefit from the protection of the Protocol until their final release. Moreover, Article 25(2) AP II provides that until their final release, the said persons continue to benefit from the protection of the Protocol even upon denunciation by the state party. Further, Common Article 3 may be deemed to continue to apply as long as persons taking no active part in the hostilities are in need of protection. When hostilities have ceased, however, it is debatable whether either Common Article 3 or the Additional Protocol can offer better protection than existing human rights obligations.⁷²

The 1995 *Tadić* Decision held that in the case of internal conflicts, IHL applies until a 'peaceful settlement is achieved'. In the *Haradinaj* Decision, the ICTY clarified that once the threshold of violence is met, a decrease in the intensity of fighting (or, one might add,

---

⁶⁷ ICTY, *The Prosecutor v Fatmir Limaj et al*, Trial Chamber Judgment, IT-03-66-T, 30 November 2005, paras 94–134.

⁶⁸ These issues are dealt with in more detail in Ch 19 of this volume.

⁶⁹ Human Rights Council, *Report of the Independent International Commission of Inquiry on the Syrian Arab Republic*, 22 February 2012, A/HRC/19/69, paras 108–9.

⁷⁰ See J.P. Rudolph, *Syrian Conflict Governed by Common Article 3 of the Geneva Conventions*, JURIST—Sidebar, 23 July 2012, available at <http://jurist.org/sidebar/2012/07/james-rudolph-syria-geneva.php>. See also ICRC Resource Centre, *Syria and Iraq: ICRC calls for better compliance with humanitarian law*, News Release 26 September 2014, at <https://www.icrc.org/en/document/syria-and-iraq-icrc-calls-better-compliance-humanitarian-law>.

⁷¹ This wording is intended to cover all possible situations, to ensure that there is no gap in protection: see ICRC Commentary APs, para 4496.

⁷² See, on the application of more favourable provisions of IHRL, David, above n 7, at 265.

degree of organization of an armed group involved) cannot end the applicability of IHL.[73] The classic method of reaching a 'peaceful settlement' is through a formal agreement sanctioning the definitive cessation of hostilities. Examples of such agreements are the Peace Agreement signed by the Government of El Salvador and the Frente Farabundo Martí in Mexico on 16 January 1992,[74] the Rome General Peace Agreement of 4 October 1992 between the Frelimo Government of Mozambique and the opposition forces of Renamo,[75] the Agreement on the Implementation, Compliance, and Verification Timetable for the Peace Agreements and the Agreement for a Firm and Lasting Peace of 29 December 1996 by the Peace Commission of the Government of Guatemala and the General Command of the Unidad Revolucionaria Nacional Guatemalteca,[76] the Lomé Peace Agreement of 7 July 1999 between the elected Government of Sierra Leone and the Revolutionary United Front,[77] and the Arusha Peace and Reconciliation Agreement for Burundi of 28 August 2000.[78] As a rule, this category of agreement includes, or is complemented by, stipulations establishing national human rights institutions and incorporating elements of transitional justice.

III. Peacekeeping operations

28   Since the last decade of the twentieth century, both UN and regional peacekeeping forces have been increasingly involved in combat situations. The beginning and end of applicability of the Geneva Conventions to peacekeeping forces will depend on the factual circumstances of the particular case and will face the related problems discussed above (MN 8–12 and 20–25).[79] Furthermore, for a number of reasons, sending states are not usually prepared to admit that their soldiers take an active part in hostilities.[80] Nevertheless, the determination of the temporal scope of application of the Geneva Conventions to peacekeeping forces is essential in establishing the status of the military personnel, as well as their liability for offences committed in the course of peacekeeping functions. Thus the discussion concerning the legal status of peacekeepers has taken place chiefly in the case law of the international criminal tribunals (see MN 35 below).[81]

29   The United Nations Secretary-General Bulletin issued on 6 August 1999[82] recapitulates the 'fundamental principles and rules of international humanitarian law' that must be respected and implemented by the UN forces, but does not further elaborate on the applicable law. In this writer's opinion, any use of force by peacekeepers directed against state armed forces or armed groups triggers the obligation to respect not only the 'fundamental principles and rules of international humanitarian law' as summarized by the

---

[73] ICTY, *The Prosecutor v Ramush Haradinaj et al*, above n 64, para 100.
[74] UN Doc A/46/863-S/23504, Annex I.   [75] UN Doc S/24635, 8 October 1992.
[76] UN Doc A/51/796-S/1997/114, Annexes I and II.
[77] See <http://www.sierra-leone.org/lomeaccord.html>.
[78] See <http://reliefweb.int/report/burundi/arusha-peace-and-reconciliation-agreement-burundi>. The Arusha Agreement did not prevent the resumption of hostilities, ending with the Global Ceasefire Agreement between the Transitional Government of Burundi and the National Council for the Defence of the Democracy-Forces for the Defence of Democracy signed in Dar-es-Salaam on 16 November 2003 (see <http://www.ucdp.uu.se/gpdatabase/peace/Bur%2020031116.pdf>).
[79] C.H.B. Garraway, 'Applicability and Application of International Humanitarian Law to Enforcement and Peace Enforcement Operations', in T. Gill and D. Fleck (eds), *The Handbook of the International Law of Military Operations* (Oxford: OUP, 2010) 129, at 130. See also Vité, above n 13, at 87–8.
[80] See Carswell, above n 66, at 155.
[81] See further Ch 1, MN 16–19; Ch 2, MN 49; and Ch 19, MN 18–20, of this volume.
[82] ST/SGB/1999/13, available at <http://www.un.org/en/ga/search/view_doc.asp?symbol=ST/SGB/1999/13>.

Bulletin, but also (at least through domestic legislation), all pertinent provisions of the Geneva Conventions.

IV. Provisions to be implemented in peacetime

Although, as a rule, the Geneva Conventions apply during armed conflict, several provisions stipulate that states parties are under an obligation to implement them in peacetime, as soon as the Geneva Conventions enter into force for them.[83] This is the case for a group of Articles common to the four Conventions, where the contracting parties undertake, 'in time of peace as in time of war', to disseminate the text of the relevant Convention

> as widely as possible in their respective countries, and, in particular, to include the study thereof in their programmes of military and, if possible, civil instruction, so that the principles thereof may become known to the entire population, in particular to the armed fighting forces, the medical personnel and the chaplains.[84]

Similarly, the obligation of the contracting parties to provide one another with the official translations of the Conventions, as well as the laws and regulations adopted to ensure their application, must clearly be satisfied in time of peace.[85] Additionally, the obligation to prosecute grave breaches based upon the principle of universal jurisdiction is, by definition, equally addressed to states not involved in an armed conflict,[86] as is the obligation to legislate on and repress misuses of the emblem of the red cross, red crescent, or red crystal.[87]

A number of provisions of the Geneva Conventions explicitly or indirectly stipulate that the contracting parties must discharge a number of obligations after either the end of hostilities or the end of the conflict. Thus, Article 119 GC III and Article 133 GC IV provide that *after the close of hostilities* the parties to the conflict may conclude an agreement establishing special commissions for the purpose of searching for dispersed POWs and internees, respectively. Article 122 GC III provides that the National Information Bureau (which must be established at the beginning of any conflict or occupation by belligerents and by neutral states with belligerents in their care) must forward all personal valuables left by repatriated POWs to the state in whose armed forces they were serving, an obligation that may also require implementation after the end of hostilities. The same applies to the obligation established by Article 26 GC IV, to facilitate enquiries made by members of families dispersed because of the war, and to encourage the work of organizations engaged in this task.[88]

The obligation to account for missing persons in both IACs and NIACs is contained in a number of national laws and military manuals, in agreements between parties to armed conflicts, and in resolutions of international organizations and conferences.[89] This

---

[83] H. Meyrowitz, 'The Functions of the Law of War in Peacetime', 26 *IRRC* 251 (1986) 77.
[84] Art 47 GC I; Art 48 GC II; Art 127 GC III; Art 144 GC IV.
[85] Art 48 GC I; Art 49 GC II; Art 128 GC III; Art 145 GC IV.
[86] Art 49 GC I; Art 50 GC II; Art 129 GC III; Art 146 GC IV.   [87] Arts 53 and 54 GC I.
[88] See Chs 13, 49, and 53 of this volume. AP I further expands the extent of humanitarian obligations to be implemented in peacetime. See Art 36 AP I relating to new weapons; Art 41(1) on the internal disciplinary system of the armed forces; Art 80 on domestic measures, orders, and instructions for the execution of the Conventions and the Protocol; Art 82 on the obligation of the contracting parties to ensure 'at all times' that legal advisers are available to counsel military commanders about the application of the Conventions and the Protocol; and, last but not least, Art 33(1) on missing persons, laying down detailed obligations on the search for persons who have been reported missing by an adverse party.
[89] See the practice and case law listed in ICRC CIHL Study, vol II, Ch 36.

obligation is based on the right of families to know the fate of their missing relatives, which is also supported by a number of international instruments. As a consequence, practice suggests that an obligation to account for missing persons has been established as a rule of customary international law applicable in both IACs and NIACs.[90]

C. Legal Consequences of a Violation

I. International responsibility

33   Determining the precise beginning and end of an armed conflict is essential to define the temporal limits of state responsibility and the related liability to make reparation. For example, the United Nations Compensation Commission (UNCC), established in 1991 by the Security Council,[91] made reference to the date of Iraq's invasion of Kuwait (2 August 1990) and to that of the cease-fire (2 March 1991) to award compensation for losses and damage suffered as a result of Iraq's invasion and occupation of Kuwait,[92] including violations of the Geneva Conventions.[93] In order to establish the temporal scope of its jurisdiction, the EECC determined the precise moment of the outbreak of hostilities between Eritrea and Ethiopia on 12 May 1998, and found that the armed conflict was formally terminated by the Algiers Peace Agreement of 12 December 2000.[94] Within this temporal framework, the Commission then adjudicated several claims relating to the treatment of protected persons under the Geneva Conventions.[95] The Commission also decided on certain claims associated with events that occurred after 12 December 2000 but nevertheless resulted from the conflict, such as delays in the release and repatriation of POWs and their mistreatment in the meanwhile.[96] Eventually, the EECC awarded compensation to Ethiopia and Eritrea, respectively, for damage incurred due to ascertained violations.[97]

II. Individual criminal responsibility

34   The prosecution of persons accused of grave breaches and other serious violations of the Geneva Conventions strictly depends on the determination of the temporal scope of applicability of IHL, in order to identify the applicable law. In the 1995 *Tadić* Decision, the ICTY Appeals Chamber recognized that, beginning in 1991, the armed conflicts in the territory of the former Yugoslavia were of a mixed character, and laid down a general framework for classification.[98] Accordingly, in dealing with subsequent cases, the various

---

[90] See Ch 13 of this volume and ICRC CIHL Study, vol I, Rule 117. Accounting for Missing Persons: 'Each party to the conflict must take all feasible measures to account for persons reported missing as a result of armed conflict and must provide their family members with any information it has on their fate.'
[91] UNSC Res 687 (1991) of 8 April 1991, paras 16 and 18.
[92] UNCC, Criteria for Expedited Processing of Urgent Claims, S/AC.26/1991/1 of 2 August 1991, para 18.
[93] See ICRC CIHL Study, vol I, Rule 150.
[94] EECC, *Jus ad Bellum—Ethiopia's Claims 1–8, Partial Award*, 19 December 2005, para 14; EECC, Decision Number 1, para B, available at <http://www.pca-cpa.org/>.
[95] See S. Sanna, 'International Humanitarian Law and the Treatment of Protected Persons', in A. de Guttry, H.H.G. Post, and G. Venturini (eds), *The 1998–2000 War between Eritrea and Ethiopia* (The Hague: T.M.C. Asser Press, 2009) 307–39.
[96] See EECC, Decision Number 1, above n 94, para C; and Sanna, above n 95, at 324–5.
[97] EECC, *Eritrea's Damages Claims*, Final Award, 17 August 2009; *Ethiopia's Damages Claims*, Final Award 17 August 2009, available at <http://www.pca-cpa.org/>.
[98] ICTY, *Tadić Decision*, n 16, paras 72–8.

Trial Chambers determined the nature of the armed conflict material to the specific indictment charges at the time.[99] Likewise, the Chambers of the International Criminal Tribunal for Rwanda (ICTR), whose temporal jurisdiction extended from 1 January to 31 December 1994, established the existence of a state of internal armed conflict in Rwanda at the times relevant to the various indictments.[100]

The existence of an internal armed conflict was also relevant in the recent case law of the international criminal tribunals dealing with crimes committed against peacekeepers. Regarding the murder of 10 Belgian peacekeepers by Rwandan soldiers on 7 April 1994, the ICTR Trial Chamber accepted that during the relevant period, a NIAC had taken place in the territory of Rwanda.[101] In the *AFRC/RUF* case, the Special Court for Sierra Leone (SCSL) Trial Chamber took note that an armed conflict had occurred in Sierra Leone from March 1991 until January 2002, covering the crimes charged in the indictment pursuant to Article 4(b) of the SCSL Statute.[102]

D. Critical Assessment

Since the purpose of the Geneva Conventions is to protect victims of armed conflict, their temporal scope of application must be measured with a view to ensuring the greatest possible value of that objective. The functional approach to the beginning as well as to the end of application, depending on the situation of the protected persons, is best suited to that aim. The provisions contained in the Geneva Conventions, however, were mainly designed to deal with inter-state armed conflicts. Thus, the beginning of application is clearly established (first shot, first person affected) for such conflicts, while the end of application gradually follows a number of expected events (the release, repatriation, return, re-establishment of protected persons). As far as today's NIACs are concerned, neither Common Article 3 nor AP II gives adequately detailed directions. On one hand, the transition from civil disturbances, riots, and unrest to a NIAC may be evaluated in retrospect, but is difficult to assess on the ground while violence increases. On the other hand, often the end of a NIAC does not change the situation of the victims, who continue to suffer from deprivation of their fundamental rights.

In recent years, the tendency to merge the law of NIAC into the law of IAC has solved some problems, but only partially, since the latter is grounded on the principle of the equality of belligerents, the application of which in NIAC is problematic, at the least. On the other hand, it is necessary for military doctrine and instructions to regulate the behaviour of the armed forces in a manner that enables them to identify the events that trigger the application of different sets of rules, and to act accordingly. This also proves crucial to the assessment of both international and individual criminal responsibility for violations of the Geneva Conventions. A further challenge is that of coordinating the application of the Geneva Conventions and IHRL, which continues to apply during armed conflict. Thus, military doctrine should incorporate principles regulating law enforcement actions, both domestically and in military operations

---

[99] Above nn 63–4 and 67.
[100] ICTR, *The Prosecutor v Jean-Paul Akayesu*, Trial Chamber Judgment, ICTR 96-4-T, 2 September 1998, para 174; *The Prosecutor v Georges Rutaganda*, ICTR-96-3-T, Judgment and Sentence, 6 December 1999, para 435; *The Prosecutor v Alfred Musema*, Trial Chamber, ICTR-96-13-T, 27 January 2000, para 971.
[101] ICTR, *The Prosecutor v Théoneste Bagosora et al*, ICTR-98-41-T, 18 December 2008, para 2230.
[102] ICTR, *The Prosecutor against Issa Hassan Sesay et al*, SCSL-04-15-T, 2 March 2009, para 969.

abroad. Not only states, but also international organizations conducting peacekeeping and peace-enforcement missions are called upon to participate in this endeavour. Defining the temporal scope of application of the Geneva Conventions to peacekeeping forces is essential, not only in order to provide military personnel with clear rules of engagement, but also to establish the responsibility of both individuals and the sending organization.

GABRIELLA VENTURINI

Chapter 4. The Geographical Scope of Application of the Conventions

	MN
A. Introduction	1
B. Meaning and Application	5
I. International armed conflicts	5
a. Territory of belligerents	5
b. Neutral territory and other areas	17
C. Relevance in Non-International Armed Conflicts	21
I. Traditional non-international armed conflicts	22
II. 'Spillover', 'multinational', 'cross-border', and 'transnational' armed conflicts	25
a. Wording, context, and object and purpose	27
b. Preparatory work	30
c. Practice	35
D. Critical Assessment	36

Select Bibliography

Daskal, J., 'The Geography of the Battlefield: A Framework for Detention and Targeting Outside the "Hot" Conflict Zone', 161 *University of Pennsylvania Law Review* (2013) 1165

Kreß, C., 'Some Reflections on the International Legal Framework Governing Transnational Armed Conflicts', 15 *Journal of Conflict and Security Law* (2010) 245

Lubell, N./Derejko, N., 'A Global Battlefield? Drones and the Geographical Scope of Armed Conflict', 11 *JICJ* (2013) 65

Milanovic, M./Hadzi-Vidanovic, V., 'A Taxonomy of Armed Conflict', in N. White and C. Henderson (eds), *Research Handbook on International Conflict and Security Law. Jus ad Bellum, Jus in Bello and Jus post Bellum* (Cheltenham: Edward Elgar Publishing, 2013) 256

Pejic, J., 'The Protective Scope of Common Article 3: More than Meets the Eye', 93 *IRRC* 881 (2011) 1

Radin, S., 'Global Armed Conflict? The Threshold of Extraterritorial Non-International Armed Conflicts', 89 *International Law Studies* (2013) 696

Vité, S., 'Typology of Armed Conflicts in International Humanitarian Law: Legal Concepts and Actual Situations', 91 *IRRC* 873 (2009) 69

Wilmshurst, E. (ed), *International Law and the Classification of Conflicts* (Oxford: OUP, 2012)

A. Introduction

The geographical scope of international humanitarian law (IHL) has increasingly become a subject of attention and debate among international legal practitioners and scholars. While armed conflicts may have always triggered reflections about the 'boundaries of the battlefield' beyond which IHL arguably does not apply, the concept of a 'geographical scope of application' is a rather recent one. When dealing with the various armed conflicts having taken place on the territory of the former Socialist Federal Republic of Yugoslavia, the International Criminal Tribunal for the Former Yugoslavia (ICTY) systematically addressed the notion for the first time, both for international armed conflicts (IACs) and for non-international armed conflicts (NIACs). However, it was operations initially labelled as being part of the so-called 'Global War on Terror', in response to the attacks against the United States (US) on 11 September 2001, which ultimately directed focus on the geographical scope of armed conflict.[1]

2   Since 11 September 2001, the geographical scope of IHL, especially of NIACs, has played a significant role in arguments on the legality of detaining 'terrorist' suspects and of resorting to their targeted killing, including through the use of armed drones.[2] While the term 'Global War on Terror' was abandoned by the US Government in 2009, the US considers itself engaged in an ongoing armed conflict against Al-Qaeda, the Taliban, and associated forces based on its inherent right to self-defence to this day. In its view, this armed conflict is global in scope and provides authority for the use of lethal force outside of 'hot battlefields'. A US Department of Justice White Paper, leaked to the press in 2013,[3] confirmed the US Government's earlier public position.[4] It stated that any US operation against Al-Qaeda and associated forces would be part of a NIAC even if it were to take place away from the zone of active hostilities. To support this position, it argued that none of the branches of the US Government had identified strict geographical limits in the domestic 'Authorization for Use of Military Force' (AUMF).[5] Furthermore, the White Paper noted that only little judicial or other authoritative precedent directly addresses the

---

[1] Whereas the debate has been profoundly shaped by reflections about the US 'Global War on Terror', other conflicts, such as that between Israel and Hezbollah in Lebanon in 2006, have considerably contributed to a commonly felt need to revisit the scopes of application of IACs and NIACs. G. Corn, 'Back to the Future: De Facto Hostilities, Transnational Terrorism, and the Purpose of the Law of Armed Conflict', 30 *University of Pennsylvania Journal of International Law* (2009) 1345, at 1348.

[2] B. Emmerson, *Report of the Special Rapporteur on the Promotion and Protection of Human Rights and Fundamental Freedoms while Countering Terrorism* (Interim Report to the General Assembly on the Use of Remotely Piloted Aircraft in Counter-Terrorism Operations), A/68/389, 18 September 2013, at 17, para 59; and B. Emmerson, *Report of the Special Rapporteur on the Promotion and Protection of Human Rights and Fundamental Freedoms while Countering Terrorism*, A/HRC/25/59, 11 March 2014, at 18, para 70. See also N. Lubell and N. Derejko, 'A Global Battlefield? Drones and the Geographical Scope of Armed Conflict', 11 *JICJ* (2013) 65; M.W. Lewis, 'Drones and the Boundaries of the Battlefield', 47 *Texas International Law Journal* (2012) 293; and R. Heinsch, 'Unmanned Aerial Vehicles and the Scope of the "Combat Zone": Some Thoughts on the Geographical Scope of Application of International Humanitarian Law', 25 *Journal of International Law of Peace and Armed Conflict* (2012) 184.

[3] US Department of Justice, *Lawfulness of a Lethal Operation Directed against a US Citizen who Is a Senior Operational Leader of Al-Qa'ida or an Associated Force*, White Paper, available at <http://msnbcmedia.msn.com/i/msnbc/sections/news/020413_DOJ_White_Paper.pdf>.

[4] See especially H. Koh, 'The Obama Administration and International Law', Annual Meeting of the American Society of International Law, 25 March 2010; J. Brennan, 'Strengthening our Security by Adhering to our Values and Laws', Harvard Law School, 16 September 2011; J. Johnson, 'National Security Law, Lawyers and Lawyering in the Obama Administration', Yale Law School, 22 February 2012; E. Holder, Speech at Northwestern University School of Law, 5 March 2012; and B. Obama, Remarks at National Defense University, 23 May 2013. See also *Fact Sheet: US Policy Standards and Procedures for the Use of Force in Counterterrorism Operations Outside the United States and Areas of Active Hostilities*, 23 May 2013, available at <http://www.whitehouse.gov/the-press-office/2013/05/23/fact-sheet-us-policy-standards-and-procedures-use-force-counterterrorism>.

[5] In the *Hamdan* case involving a Yemeni national captured during hostilities between the US and Taliban forces in Afghanistan, the US Supreme Court supported the application of Common Article 3 to the conflict with Al-Qaeda without explicitly limiting the armed conflict's geographical scope to Afghanistan. In cases in which terrorist suspects were apprehended outside 'hot battlefields', e.g. in Pakistan and Bosnia-Herzegovina, US courts have assumed a broad geographical scope. US Supreme Court, *Salim A. Hamdan v Donald H. Rumsfeld et al*, No 05-184, 29 June 2006; US Court of Appeals DC, *Mohammed Al-Adahi v Barack Obama et al*, No 09-5333, 13 July 2010; and US Court of Appeals DC, *Belkacem Bensayah v Barack Obama et al*, No 08-5537, 28 June 2010.

geographical scope of NIACs involving transnational non-state armed groups and taking place outside of a state's own territory.⁶

The applicability of the Conventions to 'transnational' armed conflicts is discussed in more detail elsewhere in this volume.⁷ Suffice it to recall that the classification of 'transnational' armed conflicts as NIACs without territorial confines is one of several proposed classifications. In 2006, the Israeli Supreme Court classified the armed conflict between Israel and various 'terrorist' organizations active in the West Bank and the Gaza Strip as an IAC because it crosses the borders of the state.⁸ Some commentators argue that 'transnational' armed conflicts should primarily be regarded as IACs between the intervening and territorial state. Others call for the recognition of a new category of armed conflict.⁹ The merits of such arguments need not be discussed here.¹⁰ It is hoped that this chapter will make a contribution not only to the debate on 'transnational' armed conflicts, for example by analysing whether Common Article 3 as treaty law can be applied outside a High Contracting Party's own territory. This chapter also discusses the application of Common Article 3 to 'traditional' NIACs inside a High Contracting Party's territory. It further provides an analysis of the geographical scope of IACs inside and outside of belligerent territory. The law of IACs is thereby presented first, before NIACs are addressed as a second step.

3

Throughout this chapter, the Conventions' scope of application *ratione loci* is referred to as their 'geographical' scope. While the term 'territorial' scope, based on the Latin word '*terra*' (translating as 'earth' or 'land'),¹¹ is also frequently used within the (academic) debate, it seems too restrictive given the Conventions' possible application in the air or at sea. In contrast, the term 'geographical' scope relates to a broader concept describing the Earth's physical features.¹² Furthermore, notions such as 'theatres of war', 'zones of conflict', or 'hot battlefields', while frequently referred to by state representatives, scholars, journalists, and others, lack legal meaning and must be considered strictly descriptive terms.¹³

4

---

⁶ US Department of Justice, above n 3, at 3.

⁷ See Ch 2 of this volume. Also note the difference between the concepts of 'transnational' and 'global' armed conflicts. While 'transnational' armed conflicts are generally analysed on a case-by-case basis, a 'global' armed conflict is sought to be established by aggregating hostilities occurring in geographically diverse locations.

⁸ Supreme Court of Israel (High Court of Justice), *The Public Committee against Torture in Israel (PCATI) and the Palestinian Society for the Protection of Human Rights and the Environment v Israel*, 769/02, 13 December 2006, para 18. For a comparison of the US and Israeli approach, see M. Milanovic, 'Lessons for Human Rights and Humanitarian Law in the War on Terror: Comparing Hamdan and the Israeli Targeted Killings Case', 89 *IRRC* 866 (2007) 373.

⁹ See R.S. Schöndorf, 'Extra-State Armed Conflicts: Is There a Need for a New Legal Regime?', 37 *New York University Journal of International Law and Politics* (2004) 1; and G. Corn and E.T. Jensen, 'Transnational Armed Conflict: A "Principled" Approach to the Regulation of Counter-Terror Combat Operations', 42 *Israel Law Review* (2009) 46. See also G. Corn and E.T. Jensen, 'Untying the Gordian Knot: A Proposal for Determining Applicability of the Laws of War to the War on Terror', 81 *Temple Law Review* (2008) 787.

¹⁰ See, e.g., C. Kreß, 'Some Reflections on the International Legal Framework Governing Transnational Armed Conflicts', 15 *Journal of Conflict and Security Law* (2010) 245.

¹¹ Oxford English Dictionaries Online, 'Territory', available at <http://www.oxforddictionaries.com/definition/english/territory>.

¹² Oxford English Dictionaries Online, 'Geography', available at <http://www.oxforddictionaries.com/definition/english/geography>.

¹³ See also K. Anderson, 'Targeted Killing and Drone Warfare: How We Came to Debate Whether There is a "Legal Geography of War"', in P. Berkowitz (ed), *Future Challenges in National Security and Law* (Online Essay Series, 2010), at 14, available at <http://www.hoover.org/sites/default/files/research/docs/futurechallenges_anderson.pdf>.

B. Meaning and Application

I. International armed conflicts

a. Territory of belligerents

i. Scope of application inside a belligerent's own territory

5   A first, fundamental question one might ask when reflecting on their geographical scope of application is whether the Conventions apply to the entire territory of states party to an IAC. At first sight, the Conventions do not provide any guidance as they do not contain specific rules on their geographical scope of application, in contrast to their temporal scope.[14] Nevertheless, one can infer from the titles of Geneva Convention (GC) I and GC II that, notwithstanding certain exceptions,[15] both Conventions generally apply only to certain geographical areas, i.e. land and sea. Given that the Conventions overlap to avoid gaps in protection,[16] the geographical scope of application of GC I and GC II can arguably be interpreted quite restrictively. In the case of hostilities between land and naval forces of parties to the conflict, GC II thus applies to forces on board ships as provided for in Article 4 GC II. If put ashore, naval forces immediately become subject to the provisions of GC I; and if they fall into enemy hands, to those of GC III.[17]

6   The general rules of public international law regarding treaties, today codified in the Vienna Convention on the Law of Treaties (VCLT), may furthermore be reverted to. While Article 4 VCLT bars the retroactive application of the Convention to treaties concluded by states before the entry into force of the Convention for those states, it can nevertheless be argued that the relevant rules contained therein may be applied to the Geneva Conventions.[18] According to Article 29 VCLT, '[u]nless a different intention appears from the treaty or is otherwise established, a treaty is binding upon each party in respect of its entire territory.' Consequently, the Geneva Conventions are generally applicable to a state's entire land territory and territorial sea appurtenant to the land (including its seabed), as well as to airspace superjacent to land territory, internal waters, and territorial sea.[19] Continental shelves, exclusive economic zones, or fishery zones, over which states exercise certain sovereign rights, are not considered part of national territory for the purposes of treaty application.[20]

---

[14] See Ch 3 of this volume and Art 5 GC I, Art 5 GC III, and Art 6 GC IV.

[15] Both GC I and GC II contain, for example, provisions on medical aircraft, thereby extending protection to medical units in the air.

[16] According to Art 20 GC I and Art 23 GC II, medical units, for example, are protected against attack from the sea and land respectively.

[17] Arts 4 para 2 and 16 GC II.

[18] Art 4 VCLT provides that the rule on non-retroactivity of the Convention is without prejudice to the application of any rules contained therein to which treaties would be subject under international law independently of the Convention. It thereby recalls that rules of the VCLT already having constituted customary international law prior to its entry into force can be applied to treaties concluded before the VCLT's entry into force. With respect to Art 29 VCLT, the International Law Commission (ILC) noted that prior to the VCLT's entry into force, '[s]tate practice, the jurisprudence of international tribunals and the writings of jurists appear to [have] support[ed] the view that a treaty is to be presumed to apply to all the territory of each party unless it otherwise appears from the treaty': ILC, 'Draft Articles on the Law of Treaties with Commentaries', *Yearbook of the International Law Commission*, 1966, vol II, at 213. With respect to the rules on treaty interpretation (Arts 31 and 32 VCLT), the International Court of Justice (ICJ) has confirmed their customary international law nature and applied them to treaties concluded well before the entry into force of the VCLT. See, e.g., ICJ, *Case concerning Kasikili/Sedudu Island, Botswana v Namibia*, 13 December 1999, 1045, at 1059, para 18.

[19] I. Brownlie, *Principles of Public International Law* (6th edn, Oxford: OUP, 2003), at 115.

[20] A. Aust, *Modern Treaty Law and Practice* (2nd edn, Cambridge: CUP, 2007), at 200.

However, can it be argued that 'a different intention appears from the treaty or is otherwise established' which would limit the Conventions' geographical scope of application? If one reasons that the Conventions' objective is to govern the humanitarian consequences of armed conflict, it seems sensible to assume that they apply to the entire territory of a state engaged in armed conflict, given that such consequences cannot necessarily be confined to a certain area of a belligerent's territory. Moreover, restricting the Conventions' application inevitably raises the question as to the criteria on which such a restriction might be based. One might consequently claim that legal certainty calls for a uniform application of the Conventions to the entire territory of belligerent states.

Yet consider cases in which hostilities take place only within certain areas of a belligerent state's territory, or are even conducted exclusively on the territory of the opposing party to an IAC.[21] An example is the initial IAC between the US-led coalition and Iraq in 2003. If accepting that '[w]hile most of Iraq became a zone of armed conflict in 2003, life for most people in the United States continued uninterrupted while its troops invaded a country on the other side of the globe',[22] one might question if the Conventions should apply to the whole of the US and, for example, govern the treatment of enemy civilians living on US territory far removed from the battlefield.[23]

Different approaches seem possible in order to restrict the Conventions' scope of application within a belligerent's territory. First, the application of the Conventions could be limited to places where actual hostilities take place. Yet despite containing numerous references to 'hostilities', conventional IHL does not define which acts or omissions qualify as such.[24] A too narrow interpretation of 'hostilities' would lead to unreasonable results if, for example, the taking of prisoners of war (POWs) was not included in this concept. But even if considering only military confrontations (e.g. exchange of fire), the approach does not seem very convincing given that the nature of contemporary warfare makes a division of territory into peaceful and hostile areas almost impossible. Secondly, the geographical scope of application of the Conventions' provisions could be determined for each rule depending on whether it has an intrinsic link to hostilities or not, thereby fragmenting the Conventions' protection. Thirdly, the Conventions could apply in the entire territory of belligerent states to all acts or omissions having a sufficient nexus to the armed conflict.

International criminal tribunals, especially the ICTY, have used different approaches in their jurisprudence. In its *Tadić* decision, the ICTY was asked to address the geographical scope of application of both IACs and NIACs.[25] The defendant argued, inter alia, that no legally cognizable armed conflict, either 'internal' or international, existed

---

[21] On the question of asymmetric warfare in IACs more generally, see, e.g., T. Pfanner, 'Asymmetrical Warfare from the Perspective of Humanitarian Law and Humanitarian Action', 87 *IRRC* 857 (2005) 149.

[22] Lubell and Derejko, above n 2, at 66.

[23] For an example of the treatment of Iraqi nationals in the UK during the 1991–2 Gulf War, see F. Hampson, 'The Geneva Conventions and the Detention of Civilians and Alleged Prisoners of War', *Public Law* (1991) 507.

[24] The ICRC's Interpretive Guidance on the Notion of Direct Participation in Hostilities under International Humanitarian Law defines, for the purposes of this study, the concept of 'hostilities' as 'the (collective) resort by the parties to the conflict to means and methods of injuring the enemy', based on Section II of the 1907 Hague Regulations, while noting that 'treaty law does not establish uniform terminology for the conduct of hostilities but refers, apart from "hostilities", also to "warfare" [...], "military operations" [...], or simply "operations"'. N. Melzer, *Interpretive Guidance on the Notion of Direct Participation in Hostilities under International Humanitarian Law* (Geneva: ICRC, 2009), at 43.

[25] ICTY, *The Prosecutor v Duško Tadić*, Appeals Chamber, Decision on the Defense Motion for Interlocutory Appeal on Jurisdiction, IT-94-1-AR72, 2 October 1995.

at the time and place the alleged offences were committed. He claimed the conflict in the Prijedor region was limited to a political assumption of power by the Bosnian Serbs and did not involve armed combat, though movements of tanks were admitted.[26] The Appeals Chamber examined the scope of application of IACs and NIACs separately, but established preliminarily that 'the temporal and geographical scope of both internal and international armed conflicts extends beyond the exact time and place of hostilities',[27] thereby rejecting an approach to armed conflict covering only the precise time and place of hostilities. With respect to IACs, the Chamber subsequently introduced a differentiated approach to the geographical application of the Conventions. It noted that '[a]lthough the Geneva Conventions are silent as to the geographical scope of international "armed conflicts," the provisions suggest that at least some of the provisions of the Conventions apply to the entire territory of the Parties to the conflict, not just to the vicinity of actual hostilities.' While, '[c]ertainly, some of the provisions are clearly bound up with the hostilities and the geographical scope of those provisions should be so limited', '[o]thers, particularly those relating to the protection of prisoners of war and civilians, are not so limited.'[28] The Tribunal eventually supported a wide geographical scope of application in concluding that '[u]ntil that moment [i.e. a general conclusion of peace/a peaceful settlement], international humanitarian law continues to apply in the whole territory of the warring States or, in the case of internal conflicts, the whole territory under the control of a party, whether or not actual combat takes place there.'[29] In applying the law to the facts, the Chamber finally concluded that

[e]ven if substantial clashes were not occurring in the Prijedor region at the time and place the crimes allegedly were committed—a factual issue on which the Appeals Chamber does not pronounce—international humanitarian law applies. It is sufficient that the alleged crimes were closely related to the hostilities occurring in other parts of the territories controlled by the parties to the conflict [...][30]

thereby applying a nexus test it previously had not referred to.

11   The ICTY Appeals Chamber's decision has been much commented on.[31] Many have recognized the Court's findings on the geographical scope as an 'interesting feature'[32] of the decision. An appraisal of the Court's ruling, however, has often been limited to its statement affirming the Conventions' application 'in the whole territory of the warring States'. To date, the Tribunal's differentiated approach to the geographical application of some of the Conventions' provisions and to its nexus test has been insufficiently developed.

12   Since its *Tadić* Appeals Chamber decision, the ICTY has held that the evaluation of the existence of a nexus between the alleged conduct of an accused and an IAC is a matter for trial.[33] It has also established criteria based on which one can examine the existence of a nexus between alleged crimes and an armed conflict. According to its jurisprudence,

---

[26] Ibid, para 66.   [27] Ibid, para 67.
[28] Ibid, para 68.   [29] Ibid, para 70.   [30] Ibid.
[31] See, e.g., C. Greenwood, 'International Humanitarian Law and the Tadić Case', 7 *EJIL* (1996) 265; and M. Sassòli, 'La première décision de la chambre d'appel du Tribunal pénal international pour l'ex-Yougoslavie: Tadić (compétence), 100 *Revue générale de droit international public* (1996) 101.
[32] A.P.V. Rogers, *Law on the Battlefield* (2nd edn, Manchester: Manchester University Press, 2004), at 219.
[33] ICTY, *The Prosecutor v Dario Kordić and Mario Čerkez*, Trial Chamber, Decision on Joint Defense Motion to Strike all Counts Arising under Article 2 or Article 3 for Failure to Allege a Nexus between the Conduct and an International Armed Conflict, IT-95-14/2, 1 March 1999.

[t]he armed conflict need not have been causal to the commission of the crime, but the existence of an armed conflict must, at a minimum, have played a substantial part in the perpetrator's ability to commit it, his decision to commit it, the manner in which it was committed or the purpose for which it was committed.[34]

To conclude that acts were closely related to an armed conflict, it is sufficient to establish that 'the perpetrator acted in furtherance of or under the guise of the armed conflict'.[35] Moreover, the ICTY noted that

[i]n determining whether or not the act in question is sufficiently related to the armed conflict, the Trial Chamber may take into account, *inter alia*, the following factors: the fact that the perpetrator is a combatant; the fact that the victim is a non-combatant; the fact that the victim is a member of the opposing party; the fact that the act may be said to serve the ultimate goal of a military campaign; and the fact that the crime is committed as part of or in the context of the perpetrator's official duties.[36]

The ICTY's jurisprudence thus gives some guidance on the required link between an alleged crime and an armed conflict for the purpose of distinguishing ordinary crimes from war crimes. However, it has not specifically addressed the nexus required for the application of IHL. After all, international law would arguably not require both standards to be the same.[37]

ii. Scope of application outside a belligerent's own territory

Resorting once more to the general rules of public international law regarding treaties, one might question the Conventions' application outside belligerent states' own territories. Article 29 VCLT binds states parties only in respect of their own territory. While proposals to include a general rule on the extraterritorial application of treaties were made during the Vienna Convention's drafting process, the ILC refrained from adopting them.[38]

Unlike international human rights law (IHRL), the extraterritorial application of which continues to be challenged,[39] conventional IHL of IAC is unanimously considered applicable outside a belligerent state's own territory.[40] Not least the nature of IACs, involving two or more states, requires the geographical scope of the Conventions to extend to extraterritorial actions by belligerent states. Excluding scenarios in which a state is initially to conduct hostilities against another state exclusively on its own territory (e.g. through attacks against embassies or military barracks), an IAC will ultimately force one of the belligerent states to act outside its own territory.

---

[34] ICTY, *The Prosecutor v Dragoljub Kunarac, Radomir Kovač, Zoran Vuković*, Appeals Chamber Judgment, IT-96-23 & 23/2, 12 June 2002, para 58.
[35] Ibid.
[36] Ibid, para 59.
[37] Similarly, a distinction has to be made between the nexus for the purposes of establishing war crimes and the belligerent nexus to determine a direct participation in hostilities. See Lubell and Derejko, above n 2, at 84.
[38] ILC, above n 18, at 213.
[39] For an overview of the extraterritorial application of international human rights law treaties, see M. Milanovic, *Extraterritorial Application of Human Rights Treaties. Law, Principles, and Policy* (Oxford: OUP, 2011) and F. Coomans and M.T. Kamminga (eds), *Extraterritorial Application of Human Rights Treaties* (Antwerp/Oxford: Intersentia, 2004).
[40] See, e.g., E. David, *Principes de droit des conflits armés* (4th edn, Brussels: Bruylant, 2008), who argues (at 256) that if, in the course of an IAC, a state is fighting on the territory of another state or on the high seas, it is 'evident' that the Conventions continue to govern the state's actions outside its own territory.

iii. Occupation

15 The Conventions also apply to cases of occupation, which are regarded and treated legally as a type of IAC.[41] One might therefore ask how the notions of 'occupation' and of the geographical scope of application of the Conventions interrelate.

16 It is important to recall that Common Article 2, while extending the Conventions' application to all cases of partial or total occupation even if it meets with no armed resistance, does not define 'occupation'. However, it has been interpreted to have a broader meaning than under Article 42 of the Hague Regulations, which requires territory to be 'actually placed under the authority of the hostile army' and which considers occupation to extend 'only to the territory where such authority has been established and can be exercised'. Common Article 2, unlike Article 42 of the Hague Regulations, arguably triggers the application of (certain provisions of) the Conventions already during the invasion phase, as soon as a civilian population comes into contact with invading forces.[42] The existence of occupation is thus determined not territorially but functionally. What consequences does this have for the geographical scope of the Conventions? If one supports a concept of occupation within the meaning of Article 42 of the Hague Regulations, the material and geographical scopes of occupation correspond. The laws of occupation then apply within a defined area over which a hostile army exercises effective control—even if such an area is limited to very small places (such as a village or small island).[43] If one accepts, however, that according to Common Article 2 the Conventions' application is triggered before territorial control is established, the material scope of occupation and the geographical scope of the Conventions differ. The Conventions' application then extends to the entire territory, while the application of the laws of occupation within such territory is restrained based on functional considerations, not territorial ones.

b. *Neutral territory and other areas*

17 The Conventions' extraterritorial application is supported not only with respect to belligerent states' territories (including cases of occupation), but also as regards the territory of neutral (i.e. non-belligerent) states and other areas, such as the high seas or outer space.

18 While the law of neutrality, together with the rules of *ius ad bellum*,[44] protects the inviolability of neutral territory, the Conventions will nevertheless apply if the law of neutrality is violated, for example in case of hostilities between belligerents on neutral territory. Similarly, while other areas, such as the high seas and outer space, have been removed from claims of sovereignty and reserved for peaceful purposes,[45] they too would have to be considered being part of the Conventions' geographical scope in case of armed conflict.

19 It is furthermore argued that a geographical distance from the belligerents' own territories or from locations of sustained combat operations is irrelevant for the application of IHL. For example, it is suggested that if during the Second World War US bombers had destroyed a Japanese aircraft carrier in a remote region of the Pacific Ocean, such an attack

---

[41] See Chs 67 and 1 of this volume.
[42] Pictet Commentary GC IV, at 21 and 60. See for a detailed discussion Ch 67, MN 41–51, of this volume.
[43] See T. Ferraro (ed), *Occupation and Other Forms of Administration of Territory* (Geneva: ICRC, 2012), at 24, and Ch 67, MN 21, of this volume.
[44] See Ch 5 of this volume.
[45] See Arts 89 and 88 United Nations Convention on the Law of the Sea; and Arts 2 and 3 Treaty on Principles Governing the Activities of States in the Exploration and Use of Outer Space, including the Moon and Other Celestial Bodies (Outer Space Treaty), respectively.

would have been considered governed by IHL despite its distance from the US, Japan, and locations of sustained combat operations.[46]

What types of acts between belligerents outside their own territories would then be considered governed by the Conventions? Surely if fighting ensued between belligerent states on neutral territory, the Conventions' protections would apply. If enemy combatants were taken prisoners on the high seas, they too would benefit from GC III. Even protected civilians fulfilling the criteria of Article 4 paragraph 1 GC IV, who find themselves neither in the territory of a belligerent state exercising control over them nor in occupied territory, would arguably be covered by GC IV.[47] If one accepts the nexus test established by the international criminal tribunals as the appropriate standard for the application of IHL to acts within a belligerent state's territory,[48] its analogous application to acts outside such territory seems plausible. The Conventions' application would thus extend to all acts closely related to the IAC—even if committed between belligerents outside their own territories.

C. Relevance in Non-International Armed Conflicts

In case of armed conflict not of an international character occurring in the territory of one of the High Contracting Parties, Common Article 3 requires each party to the conflict to apply certain minimum guarantees.[49] One might question if a distinct analysis of Common Article 3's geographical scope of application is justified. Why should it be different from the scope of application of the Conventions in which the provision is contained? Because it is the only rule within the Conventions applicable to NIACs. Due to its specificity, it has aptly been described as a 'Mini-Convention' or 'Convention within a Convention'[50] and deserves separate analysis.

I. Traditional non-international armed conflicts

Similar to IACs,[51] Common Article 3's application to the entire territory of a High Contracting Party, in case of traditional NIACs between its armed forces and a non-state armed group or between such groups, may be challenged.[52] In cases where hostilities are geographically limited to certain parts of a territory,[53] Common Article 3's application to areas remote from the battlefield may lead to counter-intuitive results. Despite being limited to some minimum guarantees (in contrast to the still moderate yet somewhat more substantive rules of Additional Protocol (AP) II), Common Article 3 contains certain rights and obligations the unqualified application of which within a High Contracting Party's entire territory may prove detrimental. In the absence of hostilities within a certain area, an obligation to collect and care for the wounded and sick (Common Article 3

---

[46] R. Chesney, 'Who May Be Killed? Anwar al-Awlaki as a Case Study in the International Legal Regulation of Lethal Force', 13 *YIHL* (2010) 3, at 34.
[47] See Ch 52 of this volume.   [48] See MN 12.
[49] See Ch 19 of this volume.   [50] Pictet Commentary GC IV, at 34.   [51] See MN 5–12.
[52] For a typology of (non-international) armed conflicts, see S. Vité, 'Typology of Armed Conflicts in International Humanitarian Law: Legal Concepts and Actual Situations', 91 *IRRC* 873 (2009) 69 and J. Pejic, 'The Protective Scope of Common Article 3: More than Meets the Eye', 93 *IRRC* 881 (2011) 1.
[53] See, e.g., the armed conflict between the Sri Lankan armed forces and Tamil Tigers, having taken place mostly in the northern and eastern regions of Sri Lanka.

paragraph 1(2) Geneva Conventions) appears simply redundant. However, an argument that in accordance with Common Article 3, members of organized non-state armed groups ('fighters') are protected only once they have disengaged from the fighting or have been placed *hors de combat*,[54] and may otherwise be directly targeted, including in areas remote from the battlefield, seems inappropriate to some. The killing of members of non-state armed groups away from the battlefield (for example in a government-controlled, peaceful capital) has thus frequently raised concerns.[55] It is crucial to note, though, that these concerns relate not only to the geographical scope of application of Common Article 3, but also to the interplay between IHL and IHRL, the legality of direct attacks against members of non-state armed groups based on their membership and the extent to which IHL not only prohibits but also allows certain conduct, such as the killing of 'fighters'.[56]

23   In its *Tadić* decision, the ICTY Appeals Chamber held that '[t]he geographical and temporal frame of reference for internal armed conflicts is similarly broad' as for IACs.[57] Given that Common Article 3 protects all those taking no (or no longer) active part in hostilities, it was found to apply 'outside the narrow geographical context of the actual theatre of combat operations'.[58] Taking into consideration Article 2 AP II, the Appeals Chamber further noted that IHL of NIACs is applicable to 'all persons affected by an armed conflict' and 'all the persons who have been deprived of their liberty or whose liberty has been restricted for reasons related to such conflict'. It thus concluded that 'the relatively loose nature of the language "for reasons related to such conflict", suggests a broad geographical scope as well', arguing that '[t]he nexus required is only a relationship between the conflict and the deprivation of liberty, not that the deprivation occurred in the midst of battle.'[59] While the Tribunal concluded its analysis with a broad observation ('international humanitarian law applies in the whole territory under the control of a party, whether or not actual combat takes place there'),[60] it may be argued that its nexus doctrine serves to limit this 'rather sweeping statement'[61] not only regarding certain provisions (i.e. Article 2 AP II), but with respect to the application of IHL of NIACs in general. Consequently, the geographical scope of IACs and NIACs within the territory of High Contracting Parties would be the same. The Geneva Conventions (including their Common Article 3) would apply to their entire territory, but be limited to acts having a sufficient nexus, i.e. being closely related to the armed conflict.

24   The ICTY's reference to 'the whole territory under the control of a party' may be regarded as a reminder of the possible parties to a NIAC, i.e. a substitution of the term 'warring States' used within its definition of the geographical scope of IACs.[62] Unlike in IACs, territory may be not under state control but the control of a non-state armed group. The reference may also, however, be seen as limiting Common Article 3's application to territories under the control of either the government or non-state armed groups, to the detriment of those

---

[54] See Melzer, above n 24, at 28.

[55] See M. Sassòli and L.M. Olson, 'The Relationship between International Humanitarian and Human Rights Law where it Matters: Admissible Killing and Internment of Fighters in Non-International Armed Conflicts', 90 *IRRC* 871 (2008) 599, at 613.

[56] For an analysis of the relationship between IHRL and IHL in NIACs, see D. Kretzmer, 'Rethinking the Application of IHL in Non-International Armed Conflicts', 42 *Israel Law Review* (2009) 8, and Ch 35 of this volume.

[57] ICTY, *Tadić*, above n 25, para 69. See also ICTR, *The Prosecutor v Georges Anderson Nderubumwe Rutaganda*, Trial Chamber Judgment, ICTR-96-3-T, 6 December 1999, para 101; and Swiss Military Court of Cassation, *Niyonteze*, 27 April 2001, at Ch 3 B.

[58] ICTY, *Tadić*, above n 25, para 69.   [59] Ibid.   [60] Ibid, para 70.

[61] Kreß, above n 10, at 266.   [62] See MN 10.

areas outside of any established control. While the application of AP II is limited to armed conflicts 'which take place in the territory of a High Contracting Party between its armed forces and dissident armed forces or other organized armed groups which, under responsible command, exercise such control over a part of its territory as to enable them to carry out sustained and concerted military operations and to implement this Protocol', Common Article 3 does not require any territorial control by a non-state armed group.[63] A limitation of the geographical scope of NIACs as suggested by the Appeals Chamber would thus be incompatible with Common Article 3's material scope.[64] So far, the ICTY's statement has not been further defined in (judicial) practice and might require clarification in the future.

II. 'Spillover', 'multinational', 'cross-border', and 'transnational' armed conflicts

In addition to traditional NIACs, in which government armed forces are fighting non-state armed groups within their territory, or in which non-state armed groups are fighting each other within the territory of a single state, various other types of armed conflicts involving non-state armed groups exist. They include 'spillover' armed conflicts between armed forces and non-state armed groups (or among non-state armed groups) spilling over into the territory of a neighbouring state, 'multinational' armed conflicts in which multinational armed forces support a state in its fight against non-state armed groups, 'cross-border' armed conflicts in which states are fighting non-state armed groups operating from the territory of a neighbouring state without the state's control over such groups, and 'transnational' armed conflicts in which states are fighting non-state armed groups in states other than neighbouring countries.

The question must therefore be raised if and to what extent Common Article 3 accommodates the possibility of NIACs outside a High Contracting Party's own territory.[65] Put differently, is the application of Common Article 3 limited to 'internal armed conflicts' and 'civil wars', or does it encompass 'spillover', 'multinational', 'cross-border', and 'transnational' armed conflicts?[66] Some consider this to be a moot question given the ICJ's finding that the substantive rules of Common Article 3 reflect 'elementary considerations of humanity' and constitute 'a minimum yardstick', which, in addition to the more elaborate rules, also apply in IACs.[67] According to these commentators, Common Article 3 today

25

26

---

[63] The control of a non-state armed group over a certain territory may, however, serve as an indicative factor to establish the degree of organization necessary in order to recognize an armed group as party to a NIAC; see ICTY, *The Prosecutor v Ramush Haradinaj, Idriz Balaj and Lahi Brahimaj*, Trial Chamber Judgment, IT-04-84-T, 3 April 2008, para 60.

[64] See also Lubell and Derejko, above n 2, at 69.

[65] A transnational application of AP II is commonly rejected because of the wording of Art 1 AP II, referring to armed conflicts 'which take place in the territory of a High Contracting Party between *its* armed forces and dissident armed forces or other organized armed groups' fulfilling certain criteria (emphasis added). However, the possibility of AP II's application to 'spillover' and 'multinational' armed conflicts is increasingly admitted. For an argument regarding the case of Afghanistan, see A. Bellal, G. Giacca, and S. Casey-Maslen, 'International Law and Armed Non-State Actors in Afghanistan', 93 *IRRC* 881 (2011) 47, at 59.

[66] For a distinction between the concepts of 'civil war' and 'non-international armed conflict', see A. Cullen, 'Key Developments Affecting the Scope of Internal Armed Conflict in International Humanitarian Law', 183 *Military Law Review* (2005) 66, who notes (at 79) that '[a]rguably one of the greatest achievements of the common Article is that it lowers the threshold for the application of international humanitarian norms' as '[i]t applies to all situations of non-international armed conflict, including situations of insurgency not reaching the threshold of a civil war.'

[67] ICJ, *Case concerning Military and Paramilitary Activities in and against Nicaragua (Nicaragua v United States of America)*, Merits, Judgment, 27 June 1986, at 114, para 218.

applies to any type of armed conflict regardless of its classification.⁶⁸ However, in the absence of a general definition of 'armed conflict' it remains worth analysing, by resorting to the rules of treaty interpretation contained in Articles 31 and 32 VCLT, whether Common Article 3 as treaty law applies to NIACs taking place extraterritorially.

a. Wording, context, and object and purpose

27   At first sight, the wording of Common Article 3 suggests its limitation to armed conflicts occurring within the territory of one state only. In accordance with its ordinary meaning, the provision's reference to the 'territory of *one* of the High Contracting Parties' (emphasis added) is to be understood in contradistinction to 'two', 'three', or 'several' High Contracting Parties' territories. However, given that Common Article 3 is not only addressed to states but equally binds non-state armed groups, it may be considered 'only logical'⁶⁹ that the provision requires a territorial link to a High Contracting Party. Thus, 'from the perspective of a newly drafted text, it appears more appropriate to interpret the phrase in question simply as emphasizing that Common Article 3 could apply only to conflicts taking place on the territory of States which had already become party to the new Conventions'.⁷⁰ The provision can therefore be interpreted to refer to the territory not of 'one' but of 'a' state party to the Conventions. Given the Conventions' universal ratification, it is moreover argued that any armed conflict today takes place on the territory of a High Contracting Party, and that the territorial reference within Common Article 3 has lost importance in practice.⁷¹

28   The existence of a NIAC is traditionally established based on positive criteria, i.e. the threshold of violence/intensity and degree of organization of the parties.⁷² According to some, these criteria presume a territorial limitation, as they are measured within a given area (e.g. intensity = frequency and severity of armed attacks within a defined space).⁷³ Yet Common Article 3's context might call for an alternative approach to defining NIACs. In order to avoid a 'gap in protection', which could not be explained by states' concerns about their sovereignty,⁷⁴ NIACs within the meaning of Common Article 3 may be defined negatively as all armed conflicts not covered by Common Article 2—regardless of their geographical extent. The US Supreme Court has applied this contextual approach to interpreting Common Article 3 in its *Hamdan* decision in 2006. It held that that the term 'armed conflict not of an international character', 'bears its literal meaning and is used […] in contradistinction to a conflict between nations'.⁷⁵

---

⁶⁸ See also Pejic, above n 52, at 204, who argues that 'to deny the applicability of Common Article 3 as treaty law based on the territorial clause but to accept its substantive application as customary law regardless of the type of conflict involved is basically a legal-technical argument with no practical consequences'.

⁶⁹ N. Melzer, *Targeted Killing in International Law* (Oxford: OUP, 2008), at 258.   ⁷⁰ Ibid.

⁷¹ ICRC, 'How is the Term "Armed Conflict" Defined in International Humanitarian Law?', Opinion Paper (2008), at 3. Nevertheless, the possibility of a NIAC occurring on the territory of a newly created state not (yet) party to the Conventions continues to exist. See also Ch 33 of this volume.

⁷² ICTY, *Tadić*, above n 25, para 70.   ⁷³ Emmerson, Interim Report, above n 2, at 18, para 63.

⁷⁴ M. Sassòli, 'Transnational Armed Groups and International Humanitarian Law', *HPCR Occasional Paper Series* 6 (2006), at 9. See also D. Jinks, 'September 11 and the Laws of War', 28 *Yale JIL* (2003) 1, noting (at 41) that 'Common Article 3 was revolutionary because it purported to regulate wholly internal matters as a matter of international humanitarian law' and arguing that '[i]f the provision governs wholly internal conflicts, as the "one state" interpretation recognizes, then the provision applies *a fortiori* to armed conflicts with international or transnational dimensions.'

⁷⁵ US Supreme Court, *Hamdan*, above n 5, at 6.

If 'the very object and purpose of IHL [...] [is] to provide relatively basic but feasible 29
standards in areas where the reality of armed conflict simply forestalls the application of
more protective (human rights) standards',[76] Common Article 3 should arguably only
be applied with territorial constraints. But the 'crowding-out' of IHRL might not be the
only reason to call for a restricted application of IHL. The assumption that IHL not only
prohibits and prescribes conduct (e.g. the treatment of detainees or the wounded and sick),
but also authorizes acts (e.g. the killing of members of organized armed groups)[77] has
caused concerns about its geographically unlimited application.[78] Nevertheless, it might
be arbitrary to limit Common Article 3's scope of application based on frontiers. After all,
the effects of armed conflicts which IHL seeks to govern do not necessarily stop at border
crossings. Following the 9/11 attacks, the debate about Common Article 3's geographical
scope of application was at first driven from a humanitarian perspective, and aimed to
extend protection to detainees captured in connection with the armed conflict between
the US and Al-Qaeda regardless of the detainees' place of capture. It has been considered
'almost unnecessary to point out that humanitarian considerations strongly militate in
favour of an expanded geographical reading of the territorial clause of Common Article 3'
and 'inconceivable' that persons captured in a NIAC could be deprived of the Article's
safeguards because its application ceases at a border.[79] The debate, however, has shifted
with the increasing resort to targeted killings, including through the use of armed drones.
From a military perspective it is argued that, if Common Article 3 is to govern the effects
of armed conflict, 'fighters' may be directly targeted regardless of their location, unless
having disengaged from the fighting or having been placed *hors de combat*. Limiting
Common Article 3's geographical scope of application to a single territory would invite
parties to use third country 'safe havens'.[80]

b. *Preparatory work*

The wording and context, as well as the object and purpose, of Common Article 3 are 30
'rather ambiguous'[81] regarding its potential extraterritorial application. The resort to supplementary means of treaty interpretation, most importantly the preparatory work of
Common Article 3, is therefore appropriate.[82]

Whereas efforts to extend the Conventions' application to NIACs were made before,[83] 31
the preparatory work for Common Article 3 was begun following the close of hostilities
of the Second World War. National Societies, having gathered at the invitation of the

---

[76] R. Geiß, 'Armed Violence in Fragile States: Low Intensity Conflicts, Spillover Conflicts, and Sporadic Law Enforcement Operations by Third Parties', 91 *IRRC* 873 (2009) 127, at 138.

[77] See US Department of Justice, above n 3, at 16; and J. Bellinger and V. Padmanabhan, 'Detention Operations in Contemporary Conflicts: Four Challenges for the Geneva Conventions and Other Existing Law', 105 *AJIL* (2011) 201, at 213.

[78] See MN 22.   [79] Pejic, above n 52, at 15.   [80] Chesney, above n 46, at 37.

[81] R. Bartels, 'Timelines, Borderlines and Conflicts. The Historical Evolution of the Legal Divide between International and Non-International Armed Conflicts', 91 *IRRC* 873 (2009) 35, at 60.

[82] In light of the importance attached to the historic circumstances surrounding the adoption of CA 3 by some commentators, it is suitable to recall the subsidiary nature of supplementary means of treaty interpretation, such as CA 3's *travaux préparatoires*. See contra, R. Ash, 'Square Pegs and Round Holes: Al-Qaeda Detainees and Common Article 3', 17 *Indiana International & Comparative Law Review* (2007) 269.

[83] See the Draft Convention on the Role of the Red Cross during Civil War submitted to the IXth International Conference of the Red Cross and Red Crescent in Washington DC in 1912, Resolution XIV adopted at the Xth International Conference in Geneva in 1921, and Resolution XIV adopted at the XVIth International Conference in London in 1938.

International Committee of the Red Cross (ICRC) in Geneva in 1946, suggested the introduction of a new provision that would extend the Conventions' application and proposed the following draft article: 'In the case of armed conflict *within the borders of a State*, the Convention shall also be applied by each of the adverse parties, unless one of them announces expressly its intention to the contrary.'[84] Several months later, the ICRC hosted a conference of governmental experts where National Societies' proposals were presented. The experts equally recommended the adoption of a provision defining the Conventions' scope of application, suggesting the following wording: 'In case of civil war, *in any part of the home or colonial territory of a Contracting Party*, the principles of the Convention shall be equally applied by the said Party, subject to the adverse Party also conforming thereto.'[85] They thus not only preferred limiting the provision's material scope of application to the Conventions' principles in case of reciprocal respect, but also amended its proposed geographical scope of application.[86]

32   After having consulted another round of governmental experts, the ICRC submitted consolidated draft conventions to National Societies and state parties, with a view to discussion and adoption at the XVIIth International Conference.[87] Accordingly, '[i]n all cases of armed conflict which are not of an international character, especially cases of civil war, colonial conflicts, or wars of religion, which may occur *in the territory of one or more of the High Contracting Parties*, the implementing of the principles of the present Convention shall be obligatory on each of the adversaries.'[88] In its comments, the ICRC addressed various issues, such as the (non) reciprocity in treaty obligations and the legal status of conflict parties,[89] but not the geographical scope of the proposed draft article. Consequently, it remains unclear why it chose to extend it from the territory of one state (possibly including its colonies) to the territory of one *or more* High Contracting Parties. The XVIIth International Conference in Stockholm in 1948 adopted the draft conventions with several amendments and requested the ICRC 'to take all necessary steps to ensure that the said draft[s], with the amendments which the Conference has made therein, be transmitted to the Governments, with a view to [their] adoption by a Diplomatic Conference'.[90] The newly amended provision then foresaw that '[i]n all cases of armed conflict not of an international character [footnote: "The words 'especially cases

---

[84] Emphasis added. Prior to the conference the ICRC had suggested that a provision be included providing that 'in case of civil war *within the frontiers of a State* the adversaries should be invited to declare their readiness to apply the principles of the Convention, subject to reciprocity being observed' (emphasis added). See ICRC, *Report on the Work of the Preliminary Conference of National Red Cross Societies for the Study of the Conventions and of Various Problems Relative to the Red Cross*, Geneva, 26 July–3 August 1946 (Geneva: ICRC, 1947), Series I, No 3a, at 15. While the approaches differ regarding the extent of legal obligation imposed, they both foresee a scope of application limited to the borders/frontiers of a state.

[85] ICRC, *Report on the Work of the Conference of Government Experts for the Study of the Conventions for the Protection of War Victims*, Geneva, 14–26 April 1947 (Geneva: ICRC, 1947), Series I, No 5b, at 8 (emphasis added).

[86] The reasons for this change of wording were not explained in the conference's report. It can only be assumed that colonial powers present at the conference considered the proposal made by National Societies (i.e. 'armed conflict within the borders of a State') to be too vague since it did not specify that a state's territory comprised both its homeland and colonies.

[87] ICRC, Draft Revised or New Conventions for the Protection of War Victims established by the International Committee of the Red Cross with the assistance of Government Experts, National Red Cross Societies and Other Humanitarian Associations (Geneva: ICRC, 1948).

[88] Ibid, at 5 (emphasis added).   [89] Ibid, at 6.

[90] Res XIX, Draft International Conventions, Report of the XVIIth International Red Cross Conference, Stockholm 1948, at 92.

of civil war, colonial conflicts or wars of religion' have been deleted."] which may occur *in the territory of one or more of the High Contracting Parties*, each of the adversaries shall be bound to implement the provisions of the present Convention.'[91] Notwithstanding the deletion of the words 'especially cases of civil war, colonial conflicts or wars of religion',[92] the provision's reference to the territory of one *or more* of the High Contracting Parties remained unchanged.

The Diplomatic Conference in Geneva in 1949 established a Special Committee to the Plenary Assembly's Joint Committee, after early discussions of the Conventions' draft common provisions showed that delegations held fundamentally different views about a possible application of the Conventions to NIACs generally and about the concept of NIACs specifically.[93] The Special Committee subsequently voted in favour of the extension of the Conventions' scope of application to NIACs, and decided further that the Stockholm draft should be abandoned and the cases of NIACs to which the Conventions would be applicable more clearly defined.[94] For this purpose, two different Working Parties were set up which subsequently presented various proposals that 'either restrict[ed] the cases of conflicts not of an international character to which the Conventions should apply, or restrict[ed] the contractual provisions to be applied in the case of a conflict which was not of an international character'.[95] Following the first Working Party's first proposal, which provided that '[i]n the case of armed conflict not of an international character occurring *in the territory of one of the High Contracting Parties*, each party to the conflict shall be bound to implement the provisions of the present Convention',[96] none of the subsequent proposals reverted to the Stockholm draft's wording. When the various proposals made by the Working Parties were presented to the Plenary Assembly, without making a recommendation as to their adoption for lack of agreement,[97] none of the draft provisions put forward thus still referred to the territory of one *or more* of the High Contracting Parties—including the second Working Party's proposal which finally received the necessary support and was adopted by 34 votes to 12 with 1 abstention.

The preparatory work of Common Article 3 has since been used to support arguments both in favour of and against a geographical limitation of the provision. Some commentators note that, possibly due to 'off-the record "hallway diplomacy"', the words 'or more' were most likely omitted because they were 'felt to be void because everyone seemed to

---

[91] ICRC, Revised and New Draft Conventions for the Protection of War Victims. Texts Approved and Amended by the XVIIth International Red Cross Conference, Revised Translation (Geneva: ICRC, 1948), at 32 (emphasis added).

[92] This deletion is generally explained by a concern of unintentionally limiting the provision's application to such conflicts. See G. Abi-Saab, 'Wars of National Liberation in the Geneva Conventions and Protocols', *Collected Courses of The Hague Academy of International Law*, 1979, vol IV (The Hague: Martinus Nijhoff Publishers, 1981), at 368.

[93] See especially the statements made by the representatives of Hungary, France, the UK, Norway, and Spain at the First Meeting of the Joint Committee, Final Record, vol II-B, at 10.

[94] Summary Record, Third Meeting of Special Committee of Joint Committee, ibid, at 45.

[95] Summary Record, Twenty-Third Meeting of Special Committee of Joint Committee, ibid, at 76.

[96] Summary Record, Fifth Meeting of Special Committee of Joint Committee, ibid, at 46 (emphasis added).

[97] Seventh Report drawn up by the Special Committee of the Joint Committee, Art 2 para 4 (Application of the Conventions to Armed Conflicts Not of An International Character), 16 July 1949, ibid, at 120–7; and Report drawn up by the Joint Committee and presented to the Plenary Assembly, ibid, at 128–33.

agree that the type of armed conflict being discussed was purely internal in character'.[98] Others argue that the Stockholm draft's reference to 'one or more' territories

> was probably lost in the subsequent attempts to restrict the application of the conventions to more narrowly and precisely defined cases of non-international armed conflict [...] without being re-introduced when it was finally decided to choose the opposite solution by restricting the applicable norms rather than their cases of applicability.[99]

Given the lack of record as to why earlier proposals extending Common Article 3's geographical scope of application to 'one or more' territories of High Contracting Parties were not adopted, both arguments remain speculative and Common Article 3's preparatory work ultimately only of limited value in assessing its geographical scope of application.

c. Practice

35 An analysis of state (and non-state) practice in applying Common Article 3 to 'spillover', 'multinational', 'cross-border', and 'transnational' armed conflicts might inform the debate.[100] State practice after the Second World War shows a significant amount of support for the application of Common Article 3 to 'spillover' armed conflicts. Uganda's military operations against members of the Lord's Resistance Army on Sudanese territory, military clashes between Colombian armed forces and Revolutionary Armed Forces of Colombia (FARC) members on Ecuadorian territory, and the spilling over of the Rwandan armed conflict onto the territory of the Democratic Republic of the Congo, for example, were widely considered covered by Common Article 3.[101] Whereas it is increasingly accepted that a renewed assessment of whether the threshold of NIACs is reached in the neighbouring country is not required (otherwise establishing a distinct NIAC),[102] it remains unclear to date to what extent the law of NIACs applies within the entire neighbouring country: '[P]resumably one would not argue that IHL applies throughout the entirety of the neighboring state on account of limited military operations chasing rebels across the border.'[103] However, the criteria based on which its application within the neighbouring country may be limited, for example a nexus approach or delimitation of a certain 'spillover area', remain to be determined in practice. In theory, the application of a nexus test, as in the case of 'traditional' NIACs, seems sensible. So far, 'cross-border' armed conflicts, as in the case of Israel's fight against Hezbollah on Lebanese territory, have not consistently been classified as NIACs—partly due to doubts as to Common Article 3's geographical scope. 'Transnational' armed conflicts have even less uniformly been regarded as NIACs covered by Common Article 3, and contextual interpretations based on the US Supreme Court's *Hamdan* decision have consistently been challenged. However,

---

[98] Bartels, above n 81, at 63. [99] Melzer, above n 69, at 258.
[100] Such analysis can either serve to establish 'subsequent practice' in the application of CA 3 within the meaning of Art 31 para 3 VCLT, or contribute to its customary modification or the creation of a corresponding customary international rule; see G. Distefano, 'La pratique subséquente des États parties à un traité', 40 *Annuaire français de droit international* (1994) 41.
[101] According to Art 1 of its Statute, the International Criminal Tribunal for Rwanda has the power to prosecute persons responsible for serious violations of IHL committed in the territory of Rwanda, and Rwandan citizens responsible for such violations committed in the territory of neighbouring states between 1 January 1994 and 31 December 1994.
[102] See *contra*, Geiß, above n 76, at 138.   [103] Lubell and Derejko, above n 2, at 78.

Common Article 3's application to 'multinational' armed conflicts has increasingly found support. Whereas it was once argued that relations between international troops involved in a NIAC in support of a territorial state and the non-state armed group should be governed by the law of IACs, such *'théorie des "conflits internationalisés à géométrie variable"'* is no longer upheld today.[104] Recent examples, such as the support of the International Security Assistance Forces to the Afghan Government, have shown that states generally accept the application of at least Common Article 3 in such cases outside their national borders.[105]

D. Critical Assessment

The lack of legal definition of the Conventions' geographical scope of application becomes apparent, first, with respect to their application within the territories of belligerent states. The general rules of public international law regarding treaties, especially Article 29 VCLT, certainly constitute a good point of departure for subsequent analyses. However, with respect both to IACs and NIACs, an unqualified application throughout a state's entire territory may be challenged. To date, state and judicial practice have not clearly established criteria on which a possible limitation could be based. Given the alternatives, that is, the restriction of the Conventions' application to places of 'hostilities' or the determination of the scope of application of individual rules, a nexus approach, according to which IHL applies throughout the entire territory to a specific act or omission if closely related to the armed conflict, seems preferable. 36

Secondly, the application of IHL outside a state's territory has received more (scholarly) attention, especially in cases of NIACs. However, it also remains largely undefined by practice. All things considered, an interpretation of Common Article 3 based on its wording, context, object, and purpose, as well as on its preparatory work, allows for either conclusion as to its geographical limitation. State and judicial practice will thus have to establish if, and to what degree, Common Article 3 is applicable outside a High Contracting Party's territory to cases of 'spillover', 'multinational', 'cross-border', and 'transnational' armed conflicts. Criteria based on which a geographically unlimited application of Common Article 3 can be restrained need to be agreed upon. While territorial approaches, e.g. the delimitation of 'spillover areas', raise concerns about the degree of arbitrariness attached to 'distance-based reasoning',[106] substantive approaches, such as the nexus test, increasingly receive support, and could form the basis for consent in the future. 37

KATJA SCHÖBERL

---

[104] G. Abi-Saab, 'Les protocoles additionnels, 25 ans après', in J.-F. Flauss (ed), *Les nouvelles frontières du droit international humanitaire* (Brussels: Bruylant, 2003) 17, at 24.

[105] See, e.g., G. Westerwelle, 'Paving the Way for a Responsible Handover: Germany's Engagement in Afghanistan after the London Conference', Policy Statement, German Parliament, 10 February 2010.

[106] Lubell and Derejko, above n 2, at 82.

Chapter 5. Rights, Powers, and Obligations of Neutral Powers under the Conventions

	MN
A. Introduction	1
B. Notion of Neutrality	5
I. Neutrality as a basic principle of international humanitarian law	5
II. Neutrality as a fundamental principle of the International Red Cross and Red Crescent Movement	8
III. 'Neutrality' as a status of states not parties to an international armed conflict	10
C. The Rights and Duties of Neutral States (Powers)	11
D. Different Possible Roles for a Neutral State under the Geneva Conventions	27
I. Obligations towards persons involved in an armed conflict who find themselves in the territory of a neutral state	28
a. Wounded, sick, and shipwrecked combatants	30
b. Permanent medical and religious personnel	36
c. Auxiliary medical personnel	37
d. Able-bodied combatants	38
e. Persons on board of vessels of belligerent parties in neutral waters or ports	42
f. Passengers of medical aircraft of a belligerent landing in a neutral state	44
g. Civilians of a party to the conflict on the territory of a neutral state	54
h. Missing and dead persons	63
II. Possibility to conclude agreements for the reception of prisoners of war in neutral territory	66
III. Possibility to conclude agreements to receive children in neutral territory	67
IV. Possibility to play the role of Protecting Power	69
E. Application in Non-International Armed Conflicts	70
F. 'War on Terror'	72
G. Concluding Remarks	73

Select Bibliography

Castren, E., *The Present Law of War and Neutrality* (Helsinki: Annales Academiae Scientiarium Fennicae, 1954)

Kussbach, E., 'Protocol I and Neutral States', 20 *IRRC* 218 (1980) 231

Michel, N., 'La neutralité suisse à l'épreuve du conflit du Kosovo', 2 *Revue suisse de droit international et de droit européen* (2000) 197

Monnier, J., 'Développement du droit international humanitaire et droit de la neutralité', *Quatre études de droit international humanitaire* (Geneva: Institut Henry Dunant, 1985)

Neff, S.C., *The Rights and Duties of Neutrals: A General History* (Manchester: Juris Publishing, 2000)

Politakis, G.P., *Modern Aspects of the Laws of Naval Warfare and Maritime Neutrality* (London and New York: Graduate Institute of International Studies/Kegan Paul International, 1998)

Schindler, D., 'Aspects contemporains de la neutralité', 121 *RCADI* (1967-II) 225

Seger, P., 'Neutrality', in A. Clapham and P. Gaeta (eds), *The Oxford Handbook of International Law in Armed Conflict* (Oxford: OUP, 2014) 248

Sersic, M., 'Neutrality in International Armed Conflict at Sea', in B. Vukas and T.M. Sosic (eds), *International Law: New Actors, New Concepts—Continuous Dilemmas* (Leiden/Boston, Mass: Martinus Nijhoff, 2010)

Skubiszewski, K., 'Law of Neutrality', in M. Soerensen (ed), *Manual of Public International Law* (London: Macmillan, 1968)

Heintschel von Heinegg, W., *Seekriegsrecht und Neutralität im Seekrieg* (Berlin: Duncker und Humblot, 1995)

A. Introduction

1   To be or not to be neutral, that is the question. It is not without reason that this chapter opens with this paraphrase of the Shakespearean query. Today, the evolution of the notion of neutrality suggests questions that cannot be easily answered. Specifically, the notion does not tell us whether states are or are not neutral in a specific armed conflict. Furthermore, it is not clear whether international law recognizes the possibility of intermediary stages between neutrality and belligerency.

2   The law of neutrality is a branch of international law which applies alongside international humanitarian law (IHL) to international armed conflicts (IACs). However, in the context of international law and the principles regulating humanitarian action, the term 'neutrality' arises in a different way from the way in which it is used in the legal framework applicable to neutral states. Specifically, neutrality is a principle of IHL to be observed by some actors operating in the context of armed conflicts, in particular by medical personnel. Neutrality is also a principle of the International Red Cross and Red Crescent Movement (IRCM). Therefore, before addressing the status of neutral states, this chapter first clarifies the meanings attached to the word 'neutrality'.

3   As for the status of neutral states, it is worth noting that when an IAC breaks out, the law of neutrality applies to states not party to that specific conflict, including those with a permanent status of neutrality. There is no difference between these types of neutrality; international law applicable to armed conflict is concerned with the rights and obligations of neutral states in a specific conflict, and with upholding their neutral status depending on whether they respect those obligations. Hereafter, the expression 'neutral state' is used to cover all states that are not party to a specific IAC.

4   Nowadays, the role of the law of neutrality in connection with IACs has lost much of its importance for two main reasons. The first is that neutrality is only linked to IAC, while the great majority of armed conflicts are non-international armed conflicts (NIACs). The second is that the adoption of the United Nations (UN) Charter has modified in depth the notion of neutrality by introducing the prohibition on the use of force by one state against another one. As Paul Seger has pointed out, 'the system of collective security, if it worked effectively, simply would leave no room for neutrality' and 'there exists general agreement among scholars that the laws of neutrality do not apply to measures of collective security adopted under Chapter VII of the UN Charter'.[1] Therefore, even states having

---

[1] P. Seger, 'The Law of Neutrality', in A. Clapham and P. Gaeta (eds), *The Oxford Handbook of International Law in Armed Conflict* (Oxford: OUP, 2014) 249, at 262.

a permanent status of neutrality are 'entitled to participate in all necessary measures, including the use of force, which the Security Council may have adopted or authorized to restore the international order, peace, and security'.[2] On the other hand, the United Nations Organization has nevertheless not considered it incompatible for a state to become a member of the Organization while keeping a permanent status of neutrality, therefore accepting implicitly that there is still room for neutrality. The reasons behind this apparent contradictory position, and the room left for neutrality, are explained below.[3]

B. Notion of Neutrality

The notion of neutrality has different meanings, which often causes confusion. We shall briefly examine these different meanings below.

I. Neutrality as a basic principle of international humanitarian law

Neutrality is a principle that has been attached to the basic idea of IHL since its origin. At first, the ambition of this body of international law was to protect and to bring assistance to wounded soldiers on the battlefield. To achieve this goal, it is indispensable that medical personnel be permitted access by the adversary to wounded soldiers. This permission is not likely to be given if the enemy fears any hostile acts from such medical personnel. The neutralization of medical personnel—being understood as the obligation imposed on such personnel to abstain from any hostile acts during the performance of their medical duties—is today part of the core of IHL. Therefore, this obligation has been extended to all IHL provisions dealing with activities devoted to the protection of, and assistance to, war victims; provisions that have developed increasingly since 1864, particularly with respect to the civilian population in conflict areas. The use of medical transports, including hospital ships and medical aircrafts, has also given rise to a new reflection on the notion of 'hostile acts', including the collection of sensitive information or other acts harmful to the enemy.

The principle of neutrality is a core element of IHL, which needs to be differentiated from two other fundamental principles, namely, the principles of humanity and impartiality. The principle of humanity requires a party or another addressee to protect the life and health of, and to ensure respect for, the human being; the principle of impartiality demands that there be no adverse distinction based on sex, race, nationality, religion, political opinions, or any other similar criteria for the victims of war. The three principles are therefore complementary but distinct.[4]

II. Neutrality as a fundamental principle of the International Red Cross and Red Crescent Movement

The book by Henry Dunant, *Un Souvenir de Solférino*,[5] written based on his experience of the aftermath of the terrible battle that took place in the vicinity of this town in 1859, was

---

[2] Ibid.   [3] See MN 18 ff and Seger, above n 1, at 262.

[4] On the principles of IHL, see in particular E. David, *Les Principes de droit des conflits armés* (5th edn, Brussels: Bruylant, 2012); and J. Pictet, *The Principles of International Humanitarian Law* (Geneva: ICRC, 1967).

[5] *Un Souvenir de Solférino* was published in 1862. A translation was published by the American Red Cross in 1939 under the title 'A Memory of Solferino'. Many other editions have been published, in French, English, and various other languages.

essential in convincing states to elaborate and adopt the first Geneva Convention (GC) in 1864 in order to improve the fate of the wounded and sick on the battlefield. But this book contains another idea which lies at the origin of the IRCM.[6] Realizing that there was a devastating lack of medical personnel, both in the French and in the Austrian armies fighting at Solferino, Dunant proposed the creation of civil societies during peacetime in order to support medical services of the armies during armed conflicts. This idea was successfully implemented, and because the red cross emblem had been chosen to identify the medical personnel and the role assigned to the National Societies to support these personnel, these Societies were given the name National Societies of the Red Cross and were authorized to use the red cross emblem. Naturally, they therefore had to comply with the same obligations as medical personnel of the armed forces in order to remain neutral while performing their activities in situations of armed conflicts. Once these Societies were created, they also became active in peacetime and started performing other humanitarian activities for all those in need of assistance. Nonetheless, they were allowed to keep their original name, as well as to use the emblem when performing those other activities. The importance of ensuring that the emblem retains its good image, and in particular for the National Societies to respect at all times the principles of humanity, neutrality, and impartiality, was then recognized by the IRCM, prompting it to adopt fundamental principles, with humanity, neutrality, and impartiality taking a central role.

9   Neutrality was basically conceived as a wartime principle. The National Societies realized that the transposition of their role, from helping all wounded and sick soldiers in the battlefield to serving the most vulnerable people in peacetime, demanded that the principle be extended. The definition of the principle of neutrality as adopted by the IRCM embraces this extension: 'In order to continue to enjoy the confidence of all, the Movement may not take sides in hostilities or engage at any time in controversies of a political, racial, religious or ideological nature.'[7] The concept of neutrality as a fundamental principle of the Red Cross therefore goes further than the requirements of the IHL's principle of neutrality. In addition, according to the IRCM, a special emphasis is put on the neutrality of the International Committee of the Red Cross (ICRC) as a 'specifically neutral and independent institution',[8] in conformity with the role and tasks attributed to it by the Geneva Conventions, and the necessity for this institution to retain the confidence of all parties to an IAC or a NIAC.[9]

III. 'Neutrality' as a status of states not parties to an international armed conflict

10   In addition to the obligation to abstain from committing, or participating in, hostile acts towards any party to an IAC, a neutral state (either with or without a permanent status of neutrality) has to observe the other requirements of the law of neutrality as set out by

---

[6] Called today 'International Red Cross and Red Crescent Movement' in the statutes of this Movement as adopted in 1986 at Geneva by the International Conference of the Red Cross. See also Ch 26 of this volume.

[7] Definition of the principle of neutrality given in Resolution VIII of the 20th International Conference of the Red Cross, Vienna, 1965.

[8] As mentioned in the present statutes of the IRCM, Art 5 para 3.

[9] On neutrality as a principle of the IRCM, see in particular J. Pictet, *The Fundamental Principles of the Red Cross Proclaimed by the 20th International Conference of the Red Cross, Vienna, 1975: A Commentary* (Geneva: Henry Dunant Institute, 1979) and M. Haroff-Tavel, 'Neutrality and Impartiality: The Importance of these Principles for the IRCM and the Difficulties Involved in Applying Them', 29 *IRRC* 273 (1989) 536.

Conventions adopted in 1907.¹⁰ For the most part, these Conventions are recognized today as reflecting customary international law on the subject. But at the same time, a neutral state remains bound by its duties as a state: in essence, it has to make political choices related to governing the country¹¹ and cannot simply abstain from taking a position in order to avoid controversy, as required from members of the IRCM.

C. The Rights and Duties of Neutral States (Powers)

It has been said that neutrality as the mere act of not participating in a war is as old as war itself.¹² However, this was a description of a fact of non-participation in hostilities, while the concept of neutrality as such developed only with the emergence of large and sovereign nation states in line with the 1648 Westphalian Treaties. The nineteenth century saw neutrality become a legal concept under customary international law. The main codification of the law of neutrality took place at the 1907 Hague Peace Conference, in particular with the adoption of the 'Convention respecting the Rights and Duties of Neutral Powers and Persons in case of War on Land'¹³ and the 'Convention concerning the Rights and Duties of Neutral Powers in Naval War'.¹⁴ For the main part, the content of those Conventions has today turned into customary international law. Without going into the detail of these two Hague Conventions, we shall briefly outline their main elements. 11

The territory of a neutral state is inviolable and may not be used by a belligerent to move troops or convoys, for military communication, or to recruit combatants. The neutral state, for its part, has the duty to prohibit such acts. Resistance of a neutral state, even by force, in response to attempts by a belligerent to violate its neutrality, cannot be regarded as a hostile act under *jus ad bellum* (but is nevertheless covered by the IHL of IACs).¹⁵ 12

Neutral states are allowed to maintain trade relationships with belligerent parties, while the latter are allowed to interfere with trade flows towards their enemy, in particular by applying the rules on prize, contraband, unneutral services, and blockade.¹⁶ 13

The supply by neutral states of ammunition or war material to a belligerent is prohibited.¹⁷ However, in the past, there was no obligation for neutral states to prevent either individuals crossing the borders and offering their services to one of the parties to the conflict, or the export of arms or munitions.¹⁸ The absence of such prohibition reflects a time when the distinction between the public and private realm was strict. International law has now evolved towards a more restrictive approach, alongside the increasing influence 14

---

¹⁰ See MN 11 ff.
¹¹ On this, see E. Castren, *The Present Law of War and Neutrality* (Helsinki: Annales Academiae Scietiarum Fennicae, 1954), at 85–6.
¹² See D. Schindler, 'Aspects contemporains de la neutralité', 121 *RCADI* (1967-II) 225, at 228; for an historical study of neutrality, see S.C. Neff, *The Rights and Duties of Neutrals: A General History* (Manchester: Juris Publishing, 2000).
¹³ Hague Convention V, signed at The Hague, 18 October 1907.
¹⁴ Hague Convention XIII, signed at The Hague, 18 October 1907.
¹⁵ See in particular Arts 1, 2, 3, 4, and 10 Hague Convention V.
¹⁶ See L. Doswald-Beck (ed), *San Remo Manual on International Law Applicable to Armed Conflicts at Sea* (Cambridge: CUP, 1995), para 150; N.L. Hill, 'The Origin of the Law of Unneutral Service', 23 *AJIL* (1929) 56, at 56–7.
¹⁷ Even if mentioned only in Art 7 Hague Convention XIII (1907), this rule is also recognized as applicable in wars on land.
¹⁸ See Arts 6–7 Hague Convention V (1907).

of states in commercial matters.[19] Nowadays, neutral states should prohibit the delivery of war material by private persons, 'in order to prevent the neutral territory concerned from becoming a base for belligerents'.[20] Whether this is an obligation in international law remains disputed.[21]

15   A chapter of Hague Convention V is devoted to the duties of neutral Powers relative to the treatment and internment of wounded or able-bodied belligerents on neutral territory, and we shall examine it below in section D.I, together with the corresponding provisions of the Geneva Conventions.

16   Similar principles, adapted to naval warfare but with more details due to the complexity of the law of the sea, are found in the 'Convention concerning the Rights and Duties of Neutral Powers in Naval War'.[22] We have seen at MN 14 the evolution of rules requiring neutral states to prevent private transfers of arms, ammunitions, or any other war material to a party to an IAC. Notwithstanding this development, the direct or indirect supply of such items by the neutral Power itself was already prohibited in 1907,[23] and even if the rule were to be found only in this Convention, it was considered valid for both land and maritime warfare. In addition, the neutral state has the obligation to prevent, within its jurisdiction, 'the fitting, arming', or 'adaptation for use in war' of any vessel, and its departure from the jurisdiction, if the state has reason to believe that such a vessel is intended 'to cruise or engage in hostile operations'.[24]

17   The Convention concerning the Rights and Duties of Neutral Powers in Naval War is complemented by the important 'Declaration concerning the laws of naval war',[25] which was adopted in 1909 in London. This Declaration was in the end not formally adopted,

---

[19] On this see, e.g., C. Rousseau, *Le droit des conflits armés* (Paris: Pedone, 1983), at 397; P. Dailler, M. Forteau, and A. Pellet, *Droit international public* (8th edn, Paris: LGDJ, 2009), at 1089, para 583; Neff, above n 12, at 145 et seq; E. David, 'Le droit de la neutralité à l'épreuve de la guerre du Golfe (1980–1988)', 11 *Cahier du Centre d'Etude de Défense et de Sécurité internationale* (1990) 43, at 44, paras 10 et seq.

[20] Castren, above n 11, at 475. In the same sense, see Dailler, Forteau, and Pellet, above n 19, at 1089, para 583.

[21] The position that 'State practice has modified the former convention rule' is also taken, inter alia, by the German 'Joint Services Regulation', 15/2 (German Bundeswehr, 1992) and for a substantial part by the doctrine. However, the Swiss Government still claims, in a report of 2 December 2005, that private companies on Swiss territory might export war material to states engaged in an armed conflict without violating the law of neutrality. The obligation of a neutral state would nevertheless demand that if the state decides to impose any restrictions on such export, those restrictions should be applied with impartiality. It needs to be recalled that Switzerland nevertheless imposes strict restrictions on the fabrication, transit, or export of war material in the framework of its *policy* of neutrality. See 'La neutralité à l'épreuve du conflit en Irak', prepared by the Swiss Government in response to a postulate of a member of the Swiss Federal Assembly (*Feuille Fédérale* 49 (13 December 2005) 6535, at 6542–55), quoted in L. Caflisch, *La pratique suisse en matière de droit international public, Compilation des chroniques de 1999 à 2010* (Bern: Direction du droit international public, 2012), at 231 ff. The *Commentary on the HPCR Manual on International Law Applicable to Air and Missile Warfare* (Program on Humanitarian Policy and Conflict Research at Harvard University: 2010) follows this Swiss line. According to the *Commentary*, even if '[s]tate practice clearly gives evidence of an increasing control of exports of arms and other military equipment […] [i]t seems that this is only a policy preference and not an expression of *opinio juris*' (at 319).

[22] Hague Convention XIII (1907).

[23] See Art 6 Hague Convention XIII (1907). On its applicability to land warfare, see G. Schwarzenberger, *International Law, as Applied by Courts and Tribunals*, II: *The Law of Armed Conflicts* (London: Stevens & Sons Ltd, 1968), at 557.

[24] See Art 8 Hague Convention XIII (1907).

[25] This Declaration can be found in D. Schindler and J. Toman, *The Laws of Armed Conflicts, A Collection of Conventions, Resolutions and Other Documents* (4th edn, Leiden/Boston, Mass: Martinus Nijhoff, 2004), at 1111 ff.

but was nevertheless broadly recognized as reflecting customary international law. It has also been completed on the regional level by the 'Havana Convention on Maritime Neutrality'.[26]

The two World Wars demonstrated the difficulty of remaining neutral in a 'total war' in which ideological and economic factors play an important role.[27] The creation of a system of collective security, in the framework of the League of Nations and subsequently in the framework of the UN, triggered the need for reconsideration of the law of neutrality. Soon after the adoption of the UN Charter, a part of the doctrine even deemed that the prohibition of war and the concept of collective security rendered obsolete the notion of neutral state.[28]

The Geneva Conventions are based on a separation between the '*jus ad bellum*' (regulations on the use of force in international relations) and '*jus in bello*' (restrictions on the means and methods of combat, and obligations towards the victims) dimensions of an armed conflict. They are founded on the principle that parties to an armed conflict have equal rights and duties according to *jus in bello*, independently of their responsibility under *jus ad bellum*. As a direct consequence, the concept of the neutral state again finds its place in the *jus in bello* system. States recognized this evolution, accepting the compatibility of being a member of the UN with having the status of permanent neutrality. In fact, this compatibility was accepted even earlier, when Sweden, as a neutral state, acceded to the UN in 1946, without any in-depth discussion.[29] The UN refused nevertheless to give such states special privileges, as demanded by Switzerland in preliminary discussions on its eventual accession. However, this demand lost its importance due to the incapacity of the UN to implement Article 43 of the UN Charter. Therefore, the Swiss Government, among others, deemed that in the absence of an agreement under Article 43, a member of the UN would not be obliged to participate in purely military actions decided under Article 42 of the UN Charter, and that participation in economic sanctions decided under Article 41 would be compatible with neutrality.[30] The Union of Soviet Socialist Republics (USSR) required Austria's permanent neutrality during the negotiations concerning the termination of Austria's occupation by the Allies, without this neutrality being considered as an obstacle to its accession to the UN.[31] Other UN member states have claimed a permanent neutral status, such as Costa Rica, Finland, Ireland, Malta, and Turkmenistan.[32]

---

[26] Ibid, at 1417 ff.

[27] See, in particular, Neff, above n 12, at 143 ff; Castren, above n 11, at 429 ff; Schindler, above n 12, at 235.

[28] This opinion was strongly defended, inter alia, by C.G. Fenwick, *International Law* (4th edn, New York: Appleton-Century-Crofts, 1965), at 727 ff. But see also Schindler, above n 12, at 237; Castren, above n 11, at 429 ff; David, above n 19, at 51.

[29] On the position of Sweden on its neutrality, see, e.g., O. Bring, 'L'influence de la Charte des Nations Unies sur le droit de la neutralité dans la guerre maritime: un point de vue suédois', 35 *Annales du droit international médical* (1991) 127; and Schindler, above n 12, at 246.

[30] See, in particular, Rapport du Conseil fédéral sur les relations entre la Suisse et l'ONU établi en réponse au postulat N.97.3320, 5 *Feuille Fédérale* 46 (24 November 1998) 4606.

[31] See I. Seidl-Hohenveldern, 'La neutralité permanente de l'Autriche', 35 *Annales de droit international médical* (1991: XIe session de la Commission médico-juridique de Monaco, 23, 24 et 25 mai 1991), at 96; and A. Verdross and B. Simma, *Universelles Völkerrecht* (Berlin: Duncker und Humblot, 1976), at 209 ff.

[32] However, the Declaration of Malta, for instance, confuses neutrality with the foreign policy of non-alignment: on this, see Dailler, Forteau, and Pellet, above n 19, at 1089, para 582; and J. Monnier, 'Développement du droit international humanitaire et droit de la neutralité', in *Quatre études de droit international humanitaire* (Geneva: Institut Henry Dunant, 1985), at 9. For details on the position of Switzerland and others vis-à-vis conflicts involving peace enforcement authorized by the UN Security Council, see Seger, above n 1, at 248.

20   The Geneva Conventions do not differentiate between states having a permanent neutral status and states without such status, but they do distinguish between states that participate and those that do not participate in a particular IAC.[33] The Geneva Conventions use the expression 'neutral Power' or 'neutral country' to cover all states not parties to a given IAC, the only exception being Article 4(B)(2) GC III, where the expression 'neutral or non-belligerent Powers' is used.[34] In fact, this Article mentions two scenarios: the first where the 'neutral or non-belligerent Power' receives persons belonging to one of the categories enumerated in Article 4 GC III from a belligerent state and the 'neutral or non-belligerent Power' has diplomatic relations with the Power on which the internees depend; the second where the two Powers do not have diplomatic relations. This precision is given in order to ensure protection for the individuals concerned by a Protecting Power or by their diplomatic representatives, not to differentiate between neutral and other non-belligerent states, where the absence of diplomatic relations is anyway not a decisive factor. It is therefore difficult to find a rational explanation for this exceptional addition of the expression 'non-belligerent' after 'neutral' Powers. The Pictet Commentary on GC III mentions it without explanation,[35] and does not conclude in any way that Article 4 meant to include states that are not covered by the provisions of the Conventions which mention exclusively 'neutral States' or 'neutral Powers'. In reality, this wording was already in the draft submitted at the 1949 Diplomatic Conference,[36] and even in the draft submitted previously at the 1948 International Red Cross Conference,[37] although this point was discussed neither in the former nor in the latter Conference. Its origin is to be found in the 1947 Conference of Government Experts, where the French Delegate made the distinction between neutral and non-belligerent states, with a reference to the Second World War, and suggested this modification, which was accepted without being discussed in earnest.[38] Logically, the acceptance of this wording should have resulted in the modification of all articles mentioning neutral states, but no one suggested this. Therefore, this reference to non-belligerent states in Article 4 GC III is a source of confusion, as it creates a dichotomy with the other Articles of the Convention, all of which mention only neutral states (or Powers). As there is no trace of any intention to distinguish between Article 4 and the other Articles referring to neutral states, we have to draw the conclusion that the entire GC III covers all states not participating in a given armed conflict under the headings 'neutral State' or 'neutral Power', without any intermediary status of 'non-belligerent state', in spite of the use of this expression in Article 4. Even an author who draws the conclusion that GC III 'a consacré, au moins indirectement, la neutralité différentielle' recognizes that 'aucun texte général

---

[33] See, e.g., Neff, above n 12, at 101 ff.

[34] The term 'neutral' (state, power, country, territory, etc) is used in Arts 4, 8, 10, 11, 37 GC I; in Arts 5, 10, 11, 17, 32, 40 GC II; in Arts 4, 10, 11, 109, 111, 123 GC III; and in Arts 4, 11, 12, 24, 36, 132, 140 GC IV.

[35] See Pictet Commentary GC III, at 69–70.

[36] See Final Record, vol I, at 74 (Draft Art 1 para 2(2)).

[37] See ICRC, Draft Revised of New Conventions for the Protection of War Victims, Document 4a of the XVIIth International Conference of the Red Cross (Stockholm, August 1948) (Geneva: ICRC, May 1948), at 53 (Art 3 para 2(2)).

[38] The Delegate of France made the following statement: 'Nous demanderions, toutefois, que le concept de pays neutre soit étendu également au pays non belligérant. En effet, certains de nos camarades ont été internés en Bulgarie, en Hongrie, ou même en Espagne, pays qui étaient non-belligérants à l'égard de la France, mais qui n'étaient pas considérés comme pays neutres': 'Sténogrammes' of the Conference of Government Experts for the Study of the Conventions for the Protection of War Victims (Geneva, 14–26 April 1947), vol IV, at 36.

SANDOZ

n'a procédé à la détermination explicite d'un véritable statut de neutralité différentielle ou de non-belligérance au sens large'.[39]

21 It is not by chance that the First Additional Protocol of 1977 (AP I) uses the expression 'neutral and other States not Parties to the conflict'.[40] To avoid misunderstanding, and to cover without ambiguity all states not a party to the IAC and not only those having the permanent status of neutrality, the draft Protocol I preferred the expression 'not engaged in the conflict'.[41] However, states having the permanent status of neutrality feared that the omission of the word 'neutral' would be a negative signal weakening their status, which is why they insisted on introducing the expression finally adopted.[42] In fact, this was a political claim, without legal or practical consequences for the rights and duties under IHL of the states concerned. Therefore, we can confirm that when an IAC breaks out, states are either belligerent or neutral.

22 This position departs from the idea of recognizing different intermediate situations between complete neutrality and belligerency[43] adopted by many states during different phases of the Second World War. Italy, Spain, Turkey, Argentina, Egypt, Bulgaria, Hungary, Romania, and even the United States before its entry into the war after the Japanese act of aggression, all declared themselves non-belligerent but not neutral, collaborating with one or several belligerents in a way that was not compatible with the law of neutrality.[44] This explains the suggestion made by the delegate of France mentioned above. However, even at that time, these positions were generally considered as a policy issue but not as introducing a new legal status.[45] We may therefore affirm the continuity of international law on this subject, or at least a return to its origin: there is no intermediate status, and no distinction is made in IHL between states having a permanent status of neutrality and states not participating in a given IAC.

23 This black and white approach must be more nuanced in practice. Depending on their degree of involvement in a given conflict, states may play some, but not all, of the roles attributed to neutral Powers. However, their humanitarian obligations remain the same. It is therefore important to investigate further the implication of various positions or types of action of states vis-à-vis other states during an armed conflict, and to draw a line between actions or positions that conform to neutral status and those which do not. In this regard, the jurisprudence of the International Court of Justice (ICJ) and the International Criminal Tribunals gives us useful indications, for instance, on the notion of participation in hostilities, control by a state of one of the belligerents, and humanitarian assistance.[46] A very delicate issue is the use of long-distance blockades, 'the prevailing view' being so far that this practice, developed during the Second World War, 'has not

---

[39] Dailler, Forteau, and Pellet, above n 19, at 1091, para 584.
[40] Expression found in Arts 2, 22, 31, 37, and 39 AP I.
[41] See ICRC Commentary APs, at 61, para 135.
[42] On this, see E. Kussbach, 'Protocol I and Neutral States', 20 *IRRC* 218 (1980) 231; and Monnier, above n 32, at 10 ff.
[43] On this, see Schindler, above n 12, at 262 ff; and Neff, above n 12, at 103 ff.
[44] Schindler, above n 12, at 264 ff; see also David, above n 19, at 51; and M. Bothe, 'Neutralité et guerre maritime', 35 *Annales du droit international medical* (1991) 60, at 60. On the debate in the US, see H.W. Briggs, 'Neglected Aspects of the Destroyer Deal', 34 *AJIL* (1940) 569, esp at 569, fn 2.
[45] See, e.g., Dailler, Forteau, and Pellet, above n 19, at 1090, para 584.
[46] On this see, e.g., V. Chetail, 'The Contribution of the International Court of Justice to International Humanitarian Law', 85 *IRRC* 850 (2003) 235 and C. Greenwood, 'The Development of International Humanitarian Law by the International Criminal Tribunal for the Former Yugoslavia', 2 *Max Planck Yearbook of United Nations Law* (1998) 97.

developed into customary law'.[47] Furthermore, it is important to recall that humanitarian assistance (with a precise list of goods which may be included in it) may not be considered as contraband.[48]

24   In practice, it is not so much the permanent or non-permanent status of neutrality that is important. The issue has more to do with, on the one hand, the willingness and ability of a given state to play the role devoted to neutral states in a given context, and, on the other hand, the perception of a belligerent as being, or not being, the victim of hostile or unfriendly acts from a state which is pretending to be neutral, even if the violation of some provisions of the law of neutrality does not have as an automatic consequence the total loss of this status. The reaction of the belligerent state towards a violation of the law of neutrality should be, first, to require an end to the illegal behaviour by the neutral state. In the event of refusal, the belligerent state should not exceed what is necessary to end the violation of the neutral state's obligation.

25   In addition, we have to distinguish cases where neutral states have a right to take the initiative from situations where certain behaviour is required on their part. The absence of involvement in an armed conflict, and the state's capacity and willingness to play a peaceful role, should be crucial factors in the former situation. The Commentary to GC IV gives a clear example of this in explaining the choice given to the parties to an IAC to accept or refuse the proposal of a neutral state as a Protecting Power: 'The enemy Power […] may consider, for political reasons for example, that the neutral Power in question is not sufficiently neutral in its eyes to carry out its protective mission in an impartial manner.'[49]

26   As for the costs of different tasks assumed by the neutral state, nothing is mentioned in the 1907 Hague Conventions. Nevertheless, the principle should be that the state 'whose nationals are benefited' bear the costs, as set out in GC IV for the accommodation of civilians who live in enemy territory and want to leave it for a neutral state when an armed conflict breaks out.[50] This principle should be applied when civilians or combatants of a party to the conflict spontaneously enter a neutral state. However, it will also depend on the economic situation of both states and the quality of their relationship; the relationship between the state of origin and its citizens who have chosen to leave; and on many other factors. The participation of the international community, individual contributions of states, or the help of regional or international organizations, such as the United Nations High Commissioner for Refugees (UNHCR), are also of importance with regard to who should bear the costs. When there are agreements, the question of cost should be part of them.

D. Different Possible Roles for a Neutral State under the Geneva Conventions

27   As mentioned above, the notion of a 'neutral state' in the Geneva Conventions includes all states not party to an IAC. Therefore, the use of this expression in this section of the

---

[47] M. Sersic, 'Neutrality in International Armed Conflicts at Sea', in B. Vukas and T.M. Sosic (eds), *International Law: New Actors, New Concepts—Continuous Dilemmas* (Leiden/Boston, Mass: Martinus Nijhoff, 2010), at 592.

[48] See Doswald-Beck (ed), above n 16, para 150.

[49] Pictet Commentary GC IV, at 87

[50] See Art 36 GC IV. It is also mentioned in Art 116 GC III that the cost of transport of POWs to, or repatriation from, a neutral state 'shall be borne […] by the Power on which the said prisoners depend'.

I. Obligations towards persons involved in an armed conflict who find themselves in the territory of a neutral state

Article 4 GC I requires any neutral Power to apply the Convention 'by analogy' to 'the wounded and sick, and to members of the medical personnel and to the chaplains of the armed forces of the Parties to the conflict, received or interned in their territory, as well as to dead persons found', and Article 5 GC II contains similar language for warfare at sea, adding the shipwrecked to the wounded and sick. This provision has been confirmed in Article 19 AP I for those persons covered by Part II of that Protocol. The Third and Fourth Geneva Conventions do not have such a general Article, but have specific provisions on hospitalization or internment in neutral states. 28

The delicate questions are the following: Does the neutral state have an obligation to accept some of those persons? If not, does the neutral state have the right to expel those who express the wish to remain, and where and under what conditions? Does the neutral state have the obligation to intern or otherwise compel some of those persons to remain on its territory? What are the legal guarantees given to these persons? In approaching these questions, we shall first see the rules applicable to different categories of people, before examining more precisely the case of medical aircraft landing in neutral states and then the case of persons belonging to one party to the conflict on board ships entering neutral waters or ports of a neutral state. 29

a. Wounded, sick, and shipwrecked combatants

With a few exceptions, wounded and sick combatants who do not meet the criteria for direct repatriation have to remain interned[51] with other military internees, to be treated as prisoners of war (POWs) if they recover, until the 'cessation of active hostilities',[52] unless an agreement is found between the neutral state and all of the parties to the conflict for an earlier repatriation. The pertinent rights and duties of POWs as prescribed by GC III[53] have to be respected by the neutral state in regard to such persons, called 'military internees'.[54] 30

The provisions mentioned above concern those wounded and sick soldiers of one of the belligerent parties who find themselves on the territory of the neutral state, either deliberately seeking shelter due to circumstances (for example, following the landing of a plane in distress or an involuntary crossing of the border), or through an organized or at least accepted transfer to a neutral state. We might ask whether wounded or sick civilians who are nationals of one of the belligerent parties are also covered by these provisions, as AP I has given a definition of the wounded and sick which covers both combatants and civilians, and which is broader than the current commonsense definition, including all persons 'in need of immediate medical assistance or care', such as newborn babies, maternity cases, expectant mothers or persons having an infirmity.[55] This definition is nowadays 31

---

[51] See Art 110 GC III.
[52] According to the expression used in Art 118 para 1 GC III. On the precise meaning of this expression, see Ch 51, MN 20–24, of this volume.
[53] On these rights and duties, see Chs 47 ff of this volume.
[54] According to Art 4B(2) GC III and, when applicable, according to Art 4 GC I and Art 5 GC II.
[55] See this definition in Art 8(a) AP I.

part of customary international law,[56] and the civilians of a party to the conflict covered by it, as well as other civilians finding themselves on the territory of a neutral state, shall benefit, *mutatis mutandis*, from the rules of Part II of AP I, as prescribed by its Article 19 mentioned at MN 28. They must in particular be treated humanely and receive the medical care and attention required by their condition. However, IHL based on classical neutrality law applies only to the military wounded and/or sick, and the duties of neutral states towards the civilian wounded and/or sick do not go beyond the obligations derived from international human rights law (IHRL). We shall see this in examining the situation of civilians on the territory of the neutral state (see section D.I.g of this chapter). In the system of the Geneva Conventions, the expression 'wounded, sick or shipwrecked' covers only members of the armed forces, and we shall examine first the specific rules of GC I and II that concern them.

32 The fate of the shipwrecked is not entirely clear. As for those who have been rescued by a merchant ship of a neutral state and brought into that state, as well as those who have been taken on board neutral warships in territorial waters of their own belligerent party or in territorial waters of the neutral state, some authors would consider that they should be released. For the former group, it is argued that the warships of the belligerent parties did not make use of the right to request the surrender of the wounded, sick, or shipwrecked on board these merchant ships (in contrast with those who are on board warships of neutral states); for the latter, it is said that they were not subject to capture by the enemy at the moment they were rescued[57] and, for these reasons, that they should be considered as escaped prisoners. This viewpoint is disputable, and we might also deem that these persons have to be treated in the same way as those who entered the neutral state by themselves and have to be interned. In the absence of clarification on this point, we consider that a margin of appreciation is left to the neutral state in question, and that it could adopt one or the other position without violating its obligations.

33 As a principle, wounded and sick combatants shall be given as a minimum the humane treatment and medical care required by GC I from the belligerent parties,[58] in addition to being treated as POWs by the neutral state in conformity with Article 4(B)(2) GC III. As soon as they have recovered from their wounds or sickness they are solely covered by GC III.[59] As soon as is feasible, the neutral state shall directly repatriate them when their state of health corresponds to the criteria given for a direct repatriation by GC III,[60] or when those criteria are reached if a deterioration in their state of health occurs later on. All decisions in these contexts are delicate, and neutral states could easily be the target of criticism by one or the other parties to the conflict. For that reason, the Convention requires the neutral state and the parties to the conflict to search for an agreement in order to determine the prisoners who may be repatriated and the establishment of a mixed medical commission.[61] This commission has to determine if the state of health

---

[56] See ICRC CIHL Database, Rule 109, at 396.
[57] In this sense, see Pictet Commentary GC II, Art 15, at 107 ff, and Art 17, at 117 ff. On a global view on maritime neutrality, see W. Heintschel von Heinegg, *Seekriegsrecht und Neutralität im Seekrieg* (Berlin: Duncker und Humblot, 1995); G.P. Politakis, *Modern Aspects of the Laws of Naval Warfare and Maritime Neutrality* (London/New York: Graduate Institute of International Studies/Kegan Paul International, 1998); and Sersic, above n 47.
[58] On those notions, see Ch 37 of this volume; and for the shipwrecked, see Ch 38.
[59] See also MN 30.   [60] See Art 110 para 1 GC III. See Ch 51, MN 7–10, of this volume.
[61] For an overview of these duties, see Art 110 paras 3 and 4 GC III.

of prisoners who are candidates for repatriation before the end of active hostilities corresponds to the criteria established by the Convention. If no agreement is found with the parties to the conflict, the neutral state should take inspiration from the criteria given by the 'Model agreement concerning direct repatriation and accommodation in neutral countries of wounded and sick prisoners of war'.[62] It would be wise for the neutral state, if no agreement can be found in the framework of the mixed medical commission, to find a solution in consultation with internationally recognized medical experts and the ICRC, in order to protect itself from accusations by one of the belligerent parties that it does not respect its duties as a neutral state.[63]

The cases of military internees who are victims of an accident during their captivity are examined for direct repatriation or internment in a neutral state according to the same criteria as other prisoners, unless they mutilate themselves voluntarily.[64] In this last hypothesis, the prisoner shall be given the necessary medical care, but is not automatically eligible for direct repatriation or internment in a neutral state. The aim of this restriction is to avoid any incentive to self-mutilate. Therefore, the neutral state should not repatriate a prisoner in such a case without the agreement of all parties to the conflict.

Direct repatriation of POWs against their will during the armed conflict is prohibited by GC III.[65] This provision had been disputed during the 1949 Diplomatic Conference, but was finally introduced in particular for the cases where, following a change of regime, the prisoner would encounter a risk of persecution after his return.[66] This provision formally concerns only wounded and/or sick combatants, but is valid for able-bodied prisoners as well.[67] Although addressed to the parties to the conflict, neutral states shall also apply it according to Article 4(B)(2) GC III. As the risk which justifies the provision depends on the situation in the country to which the prisoner is to be repatriated, nothing justifies a difference in treatment.

b. Permanent medical and religious personnel

Permanent medical personnel, as well as the religious personnel attached to the armed forces, who must anyway be 'respected and protected in all circumstances',[68] shall be freed. The possibility given to a party to the conflict to retain all or part of the permanent medical personnel of the armies[69] 'in so far as the state of health, the spiritual needs and the number of prisoners of war so require', is not really adapted to a neutral state. Even in exceptional circumstances where such a state would be confronted with the influx of a huge number of POWs in need of medical care on its territory, it is doubtful that it could compel members of the permanent medical personnel who refuse to remain on the sole basis of Article 4 GC I (and Article 5 GC II), at least without the consent of the party to the conflict on which they depend.[70] A possible request for asylum should be dealt with in

---

[62] This agreement has been adopted by the 1949 Diplomatic Conference as the Annex 1 to GC III.
[63] See Art 110 para 2 GC III. See Ch 51, MN 16, of this volume.   [64] See Art 114 GC III.
[65] See Art 109 para 3 GC III.   [66] See Pictet Commentary GC III, at 512.
[67] Ibid, at 512 ff.   [68] See Art 24 GC I and Art 36 GC II.
[69] With the exception of the medical personnel who might have been put at its disposal by the National Societies of a neutral state: those personnel may not be retained (see Arts 27 and 32 GC I).
[70] As Art 4 GC I and Art 5 GC II require neutral states to apply these Conventions by analogy, the right to retain permanent medical personnel (Art 26 GC I and Art 37 GC II) might be considered applicable. However, the situation of neutral states is different and their room for manoeuvre is broader. Such retention might even be considered as in contradiction to the human rights obligations of the neutral state concerned. In the same sense, see ICRC Commentary APs, para 1178.

conformity with international refugee law and internal laws, and a member of the permanent medical personnel who would request to leave for a third country (and who would be accepted by it) should be permitted to do so.

c. Auxiliary medical personnel

37   Members of the auxiliary medical personnel who have entered the territory of a neutral state should be kept as military internees unless such entry was effected pursuant to an agreement, or they are severely wounded and meet the conditions for direct repatriation specified in Article 110 GC III, or if an agreement providing for their repatriation is found between the neutral state and the parties to the conflict (see MN 30–35).

d. Able-bodied combatants

38   The able-bodied combatants of a party to the conflict who enter the territory or territorial waters of a neutral state, must be interned until the end of hostilities[71] and treated as POWs.[72] This is also the case for the shipwrecked who are taken on board a neutral warship or a neutral military aircraft on the high seas or in the territorial waters of a state with which their own state is in conflict.[73] The possible repatriation of soldiers who have crossed the border by mistake is envisaged by some authors, but it is at least 'uncertain whether this exception is permissible'.[74] We would opt for a negative reply to this question, which would be too difficult to clarify and would open the door to arbitrariness.

i. Escaped prisoners of war

39   Escaped POWs must be left at liberty and can leave the country. If they wish to remain and are permitted to do so, they should abstain from participation in the hostilities, even in an indirect manner, and a place of residence may be assigned to them.[75]

ii. Deserters and conscientious objectors

40   International humanitarian law and the law of neutrality also leave room for some doubts as to the treatment of deserters who enter a neutral state. Some authors think that according to the principles derived from the law of neutrality, deserters should be interned if they enter in large contingents. This seems logical, given that differentiation between those who desert and the other soldiers entering the neutral state is difficult to establish and is not justifiable. As for individual cases, some authors think that only a deserter who wishes to join the adverse party should be interned.[76] There are arguments in favour and against these solutions, and the neutral state therefore enjoys a margin of appreciation in this respect. However, international refugee law also has to be taken into consideration. The present trend is not to accord the status of refugee easily, which is anyway not automatic for deserters and conscientious objectors.[77] Nevertheless, combatants leaving a country where an IAC or a NIAC is taking place are generally not expelled by the receiving country.

---

[71] See Art 11 Hague Convention V (1907).   [72] See Art 4(B)(2) GC III.
[73] See Art 15 GC II and Pictet Commentary GC II, at 107 ff.   [74] Castren, above n 11, at 464.
[75] See Art 13 Hague Convention V (1907).
[76] These questions are discussed, inter alia, by Castren, above n 11, at 467 ff, with references to other authors.
[77] This restrictive trend is apparent, for instance, in Art 3(3) of the Swiss Asylum Law, *Recueil systématique du droit fédéral* 142.31, as revised in 2012. For a global vision on this subject, see, in particular, the *UNHCR Handbook on Procedures and Criteria for Determining Refugee Status under the 1951 Convention and 1967 Protocol relating to the Status of Refugees* (Geneva: UNHCR, 1992), paras 167–74.

e. Persons on board of vessels of belligerent parties in neutral waters or ports

42 Warships of the belligerent parties are allowed to cross neutral waters[78] and to spend a short time in ports of neutral states.[79] If they do this in conformity with the law of neutrality, those on board shall be permitted to remain on their ship and to continue their course. The warship is not subject to inspection, and it can keep on board any prisoners or wounded combatants it might be detaining. If it wishes to disembark any wounded and sick or prisoners who are on board in the neutral state, it can do so with the agreement of the neutral state. The neutral state is not obliged to agree but should take into consideration humanitarian reasons for agreeing, and should at least give a positive reply for those persons in need of urgent medical care. As for the wounded and sick members of the armed forces of a party to the conflict to which the warship belongs, they should then be interned as military internees until the end of active hostilities, unless their state of health deteriorates and renders them eligible for direct repatriation, or if there is an agreement between all parties to the conflict. The fate of the POWs is not clearly determined by the law of neutrality and the neutral state must examine the situation carefully. The party to which the warship belongs should not draw an advantage from this operation in shifting its responsibility to keep the prisoners in internment during the armed conflict onto the neutral state.[80] For this reason, latitude should be left to the neutral state either to refuse to accept the POWs, or to accept them only with the consent of the adverse party(ies), or to accept them under the condition that they shall be freed without delay (or as soon as their state of health authorizes their transfer). Nevertheless, for the POW whose state of health corresponds to the criteria laid down in GC III for possible accommodation in a neutral country,[81] an agreement for his internment until the end of active hostilities might be envisaged.

41 Another unanswered question is one concerning combatants on board vessels entering neutral waters or the port of a neutral state, as well as those who find themselves in a plane landing on the territory of a neutral state; their case is examined below.

43 If warships commit acts of hostilities in neutral waters, or if they do not respect either the prescriptions in the port or the order to leave the port, the neutral state can stop and seize them. In such cases, the sailors and crew of the warship should be interned as military internees, some of them remaining on board the immobilized vessel.[82] In such a case, the fate of the POWs who might be on board the vessel is not expressly clarified. It might be possible to consider them as if they had escaped,[83] but this solution is disputable; they should rather be considered as combatants entering a neutral state and kept until the end of active hostilities, unless an arrangement is found by the neutral states with the parties to the conflict. A prize can be brought into a neutral port only in a strictly limited number of cases ('unseaworthiness, stress of weather, or want of fuel or provisions') and 'must leave as soon as the circumstances which justified its entry are at an end'. If it does not obey the

---

[78] Which are 'internal waters, territorial sea and where applicable, the archipelagic waters of neutral States'. See Doswald-Beck (ed), above n 16, Art 14 and commentary, at 94.
[79] In conformity with Art 5 Hague Convention XIII (1907), which reflects customary international law: see also the 'Helsinki Principles of the Law of Maritime Neutrality' adopted by the International Law Association on 30 May 1998, point 2.2. These principles may be found in Schindler and Toman, above n 25, at 1425 ff.
[80] For interesting reflections and suggestions on this question, see Pictet Commentary GC II, at 125 ff.
[81] Art 110 para 2 GC III.   [82] See Art 24 Hague Convention XIII (1907).
[83] See MN 39.

order to leave, the neutral state 'must employ the means at its disposal to release it with its officers and crew', and it must intern the crew placed on board by those who seized the prize.[84]

f. Passengers of medical aircraft of a belligerent landing in a neutral state[85]

44 A medical aircraft of a party to the conflict shall not fly over the territory of a neutral state 'except by prior agreement'.[86] It is nevertheless possible that a medical aircraft will fly over the territory of a neutral state without such an agreement, 'through a navigational error or because of an emergency affecting the safety of the flight'.[87]

45 The risk for any state to have an unidentified aircraft in its aerial space is well known, and the possibility of attacking such an aircraft is not excluded.[88] The aircraft in question must make every effort to give notice of the flight and to identify itself, and must obey without delay an order to land (or to alight on water). Medical aircraft flights in conformity with an agreement may also be ordered to land (or alight on water) for inspection if the neutral state has any suspicions about them. However, this possibility should in principle be specified in the agreement and, in conformity with the principle of neutrality, 'applied equally to all Parties to the conflict'.[89]

46 In all cases, the first goal of the inspection is to determine whether the aircraft is 'in fact a medical aircraft', that is, 'exclusively employed for the removal of wounded and sick and for the transport of medical personnel and equipment',[90] or, according to the nowadays accepted definition given by AP I, 'assigned exclusively to medical transportation' (the simultaneous transport of both civilian and military wounded and sick is accepted by this Protocol and by customary international law).[91] If this is not the case, the aircraft can be seized. If the inspection discloses that it is in fact a medical aircraft, the aircraft shall be allowed to resume its flight.

47 As for the persons who are in the aircraft, the Geneva Conventions and AP I do not provide any clear answers,[92] often mentioning the requirements of international law without further elaboration. We shall therefore examine here in further detail the situation of these persons.

48 In cases where the aircraft is seized for reasons mentioned above, all passengers are placed under the responsibility of the neutral state. If there are military wounded or sick of any party to the conflict, they shall be given the necessary medical attention and care and be interned similarly to POWs, as military internees, until the end of hostilities, unless they fulfil the conditions laid down in Article 110 GC III for direct repatriation, or there is an agreement between all parties concerned. If there are civilian wounded or sick, they

---

[84] See Art 21 Hague Convention XIII (1907).

[85] See Art 37 GC I, Art 40 GC II, and Art 31 AP I.

[86] Art 31 AP I, which is part of customary international law. See ICRC CIHL Database, Rules 29 et seq; ICRC CIHL Study, at 98 ff; Doswald-Beck, above n 16, Art 181; and *Commentary of the HPCR Manual*, above n 21, at 196 ff, paras 84 et seq.

[87] Art 31(2) AP I.

[88] However, of course, only as a last resort, 'all reasonable efforts' having previously been made 'to give the order to land or to alight on water [...] or to take other measures to safeguard its own interests, and, in any case, to allow the aircraft time for compliance, before resorting to an attack' (which does not exclude but does not imply the shooting down of the aircraft, which would be only the 'last step in a series of measures'): see Art 31(2) AP I, and ICRC Commentary APs, at 328 ff, paras 1142 et seq, in particular para 1149.

[89] Art 37 para 2 GC I and Art 40 para 2 GC II.

[90] Art 36 para 1 GC I and Art 39 para 1 GC II.   [91] Art 8(g) AP I.

[92] In Art 37 para 3 GC I, Art 40 para 3 GC II, and Art 31(4) AP I.

shall be treated with humanity but they shall neither benefit from special protection, nor be submitted to any of the restrictions encompassed by the Geneva Conventions.[93]

If there are able-bodied combatants on the plane, they should be interned as military internees until the end of the hostilities, unless their state of health deteriorates to such a degree that they fulfil the requirements for direct repatriation, or if an agreement is found with all parties to the conflict. 49

The fate of the crew, if they are civilians, is not absolutely clear, unless they have participated in hostilities[94] or have committed war crimes and must be detained for that reason. We might refer to Article 4(A) subparagraph (4) or (5) GC III. However, this Article is no longer strictly applied and does not cover the situation exactly. The crew of a medical aircraft is, or at least should generally be, part of the medical personnel, and their fate, in this hypothesis, should be similar to that of the medical personnel: they should not be detained if they are 'exclusively engaged'[95] in such activities, and this solution also seems suitable for possible civilian members of the crew. Nevertheless, if they are not exclusively assigned to this task, they might be treated either as 'civilian members of military aircraft crews'[96] or as 'members of the crews of civil aircraft'.[97] The first hypothesis is not likely to occur. Nowadays it is difficult to envisage members of the crew not being part of the armed forces. The implementation of the second hypothesis leaves a certain margin of appreciation. The mention in this provision of possible 'more favourable treatment under any other provisions of international law' refers in particular to Article 6 of Hague Convention XI (1907),[98] which opens the door to the possible return of the persons concerned.[99] In fact, this provision guarantees that the neutral state will not participate in hostilities, which should determine its decision to detain these persons as POWs, or to let them go free. 50

Other able-bodied civilians should be freed and are not covered by GC III, unless it appears that they have directly participated in hostilities through use of the plane (through, for instance, the transmission of sensitive information) and/or previously, on a regular basis. If there is only a suspicion of direct participation, they should be kept in detention for further investigation. On the treatment of such civilians, see MN 56 ff. 51

Any auxiliary (military) medical personnel should be interned as military internees, and the permanent medical personnel, if they have acted in conformity with their status, should be repatriated without delay. On the exceptional possibility to retain them in conformity with Article 28 paragraph 1 GC I, see MN 36. 52

If a medical aircraft in distress, or a medical aircraft flying under an agreement but nevertheless required to land for inspection, is allowed to continue its flight after inspection, the wounded of the party to the conflict to which the aircraft belongs should remain in the aircraft unless their state of health requires an immediate transfer to a hospital, in which case their hospitalization should be the object of an agreement with their party (in general through the commander of the plane). If they are not able to return to the plane before take-off, they should remain interned in the neutral state until the end of active hostilities according to the law of neutrality,[100] unless they become eligible for direct repatriation, or an agreement is reached between the neutral state and all belligerent 53

---

[93] On this, see also MN 54 ff.   [94] On this, see MN 55.   [95] Art 24 GC I.
[96] Art 4(A)(4) GC III.   [97] Art 4(A)(5) GC III.
[98] Hague Convention XI relative to certain restrictions with regard to the exercise of the right of capture in naval war, of 18 October 1907.
[99] See Pictet Commentary GC II, at 66.   [100] See Art 14 Hague Convention V (1907).

parties. As for those wounded and/or sick soldiers who are also POWs belonging to a party to the conflict opposed to the one to which the medical aircraft is attached, they should be kept and similarly interned, applying the same rules. The question might nevertheless be delicate if they are in a plane flying with an agreement, in which case there is no obligation to control.[101] We would therefore recommend that agreements concerning flights over a neutral state by a medical aircraft of a party to the conflict exclude the transport of wounded and/or sick POWs, or, in cases where it would be justified by imperative medical reasons, make this conditional on an agreement from the party to which the soldiers belong. It is also important that the neutral state applies any measure impartially to both belligerents.[102]

g. Civilians of a party to the conflict on the territory of a neutral state

54   As a general rule, civilians of a party to the conflict on the territory of a neutral state are not directly covered by IHL,[103] which does not require, nor provide a legal basis for, their internment. They benefit from IHRL guarantees as does any person in a state, as well as from the law of diplomatic protection of foreigners, as and where applicable. They might also benefit from international refugee law, if they seek asylum and fear persecution in their country of origin. Nevertheless, there are a few cases which might concern the law of neutrality or IHL.

55   Civilians of a party to a conflict, as any persons on a neutral territory, who undertake to sustain the military effort of one party to the conflict from that neutral territory, should be prevented from doing this if such acts may be considered as contributing to an 'internationally wrongful act'. The law of neutrality is apparently not very strict on this point. It does not impose any requirement on the neutral state to prevent the crossing of its border by persons offering their services to one of the belligerents,[104] prohibiting only the transit across its territory of troops, convoys of munitions or war supplies, and the recruitment or training of persons willing to assist one of the belligerents.[105] Nevertheless, we have to note an evolution in this regard—the neutral state having the obligation to do its utmost to prevent any 'internationally wrongful act' performed from its territory in the form of assistance to a state which is using force against another state in violation of international law. In its commentary to the Articles on the Responsibility of States for Internationally Wrongful Acts, the International Law Commission recalls that if the state is not responsible, as such, for the effects of acts committed by private individuals from its territory, its responsibility is nevertheless engaged 'if it failed to take necessary measures to prevent those effects'.[106] The best way to avoid this is to prohibit such acts in national criminal legislation, so that when such acts occur, those who commit them can be pursued on a solid legal basis and according to the national rules of procedure (which, of course, should respect fundamental human rights guarantees).

---

[101] On this, see ICRC Commentary APs, at 333, para 1164.
[102] In accordance with the principle mentioned in Art 9 Hague Convention V (1907).
[103] They do not need special protection and are therefore not mentioned as 'protected persons' by Art 4 GC IV.
[104] See Art 6 Hague Convention V (1907).
[105] See Arts 2, 4, and 5 Hague Convention V (1907).
[106] *Draft articles on Responsibility of States for Internationally Wrongful Acts with commentaries*, Introductory commentary to Ch II, paras 3 and 4, at 38–9. The draft articles with commentary are found in 2 *YILC* (2001), Part 2.

The question is more delicate with regard to civilians who have previously participated 56
in hostilities directly and on a regular basis[107] against one of the belligerent parties. They
represent for the neutral state a danger similar to that resulting from soldiers of one of the
parties to the conflict, and the *ratio legis* of the rule imposing an obligation on the neutral
state to intern those soldiers might lead to the internment of these civilians as well. To
allow them to rejoin the state they have fought for or another state might be perceived as
in contradiction to the spirit of the law concerning internment of POWs, or as a violation of the obligation to prevent the crossing of the neutral state's territory by able-bodied
soldiers.[108]

However, such an internment would not have a legal basis: unless these civilians have 57
committed serious violations of IHL (war crimes),[109] they are not subject to prosecution in
the neutral state. While direct participation of civilians in hostilities is of course a violation of the internal law of the state concerned, for which prosecution and conviction is not
precluded by IHL, it is not an international crime as such. The internment of civilians for
that reason by the neutral state might therefore be in contradiction to recognized judicial
guarantees imposed by IHRL. In addition, while the status of a soldier is not too difficult
to verify, establishing that civilians have participated directly in hostilities on a regular
basis would often be an insurmountable task. For the neutral state, the only way out from
this dilemma is to watch the behaviour of those civilians carefully, to warn them, and
immediately to arrest and prosecute them if they commit any new acts of hostility against
one of the belligerent parties.

The second exception concerns civilians, regardless of whether they are covered or not 58
by the first exception, who are suspected of having committed international crimes, in
particular war crimes (war crimes consisting of grave breaches of the Geneva Conventions
and AP I are subject to a particular regime, imposing upon states parties the obligation to
prosecute those responsible for a grave breach, or to hand them over to another contracting
party having a prima facie case).[110]

Civilian internees transferred to the territory of a neutral state might be a third excep- 59
tion. The 'repatriation, the return to places of residence or the *accommodation* in a neutral
country of certain categories of internees'[111] is encouraged for, in particular, 'children,
pregnant women and mothers with infants and young children, wounded and sick, and
internees who have been detained for a long time'.[112] The word 'accommodation' might
suggest that these persons should either be hospitalized or left to go free, unless they
themselves ask to be interned for security reasons. However, this question is not clarified
by the Convention and remains open, even if the analysis is based on the French text (the
more restrictive word of 'hospitalisation' is used instead of 'accommodation'), as the fate
of those hospitalized whose health improves is also not clarified. In fact, there are two
specific questions to consider: Who has to agree to the repatriation or accommodation
in a neutral state? Would a clause specifying that the person transferred must be interned
comply with Article 132 GC IV?

---

[107] On this notion, see N. Melzer (ed), *Interpretive Guidance on the Notion of Direct Participation in Hostilities under International Humanitarian Law* (Geneva: ICRC, 2009).
[108] See Art 5 Hague Convention V (1907).   [109] See MN 58.
[110] See respectively Arts 49, 50, 129, and 146 of the GCs, and Art 85 AP I. For details of the penal aspect of IHL, see Ch 31 of this volume.
[111] Art 132 para 2 GC IV (emphasis added).   [112] Ibid.

60 As to the first question, it might seem that an agreement between the Detaining Power and this neutral state would be sufficient. However, the draft of Article 132 GC IV contained a supplementary paragraph, specifying the right of internees to refuse their repatriation to a country in which they might fear persecution for their religious or political opinions. It seems that while this paragraph was in the end deleted, it was because the delegates were of the opinion that the consent of the internees concerned was implicit,[113] as this Article should be read in conjunction with Article 109 paragraph 3 GC III, which proscribes the repatriation of POWs against their will during hostilities and, in a party's own territory, with Article 45 GC IV prohibiting transfers to a country in which the civilian may fear persecution. The necessary consent of the internees concerned is even more clearly required in occupied territories, as a transfer without that consent could constitute a forced transfer in violation of Article 49 paragraph 1 GC IV. Who can forget the famous case of Nelson Mandela, who preferred internment in his own country over liberty in a third state? However, internment could also be part of a policy to put pressure on undesirable persons in order to obtain their consent to be expelled.[114] For this reason, if the occupied territories comprise only a part of a foreign state, the government of that state should in principle also be associated with such an agreement, and other state parties, in accordance with their responsibility to ensure respect for IHL,[115] should keep an eye on any transfer, in order to avoid a disguised attempt to expel inhabitants from the occupied territories. As for the neutral state, it should be very careful, before accepting such an agreement, that its terms are at least clearly agreed upon and that no undue pressure is being exercised by any of the actors mentioned above.

61 As to the second question, the neutral state willing to 'accommodate' internees on its territory should in principle be free to do so at its convenience (while respecting IHRL obligations), and is likewise allowed to release internees who do not have to be hospitalized. However, if an agreement imposing internment in the neutral country is not mentioned by GC IV, it is also not excluded, and such internment could be preferred by the internees to the status quo, if there is no other choice. The implementation of such agreements would nevertheless not be easy. Internment of civilians is authorized only 'if the security of the detaining state makes it absolutely necessary' or 'for imperative reasons of security', and renewed consideration of a case must be made by a court or an independent administrative board at least twice a year in order to determine whether the reasons that warranted internment still exist.[116] Quite clearly, an agreement which would require that the internment lasts until the end of the hostilities (as for POWs) would be in contradiction to this requirement, as well as to IHRL obligations of the neutral state. It would be very difficult—if not impossible—for a court of a neutral state to determine whether the prolongation of the detention is 'absolutely necessary for security reasons' of the belligerent state concerned. For that reason, we would suggest that where internment is a matter of urgency for the detaining state, it should not preclude an agreement if such an agreement is in the clear interests of the person concerned, subject to the other considerations mentioned above. The detention should be limited to a definite period, with a maximum of six months, in order to avoid the suppression of the obligation to reconsider the case. Moreover, the fate of the internees after this period should also be clarified, including

---

[113] See Pictet Commentary GC IV, at 513–14.
[114] The issue of expulsion is, for instance, very sensitive in the Israeli-Palestinian context.
[115] See CA 1 of the GCs and Art 1 AP I.
[116] Condition specified as imperative (at least twice yearly) in Art 43 GC IV for parties having internees on their own territory; a bit less strict ('if possible every six months') in Art 78 GC IV for internees in occupied territories.

considerations of freedom in this or any other neutral state, or possible return to the occupied territories, with some guarantees.

Of course, the solution would be different if the person concerned were suspected of having committed a grave breach of the Geneva Conventions. The neutral state is then obliged to open an inquiry and, if justified, to bring this person before its courts or to hand him over to another state for trial.[117] In case of conviction, the person should not be released before having served his sentence.

h. Missing and dead persons

Article 4 GC I and Article 5 GC II require neutral states to apply these Conventions by analogy to, among others, 'dead persons found'. This expression must be understood as covering all persons in the neutral state who were protected by these Conventions when alive. Those civilians who are of the nationality of one of the parties to the conflict and live in the neutral state do not benefit from protection under IHL, and if they die, their case is governed by national laws and possible bilateral agreements between the states concerned. We shall not elaborate here on obligations that parties in conflict have towards the dead, which today have to be read together with provisions on the subject added in AP I.[118] This question is dealt with in another chapter of this Commentary.[119] We shall just insist on the fact that the provisions concerning, in particular, the facilitation of access to gravesites and the return of the remains of the deceased, and requiring an agreement between parties to a conflict 'as soon as the circumstances and the relations between the adverse Parties permit',[120] have to be implemented without undue delay by the neutral state, which has in principle no political obstacles to concluding such agreements. It is even a domain where the neutral state concerned could engage in useful dialogue with the aim of facilitating agreements between the conflicting parties.

As mentioned by an ICRC representative at the 1974–7 Diplomatic Conference on IHL, 'the Conventions were silent' on the important matter of missing persons.[121] Additional Protocol I mentions as a principle the duty, not only of the parties to the conflict but also of all parties to the Protocol, to implement Section III of Part II devoted to missing and dead persons, 'prompted mainly by the right of families to know the fate of their relatives'.[122] This principle is part of customary international law,[123] and a neutral state, like the parties in conflict, must 'take all feasible measures to account for persons reported missing as a result of armed conflict' and provide their family members with any information it has on their fate.[124]

Article 123 GC III provides that 'A Central Prisoners of War Information Agency shall be created in a neutral country', and Article 140 GC IV contains a similar provision for a Central Information Agency 'for protected persons, in particular internees'. The same provision nevertheless leaves open the possibility for the ICRC to 'propose to the Powers concerned the organization of such an Agency'.[125] In practice, it is the Central Tracing Agency of the ICRC which has played that role, and that practice has been recognized in AP I, which mentions it specifically.[126] The role of the Central Tracing Agency of the

---

[117] See Art 146 para 2 GC IV. [118] See ICRC CIHL Database, Ch 35.
[119] See Ch 14 of this volume.
[120] See Art 34(2) AP I. [121] Quoted in the ICRC Commentary APs, para 1188.
[122] Art 32 AP I. [123] See ICRC CIHL Database, Ch 36. [124] Ibid.
[125] See Art 123 GC III and Art 140 GC IV.
[126] See Art 33(3) AP I, and ICRC Commentary APs, para 1275.

II. Possibility to conclude agreements for the reception of prisoners of war in neutral territory

66 According to Article 109 GC III, 'seriously wounded and seriously sick' POWs 'shall be sent back to their own country', the idea being that these persons will no longer represent a threat after their repatriation and that there is therefore no valid reason to refuse this humanitarian gesture. Nevertheless, this Article also encourages parties to the conflict to conclude agreements providing for internment in a neutral state 'of able-bodied prisoners of war who have undergone a long period of captivity', and, more importantly, to make arrangements for the accommodation of wounded and sick POWs defined in paragraph 2 of Article 110 GC III. The idea behind this provision is that there may be good humanitarian reasons to send those persons to a non-hostile environment, but their potential capacity to resume hostile acts against the Detaining Power precludes their return to their own country.[127]

III. Possibility to conclude agreements to receive children in neutral territory

67 Article 24 GC IV requires all parties to an armed conflict to take special measures concerning children aged under 15 who are orphaned or separated from their families, in order not to leave them without resources for their maintenance, and to facilitate the practise of their religion and their education in conformity with their cultural traditions. When parties to a conflict are not able to fulfil these requirements, provisional transfer to a neutral state is encouraged, as far as it permits the better education of the children and with due respect to their cultural traditions. The interests of the children is the only criterion for such a transfer, which, of course, requires the agreement of both the state of the children and the neutral state accepting them. In the absence of a Protecting Power, it would be useful to assign such procedures to the ICRC.

68 The situation of children in occupied territories must be examined very carefully. Article 49 GC IV, which prohibits 'individual or mass forcible transfers' and the evacuation of children for the reasons given in Article 24, could be in contradiction to this provision. Therefore, Article 24 might be used or perceived as a pretext for the violation of Article 49. But Article 78 AP I has clarified that this provision operates in a restrictive manner. The Occupying Power may not take such a decision alone. In addition to legal representatives of the children, the agreement of the local authority of the occupied territories and, if those territories cover only a part of a state, a 'green light' from the government of that state are also necessary. In all cases, the consent of the Protecting Power is required. In the absence of a Protecting Power, it would be even more important than in the situation

---

[127] For further details, see Ch 51, MN 13–18, of this volume.

ICRC has the advantage, in comparison with the Agency created in an ad hoc manner for a single armed conflict, to be permanent, to keep information long after the end of an armed conflict (some cases of missing persons are not resolved until many years after the end of a conflict), and to keep in one place information on many, if not all, situations, with a possibility of cross-checking. The possible role of neutral states in creating Central Agencies has therefore practically vanished.

just mentioned to involve the ICRC, in order to guarantee that the best interests of the children in question are preserved. The ICRC or another institution active in the conflict could also help to search for a neutral state offering all guarantees and ready to accept these children.

IV. Possibility to play the role of Protecting Power

One important role that neutral states could play, particularly those having a permanent status of neutrality, is as a Protecting Power—an institution charged with numerous and detailed tasks according to the Geneva Conventions and AP I. However, with very few exceptions, the system of Protecting Powers has not functioned since the Second World War.[128]

E. Application in Non-International Armed Conflicts

The law of neutrality is not applicable in NIAC, the most common type of armed conflict today. The support of a state for a dissident party may be considered to be a breach of sovereignty of the state in conflict, but there are no restrictions on relations with the government side. How much support to the rebel side might constitute an act of hostility nevertheless remains a delicate question. The ICJ has helped to define which action may be considered military intervention, particularly by affirming that humanitarian assistance cannot be considered as such and clarifying the degree of involvement needed in order for a state to be considered a party to the conflict.[129] The Articles on the Responsibility of States for Internationally Wrongful Acts have also helped to clarify the issue.[130] Formally, the long-standing institution of the 'recognition of belligerency' could be utilized in some cases, but to consider on an equal footing a government and a dissident party in an internal conflict would be an unwelcome prospect for the recognizing state, one which could jeopardize its relations with the government involved. In fact, recognition could be a compromise between more radical solutions. In the recent Libyan and Syrian contexts, we saw political condemnation and military intervention in the case of the former, and military support for the parties in the case of the latter, without envisaging recognition of belligerency as a first step. In the Georgian context (2008), Russia also formally recognized South-Ossetia and Abkhazia as states, without first resorting to recognition of belligerency.

Nothing, however, prevents the UN, regional organizations, or states individually from offering their services in order to play a mitigating role in a NIAC.[131] Even if it was for just a short period and concerned only 11 combatants, the agreement concluded in 1982 between the Government of the USSR, the Afghan rebels, and the Swiss Government, to intern in Switzerland some Russian soldiers previously held by the rebels in Afghanistan, was a good example of such possible initiatives.[132] Of course, this conflict was considered an international conflict by most of the international community, but not by the USSR,

---

[128] See Ch 27 of this volume.   [129] See MN 23 and above n 46.
[130] *Draft Articles on Responsibility of States for Internationally Wrongful Acts*, above n 106, commentary on Art 8, at 47–8, paras 4–5.
[131] Keeping in mind that the obligation to 'ensure respect' for the GCs specified in CA 1 also covers CA 3, which in turn includes NIACs. For more details, see Ch 6 of this volume.
[132] See 'Africa, Latin America, Asia, Middle East, Europe', 24 *IRRC* 241 (1984) 239, and Ch 51, MN 18, of this volume.

which presented itself as supporting the Afghan Government in a NIAC. And it is with that perception in mind that the USSR nevertheless accepted the 1982 agreement.

F. 'War on Terror'

72 The recent debate on secret internment of persons suspected of being involved in terrorist activities in the 'war on terror' should lead to a very cautious attitude by the international community. The expression 'war on terror' has no legal background and gives a twofold impression: on the one hand that IHL applies, and on the other that the law of neutrality does not apply because no state is neutral towards terrorism.[133] Persons have been interned without judgment on the basis of this vague concept, which is an additional reason to oppose any further internment without a strict legal basis.[134]

G. Concluding Remarks

73 As mentioned above, there is not much practice with regard to the law of neutrality in contemporary armed conflicts. Even those states having a permanent status of neutrality do not consider themselves 'neutral' in situations of armed conflict undertaken or authorized by the UN, even accepting involvement in armed hostilities, such as the authorization of the passage of military aircraft through their national airspace. They nevertheless have to comply with the obligations under the Geneva Conventions described in this chapter. Respect for the law of neutrality often depends more on the political considerations of the states concerned than on strictly legal considerations. In practice, a new codification of the law of neutrality would logically be necessary,[135] but the complexity and ambiguity of some topics prevent states from entering into such a delicate issue with very uncertain results.

74 It is therefore important to remind states that at least for all questions linked to the treatment of belligerent soldiers on their territory, the principles of (both) IHL and of the law of neutrality remain valid—either because the Geneva Conventions are still formally applicable, or under their obligations derived from the Martens Clause and IHRL—and the idea that a 'legal black hole' might exist should be firmly rejected.[136] Numerous allegations of mistreatment, secret detentions, and even torture of prisoners transferred to different states in the framework of the so-called 'war on terror' render this reminder more pertinent than ever at the present time.

YVES SANDOZ*

---

[133] As mentioned by T. Bridgeman, 'The Law of Neutrality and the Conflict with Al Qaeda', 85 *New York University Law Review* (2010) 1186, at 1192: 'The choice to apply traditional LOAC rules by analogy to the conflict with al Qaeda (often a difficult task) is a recognition of the idea that this war, like others, should be waged according to a complete legal regime that does not allow for holes in the rule of law. To date, however, the United States has not recognized the role of neutrality in the conflict with al Qaeda.'

[134] Bridgeman speaks, for a neutral state, of 'a duty not to detain' civilians of belligerent states: ibid, at 1203.

[135] The rules of IHL have constantly been updated, but the rules on neutrality 'n'ont pas connu un processus de renouvellement et de développement comparable': Monnier, above n 32, at 14.

[136] According to the expression used by Bridgeman, above n 133, at 1196.

* With my deep gratitude to Bruno Demeyere for his valuable advice.

B. COMMON PROVISIONS

—

1. GENERAL

Chapter 6. The Obligation to Respect and to Ensure Respect for the Conventions

	MN
A. Introduction	1
B. Preparatory Works	3
C. Scope of Application	6
I. International armed conflicts and non-international armed conflicts	6
II. Addressees of the obligation	8
D. Content of the Obligation to Respect	9
E. Content of the Obligation to Ensure Respect	10
I. The internal compliance dimension of the obligation to ensure respect	10
a. An obligation to stop and prevent private actor infringements	11
b. An obligation to stop and prevent state organ infringements	13
c. Specific provisions that aim to 'ensure respect'	14
II. The external compliance dimension of the obligation to ensure respect	15
a. Does the obligation to ensure respect have an external compliance dimension?	16
b. Scope and content of the obligation to ensure respect in its external compliance dimension	20
c. The obligation not to encourage or aid or assist the commission of violations by others	37
III. 'In all circumstances'	42
F. Critical Assessment	44

Select Bibliography

Azzam, F., 'The Duty of Third States to Implement and Enforce International Humanitarian Law', 66 *NJIL* (1997) 55

Aust, H.P., *Complicity and the Law of State Responsibility* (Cambridge: CUP, 2011)

Aust, H.P., 'Complicity in Violations of International Humanitarian Law', in H. Krieger (ed), *Inducing Compliance with International Humanitarian Law: Lessons from the African Great Lakes Region* (Cambridge: CUP, 2015) 12

Benvenuti, P., 'Ensuring Observance of International Humanitarian Law: Function, Extent and Limits of the Obligations of Third States to Ensure Respect of IHL', *Yearbook of the International Institute of Humanitarian Law, 1989–90* (1992) 27

Boisson de Chazournes, L./Condorelli, L., 'Common Article 1 of the Geneva Conventions revisited: Protecting collective interests', 82 *IRRC* 837 (2000) 67

Brehm, M., 'The Arms Trade and States' Duty to Ensure Respect for Humanitarian and Human Rights Law', 12 *Journal of Conflict and Security Law* (2007) 359

Condorelli, L./Boisson de Chazournes, L., 'Quelques remarques à propos de l'obligation des Etats de "respecter et faire respecter" le droit international humanitaire "en toutes circonstances"', in C. Swinarski (ed), *Studies and Essays on International Humanitarian Law and Red Cross Principles in Honour of Jean Pictet* (Geneva/The Hague: ICRC/Martinus Nijhoff, 1984) 17

Engdahl, O., 'Compliance with International Humanitarian Law in Multinational Peace Operations', 78 *NJIL* (2009) 513

Focarelli, C., 'Common Article 1 of the 1949 Geneva Conventions: A Soap Bubble?', 21 *EJIL* (2010) 125

Gasser, H.-P., 'Ensuring Respect for the Geneva Conventions and Protocols: The Role of Third States and the United Nations', in H. Fox and M.A. Meyer (eds), *Armed Conflict and the New Law,* II: *Effecting Compliance* (London: British Institute of International and Comparative Law, 1993) 15

Geiß, R., 'Common Article 1 of the 1949 Geneva Conventions—Scope and Content of the Obligation to "Ensure Respect"—"Narrow but Deep" or "Wide and Shallow"?', in H. Krieger (ed), *Inducing Compliance with International Humanitarian Law: Lessons from the African Great Lakes Region* (Cambridge: CUP, 2015)

Kalshoven, F., 'The Undertaking to Respect and Ensure Respect in All Circumstances: From Tiny Seed to Ripening Fruit', 2 *YIHL* (1999) 3

Kessler, B., *Die Durchsetzung der Genfer Abkommen von 1949 in nicht-internationalen bewaffneten Konflikten auf Grundlage ihres gemeinsamen Art. 1* (Berlin: Duncker & Humblot, 2001)

Kessler, B., 'The Duty to "Ensure Respect" under Common Article 1 of the Geneva Conventions: Its Implications on International and Non-International Armed Conflicts', 44 *GYIL* (2001) 498

Levrat, N., 'Les Conséquences de l'engagement pris par les Hautes Parties contractantes de "faire respecter" les Conventions humanitaires', in F. Kalshoven and Y. Sandoz (eds), *Mise en œuvre du droit international humanitaire* (Dordrecht: Martinus Nijhoff, 1989) 263

Nolte, G., 'The Different Functions of the Security Council with Respect to Humanitarian Law', in V. Lowe (ed), *The United Nations Security Council and War* (Oxford: OUP, 2008) 519

Palwankar, U., 'Measures Available to States for Fulfilling their Obligation to Ensure Respect for International Humanitarian Law', 34 *IRRC* 298 (1994) 9

Pisillo-Mazzeschi, R., 'The Due Diligence Rule and the Nature of the International Responsibility of States', 35 *GYIL* (1992) 9

Ryngaert, C./Van de Meulebroucke, A., 'Enhancing and Enforcing Compliance with International Humanitarian Law by Non-State Armed Groups: An Inquiry into Some Mechanisms', 16 *Journal of Conflict & Security Law* (2012) 1

Sachariew, K., 'States' Entitlement to Take Action to Enforce International Humanitarian Law', 29 *IRRC* 270 (1989) 177

Sassòli, M., 'State Responsibility for Violations of International Humanitarian Law', 84 *IRRC* 846 (2002) 401

Tams, C., *Enforcing Obligations Erga Omnes in International Law* (Cambridge: CUP, 2005)

A. Introduction

1   Lack of respect for the rules applicable in times of armed conflict remains a persistent and central challenge to the humanitarian legal order.[1] Against this backdrop, much hope has been vested in Common Article 1 of the four Geneva Conventions. This provision arguably elevates all states to guardians over the Geneva Conventions by providing that '[t]he High Contracting Parties undertake *to respect and to ensure respect* for the present Convention *in all circumstances*.'[2] The clause, which is repeated verbatim in

---

[1] See ICRC President Jakob Kellenberger, 'Sixty years of the Geneva Conventions: Learning from the Past to Better Face the Future', Statement (Geneva, 2009), available at <http://www.icrc.org/eng/resources/documents/statement/geneva-conventions-statement-president-120809.htm>.

[2] Emphasis added. The French version of CA 1 GCs I–IV provides '[l]es Hautes Parties contractantes s'engagent à respecter et à faire respecter la présente Convention en toutes circonstances'.

Additional Protocols (APs) I and III,³ is often said to underline the 'special character of the Conventions'⁴ and to 'stress that if the system of protection of the Convention[s] is to be effective, the High Contracting Parties [...] must also do everything in their power to ensure that the humanitarian principles on which the Convention[s] [are] founded shall be universally applied'.⁵

Today, it is widely accepted that Common Article 1 is reflective of customary international law.⁶ But despite being more than 60 years old, debate over the precise scope and content of Common Article 1, in particular the obligation *to ensure respect* and the meaning of the '*in all circumstances*' formula, continues. For some authors, Common Article 1 is simply a 'soap bubble',⁷ i.e. an 'innocuous opening phrase'⁸ that serves as a recommendatory reminder of obligations and entitlements that exist regardless of Common Article 1.⁹ According to the prevailing view, however, Common Article 1 is a central provision of a 'quasi-constitutional nature'¹⁰ that obliges states to take all measures in their power, including, according to some authors, non-forcible countermeasures,¹¹ in order to induce other (contracting) states to comply with the rules of international humanitarian law (IHL).¹² The International Court of Justice (ICJ) has emphasized that the wording 'to undertake' means 'to accept an obligation [...] It is not merely hortatory or purposive'.¹³ Thus, Common Article 1 is clearly more than a recommendatory opening phrase. It is a binding provision, and whatever it is that Common Article 1 prescribes, the High Contracting Parties are obliged to do.¹⁴

---

³ Art 38(1) of the Convention on the Rights of the Child (CRC) (1989) provides that 'States Parties undertake to respect and to ensure respect for rules of international humanitarian law applicable to them in armed conflicts which are relevant to the child'.

⁴ Pictet Commentary GC I, at 25.

⁵ 'Draft Revised or New Conventions for the Protection of War Victims', XVIIth International Red Cross Conference (Stockholm, August 1948) (Geneva: ICRC, 1948), at 5.

⁶ ICJ, *Military and Paramilitary Activities in and against Nicaragua (Nicaragua v USA)*, Judgment, 27 June 1986, at 14, para 220; ICJ, *Legality of the Threat or Use of Nuclear Weapons*, Advisory Opinion, 8 July 1996, at 226, para 79; ICJ, *Legal Consequences of the Construction of a Wall on the Occupied Palestinian Territory*, Advisory Opinion, 9 July 2004, para 158.

⁷ C. Focarelli, 'Common Article 1 of the 1949 Geneva Conventions: A Soap Bubble?', 21 *EJIL* (2010) 125.

⁸ F. Kalshoven, 'The Undertaking to Respect and Ensure Respect in All Circumstances: From Tiny Seed to Ripening Fruit', 2 *YIHL* (1999) 3, at 3.

⁹ 'No such legal liability attaches to their *moral duty* to endeavor to ensure respect by their peers': ibid, at 60 (emphasis added).

¹⁰ L. Boisson de Chazournes and L. Condorelli, 'Common Article 1 of the Geneva Conventions Revisited: Protecting Collective Interests', 82 *IRRC* 837 (2000) 67, at 68.

¹¹ B. Kessler, 'The Duty to "Ensure Respect" under Common Article 1 of the Geneva Conventions: Its Implications on International and Non-International Armed Conflicts', 44 *GYIL* (2001) 498, at 506.

¹² Ibid, at 516; Boisson de Chazournes and Condorelli, above n 10, at 76 ff; P. Benvenuti, 'Ensuring Observance of International Humanitarian Law: Functions, Extent and Limits of the Obligations of Third States to Ensure Respect of IHL', *International Institute of Humanitarian Law, Yearbook 1989/90* (1992) 27, at 33; H.-P. Gasser, 'Ensuring Respect for the Geneva Conventions and Protocols: The Role of Third States and the United Nations' in H. Fox and M.A. Meyer (eds), *Armed Conflict and the New Law*, II: *Effecting Compliance* (London: British Institute for International & Comparative Law, 1993) 15; U. Palwankar, 'Measures Available to States for Fulfilling their Obligation to Ensure Respect for International Humanitarian Law', 43 *IRRC* 298 (1994) 9, at 10; F. Azzam, 'The Duty of Third States to Implement and Enforce International Humanitarian Law', 66 *NJIL* (1997) 55, at 68.

¹³ ICJ, *Application of the Convention on the Prevention and Punishment of the Crime of Genocide (Bosnia and Herzegovina v Serbia and Montenegro)* (*Bosnian Genocide Case*), Judgment, 26 February 2007, para 162.

¹⁴ L. Condorelli and L. Boisson de Chazournes, 'Quelques remarques à propos de l'obligation des états de "respecter et faire respecter" le droit international humanitaire "en toutes circonstances"', in Mélanges Pictet

B. Preparatory Works

3   Common Article 1 has no immediate predecessor. The 1864 Geneva Convention (GC), as well as the 1906 GC and the 1907 Hague Convention (X), merely contained a general provision on how the implementation of these instruments was to be achieved,[15] today reflected in Article 45 GC I and Article 46 GC II. The terms 'shall be respected […] in all circumstances', were found, for the first time, in Article 25 paragraph 1 of the 1929 Geneva Convention for the Amelioration of the Condition of the Wounded and Sick in Armies in the Field (1929 GC I) and Article 82 paragraph 1 of the 1929 Geneva Convention Relative to the Treatment of Prisoners of War (1929 GC II).[16] In light of the drafting history of these provisions, it remains debatable, however, whether states indeed intended to accord the respective first paragraph of Articles 25 and 82 of 1929 GC I and 1929 GC II any autonomous meaning, or whether these provisions merely emerged as 'by-products' of the attempt to abolish the *si omnes* clause,[17] which had dominated the discussions throughout the drafting negotiations.[18]

4   In 1949, the provision was moved to a far more prominent position. It became the very first article of all four Geneva Conventions. What is more, in 1949, the phrase 'to ensure respect' was added to the 1929 formula. The phrase originated from a draft the International Committee of the Red Cross (ICRC) had submitted in May 1948 to the XVIIth International Conference of the Red Cross in Stockholm. It is here that the formulation 'to ensure respect' made its first appearance. The draft provided that '[t]he High Contracting Parties undertake, in the name of their peoples, *to respect and to ensure respect* for the present Convention in all circumstances.'[19] The accompanying ICRC comment provided that the 'to ensure respect-clause' was meant to 'stress that if the system of protection of the Convention is to be effective, the High Contracting Parties cannot confine themselves to implementing the Convention' but 'must also do everything in their power to ensure that the humanitarian principles on which the Convention is founded shall be *universally* applied'.[20] After the deletion of the term 'in the name of their peoples' in the course of the Stockholm Conference, the draft was adopted by the Diplomatic Conference in 1949.[21]

5   At the Diplomatic Conference very little time was spent on the discussion of Common Article 1.[22] Afterwards, however, there was considerable discussion about the exact

---

17, at 24 and 26; Azzam, above n 12, at 58–9; M. Sassòli, 'State Responsibility for Violations of International Humanitarian Law', 84 *IRRC* 846 (2002) 401, at 421.

[15] 'The implementing of the present Convention shall be arranged by the Commanders-in-Chief of the belligerent armies following the instructions of their respective Governments and in accordance with the general principles set forth in this Convention.' Art 8 GC 1864; Art 25 GC 1906; Art 19 Hague Convention (X) (1907).

[16] According to Art 25 para 1 1929 GC I and Art 82 para 1 1929 GC II respectively, 'The provisions of the present Convention shall be respected by the High Contracting Parties in all circumstances.'

[17] Kalshoven, above n 8, at 7 ff.

[18] For an independent meaning, see P. Des Gouttes, *Commentaire de la Convention de Genève du 27 juillet 1929* (Geneva: ICRC, 1930), at 186: 'On a voulu souligner ici que la Convention doit s'appliquer en toutes circonstances—ce que ne disait pas celle de 1906—en temps de paix comme en temps de guerre, quant aux dispositions qui se trouvent applicables dans l'un comme dans l'autre cas. On a insisté sur son caractère d'obligation générale.' Critical: Kalshoven, above n 8, at 10; Focarelli, above n 7, at 130.

[19] 'Draft Revised or New Conventions for the Protection of War Victims', above n 5, at 4 (GC I), 34 (GC II), 51 (GC III), and 153 (GC IV) (emphasis added).

[20] Ibid, at 5 (emphasis added).   [21] Final Record, vol II-B, at 53.

[22] Kalshoven, above n 8, at 27.

meaning of the 'to ensure respect-clause'. This continues today. The controversy centres on the question whether the clause was meant to oblige states to ensure respect by their people as a whole, or whether from the outset it contained an external dimension, requiring states to ensure respect for the Conventions not only internally (i.e. by their people as a whole), but also by other states, and possibly even by organized armed groups involved in extraterritorial non-international armed conflicts (NIACs) (and in as far as they are bound by the provisions of the Geneva Conventions). Today, it is certainly plausible to accord such a meaning to Common Article 1 on the basis of a dynamic interpretation and subsequent state practice.[23] It appears rather doubtful, however, whether this could have been the case already in 1949. In view of the far-reaching, and, at least in 1949, i.e. some 20 years before the appearance of the concept of obligations *erga omnes* in the dictum of the ICJ in *Barcelona Traction*,[24] revolutionary implications of a treaty obligation to ensure respect vis-à-vis other states, one would certainly have expected at least some discussion of the issue.[25] But the debate in 1948 and 1949 focused solely on internal conflicts and states' domestic spheres.[26] Clearly, at the time of drafting, the primary rationale for the inclusion of the 'to ensure respect-clause' was to confirm an undertaking by the High Contracting Parties to guarantee respect for the Conventions not only by their organs, namely their armed forces, but also by their (civilian) populations as a whole. In light of this historic background, it cannot but be concluded that originally the words 'to ensure respect' were meant to emphasize a comprehensive internal compliance dimension rather than an external compliance dimension of Common Article 1.[27]

C. Scope of Application

I. International armed conflicts and non-international armed conflicts

Common Article 1 applies to both international armed conflicts (IACs), including situations of occupation, and NIACs.[28] It respectively refers to 'the present Convention' and thus to all the provisions contained therein, including Common Article 3. Additional Protocol II, unlike APs I and III, does not contain a provision similar to Common Article 1. Nevertheless, it is commonly held that the obligation to respect and to ensure respect in Common Article 1 also extends to AP II and states party thereto, given that its Article 1(1) provides that the Protocol 'develops and supplements Article 3 common to the Geneva Conventions of 12 August 1949'.[29] The ICRC Customary International Humanitarian Law (CIHL) Study also takes the view that a customary international

---

[23] On evolutionary legal concepts, see ICJ, *Legal Consequences for States of the Continued Presence of South Africa in Namibia (South West Africa)*, Advisory Opinion, 21 June 1971, para 53. See the detailed discussion at MN 18.
[24] ICJ, *Barcelona Traction, Light and Power Company, Limited (Belgium v Spain)*, Second Phase, Judgment, 5 February 1970, paras 33–4.
[25] 'I have not found in the records of the Diplomatic Conference even the slightest awareness on the part of government delegates that one might ever wish to read into the phrase 'to ensure respect' any undertaking by a contracting State other than an obligation to ensure respect for the Conventions by its people "in all circumstances"': Kalshoven, above n 8, at 28.
[26] Ibid.   [27] Ibid, at 60.
[28] ICJ, *Nicaragua v USA*, above n 6, paras 219–20; Kessler, above n 11, at 507 ff.
[29] Boisson de Chazournes and Condorelli, above n 10, at 69; Kessler, above n 11, at 508; Palwankar, above n 12, at 12; Benvenuti, above n 12, at 28.

law obligation to respect and to ensure respect applies in both types of conflict.[30] This chapter will focus on the obligation to ensure respect as it is contained in Common Article 1.

7   It is widely accepted that the application of Common Article 1 is not restricted to situations of armed conflict but that it also applies in times of peace. This may be inferred either from the wording of Common Article 1, which, unlike Rule 139 of the CIHL Study, is addressed not only to the parties to an armed conflict but to the 'High Contracting Parties' generally, irrespective of whether they are involved in an ongoing armed conflict or not, or from the 'in all circumstances formula'.[31] The Geneva Conventions contain certain obligations that apply not only in times of armed conflict but also in peacetime. This clearly follows from Common Article 2 paragraph 1, which explicitly refers to 'the provisions which shall be implemented in peacetime'.[32] As the Pictet Commentary explains, 'the State must of necessity prepare in advance, that is to say in peacetime, the legal, material or other means of loyal enforcement of the Convention as and when the occasion arises'.[33] There is no indication whatsoever that Common Article 1 was not meant to apply with regard to these obligations as well. In fact, already in 1929, China had pointed out that the obligation to respect should also apply with regard to peacetime obligations and not only 'in case of war' as had been suggested by the ICRC in the original draft article.[34] What is more, the peacetime application of Common Article 1 is not necessarily limited only to those few humanitarian law obligations that are specifically designed to apply in times of peace. Rather, if Common Article 1 is understood to have an external compliance dimension,[35] i.e. to contain an obligation for all High Contracting Parties to ensure respect for the Geneva Conventions by other states and other external actors, then logically the obligation is activated each time the provisions are violated, including for states that are not currently involved in an armed conflict.

II. Addressees of the obligation

8   By its wording, Common Article 1 explicitly obliges only the 'High Contracting Parties', i.e. states, to respect and to ensure respect for the Conventions. In view of the clear wording, other actors, namely organized armed groups and international organizations, are not bound by this provision.[36] Conversely, the relevant customary law rule, as formulated in the CIHL Study, extends the obligation to respect and to ensure respect (in its internal compliance dimension[37]) to 'each party to the conflict'.[38] Unlike Common Article 1, the customary humanitarian law rule thereby covers organized armed groups, as well as

---

[30] ICRC CIHL Study, vol I, Rule 139, at 495. According to Rule 139, '[e]ach party to the conflict must respect and ensure respect for international humanitarian law by its armed forces and other persons or groups acting in fact on its instructions, or under its direction or control.'

[31] Des Gouttes, above n 18, at 186. Critical: Focarelli, above n 7, at 159.

[32] See, e.g., Art 47 GC I; Art 48 GC II; Art 127 GC III; Art 144 GC IV; and ICRC CIHL Study, Rule 142, at 501.

[33] Pictet Commentary GC I, at 26.

[34] *Actes de la Conférence diplomatique de Genève de 1929* (Geneva: Journal de Genève, 1930), at 329–30.

[35] See MN 15 ff.   [36] The same holds true with regard to Art 1 AP I and AP III respectively.

[37] Notably, with regard to the external compliance dimension, Rule 144 of the ICRC CIHL Study expressly applies only to *states* and provides that '[t]hey [i.e. States] must exert their influence, to the degree possible, to stop violations [by whomever] of international humanitarian law': ICRC CIHL Study, Rule 144, at 509.

[38] Ibid, Rule 139, at 495.

international organizations to the extent that it is accepted that the organization itself could become a party to an armed conflict.[39]

D. Content of the Obligation to Respect

The obligation to respect in Common Article 1 requires High Contracting Parties to act in conformity with the provisions contained in the respective instruments. Thus, albeit formulated in the positive, it is in fact a negative obligation, requiring the High Contracting Parties not to violate the Conventions.[40] The provision has rightly been described as a truism.[41] It simply amounts to a reaffirmation of the rule expressed with the Latin tag *pacta sunt servanda* and codified in Article 26 of the 1969 Vienna Convention on the Law of Treaties (VCLT).[42] Thus, in accordance with general public international law, the obligation to respect under Common Article 1 is violated whenever conduct in breach of a provision contained in the four Geneva Conventions is attributable to a state in accordance with the rules laid out in Articles 4 to 11 of the International Law Commission's (ILC's) Articles on State Responsibility.[43]

9

E. Content of the Obligation to Ensure Respect

I. The internal compliance dimension of the obligation to ensure respect

As mentioned in section C.II of this chapter, it is undisputed that the obligation to ensure respect in Common Article 1 has an internal compliance dimension. The original rationale for the inclusion of the 'to ensure respect-clause' was to confirm an undertaking by the High Contracting Parties that they would guarantee respect for the Conventions not only by their own organs, but also by their populations as a whole.[44] Thus, by virtue of the obligation to ensure respect, the High Contracting Parties are under a positive obligation to protect the Conventions against private encroachment as well as against infringements from their own organs. The obligation to ensure respect is commonly understood broadly to comprise not only an obligation to end ongoing violations, but also an obligation 'to prevent' such violations proactively.

10

---

[39] With regard to UN forces, the applicability of IHL was acknowledged in the 1999 United Nations Secretary General's Bulletin; see UN SG Bulletin (1999), Section 1; O. Engdahl, 'Compliance with International Humanitarian Law in Multinational Peace Operations', 78 *NJIL* (2009) 513, at 519. With regard to organized armed groups, see R. Geiß, 'Humanitarian Law Obligations of Organized Armed Groups', in Proceedings of the XXXII San Remo Round Table on Current Issues of International Humanitarian Law, *Non-State Actors and International Humanitarian Law, Organized Armed Groups: A Challenge for the 21st Century* (San Remo: International Institute of Humanitarian Law, 2009) 93; S. Sivakumaran, 'Binding Armed Opposition Groups', 55 *ICLQ* (2006) 369.

[40] The corresponding customary law rule requires states not to violate customary IHL. See ICRC CIHL Study, Rule 139, at 495.

[41] Kalshoven, above n 8, at 7; Focarelli, above n 7, at 137.

[42] According to Art 26, '[e]very treaty in force is binding upon the parties to it and must be performed by them in good faith.'

[43] ILC Articles on the Responsibility of States for Internationally Wrongful Acts (2001), annexed to UN Doc A/RES/56/83 (12 December 2001).

[44] See MN 5; Kalshoven, above n 8, at 16.

a. An obligation to stop and prevent private actor infringements

11   The positive obligation to ensure respect complements the negative obligation not to violate the Geneva Conventions (i.e. to respect). States are therefore not only required not to violate the Conventions themselves (*to respect*), but they are also obliged to ensure that the Conventions are not infringed by others, namely private actors (*to ensure respect*). The obligation extends to the entire population over which a High Contracting Party exercises authority.[45] It applies to and is activated by any private activity that impairs the enjoyment of the protections granted by the Geneva Conventions. Thus, in its internal compliance dimension, the obligation to ensure respect is not limited to cases in which private actors breach humanitarian law provisions by which they are themselves directly bound, such as the criminalized humanitarian law provisions. Rather, as in the case of human rights law,[46] states are obliged to ensure that the protections granted in the Geneva Conventions as a whole can be enjoyed without any detrimental private actor interference. In the case of Common Article 1, such a broad interpretation is supported by the wording of the provision, which obliges states to ensure respect for the Geneva Conventions in their entirety. The object and purpose of Common Article 1, i.e. the aim to ensure the effective implementation of the protections granted in the Conventions as far as possible, likewise favours such an interpretation. States are therefore not only obliged to stop or prevent grave breaches committed by their citizens or other persons under their authority, they are also under an obligation to stop lower-level interferences, for example to stop persons under their authority from interfering with medical aid deliveries to the wounded and sick.

12   The obligation to ensure respect is not an obligation of result but an obligation of conduct,[47] often synonymously referred to as an 'obligation of means'. As such it is to be exercised with due diligence.[48] This means that states are obliged to take such steps as can reasonably be expected of them in the given circumstances, in order to stop or prevent private actors under their authority infringing the protections granted in the Geneva Conventions. What exactly is owed by states in a given situation depends on a variety of parameters, including the kind and extent of the harm occurring, the imminence of further violations, and available resources.[49]

b. An obligation to stop and prevent state organ infringements

13   It is widely accepted that by virtue of Common Article 1, High Contracting Parties are also under an obligation to put a stop to and proactively prevent infringements of the Geneva Conventions by their own organs, namely their armed forces.[50] Since a state cannot but

---

[45] Final Record, vol II-B, at 53.

[46] See, e.g., HRCttee, General Comment 31 (26 May 2004).

[47] Sassòli, above n 14, at 412. With regard to the structurally similar obligation to prevent genocide, see ICJ, *Bosnian Genocide Case*, above n 13, para 430.

[48] Regarding the due diligence standard, see P.M. Dupuy, 'Reviewing the Difficulties of Codification: On Ago's Classification of Obligations of Means and Obligations of Result in Relation to State Responsibility', 10 *EJIL* (1999) 371, at 384; R. Pisillo-Mazzeschi, 'The Due Diligence Rule and the Nature of the International Responsibility of States', 35 *GYIL* (1992) 9, at 41; J.A. Hessbruegge, 'The Historical Development of the Doctrines of Attribution and Due Diligence in International Law', 36 *New York University Journal of International Law & Politics* (2004) 265.

[49] ICJ, *Bosnian Genocide Case*, above n 13, para 430; Kessler, above n 11, at 506.

[50] E.g., the 1976 *Air Force Pamphlet* of the United States provides that 'the US […] *ensures* observance and enforcement through a variety of national means including close command control, military regulations, rules

act through its own organs, it is not fully clear whether this obligation already derives from the obligation to respect, or from the obligation to ensure respect. In other words, it is questionable whether the negative obligation not to violate the Geneva Conventions (i.e. to respect) also contains positive elements requiring states proactively to prevent violations by their organs, or whether the positive obligation to ensure respect extends not only to private actors, but also to state organs. It has been argued that the obligation to ensure respect in its entire internal compliance dimension is already part of, and derives directly from, the obligation to respect.[51] Thus, the ICRC Commentary to Article 1 AP I provides that 'the duty to respect implies that of *ensuring respect by civilian and military authorities, the members of the armed forces, and in general, by the population as a whole*'.[52] This interpretation has rightly been criticized.[53] Reading a positive 'ensure respect' meaning into the negative obligation to 'respect' is counter-intuitive. In view of the clear distinction between the two obligations in Common Article 1, it is more coherent to uphold an interpretation in line with the different understanding of the terms. Thus, the obligation to respect, as an obligation of result, has an exclusively negative connotation, requiring states not to violate the Conventions through their own organs and agents. Conversely, the obligation to ensure respect, in its internal compliance dimension, contains a positive obligation to put a stop to and to take proactive steps to prevent violations, not only by private actors under a state's authority but also by a state's own organs.

c. *Specific provisions that aim to 'ensure respect'*

14 The Geneva Conventions contain a number of provisions that are often depicted as specifications of the internal compliance dimension of the obligation to ensure respect contained in Common Article 1. Thus, the High Contracting Parties are required to disseminate the Conventions as widely as possible in their respective countries and to instruct their armed forces,[54] they are obliged to repress grave breaches, to take measures necessary for the suppression of all other acts contrary to the Conventions,[55] and they must prevent and suppress abuses of the emblems.[56] Although the overall object and purpose of these specific provisions is clearly to ensure better respect for the Conventions, strictly speaking, these obligations are not subcategories of the obligation to ensure respect, as it is contained in Common Article 1. Whereas the obligation to ensure respect in Common Article 1 is an obligation of conduct, the above-mentioned provisions contain obligations of result. The High Contracting Parties are obliged 'to respect' these specific provisions. Thus, states 'undertake to enact any legislation necessary to provide effective penal sanctions [for] any of the grave breaches',[57] they '*must* make legal advisers available',[58] they '*must* provide instruction in international humanitarian law to their armed forces',[59] and they '*undertake*

---

of engagement, the Uniform Code of Military Justice and other national enforcement techniques': United States Department of the Air Force, *Air Force Pamphlet 110–31*, 'International Law—The Conduct of Armed Conflict and Air Operations' (1976), para 15-2(e) (emphasis added).

[51] Pictet Commentary GC I, at 24 ff.   [52] ICRC Commentary APs, para 41 (emphasis added).
[53] Focarelli, above n 7, at 137.
[54] Arts 47/48/127/144, supplemented by Art 83 AP I, Art 18 AP I, Art 7 AP III. See also the ICRC CIHL Study, Rules 141, 142, 143.
[55] Arts 49/50/129/146 and Art 85 AP I.
[56] Art 54 GC I, Art 45 GC II, Art 18 AP I, Art 6 AP III.
[57] Arts 49/50/129/146/ and Art 85 AP I.   [58] ICRC CIHL Study, Rule 141, at 500 (emphasis added).
[59] Ibid, Rule 142, at 501 (emphasis added).

[...] to disseminate the text of the present Convention[s] as widely as possible'.[60] The due diligence obligation to ensure respect laid out in Common Article 1 is additional to these treaty-specific obligations of result. Instruction to the armed forces and dissemination of the Geneva Conventions, as well as the repression of grave breaches, are fundamental prerequisites for these instruments to be respected. However, whenever these measures prove to be insufficient, and especially where violations of the Conventions are imminent or have already occurred, the due diligence obligation contained in Common Article 1 will require states to take additional measures to ensure respect.

II. The external compliance dimension of the obligation to ensure respect

15   It remains debated,[61] however, whether Common Article 1 goes beyond the accepted 'internal compliance dimension', and whether states that have ratified the Geneva Conventions—including states that are not even party to an armed conflict—by virtue of the undertaking 'to ensure respect', are also obliged to ensure respect vis-à-vis external transgressors ('external compliance dimension').[62] The ICRC has always endorsed such an external compliance dimension.[63] This is also the prevailing view in the literature.[64] And the ICJ in its *Wall Advisory Opinion* held that 'all the States parties to the [fourth] Geneva Convention [...] are under an *obligation*, while respecting the United Nations Charter and international law, to ensure compliance by Israel [i.e. another State] with international humanitarian law'.[65] But Judges Kooijmans[66] and Higgins,[67] in their separate opinions in the *Wall Advisory Opinion*, were already rather critical about the Court's 'assertions' concerning Common Article 1.[68] Judge Kooijmans concluded that while he certainly was not in favour of a restricted interpretation of Common Article 1, he simply did 'not know whether the scope given by the Court to this Article [...] [was] correct as a statement of positive law'.[69]

a. Does the obligation to ensure respect have an external compliance dimension?

16   The wording of Common Article 1 is inconclusive as to whether the obligation to ensure respect has an external compliance dimension, and thereby extends to the violations of

---

[60] Arts 47/48/127/144; Art 83 AP I, Art 18 AP I, Art 7 AP III (emphasis added), see also the ICRC CIHL Study, Rules 141, 142, 143. With regard to the obligation to enact domestic legislation to repress grave breaches, see K. Dörmann and R. Geiß, 'The Implementation of Grave Breaches into Domestic Legal Orders', 8 *JICJ* (2009) 703.

[61] For a recent in-depth analysis of this question on which the following analysis (MN 15–41) partially relies, see R. Geiß, 'Common Article 1 of the 1949 Geneva Conventions—Scope and Content of the Obligation to "Ensure Respect"—"Narrow but Deep" or "Wide and Shallow"?', in H. Krieger (ed), *Inducing Compliance with International Humanitarian Law: Lessons from the African Great Lakes Region* (Cambridge: CUP, forthcoming 2015).

[62] Focarelli distinguishes between a 'state-compliance meaning' and an 'individual compliance meaning'; see Focarelli, above n 7, at 125.

[63] See Pictet Commentary GC I, at 25, 26; GC II at 25, 26; GC III, at 18; GC IV at 15, 16. See Focarelli, above n 7, at 134, who also points out an inconsistency, namely, the fact that the Commentary regarding GC III speaks only of 'should', whereas the Commentaries to GCs I, II, and IV speak of 'may and should'.

[64] See the works cited above n 12.

[65] ICJ, *Wall Advisory Opinion*, above n 6, para 159 (emphasis added).

[66] Ibid, Separate Opinion of Judge Kooijmans, para 50.

[67] Ibid, Separate Opinion of Judge Higgins, para 39.

[68] Cf I. Scobbie, 'Smoke, Mirrors and Killer Whales: The International Court's Opinion on the Israeli Barrier Wall', 5 *German Law Journal* (2004) 1107, at 1116 ff.

[69] ICJ, *Wall Advisory Opinion*, above n 6, Separate Opinion of Judge Kooijmans, para 50.

other states and possibly other external transgressors at large.[70] It simply leaves open whose respect exactly is to be ensured, and therefore neither supports nor excludes an external compliance dimension.[71]

Conversely, the drafting history of the Geneva Conventions, as mentioned above,[72] does not support an(y) intention of the drafters to accord this provision an external compliance meaning.[73] Moreover, contrary to a widespread assumption, the re-inclusion of Common Article 1 in APs I and III in 1977 and 2005 respectively, can hardly be qualified as a 'subsequent agreement between the parties' (Article 31(3)(b) VCLT) to accord the wording to ensure respect an external compliance dimension. Although the diplomatic conferences of 1974–7 and 2004–5 unconditionally reaffirmed the wording of Common Article 1, there was once again hardly any debate about the actual meaning of this provision.[74] Thus, the drafting history of the Additional Protocols, in and of itself, is rather inconclusive on the matter, and if viewed in combination with the *travaux préparatoires* of the 1949 Conventions, would rather seem to militate against acceptance of an external compliance dimension of the obligation to ensure respect.

17

This conclusion, however, does not forestall a dynamic interpretation of Common Article 1 and the possibility to accord a different meaning to the 'ensure respect' formula today.[75] There is an abundance of practice from states and international organizations spanning a period of over 30 years, supporting an external compliance dimension of Common Article 1.[76] The 1968 Teheran Conference on Human Rights, in the Preamble to Resolution XXIII, explicitly referred to the responsibility 'to ensure the respect of these humanitarian rules in all circumstances *by other States*'.[77] The United Nations (UN) General Assembly,[78] the Security Council,[79] and, more recently, the UN Human Rights Council[80] have accepted—albeit predominantly with regard to GC IV and the situation in the Middle

18

---

[70] See MN 27. See discussion in Geiß, above n 61.

[71] Notably, in 1993 Judge Lauterpacht, with respect to Art I of the 1948 Genocide Convention, had argued that 'the undertaking […] to prevent genocide is not limited by reference to person or place so that, on its face, it could be said to require every party positively to prevent genocide wherever it occurs': *Application of the Convention on the Prevention and Punishment of the Crime of Genocide (Bosnia and Herzegovina v Serbia and Montenegro)*, Provisional Measures—Individual Opinion Lauterpacht, 13 September 1993, para 115.

[72] See MN 3–5.

[73] ICJ, *Wall Advisory Opinion*, above n 6, Separate opinion of Judge Higgins, para 39; Separate Opinion of Judge Kooijmans, para 50.

[74] Kalshoven, above n 8, at 47, 48.

[75] See generally ICJ, *Legal Consequences for States of the Continued Presence of South Africa in Namibia (South West Africa)*, Advisory Opinion, 21 June 1971, para 53; G. Distefano, 'Dynamic Interpretation of International Treaties', 115 *RGDIP* (2011) 373.

[76] Boisson de Chazournes and Condorelli, above n 10, at 69 ff; Kessler, above n 11, at 504; Focarelli, above n 7, at 128; ICRC CIHL Study, Rule 144, at 509.

[77] International Conference on Human Rights, Teheran, 1968, Res XXIII, Preamble, para 9 (emphasis added).

[78] UNGA Res 58/97 (17 December 2003), UN Doc A/RES/58/97, para 3; UNGA Res 59/122 (10 December 2004), UN Doc A/RES/59/122, para 3.

[79] UNSC Res 681 (20 December 1990), UN Doc S/RES/681, para 5.

[80] HRC Res S-9/1 (12 January 2009), UN Doc A/HRC/RES/S-9/1, Preamble, para 9. According to the Goldstone Report: 'This provision [CA 1] entails obligations not only in relation to actors and conduct within the jurisdiction of each State but also in relation to the *international enforcement* of the Conventions.' See Human Rights Council, 'Human Rights in Palestine and other occupied Arab territories, Report of the United Nations Fact-Finding Mission on the Gaza Conflict', A/HRC/12/48 (25 Sept 2009), available at <http://www2.ohchr.org/english/bodies/hrcouncil/docs/12session/A-HRC-12-48.pdf> (emphasis added).

East—an external compliance dimension of Common Article 1.[81] Meanwhile, the ICJ has confirmed an external compliance dimension of the structurally similar obligation 'to prevent' genocide,[82] and it has done the same with regard to Common Article 1.[83] Armed conflicts, especially in the past two decades, have impelled innumerable (unilateral) calls by states on the belligerents that humanitarian law should be respected.[84] In various instances the ICRC has appealed to the international community to end violations of humanitarian law;[85] there are no records that these appeals have ever met with any criticism.[86] And while certain rules laid out in the CIHL Study have elicited considerable objections from some states,[87] as far as can be seen, no state has ever objected to customary law Rule 144 of the CIHL Study, which provides that '[t]hey [i.e. states] *must* exert their influence, to the degree possible, to stop violations of international humanitarian law'.[88]

19   Notwithstanding, there is of course no denying that in many relevant instances states have been highly selective in their sporadic reactions to breaches—including grave and egregious breaches—of IHL. Moreover, given that the precise content of the obligation to ensure respect vis-à-vis external transgressors remains debated, and in any event depends on the circumstances of each specific case,[89] it may not always be entirely clear what kind of reactions one has to look for, in order to support an obligatory external compliance dimension. The crucial question, however, is not whether reactions to violations of humanitarian law provisions have been selective, but whether they have been too selective.[90] In view of the above-mentioned practice and jurisprudential affirmations, and considering that the due diligence nature of the obligation to ensure respect allows for certain variations in states' reactions, this is no longer the case. In recent decades the selectivity has

---

[81] In Res S-9/1 of 12 January 2009, the UN Human Rights Council reaffirmed that each state party to GC IV 'is under the obligation to respect and ensure the respect for the obligations arising from that Convention', above n 80. In view of the explicit reference to CA 1 in many of the Resolutions, it is not convincing to accord merely a recommendatory character to these various statements; but see Focarelli, above n 7, at 157. For a comprehensive collection of relevant practice regarding CA 1, see ICRC CIHL Study, vol II, Practice relating to Rule 144, at 3289.

[82] ICJ, *Bosnian Genocide Case*, above n 13, para 430. The obligation to prevent is described as 'structurally similar' because, like the obligation to ensure respect, it is a due diligence obligation. With regard to the question whether the obligation 'to ensure respect' also contains a preventive dimension, i.e. an obligation to act even before a breach of the GCs actually occurs, see MN 28 ff.

[83] ICJ, *Wall Advisory Opinion*, above n 6, para 158, ICJ, *Nicaragua v USA*, above n 6, para 220.

[84] ICRC CIHL Study, vol I, at 512.

[85] Appeal of 20 March 1979, reprinted in 'Conflict in Southern Africa: ICRC Appeal', 19 *IRRC* 209 (1979) 85; Appeal of 9 May 1983, see 'Africa–Latin America–Asia–Middle East', 23 *IRRC* 235 (1983) 209, at 220; Y. Sandoz, 'L'appel du Comité international de la Croix-Rouge dans le cadre du conflit entre l'Irak et l'Iran', 29 *AFDI* (1983) 161.

[86] In fact, more recently, the High Contracting Parties have arguably supported the ICRC's consistent affirmation that states are under a legal obligation to ensure respect for humanitarian law by external transgressors. The Declaration of the Conference of High Contracting Parties to the Fourth Geneva Convention, Geneva, 2001, in para 4 provides: 'The participating High Contracting Parties call upon all parties, *directly involved in the conflict or not*, to respect and to ensure respect for the Geneva Conventions in all circumstances, to disseminate and take measures necessary for the prevention and suppression of breaches of the Conventions' (emphasis added). See also International Conference for the Protection of War Victims, Geneva, 1993, Final Declaration, Part II, para 11.

[87] J.B. Bellinger and W.J. Haynes, 'A US Government Response to the International Committee of the Red Cross Study *Customary International Humanitarian Law*', 89 *IRRC* 866 (2007) 443.

[88] The corresponding commentary emphasizes that the rule has a state compliance dimension: see ICRC CIHL Study, Rule 144, at 509 ff (emphasis added).

[89] See section E.II.b of this chapter.

[90] C. Tams, *Enforcing Obligations Erga Omnes in International Law* (Cambridge: CUP, 2005), at 234.

certainly not been such as to suggest the 'permissibility of inactivity'.[91] Thus today, it is clear that Common Article 1 also has an external compliance dimension.

b. Scope and content of the obligation to ensure respect in its external compliance dimension

The practice referred to above confirms that, by virtue of Common Article 1, states are obliged to take positive steps to induce external transgressors back into compliance with the Geneva Conventions.[92] While it is clear that this is an obligation of conduct that is to be exercised with due diligence, the precise content of the obligation is not fully settled. Of course, in part this is due to the fact that due diligence is a relative standard in so far as it requires different conduct under different circumstances.[93] In addition, however, some of the basic pre-conditions of the obligation to ensure respect vis-à-vis external transgressors have remained unclear and disputed. Does the obligation to ensure respect require states to react to each and every violation or infringement, or only to certain (serious) breaches of fundamental provisions in the Geneva Conventions? And how does Common Article 1 relate to the concept of obligations *erga omnes* (*partes*)? After all, in the past, Common Article 1 has, inter alia, been described as being itself *erga omnes*,[94] as rendering *erga omnes* all other provisions contained in the Geneva Conventions,[95] as having been a precursor of the concept of obligations *erga omnes*,[96] and as a provision that simply has nothing to do with the conception of obligations *erga omnes*.[97] Is the obligation to ensure respect in Common Article 1 limited to breaches in times of armed conflict and violations that are attributable to other states? Or is it activated also by peacetime breaches and violations by other external (non-state) actors? When exactly is the obligation to ensure respect 'triggered'? And does it even depend on any 'trigger', i.e. a previous violation of humanitarian law, or is to be construed as a continuous obligation that exists regardless of any specific violation, and that requires states not only to react, but also proactively to prevent future violations by external actors?

20

---

[91] In his individual opinion of 1993, Judge Lauterpacht, while expressing sympathy for the idea of an 'individual and collective responsibility of states for the prevention of genocide wherever it may occur', contemplated whether '[t]he limited reaction of the parties to the Genocide Convention in relation to these episodes may represent a practice suggesting the *permissibility of inactivity*'; ICJ, *Bosnian Genocide Case*, Provisional Measures—Individual Opinion Lauterpacht, para 115 (emphasis added).

[92] See MN 15, 18. This positive dimension is encompassed by the second part of Rule 144 of the ICRC's CIHL Study, according to which, '[states] must exert their influence, to the degree possible, to stop violations of international humanitarian law': ICRC CIHL Study, Rule 144 second sentence, at 509.

[93] ICJ, *Bosnian Genocide Case*, above n 13, para 430; Judge Kooijmans, in his Separate Opinion in the *Wall Advisory Opinion*, seemed to suggest that states, by virtue of CA 1, are entitled to nothing other than the issuing of political démarches; see ICJ, *Wall Advisory Opinion*, above n 6, Separate Opinion of Judge Kooijmans, paras 47 et seq. As Scobbie has already remarked, there is no justification for such a narrow approach; see Scobbie, above n 68, at 1119.

[94] Kessler, above n 11, at 501.

[95] Boisson de Chazournes and Condorelli, above n 10, at 69. Paraphrasing Michael Reismann, one might indeed wonder how all of these humanitarian norms entered into the 'magic *erga omnes* circle'; M. Reisman, 'Comment', in J. Delbrück and U. Heinz (eds), *The Future of International Law Enforcement. New Scenarios—New Law?* (Berlin: Duncker & Humblot, 1993), at 170.

[96] T. Meron, *Human Rights and Humanitarian Norms as Customary Law* (Oxford: Clarendon Press, 1989), at 190.

[97] Judge Higgins, in her Separate Opinion in the *Wall Advisory Opinion*, above n 6, held, at para 39, that CA 1, 'while apparently viewed by the Court as something to do with "the *erga omnes* principle" is simply a provision in an almost universally ratified multilateral Convention'. See also Focarelli, above n 7, at 164 ff.

i. Which kind of breaches trigger the obligation to ensure respect?

21   Absent any detailed analysis of these issues, and in view of the wording of Common Article 1 which requires states to ensure respect for the Conventions in their entirety and 'in all circumstances', there seems to be a widespread assumption that the obligation to ensure respect requires reactions to each and every breach of each and every provision of the Geneva Conventions.[98] Yet while such a broad interpretation is immediately convincing and in line with the original intention of the drafters of Common Article 1, in as far as the internal compliance dimension of the obligation to ensure respect is concerned,[99] it is less clear whether such a comprehensive scope can also be ascribed to the external compliance dimension of this obligation.

22   In an external context, it could be argued that such a sweeping interpretation of the obligation to ensure respect would simply lead to unrealistic results. If all states were indeed constantly required to react to all breaches by external transgressors, including peacetime breaches, of each and every provision of the Geneva Conventions, arguably almost all states would constantly be violating their obligations to ensure respect.[100] Wilfully denying a fair and regular trial to a single protected person (i.e. a grave breach in the legal sense, Article 147 GC IV) would activate the said obligation. What is more, on the basis of such a sweeping assumption, if taken to the extreme, it could be argued that any violation of the obligation to ensure respect itself triggers all other states' obligations to ensure respect. This would result in endless chains of breaches, and in an obligation that is largely deprived of any practical relevance.

23   In addition, it could potentially be argued that such a far-reaching conception of the obligation to ensure respect does not find sufficient support in (current) international practice.[101] The practice commonly referred to in order to support an external compliance dimension of the obligation to ensure respect, as far as can be seen, typically deals with instances of a certain gravity, and with violations that occur in times of armed conflict rather than in peacetime.[102] In this context Kessler, for example, speaks of a duty in 'exceptional cases'.[103] It is also telling that the ICJ, in the relevant part of its *Wall Advisory Opinion*, referred to the 'character and the importance of the rights and obligations involved';[104] and that the structurally related responsibility to protect (R2P) concept, ongoing debate notwithstanding, has gradually been narrowed down and is activated only by the core crimes of genocide, ethnic cleansing, war crimes, and crimes against humanity.[105] Against this backdrop, it could be argued that *de lege lata*, the obligation to ensure respect in its external compliance dimension is limited to 'serious breaches' of

---

[98] Kessler, above n 11, at 502–7; Gasser, above n 12, at 31–2. Kessler in fact argues (at 506) in favour of an even more general obligation to 'assist' and 'help' other states to comply, and that 'whenever the humanitarian crisis reaches such a degree that it amounts to a serious violation of the conventions—common Article 1 obliges the High Contracting Parties to enforce the Conventions through humanitarian measures' (at 507).

[99] See MN 5, 10–14.   [100] Focarelli, above n 7, at 156 ff.   [101] See MN 32 ff.

[102] Kessler, above n 11, at 503 ff.   [103] Ibid, at 505.

[104] ICJ, *Wall Advisory Opinion*, above n 6, para 159. Judge Simma, in his Separate Opinion in the ICJ, *Case concerning Armed Activities on the Territory of the Congo Case (DRC v Uganda)*, Judgment, 19 December 2005, stated that 'at least *the core* of the obligations deriving from the rules of international humanitarian law [...] are valid erga omnes' (para 39, emphasis added).

[105] A. Peters, 'The Responsibility to Protect: Spelling Out the Hard Legal Consequences for the UN Security Council and its Members', in U. Fastenrath et al (eds), *From Bilateralism to Community Interest* (Oxford: OUP, 2011) 297, at 300.

the Geneva Conventions.[106] Indeed, given that by virtue of Articles 40 and 41 of the ILC Articles on State Responsibility, only serious breaches of the narrow category of *jus cogens* norms trigger an obligation to 'cooperate',[107] it would prima facie seem logical to require at least a similar 'threshold of gravity' with regard to the far wider circle of norms to which the obligation to ensure respect in Common Article 1 applies, namely violations of all the provisions contained in the Geneva Conventions.

There are, however, also strong arguments in favour of a broader conception of the obligation to ensure respect in its external compliance dimension. First, concerns that a broad conception of this obligation would be unrealistically burdensome for states are attenuated by the fact that the obligation to ensure respect is a due diligence obligation, i.e. states are in any case obliged to do only what can reasonably be expected in the circumstances of each particular instance, e.g. to exert their influence. Secondly, the 'seriousness' of a violation is not a precise threshold for triggering a positive duty to act and may be criticized as creating considerable legal uncertainty.[108] Rather than affecting the application of the obligation to ensure respect, the seriousness of a breach is to be taken into consideration when determining the actual content of the obligation to ensure respect in a given case. In this regard, the due diligence nature of the obligation allows for graduated responses proportionate to the seriousness of the breach in question. As a general rule, the more serious and imminent a breach, the more will be required of states. And while it cannot reasonably be expected that states will immediately and directly react to each and every (minor, peacetime) breach of the Geneva Conventions whenever and wherever it occurs, if such (minor) breaches occur continuously and over an extended period of time, it could reasonably be expected that states will exert their influence to stop such breaches even if they do not qualify as 'serious breaches'. 24

Such a broader approach to the obligation to ensure respect, which avoids the uncertainties of determining an additional threshold of gravity, is also in line with the conception of structurally similar due diligence obligations (to prevent) in human rights law.[109] These obligations likewise do not depend on any particular threshold. The type and seriousness of the breaches in question merely affect the content of these obligations, i.e. the assessment of what it is that can reasonably be expected of states in their reactions to such breaches. The ICJ has also endorsed such a broad conception of the obligation to ensure respect in Common Article 1. In the *Wall* case, the Court held that 'all the States Parties to the Geneva Convention relative to the Protection of Civilian Persons in Time of War of 12 August 1949 are under an obligation, [...] to ensure compliance by Israel *with international humanitarian law as embodied in that Convention*'.[110] Common Article 1 makes 25

---

[106] In fact, it should be noted that if we look only at grave breaches, state practice proving the obligation to ensure respect vis-à-vis other states in the first place will appear far less selective than it is if we take into consideration states' reactions to all violations of all provisions of IHL.

[107] ILC, 'Report of the International Law Commission' (23 April–1 June and 2 July–10 August 2001) 53rd Session, UN Doc Supplement No 10 (A/Res/56/10), at 43.

[108] Nevertheless, the threshold of *serious violations* is not alien to the GCs (Arts 89, 90(2)(c)(i) AP I), nor to the ILC Articles on State Responsibility, above n 43 (Art 40(2)). As has been concluded elsewhere, on the whole it appears to be an acceptable standard to states: Tams, above n 90, at 248.

[109] HRCttee, General Comment 31 (26 May 2004).

[110] ICJ, *Wall Advisory Opinion*, above n 6, para 159 (emphasis added). The Court also said that '[i]t follows from that provision that every State party to that Convention, whether or not it is a party to a specific conflict, is under an obligation to ensure that the requirements of the instruments in question are complied with': ibid, para 158. See also *Armed Activities on the Territory of the Congo Case (DRC v Uganda)*, above n 104, Separate Opinion of Judge Simma, para 33.

it clear that the provisions contained in the Geneva Conventions are binding *erga omnes partes*,[111] and that all states parties to the Geneva Conventions share a common interest in upholding these provisions.[112] Against this backdrop, and given that in times of armed conflict even 'minor' violations of the Geneva Conventions by one party can quickly lead to an escalatory spiral of more and ever graver violations, the obligation to ensure respect in both its internal and external compliance dimensions should be construed broadly to require positive steps whenever provisions of the Geneva Conventions are breached.

26 Situated in the context of general public international law, the obligation to ensure respect in Common Article 1 may be described as containing a specification of the general concept expressed in Articles 48 and 54 of the ILC Articles on State Responsibility. According to Article 48, '[a]ny State other than an injured State *is entitled to invoke* the responsibility of another State [...] if the obligation breached is owed to a group of States [or the international community as a whole].'[113] Similarly, the savings clause contained in Article 54 of the ILC Articles does 'not prejudice the *right* of [non-injured] States [...] to take lawful measures'.[114] Common Article 1 goes further, in that it entails not only an *entitlement* to 'invoke' (Article 48) or a *right* to 'take lawful measures' (Article 54), but also an *obligation* to act if the Geneva Conventions are breached. In doing so it follows the structure of Articles 40 and 41 of the ILC Articles. However, unlike these provisions, it is not limited to *serious* breaches of obligations arising from *peremptory norms (jus cogens)* but covers all breaches of the wider circle of norms contained in the Geneva Conventions, i.e. obligations that are owed to all the states parties of the Geneva Conventions (*erga omnes partes*).[115]

ii. Whose breaches trigger the obligation to ensure respect?

27 It follows that any breach of the Geneva Conventions by another state, irrespective of where and when it occurs, activates the obligation to ensure respect. The same holds true with regard to breaches by other external (non-state) transgressors in as far as they are bound to respect the Geneva Conventions.[116] Thus, breaches by organized armed groups, given that they are bound to respect Common Article 3, will also activate the obligation to ensure respect by all the High Contracting Parties. Conversely, breaches by international organizations, albeit that they may trigger states' customary law obligation to ensure respect, will not trigger the obligation to ensure respect under Common Article 1, given that international organizations are not bound by the Geneva Conventions as such.

iii. When is the obligation to ensure respect 'triggered'?

28 With respect to the precise point in time at which the duty to take positive steps arises, it is clear that as soon as a violation has occurred, states are under an obligation to ensure respect. The question is whether the obligation to ensure respect also entails a preventive dimension, requiring states to react to threats of an imminent violation of the Geneva Conventions or even to take proactive steps—irrespective of any particular threat scenario—to ensure better compliance with the Geneva Conventions. Whereas the latter interpretation would

---

[111] See J. Crawford, *State Responsibility: The General Part* (Cambridge: CUP, 2013), at 370.
[112] Generally on the concept of obligations *erga omnes partes*, see ICJ, *Questions Relating to the Obligation to Prosecute or Extradite (Belgium v Senegal)*, Judgment, 20 July 2012, para 69.
[113] ILC Articles on State Responsibility, above n 43, Art 48 (emphasis added).
[114] Ibid, Art 54 (emphasis added). [115] Crawford, above n 111, at 370.
[116] Notably, the ICJ in the *Bosnian Genocide Case*, with regard to the obligation 'to prevent' genocide, also referred to violations by other 'actors': ICJ, *Bosnian Genocide Case*, above n 13, paras 430, 434.

seem to go far beyond what can be reasonably expected of states in an external context, in light of the object and purpose of Common Article 1, it would only seem logical to encompass scenarios in which a breach is imminent. In this latter context, guidance may be derived from the ICJ's Judgment in the *Bosnian Genocide Case*. There, the Court held, with regard to the obligation 'to prevent' genocide, that 'a State's obligation to prevent, and the corresponding duty to act, *arise at the instant* that the State learns of, or should normally have learned of, the existence of a *serious risk* that genocide will be committed'.[117] The wording of Common Article 1 certainly allows for such a broad conception of the obligation to ensure respect, and the object and purpose of this provision would seem to require it. Therefore, the ICJ's reasoning regarding the obligation to prevent genocide should also be applied to the obligation to ensure respect for the Geneva Conventions.

iv. The due diligence nature of the obligation to ensure respect: measures authorized and required by the obligation to ensure respect in its external compliance dimension

The obligation to ensure respect is an obligation of conduct that is to be exercised with due diligence. States are therefore obliged to do what can reasonably be expected of them in the given circumstances. What exactly is owed by states in a given situation therefore depends on a variety of parameters, including the kind and extent of the harm occurring, the imminence of further violations, a state's relationship with the transgressor and its capacity to exert influence, which in turn depends on factors such as geographical proximity and the strength of political links between the states concerned.[118] For example, in multinational operations, where a number of states are conducting joint operations and where states are in close and permanent contact with one another, there may be ample possibilities to influence the behaviour of other coalition members. In other constellations, a state may be rather remote from the location where the violations occur and its influence on the transgressor state may be extremely limited. But even in such a scenario, it could still reasonably be expected that the state would at least react to such occurrences, for example by condemning the violations bilaterally or, as the case may be, even publicly. Regarding the structurally related due diligence obligation to prevent genocide, the ICJ has held that states are obliged 'to employ *all means reasonably available to them*, so as to prevent genocide so far as possible'.[119] The same standard applies with regard to the due diligence obligation to ensure respect.

Measures may be taken individually and/or collectively. They could include, inter alia, acts of retorsion, such as the suspension of public aid programmes, bi- or multilateral diplomatic protests, and public denunciations. Moreover, depending on the circumstances, it may reasonably be expected of states to institute judicial proceedings,[120] to request a

---

[117] Ibid, para 431 (emphasis added). However, as far as a state's responsibility for the breach of the said obligation to prevent is concerned, the ICJ was more cautious and, in accordance with Art 14(3) of the ILC Articles on State Responsibility, held that 'a State can be held responsible for breaching the obligation to prevent genocide only if genocide was actually committed. It is at the time when commission of the prohibited act [...] begins that the breach of an obligation of prevention occurs'. For a critique, see Dupuy, above n 48, at 381 ff.

[118] ICJ, *Bosnian Genocide Case*, above n 13, para 430; Kessler, above n 11, at 506.

[119] ICJ, *Bosnian Genocide Case*, above n 13, para 430 (emphasis added). The Court also held that 'responsibility is [...] incurred if the State *manifestly failed to take all measures to prevent* genocide which were within its power, and which might have contributed to preventing the genocide': ibid (emphasis added).

[120] *Armed Activities on the Territory of the Congo (DRC v Uganda)*, above n 104, Separate Opinion of Judge Simma, paras 20–38.

meeting of the High Contracting Parties (Article 7 AP I), to resort to the Protecting Power's institution or its substitutes, and, where applicable, to submit a request to the International Fact-Finding Commission (Article 90 AP I).

31   Today, it is undisputed that, by virtue of the humanitarian law obligation to ensure respect, states are not entitled to take unilateral military action contrary to Article 2(4) of the UN Charter. The ICJ has reiterated, both with respect to the obligation to prevent genocide and with regard to the obligation to ensure respect under Common Article 1, that 'every State may only act within the limits of international law'.[121] Similarly, Resolution 3 of the 30th International Conference of the Red Cross and Red Crescent requires states to 'to exert their influence, to the degree possible, to prevent and end violations, either individually or through multilateral mechanisms, *in accordance with international law*'.[122]

32   It is less clear, however, whether or not the obligation to ensure respect entails an 'obligatory entitlement' to adopt non-forcible countermeasures in response to humanitarian law violations of other states. Such an entitlement to employ non-forcible countermeasures could potentially be construed in two ways: either every state, by virtue of Common Article 1, is rendered 'specially affected', and therefore qualifies as an 'injured state' in accordance with Article 42(b)(i) of the ILC Articles;[123] or Common Article 1, by virtue of subsequent state practice, has developed beyond the state of the law as it is described in the ILC Commentary to Article 54 of the ILC Articles on State Responsibility, by entitling non-injured states to resort to countermeasures (vis-à-vis other High Contracting Parties) in reaction to breaches of the Geneva Conventions.

33   *De lege lata*, however, neither of these approaches finds (sufficient) support. First of all, the 'specially affected clause' in Article 42(b)(i) of the ILC Articles has a factual not a legal dimension, i.e. states can qualify as 'specially affected' only because of factual circumstances, not because of legal prescription.[124] Moreover, at this stage there is no indication that—as far as countermeasures are concerned—Common Article 1 has developed beyond the general rules on state responsibility as codified by the ILC. Under Article 54 of the ILC Articles on State Responsibility, any non-injured state may only 'take *lawful measures* against that State to ensure cessation of the breach and reparation in the interests of the injured State or of the beneficiaries of the obligation breached'. The ILC thus left it deliberately open whether there exists a right of states other than the injured state to take countermeasures.[125] According to the ILC, the current state of international law on countermeasures taken in the general or collective interest is uncertain;[126] state practice is sparse and involves only a limited number of states.[127] At present there appears to be no clearly recognized entitlement of states other than the injured state to take countermeasures in the collective interest.[128] And while the law may of course be developing in the direction of a right to take countermeasures in the collective interest,[129] at present there

---

[121] ICJ, *Wall Advisory Opinion*, above n 6, para 158; ICJ, *Bosnian Genocide Case*, above n 13, para 431.
[122] 30th International Conference of the Red Cross and Red Crescent, Geneva, 2007, Res 3, para 2 (emphasis added).
[123] Sassòli, above n 14, at 423.
[124] J. Crawford, *The International Law Commission's Articles on State Responsibility. Introduction, Text and Commentaries* (Cambridge: CUP, 2002), Art 42.
[125] B. Simma, 'From Bilateralism to Community Interest in International Law', 250 *RCADI* (1994) 217; Tams, above n 90, at 249 ff.
[126] Crawford, *The International Law Commission's Articles on State Responsibility*, above n 124, Art 54, para 6.
[127] Ibid.   [128] Ibid.
[129] Tams, above n 90, at 248; C. Tams, 'Individual States as Guardians of Community Interests', in Fastenrath et al (eds), above n 105, 379, at 391.

is no indication that Common Article 1, namely the obligation to ensure respect, has already developed further than the contemporary customary international law on state responsibility. As far as can be seen, there are no instances in which states have responded to breaches of the Geneva Conventions by unilateral countermeasures on the basis of the obligation to ensure respect. The ILC Commentary to Article 54 of the ILC Articles on State Responsibility, while listing relevant instances where non-injured states have reacted to breaches by adopting economic sanctions and similar measures, does not even mention Common Article 1.[130]

According to Article 89 AP I, '[i]n situations of *serious violations* of the Conventions or of this Protocol, the High Contracting Parties undertake to act, jointly or individually, in *co-operation with the United Nations* and in conformity with the United Nations Charter.'[131] In the event of mass violations of core humanitarian law provisions, collective action through the UN, namely the Security Council, may often be the only—and certainly the most effective—way to ensure respect.[132] Indeed, over the past two decades the Security Council has developed into the 'major intergovernmental institution' in the field of IHL, its reactions to violations of IHL ranging from denunciations and focused demands for implementation, to the creation of *ad hoc* institutional mechanisms.[133] 34

Cooperation with the UN in the sense of Article 89 AP I, however, does not in and of itself relieve states of their general obligation to ensure respect. In the *Bosnian Genocide Case*, in spite of the fact that Article VIII of the Genocide Convention specifically provides for the activation of the UN collective security system, the ICJ held that the unqualified undertaking to ensure respect in Article I of the Genocide Convention has a 'separate legal existence of its own', that the duty to prevent is both 'normative and compelling', that it 'is not to be read merely as an introduction to later express references to legislation, prosecution and extradition', and that 'in particular [...] [the] undertaking to prevent, creates obligations distinct from those which appear in the subsequent Articles'.[134] In particular, the Court pointed out that '[e]ven if and when these organs [i.e. organs of the UN] have been called upon, this does not mean that the States parties to the Convention are relieved of the obligation to take such action as they can to prevent genocide from occurring.'[135] The very same reasoning may be applied concerning the humanitarian law obligation to ensure respect. Therefore, cooperation with the UN does not *per se* absolve states from their obligation to ensure respect. 35

What is more, the obligation to ensure respect could potentially influence the way in which individual members of the UN exercise their membership rights, in particular their voting rights, within the fora of the UN.[136] Thus, regarding the structurally similar concept of the responsibility to protect, it has been suggested that it may be possible to deduce an obligation at least to explain a negative vote or a veto in cases where the responsibility to protect is at issue.[137] *A fortiori*, it may be concluded that an obligation to explain 36

---

[130] Crawford, *The International Law Commission's Articles on State Responsibility*, above n 124, Art 54, paras 3 and 4.
[131] Emphasis added.   [132] Palwankar, above n 12, at 18.
[133] G. Nolte, 'The Different Functions of the Security Council with Respect to Humanitarian Law', in V. Lowe et al (eds), *The United Nations Security Council and War* (Oxford: OUP, 2008) 519, at 534.
[134] ICJ, *Bosnian Genocide Case*, above n 13, para 427.   [135] Ibid.
[136] A. Zimmermann, 'The Obligation to Prevent Genocide: Towards a General Responsibility to Protect?', in Fastenrath et al (eds), above n 105, 629, at 643.
[137] Peters, above n 105, at 323 ff.

and justify inactivity, or even potentially obstructing voting behaviour in a multilateral forum, derives from the obligation to ensure respect, the obligatory nature of which is far more established than the legal nature of the R2P concept.

c. The obligation not to encourage or aid or assist the commission of violations by others

37 It is widely accepted that, by virtue of Common Article 1, the High Contracting Parties may neither encourage,[138] nor aid or assist violations of the Conventions.[139] As mentioned above, it is less clear, however, whether these prohibited forms of conduct derive from the obligation to respect, or from the obligation to ensure respect. In *Nicaragua v USA*, the ICJ did not clearly distinguish between these two obligations.[140] The CIHL Study derives the source of the aforementioned prohibited forms of conduct from the obligation to ensure respect.[141] This appears to be the prevailing view in the literature too.[142] If states are required to take positive steps to end violations by others, so the argument goes, they must *a maiore ad minus* also be under a negative obligation not to encourage, aid, or assist such violations in the first place. Of course, a similar argument could be derived from the obligation to respect. If states are obliged not to violate the Conventions themselves, logically they should also be under an obligation not to further violations by others. Structurally, it may appear more coherent to deduce the negative obligation not to encourage, aid, or assist in violations by others from the equally negative obligation to respect (i.e. not to violate) the Conventions.[143] Otherwise, the obligation to ensure respect has to be split into a positive and a negative obligation, i.e. into an obligation of conduct (to ensure respect by others) and an obligation of result (not to encourage, aid, or assist violations by others). On the other hand, deriving an obligation not to aid or assist in violations of the law from the general '*pacta sunt servanda* obligation' would amount to an unusually broad interpretation of the obligation to respect, and would arguably render superfluous the concept of state responsibility stemming from aiding or assisting the commission of a wrongful act by another state, as laid out in Article 16 of the ILC Articles on State Responsibility. The relevance of this discussion, however, is limited because, in any case, it is undisputed that a negative obligation not to encourage, aid, or assist in violation of the Conventions flows from Common Article 1.

38 Encouragement and aiding or assisting should be distinguished.[144] Under the rules of international law on state responsibility, a state that encourages the commission of a wrongful act by another state is not internationally responsible.[145] Conversely, according to Article 16 of the ILC Articles on State Responsibility,

---

[138] ICRC CIHL Study, Rule 144, at 509: 'States may not encourage violations of international humanitarian law by parties to an armed conflict.'

[139] ICJ, *Nicaragua v USA*, above n 6, para 220; D. Schindler, 'Die erga omnes-Wirkung des humanitären Völkerrechts', in U. Beyerlin et al (eds), *Recht zwischen Umbruch und Bewahrung—Festschrift für Rudolf Bernhardt* (Berlin: Springer, 1995) 199, at 204; Azzam, above n 12, at 70; A. Imseis, 'Critical Reflections on the International Humanitarian Law Aspects of the ICJ Wall Advisory Opinion', 99 *AJIL* (2005) 102, at 115. See generally H.P. Aust, *Complicity and the Law of State Responsibility* (New York: CUP, 2011).

[140] ICJ, *Nicaragua v USA*, above n 6, para 220.   [141] ICRC CIHL Study, Rule 144, at 509.

[142] See, e.g., H.P. Aust, 'Complicity in Violations of International Humanitarian Law', in Krieger (ed), above n 61, at 12 ff.

[143] See the discussion at MN 13.   [144] Aust, above n 139, at 12.

[145] Ibid; R. Ago, 'Seventh Report on State Responsibility', II(1) *YILC* (1978) 31, at 55, para 63; ICJ, *Nicaragua v USA*, supra n 6, Dissenting Opinion Schwebel, 27 June 1986, paras 258–9.

[a] State which aids or assists another State in the commission of an internationally wrongful act […] is internationally responsible for doing so if:
(a) that State does so with knowledge of the circumstances of the internationally wrongful act; and
(b) the act would be internationally wrongful if committed by that State.[146]

Common Article 1 can thus be depicted as going beyond the general rule laid out in Article 16 of the ILC Articles on State Responsibility in two ways.[147] First, it also prescribes state responsibility in cases where violations of humanitarian law are merely encouraged. The ICJ has explicitly recognized the 'obligation not to *encourage* persons or groups engaged in the conflict in Nicaragua to act in violation of the provisions of Article 3 common to the four 1949 Geneva Conventions'.[148] This aspect of the obligation of ensuring respect is also set forth in Rule 144 of the CIHL Study, and is restated in Resolution 3 of the 30th International Conference of the Red Cross and Red Crescent in 2007.

Secondly, Common Article 1 can be said to establish a lower threshold for state responsibility, since it attenuates the rather stringent 'intent requirement' of Article 16 of the ILC Articles on State Responsibility.[149] Albeit that the intent requirement is not mentioned explicitly in Article 16, according to the ILC Commentary, '[a] State is not responsible for aid or assistance under article 16 unless the relevant State organ *intended*, by the aid or assistance given, *to facilitate* the occurrence of the wrongful conduct.'[150] This rather stringent 'intent requirement', which may often be rather difficult to establish, may be attenuated in the context of state responsibility for violations of the Geneva Conventions and other IHL provisions.[151] The rationale underlying this line of argumentation is that a specific obligation to ensure respect is more demanding and onerous than the general obligation to abstain from aiding or assisting in the commission of internationally wrongful acts.[152] Therefore, in the realm of Common Article 1, state responsibility may be established irrespective of any such specific intent. Thus, in relation to arms transfers, for example, it has been argued that once a transferring state *knows* that the receiving state systematically commits violations of IHL with certain weapons, continuing to provide assistance would be in violation of the obligation to ensure respect.[153]

The argument that the obligation to ensure respect, as it is laid out in Common Article 1, is *lex specialis* to the general rule in Article 16 of the ILC Articles, also finds support in the ICJ's reasoning in the *Bosnian Genocide Case*. There, the ICJ denied the responsibility of Serbia for complicity under Article III, lit e) of the Genocide Convention, a provision which is structurally similar to Article 16 of the ILC Articles.[154] Nevertheless, it affirmed the responsibility of Serbia under the general obligation to prevent genocide under Article I of the Genocide Convention, a provision which is structurally similar to Common Article 1 and the obligation to ensure respect.[155] In other words, even though it was not possible to establish the more stringent subjective threshold of Article III, lit e) of the Genocide Convention, in view of the continuous support by the Federal Republic of Yugoslavia of the Bosnian Serbs, the ICJ held Serbia responsible on the basis of a broader

---

[146] ILC Articles on State Responsibility, above n 43, Art 16. See also Arts 14 and 58 of the 'Draft Articles on the Responsibility of International Organizations', UN Doc A/CN.4/L.778 (30 May 2011).
[147] Aust, above n 139, at 12.   [148] ICJ, *Nicaragua v USA*, above n 6, para 220 (emphasis added).
[149] M. Brehm, 'The Arms Trade and States' Duty to Ensure Respect for Humanitarian and Human Rights Law', 12 *Journal of Conflict & Security Law* (2007) 359, at 386.
[150] Crawford, above n 124, Art 16, at 149, para 5 (emphasis added).
[151] Brehm, above n 149, at 386.   [152] Sassòli, above n 14, at 413.   [153] Ibid.
[154] ICJ, *Bosnian Genocide Case*, above n 13, para 471.   [155] Ibid. Aust, above n 139, at 14.

standard of complicity, which it derived from the general obligation to prevent genocide contained in Article I of the Genocide Convention.[156]

III. 'In all circumstances'

42 By virtue of Common Article 1, the High Contracting Parties are bound to respect the Conventions in all circumstances and to ensure respect in all circumstances. The phrase 'in all circumstances' is also used in various other provisions throughout the Geneva Conventions.[157] However, the precise meaning of the phrase has remained somewhat ambiguous. A variety of different legal meanings have been read into this term. Historically, when it first appeared in 1929, the 'in all circumstances' formula was used to mark the renouncing of the *si omnes* clause.[158] In addition, the negotiation history of the 1929 Geneva Conventions I and II indicates that the phrase also used to underline the Conventions' applicability not only in times of armed conflict, but also in times of peace.[159] But it is also argued that the formula emphasizes the non-reciprocal nature of the Geneva Conventions,[160] and that it prohibits the invocation of 'any valid pretext, legal or other, for not respecting' the Conventions, in particular *jus ad bellum* considerations or the notion of military necessity.[161] Moreover, the formula could also be interpreted as having a geographical and temporal connotation, requiring respect and ensuring respect in all places where the Geneva Conventions apply and at all times for the duration of an IAC.

43 Post-1949, many of these (original) meanings of the 'in all circumstances' formula were included in specific provisions of the Geneva Conventions. Thus, the *si omnes* clause is explicitly rejected in Common Article 2 paragraph 3, while Common Article 2 paragraph 1 clarifies that certain provisions of the Conventions also apply in times of peace. What is more, since the end of the Second World War it has become universally accepted that military necessity may not be invoked so as to override positive rules of humanitarian law.[162] Against this backdrop, it has been argued that the formula, over

---

[156] ICJ, *Bosnian Genocide Case*, above n 13, para 471.

[157] Historically see, e.g., Art 9 1906 GC and Arts 1, 9, and 25 para 1 1929 GC I. See also, e.g., Art 24 GC I, Art 12 GC II, Art14 GC III, Art 27 GC IV, as well as Arts 1(1), 10(2), 51(1), and 75(1) AP I; Arts 4(1), 7(2), and 13 AP II; and CA 3 para 1.

[158] *Actes de la Conférence diplomatique de Genève de 1929*, above n 34, Première Commission, 16 July 1929, at 321–2.

[159] Des Gouttes, above n 18, at 186.

[160] ICRC Commentary APs, para 51; ICTY, *The Prosecutor v Zoran Kupreškić et al*, Trial Chamber Judgment, IT-95-16-T, 14 January 2000, para 517; Condorelli and Boisson de Chazournes, above n 14, at 19. This finding is confirmed by Res 3 of the 30th International Conference of the Red Cross and Red Crescent, which emphasizes that the obligation to respect 'is not based on reciprocity': Preambular para 12, Geneva, 2007.

[161] Pictet Commentary GC I, at 27; GC II, at 26; GC IV, at 16; ICRC Commentary APs, para 48: '"In all circumstances" prohibits all Parties from invoking any reason not to respect the Protocol as a whole, whether the reason is of a legal or other nature. The question whether the war concerned is "just" or "unjust", one of aggression or of self-defence, should not affect the application of the Protocol [...].'

[162] See the US Military Tribunal in *US v Wilhelm List et al*, Judgment, 19 February 1948, reprinted in 15 *Annual Digest and Reports of Public International Law Cases* (1948) 632, at 647. It may be considered only where humanitarian law provisions make explicit provision for the consideration of military necessity: see R. Geiß, 'Military Necessity: A Fundamental "Principle" Fallen into Oblivion', in H. Ruiz Fabri, R. Wolfrum, and J. Gogolin (eds), *Select Proceedings of the 3rd Biennial Conference of the European Society of International Law* (Oxford: Hart Publishing, 2010) vol II, at 554.

time, may have lost part or all of its meaning.¹⁶³ However, the fact that some of the content of the 'in all circumstances' formula contained in Common Article 1 has been included in other, more specific provisions, does not compromise the catch-all purpose which the formula serves in Common Article 1. In light of the ordinary meaning of the words 'in all circumstances', and in view of the object and purpose of Common Article 1, namely to ensure compliance with the Geneva Conventions as comprehensively as possible, the formula should be interpreted broadly to encompass all of these various meanings mentioned above. Quite simply, it should be understood literally. The Geneva Conventions must be respected in all circumstances. And while circumstances of course play a role when it comes to the due diligence obligation to ensure respect and the determination of its actual content in a given situation,¹⁶⁴ when it comes to the preceding question whether the obligation to respect and to ensure respect applies at all, no factual, legal, or political circumstances whatsoever may be invoked to deny or limit its application.

F. Critical Assessment

In its reaffirmation of the *pacta sunt servanda* principle, the obligation to respect is of high symbolic value. It emphasizes the central importance of the provisions laid out in the Geneva Conventions. The obligation to ensure respect is arguably more important in that it is not merely of symbolic value but creates substantive obligations of its own. Most importantly, by virtue of this obligation, tacitly ignoring violations of fundamental humanitarian law provisions—irrespective of where they occur—today is clearly impermissible. The obligation to ensure respect contained in Common Article 1 shows that all states parties to the Geneva Conventions share a common interest in upholding these provisions. 44

Undoubtedly, the 'voice of idealism' has at times featured prominently in some of the interpretations that have been attributed to the obligation to ensure respect.¹⁶⁵ But while the obligation to ensure respect is a central component in the system of norms that aim to ensure better compliance with the provisions of the Geneva Conventions, it is of course not a panacea for solving all persistent issues of non-compliance. The scope of application of this obligation is wide. It applies to any breach of the Geneva Conventions wherever it occurs. However, this should not be perceived as an unrealistic imposition. The obligation to ensure respect is an obligation of conduct, not an obligation of result. States are not required to achieve the impossible, i.e. to stop and prevent each and every violation wherever it occurs. They are, however, obliged to react to breaches of the Geneva Conventions, and to do what can reasonably be expected of them in order to put a stop to or, in the case of an imminent threat, prevent violations of their provisions. As a general rule, the graver the violation in question, the 45

---

¹⁶³ Focarelli, above n 7, at 157–64. One indication that the formula today may indeed be of only limited relevance is contained in the ICRC CIHL Study. Notably, neither of the two customary law rules dealing with the obligation to respect and to ensure respect any longer mentions the phrase 'in all circumstances': ICRC CIHL Study, Rules 139, at 495, and 140, at 498. However, Art 1 AP III, which entered into force in January 2007, still contains the 'in all circumstances' formula.
¹⁶⁴ See MN 29 ff.
¹⁶⁵ ICJ, *Wall Advisory Opinion*, above n 6, Separate Opinion of Judge Kooijmans, para 50.

more will be expected of states to bring it to an end. In addition, the open wording of Common Article 1 helps to ensure that future developments, such as a developing right to take countermeasures in the collective interest, can be accommodated within the framework of the Geneva Conventions, and thereby underlines their character as living instruments.

ROBIN GEIß

Chapter 7. Special Agreements in International Armed Conflicts

	MN
A. Introduction	1
B. Meaning and Application	5
I. The scope of protection	10
II. The nature of protection	16
C. Relevance in Non-International Armed Conflicts	22
D. Legal Consequences of a Violation	23
E. Critical Assessment	27

Select Bibliography

Pellet, A., 'Article 38', in A. Zimmermann, C. Tomuschat, and K. Oellers-Frahm (eds), *The Statute of the International Court of Justice, A Commentary* (Oxford: OUP, 2006)

Pictet Commentary GC IV, Article 7, at 65–72

Vierucci, L., ' "Special Agreements" between Conflicting Parties in the Case-law of the ICTY', in B. Swart, A. Zahar, and G. Sluiter (eds), *The Legacy of the International Criminal Tribunal for the Former Yugoslavia* (Oxford: OUP, 2011) 401

A. Introduction

No international humanitarian law (IHL) treaty can ever claim to be comprehensive. The myriad of situations and issues that may arise during an international armed conflict (IAC)[1] are theoretically boundless, and for this reason flexibility to address unforeseen eventualities or to enhance protection may be considered a necessity. Accordingly, the notion of a special agreement covers a commitment by at least one party to an armed conflict to adopt or to refrain from certain conduct; to address certain acts; or to respond to the needs or behaviour of a specific group or specific groups above and beyond the protection afforded by the four 1949 Geneva Conventions.[2] Special agreements are also used to detail additional measures to be taken in IACs (for example, with regard to means or methods of warfare, to those entitled to special protection, or to humanitarian measures, such as mine clearance), including, specifically, during a situation of belligerent occupation.[3] A special agreement could also potentially set out the parties' understanding of applicable customary law.

1

---

[1] This chapter addresses only special agreements during IACs, including belligerent occupation. For discussion of similar agreements during armed conflicts not of an international character, see Ch 25 of this volume.

[2] Sivakumaran affirms that agreements of a similar nature date back to at least 1820. S. Sivakumaran, *The Law of Non-International Armed Conflict* (Oxford: OUP, 2012), at 124.

[3] Any such agreement must, though, respect the requirements set out in Art 47 GC IV, whereby protected persons in occupied territory 'shall not be deprived, in any case or in any manner whatsoever, of the benefits of the present Convention by [...] any agreement concluded between the authorities of the occupied territories and the Occupying Power'; see further the discussion of Art 8 GC IV at MN 12.

2   A potentially controversial issue meriting discussion at the outset is whether a special agreement that contravenes the content of either a peremptory norm of international law or a customary norm of international law may stand. In the case of the former, it appears clear that no special agreement the obligations of which run counter to a norm of *jus cogens* will be valid. Article 53 of the 1969 Vienna Convention on the Law of Treaties (VCLT) stipulates that '[a] treaty is void if, at the time of its conclusion, it conflicts with a peremptory norm of general international law.' Further, the Draft Articles on Responsibility of States for Internationally Wrongful Acts, adopted by the International Law Commission in 2001 (ILC Articles on State Responsibility), provide in Article 25:

> Nothing in this chapter [Chapter V: Circumstances Precluding Wrongfulness, one of which is found in Article 20 and is the circumstance of 'consent'] precludes the wrongfulness of any act of a State which is not in conformity with an obligation arising under a peremptory norm of general international law.

Thus, an agreement that stipulated, for instance, that 'no quarter will be given', or that torture may be used to interrogate prisoners of war (POWs) or other detainees, would almost certainly be voided by a court. Arguably, though, a single special agreement containing a series of distinct formal commitments of which only some contravene *jus cogens* may survive in part.[4]

3   More difficult to dismiss summarily is a special agreement that contravenes a customary norm of international law. As is well known, custom is a primary source of international law for the International Court of Justice (ICJ) by virtue of its Statute.[5] Although no hierarchy is explicit in Article 38(1), it is sometimes asserted that the listing of primary sources, which begins with 'international conventions, whether general or particular, establishing rules expressly recognized by the contesting states', does indeed accord the status of *primus inter pares* to a treaty (of which a special agreement may be seen as one example).[6] Alain Pellet, for example, asserts that 'customary law, except when cogens, is derogeable'.[7] Citing the ICJ's judgment in the *Elettronica Sicula* case (*United States of America v Italy*), he observes that there

> is 'no doubt that the parties to a treaty can therein either agree that' a particular customary rule 'shall not apply to claims based on alleged breaches of that treaty'; however, when the treaty is silent, it cannot be accepted 'that an important principle of customary international law should be held to have been tacitly dispensed with, in the absence of any words making clear an intention to do so'.[8]

---

[4] See, e.g., A. Cassese, *International Law* (2nd edn, Oxford: OUP, 2004), at 206.

[5] Art 38(1)(b) ICJ Statute refers to 'international custom, as evidence of a general practice accepted as law', although the tendency today is to see 'a general practice accepted as law' as directly constitutive of customary international law.

[6] Art 38(1)(a) ICJ Statute refers to 'international conventions, whether general *or particular*' (emphasis added). The terms 'convention' and 'treaty' are considered synonyms. According to Art 2(1)(a) VCLT, '"treaty" means an international agreement concluded between States in written form and governed by international law, whether embodied in a single instrument or in two or more related instruments and whatever its particular designation'. Although the VCLT explicitly limits the term to the 'purposes' of that Convention, it may be seen as a definition valid more generally. See, e.g., ICJ, *Maritime Delimitation and Territorial Questions between Qatar and Bahrain (Qatar v Bahrain)*, Jurisdiction and Admissibility, Judgment, 1 July 1994, para 23.

[7] A. Pellet, 'Article 38', in A. Zimmermann, C. Tomuschat, and K. Oellers-Frahm (eds), *The Statute of the International Court of Justice, A Commentary* (Oxford: OUP, 2006), para 243.

[8] Ibid, para 272, citing ICJ, *Elettronica Sicula* case (*USA v Italy*), Judgment, 20 July 1989, para 50.

In its judgment in 1969 in the *North Sea Continental Shelf* cases, the ICJ noted that treaties may be the basis for the formation of a new customary rule, though this approach was applied in an area where custom was absent rather than in overriding an existing rule.[9] In the later *Nicaragua* case, the ICJ held that

> customary international law continues to exist and to apply, separately from international treaty law, even where the two categories of law have an identical content. Consequently, in ascertaining the content of the customary international law applicable to the present dispute, the Court must satisfy itself that the Parties are bound by the customary rules in question; but the Court is in no way bound to uphold these rules only in so far as they differ from the treaty rules which it is prevented by the United States reservation from applying in the present dispute.[10]

Thus, the ICJ will not restrain its consideration of international law to the norms agreed in a treaty between states in contentious cases, but may look to a rule of customary international law that can, one may safely assume in the logic of the Court, apply alongside such norms. Arguably, where a collective community of states negotiates a treaty explicitly deviating from an existing customary norm, a new rule may indeed be created by the combined *usus* and *opinio juris* evidenced in the treaty-making process. But to extend the same possibility to a special agreement, which may exist between only two states, would be fundamentally flawed. Indeed, to allow such a possibility could be tantamount to voiding much of international human rights law (IHRL) and IHL. However, as we shall see later, where two customary rules conflict, states may be able lawfully to negotiate an agreement to respect one such rule while undertaking to act in contradiction to the other.

B. Meaning and Application

Numerous provisions of the Geneva Conventions address either 'agreements' or 'special agreements'. For example, in Geneva Convention (GC) I, references to agreements are made in Articles 6, 10, 15, 23, 28, 31, 36, and 37. General provisions of a similar nature are found in each of the four Conventions (Article 6 GC I, GC II, and GC III, and Article 7 GC IV). For instance, Article 6 GC I provides as follows:

In addition to the agreements expressly provided for in Articles 10, 15, 23, 28, 31, 36, 37 and 52, the High Contracting Parties may conclude other special agreements for all matters concerning which they may deem it suitable to make separate provision. No special agreement shall adversely affect the situation of the wounded and sick, of members of the medical personnel or of chaplains, as defined by the present Convention, nor restrict the rights which it confers upon them.

Wounded and sick, as well as medical personnel and chaplains, shall continue to have the benefit of such agreements as long as the Convention is applicable to them, except where express provisions to the contrary are contained in the aforesaid or in subsequent agreements, or where more favourable measures have been taken with regard to them by one or other of the Parties to the conflict.

---

[9] ICJ, *North Sea Continental Shelf Cases (Federal Republic of Germany/Denmark; Federal Republic of Germany/Netherlands)*, Judgment, 20 February 1969, para 74.
[10] ICJ, *Case concerning Military and Paramilitary Activities in and against Nicaragua (Nicaragua v USA)*, Merits, Judgment, 27 June 1986, para 179.

As evidenced by the use of the word 'may' in this provision, no general obligation is imposed on any party to the conflict to conclude a special agreement during an IAC; the regime set out in Articles 6/7 is merely permissive in nature.[11] Further, where concluded, such agreements tend to be in writing, but there is no explicit requirement in the Conventions that this be so.[12] They may also be constituted by commitments made by two parties to a third party where it is clear that the intention is to create binding obligations.[13] Certainly, as the Pictet Commentary notes, special agreements 'would not appear to be subject to formal requirements, such as signature and ratification, which are essential in the case of international treaties'.[14]

6   It appears clear that pacts between states concerning humanitarian obligations during situations of armed conflict may amount to special agreements. Pacts between states and which concern pre- and/or post-conflict humanitarian obligations, discussed below, may similarly do so. It is probably the case that agreements with neutral states, for instance those governing treatment of war victims by neutral states, may also amount to special agreements. Thus, Pictet noted:

> It is also conceivable that certain agreements could be concluded by one or more belligerent Powers with neutral States which are also party to the Convention, with a view to improving the lot of protected persons—by arranging, for example, for them to be accommodated in hospitals in a neutral country.[15]

7   It is less certain whether an agreement must be made by a minimum of two (opposing) parties to an IAC, or whether a unilateral declaration may suffice. The question of unilateral declarations was famously addressed by the ICJ in the *Nuclear Tests* cases in the following terms:

> It is well recognized that declarations made by way of unilateral acts, concerning legal or factual situations, may have the effect of creating legal obligations. Declarations of this kind may be, and often are, very specific. When it is the intention of the State making the declaration that it should become bound according to its terms, that intention confers on the declaration the character of a legal undertaking, the State being thenceforth legally required to follow a course of conduct consistent with the declaration. An undertaking of this kind, if given publicly, and with an intent to be bound, even though not made within the context of international negotiations, is binding. In these circumstances, nothing in the nature of a *quid pro quo*, nor any subsequent acceptance of the declaration, nor even any reply or reaction from other States, is required for the declaration to take effect, since such a requirement would be inconsistent with the strictly unilateral nature of the juridical act by which the pronouncement by the State was made.[16]

8   Thus, one must look to the intent behind the declaration; no 'consideration' is required, as it is for a contract to exist under some domestic legal orders. A humanitarian commitment, solemnly made, for instance not to use heavy weapons against military objectives in populated areas, could in certain circumstances meet the threshold test. Further, in

---

[11] See MN 14–15 for certain other provisions in the GCs that require special agreements to be concluded on specific issues.
[12] As the Pictet Commentary remarks (at 67) with respect to special agreements under Art 7 GC IV, '[n]o limits are placed either on the form they are to take or in regard to the time when they are to be concluded.'
[13] In this regard, Pictet refers to special agreements concluded between Italy and the UK during the Second World War: 'Testo delle Note Verbali che integrano e modificano la Convenzione di Ginevra del 1919', Rome, 1941 and 1942. Pictet Commentary GC IV, at 68.
[14] Ibid.   [15] Ibid.
[16] ICJ, *Nuclear Tests Case (New Zealand v France)*, Judgment, 20 December 1974, para 46.

contrast to treaties covered by the VCLT, there is no requirement under international law that a unilateral declaration necessarily be made in writing.[17]

More certain is that a special agreement in an IAC is not one that is concluded between a belligerent and an entity in which certain conduct is ostensibly promised or allowed. Thus, an agreement between the International Committee of the Red Cross (ICRC) and a belligerent on the rules of IHL that the latter is willing to respect is not a special agreement, nor is one in which a belligerent allows the ICRC to provide assistance to war victims.

I. The scope of protection

The potential scope of protection that may be afforded by a special agreement is extremely broad.[18] As observed in Article 6 GC I, such an agreement may cover 'all matters' concerning which High Contracting Parties 'may deem it suitable to make separate provision'. Special agreements may thus concern 'local arrangements of a purely temporary nature (evacuation)'; 'actual regulations (distribution of relief consignments)'; or may be 'a quasi-political agreement (substitute for the Protecting Power, investigations)'.[19] They could usefully concern the granting of access by civilian de-mining organizations to certain areas used by the civilian population, and authority to clear such areas, without their actions amounting to direct/active participation in hostilities. They could also reflect an agreement more generally to adopt a more narrow definition of such direct/active participation in hostilities than has been recommended by the ICRC,[20] for instance formally prohibiting use of lethal force against unarmed individuals.

Specific issues are, however, suggested in the Conventions as potential subjects for a special agreement. As the Pictet Commentary notes, with respect to GC IV these encompass the following issues:

(a) Appointment of an impartial organization as a substitute for the Protecting Power (Article 11 para. 1);
(b) Establishment of hospital and safety zones and localities (Article 14);
(c) Establishment of neutralized zones (Article 15);
(d) Evacuation of besieged areas (Article 17);
(e) Exchange and repatriation of enemy nationals (Article 36);
(f) Relief shipments for internees (Article 108);

---

[17] According to the ICJ, when addressing unilateral declarations, '[w]ith regard to the question of form, it should be observed that this is not a domain in which international law imposes any special or strict requirements. Whether a statement is made orally or in writing makes no essential difference, for such statements made in particular circumstances may create commitments in international law, which does not require that they should be couched in written form. Thus the question of form is not decisive.' ICJ, *Nuclear Tests Case (New Zealand v France)*, above n 16, para 48. Arguably, this may be applied, *a fortiori*, to agreements between states (aside, of course, from the evidentiary issue should the content of an agreement be disputed), although as noted above, a treaty is defined as a written agreement by Art 2(1)(a) VCLT.

[18] As the Pictet Commentary remarks (at 67) with respect to Art 7 GC IV, '[t]he term "special agreements" should be understood in a very broad sense. No limits are placed either on the form they are to take or in regard to the time when they are to be concluded.' The only limits set by GC IV 'concern the subject of the agreements', and are 'in the interests of the protected persons'.

[19] Pictet Commentary GC IV, at 67.

[20] See N. Melzer, *Interpretive Guidance on the Notion of Direct Participation in Hostilities under International Humanitarian Law* (Geneva: ICRC, 2009).

(g) Distribution of collective relief to internees (Article 109);
(h) Release, repatriation, return to places of residence or accommodation in a neutral country of internees during hostilities (Article 132);
(i) Search for dispersed internees (Article 133);
(j) Fixing the procedure for enquiries instituted at the request of one of the Parties in cases of alleged violation of the Convention (Article 149).

This list, though, is merely indicative.[21]

12   Arguably, special agreements may also be concluded, and may apply, even when an armed conflict is not underway. The reference to High Contracting Parties, rather than parties to the conflict, indicates that such agreements may be concluded in situations other than armed conflict, and may therefore fall within the scope of 'provisions which shall be implemented in peace-time', in accordance with Common Article 2 of the Geneva Conventions. This could cover, for instance, a situation in which the parties to the agreement reasonably determine that an armed conflict is not occurring, such as in a border incident or minor skirmish between members of armed forces of two High Contracting Parties. Given the absence of a conflict, this would not amount to a violation of Articles 7/8 common to the Geneva Conventions in which protected persons 'may in no circumstances renounce in part or in entirety the rights secured to them by the present Convention, and by the special agreements referred to in the foregoing Article, if such there be'.[22] Alternatively, one High Contracting Party may be providing support to an armed group operating in the territory of another, and fighting against the authorities of that latter state. A special agreement may be made to curtail certain forms of support (for example not to provide heavy weaponry where such weapons have been used to target medical facilities or other civilian objects), or to take additional measures to ensure respect by that armed group for the Geneva Conventions and/or other IHL rules.

13   Certain IHL obligations that continue to apply after the cessation of active hostilities may also be addressed by special agreements. Thus, the Pictet Commentary gives the example of agreements which concern arrangements to repatriate protected persons, to return them to their homes, or to resettle them.[23]

14   In contrast to the general position set out in Article 7 GC IV, however, certain provisions *require* that parties seek to make special agreements on a particular issue. Thus, for example, Article 132 requires that the parties to the conflict 'endeavour to conclude' agreements governing the release, repatriation, or return to places of residence, or accommodation in a neutral country, of certain classes of internees, in particular children, pregnant women, and mothers with infants and young children, as well as wounded and sick, or internees who have been detained for a long time.

---

[21] Pictet further observes (Pictet Commentary GC IV, at 66) that other provisions in the Convention refer to agreements between the belligerents: 'Article 22 lays down that unless there is an agreement to the contrary, medical aircraft are forbidden to fly over enemy territory. Article 23 implies the conclusion of an agreement between the Parties concerned. According to Article 83, on the marking of internment camps, the Powers concerned may agree upon a method of marking other than that laid down in the Convention. Article 135 makes a reservation in regard to any agreements concluded between the belligerents in connection with the exchange and repatriation of their nationals. Article 143 envisages the possibility of fellow-countrymen of the internees taking part in visits to internment camps by special agreement.'

[22] See, e.g., Art 8 GC IV.

[23] Pictet Commentary GC IV, at 67–8. See Art 5 para 1 GC III, in which it is stipulated that the Convention shall apply to POWs 'from the time they fall into the power of the enemy and until their final release and repatriation'. See also Art 6 para 4 GC IV, which concerns the applicability of certain conventional rules in occupied territory.

This is clearly an obligation of conduct and not of result (though good faith on the 15
part of the negotiating parties is needed). The Pictet Commentary also refers to the role
that can be played by the Protecting Power or the ICRC in suggesting and inspiring such
agreements.[24] In practice, the notion of Protecting Power has fallen into disuse in modern
IACs, and it may be incumbent on the United Nations or the ICRC to play a catalysing
and/or facilitating role in this regard.

II. The nature of protection

Consonant with the expansive scope of protection, the nature of protection that may be 16
afforded by a special agreement is also broad. The primary limitation is set out in the general
provision of each of the four Geneva Conventions, wherein it is expressly prohibited adversely
to affect 'the situation' of those to whom protection is afforded (particularly protected persons) as well as to restrict the 'rights' conferred upon them by the Convention. Thus, it is not
possible to 'contract out' of obligations undertaken by High Contracting Parties under the
Geneva Conventions or other relevant instruments, or, generally, to violate customary law.[25]

The specific proscription of restricting 'rights' conferred by the Convention is seen as an 17
important supplementary safeguard. In this regard, the Pictet Commentary opined that it

> will not always be possible to decide at once whether or not a special agreement 'adversely affects
> the situation of protected persons'. What is the position, for instance, if their situation is improved
> in certain ways and made worse in others? Some of the agreements mentioned above may have
> appeared to bring them advantages at the time of conclusion; the drawbacks only became apparent
> later. The criterion 'adversely affect the situation' is not, therefore, in itself an adequate safeguard.
> That is why the second condition is of value.[26]

The notion of 'rights conferred by the Convention' should thus be understood broadly 18
as embracing 'the whole body of safeguards which the Convention affords to protected
persons'. Moreover, according to Article 8 GC IV, protected persons 'may in no circumstances renounce in part or in entirety the rights secured to them by the present
Convention, and by the special agreements referred to in the foregoing Article, if such
there be'.[27]

It is, however, desirable to extend more generous protection or to regulate issues that 19
are not covered by the Conventions.[28] As the Pictet Commentary on GC IV points out,
'there is no doubt at all that the position of civilians under the present Convention can be
improved by means of special agreements between the belligerents. Certain Articles of the
Convention make express provision for their conclusion.'[29]

Although the Geneva Conventions rarely address the conduct of hostilities,[30] 20
there is an obvious benefit to restricting or prohibiting certain means or methods of

---

[24] Pictet Commentary GC IV, at 513.
[25] Beyond IHL, the subsequent development of IHRL would, for instance, be pertinent to the treatment of detainees; see also Ch 8 of this volume.
[26] Pictet Commentary GC IV, at 70.
[27] Similar provisions exist in Art 7 of the other three GCs (see Ch 8 of this volume for details).
[28] In this regard, it is worth recalling the Martens clause, in accordance with which, 'in cases not covered by the law in force, the human person remains under the protection of the principles of humanity and the dictates of the public conscience'. See, e.g., the fourth preambular paragraph to 1977 AP II.
[29] Pictet Commentary GC IV, at 65.
[30] One of the rare provisions regarding the conduct of hostilities is found in Art 18 GC IV, wherein '[c]ivilian hospitals organized to give care to the wounded and sick, the infirm and maternity cases, may in

warfare. Such special agreements could be general in nature—for example prohibiting the use by parties to the conflict of weapons the indiscriminate character of which is controversial—or (and arguably of more practical benefit) an undertaking not to use certain weapons in the conflict. Anti-personnel mines have been outlawed by treaty, ostensibly because of their indiscriminate effects; the same applies to cluster munitions. Scud missiles have been alleged to be inherently indiscriminate,[31] but this view is not one held by consensus.

21   More complicated is the situation where a special agreement seemingly conflicts with one customary IHL rule while seeking to respect and/or implement another. Let us consider the use of expanding bullets. The use of bullets which expand or flatten easily in the human body is prohibited under customary law in IACs (and non-international armed conflicts—NIACs) according to the ICRC,[32] and their use is explicitly criminalized as a war crime under the jurisdiction of the International Criminal Court (ICC).[33] Such bullets are, though, routinely used by numerous police forces around the world for law enforcement purposes, the reason being that they reduce the risk of 'over-penetration' and thus injury to innocent bystanders.[34] They may thus be seen as an important way to implement the customary law rule whereby '[a]ll feasible precautions must be taken to avoid, and in any event to minimize, incidental loss of civilian life, injury to civilians and damage to civilian objects.'[35] Would a special agreement between two states that were High Contracting Parties to the Geneva Conventions (but not party to the ICC Statute) necessarily be void if it were to allow for use of expanding ammunition in an armed conflict between themselves, with a view to the better protection of civilians?[36]

C. Relevance in Non-International Armed Conflicts

22   As explained in section A of this chapter, the equivalent agreements adopted in NIACs are the subject of analysis in Chapter 25 of this Commentary.

---

no circumstances be the object of attack but shall at all times be respected and protected by the Parties to the conflict'.

[31] The ICRC CIHL Study cites evidence in support of the assertion (though without necessarily endorsing the conclusion): the military manual of Canada and statements by Israel, the UK, and the US, as well as reported practice of Israel; see Rule 71, fn 42, available at <http://www.icrc.org/customary-ihl/eng/docs/v1_rul_rule71>. Solis argues that Scud missiles are 'by their nature indiscriminate': G.D. Solis, *The Law of Armed Conflict, International Humanitarian Law in War* (Cambridge: CUP, 2010), Section 14.7, at 537. The UK has argued that the V1 flying bomb and the Scud rocket 'are examples of weapons likely to be caught by this provision': UK Ministry of Defence, *The Manual of the Law of Armed Conflict* (Oxford: OUP, 2004), at 104, § 6.4.1.

[32] ICRC Customary IHL Rule 77 (Expanding bullets), available at <http://www.icrc.org/customary-ihl/eng/docs/v1_rul_rule77>.

[33] According to Art 8(2)(b)(xix), serious violations of the laws and customs applicable in IAC include '[e]mploying bullets which expand or flatten easily in the human body, such as bullets with a hard envelope which does not entirely cover the core or is pierced with incisions'.

[34] Bullets may go through the human body of the intended target and hit an unintended target behind him.

[35] ICRC Customary IHL Rule 15 (Precautions in Attack), available at <http://www.icrc.org/customary-ihl/eng/docs/v1_rul_rule15>.

[36] It might be argued that a war crime is by nature a norm of *jus cogens*; however, given the specifics of expanding ammunition and the view of US military figures (and others) on its use, that is questionable in this instance. See, e.g., Major J.F. Berry, 'Hollow Point Bullets: How History Has Hijacked their Use in Combat and Why it Is Time to Reexamine the 1899 Hague Declaration Concerning Expanding Bullets', 206 *Military Law Review* (Winter 2010) 88.

D. Legal Consequences of a Violation

What are the consequences of a violation of the terms of a special agreement in an IAC? According to Article 1 of the ILC Articles on State Responsibility, every internationally wrongful act of a state entails that state's international responsibility. Article 2 specifies that an internationally wrongful act occurs when conduct is attributable to the state under international law; and constitutes a breach of an international obligation of the state. According to the ICJ, 'refusal to fulfil a treaty obligation involves international responsibility'.[37] Thus, in so far as a special agreement amounts to a treaty, its violation will potentially found the erring state's international responsibility.

Where, though, the conduct foreseen in or required by a special agreement violates customary or conventional IHL, such as where it seeks to deprive protected persons of rights, such conduct will amount to a violation of IHL (also giving rise to state responsibility). Arguably, however, the agreement (or at least the specific provision) is not automatically voided, unless the norm being breached by the special agreement is one of *jus cogens* (see, however, Chapter 25, MN 18, of this volume).

The use of special agreements effectively to found responsibility under international criminal law has, to date, been limited. In one of the first and most quoted decisions of the International Criminal Tribunal for the former Yugoslavia (ICTY), the Appeals Chamber in the *Tadić* Appeal Decision on Jurisdiction held that its jurisdiction *ratione materiae* would also cover 'binding agreements between conflicting parties'[38] under Article 3 of the ICTY's Statute. According to Vierucci, however, in subsequent judgments it was recognized that the principle of legality required the Tribunal to apply only the rules that are beyond doubt of a customary nature.[39]

More controversially, Vierucci also suggests that the ICC 'may find it necessary to make use of special agreements concluded between conflicting parties in order to establish its jurisdiction over a certain crime'.[40] She offers, by way of illustration, 'the prohibition of the use of certain weapons, especially in non-international armed conflict'. While I would support the assertion that this is indeed 'an area where the ICC Statute is patchy',[41] her conclusion that agreements concluded between conflicting parties to prohibit use of weapons which are not banned by the ICC Statute could be used to found a prosecution in the ICC,[42] is seriously open to question. Expanding the jurisdictional reach of the ICC through recourse to special agreements is, in this author's view, highly improbable. Ad hoc or hybrid international criminal tribunals would be a far more likely venue for such a scenario given the rigidity of the ICC Statute and its amendment procedures.

23

24

25

26

---

[37] ICJ, *Interpretation of Peace Treaties with Bulgaria, Hungary and Romania*, Second Phase, Advisory Opinion, 18 July 1950, at 228.
[38] ICTY, *The Prosecutor v Duško Tadić*, Appeals Chamber Decision on the Defence Motion for Interlocutory Appeal on Jurisdiction, IT-94-1-AR72, 2 October 1995, para 143.
[39] L. Vierucci, '"Special Agreements" between Conflicting Parties in the Case-law of the ICTY', in B. Swart, A. Zahar, and G. Sluiter (eds), *The Legacy of the International Criminal Tribunal for the Former Yugoslavia* (Oxford Scholarship Online, 2011) Chapter 14, at 2, available at <http://dx.doi.org/10.1093/acprof:oso/9780199573417.003.0015>.
[40] Ibid, at 26.   [41] Ibid.   [42] Ibid.

E. Critical Assessment

27 Special agreements are potentially a valuable (if underused) means to clarify, develop, and extend, but not to undermine, applicable IHL. They may also act to implement other international legal obligations applicable in armed conflicts, such as the customary IHRL rule prohibiting arbitrary deprivation of life for those who might otherwise be deemed to be taking an active part in hostilities.

28 In IACs, there is a generally permissive authority under Article 6 of Geneva Conventions I–III and Article 7 GC IV to conclude a special agreement, although certain other Articles oblige the parties to such conflicts, with respect to specific provisions, to make reasonable efforts to negotiate successfully in this regard.

29 In sum, while the extent to which special agreements will ground individual responsibility under international criminal law—at least with respect to the ICC—may be contested, they may nonetheless prove to be a valuable addition to the corpus of *jus in bello*.

STUART CASEY-MASLEN

Chapter 8. Non-Renunciation of the Rights Provided by the Conventions

	MN
A. Introduction	1
B. Meaning and Application	5
I. Legal meaning and scope	5
II. Application	10
III. Conceptual importance	12
C. Relevance in Non-International Armed Conflicts	16
D. Legal Consequences of a Violation	17
I. Invalidity	18
II. Responsibility	20
E. Critical Assessment	22

Select Bibliography

Bugnion, F., *The International Committee of the Red Cross and the Protection of War Victims* (London: Macmillan, 2003)

Dinstein, Y., *The Conduct of Hostilities under the Law of International Armed Conflict* (2nd edn, Cambridge: CUP, 2010)

Provost, R., *International Human Rights and Humanitarian Law* (Cambridge: CUP, 2002)

Wilhelm, R.-J., 'Le caractère des droits accordés à l'individu dans les Conventions de Genève', 32 *IRRC* 380 (1950) 561

A. Introduction

According to the common provision found in Article 7/7/7/8 of the Geneva Conventions, the persons respectively protected under each Convention 'may in no circumstances renounce in part or in entirety the rights secured to them' either by the four Conventions, or by more favourable special agreements which may be concluded by the belligerents.[1]

This common provision, which enshrines what is known as the principle of the 'inalienability'[2] of the rights of protected persons, follows the common provision found in Articles 6/6/6/7 relating to the prohibition of less favourable special agreements. Together, these provisions demonstrate the 'intangible'[3] nature of the rights conferred by the Conventions: the belligerents may not relieve themselves of their duty to treat such persons in accordance with the Conventions, or at least no less favourably than as required by

---

[1] See Chs 7 and 25.

[2] H. Coursier, *Cours de cinq leçons sur les Conventions de Genève* (Geneva: ICRC, 1963), at 33; R. Kolb, *Ius in bello. Le droit international des conflits armés* (2nd edn, Basel/Brussels: Helbing Lichtenhahn/Bruylant, 2009) 400; E. David, *Principes de droit des conflits armés* (4th edn, Brussels: Bruylant, 2008) 553, at 2.408.

[3] Coursier, above n 2; Kolb, above n 2; David, above n 2. Mostly used in French, the word 'intangible' conveys the idea that those rights are inalterable and must remain untouched.

the Conventions, by agreement between the belligerents or by agreement with protected persons, or following their unilateral renunciation.[4]

3   The Pictet Commentary mentions (but with no specific details) situations where prisoners of war (POWs) were compelled to accept treatment less favourable than that required by the standard of the time.[5] It also refers to situations where POWs relinquished their status and joined the armed forces of their captor, or where the POWs' home government authorized them to choose a different status.[6] The Commentary does not refer to the renunciation of rights by other categories of protected persons. For what appear to be reasons of principle relating to a specific understanding of the very nature of the obligations enshrined in the Conventions, a general provision common to the Geneva Conventions was nevertheless considered adequate.

4   To avoid a circumstance in which protected persons in the hands of the enemy are placed under duress and forced to accept treatment less favourable than that provided by the Conventions, the International Committee of the Red Cross (ICRC) suggested the following draft provision during the 1949 negotiations: 'protected persons may in no circumstances be induced by coercion or by any other forced means, to renounce in part or in entirety the rights secured to them'[7] by the Conventions or by a more favourable special agreement. Rather than providing for a prohibition on renunciation, the draft prohibited duress leading to renunciation. Therefore, it could have been interpreted *a contrario*, as meaning that renunciation was possible if the renunciation of rights by protected persons was the result of a real and free choice. However, because of the inherent inequality between protected persons and the Power controlling them, such a free expression of will was considered by the Diplomatic Conference to be unlikely, if not impossible. Moreover, and especially amidst the inherent confusion of war, it was preferable to avoid discussions relating to the forced or free character of the renunciation of rights expressed by protected persons. Hence, and notably upon the suggestion of the Norwegian representative,[8] the Diplomatic Conference agreed on a more categorical wording, which is the one found in the Conventions.

B. Meaning and Application

I. Legal meaning and scope

5   Common Article 7/7/7/8 is literally drafted as a prohibition ('may not', i.e. an obligation not to do something) addressed to certain categories of individuals respectively protected under each Convention. However, its purpose is not so much to sanction prohibited behaviour (see MN 17–21), but rather to prevent a state from claiming to be released from its obligations under the particular Convention vis-à-vis a protected person who renounces the benefit of its corresponding rights. In other words, protected persons may not, by their own will or by any sort of agreement concluded with a state, validly dispense of the rights

---

[4] Kolb, above n 2, at 401.

[5] Bugnion is a little bit more explicit in that regard, mentioning the German practice during the Second World War, but also the immediate post-Second World War French practice: F. Bugnion, *The International Committee of the Red Cross and the Protection of War Victims* (London: Macmillan, 2003), at 437.

[6] Pictet Commentary GC I, at 78; Pictet Commentary GC II, at 57; Pictet Commentary GC III, at 88.

[7] Pictet Commentary GC IV, at 74.   [8] Ibid, at fn 2.

conferred by the Conventions, which include ICRC protection.[9] Such renunciation is deemed to be of no legal effect as far as state obligations are concerned. The Conventions do not specify what it means for protected persons to 'renounce [their] rights', nor what 'renunciation' amounts to. Relying on the 'ordinary meaning'[10] of the verb 'to renounce', one can safely conclude that this common provision refers to any expression of will by which protected persons could refuse, reject, or abandon the benefit of their rights.[11]

Common Article 7/7/7/8 prohibits any renunciation of rights by protected persons, regardless of the modality. Explicit renunciations, either unilateral or contractual, are covered by the provision. Moreover, the provision prevents any argument relating to a tacit renunciation, which might be derived, for instance, from the non-exercise of rights by protected persons. The material scope of the renunciation is immaterial, since it may not cover 'in part or in entirety' any of the rights secured to the protected persons. Furthermore, 'no circumstance' may ever legally justify such renunciation so as to render it valid; the conditions under which a renunciation may exist are irrelevant. This means, in particular, that freely expressed genuine renunciations are nevertheless devoid of any legal effect. Hence, the integrity of the Conventions is thereby protected.

From a textual point of view, the prohibition on renouncing Convention rights also applies when a more favourable treatment is conferred on protected persons by special agreement. In such a case, the provision clearly extends to the additional rights so conferred, but nevertheless continues to apply to Convention rights as a minimum standard; the legal vicissitudes that may affect the special agreement have no bearing on the protection afforded by the Conventions. Further, making more favourable treatment conferred by a special agreement conditional upon a renunciation of Convention rights is legally untenable. Similarly, the benefit of a more favourable legal regime, either claimed by protected persons or granted to them—derived for instance from international human rights law (IHRL)—can neither depend on a renunciation of the Convention rights nor entail such renunciation, even tacitly. However, protected persons are not required to relinquish a more favourable status because they may not renounce the Convention rights. Instead, the Convention rights remain in the legal background as fall-back provisions, whatever the will of the protected persons themselves might be.

Despite the fact that common Article 7/7/7/8 is drafted as a prohibition addressed to protected persons, one may derive an obligation addressed to states since they 'have pledged in advance not to accept any such renunciation'.[12] Moreover, one may consider that states have an obligation to abstain from any behaviour leading protected persons to renounce their rights. This corresponding obligation should not be limited to incitement directed at the specific categories of individuals identified in each Convention as the addressees of the rule prohibiting renunciations (i.e. 'Wounded and sick, as well as members of the medical personnel and chaplains' (GC I); 'Wounded, sick and shipwrecked persons, as well as members of the medical personnel and chaplains' (GC II); 'Prisoners of

---

[9] Bugnion, above n 5, at 438, considers that the ICRC cannot impose its protection on persons who clearly reject it, but argues that, in such a situation, the decision not to assist them has to be taken by the ICRC itself after an objective assessment of the situation, and not simply on the basis of the allegation of the Detaining Power.

[10] Art 31 para 1 VCLT.

[11] *Oxford English Dictionary*, available at <http://www.oed.com>. See also J. Salmon (ed), *Dictionnaire de droit international public* (Brussels: Bruylant–AUF, 2001), at 968.

[12] See Bugnion, above n 5, at 438.

war' (GC III); 'Protected persons' (GC IV)). While the extortion of such a renunciation under duress is of course logically prohibited, the mere suggestion of any renunciation, by the Detaining Power or even by the national state of the protected persons, should also be viewed as illegal. One might also consider that such a suggestion by any third party intervening in the conflict would be illegal. However, the obligation to abstain from inciting or inducing renunciation of rights under the Conventions should not be understood as an obligation to prevent such renunciation.

9   Whether common Article 7/7/7/8 has gained the status of a customary rule is difficult to assess. When included in the Conventions, it was certainly a purely contractual provision. Due to the lack of practice (see MN 10–11), it is doubtful that its legal nature has extended to the realm of customary international law. Further, the principle of non-renunciation is not included among the rules identified as customary international law by the ICRC Study on Customary International Humanitarian Law. That being said, it is not because this common provision lacks customary status that the 'rights' secured by the Conventions to which it applies are not of a customary nature. Moreover, the 'intangibility' principle applicable to those 'rights' and conveyed by this common provision seems to be of an axiological character, rather than of a customary nature.

II. Application

10   To date, domestic and international courts and tribunals have yet to apply common Article 7/7/7/8. Textbooks[13] and manuals[14] that mention the Article, merely restate what it provides for, sometimes recalling what is stated in the Pictet Commentary. Contemporary practice of actual, claimed, or induced renunciation by protected persons is not reported or documented.[15] The absence of reported practice can of course be considered positively and with relief; this is an international humanitarian law (IHL) provision that seems to be duly respected. However, the absence of reported practice specifically relating to common Article 7/7/7/8 does not mean that it is not relied on when breaches of other substantive provisions, including those relating to the treatment of POWs, are deplored.

11   In light of past state practice reported in the Commentary, future application of this provision may be foreseen in the event that POWs decide to join the ranks of their captors to fight against the national army in which they served (possibly due to mandatory conscription). If the forced enrolment of POWs by the Detaining Power constitutes a war crime,[16] it seems that because of the prohibition of renunciation enshrined in common Article 7/7/7/8, the Conventions do not allow POWs the possibility of joining the enemy forces by their own free will; the Detaining Power is indeed under the obligation to treat captured members of the enemy armed forces as POWs. Even where individuals have been forcibly conscripted and then wish to fight side by side with their captors to 'liberate' their country from an oppressive regime, it has been seen as forbidden under the Conventions

---

[13] In addition to other references mentioned above and below, see, e.g., Y. Dinstein, *The International Law of Belligerent Occupation* (Cambridge: CUP, 2009), at 83, para 189; M. Greenspan, *The Modern Law of Land Warfare* (Berkeley and Los Angeles, CA: University of California Press, 1959), at 70 and 160.

[14] UK Ministry of Defence, *The Manual of the Law of Armed Conflict* (Oxford: OUP, 2004), at 125, para 7.9, and 225, para 9.20.

[15] Bugnion, above n 5, at 438, briefly mentions that both Iran and Iraq have claimed that the POWs they detained were refusing ICRC protection in order to prevent it from carrying out its responsibilities during the 1980–8 war.

[16] See Art 130 GC III and Art 147 GC IV; David, above n 2, at 553, para 408.

for the Detaining Power to fulfil such a wish. The Commentary makes clear that such an 'unfortunate'[17] result (in case of POWs who had been forcibly conscripted into the army in which they served in the first place) is the consequence of the strict rule. An absolute provision allowing for the integral application of the Conventions was preferable, to protect the vast majority of victims of war due to the dangers inherent in allowing exceptions.[18] The non-renunciation clause of the Conventions prohibits radical political choice, and thus serves as a guarantee that no belligerent shall suffer from ideological betrayals within its own ranks. This clearly reflects the interests of states and the old conception according to which soldiers obey and do not question the regime they serve, nor the wisdom, morality, or legality of the war in which they are engaged. Of course, the Conventions limited that conception of obedience through the development of responsibility for war crimes. However, individual responsibility of combatants merely requires judgement on the actual military actions they are carrying out; it does not extend beyond it, so as to encompass political allegiance. The crime of aggression, recently defined in the Statute of the International Criminal Court, does not change that basic conception, as it applies only to 'person[s] in a position effectively to exercise control over or direct the political or military action of a State'.[19]

III. Conceptual importance

The meaning—or at least practical relevance—of the non-renunciation provision does not lie so much in what it commands or prohibits, but in what it reveals about the nature of the substantive rules of behaviour enshrined in the Conventions. Admittedly, the utility of this provision is the way it has allowed for various doctrinal arguments. Taking advantage of the wording of the provision, it has been argued that the Conventions not only regulate the conduct of states, but that, by doing so, they also directly confer positive rights on individuals. Moreover, those rights are not at the disposal of such individuals but are bestowed upon them as a matter of public order. In other words, two fundamental legal arguments relating to the nature of the Geneva rules have been derived from common Article 7/7/7/8: first, individuals have rights, and therefore have legal personality under IHL; secondly, such rights are inalienable, i.e. beyond the control of their beneficiaries. This second element has very often been used to affirm (or reinforce the affirmation of) the peremptory (*jus cogens*) nature of *jus in bello*. 12

The first argument, relating to the existence of rights under the Conventions for the benefit of individuals, is supposedly reinforced by the use of the verb 'secure' rather than 'confer', which is found in common Article 6/6/6/7.[20] This textual argument is certainly not of paramount importance; yet what is most significant is that through the Conventions, 'rights are bestowed directly to individuals belonging to the category indicated, and that they are not merely state rights from which individuals derive benefit'.[21] In conformity with the Commentary,[22] the vast majority of commentators hold this view, and when quoting this provision, it is not to explain its technical meaning or practical relevance, but rather to assert that the Conventions secure rights to the benefit of protected persons, 13

---

[17] As put by one delegate, not identified by Pictet Commentary GC I, at 80.
[18] Ibid. See also Greenspan, above n 13, at 101 and 104.
[19] ICC Statute, Art 8*bis*(1).
[20] Pictet Commentary GC I, at 82; Pictet Commentary GC IV, at 77.
[21] Y. Dinstein, *The Conduct of Hostilities under the Law of International Armed Conflict* (2nd edn, Cambridge: CUP, 2010), at 20, quoting Pictet Commentary GC I, at 467.
[22] Pictet Commentary GC I, at 82; Pictet Commentary GC II, at 58; Pictet Commentary GC III, at 91; Pictet Commentary GC IV, at 77.

since the very text says so.²³ Such affirmation tends to align IHL with human rights law, not as far as their application or content are concerned, but as far as their legal nature is concerned. Some have challenged this generally held view, arguing that the norms of IHL should be considered 'as standards of treatment or conduct rather than as rights of protected persons'.²⁴ This alternative view has the advantage of 'shift[ing] the emphasis from the would-be-right-holder to the person in the position of power, on whom an obligation to comply with the standard is imposed directly by public order'.²⁵ Arguably, such an 'international public order' approach of IHL is 'more consistent' with its general 'enforcement scheme' than a 'rights-based interpretation'.²⁶

14   This debate is rather abstract, if not esoteric. The conflicting views seem to depend on the choice of a theoretical conception of what one considers a 'right' under any legal system, and whether it is tenable to construct an 'obligation' vis-à-vis certain persons, without considering that those persons have a corresponding 'right' to be treated accordingly. In light of the reasoning of the International Court of Justice (ICJ) in the *LaGrand* case, regarding Article 36(1) of the Vienna Convention on Consular Relations as 'creat[ing] individual rights',²⁷ to resist the idea that the four Conventions do indeed establish rights to the benefit of protected persons—the violation of which may eventually be invoked by their national state as a matter of diplomatic protection—is a line of argument which would not likely be upheld by an international court or tribunal. That being said, confusing the purpose and nature of IHL with that of human rights law, or assimilating the former into the latter, must be avoided. Indeed, under human rights law, individuals are bestowed with rights because they are subjected to the authority of a state, i.e. they are 'subject to its jurisdiction' to use the words of the International Covenant on Civil and Political Rights.²⁸ Both historically and legally, human rights are rights of individuals aimed at limiting (or regulating) their subjection to the authority of the state concerning the organization of social life. Hence, the importance of vesting self-executing rights in individuals, i.e. rights that do not require any domestic measures of implementation to be applicable in domestic legal orders, as such measures could otherwise constrain or limit the enjoyment of those rights. Compared to the very purpose of IHRL, IHL does not aim at limiting the way states 'govern' their 'subjects'; it originally aims at humanizing the misfortunes of war. There is nothing deeply 'political' or 'constitutional' in the balance achieved by IHL, even if its humanitarian objective fulfils an essential aspiration of human beings, whether they themselves face the scourge of war or see others suffer from it. Moreover, the need for states to agree on self-executing norms, to ensure that individuals benefit from them domestically without any national measures of implementation, does not arise under IHL with the same acuteness as it does under IHRL.²⁹

---

²³ In addition to the references mentioned above, see R.-J. Wilhelm, 'Le caractère des droits accordés à l'individu dans les Conventions de Genève', 32 *IRRC* 380 (1950) 561, at 561; T. Meron, 'The Humanization of Humanitarian Law', 94 *AJIL* (2000) 239, at 251–2; G. Abi-Saab, 'The Specificities of Humanitarian Law', in Mélanges Pictet 265, at 265; P. Gaeta, 'Are Victims of Serious Violations of International Humanitarian Law Entitled to Compensation?', in O. Ben-Naftali (ed), *International Humanitarian Law and International Human Rights Law* (Oxford: OUP, 2011) 305, at 319.

²⁴ R. Provost, *International Human Rights and Humanitarian Law* (Cambridge: CUP, 2002), at 30.

²⁵ Ibid, at 32.   ²⁶ Ibid, at 32, 34.

²⁷ ICJ, *LaGrand (Germany v United States of America)*, Judgment, 27 June 2011, para 77.

²⁸ Art 2 para 1 ICCPR. See also Art 1 ECHR.

²⁹ I have argued elsewhere that individuals who are victims of IHL breaches may possibly have a right to reparation under international law if the rule breached can be considered as self-executing, but that

15 The 'rights' of protected persons—if they are considered as such—are nevertheless of a specific kind, since the prohibition on renunciation requires that they be inalienable: they are beyond the control of their beneficiaries. The strict inalienability of the 'rights' under IHL differs from the issues concerning the renunciation of rights under human rights law,[30] and has been used to affirm (or reinforce) the peremptory (*jus cogens*) nature of *jus in bello*.[31] Despite the inalienable nature of the protection afforded by the Conventions to certain individuals, it is not certain that such inalienability implies the peremptory nature (within the meaning of Article 53 VCLT) of the norms providing for such protection. Besides the fact that it would be surprising that the 1949 Diplomatic Conference had a clear and shared understanding of a notion that would only gain recognition 20 years after the Geneva Conventions, the inalienability of a treaty right by its individual beneficiaries does not necessarily mean that it cannot be derogated from by agreement between contracting parties. As opposed to common Article 7/7/7/8, common Article 6/6/6/7, on the prohibition of less favourable special agreements, rather points at the peremptory nature of the rules contained in the Geneva Conventions.[32] Admittedly, if a right conferred by treaty is inalienable by its beneficiaries, it embodies public order values that must be placed beyond the control of individuals. But, technically, this does not necessarily mean that any conflicting treaty would be considered null and void.

C. Relevance in Non-International Armed Conflicts

16 Additional Protocol II (AP II) of 1977 does not contain any similar provision. However, it has been affirmed that '[t]he principle [of non-renunciation] applies to the entirety of international humanitarian law',[33] which seems to include rules applicable in non-international armed conflicts (NIACs). To explain such an assertion, one may of course rely on the nature of the 'rights' at stake, as pointed out above. There is, however, an easier, more technical, explanation: to the extent that Common Article 3, which applies in NIACs, is part of the 1949 Conventions, all the 'rights' it confers on victims of such conflicts are to be considered as 'rights secured [...] by the [...] Convention[s]' within the meaning of common Article 7 of GC I and GC II, and therefore as under the ambit of that provision when persons protected under each Convention fulfil the condition of taking 'no active part in the hostilities' within the meaning of Common Article 3. Expanding on that construction, one could more fundamentally consider that the *ratione personae* scope of the prohibitive rule is not limited to the specific addressees of common Article 7/7/7/8, but includes any individual protected under the Geneva Conventions, so that 'persons taking no active part in the hostilities' are also prevented from validly renouncing their Article 3

---

the law governing the implementation of such reparation right in domestic courts is a domestic legal regime: P. d'Argent, 'Le droit de la responsabilité internationale complété? Examen des *Principes fondamentaux et directives concernant le droit à un recours et à réparation des victimes de violations flagrantes du droit international des droits de l'homme et de violations graves du droit international humanitaire*', 51 *AFDI* (2005) 27.

[30] P. Frumer, *La renonciation aux droits et libertés. La Convention européenne des droits de l'homme à l'épreuve de la volonté individuelle* (Brussels: Bruylant, 2001); O. De Schutter and J. Ringelheim, 'La renonciation aux droits fondamentaux. La libre disposition du soi et le règne de l'échange', in H. Dumont, F. Ost, and S. Van Drooghenbroeck (eds), *La responsabilité, face cachée des droits de l'homme* (Brussels: Bruylant, 2005) 441.

[31] See, e.g., David, above n 2, at 111, para 1.41. [32] See Meron, above n 23, at 252.

[33] H.-P. Gasser, 'Protection of the Civilian Population', in D. Fleck (ed), *The Handbook of International Humanitarian Law* (2nd edn, Oxford: OUP, 2008) 237, at 284, para 539.

rights. Moreover, as AP II 'develops and supplements Article 3 [...] without modifying its existing conditions of application',[34] arguably, the prohibition of renunciation by individuals, being one of the 'conditions of application' of Article 3, extends to the supplementary 'rights' enshrined in Protocol II.

D. Legal Consequences of a Violation

17 As the comments above make clear, common Article 7/7/7/8 is textually a prohibition addressed to individuals: protected persons 'may in no circumstances renounce [...]'. The French version of the Conventions also refers to an imperative by using the future tense ('*ne pourront en aucun cas renoncer* [...]'). Violations of the prohibition may trigger two types of legal consequences: the first concerns the validity of the renunciation as a legal act; the second concerns the responsibility of the author(s) or 'inspirator(s)' of the act, considered as an 'international wrongful act'.

I. Invalidity

18 Any renunciation of the rights of protected persons 'would be null and void'.[35] This certainly reflects a common understanding. A few comments on such an orthodox view are nevertheless useful. First, the invalidity sanctions unilateral or contractual renunciations indifferently. As recalled in MN 6, the very existence of common Article 7/7/7/8 seems to prevent any argument relating to a possible tacit renunciation. However, if need be, and despite the fact that any regime of invalidity presumes the existence of an actual legal act, one could eventually treat as invalid any 'implicit renunciation'. Secondly, the invalidity so proclaimed might rest on two different legal grounds: a renunciation might be invalid because its author is deprived of legal capacity, or because its object, i.e. the rights concerned, is a matter of public order. In light of the above, the latter view is preferred by most of the doctrine. Thirdly, the invalidity so proclaimed within international law logically relates to an act of will (the renunciation), which is considered to occur within the international legal order and is governed by it—and which, through the sanction of invalidity, is 'expelled' from it. If the renunciation is expressed in or by an act governed by a domestic legal order, its validity under domestic law is irrelevant, as its international invalidity would transcend any domestic validity because of the primacy of international law.[36] Fourthly, the invalidity so proclaimed seems to be automatic, in the sense that the very existence of a renunciation requires that it be treated immediately as null and void. This being said, there may be a controversy as to whether such renunciation exists, or whether the act of will in question actually amounts to a prohibited renunciation.

19 Entering the discourse of the (in)validity of legal acts often gives rise to more questions than answers. One might therefore consider whether it is not wiser to depart from such discourse by affirming that renunciations of rights by protected persons are simply devoid of any legal effect, rather than proclaiming that they are 'null and void'. Indeed, it is not so much the legal fate of the acts of renunciation that matters, but rather the certainty

---

[34] Art 1 para 1 AP II.   [35] Gasser and Dörmann, above n 33, at 284.
[36] J. Verhoeven, 'Les nullités du droit des gens', in P. Weil (ed), *Droit international 1, Cours et travaux de l'IHEI, 1979/1980* (Paris: Pedone, 1981) 1, at 23.

that the substantive obligations under the Conventions—or under more favourable special agreements—are duly respected and that any violator of those obligations may never successfully claim absence of responsibility on the basis of such inoperative renunciation.

II. Responsibility

If it is forbidden for protected persons to renounce their rights, they should, from a formal and logical point of view, be held responsible for any such renunciation. However, this is not what the Conventions, IHL, or general international law require. Further, no one has ever suggested that protected persons be held accountable through a formal mechanism of legal responsibility for having breached the prohibition on renunciations. Clearly, it would be shocking to hold protected persons responsible when the renunciation has been forced upon them. However, even if they have renounced freely, it would be rather awkward to do so. Besides, no existing international legal mechanism allows for invoking such individual responsibility. Moreover, it is difficult to imagine, even in a domestic setting, an instance where such an issue could arise. The only example is some form of action for indemnity against former protected persons by a war criminal claiming to have been misled by their renunciation. Almost all lawyers would see that this action would not stand any chance of success.

Since, as argued above, common Article 7/7/7/8 can be construed as implying a duty on the part of states to abstain from any behaviour which might lead protected persons to renounce their rights, any breach of such an obligation entails responsibility for the states concerned (be they the Detaining Power of the protected persons, or a third party intervening in the conflict). Such responsibility could be triggered through recourse to a diplomatic protection action by the national state of the protected persons concerned. However, no criminal responsibility is attached to the breach of this duty to abstain.

E. Critical Assessment

Common Article 7/7/7/8 is an unusual but nevertheless important provision; it is unusual because it is drafted as a prohibition addressed to protected persons themselves, rather than being addressed to the states parties. It could have forbidden any incitement or inducement to renounce the Convention rights, while clearly stating that any renunciation has no legal effect. It is an important provision because it affirms that protected persons have rights under the Conventions and that such rights are inalienable. As a provision common to the four Conventions, and despite its apparent limited practical usefulness, it has been of paramount importance to the doctrinal construction of the legal nature of obligations under IHL.

But here lies the paradox of this unusual, though important, provision: by protecting protected persons even against their own will, it concomitantly affirms their legal subjectivity under international (humanitarian) law and limits it.

PIERRE D'ARGENT[*]

---

[*] My thanks to Lindsey Cameron and Annie Hylton for their most useful comments and suggestions.

Chapter 9. Final Provisions, Including the Martens Clause

	MN
A. Introduction	1
I. The concept and role of final provisions	1
a. General features in the law of treaties	1
b. Specificities of the Geneva Conventions	4
II. The law of treaties and the Geneva Conventions: some preliminary caveats	5
B. Languages	10
I. Authentic texts	10
II. Official translations	16
C. Conclusion and Entry into Force of the Geneva Conventions	18
I. Signature	19
II. Expression of the consent of a state to be bound by the Geneva Conventions	22
a. By ratification	22
b. By accession	24
c. By succession	27
III. Entry into force	40
a. General remarks	40
b. Immediate effect	42
IV. Registration	46
a. Rationale and scope of the provision	46
b. Depositary functions and Swiss Government-specific tasks in this regard	48
D. Reservations	53
E. The Relationship with Previous Conventions: The Question of Treaties over Time on the Same Subject Matter	56
I. Application, termination, modification	56
II. Relationship with prior Hague Conventions and the earlier Geneva Conventions	58
a. Hague Conventions (1899 and 1907)	59
b. Geneva Conventions (1864, 1906, and 1929)	62
F. Denunciation	63
I. Regime	63
a. Legal effects	64
b. Procedure	67
II. Relationship with customary international law on the same subject matter	69
G. Martens Clause, International Humanitarian Law's Innovative Solution	72
I. Origins and context of the adoption of the Martens Clause	74
a. A leitmotiv of international (humanitarian) law	77
b. Impact of the specific place and wording of the Clause in the Geneva Conventions of 1949	78
II. The functions of the Martens Clause	81
a. The thesis of a simple *renvoi* to customary international law	84
b. The clause as an interpretative aid	87
c. The 'laws of humanity' as a substantive principle of international (humanitarian) law	89

Select Bibliography

Best, G., *War and Law Since 1945* (Oxford: OUP, 1994)
Corten, O./Klein, P. (eds), *The Vienna Conventions on the Law of Treaties* (Oxford: OUP, 2011)
Hollis, D.B. (ed), *The Oxford Guide to Treaties* (Oxford: OUP, 2012)
Meron, T., 'The Martens Clause, Principles of Humanity, and Dictates of Public Conscience', 94 *AJIL* (2000) 78
Pilloud, C., 'Les réserves aux conventions de Genève de 1949', 58 *Revue internationale de la Croix-Rouge* (1976) 131
de La Pradelle, P., *La Conférence diplomatique et les nouvelles Conventions de Genève du 12 août 1949* (Paris: Éditions internationales, 1951)
Rasulov, A., 'Revisiting State Succession to Humanitarian Treaties: Is There a Case for Automaticity?', 14 *EJIL* (2003) 143
Reuter, P., *Introduction to the Law of Treaties* (2nd edn, London/New York: Kegan Paul International, 1995)

A. Introduction

I. The concept and role of final provisions

a. General features in the law of treaties

1   In light of state practice with regard to the drafting of an international treaty, one may observe that most, if not all, long treaties include what are traditionally called 'final provisions'. As a quick glance at the Geneva Conventions will demonstrate, they make no exception in this respect, for they too contain a list of final provisions. The 'final provisions', as their label very clearly denotes, appear at the end of the text of the treaty, after its normative content. These clauses, which quite naturally vary from one treaty to another, may generally refer to the duration of the treaty, the means by which it is adopted, the means by which states are allowed to express their consent to be bound by it, the conditions under which a state can—perhaps—denounce it, the terms of its entry into force, the regime (if any) of reservations (and objections) to it, the official languages, the designation of the depositary (if any), its registration with the United Nations (UN) secretariat, and so on. Even where they are different in nature, scope, and aim, some provisions are generally brought together under a single heading (i.e. 'Final provisions'), even though there is no mandatory rule to this effect.

2   These provisions are instrumental for the treaty to operate, and their content aims to prevent future disputes between the parties in this regard. To this effect, in the same manner as all the other provisions of the treaty, they embody the authoritative will of the parties, which obviously prevails—in case of litigation or doubt—over their individual wills.

3   With regard to the final provisions, it is noteworthy to observe, as Article 24(4) of the Vienna Convention on the Law of Treaties (VCLT) envisages, that some of these provisions must be applied before the treaty's entry into force. In short, these are provisions which deploy their legal effects before such entry into force,[1] for they are propaedeutic to

---

[1] And even earlier, for instance those governing the modalities (i.e. voting procedure and the like) of its adoption.

it. In other words, they must be applied before the treaty's coming into force, for without their application the very entry into force of the treaty would be jeopardized.

b. *Specificities of the Geneva Conventions*

The final provisions are similar, yet not identical, within all four Geneva Conventions. The minor differences are due, among other things, to the existence or lack of prior conventions on the same subject matter the particular Geneva Convention is meant to cover. Save for the provisions relating to the official languages and authentic text, and the introduction of the Martens Clause in relation to the effect of denunciation (see section G of this chapter), the Geneva Conventions' final provisions largely resemble their 1929 counterparts. Generally, the final provisions were not discussed extensively at the International Conferences in Stockholm in August 1948, nor at the Geneva Conference in 1949. In fact, besides the question of languages and the introduction of the Martens Clause, they were already present, almost in their definitive form, in the International Committee of the Red Cross (ICRC) draft of May 1948, prepared following the Conference of Experts of April 1947.

II. The law of treaties and the Geneva Conventions: some preliminary caveats

Most of the rules governing the interpretation, application, life, modification, and death of international treaties (between states) are considered to have been codified—and progressively developed—by the VCLT 1969. State practice at large and international (as well as domestic) jurisprudence buttress the customary value of the rules contained therein. This is of paramount importance for, by virtue of its Article 4 (non-retroactivity), the VCLT cannot be applied to the Geneva Conventions, even though it is currently in force between 114 states among the High Contracting Parties to the Geneva Conventions.

Therefore, as the International Court of Justice (ICJ)—as well as other international tribunals and non-judicial bodies—has adamantly reiterated, what is applicable, then, is customary law henceforth enshrined in the VCLT. It must nonetheless be noted that the treaties in point were concluded even before the commencement of the work of the International Law Commission (ILC) with regard to the law of treaties.

Generally speaking, the legal corpus governing the Geneva Conventions as treaties is largely mirrored in the VCLT, except as regards the succession of states to treaties and the effects of armed conflicts on treaties (Article 73 VCLT). As a result, we are going to apply those rules, the content of which has been 'transcripted' into the VCLT.[2]

Moreover, and lastly, the emphasis should be put on the difference between the interpretation of a treaty and its application. Even though the Geneva Conventions were concluded in 1949, they have to be applied today by taking into account the current status of the international legal system. As the Institut de droit international stated authoritatively in 1975, in accordance with international jurisprudence, '[a]ny interpretation of a treaty must take into account all relevant rules of international law which apply between the parties at the time of application.'[3]

---

[2] For sake of simplicity, we shall mention the corresponding VCLT Articles, even though it is their customary counterparts which apply to the GCs.

[3] 'The Intertemporal Problem in Public International Law', Session of Wiesbaden (1975), Art 4.

9   It is also important to note, in regard to the Geneva Conventions, that some of their final provisions (on immediate entry into force and denunciation during an armed conflict) depart clearly from the rather formalistic solutions provided for in general international law. This is due to the acknowledgment by the High Conctracting Parties that the specific subject made it necessary to adapt some of the features of the law of treaties to the need to protect the victims of war.[4]

B. Languages

I. Authentic texts

10   The main and striking difference between the 1949 Geneva Conventions and prior Geneva Conventions, as well as the Hague Regulations, lies in the official languages of the Treaties (Article 55 GC I; Article 54 GC II; Article 133 GC III; Article 150 GC IV). In this respect, the 1949 Geneva Conventions marked the introduction of English, alongside French, as one of the official languages of the codification of international humanitarian law (IHL) (the Geneva Conventions of 1929 were drafted solely in French). French was previously the main, if not the sole, diplomatic language. In later international conferences on IHL, the authentic languages would be extended to encompass the other four official languages of the UN—Russian, Spanish, Chinese, and Arabic—in accordance with UN practice.[5] Thus the Additional Protocols (APs) I–III were drafted in the six official languages of the UN (Article 102 AP I; Article 28 AP II; Article 17 AP III). 'Authentic' in this regard means that the Geneva Conventions, couched in both the French and English languages, enshrine the true intentions of the negotiating parties.

11   Hence, French and English enjoy exactly the same formal value, and the *travaux préparatoires* were conducted in both languages with simultaneous interpretation. Indeed, the working languages within a diplomatic conference are more than often the official languages of the text eventually adopted, while the reverse is not always true.[6]

12   In the case of discrepancies, the customary rule, as reflected in Article 33(4) VCLT, provides that 'the meaning which best reconciles the texts, having regard to the object and purpose of the treaty, shall be adopted'.[7] According to some commentators, the 'role of Article 33 is precisely to rehabilitate or maintain the unity of meaning of a multilingual treaty'.[8]

---

[4] See P. de La Pradelle, *La Conférence diplomatique et les nouvelles Conventions de Genève du 12 août 1949* (Paris: Éditions internationales, 1951), at 34: 'Deux catégories de dispositions ont été insérées dans les derniers articles des quatre Conventions. Les unes, se référant au droit classique interétatique, intéressent leur applicabilité ou leur durée théorique d'application. Les autres, inspirées par des considérations humanitaires, corrigent l'automatisme des premières en fixant, dans l'éventualité d'un conflit, les conditions spéciales de leur application ou de leur durée réelle.'

[5] See Art 29 of the 1954 Hague Convention for the Protection of Cultural Property in the Event of Armed Conflict, extending the authentic languages to Russian and Spanish.

[6] As the United Nations Conference on International Organization (UNCIO) in San Francisco shows, where only English and French were the two working languages, even though the UN Charter is couched in five languages (thus adding Chinese, Spanish, and Russian), as prescribed by the Conference itself.

[7] ITLOS, *Responsibilities and Obligations of States Sponsoring Persons and Entities with Respect to Activities in the Area*, Advisory Opinion, 1 February 2011, para 57.

[8] A. Papaux and R. Samson, 'Article 33. Convention of 1969', in O. Corten and P. Klein (eds), *The Vienna Conventions on the Law of Treaties* (Oxford: OUP, 2011), vol I, 866, at 872.

According to Article 33(3) VCLT, 'the terms of the treaty are *presumed* to have the same   13
meaning in each authentic text' (emphasis added). Yet this presumption does not resolve,
by the touch of a magic wand, all the doubts, uncertainties, and divergences likely to stem
from the mere existence of two (or even more) authentic texts in different languages. First,
as the very numbering of the VCLT provisions in this respect clearly shows, in order to
reconcile the meanings flowing from the texts, the interpreter ought, at least tentatively,
to carry out interpretation of the provision concerned first in accordance with Article 31
(general *rule* of interpretation) and subsidiarily in accordance with Article 32 VCLT (supplementary *means* of interpretation). It is only then, after first resorting to the interpretation
of the text (in all the official languages), that it might be possible to ascertain the potential
divergences and eventually 'reconcile' them.[9]

If no 'reconciliation' to this effect can be achieved, Article 33(4) requires adopting the mean-   14
ing 'which *best* reconciles the texts, *having regard to the object and purpose*' (emphasis added).[10]
It is not by accident that this provision emphasizes this essential element of the general
rule of interpretation stated in Article 31(1) VCLT. As far as the Geneva Conventions are
concerned, this is of the utmost importance, taking into account the noblest purposes of
the Conventions.

A proposal was submitted by the ICRC to establish French as the language of reference   15
in case of different meanings stemming from the two official languages, as envisaged
by Article 33(1) VCLT *in fine*, but the Conference rejected this proposal.[11] It might also
be noted that an attempt to introduce a special rule preferring the interpretation most
favourable to the victims of armed conflicts ('*in dubio pro victima*' or interpretation *pro
victimis*) was abandoned.[12] Such a maxim of interpretation not confined to the question of
languages and proper to IHL, would nevertheless be an interesting tool in view of the ever
numerous attempts to water down the protections provided by the Geneva Conventions.
It could be seen as a concretization of the principle of good faith, and as one of the functions of the Martens Clause seen as an interpretative aid.[13] In fact such a rule of interpretation would be adopted later in the context of human rights protection (see Article 29(a) of
the the American Convention on Human Rights).[14]

II. Official translations

At the request of the Diplomatic Conference, the Swiss Federal Council prepared, in   16
cooperation with the interested states, an official translation of the Geneva Conventions
in Spanish and Russian,[15] the Chinese delegate expressing discontent that the Conference

---

[9] In its recent advisory opinion, the ITLOS affirmed that although there was no sensible difference of meaning between the terms used in the six authentic versions of UNCLOS, '[a] comparison between the terms used in these provisions of the Convention is nonetheless useful in clarifying their meaning'. (ITLOS, *Responsibilities and Obligations of States*, above n 7, para 63). See also ICJ, *Application of the International Convention on the Elimination of All Forms of Racial Discrimination (Georgia v Russian Federation)*, Preliminary Objections, Judgment, 1 April 2011, para 123.

[10] As has been wisely observed by Papaux and Samson, above n 8, at 882: 'The meaning of "best" in paragraph 4 remains undetermined. According to what is one interpretation judged preferable to another?'

[11] Final Record, vol II-B, at 25, 70–1, 112–13, 358.

[12] Ibid, at 68 (P. de Geouffre de La Pradelle, Monaco).   [13] See MN 87–88.

[14] See A.F. Amaya Villarreal, 'El principio *pro homine*: interpretación extensiva *vs.* el consentimiento del Estado', 5 *Revista Colombiana de Derecho Internacional* (2005) 337.

[15] 'Message du Conseil fédéral à l'Assemblée fédérale concernant l'approbation des Conventions de Genève pour la protection des victimes de la guerre du 12 août 1949', 2 *Feuille fédérale* 50 (15 December 1949) 1121, at 1144.

did not ask the Swiss Federal Council to make an official translation in the Chinese language too.[16] It is unclear whether these 'official translations' by the Swiss Federal Council enjoy any particular status for the sake of treaty interpretation. They obviously do not reach to the status of 'authentic text',[17] but arguably, the fact that they were *authorized* by the Conference provides them with an aura of multilateralism and higher reliability than purely national translations. Almost all states have translated the text of the Geneva Conventions, in realization of obligations arising from their domestic legislation as well as from the relevant provisions of the Geneva Conventions (Article 48 GC I; Article 49 GC II; Article 128 GC III; Article 145 GC IV).[18] As noted by the ICRC Commentary to AP I, purely national official translations 'are official in so far as they are established or recognized by a state; they should not be confused with official translations produced in accordance with the provisions of the treaty itself, as defined above'.[19] It might be useful to recall in this regard that the act of translating is more than a purely formal step for domestic purposes; it also has relevance as regards the application of the normative content of the Geneva Conventions, since the translation of the text and Annexes of GC III in the language of prisoners of war is part of an obligation to place those texts 'in places where all [prisoners] may read them'.[20]

17   For practical reasons, it is clear that in cases of divergent meanings between one of the official languages of the authentic texts and any of the official translations, the former will prevail. In this connection, it is not superfluous to note that, to underline the different legal status between the authentic texts, on the one hand, and the official translations, on the other, plenipotentiaries' signatures were required on the former and not—also—on the latter. This is indeed quite understandable, for the will of states is enshrined in the French and English texts (*instrumenti*) and not—technically speaking—in the official translations.

C. Conclusion and Entry into Force of the Geneva Conventions

18   The provisions covering the conclusion and entry into force of the Geneva Conventions may be found in Articles 56–58 GC I, Articles 55–57 GC II, Articles 136–138 GC III, and Articles 151–153 GC IV, respectively. The procedure regarding the making of the Geneva Conventions is, as it was for the 1929 Geneva Conventions and as it would be for the Additional Protocols, articulated in two steps, namely, signature followed by ratification. Once these two phases were accomplished, the Geneva Conventions were ready to enter into force.

I. Signature

19   According to the law of treaties, the act of signature performed by a state's plenipotentiary (Article 7 VCLT) entails *a minima* the legal effect of 'adoption of a treaty' (Article 9 VCLT), which marks the formal end of diplomatic negotiations and thus the treaty's

---

[16] Final Record, vol II-B, at 372.   [17] See, e.g., Pictet Commentary GC I, at 402.
[18] The Depositary as well as the ICRC holds a collection of national translations. These are sometimes communicated by the Depositary to High Contracting Parties, as foreseen in common Articles 48/49/128/145 of the GCs.
[19] ICRC Commentary APs, at 1122, para 3890.
[20] Art 41 para 1 GC III. See also Art 99 para 2 GC IV regarding 'places of internment' of civilians. See Ch 48, MN 91, and Ch 65, MN 29, of this volume.

birth. In fact, as from its adoption, a treaty becomes a 'living instrument' in the realm of international legal relations; at the same time, thus, the official and definitive text of the treaty is thereby drawn up. Authentication, on the other hand, is the act by which states participating in negotiations certify that the adopted text is truly the authentic one. In a way, they perform a notarial act, which is normally carried out by any procedure 'provided for in the text or agreed upon by the states participating in its drawing up' (Article 10(a) VCLT). In the case in point, the Geneva Conventions provided for the signature to entail this authentication effect. The Geneva Conventions were adopted, respectively, by 47 votes in favour without opposition and with one abstention (GC I), by 48 votes in favour without opposition and with one abstention (GC II), unanimously (49 delegations that took part in the vote, GC III), and by 47 votes in favour without opposition and with two abstentions (GC IV).[21]

All the states invited to participate at the Conference were allowed to sign the Geneva Conventions and thus participate in their formal adoption. Eighteen states signed the Conventions on 12 August 1949 (which accordingly became the date of their adoption), while 27 signed on 8 December of the same year; the remaining states signed at a later stage, before 12 February 1950, as stipulated in relevant Convention Articles.[22] Moreover, the first three Geneva Conventions were also open to signature, respectively, to the 'Powers not represented at that Conference but which are parties to the Geneva Conventions of 1864, 1906 or 1929 for the Relief of the Wounded and Sick in Armies in the Field' (Article 56 GC I),[23] to parties 'to the Tenth Hague Convention of October 18, 1907, for the Adaptation to Maritime Warfare of the Principles of the Geneva Convention of 1906, or to the Geneva Conventions of 1864, 1906 or 1929 for the Relief of the Wounded and Sick in Armies in the Field' (Article 55 GC II), and to parties 'to the Convention of July 27, 1929' (Article 136 GC III). The consolidated number of signatory states is the same for all the Geneva Conventions and stands at 61.[24] All the Geneva Conventions bear the same date of conclusion.

The adoption of a treaty marks its birth and thus, as an infant juristic act, the treaty must be protected by international law against any conduct of a signatory state 'which would defeat [its] object and purpose' before its entry into force, as provided for in Article 18 VCLT. In other words, a state which has signed the treaty before ratifying it (Article 18(a)), or a state which has already ratified it or acceded to it (Article 18(b)), must then refrain—pending its entry into force—from committing acts which would jeopardize its future operation. This provision surely constitutes one of the manifold applications of the principle of good faith, and it is thus applicable to the Geneva Conventions too. Yet the practical effect of this rule is diminished by two specificities of the Geneva Conventions.

---

[21] Final Record, vol II-B, at 519. Israel abstained from voting on GCs I, II, and IV because of the rejection by the Conference of their proposal to accept the Red Shield of David as a new emblem (ibid, at 520). On this issue, see Ch 43 of this volume and J.-F. Quéguiner, 'Commentary on the Protocol Additional to the Geneva Conventions of 12 August 1949, and Relating to the Adoption of an Additional Distinctive Emblem (Protocol III)', 89 *IRRC* 865 (2007) 175, esp at 177. Sixty-three states were present at the Conference, of which four had the status of observers. See de La Pradelle, above n 4, at 30–1.

[22] de La Pradelle, above n 4, at 13–42; G. Best, *War and Law Since 1945* (Oxford: OUP, 1994), at 80–179; J. Pictet, 'La formation du droit international humanitaire', 67 *IRRC* (1985) 3, at 9–14.

[23] 'Five States availed themselves of this opportunity, two of them having been represented at the Conference by Observers', Pictet Commentary GC I, at 403.

[24] J. Pictet, 'The New Geneva Conventions for the Protection of War Victims', 45 *AJIL* (1951) 462, at 468.

The first is embodied in a common provision which requires the signatory parties to ratify the Conventions as soon as possible,[25] thus shortening the time during which Article 18(a) is deemed to apply—an issue which has become absolutely moot. The second one stems from another common provision, according to which the Geneva Conventions shall enter into force *immediately* (thus before the elapse of the six-month period set forth in Article 58 GC I, Article 57 GC II, Article 138 GC III, Article 153 GC IV; see MN 40) if the state having ratified the Conventions (or acceded to them) is party to a conflict starting before this date.[26]

II. Expression of the consent of a state to be bound by the Geneva Conventions

a. By ratification

22 Since the Geneva Conventions have been concluded through the two-step procedure described above (see MN 18), ratification must be carried out for the signatory state to express its consent to be bound, thus paving the way for the Conventions' entry into force.[27] One of the most striking peculiarities of the Geneva Conventions with regard to the ratification process is undoubtedly the prescription directed to signatory states that the 'Convention[s] shall be ratified as soon as possible'. This 'pressing recommendation'[28] made to states pursues a two-fold purpose. The most obvious one was of course to accelerate the entry into force of the Geneva Conventions; the second one is that the accession of non-signatory states was not possible as long as the Conventions had not entered into force.

23 As already pointed out, participating states at the Conference opted for the two-step procedure. The Geneva Conventions explicitly specified that the only two means of expressing state consent to be bound were ratification and accession. Unlike other treaties, the Conventions opted for the deposit of instruments relating to them, and not for their exchange between contracting parties. Since the Geneva Conventions are multilateral and open law-making conventions striving for universal application (which they have now achieved), the solution of deposit—instead of exchange—is the most suitable one. The technique of direct exchange of instruments is more suitable for contract-treaties, whereby parties agree to *exchange* reciprocal performances. As will be shown later on (see MN 51), the Geneva Conventions enshrine values and pursue goals which transcend High Contracting Parties' individual interests. The Geneva Conventions require signatory states to deposit their instruments of ratification with the Swiss Government, i.e. the Depositary of the Geneva Conventions.[29] The Depositary (Article 57 paragraph 2 GC I; Article 56 paragraph 2 GC II; Article 137 paragraph 2 GC III; Article 152 paragraph 2 GC IV) is required to make a copy of each instrument of ratification and send it to all the other contracting parties. In this connection, it ought to be stressed that the relevant date in determining the date on which the state is bound, is that of the deposit of the instrument and not that of the authorization given by the treaty-making organ (according to the domestic law) to the Executive.

---

[25] See MN 22.   [26] See MN 42–45.
[27] ICJ, *Ambatielos case (United Kingdom v Greece)*, Preliminary Objection, Judgment, 1 July 1952, at 43.
[28] Pictet Commentary GC I, at 404.   [29] See MN 48–52.

b. By accession

This means of expressing state consent to be bound by the treaty is closely intertwined with ratification (MN 22–23). Since signature does not convey state consent in this context, an additional act is thus required; hence—as Article 11 VCLT clearly shows—accession entails the same legal effects as ratification. However, accession may be distinguished from ratification to the extent that the state concerned has not signed the treaty—in other words, has not adopted it. This may be for several reasons. For example, either—though having participated in the negotiations—the state refused to adopt the treaty while it was open for adoption (through signature), or the state was not invited to take part in the negotiations. However, for a state to accede to a treaty it is necessary that the treaty specifically provides for this possibility. In sum, it must be an 'open treaty' so that states that have not signed it can subsequently become parties to it.[30] In fact, there does not exist, under general international law, an overall right, vested in any state—or other subject of international law[31]—to become party to any treaty if the treaty does not provide for it.

24

In accordance with common provisions of the Geneva Conventions in this respect, the Conventions are thus open to accession by 'any Power' not having signed them (Article 60 GC I; Article 59 GC II; Article 139 GC III; Article 155 GC IV). As already stressed, a state can accede to the Conventions only once they have already entered into force.[32] This requirement is consonant with the general—yet not mandatory[33]—regime of the law of treaties, for it meets the need that before an outside party (to the negotiations) may become party to a treaty, the treaty must have entered into force. To this effect, signatory states must play the paramount role, for they are the true progenitors of the Conventions. At the same time, though, in order to make real the openness of the Geneva Conventions, they provide that 'the Convention shall come into force after not less than two instruments of ratification have been deposited'.[34] If the threshold had been higher, this would have delayed the 'opening' of the Geneva Conventions to potential acceding states.

25

For historical reasons, that is the expansion of the international community of states since 1949 (due primarily to the decolonization process), the number of states acceding to the Geneva Conventions is almost twice that of signatory states. But a similar disproportion had already arisen with the 1864 Geneva Convention, 'probably the earliest instance in which the original parties (not all of which exist today as independent States) became so heavily outnumbered by acceding parties'.[35]

26

---

[30] PCIJ, *Free Zones of Upper Savoy and the District of Gex*, Judgment, 7 June 1932, at 145–6.

[31] This raises the controverted question of the ability of international organizations to accede to the GCs, on which see, e.g., R. Kolb, *Droit humanitaire et opérations de maintien de la paix* (2nd edn, Geneva: Helbing & Lichtenhahn, 2006), at 113–14 and the references therein (arguing that a dynamic interpretation of the term 'Power' (*Puissances*) would permit the accession of international organizations).

[32] The APs allow for accession even prior to their entry into force (see Art 94 AP I; Art 22 AP II; Art 10 AP III). See M. Takemoto, 'The 1977 Additional Protocols and the Law of Treaties', in Mélanges Pictet 249, at 251–2 (arguing that this change reflects the evolution of the law of treaties).

[33] In fact, some multilateral treaties are open for accession the day after the treaty closes for signature. See, e.g., the 1997 Kyoto Protocol to the UN Framework Convention on Climate Change (Art 24(1)).

[34] See, e.g., Art 58 GC I.

[35] S. Rosenne, 'Participation in the Geneva Conventions (1864–1949) and the Additional Protocols of 1977', in Mélanges Pictet 803, at 804.

c. By succession

i. General remarks on succession to the Geneva Conventions

27 Lastly, it is noteworthy that another means exists for becoming a High Contracting Party to the Geneva Conventions, one that is not envisaged by the treaties themselves but which is based upon general international law—'succession'.[36] In other words, a new state can become party to the Geneva Conventions as a result of a succession of states to treaties. This matter is regulated by customary international law, codified and largely progressively developed by the 1978 Vienna Convention on Succession of States in Respect of Treaties, Article 2(1)(b) of which defines 'succession of states' as meaning 'the replacement of one State by another in the responsibility for the international relations of territory'. By way of consequence, the Geneva Conventions, like any other 'open' multilateral treaties, can still count new parties to them, provided the predecessor state (i.e. the state which has been replaced by the new state in the 'responsibility for the international relations to which the succession of States relates' (Article 2(1)(d) of the 1978 Convention)) was, at the time of the succession, party to them.

28 The Vienna Convention on Succession of States in Respect of Treaties distinguishes between different types of succession, and institutes different rules for succession to multilateral treaties according to the circumstances. That is, in the case of:

— newly independent states, i.e. those states acceding to independence in the exercise of their right to self-determination;
— the uniting of states; and
— the separation of states.

As far as newly independent states are concerned, Sections 1 and 2 of Part III of the 1978 Vienna Convention provide for an opting-in system—also called the 'clean slate' principle—according to which a newly independent state is not considered to succeed to multilateral treaties unless it expressly affirms its intention to be bound.[37] Concerning the uniting of states, the general rule said to be applicable to the Geneva Conventions is that of continuity (Articles 31 to 33).[38] Lastly, there is uncertainty as regards the separation of states outside the colonial context (or the context of the exercise of a right to secession flowing from the right to self-determination). The rule adopted by the Vienna Conference (Article 34) provides for continuity, but it remains doubtful whether the Convention reflects customary international law on this aspect.[39] Against this backdrop, some authors have advocated for so-called automatic succession to certain limited categories of multilateral treaties, such as 'law-making'[40] or 'humanitarian' treaties.[41]

---

[36] See B. Zimmermann, 'La succession d'États et les Conventions de Genève', in Mélanges Pictet 113. See also E. David, *Principes de droit des conflits armés* (4th edn, Brussels: Bruylant, 2008), at 199–206.

[37] In this respect, the Vienna Convention may be considered to reflect customary international law on the matter. See, e.g., ICJ, *Case concerning the Delimitation of Maritime Boundary between Guinea-Bissau and Senegal*, Arbitral Award of 31 July 1989, 20 *RIAA*, 119–213, at 136, para 44. See E. Henry, 'Article 16', in G. Distefano and G. Gaggioli (eds), *Commentaire de la Convention de Vienne de 1978 sur la succession d'États en matière de traités* (Brussels: Bruylant, forthcoming).

[38] A.-L. Graf-Brugère, 'Article 31' in Distefano and Gaggioli (eds), above n 37.

[39] See, e.g., International Law Association, *Rio de Janeiro Conference (2008): Aspects of the Law of State Succession, Draft Final Report*, at 4.

[40] See the seminal article by W. Jenks, 'State Succession in Respect of Law-Making Treaties', 29 *BYBIL* (1952) 105.

[41] See, e.g., ICJ, *Application of the Convention on the Prevention and Punishment of the Crime of Genocide (Bosnia and Herzegovina v Serbia and Montenegro)*, Judgment, 11 July 1996, Separate Opinion of Judge

29 While the substantive rules of the Geneva Conventions are largely considered as reflecting customary international law,⁴² there are still practical grounds for which it is necessary to determine with certainty the status of a new state as a party to the Geneva Conventions,⁴³ especially given that the behaviour of some new states in this respect sometimes remains unclear for a long time. This, as well as the frequent and sometimes long delay between the moment of independence and accession,⁴⁴ raises once again the important issue of automatic (mandatory) succession to humanitarian treaties.

30 Despite this long-standing debate, it is generally held that there is no sufficient evidence of state practice and *opinio juris* to conclude the existence of a customary rule of international law applicable to the Geneva Conventions of 1949.⁴⁵ Thus, while 54 new states have declared themselves bound by the Geneva Conventions by virtue of state succession,⁴⁶ only a handful of them have expressed the opinion that they are bound as an automatic consequence of ratification by the predecessor state.⁴⁷ The majority have declared themselves bound in more vague terms, thus leaving open the hypothesis that they became parties not through automatic succession, but pursuant to the exercise of their right to opt in. Such states as Togo, Dahomey (Benin), Ivory Coast, Congo (Léopoldville), Mauritania, Nigeria, and Upper Volta thus declared that they *confirmed* their status as parties, implying that they could have considered themselves not bound.⁴⁸ On the other side, arguably 52 new states that could have claimed to *succeed* to the Geneva Conventions⁴⁹—either by way of

---

Shahabuddeen, at 634–9, and Separate Opinion of Judge Weeramantry, at 640–55. For a critical appraisal of their arguments, see B. Stern, 'La succession d'États,' 262 *RCADI* (1996) 9, at 176–90. See also M.T. Kamminga, 'State Succession in Respect of Human Rights Treaties,' 7 *EJIL* (1996) 469, at 482.

⁴² See Ch 33, section B, of this volume.

⁴³ This is necessary for the recognition of National Societies by the Movement (see Art 4 of the Statutes of the International Red Cross and Red Crescent Movement).

⁴⁴ In the case of the Maldives, e.g., the instrument of accession to the GCs was deposited almost 26 years after its independence (see depositary notification of 12 July 1991). This problem could be solved through the acceptance of the application in conformity with CA 2 para 3 and the rules on provisional application of the Vienna Convention on Succession of States in Respect of Treaties (Art 25 VCLT). See Zimmermann, above n 36, at 119–22. The acceptance provided for in CA 2 para 3 GC does not necessarily have to be explicit (Takemoto, above n 32, at 256) and will have immediate effect (Art 62 GC I; Art 61 GC II; Art 141 GC III; Art 157 GC IV).

⁴⁵ A. Rasulov, 'Revisiting State Succession to Humanitarian Treaties: Is There a Case for Automaticity?', 14 *EJIL* (2003) 143, at 167.

⁴⁶ The practice relating to the GCs up to 1968 was set out by the Secretariat of the ILC in 'Succession of States to Multilateral Treaties: Studies Prepared by the Secretariat', UN Doc A/CN.4/200/REV.2 and A/CN.4/200/ADD. 1 and 2, in *YILC* (1968-II) 1, at 32–54. All notifications made to the Depositary from 1977 onwards are available at <http://www.eda.admin.ch/depositary>. Prior to this date, the content of notifications relating to the status of the GCs may be found in D. Schindler and J. Toman, *The Laws of Armed Conflicts* (4th edn, Leiden: Martinus Nijhoff Publishers, 2004), at 635–93. See also the information in ICRC, *Annual Report 2013* (Geneva: ICRC, 2014), at 610–16.

⁴⁷ See, e.g., the notification to the Depositary of 12 June 1978 relating to Tonga. According to its declaration, Tonga 'considers itself bound by the four [GCs] [...] *in virtue* of their former ratification by the United Kingdom' (emphasis added). See also the declarations of Tuvalu or Grenada (notification of 8 May 1981), or that of Samoa, according to which Samoa 'has declared that it considers itself bound by the four Geneva Conventions [...] *in virtue of the ratification of these Conventions by New Zealand*' (emphasis added).

⁴⁸ ICRC, *Bericht über die Tätigkeit des internationalen Komitees vom Roten Kreuz: 1962* (Geneva: ICRC, 1963), at 59–60.

⁴⁹ However, Qatar does not consider that the end of its status as a protected state should be deemed a case of state succession (CR 2000/17, at 15). Lithuania, Latvia, and Estonia, while acceding to the GCs of 1949, have in parallel issued a declaration of continuity with regard to the 1929 Convention (see Depositary notifications of 10 February 1992). This fact reflects the thesis regarding the (resurrected) continuity of the Baltic countries after the collapse of the USSR (see, e.g., M. Koskenniemi and M. Letho, 'Succession d'États dans

the so-called automatic succession or through their right to opt in—have rather chosen to *accede* to them.

31   The international case law relating to the question of automatic succession to humanitarian treaties is rather poor and inconsistent. In the *Genocide case (Bosnia Herzegovina v Serbia)*, the ICJ was asked by Bosnia to declare the Genocide Convention applicable to the Federal Republic of Yugoslavia as a result of automatic succession to humanitarian treaties, but the Court declined to decide the case on this ground.[50] While the arbitral jurisprudence is at best inconclusive in this regard,[51] the International Criminal Tribunal for the former Yugoslavia (ICTY) has applied the doctrine of automatic succession to humanitarian treaties. Confronted with the application of the Geneva Conventions to Bosnia and Herzegovina right after it became independent, the Appeals Chamber in *Delalić* expressed

> the view that irrespective of any finding as to formal succession, Bosnia and Herzegovina would in any event have succeeded to the Geneva Conventions under customary law, as this type of convention entails automatic succession, i.e., without the need for any formal confirmation of adherence by the successor State. It may be now considered in international law that there is automatic State succession to multilateral humanitarian treaties in the broad sense, i.e. treaties of universal character which express fundamental human rights.[52]

It then further asserted that '[it] is undisputable that the Geneva Conventions fall within this category of universal multilateral treaties which reflect rules accepted and recognised by the international community as a whole.'[53]

32   The practice of the Security Council is rather poor on this matter, and in any event, questions have arisen as to the competence of the Security Council to adjudicate on the applicability of IHL in concrete situations. Thus, while the Security Council has been increasingly involved in the implementation of IHL, it generally favours broad statements regarding the obligation of those involved to respect IHL, rarely mentioning specific instruments in its resolutions, as was recently illustrated in the case of South Sudan.[54] A case that supports the thesis of continuity can nevertheless be found

---

l'ex-U.R.S.S., avec examen particulier des relations avec la Finlande', 38 *AFDI* (1992) 179, at 190–8). On the concept of the resurrection of states, see G. Cansacchi, 'Identité et continuité des sujets internationaux', 130 *RCADI* (1970-II) 1, at 47–59.

[50] ICJ, *Application of the Convention on the Prevention and Punishment of the Crime of Genocide (Bosnia and Herzegovina v Serbia and Montenegro)*, Judgment, 11 July 1996, at 611–13, paras 21–3.

[51] See EECC, *Prisoners of War—Eritrea's Claim 17*, Partial Award, 1 July 2003, XXVI *RIAA* (2009), 23, at 38, para 35. The Commission did not apply or envisage the application of the rule enshrined in Art 34 of the 1978 Vienna Convention on Succession of States in Respect of Treaties (providing for continuity in cases of separation of parts of a state). This statement is not helpful, as it indicates either that Eritrea is to be considered in the eyes of the Commission as a 'newly independent state' for the sake of succession to treaties to which the 'clean slate' rule applies (Art 16 of the Vienna Convention), or that Eritrea is a separating state but that the rule of Art 34 does not reflect customary international law.

[52] ICTY, *The Prosecutor v Zejnil Delalić, Zdravko Mucić (aka 'Pavo'), Hazim Delić and Esad Landžo (aka 'Zenga')* ('*Čelebići Case*'), Appeals Chamber Judgment, 20 February 2001, IT-96-21-A, para 111.

[53] Ibid, para 112. See also ICTY, *The Prosecutor v Tihomir Blaškić*, Trial Chamber Decision of 4 April 1997 on the Defence Motion to Strike Portions of the Amended Indictment Alleging 'Failure to Punish' Liability, IT-95-14-A, para 12.

[54] See G. Nolte, 'The Different Functions of the Security Council with Respect to Humanitarian Law', in V. Lowe et al (eds), *The United Nations Security Council and War: The Evolution of Thought and Practice since 1945* (Oxford: OUP, 2008) 519. See also M. Roscini, 'The United Nations Security Council and the Enforcement of International Humanitarian Law', 43 *Israel Law Review* (2010) 330. See, lastly, Res 2047 (2012) of 17 May 2012.

in Resolution 307 (1971) of 21 December 1971, adopted shortly after the independence of Eastern Pakistan in the context of the third Indo-Pakistani war, in which the Security Council

[c]alls upon, all those concerned to take all measures necessary to preserve human life and for the observance of the Geneva Conventions of 1949 and to apply in full their provisions as regards the protection of the wounded and sick, prisoners of war and civilian population.[55]

This formulation implies that the Security Council considered that the Geneva Conventions were *de jure* applicable not only in relations between India and Western Pakistan, but also between the troops of the newly established states of Eastern Pakistan and Western Pakistan. Adding to this thesis, Bangladesh later declared itself bound by the Geneva Conventions as a matter of succession, on 4 April 1972. A comparable situation occurred 20 years later with regard to Bosnia and Herzegovina.[56]

As regards the ICRC, in the first phase it applied the continuity thesis,[57] and thus considered that the new states that had not (yet) made any declaration of continuity were nevertheless bound by the Geneva Conventions.[58] But from 1964, the ICRC started to refer to the number of states that were *expressly* bound by the Geneva Conventions,[59] and from 1980 it expressed the view that only states that had taken an explicit step as to their status as parties to the Geneva Conventions could be considered members of the International Conference of the Red Cross and Red Crescent.[60] A number of states that the ICRC considered bound as a matter of succession, such as Kenya and Guinea, later acceded to the Geneva Conventions.[61]

Beside these elements of state practice, the present authors do not have knowledge of any cases where state parties to the Geneva Conventions involved in an armed conflict with a new state have claimed that the latter was bound by the Geneva Conventions as a matter of succession to treaties. The fact that a great number of new states chose to accede to the Geneva Conventions, or made simple declarations of succession according to which no *opinio juris* may be inferred, leads to a negative answer to the question of the existence of a customary rule providing for automatic mandatory succession to the Geneva Conventions. In theory, these facts raise the question of the legal nature of the accession instrument in cases where the state is already to be considered a party to the treaty as a matter of state succession, and the (dubious) possibility for a state to accede to such a treaty. If it is considered that the law of treaties does not allow a state to accede to a

---

[55] This resolution is quoted in R. Cryer, 'The Security Council and International Humanitarian Law', in S.C. Breau and A. Jachec-Neale (eds), *Testing the Boundaries of International Humanitarian Law* (London: BIICL, 2006) 245, at 255.

[56] See UNSC Res 771 (1992) adopted on 13 August 1992 (several months before the declaration of continuity issued by Bosnia and Herzegovina in 1993) '[*reaffirming*] that all parties to the conflict are bound to comply with their obligations under international humanitarian law and in particular the Geneva Conventions of 12 August 1949'.

[57] ICRC, *Bericht über die Tätigkeit des internationalen Komitees vom Roten Kreuz: 1961* (Geneva: ICRC, 1962), at 52–3; and H. Coursier, 'L'accession des nouveaux Etats africains aux Conventions de Genève,' 7 *AFDI* (1961) 760 at 760–61.

[58] ILC, above n 46, at 37, para 151.

[59] ICRC, *Bericht über die Tätigkeit des internationalen Komitees vom Roten Kreuz: 1963* (Geneva: ICRC, 1964), at 53.

[60] See Zimmermann, above n 36, at 118–19.

[61] ICRC, *Bericht über die Tätigkeit des internationalen Komitees vom Roten Kreuz: 1965* (Geneva: ICRC, 1966), at 62.

treaty to which it is already a party as a matter of succession, then the thesis of continuity (even with an opting-out right) is put in serious doubt. On the other hand, the rare expressions of *opinio juris* have been in favour of a rule of continuity, and none of these have been expressly rebutted by other states. One might also consider that there is no explicit expression of a contrary *opinio juris*. We are thus possibly in the presence of one of these situations in which the Martens Clause could play the role of 'game changer' for the rules on the formation of customary international law.[62] Such a line of argument might provide a plausible (though doubtful) explanation of the position of the ICTY Appeals Chamber in *Delalić et al.*[63]

35   The major practical difference between cases of succession and cases of accession occurs in situations where a state neither issues a declaration of succession nor transmits an instrument of accession to the Geneva Conventions at the effective date of its independence. If the state later issues an instrument of accession, the accession 'shall take effect six months after the date on which [it is] received', while if it later issues a declaration of succession, the Geneva Conventions shall be deemed applicable retroactively as from the date of the accession to independence.

ii. Succession and accession in cases of contested statehood

36   In cases of contested statehood, the instruments of accession should be deemed valid only once the state objectively exists, which is generally proven when it has been recognized by the international community. Where (intended) 'instruments of accession' are issued prior to the date of effective independence, they should be considered non-existent, and therefore a new instrument should be deposited once statehood is established. The Depositary of the Geneva Conventions, in conformity with the law of treaties, has not been entrusted with any adjudicating function in this regard, whether in a positive way (declaring the intented accession effective) or in a negative way (declaring it void).[64] In any case where a state has an unresolved view of such a matter, it has the possibility of bringing 'the question to the attention of the signatory States and the contracting States' (Article 77(2) VCLT), which would give rise to an international dispute.

37   In the case of Algeria, for example, the Provisional Government of the Algerian Republic (GPRA) 'acceded' to the Geneva Conventions—Libya acting as an intermediary—on 20 June 1960, in the course of hostilities with France. The Swiss Federal Council transmitted to the High Contracting Parties the GPRA's intention to accede, triggering a protest by France. Algeria's status as a state party to the Geneva Conventions was thus contentious until the conclusion of the Evian Agreement in 1962. Arguably, Algeria was recognized as an independent state by no more than 17 states at the end of 1959 (29 states by April 1961), making any accession or succession impossible. The intended accession prompted the objection of France, which consequently continued to consider the Algerian War as a non-international armed conflict (NIAC).[65] The ICRC's annual report thus gives an

---

[62] See MN 88.

[63] But for Kolb, the rule of continuity flows from the principle of good faith: R. Kolb, 'Principles as Sources of International Law (With Special Reference to Good Faith)', 53 *NILR* (2006) 1, at 33.

[64] F. Ouguergouz, S. Villalpando, and J. Morgan-Foster, 'Article 77. Convention of 1969', in Corten and Klein (eds), above n 8, vol II, 1715, at 1753. But this does not stop the Depositary from expressing its opinion as a High Contracting Party.

[65] See the Swiss report of a meeting between Swiss Federal Counsellor Petitpierre and French Prime Minister Debré (Diplomatic Documents of Switzerland, DoDiS-15122 at <http://dodis.ch/15122>) and the *procès-verbal* of the Swiss Federal Council detailing its legal analysis (Diplomatic Documents of Switzerland,

additional, and allegedly effective, date of accession of the independent state of Algeria to the Geneva Conventions (3 July 1962).[66]

Following this practice, the Swiss Federal Council, in 1989, while informing the High Contracting Parties of Palestine's steps toward accession to the Geneva Conventions, refused to take further action, considering that it was 'not in a position to decide whether this communication can be considered as an instrument of accession in the sense of the relevant provisions of the Conventions and their Additional Protocols'.[67] 38

A more flexible approach has nevertheless been advocated, at least as regards declarations of accession issued by movements of national liberation from the 1960s onwards, favouring accession to the Geneva Conventions.[68] This evolution later resulted in the adoption of Article 1(4) AP I and Article 96(3) AP I,[69] which opens up the possibility for an 'authority representing a people engaged against a High Contracting Party in an armed conflict of the type referred to in Article 1, paragraph 4' to make a unilateral declaration manifesting its undertaking to apply AP I and the Conventions. Additionally, in cases where instruments of accession have been communicated before the effective birth of a new state, the Geneva Conventions seem to have been considered as binding as from the internationally recognized date of the emergence of the new state, without its having to issue a new instrument of accession. 39

III. Entry into force

a. General remarks

According to their relevant provisions (Article 58 paragraph 2 GC I; Article 57 paragraph 2 GC II; Article 138 paragraph 2 GC III; Article 153 paragraph 2 GC IV), the Geneva Conventions come into force six months after not less than two instruments of ratification have been deposited with the Swiss Government, and thereafter for each state six months after the relevant instrument of ratification is deposited. For both practical and legal reasons, the six-month period is necessary in order to allow the participant state to carry out all the appropriate steps (administrative, legislative, etc) within its domestic system to make it consonant with international obligations flowing out of the Geneva Conventions.[70] As was the case for their adoption, the date of entry into force of all the Geneva Conventions is the same, i.e. 21 October 1950, Switzerland and the Socialist Federal Republic of Yugoslavia having ratified them on 31 March 1950 and on 21 April of the same year, respectively. 40

DoDiS-15122, available at <http://dodis.ch/15163>). On the context of this intended accession, see M. Flory, 'Algérie algérienne et droit international', 6 *AFDI* (1960) 973, at 981 and 987–8; F. Perret, 'L'action du Comité international de la Croix-Rouge pendant la guerre d'Algérie (1954–1962)', 86 *IRRC* (2004) 917. But according to Michel Veuthey, the accession of 20 June 1960 can be deemed a success: M. Veuthey, 'Learning from History: Accession to the Conventions, Special Agreements, and Unilateral Declarations', in M. Vuijlsteke (ed), *Relevance of International Humanitarian Law to Non-State Actors*, Collegium, No 27 (Bruges: College of Europe, Spring 2003) 139, at 143. See also more generally on Algeria's accession to independence, J. Crawford, *The Creation of States in International Law* (2nd edn, Oxford: OUP, 2006), at 385 and 387 (with references to the works of M. Bedjaoui on the question).

[66] ICRC, *Annual Report 2011* (Geneva: ICRC, 2012), at 507.
[67] Communication of the Depositary of 13 September 1989. See also Communications of 11 December 1990 and 31 July 1991. On 10 April 2014, the Swiss Federal Council finally communicated the accession of the state of Palestine to the GCs and AP I, taking effect on 2 April 2014.
[68] G. Abi-Saab, 'Wars of National Liberation in the Geneva Conventions and Protocols', *RCADI* (1979-IV) 353, at 399–403.
[69] Ibid, at 403–15.   [70] See Ch 32 of this volume.

41 Furthermore, as regards application, a distinction must be made between those provisions which are applicable in peacetime[71] and those, on the other hand, which, though in force between the contracting parties, depend on the fulfilment of Articles 2 and 3 for their application, i.e. the existence of an armed conflict, be it international or non-international (see Chapters 1, 2, and 19 of this volume). In this respect then, application is disconnected from entry into force, since some conditions must coexist for the former to be triggered.

b. Immediate effect

42 From the outset, entry into force with immediate effect must be distinguished from the case of provisional application as encompassed by Article 25 VCLT, in so far as in the latter case a state has not necessarily expressed its consent to be bound and can thus still 'notify its intention not to become a party to the treaty' (Article 25(2)). Here, 'entry into force with immediate effect' refers to the obligation for a state to give immediate effect to some of the provisions of the Geneva Conventions, *once the state in question has already ratified them or acceded to them*, pending the six-month period set out by the Geneva Conventions, *if a war has broken out in the meantime*. In other words, the entry into force of the Geneva Conventions with respect to the state concerned is merely a matter of time, and it is moreover ineluctable.[72] In order for this immediate effect to take place, the Swiss Federal Council is required to effectuate the communication of 'ratifications or accessions received from Powers in a state of war [...] by the quickest method' (Article 62 GC I; Article 61 GC II; Article 141 GC III; Article 157 GC IV). As has been observed, the lengthy procedure established by Article 58 paragraph 2 GC I, Article 57 paragraph 2 GC II, Article 138 paragraph 2 GC III, and Article 153 paragraph 2 GC IV ought not to be followed strictly.[73] Taking into account the circumstances, the best available (and safest) means of communication should be used by the Swiss Federal Council in order to communicate to the other contracting parties the deposit by the state concerned of its instrument of ratification or accession. A possible example could have been that of the 'accession' on behalf of Algeria by the GPRA during hostilities with the French Government.[74] If that accession had been deemed possible, the Geneva Conventions should have entered into force immediately after accession by the GPRA.

43 The relevant common provision of the Geneva Conventions establishes that '[t]he situations provided for in Articles 2 and 3 shall give immediate effect to ratifications deposited and accessions notified by the Parties to the conflict before or after the beginning of hostilities or occupation' (Article 62 GC I; Article 61 GC II; Article 141 GC III; Article 157 GC IV). These two provisions envisage respectively the existence of an international armed conflict or of an occupation (even without resistance), and the existence of a NIAC.

---

[71] These include mainly CA 1 (concerning the undertaking 'to respect and to ensure respect for the present Convention in all circumstances'; see Ch 6 of this volume), Art 23 GC I and Art 14 GC IV (establishment of hospital and safety zones and localities; see Chs 18 and 41), Art 26 GC I (notification of the names of societies authorized 'to render assistance to the regular medical service of [a state's] armed forces'; see Ch 40), Art 44 GC I (rules on the use of the emblem; see Ch 43) and Art 44 GC II (on distinguishing signs), Art 47 GC I, Art 48 GC II, Art 127 GC III, and Art 144 GC IV (dissemination of IHL; see Ch 30).

[72] In fact, a state cannot, under the law of treaties, 'withdraw' its instrument of ratification or accession, no more than it can its act of signature. The only way to free itself from the bounds of the treaty is by denunciation, once it has entered into force.

[73] Pictet Commentary GC II, at 280.   [74] See MN 37.

As for practicalities, the Geneva Conventions will enter into force on the date of the 44
notification of a state's instrument of ratification (or accession) if the armed conflict (or
occupation) in which the state concerned is involved has already commenced, or, inversely,
at the moment when the armed conflict (or occupation) commences if the state concerned
has already expressed its consent to be bound.

Here again, the Geneva Conventions' specificities break in to soften the rigid techni- 45
calities inherent to the law of treaties, since the principle of effectiveness and the principle
of humanity jointly command the immediate application of the Geneva Conventions.
The Additional Protocols do not prescribe such a solution. But this principle of immediate
entry into force is arguably applicable to the Additional Protocols too, as their purpose is
to 'supplement' (Article 1(3) AP I), 'to develop and supplement' (Article 1(1) AP II), or to
'[reaffirm] and [supplement]' (Article 1(2) AP III) the Geneva Conventions.

IV. Registration

a. Rationale and scope of the provision

Article 80 VCLT embodies the obligation—for states parties—to transmit a treaty 'to 46
the Secretariat of the United Nations for registration or filing and recording, as the case
may be, and for publication' (Article 80 paragraph 1). But even if the treaty is governed by
customary international law, UN members are at any rate required to register it with the
UN Secretariat, in accordance with Article 102 of the UN Charter, to which Article 80
VCLT implicitly refers. The Geneva Conventions give effect to this obligation (Article 64
GC I; Article 63 GC II; Article 143 GC III; Article 159 GC IV).

Without going into detail, it should be noted that Article 18 of the League of Nations 47
Covenant was more stringent than its UN Charter offspring, for it provided that, failing
registration with the League of Nations Secretariat, '[n]o such treaty or international
engagement shall be binding until so registered'. The sanction now arising from the
lack of registration with the UN Secretariat entails the impossibility of invoking the
treaty concerned 'before any organ of the United Nations' (Article 102 UN Charter).
Anyway, this is not applicable in the case of the Geneva Conventions, for the Swiss
Federal Council, as Depositary, has duly registered the Geneva Conventions with the
UN Secretariat.

b. Depositary functions and Swiss Government-specific tasks in this regard

The Swiss Federal Council (i.e. Swiss Government) has been vested with the function of keep- 48
ing a record of all notifications of ratification and transmitting it 'to all the Powers in whose
name the [Conventions have] been signed, or whose accession has been notified' (Article 57
paragraph 2 GC I; Article 56 paragraph 2 GC II; Article 137 paragraph 2 GC III; Article 152
paragraph 2 GC IV). Further, the Federal Council shall communicate the accessions to all
the Powers in whose name the Conventions have been signed, or whose accession has been
notified (Article 61 paragraph 2 GC I; Article 60 paragraph 2 GC II; Article 140 paragraph 2
GC III; Article 156 paragraph 2 GC IV). The Swiss Federal Council is also assigned the task
under the Conventions of keeping the original text of the Geneva Conventions in its achives,
and of transmitting certified copies of the texts to the 'Signatory and Acceding states' (as well
as the successor states).

Beside registration, the Depositary also usually proceeds to notify cases of succession 49
and acts relating to the physiology of a treaty: reservations, objections (and withdrawals

thereof), and denunciation.[75] The Swiss Federal Council has further been designated to play the role of an intermediary in times of peace, for the communication of official translations of the text of the Conventions, 'as well as the laws and regulations which [the High Contracting Parties] may adopt to ensure the application thereof' (Article 48 GC I; Article 49 GC II; Article 128 GC III; Article 145 GC IV). Additionally, the Swiss Federal Council has issued notifications relating to changes as to the use of the emblems[76] and, in other (rare) cases, it has notified communications relating to concrete situations of application of the Conventions.[77]

50 Historically, the Swiss Federal Council has played an important role as initiator and convenor of all the diplomatic conferences for the adoption or revision of the Geneva Conventions.[78] This longstanding practice—arguably giving rise to an exclusive right to convene the diplomatic conferences under customary international law[79]—was later concretized into a formal responsibility under Article 7 AP I and Article 97 AP I, according to which the Depositary has been entrusted with the function of convening 'a meeting of the High Contracting Parties, at the request of one or more of the said Parties and upon the approval of the majority of the said Parties to consider general problems concerning the Application of the Conventions and of the Protocol'. Nothing of the kind was provided for in the Geneva Conventions, with the result that such meetings should be convened only at the request of parties to AP I.[80] Those meetings have a 'legislative' objective, with their conclusion potentially leading to amendments to AP I or the Geneva Conventions, rather than an 'executive' function of incrementing the implementation of AP I or the Geneva Conventions—especially in cases where AP I does not formally apply. The ICRC Commentary therefore rightly asserts that '[w]ith the expression "general problems," the Conference wished to exclude the discussion of specific situations, to which other provisions apply'.[81] Therefore, in 2006, in the context of the war in Lebanon, the Depositary refused to convene 'an urgent meeting of the High Contracting Parties "to discuss the serious breach of IHL in Lebanon by Israel"'.[82] Under Article 97 AP I, the Depositary has even been given the right (and responsibility) to 'decide, after consultation with all the High Contracting Parties and

---

[75] See the list of functions as codified in Art 77 VCLT.

[76] See, e.g., notification of 9 January 1989 (Decision of the People's Republic of Bangladesh 'to use henceforth the red crescent instead of the red cross as the emblem and distinctive sign'), or the notification of 20 October 1980 ('decision of the Islamic Republic of Iran to use henceforth the Red Crescent instead of the Red Lion and Sun'). Art 3(1)(b) AP III echoes this practice.

[77] See, e.g., notification of 29 January 1991, transmitting a note of the US Department of State to the Embassy of the Republic of Iraq at Washington, 'concerning the presence of two US military hospital ships in the waters of the Arabian Peninsula'.

[78] See, e.g., D. Schindler, 'Die Schweiz und das Völkerrecht', in A. Riklin, H. Haug, and R. Probst (eds), *Nouveau manuel de la politique extérieure suisse* (Berne: P. Haupt, cop., 1992) 99, at 103; M. Sassòli, 'La Suisse et le droit international humanitaire—une relation privilégiée?', 45 *Annuaire suisse de droit international* (1989) 47; or S. Gamma and L. Caflisch, 'La Suisse, dépositaire des Conventions de Genève', 165 *Beilage zur Allgemeinen schweizerischen Militärzeitschrift* (1999) 7.

[79] Sassòli, above n 78, at 69.   [80] ICRC Commentary APs, at 104, para 266.

[81] Ibid, at 106, para 274.

[82] Notification of 12 September 2006. In this notification, the Depositary noted that '[t]he Geneva Conventions do not contain any provision on the convening or the organisation of meetings of the High Contracting Parties with a view to considering alleged violations committed in a given conflict and do not provide for a particular role of the depositary in this regard. For these reasons, and without a mandate of the High Contracting Parties, the depositary replied on 11 September 2006 that it was not in a position to convene such meeting as requested.'

the International Committee of the Red Cross, whether a conference should be convened to consider' proposed amendments to AP I (see likewise Article 24 AP II and Article 13 AP III).

The establishment by the states parties to AP I of a depositary with highly advanced tasks, not merely of a notarial nature but with the mission of convening such meetings, or even diplomatic conferences, and hence dealing with questions of compliance—although the Depositary's tasks are to be clearly distinguished from those of Protecting Powers[83]—underlines the distinctive feature of the Geneva Conventions as universal law-making conventions which enshrine 'a purely humanitarian and civilizing purpose' and where 'the contracting States do not have any interests of their own'.[84]

Since 2011, the Swiss Government has also fostered the so-called 'Swiss/ICRC initiative on strengthening compliance with IHL', which aims at '[exploring and identifying] concrete ways and means to strengthen the application of international humanitarian law and reinforce dialogue on international humanitarian law issues among States and other interested actors, in cooperation with the ICRC'.[85]

D. Reservations

The Geneva Conventions do not contain a specific regime for reservations—as a matter of fact, no provision whatsoever deals with the question of reservations in the Geneva Conventions—so we are therefore entirely dependent on the customary regime on reservations to multilateral treaties as codified by the VCLT.[86] This solution was expressly confirmed in AP I and AP II, all the proposals for the introduction of a specific regime having been rejected.[87] Reservations issued at the time of signature must be confirmed at the moment of ratification, unlike accession, where the reservation is definitive by this act alone. Therefore, states ratifying or acceding to AP I or AP II may not liberate themselves from the provisions of the Geneva Conventions by issuing reservations to provisions of the Additional Protocols that are substantially equivalent to those of the Geneva Conventions.[88]

A certain number of reservations have been issued either at the time of signature, or on ratification or accession. Of the reservations issued at the time of signature, some have not been confirmed at the moment of ratification, others have been confirmed.

---

[83] Sassòli, above n 78, at 64. See generally, on the role of Protecting Powers, Ch 27 of this volume.

[84] ICJ, *Reservations to the Convention on Genocide*, Advisory Opinion of 28 May 1951, at 23.

[85] 31st International Conference of the Red Cross and Red Crescent, Geneva, Switzerland, 28 November–1 December 2011, Resolution 1, Strengthening legal protection for victims of armed conflicts, 1 December 2011, para 7. See the webpage of the Swiss–ICRC Initiative to Strengthen Compliance with International Humanitarian Law, at <http://www.eda.admin.ch/eda/en/home/topics/intla/humlaw/icrc.html>.

[86] See, e.g., C. Pilloud, 'Les réserves aux conventions de Genève de 1949', 58 *IRRC* (1976) 131 and 195, at 132; and L.S. Boudreault, 'Les réserves apportées au Protocole additionnel I aux Conventions de Genève sur le droit humanitaire', 6 *Revue québécoise de droit international* (1989/1990) 105.

[87] ICRC Commentary APs, at 1059–60, para 3666, and at 1063–4, paras 3681–5.

[88] J. Gaudreau, 'Les réserves aux Protocoles additionnels aux Conventions de Genève pour la protection des victimes de la guerre', 85 *IRRC* (2003) 143, at 150; and R. Kolb, *Ius in bello. Le droit international des conflits armés* (2nd edn, Brussels: Bruylant, 2009), at 151.

Some reservations were also withdrawn several years after their issuance.[89] Some of them are statements of non-recognition and should therefore not be considered properly as reservations.[90] Others may be considered rather as interpretative declarations or declarations of intention, or as the result of a misunderstanding. A relatively small number of them do really have a modificatory or abrogative character, and have in some cases effectively given rise to objections by third states parties (such as the US).[91] In no case has a state refused to enter into conventional relationships with a state that has issued a contentious reservation. If a state becomes party to the Geneva Conventions through a notification of succession (see MN 27–35), the generally accepted rule is that any reservations are presumed to apply unless the new state expressly renounces the benefit of the reservations (see Article 20 of the Vienna Convention on Succession of States in Matters of Treaties).[92]

55   This is not the place for an exhaustive analysis of the reservations and the controversies that some of them have engendered.[93] Let us only remind ourselves that in some cases, controversial reservations have later given rise to developments in conventional law. Thus, reservations issued by such states as Guinea-Bissau, regarding the conditions for resistance movements to be recognized as combatants, have paved the way for the compromise solution of Article 44(3) AP I. In another field, Israel's declaration on the use of the Red Shield of David eventually led to the adoption of AP III in 2005.

E. The Relationship with Previous Conventions: The Question of Treaties over Time on the Same Subject Matter

I. Application, termination, modification

56   It is material from the outset to distinguish application from termination, when dealing with relations between successive treaties. Unsurprisingly, the VCLT accurately differentiates these two scenarios by providing two separate rules for governing them. The issue of the application of treaties over time is regulated by Article 30 VCLT, whilst the topic of termination of treaties on account of the conclusion of a treaty on the same subject matter is governed by Article 59 VCLT.

57   As far as application is concerned, and leaving aside as irrelevant in this context the question of the primacy of application of the UN Charter over any other international agreement, Article 30(3) VCLT sets out the general rule according to which, if all the states are parties to the successive treaties, the 'earlier treaty applies only to the extent that its provisions are compatible with those of the later treaty'. This regime is thus established, unless, as envisaged in Article 30(2), the later treaty specifies 'that it is subject to, or that it is not to be considered as incompatible with, an earlier or later treaty'. The Geneva Conventions of 1949 do not so specify.

---

[89] See the reservations to Art 68 para 2 GC IV (death penalty in occupied territories) issued by the UK and Australia.
[90] See 'Guide to Practice on Reservation to Treaties', in ILC, *Report on the Work of its Sixty-Third Session (26 April to 3 June and 4 July to 12 August 2011)*, UN Doc A/66/10, at 12–51 and UN Doc A/66/10, Add 1, at 94–7, para 1.5.1; Gaudreau, above n 88, at 147.
[91] On the reservations of the USSR and other socialist states, and the objection by the US, see R.R. Baxter, 'The Geneva Conventions of 1949 before the United States Senate', 49 *AJIL* (1955) 550.
[92] See also G.P. Buzzini, 'Article 20', in Distefano and Gaggioli (eds), above n 37.
[93] See, for an almost exhaustive treatment of the question, Pilloud, above n 86.

II. Relationship with prior Hague Conventions and the earlier Geneva Conventions[94]

As far as termination is concerned, Article 59 VCLT envisages that the termination of a prior treaty by the conclusion of a later one can result either from an express stipulation in the latter treaty, or, failing such provision, if such an intention of the Parties can be 'otherwise established' (Article 59(1)(a)). Alternatively, the conclusion of the later treaty may lead to the termination of the prior treaty if 'provisions of the later treaty are so far incompatible with those of the earlier one that the two treaties are not capable of being applied at the same time' (Article 59(1)(b)). As far as this possibility is concerned, the VCLT's solution is in line with its other provisions, i.e. either an explicit provision contained in the treaty, or the states parties' intention to terminate the earlier treaty. In this last scenario, as elsewhere in germane VCLT provisions, the burden of proof is placed on the shoulders of the state which alleges it. Article 59(1)(b), nevertheless, puts the emphasis, failing fulfilment of the conditions set out in the previous paragraph, on the intrinsic radical incompatibility of the earlier treaty provisions with those embodied in the later treaty. 58

a. Hague Conventions (1899 and 1907)

As Article 58 GC II sets out in an uncontroversial manner, that Convention 'replaces the Xth Hague Convention of October 18, 1907, for the adaptation to Maritime Warfare of the principles of the Geneva Convention of 1906, in relations between the High Contracting Parties'. We are clearly faced with an example of the application of the aforementioned Article 59(1)(a) VCLT (see MN 58). Since nowadays all states parties to the Xth 1907 Hague Convention are parties to GC II, the latter Convention definitively applies in the relations between High Contracting Parties. 59

The situation is different as regards the relations between Geneva Conventions III and IV and the Hague Regulations. According to the relevant provisions of GC III and GC IV, those instruments are designed to be 'complementary' (Article 135 GC III) and 'supplementary' (Article 154 GC IV), respectively, to the relevant Chapters and Sections of the Hague Regulations. The slight difference of wording—only in the English text—between the relevant provisions of GC III and GC IV does not seem to have any legal consequence; the clearly expressed intention in both cases is that the new Geneva Conventions should not be seen as completely 'replacing' the Hague Regulations.[95] The cautious wording used by this provision is on a par with established international treaties' drafting techniques, in so far as it aims to stress that not only is it assumed that there is no divergence between the Conventions concerned, but also that the later treaty is founded upon the same principles as the earlier ones. 60

As far as GC IV is specifically concerned, it ought to be noted that its scope is slightly narrower than that of the 1907 Regulations, for the latter dealt not only with the treatment of civilians but also with the conduct of hostilities or the administration of occupied territories. Therefore, these aspects and issues are not addressed in GC IV unless they have an impact on the protection of civilians. In this sense, then, the term 'supplementary' must be construed so as to encompass the common scope of GC IV and the 1907 Regulations.[96] 61

---

[94] See also Ch 34, section C, of this volume.
[95] Pictet Commentary III, at 636; Pictet Commentary IV at 613.
[96] R.T. Yingling and R.W. Ginnane, 'The Geneva Conventions of 1949', 46 *AJIL* (1952) 393, at 417: 'Thus, those articles of the Hague Regulations (such as Articles 43 and 55) which have no counterpart in the Civilian

b. Geneva Conventions (1864, 1906, and 1929)

62 As regards the former Geneva Conventions, GC I and GC III are deemed to 'replace' their prior namesake conventions, although they do not abrogate them. Thus, according to its Article 59, GC I is intended to '[replace] the Conventions of 22 August 1864, 6 July 1906, and 27 July 1929, in relations between the High Contracting Parties', while GC III 'replaces the Convention of July 27, 1929, in relations between the High Contracting Parties'. As pointed out above (see MN 58), unless an explicit intention can be found, the 'replacement' of the 1929 Conventions, by GC I and GC III does not amount to the former's abrogation.[97] Therefore, states parties to both of them are simultaneously bound by them, and in the event of conflicting provisions, prior Geneva Conventions will then bow before subsequent ones.

F. Denunciation

I. Regime

63 There are many reasons why a treaty might be terminated, or why a party might wish to withdraw from it; obviously, one of them is that the treaty will cease to be applied 'in conformity with [its] provisions' (Article 54(a) VCLT). The solution embodied in the Geneva Conventions (Article 63 GC I; Article 62 GC II; Article 142 GC III; Article 158 GC IV)—and reiterated in AP I (Article 99), AP II (Article 25), and AP III (Article 14)—pertains to this provision. In this regard, the Geneva Conventions appear to be rather old-fashioned, especially if one takes into account that they clearly are law-making treaties, i.e. establishing general and abstract rules of behaviour. Therefore, at least from this angle, the Geneva Conventions are not really innovative, for they leave unaffected the High Contracting Parties' innate right to liberate themselves from them.

a. Legal effects

64 According to the law of treaties, denunciation is a means by which a state party to a treaty may show its intention not to be bound by the treaty anymore. Since the Geneva Conventions are multilateral treaties, denunciation by one or more of the parties will not, of course, lead to their termination but merely to those states' withdrawal from the Conventions. Therefore, the legal effect of denunciation impacts upon the status of the state as party to the Geneva Conventions, and not on the very existence of the Conventions, as common paragraph 4 of Articles 63/62/142/158 rightly affirms, mirroring Article 70(2) VCLT. In other words, the denouncing state merely terminates its participation in the particular treaty, without affecting the latter's existence: as the treaty has been maintained, withdrawal ultimately consists in a termination limited *ratione personarum*.[98] The breakdown of a multilateral treaty into a set of bilateral treaties founded upon the strict principle of reciprocity, allows the denouncing party to withdraw from this 'network of

---

Convention continue to bind states which are parties to both the Hague and Geneva Civilian Conventions. And states which are bound by the Hague Conventions, but not by the Civilian Convention, will remain subject to the Hague Regulations relating to occupied territory.'

[97] Pictet Commentary GC I, at 407; Pictet Commentary GC III, at 636.
[98] F. Capotorti, 'L'extinction et la suspension des traités', 134 *RCADI* (1971-III) 417, at 465.

bilateral treaties linking states parties two by two',⁹⁹ thus rendering possible the survival of the treaty between the other parties.

In spite of its neutral and uncontroversial formulation, common paragraph 4 (Articles 63/62/142/158) hides one of the most shining achievements of IHL heralded by the Geneva Conventions, namely the repudiation of the *si omnes* clause.¹⁰⁰ It was introduced (in the 1868 Saint Petersburg Declaration and later in the 1899 Hague Conventions II and III) in order to ensure a perfect equality between belligerents in the same conflict.¹⁰¹ Indeed, unlike prior Geneva Conventions and the Hague Conventions, the 1929 Geneva Conventions adamantly rejected this clause (by its sheer absence and by the introduction of the undertaking to respect the Conventions 'in all circumstances'¹⁰²), not only on humanitarian grounds but also on account of its adherence to the law of treaties as codified in Articles 54 to 56 and 70(2) VCLT, thus renouncing one of the (hardly praiseworthy) peculiarities of the Conventions dealing with the law of armed conflict.

The issue of the denunciation of the Geneva Conventions remains (and, it is hoped, is bound to remain) moot, since so far no state has ever dared to withdraw from any of the current Geneva Conventions, nor from prior ones.

b. *Procedure*

Like the traditional regime set up by centuries of treaty drafting, the Geneva Conventions establish a specific procedure for the right of denunciation to be implemented by a state party. On the one hand, it must be noted that the withdrawal will take effect one year after the notification of denunciation is made. This time span is consonant with traditional practice. On the other hand, and here the Geneva Conventions clearly depart from the orthodox path, 'a denunciation of which notification has been made at a time when the denouncing Power is involved in a conflict shall not take effect until peace has been concluded, and until after operations connected with release and repatriation of the persons protected by the present Convention have been terminated' (common paragraph 3 of the relevant provisions—see MN 63). This delayed effect of denunciation was an innovation in the general international law of the time. It mirrors the (opposite) scenario of the 'immediate effect' of some of the Geneva Conventions' provisions after ratification (or accession), pending the entry into force of the Conventions vis-à-vis the state having notified them to the Depositary, if the state in question is involved in a conflict (see MN 42–45).¹⁰³

In accordance with the law of treaties, the denunciation must be notified in writing, as for any other procedural acts relating to invalidity, termination, and suspension. Unsurprisingly, the Geneva Conventions make no exception in this respect. In accordance

---

⁹⁹ H. Ascensio, 'Article 70. Convention of 1969', in Klein and Corten (eds), above n 8, vol II, 1585, at 1601.

¹⁰⁰ In fact only GC II had the effect of 'abrogating' the *si omnes* clause of Art 18 of the 1907 Hague Convention (X) for the Adaptation to Maritime Warfare of the Principles of the Geneva; GC I and GC III only confirmed the previous corresponding provisions of 1929 GCs, and GC IV was a new Convention. See also Ch 1 of this volume at MN 11.

¹⁰¹ See S. Watts, 'Reciprocity and the Law of War', 50 *Harvard International Law Journal* (2009) 365, at 397–8 and 417.

¹⁰² C. Focarelli, 'Common Article 1 of the 1949 Geneva Conventions: A Soap Bubble?', 21 *EJIL* (2010) 125, at 130–1. See also Ch 6, section E.III., of this volume.

¹⁰³ P. Guggenheim, *Traité de droit international public* (Genève: Librairie de l'Université, 1953) vol II, at 311. But see already Art 38 para 3 of the 1929 GC I, and Art 96 para 3 of 1929 GC II. See Ch 3 of this volume for the temporal scope of application of the Conventions, and Ch 51 for the question of the repatriation of POWs.

with common paragraph 2, denunciations will be 'notified' to the Depositary, which in turn will transmit them to the other contracting parties.

II. Relationship with customary international law on the same subject matter

69 Common paragraph 4 of the relevant provisions (see MN 63) holds in clear terms that a state which has withdrawn from the Geneva Conventions 'shall remain bound to fulfil [the obligations] by virtue of the principles of the law of nations, as they result from the usages established among civilized peoples'. The international legal order is characterized by a plurality of sources as well as their equivalent normative strength. In this vein, one ought to observe that the principle of plurality of sources, and its consequences on the denunciation of a treaty, is adamantly affirmed in Article 43 VCLT, the last clause of which affirms that the termination of or withdrawal from a treaty 'shall not in any way impair the duty of any State to fulfil any obligation embodied in the treaty to which it would be subject under international law *independently* of the treaty' (emphasis added).[104]

70 Having regard specifically to the Geneva Conventions, it is significant that the ICJ, while quoting precisely common paragraph 4 of Articles 63/62/142/158, held in the *Nicaragua* case that it 'sees no need to take a position on that matter, since in its view the conduct of the United States (US) may be judged according to the fundamental general principles of humanitarian law; in its view, the Geneva Conventions are in some respects a development, and in other respects no more than the expression, of such principles'.[105] Thus, in the unlikely event that a state withdraws from any of the Geneva Conventions, it will nonetheless be bound by corresponding customary international law rules, the content of which has been authoritatively set out in the ICRC CIHL Study.

71 The existence of a right of denunciation raises the (fortunately theoretical) question of the conclusion by hypothetical (denouncing) states of other treaties differing from the Geneva Conventions in that they would provide lesser protection. According to the principle of *lex specialis ratione personarum*, such a treaty should be applied in priority to the Geneva Conventions. But this would be precluded by the *jus cogens* quality of most of the customary rules reflected in the Geneva Conventions, thus rendering any such treaty void *ab initio* (Article 53 VCLT).[106] In this connection, the Martens Clause (section G of this chapter) is often invoked to attest to the peremptory character of the principles of IHL.[107]

---

[104] See, e.g., K. Bannelier, 'Article 43. Convention of 1969', in Corten and Klein (eds), above n 8, vol II, 1031, at 1033–4. See also ICJ, *Military and Paramilitary Activities in and against Nicaragua (Nicaragua v United States of America)*, Merits, Judgment, 27 June 1986, at 95, 96, paras 178, 179.

[105] ICJ, *Nicaragua v United States of America*, above n 104, at 113, para 218.

[106] See David, above n 36, at 106–14; C. Greenwood, 'Historical Development and Legal Basis', in D. Fleck (ed), *The Handbook of International Humanitarian Law* (2nd edn, Oxford: OUP, 2009) 1, at 39; Kolb, above n 88, at 144–8; Sassòli/Bouvier/Quintin, vol I, Part I, Chapter 13, at 35. See also, e.g., P. Reuter, 'Principes de droit international public', 103 *RCADI* (1961) 425, at 466–7; A. Gómez Robledo, 'Le *ius cogens* international: sa genèse, sa nature, ses fonctions', 172 *RCADI* (1981) 9, at 179.

[107] Council of State of Belgium, *Projet de loi portant assentiment au Statut de Rome de la Cour pénale internationale*, Opinion of 21 April 1999, partly reproduced in J. Verhaegen, 'L'article 31.1.c. du statut de la Cour pénale internationale. Un autre négationnisme?', in H.-D. Bosly et al (eds), *Actualité du droit international humanitaire* (Brussels: La Charte, 2001) 93, at 118; Constitutional Court of Colombia, *Revisión de constitucionalidad del 'Protocolo adicional a los Convenios de Ginebra del 12 de agosto de 1949, relativo a la protección de las víctimas de los conflictos armados sin carácter internacional (Protocolo II)' hecho en Ginebra 8 de junio de 1977, y de la Ley 171 del 16 de diciembre de 1994, por medio de la cual se aprueba dicho Protocolo, proceso que fue*

G. Martens Clause, International Humanitarian Law's Innovative Solution

As already stated (MN 69), the denunciation of the Geneva Conventions may not liberate the denouncing state from its obligations under customary international law ('usages established among civilized peoples'). Thus, the relevant provisions of the Conventions (Article 63 paragraph 4 GC I; Article 62 paragraph 4 GC II; Article 142 paragraph 4 GC III; Article 158 paragraph 4 GC IV) operate as a reminder that customary international law binds the states independently of their conventional commitments. A few authors deny them any further function.[108] But the relevant provisions of the Geneva Conventions, inspired by the original wording of the so-called Martens Clause[109]—named after the Russian diplomat and university professor Fyodor Fyodorovich Martens (also known as Friedrich Fromhold von Martens)—previously inserted in the Preamble to the Hague Convention II of 1899, are conspicuously more expressive, stating that the denunciation 'shall in no way impair the obligations which the Parties to the conflict shall remain bound to fulfil by virtue of the principles of the law of nations, as they result from the usages established among civilized peoples, *from the laws of humanity* and *the dictates of the public conscience*' (emphasis added), thus adding two more potential 'sources' of those 'principles of the law of nations'. 72

Despite the considerable number of scholarly studies on the topic, the debate in the doctrine is still ongoing as to the exact interpretation of the Martens Clause.[110] But let us insist that the 'reminder' thesis presently represents the lowest common denominator, being the only generally accepted interpretation of the Martens Clause in the Geneva Conventions. 73

---

radicado con el No. L.A.T.-040, Sentencia No C-225/95, 18 May 1995. See also S. Miyazaki, 'The Martens Clause and International Humanitarian Law', in Mélanges Pictet 433, at 436–9.

[108] Greenwood, above n 106, at 34–5.

[109] 'Until a more complete code of the laws of war is issued, the High Contracting Parties think it right to declare that in cases not included in the Regulations adopted by them, populations and belligerents remain under the protection and empire of the principles of international law, as they result from the usages established between civilized nations, from the laws of humanity, and the requirements of the public conscience' (para 8 of the Preamble to the 1899 Hague Convention II).

[110] See esp F. Münch, 'Die Martenssche Klausel und die Grundlagen des Völkerrechts', 36 *ZaöRV* (1976) 347–73; Miyazaki, above n 107; T. Meron, 'On Custom and the Antecedents of the Martens Clause in Medieval and Renaissance Ordinance of War', in U. Beyerlin et al (eds), *Recht zwischen Umbruch und Bewahrung: Festschrift für Rudolf Bernhardt* (Berlin: Springer Verlag, 1995) 173; P. Benvenuti, 'La Clausola Martens e la tradizione classica del diritto naturale nella codificazione del diritto dei conflitti armati', in *Scritti degli allievi in memoria di Giuseppe Barile* (Padova: CEDAM, 1995) 173; V.V. Pustogarov, 'Fyodor Fyodorovich Martens (1845–1909)—A Humanist of Modern Times', 312 *IRRC* (1996) 322; R. Ticehurst, 'The Martens Clause and the Laws of Armed Conflict', 317 *IRRC* (1997) 125; V.V. Pustogarov, 'The Martens Clause in International Law', 1 *Journal of the History of International Law* (1999) 125; T. Meron, 'The Martens Clause, Principles of Humanity, and Dictates of Public Conscience', 94 *AJIL* (2000) 78; A. Cassese, 'The Martens Clause: Half a Loaf or Simply Pie in the Sky', 11 *EJIL* (2000) 188; R. Schircks, *Die Martens'sche Klausel: Rezeption und Rechtsqualität* (Baden-Baden: Nomos, 2002); D. Fleck, 'Friedrich Martens: A Great International Lawyer from Pärnu', 10 *Baltic Defence Review* (2003) 19; C. Swinarski, 'Articulation entre le droit de La Haye et le droit de Genève au lendemain des conférences de 1906 et de 1907', in Y. Daudet (ed), *Actualité de la Conférence de La Haye de 1907, Deuxième Conférence de la Paix* (Leiden/London: Martinus Nijhoff Publishers, 2008) 259, at 268; M.N. Hayashi, 'The Martens Clause and Military Necessity', in H.M. Hensel (ed), *The Legitimate Use of Military Force: The Just War Tradition and the Customary Law of Armed Conflict* (Aldershot: Ashgate, 2008) 135; T. Rensman, 'Die Humanisierung des Völkerrechts durch das *ius in bello*—Von der Martens'schen Klausel zur "*Responsibility to Protect*"', 68 *ZaöRV* (2008) 111; M. Salter, 'Reinterpreting Competing Interpretations of the Scope and Potential of the Martens Clause', *Journal of Conflict & Security Law* (2012) 1; J. von Bernstorff, 'Martens Clause', in MPEPIL, vol VI, 1143–6.

There is a consensus that the principles alluded to in the Martens Clause pertain at least to the material, as opposed to the formal, sources of IHL.[111] There also seems to be agreement that the clause does not amount to the addition of a new formal source of international law.[112] Before examining the different interpretations of the Martens Clause, let us consider its wider legal and historical context.

I. Origins and context of the adoption of the Martens Clause

74 Even though a fragmentary avatar may be found in the 1868 Saint-Petersburg Declaration's '*lois de l'humanité*',[113] the Martens Clause originated in The Hague First Peace Conference of 1899, and was inserted in the Hague Convention (II) with Respect to the Laws and Customs of War on Land. On the genesis of the clause,[114] it has been noted that the 'Russian publicist did not intend also to envisage the possibility of considering "the laws of humanity" and the "dictates of public conscience" as distinct sources of law. He used loose language for the purpose merely of solving a diplomatic problem',[115] i.e. the *levée en masse* by the population while the territory was already occupied by the invader. In order to avert a fiasco—as had happened for the same reason in Brussels (1874)—the chief of the Russian delegation designed this clause so that, even though this specific scenario of *levée en masse* was not governed by the Convention (II), 'populations and belligerents [were] to remain under the protection and empire of the principles of international law, as they result from the usages established between civilized nations, from the laws of humanity, and the requirements of the public conscience', which meant in practice that the *franc-tireurs* could no longer be summarily executed.

75 Another prominent delegate at both Hague Conferences, Baron Descamps, later indicated in a very straightforward fashion that he saw in the clause more than a verbose slogan designed to reach an empty diplomatic compromise. During the drafting of what would finally become Article 38(1)(c) of the Permanent Court of International Justice (PCIJ) Statute, to avoid the *non liquet*, the Committee of Jurists considered a third category of source of law[116] in which to look for rules to resolve the conflict and thereby accomplish

---

[111] See, e.g., IACtHR, *Barrios Altos Case—Chumbipuma Aguirre and others v Peru*, Merits, Judgment of 14 March 2001, Concurring Opinion of Judge Cançado Trindade, para 25.

[112] ICTY, *The Prosecutor v Zoran Kupreškić, Mirjan Kupreškić, Vlatko Kupreškić, Drago Kupreškić, Dragan Papić, Vladimir Šantić*, Trial Chamber, Judgment, 14 January 2000, IT-95-16-T, para 525. See also the position of the US Government in the 'Memorandum of Reservations of the USA' appended to the report of the 'Commission on the Responsibility of the Authors of the War and on Enforcement of Penalities', 14 *AJIL* (1920) 99, at 147. See also the positions of various states in the framework of the advisory proceeding on the legality of the threat or use of nuclear weapons synthesized in Ticehurst, above n 110. In this sense, see also G. Schwarzenberger, *The Frontiers of International Law* (London: Stevens & Sons Limited, 1962), at 261 and 264–9. See, though, ILC, *Summary Records of the Meetings of the Forty-Sixth Session*, 2 May–22 July 1994, II(1) *YILC*, 1994, vol II(1), at 6, para 42 (Tomuschat): 'General international law comprised rules of customary law, which in turn derived from practice and *opinio juris*. [...] General international law had a second source, the dictates of the conscience of mankind (the Martens clause), as underlined by ICJ in its judgment in the Corfu Channel case and the advisory opinion it had delivered in connection with reservations to the Convention on the Prevention and Punishment of the Crime of Genocide.'

[113] See also Art 14 of the *Tratado de Armisticio* of 1820 between Spain and Colombia, according to which the parties engage themselves to conclude 'un tratado que regularice la guerra conforme al derecho de gentes, y a las prácticas más liberales, sabias y humanas, de las naciones civilizadas'.

[114] On the preparatory works and the genesis of the clause, see Cassese, above n 110.

[115] Ibid, at 201–2.

[116] In other words, a 'topos' as evoked by G. Abi-Saab, 'Cours général de droit international public', 207 *RCADI* (1987) 9, at 186.

the goal, namely, the 'general principles of law recognized by civilized nations'. In this context, Baron Descamps tried unsuccessfully to incorporate the clause into the PCIJ Statute as a general source of international law. In the course of the discussion, he referred to the principles alluded to in the Martens Clause in explicitly jusnaturalistic terms, speaking of the 'loi fondamentale du juste et de l'injuste, profondément gravée au cœur de tout être humain et qui reçoit son expression la plus haute dans la conscience juridique des peuples civilisés', thus evoking Cicero's *recta ratio*.[117] According to other authors, these 'principles of international law' did not yet exist, thus denying the 1899 clause any norm-generating effect.[118]

It might be considered that the concept of general principles of law, along with the Martens Clause, both being products of the early twentieth century's *Zeitgeist*, pertain to the last remnants of moribund jusnaturalism vis-à-vis triumphant volontarism. According to Quadri, the general principles of law are considered as evidence of the '*status coscientiae*' of the international community.[119] That the Martens Clause and Quadri's construction of Article 38(1)(c) of the ICJ Statute are intimately related is shown, inter alia, by Shabuddeen's dissenting opinion appended to the 1996 ICJ Advisory Opinion on the *Legality of Nuclear Weapons*.[120]

a. A leitmotiv of international (humanitarian) law

After its initial adoption in the Preamble to Hague Convention II of 1899, and later in the revised version of 1907, the Martens Clause has often been reiterated—although with minor modernizing adaptations to the drafting—almost becoming a mantra of conventional humanitarian law,[121] and thus giving additional weight to the opinion of the ICJ, according to which the clause itself has become part of customary international law.[122] In 1968, the Diplomatic Conference on Human Rights requested the Secretary-General of the UN to remind the UN member states of their obligations under the Martens Clause,

---

[117] PCIJ–Advisory Committee of Jurists, *Procès-Verbaux of the Proceedings of the Committee* (The Hague: Van Langenhuysen Bothers, 1920), at 310 and 323–4. For a similar, earlier, explicitly Ciceronian reference, see G. Rolin-Jaequemyns, *La guerre actuelle dans ses rapports avec le droit international* (Gand: Imprimerie et lithographie de I.S. van Doosselaere, 1870), at 40. For a study of the links between the language of the clause and the doctrines of natural law, see Benvenuti, above n 110.

[118] F. von Liszt, *Le droit international* (transl from the 9th German edn, Paris: Pedone, 1928), at 314 (para 40). The German jurist went on to deplore the mistaken belief that confused 'les principes du christianisme et les lois de l'humanité, avec les règles positives du droit international' (at 323). *Contra*, rightly, Judge Shahabuddeen (ICJ, *Legality of the Threat or Use of Nuclear Weapons*, Advisory Opinion, 8 July 1996, Dissenting Opinion of Judge Shahabuddeen, at 406), according to whom the mere literal interpretation of the verb 'remain' would indicate the pre-existence (parallel) of other rules of international law, whatever their sources might be. Modern authors rightly point out that general principles of IHL count among the sources of IHL, independently from customary or conventional international law, under the heading of general principles of law. See, e.g., J.L. Rodríguez Villasante y Prieto, 'Las fuentes del derecho internacional humanitario', in J.L. Rodríguez Villasante y Prieto, *Derecho internacional humanitario* (Valencia: Tirant lo Blanch, 2007), at 62; V. Lowe, *International Law* (Oxford: OUP, 2007), at 283.

[119] R. Quadri, 'Cours général de droit international public', 113 *RCADI* (1964-III) 237, at 351.

[120] ICJ, *Legality of the Threat or Use of Nuclear Weapons*, above n 118, Dissenting Opinion of Judge Shahabuddeen, at 410: '[B]ut, so far as the Martens Clause is concerned, the views of States are relevant only for their value in indicating the state of the public conscience, not for the purpose of determining whether an *opinio juris* exists as to the legality of the use of a particular weapon.' The distinguished Guyanan Judge referred to the same concept by resorting to the germane formula 'state of "human conscience and reason"'.

[121] See, for a list of IHL treaties including the Martens Clause, von Bernstorff above n 110, at 1144.

[122] ICJ, *Legality of the Threat or Use of Nuclear Weapons*, above n 118, at 260, para 87; ICTY, *The Prosecutor v Zoran Kupreškić, Mirjan Kupreškić, Vlatko Kupreškić, Drago Kupreškić, Dragan Papić, Vladimir Šantić*, above n 112, para 525.

thus making official the nexus between human rights and IHL.[123] More recently, the clause has also been reproduced in the Preamble to the 2008 Oslo Convention on Cluster Munitions. On this occasion, the Diplomatic Conference stressed 'the role of public conscience in furthering the principles of humanity', and recognized 'the efforts to that end undertaken by the United Nations, the International Committee of the Red Cross, the Cluster Munition Coalition and numerous other non-governmental organisations across the world',[124] thus making plain that the manifestation of 'public conscience' in the international realm is not a purely interstate matter—although its ascertainment might well be.[125]

b. Impact of the specific place and wording of the Clause in the Geneva Conventions of 1949

78   While it is found in the Preamble to the 1899 Hague Convention II, and in Article 1(2) AP I and again in the Preamble to AP II, the Martens Clause is located in the final provisions of the Geneva Conventions which are devoid of an extended preamble stating their object and purpose. Over the years and through codifications over time, the original clause, created to meet a specific perceived need resulting from the conduct of hostilities (see MN 74), ended up encompassing all those cases not (or not sufficiently) governed by treaty rules. Article 1(2) AP I clearly belongs in this category. On the contrary, the latter's field of application seems to be different compared to that found in the Geneva Conventions, which refer to the clause in the scenario of denunciation and not in general, i.e. 'in cases not covered by this Protocol'. In other words, it may be tentatively argued that while in AP I (and in the Hague Conventions), the clause pursues the goal of supplementing treaty obligations by referring to custom, humanity, and public conscience, in the Geneva Conventions the clause addresses a specific need, arising out of their denunciation by a state party: the latter, though liberated from its treaty obligations, remains subject to other sources of law and constraints.

79   One might wonder whether any sensible consideration of its function and nature could be inferred from the different location of the Martens Clause in different instruments. Therefore, while in the Preamble the clause would be deemed to operate *failing* any regulation by the treaty (this was, by the way, one of the original roles of the clause in 1899), in the Geneva Conventions it might be argued that the clause would be triggered only by a denunciation, and thus it would be applicable to the denouncing state alone. In the same vein, could we reasonably assume that, in the case of AP I, if a state withdraws from it, it is no longer bound by the Martens Clause (due to its absence from the denunciation provision); and, conversely, that state parties to the Geneva Conventions are not bound by the Martens Clause since it is not in the Preamble, and that it applies to

---

[123] Res XXIII, 'Human Rights in Armed Conflicts', in *Final Act of the International Conference on Human Rights: Teheran 22 April to 13 May 1968*, UN Doc A/CONF./32/41, at 18.

[124] See also the Preamble to the 1997 Ottawa Convention on the Prohibition of the Use, Stockpiling, Production and Transfer of Anti-Personnel Mines and on their Destruction.

[125] See, e.g., M. Byers, *War Law: International Law and Armed Conflict* (London: Atlantic Books, 2005), at 122: 'Most international humanitarian law treaties contain something called the Martens Clause [...]. International humanitarian law is, in part, what you and I and the rest of the people on this planet determine it to be.' But see the more cautious approach of K. Anderson, 'The Ottawa Convention Banning Landmines, the Role of International Non-governmental Organizations and the Idea of Internationational Civil Society', 11 *EJIL* (2000) 91.

them only when they withdraw from the Geneva Conventions?[126] A negative answer is called for, given the established customary character of the Martens Clause. Following a black-letter law reading, it is furthermore sound to assume that since AP I completes the Geneva Conventions then, for a state party to both of the treaties, the Martens Clause eventually fulfils both functions (covering withdrawal and supplementing the two treaties).

Although it has been suggested that the slightly different wording of the clause adopted in AP I might have an impact on its meaning, 'depriving [it] of its intrinsic coherence and legal logic',[127] it seems, according to a prominent actor and witness to the drafting process of AP I, that 'a strict linguistic approach should not obscure the policy effects that were pursued and finally reached at the Diplomatic Conference'.[128]

II. The functions of the Martens Clause

As already mentioned, it is beyond doubt that the Martens Clause ranks among those principles, desiderata, and concepts—roughly grouped together under the tag 'substantive source'—which nourish and pervade the norms of IHL.[129] While, as the ICJ famously stated in the *South West Africa Cases*, 'it is necessary *not to confuse the moral ideal with the legal rules intended to give it effect*' (emphasis added),[130] it has been held by numerous authors that the Martens Clause plays a specific role in the relationships between positive international law and natural law or morals. Therefore, according to these writers, the clause would play the role of a catalytic agent—the 'positivation' of the 'Radbruch formula' in the international legal order?—allowing for certain moral imperatives to be filtered into positive law.[131] For Tomuschat, for example,

[t]he Martens Clause shows that there exists no watertight dam separating law and morals. In situations of extreme gravity, moral principles may convert themselves into positivist law if that law does

---

[126] See likewise Münch, above n 110, at 358. See also, F. Münch, 'A propos du droit spontané', in *Studi in onore di Giuseppe Sperduti* (Milan: A. Giuffrè, 1984) 149, at 161–2.

[127] Meron, 'The Martens clause,' above n 110, at 81. See also in this respect, Cassese, above n 110, at 209. Indeed, one cannot but share what this late authority wrote: 'The restrictive wording of the Preamble of the Second Additional Protocol only reflects the recalcitrance of the States gathered at Geneva in 1974–1977 in extensively regulating internal armed conflicts' (ibid, at 210).

[128] Fleck, above n 110, at 24.

[129] See *The Flick Trial*, in United Nations War Crimes Commission (UNWCC) (ed), *Law Reports of Trials of War Criminals* (London: HMSO, 1947–9) vol IX, at 33.

[130] ICJ, *South West Africa Cases (Liberia and Ethiopia v South Africa) (Second Phase)*, Judgment, 18 July 1966, paras 50, 52, at 34, 35. See also ICJ, *Legality of the Threat or Use of Nuclear Weapons*, above n 118, at 34, para 49: 'The Court must now turn to certain questions of a wider character. Throughout this case it has been suggested, directly or indirectly, that humanitarian considerations are sufficient in themselves to generate legal rights and obligations, and that the Court can and should proceed accordingly. The Court does not think so. It is a court of law, and can take account of moral principles only in so far as these are given a sufficient expression in legal form. Law exists, it is said, to serve a social need; but precisely for that reason it can do so only through and within the limits of its own discipline. Otherwise, it is not a legal service that would be rendered.' Zagor rightly pegged this passage as 'somewhat anomalous': M. Zagor, 'Elementary Considerations of Humanity', in K. Bannelier, T. Christakis, and S. Heathcote (eds), *The ICJ and the Evolution of International Law: The Enduring Impact of the Corfu Channel Case* (London/New York: Routledge, 2012) 264, at 279.

[131] In 1911, an authority construed the Martens Clause in such a way that, having in mind the incompleteness of the Laws of War, 'it is necessary to appeal to the best customs of the best peoples, and even to supplement and modify them by moral considerations, in order to fill up the gaps in the laws of war'. This author then writes of a method to which he will resort in order to expound this body of international law: see T.J. Lawrence, *The Principles of International Law* (4th edn, London: McMillan & Co Ltd, 1911), at 395. See also P.-M. Dupuy, 'Les "considérations élémentaires d'humanité" dans la jurisprudence de la Cour internationale

not provide for the necessary instruments to deal with the situation at hand. It may well be that the drafters of the Clause were not aware of its potential impact and that its actual text was the result of a diplomatic settlement.[132]

82 But caution is also called for in order not to stretch the scope of the clause too far.[133] While the clause has historically played a great role in the development of IHL, there is no certainty that future invocations will necessarily receive general acceptance. According to certain authors, the principles alluded to in the clause could be ascertained only through 'deductive logic' from established positive law.[134] While this has not necessarily been the case in the past, reference to established rules applicable in other fields, such as human rights law, might be a good way to build a solid argument on the clause.

83 Summing up, the differing functions of the Martens Clause within the Geneva Conventions and IHL at large may be grouped into three general categories, namely: the use of the clause as an interpretative tool; the clause as a principle enshrining substantive standards;[135] and the above-mentioned 'reminder of customary international law' function.

a. The thesis of a simple renvoi to customary international law

84 By reaffirming that humanity is undoubtedly one of the paramount principles which permeate and pervade the whole of IHL, the Martens Clause prevents escape clauses such as Article 62 VCLT (roughly tagged as *clausula rebus sic stantibus*) from being invoked in the light of technological or other developments undermining the imperative of respecting humanity in armed conflicts. The clause would thus strike at the very heart of any argument based on the evolution of the art of war as a ground for diluting, or even discarding, international humanitarian rules. Thus the ICJ asserted in its Advisory Opinion on the *Legality of Nuclear Weapons* that the clause 'has proved to be an effective means of addressing the rapid evolution of military technology'.[136] This function of the Martens Clause stresses its dynamic aspect: the principles of humanity being immutable, nevertheless their 'practical effect would vary from time to time'[137] according to the 'requirements of the public conscience'. From this perspective, the clause could be considered as a potent normative 'mastic', purporting to fill some holes and gaps created as a result of new technologies or new methods of waging war, while waiting for IHL to catch up by the usual modes of law-making (treaties and custom).

---

de justice', in R.-J. Dupuy and L.-A. Sicilianos (eds), *Mélanges en l'honneur de Nicolas Valticos. Droit et justice* (Paris: Pédone, 1999) 117, at 127; Salter, above n 110, at 31; Ticehurst, above n 110, at 134; and Pustogarov, 'The Martens Clause', above n 110, at 132 (writing of the clause as a 'connecting link between positive and natural law'). See also Kolb, above n 88, at 123–4, and A. Favre, *Principes du droit des gens* (Paris/Fribourg: L.G.D.J./ Éditions universitaires de Fribourg, 1974), at 718, both using the term 'positivation' of moral norms.

[132] C. Tomuschat, 'International Law: Ensuring the Survival of Mankind on the Eve of a New Century. General Course on Public International Law', 281 *RCADI* (1999) 9, at 356.

[133] Meron, 'The Martens Clause', above n 110, at 88 (stating that '[t]he Martens clause does not allow one to build castles of sand').

[134] See, e.g., A. Shibata, 'The Court's Decision *in silentium* on sources', in Bannelier, Christakis, and Heathcote (eds), above n 130, at 207. According to Shibata, the general principles contained in the ICJ's 'elementary considerations of humanity' are grounded in 'deductive logic' by reference to conventional law, and therefore 'are not natural law principles or principles of ethics or morality'. See also Cassese, above n 110, at 207.

[135] For a different approach, see, e.g., Kolb, above n 88, at 122–6.

[136] ICJ, *Legality of the Threat or Use of Nuclear Weapons*, above n 118, at 257, para 78.

[137] Ibid, Dissenting Opinion of Judge Shahabuddeen, at 406.

Therefore, the clause has the effect of discarding the application of the residual principle 85
governing public international law, according to which 'everything which is not expressively prohibited is permitted' (*Lotus*), by stressing the continuing relevance and specific legal weight of the general principles of IHL even in unforeseen situations.[138] In the same vein, it can arguably be said that, through the reversal of the *Lotus* paradigm, the clause goes beyond the prescription of Article 36 AP I by introducing a clear limitation on a state's freedom, faced with the silence of the law or its uncertainty, to resort to means and weapons not (yet) prohibited by a specific norm.

In fact, the clause would be redundant if its intended effect were to be limited to that of a 86 'reminder' of the binding character of customary international law. A clause with such a limited meaning would be pointless, since it would simply 'restate the obvious', viz a long-established and uncontroversial principle of general international law reflected in Article 43 VCLT.[139] This is attested by the discussions in the relevant Commission of the Diplomatic Conference. A much more sober drafting, with a limited reference to 'other obligations of international law', had been proposed during the discussions at the Diplomatic Conference but was discarded, the consensus being that the proposal was unsatisfactory. Shortly thereafter, the Commission decided to accept the proposal of Paul Geouffre de La Pradelle (Monaco), to insert the slightly modified text of the Martens Clause into the provisions relating to denunciation.[140] The principle of effectiveness thus requires giving full effect (or a 'value-added' effect) to the Martens Clause in addition to the reference to general international law. Furthermore, there would seem to be no reason why the general and abstract formulation of the clause should preclude it from having legal effects, as is sometimes affirmed.[141] In this context, Telford Taylor once wrote that '[w]e do not scrap the Constitution because learned judges cannot agree on its interpretation'.[142] It is thus safe to assume, as was affirmed by the prosecutors in the *Hostages* case, that 'full account must be taken of' the Martens Clause.[143]

b. *The clause as an interpretative aid*

The second broad function of the Martens Clause is that of a (substantive) principle of inter- 87 pretation in IHL. As with the 1948 Convention on the Prevention and Punishment of the Crime of Genocide, it is safe to affirm that the main object of the Geneva Conventions is to safeguard the 'most elementary principles of morality'[144] while preserving certain circumscribed state interests, and that, therefore, the Geneva Conventions should be interpreted with this in mind (Article 31(1) VCLT). The case law in which the clause has been quoted thus provides evidence that the Martens Clause allows for a flexible interpretation of humanitarian rules, notably by authorizing the interpreter to have recourse to interpretative tools such

---

[138] See, e.g., G. Abi-Saab, 'The Specificities of Humanitarian Law', in Mélanges Pictet 265, at 273–5; Miyazaki, above n 107, at 437; Kolb, above n 88, at 123.

[139] But see, Å. Hammarskjöld ('Consultation de M.Å. Hammarskjöld', in CICR, *La protection des populations civiles contre les bombardements* (Geneva: ICRC, 1930) 9, at 24–5), according to whom the process of codification amounts to the abolition of pre-existent customary international law.

[140] Final Record, vol II-B, at 72; and ibid, vol I, at 71. See also de La Pradelle, above n 4, at 35.

[141] See particularly Greenwood, above n 106, at 34–5. But see also H. Kelsen and R.W. Tucker, *Principles of International Law* (2nd edn, New York/Toronto: Holt Rinehart and Winston, 1966), at 114–16.

[142] T. Taylor, *Nuremberg and Vietnam: An American Tragedy* (Chicago, Ill: Quadrangle Books, 1970), at 16. See also ICJ, *Legality of the Threat or Use of Nuclear Weapons*, above n 118, Dissenting Opinion of Judge Shahabuddeen, at 410.

[143] *The Hostages Trial—Trial of Wilhelm List and others*, in UNWCC (ed), above n 129, vol VIII, at 82.

[144] ICJ, *Reservations to the Convention on Genocide*, above n 84, at 23.

as analogy, e.g. with human rights law,[145] or *a fortiori* arguments,[146] or ruling out *a contrario* argumentation.[147] Pierre-Marie Dupuy is thus justified in qualifying the clause as a kind of judicial 'joker'[148]—a function that does not seem to stray very far from the jusnaturalist legacy, in that it seems to allow the legal operator to choose the most favourable among the differing reasonable interpretations of a rule.[149]

88 If the contention that the Martens Clause introduces a new formal source inside IHL (not to speak of international law at large) must be rebutted, it can still legitimately be argued that it '*operates within the existing system of international sources* but, at least in the limited area of humanitarian law, *loosens* the requirement prescribed for *usus*, while at the same time *elevating opinio* (*iuris* or *necessitates*) to a rank higher than that normally admitted'.[150] The clause equally has been deemed able to facilitate the ascertainment of customary humanitarian rules by allowing the legal actor to put enhanced emphasis on the *opinio juris sive necessitatis* element rather than on state practice, notably in the cases of the prohibitions of torture[151] or serious sexual assault.[152] In the *Kupreškić* case, the Trial Chamber affirmed, with regard to reprisals against civilians, that it 'is an area where *opinio iuris sive necessitatis* may play a much greater role than *usus*, as a result of the aforementioned Martens Clause',[153] and that '*opinio necessitatis*, crystallising as a result of the imperatives of humanity or public conscience, may turn out to be the decisive element heralding the emergence of a general rule or principle of humanitarian law'.[154] Therefore, in a way, the Martens Clause does eventually have an impact on the secondary norm on the production of primary norms (to borrow Hart's concepts and terminology), not only by modifying the threshold of evidence but, even more importantly, by insisting on the paramount role of *opinio iuris* in the formation of customary law rules, to which, by the way, this same clause also refers in its wording. Alternatively, it could be maintained that if the *usus* is downgraded, or even discarded in the context of the Martens Clause, then it will not be inappropriate to refer to another 'source' of public international law, i.e. 'general principles of law recognized by civilized nations' under the terms of Article 38(1)(c) of the ICJ Statute.

---

[145] *Auditeur Militaire v Krumkamp*, 17 *ILR* (1950) 388 at 389–90. According to I. Brownlie, *Principles of Public International Law* (4th edn, Oxford: Clarendon Press, 1990), at 28: 'Considerations of humanity […] may be related to human values already protected by positive legal principles which, taken together, reveal certain criteria of public policy and invite the use of analogy. Such criteria have obvious connections with general principles of law and with equity, but they need no particular justification.' See also N. Ronzitti, *Diritto internazionale dei conflitti armati* (3rd edn, Turin: Giappichelli, 2006), at 136.

[146] *Trial of Josef Altstötter and others*, in UNWCC (ed), above n 129, vol VI, at 58.

[147] Meron, 'The Martens clause', above n 110, at 81.   [148] Dupuy, above n 131, at 128.

[149] See, for the distinction between '*choses favorables*' and '*choses odieuses*' for the sake of interpretation in the jusnaturalist tradition, L. Ehrlich, 'L'interprétation des traités', 24 *RCADI* (1928) 1, at 27–8.

[150] Cassese, above n 110, at 214.

[151] ICTY, *The Prosecutor v Anto Furundžija*, Trial Chamber, Judgment, 10 December 1998, IT-95-17/1-T, para 137.

[152] Ibid, para 168.

[153] See ICTY, *The Prosecutor v Zoran Kupreškić, Mirjan Kupreškić, Vlatko Kupreškić, Drago Kupreškić, Dragan Papić, Vladimir Šantić*, above n 112, para 527.

[154] Ibid. See also E. Wilmhurst, 'Conclusions', in E. Wilmhurst and S. Breau, *Perspectives on the ICRC Study on Customary International Humanitarian Law* (Cambridge: CUP, 2005) 401, at 412. But see the observations of Judge David Hunt as regards the opinion of the Appeals Chamber in the case *Prosecutor v Hadžihasanović, Alagić and Kubura (Decision on Interlocutory Appeal Challenging Jurisdiction in relation to Command Responsibility), Separate and Partially Dissenting Opinion of Judge David Hunt*, 133 *ILR* (2008), at 54, paras 39–40.

c. The 'laws of humanity' as a substantive principle of international (humanitarian) law

Authorities have from time to time affirmed that the 'laws of humanity' or 'elementary considerations of humanity' are nothing but a positive (general) principle of international law which 'covers any wartime activity carried out by a belligerent', whether or not the conduct in point is governed by international law.[155] According to Balladore-Pallieri, this principle of humanity (illustrated by the Martens Clause) represents incontestably the 'most general norm of the Laws of War'.[156] Indeed, references to the Martens Clause have often been made to indicate that the clause itself suffered violation as a result of certain material conduct. Indeed, the International Military Tribunal (IMT) in Nuremberg stated that '[p]risoners of war were ill-treated and tortured and murdered, not only in defiance of the well-established rules of international law, but in complete disregard of the elementary dictates of humanity. Civilian populations in occupied territories suffered the same fate.'[157]

In a considerable number of cases, criminal tribunals looked to support from the Martens Clause to provide justification for the criminalization of inhumane conduct that was allegedly not specifically and explicitly prohibited by the laws of war prior to the Second World War—such as torture,[158] arbitrary trials,[159] 'indiscriminate mass arrests for the purpose of terrorizing the population',[160] human medical experiments,[161] theft as a war crime,[162] and the killing of hostages[163]—although a tribunal once refused to adopt the same approach as regards the taking and killing of hostages.[164] There is also no scarcity of broader references to the clause[165] or of mentions of the clause as a source of obligations—although not as a source of law—overlapping with established rules of customary or treaty law rules.[166]

Most significantly, in the *Military and Paramilitary Activities in and against Nicaragua* case, the ICJ, echoing the US Military Tribunal at Nuremberg,[167] affirmed that '[the]

---

[155] G. Balladore-Pallieri, *La Guerra* (Padua: CEDAM, 1935), at 139.

[156] Ibid. See also B.V.A. Röling, *International Law in an Expanded World* (Amsterdam: Djambatan. N.V. Amsterdam, 1960), at 37–8 (esp at 38): 'Such provision presupposes that the principles of the law of nations, as they result from the usages among civilized peoples, the laws of humanity and the dictates of public conscience, contain specific rules of conduct in the event that the treaties are no longer binding'; A.A. Cançado Trindade, 'International Law for Humankind: Towards a New *Jus Gentium* (II). General Course on Public International Law', 317 *RCADI* (2005) 9, at 79. See also Salter, above n 110, at 19–30.

[157] IMT, *Trial of the Major War Criminals Before the International Military Tribunal* (Nuremberg: IMT, 1948) vol XXII, at 470.

[158] *Trial of Kriminalassisstent Karl-Heinz Hermann Klinge*, in UNWCC (ed), above n 129, vol III, at 12. See also, with reference to the UDHR, *Auditeur Militaire v Krumkamp*, above n 145, at 389–90.

[159] *Trial of Hans Paul Helmuth Latza and Two Others*, in UNWCC (ed), above n 129, vol XIV, at 58.

[160] *Trial of Gustav Becker, Wilhelm Weber and 18 Others*, in UNWCC (ed), above n 129, vol VII, at 68.

[161] *Trial of Erhard Milch*, in UNWCC (ed), above n 129, at 51.

[162] *Trial of Alois and Anna Bohmer and Their Daughters*, in UNWCC (ed), above n 129, vol IX, at 64.

[163] *Trial of Hans Albin Rauter*, in UNWCC (ed), above n 129, vol XIV, at 119.

[164] In this case, the US Military Military Tribunal at Nuremberg controversially considered that the taking of hostages could be justified in specific circumstances. For the arguments of the prosecution relying on the Martens Clause, see *The Hostages Trial—Trial of Wilhelm List and others*, above n 143, at 82.

[165] Thus in the *Altstötter* case, the court found that various provisions of the Hague Regulations and the clause had been violated (*Trial of Josef Altstötter and others*, above n 146, at 92–3).

[166] ICTY, *The Prosecutor v Martić*, Trial Chamber, Judgment, 8 March 1996, IT-95-11-R61, para 13: 'This clause has been incorporated into basic humanitarian instruments [...]. Moreover, these norms also emanate from elementary considerations of humanity which constitute the foundations of the entire body of international humanitarian law applicable to all armed conflict.'

[167] *Trial of Alfried Felix Alwyn Krupp von Böhlen und Halbach and Eleven Others*, in UNWCC (ed), above n 129, vol X, at 133–4: 'The Preamble is much more than a pious declaration. It is a general clause, making the

rules [of Common Article 3] also constitute a minimum yardstick, in addition to the more elaborate rules which are also to apply to international conflicts; and they are rules which, in the Court's opinion, reflect what the Court in 1949 called "elementary considerations of humanity".[168]

92   Again by reference to the interpretative principle of effectiveness, one of the more plausible constructions (if not the sole one) of the Martens Clause would be, borrowing Judge Shahabuddeen's words, that the source of the principles 'lay in the clause itself'. This can be argued notwithstanding the origin of the clause which concerned the need to break a diplomatic impasse. Does the Martens Clause depict a rare scenario of 'normative serendipity'? In view of the contexts in which recourse has been made to the clause, it would then be correct, although a bit ironical, to dub it as the emergency exit from voluntarist positivism.

GIOVANNI DISTEFANO   ETIENNE HENRY

---

usages established among civilised nations, the laws of humanity and the dictates of public conscience into the legal yardstick to be applied if and when the specific provisions of the Convention and the Regulations annexed to it do not cover specific cases occurring in warfare, or concomitant to warfare.'

[168] ICJ, *Nicaragua v United States of America*, above n 104, at 113–14, para 218.

2. SPECIAL RULES

Chapter 10. The Principle of Non-Discrimination

	MN
A. Introduction	1
B. Meaning and Application of the Principle of Non-Discrimination	8
I. Background	8
II. Non-discrimination in international law	11
III. Non-discrimination in the Geneva Conventions	14
IV. First Geneva Convention: wounded and sick	20
V. Second Geneva Convention: wounded, sick, or shipwrecked	24
VI. Third Geneva Convention: prisoners of war	25
VII. Fourth Geneva Convention: civilians	34
C. Relevance in Non-International Armed Conflicts	43
D. Legal Consequences of a Violation	46
I. General comments	46
II. Criminal responsibility	47
E. Critical Assessment: Areas of Future Development	52

Select Bibliography

Bayefsky, A.F., 'The Principle of Equality and Non-Discrimination in International Law', 11 *HRLJ* (1990) 117

ICRC, Customary IHL Database, 2. Practice Relating to Rule 88. Non-Discrimination, subsection III, Military Manuals, available at <http://www.icrc.org/customary-ihl/eng/docs/v2_rul_rule88_sectiond>

Moeckli, D., 'The Human Right to Non-discrimination', in *Human Rights and Non-discrimination in the 'War on Terror'* (New York: OUP, 2008)

Pictet Commentary GCs I, III, and IV

Pictet, J., 'The Fundamental Principles of the Red Cross (II)', 19 *IRRC* 211 (1979) 184

A. Introduction

The Geneva Convention of 1864 sought to guarantee humanitarian relief in armed conflict on an entirely neutral basis.[1] At the heart of the 1864 Convention was the signatories' agreement to endorse the founding mission of the International Committee of the Red Cross (ICRC): to provide care for all sick or wounded in combat, regardless of nationality. Subsequent revisions continued to prohibit discrimination against the wounded or sick on the basis of nationality.

In 1949, the Geneva Conventions were written to address the humanitarian consequences of the Second World War, in which discrimination for reasons other than nationality wrought unspeakable human tragedy. The 1949 Conventions built on the core humanitarian principle of neutrality and expanded the concept of non-discrimination: a person or an entity lawfully obliged to protect a right held by another person or entity may

---

[1] J. Pictet, 'The Fundamental Principles of the Red Cross (II)', 19 *IRRC* 211 (1979) 184.

not infringe upon that right without due justification. Specifically, the 1949 Conventions establish that parties must satisfy their humanitarian obligations without any 'adverse distinction' for reasons such as nationality, sex, and race.

3   In the Geneva Conventions, non-discrimination broadly stands for the proposition that humanitarian treatment in armed conflict, while necessarily differentiated, must never be denied without justification. The Geneva Conventions do not require identical treatment; as we shall explain, differentiated treatment is acceptable, and even required, as long as it has a reasonable and objective basis. The Conventions codify this general, overarching obligation through two specific, legally operative types of obligations. In many instances, non-discrimination appears as a *primary obligation*, requiring parties to take action to prevent the occurrence of discrimination.[2] More frequently, non-discrimination is a *subsidiary obligation*, a condition specifying that a party must satisfy its primary humanitarian obligations, such as caring for the wounded, without discrimination.

4   Each of the four Geneva Conventions includes a broad, general prohibition of discrimination against persons protected by that particular Convention. Article 12 paragraph 2 GC I requires humane treatment for the sick and wounded, without adverse distinction. Article 12 paragraph 2 GC II extends the obligation to the sick and wounded at sea, as well as to those who are shipwrecked. Article 16 GC III establishes that a party holding prisoners of war (POWs) has a primary, affirmative obligation to treat all POWs alike. The Fourth Geneva Convention sets out the general obligation twice: first, Article 13 GC IV affirms that all obligations owed to the general population must be met without adverse distinction; secondly, Article 27 GC IV affirms that there may be no adverse distinction against 'protected persons', a term to be defined at MN 35. Common Article 3, appearing in each Geneva Convention, applies the obligation to non-international armed conflict (NIAC), requiring humane treatment of those 'not taking active part in the hostilities', 'without any adverse distinction founded on race, colour, religion or faith, sex, birth or wealth, or any other similar criteria'.[3]

5   The Conventions contain additional, detailed obligations on their face concerned with discrimination. For example, the GC I obligation of humane treatment and care for the sick and wounded gives rise to two specific requirements:

— relief societies must be able to care for the sick and wounded without discrimination;[4] and
— the order of release for detained individuals must be established without discrimination.[5]

The GC III requirement that all prisoners be treated equally in all actions gives rise to other, more specific provisions. Article 14 GC III reiterates that women must receive treatment equal to that of men, which may mean that women receive special privileges. An even more specific application of this principle appears in Article 25 paragraph 4 GC III, which requires that prison camps holding both men and women must provide women-only dormitories. Where POWs are required to work, work must be managed in a non-discriminatory fashion.

6   The Conventions express non-discrimination in language that is occasionally vague and internally inconsistent. Most non-discrimination obligations neither invoke the

---

[2] See S. Besson, 'The Principle of Non-Discrimination in the Convention on the Rights of the Child', 13 *International Journal of Children's Rights* (2005) 433, at 442, citing A.F. Bayefsky, 'The Principle of Equality and Non-Discrimination in International Law', 11 *HRLJ* (1990) 117 (discussing 'subordinate clauses').

[3] Note that 'nationality' is not specified in the list of suspect classifications in non-international armed conflicts. This is a slight difference from international armed conflict, where 'nationality' is included as a suspect classification in GC I–III.

[4] Art 18 para 2 GC I.   [5] Art 31 GC I.

language of non-discrimination, nor make explicit reference to suspect classifications. In addition, the numerous lists of suspect classifications vary as to which groups are and are not included, sometimes without apparent reason for the inconsistency. Lastly, textual language requiring equal or 'the same' treatment does not always indicate a non-discrimination obligation.[6]

Non-discrimination in the context of international humanitarian law (IHL) has received little discussion, either in tribunals or in academic literature. Most consideration of non-discrimination has occurred in the context of human rights law and international investment law. Because non-discrimination, as a principle, spans various bodies of law, sources other than those of IHL help give meaning to the obligation in that context. The best explanation for the gap in coverage of non-discrimination in IHL jurisprudence and literature may be that, in times of armed conflict, the non-discrimination obligation is typically violated contemporaneously with some larger, more concrete breaches of IHL.

B. Meaning and Application of the Principle of Non-Discrimination

I. Background

The concept of 'non-discrimination' has been traced to Aristotle, who proposed a theory of equality: those in the same circumstance should be treated the same way.[7] Non-discrimination, as it appears in the Geneva Conventions, did not enter international law until the twentieth century, following the First World War.[8]

'Discrimination' may be defined as 'any exclusion, restriction or privilege that is not objective and reasonable, and which adversely affects human rights'.[9] The non-discrimination obligation is generally expressed in international documents as either an autonomous or a subordinate norm.[10] On the one hand, an autonomous norm establishes a right to equality and non-discrimination with independence from other substantive rights recognized in the document.[11] On the other hand, a subordinate norm will prohibit discrimination in relation to other substantive rights recognized in the document.[12]

Typically, an international instrument couples its non-discrimination requirement with a list of suspect classifications, which indicate prohibited discrimination when used as the basis for differentiated treatment. The most commonly listed suspect classifications are

---

[6] E.g., Art 88 para 1 GC III contains language requiring 'same' treatment: 'Officers, non-commissioned officers and men who are prisoners of war undergoing a disciplinary or judicial punishment, shall not be subjected to more severe treatment than that applied in respect of the same punishment to members of the armed forces of the Detaining Power of equivalent rank.' However, this constitutes a requirement to provide reciprocal treatment to the forces of each party to the armed conflict, rather than an application of the principle of non-discrimination.

[7] D. Moeckli, *Human Rights and Non-discrimination in the 'War on Terror'* (New York: OUP, 2008), at 59.

[8] Ibid.

[9] IACtHR, *Juridical Condition and Rights of the Undocumented Migrants*, Advisory Opinion OC-18/03, 17 September 2003, para 84. In a similar sense, see ECtHR, *Willis v United Kingdom*, App No 36042/97, 11 June 2002, para 39.

[10] Bayefsky, above n 2.

[11] Examples of autonomous norms are Art 26 ICCPR; Art 24 ACHR; and Art 1 of Protocol No 12 ECHR.

[12] Examples of subordinate norms are Art 2(1) ICCPR; Art 1(1) ACHR; and Art 14 ECHR.

race, sex, language, and religion. Such lists appear throughout the Geneva Conventions. They generally end with the phrase 'or any similar criteria', meaning that the list is illustrative, not exhaustive. Though the lists vary in terms of the classes enumerated, there is no support for the claim that groups not enumerated are any less protected from discrimination.[13]

II. Non-discrimination in international law

11 The principle of 'non-discrimination' is not unique to the Geneva Conventions. Non-discrimination serves a functionally identically role throughout contemporaneous and subsequent international agreements, including the United Nations (UN) Charter,[14] the Universal Declaration of Human Rights (UDHR),[15] the International Covenant on Civil and Political Rights (ICCPR),[16] and the International Covenant on Economic, Social, and Cultural Rights (ICESCR).[17] Within each of these instruments, non-discrimination is recognized both as a substantive right and as a subordinate norm applicable to all other substantive rights recognized therein.

12 The Permanent Court of International Justice (PCIJ), in the early twentieth century, shaped how the principle of non-discrimination should be applied. In the *Polish Upper Silesia* case,[18] the Court first applied a treaty that contained a non-discrimination guarantee.[19] It held that the mere absence of discriminatory laws (i.e. 'equality in law') did not meet obligations to minorities; there must actually be no discrimination (i.e. 'equality in fact'). This provides the conceptual basis for obligations to remedy or to prevent discrimination. In the *Minority Schools* case, the Court held that providing certain benefits to a member of a minority does not constitute discrimination, since 'equality in fact may involve the necessity of different treatment in order to attain a result which establishes equilibrium between different situations'.[20] The Court further concluded that treating groups equally might, in fact, be unequal, due to the differing 'situations and requirements' of each group.[21] A more recent judicial consideration by the Inter-American Court of Human Rights (IACtHR) endorsed this understanding of non-discrimination. In the *Undocumented Migrants Advisory Opinion*,[22] the Inter-American Court differentiated between the terms 'distinction' and 'discrimination', reserving the former for acceptable differentiated treatment. According to the Inter-American Court, in order to comply with the principle of non-discrimination, differentiated treatment must be 'reasonable, proportionate and objective'.[23] These contours of the non-discrimination principle appear in the Geneva Conventions.

---

[13] Pictet Commentary GC I, at 138.
[14] Art 1(3) UN Charter (1945) (committing the UN to 'human rights and fundamental freedoms' without discrimination).
[15] Arts 2 and 7 UDHR (1948).   [16] Arts 2(1), 4(1), and 26 ICCPR.
[17] Arts 2(2) and 3 ICESCR.
[18] R. Higgins, 'Human Rights in the International Court of Justice', 20 *LJIL* (2007) 745, at 748.
[19] PCIJ, *Case Concerning Certain German Interests in Polish Upper Silesia (Germany v Poland)*, Judgment, 25 May 1926.
[20] PCIJ, *Minority Schools in Albania*, Advisory Opinion, 6 April 1935, para 64.
[21] Ibid, para 65.
[22] IACtHR, *Juridical Condition and Rights of the Undocumented Migrants*, Advisory Opinion, OC-18/03, 17 September 2003.
[23] Ibid, para 84.

Additionally, the Inter-American Court held non-discrimination to be *jus cogens*, a peremptory norm obliging all states at all times, because equality is a fundamental principle of 'all laws' and the public order premised on law, domestic and international. The Court further asserted that non-discrimination is an obligation *erga omnes*, meaning that all states may take action against violations of the obligation. The *Migrants Opinion* does not consider armed conflict, so its interpretive value when considering the Geneva Conventions is limited to its lucid conceptual explanation of the relationship between human rights and non-discrimination.

III. Non-discrimination in the Geneva Conventions

Though 'non-discrimination' typically appears in law using fairly sweeping language, the Conventions do not explicitly or uniformly require equal treatment for all nominated classes.[24] In fact, the Conventions require parties to treat various groups differently in the provision of humanitarian care. Indeed, the Geneva Conventions are constructed upon a foundation of distinctions: all individuals related to conflict fall within different categories, sometimes designated as 'protected persons' under each Convention. These distinctions do not amount to discrimination. A party to an armed conflict owes obligations to the civilian population different from those it owes to POWs. Rather, differentiated treatment is prohibited among similarly situated individuals within a certain group, or between similarly situated groups. For example, one group of wounded combatants cannot be treated better or worse than another group of wounded combatants on the basis of religion. This does not foreclose certain legitimate distinctions, known as 'differentiation',[25] such as those made for sex and explicitly required by the Conventions.

The inclusion of the non-discrimination feature in the Geneva Conventions had significant implications. It applied a human rights principle to armed conflict, narrowing the gap between the two bodies of law.[26] This chapter considers non-discrimination as it appears in the Geneva Conventions: a condition relating to humanitarian obligations owed in armed conflict. There are other expressions of neighbouring, even overlapping, concepts that are outside the scope of this chapter.

First, the Geneva Conventions do not themselves establish positive individual rights to be free from discrimination and to enjoy equal protection of law. Other instruments do include this guarantee and, collectively, comprise the body of treaty-based human rights law. For example, the ICCPR is generally cited as *establishing* human rights in international law. Such instruments assert rights held by the individual. The Geneva Conventions only detail obligations owed by their parties. The Conventions *apply* the right to be free of discrimination to situations of armed conflicts; the existence and validity of this right is implicit in the Conventions.[27] But it might be argued that the obligations under the Geneva Conventions stem from the need to respect human personality. Pictet explains that the obligations a party owes under the Geneva Conventions to a particular person do

---

[24] Pictet Commentary GC I, 137–8.
[25] C. Lindsey, *Women Facing War* (Geneva: ICRC, 2001), at 20.
[26] See Ch 35 of this volume for a more thorough discussion of the interaction between human rights and the GCs.
[27] G.I.A.D. Draper, 'Humanitarian Law and International Armed Conflicts', 13 *Georgia Journal of International and Comparative Law* (1983) 253, at 269 (Art 3 'embodies certain principles of non-discrimination derived from the then embryonic human rights regimes, and is, indeed, ahead of some of them').

not derive from the fact that that person has become covered by the Geneva Conventions (i.e. by his or her implication in armed conflict, whether as combatant, bystander, etc). Rather, the obligations are based on the individual's humanity and, in turn, the individual's human rights.[28]

17   Secondly, the Geneva Conventions do not have, as their express purpose, the protection of minorities or marginalized groups. That goal is the object of instruments such as the Convention on the Elimination of all Forms of Racial Discrimination and the Convention on the Rights of Persons with Disabilities.[29] Such instruments establish, as primary obligations, that parties must prevent and remedy discrimination.[30] The Geneva Conventions, in contrast, have as their primary purpose the care for all persons *hors de combat* in armed conflict. The Conventions have no specific remedial objective, though many of the specific obligations included are based on the experience of previous conflicts, where members of certain groups faced types of systematic discrimination.

18   Thirdly, non-discrimination within the Geneva Conventions is distinct from the principle of the equality of the parties to armed conflict, which obliges all parties to armed conflict to apply IHL equally, without regard to the character of any other party or how it entered the conflict.[31] The principle of equality of the parties to armed conflict is fundamental to IHL, while non-discrimination is a principle derived from human rights law.

19   Each Convention provides that it may not be construed to impair the ability of the Red Cross and other 'impartial' organizations that, pursuant to an agreement of parties to armed conflict, provide humanitarian relief.[32] Impartiality, of course, is an expression of non-discrimination. Organizations that discriminate in the provision of humanitarian relief do not enjoy this broad protection.

IV. First Geneva Convention: wounded and sick

20   Under Article 12 paragraph 2 GC I, a party to armed conflict must provide humane treatment and care to the sick and wounded in its power. These obligations must be satisfied 'without any adverse distinction founded on sex, race, nationality, religion, political opinions, or any other similar criteria'.[33] The phrase 'adverse distinction' establishes that the Geneva Conventions do not require absolute, literal equality, and that the manner of treatment afforded to some people must be differentiated.[34] At times, some people will be required to enjoy differentiated treatment. The Pictet Commentary provides the example that it is necessary to afford differentiated housing or clothing to a sick individual who is accustomed to a tropical climate.[35] Article 12 paragraph 2 GC I further outlaws physical violence and attempts to kill the sick and wounded: homicide, torture,

---

[28] Pictet Commentary GC I, at 39.

[29] A. Lester, Baron Lester of Herne Hill, 'Non-Discrimination in International Human Rights Law', 119 *Commonwealth Law Bulletin* (1993) 1653, at 1653.

[30] J.L. Kunz, 'The Present Status of International Law for the Protection of Minorities', 48 *AJIL* (1954) 282, at 284–6 (identifying the UN Charter as ushering in the principle of 'non-discrimination', something different from protecting minorities).

[31] A. Roberts, 'The Equal Application of the Laws of War: A Principle under Pressure', 90 *IRRC* 872 (2008) 931, at 931.

[32] Art 9 GC I; Art 9 GC II; Art 9 GC III; Art 10 GC IV. See Pictet Commentary GC I, at 108.

[33] Art 12 para 2 GC I.   [34] Pictet Commentary GC I, at 137.   [35] Ibid, at 138.

'biological experiments', wilful denial of medical services, and the creation of 'conditions exposing them to contagion or infection'. Though each of these acts is fundamentally wrongful, they are enumerated here because, in cases of armed conflict, they are committed either with discriminatory intent or because of some concurrent, 'enabling' discrimination. Article 12 paragraph 3 GC I establishes a special rule for prioritizing the provision of medical care: 'only urgent medical reasons' may be considered to favour one person over another for treatment. Article 12 paragraph 4 GC I requires that women 'be treated with all consideration due to their sex'. Here, the Convention makes clear that the non-discrimination obligation exists concurrently with the obligation to differentiate treatment for women. It is not discrimination to provide differentiated treatment to respond to a particular need or characteristic of a group or, in this case, sex.

Article 18 paragraph 2 GC I requires parties to permit both 'inhabitants' and 'relief societies' to provide medical services to any 'wounded or sick of whatever nationality'. 21

In certain cases, the Geneva Conventions assert a primary obligation to treat similarly situated people differently. The Conventions recall the general non-discrimination obligation, while reiterating the legitimate distinctions that may be made. One such instance is in Article 31 GC I, which relates to humanitarian personnel (i.e. medical professionals and chaplains) who have fallen into enemy hands. Article 31 extends the Article 12 prohibition of discrimination against the sick or wounded to their caregivers for the purpose of their return to the party to the conflict to whom they belong. Article 31 prohibits discrimination on any of three enumerated bases, 'race, religion or political opinion', when establishing the order of those personnel to be returned. This list is exhaustive, meaning that Article 31 does not explicitly apply to any other basis for discrimination, such as sex or age.[36] The prohibition in Article 31 GC I is immediately clarified with language suggesting that release 'preferably' be made on two factors. The use of 'preferably' effectively renders this a 'should' obligation, not an absolute one. The first factor to be taken into account is when the individuals were captured (the Pictet Commentary suggests that this would be on a first in, first out basis).[37] The second factor is the individual's state of health. Article 31 further confirms that parties to the conflict may conclude agreements as to who shall be released, as well as some permissible grounds on which distinctions would be made. Even in such an agreement, parties must abide by the Article 31 prohibition of discrimination. 22

Article 37 GC I and identical Article 40 GC II, both permit each neutral Power to restrict and to regulate medical aircraft flying in its airspace or landing in its territory, provided that the neutral Power applies such rules equally to all parties to the conflict. This is a non-discrimination obligation among states. 23

V. Second Geneva Convention: wounded, sick, or shipwrecked

Article 12 paragraph 2 GC II is virtually identical to Article 12 paragraph 2 GC I. It applies a broad non-discrimination requirement to the obligations of humane treatment and care for the 'wounded, sick or shipwrecked'. The analysis is, accordingly, identical to the discussion of Article 12 paragraph 2 GC I at MN 20–23. 24

---

[36] This list is an exception; most lists relating to non-discrimination in the GCs are not exhaustive.
[37] Pictet Commentary GC I, at 266.

VI. Third Geneva Convention: prisoners of war

25 Article 14 paragraph 2 GC III requires differentiated treatment for women who are POWs. According to the Pictet Commentary, this distinction is required for three reasons:

— women's status as 'the weaker sex';
— their 'honour and modesty'; and
— for reasons relating to pregnancy and child-birth.[38]

The language recalls the Article 12 GC I/GC II formulation. Here, that requirement is qualified with a specifically mandated floor: the treatment of women must be as good as or better than that provided to men. This requirement applies to other provisions made specifically for women elsewhere in GC III.[39]

26 Article 16 GC III broadly prohibits discrimination against POWs. Here, non-discrimination is expressed both negatively and positively. Any 'adverse distinction' is prohibited, with specific reference to 'race, nationality, religious belief or political opinions'. This list is non-exhaustive, applying to 'other similar criteria', though it makes no specific mention of sex. The non-discrimination requirement is a subsidiary obligation to the requirement that 'all prisoners of war shall be treated alike'. Article 16 further specifies permissible distinctions: first, equal treatment must account for any provisions elsewhere in the Convention relating to 'rank and sex';[40] secondly, prisoners may receive 'privileged treatment' based on age, health status, and 'professional qualifications'.

27 Under Article 34 GC III, a party holding POWs must respect their freedom of religion. The only condition is that, in the practice of their religion, prisoners should respect the general routine of the day, though this is a very mild regulation that permits all but the most schedule-disruptive of religious activities to be performed.[41] The Pictet Commentary instructs that prisoners require no permission before beginning to practise their religion. Under Article 34 paragraph 2 GC III, any party holding prisoners must provide a space for them to practise their religion. These two obligations apply the more general obligation of non-discrimination against prisoners, expressed in Article 16 GC III.[42]

28 A party must provide separate dormitories for women POWs when they are interned at a camp that also interns men. Under Article 25 paragraph 4 GC III, these facilities must be equal to those supplied for male prisoners. Here, the Conventions explicitly permit distinction on the basis of sex.

29 Article 49 GC III provides that a party may require work from those POWs who are able to work, provided that this work is administered without discrimination. Article 49 enumerates specific differentiations that may be made when assigning work: 'age, sex, rank, and physical aptitude'. Article 49 further suggests that these distinctions are to be made with regard to maintaining both the physical and mental health of the prisoner. The Pictet Commentary explains that the purpose of prisoners' labour is not for any economic benefit but for the prisoners' own well-being.[43]

30 Medical personnel and religious ministers, when detained as POWs, must be treated, at a minimum, with all the privileges and benefits of their counterparts in the Detaining

---

[38] Pictet Commentary GC III, at 146.
[39] See further section E of this chapter.
[40] E.g., Part III, Section II, Chapter VII of GC III specifically concerns rank. Art 43 endeavours to 'ensure equality of treatment between prisoners of equivalent rank'.
[41] Pictet Commentary GC III, at 227–8.   [42] Ibid.
[43] Pictet Commentary GC III, at 260.

Power's own forces. Under Article 32 GC III, any prisoner who can provide medical care must be treated like an individual having equal qualifications in the Detaining Power's forces. Any prisoner who can serve as a 'minister of religion', even if he has not previously served as a chaplain, must, under Article 35 GC III, be treated like one of the Detaining Power's own 'chaplains'.

Article 23 GC III provides that POWs must receive the same level of physical protection from 'hazards of war', including air attacks, as the Detaining Power's own forces. Under Article 24 GC III, conditions in permanent 'transit or screening camps' must be equal to those of any other camp, and the prisoners must be treated the same as in any permanent camp. Further, prisoners' living quarters must at least equal those of the Detaining Power's forces 'billeted in the same area', and the quarters must allow for 'the habits and customs' of the prisoners.

Under Article 51 GC III, working conditions, work training, and safety protections for POWs must at least equal those of the Detaining Power's own nationals 'employed in similar work'. Work hours are limited to the maximum permitted for civilians of the Detaining Power by Article 52 GC III. Note that while work hours are limited by the standard for 'civilians', virtually every other aspect of the workplace is compared to that of 'nationals' in a factually similar setting.

Article 79 GC III states that prisoners are entitled to elect a representative, who must have the same nationality, language, and customs as the POWs whom he represents. Any prisoner subject to the Detaining Power's penal process must be accorded the same substantive and procedural rights the Detaining Power applies to its own forces. Under Article 87 GC III, he must receive no greater penalty for the same act. He must receive any penal dispensations made for someone of the same rank, based on his rank. Article 102 GC III provides that his sentence, to be valid, must be pronounced by the same courts, under the same procedures as in the case of members of the armed forces of the Detaining Power. He enjoys the same right to appeal his sentence, under identical procedures, by Article 106 GC III. The prisoner must serve his sentence in the same place and under the same conditions as in the case of members of the armed forces of the Detaining Power, according to Article 108 GC III. The sole exception, pronounced in Article 82 GC III, recognizes that a prisoner may be punished for an act that is not punishable within the Detaining Power's own forces, though the Detaining Power may assess only disciplinary punishment.

VII. Fourth Geneva Convention: civilians

Part II of GC IV establishes a number of general obligations concerning the protection of the civilian population during armed conflict. Article 13 states that all obligations regarding civilians function 'without adverse distinction'. Unlike its counterparts in the other Conventions, Article 13 GC IV articulates the general prohibition of discrimination without limitation. Instead, Article 13 functions as a rule of interpretation that indicates that all subsequent provisions of Part II are to be interpreted and applied without discrimination. In the other Conventions, the general non-discrimination obligation is expressed as a condition on a primary obligation, such as 'humanitarian treatment'. Non-discrimination applies to subsequent primary obligations because they express individual components of the overall humane treatment obligation. Article 13's uniqueness reflects that Part II is to be 'as general and extensive as possible'.[44] Here, the

---

[44] Pictet Commentary GC IV, at 118.

35   Article 27 GC IV guarantees humane treatment and related protections for 'protected persons', defined as any individual in the physical custody of a party to an armed conflict or occupation, where the individual is not a national of that party. The classes specified for protection are race, religion, and political opinion. Nationality does not appear in this list. The list appears to be non-exhaustive, given that these groups 'in particular' are to be protected. The drafters specifically considered and decided against including nationality here, and the Pictet Commentary declares it 'clear' that the list cannot be interpreted to include nationality.[45] The Article reaffirms that the prohibition against discrimination yields to specific provision made within the Convention for some individuals, based on age, health, and sex. Article 27 paragraph 2 further mandates that women 'shall be especially protected against any attack on their honour'. Article 27 concludes with the caveat that parties retain the right to take such measures to maintain security as are necessary in war. Custom and the decisions of jurists, however, confirm that baseline human rights, including non-discrimination, do not yield to military imperatives.[46]

nominated classes protected are race, nationality, religion, and political opinion. This list is non-exhaustive, denoted by the language that these groups 'in particular' are to be protected. While such lists typically indicate their non-exhaustive nature with the phrase 'similar criteria', the Pictet Commentary confirms that there is no functional difference.

36   Aliens in the territory of a party to the conflict are entitled to numerous protections, to the same extent as the nationals of the state where they are located: under Article 38 GC IV, these protections include medical care, relocation from war hazards, and, if applicable, whatever privileges are afforded to children aged under 15, women who are pregnant, and women with children younger than 7 years old. Article 39 GC IV stipulates that protected persons are entitled to the same 'opportunity' to find employment with pay as that enjoyed by the nationals of the Power in whose territory they are. Under Article 40 GC IV, protected persons may be 'compelled to work' only to the same extent as the state's nationals, and protected persons must always enjoy the same 'working conditions' and 'safeguards'.

37   Article 71 GC IV provides that protected persons in an occupied territory, if charged with violating criminal law, must be duly notified of the charge 'in writing, in a language they understand'. If detained, in accordance with Article 76 GC IV they must receive the same conditions of detention as obtained in the country's prisons, and must be separated from other detainees.

38   According to Article 82 GC IV, protected persons must be interned among those sharing the same nationality, language, and customs. Protected persons of the same nationality may not be separated solely because they speak different languages.

39   Under Article 91 GC IV, any interned person who requires maternity care, surgery, hospitalization, or some other 'special treatment' must be admitted to a duly equipped facility and must receive the same level of care.

40   Working conditions and salary for those interned must, according to Article 95 GC IV, be at least as good as those provided under 'the national laws and regulations' as well as 'existing practice', and as applied to the same type of work in the same area. Additionally, protected persons are entitled to worker's compensation at the national level.

41   Though all internees are entitled to allowances, under Article 98 GC IV the value of allowances need not be equal, provided that any such differences are not discriminatory.

---

[45] Ibid, at 206.   [46] Ibid, at 234.

Under Articles 99, 117, and 127 GC IV, internees are protected by the same rules regarding language, disciplinary sanctions, and transfer as POWs. 42

C. Relevance in Non-International Armed Conflicts

Common Article 3 specifically applies, and extends the requirements of Article 12 GC I to NIACs. 43

Nationality, however, is not listed among the nominated classifications in Common Article 3. The drafters, on the premise that aliens may become involved in a NIAC, specifically excluded nationality from the provision because a party may legitimately afford varying legal treatment to nationals and non-nationals.[47] The Pictet Commentary, however, suggests that, because Common Article 3 prohibits discrimination for 'any other similar criteria', it would also prohibit discrimination on the basis of nationality.[48] Given the transnational nature of many such conflicts today, any process to revise Common Article 3 to clarify this requirement would be welcome. 44

Common Article 3 reflects the two cornerstone requirements of GC I and GC II: 45

— that those *hors de combat* are to be treated humanely, including with medical care; and
— that this (and any other) obligation must be executed without discrimination.

It does not include any of the supplementary provisions that address specific situations, such as the requirement that women POWs must have separate dormitories (see MN 28). Though the issue has not been settled, one might persuasively argue that Common Article 3's humane treatment requirement includes, by analogy, all of these specific provisions because they merely clarify and specify the primary obligations of the Conventions. Whatever humanitarian obligation exists in a NIAC, there is little question that a party must satisfy that obligation without discrimination.

D. Legal Consequences of a Violation

I. General comments

It should be noted that because non-discrimination is generally a subsidiary obligation, any alleged discriminatory conduct necessarily involves another violation, which itself may have clearer means of enforcement. 46

II. Criminal responsibility

Discrimination is not a discrete war crime, that is, a serious violation of the laws and customs applicable in international armed conflict (IAC) and NIAC. However, discrimination is a necessary element in the definition of certain war crimes. For example, Additional Protocol I, Article 85(4)(c), treats apartheid and other outrages upon personal dignity based on racial discrimination both as grave breaches of the Protocol and as war crimes. 47

Similarly, the Rome Statute of the International Criminal Court (ICC Statute), which establishes jurisdiction to prosecute the 'war crimes' therein codified, does not include 48

---

[47] Pictet Commentary GC I, at 55.   [48] Ibid, at 55–6.

discrimination as an independent war crime.[49] Nevertheless, the Elements of Crimes detail discrimination as one of the possible purposes for the elements in the war crime of torture.[50] Also, some of the enumerated war crimes in the ICC Statute may be considered necessarily discriminatory (e.g. 'forced pregnancy').

49   The ICC Statute also establishes the jurisdiction of the ICC to prosecute 'crimes against humanity'.[51] Such crimes may also be perpetrated in the context of an armed conflict—whether international or non-international—therefore providing a basis for prosecution in addition to war crimes.

50   Discrimination is not defined as an independent crime against humanity. However, there are several crimes against humanity which include discrimination as a prominent element of their definition. The definition of the crime of persecution requires that such acts be carried out 'against any identifiable group or collectivity on political, racial, national, ethnic, cultural, religious, gender [...], or other grounds that are universally recognized as impermissible under international law',[52] thus requiring a discriminatory motivation. Also, the crime of apartheid presupposes racial discrimination at an institutional level, since its definition requires the perpetration of inhuman acts, 'in the context of an institutionalized regime of systematic oppression and domination by one racial group over any other racial group or groups'.[53]

51   The ICC Statute further provides broad jurisdiction for prosecuting 'genocide', the ultimate crime based on discrimination. The crime of genocide may take place in the context of an armed conflict, whether international or non-international. The charge of genocide always requires an ulterior intent,[54] 'to destroy, in whole or in part, a national, ethnical, racial or religious group', which is motivated on discriminatory grounds. This list is exhaustive and does not include political or cultural groups, or groups based on sex. There are five enumerated acts that, when targeted at a certain group or part of that group, constitute genocide:

— killing members of the group;
— causing serious bodily or mental harm to members of the group;
— deliberately forcing the group into living conditions chosen to destroy the group physically;
— imposing measures intended to prevent births within the group; and
— forcibly removing children of the group to another group.[55]

E. Critical Assessment: Areas of Future Development

52   Despite the recognition of non-discrimination within the Geneva Conventions, feminist legal scholars have strongly criticized the Conventions and IHL in general. These scholars argue that the 'rules regarding women [in IHL] are archaic and reflect the very stereotypical ideas about women that perpetuate discrimination'.[56] Indeed, as was mentioned

---

[49] Arts 5 and 8 ICC Statute.
[50] ICC Elements of Crimes, Art 8(2)(c)(i)-4.   [51] Art 7 ICC Statute.
[52] Art 7(1)(h) ICC Statute.   [53] Art 7(2)(h) ICC Statute.
[54] K. Ambos, 'What Does "Intent to Destroy" in Genocide Mean?', 91 *IRRC* 876 (2009) 833, at 834.
[55] Art 6 ICC Statute.
[56] K. Bennoune, 'Do We Need New International Law to Protect Women in Armed Conflict?' 38 *Case Western Reserve JIL* (2006–7) 363, at 364.

above (see MN 25), the Pictet Commentary justifies differentiated treatment for women by portraying them as 'the weaker sex', highlighting their role as child-bearers and emphasizing what Karima Bennoune describes as archaic notions.[57] Critics claim the Conventions and the Pictet Commentary treat women solely in terms of sexuality and reproduction.[58]

Additionally, the Geneva Conventions do not explicitly recognize rape as a grave breach, thus risking diminishing its gravity as a war crime.[59] Instead, they treat rape only as an offence against 'honour and modesty'.[60] Bennoune argues that the Conventions' characterization of victims of sexual assault as being 'dishonoured' is improper, because a victim of a crime has committed no wrongdoing. She does, however, note that many provisions specifically directed at women are beneficial.[61] That the objections largely address the sociological overtones, rather than the protections, of provisions concerning women, suggests that women do receive proper differentiation under the Conventions. As suggested by Helen Durham, these critiques must be viewed in light of IHL's fundamental limitations: it is a body of law designed to minimize the humanitarian horrors of armed conflict, which leaves no room to address the underlying inequalities in social structures pre-dating the conflict.[62]

A related, more isolated, and novel line of argument concerns claims made by advocacy groups as to the potentially discriminatory implementation of humanitarian aid delivery by the United States (US).[63] As a matter of fact, humanitarian aid delivered by the US is subject to a 'no abortion clause', which requires that this aid will not be used for abortion services.[64] Critics argue that this policy discriminatorily limits access to comprehensive medical care for women victims of sexual violence in armed conflicts.[65] In 2010, the UN Human Rights Council Working Group on the Universal Periodic Review suggested that the US '[remove] blanket abortion restrictions on humanitarian aid covering medical care given women and girls who are raped and impregnated in situations of armed conflict'.[66] The suggestion was offered by Norway,[67] citing a non-governmental organization

---

[57] Ibid, at 384.

[58] J.J. Gardam and M. Jarvis, *Women, Armed Conflict and International Law* (2001), at 94, quoted in H. Durham, 'Women, Armed Conflict, and International Law', 84 *IRRC* 847 (2002) 655, at 656.

[59] H. Durham and K. O'Byrne, 'The Dialogue of Difference: Gender Perspectives on International Humanitarian Law', 92 *IRRC* 877 (2010) 31, at 35. See also J. Prescott, 'NATO Gender Mainstreaming and the Feminist Critique of the Law of Armed Conflict', 14 *Georgetown Journal of Gender and the Law* (2013) 83.

[60] Pictet Commentary GC IV, at 206.

[61] Bennoune, above n 56, at 385.

[62] H. Durham, 'International Humanitarian Law and the Protection of Women', in H. Durham and T. Gurd (eds), *Listening to the Silences: Women and War* (Leiden: Koninklijke Brill, 2005), at 97, quoted in Durham and O'Byrne, above n 59, at 36. *Contra*, V. Oosterveld, 'Feminist Debates on Civilian Women and International Humanitarian Law', 27 *Windsor Yearbook of Access to Justice* (2009) 385.

[63] See 5 Paper Buildings, 'Letter to President Barack Obama', 1 February 2012, available at <http://globaljusticecenter.net/index.php?option=com_mtree&task=att_download&link_id=196&cf_id=34>; S.W. Seymour, 'Letter to President Barack Obama', 4 March 2011, available at <http://www.nycbar.org/pdf/report/uploads/20072069-LettertoObamaReNon-DiscriminatoryMedicalCaretoWomen.pdf>.

[64] 5 Paper Buildings, above n 63; Seymour, above n 63.

[65] Letter to President Barak Obama, 10 April 2013, available at <http://www.globaljusticecenter.net/index.php?option=com_mtree&task=att_download&link_id=321&cf_id=34>.

[66] *Report of the Working Group on the Universal Periodic Review: United States of America* (2011), available at <http://www2.ohchr.org/english/bodies/hrcouncil/docs/16session/A-HRC-16-11.pdf>.

[67] Global Justice Center, *The Right to an Abortion for Girls and Women Raped in Armed Conflict*, available at <http://globaljusticecenter.net/index.php?option=com_mtree&task=att_download&link_id=2&cf_id=34>.

report asserting that access to abortion is part of the medical treatment for rape and that the US restriction violates Common Article 3.[68] The US responded that such action would be impermissible under domestic law; the US did not advance an international law argument.[69] More recently, Louise Doswald-Beck also urged the President of the United States to lift these abortion restrictions,[70] emphasizing that this policy contravenes the prohibition of adverse distinction found in Common Article 3 of the Geneva Conventions.[71]

55   The United Kingdom Government also recently clarified its position on the issue of non-discrimination in humanitarian aid distribution, stating that abortion services may be required by Common Article 3, if they are deemed medically necessary. The spokesperson stated that such obligations under Common Article 3 must be fulfilled despite potential conflicts with domestic law.[72]

56   Scholars have raised concerns in relation to the categories of persons against whom discrimination is prohibited in the Geneva Conventions. Rory T. Hood has called for 'citizenship status' to be added to the list of protected categories in the Third and Fourth Conventions.[73] Hood argues that the US Guantánamo detentions were based on illegitimate distinctions on the basis of citizenship. As discussed above (MN 44), 'nationality' was deliberately excluded from Common Article 3 and is, perhaps, the single greatest distinction between the Conventions' treatment of NIACs and IACs.

57   There is disagreement about the number and type of categories protected from discrimination. As discussed above (MN 10), enumerated lists within various parts of the Conventions reflect the baseline prohibition against any type of adverse distinction. Some domestic laws implementing the Geneva Conventions include groups that have not previously been specifically protected. For example, Canada's law regarding the treatment of prisoners (implementing GC III) prohibits discrimination on the basis of sexual orientation.[74] The Charter of Fundamental Rights of the European Union similarly protects sexual orientation.[75] Disability is not mentioned. Additionally, the Human Rights Committee (HRCttee), the European Court of Human Rights (ECtHR), and

---

[68] Universal Periodic Review: United States of America (2011), Advance Questions to United States of America–UAdd.2, available at <http://lib.ohchr.org/HRBodies/UPR/Documents/session9/US/UnitedStatesAmerica_Add2.pdf>.

[69] Global Justice Center Legal Update, *US Position on Imposing Abortion Restrictions on Victims of War Rape is Weakening*, available at <http://globaljusticecenter.net/index.php?option=com_mtree&task=att_download&link_id=112&cf_id=34>.

[70] Letter to President Barack Obama, above n 65.

[71] There has been increasing discussion of such 'ensure respect' claims being raised by third party states. See H. Tonkin, 'Common Article 1: A Minimum Yardstick for Regulating Private Military and Security Companies', 22 *LJIL* (2009) 779.

[72] HL Deb 9 January 2013, vol 742, col 209, at <http://www.publications.parliament.uk/pa/ld201213/ldhansrd/text/130109-0002.htm#13010975000273>. See also Ch 37, MN 20–26, of this volume.

[73] R.T. Hood, 'Guantánamo and Citizenship: An Unjust Ticket Home', 37 *Case Western Reserve JIL* (2005–6) 555, at 573.

[74] Canada, Prisoner of War Handling, Detainees, Interrogation and Tactical Questioning in International Operations, B-GJ-005-110/FP-020, National Defence Headquarters, 1 August 2004, § H103.2.a, quoted in ICRC, Customary IHL Database, 2. Practice Relating to Rule 88. Non-Discrimination, subsection III, Military Manuals, available at <http://www.icrc.org/customary-ihl/eng/docs/v2_rul_rule88_sectionb>.

[75] European Union, Charter of Fundamental Rights of the European Union, 7 December 2000 (OJ C 364/01), 18 December 2000, Art 21.

the IACtHR have all stated that sexual orientation is a protected category in each of the treaties over which they exercise jurisdiction.[76] What is or is not listed may be of little functional significance because no such list in the Conventions is exhaustive.[77] As with the feminist critiques, mention of, or failure to mention, a particular protected group may be more important in terms of overtones.

Though the Geneva Conventions impose obligations on parties, they necessarily shape the behaviour of international relief organizations as well. After all, parties are obligated to permit these organizations to provide relief, when the organizations themselves do not engage in discrimination. The ICRC, having adopted non-discrimination as a cornerstone principle, may be expected to behave consistently with the Conventions. Toni Pfanner has called upon the organization to evaluate its ability to comply with non-discrimination principles when providing relief in instances of asymmetrical warfare, given the inherent complexities present in such conflicts, such as the difficulty in establishing contact with all parties to the conflict.[78]

58

GABOR RONA   ROBERT J. MCGUIRE

---

[76] The HRCttee interpreted the 'sex' category to include sexual orientation—see HRCttee, *Toonen v Australia*, Comm No 488/1992, UN Doc CCPR/C/50/D/488/1992 (1994). The ECtHR concluded that sexual orientation was protected under the 'other status' clause in Art 14 ECHR—see ECtHR, *Salgueiro da Silva Mouta v Portugal*, Judgment, 21 December 1999. More recently, the IACtHR concluded that sexual orientation was a protected category under the Convention, without specifying under which specific clause it is protected—see IACtHR, *Caso Atala Riffo y Niñas v Chile*, 24 February 2012.

[77] However, in IHRL, suspect classifications have been interpreted as creating a presumption of illegitimacy of distinctions based on those categories. Accordingly, the burden of proving that the distinction was in fact objective and reasonable would fall on the state. See M. González Le Saux and O. Parra Vera, 'Concepciones y cláusulas de igualdad en la jurisprudencia de la Corte Interamericana. A propósito del Caso Apitz', 47 *Revista Instituto Interamericano de Derechos Humanos* (2008) 127, at 132.

[78] T. Pfanner, 'Asymmetrical Warfare from the Perspective of Humanitarian Law and Humanitarian Action', 87 *IRRC* 857 (2005) 149, 166.

Chapter 11. Hospitals

	MN
A. Introduction	1
I. General remarks	1
II. Historical context	5
B. Meaning and Application	8
I. Hospitals on land	8
a. Definition of hospitals	8
b. Recognition of civilian hospitals	11
c. Identification of hospitals	15
d. Remoteness of hospitals from military objectives	18
II. Hospital ships	21
III. Scope of protection of hospitals on land and hospital ships	30
a. General remarks	30
b. Situations not depriving protection	32
c. Capture, requisition	42
C. Relevance in Non-International Armed Conflicts	46
D. Legal Consequences of a Violation	51
E. Critical Assessment	59

Select Bibliography

Bugnion, F., *The International Committee of the Red Cross and the Protection of War Victims* (Geneva/Oxford: ICRC/Macmillan, 2003), at 469–80, 529–42, 738–42

Doswald-Beck, L. (ed), *San Remo Manual on International Law Applicable to Armed Conflicts at Sea* (Cambridge: Grotius Publications, CUP, 1995)

Goodman, R.D., *Hospital Ships* (Brisbane: Boolarong Publications, 1992)

ICRC, *Health Care in Danger: Making the Case* (Geneva: ICRC, 2011)

Pictet Commentary GC I, at 194–200, 202–5

Pictet Commentary GC II, at 154–89, 193–8

Pictet Commentary GC IV, at 141–53, 316–18

Pictet, J., 'The Medical Profession and Humanitarian Law', 25 *IRRC* 247 (1985) 191

A. Introduction

I. General remarks

International humanitarian law (IHL) is based on the principle of humanity under which persons *hors de combat*, including the wounded, sick, and shipwrecked, are entitled to protection and respect for their lives and physical and moral integrity. This right would be illusory if states did not respect and take measures to ensure the protection of hospitals, other medical establishments, and units treating the wounded, sick, and shipwrecked. The special status of hospitals is a logical consequence of the principle of inviolability of the wounded, sick, and shipwrecked, and of medical personnel.[1]

---

[1] See Chs 39 and 40 of this volume.

2   The basic principles are universally recognized as binding, but some questions arise with regard to specific issues. Which establishments are considered hospitals? Do all types of hospitals enjoy identical status? How mandatory are additional criteria stipulated in IHL relating to marking hospitals with the distinctive sign and to remoteness from military objectives so that attacks against them do not imperil hospitals' safety? Is inspection and requisition of hospitals legal? How far does their inviolability extend? Does the nature of the conflict change the legal status of hospitals?

3   The universal formal recognition of principles does not ensure their respect in real life. On the contrary, hospitals are targeted, looted, encircled, deprived of essential supplies, and their premises are often violently inspected by soldiers rescuing wounded comrades or searching for wounded enemies.[2] Ensuring criminal responsibility for violations is therefore vital.

4   There is less practice with regard to the contemporary use and abuse of hospital ships. Relevant examples date back to the First and Second World Wars.[3] After the World Wars, there were few conflicts in which states' naval forces were used in full-scale naval operations; rather, they were mainly deployed to support land operations.[4] The best-known case of the use of hospital ships after the Second World War is their deployment during the Falkland-Malvinas Islands conflict. There were seven hospital ships used by the belligerent states (United Kingdom (UK) and Argentina), and all of them were originally non-hospital ships (survey vessels, icebreakers, a passenger liner) converted to serve in the required capacity.[5] At present, only the United States (US) operates vessels that are registered as hospital ships;[6] other states transform other types of vessels, as needed.

[2] For different categories of violations of hospitals' status, their practical examples and implications, see ICRC, *Health Care in Danger: Making the Case* (Geneva: ICRC, 2011), at 4, 6–9. The report on ICRC, *Violent Incidents Affecting the Delivery of Health Care* (Geneva: ICRC, 2015), published as a part of the *Health Care in Danger* project, states that from January 2012 to December 2014 the ICRC documented 1222 incidents of attacking, looting, and some other types of violence affecting health care facilities, including hospitals and health centres in 11 countries. See also UNSC Res 467, 21 April 1980 (shelling of the UNIFIL field hospital in Lebanon); UN Commission on Human Rights Res 1983/5, 15 February 1983, para 2 (border hospital in Kampuchea); UNGA Res 39/119, 14 December 1984, para 9, UNGA Res 40/139, 13 December 1985, para 3, and UNGA Res 41/157, 4 December 1986, para 4, as well as UN Commission of Human Rights Res 1987/51, 11 March 1987, para 5 (attacking military hospitals in El Salvador); UNSC Res 794, 3 December 1992 (Somalia); ICRC News Release 06/55 of 2006 (Mogadishu's Keysaney hospital in Somalia); UN Doc A/HRC/3/2, 23 November 2006 (Report of the Commission of Inquiry on Lebanon), at 42–4; Sassòli/Bouvier/Quintin, vol III, at 2534, 2557–8 (Human Rights Watch Report on Conflict over South Ossetia *Up in Flames* 2009 and Independent International Fact-Finding Mission on the Conflict in Georgia Report 2009); ICRC News Release 29/09 of 2009 and Sassòli/Bouvier/Quintin, vol III, at 1663–4 (attacks on Vanni hospital in Sri Lanka); UN Doc A/HRC/12/48, 25 September 2009 (Report of the UN Fact-Finding Mission on the Gaza Conflict), at 117–18, 141–9; UN Doc A/HRC/22/59, 5 February 2013 (Report of the Commission of Inquiry on the Syrian Arab Republic), at 21–2, 110–14; WHO *Situation Reports* on Gaza Crisis in July and August 2014 (32 hospitals in Gaza damaged and closed); ICRC CIHL Study, vol II, Part I, at 523 (Angola), 525 (Iran–Iraq), 529–30 (documents of international organizations relating to raids on hospitals on Territories Occupied by Israel, on civilian hospitals in Afghanistan in 1980s, on Liberia in 1990, on the former Yugoslavia, particularly targeting hospitals in Sarajevo, on Kislyar Hospital in Dagestan in 1996), 533 (documents of the ICRC and National Red Cross and Red Crescent Societies on the situation in Mexico and Angola in 1994 and Burundi in 1995).

[3] J.W. Garner, *International Law and the World War* (London: Longmans, Green & Co, 1920), vol I, at 505–24; J.C. Mossop, 'Hospital Ships in the Second World War: Notes', 24 *BYBIL* (1947) 398.

[4] E.g., naval operations of Korean War, Suez Crisis, Vietnam War, Indo-Pakistani War, Yom Kippur War, Iran–Iraq War, operations 'Desert Shield'/'Desert Storm', 'Enduring Freedom', 'Sharp Guard'.

[5] The case study about this conflict is presented in S.-S. Junod, *Protection of the Victims of Armed Conflict—Falkland-Malvinas Islands, 1982: International Humanitarian Law and Humanitarian Action* (Geneva: ICRC, 1984).

[6] R.J. Grunawalt, 'Hospital Ships in the War on Terror: Sanctuaries or Targets?', 58 *Naval War College Review* (2005) 89, at 111–14.

II. Historical context

The importance of the special status of hospitals in the history of IHL is obvious. The neutrality of military hospitals, their protection, and respect were provided for in the very first Article of the first IHL multilateral treaty, namely, the Convention for the Amelioration of the Condition of the Wounded in Armies in the Field adopted in Geneva in 1864. Another provision (Article 7) provided for hospitals to be marked by the red cross and national flags. The 1906 and 1929 Geneva Conventions on the wounded and sick in land warfare modified these provisions, and Geneva Convention (GC) I of 1949 develops them further. It protects military hospitals against the effects of hostilities and regulates their status in case of capture (Article 19); it confirms the protection—accorded mainly under GC II—of hospital ships in the event of attacks undertaken from the land (Article 20); and it enumerates conditions not considered as depriving hospitals of protection (Article 22), thus articulating situations that cannot be treated as 'acts harmful to the enemy' under Article 21.[7]

Protection of military hospital ships was defined for the first time in the 1899 Hague Convention (III) for the Adaptation to Maritime Warfare of the Principles of the Geneva Convention of 1864 (Articles 1–6) and developed eight years later in the 1907 Hague Convention (X) for the Adaptation to Maritime Warfare of the Principles of the Geneva Convention of 1906 (Articles 1–9). Geneva Convention II of 1949 devotes the whole of its Chapter III to regulating the legal status of hospital ships. The detailed provisions of Articles 22–33 set forth the basic obligations and protections of hospital ships and similar vessels, used not only by belligerent states but also by other actors, taking into account technical characteristics and the location of such ships. Certain conditions which do not deprive a hospital ship of protection are enumerated in Article 35. In addition, GC II confirms the protection—accorded mainly under GC I—of hospitals ashore in the event of bombardments or other attacks undertaken from the sea (Article 23).

Protection under the treaties mentioned at MN 5 and 6 was provided initially only for military hospitals, but it extended gradually to civilian hospitals. Article 27 of the Hague Regulations listed hospitals among the civilian objects to be spared 'in sieges and bombardments' unless they were used for military purposes. Their presence was to be indicated by a 'distinctive and visible sign which shall be notified to the enemy beforehand'. Civilian hospitals were also protected under Article 5 of the 1907 Hague Convention (IX) on Bombardment by Naval Forces in Time of War. Article 18 GC IV extended to civilian hospitals the humanitarian rules relating to military hospitals, but provided for additional certificates issued by states and confirming their status, as well as for specific authorization to use the protective emblem. Geneva Convention IV also regulates in detail conditions for the requisition of civilian hospitals (Article 57). At present, under Article 8(e) of Additional Protocol (AP) I and customary international law,[8] civilian hospitals enjoy the same level of protection as military ones. However, it should

---

[7] On acts depriving protection, see Ch 42 of this volume.
[8] Practice of most states does not distinguish between military and civilian hospitals, see ICRC CIHL Study, vol I, at 92, fn 82, referring to military manuals and national legislation of almost 70 states. As for more recent examples of state practice, see ICRC CIHL Database, Rule 28, III: Australia, Cameroon, Canada, Côte d'Ivoire, Israel, Peru, South Africa, Spain, UK. ICRC CIHL Study, vol I, at 92, emphasizes that such a position was adopted not only by states parties to AP I, but also by some states who were not (at that time) parties to AP I.

be noted that under Article 12 AP I, recognition by one of the parties to the conflict and appropriate authorization still constitute preconditions for such equal treatment, though this does not mean that other hospitals may be attacked, as they do not constitute military objectives.

B. Meaning and Application

I. Hospitals on land

a. Definition of hospitals

8   Geneva Convention I does not give a definition of 'hospital'. Article 19 GC I refers in general to 'fixed establishments and mobile medical units of the Medical Service' and does not mention hospitals explicitly. In the Pictet Commentary on GC I, hospitals are named as examples of fixed establishments, while field hospitals are considered mobile units, with one additional remark:

> Definitions may often be dangerous, however, and the Conference rightly refrained from any attempt to produce one. It noted that the established term 'medical units' had not in the past been the subject of divergent interpretations and […] it was at once sufficiently comprehensive and sufficiently specific.[9]

The reference to 'Medical Service' means a medical service of the armed forces (forming integral part of state's armed forces), or a medical service of a National Red Cross Society or another organization, including from a neutral country, assisting the medical services of armed forces on the basis of Articles 26 and 27 GC I.

9   Article 18 GC IV uses the term 'civilian hospital' but does not include a definition. It indicates only that the purpose of such a hospital is to 'give care to the wounded and sick, the infirm and maternity cases'. According to the Pictet Commentary to GC IV, the list of categories of persons treated is not cumulative—'[i]t will suffice if the hospital devotes itself to one category only'[10]—but in any event it must have a staff and necessary equipment, and it must be organized (not necessarily on a permanent basis) as a hospital. Institutions that serve purposes other than medical purposes are not considered to be hospitals.[11] That does not mean that they may be attacked. Their protection is inherent in the principle of the distinction between civilian objects and military objectives, which is not explicitly formulated in the 1949 Geneva Conventions themselves but was present in international law at the time of their adoption by virtue of the 1868 St Petersburg Declaration and Article 25 of the 1907 Hague Regulations.

10 In military manuals and national legislation hospitals are either mentioned separately, without additional explanation,[12] or referred to as 'medical units',[13] 'establishments and

---

[9] Pictet Commentary GC I, at 195.   [10] Pictet Commentary GC IV, at 144.
[11] See reflections on the status of different types of social care services for the old and lonely, the blind or deaf, invalids, and homes for infants and children, ibid, at 145–6.
[12] ICRC CIHL Study, vol II, Part I, at 510 (Congo), 512 (Dominican Republic, France), 514 (Mali, Morocco), 515 (Nicaragua, Nigeria), 516 (Senegal, Switzerland), 517 (USA, Air Force Commander's Handbook and Rules of Engagement for Operation 'Desert Storm'); ICRC CIHL Database, Rule 28, III: Central African Republic, Ethiopia, Greece.
[13] ICRC CIHL Study, vol II, Part I, at 510 (Agreement in Bosnia and Herzegovina), 511 (Canada), 515 (Netherlands), 517 (UK); ICRC CIHL Database, Rule 28, III, Côte d'Ivoire.

other units [...] organized for medical purposes',[14] 'medical buildings',[15] or 'protected property'.[16] In some national instruments it is confirmed that protection is afforded both to fixed and field hospitals, thus emphasizing that the most important criterion is the purpose medical units, including hospitals, serve rather than the specific way in which they are organized.[17] It may be noted that some domestic documents adopt an elaborated, wide definition of 'medical units' that includes hospitals, taking the definition more or less word for word from Article 8(e) AP I.[18]

b. Recognition of civilian hospitals

Article 18 paragraph 2 GC IV stipulates that the status of a given establishment as a civilian hospital that enjoys protection under IHL has to be confirmed by a state in the form of a special certificate. Such a requirement for official recognition is justified in view of the wealth of different types of civilian medical practice in many countries. As GC IV does not mention size or legal status under domestic law, and thus does not exclude very small units and non-state hospitals,[19] there might be a proliferation of claims for protected status, implying also the right to use the protective emblem.[20] The relevant sentence reads '[s]tates [...] shall provide all civilian hospitals with certificates', and it is still for the state concerned to set the criteria for recognition.

While the philosophy behind this rule is logical and understandable, the second part of paragraph 2 in Article 18 GC IV is not realistic. It provides that certificates confirming the status of a given establishment as a civilian hospital should also assure that such 'buildings are not used for any purpose which would deprive these hospitals of protection'. This condition is rightly criticized:

[I]t is impossible for a State at the beginning of a war or even—as this would be more often the case—during peace time, to give a cogent undertaking that in the future a hospital would in fact refrain from acts harmful to the enemy.[21]

Such an assurance may confirm only the status quo at the moment the document was issued.

Geneva Convention IV does not specify which state authority is responsible for issuing a certificate. State practice in this regard is not clear.[22] Only a few states have included the general rule on authorization in their military manuals or Geneva Conventions Acts,[23] in

---

[14] ICRC CIHL Study, vol II, Part I at 516 (Senegal); ICRC CIHL Database, Rule 28, III, Australia.
[15] ICRC CIHL Database, Rule 28, III, Chad.
[16] Ibid, US (Manual for Military Commissions).
[17] ICRC CIHL Study, vol II, Part I, at 510–3 (Argentina, Bosnia and Herzegovina, Canada, Dominican Republic, Ecuador, Germany), 515 (Kenya, New Zealand), 517 (US Naval Handbook); ICRC CIHL Database, Rule 28, III: Australia (LOAC 2006), Burundi, Chad, Mexico, Peru, South Africa, Spain, UK, US (Manual for Military Commissions 2010).
[18] ICRC CIHL Database, Rule 28, III: Australia, Canada (LOAC Manual 2001), Côte d'Ivoire, Peru, South Africa (Civic Education Manual), Spain, UK; ICRC CIHL Study, vol II, Part I, at 516 (South Africa, LOAC Manual).
[19] Pictet Commentary GC IV, at 145.   [20] See MN 16.
[21] Pictet Commentary GC IV, at 148–9.
[22] The ICRC database on national implementation of IHL does not contain a section on medical units and their authorization. This author is aware of two national documents on, among other things, authorization of civilian hospitals—Guidelines on Implementation of Arts 18–20 GC IV, issued on 6 February 1965 by the Federal Minister of Health of the Federal Republic of Germany, and Peru's IHL and Human Rights Manual of 2010, para 79, available at ICRC CIHL Database, Rule 28, III.
[23] ICRC CIHL Study, vol I, at 95, fn 103, containing six examples; and ICRC CIHL Database, Rule 28, III: Canada (2001) and UK (2004).

most cases referring to the text of Article 18 GC IV and, when applicable, Article 12 AP I. It is worthwhile mentioning that despite the fact that AP I extends civilian protection afforded under the Geneva Conventions to military wounded, sick, and shipwrecked, and to medical personnel, units, and transports, it maintains the requirement for a state's recognition of civilian medical units, including civilian hospitals, as a precondition for their protection.[24]

14   When criteria set by a state are met and this state recognizes a given institution as a civilian hospital, it should continue to supervise such an establishment in order to avoid any abuse of its status as a civilian hospital.[25]

c. Identification of hospitals

15   The effective protection of hospitals can be ensured only if an adversary is aware of their existence and location. This means there needs to be marking with the protective emblem and adequate notification.

16   Marking of military hospitals is regulated by Article 42 GC I, with the emphasis on the condition of consent from the military authorities. With regard to civilian hospitals, the requirement of a state's authorization is stipulated in Article 18 GC IV. As these questions are presented elsewhere in the present Commentary,[26] it need only be mentioned here that hospitals are obliged to receive authorization in order to have the right to display protective emblems. Authorization to use the emblem (Article 18 paragraph 3) is an act different from recognition as a civilian hospital (Article 18 paragraph 2): 'Whereas all civilian hospitals marked with the protective emblem must necessarily have been officially recognized, all recognized civilian hospitals may not necessarily be marked.'[27] National legislation often requires hospitals to be properly marked,[28] but considers it important only for the facilitation of identification and not necessary for conferring protected status.[29] With regard to international regulations adopted after the Geneva Conventions, paragraph 4 of the Preamble to AP III recalls 'that the obligation to respect [...] objects protected by the Geneva Conventions [...] derives from their protected status under international law and is not dependent on use of the distinctive emblems'. Even where a civilian hospital is not recognized, and consequently not authorized to display the distinctive emblems, it is still protected as a civilian object, as long, of course, as it does not contribute to military action.

17   Geneva Convention I and GC IV do not provide for any communication to the adverse party on the location of hospitals, nor on certification of civilian hospitals. The lack of notification of location might be understandable in the case of military field hospitals, because such information might reveal the tactical deployment of troops. However, notification relating to fixed military hospitals and civilian hospitals would enforce their security without putting at risk the security of armed forces themselves. Parties to a conflict might use Protecting Powers (in the event of their appointment) for this purpose, or, in

---

[24] See also MN 7.
[25] Pictet Commentary GC IV, at 151.   [26] See Ch 43, MN 46–48, of this volume.
[27] Pictet Commentary GC IV, at 150.
[28] ICRC CIHL Study, vol I, at 95, fn 104; and ICRC CIHL Database, Rule 28, III: Canada (2001 and 2005), UK (2004), and US (2007).
[29] Only a few military manuals attach predominant importance to marking—see ICRC CIHL Study, vol II, Part I, at 520 (Germany), 521 (Nicaragua), and 513 and 525 (Israel) (*Israel's Law of War Booklet* of 1986 'grants protection to medical facilities as long as they are clearly recognizable as such', ibid, at 513); according to the *Report on the Practice of Israel*, the implementation of the policy of not targeting medical facilities depends on whether such facilities are 'clearly recognizable': ibid, at 525. However, in *Israel's Manual on the Rules of Warfare* (2006) it is stated that '[i]t is absolutely forbidden to attack the medical facilities of the enemy', without any reference to the distinctive emblems (ibid, at 513).

view of the reluctance to designate Protecting Powers in armed conflicts after the Second World War, confer this task on the International Committee of the Red Cross (ICRC).[30] As for subsequent development of IHL, under Article 12 AP I states are invited to notify each other of the location of their medical units, but lack of notification does not entail any negative consequences; in particular the absence of notification does not deprive hospitals of protection.

d. Remoteness of hospitals from military objectives

The Geneva Conventions protect different categories of persons and objects that find themselves in the power of the enemy state, and not a state's own nationals. Therefore it is not their purpose to protect against the effects of hostilities that might endanger a state's own population, except in the case of attacks directed against the enemy. However, some provisions, including those on hospitals, serve as exceptions to this general approach, and articulate the principle of distinction between military objectives and protected objects independently of the affiliation of the protected objects.[31] Article 19 GC I on military hospitals and Article 18 GC IV on civilian hospitals emphasize that hospitals 'may in no circumstances be attacked, but shall at all times be respected and protected'.[32] 18

Both Article 19 paragraph 2 GC I and Article 18 paragraph 5 GC IV contain a recommendation to locate hospitals at a distance from military objectives so that they are not exposed to dangers resulting from the conduct of hostilities, particularly the effects of attacks undertaken against legitimate military targets. This is one of the precautionary measures to be undertaken both in peacetime and in times of armed conflict. In time of peace, area development plans should envisage the construction of hospitals far from any existing or planned infrastructure that might be considered to be of a military nature or utility in time of armed conflict. Once hostilities break out, hospitals cannot easily be moved to other locations, therefore their presence should be taken into account when decisions are taken on the placing of military objectives.[33] The notion of 'military objectives' is not defined in the Geneva Conventions and should be understood in light of subsequent developments in customary and treaty IHL on the conduct of hostilities.[34] 19

The provisions under discussion are formulated as recommendations and not strong obligations. The requirement of remoteness of hospitals from military objectives is also included in some military manuals, usually diluted by clauses like 'as far as possible' or 'to the maximum extent possible'.[35] It goes without saying that the fact that this requirement is not complied with does not affect a hospital's status, but it may nevertheless have serious consequences for its security. 20

---

[30] See examples of such notifications passed by the ICRC in different armed conflicts in F. Bugnion, *The International Committee of the Red Cross and the Protection of War Victims* (Geneva/Oxford: ICRC/Macmillan, 2003), at 740–1.

[31] See also MN 9.

[32] As for the protection of own hospitals, it might also be mentioned that Art 13 GC I makes clear that this Convention equally protects the enemy and own military wounded and sick of a party to a conflict; and Art 18 GC IV is located in Part II of GC IV, covering all civilians and not only protected persons.

[33] See examples of 'collateral damage' from attacks on military targets and damages inflicted 'in error' in *Health Care in Danger*, above n 2, at 8–9.

[34] See Arts 52(2) (definition of military objectives), 57, and 58 (precautionary measures) AP I; and Rules 7 (principle of distinction), 8 (definition of military objectives), 15, 22, 24 (precautionary measures) ICRC CIHL Study, vol I, at 25–32, 51–5, 68–71, 74–6.

[35] See ICRC CIHL Study, vol I, at 96, fn 110, and vol II, Part I, at 525 (Jordan), 527 (US, 1992); ICRC CIHL Database, Rule 28, III: Canada (2001, 2005), Netherlands (2005), Peru, UK (2004).

II. Hospital ships

21 Hospital ships are ships built or equipped by states, 'specially and solely with a view to assisting the wounded, sick and shipwrecked, to treating them and to transporting them'. This definition, contained in Article 22 GC II, clearly indicates that the main condition to be met by a ship in order to be considered a hospital ship is its exclusive use for the 'charitable mission' that must be 'entire, obvious and durable'.[36] The fact that hospital ships not only collect, assist, and treat the wounded, sick and shipwrecked after naval battles, but also evacuate and transport them, locates them both in the category of medical units (like hospitals on land) and in the category of medical transports (where land-based hospitals do not fit).[37] At present they are rather considered means of transport, and AP I regulates their status in Section II of Part II entitled 'Medical Transportation'.[38]

22 Apart from the purpose a hospital ship serves, the second important precondition for its respect and protection is notification to the parties to the conflict of the use of a given vessel as a hospital ship. Nowadays, states tend not to maintain 'official' hospital ships registered as such.[39] They operate different types of medical vessels in order to bring assistance to local populations living on rivers or lakes, to support fishing fleets at sea, or to provide humanitarian assistance in case of disasters. These ships do not function as hospital ships under IHL but can be easily converted into hospital ships. Even during the 1982 Falkland-Malvinas Islands conflict, in which as many as seven hospital ships were deployed, all of them were converted ships.[40]

23 Article 22 GC II provides for the content and timeframe of notification. Such notification is necessary both in the case of 'official' hospital ships and for vessels transformed into hospital ships, and should include the vessel's name and other characteristics, mandatory characteristics being 'registered gross tonnage, the length from stem to stern and the number of masts and funnels'.[41] Article 26 GC II recommends, 'to ensure maximum comfort and security', that states 'shall endeavour to utilize […] over long distances and on the high seas, only hospital ships of over 2,000 tons gross'. In more recent documents, such as the *San Remo Manual on International Law Applicable to Armed Conflicts at Sea*, it is emphasized that 'to provide maximum protection for hospital ships […] notification should include all available information on the means whereby the ship may be identified'.[42]

---

[36] Pictet Commentary GC II, at 159.

[37] See J. Pictet, 'The Medical Profession and Humanitarian Law', 25 *IRRC* 247 (1985) 191, at 205–6.

[38] According to ICRC CIHL Study, hospital ships fall within the category of 'Medical Transports' referred to by Rule 29, and not 'Medical Units' covered by Rule 28. See only the few direct references to hospital ships in ICRC CIHL Study, vol II, Part I, at 551 (Croatia, Ecuador), 552 (New Zealand), 554 (United States), 556 (Romania), 556–7 (national case law of Germany relating to Dover Castle hospital ship case and other national practice of Germany and the UK with regard to the Tübingen hospital ship case), 561 (ICRC press release). Some other documents refer to medical transports of all types, including sea transports—ibid, at 550 (Canada) and 551 (Hungary). At present (October 2014) the ICRC CIHL Database contains no direct references to hospital ships.

[39] Only the US Navy has two hospital ships in active service—USNS *Mercy* and USNS *Comfort*—that until the mid-1980s operated as commercial supertankers. Since 1990 they have been deployed many times to support military operations in which US has been engaged, treating both military and civilian casualties. The Royal Navy of the UK operated the hospital ship RFA *Argus*, but decided to turn it into a 'self defending primary casualty recovery ship' with defensive armament—see Grunawalt, above n 6, esp at 111–14 and 119.

[40] See above n 5 and MN 4.   [41] Art 22 para 2 GC II.

[42] L. Doswald-Beck (ed), *San Remo Manual on International Law Applicable to Armed Conflicts at Sea* (Cambridge: Grotius Publications, CUP, 1995), at 42, para 169. *San Remo Manual* is a document prepared by experts acting in 1988–94 under the auspices of the San Remo International Institute of Humanitarian Law in view of the lack of any significant development of the law on the conduct of armed

Geneva Convention II does not specify the channels to be used for such notification. As in the case of hospitals on land, the most suitable intermediaries are Protecting Powers, or, in view of states' reluctance to use the services of Protecting Powers nowadays, the ICRC.[43]

24 With regard to the timeframe, Article 22 GC II stipulates that the necessary characteristics must be notified 10 days before the ships are deployed. This was considered the minimum time limit to ensure the security of hospital ships; however, the best solution is if notification is made much further in advance (even during peacetime, and then repeated after the outbreak of hostilities) so that hospital ships are protected from the very beginning of a conflict.[44] In order to avoid the abuse of the protections afforded to hospital ships by repeated changes in the status of other vessels being converted to hospital ships, and to ensure to 'hospital ships all desirable stability and permanence',[45] Article 33 GC II stipulates that once transformed into hospital ships, merchant vessels 'cannot be put to any other use throughout the duration of hostilities'.

25 Shipwrecked persons may be picked up and treated not only by vessels assigned to the medical services of states' naval forces or transformed into such vessels and officially enjoying the status of hospital ships, but also by ships, yachts, or other small craft employed by relief societies or private persons both of belligerent and neutral states. By virtue of Articles 24 and 25 GC II, IHL extends the protection afforded to a state's hospital ships to ships 'utilized by National Red Cross Societies, officially recognized relief societies or private persons' of states parties to the conflict and neutral countries, provided they are granted an official commission by 'the Party to the conflict on which they depend' or, in the case of ships sailing under a neutral flag, have received the prior consent of their own state and the authorization of the state under whose control they will be deployed. This means that for ships from neutral countries, two permissions must be obtained. A main precondition enabling all such vessels to exercise their functions is the notification, as in the case of states' hospital ships, of the characteristics enumerated in Article 22 GC II, for the purpose of identification of the vessel as a hospital ship. Such requirements may seem to be unduly bureaucratic and burdensome, particularly in case of assistance rendered by societies from neutral countries, but their fulfilment remains, first and foremost, in the interest of the medical mission, which would be endangered if these vessels were to be sailing independently, without the fleet commander's being aware of their medical function. It should be emphasized that regulations relating to vessels from neutral countries do not apply to vessels employed by neutral international humanitarian organizations such as the ICRC. Geneva Convention II remains mute on the status of such ships. This loophole has been filled by AP I.[46]

26 Small coastal rescue craft fulfilling the conditions provided for in Articles 22 and 24 GC II may also enjoy protection, but only 'so far as operational requirements permit'— the fact that the small size of such craft implies higher risks being taken into account.[47]

---

conflicts at sea since 1913, except for 1949 GC II and some provisions of 1977 AP I that are limited to the rules on protection of persons and medical vessels and aircraft.

[43] On the ICRC practice, see Bugnion, above n 30, at 531.

[44] Pictet Commentary GC II, at 161; *San Remo Manual*, above n 42, at 42, para 169. It is worth mentioning that the US hospital ships can be fully activated and crewed within five days—in such cases early notification allows for the hospitals' deployment immediately after they are ready to undertake their tasks.

[45] Pictet Commentary GC II, at 188.

[46] Art 22(2)(b) AP I. On the ICRC status and practice in this regard, see Bugnion, above n 30, at 538–42.

[47] Art 27 GC II. Art 22(3) AP I no longer requires formal notification in the case of small craft.

Similar cautious wording is used in the case of fixed coastal installations used exclusively by coastal rescue craft.[48] Other types of vessels that are mentioned separately are lifeboats of hospital ships.[49] It should also be noted that the necessity to render medical treatment to wounded, sick, and shipwrecked persons may arise on board a warship, therefore the sick-bays are afforded protection 'as far as possible' in the event of fighting taking place on board.[50] However, hand-to-hand fighting on board a warship does not take place in today's armed conflicts, and this provision is therefore obsolete.

27   Documents adopted after 1949 simplify terminology by calling all the floating medical treatment facilities described in Articles 22, 24, 25, and 27 GC II, as well as their lifeboats and small craft, 'hospital ships and coastal rescue craft'[51] or 'hospital ships, small craft used for coastal rescue operations and other medical transports'.[52] The simplification of terminology has not been followed by a simplification of procedures, except for the relaxation of the notification requirement in the case of small craft.[53] In addition, in accordance with the approach adopted in AP I to match the status of civilian victims of armed conflicts to military ones, its Article 22(1) stipulates that hospital ships may also care for and transport civilian sick, wounded, and shipwrecked persons.

28   As in the case of hospitals on land, the effective protection of hospital ships can be ensured only if an adversary is aware of their existence and location. This can be achieved by adequate notification[54] and by marking them with protective emblems, as regulated by Article 43 GC II. These regulations were developed in Annex I to AP I, particularly Chapter III. As these questions are presented elsewhere in the present Commentary,[55] it is sufficient to note here that 'means of identification are intended only to facilitate identification and do not, of themselves, confer protected status'.[56] Not using them does not deprive hospital ships of protection. This statement is important in light of the discussion concerning whether marking hospital ships makes sense nowadays, when hospitals and other protected objects are attacked precisely because of their special status, with increased vulnerability and terror being spread in cases of destruction.[57]

29   With regard to the requirement of remoteness of hospital ships from military objectives, GC II does not contain any provision addressing precisely this problem. However, the basic philosophy is the same as in the case of hospitals on land,[58] and is expressed in Article 30 paragraph 4 GC II, specifying that 'during and after an engagement, hospital ships will act at their own risk'. The security of hospital ships would obviously be endangered in cases where they fulfil their humanitarian mission while some fighting still going on and they risk getting caught in the line of fire. 'After' means 'immediately after', in other words, when any presence in the area of engagement is still dangerous.[59] If the proximity to the military objective results from the escorting of a hospital ship by warships, the hospital ship does not lose its protected status but

---

[48] Art 27 para 2 GC II.
[49] Art 26 GC II.   [50] Art 28 GC II.   [51] Art 22 AP I.
[52] *San Remo Manual*, above n 42, at 16, 28, 34, 42, paras 47, 110, 136, 172.   [53] See above n 47.
[54] See MN 22–24.   [55] See Ch 43 of this volume.
[56] Art 173 of the 1994 *San Remo Manual*, above n 42, at 42 and explanations at 237–41. See MN 16 for similar conclusions on the marking of hospitals on land.
[57] See Grunawalt, above n 6, at 115–17.   [58] See MN 19–20.
[59] See Pictet Commentary GC II, at 180.

exposes itself to the danger of collateral damage in case an attack is undertaken against the escorting warships.[60]

III. Scope of protection of hospitals on land and hospital ships

a. General remarks

Hospitals are considered specially or specifically protected objects,[61] because their status is regulated by specific provisions and, in the case of civilian hospitals, their protection is additional to that afforded to every civilian object in accordance with the principle of distinction. Their protection is enhanced through the right to use a distinctive emblem, which is not the case for every object exempted from attack.[62] Some states and international organizations expressly recognize the special status of hospitals as a customary one, as a 'fundamental principle of humanitarian law' or as an 'elementary principle of humanity'.[63] The scope of protection depends on the category of hospitals, namely, whether they are hospitals on land or hospital ships. In the case of hospitals on land, Article 19 paragraph 1 GC I and Article 18 paragraph 1 GC IV characterize their status as follows: they may in no circumstances be attacked, but shall at all times be respected and protected by the Parties to the conflict.[64] As for hospital ships, according to Article 22 paragraph 1 GC II, they 'may in no circumstances be attacked or captured, but shall at all times be respected and protected'.

With regard to the notions of 'respect' and 'protection', including the prohibition on attacks, these are analysed elsewhere in the present Commentary.[65] Expressions such as 'in no circumstances' and 'at all times' strengthen the fundamental character and value of these regulations. They are often used in this sense in states' practice.[66] In addition, they confirm that the restrictions with regard to the scope of protection introduced by the 1864 Geneva Convention are no longer applicable. This Convention provided in its Article 1 for the neutrality, protection of, and respect for military hospitals only 'as long as they accommodate [the] wounded and sick'. The 1906 and 1929 Geneva Conventions on the wounded and sick in land warfare modified these provisions by deleting the reference to the actual presence of wounded soldiers as a precondition for protection. However, this question is still sometimes addressed in states' domestic documents.[67] Expressions

---

[60] Ibid, at 181; see also Grunawalt, above n 6, at 102.

[61] ICRC CIHL Study, vol II, Part I, at 511–16 (Benin, Croatia, France on 'special immunity', Italy, Madagascar, Nigeria, Togo), 522 (Slovenia); ICRC CIHL Database, Rule 28, III: Côte d'Ivoire, Zimbabwe, Rule 28, IV: Serbia.

[62] See comments on the notions of 'special protection' or 'specific protection' afforded to medical units, including hospitals, in *Commentary on the HPCR Manual on International Law Applicable to Air and Missile Warfare*, Program on Humanitarian Policy and Conflict Research at Harvard University, 2010, available at <http://www.ihlresearch.org/amw>, at 169.

[63] ICRC CIHL Study, vol II, Part I, at 514 (Mali, Morocco), 516 (Sweden), 524 (Egypt, Finland), 525 (Iraq, Nigeria), 527 (Zimbabwe), 528 (United Nations Commission on Human Rights); ICRC CIHL Database, Rule 28, V: Colombia.

[64] There is a meaningless difference between the two Articles in terms of their specific wording: according to Art 19 GC I, hospitals 'may in no circumstances be attacked', while under Art 18 GC IV they 'may in no circumstances be the object of attack'.

[65] See Ch 39, section B.II, of this volume.

[66] ICRC CIHL Study, vol II, Part I, at 510 (Argentina 1989, Australia), 511 (Belgium), 513 (Israel 1998), 515–17 (New Zealand, Nigeria, South Africa, UK 1958), 524 (Egypt), 526–7 (US 1987, 1991); ICRC CIHL Database, Rule 28, III: Australia, Canada, Mexico, Spain.

[67] Switzerland's Basic Military Manual of 1987 provides that medical units shall not be harmed in any way, 'even if they do not momentarily hold any wounded or sick'—see ICRC CIHL Study, vol II, Part I, at 516.

such as 'in no circumstances' and 'at all times' also serve as a decisive argument when the consequences of the lack of adequate marking of hospitals, lack of formal recognition and authorization of civilian hospitals, and the proximity of hospitals to military objectives are discussed. Such and similar situations may have negative consequences for the security of hospitals, but do not deprive them of legal protection.[68] Lastly, the wording enforces the categorical prohibition of reprisals against hospitals.[69]

b. Situations not depriving protection

32 The protection afforded to hospitals is fundamental but not absolute. International humanitarian law takes into account that parties to a conflict may be tempted to abuse their special status in order to commit acts harmful to the enemy. Such acts may result in the loss of protection of hospitals.[70] As such situations would constitute exceptions to the general rules on the protection of and respect for hospitals, they have to be subject to a restrictive interpretation. To facilitate such an interpretation, Geneva Conventions I, II, and IV enumerate cases where hospitals 'retain their character as such [...] despite certain appearances which might have led to the contrary conclusion or at least given rise to some doubt'.[71] The lists of situations not depriving hospitals of protection should not be considered comprehensive, and in a concrete case 'the good faith of the unit remains beyond question despite certain appearances to the contrary'.[72] This statement seems valid today, mainly with regard to the discussion on the arming of hospital ships and their use of encrypted communication.[73] There are also examples of domestic documents departing slightly from the language of the 1949 Geneva Conventions.[74]

33 With regard to hospitals on land, GC I provides in Article 22 for five conditions not depriving military hospital ships of protection. Article 19 paragraph 2 GC IV foresees only two such conditions with regard to civilian hospitals. These situations are not controversial, but some of them seem obsolete today. The first situation enumerated in Article 22 GC I, namely the right of the hospital's personnel to be armed and use weapons 'in their own defence, or in that of the wounded and sick in their charge', has been accepted since the 1906 Geneva Convention, and is necessary to ensure order in the hospital and to protect the wounded and sick against criminal acts like pillage, assault on members of the adversary's armed forces treated there, or assault on members of medical personnel. It has no counterpart in Article 19 GC IV; however, subsequent international regulations,[75] and some states' military manuals, confirm its relevance in the case of both military and

---

However, Chad's Instructor's Manual of 2006 states that a hospital 'may not be used for military purposes if it contains wounded people'—ICRC CIHL Database, Rule 28, III. *A contrario*, a hospital might be used for military purposes if there were no wounded people on its premises, which obviously contradicts the rules under discussion.

[68] See MN 16, 20, and 28.
[69] See Art 46 GC I, Art 47 GC II, Rule 147 ICRC CIHL Study, vol I, at 523–6.
[70] This problem is addressed in Ch 42 of this volume. [71] Pictet Commentary GC II, at 194.
[72] Ibid. See also Pictet Commentary GC I, at 203, and *Commentary on the HPCR Manual*, above n 62, at 180.
[73] See MN 39.
[74] E.g., Sierra Leone's *Instructor Manual*, listing among conditions not depriving protection 'the delivery to [a] medical unit of wounded and sick personnel [...] in non-medical transport, such as ordinary, unmarked military vehicle or helicopters'—ICRC CIHL Database, Rule 28, III.
[75] Art 13(2)(a) AP I.

civilian hospitals.[76] In AP I, the light character of individual weapons allowed is emphasized. This means weapons carried and used by a single individual, like pistols, rifles, and submachine guns.[77]

Similarly uncontroversial is the second condition not depriving a hospital of protection, namely that the unit or establishment is protected by the presence of a 'picket or by sentries or by an escort'[78] in the event of the absence of armed orderlies 'in sufficient numbers'.[79] 'In sufficient numbers' was suggested in Pictet Commentary in order to avoid an interpretation to the effect that the simultaneous presence of armed orderlies and a military guard is prohibited, even if the orderlies are not numerous enough or only few of them possess light weapons. This situation is not mirrored in GC IV, but is referred to in AP I[80] and in few domestic instruments.[81]

The third condition which does not deprive a medical unit of its protection is the presence of arms and ammunition taken from the treated combatants and not handed over to the proper service, a condition reflected in Article 19 paragraph 2 GC IV. It is here closely connected to the second condition not depriving a civilian hospital of protection, namely the treatment in its premises of sick and wounded combatants, which, at the same time, is a counterpart of the fifth condition enumerated in Article 22 GC I on the treatment in military hospitals of wounded and sick civilians. These provisions are confirmed in AP I[82] and, to a lesser degree, in states' domestic documents, and in the case law of the International Criminal Tribunal for the former Yugoslavia (ICTY).[83]

The condition listed in subparagraph 4 of Article 22 GC I, regarding the presence of personnel and material of the veterinary service, is not addressed in international instruments adopted after 1949, nor in national laws.

An additional example of a situation that might be harmful to the enemy but still not exceed the humanitarian function of medical units, and therefore not deprive them of protection, might be that of radiation emitted by x-ray apparatus, which 'could interfere with the transmission or reception of wireless messages by a military set, or with the working of a radar unit'.[84]

With regard to hospital ships, five conditions not depriving them of protection are listed in Article 35 GC II. Three of them are counterparts to subparagraphs 1, 3, and 5 in Article 22 GC I.[85] The first one—on the right of crew members to possess arms for self-defence—subsequently gave rise to an international debate on the types and quantities of arms allowed. The *San Remo Manual* specifies that '[h]ospital ships may be equipped with purely deflective means of defence, such as chaff and flares' and that '[t]he presence of such equipment should be notified'.[86] This statement is considered by the authors of the *Manual*

---

[76] ICRC CIHL Database, Rule 28, III: Belgium, Canada, Côte d'Ivoire, Switzerland. Some other states confirm the rule without special reference to either military or civilian hospitals—ibid: Bosnia and Herzegovina, Burundi, Germany, Netherlands, Sierra Leone.

[77] Art 13(2)(a) AP I.   [78] Art 22 para 1(2) GC I.   [79] Pictet Commentary GC I, at 204.

[80] Art 13(2)(b) AP I.

[81] ICRC CIHL Database, Rule 28, III: Belgium, Canada, Côte d'Ivoire, Germany, Netherlands, Nigeria, Sierra Leone, Switzerland, Ukraine.

[82] Art 13(2)(c) and (d) AP I.

[83] ICRC CIHL Database, Rule 28, III: Canada 2001, Côte d'Ivoire, Germany, Netherlands, Nigeria, Sierra Leone, US 1976. See also ICTY, *The Prosecutor v Stanislav Galić*, Appeals Chamber Judgment, IT-98-29-A, 30 November 2006, at 147, para 343.

[84] Pictet Commentary GC I, at 201.   [85] See MN 33–36.

[86] *San Remo Manual*, above n 42, at 42, para 170.

to be purely confirmatory of GC II.[87] States' practice is not uniform. Prior to the deployment of USNS *Comfort* in support of 'Operation Iraqi Freedom', 50-caliber machine guns were installed on this hospital ship, 'exclusively for defence, to fend off attacks by swarming, heavily armed speed boats or suicide craft'.[88] The US adopted the position that this was legal because of the purely defensive character of these guns. However, when the UK decided to install defensive armaments on its hospital ship RFA *Argus*, it changed its status from a hospital ship to a self-defending primary casualty recovery ship.[89]

39   The other conditions listed in Article 35 are not controversial, including the two that do not have counterparts in GC I and relate to '[t]he transport of equipment and personnel intended exclusively for medical duties' in quantities exceeding normal requirements, and '[t]he presence of apparatus exclusively intended to facilitate navigation and communication'.[90] What is controversial nowadays is an attempt to add, through states' practice and 'soft law' documents, a sixth condition to the catalogue formulated in Article 35 GC II. Namely, it is argued that hospital ships should be permitted to use cryptographic communications equipment in order to be able to communicate directly with warships without revealing warships' positions to enemy forces. 'Most modern communications and navigation systems, including satellite systems, use some form of encryption even at the most basic level.'[91] Paragraph 171 of the *San Remo Manual* states that 'hospital ships should be permitted to use cryptographic equipment', but this equipment 'shall not be used in any circumstances to transmit intelligence data nor in any other way to acquire any military advantage'.[92] This provision departs sharply from Article 34 GC II, which specifically prohibits the possession or use of secret codes by hospital ships and expressly considers such acts as harmful to the enemy. Drafters of the *Manual* emphasized that paragraph 171 reflects what they considered the law ought to be and not what it is.[93] Hence the possession and use of secret codes still form the basis for loss of protection,[94] but do not necessarily turn hospital ships into legitimate targets for attacks.

40   In order to assure themselves that hospital ships and coastal rescue craft—both belonging to the adversary and neutral—are used in conformity with the rules set out in IHL and hence enjoy protection, parties to the conflict have the right to control them. Article 31 GC II enumerates a few means to exercise this control. First and foremost, states can search a hospital ship and its equipment, and check the identity of the sick and wounded as well as crew members. In this context, control of the use of communications is mentioned explicitly.[95] States are not obliged to accept medical assistance, they can give certain orders with regard to a hospital ship's course, and even put a commissioner on board who would see that such orders were carried out. Independently of the possibility of a commissioner's temporary presence for the verification of the execution of concrete orders, neutral observers may be put on board hospital ships, 'unilaterally or by particular agreement',[96] to verify

---

[87] Ibid, at 41, para 159.   [88] US position quoted after Grunawalt, above n 6, at 116.
[89] See above n 39.
[90] See Pictet Commentary GC II, at 195–9; and Grunawalt, above n 6, at 104.
[91] US position quoted after Grunawalt, above n 6, at 114. See *contra* A.M. Smith, 'Has the Red Cross-Adorned Hospital Ship Become Obsolete?', 58 *Naval War College Review* (2005) 121—the author argues that encrypted communications are not necessary.
[92] *San Remo Manual*, above n 42, at 42, para 171.   [93] See stipulation ibid, at 41, para 159.
[94] See Ch 42, MN 7 and 9–13, of this volume.
[95] See MN 39 on the contemporary discussion concerning the legality of the use of encrypted communication.
[96] Art 31 para 4 GC II. On the practical application of this provision, see Bugnion, above n 30, at 533–4.

the strict observation of IHL and thus to prevent the improper use of hospital ships in violation of GC II. 'If the gravity of circumstances so requires',[97] for example in order to ensure the secrecy of military operations, states can detain hospital ships temporarily, for a period not exceeding seven days. Obviously this measure is truly exceptional and cannot lead to a hospital ship's capture, which would contradict the clear prohibition against capture contained in Article 22 GC II.[98] However, these complex provisions cannot be applied in practice unless belligerent naval forces are more or less equal. 'Otherwise, the only belligerent able to [exercise supervision] will be the one that succeeds in clearing the war zone of all surface vessels belonging to the enemy. [...] [T]he latter will then probably denounce all sorts of nefarious abuses and, since it derives so little benefit from the Convention, will cease to observe it.'[99]

41 Geneva Convention I and AP I do not contain any provision similar to Article 31 GC II, but states' practice allows for the inspection of land hospitals without, however, specifying concrete procedures.[100]

c. Capture, requisition

42 As clearly expressed in Article 19 GC I and Article 22 GC II, the scope of protection for military hospitals on land and for hospital ships differs, in that the former may be captured by the adverse party, while capture of the latter is strictly prohibited.

43 If a military hospital on land is captured, it shall continue to treat its patients 'as long as the capturing Power has not itself ensured the necessary care of the wounded and sick found in such establishments'.[101] This provision does not introduce a new concept, it simply confirms the principle of humanity that includes protection of combatants *hors de combat*. The reason for this repetition is convincingly explained in the Pictet Commentary:

> After capture the ultimate fate reserved for the various elements which go to make up a [...] medical unit (building, personnel and equipment) varies according to their nature and existing circumstances [...] But there is a period during which its elements cannot be separated [...] the period, namely, during which the wounded and sick [...] need its help.[102]

In the course of the subsequent development of IHL, this rule was not amended, which confirms its fundamental nature, deeply rooted in the principle of humanity.

44 The rule regarding the prohibition of capture of hospital ships (and the corresponding one on the prohibition of their detention for the period exceeding seven days)[103] is motivated by the fact that ships (and hospital ships in particular) were considered to be in short supply in times of war.[104] It is much easier to build or equip a hospital on land than a floating one. The right of belligerents to capture hospital ships, even under the similar conditions that apply in the case of capture of hospitals on land, might deprive new casualties of any chance to be collected and cared for. Geneva Convention II repeats this prohibition in Article 29 with regard to hospital ships in occupied ports. It might be mentioned in this context that, while in neutral ports, hospital ships cannot be subjected

---

[97] Art 31 para 1 GC II.
[98] See MN 30 and 42.
[99] Bugnion, above n 30, at 532. See also practical examples referred to therein.
[100] ICRC CIHL Study, vol I, at 96, fn 108.   [101] Art 19 para 1 GC I.
[102] Pictet Commentary GC I, at 197–8. As for the status of buildings, personnel, and equipment, see Chs 40–1 of this volume.
[103] See MN 40.   [104] Pictet Commentary GC II, at 158.

to the restrictions that are applicable to warships with regard to the length of their stay, the provision of supplies, and other rules that a neutral state is obliged to apply towards warships in accordance with the 1907 Hague Convention (XIII) concerning the Rights and Duties of Neutral Powers in Naval War.[105] Another regulation that does not relate directly to the capture of hospital ships, but which deserves mention here in order to have a comprehensive overview of situations similar from a humanitarian point of view, though formally different, is the rule on the treatment of sick-bays of warships in the event of their capture.[106] They 'may not be diverted from their purpose so long as they are required for the wounded and sick', although urgent military necessity may justify other decisions of the commander into whose power they have fallen.[107] The *San Remo Manual* confirms that hospital ships and small craft used for coastal rescue operations are exempt from capture,[108] but at the same time formulates conditions which need to be fulfilled to ensure such exemption.[109] These conditions are very similar to those for the exemption of hospital ships from attack,[110] in other words they reflect the situation in which a hospital ship is considered to act in accordance with its mission and hence enjoy protection.

45 With regard to civilian hospitals, the question of the scope of their protection in the event of capture by the adversary can arise within the legal framework of occupation. The crucial provision in this context is contained in Article 56 paragraph 1 GC IV, imposing a duty on the occupying state of 'ensuring and maintaining [...] hospital establishments and facilities'. However, Article 57 GC IV introduces an exception to this rule, by allowing the occupying state to requisition civilian hospitals under certain cumulative conditions. The first condition is that such requisition must be temporary, and after the change of circumstances the hospital has to serve the medical needs of the civilian population once more. The second condition is that such a requisition may take place only when it is urgently necessary for the medical (and no other) purposes of the armed forces of the occupying state, namely, for the care of its military wounded and sick. The third condition is that 'suitable arrangements are made in due time for the care and treatment of the patients and for the needs of the civilian population for hospital accommodation'.[111] This provision is developed by Article 14 AP I, which emphasizes the rule of non-requisition of civilian hospitals and maintains the above three conditions as those justifying exception. The possibility of the requisition of hospitals is closely related to the legal status of materials and stores of civilian hospitals, and, by virtue of Article 56 of the Hague Regulations 1907, to the question of the protection of private property. States' practice is not well developed in this area.[112]

C. Relevance in Non-International Armed Conflicts

46 The problem of protection of hospitals is extremely relevant not only in international armed conflicts (IACs), but also in non-international armed conflicts (NIACs). Most of the cases of violence against hospitals, including direct attacks, collateral damage, forced

---

[105] On neutrality, see Ch 5, esp MN 42–43, of this volume.
[106] See MN 26 and Ch 41, MN 22 and 38, of this volume regarding sick-bays.
[107] Art 28 GC II.   [108] *San Remo Manual*, above n 42, at 34, para 136.   [109] Ibid, para 137.
[110] Ibid, at 17, para 48.   [111] Art 57 para 1 GC IV.
[112] See ICRC CIHL Database, Rule 28, III: Cameroon 2006, Netherlands 2005, and Spain 2007; Rule 28, IV: Croatia and Ethiopia.

entries, and looting, take place during NIACs.[113] Common Article 3 does not explicitly provide for the protection of hospitals or—more generally—medical units. However, such protection is implied in Common Article 3 paragraph 1(2), where it is stated that '[t]he wounded and sick shall be collected and cared for'. Such persons could not receive medical care if hospitals were lawfully attacked, therefore the only logical conclusion is that hospitals are protected in NIACs as in IACs, despite the lack of express provision to this effect in Common Article 3. It might be called 'a subsidiary form of protection' inferred from Common Article 3.[114]

There is no doubt that there exists a norm of customary IHL providing for the protection of and respect for hospitals in NIAC. It is confirmed in unanimous state practice, expressed in military manuals[115] and national legislation providing for the prosecution of breaches,[116] as well as in *opinio iuris* mirrored in states' official statements condemning attacks whenever this rule has been violated.[117] Such condemnations have also been expressed by the United Nations and by the ICRC.[118] Codes of conduct issued by some non-state armed groups contain obligations similar to those binding upon states on the basis of international treaties. For example, guidelines issued by the National Transition Council in Libya in May 2011 state as follows: 'Do not target medical personnel, facilities, transports or equipment. These may be searched if you need to verify they are genuine [...].'[119] However, it should be noted that although the practice of military forces entering hospitals to 'verify they are genuine' and to check the wounded and sick who are staying in the hospital is formally allowed in IAC[120] and in NIAC, it presents a more and more serious problem. Treatment of wounded fighters becomes impossible because they do not dare go to a hospital. Only a few states provide in their national legislation for the wide obligation to 'safeguard hospitals from violence' and ensure 'unimpeded continuation of their work'.[121]

47

---

[113] See above n 2, NIACs in Afghanistan, Angola, Bosnia and Herzegovina, Burundi, Chechnya, Kampuchea, Kyrgyzstan, Lebanon, Liberia, Mexico, Libya, Rwanda, El Salvador, Somalia, Sri Lanka, Syria. It is not possible to draft a comprehensive list of acts directed against hospitals, taking into account their frequency and different forms.

[114] ICRC CIHL Study, vol I, at 93. See also K. Dörmann, *Elements of War Crimes under the Rome Statute of the International Criminal Court. Sources and Commentary* (Cambridge: CUP, 2003), at 215.

[115] ICRC CIHL Study, vol I, at 94, fn 93; and ICRC CIHL Database, Rule 28, III: UK 2004.

[116] ICRC CIHL Study, vol I, at 94, fn 94; and ICRC CIHL Database, Rule 28, IV: Australia 2007, Burundi, France, Iraq, Peru, Republic of Korea, Senegal, South Africa, Uruguay.

[117] ICRC CIHL Study, vol I, at 94, fnn 95–6.

[118] Ibid, fnn 97–8. See also the *Report of the Secretary General on the Protection of Civilians in Armed Conflict*, 22 May 2012, S/2012/376, para 11, at 3 (on Syria), para 13, at 4 (on Libya), para 32, at 8 (on the value of the ICRC study on *Health Care in Danger*), and para 41, at 10 (on non-state armed groups committing violations of IHL by attacking health care services in NIAC).

[119] 'A Collection of Codes of Conduct Issued by Armed Groups', 93 *IRRC* 882 (2011) 483, at 500. See also 'Directory of Armed Non-State Actors Humanitarian Commitments', posted on the website of Geneva Call—NGO dedicated to engaging armed non-state actors with a view to compliance with the norms of IHL and IHRL, available at <http://www.theirwords.org/>, in particular Code of War of ELN in Colombia of 1992 and agreement concluded between ELN and National Peace Committee in 1998—*Acuerdo de Puerta del Cielo*, para 14; *Comprehensive Agreement on Respect for Human Rights and International Humanitarian Law* between the Government of the Republic of the Philippines and the National Democratic Front of the Philippines of 1998, Art 4 para 3; *Internal Rules and Regulations of Moro Islamic Liberation Front of Philippines* of 2006, Art 34 para 7.

[120] See MN 40–41.

[121] See MN 50. On the consequences of disruptive armed entry, see the report on *Violent Incidents Affecting the Delivery of Health Care* (Geneva: ICRC, 2014), at 11–12, published as part of the ICRC *Health Care in Danger* project.

48   The subsequent development of treaty law confirms the protection of hospitals in NIACs to the same extent as in IACs. Article 11(1) AP II repeats the principle of respect for and protection of medical units at all times. The Statute of the International Criminal Court (ICC Statute) qualifies as war crimes, both in IAC and in NIAC, '[i]ntentionally directing attacks against [...] hospitals and places where the sick and wounded are collected, provided they are not military objectives' and '[i]ntentionally directing attacks against [...] medical units [...] using the distinctive emblems of the Geneva Conventions in conformity with international law.'[122] The ICC Elements of Crimes have identical wording with regard to these war crimes, independently of whether they are committed in an IAC or in a NIAC.[123] The International Criminal Tribunal for Rwanda (ICTR) referred to the protection of hospitals in a few cases on the basis of Common Article 3 and AP II, although this was not reflected in its judgments due to fact that the Tribunal did not establish that the accused had violated their protected status.[124]

49   There are some other instruments pertaining to NIAC that confirm the principles of respect for and protection of hospitals.[125] The prohibition of attacks against medical units, facilities, and transports in NIAC is also clearly formulated in 'soft law' international documents like the *San Remo Manual on the Law of Non-International Armed Conflict*.[126] Its Commentary explains that attacks are forbidden due to the status of these as objects 'entitled to special protection' in NIAC.[127] There are no statements known to this author claiming the legality of depriving hospitals of protection in NIAC because of the qualification of the conflict. In the event that hospitals are attacked, allegations are denied, and such denials support the existence of the rule on the protection and respect owed to hospitals.[128]

50   The scope of regulation on the protection of and respect for hospitals in NIAC is narrower than in IAC. The ICC Statute criminalizes only 'attacks' against hospitals both in IAC and NIAC. The national legislation of states usually forbids the same type of acts, sometimes adding a prohibition on the 'destruction of hospitals'.[129] There are only a few examples of wider references to the need to 'respect', 'safeguard from violence', ensure 'unimpeded continuation of work', or prohibit 'breaches of norms of IHL against medical units' as long as those units are not used to commit hostile acts.[130] There are no examples

---

[122] See identical texts of Art 8(2)(b)(ix)/Art 8(2)(e)(iv) and Art 8(2)(b)(xxiv)/Art 8(2)(e)(ii) ICC Statute.

[123] ICC Elements of Crimes, Art 8(2)(b)(ix)/Art 8(2)(e)(iv) and Art 8(2)(b)(xxiv)/Art 8(2)(e)(ii).

[124] ICTR, *The Prosecutor v Casimir Bizimungu et al*, Trial Chamber Judgment, ICTR-99-50-T, 30 September 2011, at 227, para 917, and ICTR, *The Prosecutor v Pauline Nyiramasuhuko et al*, Trial Chamber Judgment, ICTR-98-42-T, 24 June 2011, at 521, para 2143, with the exception of the accused, Joseph Kanyabashi, whose responsibility for the massacre of Tutsis in Matyazo Clinic has been established by the Tribunal (ibid, at 485–512, paras 2012–13).

[125] *Bosnia and Herzegovina, Agreement No 1* of 22 May 1992 concluded between parties to the conflict under the auspices of the ICRC, para 2.2—Sassòli/Bouvier/Quintin, vol III, 1717–21, at 1719.

[126] M.N. Schmitt, C.H.B. Garraway, and Y. Dinstein (eds), *The Manual on the Law of Non-International Armed Conflict with Commentary* (San Remo: International Institute of Humanitarian Law, 2006), available at <http://www.iihl.org/iihl/Documents/The Manual on the Law of NIAC.pdf>, Rule 4.2.1, at 56.

[127] Ibid.

[128] S. Sivakumaran, *The Law of Non-International Armed Conflict* (Oxford: OUP, 2012), at 373–5. See also ICRC CIHL Study, vol II, Part I, at 535 (unnamed armed opposition groups).

[129] ICRC CIHL Study, vol II, Part I, at 518–23 (Australia, Azerbaijan, Congo, El Salvador, Germany, Netherlands, New Zealand, Nicaragua, Trinidad and Tobago, UK); ICRC CIHL Database, Rule 28, IV: Burundi, Iraq, Peru, Republic of Korea, Senegal, South Africa, Uruguay.

[130] ICRC CIHL, vol II, at 520 (Georgia), 522 (Tajikistan), 530 (European Community on Liberia, Council of Europe on Chechen attack on hospital in Dagestan), 533 (ICRC on Angola and Mexico); ICRC CIHL Database, Rule 28, XI: 1978 ICRC statement on Lebanon.

known to this author of norms or practical steps undertaken in NIAC that are required in IAC with regard to the recognition of civilian hospitals or their authorization to use protective emblems;[131] nor is there practice confirming in NIAC the special status and protection of hospital ships, comprehensively regulated under the law of IAC.[132]

D. Legal Consequences of a Violation

As in the case of many other rules of IHL, one of the means of inducing compliance with the obligation to respect and protect hospitals is criminal accountability of those responsible for its violation under national and international law.

51

Neither the Geneva Conventions nor AP I explicitly qualify violations of a hospital's status as grave breaches. However, the expression 'extensive destruction and appropriation of property' protected by the given Geneva Convention, used in the provisions on grave breaches,[133] suggests that the extensive destruction of hospitals and hospital ships, not justified by military necessity, would constitute a grave breach of the Geneva Conventions.[134] According to the ICTY, the notion of 'extensive' should be 'evaluated according to the facts of the case', and even a single act of destruction of a hospital 'may suffice to characterize an offence'.[135] In addition, one might argue that such destruction will often lead to 'wilful killing' or 'wilfully causing great suffering or serious injury to body or health', thus meeting other criteria contained in the definition of grave breaches.[136] This interpretation is not universally accepted.[137]

52

The domestic law of many states qualifies as war crimes certain acts that could amount to attacks against hospitals.[138] Material elements of these crimes are often based on Article 8 of the ICC Statute,[139] but in some domestic regulations the catalogue of such acts is more detailed, for example 'use of a privileged building for improper purposes',[140] 'attacks, misappropriation and destruction',[141] 'burning, destroying or attacking hospitals on land

53

---

[131] See MN 11–17.

[132] See MN 21–29. The possibility of naval hostilities in NIAC was considered probable in *Bosnia and Herzegovina. Agreement No 1*, above n 125, para 2.1 referring to GC II, at 1719.

[133] Art 50 GC I, Art 51 GC II, Art 147 GC IV.

[134] See Pictet Commentary GC II, at 269; Pictet Commentary GC IV, at 597, 601. Pictet Commentary GC I, at 371–2 does not mention hospitals expressly but refers to property defined in Arts 33–36 GC I, i.e. buildings, material, stores of medical establishments, as well as medical transports.

[135] ICTY, *The Prosecutor v Tihomir Blaškić*, Trial Chamber Judgment, IT-95-14, 3 March 2000, at 53. The ICTY referred to Pictet Commentary GC IV, at 601, where it is stated that 'an isolated incident would not be enough', but at the same time it is admitted that in the case of a single civilian hospital bombed intentionally, not considering its destruction as a grave breach 'would be an inadmissible inference to draw'.

[136] Pictet Commentary GC II, at 270.

[137] See the very cautious formulation in Pictet Commentary GC IV, at 597 and ICRC CIHL Database, Rule 28 III: UK (1958), US (1976)—in these military manuals it is assumed that the list of grave breaches does not include some acts directed against hospitals, and that their criminalization is additional to the grave breaches regime.

[138] ICRC CIHL Study, vol II, Part I, at 512 (Ecuador), 513 (Italy), 518–23 (Azerbaijan, China, Congo, El Salvador, Netherlands, New Zealand, Nicaragua, Trinidad and Tobago, UK); ICRC CIHL Database, Rule 28 III: Australia (2006), Canada (2001), Chad, Rule 28, IV: Australia (2007), Belgium, Bosnia and Herzegovina, Burundi, Croatia, Ethiopia, France, Republic of Korea, Senegal, Serbia, South Africa, US, Uruguay.

[139] See MN 48.

[140] ICRC CIHL Study, vol II, Part I, at 515 (New Zealand, Nigeria); ICRC CIHL Database, Rule 28 III: Canada (2001), UK (1958 and 2004), US (1976, 1985).

[141] ICRC CIHL Study, vol II, Part I, at 512 (Colombia 1995), 516 (Switzerland).

and sea'.[142] In a few cases, domestic law clearly refers to the customary nature of such war crimes.[143] The mental element is defined by different expressions, probably most consistent with the definitions applied in the criminal law of a given state, for example attacks are 'unjustified', they are committed 'wilfully', 'intentionally', 'deliberately', 'arbitrarily', 'knowingly', 'maliciously', 'without proper cause', or 'without any necessity'. In one criminal code there is a particularly comprehensive definition, 'in a manner which is unlawful, arbitrary or disproportionate to the requirements of strict military necessity'.[144] The penalty stipulated under national laws varies considerably, from death or life imprisonment[145] to 'imprisonment for at most four years'.[146]

54 The ICC Statute qualifies attacks against hospitals as war crimes, both in IAC and in NIAC.[147] As discussed above,[148] in IAC, both enemy and own hospitals are protected. Article 8 of the ICC Statute does not distinguish between these two categories of situations, therefore the only conclusion must be that attacking one's own hospital constitutes a war crime in the same way as attacking an enemy one. The ICC Elements of Crimes define the material element of this war crime as follows: the perpetrator directed an attack in the context of an armed conflict and the object of the attack was one or more hospital buildings; in the case of Article 8(2)(b)(xxiv) and Article 8(2)(e)(ii), the additional necessary element is the identification indicating protected status.[149] The concept of attack 'refers to the use of armed force to carry out a military operation during the course of an armed conflict'.[150] It is clear that this war crime does not require actual damage as a result of the attack.[151] The mental element of the crime is defined as the intention of the perpetrator, being aware of factual circumstances that have established the existence of an armed conflict, that the hospital would be the object of the attack.[152]

55 The case law specifically addressing violations of the protections afforded to hospitals, and more precisely to hospital ships, dates back to the First World War. The most famous cases were those relating to *Llandovery Castle* and *Dover Castle*, which came before the German Supreme Court in Leipzig in 1921.[153] In both cases, hospital ships (Canadian and British respectively) were torpedoed and sunk by German submarines. In the former case, survivors remaining in the water and in the lifeboats were machine-gunned, while in the latter case the German commander allowed some time to elapse between the firing of the first and second torpedoes, to allow for the rescue of the wounded and sick by another ship. In both cases, the commanders were convinced that the hospital ships were being used for military purposes. In the *Dover Castle* case, the German commander successfully raised the defence of superior (German Government and admiralty) orders and was acquitted.[154] In the *Llandovery Castle* case, two lieutenants (in the absence of their commander who had escaped) were convicted and sentenced. However, they were punished not for torpedoing the hospital ship, but for firing at the shipwrecked in the lifeboats and in the water.

---

[142] Ibid, at 523 (Venezuela).
[143] Ibid, at 519 (Canada); ICRC CIHL Database, Rule 28 III: Australia (2006), UK (2004).
[144] ICRC CIHL Database, Rule 28, IV, Ethiopia 2004.   [145] Ibid, Ethiopia.
[146] Sweden, ICRC CIHL Study, vol II, Part I, at 522.   [147] See MN 48.   [148] MN 18.
[149] ICC Elements of Crime, Art 8(2)(b)(ix)/Art 8(2)(e)(iv) and Art 8(2)(b)(xxiv)/Art 8(2)(e)(ii).
[150] Dörmann, above n 114, at 216 and 350.
[151] Ibid, at 215 and 350.   [152] See above n 149.
[153] 16 *AJIL* (1921) 704. See also Editorial, 'The Hospital Ship *Llandovery Castle*', 8(8) *The Canadian Medical Association Journal* (1918) 734.
[154] J.A. Williamson, 'Some Considerations on Command Responsibility and Criminal Liability', 90 *IRRC* 870 (2008) 303, at 314.

There seems to be no present-day case law on such violations. As mentioned above,[155] certain persons were accused before the ICTR of acts violating hospitals' status, in the form of charges not relating to attacks against the hospitals themselves, but relating to the kidnapping and killing of Tutsis who had sought medical treatment there. Hence, these acts were rather acts directed against the wounded and sick, although the cases implied a lack of respect for hospitals as well. With the exception of one accused,[156] all were found not guilty of these particular crimes because of the lack of sufficient evidence with regard to their personal involvement in the killings of the Tutsis who were in the hospitals.[157]

In the practice of the ICTY there have been a few cases relating to some degree to the status of hospitals, but none of them has given the Tribunal occasion to analyse the status of hospitals in depth. The *Vukovar Hospital Case* did not—contrary to its name—refer to an attack against the Vukovar hospital, but to the massacre of Croat wounded, sick combatants and civilians, as well as other civilians who sought refuge there after their transfer by the Yugoslav People's Army (JNA) from the Vukovar hospital to a farm in Ovčara.[158] The transfer itself was legal, based on the agreement concluded in Zagreb between the JNA and the Croatian Government. The main offence, namely the killing of these victims by Serb irregular forces after JNA withdrawal, was not at all related to the status of the Vukovar hospital.[159]

In the case of *Stanislav Galić*, concerning events surrounding the siege of Sarajevo by Bosnian Serb forces, the ICTY considered attacks on the Koševo hospital in Sarajevo as examples of the campaign of attacks on civilians, and not as attacks on an object enjoying special protection under IHL. In view of the contention made by the accused that the Sarajevo Romanija Corps forces (part of the Army of the Republika Srpska) could fire at the hospital because the Army of Bosnia and Herzegovina was using it as a military base, and weapons were being fired from hospital grounds,[160] the Tribunal analysed the conditions that justify a loss of protection for medical units,[161] as well as the conditions under which hospitals retain their protection.[162] Some references were also made in other cases[163] to targeting hospitals in the context of attacking civilians.

E. Critical Assessment

The legal status of hospitals as specially protected objects enforces the rule that the wounded, sick, and shipwrecked should be collected and cared for, shielded from attacks and the other effects of hostilities. There are rules in the Geneva Conventions

---

[155] MN 48.

[156] Joseph Kanyabashi, found guilty of, among other things, serious violations of CA 3 and AP II; see ICTR, *Nyiramasuhuko et al*, above n 124, at 1462, sentence para 6244, and the references to the massacre at Matyazo Clinic, at 485–512, paras 2012–103.

[157] See above n 124 and MN 48.

[158] ICTY, *The Prosecutor v Mile Mrkšić, Miroslav Radić, Veselin Šljivančanin*, Appeals Chamber Judgment, IT-95-13/1-A, 5 May 2009.

[159] On the Zagreb Agreement, see ICTY, *The Prosecutor v Mile Mrkšić, Miroslav Radić, Veselin Šljivančanin*, Trial Chamber Judgment, IT-95-13/1-T, 27 September 2007, at 52, paras 130–1.

[160] *Galić*, above n 83, at 145–8, paras 338–46.   [161] Ibid, at 146, para 342.

[162] Ibid, at 147, para 343. For further detail, see MN 32–37.

[163] E.g., ICTY, *The Prosecutor v Milan Martić*, Trial Chamber Judgment, IT-95-11-T, 12 June 2007, at 116–17, paras 309–13.

confirming and developing this principle, there are rules that are outdated and useless, and there are controversial rules that require further clarification through international practice.

60   The basic rules of protection and respect are universally recognized, and there is no official practice questioning their validity. It is also now universally recognized that civilian hospitals enjoy the same level of protection as military ones (established in GC I and in GC II), after they are formally recognized by one of the parties to the conflict. While this condition of formal recognition might seem bureaucratic, and in practice most states do not comply with it, the importance of the rule should not be neglected. Taking into account the different forms of civilian medical practice in times of peace, the lack of any requirement for formal state support might result in claims for special protection to the extent of almost paralysing military activities, and as a corollary diminishing the will of belligerents to respect the special status of hospitals. Other conditions formulated in the Geneva Conventions, namely those relating to the marking of hospitals and their remoteness from military objectives, are also important, although not mandatory. Hospitals are today protected both in IAC and in NIAC, although state practice does not indicate to what extent rules providing for different formal requirements are applicable in NIAC.

61   There are also a few rules contained in the Geneva Conventions that are now no longer relevant and may be considered obsolete. Particularly outdated are the provisions of Article 28 GC II on sick-bays. More numerous are those provisions that are redundant, simply repeating principles formulated elsewhere in IHL. Here we might mention Article 29 GC II on the status of hospital ships in occupied ports, or Article 20 GC I and Article 23 GC II on the protection of hospital ships from attacks from the land and on the protection of hospitals ashore from attacks from the sea. One might argue, however, that repetitions do no harm. The rules on the control and search of hospital ships, and those provisions which rely on commissioners and neutral observers, no longer seem relevant in light of modern means of collecting intelligence, including satellite remote sensing. And more generally, as naval warfare is less and less frequent, some provisions of GC II, particularly on the different types of vessels and their detailed status, are too elaborate and unnecessarily complicated.

62   Some provisions on hospitals contained in the Geneva Conventions are not considered obsolete but as controversial, particularly with regard to situations which do not deprive hospitals of protection. These doubts arise mainly in the context of naval warfare. There is no uniform approach to the question of legitimate means of defence and modes of communications of hospital ships. Some states and authors claim that the provisions of the 1949 Geneva Conventions on weapons on board a ship and on encrypted communication are not only outdated but even harmful to the safety of hospital ships today, while others consider these conventional provisions still to be relevant. The solution proposed by the 1994 *San Remo Manual*, regarding the flexible interpretation of rules on encrypted communications, has not been universally accepted so far, and the controversy continues.

63   Taking into account the frequent violations of the status of hospitals in contemporary armed conflicts, it has to be accepted that the weakness of the regime set out in the Geneva Conventions is less about outdated or controversial provisions, and much more about the lack of efficient means for their implementation. Apart from the methods of ensuring

better compliance that are provided for in the Geneva Conventions,[164] it is worthwhile mentioning an interesting initiative taken by the World Health Organization (WHO) that may help to avoid impunity for attacks directed against hospitals. The WHO intends to collect and report data specifically on attacks against medical services, including hospitals.[165] In any event, it is the role of the whole international community, including the ICRC as the guardian of the Geneva Conventions, to enhance respect for hospitals by engaging with states, their armed forces, and health care institutions, as well as with non-state armed groups.

ELŻBIETA MIKOS-SKUZA

---

[164] See Chs 26–32 of this volume.

[165] WHO Executive Board Resolution EB 130.R14, referred to by the UN Secretary General in his report S/2012/376, above n 118, at 9, para 34. In July–September 2014, during the Gaza Crisis, WHO issued 11 reports on health facilities damaged and closed, and on the situation of their staff and patients. These reports are available at <http://www.emro.who.int/pse/publications-who/gaza-situation-report-update-july-september-2014.html?format=html>. Similar reports were issued about the conflict in Syria, see <http://www.emro.who.int/images/stories/syria/SituationReport_20140615.pdf?ua=1>.

Chapter 12. Humanitarian Assistance

	MN
A. Introduction	1
I. The notion of humanitarian assistance	1
II. Historical background	7
III. Relevant provisions	17
B. Meaning and Application	20
I. Beneficiaries of relief	20
II. Providers of relief activities	27
a. States	28
b. United Nations forces	30
c. Impartial humanitarian organizations	33
III. The consent requirement	38
IV. Specific relief obligations of parties to an international armed conflict	49
a. Relief obligations of Detaining Powers	50
b. Relief obligations of the Occupying Power	58
V. The free passage obligation	65
C. Relevance in Non-International Armed Conflicts	72
D. Legal Consequences of a Violation	82
E. Critical Assessment	90

Select Bibliography

Abril Stoffels, R., 'Legal Regulation of Humanitarian Assistance in a Conflict: Achievements and Gaps', 86 *IRRC* 855 (2004) 515

Blondel, J.-L., 'Assistance to Protected Persons', 27 *IRRC* 260 (1987) 451

Cubie, D., 'An Analysis of Soft Law Application to Humanitarian Assistance: Relative Normativity in Action?', 2 *Journal of International Humanitarian Legal Studies* (2011) 177

Fortsythe, D.P./Rieffer-Flanagan, B.A.J., *The International Committee of the Red Cross: A Neutral Humanitarian Actor* (London/New York: Taylor & Francis Ltd, 2007)

Heintze, H.-J./Zwitter, A. (eds), *International Law and Humanitarian Assistance: A Crosscut through Legal Issues Pertaining to Humanitarianism* (Berlin/Heidelberg: Springer-Verlag, 2011)

McGoldrick, C., 'The Future of Humanitarian Action: An ICRC Perspective', 93 *IRRC* 884 (2011) 983

OECD, 'Civilian and Military Means of Providing and Supporting Humanitarian Assistance during Conflict: A Comparative Analysis: Note by the Secretariat', DCD/DAC(97)19/*REV1*

Williamson, J.A., 'Using Humanitarian Aid to "Win Hearts and Minds": A Costly Failure?', 93 *IRRC* 884 (2011) 1035

A. Introduction

I. The notion of humanitarian assistance

To this day, no hard law definition of 'humanitarian assistance' exists in international law. Yet the definition can be deduced from some international instruments and international practice. Roughly defined, we can say that 'humanitarian assistance' means providing emergency relief for people affected by natural or man-made disasters.[1]

2   Humanitarian assistance seems to cover a range of humanitarian activities, which are broader than those falling under analogous expressions like 'humanitarian aid', 'humanitarian relief', 'relief assistance', and 'relief aid'. While the Geneva Conventions, as well as the Additional Protocols, tend to use the term 'relief', the term 'assistance' refers, in this context, to specific activities, particularly in the religious or medical spheres.[2] In this chapter, the expressions 'humanitarian assistance' and 'humanitarian relief' will be referred to interchangeably.

3   The expression 'humanitarian assistance' is more frequently used in United Nations (UN) documents generally dealing with 'natural disasters or other emergencies'. It first and foremost refers to the relief responsibilities/obligations of a state (or a non-state party to a non-international armed conflict (NIAC)) vis-à-vis the population under its control, and is regarded as a subsidiary 'responsibility' devolving upon third states and the 'international community as a whole' only when the authority concerned is unwilling or unable to provide assistance.[3] The expression therefore seems to have acquired a legal meaning encompassing all international 'responsibilities' relating to collective relief.[4]

4   As we shall see further, today these responsibilities consist of duties and rights operating in the relations between states *inter se*, and between states and armed groups.[5] Concerning the providers of relief, Geneva law regards their activity as a matter of their functional capacity to deliver aid, rather than as a right and duty to assist people in distress.[6]

5   'Humanitarian assistance' needs to be distinguished from 'humanitarian intervention', a coercive action of a state carried out in the territory of another state—or in territory controlled by a rebel group in the affected state—in order to protect and relieve a population whose survival is at risk. In such instances, relief is delivered through an operation carried out, at times under UN Security Council 'authorization' according to Chapter VII of the UN Charter, by the military forces of a state—or by a military coalition—without the consent of the

---

[1] For a hard definition in force at the national level of the EU member states, see the Preamble to the EU Council Regulation on humanitarian aid (1996, modified in 2003 and 2009). A soft law definition is given by the Institute of International Law in its Resolution on 'Humanitarian Assistance' (para I(1)), 70-I *Yearbook of the Institute of International Law* (2003), at 536 ff.

[2] Arts 12, 26, 27 GC I; Arts 12, 13, 21, 22, 30 GC II; Arts 34, 37 GC III; Arts 38, 58 GC IV.

[3] UNGA Resolutions refer to responsibilities more than to obligations, whereas UNSC Resolutions affirm the IHL obligations or even create, under Ch VII of the UN Charter, new relief obligations, both for warring states and armed groups, as well as for third states.

[4] See the almost annual Reports of UN Secretary-General on 'Assistance in cases of natural disaster', in particular A/5845 of 1965 and E/4994 of 1971. See also UNGA Resolutions, in particular Res 2816/XXVI of 1971, creating the 'United Nations Disaster Relief Organization' and, among the most relevant, Res 43/131 of 1988, Res 45/100 of 1990, Res 46/182 of 1991 (the last containing *Guiding Principles on Humanitarian Assistance*).

[5] The IIL Resolution (above n 1) correctly states that the primary responsibility in the relief field falls not only on states, but also on 'any other authority exercising jurisdiction or *de facto* control over the victims of a disaster' (para III(2)). Indeed, much like states, certain insurgent groups identifiable through their unifying organization and effective control of territory are the addressees of international customary law. These groups may also become addressees of some IHL conventional rules should they conclude agreements provided for in CA 3 para 3.

[6] In this sense, see Pictet Commentary GC I, at 832. Moreover, provisions of the GCs seem to acknowledge the freedom of impartial organizations to act in the humanitarian field rather than an ability or a right granted them by law. For a different perspective, see H. Spieker, 'The Right to Give and to Receive Humanitarian Assistance', in H.-J. Heintze and A. Zwitter (eds), *International Law and Humanitarian Assistance: A Crosscut Through Legal Issues Pertaining to Humanitarianism* (Berlin/Heidelberg: Springer-Verlag, 2011) 7.

territorial power. Humanitarian assistance independent of such an intervention, on the other hand, may be delivered to those people in need only at the request or with the consent—in the form of an agreement or an authorization—of the recipient state or the armed group controlling the territory concerned.

Even if the goal pursued by these two kinds of 'missions' could in principle be the same—helping people in distress—the need for such consent/agreement/authorization is a key reason for keeping the two notions completely distinct.

II. Historical background

The international legal history of humanitarian assistance to anyone in distress independently of armed conflicts is comparatively recent. Its emergence on the scene of international law is linked with the development of international human rights law (IHRL), although human rights instruments do not specifically refer to the right to humanitarian assistance.[7] They rather affirm individual rights, some of which do indeed constitute the basis of humanitarian assistance, such as the rights to life, to food, to health, to housing, and to human dignity. Yet humanitarian assistance, as a corollary of these individual rights, is rather to be conceived of as a collective right.[8]

Unlike humanitarian assistance for victims of natural disasters, relief for victims of armed conflicts developed gradually at the normative level starting from the middle of the nineteenth century, influenced by the then modest humanization of the law of armed conflicts. However, relief was always and is still intended, in this context, as a benefit that states are obliged to ensure to some classes of protected persons, rather than a right to which those persons would be entitled individually.

As is well known, for a long time the law of armed conflict protected only enemy combatants in inter-state wars, based on the logic of reciprocity essentially inspired by the strict inter-governmental interest of facilitating, after the war, new peaceful (commercial) relations. Humanitarian considerations were distant from this logic, thus humanitarian relief of war victims did not have any place in it.

Only the compassion of a good Samaritan could have opened the door to the expression of interest by the international community in aiding war victims. Indeed, the sporadic rules on relief in armed conflicts in force before 1949 appeared only after Henry Dunant became aware of the terrible suffering of wounded soldiers on the battlefield of Solferino in 1859. This brought him to propose the creation of national relief societies, with the aim of alleviating this suffering regardless of to which side of the conflict the combatants belonged. The Geneva Society of Public Welfare took up this proposal and in 1863 created the 'International Relief Committee for Injured

---

[7] The CRC actually affirms the right to humanitarian assistance for children in a particular position, namely those who are seeking refugee *status* or are already considered as refugees (Art 22). However, this right may most effectively be implemented as a collective right according to refugee instruments, rather than as an individual right under the CRC.

[8] The CESCR, in referring in General Comment 12 to the obligation of every state 'to ensure for everyone under its jurisdiction access to the minimum essential food' (para 14), affirms that 'this obligation also applies for persons who are victims of natural or other disasters' (para 15). It further underlines that '[t]he prevention of access to humanitarian food aid in internal conflicts or other emergency situations' is a violation of the right to food (para 19), but it does not directly refer to the right to humanitarian assistance. According to the Committee, '[t]he right to adequate food will have to be realized progressively', which is not appropriate for people in distress.

Combatants' (from 1875, the International Committee of the Red Cross (ICRC)). The Relief Committee immediately convened an International Conference, which adopted a number of resolutions for the purpose of creating national relief societies. Thus, the predecessor of the ICRC was intended not for monitoring the implementation of the *protective rules* of armed conflicts, which had already been in force for a long time, but rather for operating in the domain of *relief,* particularly for the benefit of the wounded and sick.[9] These resolutions may be considered the foundation of the International Red Cross and Red Crescent Movement (IRCM), and as the initial starting point of its engagement in the adoption of specific treaty rules on relief for any victim of any armed conflict.

11   Thanks to the commitment of the IRCM and of the ICRC,[10] the first provision regarding humanitarian relief for wounded or sick combatants in international armed conflicts (IACs), to 'whatever nation they may belong', was inserted in Article 6 of the 1864 Geneva Convention for the Amelioration of the Condition of the Wounded in Armies in the Field. The same goal was pursued by Article 1 of the 1906 Geneva Convention. On the other hand, the Hague Convention of 1899 on the Laws and Customs of War on Land, in particular its annexed Regulations, dealt with relief for two classes of victims: the wounded or sick and prisoners of war (POWs).

12   As far as populations under military occupation were concerned, the Hague Regulations merely prescribed the obligations of the Occupying Powers of 'restoring and assuring, in so far as possible, order and public life',[11] without any mention of protection or relief. After all, until the First World War the real victims of armed conflicts were either wounded and sick soldiers or POWs, while civilians, being scarcely involved in the classic method of warfare, remained under the sole residual and weak protection of the Martens Clause (see Chapter 9 of this volume). However, in the author's view, by not referring to any affirmative humanitarian activity, this clause bears only a *protective potential* for the benefit of all war victims in any 'circumstance', but it has scant relevance in the field of relief. The subsequent Geneva Conventions of 1929 merely dealt with protection and relief for wounded and sick combatants and POWs, as the ICRC failed in its attempts to extend the law of armed conflicts to civilians, despite their involvement in the hostilities of the First World War.[12]

13   Furthermore, all the Conventions mentioned above applied only to inter-state conflicts. Indeed, notwithstanding the engagement of the ICRC on the operational level in providing protection and relief for victims of certain internal armed conflicts and, on the legal level, in promoting international rules in favour of all victims of any war, the proposal to adopt an international convention for the context of civil wars failed in 1912.[13] In this

---

[9] Through the obligations restricting the means and methods of warfare, IHL protects victims of armed conflicts from the harmful effects of hostilities; through the 'relief' provisions, IHL provides for care and assistance to the same victims. A clear distinction between these two goals does not always exist, but there is certainly a clear priority in the quality and quantity of IHL stipulations in the area of protection compared with those in the relief domain (on this distinction and interaction, see J.-L. Blondel, 'Assistance to Protected Persons', 27 *IRRC* 260 (1987) 451.

[10] See D. Palmieri, 'An Institution Standing the Test of Time? A Review of 150 Years of the History of the International Committee of the Red Cross', ICRC: 150 Years of Humanitarian Action, 94 *IRRC* 888 (2012) 1273.

[11] Art 43 Hague Regulations.

[12] The ICRC only managed to lobby successfully for a mention for civilians in the Final Act of the Conference (point VI).

[13] The Draft Convention on civil wars submitted to the ICRC Conference of 1912 was not even discussed.

realm, the ICRC merely succeeded in adopting certain resolutions: during its Conference of 1921, the Resolution on the right to relief for all victims of civil wars or social or revolutionary disturbances, and, during its 1938 Conference, the Resolution on the extension to civil wars of the humanitarian principles of the 1929 Geneva Conventions. This 'law-making' deployed before the Second World War allowed the ICRC, during that war, to carry out large relief operations.[14]

These Resolutions also represent the origin of Common Article 3, in both its protective and its relief provisions, which were influenced by the new humanitarian spirit following the large-scale massacres perpetrated during the Second World War. Yet although the humanization process of the law of armed conflicts was revolutionary in 1949, even in light of the new qualification of this body of law as international humanitarian law (IHL), the drafting of Common Article 3 was subject to many constraints founded on pure governmental interests. It was particularly difficult for states to accept that humanitarian protection and relief could be intended for individuals considered to be no more than criminals by the state affected by an insurrection. Common Article 3 was finally adopted, and it subsequently proved its 'revolutionary' potential in protecting all those not participating—or no longer participating—in hostilities.

The human rights values that became imperative after the Second World War, in 1949 also led to some limited improvements in the rules applicable to inter-state conflicts, particularly in favor of POWs and civilian internees. Furthermore, civilians as such were finally taken into consideration as war victims needing both protection and humanitarian relief.

These values, which gradually penetrated every sphere of international law, also led to the development, in the 1970s, 1980s, and especially in the 1990s, of international rules—mostly in the form of soft law instruments—on humanitarian relief for victims of natural disasters.[15] This trend also had an immediate impact on the rules relating to humanitarian assistance found in Additional Protocol (AP) I and, in a more limited way, in AP II, as well as on the development in this field of a new general IHL. Therefore, an analysis of the Geneva Conventions rules on humanitarian relief cannot be conducted without considering other humanitarian obligations binding the same state parties.[16] In particular, these rules cannot be interpreted in isolation from the other rules arising out of the progressive development of customary international law (CIL), from human rights instruments, or from UN Security Council resolutions adopted under Chapter VII when the goal of the restoration and maintenance of international peace is involved. Furthermore, it needs to be taken into account that treaty rules cannot derogate from any *jus cogens* norm, even if the latter has emerged after

---

[14] See *Rapport du Comité international de la Croix-Rouge sur son activité pendant la seconde guerre mondiale*, vol III: *Actions de secours* (Geneva: ICRC, 1948).

[15] UNGA Resolutions in particular represent a source for these soft rules. Another important source is the Draft Articles on 'The Protection of Persons in the Event of Disasters', adopted on the first reading by the Drafting Committee of the ILC during the 2014 session (A/CN.4/L.831). However, a UNGA 'declaration', as soft codification of general international law on humanitarian assistance, was never adopted. Regrettably, the attempt to agree on a convention at the universal level also failed (see the UN Draft Convention on expediting the delivery of emergency assistance, UN Doc A/39/267/Add.2, 1984). Some successes were reached at regional level, however, with the adoption of the Inter-American Convention to Facilitate Disaster Assistance and the EU Regulation on humanitarian aid (above n 1). Concerning hard and soft law sources in this field, see the *Preliminary Report* by the ILC Special Rapporteur, A/CN.4/598, 2008.

[16] See Art 31(3)(c) VCLT.

the adoption of the treaty.[17] With respect to the field of relief, in the author's view this is precisely the case as regards the prohibition of starvation, now codified in the 1977 Protocols (see MN 44–45).

III. Relevant provisions

17 Some provisions specific or common to the four Geneva Conventions deal directly—albeit not always exclusively—with relief for victims of armed conflicts. Some other provisions of these Conventions may have only an indirect relevance.

18 A general provision concerning IACs, contained in common Articles 9/9/9/10, leaves the initiatives for humanitarian activities to impartial organizations. The obligation to 'care for' the wounded, sick, and shipwrecked is also relevant to the domain of relief (Article 12 GC I and GC II). Various other provisions of GC III and GC IV deal in detail with relief obligations in favour of the respective class of victims of IACs. These obligations are imposed either upon warring parties—that is the Detaining Power (MN 50–57), or the Occupying Power (MN 58–64)—or upon all High Contracting Parties (MN 65–71). In addition, some other Geneva Conventions obligations that have an indirect relevance to the field of relief, such as those requiring parties to ensure respect for and to execute these Conventions, also deserve to be taken into account (see Chapter 6 of this volume).

19 As for NIACs, Common Article 3 essentially lays down fundamental protective and binding rules in favour of NIAC victims; while as far as their relief is concerned, it provides only that impartial humanitarian organizations may 'offer their services' (MN 73–74; see also Chapter 24 of this volume).

B. Meaning and Application

I. Beneficiaries of relief

20 The beneficiaries of humanitarian activities 'allowed' by the common general provision are different in each of the four Conventions: 'wounded and sick, medical personnel and chaplains' (Article 9 GC I); 'wounded, sick and shipwrecked persons, medical personnel and chaplains' (Article 9 GC II); 'prisoners of war' (Article 9 GC III); and civilian persons (Article 10 GC IV). These same classes of persons also benefit from some specific obligations set out in each of the four Conventions.

21 In Article 13, GC I identifies the wounded and sick as those who would benefit from POW treatment under GC III if they fell into the power of the enemy. Unlike the protection required by GC III for POWs, the protection and relief required by GC I is not limited to the wounded and sick who have fallen into the power of the enemy. Article 13 GC II is specular, *mutatis mutandis*, to Article 13 GC I, merely adding the reference to the shipwrecked 'from any cause', including 'forced landings at sea by or from aircraft' (Article 12 GC II). As already noted, both classes of persons dealt with by GC I and GC II are also beneficiaries of the general obligation to be cared for (Article 12). According to GC III, POWs who benefit from protection and relief are, in simplified terms, all captured

---

[17] In fact the content of Art 64 VCLT is even more radical: 'If a new peremptory norm of general international law emerges, any existing treaty which is in conflict with that norm becomes void and terminates.'

persons who were fighting with the official armed forces of the enemy state as prescribed by Article 4.[18]

If the classes of persons who are the beneficiaries of relief activities according to the first three Geneva Conventions are clearly identified in each of them, the identification of the beneficiaries under GC IV, in particular under Article 10, is more problematic, as the term 'civilian persons' is not defined.[19] Article 4 GC IV merely identifies the 'protected persons' as those who are in the hands of a party to the conflict or Occupying Power of which they are not nationals.

The lack of a definition of 'civilians persons' entails two problems linked *inter se*: (i) the distinction between 'protected persons' and 'civilians'; (ii) the question of whether Article 10 GC IV applies only to enemy civilians, more generally to civilians who are not nationals, or even to civilians of the warring party concerned.

The title of GC IV, 'Geneva Convention Relative to the Protection of Civilian Persons in Time of War', could prima facie lead one to consider that the two categories—'civilian persons' and 'protected persons'—coincide. However, it is a fact that the protective rules of GC IV refer always and only to 'protected persons'. This class of persons is also the beneficiary of specific provisions on relief (Articles 30 and 38), which therefore apply to non-nationals with respect to the state concerned, including 'civilian internees' but not civilians *tout court*. Hence, the recourse to two different expressions can only imply that the 'civilian persons' of Article 10 do not coincide with the reductive definition of 'protected persons', the first class of persons being broader than the second one and encompassing it (see Chaper 55 of this volume).

The broad meaning of the expression 'civilian persons' used in Article 10 is also implicitly confirmed by the fact that when the Geneva Conventions need to limit the scope of the word 'civilian', they do it expressly, as in the case of the wording of Article 23 GC IV concerning the obligation to allow free passage of consignments in favour of 'civilians of another Contracting Party, even if the latter is its adversary' (see MN 65–71). In contrast, the general reference made in Article 10 to 'civilian persons' without any limitation implies that GC IV should not lead to a civilian's being excluded from being the beneficiary of any humanitarian activities undertaken with the consent of the parties. The negotiators of the Geneva Conventions, departing from the presumption of inherent responsibilities (not yet proper obligations) of a state vis-à-vis its own population,[20] were indeed very cautious when dealing with civilians belonging to the warring parties: they avoided imposing *obligations* on states resulting in favour of their own civilian population.

Concerning the situation of occupation, for which GC IV provides a highly protective *lex specialis* regime, the population *tout court* is identified as the beneficiary of obligations to provide relief imposed on the Occupying Power. Here, the exclusion of the population belonging to the Occupying Power from the protections accorded is *in re ipsa*. However, the utilization of the term 'population' without qualifying it as civilian implies that the

---

[18] See Ch 48 and Ch 49, section B.VI, of this volume. [19] As it is in AP I (Art 50).
[20] UNGA Resolutions on humanitarian assistance reiterate this principle: '[E]ach State has the responsibility first and foremost to take care of the victims of natural disasters and other emergencies occurring on its territory. Hence, the affected State has the primary role in the initiation, organization, coordination and implementation of humanitarian assistance within its territory' (*Guiding Principles on Humanitarian Assistance*, above n 4).

benefit also extends to members of the armed forces belonging to the occupied state and detained in the occupied territory.[21]

II. Providers of relief activities

27 Humanitarian assistance in armed conflicts is provided by states, international organizations (such as, *in primis*, UN institutions), the ICRC, the International Federation of the Red Cross and Red Crescent, National Societies of the Red Cross and Red Crescent, and non-governmental organizations (NGOs). All of these providers of humanitarian assistance are explicitly or implicitly referred to in the Geneva Conventions. They deliver humanitarian assistance not only in the context of IACs, but also in the context of NIACs. The discussion in this section therefore is applicable, *mutatis mutandis*, to NIACs too. The specifics of humanitarian assistance for NIACs are dealt with below (MN 72–81).

a. States

28 States as providers of relief are mentioned only in the rule providing for relief schemes on behalf of the population of an occupied territory that is inadequately supplied (Article 59 paragraph 2 GC IV).

29 Despite this sole consideration by the Geneva Conventions of states as providers of relief, they are frequently involved in relief activities through their civilian and military personnel, both of which are increasingly trained and specialized in providing assistance in situations of both natural disaster and armed conflict, even abroad. Their logistical means, the rapidity of and capacity for their deployment, and the discipline and preparedness of such personnel, certainly constitute some of the most valued attributes in this realm.[22] However, the utilization of national military forces might not always appear to be a neutral and impartial solution for both sides in a conflict, in particular when those forces access the territory with the 'consent' of one side only. After all, the Geneva Conventions and the Additional Protocols completely ignore the channelling of humanitarian assistance from the outside by military forces, and Article 63 paragraph 2 GC IV, which refers to local relief organizations, expressly mentions their *non-military character*.

b. United Nations forces

30 Some of the problems identified with regard to national military operations for humanitarian assistance are solved by assigning humanitarian tasks, in addition to the traditional ones, to UN peacekeeping forces. These forces benefit not only from their logistic and operational abilities in the field, but also from a certain moral authority, which could function as a deterrent against violent attacks. Moreover, the Convention of 1994 on the Safety of United Nations and Associated Personnel (Safety Convention) also gives

---

[21] See Pictet Commentary GC IV, at 310, and the *travaux préparatoires*, according to which 'The Working Party had omitted the word "civilian" before the word "population" […], being of the opinion that the case of relief intended for troops in camps in occupied territory must also be provided for' (Final Record, vol II-A, at 745).

[22] This kind of force was first organized by France in 1983 ('Force d'action humanitaire militaire d'intervention rapide'). Since that time, other analogous forces have been organized in several states for relief missions abroad: see *Civilian and Military Means of Providing and Supporting Humanitarian Assistance During Conflict: a Comparative Analysis*, Note by the Secretariat of OECD, DCD/DAC(97)19/REV1, *passim*.

protection to this kind of humanitarian operator, at least against unlawful conduct by the contracting territorial state.[23]

However, pursuant to the original intention for such missions, UN peacekeeping forces are equipped with light weapons to be used only for the purposes of self-defence. They are not equipped for protecting humanitarian operators or a population in distress suffering from attacks by armed groups. The security problems of humanitarian personnel could be better faced by the new practice of *enforcement* operations, which the UN Security Council frequently mandates to aid civilian populations and to protect humanitarian operators in situations of armed conflict.[24] However, the numbers of UN enforcement staff are usually insufficient, and they are still hardly equipped to be able to carry out security tasks in very dangerous situations, as the tragic events of Srebrenica and Darfur, among others, clearly showed.[25]

In addition to the above-mentioned problems UN forces face in the field, the Organization also needs to overcome several obstacles when envisaging recourse to both peacekeeping and enforcement missions, in particular the need to accommodate the 'veto' procedure with regard to UN Security Council resolutions,[26] the necessity to solve the financing problems, to obtain the transfer of national military contingents, and to organize a unified command, as well as the need to obtain from the host state not merely consent for the operation, but sometimes also '*agrément*' for that specific national contingent (see MN 38–48). Therefore, the UN forces are also far from being the best means to achieve a relief mission that would be both rapid and effective in providing aid to victims in distress.[27]

c. Impartial humanitarian organizations

Some of the above considerations on using military forces for humanitarian assistance lead to the conclusion that, even during armed conflicts, impartial organizations that have recourse only to civilian means of delivering assistance are the most appropriate providers of relief. Indeed, field experience demonstrates that their relief personnel are exposed to the lowest possible level of risk, particularly if such organizations maintain their strict neutrality and impartiality and act exclusively for humanitarian goals, refraining from being involved in the larger political agenda.[28] It is therefore not surprising that the Geneva Conventions (and the Protocols) recognize that the sole role of these

---

[23] The Convention has been ratified or acceded to by 91 states only. Furthermore, its protective scope excludes the majority of humanitarian operations as well as UN enforcement operations (Art 21).

[24] See N. Currier, 'Protecting Protectors—Strengthening Staff Security: Priority and Challenges', *UN Chronicle online*, available at <http://www.redcross.ca/cmslib/general/oteoc_ben_perrin.pdf>.

[25] Consider, among many similar events, the relatively recent attack against the Tanzanian contingent of UN forces deployed in Darfur with an enforcement and humanitarian mandate (S/RES/1769(2007) and S/RES/2113(2013)): in July 2013, seven members of the forces were killed and another 17 were wounded in an ambush by rebels.

[26] Thus, for instance, the UNSC Res 2043(2012) on the Syrian situation could only call 'upon all parties to cease all armed violence' and establish a mission of 300 unarmed military observers for monitoring the situation. In successive Resolutions, the UNSC merely affirmed that obstructions to humanitarian relief for the population in desperate need 'can violate' IHL, and expressed its intent to take 'further steps' in case of non-compliance (see, e.g., Res 2139 (2014)). Lacking unanimity on this, it did not refer to 'all necessary means', like in other situations.

[27] See on this the view expressed in the ICRC *Rapport d'opérations*, 1991/92, at 53 ff.

[28] See on this J.A. Williamson, 'Using Humanitarian Aid to "Win Hearts and Minds": A Costly Failure?', 93 *IRRC* 884 (2011) 1035.

organizations should be as providers of humanitarian assistance, leaving the management of security to the Detaining and Occupying Powers.[29]

34 However, in the Geneva Conventions, as in any other binding international instrument, one cannot find a definition of 'impartial humanitarian organization' ('body' or 'agency', as the rules usually refer to it).[30] The Geneva Conventions rules merely refer to a model allowing one to identify the humanitarian and impartial character of the organization, namely the ICRC (see Chapter 24 of this volume), which seems to be the most appropriate body for providing relief to victims of IACs and NIACs.[31] In addition to being a model of reference, a particular position is accorded to the ICRC in performing its humanitarian activities.[32]

35 The reference to the model of the ICRC makes it necessary to look at the characteristics of this organization as enshrined in its Statute, which governs all of its activities in the field.[33] First, the ICRC activities must aim solely at the interests of human beings and their needs, completely aside from any other considerations; in particular, they should be carried out with no discrimination on the basis of uniform, allegiance, nationality, race, religion, or beliefs. Secondly, the ICRC should maintain complete neutrality vis-à-vis parties to an IAC or a NIAC. Thirdly, to reach its intended beneficiaries, the ICRC must procure the consent or authorization not only of state authorities, but also of the armed group—or armed groups—controlling the territory affected by the emergency situation. This approach enables the ICRC to enter into dialogue with all parties to the conflict, and thus to operate in conditions of essential security.[34] Fourthly, governmental or rebels' armed escorts are to be avoided, if possible, not only for the purpose of maintaining an absolute distance from the different parties to the conflict, but also in order not to put at risk the humanitarian staff in the event of an armed confrontation involving official escorts;[35] the ICRC would have recourse to military escorts only in some specific situations where relief activities are likely to be

---

[29] Indeed, while GCs also envisage foreign and international actors as providers of relief, their security in the field is still intended to remain in the hands of Detaining Powers or Occupying Powers (see, particularly, Art 125 GC III, Art 142 para 1 GC IV, and Art 70(4) AP I). The same approach is followed in UNGA and UNSC Resolutions as in the Safety Convention (Art 7).

[30] UN Resolutions also do not define the humanitarian and impartial character of the organizations able to provide humanitarian assistance, merely referring to those features in addition to that of neutrality: see, among others, UNGA Res 46/182 of 1991 as well as UNSC Res 1296/2000.

[31] ICJ, when dealing with the impartiality of humanitarian aid in relation to the principle of non-intervention, referred to the ICRC principles and practice (see ICJ, *Military and Paramilitary Activities in and against Nicaragua*, Judgment, 27 June 1986, paras 242–43; MN 48; see also Ch 24, MN 11, of this volume).

[32] See Art 126 GC III and Art 142 GC IV.

[33] See on this D.P. Fortsythe and B.A.J. Rieffer-Flanagan, *The International Committee of the Red Cross: A Neutral Humanitarian Actor* (London/New York: Taylor & Francis Ltd, 2007), *passim*; C. McGoldrick, 'The Future of Humanitarian Action: An ICRC Perspective', 93 *IRRC* 884 (2011) 983; V. Bernard, Editorial 'The Quest for Humanity', 94 *IRRC* 888 (2012) 1195, at 1199 ff; 'Interview with Peter Maurer President of the ICRC', 94 *IRRC* 888 (2012) 1209, esp at 1216 ff; M. Schmale, 'Reflections on the ICRC's Present and Future Role in Addressing Humanitarian Crises', 94 *IRRC* 888 (2012) 1263, at 1265; ICRC, 'The International Committee of the Red Cross's (ICRC's) Confidential Approach', 94 *IRRC* 887 (2012) 1135.

[34] Thus, the ICRC, which avoids denouncing specific IHL violations, prefers a cautious diplomatic and confidential approach. This approach was often questioned by certain NGOs, like *Médecins sans frontières*: R. Brauman, 'Médecins Sans Frontières and the ICRC: Matters of Principle', 94 *IRRC* 888 (2012) 1523.

[35] Nonetheless, in 2003, ICRC delegates and personnel were attacked in Baghdad. The Committee decided to close its seat temporarily rather than to have recourse to military protection: see *Report on the Use of Armed Protection for Humanitarian Assistance*, Working Paper 95/CD/12/1, available at <http://www.icrc.org/Web/eng/siteeng0.nsf/html/57JNEG>.

put at risk by banditry. Similarly, private military escorts are likewise usually avoided by the ICRC.[36]

The above-mentioned features of the ICRC as a model of reference, read in the light of Geneva Conventions relief rules, entail that:

— in so far as the term 'humanitarian' is concerned, the relief organization must take into account human beings as such, regardless of any military, political, professional, national, or other status; humanitarian assistance cannot be used for political purposes or in exchange for receiving support from the victims;
— impartiality represents a feature to be considered only in respect of victims; it does not refer to absolute equality, since, for instance, the gravity of wounds or the status of children, expectant mothers or maternity cases, as well as the inability to reach certain prisoner camps, might have relevance in delivering relief;[37]
— formal neutrality vis-à-vis parties to the conflict, evoked by the ICRC Statute and some UN Security Council Resolutions, is not explicitly required by the Geneva Conventions; indeed, it could represent an obstacle to the activities of some national Red Cross Societies.[38] However, provided that merely humanitarian considerations motivate these activities, neutrality as a material approach is *in re ipsa*; its relevance may also be deduced by reference to the Geneva Conventions' stipulations that provide, for some humanitarian activities, for the involvement of Protecting Powers as neutral entities[39] or of 'neutral powers';[40]
— the relief organization is not required to be international in nature, since National Societies are also able to be impartially engaged in humanitarian assistance abroad;[41]
— the concrete modalities for carrying out relief activities are left in the hands of impartial organizations, albeit under a certain level of supervision by the state concerned and any non-state entity, sometimes in accordance with special agreements between states/armed groups and relief providers.

The potential scope of humanitarian activities according to the common general provision applicable in IACs is very broad. Indeed, this provision represents a *chapeau* rule for all of the Geneva rules referring to such activities by any impartial organization, thus excluding

---

[36] On the practice of using private contractors for the protection of humanitarian operators, see B. Perrin, *Humanitarian Assistance and the Private Security Debate: An International Humanitarian Perspective*, 2008, available at <http://www.croixrouge.ca/cmslib/general/oteoc_ben_perrin.pdf>, at 15 ff. In performing such a function, they should not be regarded as directly participating in hostilities (on this, *Second Expert Meeting: DPH*, ICRC and T.M.C. Asser Institute, October 2004, at 14, available at <http://www.icrc.org>), on condition that they operate in compliance with applicable domestic law and IHL (B. Perrin, 'Promoting Compliance of Private Security and Military Companies with International Humanitarian Law', 88 *IRRC* 863 (2006) 613).

[37] Art 2 Annex III to GC III, after providing some possibilities of unequal distribution of collective relief, states that '[w]ithin the limits thus defined, the distribution shall always be carried out equitably'.

[38] Some National Red Cross Societies, such as the Italian one, also have a military component, which, however, does not take part in hostilities while, together with the para-medical component (the 'Red Cross Nurses'), it carries out, with impartiality and merely for humanitarian purposes, the tasks provided for by Arts 24–26 GC I. This Society is recognized as an impartial organization according to the conditions stipulated in Art 4 of the 'Statutes of the International Red Cross and Red Crescent Movement', as well as in GCs and Protocols.

[39] The several references in the GCs to Protecting Powers' tasks became obsolete, as by now these functions are routinely fulfilled by the ICRC (see Ch 27, MN 17 and 25, of this volume).

[40] See, e.g., Art 61 para 1 GC IV.

[41] Art 125 GC III *in fine* mentions this feature, but only in order to allow international organizations, in addition to national ones, to assist POWs.

these rules from being interpreted restrictively (see Article 123 paragraph 4 GC III and Article 140 paragraph 4 GC IV). It also opens the door to any further humanitarian activity, although only optional, thus representing a reserve rule in this field.

III. The consent requirement

38   The *optional* humanitarian activities, according to the common general provision applicable in IACs, are further affected by their being subject to the requirement of 'consent'[42] of the parties concerned.[43] The Geneva Conventions' French and English wording is mostly interpreted in the sense that consent cannot be refused without 'good reasons', an expression that may be viewed as too undetermined and abstract.[44]

39   By contrast, as regards the population under occupation, a special regime established by GC IV stipulates an obligation *de contrahendo* upon the Occupying Power with respect to relief schemes undertaken by states and impartial organizations. Such an obligation is not subject to any condition; the schemes 'shall be agreed' upon and relief shall be facilitated 'if the whole or part of the population of an occupied territory is inadequately supplied' (Article 59 paragraphs 1 and 2 GC IV) (MN 53).

40   In this situation, therefore, the object of the obligation *de contrahendo* is not the relief as such, nor the access to affected territory and victims, but only the relief schemes. A refusal to negotiate relief schemes entails a violation of GC IV. Once the schemes are agreed upon, relief operations should be carried out automatically, as the states may no longer call them into question.

41   A mandatory relief regime is also stipulated in AP I for situations of IAC other than occupation, but only in favour of the civilian population 'not adequately provided with supplies essential to its survival'. In such instances, 'relief actions […] *shall* be undertaken subject to the *agreement* of the Parties concerned' (Article 70(1) read in conjunction with Article 69(1) AP I, emphasis added). Thus, the mandatory relief actions in favour of such a population, and access to victims, are merely submitted to the *agreement* of the parties concerned. Indeed, the word 'consent', used in the Geneva Conventions provision without any distinction between the beneficiaries, is replaced in Article 70 AP I by the word

---

[42] In this chapter the term *consent* is used in a general sense, even when considering the '*agrément/agreement*' condition.

[43] The 'consent requirement' in the GCs has its origin in Art 88 1929 GC II, which states that its provisions 'do not constitute any obstacle to the humanitarian work which the International Red Cross Committee may perform for the protection of prisoners of war with the consent of the belligerents concerned'. In 1929, the language used in international negotiations, as well by the ICRC, was French. It is therefore noteworthy that in the French version of the Convention, the only authentic text, the term used is *agrément* and not *consentement*. In the author's view, the translation of the term '*agrément*' as 'consent' was at that time not accurate; regrettably, such a translation was inherited by the GCs, while in the French version of the GCs' common general provision, as in the draft of the GCs elaborated in French by the Red Cross Conference in 1948, the term '*agrément*' remained, although in other provisions of the GCs the term 'consent' is still used (see, e.g., Art 37 GC I, Art 24 GC VI).

[44] According to Pictet Commentary GC I, at 110–11, '[t]he Powers do not have to give a reason for their refusals. The decision is entirely theirs. But being bound to apply the Convention, they alone must bear the responsibility if they refuse help in carrying out their engagements.' This state-centric approach—only slightly limited by the last sentence—to the interpretation of the GCs is not surprising. In the 1950s, when the humanization of international law was just taking shape, the 1948 Universal Declaration of Human Rights essentially reflected the West's humanitarian approach, while the UN 1966 international covenants were not yet adopted and the principle of non-interference was at the centre of the confrontation between East and West.

'agreement', although it is still used in Article 18(2) AP II,[45] as well as in various other provisions of AP I referring to the same or analogous aspects of humanitarian activities.[46]

Although the distinction between the two English words is not as obvious as if comparing the old diplomatic French term *'agrément'* with *'consentement'*, it may be assumed that the contracting parties, by using in the English version of Article 70 of AP I a term different from the one used in the common general provision of the Geneva Conventions—and more consistent with the French term *'agrément'*— intended that the two terms should have different legal meanings.[47] Indeed, the words *consentement/consent* habitually refer, in international law, to the expression of the 'will' as a formal element for assuming international obligations by the act of ratification of a treaty, or by an ad hoc consent in other cases of acceptance of international obligations. By contrast, the word *agrément* rather means approval, i.e. the authorization by a state for a specific foreign officer or delegate (or entity) to enter its territory in accordance with the obligation previously assumed in general terms by the state. Therefore, despite the obligation previously assumed in a treaty establishing diplomatic or consular relations with another state, the *'agrément'* for a specific diplomatic or consular officer to deploy such a function in a foreign territory could be refused by the territorial state on the basis of a *persona non grata* claim.[48] In the same way, a party to an IAC could refuse, on the basis of an alleged lack of independence/neutrality/impartiality, the authorization for a specific humanitarian organization to deploy relief activities, although this party, by ratifying AP I, has already consented *ex ante* and in the abstract to these activities. Refusing access to victims would result in a violation of the Protocol. The use of the term *'agreement'*, rather than *consent*, seems after all more consistent with the *obligation* to undertake humanitarian relief. Indeed, the French term *agrément* and its English equivalent 'agreement' reflect, in the author's view, a more open approach to humanitarian exigencies than the term *'consentement'* and its English counterpart 'consent'.[49]

42

---

[45] It is noteworthy that the French version of Art 18(2) AP II uses the term *'consentement'* and not the term *'agrément'*, unlike AP I (and the common general provision of the GCs).

[46] See, e.g., Arts 64(1) and 81(1), which respectively concern civil defence and humanitarian activities by the ICRC.

[47] Actually, draft Art 62(2) AP I, elaborated by the ICRC in 1973, merely proposed that the parties 'shall agree and facilitate […] relief actions' (*Official Records of the Diplomatic Conference* of 1974–7, vol I, Part Three, at 20). Similar wording was proposed by the ICRC for AP II (only limiting it by the addition of the sentence 'to the fullest possible extent', ibid, vol I, at 165). The consent requirement in both contexts appeared during the Diplomatic Conference (ibid, vol III). It was also inserted in a proposal of a new Article 70*bis* filed on 24 March 1975 by a group of states (ibid, vol III, at 311) and approved by the Working Group by *consensus* (ibid, vol X, at 45). Later, the word 'consent' was replaced by the word 'agreement' in the provision on relief of AP I, but it remained in the rules indicated above n 43 and in the relief provision of AP II. Nonetheless, some delegates expressed their dissatisfaction with the 'agreement' condition, while others simply observed that it did not imply the freedom of the parties to refuse relief actions (see, e.g., *Official Records*, vol XII, at 336, and vol VII, at 156). In any event, all of the problems of compatibility between the different authentic texts of the Protocols—French, English, Russian, Spanish, and Arabic—were confronted and solved by joint efforts (see, e.g., ibid, vol XII, at 334), which could not be achieved in 1929 when the Conventions were drafted only in French.

[48] The term *agrément* in this sense is also used in common Arts 8 of GC I, GC II, and GC III, and in Art 9 GC IV, as well as in Art 126 GC III. In all these provisions it was translated into English as 'approval'.

[49] The term 'agreement' certainly has weaker force than the term 'consent'. Indeed, whereas the term 'consent' evokes a unilateral act, the term 'agreement' rather evokes the result of bilateral (or multilateral) negotiations (in the case *sub judice*, the negotiations on the modalities of relief operations, according to the obligation to undertake them).

43 In sum, in the author's view, state parties to AP I assumed the obligation to accept outside humanitarian assistance for a civilian population whose survival was at risk, retaining only their right to verify certain conditions concerning the features of the organizations involved and certain modalities for the concrete relief operation to be carried out.[50]

44 In addition, there is another development that comes into play. The rules on the prohibition of starvation as a method of combat and the prohibition of attacks against 'objects indispensable to the survival of the civilian population' (clearly stipulated in both AP I and AP II)[51] have now become part of CIL.[52] The prohibition of starvation is even considered to be a peremptory rule that cannot be derogated from by treaty rules nor restricted 'whatever the motive' (as stipulated in Article 54(2) AP I).[53] This has an impact on the interpretation of the rules of the Geneva Conventions concerning humanitarian relief. Arguably, these rules represent the recognition and the synthesis, in the context of IHL, of some fundamental rights protected by IHRL, such as the rights to life and the right not to be submitted to torture or cruel, inhuman, or degrading treatment or punishment; in short, the rights that cannot be derogated from in any public emergency.[54]

45 The rules of CIL on the prohibition of starvation demand that any civilian population at risk of starvation *must* receive the relief supplies necessary for its survival.[55] Thus, the

---

[50] In this respect, see also Rule 55 ICRC CIHL Study, stating that the obligation to 'allow and facilitate rapid and unimpeded passage of humanitarian relief' refers to 'civilians in need' *tout court* and not only to civilians whose survival is at risk, but without referring to the consent condition.

[51] See Art 54 AP I and Art 14 AP II. Already during the war in Biafra, the *opinio juris* about the illegality of starvation was largely expanded in the international community, see G.A. Mudge, 'Starvation as a Means of Warfare', *International Lawyer* (1969/1970), at 228 ff. In the Eichmann case, for instance, the District Court of Jerusalem held that starvation caused serious bodily or mental harm, and therefore amounted to an act of genocide (Judgment, 12 December 1961, referred to in ICRC CIHL Database, A V (Israel)).

[52] See Rules 53 and 54, as well as the respective underlying practice as described in the ICRC CIHL Study.

[53] The ICRC Commentary on APs underlines that a proposed 'exception in case of imperative military necessity was not adopted' for the prohibition in AP II (at 1456, para 4795). And the UNSC, when imposing, under Ch VII of the UN Charter, *embargo* measures against a state or insurgent group, always takes into account humanitarian safeguards, namely in exempting from these measures the supplies essential for the survival of local populations. See, among others, Res 1296/2000, para 8. On this, B. Kondoch, 'The Limits of Economic Sanctions under International Law', in M. Bothe and B. Kondoch (eds), *International Peacekeeping: The Yearbook of International Peace Operations* (The Hague: Kluwer Law International, 2002) vol VII, 267, at 284 ff.

[54] This peremptory limit is imposed upon states when adopting emergency measures pursuant to every human rights instrument (see, in particular, Art 4 ICCPR). It acknowledges the existence of a link between IHRL and IHL, notwithstanding their independence from each other, when the public emergency is represented by an armed conflict, as also appears evident in CA 3; see F. Lattanzi, 'La frontière entre droit international humanitaire et droits de l'homme', in E. Decaux, A. Dieng, and M. Sow (eds), *Des droits de l'homme au droit international pénal. Etudes en l'honneur d'un juriste africain, feu le Juge Laity Kama* (Leiden: Martinus Nijhoff Publisher, 2007) 519.

[55] The UNSC, in situations of grave distress caused by armed conflicts, by assuming the GCs as additional legal basis for its assessments, affirms the obligation of all belligerents to ensure relief for, and access to, all civilians. It also considers the deliberate denial of access to victims as an act of violence or abuse (UNSC Res 1674(2006), on *Protection of civilians in armed conflicts*, para 5) and thus as a serious violation of IHL, a crime against humanity (Res 2139 (2014) on Syria), and even a threat to international peace and security (see, e.g., Res 1296/2000, para 8). These Resolutions also call on the entire international community to cooperate in relief actions, clearly assuming the *erga omnes* effect of relief obligations in dramatic situations: in this sense see the *Preliminary Report*, above n 15, para 16; the *Fourth Report* (A/CN.4/643), paras 78–91; and *Guiding Principles on Humanitarian Assistance*, above n 4, point 7. On the practice related to the general obligation to provide for the basic needs of people in grave distress under IHRL and IHL, see F. Zorzi Giustiniani, *Le Nazioni Unite e l'assistenza umanitaria* (Naples: Scientifica, 2008), at 26–27.

Geneva Conventions' 'consent requirement' for IACs, as frequently interpreted according to an excessive concern about state prerogatives, is not applicable in every circumstance.[56] It cannot be used to justify a lack of concern for a population, or part of it, whose survival is in acute danger. This means that relief activities in the gravest situations can only be subject to certain conditions and modalities regarding the delivery of relief supplies in the field. They cannot be subject to a strict 'overall' condition of consent. Conversely, when a situation does not involve civilians whose survival is at risk, the relief activities in the IAC context remain optional, and they may thus also be refused.

A final remark concerns the relationship between the 'consent requirement', as discussed in connection with the different expressions and limitations set out above, and the principle of non-intervention in internal affairs.[57] This principle was very often presented in opposition to even a simple offer of relief during the First World War, and especially during the Second World War. Only in 1977 could the following mild provision be inserted in Article 70(1)AP I: 'Offers of [...] relief shall not be regarded as interference in the armed conflict or as unfriendly acts.'[58]

The issue of the relationship between humanitarian assistance and the principle of non-intervention was definitively solved in 1986 by a clear position taken by the International Court of Justice (ICJ) in the *Nicaragua* case, where the Court held, '[t]here can be no doubt that the provision of strictly humanitarian aid to persons or forces in another country, whatever their political affiliations or objectives, cannot be regarded as unlawful intervention, or as in any other way contrary to international law.'[59]

Importantly, the stand taken by the ICJ has a general purport and applies equally to humanitarian assistance delivered in the context of NIACs. This must be taken into account when analysing the issue of consent for activities of humanitarian assistance which take place in a situation of NIAC (MN 72–81; see also Chapter 24, MN 26–28, of this volume).

---

[56] Although Rule 55 of the ICRC CIHL Database does not mention the consent condition (see above n 50), the Database Summary underlines that 'a humanitarian organization cannot operate without the consent of the party concerned', which, however, 'must not be refused on arbitrary grounds'. In the author's view, a certain contradiction between the wording of the Rule and the comments reveals that the analysis of the underlying practice lacks distinction between civilians in need *tout court* and civilians in essential need for their survival; a distinction which is very clear in the practice referred to in ICRC CIHL Database (see, e.g., the reference to Res II of the 26th International Conference of the Red Cross and Red Crescent (1995), Practice related to Rule 55, Section A IX).

[57] This link is evoked in the Reports of the ILC Special Rapporteur on humanitarian assistance (A/CN.4/598, A/CN.4/615, A/CN.4/629, A/CN.4/643, A/CN.4/652): see particularly the *Preliminary Report*, above n 15, at 20 ff. The debate in the UNGA on these Reports showed how states are still jealous of their sovereign prerogative to decide whether external humanitarian assistance is needed. Nonetheless, all agreed that there are some limits to the denial of access to victims, albeit that these limits could not be defined (the debate focused on the unclear notion of 'arbitrary' refusal without underlining the particular situation of a population at risk as to its survival).

[58] The same weak wording is present in IIL Resolution on the 'Protection of Human Rights and the Principle of Non-Intervention in Internal Affairs of States' (Art 5), 13 September 1989, in 63 *Yearbook Institute of International Law* (1989) part I, at 338.

[59] ICJ, *Military and Paramilitary Activities in and against Nicaragua*, above n 31, para 242. Although the US humanitarian assistance was provided to Nicaraguan territory through a coercive intervention, the quoted statement strictly dealt with pure humanitarian activities—and not merely with humanitarian offers such as those envisioned by the AP I provision—but it did not deal with humanitarian intervention as a coercive measure. On this issue, what the ICJ also said *en passsant* might be considered relevant, i.e. 'the use of force could not be the appropriate method to monitor or ensure [...] respect' for human rights (ibid, para 268).

IV. Specific relief obligations of parties to an international armed conflict

49 In addition to the obligations to ensure essential relief to a population lacking in basic needs and to accept such relief coming from abroad, as discussed above in connection with the 'consent requirement', further obligations, which become operative when parties to the Geneva Conventions are involved in an IAC, essentially address the Detaining and Occupying Powers with respect to POWs and civilian internees.

a. Relief obligations of Detaining Powers

50 According to GC III, Detaining Powers must allow POWs to receive by any means individual parcels or collective relief, consisting in particular of foodstuffs, clothing, medical supplies, and articles of a religious, educational, or recreational character, as prescribed by a non-exhaustive list in Article 72 paragraph 1.

51 Books may not be included in parcels of clothing and foodstuffs. Medical supplies should, as a rule, be sent in collective parcels. By way of this limitation, the negotiators of the Geneva Conventions tried to reduce the risk of some inequality between POWs receiving and those not receiving individual parcels. This issue was debated at length during the Conference, because during the Second World War individual parcels sent to POWs had resulted in problems of inequality. The proposal to prohibit them eventually failed, and the more permissive approach prevailed subject to the said limitation and further restrictions, which might be proposed by the relief operator in the sole interest of POWs (Article 72 paragraph 3 GC III).[60]

52 Fulfilment of collective and individual relief obligations does not free the Detaining Powers from their obligations in respect of POWs provided in GC III (Article 72 paragraph 2).

53 An obligation *de contrahendo* to adopt special agreements on the conditions for sending and receiving individual and collective relief is imposed upon the Detaining Power and the state to which the prisoners belong, so long as these agreements do not delay the receipt of relief supplies (Article 72 paragraph 4).[61] Article 73 set out some restrictions for these agreements: they need to leave untouched the 'right' of prisoners' representatives to organize the distribution of collective relief in the interest of POWs, as well as the 'right' of representatives of the provider of relief to supervise its distribution. In the absence of such agreements, the specific regulations in Annex III to GC III apply.

54 Under Article 125 GC III, the Detaining Power has the obligation to grant humanitarian organizations all necessary facilities for visiting POWs, and for distributing relief supplies coming from any source. The same rules apply in the labour detachments of POWs (Article 56 GC III). The number of impartial humanitarian organizations assisting POWs may be limited, but 'such limitation shall not hinder the effective operation of adequate relief', and the ICRC's special position in this field shall be recognized (Article 125 paragraph 3).

55 Independently of the limited permissibility of interning protected civilians for imperative security reasons (Article 79), several rules of GC IV deal with individual and collective relief for civilian internees (Articles 108–111). They are analogous to those provided

---

[60] See Pictet Commentary GC III, at 351–53.
[61] See, e.g., the agreements 'On Ground Rules' stipulated in 1995 between UN Operation Lifeline Sudan and the Sudan People's Liberation Movement/Army.

for POWs, albeit less extensive and detailed. In the absence of special agreements, the modalities and conditions for receiving relief supplies are regulated by an Annex to GC IV. The providers of humanitarian assistance need to be informed, should military necessity require limiting the quantity of shipments. They may also undertake the conveyance of shipments, should military operations prevent the Powers concerned from ensuring delivery.

In addition to the stipulation that protected persons 'shall continue to be regulated, in principle, by the provisions concerning aliens in time of peace' (Article 38 paragraph 1 GC IV), some relief obligations are addressed by GC IV to the Powers detaining these persons for whatever reason (other than internment). These Powers have the obligation to enable foreign civilians to receive individual or collective relief (Article 38 paragraph 1). Under these accessory obligations, those persons should be granted all facilities to allow them to make application to and receive visits from any national or international relief organization, which, in turn, should be granted all facilities for these purposes (Article 30 GC IV). The visits are subject to the security or other reasonable needs of the Detaining Power, which may also limit the number of these organizations, but only in a way not prejudicial to ensuring effective and adequate relief for all protected persons (Article 142 GC IV). 56

A general provision complementary to all previous obligations of Detaining Powers provides that representatives and delegates of the Protecting Power and the ICRC must be authorized—except, temporarily, for reasons of imperative military necessity—to go to all places freely selected, 'particularly to places of internment, detention and work' (Article 143 paragraph 3). 57

b. *Relief obligations of the Occupying Power*

Based on the exercise of its power on the enemy's occupied territory, the Occupying Power has the duty to ensure, by all the means at its disposal, the needs of the entire population as regards food and medical stores. Requisition of these relief supplies in favour of the occupying army is allowed only after the needs of the population have been satisfied (Article 55 paragraphs 1 and 2 GC IV). 58

If local resources are inadequate, the Occupying Power 'should bring in' these supplies (Article 55 paragraph 1 GC IV). Hence, this obligation, albeit rather weak—'should' and not 'shall'—concerns external relief for the population under occupation as a subsidiary means of relief that the Occupying Power has the obligation to ensure. The expression 'bring in', instead of 'import', seems to suggest the need for the Occupying Power to bring relief supplies from its national territory, as relief from other external sources is subject to a relief scheme agreement, which needs to be reached with the provider of relief. 59

Indeed, the Occupying Power should agree to relief schemes undertaken either by states or by impartial humanitarian organizations if the whole or part of the population is inadequately supplied, *particularly* as regards foodstuffs, medical supplies, and clothing. It also has the obligation to facilitate such relief schemes 'by all the means at its disposal', and to accept the cooperation of and supervision by the Protecting Power for the distribution of consignments (Article 59 GC IV). Such a function may be delegated 'to a neutral Power, to the ICRC or to any other impartial humanitarian body' (Article 61 paragraph 1 GC IV). 60

Consignments of relief supplies cannot be diverted by the Occupying Power, except in cases of urgent necessity, in the interests of the population of the occupied territory, and 61 with the consent of the Protecting Power (Article 60 GC IV). Their rapid distribution has to be facilitated by the Occupying Power, which is also under an obligation to exempt such supplies from all charges, taxes, and custom duties, subject to the economic needs of the occupied territory (Article 61 paragraph 2 GC IV).

62   Complementary to all of the above-mentioned obligations is the faculty granted to the Protecting Power to verify the state of the needs of the population with regard to food and medical supplies. This ability may be temporarily restricted only for imperative military reasons (Article 55 paragraph 3 GC IV).

63   The Occupying Power must also permit national Red Cross Societies to continue to carry out their activities according to the Red Cross principles, except in cases of urgent reasons of security (Article 63 paragraph 1(a) GC IV). Further, it cannot demand changes in the personnel staffing of these societies which would prejudice such activities (Article 63 paragraph 1(b) GC IV). In the same spirit, it is provided that the Occupying Power, in cooperation with national and local authorities, should ensure medical and hospital establishments and services, and should allow medical personnel of all categories to carry out their duties (Article 56 GC IV).

64   In addition to the obligations imposed upon Occupying Powers for the benefit of all the segments of a population under occupation, there is a specific obligation aimed at protected persons: Occupying Powers have to permit them to receive individual relief, subject to an exception for imperative reasons of security (Article 62 GC IV). Furthermore, protected persons accused of a crime and detained in the country under occupation are entitled 'to receive at least one relief parcel monthly' and to be visited by the entities provided for in Article 143 (Article 76 paragraphs 6 and 7 GC IV).

V. The free passage obligation

65   The obligation to allow free passage of relief consignments is imposed in Article 23 GC IV upon all contracting parties irrespective of their involvement in an IAC other than occupation.[62] The material scope of this free passage obligation is determined in a selective way: while it is generally limited to 'medical and hospital stores and objects necessary for religious worship', it also extends to essential foodstuffs, clothing, and tonics for selected persons, namely 'children under fifteen, expectant mothers and maternity cases'.

66   Such a restrictive approach also inspires the conditions stipulated in paragraphs 2 and 3 of Article 23. First, the party concerned needs to be satisfied that there are no serious reasons for fearing the diversion of the consignments from their destination or the inefficacy of control. Secondly, it may also refuse free passage should the above-mentioned consignments of goods replace those provided or produced by the enemy, where a definite advantage 'may accrue to the military efforts or economy of the enemy'. Thirdly, the distribution of relief goods will be made under the local supervision of the Protecting Power. Lastly, the Power allowing free passage has the right to prescribe the technical arrangements for that passage.

67   These conditions, essentially left to the unilateral evaluation of the state concerned, make the already limited obligation of free passage too subjective, despite the requirement

---

[62] It is worth noting that in light of its origin, the free passage obligation is usually intended to bring relief to civilians under blockade or under siege (see Pictet Commentary GC IV, at 178), but in fact the scope of its beneficiaries is clearly broader, covering the free passage of relief to civilians in any situation of conflict other than occupation.

that consignments 'shall be forwarded as rapidly as possible' (Article 23 paragraph 4). Furthermore, tasking the Protecting Power, which is in fact the ICRC, with the duty of supervision might contribute to the failure of relief activities of other impartial organizations should Red Cross personnel not be present in the field.[63]

The restrictive scope of Article 23, both objectively and subjectively, and the related conditions are not present in AP I, which provides that 'each Contracting Party shall allow and facilitate rapid and unimpeded passage of all relief consignments, equipment and personnel [...] even if such assistance is destined for the civilian population of the adverse Party' (Article 70(2) AP I). 68

In the author's view, the humanitarian developments reflected in Article 70(1) and (2) AP I cannot but have an impact on the obligation of free passage. This obligation must extend to all essential relief supplies—essential foodstuffs in particular—for any civilian whose survival is in danger in an IAC other than occupation. 69

A separate, larger obligation of free passage is imposed by GC IV on all contracting parties in the situation of occupation (Article 59). This specific obligation is applicable to the relief 'consignments of foodstuffs, medical supplies and clothing', for the benefit of the whole or part of the population of an occupied territory which is 'inadequately supplied'. This wording is consistent with the primary obligation imposed on the Occupying Power, directly and adequately to relieve the population (see MN 58–61). Indeed, it does not refer to beneficiaries in a selective way but imposes the obligation to allow free passage of supplies necessary for ensuring adequate conditions of life of the whole population or part of it. Hence, the adequacy of supplies is to be commensurate with the needs of the different classes of persons composing the population and residing in different localities.[64] 70

This obligation is subject to the faculty accorded to the state granting free passage to search the consignments, to prescribe times and routes for the passage, and to verify, through the Protecting Power, that these consignments are not diverted for the benefit of the Occupying Power (Article 59 paragraph 4 GC IV). 71

C. Relevance in Non-International Armed Conflicts

Whereas until 1949 the wounded and sick beneficiaries of the obligation to be collected and cared for were only those military personnel engaged in inter-state conflicts, from 1949 onwards the wounded and sick among the shipwrecked, captured insurgents, and civilians residing on the territory of a state being the theatre of a NIAC, also became beneficiaries of such a specific obligation (Common Article 3, paragraph 1(2)). 72

On the other hand, whereas Common Article 3 grants persons not taking part—or no longer taking part—in hostilities mandatory protection, as far as relief in general is 73

---

[63] Pictet Commentary GC IV, at 184, recalls that, during the Second World War, the Allies authorized relaxation of the blockade only in cases where the Committee was able to supervise the forwarding and distribution of consignments.
[64] Such a free passage obligation is also applicable to the Occupied Palestinian Territories. Some doubts might arise with regard to the Gaza Strip, given that it rather seems a territory under blockade. There would be a notable difference whether one regime or the other were applied. The occupation regime appears to encompass the situation considered in Res 1860 of 2009, where the UNSC called for 'an immediate ceasefire in Gaza leading to a full Israeli withdrawal, unimpeded provision through Gaza of food, fuel and medical treatment'. The position taken by the Israeli High Court of Justice in the *Albasyouni* case could be interpreted similarly (HCJ, Judgment, 30 January 2008, ICRC CIHL Database, A V (Israel)).

concerned, these persons are only the beneficiaries of humanitarian services offered by any impartial body (Common Article 3 paragraph 2).

74 As for the providers of humanitarian relief in NIAC, the analysis carried out above for situations of IACs equally applies, *mutatis mutandis*, to NIACs. It is worth underlining here, however, that the formulation of Common Article 3 paragraph 2 merely provides for the possibility of an impartial organization offering its humanitarian services, and thus is more restrictive than the provisions concerning providers of humanitarian assistance in IAC. In Common Article 3, humanitarian operators seem to be put at the complete service of the parties involved in the conflict, rather than being intended as effective providers of any humanitarian initiative and activity.

75 However, Common Article 3 does not make reference to the need for the consent of the party receiving humanitarian relief. This is understandable in light of the reference to *offers* of services and not to *activities/actions/work*, which, by contrast, are usually subject to the requirement of consent. Indeed, the liberty of the parties to a NIAC to accept or not the 'offers' of services by 'any impartial organization' is *in re ipsa*.[65]

76 Such an approach remains in Article 18(1) AP II, which, similar to Common Article 3, refers only to the 'offer of humanitarian services' by 'relief societies located in the territory' of the state party, which have direct access to victims and operate under the control of local authorities. As in Common Article 3, such an offer is not made conditional on any form of consent. However, consent to the humanitarian relief is requested by the following paragraph, which refers to relief *actions*—although here by *any* impartial organization—in favour of 'the civilian population [...] suffering undue hardship owing to a lack of the supplies essential for its survival'. The *consent* shall be given by the 'High Contracting Party concerned'; thus by the sole state party to a NIAC. Furthermore, here the term *consent*, instead of *agreement*, is used in spite of the mandatory character of these actions as provided in Article 70 AP I, where, however action is more coherently linked to the term *agreement* (see MN 38–48).

77 Article 18(2) AP II thus follows a state-centric approach not present in Common Article 3, as it mentions only the 'High Contracting Party', which is the 'state party' to the conflict, as the addressee of offers by 'local organizations', and even of offers of only 'traditional services' (Common Article 3 instead refers in general to the 'Parties to the conflict'). This state-centric claim, espoused at the Conference by the large majority of states, completely ignored the realities of international relations. Indeed, the situation in practice may frequently allow for relief without the consent—or agreement—of the High Contracting Party, when the affected territory may be reached without passing through areas under governmental control. In such a situation, in order to avoid, in so far as possible, a relief operation that will be unsafe for the humanitarian personnel, and the risk of humanitarian aid not reaching the victims, the rebels' 'consent' could be needed more than that of the government.[66]

---

[65] See Art 88 1929 GC II, the GCs' common provision 9/9/9/10, and Art 70 AP I, as well as Art 18(2) AP II. As the Mexico Delegation explained at the Conference, 'offers of foreign relief could be made in internal conflicts and were not subject to the consent of the High Contracting Party concerned. In fact, it was difficult to see how an offer, which was a spontaneous act could be subject to consent' (*Official Records*, above n 47, vol VII, at 147).

[66] In the case of enforcement operations under Ch VII in a situation of NIAC, the UN also tries to obtain the consent of the non-state party—or parties—involved in the conflict, being thus forced at times to limit its intervention to dealing with bandits and rebel groups of minor importance. It is worth recalling that the UN, in order to deploy UNOSOM I and II in Somalia in the early 1990s for delivering humanitarian assistance in a situation of complete anarchy, needed to negotiate with 15 armed warlords!

The discrepancies between Common Article 3 and Article 18 AP II, for parties to both 78
the Geneva Conventions and AP II, must be solved according to the stipulation that the
Protocol 'develops and supplements Common Article 3 to the Geneva Conventions of
12 August 1949 *without modifying its existing conditions of application*' (Article 1(1) AP
II (emphasis added)).[67] Hence, they are to be solved, in the author's view, in conformity
with the more liberal and realistic approach followed by Common Article 3 with respect
to the equality of all the parties to a NIAC as regards receiving offers of services by *any*
humanitarian organization.

Furthermore, as the statement of ICJ in *Nicaragua* case, referred to above, was intended 79
to apply in both contexts, IAC and NIAC (see MN 48), the respect due to the principle of
non-intervention expressly stated in AP II may not be used to oppose offers of humanitarian activities by *any* impartial organization to *any* party of the conflict, notwithstanding
the silence on this of AP II, unlike AP I (see MN 46).

In addition, the conclusions reached above as regards the impact of the prohibition 80
of starvation as a method of warfare (MN 44–45) are also applicable to NIAC. The *consent* requirement stipulated in Article 18(2) AP II cannot prevent humanitarian relief in
order to ensure the basic needs of a population or parts of it suffering from a lack of supplies essential for its survival during a NIAC. Moreover, both the state and the non-state
entity parties to the NIAC shall be considered as the addressees of the relief obligation in
favour of the local population in need—regardless of its allegiance to either party to the
conflict—and of the obligation to accept foreign or international humanitarian assistance
should these parties be unable to carry out such activities directly. Thus, in NIAC as well,
when the survival of a civilian population is at risk, it is more a question of 'authorizing'
a specific humanitarian operator to carry out relief activities in the field and of negotiating the related modalities, rather than a question of giving 'overall consent' for the relief
mission.

It should be mentioned that no obligation to allow free passage exists in the Geneva 81
Conventions as regards NIAC. Additional Protocol II is also silent on this matter.[68]
However, in the author's view, such an obligation is the implicit consequence of the
humanitarian developments with respect to any civilian population that is suffering
undue hardship owing to a lack of supplies essential for its survival.

D. Legal Consequences of a Violation

No specific violations of the rules on humanitarian assistance are included in the lists of 82
grave breaches contained in each Geneva Convention as well as in AP I.[69] However, among
the measures required for the suppression of any act contrary to the Geneva Conventions
(Article 49 GC I; Article 50 GC II; Article 129 GC III; Article 146 GC IV), states may also
have recourse, as an optional measure, to the penal repression of these acts (see Chapter
36, MN 10, of this volume).

---

[67] See Ch 34, section D.I.b, of this volume.
[68] A free passage obligation was instead provided in the ICRC Draft of AP II (Art 33), but, astonishingly, it 'was deleted at the last moment as part of a package aimed at the adoption of a simplified text' (ICRC CIHL Database, Summary to Rule 55).
[69] By contrast, the UN Safety Convention imposes the obligation to repress attacks against UN and associated operations according to the territorial and national link, while the residency active link and the national passive one are optional (Art 9). It also provides the principle *judicare aut dedere*.

83 In addition, although the Statutes of the two ad hoc international criminal tribunals—the International Criminal Tribunal for the former Yugoslavia (ICTY) and the International Criminal Tribunal for Rwanda (ICTR)—unlike the International Criminal Court (ICC) Statute (e.g. Article 8(2)(b)xxv), do not specifically refer to violations in the domain of relief, such violations assume relevance in the activity of those two tribunals.

84 First, the relevance of such violations appears evident in two grave breaches listed in the Geneva Conventions and expressly mentioned in both the Statutes of the ICTY and ICTR: inhuman treatment, and wilfully causing great suffering or serious injury to body or health. This relevance is amplified by the reference to 'deprivation of access to food and medicine' contained in the definition of extermination as a crime against humanity, elaborated by the ICTY and codified in the ICC Statute.[70] Furthermore, among acts of genocide provided in the Genocide Convention of 1948 and appearing in both Statutes, the crime of 'deliberately inflicting on the group conditions of life calculated to bring about its physical destruction in whole or in part' is also relevant in the field of relief.

85 It is also noteworthy that Article 3 of the ICTY Statute, while criminalizing the grave breaches contained in the Geneva Conventions, also adds an open clause, 'these violations shall include, but shall not be limited to'. Furthermore, Article 4, in referring to 'the laws and customs of war', enumerates some serious violations of these laws and customs with the same open clause. Moreover, the ICTR Statute refers to violations of Common Article 3 and AP II, and enumerates some of them, again leaving the list open. Thus, the open clause leaves the possibility, in the context of these tribunals, to charge and convict individual defendants of serious violations of rules concerning humanitarian relief.

86 However, the prosecutors of the two ad hoc Tribunals have not specifically charged anyone for crimes in the relief domain. In fact, in their indictments, they usually allege violations of relief rules in the context of counts related to other grave violations of IHL.[71] The Chambers can only convict on charges contained in indictments, thus there are no convictions specifically for crimes in the relief domain.[72] Nonetheless, judgments of the Tribunals contain frequent findings of violations of relief rules, such as starvation of civilians,[73] restrictions and obstruction of deliveries of humanitarian aid,[74] destruction

---

[70] Art 7(2)(b) ICC Statute.

[71] So, e.g., violations of relief rules, in particular obstructions to humanitarian aid, were alleged in the *Milosevic* Indictment as a 'crime of persecutions' [*sic*]: see para 35(k) of the Amended Indictment of 22 November 2002 (in para 35(c) starvation was also alleged). Allegations of violations of relief rules are also present in the Indictments against *Karadžić* and *Mladić*. Indeed, they are both accused of having directed and/or authorized 'the restrictions of humanitarian aid destined to the enclave of Srebrenica' (see *Karadžić* Indictment of 19 October 2009 and *Mladić* Indictment of 16 December 2011, para 14(j) and para 13(k) respectively). This charge is in particular alleged in the context of the counts 'persecutions' and 'inhuman acts' as 'crimes against humanity': see *Karadžić* paras 57, 74 and *Mladić*, paras 56, 73.

[72] The findings of inadequate living conditions in POW camps and in civilian detention facilities resulted in numerous convictions for the crimes of extermination, torture, cruel and inhuman treatment, etc. For instance, in *Blaškić*, it was affirmed that the deprivation of food and water from Bosnian Muslim civilian detainees 'rose to the level of gravity of the other crimes enumerated in Art 5' (ICTY, *The Prosecutor v Tihomir Blaškić*, Appeals Chamber Judgment, IT-95-14-A, 29 July 2004, para 155). However, the issue concerned more the violation by the Detaining Power of IHL rules relating to the protection of detainees rather than those concerning the provision of relief.

[73] See ICTY, *The Prosecutor v Mićo Stanišić and Stojan Župljanin*, Trial Chamber Judgment, IT-08-91-T, 27 March 2013, paras 584, 598.

[74] In *Blagojević*, the Trial Chamber referred to 'blocking humanitarian supplies and convoys from entering Srebrenica enclave at Žuti Most' in order to assess the crime of forcible transfer of civilians (ICTY, *The Prosecutor v Vidoje Blagojević and Dragan Jokić*, Trial Chamber Judgment, IT-02-60-T, 17 January 2005,

of supplies essential for the survival of the protected persons under each Convention,[75] and attacks against humanitarian personnel or against civilian objects used for relief for victims.[76]

However, attacks against humanitarian personnel and against essential relief supplies are not merely considered by the jurisprudence of the Tribunals in the context of certain elements of crimes expressly listed in the Statutes; they are also directly repressed as crimes, although not in their specific characterization as crimes in the domain of relief. They are considered war crimes as long as members of the relief personnel are entitled to protection as civilians not taking a direct part in hostilities, and as long as the supplies they are delivering are not military objectives.[77] This indirect protection does not undermine, in the author's view, the important role that humanitarian operators and relief installations and supplies play in the survival of victims of war. Indeed, this role acquires a specific relevance in the Chambers' determination of the civilian status of both relief personnel and supplies.[78]

The jurisprudence of the two ad hoc Tribunals has led to the inclusion of some relief-related violations in the Statute of the Special Court for Sierra Leone (SCSL)[79] and in the ICC Statute. In the latter, starvation is directly criminalized as a war crime among 'other serious violations of the laws and customs applicable in international armed conflict',[80] while intentional attacks against personnel, installations, material, units, or

---

paras 98, 111, 138, 155, 213, 264). For the same approach, see also the convictions of *Popović* et al for, inter alia, the forcible transfer—inhuman acts as crime against humanity—of Bosnian Muslims from the Zepa and Srebrenica enclaves. In particular, the denial of clearance to UNPROFOR humanitarian convoys destined to Srebrenica was considered as a means for the commission of that crime (ICTY, *The Prosecutor v Vujadin Popović*, Trial Chamber Judgment, IT-05-88-T, 10 June 2010, paras 214–15, 219 ff, 231 ff, 240, 766–67, 777, 782, 939, 1085, 1701, 1707–10, 1716, 1738, 1803, 1808–10, 2195, 2197) or for terrorizing the population (ibid, paras 196–200). In *Galić*, it was ascertained that UN troops in Sarajevo frequently had to modify the locations where citizens gathered to receive humanitarian aid in order to avoid being targeted by shells, although 'it was well known' that humanitarian aid was distributed (ICTY, *The Prosecutor v Stanislav Galić*, Trial Chamber Judgment, IT-98-29-T, 5 December 2003, para 223). In *Krstić*, the Court considered the blocking of humanitarian aid in the overall context of reconstructing the 'humanitarian crisis', and in the assessment of the terror spread among the civilian population as a means to effect the forcible transfer of the enemy ethnic group (ICTY, *The Prosecutor v Radislav Krstić*, Trial Chamber Judgment, IT-98-33-T, 2 August 2001, para 615 and 653). For the violations of rules concerning the ICRC visits to POWs, see, among others, ICTY, *The Prosecutor v Zdravko Tolimir*, Trial Chamber Judgment, IT-05-88/2-T, 12 December 2012, para 1152.

[75] The destruction of Srebrenica's water supply had great relevance in the determination of the crime of persecution in *Tolimir*, above n 74, para 174. See also *Blagojević*, above n 74, and ICTY, *The Prosecutor v Vlastimir Đorđević*, Trial Chamber Judgment, IT-05-87/1-T, 23 February 2011, para 337, concerning crimes committed in other ex-Yugoslav locations.

[76] ICTY Chambers have made frequent findings on the gravest consequences of attacks on and destructions of objects indispensable to the survival of the civilian population, in particular when dealing with the destruction of Bosnian villages (which always entailed the destruction of foodstuffs and other relief supplies essential for the survival of their inhabitants), or with the blockade of Dubrovnik and the overall context of the attack against Dubrovnik civilians as a war crime (ICTY, *The Prosecutor v Pavle Strugar*, Trial Chamber Judgment, IT-01-42-T, 31 January 2005, paras 26, 48, 176).

[77] See, e.g., *Strugar*, above n 76, para 244.

[78] Indeed, the assessment by the Chambers of war crimes against civilians may benefit from a *presumptio hominis*, i.e. the simple presumption of the civilian status of personnel and of relief supplies and installations, and so render easier the task of the Judges.

[79] Regarding the criminalization of attacks against humanitarian personnel and objects, although only 'as long as they are entitled to the protection given to civilians or civilian objects', see Art 4.

[80] Art 8(2)(b)(xxv). During the negotiations on the ICC Statute, many proposals were put forward to also include starvation for the context of NIAC. This would have been consistent with the criminalization of attacks against humanitarian personnel and installations, also in NIAC (Art 8(2)(e)(iii) ICC Statute), and the

vehicles involved in a humanitarian assistance or UN peacekeeping mission are equally criminalized in both IAC and NIAC, although under the same conditions discussed in the previous paragraph.

89   The jurisdiction of the ICC, limited to statutory crimes according to the *lex specialis* principle, may be 'overcome' by reading serious violations of relief rules into conduct expressly prohibited in the Statute as a war crime, or crime against humanity or an act of genocide, as was done by the two ad hoc Tribunals. Furthermore, the *lex specialis* ICC competence might be 'overcome' by interpreting the Statute in a way 'consistent with internationally recognized human rights' (Article 21(3)), in particular through the open clause addressing '[o]ther inhumane acts of a similar character intentionally causing great suffering, or serious injury to body or to mental or physical health' as a crime against humanity (Article 7(1)(k)). Thus, for instance, the ICC Prosecutor and the Chambers might extend the criminalization of starvation to the context of NIAC by adopting, in application of the above-quoted provision, the coherent solution of the ICTY and ICTR, which have frequently resorted to it, beginning with the decision in *Tadić*.[81] After all, in the author's view, the impunity of an individual responsible for starvation in a NIAC would be inconsistent with internationally recognized human rights, and incoherent if compared with the criminalization of starvation in the context of an IAC.

E. Critical Assessment

90   The sovereign-based approach, recently adopted in the matter of humanitarian assistance by some states' delegations during the debates in the UNGA on ILC Reports concerning 'The Protection of Persons in the Event of Disasters', shows that claims about state sovereign prerogatives are still strong.

91   As a matter of fact, when moving on to discussing new rules in the present extended composition of the international community, the old ghosts, which characterized the Cold War period—such as the principle of non-intervention in the internal affairs of states (or, using different wording, in domestic jurisdiction)—reappear in the humanitarian realm.[82] However, at the same forum, the majority of states' delegations have shown themselves to be particularly sensitive to considerations of solidarity as regards the needs of victims of natural or man-made disasters, the same considerations that both inspire the best practices in the field in the matter of humanitarian assistance referred to in this chapter and represent a leading tool for the interpretation of IHL relief rules applicable in IAC and NIAC contexts.

92   In particular, the overall picture on humanitarian assistance in the Geneva Conventions shows that whereas different specific rules apply in IACs and NIACs, some fundamental humanitarian principles equally govern relief for victims in both contexts. Indeed, the

---

prohibition of starvation in AP II. Regrettably, the claims of sovereign prerogatives of states during negotiations outweighed these proposals.

[81] ICTY, *The Prosecutor v Duško Tadić*, Appeals Chamber Decision on the Defence Motion for Interlocutory Appeal on Jurisdiction, IT-94-1, 2 October 1995, para 127.

[82] As was also expressed by a 'group of lawyers' in a statement attached to the letter sent by the Permanent Syrian Representative to the UN. It stated, 'in order to import any type of humanitarian aid to a Member State of the United Nations, prior consent must be obtained from that State. The decision whether to agree or refuse is a matter of national jurisdiction' (18 June 2014, S/2014/426).

rhetorical question posed in 1995 in an ICTY decision—'Why protect civilians from belligerent violence [...] when two sovereign States are engaged in war, and yet refrain from enacting the same bans or providing the same protection when armed violence has erupted "only" within the territory of a sovereign State?'—cannot but have the same coherent response in the relief domain as that achieved in the *Tadić* case with regard to the domain of protection. In particular, in both contexts, delivering essential supplies to a population whose survival is at risk is mandatory, and the denial of access to victims amounts to a serious violation of IHL.

93 This picture also gives rise to the conclusion that the pragmatic approach followed by international humanitarian organizations in negotiating access to victims with each party to the conflict which has control over the territory affected by the emergency, in the spirit of Common Article 3, is the best way for the relief to reach any population in need rapidly and efficiently. This also means that the best way to ensure external help to all victims of emergencies in times of armed conflicts is to avoid channelling humanitarian assistance through military operations and rather to support and facilitate the activities of impartial humanitarian organizations, according to the letter and spirit of the Geneva Conventions.

94 It can after all be concluded that the relief regulations contained in the Geneva Conventions may prove to be sufficiently developed, and even endowed with a potential that is broader than appears at first sight. These regulations need to be complied with in all their potential rather than amended, but they also need to be read in light of the humanization process of domestic laws and international law, without any compromise on fundamental humanitarian principles in the name of a fake notion of 'sovereign prerogatives'.[83] The first authentic prerogative of a 'sovereign' is to act, even accepting external help, to avoid serious suffering for any people in its power, in wartime as in peacetime. There does not exist a higher interest to protect. The centuries-old Roman maxim '*hominum causa omne jus constitutum est*' has to be the leading principle in the domain of relief as well.

FLAVIA LATTANZI

---

[83] ICRC President P. Maurer, IHL and Humanitarian Principles are Non-negotiable—Syria is no exception, Editorial, *IRRC* (15 February 2014), available at <https://www.icrc.org/eng/resources/documents/article/editorial/2014-02-15-syria-maurer-humanitarian-principles.htm>.

Chapter 13. Search for Missing Persons

	MN
A. Introduction	1
I. Definition and phenomenon	1
II. Applicable legal framework and its development	6
B. Meaning and Application	14
I. Providing identity documents	15
II. Collecting and recording information	19
III. Forwarding of information, documents, and objects to the National Information Bureau	29
IV. Transmission of information to the power on which a person depends	34
V. Search for missing persons	40
C. Relevance in Non-International Armed Conflicts	51
D. Legal Consequences of a Violation	54
I. State responsibility	54
II. Criminal responsibility	60
E. Critical Assessment	65

Select Bibliography

Blumenstock, T., 'Legal Protection of the Missing and Their Relatives: The Example of Bosnia and Herzegovina', 19 *LJIL* (2006) 773

Boutruche, T., 'Missing and Dead Persons', in MPEPIL

ICRC, *Missing Persons: A Handbook for Parliamentarians* (No 17, Geneva: ICRC and Inter-Parliamentary Union, 2009)

ICRC Advisory Service on International Humanitarian Law, *Guiding Principles/Model Law on the Missing*, available at <http://www.icrc.org/eng/assets/files/other/model-law-missing-0209-eng-.pdf>

ICRC CIHL Study, Rules 117 and 123 (rules and practice)

ICRC Commentary APs, Arts 32 and 33 AP I

OHCHR, *Study on the Right to Truth*, UN Doc E/CN.4/2006/91 (8 February 2006)

Pictet Commentary GC I, Art 16

Pictet Commentary GC II, Art 19

Pictet Commentary GC III, Arts 17, 119(7), 122, and 123

Pictet Commentary GC IV, Arts 16, 133 para 3, 136–40

Sassòli, M., 'The National Information Bureau in Aid of the Victims of Armed Conflicts', 27 *IRRC* 256 (1987) 6

Sassòli, M./Tougas, M., 'The ICRC and the Missing', 84 *IRRC* 848 (2002) 727

Scovazzi, T./Citroni, G., *The Struggle against Enforced Disappearance and the 2007 United Nations Convention* (Leiden: Martinus Nijhoff Publishers, 2007)

A. Introduction

I. Definition and phenomenon

1   The notion of 'missing persons'—even though appearing in the First Additional Protocol to the Geneva Conventions (AP I)[1]—is not specifically defined by any legal instrument of international humanitarian law (IHL). Rather, the definition accrues from the various provisions dealing with the phenomenon, most notably from the 'right of families to know the fate of their relatives' as stipulated in Article 32 AP I. From these provisions it follows that persons are considered missing if their relatives or the Power on which they depend have no information on their fate and whereabouts.[2] While persons can go missing in various contexts, such as situations of internal violence or disturbances, and natural catastrophes,[3] the relevant rules of IHL apply only if the person is missing in connection with an armed conflict or a situation of occupation.[4] One specific and reoccurring instance where a person may go missing is that of an enforced disappearance. However, enforced disappearance is predominantly regulated in international human rights law (IHRL) and international criminal law, a fact to be remembered when discussing the concept of missing persons under IHL.[5] In the following, the term 'enforced disappearance' is used exclusively to denote the specific human rights violation or the criminal offence of enforced disappearance. By contrast, the more inclusive notions of 'missing person' or 'to go missing' refer to the broader concept, taking into account that in armed conflicts or situations of occupation the reasons for a person being unaccounted for are manifold.

2   Persons who have gone missing in a situation of armed conflict or occupation are either dead[6] or alive, and in the latter case deprived of their liberty by the enemy or free, but separated from their relatives by borders or frontlines.[7] In the past, it was mainly combatants who were at risk of going missing, the so-called 'missing in action'. However, starting with the Second World War, civilians increasingly became caught up in the violence or were often the very target of violence. With civilians becoming the overwhelming majority of victims of armed conflicts,[8] the number of civilian missing increased as well.[9] Despite a

---

[1] Section III of Part II AP I.
[2] Sassòli/Bouvier/Quintin, at 206; see, e.g., Art 2 Law on Missing Persons of Bosnia and Herzegovina (Official Gazette of BiH, 9 November 2004), unofficial English translation provided by the International Commission on Missing Persons, available at <http://www.ic-mp.org/wp-content/uploads/2007/11/lawmp_en.pdf> (hereinafter BiH Law on Missing Persons).
[3] See the broad definition of 'missing person' in Art 2 Model Law on the Missing (ICRC Advisory Service on International Humanitarian Law, *Guiding Principles/Model Law on the Missing*), available at <http://www.icrc.org/eng/assets/files/other/model-law-missing-0209-eng-.pdf>.
[4] CA 2. See also the relevant chapters of this volume, in particular Chs 1, 2, and 67.
[5] According to the definition provided in the International Convention for the Protection of All Persons from Enforced Disappearance of 2006 (ICED), 'enforced disappearance' essentially denotes arrest, detention, abduction, or any other form of deprivation of liberty committed by state actors or with the authorization, support, or acquiescence of the state, which is followed by a refusal to acknowledge the deprivation of liberty or by concealing the fate and whereabouts of the disappeared person. See, e.g., Art 2 ICED. The ICC Statute defines 'enforced disappearance' in similar terms: Art 7(2)(i). The main differences between the ICC Statute and Art 2 ICED are that the offence can also be committed by a 'political organization', and that the perpetrator must act with the intention of removing the victim from the protection of the law for a prolonged period of time.
[6] On the dead in armed conflicts, see also Ch 14 of this volume.
[7] M. Sassòli and M. Tougas, 'The ICRC and the Missing', 84 *IRRC* 848 (2002) 727, at 730; Sassòli/Bouvier/Quintin, at 206.
[8] UNICEF, 'Patterns in conflict: Civilians are now the target', available at <http://www.unicef.org/graca/patterns.htm>.
[9] S. Martin, 'The Missing', 84 *IRRC* 848 (2002) 723, at 724.

more complete and elaborate normative framework applying to persons who go missing during armed conflicts or situations of occupation,[10] recent conflicts have left thousands of persons unaccounted for.[11]

The phenomenon of missing persons displays its negative effects on various levels. First of all, the person who is unaccounted for, if alive, suffers because he or she is cut off from the outside world,[12] the most notable consequence of which is being unable to contact his or her family.

Furthermore, as is expressed by Article 32 AP I, which refers to the right of families to know the fate of their loved ones, the relatives of the missing person also suffer from the lack of information concerning the fate and whereabouts of their next of kin. For them, the absence of information principally has a psychological and emotional dimension, in that they 'endure the agony of not knowing whether family members were killed in the conflict or are still in detention or, if detained, have since died'.[13] It is often only the official notification of death that can close the circle of uncertainty and put an end to their false hope. Without this acknowledgement of the loss of life, the mourning process can seldom be initiated.[14] Being in possession of information about the fate of relatives is also of great legal and administrative significance. In many jurisdictions, only the legal consequences flowing from the death of a relative are regulated and the missing person has no legal status. Hence, relatives of persons who have gone missing cannot claim support, or are prevented from exercising rights in a number of matters, such as social welfare, inheritance, property rights, and marital and family law. In addition, economic hardship may arise if it is the primary breadwinner of the family who has gone missing. Ideally, states should adopt legislation governing the legal status of missing persons and the rights of family members.[15]

The issue of missing persons has a collective dimension as well. Parties to a (former) conflict may manipulate and exploit the issue of missing persons, to perpetuate hate and national or ethic exclusion, or to rally support for their cause.[16] Furthermore, not establishing and making the fate and whereabouts of victims known may hinder reconciliation and sustainable peace. Therefore, as a general rule, clarifying the issue of missing persons to the extent possible is one of the objectives of truth and reconciliation commissions.[17]

---

[10] See section A.II of this chapter.
[11] As just one example, a total of 34,325 persons were reported missing to the ICRC following the conflicts in the former Yugoslavia in the 1990s: ICRC, 'Missing Persons in the Territory of Former Yugoslavia,' ICRC Field Newsletter (25 April 2008), available at <http://www.icrc.org/eng/resources/documents/field-newsletter/serbia-missing-newsletter-010408.htm>.
[12] HRCttee, *Sarma v Sri Lanka*, Comm No 950/2000, 16 July 2003, para 9.5.
[13] ECtHR, *Cyprus v Turkey*, Grand Chamber Judgment, 10 May 2001, para 157.
[14] A. Petrig, 'The War Dead and Their Gravesites', 91 *IRRC* 874 (2009) 341, at 351.
[15] ICRC, *Missing Persons: A Handbook for Parliamentarians* (No 17: ICRC and Inter-Parliamentary Union, 2009) (hereinafter ICRC Handbook), at 10–11; see Arts 8–10 Model Law on the Missing and related commentary; Arts 11–19 BiH Law on the Missing; Art 6 Law on Missing Persons of Kosovo (*Official Gazette of the Republic of Kosovo*, 14 September 2011), unofficial translation provided by the International Commission on Missing Persons, available at <http://www.ic-mp.org/wp-content/uploads/2007/11/law-on-missing-persons-republic-of-kosovo.pdf>; Art 24(6) ICED.
[16] Sassòli and Tougas, above n 7, at 727–8.
[17] Section 3 para 1(c) South African Promotion of National Unity and Reconciliation Act No 34 of 1995, cited by M. Crettol and A.-M. La Rosa, 'The Missing and Transitional Justice: The Right to Know and the Fight against Impunity', 88 *IRRC* 862 (2006) 355, at 356.

II. Applicable legal framework and its development

6   Various rules of IHL aim at preventing persons from going missing and ensuring that persons do not remain unaccounted for. However, these rules do not cover the situation where persons voluntarily abscond because they wish to sever all ties with their family or state.[18]

7   International humanitarian law had already begun addressing the issue of missing persons in the nineteenth century, albeit only with regard to combatants. For instance, the institution of a bureau of information for prisoners of war (POWs), to centralize information and answer enquiries about combatants in the hands of the enemy, was foreseen in the Hague Regulations of 1899 and 1907.[19] Moreover, the Oxford Manual on *The Laws of War on Land* of 1880 stipulates that the dead should not be buried until all articles on them serving to establish their identity have been collected.[20] Furthermore, the Geneva Conventions for the Amelioration of the Condition of the Wounded and Sick in Armies in the Field of 1906 and 1929[21] respectively, set forth obligations pertaining to the identification of the dead, and the collection and forwarding of information on POWs.

8   The large-scale interment of civilians during the Second World War evidenced the need to adopt IHL rules in order to prevent civilians from going missing, and to elucidate their fate and whereabouts if persons nevertheless remain unaccounted for. Also, the existing rules of IHL obliging the enemy Power to account for combatants in its hands proved insufficient in many respects. These two shortcomings were, to some extent, remedied by the adoption of the four Geneva Conventions in 1949.[22]

9   Under the Geneva Conventions, missing persons are first of all entitled to the protection offered to the respective category of protected persons to which they belong. What is more, each Geneva Convention (GC) contains specific rules aimed at preventing persons from going missing, and to clarify their fate and whereabouts. Essentially, they stipulate that each party to the conflict must collect and record information on the identity and whereabouts of protected persons,[23] and centralize such information at the National Information Bureau (NIB),[24] which must be established by states party to the Geneva Conventions at the outbreak of hostilities or the commencement of a situation of occupation at the very latest.[25] For its part, the NIB is obliged to forward the said information either through the intermediary of the Central Agency,[26] or via the Protecting Power to the Power on which the protected person depends.[27] The NIB must also collect and forward specific documents and objects belonging to the protected person to the Power on which he or she depends.[28] In order to clarify the fate and whereabouts of specific

---

[18] Sassòli/Bouvier/Quintin, at 206. An exception constitutes Art 137 para 2 GC IV, stipulating that information should not be transmitted if it might be detrimental to the person concerned. On this situation, see MN 37–39.

[19] Art 14 Regulations concerning the Laws and Customs of War on Land, Annexed to Convention (II) with Respect to the Laws and Customs of War on Land (1899); Art 14 Hague Regulations.

[20] Art 20 *The Laws of War on Land* (Oxford: manual published by the Institute of International Law, adopted by the Institute of International Law, 1880).

[21] Arts 3 and 4 Convention for the Amelioration of the Condition of the Wounded and Sick in Armies in the Field (1906) [no longer in force]; Art 4 1929 GC I [no longer in force]: see Ch 34, MN 16–22, of this volume.

[22] GC I, GC II, GC III, and GC IV.   [23] Arts 16 para 1 GC I; Art 19 para 1 GC II.

[24] Art 16 para 2 GC I; Art 19 para 2 GC II; Art 122 para 2 GC III; Art 136 para 2 GC IV.

[25] Art 122 para 1 GC III; Art 136 para 1 GC IV.   [26] Art 123 GC III; Art 140 GC IV.

[27] Art 16 para 2 GC I; Art 19 para 2 GC II; Art 122 para 3 GC III; Art 137 para 1 GC IV; on the NIB and the Central Agency, see also Ch 53, section B.V, of this volume.

[28] Art 16 para 3 GC I; Art 19 para 3 GC II; Art 122 para 9 GC III; Art 139 GC IV.

protected persons, the Geneva Conventions stipulate that enquiries regarding a person reported missing must be answered by the NIB,[29] and provide for the setting up by way of agreement of bodies tasked with searching for dispersed POWs and internees.[30] Lastly, in order to prevent persons from going missing, each party to the conflict must issue identity cards to the persons under its jurisdiction who are at risk of becoming POWs.[31]

10 A section on missing and dead persons can be found in AP I, which notably extends the obligation to search for missing persons to persons not covered *ratione personae* by the Geneva Conventions, and reinforces the duty to furnish and exchange information on the missing and the dead in order to facilitate the search for them.[32] What is more, the rules of IHL pertaining to the missing are supplemented by IHRL, namely the right to know the truth about the fate and whereabouts of persons who have disappeared.[33]

11 The right to truth is also implicitly contained in Article 26 GC IV, which stipulates that the parties to the conflict must facilitate enquiries made by members of families dispersed as a result of armed conflict. It is expressly mentioned in Article 32 AP I stating that implementation of the rules on missing persons 'shall be prompted mainly by the right of families to know the fate of their relatives'.

12 It has been contended that the obligation to search for missing persons under IHL[34] contributed to the development of a human right to truth.[35] Yet it was not until the International Convention for the Protection of All Persons from Enforced Disappearances (ICED) entered into force in 2010 that the right to truth was expressly recognized as an autonomous right in a binding human rights treaty[36] and not merely as a component of other human rights.[37]

13 The growing recognition of the right to know the truth under IHRL not only supplements IHL, which is of special importance in non-international armed conflicts (NIACs), but is cited in examples of state practice as a necessary component of a customary IHL rule requiring that parties to a conflict must take all feasible measures to account for persons reported missing and provide the families with information on the fate of missing persons.[38]

B. Meaning and Application

14 What follows is a presentation of the core articles of the Geneva Conventions and AP I dealing with the issue of missing persons, that is, Article 16 GC I, Article 19 GC II, Articles 17, 119, 122, and 123 GC III, Articles 133 and 136–140 GC IV, and Articles 32 and 33 AP I. These rules are explained in the context of the different obligations in IHL to prevent persons from going missing and to account for persons reported missing in

---

[29] Art 122 para 7 GC III; Art 137 para 1 GC IV.
[30] Art 119 para 7 GC III; Art 133 para 3 GC IV.   [31] Art 17 para 3 GC III.
[32] ICRC Commentary APs, para 1222.
[33] This right has been developed by various domestic, regional, and international courts and bodies in recent decades, and is today a widely recognized concept in international law: see, e.g., OHCHR, *Study on the Right to Truth*, UN Doc E/CN.4/2006/91 (8 February 2006), especially as regards enforced disappearance; see, e.g., UNWGEID, 'General Comment on the right to the truth in relation to enforced disappearance', in HRCouncil, *Report of the Working Group on Enforced or Involuntary Disappearances*, UN Doc A/HRC/16/48 (26 January 2011).
[34] Art 33(1) AP I.   [35] OHCHR, *Study on the Right to Truth*, above n 33, paras 4–5.
[36] Art 24(2) ICED.   [37] On the right to truth, see also section D.I of this chapter and MN 66.
[38] ICRC CIHL Study, Rule 117, and vol II, Chapter 36, paras 143–95. See also Ch 14 of this volume.

situations of armed conflict or occupation. First, the IHL framework on missing persons contains important rules regarding the issuance of means of personal identification, most notably identity cards and discs. Correct identification is crucial for parties to the conflict properly to discharge their obligation to record and collect information relating to, inter alia, the identity of, state of health of, and measures taken against protected persons under their power. Furthermore, all four Geneva Conventions provide that the collected information shall be forwarded without delay to the NIB, which allows the information to be centralized and ultimately transmitted to the Power on which the protected persons depend. Lastly, IHL sets out an obligation to conduct investigative searches for persons who remain unaccounted for.

I. Providing identity documents

15 The issuance of means of personal identification—notably identity cards[39]—is of considerable importance in preventing a person from going missing.[40] Correctly discharging the obligation to equip persons who risk becoming protected persons with identity documents, also facilitates the proper functioning of the authorities and bodies tasked by the Geneva Conventions—notably the NIB and the Central Tracing Agency (CTA)—to centralize and forward information about protected persons in the hands of the enemy to the Power on which they depend, and ultimately to the families. Identification is thus in the mutual interest of the parties to a conflict. The Geneva Conventions not only set forth what type of identification measures must be undertaken, but also provide a number of models by which a certain level of standardization can be reached, which, in turn, facilitates the task of establishing the identity of protected persons.[41]

16 Identity cards are the basic document by which the status and identity of a protected person may be established.[42] Each party to a conflict is therefore obliged to furnish 'the persons under its jurisdiction who are liable to become prisoners of war' with an identity card,[43] regardless of their nationality.[44] The identity card *must* bear the type of information which the prisoner is required to give when questioned.[45] It *may* contain additional information, such as a signature, fingerprints, the religious denomination of its holder, or a photograph, which makes it more difficult to exchange cards.[46]

17 Since identity cards and other means of identification must be issued at the outbreak of hostilities at the very latest, states party to the Geneva Conventions must have already established the necessary legal and institutional framework for the issuance of these

---

[39] Art 16 para 1(f) GC I; Art 19 para 1(f) GC II; Art 17 para 3 GC III.

[40] ICRC Advisory Service on International Humanitarian Law, *Means of Personal Identification*, available at <http://www.icrc.org/eng/assets/files/other/means_of_personal_id_eng.pdf>, at 1; Commentary on Art 11 Model Law on the Missing.

[41] ICRC, *Means of Personal Identification*, above n 40, at 1.   [42] Ibid.

[43] Art 17 para 3 GC III. State parties are, in addition, required to issue specific identity cards for personnel of the armed forces carrying out special tasks, e.g. to persons accompanying the armed forces (Art 4(A)(4) and Annex IV.A. GC III; see also Art 40 paras 2 and 3 and Annex II GC I; Art 42 paras 2 and 3 and Annex GC II; Art 67(1)(c) AP I). They must also do so with regard to certain civilians, namely permanent or temporary staff of civilian hospitals, or civilian civil defence personnel (Art 20 paras 2 and 3 GC IV; Arts 18(3), 66(3), 79(3), and Annex I AP I). From the wording of some of these provisions it follows that the rationale behind this obligation is not to prevent these persons from going missing but to ensure that they receive the proper status and treatment when falling into the power of the enemy.

[44] Pictet Commentary GC III, at 161.

[45] Art 17 paras 1 and 3 GC III; Pictet Commentary GC III, at 161.   [46] Ibid, at 161–2.

documents in peacetime.[47] Indeed, Common Article 2 recognizes that some of the provisions of the Geneva Conventions need to be implemented in peacetime, which notably include those regarding the taking of preparatory measures, such as those pertaining to identification.[48]

Another important means of identification is the issuance of identity discs to combatants, especially for later identification of dead persons buried by the enemy.[49] While the Geneva Conventions do not explicitly stipulate an obligation to issue such discs and do not describe a model identity disc,[50] different provisions refer to this additional means of identification.[51] However, the issuance of identity discs was generalized, at least in principle, during the XIIIth International Red Cross Conference in 1928.[52] Furthermore, in 1981, the International Conference of the Red Cross issued a Resolution on the wearing of identity discs, which urges parties to a conflict to take all necessary measures to provide members of their armed forces with an identity disc and to ensure that these discs are worn during service. In addition, the Resolution recommends that these discs, which should be made out of material resistant to battlefield conditions and be composed of two separable parts, contain all information necessary for a precise identification of the person wearing the disc.[53]

II. Collecting and recording information

To prevent persons from going missing, and in any case to help to clarify their fate and whereabouts during an armed conflict or occupation, it is of prime importance that information relating to their identity and their state of health, as well as measures taken against them, is collected and recorded.[54] All four Geneva Conventions explicitly or implicitly contain an obligation to collect and record such information on the persons they protect.[55] With the adoption of AP I, the obligation to record was extended *ratione personae* to all those who were inadequately protected by the Geneva Conventions.[56] The obligation to record personal details of persons deprived of their liberty during an armed conflict or occupation is considered to have attained the status of customary international law.[57]

From the introductory words of Article 16 paragraph 1 GC I and Article 19 paragraph 1 GC II, it follows that the obligation to collect and record information is mandatory and not at the discretion of the parties to the conflict.[58] However, the obligation to collect and record information is not one of result but rather one of means.[59] This implies that

---

[47] Pictet Commentary GC III, at 161; ICRC Commentary APs, para 3972; Art 11(3) Model Law on the Missing; ICRC, *Means of Personal Identification*, above n 40, at 2.
[48] ICRC Commentary APs, para 149; Petrig, above n 14, at 363–5.
[49] See, e.g., Art 20 para 1 GC II.
[50] ICRC Commentary APs, Annex I, fn relating to para 3972.
[51] See, e.g., Arts 16 paras 1(f) and 3, 17 para 1, and 40 para 2 GC I; and Arts 19 paras 1(f) and 3, 20 para 1, and 42 para 2 GC II.
[52] ICRC, *The Geneva Conventions of August 12, 1949: Analysis for the Use of National Red Cross Societies* (Geneva: ICRC, 1950), vol I, at 19.
[53] Resolution I: Wearing of identity discs, in 'Resolutions of the XXIVth International Conference of the Red Cross', 63 *IRRC* 225 (November–December 1981) 318, at 318–19.
[54] ICRC Handbook, above n 15, at 18.
[55] See, e.g., Art 16 para 1 GC I; Art 19 para 1 GC II; Art 122 paras 2–7 GC III; and Arts 136 para 2 and 138 GC IV; see also Art 50 para 4 GC IV.
[56] Art 33(1) and (2) AP I; ICRC Commentary APs, para 1247.
[57] ICRC CIHL Study, Rule 123.   [58] Pictet Commentary GC I, at 161.
[59] ICRC CIHL Study, vol I, at 426.

the obligation is fulfilled if a party to the conflict makes every possible effort and uses all means at its disposal to discharge the obligation—even if it ultimately fails to collect and record all information about each and every person in its hands. A party's use of its best effort to fulfil the obligation includes taking all necessary preparatory steps in good time, and even before the outbreak of hostilities.[60]

21   As regards sick, wounded, shipwrecked, or dead combatants, Article 16 paragraph 1 GG I and Article 19 paragraph 1 GC II explicitly stipulate that each party to the conflict shall record 'any particulars' assisting in the identification of such combatants who have fallen into its hands. When persons are picked up at sea, the obligation to collect and record information is based on GC II until they are landed.[61] The recording may take various forms, such as lists or card indexes, but must be sufficient to enable the keeping of an accurate account of POWs and ultimately to forward the information to the adverse Power.[62]

22   The obligation 'to record any particulars' that may assist in the person's identification[63] is complemented by a suggestive, rather than limited or imperative,[64] list of particulars which the records should, if possible, contain. The information can generally be obtained without questioning the person who falls into the hands of the enemy, who will often not be in a position to reply, since it is either contained in the identity card or is in the possession of the Detaining Power.[65]

23   The obligation to record must be discharged 'as soon as possible'.[66] While the wording allows the specificities of each case to be taken into account, the overarching principle of the provisions on missing persons—the right of families to know the fate of their relatives—suggests speedy fulfilment of the obligation.[67] In the context of naval warfare, it is argued that the information should be collected and recorded as soon as the persons concerned are taken on board the enemy Power's vessel.[68]

24   As regards POWs, the establishment of their identity immediately following capture is the first duty of the Detaining Power.[69] In addition, information must be collected pertaining to the individual POW's whereabouts, namely information on transfer, release, repatriation, escape, or admission to a hospital, and relating to his or her state, especially poor health or death.[70] Overall, the type and nature of information to be collected and recorded shall be such as to 'make it possible quickly to advise the next of kin concerned'.[71]

25   Certain information can be obtained from POWs only by questioning them—in a language they understand[72]—or by consulting their identity cards.[73] Against this background, POWs are obliged to show their identity cards upon request, which may in no case be taken away from them,[74] and to provide the Detaining Power with specific types of information.[75] The latter obligation, which is independent from the former,[76]

---

[60] Ibid; Pictet Commentary GC I, at 161.
[61] Pictet Commentary GC II, at 137–8; after they have been landed, GC I will apply to them.
[62] Pictet Commentary GC I, at 162.   [63] Art 16 para 1 GC I; Art 19 para 1 GC II.
[64] Pictet Commentary GC I, at 162; Pictet Commentary GC II, at 139.
[65] Pictet Commentary GC I, at 162.   [66] Art 16 para 1 GC I; Art 19 para 1 GC II.
[67] Pictet Commentary GC I, at 161.   [68] Pictet Commentary GC II, at 139.
[69] Pictet Commentary GC III, at 156–7.   [70] Art 122 paras 4–6 GC III.
[71] Introductory sentence of Art 122 para 4 GC III; Pictet Commentary GC III, at 576.
[72] Art 17 para 6 GC III.   [73] Pictet Commentary GC III, at 157.   [74] Art 17 para 3 GC III.
[75] Art 17 para 1 GC III; on the rationale behind this limitation, see Pictet Commentary GC III, at 156.
[76] Ibid, at 162.

is reinforced by a sanction: if POWs wilfully fail to provide the said information, or wilfully make incorrect statements, the privileges accorded to them by virtue of their rank or status[77] may be restricted. Since only wilful infringement of the rule triggers this sanction, a POW cannot be held liable if the lack of correctness of the statement is due to his or her physical or mental condition. In such cases, the Detaining Power is obliged to hand over the POW to the medical service and to establish his or her identity by means other than direct questioning.[78] The Detaining Power is prohibited from using physical or mental torture, or any other form of coercion in order to secure the information listed in Article 17 paragraph 1 GC III—and any other type of information—from the POW.[79]

As regards civilians, Article 136 paragraph 2 GC IV defines the circle of protected civilians[80] on whom information must be collected and later forwarded to the NIB. First of all, the obligation extends to civilians who are in custody for more than two weeks. Thereby, the nature of detention is irrelevant and can, for example, be detention for political reasons or for the (alleged) commission of an offence.[81] Furthermore, the obligation pertains to civilians who are subject to assigned residence or interned.

Among the information to be collected are the particulars that 'make it possible to identify the protected person exactly and to advise his next of kin quickly'. This general indication guiding the collection of information is followed by a list of particulars, which shall allow for accurate identification of the person.[82] Even though some of this information can be obtained only from the protected persons, unlike POWs they are not required to provide certain particulars. Rather, the Detaining Power must try to secure the information from another source or abandon the attempt.[83] A refusal by the person in the hands of the enemy to share this information may notably be driven by fear that relatives will be subject to reprisals.[84]

In addition to identity particulars, the list includes the date, place, and nature of the action taken vis-à-vis the individual, and the address to which correspondence may be sent to him or her.[85] Furthermore, information relating to the person's state of health must be collected. Lastly, the Detaining Power is explicitly obliged to collect information about any and all changes pertaining to protected persons, such as transfers, releases, repatriations, escapes, births, admittances to hospital, or death.[86] This is of utmost importance in order to ascertain the whereabouts of protected civilians.

III. Forwarding of information, documents, and objects to the National Information Bureau

All four Geneva Conventions provide that the information collected and recorded shall be forwarded without delay to the NIB.[87] This allows for the centralizing of information on

---

[77] Regarding privileges accorded by virtue of status or rank, see, e.g., Arts 16, 39 para 3, 40, 44, 45, 49, 79 paras 2 and 3, 87 para 4, and 97 para 3 GC III.
[78] Art 17 para 5 GC III.   [79] Pictet Commentary GC III, at 163.   [80] Art 4 GC IV.
[81] Pictet Commentary GC IV, at 525–6.
[82] Art 138 para 1 GC IV.
[83] Art 31 GC IV prohibits exercising any coercion of a civilian to obtain information.
[84] Pictet Commentary GC IV, at 535.   [85] Art 138 para 1 GC IV.
[86] Art 138 paras 1 and 2 GC IV.
[87] Art 16 para 2 GC I; Art 19 para 2 GC II; Art 122 para 3 GC III; and Art 136 para 2 GC IV. See also Art 50 para 4 GC IV.

30   For sick, wounded, shipwrecked, and dead combatants, as well as for POWs, one and the same NIB is competent to receive, centralize, and transmit information collected and recorded.[90] The Power in whose hands protected persons are is free to choose the most appropriate means by which its military authorities may transmit the information to the NIB.[91] Even though this obligation must be discharged as soon as possible, it is argued that in naval warfare it is sufficient if the information is forwarded only once the naval unit is in port, i.e. once the persons have landed.[92] Such an interpretation accommodates the concern that a warship will try to limit its communication over the radio to a bare minimum.[93]

31   With regard to protected persons under GC IV, the parties to the conflict are required 'within the shortest possible period' to forward information to the NIB on measures taken vis-à-vis persons who are in their custody for more than two weeks, subject to assigned residence, or interned. Any changes pertaining to these persons must be communicated to the NIB promptly.[94]

32   In addition, the Power in whose hands protected persons are is obliged to forward certain documents to the NIB, such as death certificates or duly authenticated lists of the dead, last wills, or other documents of importance to the next of kin.[95] The Geneva Conventions also refer to certain objects that must be transmitted to the NIB, namely personal valuables left by protected persons, or money and articles of intrinsic or sentimental value found on dead combatants.[96]

33   Since the NIB plays a key role in preventing persons from going missing and resolving cases of persons unaccounted for,[97] it must be operational as soon as hostilities break out or a situation of occupation begins,[98] and cannot be improvised at that moment. Therefore, state parties should[99] lay the groundwork for its establishment in peacetime.[100] The Geneva Conventions do not contain any indication as to the nature, composition, or working methods of the NIB, or which body shall be responsible for running it.[101]

---

[88] Art 13(2) Model Law on the Missing; Pictet Commentary GC I, at 165.

[89] See section B.IV of this chapter.

[90] Art 16 para 2 GC I; Art 19 para 2 GC II; and Art 122 para 2 GC III. Pictet Commentary GC I, at 166.

[91] Pictet Commentary GC III, at 574–5.

[92] In application of Art 16 para 2 GC I in the case of wounded, sick, or shipwrecked combatants, or Art 122 para 2 GC III in the case of able-bodied persons.

[93] Pictet Commentary GC II, at 138–9.

[94] Art 136 para 2 GC IV.

[95] Art 16 para 3 GC I; Art 19 para 3 GC II; Arts 120 para 2 and 122 para 9 GC III.

[96] Art 16 para 3 GC I; Art 19 para 3 GC II; Art 122 para 9 GC III; Art 139 GC IV.

[97] In addition to centralizing information, it transmits it to the Power on which the protected persons depend (see section B.IV of this chapter) and plays a role in the search for protected persons reported missing (see section B.V).

[98] Art 122 para 1 GC III; Art 136 para 1 GC IV.

[99] M. Sassòli, 'The National Information Bureau in Aid of the Victims of Armed Conflicts', 27 *IRRC* 256 (1987) 6, at 14–15.

[100] See, e.g., Resolution 14 (National Information Bureau), adopted at the 25th International Conference of the Red Cross, which urges state parties to the GCs 'to consider taking such measures as may be necessary to institute their National Information Bureau in peacetime in order for it to fulfil its tasks as soon as possible at the outbreak of hostilities': see ICRC, *National Information Bureau (NIB)*, available at <http://www.icrc.org/eng/resources/documents/misc/57jmdh.htm>; see also Art 13(1) Model Law on the Missing and related commentary.

[101] Sassòli, above n 99, at 8.

It is suggested that the NIB's independence vis-à-vis the state should not be too great since it is the latter's international responsibility to ensure that the NIB discharges its obligations properly.[102] To charge a body, which is part of the administration, with the task of running the NIB may be preferable to entrusting it to the National Society, since a state authority may have an easier time gathering information from uncooperative departments than a body outside the administration, and a Detaining Power may be reluctant to share information with a non-governmental authority due to security concerns. Members of the National Society working for the NIB may also be confronted with a dilemma as between their humanitarian duty and their duty as citizens of the Detaining Power. Lastly, outsourcing the running of the NIB may diminish the state party's sense of responsibility.[103] The duties of the NIB set out in GC III and GC IV may be assumed by two separate bodies or by one alone. In those cases where the NIB is run by a government authority, it may be preferable to assign two separate bodies, since the administrative units responsible for civilians under its power are generally not the same as those responsible for POWs.[104]

IV. Transmission of information to the power on which a person depends

The NIB is under an obligation immediately to transmit the information it receives by the most rapid means available to the Power on which the protected persons depend.[105] The Geneva Conventions envisage two channels by which the information may be forwarded to that Power: either through the intermediary of the Protecting Power, or via the Central Agency.[106]

The first option is of a rather theoretical nature, given that a Protecting Power has been designated in only five of the numerous armed conflicts that have broken out since the Second World War.[107] The usual method of forwarding information from the NIB to the Power on which the protected persons depend is via the Central Agency referred to in all four Geneva Conventions. In practice, it is the CTA of the International Committee of the Red Cross (ICRC), which is a permanent body working closely with National Societies, that plays the role of the central information agencies referred to in the Geneva Conventions.[108] Hence, the wording of Article 33(3) AP I, explicitly mentioning the CTA and referring to National Societies, better reflects the current institutional reality than the wording of the Geneva Conventions.[109]

---

[102] Ibid. [103] Ibid, at 9.
[104] Ibid; thus, e.g., the NIB in the UK is split into two sections, the Prisoner of War Information Bureau (PWIB), run by the Ministry of Defence, and the Civilian Information Bureau (CIB), dealing with civilian internees within the UK national boundaries, which is run by the Home Office: ICRC Handbook, above n 15, at 18.
[105] Art 122 para 3 GC III and Art 137 para 1 GC IV; even absent a time requirement, Art 16 para 2 GC I and Art 19 para 2 GC II are interpreted this way: Pictet Commentary GC I, at 166, and Pictet Commentary GC II, at 141.
[106] Art 16 para 2 GC I, Art 19 para 2 GC II, and Art 122 para 3 GC III (referring to the Central Prisoners of War (Information) Agency); Art 137 para 1 GC IV (referring to the Central Information Agency in cases of civilians); as per Art 140 para 1 GC IV, these two agencies may be the same.
[107] Sassòli/Bouvier/Quintin, at 366; ICRC Commentary APs, para 1274; see Ch 27 of this volume.
[108] See Ch 49 of this volume; Sassòli, above n 99, at 11–12; ICRC, 'ICRC Protection Policy', 90 *IRRC* 871 (2008) 751, at 756.
[109] ICRC Commentary APs, para 1275.

36   In cases where combatants are in the hands of the enemy, the CTA forwards their information, documents, and objects to their country of origin and/or to the Power on which they depend.[110] For civilians, the receiving entity is either their country of origin and/or their country of residence.[111] From the wording of the relevant provisions—'shall make it possible quickly to advise the next of kin concerned'[112] and 'to advise his next of kin quickly'[113]—it follows that the state must forward the information, documents, and valuables to the families concerned as soon as possible.[114]

37   In some situations, the protected persons may consider it prejudicial to themselves or their relatives if information is forwarded to the Power on which they depend. For instance, a person who has fled his or her country due to persecution may prefer that his or her whereabouts remain unknown to the authorities of the state in question.[115] Furthermore, there may be situations where a protected person wishes to sever all links with his or her immediate family and relatives.[116]

38   Article 137 paragraph 2 GC IV takes this situation into account by providing an exception to the obligation of the NIB to forward information if it would be detrimental to the person concerned or his or her relatives. Yet even in such a case, the NIB must forward the information—with an indication of its confidential nature—to the CTA. However, the CTA is prohibited from transmitting the information to the Power on which the protected person depends.[117]

39   As regards combatants in the hands of the enemy, no similar provision exists in Geneva Conventions I, II, or III. Arguably, given the humanitarian character of the tasks assigned to the CTA, it should be possible for it to forward information to the family only and not to the authorities, as is the practice for information concerning civilians.[118] While the Power on which combatants depend may also have an interest in knowing the fate of its soldiers,[119] it is rather the individual who is at the centre of the Geneva Convention rules on the missing. As expressed by Article 32 AP I, activities implementing the rules on missing persons shall mainly be guided by the right of families to know the fate of their relatives. While this guiding principle may help solve the conflict of interest that arises when a person wishes for information to be given to his or her family alone, and not to the state authorities, it accentuates the conflict of interest when the combatant does not want information on his or her whereabouts to be shared with his or her next of kin. It is argued that in such situations, one might attempt to make the protected person understand the value of providing his or her family with the requisite information, yet such a course of action cannot be imposed on him or her.[120] This seems in line with the idea that actions taken in relation to missing persons should be prompted primarily,[121] but not exclusively, by the right of families to know the fate of their loved ones.

V. Search for missing persons

40   As regards the search for protected persons, it is necessary to distinguish between two types of searches:

---

[110] Art 123 para 2 GC III; Sassòli, above n 99, at 12, fn 26.   [111] Art 140 para 2 GC IV.
[112] Art 122 para 4 GC III.   [113] Art 138 para 1 GC IV.   [114] Sassòli, above n 99, at 13.
[115] Pictet Commentary GC IV, at 531–2.   [116] Sassòli/Bouvier/Quintin, at 206.
[117] Art 137 para 2 GC IV, read together with Art 140 para 2 GC IV.
[118] Art 140 GC IV; Pictet Commentary GC IV, at 546.
[119] ICRC Commentary APs, para 1218.   [120] Ibid, para 1219.
[121] See wording of Art 32 AP I.

— the search for casualties and their collection and evacuation, i.e. the physical search for persons by combing a certain area;[122] and
— searches of an investigative character, i.e. searches ranging from an enquiry into the whereabouts of a protected person to conducting a true investigation.[123]

While the physical search for persons is a precondition to collecting, recording, and forwarding information pertaining to their identity and whereabouts, and thus to preventing persons from going missing later on, the following considerations relate only to investigative searches.

41 While Article 33(1) AP I explicitly stipulates an obligation to search for persons who have been reported missing, the Geneva Conventions only implicitly contain such an obligation, providing that the NIB must reply to all enquiries about protected persons it receives,[124] which may sometimes necessitate a search.[125] Indeed, the idea that a satisfactory reply to a request can often be provided only after a careful search, is expressed by Article 122 paragraph 7 GC III, which obliges the NIB to take the necessary steps to receive information not yet in its possession but needed in order to answer an enquiry. Even absent an explicit counterpart in GC IV, the obligation to gather the necessary information is understood as being encompassed by the wording of Article 137 paragraph 1 GC IV, for otherwise it would be impossible to reply to *all* enquiries.[126]

42 A proposal to specify which individuals or entities may submit a request was rejected during the drafting process. From the retained wording, it is concluded that a broad spectrum of persons, institutions, and authorities may do so, notably the CTA but also private persons.[127] The NIB is only obliged to reply to enquiries sent to it concerning POWs[128] and persons protected by GC IV.[129]

43 The provisions setting out the obligation to reply to all enquiries do not contain any indication as to their application in time. However, among the provisions that apply in peacetime are those that regulate phenomena originating in or resulting from an armed conflict or occupation, but the effects of which extend beyond the conclusion of these situations. This criterion for applying an IHL provision in peacetime seems to be met regarding the search for persons who went missing in connection with an armed conflict or occupation and who are still missing even after these situations have ended.[130] This also follows from the fact that the drafters of Article 33(1) AP I, which pertains to the search for persons reported missing, did not retain a proposal explicitly stating that searches must be carried out without any time limit, because they considered this idea to be implicit in the provision.[131]

44 The obligation to search as set out in GC III and GC IV is limited in various respects, notably as to the categories of persons regarding whom a request may be submitted. Since these categories comprise only POWs and protected civilians, the obligation to reply to enquiries does not apply to combatants, for instance, who do not appear on lists of captured

---

[122] See, e.g., Art 15 GC I, Art 18 GC II, and Art 16 para 2 GC IV.
[123] ICRC Commentary APs, paras 1224 and 1233.
[124] Art 122 para 7 GC III and Art 137 para 1 GC IV; see also Art 26 GC IV.
[125] Pictet Commentary GC III, at 578. In other cases, the NIB may already be in possession of the relevant information, e.g., a death certificate that may be forwarded to the family concerned: Sassòli, above n 99, at 13.
[126] Pictet Commentary GC IV, at 530–1.   [127] Ibid, at 531.   [128] Art 122 para 7 GC III.
[129] Art 137 para 1 GC IV.
[130] Regarding Arts 33 and 74 AP I, see ICRC Commentary APs, para 149.   [131] Ibid, para 1239.

or deceased persons,[132] or to civilians who fail to meet the definition of a protected person in Article 4 GC IV. In comparison, the obligation to search stipulated in Article 33(1) AP I has a much broader personal scope of application, in that it relates to 'persons who have been reported missing by an adverse Party'. While the wording of the provision requires only that the request stems from an adverse party, it is argued that this party must possess a genuine interest in enquiring into the fate and whereabouts of a person because, for instance, the missing person or his or her relatives is/are its national(s) or resident(s). In cases where the legitimacy of a request is contested, the interests of the families, i.e. their right to know, should prevail and the request be followed up.[133]

45   Furthermore, the Geneva Convention provisions intended to account for persons reported missing are limited in that they envisage only one specific way of obtaining information about the fate of a missing person—to address an enquiry to the NIB, which, in turn, is obliged to answer it. By comparison, the rather open-ended wording of Article 33(1) AP I allows for more leeway in determining the most appropriate way to account for a person who has gone missing, and it is addressed to the state in general and not only to the NIB, which may even be a non-governmental organization.[134] Lastly, unlike the Geneva Conventions, Article 33(1) AP I explicitly stipulates the duty of the requesting state to furnish and exchange information concerning missing persons, which facilitates the search. Overall, Article 33(1) AP I adds an important protective layer to the Geneva Conventions' provisions pertaining to the search for missing persons.

46   A more general obligation to search for missing persons arguably exists by virtue of customary international law. For example, Rule 117 of the ICRC Customary International Humanitarian Law Study stipulates that each party to the conflict 'must take all feasible measures to account for persons reported missing as a result of armed conflict'. This notably encompasses the obligation to search for missing persons and to provide the relatives with relevant information about them.[135] A general obligation to investigate the fate and whereabouts of missing persons, and to inform their relatives accordingly, may also be derived from IHRL.[136]

47   Various mechanisms and institutions exist that are designed to prevent persons from going missing, or which are tasked with processing and resolving cases of missing persons. They include the NIB and CTA, which derive their mandate directly from the Geneva Conventions. Furthermore, the Geneva Conventions provide for the setting up of bodies by way of agreement, in order to search for dispersed POWs and civilian internees. Thus, in order to assure the repatriation of POWs with as little delay as possible, parties to the conflict shall establish, by way of agreement, commissions tasked with the purpose of searching for dispersed POWs.[137] Meanwhile, in order to realize the goal that interment shall cease as soon as possible after the close of hostilities,[138] which is predicated on knowledge of who is interned where, GC IV stipulates that committees tasked with searching for dispersed internees may be set up.[139] While the provision pertaining to POWs is couched in more mandatory language than that pertaining to civilians, both provisions make the creation of such bodies dependent on an *agreement* between the respective parties, which is not always easy to reach given that their relationship is often marked by

---

[132] Ibid, paras 1188 and 1229.   [133] Ibid, paras 1225–7.   [134] See MN 33.
[135] For relevant state practice, see ICRC CIHL Study, vol II, Chapter 36, paras 1–94.
[136] See section D.I of this chapter.   [137] Art 119 para 7 GC III.   [138] Art 133 para 1 GC IV.
[139] Art 133 para 3 GC IV; Pictet Commentary GC IV, at 516.

animosity and distrust. However, practice demonstrates that—often in pursuance of a peace agreement—tracing bodies are established by way of agreement, and that their mandate *ratione personae* is often wider than that pertaining to dispersed POWs and internees.[140]

The United Nations Working Group on Enforced or Involuntary Disappearances deserves mention as an example of an international body[141] facilitating the search for missing persons not rooted in IHL.[142] Its mandate is, inter alia, of a humanitarian nature in that it assists families in determining the fate or whereabouts of relatives who have disappeared. To this end, the Working Group receives reports submitted by the relatives of missing persons, directly or indirectly, and transmits them to the governments concerned.[143] It acts on a purely humanitarian basis, serving as a channel of communication between relatives of missing persons and the government concerned. Hence, its activities are not conditional on the ratification of a specific treaty by the respective states.[144] Furthermore, the Working Group's role ends when the fate or whereabouts of the missing person are clearly established, and it is not part of its mandate to establish responsibility for the disappearance.[145] Until recently, the mandate of the Working Group did not extend to disappearances occurring in international armed conflicts (IACs) given the competence of the ICRC in these situations.[146] However, in 2011, it decided to deal with all enforced disappearances, regardless of the type of armed conflict in which they arise. The Working Group's methods of work were amended accordingly, and went into effect on 1 January 2012.[147] 48

Lastly, the emergency procedure to seek and find a disappeared person established under the ICED bears mention. A request for urgent action may be filed with the Committee on Enforced Disappearance[148] by any person who has a legitimate interest in the disappeared person. If the request to seek and find a specific person is in line with certain criteria, the Committee requires the respective state party to provide it with information on the person being sought. The Committee is competent to issue recommendations to the state, including the taking of necessary measures to locate and protect the person being sought. The Committee transmits information obtained by the state to the requesting party.[149] 49

---

[140] See, e.g., the Working Group on the Process of Tracing Persons Unaccounted for in Connection with the Conflict on the Territory of Bosnia and Herzegovina set up pursuant to the Dayton Peace Agreement: T. Blumenstock, 'Legal Protection of the Missing and Their Relatives: The Example of Bosnia and Herzegovina', 19 *LJIL* (2006) 773, at 779.

[141] National tracing bodies are not mentioned here; but see, e.g., Art 7 BiH Law on Missing Persons.

[142] Its original mandate derives from HRComm, Res 20 (XXXVI) Question of Missing and Disappeared Persons (29 February 1980); since then, its mandate has been constantly renewed, most recently in 2011 for three years with HRCouncil, Res 16/16: Enforced or Voluntary Disappearances, UN Doc A/HRC/RES/16/16 (12 April 2011).

[143] HRCouncil, *Report of the Working Group on Enforced and Involuntary Disappearances*, UN Doc A/HRC/19/58/Rev.1 (2 March 2012) (hereinafter Report of the UNWGEID (2012)), Annex II, para 2.

[144] OHCHR, *Enforced or Involuntary Disappearances: Fact Sheet, No 6 (Rev 3)*, available at <http://www.ohchr.org/Documents/Publications/FactSheet6Rev3.pdf>, at 12–13.

[145] Ibid, at 15.

[146] HRCouncil, *Report of the Working Group on Enforced and Involuntary Disappearances*, UN Doc A/HRC/16/48 (26 January 2011) Annex I, para 11.

[147] Report of the UNWGEID (2012), above n 143, para 4.

[148] On the Committee on Enforced Disappearances, see also MN 54.

[149] Art 30 ICED.

50   Mechanisms and institutions tasked with processing and resolving cases of missing persons increasingly rely on information technology and electronic tools for collecting, storing, and analysing data relating to persons who are unaccounted for. Thus, for instance, more than 50 institutions—among them NIBs—work with the Ante-Mortem/Post-Mortem database developed by the ICRC.[150] The development of forensic science, most notably in the field of DNA-based identification, has also opened up new avenues in the search for missing persons. The International Commission on Missing Persons, for instance, which operates a DNA human identification facility, identified over 17,000 persons who went missing in the conflicts taking place in the former Yugoslavia, by matching DNA profiles of missing persons with those of family members.[151] While DNA-based identification methods greatly enhance the likelihood that persons do not remain unaccounted for, the processing of this very sensitive data may involve data protection issues. Absent any binding rules on protecting genetic data in international law,[152] the issue is mainly governed by domestic law and general human rights norms relating to privacy, non-discrimination, or human dignity.[153]

C. Relevance in Non-International Armed Conflicts

51   Neither Common Article 3 nor AP II contains explicit provisions relating to missing persons. Yet even absent such rules, various obligations aimed at preventing persons from going missing in NIACs, or to clarify the fate and whereabouts of persons who have gone missing in a NIAC, exist by virtue of customary IHL and IHRL.

52   The obligation to record personal details of persons deprived of their liberty is said to be a norm of customary international law applicable in NIACs.[154] What is more, various binding human rights instruments contain an obligation to record details of persons deprived of their liberty, which contributes to the prevention of enforced disappearances specifically.[155] As regards the centralized collection of information and the forwarding of such information to families, it bears mentioning that the NIB may also assume this task in the case of a NIAC.[156] Also, the CTA's activities extend to NIACs.[157]

53   As regards the search for missing persons, Article 8 AP II is not applicable because the provision pertains to physical searches rather than to those of an investigative nature.[158] However, the obligation to take all feasible steps to account for persons reported missing, and to inform families of their fate and whereabouts, is arguably a customary IHL rule.[159] What is more, that states must clarify and investigate cases of persons who are

---

[150] ICRC Resource Centre, 'The Ante-Mortem/Post-Mortem Database, An Information Management Application for Missing Persons/Forensic Data' (September 2012), available at <http://www.icrc.org/eng/assets/files/2013/ampm-database-information-sheet-icrc-2012.pdf>, at 2.

[151] International Commission on Missing Persons, 'About Us', available at <http://www.ic-mp.org/about-us/> and 'DNA analysis: Only Way in Identification Process' <http://www.ic-mp.org/activities/technical-assistance/dna>.

[152] For soft law, see International Declaration on Human Genetic Data (adopted 16 October 2003), Records of the General Conference (UNESCO), 32nd Session, vol I: Resolutions, Ch IV, at 39–48.

[153] ICRC, *Missing People, DNA Analysis and Identification of Human Remains* (2nd edn, Geneva: ICRC, 2009), available at <http://www.icrc.org/eng/assets/files/other/icrc_002_4010.pdf>, at 39.

[154] ICRC CIHL Study, Rule 123, and vol I, at 439.

[155] Art XI para 2 Inter-American Convention on Forced Disappearance of Persons (1994); Art 17(3) ICED.

[156] ICRC Handbook, above n 15, at 31; Art 13(1) Model Law on the Missing.

[157] ICRC Protection Policy, above n 108, at 756.

[158] ICRC Commentary APs, para 4648, which refers to provisions on physical searches discussed at MN 40.

[159] See ICRC CIHL Study, Rule 117; on its application in NIACs, see ibid, vol I, at 421.

unaccounted for, and impart information about their fate and whereabouts to their families, is clearly required by virtue of various human rights norms. Further, regarding enforced disappearances specifically, the right to know the truth is explicitly stipulated in Article 24(2) ICED.[160]

D. Legal Consequences of a Violation

I. State responsibility

As mentioned, enforced disappearances are an important—albeit not the sole—reason for persons going missing in situations of armed conflict or occupation.[161] When the ICED was adopted in 2006, a distinct and autonomous human right not to be subjected to enforced disappearance was created, one which had never existed before at the universal level, and the violation of which may engage state responsibility. The Committee on Enforced Disappearances, the monitoring body of the ICED, assumes the two rather traditional roles of receiving and examining individual and inter-state communications concerning enforced disappearances.[162] Moreover, it has also the power to bring the practice of widespread or systematic enforced disappearances to the attention of the United Nations (UN) General Assembly, after seeking information on the matter from the state.[163]

Relatives of persons who are unaccounted for have a right to know the fate and whereabouts of their next of kin. Various domestic,[164] regional, and international courts and human rights bodies have, by virtue of different human rights norms, affirmed the existence of a positive obligation of the state to account for the fate and whereabouts of persons who went missing due to acts amounting to enforced disappearance specifically or because of other state conduct.

At the universal level, the United Nations Human Rights Committee (HRCttee) has construed a positive obligation of the state to investigate cases of persons who are unaccounted for by virtue of a series of rights. In its General Comment on the right to life, it held that states should establish 'effective facilities and procedures to investigate thoroughly cases of missing and disappeared persons in circumstances which may involve a violation of the right of life'.[165] Furthermore, the continuing uncertainty as to the fate or whereabouts of a missing person due to the absence of a full investigation into his or her disappearance causes anguish and stress on the part of relatives that may amount to inhuman treatment.[166] Moreover, the failure to conduct a thorough and effective investigation into the whereabouts and fate of a person, or inadequately to share information gathered from such an investigation, is in violation of the right to an effective remedy.[167]

---

[160] On the right to truth, see sections A.II and D.I of this chapter and MN 66.   [161] See MN 1.
[162] Arts 31–32 ICED.
[163] Art 34 ICED. On its competence regarding the emergency procedure to seek and find disappeared persons, see MN 49.
[164] See, e.g., the case law of the Human Rights Chamber for Bosnia and Herzegovina discussed in Blumenstock, above n 140, at 780–92.
[165] Art 6 ICCPR (1966); HRCttee, *General Comment 6: The Rights to Life (Art 6)* (30 April 1982), para 4; see also HRCttee, *Bousroual v Algeria*, Comm No 1085/2002, 15 March 2006, paras 9.10–9.11.
[166] Art 7 ICCPR; HRCttee, *Quinteros v Uruguay*, Comm No 107/1981, 21 July 1983, para 14; HRCttee, *Sarma v Sri Lanka*, above n 12, para 9.5; HRCttee, *Bousroual v Algeria*, above n 165, para 9.8.
[167] Art 2(3) ICCPR; HRCttee, *Sarma v Sri Lanka*, above n 12, para 11; HRCttee, *El Hassy v The Libyan Arab Jamahiriya*, Comm No 1422/2005, 24 October 2007, para 6.9.

57   At the regional level, the European Court of Human Rights has established a positive obligation of the state to investigate the facts surrounding the fate and whereabouts of a person who has disappeared, and to bring such facts to the attention of the victim's relatives by virtue of various rights. The absence of a prompt and effective investigation into an arguable claim that a person had been taken into custody and had not been seen since was found to be in breach of the procedural dimension of the right to liberty.[168] Furthermore, the procedural dimension of the right to life requires state authorities 'to conduct an official investigation into an arguable claim that a person, who was last seen in their custody, subsequently disappeared in a life-threatening context'.[169] The ongoing failure to provide the requisite investigation—an obligation that potentially exists as long as the fate of the person who is unaccounted for is unknown—constitutes a continuing violation of the right to life.[170] Lastly, the Court has found that a failure on the part of state authorities to investigate the fate and whereabouts of a person who disappeared may amount to inhuman treatment of the missing person's relatives, who are kept in the dark as to the fate of their next of kin and who suffer the anguish of uncertainty.[171]

58   The Inter-American Court of Human Rights affirmed a duty to investigate cases of missing persons, which continues as long as there is uncertainty about the fate of the person who has disappeared, and to inform the relatives accordingly.[172] The Court decided that a lack of effective investigation to ascertain the fate of a person who is unaccounted for, and a failure to provide information, generates feelings of insecurity, frustration, and impotence, in addition to suffering and anguish, which may violate the right to mental and moral integrity of the next of kin.[173] In addition, it found that by virtue of the rights to a fair trial and judicial protection, relatives have a right to have disappearances investigated effectively, and a right to seek and receive information.[174] What is more, the Court held that the right to freedom of thought and information protects not only the expression of opinions, but also the right to seek, receive, and impart information and ideas of all kinds, notably where disappearances are concerned.[175]

59   For its part, the African Commission on Human and Peoples' Rights decided that the refusal to inform the family if and where an individual is held, amounts to inhuman treatment of the family concerned.[176]

---

[168] Art 5 ECHR (1950); ECtHR (GC), *Cyprus v Turkey*, above n 13, para 150; ECtHR, *Palić v Bosnia and Herzegovina*, Judgment, 15 February 2011, para 79; ECtHR, *Imakayeva v Russia*, Judgment, 9 February 2007, para 171; ECtHR, *Bazorkina v Russia*, Judgment, 11 December 2006, para 146.

[169] Art 2 ECHR; ECtHR, *Palić v Bosnia and Herzegovina*, above n 168, para 63. See also ECtHR (GC), *Cyprus v Turkey*, above n 13, paras 131–2; and ECtHR (GC), *Varnava and others v Turkey*, Judgment, 18 September 2009, para 148.

[170] ECtHR (GC), *Varnava and others v Turkey*, above n 169, para 148.

[171] Art 3 ECHR; see, e.g., ECtHR (GC), *Cyprus v Turkey*, above n 168, paras 156–7; ECtHR, *Kurt v Turkey*, Judgment, 25 May 1998, paras 130–4; ECtHR, *Timurtaş v Turkey*, Judgment, 13 June 2000, paras 91–8; ECtHR, *Bazorkina v Russia*, above n 168, paras 137–42; ECtHR (GC), *Varnava and others v Turkey*, above n 169, para 200.

[172] IACtHR, *Case of Velásquez-Rodríguez v Honduras*, Judgment (Merits), 29 July 1988, para 181.

[173] Art 5(1) ACHR (1969); IACtHR, *Gomes Lund et al ('Guerrilha do Araguaia') v Brazil*, Judgment (Preliminary Objections, Merits, Reparations, and Costs), 24 November 2010, paras 241–3.

[174] Arts 8(1) and 25 ACHR; IACtHR, *Blake v Guatemala (Blake case)*, Judgment, 24 January 1998, para 97; IACtHR, *Case of Bámaca-Velásquez v Guatemala*, Judgment (Reparations and Costs), 22 February 2002, paras 74–6; *Gomes Lund et al*, above n 173, para 212.

[175] Art 13 ACHR; *Gomes Lund et al*, above n 173, paras 196–202 and 212.

[176] Art 5 ACHPR, 27 June 1981; ACHPR, *Amnesty International and others v Sudan*, Comm Nos 48/90, 50/91, 89/93 (1999), para 54.

II. Criminal responsibility

In cases where a national legislature has criminalized acts amounting to a systematic and deliberate denial of the right to know the fate of one's relative, criminal liability may arise under domestic law for a failure to fulfil the obligations relating to the search for missing persons. As regards missing persons in general, the Model Law on the Missing stipulates that states shall adopt legislation in order to criminalize acts amounting to such conduct, notably the unjustified refusal by an official to provide data on a missing person, the undue or delayed provision of information on a missing person, the intentional provision of false and unverified data, and the systematic and deliberate denial of the right to inform relatives of one's capture, arrest, address, and state of health, and to exchange news with relatives in detention.[177]

Such provisions may, for instance, be found in the Law on Missing Persons of Bosnia and Herzegovina of 2004. An official is liable to a fine if he or she blocks access to information by a relative or an institution in charge of tracing, delays or hinders, without justified cause, the availability of the requested information, or delivers incorrect or outdated information, thus hindering a search or making it impossible to trace a person.[178] Interestingly enough, the BiH Law on Missing Persons goes beyond criminal responsibility of natural persons and provides for institutions or competent authorities to be held criminally liable if they impede access to information, be it a relative's access or that of an institution tasked with tracing missing persons, or if they enable any form of discrimination against family members of a person reported missing.[179]

In the context of state responsibility, we concluded that the systematic and persistent failure to search for missing persons, and the resulting continued uncertainty about their fate, may amount to 'inhuman treatment' of the relatives of missing persons.[180] Inhuman treatment, in turn, is an act listed as a grave breach in the Geneva Conventions if committed against protected persons.[181] Hence, the persistent and systematic failure to search for missing persons arguably qualifies as a grave breach if a Power could find the missing person, has control over the relatives who are protected persons, and deliberately chooses not to search for the person who went missing in order to inflict suffering on his or her relatives.

Turning now to the narrower concept of enforced disappearances specifically, the ICED obliges state parties to criminalize the failure to record instances of deprivation of liberty and the recording of false information. Hence, the Convention requires legislation criminalizing a failure to prevent persons from disappearing by duly recording certain information. Furthermore, the refusal to provide information on the deprivation of liberty or the provision of inaccurate information must carry a criminal sanction. In addition, states must impose sanctions for the delay or obstruction of two specific remedies—the judicial remedy to obtain certain information regarding a person deprived of his or her liberty, and the right have the lawfulness of detention reviewed by a court—both of which are granted to persons who have a legitimate interest in such information.[182]

---

[177] Arts 24 and 25 Model Law on the Missing.   [178] Art 25 para 1 BiH Law on Missing Persons.
[179] Art 25 para 2 BiH Law on Missing Persons.
[180] See MN 56, 57, and 59; see also ICRC Report, *The Missing and their Families, Summary of the Conclusions arising from Events Held Prior to the International Conference of Governmental and Non-Governmental Experts (19–21 February 2003)*, available at <http://www.icrc.org/eng/assets/files/other/icrc_themissing_012003_en_10.pdf>, at 29.
[181] Art 50 GC I; Art 51 GC II; Art 130 GC III; Art 147 GC IV.   [182] Art 22 ICED.

64 Enforced disappearance is among the punishable acts that may amount to a crime against humanity when committed as part of a widespread or systematic attack against the civilian population. While the definition of 'crimes against humanity' of the International Criminal Court (ICC) Statute includes enforced disappearance in the list of punishable acts,[183] the International Criminal Tribunal for the former Yugoslavia (ICTY) Statute does not. However, the ICTY stated in dicta that enforced disappearance may amount to inhuman treatment, which is among the punishable acts of the crime against humanity definition of the ICTY Statute.[184] The ICED simply states that the widespread or systematic practice of enforced disappearance constitutes a crime against humanity as defined in applicable international law.[185]

E. Critical Assessment

65 In 1949, the adoption of the Geneva Conventions' provisions on the missing constituted a major step forward as regards the protection of persons at risk from disappearing and the ascertainment of their fate—especially for civilians. And yet the whole of the population of countries in conflict does not come within the protective ambit of these rules. This shortcoming of the Geneva Conventions *ratione personae* is accentuated by the fact that over the last decades, civilian populations have increasingly become the target of violence, and sometimes control over a civilian population is itself at stake in conflicts.

66 An important normative development pertaining to the issue of missing persons took place in 1977 with the adoption of AP I, which is today rather widely ratified. Not only does one find the idea of the right of families to know the fate of their relatives expressly mentioned for the first time in a multilateral treaty, but one also finds IHL rules on missing persons applied to an enlarged circle of persons. In addition, domestic, regional, and international courts and human rights bodies have developed the right to truth in relation to disappearances, with considerable resolve. Hence, as regards IACs, a solid body of norms aimed at preventing persons from going missing and clarifying cases of persons who have disappeared exists today. Also in NIACs, despite the silence of treaty-based IHL in respect of the missing, a number of obligations requiring that persons are accounted for flow from IHRL and customary IHL.

67 These normative developments and the current state of law regarding missing persons in armed conflict stands in stark contrast to the notable number of persons who have disappeared in more recent conflicts. This demonstrates that the prevention of disappearances and the search for missing persons is not an issue solely predicated on law and the completeness of the legal framework; it is rather an issue highly influenced by political and humanitarian choices, in particular those of the parties to the conflict. Hence, if the rules on the missing are to overcome their aspirational character, it seems necessary to work towards the dissemination of these rules and convince parties to the conflict that it is in their mutual interest to comply with them.

ANNA PETRIG

---

[183] Art 7(1)(i) ICC Statute.
[184] ICTY, *The Prosecutor v Zoran Kupreškić et al*, Trial Chamber Judgment, IT-95-16-T, 14 January 2000, para 566 (dicta).
[185] Art 5 ICED.

Chapter 14. The Dead

	MN
A. Introduction	1
B. Meaning and Application	7
I. Search for and collection of the dead	7
II. Identify and record	10
III. Investigate and prosecute	21
IV. Burial	30
V. According to the rites of the religion	34
VI. Burial at sea and cremation	39
VII. Returning the remains	43
VIII. Respect for gravesites	48
C. Relevance in Non-International Armed Conflicts	51
D. Legal Consequences of a Violation	57
E. Critical Assessment	64

Select Bibliography

ICRC CIHL Study, Chapter 35, Rules 112–16 and Chapter 36, Rule 117
ICRC, *Operational Best Practices Regarding the Management of Human Remains and Information on the Dead by Non-Specialists, For All Armed Forces, For All Humanitarian Organizations*
Krähenmann, S., 'Positive Obligations in Human Rights Treaties' (unpublished PhD thesis, Graduate Institute of International and Development Studies, Geneva, 2012), at section 1.3 and Chapter 3
Naqvi, Y., 'The Right to the Truth in International Law: Fact or Fiction', 88 *IRRC* 862 (2006) 245
Petrig, A., 'The War Dead and their Gravesites', 91 *IRRC* 874 (2009) 341
Pictet Commentary GC I, 143–83

A. Introduction

For as long as armed conflicts have existed, death has been an inevitable result. In addition to being a legal issue, the treatment of the war dead is a sensitive and personal matter. Without knowing the extent of the law with regard to the dead, it is clear that people feel passionately about the significance of honouring the remains and memory of the deceased. There are numerous war memorials and cemeteries that recognize those who have died during wars, and anger and devastation are often expressed when the dead or

1

people's remains are not treated respectfully.[1] Similar issues exist if people are not told the fate of their relatives.[2]

2 How to treat those who have fallen, as well as what and how information must be communicated to their country of origin and their family, is codified in numerous areas of international law, domestic law, bilateral and multilateral agreements such as peace agreements, as well as in emerging fields such as transitional justice. Of particular relevance is international humanitarian law (IHL), and in particular the Articles of the Geneva Conventions that cover issues such as collecting the remains of the dead, examining them, recording the findings, investigating and prosecuting any wrongdoing, sharing the information with relevant parties, and respectfully dealing with dead bodies. These acts are important on many levels: for the memory and dignity of the deceased person; for protection of combatants involved in active combat; for the family's healing process; for national healing; for criminal investigations and prosecutions; and for historical records and understanding.

3 With respect to the dead, the Geneva Conventions and their Additional Protocols contain a number of substantive obligations that address some of these concerns and needs. This includes the obligation to search for and collect the dead.[3] Parties have an obligation to identify and record information on the dead,[4] and in some instances to create a register of particulars,[5] and in others to issue death certificates or certified lists with the relevant particulars.[6] The Geneva Conventions also set out how this information should be passed between the parties.[7] These provisions on identifying, recording, and passing on information relating to the deceased imply a right of the families to know the fate of their relatives.[8] Whether this right is in fact a legal requirement, and how far it extends, will be discussed below.

4 Further to this, every death of a prisoner of war (POW) or interned protected person that is caused or suspected to be caused by another person, or the cause of which is unknown, must be investigated and the information given to the Protecting Power; and if there is any question of guilt, measures must be taken to prosecute the relevant people.[9] These provisions raise questions relating to whose death is covered by this requirement, and the potential risk that an obligation to enquire about causes of death may diminish the chances of identifying and informing the family, and the willingness of parties to do so.

5 There is also a clear obligation to prevent the dead from being despoiled,[10] and to respect mortal remains.[11] Included in this requirement for respect is the way in which

---

[1] E.g., see the outrage expressed when Second World War graves were vandalized in Benghazi in early 2012: 'Fury Over Attack on British War Graves in Benghazi', BBC, 4 March 2012, available at <http://www.bbc.co.uk/news/uk-17244211>; or when information surfaced in January 2012 about US troops in Afghanistan urinating on deceased members of the Taliban.

[2] See, e.g., where women spoke about the distress of not knowing the fate of their sons in J. Fangalasuu et al, 'Herem Kam: Stori Blong Mifala Olketa Mere', Women's Submission to the Solomon Islands Truth and Reconciliation Commission (2009), at 25. See also Ch 13, esp MN 4–5, of this volume.

[3] Art 15 GC I; Art 18(1) GC II; Art 16(2) GC IV; Art 8 AP II. This obligation is considered to be of a customary nature by ICRC CIHL Study, Rule 112.

[4] Art 17 para 1 GC I; Art 20 para 1 GC II; Art 120 para 3 GC III; Art 129 para 2 GC IV.

[5] Art 16 GC I; Art 19 para 1 GC II. [6] Art 120 para 2 GC III; Art 129 GC IV.

[7] Art 16 paras 2 and 3 GC I; Art 19 paras 2 and 3 GC II; Art 120 paras 1 and 2 GC III; Art 129 paras 1 and 3 GC IV.

[8] See Ch 13, esp MN 14–39, of this volume. [9] Art 121 GC III; Art 131 GC IV.

[10] Art 15 GC I; Art 18 para 1 GC II; Art 16 para 2 GC IV; Art 8 AP II. This obligation is considered to be of a customary nature by ICRC CIHL Study, Rule 113.

[11] Art 34 (1) AP I.

the dead are disposed of, that is, the dead must be buried in individual marked graves, and this must be done where possible according to religious beliefs.[12] What will necessarily be considered, however, is what exactly is meant by the phrase 'according to the rites of the religion',[13] and what the consequences are of not respecting this obligation. Controversy may arise when religious rites seemingly conflict with other legal necessities, for example further investigation as to cause of death, or when different legal principles are competing with each other or even with political imperatives, for example the burials of Osama bin Laden at sea and Muammar Gaddafi in an unmarked grave. There are also some instances where mass graves may be acceptable,[14] and this will be discussed further, along with whether and when cremation is permissible,[15] and whether and when burial at sea is permissible.[16]

In terms of respecting the dead, this also extends to gravesites and other burial locations.[17] However, the extent to which a party must do this, and for how long after a conflict this obligation exists, is unclear. Geneva Convention (GC) I and GC II specifically refer to the possible return of mortal remains to the home country, whereas GC III refers only to who has responsibility for keeping records regarding any moving of bodies in general.[18] Both GC III and GC IV make specific reference to the returning of ashes to the home country.[19] The Geneva Conventions also obligate parties to return the personal effects of the dead.[20]

B. Meaning and Application

I. Search for and collection of the dead

According to Article 15 paragraph 1 GC I, at all times (on land), as well as following a military engagement in cases on both land and sea (Article 18 paragraph 2 GC II), parties are under an obligation to search for the dead. The obligation to search 'at all times' is limited to land warfare in recognition of the special circumstances that prevail at sea.[21] The obligation to do this in all cases is 'without delay', but the detail of what is actually required to be done recognizes the reality of warfare and the possible threat to those who may be involved in search and collection, by simply obliging the parties to take 'all possible measures'.[22] This obligation to search for the dead relates to civilians too, but in GC IV reference is made to searching for and collecting the dead to the extent allowed by military considerations.[23] It appears that this qualification does not create a significant material difference with regard to the Articles in GC I and II but rather is related to the actors (military or civilian) responsible for the search for and collection of dead combatants versus dead civilians.[24] Under GC IV, it is not military commanders who are responsible for searching for the dead but rather civilian authorities. As such, it is not possible to send civilian relief teams into a battle zone without considering the military situation.[25] There is

---

[12] Art 17 para 3 GC I; Art 120 para 4 GC III; Art 130 para 1 GC IV.
[13] Ibid.   [14] Art 120 para 5 GC III; Art 130 para 2 GC IV.
[15] Art 17 para 2 GC I; Art 120 para 5 GC III; Art 130 para 2 GC IV.   [16] Art 20 GC II.
[17] Art 17 para 3 GC I; Art 120 para 4 GC III; Art 130 para 1 GC IV; Art 34 para 1 AP I.
[18] Art 17 para 3 GC I and Art 20 para 2 GC II, referring to the provisions on the dead contained in GC I; and Art 120 para 6 GC III.
[19] Art 120 para 6 GC III; Art 130 para 2 GC IV.
[20] Art 16 para 3 GC I; Art 19 para 3 GC II; Art 122 para 9 GC III; Art 139 GC IV.
[21] Pictet Commentary GC II, at 131.   [22] Pictet Commentary GC I, at 151.
[23] Art 16 para 2 GC IV.   [24] Pictet Commentary GC IV, at 136–7.   [25] Ibid.

8   There is no specific mention in GC I and GC II regarding to whom exactly the provisions on search and collection apply. As GC I and GC II by their very nature refer to enemy combatants, it is clear that such persons are covered by these Articles. It is also assumed that a party's own fallen combatants should be searched for and collected in accordance with Article 15 GC I and Article 18 GC II respectively. This is deduced from the language used in Article 15, where there is simply mention of 'dead' persons, as compared to Article 16 GC I which refers to a 'dead person of the adverse Party'.[27] This interpretation is supported by the commentary to Article 16,[28] and is allegedly confirmed by the existence of a corresponding rule of customary international law, which states that this obligation to search for and collect the dead should apply 'without adverse distinction'.[29] In terms of fallen civilians, it is clear that Article 16 GC IV applies to all civilians as it is contained within Part II of GC IV, which covers 'the whole of the populations of the countries in conflict, without any adverse distinction'.

no clear indication of when this duty to search for remains would cease, but human rights law suggests that the obligation to search for the bodies of people who disappear or die during an armed conflict, and the corresponding duty to account for their fate, continues well beyond the end of the armed conflict.[26]

9   The Articles on searching for and collecting the dead are not only important in their own right, they are a prerequisite to fulfilling other obligations under the Geneva Conventions, namely identifying bodies and recording relevant information, and providing appropriate burials and returning personal effects, issues that will be discussed below.

II. Identify and record

10   Parties are obliged to identify and record information on the dead before they are interred.[30] This includes an examination, preferably by a medical practitioner, to confirm the death and the identity of the deceased.[31] Geneva Convention I and GC II also require parties to record all particulars that may assist with the identification of the deceased.[32] All Geneva Conventions require that death certificates (or duly authenticated or certified lists) be issued, whether for those collected from the battlefield or those who die while in the hands of the enemy.[33] In particular, GC III sets out what a death certificate should include,[34] and both GC III and GC IV mandate that the cause of death must be included on the certificate. The Geneva Conventions also set out how this information should be passed between the parties—for fallen combatants, through the Information Bureaux for

---

[26] ECtHR, *Varnava and others v Turkey*, Grand Chamber, 18 September 2009, at 148. If the death of the victim is known to be a certainty (as opposed to being presumed), the procedural obligation to investigate is not a continuing obligation, even if the exact cause, circumstance, or responsibility for the death is not established. If death took place before entry into force of the relevant treaty, there must be a 'genuine connection' between the death and entry into force of the treaty for the duty to investigate to arise. The Grand Chamber of the ECtHR recently rejected as inadmissible the case against Russia for its failure to investigate the circumstances of the Katyn massacre in 1940 (ECtHR, *Janowiec and others v Russia*, Grand Chamber, 21 October 2013, paras 159–60). However, it is not clear whether the same reasoning would be applied to enforced disappearances that took place before adoption of the ECHR. See also Ch 13, MN 54–59, of this volume.

[27] Art 16 para 1 GC I; Art 19 GC II.   [28] Pictet Commentary GC I, at 160.
[29] See ICRC CIHL Study, Rule 112.
[30] Art 17 para 1 GC I; Art 20 para 1 GC II; Art 120 para 3 GC III; Art 129 para 2 GC IV.
[31] Ibid.   [32] Art 16 GC I; Art 19 para 1 GC II.
[33] Art 16 para 3 GC I; Art 19 para 3 GC II; Art 120 para 2 GC III; Art 129 GC IV.
[34] Annex 4D GC III.

POWs and protected civilians, in particular internees, who have died, and in both cases through the Protecting Power as well as the Central Information Agency.[35]

It is clear from the wording that the provisions in GC I and GC II on parties to a conflict recording the particulars of the deceased apply only to a 'dead person of the adverse Party falling into their hands'.[36] This does not, of course, preclude a party from having its own regulations on recording particulars of its deceased combatants. With respect to deceased civilians, the relevant Articles on identifying and recording deaths are in Section IV GC IV ('Regulations for the treatment of internees'), as well as in Article 136 GC IV, which is in Section V ('Information Bureaux and Central Agency'). The relevant regulations in Section IV apply only to protected persons interned in their own or occupied territory. Article 136 GC IV makes it clear that in addition, the death of 'any protected persons who are kept in custody for more than two weeks, who are subjected to assigned residence or who are interned', must be reported to the Information Bureaux. Again, this does not preclude a party establishing regulations with respect to its own nationals who are killed during the course of a conflict.

These Articles contained in the four Geneva Conventions on identifying and recording information of the deceased do not expressly state that there is a right of families to know the fate of their loved ones. Nonetheless, the requirement to examine, collect, record, and transfer information regarding the dead, and the requirement to establish Information Bureaux and the like, suggest a definite right of families to know the fate of their relatives, at least with respect to deceased relatives in the hands of the enemy. Additional Protocol (AP) I has gone further than the Geneva Conventions, and indeed expressly states that there is a 'right of families to know the fate of their relatives'.[37]

As also noted elsewhere in this Commentary (see Chapter 13, MN 6–13 and 54–59), there is increasing discussion[38] and a growing consensus that a right to know and/or a right to the truth exists in international law.[39] The right is said to stem from IHL[40]—from both the explicit[41] and the implicit[42] provisions. Aside from the right to know as set out in IHL, the only explicit legal provision with respect to a right to know in a human rights treaty is Article 24(2) of the International Convention for the Protection of All Persons from Enforced Disappearances. International human rights bodies have, nevertheless, inferred a right to know based on other explicit rights contained in human rights treaties. For example, the Human Rights Committee found that the right to an effective remedy and reparation means that states are required to provide information about the violation of any such right and, in the case of death while in the hands of the adverse party, the location of the burial site.[43] Additionally, in some circumstances, international human rights bodies have found that the right to know stems from the prohibition of inhuman and degrading treatment

---

[35] Art 16 para 3 GC I; Art 19 para 3 GC II; Arts 120 para 2, 122 para 1, and 123 GC III; Arts 129 para 3, 136 para 1, and Art 140 para 1 GC IV.
[36] Art 16 GC I; Art 19 GC II.
[37] Art 32 AP I; Ch 13 of this volume.
[38] See Y. Naqvi, 'The Right to the Truth in International Law: Fact or Fiction', 88 *IRRC* 862 (2006) 245.
[39] OAS Res AG/RES 2595 (XL-O/10), *Right to the Truth*, adopted at the fourth plenary session, held on 8 June 2010; HRCouncil Res 9/11, *Right to the Truth*, A/HRC/9/L.12.
[40] Naqvi, above n 38, at 248.   [41] Arts 32 and 33 AP I.
[42] See GC Arts already discussed on searching for, recording, and reporting the dead.
[43] Views of 3 April 2003, *Case of Lyashkevich v Belarus*, Comm No 887/1999, UN Doc CCPR/C/77/D/950/2000, para 11. Although this case does not pertain to armed conflict, it demonstrates the link the HRCttee makes between the right to know and the right to an effective remedy.

(in particular in cases of enforced disappearance). Pursuant to international human rights law, this right to know would pertain to all persons, not just those who have died in the hands of the enemy.[44]

14   In addition to IHL and international human rights bodies, the right to know has been recognized by a number of international organs,[45] international and domestic courts,[46] and international organizations,[47] and is a guiding principle for many truth commissions and commissions of inquiry,[48] so much so that some contend it has become a customary right—in particular with respect to the missing.[49]

15   If it is to be accepted that under customary international law there is a right to know, at least in some circumstances, what this right actually entails, and how this may affect the interpretation of IHL principles on the dead, remains to be determined. For example, one might question the extent of the right to know with regard to the provisions covering lawful deaths during conflict. Although the provisions highlight the requirement to establish basic information, suggesting a basic right to know, they do not outline the detail that is required in identifying the body and recording particulars. For instance, it is unclear whether looking into the cause of death extends to investigating the circumstances of death and identifying the person or persons who may be responsible for this death, and then communicating this information to the next of kin. Given the mass of casualties that can sometimes occur during lawful military operations, it would seem that acquiring such detailed information regarding each individual death would be incredibly burdensome for the parties. Also, detailed information may be hampered by the reality of warfare, with information and evidence impossible to retrieve or inadvertently destroyed as a result of ongoing combat operations. International humanitarian law certainly recognizes the reality of warfare, as seen in the qualifications contained in the provisions on the collection of the dead, but such realities and qualifications can result in less information regarding the fate of deceased relatives.

16   For those who have died while being interned, the right of their families to know what happened would more easily be satisfied because of the investigation requirements of Article 121 GC III and Article 131 GC IV. Whether the right then extends to requiring relatives to be told the location of the deceased's grave is unclear. As will be discussed, the provisions of the Geneva Conventions and AP I requiring that graves be marked, and limiting the circumstances in which mass burial, burial at sea, and cremation are acceptable, all point in the direction of supporting the right of the family to be able to know as much as possible.

---

[44] ECtHR, *Varnava*, above n 26, at 186, particularly with respect to combatants in an IAC: 'Whether they died, in the fighting or of their wounds, or whether they were captured as prisoners, they must still be accounted for.'

[45] E.g., see HRCouncil and the UNGA Resolutions referred to above n 39.

[46] E.g., the ECtHR has inferred a right to the truth as part of other explicit rights, including the right to an effective investigation and to be informed of the results. See ECtHR, *Cyprus v Turkey*, 10 May 2001.

[47] ICRC, *Operational Best Practices Regarding the Management of Human Remains and Information on the Dead by Non-Specialists, For All Armed Forces, For All Humanitarian Organizations* (November 2004), at 10, 2.3, available at <http://www.icrc.org/eng/assets/files/other/icrc-002-858.pdf>.

[48] E.g., see the objectives of the South African Truth and Reconciliation Commission, South African Promotion of National Unity and Reconciliation Act No 34 of 1995, s 3(1)(c).

[49] See the meeting referenced by L. Despouy, Special Rapporteur on States of Emergency, in his 8th Annual Report, UN Doc E/CN.4/Sub.2/1995/29 Corr.1, according to which experts concluded that the right to truth has achieved the status of a norm of customary international law; and this right is also considered to be of a customary nature by the ICRC CIHL Study, Rule 117.

Nonetheless, in addition to the right to know being hampered by the realities of warfare, and the lack of specificity in IHL, there are also instances where the right to know is arguably trumped by other imperatives, such as the need to encourage a cessation of hostilities, or by criminal investigations. In negotiating peace settlements, the idea of amnesties is often put on the table and, in many cases, negotiated into peace agreements. Those who criticize amnesties, amongst other things, say that they are incompatible with IHL and with a right to know. While it is generally accepted that an amnesty cannot be provided for international crimes, the inability to initiate investigations and criminal proceedings for crimes that are covered by an amnesty means that less information will be uncovered regarding what actually happened. On the other hand, in the past, amnesties have been provided for individuals who have agreed to share the truth about their crimes.[50] As one author puts it, this leaves one to question whether a legal judgment is required in order to establish 'the truth'.[51] As such, although highly controversial, a 'truth for amnesty' formula can, in some instances, arguably aid in the recovery of facts about a death during armed conflict.

The right to know the fate of relatives during a conflict can at times be hindered and at other times aided by criminal investigations. Some criminal tribunals will have the resources to conduct exhumations and to identify various patterns of violence that may help in the establishment of guilt for an international crime. However, these tribunals will often lack the resources to identify the individual bodies being exhumed. In such instances, families will be prevented from knowing exactly what happened to their specific relative, and will not be able to receive confirmation of the whereabouts of the remains of their next of kin or have the remains returned to them.

In situations where alleged killings during conflict are prosecuted in civil domestic judicial systems or international tribunals, in some cases victims' families are able to join the proceedings in various capacities and at various stages of a trial.[52] Such systems allow victims increased access to and control over information; however, they still do not adequately satisfy a victim, or a victim's family's right to know. For example, in a situation like the International Criminal Court (ICC), even if victims' families can join proceedings, this will apply only to those who can link the alleged crime to that which is under the ICC's jurisdiction—this also presupposes that the family members have some basic knowledge about what happened to their next of kin.

Identifying and recording information about the dead during armed conflict is an integral part of IHL, which is, in many instances, reinforced and expanded upon by other bodies of law such as human rights and international criminal law. Despite the lack of clarity regarding the content of the right for those who die but were not interned, it may be presumed that this right would include at least knowing the circumstances and cause of the death, although, as mentioned, sometimes it will be hard to establish necessary details when there are mass casualties, or when death occurs in the course of intensive military operations.[53]

---

[50] See the 'truth for amnesty' formula implemented by the South African Truth and Reconciliation Commission, South African Promotion of National Unity and Reconciliation Act No 34 of 1995.

[51] Naqvi, above n 38, at 247.

[52] In civil systems victims can join as *parties civiles*; for an example in an international tribunal, see ICC Statute, Arts 68(3) and 75.

[53] ECtHR, *Al-Skeini and others v United Kingdom*, Judgment, 7 July 2011, at 164; ECtHR, *Ergi v Turkey*, 28 July 1998, at 85. See also the ECtHR cases of *Hassan v United Kingdom*, Judgment, 16 September 2014,

III. Investigate and prosecute

21 The right to know is also linked to a large degree to the duty to investigate—one can only 'know' what happened if and when the facts surrounding the death are established, and often this information only follows from an investigation. The IHL requirement to investigate deaths comes under Article 121 GC III and Article 131 GC IV. According to these Articles, deaths of POWs or civilian internees that *may* have been caused by a sentry, another POW or internee, or any other person, or where the death of such persons is unknown, must be investigated and the information given to the Protecting Power; and if there is any question of guilt, measures must be taken to prosecute those accused of causing the deaths.[54]

22 First, it is important to be clear about to whose deaths these Articles refer. Article 121 GC III is relatively straightforward in this sense, as it clearly states that it applies to POWs—combatants who are *hors de combat*, in the hands of the enemy, and who have died during this time, whether from a violent attack or as a result of illness.[55] The purpose of this Article was to protect POWs both from wrongdoing committed by the Detaining Power and from wrongdoing committed by other POWs or civilians of any nationality.[56] Article 131 GC IV is also relatively clear, in that it refers to 'internees' and appears in Section IV of GC IV which relates to interned protected persons in own or occupied territory. As with the corresponding GC III provision, it is believed to cover violent death and unexplained illness, and is intended to protect civilians from both the Detaining Power and other internees.[57]

23 The degree to which deaths not covered by these two Articles should be investigated is not made clear in the Geneva Conventions. Unlike many of the other provisions on the dead, these Articles appear to apply only to enemy combatants and protected persons. It does not seem that they extend to all those who have died in the power of the enemy, or even to all those who have died in suspicious circumstances even if not in the hands of the enemy at the time.[58] A duty to investigate may, however, be inherent in the duty to search for persons alleged to have committed grave breaches, such as wilful killing.[59] Nevertheless, it would appear that beyond the requirement to establish cursory information about these other people, and to search for alleged perpetrators of wilful killing, the duty to investigate deaths of a country's own nationals, or of those dead who do not fall into the categories of Article 121 GC III or Article 131 GC IV, falls rather under other bodies of law, in particular, human rights law and domestic criminal and military law.

24 While international human rights treaties do not contain a specific provision saying that states must investigate deaths, the various regional human rights courts and the Human Rights Commission have come to the conclusion that in order to protect the right to life, alleged breaches of this right must be investigated.[60] As such, human rights courts

---

and *Jaloud v the Netherlands*, Judgment, 20 November 2014. See also Ch 35 of this volume for a discussion of the *Hassan* Judgment.

[54] Art 121 GC III; Art 131 GC IV.
[55] Pictet Commentary GC III, at 570. [56] Ibid. [57] Ibid, at 509.
[58] This is, however, different from an investigation into a breach of the laws relating to conduct of hostilities.
[59] Art 146 para 2 GC IV. For a contrary view, see, however, Ch 31, MN 40, of this volume.
[60] E.g., see ECtHR, *Isayeva, Yusupova and Bazayeva v Russia*, Judgment, 24 February 2005, paras 201–25; and P. Alston, Special Rapporteur on extra-judicial, summary, or arbitrary executions, *Report to the Human Rights Commission*, UN Doc E/CN.4/2006/53 (2006), paras 20–7, 33–43.

have maintained the duty of a state to investigate the operations of armed forces in order to ascertain whether their planning and conduct are in keeping with the right to life.[61] This is not to say that there cannot or will not be civilian deaths in a military operation, but rather in circumstances where the relevant human rights treaty applies, it reinforces IHL principles of distinction and proportionality by insisting that operations are planned and executed with the requisite care for the lives of the civilian population.[62]

In addition to the duty to investigate operations of armed forces, pursuant to recent decisions of the European Court of Human Rights (ECtHR), states have to investigate deaths within their own armed forces that have occurred in suspicious circumstances, namely suicides. The ECtHR has heard a series of cases concerning the suicide of conscripts during their service, and in all these cases, the Court affirmed the duty to investigate the suicide.[63] 25

It has yet to be decided whether the duty to investigate extends to a party's own combatant who dies during military operations while abroad.[64] Following the Strasbourg Court's unambiguous finding that the European Convention on Human Rights (ECHR) applies extraterritorially in Iraq,[65] the United Kingdom (UK) Supreme Court confirmed that the ECHR applies to British soldiers deployed abroad in 2013. This decision may well impact future decisions of the ECtHR and therefore the duty to investigate deaths of a party's own combatants. 26

Given, therefore, that an investigation is required when individuals have been killed as a result of the use of force, it is important to establish the content of the duty. According to the case law of the ECtHR, such investigations require that authorities act on their own motion; those carrying out the investigation must be independent; the investigation must be capable of leading to a determination of whether the force used was or was not justified; the investigation must be prompt; and there must be an element of public scrutiny.[66] 27

Depending on the outcome of the investigation, the relevant provisions of the Geneva Conventions and human rights law point to a follow-up prosecution.[67] As mentioned earlier in this section, in relation to POW deaths and civilian internee deaths, if an investigation sheds light on a wrongdoing, 'all measures' shall be taken for the prosecution of the alleged responsible person.[68] In terms of those unlawfully killed during armed conflict but not covered by these two provisions of the Geneva Conventions, human rights law fills the gap. International human rights bodies have asserted the obligation to prevent and investigate violations of the right to life, impose appropriate punishment, and provide for compensation.[69] The aim of investigations under human rights law, however, is not purely 28

---

[61] ECtHR, *Isayeva, Yusupova and Bazayeva v Russia*, above n 60, paras 155–200.
[62] E.g., provided that the ECHR applies extraterritorially, the ECtHR has confirmed the duty to investigate deaths occurring during military operations. For more detail, see ECtHR, *Al-Skeini and others v United Kingdom*, above n 53, at 150.
[63] E.g., see ECtHR, *Abdullah Yilmaz v Turkey*, Judgment, 17 June 2008.
[64] See ECtHR, *Pritchard v United Kingdom* (App No 1573/11), communicated on 8 September 2011.
[65] ECtHR, *Al-Skeini and others v United Kingdom*, above n 53.
[66] ECtHR, *Isayeva, Yusupova and Bazayeva*, above n 60, paras 208–14.
[67] Alston, above n 60, paras 20–7, 33–43.   [68] Art 121 GC III; Art 131 GC IV.
[69] E.g., see HRCttee, *General Comment 6: Article 6 (Right to Life)*, 27 July 1982, para 3; HRCttee, *General Comment 31: The Nature of the General Legal Obligation Imposed on States*, 29 March 2004, para 8; IACtHR, *Velásquez Rodríguez Case*, 29 July 1988, para 14; IACtHR, *'Las Dos Erres' Massacre v Guatemala*, 24 November 2009, para 148; ECtHR, *Al-Skeini and others v United Kingdom*, above n 53, paras 165–6.

punitive but also serves as an opportunity to identify patterns of violations.[70] Human rights courts have found that when a state fails to do this, it falls short in its duty to investigate.[71]

29 It is also worth noting that armed forces generally have their own policy on inquiry and/or investigation into combat-related deaths of both their own and enemy combatants. In most cases, the outcome of such inquiries/investigations may be passed on to the deceased's family, with some censorship relating to national security and/or issues of privacy. In addition to this, domestic military law or policy will also address cases where prosecution of a suspicious death of a party's own combatant is required.[72] The concern, however, with the obligation of a state to inquire into the cause of death and to seek the person responsible and punish him or her, is that it can simultaneously diminish the chances of the family's being informed and the state's willingness to do so. If an inquiry is held, depending on the findings, those carrying out the inquiry may be less inclined to share the information with the family if the results reflect badly on the party holding the inquiry. Nonetheless, despite any inclination to keep wrongdoings confidential, the withholding of information and any decisions regarding investigations and prosecutions should be made in a manner consistent with a state's international obligations.

IV. Burial

30 Part of the obligation to search for and collect the dead is to 'prevent their being despoiled' or pillaged.[73] This has been understood to mean that the dead must be guarded and, where necessary, protected from anyone seeking to lay hands on them or to steal their possessions.[74] So important is this protection that those called upon to prevent the despoiling of dead bodies may, if necessary, use arms for that purpose.[75] While these Articles do not specifically refer to those interned either as POWs or civilians (they refer to all those who have died on the battlefield or at sea), other Articles in the relevant Conventions (for example, Article 13 GC III) make it clear that while in enemy hands, POWs and interned civilians must be treated humanely and with respect, which, given the extensive laws on the treatment of the dead, means it is assumed that by extension, these Articles on humane treatment would include those who have died in enemy hands. Further to this, it will be important to consider what the consequences are for not protecting the dead against pillage, or their place of burial from being despoiled. This will be discussed in section D of this chapter.

31 One way to ensure that dead bodies are protected and respected, at least once collected, is to prescribe the way in which bodies are disposed of. Such detail is laid out in all the Geneva Conventions, thereby making the rules on disposal of the body relevant to those who die on the battlefield as well as to those who die in the hands of the Detaining Power.

32 To the extent permitted by the circumstances, or unless the circumstances are unavoidable, the dead must be buried in individual marked graves.[76] Although, in recognition

---

[70] See discussion in S. Krähenmann, *Positive Obligations in Human Rights Treaties* (unpublished PhD thesis, Graduate Institute of International and Development Studies, Geneva, 2012), at 3.1.2.

[71] Ibid.

[72] E.g., see the case of the death of US soldier Private Danny Chen in Afghanistan, at <http://www.nytimes.com/2012/04/12/nyregion/any-trials-in-pvt-danny-chens-death-will-be-in-us-military-says.html?_r=1>.

[73] Art 15 GC I; Art 18 para 1 GC II; Art 16 para 2 GC IV; Art 8 AP II. This obligation is also considered to be of a customary nature by ICRC CIHL Study, Rule 113.

[74] Pictet Commentary GC I, at 152.   [75] Ibid.

[76] Art 17 para 1 GC I; Art 20 para 1 GC II; Art 120 para 5 GC III; Art 130 para 2 GC IV.

of the reality of warfare, no absolute obligation has been imposed, a common grave should always be an exceptional measure.[77] Circumstances that might dictate its necessity include climatic or military considerations, or, for example, if it were in the interests of public health.[78] It is worth noting, however, that if death resulted from trauma (as opposed to illness), as is most likely in a conflict situation, there is a negligible risk of dead bodies causing outbreaks of disease.[79] This therefore minimizes the justification for a quick mass burial from the perspective of the physical health risks, although it is acknowledged that there are psychological impacts caused by long delays in people being buried or cremated.[80] Furthermore, mass graves are considered contrary to the notion of respecting the dead, and they also make the opportunity for future exhumations almost impossible, which, amongst other things, can aid in concealing the commission of a crime.[81]

There is no specific explanation as to what is required in order to mark a grave, but the point is that it should always be possible to locate the precise resting place of a fallen combatant.[82] In the case of the burial of Muammar Gaddafi in an unmarked grave, competing reasons were given—some claimed it was to prevent his grave becoming a shrine or a site of pilgrimage for his supporters, and others claimed it was to prevent his gravesite becoming a target for his enemies. The latter is a legitimate legal concern but the former is not, and it should not be a factor when deciding how someone who has died during conflict should be buried (this will be discussed further in relation to Osama bin Laden in section B.V of this chapter).[83] 33

V. According to the rites of the religion

Disposing of the body must be done, where possible, 'according to the rites of the religion' of the deceased.[84] What exactly is meant by 'according to the rites of the religion',[85] and what the consequences are of not respecting this obligation, remain open questions. At the time of drafting the Geneva Conventions, it appears that this phrase was added in recognition that some religious burial practices can be quite arduous, involving, for example, sacrificing an animal or using some rare ingredient.[86] It is worth considering, however, the possibility that perhaps today this requirement may compete with other demands. 34

Controversy may arise when religious rites seemingly conflict with other legal obligations, for example further investigation as to cause of death, or when different legal principles are competing with each other or even with political priorities, for example the burial of Muammar Gaddafi in an unmarked grave after a lengthy period, or the burial of Osama bin Laden at sea.[87] 35

Gaddafi's body was on display for five days, after which his body was apparently washed and prepared according to Islamic practice. This is contrary to the usual Islamic practice, which requires burial within 24 hours. The justification for the extended time above ground was reported as being to give the Libyan people an opportunity to have some closure and to 36

---

[77] Pictet Commentary GC I, at 177. [78] Ibid.
[79] World Health Organization, Technical Note, 'Disposal of Dead Bodies in Emergency Conditions', available at <http://www.who.int/water_sanitation_health/hygiene/envsan/tn08/en/>.
[80] Ibid. [81] Pictet Commentary GC I, at 177. [82] Ibid, at 180.
[83] Art 15 GC 1. [84] Art 17 para 3 GC I; Art 120 para 4 GC III; Art 130 para 1 GC IV.
[85] Ibid. [86] Pictet Commentary GC I, at 179.
[87] It is acknowledged that the conflict in which the death of Muammar Gaddafi occurred may be classified as a NIAC, in which case the GCs (other than CA 3) would not apply; however, see section C of this chapter for a discussion of the application of these laws in a NIAC.

see for themselves that Gaddafi's lengthy reign was over.[88] Although, as mentioned, the provisions on burying bodies according to the 'rites of the religion' may be qualified by what is possible, it would seem that such emotional and political justifications for not following ordinary religious practice are contrary to what the drafters had in mind. As such, it is important that the laws on treatment of the dead are not interpreted in a way that could amount to 'victor's justice'.

37   Conversely, according to the information provided by the United States (US) Government, Osama bin Laden was buried at sea precisely because the burial needed to be done within 24 hours in accordance with Islamic law.[89] The US claimed that it complied with Islamic religious rites by providing Osama bin Laden with a swift burial, which was preceded by ritual washing, the body being covered in the ritual white shroud and prayers being recited.[90] Nonetheless, many did question whether burial at sea complied with Islamic tradition, as usually Islamic burials take place on land, particularly if the death occurred on land.[91] Similar to the situation mentioned earlier with regard to Gaddafi, some commentators have suggested that the burial of Osama bin Laden at sea by the US was for political reasons, as the US would have wanted to avoid his gravesite becoming a type of shrine.[92] If this was a factor, and given the conflicting views on Islamic practice in this area it appears questionable that the reason for burial at sea was purely because of religious rites, it may be that political interests played a part in determining the method of burial.

38   An argument could be put forward, however, that the burial of Osama bin Laden at sea prevented any potential despoiling of his body by enraged enemies (similar to the argument regarding the burying of Gaddafi in an unmarked grave). If this was the case, and if Islamic law required him to be buried where the death occurred, then the US Government was obliged to make a decision between two competing legal principles—preventing a dead body from being despoiled, and interring the body according to the rites of the deceased's religion. Both these provisions come with qualifications—the first requires parties to 'take all possible measures',[93] and the second is qualified by the words 'if possible'[94]—and so it is not certain which would prevail, although the former obligation on the prevention of despoliation would seem to take priority. Nevertheless, to bury a person at sea, hundreds or thousands of kilometers away from the place of death, would appear to be an abuse of this qualification and the rules relating to burial at sea which are discussed below. Any evaluation of these two legal principles and decisions around burial should be made absent the political desires of the parties.

---

[88] There are numerous news articles that have reported on this and reference statements by Libyan officials. See, e.g., 'Gaddafi Buried in Unmarked Grave in Libya DESERT to Avoid Creating Shrine', *Guardian*, 25 October 2011, available at <http://www.guardian.co.uk/world/2011/oct/25/gaddafi-buried-in-unmarked-grave>.

[89] See White House Press Conference on 2 May 2011, comments by John Brennan, White House Homeland Security and Counter Terrorism Advisor.

[90] See Office of the Press Secretary, The White House, Press Briefing by Press Secretary Jay Carney, 5 March 2011, James S. Brady Press Briefing Room, available at <http://www.whitehouse.gov/the-press-office/2011/05/03/press-briefing-press-secretary-jay-carney-532011>.

[91] There are numerous news articles that have reported on this and quote a variety of Islamic leaders and websites. See, e.g., 'Bin Laden Sea Burial Not in Line with Islam, Clerics Say', Reuters, 3 May 2011, available at <http://af.reuters.com/article/egyptNews/idAFLDE7420A020110503?sp=true>.

[92] Ibid. There are numerous news articles that have reported on commentators putting forward this idea.

[93] Art 15 GC I.   [94] Art 17 GC I.

VI. Burial at sea and cremation

Aside from religious considerations, burial at sea can be problematic as it provides no real opportunity for families subsequently to visit the gravesite of the deceased, or for a later return of the deceased's remains to his or her home country or family. This will be discussed in more detail in the following sections on returning the remains and gravesites, respectively. There are some circumstances in which burial at sea will, however, be deemed acceptable. According to Article 20 GC II, combatants who have died at sea may be buried at sea, ideally individually, which burial should be preceded by a medical examination in order to confirm the death and the identity of the person. There is no mention that this Article applies specifically to a 'dead person of the adverse Party', so it would presumably apply to all deceased combatants. The Article clearly states that if the dead person is on land then GC I should apply. Here there is no mention of religious rites, although there is a reference to GC I in cases where a ship has landed, and GC I does refer to religious rites. This, however, invites the question whether religious rites must be followed in the case of a lawful burial at sea. It is assumed that at sea there is less likely to be the range of religious personnel on board the naval vessel, and in many cases there is the possibility that the necessary religious provisions are harder to obtain. Perhaps this is the reason for omitting the reference to religious rites. Either way, given the spirit of the Geneva Conventions, where possible, a burial at sea should still comply with religious rites so as to afford the deceased, to the extent possible, the dignity and respect which would be afforded to him or her on land.

No reference is made in the Geneva Conventions to burial at sea for civilians who have died at sea or aboard a ship during armed conflict. This could be because there are less likely to be civilians in such a predicament. Nonetheless, it has been accepted that the rules applying to the dead at sea will apply, where possible, to civilian dead at sea.[95]

The Geneva Conventions also prescribe whether and when cremation is permissible.[96] The provisions reflect a strong preference in favour of burial over cremation, with cremation being accepted for 'imperative reasons of hygiene' or for religious reasons.[97] In the case of POWs and interned civilians who die, they may be cremated if this is in accordance with an express desire.[98] In cases where the dead are exceptionally cremated, the circumstance and reasons for the cremation must be stated in the death certificate.[99] In cases of cremated POWs or fallen combatants, their ashes shall be kept by the Graves Registration Service until they can be disposed of in accordance with the home country's wishes.[100] In the case of deceased civilian internees, the ashes must be kept and transferred as soon as possible to the deceased's family upon their request.[101]

There is no specific mention in Article 17 GC I regarding to whom exactly the provision on cremation applies. Reference is simply made in this Article to 'the dead', and so it is assumed that this applies to enemy combatants (based on the nature and purpose of GC I) and to a party's own combatants (when compared with the wording in Article 16 GC I, which refers to a 'dead person of the adverse Party'). Other provisions in GC I that relate to respectful treatment of the deceased, marking graves, and returning remains (to

---

[95] Pictet Commentary GC II, at 150.
[96] Art 17 para 2 GC I; Art 120 para 5 GC III; Art 130 para 2 GC IV. [97] Ibid.
[98] Art 120 para 5 GC III; Art 130 para 2 GC IV.
[99] Art 17 para 2 GC I; Art 120 para 5 GC III; Art 130 para 2 GC IV.
[100] Art 17 para 3 GC I; Art 120 para 6 GC III. [101] Art 130 para 2 GC IV.

be discussed in more detail in section B.VII of this chapter), would suggest that a party's own fallen combatants should be cremated only in accordance with Article 17 GC I, and that remains should be marked, and where there is no legitimate home country objection, returned to families upon request. In any case, most armed forces would have their own internal policies with regard to mortuary affairs, but these should be consistent with their obligations under international law. As such, even if a deceased combatant is cremated in accordance with the Geneva Conventions, practices that include dumping the ashes of one's own combatants in landfill are highly problematic, as they contradict other provisions of the Geneva Conventions discussed earlier.

VII. Returning the remains

43 Returning the remains of those who have died during an armed conflict is very important for the mourning process of the deceased's family. Geneva Convention I and GC II refer specifically to the possible return of mortal remains to the home country. The reason given for these provisions being optional is that different countries traditionally took different approaches to the burial of war dead—some required them to be buried where they had fallen, and others liked to bring the dead home.[102] It seems that now, states prefer to have the remains of their deceased repatriated, although there is some acknowledgement that this may not always be possible.[103] As mentioned in section B.VI of this chapter, all Geneva Conventions refer to disposing of ashes in accordance with the home country's wishes,[104] although GC IV actually states that the ashes shall be kept and transferred as soon as they are requested by the deceased's next of kin. In GC III and GC IV, there is no mention of returning bodies or other remains, but GC III does state that the party controlling the territory is responsible for maintaining records of any subsequent moves of the bodies.[105] This therefore does not preclude the possibility of returning POW remains to their home country, but there is no discussion as to in what circumstances such transfers may occur.

44 In a case where the deceased combatant's or POW's family and the home country have conflicting wishes, the commentaries to the Geneva Conventions are silent; however, the commentary to AP I states that both the family and the home country can request the remains, but the home country may veto any request made by the family.[106] Although not included in the commentary to AP I, one example where the state interests and the family's desires may conflict is in the case of a criminal trial. In a situation where a criminal investigation and trial are taking place, personal effects or remains may be kept by the relevant authorities for evidentiary purposes.

45 There is no question that these provisions apply to combatants of the adverse party, POWs, and civilian internees in their own and occupied territory. Again, though, the question is raised as to whether they apply to a party's own combatants, that is, what the obligations are on a party with respect to its own fallen combatants. As has been mentioned in previous sections, Article 17 GC I refers to 'the dead' as opposed to the dead 'of the adverse Party'. This suggests that it applies to all dead combatants. In any case, Article 34 AP I has a much larger personal field of application. However, many militaries have domestic laws regarding military cemeteries and returning remains that would govern

---

[102] Pictet Commentary GC I, at 181.
[103] See practice relating to ICRC CIHL Study, Rule 114.
[104] See provisions referred to above n 18, and Art 130 para 2 GC IV.
[105] Art 120 para 6 GC III.   [106] ICRC Commentary APs, para 1346.

their conduct with respect to the next of kin. Nonetheless, the basic principle of respecting remains, as discussed, would need to be applied.

There is no time limit on these provisions. While reference is made to returning ashes 'as soon as possible'[107] in the case of deceased and cremated internees, often the return of remains may take place long after the close of hostilities. For example, the ashes of 3,500 Japanese soldiers who died during the Second World War in Irian Java were returned to Japan only in 1991.[108]

The Geneva Conventions also obligate parties to return the personal effects of the dead.[109] Such effects include the deceased's identity disc or part thereof, any last will or other important documentation, money, and any other sentimental materials found on the dead person's body.[110] The transfer should be done through the relevant official Information Bureaux.[111] Weapons and other items that might be used in a military operation do not need to be returned and may be kept as war booty.[112]

VIII. Respect for gravesites

The obligation to respect the dead extends to their gravesites and other burial locations.[113] Parties must 'ensure' that graves are properly maintained and marked, and to this end there is a positive obligation to set up an Official Graves Registration Service at the commencement of hostilities. This is to enable bodies of fallen combatants or POWs to be identified; to enable later exhumations where required;[114] and to aid with potential transfers of the bodies back to the home country.[115] The Graves Registration Service is also the primary body responsible for preventing graves from being violated and sacrilege of all kinds.[116] However, the extent to which a party must maintain and protect gravesites, and how long after a conflict this obligation exists, remains unclear, as such an obligation is seemingly endless and also immensely costly.

The wording of the Geneva Conventions arguably suggests that the obligation is ongoing, requiring that graves are 'always' able to be found.[117] The commentators on AP I, however, consider that the lack of a time limit on this obligation is an 'obvious gap' which has been addressed by AP I.[118] Additional Protocol I states that as soon as relations between the conflicting parties permit, agreements should be made with countries in whose territory graves are located regarding access to, and the permanent protection and maintenance of, gravesites.[119] Additional Protocol I also sets out the procedure for cases where an agreement has not been reached and the deceased's home country is not willing to maintain the gravesite at its own expense. This includes offering to facilitate the return of the remains, and if this offer is not accepted, after five years from the date of the offer and with due notice, the party in whose territory the deceased is located may adopt arrangements regarding the gravesites pursuant to its domestic law.[120] Many countries, or even

---

[107] Art 130 para 2 GC IV.   [108] ICRC CIHL Study, Rule 114.
[109] Art 16 para 3 GC I; Art 19 para 3 GC II; Art 122 para 9 GC III; Art 139 GC IV.   [110] Ibid.
[111] Ibid.   [112] See ICRC CIHL Study, Commentary to Rule 114.
[113] Art 17 para 3 GC I; Art 120 para 4 GC III; Art 130 para 1 GC IV; Art 34(1) AP I.
[114] Exhumations are referred to in the GCs and are also addressed in Art 34 AP I. Generally, exhumations are prohibited; however, in cases where the purpose is to return the remains to the home country, or if there is overriding public necessity, then they are permitted.
[115] Art 17 para 3 GC I; Art 120 para 4 GC III.   [116] Pictet Commentary GC III, at 180.
[117] Art 17 para 3 GC I; Art 120 para 4 GC III.   [118] ICRC Commentary APs, para 1328.
[119] Art 34 para 2 AP I.   [120] Art 34 para 3 AP I.

groups of countries, have existing bodies that are mandated to oversee war graves. These bodies or commissions often exist to maintain war graves both on a country's own territory and overseas.[121]

50   The rules for deceased internees are slightly different, in that they require that graves are respected, maintained, and marked in such a way 'that they can always be recognised'.[122] The responsibility for ensuring this rests on the detaining 'authorities'.[123] Additional Protocol I appears to enlarge this by referring to High Contracting Parties in whose territory graves and remains are situated,[124] thereby not limiting the responsibility of maintaining graves to parties to the conflict. In terms of the duration of the obligation to maintain gravesites of deceased internees, the same rules discussed above would apply.

C. Relevance in Non-International Armed Conflicts

51   There is only one written IHL rule that specifically covers the dead in non-international armed conflicts (NIACs). It is Article 8 AP II. This Article simply states that the dead should be searched for, and that all possible measures should be taken to prevent their being despoiled and to ensure that they are decently disposed of. According to the Customary International Humanitarian Law (CIHL) Study, the obligation to search for, collect, and evacuate the dead, as well as the obligations to dispose of the dead respectfully and to maintain gravesites, are in fact customary international law, with no official contrary practice being found.[125]

52   The obligation to search for and collect the dead is also a prerequisite to other rules which were found to be customary international law in NIACs as well, namely, the obligations to respect dead bodies and to ensure they are not despoiled.[126] In fact, the obligation to respect dead bodies is also considered to be inherent in Common Article 3. While this Article does not refer to the dead specifically, it prohibits 'outrages upon personal dignity', which may be understood as including respect for the dead. In addition to this, the requirement that dead bodies are respected can be found in the Elements of Crimes of the International Criminal Court (ICC), which includes the mutilating of dead bodies in NIACs as a war crime of 'committing outrages upon personal dignity'.[127] International human rights bodies have similarly addressed the importance of respecting the dead by finding that mutilation by state agents of dead bodies or disrespectful treatment of their bodies is considered inhuman and degrading treatment of the next of kin.[128] Thus respecting personal dignity should be the guiding principle for the treatment of dead bodies in a NIAC in the absence of any other more prescriptive rules in IHL.

---

[121] See, e.g., the Office of Australian War Graves at <http://www.dva.gov.au/commemorations-memorials-and-war-graves/office-australian-war-graves>, or the German War Graves Commission at <http://www.volksbund.de/en/volksbund.html>.

[122] Art 130 para 1 GC IV.   [123] Ibid.   [124] Art 34 para 2 AP I.

[125] See ICRC CIHL Study, Commentary to Rule 112.

[126] See ICRC CIHL Study, Commentary to Rule 113.

[127] ICC Elements of Crimes, Definition of committing outrages upon personal dignity as a war crime (ICC Statute, fn 57 relating to Art 8(2)(c)(ii)).

[128] ECtHR, *Akkum and others v Turkey*, Judgment, 24 March 2005, para 250; ECtHR, *Arzu Akhmadova and others v Russia*, Judgment, 8 January 2009, para 205.

53 In NIACs, there is no treaty provision specifically outlining measures required to identify the dead prior to their being interred and to investigate the circumstances of the death. Nevertheless, there has been consistent practice found to suggest the measures discussed above are applicable in NIACs. In addition, international human rights law requires the dead to be identified and the circumstances investigated. As mentioned earlier (at MN 24), international human rights treaties do not contain a specific provision that requires states to investigate deaths, but the various regional human rights courts have come to the conclusion that in order to protect the right to life, breaches of this right must be investigated.[129] For example, in the case of *Isayeva, Yusupova and Bazayeva v Russia*,[130] which related to a NIAC, the ECtHR said that the implication of the right to life is that there should be some form of effective official investigation when individuals have been killed as a result of the use of force.[131] Additionally, a handful of international resolutions, all of which have garnered widespread support, uphold the principle of accounting for the dead in NIACs by identifying and providing information about them.[132]

54 The IHL rule that appears to have less certain application in NIACs is that relating to the return of the mortal remains and personal effects of the dead, possibly because in a NIAC there is often no question of 'return'. It is not referred to in AP II, but there is some indication that state practice supports the rule's application in NIACs.[133] In addition, the rules on burial according to religious rites seem to receive no specific mention in relation to NIACs—neither in AP II, nor in customary international law. If the conflict in Libya in which Colonel Gaddafi was ousted and killed is classified as a NIAC, it raises the question whether the disposal of Gaddafi's body, which was not buried immediately (contrary to Islamic law), contradicted any IHL principle for NIACs. Although there is no specific mention of religious rites and burials, these rules could nevertheless be considered to come under the principles set forth in Common Article 3 in relation to personal dignity. Respect for personal dignity should be the guiding measure when there are no clear provisions prescribing the conduct.

55 In terms of to whom the provisions would apply in NIACs, it seems that they would apply without adverse distinction based on Article 2(1) AP II. That is, they would apply to all persons affected by the conflict as defined in Article 1 AP II. In terms of when the rules on the dead apply and the extent to which they apply, following AP II and the CIHL Study, it is similar to the situation in international armed conflicts (IACs), i.e. 'whenever circumstances permit, and particularly after an engagement', but there is a recognition that the obligation is not unlimited and endless, as the provision states that 'all possible measures shall be taken'.[134]

56 The obligations will extend to both parties to the conflict—both the state party (if a state is involved in the NIAC) and the rebel groups, in accordance with Common Article 3. Nonetheless, the extent to which rebel groups will be able to comply with all these rules will vary, depending, for example, on their degree of control over the territory.

---

[129] See, e.g., ECtHR, *Isayeva, Yusupova and Bazayeva*, above n 60, paras 201–25; and Alston, above n 60, paras 20–7, 33–43.
[130] ECtHR, *Isayeva, Yusupova and Bazayeva*, above n 60, paras 201–25.   [131] Ibid, paras 209–14.
[132] See ICRC CIHL Study, Commentary to Rule 116.
[133] See ICRC CIHL Study, Commentary to Rule 114.   [134] Art 8 AP II.

D. Legal Consequences of a Violation

57 The basic rules on searching for and collecting the dead do not seem to carry with them any explicit specific legal consequences if violated. As these provisions acknowledge the realities of the conflict and require parties to comply with them to the extent possible, it would be difficult, for example, to find individuals criminally responsible for not collecting bodies if they were able to claim that they did take all possible measures. However, under human rights law, in such circumstances the state may be responsible in some instances for the violation of the right to an effective remedy[135] if bodies are not searched for and collected. In cases where a life has been lost, actualizing the right to a remedy can entail undertaking an investigation and providing the next of kin with information on what happened to the deceased.[136] In such an instance, searching for and collecting the dead may form part of the investigation. In addition to this, in some cases, not providing families with information of what happened to their next of kin has been deemed to amount to inhuman and degrading treatment.[137] The ECtHR has found that even in an armed conflict, conducting an investigation is still an important procedural aspect of the right to life. When normal investigative procedures are not possible, such investigations may be conducted by special bodies set up for this very purpose, for example, by the government and/or the UN.[138] Nonetheless, without searching for and collecting bodies, such investigations are often severely limited.

58 Once bodies have been searched for and collected, if some of the rules that follow relating to treatment of the bodies are not complied with, there is the possibility that those responsible will incur legal consequences, including criminal sanctions. Under the ICC Statute, it is a war crime, in both an IAC and a NIAC, to commit 'outrages upon personal dignity'.[139] According to the ICC Elements of Crimes, to be guilty of this war crime, the perpetrator must have 'humiliated, degraded or otherwise violated the dignity of one or more persons'.[140] This includes dead persons, as the victim does not need to be personally aware of the violation.[141] This element of the crime also takes into consideration, where relevant, the cultural background of the victim.[142] As such, it is clear that there could be criminal sanctions for pillaging and/or despoiling dead bodies. Furthermore, given the reference to cultural considerations, if a dead person's religious practices are not respected in the treatment of the corpse, a case could be made that a war crime has been committed.

59 Even prior to the ICC Statute, mistreatment of dead bodies during conflict was prosecuted as a war crime. In 1947, in the United States General Military Government Court at Dachau, Max Schmid was found guilty of a war crime for 'wilfully, deliberately and wrongfully encourag[ing], aid[ing], abet[ting] and participat[ing] in the maltreatment of a dead unknown member of the United States Army'.[143] Furthermore, the judgment

---

[135] See, e.g., Art 13 ECHR.   [136] See Krähenmann, above n 70, at 3.1.2.
[137] See ECtHR, *Varnava*, above n 26, para 201.
[138] Ibid, paras 170–7.
[139] Art 8(2)(b)(xxi) (for IACs) and Art 8(2)(c)(ii) (for NIACs) ICC Statute.
[140] ICC Elements of Crimes, UN Doc PCNICC/2000/1/Add.2 (2000), at 29 and 35.
[141] Ibid, 27 fn 49 and 33 fn 57, which state: 'For this crime, "persons" can include dead persons. It is understood that the victim need not personally be aware of the existence of the humiliation or degradation or other violation. This element takes into account relevant aspects of the cultural background of the victim.'
[142] Ibid.
[143] See *Trial of Max Schmid*, United States General Military Government Court, Dachau, 1947, UNWCC Law Reports, vol XIII, at 151, para 1, 'The Charges'.

went on to list examples of other military courts of various other countries that had found defendants guilty of similar offences.[144]

More recently, in a case before the International Criminal Tribunal for Rwanda (ICTR),[145] the Appeals Chamber referred to the notion that desecrating a dead body is condemned under international law. It went on to set out an extensive list of the domestic jurisdictions that have criminalized degrading the dignity of the corpse or interfering with dead bodies, thus suggesting that such violations are condemned under customary international criminal law.[146] 60

As mentioned earlier (see MN 52), various international human rights bodies have also found that the mistreatment of a dead body can lead to inhuman and degrading treatment of the relatives of the deceased.[147] 61

There is therefore little question that mistreating a dead body can amount to a war crime, and even to a human rights violation of the deceased's next of kin. What is less clear, however, is what constitutes this mistreatment. Many of the earlier cases referred to in the preceding paragraphs related to cannibalism or mutilation of bodies. Disrespectful treatment of bodies has also been deemed ill-treatment.[148] In the *Tadić* case, the prosecution argued that a crime against humanity had been committed under Article 5(i) (other inhumane acts) of the Statute of the International Criminal Tribunal for the former Yugoslavia (ICTY), by the discharging of the contents of a fire extinguisher into a dead body.[149] The Trial Chamber conceded that in the past, certain acts against dead bodies had been considered to be war crimes, including failure to comply with IHL on treatment of the war dead.[150] Furthermore, it accepted that an 'inhumane act' can ordinarily refer to a living or a dead person.[151] Nevertheless, it took the view that in light of the acts listed in Article 5(i) of the ICTY Statute, 'other inhumane acts' must relate to living individuals so as to be in keeping with the other types of acts enumerated, in accordance with the *ejusdem generis* rule.[152] 62

It is also worth considering whether acts such as taking photographs of, or with, dead bodies, or even of coffins returning home, would violate the prohibition of ill-treatment of dead bodies such as to amount to a war crime. Other provisions of the Geneva Conventions, namely Article 13 GC III and Article 27 GC IV, regulate this via the prohibition on subjecting POWs and protected persons to 'public curiosity'. Often violations of this kind are treated by domestic military tribunals, as can be seen in the case of the photographs taken at Abu Ghraib prison in Iraq. Furthermore, even if the taking of a photo or video is not unlawful per se, it may in fact be evidence of unlawful behaviour. For example, in January 2012, footage of US marines urinating on the dead bodies of Afghanis was widely reported in the media and, although also likely to be a violation of IHL, the men involved were charged under domestic military law. For violations of IHL relating to the dead, such as the mistreatment of dead bodies, domestic legal rules are likely to be used most frequently. 63

---

[144] Ibid, at 151–2 and notes thereto.
[145] ICTR, *Théoneste Bagosora and Anatole Nsengiyumva v The Prosecutor*, Appeals Chamber Judgment, ICTR-98-41-A, 14 December 2011, para 82.
[146] Ibid, at 729.   [147] See cases referred to above n 128.
[148] E.g., ibid.
[149] ICTY, *The Prosecutor v Duško Tadić*, Trial Chamber Judgment, IT-94-1T, 7 May 1997, para 748.
[150] Ibid.   [151] Ibid.   [152] Ibid.

E. Critical Assessment

64 The rules on the fate and humane treatment of the deceased safeguard their dignity; they also impact upon the families' experience of loss, as well as on the narrative and healing of a country. Like most of the other laws of armed conflict, they remind those engaged in the theatre of war that the enemy is still a person and must be treated with respect. It is unclear whether there is more or less respect for these laws today than when the Geneva Conventions were first conceived, but what is apparent is that violations, or even questionable conduct, especially that relating to the treatment of the dead, are far more likely to enter the public domain. The proliferation of the media and the Internet has meant that when soldiers forget or dismiss the humanity of their enemy by urinating on dead bodies or defacing them in other ways, the world is made aware of it, and the offenders are forced to account for their behaviour in one way or another.

65 Another interesting phenomenon today is the interaction of IHL, criminal law, politics, and emerging fields like transitional justice. In recent times there have been a handful of leaders who have been painted as enemies of 'the West' or 'democracy'. Such leaders, like Saddam Hussein, Osama bin Laden, and Muammar Gaddafi, have been hunted down and either captured or killed. The problem, however, is what to do with them once found or captured—to put them on trial, where, under what law, and so on. Countries engaged in such operations are required, of course, to follow international law, but often there are competing interests. Even if such leaders are killed in the course of war, as has been discussed, the question of what to do with their bodies becomes paramount. Should there be a different set of laws for 'tyrannical' leaders who have died during combat? Should there be laws that take into account the risk of their graves becoming shrines, or conversely the risk of their graves being defaced, or even the need for a population to heal and how best this may be facilitated (for example, putting the dead body on display, dumping the body at sea, or burying the body in an undisclosed unmarked grave)? It seems that at least with the more recent examples, there have been attempts to justify the treatment of dead leaders as being in compliance with IHL, but it is not clear whether this is just a retrospective justification once the political decision of how to treat the deceased has been made. It is impossible to pass conclusive judgment on this, but what must be reiterated is that, regardless of the actions of the deceased prior to their deaths, basic principles of justice must be followed as set out in international law.

DANIELA GAVSHON*

---

* I would like to thank Sandra Krähennman, PhD Graduate Institute of International and Development Studies, for her revision of this chapter.

Chapter 15. Taking of Hostages

	MN
A. Introduction	1
I. Historical context	4
II. Hostage-taking in international law	11
a. International humanitarian law treaties	12
b. International human rights law	17
B. Meaning and Application	21
I. Victims of hostage-taking	21
II. The core elements of hostage-taking	26
a. '[S]eized, detained or otherwise held hostage one or more persons'	28
b. '[T]hreatened to kill, injure or continue to detain such […] persons'	34
c. '[I]ntended to compel [a third party] to act or refrain from acting'	38
d. The elements of hostage-taking: express or implicit?	41
III. Unlawful deprivation of liberty: an element of hostage-taking?	45
C. Relevance in Non-International Armed Conflicts	54
D. Legal Consequences of a Violation	58
I. The International Convention against the Taking of Hostages	60
II. Statutes of international criminal courts and tribunals	65
III. Other international treaties	68
E. Critical Assessment	69

Select Bibliography

Burgos, H.S., 'The Taking of Hostages and International Humanitarian Law', 29 *IRRC* 270 (1989) 196

Carrillo-Suarez, A., '*Hors de logique*: Contemporary Issues in International Humanitarian Law as Applied to Internal Armed Conflict', 15 *American University International Law Review* (1999-2000) 1

Elliott, W., 'Hostages or Prisoners of War: War Crimes at Dinner', 149 *Military Law Review* (1995) 241

Dörmann, K. et al, *Elements of War Crimes under the Rome Statute of the International Criminal Court: Sources and Commentary* (Cambridge: CUP, 2003), at 124–7 and 406–7

Hammer, E./Salvin, M., 'The Taking of Hostages in Theory and Practice', 38 *AJIL* (1944) 1

Herrman, I./Palmieri, D., 'A Haunting Figure: The Hostage Through the Ages', 87 *IRRC* 857 (2005) 135

Rosenstock, R., 'The International Convention against the Taking of Hostages: Another International Community Step against Terrorism', 9 *Denver Journal of International Law and Policy* (1980) 169

Verwey, W., 'The International Hostages Convention and National Liberation Movements', 75(1) *AJIL* (1981) 69

Wilder, S., 'International Terrorism and Hostage-Taking: An Overview', 11 *Manitoba Law Journal* (1981) 367

Lord Wright, 'The Killing of Hostages as a War Crime', 25 *BYBIL* (1948) 296

A. Introduction

1 Article 34 of the Fourth Geneva Convention (GC IV), which is applicable during international armed conflict (IAC), states that '[t]he taking of hostages is prohibited'. This proscription is articulated in similarly concise terms in Article 75(2)(c) of the First Additional Protocol (AP I). For non-international armed conflict (NIAC), it is stated in Common Article 3 of the four Geneva Conventions of 1949 and in Article 4(2)(c) of the Second Additional Protocol (AP II). Notably, however, GC III does not expressly protect prisoners of war (POWs) from being treated as hostages during IAC: an omission that is irreconcilable with the humanitarian intent of this absolute prohibition during armed conflict.

2 The fundamental issue of hostage-taking is that its meaning 'has never acquired any real degree of precision and the vagaries in its application have been carried over, almost unconsciously, into legal issues'.[1] International humanitarian law (IHL) does not define hostage-taking, which results in its constituent elements—and the content of each—being subject to varied interpretations. The definition of hostage-taking has, however, been refined by, inter alia, the decisions of international criminal tribunals and scholarly opinion, which help to clarify the meaning of the prohibition for the purposes of the Geneva Conventions and their Additional Protocols.

3 Ultimately, this commentary proposes a definition of hostage-taking for the purposes of its prohibition under the Geneva Conventions and their Protocols, which govern the conduct of parties to armed conflict. By this definition, hostage-taking occurs where one or more persons were seized, detained, or otherwise held hostage in order to compel a third party to act or refrain from acting, and these person(s) were threatened, expressly or implicitly, with *death* or *injury* or *unlawful deprivation of liberty* as a consequence of the third party's failure to act or refrain from acting. With this definition, this commentary hopes to clarify the meaning of the prohibition of hostage-taking under the Geneva Conventions and their Additional Protocols, and to ensure its consistency with the historical foundation of the prohibition, as well as with contemporary IHL, and, where appropriate, with other bodies of law and scholarly writing. Notably, under this definition—and provided that all of the requisite criteria are fulfilled—persons may be considered to be hostages even where they are otherwise *lawfully* deprived of their liberty. Likewise, a person may be considered to be a hostage if—in order to extract concessions from a third party—he or she is threatened with detention that continues to be, or that will become, unlawful.

I. Historical context

4 Hostage-taking during armed conflict is known to have occurred since the fourth century BCE. Historically, the hostage was offered, one state to another, as a guarantee of the performance of treaty obligations in force between the two, or as a symbol of 'submission on the part of the vanquished' *post bello*.[2] Such 'surety hostages'[3] were selected for their symbolic value as representatives of the state, were offered 'voluntarily',[4] and were treated

---

[1] H. Cooper, 'Law and Practice in Throes of Evolution', 15 *Case Western Reserve JIL* (1983) 61, at 64.
[2] I. Herrman and D. Palmieri, 'A Haunting Figure: The Hostage through the Ages', 87 *IRRC* 857 (2005) 135, at 137.
[3] W. Elliott, 'Hostages or Prisoners of War: War Crimes at Dinner', 149 *Military Law Review* (1995) 241, at 243–4.
[4] Herrman and Palmieri, above n 2, at 137–8.

in a manner befitting their status.[5] Commonplace until the mid-eighteenth century,[6] hostages as a guarantee of treaty obligations were gradually abandoned in favour of security established by the 'temporary transfer of control of territory'.[7]

From the heyday of the Roman Empire[8] until the conclusion of the Second World War, hostages have been taken by the Occupying Power from amongst the occupied population to ensure security and compliance with the occupier's laws.[9] To this end, there have been two principal and distinguishable forms of hostage-taking. In the first, so-called 'prophylactic hostage taking',[10] prominent persons have been taken into custody and 'punished'—often executed—upon the *subsequent* wrongdoing of members of the community concerned.[11] In the second, persons have been taken captive *after* the alleged wrongdoing, and their release or continued well-being has been made contingent upon surrender of the culprits by the local community.[12]

The term 'hostage-taking' has also been used to describe a scenario in which the Occupying Power has responded to criminal activity by executing members of the community.[13] In this situation, which has also been referred to as the taking of 'reprisal prisoners', inhabitants of occupied territory have been 'seized and shot *after* the occurrence of [criminal] acts without being held in detention'.[14] In such cases, however, the victim has, prima facie, not been treated as a hostage because, as considered in MN 28–33 of this chapter, deprivation of liberty is an essential precondition to hostage-taking.

Since at least the Middle Ages, there is evidence that persons 'captured in combat' have been held in exchange for ransom.[15] This practice persists to date. Hostages have also been used to deter attacks, including attacks otherwise permitted by humanitarian law,[16] to ensure reciprocal good treatment of persons deprived of liberty,[17] and to achieve various tactical and political ends, such as to induce the opposing party to the conflict to release detainees within its power.

Lastly, the term 'hostage' has also been used to describe apparently arbitrary and anarchic capture and executions.[18] This situation, illegal though it is,[19] may be difficult to reconcile with the definition of hostage-taking under humanitarian law for lack of a discernible intention on the part of the hostage-taker to extract a concession from a third party (see MN 38–40).

---

[5] Elliott, above n 3, at 243–4.
[6] Although some isolated examples also occurred in the nineteenth century. See Herrman and Palmieri, above n 2, at 138 and 141. There are indications too that the British withheld Argentinean POWs to 'guarantee the armistice' following the Falkland Islands war (Cooper, above n 1, at 62, fn 4). See Pictet Commentary GC IV, at 230.
[7] Elliott, above n 3, at 244.   [8] Ibid.
[9] E. Hammer and M. Salvin, 'The Taking of Hostages in Theory and Practice', 38 *AJIL* (1944) 1, at 20–1.
[10] Elliott, above n 3, at 244.   [11] Herrman and Palmieri, above n 2, at 141–2.
[12] Elliott, above n 3, at 245–6.
[13] Lord Wright, 'The Killing of Hostages as a War Crime', 25 *BYBIL* (1948) 296, at 298.
[14] Ibid (emphasis added). See also Elliott, above n 3, at 248. Contrast, however, Dinstein, who describes 'reprisal prisoners' as 'taken into custody for the purposes of guaranteeing with their lives the future good conduct of the population of the community from which they were taken': Y. Dinstein, *The Conduct of Hostilities under the Law of International Armed Conflict* (Cambridge: CUP, 2004), at 227, referring to the *Hostage Case (US v List et al)*, American Military Tribunal, Nuremberg, 1948, UNWCC Law Reports, vol VIII, paras 1230 and 1253.
[15] Elliott, above n 3, at 244.   [16] Hammer and Salvin, above n 9, at 31–2.
[17] H.S. Burgos, 'The Taking of Hostages and International Humanitarian Law', 29 *IRRC* 270 (1989) 196, at 200.
[18] Herrman and Palmieri, above n 2, at 142 and 145.
[19] See, e.g., CA 3; Art 4 AP II; Arts 12 and 50 GC I; Arts 12 and 51 GC II; Arts 13, 99–108, and 130 GC III; Arts 27, 71–76, and 147 GC IV; and Arts 11, 75, and 85 AP I.

9   Until the end of the Second World War, hostage-taking was 'an accepted part of warfare'[20] and, within certain parameters, lawful. In the seminal case on the legality of hostage-taking during the Second World War, *Wilhelm List*,[21] the United States (US) Military Tribunal deemed, first, that the taking of hostages was permissible only under 'very restrictive conditions and subject to certain rather extensive safeguards [...] [and, secondly, that] after a judicial finding of strict compliance with all pre-conditions and as a last desperate remedy hostages may even be sentenced to death'.[22]

10   The first element of the Tribunal's finding in *Wilhelm List*, that hostage-taking was not prohibited per se, finds support in the literature of the time.[23] It is evident that hostage-taking had a 'legal form' during the Second World War,[24] which included hostage-taking in occupied territory to maintain law and order.[25] Against this background, the proscription of hostage-taking in the Geneva Conventions was 'to some extent a departure from international law as it stood at the time, [according to which] the possibility of an Occupying Power taking hostages as a measure of last resort and under certain strict conditions [remained open]'.[26] Departure though it was, the effect of the Geneva Conventions is an absolute prohibition on hostage-taking, thus concluding, *a fortiori*, any lingering debate as to the legality of putting such hostages to death.[27]

II. Hostage-taking in international law

11   The present commentary is concerned with hostage-taking under the Geneva Conventions and their Additional Protocols; it seeks to elucidate the prohibition of hostage-taking as it binds parties to armed conflict. To do so, however, this commentary relies upon international criminal law (ICL)—including the International Criminal Court (ICC) Statute and the Statutes and case law of international criminal tribunals—which contains established definitions and interpretations of hostage-taking as a war crime. Where differences are manifest between elements of a definition that would govern the conduct of parties to a conflict and that which would determine the conduct of individuals for criminal law purposes, this commentary attempts to identify the disparity and emphasize the former.

a. *International humanitarian law treaties*

12   With regard to IAC,[28] Article 34 GC IV prohibits in absolute terms[29] taking as hostage a protected civilian within the meaning of Article 4 of the same Convention. Consequently, certain categories of persons are excluded from protection on the basis of their nationality.[30]

---

[20] Elliott, above n 3, at 243.   [21] *Hostage Case (US v List et al)*, above n 14, para 1230.
[22] Wright, above n 13, at 308. See also the *US Basic Field Manual of Law Warfare*, '[h]ostages taken and held for the declared purpose of insuring against unlawful acts by the enemy forces or people may be punished or put to death if the unlawful acts are nevertheless committed. Reprisals against prisoners of war are expressly forbidden by the Geneva Convention of 1929' (Wright, at 304).
[23] Hammer, above n 9, at 20 and 29–32; and Wright, above n 13, at 296, 302, and 310.
[24] Hammer, above n 9, at 27.   [25] Ibid, at 26–9.
[26] ICRC CIHL Study, vol I, at 334.
[27] '[N]ot only the execution but even the taking of hostages is prohibited': H-P. Gasser and K. Dörmann, 'Protection of the Civilian Population', in D. Fleck (ed), *The Handbook of International Humanitarian Law* (3rd edn, Oxford: OUP, 2013) 231, at 279. See also Pictet Commentary GC IV, 231. See further ICTY, *The Prosecutor v Dario Kordić et al*, Appeals Chamber Judgment, IT-95-14/2-A, 17 December 2004, paras 687–9.
[28] Art 2 GC I–GC IV; and Art 1 AP I. For NIAC, see MN 54–57.
[29] Pictet Commentary GC IV, Art 34, at 231.   [30] See Ch 55 of this volume.

The reach of the prohibition on hostage-taking in IAC is extended by Article 75(2)(c) 13
AP I, which covers 'persons who are in the power of a Party to the conflict, affected by
conflict or occupation and who do not benefit from more favourable treatment under
the Conventions'. As such, it extends protection to '[r]efugees and stateless persons [...]
[m]ercenaries [...] [o]ther persons denied prisoner-of-war status [and] [p]rotected persons
subject to Article 5 of the Fourth Convention'.[31]

Lastly for IAC, Article 147 GC IV designates violation of the prohibition of 14
hostage-taking as amounting to a grave breach, which is subject to the mechanism that is
established for the criminal prosecution of alleged perpetrators.[32]

In NIAC—considered in more detail at MN 54–57—Common Article 3 and Article 15
4(2)(c) AP II expressly prohibit the taking of hostages.

Importantly, the term 'hostage' does not connote a classification of persons for the 16
purposes of IHL.[33] Rather, under the IHL of IAC and NIAC, persons deprived of their
liberty are classified as either protected civilians[34] or POWs in the former,[35] and as persons
hors de combat in the latter. Hostage-taking, by contrast, is a treatment to which persons
are subject.[36]

b. International human rights law

Human rights treaties do not refer expressly to hostage-taking. This, however, does not 17
preclude the latter's proscription by one or more of the provisions of the former. The United
Nations (UN) High Commissioner for Human Rights has '[e]mphasize[d] that the taking
of hostages, wherever and by whomever committed, constitutes a serious obstacle to the
full enjoyment of all human rights'.[37] Such 'rights' may be divided into two categories:

— rights that prohibit the taking of hostages per se, in particular the prohibition on
arbitrary detention;
— rights which protect the hostage from certain treatment *after* he or she has been
deprived of liberty, such as the right to life.

Article 9 of the International Covenant on Civil and Political Rights (ICCPR)—which 18
is used here as *indicative* also of the rule included in regional human rights instruments—
protects individuals from detention, 'except on such grounds and in accordance
with such procedure as are established by law'.[38] Whether an identified instance of

---

[31] ICRC Commentary APs, at 869–71, paras 3022–66. In relation to the protection under Art 75 of 'nationals of a State Party to the conflict vis-à-vis that State', see also para 2926 (concerning Art 72) and paras 3017–18.

[32] Art 146 GC IV. See Ch 31 of this volume.

[33] Art 34 GC IV prohibits taking protected civilians as hostages. Thus, implicitly, 'protected civilian' is the individual's status, hostage-taking the treatment to which he or she is subject.

[34] Art 4 GC IV.   [35] Art 4 GC III.

[36] On the distinction between the right to personal liberty and 'mistreatment', see M. Nowak, *UN Covenant on Civil and Political Rights: CCPR Commentary* (2nd edn, Kehl: N.P. Engel Verlag, 2005), at 212–13. See also Ch 35 of this volume.

[37] UNHCHR, 'Hostage-Taking', Res 1996/62, 58th meeting, 23 April 1996.

[38] Art 9(1) ICCPR. Note that Art 9 may be subject to derogation 'in time of public emergency which threatens the life of the nation', but 'no measure derogating from the provisions of the Covenant may be inconsistent with the State Party's other obligations under international law, particularly the rules of international humanitarian law'. See Art 4 ICCPR; HRCttee, *CCPR General Comment 29, Article 4: Derogations during a State of Emergency*, CCPR/C/21/Rev.1/Add.11, 31 August 2001, 3, 9, and 16.

hostage-taking will be in violation of Article 9 ICCPR is best understood by consideration of two principal contexts:

— In the first context the detaining authority has no legislative basis or other authority for the deprivation of liberty. Here, the hostage-taking is not, or ceases to be, pursuant to legislation describing 'the grounds on which an individual may be deprived of his liberty and the procedures to be used',[39] and consequently is in violation of Article 9.

— In the second context, the detaining authority has sought to establish a legislative basis for hostage-taking per se. That is, it has enacted legislation that foresees detention in pursuance of concessions from a third party, which are compelled by threats against the person deprived of his or her liberty. Here, it is important to note that the Human Rights Committee has recognized that legislative prescription in and of itself does not authorize the state to engage in detention of all types.[40] Hostage-taking cannot fall within the ambit of permissible detention under international human rights law, both because it is otherwise prohibited by international law[41] and because it is characterized by violations of accompanying rights, such as the principle of individual criminal responsibility.[42] As such, under Article 9 ICCPR, a state cannot purport to enact law to authorize hostage-taking per se.

19   Also noteworthy is the situation in which persons have been deprived of their liberty in accordance with a legal basis, have been afforded all of the requisite safeguards of Article 9, and have subsequently been treated as hostages. Here, the fact of the hostage-taking does not, *ipso facto*, render the deprivation of liberty in violation of Article 9, because, as discussed in this chapter, hostage-taking is a treatment to which persons are subject and, as such, does not necessarily affect the underlying legality of the detention.

20   In addition to Article 9, hostage-taking may threaten certain rights of the individual in the course of his or her deprivation of liberty. These include the rights to life,[43] freedom of movement,[44] humane treatment in detention,[45] fair trial,[46] and the prohibitions on torture[47] and enforced disappearance.[48] These rights, which do not prohibit hostage-taking per se, are not recalled in detail in this commentary.

---

[39] R. Lillich, 'Civil Rights', in T. Meron (ed), *Human Rights in International Law: Legal and Policy Issues* (Oxford: OUP, 1984) 115, at 138.

[40] HRCttee, *A v Australia*, Comm No 560/1993, UN Doc CCPR/C/59/D/560/1993 (1997), 9.2. The deprivation of liberty must also be both reasonable and necessary (HRCttee, *Womah Mukong v Cameroon*, Comm No 458/1991, UN Doc CCPR/C/51/D/458/1991 (1994), 9.8).

[41] HRCttee, *A v Australia*, above n 40, 9.2.

[42] That is, by the very character of hostage-taking, the hostage is not deprived of his or her liberty for his or her own personal wrongdoing. Neither the ICCPR nor the ECHR expressly includes the principle of individual criminal responsibility, but the ECtHR has recognized it as a corollary to the presumption of innocence. See ECtHR, *AP, MP, and TP v Switzerland*, Judgment, 29 August 1997, paras 37–9. The principle—defined as a right not to be punished for the acts of others—is, however, enshrined in Art 5(3) ACHR, concerning 'humane treatment', and Art 7(2) ACHPR. Under IHL, see Art 33 GC IV; Art 75(4)(b) AP I; and Art 6(2)(b) AP II.

[43] Art 6 ICCPR.   [44] Art 12 ICCPR.   [45] Art 10 ICCPR.   [46] Art 14 ICCPR.

[47] Art 7 ICCPR. See also Art 1 CAT. It might be argued that hostage-taking by definition violates the prohibition on torture. Consider as indicative the HRCttee's Communications in relation to capital punishment and Art 7 ICCPR. See, e.g., HRCttee, *Francis v Jamaica*, Comm No 606/1994, UN Doc CCPR/C/54/D/606/1994 (1995).

[48] International Convention for the Protection of All Persons from Enforced Disappearances.

B. Meaning and Application

I. Victims of hostage-taking

From among the four Geneva Conventions, only GC IV contains the prohibition of the taking of hostages during IAC. That is, persons other than protected civilians under GC IV are not envisaged as the victims of hostage-taking. Consequently, under the Geneva Conventions alone, POWs cannot be considered to be treated as hostages.[49]

A logical response to the exclusion of POWs from protection against hostage-taking is that POWs are so protected by Common Article 3 paragraph 1(1)(b), despite its applicability, prima facie, only to NIAC.[50]

Alternatively, POWs may be protected against hostage-taking by way of customary IHL. The International Committee of the Red Cross (ICRC) Customary International Humanitarian Law (CIHL) Study contends that the victims of hostage-taking are not limited to protected civilians.[51] To arrive at this conclusion, the authors cite Common Article 3, the Elements of Crimes of the ICC, and the International Convention against the Taking of Hostages (Hostages Convention).[52] As considered below (see MN 60–64), under the Hostages Convention, which to date has been ratified or acceded to by 167 states, POWs *can be* considered to be hostages during IAC. Adding further support to this contention, few national military manuals preclude POWs' being understood as hostages,[53] and several expressly contemplate such persons as objects of the prohibition.[54]

There is evidence that the International Criminal Tribunal for the former Yugoslavia (ICTY) concurs with this result. The Trial Chamber in *Blaškić* found that Article 3 ICTY Statute, applicable to both IAC and NIAC,[55] 'includes' a prohibition on 'hostage-taking'[56] that extends to the objects envisaged by Common Article 3.[57] The Tribunal distinguished this crime from 'taking civilians as hostage'[58]—a grave breach, as per Article 2 ICTY Statute—and determined that both had been violated in a single instance of hostage-taking[59] during IAC.[60] In the hostage-taking under consideration, 'not all [the

---

[49] Amongst others, without explanation, Dinstein finds to the contrary: 'Although in practice the victims of hostage taking in wartime are usually civilians, there is no reason to regard them as the sole beneficiaries of the norm. No hostage can be taken, whether civilians, combatants (especially, prisoners of war), or even neutrals': Y. Dinstein, *The Conduct of Hostilities under the Law of International Armed Conflict* (2nd edn, Cambridge: CUP, 2010), at 227.

[50] The ICJ in the *Nicaragua* case determined that the protections afforded by CA 3 also apply to the benefit of persons placed *hors de combat* during IAC: ICJ, *Case concerning Military and Paramilitary Activities in and against Nicaragua (Nicaragua v USA)*, Judgment, 27 June 1986, para 218, borrowing from *Corfu Channel (United Kingdom v Albania)*, Judgment, 9 April 1949, para 22. See Ch 4 of this volume.

[51] ICRC CIHL Study, vol I, 336.   [52] Ibid.

[53] Mirroring IHL, many military manuals prohibit only the 'taking of hostages'. See ibid, vol II, 2264–8. Some manuals do, however, limit the prohibition to 'taking civilian hostages', thus excluding POWs. See, e.g., ibid, vol II, 2265.

[54] See, e.g., ibid, vol II, 2267.

[55] ICTY, *The Prosecutor v Tihomir Blaškić*, Trial Chamber Judgment, IT-95-14-T, 3 March 2000, para 161; and Jurisdiction, ICTY, *The Prosecutor v Duško Tadić*, Appeals Chamber Decision, IT-94-1, 2 October 1995, para 137.

[56] Art 3 ICTY Statute does not include an express prohibition on hostage-taking, but the acts identified are indicative, not exhaustive.

[57] *Blaškić*, Trial Chamber, above n 55, para 177.   [58] Described succinctly ibid, para 701.

[59] Ibid, para 708.

[60] On account of Croatia's direct involvement, ibid, para 94, and on account of overall control by Croatia, paras 122–3.

hostages] were necessarily civilians, [but] all were persons placed *hors de combat*'.[61] Put simply, for the ICTY the 'laws and customs of war' prohibit the use of persons placed *hors de combat* during IAC as hostages, thus establishing that POWs may be the victims of hostage-taking. This finding was not challenged upon appeal.[62]

25   Despite these compelling arguments, a POW cannot also be treated as a hostage if, as some sources suggest, hostage-taking is necessarily evidenced by an existing *unlawful* deprivation of liberty (see MN 45–52).

II. The core elements of hostage-taking

26   Although the Geneva Conventions and their Additional Protocols do not themselves contain a definition of hostage-taking, other bodies of law are more illuminating. The Hostages Convention, Article 1, for example, provides a comprehensive definition:

> Any person who seizes or detains and threatens to kill, to injure or to continue to detain another person [...] in order to compel a third party, namely, a State, an international intergovernmental organization, a natural or juridical person, or a group of persons, to do or abstain from doing any act as an explicit or implicit condition for the release of the hostage commits the offence of taking of hostages [...] within the meaning of this Convention.

The ICC Elements of Crimes, which were informed by the definition of hostage-taking in Article 1 of the Hostages Convention, describe the three principal elements of hostage-taking:

1. The perpetrator seized, detained or otherwise held hostage one or more persons.
2. The perpetrator threatened to kill, injure or continue to detain such person or persons.
3. The perpetrator intended to compel a State, an international organization, a natural or legal person or a group of persons to act or refrain from acting as an explicit or implicit condition for the safety or the release of such person or persons.[63]

Although sourced directly from ICL, these elements provide a basis from which to understand the prohibition of hostage-taking under IHL with—as noted below—adjustment to accommodate the particularities of the prohibition as it is applicable to the parties to an armed conflict.

27   These elements are equally applicable to hostage-taking for both IAC and NIAC.[64] This is supported by the jurisprudence of the ICTY.[65] For the purposes specifically of IHL, the Commentaries to AP I and AP II, Articles 75 and 4 respectively, being *ostensibly* the same, suggest that the elements of the prohibition ought also to be considered the same in each of the two forms of armed conflict.[66] In the following paragraphs, each of these elements is considered in turn.

---

[61] Ibid, para 708.
[62] ICTY, *The Prosecutor v Tihomir Blaškić*, Appeals Chamber Judgment, IT-95-14-A, 29 July 2004, paras 640–6.
[63] ICC Elements of Crimes, Arts 8(2)(a)(viii) and 8(2)(c)(iii).
[64] Compare ibid, Arts 8(2)(a)(viii) and 8(2)(c)(iii), 129, and 147.
[65] ICTY, *The Prosecutor v Dario Kordić et al*, Trial Chamber Judgment, IT-95-14/2-T, 26 February 2001, para 320. This finding was not challenged upon appeal: see *Kordić Appeals Chamber*, above n 27, particularly paras 932–9.
[66] ICRC Commentary APs, Art 75 AP I, at 874, para 3052; and Art 4 AP II, at 1375, para 4537. The requirement of an unlawful deprivation of liberty is, however, premised on the Pictet Commentary GC IV, Art 147, applicable exclusively to IAC.

a. '[S]eized, detained or otherwise held hostage one or more persons'

Central to the act of hostage-taking is the deprivation of the victim's liberty. For IHL, the Pictet Commentary to Article 34, borrowing wording from Article 4 GC IV, portrays the hostage as being 'in the hands of the enemy'.[67] This describes, on the narrowest possible interpretation, any deprivation of liberty akin to that of imprisonment.[68] Under the Hostages Convention the phrase 'seizes or detains'—which is reproduced and broadened by the Elements of Crimes as 'seized, detained or *otherwise held hostage*'[69]—connotes the same requirement. Similarly, the ICTY has expressly defined hostage-taking as entailing a 'deprivation of liberty'.[70] Using varying terminology, sometimes simply replicating the wording of the Hostages Convention,[71] domestic legislation too outlines this requirement.[72] On the basis of these formative sources, the first element of the definition of hostage-taking for the purposes of IHL, which is proposed herein, is: *One or more persons were seized, detained, or otherwise held hostage.*

28

The difficult question associated with this element is whether, for the purposes exclusively of state responsibility, large populations, whole countries, or all of the inhabitants of an occupied territory can be held hostage *en masse* by an Occupying Power? This was the assertion of several states during the drafting of the Hostages Convention:[73] an assertion that finds some support in the Pictet Commentary to Article 34 GC IV, which describes the hostage as being 'in the hands of the enemy'.[74] This phrase, 'in the hands of the enemy', is that of the text of Article 4 GC IV, used to identify protected persons; the Pictet Commentary, in turn, reads:

29

> The expression 'in the hands of' is used in an extremely general sense. It is not merely a question of being in enemy hands directly, as a prisoner is. The mere fact of being in the territory of a Party to the conflict or in occupied territory implies that one is in the power or 'hands' of the Occupying Power.[75]

There is thus a contention—*lex ferenda*—that the hostage need merely be 'in occupied territory', and not deprived of liberty in the narrower sense connoted by the term 'imprisonment'. Indeed, this interpretation would be consistent with the historical context in which the absolute prohibition of hostage-taking under humanitarian law abruptly arose. That is, it would serve to protect the population of occupied territory from threats to their life or well-being where the Occupying Power purports to extract security assurances or other concessions.

30

For the purposes of the elements of hostage-taking, this situation would be best described by the phraseology employed by the ICC Statute—'otherwise held hostage'[76]—which

31

---

[67] Pictet Commentary GC IV, Art 34, at 228.   [68] Ibid, Art 4, at 47.
[69] Emphasis added. See K. Dörmann et al, *Elements of War Crimes under the Rome Statute of the International Criminal Court: Sources and Commentary* (Cambridge: CUP, 2003), at 125.
[70] *Kordić*, Trial Chamber, above n 65, para 312; and *Blaškić*, Trial Chamber, above n 55, para 158.
[71] See, e.g., Australia's Crimes (Hostages) Act 1989 (Cth), s 7(a).
[72] In some national legislation, the deprivation of liberty is inherent in the notion of hostage-taking. E.g., this element is described as the 'taking or holding a person as hostage' in the Criminal Code of the Republic of Uzbekistan, 1994, Art 245, and as 'kidnapping or keeping hostage' in the Criminal Code of the Republic of Albania, 1995 (consolidated version as of 1 December 2004), Art 109.
[73] R. Rosenstock, 'The International Convention against the Taking of Hostages: Another International Community Step against Terrorism', 9 *Denver Journal of International Law and Policy* (1980) 169, at 177.
[74] Pictet Commentary GC IV, Art 34, at 229.   [75] Ibid, Art 4, at 47.
[76] This phrase is described by Dörmann et al, above n 69, at 124, as being 'adapted [from the Hostages Convention] to the context of armed conflict'.

would encompass circumstances other than detention or imprisonment in the narrow sense. This phrase is retained in the definition of hostage-taking proposed herein.

32   There remain, however, two principal limitations to the contention that 'otherwise held hostage' may encompass all persons in occupied territory for the purposes of hostage-taking under IHL:

— First, the contention is contingent upon demonstrating—contrary to some robust indicators (see MN 45–52)—that hostage-taking does not necessarily require an *unlawful* seizure, detention, or 'otherwise holding'. International humanitarian law does not prohibit occupation but seeks to regulate the conduct of the Occupying Power, and in doing so to protect the local population therein. Thus, whether or not a particular instance of occupation violates *jus ad bellum*, the situation of the general population of occupied territory cannot be equated with *unlawful* seizure, detention, or 'otherwise holding' under *jus in bello*.

— Secondly, the contention is incompatible with the fact that a threat of *continued* detention or 'otherwise holding' (see MN 34–37) in pursuance of concessions from a third party would suffice to establish hostage-taking. In particular, an Occupying Power would violate the prohibition of hostage-taking for threatening to continue the occupation in the course of otherwise bona fide negotiations to end it.

To overcome these challenges, the definition of hostage-taking proposed herein (see MN 3 or 69) foresees that (i) hostage-taking may encompass situations of lawful deprivation of liberty or 'otherwise holding', where threats are made against the life or well-being of the hostage; and that (ii) a threat of continued lawful detention or 'otherwise holding' would not suffice to amount to hostage-taking. Thus, for the purposes of the inhabitants of occupied territory, the threat would necessarily need to be against their life or well-being, not merely a threat of continued occupation.

33   In any event, were this contention to succeed, the mere fact of an individual's presence in occupied territory would be insufficient to conclude that he or she is a hostage. To amount to hostage-taking, the other elements of the prohibited act—namely, a threat against the individual in order to extract concessions from a third party—must also be demonstrable.

b. '[T]hreatened to kill, injure or continue to detain such [...] persons'

34   To amount to hostage-taking, the deprivation of liberty must be accompanied by a threat against the hostage. The Commentaries to both Article 34 GC IV and Article 75 AP I contemplate this requirement with the phrase 'answer with their freedom or their life'.[77] This short phrase is further developed by the ICRC Commentary to AP II to read 'answer with their freedom, their physical integrity or their life'.[78] Humanitarian law thus envisages that a threat to the well-being of the hostage, such as torture, cruel, inhuman, or degrading treatment, would suffice to trigger hostage-taking. Noting, in particular, that since the definition of torture in Article 1 of the Convention against Torture encompasses mental pain or suffering, it is reasonable to conclude that a threat of psychological harm would suffice for the purposes of this element of hostage-taking.

---

[77] Pictet Commentary GC IV, Art 34, at 228; and ICRC Commentary APs, Art 75 AP I, at 874, para 3052.
[78] ICRC Commentary APs, Art 4 AP II, at 1375, para 4537.

In international criminal law, the ICTY, in its decision in *Blaškić*, describes hostages 35
as 'sometimes under threat of death',[79] but references the Pictet Commentary to Article
147 GC IV, which itself adds a 'threat [...] to prolong the hostage's detention'.[80] The
Appeals Chamber finds that 'a situation of hostage-taking exists when a person seizes or
detains and threatens to kill, injure or continue to detain another person'.[81] In *Kordić*, the
Tribunal also considers the Pictet Commentary but goes further, describing this element
of hostage-taking as a 'conditional threat in respect of the physical and mental well-being
of civilians'.[82]

It is thus established that hostage-taking entails, in the words of the Hostages 36
Convention—from which the ICC Elements of Crimes borrow verbatim—a threat 'to
kill, to injure or to continue to detain'.

For the purposes of hostage-taking under IHL, this element is best described as: *The* 37
person(s) were threatened [...] with death or injury or unlawful deprivation of liberty as a
consequence of the third party's failure to act or refrain from acting. Notably, this commentary proposes that 'unlawful' ought to modify the phrase 'deprivation of liberty'. Thus,
whereas a threat of continued lawful detention would not suffice for hostage-taking, a
threat of continued unlawful detention, or a threat to detain the individual unlawfully
in the future, would meet the requirements of this element of the prohibition (see MN
45–52).

c. '[I]ntended to compel [a third party] to act or refrain from acting'

The 'intention'—borrowing the lexis of criminal law—on the part of the hostage-taker 38
that a third party act or refrain from acting in a particular fashion, is a fundamental component of hostage-taking. The Pictet Commentary, reflecting the form of hostage-taking
most prevalent immediately prior to the drafting of the Geneva Conventions, defines this
element as making the hostage 'answerable [...] for the execution of [the hostage-taker's]
orders and the security of his armed forces'.[83]

Article 1 of the Hostages Convention conveys the same sentiment, referring to an inten- 39
tion 'to compel a third party [...] to act or refrain from acting as an explicit or implicit
condition for the safety or the release of [the hostage]'. This wording has been embraced
by the ICC Elements of Crimes,[84] and is cited with approval by the ICRC CIHL Study,
albeit with the word 'intention' replaced by 'in order to'.[85] This change of wording serves
to distinguish the objective of criminal sanction—complete with *mens rea*—of the ICC
Elements of Crimes from the broader scope of hostage-taking as an international wrongful act of the state or any other party to an armed conflict.

Thus, in IHL, the phrase 'in order to compel' a third party to act or refrain from 40
acting—evidenced by a demand—is firmly established as a component of the definition.
For the purposes of the definition proposed herein, this element is retained simply as:
in order to compel a third party to act or refrain from acting.

---

[79] *Blaškić*, Trial Chamber, above n 55, para 158.
[80] Pictet Commentary GC IV, Art 147, at 600–1.
[81] *Blaškić*, Appeals Chamber, above n 62, para 639.
[82] *Kordić*, Trial Chamber, above n 65, para 312. The Appeals Chamber recognizes the importance of a 'threat' for the elements of hostage-taking in criminal law, above n 27, paras 936–8.
[83] Pictet Commentary GC IV, Art 34, at 229.
[84] ICC Elements of Crimes, Arts 8(2)(a)(viii) and 8(2)(c)(iii).
[85] ICRC CIHL Study, vol I, at 336.

d. The elements of hostage-taking: express or implicit?

41 Hostage-taking, as envisaged by the ICC Elements of Crimes and the Hostages Convention, recognizes that the intent to compel a third party may be an *'explicit or implicit* condition for the safety or the release of' the hostage.[86] Considering this element of the definition—albeit outside of the context of armed conflict—the US Court of Appeals, in the case *Simpson v Libya*, concluded that

> [t]he plain text of [...] the [Hostages] Convention [...] reflect[s] that a plaintiff need not allege that the hostage taker had communicated its intended purpose to the outside world [...] '[D]emands' are not required to establish the element of hostage taking: The words 'in order to compel' do not require more than a motivation on the part of the offender.[87]

42 Despite the conclusion of the US Court of Appeals, the Hostages Convention itself suggests another 'plain text' interpretation: whereas it is sufficient that the threat and its link to the ill-treatment or continued detention of the hostage—that is, its being a *'condition'*—be implicit, the 'demand' *itself* ought necessarily remain express. Textually, this is justified, because in the Convention 'explicit or implicit' modifies the term 'condition'. It is this alternative interpretation that Burgos describes most succinctly:

> The attempt to compel a third party to act in a given way [...] is explicit when the perpetrators demand as a condition for the release of the hostage that the government release political prisoners, pay a ransom or extradite a political figure; it is implicit when certain *demands are made* on the government without the express statement that they are a condition for the release for the hostage.[88]

43 On this distinction, the law and its interpretation appear at first inconclusive. In *Blaškić*, for example, the ICTY was not compelled to determine whether the demand as such may be implicit. Rather, it found evidence indicating that the demand—for the armed forces of Bosnia Herzegovina to cease their advance—the threat—against the lives of the Bosnian Muslims held—and the fact of the latter being conditional upon the former were all explicitly conveyed to the third party concerned.[89] The Trial Chamber of the Special Court for Sierra Leone (SCSL) is, however, more informative. The Chamber stated categorically that '[t]he threat can be either explicit or implicit'; but, contradictorily, subsequently found that

> these threats made to the captives do not suffice [for the purposes of hostage-taking]. The offence of hostage taking requires the threat to be communicated to a third party, with the intent of compelling the third party to act or refrain from acting as a condition for the safety or release of the captives.[90]

44 At a minimum, it is clear that, as noted above, a 'mere' deprivation of liberty cannot amount to hostage-taking. Truly 'symbolic hostages',[91] or anarchic deprivations of liberty (see MN 8) that are devoid of any evident third-party compulsion, fundamentally lack the

---

[86] ICC Elements of Crimes, Arts 8(2)(a)(viii) and 8(2)(c)(iii) (emphasis added); and Art 1 Hostages Convention. The ICRC CIHL Study also adopts this element.

[87] *Simpson v Socialist People's Libyan Arab Jamahiriya*, US Court of Appeals, District of Columbia Circuit, 470 F 3d 356, No 05-7048, 21 November 2006, paras 15–16.

[88] Burgos, above n 17, at 198 (emphasis added).

[89] *Blaškić, Trial Chamber*, above n 55, paras 705–8.

[90] SCSL, *The Prosecutor v Issa Hassan Sesay*, Trial Chamber Judgment, SCSL-04-15-T, 2 March 2009, paras 242 and 1964.

[91] Herrman and Palmieri, above n 2, at 135, abstract and 142.

character of hostage-taking. Favouring Burgos's interpretation, and seeking to clarify the decision of the SCSL, it is the author's contention that it is the 'demand'—not the threat as such—that must be express. The threat against the hostage and the link between the demand and the consequences of its non-fulfilment—i.e. the conditional nature of the threat—may be implicit.

III. Unlawful deprivation of liberty: an element of hostage-taking?

Several influential sources have stated that, in addition to the principal elements of hostage-taking (see MN 26–40), the existing deprivation of liberty needs necessarily to be *unlawful* to trigger hostage-taking. The foundation for this contention is the Pictet Commentary to GC IV, Article 147: 'Hostages might be considered as persons *illegally* deprived of their liberty [...]'[92] In their analysis, the authors of the *Elements of War Crimes under the Rome Statute* indicate that the unlawful character of the deprivation of liberty is a prerequisite to hostage-taking.[93] Moreover, notwithstanding that Article 147 is concerned exclusively with IACs, and that the element of an unlawful deprivation of liberty is not replicated in Common Article 3 and Article 4(c) AP II, nor in their Commentaries, they conclude that the elements—including an unlawful deprivation of liberty—are identical in IAC and NIAC.[94]

The jurisprudence of the ICTY is inconclusive in respect of the requirement that, to amount to hostage-taking, the deprivation of liberty must be unlawful. Initially, the ICTY Trial Chamber in *Blaškić* indicated that the deprivation of liberty should be, *but need not necessarily be*, unlawful for the prohibition on hostage-taking to be violated.[95] More categorically, the Trial Chamber in *Kordić*, quoting the Pictet Commentary,[96] subsequently found that the 'crime of taking civilians as hostages consists of the unlawful deprivation of liberty'.[97] This interpretation was later quoted—seemingly with approval—by the Appeals Chamber in *Blaškić*,[98] but in the following paragraph the Tribunal omits the requirement of an unlawful deprivation of liberty in its restatement of the elements of hostage-taking. Referencing the Hostages Convention, the Appeals Chamber found that

a situation of hostage-taking exists when a person seizes or detains and threatens to kill, injure or continue to detain another person in order to compel a third party to do or to abstain from doing something as a condition for the release of that person.[99]

One interpretation of the formative statements, noted in the preceding paragraphs, that hostages are 'illegally deprived of their liberty', or that hostage-taking 'consists of an unlawful deprivation of liberty', is that these authors intended to convey that the *consequence* of hostage-taking is an unlawful deprivation of liberty. This interpretation is, however, inconsistent with the fact that, as noted above, hostage-taking is a treatment to which individuals are subject; hostage-taking does not render unlawful the deprivation of liberty per se. Thus, these statements can only be understood to have intended to mean that, in the authors' views, unlawful detention is a necessary precursor to—a constituent element of—hostage-taking.

In light of the uncertainty on the existence of a prerequisite that the deprivation of liberty needs first to be unlawful in order to amount to hostage-taking, the influential

---

[92] Pictet Commentary GC IV, Art 147, at 600 (emphasis added).
[93] Dörmann et al, above n 69, at 127.
[94] Ibid, at 407.   [95] *Blaškić*, Trial Chamber, above n 55, para 158.
[96] *Kordić*, Trial Chamber, above n 65, para 311.   [97] Ibid, para 312.
[98] *Blaškić*, Appeals Chamber, above n 62, para 638.   [99] Ibid, para 639.

definition of hostage-taking in Article 1 of the Hostages Convention is revealing in its silence on such a requirement. This omission is also true as regards the text of the Elements of Crimes under the ICC Statute[100] and some academic consideration of the elements.[101]

49   If the deprivation of liberty needs be unlawful to amount to hostage-taking, the implications are that certain categories of persons under IHL cannot be considered hostages, regardless of the fact that the treatment to which they are subject may resemble hostage-taking. Prisoners of war may be lawfully deprived of liberty according to Article 21 GC III, which is both prohibitive and permissive. Article 21 restricts the use of 'detention' as a method of depriving enemy combatants of their liberty, except as a disciplinary sanction, and, in doing so, authorizes the use of internment. Similarly, parties to an IAC have an authority to intern protected civilians by virtue of GC IV.[102] That is, protected civilians may—for 'imperative reasons of security'[103]—be deprived of their liberty *lawfully*. If an unlawful deprivation of liberty is considered to be a necessary precondition to hostage-taking, an individual may not also be considered to be treated as a hostage where such criteria for his or her lawful detention under IHL are satisfied. It should be noted, however, that even in these circumstances, the authority for the deprivation of liberty is liable to expire: in the case of POWs, at the 'cessation of active hostilities' in accordance with Article 118 paragraph 1 GC III;[104] and in the case of protected civilians, when the reasons for the internment cease to exist.[105]

50   Although more contentious, parties to a NIAC may also lawfully deprive persons of liberty for reasons relating to the armed conflict. Common Article 3 and Article 5 AP II[106] may amount to implicit authorities to detain and intern respectively, without which reference to 'persons, *hors de combat* by [...] detention', 'regularly constituted courts', and 'internment' would be superfluous. If true, the effect would be to locate 'persons taking no active part in the hostilities, including members of armed forces [...] placed *hors de combat* by [...] detention'—and *expressly* protected from hostage-taking by Common Article 3 paragraph 1(1)(b)—outside of the scope of hostage-taking by virtue of their deprivation of liberty being lawful.

51   If, conversely, the requirement of an unlawful deprivation of liberty is forgone, a threat of continued lawful detention or internment would suffice to trigger hostage-taking where any concessions are sought from a third party. For example, a threat of continued *lawful* internment is an inevitable consequence of the negotiations in pursuance of a prisoner exchange agreement. The absurd result is that the prohibition on hostage-taking would render unlawful an act otherwise 'encouraged' by humanitarian law: prisoner exchanges are an activity foreseen by, and permissible under, Article 109 GC III.[107] Further to the

---

[100] ICC Elements of Crimes, Arts 8(2)(a)(viii) and 8(2)(c)(iii). As noted above, however, Dörmann et al, above n 69, at 127, interpreting the ICC Elements of Crimes in light of, inter alia, the *Kordić* Trial Chamber Judgment, above n 65, arrive at the conclusion that the deprivation of liberty ought, in fact, to be unlawful.

[101] Burgos, above n 17, at 198.   [102] Arts 42 and 78 GC IV.

[103] Art 78 GC IV. In own territory, 'only if the security of the Detaining Power makes it absolutely necessary' (Art 42 GC IV).

[104] Burgos, above n 17, at 198–204. See Ch 51 of this volume.   [105] Art 132 GC IV.

[106] See also AP II, Art 6(5).

[107] Art 132 GC IV extends a similar proposal to parties to the conflict vis-à-vis civilian internees: 'The Parties to the conflict shall [...] *endeavour* during the course of hostilities, to conclude agreements for the release, the repatriation [...] of certain classes of internees [...]' (emphasis added)

legal permissibility, the exchange of persons deprived of their liberty during armed conflict has both humanitarian utility[108] and historical precedent.[109]

Thus it is tenable neither to retain the requirement of an *unlawful* deprivation of liberty, 52 nor to remove it completely from the definition of hostage-taking. To resolve this conundrum, the definition proposed herein (see MN 3 or MN 69) abandons the requirement of an unlawful deprivation of liberty as a prerequisite to hostage-taking, but recognizes that a threat of unlawful detention—levied against an individual in pursuance of concessions from a third party—could amount to hostage-taking. Consequently, where a threat is made against the individual's life or well-being, or to continue/commence an unlawful deprivation of liberty, hostage-taking may occur regardless of the threshold legality of capture, seizure, or detention. By contrast, however, hostage-taking may not occur where a threat is made—or implied—to continue a lawful deprivation of an individual's liberty, even where the circumstances may otherwise resemble hostage-taking.

Importantly, contrary to popular and political discourse, not every unlawful dep- 53 rivation of liberty—including those by armed groups—equates to hostage-taking. Hostage-taking arises only where its three core elements are present. Absent these elements, the deprivation of liberty may nonetheless be in violation of the prohibition of arbitrary detention (see MN 17–20).

C. Relevance in Non-International Armed Conflicts

Common Article 3, applicable to conflicts 'not of an international character', proscribes the 54 taking as hostage of any 'person taking no active part in hostilities, including members of armed forces who have laid down their arms and those placed *hors de combat* by sickness, wounds, detention or any other cause'. Article 4(2)(c) AP II reinforces this prohibition, protecting ostensibly the same categories of persons during the 'higher threshold' NIACs to which it applies.[110] In sum, in NIAC, any person placed '*hors de combat* by [...] detention', is within the ambit of the prohibition of hostage-taking under Common Article 3 paragraph 1(1)(b).[111]

The elements of hostage-taking, as described at MN 26, are the same in both IAC 55 and NIAC.

A cursory examination of contemporary news media suggests that hostage-taking has 56 been, to date, frequently utilized by armed groups,[112] which may challenge the customary status of the prohibition of hostage-taking in NIAC. The present commentary does not purport to resolve the question of the value of the practice of armed groups for the development of customary law. It suffices to note that, for IHL, the principle of the equality of belligerents—insecure though it may be in NIAC[113]—requires the practice and '*opinio juris*' of both to contribute to the existence of a single rule applicable to *all* parties to the armed

---

[108] Pictet Commentary GC IV, Art 132, at 512.
[109] See, e.g., W. Mason, 'Prisoners of War', in H.K. Kippenberger (ed), *Official History of New Zealand in the Second World War 1939–45* (Wellington, NZ: War History Branch, 1954), at 321.
[110] In regard to the criteria for the application of AP II, see Art 1.
[111] The same would be true under Art 4(2)(c) AP II.
[112] E.g., A. Carrillo-Suarez, '*Hors de logique*: Contemporary Issues in International Humanitarian Law as Applied to Internal Armed Conflict', 15 *American University International Law Review* (1999-2000) 1, at 25.
[113] J. Somer, 'Jungle Justice: Passing Sentence on the Equality of Belligerents in Non-International Armed Conflict', 89 *IRRC* 867 (2007) 655, esp 655–64.

conflict.[114] To otherwise find that states, but not the armed groups in opposition to them,[115] are prohibited from taking hostages is an untenable solution in practice.

57 For armed groups, codes of conduct, unilateral declarations,[116] and tools foreseen by IHL, such as agreements between the conflicting parties to adhere to all, or parts, of the law,[117] are indicative of the existence of a customary rule[118] and the extent to which groups consider themselves to be bound.[119] For the purposes of hostage-taking, these 'indicators' are best considered in four general categories:

— First, some armed groups have expressed their intention to respect the prohibition of hostage-taking, either in full or in part.[120]
— Secondly, without specifically referring to hostage-taking, many armed groups have indicated their commitment to abide by Common Article 3.[121]
— Thirdly, armed groups have demonstrated their willingness to be bound by the full corpus of IHL applicable to IAC.[122]
— Lastly, armed groups have committed to the respect of persons deprived of liberty,[123] including disseminating an interdiction on their execution.[124]

For the last of these, it is unclear that 'respect' per se is foreseen to constitute an absolute prohibition on hostage-taking, but at a minimum, the practices of ill-treatment and execution historically associated with hostage-taking are forbidden. Ultimately, despite

---

[114] This is particularly true of 'fundamental humanitarian protections' such as the prohibition on the taking of hostages. See ibid, at 656, 663–4.

[115] Where the armed conflict is not between two armed groups. See CA 3.

[116] See generally M. Mack and J. Pejic (ICRC), *Increasing Respect for International Humanitarian Law* (Geneva: ICRC, 2008), at 16–28.

[117] CA 3 para 3; see Ch 25 of this volume.

[118] These indicators correspond to the evidence of custom applicable to states. See I. Brownlie, *Principles of Public International Law* (7th edn, Oxford: OUP, 2008), at 6–7.

[119] That is, the '*opinio juris*' of the armed groups. See generally ICJ, *Continental Shelf Case (Libyan Arab Jamahiriya v Malta)*, Judgment, 3 June 1985.

[120] See, inter alia, *The Comprehensive Agreement on Respect for Human Rights and International Humanitarian Law Between the Government of the Republic of the Philippines and the National Democratic Front of the Philippines*, 16 March 1998, available at <http://www.incore.ulst.ac.uk/services/cds/agreements/pdf/phil8.pdf>, Part IV, Art 3(1)); and *Code of Rules and Attitudes of the Organisation for the Successful Conduct of Fighting*, Libyan Liberation Army, 2011, available at <http://theirwords.org/media/transfer/doc/ly_ntc_2011_04_eng-37607a6aa5ec5080127c21e730a8f9e9.pdf>, Art 2(2)(c).

[121] E.g., the Revolutionary People's Front in India made a declaration during the 49th Session of the Human Rights Sub-Commission of its '"unequivocal intention to comply" with Article 3 common of the Geneva Conventions' (Human Rights Watch, '"These Fellows Must be Eliminated": Relentless Violence and Impunity in Manipur' (2008) 19, available at <http://www.hrw.org/en/node/75175/section/1>, fn 33).

[122] See, as examples, the statement of the leader of the Communist Party of Nepal (Maoists) of March 2006, Human Rights Watch, 'Between a Rock and a Hard Place: Civilians Struggle to Survive in Nepal's Civil War', October 2004, available at <http://www.hrw.org/reports/2004/10/06/between-rock-and-hard-place>, 22, fn 58; and the letter from the Palestinian Liberation Organization to the Swiss Federal Department of Foreign Affairs, reproduced in the *International Review of the Red Cross*: 72 *IRRC* 781 (1990) 69, at 69–70.

[123] The Chinese Workers' and Peasants' Red Army's eighth point of action requires that fighters '[d]o not ill-treat captives' (Chinese Workers' and Peasants' Red Army, *Three Main Rules of Discipline and the Eight Points for Attention* (1947), available at <http://english.peopledaily.com.cn/dengxp/vol2/note/B0060.html>). The Code of Conduct of the Sendero Luminoso in Peru prohibits its members from mistreating prisoners (J. Weinstein, *Inside Rebellion, The Politics of Insurgent Violence* (Cambridge: CUP, 2007), at 152). See also the *Rules for the Conduct of Warfare*, Kurdistan Workers' Party, 2004, available at <http://theirwords.org/media/transfer/doc/tr_pkk_hpg_2004_03-3ce0498c8cf99a351666bad48ff65fc8.pdf>, Part B, 'With Regard to Civilians and Captives'.

[124] The Code of Conduct of the National Resistance Army in Uganda prohibits the killing of 'any captured prisoner' (Weinstein, above n 123, at 246–51).

popular discourse, these indicators suggest broad acceptance by armed groups of the inviolable character of the prohibition of hostage-taking.

D. Legal Consequences of a Violation

As for other rules of IHL, the violation of the prohibition of hostage-taking engages the responsibility of states. A state will be responsible under IHL for hostage-taking by persons attributable to it—including but not limited to members of its armed forces[125]—where there is a nexus between the hostage-taking and an armed conflict to which the state is party. The state will be required, in turn, to cease the unlawful act and to make reparations: in any event, the state must ensure that hostages are released. Further, in accordance with Common Article 1 to the Geneva Conventions, all states parties are required to ensure respect for IHL.[126] That is, at an absolute minimum, a state must not encourage hostage-taking, even where it is undertaken by persons who are not attributable to it under the law of state responsibility (see Chapter 6 of this volume).[127]

58

As noted above, in the consideration of the elements of hostage-taking (MN 26), ICL, including the decisions of international criminal tribunals, clarifies the meaning of the prohibition for the purposes of the Geneva Conventions and their Additional Protocols. Indeed, the criminal prohibition of hostage-taking is well established in international law. Importantly, under Article 147 GC IV, treating protected persons as hostages during IAC amounts to a grave breach of the Geneva Conventions, for which states must undertake to enact legislation to provide effective penal sanctions.[128] Various other international instruments also criminalize the taking of hostages, and require states parties to enact legislation to punish the act and prosecute or extradite alleged perpetrators. The following paragraphs offer a non-exhaustive record of the sources of the criminal prohibition of hostage-taking.

59

I. The International Convention against the Taking of Hostages

The Hostages Convention—and thus the definition in Article 1 (see MN 26)—is applicable at all times, including during armed conflict. It expressly refers to, but does not substitute for, the provisions of IHL. Article 12 states that

60

the present Convention shall not apply to an act of hostage-taking committed in the course of armed conflicts as defined in the Geneva Conventions of 1949 and the Protocols thereto, including armed conflicts mentioned in article 1, paragraph 4, of Additional Protocol I of 1977 [...]

Rosenstock summarizes the consequences of Article 12, and describes the intersection of the Hostages Convention and the Geneva Conventions—and thus the applicability of the former to armed conflict—succinctly:

These [Geneva] conventions will take precedence over the Hostages Convention when and only when (1) the former prohibit the particular act and provide for an explicit obligation to prosecute or

---

[125] The state will be responsible even if members of its armed forces are acting in excess of authority or in contravention of instructions. See ILC Articles on State Responsibility, Arts 4 and 7. See also Art 90 AP I.
[126] CA 1 and ICRC CIHL Study, Rule 139, at 495. In regard to non-state actors, see ibid, at 498.
[127] See, inter alia, ICJ, *Advisory Opinion concerning Legal Consequences of the Construction of a Wall in the Occupied Palestinian Territory*, 9 July 2004, paras 158–9; and *Nicaragua v USA*, above n 50, paras 219, 220, and 255.
[128] Art 146 GC IV. See Ch 31 of this volume.

hand over the actor and (2) the state party to the Hostages Convention is legally bound to prosecute the actor or extradite him.[129]

61 Consequently, for states parties, the Hostages Convention is applicable to all acts of hostage-taking during NIAC and to such acts during IAC, except those as regards which GC IV and AP I establish the system of repression of grave breaches. Thus excluded from the Hostages Convention is the taking as hostage of protected civilians within the meaning of Article 4 GC IV[130] and, by virtue of the extended definition of protected persons in Article 73 AP I, refugees and stateless persons.[131] Thus, in effect, the Hostages Convention fills gaps in terms of 'universal jurisdiction', which the Geneva Conventions address only in relation to grave breaches.[132]

62 This interpretation underpinned the decision of the UK's Central Criminal Court in *R v Zardad*[133] after the defence sought to argue, erroneously, that the Geneva Conventions excluded the Hostages Convention in situations of NIAC.[134] The Court concluded in favour of the prosecution's response that for Article 12 to preclude the application of the Hostages Convention, 'two preconditions must be satisfied: (i) the hostage-taking alleged must come within the Geneva Conventions or Additional Protocols; (ii) the [respondent state] must be bound under the Geneva Conventions to prosecute or hand over the hostage taker'.[135] Here, the Court noted, no duty arose to 'prosecute or hand over a hostage taker in internal armed conflict'.[136]

63 Notably, treating as hostage a POW—within the meaning of Article 4 GC III—*does not* oblige states to prosecute or extradite the alleged responsible person. Consequently, in accordance with Article 12, POWs may be victims within the meaning of the prohibition of hostage-taking under the Hostages Convention, despite not being foreseen as such by treaty IHL (see MN 21–25).[137]

64 Where the requirements of the definition of the Hostages Convention are met, the Convention requires states parties, inter alia, to 'take all measures […] to ease the situation of the hostage' (Article 3) and to take alleged offenders 'into custody […] for such time as is necessary to enable any criminal or extradition proceedings to be instituted' (Article 6).

II. Statutes of international criminal courts and tribunals

65 In addition to the Hostages Convention, the statutes of international criminal courts and tribunals include, as a war crime, the taking of hostages during armed conflict. Article 8(1) ICC Statute, affords the Court 'jurisdiction in respect of war crimes', which include hostage-taking as a grave breach of the Geneva Conventions.[138] As such,

---

[129] Rosenstock, above n 73, at 184.
[130] GC IV, Arts 4, 34, 146 and 147. On GC IV, Art 4, see Ch 31 of this volume.
[131] AP I, Arts 73 and 85(2).
[132] GC IV, Arts 34 and 147. Limited also to the taking of protected civilians as hostage. See Ch 35 of this volume.
[133] *R v Zardad*, Central Criminal Court of the UK, concerning 'Ruling on the Taking of Hostages Act 1982', 5 October 2004, unapproved judgment, available at <www.redress.org/downloads/news/zardad%205%20oct%202004.pdf>.
[134] Ibid, para 2.
[135] Ibid, paras 10 and 15.   [136] Ibid, para 15.
[137] Art 12 'leaves no doubt at all that the *Hostages Convention* will be applicable to all cases of hostage-taking *not prohibited under a previous convention*': W. Verwey, 'The International Hostages Convention and National Liberation Movements', 75 *AJIL* (1981) 69, at 86 (emphasis added).
[138] Art 8(2)(a)(viii) ICC Statute.

and as acknowledged in the chapeau of Article 8(2)(a), the crime requires that the hostage is a person protected by the Geneva Conventions, that is, within the meaning of Article 4 GC IV. Further, to come within the ambit of Article 8(1) and (2)(a) ICC Statute, the hostage-taking must necessarily have been committed in the course of an IAC.

In NIAC the ICC Statute grants the Court jurisdiction over the crime of hostage-taking as envisaged by Common Article 3, that is, hostage-taking 'committed against persons taking no active part in the hostilities, including members of armed forces who have laid down their arms and those placed *hors de combat* by sickness, wounds, detention or any other cause'.[139]

The taking of hostages is also prohibited under Articles 2(h)[140] and 3 of the ICTY Statute,[141] Article 4(c) of the Statute of the International Criminal Tribunal for Rwanda, and Article 3(c) of the SCSL Statute. Neither the ICC Statute, nor the statutes of the three international criminal tribunals develop the definition of hostage-taking.

III. Other international treaties

Beyond the Hostages Convention and the statutes of international criminal courts and tribunals, other multilateral treaties, international and regional, have a role in prohibiting acts—or regulating international cooperation in respect of those acts—that may also amount to hostage-taking in relation to specific situations and/or groups of persons. International treaties of this kind include the Convention on the Prevention and Punishment of Crimes against Internationally Protected Persons, Including Diplomatic Agents.[142] Regional treaties encapsulating similar prohibitions include the Convention to Prevent and Punish the Acts of Terrorism taking the form of Crimes against Persons and Related Extortion that are of International Significance,[143] the Organization of African Unity (OAU) Convention on the Prevention and Combating of Terrorism,[144] and the European Convention on the Suppression of Terrorism.[145] Although generally applicable during armed conflict, these treaties do not, however, offer a comprehensive definition of hostage-taking.

E. Critical Assessment

To reconcile the elements and objects of hostage-taking, ensure consistency with the historical context of the prohibition of hostage-taking, other bodies of law, and scholarly

---

[139] Ibid, Art 8(2)(c)iii.

[140] Art 2 ICTY Statute affords the Tribunal the 'power to prosecute persons committing or ordering to be committed grave breaches of the Geneva Convention [...] namely the following acts against persons or property protected under the provision of the relevant Geneva Convention: [...] (h) taking civilians as hostages'.

[141] *Blaškić*, Trial Chamber, above n 55, para 177, fn 337.

[142] Convention on the Prevention and Punishment of Crimes against Internationally Protected Persons, Including Diplomatic Agents (1973). Art 2 requires State Parties to make the crime of 'kidnapping' punishable by appropriate penalties.

[143] Convention to Prevent and Punish the Acts of Terrorism taking the form of Crimes against Persons and Related Extortion that are of International Significance (OAS) (1971). See Art 2, which refers to 'kidnapping'.

[144] OAU Convention on the Prevention and Combating of Terrorism (1999). See the definition of 'terrorist act' in Art 1.

[145] European Convention on the Suppression of Terrorism (1977). See particularly Art 1, which refers to 'kidnapping, the taking of a hostage or serious unlawful detention'.

opinion, it is the author's contention that hostage-taking under IHL is most accurately articulated as follows:

— One or more persons were seized, detained or otherwise held hostage;
— in order to compel a third party to act or refrain from acting; and
— the person(s) were threatened, expressly or implicitly, with *death* or *injury* or *unlawful deprivation of liberty* as a consequence of[146] the third party's failure to act or refrain from acting.

70   In this definition a person is deprived of liberty in order to compel a third party to act or refrain from acting, and threats have been levied against him or her. The second element of the definition, namely that the deprivation of liberty 'be in order to compel the third party to act or refrain from acting', will generally be manifested by a demand, which, in the author's opinion, ought necessarily to be express (see MN 44). By contrast, the third element—the threat against the hostage, *and/or its nexus to the demand*[147]—need only be implicit. In practice, implicit threats are more likely to occur where the threat is of an—often ongoing—unlawful deprivation of liberty.

71   Under this definition, regardless of the legality of the detention, the threat is against the individual's life or well-being, or, alternatively, the threat is to continue or to commence an *unlawful* deprivation of liberty. This definition best describes hostage-taking for the purposes of its prohibition under IHL for three principal reasons:

— By omitting the threshold requirement of an existing, *unlawful* deprivation of liberty, this definition secures protection from hostage-taking for the objects of the prohibition in both IAC—including POWs—and NIAC where a threat is made against their lives or well-being. Importantly, however, under this definition, a threat of a deprivation of liberty that is or will become unlawful—such as that which exceeds the parameters for detention or internment under IHL, including the continued internment of POWs beyond the cessation of active hostilities—will also suffice to establish hostage-taking.
— This definition would, moreover, enable hostage-taking to encompass the situation of the inhabitants of occupied territory if, in accordance with the requirements of the first element of the definition, they are 'otherwise held hostage' (which was proposed, *lex ferenda*, see MN 29–33). That is, an Occupying Power would be in violation of the prohibition of hostage-taking for threats against the lives or well-being of the population of occupied territory in order to compel a third party to grant concessions. By contrast, however, the Occupying Power would not be in violation of the prohibition for engaging in other negotiations, such as those necessary to conclude the occupation, where the threat to the population is 'only' that of continued occupation.
— Indeed, this definition does not prohibit a party to the conflict from engaging in any bona fide negotiations for which an individual's continued, lawful deprivation of liberty is an implicit—if not express—condition for the concessions sought. It thus would generally not render negotiations in pursuance of a prisoner exchange illegal, except, importantly, where such negotiations are premised upon a threat to the life or well-being of persons deprived of liberty.

DAVID TUCK

[146] In this definition, 'as a consequence of' may also be understood as 'conditional upon'.

[147] In other words, the fact that the threat will be a consequence of the non-fulfilment of the demand may be implicit.

Chapter 16. Torture, Cruel, Inhuman, or Degrading Treatment or Punishment

		MN
A.	Introduction	1
B.	Meaning and Application	5
	I. Four types of ill-treatment under international human rights law, international humanitarian law, and international criminal law	5
	II. Torture	13
	a. The involvement of a public official or another person acting in an official capacity	18
	b. The threshold of severity	25
	c. Purposes	31
	d. Intent	36
	e. Conduct	37
	III. Inhuman or cruel treatment	38
	a. The threshold of severity	43
	b. Intent	45
	IV. Degrading or humiliating treatment	48
	a. The threshold of severity	49
	b. Intent	54
	V. Inhuman or degrading punishment in international humanitarian law and international criminal law	60
C.	Relevance in Non-International Armed Conflicts	62
D.	Legal Consequences of a Violation	71
	I. State responsibility	72
	II. Criminal responsibility	79
	III. Legal remedies for victims	88
E.	Critical Assessment	92

Select Bibliography

Burgers, J.H./Danelius, H., *The United Nations Conventions against Torture: A Handbook on the Convention against Torture and Other Cruel, Inhuman, or Degrading Treatment or Punishment* (Leiden: Martinus Nijhoff Publishers, 1988)

Droege, C., '"In Truth the Leitmotiv": The Prohibition of Torture and other Forms of Ill-Treatment in International Humanitarian Law', 89 *IRRC* 867 (2007) 515

Evans, M.D., 'Getting to Grips with Torture', 51 *ICLQ* (2002) 365

Human Rights Commission, Joint Report on the Situation of Detainees at Guantánamo Bay, 27 February 2006, UN Doc E/CN.4/2006/120

Marshall, J., 'Torture Committed by Non-State Actors: The Developing Jurisprudence from the Ad Hoc Tribunals', 5 *Non-State Actors and International Law* (2005) 171. Reprinted in A. Bianchi (ed), *Non-State Actors and International Law* (Farnham: Ashgate, 2009) 493

Mowbray, A., *Cases, Materials, and Commentary on the European Convention on Human Rights* (Oxford: OUP, 2012)

Nowak, M., 'Challenges to the Absolute Nature of the Prohibition of Torture and Ill-Treatment', 23 *NQHR* (2005) 674

Nowak, M., *UN Covenant on Civil and Political Rights: CCPR Commentary* (2nd edn, Kehl: Norbert Paul Engel Verlag, 2005)

Nowak, M., 'What Practices Constitute Torture? US and UN Standards', 28 *HRQ* (2006) 809

Nowak, M./McArthur, E., *The United Nations Convention against Torture: A Commentary* (Oxford: OUP, 2008)

Reidy, A., *The Prohibition of Torture. A Guide to the Implementation of Article 3 of the European Convention on Human Rights*, Human Rights Handbooks No 6 (Strasbourg: Council of Europe, 2003)

Rodley, N.S., 'The Definition(s) of Torture in International Law', 55 *Current Legal Problems* (2002) 467

Schabas, W., 'The Crime of Torture and the International Criminal Tribunals', 37 *Case Western Reserve JIL* (2006) 349

A. Introduction

1   Ever since Augustinus' and Thomas Aquinas' findings on just war, and as late as Gentili's *De Iure Belli Libri Tres*, it is clear that the state of war, irrespective of being just or unjust, does not serve as a blank cheque for military recklessness; however, as these early thoughts on restricting conduct during just wars were still somewhat hesitant, it was the divide between *jus ad bellum* and *jus in bello* which paved the way for the notion of humanity regardless of the cause of wars. On this basis, upholding human dignity and human integrity has been one of the main elements of the modern quest to regulate warfare, from the 1863 Lieber Code onwards. Extensive references to the general notions of humanity and human treatment were subsequently made in the St Petersburg Declaration and the Hague Conventions, most notably their famous Martens Clause.[1]

2   After the horrors of the Second World War, humane treatment was finally placed at the very core of the law on armed conflict—as it was succinctly noted in the 1958 Pictet Commentary, '[t]he obligation to grant protected persons humane treatment is in truth the "leitmotiv" of the four Geneva Conventions.'[2] Accordingly, if not for disagreement over minor additions to it, the Geneva Conventions would have included the following text in their Preamble:

Respect for the personality and dignity of human beings constitutes a universal principle which is binding even in the absence of any contractual undertaking.

Such a principle demands that, in time of war, all those not actively engaged in the hostilities and all those placed 'hors de combat' by reason of sickness, wounds, capture, or any other circumstance, shall be given due respect and have protection from the effects of war, and that those among them who are in suffering shall be succoured and tended without distinction of race, nationality, religious belief, political opinion or any other quality […][3]

---

[1] The Martens Clause is part of the Preamble to the Hague Convention II of 1899; it was formulated as a reaction to the failure of the delegates to determine the status of civilians taking part in battling occupation. It reads as follows: 'Until a more complete code of the laws of war has been issued, the High Contracting Parties deem it expedient to declare that, in cases not included in the Regulations adopted by them, the inhabitants and the belligerents remain under the protection and the rule of the principles of the law of nations, as they result from the usages established among civilized peoples, from the laws of humanity, and the dictates of the public conscience.' See also Ch 9, section G, of this volume.

[2] Pictet Commentary GC IV, at 204.   [3] Ibid, at 21.

The strong notion of humane treatment has thus been enshrined in the set of minimum humanitarian standards to be respected in both non-international armed conflicts (NIACs) and international armed conflicts (IACs), as stipulated in Common Article 3 and its corresponding customary international law rule.

Apart from this minimum threshold, each of the Geneva Conventions entails its own regime on that matter. Article 12 paragraph 2 GC I and GC II prescribe standards of humane treatment and care. Since inhumane treatment is all too likely if a warring party exercises control over persons who are prisoners of war (POWs), GC III is the most detailed of the Conventions. Aside from general obligations providing for humane treatment (Article 13) and the entitlement of POWs to respect for their honour (Article 14), it contains the prohibition against torture and coercion (Article 17 paragraph 4 and Article 87 paragraph 3), as well as various inhuman acts POWs may face (Articles 87 paragraph 3, 89, and 108). The Fourth Geneva Convention too sets out a general provision regarding respect and honour (Article 27), while also proscribing all forms of torture and cruel, inhuman or degrading treatment (Articles 31 and 32 GC IV).

B. Meaning and Application

I. Four types of ill-treatment under international human rights law, international humanitarian law, and international criminal law

At the outset, and as will be shown, it must be stated that the general structure of the Geneva Conventions and their drafting history reveal that they were never intended to create an elaborate system covering different and distinct types of torture and cruel, inhuman or degrading treatment or punishment (CIDT) as we find it in international criminal law (ICL) and international human rights law (IHRL). This, however, has come at the expense of coherence; for instance, torture as a grave breach is defined differently from torture in connection with the questioning of prisoners. The meaning of the various terms as discussed here ultimately often depends on the structure of the provision in the context of the respective article in its entirety, or even the Geneva Convention in which it appears.

Furthermore, the various forms of inhuman treatment usually appear together, or at least in a manner that *a fortiori* prohibits all forms of torture and CIDT by setting a rather high standard of conduct. The drafters seem to have been driven by the ambition to broaden the scope of the provisions' application so as to prevent any possible legal loopholes allowing crude justifications to consider a particular form of ill-treatment as lawful, without concerning themselves with the question whether a particular act amounts to torture or any of the other forms of mistreatment discussed here—there would basically be no difference in the consequences. Therefore, the distinction could be seen as less important for international humanitarian law (IHL) than for IHRL and ICL. However, applying the scheme as developed in these last two branches of law serves as a means to provide coherence not only in ICL, where the case law reveals a certain amount of confusion and misapplications, but also under the grave breaches regime. Further, it must not be forgotten that torture, inhuman, and degrading treatment are also mentioned together in multiple human rights treaties, including the International Covenant on Civil and Political Rights (ICCPR) and the European Convention on Human Rights (ECHR). However, the exact type of violation of IHRL and, equally, IHL is not irrelevant from a moral point of view—a violation of the prohibition of degrading treatment is obviously highly reprehensible, but not to the same extent as violation of the prohibition against acts of torture. On this basis, the European Court of Human Rights (ECtHR) has distinguished between torture and inhuman or degrading treatment from the beginning of its jurisprudence on Article 3 ECHR.[4] The Human Rights Committee (HRCttee), while it has rejected the necessity 'to establish sharp distinctions between the different kinds of punishment or treatment',[5] also distinguished between torture and CIDT in a variety of cases.[6]

7 Thus, reference needs to be made to the relationship between IHRL and IHL.[7] Owing to the fact that both of these branches of international law serve the protection of human beings and their dignity, and due to their parallel validity in times of armed conflict,[8] a high level of convergence may be observed. It follows that the pertinent rules of the Geneva Conventions can and should be interpreted in light of IHRL and vice versa.[9] On this basis, and also given the lack of definitions and a sufficiently clear classification scheme of the various forms of ill-treatment under IHL, their meaning as distinguished in IHRL, namely torture, cruel, inhuman, and degrading treatment or punishment, will be discussed first. Then we shall analyse which terms in IHL correlate with the respective expressions in IHRL, and whether there are differences in the definition and interpretation of these terms. In addition to the respective literature in IHL, we shall also make use of ICL with respect to torture as a war crime and a crime against humanity, and the relevant case law of international criminal tribunals.

8 *Torture* is the intentional infliction of severe pain or suffering, whether physical or mental, on a powerless person for a specific purpose, such as the extraction of information or a confession, intimidation, discrimination, or punishment.[10] According to IHRL, torture must be inflicted by or at the instigation of, or with the consent or acquiescence of, a *public official* or other person acting in an official capacity. This means that certain harmful traditional practices, such as female genital mutilation, can be considered as torture if the state does not take sufficient measures, in accordance with the principle of due diligence, to prevent and eradicate them. But in most cases, torture is inflicted by the police, military, intelligence, and other state security officers. Torture usually takes place in detention, typically in an interrogation room, where the perpetrators, by means of threats and violence, convey the message to the victim that he or she is totally under their control and therefore is advised to 'cooperate'. This situation of *powerlessness* is often underlined by handcuffing, hooding, and/or stripping the victim naked, by the suspension of the victim in a painful position, and by similar methods of humiliation emphasizing the unequal power relationship. In addition to beatings, a broad variety of physical and mental methods of torture have been developed over time, ranging from electric shocks and branding, to water boarding and highly sophisticated methods of sensory deprivation. If these methods are applied for one of the purposes mentioned above and reach the level of

---

[4] ECtHR, *Ireland v United Kingdom*, Judgment, 18 January 1978, para 167.
[5] HRCttee, General Comment 20, Art 7 (Prohibition of torture, or other cruel, inhuman or degrading treatment or punishment), 10 March 1992, para 4.
[6] M. Nowak, *UN Covenant on Civil and Political Rights: CCPR Commentary* (2nd edn, Kehl: Norbert Paul Engel Verlag, 2005), at 162–3.
[7] See Ch 35 of this volume on that subject.
[8] ICJ, *Legality of the Threat or Use of Nuclear Weapons*, Advisory Opinion, 8 July 1996, para 25.
[9] Cf A. Orakhelashvili, 'The Interaction between Human Rights and Humanitarian Law: Fragmentation, Conflict, Parallelism, or Convergence?', 19 *EJIL* (2008) 161.
[10] See the definition of torture in Art 1 of the Convention against Torture and other Cruel, Inhuman or Degrading Treatment and Punishment (CAT): see CAT-Commentary, at 66 ff, with further references.

severe physical or mental pain or suffering, either objectively or at least in the subjective perception of the victim, we speak of torture. According to Article 2 of the Convention against Torture and other Cruel, Inhuman or Degrading Treatment and Punishment (CAT), '[n]o exceptional circumstances whatsoever, whether a state of war or a threat of war, internal political instability or any other public emergency, may be invoked as a justification of torture.' This means that the prohibition of torture is one of very few absolute human rights which can never be restricted or derogated from, even for a 'good purpose' such as the extraction of the secret code to a 'ticking bomb' in the fight against terrorism.

Despite the original approach of the ECtHR in the Northern Ireland case, which considered the intensity of the pain and suffering as the decisive criterion for distinguishing torture from other forms of ill-treatment,[11] there is a growing consensus among scholars and in the jurisprudence that torture requires the same intensity of severe pain or suffering as cruel and inhuman treatment or punishment.[12] The threshold is lower only for degrading treatment or punishment, which requires, however, a particularly humiliating attitude. The decisive criteria which distinguish torture, as defined in Article 1 CAT, from other forms of ill-treatment, are therefore the requirements of *intention*, a specific *purpose*, and the *powerlessness* of the victim. 9

It is difficult to distinguish *cruel treatment* from *inhuman treatment*. Every infliction of severe pain or suffering by, or at least with the acquiescence of, a public official, which does not entail any of the additional definitional criteria for torture (intention, purpose, and powerlessness), can be considered as cruel or inhuman treatment. Since torture requires intention and purpose, negligent infliction of severe pain or suffering can never constitute torture. Even gross negligence, such as forgetting a detainee in a remote cell, who is slowly starving to death, does not amount to torture, although the detainee is in a powerless situation and subjected to the most severe physical and mental suffering. In times of a global prison crisis, the general conditions of detention in many countries of the world (overcrowding, appalling hygienic conditions, high level of inter-prisoner violence, lack of food, medicine, privacy and other basic needs, and human rights) can be regarded only as cruel and inhuman treatment.[13] At the same time, cruel and inhuman treatment may also be inflicted outside detention and a situation of powerlessness. Typical examples are the excessive use of force by the police when arresting a person, quelling a riot or insurrection, dissolving a public gathering, or acting in self-defence or the defence of others. Since the security forces are entitled to use physical force and arms for purposes of law enforcement, the principle of proportionality must be applied in order to determine whether the use of force is excessive or not. Only use of force resulting in severe pain or suffering, and which, in the particular circumstances of a given case, is considered to be excessive and non-proportional in relation to the lawful 10

---

[11] ECtHR, *Ireland v United Kingdom*, above n 4, para 162.

[12] See ibid, Separate Opinion of Judge Matscher cf also N.S. Rodley, 'The Definition(s) of Torture in International Law', 55 *Current Legal Problems* (2002) 467; M.D. Evans, 'Getting to Grips with Torture', 51 *ICLQ* (2002) 365; M. Nowak, 'Challenges to the Absolute Nature of the Prohibition of Torture and Ill-Treatment', 23 *NQHR* (2005) 674; A. Cullen, 'Defining Torture in International Law: A Critique of the Concept employed by the European Court of Human Rights', 34 *California Western International Law Journal* (2003) 29; Report of the UN Special Rapporteur on Torture and other Cruel, Inhuman or Degrading Treatment, UN Doc E/CN.4/2006/6; CAT-Commentary, at 69.

[13] See, e.g., The global study of the UN Special Rapporteur on Torture, UN Doc A/HRC/13/39/Add.5 of 5 February 2010, paras 229–37, as well as case law of the UN HRCttee, the UN Committee against Torture, the ECtHR, and the IACtHR: cf Nowak, above n 6, at 172 ff; CAT-Commentary, at 559 ff; P. van Dijk et al (eds), *Theory and Practice of the European Convention on Human Rights* (4th edn, Antwerp/Oxford: Intersentia, 2006), at 419 ff.

purpose to be achieved, amounts to inhuman or cruel treatment.[14] If a person suspected of having committed a crime is resisting arrest by the police with force, even the intentional infliction of severe pain or suffering may be justified if absolutely necessary and proportional to perform the arrest. If excessive force is used, the infliction of severe pain amounts to cruel or inhuman treatment. As soon as the person is arrested, handcuffed, and therefore in a powerless position, further beatings that inflict severe pain or suffering for a specific purpose may be considered as torture, even outside any place of detention.

11   *Degrading treatment* constitutes the least severe form of ill-treatment, and therefore does not need to reach the level of severe pain or suffering. The severity of the suffering imposed is of less importance than the humiliation of the victim, regardless of whether this is in the eyes of others or those of the victim himself or herself.[15] Degrading treatment may be inflicted by law enforcement officials both inside and outside detention. Emptying urine buckets over the heads of prisoners, throwing their food and water on the floor, soaking their bedding, or pulling them by their hair have all been found to constitute degrading treatment. Nudity and sexual harassment have often been used as means to humiliate detainees. Similarly, chain-gangs, exposing persons in cages to the public, pillorying, and other forms of public humiliation amount to degrading treatment.

12   The most typical example of *cruel, inhuman* or *degrading punishment* is corporal punishment, whether as a form of judicial or disciplinary punishment, in detention, in the military, or in schools. After a landmark judgment of the ECtHR, in which the birching of a juvenile as a traditional judicial punishment on the Isle of Man had been found to be degrading punishment in violation of Article 3 ECHR,[16] similar case law has been developed by the UN HRCttee,[17] the Inter-American Court of Human Rights (IACtHR),[18] the European Committee of Social Rights, the UN Committee against Torture, the UN Special Rapporteur on Torture, and other international and regional monitoring bodies.[19] Since capital punishment constitutes an aggravated form of corporal punishment, an increasing number of judicial bodies also regard the death penalty, or at least the death row phenomenon and certain forms of execution, as cruel, inhuman and degrading punishment, and there is a clear trend towards universal abolition of capital punishment.[20] The UN Committee against Torture has also considered life imprisonment for children, certain forms of hard labour, internal exile, and solitary confinement as constituting cruel, inhuman, or degrading punishment.[21]

II. Torture

13   This section of the chapter discusses torture without distinguishing the criminal nature of the act and the prohibition upon belligerents.

---

[14] CAT-Commentary, at 568.
[15] ECtHR, *Tyrer v United Kingdom*, Judgment, 25 April 1978, para 32. See also Nowak, above n 6, at 165.
[16] ECtHR, *Tyrer v United Kingdom*, above n 15.
[17] HRCttee, *Osborne v Jamaica*, Communication No 759/1997, UN Doc CCPR/C/68/D/759/1997 (2000).
[18] IACtHR, *Winston Caesar v Trinidad and Tobago*, 11 March 2005, Series C No 123 (2005).
[19] Cf CAT-Commentary, at 561 ff.
[20] Cf W. Schabas, *The Abolition of the Death Penalty in International Law* (Cambridge: CUP, 2002); Nowak, above n 6, at 168 ff; CAT-Commentary, at 564 ff; Report of the UN Special Rapporteur on Torture, UN Doc A/HRC/10/44, 14 January 2009, paras 29–48; UNGA Res A/RES/62/149, A/RES/63/168, A/RES/65/206; Amnesty International, *Death sentences and executions in 2011* (London: Amnesty International, 2012, available at <http://www.amnesty.org/en/library/info/ACT50/001/2012/en>.
[21] CAT-Commentary, at 566.

14 International humanitarian law has provided for the prohibition of torture from its very beginnings.[22] The Lieber Code from 1863 held in its Article 16 that military necessity does not provide justification for the infliction of torture aimed at the extortion of confessions, while the prohibition on occupying powers torturing civilians was likely to have been established as customary international law at least by the time of the Hague Conventions.[23] Articles 4 and 46 of the Regulations annexed to Hague Convention IV of 1907, together with the Martens Clause, have special importance in this regard.[24] The Geneva Conventions, apart from the provisions imposing a general duty of humane treatment, which obviously also includes the prohibition of torture, explicitly proscribe the infliction of torture in Common Article 3 paragraph 1(1)(a), Article 12 paragraph 2 GC I and GC II, Article 17 paragraph 3 GC III, Article 87 GC III, and Articles 31 and 32 GC IV.

15 It is important to note that neither the Geneva Conventions nor the Additional Protocols (APs) provide a definition of 'torture'. The Pictet Commentary is also not particularly helpful, as it does not apply a general definition of 'torture' throughout the respective discussions of the various provisions on torture in the Geneva Conventions. Depending on the article being discussed, it either refers to a broad definition, including 'judicial torture to extort confessions and extrajudicial torture', or to 'judicial torture' only.[25]

16 The same is true for the statutes of the International Criminal Tribunal for the former Yugoslavia (ICTY) and the International Criminal Tribunal for Rwanda (ICTR), that relied in their case law extensively on IHRL and on the definition of 'torture' provided in Article 1 CAT. But the International Criminal Court (ICC) Statute, which was adopted on 17 July 1998, i.e. before the two ad hoc tribunals had provided any significant judicial interpretation of the term 'torture',[26] sets out in Article 7(2)(e) the following legal definition of torture as a crime against humanity:

'Torture' means the intentional infliction of severe pain or suffering, whether physical or mental, upon a person in the custody or under the control of the accused [...]

The term 'crime against humanity' is defined in Article 7(1) ICC Statute as meaning

any of the following acts [e.g. torture, rape, or '[o]ther inhumane acts of a similar character intentionally causing great suffering, or serious injury to body or to mental or physical health'] when committed as part of a widespread or systematic attack directed against any civilian population, with knowledge of the attack [...]

In this regard, it is crucial that crimes against humanity, and thus torture as part of such an attack, can be committed both in peacetime and during armed conflicts.[27]

17 A short comparison between the legal definitions in Article 1 CAT and in Article 7(2)(e) ICC Statute reveals the following differences. First, neither the involvement of a public

---

[22] Cf W.A. Schabas, 'The Crime of Torture and the International Criminal Tribunals', 55 *Case Western Reserve JIL* (2006) 349.
[23] A. Cassese, 'The Martens Clause: Half a Loaf or simply a Pie in the Sky?', 11 *EJIL* (2000) 187, at 203.
[24] See ICTY, *The Prosecutor v Anto Furundžija*, Trial Chamber Judgment, 10 December 1998, IT-95-17/1-T, para 137.
[25] Pictet Commentary GC IV, at 223. See the discussion below on severity and purposes in sections B.II.b and c respectively.
[26] See Schabas, above n 22, at 354.
[27] See, e.g., ICTY, *The Prosecutor v Duško Tadić*, Appeals Chamber, Decision on the Defence Motion for Interlocutory Appeal on Jurisdiction, 2 October 1995, IT-94-1-I, para 70.

official nor a specific purpose, as required by Article 1 CAT, can be found in Article 7 ICC Statute. On the other hand, the ICC Statute explicitly demands that the victim must be in the custody or under the control of the accused. Detention or direct control of the victim by the perpetrator (powerlessness of the victim) must be read into the CAT definition, and in fact constitutes the most important element of distinguishing torture from other forms of ill-treatment.[28] In the following, we provide a short analysis of some of the key decisions of the ICTY and ICTR relating to the involvement of a public official, the purpose of torture, the threshold of severity, and other definition criteria of torture as a war crime or a crime against humanity under ICL.

a. *The involvement of a public official or another person acting in an official capacity*

18 Article 1(1) CAT provides that for an act to constitute torture, one of the requirements is that it needs to be 'inflicted by or at the instigation of or with the consent or acquiescence of a public official or other person acting in an official capacity'. There are different reasons why Article 1 CAT demands the involvement of a public official. Most importantly, this provision reflects the traditional view of IHRL that states can be held accountable for human rights violations only if those violations are committed by state actors.[29] During the drafting of the CAT, this traditional view was challenged by a number of states with the argument that the requirement of states to use domestic criminal law for the purpose of punishing the perpetrators of torture was one of the main reasons why the Convention had been developed, thereby rendering the involvement of a state actor unnecessary.[30] Other states took the view, however, that torture was particularly reprehensible if committed with the full power and authority of a state official. As a compromise, the involvement of a public official by acquiescence and the phrase 'other person acting in an official capacity' were added. This means, first, that by applying the principle of due diligence, states can also be held accountable for private acts of torture, such as female genital mutilation, if they fail to take the necessary steps to prevent such practices. Secondly, in fragile states or during armed conflicts, other persons 'acting in an official capacity' might also include members of rebel, guerrilla, or insurgent groups who exercise *de facto* authority.[31]

19 Drawing from this definition, the ICTY and ICTR have always been clear in holding that individuals may be held accountable for torture as a war crime or a crime against humanity regardless of whether they acted *qua* state officials or as members of a non-state actor. It was, however, debated in the jurisprudence whether the individual needed to have the status of an 'official' resembling that of public officials of the state, within a non-state armed group. At first, this was answered in the affirmative, as the ICTR in *Akayesu* strictly adhered to the wording of the CAT and thus stated that, for an act to constitute torture, one of the requirements was that '[t]he perpetrator was himself an official, or acted at the instigation of, or with the consent or acquiescence of, an official or person acting in an official capacity.'[32] Jean-Paul Akayesu had been convicted of torture as a crime against humanity because of having used

---

[28] Report of the UN Special Rapporteur on the question of torture, above n 12.
[29] Cf ICTY, *The Prosecutor v Radoslav Brđanin*, Trial Chamber Judgment, 1 September 2004, IT-99-36-T, para 489.
[30] See CAT-Commentary, at 41 ff and 77.   [31] Ibid, at 78 ff.
[32] ICTR, *The Prosecutor v Jean-Paul Akayesu*, Trial Chamber Judgment, ICTR-96-4-T, 2 September 1998, para 593.

threats and brutality during interrogations. However, since he was a mayor of a Rwandan town, the question of non-state officials did not arise.

In November 1998, a Trial Chamber of the ICTY followed the approach of the ICTR in a well-known case concerning torture administered by Bosnian Muslims in the Čelebići prison camp between Sarajevo and Mostar. In its discussion of torture in customary international law on the basis of IHRL, it noted that, for the prohibition to have teeth in armed conflicts not conducted between state armies only, be they international or non-international in character, it obviously had to be interpreted as including officials of non-state actors as well.[33] The Trial Chamber further emphasized, in accordance with the IHRL-related findings outlined above, the 'very broad terms' of the CAT definition as also including 'officials who take a passive attitude or turn a blind eye to torture, most obviously by failing to prevent or punish torture under national penal or military law, when it occurs'.[34]

One month later, a Trial Chamber of the ICTY convicted Anto Furundžija, the local commander of a special unit within the armed forces of the Croatian Defence Council (HVO) in Bosnia and Herzegovina, of the crime of torture as a war crime.[35] The HVO was one of the three main armed forces during the armed conflict in Bosnia and Herzegovina, fighting the regular army of the State of Bosnia and Herzegovina. Mr Furundžija, therefore, was clearly not a state official. Concerning the elements of the crime of torture as a war crime, the ICTY stressed that 'at least one of the persons involved in the torture process must be a public official or must at any rate act in a non-private capacity, e.g. as a *de facto* organ of a State or any other authority-wielding entity'.[36]

While these early rulings had accepted the individual criminal responsibility of non-state actors, they still adhered to the 'public official' requirement of the definition in Article 1 CAT. In later judgments, the ICTY started to rely more on the definition of 'torture' as a crime against humanity in Article 7(2)(e) ICC Statute, which does not contain any reference to a public official. In *Kvočka*, an ICTY Trial Chamber explained with reference to the ICC Statute that 'the state actor requirement imposed by international human rights law is inconsistent with the application of individual criminal responsibility for international crimes found in international humanitarian law and international criminal law'.[37] In its discussion on the different nature of torture in IHRL and IHL, the ICTY Trial Chamber in *Kunarac et al* observed the necessity to draw a clear distinction between provisions that are addressed to states and persons whose acts are attributable to states, and provisions addressing individuals. It then stated that 'the identity and official status of the perpetrator is irrelevant insofar as it relates to accountability',[38] and hence concluded that 'the presence of a state official or of any other authority-wielding person in the torture process is not necessary for the offence to be regarded as torture under international humanitarian law'.[39]

---

[33] ICTY, *The Prosecutor v Zejnal Delalić et al*, Trial Chamber Judgment, 16 November 1998, IT-96-21-T, para 473.
[34] Ibid, para 474. See also ICTY, *Furundžija*, above n 24, para 162.
[35] See ICTY, *Furundžija*, above n 24.   [36] Ibid, para 162.
[37] ICTY, *The Prosecutor v Miroslav Kvočka et al*, Trial Chamber Judgment, 2 November 2001, IT-98-30/1-T, para 139.
[38] ICTY, *The Prosecutor v Dragoljub Kunarac, Radomir Kovač, and Zoran Vuković*, Trial Chamber Judgment, 22 February 2001, IT-96-23-T & IT-96-23/1-T, para 494.
[39] Ibid, para 496, further confirmed by the Appeals Chamber Judgment, 12 June 2002, para 148. See also ICTR, *The Prosecutor v Laurent Semanza*, Trial Chamber Judgment, 15 May 2003, ICTR-97-20-T, para 342.

23   Overall, it is safe to conclude that the definition of the offence of torture in armed conflicts no longer depends upon the involvement of a public official or any other person acting in an official capacity. Members of non-state armed groups and other individuals may also commit torture, and holding any individual perpetrator of such acts accountable for torture as a war crime or a crime against humanity does not face any obstacles. The only effect of having the status of a commander of an armed group or other official is that it may 'constitute an aggravating circumstance when it comes to sentencing, because the official illegitimately used and abused a power which was conferred upon him or her for legitimate purposes'.[40]

24   Consistent with this discussion on the necessity of the involvement of a public official, the *Kunarac et al* Trial Chamber provided a conclusive and generally valid definition of torture as a crime in IHL on the basis of customary international law, as being constituted by the following elements, which will be addressed in detail below (MN 25–37):

(i)   The infliction, by act or omission, of severe pain or suffering, whether physical or mental.
(ii) The act or omission must be intentional.
(iii) The act or omission must aim at obtaining information or a confession, or at punishing, intimidating or coercing the victim or a third person, or at discriminating, on any ground, against the victim or a third person.[41]

b. *The threshold of severity*

25 It is unclear whether an act constitutes torture under the Geneva Conventions only if it reaches a certain level of severity. On the one hand, Article 17 paragraph 3 GC III distinguishes between 'physical or mental torture' and 'any other form of coercion' as prohibited means of obtaining information from POWs, while further stipulating that a POW 'may not be threatened, insulted, or exposed to any unpleasant or disadvantageous treatment of any kind' as a consequence of a refusal to answer such questions. In similar fashion, Article 31 GC IV mentions the prohibition of 'physical or moral coercion […] in particular to obtain information', without explicitly referring to torture, which is nevertheless mentioned in Article 32 GC IV. The structure of these Articles could thus be read as establishing a classification of prohibited acts in connection with interrogations on the basis of the grade of severity, with torture being at the highest level. On the other hand, Pictet Commentary GC IV does not refer to a specific level of severity, merely stating that '[t]here need not necessarily be any attack on physical integrity since the "progress" of science has enabled the use of procedures which, while they involve physical suffering, do not necessarily cause bodily injury.'[42] Also, it must not be forgotten that the inclusion of torture in Article 17 paragraph 3 GC III was aimed at making the provision 'more categorical' by establishing a prohibition additional to that of mere coercion, rather than including a different and particularly severe form of ill-treatment.[43] Hence, if one wants to interpret this provision as requiring a higher level of severity for torture than for other actions taken as a means to extract confessions, the authors of the Geneva Conventions would not have felt

---

[40] ICTY, *Kunarac et al*, Appeals Chamber, above n 39, para 181.
[41] ICTY, *Kunarac et al*, above n 38, para 497, subsequently discussed and largely confirmed by the Appeals Chamber, above n 39, paras 142–8.
[42] Pictet Commentary GC IV, at 223.   [43] Pictet Commentary GC III, at 163.

the urge to make a specific reference to torture since, *a fortiori*, it would have been already covered by the prohibition of coercion (as is the case with Article 31).

26 Furthermore, since Article 17 paragraph 3 GC III is an example of the general pattern in IHL of mentioning the prohibition of torture together with other forms of ill-treatment, the issue of severity is less important in IHL than in IHRL and ICL. Again, we must not forget that Article 17 paragraph 3 GC III aims at protecting POWs against pressure, whatever its form, to the widest extent possible, and thus without paying much attention to detailed differentiations between the proscribed acts on the basis of severity or other requirements. In sum, it can thus be stated that the Geneva Conventions do not contain a clear and stringent position on this requirement. It is thus pertinent to apply the scheme as developed in IHRL, where severity is not one of the criteria that distinguishes torture from other acts of CIDT in IHL.

27 Things are different in the case law of the ECtHR and the ICTY, however. On the question of assessing the severity of the infliction of pain or suffering, the ICTY Trial Chamber in *Krnojelac* stated that it regarded 'the general reasoning and criteria used by the European Court of Human Rights in order to assess the gravity of the act of torture, as well as its relationship with other less serious offences, as sufficiently compelling as to warrant adopting it in the present case',[44] and thus, by using a formulation resembling the one usually given by the ECtHR in torture-related cases from early on,[45] held that

> [w]hen assessing the seriousness of the acts charged as torture, the Trial Chamber must take into account all the circumstances of the case, including the nature and context of the infliction of pain, the premeditation and institutionalisation of the ill-treatment, the physical condition of the victim, the manner and method used, and the position of inferiority of the victim. In particular, to the extent that an individual has been mistreated over a prolonged period of time, or that he or she has been subjected to repeated or various forms of mistreatment, the severity of the acts should be assessed as a whole to the extent that it can be shown that this lasting period or the repetition of acts are inter-related, follow a pattern or are directed towards the same prohibited goal.[46]

28 The reliance of the ICTY on the case law of the ECtHR essentially means that it follows the approach of requiring a higher threshold of suffering for torture than for cruel or inhuman treatment.[47] However, it should be noted that the ICTY, by also including outrages upon personal dignity in the category of inhuman treatment,[48] has set a lower threshold for the term than generally understood in IHRL.

29 The Elements of Crimes adopted in relation to the ICC Statute follow the generally accepted view that the same threshold, of 'severe physical or mental pain or suffering upon one or more persons', applies to the different offences of torture as a crime against humanity and as a war crime, as well as to inhuman or cruel treatment.[49]

---

[44] ICTY, *The Prosecutor v Milorad Krnojelac*, Trial Chamber Judgment, 15 March 2002, IT-97-25-T, para 181; see also *Delalić et al* above n 33, paras 462–4.

[45] ECtHR, *Ireland v United Kingdom*, above n 4, para 162.

[46] ICTY, *Krnojelac*, above n 44, para 182.

[47] ICTY, *Delalić et al*, above n 33, para 442, which, in order to avoid confusion, should be read in combination with the Appeals Chamber Judgment, 20 February 2001, IT-96-21-A, para 424; ICTY, *Kvočka et al*, above n 37, para 161; *Brđanin*, above n 29, para 483; ICTY, *Krnojelac*, above n 44, para 180.

[48] See ICTY, *Delalić et al*, above n 33; ICTY, *The Prosecutor v Dario Kordić and Mario Čerkez*, Trial Chamber Judgment, 26 February 2001, IT-95-14/2-A, para 245; ICTY, *The Prosecutor v Zlatko Aleksovski*, Trial Chamber Judgment, IT-95-14/1-T, 25 June 1999, para 54; see also Pictet Commentary GC IV, at 598.

[49] ICC Elements of Crimes, torture as crime against humanity, Art 7(1)(f): '1. The perpetrator inflicted severe physical or mental pain or suffering upon one or more persons […]'; torture as war crime, Art 8(2)(a)(ii): '1. The perpetrator inflicted severe physical or mental pain or suffering upon one or more persons […]'.

30   The effect of the approach of the ICTY following the higher threshold requirement of the ECtHR was that acts clearly constituting torture were sometimes qualified only as inhuman treatment.[50] It thus remains to be seen whether future jurisprudence will follow the generally accepted definition of 'torture' in IHRL as outlined above and the ICC Elements of Crimes; although this would naturally be highly welcome, such a change must nevertheless not take place 'at the cost of raising the threshold of severity required for treatment to be deemed cruel or inhuman'.[51]

c. Purposes

31   The Geneva Conventions also lack coherence regarding the inherent link between torture and a specific purpose. The findings on Article 17 paragraph 3 GC III and Articles 31 and 32 GC IV are also relevant here. The former in broad terms prohibits not only the infliction of torture 'to secure from [POWs] information of any kind whatever', but also coercion and 'any unpleasant or disadvantageous treatment of any kind'. A contextual interpretation thus seems to imply that torture under this provision is not set apart from these other forms of ill-treatment, in particular inhuman treatment, by its purpose. An equal approach is found in GC IV, where Article 31 mentions the purpose of obtaining information without referring to torture, while the Pictet Commentary to Article 32 GC IV contains a broad definition which covers not only judicial torture, i.e. torture linked to the specific purpose of extracting confessions, but also acts under the notion of 'extrajudicial confessions'.[52] However, this would essentially mean that neither the purpose nor the severity of the act is an essential element. Taking note of this problem, the commentaries to torture as a grave breach add to the confusion by using only the narrow definition of 'judicial torture' as outlined above.[53] The Commentary to Article 130 GC III mentions a more restrictive set of purposes than Article 1(1) CAT, as it distinguishes 'wilfully causing great suffering', for motives such as punishment, revenge, or pure sadism, from the notion of torture. The Commentary to torture in Article 147 GC IV in particular refers to the necessity of applying only its 'legal meaning—i.e., the infliction of suffering on a person to obtain from that person, or from another person, confessions or information'—in order to distinguish torture from inhuman treatment, and explicitly states that '[i]t is more than a mere assault on the physical or moral integrity of a person. What is important is not so much the pain itself as the purpose behind its infliction.'[54] Seen in this light, the above-mentioned Article 31 GC IV, notwithstanding the referral to coercion only, should rather be understood as essentially containing a prohibition of torture. Similarly, wilfully causing great suffering as a means of punishment also amounts to torture.[55]

32   International human rights law and ICL also clearly follow this latter definition, and equally require a specific purpose, as mentioned in Article 1(1) CAT.

33   At the same time, the ICTY emphasized that the list of purposes in customary IHRL, and thus in Article 1(1) CAT, is not exhaustive but merely representative.[56] However, the

---

[50] See the discussion below on inhuman treatment in section B.III.
[51] C. Droege, '"In Truth the Leitmotiv": The Prohibition of Torture and other Forms of Ill-Treatment in International Humanitarian Law', 89 *IRRC* 867 (2007) 515, at 528.
[52] Pictet Commentary GC IV, at 223.
[53] Pictet Commentary GC II, at 268; Pictet Commentary GC III, at 627. Pictet Commentary GC I explicitly abstains from discussing the notion of torture.
[54] Pictet Commentary GC IV, at 598.   [55] ICTY, *Delalić et al*, above n 33, para 508.
[56] Ibid, para 470.

necessity of a specific purpose has to be interpreted narrowly, in the sense that any further purpose needs to have 'something in common with the purposes expressly listed'.[57] Thus, the ICTY Trial Chamber in *Furundžija* introduced the addition of the purpose of humiliation not only on the basis of 'the general spirit of international humanitarian law [...] [the] primary purpose [of which] [...] is to safeguard human dignity' and the formulation of outrages upon personal dignity in the Geneva Conventions, but also by reference to the close relation of humiliation to the explicitly mentioned purpose of intimidation.[58] However, the purpose of humiliation was discarded by the Trial Chamber in *Krnojelac*, which argued that while there may be a tendency to enlarge the list of prohibited purposes, particularly in IHRL, this additional purpose had not been part of customary international law at the time when the alleged acts were committed, while also stating that the above-cited finding regarding the primary aim of IHL would not suffice from the standpoint of the principle of legality.[59]

In sum, adding this further purpose was not of pressing necessity, particularly since, as was correctly pointed out in *Delalić et al*, several of the explicitly listed purposes—namely, intimidation, punishment, coercion, discrimination—are almost inevitably involved whenever rape occurs at the instigation of, or with the consent or acquiescence of, a public official, particularly during armed conflicts, and thus rape and other forms of sexual violence always constitute torture if the other necessary requirements are present.[60] This finding necessarily extends to rape committed by members of non-state armed groups as well.

34

In any case, for the ICTY and ICTR, the requirement of a certain purpose for the qualification of an act of ill-treatment as torture, as defined in Article 1 CAT, was never put in question. It is, therefore, surprising that the purpose requirement was deleted from the definition of torture as a crime against humanity in the ICC Statute.[61] While the ICC Elements of Crimes for torture as a war crime as mentioned in Article 8(2)(a)(ii) and (c)(i) list the same purposes as those set out in the CAT definition, this element is lacking in the definition of torture as a crime against humanity in Article 7(2)(e) ICC Statute. The rationale behind this approach is still unclear. It might perhaps have been an oversight during the drafting process. But since the definition requires the intentional infliction of severe pain or suffering, the intent may be interpreted to cover a certain purpose too, as we shall explain below (MN 36).

35

d. Intent

A further condition regarding the *mens rea* of torture is that the pain or suffering has to be inflicted intentionally, i.e. it must be 'deliberate and not accidental'.[62] This has to be assessed from an objective viewpoint. It follows that pure negligence can in no

36

---

[57] J.H. Burgers and H. Danelius, *The United Nations Conventions against Torture: A Handbook on the Convention against Torture and Other Cruel, Inhuman, or Degrading Treatment or Punishment* (Dordrecht: Martinus Nijhoff Publishers, 1988), at 118; see also CAT-Commentary, at 75.

[58] ICTY, *Furundžija*, above n 24, para 162. See also ICTY, *Kvočka et al*, above n 37, paras 140 ff, 152, and 157.

[59] ICTY, *Krnojelac*, above n 44, para 186; see also ICTY, *Kunarac et al*, above n 38, para 497; or ICTY, *The Prosecutor v Blagoje Simić, Miroslav Tadić, and Simo Zarić*, Trial Chamber Judgment, 17 October 2003, IT-95-9-T, para 79.

[60] ICTY, *Delalić et al*, above n 33, para 495 ff.

[61] See also M. Nowak, 'The Crime of Torture', in M. Odello and G.L. Beruto (eds), *Global Violence: Consequences and Responses, Forty years of excellence in Humanitarian Dialogue: The 40th Anniversary of the International Institute of Humanitarian Law, 33rd Round Table on Current Issues of International Humanitarian Law*, San Remo, 9–11 September 2010 (Milan, 2011), 157.

[62] ICTY, *Delalić et al*, above n 33, para 468.

circumstances be sufficient for an act to constitute torture. Appalling prison conditions or forgetting a prisoner in his cell may, therefore, 'only' amount to CIDT. According to the case law of the ICTY, the intention has to be directed both at the act of infliction of severe pain or suffering *and* at the purpose it aims to achieve. The crime of torture without any purpose, as indicated by the definition of torture as a crime against humanity in Article 7(2)(e) ICC Statute, is therefore difficult to imagine. Yet it is clear that it is sufficient if the prohibited purpose is part of the motivation; it does not have to be the primary or the sole purpose behind the act.[63]

e. Conduct

37 Given its very nature, the majority of incidents of torture are the consequence of the active infliction of pain or suffering; nevertheless, it would be absurd to assume that omissions meeting all of the necessary requirements do not constitute torture solely because of the passive nature of the act. It is thus clear that torture may also be committed through omissions,[64] such as the deliberate deprivation of a sufficient amount of food.[65]

III. Inhuman or cruel treatment

38 As outlined in section A of this chapter, humane treatment has gradually evolved from being one among several aspects of regulation of armed conflicts to becoming its very essence. Thus, the Geneva Conventions entail not only a negative duty to abstain from certain acts, but also, more importantly, a positive obligation upon the states parties as well as other actors taking part in the hostilities, in a wide range of provisions according to which they have to treat the numerous categories of persons possibly affected by armed conflicts—with the exception of combatants who are not in the power of the enemy—in a humane manner. Common Article 3 stipulates that all parties to a conflict are obliged to offer humane treatment towards all such persons, and includes a list of acts which are prohibited at all times and in all circumstances, such as 'violence to life and person' and mutilation.

39 The other provisions found in Geneva Conventions I–IV prescribe in general and sometimes specific terms the humane treatment of the persons addressed in the respective Convention, namely wounded and sick forces in the field (Article 12 paragraph 2 GC I) and at sea (Article 12 paragraph 2 GC II), while obviously containing more detailed and specific provisions with regard to particularly vulnerable categories of persons, i.e. POWs (Articles 13 paragraph 1, 14 paragraph 1, 87 paragraph 3, 89 paragraph 4, 108 GC III) and civilians (Articles 27, 32, 118, and 119 GC IV). Additionally, Common Article 3 paragraph 1(1)(a), Article 87 paragraph 3 GC III, and Article 118 GC IV refer to 'cruel treatment' or 'all forms of cruelty'. This category, however, is essentially the same as 'inhuman treatment'.[66]

40 From the perspective of consequences, inhuman treatment constitutes a grave breach of the Geneva Conventions (Articles 50 GC I and II respectively, Article 130 GC III, and Article 147 GC IV).

41 The jurisprudence on inhuman treatment does not clearly distinguish between torture on the one hand and inhuman or cruel treatment on the other. The most profound

---

[63] Ibid, para 470.   [64] Ibid, para 468.
[65] ICTY, *Krnojelac*, above n 44, para 183. See also CAT-Commentary, at 66.
[66] See, e.g., ICTY, *Delalić et al*, above n 33, para 551, or ICTY, *The Prosecutor v Tihomir Blaškić*, Trial Chamber Judgment, 3 March 2000, IT-95-14-T, para 186.

definition of 'inhuman treatment' was advanced in *Delalić et al*,[67] where the ICTY Trial Chamber, due to the lack of any definition in the IHRL documents, undertook a lengthy survey which covered considerations of the International Committee of the Red Cross (ICRC) Commentaries on the Geneva Conventions and Additional Protocol II (AP II), the lists of prohibited acts under the Nuremberg Charter, the International Law Commission (ILC) Draft Code of Crimes against the Peace and Security of Mankind, the jurisprudence of the ECtHR as well as of the Human Rights Committee, and legal scholarship. The outcome of these extensive deliberations was the finding that

> inhuman treatment is an intentional act or omission, that is an act which, judged objectively, is deliberate and not accidental, which causes serious mental or physical suffering or injury or constitutes a serious attack on human dignity. The plain and ordinary meaning of the term inhuman treatment in the Geneva Conventions confirms this approach and clarifies the meaning of the offence. Thus, inhuman treatment is intentional treatment which does not conform with the fundamental principle of humanity, and forms the umbrella under which the remainder of the listed 'grave breaches' in the Convention fall. Hence, acts characterised in the Conventions and Commentaries as inhuman, or which are inconsistent with the principle of humanity, constitute examples of actions that can be characterised as inhuman treatment.[68]

This definition of inhuman treatment, which resembles the definition of torture by including the requirement of intent, clearly contradicts the meaning of 'cruel or inhuman treatment' under IHRL (see MN 8–10). On the basis of this definition, perpetrators of obvious acts of torture were sometimes found guilty only of inhuman treatment. 42

a. The threshold of severity

By following the jurisprudence of the ECtHR in relation to the threshold of severity requirement, the ICTY blurred the distinction between torture and cruel or inhuman treatment. Rather than identifying intent, purpose, and the powerlessness of the victim as the essential distinguishing criteria, the ICTY introduced the threshold of *serious* pain or suffering for inhuman treatment, as opposed to the *severe* pain or suffering required for torture. 43

Essentially, the Trial Chamber in *Delalić et al* defined inhuman treatment 'in relative terms' as 'treatment which deliberately causes serious mental and physical suffering that falls short of the severe mental and physical suffering required for the offence of torture'.[69] Thus, to cite just one example, the fact that persons were not aware that they had been used as human shields was found as not constituting inhuman treatment.[70] On the assessment of severity, the Trial Chamber in *Krnojelac*, again in a similar fashion to the general formulation of the ECtHR in cases involving ill-treatment, repeated *mutatis mutandis* its findings on the assessment of the severity of acts alleged as constituting torture; furthermore, it also stated that real and serious suffering was sufficient, and also explicitly denied the need for any minimum length of the suffering,[71] while the actual presence of long-term effects nevertheless constitutes a factor when determining the seriousness of an act.[72] Going a bit 44

---

[67] See the wide-ranging endorsement of the findings in subsequent cases, e.g., ICTY, *Blaškić*, above n 66, para 154; ICTY, *Kunarac et al*, above n 38, para 502; ICTY, *Kordić and Čerkez*, above n 48, para 256.
[68] ICTY, *Delalić et al*, above n 33, para 543.
[69] Ibid, para 542.   [70] ICTY, *Blaškić*, above n 66, para 715.
[71] ICTY, *Krnojelac*, above n 44, para 131   [72] ICTY, *Simić et al*, above n 59, para 75.

further and into more detail with regard to the requirement of long-term effects, the Trial Chamber in *Krstić* held that

> serious harm need not cause permanent and irremediable harm, but it must involve harm that goes beyond temporary unhappiness, embarrassment or humiliation. It must be harm that results in a grave and long-term disadvantage to a person's ability to lead a normal and constructive life.[73]

b. Intent

45   Since the Geneva Conventions in general impose a positive duty relating to humane treatment, it follows that a specific intent is not necessary. Cases of intentional inhuman treatment nevertheless *additionally* fall under the distinct notion of 'wilfully causing great suffering or serious injury to body or health', which, by its very wording, obviously requires a specific *mens rea*.

46   Under IHRL, intent, or lack thereof, is one of the criteria distinguishing torture from cruel or inhuman treatment.[74] Even negligent conduct amounting to the infliction of severe pain or suffering, such as excessive use of force by negligence or appalling conditions of detention, may qualify as cruel or inhuman treatment.[75] In ICL, the requirement that inhuman treatment requires 'an act which, judged objectively, is deliberate and not accidental', in the early judgment of the ICTY in the Čelebići prison camp case,[76] has rendered this distinction fuzzy. In later judgments, the required level of intentionality was, however, set at a comparatively low level. In *Vasiljević*, the Trial Chamber held, for example, that

> [t]he *mens rea* of inhumane acts is satisfied where the offender, at the time of the act or omission, had the intention to inflict serious physical or mental suffering or to commit a serious attack on the human dignity of the victim or where he knew that his act or omission was likely to cause serious physical or mental suffering or a serious attack upon human dignity and was reckless thereto.[77]

47   In relation to crimes against humanity, the requirement of intent seems to be supported by Article 7(1)(k) ICC Statute, which defines inhuman treatment as other 'inhumane acts of a similar character intentionally causing great suffering, or serious injury to body or to mental or physical health'. In relation to war crimes, however, neither Article 8(2)(a)(ii) and (c)(i) ICC Statute, nor the Elements of Crimes require intent for the crimes of inhuman or cruel treatment.

IV. Degrading or humiliating treatment

48   The equivalent of the prohibition of degrading treatment in IHRL is the category of 'outrages upon personal dignity', as mentioned in Common Article 3 paragraph 1(1)(c). As will be shown below (see MN 49–59), the fact that this provision explicitly mentions 'humiliating and degrading treatment' as an example may lead to some confusion

---

[73] ICTY, *The Prosecutor v Radislav Krstić*, Trial Chamber Judgment, 2 August 2001, IT-98-33-T, para 513.
[74] Cf CAT-Commentary, at 73 ff.
[75] Ibid, at 557 ff. See also, e.g., European Committee for the Prevention of Torture, 2nd General Report, at paras 44–6; HRCttee, *Deidrick v Jamaica*, Comm No 619/1995, 9 April 1998, para 9.3.
[76] ICTY, *Delalić et al*, above n 33, para 543.
[77] ICTY, *The Prosecutor v Mitar Vasiljević*, Trial Chamber Judgment, 29 November 2002, IT-98-32-T, para 236; see also ICTY, *Krnojelac*, above n 44, para 132; or ICTR, *The Prosecutor v Clément Kayishema and Obed Ruzindana*, Trial Chamber Judgment, 21 May 1999, ICTR-95-1-A, para 153.

regarding the severity of the suffering involved. Apart from this provision, Article 13 GC III and Article 27 GC IV enshrine the protection against insults and exposure to public curiosity, while the latter and Article 14 GC III implicitly outlaw degrading treatment by enshrining the general obligation to respect a person and his or her honour. Article 27 GC IV also includes a provision guaranteeing a broad regime of special protection for women, first and foremost against 'rape, enforced prostitution or any form of indecent assault'.

a. The threshold of severity

Under IHRL, even the infliction of pain or suffering which does not reach the threshold of 'severe' may be considered as degrading treatment if it contains a particularly humiliating element.[78] At the ICTY, the jurisprudence on the concept of 'outrages upon personal dignity' has been somewhat confusing. It was first referred to by the ICTY Trial Chamber in the *Furundžija* case, where it dealt with rape under the prohibition of outrages upon personal dignity in Article 4(2)(e) AP II and as being implicitly covered by Common Article 3 paragraph 1(1)(c).[79] Focusing on the issue of rape, however, there was no substantial analysis of the requirements of the offence of outrages upon personal dignity as such. 49

This issue was taken up by the ICTY Trial Chamber in *Aleksovski*, which went as far as identifying outrages upon personal dignity as a 'species of inhuman treatment that is deplorable, occasioning more serious suffering than most prohibited acts falling within the genus'.[80] With regard to the objective element, the ICTY thus focused on the effects upon the victim in describing such an outrage as 'an act which is animated by contempt for the human dignity of another person. The corollary is that the act must cause serious humiliation or degradation to the victim', while further adding that such an act does not necessarily have to cause mental or physical harm but at least 'real and lasting suffering arising from the humiliation or ridicule'.[81] In its conclusion regarding the evaluation of the seriousness of the act, it thus identified '[t]he form, severity and duration of the violence, the intensity and duration of the physical or mental suffering' as the relevant factors.[82] 50

Later, the ICTY Trial Chamber in *Kunarac et al* rejected the requirement of 'lasting suffering' and that of any minimum long-term effect at all, which was identified as nevertheless having an indicatory role in proving the existence of outrages upon personal dignity. Overall, it held that, in line with IHRL, 'real and serious' humiliation or degradation was sufficient.[83] Regarding the question of whether or not a person had to be seen as having been humiliated by certain acts, the Trial Chamber in *Aleksovski* stated that this assessment could not be undertaken on a subjective basis alone, as individuals have different perceptions as to what constitutes humiliation, and also vary in how they cope with possibly degrading acts. Thus, in order to avoid the unjust result of the culpability depending solely on the character of the victim, the Trial Chamber further included a mitigating objective yardstick, stating that 'the humiliation to the victim must be so intense that the reasonable person would be outraged'.[84] 51

The notion of an objective assessment along with evaluating the individual concerned was re-emphasized by the Appeals Chamber in *Aleksovski* when it held that 'any human being' would have felt more than inconvenience and discomfort caused by the perpetrated 52

---

[78] See CAT-Commentary, at 558.   [79] ICTY, *Furundžija*, above n 24, para 166.
[80] ICTY, *Aleksovski*, above n 48, para 54.   [81] Ibid, paras 52–6.
[82] Ibid, para 57.   [83] ICTY, *Kunarac et al*, above n 38, para 501.
[84] ICTY, *Aleksovski*, above n 48, para 54.

acts.⁸⁵ In *Kunarac et al*, however, the Trial Chamber took a different approach and went as far as completely leaving aside the particular victim's feelings, holding that an outrage upon dignity was 'any act or omission which would be generally considered to cause serious humiliation, degradation or otherwise be a serious attack on human dignity'.⁸⁶ This approach is in conformity with the ICC Elements of Crimes on outrages upon personal dignity of Article 8(2)(b)(xxi) and (c)(ii), which require that 'the severity of the humiliation, degradation or other violation was of such degree as to be generally recognized as an outrage upon personal dignity'.

53   In sum, the case law of the ICTY in principle confirms the understanding of IHRL and IHL, according to which the threshold for degrading treatment may be lower than the severe pain or suffering required for cruel or inhuman treatment (see MN 43–44). It is the humiliation inflicted upon the victim which is decisive.

b. Intent

54   In its determination of the subjective element of degrading treatment, the ICTY Trial Chamber in *Aleksovski* relied heavily on the ICRC Commentary to the Additional Protocols, according to which the acts of the accused had to be carried out with the intent to humiliate or ridicule the victim. In somewhat unclear fashion, however, it then stated that

> [t]he ICRC, in proposing the mental element for the offence of 'inhuman treatment' accepted a lower degree of *mens rea*, requiring the perpetrator to act willfully. Recklessness cannot suffice; the perpetrator must have acted deliberately or deliberately omitted to act but deliberation alone is insufficient. While the perpetrator need not have had the specific intent to humiliate or degrade the victim, he must have been able to perceive this to be the foreseeable and reasonable consequence of his actions.⁸⁷

55   Given the slightly confusing overall impression left by the paragraph, it is not surprising that the ICTY Appeals Chamber in *Aleksovski* noted that this reasoning was somewhat unclear and, on the basis of its own interpretation of the ICRC Commentary, rejected the need for a specific intent to humiliate.⁸⁸

56   Agreeing on the finding that the *Aleksovski* Trial Chamber was not fully comprehensible in its judgment, and outlining that it had not sufficiently distinguished its own findings from that of the ICRC, the Trial Chamber in *Kunarac et al* took up the remaining open question (since the Appeals Chamber in *Aleksovski* had not addressed this issue) as to whether knowledge of the foreseeable consequences was required. It answered this question in the affirmative, stating that

> [a]s the relevant act or omission for an outrage upon personal dignity is an act or omission which would be generally considered to cause serious humiliation, degradation or otherwise be a serious attack on human dignity, an accused must know that his act or omission is of that character—i.e., that it could cause serious humiliation, degradation or affront to human dignity.⁸⁹

57   However, the Trial Chamber mitigated this finding by stating that it did not demand that the accused has to be aware of the actual consequences of the act as such. It rightfully observed that the accused's actual knowledge of the specific character of the proscribed

---

⁸⁵ ICTY, *The Prosecutor v Zlatko Aleksovski*, Appeals Chamber Judgment, IT-95-14/1-A, 24 March 2000, para 37. See also the discussion on the threshold for torture, MN 25–30.
⁸⁶ ICTY, *Kunarac et al*, above n 38, para 507.   ⁸⁷ ICTY, *Aleksovski*, above n 48, para 56.
⁸⁸ ICTY *Aleksovski*, Appeals Chamber, above n 85, para 27.
⁸⁹ ICTY, *Kunarac et al*, above n 38, para 512.

behaviour had little practical significance, since the objective element would usually imply the presence of the subjective element as well.[90]

In its conclusions, the Trial Chamber in *Kunarac et al* thus identified outrages upon personal dignity as being comprised of the following elements:

(i) that the accused intentionally committed or participated in an act or omission which would be generally considered to cause serious humiliation, degradation or otherwise be a serious attack on human dignity, and
(ii) that he knew that the act or omission could have that effect.[91]

Altogether, it needs to be stated that the way in which the ICTY has addressed the concept of outrages upon personal dignity in these two cases is questionable, due to the lack of precision in distinguishing it from inhuman or cruel treatment and the 'ordinary-language approach to the [ICTY] statute, mixing intuition in liberally with their literal method, while making few external references which would root the offence in legal history'.[92] Nevertheless, since the decisive criterion distinguishing 'outrages upon personal dignity' from inhuman or cruel treatment is the element of humiliation, we agree with the finding that the accused must either intentionally humiliate the victim, or at least know that the act or omission in which he or she participated could have a humiliating effect. Pure negligence, as with respect to inhuman treatment, is therefore not sufficient.

V. Inhuman or degrading punishment in international humanitarian law and international criminal law

Apart from the general provisions on inhuman and degrading treatment, which are obviously also applicable with regard to punishments of all forms, several of the provisions in the Geneva Conventions explicitly outlaw certain forms of punishment, namely Articles 17, 87, 89, and 108 GC III on POWs, as well as Articles 32 and 118 GC IV on civilians. In general, these provisions make it clear that coercion, collective punishment, corporal punishment, deprivation of sunlight, and violent punishment or punishment endangering the health of a POW are forbidden, while women have to be confined apart from men and under female supervision when serving a sentence.

In contrast to IHRL, the statutes of the main international criminal tribunals do not contain a specific reference to 'cruel, inhuman or degrading punishment'. The tribunals therefore have discussed these acts in the context of the three general categories of ill-treatment in IHL. Examples of punishment that was held as being degrading and/or inhuman include systematic beatings and kicking, solitary confinement, collective punishment, and the combination of beatings, short solitary confinement, and food deprivation.[93]

C. Relevance in Non-International Armed Conflicts

There can be no doubt that torture and CIDT are prohibited in both IACs and NIACs. From the perspective of the victim, the legal status of the person inflicting harm is

---

[90] Ibid, para 513.   [91] Ibid, para 514.
[92] A. Zahar and G. Sluiter, *International Criminal Law: A Critical Introduction* (Oxford: OUP, 2008), at 131 and 134.
[93] ICTY, *Krnojelac*, above n 44, paras 216–36.

irrelevant. Non-state actors are equally obliged to act in conformity with the various provisions on ill-treatment.

63   Furthermore, states are responsible for exercising due diligence in the prevention and punishment of violations of IHL by such actors.⁹⁴

64   This is already clear from the fact that these violations of IHL are to be found in Common Article 3, which is the minimum yardstick not only for NIACs but for IACs as well. As has been noted by the ICTY in the landmark Decision on the Defence Motion for Interlocutory Appeal on Jurisdiction in *Tadić*:

> [I]n the area of armed conflict the distinction between interstate wars and civil wars is losing its value as far as human beings are concerned. Why protect civilians from belligerent violence, or ban rape, torture or the wanton destruction of hospitals, churches, museums or private property, as well as proscribe weapons causing unnecessary suffering when two sovereign States are engaged in war, and yet refrain from enacting the same bans or providing the same protection when armed violence has erupted 'only' within the territory of a sovereign State? If international law, while of course duly safeguarding the legitimate interests of States, must gradually turn to the protection of human beings, it is only natural that the aforementioned dichotomy should gradually lose its weight.⁹⁵

65   On this basis, the Tribunal stated that 'at least with respect to the minimum rules in Common Article 3, the character of the conflict is irrelevant'.⁹⁶ In the same vein, the ICTY also came to its often-repeated conclusion regarding the fundamental purpose of IHL and its effects upon the applicability of distinct rules in IACs and NIACs, when it stated that '[w]hat is inhumane, and consequently proscribed, in international wars, cannot but be inhumane and inadmissible in civil strife'.⁹⁷

66   Most prominently, the ICTY also undertook a short survey of state practice, on the basis of which it concluded that customary international law provided for criminal liability for serious violations of Common Article 3.⁹⁸

67   Altogether, it is clearly established that no substantial difference exists between IACs and NIACs with regard to CIDT and torture, and there are no difficulties in applying the above-discussed norms to NIACs and IACs alike,⁹⁹ especially given the character of the norms relating to the latter type as merely substantiating the general prohibition of ill-treatment.

68   It follows that all parties to a NIAC and their individual members, above all those acting in official capacity, are under an obligation to abstain from any act of ill-treatment, and those members will be held personally accountable for any failure to fulfil that obligation.¹⁰⁰

69   Also, given the tremendous importance of non-state armed groups as one of the main actors in the vast majority of armed conflicts, addressing them in a mode somewhat similar to that of states would serve as a further form of pressure on them to have them adhere at least to the very core of IHL—upholding a person's dignity to the widest extent possible.¹⁰¹

---

⁹⁴ See the discussion on state responsibility at MN 72ff.   ⁹⁵ *Tadić*, above n 27, para 97.
⁹⁶ Ibid, para 102.   ⁹⁷ Ibid, para 119.
⁹⁸ Ibid, para 134; see also ICRC CIHL Study, vol I, Rule 158, at 607–10.
⁹⁹ See E. David, 'Internal (Non-International) Armed Conflict', in A. Clapham and P. Gaeta (eds), *The Oxford Handbook of International Law in Armed Conflict* (Oxford: OUP, 2014) 353.
¹⁰⁰ See ICTY, *Furundžija*, above n 24, para 140; see also Chs 19 and 20 of this volume.
¹⁰¹ On the proposal regarding holding non-state armed groups accountable, see L. Zegveld, *The Accountability of Armed Opposition Groups in International Law* (Cambridge: CUP, 2002); on human rights

As a side note, these provisions have to be interpreted in good faith. For instance, while non-state armed groups may basically take prisoners without violating Common Article 3,[102] the generally accepted view that the provisions on the status of POWs are not applicable to NIACs obviously does not serve as a legal justification for such groups to mistreat or even torture captured soldiers or other persons in their power.

D. Legal Consequences of a Violation

Given the severity of their very nature, violations of the right to human dignity, i.e. instances of torture and CIDT, trigger a variety of legal consequences. These may be assessed from the perspectives of individual and state responsibility, in times both of peace and armed conflicts.

I. State responsibility

Apart from the general rules on state responsibility, Article 3 of the Fourth Hague Convention 1907 and Article 91 AP I make it clear that states bear responsibility under IHL in times of armed conflict. As it was succinctly summarized by the ICTY Trial Chamber in *Furundžija*:

> Under current international humanitarian law, in addition to individual criminal liability, State responsibility may ensue as a result of State officials engaging in torture or failing to prevent torture or to punish torturers. If carried out as an extensive practice of State officials, torture amounts to a serious breach on a widespread scale of an international obligation of essential importance for safeguarding the human being, thus constituting a particularly grave wrongful act generating State responsibility.[103]

Equally important, since the obligation to grant protected persons humane treatment in times of armed conflict is at the heart of the four Geneva Conventions, they contain many provisions that are more detailed than the respective provisions of IHRL. At the same time, the prohibition of torture and CIDT under IHRL, as provided for in Article 7 ICCPR and comparable provisions in regional human rights treaties, constitutes an absolute human right, which, according to Article 4(2) ICCPR and relevant provisions in regional human rights treaties, cannot be derogated from even in times of public emergency, including internal disturbances and armed conflicts. It follows that the respective provisions of IHRL continue to be fully applicable in both IACs and NIACs.

International human rights law provides a variety of state obligations as regards respecting, protecting, and fulfilling the right to human dignity. The general obligation to protect means that states must also take all necessary measures to protect individuals against torture or CIDT inflicted by private actors, in accordance with the principle of due diligence.[104] One of the obligations to fulfil the right to human dignity derives from Article 4 CAT, which requires states parties to criminalize torture (but not CIDT) with adequate penalties, to investigate every single act of torture, and to bring the perpetrators

---

obligations of non-state actors in general, see A. Clapham, *Human Rights Obligations of Non-State Actors* (Oxford: OUP, 2006); and P. Alston (ed), *Non-State Actors and Human Rights* (Oxford: OUP, 2005).

[102] Zegveld, above n 101, at 65.
[103] ICTY, *Furundžija*, above n 24, para 142.   [104] See, e.g., Art 16 CAT.

to justice regardless of whether their acts are attributable to the state or not in accordance with the principles of territorial, active nationality and universal jurisdiction.

75   International humanitarian law also contains an analogous obligation to respect IHL under Common Article 1 and Article 1(1) AP I. The IHRL obligations to protect and fulfil the right to human dignity can also be applied *mutatis mutandis* to the field of IHL. A state is generally responsible not only to prevent and punish war crimes by its own forces or attributable actors, but also to exercise due diligence in the prevention and punishment of IHL violations by other non-state armed groups.[105]

76   It follows that, in any event, if all of the elements are present and if the perpetrators' acts can be attributed to the state, that state is responsible for the violation of the prohibition of torture or CIDT. However, it also needs to be reiterated that state responsibility does not necessarily require individual criminal responsibility and subsequent attribution of the acts of liable perpetrators to the state. Human rights bodies, because of their very mission, obviously follow a different approach from ICL courts and tribunals when it comes to the *mens rea* requirement. When assessing whether a state has violated its obligation to respect the prohibition of torture and CIDT, the focus of human rights bodies generally lies not on the individual perpetrators, but with the circumstances of the case and the conduct of the state as a whole. On the question of torture, the ECtHR, although it pays due regard to defining torture as a deliberate act, usually does not embark upon ascertaining whether the specific perpetrator acted with a particular intent, but rather examines the context in which the acts took place. 'Deliberately' can thus also be understood as 'systematic' and 'calculated'.[106] This is due in part to this Court's different interpretation of torture as being distinguished by the intensity of suffering instead of the specific purpose, which renders a profound discussion on the intent of the perpetrator more or less obsolete by shifting the focus towards the impact of certain acts on the victim. Also, and more generally when it comes to the jurisprudence of human rights bodies, the circumstances of the case are pivotal; it must not be forgotten that most of the main ECtHR cases, and the majority of HRCttee views, that led to an explicit finding that torture had occurred, related to interrogations and the accompanying detentions.[107]

77   Lastly, the consequences of the special status of the prohibition of torture as *jus cogens* must not be forgotten. A violation of such a norm renders the special regime of the ILC Articles on State Responsibility for Internationally Wrongful Acts applicable.[108] First and foremost, violations of *jus cogens* also affect other states, as these are obliged to abstain from recognizing as lawful any situation arising from such a breach, and from assisting or providing aid to the responsible state in maintaining this situation, and to cooperate in order to end the breach.[109]

78   Since any *jus cogens* rule is also an obligation *erga omnes*,[110] every state is entitled to invoke the responsibility of the state acting in violation of the prohibition of torture.[111] More specifically, the International Court of Justice (ICJ) held in *Belgium v Senegal* that

---

[105] See the discussion in the ICRC CIHL Study, at 532.
[106] *Ireland v United Kingdom*, above n 4, Separate Opinion of Judge Matscher, para 1.
[107] Nowak, above n 6, at 162–3; van Dijk et al (eds), above n 13, at 406–7.
[108] Art 40 ILC Articles on State Responsibility.
[109] Art 41 ILC Articles on State Responsibility.
[110] See, e.g., M. Byers, 'Conceptualising the Relationship between *Jus Cogens* and *Erga Omnes* Rules', 66 *NJIL* (1997) 211.
[111] Art 48(1)(b) ILC Articles on State Responsibility.

II. Criminal responsibility

To begin with the IHL regime on individual criminal responsibility, every single act of torture, inhuman treatment, and outrages upon personal dignity (which is included in the notion of inhuman treatment[113]) falls under the Geneva Conventions' grave breaches regime in Articles 50 GC I and GC II, Article 130 GC III, and Article 147 GC IV, with all the consequences arising therefrom. These provisions provide for rules on the penalization of the perpetrators regardless of their nationality,[114] and for the duty to search for and bring those perpetrators before a state's own courts or extradite them to other states.[115]

In the case of NIACs, torture and CIDT are considered to be serious violations of Common Article 3. Yet, such conflicts are are not part of the grave breaches regime, and Common Article 3 in general does not include any provision on its enforcement. This means that there is no express obligation to prosecute every individual act of torture and CIDT. Rather, Article 49 GC I, Article 50 GC II, Article 129 GC III, and Article 146 GV IV provide that states parties 'shall take measures necessary for the suppression of all acts contrary to the provisions of the present Convention other than the grave breaches'. The prosecution of such acts as war crimes in NIACs by a state's domestic courts is within the discretion of every state.[116] In practice, states and their domestic courts have often proved to be either incapable of trying and punishing perpetrators, or reluctant to do so.[117]

If states are unwilling or unable genuinely to carry out such investigation or prosecution, the ICC may be competent to investigate and prosecute under the principle of complementarity, as stipulated in Article 17 ICC Statute, while all of the statutes of the main international criminal tribunals cover all of the forms of ill-treatment discussed here.

The Statutes of the ICTY and ICTR, as well as the Statute of the ICC, explicitly include torture in their provisions on war crimes/grave breaches of the Geneva Conventions (Article 2(b) ICTY Statute; Article 8(2)(a)(ii)) and (c)(i) ICC Statute or on violations of Common Article 3 and AP II (Article 4(a) ICTR Statute). At the same time, torture is included in their respective lists of crimes against humanity (Article 5(f) ICTY Statute; Article 3(f) ICTR Statute; Article 7(1)(f) ICC Statute).

The statutes of the main international criminal tribunals also include the power to prosecute those responsible for inhuman or cruel treatment during armed conflicts (Articles 2(b) and 3 ICTY Statute; Article 4(a) ICTR Statute—again as a violation of Common Article 3 and AP II; Article 8(2)(a)(ii) and (c)(i) ICC Statute). At the same

---

[112] ICJ, *Questions relating to the Obligation to Prosecute or Extradite (Belgium v Senegal)*, Judgment, 20 July 2012, paras 68–70.

[113] Pictet Commentary GC IV, at 598.

[114] K. Zemanek, 'New Trends in the Enforcement of *Erga Omnes* Obligations', 4 *Max Planck Yearbook of United Nations Law* (2000) 1, 19.

[115] See Ch 31 of this volume.

[116] Cf, however, the Arbitral Tribunal in the *British Claims in the Spanish Zone of Morocco* case, Arbitral Award, 1 May 1925, reprinted in *Reports of International Arbitral Awards* (New York: United Nations, 1949), vol II, Section III(II), at 642, §§ 3–6.

[117] See, e.g., E. La Haye, *War Crimes in Internal Armed Conflicts* (Cambridge: CUP, 2008), at 121.

time, inhuman treatment may constitute a crime against humanity (Article 5(f) ICTY Statute; Article 3 ICTR Statute; Article 7(1)(k) ICC Statute). The Statute of the ICTY further provides, in accordance with the grave breaches regime, for the offence of wilfully causing great suffering or serious injury to body or health in Article 2(c); the ICC Statute refers to this category in Article 8(2)(a)(iii), while, in connection with crimes against humanity, it subsumes this category of crimes under its Article 7(1)(k); the ICTY Statute, however, does not refer explicitly to wilfully causing great suffering in its provision on crimes against humanity.

84 While the ICTY Statute does not explicitly mention degrading treatment, the ICTR Statute lists '[o]utrages upon personal dignity' and explicitly mentions 'humiliating and degrading treatment, rape, enforced prostitution and any form of indecent assault' under its competence for violations of Common Article 3 and of AP II in Article 4(e). Article 8(2)(b)(xxi) and (c)(ii) of the ICC Statute refer to 'outrages upon personal dignity, in particular humiliating and degrading treatment' as distinct war crimes in both IACs and NIACs.

85 Also, it is generally contended that all states are entitled to try such suspected war criminals in their national courts on the basis of the principle of universal jurisdiction.

86 The CAT also entails an obligation to criminalize and investigate acts of torture *ex officio*, and further provides for jurisdiction on territorial grounds, on the basis of active and passive nationality jurisdiction, as well as universal jurisdiction.

87 *Crimes against humanity*, i.e. certain acts and omissions 'committed as part of a widespread or systematic attack directed against any civilian population, with knowledge of the attack' as per the wording of the ICC Statute, also apply both in times of peace and during armed conflicts. They comprise, inter alia, torture, rape, and other forms of sexual violence, and other inhuman acts of a similar character, i.e. cruel and inhuman treatment and punishment.

III. Legal remedies for victims

88 From the perspective of the victim, it is difficult to hold states accountable under IHL and to exercise the right to an effective remedy and adequate reparation for the harm suffered. Although Article 3 of the Fourth Hague Convention 1907 and Article 91 AP I, as well as customary international law, may be seen as endowing individuals with the right to compensation for violations of IHL, no secondary rights arise out of these provisions. As a consequence,

[v]ictims of violations of IHL can hardly claim compensation through national courts on the basis of Article 3 […] or any other provisions. At the international level, more channels are available to victims to claim compensation. But a general remedy does not exist.[118]

89 It follows that states are not obliged to establish a system of remedies for violations of IHL in their domestic order, thereby often leaving victims 'empty-handed' in seeking redress for violations.[119]

90 In the meantime, IHRL is of crucial importance in filling this gap. Under the CAT, all victims of torture and CIDT have a right to an effective remedy and adequate reparation for the harm suffered in their domestic legal order.[120]

---

[118] L. Zegveld, 'Remedies for Victims of Violations of International Humanitarian Law', 85 *IRRC* 851 (2003) 497, at 507.

[119] Ibid.   [120] Arts 13 and 14 CAT; cf CAT-Commentary, at 439 ff.

Since the mechanisms of IHRL continue to apply during armed conflicts, victims have 91 the possibility to address the various regional and international human rights bodies. In this regard, the jurisprudence of the ECtHR has broken ground in showing its willingness to assess situations of NIACs on the basis of IHRL alone, thereby enabling it to exercise jurisdiction even if the state responsible for violations of IHL/IHRL strictly denies the existence of an armed conflict on its territory for political reasons.[121] Other regional IHRL tribunals have shown a general tendency or willingness to apply IHL in combination with, or as being implicitly part of, IHRL.[122] Under Article 22, the CAT also provides for an individual complaints procedure to the UN Committee against Torture in connection with all acts of ill-treatment. Special reference also needs to be made to the possibility of urgent action by the Special Rapporteur on Torture, upon receipt of credible information that persons are at risk of being subjected to torture or CIDT.

E. Critical Assessment

Given the common aim of IHRL and IHL of protecting the dignity and well-being of 92 individuals, it is no wonder that there are no essential differences in their respective provisions on torture, cruel, inhuman or degrading treatment and punishment. It is clear that, due to their absolute prohibition, acts that constitute torture or CIDT in times of peace cannot become tolerable in exceptional situations, above all in times of armed conflict. Applying the IHRL regime on this matter to IHL serves as a means to secure coherence in the application of the respective Articles in the Geneva Conventions.

In principle, the case law of the main international criminal tribunals relies on the 93 meaning of the three types of violations of the right to human dignity as developed by IHRL. *Torture* is the deliberate infliction of severe pain or suffering, whether physical or mental, on a powerless person in the custody or under the direct control of the perpetrator for a certain purpose, such as the extraction of a confession or information, intimidation, coercion, or discrimination. *Cruel or inhuman treatment or punishment* is the infliction of severe pain or suffering that lacks one or more of the definitional criteria for torture, namely intent, purpose, and powerlessness. *Degrading or humiliating treatment or punishment (outrages upon personal dignity)* includes the infliction of pain or suffering not reaching the threshold of being 'severe', if applied in a particularly humiliating way.

Although the case law of international criminal tribunals in principle follows the estab- 94 lished meaning of torture and CIDT under IHRL, there are certain differences. First of all, the involvement of a *'public official or other person acting in an official capacity'*, at least by acquiescence, as required by Article 1 CAT, does not apply for torture as a war crime or a crime against humanity. Secondly, the ICTY, in principle, also requires *intent* for the crime of cruel or inhuman treatment, unlike IHRL. This case law seems to exclude criminal responsibility for negligent conduct. In relation to crimes against humanity, this interpretation is supported by Article 7(1)(k) ICC Statute, which refers to other 'inhumane acts of a similar character intentionally causing great suffering'. Thirdly, the definition of torture as a crime against humanity in Article 7(2)(e) ICC Statute lacks the requirement

---

[121] See, on the ECtHR case law on the armed conflict in Chechnya, W. Abresch, 'A Human Rights Law of Internal Armed Conflict: The European Court of Human Rights in Chechnya', 16 *EJIL* (2005) 741.

[122] Zegveld, above n 118, at 515 ff; see also H.-J. Heintze, 'On the Relationship between Human Rights Law Protection and International Humanitarian Law', 86 *IRRC* 856 (2004) 789, at 802 ff.

of *purpose*, whereas under IHRL and in the definition of torture as a war crime in the ICC Elements of Crimes, the purpose constitutes an essential element distinguishing torture from cruel or inhuman treatment. Lastly, the international criminal tribunals further blur the distinction between torture and cruel or inhuman treatment by following the jurisprudence of the ECtHR, which requires a higher *threshold for the severity of pain or suffering* in relation to torture. Altogether, these differences lead to certain inconsistencies, and to the fact that certain acts of torture have been prosecuted only as the crime of inhuman treatment.

95   The differences between IHRL and ICL are thus mainly due to the different viewpoints of these two branches of international law, i.e. state responsibility in contrast to individual criminal responsibility. On this basis, the relatively young international criminal tribunals, especially at the beginning of their jurisprudence, had the benefit of being able to resort to a significant amount of jurisprudence and scholarship in IHRL law, and could often apply these findings to the special necessities of judging the exceptional situation of armed conflicts and holding individuals responsible instead of states.

96   While inter-state wars have decreased constantly ever since the Second World War, internal conflicts have been on the rise ever since. This has had a significant impact on the principle of humanity. First of all, NIACs, regardless of whether they are fought between a state and one or several armed groups, or only among armed groups with no real state actor identifiable, often rage among ethnic, cultural, tribal, and/or religious communities, with the tragic consequence of being marked by a high level of violence which particularly affects civilians. At the same time, the various actors involved are in most cases not particularly keen on acting in conformity with IHL, or do not even know of its existence. Hence, the problem is not the lack of rules but lack of knowledge and, above all, of observance, a phenomenon that has already been identified by Cicero's famous words, *silent enim leges inter arma*.

97   One of the principal problems in this connection is the simple fact that the regional human rights regimes are uneven in their quality, with those parts of the world in which the majority of contemporary armed conflicts are taking place having the weakest human rights regime, while the international human rights bodies are often either toothless or not competent at all. This is one of the main reasons in favour of the establishment of a World Court of Human Rights, with universal jurisdiction over human rights abuses by states, international organizations, and non-state actors, including armed groups.[123]

98   Lastly, the significant progress in international criminal law has clearly sent the message to individuals that the times of impunity are over. The success of the ICC and its jurisdiction, be it by an increase in states parties or referrals by the Security Council, will thus be of crucial importance in the years that follow.

MANFRED NOWAK   RALPH JANIK

---

[123] Cf J. Kozma, M. Nowak, and M. Scheinin, *A World Court of Human Rights—Consolidated Statute and Commentary* (Wien/Graz: Neuer Wissenschaftlicher Verlag, 2010).

Chapter 17. Rape and Other Sexual Violence

	MN
A. Introduction	1
B. Meaning and Application	7
I. Article 27 paragraph 2 GC IV	7
a. The antecedents of Article 27 GC IV	11
b. Attacks on honour	16
c. Rape	25
d. Enforced prostitution	30
e. Indecent assault	37
II. Protections for prisoners of war, the wounded, and child detainees	43
C. Relevance in Non-International Armed Conflicts	54
D. Legal Consequences of a Violation	62
I. Rape and other forms of sexual violence as war crimes	62
II. The role of the Security Council	70
E. Critical Assessment	73

Select Bibliography

Askin, K.D., *War Crimes against Women: Prosecution in International War Crimes Tribunals* (The Hague: Martinus Nijhoff, 1997)

de Brouwer, A., 'Supranational Criminal Prosecution of Sexual Violence: The ICC and the Practice of the ICTY and the ICTR', 20 *School of Human Rights Research Series* (2006)

de Brouwer, A. et al (eds), *Sexual Violence as an International Crime: Interdisciplinary Approaches* (Cambridge: Intersentia, 2013)

Charlesworth, H./Chinkin, C., *The Boundaries of International Law: A Feminist Analysis*, (Manchester: Manchester University Press, 2000)

Durham, H./Gurd, T. (eds), *Listening to the Silences; Women and War* (Leiden: Martinus Nijhoff, 2005)

Durham, H./O'Byrne, K., 'The Dialogue of Difference: Gender Perspectives on International Humanitarian Law', 92 *IRRC* (2010) 31

Edwards, A., *Violence against Women under International Human Rights Law* (Cambridge: CUP, 2010)

Gardam, J./Jarvis, M., *Women, Armed Conflict and International Law* (The Hague: Kluwer Law International, 2001)

Lewis, D.A., 'Unrecognized Victims: Sexual Violence against Men in Conflict Settings under International Law', 27 *Wisconsin International Law Journal* (2009) 1

Ni Aolain, F./Valji, N. (eds), *Gender and Conflict Handbook* (Oxford: OUP, 2014)

Sellers, P., 'The Context of Sexual Violence: Sexual Violence as Violations of International Humanitarian Law', in G. McDonald and O. Swak Goldman (eds), *Substantive and Procedural Aspects of International Criminal Law* (The Hague: Kluwer Law International, 2000) 265

Sellers, P., 'The "Appeal" of Sexual Violence: Akayesu/Gacumbitsi' in K. Stefisyn (ed), *Gender-based Violence in Africa* (Pretoria: University of Pretoria, 2007) 51

A. Introduction

1 Despite long-standing and clear prohibitions under international humanitarian law (IHL), conflict-related rape and other forms of sexual violence, often committed with unspeakable brutality, persist. Most reports recount sexual attacks against women and girls, but the targeting of men and boys for sexual violence is increasingly gaining visibility. Whether employed as a military tactic to terrorize, humiliate, and dehumanize individuals or communities, as a means to force whole populations to flee, or as a method to punish detainees or to commit genocide, sexual violence violates the fundamental tenet of the Geneva Conventions—humane treatment.

2 The point of departure for the commentary in this chapter is that protection from sexual violence, expressly provided in the Geneva Conventions under Article 27 paragraph 2 Geneva Convention (GC) IV and impliedly elsewhere, for example, Article 14 GC III, and Common Article 3, is inherent to the guarantee of humane treatment without adverse distinction that underpins the Conventions. It is the standard of duty owed to all victims of war at all times. The Preliminary Remarks of the International Committee of the Red Cross (ICRC) to the Geneva Conventions of 1949 confirm this, pointing out that each of the Conventions was 'inspired by the respect for the human personality and dignity'.[1] On GC IV, under which civilians on the territories of a party to the conflict and in occupied territories are explicitly to be protected from rape, enforced prostitution, and indecent assault of any kind in accordance with Article 27, the ICRC notes in its Preliminary Remarks that

> [s]trictly speaking, the (Fourth) Convention introduces nothing new in a field where the doctrine is sufficiently well-established. It adds no specifically new ideas to International Law on the subject, but aims at ensuring that, even in the midst of hostilities, the dignity of the human person, universally acknowledged in principle, shall be respected.[2]

3 Pictet ventured further. He commented that Article 27 'proclaims the principle of respect for the human person and the inviolable character of the basic rights of men and women', and is the 'basis on which the Convention rests, the central point in relation to which all its other provisions must be considered'.[3]

4 The fact that Article 27 paragraph 2 GC IV uses dated, sexist, and legally imprecise language should not inhibit its progressive interpretation (see further Chapter 10 of this volume, MN 25, and MN 52–55). This chapter espouses the view that the Geneva Conventions' shielding of protected persons from rape and other forms of sexual violence in such provisions is not only fundamental to the enforcement of IHL, but also vital to ensure the evolution of the doctrine of humane treatment, the overarching principle of humanitarian law.[4]

---

[1] ICRC, Preliminary Remarks to 1949 Geneva Conventions in *The Geneva Conventions of August 12, 1949* (Geneva: ICRC, 1994), at 29.
[2] Ibid.   [3] Pictet Commentary GC IV, at 200–1.
[4] See Rule 87 ICRC CIHL Study on humane treatment, which affirms that humane treatment is a long-standing core IHL concept owed to all protected persons and persons *hors de combat*. Humane treatment entails provision of a concrete duty to ensure the respect and 'dignity of a person', yet the notion of its execution constantly develops to incorporate the 'influences of changes in society'.

The protection against rape and other forms of sexual violence is also ensured by international human rights instruments and customary international law (CIL).[5] Unbelievably, protection of women and girls from sexual violence is not explicitly provided for in the Convention on the Elimination of All Forms of Discrimination against Women (CEDAW),[6] and this omission highlights some of the limitations international human rights law (IHRL) shares with IHL in addressing women's and girls' particular experiences.[7] However, IHRL prohibits violence, including sexual violence, against any person during armed conflict and in peacetime. It also prohibits violence against women as unlawful sex discrimination,[8] which, like the IHL principle of 'non-adverse treatment', is a customary norm of international law.[9]

This chapter examines the historical policy origins and modern scope of the application of the protection from rape and other forms of sexual violence under the Geneva Conventions. Reference is made to the relevant provisions in Additional Protocol (AP) I and AP II, and in

---

[5] Human rights violations have IHL counterparts, including protections against torture and cruel, inhuman, or degrading treatment or punishment, slavery and slavery-like practices such as trafficking, and the right to life. On the relationship between IHL and IHRL see Ch 35 of this volume. On rape as torture, see Ch 16 of this volume. See also, e.g., Special Rapporteur on Torture Report before the Human Rights Council, 15 January 2008, A/HRC/7/3, para 36; also ECtHR, *Aydin v Turkey*, Judgment, 25 September 1997, holding that 'rape was constitutive of torture'. In the context of armed conflict, see also Rule 8 ICRC CIHL Study; ICTR, *The Prosecutor v Jean-Paul Akayesu*, Trial Chamber Judgment, ICTR-96-4-T, 2 September 1998, para 596. In relation to females specifically, see, e.g., UN Declaration on the Elimination of Violence against Women, UNGA Res 48/104, 20 December 1993; CEDAW General Recommendations 19 and 30; Art 11 of the Protocol to the ACHPR on the Rights of Women in Africa; Council of Europe Convention on Preventing and Combating Violence against Women and Domestic Violence, 2011 (Istanbul Convention) (e.g., Arts 2 and 36).

[6] Note, however, the work of the UN CEDAW Committee. General Recommendation 19 on violence against women provides that violence against women is also sex-based discrimination that violates Art 1 of the Convention and, as such, 'impairs or nullifies the enjoyment by women of human rights and fundamental freedoms under general international law or under human rights conventions', including 'the *right to equal protection* according to humanitarian norms in times of international or internal armed conflict' (General Recommendation 19, Violence against Women, 1992, CEDAW/C/GC/19, para 7(c) (emphasis added)). The UN CEDAW Committee's General Recommendation 30 on women in conflict prevention, conflict, and post-conflict situations (2013) further clarifies states' human rights obligations towards women and girls in armed conflict, reiterating that 'in situations that meet the threshold definition of non-international or international armed conflict, the [CEDAW] and international humanitarian law apply concurrently and their different protections are complementary, not mutually exclusive'. Note that this General Recommendation, broad in scope, covers 'the application of the Convention to conflict prevention, international and non-international armed conflicts, situations of foreign occupation, as well as other forms of occupation and the post-conflict phase'. It also covers 'other situations of concern' not necessarily classified as armed conflict under international law, 'such as internal disturbances, protracted and low-intensity civil strife, political strife, ethnic and communal violence, states of emergency and suppression of mass uprisings, war against terrorism and organized crime'. The CEDAW Committee acknowledged that, at times, an unclear delineation exists between periods of pre-conflict, conflict and post-conflict (CEDAW/C/GC/30, para 4). For a comprehensive discussion of CEDAW, see M. Freeman, C. Chinkin, and B. Rudolf (eds), *The UN Convention on the Elimination of All Forms of Discrimination against Women, A Commentary* (Oxford: OUP, 2012).

[7] See critical commentaries, C. Bunch, 'Women's Rights as Human Rights: Towards a Re-vision of Human Rights', 12 *HRQ* (1990) 486; H. Charlesworth, 'What Are Women's Human Rights?', in R. Cook (ed), *Human Rights of Women: National and International Perspectives* (Philadelphia, PA: University of Pennsylvania Press, 1994) 58.

[8] See UN CEDAW Committee, General Recommendation 19, above n 6; Istanbul Convention, above n 5, Art 3; Inter-American Convention on the Prevention, Punishment and Eradication of Violence against Women. For prohibition of violence, including sexual violence, elsewhere in IHRL instruments, see CRC (e.g., Arts 34 and 38); CRC-OPAC; and Convention on the Rights of Persons with Disabilities (e.g., Art 11).

[9] The prohibition of discrimination, at a minimum on racial grounds, is also a peremptory norm of international law. See, e.g., the US (Third) Restatement of the Foreign Relations Law. On IHL, see ICRC CIHL Study, Rule 88: Adverse distinction in the application of international humanitarian law based on race, colour, sex, language, religion or belief, political or other opinion, national or social origin, wealth, birth or other status, or on any other similar criteria is prohibited.

B. Meaning and Application

I. Article 27 paragraph 2 GC IV

7 Article 27 GC IV safeguards protected civilians who are on the territory of a party to the conflict, as well as enemy inhabitants of occupied territory. Its origin may be traced to a proposal submitted to the ICRC by the International Women's Congress and the International Federation of Abolitionists.[10] Article 27, inter alia, recognizes civilians' express entitlement to respect for their persons, their honour, and family rights. It guarantees humane treatment, which precludes violence, threats, insults, or acts of public curiosity. The provision goes beyond prohibition by affirmatively requiring humane treatment and, in paragraph 2, that women '*shall be* especially protected against any attack on their honour, in particular against rape, enforced prostitution, or any form of indecent assault'.[11] It is the only Article in the Geneva Conventions explicitly to refer to, and require protection from, acts of sexual violence.[12]

8 The drafters of the Geneva Conventions in 1949, with the particular crimes committed against women during the Second World War in mind, and probably lacking awareness of the extent to which males are also targeted for sexual and gender-based violence, limited the explicit prohibitions against sexual assault under Article 27 paragraph 2 to attacks against females. However, the principle of humane treatment without adverse distinction extends Article 27's prohibitions to all protected persons similarly situated, and Article 27 paragraph 1 mandates that male civilians, irrespective of personal circumstance, shall enjoy respect for their 'person and honour'. This necessarily includes protection from sexual violence.[13]

9 The protection of women against rape, forced prostitution, and indecent assault was included in Article 76 AP I, and thus extended to all women in the territory of parties involved in the conflict. As the ICRC Commentary explains, Article 76 AP I 'thus […] applies both to women affected by the armed conflict, and to others, that is women protected by the fourth Convention and those who are not'.[14] In this way, Article 76 'develops the fourth Convention by extending the circle of its beneficiaries'[15] in keeping with the intention of the drafters of that Convention 'to proscribe such acts in general', as a response to the 'abuses perpetrated particularly during the Second World War, when countless women of all ages had been subjected to terrible outrages'.[16] The much-criticized

---

[10] Pictet Commentary GC IV, at 205, citing the Final Record, vol II-A, at 821.

[11] The special protections to be afforded women under Art 27 para 2 and other provisions extend to girls as well.

[12] See the discussion of the omission of rape as an explicit provision of the grave breaches regime at MN 62–65. On the protection against other forms of sexual violence under Art 27 GC IV see *amplius* Ch 61 of this volume.

[13] Cf D.A. Lewis, 'Unrecognized Victims: Sexual Violence against Men in Conflict Settings under International Law', 27 *Wisconsin International Law Journal* (2009) 1, at 23.

[14] ICRC Commentary APs, para 3151.   [15] Ibid, para 3154.   [16] Ibid, para 3152.

connection made in Article 27 paragraph 2 GC IV between crimes of sexual violence and women's 'honour' (see MN 16–24) was not repeated in Article 76 AP I, which requires instead that women 'shall be the object of special respect and shall be protected in particular against rape, forced prostitution and any other form of indecent assault'.

The prohibition on enforced prostitution and any form of indecent assault is also contained in Article 75(2)(b) AP I, which expressly provides that these are among the acts that 'are and shall remain prohibited at any time and in any place whatsoever, whether committed by civilians or by military agents'. This provision is applicable to persons of any gender affected by the situations covered by AP I in so far as they are 'in the Power of a Party to the conflict' and 'do not benefit from a more favourable treatment' under the Geneva Conventions and AP I. It thus expands the protection against enforced prostitution and indecent assault already mandated in Article 27 paragraph 2 GC IV.

a. The antecedents of Article 27 GC IV

While GC IV's singular focus on codifying the protection of civilians from the excesses of war was an historical first, earlier instruments also gave protection to civilians trapped by war or under occupation, including from rape and other sexual abuse.

The United States Army General Order No 100 of 1863, commonly known as the Lieber Code,[17] was derived in part from CIL. Article 44 of the Code expressly outlawed, 'all rape', along with killing of persons in the invaded country, designating such conduct as wanton violence. Article 22 provided that 'unarmed citizens were to be spared in person, property and honor', while Article 37, applicable during occupation, required the protection of 'persons of the inhabitants, especially those of women; and the sacredness of domestic relations'. The maximum penalty for violations of Articles 44 and 37 was death.[18]

The Geneva Convention of 1864 quickly followed the promulgation of the Lieber Code. However, Hague Convention IV Respecting the Laws and Customs of War on Land[19] proved more influential on Article 27 GC IV. Drafted in 1899 and revised in 1907, the Regulations in the Annex revisited the protection of persons in occupied territories.[20] It required occupying forces to respect 'family honour and rights',[21] which implicitly includes a prohibition against rape and other forms of sexual violence.[22] The Commission of Government Experts cited Article 46 of the Hague Regulations when urging delegates drafting the 1949 Geneva Conventions to incorporate a provision to respect the decency

---

[17] Lieber Code (1863), US War Department, *The War of the Rebellion: A Compilation of the Official Records of the Union and Confederate Armies* (Washington, DC: Government Printing Office, 1899), Series III, vol 3, at 148–64.

[18] Ibid, Arts 44 and 47.

[19] Convention Respecting the Laws and Customs of War on Land (Hague Convention IV), The Hague, 18 October 1907.

[20] Art 1 Hague Regulations: 'The laws, rights, and duties of war apply not only to armies, but also to militia and volunteer corps fulfilling the following conditions: [...] (4) to conduct their operations in accordance with the laws and customs of war.' The authors contend that this prohibited combatants from committing sexual violence, even in circumstances of non-occupation under 'the laws and customs of war'. See P. Sellers, 'The Context of Sexual Violence: Sexual Violence as Violations of International Humanitarian Law', in G. McDonald and O. Swak Goldman (eds), *Substantive and Procedural Aspects of International Criminal Law* (The Hague: Kluwer Law International, 2000) 265, at 274.

[21] Art 46 Hague Regulations.

[22] At the time of the drafting of the GCs, the common meaning of Art 46's protection of 'family honour' prohibited rape, Pictet Commentary GC IV, at 202.

and dignity of women, given the widespread 'rapes, indecent assaults and placement of women in disorderly houses' during the Second World War.[23] Unlike Article 46, Article 27 GC IV protects civilians on the territory of a party to the conflict, irrespective of whether military occupation exists.

14 The extensive rapes and other acts of sexual violence against civilian females in the First World War, particularly in Belgium, were considered by the Commission on the Responsibility of the Authors of the War and the Enforcement of Penalties[24] to constitute violations of the laws of war and the 'clear dictates of humanity'. Because of their conspicuous position on the list of war crimes that Central Power defendants could have faced if an international criminal tribunal had been established, prosecution of rape and for the abduction of women and girls for the purposes of prostitution is likely to have figured prominently. The post-war international criminal prosecutions foreseen by Article 227 of the Treaty of Versailles failed to materialize.[25] However, the Report of the Commission recognized that civilians were to be shielded from rape and enforced prostitution during war and periods of military occupation. This view ultimately informed the drafting of Article 27.

15 The third antecedent was the 1929 Geneva Convention Relative to the Treatment of Prisoners of War (1929 GC II), especially Article 3, which gave unprecedented attention to the treatment of female prisoners of war (POWs). It declared that female prisoners shall 'be treated with all consideration due to their sex',[26] providing for a duty to accord humane treatment—plainly intended to protect against sexual violence. Article 27 GC IV reprises this provision and articulates this intention by expressly prohibiting rape, enforced prostitution, and *any* form of indecent assault.

b. Attacks on honour

16 Article 27 paragraph 2 GC IV provides that women are to be especially protected from sexual and gender-based violence as an 'attack on their honour' (see Chapter 61, MN 12–13, of this volume). Protection from all other kinds of attacks against their honour, and all attacks against the honour of all protected persons, is provided in Article 27 paragraph 1.

17 'Honour' is not defined in the Conventions. The ICRC Commentary calls honour 'a moral and social quality', with the right to respect for it 'invested in man' because of inherent human characteristics of 'reason' and 'conscience'. Honour is a quality present in all, and respect for it must be accorded at all times and without discrimination on any ground, as is made clear in Article 27 paragraph 3 GC IV.[27] The content of honour is not fixed. It is

---

[23] The Commission of Government Experts' Study of Conventions for the Protection of War Victims, Condition and Protection of Civilians in Time of War, Chapter III, at 47 (14–26 April 1947).

[24] Commission on the Responsibility of the Authors of the War and on Enforcement of Penalties, Report presented to the preliminary Peace Conference, 29 March 1919, Pamphlet No 32, Division of International Law, Carnegie Endowment for Peace.

[25] See K.D. Askin, *War Crimes against Women: Prosecution in International War Crimes Tribunals* (The Hague: Martinus Nijhoff, 1997), at 42–4; K.D. Askin, 'Treatment of Sexual Violence in Armed Conflict: A Historical Perspective and the Way Forward', in A-M. de Brouwer et al (eds), *Sexual Violence as an International Crime: Interdisciplinary Approaches* (Cambridge: Intersentia, 2013). A descriptive account of the widespread rapes during the First World War is found in S. Brownmiller, *Against Our Will, Men, Women and Rape* (London: Secker & Warburg, 1975), at 43.

[26] Discussion of common Arts 12 GC I and GC II and Art 14 GC III, at MN 43–53.

[27] Pictet Commentary GC IV, at 202. Also, at 206, on the equality/non-discrimination principle in Art 27 para 3, the Pictet Commentary notes that 'any protected person is entitled to all the rights and liberties proclaimed by the Convention under a general principle common to all the Geneva Conventions. It is clear from

dependent on context—at least location, time, and gender—the influence of which is evident in the meanings ascribed to women's honour under Article 27 paragraph 2. Although the relationship between honour in paragraph 1 and paragraph 2 is not addressed in the Conventions, Pictet claims that women have special protection '*in addition* to the safeguards laid down in paragraph 1, which they enjoy equally with men'.[28]

This reference to 'honour' has not been replicated elsewhere. For example, the Universal Declaration of Human Rights, which is contemporaneous with the Geneva Conventions, refers to the inherent 'dignity' of every person rather than to their 'honour'.[29] The 1977 Additional Protocols also refer to 'dignity' not honour, prohibiting 'outrages upon personal dignity' and extending the protection against such attacks to men and boys.[30] Accordingly, IHL protects non-combatant females from sexual and gender-based violence as an 'attack on their honour' (Article 27 paragraph 2 GC IV) and all persons from 'outrages upon personal dignity' (Articles 75(2)(b) and 76 AP I) in the context of an IAC. In NIACs sexual violence comprising 'outrages upon personal dignity' is also prohibited (Common Article 3; Article 4(2)(e) AP II), whether committed against males or females. These Additional Protocol provisions also repeat the examples of violations listed in Article 27 paragraph 2 GC IV.[31]

Article 27 paragraph 2 is a direct response to the sexual attacks against women and girls committed during the Second World War, which 'revolt the conscience of all mankind' and which 'underline the necessity of proclaiming that women must be treated with special consideration'.[32] Article 27 also ostensibly echoes the concern for the duty owed to female detainees addressed in Article 3 1929 GC II, and carried over subsequently into the protections for women internees under the Geneva Conventions. These detail special measures to protect women detainees from attacks on their honour, including protecting against 'attacks' from the detaining party and from other protected persons,[33] the provision of separate sleeping quarters and sanitary conveniences for women temporarily interned with men who are not family members,[34] and searches of women internees by women only.[35] Other measures address protection of females in recognition of needs arising from their reproductive role, including requiring that 'expectant and nursing mothers [...] be given additional food'

18

19

---

the wording of the provision that the list of various criteria on which discrimination might be based—race, religion and political opinion—is only given by way of example. The criteria of sex and gender, language, colour, social position, financial circumstances and birth might be added. In a word, any discriminatory measure whatsoever is banned, unless it results from the application of the Convention. Nationality is not among the various criteria mentioned (it was mentioned in Article 13) and the discussions at the Diplomatic Conference make it clear that it cannot be regarded as implicitly included.'

[28] Pictet Commentary GC IV, at 205. This chapter does not discuss the gendered meaning of honour of males under IHL, although it is a matter warranting further examination. Also, there is some discussion in J.G. Gardam and M.J. Jarvis (eds), *Women, Armed Conflict and International Law* (The Hague: Kluwer Law International, 2001), e.g., at 107–12.

[29] See Art 1 UDHR: 'All human beings are born free and equal in dignity and rights.'

[30] See Art 75(2)(b) AP I and Art 4(2)(e) AP II. See also H. Durham and K. O'Byrne, 'The Dialogue of Difference: Gender Perspectives on International Humanitarian Law', 92 *IRRC* 877 (2010) 31.

[31] Art 75(2)(b) AP I; Art 4(2)(e) AP II. Under the APs, sexual violence is also implicitly prohibited as, e.g., acts of violence to the life, health, or physical or mental well-being of persons, or torture and mutilation. These acts are prohibited at any time, in any place whatsoever, and against any protected person, regardless of gender (Art 75(2) AP I). However, by contrast to the Conventions, the APs also expressly prohibit sexual and gender-based violence, naming rape, enforced prostitution, and other forms of indecent assault as outrages upon personal dignity against all protected persons, of any gender.

[32] Pictet Commentary GC IV, at 205. See also discussion of Art 14 GC III, at MN 43–53.

[33] E.g., Art 14 GC III.   [34] Art 85 GC IV.   [35] Art 97 GC IV.

(Article 89), and that 'maternity cases [...] can be given and shall receive care not inferior to that provided the general population' (Article 91). Many of these special measures, while perhaps well-meaning, are based on the stereotype of women as inherently weak relative to men[36] and susceptible to sexual violence.

20   Nonetheless, women and girls are disproportionately targeted for sexual attack, but this is attributable to gender inequality throughout the world and not to some inherent characteristic. In the context of war, they are frequently vulnerable to sexual violence as unarmed civilians in a context of generalized violence and disorder. Women also continue to carry out gender-prescribed activities during armed conflict, such as collecting water, which might take them outside safer zones or otherwise expose them to risk. Increasingly, they are also targeted as a deliberate tactic of war, 'a systemic part of the strategy of political control'.[37] The reductionist approach taken in Article 27 of equating female honour with modesty and chastity, is based on a mischaracterization of the harm caused by sexual and gender-based violence, and perpetuates the discriminatory gender stereotypes that make women vulnerable to such attacks.

21   Protecting honour from attack, rather than the person, as in Article 27 paragraph 2, is, therefore, troublesome, and has been the subject of considerable and justifiable feminist criticism. For instance, the linking in Article 27 paragraph 2 of sexual violence to honour may make it seem as if 'the provision is more about the social value traditionally attached to a woman's chastity' than her physical protection.[38] On the other hand, it is undoubtedly the case that in some states, and amongst conservative military officials, the concept of 'honour', as used in Article 27 paragraph 2, resonates strongly. It can therefore be useful in promoting observance of the prohibitions against sexual violence in armed conflict. The authors acknowledge the tension this raises, especially for feminist lawyers, given the imperative of preventing, prohibiting, and punishing sexual violence in armed conflict.

22   Article 27 paragraph 2 has also been criticized for being couched in notions of family honour, rather than physical and psychological safeguards for the protected person.[39] An extreme example of the impact of this is evident where women's honour, understood as inseparable from chastity, is considered the property of the family or community. Here, so-called 'honour crimes', such as killing, or 'chastity' reparations, such as marriage to the offender, are encouraged or forced to avenge perceived transgressions and to prevent any further shaming of the family. This same confusion, a belief in a 'collective honour' residing in the chastity of women, is also behind the deliberate military and political strategy that uses rape as a 'weapon of war'.

23   International humanitarian law, like much of international law in general, is criticized for being a 'thoroughly gendered system' in which the 'characteristics of men and women are assumed and serve as a basis on which to construct the regime'. Here, honour for men means 'bravery, fortitude, self-reliance; for women: chastity, modesty, frailty and dependence'.[40] On this basis, Article 27 paragraph 2 and the other special protections for

---

[36] This is clear from the special protections for women POWs. E.g., Arts 14, 16, and 49 GC III assume women's relative physical weakness compared to men, which should be taken into account in requiring POWs to work. See Pictet Commentary GC III, at 146–7, which explains the adoption of special measures here on the basis of women as 'the weaker sex'.

[37] C. Chinkin and M. Kaldor, 'Gender and New Wars', 67 *Journal of International Affairs* (2013) 167.

[38] C. Lindsey, 'The Impact of Armed Conflict on Women', in H. Durham and T. Gurd (eds), *Listening to the Silences: Women and War* (Leiden: Martinus Nijhoff, 2005) 21, at 33, referring to the critiques of others and not necessarily her own.

[39] Gardam and Jarvis (eds), above n 28, at 108–10.   [40] Ibid, at 11.

women 'take the male perception of not only what it is to be a woman, but also what it is about a woman that warrants protection. In doing so, a picture of a woman is presented that is distorted and far from the reality of their lives.'[41] The assumptions that follow, evident in Article 27 paragraph 2, include that chastity and modesty are inherent qualities of women's honour, but not necessarily of men's, and that women's dignity equates with their sexual purity. As Pictet comments, 'women […] have an absolute right to respect for their honour and their *modesty*, in short, for their dignity as women'.[42] Under this framework, sexual violence in conflict is erroneously viewed as something that happens only to female 'victims', while males' experience of sexual violence is assumed to be that of a perpetrator.

While there have been convictions for war crimes of rape and other forms of sexual violence before international criminal tribunals, especially by the International Criminal Tribunal for Rwanda (ICTR), the International Criminal Tribunal for the former Yugoslavia (ICTY), and the Special Court for Sierra Leone (SCSL), there have been no cases citing 'attacks upon honour' as a basis for gender-based charges. It now seems unlikely that a criminal prosecution would be pursued as an attack against a woman's or a girl's honour. The prohibition has been superseded by the 1977 Additional Protocols and by the adoption of the Statute of the International Criminal Court (ICC), which contains the most comprehensive list of sexual and gender-based crimes under international law but does not include the war crime of attacking a woman's honour.[43] It seems to be largely redundant, even if its underlying assumptions are more enduring. 24

c. *Rape*

The International Military Tribunal for the Far East (IMTFE) Judgment[44] condemned rape in several instances as a 'Conventional War Crime', citing in the indictment Article 3 of the 1929 GC II, Article 46 of the Annex to the 1907 Hague Convention, and the laws and customs of war.[45] The Judgment did not, however, define the conduct that amounts to rape. Subsequent Second World War cases in the Pacific theatre, such as the *Yamashita*,[46] *Awochi*,[47] and *Sakai*[48] cases, entered convictions for, but likewise did not define, rape. In the Dutch-led Temporary Court Martial in Batavia, the Judge-Advocate characterized rape as forcibly causing a woman to have 'extra-marital carnal intercourse'.[49] 25

The Geneva Conventions do not define rape, and neither does Article 76 AP I. By the time the two ad hoc international criminal tribunals for the former Yugoslavia and Rwanda were established in the 1990s, there was still no accepted definition of rape under international law. 26

---

[41] Ibid, at 10–11.   [42] Pictet Commentary GC IV, at 206 (emphasis added).

[43] Art 8(2)(b)(xxi) and (xxii) ICC Statute.

[44] See IMTFE, *United States et al. v Araki et al.*, Judgment, 4 November 1948, in R.J. Pritchard and S. Saide (eds), *The Tokyo War Crimes Trial: The Complete Transcripts of the Proceedings of the International Military Tribunal for the Far East* (New York: Garland, 1981), vol 22, 31, also available at <http://werle.rewi.hu-berlin.de/tokyo.anklageschrift.pdf>. See also Pritchard and Saide (eds) for transcripts of the proceedings as well as documents.

[45] Indictment, App D, reprinted in *Trial of Japanese War Criminals*, US Dept of State Publication No 2613, at 93–6.

[46] *Trial of General Tomoyuki Yamashita*, United States Military Commission, Manila, 1946, UNWCC Law Reports, vol IV, at 4, 6, 35.

[47] *Trial of Washio Awochi*, Netherlands Temporary Court-Martial, Batavia, 1946, UNWCC Law Reports, vol XIII, at 123, 125.

[48] *Trial of Takashi Sakai*, Chinese War Crimes Military Tribunal, Nanking, 1946, UNWCC Law Reports, vol XIV, at 7.

[49] See *Judge-Advocate v X et al*, Netherlands Temporary Court-Martial in Batavia, 1948, Case No 72/1947 (Verdict 231), available at <http://tinyurl.com/pzsnfwp>, at 2–5.

27   It required several trials at the ICTR and ICTY for a consensus on the legal elements of rape to emerge. The ICTR Trial Chamber first defined rape in the *Akayesu* case,[50] closely followed by definitions in the ICTY in *Delalić*[51] and then in *Furundžija*.[52] Finally, the ICTY Appeals Chamber in *Kunarac* settled on a definition for rape as a war crime[53] and as a crime against humanity in 2002.[54] This decision introduced the requirement for proof of the victim's lack of consent and the perpetrator's knowledge of the lack of consent. Importantly, the Appeals Chamber stated that consent must be given voluntarily and as a result of the person's own free will, and hence is to be 'assessed in the context of the surrounding circumstances'.[55]

28   Although binding only on the ICTY and ICTR, the *Kunarac* definition has been influential. The SCSL applied a slight variation of it in assessing the charge of rape as a crime against humanity in the *Charles Taylor* case,[56] and key elements were incorporated into the Elements of Crimes for the ICC.[57] At the time of writing, the ICC had not rendered a conviction for rape either as a war crime or as a crime against humanity. However, the definition in the Elements of Crimes is highly persuasive and has been copied into the laws establishing the Extraordinary Chambers in the Courts of Cambodia (ECCC)[58] and the Special Panels for Serious Crimes in East Timor, which entered a conviction for rape in the *Cardoso* case.[59] A number of states parties to the ICC Statute have also incorporated these elements for rape into their national laws.[60]

---

[50] The Trial Chamber acknowledged that it 'must define rape as there is no commonly accepted definition of this term in international law': ICTR, *Akayesu*, above n 5, paras 596 and 597. Note that the definition adopted was in relation to a charge of rape as a crime against humanity. Despite the differences in the contextual elements for rape as a crime against humanity or a war crime, the *actus reus* elements apply equally to both.

[51] ICTY, *The Prosecutor v Zejnil Delalić et al*, Trial Chamber Judgment, IT-96-21-T, 16 November 1998, para 479.

[52] ICTY, *The Prosecutor v Anto Furundžija*, Trial Chamber Judgment, IT-95-17/1-T, 10 December 1998, para 180.

[53] The definition for rape applies to IAC as well as to NIAC.

[54] In the *Kunarac* case (also known as *Foča*), the definition of rape, confirmed on appeal, was the penetration, however slight: (a) of the vagina or anus of the victim by the penis of the perpetrator or any other object used by the perpetrator; or (b) of the mouth of the victim by the penis of the perpetrator; where such sexual penetration occurs without the consent of the victim. Consent for this purpose must be consent given voluntarily, as a result of the person's free will, assessed in the context of the surrounding circumstances. The *mens rea* is the intention to effect this sexual penetration, *and* the knowledge that it occurs without the consent of the person. ICTY, *The Prosecutor v Dragoljub Kunarac et al*, Appeals Chamber Judgment, IT-96-23 & IT-96-23/1-A, 12 June 2002, para 128.

[55] Ibid, para 460. An unsuccessful appeal to the ICTR Appeals Chamber was lodged in *Gacumbitsi*, in which the prosecutor argued in favour of retaining the *Akayesu* definition of rape which did not require proof of the victim's lack of consent or the perpetrator's knowledge of the victim's lack of consent. ICTR, *The Prosecutor v Sylvestre Gacumbitsi*, Appeals Chamber Judgment, ICTR-2001-64-A, 7 July 2006, para 153.

[56] SCSL, *The Prosecutor v Charles Taylor*, Trial Chamber Judgment, SCSL-03-01-T, 18 May 2012, para 415.

[57] Rape as a war crime, Art 8(2)(b)(xxii)-1, ICC Elements of Crimes, UN Doc PCNICC/2000/1/Ass 2(2000), Art 8(2)(b)(xxii)-1. Also, e.g., Art 7(1)(g)-1 for identical *actus reus* elements for rape as a crime against humanity and Art 8(2)(e)(vi)-1, rape as a war crime in a NIAC.

[58] In the case against *Kaing Guek Eav* (alias 'Duch'), the Court convicted Duch of the crime against humanity of torture, including an act of rape. It held that, with respect to the *actus reus* of torture, '[c]ertain acts are considered by their nature to constitute severe pain and suffering. These acts include rape [...].' See ECCC, Case No 001/18-07-2007-ECCC-TC, Judgment, 26 July 2010, 99, at 85, para 355. This decision has sometimes been misunderstood as a conviction for the crime against humanity of rape. See Trial Chamber discussion, para 366, and the Supreme Court Chamber's discussion on appeal in Case No 001/18-07-2007-ECCC/SC, 3 February 2012, paras 208–13.

[59] *The Prosecutor v Jose Cardoso Fereira*, Case No 04/2001, 5 April 2003.

[60] See, e.g., Coalition for the International Criminal Court, *Chart on the Status of Ratification and Implementation of the Rome Statute and the Agreement on Privileges and Immunities*, available at <http://www.iccnow.org/documents/Global_Ratificationimplementation_chart_May2012.pdf>.

Unlike Article 27 paragraph 2 GC IV (and Article 76 AP I), the crime is gender neutral 29
under the ICC Statute and in the legal instruments which reformulated the provision
contained therein. However, there is no clash with Article 27 paragraph 2 GC IV since
the protection against rape expressly mandated in favour of females equally applies to
males under the principle of humane treatment and under other specific prohibitions that
apply implicitly to rape, such as the prohibition of torture as a grave breach (e.g., Article
146 GC IV).[61]

d. Enforced prostitution

The protection against enforced prostitution was included in Article 27 paragraph 2 GC 30
IV as it was one of the crimes committed against women in the Second World War that the
Conference particularly wanted to address (see also Chapter 61, MN 15, of this volume),[62]
although the Geneva Conventions fail to define it. Pictet reports that when drafting Article
27, the Conference had in mind the many thousands of women and girls forced into military
brothels during that war,[63] and refers to the practice as 'the forcing of a woman into immorality by violence or threats'.[64] A well-known example of enforced prostitution from this time is
the Japanese military brothels of the 1930s and 1940s, known as 'comfort stations', in which
hundreds of thousands of women and girls across the Asia-Pacific region were held and raped
repeatedly for the duration of their detention, or until they were killed.[65]

The Dutch Temporary Court Martial in Batavia (Jakarta) in Indonesia conducted the 31
only prosecutions for enforced prostitution in the context of armed conflict in 1948. They
convicted a number of Japanese military of the war crimes of coercion to prostitution,
abduction of women and girls for enforced prostitution and rape, and ill-treatment of
prisoners in relation to 35 Dutch nationals who had been interned by the Japanese and
then forced to become 'comfort' women.[66] One accused was sentenced to death, and the
others to terms of imprisonment ranging from two to 20 years.[67]

At the Nuremberg Tribunal, the Russian Prosecutor submitted evidence that in the 32
city of Smolensk, 'the German Command opened a brothel for officers in one of the
hotels into which hundreds of women and girls were driven'.[68] At the Tokyo Tribunal, evidence of the Japanese military forces setting up brothels in areas under their occupation,
such as Kweilin in China, formed part of the judgment.[69] However, evidence of forced

---

[61] See S. Sivakumaran, 'Prosecuting Sexual Violence against Men and Boys', in de Brouwer et al (eds), above n 25, 79 at 79–82. Also discussion at MN 7–10 and throughout.

[62] Pictet Commentary GC IV, at 205.   [63] Ibid.   [64] Ibid, at 206.

[65] There were also German military brothels across Europe during the Second World War, in which tens of thousands of women and girls were forced into prostitution. See, e.g., Askin, *War Crimes against Women*, above n 25, at 79.

[66] The Court Martial applied the definition of 'enforced prostitution' as a war crime from Dutch law, i.e. 'the abduction of girls and women for the purpose of enforced prostitution'.

[67] See Batavia Case No 72/1947 (Verdict 231), above n 49, at 21–2. Also see A.-M. de Brouwer, 'Supranational Criminal Prosecution of Sexual Violence: The ICC and the Practice of the ICTY and the ICTR', 20 *School of Human Rights Research Series* (2006), at 103; K.D. Askin, 'Prosecuting Wartime Rape and Other Gender-Related Crimes under International Law: Extraordinary Advances, Enduring Obstacles', 21 *Berkeley JIL* (2003) 288, at 302.

[68] *Trial of the Major War Criminals before the International Military Tribunal*, Nuremberg, 14 November 1945–1 October 1946 (Nuremberg, 1947), vol VII, at 455–6.

[69] IMTFE Judgment, above n 44, vol I, at 1125. Nevertheless, the Tokyo Tribunal did not pursue the enforced prostitution or sexual enslavement of the upwards of 100,000 other women and girls compelled into the 'comfort' system. See P. Sellers, 'Wartime Female Slavery: Enslavement?', 44 *Cornell International Law Journal* (2011) 118, at 117–19.

prostitution that could have been the basis for separate convictions of the war crime of enforced prostitution was instead incorporated into the charges for rape as a violation of the laws and customs of war and into charges of ill-treatment.[70]

33   There had been no prosecutions for enforced prostitution before the more recently established international and internationalized criminal tribunals. The crime is not expressly listed in the ICTY Statute, although it is included in the Statute for the ICTR as an example of an outrage upon personal dignity and a violation of Common Article 3 and of Article 4 AP II.[71] In the Statute of the SCSL, enforced prostitution is expressly included as a crime against humanity against the person (not against a person's 'honour') (Article 2(g)), and as an outrage upon personal dignity as a violation of Common Article 3 (Article 3(e)). The SCSL did not charge enforced prostitution (although sexual slavery as a crime against humanity was charged).[72] The law establishing the ECCC does not expressly include this crime either.[73]

34   Under the ICC regime, enforced prostitution is a war crime and a crime against humanity.[74] It is a crime against the person and not against a person's 'honour'. Like all crimes within the jurisdiction of the ICC, except forced pregnancy, this crime is gender neutral.[75] At the time of writing, the ICC had not issued indictments for enforced prostitution.

35   A number of commentators take the view that the conduct that constitutes enforced prostitution is better characterized and prosecuted as sexual slavery.[76] They consider that, in the context of armed conflict, most, if not all, factual scenarios that could be described as enforced prostitution would also amount to sexual slavery.[77] Furthermore, while the conduct might essentially be the same, characterizing it as sexual slavery rather

---

[70] IMTFE Judgment, above n 44, vol I, at 1178. General Shunroko Hata, Commander of the Chinese Expeditionary Forces between 1941 and 1944, was convicted upon Count 55 of the indictment that alleged disregard of the legal duty to secure the observance and prevent the breaches of the laws of war that occurred when large numbers of the inhabitants were murdered, tortured, raped, and otherwise ill-treated. Hata's troops invaded and occupied the Kweilin, committing rapes and setting up a brothel.

[71] The ICTY has prosecuted individuals for the crimes against humanity of rape and enslavement for conduct amounting to 'sexual slavery', in *The Prosecutor v Dragoljub Kunarac et al*, Trial Chamber Judgment, ICTY-IT-96-23-T & IT-96-23/1, 22 February 2001.

[72] Indictments for crimes against humanity of sexual slavery—SCSL, *The Prosecutor v Alex Tamba Brima et al*, Trial Chamber Judgment, SCSL-04-16-T, 20 June 2007 ('*AFRC case*'); and convictions for sexual slavery as a crime against humanity—SCSL, *The Prosecutor v Issa Hassan Sesay et al*, Trial Chamber Judgment, SCSL-04-15-T, 2 March 2009 ('*RUF case*'). Also V. Oosterveld, 'The Gender Jurisprudence of the Special Court for Sierra Leone: Progress in the Revolutionary United Front Judgments', 44 *Cornell International Law Journal* (2011) 49.

[73] Law on the Establishment of the Extraordinary Chambers in the Courts of Cambodia (2004).

[74] Crime against humanity—Art 7(2)(g); serious violations of the laws and customs applicable in IAC—Art 8(2)(b)(xxii)—and NIAC—Art 8(2)(e)(vi). Panels with Jurisdiction over Serious Criminal Offences for East Timor have jurisdiction over the same crimes against humanity and war crimes as the ICC (ss 5 and 6 Regulation No 2000/15, UNTAET/REG/2000/15, 6 June 2000).

[75] The non-contextual elements of the crime, as established in the ICC Elements of Crimes, are: (1) The perpetrator causes a person to engage in sexual acts including by force or threat of force or coercion, by an abuse of power or by taking advantage of a coercive environment in which the person cannot give genuine consent. (2) The perpetrator must also obtain or expect to obtain pecuniary or other advantage in exchange for, or in connection with the sexual acts. E.g., Art 8(2)(b)(xxii)-3, ICC Elements of Crimes.

[76] E.g., Final Report of the UN Special Rapporteur of the Working Group on Contemporary Forms of Slavery: Systematic rape, sexual slavery and slavery-like practices during armed conflict, 22 June 1998, UN Doc E/CN.4/Sub.2/1998/13 ('McDougall Report'), para 31; K.D. Askin, 'The Jurisprudence of International War Crimes Tribunals: Securing Gender Justice for Survivors', in Durham and Gurd (eds), above n 38, at 129; see also de Brouwer, above n 67, at 142–3.

[77] McDougall Report, above n 76, para 33.

than enforced prostitution 'responds to the concern expressed by survivors of the "comfort system" that the term "forced prostitution" obscures the terrible gravity of the crime, suggests a level of voluntariness, and stigmatizes its victims as immoral or "used goods" '.[78] Indeed, the legal description of the crimes committed against the 'comfort' women factually are more accurately and appropriately termed sexual slavery.[79]

Nonetheless, the drafters of the ICC Statute decided to retain enforced prostitution as a crime distinct from sexual slavery (see also Chapter 61, MN 15, of this volume), because of its historical significance—its explicit prohibition in the 1919 War Crimes Commission Report, Geneva Conventions, and Additional Protocols. After extensive debate, they included the second *actus reus* element—the perpetrator gets, or expects to get, a pecuniary or other advantage—to distinguish enforced prostitution from sexual slavery, and because it was consistent with a common understanding of the crime.[80] However, on the basis of this element, it is questionable whether the crimes committed against many of the 'comfort' women and girls and others forced into prostitution during the Second World War, which the Conference intended Article 27 paragraph 2 to protect against, would amount to enforced prostitution under the ICC Statute (although they would constitute sexual slavery). Nonetheless, including enforced prostitution in the jurisdiction of the ICC might allow prosecution of conduct that lacks slavery-like conditions,[81] making it another potential 'tool for future prosecutions of sexual violence in armed conflict situations'.[82]

36

e. Indecent assault

Besides Article 27 paragraph 2 GC IV (see Chapter 61, MN 16, of this volume), the protection against indecent assault is expressly mandated in three provisions of AP I. First, in Article 75(2)(b), which includes 'any form of indecent assault' among the acts that 'are and shall remain prohibited at any time and in any place whatsoever, whether committed by civilians or by military agents'. Secondly, in Article 76(1), which provides that women shall be protected from 'rape, forced prostitution and any other form of indecent assault'. Thirdly, in Article 77(1), which provides that children shall be protected 'against any form of indecent assault' (but without any reference to rape or enforced prostitution). The fundamental guarantees listed in Article 4(e) AP II combine 'any form of indecent assault', with rape, enforced prostitution, and humiliating and degrading treatment, with all types of outrages against personal dignity. Article 4 of the Statute for the ICTR and Article 3 of the Statute of the SCSL incorporate the language 'any form of indecent assault' as an outrage upon personal dignity, following verbatim the language of Article 4 AP II. However, the ICTY Statute does not include 'indecent assault'. Likewise, the ICC Statute does not include indecent assault as an outrage upon personal dignity in either IAC or NIAC.

37

Article 27 paragraph 2 does not define 'any form of indecent assault'. However, the ICRC Study on Customary International Humanitarian Law (ICRC CIHL Study)

38

---

[78] Judgment of the Women's International War Crimes Tribunal on Japan's Military Sexual Slavery 2001, para 634, reproduced at <http://www.alpha-canada.org/wp-content/themes/bcalpha-theme/resources/Sexual-Slavery/judgement_e01_optz.pdf>.

[79] Ibid, paras 634–9.

[80] de Brouwer, above n 67, at 142; also K. Dörmann, *Elements of War Crimes under the Rome Statute of the International Criminal Court, Sources and Commentary* (Cambridge: ICRC/CUP, 2003), at 329.

[81] B. Bedont and K. Martinez, 'Ending Impunity for Gender Crimes under the International Criminal Court', 6 *Brown Journal of World Affairs* (1999) 65, at 73. Also de Brouwer, above n 67, at 143, who posits that 'survival sex', in which women and girls, in the context or aftermath of armed conflict, exchange sex for essential goods and services (e.g., food, medicine, and health care) for themselves or family members, is an example of conduct better prosecuted as enforced prostitution rather than sexual slavery.

[82] McDougall Report, above n 76, para 32.

makes it clear that 'any form of indecent assault' equates to any form of sexual violence.[83] The ICTY Trial Chamber in *Stakić*, for example, took the same view, holding that the offence of sexual assault, other than rape, is punishable and embraces 'all serious abuses of a sexual nature inflicted upon the integrity of a person by means of coercion, threat of force or intimidation in a way that is humiliating and degrading to the victim's dignity'.[84] The *Milutinović* Trial Judgment[85] held 'sexual assault' to constitute an act of persecution as a crime against humanity that denied or infringed upon a person's fundamental rights.

39   What conduct, therefore, constitutes indecent acts? To paraphrase Pictet's famous caveat concerning torture, concrete acts depend on the imagination of future perpetrators, therefore rendering any list purporting to be complete restrictive over time. Nonetheless, the present authors' incomplete list,[86] included for illustration, highlights conduct that would amount to indecent assault. Whether the prohibition of 'any form of indecent assault' incorporates rape and enforced prostitution depends on standard treaty interpretation principles, including whether these crimes are specifically prohibited separately. For example, in Article 77(1) AP I, only 'indecent assault' is listed in relation to the protection of children, hence the prohibition must be read to cover rape, enforced prostitution, and all other sexual and gender-based violence.

40   Article 77(1) AP I requires that children 'shall be the object of special respect and shall be protected against any form of indecent assault'. The obligation applies to all parties to a conflict, requiring protection of children from indecent assault by members of their own party or the opposing party. Article 77(3) thus requires an adverse party into whose hands children taking part in the hostilities may fall, to *continue* to afford them this special protection, whether detained as POWs or not.[87]

---

[83] See ICRC CIHL Study, Rule 93.
[84] ICTY, *The Prosecutor v Milomir Stakić*, Trial Chamber Judgment, IT-97-24, 31 July 2003, para 757.
[85] ICTY, *The Prosecutor v Milan Milutinović et al*, Trial Chamber Judgment, IT-05-87-T, 26 February 2009, para 1767.
[86] Indecent assault conduct would encompass, inter alia: vaginal, labial, penile, testicular, breast, and anal mutilations; insertions of objects and liquids into the genitals and anus; burning of pubic hair; insertion of genitalia into one's own or another person's orifice, or into an animal, plant, tree, or inanimate object; rape (e.g., gang rapes, rape of children, rape of pregnant women, rapes prior to executions); compelled sexual acts between protected persons, especially family members, members of the same sex, internees, the aged, sick, disabled, military comrades or with the deceased; forced nudity, forced public display while nude, forced performance of duties while nude; forced masturbation, forced masturbation of other protected persons or members of Detaining Power; being compelled to watch infliction of sexual violence on others; or sexual insults, threats, intimidation, coercion, punishment, or threats of sexual violence; forced circumcision; forced abortion; forced pregnancy; forced birth; or mutilation of a pregnant womb.
[87] This is a crucial protection for child soldiers, who are not only routinely subjected to sexual and gender-based violence, such as rape, sexual slavery, forced pregnancy and forced abortion, but, especially in the case of girls, who are often 'recruited' specifically for the purpose of sexual slavery and forced (domestic) labour by 'fellow' members of their armed forces. See ICC, *The Prosecutor v Thomas Lubanga Dyilo*, Trial Chamber Judgment pursuant to Article 74 of the Statute, Separate and Dissenting Opinion of Judge Odio-Benito, ICC-01/04-01/06, 14 March 2012. In addition to being subjected to sexual abuse, boys are also often forced to perpetrate sexual abuse against the enemy, or even within their own group, in order, for example, to gain status within the masculine hierarchy of the armed group and thus increase their chance of survival. See also ICC, *The Prosecutor v Bosco Ntaganda*, Decision Pursuant to Article 61(7)(a) and (b) of the Rome Statute on the Charges of the Prosecutor against Bosco Ntaganda, ICC-01/04-02/06-309, 9 June 2014, at paras 76–80. Ntaganda was a commander of the militia UPC/FPLC in the conflict in the Democratic Republic of Congo and was charged, inter alia, with rape and sexual slavery of members of his own militia, namely child soldiers under the age of 15 years. The Chamber confirmed this charge after finding that, when read in the context of the prohibition against the use of child soldiers under 15 years in hostilities (Art 4(3)(c) AP II as reflected in Art 8(2)(e)(vii) ICC Statute), the child soldiers were not actively or directly taking part in hostilities at

41 The phrase 'any indecent assault' performs a residual function and covers any form of sexualized conduct that contravenes humane treatment and is not expressly listed. Its inclusion in Article 27 and in the fundamental guarantee provisions of the Additional Protocols, signals that the prohibition is central to assurances of humane treatment for all persons, at all times, irrespective of the circumstances or the characterization of the armed conflict.

42 Note that the equivalent residual clause in the ICC Statute (Article 8(2)(b)(xxii)) criminalizes 'any *other* form of sexual violence *also constituting a grave breach* of the Geneva Conventions'. The ICRC CIHL Study Rule 156 (definition of war crimes of sexual violence) notes that this additional prerequisite in Article 8 was necessary to reassure delegates at the Rome Diplomatic Conference, some of whom were concerned that alternative wording proposed for this residual clause—'any other form of sexual violence'—was too vague.[88]

II. Protections for prisoners of war, the wounded, and child detainees

43 Article 14 GC III provides for the general protection owed to POWs. It complements the general requirement that POWs 'be humanely treated' at all times, and 'be protected, particularly against acts of violence or intimidation and against insults and public curiosity' (Article 13 GC III). Specifically, Article 14 requires that states respect POWs in their 'person and honour', and expressly provides, in paragraph 2, that humane treatment, the *sine qua non* of IHL, be extended to female POWs: 'Women shall be treated with all the regard due to their sex and shall in all cases benefit by treatment as favourable as that granted to men.'

44 This approach follows Article 3 1929 GC II, which required respect for the 'person and honour' of all prisoners, and that 'women be treated with all consideration due to their sex'. The Rasmussen Commentary to 1929 GC II recalls that the German Delegate, who proposed including 'consideration due their sex', was motivated by the participation of female combatants in the First World War, their growing incorporation into the national defence, and thus the likelihood of female POWs in the future.[89]

45 The provision was invoked during the war crimes trials following the Second World War. At Nuremberg, the Tribunal cited Article 3 1929 GC II in its Judgment, as part of the law relating to war crimes that guided their deliberation.[90] Furthermore, subparagraph

---

the specific time these crimes were committed against them: 'The sexual character of these crimes, which involve elements of force/coercion or the exercise of rights of ownership, logically preclude active participation in hostilities at the same time.' (para 79) Accordingly, the Pre-Trial Chamber held that the requirement for humane treatment of persons taking no active part in the hostilities under CA 3 and Art 4(1) and (2) AP II applied, and the 'UPC/FPLC child soldiers under the age of 15 years continue to enjoy protection under IHL from acts of rape and sexual slavery' (para 79).

[88] See, ICRC CIHL Study, Rule 156. The ICRC states that '[i]t was solved by introducing the words "also constituting a grave breach of the Geneva Conventions". Although the intention of some of the groups that pressed for the inclusion of this crime was to stress that *any* form of sexual violence should be considered to be a grave breach, this phrase has been interpreted by states in the Elements of Crimes for the International Criminal Court as requiring that "the conduct was of a gravity comparable to that of a grave breach of the Geneva Conventions".' See also Dörmann, above n 80, at 331–2; O. Triffterer (ed), *Commentary on the Rome Statute of the International Criminal Court* (2nd edn, Oxford: Hart Publishing, 2008), at 451–4.

[89] G. Rasmussen, *Code des prisonniers de guerre: Commentaire de la Convention du 27 juillet 1929 relative au traitement des prisonniers de guerre* (Copenhagen: Levin & Munksgaard, 1931).

[90] *Trial of the Major War Criminals*, above n 68, vol I, at 253.

C of the factual allegation of Count Three, war crimes, included 'ill-treatment of prisoners of war'.[91] At the Tokyo Tribunal, Count 54 (ordering, permitting, or authorizing of war crimes) and Count 55 (alleged disregard of the legal duty to observe and prevent breaches of the laws of war) alleged: 'Inhumane treatment [...] [of] prisoners of war'; 'Mistreatment of the sick and wounded, medical personnel and female nurses'; and '(c) *female nurses were raped*, murdered and ill-treated'.[92]

46   The widespread rape of female POWs during the Second World War led the drafters of the 1949 Geneva Conventions to retain verbatim the requirement that women prisoners be accorded 'consideration due to their sex'. However, they also added the requirement that female prisoners 'shall in all cases benefit by treatment as favourable as that granted to men', regardless of any customary practices of the Detaining Power.

47   Pictet advises that these two conjunctive phrases must be read in reverse, with the emphasis placed on the according of equal treatment to all POWs and not on the 'vague idea of regard',[93] since it was the consternation that, in many countries, 'much prejudice still remained which sometimes placed women on an inferior footing' that led members of the Diplomatic Conference to insert this equality provision into Article 14.[94]

48   Pictet comments that the principle of equal treatment of prisoners regardless of gender is weakened to some extent by provision for special measures for female POWs and by unspecified special treatment required to give females 'regard due to their sex'. Special measures for female prisoners under GC III require female guards, separate detention quarters and sanitation facilities, special work assignments, nutritional allocation for pregnant or nursing mothers, repatriation preference, and a penal sanctions regime for pregnant prisoners.[95] However, taken as a whole, these measures should be interpreted as strengthening the principle of equality by recognizing the different needs of prisoners because of their sex, gender, or other status (e.g., pregnancy).

49   Article 14 does not define 'regard due to their sex'. According to Pictet, it refers to the (assumed) feminine attributes of weakness, honour, and modesty, as well as pregnancy and childbirth,[96] that are the basis for the Convention's differential treatment of female POWs. Pictet also comments that the connotation of weakness, and the description 'weaker sex', 'has a bearing on' rules regarding labour by, and food rations for, female prisoners,[97] while attributes such as 'honour' and 'modesty' require protection of women prisoners from 'rape, enforced prostitution and indecent assault'. 'Regard' due to women's honour and modesty therefore unequivocally proscribes any form of sexual violence against women POWs.

50   Geneva Convention III sets out other prohibitions and measures, including against 'insults and public curiosity' directed at POWs (Article 13 GC III), coercion and physical

---

[91] Nuremberg defendants Rosenberg, the Reich Minister for Occupied Eastern Territories including Russia, and Keitel, Chief of Command of the High Command, were convicted of Counts 3 and 4 based upon the ill-treatment inflicted on persons in occupied territories, substantiated inter alia by evidence of sexual violence; see *Trial of the Major War Criminals*, above n 68, vol I, at 43, 51–2.

[92] Indictment, App D, reprinted in *Trial of the Japanese War Criminals*, US Dept of State Publication No 2613, at 93–6 (1946) (emphasis added); see also IMTFE Judgment, above n 44, at 113.

[93] Pictet Commentary GC III, at 146.

[94] Report on the Work of the Conference of Government Experts, 119, cited in Pictet Commentary GC III, at 146.

[95] See Arts 25, 29, 49, 97, 88, and 108 GC III, respectively. See also Ch 61 of this volume.

[96] Pictet Commentary GC III, at 147.   [97] Ibid.

or mental torture during interrogation of POWs (Article 17 GC III), and the requirement for sex-segregated accommodation (Article 25 paragraph 4 GC III), which Pictet comments was intended to ensure that male POWs could not access female quarters, irrespective of the consent of the female prisoners.[98]

51 The duty to protect women from all forms of sexual violence as part of giving them due 'regard', is also expressly owed to those women who are wounded or sick on land (Article 12 GC I) or shipwrecked (Article 12 GC II). These provisions do not include equal treatment language, but do extend the requirement for humane treatment to all protected persons.[99]

52 Rule 134 of the ICRC CIHL Study (Women) cites these provisions to assert that IHL affords women the same protection as men without discrimination. State practice on protections based upon consideration of 'regard due to their sex', together with the provision of special measures to ensure no adverse discrimination, is discernible in national military manuals.[100] For example, some states have replicated the language of these provisions and specified the intention to prohibit rape, enforced prostitution, and indecent assault.[101] However, to date, no one has been convicted by a modern international criminal tribunal or court for sexual violence as a violation of Article 14.[102]

53 Article 77 AP I echoes Article 14 GC III, providing that 'children shall be the object of special respect and shall be protected against any form of indecent assault'. They are to be provided 'with the care and aid they require, whether because of their age or for any other reason'. Article 77(3) expressly requires a Detaining Power to continue to protect children throughout the period of detention, including children under 15 years of age who have taken direct part in hostilities, even if unlawfully so under international law, and irrespective of their POW status. The special protection must include the same kinds of measures to which adult POWs are entitled, including protection from members of their own party, as well as from members of the Detaining Party. For instance, Article 77(4) AP I, following the approach in Article 25 GC III, requires segregated quarters to protect children from a range of potential abuses, including sexual, by adult members of their own side and of the Detaining Party.

C. Relevance in Non-International Armed Conflicts

54 Common Article 3 to the Geneva Conventions[103] extended fundamental IHL objectives, namely the principle of respect for the human personality and guarantees of humane treatment, to situations of non-international or internal armed conflict.

---

[98] Pictet Commentary GC III on Art 25 (Quarters), at 195. See also Ch 61 of this volume.
[99] The language of 'regard due to their sex' is not found in the APs. E.g., Art 76(1) AP I states instead that women are the 'object of special respect', an equally vague, and arguably patronizing, term.
[100] ICRC CIHL Study, Rule 134, Section A, III, National Military Manuals.
[101] See ICRC CIHL Study, Rule 134, State Practice.
[102] In *Mrškić*, the ICTY Trial and Appeal Chambers examined the killing and torture of POWs based upon CA 3, as interpreted under Art 3 ICTY Statute. ICTY, *The Prosecutor v Mile Mrškić et al*, Trial Chamber Judgment, IT-95-13/1-T, 27 September 2007, and Appeals Chamber Judgment, IT-95-13/1-A, 5 May 2009.
[103] CA 3 reads in part: 'In the case of armed conflict not of an international character occurring in the territory of one of the High Contracting Parties, each Party to the conflict shall be bound to apply, as a minimum, the following provisions: (1) Persons taking no active part in the hostilities shall in all circumstances be treated humanely, without any adverse distinction [...]'. Various prohibited acts are then listed, including torture and outrages upon personal dignity, discussed below.

Common Article 3 is unconditionally the minimum standard of humane treatment to be given to persons taking no active part in hostilities. No excuse or extenuating circumstances prevent its application. It is operable at any time, in any place whatsoever. The obligation for all parties is absolute.[104] While Common Article 3 does not specify rape or other types of sexual violence, these acts are implicitly covered by the listed prohibitions, in particular under subparagraphs 1(1)(a) ('violence to life and person, in particular murder of all kinds, mutilation, cruel treatment and torture'), and 1(1)(c) ('outrages upon personal dignity, in particular humiliating and degrading treatment'). Those provisions have proved central to addressing rape and other sexual violence in international jurisprudence.[105]

55   Common Article 3 paragraph 1(1)(c) does not define what constitutes 'outrages upon personal dignity'. Clearly, however, the drafters intended the provision to cover, at a minimum, the sexual violence conduct set out in Article 27 GC IV—rape, enforced prostitution, and indecent assault. Pictet reports that Common Article 3 paragraph 1(1)(a) and (1)(c) '[concern] acts which world public opinion finds particularly revolting—acts which were committed frequently during the Second World War'.[106] Furthermore, Pictet opines that the drafters rejected the idea of an exhaustive list of acts, noting that the 'more specific and complete a list tries to be, the more restrictive it becomes'. Hence, Pictet states, '[t]he form of wording adopted is flexible, and at the same time precise'.[107]

56   Sexual violence prohibited under Common Article 3 paragraph 1(1)(a) includes sexual mutilations, reproductive experiments, sexualized killings, and rape. Subparagraph (1)(c), prohibiting outrages upon personal dignity, provides a legal basis for proscriptions of sexual abuse in NIAC. This illustrates a tension in the Geneva Conventions protection regime that links dignity and honour with crimes of sexual violence against females, rather than emphasizing the violent nature of the acts as attacks against a person. Significantly, Common Article 3 provides the basis for sexual violence safeguards in the fundamental guarantees provisions of AP I and AP II. Notably, Article 4 AP II contains the entirety of Common Article 3.[108] Each fundamental guarantee provision proscribes 'outrages upon personal dignity' and lists explicit forms of outrages, such as 'degrading treatment, enforced prostitution and any form of indecent assault' (Article 75(2)(b) AP I; Article 4(2)(e) AP II).

57   The Common Article 3 interdictions have also been incorporated into the Statutes of the ICTR (Article 4) and SCSL (Article 3). Even though the ICTY Statute does not expressly include 'outrages upon personal dignity' per se, the *Tadić* appeals decision held that violations of Common Article 3 were within its subject matter jurisdiction under violations of the laws and customs of war (Article 3 ICTY Statute).[109] The jurisprudence moreover confirmed that Common Article 3 encompasses rape.[110]

---

[104] E.g., Pictet Commentary GC IV, at 37.   [105] E.g., *Furundžija*, above n 52.
[106] Pictet Commentary GC IV, at 38.
[107] Ibid.
[108] Art 1(1) AP II clarifies that this Protocol 'develops and supplements [Common] Article 3 without modifying its existing conditions of application'.
[109] ICTY, *The Prosecutor v Duško Tadić*, Decision on the Defence Motion for Interlocutory Appeal on Jurisdiction, 2 October 1995, para 91.
[110] ICTY, *The Prosecutor v Anto Furundžija*, Decision on the Defendant's Motion to Dismiss Counts 13 and 14 of the Indictment, IT-95-17/1-PT, 29 May 1998, at 6(d), stating that the Appeals Chamber in *Tadić* did not preclude charging outrages upon personal dignity, including rape, thereunder.

58 The ICC Statute incorporates the original wording of Common Article 3, but de-links 'outrages upon personal dignity' from rape, enforced prostitution, and indecent assault (Articles 8(2)(b)(xxi) and 8(2)(c)(ii)), which are covered in separate provisions.[111]

59 The ICRC CIHL Study Rule 90 readily associates outrages upon personal dignity with torture and inhuman treatment. The 'outrages upon personal dignity' umbrella of protections has been a rich source of jurisprudence. For instance, in *Furundžija*, in which Witness A testified that she was raped vaginally and orally, the Trial Chamber found that

> [s]exual assaults were committed publicly; Members of the Jokers were watching and milling around the door of the pantry. They laughed at what was going on. The Trial Chamber finds that Witness A suffered severe physical and mental pain, along with public humiliation, at the hand of the accused in what amounted to outrages upon her personal dignity and sexual integrity.[112]

60 The *Kunarac* ICTY Trial Chamber held that forcible naked dancing on tables constitutes an outrage on personal dignity. The accused, Kovač, knew that 'having to stand naked on a table, while the accused watched them was a painful and humiliating experience for the three women involved, even more so because of their young age'.[113]

61 Common Article 3 paragraph 1(1)(c) has also been relied on to charge 'degrading treatment', especially sexual abuse, including rape, by the ICTR,[114] and acts of sexual slavery before the SCSL.[115] State practice has also relied upon Common Article 3 paragraph 1(1)(c).[116]

D. Legal Consequences of a Violation

I. Rape and other forms of sexual violence as war crimes

62 Despite the inclusion of express protections in Article 27 paragraph 2 GC IV, the omission of rape and other forms of sexual violence from the list of crimes under the Geneva Conventions' grave breaches provisions, especially under Article 147 GC IV, has caused controversy and confusion. The Preliminary Remarks to the Convention have done little to reduce this confusion by commenting that grave breaches would make an 'important contribution toward defining war crimes', arguably implying that only those grave breaches that were listed were war crimes under the Conventions. The omission of rape as an explicit grave breach created a misperception in the minds of some that rape was not a war crime *and* not justiciable under the grave breaches provisions. The omission was compounded by the failure of the drafters of the fundamental guarantees provision in Article 75 AP I to include rape.

---

[111] See Art 8(2)(b)(xxii) ICC Statute.   [112] ICTY, *Furundžija*, above n 52, para 272.

[113] ICTY, *Kunarac*, above n 71, paras 772–74.

[114] See ICTR, *The Prosecutor v Augustin Ndindiliyimana*, Trial Chamber Judgment and Sentence, ICTR-00-560T, 17 May 2011; *The Prosecutor v Idelphonse Hategekimana*, Trial Chamber Judgment and Sentence, ICTR-00-55BT, 6 December 2010; *The Prosecutor v Tharcisse Renzaho*, Trial Chamber Judgment, ICTR-97-31-T, 14 July 2009; *The Prosecutor v Théoneste Bagosora*, Trial Chamber Judgment, ICTR-98-41-T, 18 December 2008.

[115] SCSL, *AFRC case*, above n 72, paras 718–19; see also SCSL, *Taylor*, above n 56, para 1196.

[116] See Court of Bosnia and Herzegovina, Section I for War Crimes, *The Prosecutor v Zrinko Pinčić*, Verdict and Sentence, Case No X-KR-08/502, 28 November 2008; *The Prosecutor v Velibor Bogdanović*, Verdict and Sentence, Case No S1 1K003336 10 Krl, 29 August 2011.

63 In the early 1990s, the disclosure of widespread, conflict-related sexual violence in Bosnia and Herzegovina led to persistent demands by the international community, particularly feminist activists, to have rape explicitly 'recognized' as a war crime. Although rape had long been a violation of IHL, as outlined above, it was rarely, if ever, explicitly listed as a war crime in treaties. There was further concern that because rape was not an explicit grave breach of the Geneva Conventions, it was not treated as a war crime. To clarify the status of rape under IHL, the ICRC issued an Aide-Mémoire in 1992, stating that the grave breach regime in Article 147 GC IV 'obviously not only covers rape, but also any other attack on a woman's dignity'.[117] While the Aide-Mémoire did not completely quell concerns, it impelled the ICRC to take greater strides to inform parties to all armed conflicts that rape under Article 27 was indeed a serious violation of IHL and could amount to a grave breach. It also prompted the ICRC to deepen its analysis of the Geneva Conventions and the CIL bases for the prohibition of rape and other forms of sexual violence, as evidenced, inter alia, by the ICRC's CIHL Study Rule 93.[118] In the commentary to Rule 156 of the CIHL Study on the definition of war crimes, the ICRC acknowledges that the listing of rape, sexual slavery, enforced prostitution, and enforced pregnancy as war crimes in the ICC Statute 'reflects changes in society'. It also reiterated that

[a]lthough rape was prohibited by the Geneva Conventions, it was not explicitly listed as a grave breach either in the Conventions or in Additional Protocol I but would have to be considered a grave breach on the basis that it amounts to inhuman treatment or wilfully causing great suffering or serious injury to body or health.[119]

64 Critically, the convictions for war crimes committed in the former Yugoslavia confirmed that rape and other forms of sexual violence do indeed constitute serious and enforceable violations of IHL that could amount to grave breaches under the charges of torture or inhuman treatment,[120] as well as violations of Common Article 3.

---

[117] ICRC, Aide-Mémoire, para 2 (3 December 1992). For discussion on feminist activism on this issue, see, e.g., K. Engle, 'Feminism and its (Dis)Contents: Criminalizing Wartime Rape in Bosnia and Herzegovina', 99 *AJIL* (2005) 778; H. Charlesworth, 'Feminist Methods in International Law', 93 *AJIL* (1999) 379; C. Chinkin, '"Reconceiving Reality": A Ten-Year Perspective', 97 *ASIL PROC* (2003) 55. Note also Y. Kushalani, *Dignity and Honour of Women as Basic Human Rights* (The Hague: Martinus Nijhoff Publishers, 1982), at 148–53, arguing that the dignity and honour of women is a basic human right and a long-standing general principle of international law, including the laws of war.

[118] In the 1990s, the ICRC strengthened its analysis of IHL prohibitions of sexual violence. See ICRC Statement before the Commission for the Rights of Women, European Parliament, 18 February 1993 (Brussels); Resolution 2B, 26th International Red Cross and Red Crescent Conference (Geneva, 1995), wherein the Conference conveyed outrage at sexual violence in armed conflicts, in particular rape used as an instrument of terror, and forced prostitution; ICRC Update on the Aide-Mémoire on rape committed during the armed conflict in ex-Yugoslavia, of 3 December 1992. In 1998, the ICRC conducted a study to better identify the ways in which women are affected by armed conflicts, and to determine how to improve its own response: see Resolution 1: Plan of Action for the years 2000–3, 27th International Red Cross and Red Crescent Conference (Geneva, 1999); in 1999, at the same Conference, the President pledged a four-year commitment to reiterate the ICRC's concern about sexual violence in armed conflict, available at <http://www.icrc/eng/women>. Also in 1999, the ICRC integrated inquiries about rape and other sexual violence into a survey marking the 50th Anniversary of the Geneva Conventions: *People on War Report: ICRC Worldwide Consultation on the Rules of War* (Geneva: ICRC, 1999); in 2000, the ICRC's *Project on Women and War* described the ICRC commitment to focus on issues affecting females in armed conflict, C. Lindsey, 'Women and War—An Overview' 89 *International Review of the Red Cross* (30 September 2000), available at <http://www.icrc.org/eng/resources/documents/misc/57jqq3.htm>.

[119] ICRC CIHL Study, Rule 156 Definitions of War Crimes.

[120] See, the ICTY's first case, *The Prosecutor v Duško Tadić*, Trial Chamber Judgment, IT-94-1-T, 7 May 1997, where the Tribunal held that acts of male sexual assault, including mutilation, fellatio, and indecent assault, constituted the war crimes of inhuman and cruel treatment, and the crimes against humanity of other

In April 2013, the Foreign Ministers of the Group of Eight (G8) adopted a declaration that included a statement 'recall[ing] that rape and other forms of serious sexual violence in armed conflict are war crimes and also constitute grave breaches of the Geneva Conventions and their first Protocol'.[121] Moreover, confirming the gravity of sexual violence crimes by re-stating their grave breaches status, the G8 reiterated that this status triggers state obligations to prevent, investigate, and prosecute or extradite suspects under for example Article 146 GC IV, and obliges third states to exercise universal jurisdiction over suspects. For a genre of war crimes that has been spectacularly under-investigated and under-prosecuted, such reiteration is significant.[122]

To date, no international criminal cases have relied solely on Article 27 paragraph 2 as a legal basis for prosecution of sexual violence. Moreover 'indecent assault' is not listed as a war crime in Article 8 of the ICC Statute, nor in the Statutes of the ICTY, ICTR, SCSL, or the ECCC. Rape and enforced prostitution[123] are expressly listed as war crimes in the ICC Statute (Article 8(2)(b) and (c)).[124]

However, Article 27 GC IV has been cited in ICTY decisions. In *Furundžija*, the Trial Chamber held that 'attention must be drawn to the fact that there is a prohibition of rape and any form of indecent assault on women in Article 27 of Geneva Convention IV'.[125] In *Kvočka*, the Trial Chamber recognized that rape was not only prohibited by Common Article 3, but that it was also 'a crime explicitly protected against in Article 27 of the Fourth Geneva Convention'.[126] In *Đorđević*[127] and the

---

inhuman acts; ICTY, *Furundžija*, above n 52, convicted for forced nudity and humiliation, in addition to acts of rape; see also ICTY, *The Prosecutor v Miroslav Kvočka et al*, Trial Chamber Judgment, IT-98-30/&-T, 2 November 2001, and ICTY, *Delalić*, above n 51. Similarly, the SCSL has held perpetrators of rape guilty of a war crime, see *AFRC* case, above n 72, paras 1068–188. In most situations in which rape and other forms of sexual violence occur in armed conflict, victims will be in the custody or control of the perpetrator, or the perpetrator will be taking advantage of 'a coercive environment' to commit the crime. For this reason, war crimes of rape, etc invariably will be factually and legally contiguous with the grave breach of torture. For analysis, see ICTY, *Kunarac* Appeals Chamber, above n 54; Amnesty International, *Rape and Sexual Violence: Human Rights Law and Standards in the International Criminal Court* (IOR 53/001/2011), at 38; REDRESS, *Redress for Rape, Using International Jurisprudence on Rape as a Form of Torture or Other Ill-treatment* (October 2013), available at <http://redress.org/downloads/publications/FINAL%20Rape%20as%20Torture%20%281%29.pdf>.

[121] *Declaration on Preventing Sexual Violence in Conflict*, adopted at the G8 Foreign Ministers Meeting, London, 11 April 2013 ('G8 Declaration'). The statement was based on analysis by the UK, then holding the Presidency of the G8, confirming that although 'sexual violence and rape are not specifically listed as "grave breaches" of the [Geneva Conventions] or [Additional Protocol I] […] as a matter of treaty interpretation, serious sexual violence and rape should be regarded as "grave breaches" on the basis that they will always amount in practice to torture or inhuman treatment, or wilfully causing great suffering, which are so listed. This position can be taken whether or not it is accepted that sexual violence is a grave breach as a matter of customary international law. International practice supports this interpretation.' *Preventing Sexual Violence in Conflict: Sexual Violence as a Grave Breach of the Geneva Conventions*, Paper by the United Kingdom, 3 February 2013, copy on file with the authors. The Declaration was subsequently launched during the 2013 UNGA and, at the time of writing, 140 states had endorsed it.

[122] See also discussion of consequences of violations of Art 27 GC IV in Ch 61 of this volume. See further Ch 31, MN 56–61, of this volume, on the system of universal jurisdiction over grave breaches. Cf, G8 Declaration, above n 121: 'States have an obligation to search for and prosecute (or hand over for trial) any individual alleged to have committed or ordered a grave breach regardless of nationality. Accordingly, those accused of grave breaches should be brought to trial, in a manner consistent with international norms. There should be no safe haven for perpetrators of sexual violence in armed conflict.'

[123] See the discussion of Art 27 GC IV and enforced prostitution at MN 30–36.

[124] See ICRC CIHL Study, Rule 156, discussion of the war crime of committing sexual violence.

[125] ICTY, *Furundžija*, above n 52, para 175.

[126] ICTY, *Kvočka*, above n 120, para 234, fn 409. See also ICTY, *Delalić*, above n 51, para 476.

[127] ICTY, *The Prosecutor v Vlastimir Đorđević*, Trial Chamber Judgment, IT-05-87/1, 23 February 2011, para 1767, fn 6238.

Milutinović case,[128] the Trial Chambers cited Article 27 approvingly as the CIL basis for prohibitions against sexual assault.

68 States' practice has incorporated the Article 27 prohibitions, including rape, enforced prostitution, and indecent assault, into national military manuals, recognizing them as crimes, subject to individual criminal responsibility by members of the armed forces, including commanders.[129]

69 Individual criminal responsibility for direct and indirect perpetrators (including civilian superiors and military commanders) attaches for crimes under international law, including grave breaches of the Geneva Conventions and other serious violations of IHL. As yet, no ICC convictions have been recorded for sexual violence amounting to grave breaches.[130] However, numerous individuals, including combatants, military commanders, and civilians, have been convicted of war crimes of sexual violence before international criminal tribunals, such as the ICTY and ICTR, the SCSL, and the Special Panel for Serious Crimes (East Timor).[131]

II. The role of the Security Council

70 Extensive campaigning by women's rights organizations throughout the 1990s led the Security Council to join other United Nations (UN) organs in condemning sexual violence in armed conflict, particularly against women and children, identifying it as a threat to international peace and security. In 2000, it adopted Resolution 1325,[132] the first in a series of resolutions on the Security Council's Women, Peace and Security agenda, which reaffirmed the *Beijing Declaration's conclusions* and underscored the CEDAW Committee's General Recommendation No 19.[133] Six subsequent resolutions[134] address the continuing prevalence of sexual violence in conflict and highlight the connection between such violence, women's exclusion from peace and transitional processes, and continuing insecurity. They call on UN member states to fulfil their obligations 'to implement fully, international humanitarian and human rights law that protects the rights of

---

[128] ICTY, *Milutinović*, above n 85, para 196, fn 355.

[129] See ICRC CIHL Study, Rule 93 (Rape and other Forms of Sexual Violence), fn 10.

[130] See, e.g., ICC, *The Prosecutor v Germain Katanga*, Judgment pursuant to Article 74, ICC-01/04-01/07-3436, 7 March 2014, prosecuted for committing through other persons crimes against humanity and war crimes, including rape and sexual slavery—he was found not guilty of rape or sexual slavery charges; ICC, *The Prosecutor v Omar Hassan Ahmad Al Bashir*, Second Warrant of Arrest for Omar Hassan Ahmad Al Bashir, ICC-02/05-01/09, 12 July 2010, including charges as an 'indirect co-perpetrator' of the crime against humanity of rape; ICC, *The Prosecutor v Francis Kirimi Muthaura and Uhuru Muigai Kenyatta*, ICC-01/09-02/11, as indirect co-perpetrators of the crime against humanity of rape. Note the charges against Muthuaura were withdrawn on 11 March 2013 and against Kenyatta on 13 March 2015.

[131] These cases are well documented elsewhere in this chapter and on the websites for each tribunal. Also see the ICTY website on its work prosecuting crimes of sexual violence, available at <http://www.icty.org/sid/10312>. Note further the *International Protocol on the Documentation and Investigation of Sexual Violence in Conflict, Basic Standards of Best Practice in the Documentation of Sexual Violence as a Crime under International Law*, 1st edn, June 2014. This initiative of the Government of the UK is intended to assist in better and more investigations and prosecutions of these crimes at national and international levels. Available at <https://www.gov.uk/government/publications/international-protocol-on-the-documentation-and-investigation-of-sexual-violence-in-conflict>.

[132] UNSC Res 1325 (2000).

[133] Beijing Declaration and Platform for Action, 1995, e.g., para 133. On CEDAW General Recommendation 19, see above n 6.

[134] UNSC Res 1820 (2008), 1888 (2008), 1889 (2009), 1960 (2010), 2106 (2013), and 2122 (2013).

women and girls during and after conflicts',[135] and 'to comply with their obligations for prosecuting persons responsible for such acts',[136] including civilian superiors and military commanders, in accordance with IHL.[137] Further, 'to ensure that all victims of sexual violence, particularly women and girls, have equal protection under the law and equal access to justice'.[138] They also call on 'all parties to armed conflict to take special measures to protect women and girls from gender-based violence, particularly rape and other forms of sexual abuse'.[139]

Security Council Resolution 1960 establishes a mechanism to sanction parties to armed conflict who perpetrate sexual violence against any person in violation of their IHL obligations. Security Council Resolution 1960 asks for the Annual Reports of the UN Secretary-General to detail 71

> information on parties to armed conflict that are credibly suspected of committing, or being responsible for acts of rape or other forms of sexual violence, and to list [...] the parties that are credibly suspected of committing or being responsible for patterns of rape and other forms of sexual violence in situations of armed conflict on the Security Council agenda; [and the UN] expresses its intention to use this list as a basis for more focused United Nations engagement with those parties, including, as appropriate, measures in accordance with the procedures of the relevant sanctions committees [...][140]

Resolution 1882, mirroring the Women, Peace and Security suite of Security Council Resolutions, also calls on UN Member States to 'take decisive and immediate action against persistent perpetrators of violations and abuses committed against children in situations of armed conflict', including bringing to justice those responsible 'through national justice systems, and where applicable, international justice mechanisms and mixed criminal courts and tribunals, with a view to ending impunity' for such violations.[141]

The Security Council Resolutions on Women, Peace and Security, and Children in Armed Conflict are binding on UN member states and reiterate their obligations and duties under international law, including IHL and, in particular, under the Geneva Conventions and their Additional Protocols. 72

E. Critical Assessment

The prohibition of rape and other forms of sexual violence, however described, falls squarely within the duty of a party to an armed conflict to provide humane treatment to protected and other persons, regardless of sex, age, or other distinction. This is an 73

---

[135] E.g., UNSC Res 1325 (2000), para 9, which 'Calls upon all parties to armed conflict to respect fully international law applicable to the rights and protection of women and girls as civilians, in particular [...] under the Geneva Conventions [1949], Additional Protocols thereto [1977], Refugee Convention [1951] and the Protocol thereto [1967], the Convention on the Elimination of All Forms of Discrimination against Women [1979], Optional Protocol thereto [1999], the United Nations Convention on the Rights of the Child [1989], and the two Optional Protocols thereto [2000], and to bear in mind the relevant provisions of the Rome Statute of the International Criminal Court.'
[136] E.g., UNSC Res 1820, para 4.   [137] E.g., UNSC Res 1888, para 7.
[138] E.g., UNSC Res 1820, para 4.   [139] E.g., UNSC Res 1325, para 10.
[140] UNSC Res 1960, para 3.   [141] E.g., UNSC Res 1882, para 16.

obligation that is owed irrespective of the characterization of the armed conflict, and at all times and in all places.

74   Efforts in recent decades to reinterpret the outdated and sexist approach of the Geneva Conventions and Additional Protocols to the protection of women and girls from sexual and gender-based violence, have eliminated any remaining doubt that such acts violate IHL and may amount to grave breaches or crimes under international law (as war crimes, crimes against humanity, or genocide), engendering individual criminal liability as well as state responsibility. No doubt can remain either that the prohibitions against sexual and gender-based violence in armed conflict are *jus cogens* norms,[142] and that states are duty-bound to investigate and prosecute or extradite to a third state those credibly suspected of committing such crimes.[143]

75   Despite these clear obligations, war crimes of rape and other forms of sexual violence continue unabated during armed conflicts of all kinds. Meanwhile, the extensive lack of compliance with the obligations to prevent and diligently investigate and prosecute violations when they occur, and to provide full reparation to victims, creates a cycle of impunity.

76   The factors behind this gross lack of compliance are complex and varied, but significantly include fundamental gender inequalities found in all societies. The failure of the drafters to include express provisions addressing sexual violence in each Convention, including in the grave breaches provisions, is symptomatic of this and has led to the creation of the 'gendered hierarchy that permeates IHL'.[144] In this hierarchy, gender stereotypical ideals of female honour are shrouded in 'chastity and modesty', which impedes women's independent personhood. Masculine privilege and notions of warrior honour and duty obscure, even preclude the possibility of males being subjected to conflict-related sexual and gender-based violence. This is further reflected in the lack of express prohibitions against male sexual violence, rendering the fact of such violations invisible. The failure to confront the innate realities of female and male wartime sexual violence in full[145] results in protections that are ambiguous, incoherent, and insufficient. This is an outmoded and unprincipled approach. A modern, gendered analysis and application of the Geneva Conventions, and a more lucid articulation of how war-related sexual and gender-based violence contravenes the fundamental principle of humane treatment, are overdue.

77   Suggestions have been advanced for a new legal instrument, whether a stand-alone convention or a protocol, that fully integrates a gender perspective.[146] At a minimum, such an instrument should update the Geneva Convention grave breaches regime and the fundamental guarantee articles of the Additional Protocols, to include rape and all forms of sexual violence, including a residual phrase (e.g., 'other forms of sexual violence'). The list of acts in the ICC Statute is the best guide as it is currently the most

---

[142] See, e.g., P. Viseur Sellers, 'Sexual Violence and Peremptory Norms: The Legal Value of Rape', 34 *Case Western Reserve JIL* (2002) 287, at 292; D.S. Mitchell, 'The Prohibition of Rape in International Humanitarian Law as a Norm of Jus Cogens: Clarifying the Doctrine', 15 *Duke Journal of Comparative and International Law* (2005) 219, at 228; Lewis, above n 13, at 11.

[143] Refer, e.g., to para 4 of the G8 Declaration, above n 121.

[144] Gardam and Jarvis, above n 28, at 251.

[145] Ibid, for a comprehensive discussion of the shortcomings of IHL from a gender perspective. See also H. Charlesworth and C. Chinkin, *The Boundaries of International Law: A Feminist Analysis* (Manchester: Manchester University Press, 2000).

[146] Gardam and Jarvis, above n 28, at 256–7.

comprehensive.¹⁴⁷ Prohibitions against sexual violence must be gender-neutral (with the exception of gender-specific violations such as forced pregnancy) and not replicate problematic language, such as 'regard due to their sex', or concepts, such as treating sexual violence as an attack on female honour.

78 Consistent with the non-adverse distinction principle, any new instrument must expressly include prohibitions of sexual violence against all people regardless of gender, sex, gender identity, sexual orientation, or, indeed, any other status. Consistent with the requirement for states to accord children special respect, it must also fully safeguard them from sexual violence irrespective of their circumstances, and from all parties, including those of their own side. Express protection should include child soldiers¹⁴⁸ and all children born as a result of conflict-related rape.

79 Such an instrument could draw upon IHRL, international criminal law, and IHL¹⁴⁹ to create a protection regime to redress the entirety of sexual and gender-based violence committed during armed conflict, including in 'new wars',¹⁵⁰ wherein sexual violence is commonly used as a deliberate political or military tactic.

80 A new instrument may be an unlikely short-term prospect, and there is a risk that prohibitions, protections, and norms might be weakened or removed rather than strengthened.¹⁵¹ Nevertheless, a binding instrument that comprehensively addresses protection from sexual and gender-based violence for everyone in every type of armed conflict could outweigh these risks, and merits further consideration.

81 In any event, a strong commitment to the dissemination, implementation, and enforcement of existing protections is vital, as is regular training of armed forces, especially commanders. Political leadership committed to meeting IHL and IHRL obligations in relation to the suppression, investigation, and prosecution of violations involving sexual violence in every case is indispensable and urgently required. Dissemination of and adherence to authoritative guidance from UN human rights treaty bodies on state responsibilities, such as the CEDAW General Recommendation 30, are imperative. Similarly, guidance on the interpretation of Article 38 of the Convention on the Rights of the Child is warranted.¹⁵²

82 Meanwhile, a strenuous execution of regional IHRL instruments that address sexual violence in armed conflict, such as the Protocol to the African Charter on Human and Peoples' Rights of Women in Africa and the Istanbul Convention on Preventing and Combating Violence against Women and Domestic Violence,¹⁵³ is needed to guide states' wartime protection of males and females. Lastly, a more concerted effort by

---

¹⁴⁷ Art 8(2)(b)(xxii) and (2)(e)(vi) ICC Statute.
¹⁴⁸ Consistent with the decision on the confirmation of charges, ICC, *Ntaganda*, above n 87.
¹⁴⁹ There is precedent for this, e.g., in the ICC Statute.
¹⁵⁰ 'New wars' is a term used 'to distinguish contemporary political violence from the predominant "old war" conception' on which the Geneva Conventions and much of IHL in general are based. See, e.g., Chinkin and Kaldor, above n 37.
¹⁵¹ There are many examples of efforts to wind back or limit women's rights in the negotiation of international instruments, both 'hard' and 'soft'. Examples include proposals to use 'gender' in the ICC Statute and to include the crime of enforced pregnancy. Both proposals were vigorously opposed by conservative states and civil society organizations, and by the Holy See. On this point, see Bedont and Martinez, above n 81. See also ICRC Commentary on AP II, which has a narrower scope of application than CA 3, which it was originally intended to expand.
¹⁵² On CEDAW General Recommendation 30, above n 6. See the Secretary General's Annual Report to the Security Council on the implementation of UNSC Res 1882 in relation to children in armed conflict.
¹⁵³ The Istanbul Convention (Council of Europe) 2011 applies during periods of armed conflict and non-conflict (Art 2(2)), above n 5.

UN member states and UN agency engagement is needed to implement UN Security Council Resolutions on Women, Peace and Security, including prioritizing measures for women's participation on an equal basis with men in peace talks and other transitional processes.

83 When interpreting, implementing, and enforcing the existing protections under the Geneva Conventions, Additional Protocols, and IHL in general, or in the development of new instruments or standards purporting to strengthen such protections, the single guiding question ought to be: what approach best enables IHL to effectively safeguard all persons from sexual and gender-based violence in full accordance with the fundamental principle of humane treatment without adverse distinction?

PATRICIA VISEUR SELLERS   INDIRA ROSENTHAL*

---

* This commentary is written in the authors' personal capacities.

Chapter 18. Protected Areas

	MN
A. Introduction	1
B. Meaning and Application	6
I. Hospital zones and localities	6
II. Hospital and safety zones and localities	21
III. Neutralized zones	24
IV. Red Cross box in sea warfare	29
V. Non-defended localities and demilitarized zones under Additional Protocol I	30
a. Non-defended localities	31
b. Demilitarized zones	34
C. Relevance in Non-International Armed Conflicts	36
D. Protected Areas Established by the UN Security Council	38
I. The legal basis for the establishment of protected areas and safe corridors	40
II. The protection of the protected areas and safe corridors	44
E. Protected Area Recent Practice	47
I. Sri Lanka	48
II. Iraq	49
III. Somalia	50
IV. Bosnia-Herzegovina	51
V. Rwanda	55
VI. Darfur	56
F. Legal Consequences of a Violation	57
G. Critical Assessment	61

Select Bibliography

Bothe/Partsch/Solf, at 375–89

Bouvier, A., 'Zones protégées, zones de sécurité et protection de la population civile', in K. Boustany and D. Dormoy (eds), *Perspectives humanitaires entre conflits, droit(s) et action* (Brussels: Bruylant, 2002) 251

ICRC Commentary APs, paras 2263–318

Lavoyer, J.-P., 'International Humanitarian Law, Protected Zones and the Use of Force', in W. Biermann and M. Martin (eds), *UN Peacekeeping in Trouble: Lessons Learned from the Former Yugoslavia* (Aldershot: Ashgate, 1998) 262

Pictet Commentary GC I, at 206–15, 415–29

Pictet Commentary GC IV, at 120–8, 129–33

Sandoz, Y., 'The Establishment of Safety Zones for Persons Displaced within their Country of Origin', in N. Al-Nauimi and R. Meese (eds), *International Legal Issues Arising under the United Nations Decade of International Law* (The Hague/London/Boston: Kluwer Law International, 1995) 899

Torelli, M., 'Les zones de sécurité', 99 *RGDIP* (1995) 787

A. Introduction

1 Within the category of protected areas, international humanitarian law (IHL) encompasses a number of zones which have a different nomenclature. They have in common the removal of the area from the hostilities, and have the aim of providing shelter and care to the wounded and sick, pregnant women, and to civilians generally. The conditions governing protected areas are laid down in both Geneva Convention (GC) I and GC IV.

2 Article 23 GC I addresses protected areas, naming them 'hospital zones and localities'. Two provisions dedicated to protected areas are set out in GC IV: Article 14, dedicated to 'hospital and safety zones and localities'; and Article 15, regulating the establishment of 'neutralized zones'.

3 Of utmost importance is the Draft Agreement contained in Annex I to GC I, which sets out a blueprint from which the parties may draw elements for establishing a protected area. A Draft Agreement is also annexed to GC IV, which is construed in the same terms as that annexed to GC I.

4 Protected areas are also envisaged by Additional Protocol (AP) I to the Geneva Conventions. This embodies two provisions: Article 59, relating to non-defended localities; and Article 60, addressing demilitarized zones.

5 There is no express provision for non-international armed conflicts (NIACs). However, Common Article 3 states that the parties to the conflict may bring into force between them all or part of the provisions relating to international armed conflicts (IACs), and thus also those relating to safety zones and localities. They may also use the provisions of the Draft Agreement for inspiration when setting up an agreement. There is no provision on this matter in AP II. However, the parties may always apply Common Article 3, which is not abrogated but only supplemented by AP II. The question is whether the parties may bring into force not only the provisions of the Geneva Conventions, but also those of AP I as far as they may be applicable to NIACs. It is preferable to affirm that the parties may freely aspire to those provisions, since the application of AP I via Common Article 3 seems barred because there is a specific Protocol for NIACs, i.e. AP II.[1] The United Nations (UN) may establish protected areas in the framework of peacekeeping or peace-enforcement operations. They may be mandatory if the Security Council so decides. Generally, protected areas established by the Security Council differ from those established under the Geneva Conventions, and may encompass different modalities for their enforcement. Their size may also differ, and a protected area may contain the entire territory of a belligerent. Usually they are unilaterally imposed on one belligerent, for instance by a no-fly zone. They may be established during both an IAC and a NIAC.

B. Meaning and Application

I. Hospital zones and localities

6 The main features of hospital zones and localities are addressed by Article 23 GC I, which spells out when a zone may be established, the territory in which the zone may be established, and the category of individuals who may reside in the zone. The creation of the zone is optional and strengthens the obligation, already enshrined in IHL, not to subject

---

[1] For a contrary view, see, however, Ch 25, MN 9, of this volume.

objects which are specially protected, for instance hospitals, to hostilities. Thus hospital zones and localities should be protected and not be subject to any attack.

As far as timing is concerned, under Article 23 paragraph 1, hospital zones and localities may be established in peacetime as well as after the outbreak of hostilities. The creation of a zone in peacetime is quite unrealistic, since it foresees a possible conflict with a neighbouring state that a country will usually not wish to emphasize. As Pictet points out, a state may carry out all preparatory work for the creation of the zone, which will take effect at the outbreak of hostilities after notification to the enemy and recognition of the zone. Such zones may be established in the territory of the belligerent and in occupied areas, if the need arises.[2] Obviously, the only part of the territory concerned in peacetime is the national territory of the power establishing the zone. In time of war, as already mentioned, a zone may be established if the need arises. The establishment of the zone is at the discretion of the belligerent, and the need for such a zone should be considered according to circumstances, for instance the necessity to remove a number of people from the reach of hostilities. The notion of occupied territory implies the established presence of the occupying army; a temporary presence, for instance during an invasion, cannot be a valid element for establishing the zone. (However, a neutralized zone of temporary character may always be established where the actual combat is taking place.) The hospital zones are established outside the zone of combat and have in principle a stable character.[3]

The people who may reside in the zone or locality are, first, the wounded and sick. In addition, those who are entrusted with the organization and the administration of the zone and locality, as well as personnel entrusted with the care of the wounded and sick, may reside in the zone. Those who have no right to reside in the zone should be prevented from entering it.

The establishment of protected zones depends on their recognition by the parties. Under Article 23 paragraph 2 GC I, the parties may conclude an agreement on mutual recognition of their zones. Recognition is required even if the zone was constituted in a time of peace and before the outbreak of hostilities. On this point GC I provides a tool for helping parties to conclude the agreement. A Draft Agreement is annexed to the Convention, and the parties are free to refer to it. They also may modify the clauses of the model as they deem necessary.

A role is given to the Protecting Powers and to the International Committee of the Red Cross (ICRC) by Article 23 paragraph 3 GC I. They may lend their good offices for facilitating the conclusion of the agreement. The ICRC's role is paramount, since the system involving the Protecting Powers has not proven to be very effective.

The Draft Agreement annexed to GC I contains useful elements for the creation of the zone. It integrates the content of Article 23, even though it is just a model and does not have the same cogency as the GC I provision. The Draft Agreement applies to hospital zones, as well as to localities regulated by Article 23.

As far as the persons entitled to reside in the zone are concerned, the Draft Agreement specifies that those who had permanent residence in the zone before its creation are permitted to stay. The conditions for residing in the zone are very strict, and the responsible power is obliged to take all necessary measures in order to impede the access of persons

---

[2] Pictet Commentary GC I, at 213.
[3] A. Bouvier, 'Zones protégées, zones de sécurité et protection de la population civile', in K. Boustany and D. Dormoy (eds), *Perspectives humanitaires entre conflits, droit(s) et action* (Brussels: Bruylant, 2002), at 255.

who have no right to stay in the zone. Persons residing in the zone 'in whatever capacity' should not take part in the hostilities in any manner, nor perform any function connected with military operations or the production of war material within or outside the zone.[4] This means that persons residing in the zone cannot perform any job connected with war material even though it takes place outside the zone. The same is true for other functions, for instance any intelligence function.

13   The Draft Agreement also specifies the location of the zone and its size. The zone should be far removed from all military objectives or larger industrial or administrative establishments. Moreover, the zone should not be situated in areas which may become important for the conduct of war. This may create a problem given the mobility of the frontline. One might speculate that the zone should be moved if the frontline comes close to the zone. However, this would require the agreement of the adverse party.

14   As for the size, the Draft Agreement contains useful indications. The zone should comprise only a small part of the territory governed by the Power establishing it. This formulation is valid not only for national territory, but also for any territory under occupation. It follows that a zone may be established in occupied territory only if large areas of the enemy territory have been occupied. The other condition is represented by the size of the population residing in the area where the zone is established. The area should be thinly populated in relation to the possibility of accommodation.

15   The hospital zone should be completely free from hostilities. To this end, Article 3 of the Draft Agreement stipulates that lines of communication and means of transportation cannot be used for transport of military personnel or material, even in transit. It is added that the zone must in no circumstances be defended by military means. This presupposes that the zone will not become the object of attack—even by way of reprisal, since Article 11 of the Draft Agreement specifies that hospital zones may not be attacked 'in any circumstances'—and that the parties to the conflict should protect and respect the zone. There is no provision on the maintenance of law and order within the zone. Is light armament for this purpose allowed? The problem has been addressed positively in Article 60 AP I on demilitarized zones. It may be clarified in the agreement establishing and recognizing the zone.

16   The marking of the zone is important, since belligerents need to know where it is located if they are obliged to respect it. The signs are those in use for marking protected objects, e.g. red crosses on a white background placed on the outer precincts and on the buildings, and at night appropriate illumination can be used.

17   The establishment of the zone is consensual. One must distinguish between peacetime and wartime establishment. If the zone is instituted in peacetime, the instituting party must communicate its establishment to all contracting parties, but as already noted, it will take effect only after the outbreak of hostilities and its recognition by the adverse party. The zone may also be established after the outbreak of hostilities. The instituting party should notify the adverse party of the zones established in peacetime, as well as of those instituted in wartime. The zone is regularly constituted as soon as it is recognized by the adverse party, which may object to the existence of the conditions required for its establishment. The adverse party may make its recognition conditional upon appropriate controls, which may be discharged by one or more special commissions which are always

---

[4] Draft Agreement Art 2.

entitled to have free access to the zone and are entitled to inspect it to see whether the party is abiding by the terms of the agreement. The special commissions may make random inspections, and may come from outside the zone or reside therein.

The control exercised by the special commission has an influence on how long the agreement remains in force. If there is any deviation from its content, the commission will immediately bring it to the attention of the power governing the zone and fix a time limit for its rectification. The recognizing party is made aware that there is conduct taking place contrary to the obligations of the governing power. If the latter does not comply with the measures necessary to redress the situation, the former may declare that it is no longer bound by the agreement. Thus the agreement is terminated. Given the fact that the agreement applies in time of hostilities, it is obvious that no procedure is indicated to settle a disagreement regarding non-compliance by the party that has created the zone. 18

The procedure for nomination of the members of the commission is very elementary. The governing power and the adverse party nominate the commission members. The names may also be suggested by neutral Powers. However, the Draft Agreement does not say how many members should be nominated, what happens if an objection is raised by the other party, and whether the ICRC may take over the task of the special commission. 19

The Draft Agreement also regulates the destiny of the zone situated in a territory which is later occupied by the adverse party. In principle, the zone should continue to be respected and utilized as such. Should its function be modified, the Occupying Power is obliged to ensure the safety of the persons accommodated in the zone. 20

II. Hospital and safety zones and localities

As noted above (MN 2), GC IV contains two provisions on protected zones, Articles 14 and 15. They are located in Part II of the GC IV, which is dedicated to the general protection of populations against certain consequences of war, and thus extends the protection of the Convention to the territory of the parties even if it is not under occupation and to persons who are not protected persons as defined in Article 4. 21

Article 14 almost repeats Article 23 GC I, being dedicated to the same topic: hospital and safety zones and localities. The nomenclature is slightly different since Article 14 GC IV deals with 'hospital and safety zones' and localities, while Article 23 GC I encompasses only 'hospital zones' and localities. The procedures for concluding the agreement establishing the zone, its recognition, and control are the same. Article 14 paragraph 3 also includes a reference to the Protecting Powers and to the ICRC, who are invited to lend their good offices to facilitate the establishment of hospital and safety zones and localities. For facilitating their institution, a Draft Agreement like the one annexed to GC I is annexed to GC IV. The main difference between Article 23 GC I and Article 14 GC IV is as regards the category of protected persons: Article 14 protects not only the wounded and sick, but also aged persons, children under 15 years old, expectant mothers, and mothers of children aged under 7. Persons entrusted with the administration of the zones are not mentioned. Note, however, that the Annex to GC IV repeats the wording of the Annex to GC I verbatim, making reference to Article 23, including the category of persons indicated therein which comprises persons entrusted with the administration of the zone. A reasonable interpretation of Article 14 GC IV supports the conclusion that those who are entrusted with the administration of the zone, and medical personnel taking care of 22 the wounded and sick, are allowed to reside in the zone. Parties are called to indicate in their agreement the category of persons who will reside in the zone in addition to those indicated under Article 14 paragraph 1.

23   As already noted by Kalshoven in 1987, the concept of hospital and safety zones under Article 14 GC IV is no more than a 'theoretical possibility', since such zones should be situated at considerable distance from the battle area and are difficult to implement in densely populated regions with industrial infrastructure where the fighting is presumed to take place.[5] As a matter of principle, the zone should be away from large industrial establishments.

III. Neutralized zones

24   Article 15 GC IV introduces another type of protected zone: the neutralized zone. While the zones envisaged in Article 14 GC IV are distant from the frontline and may also be established in peacetime, by definition neutralized zones are instituted while the armed conflict is ongoing. As Article 15 points out, such zones are established 'where fighting is taking place' and thus are not far from the frontline, but they may be established in a locality which may be isolated from the combat zone. The purpose of the zone is to shelter the following persons from the effects of war:

— wounded and sick combatants or non-combatants;
— civilian persons not taking part in the hostilities and who do not perform any work of a military character while they reside in the zone.

Thus the category of people who are sheltered in the zone is broader than that encompassed by Article 14 GC IV (see MN 22).

25   Article 15 paragraph 1 adds that shelter is offered to these persons 'without distinction'. What is meant by this? One possible interpretation is that all persons belonging to the category of people mentioned in the provision should be offered shelter without discrimination, as affirmed in Article 13 GC IV, which covers the whole of the populations of the countries in conflict, even enemy civilians who have been wounded and are in need of care.

26   The source of the neutralized zone is the agreement of the parties. The agreement should be in writing, and should be concluded and signed by the representatives of the parties to the conflict. Article 15 does not indicate any other formality, for instance it does not spell out who the representatives of the parties entitled to sign the agreement should be. Customary international law empowers the organs of belligerent parties to stipulate conventions and agreements between them. The law of armed conflict requires few formalities, and the agreement is valid upon signature and does not need to be ratified. The belligerent representatives may be the military commanders, and they do not need to prove their full powers even though they do not belong to the category of persons whose full powers are presumed as indicated by Article 7(2) of the Vienna Convention on the Law of Treaties (VCLT). The agreement should contain the geographical coordinates of the neutralized zone and indicate how it will be administered and supplied with food, as

---

[5] F. Kalshoven, *Constraints on the Waging of War* (Geneva: International Committee of the Red Cross, 1987), at 51–2.

well as its beginning and duration. The modalities of supervision are of utmost importance. Article 15 GC IV does not spell out the institution entrusted with the task of controlling the neutralized zone. That task might be given to the Protecting Powers, or to the ICRC. The task of supervision may fall under the general functions performed by the Protecting Powers and by the ICRC under Articles 9 and 10 GC IV. Such tasks may also be given to any other impartial humanitarian organization under Article 10. Obviously the parties may agree on the establishment of several neutralized zones in the regions where the fighting is going on. Article 15 does not say anything about the fate of the agreement in the case of a violation of it. The issue is governed by the law of treaties, and one might consider that agreements on neutralized zones fall within the category of treaties relating to the protection of human persons and thus are excluded from the operation of the clause *inadimplenti non est adimplendum* as a ground for their suspension or termination, as set out in Article 60(5) VCLT.

Neutralized zones were created before the conclusion of Geneva Conventions on a few occasions, for instance in a quarter of Madrid at the time of Spanish Civil War (1936), in Shanghai during the conflict between China and Japan (1937), and in Jerusalem in 1948 at the time of the Arab–Israeli conflict. After the entry into force of the Geneva Conventions, neutralized zones were established in Dacca during the Indo-Pakistani war (1971), at the time of invasion of northern Cyprus by Turkey (1974), and shortly before the fall of Saigon during the Vietnam War, and in Phnom Penh (1975), Chad (1980), and Lebanon (1983). The institution of each zone was made possible thanks to the good offices of the ICRC. In all these cases the wounded and sick, as well as civilians and children, benefitted from the zone, and this shows that the distinction between safety zones and neutralized zones is often blurred. During the Falkland/Malvinas conflict (1982) it was decided to create a neutralized zone around the Cathedral at Port Stanley. This decision was made possible thanks to the initiative of the ICRC and the agreement of Argentina and the United Kingdom (UK). However, the zone was created very close to the end of hostilities and consequently was never used.

As Sandoz has explained:

Formalization of the system of protected zone in the Geneva Conventions has not led to any proliferation of such zones during conflicts that have arisen since the Conventions were adopted. Moreover, in the few instances where protected zones have since been created, they have been established in dire emergency and fall very roughly into the category envisaged in the Geneva Conventions, if at all.[6]

Be that as it may, the notion of protected zones (both safety zones and localities, and neutralized zones) is incorporated in numerous military manuals, and also into national legislation.[7] The prohibition of attacks against a zone established to shelter the wounded, the sick, and civilians from the effect of hostilities, as well as against a demilitarized zone agreed upon between the parties to the conflict, is regarded as a customary norm.[8]

---

[6] Y. Sandoz, 'The Establishment of Safety Zones for Persons Displaced within their Country of Origin', in N. Al-Nauimi and R. Meese (eds), *International Legal Issues Arising under the United Nations Decade of International Law* (The Hague/London/Boston: Kluwer Law International, 1995) 899, at 908.

[7] For the relevant practice and legislation, see ICRC CIHL Study, vol II, at 672–722.

[8] Ibid, at 119–21.

IV. Red Cross box in sea warfare

29   The IHL Conventions on the law of the sea do not envisage safety or neutralized zones. Such zones are not regulated either in the Hague Conventions of 1907, or in GC II dedicated to armed conflict at sea and to hospital ships. In practice, however, a way has been found to apply the notion of protected zones to sea warfare. During the Falkland/Malvinas Conflict, Argentina and the UK agreed to establish a safety Red Cross 'box' in a sea area adjacent to the Islands, where hospital ships (hospital warships and ships converted into hospital ships) were stationed ready to rescue shipwrecked sailors and evacuate them with helicopters. The agreement, which was not made in writing, was concluded by the two countries soon after the British moved towards the Falkland/Malvinas. The zone was around 20 miles wide. Any military activity within the zone was banned.[9]

V. Non-defended localities and demilitarized zones under Additional Protocol I

30   Part IV, Section I, Chapter V of AP I deals with localities and zones under special protection. It regulates two kinds of protected zones: non-defended localities (Article 59); and demilitarized zones (Article 60). Article 59 AP I goes back to the notion covered by Article 25 of the Regulations appended to Hague Convention IV on undefended towns, while Article 60 AP I is a kind of development of Article 15 GC IV (MN 24–28).[10] There are similarities and differences between non-defended localities and demilitarized zones under AP I, and protected zones under GC I and GC IV. The main difference is that the former protect the entire population within the locality/zone and not just a special category of civilians such as those protected by the latter, i.e. the wounded and sick, and, by way of extension, the resident population.[11] According to Sandoz, the Additional Protocols 'tend to remove the division between military and civilian wounded and sick and lessen the distinction between military and civilian hospital personnel and establishments', with the consequence of rendering obsolete the distinction between hospital zones envisaged by GC I and hospital and safety zones regulated by Article 14 GC IV.[12]

a. Non-defended localities

31   Non-defended localities find their source in a unilateral declaration of the controlling power that becomes effective without any express agreement by the enemy. Its acknowledgement by the other side produces a kind of estoppel, rendering it legally impossible to question whether all conditions laid down by Article 59 AP I are fulfilled.[13] The declaration should emanate from the government, but also from the military commander controlling the place. It is not specified whether mere acquiescence by the enemy is enough, or whether a formal acknowledgement is required. Article 59 AP I employed the notion of 'undefended locality' instead of 'undefended town' since the concept may also apply to

---

[9] Cf S.S. Junod, *Protection of the Victims of Armed Conflict Falkland-Malvinas Islands (1982): International Humanitarian Law and Humanitarian Action* (2nd edn, Geneva: ICRC, 1985), at 23–4, 26.
[10] Bothe/Partsch/Solf, at 387.
[11] F. Kalshoven, *The Law of Warfare* (Leiden: Sijthoff, 1973), at 73.
[12] Sandoz, above n 6, at 913.
[13] According to Bothe/Partsch/Solf, the unilateral declaration establishing a non-defended locality is not an offer to conclude an agreement and it is binding on the adverse party provided that all conditions laid down by Protocol I are met (at 383–4).

a small section of a town. A party to the conflict may declare as a non-defended locality 'any inhabited place near or in a zone where armed forces are in contact which is open for occupation by an adverse Party'.[14] As a matter of fact, the non-defended locality cannot be located away from the frontline and in anticipation of a future event.[15] A non-defended locality is open to occupation by the adverse party as the power controlling the locality will not put up any resistance (this is the well-known practice of 'open cities' according to the terminology in use before the adoption of AP I). The declaration should be acknowledged by the adverse party to which it is addressed. The declaration should define and fix the limit of the non-defended locality. Supervision is welcomed, but it is not a necessary ingredient of the agreement.

Under Article 59 AP I a number of conditions are required for the establishment of a non-defended locality, namely:

— evacuation of all combatants, as well as of weapons and military equipment;
— no hostile use of fixed military equipment;
— no act of hostility by the authorities or by the population;
— no activity in support of military operations.

The above conditions may be derogated from if the parties so wish. The presence of protected persons, for instance wounded soldiers, as well as police forces entrusted with the task of maintaining law and order, is permitted. The non-defended locality should be appropriately marked, and the way this is carried out should be set out in the declaration establishing the non-defended locality.

Like protected zones under the Geneva Conventions, a non-defended locality may lose its status if the conditions for its existence are not fulfilled, for instance its status ends as soon it is occupied by the enemy. Nevertheless, the locality shall continue to enjoy the protection given by other norms of IHL. Thus the invading power should take care of the wounded and sick, and the civilian population and civilian objects cannot be attacked.

b. *Demilitarized zones*

Demilitarized zones may be established by the agreement of the parties. However, unlike non-defended localities, which are to be established in the zone close to the hostilities and in the contact zone, demilitarized zones may be established anywhere. Moreover non-defended localities are open to the occupation of the enemy and their existence is only temporary, while the status of demilitarized zones ends according to the term of the agreement, unless their existence is questioned because they do not continue to fulfil the conditions of their establishment. The requirements for setting out a demilitarized zone under Article 60 AP I are the same as those listed under Article 59 for non-defended localities (see MN 32), with the addition of one more condition, i.e. that the party controlling the zone should cease any activity in the zone linked to the military effort. The content of this obligation should be spelled out in the agreement establishing the zone. Even if the demilitarized zone is far from the frontline, it may happen that fighting is taking place close to the zone. This notwithstanding, it cannot be used for purposes related to the conduct of hostilities or its status will be unilaterally revoked, provided

---

[14] Art 59(2) AP I.
[15] Y. Dinstein, *The Conduct of Hostilities under the Law of International Armed Conflict* (2nd edn, Cambridge: CUP, 2010), at 110 and authorities quoted therein.

that the parties have so agreed. In principle, a demilitarized zone does not end if the area in which it is located is occupied by the enemy. However, in the agreement creating the zone it might be foreseen that if the area in which the zone is located falls into enemy hands, the zone may continue to exist or, on the contrary, may be occupied with the loss of its status.[16]

35   Formalities for concluding the agreement on the establishment of a demilitarized zone are very limited. The agreement may be concluded orally or in writing, and may consist of reciprocal and concordant declarations, for instance an exchange of notes. This is in keeping with the law of treaties, which allows for the conclusion of agreements orally or through any instrument clearly showing the will of the parties. The Protecting Powers or any impartial humanitarian organization might help in concluding the agreement, which should also contain the method of its supervision if the parties agree. The ICRC is not mentioned, but no doubt it may lend its good offices to assist in concluding the agreement. If there is a material breach of the agreement, comprising a violation of the conditions established for proclaiming the demilitarized zone, the obligation imposed on the other party will cease to exist, a classic case of *inadimplenti non est adimplendum*. Demilitarized zones may also be established in peacetime, unlike non-defended localities which presuppose the existence of hostilities. The demilitarized zones regulated by Article 60 AP I are a species of a broader genus represented by demilitarized zones established by peace treaties or armistice agreements. This last category has a permanent character and is often referred to as an example of servitude in international law. Moreover, demilitarized zones established by peace treaties do not have a fixed content like those developed under Article 60 AP I.

C. Relevance in Non-International Armed Conflicts

36   Common Article 3 does not contain any provision regarding hospital zones and localities. However, the parties may conclude an agreement to bring the provisions of the Conventions into force in whole or in part. For instance, an agreement was concluded between Croatia and the Socialist Federal Republic of Yugoslavia (SFRY) on a protected zone around the Osijek hospital (27 December 1991) which was put under ICRC supervision. A few days before, a protected zone was instituted in Dubrovnik (6 December 1991). In both cases, the regime of the zone was drawn from Article 23 GC I and Articles 14 and 15 GC IV, and the content of the Osijek protected zone was precisely defined in its constitutive agreement.[17] Note that the conflict was regarded as non-international by the SFRY. The parties are free to conclude agreements outside the framework of the Conventions but aspiring to their provisions, as happened with the zones created near to Managua Airport and inside hospitals and churches during the civil war in Nicaragua in 1979, in order to shelter those who had laid down arms.[18] This does not impede the ICRC from lending its services. According to the ICRC Study on Customary International

---

[16] UK Ministry of Defence, *The Manual of the Law of Armed Conflict* (Oxford: OUP, 2004), at 93, fn 254.
[17] See its content in J.-P. Lavoyer, 'International Humanitarian Law, Protected Zones and the Use of Force', in W. Biermann and M. Martin (eds), *UN Peacekeeping in Trouble: Lessons Learned from the Former Yugoslavia* (Aldershot: Ashgate, 1998), at 268–9. The ICRC intervened with formal representations to the belligerent parties when the protected zone was hit by shells: ibid, at 269.
[18] Sandoz, above n 6, at 914.

Humanitarian Law, the prohibition on attacking undefended localities also applies to NIAC, which is in keeping with Article 3 of the Statute of the International Criminal Tribunal for the former Yugoslavia (ICTY) as well as the prohibition inserted in several military manuals.[19] Additional Protocol II does not contain any formal prohibition. However, Article 13(2) states that the civilian population as such, and individual civilians, may not be the object of an attack. In *Public Prosecutor v Perišić*, a Croatian Court applied not only Article 25 of the Hague Regulations, but also Common Article 3, and Articles 13 and 14 AP II to the Zadar shelling.[20] The ICRC may take the initiative to invite the parties to establish a hospital zone. On 6 November 1990 the ICRC notified the parties involved in the conflict in Sri Lanka of the intention to reopen the Jaffna Teaching Hospital and to declare the area around it a hospital zone.[21]

As already noted, AP II does not contain provisions on non-defended localities and demilitarized zones. Those provisions presuppose the sovereignty of the parties to the conflict, a condition which is not compatible with the status of rebels in a civil war. It is also to be pointed out that a demilitarized zone may be established in times of peace, and this is a nonsense in a NIAC. Therefore even if it is assumed that Common Article 3 may be applied to the provisions of AP I, there is in principle a material non-applicability of Articles 59 and 60 to NIAC. If, however, the conflict escalates and the rebels have stable territorial control, there is no obstacle to the parties freely concluding agreements inspired by the provisions of AP I, in particular by Article 59 on non-defended localities. It is doubtful that the constituted government would enter such an agreement, though, since this might imply a kind of recognition of belligerency on its part. Note that even the Draft Protocol which was submitted by the ICRC to the Diplomatic Conference in 1973, and which often replicated provisions on IACs, did not contain any provision on non-defended localities and demilitarized zones for NIACs.

D. Protected Areas Established by the UN Security Council

The terminology referred to by the Geneva Conventions and AP I has a precise meaning, and the notion of each protected zone is construed within defined legal parameters. In contrast, the UN Security Council terminology is very broad and encompasses a variety of concepts, such as safe areas, safe havens, neutralized zones, UN protected areas, temporary corridors, security corridors, humanitarian corridors, and safe corridors. While the notion of 'zone' or 'area' implies a locality in which the population in need of protection is living, 'corridor' describes a route within the territory which should be used in order to bring assistance and relief to a population in danger, for instance in response to a shortage of food and water. Since the Gulf War the concept of a no-fly zone has gained currency. The latest application was the no-fly zone over Libya (2011). However, no-fly zones are more a device connected to the conduct of hostilities than an instrument for building a protected area. Occasionally they may be employed for the latter purpose in addition to the attainment of other strategic objectives. For instance, the no-fly zones over the Bosnian skies (1994), or over Northern and Southern Iraq after the Iraq–Kuwait

---

[19] See ICRC CIHL Study, vol I: Rules, at 123.
[20] See ibid. [21] Sassòli/Bouvier/Quintin, at 1652–3.

war, were created, respectively, for impeding the bombardment of the Bosnian cities of Sarajevo, Bihac, and Goradze, and for blocking air operations by Saddam Hussein against the Kurds in the North (operation Provide Comfort, 1991–6) and the Shi'ite Muslims in the South (operation Southern Watch, 1992–6). As far as Gaddafi's Libya was concerned, Security Council Resolution 1973 (2011) affirmed in paragraph 6 that the no-fly zone was established 'in order to protect civilians'.

39 The creation of safe zones and humanitarian corridors has become an important issue for the Security Council, as proven by Resolution 1296 (2000) on protection of victims of armed conflict, which in paragraph 15 'indicates its willingness to consider the appropriateness and feasibility of temporary security zones and safe corridors for the protection of civilians and the delivery of assistance in situations characterized by the threat of genocide, crimes against humanity and war crimes against the civilian population'. Pursuant to Resolution 1894 (2009) the UN Secretary-General submitted a series of reports on the protection of civilian populations in armed conflict, which include the notion of safe areas and safe access for humanitarian purposes.[22]

I. The legal basis for the establishment of protected areas and safe corridors

40 The main problem with protected areas or safe corridors created outside the framework of the Geneva Conventions and the Additional Protocols, is the mode of their establishment. While the agreement of the parties is a necessary requirement for establishing protected areas under the Geneva Conventions, the same is not always true for protected areas established under a Security Council Resolution, adopted under Chapter VII of the UN Charter. Usually those kinds of areas are protected by an external force, and the entry into foreign territory is conditional upon a clear mandate by the Security Council. Humanitarian emergencies may be considered to constitute a threat to peace, and the Security Council may act under Chapter VII and Article 39. In the absence of a Security Council Resolution giving permission to enter foreign territory, the consent of the territorial sovereign functions as a circumstance precluding wrongfulness under the law of state responsibility. The Security Council may dispatch a force on its own, or may allow member states willing to do so to enter the foreign territory. As experience shows, the main problem of safe areas proclaimed by a Security Council Resolution is their protection. Robust peacekeeping is needed if the dispatch of a peace-enforcing operation is not politically feasible. A minor form of interference with the territorial sovereign takes place if the safe area is established as a provisional measure under Article 40 of the UN Charter, for instance for opening humanitarian corridors having a temporary nature. A safe area may be established by a regional organization acting under Chapter VIII of the UN Charter. In this case the mandate of the Security Council is also necessary unless the consent of the territorial sovereign is sought and given. The regional organization may be empowered to act by its constitutive instrument vis-à-vis member states, and in this case the mandate of the Security Council is no longer necessary since the consent of the territorial sovereign is enshrined in the constitutive act of the organization and it is given *a priori*. For instance, Article 4 of the Constitutive Act of the African Union, as amended in 2003, gives a right

---

[22] See, e.g., UN Doc S/2010/579.

to the Union to intervene in a member state pursuant a decision of the Assembly in case of war crimes, genocide, and crimes against humanity.

Does the doctrine of responsibility to protect (R2P) have any impact on establishing 41 safe havens or humanitarian corridors? According to a number of authors, R2P allows forces to enter foreign territory even without the consent of the sovereign and without a mandate of the Security Council.[23] It is the old doctrine of humanitarian intervention which affirms that the entry into foreign territory is permitted when the sovereign is unable or unwilling to protect its own population or part of it. According to the present writer, the doctrine of R2P as a valid excuse to enter foreign territory without the consent of the sovereign or a mandate by the Security Council is not endorsed by the current practice and general *opinio juris*. Only a minority of members of the international community, namely some Western states, share the view that humanitarian intervention may be carried out even without a mandate by the Security Council; the majority of states in the world community deem a Security Council resolution to be necessary.

The practice of safe areas has been developed not only for helping war-torn populations, 42 but also to stop refugees fleeing from a territory experiencing hostilities. People fleeing a territory devastated by war may enter a neighbouring country and create security problems. In addition, it is not clear whether those people may claim the status of 'refugee' under the 1951 Refugee Convention. A solution has been found with the creation of safe havens close to the border, or in areas straddling the border.

While GC I, GC IV, and AP I apply to IACs, the safe havens created outside the Geneva 43 Conventions have mostly been applied during NIACs, even though examples of application during an IAC may be counted. A UN-created safety zone differs from the zones created under the Geneva Conventions, since it is not open to occupation by the hostile army as undefended towns are. In a NIAC the consent of all parties to the conflict might facilitate the protection of the area, even if the consent of the constituted government is necessary only from a formal point of view. Note, however, that whenever the zone is established by a mandatory Security Council resolution, it can create obligations for all the parties to the conflict, i.e. rebels and the constituted government.

II. The protection of the protected areas and safe corridors

As has already been noted (MN 40), the main problem with the establishment of pro- 44 tected areas created outside the scheme of the Geneva Conventions is their defence and the choice of the best means to achieve that objective. They concentrate a large number of civilians in a small area, and in the event of a violation the civilians are in mortal danger. The concentration of minorities might be an attraction for a criminal belligerent pursuing a policy of genocide. The issue is being considered by the UN Secretary-General in the context of the reports on the protection of civilian populations in time of armed conflict. The presence of UN troops is essential, as well as their will and capacity to react in the event of a violation of the zone, as is proper interpretation of their mandate, in order not to repeat the Srebrenica case where the Dutch contingent was powerless in the face of the massacre perpetrated by the Bosnian Serb forces. It is also crucial to outline the main

---

[23] See, e.g., C. Greenwood, 'Humanitarian Intervention: The Case of Kosovo', 10 *Finnish Yearbook of International Law* (1999) 141; F.R. Teson, 'The Liberal Case for Humanitarian Intervention', in J.L. Holzgrefe and R.O. Kehoane (eds), *Humanitarian Intervention* (Cambridge: CUP, 2003) 93. Cf also G.P. Fletcher and J.D. Ohlin, *Defending Humanity: When Force is Justified and Why* (Oxford: OUP, 2008) 129.

features of the zone clearly—for instance if it should be demilitarized—and to establish whether the UN troops should stay outside the perimeter of the zone or should be allowed to station themselves in the zone.

45   The lack of a common terminology for addressing the notion of protected areas may hinder the development of a common definition and of agreement on the law to be applied, namely in connection with the application of IHL and international human rights law. An additional difficulty is represented by the fact that the notion of protected areas outside the Geneva Conventions belongs both to *jus ad bellum* and to *jus in bello*: the establishment of the zones belongs to the former, while their content belongs to the latter. Usually such zones are created by mandate of the Security Council, or might be set up unilaterally by states without the consent of the territorial sovereign, if one shares the doctrine of humanitarian intervention/R2P (which is not the case with the present author).[24] This implies that the intervening force takes side against a belligerent and that the principle of neutrality is not endorsed.

46   People living in a UN security zone should be protected from the effects of hostilities and should not be removed. It is open to question whether war criminals living in the zone may be apprehended and handed over to an international criminal tribunal.

E. Protected Area Recent Practice

47   Recent practice on protected areas is mainly due to the UN Security Council and its peacekeeping/peace-enforcement operations. The involvement of the Security Council does not mean, however, that the ICRC does not have any role to play. For instance, the ICRC intervened with a position paper distributed to various international authorities, in which it offered its services to meet the tragedy of Bosnia-Herzegovina and to establish protected zones for endangered civilians. The effectiveness of protected areas established by the Security Council is nevertheless open to doubt. It has been questioned whether the protected zones provide a real safe haven against external action, and whether in fact they are really impermeable to external threats, or whether on the contrary they generate opportunities for hostile militias to launch attacks on a concentration of civilians who were previously more scattered across the territory.[25] There is also the problem of displaced persons, making it necessary that those establishing the area take care that the people living there receive the necessary humanitarian assistance.

I. Sri Lanka

48   Since 1990 three Open Relief Centres have operated in the region for a number of years, with the consent of the parties to the conflict. A kind of demilitarized zone was established, and the Centres were a sanctuary for refugees and people in need of assistance. The Centres were instituted outside the framework of humanitarian law. The civil war in Sri Lanka terminated in May 2009 after 25 years in which abuses and widespread violations of both humanitarian and human rights law amounting to war crimes were committed by

---

[24] The Syrian civil war, which erupted in 2011, has already been the subject of a number of Security Council Resolutions (2042 (2012), 2043 (2012), 2118 (2013), 2139 (2014), 2165 (2014)).

[25] Recent and past practice is reviewed by M. Torelli, 'Les zones de sécurité', 99 *RGDIP* (1995) 787; Lavoyer, above n 17, at 262–79; Sandoz, above n 6, at 899–927; Bouvier, above n 3, at 251–64.

both parties, in particular during the final stage of the conflict. According to a report of Human Rights Watch released in February 2009, the government in power unilaterally declared a safe zone of 35 square kilometres in rebel-controlled territory, inviting civilians to settle there. The rebels operated in the zone, claiming that it was not created under an agreement but only declared unilaterally by the Government. The consequence was that the Government forces attacked the rebels in the safety zone and the life of civilians was put at risk. The lack of respect for the safety zones by the government forces was confirmed by the Report of the Secretary-General's Panel of Experts on Accountability in Sri Lanka released on 31 March 2011.[26]

II. Iraq

Security Council Resolution 688 (1991) requested Iraq to allow immediate access by international humanitarian organizations to all those in need of assistance in all parts of Iraq, and to make available all necessary facilities for their operation. In effect the UK and the United States (US) and other allies entered Northern Iraq with the operation Provide Comfort. The mission is not easily classified under the practice of safe areas, and was rather a mission to escort humanitarian convoys to bring relief to the Kurdish population. As noted above (MN 38), the no-fly zone subsequently established, which did not have its foundations in Resolution 688 (1991), belongs more to *jus ad bellum* than to *jus in bello*. The safe havens established in Northern Iraq were also due to the policy of the Western powers that allowed for a mass of Kurdish refugees to return from Turkey.

49

III. Somalia

In 1992, Operation Restore Hope landed in Somalia to supply relief to the civilian population. The mission, led by the US, was under the cover of UN Security Council Resolution 794 (1992). In reality the peacekeeping troops also created a preventive zone, near to the border with Kenya, aimed at containing the flux of refugees and preventing the creation of new refugees.[27]

50

IV. Bosnia-Herzegovina

Security Council Resolution 762 (1992) established three UN Protected Areas (UNPAs) in Bosnia-Herzegovina, which included the Krajina, Eastern Slavonia, and Western Slavonia. The supervision of the UNPAs was entrusted to the United Nations Protection Force (UNPROFOR), which was tasked with their demilitarization and the protection of ethnic minorities under Resolution 743 (1992). According to an unofficial UN Report,

51

UNPROFOR's mandate is to ensure that the UNPAs are demilitarized, through the withdrawal or disbandment of all armed forces in them, and that all persons residing in them are protected from fear of armed attack. To this end, UNPROFOR is authorized to control access to the UNPAs, to ensure that the UNPAs remain demilitarized, and to monitor the functioning of the local police there to help ensure non-discrimination and the protection of human rights. Outside the UNPAs,

---

[26] Report of the Secretary-General's Panel of Experts on Accountability in Sri Lanka, 31 March 2011, available at <http://www.un.org/News/dh/infocus/Sri_Lanka/POE_Report_Full.pdf>. See, in particular, paras 74 and 80.

[27] See the critical remarks regarding Somalia and other protected zones by J. Hyndeman, 'Preventive, Palliative or Punitive? Safe Spaces in Bosnia-Herzegovina, Somalia and Sri Lanka', 16 *Journal of Refugee Studies* (2003) 167.

UNPROFOR military observers are to verify the withdrawal of all the JNA [Jugoslav National Army] and irregular forces from Croatia, other than those disbanded and demobilized there. In support of the work of the humanitarian agencies of the United Nations, UNPROFOR is also to facilitate the return, in conditions of safety and security, of civilian displaced persons to their homes in the UNPAs.[28]

The Croatian army, however, carried out hostilities within the UNPAs and adjacent areas.

52   Security Council Resolution 819 (1993) declared Srebrenica a safe area, free from any attack and any hostile act. A trilateral agreement to demilitarize Srebrenica was signed by the UNPROFOR force commander, the commander of the Bosnian Serb forces, and the Commander of Bosnian Muslim forces. This notwithstanding, Srebrenica was placed under siege and heavily bombed.

53   In addition to Srebrenica, other cities were declared safe areas by Resolution 824 (1993), free from armed attacks and from any other hostile act: Sarajevo, Goradze, Tuzla, Zepa, and Bihac. They were not in fact demilitarized, however, since the Bosnian Muslims feared that the Bosnian Serbs would not have abided by the declaration of safe areas and that UNPROFOR was not able to defend them. The safe areas were not respected by Bosnian Serbs, and Resolution 941 (1994) condemned the indiscriminate shelling of those cities and of Sarajevo. The North Atlantic Treaty Organization (NATO) was authorized to take action by the Security Council.

54   The record of safe areas in Bosnia is very poor.[29] In 1995 Bosnian Serb forces entered Srebrenica and Zepa, killing and committing atrocities without any impediment from the UNPROFOR troops.

V. Rwanda

55   Security Council Resolution 929 (1994) allowed member states to contribute to the security and the protection of displaced persons, refugees, and civilians at risk, including by the establishment of secure areas and humanitarian zones. However, genocide had already been perpetrated. France, which intervened with *Opération Turquoise* for almost a year, created a number of *zones sûres* which covered a large part of the Rwandan territory. After the French withdrawal the operation was taken over by a full-fledged UN Assistance Mission for Rwanda (UNAMIR). The results of *Opération Turquoise* were very poor, since the Hutu militia were not disarmed and the people in the safe areas were not protected militarily. The UNAMIR, too, was not able to prevent the massacre of people stationed in refugee camps. The safe haven policy was also criticized, since it prevented refugees from fleeing into neighbouring countries, mainly the Democratic Republic of the Congo.

VI. Darfur

56   The Plan of Action for Darfur, agreed on 7 August 2004 by Sudan and the UN following Security Council Resolution 1556 (2004), foresaw the identification of safe areas where hostilities should be terminated. The Agreement of 20 June 2011 between the Government of Sudan and the Sudan People's Liberation Movement envisaged the deployment of the

---

[28] Available at <http://www.un.org/en/peacekeeping/missions/past/unprof_b.htm>.
[29] For a critical assessment, see C. Ingrao, 'Safe Areas', in C. Ingrao and T.A. Emmert (eds), *Confronting the Yugoslav Controversies: A Scholar's Initiative* (2nd edn, West Lafayette, IN: Purdue University Press, 2010) 203.

F. Legal Consequences of a Violation

Grave breaches of the Geneva Conventions do not include as a specific crime the violation of protected zones. Article 50 GC I lists a number of grave breaches, such as wilful killing or torture, but does not qualify the violation of Article 23 GC I as a grave breach. The same is true for Article 147 GC IV in relation to Articles 14 and 15 of that Convention. Even the Statutes of the International Criminal Tribunal for the Former Yugoslavia (ICTY) and of the International Criminal Tribunal for Rwanda (ICTR) do not list an attack against a protected zone as a war crime. Likewise the Statute of the International Criminal Court (ICC) does not include an attack against a protected zone as a war crime or as a crime against humanity.[30] 57

An attack against a protected zone may nevertheless qualify as a war crime under a different heading. Such zones may fall within the category of undefended towns or dwellings which are not military objectives, and thus an attack on them will constitute a war crime under a number of provisions (Article 3(c) ICTY Statute; Article 8(2)(b)(v) ICC Statute). An attack against a protected zone may qualify as an attack against the civilian population and/or against civilians not taking part in the hostilities (Article 8(2)(b)(i) ICC Statute),[31] or as an attack against hospitals or localities where the wounded and sick are located (Article 8(2)(b)(ix) ICC Statute).[32] In *The Prosecutor v Stanislav Galić*, Commander Galić was held responsible for war crimes under Article 3 of the ICTY Statute for attacks on civilians and acts of violence with the primary aim of spreading terror among the civilian population.[33] An attack against the population residing in a protected area may also constitute the crime of genocide, as was held by the ICTY in the *Krstić* case.[34] 58

A different approach has been taken by AP I. It contains an explicit provision defining attacks against non-defended localities and demilitarized zones as grave breaches of the Protocol, provided that such attacks are committed wilfully, in violation of the relevant provisions of the Protocol, and causing death or serious injury to body or health (Article 85(3)(d) AP I). 59

What kind of measures might be envisaged in the event of a violation of protected zones established by the Security Council? One option would be to take enforcement measures. On the premise that the violation qualifies as an Article 39 UN Charter situation, the Security Council may authorize states to intervene with forceful measures, as happened in the former Yugoslavia following the violation of safe areas established around Srebrenica and other cities of Bosnia-Herzegovina.[35] Another possibility is to set 60

---

[30] See, however, J.K. Kleffner, 'Protection of the Wounded, Sick, and Shipwrecked', in D. Fleck (ed), *The Handbook of International Humanitarian Law* (2nd edn, Oxford: OUP, 2008) 325, at 358, fn 178.
[31] See also Art 8(2)(e)(i) ICC Statute for NIACs.
[32] See also Art 8(2)(e)(iv) ICC Statute for NIACs.
[33] ICTY, *The Prosecutor v Stanislav Galić*, Trial Chamber Judgment, IT-98-29-T, 5 December 2003, paras 595–7; ICTY, *The Prosecutor v Stanislav Galić*, Appeals Chamber Judgment, IT-98-29-A, 30 November 2006, para 87.
[34] ICTY, *The Prosecutor v Krstić*, Appeals Chamber Judgment, IT-98-33-A, 19 April 2004. Srebrenica, where the crimes were committed, was referred to by the Tribunal as a 'United Nations so-called safe area which was intended as an enclave of safety set up to protect its civilian population from the surrounding war' (para 2).
[35] UNSC Res 836 (1993), 837 (1993), and 844 (1993).

out sanctions, namely an embargo on weapons. A further measure is represented by action aimed at obtaining reparation for violation of the laws of war.[36] A duty of reparation is expressly envisaged by Article 3 of the Hague Convention IV of 1907 and by Article 91 AP I. However, both Articles cover relations between states, and the right of individuals to obtain compensation is often frustrated by the principle of sovereign immunity of foreign states, a principle which also is often endorsed by the statute or the headquarters agreements of international organizations. In the case *The State of the Netherlands v Hasan Nuhanović*, The Hague Court of Appeal, in its judgment of 5 July 2011, held the Dutch Government responsible for not giving protection to those who had taken refuge with the Dutch contingent serving as members of the UN peacekeeping forces. The judgment was confirmed by the Supreme Court of the Netherlands (6 September 2013).[37] As to the alleged responsibility of the UN, in the case *Mothers of Srebrenica and others v The Netherlands and the United Nations* (13 April 2012), the Dutch Supreme Court upheld the decision of the Hague Court of Appeal (30 March 2010) that the UN could not be summoned, since that body enjoyed immunity from legal proceedings. According to the Dutch Supreme Court, the rule might not be disregarded even if a violation of an international rule of *jus cogens* had occurred. The European Court of Human Rights also held that the UN enjoyed immunity from national jurisdiction, and that the claimants were not entitled to proceed against the UN before a Dutch tribunal.[38]

G. Critical Assessment

61 The establishment of protected zones is beneficial for the wounded, sick, and civilian populations. The risk is connected with the unwillingness of the enemy to respect IHL. Protected areas often imply a displacement of civilians and their concentration in a designated locality. If the enemy does not respect IHL, the danger is that such a concentration becomes a trap for the civilians and facilitates the commission of war crimes, especially when the conflict is motivated by racial considerations and ethnic cleansing. Another danger is the fact that those who reside outside the zone are exposed to an increased risk. This is unacceptable, since the whole civilian population must be respected and the protected zone aims at giving additional protection.

62 While the notions of hospital zones and localities, hospital and safety zones and localities, neutralized zones, non-defended localities, and demilitarized zones are well regulated in the Geneva Conventions and in AP I, the same is not true for security zones established by the UN. Practice regarding UN security zones is often inconsistent,[39] and these zones are radically different from the protected zones under the Geneva Conventions, even though they have in common the purpose of removing from the path of hostilities persons who may not be targeted according to the law of armed conflict. The other criticism raised is that it is difficult to implement a security zone without the agreement of the parties to

---

[36] See the Declaration of International Law Principles on Reparation for Victims of Armed Conflict, adopted by the International Law Association at The Hague in 2010, available at <http://www.ila-hq.org>.

[37] Cf T. Dannenbaum, 'Killings at Srebrenica, Effective Control and the Power to Prevent Unlawful Conduct', 61 *ICLQ* (2012) 713. See also The Hague District Court, *Mothers of Srebrenica v The State of the Netherlands and the United Nations*, Judgment, 16 July 2014.

[38] ECtHR, *Stichting Mothers of Srebrenica and others v The Netherlands*, Judgment, 11 June 2013, para 169.

[39] Torelli, above n 25, at 809. See also W.C.H. Chau, 'Creating Refuge in Hell: The Coming of Age of Safe Areas for the Protection of Civilians in Armed Conflict', 18 *Te Mata Koi Auckland University Law Review* (2012) 191.

the conflict.⁴⁰ In practice, the Security Council can do away with the consent of the parties and impose safety zones on them.⁴¹ Then armed personnel must be dispatched for their defence. Too often the security zones are linked to peace support operations, and their neutrality is consequently open to question, since the Security Council gives the impression of taking the side of one belligerent, attempting to influence the course of the conflict,⁴² or of being motivated by political intent, such as with the safety zone in North Iraq.⁴³

As has been affirmed, on the one hand the UN security zones are a response to violations of IHL and aim to remove from the path of hostilities the civilian population or a group of people who are in principle protected by IHL since they must not be attacked or persecuted.⁴⁴ On the other hand, the model of protected areas envisaged by GC I and GC IV is not formally applicable to the UN, since that body cannot be a formal addressee of the Geneva Conventions. This said, it is true that the application in practice of protected areas under the Geneva Conventions and AP I has been very modest, and their effectiveness is questionable, while recourse to protected areas as designated by the Security Council is gaining currency, even more so since such protected areas are designed to protect a large geographical area in comparison with the small scope of the safe areas. The two sets of notions adhere to a different philosophy. While the rationale behind the codification on protected areas under the Geneva Conventions and AP I is to afford special protection in addition to the general protection given by IHL to the category of people mentioned in the relevant provisions, the safe areas established by the Security Council are designed to offer the civilian population protection which is not given by belligerents who are not abiding by IHL. For this purpose a clear mandate is needed, and UN troops should be ready to use force to defend the civilian population, and not remain inactive as happened in Srebrenica.

In conclusion, IHL tries to protect the wounded, sick, or civilians by placing on combatants the obligation to positively identify military objectives and to attack only those objectives, respecting the wounded, sick, and civilians wherever they happen to be. From this perspective, protected zones and safe areas are only a second-best solution from the point of view of IHL, since they are aimed at giving a form of protection which should already be provided by the basic principles of humanitarian law.

NATALINO RONZITTI

---

⁴⁰ Torelli, above n 25, at 845. ⁴¹ Sandoz, above n 6, at 919.
⁴² Lavoyer, above n 17, at 272. ⁴³ Sandoz, above n 6, at 919.
⁴⁴ Cf Bouvier, above n 3, at 260–1.

3. COMMON ARTICLE 3

COMMON ARTICLES

Chapter 19. The Concept of Non-International Armed Conflict

	MN
A. Introduction	1
B. Categories of Non-International Armed Conflicts	5
C. 'Not of an International Character'	12
I. Parties to the conflict	12
II. Armed conflict in occupied territory	14
III. Third party involvement	17
a. Third state involvement	17
b. United Nations and/or other international involvement	18
D. Geographical Scope	21
I. 'Territory of a High Contracting Party'	22
II. Extent of IHL's application	32
E. Existence of Armed Conflict	34
I. Organization of the parties	35
a. Territorial control	40
b. Responsible command	43
c. Political motivation	46
II. Intensity of the hostilities	48
a. Internal disturbances and tensions	49
b. Protracted armed violence	53
c. The threshold of intensity	58
F. Critical Assessment	62

Select Bibliography

Cullen, A., *The Concept of Non-International Armed Conflict in International Humanitarian Law* (Cambridge: CUP, 2010)

Moir, L., *The Law of Internal Armed Conflict* (Cambridge: CUP, 2002)

Pejić, J., 'Status of Armed Conflicts', in E. Wilmshurst and S. Breau (eds), *Perspectives on the ICRC Study on Customary International Humanitarian Law* (Cambridge: CUP, 2007) 77

Pictet Commentary GC I, at 37–50

Pictet Commentary GC IV, at 25–36

Sivakumaran, S., *The Law of Non-International Armed Conflicts* (Oxford: OUP, 2012), at 155–235

Vité, S., 'Typology of armed conflicts in International Humanitarian Law: Legal Concepts and Actual Situations', 91 *IRRC* 873 (2009) 69

Wilmshurst, E. (ed), *International Law and the Classification of Conflicts* (Oxford: OUP, 2012)

A. Introduction

Common Article 3 represented the first legal regulation of non-international armed conflict (NIAC) in an international instrument.[1] The text of the Article itself, however,

---

[1] For discussion of the historical background regarding the regulation of NIAC, and the drafting process of CA 3, see L. Moir, *The Law of Internal Armed Conflict* (Cambridge: CUP, 2002) 1–29; A. Cullen,

stipulates only that it applies to cases of 'armed conflict not of an international character occurring in the territory of one of the High Contracting Parties'. No further guidance is provided as to precisely what constitutes NIAC and, as such, the issue of identifying those armed conflicts falling within its scope of application has been both difficult and controversial. Several delegations at the 1949 Diplomatic Conference had favoured the enumeration of certain criteria, but this approach was ultimately abandoned. Whilst it has often been argued that the failure of Common Article 3 to define NIAC was ultimately beneficial,[2] permitting efforts to apply Common Article 3 to as broad a range of circumstances as possible, another consequence is that states can seek to avoid international humanitarian law (IHL) obligations by simply denying the existence of an armed conflict (although the impact of such denials has been at least partially diminished by the development of human rights law).[3]

2 The Pictet Commentary accordingly suggested that the criteria discussed at the Diplomatic Conference could still be useful in determining when Common Article 3 should apply. Although not quite identical in each of the Commentaries,[4] they are summarized as follows:

(1) That the Party in revolt against the *de jure* Government possesses an organized military force, an authority responsible for its acts, acting within a determinate territory and having the means of respecting and ensuring respect for the Convention.
(2) That the legal Government is obliged to have recourse to the regular military forces against insurgents organized as military and in possession of a part of the national territory.
(3) (a) That the *de jure* Government has recognized the insurgents as belligerents; or
    (b) that it has claimed for itself the rights of a belligerent; or
    (c) that it has accorded the insurgents recognition as belligerents for the purposes only of the present Convention; or
    (d) that the dispute has been admitted to the agenda of the Security Council or the General Assembly of the United Nations as being a threat to international peace, a breach of the peace, or an act of aggression.
(4) (a) That the insurgents have an organization purporting to have the characteristics of a State.
    (b) That the insurgent civil authority exercises *de facto* authority over persons within a determinate territory.

The Concept of Non-International Armed Conflict in International Humanitarian Law (Cambridge: CUP, 2010) 7–51.

[2] Pictet Commentary GC I, at 49; J. Pejić, 'Status of Armed Conflicts', in E. Wilmshurst and S. Breau (eds), *Perspectives on the ICRC Study on Customary International Humanitarian Law* (Cambridge: CUP, 2007) 77, at 85, 'no definition would be capable of capturing the factual situations that reality throws up and [...] a definition would thus risk undermining the protective ambit of humanitarian law'.

[3] T. Meron, 'The Humanization of Humanitarian Law', 94 *AJIL* (2000) 239, at 261; L. Moir, 'The European Court of Human Rights and Humanitarian Law', in R. Kolb and G. Gaggioli (eds), *Research Handbook on Human Rights and Humanitarian Law* (Cheltenham: Edward Elgar Publishing, 2013) 480, at 481; M. Sassòli, 'Use and Abuse of the Laws of War in the "War on Terrorism"', 22 *Law and Inequality* (2004) 195, at 195–6.

[4] There are slight differences between Pictet Commentary GC I, at 49–50, Pictet Commentary GC IV, at 36, and Pictet Commentary GC III, at 36. The list is completely absent from Commentary GC II. See Cullen, above n 1, at 52–3.

(c) That the armed forces act under the direction of the organized civil authority and are prepared to observe the ordinary laws of war.
(d) That the insurgent civil authority agrees to be bound by the provisions of the Convention.

Evidently, these criteria represent a relatively high threshold. Perhaps mindful of this, however, the Commentaries are careful to clarify that the list is 'in no way obligatory'[5] and is, instead, suggested simply as a 'useful [...] means of distinguishing a genuine armed conflict from a mere act of banditry or an unorganized and short-lived insurrection'.[6] In fact, they assert that Common Article 3 should be applied as widely as possible—even 'where armed strife breaks out in a country, but does not fulfil any of the above conditions'.[7]

This may appear somewhat contradictory, in that low-intensity disturbances and tensions are accepted as being beyond the reach of Common Article 3.[8] Indeed, the claim that Common Article 3 merely requires respect for 'a few essential rules which [a government] in fact respects daily, under its own laws, even when dealing with common criminals',[9] fails to explain the levels of support for—or opposition to—Common Article 3, or to appreciate that it actually imposes only limited legal obligations in a limited range of situations.[10] At any rate, whilst influential, the criteria enumerated by Pictet have 'failed to crystallise into customary international law'.[11] Instead, the required elements of NIAC have been developed through case law. To complicate matters, however, additional (and not necessarily consistent) definitions of NIAC are provided in Additional Protocol II (AP II) and in the International Criminal Court (ICC) Statute. It is, then, necessary to consider these different expressions of the concept and their impact on the Geneva Conventions.

B. Categories of Non-International Armed Conflicts

Adopted in 1977 and aimed at the 'elaboration and completion' of Common Article 3,[12] AP II offers greater precision regarding its scope of application. It indicates in Article 1(1) that it applies to all armed conflicts not otherwise covered by Additional Protocol I (AP I), and

> which take place in the territory of a High Contracting Party between its armed forces and dissident armed forces or other organized armed groups which, under responsible command, exercise such control over a part of its territory as to enable them to carry out sustained and concerted military operations and to implement this Protocol.

Not only is this considerably more detailed than Common Article 3, it is also much more demanding. Impact on the scope of Common Article 3 is, however, limited in that, whilst AP II 'develops and supplements' Common Article 3, it does so 'without modifying its existing conditions of application'.[13] As the International Committee of the Red Cross (ICRC) Commentary explains, 'Keeping the Protocol separate from common Article 3

---

[5] Pictet Commentary GC I, at 49. [6] Ibid, at 50. [7] Ibid. [8] See MN 49–51.
[9] Pictet Commentary GC I, at 50.
[10] Moir, above n 1, at 37–8; J.E. Bond, 'Internal Conflict and Article 3 of the Geneva Conventions', 48 *Denver Law Journal* (1971) 263, at 270.
[11] S. Boelaert-Suominen, 'Commentary: The Yugoslavia Tribunal and the Common Core of Humanitarian Law Applicable to All Armed Conflicts', 13 *LJIL* (2000) 619, at 633–4.
[12] *Official Records of the Diplomatic Conference on the Reaffirmation and Development of International Humanitarian Law Applicable in Armed Conflicts, Geneva (1974–1977)* (Bern: ICRC, 1978), D. Bujard (ICRC), CDDH/I/SR.22, vol VIII, at 201.
[13] Art 1(1) AP II.

was intended to prevent undercutting the scope of Article 3 itself by laying down precise rules. In this way common Article 3 retains an independent existence.'[14]

6   There is, therefore, a clear contrast in the material field of application between AP II and Common Article 3. This has important consequences, and results in two separate categories of NIAC. Common Article 3 accordingly applies once NIAC exists (and so to *all* situations of NIAC, including those also covered by AP II), whereas AP II applies only to that subset of NIAC comprising those conflicts crossing its own, higher threshold.[15]

7   Neither Common Article 3 nor AP II indicates when an armed conflict exists per se. In 1995, however, the International Criminal Tribunal for the former Yugoslavia (ICTY) Appeals Chamber determined that 'an armed conflict exists whenever there is a resort to armed force between States or protracted armed violence between governmental authorities and organized armed groups or between such groups within a State'.[16] This statement (the '*Tadić* formula') refers to armed conflict in general, providing clearly defined parameters in relation to both international armed conflict (IAC) (resort to armed force between states) and NIAC (protracted armed violence involving organized armed groups), and, in the context of NIAC, has been widely accepted and consistently used in international law since—not only in subsequent ICTY and International Criminal Tribunal for Rwanda (ICTR) cases,[17] but also by the ICC,[18] and (admittedly, with varying degrees of accuracy)[19] in relation to Somalia,[20] Palestine,[21] Sierra Leone,[22] Sudan,[23] East Timor,[24] Lebanon,[25] etc.[26]

---

[14] ICRC Commentary APs, para 4454.

[15] Moir, above n 1, at 100–3; ECtHR, *Korbely v Hungary*, Judgment, 19 September 2008, para 87: 'Article 3 of the Geneva Conventions had an original scope of application which could not be considered to have been retroactively restricted by Protocol II. Consequently, any civilian participating in a conflict of a non-international character, irrespective of the level of intensity of the conflict or the manner in which the insurgents were organised, enjoyed the protection of Article 3 of the Geneva Conventions.'

[16] ICTY, *The Prosecutor v Duško Tadić*, Appeal on Jurisdiction, IT-94-1-AR72, 2 October 1995, para 70.

[17] ICTY, *The Prosecutor v Fatmir Limaj, Haradin Bala and Isak Musliu*, Trial Chamber Judgment, IT-03-66-T, 30 November 2005, para 84, indicates that the test 'set out in the *Tadić* Jurisdiction Decision […] has been applied consistently by the Tribunal', whilst in ICTY, *The Prosecutor v Naser Orić*, Trial Chamber Judgment, IT-03-68-T, 30 June 2006, para 254, the jurisprudence on this point was considered 'well settled'. For ICTR jurisprudence, see, e.g., *The Prosecutor v Jean-Paul Akayesu*, Trial Chamber Judgment, ICTR-96-4-T, 2 September 1998, paras 619–21; *The Prosecutor v George Rutaganda*, Trial Chamber Judgment, ICTR-96-3-T, 6 December 1999, para 92.

[18] ICC, *The Prosecutor v Thomas Lubanga*, Trial Chamber Judgment Pursuant to Art 74 of the Statute, ICC-01/04-01/06, 14 March 2012, para 533.

[19] See, e.g., *Report of the International Commission of Inquiry on Darfur to the United Nations Secretary-General*, 25 January 2005, where, despite indicating at para 74 its reliance on the *Tadić* formula, para 75 asserted that the situation in Darfur constituted NIAC because 'the requirements of (i) […] organized armed groups fighting against the central authorities, (ii) control by rebels over part of the territory and (iii) protracted fighting, in order for this situation to be considered an internal armed conflict under Common Article 3 of the Geneva Conventions are met'. A similar approach was taken in the *Report of the International Commission of Inquiry to Investigate All Alleged Violations of International Human Rights Law in the Libyan Arab Jamahiriya*, UN Doc A/HRC/17/44, 1 June 2011, paras 63–4. Both actually set a higher threshold than that indicated by the ICTY. See MN 40–42.

[20] *Report on the Situation of Human Rights in Somalia, pursuant to Commission Resolution 1996/57 of 19 April 1996*, UN Doc E/CN.4/1997/88, 3 March 1997, para 54.

[21] *Report of the Special Rapporteur of the Commission on Human Rights on the Situation of Human Rights in the Palestinian Territories Occupied by Israel since 1967*, UN Doc E/CN.4/2002/32, 6 March 2002, para 18.

[22] *Report of the Sierra Leone Truth and Reconciliation Commission* (Accra: GPL Press, 2004) 39, para 57.

[23] *Report of the International Commission of Inquiry on Darfur*, above n 19.

[24] *Report of the Commission for Reception, Truth and Reconciliation in Timor-Lieste (CAVR)*, October 2005, Part 2, 29, para 141.

[25] *Report of the Commission of Inquiry on Lebanon pursuant to Human Rights Council Resolution S-2/1**, UN Doc A/HRC/3/2, 23 November 2006, para 51.

[26] See discussion in Cullen, above n 1, at 137–9 and, more recently, *Report of the Independent International Commission of Inquiry on the Syrian Arab Republic*, UN Doc A/HRC/21/50, 15 August 2012, para 12.

Determining when the threshold of armed conflict has been crossed remains the primary difficulty, however, and it is also necessary in this context to consider the ICC Statute which, in the provisions devoted to war crimes in NIAC (i.e. Article 8(2)(c)–(f)), distinguishes between serious violations of Common Article 3 and other serious violations of the applicable laws and customs of war.[27] That neither can be committed in 'situations of internal disturbances and tensions, such as riots, isolated and sporadic acts of violence and other acts of a similar nature' (since in such cases IHL simply does not apply) is uncontroversial.[28] Perhaps more problematic is that whilst Article 8(2)(d) stipulates that serious violations of Common Article 3 are subject to the jurisdiction of the ICC when committed in the context of 'armed conflicts not of an international character' (therefore retaining the formula that appears in Common Article 3 itself), Article 8(2)(f) provides that the acts listed in Article 8(2)(e) constitute war crimes for the purpose of the jurisdiction of the ICC when committed in the context of 'armed conflicts that take place on the territory of a State when there is *protracted armed conflict between governmental authorities and organized armed groups or between such groups*' (emphasis added). This requirement clearly falls short of the AP II threshold and, although referring to 'protracted armed *conflict*' rather than 'protracted armed *violence*', has its basis in the *Tadić* formula.[29] Nonetheless, the enumeration of two separate categories of crimes, each followed by their own threshold for application, and the apparent association of the *Tadić* formula with Article 8(2)(e) alone, has led to suggestions that Article 8(2)(f) indicates a new, third category of NIAC, separate from that in Article 8(2)(d) and containing an additional (compulsory) temporal criterion.[30] Attempts to demarcate two separate categories of NIAC within the ICC Statute are understandable but misguided. The better view is to consider the thresholds stated in Article 8(2)(d) and (f) as the same, with the latter merely clarifying the former's scope of application—i.e. that of Common Article 3.[31] It is, after all, clear that most states involved in drafting the ICC Statute initially envisaged a single threshold to cover *all* crimes committed during NIAC.[32]

Article 8(2)(c) and (e) both expressly apply to 'armed conflicts not of an international character', a term taken *verbatim* from Common Article 3 rather than AP II and which, by the time of the ICC Statute's adoption, was widely accepted as indicating those situations falling under Common Article 3. The phrase thereby represented the 'established lower threshold' for the application of IHL,[33] and it would have been 'peculiar' for it to be interpreted differently in the context of the ICC Statute, suggesting a 'uniformity of application for sections 2(c) and 2(e) of Article 8'.[34]

---

[27] Art 8(2)(c) and (e) ICC Statute. [28] Art 8(2)(d) and (f) ICC Statute. See MN 49–51.
[29] The ICTY sees the provision as defining armed conflict by 'the same two characteristics'. See ICTY, *The Prosecutor v Limaj*, above n 17, para 87; and ICTY, *The Prosecutor v Ljube Boškoski and Johan Tarčulovski*, Trial Chamber Judgment, IT-04-82-T, 10 July 2008, para 197, indicating that the Art 8(2)(f) test was considered 'distinct from, and a lower threshold than, the test under Additional Protocol II'.
[30] S. Vité, 'Typology of Armed Conflicts in International Humanitarian Law: Legal Concepts and Actual Situations', 91 *IRRC* 873 (2009) 69, at 81–3; Cullen, above n 1, at 174 and 177–8.
[31] Meron, above n 3, at 260, insists that whilst Art 8(2)(f) exacerbates the previous lack of clarity, it 'should not be considered as creating yet another threshold of applicability'. See also T. Meron, 'Crimes Under the Jurisdiction of the International Criminal Court', in H.A.M. von Hebel et al (eds), *Reflections on the International Criminal Court* (The Hague: T.M.C. Asser, 1999) 47, at 54; Vité, above n 30, at 81; Cullen, above n 1, at 174–85.
[32] Cullen, above n 1, at 175–6. [33] Ibid, at 180.
[34] Ibid, at 182. It is true that Art 8(2)(f) refers to conflict that takes place 'in the territory of a State', whereas (unlike Common Article 3) Art 8(2)(d) does not. This discrepancy has no practical relevance,

10 The conclusion must therefore be that the ICC Statute provides for a single category of NIAC, and that the only distinctions required are those (i) between IAC and NIAC, and (ii) between NIAC and internal disturbances and tensions.[35] It is the latter threshold (i.e. the *Tadić* formula/Common Article 3 threshold) that must be crossed in order for the customary international law rules of NIAC to become applicable.

11 Of course, given that the *Tadić* formula presents the concept 'in an abstract manner, [...] it is apparent that whether a conflict meets the criteria of Common Article 3 is to be decided on a case by case basis'.[36] Precisely how this is to be achieved in terms of assessing (i) the level of organization of armed groups, and (ii) the protracted nature of armed violence is addressed below. First, however, it is necessary to consider the two criteria explicitly included in Common Article 3 itself, namely: (i) that the armed conflict be non-international in character; and (i) that it take place on the territory of a High Contracting Party.

C. 'Not of an International Character'

I. Parties to the conflict

12 Common Article 2 provides that the Geneva Conventions are applicable 'to all cases of declared war or of any other armed conflict which may arise between two or more of the High Contracting Parties'. Only states can be High Contracting Parties, and the Conventions as a whole therefore apply only to conflicts occurring between states, i.e. *international* armed conflicts.[37] Similarly, AP I (relating to the protection of victims of IAC), provides in Article 1(3) that it applies to those 'situations referred to in [Common] Article 2', whilst Article 1(4) develops this categorization by indicating that the IACs referred to in the preceding paragraph include 'armed conflicts in which peoples are fighting against colonial domination and alien occupation and against racist regimes in the exercise of their right of self-determination'.[38] In terms of classification, armed conflict can only be international or non-international in character. As such, any other armed conflict (i.e. which is neither inter-state nor a war of national liberation) must be considered a NIAC: 'Legally speaking, no other type of armed conflict exists.'[39] So-called

---

however, in that the reference in Art 8(2)(e) to '*other* serious violations' of IHL in NIAC indicates that these must necessarily take place in 'the same category of armed conflict as that of common Article 3'. See ibid, at 182–3: 'It follows by rule of logic [...] that the "serious violations of [common] article 3 [...]" listed in Article 8(2)(c) form a subset of "serious violations of the laws and customs applicable to armed conflicts not of an international character".'

[35] M. Bothe, 'War Crimes', in A. Cassese et al (eds), *The Rome Statute of the International Criminal Court: A Commentary* (Oxford: OUP, 2002) 379, at 418; Cullen, above n 1, at 179. Even some advocates of an intermediate threshold accept that it relates only to the ICC's jurisdiction, and that the Statute 'does not establish a category that is more generally applicable'. See Vité, above n 30, at 83.

[36] ICTR, *The Prosecutor v Alfred Musema*, Judgment and Sentence, ICTR-96-13-A, 27 January 2000, para 249; ICTR, *The Prosecutor v Rutaganda*, above n 17, para 92.

[37] In the absence of an agreement to apply all of the Conventions under CA 3. See Moir, above n 1, at 63–5. On the notion of IAC, see Ch 1 of this volume.

[38] This, perhaps controversially, transforms what would otherwise have been NIAC into IAC. It has, however, had little impact in practice. See MN 46 below; C. Greenwood, 'Customary Law Status of the 1977 Geneva Protocols', in A.J.M Delissen and G.J. Tanja (eds), *Humanitarian Law of Armed Conflict: Challenges Ahead* (Dordrecht: Martinus Nijhoff, 1991) 93, at 111–12. See also Ch 2, MN 43–44, of this volume.

[39] ICRC, 'How Is the Term "Armed Conflict" Defined in International Humanitarian Law?', Opinion Paper (March 2008), at 1, available at, <http://www.icrc.org/eng/assets/files/other/opinion-paper-armed-conflict.pdf>.

'mixed armed conflicts' raise specific issues that are discussed elsewhere in this volume (see Chapter 2 of this volume). The accepted position in such circumstances, however, is that IAC and NIAC can coexist, with the applicable body of IHL determined by the nature of the parties to the particular hostilities in question.[40]

A non-international armed conflict does not require the participation of governmental forces, and can exist between competing non-state armed groups. Although explicitly required by Article 1(1) AP II, which applies only to conflicts on the territory of a state party 'between *its armed forces* and dissident armed forces or other organized armed groups' (emphasis added), this is one of the aspects serving to limit the application of AP II, and does not impact upon the broader scope of Common Article 3—which makes no reference to the parties to the conflict whatsoever.[41] Indeed, to require state involvement would be extremely problematic from a humanitarian standpoint, leaving situations such as those existing in 'failed states' unregulated by IHL. Accordingly, NIAC also refers to 'the crumbling of all governmental authority in the country, as a result of which various groups fight each other in the struggle for power'.[42]

II. Armed conflict in occupied territory

Perhaps more difficult is the question of how to characterize armed conflict taking place in occupied territory. As discussed, Common Article 2 indicates the applicability of the Conventions in their entirety to 'all cases of partial or total occupation of the territory of a High Contracting Party, even if the said occupation meets with no armed resistance'. As such, suggestions that occupation and NIAC are 'mutually exclusive concepts', and that any armed conflict taking place in the context of an occupation must be international in character, are understandable.[43] The situation is, however, slightly more nuanced than this. It is, after all, possible that armed conflict could exist in occupied territory between two (or more) non-state parties without any involvement on the part of the Occupying Power,[44] which is difficult to perceive as anything other than NIAC. Even where hostilities involve the Occupying Power, however, there may still be a question as to the characterization of the conflict.

Although it has been suggested that '[a]n armed conflict which takes place between an Occupying Power and rebel or insurgent groups [...] in occupied territory, amounts to an international armed conflict',[45] the position seems to turn more precisely on the relationship between the insurgent group and the occupied state. General agreement exists that hostilities involving the Occupying Power and organized armed groups belonging to the occupied state (in terms of Article 4(A)(2) GC III) are international

---

[40] Vité, above n 30, at 86; Moir, above n 1, at 47; D. Schindler, 'International Humanitarian Law and Internationalized Armed Conflicts', 22 *IRRC* 230 (1982) 255; ICC, *The Prosecutor v Lubanga*, above n 18, para 540; ICTY, *The Prosecutor v Duško Tadić*, Appeals Chamber Judgment, IT-94-1-A, 15 July 1999, para 84.
[41] See MN 5–6.
[42] H.P. Gasser, 'International Humanitarian Law', in H. Haug (ed), *Humanity for All* (Berne: Paul Haupt, 1993) 491, at 555.
[43] See, e.g., ICRC, *Expert Meeting on Occupation and Other Forms of Administration of Foreign Teritory* (Geneva, March 2012), at 127.
[44] A. Paulus and M. Vashakmadze, 'Asymmetrical War and the Notion of Armed Conflict: A Tentative Conceptualization', 91 *IRRC* 873 (2009) 95, at 115, suggesting conflict in Israeli Occupied Territory between Hamas and the Palestinian Authority or Fatah, or else between Bosnian Muslims and Croats during the Bosnian conflict between Muslims and Serbs.
[45] Ibid; A. Cassese, *International Law* (2nd edn, Oxford: OUP, 2005), at 420.

in character by virtue of Common Article 2.⁴⁶ Similarly, where the occupied state has overall control of the insurgent group,⁴⁷ the situation would seem to be one of IAC. Conflict between an Occupying Power and insurgents not connected to the occupied state would be NIAC. Few armed groups, however, are likely to meet the requirements of 'belonging' under Article 4(A)(2) GC III. Nor may 'overall control' be easily demonstrated,⁴⁸ and it is more probable that hostile acts will be carried out against occupying forces by armed groups connected with the occupied state in some way—or claiming to fight on its behalf—but not necessarily 'belonging to' or 'controlled by' the state as required by international law. In such circumstances, classification of the conflict remains difficult.

16 Some maintain that these conflicts are international in character:

> Since the original international armed conflict and the resulting occupation would necessarily have created the conditions for the occupied government's breakdown and the appearance of armed resistance groups fighting on behalf of the occupied State [...] the armed confrontation [...] [is] a continuation of the original international armed conflict [and there is] no need to legally reclassify the situation.⁴⁹

This appears to lose sight of the overriding importance of the nature of the parties involved, and the influence that this exerts on the characterization of a conflict.⁵⁰ Put simply, unless the armed group belongs to, or is controlled by, the occupied state, it is difficult to envisage the conflict as anything other than between a state and a non-state party—and thus as non-international. Occupation does not internationalize armed conflict per se, and it is entirely possible for a NIAC and an occupation to coexist. The ICC Trial Chamber confirmed this position in *Lubanga*, finding 'insufficient evidence to establish (even on a prima facie basis) that either Rwanda or Uganda exercised overall control over the UPC/FPLC',⁵¹ and that since this did not result in an inter-state conflict, 'it remained a non-international conflict notwithstanding any concurrent international armed conflict between Uganda and the DRC'.⁵²

III. Third party involvement

a. Third state involvement

17 Complications are possible in terms of the parties to an armed conflict which is seemingly not of an international character, and the impact that the participation of additional states may have on its classification. Provided it is borne in mind, however, that only inter-state hostilities constitute IAC, and that different legal regimes apply according to the particular parties in question, it is clear that armed intervention by third states in support of the insurgents and against the government party constitutes a Common Article 2 armed conflict as between the two states, and may serve to internationalize the conflict per se should the third state equally exercise overall control in relation to the insurgent party.

---

⁴⁶ ICRC, *Expert Meeting*, above n 43, at 124.
⁴⁷ As per the 'overall control' test set out in ICTY, *The Prosecutor v Tadić*, above n 40, para 137, whereby the state plays a role in 'organising, co-ordinating or planning the military actions of the military group, in addition to financing, training and equipping or providing operational support'.
⁴⁸ ICRC, *Expert Meeting*, above n 43, at 126.
⁴⁹ Ibid.   ⁵⁰ See MN 12.   ⁵¹ ICC, *The Prosecutor v Lubanga*, above n 18, para 561.
⁵² Ibid, para 563.

Direct armed intervention on behalf of the government, in contrast, has no impact on the non-international character of the conflict.[53]

b. United Nations and/or other international involvement

It is also relatively common for United Nations (UN) or other multinational forces to be present during NIAC, especially in the context of peacekeeping operations carried out with the consent of the host state. When this is the case, the multinational forces are impartial and not actively engaged in hostilities,[54] and therefore the characterization of the conflict as NIAC is unaffected. Members of peacekeeping forces should therefore be seen as 'persons taking no active part in hostilities' in terms of Common Article 3, so that attacks on them by a party to NIAC would be unlawful.[55] Where multinational troops actively participate in hostilities in support of one side or the other, however,[56] such as in the case of UN peace enforcement operations under Chapter VII, the character of the conflict can change.

Indeed, some argue that any direct involvement of multinational forces automatically renders a conflict international.[57] Again, however, the critical question should be that of which forces are in direct conflict in any given situation; and a consistent application of the principle whereby only inter-state hostilities constitute IAC makes this position difficult to sustain. Thus, hostilities between state and non-state forces, or between different non-state forces, remain NIACs, as do hostilities between UN or other multinational troops and rebel forces. Only hostilities arising between UN troops and the host state would be international in character.[58]

That is not to say that difficult issues do not continue to arise in this area of the law, such as whether the system of pairings 'implies the equalization of parties who are not, in fact, equal',[59] and whether the undeniable 'international dimension' of UN involvement requires its forces to apply the rules of IAC in hostilities with parties to the conflict (and

---

[53] D. Jinks, 'The Temporal Scope of Application of International Humanitarian Law in Contemporary Conflicts', Harvard University Program on Humanitarian Policy and Conflict Research, Background Paper prepared for the Informal High-Level Expert Meeting on the Reaffirmation and Development of International Humanitarian Law, Cambridge, 27–9 January 2003, available at <http://www.hpcrresearch.org/sites/default/files/publications/Session3.pdf>, at 9; Moir, above n 1, at 50–1. For more detailed consideration of 'internationalized' armed conflict, see Ch 2 of this volume.

[54] Resort to force being limited to situations of self-defence.

[55] C. Greenwood, 'International Humanitarian Law and United Nations Military Operations', 1 *YIHL* (1998) 3, at 31.

[56] See, e.g., MONUC forces acting in support of the DRC and against insurgent attacks, referred to in Vité, above n 30, at 87.

[57] See Ch 1, in particular n 25, of this volume. See also D. Shraga, 'The UN as an Actor Bound by International Humanitarian Law', in L. Condorelli et al (eds), *The United Nations and International Humanitarian Law* (Paris: Editions Pedone, 1996) 317, at 333; D.W. Bowett, *United Nations Forces* (London: Stevens, 1964), at 509; R.D. Glick, 'Lip Service to the Laws of War: Humanitarian Law and United Nations Armed Forces', 17 *MJIL* (1995–6) 53, at 89–90.

[58] See Ch 1, MN 18, of this volume. See also ICRC, *International Humanitarian Law and the Challenges of Contemporary Armed Conflicts*, Report prepared for the 31st International Conference of the Red Cross and Red Crescent, October 2011, 31IC/11/5.1.2, at 31; H. McCoubrey and N.D. White, *The Blue Helmets* (Aldershot: Dartmouth, 1996), at 172; Pejić, above n 2, at 94; B.D. Tittermore, 'Belligerents in Blue Helmets: Applying International Humanitarian Law to United Nations Peace Operations', 33 *Stanford JIL* (1997) 61, at 110. The same applies where the host state withdraws consent, although perhaps 'with some caution', especially where there is a significant degree of territorial control by the insurgent group(s). See R. Murphy, 'United Nations Military Operations and International Humanitarian Law: What Rules Apply to Peacekeepers?', 14 *Criminal Law Forum* (2003) 153, at 185.

[59] J. Saura, 'Lawful Peacekeeping: Applicability of International Humanitarian Law to United Nations Peacekeeping Operations', 58 *Hastings Law Journal* (2006–7) 479, at 514.

vice versa), irrespective of how the conflict is legally classified—and without affecting that classification.[60] Thus, it may be the case that UN involvement renders the rules of IAC applicable to all situations involving the active participation of its troops (in relation to operations against both state and non-state parties), but without changing the non-international character of the armed conflict for the state and insurgent parties involved in their mutual relations.[61] To that end, however, the relevant IHL obligations in those hostilities involving multinational forces and the legal classification of the conflict per se can be seen as distinct questions.[62]

D. Geographical Scope

21 Common Article 3 provides not only that conflicts within its purview must be non-international in character, but also, as far as geographical scope is concerned, that the conflict must take place 'in the territory of one of the High Contracting Parties'. Prima facie, this somewhat limited requirement is straightforward. According to the ICRC, universal ratification of the Conventions means that the requirement 'has lost its importance in practice. Indeed, any armed conflict between governmental armed forces and armed groups or between such groups cannot but take place on the territory of one of the Parties to the Convention'.[63] Questions nonetheless remain as to:

— whether a NIAC must be *limited* to the territory of a single High Contracting Party; and
— the geographical extent of IHL's application where hostilities are limited to part of a state's territory.

I. 'Territory of a High Contracting Party'

22 The first issue is whether Common Article 3 applies only to those armed conflicts which are non-international in the sense of being *internal*, i.e. limited to the territory of a single High Contracting Party. Pictet's Commentaries suggest that it was intended to refer to conflicts similar to IAC, but which occur 'within the confines of a single country'.[64] More recently, the *San Remo Manual on Non-international Armed Conflicts* has similarly provided that '[n]on-international armed conflicts are armed confrontations occurring *within the territory of a single State* and in which the armed forces of no other State are engaged against the central government.'[65]

23 This approach is highly problematic given the emergence of non-state actors capable of independently inflicting significant damage abroad, and the consequent increase in the number of contemporary armed conflicts between states and those non-state actors

---

[60] Murphy, above n 58, at 180.
[61] Saura, above n 59, at 515. This has not necessarily been the consistent approach of the UN, however. See Greenwood, above n 55, at 26.
[62] See discussion of the applicability of the Conventions to UN forces in Ch 1, MN 16–19, of this volume.
[63] ICRC, above n 39, at 3.
[64] Pictet Commentary GC IV, at 36. See also Pictet Commentary GC III, at 37; Pictet Commentary GC II, at 33. There is no similar explanation in Pictet Commentary GC I.
[65] Emphasis added. It further explains that they do not include 'conflicts extending to the territory of two or more States'. See International Institute of Humanitarian Law (drafting committee M.N. Schmitt et al), *The Manual on the Law of Non-International Armed Conflict with Commentary* (2006), at 2, available at <http://www.dur.ac.uk/resources/law/NIACManualIYBHR15th.pdf>.

operating from within the territory of a third state. It is unlikely that such situations were contemplated by the drafters of the Geneva Conventions, but to maintain that the Conventions as a whole apply only to IAC, and Common Article 3 only to wholly internal NIAC, would leave conflicts between a state and a foreign-based (or transnational) armed group—or, indeed, an internal NIAC that spills over into the territory of a neighbouring state—beyond the ambit of IHL.[66] As Sassòli explains:

> If such wording meant that conflicts opposing states and organized armed groups and spreading over the territory of several states were not 'non-international armed conflicts', there would be a gap in protection, which could not be explained by states' concerns about their sovereignty. Those concerns made the law of non-international armed conflict more rudimentary. Yet concerns about state sovereignty could not explain why victims of conflicts spilling over the territory of several states should benefit from less protection than those affected by conflicts limited to the territory of only one state.[67]

Jinks agrees that there is 'no principled (or pragmatic) rationale for this regulatory gap',[68] and recalls that Common Article 3 was considered revolutionary due to its regulation of wholly internal matters through the reach of IHL, asserting that, if it governs wholly internal conflicts, it must apply '*a fortiori* to armed conflicts with international or transnational dimensions'.[69] Indeed, as per the *Nicaragua* case,[70] not only does Common Article 3 apply to all conflicts not covered by Common Article 2, in practical terms it applies to *all* armed conflicts, in that '*international* armed conflicts trigger protections equal to, and in most areas greater than, those accorded by [C]ommon Article 3. Therefore, because armed conflicts are either international or "not of an international character", the minimum humanitarian protections recognized in [C]ommon Article 3 extend to all armed conflicts.'[71] As such, the apparent geographical restriction set out in Common Article 3 cannot be accepted as representative of the current state of IHL. 24

Looking first at the scenario whereby NIAC initially limited to the territory of a single state extends onto the territory of another (or others),[72] it should be noted that the ICTR Statute, clearly concerned with NIAC (its provisions regarding violations of the laws of war in Article 4 were limited to violations of Common Article 3 and AP II), explicitly asserts the Tribunal's jurisdiction over violations of the relevant rules of IHL not only in the territory of Rwanda, but also over 'Rwandan citizens responsible for such violations committed in the territory of neighbouring States'.[73] Assuming that consent exists on the 25

---

[66] D. Jinks, 'September 11 and the Laws of War', 28 *Yale JIL* (2003) 1, at 40–1. This had been the approach taken by the US Court of Appeals in *Hamdan v Rumsfeld*, 415 F 3d 33 (2005), at 41.
[67] M. Sassòli, 'Transnational Armed Groups and International Humanitarian Law', Harvard University Program on Humanitarian Policy and Conflict Research, *Occasional Paper Series*, Winter 2006 (No 6), at 9.
[68] Jinks, above n 66, at 41.   [69] Ibid.
[70] ICJ, *Case concerning Military and Paramilitary Operations in and against Nicaragua (Nicaragua v United States of America)*, Merits, Judgment, 27 June 1986, para 218, describing CA 3 as a 'minimum yardstick', even in the event of IAC, representing 'elementary considerations of humanity'. The ICJ went on, at para 219, to hold that '[b]ecause the minimum rules applicable to international and to non-international armed conflicts are identical, there is no need to address the question whether those actions must be looked at in the context of the rules which operate for the one or for the other category of conflict'.
[71] Jinks, above n 66, at 41.   [72] Described by Vité, above n 30, at 89, as an 'exported' NIAC.
[73] ICTR Statute, Art 1. See also Art 7, indicating that the territorial jurisdiction of the Tribunal extended not only to the territory of Rwanda itself, but also 'to the territory of neighbouring States in respect of serious violations of international humanitarian law committed by Rwandan citizens'.

26 part of the neighbouring state in relation to the use of force against the non-state armed group seeking refuge in its territory, there is no Common Article 2 armed conflict, and so the situation must be classified as NIAC.[74]

26 The situation where government forces engage in cross-border military activity with non-state armed actors located in a third state without that state's consent requires more detailed consideration and has been high on the international legal agenda since 11 September 2001.[75] It is perhaps useful to consider two separate scenarios here: the first being where the non-state armed actors are considered to be acting on behalf of the host state. If this can be demonstrated in terms of overall control by the host state then the situation is, in effect, a Common Article 2 IAC.[76] The second scenario involves a non-state armed group acting independently of the host state, or where any host state involvement is insufficient to cross the relevant 'control' threshold. It has been suggested that this represents a novel type of armed conflict, requiring the development of a new and specific legal regime,[77] which seems unnecessary. Again, it is the character of the belligerents (and not the territorial reach of the conflict) that determines the applicable rules.

27 To illustrate, in terms of the military reaction to 9/11, it is probably true that Al-Qaeda's lack of organization and methods of operation meant that it could not reasonably be considered a party to an armed conflict, even if a 'global non-international conflict' were possible.[78] That does not mean that such a conflict could not exist, however, which was the approach taken by the US Supreme Court in *Hamdan v Rumsfeld*,[79] holding that 'the phrase "not of an international character" bears its literal meaning', i.e. not between sovereign states.

28 Granted, the approach to such situations may not appear consistent. In the context of Israel's 2006 military operations against Hezbollah within Lebanon, for example, Sassòli has suggested that the absence of Lebanese consent rendered them an IAC under Common Article 2.[80] The Human Rights Council's Commission of Inquiry also considered the situation to constitute an IAC. Nonetheless, a body of opinion insists, on the contrary, that combat operations between Israel and Hezbollah—even on Lebanese territory—represented a NIAC. Closer inspection reveals that much depends on the approach taken to the relationship between Hezbollah and Lebanon. Thus, despite accepting that hostilities were carried out only between Israel and Hezbollah,[81] the UN Commission of Inquiry believed that Hezbollah should be seen as agents of

---

[74] Vité, above n 30, at 89.

[75] Paulus and Vashakmadze, above n 44, at 110, state that CA 3 seems to exclude conflicts on the territory of more than one state, and explain that whilst '[i]n 1949 this omission may have been due to the relative obscurity of such conflicts […] since 11 September 2001 at the latest, they are at the forefront of international debate'.

[76] See discussion in Ch 2 of this volume.

[77] See, e.g., G.S. Corn, 'Hamdan, Lebanon and the Regulation of Hostilities: The Need to Recognize a Hybrid Category of Armed Conflict', 40 *Van JTL* (2007) 295.

[78] Vité, above n 30, at 93; Pejić, above n 2, at 85; Sassòli, above n 67, at 10–11. See also the discussion of organization below at MN 35–39.

[79] 548 US 557 (2006), at 628–31.

[80] Especially in light of the lower threshold for IAC (as discussed in Chs 1 and 2). See Sassòli, above n 67, at 5. Paulus and Vashakmadze, above n 44, at 112, agree: 'If the Lebanese government had consented to Israel's intervention on its territory, the conflict would have constituted a non-international armed conflict between the state of Israel and Hezbollah. However, the Israeli military intervention occurred without Lebanon's consent and resulted in large-scale destruction of the Lebanese infrastructure.'

[81] *Report of the Commission of Inquiry on Lebanon*, above n 25, para 53.

Lebanon. To the extent that Lebanon had been a direct target of Israeli action,[82] it was a party to the conflict, and Hezbollah was a group 'belonging to a Party to the conflict' in terms of Article 4A(2) GC III. As such, the conflict was international in character.[83] Opposing views are based on the premise that the link between Hezbollah and Lebanon seemed less certain, so that the conflict between Israel and Hezbollah was non-international.[84]

The Israeli Supreme Court nonetheless held in *Public Committee against Torture in Israel v Israel*,[85] that Israel Defense Forces (IDF) action against militant Palestinian organizations in the Occupied Palestinian Territories was an IAC; first, because the conflict crossed the frontiers of the state[86] and, secondly, because contemporary terrorist organizations have massive capability. It believed that

> the fact that the terrorist organizations and their members do not act in the name of a state does not turn the struggle against them into a purely internal state conflict. Indeed, in today's reality, a terrorist organization is likely to have considerable military capabilities. At times they have military capabilities that exceed those of states. Confrontation with those dangers cannot be restricted within the state and its penal law. Confronting the dangers of terrorism constitutes a part of the international law dealing with armed conflicts of international character.[87]

Most of this is true, and the Court was correct to indicate that such situations are regulated by IHL. Where two states are not in conflict with each other, however, the appropriate regime is that of NIAC, i.e. Common Article 3.[88] The ICC recently confirmed this position, holding that

> when a State enters into a conflict with a non-governmental armed group located in the territory of a neighbouring State and the armed group is acting under the control of its own State, "the fighting falls within the definition of an international armed conflict between the two States". However, if the armed group is not acting on behalf of a government, in the absence of two States opposing each other, there is no international armed conflict.[89]

As such, and despite the approach of Pictet's Commentaries, reference in Common Article 3 to conflicts occurring on the territory of a High Contracting Party should be seen as a general geographical requirement, easily fulfilled, and recalling simply that Common Article 3 applies only in the territory of those states that have ratified the Conventions. It does not require that hostilities be limited geographically to the territory of a single state.[90] The concepts of NIAC and IAC 'are distinguished [...] by the parties involved rather than by the territorial scope of the conflict'.[91]

---

[82] Ibid, para 58.   [83] Ibid, paras 50–62, and 65–8.
[84] Vité, above n 30, at 91–2, asserts that this existed alongside a separate IAC between Israel and Lebanon.
[85] HCJ 769/02, *Public Committee against Torture in Israel v Government of Israel* [2006].
[86] Ibid, para 18. The Court further asserted that hostilities took place in the context of belligerent occupation, thus by definition constituting IAC. See, however, discussion at MN 14–16.
[87] HCJ 769/02, *Public Committee against Torture in Israel v Government of Israel* [2006], para 21.
[88] See D. Turns, 'The "War on Terror" through British and International Humanitarian Law Eyes: Comparative Perspectives on Selected Legal Issues', 10 *New York City Law Review* (2007) 435, esp at 466–73; Paulus and Vashakmadze, above n 44, at 112.
[89] ICC, *The Prosecutor v Lubanga*, above n 18, para 541. The ICC also asserted that 'overall control', rather than 'effective control', was the appropriate test for internationalization of a conflict. See Ch 2 of this volume.
[90] Sassòli, above n 67, at 9; Jinks, above n 66.
[91] L. Zegveld, *Accountability of Armed Opposition Groups in International Law* (Cambridge: CUP, 2002), at 136, as quoted in Sassòli, above n 67, at 9; ICRC Commentary APs, para 4458.

II. Extent of IHL's application

32   Case law makes clear that there is a broad geographical scope in terms of IHL's application to NIAC, which is not only relevant to those areas where hostilities are actually in progress, but also extends to the entire territory of the parties involved. The *Tadić* formula provides that IHL applies to 'the whole territory under the control of a party, whether or not actual combat takes place there',[92] and this has been reiterated in subsequent jurisprudence to the extent that it is now 'settled'.[93] In *Prosecutor v Kunarac*, for example, the ICTY Appeals Chamber held:

> There is no necessary correlation between the area where the actual fighting is taking place and the geographical reach of the laws of war. The laws of war apply in the whole territory of the warring states or, in the case of internal armed conflicts, to the whole territory under the control of a party to the conflict, whether or not actual combat takes place there […] A violation of the laws or customs of war may therefore occur […] in a place where no fighting is actually taking place.[94]

33   The ICTR similarly held that 'the mere fact that Rwanda was engaged in an armed conflict meeting the threshold requirements of [C]ommon Article 3 and Additional Protocol II means that these instruments would apply over the whole territory hence encompassing massacres which occurred away from the "war front"'.[95]

E. Existence of Armed Conflict

34   Common Article 3 does not address the fundamental question of precisely what constitutes an *armed conflict*. In order to determine whether an armed conflict exists, it is instead necessary to consider the *Tadić* formula of (i) organized armed groups, and (ii) protracted armed violence.

I. Organization of the parties

35   It is universally accepted that a certain level of organization is required on the part of insurgents in order for a NIAC to exist. It is, after all, difficult to see a disorganized group of individuals being a 'party' to an armed conflict in the context of IHL. Security Council resolutions may have 'called upon "all parties to the conflict" to respect international humanitarian law, [even] in the context of such "anarchic conflicts" as those in Somalia and Liberia',[96] but international criminal courts and tribunals have consistently adhered to the *Tadić* formula, requiring the participation of 'organized armed groups'. The ICRC has similarly maintained that 'an armed conflict exists when the armed action is taking place between two or more parties and reflects a minimum of organization'.[97]

---

[92] ICTY, *The Prosecutor v Tadić*, above n 16.   [93] ICTY, *The Prosecutor v Limaj*, above n 17.

[94] ICTY, *The Prosecutor v Dragoljub Kunarac, Radomir Kovač and Zoran Vuković*, Appeals Chamber Judgment, IT-96-23 and IT-96-23/1-A, 12 June 2002, para 57.

[95] ICTR, *The Prosecutor v Akayesu*, above n 17, para 636. See also *Niyonteze Case*, Swiss Military Appeals Chamber 1A, Decision of 26 May 2000, reproduced in Sassòli/Bouvier/Quintin, vol III, 2221, at 2224–5. For discussion of the geographical scope of application of the Conventions more generally, see Ch 4 of this volume. For discussion of the issue of temporal scope of the application of CA 3, see Ch 3 of this volume.

[96] ICRC, 'Armed Conflicts Linked to Disintegration of State Structures', Preparatory Document Drafted by the International Committee of the Red Cross for the First Periodical Meeting on International Humanitarian Law, Geneva, 19–23 January 1998, III(1)(a).

[97] 'Agreement on the Organisation of the International Activities of the Components of the International Red Cross and Red Crescent Movement', 38 *IRRC* 322 (1998) 159. See also K. Dörmann, *Elements of War*

Requiring that the parties to NIAC be organized is not, then, controversial. More **36** difficult is the question of how to determine the appropriate level of organization. There seems to be a general consensus that this level would enable the parties to carry out the obligations imposed by Common Article 3. Whilst it is assumed that government armed forces would cross this threshold, the 'minimum degree of organization and discipline' required of armed groups would be such as to permit them to 'respect international humanitarian law'.[98]

Jurisprudence of the ICTY confirms this approach, most clearly in a series of decisions **37** regarding the Kosovo Liberation Army (KLA), and whether it was sufficiently organized to constitute an organized armed group under the *Tadić* formula.[99] In basic terms, it is settled that in order for an armed group to be organized, 'it would need to have some hierarchical structure and its leadership requires the capacity to exert authority over its members',[100] to the point whereby, 'as a minimum [...] the basic obligations of Common Article 3 [...] may be implemented'.[101] This does not imply the same level of organization as state forces, nor the level required for AP II to apply (i.e. that of responsible command and territorial control sufficient to permit sustained and concerted military operations as well as implementation of AP II).[102]

A detailed and wide-ranging survey of how organization had been evaluated by the **38** ICTY was provided by the Trial Chamber in *The Prosecutor v Boškoski*.[103] Explaining that—whilst neither exhaustive nor concurrent/cumulative—a number of indicative factors, falling into five broad groups, had been considered, the passage merits quotation at length:

In the first group are those factors signalling the presence of a command structure, such as the establishment of a general staff or high command, which appoints and gives directions to commanders, disseminates internal regulations, organises the weapons supply, authorises military action, assigns tasks to individuals in the organisation, and issues political statements and communiqués, and which is informed by the operational units of all developments within the unit's area of responsibility. Also included in this group are factors such as the existence of internal regulations setting out the organisation and structure of the armed group; the assignment of an official spokesperson; the communication through communiqués reporting military actions and operations undertaken by the armed group; the existence of headquarters; internal regulations establishing ranks of servicemen and defining duties of commanders and deputy commanders of a unit, company, platoon or

---

Crimes under the Rome Statute of the International Criminal Court (Cambridge: CUP, 2002), at 442, requiring that parties be 'organised to a greater or lesser extent'.

[98] ICRC, above n 96. The group need not act under the control of a civilian authority—see ICTY, *The Prosecutor v Slobodan Milošević*, Trial Chamber Decision for Motion on Judgment of Acquittal, IT-02-54-T, 16 June 2004, para 34.

[99] Briefly in ICTY, *The Prosecutor v Milošević*, above n 98, paras 23–5; and applying indicative criteria to factual scenarios more fully in ICTY, *The Prosecutor v Limaj*, above n 17, paras 94–134, ICTY, *The Prosecutor v Ramush Haradinaj, Idriz Balaj and Lahi Brahimaj*, Trial Chamber Judgment, IT-04-84-T, 3 April 2008, paras 63–89, and ICTY, *The Prosecutor v Vlastimir Đorđević*, Trial Chamber Judgment, IT-05-87/1-T, 23 February 2011, paras 1537–78.

[100] ICTY, *The Prosecutor v Boškoski*, above n 29, para 195.

[101] Ibid, para 196. A lack of the requisite organization is not, however, to be inferred from even frequent violations of IHL (ibid, para 205).

[102] Ibid, para 197: 'Additional Protocol II requires a higher standard than Common Article 3 for establishment of an armed conflict. It follows that the degree of organisation required to engage in "protracted violence" is lower than the degree of organisation required to carry out "sustained and concerted military operations"'. See also discussion above (MN 5–6).

[103] Ibid, paras 199–203 (references omitted).

squad, creating a chain of military hierarchy between the various levels of commanders; and the dissemination of internal regulations to the soldiers and operational units.

Secondly, factors indicating that the group could carry out operations in an organised manner have been considered, such as the group's ability to determine a unified military strategy and to conduct large scale military operations, the capacity to control territory, whether there is territorial division into zones of responsibility in which the respective commanders are responsible for the establishment of Brigades and other units and appoint commanding officers for such units; the capacity of operational units to coordinate their actions, and the effective dissemination of written and oral orders and decisions.

In the third group are factors indicating a level of logistics have been taken into account, such as the ability to recruit new members; the providing of military training; the organised supply of military weapons; the supply and use of uniforms; and the existence of communications equipment for linking headquarters with units or between units.

In a fourth group, factors relevant to determining whether an armed group possessed a level of discipline and the ability to implement the basic obligations of Common Article 3 have been considered, such as the establishment of disciplinary rules and mechanisms; proper training; and the existence of internal regulations and whether these are effectively disseminated to members.

A fifth group includes those factors indicating that the armed group was able to speak with one voice, such as its capacity to act on behalf of its members in political negotiations with representatives of international organisations and foreign countries; and its ability to negotiate and conclude agreements such as cease fire or peace accords.[104]

39   Since Common Article 3 does not require government participation, the organization test must be applied to each armed group involved in hostilities. Where several armed groups engage state forces, but without coordinating their activities, provided that the requisite level of organization can be demonstrated for each group, a lack of overall organization between these groups would not seem to preclude the existence of a NIAC (or, indeed, several conflicts) in the context of Common Article 3.

a. Territorial control

40   It has been suggested that the ability of armed groups to implement their obligations under Common Article 3 also requires some possession of, and control over, national territory.[105] As mentioned, territorial control was one of the indicative criteria suggested at the 1949 Diplomatic Conference[106] and is an explicit requirement for the application of AP II, although it has been criticized even in the context of the latter's higher threshold.[107] Indeed, it was argued at the 1974–7 Diplomatic Conference that the requirement is

too restrictive in view of the nature of modern, and particularly guerrilla, warfare. In armed conflict situations characterised by high mobility, territorial control continuously changes hands, sometimes altering between day and night, to the point of becoming meaningless. Other forms of intense armed conflict, such as urban guerrilla armed conflict, would not fulfil the requirement

---

[104] More recently reaffirmed by the UN Commission of Inquiry on Libya, above n 19, para 64, and ICC, *The Prosecutor v Lubanga*, above n 18, para 537, noting that these factors should be 'applied flexibly', given that the requirement of organization in Art 8(2)(f) of the ICC Statute is 'limited'.

[105] G.I.A.D. Draper, 'The Geneva Conventions of 1949', 114 *RCADI* (1965-i) 59, at 90. See also above n 19.

[106] See MN 2.

[107] R. Abi-Saab, 'Humanitarian Law and Internal Conflicts: The Evolution of Legal Concern', in Delissen and Tanja (eds), above n 38, 209, at 216; G. Herczegh, 'Protocol Additional to the Geneva Conventions on the Protection of Victims of Non-international Armed Conflicts', in G. Haraszti (ed), *Questions of International Law* (Budapest: Akadémiai Kiadó, 1981) 71, at 77–8.

of territorial control. Such a requirement would then exclude from the ambit of Protocol II many, if not most, of the contemporary types of internal armed conflict and would confine it to the relatively rare cases of characterised civil war; it would thus severely limit its real significance and usefulness.[108]

A degree of territorial control on the part of insurgents would certainly strengthen the case for determining that a Common Article 3 conflict is taking place. Likewise, the ability to perform certain humanitarian obligations (e.g., the collection and care of the sick and wounded, the provision of justice according the necessary guarantees of due process,[109] etc) may be difficult without a secure territorial base. Territorial control may therefore be one possible indicator of NIAC, but that does not mean that Common Article 3 *cannot* apply where territorial control is absent; and the ICTY has confirmed that control over territory is not required for NIAC to exist.[110]

Futhermore, the ICC Statute does not require territorial control in relation to war crimes committed during NIAC. Although initially proposed,[111] several states argued that it would have unacceptably restricted the Court's jurisdiction. Sierra Leone, for example, pointed out that a territorial control requirement would 'exclude the type of conflict currently taking place in Sierra Leone',[112] whilst Uganda asserted that '[w]hether or not the perpetrators [of a war crime in the context of NIAC] controlled territory was immaterial: they might be operating from a neighbouring country, with or without that country's consent, as was currently the case in Uganda'.[113] The Trial Chamber has accordingly held that the ICC Statute requires only a protracted armed conflict between organized armed groups, and that it is 'therefore unnecessary for the prosecution to establish that the relevant armed groups exercised control over part of the territory of the State'.[114]

b. Responsible command

Command responsibility clearly exists in terms of individual criminal responsibility for violations of IHL amounting to war crimes committed during NIAC.[115] That is not to say, however, that responsible command is a necessary indicator of the organization of an armed group, and therefore required for an armed conflict to exist, as under the more exacting terms of Article 1(1) AP II.[116]

---

[108] Per G. Abi-Saab in *Official Records*, above n 12, CDDH/I/SR.24, VIII, 229 at 235. ICRC Commentary APs, para 4467, accepts that territorial control can change hands rapidly, and suggests a relative assessment in relation to the level of control exerted by the opposing party.

[109] See, e.g., S. Sivakumaran, 'Courts of Armed Opposition Groups: Fair Trials or Summary Justice?', 7 *JICJ* (2009) 489. The LTTE court system, referred to at 493–5, was extensive, comprising 17 courts in a hierarchical structure, which would have been impossible to achieve without stable territorial control.

[110] ICTY, *The Prosecutor v Milošević*, above n 98, para 36, where the *amici curiae* argument that armed conflict did not exist in Kosovo because the KLA did not exercise territorial control sufficient to carry out sustained and concerted military operations, was dismissed as legally irrelevant.

[111] See Cullen, above n 1, at 167–74.

[112] UN Doc A/CONF.183/C.1/SR.35, 13 July 1998, para 8.   [113] Ibid, para 23.

[114] ICC, *The Prosecutor v Lubanga*, above n 18, para 536.

[115] ICTY Statute Art 7(3); ICTR Statute Art 6(3); ICC Statute Art 38; Statute of the Special Court for Sierra Leone Art 6(3); UN Transitional Administration in East Timor Regulation 2000/15 on the Establishment of Panels with Exclusive Jurisdiction over Serious Criminal Offences, UN Doc UNTAET/REG/2000/15, 6 June 2000, Section 16; ICTY, *The Prosecutor v Enver Hadžihasanović, Mehmed Alagić and Amir Kubara*, Appeals Chamber Decision on Interlocutory Appeal Challenging Jurisdiction in Relation to Command Responsibility, IT-01-47-AR72, 16 July 2003, para 31.

[116] It will be recalled that AP II applies to conflicts taking place 'in the territory of a High Contracting Party between its armed forces and dissident armed forces or other organized armed groups which, *under*

44 The ICTY Appeals Chamber had suggested that this may be the case in *The Prosecutor v Hadžihasanović*, asserting that command responsibility was a 'corollary' of responsible command,[117] and that the latter was an 'integral notion' of Common Article 3.[118] Relying on the suggestion that Common Article 3 applies where an armed group possesses 'an organized military force, an authority responsible for its acts, acting within a determinate territory and having the means of respecting and ensuring respect for the Convention',[119] whilst Article 1(1) AP II 'likewise' refers to organization and responsible command, the ICTY Appeals Chamber went on to state that 'there cannot be an organized military force save on the basis of responsible command' and that this, in turn, leads to command responsibility.[120] Not only does this conflate the threshold of Common Article 3 with that of AP II, effectively imposing the latter's higher threshold on both,[121] it ignores the fact that the Pictet Commentary GC IV requirement referred to was explicitly qualified as being 'in no way obligatory',[122] and that the accepted application of Common Article 3 is now considerably wider than had been envisaged in 1949.[123]

45 The level of organization required for NIAC therefore falls short of both territorial control and/or responsible command. Thus, as indicated in *The Prosecutor v Limaj*, 'some degree of organisation by the parties will suffice to establish the existence of an armed conflict. This degree need not be the same as required for establishing the responsibility of superiors for the acts of their subordinates'.[124]

c. Political motivation

46 Political motivation is clearly relevant in terms of Article 1(4) AP I which, it will be recalled, renders hitherto NIACs international where the insurgent party is 'fighting against colonial domination and alien occupation and against racist regimes in the exercise of their right of self-determination'.[125] Given the underlying basis of many NIACs, it may appear equally relevant in that context, and the ICRC has suggested that armed groups 'would normally seek to overthrow the government in power or alternatively to bring about a secession so as to set up a new state'.[126]

47 That may be true, but the requirement is absent from both Common Article 3 and the *Tadić* formula, and the ICTY has taken a firm stance in relation to the importance

---

responsible command, exercise such control over a part of its territory as to enable them to carry out sustained and concerted military operations and to implement this Protocol' (emphasis added).

[117] ICTY, *The Prosecutor v Hadžihasanović*, above n 115, para 14. [118] Ibid, para 15.

[119] Pictet Commentary GC IV, at 35.

[120] ICTY, *The Prosecutor v Hadžihasanović*, above n 115, para 16. The Trial Chamber had already indicated its view that responsible command entails 'an organization that is both capable of planning and carrying out sustained and concerted military operations, *and* imposing discipline in the name of the *de facto* force or government'. See ICTY, *The Prosecutor v Enver Hadžihasanović, Mehmed Alagić and Amir Kubara*, Trial Chamber Decision on Joint Challenge to Jurisdiction, IT-01-47-PT, 12 November 2002, para 161, referring to ICRC Commentary APs, para 4463.

[121] Cullen, above n 1, at 151–7.   [122] Pictet Commentary GC IV, at 35.

[123] Cullen, above n 1, at 151–3; MN 22–31.

[124] ICTY, *The Prosecutor v Limaj*, above n 17, para 89. See also ICC, *The Prosecutor v Lubanga*, above n 18, para 536, noting that the ICC Statute 'does not incorporate the requirement that the organised armed groups were "under responsible command", as set out in [AP II]. Instead, the "organized armed groups" must have a sufficient degree of organisation, in order to enable them to carry out protracted armed violence'.

[125] This politically driven development was controversial. See G.I.A.D. Draper, 'Wars of National Liberation and War Criminality', in M. Howard (ed), *Restraints on War* (Oxford: OUP, 1979) 135, at 150; Cullen, above n 1, at 73–9; MN 12.

[126] ICRC Commentary APs, para 4341.

(or otherwise) of the aims of the parties involved. Thus, in addressing the argument that armed conflict could not exist in Kosovo because Serbian operations had been aimed at 'ethnic cleansing' rather than defeat of the enemy army, it held that the existence of an armed conflict was assessed solely on the criteria of intensity and organization, and that 'the purpose of the armed forces to engage in acts of violence or also achieve some further objective is, therefore, irrelevant'.[127] This must be correct, in that the particular motives or objectives of any party to any given conflict 'are never uniform and cannot always be clearly identified'.[128] To deny that an armed conflict could exist on this basis would therefore raise innumerable practical problems.

II. Intensity of the hostilities

Common Article 3 does not indicate the level of intensity required for a situation to constitute an armed conflict. It seems clear, however, that, when adopted, it was envisaged as covering situations that would traditionally have been termed 'civil war', i.e. relatively high threshold situations, essentially the same as international armed conflict, but taking place within a single state.[129] As indicated above, the situation has developed considerably since 1949. Common Article 3 is now seen as possessing a much lower threshold, and as being applicable to a broader range of situations. That being said, clearly there is still a threshold to be crossed before internal unrest can properly be characterized as armed conflict. 48

a. Internal disturbances and tensions

Unlike Common Article 3, AP II states that it does not apply to 'situations of internal disturbances and tensions, such as riots, isolated and sporadic acts of violence and other acts of a similar nature, as *not being armed conflicts*'.[130] Whether it is necessary for it to do so in light of the objective criteria set out in Article 1(1) seems doubtful;[131] and the provision seems to be a remnant of earlier drafts giving AP II the same threshold of application as that of Common Article 3, although without specifying that internal disturbances and tensions were not armed conflicts.[132] It is therefore difficult to avoid the conclusion that the phrase was intended to 'define the lower threshold of the concept of armed conflict' in general terms.[133] Thus, although Article 1(2) AP II does not change the scope of Common Article 3,[134] the provision is hugely significant for its interpretation and application in that, because Common Article 3 applies only to NIAC, it does not regulate scenarios falling short of this. 49

Precisely what constitutes internal disturbances and tensions as compared to armed conflict is, perhaps, open to question. Neither term has been defined authoritatively as a legal concept, although the ICRC considers internal disturbances to be 50

situations in which there is no non-international armed conflict as such, but there exists a confrontation within the country, which is characterized by a certain seriousness or duration and which involves acts of violence. These latter can assume various forms, all the way from the spontaneous

---

[127] ICTY, *The Prosecutor v Limaj*, above n 17, para 170.   [128] Vité, above n 30, at 78.
[129] Pictet Commentary GC IV, at 36; Cullen, above n 1, at 54; and discussion above (MN 22–31).
[130] Art 1(2) AP II, emphasis added.   [131] Cullen, above n 1, at 108.   [132] ICRC, Draft Protocol Additional to the Geneva Conventions of 12 August, 1949, and Relating to the Protection of Victims of Non-international Armed Conflicts, Art 1(2), in *Official Records*, above n 12, vol I, at 33.
[133] ICRC Commentary APs, para 4473.   [134] See MN 5–6.

generation of acts of revolt to the struggle between more or less organized groups and the authorities in power. In these situations, which do not necessarily degenerate into open struggle, the authorities in power call upon extensive police forces, or even armed forces, to restore internal order.[135]

The Inter-American Commission on Human Rights (IACommHR) has subsequently held that internal disturbances include 'large scale violent demonstrations, students throwing stones at the police, bandits holding persons hostage for ransom, or the assassination of government officials for political reasons—all forms of domestic violence not qualifying as armed conflicts'.[136]

51   Internal tensions, on the other hand, are stated by the ICRC to include less violent circumstances involving, for example, mass arrests, large numbers of political detainees, torture or other kinds of ill-treatment, forced disappearances, and/or the suspension of fundamental judicial guarantees;[137] whilst 'internal strife' more broadly implies

> serious acts of violence over a prolonged period or a latent situation of violence, whether of political, religious, racial, social, economic or other origin, accompanied by one or more features such as: mass arrests, forced disappearances, detention for security reasons, suspension of judicial guarantees, declaration of state of emergency, declaration of martial law.[138]

52   Maintaining that internal unrest does not constitute NIAC, and that some threshold of intensity must be crossed before IHL applies, may not be problematic in theory. Such demarcation nevertheless remains difficult in practice, and a great deal of work has gone into judicial and other international efforts aimed at 'distinguishing an armed conflict from banditry, unorganized and short-lived insurrections, or terrorist activities, which are not subject to international humanitarian law'.[139] It is to this exercise that we now turn.

b. Protracted armed violence

i. Duration

53   Intimately linked to the question of the intensity of violence required for armed conflict to exist, is that of the duration of hostilities necessary to trigger the application of Common Article 3. The *Tadić* formula requires 'protracted armed violence',[140] but offers no further guidance. As such, the 'parameters of reasonable interpretation' are open to question,[141] and the test will necessitate assessment on a case-by-case basis. This may not always be straightforward, however, and it has been suggested that this aspect of the *Tadić* formula serves to present the military with 'an irreconcilable contradiction', in that, '[i]f IHL applies "from the initiation" of a non-international armed conflict, but a situation can only be gauged as an armed conflict at such time as the violence in question becomes "protracted", how is the foot soldier to know at what point IHL begins to apply?'[142]

---

[135] ICRC Commentary APs, para 4475.
[136] IACommHR, *Abella v Argentina*, 17 February 1998, para 154.
[137] ICRC Commentary APs, para 4476. See further A. Eide, 'Internal Disturbances and Tensions', in UNESCO, *International Dimensions of Humanitarian Law* (Dordrecht: Martinus Nijhoff, 1988) 279.
[138] Agreement Adopted by Consensus in Resolution 6 of the Council of Delegates in Seville, 27 November 1997, Art 5.2(b), available at <http://www.icrc.org/eng/resources/documents/article/other/57jp4y.htm>.
[139] ICTY, *The Prosecutor v Duško Tadić*, Trial Chamber Judgement, IT-94-1-T, 7 May 1997, para 562.
[140] ICTY, *The Prosecutor v Duško Tadić*, above n 16. It should be noted that this applies only to NIAC, and that IAC apparently has a somewhat lower threshold. See Ch 1, MN 20–38, of this volume.
[141] Cullen, above n 1, at 143.
[142] A.J. Carswell, 'Classifying the Conflict: A Soldier's Dilemma', 91 *IRRC* 873 (2009) 143, at 151.

Jinks argues that, in fact, 'most instances of internal strife would satisfy this requirement', because the evaluation of whether a conflict is protracted or not takes place with 'reference to the entire period from initiation to the cessation of hostilities':

> [T]he laws of war apply to all acts committed in an armed conflict even if committed prior to the point at which the 'protracted' threshold was crossed. That is, the 'protracted' requirement does not immunize acts committed in the early stages of an internal armed conflict. In short, the 'protracted' armed violence requirement is best understood as little more than a restatement of the general rule excluding 'isolated and sporadic acts of violence' […][143]

This perhaps approaches things with the benefit of hindsight, and would probably fail to assuage the concerns of military commanders at the onset of hostilities. It is nonetheless clear that the 'protracted' threshold is crossed much more easily than the 'sustained and concerted' threshold of AP II. The ICRC has accepted that '[a]t the beginning of a conflict military operations rarely have such a character; thus it is likely that only common Article 3 will apply to the first stage of hostilities'.[144]

In more concrete terms, the ICTR case law has established that 'armed violence extending over only a few months satisfies the "protracted" requirement',[145] whilst the IACommHR held in *Abella v Argentina* that a military engagement lasting less than 48 hours constituted a Common Article 3 NIAC, based upon

> the concerted nature of the hostile acts undertaken by the attackers, the direct involvement of government armed forces, and the nature and level of the violence attending the events in question. More particularly, the attackers involved carefully planned, coordinated and executed an armed attack, i.e., a military operation, against a quintessentially military objective—a military base […][146]

This suggests a low threshold for the duration of hostilities required to constitute armed conflict. As such, the application of IHL as determined by the temporal aspect of 'protracted armed violence' should not be interpreted restrictively.

ii. Intensity

Although, prima facie, 'protracted armed violence' seems to represent a temporal requirement, referring to the duration rather than the intensity of hostilities, these two concepts have become inextricably linked in ICTY case law. Thus, whilst accepting that the 'protracted' violence requirement 'adds a temporal element to the definition of armed conflict',[147] it has consistently been asserted that the test for NIAC consists of only 'two criteria, namely (i) the intensity of the conflict and (ii) the organisation of the parties to the conflict'.[148] Indeed, in *The Prosecutor v Haradinaj*, the Trial Chamber undertook a survey of 'how the criterion of "protracted armed violence" has been interpreted in practice',[149]

---

[143] Jinks, above n 53, at 6.
[144] ICRC Commentary APs, para 4469. [145] Jinks, above n 53, at 6.
[146] IACommHR, *Abella v Argentina*, above n 136, paras 154–6.
[147] ICTY, *The Prosecutor v Boškoski*, above n 29, para 186. See also ICTY, *The Prosecutor v Dario Kordić and Mario Čerkez*, Appeals Chamber Judgment, IT-95-14/2-A, 17 December 2004, para 341, referring to 'serious fighting *for an extended period of time*' (emphasis added), and ICC, *The Prosecutor v Lubanga*, above n 18, para 234, noting that the ICC Statute's reference to 'protracted armed conflict' indicates 'the need for the armed groups in question to have the ability to plan and carry out military operations *for a prolonged period of time*' (emphasis added).
[148] ICTY, *The Prosecutor v Boškoski*, above n 29, para 175. See also, e.g., ICTY, *The Prosecutor v Rutaganda*, above n 17, para 92; ICTY, *The Prosecutor v Limaj*, above n 17, para 84.
[149] ICTY, *The Prosecutor v Haradinaj*, above n 99, para 39.

finding that the Tribunal had treated it as 'referring more to the *intensity* of the armed violence than to its duration'.[150] As such, it would appear that the duration of hostilities is simply considered to be one factor, albeit an important one,[151] relevant in assessing the intensity requirement.

c. *The threshold of intensity*

58 Distinguishing NIAC from internal disturbances and tensions on the basis of intensity is a difficult task, exacerbated by the fact that, in contrast to international relations, it is not uncommon for states to employ armed force within their own borders and against their own citizens—not to mention the reluctance of states to admit that they are facing internal difficulties beyond their control, amounting to armed conflict.[152] The problems faced by the international community in determining whether, and when, NIAC existed in Libya and Syria illustrate the point well.[153] Thus, despite protracted unrest in Syria, and over 16,000 deaths since the initial uprising in March 2011, only on 15 July 2012 did the ICRC indicate that the situation had reached the threshold for NIAC.[154]

59 As with the organization test, the ICTY has considered how intensity should be assessed in a number of cases,[155] with the *Boškoski* Trial Chamber again providing an extremely valuable overview and crystallization of the approach in the following terms:

> Various indicative factors have been taken into account by Trial Chambers to assess the 'intensity' of the conflict. These include the seriousness of attacks and whether there has been an increase in armed clashes, the spread of clashes over territory and over a period of time, any increase in the number of government forces and mobilisation and the distribution of weapons among both parties to the conflict, as well as whether the conflict has attracted the attention of the United Nations Security Council, and whether any resolutions on the matter have been passed. Trial Chambers

---

[150] Ibid, para 49 (emphasis added).

[151] ICTY, *The Prosecutor v Boškoski*, above n 29, para 175, 'care is needed not to lose sight of the requirement for protracted armed violence [...] when assessing the intensity of the conflict'.

[152] See above n 3.

[153] The ICRC asserted the existence of an armed conflict in Libya on 10 March 2011, but without indicating how the decision had been arrived at, or classifying the conflict ('Libya: Urgent to apply the rules of war', ICRC news release 11/53, 10 March 2011), whilst the ICC Prosecutor asserted the existence of armed conflict since 'the end of February', and the UN Commission of Inquiry suggested February 24 as the date by which 'a non-international armed conflict had developed sufficient to trigger the application of AP II and Common Article 3'. See *First Report of the Prosecutor of the International Criminal Court to the UN Security Council Pursuant to UNSCR 1970* (2011), para 37; *Report of the International Commission of Inquiry on Libya*, above n 19, para 65.

[154] BBC News, 'Syria in Civil War, Red Cross Says', 15 July 2012, available at <http://www.bbc.co.uk/news/world-middle-east-18849362>. Apparently based on relative territorial control (see MN 40 and above n 108), UN Under-Secretary for Peacekeeping Operations, Hervé Ladsous, had voiced this opinion on 12 June (<http://www.bbc.co.uk/news/world-middle-east-18417952>), whilst President al-Assad admitted the existence of a state of war on 26 June (<http://www.bbc.co.uk/news/world-middle-east-18598533>). In May 2012, the Security Council stated that Syria's 'outrageous use of force against [its] civilian population constitutes a violation of applicable international law', but without characterizing the situation as an armed conflict, or identifying the 'applicable international law'. See Security Council Press Statement on Attacks in Syria, SC/10658, 27 May 2012. There were, of course, also questions as to the organization of armed groups.

[155] ICTY, *The Prosecutor v Tadić*, above n 139, paras 565–7; ICTY, *The Prosecutor v Limaj*, above n 17, paras 135–73; ICTY, *The Prosecutor v Zejnil Delalić et al*, Trial Chamber Judgment, IT-96-21-T, 16 November 1998, paras 186–90; ICTY, *The Prosecutor v Milošević*, above n 98, paras 28–31; ICTY, *The Prosecutor v Kordić and Čerkez*, above n 147, paras 340–1; ICTY, *The Prosecutor v Haradinaj*, above n 99, paras 91–7; ICTY, *The Prosecutor v Sefer Halalović*, Trial Chamber Judgment, IT-01-48-T, 16 November 2005, paras 161–72; ICTY, *The Prosecutor v Hadžihasanović*, above n 115, paras 20–3; ICTY, *The Prosecutor v Milan Martić*, Trial Chamber Judgment, IT-95-11-T, 12 June 2007, paras 344–5; ICTY, *The Prosecutor v Đorđević*, above n 99, paras 1532–77.

have also taken into account in this respect the number of civilians forced to flee from the combat zones; the type of weapons used, in particular the use of heavy weapons, and other military equipment, such as tanks and other heavy vehicles; the blocking or besieging of towns and the heavy shelling of these towns; the extent of destruction and the number of casualties caused by shelling or fighting; the quantity of troops and units deployed; existence and change of front lines between the parties; the occupation of territory, and towns and villages; the deployment of government forces to the crisis area; the closure of roads; cease fire orders and agreements, and the attempt of representatives from international organizations to broker and enforce cease fire agreements.[156]

The suitability of these criteria has been reaffirmed in the context of NIAC under the ICC Statute, with the ICC Trial Chamber in *Lubanga* outlining the elements identified by the ICTY in broad terms before indicating its view that 'this is an appropriate approach'.[157]

As is also the case with the various criteria/elements for organization, it should be noted that, whilst these factors assist in determining whether the necessary level of intensity has been reached, they are to be applied on a case-by-case basis. They are neither exhaustive (territorial control and responsible command, for example, may serve equally to illustrate the intensity of hostilities as well as the organization of armed groups despite going beyond the *Tadić* formula),[158] nor are they 'factors that need to exist concurrently'.[159]

Nor must the intensity of NIAC be constant. Thus, where insurgents, having gained stable control over a portion of territory, are able to repel sporadic government attacks such that there is a reduction in the scale and extent of hostilities, an armed conflict still exists. The continued application of Common Article 3 is appropriate not only by reason of evident territorial control,[160] but also via the *Tadić* formula's insistence that IHL applies throughout the whole territory until a peaceful settlement is achieved.[161] As such, once the threshold of intensity has been crossed, it can undulate without affecting the existence of an armed conflict and the application of IHL.[162] Equally, given the geographical scope of the application of IHL to NIAC,[163] it seems unnecessary to assess the intensity of hostilities in each separate territory where a conflict extends beyond the confines of a single state.

---

[156] ICTY, *The Prosecutor v Boškoski*, above n 29, para 177 (references omitted). It went on to provide, at para 178, that another indicative factor is 'the way that organs of the State, such as the police and military, use force against armed groups. In such cases, it may be instructive to analyse [...] in particular, how certain human rights are interpreted, such as the right to life and the right to be free from arbitrary detention, in order to appreciate if the situation is one of armed conflict'. On different approaches to proportionality by IHRL and IHL in this respect, see Moir, above n 3, at 485–6.

[157] ICC, *The Prosecutor v Lubanga*, above n 18, para 538. The ICC *Lubanga* Pre-Trial Chamber, in its Decision on Confirmation of Charges, ICC-01/04-01/06, 29 January 2007, para 235, had held that a conflict of sufficient intensity existed due to the number of armed attacks, the number of victims, and the fact that the UNSC was actively seized of the matter. For a more detailed indication of how these elements have been applied to specific factual circumstances, see ICTY, *The Prosecutor v Limaj*, above n 17, paras 135–73, and ICTY, *The Prosecutor v Boškoski*, above n 29, paras 208–49.

[158] Cullen, above n 1, at 153–4. In *The Prosecutor v Haradinaj*, above n 99, para 49, the Trial Chamber stated that these indicative factors are not, 'in themselves, essential to establish that the criterion is satisfied'.

[159] Vité, above n 30, at 77.   [160] See above, MN 41.

[161] See discussion in Ch 3 of this volume, and above n 16.

[162] ICTY, *The Prosecutor v Haradinaj*, above n 99, para 100, 'since according to the *Tadić* test an internal armed conflict continues until a peaceful settlement is achieved, and since there is no evidence of such a settlement during the indictment period, there is no need for the Trial Chamber to explore the oscillating intensity of the armed conflict'.

[163] See MN 32–33.

F. Critical Assessment

62 The characterization of an armed conflict as being either international or non-international in nature remains a vital exercise for determining the applicability of different rules of IHL. Despite what seems to be a growing overlap of the (particularly customary) legal regulation of hostilities, IAC and NIAC are governed by different bodies of IHL. Consequently, the effective legal regulation of armed conflict according to the relevant set of humanitarian norms is still dependent upon the accurate identification of (i) whether an armed conflict exists, and (ii) whether that armed conflict is to be classified as international or non-international.

63 As demonstrated above, however, the identification of NIAC is not necessarily a straightforward exercise: Common Article 3 is vague in relation to its scope of application, and alternative/competing definitions of the concept of NIAC in AP II, the ICC Statute, international (and national) case law, and by other international bodies do not always appear entirely consistent. In addition, it is important to recall that the neat classification of armed conflict as either IAC or NIAC is not always possible due to the complex nature of many contemporary conflicts. Such conflicts may involve numerous state and non-state parties with a variety of different relationships, or may take place in the context of occupied territory and may involve the active participation of UN or other multinational troops. The emergence of non-state armed groups operating from the territory of third states poses similarly complex questions in relation to the classification of armed conflict as either international or non-international, particularly in the context of the geographical scope of hostilities.

64 The law can, perhaps, be interpreted fairly simply, in that whether an armed conflict is IAC or NIAC depends on the parties to that conflict. Any armed conflict not regulated by Common Article 2 (i.e. an armed conflict between states, with due regard to the nature of the relationship between third states and armed non-state groups) is necessarily a Common Article 3, or non-international, armed conflict—provided that the threshold separating NIAC from internal disturbances and tensions has been duly crossed. In other words, the existence of NIAC depends upon the necessary levels of organization on the part of insurgents, and intensity of hostilities having been reached. More stringent requirements of territorial control, etc, may be suggested by AP II, but it must be recalled that the threshold of applicability set out in AP II is specific to that instrument, and it is the lower threshold as contained in Common Article 3 and customary IHL (i.e. the *Tadić* formula) that determines the existence of NIAC per se.

65 Of course, it should not be expected that a critical measurement of the relevant levels of organization and intensity in question will necessarily be easy—as with any objective assessment of stipulated criteria—judgments as to whether these criteria have, in fact, been met or not will inevitably be the subject of debate. In this respect, the illustrative indicia identified by the ICTY are particularly helpful. They may be neither exhaustive nor definitive, but the detailed way in which they have been enumerated, discussed, and applied by the Tribunal in the context of difficult, and changing, factual circumstances does provide some evidence that the legal concept of NIAC is capable of identification in practice, and that the accurate (and objective) classification of an armed conflict as non-international in character is possible, despite the inherent complexities.

LINDSAY MOIR

Chapter 20. The Addressees of Common Article 3

	MN
A. Introduction	1
B. Meaning and Application	3
I. Parties to non-international armed conflicts	3
II. The binding nature of Common Article 3 on the addressees	7
a. State ratification	10
b. National law	14
c. Treaties and third parties	17
d. Consent of the armed group	21
e. Claims of the armed group to represent the state	27
f. Armed group exercising state-like functions	31
g. Customary international law	35
h. Final remarks	39
III. Tension between binding nature and legal status	41
IV. Engaging addressees on Common Article 3 and obstacles thereto	45
C. Applicability in International Armed Conflicts	51
D. Legal Consequences of a Violation	55
E. Critical Assessment	64

Select Bibliography

Cassese, A., 'The Status of Rebels under the 1977 Geneva Protocol on Non-International Armed Conflicts', 30 *ICLQ* (1981) 416

Harvard Program on Humanitarian Policy and Conflict Research, 'Humanitarian Action under Scrutiny: Criminalizing Humanitarian Engagement', *HPCR Working Paper*, February 2011

Kleffner, J.K., 'The Collective Accountability of Organized Armed Groups for System Crimes', in A. Nollkaemper and H. van der Wilt (eds), *System Criminality in International Law* (Cambridge: CUP, 2009)

Kleffner, J.K., 'The Applicability of International Humanitarian Law to Organized Armed Groups', 93 *IRRC* 882 (2011) 443

Moir, L., *The Law of Internal Armed Conflict* (Cambridge: CUP, 2002)

Pictet Commentaries Geneva Conventions I–IV

Sivakumaran, S., 'Binding Armed Opposition Groups', 55 *ICLQ* (2006) 369

Sivakumaran, S., *The Law of Non-International Armed Conflict* (Oxford: OUP, 2012)

Zegveld, L., *The Accountability of Armed Opposition Groups in International Law* (Cambridge: CUP, 2002)

A. Introduction

As seen throughout this Commentary, the Geneva Conventions largely regulate armed conflicts of an international character.[1] Of the hundreds of Articles that comprise the Conventions, only one, Common Article 3, regulates armed conflicts not of an international character (NIACs). Nonetheless, the adoption of Common Article 3 in 1949 was

---

[1] See also Chs 1, 2, and 19 of this volume.

a significant breakthrough, representing the first time a provision of a multilateral treaty sought to regulate NIACs. Prior to 1949, NIACs were regulated by international law, but only in an ad hoc manner.

2   Common Article 3 provides that in NIACs, 'each Party to the conflict shall be bound to apply' certain listed provisions. The Article is thus addressed to the parties to the conflict. Two principal issues arise from the construction:

— Who are the parties to a NIAC?
— How are the parties bound by Common Article 3?

B. Meaning and Application

I. Parties to non-international armed conflicts

3   As mentioned, Common Article 3 provides that 'each Party to the conflict shall be bound to apply' certain listed provisions. This phrase bears its literal meaning, namely, that upon the outbreak of an armed conflict not of an international character,[2] all the parties to that conflict are bound by the provision.

4   Precisely who is bound by the provision will thus turn on the specificities of the NIAC in question.[3] Non-international armed conflicts are fought between a state and a non-state armed group, or between armed groups. In a conflict that is fought between a state and a non-state armed group, Common Article 3 will bind both the state and the armed group. In a conflict that is fought between two or more armed groups, the armed groups will be bound by the provision. Where an outside state is a party to the conflict and the conflict remains non-international in character—for example, where an outside state intervenes on the side of the state party to the conflict—the outside state will also be bound by Common Article 3. In sum, Common Article 3 will bind the entity in question, provided it is a party to the conflict.

5   Entities that are involved in a NIAC, but which are not parties to the conflict, also bear certain obligations under international humanitarian law (IHL). Where an outside state is involved in the armed conflict but is not a party to the conflict, for example because its involvement is not such as to give it overall control over the armed group and thus internationalize the conflict, the outside state bears obligations under Common Article 1 of the Geneva Conventions 'to respect and to ensure respect' for the Conventions. Indeed, Common Article 1 binds states that are not involved in the conflict.[4]

6   In order for Common Article 3 to apply, the situation must amount to an armed conflict. However, states may make a commitment to apply aspects of Common Article 3 whilst simultaneously taking the view that the situation does not reach the threshold of an armed conflict and amounts only to internal tensions and disturbances. There are numerous examples of such practice, usually relating to the acceptance of the offer of services on the part of the International Committee of the Red Cross (ICRC), made pursuant to Article 5(3) of the Statutes of the International Red Cross and Red Crescent Movement.[5]

---

[2] See MN 51–54 for application of the provision to armed conflicts of an international character.
[3] See Ch 19 of this volume.   [4] See Ch 6 of this volume.
[5] See M. Veuthey, 'Les conflits armés de caractère non-international et le droit humanitaire', in A. Cassese (ed), *Current Problems of International Law: Essays on UN Law and on the Laws of Armed Conflict* (Milan: Giuffrè, 1975) 179, at 246–7.

In such a situation, certain norms of Common Article 3 may be applied without the qualification of the situation as a NIAC.

II. The binding nature of Common Article 3 on the addressees

The binding nature of Common Article 3 on states is uncontroversial. States parties to the Geneva Conventions are bound by Common Article 3 by virtue of their party status. This is the principle of *pacta sunt servanda*.[6] At the time of writing, all states were parties to the Geneva Conventions. States are also bound by the provisions enshrined in Common Article 3 through customary international law, as the article has been, at least since 1986, considered to reflect customary international law.[7]

Slightly more difficult to explain is the binding nature of Common Article 3 on a non-state party to a NIAC. Non-state armed groups may be parties to NIACs, but they cannot be parties to the Geneva Conventions. Accordingly, the principle of *pacta sunt servanda* is not applicable to them. Historically, this led some to opine that armed groups were not bound by Common Article 3.[8] However, this is not the conclusion to be drawn; rather, armed groups are bound by Common Article 3 for reasons other than *pacta sunt servanda*. These reasons include:

— through ratification by the state;
— through domestic law;
— the binding nature of treaties on third parties;
— consent of the armed group to be bound by Common Article 3;
— claims of the armed group to represent the state;
— the armed group's exercising state-like functions; and
— on the basis of customary international law.

Some of these rationales serve to explain how Common Article 3 binds non-state armed groups that are parties to conflicts but cannot apply more broadly to all other norms of IHL. Other rationales apply to all norms of IHL but only to a subset of armed groups. Together, however, they explain how non-state parties to NIACs are bound by IHL. The focus of the section that follows will be on the explanatory value of the binding nature of Common Article 3 on non-state armed group parties to NIACs; the applicability to other norms of IHL will be touched on briefly.

a. State ratification

When a state ratifies a treaty,[9] it does so not just on behalf of the state but also on behalf of all individuals within its jurisdiction. This approach thus considers non-state armed groups bound by Common Article 3 because the state, in ratifying the Geneva Conventions, binds all individuals within its jurisdiction to the Conventions, even those who may later rebel against it. The principal advantage of this explanation is its applicability to armed groups

---

[6] Art 26 VCLT provides: 'Every treaty in force is binding upon the parties to it and must be performed by them in good faith.'
[7] ICJ, *Military and Paramilitary Activities in and against Nicaragua (Nicaragua v United States of America)* Merits, Judgment, 27 June 1986, para 218.
[8] See, e.g., Final Record, vol II-B, at 79 (USA, France), 94 (UK, Australia); ICRC, *The Geneva Conventions of August 12, 1949: Analysis for the Use of National Red Cross Societies* (Geneva: ICRC, 1950) vol II, at 6–7.
[9] The notion of ratification in this context refers to ratification, including accession, at the international level and not ratification in domestic law. See Arts 2(1)(b) and 11 VCLT.

418   *Common Provisions*

generally and, depending on the wording of the provision, in respect of rules of IHL other than Common Article 3 alone.

11   This rationale was supported by some of the delegates at the 1949 Diplomatic Conference.[10] It is also the explanation that has been used by the ICRC, on at least one occasion, in considering a non-state armed group bound by Common Article 3. When the National Liberation Front (FLN) of Vietnam informed the ICRC that it did not consider itself bound by the Geneva Conventions, the ICRC responded that the 'Front national de libération, [...] se trouve également lié par les engagements souscrits au nom du Vietnam'.[11] Indeed, the ICRC had suggested for inclusion in Common Article 1 the language: 'The High Contracting Parties undertake, *in the name of their peoples*, to respect and to ensure respect for the present Convention in all circumstances.'[12]

12   Two objections are commonly raised as criticisms of this explanation. First, it is sometimes suggested that this explanation fails to appreciate the divergence in the practice of states concerning the implementation of treaties in the domestic legal order. Accordingly, were the state not to incorporate Common Article 3 into its domestic law, the armed group would not be bound. However, it is well accepted that certain treaties—depending on their wording and the intention of the parties—create rights for and obligations on individuals directly upon their ratification by the state, i.e. directly through international law, irrespective of whether or not they have been incorporated into domestic law.[13] The rights and obligations may not be enforceable at the domestic level, but their binding nature on the individuals is not in doubt. Therefore, it is possible to hold that Common Article 3 and other conventional rules of IHL are binding on a non-state armed group not through domestic law but directly through international law.

13   The second objection is less a legal objection and more a practical one, namely, that armed groups are unlikely to comply with rules that have been formulated by the very governments with which they are in conflict. Although intuitively appealing, the concern is overstated and unsupported by evidence. Even if armed groups reject national law—and not all armed groups do—they tend not to reject Common Article 3 or IHL. This is evident from the numerous commitments made by armed groups to respect IHL (see MN 22). Furthermore, in respect of those armed groups that have rejected IHL or aspects thereof, this was not because it was formulated by the opposing party to the conflict, but rather because the armed group was not involved in its formation.[14]

b. *National law*

14   Common Article 3 may also bind parties to conflicts through the lens of national law. This will depend on the interplay between national law and international law in the state

---

[10] Final Record, vol II-B, at 94 (Greece). See also, at the 1974–7 Diplomatic Conference: *Official Records*, vol VIII, at 239, para 55 (ICRC); vol IX, 234, para 54 (ICRC), 238, para 9 (Mongolia); vol XIV, 314, paras 22 and 24 (USSR).

[11] Letter from the Vice-President of the ICRC to Président, Front National de Libération du Sud-Vietnam, 14 June 1965, ICRC Archives B AG 202 223-005

[12] ICRC, Draft Revised or New Conventions for the Protection of War Victims (Geneva, May 1948), at 4 (emphasis added).

[13] See *Jurisdiction of the Courts of Danzig* (1928) PCIJ Series B, No 15, p 17; ICJ, *LaGrand (Germany v United States of America)*, Judgment, 27 June 2001, para 77. See also Report of the International Law Commission covering its second session, 5 June–29 July 1950, A/1316 (1950), Formulation of the Nurnberg Principles, para 99.

[14] This was the case with the Fuerzas Armadas Revolucionarias de Colombia (FARC), the Frente Farabundo Martí para la Liberación Nacional (FMLN) of El Salvador, and the FLN of Vietnam, on particular norms of

in question. In some states, treaties are directly applicable in the national legal system, for example by virtue of a constitutional provision; in other states, treaties are required to undergo some form of implementation in national law, on a treaty by treaty basis, before they can be considered directly applicable in that system. In so far as customary international law is concerned, in many states, customary international law automatically forms part of national law. However, the precise status of the international legal norm, in particular whether it can take precedence over conflicting national legislation, varies from state to state.

The consequence of this is that, in certain states, Common Article 3 will be given effect in national law only if there is domestic legislation that implements the Geneva Conventions, or, with regard to Common Article 3 as reflective of rules of customary international law, if customary international law is directly applicable in the national legal system. Should there not be any such implementing legislation and should customary international law not be part of domestic law, Common Article 3 will not be considered directly applicable in the national legal system, for example before a domestic court.

Thus, it is necessary to distinguish between the application of Common Article 3 at the international level and at the national level. As discussed above, Common Article 3 and other norms of IHL are binding on parties to conflicts directly through international law. Indeed, when considering the application of Common Article 3, international courts and tribunals do not look into the binding nature of the Article through domestic law. Instead, their focus is entirely on Common Article 3 as a norm of international law, and it may be applied at the international level irrespective of its implementation in national law. Accordingly, this national law explanation is important only in so far as application in the domestic legal system is concerned.

c. *Treaties and third parties*

Common Article 3 (and other rules of conventional IHL) may be binding on armed groups through the binding nature of treaties on third parties.[15] The general rules concerning the binding nature of treaties on third states may be found in the Vienna Convention on the Law of Treaties (VCLT). Article 34 VCLT provides that '[a] treaty does not create either obligations or rights for a third State without its consent.' This is the corollary to the principle of *pacta sunt servanda*. However, a treaty may, in some instances, apply to third states, as recounted in Articles 35 and 36 VCLT. Article 35 provides that a third state may be subject to obligations that are contained in a treaty to which it is not party, provided that those states that are parties 'intend the provision to be the means of establishing the obligation' and the third state 'expressly accepts that obligation in writing'. Article 36 provides that third states may receive rights that are contained in a treaty to which they are not party, provided that the parties to the treaty 'intend the provision to accord that right' to the third states and the third states 'assent thereto'. Unlike the case of obligations, the assent of the third states is to be presumed unless there is an indication to the contrary, or the treaty provides otherwise.

---

international humanitarian law. See, respectively, Human Rights Watch, *War Without Quarter: Colombia and International Humanitarian Law* (1998), text at fn 34, available at <http://www.hrw.org/legacy/reports98/colombia/>; Second Report of the United Nations Observer Mission in El Salvador, A/46/658, 15 November 1991, paras 64–5; Letter from Chef de la Représentation Permanente du FLN du Sud-Vietnam en URSS to Representative of the ICRC, 16 October 1965, ICRC Archives B AG 202 223-005. An exception is Islamic State (IS).

[15] See, in particular, A. Cassese, 'The Status of Rebels under the 1977 Geneva Protocol on Non-International Armed Conflicts', 30 *ICLQ* (1981) 416.

18   In order for Common Article 3 to be binding on armed groups through the principles set out above, a series of hurdles must be overcome. Articles 35 and 36 VCLT relate to treaties that are binding on third states,[16] rather than on third parties more broadly. As such, the rules in those Articles cannot be applied *qua* treaty to armed groups. It is unclear whether the rules may apply as a matter of custom.[17] Even if Articles 35 and 36 VCLT have customary status, it is less than clear that the scope of the customary rules extends to third parties and not only to third states.

19   Assuming that Articles 35 and 36 VCLT are applicable to entities other than states *qua* customary rules, the states parties to the treaty must intend the treaty to vest rights and obligations in third parties. In this case, the states parties to the Geneva Conventions must intend Common Article 3 to grant rights and obligations to armed groups. This can readily be satisfied. Common Article 3 provides that 'each Party to the conflict shall be bound to apply' certain listed rules. As the parties to a NIAC are states and armed groups, or armed groups alone, states parties to the Geneva Conventions must be taken as intending that armed groups parties to conflicts are bound by Common Article 3. More difficult is the second prerequisite of Article 35 VCLT or its customary equivalent, namely, that the third party must accept the obligations in writing. Leaving aside the written confirmation—it not clear whether the form in which the commitment is to manifest itself is also a customary one[18]—in this case the armed group must accept the obligations of Common Article 3. Should the armed group not accept the obligations, this line of reasoning would not suffice to bind it to Common Article 3. As such, everything turns on whether or not the armed group accepts to be bound by Common Article 3.

20   As consent is determinative, the rationale of armed groups being bound by Common Article 3 is best argued through their consent to be bound and the consent of states parties to the Geneva Conventions.

d. Consent of the armed group

21   Armed groups frequently undertake to apply IHL, the Geneva Conventions, or specific norms. This usually takes place through the issuance of a unilateral declaration by which the group consents to be bound. It also arises through the conclusion of an agreement between the state and the armed group that brings into force particular humanitarian norms. Such an agreement is envisaged in Common Article 3, which exhorts the parties 'to bring into force, by means of special agreements, all or part of the other provisions' of the Geneva Conventions.[19]

22   There are numerous examples of ad hoc commitments of armed groups.[20] Often, the commitment references the 'Geneva Conventions' or 'international humanitarian law' generally. On occasion, the commitment mentions Common Article 3 specifically, as is the case with the declarations made to the ICRC by the parties to the conflict in Lebanon in June 1958; the unilateral declaration of the National Democratic Front of the

---

[16] Or third organizations in the case of the 1986 Vienna Convention on the Law of Treaties between States and International Organizations or between International Organizations. See Art 34.

[17] In favour: C. Laly-Chevalier, 'Article 35', in O. Corten and P. Klein (eds), *The Vienna Conventions on the Law of Treaties: A Commentary* (Oxford: OUP, 2011) 902, at 904–5.

[18] R. Jennings and A. Watts, *Oppenheim's International Law*, vol I: *Peace* (London: Longman, 1992), at 1262, fn 12; Laly-Chevalier, above n 17, at 905, considers this 'an act of progressive development of the law'.

[19] See Ch 25 of this volume.

[20] See, e.g., S. Sivakumaran, *The Law of Non-International Armed Conflict* (Oxford: OUP, 2012), Chapter 4. See, for a searchable database, Geneva Call, *Their Words, Directory of Armed Non-State Actor Humanitarian Commitments*, available at <http://theirwords.org/>.

Philippines in August 1991; the 22 May 1992 Agreement concluded between the parties to the conflict in Bosnia; and the Agreement on the Protection of Civilians and Civilian Facilities concluded between the Government of Sudan and the Sudan People's Liberation Movement (SPLM) in 2002.[21]

The nature of these commitments is not altogether clear. Some take the view that they are mere propaganda tools; others that they ought to be taken seriously. This author is of the view that each commitment must be considered individually to ascertain whether or not it amounts to propaganda. This, in turn, will depend on such things as the identity of the actor that makes the commitment, and whether or not the commitment is actually followed in practice. It is difficult to make generalizations.

The normative status of these commitments is also unsettled. Ad hoc agreements concluded between the parties to the conflict have been considered 'binding', and demands have been made for their compliance.[22] They have also been used in a myriad of other ways.[23] However, on occasion, they have been considered as 'not, strictly speaking, treaties', and as 'not creat[ing] an obligation in international law', only domestic law.[24] The circumstances in which unilateral declarations are binding on states are less than clear,[25] and this question can be considered even more open in the case of armed groups. However, unilateral declarations of armed groups have been utilized by international criminal courts and tribunals, and have been considered binding by influential actors.[26] It thus seems that ad hoc commitments may be treated as binding on armed groups. Indeed, this author is of the view that, with respect to ad hoc commitments on IHL that are issued during a conflict, which are clear and precise, there should be a presumption that they are binding.

Consent is useful as a means of engaging with armed groups on their obligations under IHL (see further MN 40). As a practical matter, it may be of greater utility to engage with an armed group on a commitment that it has made, rather than a commitment that was entered into by the state some decades ago, as a rationale to explain the mandatory character of Common Article 3 on non-state armed groups. Furthermore, ad hoc commitments

---

[21] Note of ICRC Delegate de Traz to ICRC, 16 June 1958; Note, 20 June 1958, ICRC Archives B AG 200 115-001; NDFP Declaration of Adherence to International Humanitarian Law, 15 August 1991, reproduced in NDFP, *Declaration of Undertaking to Apply the Geneva Conventions of 1949 and Protocol I of 1977* (NDFP Human Rights Monitoring Committee Booklet No 6), at 98; Agreement No 1 of 22 May 1992, reproduced in Sassòli/Bouvier/Quintin, at 1717; Agreement between the Government of the Republic of Sudan and The Sudan People's Liberation Movement to Protect Non-Combatant Civilians and Civilian Facilities from Military Attack, 10 March 2002.

[22] See, e.g., Report of the International Commission of Inquiry on Darfur to the Secretary-General, S/2005/60, 1 February 2005, para 174; UNSC Res 1127 (1997).

[23] For the varying uses of the 22 May 1992 agreement by the ICTY, see L. Vierucci, '"Special Agreements" between Conflicting Parties in the Case-law of the ICTY', in B. Swart, A. Zahar, and G. Sluiter (eds), *The Legacy of the International Criminal Tribunal for the Former Yugoslavia* (Oxford: OUP, 2011) 401.

[24] Colombian Constitutional Court, Constitutional Case No C-225/95, 18 May 1995, reproduced in Sassòli/Bouvier/Quintin, 2240, at para 17. See also SCSL, *The Prosecutor v Morris Kallon and Brima Bazzy Kamara*, Appeals Chamber Decision on Challenge to Jurisdiction: Lomé Accord Amnesty, SCSL-2004-15-AR72(E) and SCSL-2004-16-AR72(E), 13 March 2004, para 49.

[25] But see ICJ, *Nuclear Tests (New Zealand v France)*, Judgment 20 December 1974, paras 46–7; International Law Commission's 2006 Guiding Principles applicable to unilateral declarations of States capable of creating legal obligations and its Commentaries thereto, in International Law Commission, Report on the work of its fifty-eighth session (1 May to 9 June and 3 July to 11 August 2006), UN Doc A/61/10, Ch IX.

[26] See, e.g., ICTR, *The Prosecutor v Jean-Paul Akayesu*, Trial Chamber Judgment, ICTR-96-4-T, 2 September 1998, para 627; Report of the Special Rapporteur on Extrajudicial, Summary or Arbitrary Executions, Mission to Sri Lanka, UN Doc E/CN.4/2006/53/Add.5, 27 March 2006, para 30.

may extend to bring into force IHL norms that would not otherwise be applicable, such as a commitment not to use certain weapons that have not been prohibited, or a commitment to abide by international human rights law (IHRL). Thus, ad hoc commitments are useful tools by which to build on pre-existing baseline obligations.

26 One potential drawback of this rationale is that it could suggest that without consent on the part of the armed group, the armed group would not be bound by Common Article 3 or other IHL norms. As is evident from the other explanations, this is not correct.

e. *Claims of the armed group to represent the state*

27 A further rationale is that non-state armed groups are bound by Common Article 3, and other IHL norms, through their claim to represent the state against which they are fighting. As is well known, in international law, ratification of a treaty by a government binds the state as such and not just the particular government that ratifies it. An armed group that wins the insurrection and becomes the new government of the state is bound by a treaty, even if it was previously fighting against the very government that ratified the treaty.[27] The present rationale takes this principle one stage further and holds that an armed group that claims to be the government or to represent the state is also bound by the relevant treaty. The ICRC Commentaries to the Geneva Conventions put it this way: '[I]f the responsible authority at [its] head exercises effective sovereignty, it is bound by the very fact that it claims to represent the country, or part of the country.'[28]

28 This is reflected in the practice of some armed groups. A number of these have taken the view that as they are seeking to represent the state on the international plane, they will follow certain international rules that are part of the international system.[29]

29 The difficulty with this rationale is the extension of the binding nature of a treaty, on an armed group that becomes the new government, to the armed group that claims to be the government. Armed groups that become governments are bound because they are the new government, not because of their status as a former armed group. In respect of the armed group that never becomes the government, obligations of the state are purportedly assigned to those who merely claim to represent the state, no matter how ridiculous or unlikely the claim may be. It is questionable why a bare assertion of state representation should bring into play the rules governing NIACs.

30 This rationale is also limited in its explanatory value. The ICRC Commentary notes that '*if* the responsible authority [...] exercises effective sovereignty, it is bound' (emphasis added), which cannot serve to explain how the responsible authority that does not exercise effective sovereignty is bound. Likewise, it fails to explain how armed groups that do not claim to represent the state but fight for secession are bound. Further, where the armed group does not purport to represent the state, for example if it is fighting for control over natural resources or to displace the government in favour of elections, it would not

---

[27] This follows from the *forma regiminis mutata non mutatur ipsa civitas* principle by which extra-constitutional changes to the government do not affect the person of the state.

[28] Pictet Commentary GC III, at 37. This is the only explanation that is included in each of the four of the commentaries to CA 3.

[29] See, e.g., Interim National Council [National Transitional Council], *A Vision of a Democratic Libya*, 29 March 2011, referring to '[a] state which will uphold the values of international justice, citizenship, the respect of international humanitarian law and human rights declarations, as well as condemning authoritarian and despotic regimes'.

be bound by Common Article 3 through this explanation. Therefore, at the very most, this rationale explains only why those armed groups that purport to represent the state are bound.

f. Armed group exercising state-like functions

A variation of the above rationale relates to the armed group that exercises state-like functions. Unlike the previous rationale, which focuses on the claim of the group, this rationale is usually manifested through the exercise of effective control over territory. In this version, as the armed group is akin to a state, it is bound by certain obligations that attach to states.

Arguments along these lines have been used to explain how non-state armed groups are bound by IHRL.[30] Although potentially useful for IHRL, they are far less useful in so far as IHL is concerned. Historically, at a time when the law of war regulated NIACs upon recognition of belligerency, this rationale may have been instructive. In such instances, the armed group was required inter alia to occupy and maintain 'a measure of orderly administration of a substantial part of national territory'.[31] However, today, with the decline of recognition of belligerency, this rationale is less persuasive.

This rationale could suggest, in a rather misleading manner, that in order for an armed group to apply IHL, it must be state-like in character. State-like entities are not required for Common Article 3 to apply, nor are they required for the possibility to comply with the obligations contained therein. Indeed, in order for Common Article 3 to apply, the armed group in question need not exercise any territorial control at all.[32] Conversely, Additional Protocol II (AP II) does require the armed group to exercise territorial control, but only such territorial control as to enable the group to carry out sustained and concerted hostilities and to implement the Protocol. Most norms do not require territorial control in order for them to be implemented. Some norms do require some measure of territorial control and certain capabilities on the part of the armed group, principally those relating to detention and trial; however, armed groups are not obliged to detain or to try, and if they choose to do so, they may do so without being of a state-like character.

In any event, this rationale is limited in its explanatory value. It purports to explain why groups that exercise state-like functions are bound by Common Article 3. At most, it could explain why groups such as the Liberation Tigers of Tamil Eelam (LTTE) in Sri Lanka, the Fuerzas Armadas Revolucionarias de Colombia (FARC) in Colombia, and the SPLM in Sudan, all of which exercised control over a significant degree of state territory and established a state-like apparatus, were bound by Common Article 3. However, the majority of NIACs are not of this sort, and the binding nature of Common Article 3 on armed groups that are parties to such conflicts cannot be explained by this rationale.

---

[30] See, e.g., Report of the Secretary-General's Panel of Experts on Accountability in Sri Lanka, 31 March 2011, para 181. See generally A. Clapham, *Human Rights Obligations of Non-State Actors* (Oxford: OUP, 2006).

[31] L. Oppenheim, *International Law: A Treatise*; ed H. Lauterpacht (London: Longman, 1952), vol II, at 249–50. See also Special Message of President Grant, 13 June 1870, issued in respect of the violence in Cuba, reproduced in J.B. Moore, *Digest of International Law* (Washington, DC: Government Printing Office, 1906), vol I, at 194–5.

[32] ICTY, *The Prosecutor v Slobodan Milošević*, Trial Chamber Decision on Motion for Acquittal, IT-02-54-T, 16 June 2004, para 36. Contra ICTR, *The Prosecutor v Akayesu*, above n 26, para 619; ICC, *The Prosecutor v Omar Hassan Ahmed Al-Bashir*, Decision on the Prosecution's Application for a Warrant of Arrest against Omar Hassan Ahmed Al Bashir, ICC-02/05-01/09, 4 March 2009, paras 59–65.

g. Customary international law

35 According to this explanation, IHL binds non-state armed groups through customary international law. Thus, the armed group need not be party to the relevant treaty to be bound by the provisions that reflect customary international law.

36 It was on this basis that the Special Court for Sierra Leone (SCSL) held the Revolutionary United Front (RUF) bound by IHL. Likewise, it was by referring to customary international law that the International Court of Justice (ICJ) considered the Contras of Nicaragua to be bound; and the International Commission of Inquiry on Darfur held the Sudan Liberation Movement/Army (SLM/A), and the Justice and Equality Movement (JEM) bound.[33]

37 The norms contained in Common Article 3 are unquestionably of a customary international law status. In *Nicaragua v United States of America*, the ICJ held:

> There is no doubt that, in the event of international armed conflicts, these rules [of Common Article 3] also constitute a minimum yardstick, in addition to the more elaborate rules which are also to apply to international conflicts; and they are rules which, in the Court's opinion, reflect what the Court in 1949 called 'elementary considerations of humanity' […][34]

The International Criminal Tribunal for the former Yugoslavia (ICTY), the International Criminal Tribunal for Rwanda (ICTR), the SCSL, and domestic courts have also confirmed that Common Article 3 has passed into the corpus of rules that reflect customary international law.[35]

38 As will be evident from the above, this rationale cannot explain how non-state armed groups are bound by rules of IHL that do not have customary status. This is less important today in light of the extensive body of customary IHL rules that are applicable in NIACs.[36] However, some conventional rules have not yet passed into the corpus of customary IHL. Were this rationale alone to be used, the rules would seemingly not be binding on armed groups. Furthermore, this rationale cannot explain how rules were binding on armed groups before they gained customary status. For example, for a time, only 'the core' of AP II was considered part of customary international law,[37] yet AP II itself was considered binding on armed groups. Accordingly, this explanation, too, is a useful but limited one.

h. Final remarks

39 The idea that Common Article 3 binds non-state armed groups that are parties to NIACs is uncontroversial. As is evident from the above, the legal explanation behind the binding nature is more open to dispute, but the fact of its binding nature is not. Indeed, courts have generally been satisfied to note that Common Article 3 is binding, without delving

---

[33] SCSL, *The Prosecutor v Kallon and Kamara*, above n 24, para 47; Report of the International Commission of Inquiry on Darfur to the Secretary-General, UN Doc S/2005/60, 1 February 2005, para 172; ICJ, *Nicaragua v United States of America*, above n 7, paras 218–19.

[34] ICJ, *Nicaragua v United States of America*, above n 7, para 218.

[35] ICTY, *The Prosecutor v Duško Tadić*, Appeals Chamber Decision on the Defence Motion for Interlocutory Appeal on Jurisdiction, IT-94-1-AR72, 2 October 1995, para 98; ICTR, *The Prosecutor v Akayesu*, above n 26, para 608; SCSL, *The Prosecutor v Kallon and Kamara*, above n 24, para 47; Colombian Constitutional Court, Constitutional Case No C-225/95, 18 May 1995, reproduced in Sassòli/Bouvier/Quintin, at 2240.

[36] See, in particular, ICRC CIHL Study.

[37] ICTY, *The Prosecutor v Tadić*, above n 35, para 98; ICTR, *The Prosecutor v Akayesu*, above n 26, paras 609–10.

into the international law basis behind its binding nature. However, this makes it more difficult to establish precisely how it is that other IHL provisions bind non-state armed groups.

Lastly, it should be recalled that different explanations may be used to satisfy different audiences. For example, when engaging a non-state armed group that has indicated its consent to be bound by Common Article 3, it may be preferable to use the consent-based rationale to engage the group, rather than the fact that the group is bound through state ratification of the Geneva Conventions or on the basis of the customary international law nature of the provisions of Common Article 3. This does not mean that should the group withdraw its consent, it is no longer bound. Rather, it will sometimes be useful to draw a distinction between explanations that are used to bind a party as a matter of law and explanations that are used to engage with a party to further its compliance with the law.

III. Tension between binding nature and legal status

The final sentence of Common Article 3 provides that 'The application of the preceding provisions shall not affect the legal status of the Parties to the conflict.' Although formulated in terms of 'legal status', the provision was originally drafted to vitiate the claim that application of Common Article 3 resulted in recognition of belligerency.[38] Historically, recognition of belligerency brought into play the law of war (the law of international armed conflict (IAC)). Through the final sentence of Common Article 3, states wanted to guard against the reverse proposition, that application of the law of armed conflict would be tantamount to recognition of belligerency. However, the clause is broader than recognition of belligerency alone, as indeed is reflected in the language of the provision, and has even been interpreted to extend to a denial of legitimacy.

At its adoption in 1949, not all states felt that the clause served its purpose. The Delegate of Burma, who was particularly outspoken in his opposition to the regulation of NIACs, stated that the final sentence of Common Article 3 was 'an attempt to safeguard the legal status of the de jure government'. However, in his view, it was

> only a bait [...] Whether or not you safeguard the legal status of the de jure government, the mere inclusion of this Article in an international Convention will automatically give the insurgents a status as high as the legal status which is denied to them. It can easily be imagined that this paragraph is going to be an encouragement and an incentive to the insurgents.[39]

Contrasted with Burma's view was that of the Union of Soviet Socialist Republics (USSR), whose Delegate took the view that the clause was 'redundant [...] since the legal status of [the] Parties would in no way be affected'.[40] For its part, Norway praised the 'sound innovation' of the clause, stating that '[i]f the application of the Convention entailed no consequence as regards the legal status of opposing parties, that meant that the Convention must be applied even where the opposing parties were not recognized as belligerents.'[41]

Over time, the idea has become increasingly accepted, and a similar clause now appears in many instruments that are applicable in NIACs. For example, the clause, or its equivalent, has been included in numerous IHL treaties, treaties in associated areas,

---

[38] See Sivakumaran, above n 20, at 205–7.
[39] Final Record, vol II-B, 330 (Burma).   [40] Ibid, 98 (USSR).   [41] Ibid, 11 (Norway).

ad hoc agreements between parties to conflicts, and even unilateral declarations of armed groups.[42] It would seem that, provided such a clause is present, states are increasingly willing to regulate NIACs. More difficult, and still controversial, is engagement with non-state armed groups (see MN 48, 50).

44   There is, then, a tension between the fact that Common Article 3 is binding on parties to the conflict *qua* treaty rules, including non-state armed groups, and the statement in the clause that the fact that they are bound does not affect their legal status. The sentence has been aptly described as an 'enigma' and Article 3 as having 'two souls: one is humanitarian and open to insurgents; the other favours respect for state sovereignty and is thus opposed to the rebels'.[43]

IV. Engaging addressees on Common Article 3 and obstacles thereto

45   This author shares the view that respect for Common Article 3 on the part of certain parties to conflicts can be increased if there is engagement with those parties. United Nations (UN) Secretary-General Ban-Ki Moon has stated that 'while engagement with non-State armed groups will not always result in improved protection, the absence of systematic engagement will almost certainly mean more, not fewer, civilian casualties in current conflicts'.[44] At the very least, knowledge of IHL in general, and of Common Article 3 in particular, will be increased if there is engagement with parties to conflicts on humanitarian norms. There will be little compliance with IHL if parties are unaware of their obligations under it, and ignorance of parties as to their obligations is all too frequent. However, it is contentious to engage with non-state armed group parties to conflicts, which opposing states often characterize as criminals and terrorists.

46   International humanitarian law envisages engagement with non-state armed groups in certain respects. Common Article 3 provides that an impartial humanitarian body, such as the ICRC, may 'offer its services' to parties to conflicts, such parties including non-state armed groups. Parties to conflicts are required to disseminate IHL,[45] and outside entities, in particular the ICRC, assist with these dissemination efforts. Parties to conflicts are also under a customary international law obligation to provide instruction on IHL to their forces.[46] As noted above (MN 21), Common Article 3 exhorts parties to conclude 'special agreements', bringing into force other rules of IHL. This too is usually done with the assistance of outside actors.

47   The Security Council has recognized the importance of providing instruction to parties to conflicts, including non-state armed groups. Security Council Resolution 1894 (2009)

---

[42] See, e.g., Hague Convention for the Protection of Cultural Property in the Event of Armed Conflict (1954), Art 19(4); Second Hague Protocol for the Protection of Cultural Property in the Event of Armed Conflict (1999), Art 22(6); Convention on Certain Conventional Weapons (1980), Amended Art 1(6); Amended Protocol II on Prohibitions or Restrictions on the Use of Mines, Booby-Traps and Other Devices (1996), Art 1(6); Optional Protocol to the Convention on the Rights of the Child on the Involvement of Children in Armed Conflicts (2000), Art 4(3); African Union Convention for the Protection and Assistance of Internally Displaced Persons in Africa (2009), Art 7; Government–FARC Humanitarian Exchange Accord, 2 June 2001; Agreement of 22 May 1992 [Bosnia], reproduced in Sassòli/Bouvier/Quintin, at 1717; Deed of Commitment under Geneva Call for Adherence to a Total Ban on Anti-Personnel Mines and for Cooperation in Mine Action, Art 6.

[43] A. Cassese, 'Civil War and International Law', in A. Cassese (ed), *The Human Dimension of International Law: Selected Papers* (Oxford: OUP, 2008) 110, at 119 (emphasis omitted).

[44] UN Doc S/2009/277, 29 May 2009, para 40.   [45] See, e.g., Art 19 AP II.

[46] ICRC CIHL Study, Rule 142.

calls for 'all parties concerned [...] to provide training for [...] members of armed forces and armed groups [...] on relevant international humanitarian, human rights and refugee law'. Pursuant to various Security Council resolutions, certain listed armed groups are required to conclude action plans with UN entities on humanitarian norms, under threat of sanction.[47] This, too, necessitates engagement with the listed groups. The Security Council has also called upon parties to conflicts to facilitate humanitarian relief efforts.[48]

At the same time as the increasing recognition of the importance of engaging with non-state armed groups on humanitarian norms, there is a growing hesitancy over engagement with non-state armed groups. Traditionally, concerns have related to the potential of affording legitimacy to these groups. Certain states link engagement of non-state armed groups with affording them a degree of legitimacy,[49] thus presenting an obstacle to their engagement. Entities that do engage with non-state armed groups have accordingly stressed that engagement and legitimacy should be divorced from one another, and that engagement operates without affording the groups any legitimacy.[50] Such a caveat should operate in the same way as the legal status caveat operates in the context of Common Article 3 (see MN 41–43). However, states do not always hold this view.

Considered less often is the notion of legitimacy itself, whether it is political legitimacy, legitimacy in law, or some other construct of legitimacy. Also critical, but asked less frequently, is from whose perspective legitimacy is being assessed. The issue is usually presented as a comparison between the legitimacy of the armed group and the legitimacy of the state, with the armed group being considered inherently illegitimate and the state inherently legitimate. From the perspective of the beneficiaries of Common Article 3, things may be judged differently.

More recently, concerns have been espoused in relation to engaging with non-state armed groups that have been characterized as terrorist groups. A number of states have listed certain groups as terrorist groups and prohibit the provision of material support to them.[51] Depending on the domestic legislation in question, material support may include such things as training on humanitarian norms. One national court has explained that, for the purposes of its legislation, material support even for peaceful purposes can lend legitimacy to the group and free up resources within the group that may be used for violent purposes.[52] Terrorist lists are also maintained at the regional level and by the UN.[53] The Security Council has called on states to '[r]efrain from providing any form of support, active or passive, to entities or persons involved in terrorist acts'.[54] There is thus a tension between engaging with armed groups, even on humanitarian norms, and terrorist listings. (see for a detailed discussion Chapter 24, MN 29–33, of this volume).

---

[47] UNSC Res 1612 (2005), 1882 (2009), and 1960 (2010).
[48] See, e.g., UNSC Res 1964 (2010).
[49] See, e.g., Security Council, 6151st meeting, 26 June 2009, Protection of Civilians in Armed Conflict, UN Doc S/PV.6151, 26 June 2009, 9 (Vietnam) and 17 (Russian Federation).
[50] See, e.g., Report of the Special Representative of the Secretary-General for Children and Armed Conflict, UN Doc A/60/335, 7 September 2005, para 51.
[51] See, e.g., in the US, 18 USC §2339B. The UK maintains a list of 'proscribed terrorist organizations' pursuant to the Terrorism Act 2000. Likewise, Canada maintains a list of 'listed entities' pursuant to its Anti-Terrorism Act 2001. See for a more complete list Ch 24, nn 52 and 53, of this volume.
[52] US Supreme Court, *Holder, Attorney-General et al v Humanitarian Law Project et al* (2010) 130 S Ct 2705, 2725.
[53] See, e.g., the list maintained by the 1267 Committee of individuals, groups, undertakings, and entities associated with Al-Qaeda. The EU maintains a list of 'persons, groups and entities involved in terrorist acts': 2001/931/CFSP (2001).
[54] UNSC Res 1373 (2001).

C. Applicability in International Armed Conflicts

51 When originally drafted, Common Article 3 was designed for application in NIACs. The opening clause of the Article reads, '[i]n the case of armed conflict not of an international character occurring in the territory of one of the High Contracting Parties […]'.[55] At the level of conventional law, Common Article 3 remains limited to NIACs.

52 As a matter of customary international law, Common Article 3 applies also to IACs. In the 1986 case *Nicaragua v United States of America*, the ICJ held that it need not judge the conflict between the Contras and the Government of Nicaragua, which it considered a NIAC, and the conflict between the United States and Nicaragua, which it considered an IAC, by different sets of rules. Instead, it considered that '[t]he relevant rules are to be looked for in the provisions of [Common] Article 3'.[56]

53 In the *Nicaragua* case itself and in the period that followed the *Nicaragua* judgment, this matter was not entirely settled.[57] However, this was largely due to the failure of the Court to set out the state practice and *opinio juris* that led to its conclusion, rather than the conclusion itself. Since that time, the matter has become well settled and now reflects the unchallenged orthodoxy. The applicability of Common Article 3 in IACs as a matter of customary international law has been followed by the ICTY in the *Tadić* case and in the Tribunal's later jurisprudence.[58] It has also been referred to in judgments of influential national courts.[59] Indeed, the Customary International Humanitarian Law Study accepted this to the extent that it did not consider it necessary to reference Common Article 3 in its commentaries to the rules.[60] The conclusion that Common Article 3 reflects customary international law is sound, especially given that Common Article 3 was taken from an intended preamble to GC IV,[61] reflecting its basic provisions and general themes that underlie all of IHL.

54 As a matter of caution and without advocating the possibility, should any 'new' types of armed conflicts be recognized in the future, Common Article 3 would be applicable to them too.

D. Legal Consequences of a Violation

55 Violation of the norms contained in Common Article 3 can result in the responsibility of the party to the conflict, individual criminal responsibility, and certain other measures.

56 If the state party to the conflict commits a violation, the violation may result in state responsibility. This will be judged against the usual rules on state responsibility. Actions brought against a state for violations of IHL are not commonplace, largely for lack of

---

[55] On the concept of a non-international armed conflict, see Ch 19 of this volume.

[56] ICJ, *Nicaragua v United States of America*, above n 7, para 219. The ICJ considered the customary status of the rules as the US had reserved 'disputes arising under a multilateral treaty', unless certain conditions were present, from its Optional Clause Declaration. By virtue of looking at the customary rules, the Court did not have to consider the role, if any, of the reservation.

[57] See ICJ, *Nicaragua v United States of America*, above n 7, Dissenting Opinion of Judge Sir Robert Jennings, at 537. See also ibid, Separate Opinion of Judge Ago, at 184, para 6.

[58] ICTY, *The Prosecutor v Tadić*, above n 35, 2 October 1995, para 102. See also ICTY, *The Prosecutor v Zejnil Delalić et al*, Judgment, IT-96-21-T, 16 November 1998, para 303.

[59] *Hamdan v Rumsfeld, Secretary of Defense et al*, 548 US 557 (2006), at 631 fn 63.

[60] ICRC CIHL Study, at xliv.

[61] Final Record, vol II-A, 696. See also Pictet Commentary GC I, at 52.

jurisdiction and an available forum. However, states are sometimes held to have violated Common Article 3.[62]

States may also be held responsible, in certain situations, for the acts of armed groups. For example, an act of an armed group is to be considered an act of the state if the armed group is acting under the direction and control of the state.[63] 57

In theory, if the non-state armed group, party to the conflict, commits a violation, this could attract the responsibility of the armed group,[64] and lead to remedies such as reparations.[65] However, responsibility of the non-state armed group as such is an underdeveloped area of the law. It is not possible, for example, to apply the same elements of attribution in the law of state responsibility, without more, to the non-state armed groups, given the differences between the two groups. Provision will also have to be made to account for greater fragmentation and disintegration of armed groups. Furthermore, an available forum before which to bring a claim will prove difficult. 58

More developed is the responsibility of an armed group that later becomes the new government of a state or of a new state. Pursuant to the ILC Articles on State Responsibility, the conduct of the armed group in such circumstances is to be considered an act of the state or the new state, respectively.[66] This means that acts that were committed by the armed group whilst it was not a representative of a state, indeed whilst it was fighting against the state, can nonetheless be attributed retrospectively to the state. Consequently, both the acts of the then armed group (now government) and the acts of the old government are attributable to the state. The rationale behind such a proposition is that it would be 'anomalous if the new regime or new State could avoid responsibility for conduct earlier committed by it'.[67] For the same reason, private acts of individuals who made up the then armed group (now government) cannot be attributed to the state. 59

Violation of the norms contained in Common Article 3 may also lead to belligerent reprisals by the adverse party. This may be done, provided the conditions for the use of belligerent reprisals are met and the specific belligerent reprisal to be used is not prohibited.[68] 60

In addition to state or armed group responsibility, violation of the norms contained in Common Article 3 may also result in individual criminal responsibility on the part of the individual who commits the violation or through other modes of liability. State or armed group responsibility does not negate individual criminal responsibility, and vice versa. Historically, it had been thought that violations of IHL applicable in NIAC, such as Common Article 3, did not give rise to individual criminal responsibility under 61

---

[62] See, e.g., IACtHR, *Avilan et al v Colombia*, Case 11.142, Report No 26/97, 30 September 1997, OEA/Ser.L/V/II.98, doc.6 rev, 13 April 1998, para 202; IACtHR, *Hugo Bustios Saavedra v Peru*, Case 10.548, Report No 38/97, 16 October 1997, OEA/Ser.L/V/II.98, doc.6 rev, 13 April 1998, para 88; IACtHR, *Lucio Parada Cea et al v El Salvador*, Case 10.480, Report No 1/99, 27 January 1999, para 82.

[63] ILC Articles on State Responsibility, Art 8.

[64] See ILC Articles on State Responsibility, Commentary to Article 10, in Report of the International Law Commission, Fifty-third session, A/56/10, p 118; Report of the International Commission of Inquiry on Darfur, para 600.

[65] See the cautious statement in the ICRC CIHL Study, Commentary to Rule 150. See also, taking a stronger view, Report of the International Commission of Inquiry on Darfur, paras 590–600.

[66] ILC Articles on State Responsibility, Art 10.

[67] ILC Articles on State Responsibility, Commentary to Article 10, in Report of the International Law Commission, above n 64, at 110.

[68] See Ch 29, in particular MN 37–50, of this volume.

international law.⁶⁹ At least since 1995, following the holding of the ICTY in *Tadić*, this is no longer the case.⁷⁰ *Serious* violations of Common Article 3 are explicitly criminalized in the Statute of the ICTR and the Statute of the SCSL.⁷¹ In so far as the International Criminal Court (ICC) is concerned, the ICC Statute largely reproduces Common Article 3.⁷² Serious violations of Common Article 3 may also be prosecuted at the domestic level.

62   The criminalized version of Common Article 3 binds individuals directly through international criminal law. The individual in question may be a member of the state armed forces, the non-state armed group, or a civilian not linked to a party to the conflict. Parties to conflicts are abstract entities. Thus, the criminalized version of Common Article 3 necessarily binds individuals who comprise the parties to the conflict. In a well-known passage, the International Military Tribunal at Nuremberg held, 'Crimes against international law are committed by men, not by abstract entities, and only by punishing individuals who commit such crimes can the provisions of international law be enforced.'⁷³ Individuals who do not comprise the parties to the conflict but who have a nexus to a party to the conflict have also long been prosecuted for war crimes.⁷⁴ Furthermore, the binding nature of international criminal law on persons without a connection to a party to the conflict has also been confirmed. According to the ICTR Appeals Chamber in *Akayesu*, 'international humanitarian law would be lessened and called into question if it were to be admitted that certain persons be exonerated from individual criminal responsibility for a violation of common Article 3 under the pretext that they did not belong to a specific category'.⁷⁵

63   These cases may be read as holding that it is Common Article 3, *qua* IHL, that binds individuals directly and not only the criminalized version of Common Article 3, *qua* international criminal law. For example, although the *Akayesu* Appeals Chamber, in the

---

⁶⁹ See, e.g., 'Some Preliminary Remarks by the International Committee of the Red Cross on the Setting-Up of an International Tribunal for the Prosecution of Persons Responsible for Serious Violations of International Humanitarian Law Committed on the Territory of the Former Yugoslavia', DDM/JUR/442b, 25 March 1993, para 4, reprinted in V. Morris and M.P. Scharf, *An Insider's Guide to the International Criminal Tribunal for the Former Yugoslavia* (Irvington-on-Hudson, NY: Transnational, 1995), vol II, at 391, 392; Final Report of the Commission of Experts established pursuant to UNSC Res 780 (1992), S/1994/674, 27 May 1994, para 52.
⁷⁰ ICTY, *The Prosecutor v Tadić*, above n 35, paras 128–36.
⁷¹ Art 4 ICTR Statute; Art 3 SCSL Statute.   ⁷² Art 8(2)(c) ICC Statute.
⁷³ *Trial of the Major War Criminals before the International Military Tribunal, Nuremberg, 14 November 1945–1 October 1946* (Nuremberg, 1947), vol I, at 171, 223.
⁷⁴ See, e.g., *The Hadamar Trial* [1947] I LRTWC 46; *The Essen Lynching Case* [1947] I LRTWC 88; *The Zyklon B Case* [1947] I LRTWC 93. The Military Commissions in question did not require a nexus between the civilian and a party to the conflict. Indeed, the 'notes' on the *Hadamar* case indicate that the decision of the Commission was 'an application of the rule that the provisions of the laws and customs of war are addressed not only to combatants but also to civilians, and that civilians, by committing illegal acts against nationals of the opponent, may become guilty of war crimes' (53–4). However, a nexus did exist in each of the cases, and trial chambers of the ICTR have read the cases in this manner: ICTR, *The Prosecutor v Akayesu*, above n 26, para 633; ICTR, *The Prosecutor v Alfred Musema*, Trial Chamber Judgment, ICTR-96-13-T, 27 January 2000, para 274. An ICTY Trial Chamber in *Kunarac* also observed that '[i]t would appear to the Trial Chamber that common [a]rticle 3 may also require some relationship to exist between a perpetrator and a party to the conflict.' However, the Trial Chamber went on to note that it need not consider the point. ICTY, *The Prosecutor v Dragoljub Kunarac, Radomir Kovač and Zoran Vuković*, Trial Chamber Judgment, IT-96-23-T and IT-96-23/1-T, 22 February 2001, para 407.
⁷⁵ ICTR, *The Prosecutor v Jean-Paul Akayesu*, Appeals Chamber Judgment, ICTR-96-4-A, 1 June 2001, para 443. See also the jurisprudence above n 74.

passage quoted immediately above, referenced individual criminal responsibility—that being the context in which the issue arose—the Appeals Chamber came to its conclusion in respect of Common Article 3 as a norm of IHL, having found the relevant international criminal law on the point inconclusive.[76] This reading has important consequences for rules of IHL, the violation of which do not give rise to criminal sanction. However, the position is not altogether clear, with judicial statements on the point being rather opaque and commentators taking different positions on the issue.[77]

E. Critical Assessment

International law remains state-centric by its nature. As such, the manner in which IHL binds non-state armed groups is somewhat unsettled. What is not contentious, however, is that IHL in general, and Common Article 3 in particular, does bind parties to conflicts, including non-state armed group parties to conflicts. Different explanatory rationales may be used for different purposes with different audiences. Over time, the binding nature of Common Article 3 has been extended to include parties to IACs. 64

The regulation of NIACs sometimes proves controversial for reasons of state sovereignty and purported interference in the internal affairs of the state. It was only in 1949, through Common Article 3, that NIACs were regulated systematically for the first time by IHL. Today, the regulation of NIACs remains difficult but is far less controversial. This is evident from the numerous rules of conventional IHL that apply to such conflicts aside from Common Article 3. This is due, in no small part, to the caveat contained in Common Article 3 that the legal status of the parties to the conflict remains unchanged by application of the provision. Such a caveat can be found in many of the other instruments that regulate NIACs. 65

There remain, however, very real difficulties with engaging non-state armed groups on humanitarian norms. Engagement with non-state armed groups is sometimes considered to legitimize them. Yet there is no reason why this should be the case. Engagement is often carried out by humanitarian actors with the express caveat that it does not amount to legitimization. Such a caveat should operate in the same way as the Common Article 3 clause operates in respect of legal status. Engagement with groups that are listed as terrorist groups might be considered provision of material support to them, and, as such, constitutes prohibited conduct in certain national systems. This means that engagement with a certain class of non-state armed groups on their obligations under Common Article 3 is prohibited. While prohibiting support to terrorist groups is of undoubted importance, if engagement does lead to improved compliance with humanitarian norms, a better balance must be found between the two competing objectives of the international community. 66

SANDESH SIVAKUMARAN

---

[76] ICTR, *The Prosecutor v Akayesu*, above n 75, para 436. See also the notes on *Hadamar*, above n 74.

[77] Compare J.K. Kleffner, 'The Applicability of International Humanitarian Law to Organized Armed Groups', 93 *IRRC* 882 (2011) 443, at 449–51, with R. Arnold, 'The Liability of Civilians under International Humanitarian Law's War Crimes Provisions', 5 *YIHL* (2002) 344. See also Sassòli/Bouvier/Quintin, at 26, describing the matter as 'unclear'.

Chapter 21. The Beneficiaries of the Rights Stemming from Common Article 3

	MN
A. Introduction	1
B. Meaning and Application	7
I. Persons taking no active part in the hostilities	7
II. Members of armed forces who have laid down their arms	14
III. Those placed *hors de combat* by sickness, wounds, detention, or any other cause	19
IV. The wounded, sick, and shipwrecked	25
V. Impartial humanitarian bodies	27
C. Legal Consequences of a Violation	28
D. Critical Assessment	29

Select Bibliography

Kleffner, J.K., 'From "Belligerents" to "Fighters" and Civilians Directly Participating in Hostilities—On the Principle of Distinction in Non-International Armed Conflicts One Hundred Years after the Second Peace Conference', 54 *NILR* (2007) 315

Kleffner, J.K., 'Friend or Foe? On the Protective Reach of the Law of Armed Conflict', in M. Matthee, B. Toebes, and M. Brus (eds), *Armed Conflict and International Law, in Search of the Human Face—Liber Amicorum in Memory of Avril McDonald* (The Hague: T.M.C. Asser Press, 2013) 285

Melzer, N., 'The Principle of Distinction between Civilians and Combatants', in A. Clapham and P. Gaeta (eds), *The Oxford Handbook of International Law in Armed Conflict* (Oxford: OUP, 2014) 296

Moir, L., *The Law of Internal Armed Conflict* (Cambridge: CUP, 2002)

Pictet Commentaries to GC I–GC IV

Sivakumaran, S., *The Law of Non-International Armed Conflict* (Oxford: OUP, 2012)

A. Introduction

Common Article 3 of the Four Geneva Conventions is the first treaty provision that expressly regulates the protection of certain persons from a number of acts in non-international armed conflicts (NIACs). That protection is conditional upon the persons concerned 'taking no active part in the hostilities'. The protection of persons who do not (or no longer) actively participate in hostilities is one of the cornerstones of the law of armed conflict, with a long historical pedigree. Indeed, such protection can be traced back over the centuries to ancient cultural, religious, and philosophical sources.[1] Some of the historical precedents of legal rules that provide for the protection of persons who take no active part in the hostilities were applicable in what today would be called armed conflicts

---

[1] M.E. O'Connell, 'Historical Development and Legal Basis', in D. Fleck (ed), *The Handbook of International Humanitarian Law* (3rd edn, Oxford: OUP, 2013) 1, at 15–18.

'not of an international character' in the sense of Common Article 3. Thus, the 1863 Lieber Code that detailed the 'Instructions for the Government of Armies of the United States in the Field' during the American Civil War (1861–5) against the secessionist Confederacy of states supporting slavery, contained a number of provisions on the protection of 'persons in the invaded country' (Article 44), 'prisoners of war' (Article 49), an 'enemy already wholly disabled' (Article 71), and captured wounded enemies (Article 79).[2]

2   While such provisions confirm the long-standing idea that those who do not take an active part in the hostilities enjoy protection, the actual meaning of 'taking no active part in the hostilities' has evolved considerably over time. A very ancient source, the Indian 'Laws of Manu' (1500 BCE), for instance, extend protection to members of the opposing armed forces who are fleeing or sleeping, who are fighting with another foe, whose weapons are broken, and enemies who are 'afflicted with sorrow' or are in fear.[3] More recently, the Lieber Code made a distinction between 'loyal' and 'disloyal' citizens, with the latter being deprived of some of the protections enjoyed by the former (Articles 155 and 156 Lieber Code). In comparison to such earlier sources, the meaning of 'taking no active part in the hostilities' in Common Article 3—and, as a consequence, also the group of beneficiaries granted protection under the provision in a NIAC—is more restrictive in certain respects, while being more expansive in others.

3   The International Court of Justice (ICJ) has identified that the protections afforded to persons taking no active part in hostilities under Common Article 3 'constitute a minimum yardstick' and correspond to 'elementary considerations of humanity'.[4] That assertion confirms both the centrality of the protection granted by Common Article 3, as well as its rudimentary nature. Against this background, the provision must be considered in the context of additional rules pertaining to the protection of (certain groups of) persons taking no active part in the hostilities under applicable treaty and customary international law (CIL) pertaining to NIAC. Such additional rules include those regulating specific protections of the wounded, sick, and shipwrecked,[5] the dead,[6] medical and religious personnel,[7] persons deprived of their liberty,[8] women,[9] children,[10] the elderly, disabled, and infirm,[11] displaced,[12] and missing persons,[13] humanitarian relief personnel,[14] personnel involved in a peacekeeping mission who are entitled to the protection given to civilians under international humanitarian law (IHL),[15] and journalists.[16] As is clear from the wording of the provision that provides that parties to a NIAC are

---

[2] See Lieber Code.

[3] Laws of Manu, Chapter VII, Rules 91–3, available at <http://www.fordham.edu/halsall/india/manu-full.asp>.

[4] ICJ, *Corfu Channel (United Kingdom of Great Britain and Northern Ireland v Albania)*, Merits, 9 April 1949, at 22, para 215; ICJ, *Case concerning Military and Paramilitary Activities in and against Nicaragua (Nicaragua v United States)*, Merits, Judgment, 27 June 1986, at 114, para 218.

[5] Cf Part III AP II; Rules 109–11 ICRC CIHL Study.
[6] Art 8 AP II; Rules 112, 113, 115, 116 ICRC CIHL Study.
[7] See, e.g., Art 9 AP II; Rules 25 and 27 ICRC CIHL Study.
[8] Arts 5–6 AP II; Rules 118–23, 124 (B), 125–7, 128 (C) ICRC CIHL Study.
[9] See, e.g., Arts 5(2)(a) and 6(4) AP II; Rule 134 ICRC CIHL Study.
[10] See, e.g., Arts 4(3) and 6(4) AP II; Art 38 CRC; Rules 135–7 ICRC CIHL Study.
[11] See, e.g., Rule 138 ICRC CIHL Study.
[12] See, e.g., Art 17 AP II; Rules 129 (B), 131–3 ICRC CIHL Study.
[13] See, e.g., Rule 117 ICRC CIHL Study.
[14] See, e.g., Art 18(2) AP II; Rule 56 ICRC CIHL Study.   [15] Cf Rule 33 ICRC CIHL Study.
[16] Cf Rule 34 ICRC CIHL Study.

bound to apply Common Article 3 'as a minimum', and that they should endeavour to bring into force the other provisions of the Geneva Conventions (or, for that matter, additional rules of the law of armed conflict more generally), parties to a NIAC can extend the protections. They can also choose explicitly to mention additional categories of persons taking no active part in the hostilities as beneficiaries, by way of a special agreement or unilaterally. Mentioning additional categories of persons does in no way diminish the protective reach of Common Article 3 as a matter of treaty and CIL: due to its open-ended reference to 'persons taking no active part in the hostilities', an explicit mentioning of, for instance, women and children would be declaratory rather than constitutive of the protections that such persons enjoy under Common Article 3, provided they do not take an active part in the hostilities.

According to its wording, Common Article 3 protects persons taking no active part in the hostilities 'in the case of armed conflict not of an international character' (see Chapter 19 of this volume). The explicit limitation to NIACs may be understood to exclude as beneficiaries of Common Article 3 those who take no active part in the hostilities in international armed conflicts (IACs). However, it has been suggested that because it constitutes a minimum yardstick applicable in NIACs, which are regulated in only a rudimentary way, the protections granted by the provision must *a fortiori* be respected during IACs. 'For "the greater obligation includes the lesser [...]".'[17] According to this view, Common Article 3 is applicable to armed conflicts in general.[18] Persons taking no active part in the hostilities in IACs are thus included in the group of beneficiaries enjoying protection from the acts prohibited under Common Article 3, notwithstanding the fact that they are also cumulatively protected by more detailed and/or extensive rules of the law of armed conflict applicable in IACs.

The partial overlap in NIACs of the protection under Common Article 3, on the one hand, and the rules of the Geneva Conventions the application of which is limited to IACs, on the other hand, should not obscure the fact that important differences exist between these two (sets of) protective rules. Such differences concern not only the extent to which persons taking no active part in the hostilities are protected; rather, it is the very conceptual basis for being considered a person who benefits from the respective protections that is distinct. The assessment of whether or not a person enjoys protection under Common Article 3 is conduct-based, in as much as that protection attaches to the actual activities of a person, or, to be more precise, his or her abstaining from certain activities, namely those that amount to active participation in the hostilities. In contrast, the law of IAC enshrined in the Geneva Conventions bases its protection, by and large,[19] on the status of the person.[20] The latter, status-based protection attaches to a person who falls into one of the categories that the Geneva Conventions define positively (chiefly the wounded,

---

[17] Pictet Commentary GC III, at 38.
[18] In this vein, see, e.g., the ICJ, *Nicaragua Case*, above n 4, at 114, para 218 (asserting that '[t]here is no doubt that, in the event of international armed conflicts, these rules [of Common Article 3] also constitute a minimum yardstick, in addition to the more elaborate rules which are also to apply to international conflicts' as a matter of CIL); ICTY, *The Prosecutor v Duško Tadić*, Appeals Chamber Defence Motion for Interlocutory Appeal on Jurisdiction of the Appeals Chamber, Decision, 2 October 1995, para 102 ('at least with respect to the minimum rules in common Article 3, the character of the conflict is irrelevant'); ICTY, *The Prosecutor v Duško Tadić*, Trial Chamber Judgment, IT-94-1-T, 7 May 1997, paras 559, 568, 607.
[19] An important exception in that respect are the fundamental guarantees stipulated in Art 75 AP I and CIHL, see Rules 87–105 ICRC CIHL Study.
[20] Sassòli/Bouvier/Quintin, at 328, with further references.

sick, and shipwrecked; medical and religious personnel; prisoners of war; and 'protected persons' in the sense of Geneva Convention (GC) IV).[21]

6   No requirement, other than that the person concerned abstains from actively participating in hostilities, conditions the protection under Common Article 3. Indeed, Common Article 3 affirms such an understanding when it stipulates that humane treatment shall be granted 'without any adverse distinction founded on race, colour, religion or faith, sex, birth or wealth, or any other similar criteria'.[22] Pictet recalls that states considered it desirable to draft the non-discrimination clause with specific criteria on the basis of which it is prohibited to make an adverse distinction in NIACs, to ensure that there are no possible loopholes.[23] (See further Chapter 10 of this volume on the principle of non-discrimination.) Such an understanding militates against the view that the extent of the notion of 'persons taking no active part in the hostilities' is limited in any way. It has nevertheless been suggested that Common Article 3 does not protect persons taking no active part in the hostilities who are 'members of armed groups from acts of violence directed against them by their own forces'.[24]

B. Meaning and Application

I. Persons taking no active part in the hostilities

7   The overarching category of those benefiting from the protection of Common Article 3 is 'persons taking no active part in the hostilities'. That broad category encompasses the persons specifically mentioned in Common Article 3, i.e. members of the armed forces who have laid down their arms and those placed *hors de combat*. Yet the notion of 'persons taking no active part in the hostilities' is broader than the sum of the subcategories that are specifically identified as enjoying protection. That is clear from the wording of the provision, which stipulates that '[p]ersons taking no active part in the hostilities [...] includ[e]' the mentioned subcategories. Most notably, the specified groups of persons include 'members of armed forces', whereas 'persons taking no active part in the hostilities' quintessentially include those who are not members of the armed forces, i.e. civilians. While Common Article 3 does not mention, let alone define, the notion of 'civilian', the notion is a consequence of the implicit juxtaposition in Common Article 3 of those persons who are 'members of the armed forces' and those who are not.

8   The definition of the notion of 'active participation' in hostilities is central to the determination of whether or not a person enjoys protection under Common Article 3. Some authorities consider the notion of 'active participation' to be synonymous with the notion of 'direct participation' in hostilities.[25] That view finds support in the—equally authentic—French-language texts of those treaties that employ the notions since the

---

[21] See, on the distinction between positive and negative definitions of who enjoys protection in IACs and under CA 3, respectively, ICTY, *Tadić*, Trial Chamber, above n 18, para 615.

[22] Cf CA 3 para 1(1).   [23] Pictet Commentary GC I, at 55 et seq.

[24] SCSL, *The Prosecutor v Issa Hassan Sesay, Morris Kallon and Augustine Gbao*, Trial Chamber Judgment, SCSL-04-15-T, 2 March 2009, para 1451. Contra J.K. Kleffner, 'Friend or Foe? On the Protective Reach of the Law of Armed Conflict', in M. Matthee, M. Toebes, and M. Brus (eds), *Armed Conflict and International Law, in Search of the Human Face—Liber Amicorum in Memory of Avril McDonald* (The Hague: T.M.C. Asser Press, 2013) 285, at 296.

[25] E.g., ICTR, *The Prosecutor v Jean-Paul Akayesu*, Trial Chamber Judgment, ICTR-96-4-T, 2 September 1998, para 629.

pertinent French texts use identical terms for both.[26] In contrast to the view that 'direct participation' and 'active participation' are synonymous concepts, it has on occasion been asserted that they have distinct meanings. Notably, this latter view has gained some prominence in the jurisprudence of international criminal courts and tribunals, starting with the Special Court for Sierra Leone (SCSL) and later the International Criminal Court (ICC), that were called upon to adjudicate cases in which individuals were accused of the war crime of using children to participate actively in hostilities.[27] More specifically, the SCSL and the ICC held that—in the context of that war crime—the notion of 'active' participation is broader than, and encompasses, 'direct' participation. In their view, 'direct' participation in hostilities denotes combat activities, whereas 'active' participation also encompasses combat-related support activities such as scouting, spying, sabotage, acting as decoys or couriers, and manning military check-points.[28] However, it cannot be discerned from the reasoning leading the SCSL and ICC to conclude that the notions of 'active' and 'direct' participation are not co-extensive, that these courts were of the view that the purported differences also apply outside the context of the specific war crime of using children to participate actively in hostilities that they were called upon to adjudicate. Accordingly, the better view appears to be the one expressed in the 2009 'Interpretive Guidance on the Notion of Direct Participation in Hostilities under International Humanitarian Law'[29] of the International Committee of the Red Cross (ICRC), which treats 'direct participation' and 'active participation' as synonymous.[30] The Guidance is the result of a six-year process that brought nearly 50 legal experts together from military, governmental, and academic circles, from international organizations and non-governmental organizations, all participating in their private capacity.[31] The Guidance does not necessarily reflect a unanimous or majority opinion of the participating experts, but instead provides the ICRC's official recommendations on how IHL relating to the notion of active/direct participation in hostilities should be interpreted. Indeed, the Guidance has proved to be controversial in a number of respects. However, it has an undeniable value as a reference point in the quest to determine what it means to actively participate in the hostilities for the purpose of interpreting Common Article 3.

The Guidance identifies three constitutive elements of direct/active participation in hostilities. First, in order for a person to be considered as actively participating in the hostilities, he or she must engage in an act that reaches a certain threshold of harm. Accordingly, the act 'must be likely to adversely affect the military operations or military capacity of a party to an armed conflict or, alternatively, to inflict death, injury, or destruction on persons or objects protected against direct attack'.[32] Secondly, there must be 'a direct causal link between the act and the harm likely to result either from that act, or from a coordinated military operation of which that act constitutes an integral part', referred

---

[26] Cf French language version of CA 3, Art 51 AP I, and Art 13(3) AP II, all of which refer to persons who do not or do 'participent directement aux hostilités'.

[27] Cf Art 4(c) SCSL Statute; Art 8(2)(b)(xxvi) and (e)(vii) ICC Statute.

[28] SCSL, *The Prosecutor v Alex Tamba Brima, Ibrahim Bazzy Kamara and Santigie Borbor Kanu (AFRC case)*, Trial Chamber Judgment, SCSL-04-16-T, 20 June 2007, paras 736–7; ICC, *The Prosecutor v Thomas Lubanga Dyilo*, Trial Chamber Judgment, ICC-01/04-01/06, 14 March 2012, paras 619–28.

[29] DPH Guidance.

[30] Ibid, at 43–4.   [31] The present author was one such participant.

[32] DPH Guidance, at 47–50.

to as the requirement of 'direct causation'.³³ Thirdly, 'the act must be specifically designed to directly cause the required threshold of harm in support of a party to the conflict and to the detriment of another (belligerent nexus)'.³⁴

10   The three aforementioned constitutive elements are cumulatively determinative of active/direct participation in hostilities. Put differently, if one of the requirements is not met, the person concerned falls within the protective reach of Common Article 3 as a person who is taking no active part in the hostilities. For instance, even if a person engages in an act that is likely to cause damage to a military object, such a person would still be protected against the acts that Common Article 3 prohibits if one or both of the remaining two requirements of direct causation and belligerent nexus are missing. That could be the case, for instance, when the act in question that is likely to adversely affect the military operations or capacity of a party to an armed conflict consists of the production of ammunition. Here, the causal connection between the act and the likely adverse effect is too remote to satisfy the second constitutive element of active participation in the hostilities. Likewise, if information reasonably available at the relevant time clearly suggests that the damage to a military objective is done for the purpose of personal, financial gain (for instance, disassembling a military vehicle to sell parts of it on to car owners or garages), the person concerned would still have to be considered a person taking no active part in the hostilities who enjoys the protection of Common Article 3 due to the absence of a belligerent nexus of his or her acts.

11   The language of Common Article 3 does not further specify the temporal scope of the protection of persons taking no active part in the hostilities. At face value, the provision suggests that any person enjoys the protection as soon as, and for as long as, he or she takes no active part in the hostilities by engaging in acts that fulfil the constitutive criteria referred to above. No distinction is made between, on the one hand, members of the armed forces and, on the other hand, persons who are not members of the armed forces (civilians) as far as their entitlement to protection is concerned (see also MN 13 below). In that way, the loss of protection under Common Article 3 is more restrictive than that provided for in Additional Protocol (AP) II (Article 13(3)) and in customary IHL (evidenced by the ICRC Customary International Humanitarian Law (CIHL) Study, Rule 6). For the loss of protection under AP II and customary IHL, including the 'unless and for such time' element of such a loss, is limited to *civilians* who participate directly in hostilities, to the exclusion of members of the armed forces.

12   The inclusion of both civilians and members of the armed forces within the group of persons enjoying protection under Common Article 3, provided they do not take an active part in the hostilities, has led some to conclude that these two categories of persons have to be treated on an equal footing as far as the temporal scope of the loss of protection is concerned.³⁵ According to such a view, both members of the armed forces and civilians lose their protection only if and for as long as they actively participate in hostilities. The opposite view, which is referred to as the 'membership approach', holds that a distinction is to be made between those who are members of the armed forces and civilians. While the former lose their protection for the entire duration of their membership unless they have laid down their arms or are placed *hors de combat*, civilians do so only if and for as long

---

[33] Ibid, at 51–8.   [34] Ibid, at 58–64.
[35] Special Rapporteur on Extrajudicial, Summary, or Arbitrary Executions, *Study on Targeted Killings*, UN Doc A/HRC/14/24/Add.6 (28 May 2010), paras 58, 65–6.

as they actively participate in hostilities.³⁶ A more restrictive variation of the latter view is expressed by the ICRC in its *Interpretive Guidance on the Notion of Direct Participation in Hostilities under International Humanitarian Law*, where the continuous loss of protection does not extend to all members of the armed forces of a party to a NIAC, but only to members of the state armed forces and those members of the armed forces of a non-state organized armed group who are fulfilling a continuous combat function, i.e. a continuous function involving their direct participation in hostilities.³⁷

It is submitted that the better view on the temporal scope of the loss of protection is to 13 distinguish between those who are not and those who are members of the armed forces of a party to a NIAC. Those who are not members of the armed forces of a party to a NIAC, i.e. civilians, should be presumed not to take an active part in the hostilities. Accordingly, the rule is that they enjoy the protection of Common Article 3, with the exception of active participation in the hostilities. In other words, civilians would be entitled to protection from direct attack unless and for such time as they take an active part in hostilities. Such an approach would reconcile Common Article 3 with the pertinent treaty and customary law on the loss of protection of civilians.³⁸ The reverse logic may reasonably be applied vis-à-vis those who have been reliably determined to be members of the armed forces of a party to a NIAC. The fact that they are members of the armed forces justifies that they enjoy the protection of Common Article 3 only if and when they have laid down their arms or are *hors de combat*, but that they are otherwise not protected from direct attack because they may be presumed to engage in acts that fulfil the three constitutive criteria for active participation in the hostilities referred to above. Indeed, the specific mentioning of members of the armed forces in Common Article 3 and of the conditions under which they enjoy protection (surrender or being placed *hors de combat*) hints at such a presumptive distinction between those who are not members of the armed forces (i.e. civilians) and those who are.³⁹ It is nevertheless acknowledged that the precise contours of the suggested presumptive loss of protection of members of the armed forces is subject to considerable controversy, especially as far as members of non-state organized armed groups are concerned. As noted, one such controversy centres around the question whether the presumptive loss of protection should be applied only to members of non-state organized armed groups who fulfil a continuous combat function. Another debate relates to the question what is required for such members to be considered to 'have laid down their arms'. We shall return to both issues below.

II. Members of armed forces who have laid down their arms

The first subgroup of persons specifically mentioned as enjoying the protection of Common 14 Article 3 are 'members of armed forces who have laid down their arms'. Common Article 3 thus confirms the existence of, and membership in, 'armed forces' in NIACs, while not distinguishing between state armed forces and non-state armed forces. Furthermore, the

---

³⁶ S. Sivakumaran, *The Law of Non-International Armed Conflict* (Oxford: OUP, 2012), at 365–7.
³⁷ DPH Guidance, at 70; on the notion of 'continuous combat function', see also ibid, at 33–6.
³⁸ Cf Art 13(3) AP II; Rule 6 ICRC CIHL Study.
³⁹ N. Melzer, 'The Principle of Distinction between Civilians and Combatants', in A. Clapham and P. Gaeta (eds), *The Oxford Handbook of International Law in Armed Conflict* (Oxford: OUP, 2014) 296, at 310: ' "[M]embers of the armed forces" are to be considered as "persons taking no active part in the hostilities" only once they have definitely disengaged or have been placed *hors de combat*. Mere suspension of combat is insufficient.'

provision is addressed to 'each Party to the conflict', thereby recognizing the existence of collective entities that face each other, at least one of which is a non-state actor. Indeed, it is the existence of these collective entities—organized armed groups—together with the intensity of the armed violence that is central in distinguishing genuine armed conflicts from mere internal disturbances, sporadic acts of violence and the like, which are beyond the reach of the laws of armed conflict.[40] What is more, Common Article 3 extends to NIACs that occur exclusively between opposing organized non-state armed groups, without the involvement of the armed forces of a state.[41] Accordingly, 'members of the armed forces' need to be understood to include members of armed forces of a state and those of an organized non-state armed group. A comparison between the wording of Common Article 3 and Article 1 AP II corroborates such a conclusion. Article 1 AP II distinguishes the 'armed forces' of a High Contracting Party (i.e. state armed forces) from 'dissident armed forces' (i.e. 'where there is a rebellion by part of the government army'[42]) and 'other organized armed groups' (i.e. 'insurgents'[43]). Such a distinction is absent from Common Article 3.

15   One of the questions that arise in the present context is how a person's membership in the armed forces is to be determined. As far as the regular armed forces of a state and those forces (police, paramilitary, etc) that are formally incorporated into the regular armed forces of a state are concerned, membership may be determined on the basis of applicable domestic laws and regulations.[44] However, the notion of 'armed forces' in Common Article 3 is not limited to 'regular armed forces'.[45] Accordingly, where no domestic laws and regulations are available, the 'armed forces' of a state or non-state party to a NIAC governed by Common Article 3 need to be identified on the basis of the function assumed by the entity in question. If an entity assumes the function of the armed forces of a party to such a NIAC, regardless of whether that party is a state or a non-state armed group, it should be regarded as an 'armed force' for the purposes of Common Article 3.[46] In a similar vein, the membership of a person in such irregular armed forces of a state party to a NIAC and in the armed forces of a non-state party to a NIAC, also needs to be determined on a functional basis. This functional test has led the ICRC to conclude that, for the purpose of the principle of distinction, only those persons who assume a continuous combat function should be considered to be members of the armed forces of non-state parties to NIACs.[47] If one were to adopt the same approach in the present context for the purpose of determining who is to be considered a member of the armed forces entitled to humane treatment because he or she has laid down his or her arms, it would mean that only those members who assume a continuous combat function are required to lay down their arms (provided they are not being placed *hors de combat*) in order for them to be entitled to the protections of Common Article 3. Persons who fulfil other functions in the armed forces (for example, medical and religious personnel, or those who assume combat functions on only an intermittent basis) would be entitled to the protections of Common Article 3 unless they take an active part in the hostilities. If one instead adopted an unqualified

---

[40] J.K. Kleffner, 'From "Belligerents" to "Fighters" and Civilians Directly Participating in Hostilities—On the Principle of Distinction in Non-International Armed Conflicts One Hundred Years after the Second Peace Conference', 54 *NILR* (2007) 315, at 324.
[41] Sivakumaran, above n 36, at 181 (with further references).
[42] ICRC Commentary APs, at 1351, para 4460.   [43] Ibid.   [44] DPH Guidance, at 31.
[45] Sivakumaran, above n 36, at 180; ICRC APs Commentary, para 4462.
[46] DPH Guidance, at 25, 31–5.   [47] DPH Guidance, at 33–6.

membership approach, every member—except medical and religious personnel who (are expected to) exclusively assume non-combatant functions—would have to engage in an act amounting to the 'laying down [of his or her] arms', irrespective of whether the person concerned is assuming a continuous or an intermittent combat function. The difference between such an unqualified membership approach and the continuous combat function approach would hence be, for instance, that a person who serves as a cook in the armed forces of a non-state organized armed group, but who also (at least occasionally) actively participates in the hostilities, would be required to lay down his or her arms before being entitled to the protections of Common Article 3 according to the unqualified membership approach (unless that person is placed *hors de combat*). The same person would be entitled to these protections when adopting the continuous combat function approach, unless he or she takes an active part in the hostilities.

Whether a person is to be considered to have ceased to be a member of the armed forces has to be approached in the same way as the question whether a person is a member. In other words, as far as members of the regular armed forces of a state party to a NIAC are concerned, the matter may be determined on a formal basis, namely the applicable domestic laws and regulations. As far as irregular armed forces of both state and non-state parties to a NIAC are concerned, the end of a person's membership has to be determined by drawing on functional criteria. Accordingly, a person is to be considered to have ceased to be a member of such armed forces if and when that person can reliably be determined to have ceased to assume the function of a member of the armed forces. Such determination is inherently contextual, but it has been pointed out that **16**

[d]isengagement from an organized armed group need not be openly declared; it can also be expressed through conclusive behaviour, such as a lasting physical distancing from the group and reintegration into civilian life or the permanent resumption of an exclusively non-combat function (e.g., political or administrative activities).[48]

While the wording of Common Article 3 is open to different constructions, it is understood that the laying down of arms by an individual member triggers his or her protection. It is not necessary for the armed force as a whole to have done so.[49] In the legal sense, the 'laying down of arms' means that the person concerned is surrendering to the enemy armed forces. However, the process of surrendering is not effectuated by the mere act of laying down arms, for example, putting one's weapon on the ground while loading a truck. Rather, in order to be protected by Common Article 3, the person concerned must clearly express an intention to surrender.[50] Common expressions that indicate such an intention are the waving of a white flag, or placing one's hands on one's head. Nevertheless, the law does not prescribe precise modalities for expressing such an intention, and much will depend on the context in which the surrender is taking place. In air warfare, for instance, waggling the aircraft's wings while opening the cockpit, and in sea warfare ceasing fire and lowering the flag, may constitute a way to express an intent to surrender. When such an intention has been expressed and the person concerned has ceased to engage in hostile acts, the protection of Common Article 3 starts to apply. That protection continues after the process of surrendering is completed and the person concerned finds himself or herself in the hands of the opposing armed force. However, by that point, the person concerned has **17**

---

[48] DPH Guidance, at 72.   [49] Pictet Commentary GC I, at 53.
[50] Cf Rule 47(c) ICRC CIHL Study.

transitioned from being a member of the armed force who has laid down his or her arms, to being a member placed *hors de combat* (see section B.III of this chapter). The wording of Common Article 3 suggests that 'members of armed forces who have laid down their arms' are distinct from 'those placed *hors de combat* by sickness, wounds, detention, or any other cause'. This is in contrast to AP I and customary IHL, which include persons who clearly express an intention to surrender within the category of persons *hors de combat*.[51] However, that distinction is immaterial as far as the protection of Common Article 3 is concerned, because the prohibitions of the enumerated acts pertain to both categories of persons. It is nevertheless worth noting that for factual reasons, some of the prohibitions, in particular mutilation, cruel treatment and torture, the taking of hostages, and the due process requirements flowing from Common Article 3 paragraph 1(1)(d), presuppose that the person concerned is in the hands of the adverse party.

18   The protection of members of the armed forces who are surrendering is intrinsically linked to the prohibited method of warfare to order that there shall be no survivors, as stipulated in conventional and customary IHL, and applicable in IACs and NIACs.[52] It would be incompatible with the general idea that members of armed forces who have laid down their arms are entitled to protection, if the parties to an armed conflict or individual commanders were allowed to exclude categorically any possibility for members of opposing armed forces to surrender. Conversely, the protection of the institution of surrender is reinforced by a number of rules that prohibit certain forms of deception. These rules include the prohibition of making improper use of the white flag,[53] and of killing, injuring, or capturing an adversary by resort to perfidy.[54]

III. Those placed *hors de combat* by sickness, wounds, detention, or any other cause

19   The second subgroup of persons who are explicitly identified as enjoying the protection of Common Article 3 are 'those placed *hors de combat* by sickness, wounds, detention or any other cause'. The wording of Common Article 3 paragraph 1(1) is somewhat ambiguous as to whether 'those placed *hors de combat*' are to be understood to constitute a subcategory of 'members of the armed forces' or of all persons taking no active part in the hostilities, thus including civilians 'placed *hors de combat*'. The question arises whether the relevant parts of the provision are to be construed effectively to read '[p]ersons taking no active part in the hostilities, including […] those placed *hors de combat*', or rather 'including members of the armed forces […] placed *hors de combat*'. The provision in French in the other authentic language version is also unclear when it refers to 'les personnes qui ont été mises hors de combat', which could mean to reference back to 'personnes qui ne participent pas directement aux hostilités' as the umbrella category of persons who enjoy the protection of Common Article 3. Indeed, in the French version, such an interpretation would find support in the way the two specifically mentioned subcategories of 'personnes qui ne participent pas directement aux hostilités' are identified, namely as 'les membres de forces armées qui ont déposé les armes et les personnes qui ont été mises hors de combat'. The distinction between 'les membres de forces armées' and 'les personnes' could be understood to mean that the latter constitute a category that is separate from members of the armed

---

[51] Cf Art 41(2) AP I; Rule 47 ICRC CIHL Study, at 167–8.
[52] Cf Art 40 AP I, Art 4 AP II, Rule 46 ICRC CIHL Study.   [53] Cf Rule 58 ICRC CIHL Study.
[54] Cf Rule 65 ICRC CIHL Study.

forces, rather than being a subcategory of such members. The English and the French wording of Common Article 3 is more ambiguous in that respect than subsequent rules that pertain to the protection of persons *hors de combat*. These other rules include Article 41 AP I, which is concerned with the safeguard of 'an enemy' *hors de combat* (Article 40 AP I). The deliberate choice of the drafters of the provision to include the word 'enemy' rather than 'member of the armed forces' or 'combatant', supports the view expressed in the ICRC Commentary that the notion of 'enemy' is distinct from 'members of the armed forces'. According to that view, Article 41 AP I 'protects both regular combatants and those combatants who are considered to be irregular, both those whose status seems unclear *and ordinary civilians*'.[55] This would seem to contrast with Rule 87 of the ICRC CIHL Study, which distinguishes between civilians, on the one hand, and persons *hors de combat*, on the other hand, when specifying the entitlement to humane treatment. Such a distinction indicates that persons *hors de combat* are presumed to be members of the armed forces, not civilians.

The wording in Common Article 3, 'placed *hors de combat*', which literally translates as 'placed out of combat', presupposes that those to whom reference is made were involved in combat prior to becoming sick, wounded, being detained, etc. It is the fact that persons who posed a military threat have ceased to do so because they are incapacitated, which is the central consideration underlying the protection of those placed *hors de combat*. Persons who constitute such a threat may be members of armed forces, but may also be those who are not members of armed forces (i.e. civilians) who were actively participating in the hostilities. It is therefore submitted that it would better conform to the underlying idea of being 'placed *hors de combat*' if Common Article 3 were to be construed to encompass all those persons who were, but are *no longer*, taking an active part in the hostilities due to the above-mentioned reasons (sickness, being wounded or detained, etc).[56] While such a construction would thus exclude civilians who neither are nor were actively participating in hostilities from the notion of those who are considered *hors de combat*, those civilians do, of course, remain under the protection of Common Article 3 because they squarely fall into the broad, overarching category of persons taking no active part in the hostilities. The important conclusion from the foregoing analysis is, however, that the notion of 'those *hors de combat*' includes civilians who directly participated in hostilities. While that conclusion does not add to or diminish the protection to which all persons taking no active part in the hostilities are entitled under Common Article 3—including civilians who did so participate, but have ceased to do so—it serves to clarify the concept of 'being *hors de combat*', not least in the light of the differences in the meaning of the notion expressed in Rule 87 of the CIHL Study.

Common Article 3 does not further define the causes of being placed *hors de combat* by 'sickness, wounds, detention or any other cause'. However, as far as 'sickness' and 'wounds' are concerned, the interpretation of these notions is informed by other relevant rules of the law of armed conflict provided they are applicable between the parties[57], most pertinently CIL as evidenced by Rule 47 of the CIHL Study. The latter provision specifies that one way in which a person is to be considered *hors de combat* is if he or she 'is defenceless because of

---

[55] ICRC Commentary APs, at 483, para 1606 (emphasis added).
[56] See, in a similar vein, HPCR, *Manual on International Law Applicable to Air and Missile Warfare Commentary* (2010), at 95, para 4.
[57] Cf Art 31(3)(c) VCLT.

unconsciousness, shipwreck, wounds or sickness'. An interpretation of Common Article 3 in the light of CIL suggests that it is not enough to be wounded or sick for a person to be considered *hors de combat*. Rather, in order to enjoy the protection of Common Article 3, it is further required that the sickness or wound(s) (i.e. trauma, disease, or other physical or mental disorder or disability)[58] renders him or her defenceless.

22   'Detention', in turn, should be understood broadly to encompass any deprivation of physical liberty of a person. The duration of the deprivation of physical liberty is immaterial. The apprehension of a person, however short, or his or her confinement to a detention centre or internment camp are clear-cut examples. Whether other limitations placed upon the freedom of movement of a person amount to the actual deprivation of physical liberty depends on their degree and intensity. Whether restricting the freedom of movement of a person reaches the required threshold depends on certain criteria, including the type, effects, and manner of implementation of the measure in question.[59] At the same time, the concept of 'detention' as a ground for a person to be placed *hors de combat* in Common Article 3 does not seem to be as wide as the concept of 'being in the power of the adverse Party' in Article 41(2)(a) AP I, if one considers that this latter provision has been interpreted to also cover cases in which the person concerned is at the mercy of a party to the armed conflict 'by means of overwhelming superior firing power to the point where they can force the adversary to cease combat' and a formal surrender is impossible.[60]

23   The residual ground for being placed *hors de combat* by 'any other cause' might nevertheless arguably cover the last-mentioned situation. In fact, the open-ended nature of Common Article 3 contrasts starkly with the exhaustive definition of what it means to be *hors de combat* in Article 41(2) AP I. Notwithstanding the resulting flexibility in Common Article 3, it is not immediately obvious what causes lead to a person being placed *hors de combat* other than those examined above.

24   Common Article 3 does not include further detail on the conditions for granting protection to persons *hors de combat*. However, such protection does not apply, or ceases to apply, if a wounded or sick or detained person engages in hostile acts or attempts to escape. As far as wounded and sick persons are concerned, this would already be the consequence of such persons manifestly not being defenceless, as is required for a wounded or sick person to be considered *hors de combat*.[61] However, beyond the specific requirement of defencelessness that pertains to wounded and sick persons, the notion of being *hors de combat* is subject to the general condition that the person concerned abstains from any hostile act and does not attempt to escape. Such an understanding is confirmed by customary IHL, as evidenced by Rule 47 of the CIHL Study. Hostile acts certainly include the firing of weapons, an attempt to communicate with one's own side, the destruction of installations in one's own possession or of one's own military equipment,[62] and other acts that do amount to active participation in the hostilities (see MN 9–11). As far as attempts to escape are concerned, there may be clear-cut instances, for example, if a detainee is running away after having broken through the parameters of a detention camp, or if he or she breaks loose and runs away from the military unit that has detained him or her. However,

---

[58] The definitions of the notions of being 'wounded' and 'sick' in Art 8(a) AP I are applicable in NIAC too: see Sivakumaran, above n 36, at 274 (with further references).
[59] ECtHR, *Guzzardi v Italy*, Judgment, 6 November 1980, para 92.
[60] Cf ICRC Commentary APs, at 484, para 1612.   [61] See MN 21.
[62] Cf ICRC Commentary APs, at 488, para 1622.

due to the serious consequences of such attempts (the loss of protection as a person *hors de combat*), it stands to reason that only those acts should be treated as attempts to escape that have, on the basis of the information that would be reasonably available at the time, at least some prospect of being successful. In other words, if a person *hors de combat* engages in an act that is manifestly bound to be futile in the quest to escape, such act should not be treated as an attempt to escape which leads to the loss of protection as a person *hors de combat* under Common Article 3. An example would be a seriously wounded person who slowly crawls away, abstains from hostile acts, and can be apprehended without exposing one's own forces to any increased risk.

IV. The wounded, sick, and shipwrecked

Paragraph 1(2) of Article 3 of Geneva Conventions I, III, and IV identifies the 'wounded   25
and sick' as a separate group of beneficiaries, and stipulates the obligation of parties to NIACs to collect and care for them. Only Article 3 of GC II adds the 'shipwrecked'. Hereafter, only the obligations towards the wounded and sick will be discussed (for the shipwrecked, see Chapter 38, in particular section C). The two notions of 'wounded' and 'sick' have an identical meaning to those found in the law of IACs (see further Chapter 37 of this volume). Thus, they encompass all those who are in need of medical assistance or care because of trauma, disease, or other physical or mental disorder or disability, provided that they refrain from any act of hostility.[63] Accordingly, the abstention from acts of hostility is a constitutive element of the status of being 'wounded' or 'sick' in the sense of Common Article 3 paragraph 1(2) as much as it is in the law of IACs.[64] The definition in the law of IAC (Article 8(a) AP I) also extends to persons who are neither 'sick' nor 'wounded' in the ordinary meaning of these words, but who are in need of immediate medical assistance or care, such as new-born babies and expectant mothers. Although this express specification is absent from the law of NIAC, it stands to reason to interpret the notions of 'wounded' and 'sick' uniformly and equally broadly in the law of NIAC[65] during which Common Article 3 paragraph 1(2) applies. The two notions of 'wounded' and 'sick' in Common Article 3 paragraph 1(2) are therefore significantly broader than the notion of 'those placed *hors de combat* by sickness [and] wounds' in Common Article 3 paragraph 1(1). As previously mentioned, the latter notion is limited to those who were, but are *no longer*, taking an active part in the hostilities. In contrast, the notions of 'wounded' and 'sick' in Common Article 3 paragraph 1(2) also extend to those who neither were nor are taking an active part in the hostilities, whether civilians or members of the armed forces of a party to the conflict.

Whereas the prohibitions in Common Article 3 paragraph 1(1), first and foremost,   26
impose negative obligations of result, such as abstaining from violence to life, from the taking of hostages, and from outrages upon personal dignity, subparagraph (2) imposes positive obligations of conduct: the collection of and care for the wounded and sick. This obligation differs from the conventional law of IAC and AP II in as much as these impose an obligation to 'respect' and 'protect' the wounded, sick, and shipwrecked.[66] While 'to respect' is understood to refer to the negative obligation to abstain from hostile acts and

---

[63] Cf Art 8 AP I.
[64] J.K. Kleffner, 'Protection of the Wounded, Sick and Shipwrecked', in Fleck (ed), above n 1, 321 at 324–5.
[65] In this vein, ICRC Commentary APs, at 1408–9, paras 4636–9.
[66] Cf Art 12 GC I and GC II; Art 10 AP I; Art 7(1) AP II.

to spare the wounded, sick, and shipwrecked, 'to protect' means 'to come to someone's defence, to lend help and support', and implies

> taking measures to remove the wounded, sick and shipwrecked, if possible, from the scene of combat and shelter them, and to ensure that they are effectively respected, i.e., that no one takes advantage of their weakness in order to mistreat them, steal their belongings, or harm them in any other way.[67]

Thus understood, it is clear that the obligations to collect and care for the wounded and sick are undoubtedly part and parcel of the obligation to protect them, but the former does not exhaust the latter obligation. Rather, collection and care constitute only specific aspects of the protection. In other words, the obligation to collect and care for the wounded and sick in Common Article 3 paragraph 1(2) is narrower than the obligation under GC I and GC II, AP I and AP II to respect and protect the wounded, sick, and shipwrecked.[68] It has been suggested, for instance, that the obligation to collect in Common Article 3 paragraph 1(2) implies neither an obligation to *search* for the wounded, sick, and shipwrecked, nor an obligation to *evacuate* them, as provided for in other pertinent rules of the law of armed conflict.[69]

V. Impartial humanitarian bodies

27 According to paragraph 2 of Common Article 3, impartial humanitarian bodies, such as the ICRC, may offer their services to the parties to the conflict. That provision makes such humanitarian bodies the beneficiaries of a right of initiative. See, for further discussion, Chapter 24 of this volume.

C. Legal Consequences of a Violation

28 As far as legal consequences of a violation of the rules in Common Article 3 pertaining to the protection of the aforementioned beneficiaries are concerned, reference is made to the relevant section of Chapters 20, 22–4 and 25, MN 36, of this volume.

D. Critical Assessment

29 Due to its broad reference to persons taking no active part in the hostilities, and because of the open-ended nature of the concept of persons *hors de combat*, Common Article 3 paragraph 1(1) captures the essence of humanitarian protection during armed conflicts. Indeed, it is hard to contemplate a situation in which a person who on a normative level should be entitled to the protections under Common Article 3 paragraph 1(1) would be deprived of such protections as a matter of law. At the same time, subsequent developments in conventional and customary IHL, applicable in NIACs, bear witness to the fact that Common Article 3 constitutes the beginning rather than the last word, not

---

[67] ICRC Commentary APs, at 1408, para 4635.
[68] On the underlying reason for drafting CA 3 in this narrower way, see Pictet Commentary GC I, at 57.
[69] J.P. Benoit, 'Mistreatment of the Wounded, Sick and Shipwrecked by the ICRC Study on Customary International Humanitarian Law', 11 *YIHL* (2008) 175, at 199–203, who posits that the ICRC fails convincingly to show the customary nature of Rule 109, thereby suggesting the obligation to search for and to evacuate the wounded and sick cannot be deduced from CA 3. But see Sivakumaran, above n 36, at 277.

only concerning the substance of relevant prohibitions that govern the conduct of parties to a NIAC, but also concerning the categories of beneficiaries. While in no way does that diminish the central importance of Common Article 3 as the base-line of the law of NIACs, it underlines its inherent limitations. One such limitation is the silence in Common Article 3 about medical and religious personnel. They certainly do enjoy the protection from the acts enumerated in Common Article 3 paragraph 1(1), but nothing in Common Article 3 pertains to the important aspect of their being enabled to perform their duties, a gap that has been filled by AP II (Article 9) and customary IHL (Rules 25–7 of the ICRC CIHL Study). In a similar vein, Article 7 AP II and customary IHL (Rules 109–11 of the ICRC CIHL Study) impose upon parties to an armed conflict obligations pertaining to the shipwrecked that go well beyond the obligations stipulated in Common Article 3 paragraph 1(1) GC II. Last but not least, the law of NIACs has also evolved beyond Common Article 3 to take account of the specific needs of certain categories of persons, such as persons deprived of their liberty,[70] women,[71] children,[72] the elderly, disabled, and infirm,[73] displaced,[74] and missing persons,[75] humanitarian relief personnel,[76] personnel involved in a peacekeeping mission who are entitled to the protection given to civilians under IHL,[77] and journalists.[78]

JANN K. KLEFFNER

---

[70] Arts 5–6 AP II; Rules 118–23, 124 (B), 125–7, and 128(C) ICRC CIHL Study.
[71] See, e.g., Arts 5(2)(a) and 6(4) AP II; Rule 134 ICRC CIHL Study.
[72] See, e.g., Arts 4(3) and 6(4) AP II; Art 38 CRC; Rules 135–7 ICRC CIHL Study.
[73] See, e.g., Rule 138 ICRC CIHL Study.
[74] See, e.g., Art 17 AP II; Rules 129 (B) and 131–3 ICRC CIHL Study.
[75] See, e.g., Rule 117 ICRC CIHL Study.
[76] See, e.g., Art 18(2) AP II; Rule 56 ICRC CIHL Study.   [77] Cf Rule 33 ICRC CIHL Study.
[78] Cf Rule 34 ICRC CIHL Study.

Chapter 22. Murder in Common Article 3

	MN
A. Introduction	1
B. Meaning and Application	5
I. Protected persons and circumstances of protection	5
a. Members of the armed forces *hors de combat*	6
b. Civilians taking no active part in hostilities	7
II. Requirement for an intent to kill a person protected by Common Article 3	13
a. Intent to kill	14
b. Intent to kill a person protected	23
III. Murder by act or omission	27
IV. Proof of death and unidentified victims	29
V. Murder and summary execution	31
C. Legal Consequences of a Violation: Murder, Arbitrary Deprivation of Life, and Human Rights Law	36
D. Critical Assessment	41

Select Bibliography

Akhavan, P., 'Reconciling Crimes against Humanity with the Laws of War', 6 *JICJ* (2008) 21

Badar, M.E., 'Rethinking *Mens Rea* in the Jurisprudence of the International Criminal Tribunals for the Former Yugoslavia and Rwanda', in O. Olusanya (ed), *Rethinking International Criminal Law* (Amsterdam: Europa Law Publishing, 2007) 13

Cassese, A., *International Criminal Law* (2nd edn, Oxford: OUP, 2008)

Cumes, G., 'Murder as a Crime against Humanity in International Law: Choice of Law and Prosecution of Murder in East Timor', 11 *European Journal of Crime, Criminal Law & Criminal Justice* (2003) 40

Dörmann, K., *Elements of War Crimes under the Rome Statute of the International Criminal Court: Sources and Commentary* (Cambridge: CUP, 2003)

Eboe-Osuji, C., 'Murder as a Crime against Humanity at the Ad Hoc Tribunals: Reconciling Different Languages', 43 *CanYIL* (2005) 145

Melzer, N., *Targeted Killing in International Law* (Oxford: OUP, 2008)

A. Introduction

Common Article 3 paragraph 1(1)(a) prohibits 'violence to life and person, in particular murder of all kinds'.[1] Murder is recognized as a fundamental violation of the laws and customs of war, is prohibited at customary international law, and is a clearly established underlying offence for war crimes.[2] At its core, Common Article 3 murder prohibits intentional,

---

[1] The French text reads, 'les atteintes portées à la vie et à l'intégrité corporelle, notamment le meurtre sous toutes ses formes'.

[2] *Trial of Susuki Motosuke*, Netherlands Temporary Court-Martial, Amboina, 1948, UNWCC Law Reports, vol XIII, at 129 (the Notes on the Case state: 'Murder is one of the offences which have long been

unjustified killings of those not actively participating in armed conflict, including civilians and members of the armed forces *hors de combat*. It outlaws those acts which 'world public opinion finds particularly revolting',[3] and constitutes explicit legal recognition of the international community's desire to prevent and punish acts considered to violate basic humanitarian principles.[4]

2   Murder and related unlawful killing offences in armed conflict have been prohibited in numerous treaties,[5] statutes of international criminal tribunals and courts,[6] domestic legislation on war crimes, and military codes and manuals.[7] Such offences have been charged and prosecuted in a wide range of fora, including national military tribunals; the post-Second World War tribunals set up by numerous countries; and in the international criminal tribunals and courts, including the International Criminal Court (ICC).[8] Violations against life committed during war are routinely condemned by states

---

recognised as a criminal violation of the laws and customs of war ever since these violations were defined.'); *Trial of Franz Holstein and Twenty-Three Others*, Permanent Military Tribunal, Dijon, 1947, UNWCC Law Reports, vol VIII, at 27 (murder 'has had a long recognition in the laws and customs of war'); *United States of America v Otto Ohlendorf et al (Einsatzgruppen Case)*, 10 April 1948, at 459 ('Without exception these rules [of war] universally condemn wanton killing of noncombatants. In the main, the defendants in this case are charged with murder. Certainly no one can claim with the slightest pretense at reasoning that there is any taint of *ex post factoism* in the law of murder. [...] [I]t cannot be said that prior to Control Council Law No 10, there existed no law against murder. The killing of a human being has always been a potential crime which called for explanation. The person standing with drawn dagger over a fresh corpse must, by the very nature of justice, exonerate himself.'); ICTY, *The Prosecutor v Zejnil Delalić et al ('Čelebići Case')*, Appeals Chamber Judgment, IT-96-21-A, 20 February 2001, para 143 (the principles in CA 3 had 'already become customary law at the time of the adoption of the Geneva Conventions'); Colombia, Constitutional Court (Plenary Chamber), *Constitutional Case No C-291/07*, Judgment of 25 April 2007, at 112 (describing the prohibition against murder in CA 3 as a *jus cogens* norm and 'one of the first guarantees under international humanitarian law'). See also Lieber Code, Arts 23, 47, 71, 148; Commission on the Responsibility of the Authors of the War and on Enforcement of Penalties, Report Presented to the Preliminary Peace Conference, 29 March 1919, at 113 (listing '[m]urders and massacres' as among the 'cruel practices' and 'barbarism' committed by Germany and its allies during the First World War in violation of the rights of civilians and combatants).

[3] Pictet Commentary GC I, at 53–54.

[4] See, e.g., Final Record, vol II-A, at 184, 645, 647; vol II-B, at 331–5, 337, 355–6, 375–7, 387; Pictet Commentary GC IV, at 34, 36.

[5] IMT Charter, Art 6(b) ('murder' of the civilian population and of prisoners of war as a violation of the laws or customs of war); Control Council Law No 10, Punishment of Persons Guilty of War Crimes, Crimes against Peace and against Humanity, 20 December 1945, Art II(1)(b); Art 50 GC I; Art 51 GC II; Art 130 GC III; Art 147 GC IV; Art 75(2)(a)(i) AP I; Art 4(2)(a) AP II.

[6] Art 4 ICTR Statute; Art 3(a) SCSL Statute; Art 8(2)(c)(i) ICC Statute. 'Murder' is not specifically listed as a war crime in the ICTY Statute, but the ICTY has held that Art 3 of its Statute includes CA 3 violations: ICTY, *The Prosecutor v Milorad Krnojelac*, Trial Chamber Judgment, IT-97-25-T, 15 March 2002, para 52.

[7] See, e.g., Australia, *The Manual of the Law of Armed Conflict* (2006), §9.46; Belarus, Criminal Code (1999), Art 135(3); Cameroon, *Règlement de discipline générale dans les Forces de defense* (2007), Art 32; Colombia, *Derecho Internacional Humanitario—Manual Básico paras las Personerías y las Fuerez Armadas de Colombia* (1995), at 42; Germany, Law Introducing the International Crimes Code (2002), Art 1, §8(1)(1); Kenya, Law of Armed Conflict, Military Basic Course, at 5; Netherlands, *Toepassing Humanitair Oorlogsrecht* (1993), at XI1–XI4; Republic of Korea, *ICC Act* (2007), Art 10(1); Russian Federation, Regulations on the Application of the Rules of International Humanitarian Law by the Armed Forces of the Russian Federation (2001), §81; UK, *The Manual of the Law of Armed Conflict* (2004), §15.4; Yemen, Military Criminal Code (1998), Art 21(1).

[8] The relevant jurisprudence is discussed in detail below (section B). 'Murder' has been one of the most common charges in war crimes jurisprudence. See, e.g., US Army, Office of the Judge Advocate, European Command, War Crimes Branch, *Statistical Report on War Crimes Activities*, 20 June 1948 (recording 578 accused tried for murder).

and civil society,[9] and are reported by United Nations (UN) country missions, Special Rapporteurs, and international commissions of inquiry.[10]

Yet, curiously, the prohibition against 'murder' is only minimally explored in the literature and commentary on Common Article 3 specifically, and in humanitarian law or international criminal law generally.[11] Murder has often been assumed to be so self-evident as to need little explanation: its constituent elements have been little discussed during treaty drafting, and it frequently receives only limited and perfunctory exposition in the relevant jurisprudence.[12] However, and while numerous forms of killings fall clearly within the core of 'murder', the scope of the prohibition is not always readily apparent. In addition, murder in Common Article 3 overlaps with other international legal prohibitions against unlawful killing, and it is important to consider how or whether to distinguish murder. A range of different terms have been used across treaties and jurisprudence to describe killings prohibited by international law.[13] Many of the terms have distinct histories, connotations, or spheres of application. Some have now been intentionally harmonized, such as murder as a war crime and murder as a crime against humanity, as well as murder in non-international armed conflict (NIAC) and 'wilful killing' in international armed conflict (IAC).[14] Others describe killing prohibitions which share similar characteristics with murder but which have been split into separate offences (summary execution), or which may apply in domains that are distinct (killings prohibited by conduct of hostilities rules) or overlapping (killings prohibited by human rights law).

---

[9] See, e.g., UNSC Res 1296, S/RES/1296 (2000); UNSC Res 1894, S/RES/1894 (2009).

[10] See, e.g., Special Rapporteur on extrajudicial, summary, or arbitrary executions, *Mission to Afghanistan*, A/HRC/11/2/Add.4, 6 May 2009; *Mission to the Central African Republic*, A/HRC/11/2/Add.3, 27 May 2009; *Mission to the Democratic Republic of the Congo*, A/HRC/14/24/Add.3, 1 June 2010; and see UN reports cited below nn 16, 30, 35, 39, 40, 47, 87, and 92.

[11] *Report of the International Law Commission on the Work of its Forty-eighth Session*, 'Art 18 Crimes against Humanity, Commentary', A/51/10/11, 1996, para 7 ('Murder is a crime that is clearly understood and well defined in the national law of every State. This prohibited act does not require any further explanation.'). This has, accurately, been described as a 'misconception': L.J. van den Herik, *The Contribution of the Rwanda Tribunal to the Development of International Law* (Leiden: Martinus Nijhoff, 2005), at 180. The Pictet Commentaries also do not further define or explain 'violence to life' or 'murder', except to state generally that subparagraph (a) sets out 'absolute prohibitions', in 'definite wording' without any 'possible loophole [...] no excuse, no attenuating circumstances', and that the language was left intentionally general so as to be 'flexible' and not unnecessarily 'restrictive': Pictet Commentary GC I, at 53–54.

[12] During the drafting of the GCs, murder was often mentioned, but not explained in any depth. See Final Record, vol II-A, at 191 ('murdered' is 'self-explanatory'), and references cited above n 4. Longer references to murder during the debates include: vol II-B, at 329 (the representative of Burma, stating that CA 3 contained 'the most obvious rules of the Convention' and reading aloud the prohibition of murder 'of all kinds', added, parenthetically, 'I do not know how many kinds of murder there are'), at 427 (the representative of Bulgaria, discussing murder in another context, gives as a clear example a case in which a husband 'draws his revolver and shoots' a soldier who insulted his wife), at 429 (the representative of Canada gives as an obvious example of a '[brutal murder] in cold blood' a 'shot in the back—for no reason at all'); K. Dörmann, *Elements of War Crimes under the Rome Statute of the International Criminal Court: Sources and Commentary* (Cambridge: CUP, 2003), at 38 (the elements of wilful killing 'did not provoke long discussions' in the ICC Preparatory Committee); ICTY, *The Prosecutor v Zoran Kupreškić et al*, Trial Chamber Judgment, IT-95-16-T, 14 January 2000, para 560 (the elements of murder are 'well known').

[13] Including: violence to life, killing in violation of the laws and customs of war, murder (*meurte*), manslaughter, wilful killing, premeditated killing (*assassinat*), unlawful killing, summary execution, execution without due process, extrajudicial execution, arbitrary killing, mass killing, massacre, felonious killing, deliberate killing of civilians, killing with malice aforethought, murder as a crime against humanity, unlawful attacks on civilians, arbitrary deprivation of life.

[14] See MN 19–22.

4   This chapter provides commentary on the application of the prohibition against murder in Common Article 3, explains the elements of this offence, and compares 'murder' to other prohibitions against killing in international humanitarian law (IHL), international criminal law, and human rights law.

B. Meaning and Application

I. Protected persons and circumstances of protection

5   Under the terms of Common Article 3, persons not actively participating in hostilities, including members of the armed forces who have laid down their arms and persons who have been placed *hors de combat* by sickness, wounds, detention, or any other cause, are protected by the prohibition against murder. There is no legal concept of murder in relation to those actively participating in hostilities.[15]

a. *Members of the armed forces* hors de combat

6   Violations of the prohibition against murdering members of the armed forces who are *hors de combat* have been widely prosecuted and condemned.[16] In cases which turned on whether the individuals were in fact *hors de combat* at the time of the killing, courts have found that if the accused had reasonable grounds for believing that they were not, then the killing would not be a murder.[17]

b. *Civilians taking no active part in hostilities*

7   Civilians often bear the brunt of violence in armed conflict, and are frequently caught between and targeted by the warring parties. Common Article 3, on its face, prohibits *all* violence to life and murders of 'persons' not actively participating in hostilities, 'at any time and in any place whatsoever'. While the term 'civilian' does not appear in Common Article 3, it is used here to describe and distinguish those who are protected by Common Article 3 but are not members of armed forces or armed groups.

8   Active participation, not defined in Common Article 3, and now generally referred to as 'direct participation',[18] has in recent years been the subject of extensive commentary

---

[15] See, e.g., SCSL, *The Prosecutor v Issa Hassan Sesay et al*, Trial Chamber Judgment, SCSL-04-15-T, 2 March 2009, para 1108 (the deceased were not civilians and thus their killing was not a war crime). The permissibility of killing fighters is not often stated explicitly in national laws or treaties prohibiting murder, but for an example of a law that does so state, see Cote d'Ivoire, Ministry of Defence, *Droit de la guerre, Manuel d'instruction, Livre IV* (November 2007), at 50: 'Murder is prohibited. However, it is not prohibited to kill an enemy during combat.'

[16] E.g., *United States v Hatley*, US Army Court of Criminal Appeals, 30 June 2011 (US soldier convicted of premeditated murder for involvement in the killing of detainees in Iraq, when he shot each of them 'point blank in the back of the head'); ICTY, *The Prosecutor v Fatmir Limaj et al*, Trial Chamber Judgment, IT-03-66-T, 20 November 2005; *Report of the Secretary-General's Panel of Experts on Accountability in Sri Lanka*, 31 March 2011, para 193 ('*Sri Lanka Report*') (killings by the Sri Lankan Army of unarmed and detained fighters).

[17] E.g. *Trial of Karl Amberger (The Dreierwalde Case)*, British Military Court, Wuppertal, 1946, UNWCC Law Reports vol I, at 82–87. The court did not accept the accused's argument that the prisoners were trying to escape, and he was found guilty of committing a war crime. The Notes on the Case state that a prisoner would lose protection 'on the rise of any set of circumstances which caused his captors reasonably to believe that he was attempting to escape […] [I]t is not enough for the captor to have a merely subjective fear that an attempt to escape is being made […].'

[18] ICTR, *The Prosecutor v Jean-Paul Akayesu*, Trial Chamber Judgment, ICTR-96-4-T, 2 September 1998, para 629.

and debate.¹⁹ In its detailed 2009 study, the International Committee of the Red Cross (ICRC) defines direct participation as having three 'cumulative criteria': the act must (i) meet a required threshold of harm to the enemy's military operations or capacity, or to protected persons or objects; (ii) have a direct causal link to the harm; and (iii) have the requisite belligerent nexus.²⁰ Civilians not engaging in such acts are protected, and killing them could constitute murder.

Common Article 3's terms of protection against killing civilians appear broad and do not provide explicit guidance as to whether the prohibition applies to or has implications for killings committed *in the conduct of hostilities*. Common Article 3 does not, for example, specifically state that a killing of a civilian is not 'murder' if it resulted from an attack carried out in accordance with the rules for the conduct of hostilities.²¹ While such a broad reading of murder would clearly be fundamentally at odds with IHL,²² it is not immediately clear from the text specifically what scope-limiting legal principles do apply to Common Article 3 murder.²³ Could 'murder' include the intentional targeting of civilians by aerial bombardment in enemy-controlled territory, a military attack on an entirely civilian neighborhood, or the killing of civilians resulting from an intentionally disproportionate attack on a military target? 9

Two different interpretations have been advanced to resolve these questions. First, much commentary has stated or assumed that Common Article 3 does not address the conduct of hostilities but, rather, governs conduct in relation to individuals 'in the power 10

---

¹⁹ DPH Guidance. For commentary on and disagreement with the ICRC's DPH Guidance, see the collection of articles in 42 *NYU Journal of International Law and Policy* (2009–10). The Pictet Commentaries defined civilians simply as 'people who do not bear arms'. See Pictet Commentary GC IV, at 40. See Ch 21, MN 8–10, of this volume.

²⁰ DPH Guidance, at 41–64. See also M. Schmitt, 'The Interpretive Guidance on the Notion of Direct Participation in Hostilities: A Critical Analysis', 1 *Harvard National Security Journal* (2010), at 26–27 (noting that this aspect of the ICRC guidance is the subject of more widespread agreement).

²¹ The Pictet Commentaries to CA 3 do not clearly resolve this point. In the Pictet analysis of the grave breach of 'wilful killing', that prohibition's relevance to the conduct of hostilities is also unclear. See Pictet Pictet Commentary GC III, at 627 ('cases in which prisoners of war are killed as a result of acts of war—for example the bombardment of a hospital—are perhaps in a different category: the question is left open'); Pictet Commentary GC IV, at 597 (giving the example of the bombardment of a civilian hospital as a case 'more difficult to class as wilful killing', but similarly stating that the question is 'left open').

²² See, e.g., Israel, *The Public Committee against Torture in Israel v Israel*, HCJ, 769/02, 11 December 2005, para 35 (civilian deaths properly described as collateral or incidental would likely not lead to state liability); P. Akhavan, 'Reconciling Crimes against Humanity with the Laws of War', 6 *JICJ* (2008) 21, at 28 (arguing that 'if civilian deaths were incidental to a military attack that was neither indiscriminate nor disproportionate contrary to the laws of war, the constituent elements of "murder" would not be satisfied'); M. Boot, *Genocide, Crimes against Humanity, War Crimes: Nullem Crimen Sine Lege and the Subject Matter Jurisdiction of the International Criminal Court* (Antwerp: Intersentia, 2002), at 579, fn 137 (killing civilians may be a war crime, but civilian deaths 'caused by an armed attack may, however, be justified as "collateral damage" when in conformity with the principle of proportionality'); United States, *Manual for Military Commissions* (2007), 'Murder of Protected Persons' (a Comment to the offence states: 'The intent required for this offense precludes its applicability with regard to collateral damage or death, damage, or injury incident to a lawful attack'); IACtHR, *Case of the Massacres of El Mozote and Nearby Places v El Salvador,* Judgment, 25 October 2012, para 154 (referring to the lack of evidence that civilians were killed in the context of combat).

²³ See G. Abi-Saab, 'Non-International Armed Conflicts', in UNESCO, *International Dimensions of Humanitarian Law* (Dordrecht: Martinus Nijhoff Publishers, 1988) 217, at 223 ('numerous critical issues which proved to be of frequent recurrence and great practical consequence (such as […] the protection of civilian populations against indiscriminate attacks) are not, or only obliquely, addressed by [CA 3]').

of', 'in the hands of', or 'captured by' a party to an armed conflict.[24] In *Abella v Argentina*, for example, the Inter-American Commission on Human Rights stated that civilians are 'covered by Common Article 3's safeguards when they are captured by or otherwise subjected to the power of an adverse party'.[25] Zegveld argues that this limitation follows from the word 'treatment' in Common Article 3, which 'presupposes a degree of control over the person'.[26] The limitation also appears evident in some statements made during the drafting of Geneva Convention (GC) IV,[27] as well as from the kinds of cases prosecuted after the Second World War.[28] On this reading, the scope of murder (or the extent of or circumstances of protection provided to civilians) depends substantially on the threshold of control necessary for Common Article 3 to govern a killing. Murder would clearly include cases in which power was directly and physically exercised over civilians, such as killings of civilian prisoners held in concentration camps or detention centres.[29] It has also been held to include cases in which the attacking party takes physical custody or is in control—through force and proximity—of civilians during or after an operation or attack, including where civilians are rounded up and deliberately shot,[30] or where the

---

[24] ICRC Commentary APs, para 4365 (explaining that a gap in CA 3 is that it contains 'no rules on the conduct of hostilities for sparing the civilian population as such'); ICRC CIHL Study, vol I, at 299, 313–14 (the fundamental guarantees, such as the prohibition against murder, apply to civilians 'in the power of' a party); DPH Guidance, at 28, 62; G.I.A.D. Draper, 'The Geneva Conventions of 1949', 114 *RCADI* (1965-I) 59, at 84–85 (The Geneva Conventions 'adopted the solution of eschewing any direct attempt to legislate for the conduct of hostilities [...] the prohibitions relate to treatment outside of combat'); J. Pejic, 'The Protective Scope of Common Article 3: More than Meets the Eye', 93 *IRRC* 881 (2011) 189, at 203, 205–6, 219 (CA 3 protects persons in the 'power' of or 'captured', and 'deals with' the 'protection of persons in enemy hands'); N. Melzer, *Targeted Killing in International Law* (Oxford: OUP, 2008) at 216; Y. Arai-Takahashi, *The Law of Occupation: Continuity and Change of International Humanitarian Law, and its Interaction with International Human Rights Law* (Leiden: Martinus Nijhoff Publishers, 2009), at 299 (CA 3 applies to persons 'captured in armed conflict'; murder can only be committed in the law and order, rather than the hostilities, context); T. Meron, 'Application of Humanitarian Law in Non-International Armed Conflicts, Remarks', 85 *ASIL* (1991), at 84; UK Ministry of Defence, *The Manual of the Law of Armed Conflict* (Oxford: OUP, 2004), at 215. See also *Einsatzgruppen Case*, above n 2, at 111 (distinguishing civilian collateral harm in a military attack as 'entirely different, both in fact and in law, from an armed force [entering civilian homes and] dragging out the men, women and children and shooting them').

[25] IACommHR, *Abella v Argentina*, Case 11.137, Rep No 55/97, 18 November 1997, para 176.

[26] L. Zegveld, *Accountability of Armed Opposition Groups in International Law* (Cambridge: CUP, 2002), at 83–84 (arguing that only 'detention' killings are prohibited).

[27] Final Record, vol II-A, at 716–719, vol II-B, at 408.

[28] B.V.A. Röling, 'The Law of War and the National Jurisdiction since 1945', *RCADI* (1960-II), at 397–98 (noting that the cases were all about treatment, and that violations of hostilities rules were not prosecuted).

[29] See, e.g., *Trial of Wilhelm List and others (The Hostages Trial)*, US Military Tribunal, Nuremberg, 1948, UNWCC Law Reports, vol VIII (charges included the murder of individuals in concentration camps); *Trial of Josef Kramer and 44 others (The Belsen Trial)*, British Military Court, Luneburg, 1945, vol II (accused found guilty of killing as a war crime Allied military personnel and civilians in Belsen and Auschwitz concentration camps); ECCC, *Guek Eav Kaing*, Trial Chamber Judgment, 001/18-07-2007/ECCC/TC, 26 July 2010, at 431–7 (executions at S-21 prison).

[30] SCSL, *Sesay et al*, above n 15, para 1020 (14 civilians executed in a house); *Report of the Independent International Commission of Inquiry on the Syrian Arab Republic*, A/HRC/22/59, 5 February 2013, at Annex IV, para 25 ('*Syria Report*') (credible evidence indicated that 'fighting aged males were sought out for execution, in violation of common Article 3'). See also *Trial of Franz Holstein*, above n 2 (murder as a war crime was found when German forces arrested French men from their homes, and then lined them up and shot them; when German forces shot farmers working in their fields; when German forces shot residents in their homes, including those accused of being 'terrorists'); *Trial of General von Mackensen and General Maelzer*, British Military Court, Rome, 1945, UNWCC Law Reports, vol VIII (killing of 335 Italians); the Commission on the Truth for El Salvador, *From Madness to Hope: The 12-year War in El Salvador*, S/25500 (1993); SCSL, *The Prosecutor v Moinina Fofana and Allieu Kondewa*, Trial Chamber Judgment, SCSL-04-14-T, 2 August 2007, para 787 (targeting of civilians thought to be rebel 'collaborators').

attackers enter a camp for internally displaced persons (IDPs) and kill its residents.[31] And if 'in the hands of' is interpreted as it is in GC IV generally, murder could include intentional killings of civilians on territory controlled by the party, even absent direct physical custody of the individual.[32] But on this first interpretation, it would be difficult, for example, for murder to encompass the killing of civilians resulting from an aerial bombardment of enemy-controlled territory, or territory on which active hostilities were taking place, even if that attack were knowingly directed at civilians and violated the rules of precaution, distinction, or proportionality. Such killings would be governed by the rules of IHL for the conduct of hostilities, and might constitute, for example, a violation of the prohibition against intentionally directing attacks against civilians.

Secondly, and in the alternative, some commentary and jurisprudence suggests that the prohibition against violence to life in Common Article 3 not only covers killings 'in the power of', but also implies rules for the conduct of hostilities.[33] Cassese, for example, while noting that Common Article 3 'on the face of it' does not 'have any direct bearing on the actual conduct of hostilities', argues that on 'close scrutiny' it has 'some indirect regulation'.[34] For instance, he contends that a rule that civilians should not be the object of attack must follow from Common Article 3's prohibition on violence to life. Similarly, the UN Mission to El Salvador cited Common Article 3 for the rules of distinction, proportionality, and precautions in attack, and the International Commission of Inquiry on Libya cited Common Article 3 for the prohibition against intentionally targeting civilians.[35] The International Criminal Tribunal for the former Yugoslavia (ICTY) Trial Chamber appeared to classify conduct of hostility killings as murder in *Galić*[36] and *Kordić*,[37] and explicitly did so in *Strugar*.[38] These cases do not discuss whether or not a limiting principle of 'in the power of' is relevant; rather, *Strugar* framed the legal issue as one of the requisite intent to kill civilians. On this interpretation, murder could describe killings with intent to kill and which violated the rules for the conduct of hostilities. An intentional attack on civilians, even where not captured or in the power of the attacking party, might thus constitute murder. This

11

---

[31] ICC, *The Prosecutor v Joseph Kony*, Pre-Trial Chamber Warrant of Arrest, ICC-02/04-01/05, 27 September 2005 (unlawful killings of civilians during attack on Ugandan IDP camp charged as murder).

[32] Pictet Commentary GC IV, at 47 (interpreting 'in the hands of' in an 'extremely general sense'); ICTY, *The Prosecutor v Duško Tadić*, Trial Chamber Judgment, IT-94-1-T, 7 May 1997, paras 579–80, 615 (citing Pictet, interpreting 'in the hands of' in GC IV to mean in areas under effective control or occupation, and arguing that those protected by CA 3 includes 'at least' those protected in international armed conflict by GC IV's grave breaches regime). See also Final Record, vol II-B, at 407 (the representative of the US defines 'in their hands' as under occupation, or 'in control' of that state and not another, and argues that the expression is intended to 'limit' protections and to clarify that the 'conduct of military operations' are not being regulated).

[33] Cf Ch 21 of this volume.

[34] A. Cassese, 'The Geneva Conventions of 1977 on the Humanitarian Law of Armed Conflict and Customary International Law', 3 *UCLA Pacific Basin Law Journal* (1984) 55, at 107. See similarly J.E. Bond, 'Application of the Law of War to Internal Conflicts', 3 *Georgia Journal of International and Comparative Law* (1973) 345, at 348; A.P.V. Rogers, *Law on the Battlefield* (2nd edn, Manchester: Manchester University Press, 2004), at 221; W.H. Boothby, *The Law of Targeting* (Oxford: OUP, 2012), at 433.

[35] UN Observer Mission in El Salvador, A/46/876 (19 February 1992), para 131; *Report of the International Commission of Inquiry to investigate all alleged violations of international human rights law in the Libyan Arab Jamahiriya*, A/HRC/17/44 (12 January 2012), para 146 ('*Libya Commission*').

[36] ICTY, *The Prosecutor v Stanislav Galić*, Trial Chamber Judgment, ICTR-98-29-T, 5 December 2003, paras 331–45.

[37] ICTY, *The Prosecutor v Dario Kordić and Mario Čerkez*, Trial Chamber Judgment, IT-95-14/2-T, 26 February 2001, para 723.

[38] ICTY, *The Prosecutor v Pavle Strugar*, Trial Chamber Judgment, IT-01-42-T, 31 January 2005, para 240.

broader approach to Common Article 3 seems to have been adopted by a number of UN country missions and commissions of inquiry. The UN Secretary-General's Panel of Experts on Accountability in Sri Lanka included within murder the 'indiscriminate shelling' of civilians, as well as suicide attacks against civilians, 'both in and outside of the conflict zone'.[39]

12   The question of whether Common Article 3 murder can regulate killings in the conduct of hostilities—or whether intentional attacks on civilians not complying with the rules for the conduct of hostilities can be characterized as murder—is not clearly resolved. In the author's view, the weight of expert opinion and the history of the Geneva Conventions tend towards the narrower interpretation of Common Article 3 murder. Generally, the conceptually clearer approach might be to maintain a distinction between Common Article 3 murders of persons in the power of the relevant party, and unlawful killings governed by conduct of hostilities prohibitions against direct attacks on civilians, indiscriminate attacks, and so on. A recent example demonstrating conceptual clarity on this issue is the reporting of the Independent International Commission of Inquiry on the Syrian Arab Republic. The Commission clearly distinguishes between violations in the conduct of hostilities (such as indiscriminate or disproportionate attacks via aerial bombardment or shelling, as well as sniper attacks and suicide bombings) and violations of the treatment of civilians—under which the report addresses murder, a category in which the Commission included killings of civilians arrested or abducted at checkpoints or in raids on their homes.[40] This approach also has the benefit of distinctly naming and accounting for the different forms of killings committed in armed conflict. It is the case, however, that the different forms of unlawful killing may occur in close succession, or, in some instances, may be very difficult to separate in practice.[41]

II. Requirement for an intent to kill a person protected by Common Article 3

13   The element of murder most subject to judicial and scholarly discussion has been the required *mens rea*. This has been especially discussed in the context of assessing individual criminal liability, but intent is also relevant to assessing whether there has been a violation of the prohibition of murder in Common Article 3. The development and contours

---

[39] *Sri Lanka Report*, above n 16, paras 193, 206, 242 (citing ICTY, *Strugar*). See also *Libya Commission*, above n 35, para 140, fn 174 (contemplating the applicability of 'wilful killing' to airstrikes, but finding no evidence of the necessary intent); *Report of the International Commission of Inquiry on Darfur to the United Nations Secretary-General*, 25 January 2005, paras 269–83 ('*Darfur Commission*') (listing separately the violations of indiscriminate attacks on civilians from 'killings of civilians', but also using 'killing' and 'murder' interchangeably, and to describe killings following confinement, as well as attacks on villages, shelling, and indiscriminate air attacks); UN Assistance Mission in Afghanistan, *Afghanistan Annual Report on Protection of Civilians in Armed Conflict 2013* (February 2014), at xii, 24–26 (defining murder as the 'deliberate killing of civilians', and appearing to include not only cases of killings by the Taliban after abduction or other physical control, but also cases in which civilians were not in the physical control of the party); UN Assistance Mission in Afghanistan, *Afghanistan: Annual Report on Protection of Civilians in Armed Conflict 2012* (February 2013), at 22 ('*Afghanistan Report*') (detailing suicide attacks).

[40] *Report of the Independent International Commission of Inquiry on the Syrian Arab Republic*, A/HRC/25/65 (12 February 2014), paras 20–28, 85–106; *Syria Report*, above n 30, paras 49–50, and Annex, paras 31, 36 (clearly differentiating murder from making the civilian population the object of attack).

[41] See, e.g., ICC, *The Prosecutor v Bosco Ntaganda*, Pre-Trial Chamber Decision, ICC-01/04-02/06, 13 July 2012 (alleging, on the same sets of facts regarding the deliberate killing of hundreds of civilians, murder as war crime, murder as a crime against humanity, and the war crime of attacking a civilian population).

of murder in international law have been closely connected to and informed by domestic criminal law killing prohibitions.⁴²

a. Intent to kill

It is broadly accepted that premeditation is not necessary. However, there has been ambiguity about the scope or necessity of 'intention', and whether murder can be committed through—as variously formulated in numerous cases—recklessness, *dolus eventualis*, indirect intent, or knowledge (or knowledge and acceptance) of death as a near certain, probable, foreseeable, or likely result of an act or omission.

There has been dispute in the ICTY and the International Criminal Tribunal for Rwanda (ICTR) about whether premeditation was required for murder as a crime against humanity,⁴³ but premeditation is not required for Common Article 3 murder.⁴⁴ Many war crimes cases have stated explicitly that premeditation is not necessary, and, further, that the laws of war do not recognize any domestic law distinction between murder and manslaughter: both violate international law.⁴⁵

---

⁴² See, e.g., *Trial of Carl Bauer, Ernst Schrameck and Herbert Falten*, Permanent Military Tribunal, Dijon, 1945, UNWCC Law Reports, vol VIII, at 19 (equating murder under the French Penal Code with international law prohibitions on killing captured prisoners of war); *Trial of Franz Holstein*, above n 2, at 27 (murder is a war crime, 'found in the municipal law of many nations dealing with war crimes, as it emerged during or after the war 1939–45'); Final Record, vol II-A, at 647, vol II-B, at 355; *United States v John G. Schultz*, 1952 WL 2700, para 11 ('[C]ertain crimes are universally recognized as properly punishable under the law of war. These include murder, manslaughter [...] The test bringing these offenses within the common law of war has been their almost universal acceptance as crimes by the nations of the world'); ICTY, *The Prosecutor v Goran Jelisić*, Trial Chamber Judgment, IT-95-10-T, 14 December 1999, para 35 (referring to the 'legal ingredients of the offence as generally recognised in national law'); *Libya Commission*, above n 35, para 141 ('Interpretations given by the international courts to the elements of murder largely mirror those of traditional criminal law'); J.B. Keenan and B.F. Brown, *Crimes against International Law* (Washington, DC: Public Affairs, 1950), at 118 (domestic law murder and murder under international law have the same 'physical act of the unjustified taking of human life'). But see ICTY, *The Prosecutor v Zejnil Delalić*, Trial Chamber Judgment, IT-96-21-T, 16 November 1998, paras 424, 431, 437 (taking into account the *actus reus* and *mens rea* of murder in national legal systems, but warning against an approach to murder that 'confines itself to the specificities of particular national jurisdictions' which can 'lead to confusion').

⁴³ For the view that premeditation is necessary for murder as a crime against humanity, see ICTR, *The Prosecutor v Laurent Semanza*, Trial Chamber Judgment, ICTR-97-20-T, 15 May 2003, paras 335–9; ICTR, *The Prosecutor v Clément Kayishema and Obed Ruzindana*, Trial Chamber Judgment, ICTR-95-1-T, 21 May 1999, paras 137–40. For the view that customary international law never required premeditation, see ICTR, *Akayesu*, above n 18, para 588; ICTY, *The Prosecutor v Tihomir Blaškić*, Trial Chamber Judgment, IT-95-14-T, 3 March 2000, para 216; ICTY, *Kordić and Čerkez*, above n 37, para 236. For discussion, see C. Eboe-Osuji, 'Murder as a Crime against Humanity at the Ad Hoc Tribunals: Reconciling Different Languages', 43 *CanYIL* (2005) 145.

⁴⁴ ICTR, *The Prosecutor André Ntagerura et al*, Trial Chamber Judgment, ICTR-99-46-T, 25 February 2004, para 765; ICTR, *The Prosecutor v Augustin Ndindiliyimana et al*, Trial Chamber Judgment, ICTR-00-56-T, 17 May 2011, para 2143; SCSL, *The Prosecutor v Alex Tamba Brima et al*, Trial Chamber Judgment, SCSL-04-16-T, 20 June 2007, para 690; ICTR, *Semanza*, above n 43, para 373; *Libya Commission*, above n 35, para 141; *Sri Lanka Report*, above n 16, para 251.

⁴⁵ *Trial of Franz Holstein*, above n 2, at 27 (murder, 'premeditated or not', is a war crime); *Trial of Heinrich Gerike and Seven Others (The Velpke Children's Home Case)*, British Military Court, Brunswick, 1946, UNWCC Law Reports, vol VII, at 79 (Notes on the Case state that '[i]n general it is recognized that the distinction made in English Law between murder and manslaughter is not relevant in trials of war criminals'); *Trial of Kapitänleutnant Heinz Eck and four others (The Peleus Trial)*, British Military Court, Hamburg, 1945, UNWCC Law Reports, vol I, at 20 (Notes on the Case state: 'The acts committed by the accused were therefore considered to be crimes, namely war crimes, irrespective of whether in municipal jurisprudence they should correctly be classified either as murder or as manslaughter or as any other offence against life and limb.'). See also *United States v John G. Schultz*, 1952 WL 2700 (CMA), para 11 ('[C]ertain crimes are universally recognized as properly punishable under the law of war. These include murder [and] manslaughter'); *Trial of James W. Duncan*, GCMO 153, 8 June 1866 (a prison guard was charged with '[m]urder, in violation of

16   The requirement of 'intention' is more complicated. Numerous cases and commissions have explicitly excluded from murder those killings that result from negligence or gross negligence,[46] or genuine mistakes in targeting.[47] However, cases have differed with respect to whether murder is committed only where a killing is carried out with deliberate purpose or 'specific' and 'direct' intent, or whether the *mens rea* may include a lower standard, such as of recklessness, *dolus eventualis*, or indirect intent.

17   The international criminal tribunal jurisprudence often states that the murder test has been formulated with just 'slight variations in expression',[48] and that the test is settled.[49] However, some of the common formulations are ambiguous, or may only permit a recklessness or *dolus eventualis* standard where death resulted from an intention to cause serious bodily harm, but not for other acts more broadly. This is because the *mens rea* test is often separated into two clauses: (i) intent to kill and (ii) intent to cause serious bodily harm, together with—depending on the case—knowledge of the likelihood of death, acceptance that the harm would likely cause death, or with recklessness as to death.[50] On such formulations, the lower *mens rea* to kill is clearly relevant only where paired with direct intent to cause grievous physical harm.

18   Some cases have stated explicitly that intent does not include recklessness, but have allowed a 'knowledge and acceptance' test.[51] Some use recklessness or *dolus eventualis* to infer intention.[52] Others suggest that intent may include *dolus eventualis* or recklessness.[53]

the laws of war' for 'willfully, feloniously, and with malice aforethought' beating a prisoner, who subsequently died. He was found to have acted not 'with malice aforethought' and was thus found guilty not of murder but of manslaughter, 'in violation of the laws of war').

[46] See, e.g., ICTY, *The Prosecutor v Milomir Stakić*, Trial Chamber Judgment, IT-97-24-T, 21 July 2003, paras 584–7; ICTY, *The Prosecutor v Radoslav Brđanin*, Trial Chamber Judgment, IT-99-36-T, 1 September 2004, paras 386–7. See also Pictet Commentary GC I, at 372 ('mere negligence' is not covered by 'wilful killing'); ICRC Commentary APs, para 3474 (excluding 'ordinary negligence').

[47] See, e.g., *Report of the United Nations Fact-Finding Mission on the Gaza Conflict*, A/HRC/12/48, 25 September 2009, para 47 ('*Gaza Report*') (discussing an alleged Israeli strike on a house resulting in the deaths of 22 family members, and noting that 'if a mistake was indeed made, there could not be said to be a case of willful killing').

[48] ICTY, *Krnojelac*, above n 6, para 323.

[49] ICTY, *Stakić*, above n 46, para 584; ICTY, *The Prosecutor v Enver Hadžihasanović and Amir Kubura*, Trial Chamber Decision on Motions for Acquittal Pursuant to Rule 98 *Bis* of the Rules of Procedure and Evidence, IT-01-47-T, 27 September 2004, para 37 (the definition is 'widely established').

[50] See, e.g., ICTY, *The Prosecutor v Radislav Krstić*, Trial Chamber Judgment, IT-98-33-T, 2 August 2001, para 485; ICTY, *Stakić*, above n 46, para 584; ICTY, *The Prosecutor v Miroslav Kvočka et al*, Appeals Chamber Judgment, IT-98-30/1-A, 28 February 2005, para 259; ICTY, *Krnojelac*, above n 6, para 324; ICTR, *The Prosecutor v Joseph Nzabirinda*, Sentencing Judgment, 2000-77-T, 23 February 2007, para 25; ICTR, *The Prosecutor v Mikaeli Muhimana*, Trial Chamber Judgment, ICTR-95-1B-T, 28 April 2005, para 568; ICTY, *The Prosecutor v Naser Orić*, Trial Chamber Judgment, IT-03-68-T, 30 June 2006, para 346; ICTR, *Akayesu*, above n 18, para 589.

[51] ICTY, *Orić*, above n 50, at fn 1020 (agreeing with the defence submission that 'intent does not include recklessness').

[52] ICTY, *Delalić*, above n 42, para 437: '[I]t is clear that some form of intention is required. However, this intention may be inferred from the circumstances, whether one approaches the issue from the perspective of the foreseeability of death as a consequence of the acts of the accused, or the taking of an excessive risk which demonstrates recklessness.'

[53] See, e.g., ICTY, *Stakić*, above n 46, paras 584–7 (using the split clause test, but also finding that both a *dolus directus* and a *dolus eventualis* suffice, with the latter meaning, 'if the actor engages in life-endangering behavior, his killing becomes intentional if he "reconciles himself" or "makes peace" with the likelihood of death. Thus if the killing is committed with "manifest indifference to the value of human life", even conduct of minimal risk can qualify as intentional homicide'); ICTY, *Hadžihasanović and Kubura*, above n 49, para 37 (citing *Stakić*); ICTY, *Brđanin*, above n 46, paras 386–87 (holding that intent includes both *dolus directus* and *dolus eventualis*—entailing recklessness, but not negligence or gross negligence—but then concluding with the test, 'it must be established that the accused had an intention to kill or to inflict grievous bodily harm or serious injury in the reasonable knowledge that it would likely lead to death').

Still others do not use the split clause formulation, and use an arguably broader test that incorporates indirect intent, or knowledge of death as a probable consequence, in relation to any act. *Halilović*, for example, agreed with *Strugar* that it 'is now settled that the *mens rea* is not confined to cases where the accused has a direct intent to kill or to cause serious bodily harm, but also extends to cases where the accused has what is often referred to as an indirect intent'.[54]

Importantly, international tribunals and commissions have now clearly sought to harmonize murder in its different spheres of application: murder as a war crime and as a crime against humanity, as well as murder or 'wilful killing' in either IAC or NIAC.[55] This latter harmonization has particular importance for the *mens rea*, as the commentary to Article 85 of Additional Protocol (AP) I provides that 'wilfully' means 'with intent' which 'encompasses [...] "recklessness", viz, the attitude of an agent who, without being certain of a particular result, accepts the possibility of it happening'.[56]

However, the Statute of the International Criminal Court (ICC) arguably provides for a stricter *mens rea* than some of the tribunal cases.[57] Some early ICC jurisprudence, discussing the mental element necessary for crimes generally, has excluded *dolus eventualis* and recklessness,[58] which may put it at odds with the national-level crime upon which murder was originally developed.[59]

In contrast, recent international UN-mandated inquiries, including on the Sri Lanka and Gaza conflicts, have held that murder can be committed through recklessness.[60]

---

[54] ICTY, *The Prosecutor v Sefer Halilović*, ICTY, Trial Chamber Judgment, IT-01-48-T, 16 November 2005, at fn 80; ICTY, *Strugar*, above n 38, para 236: 'The following formulation appears to reflect the understanding which has gained general acceptance in the jurisprudence of the Tribunal: to prove murder, it must be established that death resulted from an act or omission of the accused, committed with the intent either to kill or, in the absence of such a specific intent, in the knowledge that death is a probable consequence of the act or omission. In respect of this formulation it should be stressed that knowledge by the accused that his act or omission might *possibly* cause death is not sufficient to establish the necessary *mens rea*. The necessary mental state exists when the accused knows that it is *probable* that his act or omission will cause death.' Also see ICTY, *The Prosecutor v Mile Mrkšić et al*, Trial Chamber Judgment, IT-95-13/1-T, 27 September 2007, para 486; ICTY, *Limaj et al*, above n 16, para 241; ECCC, *Kaing*, above n 29, para 437; Melzer, above n 24, at 149 (the test is intentional or reckless acts or omissions).

[55] ICTY, *Halilović*, above n 54, para 35, fn 80; SCSL, *Brima et al*, above n 44, para 688; SCSL, *The Prosecutor v Charles Taylor*, Trial Chamber Judgment, SCSL-03-01-T, 18 May 2012, para 412; SCSL, *Sesay et al*, above n 15, para 142; ICTY, *Orić*, above n 50, para 345; ICTY, *Brđanin*, above n 46, para 380; ICTY, *Delalić*, above n 42, para 422 ('there can be no line drawn between "wilful killing" and "murder" which affects their content'); ECCC, *Kaing*, above n 29, para 430; *Libya Commission*, above n 35, para 140; *Darfur Commission*, above n 39, para 271, fn 134; Dörmann, above n 12, at 394 (noting the views of the Preparatory Committee that 'there can be no difference' between murder and wilful killing).

[56] ICRC Commentary APs, para 3474; ICTY, *Halilović*, above n 54, para 35, fn 80 (citing the Commentary to interpret murder).

[57] Boot, above n 22, at 583. But for contrary views, see A. Cassese, *International Criminal Law* (2nd edn, Oxford: OUP, 2008), at 73; Dörmann, above n 12, at 43.

[58] ICC, *The Prosecutor v Jean-Pierre Bemba Gombo*, Pre-Trial Chamber Decision, ICC-01/05-01/08, 15 June 2009, para 369; ICC, *The Prosecutor v Thomas Lubanga Dyilo*, Trial Chamber Judgment, ICC-01/04-01/06, 14 March 2012, para 1011.

[59] See, e.g., discussion of the *mens rea* for murder in common and civil law systems in ICTY, *The Prosecutor v Tihomir Blaškić*, Appeals Chamber Judgment, IT-95-14-A, 29 July 2004, paras 34–39.

[60] *Sri Lanka Report*, above n 16, paras 206, 251 (stating that the *mens rea* 'encompasses reckless disregard for life' and reporting credible allegations of attacks on hospitals and humanitarian objects as possible murder, whether the targeting was 'direct or reckless'); *Gaza Report*, above n 47, para 1433 (referring to an incident as indicating 'an intention, or at least recklessness, to cause harm to civilians, which may amount to willful killing'). However, in the UN's Libya Inquiry, the Commission stated that it did not receive any evidence suggesting that civilian deaths caused by NATO were 'deliberate', and thus

22 In the author's view, a *mens rea* that incorporates indirect intent or recklessness better comports with the broad protection for life provided by the language of Common Article 3, domestic criminal law, and early war crimes cases. Whether or not this is used specifically for the purpose of defining the war crime of murder and in prosecutions of individuals, it should in any case be sufficient to establish a violation of Common Article 3 by a state or an armed group.

b. Intent to kill a person protected

23 The circumstances of many of the killings brought before courts or investigated by commissions—the large number of dead, the brutal manner of killing, women and child victims, the absence of combat in the vicinity—often leave little doubt that the victims were deliberately and unlawfully killed as civilians. There has generally been little need for the investigating or assessing mechanism to address in detail the relevant law in cases of doubt as to civilian status, or doubt as to the perpetrator's knowledge of civilian status or knowledge of whether or not the targeted individual was actively participating in hostilities. Yet these are crucial legal questions, particularly for asymmetrical conflicts. While an intention to kill may be readily discernible in a particular case (thus satisfying any of the above-discussed *mens rea* tests), it is the *mens rea* as to protected status that would become crucial in categorizing a killing as a murder.

24 Numerous cases have referred simply to the objective fact of a victim's protected status, and found murder on that basis;[61] others have found facts of protected status and held that the perpetrators 'were aware' of the victim's status, without clearly addressing whether the knowledge test is entirely subjective, or setting out the nature of any objective or reasonableness element.[62] A number of cases, addressing the question in more detail, have held that because protected status is an element of the offence, the prosecution 'must show that the *mens rea* of the Accused encompassed the fact that the victim was a person not taking direct part in the hostilities'.[63] The Special Court for Sierra Leone (SCSL) held in *Sesay* that the proper test was whether 'the perpetrators knew or had reason to know of the factual basis for the protection: that is, that the [victims] were not taking a direct part in hostilities at the time of the attack', and considered whether the belief in direct participation had a reasonable basis.[64] In *Halilović*, the ICTY held that the test is whether 'the perpetrator was aware or should have been aware of the fact that the victims were persons taking no active part in the hostilities'.[65]

---

it did not discuss whether the crime of wilful killing had been committed: *Libya Commission*, above n 35, at 140, fn 174.

[61] See, e.g., ICTY, *Orić*, above n 50, para 258 ('To fulfill this requirement [of killing a protected person], it is sufficient to examine the relevant facts of each victim and to ascertain whether that person was actively involved in the hostilities at the relevant time'); ICTR, *The Prosecutor v Pauline Nyiramasuhuko et al*, Trial Chamber Judgment, ICTR-98-42-T, 24 June 2011, paras 6160–2 (the Tribunal, '[c]onsidering the evidence in its totality', concluded that the victims were civilians, and did not expressly consider the accused's state of mind); ICTR, *The Prosecutor v Théoneste Bagosora et al*, Trial Chamber Judgment, ICTR-98-41-T, 18 December 2008, paras 2237–40 (examining objective criteria, and not discussing state of mind); ICTR, *Ndindiliyimana*, above n 44, paras 2139–41; ICTY, *Tadić*, above n 32, para 616.

[62] ICC, *Bemba Gombo*, above n 58, para 279.   [63] SCSL, *Sesay et al*, above n 15, para 105.

[64] Ibid, paras 93, 1447–8, 1942, 1959. See also SCSL, *Taylor*, above n 55, para 574.

[65] ICTY, *Halilović*, above n 54, para 36; ICTY, *The Prosecutor v Strugar*, Appeals Chamber Judgment, IT-01-42-A, 17 July 2008, para 271.

However, and although some states' military manuals also use a similar 'knew or should have known' test,[66] the ICC's Elements of Crimes are arguably more restrictive. While they do not require that the perpetrator made a *legal* evaluation,[67] they do require that the 'perpetrator be aware of the factual circumstances that establish the protected status'.[68]

There are strong legal and policy reasons for adopting a 'reasonable basis' (for believing that the killed person was not protected by Common Article 3) or 'reckless disregard' (for protected status or for facts indicating that the killed person was protected by Common Article 3) test for Common Article 3 murder. A purely subjective test undermines the protection of civilians, rewards failures to presume civilian status in cases of doubt, and is at odds with the fundamental humanitarian law principle of distinction.

III. Murder by act or omission

It is undisputed that murder may be committed by either act or omission.[69] The level of causation necessary is generally described as a 'substantial cause'.[70] However, almost all of the international murder jurisprudence concerns unambiguously positive and direct acts, such as shootings, brutal physical and sexual assaults, and civilians forcibly trapped inside burning homes. Few cases exist to demonstrate the scope of murder by omission. The omission cases that have been brought have generally concerned the deaths of detained fighters or civilians, and the kinds of omissions have generally concerned a failure to provide or ensure basic conditions in detention necessary for life,

---

[66] United States, *Manual for Military Commissions* (2007), 'Murder of Protected Persons' ('[t]he accused knew or should have known of the factual circumstances that established that person's protected status'); Australia, Criminal Code Act (1995), ss 268.24, 268.70 (listing, as one of the elements of the war crime of both murder and wilful killing, 'the perpetrator knows of, or is reckless as to, the factual circumstances that establish that the person or persons are so protected').

[67] ICC, *The Prosecutor v Germain Katanga and Mathieu Ngudjolo Chui*, Pre-Trial Chamber Decision on the Confirmation of Charges, ICC-01/04-01/07, 30 September 2008, para 297.

[68] See, e.g., G. Werle, *Principles of International Criminal Law* (2nd edn, The Hague: T.M.C. Asser Press, 2009), at 328 (noting the contrast with the ICTY cases); ICC, *The Prosecutor v Thomas Lubanga Dyilo*, Pre-Trial Chamber Decision on the confirmation of charges, ICC-01/04-01/06, 29 January 2007, paras 356–60 (discussing the 'should have known' standard as applicable only where explicitly provided for in the Elements of Crimes). But see Dörmann, above n 12, at 41 (arguing that under the ICC Statute, the accused may be responsible if, 'due to his position or skills, he must have known the facts'); DRC, Military Court of the Eastern Province, *Bongi Massaba Case*, Judgment on Appeals, 4 November 2006 (the accused was found guilty of the war crime of murder, for killing, after capture, five students; the Court, applying the ICC elements, stated that the defendant 'could not have been mistaken about' their civilian status).

[69] ICRC Commentary APs, para 4532 ('[m]urder covers not only cases of homicide, but also intentional omissions which may lead to death'); ICTY, *The Prosecutor v Stanislav Galić*, Appeals Chamber Judgment, IT-98-29-A, 30 November 2006, para 149 (rejecting Galić's argument that murder cannot be committed by omission); ICTY, *Kvočka et al*, above n 50, para 261; ICTY, *Orić*, above n 50, para 302; ICTR, *Nzabirinda*, above n 50, para 25 ('[t]he commission of a positive act is not an absolute requirement of criminal responsibility'); ICTY, *Krnojelac*, above n 6, para 324; ICTY, *Delalić*, above n 42, para 424 (finding it 'unnecessary to dwell' on the *actus reus* of murder, but noting that it includes 'omissions as well as concrete actions'); SCSL, *Brima et al*, above n 44, para 688; SCSL, *Sesay et al*, above n 15, para 142; ICC, *Bemba Gombo*, above n 58, paras 132, 274; ECCC, *Kaing*, above n 29, para 331; ICC, *Katanga and Chui*, above n 67, para 287; *Sri Lanka Report*, above n 16, para 251 (following the tribunals).

[70] Few cases have turned on the meaning of 'substantial', although the formulation is common. See ICTY, *Brđanin*, above n 46, para 382; ICTY, *Orić*, above n 50, para 347; SCSL, *Brima et al*, above n 44, para 689; ICTY, *Delalić*, above n 42, para 424, fn 435 (discussing 'substantial cause' and other formulations in national systems); ICC, *Katanga and Chui*, above n 67, para 296 (following the ICTY); *Sri Lanka Report*, above n 16, para 251 (following the tribunals); *Libya Commission*, above n 35, para 141.

including food, general sanitation, and medical care.[71] One ICTY case found that a suicide of a detainee could constitute murder, so long as the requisite intent and causation existed.[72]

28   In *Orić*, the ICTY provided an important elaboration on murder by omission. The Tribunal held that omissions only incur legal responsibility if there was a duty to act, a requirement it said was 'obvious', although it correctly noted that this was not usually 'explicitly stated' in prior case law.[73] Such duties could

> arise out of responsibility for the safety of the person concerned, [be] derived from humanitarian law or based on a position of authority, or can result from antecedent conduct by which the person concerned has been exposed to danger.[74]

IV. Proof of death and unidentified victims

29   The death of the victim is an element of murder, but it is not necessary to prove that the body of the deceased was recovered.[75] Death may be shown through circumstantial evidence (such as proof of mistreatment of the victim, and the time since the person disappeared) where the death is the 'only reasonable inference'.[76]

30   In many cases, large numbers of civilians have been killed together, and these large-scale multiple murders have often been termed 'mass killing' or 'massacre'.[77] The international criminal tribunal jurisprudence has also accommodated the realities of armed conflict, in which violence and insecurity cause significant evidentiary difficulties by inhibiting the recollection or gathering of precise and complete information. The tribunals have held that murder may be found without clear evidence of the identity of each individual victim

---

[71] *Trial of Heinrich Gerike and seven others*, above n 45, at 81 (the accused were charged with a 'war crime [...] in violation of the laws and usages of war', for being 'concerned in the killing by willful neglect' of Polish children forcibly taken from their mothers and put in the accused's care); ICTY, *Kvočka et al*, above n 50, para 270 (an individual held in a detention camp and who died 'as a result of willful omission to provide medical care' was murdered); ECCC, *Kaing*, above n 29, para 437 (lack of food and medical care at S-21 prison).

[72] ICTY, *Krnojelac*, above n 6, paras 328–42. The accused was charged with the murder of a person who committed suicide after being beaten and placed in an isolation cell. The prosecution argued that it was reasonably foreseeable that the situation would lead to suicide. The Trial Chamber stated that the 'crucial issues are causation and intent [...] the relevant act or omission [...] must have caused the suicide [...] and the [perpetrator] must have intended by that act or omission to cause the suicide of the victim, or have known that the suicide of the victim was a likely and foreseeable result of the act or omission'. The Trial Chamber considered evidence that the deceased had been 'depressed about his family situation and committed suicide for that reason', and held that the prosecution had not established beyond a reasonable doubt that the beating was the cause of the suicide.

[73] ICTY, *Orić*, above n 50, para 304, fn 859.

[74] Ibid, para 304 (footnotes omitted).

[75] ICTY, *Mrkšić et al*, above n 54, para 486; ICTY, *Kvočka et al*, above n 50, para 260; ICC, *Bemba Gombo*, above n 58, para 133.

[76] SCSL, *Brima et al*, above n 44, para 689. See also ICTY, *Krnojelac*, above n 6, para 327 (setting out relevant factors, and referring to ECtHR, IACtHR, and national-level jurisprudence in support); ICTY, *Brđanin*, above n 46, paras 383–5; ICTY, *Kvočka et al*, above n 50, para 260; ICTY, *Halilović*, above n 54, para 37 (listing additional factors); ICTY, *Limaj et al*, above n 16, paras 342–4, 350, 372, 378 (finding the factors not satisfied).

[77] See, e.g., Chinese War Crimes Military Tribunal of the Ministry of National Defence (Nanking), *Trial of Takashi Sakai*, 29 August 1946 (Japanese military commander convicted of the massacre of over 100 civilians); *Darfur Commission*, above n 39, paras 272–73 (mass killings of civilians in various villages); *Syria Report*, above n 30, para 42 ('intentional mass killing' or the 'massacre' of civilians constitutes 'multiple instances of the war crime of murder').

or the precise date of a killing;[78] and in the context of a mass killing, it is not necessary to prove a confirmed total number of victims.[79]

V. Murder and summary execution

Common Article 3 lists 'murder' in subparagraph (a), and executions without a proper trial (summary execution) as a separate prohibited act in subparagraph (d). The ICC Statute and the international criminal tribunal statutes follow this separation.

In numerous Second World War era cases, murder and summary execution were merged concepts. In *The Almelo Trial*, for example, a Dutch civilian and a British soldier were captured, interrogated, and ordered executed. The defence argued that the executions were lawful, as the accused had a reasonable basis to believe that the victims had committed offences (spying and treason) to which the death penalty could lawfully be applied. The prosecution argued that it was a 'so-called execution' that 'had no connection with any legal process and was in fact cold-blooded murder'.[80] The court found that there had been no regular trial, that the accused had reason to believe this fact, and that the accused were guilty of war crimes for killing in violation of the laws and usages of war. Similarly, in the *Trial of Susuki Motosuke*, the accused was found guilty of the 'war crime of murder' where he ordered the execution of Indonesians following a trial process the military court deemed improper.[81]

More recent cases and inquiries have also highlighted the similarity between murder and summary execution. The International Court of Justice (ICJ) has held that the same

---

[78] SCSL, *Sesay et al*, above n 15, para 1045 (the Chamber could not 'determine the specific dates of each incident' but was 'satisfied that the acts described [...] occurred within the Indictment period'); ICC, *Bemba Gombo*, above n 58, para 133 (there is no need to find or identify the corpse, but the 'Prosecutor is still expected to specify, to the extent possible, inter alia, the location of the alleged murder, its approximate date, the means by which the act was committed with enough precision, the circumstances of the incident and the perpetrator's link to the crime').

[79] In *Sesay*, for example, fighters were prosecuted for shooting, hacking, beheading, eviscerating, and burning to death 'an unknown number of civilians': SCSL, *Sesay et al*, above n 15, para 1017. The Court found the accused guilty of murder where it was shown that many civilians were unlawfully killed, and where a witness testified to burying over 200 bodies after an attack. Also see ICC, *Bemba Gombo*, above n 58, para 134 (at least for the evidentiary threshold at the pre-trial stage, and citing to ICTY and ICTR jurisprudence, that 'in case of mass crimes, it may be impractical to insist on a high degree of specificity [...] [I]t is not necessary for the Prosecutor to demonstrate, for each individual killing, the identity of the victim and the direct perpetrator. Nor is it necessary that the precise number of victims be known [...] This allows the Chamber to consider evidence referring to "many" killings or "hundreds" of killings without indicating a specific number'); ECCC, *Kaing*, above n 29, para 436 (noting that the 'inaccuracy of the existing record' meant that it was 'not possible to quantify the precise number' who died at S-21 prison).

[80] *Trial of Otto Sandrock and three others (The Almelo Trial)*, British Military Court, Almelo, 1945, UNWCC Law Reports, vol I, at 37.

[81] *Trial of Susuki Motosuke*, above n 2, at 127. See also *Trial of Sergeant-Major Shigeru Ohashi and six others*, Australian Military Court, Rabaul, 1946, UNWCC Law Reports, vol V, at 30 (the Japanese accused were found guilty of murder when the deceased were beheaded after an unfair trial for acts of sabotage; the Judge Advocate advised the Court that the Japanese accused should be acquitted if the summary trials had in fact been 'fair and reasonable'); *Trial of Captain Eikichi Kato*, Australian Military Court, Rabaul, 1946, UNWCC Law Reports, vol V (defendant found guilty of the murder of six civilians for executing them after an unfair trial); Holland, Special Court (War Criminals) of Arnhem, *In re Enkelstroth*, 20 February 1948 (police officer found guilty of war crimes for shooting to death four civilians suspected of being saboteurs; the Court found that the shooting 'was so clearly at variance with international law that even a police officer of inferior rank must have known that it was unlawful').

facts could violate both prohibitions,[82] and the UN Inquiry on Syria equated the war crime of murder with that of execution without due process.[83]

34   These cases reflect the fact that, as the 'process' offered the victim nears zero, it is difficult to maintain a clear line between a murder and a summary execution. In this sense, summary execution could be classed either as a species of murder, or as a separate but overlapping offence. There is, however, an important conceptual difference between summary executions and other intentional unlawful killings. Because international law does not currently prohibit the death penalty for certain serious offences, a summary execution is an intentional killing that would be lawful but for the lack of proper judicial process.

35   For this reason, for those cases where the victim allegedly committed a capital offence and where some form of 'process' was offered before the execution, the author's view is that a charge of summary execution would generally better capture the factual circumstances and the distinct basis of illegality.

C. Legal Consequences of a Violation: Murder, Arbitrary Deprivation of Life, and Human Rights Law

36   As discussed, a violation of the prohibition against murder under Common Article 3 is generally accepted as giving rise to individual criminal responsibility for war crimes, and any Common Article 3 violation would also give rise to either state or non-state actor liability. In addition, as is well known, human rights law protects each individual's right to life, and prohibits the arbitrary deprivation of life.[84] Any killing prohibited by Common Article 3 murder would also clearly violate human rights law.[85] However, the scope of the human rights law protection is wider in certain respects, whether applied during armed conflict or in peacetime.

37   Outside armed conflict, human rights law is broader than the war crime of murder, both as regards whom it protects and the extent of the legal protection. Human rights law protects all persons, and does not recognize the status-based protections found in humanitarian law.[86] It requires the state both to respect and to ensure the right to life: the state has a negative obligation to refrain from committing unlawful killings, and a positive obligation to ensure the right and prevent violations.[87]

---

[82] ICJ, *Case concerning Military and Paramilitary Activities in and against Nicaragua (Nicaragua v United States of America)*, Judgment, 27 June 1986, para 255.

[83] *Syria Report*, above n 30, at Annex V, para 33. Similarly, see *Afghanistan Report*, above n 39, at 22–3 (discussing executions by Anti-Government Elements in Afghanistan after purported 'trials' as 'murder').

[84] Art 4 ACHPR; Art 4 ACHR; Art 4 Arab Charter on Human Rights; Art 11 ASEAN Human Rights Declaration; Art 2(1) ECHR; Art 6(1) ICCPR; Art 3 UDHR.

[85] See, e.g., *Syria Report*, above n 30, para 58 (cases of 'arbitrary deprivation of life, contrary to international human rights law, such as extrajudicial or summary executions, were reported throughout the period under review, frequently overlapping with the war crime of murder'); *Colombia Constitutional Case*, above n 2, at 112 (the homicide prohibition in humanitarian law 'corresponds' to the right to life in human rights law). See also IACommHR, *Abella*, above n 25, paras 158–61.

[86] Similar kinds of perpetrator actions in both armed conflict or in peacetime could legally justify killing the perpetrator, although the legal basis under humanitarian and human rights law would differ. For example, a civilian actively participating in armed conflict by lethally attacking innocent civilians may be lawfully killed under humanitarian law because that person's actions remove him from protected status. An individual similarly attacking others during peacetime may be lawfully killed under human rights law where the killing was necessary in self-defence in the face of an imminent threat.

[87] HRCttee, General Comment 6, 1982, para 3; UN Special Rapporteur on extrajudicial, summary, or arbitrary executions, P. Alston, *Report to the Human Rights Council (2010)*, A/HRC/14/24, 20 May 2010, paras

Any use of state force must be both necessary and proportionate, and the intentional use of lethal force is lawful only where strictly necessary to protect life.[88] Further, and as stated clearly in *McCann v United Kingdom*, while the right to life 'extends to' intentional killing, it is not 'concerned exclusively' with such violations.[89] The state may also be liable for violating the right to life where it fails to take 'appropriate care in the control and organization' of its military or police operations, even where the immediate act of killing itself did not give rise to a violation.[90] State responsibility may be engaged where a state is 'negligent' or fails 'to take all feasible precautions' to protect civilians,[91] or where it fails to meet its due diligence obligation to protect individuals from violations by private actors (e.g. criminals).[92]

In addition, to the extent human rights law permits killings akin to the 'collateral' harm of armed conflict, the scope of legality is considerable narrower than in humanitarian law. The death of an innocent bystander in a lawful police operation might not violate human rights law where the use of force strictly complied with the necessary and proportionate test, but human rights law does not countenance humanitarian law's 'proportionate to a military advantage' test.

In an armed conflict, it is generally accepted that human rights law continues to apply (see Chapter 35 of this volume), and that the content of the human rights law prohibition against the 'arbitrary deprivation of life' is determined by IHL.[93] Thus, during armed

---

45–47; *Case of the Massacres of El Mozote*, above n 22, para 145; IACtHR, *Case of the Ituango Massacres v Colombia*, Judgment, 1 July 2006, paras 129–31; ECtHR, *Ergi v Turkey*, Judgment, 28 July 1998, para 79; ACommHPR, *Commission Nationale des Droits de l'Homme et des Liberties v Chad*, 74/92, 1995, para 22; ACommHPR, *Mouvement Burkinabé des Droits de l'Homme et des Peuples v Burkina Faso*, 204/97, 2001, para 42.

[88] UN Special Rapporteur on extrajudicial, summary, or arbitrary executions, P. Alston, *Study on Targeted Killings*, A/HRC/14/24/Add.6, 28 May 2010, para 32; Code of Conduct for Law Enforcement Officials, A/34/46, 1979, Art 3; Basic Principles on the Use of Force and Firearms by Law Enforcement Officials, A/Conf.144/28/Rev.1, 1990, Art 9; *Libya Commission* (2012), above n 35, para 144.

[89] ECtHR, *McCann and others v United Kingdom*, Judgment, 27 September 1995, para 148. See also ECtHR, *Isayeva v Russia*, Judgment, 24 February 2005, para 173; ECtHR, *Ergi*, above n 87, para 79; ECommHR, *Stewart v United Kingdom*, Judgment, Decision on Admissibility, 10 July 1984, para 15.

[90] ECtHR, *McCann*, above n 89, paras 200, 212; ECtHR, *Ergi*, above n 87, para 79; ECtHR, *Isayeva*, above n 89, paras 175–202 (finding a violation of the right to life where the state had not 'planned and executed [a military bombing in Chechnya] with the requisite care for the lives of the civilian population'); ECtHR, *Khamzayev and others v Russia*, Judgment, 31 May 2011, paras 178–90 (finding a breach of the right to life where the Russian authorities did not 'take the necessary degree of care [...] in preparing the operation'). The Russia cases are discussed here under human rights law, although they represent a confused approach to humanitarian and human rights law. The decisions do not make explicit references to humanitarian law, but their language and legal conclusions appear to borrow heavily from it, and may be better understood as applications of humanitarian law within a human rights framework.

[91] ECtHR, *Isayeva*, above n 89, paras 175–6; ECtHR, *Ergi*, above n 87, para 79.

[92] *Study on Targeted Killings*, above n 88, para 33; UN Special Rapporteur on extrajudicial, summary, or arbitrary executions, P. Alston, *Report to the Commission on Human Rights (2005)*, E/CN.4/2005/7, 22 December 2004, paras 71–4.

[93] ICJ, *Legality of the Threat or Use of Nuclear Weapons*, Advisory Opinion, 8 July 1996, para 25 ('The test of what is an arbitrary deprivation of life [...] falls to be determined by the applicable *lex specialis*, namely the law applicable in armed conflict [...] Thus whether a particular loss of life, through the use of a certain weapon in warfare, is to be considered an arbitrary deprivation of life contrary to Article 6 of the Covenant, can only be decided by reference to the law applicable in armed conflict and not deduced from the terms of the Covenant itself'); IACommHR, *Abella*, above n 25, para 161 (referring to the rules of humanitarian law in order to 'define or distinguish civilians from combatants and other military targets [and] specify when a civilian can be lawfully attacked or when civilian casualties are a lawful consequence of military operations'); IACtHR, *Case of the Santo Domingo Massacre v Colombia*, Judgment, 30 November 2012, para 187; HRCttee, *General Comment 31*, 26 May 2004, para 11. See discussion of this and contrary views in

conflict, human rights law incorporates humanitarian law's (in certain circumstances, more permissive) rules of killing (see Chapter 35, MN 32, 51–53, and 80–81, of this volume). Human rights law protections, however, remain broader than Common Article 3 murder, and clearly apply during the conduct of hostilities.[94] In other words, the prohibition on the violation of the right to life in human rights law encompasses all of IHL's rules against unlawful killings, and not only 'murder' specifically. A state's responsibility for a violation of the right to life has been found, for example, where the state's security forces failed to take adequate precautions in attack, or where military actions failed to comply with the principles of proportionality and distinction.[95] Assessing the humanitarian law violation within the human rights framework may also have implications for the burden of proof.[96]

D. Critical Assessment

41   International law regulates all killings committed during peacetime or armed conflict, and killings of many different forms are prohibited by a variety of distinctly named international violations and crimes. The different constructions often capture a key characteristic of a particular form of unlawful killing. Terminology and the elements of different unlawful killing offences often overlap, however, and clearly separating legal offences, as well as conceptually separating forms of killings, can in practice be challenging. The content of offences and names of killings have also shifted over time, and there have been explicit attempts to both harmonize and distinguish.

42   'Common Article 3 murder' is one particular species of unlawful killing, and also one form of 'murder'. It was drafted against the background of the types of unlawful killings of prisoners of war and of civilians in occupied territories committed during the Second World War, and out of concern that such killings, considered to violate basic and shared moral codes, should also be explicitly prohibited in NIACs. Despite its fundamental importance, Common Article 3 murder has been the subject of surprisingly little study.

43   Common Article 3 murder clearly includes killings committed with direct intent, whether by act or omission, of both civilians and members of the armed forces taking no active part in hostilities who are physically captured, detained, or otherwise in the physical control of the relevant party to the armed conflict. There is also a strong argument that murder includes killings of such persons where the death resulted from recklessness or was committed with indirect intent. Murder may also include, more broadly, the killing of civilians who are in territory controlled by the party who used force. While Common Article 3 murder may be argued to include any intentional killing that violates the conduct of hostilities rules of IHL, the weight of authority seems to tend to adopt a somewhat

---

M. Forowicz, *The Reception of International Law in the European Court of Human Rights* (Oxford: OUP, 2010), at 316–21.

[94] ICRC CIHL Study, vol I, at 313–14.

[95] IACtHR, *Santo Domingo Massacre*, above n 93, paras 196–235 (finding that the Colombian Air Force launched bombs into and fired machine guns at individuals in a village in 1998, resulting in deaths in violation of the right to life). Also see IACtHR, *Case of the 'Mapiripán Massacre' v Colombia*, Judgment, 15 September 2005, para 110.

[96] IACommHR, *Abella*, above n 25, para 195 (holding that if any fighters die while in the custody of the state, 'the State must bear the burden of proving' that it was not responsible for their deaths).

narrower approach, requiring the victim to be in the attacker's control for 'murder' to apply. The development of customary law clearly regulating the conduct of hostilities in NIACs, together with the growth of international criminal law since the drafting of Common Article 3, arguably reduces the practical significance of delineating the precise scope of Common Article 3 specifically. Nevertheless, the cases and commentary examined in this chapter indicate that there has been analysis and ad hoc developments of the law relating to unlawful killings in different spheres, sometimes carried out without regard to or in recognition of other applications. This has undermined clarity about murder and related offences, and future legal developments in this area should aim to apply, analyse, and articulate the law relating to killings consistently across, and in light of, the various applicable regimes.

SARAH KNUCKEY

Chapter 23. Judicial Guarantees under Common Article 3

	MN
A. Introduction	1
B. Meaning and Application of Common Article 3 paragraph 1(1)(d)	6
I. Nature of the court required to pronounce judgment	6
a. Regularly constituted	6
b. Independent and impartial	10
II. Guarantees recognized as 'indispensable'	16
a. Evaluation of which guarantees fall into this category	16
b. Principle of legality	19
c. Individual criminal responsibility	22
d. Presumption of innocence	23
e. Information on the particulars of the offence	26
f. Necessary rights and means of defence	27
g. Public trial	45
h. Right of an accused to be present at the trial	49
i. Right not to be compelled to testify against oneself or to confess guilt	51
j. Information on possible appeal	53
k. Limits on the death penalty	57
l. Prohibition of trial more than once for the same offence	60
III. Other important judicial guarantees	62
a. Trial within a reasonable time	62
b. Non-transfer to a trial representing a flagrant denial of justice	64
IV. Pre-trial judicial guarantees for detainees	66
a. Right to fair trial includes pre-trial guarantees	66
b. Appearance before a judicial officer	68
c. Trial within reasonable time or release	73
C. Rights and Duties of Rebels	77
I. Duty not to convict or sentence a person without respecting judicial guarantees	77
a. All state fair trial obligations apply to rebel trials	78
b. A more lenient standard for rebel trials?	81
II. Do rebel groups have the right to try persons?	86
a. Trying persons with existing courts and legislation	87
b. The creation of courts by rebel groups	88
D. Legal Consequences of a Violation	91
I. State responsibility: right to reparation/remedy	91
II. Individual criminal responsibility for an international wrong	94
III. Criminal responsibility at the national level	98
E. Critical Assessment	100

Select Bibliography

Barela, S., 'Judicially Moderated Dialogue and the "War on Terror"', in L. Hennebel and H. Tigroudja (eds), *Balancing Liberty and Security: The Human Rights Pendulum* (Nijmegen: Wolf Legal Publishers, 2012) 87

Clapham, A., *Human Rights Obligations of Non-State Actors* (Oxford: OUP, 2006), Chapter 7

Doswald-Beck, L., *Human Rights in Times of Conflict and Terrorism* (Oxford: OUP, 2011), Chapters 9–13

Somer, J., 'Jungle Justice: Passing Sentence on the Equality of Belligerents in Non-International Armed Conflict', 89 *IRRC* 867 (2007) 655

A. Introduction

1 The prohibition of sentences and executions without a trial respecting judicial guarantees was motivated by the preponderance of summary trials. As explained in the Pictet Commentary to Common Article 3 paragraph 1(1)(d), such trials 'are too open to error' and they add 'too many further victims to all the other innocent victims of the conflict'.[1]

2 Article 6 of Additional Protocol (AP) II is the main provision that gives more detail to Common Article 3 paragraph 1(1)(d). As explained in the Commentary, this provision clarifies the basic customary rule and represents 'some principles of universal application which every responsibly organized body must, and can, respect'.[2] Some of its provisions were included to reflect details found in Geneva Conventions III and IV, whereas others were included to reflect human rights treaty provisions that did not exist in 1949.[3] As will be shown below, these treaty provisions are now accepted as basic standards, set forth not only in the United Nations (UN) treaties, but also in the regional treaties of Europe, America, Africa, and the Arab world. The provisions are also reflected in Article 75 AP I, which the United States (US) Supreme Court referred to as customary law standards required by Common Article 3.[4]

3 Since the drafting of AP II, there have been further developments. These include more recent human rights treaties, as well as the case law and general comments of the relevant human rights treaty bodies. These are valuable because they interpret the provisions of human rights treaties which are the same as those in Article 6 AP II. A number of these developments are also reflected in resolutions adopted by the UN since 1977. Other developments have taken place in the context of international criminal law, in particular the International Criminal Court (ICC) Statute and its Elements of Crimes.

4 The rules that reflect 'indispensable' judicial guarantees have developed in the context of state obligations, as human rights treaty provisions formally apply only to states. However, Common Article 3 expressly applies to all parties to a non-international armed conflict (NIAC), and therefore also to the rebel armed groups. What this means for judicial guarantees is more fraught with difficulty than for the other provisions of Common Article 3, and does not seem to have been considered in depth in 1949. The application of Common Article 3 paragraph 1(1)(d) to rebel groups is discussed in MN 77–90.

5 It only became generally accepted in the 1990s that serious violations of international humanitarian law (IHL) in NIACs could amount to war crimes. The extent to which such crimes can stem from a lack of fair trial is addressed in MN 94–99.

---

[1] Pictet Commentary GC IV, at 39.   [2] ICRC Commentary APs, para 4597.
[3] The wording was taken from Arts 14 and 15 ICCPR.   [4] See MN 17.

B. Meaning and Application of Common Article 3 paragraph 1(1)(d)

I. Nature of the court required to pronounce judgment

a. Regularly constituted

Common Article 3 of the Geneva Conventions prohibits the 'passing of sentences or carrying out of executions' unless there is a previous judgment 'pronounced by a regularly constituted court'. 'Regularly constituted' has its equivalent in the term 'competent' in several human rights treaties,[5] which has been interpreted as meaning that the tribunal has been established by law in order to decide cases relating to certain subject matters. In other words, the jurisdictional power of a tribunal is not created for a specific case, nor by an arbitrary administrative act.[6] 6

States have had resort to special or military courts in order to hear cases concerning national security, but they have often been found to lack independence and impartiality.[7] The UN Basic Principles on the Independence of the Judiciary state that '[e]veryone shall have the right to be tried by ordinary courts or tribunals using established legal procedures'.[8] 7

The US Supreme Court, in the case of *Hamdan v Rumsfeld, Secretary of Defense et al*,[9] considered the meaning of 'regularly constituted court' in the context of the military commissions created by the US Government to try people held at Guantánamo Bay. The international law rule considered relevant was Common Article 3 as a minimum for any armed conflict. The Court quoted the International Committee of the Red Cross (ICRC) Commentary to Article 66 of Geneva Convention (GC) IV, as follows: '[R]egularly constituted tribunals [...] include "ordinary military courts" and "definitely exclud[e] all special tribunals".'[10] The Court went on to quote from the ICRC's Customary Law Study, which describes 'regularly constituted court' 'to mean "established and organized in accordance with the laws and procedures already in force in a country"'.[11] The Supreme Court then noted that the normal court would be the regular 'courts-martial established by congressional statutes' and that another system, namely the military commission, can be '"regularly constituted" by the standards of our military justice system only if some practical need explains deviations from court-martial practice [...] [N]o such need has been demonstrated here.'[12] 8

Similarly, the UN Human Rights Committee (HRCttee) does not rule out the existence of special courts but insists that they comply with the requirements for independence and impartiality.[13] Further, there must be some valid reason why the normal court is unable to 9

---

[5] Art 14 ICCPR; Art 8 ACHR; Art 7 ACHPR; Art 13 Arab Charter.

[6] See, e.g., M. Nowak, *UN Covenant on Civil and Political Rights: CCPR Commentary* (2nd edn, Kehl: N.P. Engel Publisher, 2005), at 319, para 24.

[7] E.g. IACtHR, *Castillo Petruzzi et al v Peru*, Judgment, 30 May 1999, para 129; IACommHR, *Report on Terrorism and Human Rights*, 2002, para 230; ACommHPR, *Media Rights Agenda v Nigeria*, Com 224/98, 6 November 2000, para 62.

[8] Principle 5, *Basic Principles on the Independence of the Judiciary*, endorsed by UNGA in Res 40/32, 29 November 1985, and Res 40/146, 13 December 1985; HRComm, *Situation of Detainees at Guantánamo Bay*, UN Doc E/CN.4/2006, 120, 15 February 2006, paras 30–1.

[9] US Supreme Court, *Hamdan v Rumsfeld*, 548 US 557 (2006).   [10] Ibid, at 69.   [11] Ibid.

[12] Ibid, at 70.   [13] Ibid; and HRCttee, General Comment 32, 23 August 2007, para 22.

hear the case, for otherwise there is a violation of the right to equality before the law under Article 26 of the International Covenant on Civil and Political Rights (ICCPR).[14]

b. Independent and impartial

10 Article 6(2) AP II does not repeat the requirement of 'regularly constituted' but instead prohibits convictions that are not pronounced by 'a court offering the essential guarantees of independence and impartiality'. The ICRC Commentary explains that during the negotiations, 'some experts argued that it was unlikely that a court could be "regularly constituted" under national law by an insurgent party'. The alternative formula was proposed by the ICRC and 'accepted without opposition'.[15]

i. Meaning of 'independent'

11 Judges must be able to decide cases independently of the executive, and be seen to be free of influence or pressure from it. The HRCttee expressed this concept as follows: 'A situation where the functions and competences of the judiciary and the executive are not clearly distinguishable or where the latter is able to control or direct the former is incompatible with the notion of an independent tribunal.'[16] It then listed the following factors that help ensure the independence of a tribunal:

— procedure and qualifications for the appointment of judges;
— guarantees relating to their security of tenure until a mandatory retirement age or the expiry of their term of office;
— conditions governing promotion, transfer, suspension, and cessation of their functions;
— lack of political interference by the executive branch and legislature;
— protection against conflicts of interest and intimidation.[17]

12 In order to ensure the above, judges' term of office, adequate remuneration, and pensions on retirement need to be secured by law.[18] One of the most important elements is to ensure that judges cannot be dismissed except on 'serious grounds of misconduct or incompetence', and even here effective judicial protection must be available to contest the dismissal.[19] Dismissal of judges, or pressure on them to resign before the end of their term of office, is the most obvious indicator of lack of independence, especially if it occurs during a sensitive case.[20] The same elements are found in the UN Basic Principles on the Independence of the Judiciary.[21]

ii. Meaning of 'impartial'

13 The HRCttee, the European Court of Human Rights (ECtHR), and the Inter-American Commission on Human Rights (IACommHR) have specified that there are two aspects

---

[14] HRCttee, *Joseph Kavanagh v Ireland*, Com 819/1998, Views, 26 April 2001, para 10.3. Human rights bodies are of the view that civilians should not be tried before military courts; see, e.g., HRCttee, General Comment 32, para 22.

[15] ICRC Commentary APs, para 4600.

[16] HRCttee, General Comment 32, para 19.   [17] Ibid.   [18] Ibid.   [19] Ibid, para 20.

[20] See, e.g., *Opinion concerning Mr Sadam Hussein Al-Tikrit*, UN Working Group on Arbitrary Detention, Opinion No 31/2006, UN Doc A/HRC/4/40Add.1, 114–19, § 9.

[21] *Basic Principles on the Independence of the Judiciary*, endorsed by UNGA Res 40/32, 29 November 1985, and 40/146, 13 December 1985, Principles 1, 2, 7, 11–14, 17–20. Rulings by other human rights bodies to the same effect: ECtHR, *Incal v Turkey*, Judgment, 9 June 1998, para 65; IACommHR, *Garcia v Peru*, Case No 11.006, Report No 1/95, 7 February 1995; also IACommHR, *Report on Terrorism and Human Rights*, 2002, para 229.

to the requirement of impartiality: the first is referred to as 'subjective impartiality', and the second as 'objective impartiality'.[22]

The HRCttee described 'subjective impartiality' as follows:

[J]udges must not allow their judgment to be influenced by personal bias or prejudice, nor harbour preconceptions about the particular case before them, nor act in ways that improperly promote the interests of one of the parties to the detriment of the other.[23]

Subjective impartiality depends, therefore, on the real state of mind of the judge or jury.[24] The ECtHR has stated that this type of impartiality is to be presumed, unless there is proof to the contrary.[25]

As regards 'objective impartiality', the HRCttee stated that the 'tribunal must also appear to a reasonable observer to be impartial'.[26] Objective impartiality will be lacking if the situation of the judge or jury members is such that bias may well be feared, such as where there is an overlap between the functions of the prosecution and those of the judge. Not surprisingly, tribunals which include members of the military have frequently been perceived as lacking in objective impartiality because, in trials of rebels, it is often the military that is involved in fighting such rebels. Special courts comprising mixed military and civilian judges similarly have been found to lack objective impartiality.[27]

II. Guarantees recognized as 'indispensable'

a. Evaluation of which guarantees fall into this category

i. Guarantees listed in international human rights treaties

The reference in Common Article 3 to 'all the judicial guarantees which are recognised as indispensable by civilized peoples' makes it clear that this provision is not referring to a specialized list created for trials during armed conflict, but rather to fair trial guarantees that the negotiators of the 1949 Conventions considered to be normal in their own countries for criminal trials. The list of judicial guarantees listed in the European Convention on Human Rights (ECHR), adopted just a year later, is a good indication of the kind of rules that negotiators would have had in mind as normal criminal trial procedures. These rules have since been reproduced in the ICCPR and in the other main regional human rights treaties. Indeed, it is generally accepted that, when evaluating the meaning of 'judicial guarantees' in IHL, it is appropriate to refer to the judicial guarantees listed for criminal trials in international human rights treaties.[28]

---

[22] E.g., ECtHR, *Findlay v United Kingdom*, Judgment, 25 February 1997, para 73; IACommHR, *Report on Terrorism and Human Rights*, 2002, para 229.
[23] HRCttee, General Comment 32, para 21.
[24] IACommHR, *Andrews v United States*, Case No 11.139, Report No 57/96, paras 159–72.
[25] ECtHR, *Thorgeir Thorgeirson v Iceland*, Judgment, 25 June 1992, para 50.
[26] HRCttee, General Comment 32, para 21.
[27] E.g., ECtHR, *Incal v Turkey*, above n 21, paras 68 and 71–3; ACommHPR, *Constitutional Rights Project et al v Nigeria*, Com 60/91, 3 November 1994. The Commission stated, in para 14, that '[r]egardless of the character of the individual members of such tribunals, its composition alone creates the appearance, if not the actual lack, of impartiality'.
[28] E.g., F. Hampson, 'The Relationship between International Humanitarian Law and Human Rights Law from the Perspective of a Human Rights Body', 90 *IRRC* 871 (2008) 549, at 561; H.-J. Heintze, 'On the Relationship between Human Rights Law Protection and International Humanitarian Law', 86 *IRRC*

17   Another approach, taken by the ICRC in 2011, is to refer to Article 75(4) AP I, itself based on the judicial guarantees in Article 14 ICCPR, as 'reflect[ing] customary law applicable in all types of armed conflict'.[29] It is also significant that the US Supreme Court, in evaluating which judicial guarantees are required by Common Article 3, stated that '[m]any of these are described in Article 75 [AP I]' and that this Article was 'indisputably part of [...] customary international law'.[30]

ii. Judicial guarantees listed in Article 6 AP II

18   The chapeau to Article 6(2) makes it clear that the guarantees listed in that provision are not exhaustive, but those which are listed there are obviously considered to be fundamentally important.[31]

b. Principle of legality

19   Article 6(2)(c) AP II specifies the basic principle that no one may be held guilty of an offence that was not criminal at the time of the commission of the act concerned, nor may a heavier penalty be imposed than that applicable at that time.[32] The principle of legality is not limited to prohibiting a criminal conviction with no existing legal norm. A norm that is not clearly articulated, but which is vague or ambiguous, also violates this rule. The point is that a person must be able to know in advance what behaviour represents offences and with which type of punishments.[33]

20   A conviction despite amnesty legislation does not violate the principle of legality, if the crime is a violation of international human rights law (IHRL) or an international crime.[34] Unlike AP II, which simply uses the expression 'under the law', human rights provisions specify that the principle of legality will be violated if there is no prior 'national or international law' criminalizing the act concerned. It would seem reasonable to include an international offence within the meaning of Article 6(2)(c) AP II, which would now cover war crimes.

21   The ECtHR has on several occasions considered cases in which persons were convicted by their national court for international crimes (genocide, crimes against humanity, and war crimes) which had occurred many years previously. The ECtHR specified that there would not be a violation of the principle of legality if the national court's interpretation was

---

856 (2004) 789, at 795; N. Lubell, 'Challenges in Applying Human Rights Law to Armed Conflict', 87 *IRRC* 860 (2005) 737, at 739. These authors treat this point as self-evident. See also *Expert Meeting on Procedural Safeguards for Security Detention in Non-International Armed Conflict*, Chatham House and ICRC, London, 22–3 September 2008, at 5. It was agreed that a person may be detained on suspicion of having committed a crime only if this 'is in accordance with the applicable criminal law procedure and relevant human rights law'.

[29]   ICRC, *International Humanitarian Law and the Challenges of Contemporary Armed Conflicts*, Report prepared for the 31st International Conference of the Red Cross and Red Crescent, Geneva, October 2011, at 16.
[30]   US Supreme Court, *Hamdan v Rumsfeld*, above n 9, at 70–1.
[31]   Although the right to a fair trial is not listed as non-derogable in those human rights treaties that allow for derogation during states of emergency, the relevant treaty bodies have specified that essential judicial guarantees cannot be derogated from in the case of criminal trials. See, e.g., IACtHR, *Zembrano Velez and others v Ecuador*, Judgment, 4 July 2007, paras 64–7; IACommHR, *Lindo et al v Peru*, Case 11.182, Report 49/00, 13 April 2000, para 86; HRCttee, General Comment 29, 24 July 2001, para 16. See also the ICRC CIHL Study, where Rule 100 specifies that '[n]o one may be convicted or sentenced, except pursuant to a fair trial affording all essential judicial guarantees'.
[32]   The principle of legality is non-derogable under human rights treaties.
[33]   IACtHR, *Petruzzi et al v Peru*, above n 7, para 121; ECtHR, *Kokkinakis v Greece*, Judgment, 25 May 1993, para 52.
[34]   ECtHR, *Ely Ould Dah v France*, Admissibility Decision (only in French), 17 March 2009.

c. Individual criminal responsibility

Article 6(2)(b) AP II, which specifies that a conviction can take place only on the basis of 'individual penal responsibility', is closely linked with the prohibition of collective punishments provided for in Article 4(2)(b) AP II. Both are rules of customary international law.[36]

d. Presumption of innocence

The presumption of innocence is specified in Article 6(2)(d) AP II. It is in all the human rights treaties,[37] and means that the burden is on the prosecution to prove the guilt of the accused beyond reasonable doubt.[38]

Human rights treaty bodies have specified that the presumption of innocence also binds the executive. There is therefore a violation of this rule if officials publicly express their view of the guilt of any suspect.[39] This is important, in that it is tempting for officials to indicate their view that 'terrorism' suspects and others accused of abuses during armed conflict are guilty before a trial or before the outcome of a trial.

Human rights treaty bodies have indicated that lengthy pre-trial detention can violate the presumption of innocence, and also that such detention can adversely affect the court into assuming guilt.[40]

e. Information on the particulars of the offence

Information on the particulars of the offence is provided for in Article 6(2)(a) AP II and is essential in order to give an accused person any possibility for an effective defence. This is not quite the same as the requirement, in all human rights treaties, that all arrested persons are to be notified of the reasons for their arrest (in addition to any charge) without delay.[41] The reason for the arrest (which is not limited to criminal matters and can include administrative detention) must be given either immediately or at least on the same day, and not more than a few hours later.[42] If a person is detained after arrest, the notification

---

[35] E.g., ECtHR, *Kononov v Latvia*, Judgment, 17 May 2010, paras 211–13 and 235–8. For a discussion of these cases, see L. Doswald-Beck, *Human Rights in Times of Conflict and Terrorism* (Oxford: OUP, 2011), at 306–15.

[36] ICRC CIHL Study, Rules 102 and 103.

[37] Art 14(2) ICCPR; Art 6(2) ECHR; Art 8(2) ACHR; Art 7(1)(b) ACHPR; Art 16, chapeau, Arab Charter.

[38] HRCttee, General Comment 32, para 30.

[39] HRCttee, *Gridin v Russia*, Com 770/1997, Views, 20 July 2000, para 8.3; ECtHR, *Allenet de Ribemont v France*, Judgment, 10 February 1995, paras 35–6 and 41; ACommHPR, *Principles and Guidelines on the Right to a Fair Trial and Legal Assistance in Africa*, 2003, Section N.6(e)2.

[40] IACtHR, *Suárez Rosero v Ecuador*, Judgment, 12 November 1997, paras 77–8; IACommHR, *Bronstein and others v Argentina*, Case No 11.205 and 22 others, Report No 2/97, paras 46–8.

[41] Art 14(3)(a) ICCPR; Art 6(3)(a) ECHR; Art 8(2)(b) ACHR; Art 16(1) Arab Charter. The ACommHPR has stated that the right of defence includes the right to understand the charges: *Malawi African Association and others v Mauritania*, Coms 54/91 et al, 11 May 2000, para 97.

[42] ECtHR, *Fox, Campbell and Hartley v United Kingdom*, Judgment, 30 August 1990, para 40; IACtHR, *Humberto Sanchez v Honduras*, Judgment, 7 June 2003, para 82; HRCttee, *Grant v Jamaica*, Views, 22 March 1996, para 8.1; ACommHPR, *Rights International v Nigeria*, Com 215/98, 15 November 1999, para 29.

of a formal criminal charge should not be delayed beyond a few days. Thus in cases before the HRCttee, a delay of three days was found to be acceptable,[43] but ten days was not.[44] The purpose of these short time spans is to enable detainees to exercise their right to contest the lawfulness of their detention. The indication 'without delay' in AP II indicates that this notification needs to be speedy and, as detention is the likely scenario in armed conflict, the short time spans indicated above would apply. It is evident that information on the charge needs to be sufficiently clear and precise to enable an adequate defence. Article 14(3)(a) ICCPR specifies, for example, that the individual must be informed 'in detail in a language which [the accused] understands of the nature and cause of the charge against him'.

f. Necessary rights and means of defence

27 Article 6(2)(a) AP II specifies that the necessary rights and means of defence must be provided both before and during the trial. Given that no further detail is provided in this provision, the necessary procedures to ensure that it is respected are best taken from the details provided in international human rights law.

i. Right of the accused to defend themselves personally or to be defended by a lawyer of their own choice

28 This right is set forth in all the human rights treaties.[45] Although the treaty provisions state that a person has the right to defend himself or herself *personally*, this does not necessarily mean that a court must accept a lack of legal assistance. The HRCttee has stated that

> [t]he interests of justice may, in the case of a specific trial, require the assignment of a lawyer against the wishes of the accused, particularly in cases of persons substantially and persistently obstructing the proper conduct of trial, or facing a grave charge but being unable to act in their own interests, or where this is necessary to protect vulnerable witnesses from further distress or intimidation if they were to be questioned by the accused. However, any restriction of the wish of accused persons to defend themselves must have an objective and sufficiently serious purpose and not go beyond what is necessary to uphold the interests of justice.[46]

The ECtHR has specified that it would be possible to accept a waiver of an accused's right to a lawyer only if the accused could reasonably foresee the consequences of this, and if it was a 'knowing and intelligent relinquishment'.[47] This would appear to put the stress on the need to avoid allowing an accused to defend himself or herself, at least at the interrogation stage, rather than on making the compulsory assistance of a lawyer an exception, as implied by the HRCttee. The more serious the alleged offence, the more likely it is that either treaty body would consider that a lawyer should be provided, even against the wishes of the accused.[48]

---

[43] HRCttee, *Pennant v Jamaica*, Com 647/1995, Views, 3 December 1998, para 8.1. The ECtHR also implied that a delay of a few days before the formal charge, unlike such a delay before giving the reasons for arrest, would not be a violation: ECtHR, *Brogan and others v United Kingdom*, Judgment, 29 November 1988, para 53.

[44] HRCttee, *Fillastre v Bolivia*, Com 336/1988, Views, 6 November 1991, para 6.4.

[45] Art 14(3)(d) ICCPR; Art 6(3)(c) ECHR; Art 8(2)(d) ACHR; Art 16(3) Arab Charter; and Art 7(1)(c) ACHPR.

[46] HRCttee, General Comment 32, para 37.

[47] ECtHR, *Pishchalnikov v Russia*, Judgment, 24 September 2009, paras 77–8.

[48] A lawyer additional to the one chosen by the accused is possible if needed, e.g. in a long and complex case: ECtHR, *Croissant v Germany*, Judgment, 25 September 1992, paras 29–30. This is not the same as having

Quite another issue is involved with the assignment of an additional lawyer when the 29
accused's own lawyer is not allowed access to all relevant prosecution material. In such a
case, the ECtHR has stated that

the special advocate could perform an important role in counterbalancing the lack of full disclosure
and the lack of a full, open, adversarial hearing by testing the evidence and putting arguments on
behalf of the detainee during the closed hearings. However, the special advocate could not perform
this function in any useful way unless the detainee was provided with sufficient information about
the allegations against him to enable him to give effective instructions to the special advocate.[49]

This would seem to imply that the existence of such special advocates, in addition to
the accused's own lawyer, would not of itself be a violation of the right to a lawyer of
the accused's own choice. The extent to which such material may be kept confidential is
addressed in MN 42.

The ability to benefit from the services of a lawyer is adversely affected if states prosecute 30
lawyers who defend persons seen by the state as subversive. This is contrary to accepted
principles relating to the respect of lawyers' functions. The UN Basic Principles on the
Role of Lawyers specify that '[l]awyers shall not be identified with their clients or their
clients' causes as a result of discharging their functions'.[50]

ii. Right to services of a lawyer free of charge if the interests of justice so require

Given the expense of legal counsel, it is not surprising that human rights treaties provide 31
that legal assistance in criminal cases must be provided free of charge if the 'interests of
justice so require'.[51] This has been interpreted as meaning that a lawyer must be provided
free of charge if the lack of a lawyer would adversely affect the fairness of the trial.[52] The
most important element is the gravity of the offence, including severity of sentence. Other
factors could be the legal complexity of the case and whether the accused are able to defend
themselves.[53] It is evident that the interests of justice will be pertinent in most cases related
to armed conflict, as the offences will often be serious and carry heavy penalties.

iii. Right of lawyer to unimpeded access to and private communication with the accused

The ability for an accused to benefit effectively from a lawyer's aid depends on proper 32
access. It is well established that communications with a detainee's lawyer are to be confidential, at whatever stage of proceedings.[54] Face-to-face 'communications may be within
sight, but not within the hearing, of a law-enforcement official'.[55] Confidentiality includes

---

a lawyer forced on an accused who is prevented from choosing his own lawyer, e.g., HRCttee, *Antonio Viana Acosta v Uruguay*, Com 110/1981, Views, 29 March 1984, paras 2.6 and 15; ACommHPR, *Civil Liberties Organisation, Legal Defence Centre, Legal Defence and Assistance Project v Nigeria*, Com 218/98, 7 May 2001, paras 28–9.

[49] ECtHR, *A and others v United Kingdom*, Judgment, 19 February 2009, para 220.

[50] Principle 18 of the UN *Basic Principles on the Role of Lawyers*, endorsed by UNGA Res 45/166, 18 December 1990.

[51] Art 14(3)(d) ICCPR; Art 6(3)(c) ECHR; Art 16(4) Arab Charter. The ACHR words it slightly differ-
ently, but it has been interpreted in the same way as the other treaty bodies. It is also included in the African Commission's *Fair Trial Principles*, Section H.(a).

[52] E.g., IACtHR, Advisory Opinion 11/90, 10 August 1990, paras 25–7.

[53] HRCttee, General Comment 32, para 38; ACommHPR, *Fair Trial Principles*, Section H.(b) and (c); ECtHR, *Quaranta v Switzerland*, Judgment, 24 May 1991, paras 32–37.

[54] This is spelled out in Art 8(2)(d) ACHR and Art 7(1)(c) ACHPR.

[55] Principle 18(4) of the *Body of Principles for the Protection of All Persons under Any Form of Detention or Imprisonment*, UNGA Res 43/173, 9 December 1988; ECtHR, *Öcalan v Turkey*, Judgment, 12 May 2005,

correspondence.[56] The only exception is where letters could 'endanger prison security or the safety of others or are otherwise of a criminal nature'.[57] Such an exception could include an official unconnected with the case reading mail, where there is a genuine fear that such communications are being used to prepare new offences.[58]

iv. Presence of a lawyer during all interrogations

33   A detainee needs to have access to an independent lawyer in order to help prevent ill-treatment and in order to ensure proper preparation of his or her defence. Often the two aims are combined, because a confession extracted under torture or other ill-treatment is all too often used by national courts as a basis for conviction. This evidently has a fundamentally negative effect on the fairness of the trial.[59]

34   The first days of detention are the most dangerous as regards ill-treatment, in particular during interrogation.[60] In Resolution 13/19, adopted in March 2010, the UN Human Rights Council stressed that, in order to prevent torture and other inhuman or degrading treatment, states are to 'ensure access to lawyers from the outset of custody and during all interrogations'.[61]

35   The initial interrogation is also the time when a detainee may make statements being unaware of the effect that these might have on the preparation of the defence as a whole. An intimidating atmosphere, repeated intensive interrogations with leading questions, and the complexity of some legal aspects of a case, can lead to self-incriminating statements that cause irreparable damage to the defence, and so undermine the overall fairness of the trial.[62] It is for this reason that human rights treaty bodies have held that interrogations without the presence of a lawyer violate the right to a fair trial. These have included the lack of a lawyer during the initial stages of police interrogation.[63]

v. Enough time and facilities before the trial to prepare the defence

36   The ability to prepare a defence adequately will include sufficient time, sufficient access to relevant material, and sufficient consultation with one's lawyer.

---

para 132. The ACommHPR's *Fair Trial Principles* state, in Section N.3(e), that '[a]ll arrested, detained or imprisoned persons shall be [able] to communicate with a lawyer, without delay, interception or censorship and in full confidentiality'.

[56] ECtHR, *Campbell v United Kingdom*, Judgment, 25 March 1992, paras 46–7.

[57] Ibid, para 48. The ECtHR specified in this case that letters may be opened to ensure there is no illicit enclosure, such as drugs or explosives, but may not be read.

[58] ECtHR, *Erdem v Germany*, Judgment, 5 July 2001, paras 34, 65, 68–9.

[59] E.g., ECtHR, *Salduz v Turkey*, Judgment, 27 November 2008, para 57. The applicant had made a statement during interrogation without the presence of a lawyer. It was used as the basis for his conviction, despite the fact that he insisted that it was made under duress. The ECtHR found a violation of the right to a fair trial.

[60] See, e.g., Committee for the Prevention of Torture: CPT, 12th Annual Report, CPT/Inf (2002) 15, para 41.

[61] HRC, Res 13/19, adopted 26 March 2010 without a vote, para 6. See also, to the same effect: ACommHPR, Res 61 (XXXII) 2002, para 20(c); IACommHR, *Report on Terrorism and Human Rights*, 2002, para 237. The need for early access to a lawyer for all detainees is also specified in: UN *Body of Principles for the Protection of All Persons under Any Form of Detention or Imprisonment*, UNGA Res 43/173, 9 December 1988, para 17; Council of Europe *Recommendation of the Committee of Ministers on the European Prison Rules*, 11 January 2006, para 98.

[62] E.g., ECtHR, *Öcalan v Turkey*, above n 55, para 131.

[63] HRCttee, *Marlem Carranza Alegre v Peru*, Com 1126/2002, Views, 17 November 2005, paras 2.10 and 7.5; ECtHR, *John Murray v United Kingdom*, Judgment, 8 February 1996, para 63: the accused was denied a lawyer during the first 48 hours of detention.

37 The time required will depend on the complexity of the case and on the seriousness of the offence. Reasonable requests for an adjournment should be granted.[64] Potentially long prison sentences, or the possibility of the death penalty, automatically require a significant amount of time to prepare the defence.[65]

38 Access must be granted to all the relevant documents and other evidence that the prosecution intends to use in court.[66] It might not be necessary for the accused to see all the documents, because the lawyer can consult with the client with regard to those documents the lawyer considers relevant.[67] Very voluminous files will require significant time for lawyers to read the material and consult with their clients.[68]

39 Adequate communication with one's lawyer means that such communication must be prompt and must be available at all relevant stages,[69] including during the preparation of any appeal.[70] The aid of a defence lawyer will not be adequate if that lawyer is so incompetent that the accused has been without an effective defence in practice.[71] Sufficient opportunity for the lawyer and the client to consult with each other is also relevant. Thus a complex and detailed case will require extensive consultation in order to discuss the charges.[72]

vi. Assistance of an interpreter if the accused cannot speak or understand the language used in court

40 This right to an interpreter is provided for as part of the right to a fair trial in criminal proceedings.[73] It applies to aliens as well as to nationals, and at all stages of oral proceedings.[74] The ECtHR has additionally specified that it includes the obligation to translate documents that the accused needs to understand in order to be able to defend himself or herself.[75]

vii. Equality of arms

41 The principle of equality before a tribunal is spelled out in the ICCPR and the ACHR,[76] and is reflected in provisions requiring an accused person to be able to produce and question witnesses on the same basis as the prosecution.[77] All human rights bodies have insisted on 'equality of arms', namely, equality in procedural rights, including presentation and

---

[64] HRCttee, General Comment 32, para 32.
[65] IACommHR, *Aguado Montealegre v Nicaragua*, Case No 10.198; Report No 29/89, at 348: a procedure lasting six weeks in total was insufficient to prepare a defence to a charge of an offence resulting in a 30-year sentence. On the death penalty, see, e.g, HRCttee, *Philip v Trinidad and Tobago*, Com 594/1992, Views 20 October 1998, para 7.2.
[66] HRCttee, General Comment 32, para 33.
[67] E.g., ECtHR, *Kremzow v Austria*, Judgment, 21 September 1993, para 52.
[68] ECtHR, *Öcalan v Turkey*, above n 55, paras 140–7: two weeks for Öcalan's lawyers to examine the case file of 17,000 pages, and 20 days for Öcalan to examine the file, were insufficient.
[69] HRCttee, General Comment 32, para 34.
[70] E.g., HRCttee, *J. Campbell v Jamaica*, Com 307/1988, Views, 24 March 1993; ACommHPR, *Avocats Sans Frontières v Burundi*, Com 231/99, 6 November 2000, para 30. See also HRCttee, General Comment 32, para 38.
[71] E.g., ECtHR, *Daud v Portugal*, Judgment, 21 April 1998, para 38; HRCttee, *Whyte v Jamaica*, Com 732/1997, Views, 27 July 1998, para 9.2.
[72] See, e.g., ECtHR, *Öcalan v Turkey*, above n 55, para 135.
[73] Art 14(3)(f) ICCPR; Art 6(3)(e) ECHR; Art 8(2)(a) ACHR; Art 16(4) Arab Charter; ACommHPR, *Fair Trial Principles*, Section A.(2)(g).
[74] HRCttee, General Comment 32, para 40.
[75] ECtHR, *Kamasinski v Austria*, Judgment, 19 December 1989, para 74.
[76] Art 14(1) ICCPR; Art 8(2) ACHR.
[77] Art 14(3)(e) ICCPR; Art 6(3)(d) ECHR; Art 16(5) Arab Charter.

examination of evidence.[78] Violations include insufficient detail in an indictment,[79] a court's refusing to take into account a document filed after the others,[80] and lack of access to relevant documents submitted by the other party.[81] The ECtHR has specified that there must be some form of 'adversarial proceedings'. This does not mean that all criminal trials are required to use the Anglo-American common law system, but only that an accused must be entitled to question and challenge statements made in court, whether by the adversary or by a public official.[82]

42   The use of confidential material by the prosecution, which cannot be contested by the defence, has arisen before the ECtHR in cases relating to drug-dealing or terrorism where the prosecution did not wish to reveal to the defence its sources of information. The Court accepted that it may be necessary to keep information from the accused for the purposes of 'national security or the need to protect witnesses at risk of reprisals or [to] keep secret police methods of investigation of crime'.[83] In the interests of justice, 'the judge should continue to assess the need for disclosure throughout the progress of the trial'.[84] In cases where information needs to be kept confidential, there will nevertheless not be a fair trial, and therefore a violation of the ECHR, where 'a conviction is based solely or to a decisive degree on depositions that have been made by a person whom the accused has had no opportunity to examine or to have examined'.[85]

viii. Examination of witnesses

43   Article 75(4)(g) AP I uses the same wording as the ICCPR, which specifies that an accused's rights of defence include the rights '[t]o examine, or have examined, the witnesses against him and to obtain the attendance and examination of witnesses on his behalf under the same conditions as witnesses against him'.[86] Other human rights treaties have equivalent provisions.[87]

44   National courts may not refuse witnesses who are relevant for the defence, or who are needed to ensure equality of arms.[88] The use of anonymous witnesses raises the same potential problem of lack of equality of arms as the use of confidential information (discussed in MN 42). In principle, witnesses should be examined at a public hearing. Exceptions are possible only if there is sufficient need to protect witnesses' identity and if measures are taken to ensure an adequate defence. Such measures include, 'an adequate and proper opportunity [for the accused] to challenge and question a witness against him, either at the time the witness was making his statement or at some later stage of the proceedings'.[89] Additionally, there will not be a fair trial if the judges do not evaluate

---

[78] HRCttee, General Comment 32, para 13; ACommHPR, *Fair Trial Principles*, Section N.6(a).
[79] HRCttee, *Wolf v Panama*, Com 289/1988, Views, 26 March 1992, para 6.6.
[80] HRCttee, *Jansen-Gielen v Netherlands*, Com 846/1999, Views, 3 April 2001, para 8.2.
[81] HRCttee, *Äärelä and Näkkäläjärvi v Finland*, Com 779/1997, Views, 24 October 2001, para 7.4.
[82] E.g., ECtHR, *Belziuk v Poland*, Judgment, 25 March 1998, para 37.
[83] ECtHR, *Jaspar v United Kingdom*, Judgment, 16 February 2000, para 52.   [84] Ibid, para 56.
[85] ECtHR, *Lucà v Italy*, Judgment, 27 February 2001, para 40. The same criteria are used for cases concerning decisions on lawfulness of detention: ECtHR, *A and others v United Kingdom*, above n 49, paras 216–20.
[86] Art 14(3)(e) ICCPR.
[87] Art 6(3)(d) ECHR; Art 16(5) Arab Charter; Art 8(2)(f) ACHR; ACommHPR, *Fair Trial Principles*, Section A.2(e).
[88] HRCttee, General Comment 32, para 39; ECtHR, *Vidal v Belgium*, Judgment, 22 April 1992, paras 33–4.
[89] ECtHR, *Kostovski v Netherlands*, Judgment, 20 November 1989, para 41.

whether the witnesses really needed protection, or if a conviction is based to a decisive extent on anonymous statements.[90]

g. Public trial

Article 75(4)(i) AP I specifies that the judgment of a conviction must be pronounced publicly. Human rights treaties are wider, in that they require trials to be conducted in public. They do provide for a possible exception to this for reasons of national security, but judgments in criminal cases must be public (unless this is not in the interests of children being tried).[91] A judgment must be written, including the essential findings of fact and evidence, and an explanation of the legal reasoning.[92] 45

The purpose of publicity is to prevent secret trials, which are a significant danger in any armed conflict, especially as such trials are likely to violate fair trial rules. As explained by the HRCttee, 'The publicity of hearings ensures the transparency of proceedings and thus provides an important safeguard for the interest of the individual and of society at large.'[93] It is only the trial itself, and any appeal that reconsiders the facts, that need to be public, and not necessarily pre-trial procedures or appeals on points of law.[94] 46

In order to ensure that the proceedings are public, courts 'must make information regarding the time and venue of the oral hearings available to the public and provide for adequate facilities for the attendance of interested members of the public [...] including members of the media, and [attendance] must not, for instance, be limited to a particular category of persons'.[95] 47

The treaty texts specify that exceptions to the presence of the public and press are possible only if the interests of justice so require. The dangerous nature of the accused is not a reason to prevent a public trial.[96] Relevant cases so far have concerned proceedings before a military or special court held in places off-limits to the public. These cases made it quite clear that entire trials may not be held in secret.[97] On the other hand, it is evident that if certain information or witnesses are to be kept confidential, then to the degree that this is acceptable, as explained in MN 42 and 44, for those parts of the trial, the public may be excluded. 48

h. Right of an accused to be present at the trial

The right of an accused to be present at his or her own trial is provided for in Article 6(e) AP II. This reflects the rule in the ICCPR, which states that an accused person is entitled to be 'tried in his presence'.[98] The ECHR and the ACHR do not specify this directly, but 49

---

[90] ECtHR, *Van Mechelen and others v Netherlands*, Judgment, 23 April 1997, paras 56, 59–60, and 63; IACommHR, *Report on Terrorism and Human Rights*, 2002, para 251; *Report of the Special Rapporteur on the promotion of human rights and fundamental freedoms while countering terrorism*, 4 February 2009, UN Doc A/HRC/10/3, § 63.

[91] Art 14(1) ICCPR; Art 6(1) ECHR; Art 8(5) ACHR; Art 13(2) Arab Charter; ACommHPR, *Fair Trial Principles*, Section A.3(f).

[92] HRCttee, General Comment 32, para 29; ECtHR, *Campbell and Fell v United Kingdom*, Judgment, 28 June 1984, para 91.

[93] HRCttee, General Comment 32, para 28. See also, to the same effect, ECtHR, *Stefanelli v San Marino*, Judgment, 8 February 2000, para 19.

[94] HRCttee, General Comment 32, para 28; ECtHR, *Helmers v Sweden*, Judgment, 29 October 1991, para 38.

[95] HRCttee, General Comment 32, paras 28–9; ACommHPR, *Fair Trial Principles*, Section A.3(a)–(e).

[96] ECtHR, *Campbell and Fell v United Kingdom*, above n 92, para 87.

[97] E.g., IACtHR, *Petruzzi et al v Peru*, above n 7, para 172.

[98] Art 14(3)(d) ICCPR; also in Art 16(3) Arab Charter.

as they include the right of an accused person to defend himself or herself in person, this right must be implied. Although a person may choose not to be present at the trial, such a choice must be based on unequivocal evidence.[99] A trial *in absentia* is possible only when notice has been given of the trial sufficiently in advance, and where the necessary steps have been taken to inform the accused person of the date and place of the trial, including a request for his or her attendance.[100] There is also a right to be present at appeal proceedings, provided that these concern questions of both fact and law, and not questions of law only.[101]

50 An exception to this right has been accepted in the case of hearings that include confidential evidence, where the accused—and sometimes even the accused's own lawyer—is not present. This possibility, which occurs most typically in cases relating to under-cover informants, is addressed in MN 42 and 44. However, this exception will cover only that part of the trial where this specific information is being presented to and discussed before the judges, not the entire trial.

i. Right not to be compelled to testify against oneself or to confess guilt

51 The right not to be compelled to testify against oneself or to confess one's guilt is specified in Article 6(2)(f) AP II and in human rights treaties.[102] It is very closely connected with the prohibition against ill-treatment during interrogation and the requirement of the presence of a lawyer during such interrogation, as described above. The HRCttee has confirmed that this provision is to be understood as prohibiting the use of 'physical or undue psychological pressure from the investigating authorities on the accused, with a view to confessing guilt', and that statements or confessions obtained as a result of torture or inhuman treatment are to be excluded from evidence at a trial.[103] This includes self-incriminating statements being made under duress without the presence of a lawyer.[104]

52 This provision means that evidence for criminal trials must not rely on confessions but rather on accurate and reliable evidence.[105] The UN Special Rapporteur on torture has pointed out that interrogators need to 'receive training in order to ensure that they have the necessary skills to conduct interrogations and interview victims and witnesses'.[106] With regard to the possibility of inferences being drawn from remaining silent, the ECtHR stated that this does not prevent a court from taking silence into account,[107] but such silence may not be the sole or principal basis for conviction.[108]

---

[99] ECtHR, *Zana v Turkey*, Judgment, 25 November 1997, para 70.
[100] HRCttee, General Comment 32, para 36; ECtHR, *Colozza v Italy*, Judgment, 12 February 1985, para 28.
[101] HRCttee, *Karttunen v Finland*, Com 387/1989, Views, 23 October 1992, para 7.3; ECtHR, *Kremzow v Austria*, above n 67, paras 58–67.
[102] Art 14(3)(g) ICCPR; Art 8(3) ACHR; Art 16(6) Arab Charter.
[103] HRCttee, General Comment 32, para 41.
[104] IAComHR, *Aguado Montealegre v Nicaragua*, above n 65.
[105] ECtHR, *Pishchalnikov v Russia*, above n 47, para 71. The same point has been stressed by the European Committee for the Prevention of Torture, *12th General Report*, CPT/Inf (2002) 15, para 34.
[106] HRCttee, Report, 23 December 2003, UN Doc E/CN.4/2004/56, para 35.
[107] ECtHR, *John Murray v United Kingdom*, above n 63, para 47.
[108] ECtHR, *Condron v United Kingdom*, Judgment, 2 May 2000, para 66.

j. Information on possible appeal

Article 6(3) AP II states that a convicted person is to be advised of possible judicial or other remedies as well as possible time limits, which means that if there is the possibility of appeal under national law, it must not be denied.[109]

The ICRC Commentary to the APs specifies that at the time of the adoption of the Protocols in 1977, the right to an appeal was not sufficiently widespread in national legislation to include it as an absolute right.[110] More recently, however, it has been consistently included in human rights treaties.[111] Although human rights provisions refer to the right of appeal's being governed 'according to law', this phrase refers to the modalities of its exercise and not to the very existence of the right of appeal.[112] This right is not reserved for only the most serious offences.[113] Although an exception may be possible for minor offences,[114] this exception is not likely to be relevant for offences associated with armed conflict.[115]

The human rights treaty bodies have specified that the right of appeal must include at least one appeal to another higher tribunal that reviews both facts and law, not just law.[116] In order for an appeal not to be illusory, the lower court delivering the conviction must provide a written reasoned judgment within a reasonable time.[117]

It would be difficult to assert that IHL now requires the right to appeal, but as such a right exists in human rights law, the assumption will be that a person convicted by a state tribunal must be able to access a higher tribunal.

k. Limits on the death penalty

Article 6(4) AP II specifies that persons who were under 18 at the time of the offence, as well as mothers of young children and pregnant women, may not be subjected to the death penalty. This provision reflects the rules applicable to international conflicts contained in the Geneva Conventions and AP I,[118] as well as those in human rights treaties,[119] and may be seen as reflecting customary international law.[120]

It is worth noting that under IHRL, there is a progressive move to eliminate the death penalty altogether, and although this has not yet achieved universal acceptance, a trend towards this effect can be seen. The ICCPR, the ACHR, and the Arab Charter specify that

---

[109] This is expressly stated in Art 106 GC III; Art 73 GC IV for international conflicts.
[110] ICRC Commentary APs, para 3587.
[111] Art 2(2) ECHR Protocol 7 (1984); Art 14(5) ICCPR; Art 8(2)(h) ACHR; Art 16(7) Arab Charter; ACommHPR, *Fair Trial Principles*, Section N.10.
[112] HRCttee, General Comment 32, para 45.   [113] Ibid.
[114] Art 2(2) ECHR Protocol 7 (1984).
[115] The Council of Europe Explanatory Report to Protocol 7 states that '[w]hen deciding on whether a defence is of a minor character, an important criterion is the question of whether the offence is punishable by imprisonment or not', Doc ETS No 117, para 21.
[116] HRCttee, General Comment 32, para 48; ACommHPR, *Malawi African Association*, above n 41, para 94; IAComHR, *Abella v Argentina*, Case 11.137, Report No 55/97, 18 November 1997, para 261.
[117] HRCttee, *Frances v Jamaica*, Com 320/1988, Views, 24 March 1993, para 12.2; ECtHR, *Hadjianastassiou v Greece*, Judgment, 16 December 1992, paras 29–37; ACommHPR, *Marcel Wetsch o'konda Koso and others v Democratic Republic of Congo*, Com 281/2003, 24 November 2008, para 90.
[118] Art 68 para 4 GC IV; Art 76(3) and Art 77(5) AP I.
[119] Arts 6(2), (4), and (5) ICCPR; Art 4(2), (5), and (6) ACHR; Arts 6 and 7 Arab Charter; Art 37 CRC.
[120] ICRC CIHL Study, Commentary to Rules 134 and 135. See also the US Supreme Court case of *Roper v Simmons*, No 03-633, Decided 1 March 2005, in which the majority judgment referred to the fact that most states prohibited the juvenile death penalty.

the death penalty may be imposed for only the most serious crimes.[121] Several Protocols prohibit the death penalty, although—aside from Protocol 13 to the ECHR—an exception is made for crimes committed in time of 'war'.[122] It is unlikely that 'war' includes non-international conflicts, as the intention was almost certainly to refer either to formal 'war' or at least to major international armed conflicts.

59   The extradition of a person for trial where there is a real risk of that person's being subjected to the death penalty has been considered in certain circumstances to amount to a violation of the right to life or to inhuman treatment, and therefore prohibited.[123] Although it cannot yet be asserted that these human rights developments have become universal and therefore applicable to IHL, it can be postulated that it would be prohibited to extradite a person to a country where there is a risk that he or she would be subjected to the death penalty in violation of Article 6(4) AP II.

l. Prohibition of trial more than once for the same offence

60   Article 75(4)(h) AP I sets forth a prohibition on trying someone more than once for the same offence (*ne bis in idem*), which is virtually the same as the prohibition in the ICCPR and similar to those in other human rights treaties.[124] It applies to an offence for which a person has already been finally convicted or acquitted, although the ACHR limits the rule to persons acquitted by final judgment.[125]

61   The rule does not apply to cases where new facts come to light, or where there has been a fundamental defect in the trial that could affect the outcome of the case.[126] The HRCttee also included as an exception the retrial of a person convicted *in absentia*, if that person requests it.[127] This is evidently important, because trials *in absentia* would normally suffer from a lack of adequate preparation of the defence.

III. Other important judicial guarantees

a. Trial within a reasonable time

62   Human rights treaties state that accused persons are entitled 'to be tried without undue delay',[128] or 'within a reasonable time'[129] after arrest or first official notification. The criteria that are taken into account are: the complexity of the case; the procedural activity of the applicant/petitioner; and the conduct of the judicial authorities.[130] The length of the proceedings is unreasonable when there is no valid reason for the delay, such as in cases

---

[121] For an analysis of the meaning of this term, see UN Doc A/HRC/4/20, 29 January 2007, paras 39–53.

[122] Art 2 ECHR Protocol 6 (1983) (Art 3 specifies that no derogation is possible from this Protocol); Arts 1, 2, and 3 ECHR Protocol 13 (2002); Arts 1 and 2 ICCPR Second Optional Protocol (1989); Arts 1 and 2 Protocol to the ACHR to abolish the death penalty (1990).

[123] E.g., ECtHR, *Al-Saadoon and Mufdhi v United Kingdom*, Judgment, 2 March 2010, para 123; HRCttee, *Roger Judge v Canada*, Com 829/1998, Views, 20 October 2003, paras 10.3–10.6.

[124] Art 14(7) ICCPR; Art 4 ECHR Protocol 7 (1984), which provides that this rule is non-derogable; Art 19(1) Arab Charter; ACommHPR, *Fair Trial Principles*, Section N.8.

[125] Art 8(4) ACHR.

[126] Art 4(2) ECHR Protocol 7 (1984); HRCttee, General Comment 32, para 56.

[127] HRCttee, General Comment 32, para 54.   [128] Art 14(3)(c) ICCPR.

[129] Art 6(1) ECHR; Art 8(1) ACHR; Art 7(1)(d) ACHPR.

[130] See, e.g., HRCttee, General Comment 32, para 35; ECtHR, *König v Germany*, Judgment, 28 June 1978, para 99; ACommHPR, *Fair Trial Principles*, Section N.5(c); IACtHR, *Valle Jaramilllo et al v Columbia*, Judgment, 27 November 2008, para 155.

which are not particularly complicated or where there are significant periods of inactivity which show a lack of diligence by the authorities.[131]

Although the disorder created by armed conflict can genuinely delay trials, the existence of an armed conflict will not necessarily, of itself, provide a valid excuse for excessive delay. In a case against Eritrea, the Government blamed the war for a delay of over five years. The African Commission on Human and Peoples' Rights (ACommHPR) expressly refused to accept this reasoning, stating that certain minimum standards must be maintained.[132]

b. Non-transfer to a trial representing a flagrant denial of justice

This is an issue that has arisen relatively recently in IHRL. The ECtHR found a violation of the right to fair trial in the context of an extradition to a state where the applicant would face a trial that included evidence against him obtained through torture. Such a trial would represent a 'flagrant denial of justice'.[133] It is generally accepted by human rights treaty bodies that it is unlawful to extradite or deport a person to a place where he faces a real risk of torture or inhuman treatment.[134] In this regard, both the HRCttee and the ECtHR have stated that a trial that does not respect judicial guarantees, and in which the accused faces the death penalty, amounts to subjecting the accused to 'inhuman treatment'.[135]

Although not expressly stated in IHL treaties in relation to non-international conflicts, it is significant that GC III and GC IV prohibit handing over persons to authorities that cannot be trusted to respect their IHL obligations.[136] There is no obvious reason why this should not also apply to non-international conflicts. In particular, recent and existing conflicts which began as international conflicts, have been recategorized as non-international conflicts further to the installation of a new government supported by the foreign forces. In principle it should not be acceptable to hand over persons to the new government if such government does not yet respect the necessary judicial guarantees. A relevant judgment is that of *Al-Saadoon and Mufdhi v United Kingdom*, in which handing over detainees to the Iraqi Government was found to violate the prohibition of inhuman treatment because the death penalty was possible.[137] The ECtHR specified that international obligations overrode the bilateral agreement requiring such transfer that had been made between the United Kingdom and Iraqi authorities.[138]

---

[131] E.g., IACtHR, *Genie Lacayo v Nicaragua*, Judgment, 29 January 1997, para 81; ACommHPR, *Alhassan Abubakar v Ghana*, Com 103/93, 31 October 1996, para 12; ECtHR, *Yagci and Sargin v Turkey*, Judgment, 8 June 1995, paras 63–9.

[132] ACommHPR, *Article 19 v Eritrea*, Com 275/2003, 30 May 2007, paras 99–100, in which a violation of Art 7(1)(d) ACHPR was found.

[133] ECtHR, *Othman v United Kingdom*, Judgment, 17 January 2012, para 263.

[134] This is also specified in Art 3 of the Convention against Torture and other Cruel, Inhuman or Degrading Treatment and Punishment. See generally Ch 58, MN 63–74, of this volume.

[135] HRCttee, *Francisco Juan Larrañaga v The Philippines*, Com 1421/2005, Views, 14 September 2006, para 7.11; ECtHR, *Öcalan v Turkey*, above n 55, para 207.

[136] Art 12 para 2 GC III; Art 45 paras 3 and 4 GC IV.

[137] ECtHR, *Al-Saadoon and Mufdhi v United Kingdom*, above n 123, paras 120–2 and 144.

[138] Ibid, para 138. See also S.E. Hendin, 'Detainees in Afghanistan: The Balance between Human Rights Law and International Humanitarian Law for Foreign Military Forces', 14 *Tilburg Law Review* (2007–8) 249, at 266–8, in which the author argues that persons may not be handed over to Afghan authorities if it is not clear that the authorities are able and willing to respect human rights requirements.

IV. Pre-trial judicial guarantees for detainees

a. Right to fair trial includes pre-trial guarantees

66 A number of judicial guarantees, most notably those referred to in MN 26–42 and 64–65, are not only essential for a fair trial but must also be provided before the trial itself. Indeed some of these are to be available almost immediately after arrest, and others are important right up until the actual trial takes place.

67 The UN Working Group on Arbitrary Detention has stressed that persons who are detained have less chance than those who are not confined to organize their defence effectively.[139] It is therefore important that people are not detained arbitrarily. Certain procedures in GC III and GC IV help prevent the unlawful confinement of people, and IHRL provides specific rules that help prevent the arbitrary detention of persons arrested with a view to a criminal trial. These are examined further below.

b. Appearance before a judicial officer

68 Although not specified as such in Common Article 3, it is standard practice in the national criminal procedure of virtually all states that persons arrested on suspicion of having committed a criminal offence are to be brought before a judicial officer within 24 or 48 hours. This requirement, to bring detainees promptly before a judicial officer, is reflected in human rights treaties.[140]

69 This procedure is important for a number of reasons. In particular, the judicial officer will assess whether sufficient legal reason exists for the arrest and whether detention before trial is necessary. The fact of being presented to the judiciary means that the arrested person is not at the complete mercy of the police, and is therefore less likely to be ill-treated or forcibly 'disappeared'.

70 Human rights treaty bodies have specified that the word 'promptly' in the treaty texts means that an arrested person must be personally presented to a judicial officer within two to three days, unless there is a genuine physical reason preventing this.[141] The officer concerned does not necessarily have to be a judge, but must be independent of the executive and must be able to release the person if there was no valid reason for holding him or her.[142] There also needs to be a minimal judicial procedure.[143]

71 This provision is not listed as non-derogable. There have been cases of genuine states of emergency where derogations from this right were undertaken and then contested before international human rights treaty bodies. A short delay beyond the two- to three-day time limit was accepted because the state concerned fully explained the need for this, and safeguards in the form of contact with family, doctor, and lawyer were available within two days or less of the arrest.[144] On the other hand, long delays of

---

[139] Report of the Working Group on Arbitrary Detention, 12 December 2005, UN Doc E/CN.4/2006/7, para 66.

[140] Art 9(3) ICCPR; Art 14(5) Arab Charter; Art 5(3) ECHR; Art 7(5) ACHR; ACommHPR, *Fair Trial Principles*, Section M.3(a) and (b).

[141] HRCttee, *Borisenko v Hungary*, Com 852/1999, Views, 6 December 2002; ECtHR, *Öcalan v Turkey*, above n 55, para 103; IACtHR, *Tibi v Equador*, Judgment, 7 September 2004, paras 117–18.

[142] HRCttee, *Kulomin v Hungary*, Com 521/1992, Views, 22 March 1996, para 11.3; IACtHR, *Suárez Rosero v Ecuador*, above n 40, paras 34 and 53–6; ACommHPR, *Constitutional Rights Project v Nigeria*, Com 153/96, 15 November 1999, paras 15–16.

[143] ECtHR, *Branningan and McBride v United Kingdom*, Judgment, 25 May 1993, para 58.

[144] Ibid, where a delay of up to seven days was accepted because of adequate safeguards.

11 days or more (still less elimination of the right) have not been accepted.¹⁴⁵ Following the same line of reasoning, totally arbitrary arrests cannot be justified during a state of emergency.¹⁴⁶

A distinction needs to be made between an inability to respect this provision because of *force majeure* (for example, active hostilities in the region) and a decision by the government to delay presentation to a judicial authority. The latter would be subject to the limitations to derogation just described. Cases of genuine *force majeure* will turn on when a return to the normal, or at least adequate, procedure is practically possible. 72

c. Trial within reasonable time or release

The same legal provisions that specify that arrested persons are to be brought before a judicial officer, state that such persons are to have a trial within a reasonable time or be released.¹⁴⁷ The purpose of this provision is to prevent unnecessary pre-trial detention, which is all too common. Such detention creates overcrowding, stress for family members, and difficulties in preparing an adequate defence.¹⁴⁸ 73

The human rights treaty bodies have specified that a person may not be kept in pre-trial detention unless there is a genuine danger of his or her absconding, the commission of new offences, collusion, intimidation of witnesses, suppression of evidence, or serious public disorder.¹⁴⁹ The existence of one or more of such grounds must be genuinely established and not just presumed.¹⁵⁰ 74

The evaluation of whether a person is kept too long in pre-trial detention, even if one or more of these grounds was present when first detained, will depend on whether the ground is still in existence and whether the authorities have been sufficiently diligent in pursuing the case. In this regard, although the complexity of the case and the procedural remedies pursued by the detainee may be taken into account, it is important to keep in mind that a person detained prior to trial must be presumed innocent.¹⁵¹ Therefore the trials of persons in detention need to be given priority, to avoid an abuse of the presumption of innocence.¹⁵² 75

Once required to be held in detention by the judicial officer, the only way that a detainee awaiting trial can contest his or her continued detention is by having the lawfulness of the 76

---

¹⁴⁵ IACtHR, *Petruzzi et al v Peru*, above n 7, paras 109-11; ECtHR, *Aksoy v Turkey*, Judgment, 18 December 1996, para 78; ECtHR, *Nuray Sen v Turkey*, Judgment, 17 June 2003, paras 27–8.
¹⁴⁶ IACommHR, *Lindo et al v Peru*, above n 31, paras 83–5.
¹⁴⁷ Art 9(3) ICCPR; Art 14(5) Arab Charter; Art 5(3) ECHR; Art 7(5) ACHR; ACommHPR, *Fair Trial Principles*, Section M.3(a). The ICCPR specifies that pre-trial detention 'shall not be the general rule'.
¹⁴⁸ Report of the Working Group on Arbitrary Detention, 12 December 2005, UN Doc E/CN.4/2006/7, paras 63–6.
¹⁴⁹ See, e.g., IACommHR, *Bronstein et al v Argentina*, Cases 11.205, 11.236, 11.238, 11 March 1997, Report No 2/97, 11 March 1997, paras 26–37; HRCttee, *Juan Peirano Basso v Uruguay*, Com 1887/2009, Views, 19 October 2010, para 10.2.
¹⁵⁰ E.g., ECtHR, *Istratii and others v Moldova*, Judgment, 27 March 2007, paras 9–16 and 73–8. The ECtHR's approach in this matter has been directly referred to and applied by the IACommHR in, e.g., *Jorge A. Giménez v Argentina*, Case 11.245, Report No 12/96, 1 March 1996, paras 82–3.
¹⁵¹ E.g., ACommHPR, *Fair Trial Principles*, Section N.5(b)–(c); IACtHR, *Suárez Rosero v Ecuador*, above n 40, para 72; HRCttee, *Fillastre v Bolivia*, above n 44, para 6.5; ECtHR, *Toth v Austria*, Judgment, 12 December 1991, para 67. See also Report of the Working Group on Arbitrary Detention, 12 December 2005, UN Doc E/CN.4/2006/7, para 64.
¹⁵² E.g., IACommHR, *Giménez v Argentina*, above n 150, paras 99–102.

detention reviewed. This is a right, often referred to as the 'writ of habeas corpus', that is available to any detainee, whether awaiting trial or not.

C. Rights and Duties of Rebels

I. Duty not to convict or sentence a person without respecting judicial guarantees

77   As Common Article 3 imposes obligations on rebel groups, it is evident that this obligation, contained in paragraph 1(1)(d), equally applies to them. A failure to respect the obligation not to convict or sentence a person without respecting judicial guarantees will result in a violation of IHL. The major question is whether rebel groups could in fact respect the duties outlined in section B of this chapter. There are two possible approaches to this: first, that all the obligations expected of state institutions must apply to rebels; or, secondly, that a more lenient standard might be applied to them.

a. *All state fair trial obligations apply to rebel trials*

78   The view that the rules must apply to all parties equally in non-international conflicts is a dogma borrowed from IHL applicable in international conflicts. It has been expressed as being based on equality of obligations between belligerents, or alternatively on the basis that persons affected have equal rights under IHL.[153] The dogma is not without difficulty, but there is some international practice to support it. During the El Salvador conflict of the 1980s and 1990s, the Farabundo Martí National Liberation Front (FMLN) established courts through which it passed sentences and executed suspected government agents and collaborators. In its report on El Salvador, the UN Observer Mission in El Salvador (ONUSAL) confirmed that the FMLN must respect Article 6 AP II, even though a rebel group might have difficulty in doing so. The report found that the courts were not independent and impartial, because of the political differences between the judges and accused; that the principle of legality had not been respected, as the supposed legal code used was seriously defective; and that the procedure, which lasted five days, was clearly so summary that it did not afford the necessary rights and means of defence.[154] Americas Watch also insisted that the same standards must apply to a rebel group.[155] During the Nepal conflict, the Communist Party of Nepal-Maoist (CPN-M) established 'peoples' courts'. The Office of the High Commissioner for Human Rights (OHCHR) criticized these courts because they failed to provide 'minimum guarantees of due process and fair trial by an independent court', stating that investigations of abuses by their own members 'cannot substitute for prosecutions carried out by a state court'.[156]

79   Practice so far therefore seems to suggest that full guarantees are required, although these have yet to be seen by a rebel court. It would appear to be accepted that such guarantees could be respected only if a rebel group has sufficient control of territory that it can,

---

[153] E.g., on the basis that all parties to armed conflicts have the same obligations: Institute of International Law, *Berlin Resolution*, 1999, Art II; ICRC CIHL Study, Rule 100 and Commentary.

[154] UN Doc A/46/876–S/23580, 19 February 1992, paras 111–15.

[155] Related in J. Somer, 'Jungle Justice: Passing Sentence on the Equality of Belligerents in Non-International Armed Conflict', 89 *IRRC* 867 (2007) 655, at 680.

[156] OHCHR-Nepal, *Human Rights Abuses by the CPN-M, Summary of Concerns*, 9/2006, at 4.

and does, behave like a government authority in that area.[157] Support for this approach is found in the requirement, under AP II, that sufficient control of territory exists for a party to be able to respect its provisions.[158]

United Nations Special Rapporteurs have pointed out that the 'Security Council has 80 long called upon various groups [...] to formally assume international obligations to respect human rights' and that '[i]t is especially appropriate and feasible to call for an armed group to respect human rights norms when it "exercises significant control over territory and population and has an identifiable political structure" '.[159] Both the Security Council and the General Assembly have adopted resolutions calling on named rebel groups that are *de facto* authorities to respect human rights.[160] This understanding includes pre-trial guarantees, as explained in MN 66–76. The OHCHR, for example, complained of the CPN-M peoples' courts abducting suspects and holding them in private houses for investigation.[161]

b. A more lenient standard for rebel trials?

Common Article 3 does not necessarily require rebel groups to control territory in order 81 for it to apply, and yet paragraph 1(1)(d) applies to them. It is evident that executing or passing sentence without any trial at all will be an automatic violation. The question, rather, is whether, in situations where rebel groups do not possess sufficient territory and/or are not sufficiently organized to exercise governmental authority, they could hold trials without being automatically in violation of this provision. If the standard to be required is that expected of state authorities, the response would be that any attempt at holding a trial is bound to result in a violation. Therefore, one approach would be that Common Article 3 prevents such trials altogether.

An alternative approach is to assume that Common Article 3 does presuppose that fair 82 trials could be possible, and therefore a less rigid standard might be applied. It has been suggested that it would be enough that rebel courts adopt 'appropriate standards', in particular, prompt notice of charges, adequate time and facilities to prepare a defence, right to counsel, and the assistance, if necessary, of an interpreter. This proposed list represents fundamental elements, but, as the author admits, it is not clear that even these could be respected.[162] On the other hand, these standards are less onerous than those listed in section B.II of this chapter, and therefore might at least avoid simple extra-judicial executions or totally summary trials without any guarantees at all. This approach is also supported by

---

[157] On this point see, in particular, C. Tomuschat, 'The Applicability of Human Rights Law to Insurgent Movements', in H. Fischer et al (eds), *Krisensicherung und Humanitärer Schutz—Crisis Management and Humanitarian Protection: Festschrift für Dieter Fleck* (Berlin: Berliner Wissenschafts-Verlag, 2004) 573, at 578. This approach can also be supported by the argument that control of territory creates the capacity to respect fair trial guarantees, and therefore the obligation to respect them. For a discussion of rights and obligations based on capacity, see A. Clapham, *Human Rights Obligations of Non-State Actors* (Oxford: OUP, 2006), at 70–3.

[158] ICRC Commentary APs, paras 4457 and 4464–7.

[159] Report of the Mission to Lebanon and Israel, UN Doc A/HRC/2/7, 2 October 2006, para 19.

[160] E.g., UNSC Res 1333, 19 December 2000; Res 1574, 19 November 2004; Res 2067, 18 September 2012; Res 2071, 12 October 2012; Res 2098, 28 March 2013. UNGA Res 56/176, 19 December 2001; and Res 57/234, 18 December 2002.

[161] OHCHR-Nepal, above n 156, at 4. The fact that judicial guarantees must include pre-trial guarantees was also stated in ONUSAL's report on the behaviour of the FLMN in El Salvador: UN Doc A/46/876–S/23580, 19 February 1992, para 111.

[162] J. Bond, 'Application of the Laws of War to Internal Conflict', 3 *Georgia Journal of International and Comparative Law* (1973) 372.

the notion that rebel commanders are required to try members of their own armed forces for war crimes, as handing them over to state authorities for trial would be unrealistic.[163]

83 Would Common Article 3 allow for such an approach? This depends on which rights are considered 'indispensable' and whether these could be different from those listed in section B.II of this chapter. It is also clear that a court has to be at least 'independent and impartial', which is not self-evident for a rebel group which is not a *de facto* government.

84 Another method might be to require all the 'indispensable' rights, but to accept some flexibility in their implementation in order to take into account the realities of the situation. To a limited degree, this has been adopted in human rights jurisprudence: the physical impossibility of presenting a person before a judicial officer within the normal two- to three-day time limit has been accepted by the ECtHR.[164] Therefore, the physical impossibility of respecting some of the duties within the normal required times should be seen as not violating IHL. However, to do away with guarantees that render fair trial meaningful, such as the right to a lawyer during interrogations (which could be postponed), would be problematic. The argument that requiring a lawyer for an accused is unrealistic in certain circumstances undermines the idea that a fair trial is possible in those circumstances. Better perhaps to have no trial at all, and to accept security detention instead.[165]

85 There is a human rights consideration that is directly relevant to this point. States are required to ensure[166] that all persons accused of a criminal offence receive a fair trial. This obligation exists within a state's entire jurisdiction, which automatically includes all of its national territory.[167] It would not be consistent with this duty if states were to accept that persons could be tried by courts that do not properly respect judicial guarantees. It might be objected that this does not concern IHL; but it does: states have expressly included in Common Article 3 and AP II that no one may be convicted without the respect of such guarantees. As we shall see in MN 90, states have shown significant concern about the idea that rebels may set up their own courts. Whatever their real motivation, this concern does accord with their human rights obligations!

II. Do rebel groups have the right to try persons?

86 It has been argued that the obligation not to convict anyone without a fair trial automatically implies a right to conduct trials, including the creation of courts, and legislation if necessary, for this purpose.[168] Although attractive as a proposition, it is submitted that this does not necessarily follow. If a body is given obligations which it has to carry out, for example the ICRC's mandate under the Geneva Conventions to create the Central Tracing Agency, it is clear that sufficient rights must have been given to carry out such mandates adequately. The same is not true for rebel groups: Common Article 3 and AP II do not actually require them to conduct trials; they only prohibit trials without adequate guarantees. A more careful analysis is therefore called for.

---

[163] Somer, above n 155, at 685.
[164] ECtHR, *Medvedyev and others v France*, Judgment, 29 March 2010, paras 128–33.
[165] See, e.g., a case in which the ECtHR accepted the argument of Ireland that, in the emergency situation concerned, administrative detention (with safeguards) was preferable to trials without proper evidence being available: ECtHR, *Lawless v Ireland*, Judgment, 1 July 1961, para 36 of 'The Law'.
[166] All human rights treaties require that states 'ensure' or 'secure' the rights contained therein.
[167] Stressed, e.g., in ECtHR, *Ilaşcu and others v Moldova and Russia*, Judgment, 8 July 2004, para 333.
[168] J.K. Kleffner, 'The Applicability of International Humanitarian Law to Organized Armed Groups', 93 *IRRC* 882 (2011) 443, at 451.

a. Trying persons with existing courts and legislation

87 In cases where rebel groups control sufficient territory, there seems to be no reason why normal courts should not continue to work, using pre-existing legislation, on crimes that are unrelated to the armed conflict. This would include everything from privately motivated murders to traffic offences. This would be in accord with states' positive human rights obligations to ensure that people under their jurisdiction are protected from arbitrary deprivation of life, loss of property, etc through the trial of common criminals.

b. The creation of courts by rebel groups

88 The FMLN in El Salvador and the Maoist group in Nepal created courts on the basis of a new a penal code. This raises the whole issue of whether rebel groups have the right to create new law, and then to try persons on the basis of such law. The assumption of the UN reports appeared to be that rebel courts could be created, because all the criticism was aimed at their lack of independence, impartiality, and adequate judicial guarantees.[169] In these cases the rebel groups did have sufficient control of territory and acted like a government in that region.[170]

89 The most serious problem is the creation of special courts to try government personnel and other 'enemies'. It is doubtful whether such courts could be independent and impartial. The pressure on the judges to reach the desired result would be overwhelming.[171] Equally, an ad hoc court for a particular individual or group, hastily put together for the purpose, will not respect the guarantees required by Common Article 3. A different scenario could be the creation of courts to replace corrupt and inefficient government courts. In such a case there might not be an automatic problem of lack of fair trial guarantees. The 'peoples' courts' created by the Maoist group in Nepal were given the task of hearing the whole range of criminal offences, including war crimes committed by their own personnel. If judicial guarantees had been respected, there would not have been a violation of IHL.

90 There remains, nevertheless, a suspicion of rebel courts, even if they try their own members for war crimes, as indicated by the reaction of the OHCHR, which stated that such trials 'cannot substitute for prosecutions carried out in a state court'.[172] State practice on this issue is primarily negative. During the negotiations of AP II, the ICRC argued in favour of the equality of rights and obligations of all parties to a non-international conflict, and proposed a treaty provision to this effect.[173] In this context it specified that rebels should be able to create their own courts. However, with the exception of one state,[174] all the others were either wary, or positively hostile to this notion.[175] The problem is that the creation of a criminal justice system is a fundamental function of government, and states are vehement in their rejection of any kind of status for rebel groups. On the other hand, it is clearly the case that the creation of courts that respect judicial guarantees is not a

---

[169] Described in MN 78.
[170] The assumption that such courts are possible in the right circumstances is confirmed by the ICRC Commentary APs, para 4597: 'every responsibly organised body' must respect Art 6 AP II; the footnote attached specifies that this also applies to organized armed groups within the meaning of Art 1 of the Protocol, i.e. that they control territory and are able to apply the Protocol.
[171] As pointed out in relation to FMLN courts: UN Doc A/46/876–S/23580, 19 February 1992, para 112.
[172] OHCHR-Nepal, above n 156, at 4.   [173] Draft Art 5.   [174] Belgium.
[175] A description of the discussion during the negotiations of AP II can be found in Somer, above n 155, at 660 and 677–8.

violation of IHL. A conclusion might be that international law neither expressly allows, nor prohibits the creation of rebel courts.

D. Legal Consequences of a Violation

I. State responsibility: right to reparation/remedy

91 As a lack of judicial guarantees during or before trial, or the execution of a person without a fair trial, represents various human rights violations,[176] the procedures available under human rights bodies would be relevant. Of course, both IHL and human rights violations may be submitted to the International Court of Justice (ICJ) in an inter-state dispute.

92 Several forms of reparation might be suitable in response to a conviction which failed to respect judicial guarantees. Restitution would require quashing the conviction, and rehabilitation could help the person be re-established in society. Compensation would be expected for loss of income and for the pain and suffering concerned. Guarantees of non-repetition may also be appropriate, depending on the circumstances. Satisfaction could be required in the form of finding and publicizing the truth about how the wrong occurred.

93 If a person has been executed without a trial, or without respecting judicial guarantees, then full restitution is clearly impossible. Quashing the conviction would still be appropriate if a trial had taken place, and all the other forms of reparation would be appropriate for family members. In addition, the state needs to investigate and punish those responsible for the wrongful execution as a form of satisfaction for the relatives.[177]

II. Individual criminal responsibility for an international wrong

94 A violation of Common Article 3 paragraph 1(1)(d) is listed in Article 8(2)(c)(iv) of the ICC Statute and in Article 4(g) of the International Criminal Tribunal for Rwanda (ICTR) Statute as an international crime. Also pertinent is Article 7(1)(e) of the ICC Statute, which includes, as a crime against humanity, 'imprisonment or other severe deprivation of physical liberty in violation of fundamental rules of international law' if carried out as part of a widespread or systematic attack against any civilian population. The same is true for the crime against humanity of 'imprisonment' in the Statutes of the International Criminal Tribunal for the former Yugoslavia (ICTY) and ICTR.[178] Executions without trial would amount to murder,[179] which is the subject of Chapter 22 of this volume. Murder is a violation of Common Article 3 paragraph 1(1)(a) and listed as a war crime in Article 8(2)(c)(i) of the ICC Statute.

---

[176] The principle of legality, the right to fair trial, right to liberty and security of person, and, in the case of execution, the right to life. An unfair trial potentially resulting in the death penalty amounts to inhuman treatment.

[177] HRCttee, General Comment 31, paras 16–18; UN Basic Principles and Guidelines on the Right to a Remedy and Reparation for Victims of Gross Violations of International Human Rights Law and Serious Violations of International Humanitarian Law, adopted by UNGA Res 60/147, 16 December 2005, paras 22(b) and (f).

[178] ICTY Statute Art 5(e); ICTR Statute Art 3(e).

[179] E.g., the Independent International Commission of Inquiry on the Syrian Arab Republic categorised the executions ordered by summary trials carried out by anti-government armed groups as 'unlawful killings': UN Doc A/HRC/20/CRP.1, 26 June 2012, paras 90 and 93.

The Elements of Crimes of the ICC interpret the lack of a 'regularly constituted court' 95
as meaning a court that 'did not afford the essential guarantees of independence and
impartiality'.[180] This means that this crime uses the definition of the nature of the court
that is required from Article 6 AP II, rather than Common Article 3. As noted in MN 10,
this was adopted to take into account possible rebel group courts, but it now applies to
both parties from the point of view of what amounts to a war crime. In any event, special
courts are frequently not independent and impartial, and this is the most serious violation
of the right to a fair trial.

With regard to the other judicial guarantees, these were intentionally not listed in 96
the Elements of Crimes. There was disagreement amongst the negotiators as to whether
a list would exclude important rights, and also whether the absence of respect for one
right would be enough to create a war crime. A footnote to this provision states that an
assessment needs to be made by the ICC as to whether the cumulative effect of any lack
amounted to the deprivation of a fair trial.[181]

In the case of *Kordić and Čerkez*, the ICTY was of the view that the crime against 97
humanity of 'imprisonment' and the grave breach of 'unlawful confinement' had common elements. The Court defined the crime of 'arbitrary imprisonment' as 'the deprivation
of liberty of the individual without due process of law'.[182] Although this case concerned
security detention, there is no reason why detention before or after trial without judicial
guarantees should not also be pertinent to this crime.

III. Criminal responsibility at the national level

Rebels remain subject to prosecution under national law, even when they have not committed any offences under IHL. Article 6(5) AP II encourages governments to grant the widest 98
possible amnesty to persons convicted for having taken part in the armed conflict, as well
as for those detained for security reasons. This is frequently done in the context of peace
agreements at the end of such conflicts. It is understood, however, that this amnesty must
not apply to persons who have committed international crimes, including war crimes.[183]

The requirement for states to try persons responsible for war crimes means that not 99
only rebel groups, but also state personnel wrongfully convicting persons or arbitrarily
detaining persons must be investigated and prosecuted.[184] Nevertheless, it has been noted
that rebel groups will have great difficulty in conducting trials that respect all relevant
judicial guarantees. It is therefore suggested that if such a rebel court imposes a sentence
of imprisonment, rather than execution, this should be taken into account in mitigation
of sentence in the event that an individual is tried for such a denial of judicial guarantees.

E. Critical Assessment

Although the requirement for a state to respect judicial guarantees does not, in principle, 100
present difficulties of capacity, the same is not true for rebel groups. Even for states, it

---

[180] UN Doc ICC-ASP/1/3 (part II-B), 9 September 2002; in Element 4 of Art 8(c)(iv).
[181] See commentary on the elements of this crime and the understandings of the states in K. Dörmann, *Elements of War Crimes under the Rome Statute of the International Court: Sources and Commentary* (Cambridge: CUP, 2003), at 408–38.
[182] ICTY, *The Prosecutor v Dario Kordić and Mario Čerkez*, Trial Chamber, Judgment, 26 February 2001, IT-95-14/2-T, paras 301–2.
[183] ICRC CIHL Study, Rule 159 and Commentary.   [184] Ibid, Rule 158 and Commentary.

101   The basic problem for IHL is the dogma of equality of obligations between belligerents which is fundamental for international conflicts.[185] Various suggestions have been made on how to deal with inequalities of capacity in non-international conflicts, ranging from a sliding scale of obligations to nuanced enforcement practices.[186] It has been suggested that although states are required to respect IHL and IHRL in full, the obligations of rebel groups should be limited to those IHL requirements that groups are capable of respecting in practice.[187] The problem with this is that existing IHL treaty obligations refer to guarantees considered indispensable by states; and furthermore this suggestion would be really unfortunate in contexts where human rights either are not well respected, or their application is disputed during conflict. There is also an increasing tendency, outside treaty law, to require non-governmental authorities to respect human rights.

102   If rebel groups cannot in practice respect judicial guarantees required for trials, detention without trial might be the better option. Although Common Article 3 does not regulate such administrative detention, IHRL automatically applies to detention by state authorities.[188] This is not evidently the case for rebel groups, although, as described in MN 80, there is an increasing tendency for states to insist that groups that control territory respect human rights. Attempts are being made to find a solution for IHL, in order to ensure that administrative detention by all parties respects certain standards and safeguards.[189] At stake is the fundamental axiom of IHL that no one is to suffer arbitrary treatment. If this can be achieved for any type of detention then it would be possible to maintain the same standard for trials, required by Common Article 3 and Protocol II, for all parties to a non-international conflict. In the view of this author, this is the better approach.

LOUISE DOSWALD-BECK

---

[185] See, e.g., series of articles in 93 *IRRC* 882 (2011) devoted to the theme, 'Understanding Armed Groups and the Applicable Law'.

[186] E.g., Debate between M. Sassòli and Y. Shany, 'Should the Obligations of States and Armed Groups under International Law Really Be Equal?', 93 *IRRC* 882 (2011) 425; R. Provost 'The Move to Substantive Equality in International Humanitarian Law: A Rejoinder to Marco Sassòli and Yuval Shany', 93 *IRRC* 882 (2011) 437.

[187] Suggested by L. Olson, 'Practical Challenges of Implementing Complementarity between International Humanitarian Law and Human Rights Law—Demonstrated by the Procedural Regulation of Internment in Non-International Armed Conflict', 40 *Case Western Reserve JIL* (2009) 437, at 454.

[188] These obligations are described in Doswald-Beck, above n 35, Chapter 9, and also at 95–7.

[189] ICRC, above n 29, at 18, and annexed document which represents the ICRC's institutional position: J. Pejic, 'Procedural Principles and Safeguards for Internment/Administrative Detention in Armed Conflict and Other Situations of Violence', 87 *IRRC* 858 (2005) 375.

Chapter 24. The Right of Initiative of the ICRC and Other Impartial Humanitarian Bodies

	MN
A. Introduction	1
B. Meaning and Application	8
I. Nature of the organization	8
II. Addressee of the initiative	14
III. Consequences of making an offer	17
a. Right to offer without an obligation to accept	17
b. Acceptance by one party only	20
c. Non-interference	26
d. Relationship with counterterrorism legislation	29
e. Services which may be offered	34
C. Relevance Outside Non-International Armed Conflicts	36
I. The right of initiative in international armed conflict	36
II. The ICRC in international armed conflict	37
III. The ICRC's right of initiative in situations not amounting to an armed conflict	38
D. Legal Consequences of a Violation	41
E. Critical Assessment	42

Select Bibliography

Bugnion, F., *The International Committee of the Red Cross and the Protection of War Victims* (Geneva/Oxford: ICRC/Macmillan, 2003)

Kalshoven, F., 'Impartiality and Neutrality in Humanitarian Law and Practice', 29 *IRRC* 273 (1989) 516

Mackintosh, K., 'Holder v. Humanitarian Law Project: Implications for Humanitarian Action: A View from Medecins Sans Frontières', 34 *Suffolk Transnational Law Review* (2011) 501

Modirzadeh, N.K., Lewis, D.A., and Bruderlein, C., 'Humanitarian Engagement under Counter-Terrorism: A Conflict of Norms and the Emerging Policy Landscape', 93 *IRRC* 883 (2011) 623

Pictet Commentary GC I, at 57–9

Sandoz, Y., 'Le droit d'initiative du Comité international de la Croix-Rouge', 22 *GYIL* (1979) 352

Spieker, H., 'The Right to Give and Receive Humanitarian Assistance', in H.-J. Heintze and A. Zwitter (eds), *International Law and Humanitarian Assistance* (Berlin/Heidelberg: Springer, 2011) 7

van Steenberghe, R., 'Non-State Actors from the Perspective of the International Committee of the Red Cross', in J. d'Aspremont (ed), *Participants in the International Legal System: Theoretical Perspectives* (New York: Routledge, 2010) 204

A. Introduction

1 The 'right of initiative' traditionally refers to the right of impartial humanitarian organizations to offer their services to parties to a non-international armed conflict (NIAC), without such an offer being deemed interference in the internal affairs of the state in question. Despite the fact that, strictly speaking, the Common Article 3 right of initiative does not exclusively belong to the International Committee of the Red Cross (ICRC), it seems apt to begin by discussing the history of the Red Cross Movement. At their inception, Red Cross National Societies were, by definition, associated with their respective governments, as they were auxiliaries to the medical services of the armed forces of the state. In the context of a NIAC, particularly one involving the government, they were necessarily affiliated with one party to the conflict. Nevertheless, Red Cross National Societies found ways to assist all the wounded in cases of NIAC. For instance, the French Society for the Relief of Wounded Soldiers cared for the wounded of both sides during the Paris Commune in 1871.[1] Similarly, the Spanish Red Cross National Society was able to assist all the wounded during the Third Carlist War in 1872, after its neutrality was recognized by both sides.[2] However, the first incidence of a foreign National Society assisting in the context of a NIAC was in 1895, when the American Red Cross Society obtained permission from the Spanish Government to deliver food and medical aid in the course of the conflict in Cuba.[3]

2 At this time, however, the ICRC was slightly ambivalent about its role in NIACs. It was not until 1938, during the 16th International Conference of the Red Cross and Red Crescent, that the right of initiative, as we now know it, started to emerge. Partly due, perhaps, to its rather traumatic experience in Russia (1917–21), where its activities were challenged as interference in internal affairs,[4] as well as its experiences in Upper Silesia, Ireland, and Spain, the ICRC submitted a Draft Resolution to the 16th International Conference, which addressed the issue of ICRC activities in situations outside of international armed conflict (IAC).[5] Article IV, paragraph 3 of this Resolution read:

Independently of direct requests for assistance, the International Committee is empowered, when the National Red Cross is divided between both parties, or when foreign societies are co-operating, to act as intermediary and thus facilitate the organization or co-ordination of the relief action.

Acting spontaneously and on its own authority, the International Committee may also offer its services and the collaboration of its appointed delegates, in order to ensure the best possible care of the sick and wounded, and assistance for POWs and for families separated by the events of war.

Such steps shall only be taken with the consent of the interested parties.

The International Red Cross Committee may, as in time of international war, request the direct or indirect co-operation of foreign Red Cross Societies.

---

[1] F. Bugnion, *The International Committee of the Red Cross and the Protection of War Victims* (Geneva/Oxford: ICRC/Macmillan, 2003), at 246.
[2] Ibid, at 246.
[3] *Bulletin international des Sociétés de secours aux militaires blessés*, later *Bulletin international des Sociétés de la Croix-Rouge*, 112 (October 1897), at 265–6.
[4] See Bugnion, above n 1, at 250–8. [5] Ibid, at 284.

Such action, whatever form it may take, shall in no case be considered as the recognition of a state of war or belligerence, nor as help furnished to one or other of the hostile parties.[6]

While the Resolution that was ultimately adopted did not contain this language at all, but rather a watered-down version of the substance, this paragraph of the Draft Resolution is nevertheless interesting for our purposes. Four of the main aspects of the right of initiative as it appears in Common Article 3 are evident even here. First, the draft provides that the ICRC may act spontaneously without having to be approached by any of the parties. Secondly, the ICRC may offer its services for certain humanitarian purposes. Thirdly, the action of the ICRC is contingent only on the consent of the party to which the request is addressed. Lastly, the ICRC's actions have no bearing on the legal status of the parties or the conflict.

A few years later, during the Diplomatic Conference, while Common Article 3 remained generally controversial—particularly in relation to its field of application—the right of initiative of the ICRC or any other impartial humanitarian body appeared in all the drafts proposed by both Working Parties.[7] The importance placed on the right of initiative is also reflected in the arguments of the Swiss delegate (Mr Bolla), who argued in favour of keeping Article 2A (now Common Article 3) based on the fact that this would allow the ICRC to carry out its work in 'civil wars'. Responding to suggestions that no provision referring to conflicts not of an international character be included, Mr Bolla argued that

[i]f as a result of these the Conventions we are engaged in establishing should be found not to contain a single word relating to civil war, it would be natural to conclude that the Diplomatic Conference of Geneva actually did not wish to frame any regulations whatever for the purpose of protecting the victims of civil war. And in that event I fear that the generous offers of service made by the International Committee of the Red Cross would meet with a categorical refusal, based on this *a contrario* argument.

[...] It would be extremely regrettable if activity of this kind should be rendered impossible by the deletion of the text of Article 2A as it now stands, from all the four Conventions.[8]

Thus, not only was ICRC activity in NIAC based on the right of initiative seen to be a crucial part of Common Article 3, but Common Article 3 was seen to be crucial in order to ensure the ICRC's work.

Mr Carry, representing the ICRC, said of the draft Article that despite not 'being a complete expression of the ideal which the International Committee has in view, [the text] ensures a minimum protection and—which is still more important—gives impartial international bodies, such as the International Committee of the Red Cross, means of intervention'.[9]

The right of initiative as contained in Common Article 3 is a reflection of the same right in times of IAC as contained in common Articles 9/9/9/10, and is the reduction of those Articles to fit into the 'Convention in miniature'.[10] As expressed in the second paragraph of Common Article 3, the right of initiative essentially allows impartial humanitarian organizations to offer their services to the parties to a NIAC.

---

[6] Ibid.   [7] Final Record, vol II-B, at 124–6.
[8] Ibid, at 335–6.   [9] Ibid, at 336.   [10] Pictet Commentary GC I, at 58.

B. Meaning and Application

I. Nature of the organization

8 Under Common Article 3, the right of initiative is enjoyed by impartial humanitarian organizations. The organization need not be an 'international' organization. In the course of the discussion of the very same phrase in what are now common Articles 9/9/9/10, the proposal to include the 'international' qualification was rejected.[11]

9 However, the organization must be both humanitarian and impartial. The ICRC is cited by the provision as an example of such a body. Therefore, while other organizations fulfilling these conditions may also offer their services, the ICRC may not be denied this right on the grounds that it is not an impartial humanitarian organization.

10 Given the reference to the ICRC as an impartial humanitarian organization in the text, the obvious starting point to determine whether an organization is impartial and humanitarian is by reference to the principles of impartiality and humanity as two of the fundamental principles of the Red Cross. According to the Preamble to the Statutes of the International Red Cross and Red Crescent Movement,[12] which is based on Jean Pictet's Commentary on these principles, 'humanity' encompasses three elements: the prevention and alleviation of suffering; the protection of life and health; and the assurance of respect for the individual.[13] Impartiality, in turn, involves non-discrimination on the basis of nationality, race, religious beliefs, class, or political opinion, as well as giving assistance that is proportionate to needs, in other words, giving priority to cases on the basis of urgency.[14] Additionally, at least according to Pictet, impartiality implies the application of non-discrimination by the individuals acting on behalf of the organization.[15]

11 The International Court of Justice confirmed this understanding of humanity and impartiality by referring to the Fundamental Principles of the Red Cross in its discussion about circumstances in which humanitarian assistance cannot be considered intervention in internal affairs.[16]

12 Therefore, it may be said that in order to fall within paragraph 2 of Common Article 3 such as to enjoy the right of initiative, an organization must be one that is primarily engaged in alleviating suffering without any adverse distinction except on the basis of need.

13 In this regard, the reference to the ICRC is merely by way of example of such an organization, the ICRC's humanitarian and impartial nature being uncontroversial. Other organizations may also claim the right of initiative, though a state may not deny that the ICRC enjoys this right. Unfortunately, practice of this is difficult to discern, since it seems that organizations only rarely refer to the right of initiative publicly.[17] One difference between the ICRC and other organizations remains that the ICRC has explicitly and

---

[11] Final Record, vol II-B, at 61.
[12] Preambular para 2 of the Statutes of the International Red Cross and the Red Crescent Movement, adopted by the 25th International Conference of the Red Cross at Geneva in October 1986.
[13] J.S. Pictet, *The Fundamental Principles of the Red Cross: Commentary* (Geneva: The International Federation of the Red Cross and Red Crescent Societies, 1979), at 14–17.
[14] Ibid, at 24–7.   [15] Ibid, at 31–3.
[16] ICJ, *Case concerning Military and Paramilitary Activities in and against Nicaragua (Nicaragua v United States of America)*, Merits, para 242.
[17] See, however, Geneva Call, *Armed Non-State Actors and Landmines*, vol II: *A Global Report on NSA Mine Action* (Geneva: Geneva Call and Program for the Study of International Organization(s), 2006), at 38.

publicly claimed the right of initiative for itself in the Statutes of the International Red Cross and Red Crescent Movement, which was adopted by the International Conference of the Red Cross and the Red Crescent, which includes all states parties to the Geneva Conventions.[18]

II. Addressee of the initiative

Under Common Article 3, an impartial humanitarian organization may offer its services to the *parties* to the conflict. Since Common Article 3 covers conflicts between governmental forces and non-state armed groups, as well as conflicts between non-state armed groups, this means that humanitarian organizations exercising their right of initiative may address themselves to non-state armed groups as well as to the government of the state. It might be asked whether an organization may offer its services to only one party to a NIAC. The answer to this is not immediately evident from the text of the provision itself. In his discussion of the matter in relation to the National Societies not located in the territory of the state involved in the conflict, Kalshoven argues that they are not under an obligation to offer their services to both parties to the conflict, and may make the offer to one side only without breaching the principles of impartiality and humanity.[19] One might also point to the Record of the Diplomatic Conference, where the ICRC said that its independence would be jeopardized if it were mentioned in any mandatory clause.[20]

Bugnion, on the other hand, argues for the extreme version of precisely the opposite view. According to him, the ICRC may not even exercise its discretion about whether to offer its services to parties to an armed conflict—it is obliged to do so.[21] His argument is based on the ICRC's 'tradition, its consistent practice, the Fundamental Principles of the Red Cross and its own ethos'.[22] Incidentally, he also points to comments made by the ICRC during the Diplomatic Conference, in which the delegate refers to the 10th International Conference to support his view.[23] For our purposes here, his arguments lead to the position that in a NIAC, the ICRC is obliged to offer its services to both parties to the conflict.

While Kalshoven and Bugnion's views are undoubtedly interesting, they are also specific to the Red Cross Movement. Even if Bugnion's position is accepted, it would mean that the *ICRC* is under an obligation to offer its services to both parties in a NIAC due to reasons that are specific to it and not related to international humanitarian law (IHL). However, the relevant question for IHL lawyers looking at the right of initiative of all impartial humanitarian bodies under Common Article 3, is whether Common Article 3 imposes such an obligation. Nothing in the plain meaning of Common Article 3 seems to indicate that an organization must offer its services to both parties to the conflict. Indeed, the word 'may' indicates discretion on the part of the body. Moreover, in certain cases, it

---

[18] Art 5(3) Statutes of the ICRM, above n 12, and amended by the 26th International Conference of the Red Cross and Red Crescent at Geneva in December 1995 and by the 29th International Conference of the Red Cross and Red Crescent at Geneva in June 2006.

[19] F. Kalshoven, 'Impartiality and Neutrality in Humanitarian Law and Practice', 29 *IRRC* 273 (1989) 516, at 525.

[20] Final Record, vol II-B, at 95.   [21] Bugnion, above n 1, at 408–9.   [22] Ibid, at 409.

[23] 'M Pilloud […] rappelle qu'en vertu d'un mandat qui lui a été conféré par la Xe Conférence internationale de la Croix Rouge, le CICR est tenu d'étendre son activité humanitaire aux conflits civils': *Actes de la Conférence diplomatique de Genève de 1949*, Départment politique fédéral, Berne, 1949, Final Record, vol II-B, at 41. According to Bugnion, the English record is misleading: see Bugnion, above n 1, at 409.

might make no sense to offer services to both parties. For instance, it is not inconceivable that only one party to an armed conflict has the resources to hold detainees. In such a case, an impartial humanitarian organization which is exclusively engaged in visiting detainees would logically offer its services only to that party.

III. Consequences of making an offer

a. Right to offer without an obligation to accept

17 While the right of initiative in Common Article 3 gives impartial humanitarian bodies a right to offer their services, it does not impose any corresponding obligation on the parties to accept such services.[24] Nothing in the language of Common Article 3 suggests this. Further, this position is based on the fact that such an obligation was proposed by the delegate of the United States (US) at the Diplomatic Conference and rejected.[25] Unfortunately, it is difficult to get a sense of whether this position is also supported by practice. This is because, as mentioned above, practice on this subject is notoriously difficult to analyse since humanitarian organizations apart from the ICRC do not explicitly refer to the right of initiative as a basis for their actions, and while we might assume that the ICRC does this in its communications with the parties, its commitment to confidentiality means that it does not often say so publicly. Instances of the ICRC's services being publicly refused in contexts where the state has acknowledged the existence of a NIAC are even rarer. In the last ten years, the only context in which it has publicly declared the existence of a NIAC and where it has admitted facing opposition to its activities is in Myanmar. The ICRC's activities (as well as those of other humanitarian organizations) were restricted in late 2005, with the restrictions becoming very severe by the end of 2006.[26] As a consequence of being able neither to carry out activities in favour of those affected by the armed conflict (i.e. having its offer of services refused), nor to engage in a meaningful dialogue with the Government, the ICRC issued a rare press release denouncing violations of IHL.[27] However, while it reminded the Government that it 'stands ready to do everything it can to pursue its humanitarian activities for people in Myanmar who require assistance, in accordance with its internationally recognized mandate',[28] it did not claim that not accepting such humanitarian activities constituted a violation of IHL.

18 Of course, there are also other ways of reading this practice. For instance, one could claim that the fact that the ICRC mentions the restrictions placed on it in a media release about violations of IHL somehow implies that this is also a violation of IHL. Further, one could also point to the scarcity of practice on public refusal of services by states which acknowledge NIACs on their territory as an indicator of a practice of acceptance.

19 However, both of these arguments suffer from the same shortcoming from which most arguments concerning public ICRC practice in relation to NIACs suffer—it is not clear what is an indication of a legal opinion and what is merely a political choice. If it were possible reliably to claim that the ICRC always publicly declares every NIAC to be such, and that it then offers its services to all parties and makes public the result of its efforts each time, then its practice would serve as a useful indication of the state of the law. However, given that this is not the case, the most sound position is one based on the explicit rejection

---

[24] Pictet Commentary GC I, at 58. [25] Final Record, vol II-B, at 95.
[26] ICRC Annual Reports 2006, at 185–8. [27] ICRC News release 82/07 of 29 June 2007.
[28] Ibid.

of a corresponding obligation during the Diplomatic Conference, combined with the absence of explicit assertions from the ICRC, states, or other international bodies that refusing an offer of services from an impartial, humanitarian organization constitutes a violation of Common Article 3. (Whether this argument may be made by reference to 'the right to humanitarian assistance' is explored in MN 43, below).

b. Acceptance by one party only

Another aspect crucial to the right of initiative is that while a party is not obliged to consent to receiving services, its denial of consent is only for itself. This position finds its roots in the first articulation of the right of initiative—the Draft Resolution submitted by the ICRC to the International Conference in 1938. This Draft referred to 'the consent of the interested parties'. In the course of the Diplomatic Conference, the delegate from Burma, General Oung, explicitly drew the Conference's attention to the fact that accepting the right of initiative as drafted would allow the ICRC (or another organization) to offer its services to the non-state armed group even where the state has denied consent.[29] Yet the text was adopted as proposed, indicating that states consciously accepted that they would not be able to control the relationship between the ICRC and the armed non-state actors (NSAs).

Nevertheless, a situation in which the government has refused the ICRC's services but the NSA wishes to collaborate, presents a formidable challenge for the ICRC (or any other body acting under Common Article 3). In their discussions of this issue, Bugnion[30] and van Steenberghe[31] distinguish between two scenarios—one in which it is not possible to access the territory controlled by the NSA without passing through territory controlled by the government, and one in which it is possible to access the territory controlled by the NSA without having to pass through that controlled by the government, perhaps because it can be accessed through another state.[32] Both authors say that while the first of these presents the ICRC with an impossible situation, where it has no choice but to continue negotiations with the government, in the latter, the ICRC may carry out its services.[33] Indeed, Bugnion cites past ICRC practice in this regard.[34]

What remains slightly unclear from what both authors say, however, is whether this is the legal situation or merely an appraisal of the practical constraints. It is clear that from a practical perspective, the ICRC is in a difficult situation. Regardless of its legal position, it would be faced with a politically sensitive situation, and would risk rupturing any future relationship with the government, were it to pass through areas controlled by the government even if it were legally entitled to do so. Additionally, there would be some very real security risks for its staff.

From a legal perspective, however, this distinction seems indefensible. Arguably, if the consent of the government is decisive for territory under its control, it is equally decisive for territory it claims but which is not under its control. After all, control over part of a state's territory by an NSA does not affect the state's sovereignty. However, if a state's consent to be on its territory, even where that territory is not under its control, were a

---

[29] Final Record, vol II-B, at 337.
[30] Bugnion, above n 1, at 520.
[31] R. van Steenberghe, 'Non-State Actors from the Perspective of the International Committee of the Red Cross', in J. d'Aspremont, *Participants in the International Legal System* (New York: Routledge, 2011) 204, at 207.
[32] Bugnion, above n 1, at 520; van Steenberghe, above n 31, at 207.   [33] Ibid.
[34] Algeria (1958), Iraqi Kurdistan (1974), Eritrea and Southern Angola: Bugnion, above n 1, at 522–3.

requirement, this would mean that in every instance of an offer of services, the state's consent would be a requirement. This would then mean that when services are offered to the state, only its consent is required, while if they are offered to the NSA, both the state's consent and the NSA's consent are required. This clearly goes against the principle that each party consents only for itself.

24 Further, in order to be effective, the right of initiative must necessarily involve, at a minimum, consent to passing through territory to carry out activities on territory controlled by the other party. By virtue of being a party to the Geneva Conventions, a state would have agreed to be legally bound to allow the ICRC some minimum level of access to its territory where the other party consents. While the ICRC sometimes works with NSAs outside the territory of the state they are fighting,[35] this is an exceptional circumstance. Certainly at the time this provision was adopted by the Diplomatic Conference, the vast majority of the ICRC's work with parties to NIACs was on the territory of the state involved.[36] This means that the typical situation which was being addressed by the right of initiative was one in which services and access to territory were coupled. Given the wording of this part of Common Article 3, and that it is generally accepted that it is only the consent of the party which is offered the services which matters, the insistence on also requiring the territorial state's consent would be to render the right of initiative devoid of any meaningful content.

25 Therefore, it must be assumed that by virtue of ratifying the Geneva Conventions, which include Common Article 3, states have bound themselves to allowing an organization access to territory which legally continues to belong to the state but is under the effective control of a NSA, even if they are not willing to allow the same organization access to territory which is under their control.

c. Non-interference

26 While a party to a NIAC may not be obliged to accept an offer of services, one part of the right of initiative which is clear is that the state may not consider such an offer as interference in its domestic affairs.[37] Indeed, this is the very essence and rationale of the 'right' of initiative, since without such a stipulation—that an offer of services does not constitute interference in domestic affairs—this part of Common Article 3 would be meaningless.[38]

27 The idea that the offer of an impartial humanitarian organization cannot be construed as interference in domestic affairs is uncontroversial. However, what seem unclear is what exactly this means. Going back to the Draft Resolution proposed by the ICRC in 1921, the final part of Article IV paragraph 3 gives an indication as to what non-interference into domestic affairs might be in relation to an organization as opposed to another state. This paragraph specified that actions taken by the ICRC 'shall in no case be considered as the recognition of a state of war or belligerence, nor as help furnished to one or other of the hostile parties'.[39] Thus, it could be said that offering services cannot be seen by a state party to the conflict as an action directed against its internal sovereignty, or by either party as providing aid and assistance to the military activities of the other side.

---

[35] E.g., in 2011 the ICRC met with armed groups from Myanmar in Thailand to discuss IHL issues such as the use of child soldiers and anti-personnel mines: *ICRC Annual Report* 2011, at 254.

[36] Bugnion, above n 1, at 284.

[37] Pictet Commentary GC I, at 58.   [38] Ibid.   [39] Bugnion, above n 1, at 284.

It could be argued that the question of interference in domestic affairs would not even 28
arise in situations of NIAC which involve violations of IHL and human rights law, since
the practice of the United Nations (UN) Security Council has been consistently to find
such situations matters of '*international* peace and security', most famously in the former
Yugoslavia.[40]

d. Relationship with counterterrorism legislation

Recent developments in the fight against terrorism, in particular in the US, seem to be 29
directly at odds with what seemed to be an uncontroversial aspect of Common Article 3:
that a state may not hinder an impartial humanitarian organization to offer its services
to an armed group. Section 2339B, title 18 of the United States Code (USC)[41] made it a
crime to 'knowingly provid[e] material support or resources' to certain foreign organizations designated as 'terrorist organizations' by the Secretary of State of the US.[42] 'Material
support and resources' was defined as

> any property, tangible or intangible, or service, including currency or monetary instruments or
> financial securities, financial services, lodging, training, expert advice or assistance, safehouses,
> false documentation or identification, communications equipment, facilities, weapons, lethal substances, explosives, personnel […] and transportation, except medicine or religious materials.[43]

Between 1998 and 2010, in the course of having the law challenged on constitutional
grounds, it was amended twice. In 2001, 'expert advice or assistance' was included in
the definition of 'material support or resources'.[44] In 2004, the law was amended again
to include the requirement of knowledge that the group was designated as a terrorist
group.[45] This same amendment also added 'service' to the definition of 'material support
or resources',[46] defined 'training' as 'instruction or teaching designed to impart a specific skill, as opposed to general knowledge',[47] and defined 'expert advice or assistance' as
'advice or assistance derived from scientific, technical or other specialized knowledge'.[48]

In *Holder v Humanitarian Law Project*, §2339B was challenged on constitutional grounds. 30
In the final Supreme Court decision of 2010, the law was upheld as constitutional.[49]
While the implications of the decision for US constitutional law are not crucial in
this context, the decision has grave implications for the right of initiative. Among the
activities that the plaintiff was carrying out was 'train[ing] members of [the Kurdistan
Workers' Party] on how to use humanitarian and international law to peacefully
resolve disputes'.[50] According to the Court, '[m]ost of the activities in which plaintiffs
seek to engage readily fall within the scope of the terms "training" and "expert advice
or assistance" '.[51] Arguably, other, more clearly material forms of support, such as food,

---

[40] UNSC Res 808 at 2, UN Doc S/RES/808 (22 February 1993).
[41] §2339B (a)(1), Antiterrorism and Effective Death Penalty Act of 1996. It was amended by the Uniting and Strengthening America by Providing Appropriate Tools Required to Intercept and Obstruct Terrorism Act of 2001 (Patriot Act), and the Intelligence Reform and Terrorism Prevention Act of 2004.
[42] The authority is bestowed on the Secretary of State by virtue of 8 USC §§1189(a)(1), (d)(4).
[43] Ibid, §2339A(b)(1); see also §2339B(g)(4).   [44] Patriot Act, above n 41, §805(a)(2)(B).
[45] Intelligence Reform and Terrorism Prevention Act of 2004, §6603.
[46] 18 USC §2339A(b)(1).   [47] 18 USC §2339A(b)(2).   [48] 18 USC §2339A(b)(3).
[49] *Holder v Humanitarian Law Project*, 130 S Ct (2010) 2705, at 2725.
[50] Ibid, at 2706. The plaintiff was also providing assistance to the Liberation Tigers of Tamil Eelam (LTTE), but since the conflict in Sri Lanka had ended by 2010, this is not relevant for our purposes.
[51] Ibid, at 2720.

clothes, and winter supplies, would even more readily fall within the definition of 'material support of terrorism'.

31   It could be argued that the humanitarian and impartial nature of the Humanitarian Law Project might be questioned. However, this law does not draw a distinction between impartial humanitarian organizations and others. Therefore, given that many of the 58 groups currently designated as terrorist organizations are parties to NIACs,[52] members of an impartial organization that were to offer services to one of these parties to a conflict would run the risk of facing criminal prosecution in the US, even if they were to conduct an IHL dissemination session without providing any physical assistance.

32   This legislation, and other anti-terrorism legislation criminalizing the provision of support of terrorism,[53] is frequently considered to implement Security Council Resolution 1373 (2001),[54] whereby the Security Council decided that states are to criminalize various acts related to funding for terrorism by their nationals or in their territory. If this is the case, such legislation could be said to prevail over Common Article 3, by virtue of a

---

[52] US Department of State, Bureau of Counterterrorism, Designated Foreign Terrorist Organizations, 28 September 2012, available at <http://www.state.gov/j/ct/rls/other/des/123085.htm>. On 10 April 2014, these groups were (chronologically in the order in which they were added to the list): Abu Nidal Organization (ANO), Abu Sayyaf Group (ASG), Aum Shinrikyo (AUM), Basque Fatherland and Liberty (ETA), Gama'a al-Islamiyya (Islamic Group) (IG), HAMAS, Harakat ul-Mujahidin (HUM), Hizballah, Kahane Chai (Kach), Kurdistan Workers Party (PKK) (Kongra-Gel), Liberation Tigers of Tamil Eelam (LTTE), National Liberation Army (ELN), Palestine Liberation Front (PLF), Palestinian Islamic Jihad (PIJ), Popular Front for the Liberation of Palestine (PFLF), PFLP-General Command (PFLP-GC), Revolutionary Armed Forces of Colombia (FARC), Revolutionary Organization 17 November (17N), Revolutionary People's Liberation Party/Front (DHKP/C), Shining Path (SL), al-Qaeda (AQ), Islamic Movement of Uzbekistan (IMU), Real Irish Republican Army (RIRA), United Self-Defense Forces of Colombia (AUC), Jaish-e-Mohammed (JEM), Lashkar-e Tayyiba (LeT), Al-Aqsa Martyrs Brigade (AAMB), Asbat al-Ansar (AAA), al-Qaida in the Islamic Maghreb (AQIM), Communist Party of the Philippines/New People's Army (CPP/NPA), Jemaah Islamiya (JI), Lashkar i Jhangvi (LJ), Ansar al-Islam (AAI), Continuity Irish Republican Army (CIRA), Libyan Islamic Fighting Group (LIFG), al-Qaida in Iraq (AQI), Islamic Jihad Union (IJU), Harakat ul-Jihad-i-Islami/Bangladesh (HUJI-B), al-Shabaab, Revolutionary Struggle (RS), Kata'ib Hizballah (KH), al-Qa'ida in the Arabian Peninsula (AQAP), Harakat ul-Jihad-i-Islami (HUJI), Tehrik-e Taliban Pakistan (TTP), Jundallah, Army of Islam (AOI), Indian Mujahedeen (IM), Jemaah Anshorut Tauhid (JAT), Abdallah Azzam Brigades (AAB), Haqqani Network (HQN), Ansar al-Dine (AAD), Boko Haram, Ansaru, al-Mulathamun Battalion, Ansar al-Shari'a in Benghazi, Ansar al-Shari'a in Darnah, Ansar al-Shari'a in Tunisia, Ansar Bayt al-Maqdis.

[53] National legislation that goes beyond criminalizing the provision of financial assistance and services and which risks threatening the activities of humanitarian organizations includes: Australia—Criminal Code (1995), Art 101.2; Bulgaria—Criminal Code, Art 108; Cambodia—Law on Counter Terrorism (2007), Art 77; Canada—Criminal Code, Art 83.18; Cape Verde—Penal Code (2003), Art 316; Cyprus—Federal Law on Terrorism (2004), Art 9; Denmark—Criminal Code (2005), para 114b; Ethiopia—Criminal Code (2005), Art 479; Gambia—Anti-terrorism Act (2002), Art 6; Georgia—Law on Amendments to the Criminal Code of Georgia (2007), Art 328; Ghana—Anti-terrorism Bill (2005), Art 6; Grenada—The Terrorism Act (2003), Art 6; Iceland—Penal Code, s 22; India—Prevention of Terrorism Act (2002), Art 21; Indonesia—Government Legislation in Lieu of Legislation No 1/2002 on Combating Criminal Acts of Terrorism (2002), s 16; Italy—Penal Code (1930), Art 270ter; Jamaica—Terrorism Prevention Act (2005), Art 7; Kenya—Anti-terrorism Bill (2003), Art 9; Malaysia—Penal Code (1997), s 130J; Mauritius—Prevention of Terrorism Act (2002), Art 6; Palau—Counter-Terrorism Act (2007), s 2(h)(7); Papua New Guinea—Internal Security Act (1993), Art 6; Philippines—Anti-terrorism Act (2005), s 4; Republic of Moldova—Criminal Code, Art 279; Saint Kitts and Nevis—Anti-terrorism Act (2002), Art 10; Saint Vincent and the Grenadines—United Nations (Anti-terrorism Measures) Act (2002), Art 6; Slovakia—Criminal Code (2005), s 297; South Africa—Anti-terrorism Bill (2003), Art 3; Sri Lanka—Emergency (Prevention and Prohibition of Terrorism and Specified Terrorist Activities) (2006), Reg 7; Tanzania—Prevention of Terrorism Act (2002), Art 18; Trinidad and Tobago—Anti-terrorism Act (2005), Art 9; Uganda—Penal Code Act, Art 26; Uganda—Anti-terrorism Act (2002), Art 89; Zambia—Anti-terrorism Act (2007), para 13.

[54] UN Doc S/RES/1373 (28 September 2001).

combination of Article 103 of the UN Charter and Resolution 1373. However, given the importance of Common Article 3, Resolution 1373 ought rather to be read so that it is consistent with the Geneva Conventions. Such a reading would exclude the services of an impartial humanitarian organization provided to a party to a NIAC from the ambit of the sort of support targeted by the Resolution.

Legislation which effectively criminalizes the offer of services to a party to a NIAC by an impartial humanitarian organization clearly contravenes the obligations of states not to regard such offers or services as unfriendly acts. If the reading of Resolution 1373 proposed above is accepted, this means that states that apply their legislation in this way are in violation of their obligations under the Geneva Conventions.

e. Services which may be offered

The text of Common Article 3 does not specify or limit the kinds of services which may be offered. Arguably, in order to fall under this provision, there must be a link between the conflict and the services offered. The practice of the ICRC serves to illustrate the kinds of services at issue. In 2011 (which was a typical year in terms of ICRC activities), for instance, the ICRC carried out a range of activities in situations that it acknowledged as NIACs, such as: assistance activities, including distributing food and essential household items to persons displaced by the conflict;[55] assisting people, including those returning after being displaced by the conflict, and communities to survive economically by providing tools, seeds, and animal health services and loans;[56] establishing programs relating to health, including access to clean water;[57] helping to re-establish family links and trace missing persons;[58] visiting persons deprived of liberty to monitor whether the conditions in which they are detained meet internationally recognized standards, and in some cases assisting the authorities to shorten trial periods and meet the nutritional and health needs of detainees;[59] maintaining dialogue with parties to the conflict with a view to addressing violations of IHL, including through the provision of IHL training;[60] helping to boost local capacity to care for the wounded and sick;[61] assisting in the management of risks to

---

[55] *ICRC Annual Report* 2011, at 100 (Central African Republic); at 112 (Democratic Republic of Congo); at 139 (Libya); at 152 (Somalia); at 157–8 (Sudan and South Sudan); at 168 (Côte d'Ivoire); at 177 (Senegal); at 241–2 (Philippines); at 305 (Russia); at 381 (Iraq); at 405–6 (Yemen).

[56] Ibid, at 100 (Central African Republic); at 112 (Democratic Republic of Congo); at 139 (Libya); at 152 (Somalia); at 158 (Sudan and South Sudan); at 169 (Côte d'Ivoire); at 177–8 (Senegal); at 241–2 (Philippines); at 305 (Russia); at 334 (Colombia); at 381 (Iraq); at 405–6 (Yemen).

[57] Ibid, at 100 (Central African Republic); at 112 (Democratic Republic of Congo); at 139 (Libya); at 152–3 (Somalia); at 158 (Sudan and South Sudan); at 168–9 (Côte d'Ivoire); at 178–9 (Senegal); at 306 (Russia); at 334–5 (Colombia); at 381 (Iraq); at 405–6 (Yemen).

[58] Ibid, at 101 (Central African Republic); at 112–13 (Democratic Republic of Congo); at 138 (Libya); at 153 (Somalia); at 158–9 (Sudan and South Sudan); at 168 (Côte d'Ivoire); at 179 (Senegal); at 305 (Russia); at 335 (Colombia); at 382 (Iraq); at 406 (Yemen).

[59] Ibid, at 101 (Central African Republic); at 113 (Democratic Republic of Congo); at 139 (Libya); at 159 (Sudan and South Sudan); at 169–70 (Côte d'Ivoire); at 179 (Senegal); at 243 (Philippines); at 306 (Russia); at 382 (Iraq); at 406–7 (Yemen).

[60] Ibid, at 101–3 (Central African Republic); at 114 (Democratic Republic of Congo); at 138 and 140 (Libya); at 153 (Somalia); at 159–60 (Sudan and South Sudan); at 170 (Côte d'Ivoire); at 179 (Senegal); at 244 (Philippines); at 305, 306–7 (Russia); at 336 (Colombia); at 383 (Iraq); at 407 (Yemen).

[61] Ibid, at 113 (Democratic Republic of Congo); at 139 (Libya); at 153 (Somalia); at 159 (Sudan and South Sudan); at 170 (Côte d'Ivoire); at 179 (Senegal); at 243–4 (Philippines); at 306 (Russia); at 335–6 (Colombia); at 382–3 (Iraq); at 407 (Yemen).

civilians from mines and explosive remnants of such mines;[62] and assisting civilians who have been affected by violence to find protection.[63]

35   Thus, it might be said that a wide range of activities could fall under the right of initiative, including those which aim to assist and protect people affected by NIAC, as well as those which aim to curtail violations of IHL.

C. Relevance Outside Non-International Armed Conflicts

I. The right of initiative in international armed conflict

36   As mentioned above, the right of humanitarian initiative in NIAC is based on a similar provision in IAC. This is contained in common Articles 9/9/9/10.[64] Since Common Article 3 sought to mimic these provisions for application in situations of NIAC,[65] the content of the humanitarian right of initiative is largely identical.[66]

II. The ICRC in international armed conflict

37   There is, however, a difference between IAC and NIAC in relation to the ICRC specifically. While the ICRC enjoys a general right of initiative as an impartial humanitarian body in both types of conflict (under Common Article 3 in NIAC and under common Articles 9/9/9/10 in IAC), in IAC it also enjoys a conventional mandate which the states must respect. Thus, unlike visits to persons deprived of their liberty in relation to a NIAC, where a state enjoys the discretion to refuse the ICRC's offer, a state is obliged to allow the ICRC to visit prisoners of war and protected civilians in the event of an IAC.[67]

III. The ICRC's right of initiative in situations not amounting to an armed conflict

38   Under the Statutes of the International Red Cross and Red Crescent Movement, not only does the ICRC enjoy the right of initiative in IAC and NIAC, but by virtue of Article 5(3), it has also claimed such a right for itself in situations that do not amount to an armed conflict. Indeed, it has been ICRC practice to offer its humanitarian services to states even where there is no armed conflict, and there is corresponding practice of states to accept this. For instance, in 2011, the ICRC visited detention facilities in several states without invoking IHL. In Egypt[68] and Iran,[69] for instance, it used the language of civil unrest, and in Zimbabwe it visited police stations.[70]

39   The advantage of having a right of initiative in the absence of armed conflict as well as in IAC and NIAC, is that the ICRC can offer its services without communicating its legal reading of the situation. Leaving aside the question of whether it ought to announce publicly the beginning and end of armed conflicts in light of its role as the guardian of IHL (after all, the first step to ensuring that IHL is respected is to insist that IHL applies), there may be times when such communication is politically sensitive. Further, from a humanitarian perspective, if the ICRC has a right to offer its services at all times, then it could

---

[62] Ibid, at 139 (Libya); at 382 (Iraq).
[63] Ibid, at 334 (Colombia).   [64] See also Ch 26, section C, of this volume.
[65] Pictet Commentary GC I, at 58.
[66] See generally Ch 12, MN 35–37, and Ch 26, MN 23, of this volume.
[67] See Ch 26, section C, of this volume.   [68] *ICRC Annual Report* 2011, at 373.
[69] Ibid, at 378.   [70] Ibid, at 181.

make such an offer in general terms in the absence of armed conflict, and then amend its offer if the situation evolves into a NIAC or an IAC. This would mean that there would be certain humanitarian activities that could continue uninterrupted regardless of changes in the legal classification of the situation.

However, in the course of the 31st International Conference of the Red Cross and Red Crescent, some states seemed to display a certain amount of discomfort with the ICRC discussing situations which do not amount to armed conflict. This is evident in the fact that the Draft Resolution submitted to the Conference by the Committee was entitled 'Health Care in Danger: Respecting and Protecting Health Care in Armed Conflict and Other Situations of Violence', while the one eventually adopted was entitled 'Health Care in Danger: Respecting and Protecting Health Care'. The Draft[71] contained 12 references to such situations; the Resolution, none.[72] To the extent that this indicates a suspicion on the part of states towards ICRC activities in situations which do not amount to armed conflict, it might mean that the ICRC will have to be more diligent in its classification of NIACs and its communication of such a classification. After all, in NIAC, its right of initiative is regulated by the Geneva Conventions which states have freely ratified.

D. Legal Consequences of a Violation

Since the right of initiative imposes no duty apart from not considering an offer to be an unfriendly act, it is not immediately clear whether the notion of 'violation' is relevant. Nevertheless, given the above discussion regarding anti-terrorism legislation which arguably does violate the norm in this way, it is theoretically possible that states with such legislation expose themselves to the usual consequences of violating an international obligation. In theory, if Common Article 1 is interpreted as making every state party injured by any violation of IHL, it is possible for another state party to the Geneva Conventions to take proportionate countermeasures against a state with offending legislation, relying on Article 49 of the ILC Articles on State Responsibility.[73] In any case, every state party could invoke such a violation and demand its cessation, as Common Article 1 clearly implies that Common Article 3 constitutes an obligation *erga omnes*.[74]

E. Critical Assessment

Curiously, there are two (seemingly) contradictory trends emerging with regard to the services of humanitarian organizations in situations of NIAC which could shape the development of the right of initiative. On the one hand, arguments that states are obliged to grant access to humanitarian agencies which deliver aid are invoked with increasing frequency, including by intergovernmental organizations.[75] On the other hand, states

---

[71] ICRC, *Health Care in Danger: Respecting and Protecting Health Care in Armed Conflict and Other Situations of Violence—Draft Resolution and Background Document* (Geneva, October 2011).
[72] *Resolution 5—Health Care in Danger: Respecting and Protecting Health Care*, 31st International Conference of the Red Cross and Red Crescent, adopted 1 December 2011.
[73] ILC Articles on State Responsibility. [74] Ibid, Art 48. [75] See Ch 12 of this volume.

43   The first of these trends is marked by increasing insistence that states grant humanitarian actors access to their territories to carry out activities in favour of the civilian population.[76] While it is hard to imagine that such insistence will extend to all humanitarian initiatives (for instance, it is not likely that states will accept that they have an obligation to allow all impartial humanitarian agencies to visit persons deprived of their liberty in connection with a NIAC, absent a specific treaty obligation), it is conceivable that under the pressure of practice and existing obligations under other branches of law, such as human rights law, states will accept an obligation to allow food and medical aid. Indeed, in UN Security Council Resolution 2139 (2014), the Council demanded that 'all parties, in particular the Syrian authorities, promptly allow rapid, safe and unhindered humanitarian access for UN humanitarian agencies and their implementing partners'.[77] This Resolution thus 'imposes' humanitarian access, be it only for UN agencies and their implementing partners. It even recalled 'that arbitrary denial of humanitarian access […] can constitute a violation of international humanitarian law'.[78]

44   The competing trend is marked by moves made by states to criminalize humanitarian assistance to and engagement with parties to NIACs discussed above.[79] Since providing humanitarian assistance to civilians living in areas controlled by a non-state party to a NIAC would necessarily involve contacting this party and negotiating with it, any organization undertaking this task opens itself up to the risk of criminal prosecution. This risk is graver if there is any chance that even some of this aid might be diverted—a possibility that no organization can rule out completely.

45   The crystallization of both these trends could lead to an unfortunate situation where states are obliged to grant access to humanitarian agencies which are delivering aid on to the territory under their control, but at the same time could effectively deprive populations living in parts controlled by a non-state armed group from benefitting from such aid under the threat of criminal sanctions for those negotiating with such groups. Even medical assistance, traditionally an area protected by IHL even where it benefits combatants, is complicated by these competing trends. Security Council Resolution 2139 demands that the parties in Syria 'facilitate free passage to all areas for medical personnel, equipment, transport and supplies',[80] while under US case law, 'medical support, such as volunteering to serve as an on-call doctor for a terrorist organization, constitutes a provision of personnel and/or scientific assistance' which would fall foul of the Patriot Act.[81] So while the Syrian Government is under an obligation to facilitate the work of medical personnel, even if they are helping the opposition, the only thing that prevents the US Government from prosecuting the same medical personnel is the fact that most groups of the Syrian opposition are not on its list of terrorist organizations.

NISHAT NISHAT*

---

[76] See, e.g., ICRC CIHL Database, Rule 55.   [77] UNSC Res 2139 (2014), para 6.
[78] Ibid, Preambular para 10.   [79] MN 29–33.
[80] Above n 77, para 6.   [81] *United States v Sabir*, F 3d (2d Cir Feb 4, 2011), 27.

* I am greatly indebted to the editors and Ms Annie Hylton for their invaluable comments on an earlier draft of this chapter. Any errors, of course, remain my own responsibility.

Chapter 25. Applicability of the Conventions by Means of Ad Hoc Agreements

	MN
A. Historical Background and Meaning of the Provision	1
B. Practice and Content of the Ad Hoc Agreements	5
C. Legal Status of the Ad Hoc Agreements	19
D. Legal Consequences in Case of a Violation	31
I. Compliance mechanism	33
II. Enforcement mechanism	39
a. Individual criminal responsibility	41
b. State responsibility	47
E. Critical Assessment	49

Select Bibliography

Bell, C., 'Peace Agreements: Their Nature and Legal Status', 100 *AJIL* (2006) 372

Bell, C., *On the Law of Peace: Peace Agreements and the* Lex Pacificatoria (Oxford: OUP, 2008)

Corten, O./Klein, P., 'Are Agreements between States and Non-State Entities Rooted in the International Legal Order?', in E. Cannizzaro (ed), *The Law of Treaties beyond the Vienna Convention* (Oxford: OUP, 2011) 3

Ewumbue-Monono, C., 'Respect for International Humanitarian Law by Armed Non-State Actors in Africa', 88 *IRRC* 864 (2006) 905

Jakovljevic, B., 'The Agreement of May 22, 1992, on the Implementation of International Humanitarian Law in the Armed Conflict in Bosnia-Herzegovina', 2–3 *Yugoslovenska Revija za Medunarodno Pravo* (1992) 212

Roucounas, E., 'Peace Agreements as Instruments for the Resolution of Intrastate Conflict', in UNESCO, *Conflict Resolution: New Approaches and Methods* (Paris: UNESCO, 2000) 113

Sandoz, Y., 'Réflexions sur la mise en oeuvre du droit international humanitaire et sur le rôle du Comité international de la Croix-Rouge en ex-Yougoslavie', 4 *Revue suisse de droit international et de droit européen* (1993) 461

Sivakumaran, S., 'Binding Armed Opposition Groups', 55 *ICLQ* (2006) 369

Sivakumaran, S., *The Law of Non-International Armed Conflict* (Oxford: OUP, 2012)

Veuthey, M., 'Learning from History: Accession to the Conventions, Special Agreements, and Unilateral Declarations', in *Relevance of International Humanitarian Law to Non-State Actors: Proceedings of the Bruges Colloquium: 25th–26th October 2002* (Bruges [etc]: College of Europe [etc], 2003) 139

Vierucci, L., ' "Special Agreements" between Conflicting Parties in the Case-law of the ICTY', in B. Swart, G. Sluiter, and A. Zahar (eds), *The Legacy of the International Criminal Tribunal for the Former Yugoslavia* (Oxford: OUP, 2011) 401

Vierucci, L., *Gli accordi fra governo e gruppi armati di opposizione nel diritto internazionale* (Naples: Scientifica, 2013)

A. Historical Background and Meaning of the Provision

1 According to Common Article 3 paragraph 3 the parties to a non-international armed conflict (NIAC), 'should [...] endeavour to bring into force, by means of special agreements, all or part of the other provisions of the [...] Convention[s]'. The wording of this paragraph testifies to the reluctance of the states that participated in the 1949 Diplomatic Conference to make the provisions of each or any of the four Geneva Conventions applicable in their entirety to all NIACs. Accordingly, the parties to a NIAC are encouraged to stipulate agreements supplementing Common Article 3.[1] The interest in concluding such agreements lies in the fact that, beyond the rules that are applicable between the parties via custom or treaty, they also become bound by ad hoc rules for the specific conflict the agreement covers.

2 In 1949, the drafters of the Geneva Conventions feared that a special agreement concluded by virtue of Common Article 3 would constitute an implicit recognition of the belligerency rights of an opposing party. This led to the specification included in the fourth paragraph of Common Article 3, that the legal status of the parties to the conflict would not be affected by the adoption of such an agreement.

3 Common Article 3 paragraph 3 does not specify whether an ad hoc agreement may be concluded only between the parties to a conflict, or whether it may also be concluded with third parties, e.g. the United Nations (UN) and the International Committee of the Red Cross (ICRC).[2] It is submitted that an agreement between one party to a conflict and a third party comes under the purview of Common Article 3 only if it concerns the rights and obligations of all the contracting parties in terms of international humanitarian law (IHL). This means that if an agreement contains only a unilateral (not bilateral) undertaking by one party to the conflict to respect IHL, or specifies only the rights and obligations of the third party,[3] it cannot be considered as covered by Common Article 3.

4 Common Article 3 paragraph 3 also leaves open the question of the form that an ad hoc agreement ought to take. As a consequence, not only written but also oral agreements might be considered to come within the purview of this provision, provided they contain parallel (not unilateral) commitments between the parties.

B. Practice and Content of the Ad Hoc Agreements

5 Practice shows that ad hoc agreements that are expressly grounded in Common Article 3[4] are very few. Reference may be made to the Agreement on the Application and the

---

[1] According to a literal interpretation of CA 3, para 3, the parties to a conflict are merely invited to conclude special agreements. *Contra*, Pictet Commentary GC I, at 59, referring to an obligation *de contrahendo* ('The provision does not merely offer a convenient possibility, but makes an urgent request, points out a duty').

[2] The Pictet Commentary GC I seems to assume that special agreements were to be concluded between the government and one (or more) armed opposition groups only (ibid, at 59–60 and esp at 48). L. Zegveld, *The Accountability of Armed Opposition Groups in International Law* (Cambridge: CUP, 2002), at 29, envisages the possibility that a special agreement might be concluded between armed groups, or between an armed group and an international organization or the ICRC.

[3] For examples of agreements concluded by one party to a NIAC and the ICRC, see C. Ewumbue-Monono, 'Respect for International Humanitarian Law by Armed Non-State Actors in Africa', 88 *IRRC* 864 (2006) 905, at 911–13 (these agreements mainly concern the creation of humanitarian corridors to evacuate vulnerable persons, and the liberation of persons deprived of their freedom for reasons connected with the conflict).

[4] We are referring to those agreements that are expressly concluded on the basis of CA 3 para 3.

Implementation of International Humanitarian Law within the Context of the Conflict in Bosnia-Herzegovina, signed on 22 May 1992;[5] the Humanitarian Agreement between the Government of Colombia and the Revolutionary Armed Forces of Colombia–People's Army (FARC–EP), concluded on 2 June 2001;[6] and the Agreement between the Government of the Republic of Sudan and the Sudan People's Liberation Movement (SPLM) to Protect Non-Combatant Civilians and Civilian Facilities from Military Attack, of 10 March 2002.[7] The small number of the ad hoc agreements expressly covered by Common Article 3 is striking in view of the large number of NIACs that have taken place since the entry into force of the Geneva Conventions. This testifies to the difficulties for the parties to a NIAC to negotiate ad hoc humanitarian rules in the course of the armed confrontation.[8]

However, in our view also those agreements that, though formally not stipulated by virtue of Common Article 3, aim at putting in place additional humanitarian rules between the parties to the conflict, should qualify as ad hoc agreements since they fulfil the same objective pursued by Common Article 3 paragraph 3.[9] Reference is here made to those special agreements the object and purpose of which is humanitarian, such as the Comprehensive Agreement on Respect for Human Rights and International Humanitarian Law concluded between the Government of the Philippines and the National Democratic Front of the Philippines, on 16 March 1998 (CARHRIHL),[10] and the Protocol between the Government of the Sudan, the Sudan Liberation Movement/Army, and the Justice and Equality Movement on the Improvement of the Humanitarian Situation in Darfur, of 9 November 2004.[11] It should be noted that several distinct agreements concluded between the same parties to the conflict might aim at addressing humanitarian issues.[12]

More debatable is the qualification as ad hoc agreements within the meaning of Common Article 3 of those mutual engagements that, though pursuing other than humanitarian aims, for example a ceasefire or peace proper, also contain rules of a humanitarian nature. The most correct view seems to be that these agreements do not fall within the category envisaged by Common Article 3, since their prevailing object and purpose are not humanitarian. In any case, the humanitarian rules of these agreements, if any, should be taken into account as IHL norms binding the parties to that specific armed conflict.[13]

---

[5] The agreement was signed by the representatives of the various factions of the conflict in Bosnia-Herzegovina, namely a representative of Alija Izetbegović (President of the Republic of Bosnia-Herzegovina and the Party of Democratic Action), Radovan Karadžić (President of the Serbian Democratic Party), and Miljenko Brkić (President of the Croatian Democratic Community). The text of the agreement is on file with the author.

[6] The agreement, labelled as the Acuerdo entre el Gobierno Nacional y las FARC-EP (Acuerdo Humanitario), is available at <http://www.ideaspaz.org/secciones/publicaciones/download_boletines/boletindepaz01.htm>.

[7] The Agreement is available at <http://peacemaker.un.org/node/1259>.

[8] It is plausible that *durante bello* the parties prefer to commit themselves to humanitarian rules without having to negotiate with the enemy, e.g., by issuing unilateral declarations of respect for IHL rules. However, the conclusion of an ad hoc agreement has the advantage of binding all the parties to the same rules.

[9] In this sense, see also S. Sivakuraman, *The Law of Non-International Armed Conflict* (Oxford: OUP, 2012), at 125.

[10] The Agreement is available at <http://peacemaker.un.org/node/1537>.

[11] See also the Acuerdo de La Puerto del Cielo between some representatives of the Colombian civilian society and the Ejercito de Liberación Nacional, 15 July 1998.

[12] E.g., during the conflict in Bosnia-Herzegovina, beyond the one expressly grounded in CA 3 (above MN 5 and n 5), four other agreements were concluded under the auspices of the ICRC between 23 May and 1 October 1992 [agreements on file with author], all of which have an exclusively humanitarian object and purpose.

[13] Practice indicates that these humanitarian rules contained in non-CA 3 agreements mainly concern the release of persons deprived of their freedom in connection with the armed conflict, the amnesty for certain

8   Common Article 3 agreements are usually negotiated by intermediaries, often the ICRC. Indeed, it would probably be unrealistic to expect that a party to an armed conflict would be willing to take the initiative to negotiate directly with its adversary.

9   As to content, ad hoc agreements should not only restate the applicability of Common Article 3,[14] but also extend the law binding the parties beyond that provision, because the rationale underlying the Article is to bring into force IHL rules that would not otherwise bind the parties. This means that through the ad hoc regulation, the rules contained in Additional Protocol (AP) I of 1977 may also become applicable.[15] Denying this possibility would prevent the parties from agreeing on detailed rules on the conduct of hostilities for a specific NIAC. Similarly, the rules of AP II of 1977 may also become the object of an ad hoc agreement, in case the state is not a party to the Protocol, as well as human rights concerns not addressed by IHL rules.[16] At the same time, some provisions of the Geneva Conventions are difficult to apply in NIACs as they relate to notions attached exclusively to international armed conflicts (IACs).[17]

10 According to the Pictet Commentary to GC I,[18] 'the most practical way' to extend the application of IHL through ad hoc regulation 'is not to negotiate special agreements in great detail, but simply to refer to the Convention[s]' as they stand, or to specific provisions thereof. In practice, the ad hoc agreements, both those expressly grounded in Common Article 3 and those having a humanitarian object and purpose, mainly reformulate the obligations already contained in the Geneva Conventions rather than making a *renvoi* to the latter. For example, on 22 May 1992, the three factions combating each other in Bosnia-Herzegovina agreed in writing, inter alia, to allow 'the free passage of medicines and medical supplies, essential foodstuff and clothing that are exclusively destined to the civilian population';[19] while on 10 March 2002, the Government of Sudan and the SPLM undertook 'to refrain from targeting or intentionally attacking non-combatant civilians' and 'civilian objects or facilities'.[20] In short, practice indicates that the parties are free to choose whether to bring into force humanitarian rules between themselves by referring generally to the Geneva Conventions, to some specific provisions of one or more of the Geneva Conventions, or by reformulating all or part of one or more Conventions.

---

offences relating to the armed conflict, and provisions on the delivery of humanitarian assistance. For details on the content of these agreements, see L. Vierucci, 'International Humanitarian Law and Human Rights Rules in Agreements Regulating or Terminating an Internal Armed Conflict', in R. Kolb and G. Gaggioli (eds), *Research Handbook on Human Rights and Humanitarian Law*' (Cheltenham: Edward Elgar, 2013) 416, at 424–8. E.g., in the 1976 Tripoli Agreement, the Government of the Philippines and the Moro National Liberation Front agreed on the return of all 'refugees' who had abandoned their areas of residence in the south of the country; whereas under Art II, para 3 of the Peace Accords between the Government of Angola and UNITA, 1 May 1991, all civilian and military prisoners held in connection with the conflict were to be released.

[14] This is the case for the Nairobi Peace Agreement signed on 17 December 1985 between the Government of Uganda and the National Resistance Movement.

[15] Some practice testifies to this possibility (see, e.g., Art 2 para 3 of the Bosnia-Herzegovina Agreement, signed on 22 May 1992, above n 5, requiring that the civilian population be treated in accordance with Arts 72 and 79 AP I).

[16] M. Sassòli, 'Possible Legal Mechanisms to Improve Compliance by Armed Groups with International Humanitarian Law and International Human Rights Law', at 10 (paper on file with author).

[17] E.g., the notions of occupied territory and protected person adopted in the Geneva Conventions cannot be ipso facto transposed to non-international armed conflicts. However, some provisions of an exclusive humanitarian nature, such as the rule prohibiting the transfer of all or part of the population of the occupied territory within or outside this territory, might be suitable also to non-international conflicts.

[18] Pictet Commentary GC I, at 59.

[19] Art 2, para 6 of the 1992 Agreement on Bosnia-Herzegovina, above n 5.

[20] Art 1(a) and (b) of the 2002 Government of Sudan and SPLM/A Agreement, above n 7.

One might wonder whether a Common Article 3 agreement can derogate from the 11
protection that the provision affords to persons taking no active part in hostilities. In
our opinion this possibility is excluded by the very letter of the Article.[21] Its first paragraph clearly refers to the 'minimum' protective measures that shall be ensured in a
NIAC,[22] thereby implying that further protections are due, while paragraph 3 clarifies
that an agreement should aim at bringing into force 'all or part of the other provisions'
of the Geneva Conventions, thus preventing any protection below that envisaged in the
Article. This conclusion may also be reached on account of the *jus cogens* nature of the
protection set out in Common Article 3, since no treaty may derogate from a *jus cogens*
rule.[23]

More controversial is whether a Common Article 3 agreement may derogate from the 12
international customary rules applicable in NIAC. By virtue of the principle *lex posterior
derogat priori*, the answer would have to be in the affirmative. Nevertheless, this principle
becomes inapplicable where the preceding regulation amounts to *jus cogens*. Although it
is undeniable that Article 3 does qualify as *jus cogens*,[24] doubts exist as to whether (and
eventually what) other customary IHL rules have attained a similar status.[25] In light of
this, the question can only be answered on a case-by-case basis.

This question is further complicated by the possible application, to a NIAC, of rules of 13
international human rights law (IHRL) in place of, or in complementarity to, IHL rules.
A case in point is the attribution, by way of a Common Article 3 agreement, of POW
status to enemy fighters during a NIAC: might such a status deprive the fighters of the
habeas corpus rights that they enjoy by virtue of IHRL? In our view the question has to be
solved according to the body of law (IHRL or IHL) that, in a specific case, is found to be
applicable.

In general, the ad hoc agreements that have been concluded so far pursue protective 14
purposes by requiring the parties to respect the wounded, the sick, the civilian population,
and those persons deprived of their freedom. However, some also set out provisions on the
conduct of hostilities, a commitment to disseminate IHL rules, and the reiteration of the
principle that the legal status of the parties remains unaffected by the ad hoc regulation.

---

[21] This interpretation of CA 3 is in line with the provisions of Arts 6/6/6/7 of the GCs, concerning IACs, according to which a special agreement concluded on the basis of one of those Articles shall not 'adversely affect the situation' of the sick, wounded, or shipwrecked, or of prisoners of war (POWs) or protected persons, or 'restrict the rights' that the relevant GC confers upon each of the above-mentioned categories of persons (see Ch 35, MN 16–18, of this volume).

[22] According to CA 3, para 1, 'each Party to the conflict shall be bound to apply, *as a minimum*, the following provisions […]' (emphasis added).

[23] The *jus cogens* nature of the protection set forth in CA 3 was recognized by the ICJ, *Case concerning Military and Paramilitary Activities in and against Nicaragua*, Judgment, 27 June 1986, para 218, and made explicit by the ICTY, *The Prosecutor v Zejnil Delalić et al*, Appeals Chamber Judgment, IT-96-21-A, 20 February 2001, para 143 (CA 3 'sets forth a minimum core of mandatory rules [and], reflects the fundamental humanitarian principles which underlie international humanitarian law as a whole, and upon which the Geneva Conventions in their entirety are based. These principles, the object of which is the respect for the dignity of the human person, developed as a result of centuries of warfare and had already become customary law at the time of the adoption of the Geneva Conventions because they reflect the most universally recognised humanitarian principles').

[24] See the case law referred to above n 23.

[25] On this issue see R. Nieto-Navia, 'International Peremptory Norms ("Jus Cogens") and International Humanitarian Law', in L.C. Vohrah et al (eds), *Man's Inhumanity to Man: Essays on International Law in Honour of Antonio Cassese* (Alphen aan den Rijn: Kluwer, 2003) 627.

15 In view of the fact that Common Article 3 notably lacks an express provision concerning the modality of its implementation and enforcement, it would be appropriate for the ad hoc agreements to fill this crucial gap. Ideally, the agreements should detail both the specific steps the parties must take to ensure compliance with the new regulation and the consequences in case of violation. According to the dominant practice, ad hoc agreements do not provide for compliance measures in case of a dispute concerning interpretation or implementation issues.[26] By contrast, the agreements usually set out the measures to be taken in case of violation (see section D of this chapter).

16 All in all, practice shows that Common Article 3 agreements do not contain rules on the protection due to special objects, such as historical monuments, and on the individual responsibility of those persons responsible for a breach of the agreed regulation.

17 Lastly, the question may arise concerning the impact that a special agreement may have on the classification of the conflict. In other words, is an agreement drafted according to Common Article 3 paragraph 3 evidence of the non-international nature of an armed conflict? This question has arisen before the Chambers of the International Criminal Tribunal for the former Yugoslavia (ICTY), which have used the special agreement of 22 May 1992 concluded between the representatives of the three factions of the armed conflict in Bosnia-Herzegovina as evidence, alternatively, of the international and non-international nature of that conflict.[27] The wavering in the case law of the ICTY not only reflects the very nature of the conflict in Bosnia-Herzegovina, which did contain elements of both international and non-international conflict, but also highlights the judges' specific competence to qualify a certain conflict. As rightly spelt out by the ICTY Trial Chamber in the *Tadić* Judgment, the signing of special agreements between conflicting parties, such as that of 22 May 1992, 'does not in any way affect the independent determination of the nature of that conflict by this Trial Chamber'.[28] The approach taken by the Chamber in this Judgment is in line with the prevailing opinion whereby the determination of the nature of an armed conflict has to be based on a *de facto* standard and not on the intention of the parties.

18 The above is linked to the question of the eventual violation of Articles 6/6/6/7 of the Geneva Conventions in the event that an agreement grounded in Common Article 3 regulates a conflict, which is later determined to be international, and the agreement therefore falls short of the safeguards required by the Geneva Conventions for an international armed conflict. In this case, it seems that the most reasonable conclusion is to consider the Common Article 3 agreement null and void because it is in conflict with the safeguard clause contained in Articles 6/6/6/7.[29]

---

[26] E.g., no organ is created to ascertain the content of a specific provision of the agreement or to verify respect for the agreement. The inclusion of a provision for such a body is typical of ceasefire and peace agreements.

[27] In ICTY, *The Prosecutor v Duško Tadić*, Appeals Chamber Decision on Jurisdiction, IT-94-1-T, 2 October 1995, para 73, the ICTY Appeals Chamber stated that the 22 May Agreement 'reflect[ed] the internal aspects of the conflict' because it was explicitly grounded in CA 3 and on account of the support it received from the ICRC; whereas in ICTY, *The Prosecutor v Tihomir Blaškić*, Trial Chamber Judgment, IT-95-14-T, 3 March 2000, para 81, the same agreement was used by the ICTY Trial Chamber to conclude in favour of the international nature of the conflict. For the details of this case law, see L. Vierucci, '"Special Agreements" between Conflicting Parties in the Case-Law of the ICTY', in B. Swart, G. Sluiter, and A. Zahar (eds), *The Legacy of the International Criminal Tribunal for the Former Yugoslavia* (Oxford: OUP, 2011) 401, at 426–7.

[28] ICTY, *The Prosecutor v Duško Tadić*, Trial Chamber Judgment, IT-94-1-T, 7 May 1997, para 583.

[29] See however Ch 35, MN 24, of this volume. For the safeguard clause, see above n 21. The view of invalidity is propounded also by C. Greenwood, 'International Humanitarian Law and the *Tadić* Case', 7 *EJIL* (1996) 265, at 272.

C. Legal Status of the Ad Hoc Agreements

Minimal attention has been paid by legal scholarship and judicial bodies to the question 19 of the legal status of Common Article 3 agreements.[30] By contrast, the more general issue of the status of agreements concluded between a government and an armed opposition group has raised greater attention. We shall focus on the debate concerning the latter category of agreements, since it also encompasses the engagements taken in pursuance of Common Article 3.

The doctrine has underlined the complexity of defining the legal status of agreements 20 stipulated by a government with an armed opposition group, given the close interconnection, within each agreement, of elements of an international and an internal nature. This feature would render the determination of the legal status of such agreements an enigma. The complexity of the question has given rise to a wide array of views that can be referred to only briefly here.

One view holds that an agreement between a government and an armed opposition 21 group is regulated by the national legal order, because the non-state party has no international legal personality.[31] Only if the opposition group satisfies the conditions to be recognized as an 'insurgent movement' may these agreements be governed by international law and therefore qualify as treaties.[32]

According to another view, these agreements are mixed or hybrid, in that they are 22 internal on account of the nature of the parties to them, but international because their implementation is guaranteed by an international subject (a state or an international organization).[33]

---

[30] The Constitutional Court of Colombia has specifically tackled the question of the legal status of a CA 3 agreement. See below n 31.

[31] This is the position taken by the SCSL, *Prosecutor v Morris Kallon and Brima Bazzy Kamara*, Appeals Chamber, Decision on Challenge to Jurisdiction: Lomé Accord Amnesty, SCSL-2004-15-AR72(E) and SCSL-2004-16-AR72(E), 13 March 2004. While reviewing the constitutionality of AP II, the Constitutional Court of Colombia stated that CA 3 agreements are not, strictly speaking, treaties (i.e. agreements regulated by international law) because they are not concluded between subjects of international law but between the parties to an internal armed conflict: see Corte Constitucional de la República de Colombia, sentencia C-225/95, 18 May 2005, para 17. The decision is partially reproduced in English in Sassòli/Bouvier/Quintin, at 2240.

[32] G. Schwarzenberger, *International Law as Applied by International Courts and Tribunals* (London: Stevens & Sons, 1968), at 729. This view certainly reflects international law on the point. The Appeals Chamber of the SCSL has accepted that the Revolutionary United Front (RUF) was a 'Party to the conflict' in the meaning of CA 3, but has denied it international personality as an insurgent movement both on account of the last paragraph of CA 3, whereby that provision does not modify the legal status of the parties to the conflict, and because there is nothing to show that the Government of Sierra Leone or any other state had granted the RUF recognition as an entity other than a faction within Sierra Leone: SCSL, *Kallon and Kamara*, above n 31, paras 45–9. This position has been reiterated by the Appeals Chamber in the four decisions issued on 25 May 2004, namely *The Prosecutor v Allieu Kondewa*, Decision on Lack of Jurisdiction/Abuse of Process: Amnesty Provided by the Lomé Accord, SCSL-2004-14-AR72(E); *The Prosecutor v Moinina Fofana*, Decision on Preliminary Motion on Lack of Jurisdiction: Illegal Delegation of Jurisdiction by Sierra Leone, SCSL-2004-14-AR72(E); *The Prosecutor v Moinina Fofana*, Decision on Preliminary Motion on Lack of Jurisdiction Materiae: Nature of the Armed Conflict, SCSL-2004-14-AR72(E); and *The Prosecutor v Moinina Fofana*, Decision on Preliminary Motion on Lack of Jurisdiction Materiae: Illegal Delegation of Powers by the United Nations, SCSL-2004-14-AR72(E).

[33] R. Goy, 'Quelques accords récents mettant fin à des guerres civiles', 38 *AFDI* (1992) 112, at 126, defines such agreements as 'accords partiellement internationalisés', while for P. Kooijmans, 'The Security Council and Non-State Entities as Parties to Conflicts', in K. Wellens (ed), *International Law: Theory and Practice*,

23   Lastly, some scholars affirm that these consensual engagements are international non-binding agreements because, though both parties enjoy international personality,[34] the agreements lack implementation guarantees regulated by international law.[35]

24   The variety of opinions expressed on the legal status of these agreements reflects the intricacy of the question. However, it also shows the insufficient consideration devoted to the very aspect that, in our opinion, is determinative of the question, namely, the notion of international personality. The notion of international personality propounded by scholars who have analysed the legal status of an agreement between the government and an armed opposition group is a formalistic one. Accordingly, the subject of the international legal order is pre-determined by the latter. The consequence of this approach is that no new subject can emerge unless the legal order has preventively envisaged this possibility for a specific entity.

25   However, there is a second, well-established notion of international personality that privileges the fact that title to legal rights and duties is directly established by the international legal order. This means that an entity that is the addressee of international rights and duties enjoys international personality, irrespective of the pre-determination of the personality of that very entity by the legal order.[36]

26   If we embrace this second notion of international personality, the crucial question in determining the legal status of a special agreement becomes the nature of the rights and duties set forth in these consensual engagements. Only if these rights and duties are international can the entity upon which the former are incumbent enjoy international personality.

27   Limiting our analysis to the legal status of Common Article 3 agreements, the fact that their content consists in the very obligations set out in treaties concluded between states (i.e. the four Geneva Conventions of 1949) leaves little doubt as to the international nature of these obligations. Indeed, these obligations are owed to the High Contracting Parties of the Conventions, and not only to the Parties to the NIAC who have stipulated the agreement. In light of this reasoning, one can only conclude

---

Essays in Honour of Eric Suy (The Hague: Nijhoff, 1998) 333, at 388, only those agreements concluded with the participation of the UN, namely 'internationalized peace-agreements', are regulated by international law. Cf also E. Roucounas, 'Peace Agreements as Instruments for the Resolution of Intrastate Conflict', in UNESCO, *Conflict Resolution: New Approaches and Methods* (Paris: UNESCO, 2000) 113, at 116–20. A more articulated argument is propounded by C. Bell, 'Peace Agreements: Their Nature and Legal Status', 100 *AJIL* (2006) 372, esp at 391, for whom agreements between a government and an armed opposition group are regulated by an intricate web of international and national rules that the author defines, by analogy to the *lex mercatoria*, as *lex pacificatoria*.

[34] Their international personality stems from the fact that the government is an expression of the state at the international level, while the armed opposition group is the expression of the 'community' dimension of the state; see M. Starita, *Processi di riconciliazione nazionale e diritto internazionale* (Naples: Scientifica, 2003), at 289 f.

[35] In Starita's view, the power of the UN to suspend or cancel the assistance activity carried out in a specific country by virtue of the agreement is the only guarantee present in the agreements, and it is not enough to conclude that a particular instrument is regulated by international law: ibid, at 302.

[36] ICJ, *Reparations for Injuries Suffered in the Service of the United Nations*, Advisory Opinion, 11 April 1949, at 178. See also J. Barberis, 'Nouvelles questions concernant la personnalité juridique internationale', 179 *RCADI* (1983-I) 145, at 165 f; and P.M. Dupuy, 'L'unité de l'ordre juridique international', 297 *RCADI* (2002) 9, at 110 f.

that Common Article 3 agreements are treaties in the meaning of the 1969 Vienna Convention on the Law of Treaties (VCLT), namely, 'international agreements [...] governed by international law'.[37]

Considerations of logic corroborate this conclusion. During a NIAC, the national legal order is unable to ensure pacific coexistence between citizens. As rightly pointed out, 'insurgency and civil war either cause domestic public law and order to collapse, or make it inoperative'.[38] Indeed, had the national legal order been able to bind the armed opposition group during the conflict, there would have been no need for an ad hoc regulation. In addition, if the ad hoc agreements were subject to domestic law, the governmental party could make them void, or modify them by changing the domestic legislation—a circumstance that would violate the principle of equality of belligerents before IHL.

The qualification of Common Article 3 agreements as treaties has major legal consequences. Since treaties are one of the sources of international law, these agreements can be relied upon by international adjudicatory bodies.[39]

In short, to the extent that a Common Article 3 agreement contains *international* obligations, it qualifies as a treaty irrespective of the international personality enjoyed by the parties.

D. Legal Consequences in Case of a Violation

One of the shortcomings of Common Article 3 is the lack of a compliance and enforcement mechanism in the event of violation of its provisions or disputes concerning its interpretation and implementation.[40] This lacuna should be filled by providing the special agreements with a compliance and enforcement scheme, taken, for example, from the Geneva Conventions' provisions on individual responsibility.

Practice is only partially consonant with this. Let us distinguish between the compliance mechanisms and the enforcement mechanisms that ought to be, or actually have been, included in the special agreements.

---

[37] Art 2 para 1(a) VCLT. Art 3 of the Convention does not preclude the possibility that non-state entities may conclude 'treaties'. However, according to the notion of 'treaty' adopted by the Convention, only those agreements stipulated in writing come under this definition.

[38] Roucounas, above n 33, at 120.

[39] This was implicitly done in the *Tadić* case, above n 27, where the ICTY Appeals Chamber established that the international agreements between conflicting parties could qualify as 'treaties' (the Chamber reached this conclusion without giving reasons). Both in *The Prosecutor v Stanislav Galić*, Trial Chamber Judgment, IT-98-29-T, 5 December 2003, and in *Blaškić*, above n 27, the Trial Chamber qualified the May 1992 Agreement on Bosnia-Herzegovina, above n 5, as a treaty (respectively at paras 96–8 and paras 172–3). Although we believe that this determination is correct for the reasons spelt out in the text, these judgments are not flawless as to the qualification of the agreement as a treaty in the case before them; see Vierucci, above n 27, at 405–16. See also UN Doc S/2005/60, Report of the Independent Commission of Inquiry on Darfur to the Secretary-General, 1 February 2005, para 174, stating that two insurgent movements, the Sudan Liberation Movement/Army and the Justice and Equality Movement, 'possess under customary international law the power to enter into binding international agreements (*jus contrahendi*), and have entered into various internationally binding agreements with the Government'.

[40] G. Draper, 'The Geneva Conventions of 1949', 144 *RCADI* (1965) 59, at 97.

I. Compliance mechanism

33 An ad hoc agreement should not only set out the measures aimed at establishing the facts concerning IHL violations when the conflict is ongoing, but should also provide for a mechanism to solve disputes concerning its interpretation and implementation. The importance of a compliance mechanism of this sort cannot be overstated, given the difficulty between the parties to a conflict to find a common position on fact-finding concerning IHL breaches.

34 According to the prevailing practice, the special agreements set up ad hoc compliance commissions on which both parties to the conflict are jointly represented,[41] often together with a third participant in order to ensure the impartiality of the organ. The choice of the third party depends on the specific content of the agreement: it might be the ICRC (1992 Bosnia-Herzegovina Agreement), the UN (2004 Protocol between the Government of Sudan and the SPLM/A), or one or more third states (2002 Government of Sudan and SPLM/A Agreement). Indeed some agreements are entirely devoted to detailing the composition of such a commission; a case in point is the Agreement on the Civilian Protection Component of the International Monitoring Team between the Government of the Philippines and the Moro Islamic Liberation Front, signed on 27 October 2009.

35 The compliance commission is competent to act in case of violation of the obligations contained in the agreement by virtue of its fact-finding power. It also has the power to inform the parties of its findings. Additionally, it may be tasked to make recommendations to the parties on the steps to be taken to end the violation, to prevent its recurrence, and to punish those responsible for it.[42]

36 Nothing prevents the parties from agreeing to a mechanism addressing not only the violations of the agreement, but also any violation of IHL which occurs during the conflict. This was the case for the 1992 Agreement concerning Bosnia-Herzegovina,[43] and for the 1998 CARHRIHL Agreement relating to the Philippines.[44]

37 Importantly, practice shows that the compliance commission has no enforcement powers. The decision on what measures to take following the recommendations of this body lies exclusively within the parties to the agreement. At most, the commission may make public the report.[45]

38 Despite the regrettable lack of enforcement powers, the provision concerning the establishment of a compliance body is an important achievement due to the difficulty in ascertaining the facts regarding IHL breaches when the armed conflict is in full swing.

II. Enforcement mechanism

39 Although an enforcement mechanism ought to be provided for in an ad hoc agreement, this is a rare occurrence. Exceptionally, Article 3 of the 1992 Bosnia-Herzegovina Agreement

---

[41] E.g. the CARHRIHL provides for a joint monitoring committee composed of the parties to the agreement only.

[42] See Art 3 of the 1992 Agreement on Bosnia-Herzegovina, above n 5; and Art 2 para 1 of the 2002 Government of Sudan and SPLM/A Agreement, above n 7.

[43] See Art 3 of the 1992 Agreement on Bosnia-Herzegovina, above n 5.

[44] See Art 6 of CARHRIHL, above n 10.

[45] See Art 4(b) of the 2002 Government of Sudan and SPLM/A Agreement, above n 7, according to which the final report relating to each incident, including the comments and explanations of the parties, will be made public.

established that the persons responsible for any violation of IHL should be punished 'in accordance with the law in force'.[46]

In general, an enforcement mechanism may encompass both individual criminal responsibility and state responsibility, both of which are addressed below (MN 41–48). However, nothing precludes the parties from also providing for the responsibility of the non-governmental party to the agreement, namely, the armed opposition group as such.

a. Individual criminal responsibility

Reliance by criminal tribunals on ad hoc agreements as partial factual evidence does not pose any thorny issues from an international law perspective. Indeed, ad hoc agreements may be used by international criminal tribunals as evidence in several respects. First, as evidence of the existence of an armed conflict in a given area. In this regard the ICTY has frequently relied on ceasefire agreements,[47] but nothing prevents the use of Common Article 3 agreements to the same effect. More troublesome is the use of an ad hoc agreement by a tribunal with a view to establishing the nature of an armed conflict. Reliance on an ad hoc agreement as evidence of the parties' intention to define a certain conflict as non-international would contravene Common Article 2 to the Geneva Conventions, which has introduced a *de facto* standard relating to the existence of the conflict. Indeed, the judges are the sole organ that may establish the nature of an armed conflict, and they must do so independent of the qualification given by the parties, including the one contained in a Common Article 3 agreement.[48]

Secondly, an ad hoc agreement may be used to reconstruct the position held by a defendant in a chain of command at the time of commission of the alleged offence. For example, the role played by a defendant in the stipulation or implementation of an ad hoc agreement may indicate that he held a position of command at the relevant time.[49]

Thirdly, the breach of a Common Article 3 agreement may be relied upon as one of the factual elements useful to determine the intention of the defendant to commit a specific offence.[50]

---

[46] For remarks concerning the meaning of the expression punishment 'in accordance with the law in force', see Vierucci, above n 27, at 418–21.

[47] See, e.g., ICTY, *The Prosecutor v Enver Hadžihasanović and Amir Kubura*, Trial Chamber Judgment, IT-01-47-T, 15 May 2006, paras 20 and 23. The ICC has relied on an inter-state agreement to determine the existence of an armed conflict (*The Prosecutor v Thomas Lubanga Dyilo*, Decision on Confirmation of Charges, ICC-01-/04-01/06, 29 January 2007, referring to the Luanda agreement of September 2002 concluded between Uganda and the Democratic Republic of Congo, para 193), but in the future it could also rely on CA 3 agreements.

[48] See the case law referred to above n 27.

[49] The ICTY judges have often used the role played in the implementation of a ceasefire and peace agreement as evidence of the position of command held by the defendant; see, e.g., *The Prosecutor v Mladen Naletilić and Vinko Martinović*, Trial Chamber Judgment, T-98-34-T, 21 March 2003, para 130. The ICC Pre-trial Chamber has used the signing of peace agreements such as the Accord de Cessation des Hostilités en Ituri, 18 March 2003, to substantiate the conclusion that the accused persons were in charge of the organization at the relevant time; see ICC, *The Prosecutor v Germain Katanga and Mathieu Ngudjolo Chui*, Decision on Confirmation of Charges, ICC-01/04-01/07, 30 September 2008, para 542.

[50] See, e.g., ICTY, *The Prosecutor v Mile Mrkšić et al*, Trial Chamber Judgment, IT-95-13/1, 27 September 2007, para 604, where the Trial Chamber relied on the violation of the Agreement concluded on 18 November 1991 between the Yugoslav People's Army, the Croatian Government, and a representative of the European Community Monitoring Mission to evacuate the sick and wounded from the Croatian hospital of Vukovar in order to show the *mens rea* of the defendant.

44 The crucial issue concerning the use of ad hoc agreements by international criminal tribunals regards the reliance on such engagements by the judges as a source of law both *ratione materiae* and *ratione personae*. If the tribunal is expressly competent to adjudicate upon an ad hoc agreement, and if the latter establishes the individual responsibility of the author for a certain offence,[51] the situation is clear-cut. If this is not the case, reliance on an ad hoc agreement depends on the scope of the tribunal's jurisdiction.

45 For example, in the *Tadić* decision on jurisdiction of 2 October 1995, the ICTY Appeals Chamber held itself to be competent to adjudicate not only crimes that were beyond doubt of a customary nature, but also violations of 'international agreements binding upon the conflicting parties',[52] provided such violations qualified as crimes under Article 3 of the Statute of the Tribunal[53] and 'the violation [...] entail[ed], under customary or conventional law, the individual criminal responsibility of the person breaching the rule'.[54] However, the ICTY Appeals Chambers have never relied exclusively on a special agreement to ground their jurisdiction in a specific case.[55]

46 Turning to the International Criminal Court (ICC), one might wonder whether the Statute allows the Court to ground its jurisdiction on an ad hoc agreement. This possibility is excluded by several provisions of the Statute that limit the jurisdiction of the Court to the crimes expressly provided for in the Statute.[56]

b. State responsibility

47 Common Article 3 agreements are one of the means available to the High Contracting Parties to the Geneva Conventions to discharge their obligation 'to respect and to ensure respect' for the provisions of the Conventions as set out in Common Article 1. They may also be relied upon by international courts and tribunals competent to adjudicate the conduct of a state. In this respect, the issue concerning the legal status of the agreement is likely to arise before these judicial bodies too.

48 In addition, both judicial and non-judicial bodies may rely on these agreements to intervene between the parties to a conflict with respect to a specific issue.[57] For example, ad hoc agreements contain provisions constituting 'applicable international humanitarian law' for the purpose of the Universal Periodic Review before the UN Human Rights

---

[51] Practice shows that nearly no agreement has so far established individual criminal responsibility for particular conduct. Art 3 of the 1992 Agreement on Bosnia-Herzegovina (above n 5) is probably the only exception.

[52] ICTY, *Tadić*, above n 27, para 143. For concerns relating to respect for the principle of legality, this approach was better explained in subsequent case law, when it was held that the ICTY Chambers could apply not only rules of a customary nature but also treaty rules. In particular in *The Prosecutor v Dario Kordić and Mario Čerkez*, Appeals Chamber Judgment, IT-95-14/2-A, 17 December 2004, para 46, the Appeals Chamber has clarified, by relying on the 1995 *Tadić* holding, that the ICTY has jurisdiction both over crimes based on customary international law at the time of their commission and over treaty-based crimes.

[53] According to Art 3 of the Statute, the ICTY is competent to adjudicate violations of the laws and customs of war.

[54] ICTY, *Tadić*, above n 27, para 94.

[55] By contrast, a Trial Chamber has grounded its jurisdiction *ratione materiae* and *ratione personae* on the 22 May 1992 Agreement on Bosnia-Herzegovina, in *Galić*, above n 39, paras 96–8 and 124–9. This approach was set aside in the Appeals Judgment of 30 November 2006 that asserted the customary nature of the offence and related individual criminal responsibility.

[56] See in particular Art 5(1) and Art 25(2) ICC Statute.

[57] In this sense see ICRC, 'Increasing Respect for International Humanitarian Law in Non-International Armed Conflict', February 2008, at 18, available at <http://www.icrc.org/eng/assets/files/other/icrc_002_0923.pdf>.

Council;[58] and the UN Special Rapporteurs may take such agreements as evidence of the obligations accruing to the parties to a specific conflict.

E. Critical Assessment

Common Article 3 agreements are noticeably few if compared to the number of NIACs that have occurred since the adoption of the four Geneva Conventions. Although this paucity may be explained by the difficulty of achieving the consent of conflicting parties once an armed struggle is underway, the advantages of this method of ad hoc regulation justify increased efforts both by the parties to a specific conflict and by third parties to conclude more such agreements in the future. 49

These agreements help to clarify the law applicable to a specific NIAC, and may also create new obligations between the parties. Their adoption is especially crucial to shed light on the IHL rules that bind an armed opposition group and to create a sense of ownership of the IHL rules the group has agreed to respect. The importance of such regulation is crystal clear when an enforcement mechanism is also established to tackle violations of the agreed obligations. 50

The disadvantages consist in the limited applicability of the agreements, since they bind only the parties having entered into them and only for the duration of the specific conflict. This in turn increases the risk of fragmentation of the applicable law, because the various parties to the same conflict may be bound by different rules.[59] In addition, the parties may be led to believe that the ad hoc agreement is the only regulation in force between them, to the detriment of the customary and treaty rules that are otherwise binding. 51

In any case, these disadvantages do not outweigh the benefits of having clear rules. Most importantly, such a clarity is conducive to better identification of the party responsible for eventual violations. 52

LUISA VIERUCCI

---

[58] UN Doc A/HRC/Res. 5/1, 18 June 2007, 'Institution-building of the United Nations Human Rights Council', Annex, Art A para 2, according to which the Universal Periodic Review shall take into account also 'applicable international humanitarian law'.

[59] R. Kolb and R. Hyde, *An Introduction to the Law of Armed Conflict* (Oxford: Hart Publishing, 2008), at 111.

C. ENSURING COMPLIANCE WITH THE CONVENTIONS

Chapter 26. The Role of the International Committee of the Red Cross

	MN
A. Introduction	1
B. What is the ICRC?	3
I. History and structure	3
II. International legal status	10
III. Impartiality, neutrality, and independence	14
C. Functions under the Geneva Conventions	17
I. General	17
II. Protection	24
III. Assistance	33
D. The ICRC's Role in the Implementation of International Humanitarian Law	37
I. General	37
II. Technical assistance	38
III. Promoting compliance globally	40
IV. Persuading parties to comply through confidential communications	44
a. Doctrine 15 and practice	45
b. Confidentiality as a tool	47
c. The role of legal argumentation	50
d. Results	53
e. Reconciling the guardian and operational roles	56
E. The ICRC and International Criminal Courts	58
F. Critical Assessment	65

Select Bibliography

Bugnion, F., *The International Committee of the Red Cross and the Protection of War Victims* (Oxford: Macmillan, 2003)

Forsythe, D.P., *The Humanitarians: The International Committee of the Red Cross* (Cambridge: CUP, 2005)

Gazzini, T., 'A Unique Non-State Actor: The International Committee of the Red Cross', 4 *Human Rights and International Legal Discourse* (2010) 32

Giladi, R., 'The Utility and Limits of Legal Mandate: Humanitarian Assistance, the International Committee of the Red Cross, and Mandate Ambiguity', in A. Zwitter et al (eds), *Humanitarian Action: Global, Regional and Domestic Legal Responses* (Cambridge: CUP, 2014) 81

Krähenbühl, P., 'The ICRC's Approach to Contemporary Security Challenges: A Future for Independent and Neutral Humanitarian Action', 86 *IRRC* 855 (2004) 505

Moorehead, C., *Dunant's Dream: War, Switzerland and the History of the Red Cross* (New York: HarperCollins, 1998)

Ratner, S., 'Law Promotion beyond Law Talk: The Red Cross, Persuasion, and the Laws of War', 22 *EJIL* (2011) 459

Sandoz, Y., 'Le droit d'initiative du Comité international de la Croix-Rouge', 22 *German Yearbook of International Law* (1979) 352

A. Introduction

1   In the absence of a serious implementation mechanism in the Geneva Conventions, much of the leading responsibility for promoting their observance falls upon the International Committee of the Red Cross (ICRC), the 150-year-old institution that is a *sui generis* hybrid between a Swiss non-governmental organization (NGO) and an international organization. With its secretariat in Geneva and delegations throughout the world, the ICRC is, in many conflicts, the most direct voice for the Conventions. The central role of the ICRC pre-dates the Conventions, for the ICRC has been the driving force behind the codification of international humanitarian law (IHL) since the mid-nineteenth century.

2   As a result, the Geneva Conventions, like their predecessors, contemplate, or even assign, certain responsibilities to the ICRC (or an equivalent organization that does not currently exist). Yet there is an enormous gap between the discrete and ultimately limited role of the ICRC under the Conventions and its actual operations, accepted as legitimate by most states and non-state actors. Today, the bulk of ICRC activities are not even mentioned in the Conventions, and the legal duty on states to cooperate with the ICRC is highly circumscribed. Rather, the institution has, in its long existence, succeeded in bypassing a weak treaty mandate through a process and identity characterized by discretion and flexibility. As a result, states now expect the ICRC to insert itself in situations of international armed conflict (IAC) and non-international armed conflict (NIAC), as well as in other non-conflict situations, and warring parties are expected to allow the ICRC to carry out its mandate. Both the ICRC's operations and the expectations by and on states regarding its work demonstrate the limitations of relying upon the Conventions' texts for understanding contemporary IHL.

B. What is the ICRC?

I. History and structure

3   The idea for what eventually became the ICRC dates back to 1859, when Henri Dunant, a Swiss businessman, witnessed the horrendous fate of wounded soldiers at the 1859 Battle of Solferino between French-Sardinian forces and Austria. Four years later, in February 1863, Dunant, joined by four other prominent Swiss men—Gustave Moynier, General Guillaume-Henri Dufour, Louis Appia, and Théodore Maunoir—created the International Committee for the Relief of Wounded in the Event of War.[1] That same year, the new Committee convinced 16 states to participate in the first Geneva conference on the treatment of war wounded; it adopted a key resolution setting up national committees to provide humanitarian and medical aid to armies in wartime. The personnel involved in relief would be identified by a distinctive sign, comprising a red cross on a white background, which was designed as the reverse of the Swiss flag.[2] A more ambitious achievement took place the following year, when the Swiss Government, pressured by the

---

[1] See generally D.P. Forsythe, *The Humanitarians: The International Committee of the Red Cross* (Cambridge: CUP, 2005), at 15–29; F. Bugnion, *The International Committee of the Red Cross and the Protection of War Victims* (Oxford: Macmillan, 2003), at 11–28.

[2] Resolutions of the International Conference, Geneva, 26–9 October 1863, available at <http://www.icrc.org/IHL.nsf/FULL/115?OpenDocument>.

Committee, convened a 16-nation diplomatic conference that adopted the First Geneva Convention on Wounded in Armies in the Field.[3] In 1875, the Committee renamed itself the ICRC.

In its 150 years of activity, the ICRC has steadily expanded its operations, often relying on the thinnest of international legal mandates. During the First World War, it took advantage of its neutral Swiss identity and created an International Prisoners of War Agency that provided information to families about their prisoner of war (POW) relatives; it also began visiting detainees, both military and civilian, delivering relief packages and reporting on their conditions both publicly and privately. This practice continued during the Second World War on a more global scale, to include operations in Africa and Asia. Yet despite the brave work of many delegates and the important humanitarian assistance provided at the margins, the War also revealed severe shortcomings in both the ICRC's *modus operandi* and its institutional identity. Its preference for confidential communications, combined with fear among its Swiss leaders concerning the implications for Switzerland of the ICRC's activities, contributed to a failure to speak publicly about the Holocaust, despite knowledge of the conditions in concentration camps and the fate of those deported for extermination.[4] The ICRC took many years to acknowledge its failures, and indeed the Second World War continues to cast a shadow over the organization and highlights the moral questions associated with the ICRC's approach. Since the end of the War, the ICRC further expanded its operations to include conflicts associated with decolonization and the Cold War, and eventually the break-up of various states and untraditional conflicts that have characterized this period.

Since its inception, the ICRC has sought to push states toward concluding legal agreements to expand the scope of IHL. It carried out intensive preparatory work for the Geneva Conventions and Protocols and prepared drafts that provided the basis for the two diplomatic conferences. It remains a major participant and source of technical and legal expertise in negotiating processes, including in the United Nations (UN) conference on conventional weapons and other meetings on weapons systems. Further, the ICRC continues to promote the relevance of customary international law.[5]

Despite its expansion and global presence, the ICRC remains formally a committee, currently composed of 16 Swiss citizens.[6] The Committee works at different levels, including the Assembly (composed of all members), the Assembly Council (composed of five members), and the Presidency (composed of the President and two Vice-Presidents). The ICRC's directorate, comprising a Director-General and department heads, oversees the permanent staff, which carries out its daily work in Geneva and abroad.[7] The staff has long included non-Swiss nationals, especially as local staff: today the ICRC has about 1,400

---

[3] Convention for the Amelioration of the Condition of the Wounded in Armies in the Field, Geneva (1864).

[4] For the key work of historical research, see J.-C. Favez, *Une mission impossible? Le CICR, les déportations et les camps de concentration Nazis* (Lausanne: Payot, 1988) (English version published as *The Red Cross and the Holocaust* (Cambridge: CUP, 1999)).

[5] On the last of these, see ICRC CIHL Study and ICRC CIHL Database, 2. Practice, available at <http://www.icrc.org/customary-ihl/eng/docs/v2_rul>.

[6] See Statutes of the International Committee of the Red Cross (Statutes of the ICRC), Arts 2 and 7, 3 October 2013, available at <http://www.icrc.org/eng/resources/documents/misc/icrc-statutes-080503.htm>.

[7] For the evolution of the current structure, see Forsythe, above n 1.

so-called expatriate staff, some 800 of whom work in Geneva; nearly 60 per cent of the expatriates are non-Swiss.[8] At the same time, until 2010 the heads of all the departments were Swiss, creating a 'chocolate ceiling' for non-Swiss nationals in the ICRC.

7   Legally, the ICRC is a private association under the Swiss Civil Code.[9] Its internal structure is governed by the Statutes of the ICRC, a document created, and subject to revision, by the ICRC Assembly.[10] The ICRC is also one of three entities in an umbrella organization, the International Red Cross and Red Crescent Movement. The Movement's other members are the National Red Cross and Red Crescent Societies, and the International Federation of Red Cross and Red Crescent Societies, which coordinates activities of the national societies.[11] The Movement is governed by its own set of Statutes,[12] adopted by an international conference consisting of representatives of the ICRC, each national society, the Federation, and states parties to the Geneva Conventions. (The current Statutes date from 1986, with amendments made in 1996 and 2006.) Under its own Statutes and the Statutes of the Movement, the ICRC must carry out any mandate given to it by the Movement's international conference.[13] However, it is not otherwise accountable to the Movement, whose Statutes recognize it as 'an independent humanitarian organization having a status of its own'.[14] With respect to its most politically sensitive work—protection activities during armed conflict and other related situations—the ICRC acts quite independently of the Federation and the national societies, many of which are government-controlled.

8   The ICRC is funded by the states parties to the Geneva Conventions, the national societies, other international organizations, and private sources. Additionally, the ICRC often seeks and obtains special contributions through emergency appeals. The budget of the ICRC for 2015 was SFr 1.6 billion.

9   The ICRC thus represents a *sui generis* entity. Its status under Swiss law as a private association makes it akin to an NGO. Its treaty-based functions, the role of states in the Movement and the international conferences, the funding by governments, and the ICRC's image through its delegations resemble the workings of an international organization. Its close ties to Switzerland—Geneva, the nationality of Committee members and senior staff, and frequent contacts with the Swiss Foreign Ministry[15]—give it a profile unique among international organizations and NGOs; and the ICRC clearly benefits from Switzerland's reputation for neutrality in international affairs. Governments and armed groups suspicious of the motives of NGOs based in the UK, the US, or France, will be less likely to attack the motives of the ICRC.

---

[8] 'Working for the ICRC: a Wide Range of Profiles and Missions', 1 January 2009, available at <http://www.icrc.org/eng/resources/documents/misc/5r4j73.htm>.

[9] See Swiss Civil Code Arts 60–69, available at <http://www.admin.ch/ch/e/rs/2/210.en.pdf>.

[10] Above n 6.

[11] The Red Crescent emblem was adopted by national societies not wishing to use a cross. In 2005, states recognized a third emblem, the Red Crystal, permitting the entry into the Federation of the Israeli Magen David Adom (which will use the crystal with the Star of David within it). See Additional Protocol (AP) III.

[12] Statutes of the International Red Cross and Red Crescent Movement 1986 (Statutes of the Movement), available at <http://www.icrc.org/eng/assets/files/other/statutes-en-a5.pdf>.

[13] Art 4(h) ICRC Statutes; Art 5(2)(h) Statutes of the Movement. The ICRC plays a leadership role in the conference, preparing papers and proposals on ongoing issues of IHL and seeking the endorsement of states (and, to a lesser extent, the national societies) for its priorities.

[14] Art 5(1) Statutes of the Movement.

[15] See Forsythe, above n 1, at 202–27; C. Moorehead, *Dunant's Dream: War, Switzerland and the History of the Red Cross* (New York: HarperCollins, 1998), at 371–470.

II. International legal status

Neither the Conventions nor the Statutes of the ICRC or the Movement address the ICRC's international legal status. Commentators have pondered whether the ICRC possesses so-called international legal personality in the sense of enjoying rights and duties under international law, although the practical utility of that concept (and in particular its binary character) has been seriously undermined.[16] The canonical discussion of international legal personality elaborated by the International Court of Justice (ICJ) in the *Reparation for Injuries Case*—which asks whether an entity was 'intended to exercise and enjoy, and is in fact exercising and enjoying, functions and rights which can only be explained on the basis of the possession of a large measure of international personality and the capacity to operate upon an international plane'[17]—is somewhat tautological, and moreover was focused on an intergovernmental body.[18] Although the ICRC is governed by Statutes approved by, among others, the states parties to the Conventions, it is not an agent of states. Nor does its international mandate mean that it has rights and obligations under international law.

With respect to particular prerogatives and implications often associated with international legal personality, practice is not particularly conclusive. The ICRC enjoys UN observer status;[19] it certainly conducts diplomacy directly with states; and it has concluded numerous agreements with states or international organizations regarding operational matters.[20] These include accreditation procedures and agreements with states where the ICRC operates, which grant it privileges and immunities.[21] Even where no such agreement exists, the ICRC often receives lenient treatment akin to a de facto grant of privileges and immunities by the host state. Yet it remains unclear whether these accords are *governed* by international law,[22] even if their subject matter relates to a Convention-based mandate.[23] Further, agreements or national legislation granting the ICRC privileges and immunities do not imply that the ICRC has any international legal right to such treatment. A state's refusal to admit the ICRC into its territory or deny it access to POWs violates the rights of the state on which the POWs depend (or perhaps obligations vis-à-vis the international community), but it does not violate legal rights of the ICRC or give it international legal claims.[24] One rare, 'most relied upon episode' of UN *ex gratia* compensation following the

---

[16] See R. Higgins, *Problems and Process: International Law and How We Use It* (Oxford: OUP, 1994), at 50.

[17] ICJ, *Reparation for Injuries Suffered in the Service of the UN*, Advisory Opinion, 11 April 1949, at 179.

[18] Ibid, at 180.

[19] UNGA Res 45/6, 16 October 1990; see also UN, 'Intergovernmental organizations having received a standing invitation to participate as observers in the sessions and the work of the General Assembly and maintaining permanent offices at Headquarters', available at <http://www.un.org/en/members/intergovorg.shtml>.

[20] E.g., Agreement between the ICRC and the Swiss Federal Council to Determine the Legal Status of the Committee in Switzerland, 33 *IRRC* 293 (1993) 150, Art 22; and ibid, Art 1 (ICRC 'international juridical personality').

[21] J.-P. Lavoyer, 'The International Committee of the Red Cross: Legal Status and Headquarters Agreements', in D. Fleck (ed), *The Handbook of the Law of Visiting Forces* (Oxford: OUP, 2001) 471; C. Sommaruga, 'Swiss Neutrality, ICRC Neutrality: Are They Indissociable? An Independence Worth Protecting', 32 *IRRC* 288 (1992) 264, at 268.

[22] Lavoyer, above n 21, at 478; A.-K. Lindblom, *Non-Governmental Organisations in International Law* (Cambridge: CUP, 2005), at 496, 509.

[23] Vienna Convention on the Law of Treaties between States and International Organizations or between International Organizations (1986) Art 2.1(h); *contra*, Report on 26th Session, *YILC* 1974, vol II(1), 290, at 297.

[24] *Contra* G. Abraham, 'Yes, ... but Does It Have Personality? The International Committee of the Red Cross and Sovereign Immunity', 124 *South African Law Journal* (2007) 499, at 503.

1961 death of an ICRC delegate in the Congo does not confirm ICRC capacity to bring international claims against international persons.[25]

12 The ICRC's tendency to avoid focusing on these legal questions fosters ambiguity. As it sets its priorities on operations, it often relies on pragmatic or even informal arrangements with the states where it operates. It frequently invokes its dual legal character and, at times, emphasizes its private law status to bolster its non-partisanship claims.[26] It has rarely invoked a claim of international legal personality.[27] Similarly, it is hard to imagine the ICRC bringing any sort of formal claim against a state, as this would be incongruent with its institutional culture. It is as difficult to envisage a state bringing a legal claim to compel the ICRC to offer its services or to refrain from doing so. The ICRC's preference to operate with an ambiguous legal status indicates that international personality is, at times, convenient or 'useful'[28] for discharging its mandate, but not functionally necessary. More important is that the ICRC's character as a neutral intermediary presupposes that, in times of war, it must act on its own resolve, much like any other NGO.

13 At the same time, the special recognition and responsibilities afforded to the ICRC by the Geneva Conventions, discussed below, enable it, unlike most NGOs, to make requests and even demands upon states—though not formal legal claims. The ICRC uses that special status as needed to carry out its protection and assistance functions. That status, while not conferring the rights and duties often associated with international legal personality, remains a useful tool.

III. Impartiality, neutrality, and independence

14 The ICRC describes itself as 'an impartial, neutral and independent organization', with an 'exclusively humanitarian mission' to protect and assist victims of armed conflict and other violent situations.[29] Neutrality, impartiality, and independence also comprise three of the Movement's 'Fundamental Principles'.[30] Some provisions of the Geneva Conventions assume or imply ICRC impartiality and neutrality (but not independence): under Common Article 3, an offer of services to parties to a NIAC may come from '[a]n impartial humanitarian body, such as the [ICRC]'. Article 9/9/9/10 states that the Conventions ought not to impede 'the humanitarian activities which the [ICRC]' undertakes with the parties' consent.[31] The ICRC points to positive acceptance, direct or indirect, of these characteristics by states: in the Conventions, in the Movement's Statutes, and by acquiescence.[32]

---

[25] T. Gazzini, 'A Unique Non-State Actor: The International Committee of the Red Cross', 4 *Human Rights and International Legal Discourse* (2010) 32; Y. Beigbeder, *The Role and Status of International Humanitarian Volunteers and Organizations* (Dordrecht: Martinus Nijhoff, 1991), at 321 (ICRC asking Switzerland to bring claims).

[26] Bugnion, above n 1, at 955.

[27] The ICRC's submission to the ICTY was an exception: S. Jeannet, 'Recognition of the ICRC's Long-Standing Rule of Confidentiality: An Important Decision by the ICTY', 82 *IRRC* 838 (2000) 403. See further MN 58–64.

[28] Lavoyer, above n 21, at 477. The first agreement was concluded only in 1973.

[29] ICRC, *The International Committee of the Red Cross: Its Missions and Work* (Geneva: ICRC, 2009), at 4.

[30] Statutes of the Movement, Preamble.

[31] Art 10/10/10/11 (neutrality and impartiality); Art 11/11/11/12 (neutrality); Art 5 AP I; ICRC–Swiss Agreement, above n 20, Art 2.

[32] ICRC, *Missions and Work*, above n 29, *passim*; Sommaruga, above n 21, at 267.

At the same time, the Conventions leave it to the ICRC to assert, formulate, and apply 15 its own understanding of these terms.[33] In asserting these characteristics, the ICRC seeks to shape how others with whom it interacts perceive it. Assertions of neutrality, impartiality, and independence aim at carving a space where the ICRC and its operations are neither ignored nor politically manipulated by the parties to a conflict. In the ICRC's words, impartiality is 'a principle that rejects any form of discrimination, [and] calls for equal treatment [...] according to [...] needs'.[34] Neutrality denotes abstention from 'taking sides in hostilities or controversies of a political, racial, religious or ideological nature'. Remaining neutral enables the ICRC to 'keep everyone's trust [...] to make more contacts and gain access to those affected'.[35] Independence, reflected in the ICRC composition and Swiss membership (though not funding, which remains quite dependent on others), means detachment from 'national and international politics'; the ICRC sees it as giving the institution the 'autonomy [...] to accomplish the exclusively humanitarian task entrusted to it with complete impartiality and neutrality'.[36] It allows the ICRC to position itself as distinct 'from political decision-making processes', espousing no 'ulterior political motives'.[37]

These characteristics are no abstract principles. Rather, they underscore the ICRC's 16 approach to its operations.[38] Ultimately, all three are geared toward access and acceptability.[39] Grounded in long experience and institutional culture more firmly than in any formal source, these assertions now form the backbone of ICRC identity. These principles, and neutrality in particular, also imply for the ICRC a reverential insistence on the complete separation of *jus ad bellum* and *jus in bello*. By refusing to venture itself, in any circumstances, into the underlying causes, justifications, or legality of any armed conflict, the ICRC hopes to convey to the parties the idea that they are bound to comply with IHL regardless of the legality of the recourse to force.[40]

C. Functions under the Geneva Conventions

I. General

An inquiry into the role of the ICRC under the Geneva Conventions immediately runs 17 into a double discrepancy. First, a wide gap separates the meagre language of the Conventions' provisions mandating ICRC operations from the broad perception and exercise in practice of that mandate by the ICRC. Secondly, this very gap appears incongruent with a prevalent perception of the ICRC as an essentially conservative organization.[41] There is a markedly un-conservative strain about the common description according to

---

[33] Arts 1 and 4 ICRC Statutes; J. Pictet, *The Fundamental Principles of the Red Cross: Commentary* (Geneva: Henry-Dunant Institute, 1979).

[34] ICRC, *Missions and Work,* above n 29, at 10.

[35] Ibid; L. Minear, 'The Theory and Practice of Neutrality: Some Thoughts on the Tensions', 81 *IRRC* 833 (1999) 63.

[36] ICRC, *Missions and Work,* above n 29, at 10.

[37] P. Krähenbühl, 'The ICRC's Approach to Contemporary Security Challenges: A Future for Independent and Neutral Humanitarian Action', 86 *IRRC* 855 (2004) 505, at 512.

[38] M. Harroff-Tavel, 'Does It Still Make Sense to Be Neutral?', 25 *Humanitarian Exchange* (2003), at 2–4, available at <http://www.odihpn.org/download/humanitarianexchange025pdf>.

[39] Krähenbühl, above n 37, at 510; Sommaruga, above n 21, at 268. On past departures, see D.P. Forsythe, 'The ICRC: A Unique Humanitarian Protagonist', 89 *IRRC* 865 (2007) 63.

[40] See, e.g., T. Pfanner, 'Editorial', 88 *IRRC* 864 (2004) 717.   [41] Forsythe, above n 39, at 63.

which 'every activity [...] by the ICRC can be traced back to an initiative taken by it on some occasion'.[42] This tension between conservatism and sometimes radical innovation, as between the formal and the actual, calls for a thematic focus rather than a clause-by-clause interpretation.

18 The broadest statement of the ICRC's mandate can be found in Article 4 of its own Statutes, providing that its role 'in particular' is:

> c) to undertake the tasks incumbent upon it under the Geneva Conventions, to work for the faithful application of international humanitarian law applicable in armed conflicts and to take cognizance of any complaints based on alleged breaches of that law;
> d) to endeavour at all times—as a neutral institution whose humanitarian work is carried out particularly in time of international and other armed conflicts or internal strife—to ensure the protection of and assistance to military and civilian victims of such events and of their direct results [...]

That Article then adds:

> 2. The ICRC may take any humanitarian initiative which comes within its role as a specifically neutral and independent institution and intermediary, and may consider any question requiring examination by such an institution.[43]

19 Although these provisions begin with a reference to the Conventions, the latter consist merely of 'a series of disconnected obligations which, together, do not make up a coherent whole'.[44] They hardly envisage a robust role for the ICRC. Instead, under various Articles of the Geneva Conventions, the ICRC can lend its 'good offices' to facilitate the creation of hospital zones and localities in peacetime;[45] it can receive an up-to-date record of the labour detachments of POWs;[46] it has a role in the appointment of Mixed Medical Commissions;[47] it can discuss the modalities of its relief operations for POWs and civilians;[48] it can receive representations by POW representatives and civilian Internees Committees;[49] and it may also make proposals on the organization of the Central Prisoners of War Information Agency. These and other Articles alluding to the activities of the ICRC do not quite assert a broad conventional mandate as implied in the Statutes. Furthermore, they rarely allude to the ICRC exclusively.[50]

20 In some cases, ICRC activities in specific fields go well beyond its role as envisaged in the Conventions: Article 123 GC III only empowers the ICRC to propose, 'if it deems necessary', the organization of a 'Central Prisoners of War Information Agency' to be created in a neutral country. In practice, the ICRC operates the Central Tracing Agency itself.[51] Likewise, its offers of good offices cover far broader grounds than the treaty text suggests.[52]

---

[42] Bugnion, above n 1, at 351; J.D. Armstrong, 'The International Red Cross Committee and Political Prisoners', 39 *International Organization* (1985) 615, at 621; Sassòli/Bouvier/Quintin, vol I, at 465.

[43] Art 4 ICRC Statutes.   [44] Bugnion, above n 1, at 350.

[45] Art 23 GC I; Art 14 GC IV. See Ch 18 of this volume.   [46] Art 56 GC III; Art 96 GC IV.

[47] Art 112, Annex II GC III.   [48] Arts 72, 73, 75 GC III; Arts 59, 61, 108, 111, 142 GC IV.

[49] Art 79 GC III; Arts 102, 104 GC IV.

[50] E.g., Art 9/9/9/10 ('or any other impartial humanitarian organization'), and CA 3. K. Mackintosh, 'Beyond the Red Cross: The Protection of Independent Humanitarian Organizations and their Staff in International Humanitarian Law', 89 *IRRC* 865 (2007) 113.

[51] See further MN 29–31.

[52] See above n 45. T. Fischer, 'The ICRC and the 1962 Cuban Missile Crisis', 83 *IRRC* 842 (2001) 287, at 294; ICRC, 'ICRC Position on Hostage-Taking', 84 *IRRC* 846 (2002) 467.

The key exception, one that overshadows these rather paltry responsibilities, is the 21 explicit ICRC right to visit persons deprived of liberty, discussed further in MN 25–27. Another exception, enabling it to operate as a Protecting Power substitute, has been moribund since before the Second World War.[53] A state's refusal to allow the ICRC to visit protected persons in an IAC is the rare situation where a refusal to let the ICRC fulfil its treaty-based functions amounts to a violation of the Conventions.

As for the savings clause in Article 9/9/9/10—that the Conventions 'constitute no 22 obstacle to the humanitarian activities which the [ICRC] or any other impartial humanitarian organization may, subject to the consent of the Parties to the conflict concerned, undertake for the protection of civilian persons and for their relief'—it is similarly not a positive mandate for action. Rather, it suggests that the ICRC may undertake, with the consent of parties to an IAC, humanitarian protection and relief activities in favour of protected persons. This clause acknowledges an ICRC role pre-dating the Conventions and ensures that the Conventions will not limit that role.[54]

Yet in the ICRC's doctrine, that clause, along with the above-quoted provisions in its 23 Statute, are at the root of what it refers to as its 'right of initiative'—to offer its unique operations to the parties to a conflict in the hope that they will consent to them. That right has a more affirmative conventional basis for NIACs, as Common Article 3 provides for the right of '[a]n impartial humanitarian body, such as' the ICRC to 'offer its services' to the parties.[55] The right of initiative thus allows for a mandate broader than that in the Conventions, but it is also more restricted in that the parties may always refuse an offer. Thus, its classification as a 'right' may be dubious. Nonetheless, the right of initiative places the ICRC in a position to defend its involvement in specific conflicts, in particular NIACs, where it may approach and deal with the non-state party even against the wishes of the state, and yet still assert that it is not interfering in the internal affairs of that state.[56] With this basic framework laid out, we now turn to the two core functions of the ICRC.

II. Protection

The ICRC's protection function lies at the core of its mandate and activities. As used by 24 the ICRC, protection is a process aimed at ensuring that actors 'respect their obligations and the rights of individuals in order to preserve the safety, physical integrity and dignity of those affected by armed conflict and other situations of violence'. It includes preventing and putting a stop to 'actual or potential' violations of pertinent norms. Protection also includes activities that reduce vulnerability and exposure to risks.[57]

Convention rules regarding ICRC visits impose obligations on parties to an IAC in 25 whose power protected persons are found. In this area, they seem to confer corresponding

---

[53] Arts 10/10/10/11; Art 5(4) AP I. Sassòli/Bouvier/Quintin, vol I, at 365. See Ch 27 of this volume.

[54] Pictet Commentary GC IV, at 94; Pictet Commentary GC III, at 106. See also 1929 GC II, Art 88.

[55] See Art 4(1)(d)–(2) ICRC Statutes; Art 5(2)(d)–(3) Statutes of the Movement (also in internal strife); see also Y. Sandoz, 'Le droit d'initiative du Comité international de la Croix-Rouge', 22 *German Yearbook of International Law* (1979) 352.

[56] Notwithstanding the state consent requirement, 'practice has transcended this conventional limit': G. Torreblanca, 'The International Committee of the Red Cross and Human Rights Law', in G. Gaggioli and R. Kolb (eds), *Research Handbook on Human Rights and Humanitarian Law* (Cheltenham: Edward Elgar, 2013) 540, at 544. Please see Ch 24 of this volume.

[57] ICRC, 'ICRC Protection Policy', 90 *IRRC* 871 (2008) 751, at 751–2

rights on the ICRC.[58] In IAC, the ICRC's right to visit POWs and protected civilians, whether detained, living in an occupied territory or on the enemy's own territory, is discussed in Article 126 GC III and Article 143 GC IV.[59] Both extend the 'prerogative' of 'representatives or delegates of the Protecting Powers' to visit protected persons to ICRC delegates whose appointment was submitted for the Detaining Power's approval. This obligation on states effectively grants detainees a corresponding right to receive visits.[60]

26 This right of visitation in an IAC is broad and nearly absolute. The language is deliberately inclusive ('all places'; 'all premises'): it emphasizes the ICRC's 'full liberty' 'to select the places […] to visit'; it also prohibits restrictions to the 'duration and frequency' of visits. Other provisions support this conclusion.[61] The Detaining Powers may 'prohibit' ICRC visits only 'for reasons of imperative military necessity', and 'only as an exceptional and temporary measure'.[62] The two visitation provisions contain their own exceptions and therefore admit no additional grounds of limitation.[63] The high potential for abuse suggests that 'reasons of imperative military necessity' cannot legitimately relate to the visit itself, but only to extraneous causes.[64] Another crucial aspect specifically provided for by Article 126 GC III and Article 143 GC IV is that ICRC visits are to be conducted 'without witnesses' (although the ICRC would have in all likelihood insisted on this condition anyway). Beyond these provisions, the complex modalities governing ICRC detention visits are not addressed in the Conventions but rather entrenched in ICRC practice.

27 The Conventions do not address ICRC visits in NIACs. Yet it has long been accepted by states that the ICRC's right of initiative under Common Article 3 includes the possibility for the ICRC to offer to conduct visits, under essentially the same conditions. The offer may be, and often is, rejected by one or both sides to a NIAC.[65] Moreover, the ICRC frequently relies on the power of initiative to visit people in situations not amounting to armed conflict. This significant assertion of authority, though equally conditioned on the state's consent, has permitted delegates to visit detainees in countries not experiencing war, and to work on issues where human rights law, not IHL, is the governing legal framework. These efforts have included visits to detainees in South Africa under apartheid, to Argentina and Chile during their military regimes, and to numerous countries today, such as Jordan, Sri Lanka, and Haiti.[66] Of 756,158 detained persons visited by the ICRC worldwide in 2013, only 128 were POWs; 2,690 were civilians protected under GC IV,[67] meaning that the vast majority of visits were not based upon a right enshrined in the Conventions to conduct such visits, but were completely outside the Conventions' framework.

---

[58] Pictet Commentary III, at 604.   [59] See also ICRC CIHL Study, Rule 124.
[60] Art 76 GC IV; Art 125 bars the use of disciplinary punishment to deprived detainees 'of the benefit of the provisions of […] Article 143'. GC III does not explicitly provide for such a 'right' of POWs, but retains the 'benefit' of ICRC visit in Arts 98, 108.
[61] Arts 98, 108 GC III; Art 125 GC IV.
[62] In effect, only postpone: Pictet Commentary GC III, at 608, 611.
[63] Cf Supreme Court of Israel, *Obeid & Dirani v Defence Minister et al*, HCJ 794/98, Judgment, 23 August 2001.
[64] E.g., hostilities in the vicinity of the place of visit, following Arts 19, 50 GC III; Arts 28, 40, 83, 95 GC IV. Bugnion, above n 1, at 583; *contra*, Pictet Commentary GC III, at 611. Eritrea did not invoke the exception in EECC, *Prisoners of War—Ethiopia's Claim 4*, Partial Award, 1 July 2003.
[65] Bugnion, above n 1, at 585–6; see Ch 24 of this volume.
[66] See ICRC, *Annual Report 2013*, available at <http://www.icrc.org/eng/assets/files/annual-report/icrc-annual-report-2013.pdf>. For the Legal Division's unofficial position on this issue, see C. Droege, 'The Interplay between International Humanitarian Law and International Human Rights Law in Situations of Armed Conflict', 40 *Israel Law Review* (2008) 310.
[67] ICRC, *Annual Report*, above n 66, at 528; see Ch 35 of this volume.

The extension of the ICRC's work beyond cases of armed conflict has elicited different reactions within the ICRC, with some officials welcoming the opportunity for the ICRC to become a player in the implementation of human rights law, whether regarding detention, fair trial guarantees, or non-refoulement. They believe that the needs of victims must be examined broadly, and that the ICRC should take advantage of its access to those in need of protection. Others recoil at this move into the human rights field, arguing that it detracts from the fundamental purpose of the ICRC, risks perceptions that the ICRC is interfering in a state's internal affairs (and thus is no different from other NGOs) and overlaps with the work of human rights NGOs.

Other key ICRC protection functions—often carried out in close cooperation with other Movement components—involve the restoration of family links (RFL), gathering of information about missing persons, and the operation of the Central Tracing Agency (CTA).[68] These all address the debilitating uncertainties attending war, strife, and natural disasters, by establishing and transmitting information about the fate of soldiers and civilians.

Like other ICRC activities, these find inspiration in Dunant's impulsive actions at Solferino. Here, too, some conventional bases for ICRC activities may be cited; these also bear little relation to the scope and diversity of actual ICRC operations. This actuality reflects past initiative and occasional state consent, incrementally coalescing into a tradition to which states have long acquiesced. Provisions of the Geneva Conventions attest to, rather than constitute, the ICRC's functions in this area.[69]

The CTA is envisioned by Geneva Conventions III and IV, for example, as a worldwide clearinghouse for restoring family news and contacts, based on information received from national 'Information Bureaux'.[70] Both Conventions specify the particulars to be transmitted to the CTA, yet the only function they assign to the ICRC is proposing 'to the Powers concerned the organization of such an Agency'—'if it deems necessary'.[71] While under the Geneva Conventions, anyone could in theory establish the CTA, the ICRC operates the CTA that takes charge of this process.[72]

The gap between conventionally assigned functions and actual ICRC activities is even greater in the case of RFL and the missing.[73] The Conventions do impose obligations on parties to a conflict in these matters; they do not, however, entrust the ICRC with explicit or concrete protection functions in this respect.

---

[68] ICRC, *The Need to Know: Restoring Links between Dispersed Family Members* (Geneva: ICRC, 2010), available at <http://www.icrc.org/eng/assets/files/publications/icrc-002-4037.pdf>; M. Sassòli and M.-L. Tougas, 'The ICRC and the Missing', 84 *IRRC* 848 (2002) 727. RFL refers to 'a range of activities that aim to prevent separation and disappearance, restore and maintain contact between family members, and clarify the fate of persons reported missing'. ICRC, *Restoring Family Links Strategy, Including Legal References* (Geneva: ICRC, 2009), at 15, available at <http://www.icrc.org/eng/assets/files/other/icrc_002_0967.pdf>.

[69] Bugnion, above n 1, esp at 84–90, 498–507, 537, 555–79, 772–92.

[70] Art 122 GC III; Arts 136, 138 GC IV; G. Djurovic, *The Central Tracing Agency of the International Committee of the Red Cross: Activities of the ICRC for the Alleviation of Mental Suffering of War Victims* (Geneva: Henry-Dunant Institute, 1981); and Ch 53 of this volume.

[71] E.g., Arts 30, 54, 68, 70, 74, 75, 77, 120, 122 GC III. Art 123 GC III states only that that a CTA 'shall be created in a neutral country'. Cf Art 122 ('each of the Parties to the conflict shall institute an official Information Bureau').

[72] H.-P. Gasser, 'Protection of the Civilian Population', in Fleck (ed), above n 21, 209, at 251. See also Art 33(3) AP I (referring to the CTA 'of' the ICRC).

[73] For NIACs, neither CA 3 nor AP II addresses these issues: cf, however, ICRC CIHL Study, Rules 105, 116, 117, 125, 126.

III. Assistance

33   Assistance, the ICRC's other principal mandate, aims at preserving life and restoring 'the dignity of individuals and communities affected by armed conflict or other situations of violence' by addressing their essential needs. The ICRC assistance programmes provide mainly food, shelter, water, and medical care; in addition, they seek to ensure access to such essentials, as well as to preserve income and means of production.[74] Because, as noted, protection includes activities to reduce exposure to risk, it is at times difficult to distinguish between protection and assistance; the two notions under ICRC policy are 'intrinsically linked'.[75]

34   The assistance mandate is addressed by broad assertions in both the Statutes[76] and a scattered set of conventional provisions on 'relief', which rarely allude to the ICRC exclusively.[77] Its treaty-based right to provide assistance is implicit in its entitlement to propose limits on shipment of relief to POWs only 'in respect of [its] own shipments';[78] its right 'to supervise' distribution of relief to POWs is implied in the rule that special agreement cannot restrict such supervision.[79] The ICRC's 'special position [...] in this field', 'to be recognized and respected at all times', does not quite amount to an explicit right: Article 125 GC III mentions it only concerning the right of the Detaining Power to limit the numbers and supervise the activities of other organizations 'distributing relief supplies'.[80]

35   The ICRC's right to provide relief to civilians under occupation is more explicit, yet also more qualified: the Occupying Power is obliged to 'agree to relief schemes on behalf of the [occupied] population', and 'to facilitate them by all the means at its disposal'.[81] The ICRC is one of the entities that may undertake such schemes. But this duty applies only if 'the whole or part of the population of an occupied territory is inadequately supplied'.[82] A broader right is implicit in Article 30 GC IV, giving protected civilians 'every facility for making application' to the ICRC and other organizations, and obliging the authorities to grant 'all facilities for that purpose'.[83] The ICRC may also play a role in the distribution of relief consignments, if so empowered by agreement.[84] Its position on relief to civilian internees is similar to that governing POWs.[85] Outside IAC, ICRC assistance operations rely exclusively on its Common Article 3 or statutory right of initiative.[86]

36   Yet in practice, treaty-based sources of authority matter very little to the ICRC's daily work. Even with regard to POWs and civilian detainees, assistance operations rely mostly

---

[74] ICRC, *Assistance for People Affected by Armed Conflict and Other Situations of Violence* (2nd edn, Geneva: ICRC, 2012), at 2.

[75] ICRC Protection Policy, at 752.

[76] ICRC Statutes, Art 4(1)(d); Statutes of the Movement, Art 5(2)(d).

[77] For a critical account, see R. Giladi, 'The Utility and Limits of Legal Mandate: Humanitarian Assistance, the International Committee of the Red Cross, and Mandate Ambiguity', in A. Zwitter et al (eds), *Humanitarian Action: Global, Regional and Domestic Legal Responses* (Cambridge: CUP, 2014) 81.

[78] Art 72 GC III. Under Art 75, the ICRC may undertake to convey relief shipments where 'military operations' prevent the parties from meeting their obligation to assure their transport.

[79] Art 73 GC III.   [80] Pictet Commentary GC III, at 600–1.   [81] Art 59 GC IV.

[82] Ibid.   [83] See also Art 142 GC IV; Art 125 GC III.   [84] Art 61 GC IV.

[85] Arts 108, 109, 111, 142 GC IV, comparable to Arts 72, 73, 75, 125 GC III, respectively; Annex II.

[86] Arts 5 and 18 AP II do not mention the ICRC. See also Seville Agreement Art 6: 38 *IRRC* 322 (1998) 159.

on ICRC internal doctrine and practices. The Conventions lack instruction on needs assessment and exit strategies, coordination and cooperation with other relief actors, or navigation through the complex security and political environments where the ICRC runs assistance programmes. Thus, ICRC assistance practice is much broader than its conventional mandate suggests.[87] It includes, for example, the provision of vaccination and prosthetics; the building and maintenance of sewage facilities; micro-economic initiatives; and the treatment of unexploded or abandoned ordnance.[88] In armed conflict, other violent situations, and even natural disasters, the ICRC now operates in the face of diverse needs, among multiple relief actors, and where law counts little. Its current assistance policy, which includes health and economic security, does not even mention the Conventions.[89]

D. The ICRC's Role in the Implementation of International Humanitarian Law

I. General

The ICRC's two key operational roles must be seen in the context of a much more ambitious goal it has set for itself—as the 'guardian of international humanitarian law'.[90] More than simply helping the victims of armed conflict, the ICRC constantly seeks to elicit compliance by actors with the rules of IHL. Such a role is not mentioned in the Conventions, but it has become a core, parallel mission, now widely accepted by states and non-state actors. Indeed, this complements the leadership role the ICRC has assumed in the codification of IHL. That action takes place before and during armed conflict, with states and non-state actors, in venues ranging from the chambers of international organizations to secretive meetings with warring parties.[91] The ICRC's activities in this regard can be grouped into three categories, set out below in MN 38–57.

37

II. Technical assistance

First is the ICRC's technical assistance, which is focused on capacity-building—enabling states and, to an increasing extent, non-state actors to create the regulatory frameworks and institutions that may increase their ability to comply with IHL. Thus, the ICRC targets governments, with a view to their ratifying various treaties and enacting implementing legislation. It offers so-called advisory services, overseen by lawyers, entailing hands-on assistance to foreign ministries, legislatures, and other domestic decision makers.[92] Officially, the ICRC seems to assume that ratification and domestic legislation is necessary for state compliance with the rules of IHL.[93] Indeed, delegates have noted that

38

---

[87] D.P. Forsythe, 'The International Committee of the Red Cross and Humanitarian Assistance: A Policy Analysis', 36 *IRRC* 314 (1996) 512.
[88] ICRC, *Assistance*, above n 74.   [89] ICRC, 'ICRC Assistance Policy', 86 *IRRC* 855 (2004) 677.
[90] ICRC, *Missions and Work*, above n 29; see also D. Rieff, *A Bed for the Night: Humanitarianism in Crisis* (New York: Simon & Schuster, 2002), at 19 ('custodian of the laws of war').
[91] For a comprehensive study, in part based on interviews with ICRC officials, see S. Ratner, 'Law Promotion beyond Law Talk: The Red Cross, Persuasion, and the Laws of War', 22 *EJIL* (2011) 459.
[92] See Advisory service on international humanitarian law, available at <http://www.icrc.org/eng/what-we-do/building-respect-ihl/advisory-service/index.jsp>; see Ch 32 of this volume.
[93] ICRC, *Annual Report*, above n 66, at 16, 66–7.

convincing a state to comply is sometimes aided by the presence of a domestic law requiring military personnel to follow IHL and containing sanctions for breaches. Yet the ICRC devotes few resources to this process, suggesting that the institution realizes that a legal framework forms only a small part of the process leading to compliance.

39   Beyond assistance in drafting legislation, the ICRC organizes education and training for participants in armed conflicts, helping to translate the norms of IHL (regardless of the state's ratification status or domestic law) into doctrine, operational policies, and rules of engagement. It helps prepare military manuals and organizes educational programs for various levels of the armed forces. Having recognized the need for contact with non-state armed groups, for at least a decade the ICRC has attempted to educate them about IHL. Such an initiative presents special challenges because the groups typically operate clandestinely, often have unusual hierarchical structures, and may prove unfamiliar with or suspicious about IHL (e.g., seeing it as a tool of states against rebel groups).[94]

III. Promoting compliance globally

40   In addition to technical assistance, the ICRC undertakes a global, non country-specific set of activities aimed at the development, interpretation, and promotion of IHL. It seeks to influence states, international organizations, and non-state actors to take IHL more seriously, and—equally important—to take the ICRC's interpretations of IHL more seriously, in the belief that such awareness of the law will promote observance of it when conflicts arise.

41   First, building on its critical role in the preparation of the Geneva Conventions and Protocols, the ICRC has authored, or participated closely in the preparation of, interpretive documents on IHL, each with different legal valences. Most of these documents are primarily addressed at experts in IHL and human rights law. Although they are not tailored to particular country situations, the ICRC often prepares these documents with certain states in mind. Thus, its proposal for procedural safeguards for detainees and its elaboration of the notion of direct participation in hostilities (DPH) were sparked by ICRC concerns over US use of force against suspected terrorists.[95]

42   Secondly, the ICRC engages in so-called 'humanitarian diplomacy' in multilateral fora. This process involves lobbying international institutions whose work includes issues of relevance to the ICRC. Some of the multilateral diplomacy work is targeted at country situations, for example where a regional organization is following a war and ICRC input would be useful. But much of the work is non-country-specific.[96] The audience extends beyond the specialists in IHL to diplomats. The process aims both to impart expertise where it is lacking and to convince decision makers to take into account the ICRC's interpretation of the law or its operational needs. The ICRC relies on friendly

---

[94] Regarding an effort to explain the consistency of IHL with Sharia to Muslim religious scholars with ties to armed groups in Iraq, Lebanon, and Afghanistan, see, e.g., *Iran: Dialogue on Islam and International Humanitarian Law in Qom*, 1 December 2006, available at <https://www.icrc.org/eng/resources/documents/feature/2006/ihl-islam-event-011206.htm>.

[95] See J. Pejic, 'Procedural Principles and Safeguards for Internment/Administrative Detention in Armed Conflict and Other Situations of Violence', 87 *IRRC* 858 (2005) 375; ICRC, *Interpretive Guidance on the Notion of Direct Participation in Hostilities under International Humanitarian Law* (Geneva: ICRC, 2009). For other examples, see Montreux Document on Private Military and Security Companies (2008), UN Doc A/63/467-S/2008/636; ICRC CIHL Study.

[96] See ICRC, *Annual Report*, above n 66, at 68–9.

states to inject its views in fora open only to states. It has thus closely followed UN debates about protection of civilians in armed conflict and has offered views reflected in UN resolutions and documents.[97] Additionally, the ICRC joins in the preparation of treaties or encourages their ratification, as with the Convention on the Prohibition of the Use, Stockpiling, Production and Transfer of Anti-Personnel Mines and on their Destruction, 1997; the Statute of the International Criminal Court (ICC), 1998; and the Convention on Cluster Munitions, 2008.

Lastly, the ICRC develops educational curricula for IHL, runs the ICRC website, and organizes commemorations on significant anniversaries. This strategy casts the widest net of all, to legislators, educators, civil society, and ordinary citizens. International humanitarian law is explained at a very basic level, with focus on the most elementary rules.[98] 43

IV. Persuading parties to comply through confidential communications

At the core of the ICRC's compliance strategy are confidential communications with the parties to an armed conflict or other security situation. 44

a. Doctrine 15 and practice

The ICRC's approach to IHL violations is spelled out in formal doctrine—confidential internal ICRC policy adopted at a high level within the institution.[99] Doctrine 15, entitled 'Action by the ICRC in the Event of Violations of International Humanitarian Law or of Other Fundamental Rules Protecting Persons in Situations of Violence',[100] as well as practice, point to four steps in the ICRC's country-specific communications: 45

— *Phase 1: Reminder of obligations.* When an IAC breaks out, the ICRC deposits a confidential aide-memoire with the warring parties (including non-state actors), reminding them of their core obligations under IHL. When internal hostilities reach a certain threshold, such memoranda will be sent to the government and insurgent forces as well.[101]

— *Phase 2: Bilateral confidential memoranda and discussions.* Once a conflict is underway, or in non-conflict situations where the ICRC is invited by government to operate, the ICRC gathers information on the situation of victims. Its primary method is through visits by delegation members to prisons, war zones, refugee camps, hospitals, and other venues. Once it is able to gather a fuller picture of the violations, the ICRC typically submits a detailed report to the parties during the conflict or thereafter.[102]

---

[97] See, e.g., UNSC Res 1882, 4 August 2009; GA Res 63/125, 15 January 2009. See also *Report of the Secretary-General on the Protection of Civilians in Armed Conflict*, 29 May 2009, paras 41–5, UN Doc S/2009/277 (commending ICRC).

[98] See, e.g., ICRC, *The Basics of International Humanitarian Law* (Geneva, ICRC: 2010), available at <http://www.icrc.org/eng/assets/files/publications/icrc-002-0850.pdf>; ICRC, *International Humanitarian Law: A Universal Code* (2009), video at <http://www.icrc.org/eng/resources/documents/film/f00981.htm>.

[99] Most doctrine is confidential. The ICRC has stated its hope to have public versions of all doctrines, though the culture of the institution suggests that this will be a difficult task.

[100] Reprinted at 87 *IRRC* 858 (2005) 393 (hereinafter Doctrine 15).

[101] Doctrine 15 does not include Phase 1, as these memoranda are issued before violations are suspected or established. See also T. Pfanner, 'Various Mechanisms and Approaches for Implementing International Humanitarian Law and Protecting and Assisting War Victims', 91 *IRRC* 874 (2009) 279, at 292–3.

[102] For one leaked report, see *ICRC Report on the Treatment of Fourteen 'High Value' Detainees in CIA Custody* (February 2007), available at <http://www.nybooks.com/icrc-report.pdf>.

The ICRC hopes that its confidential reports will lead to a dialogue with states and armed groups to improve the plight of victims. The prospects for such discussions vary significantly across targets. Some will sit down with ICRC officials to consider solutions; others are not interested in follow-up. Interlocutors range from senior governmental officials, aided by lawyers, to leaders of insurgent forces, to prison administrators.

— *Phase 3: Mobilization of other actors.* If the ICRC believes that confidential dialogue is not improving the situation of victims, it will cultivate other actors who may have influence on the parties. These efforts will focus on governments friendly with the target state or armed group (including those giving them funds), but might also include international organizations or NGOs.

— *Phase 4: Public criticism.* In rare cases, the ICRC will abandon confidentiality and issue a public statement of censure. Doctrine 15 identifies two forms of such criticism—a public expression of concern over the quality of its dialogue with the target state or group; and a 'public condemnation of specific violations of international humanitarian law'.[103]

46 The four phases of action are carried out primarily at the level of country delegations and sub-delegations outside a national capital. Delegation heads seek Geneva's approval for overall strategy, as well as for the content of written communications (typically vetted by the Legal Division). Officials in Geneva will become involved in high-level diplomacy. The ICRC has a long tradition of acting as a bottom-up and consensus-driven organization, with the head of delegation's judgement on the strategy generally receiving deference in Geneva.

b. Confidentiality as a tool

47 The doctrine and practice of the ICRC treat confidentiality as the baseline for communications with governments and armed groups, one deemed essential to gain the trust of the parties and access to the victims. As a result, those outside the ICRC's channel of communications generally will not know: (i) the facts of the particular violation, including the type of abuses, their location, their perpetrators, or their victims; or (ii) the ICRC's opinion as to whether that conduct violates IHL or other legal norms. Yet confidentiality is really a tool, not a principle (and is not mentioned among the three core principles)—and one calibrated to match operational needs. While confidentiality is often crucial for access, the parties may be more motivated to grant access due to trust in the even-handedness and experience of the ICRC.

48 Moreover, the ICRC may, with the consent of the parties, share information.[104] Regarding conditions of confinement in prisons, states frequently want potential donors to know about their limitations and provide aid towards remedying the situation. Even without a state's permission to go public, ICRC doctrine allows for mobilization and denunciation. Moreover, the ICRC has issued statements of concern during a conflict

---

[103] Doctrine 15, above n 100, paras 3.2, 3.3.

[104] Though it need not do so. See EECC, *Prisoners of War—Ethiopia's Claim 4*, above n 64, paras 46–8, and *Eritrea's Claim 17*, 1 July 2003, paras 50–3 (criticizing the ICRC's refusal to hand over to the Commission reports on POW visits despite the permission of the two states).

that identify violations but conspicuously avoid identifying the violator.[105] It can also make statements that effectively blame one side and urge better behaviour without formally condemning it.[106] The ICRC has a communication infrastructure to inform the world—up to a point—of its activities.

The result is thus a spectrum of approaches to confidentiality. In each episode, the ICRC's determination regarding dissemination of its views is driven by an internal judgement as to what will be most effective for the victims.[107] Generally, it tilts in favour of fairly strict confidentiality, out of a belief that it is necessary for access; public criticism (or even the threat of it) is viewed as not aiding the victims but risking withdrawal of cooperation by the state or armed group, or, worse, removal of or harm to ICRC staff. Internally, delegates are acculturated, through training and field experience, to accept the starting point of confidentiality; indeed, most presumably endorse the ICRC's *modus operandi* even before signing up. Decisions to move to mobilization or public denunciation generally require higher-level approval, either by the head of delegation or by officials in Geneva.

c. The role of legal argumentation

The ICRC deploys law quite flexibly in its interactions with parties. In most situations, the ICRC shares its legal views with the parties and advises them of their obligations under IHL. Yet it sometimes keeps its position on legal matters ambiguous. It will sometimes refuse to state, even to the parties to a conflict, whether it has determined that the level of violence has risen to the threshold which would trigger Common Article 3 or AP II, as addressed in Chapter 19 of this volume. The ICRC has also often refrained from informing parties whether it regards one state's control of foreign territory as an occupation, which triggers the protections of Convention IV. In these cases, the ICRC justifies this ambiguity by a concern that states might react adversely to the ICRC's opinions and withhold cooperation. Thus, in the case of the threshold for armed conflict, the government may want to maintain its official line that an opposition group is merely a criminal band, or that fighting is only at the level of skirmishes. In the case of occupation, a state will generally wish to deny strongly that it is occupying another state. Thus, rather than telling the state that it is legally an occupier, the ICRC presents it with a generic set of expectations for the treatment of civilians.

Indeed, sometimes the ICRC avoids IHL arguments with the parties in favour of other arguments that one of the authors has organized as follows:

— humanitarian arguments, i.e., that changed behaviour will reduce the suffering of innocent victims of the conflict;
— political arguments, i.e., that changed behaviour will improve the target's domestic or international reputation;
— economic arguments, i.e., that changed behaviour will lead to additional sources of foreign or domestic revenue;
— pragmatic arguments, i.e., that changed behaviour will improve the efficiency, discipline, or internal functioning of the target's armed or security forces;

---

[105] See, e.g., 'ICRC condemns the shelling of Gaza's Al Aqsa Hospital', 21 July 2014, available at <http://www.icrc.org/eng/resources/documents/news-release/2014/07-21-gaza-al-aqsa-hospital.htm>.

[106] 'US Detention Related to the Fight against Terrorism—the Role of the ICRC', 4 March 2009, available at <http://www.icrc.org/eng/resources/documents/misc/united-states-detention-240209.htm>; see also 'Gaza: ICRC Demands Urgent Access to Wounded as Israeli Army Fails to Assist Wounded Palestinians', 8 January 2009 (de facto denunciation).

[107] See Ratner, above n 91, at 472–4; Pfanner, above n 101.

— moral arguments, i.e., that changed behaviour is the morally right way to respond, in the sense of the way a decent or professional military or security force should act; and
— customary arguments, i.e., that changed behaviour is demanded by the customs and mores of the society.

Sometimes those six arguments are offered as reasons to comply with an IHL norm; at other times they simply replace any discussion of the norm.[108]

52   This practice reflects an evolving policy that the ICRC needed to move beyond integrating the law into training, military codes, unilateral declarations, and ceasefire agreements, and rather to engage in what it called 'strategic argumentation'.[109] The ICRC has thus, at times, pushed legal argumentation into the shadows. It seems as if such alternative argumentation is critical when interlocutors: (i) are ignorant of, or might be confused by, the law's content; or (ii) see the law as a creation or tool of their enemy (as is common among rebel groups, who do not become parties to IHL treaties). As a result, one witnesses a spectrum of dialogues with respect to their legal component. At one end might be highly legalized and lawyered exchanges with the US or Israeli military; at the other might be conversations with the Lord's Resistance Army or elements of the Taliban.

d. Results

53   The effectiveness of the ICRC's bilateral communications in inducing compliance with IHL is difficult to gauge. That process is just one of the methods used by the ICRC, along with the other methods discussed above. Moreover, ICRC interventions may have a delayed effect on compliance by the targeted actors, or affect the compliance of other actors.[110] If success were measured by comparing compliance by targets with IHL norms in the presence of the ICRC compared with its absence, the ICRC would be able to point to many instances where its responses appear to have been the proximate cause of improvement in the situations of victims and IHL compliance, for example in informing families of the fate of missing relatives, establishing communication between detainees and relatives, and improving detainee conditions. Delegates and victims have many stories suggesting that the ICRC is indispensable due to its often unique access to victims.[111] Governments and armed groups are generally at least willing to meet ICRC delegates and hear their concerns. At the same time, governments can use the presence of an ICRC delegation as a public fig leaf to claim that their practices conform to IHL. The added value of the ICRC's presence, controlling for all other factors, seems impossible to determine robustly.

54   If the metric is switched to a comparison with the work of other actors—states and NGOs—evaluation becomes even harder. States can sometimes exert more pressure

---

[108] Ratner, above n 91, at 477–81. See also O. Bangerter, 'Reasons Why Armed Groups Choose to Respect International Humanitarian Law or Not', 93 *IRRC* 882 (2011) 353.

[109] For a public summary of the still-confidential document, see ICRC, *Increasing Respect for International Humanitarian Law in Non-international Armed Conflicts* (Geneva, ICRC: 2008), at 30, available at <http://www.icrc.org/eng/assets/files/other/icrc_002_0923.pdf>.

[110] See generally R. Howse and R. Teitel, 'Beyond Compliance: Rethinking Why International Law Really Matters', 1 *Global Policy* (2010) 127–36.

[111] See generally ICRC, *Annual Report*, above n 66; 'ICRC Detention Visits: Ex-Detainees Share their Experiences', 31 December 2005, available at <http://www.icrc.org/eng/resources/documents/misc/detention_testimonies_040713.htm>; 'Aline: "Many former detainees speak of a moral debt to the ICRC"', 25 May 2005, available at <http://www.icrc.org/eng/resources/documents/misc/rwanda-testimony-250505.htm>.

on violators than the ICRC, and with better results. Human rights NGOs can point to instances where the public shaming of a state pushed that state to act where private communications failed. Yet again, this comparison seems impervious to robust testing.

In the end, the confidentiality that undergirds the ICRC's work makes it resistant to assessments of its success, leaving us mostly with stories from delegates or victims. The camps, prisons, and theatres of operations it visits; the warriors, detainees, and civilian victims it sees; the legal and other arguments it uses; and the behaviour of states and non-state actors before and after ICRC overtures—all are mostly hidden from outside scrutiny. Governments rarely acknowledge that their actions result from ICRC interventions. The growth of the institution over time, including its support from donors, suggests that its reputation as the central NGO in the protection of victims of armed conflict is secure. It is difficult to appraise, however, whether that support reflects any international consensus on the ICRC's success regarding IHL, or is based on a desire—from empathy, guilt, or self-interest—to fund, and be seen as funding, the work of the ICRC.

e. *Reconciling the guardian and operational roles*

The ICRC's protection work thus entails direct efforts to persuade parties to comply with IHL, yet its methods seem to create a tension with its self-professed role as the 'guardian' of IHL. The secrecy of its legal conclusions means that a particularly authoritative interpreter of a corpus of international law is refraining from telling the world its view of the law in specific cases. The ambiguity in withholding those legal views even from the warring parties seems even more at odds with the guardian role, for without legal guidance, the prospects for convincing them to understand and follow the norms seem all the more difficult. The decision in some situations to avoid (rather than simply supplement) legal argumentation in favour of other arguments seems to be giving a party reasons to act a certain way *without regard to* whether the party would then be following a rule.

All of these aspects of its work demonstrate that the ICRC is fundamentally concerned with changing the behaviour of actors in order to conform with the rules of IHL, and that it will use whatever combination of secrecy, ambiguity, and directness of legal argumentation advances that goal. While it would certainly prefer those actors to 'internalize' the rules and comply with them out of a sense of legal obligation, the ICRC is ultimately satisfied if the actors follow the rules for whatever reason. Given the obstacles to internalization during armed conflict, the gravity of the violations and thus the urgency of terminating them, and the actors with whom ICRC delegates interact—not typically lawyers in foreign ministries or legislatures—compliance, for whatever reason, is hard enough. By seeking compliance rather than internalization (sometimes called obedience),[112] the ICRC reconciles its guardian role and its humanitarian/protection role, though not in the rather simplistic way suggested in its official doctrine.[113] Rather, the institution interprets

---

[112] H. Koh, 'Why Do Nations Obey International Law?', 106 *YLJ* (1997) 2599, at 2600–1, fn 3.
[113] Ratner, above n 91, at 498–501; for the doctrine, see ICRC, *Missions and Work*, above n 29, at 6 ('These two lines [helping victims and law promotion] are inextricably linked because the first operates within the framework provided by the second, and the second draws on the experience of the first and facilitates the ICRC's response to the needs identified').

its role as guardian of IHL as one in which it seeks to address the behaviour of actors, and not their words or internal thoughts.

E. The ICRC and International Criminal Courts

58   The idea of judicial enforcement of IHL is not new to the ICRC. Gustave Moynier, its second President, proposed it in 1872, but with some ambivalence: first, he had hoped that public opinion would 'compel obedience' to the 1864 Convention. The conduct of the Franco-Prussian War, however, led him to propose the creation of a permanent court to 'prevent and suppress' infractions of the Convention.[114]

59   Some of Moynier's ambivalence persists today. The ICRC's unique method for promoting compliance does not preclude an awareness of that method's limits. Thus, it has supported other efforts to promote respect for IHL, including punishment of war crimes. It welcomed the establishment of the ad hoc tribunals in the 1990s, and played an active and public role in negotiations leading to the ICC.[115] It promotes ratification of the ICC Statute, attends its Assembly of States Parties' meetings, and encourages these states to implement their ICC obligations, including by technical support.[116]

60   On the other hand, the operation of international criminal tribunals gives new form to the tension between assisting victims and protecting them by punishing perpetrators, between the protection and guardianship roles, and between operations and law. Judicial enforcement of IHL, equipped with an authoritative voice and coercive force, can help enforce IHL, expand its scope, and bolster the legal interpretations promoted by the ICRC. It can also, however, compete with the ICRC as authoritative interpreter of IHL and produce more rigid law limiting the ICRC's latitude for persuasion. A clash of mandates can harm the ICRC's position and operations.

61   A clash can also harm ICRC operational principles and working methods. The International Criminal Tribunal for the former Yugoslavia (ICTY) Prosecutor's early request to hear the testimony of a former ICRC interpreter threatened the ICRC's control of information obtained through confidential dialogue and challenged its policy of abstaining from participation in judicial proceedings.[117] It would have violated the confidentiality of past ICRC dialogue and compromised the trust necessary to persuade future interlocutors. Taking part in court proceedings would also have the appearance of taking sides, impairing the ICRC's neutral image, threatening its independence, and even affecting the security of delegates in the field.[118] Another challenge presented by the operation of criminal tribunals concerned those courts' treatment and detention of

---

[114] C.K. Hall, 'The First Proposal for a Permanent International Criminal Court', 80 *IRRC* 322 (1998) 57.
[115] ICRC Advisory Service, *Punishing War Crimes: International Criminal Tribunals*, 01/2003.
[116] 'Establishment of the International Criminal Court', ICRC Statement, 14 October 2002, available at <http://www.icrc.org/eng/resources/documents/misc/5f2j22.htm>.
[117] ICRC, International Criminal Court: Overview (29 October 2010) ('total control over the information'); ICTY, *The Prosecutor v Blagoje Simić et al*, Trial Chamber, Decision on the Prosecution Motion under Rule 73 for a Ruling concerning the Testimony of a Witness, IT-95-9, 27 July 1999.
[118] Interview: 'ICRC and ICC: two separate but complementary approaches to ensuring respect for international humanitarian law', available at <http://www.icrc.org/eng/resources/documents/interview/international-criminal-court-interview-101008.htm>; A.-M. La Rosa, 'Humanitarian Organizations and International Criminal Tribunals, Or Trying to Square the Circle', 88 *IRRC* 861 (2006) 169, at 170.

persons accused, who often fall under the ICRC mandate. Here, criminal tribunals are the object of ICRC dialogue and persuasion, just like states, armed groups, and international forces.

The ICRC has responded to these challenges by selective engagement. It promotes a vision of the 'separate but complementary' roles of the ICRC and the tribunals,[119] enabling it to choose whether to cooperate with the tribunals or confront them. On the one hand, it works to underscore the IHL components of the ICC Statute and promulgates its own interpretation of these.[120] On the other hand, it participated, backed by expert opinions, in the ICTY proceedings to preserve its right not to participate in such proceedings,[121] and it battled to preserve the confidentiality of its submissions.[122] This produced an ICTY ruling upholding ICRC immunity from testimony and disclosure,[123] which was followed by other ad hoc tribunals. Engagement by the ICRC produced Rule 73 of the ICC Rules of Procedure and Evidence,[124] which obliges the ICC to 'regard as privileged' and not subject to disclosure any information obtained by the ICRC and its employees, past and present, in the course of 'performance by ICRC of its functions'. Lastly, the ICRC negotiated agreements under which it conducts visits to persons under the ICC's jurisdiction.[125]

Finally, the deterioration in the security of humanitarian operations in recent decades has led to efforts to criminalize attacks on ICRC personnel, buildings, vehicles, and other objects. In IACs, such acts fit easily into the ICC Statute's list of war crimes as attacks on civilians and civilian objects.[126] Some, however, qualify as more particular war crimes, for example under Articles 8(2)(b)(iii) (attacks on humanitarian assistance) and 8(2)(b)(xxiv) (attacks on objects and personnel 'using the distinctive emblems of the Geneva Conventions in conformity with international law'). In NIACs, in addition to comprising attacks against civilians,[127] intentional attacks against the ICRC qualify as war crimes under Article 8(2)(e)(ii)–(iv), concerning humanitarian-related persons and objects. The inclusion of attacks on humanitarian personnel in the Rome Statute is clearly a recognition by states of the importance of the ICRC's mission, though it does not confer any new sort of new personality or status on the ICRC (MN 10–13). Whether the ICC Prosecutor will devote resources to prosecuting such attacks remains, however, an open question.

Even with this criminalization, one must recall ICRC reticence toward participation in judicial, let alone criminal, proceedings, and its traditional sensitivity regarding

---

[119] ICTY, *Simić*, above n 117, para 79.

[120] K. Dörmann, *Elements of War Crimes under the Rome Statute of the International Criminal Court: Sources and Commentary* (Cambridge: ICRC and CUP, 2003).

[121] ICTY, *Simić*, above n 117; G. Rona, 'The ICRC Privilege Not to Testify: Confidentiality in Action', 84 *IRRC* 845 (2002) 207.

[122] ICTY, *The Prosecutor v Blagoje Simić et al*, Trial Chamber, Decision on Application by Stevan Todorović to Reopen the Decision of 27 July 1999 etc, 28 February 2000.

[123] ICTY, *Simić*, above n 117.   [124] ICC-ASP/1/3, *Official Records* (3–10 September 2002).

[125] Agreement between the International Criminal Tribunal for the Former Yugoslavia and the ICRC on Procedures for Visiting Persons Held on the Authority of the Tribunal, 36 *IRRC* 311 (1996) 238; Agreement between the International Criminal Court and the International Committee of the Red Cross on Visits to Persons deprived of Liberty Pursuant to the Jurisdiction of the International Criminal Court (2006).

[126] Art 8(2)(b)(i)–(ii) ICC Statute. O. Triffterer (ed), *Commentary on the Rome Statute of the International Criminal Court* (2nd edn, Munich: C.H. Beck, 2008), at 323. See also UNSC Res 1502, 26 August 2003 (noting 'prohibitions under international law against attacks knowingly and intentionally directed against personnel involved in a humanitarian assistance [...] which in situations of armed conflicts constitute war crimes').

[127] E.g. Art 8(2)(e)(i) ICC Statute, but not objects.

perceptions of its independence and neutrality. It is thus unlikely that the ICRC would openly campaign for or cooperate with such proceedings as part of its own security strategy.[128]

F. Critical Assessment

65   The ICRC remains among the most unusual of international institutions. By dint of its pedigree and *modus operandi*, states have, at times directly but mostly through tacit consent, entrusted it with responsibilities that they themselves seem unable to accept jointly as parties to the Geneva Conventions. Whereas in other global regimes, states create or assign intergovernmental bodies or their staff to address violations of their rules—to investigate, persuade, mediate, and mobilize support for strategies that will push or pull a violating entity to reverse course—in IHL the task falls to a Swiss NGO acting independently of states, with only financial accountability to them. The ICRC has certainly welcomed and encouraged this increased level of responsibility. Moreover, it has pulled off an impressive feat: knowing it lacks political power, it takes advantage of the trust states have in it to provide important relief to victims of armed conflict, whether soldiers *hors de combat* or civilians. It gains access to zones closed to, or too inhospitable for, most NGOs, diplomats, and the functionaries of international organizations, relying upon its emblem and the skill of its staff to wrench small and occasionally big victories for IHL from the hardest of armies.

66   Yet in the end, the very broad responsibilities of the ICRC are also an important sign of failure by the states parties to the Geneva Conventions—failure to assume true ownership of them. While states and NGOs have called for decades for an enforcement mechanism linked to and controlled by those states parties, most recently at the 2011 international conference of the Movement,[129] powerful states remain hesitant to strengthen the Conventions through such a mechanism. Since 2011, the ICRC has been working alongside the Swiss Government to forge some kind of consensus among the Conventions' parties on the modalities of such a mechanism. This new effort, mostly behind the scenes for now, to nudge states toward addressing some longstanding shortcomings of the Geneva Conventions, in many ways flows from earlier campaigns by the ICRC to develop and codify IHL. The process is proceeding slowly, with a focus on getting agreement on new procedures of periodic reporting of national implementation of IHL, regular thematic discussions, and fact-finding.[130]

---

[128] Note the narrow confines of §6, 'Health Care in Danger', Resolution adopted at the 31st International Conference of the Red Cross and Red Crescent (2011), Res 31IC/11/R5, available at <http://rcrcconference.org/wp-content/uploads/sites/3/2015/03/R5_HCiD_EN.pdf>, calling upon 'States to ensure effective investigation and prosecution of crimes committed against health care personnel—including Movement personnel—their facilities and their means of transportation, especially attacks carried out against them, and to cooperate to this end [...] with international criminal tribunals and courts'.

[129] See Strengthening the legal protection for victims of armed conflicts, Resolution adopted at the 31st International Conference of the Red Cross and Red Crescent (2011), Res 31IC/11/R1, available at <http://rcrcconference.org/wp-content/uploads/sites/3/2015/03/R1_Strengthening_IHL_EN.pdf>.

[130] For public documents on the process, see Swiss Federal Department of Foreign Affairs, Joint Initiative of Switzerland and the International Committee of the Red Cross (ICRC) on Strengthening Compliance with International Humanitarian Law, available at <http://www.eda.admin.ch/eda/en/home/topics/intla/humlaw/icrc.html>.

Until such a mechanism is in force, and, given its rather modest reach, even after it is, 67
states still would rather, it seems, rely upon a group of Swiss notables, bolstered by an international staff, to promote observance of IHL and aid war victims, than attempt to build an institution within the Conventions that they would control and deploy against violating parties. Although occasionally other institutions—the UN or the European Union—will fill this gap by taking action against violators, the states parties themselves seem to fear the divisiveness associated with implementation of IHL. While the ICRC may well consider itself the guardian of the Geneva Conventions, the result is an outsourcing of the responsibilities for compliance with those treaties that should give us all pause.

ROTEM GILADI   STEVEN RATNER

Chapter 27. Protecting Powers

	MN
A. Introduction: Historical Evolution of the Institution of Protecting Powers	1
B. Meaning and Application	5
I. Definition of a Protecting Power	5
II. Modalities of appointment of a Protecting Power	8
III. Functions of the Protecting Power	9
a. General functions	10
b. Specific functions	11
c. Additional Protocol I	14
d. Other Conventions	15
IV. Practice since 1949	16
V. Reasons for the Decline of the Institution of Protecting Powers	18
C. Relevance in Non-International Armed Conflicts	27
D. Legal Consequences of a Violation	28
E. Critical Assessment	29

Select Bibliography

There is a short chapter on Protecting Powers in all the manuals of IHL, including those mentioned in the general Bibliography of the present Commentary. For further bibliographical references, see *Bibliography of International Humanitarian Law Applicable in Armed Conflicts* (2nd edn, Geneva: ICRC, 1987), at 556. On Protecting Powers, one might also refer to the following literature:

Bertschy, R., *Die Schutzmacht im Völkerrecht* (Fribourg: (without editor's notice), 1952)

Bugnion, F., *Le comité international de la Croix-Rouge et la protection des victimes de la guerre* (Geneva: ICRC, 1994) Protecting Power, at 1413

Cortese, G., *La potenza protettrice nel diritto internazionale* (Rome: Edizioni Bizzarri, 1972)

Cortese, G., 'La potenza protettrice in caso di rottura delle relazioni diplomatiche', 54 *Revue de droit international, de sciences diplomatiques et politiques* (1976) 96

Dominicé, C./J. Patrnogic, 'Les puissances protectrices dans les Conventions de 1949', *Annales de droit médical* (1977) 24

Franklin, W.M., *Protection of Foreign Interests: A Study in Diplomatic and Consular Practice* (Washington, DC: US Government Printing Office, 1946)

Heintze, H.J., 'Protecting Power' in MPEPIL

Henn, C., *The Origins and Early Development of the Idea of Protecting Power* (Cambridge: PhD, University of Cambridge, 1986)

Janner, A., *La puissance protectrice en droit international d'après les expériences faites par la Suisse pendant la Seconde Guerre mondiale* (Basel: Helbing & Lichtenhahn, 1948)

Laitenberger, B., 'Die Schutzmacht', 21 *German Yearbook of International Law* (1978) 180

Lowe, V., 'Diplomatic Law: Protecting Powers', 39 *ICLQ* (1990) 471

Peirce, G., 'Humanitarian Protection for the Victims of War: The System of Protecting Powers and the Role of the ICRC', 90 *Military Law Review* (1980) 89

De La Pradelle, P.G., 'Une institution en question du droit international humanitaire: la puissance protectrice', *Essays in Honor of M. Udina* (Milan: Giuffrè, 1975) vol I, at 409–19

De Preux, J., 'Puissance protectrice', 67 *IRRC* 752 (1985) 86

Sassòli/Bouvier/Quintin, vol I, at 365–7

Wolfrum, R./Fleck, D., 'Enforcement of International Humanitarian Law', in D. Fleck (ed), *The Handbook of International Humanitarian Law* (2nd edn, Oxford: OUP, 2008) 675, at 709–11

Wylie, R.N., 'Protecting Powers in a Changing World', 1 *Politorbis* (2006) 6

A. Introduction: Historical Evolution of the Institution of Protecting Powers

1   This is not the place to discuss the historical evolution of the institution of Protecting Powers at length, since the focus must be on developments since 1949. It may simply be recalled that the system of Protecting Powers for diplomatic purposes has existed since the sixteenth century. It was for the first time transferred to, and implemented in, a situation of belligerency during the Franco-Prussian War of 1870–1.[1] It came to full maturity in the First World War, and later in the Second World War, before it quickly declined. The rule initially rested on the practice of states, and hence on customary international law. It was then codified in Article 86 of the 1929 Geneva Convention relative to the Treatment of Prisoners of War.[2] Some inadequacies with this provision became apparent. First, it was too limited in scope: it applied only to prisoners of war (POWs), and thus left enemy civilians or persons in occupied territories without protection. Secondly, there was no obligation to appoint a Protecting Power; the 1929 Convention only underscored the 'possibility' of such an appointment, limiting itself to recommending it. Thirdly, the question of the replacement of a Protecting Power not living up to its obligations, and the whole question of a substitute for a Protecting Power, was not addressed. This was to some extent in line with the basic tenet whereby there was no obligation at all to appoint a Protecting Power. Fourthly, there was an absence of any regulation as to non-recognized governments being appointed as Protecting Powers; such a nomination might be rejected by the opposing belligerent on the grounds of non-recognition.

2   Common Articles 8/8/8/9 and 10/10/10/11 of Geneva Conventions (GCs) I–IV of 1949 improved the legal regulation relating to Protecting Powers on several—but not all—points. First, the institution was broadened to include all protected persons, the wounded, sick, shipwrecked or captured military personal, and the protected civilians (the so-called 'Hague Law' is not included here[3]). Secondly, the appointment of a Protecting Power was made a legal obligation for each belligerent. Its opponent must accept the protection of a Protecting Power, even if it may resist a particular appointment, for example if it does not hold the proposed state to be sufficiently neutral or independent (see further MN 4). Thirdly, provision was made for the substitution of an absent or a defaulting Protecting Power, by allowing an 'impartial organization' or the ICRC to step in and carry out the functions of a Protecting Power.

3   Article 5 of Additional Protocol (AP) I develops the system further. First, it strengthens the duty to appoint a Protecting Power from the very 'beginning' of the armed conflict

---

[1] G. Cortese, *La potenza protettrice nel diritto internazionale* (Rome: Bizzarri, 1972). See also C. Henn, *The Origins and Early Development of the Idea of Protecting Power* (Cambridge: PhD University of Cambridge, 1986).

[2] All the quoted provisions may be consulted either on the website of the ICRC, at <http://www.icrc.org>, or in D. Schindler and J. Toman, *The Law of Armed Conflicts* (4th edn, Leiden/Boston: Martinus Nijhoff, 2004).

[3] Hague Law issues are covered by the customary limb of the institution of the Protecting Power. A state may nominate a Protecting Power with the task to perform various functions, including in the field of the Hague Law. But this extends beyond the GCs, which are the object of this Commentary.

(Article 5(2)). Secondly, it lays out a procedure by which the ICRC can, and indeed must, aid the belligerent parties in attempting to nominate a Protecting Power. The belligerent parties are under an obligation to cooperate with the ICRC on this issue, as set out in the provision. This involvement of the ICRC having been explicitly recognized and made mandatory, no state party to AP I can complain of undue 'intervention' by the ICRC in this delicate matter. Thirdly, Article 5 underlines that the maintenance of diplomatic relations is no 'obstacle' to the appointment of a Protecting Power, thus inviting the parties to make such appointments in such a situation (Article 5(6)).

4   Throughout these regulations, the necessity for consent of the belligerents involved to the appointment of the Protecting Power is stressed. No state can unilaterally appoint its Protecting Power and impose that Protecting Power on the opposing belligerent. Moreover, the Protecting Power itself must obviously accept the appointment. This state of affairs could be considered as unfortunate, and even as a fatal shortcoming. It might be considered to be the main reason preventing the implementation of the institution of Protecting Powers. However, the need for consent is but a systemic condition for the Protecting Power to perform its functions correctly. It would not serve any purpose to force an unwelcome Protecting Power upon an unwilling state. The state not having accepted the appointment would then constantly hamper the Protecting Power's activities by putting obstacles in its way, thus ultimately leading to the failure of the enterprise. From this perspective, the consent requirement is a realistic condition for the proper implementation and unfolding of the institution of Protecting Powers.

B. Meaning and Application

I. Definition of a Protecting Power

5   A Protecting Power is a neutral state or a state not party to an international armed conflict (IAC), which is nominated in order to safeguard the interests of one or more states parties to that armed conflict, notably when direct diplomatic relations are severed, and to contribute to the control of implementation and respect for the applicable international humanitarian law (IHL). A humanitarian mandate of a Protecting Power is thus added to a diplomatic mandate. A Protecting Power may be nominated to perform one of either tasks, or both tasks at once. The functions of the Protecting Power in the humanitarian limb are not set out anew in each case, by way of special agreement. Rather, they are defined in the body of modern IHL itself, through a series of rules mentioned below. In this chapter, only the humanitarian aspect of the nomination and tasks of a Protecting Power will be considered. It should be stressed, however, that a Protecting Power may be nominated to perform humanitarian law tasks even when diplomatic representation is unnecessary. If diplomatic relations between the belligerents are not severed, there will be no need to nominate a Protecting Power for such purposes. However, in such a case, the appointment as regards the humanitarian tasks is not hampered in any way, since a Protecting Power *may* here be nominated (but need not be nominated), notwithstanding that the belligerent states continue to entertain restricted or ordinary diplomatic intercourse.

6   In Article 5(6) AP I,[4] the words 'is no obstacle' underline that, for humanitarian purposes, a Protecting Power can be nominated even if diplomatic intercourse is not severed.

---

[4] Art 5(6) AP I reads: 'The maintenance of diplomatic relations between Parties to the conflict or the entrusting of the protection of a Party's interests and those of its nationals to a third State in accordance with

These words might also be interpreted to mean that the ordinary rule of Article 5(1) AP I applies, whereby there is also a *duty* to appoint a Protecting Power. To some extent this would indeed be the better interpretation, since the ordinary functioning of diplomacy during an armed conflict is to some extent always reduced. Such a state of affairs operates to the detriment of the protected persons. However, the states represented at the Conference of 1977 leading to the adoption of AP I did not want to assume any obligation to appoint a Protecting Power when diplomatic relations between the belligerents continue.[5] There is some room for holding that if diplomatic relations are not severed, but are reduced or otherwise not working to full efficacy with regard to the humanitarian tasks, the duty to appoint a Protecting Power according to Article 5(1) AP I remains. This view would be most in line with the wording and aim of that provision. The point need not be further canvassed here, however. Indeed, the subsequent practice of state parties to the Geneva Conventions of 1949 has abrogated that duty and turned the appointment of a Protecting Power into a simple option. This aspect will be addressed in MN 28.

7   It should be underscored that, in the past, the nomination of more than one Protecting Power by the same state was not uncommon. Thus, in the Greco-Turkish War of 1897, Great Britain, France, and Russia acted jointly for Greece in Turkey. These states had indeed been the protectors of Greece's independence. Therefore, it was diplomatically understandable that Greece elected them jointly to safeguard its interests in that war. In the twentieth century, this practice of nominating more than one Protecting Power completely disappeared. Rather, the salient problem became that states refrained from nominating any Protecting Power at all. Conversely, as a Protecting Power, a state can represent more than two parties to an armed conflict. Switzerland has done so in more than one case, especially during the World Wars.

II. Modalities of appointment of a Protecting Power

8   The modalities of appointment of a Protecting Power are left to the discretion of the states concerned. International law has not erected any formalism in this area, a course which in any case would hardly be advisable. There are simply optional procedures for such a nomination.[6] These procedures were enriched by Article 5(3) AP I. First, an appointment may ensue from an agreement between the opposing belligerents and the Protecting Power. Secondly, if direct agreement proves to be difficult, the ICRC may offer its good offices and mediate between the parties. Agreement may then flow from these efforts. Thirdly, the procedure set out under Article 5(3) AP I may be followed. The ICRC can require each party to the conflict to provide it with a list of at least five states which that party would accept as the Protecting Power. The ICRC will then compare the lists to see if there is any convergence. Such a procedure may give some fresh impetus to the mediation of the ICRC. Fourthly, to the extent that no agreement can be reached, the belligerents may designate the ICRC or any other international organization offering all due guarantees of impartiality and efficacy, to act as a substitute for the Protecting Power. It is now common practice for the ICRC not to insist on the nomination of a Protecting Power, precisely because states

---

the rules of international law relating to diplomatic relations is no obstacle to the designation of Protecting Powers for the purpose of applying the Conventions and this Protocol.'

[5] See ICRC Commentary APs, para 229.

[6] See R. Wolfrum and D. Fleck, 'Enforcement of International Humanitarian Law', in D. Fleck (ed), *The Handbook of International Humanitarian Law* (2nd edn, Oxford: OUP, 2008) 675, at 710.

have proven very reluctant to proceed on such lines. The reasons for this are considered below (MN 18–26).

III. Functions of the Protecting Power

Under IHL, the functions of the Protecting Power are set out in the relevant Conventions, namely, the Geneva Conventions of 1949 and AP I of 1977. These functions are of a general nature, and also consist of a series of particular tasks. 9

a. General functions

On the general plane, the Protecting Power represents the Protected Power. It has to safeguard the interests of the Protected Power which designated it. This means that it can venture into various diplomatic situations, not only for the implementation of IHL duties by the belligerent which it should control, but also for the improvement of the situation on the ground. It can thus, for example, propose new special agreements addressing and potentially solving this or that problem encountered on the ground. Moreover, the Protecting Power can entertain mediation efforts between the Power it protects and the opposing belligerent. With the agreement of the parties, it may also investigate violations of IHL by undertaking concrete action on the territory of a belligerent. In all these situations, the Protecting Power must exercise a certain degree of diplomacy. It must ponder how much is acceptable at what time, always seeking the agreement of the party (or parties) concerned. Moreover, the Protecting Power has to make sure that it never departs from its duty of impartiality, nor from its ostensible impartiality; that is, the Protecting Power must not only be impartial, but must also be seen to be impartial. 10

b. Specific functions

As already mentioned in MN 9, these specific functions are set out in some detail by the relevant Conventions. First, the Protecting Power is the beneficiary of several duties of information imposed on the Detaining or Protected Power. Secondly, the Protecting Power is required actively to perform a series of functions. 11

i. Duties regarding information

The Protecting Power is the beneficiary of the following information duties imposed on the belligerent concerned: 12

— transmission of information as to the particulars of any wounded, sick, shipwrecked, or dead military personnel of the protected party who have fallen into the hands of the adverse belligerent (Article 16 paragraph 3 GC I and Article 19 paragraph 2 GC II);
— transmission of information about the geographical location of POW camps (Article 23 paragraph 3 GC III) and about labour detachments among the POWs (Article 56 paragraph 3 GC III; see also analogously for labour detachments of interned civilians, Article 96 GC IV);
— transmission of information about limitations on the credit accounts of POWs (Article 60 paragraph 4 GC III);
— information on the Detaining Power's reasons for not recognizing a representative elected by POWs (Article 79 paragraph 4 GC III; and analogously for interned civilians, Article 102 paragraph 1 GC IV) or for dismissing that representative (Article 81 paragraph 6 GC III);

- information on offences which are punishable by the death penalty under the laws of the Detaining Power (Article 100 paragraph 1 GC III);
- notification of any death sentence, which carries a mandatory stay of execution of six months (Articles 101 and 107 GC III; and see analogously Article 75 paragraph 2 GC IV);
- notification of judicial proceedings against a POW instituted by the Detaining Power (Article 104 paragraph 1 GC III);
- transmission of the wills of POWs in case of their death (Article 120 paragraph 1 GC III);
- transmission of reasons regarding refusal of permission for enemy civilians to leave the territory of a belligerent, unless reasons of security prevent it or the protected person objects (Article 35 paragraph 3 GC IV);
- receipt of information about any transfers or evacuations of protected civilians (Article 49 paragraph 4 GC IV);
- notification of and information about judicial proceedings against protected civilians (Article 71 paras 2 and 3 GC IV);
- notification of and information about any criminal sentence involving the death penalty or imprisonment for more than two years (Article 74 paragraph 2 GC IV);
- transmission of information about the measures taken by the Detaining Power for executing the provisions of GC IV regarding relations of interned civilians with the exterior (Article 105 GC IV);
- transmission of the official record of death of an interned civilian (Article 129 paragraph 3 GC IV).

ii. Activities of the Protecting Power

13   The Protecting Power may be called on to perform the following functions, according to what is required in a particular situation:

- lending its good offices in order to facilitate the institution and recognition of hospital zones and localities (Article 23 paragraph 3 GC I);
- communication between the belligerents of official translations of the relevant Convention (Article 48 GC I, Article 49 GC II, Article 128 GC III, and Article 145 GC IV; see also Article 84 AP I);
- transmission of information on the rate of wages fixed for POWs by the Detaining Power, through the Protecting Power, to the Power on which POWs depend (Article 62 paragraph 1 GC III);
- transmission of information about and notifying transfers of funds of POWs (Article 63 paragraph 3 GC III);
- inspection of copies of POWs' accounts (Article 65 paragraph 2 GC III);
- transmission of lists giving detailed information on the winding up of POWs' accounts at the moment of their release (Article 66 paragraph 1 GC III);
- transmission of information about claims for compensation made by POWs (Article 68 paragraph 1 GC III);
- transmission of information about the capture of POWs and their relations with the exterior (Article 69 GC III);
- supervision of limitations imposed on POWs regarding their correspondence (Article 71 paragraph 1 GC III);
- supervision of limitations on relief shipments for the benefit of POWs (Article 72 paragraph 3 GC III);

- assistance given to POWs in the context of collective relief shipments (Article 73 paragraph 3 GC III);
- organizing the conveyance of such shipments by suitable means of transport (Article 75 paragraph 1 GC III);
- aiding in the preparation, execution, and transmission of legal documents concerning POWs (Article 77 paragraph 1 GC III);
- receiving complaints and requests from POWs (Article 78 paragraph 2 GC III);
- inspection of the record of disciplinary punishments of POWs maintained by the camp commander (Article 96 paragraph 5 GC III; and analogously for interned civilians, Article 123 paragraph 5 GC IV);
- finding an advocate or counsel for POWs if judicial proceedings are instituted against them and they do not make such a choice themselves (Article 105 paragraph 2 GC III);
- transmission of information relating to the 'information bureau' for POWs (Article 122 paragraph 3 GC III) or interned civilians (Article 137 paragraph 1 GC IV);
- visiting POWs in their camps and controlling implementation of GC III (Article 126 paragraphs 1 and 2 GC III; and analogously the same functions for interned civilians, Article 143 GC IV);
- supervision of distribution of medical supplies, food, and clothing for civilians (Article 23 paragraph 3 GC IV);
- receiving applications by protected civilians under GC IV (Article 30 paragraph 1 GC IV)
- transmitting allowances from their home country, or itself paying funds to civilians in the hostile territory (Article 39 paragraph 3 GC IV; and analogously for interned civilians, Article 98 paragraph 2 GC IV);
- transmission of information about the will of a civilian to be interned, while he or she is in the hostile territory (Article 42 paragraph 2 GC IV);
- receiving applications for protection in the context of working arrangements of protected civilians in occupied territories (Article 52 paragraph 1 GC IV);
- verifying the state of food and medical supplies in occupied territories, except for temporary restrictions due to imperative military requirements (Article 55 paragraph 4 GC IV);
- control of relief consignments and their proper destination (Article 59 paragraph 4 GC IV);
- supervising the distribution of relief consignments (Article 61 paragraph 1 GC IV; and analogously in the context of interned civilians, Article 109, paragraph 3 GC IV);
- providing an accused civilian, in criminal judicial proceedings, with an advocate or counsel (Article 72 paragraph 2 GC IV);
- attending the trial of any protected civilian (Article 74 paragraph 1 GC IV; and analogously for POWs, Article 105 paragraph 5 GC III);
- visiting of protected persons who are detained (Article 76 paragraph 6 GC IV);
- transmission to the Protected Power of information about the geographical location of places of internment of civilians (Article 83 paragraph 2 GC IV);
- requiring statements about accounts of interned civilians (Article 98 paragraph 3 GC IV);
- organizing and conveying relief shipments by suitable means, for the benefit of interned civilians (Article 111 paragraph 1 GC IV).

c. Additional Protocol I

14 Additional Protocol I adds certain functions to those listed above, including:

— access to medical records of persons in the power of the adverse party according to Article 11(6) AP I;
— transmission of information relating to missing persons according to Article 33(3) AP I;
— transmission of the claim of the Protected Power that a particular person is entitled to POW status according to Article 45(1) AP I;
— facilitation of the conclusion of agreements between the belligerents relating to demilitarized zones according to Article 60(2) AP I;
— supervising the distribution of assistance to the civilian population in a territory not occupied according to Article 70(3)(b) AP I;
— supervising the evacuation of children according to the conditions of Article 78(1) AP I.

d. Other Conventions

15 It might be worth mentioning that a Protecting Power also has functions under other Conventions, for example:

— the Hague Convention on the Protection of Cultural Property in Times of War (1954), according to Articles 21–22;
— the Regulations for the Execution of the above Convention, annexed to the 1954 Convention, in Article 6;
— the Second Protocol to the Hague Convention of 1954 (1999), under Articles 34 and 36.

IV. Practice since 1949

16 Since the adoption of the Geneva Conventions of 1949, Protecting Powers have been nominated in only five armed conflicts:[7]

— In the *Suez war* (1956), between France and the United Kingdom (UK) on the one side, and Egypt on the other. Switzerland was nominated on behalf of France and the UK; India was appointed for Egypt.
— In the *Bizerte conflict* (1961), between France and Tunisia. Switzerland was appointed on behalf of France, Sweden on behalf of Tunisia.
— In the *Goa conflict* (1961), between India and Portugal. The United Arab Republic was appointed Protecting Power on behalf of India, Brazil was so appointed on behalf of Portugal.
— In the *Indo-Pakistani war* of 1971, where both states elected Switzerland as Protecting Power.
— In the *Falklands/Malvinas conflict* (1982), between the UK and Argentina. Switzerland represented the UK and Brazil represented Argentina. In this case, both states acted as diplomatic Protecting Powers and were not nominated under the scheme of the

---

[7] The statement of F. Bugnion, *Le comité international de la Croix-Rouge et la protection des victimes de la guerre* (Geneva: ICRC, 1994), at 1009, remains true today.

Geneva Conventions. However, both states also accomplished the tasks delegated to Protecting Powers under to the Conventions, for example regarding the required notification of hospital ships in accordance with Article 22 GC II.[8]

In all other cases, the ICRC has acted as a sort of *de facto* substitute for a Protecting Power. However, it has performed the functions in its own name and according to its own mandate, rather than stressing that it acted as the representative of a particular state. Its annual reports of activities provide the necessary information as to its actions on the ground in the various conflicts.

V. Reasons for the Decline of the Institution of Protecting Powers

Since 1949, the time of adoption of the Geneva Conventions, there have been only five armed conflicts of an international character in which Protecting Powers were appointed (see MN 16). This is an almost insignificant figure, if compared with the total number of IACs since that date. The reasons for the decline of the institution have been manifold.

First, there is the difficulty of agreement on an impartial Protecting Power in a situation where the belligerents are often at the height of mutual hostility and not likely to agree on anything. Moreover, the successful appointment of a Protecting Power is not felt as being a high priority, especially since the ICRC almost always plays the role of a *de facto* substitute for a Protecting Power.

Secondly, it is sometimes feared that the acceptance of a Protecting Power might be interpreted as a recognition of the adverse party whose legal existence may be contested (e.g. in the Israeli–Arab wars).

Thirdly, it may happen that a belligerent denies the applicability of the Geneva Conventions to the armed conflict in which it is engaged. It may then quite straightforwardly refrain from nominating a Protecting Power in case this might be seen as equating to implementation of the Conventions. Similarly, it may be that a state denies the existence of an IAC, or denies being a party to it. Or, alternatively, a state may maintain that an armed conflict has remained purely non-international, in spite of massive foreign intervention. If it does not want to be seen as contradicting itself, it may be unable to appoint a Protecting Power. There is thus a series of 'denying strategies' which may impede the appointment of a Protecting Power.

Fourthly, the argument has been made that it is increasingly difficult to find any truly neutral or non-engaged state in a post-1945 world dominated by profound ideological rivalries.

Fifthly, from the perspective of the Protecting Power, its tasks are onerous, demanding, and politically sensitive. It risks becoming entangled in the conflict, being accused of 'non-neutral' services, intervention in internal affairs, excessive insistence, etc. All of these factors may embarrass the Protecting Power in its foreign policy. A state may thus be reluctant to accept such a burdensome task, for which it will not earn much gratitude but risks being branded, grudgingly or openly, as a quasi foe.

Sixthly, the services of a Protecting Power are often quite costly. A state may hesitate to undertake such expenditure at a time of constrained national budgets. This is all the more

---

[8] S. Junod, *La protection des victimes du conflit armé des îles Falkland/Malvinas (1982)* (Geneva: ICRC, 1984), at 20–1.

25 As already suggested, the very fact that the ICRC has taken on the role of a substitute Protecting Power acts as a further disincentive for states who might otherwise appoint a Protecting Power, or for other states who need to accept the function of a Protecting Power. Indeed, the expectation is that the ICRC will in any event—and in a perfectly impartial way—undertake the necessary action, as the Protecting Power would have done, and indeed often perhaps even more efficiently. This positive expectation has much to do with the ICRC's uncontested status, but also with its quite extensive experience in the field in such matters. The ICRC assumes, without difficulty, protective tasks like those assigned to a Protecting Power. However, it does not like nominally to perform the function of a *de facto*, and more so a *de jure*, substitute for a Protecting Power. It prefers to fulfil almost all of the latter's functions in its own right, without giving the impression that it represents a state to the armed conflict rather than taking its own impartial stand, geared towards the interests of the protected persons.

26 Lastly, the state of neutrality (which was an active basis of the institution of Protecting Powers) has itself declined after 1945, under pressure of the *jus contra bellum* of collective security. The fact of remaining aloof from a conflict is now frequently cast in the categories of 'right' and 'wrong', and thus increasingly is viewed with suspicion. This has not favoured the institution of Protecting Powers.

C. Relevance in Non-International Armed Conflicts

27 From the point of view of the legal scope of application, the appointment of a Protecting Power is limited to IACs. There is no equivalent regulation in NIACs, neither in the Geneva Conventions, nor in Additional Protocol (AP) II. This is but one more testament to the fact that the implementation of the law of NIAC (as well as its substance) is less developed than that of IAC. In the case of the latter, belligerent states confront other belligerent states on an inherently international plane. Thus, these states more easily accept the idea of equality of entitlements and the necessity to enter into a network of mutual dealings. Conversely, NIACs are still seen by most states as involving the rising of seditious forces on their own territory. States continue to view such forces as law-breakers; they utterly resist considering them as equals in any way (to wit, no status of regular combatants exists in NIACs). States do not want to see international involvement through requests for respect of IHL norms. The preceding developments, however, just mean that there is no *statutory* Protecting Power in NIACs. Nothing prevents the parties from accepting a Protecting Power by special agreement. To date, this has apparently never happened. The ICRC has nonetheless more than once offered its services as a sort of non-official Protecting Power in NIACs.[9]

D. Legal Consequences of a Violation

28 Overall, there is an impressive array of reasons that explain why the institution of Protecting Powers has fallen into disuse. Legally, this clearly does not connote any idea

---

[9] See Ch 26 of this volume.

of obsolescence or desuetude. The legal institution of Protecting Power has not, to any extent, been abrogated. Hence, a state could perfectly well appoint a Protecting Power today and seek the agreement of the opposing party. However, state practice has turned the original duty to nominate a Protecting Power into a *mere option*. States have not refrained from nominating Protecting Powers with the conviction that they were breaching a rule enshrined in the Geneva Conventions and other IHL conventions. Indeed, no claim of responsibility for breach of international law has ever been formulated, nor has the ICRC itself insisted on the implementation of the duty as a matter of legal obligation. On the contrary, states have progressively considered that the duty to make such a nomination, as enshrined in the Geneva Conventions and AP I,[10] should not be imposed on them. What they conceded at the Conferences was not borne out in practice. This subsequent practice of abstention was doubtlessly accompanied by a sense of *opinio juris* or *non juris*: namely, that the belligerents were not obliged to appoint or accept such Protecting Powers, and that hence the duty postulated in the Conventions had become a simple option of nomination.[11] The conventional duty of nomination was thus abrogated by consonant subsequent practice, which was accorded legal weight. This state of affairs may be regretted, but it should not be ignored. This is the true legal meaning of the frequently made contention that the institution of the Protecting Power has not 'functioned' in modern armed conflicts, or even that it has been 'ineffective'.

E. Critical Assessment

Since 1945, the fate of the institution of the Protecting Power shows graphically that the law is bound to remain ineffective if the Conventions are applied too boldly beyond what states are ready to accept, or beyond what is, in any event, unavoidable in situations of war. What has been agreed in the generous enthusiasm of a Diplomatic Conference, or grudgingly conceded under the unrelenting pressure of public opinion, will be flouted thereafter in actual practice. This consideration certainly applies to the 'duty' to nominate and accept Protecting Powers, as enshrined in the Geneva Conventions and AP I. States have not been ready to go further than to accept an option for such action. The fact that the option has not been used very much is due to important changes in international society after 1945. The general conditions favourable to that traditional institution have quickly been fading away. 29

There is, for the time being, no realistic prospect of revitalizing the institution of Protecting Powers. This state of affairs also reflects the fact that the system of implementation of IHL has tended to shift to some extent away from 'subjective' mechanisms, dependent on the will of the belligerents, to 'objective' mechanisms, independent of their will and sometimes even of their cooperation. The focus today is geared towards criminal international law and its tribunals; the intervention of the Security Council; plans for a sort of High Commissioner for IHL; efforts to strengthen the work of the ICRC; stress being laid on the role of third parties under Article 1 of the Conventions, etc. Conversely, 30

---

[10] The 'duty' was already heavily qualified by the overriding requirement of consent to the concrete nominations (see MN 4).

[11] The argument of subsequent practice may not be without dangers in the field of IHL, but there are situations where there can be hardly any doubt as to the generality of a practice (here: abstention) and the legal significance which is ascribed to it.

the rather old-fashioned mechanisms of inter-belligerent cooperation are no longer in the limelight. This situation could—and certainly will—change over time. However, if there is much to be said for the direct cooperation between states in almost all areas of international law, where it is more often than not the key to any true progress, the same cannot be said in the field of IHL. During armed conflicts, the belligerent states are pitched one against the other in deepest hostility. Any attempt to make significant progress while relying on their readiness to cooperate, has proved to be doomed to failure. From this perspective, there is little prospect for a revival of the Protecting Powers. However, there remains the possibility that some states might appoint Protecting Powers, their opponents accept them, and the institution proves quite useful in that particular conflict; and hence such examples could in turn stimulate other states in other conflicts to nominate Protecting Powers too. In that limited context, the institution might undergo some form of rather limited blossoming. It must be admitted, however, that there are no signs of any such developments, and the future of the institution of the Protecting Powers remains at best quite uncertain.

ROBERT KOLB

Chapter 28. Good Offices, Conciliation, and Enquiry

	MN
A. Introduction	1
B. Meaning and Application	10
I. Conciliation procedure	10
a. Scope and modalities	10
b. Limitations on the use of conciliation	16
II. Enquiry	18
a. Fact-finding as a means to ensure further compliance with international humanitarian law	19
b. Modalities and scope of the enquiry procedure	20
c. The International Humanitarian Fact-Finding Commission	25
C. Relevance in Non-International Armed Conflicts	27
D. Critical Assessment: The Proliferation of Fact-Finding and Inquiry Missions	28

Select Bibliography

Bothe, M., 'Fact-Finding as a Means of Ensuring Respect for International Humanitarian Law', in W. Heintschel von Heinegg and V. Epping (eds), *International Humanitarian Law Facing New Challenges* (Berlin: Springer, 2007) 249

Boutruche, T., 'Credible Fact-Finding and Allegations of International Humanitarian Law Violations: Challenges in Theory and Practice', 16 *Journal of Conflict and Security Law* (2011) 105

Condorelli, L., 'The International Humanitarian Fact-Finding Commission: An Obsolete Tool or a Useful Measure to Implement International Humanitarian Law?', 83 *IRRC* 842 (2001) 393

Cot, J-P., 'Conciliation', in MPEPIL

Frulli, M., 'UN Fact-Finding Commissions and the Prosecution of War Crimes: An Evolution towards Justice-Oriented Missions?', in F. Pocar, M. Pedrazzi, and M. Frulli (eds), *War Crimes and the Conduct of Hostilities: Challenges to Adjudication and Investigation* (Cheltenham: Edward Elgar Publishing, 2013) 331

Jachec-Neale, A., 'Fact-Finding', in MPEPIL

Lapidoth, R., 'Good Offices', in MPEPIL

Pictet Commentary GC I

Pictet Commentary GC IV

Sassòli, M., 'The Implementation of International Humanitarian Law: Current and Inherent Challenges', 10 *YIHL* (2007) 45

Stewart, J.G., 'The UN Commission of Inquiry on Lebanon: A Legal Appraisal', 5 *JICJ* (2007) 1039

Vezzani, S., 'Fact-Finding by International Human Rights Institutions and Criminal Prosecution', in F. Pocar, M. Pedrazzi, and M. Frulli (eds), *War Crimes and the Conduct of Hostilities: Challenges to Adjudication and Investigation* (Cheltenham: Edward Elgar Publishing, 2013) 349

Vité, S., *Les procédures internationales d'établissement des faits dans la mise en œuvre du droit international humanitaire* (Brussels: Bruylant, 1999) 485

Waldman, A., *Arbitrating Armed Conflict: Decisions of the Israel–Lebanon Monitoring Group* (Huntington, NY: Juris, 2003) 320

A. Introduction

1 The issue of compliance with international humanitarian law (IHL) and the related question of the limitations of IHL's existing compliance mechanisms have been constant reminders of the weakness of this body of law. The launch of the Swiss/ICRC Initiative on Strengthening Compliance with International Humanitarian Law in 2012 aimed at reinforcing dialogue among states and other actors to identify concrete ways and means of improving respect for IHL, with a particular focus on the question of compliance mechanisms.[1] Unlike the complementary notion of enforcement of IHL that focuses on the ways to restore observance of IHL when it has been violated, compliance pertains to ensuring that belligerents act in conformity with IHL. The key challenge lies in how to guarantee effective compliance by belligerents in times of war, a period characterised by the lack of trust between the parties to the conflict accompanied by mutual accusations of violations. If the question of ensuring compliance is problematic, the issue of the peaceful settlement of disputes as an obligation for states is even more difficult, especially with regard to disputes arising from a difference of views about whether a violation has occurred. Armed conflict presents a fundamental obstacle for those mechanisms designed for the peaceful settlement of disputes to be efficient in relation to IHL disputes between parties to a conflict, who, by definition, have failed to resolve their dispute by peaceful means. On the other hand, the very purpose of IHL, i.e. to regulate the conduct of hostilities and protect those who do not or no longer take part in hostilities, calls for effective mechanisms to ensure its consistent interpretation, application, and respect by all parties, in order to provide better protection to victims in times of war.

2 The Geneva Conventions address conciliation and enquiry procedures that fall within the range of mechanisms that contribute to ensuring compliance with those Conventions under their common provisions. More generally IHL's procedures should be considered in relation to the broader realm of international law compliance and dispute settlement mechanisms. Under international law, conciliation is traditionally seen as a means of dispute settlement, standing between diplomatic methods, including good offices, on the one hand, and judicial settlements on the other hand. Conciliation may be defined as

> a method for the settlement of international disputes of any nature according to which a commission set up by the parties, either on a permanent basis or on *ad hoc* basis to deal with a dispute, proceeds to the impartial examination of the dispute and attempts to define the terms of a settlement susceptible of being accepted by them, or of affording the parties, with a view to its settlement, such aid as they may have requested.[2]

Under this understanding, conciliation is a specific technical mechanism characterized by various features. Historically, conciliation, as a method of settlement of international disputes, developed after the First World War and traditionally addressed inter-state political disputes. While absent from The Hague Peace Conferences Conventions in 1899 and

---

[1] Swiss/ICRC Initiative on Strengthening Compliance with International Humanitarian Law, Fact Sheet, available at <http://www.eda.admin.ch/etc/medialib/downloads/edazen/topics/intla.Par.0031.File.tmp/Factsheet_Compliance_October%202013_EN.pdf>.

[2] Institute of International Law, Resolution on International Conciliation (Institute of International Law [IDI]) IDI Resolution II/1961, (1961) 49(II) Ann IDI 385, Art 1.

1907, that only contained provisions on mediation and commissions of inquiry, numerous bilateral treaties, such as the 1921 German–Swiss Arbitration Treaty or the 1925 Treaty between France and Switzerland, contained provisions on conciliation. It became common practice to include a conciliation procedure in international treaties, irrespective of their subject matter, as a means to resolve disputes arising from their interpretation and application.

On the other hand, enquiry, while also commonly recognized as a form of international dispute settlement, refers to the general 'process of elucidating facts, given that it is the varied perceptions of these facts that often give rise to the dispute in the first place'.[3] It is at times used as a synonym for fact-finding.

In light of these definitions, it is essential first to highlight that the provisions of the Geneva Conventions on conciliation (Article 11 of Geneva Conventions (GCs) I, II, and III, and Article 12 GC IV) may be misleading, as they do not establish a conciliation procedure according to the technical meaning of the term spelled out earlier. Those Articles are included within the Chapter on General Provisions, following the Articles on Protecting Powers, the Activities of the International Committee of the Red Cross (ICRC), and the Substitutes for Protecting Powers. Rather, they primarily envisage the role of Protecting Powers to offer good offices. While such an offer could involve conciliation, in that 'Protecting Powers shall lend their good offices with a view to settling the disagreement', it does not cover all the characteristics of a conciliation procedure as defined in international law. The reference to the term 'conciliation' in this contribution will be made only as used in the terminology of the Geneva Conventions; it will not imply the full meaning of this mechanism under international law.

Within the IHL framework, the procedures on conciliation and enquiry are complementary, as the scope of conciliation is broadly conceived to cover issues arising from the application and interpretation of the provisions of the Geneva Conventions, while the enquiry procedure relates to cases of alleged violations of those Conventions. Furthermore, conciliation and enquiry are two specific procedures provided for by separate Articles of the Geneva Conventions. However, conciliation is also envisaged to operate within the wider context of other compliance mechanisms under the Conventions (see Chapters 26 and 27 of this volume). The modalities of the conciliation procedure specifically provide for a role to be played by the Protecting Powers and the ICRC.

With regard to IHL treaties, the first provisions to spell out the principles of a conciliation procedure, used in the sense of conferring a role on Protecting Powers, were Article 83 paragraph 3 and Article 87 of the 1929 Geneva Convention Relative to the Treatment of Prisoners of War (1929 GC II). This Convention envisaged the possibility for the belligerents, at the commencement of hostilities, to authorize meetings of representatives of the respective authorities in charge of the administration of prisoners of war (POWs), and provided that, in the event of a dispute between the belligerents regarding the application of the Convention, the Protecting Powers should, as far as possible, lend their good offices to the parties with the object of settling the dispute. Beside the Geneva Conventions (which will be examined below), the 1954 Hague Convention for the Protection of Cultural Property in the Event of Armed Conflict also includes a similar procedure, under the heading 'Conciliation procedure', in its Article 22.

---

[3] A. Jachec-Neale, 'Fact-Finding', in MPEPIL.

7   Unlike conciliation as a technical procedure in international law, which over the last decades has been revived, at least in treaties,[4] enquiry has met with more resistance from states,[5] especially in the field of IHL. While Article 30 of the 1929 Geneva Convention for the Amelioration of the Condition of the Wounded and Sick in Armies in the Field (1929 GC I) provided for the institution of an enquiry, this gave rise to significant discussions, as states feared it might lead to possible sanctions by other states as a result of the enquiry.[6] This reluctance may be explained by the very purpose of the enquiry, relating to alleged violations of an IHL treaty that might require establishing the facts as well as drawing legal conclusions. In light of those potential far-reaching consequences for states in cases of allegations of violations, any attempt to create an automatic procedure of enquiry in the Geneva Conventions failed, and the mechanism adopted in 1949 relies on the ad hoc consent of the parties.[7] An enquiry procedure is envisaged by Article 52 GC I, Article 53 GC II, Article 132 GC III, and Article 149 GC IV as part of the Chapter on 'Repression of Abuses and Infractions'. The negotiations on the creation of an International Fact-Finding Commission within Additional Protocol (AP) I during the Diplomatic Conference of 1974–7, gave rise to similar difficult debates, partly due to some efforts to address the weaknesses of the enquiry procedure under the Geneva Conventions. While the establishment of the International Humanitarian Fact-Finding Commission (IHFFC) pursuant to Article 90 AP I is a significant step forward, this mechanism, like the enquiry procedure under the Geneva Conventions, has never actually been used in practice.

8   Conciliation and enquiry have a common aim of clarifying disputes, and they involve establishing the veracity of claims. Enquiry focuses specifically on cases of violations of the Geneva Conventions, whereas conciliation covers all disputes pertaining to their application and interpretation. Conceptually, conciliation would tend to seek a solution for the future, while enquiry looks at what has happened. But the two processes overlap, in that an enquiry, which may be about establishing facts or fact-finding, can be a component of a conciliation procedure in the technical sense of the term.[8] Enquiry and related fact-finding activities may also be seen as a distinct means of dispute settlement, independent from ascertaining facts in the context of conciliation mechanisms. In that respect enquiry may also be part of a judicial dispute settlement.[9] Under the Geneva Conventions both conciliation and enquiry procedures require the ad hoc agreement of the parties after the dispute has arisen or the alleged violation occurred, which is a traditional approach under IHL and traditional public international law but which constitutes a key weakness for the working of these procedures in the context of an armed conflict. Indeed in war, characterized by violence and distrust between belligerents, it is very difficult to rely on mechanisms that require the consent and cooperation of the parties.

9   The reluctance of states parties to the Geneva Conventions to resort to those two procedures highlights the current ongoing discussions among IHL scholars and practitioners on ways to improve compliance with IHL obligations. This debate is obviously relevant in the context of international armed conflicts covered by the provisions on conciliation and enquiry under the Geneva Conventions, but also relates to contemporary efforts to

---

[4] J-P. Cot, 'Conciliation', in MPEPIL.   [5] Pictet Commentary GC I, at 375.   [6] Ibid.
[7] Pictet Commentary GC I, at 376–7.
[8] M. Bothe, 'Fact-finding as a Means of Ensuring Respect for International Humanitarian Law', in W. Heintschel von Heinegg and V. Epping (eds), *International Humanitarian Law Facing New Challenges* (Berlin: Springer, 2007) 249, at 254.
[9] Ibid, at 254–5.

design mechanisms for encouraging compliance by non-state actors with IHL in time of non-international armed conflicts (NIACs). As a result of the institutional limitations of the Geneva Conventions' enquiry procedure, fact-finding activities on alleged violations of IHL have been carried out using mechanisms created outside the IHL treaties framework. While the development of international criminal law institutions and substantive law over the past two decades has attracted much attention in the field of the means to enforce IHL, it is important to address the contribution of the parallel phenomenon of the proliferation of fact-finding bodies mandated to establish facts about alleged IHL violations, a task that may be part of the traditional procedure of enquiry. These range from the increasing resort to commissions of inquiry, such as those established by the United Nations (UN) Human Rights Council, to initiatives aimed at harmonizing methodological guidelines to carry out fact-finding activities, including the growing role of social media in documenting war crimes, and the related issues of the reliability and admissibility of such material as possible evidence. However fact-finding missions and commissions of inquiry differ from the enquiry procedure envisaged in the Geneva Conventions, through distinct purpose and scope.

B. Meaning and Application

I. Conciliation procedure

a. Scope and modalities

As highlighted in section A of this chapter, the conciliation procedure envisaged in the Geneva Conventions does not correspond to conciliation in its technical meaning, characterized by specific features such as the establishment of a commission to review the dispute impartially and that is entrusted with the role of proposing elements of the settlement. In that regard, the term 'conciliation' is not even used in the operative text of the common Articles of the Geneva Conventions, which instead refer to the role of Protecting Powers having the opportunity to lend their 'good offices' in certain situations. In that respect Protecting Powers are an institutionalization of 'good offices' under IHL. In general terms, providing 'good offices' is one of the diplomatic methods for the settlement of disputes. In broad terms this refers to the efforts of a third party—in this case a Protecting Power—to find a solution to a dispute between two or more states, through opening dialogue between them. However, strictly speaking, good offices only cover the mere involvement of a third party in encouraging the parties to a dispute to talk to each other. As such, the role played by the third party would not include helping them to reach a compromise, which would practically amount to mediation.[10]   10

Recourse to this 'conciliation' procedure under the Geneva Conventions by Protecting   11
Powers covers all cases where this is 'advisable in the interest of protected persons' as defined by the four Conventions. The common Articles on the conciliation procedure specifically refer to disagreement between parties to the conflict as to the application and interpretation of the Geneva Conventions as one of the situations where the interests of the protected persons may be at stake. In that respect they offer broader opportunities than the Articles of 1929 GC II, which were limited to cases of dispute relating to the

---

[10] R. Lapidoth, 'Good Offices', in MPEPIL.

application, but not the interpretation, of the Convention. Furthermore, the interests of the protected persons as an overarching and primary goal of conciliation can potentially require the lending of good offices to address the modalities of the implementation of certain obligations under the Geneva Conventions, as well as issues that may not be regulated per se by the Conventions. Thus one might envisage that when exercising their 'good offices', Protecting Powers may consider additional concerns in order to settle a disagreement in the interests of the protected persons. However, this does not mean that the Protecting Powers are entrusted with a general authority to interpret the Geneva Conventions; rather, they may intervene when there is a disagreement between parties to a conflict on a particular aspect.

12   It is commonly noted that the Geneva Conventions provide more rights and duties to the Protecting Powers than those of mere agents acting under the instructions of the state whose interests they safeguard.[11] The conciliation procedure illustrates this proactive role, in that Protecting Powers may act solely in the interest of the protected persons. Protecting Powers additionally have the right to act on their own initiative, and this contributes to widening the possibilities of resorting to the conciliation procedure in any form which good offices may take.

13   The Geneva Conventions offer a possible meeting between the representatives of the parties to the conflict as a way to settle a dispute. However, Protecting Powers may resort to other methods to reach a solution agreeable to all. According to the Geneva Conventions, a meeting may be convened at the initiative of the Protecting Powers or at the invitation of one party. The Geneva Conventions specify that this meeting may take place on suitably chosen neutral territory. This stems directly from the practice developed during the First World War. According to Article 11 GC I–III and Article 12 GC IV, the representatives of the parties to the conflict would include particular representatives of authorities responsible for the categories of persons covered respectively by each of the four Conventions.

14   The conciliation procedure and related meetings to address disputes were meant to facilitate the better application of the Geneva Conventions for the benefit of protected persons, in particular with regard to the modalities for the implementation of certain obligations that might give rise to dispute, such as the routes for the repatriation of the seriously wounded and sick.[12] A question arises as to the extent to which the Protecting Powers are entitled to play a more active role, within the more technical sense of the term 'conciliation'. Under the strict definition of 'good offices', the potential role to be played seems very limited. However, in as much as Protecting Powers can lend their good offices with a view to 'settling the disagreement', they may suggest a solution to the dispute, or even present a conciliation report. While Protecting Powers were conceived of more as mere agents in the framework of the 1929 GC II, it has been argued that the general trend under the Geneva Conventions is to grant them more extensive rights and duties.[13] Therefore, and provided that they respect the purpose of the 'conciliation' procedure, they may be more involved in proposing solutions.

15   The only element of the conciliation procedure that departs from an approach based on the consent of parties is the requirement that the parties to the conflict are bound to give effect to the proposals formulated by the Protecting Powers with a view to a meeting. The possibility to invite a person belonging to a neutral Power or delegated by the ICRC

---

[11] Pictet Commentary GC I, at 127–8.   [12] Ibid, at 129.   [13] Ibid, at 114–15.

also depends on the consent of the parties. The second part of this conciliation procedure under the four Conventions, with regard to the outcome, corresponds to the classical notion of conciliation as a non-compulsory procedure, as parties are not bound by the proposals made by the Protecting Powers.

b. Limitations on the use of conciliation

While meetings between representatives of the parties to the conflict were frequent during the First World War, according to the ICRC, none occurred during the Second World War. This presents a fundamental challenge to the use of conciliation relating to the application of IHL in the context of an armed conflict. Furthermore, the Geneva Conventions do not provide for a solution in the absence of Protecting Powers, unlike Article 36 of the Second Protocol to the Hague Convention of 1954 for the Protection of Cultural Property in the Event of Armed Conflict, which states that '[i]n a conflict where no Protecting Powers are appointed the Director-General [of UNESCO] may lend good offices or act by any other form of conciliation or mediation, with a view to settling the disagreement'. 16

The lack of resort to the conciliation procedure foreseen in the Geneva Conventions is linked to the reluctance of states to use any type of compliance mechanism to resolve inter-state disputes in times of war. All attempts failed during the Diplomatic Conference to include a mechanism for the legal settlement of disputes based on the growing practice in international law conventions, which refer to the jurisdiction of the International Court of Justice. Despite its flexible and diplomatic features, the conciliation procedure envisaged in the Geneva Conventions has never been used. The nature of disputes arising from the application and interpretation of IHL treaties makes any mechanism based on the consent of parties concerned potentially inefficient. The inter-state complaint mechanisms established under several human rights treaties suffered from the same limitations. For example, Articles 11–13 of the Convention on the Elimination of All Forms of Racial Discrimination and Articles 41–43 of International Covenant on Civil and Political Rights established a procedure for the resolution of disputes between state parties over a state's fulfilment of its obligations under the relevant Convention/Covenant through the establishment of an ad hoc Conciliation Commission. These procedures have never been used. 17

II. Enquiry

In broad terms, 'enquiry' and 'fact-finding' are synonymous, and are generally considered as one of the methods of international dispute settlement that may be combined with other means such as conciliation and good offices. In the context of disputed versions of events and conflicting accounts, 'fact-finding' and 'enquiry' aim at ascertaining and clarifying facts through an impartial process. They serve to illuminate the circumstances, causes, consequences, and aftermath of an event from a systematic collection of facts. The enquiry procedure envisaged by the Geneva Conventions is therefore the formal institutionalization of a traditional dispute settlement method, but it needs to be analysed in the context of the recent proliferation of international fact-finding bodies created outside the IHL treaty framework. 18

a. Fact-finding as a means to ensure further compliance with international humanitarian law

During or in the aftermath of an armed conflict, all actors argue that violations of IHL have occurred. Fact-finding serves a primary purpose of objectively establishing 'what 19 really happened' and ensuring that the facts are not lost in the streams of false accusations. The importance of fact-finding to ensure compliance with IHL therefore lies at different levels. First, ascertaining facts plays a key role in ensuring compliance with IHL, as it contributes to establishing the facts about the actual behaviour of parties to a conflict and on this basis helps to determine whether IHL violations took place. Secondly, fact-finding mechanisms play a role in determining the responsibility of states, armed groups, and individuals for IHL violations, and may serve to initiate subsequent legal proceedings.[14] Additionally, fact-finding may help to facilitate the interpretation and application of general IHL rules. Fact-finding can play a preventive role by contributing to the establishment of facts about past abuses, as well as debunking unfounded allegations of IHL violations. Conversely, if the record on false allegations is not settled for a prolonged period of time by an impartial enquiry, this may fuel resentment between communities and belligerents, and lead to acts of vengeance, including further violations of IHL in the case of renewed armed conflict.[15] Lastly, fact-finding contributes to ensuring better understanding and dissemination of IHL, as well as to enhanced credibility. In a violent context such as an armed conflict, an inevitable tension exists between moral evaluation by public opinion and evaluation according to the application of IHL to certain acts. The same incident may be perceived as a violation of IHL by some observers, while a strict application of the law to the facts may reveal that it is not. Elucidating facts related to allegations of IHL violations through an impartial and independent body would help reduce the 'gap'[16] between the legal evaluation of a given act in times of war and the perceived reality, strengthening the credibility of IHL within public opinion.

b. Modalities and scope of the enquiry procedure

20 The enquiry procedure in the Geneva Conventions is conceived as a mechanism to solve inter-state disputes between parties to a conflict concerning any alleged violation of the Conventions. From the outset it is fundamental to note that such disputes can be purely factual, with conflicting views on a given incident and on which party is responsible, a contention as regards the legal assessment of the facts, with contradictory claims as to whether a given act constitutes a violation of the Geneva Conventions, or a combination thereof. This complements other means of dealing with violations, such as prosecutions relating to individual criminal responsibility for graves breaches (see Chapter 31 of this volume). Article 30 of 1929 GC I had already introduced a similar enquiry procedure, based on the agreement between the parties to the conflict. The main contentious point during the negotiations of the Geneva Conventions revolved around the possibility of establishing an automatic procedure to address the issue of consent (seen as the key weakness as regards the application of this mechanism). Unsurprisingly, no agreement was found and a conservative approach was adopted,

---

[14] E.g., see M. Frulli, 'UN Fact-Finding Commissions and the Prosecution of War Crimes: An Evolution towards Justice-Oriented Missions?', in F. Pocar, M. Pedrazzi, and M. Frulli (eds), *War Crimes and the Conduct of Hostilities: Challenges to Adjudication and Investigation* (Cheltenham: Edward Elgar Publishing, 2013) 331, at 331; and S. Vezzani, 'Fact-Finding by International Human Rights Institutions and Criminal Prosecution', ibid, at 349.

[15] Report of the Independent International Fact-Finding Mission on the Conflict in Georgia, vol II, September 2009, at 430.

[16] M. Sassòli, 'The Implementation of International Humanitarian Law: Current and Inherent Challenges', 10 *YIHL* (2007) 45, at 67.

in that the four Conventions refer to a procedure similar to the enquiry procedure envisaged in 1929 GC I (Article 52 GC I, Article 53 GC II, Article 121 GC III, and Article132 GC IV).

The enquiry procedure may be triggered by one of the parties to the conflict. Pursuant to paragraph 1 of the relevant provisions in the four Conventions, it is upon the request of a belligerent state that the enquiry is to be instituted, and once a request has been made, the holding of the enquiry is mandatory. At least in theory, the enquiry procedure is meant to be part of the set of provisions detailing the system put in place by the Geneva Conventions to repress abuses and infractions. While state parties to the Geneva Conventions undertake to suppress all breaches of the Conventions, according to Article 49 GC I, Article 50 GC II, Article 129 GC III, and Article 146 GC IV, regardless of whether an enquiry has been instituted, an enquiry is envisaged only where a violation is alleged. This reference to alleged violations as the main scope of the enquiry raises an important issue. The enquiry procedure primarily focuses on disputes revolving around the need to establish facts to determine the international responsibility of a state party to the conflict. However, considering that it addresses alleged violations, it may also be relevant to cover disputes arising from legal issues and claims related to certain facts. In that regard, the general obligation to put an end to breaches of the Geneva Conventions also arises when it comes to the effects of the findings of an enquiry. Once a violation has been established as a result of an enquiry procedure, a series of actions must be taken by the party concerned depending on the nature of the violation. The provisions of the Geneva Conventions refer to the obligation to put an end to the violation, in the event that it is of a continuous nature, and to repress violations, stating explicitly that the purpose of an enquiry is to ensure respect for IHL. However, it is important to note that in addition to those two obligations, putting an end to violations and repressing them, the obligations of states with regard to the rights of victims to a remedy and to reparation have been developing since the adoption of the four Conventions for certain types of violations. The obligations arising from the findings of an enquiry in cases of serious IHL violations should therefore be interpreted in the context of the emerging body of norms relating to victims' rights.[17] 21

The wording of the provisions on enquiry in the Geneva Conventions raises an interesting question as to the scope of the enquiry, and the relationship between ascertaining facts and making a legal determination of whether those facts constitute a violation under IHL. The Geneva Conventions provide only that the enquiry relates to any alleged violation. This implies, first, ascertaining the facts in relation to the alleged violation that gave rise to the enquiry procedure and, secondly, then deciding whether the violation has been established. However, this invites the question whether it is ever possible for a fact-finding or investigative body to distinguish between establishing facts related to alleged violations on the one hand, and their legal assessment, on the other hand. 22

By definition, fact-finding requires the comparison and clarification of facts. In this regard, a fact can never be considered on its own, in isolation, but needs systematically to be linked to other facts and information, and put into a context. When ascertaining facts on alleged violations of IHL or human rights law, one is also faced with the interface 23

---

[17] E.g., see Basic Principles and Guidelines on the Right to a Remedy and Reparation for Victims of Gross Violations of International Human Rights Law and Serious Violations of International Humanitarian Law, adopted and proclaimed by the UNGA Res 60/147 of 16 December 2005, A/RES/60/147.

between the facts and the law. It seems virtually impossible to conduct fact-finding without knowledge of the law, notably in cases where the fact-finding mandate relates to alleged IHL violations. The question is rather to what extent the two operations should be strictly independent of one another. According to Salmon, the expression 'ascertaining' facts is misleading, as it suggests that the operation is about ascertaining an objective phenomenon that would then be 'confronted' with the legal norm. On the contrary, Salmon stresses the influence of law on facts in several respects: for example, he suggests that the relevance of a fact is linked to the choice of the applicable law.[18] Ultimately, the facts covered through the inquiry are framed by the elements of the very rule allegedly violated. The greatest challenge to separating the findings on facts from legal assessment lies in the context of fact-finding missions that are not entitled to formally conclude in law, even though their work is related to alleged violations. In this regard, one can assume that it is virtually impossible to exclude all legal considerations from the fact-finding process because of the inherent influence of the law over facts. To inquire about allegations of torture requires addressing the facts that are relevant to the components of the legal definition of torture. This challenge is exemplified by the interpretation of the mandate of the IHFFC discussed further in section B.II.c of this chapter. The ICRC Commentary on Additional Protocol I of 1977 states that '[i]n principle it is only concerned with facts, and essentially has no competence to proceed to a legal assessment', with however a nuance in that 'the Commission may be called upon to provide a legal evaluation of the extent of its mandate'.[19] On the other hand, some have argued that the IHFFC is entrusted with a legal evaluation of facts,[20] precisely on the basis that establishing facts vis-à-vis alleged unlawful acts cannot be done otherwise than in light of the pertinent rules of IHL.[21] Investigating facts with an explicit or implicit link to violations requires, to a certain extent, a minimum amount of legal evaluation, for the mere purpose of defining the scope of the facts to be reviewed.

24   The sensitive nature and subject matter of the enquiry procedure—investigating alleged violations of the Geneva Conventions by a party to a conflict and its possible corresponding responsibility—may account for the fact that no enquiry has ever been instituted. For example, in 1973, following allegations of violations made in the context of the conflict between Israel and some Arab States, the ICRC sought to set up an enquiry based on the procedure in the Geneva Conventions, but this attempt failed due to lack of agreement among the parties.[22]

c. The International Humanitarian Fact-Finding Commission

25   Following the failure of the enquiry procedure to function as an efficient IHL monitoring or compliance mechanism, renewed interest emerged during the negotiations for the adoption of AP I for the creation of another institution. This treaty eventually provided for the establishment of the IHFFC pursuant to Article 90. This Commission is competent to 'enquire into any facts alleged to be a grave breach as defined in the Conventions and this

---

[18] J. Salmon, 'Le fait dans l'application du droit international', 175 *RCADI* (1982) 261, at 296.
[19] ICRC Commentary APs 1037, at 1041.
[20] K.J. Partsch, 'Fact-Finding and Inquiry', in R. Bernhardt (ed), *Encyclopedia of Public International Law* (Amsterdam–London: North-Holland, 1992) 343, at 344.
[21] L. Condorelli, 'The International Humanitarian Fact-Finding Commission: An Obsolete Tool or a Useful Measure to Implement International Humanitarian Law?', 83 *IRRC* 842 (2001) 393, at 399.
[22] F. Bugnion, *Le comité international de la Croix-Rouge et la protection des victimes de la guerre* (Geneva: ICRC, 1994) 1099.

Protocol or other serious violation of the Conventions or of this Protocol', and to 'facilitate, through its good offices, the restoration of an attitude of respect for the Conventions and this Protocol'.

Unlike the enquiry procedure under the Geneva Conventions, the IHFFC is a permanent body, which was officially constituted in 1991. In that respect this is a new IHL compliance mechanism, with the potential to fill the existing institutional gap in the field of investigating IHL violations. However, the IHFFC may conduct its work only with the consent of the parties involved. The modalities of consent are twofold: either states accept the competence of the IHFFC in relation to other states doing the same, by way of declaration, similar to the optional clause on recognition of compulsory competence pursuant to Article 36 paragraph 2 of the Statute of the International Court of Justice; or, for states that did not make a general declaration, a state party to an armed conflict may accept the IHFFC's competence on a temporary basis, for the specific conflict it is a party to or in relation to a specific allegation of a serious violation. While this constitutes an improvement compared to the mechanism under the Geneva Conventions, it does not create an automatic compulsory procedure. As a result of a combination of lack of political will, reluctance of states regarding independent investigative institutions, and the condition of consent, and despite the contribution of the IHFFC to the ongoing debate on strengthening compliance with IHL and some 72 states having made a declaration accepting the competence of the IHFFC, this mechanism has never been used to conduct an investigation. It still remains a valuable tool, though, as it is a permanent body available to the parties to the conflict.

C. Relevance in Non-International Armed Conflicts

The large majority of contemporary armed conflicts being of a non-international character, the relevance of an enquiry procedure in those contexts is even more acute. However, the enquiry Articles of the Geneva Conventions formally do not apply to violations of Common Article 3 that applies in such types of conflict. The enquiry being based on the consent of parties, it might be possible to consider that parties to a NIAC would agree to set up an enquiry procedure. And just as it has been argued that the IHFFC may intervene to enquire into alleged violations of humanitarian law arising in NIACs, so long as all parties to the conflict agree,[23] the same could be envisaged for the creation of any other enquiry based on mutual consent. The key challenge lies in the greater difficulty in securing the consent of parties to an internal armed conflict.

D. Critical Assessment: The Proliferation of Fact-Finding and Inquiry Missions

In light of the very limited use of enquiry mechanisms under IHL treaties, the proliferation of fact-finding missions and commissions of inquiry created outside the scope of the IHL treaties constitutes a key development. The lack of agreement between parties to a conflict to set up an enquiry procedure has led to states imposing investigative bodies through the UN system. In as much as the development of international criminal law

---

[23] Condorelli, above n 21, at 401–2.

both substantively and procedurally occurred through the establishment of international courts and tribunals and their related jurisprudence, the increasing resort to fact-finding missions and commissions of enquiry to investigate IHL violations has given rise to a new set of institutions and an emerging practice, contributing to better compliance with and implementation of IHL.

29   However, while the enquiry procedure of the Geneva Conventions pertains to establishing facts, the UN-created fact-finding missions and commissions of inquiry vary in nature, scope, and purpose. For example, although it has been argued that the enquiry procedure 'deals only with violations of a certain degree of seriousness which cause disagreement between the Parties',[24] UN commissions of inquiry tend to focus primarily on the most serious or systematic violations but do not exclusively address allegations causing a dispute between parties to the conflict. As a result, they do not necessarily constitute an alternative to other means of settlement of disputes or enforcement. They rather seek to investigate patterns of violations to avoid further abuses and to clarify the facts, but not in a logic of inter-state dispute settlement. In practice they also tend to be created in the context of a NIAC.

30   Recent years have seen the UN Human Rights Council and the Security Council create fact-finding missions and commissions of inquiry specifically mandated to investigate alleged violations of international human rights and humanitarian law in conflict or post-conflict contexts. For example, the Security Council created the International Commission of Inquiry on Darfur in 2004, and the Human Rights Council established fact-findings missions and commissions of inquiry to address alleged violations committed during the war in Lebanon in 2006, the Gaza conflict in 2009, and the conflicts in Libya and Syria in 2011. Similar missions were also created by the UN Secretary-General, such as the Panel of Experts on Accountability in Sri Lanka, and by the European Union, with the International Independent Fact-Finding Mission on the Conflict in Georgia, in 2011 and 2008 respectively. The case of the Israel–Lebanon Monitoring Group, established by the April Cease-Fire Understanding between Israel and Hezbollah, is particularly interesting as it combined elements of conciliation and of fact-finding.[25]

31   While these ad hoc mechanisms have mostly been created by UN human rights or political organs, they have been tasked with addressing allegations of IHL violations in addition to human rights violations in relation to a specific armed conflict. Even in the case of Libya, where the mandate only called for the Commission 'to investigate all alleged violations of international human rights law in the Libyan Arab Jamahiriya, establish the facts and circumstances of such violations and of the crimes perpetrated and where possible, to identify those responsible', the International Commission of Inquiry on Libya interpreted its mandate as including IHL violations too, as a matter of law, given the applicability of this body of norms in situations of armed conflict.

32   The recent proliferation of such missions has renewed debate around the role played by those commissions in relation to the issue of compliance with IHL, leading some scholars to ask whether they constitute a new form of adjudication in the absence of universal compulsory jurisdiction by international judicial bodies.[26] This is so, not least

---

[24] Pictet Commentary GC IV, at 604.
[25] A. Waldman, *Arbitrating Armed Conflict: Decisions of the Israel–Lebanon Monitoring Group* (Huntington, NY: Juris, 2003).
[26] D. Akande and H. Tonkin, 'International Commission of Inquiry: A New Form of Adjudication', 6 April 2012, available at <http://www.ejiltalk.org/international-commissions-of-inquiry-a-new-form-of-adjudication/>.

because the mandate of fact-finding missions and commissions of inquiry usually goes far beyond the mere factual assessment of a series of allegations. As highlighted earlier, such bodies, through fact-finding on alleged IHL violations, address key IHL issues and make legal determinations, ranging from classifying a situation as an armed conflict or legally assessing the aspects of control by a state over an armed group, to interpreting certain rules of IHL, the meaning and scope of which may be unsettled under IHL, and consequently contributing to the progressive interpretation of IHL norms. Furthermore, some fact-finding missions and commissions of inquiry are specifically mandated to identify those responsible for IHL violations, be they state security forces, armed groups, or individuals. While identifying individuals may raise important issues of due process and fairness, such findings can serve to support international or national prosecutions in particular cases and accountability processes in general, contributing to a better enforcement of IHL. Lastly, fact-finding missions may also identify patterns of IHL violations resulting from certain dubious practices in warfare, such as the use of explosive weapons in densely populated areas, and thereby help to enhance compliance with IHL in the future.

On the other hand, the proliferation of fact-finding bodies tasked with looking into alleged IHL violations raises numerous challenges. First, as matter of principle, it highlights the difficulty of ascertaining facts pertaining to certain IHL rules, including the law on the conduct of hostilities. The way norms regulating the conduct of hostilities are designed necessitates that certain facts which are particularly hard to verify are established. Moreover, fact-finding must cover all components of these norms in order to be able to reach a legal conclusion. Such components relate to factual elements that pertain to an array of different aspects, such as the intention of the attacker, the way weapons were used, the nature of the target, the effects of the attack, and the likely behaviour of the defender. There is the constant challenge of taking into account two different perspectives. The first one concerns the issue of time: the legality of an attack depends on an *ex ante* evaluation by the attacker, while the facts are established *ex post*. The other perspective is about the actor involved, the attacker or the defender. For example, the concept of 'military objective' depends on the plans of the attacker and the perceived behaviour of the defender. 33

The increasing task given to fact-finding missions to identify individual perpetrators also raises methodological and legal issues pertaining to the relationship between IHL and international criminal law standards, such as the question of the standards of proof to be used by those bodies.[27] For example, a commission entrusted with a mixed mandate of not only establishing the facts of alleged violations committed by a state and by non-state actors, but also identifying individuals, may have to apply different standards of proof, and not just a mere 'balance of probabilities' evidentiary threshold, to make its determinations concerning individuals. For example, the International Commission of Inquiry on Darfur had to identify individual perpetrators, and therefore resorted to a combined formula without reaching the higher standard of proof used by criminal tribunals.[28] 34

---

[27] E.g., see S. Wilkinson, 'Standards of Proof in International Humanitarian and Human Rights Fact-Finding and Inquiry Missions', Geneva Academy of International Humanitarian Law and Human Rights, available at <http://www.geneva-academy.ch/docs/Standards%20of%20proo%20report.pdf>; Frulli, above n 14, at 331–48; Vezzani, above n 14, at 349–68.

[28] Report of the International Commission of Inquiry on Darfur to the United Nations Secretary-General, 25 January 2005, para 15.

35 The proliferation of these institutions also raises numerous practical issues calling for a better harmonization of methodology and practices, notably where the information gathered is to be used to support criminal prosecutions. These include: ways to overcome the impossibility of accessing the territory where the IHL violations are taking place; the methodology to assess the reliability and admissibility of evidence; respect for ethical principles, such as the 'do no harm' standard when interviewing victims and witnesses to avoid re-traumatization, the protection of persons coming into contact with the fact-finding mission, and specific requirements when investigating certain types of violations such as sexual and gender-based violence.

36 These developments do not supersede the need to strengthen efforts for IHL-specific existing enquiry mechanisms to be used, or for new ones to be created. However, in the event that an enquiry procedure under the Geneva Conventions is instituted, its work will undoubtedly be influenced by the emerging practice of fact-finding and inquiry missions created outside the IHL framework.

THÉO BOUTRUCHE[*]

---

[*] Théo Boutruche is an Independent Consultant in International Human Rights and Humanitarian Law. The views expressed in this chapter are solely those of the author and do not necessarily reflect those of the organizations he worked for or currently works for.

Chapter 29. Prohibition of Reprisals

	MN
A. Introduction	1
B. Meaning and Application	7
I. Definition and related concepts	7
II. Scope of application	13
III. Conditions of exercise	20
a. Purpose	21
b. Subsidiarity	27
c. Proportionality	30
d. High-level authorization	33
e. Termination	34
IV. Status under customary law	35
C. Relevance in Non-International Armed Conflicts	37
D. Legal Consequences of a Violation	51
I. Violation of legal requirements	53
II. Circumstance precluding wrongfulness and justification	55
E. Critical Assessment	61

Select Bibliography

Bierzanek, R., 'Reprisals as a Means of Enforcing the Laws of Warfare: The Old and the New Law', in A. Cassese (ed), *The New Humanitarian Law of Armed Conflict* (Naples: Editoriale Scientifica, 1979) 232

Bílková, V., 'Belligerent Reprisals in Non-International Armed Conflicts', 63 *ICLQ* (2014) 31

Bristol, M., 'The Laws of War and Belligerent Reprisals against Enemy Civilian Populations', 21 *The Air Force Law Review* (1979) 397

Cassese, A., 'Justifications and Excuses in International Criminal Law', in A. Cassese, P. Gaeta, and J.R.W.D. Jones (eds), *The Rome Statute of the International Criminal Court: A Commentary* (Oxford: OUP, 2002) 951

Darcy, S., 'The Evolution of the Law of Belligerent Reprisals?', 175 *Military Law Review* (2002) 184

Darcy, S., 'What Future for the Doctrine of Belligerent Reprisals?', 5 *YIHL* (2002) 107

Greenwood, C., 'The Twilight of the Law of Belligerent Reprisals', 20 *Netherlands Yearbook of International Law* (1989) 35

Greenwood, C., 'Belligerent Reprisals in the Jurisprudence of the International Tribunal for the Former Yugoslavia', in H. Fischer, C. Kreβ, and S.R. Lüder (eds), *International and National Prosecution of Crimes Under International Law—Current Developments* (Berlin: Verlag Arno Spitz GmbH, 2001) 539

Hampson, F., 'Belligerent Reprisals and the 1977 Protocols to the Geneva Conventions of 1949', 37 *ICLQ* (1988) 818

Kalshoven, F., *Belligerent Reprisals* (The Hague: Martinus Nijhoff, 1971, republished 2005)

Kalshoven, F., 'Belligerent Reprisals Revisited', 21 *Netherlands Yearbook of International Law* (1990) 43

Kalshoven, F., 'Reprisals and the Protection of Civilians: Two Recent Decisions of the Yugoslavia Tribunal', in L. Vohrah et al (eds), *Man's Inhumanity to Man: Essays on International Law in Honour of Antonio Cassese* (The Hague: Kluwer Law International, 2003) 481

Nahlik, S.E., 'Belligerent Reprisals as Seen in the Light of the Diplomatic Conference on Humanitarian Law, Geneva, 1974–1977', 42 *Law and Contemporary Problems* (1978) 36

Price, A., *Towards a Conceptualization of Belligerent Reprisals in Contemporary Armed Conflicts* (LLM Thesis on file at the Graduate Institute of International and Development Studies, Geneva, 2012), at 55

Ruffert, M., 'Reprisals', in MPEPIL

Sutter, P., 'The Continuing Role for Belligerent Reprisals', 13 *Journal of Conflict and Security Law* (2008) 93

A. Introduction

1   Belligerent reprisals have long been considered an essential mean of securing compliance with international humanitarian law (IHL). There is, however, a growing tendency to outlaw them altogether.[1] Those that may still be lawful are subject to stringent conditions.[2] This trend is grounded on the fact that enforcing IHL through reprisals is increasingly perceived as ineffective, unjust, and open to abuse, in particular because it risks leading to an escalation of violence.[3] Reprisals are also viewed as being anachronistic in a modern international order which offers more equitable alternative methods of law enforcement. In this spirit, as early as 1934, N. Politis, Rapporteur of the Institut de droit international, stated that reprisals 'relèvent du système archaïque et barbare selon lequel chacun pourvoit de son mieux, par ses propres moyens, à la sauvegarde de ses droits et à la défense de ses intérêts'.[4] Moreover, mutual deterrence, on which the logic of reprisals is based, is fundamentally alien to contemporary international human rights law (IHRL) which increasingly applies in armed conflicts.[5] Nonetheless, the prohibitions of certain reprisals—in particular those contained in Additional Protocol (AP) I against civilians and civilian objects—still provoke controversy among states and scholars. Indeed, some consider that reprisals—and the threat of them—offer strong deterrent effects.[6] They also argue that,

---

[1] ICRC CIHL Study, at 513.   [2] Ibid.

[3] For a summary of the arguments in favour of the prohibition of reprisals, see S. Darcy, 'What Future for the Doctrine of Belligerent Reprisals?', 5 *YIHL* (2002) 107, at 111–20. See also C. Greenwood, 'The Twilight of the Law of Belligerent Reprisals', 20 *Netherlands Yearbook of International Law* (1989) 35, at 36; S. Oeter, 'Methods and Means of Combat', in D. Fleck (ed), *The Handbook of Humanitarian Law in Armed Conflicts* (2nd edn, Oxford: OUP, 2008) 119, at 232, para 476. For a detailed study of the concept of belligerent reprisals, see F. Kalshoven, *Belligerent Reprisals* (The Hague: Martinus Nijhoff, first published in 1971, republished in 2005).

[4] *Annuaire de l'Institut de Droit international*, 1934, at 26. See also G.I.A.D. Draper, *The Red Cross Conventions* (New York: Praeger, 1958), at 98.

[5] T. Meron, 'Convergence of International Humanitarian Law and Human Rights Law', in D. Warner (ed), *Human Rights and Humanitarian Law: The Quest for Universality* (The Hague: Martinus Nijoff, 1997), at 100; Y. Dinstein, *The Conduct of Hostilities under the Law of International Armed Conflict* (2nd edn, Cambridge: CUP, 2004), at 258–9.

[6] For a summary of the arguments against a general prohibition of reprisals, see Darcy, above n 3, at 121–8. See also A. Roberts, 'The Laws of War: Problems of Implementation in Contemporary Conflicts', 6 *Duke Journal of Comparative & International Law* (1995) 11, at 78; M. McDougal and F. Feliciano, *Law and Minimum World Public Order: The Legal Regulation of International Coercion* (New Haven, CT: Yale University Press, 1962), at 682.

in the absence of adequate sanctions in the event of IHL violations, reprisals constitute the only efficient means of ensuring respect for the laws of war.[7]

Due to these divergent interests, states have not been able to agree on a general and absolute prohibition of reprisals in international armed conflict (IAC).[8] However, concerned by their dangerous repercussions on the conduct of hostilities, they have gradually limited the scope of application of reprisals and their conditions of exercise. The conventional rule prohibiting reprisals was first introduced in 1929 to protect prisoners of war (POWs), after the sufferings they had endured during the First World War.[9] It was then supplemented in 1949 by a similar provision in Geneva Convention (GC) III.[10] Similarly, GC I,[11] GC II,[12] and GC IV[13] added provisions prohibiting reprisals against certain persons and goods protected by these conventions, such as the wounded, sick, shipwrecked, and protected civilians and their properties.

Even though it falls outside the ambit of this Commentary, it should nevertheless be noted that AP I considerably expanded the categories of persons and objects protected by the Geneva Conventions from reprisals, in particular civilian persons and objects during the conduct of hostilities.[14] For the sake of completeness, it is also worth noting that other IHL conventions—i.e. the Convention for the Protection of Cultural Property in the Event of Armed Conflict of 14 May 1954,[15] and the Protocol on Prohibitions or Restrictions on the Use of Mines, Booby-Traps and Other Explosive Devices (Protocol II) to the Convention on Certain Conventional Weapons of 10 October 1980 as amended on 3 May 1996[16]—contain specific restrictions on the recourse to reprisals.

In addition to becoming progressively limited in scope, reprisals against those persons and objects which remain lawful targets have been submitted to strict customary requirements of purpose, proportionality, subsidiary, authorization, and termination. The precise content of some of these conditions remains, however, unsettled and controversial.[17]

With regard to non-international armed conflict (NIAC), neither Common Article 3 nor AP II bans reprisals as such. This lacuna generates discord.[18] According to the International Committee of the Red Cross (ICRC), the absolute character of these provisions does not allow room for reprisals. Moreover, the institution of reprisals—which appeared in the nineteenth and early twentieth centuries—governs traditional inter-state relations.[19] The regime regulating this institution has, therefore, developed almost exclusively within the framework of IHL regulating IAC and ignores the context of NIAC. Nonetheless, the apparent silence of Common Article 3 and AP II on reprisals has led certain scholars to dispute the applicability of the prohibition of reprisals in NIAC.[20]

---

[7] Greenwood, above n 3, at 56. See also P. Sutter, 'The Continuing Role for Belligerent Reprisals', 13 *Journal of Conflict and Security Law* (2008) 93, at 119–20.

[8] ICRC Commentary APs, para 810.   [9] Art 2(3) of 1929 GC II.

[10] Art 13 para 3 GC III.   [11] Art 46 GC I.   [12] Art 47 GC II.

[13] Art 33 para 3 GC IV.

[14] Art 20 AP I; Art 51(6) AP I; Art 52 AP I; Art 53 AP I; Art 54 AP I; Art 55 AP I; Art 56 AP I.

[15] Art 4(4).   [16] See Art 3(2) of original Protocol II and Art 3(7) of amended Protocol II.

[17] A. Price, *Towards a Conceptualization of Belligerent Reprisals in Contemporary Armed Conflicts* (LLM Thesis on file at the Graduate Institute of International and Development Studies, Geneva, 2012), at 55.

[18] For an in-depth analysis of the concept of reprisals in NIAC, see V. Bílková, 'Belligerent Reprisals in Non-International Armed Conflicts', 63 *ICLQ* (2014) 31.

[19] See ICRC CIHL Study, at 527; ICRC Commentary APs, para 4529.

[20] S. Darcy, 'The Evolution of the Law of Belligerent Reprisals?', 175 *Military Law Review* (2002) 184, at 218–19; Kalshoven, above n 3, at 269; F. Kalshoven, 'Reprisals and the Protection of Civilians: Two Recent Decisions of the Yugoslavia Tribunal', in L. Vohrah et al (eds), *Man's Inhumanity to Man, Essays on International Law in Honour of Antonio Cassese* (The Hague: Kluwer Law International, 2003) 481, at 505.

Some commentators have also queried whether reprisals could constitute an enforcement mechanism available to armed groups as well as states.[21]

6   In light of the above considerations and ambiguities, the prohibitions of reprisal pose delicate questions of interpretation which revolve around the following five main issues: (i) the exact meaning and scope of application of these prohibitions; (ii) the determination of the conditions under which specific reprisals may be taken; (iii) the status under customary law of the prohibitions of reprisals and their exceptions; (iv) the application of these prohibitions in NIAC; and (v) the possibility of invoking reprisal as a 'circumstance precluding wrongfulness', or as a defence to charges of war crimes.

B. Meaning and Application

I. Definition and related concepts

7   The concept of a 'reprisal' is not defined in IHL treaties. However, it is commonly agreed that it consists of an action that would otherwise be breaching IHL but that, in exceptional cases, is considered lawful under international law when used to enforce the laws of war.[22] This concept must be distinguished from the following notions with which it has often been associated: retorsion, countermeasures, termination or suspension of treaties, and collective punishment.

8   A clear distinction must be drawn between acts of *retorsion* and reprisals. Acts of retorsion constitute reactions of a state, which is not breaching its international obligations, to the acts of another state which may be internationally wrongful.[23] Like reprisals, acts of retorsion aim at ending a prejudicial course of action undertaken by another state.[24] In contrast to reprisals, these acts are 'unfriendly' but not necessarily in violation of a rule of international law. They may include the prohibition of or limitations upon normal diplomatic relations, embargoes, or withdrawal of voluntary aid programmes.[25]

9   According to some, reprisals are also to be contrasted with *countermeasures*, while others consider them as a special case of countermeasures, subject to special rules.[26] The International Law Commission (ILC) is ambiguous on this controversy.[27] According to the first view, preferred by this author, while the former apply only in IACs and are regulated by the specific regime of IHL, the latter operate in times of peace, are governed, as circumstances precluding wrongfulness, by the secondary rules of the law on state responsibility, in particular by Articles 49 to 54 of the ILC Articles on State Responsibility, and are subject to certain specific procedural requirements which cannot apply in situations of war, such as those envisaged in Article 52 of the ILC Articles on State Responsibility. Furthermore, reprisals are usually described as measures designed to induce a state to comply with IHL (cessation of violations) or to prevent further violations (deterrence

---

[21] L. Zegveld, *The Accountability of Armed Opposition Groups in International Law* (Cambridge: CUP, 2002), at 89–90.
[22] ICRC CIHL Study, at 513.
[23] ILC Commentary, at 128, para 3; ICRC Commentary APs, para 815. See also L.-A. Sicilianos, *Les réactions décentralisées à l'illicite* (Paris: LGDJ, 1990), at 7.
[24] F. Hampson, 'Belligerent Reprisals and the 1977 Protocols to the Geneva Conventions of 1949', 37 *ICLQ* (1988) 818, at 820.
[25] ILC Commentary, at 128, para 3.   [26] Bílková, above n 18, at 33; Kalshoven, above n 3, at 1.
[27] ILC Commentary, at 128, para 3.

of violations).²⁸ In contrast, countermeasures aim not only at ensuring cessation of the internationally wrongful conduct, but also at providing reparation to the injured state.²⁹

Both concepts share similarities however. They both constitute responses to a state 10 allegedly responsible for a wrongful act.³⁰ Moreover, both measures are subject to certain similar conditions of exercise: they are actions of last resort, and they must respect the general requirements of proportionality and termination. It should nonetheless be noted that Article 50(1)(c) of the ILC Articles on State Responsibility precludes taking countermeasures in certain circumstances, in particular when they affect 'obligations of a humanitarian character prohibiting reprisals'. The ILC Commentary on Articles on State Responsibility refers in this regard to 'the basic prohibition of reprisals against individuals, which exists in international humanitarian law', and observes that, under IHL, 'reprisals are prohibited against defined classes of protected persons, and these prohibitions are very widely accepted'.³¹ Accordingly, the right to take countermeasures cannot be invoked in order to justify the (temporary) violation of any international legal obligations prohibiting reprisals.

Reprisals are distinct from acts of *termination or suspension of the operation of a treaty* 11 resulting from its breach. Indeed, in case of reprisal measures, the IHL obligation which is not respected does not cease to exist or to be binding upon the state which took these measures. As the ILC Commentary stated in relation to countermeasures, one could argue that this obligation becomes temporarily 'ineffective' only until the state targeted by way of reprisals has brought its own conduct into line with IHL.³² While the termination or suspension is governed by the law of treaties, in particular Article 60 of the Vienna Convention on the Law of Treaties (VCLT) (1969), reprisals are regulated by IHL. In any event, Article 60(5) VCLT, echoing Article 50 of the ILC Articles on State Responsibility, expressly states that the provision regulating the termination or suspension of the operation of a treaty as a consequence of its breach does 'not apply to provisions relating to the protection of the human person contained in treaties of a humanitarian character, in particular to provisions prohibiting any form of reprisals against persons protected by such treaties'. This exception is based on the customary principle according to which the obligation to respect IHL and to ensure respect for it does not depend on reciprocity.³³ As clearly explained by Hampson,

> if an object in employing reprisals is to encourage the offending party to return to lawful ways, it will hardly be assisted by the suspension of the Geneva Conventions in its relations with victim States. The only way to give any meaning to provisions prohibiting certain reprisals is to say that the victim State cannot suspend them, even in the face of material breach of the treaty by the offending State.³⁴

---

²⁸ Greenwood, above n 3, at 37; Hampson, above n 24, at 820. It should be noted, however, that the exact purposes of reprisals have raised many debates among scholars. For a summary of these debates, see S. Darcy, 'Retaliation and Reprisal', in M. Weller (ed), *Oxford Handbook on the Use of Force* (Oxford: OUP, 2013), available at <http://ssrn.com/abstract=2172573> or <http://dx.doi.org/10.2139/ssrn.2172573>.

²⁹ ILC Commentary, at 128, para 1, and at 130, para 1.
³⁰ Art 49(1) of the ILC Articles on State Responsibility.   ³¹ ILC Commentary, at 128, para 3.
³² Ibid, at 71, para 3.
³³ ICRC CIHL Study, Rule 140, at 374. See also ICTY, *The Prosecutor v Zoran Kupreškić et al*, Trial Chamber Judgment, IT-95-16-T, 14 January 2000, paras 514–20.
³⁴ Hampson, above n 24, at 831.

12 Lastly, *collective punishment* and reprisals should be differentiated.[35] They pursue different purposes. On the one hand, collective punishment aims at making a group of persons pay the price for the behaviour of one or more other individuals or groups, and is strictly prohibited in both IAC and NIAC.[36] On the other hand, reprisals are not punitive in nature.[37] As an enforcement mechanism, they seek to force the adversary to comply with IHL.[38]

II. Scope of application

13 As recalled in the introduction to this chapter, over the course of the twentieth century, IHL has progressively limited the circumstances in which reprisals may be taken.[39] The 1929 Convention Relative to the Treatment of Prisoners of War (1929 GC II) was the first treaty which explicitly prohibited reprisals (against POWs). The Geneva Conventions and AP I then further strengthened this prohibition by including specific rules banning reprisals against numerous categories of persons and objects.

14 Regarding individuals, Article 13 paragraph 3 GC III reiterates the prohibition of reprisals against POWs contained in Article 2(3) of 1929 GC II.[40] Moreover, Article 46 GC I and Article 47 GC II grant protections against reprisals to the following protected persons in the power of a party to the conflict: the wounded, sick, shipwrecked, and medical and religious personnel. Although neither the 1907 Hague Regulations nor the 1929 Geneva Convention protected civilians, Article 33 paragraph 3 GC IV prohibited, for the first time, reprisals against those who qualified for protected person status under GC IV. This means that, according to GC IV's scope of application *ratione personae*, reprisals have been banned only against civilians in occupied territories and other categories of civilians in the hands of the enemy, such as enemy nationals within the territory of one of the belligerents.[41]

15 As to objects, Article 46 GC I and Article 47 GC II prohibit reprisals against medical buildings, vessels, and equipment protected thereby. In addition, Article 33 paragraph 3 GC IV forbids the taking of reprisals against the property of protected persons, i.e. civilians in the power of the adverse party. A further limitation has been introduced by Article 4(4) of the Convention for the Protection of Cultural Property in the Event of Armed Conflict, which provides that states 'shall refrain from any act directed by way of reprisals against cultural property' of great importance to the cultural heritage of people.

16 Among these provisions, Article 33 paragraph 3 GC IV constitutes an important innovation. Indeed, as stated by Greenwood, it 'represented a substantial departure from the

---

[35] F. Kalshoven, 'Belligerent Reprisals Revisited', 21 *Netherlands Yearbook of International Law* (1990) 43, at 78.

[36] See Art 87(3) GC III; Art 33(1) GC IV; Art 75(2)(d) AP I; Art 4(2)(b) AP II.

[37] ICRC CIHL Study, at 515.

[38] C. Greenwood, 'Belligerent Reprisals in the Jurisprudence of the International Tribunal for the Former Yugoslavia', in H. Fischer, C. Kreß, and S.R. Lüder (eds), *International and National Prosecution of Crimes under International Law—Current Developments* (Berlin: Verlag Arno Spitz GmbH, 2001) 542.

[39] While it is referred to in the 1863 Lieber Code (Art 28) and in the 1880 *Oxford Manual* (Art 85; Art 86), the notion of reprisals was not mentioned in any of the texts adopted at the international conferences at Brussels in 1874 or at The Hague in 1899 and 1907. See S.E. Nahlik, 'Belligerent Reprisals as Seen in the Light of the Diplomatic Conference on Humanitarian Law, Geneva, 1974–1977', 42 *Law and Contemporary Problems* (1978) 36, at 38–9.

[40] Art 2(3) of 1929 GC II states that '[m]easures of reprisal against them [POWs] are forbidden'.

[41] Art 4 GC IV.

law relating to belligerent occupation which had been in force during the Second World War'.[42] Accordingly, Pictet Commentary GC IV affirmed that

[t]he prohibition of reprisals is a safeguard for all protected persons, whether in the territory of a Party to the conflict or in occupied territory. It is absolute and mandatory in character and thus cannot be interpreted as containing tacit reservations with regard to military necessity. The solemn and unconditional character of the undertaking entered into by the States Parties to the Convention must be emphasized. To infringe this provision with the idea of restoring law and order would only add one more violation to those with which the enemy is reproached. [...] This paragraph, like the first one, marks a decisive step forward in the affirmation and defence of rights of individuals and there is no longer any question of such rights being withdrawn or attenuated as a result of a breach for which those individuals bear no responsibility.[43]

In sum, the Geneva Conventions outlaw reprisals against specific categories of individuals and objects. However, none of these Conventions contains any general prohibition against reprisals. Therefore, reprisals amounting to violations of provisions of the Geneva Conventions that do not directly cause harm to protected persons or objects could theoretically be considered lawful when the conditions for exercising them are met. Moreover, as the remit of Article 33 is limited primarily to enemy aliens who find themselves in the territory of a party to the conflict and to civilians in occupied territory, GC IV does not offer any protection from belligerent reprisals affecting the civilian population or civilian objects of a party to an IAC when they are located in territory still controlled by their own party. As shown below, however, attempts were made to remedy this lacuna in 1977.[44] 17

Without examining in detail the provisions of AP I on reprisals, which fall outside the scope of this Commentary, it should be mentioned that after considerable debate during the Diplomatic Conference on the Reaffirmation and Development of International Humanitarian Law Applicable in Armed Conflicts of 1974 to 1977,[45] AP I has confirmed the tendency towards banning reprisals against a broader category of civilians and civilian objects. Indeed, it has reaffirmed the protection of the wounded, sick, and shipwrecked, widened the definition of those categories, and added new protected objects and persons (Articles 20 and 8 AP I). Furthermore, AP I has added rules on the prohibition of reprisals against civilians (Article 51(6)) as well as civilian objects (Article 52) during the conduct of hostilities. Specific objects have also been protected: cultural objects and places of worship (Article 53), objects indispensable to the survival of the civilian population (Article 54), the natural environment (Article 55), and works and installations containing dangerous forces (Article 56). 18

The protection granted by Article 51(6) to 'the civilian population or civilians' is certainly an essential provision of AP I.[46] As of 1977, not only civilians who found themselves 'in the hands of a Party to the conflict or Occupying Power of which they are not nationals', but also all civilians affected by hostilities, have been fully protected against reprisals under this Protocol. In light of these developments, the residual scope for taking reprisals is now tightly circumscribed. Indeed, there are only a few instances where IHL treaties have not outlawed them. The majority of the literature on this issue agrees that the only lawful targets of such measures are military objectives and enemy armed forces.[47] As 19

---

[42] Greenwood, above n 3, at 51.   [43] Pictet Commentary GC IV, at 228.
[44] Darcy, above n 20, at 201.   [45] Nahlik, above n 39, at 45–64.
[46] Oeter, above n 3, at 234, para 479.
[47] See, e.g., M. Bristol, 'The Laws of War and Belligerent Reprisals against Enemy Civilian Populations', 21 *The Air Force Law Review* (1979) 397, at 418; Darcy, above n 20, at 210; Greenwood, above n 3, at 65; Hampson, above n 24, at 828–9.

these targets are in principle legitimate anyway, reprisals may be envisaged only following recourse to certain unlawful methods of combat or weapons[48] (unless a treaty banning the use of these weapons expressly prohibits reprisals).[49]

III. Conditions of exercise

20 In order to avoid any abuse which might occur in environments characterized by inequalities between belligerent forces, reprisals may be taken only under five stringent conditions. These are not laid down in the Geneva Conventions or in AP I. In fact, attempts to codify them were unsuccessful. These conditions stem mainly from military manuals, judicial decisions,[50] and official statements. To a certain extent, they can also be deduced from the limits imposed on countermeasures by Articles 49 to 54 of the ILC Articles on State Responsibility.[51] However, defining their precise content still raises controversies.[52]

a. Purpose

21 It flows from the definition of reprisals that such measures may be taken only in reaction to a prior violation of IHL, and only for the purpose of inducing one's adversary to comply with the laws of war, namely to end and/or deter the recurrence of the original, or similar, offending acts.[53] From this principle, which is well established in state practice—including military manuals, national legislation, and case law[54]—there are five consequences to be addressed.

22 First, to be lawful, a reprisal measure which breaches IHL may be taken only in reaction to a prior violation of the same 'type of law', that is of *jus in bello*.[55] Thus, a violation of a norm of *jus ad bellum* cannot justify, as a reprisal, the infringement of any of the laws of armed conflict.[56] This consequence flows from the fundamental principle of the

---

[48] ICRC Commentary APs, para 1985. See also Darcy, above n 20, at 211–16; Hampson, above n 24, at 829.
[49] See Art 3(7) of the Protocol on Prohibitions or Restrictions on the Use of Mines, Booby-Traps and Other Devices (Protocol II) to the Convention on Certain Conventional Weapons of 10 October 1980, as amended on 3 May 1996.
[50] See, in particular, the case law from the aftermath of the Second World War and, in particular: *Trial of Wilhelm List and others*, United States Military Tribunal, Nuremberg, 1947–8, UNWCC Law Reports, vol VIII, at 34 ('*Hostages case*'); *The United States of America v Otto Ohlendorf and others*, 1946–9, Nuremberg Military Tribunals, Nuremberg, UNWCC Law Reports, vol IV, at 3; *Trial of Kriminalsekretar Richard Wilhelm Hermann Bruns and two others*, Eidsivating Lagmannsrett and the Supreme Court of Norway, 1946, UNWCC Law Reports, vol III, at 12 ('*Bruns case*'); *Trial of General von Mackenson and General Maelzer*, British Military Courts, Rome, 1946, UNWCC Law Reports, vol VIII, at 15 ('*von Mackenson case*'). See also the early arbitral jurisprudence in the *Naulilaa* case (*Responsibility of Germany for damage caused in the Portuguese colonies in the south of Africa (Portugal v Germany)*, 31 July 1928, 2 *United Nations Reports of International Arbitral Awards*, at 1011) and in the *Cysne* case (*Responsibility of Germany for acts committed subsequent to 31 July 1914 and before Portugal entered into the war (Portugal v Germany)*, 30 June 1930, 2 *United Nations Reports of International Arbitral Awards*, at 1035).
[51] M. Ruffert, 'Reprisals', in MPEPIL (2012) 927, at 929. See also the substantive and formal conditions imposed by the ICJ on the taking of countermeasures (ICJ, *Gabčikovo-Nagymaros Project (Hungary/Slovakia)*, Judgment, 25 September 1997, para 83).
[52] Price, above n 17, at 55.
[53] ICRC CIHL Study, at 515; Darcy, above n 20, at 188; McDougal and Feliciano, above n 6, at 682.
[54] See practice cited in ICRC CIHL Study, at 515.
[55] ICRC CIHL Study, at 515; Darcy, above n 20, at 189; Greenwood, above n 3, at 40–1; A. Mitchell, 'Does One Illegality Merit Another? The Law of Belligerent Reprisals in International Law', 170 *Military Law Review* (2001) 155, at 159–60.
[56] M. Sassòli, 'State Responsibility for Violations of International Humanitarian Law', 84 *IRRC* 846 (2002) 401, at 426. Sassòli states in this regard: 'Once it is, however, admitted that even the most egregious

separation of and distinction between *jus in bello* and *jus ad bellum*: IHL must apply equally to all parties, regardless of the legality of their resort to force.[57] Furthermore, as underlined by Sassòli, '[i]f any rules of international humanitarian law could be violated as a countermeasure against an act of aggression, those rules would be meaningless'.[58]

Secondly, according to the ICRC, only violations which are considered to be 'serious' may justify reprisals.[59] This condition, rarely evoked by academic commentaries, is most likely intended to preclude reliance on each and every minor infringement in order to justify a breach, even minor, of IHL. That said, determining precisely what a 'serious' violation is may raise questions to which no clear answers can be given. What criteria should be used to qualify a violation as 'serious'? The interest protected by the rule infringed? The number of victims? The nature and extent of the damages suffered? It is submitted that a combination of these elements must be assessed in light of the individual circumstances of each situation.

Thirdly, belligerent reprisals may never be pursued for revenge or punishment. Above all, they must aim at securing observance of IHL.[60] Assessing the genuine motive justifying recourse to reprisals may prove difficult, especially in 'real-war conditions'. Such a problem is aggravated by the fact that, in the absence of an independent monitoring body, we are faced with the unilateral decision of the authorities of the injured state.[61] However, as examined below, before taking reprisals, belligerents should make public their willingness to take retaliatory measures. This element should facilitate the exercise of some sort of control over respect for this condition.

Fourthly, reprisals may be directed against a state only for its own violations or those perpetrated by an entity under its control. As stated in 1948 by the Rome Military Tribunal, 'the right to take reprisals arises only in consequence of an illegal act which can be attributed, directly or indirectly, to a State'.[62] This leads to two consequences. On the one hand, reprisals cannot, in principle, be targeted against a state for violations of IHL committed by independent non-state actors.[63] Such an assertion is grounded on the traditional view that reprisals govern inter-state relations, and therefore apply only in IAC. This issue will be revisited later. On the other hand, reprisals cannot be taken against a state other than the state responsible for the initial violation of IHL.[64] Even if most military

---

violation of international law, i.e. aggression, cannot justify violations of international humanitarian law as a countermeasure, it is suggested that no other violation of the law of peace may be met by countermeasures violating international humanitarian law. If this is true, even violations of international humanitarian law not prohibited by way of reprisals may be justified only as countermeasures in reaction to violations of international humanitarian law.' See also Sutter, above n 7, at 95–6.

[57] Greenwood, above n 3, at 40–1.   [58] Sassòli, above n 56, at 425.
[59] ICRC CIHL Study, at 515. See also Sutter, above n 7, at 96.
[60] Price, above n 17, at 55; Darcy, above n 20, at 191; Greenwood, above n 3, at 46.
[61] Hampson, above n 24, at 822; Bristol, above n 47, 418.
[62] Military Tribunal of Rome, *In Re Kapler*, 20 July 1948, in H. Lauterpacht (ed), 1948 *Annual Digest & Report of Public International Law Cases* 471, at 472 ('*Ardeatine Cave Massacre case*').
[63] Darcy, above n 20, at 190.
[64] Conversely, one might ask whether third states—'outsiders' or cobelligerent states—are entitled to take measures of reprisal in light of the *erga omnes* nature of most IHL obligations. It is, however, the position of this author that the bilateral nature of the mechanism of reprisals entails that only those states whose rights have been directly violated, and which are in a position accurately to assess the extent to which the conditions for taking reprisals have been met, should be allowed to take such measures. Permitting third states, even if they are cobelligerents, to take reprisals would have grave consequences: an escalation of violence would in most cases be inevitable.

manuals remain silent on the matter, and despite limited contrary practice and opinion,[65] it is generally agreed that reprisals against allies of the violating state are forbidden.[66] By comparison, it is interesting to note that, according to Article 49 of the ILC Articles on State Responsibility, countermeasures are legitimate only 'against a State which is responsible for an international wrongful act'. Moreover, conducting reprisals against third states would considerably increase the risk of an escalation of violence on a large scale.

26   Fifthly, as reprisals require a previous breach of IHL before being taken, 'anticipatory' reprisals and 'counter-reprisals' are not allowed.[67] The former are unlawful since they are decided upon in response to a violation which has not yet occurred or which may never take place. The latter are equally illegal, at least when they constitute reactions to lawful reprisals which, by definition, do not constitute violations of IHL.[68] Any other interpretation of the law of belligerent reprisals would inexorably lead to an endless chain of violent conduct and IHL violations.

b. Subsidiarity

27   As detailed in many manuals and confirmed by national case law, reprisals may be undertaken only as measures of last resort, when no other lawful means can be used to induce the adversary to comply with IHL, such as addressing a formal complaint to the adversary through bilateral diplomatic protests, threatening the adversary with criminal investigations or prosecutions, or with taking reprisals, appealing to an international forum, like the United Nations (UN) Security Council or other international bodies, or waiting for the conclusion of peace negotiations.[69]

28   It flows from this principle that the injured state must warn the adversary of its intention to have recourse to reprisals in advance. Indeed, prior to any action, the adverse party must be aware of the nature of and reasons for the retaliatory measures envisaged against it, and in particular of the fact that these measures are aimed at enforcing IHL. After such a warning has been given, reprisals should be taken at an appropriate time—neither too soon, in order to give an opportunity to the adversary to resume compliance with IHL, nor too late, in order effectively to prevent the adversary from committing further violations.[70]

29   Some scholars have expressed the view that, in exceptional circumstances, the principle of subsidiarity should be set aside.[71] According to them, these circumstances include the existence of an immediate risk of further violations and graver dangers if alternative measures have to be exhausted prior to any action, or the apparent futility of these measures. It is submitted that the requirement of subsidiarity should not be ignored.[72] Indeed,

---

[65] See M. Akehurst, 'Reprisals by Third States', 44 *BYBIL* (1970) 1, at 15–18; Dinstein, above n 5, at 255.
[66] ICRC CIHL Study, at 515.   [67] Ibid; Ruffert, above n 51, at 928.
[68] Darcy, above n 20, at 191.
[69] See practice cited in ICRC CIHL Study, at 516. For instance, in the ICTY *Martić* case, the Trial Chamber held that reprisals were not justified because the shelling was not a measure of last resort. Indeed, peace negotiations were ongoing when these measures were taken (ICTY, *The Prosecutor v Milan Martić*, Trial Chamber Judgment, IT-95-11-T, 12 June 2007, para 468). This conclusion was confirmed by the ICTY Appeals Chamber (ICTY, *The Prosecutor v Milan Martić*, Appeals Chamber Judgment, IT-95-11-A, 8 October 2008, para 265).
[70] See Hampson, above n 24, at 823. See also *Bruns case*, above n 50, at 22; *Ardeatine Cave Massacre case*, above n 62, at 472; ICTY, *The Prosecutor v Martić*, Trial Chamber Judgment, above n 69, para 468; ICTY, *The Prosecutor v Martić*, Appeals Chamber Judgment, above n 69, para 265.
[71] Hampson, above n 24, at 823; Kalshoven, above n 3, at 341; McDougal and Feliciano, above n 6, at 686–7.
[72] Greenwood, above n 3, at 47.

allowing exceptions to it would encourage states to violate IHL in order to enforce it, instead of using the numerous collective and individual lawful means of action currently offered by the international legal system.

c. Proportionality

Reprisals are governed by a third essential limiting factor based on considerations of proportionality. The principle of proportionality is relevant in determining what measures may be taken in reprisal and their degree of intensity.[73] Even if it is well established in state practice,[74] doctrine and jurisprudence, it raises sensitive questions of evaluation.

The benchmark by which proportionality has to be determined has generated controversies among scholars. The predominant view, endorsed by the ICRC and most of the case law on the issue, is that reprisals must be proportionate to the initial violations.[75] Other criteria—such as the 'damage suffered' or the 'legitimate end to be achieved'—have also been put forward.[76] Greenwood has proposed a combination of two criteria: 'reprisals should exceed neither what is proportionate to the prior violation nor what is necessary if they are to achieve their aim of restoring respect for the law'.[77] Measuring reprisals with the aim to be achieved has some merit. However, this element is difficult—if not impossible—to quantify concretely, relies highly on the subjective evaluation of the belligerents, and is thus open to abuse.[78] While the 'damage caused to the victims' could constitute another point of reference, the most precise, objective, and measurable yardstick remains the initial violation that the reprisal purports to remedy.

Determining precisely what constitutes a proportionate measure may also prove difficult. It can at best be achieved by approximation. Indeed, on a theoretical level, as stated by the ILC Commentary, this process requires 'taking into account not only the purely "quantitative" element of the injury suffered, but also "qualitative" factors such as the importance of the interest protected by the rule infringed and the seriousness of the breach'.[79] Moreover, as seen above, the scope of lawful reprisals is now strictly limited.[80] Consequently, measures of reprisal will rarely take the form of retaliation in kind, that is, resorting to the same unlawful measures as the original offence.[81] Often, the norm violated by these measures will be of a different nature from the initial breach of IHL. Such difficulties are exacerbated by practical considerations. Indeed, in modern asymmetrical armed conflicts, belligerents do not have access to the same means of warfare: some have at their disposal very accurate, modern, and sophisticated weapons, while others are obliged to use guerrilla methods.[82] In these circumstances, comparing reprisal measures with the initial violations which may justify them is not an easy task.[83] However, these theoretical and practical considerations should not imply that the principle of proportionality has

---

[73] ILC Commentary, at 134, para 1.
[74] See practice cited in ICRC CIHL Study, at 517. The requirement of proportionality has led to many discussions before war crimes tribunals. See, e.g., *Hostages case*, above n 50, at 65; *von Mackenson case*, above n 50, at 45; *Ardeatine Cave Massacre case*, above n 62, at 472.
[75] ICRC CIHL Study, at 517. [76] McDougal and Feliciano, above n 6, at 682.
[77] Greenwood, above n 3, at 44. [78] Darcy, above n 20, at 19; Sutter, above n 7, at 101.
[79] ILC Commentary, at 135, para 6. [80] See Hampson, above n 24, at 824.
[81] Dinstein, above n 5, at 255.
[82] R. Bierzanek, 'Reprisals as a Means of Enforcing the Laws of Warfare: The Old and the New Law', in A. Cassese (ed), *The New Humanitarian Law of Armed Conflict* (Naples: Editoriale Scientifica, 1979) 232, at 244.
[83] L. Moir, *The Law of Internal Armed Conflict* (Cambridge: CUP, 2002), at 238.

lost its relevance and can thus be disregarded. As rightly pointed out by Bothe, '[i]n the final analysis [...] most decisions on the major political, economic, and social affairs of societies as well as major military decisions rest on the subjective judgement of decision makers based on the weighing of factors which cannot be quantified'.[84] In this context, the ultimate test will be whether any 'reasonable competent person', placed in the same circumstances, would have taken reprisal measures of a similar nature and degree of intensity in reaction to the same violation of IHL. This test should nevertheless take into account the fact that every competent authority must enjoy a certain margin of appreciation when deciding on the matter.[85]

d. High-level authorization

33   It is well established in state practice—including military manuals, as well as national legislation and official statements[86]—that reprisals must be authorized at the highest level of authority. There is, however, no agreement on whether the competent authority must necessarily be military or political. Indeed, according to some authors[87] and recent practice,[88] reprisals can be undertaken only with the authorization of the highest political actors. For others, a military commander-in-chief is entitled to take such a decision.[89] As emphasized by Sutter, '[b]y limiting the power to authorize reprisals to a small number of senior commanders, it may well serve to limit hasty or ill-conceived acts of reprisal by subordinate commanders in the heat of the moment'.[90] However, prior to ordering a measure of reprisal, a complex assessment of not only legal and military but also political factors has to be undertaken. Furthermore, the highest political authority is frequently detached from the conduct of the hostilities and takes political responsibility for his or her acts, while a commander-in-chief might be more inclined to retaliate against the enemy attacks which inflicted losses among his or her soldiers. Nevertheless, recent events have shown that, as they are not directly at risk and heavily influenced by public opinion, Heads of State are not necessarily cautious in respecting the interests and rights of the adversary. Thus, some degree of coordination at the highest level, both political and military, is necessary. In any event, the decision to take reprisals must rest with a person whose level of experience and responsibility is such that he or she is able to ensure that all required conditions are met in full.[91]

e. Termination

34   Once the adverse party has resumed compliance with IHL and the violations have ceased, reprisal measures must be terminated immediately.[92] Indeed, in such cases, there is no justification for prolonging these measures. This requirement derives from the inherent nature of reprisals, which may be ordered only to induce an adversary to comply with the laws of war.

---

[84] Bothe/Partsch/Solf, at 310. [85] Kalshoven, above n 3, at 341–2.
[86] See practice cited in ICRC CIHL Study, at 518. *Contra* see Sutter, above n 7, at 100.
[87] See Oeter, above n 3, at 233, para 477. [88] See practice cited in ICRC CIHL Study, at 518.
[89] G. Draper, 'The Enforcement and Implementation of the Geneva Conventions of 1949 and the Additional Protocols of 1977', 163 *RCADI* (1978) 9, at 34; 1880 *Oxford Manual*, above n 39, Art 86.
[90] Sutter, above n 7, at 100. See also Oeter, above n 3, at 233, para 477.
[91] Darcy, above n 20, at 19. [92] ICRC CIHL Study, at 518.

IV. Status under customary law

In light of extensive state practice (as reflected in multiple military manuals, national legislation, and official statements), it is generally accepted that the various provisions banning reprisals against protected persons contained in GCs I, II, III, and IV—including those against civilians in occupied territory—are regarded as constituting customary international law.[93] The same conclusion may be drawn with regard to objects protected by these Conventions—including those belonging to civilians in the power of the adverse party—as well as objects protected by the 1954 Convention for the Protection of Cultural Property.[94] The customary status of a prohibition of reprisals against civilian persons and objects during the conduct of the hostilities is, however, far more controversial.[95]

As to the five conditions examined above (at MN 20–26), and upon which reprisals may be imposed, it is generally agreed that they constitute norms of customary international law.[96] It should nonetheless be recalled that the exact meaning of some of these requirements—such as the existence of possible exceptions to the principle of subsidiarity, the nature of the authorities (political or military) entitled to decide on the taking of reprisals, or the content of the principle of proportionality—remain controversial.

C. Relevance in Non-International Armed Conflicts

Common Article 3 does not expressly provide for the prohibition of reprisals. Additional Protocol II is also silent on the matter. These gaps raise disagreements in the legal literature and jurisprudence on whether and, if so, under what conditions the prohibition of reprisals applies in NIAC with regard to the protections in Common Article 3 (and AP II). On the one hand, some, including the ICRC, argue that reprisals are incompatible with the 'absolute nature' of the prohibitions contained in these texts, and that their ban is corroborated by state practice and justified on several historical, political, and substantive grounds. On the other hand, some commentators underline that such a conclusion cannot be drawn either from the text of Common Article 3 or from its *travaux préparatoires*. They consider that the status of reprisals in NIAC is, at a minimum, unclear.

According to the first approach, the prohibition of reprisals may be deduced from the wording of Common Article 3, which prohibits violence to life and person, the taking of hostages, outrages upon personal dignity, in particular humiliating and degrading treatment, and the denial of a fair trial. Indeed, these prohibitions apply and remain applicable 'at any time and in any place whatsoever'. In addition, Common Article 3 provides that

---

[93] Ibid, Rule 146, at 519–20.

[94] Ibid, Rule 147, at 523–5.

[95] Given the limited scope of this chapter, it suffices to note that, while two decisions of the ICTY have affirmed the customary nature of the rules prohibiting reprisals contained in AP I based largely on the imperatives of humanity and public conscience (see ICTY, *The Prosecutor v Kupreškić*, above n 33, para 531; ICTY, *The Prosecutor v Milan Martić*, Trial Chamber Decision on Review of Indictment Pursuant to Rule 61, IT-95-11-R61, 8 March 1996, para 10), limited contrary state practice points in the other direction, as illustrated by the reservations made by the United Kingdom and France upon ratification of AP I or the declarations of the United States that it does not accept such a prohibition (see practice cited in ICRC CIHL Study, Rule 146, at 521–3; Rule 146, at 525).

[96] ICRC CIHL Study, Rule 145, at 513–18.

all persons who do not, or who no longer, take a direct part in hostilities must be treated humanely 'in all circumstances'. Accordingly, Pictet Commentary GC IV states that

> the acts referred to under items (a) to (d) are prohibited absolutely and permanently, no exception or excuse being tolerated. Consequently, any reprisal which entails one of these acts is prohibited, and so, speaking generally, is any reprisal incompatible with the 'humane treatment' demanded unconditionally in the first clause of sub-paragraph (1).[97]

39 In other words, the absolute nature of the acts prohibited and the obligations imposed by Common Article 3—which, according to the International Court of Justice (ICJ), reflects 'elementary considerations of humanity'[98]—does not leave any place for reprisals in NIAC[99] since these obligations must apply respectively 'at any time and in any place' or 'in all circumstances'. The case law of the International Criminal Tribunal for the former Yugoslavia (ICTY)[100] endorses this approach. It is worth noting that the ICRC[101] and the ICTY[102] also infer the prohibition of reprisals in NIAC from Article 4(2) AP II, which forbids in the same absolute terms as Common Article 3—that is to say, 'at any time and in any place whatsoever'—several inhumane acts, including collective punishments. The ICRC Commentary to the Additional Protocols attaches particular weight to the banning of collective punishments, which is described as 'virtually equivalent to prohibiting "reprisals" against protected persons'.[103]

40 The ICRC,[104] some states,[105] and some scholars[106] have also developed another line of reasoning to outlaw reprisals in NIAC: this measure is, according to them, conceived to govern relations between states, and therefore does not apply between states and armed groups or between armed groups. Indeed, few governments would be ready to grant these groups such exorbitant powers that could be exercised against their own population.[107] Moreover, during the Diplomatic Conference on the Reaffirmation and Development of International Humanitarian Law Applicable in Armed Conflicts, several delegations argued that states can take enforcement measures because only they are 'subjects of international law possessing "facultas bellandi" '.[108] This explains why certain military manuals define reprisals as measures of enforcement by one state against another.[109]

---

[97] Pictet Commentary GC IV, at 39–40. See also ICRC CIHL Study, Rule 148, at 526.
[98] *Military and Paramilitary Activities in and against Nicaragua (Nicaragua v United States of America)*, Merits, Judgment, 26 June 1986, para 218.
[99] Moir, above n 83, at 240.
[100] ICTY, *The Prosecutor v Martić*, above n 95, para 15; ICTY, *The Prosecutor v Kupreškić*, above n 33, paras 526–7.
[101] ICRC Commentary APs, at 1372, para 4530; ICRC CIHL Study, Rule 148, at 527.
[102] ICTY, *The Prosecutor v Martić*, above n 95, para 16.
[103] ICRC Commentary APs, at 1374, para 4536.   [104] ICRC CIHL Study, Rule 145, at 527–8
[105] See military manuals cited in ICRC CIHL Study, Rule 145, at 528, fn 112.
[106] See S. Jones, 'Has Conduct in Iraq Confirmed the Moral Inadequacy of International Humanitarian Law? Examining the Confluence between Contract Theory and the Scope of Civilian Immunity during Armed Conflict', 16 *Duke Journal of Comparative & International Law* (2006), at 293.
[107] See Nahlik, above n 39, at 63. Moreover, as recalled by Eide, during the negotiation which led to the adoption of AP II, '[t]he representatives of many States felt that the notion of reprisals is inappropriate in the context of internal armed conflicts. Underlying this position was the view that the system of sanctions in international law still remains de-centralized, whereas in internal conflicts there is a centralized system of sanctions': A. Eide, 'The New Humanitarian Law in Non-International Armed Conflict', in Cassese (ed), above n 82, 278, at 298. Experience has demonstrated, however, that this reason is no longer valid. Indeed, in the case of NIAC, states are often incapable of guaranteeing the existence of an effective 'system of sanctions'.
[108] ICRC Commentary APs, at 1372, fn 18.
[109] See military manuals cited by ICRC CIHL Study, Rule 145, at 528, fn 112.

41 It should be observed that the UN has occasionally condemned acts of reprisal against civilians in NIAC, as demonstrated by some resolutions adopted by the General Assembly (UNGA)[110] or the Human Rights Commission (HRComm).[111] On a substantive level, similar arguments to those raised in the context of IAC are put forward to justify the exclusion of reprisals in NIAC: the necessity to promote non-violent means of enforcing IHL, the inefficiency of reprisals, as well as the potential of abuse and the risk of escalation of violence that such measures entail.[112]

42 Nevertheless, some scholars remain sceptical about this approach.[113] Their arguments should be recalled briefly. First, the prohibition of reprisals cannot be logically deduced from the absolute character of a norm. Indeed, a reprisal constitutes, by definition, a violation of that norm.[114] Outlawing reprisals thus requires the adoption of specific rules banning them,[115] similar to those existing in IAC. Secondly, the prohibition of reprisals cannot be inferred from the interdiction of collective punishment enshrined in Article 4(2) AP II. As outlined earlier, they are two different concepts: reprisals are designed to enforce IHL, while collective punishment imposes sanctions on a group of individuals.[116] Thirdly, the *travaux préparatoires* of Common Article 3 are not conclusive. Diametrically opposed views were expressed during the negotiation of this provision—some supporting the implicit prohibition of reprisals, others running against it.[117] Fourthly, other provisions of the Geneva Conventions refer to the expression 'at any time' and have never been interpreted as addressing reprisals.[118] Fifthly, on a political level, according to certain scholars, states would not agree implicitly that their capacity to combat rebels or insurgents on their own territories be limited.[119] As Kalshoven noted, the 'implicit waiver of such a power cannot lightly be assumed'.[120] Lastly, several substantial arguments—based on, inter alia, the effectiveness of reprisals against armed groups, or the absence of alternative enforcement mechanisms with a real impact on the conduct of the hostilities in NIAC—militate in favour of allowing reprisals in limited circumstances.

43 Notwithstanding these arguments and the absence of an explicit reference to the notion of reprisals in Common Article 3 (and AP II), the ICRC concluded, on the basis of the interpretation described above, that there is a customary principle according to which '[t]he parties to non-international armed conflicts do not have the right to resort to belligerent reprisals'.[121] It is our view that the legitimacy of this conclusion is reinforced by the following considerations.

44 First, the ban of reprisals in NIAC corresponds to the growing tendency towards outlawing them altogether in IAC. It is also consistent with the current trend initiated by international criminal tribunals, the ICRC, and scholars to bring the IHL applicable in NIAC into line with that applicable in IAC.

45 Secondly, the argument according to which Common Article 3 (and AP II) might allow reprisals in NIAC because these rules do not expressly prohibit them is inapt. Indeed, it is

---

[110] See UNGA Res 48/52 and 49/207.
[111] HRComm Res 1993/66 and 1994/84, and Res 1995/74.
[112] See Kalshoven, above n 35, at 78.
[113] Darcy, above n 20, at 216–20; Kalshoven, above n 3, at 269.
[114] Price, above n 17, at 77; Darcy, above n 20, at 218.   [115] Darcy, above n 20, at 191.
[116] See section B.I above. See also Kalshoven, above n 35, at 78.
[117] Kalshoven, above n 3, at 279; Bílková, above n 18, at 44–7.   [118] Bílková, above n 18, at 55.
[119] Darcy, above n 20, at 217.   [120] Kalshoven, above n 3, at 279.
[121] ICRC CIHL Study, Rule 148, at 527.

tantamount to saying that the prohibition against violations of the laws of war—which is, by definition, binding—does not apply in certain circumstances because it is not specifically stated. In fact, the silence of IHL in NIAC can be attributed to the fear expressed by some states that any explicit reference to the notion of reprisals, even by way of prohibition, could give the impression *a contrario* that they are permissible in this context.[122]

46 Thirdly, the risk that reprisals will generate a cycle of vengeance is reinforced in NIACs, which often lead to highly confused situations. A wide variety of actors is generally involved in these types of conflicts.[123] Some armed groups are well organized and structured, control a large part of the territory, and are widely supported by the local population. Others lack structure and organization, and act independently of any popular support and land base. Some are more sensitive than others to the pressure exercised on them by their adversaries, and to the necessity of protecting the population surrounding them. In these circumstances, it may prove difficult for states to figure out how the geo-strategic interests and economic and social ties of such groups might be adversely affected by reprisals, and, ultimately, to assess precisely whether taking these measures will induce compliance with IHL.

47 Fourthly, if reprisals were authorized in NIAC and states were able to target armed groups with precision then, according to the principle of equality of belligerents, these groups should also be allowed to take such measures. Clearly, reprisals would be an inefficient mechanism for inducing respect for IHL if they were available to only one party to the conflict. Furthermore, states are not the only ones bound by IHL. Whatever might have been the point of view expressed by certain delegations during the negotiation of AP II,[124] it is now widely recognized that armed groups are also subjects of international law, in that they have an international legal personality (albeit limited) in order to exercise certain rights and duties deriving from Common Article 3, AP II, and customary norms.[125] Accordingly, they should, in theory, be able to enforce an opposing party's compliance with these norms, including by resorting to reprisals.[126] Obviously, this approach could entail dangerous consequences and raise delicate questions. Should every armed group participating in a NIAC be entitled to have recourse to reprisals? Only certain armed groups? In that case, which ones? Only quasi-states which control part of the territory and have established an administration similar to that of a state? Or only those that are structured and organized in such way that they are capable of exercising strict control over any reprisals they initiate? It would seem that, given today's conflict dynamics, if non-state armed groups involved in NIAC were authorized to take retaliatory measures against states or other armed groups, an escalation of violence would in most cases be inevitable.

48 Fifthly, should reprisals be authorized in NIAC, the conditions in which they could be exercised would need to be clarified. However, precisely determining these conditions and their scope would not be a simple matter: Common Article 3 (and AP II) are silent on

---

[122] See ICRC CIHL Study, Rule 148, at 528, and the statements referred to in fn 118.

[123] M. Sassòli, 'Taking Armed Groups Seriously: Ways to Improve their Compliance with International Humanitarian Law', 1 *International Humanitarian Legal Studies* (2010) 5, at 14–15.

[124] See MN 40.   [125] Zegveld, above n 21, at 89. See also Sassòli, above n 123, at 13.

[126] A. Cassese, 'The Status of Rebels under the 1977 Geneva Protocol on Non-International Armed Conflicts', 30 *ICLQ* (1981) 416, at 430–1; Zegveld, above n 21, at 89–90. As observed by Ruffert, 'modern warfare against private belligerents such as terrorist groups is not covered by the law of reprisals unless violations that have occurred, either inadvertently or with intent, may be attributed to a certain state. It is submitted that the general shift in the recognition of private actors as subjects of public international law might trigger a future change in the pertinent rules, which has not yet emerged' (Ruffert, above n 51, at 930).

this issue, and the limited practices of states do not easily assist in addressing the lacuna. Indeed, states are reluctant to declare openly that their actions constitute reprisals in NIAC, since they remain wary of their potentially disastrous effects on the state's own population and armed forces. Moreover, military manuals do not shed much light on the matter. On the contrary, as seen above, several of them preclude recourse to reprisals in NIAC. It should also be noted that certain requirements—such as the fact that reprisals must be ordered at the highest political or military level—might not be easily applicable to every armed group, especially those which lack structural and hierarchical foundations. In the same vein, imputing the originally unlawful action to the party against whom reprisal actions are taken may be tested in light of the diversity and mobility of actors involved in NIAC. The theoretical and practical difficulties raised by the application of the principle of proportionality would also be increased given the *de facto* inequality of belligerents that characterizes such environments. Thus, the conditions for exercising reprisals would need to be adapted to the specificities of armed groups participating in NIAC. The wide diversity of these groups would mean that clarity would be very difficult to establish.

Sixthly, authorizing reprisals in NIAC would contradict the efforts invested by the UN, the ICRC, non-governmental organizations, and some states in promoting respect for IHL. A dangerous—not to say contradictory or incomprehensible—signal would be sent to non-state actors if they were told, on the one hand, that they must respect IHL in all circumstances and, on the other, that they are legally entitled to breach it when their adversary does not respect it. This danger is increased by the fact that 'individual and collective behaviour in time of war is [already] generally governed by the *lex talionis*', and the 'frequent recourse to the argument of reciprocity so as not to comply with IHL'.[127]

Lastly, it should be emphasized that several collective bodies that operate at the international level have now been entrusted with the competence to enforce IHL in both IAC and NIAC. In other words, guaranteeing respect for IHL in NIAC is no longer the reserve of states. This observation must be qualified, however, and will be re-examined in section E of this chapter.

D. Legal Consequences of a Violation

It should be recalled at the outset that reprisals are acts that would be in breach of IHL but which are lawful in certain circumstances and under specific conditions. This means that if these circumstances exist and if these conditions are met, such acts are considered 'not wrongful'.[128]

It is also worth noting that, in principle, the legal regimes governing state responsibility and individual responsibility are distinct.[129] In other words, they are both governed by separate sets of norms, respectively, the international rules on laws of state responsibility, regulating, inter alia, the 'circumstances precluding wrongfulness',[130] and international

---

[127] D. Munoz-Rojas and J.-J. Frésard, 'The Roots of Behaviour in War: Understanding and Preventing IHL Violations', 86 *IRRC* 853 (2004) 189, at 201–2.
[128] For a discussion on whether an individual can escape individual criminal responsibility in international criminal law by claiming that the action was taken in reprisal, see Ch 36 of this volume.
[129] P.-M. Dupuy, 'International Criminal Responsibility of the Individual and International Responsibility of the State', in A. Cassese, P. Gaeta, and J.R.W.D. Jones (eds), *The Rome Statute of the International Criminal Court: A Commentary* (Oxford: OUP, 2002) 1085, at 1091.
[130] See Arts 20–27 ILC Articles on State Responsibility.

criminal law, including the rules on 'defences' or 'grounds for excluding criminal responsibility'.[131] Thus, the application of one set of norms does not per se depend on the other. That being said, these two bodies of law share elements in common. Indeed, norms governing state and individual responsibility in case of reprisals are grounded in IHL, which, to a certain extent, forms a coherent whole.[132] Overall, a proper balance needs to be found between the necessity of maintaining the specificities of each set of norms and the imperative of ensuring a degree of consistency between them.

I. Violation of legal requirements

53 A state and an individual may be held accountable if they ordered or carried out measures which constitute belligerent reprisals prohibited by the Geneva Conventions (and AP I), or if they violated the strict customary requirements under which belligerent reprisals may be exercised. Accordingly, they are prevented from arguing that their illegal acts were 'not wrongful' or were 'justified' because they constitute reactions to prior serious violations of IHL. Both the state and the individual may be liable for such acts.

54 However, as a result of the distinction between the legal regimes of state responsibility and individual responsibility, a state could be held accountable for violating the laws governing belligerent reprisals, while, at the same time, an individual might escape conviction for the same violation. For example, a state could be declared responsible for ordering illegal belligerent reprisals, while the commander executing them might have a valid defence if he or she could reasonably believe that the reprisal order he or she carried out was not manifestly illegal.[133] On the other hand, the reverse case—where a state is exonerated from responsibility for reprisals and the individual who executed them is found responsible—can occur only if the individual is unaware of the decision of a state upon which he or she is depending to resort to reprisals.

II. Circumstance precluding wrongfulness and justification

55 An act of reprisal taken by an injured state in order to induce the target state to comply with IHL is precluded from being considered wrongful when committed in accordance with the laws of war and, in particular, with the requirements of purpose, proportionality, subsidiary, authorization, and termination discussed in section B.III above. But in contrast to justifications in international criminal law, circumstances precluding wrongfulness (such as reprisals) do not make the act in question lawful: they merely render definitively or temporarily ineffective the obligations violated, thereby exonerating the state from its international responsibility.[134] In addition, it could be inferred, by analogy with Article 27 of the ILC Articles on State Responsibility, that invoking reprisals, like any other circumstances precluding wrongfulness, 'is without prejudice to the question of compensation for any material loss caused by the act in question'.[135] Thus, not only the targeted state but also

---

[131] See Art 31 ICC Statute.

[132] B. Bonafè, *The Relationship between State and Individual Responsibility for International Crimes* (The Hague: Martinus Nijhoff, 2009), at 163.

[133] A. Zimmermann, 'Superior Orders', in Cassese, Gaeta, and Jones (eds), above n 129, 957, at 969–70.

[134] J. Salmon, 'Les circonstances excluant l'illicéité', in K. Zemanek and J. Salmon, *La responsabilité internationale* (Paris: Pedone, 1988) 89, at 92. For a summary on the doctrinal debates over this controversial issue, see S. Szurek, 'The Notion of Circumstances Precluding Wrongfulness', in J. Crawford, A. Pellet, and S. Olleson (eds), *The Law of International Responsibility* (Oxford: OUP, 2010) 427, at 435.

[135] Art 27 ILC Articles on State Responsibility.

the state resorting to reprisals may be under an obligation to compensate for the material loss caused. One might consider that such an obligation to provide compensation applies only when a circumstance precluding wrongfulness (such as necessity or duress) is not caused by the conduct of the state against which it is invoked.[136] In the case of reprisals, the state claiming compensation would, through its own unlawful conduct, have initially triggered the reprisal which resulted in the material loss. If, on the contrary, an obligation of compensation is considered to exist, the legal basis of such an obligation for losses caused by acts the wrongfulness of which is precluded remains controversial among commentators on the Articles on state responsibility.[137] In IHL, it could be considered to be in line with the obligation of Article 91 AP I, which imposes on belligerents that violate IHL an obligation to pay compensation 'if the case demands'. Grounded in considerations of justice, such an obligation is even more justified given that measures of reprisal can bring with them severe material loss and that, as will be seen below, the person who engages in them (and is allowed to invoke them as a criminal defence) is not personally bound to provide compensation.

Since the regimes governing the responsibility of the state and of the individual are distinct, the existence of a circumstance precluding wrongfulness of state conduct should not have any influence on the issue of individual responsibility, unless it is shown that a corresponding defence exists under international criminal law.[138] In this regard, it should be noted that reprisals are not listed in Article 31 of the Statute of the International Criminal Court (ICC Statute) among the '[g]rounds for excluding criminal responsibility'. The Statutes of the ICTY, the International Criminal Tribunal for Rwanda, and the Special Court for Sierra Leone are also silent on the matter. This is not surprising given the incertitude surrounding the scope of these measures and their conditions of exercise. In fact, some states expressed concern during ICC Statute negotiations 'over the inclusion of reprisals under defences', and 'question[ed] […] which set of rules governing reprisals should apply'.[139] Notwithstanding this silence, ICTY jurisprudence implicitly recognizes that reprisals may be invoked, albeit in limited circumstances, as a defence to a charge of war crimes. Indeed, the ICTY has spelled out the IHL requirements that reprisals must satisfy, and examined whether they had been met in certain cases.[140] The justification of reprisal had also been pleaded as a defence in many cases from the aftermath of the Second World War.[141] This had led some scholars to assert that reprisals could be raised as a defence.[142] On a substantive level, it should be recalled that recourse to these measures is

---

[136] ILC Commentary, at 86, para 5.
[137] M. Forteau, 'Reparation in the Event of a Circumstance Precluding Wrongfulness', in Crawford, Pellet, and Olleson (eds), above n 134, 887, at 891.
[138] Bonafè, above n 132, at 150.
[139] *Report of the Preparatory Committee on the Establishment of an International Criminal Court*, GA OR, 51st session, Supp No 22, UN Doc A/51/22, vol I (1996), para 209; *Report of the Preparatory Committee on the Establishment of an International Criminal Court*, UN Doc A/51/22, vol II (1996), at 103.
[140] See ICTY, *The Prosecutor v Kupreškić*, above n 33, para 531; ICTY, *The Prosecutor v Martić*, above n 95, para 10; ICTY, *The Prosecutor v Martić*, Trial Chamber Judgment, above n 69, para 468; ICTY, *The Prosecutor v Martić*, Appeals Chamber Judgment, above n 69, para 265. See also jurisprudence cited above n 50.
[141] See jurisprudence cited above n 50.
[142] M. Bothe, 'War Crimes', in Cassese, Gaeta, and Jones (eds), above n 129, 379, at 387; A. Cassese, 'Justifications and Excuses in International Criminal Law', in Cassese, Gaeta, and Jones (eds), above n 129, 951, at 951–2; S. Darcy, 'Defences to International Crimes', in W. Schabas and N. Bernaz (eds), *Routledge Handbook of International Criminal Law* (London: Routledge, 2011) 231, at 239; E. van Sliedregt, *The Criminal Responsibility of Individuals for Violations of International Humanitarian Law* (The Hague: T.M.C. Asser Press, 2003), at 291–4.

warranted by the necessity to stop serious violations of IHL or to prevent their recurrence. As rightly pointed out by Cassese,

> [i]n these and other, similar cases, society and the legal order make a positive appraisal of what would otherwise be misconduct. Society and law want the person so to behave, because in weighing up two conflicting values (the need not to use prohibited weapons and the necessity to impose on the enemy belligerent compliance with law) they give pride of place to one of them, although this entails the infringement of the legal rules designed to satisfy the other need.[143]

57 In line with this approach, the conduct of individuals taking reprisals in accordance with IHL requirements is lawful. Thus, no obligation of compensation arises.[144] This is unlike the case of a state where, as stated above, reprisals which are allowed might arguably still entail compensation.

58 For the sake of completeness, three final remarks should be made. First, it remains to be seen whether, despite the silence of the ICC Statute, ICC judges will allow resort to the defence of reprisal under Articles 31(3)[145] and 21 of that instrument and, accordingly, accept that such defence is in accordance with 'established principles of international law of armed conflict'[146] or with 'general principles of law'.[147] Should the ICC take a different position, a gap would exist between, on the one hand, the ICC system and, on the other hand, IHL and the jurisprudence of the ad hoc Tribunals (under which reprisals can be invoked). Obviously, such a gap could be the source of considerable tension between the ICC and a number of states, since the possibility of having recourse to limited forms of reprisals remains a highly sensitive topic. Moreover, as argued above, this lacuna would prevent the guarantee of a consistent application of the principles governing state and individual responsibility.

59 Secondly, the justification of reprisals must be distinguished from the defence of *tu quoque*. According to the latter, a violation of IHL by an individual might be justified by the fact that the adversary (prosecuting the individual in question) has also committed a similar crime.[148] However, this argument runs against the 'non reciprocal' nature of IHL obligations and is declared invalid, at least as a defence to a crime.[149]

60 Lastly, reprisals may not be raised as a circumstance precluding wrongfulness or as a defence to charges of certain international crimes, such as torture, crimes against humanity, or genocide. Indeed, the last two crimes—which may also be committed in times of peace—are characterized by the commission of criminal acts mainly directed against the civilian population which, as seen above, can never be targeted by way of reprisals. These crimes are also of such magnitude and seriousness that no one could reasonably argue that committing similar acts constituting crimes against humanity or genocide in reprisal could contribute to the ending of the original violations. In addition, Article 50(1)(b) of the ILC Articles on State Responsibility precludes taking countermeasures when

---

[143] Cassese, above n 142, at 951–2.   [144] Ibid, at 952–3.

[145] Art 31(3) ICC Statute provides that '[a]t trial, the Court may consider a ground for excluding criminal responsibility other than those referred to in paragraph 1 where such a ground is derived from applicable law as set forth in article 21'.

[146] Art 21(1)(b) ICC Statute. See Darcy, above n 142, at 240.   [147] Art 21(1)(c) ICC Statute.

[148] ICTY, *The Prosecutor v Kupreškić*, above n 33, para 515.

[149] The question as to whether the defence of *tu quoque* can have an impact on punishment is subject to debate. For a detailed analysis of the concept of *tu quoque*, see S. Yee, 'The Tu Quoque Argument as a Defence to International Crimes, Prosecution or Punishment', 3 *Chinese Journal of International Law* (2004) 87, at 124–33; A. Cassese et al, *International Criminal Law, Cases & Commentary* (Oxford: OUP, 2011), at 516–22.

they affect 'obligations for the protection of fundamental human rights'. In the same vein, at the individual level, Article 21(3) of the ICC Statute states that '[t]he application and interpretation of law pursuant to this article must be consistent with internationally recognised human rights'. It goes without saying that the commission of acts of torture, crimes against humanity, or genocide by way of reprisals would violate fundamental (or internationally recognized) human rights.

E. Critical Assessment

A consensus is progressively emerging in favour of a general prohibition of belligerent reprisals in both IAC and NIAC. This trend must be welcomed. Indeed, the efficiency of such measures in enforcing IHL is far from being proven. Belligerent reprisals often lead to an escalation of violence, especially if armed groups are implicated. Also, their legitimacy and fairness are more than doubtful. As forcefully stated by the ICTY, 61

> [i]t cannot be denied that reprisals against civilians are inherently a barbarous means of seeking compliance with international law. The most blatant reason for the universal revulsion that usually accompanies reprisals is that they may not only be arbitrary but are also not directed specifically at the individual authors of the initial violation. Reprisals typically are taken in situations where the individuals personally responsible for the breach are either unknown or out of reach. These retaliatory measures are aimed instead at other more vulnerable individuals or groups. They are individuals or groups who may not even have any degree of solidarity with the presumed authors of the initial violation; they may share with them only the links of nationality and allegiance to the same rulers.[150]

Furthermore, an inherent contradiction is at the heart of the concept of reprisals: how can a violation of IHL by one belligerent contribute to respect for the same body of law by its adversary? This paradox underlies all the ambiguities studied above regarding the scope of application of reprisals, the conditions of their exercise, their applicability in NIAC, and their use as a defence in criminal proceedings. One might also ask, however, whether the powers of certain collective international bodies—such as the Security Council, the UN Commission on Human Rights, international criminal tribunals, international commissions of investigation, the International Humanitarian Fact-Finding Commission (IHFFC), or the ICRC—could constitute adequate substitutes for reprisals. Clearly, the international system of enforcing IHL is less than perfect. The deterrent and coercive effects of international tribunals are limited. The organs especially designed to monitor the conduct of belligerents, such as the IHFFC, have rarely been used in practice and are mainly geared towards states.[151] The bodies created under the legal frameworks other than IHL also have their limits.[152] Such deficiencies should not, however, lead to the revival of the institution of belligerent reprisals. On the contrary, they should prompt states to find adequate solutions to curtail reprisals by strengthening existing mechanisms and improving their functions, or by studying alternative solutions.[153] 62

Accordingly, new ways of encouraging, monitoring, and controlling respect for IHL by states and armed groups[154] should be devised, including setting up an international 63

---

[150] ICTY, *The Prosecutor v Kupreškić*, above n 33, para 528.
[151] See *ICRC Report on 'Strengthening Legal Protection for Victims of Armed Conflicts'*, 31st International Conference on the Red Cross and Red Crescent (2011), at 26.
[152] Ibid.   [153] Ibid, at 27.   [154] Sassòli, above n 123, at 41–2.

institution entrusted with the main task of overseeing compliance with IHL. However, such an institution would be effective only if several conditions were met. For instance, all guarantees should be put in place in order that it might be fully independent and neutral, able to act without the consent of belligerents and to impose binding decisions on them. Such an organ should also benefit from wide-ranging powers and be allowed to decide freely how to exercise them in a given situation. These powers might include:

— classifying the nature of the hostilities;
— negotiating agreements with armed forces;
— inviting states and armed groups to report periodically on respect for and implementation of IHL;
— gathering evidence on IHL breaches;
— identifying alleged perpetrators;
— if necessary, publicly denouncing these breaches;
— imposing upon belligerents measures to prevent further violations; and
— reporting on regular basis to the Security Council and recommending to it appropriate measures.

64 It is only if new solutions are put in place to reinforce respect for IHL and, in particular, if a truly neutral and powerful mechanism is offered to states and armed groups to monitor compliance with international norms, that the temptation of these actors to resort to reprisals will subside and that, ultimately, the lack of legitimacy of this archaic method in contemporary reality will be exposed.

JÉRÔME DE HEMPTINNE*

* I would like to thank the editors of this chapter, Mr Guido Acquaviva, Mr Christopher Black, Ms Mariya Nikolova, and Ms Iris van der Heijden, for their revision of the text and their useful comments. All errors are mine.

Chapter 30. Dissemination of the Conventions, Including in Time of Armed Conflict

	MN
A. Introduction	1
I. General remarks	1
II. Historical context	7
B. Meaning and Application	11
I. Who disseminates the Conventions?	11
II. Time factor in dissemination	20
III. Categories of addressees of dissemination	22
a. Armed forces	23
b. Civilian population	30
IV. Methods and content of dissemination	38
C. Relevance in Non-International Armed Conflicts	47
D. Legal Consequences of a Violation	57
E. Critical Assessment	60

Select Bibliography

David, E., 'Dissemination of International Humanitarian Law at University Level', 27 *IRRC* 257 (1987) 155

Hampson, F., 'Fighting by the Rules: Instructing the Armed Forces in Humanitarian Principles', 29 *IRRC* 269 (1989) 111

ICRC, *Exploring Humanitarian Law, IHL Guide: A Legal Manual for EHL Teachers* (Geneva: ICRC, 2009)

Klenner, D., 'Training in International Humanitarian Law', 82 *IRRC* 839 (2000) 653

de Mulinen, F., *Handbook on the Law of War for Armed Forces* (Geneva: ICRC, 1989)

Pictet Commentary GC I, at 347–9

Pictet Commentary GC II, at 257–9

Pictet Commentary GC III, at 613–15

Pictet Commentary GC IV, at 580–2

Surbeck, J.-J., 'La diffusion du droit international humanitaire, condition de son application', in Mélanges Pictet 537

Verri, P., 'Institutions militaires: le problème de l'enseignement du droit des conflits armés et de l'adaptation des règlements à ses prescriptions humanitaires', in Mélanges Pictet 603

Zys, D. (ed), *Practical Guide on Dissemination for National Societies* (Geneva: Henry-Dunant Institute, 1983)

A. Introduction

I. General remarks

1   Each Geneva Convention (GC) of 1949 contains one Article providing for the obligation of states to disseminate its text 'in time of peace as in time of war […] as widely as possible […] so that the principles thereof may become known to the entire population' (Article 47

GC I, Article 48 GC II, Article 127 GC III, Article 144 GC IV). It emphasizes the duty of states to include the study of the Geneva Conventions in their programmes of military and, if possible, civil instruction. Geneva Convention III adds that any military or other authorities who in time of war are responsible for prisoners of war (POWs) must possess the text of the Convention and be specially instructed as to its provisions (Article 127 paragraph 2). The officers in charge of POW camps have to ensure that these provisions are made known to the camp staff and the guards, and are held responsible for their application (Article 39). Furthermore, the Convention must be posted in places where the POWs can read it (Article 41). Geneva Convention IV provides for the same obligations with regard to any civilian, military, police, or other authorities who assume responsibilities in respect of civilians, particularly in places of internment (Articles 99 and 144 paragraph 2).

2   The obligation to disseminate texts of the Geneva Conventions is included in the chapters on the execution of the Conventions. It clearly demonstrates the conviction of the states parties that the effective application of these treaties would not be possible without making their rules known first and foremost to the armed forces and civilian authorities, but also to the civilian population as a whole. The obligation to spread knowledge of the Geneva Conventions is one of the measures of their national implementation, referred to in Article 45 GC I and Article 46 GC II, and is a corollary to the commitment, confirmed in Common Article 1 of the Geneva Conventions, to respect and to ensure respect for their provisions in all circumstances.[1] There is not much likelihood that the rules will be observed if they are not known by those responsible for applying them. In this context the famous axiom from the Pictet Commentary is often quoted: 'One of the worst enemies of the Geneva Conventions is ignorance.'[2] This ignorance cannot be excused in the light of clear legal obligations to provide instruction in international humanitarian law (IHL): 'Whilst ignorance of the law is not generally accepted as a defence, the first step to enforcement of the law of armed conflict must be to ensure as wide a knowledge of its terms as possible'.[3]

3   In more concrete terms, the primary purpose of dissemination of the Geneva Conventions is to prevent violations of their norms. 'As the old saying goes—an ounce of prevention is worth a pound of cure—the training in the Conventions given today may prevent prosecution of the war crime of tomorrow';[4] education is a better guarantee of respect for humanitarian rules than any sanction could ever be. This preventive aspect of dissemination is emphasized in military manuals and other national documents.[5] Some states formulate this purpose simply as to 'develop an awareness of soldiers of what is right and what is wrong',[6] and to ensure that they know that violations lead to penal and disciplinary sanctions.

---

[1] See in detail Ch 6, MN 14 and 18 and Ch 32, section C.IV, of this volume.
[2] Pictet Commentary GC I, at 348. See also ICRC CIHL Study, at 3216; and ICRC CIHL Database, Rule 142, Section B, III.
[3] The UK *Manual of the Law of Armed Conflict*, ICRC CIHL Database, Rule 142, Section B, III.
[4] J.J. McGowan, 'Training in the Geneva and Hague Conventions: A Dead Issue?', XIV *Revue de droit pénal militaire et de droit de la guerre* (1975) 51, at 57. See also ICRC Commentary APs, at 961.
[5] ICRC CIHL Study, at 3211, 3214–17, 3220–1, 3227; ICRC CIHL Database, Rule 142, Section A, III and VI, and Section B, III. See also Israel Supreme Court sitting as the High Court of Justice, *Physicians for Human Rights v The Commander of the IDF in the West Bank, The Commander of the IDF Forces in Gaza*, case HCJ 2117/02, Judgment of 28 April 2002; and *Report of the Winograd Commission*, Chapter 14, para 20, 30 January 2008, in Sassòli/Bouvier/Quintin, at 1278.
[6] ICRC CIHL Study, at 3215, 3216–17; and ICRC CIHL Database, Rule 142, Section A, VI.

For armed forces, respect for IHL is a matter of order and discipline. Anyone who wants 'his troops to display tactically efficient, correct and disciplined behavior in combat must continuously invest in instruction and training, which must include [IHL]'.[7]

There are also other purposes of widespread dissemination of the Geneva Conventions. It is not only a factor for their effective application by combatants and civilians, but also—by spreading the moral principles of humanity—a factor for developing the spirit of peace in the whole population,[8] for the 'rejection of violence and the refusal of indifference to suffering'.[9] As stated in one military manual, 'Providing information about [IHL] is the necessary basis to create common consciousness and to further the attitude of the peoples towards a greater acceptance of these principles as an achievement of the social and cultural development of mankind.'[10]

It is interesting to note that many states refer simply to their explicit legal obligation to disseminate the Geneva Conventions with respect to both the armed forces and the civilian population.[11] Some states even repeat the text of Article 47 GC I in their military manuals and national legislation.[12] It is very rare that the value of IHL dissemination is questioned.[13]

II. Historical context

The obligation of states to 'take the necessary steps to acquaint their troops [...] with the provisions of [law] and to make them known to the people at large' was laid down for the first time in the 1906 GC (Article 26). This provision was repeated in the 1929 GC I (Article 27). The 1929 GC II contained a less concrete obligation in this respect, merely stating that the text of the Convention should be posted to enable POWs to inform themselves of it (Article 84). The 1899 Hague Convention II and 1907 Hague Convention IV should also be mentioned as documents that provided for the obligation of states to 'issue instructions to their armed land forces which shall be in conformity with the [Hague] Regulations' (Article 1). However, this obligation was more vague than the one contained in the 1906 GC: issuing instructions is not the same as the obligation to ensure that armed forces receive them.[14] In addition, the Hague Regulations did not mention dissemination

---

[7] D. Klenner, 'Training in International Humanitarian Law', 82 *IRRC* 839 (2000) 653, at 656. See also ICRC CIHL Database, Rule 142, Section B, III.

[8] Pictet Commentary GC I, at 349.

[9] D. Zys (ed), *Practical Guide on Dissemination for National Societies* (Geneva: Henry-Dunant Institute, 1983), Chapter 1, at 2.

[10] Germany's *Military Manual*, ICRC CIHL Study, at 3215. References to values, ethical dimensions of military professionalism, sensitization of the population, and promotion of culture of peace are also present in national documents adopted by, e.g., South Africa, Slovakia, Niger (ICRC CIHL Study, at 3239, 3275, 3280), and Philippines (ICRC CIHL Database, Rule 142, Section B, III). Other, more detailed reasons for dissemination are discussed in K. Dörmann, 'Dissemination and Monitoring Compliance of International Humanitarian Law', in W. Heintschel von Heinegg and V. Epping (eds), *International Humanitarian Law: Facing New Challenges* (Berlin, Heidelberg: Springer, 2007) 225, *passim*; Pictet Commentary GC I, at 349.

[11] ICRC CIHL Study, at 3212, 3214–15, 3217, 3219–20, 3222, 3224, 3227, 3232, 3243; ICRC CIHL Database, Rule 142, Section A, III, and VI. This obligation is referred to in numerous documents adopted by the components and bodies of the IRCM, see ICRC CIHL Study, at 3257 (ICRC and Council of Delegates).

[12] ICRC CIHL Study, at 3218, 3220; ICRC CIHL Database, Rule 142, Section A, III and IV: Sri Lanka.

[13] Cf ICRC CIHL Study, at 3244–5 (anonymous states, paras 479 and 482).

[14] F. Hampson, 'Fighting by the Rules: Instructing the Armed Forces in Humanitarian Principles', 29 *IRRC* 269 (1989) 111, at 112.

to the civilian population. The above provisions were developed and made more specific in the Geneva Conventions of 1949.

8   International humanitarian law treaties adopted after 1949 usually provide for the obligation of states parties to disseminate them. One might mention the 1954 Hague Convention for the Protection of Cultural Property in the Event of Armed Conflict (Article 25), the 1999 Second Protocol to that Convention (Article 30), the 1980 Convention on Certain Conventional Weapons (Article 6), its Second Amended Protocol (Article 14) and Fourth Protocol (Article 2), and the Convention on the Rights of the Child (Article 42) and its Optional Protocol of May 2000 on the involvement of children in armed conflict (Article 6).

9   The obligation to disseminate IHL is reiterated and developed in the Additional Protocols of 1977. Article 83 of Additional Protocol (AP) I basically repeats the text of the respective Articles of the Geneva Conventions, putting more emphasis on encouraging civilians to study them, and introducing the obligation of civilian authorities, responsible for their application in time of armed conflict, to be fully acquainted therewith. However, dissemination to civilians is still dealt with in less strict terms than instruction to armed forces. The difference between AP I and the Geneva Conventions is that AP I provides for new measures, such as qualified personnel (Article 6), legal advisers (Article 82), obligations of commanders (Article 87(2)), and implementing legislation (Article 84), to strengthen, inter alia, the obligation to disseminate. As for AP II, its Article 19 contains a very general obligation to disseminate the Protocol as widely as possible. Despite its vagueness, it still represents progress in comparison to Common Article 3 of the Geneva Conventions, which makes no reference to dissemination in non-international armed conflicts (NIACs).

10   That states and other parties to armed conflicts carry out dissemination activities in practice and consider themselves legally bound to do so, attests to the fact that this rule has become a norm of customary international law.[15]

B. Meaning and Application

I. Who disseminates the Conventions?

11   The Geneva Conventions state in clear terms that it is first and foremost the duty of states to disseminate IHL. This rule is confirmed by an extensive practice of states, and has been reiterated on numerous occasions by international organizations and at international conferences.[16]

12   Different subjects and entities are engaged when states fulfil their task of disseminating IHL. Article 45 GC I and Article 46 GC II stipulate that in the execution of the Conventions, states act through their Commanders-in-Chief. This rule is further developed in AP I. Under the terms of its Article 87(2), it is the commanders at all levels of the chain of command who, 'commensurate with their level of responsibility [...] ensure that members of the armed forces under their command are aware of their obligations under the Conventions'. Article 82 AP I contains a specific requirement to ensure that legal

---

[15] See ICRC CIHL Study, Rules 142 and 143, at 501–8.
[16] Ibid, see in particular fns 39–41, 43–4, 67–8, 72–5; UNGA Res 63/125 of 2008, para 5; and Res 67/93 of 2012, para 6.

advisers in armed forces are available to advise military commanders 'on the appropriate instruction to be given to the armed forces' on the application of the Geneva Conventions and AP I.[17] Under Article 6 AP I, states should 'endeavour [...] to train qualified personnel to facilitate the application of the Conventions'. Although potential dissemination activities of qualified persons are not explicitly mentioned in this provision, there seems to be no doubt that Article 6 encompasses such activities as well.[18]

In more than 100 states a special mechanism has been set up, namely an inter-ministerial IHL committee, aiming at the better fulfilment of the state's obligations under the Geneva Conventions, including in the field of dissemination. Although such committees are not provided for in any IHL treaty, their number is growing systematically, and one of their usual tasks is drawing up and implementing a national dissemination programme.[19]

States are assisted in carrying out dissemination activities by their National Red Cross or Red Crescent Societies. In accordance with the Statutes of the International Red Cross and Red Crescent Movement (IRCM) of 2006 (Article 3(2)) and their own statutes adopted domestically, National Societies have a mandate to disseminate, and to help their governments to disseminate, knowledge of IHL. They must take initiatives to that effect, and recruit, train, and assign the necessary staff.[20] Their International Federation also helps promote IHL and cooperates with National Societies in this field.[21] The role of National Red Cross and Red Crescent Societies in dissemination of IHL is officially recognized by many countries.[22] Some states provide National Societies with funds for this purpose.[23]

The International Committee of the Red Cross (ICRC) is the most important international ally of states and their National Red Cross and Red Crescent Societies in the field of dissemination of the Geneva Conventions.[24] It has delegates all over the world who are assigned to dissemination tasks, it draws up dissemination programmes and special teaching materials for different types of audience, organizes numerous courses, seminars, and workshops, and runs campaigns to raise public awareness of the existing regulations.[25] The need to cooperate with the ICRC in the field of dissemination of IHL both for armed

---

[17] As for the obligations of commanders and the role of their legal advisers in the field of dissemination of IHL, see in more detail MN 24–25.

[18] ICRC Commentary APs, at 94.

[19] Information on these committees, including their mandate, is regularly updated by the ICRC Advisory Service on International Humanitarian Law, available as 'National Committees and Other National Bodies on International Humanitarian Law' (31 August 2014), available at <https://www.icrc.org/en/document/table-national-committees-and-other-national-bodies-international-humanitarian-law>.

[20] J.-L. Chopard, 'Dissemination of the Humanitarian Rules and Cooperation with National Red Cross and Red Crescent Societies for the Purpose of Prevention', 35 *IRRC* 306 (1995) 244. There are many examples of activities undertaken by National Societies in this field—for practical tools see, e.g., Zys, above n 9, and a trainer's book T. Morris, *Learning about International Humanitarian Law* (Copenhagen: Danish Red Cross, 2011).

[21] Art 5(1)(B)(c) of the Constitution of the International Federation of Red Cross and Red Crescent Societies of 2007.

[22] ICRC CIHL Study, at 3235–6, 3241–2, 3276–8, 3281; ICRC CIHL Database, Rule 142, Section A, VI.

[23] ICRC CIHL Study, at 506.

[24] Art 5 para 2(g) and para 4(a) IRCM Statutes of 2006; Art 4 para 1(g) and Art 5 para 1(a) of the Statutes of the ICRC of 2003.

[25] It is not possible to describe the countless activities of the ICRC in the field of dissemination of IHL. They are presented on the ICRC website, at <http://www.icrc.org/eng/what-we-do/building-respect-ihl/index.jsp>.

forces and civilians is formally recognized by states in their national regulations,[26] as well as by the United Nations (UN).[27]

16   United Nations organs and bodies, specialized agencies, and intergovernmental and non-governmental organizations are also encouraged to initiate, coordinate, and support dissemination programmes, thus supplementing states' activities in this field.[28] The UN Secretary-General has been invited a number of times to encourage the study and instruction of the relevant principles by the means at his disposal.[29]

17   One should also recognize the role of the International Institute of Humanitarian Law in San Remo in organizing international courses for officers and in the publication of instruction materials supporting national dissemination activities.[30]

18   The role of the media in spreading knowledge of the Geneva Conventions cannot be overestimated. They have an important part to play in making the population aware of certain rules, even if their preventive capacity is limited.[31]

19   In the case of NIACs, armed opposition groups must disseminate IHL to their armed forces.[32]

II. Time factor in dissemination

20   To be effective, dissemination must take place in peacetime. 'Just as the preparations for the military and economic aspects of a possible armed conflict are made in peacetime, so must the groundwork for the humanitarian aspects, in particular respect for IHL, be laid before war breaks out.'[33] If something is not practised in times of peace, it cannot be expected to work in times of armed conflict. The importance of starting dissemination in peacetime is acknowledged in states' national legislation and military manuals.[34] As stated in one of them, 'once a conflict has started [...] the authorities concerned have by then turned to questions of greater priority that may overwhelm any argument in favour of humanitarian conduct'.[35]

21   While instruction in the content of the Geneva Conventions is required in time of peace, there is still more specific instruction that is needed in time of war. This may be deduced from the expression 'armed fighting forces' used in Article 47 GC I and Article 48 GC II. In addition, Article 127 GC III and Article 144 GC IV clearly provide for special instruction to some specific branches of military authorities (like military police and intelligence) and civilian authorities (including civilian police), who, in time of war, assume responsibilities in respect of POWs and protected civilians. They must possess the text of the Conventions, ensure that it

---

[26] ICRC CIHL Study, at 3217, 3220, 3226–7, 3230–1, 3233–5, 3237–40, 3274–81; ICRC CIHL Database, Rule 142, Section A, VI, and Rule 143, IV.

[27] ICRC CIHL Study, practice of UN General Assembly at 3246, UN Secretary-General at 3248, UN Commission on Human Rights at 3247 and 3249. See also ICRC CIHL Database, Rule 143, VII and UNSC Res 1894 of 2009, para 7.

[28] Cf UNGA Res 59/197 of 2004, 59/211 of 2004, 61/30 of 2006; UN Commission on Human Rights Res 2003/53, Res 2004/37, Res 2005/39.

[29] Cf UNSC Res 1208 of 1998, 1296 of 2000; UNGA Res 59/197 of 2004, 59/211 of 2004, 60/123 of 2005, 61/30 of 2006.

[30] E.g., ICRC CIHL Study, at 3230–1, 3236–7. See also ICRC Commentary APs, at 964.

[31] C. Plate, 'Journalists' reports cannot prevent conflict', 82 *IRRC* 839 (2000) 617.

[32] See more in detail MN 51.

[33] Sassòli/Bouvier/Quintin, at 356. See also Klenner, above n 7, at 655.

[34] ICRC CIHL Study, at 3211–12, 3214, 3216, 3218, 3234, 3264, 3266; ICRC CIHL Database, Rule 142, Section A, III and VI, and Section B, III, Rule 143, III. See also *Report of the Winograd Commission*, above n 5, para 30.

[35] Kenya's LOAC Manual of 1997, ICRC CIHL Study, at 3216.

is 'known to the camp staff and the guard',[36] and make it available to the POWs and internees in a language which they understand.[37] However, while many internal regulations provide for dissemination of IHL in time of peace,[38] there are only a few that expressly refer to IHL training in times of armed conflict, for both armed forces and civilians.[39]

III. Categories of addressees of dissemination

There are two main types of addressees at whom dissemination activities should be directed—armed forces and the civilian population. The obligation to include the study of the Conventions in the programmes of military instruction is formulated in a more categorical manner than the obligation to disseminate the texts among the civilian population, nevertheless both obligations constitute treaty obligations.

a. Armed forces

Incorporating the study of IHL into programmes of military instruction is the fundamental measure set forth in the treaties with a view to making the law known to the armed forces who bear primary responsibility for its application. It is confirmed in military manuals, other national legislation,[40] and in some states even in the Constitution.[41]

This obligation is strengthened by Article 45 GC I and Article 46 GC II emphasizing the responsibility of commanders for the execution of the Conventions. The subsequent development of IHL made this responsibility even more explicit. Article 87(2) AP I states that commanders must ensure that the military personnel under their command are aware of their obligations under these instruments. This rule is set forth in numerous military manuals[42] and supported by official statements.[43] Some of them mention it jointly and equally with commanders' responsibility to ensure that their troops respect IHL, thus clearly indicating that dissemination is one of the methods of ensuring compliance with the law.[44] This authority is exercised 'commensurate with [a commander's] level of responsibility'.[45] In a few manuals it is stated that 'the superior is the normal instructor of his subordinates for LOAC [law of armed conflict] training'.[46] Some manuals contain a detailed list of a commander's obligations in this respect.[47] The criminal responsibility of superiors for the violations committed by their subordinates should incite military authorities to fulfil their obligations in this field.[48]

Additional Protocol I provides, in addition, for the necessity of training legal advisers to assist commanders in the application of the Geneva Conventions and Additional

---

[36] Art 39 GC III. See similar wording in Art 99 GC IV.   [37] Art 41 GC III and Art 99 GC IV.
[38] See above n 34.
[39] ICRC CIHL Study, at 3222, 3273; ICRC CIHL Database, Rule 142, Section B, III, Rule 143, III.
[40] See the legislation as listed by the ICRC CIHL Study, above nn 5–6, 11–12, and 16.
[41] Constitutions of Burundi and of Democratic Republic of the Congo, ICRC CIHL Database, Rule 142, Section A, IV.
[42] These manuals are enumerated in ICRC CIHL Study, at 504, fn 52. See other examples in ICRC CIHL Database, Rule 142, Section B, III.
[43] ICRC CIHL Study, at 504, fn 55.
[44] Ibid, fn 54. See also ICRC CIHL Database, Rule 142, Section B, III.
[45] Art 87(2) AP I. See reference to 'respective spheres of authority', ICRC CIHL Study, at (respectively) 3261, 3264; and ICRC CIHL Database, Rule 142, Section B, III.
[46] ICRC CIHL Study, at 3262–4.
[47] Russian Federation's Regulations on the Application of IHL of 2001 and Ukraine's IHL Manual of 2004, ICRC CIHL Database, Rule 142, Section B, III.
[48] Y. Sandoz (ed), *Les moyens de mise en oeuvre du droit international humanitaire* (Geneva: International Institute of Humanitarian Law, 2005), at 26; ICRC CIHL Study, at 504.

Protocols, and to advise them on the appropriate instruction to be given to the armed forces on this subject.[49] Similar tasks are vested in 'qualified persons' under Article 6 AP I. The latter provision does not mention explicitly the dissemination activities of these personnel, but it is understood this way in states' practice. The importance of training qualified personnel and legal advisers, and then of commanders using their skills and knowledge to organize training within armed forces, is expressly recognized in military manuals and other documents of some states.[50] One manual even provides for the responsibility of a legal adviser 'to report to the command cases of unsatisfactory knowledge of the laws of armed conflict by the personnel and reasons for that'.[51]

26   The study of the Geneva Conventions should find a place in the training programmes of the whole of the armed forces, the instruction given being adapted to the rank of those for whom it is intended.[52] The necessity to train every single soldier in essential rules of the Geneva Conventions is very widely accepted by states.[53] As noted in military manuals, '[t]he overall aim of LOAC training is to ensure respect for LOAC by all members of the armed forces, irrespective of their function, time, location and situation'.[54] The obligation to educate applies above all, but not exclusively, to active duty personnel. International humanitarian law should be also included in programmes of instruction of reservists.[55]

27   In accordance with Article 127 GC III and Article 144 GC IV, any military authorities who assume responsibilities with regard to persons protected by these instruments should be 'specially instructed as to their provisions'. This rule is repeated in Article 83(2) AP I with slightly different wording ('shall be fully acquainted with the text' of the Conventions), and it extends the obligation of being 'fully acquainted' to authorities exercising responsibilities in respect of any of the four Geneva Conventions, not only GC III and GC IV. As mentioned above, this category of military personnel also has some responsibilities as providers, not only as receivers, of instruction.[56]

28   Article 47 GC I and Article 48 GC II expressly mention two classes of persons other than combatants who require special instruction, namely, medical personnel and chaplains. As these persons enjoy special status under IHL, 'they ought to make a special point of scrupulously observing the corresponding duties which the Convention imposes on them',[57] even though it may not be that easy to familiarize all medical personnel with IHL 'in view of the variety of people for whom it is intended and the diverse situations in which their services may be required'.[58]

29   Peacekeeping, peace-enforcement, and peace-building troops comprise another category of staff that should be trained in IHL. They are not specifically mentioned in the

---

[49] Art 82 AP I. See ICRC Commentary APs, at 953.
[50] ICRC CIHL Study, at 3215, 3218–19, 3225, 3260; ICRC CIHL Database, Rule 142, Section A, VI, Section B, III.
[51] ICRC CIHL Database, Rule 142, Section B, III.   [52] See in more detail MN 43.
[53] ICRC CIHL Study, at 3211–12, 3215, 3217–22, 3226–7, 3230–7, 3244, 3267; ICRC CIHL Database, Rule 142, Section A, III and VI, Section B, III. See also *Report of the Winograd Commission*, above n 5, para 52, Recommendation No 1, at 1283–4.
[54] Chad's *Instructor's Manual* and South Africa's *Revised Civic Education Manual*, ICRC CIHL Database, Rule 142, Section B, III.
[55] McGowan, above n 4, at 52.   [56] See MN 21.
[57] Pictet Commentary GC I, at 349. The obligation to disseminate IHL to medical personnel (and to chaplains) is emphasized in national documents of some states and in their official statements, e.g., ICRC CIHL Study, at 3225, 3279; ICRC CIHL Database, Rule 142, Section A, III and Section B, III.
[58] A. Baccino-Astrada, *Manual on the Rights and Duties of Medical Personnel in Armed Conflicts* (Geneva: ICRC and the League of Red Cross Societies, 1982), at 9.

Geneva Conventions or Additional Protocols, but the obligation of the UN organs and bodies to ensure that the military personnel of the UN forces are fully acquainted with IHL rules is clearly set forth in other documents.[59] The UN General Assembly used to emphasize that dissemination to the UN personnel enhances their security and effectiveness in accomplishing their function.[60] As these forces should be trained before any deployment, many states providing contingents to the UN consider it their duty to ensure adequate instructions before making them available.[61]

b. Civilian population

In accordance with Article 47 GC I, Article 48 GC II, Article 127 GC III, and Article 144 GC IV, states should disseminate the Geneva Conventions 'as widely as possible' and include, if possible, 'the study thereof in their programmes of [...] civil instruction', so that their principles may become known to the entire population. Civilians must understand that 'certain rules apply independently of who is right and who is wrong, protecting even the worst enemy, police forces, civil servants, politicians, diplomats, judges, lawyers, journalists, students who fulfill those tasks in the future, and the public at large must know the limits constraining everyone's actions in armed conflicts, the rights everyone may claim'.[62] In addition, Article 127 GC III and Article 144 GC IV provide that any civilian authorities who in time of armed conflict assume responsibilities in respect of protected persons, must be specially instructed in IHL. Article 83 AP I obliges states to encourage the study of IHL by the civilian population. According to the ICRC Customary International Humanitarian Law Study, this rule is of a customary character.[63] States' recognition of this obligation is expressed, as in the case of dissemination to armed forces, in military manuals, national legislation,[64] and even in a national Constitution.[65] It is very seldom that states admit they have no dissemination activities aimed at their civilian population.[66] The UN, other inter-governmental organizations, and the IRCM have called on states on numerous occasions to promote the teaching of IHL to the civilian population.[67]

The obligation to disseminate the knowledge of the Geneva Conventions among the civilian population is formulated in a less strict manner than the obligation regarding instruction of the armed forces. All four Geneva Conventions include expressions like 'as possible' and 'if possible', which imply less stringent obligations. The use of the latter expression is explained not by the need to make civilian instruction optional, but by the necessity to take into account the possibility that in federal countries, the central government may have no authority over local institutions with regard to the education system.[68] As for the expression 'as widely as possible', it has been pointed out that this formula is

---

[59] UN Secretary-General's Bulletin on observance by UN forces of IHL, UN Doc ST/SGB/1999/13 of 1999, Section 3. See also UNSC Res 1296 of 2000, Res 1674 of 2006, Res 1756 of 2007, Res 1894 of 2009 and documents referred to above nn 28 and 29.
[60] Cf UNGA Res 58/122 of 2003, Res 59/197 of 2004, Res 59/211 of 2004, Res 60/123 of 2005.
[61] ICRC CIHL Study, at 503 including fns 46 and 47, ICRC CIHL Database, Rule 142, Section A, VI.
[62] Sassòli/Bouvier/Quintin, at 356.
[63] ICRC CIHL Study, Rule 143.
[64] See examples in ICRC CIHL Study, at 506, fns 67 and 68, at 3234, 3277, 3281; ICRC CIHL Database, Rule 143, III and IV, and VI.
[65] Constitution of the Democratic Republic of the Congo, ICRC CIHL Database, Rule 143, IV.
[66] ICRC CIHL Study, at 3279, 3281.   [67] Ibid, at 507, fns 72–5.
[68] Pictet Commentary GC I, at 349; ICRC Commentary APs, at 965; ICRC CIHL Study, at 506; S.-S. Junod, 'La diffusion du droit international humanitaire', in Mélanges Pictet 359, at 359–60.

rather vague and ambiguous.[69] Nevertheless, it implies that states should at least take measures conducive to the study of IHL by the civilian population.

32   The Geneva Conventions stipulate that instruction in IHL should be provided primarily to the public authorities responsible for its application in respect of protected persons. This obligation is reinforced in Article 83 AP I. Many states introduce the obligation of IHL training for civil servants with special responsibilities in case of emergency (e.g., civil defence) and for law enforcement personnel (judiciary, prison personnel, border guards).[70] Resolutions of the UN organs and bodies support this requirement.[71] Police and security forces deserve special attention in all dissemination activities.[72] They are sometimes engaged in situations the legal qualification of which is difficult, therefore they should be familiar both with human rights law applicable during internal disturbances and tensions, and with IHL applicable in NIAC, and be able to respect them in the context of operational situations. Obviously, they should also be aware of their status in international armed conflict (IAC). International documents refer sometimes not directly to the IHL instruction for police and security forces, but to their training in 'police ethics and human rights' with a view to limiting the use of force and firearms.[73]

33   Training in IHL should ideally be addressed to all levels of civil servants, including policy makers in the Ministries of Foreign Affairs, National Defence, Justice, Health and Social Affairs, and Education, as well as towards politicians, diplomats, and international officials.[74]

34   Another category of civilians that should receive instruction in IHL comprises the medical and paramedical professions. All members of the health services should be conversant with the basic principles of IHL, in particular with the provisions of the Geneva Conventions concerning medical personnel and equipment, medical missions, and the use of the protective emblems. The importance of such instruction is recognized by some states.[75] Personnel from social services and humanitarian organizations should be also familiar with IHL rules relating to their status and the legal status of protected persons.[76]

35   The Geneva Conventions do not provide explicitly for the obligation to disseminate to the youth of states parties, but the most fundamental principles of IHL should be taught at

---

[69] Sandoz, above n 48, at 24–5.

[70] ICRC CIHL Study, at 507, fn 77, at 3223, 3237; ICRC CIHL Database, Rule 142, Section A, III, Rule 143, IV and VI.

[71] ICRC CIHL Study, at 508, fn 78; UNGA Res 59/197 of 2004 and Res 61/30 of 2006; UN Commission on Human Rights, Res 2005/34, Res 2005/39 and Res 2005/81.

[72] Cf ICRC CIHL Study, at 3214, 3222, 3233, 3236–9, 3242, 3280; ICRC CIHL Database, Rule 142, Section A, IV, Rule 143, IV; UN Commission on Human Rights Res 2004/43, Res 2004/72, Res 2005/34, Res 2005/39, Res 2005/81.

[73] Basic Principles on the Use of Force and Firearms by Law Enforcement Officials of 1990, UN Doc A/CONF.144/28/Rev.1, 1990, at 112, para 20. See also, e.g., Code of Conduct for Law Enforcement Officials—UNGA Res 34/169 of 1979, Arts 2 and 3; The European Code of Police Ethics—Rec(2001)10 of 2001 adopted by the Committee of Ministers of the Council of Europe, para 29. For more on dissemination to police and security forces, see C. de Rover, *To Serve and to Protect* (Geneva: ICRC, 1998), *passim*.

[74] See *Respect for International Humanitarian Law. Handbook for Parliamentarians* (Geneva: ICRC, Inter-Parliamentary Union, 1999); 'Geneva, New York, Washington—Dissemination of International Humanitarian Law to Diplomats and International Officials', 35 *IRRC* 306 (1995) 356.

[75] ICRC CIHL Database, Rule 143, IV. See also Res 2005/39 of the UN Commission on Human Rights. A model dissemination programme for medical and social circles is drafted by Zys, above n 9, Chapter VI, at 3.

[76] ICRC CIHL Database, Rule 143, IV and VI; UNSC Res 1265 of 1999.

an appropriate level in schools.[77] Such education should obviously convey the spirit rather than the letter of the Geneva Conventions, and should be adapted to the age of children and adolescents, and to their historical and cultural background.[78] States recognize the importance of teaching IHL to their youth, particularly in secondary education.[79]

It is also widely accepted that the Geneva Conventions should be disseminated in institutions of higher education, especially in universities.[80] In this context faculties of law are emphasized,[81] but IHL should also be included in programmes run by other faculties, for example international relations,[82] political science, journalism,[83] and medicine. Principles of IHL might also be attractive for students of philosophy, history, sociology, and anthropology too.

The media play a special role in dissemination of the Geneva Conventions 'as widely as possible' among the general public, particularly if there is an interest provoked by some events. Therefore, they should also be given some training in order to be able to comment on news in a legally correct way.[84]

IV. Methods and content of dissemination

The Geneva Conventions state that dissemination must be as wide as possible, but remain mute with regard to the methods to be used. The manner in which dissemination is effected is left to states.

Dissemination cannot be perceived only in terms of passing on information. Particularly with regard to the armed forces, taking into account the considerable stress to which combatants are subjected during hostilities, as well as the need to take decisions very quickly, the most fundamental rules have to be 'imprinted' on soldiers' minds. Training has to trigger spontaneous humanitarian reactions and develop instinctive behaviour that meets the standards of the Geneva Conventions even in the most stressful situations.[85] International humanitarian law should not be 'taught' but discussed in terms that are concrete and operational, made part of a continuous process of establishing automatic responses.

With regard to soldiers, rules should be considered an integral part of exercises and routine training. Training in IHL should form part of military instruction, along with other

---

[77] Resolution 21 para 2(d), adopted by the Diplomatic Conference leading to the adoption of the APs, ICRC CIHL Study, at 3284.

[78] For more on dissemination among youth, see *Exploring Humanitarian Law, IHL Guide: A Legal Manual for EHL Teachers* (Geneva: ICRC, 2009); E. Baeriswyl, 'Teaching Young People to Respect Human Dignity—Contribution of the International Red Cross and Red Crescent Movement', 37 *IRRC* 319 (1997) 357; S. Tawil, 'International Humanitarian Law and Basic Education', 82 *IRRC* 839 (2000) 581; Zys, above n 9, Chapter VII, at 3–15.

[79] ICRC CIHL Study, at 508, fn 80, at 3277, 3280; ICRC CIHL Database, Rule 143, VI.

[80] ICRC CIHL Study, at 507, fn 71 and at 3271, 3274–5, and 3278–80.

[81] For a detailed description of ways of presenting IHL at law faculties, see E. David, 'Dissemination of International Humanitarian Law at University Level', 27 *IRRC* 257 (1987) 155; H.S. Levie, 'Teaching Humanitarian Law in Universities and Law Schools', 31 *The American University Law Review* (1982) 1005; Sassòli/Bouvier/Quintin, CD, Part III; Zys, above n 9, Chapter V, at 5–13.

[82] W.V. O'Brien, 'The *Jus in Bello* in International Relations Studies', 31 *The American University Law Review* (1982) 1011.

[83] Sassòli/Bouvier/Quintin, Part III.

[84] See Model Programme of a seminar for journalists in Zys, above n 9, Chapter VIII, at 3. There are reports on state practice in this area in ICRC CIHL Study, at 3278; ICRC CIHL Database, Rule 143, IV and VI.

[85] See the purposes of training specified in documents in the ICRC CIHL Study, at 3217, 3219–20, 3236; and the ICRC CIHL Database, Rule 142, Section A, III and Section B, III.

elements relating to preparation for combat.⁸⁶ In states' practice it is recognized that IHL should be incorporated into military manuals that serve as a main source of authoritative guidance,⁸⁷ handbooks,⁸⁸ and other publications or materials.⁸⁹ Although the most popular method of training still seems to be classroom-type instruction in the form of courses and seminars,⁹⁰ it is nevertheless understood more and more widely that this may not be sufficient to ensure full respect for IHL during the stress of combat, and that training in the practical application of the Geneva Conventions is required. Scenarios including IHL should be integrated into normal military activities, systematic combat exercises, and manoeuvres,⁹¹ and into rules of engagement and standard operating procedures,⁹² as well as concrete orders given in the combat situation.⁹³ '[T]raining should not just address the rules, but case studies from recent and past [...] operations';⁹⁴ the instructor has to translate more than 400 Articles of the Geneva Conventions into concrete situations and experience relating to IHL. The importance of refresher courses should not be underestimated either.⁹⁵

41   The role and qualifications of the instructor cannot be overestimated. He must be truly committed to training and able to present the law in a credible way as a very relevant subject, to be well understood in the best interests of every soldier.⁹⁶ In addition, '[i]t is necessary to overcome skepticism towards IHL as a potential obstacle in achieving the main objective, namely winning the war',⁹⁷ in order to overcome perception that respect for the Geneva Conventions may contradict political or military objectives.

42   As regards civil instruction, in contrast to instruction of armed forces, there is less need to instil automatic reflexes ensuring effective application of the Geneva Conventions in the extreme stress of combat. Civil instruction focuses more on imparting knowledge and modifying attitudes. Military manuals and scenarios during manoeuvres are obviously less relevant, and priority should be given to the availability of the Geneva Conventions in national languages,⁹⁸ publication of supporting materials like audiovisual products,

---

⁸⁶ Sassòli/Bouvier/Quintin, at 356. See also P. Verri, 'Institutions militaires: le problème de l'enseignement du droit des conflits armés et de l'adaptation des règlements à ses prescriptions humanitaires', in Mélanges Pictet 603, at 614–16.

⁸⁷ See the practice of some states in this respect in ICRC CIHL Study, at 3213–15, 3220–1, 3237; and the ICRC CIHL Database, Rule 142, Section A, III.

⁸⁸ On the role of handbooks, see F. de Mulinen, *Handbook on the Law of War for Armed Forces* (Geneva: ICRC, 1989), at 14–16.

⁸⁹ ICRC CIHL Study, at 3218, 3221, 3226, 3229, 3235–41, 3267; ICRC CIHL Database, Rule 142, Section A, VI.

⁹⁰ ICRC CIHL Study, at 3228, 3236, 3238, 3240; ICRC CIHL Database, Rule 142, Section A, III and VI: Belgium, and Section B, III.

⁹¹ ICRC CIHL Study, at 3212, 3216–21, 3225, 3228, 3236–7; ICRC CIHL Database, Rule 142, Section A, III and VI, and Section B, III and, IV.

⁹² See the Philippines' AFP Standing Rules of Engagement of 2005, ICRC CIHL Database, Rule 142, Section B, III. Cf ICRC CIHL Study, at 3267; ICRC CIHL Database, Rule 142, Section A, VI.

⁹³ D. Muñoz-Rojas and J.-J. Frésard, *The Roots of Behaviour in War: Understanding and Preventing IHL Violations* (Geneva: ICRC, 2004), at 16.

⁹⁴ United States, The Fay Report of August 2004, ICRC CIHL Database, Rule 142, Section A, VI.

⁹⁵ Pictet Commentary GC I, at 348.

⁹⁶ On concrete problems of training armed forces in IHL and on examples of courses run by the ICRC, see D.L. Roberts, 'Training the Armed Forces to Respect International Law: The Perspective of the ICRC Delegate to the Armed and Security Forces of South Asia', 37 *IRRC* 319 (1997) 433; Verri, above n 86, at 613–14.

⁹⁷ Hampson, above n 14, at 119–21.

⁹⁸ See Art 48 GC I, Art 49 GC II, Art 128 GC III, Art 144 GC IV.

and the use of the Internet for the promotion of these materials as well as for organization of e-courses. National and international IHL courses and competitions, for example the J. Pictet Competition, are widely recognized by the student community as valuable experiences. As an example of an interesting national initiative, we might highlight the Philippines' declaration of 12 August (date of the adoption of the Geneva Conventions) as a national IHL Day in order to 'raise the people's consciousness and promote greater awareness of the principles of IHL' through seminars, symposia, and other nationwide activities coordinated by the Departments of Foreign Affairs and National Defence, with the support of the National Red Cross Society and the ICRC.[99]

With regard to the content of the instruction, it varies depending on whether it is intended for civilians or combatants. For the latter, it should be adapted to the rank and actual responsibilities of those to whom it is addressed.[100] The fundamental rules of the Geneva Conventions can be taught at any level, and the training received by every soldier should be simple (but not simplistic) in its form, using elementary notions understood by everyone.[101] The extent of knowledge and the need for a wider perspective increases with seniority. Internal regulations of some states clearly recognize the important role of enhanced training for officers.[102] Several manuals provide for concrete programmes of instruction for different levels and ranks.[103]

43

Apart from traditional IHL topics, some states attach particular importance to numerous concrete issues to be specially included in the training programmes, e.g. relations between the military and humanitarian workers,[104] arrest and other forms of detention,[105] the prohibition of torture,[106] the protection of children.[107] United Nations organs and agencies also insist on more training on the protection of children in armed conflicts, as well as with regard to gender-related problems[108] and the protection of the environment.[109]

44

The interrelation between the Geneva Conventions, international human rights law (IHRL) and international criminal law should also be addressed adequately in dissemination activities.[110] On the one hand, it is a question of a general awareness of the legal ramifications of human dignity and the consequences of any violation. On the other hand, the importance of such an approach results from the interdependence of these branches of law during armed conflicts, as well as from the increasing engagement of armed forces

45

---

[99] Philippines, ICRC CIHL Database, Rule 143, IV.
[100] See ICRC CIHL Study, at 3221, 3232, 3239; ICRC CIHL Database, Rule 142, Section A, VI. Cf also H.H. Almond, 'The Teaching and Dissemination of the Geneva Conventions and International Humanitarian Law in the United States', 31 *The American University Law Review* (1982) 981, at 982; de Mulinen, above n 88, *passim*; F. de Mulinen, 'Law of War Training within the Armed Forces: Twenty Years of Experience', 27 *IRRC* 257 (1987) 168, at 174–6.
[101] This aspect of IHL training is sometimes emphasized in states' domestic documents: see ICRC CIHL Study, at 3214, 3217, 3224–5, 3230–1, 3234, 3239; ICRC CIHL Database, Rule 142, Section A, III and VI.
[102] ICRC CIHL Study, at 3215, 3218, 3219, 3240, 3242; and the ICRC CIHL Database, Rule 142, Section A, VI.
[103] E.g., Canada's *Prisoner of War Handling and Detainees Manual* of 2004 or Canada's Code of Conduct of 2005, referred to in ICRC CIHL Database, Rule 142, Section A, III; Spain's LOAC Manual of 1996, ICRC CIHL Study, at 3219; and numerous military teaching manuals which serve as educational tools for armed forces, referred to in the list annexed to the ICRC CIHL Study, at 4196–207.
[104] ICRC CIHL Study, at 3225, 3233, 3236, 3242.
[105] ICRC CIHL Database, Rule 142, Section A, VI.   [106] Ibid.   [107] Ibid.
[108] E.g., *UN Secretary-General Report on the Protection of Civilians in Armed Conflict of 1999*, UN Doc S/1999/957; UNSC Res 1296 of 2000, 1756 of 2007; UNGA Res 59/197 of 2004, 61/30 and 61/173 of 2006; UN Human Rights Commission Res 2005/39.
[109] UNGA Res 47/37 of 1992 and 49/50 of 1994.   [110] See Chs 35 and 36 of this volume.

in law enforcement operations. The necessity of integrating IHL and IHRL in training armed forces is noted by many states.[111] Sometimes states emphasize the role of additional teaching in criminal law in order to prevent war crimes.[112] The need to teach both IHRL and IHL is also clearly expressed in documents adopted by the UN organs and bodies.[113] In UN documents refugee law is often mentioned separately from IHRL, as a branch of law that should receive extra attention in dissemination activities.[114]

46   While presenting the content of the Geneva Conventions, one should take into consideration that there are significant differences between combatants and civilians in terms of their behaviour and their attitudes towards IHL. Soldiers carry out orders, sometimes even if these are in conflict with their conscience; hence dissemination activities should be focused more on the norms than on their underlying values. '[T]he perception that there are legal norms is more effective than the acknowledgement of moral requirements [...] which can be more easily relativized than the rules of law.'[115] The norm draws easily identifiable limits. With regard to civilians, the content of the message should—on the contrary—be based on values.[116] The fundamental rules of IHL are often mirrored in the ethics or morality of local cultures and traditions, and this aspect should be very much exploited in dissemination activities intended for civilians. It should be tailored to local circumstances.

C. Relevance in Non-International Armed Conflicts

47   Common Article 3 of the Geneva Conventions does not expressly provide for the obligation to spread knowledge about its content. Such an obligation results, however, from the general formula of Article 47 GC I on dissemination of 'the text of the present Convention' without any exceptions, and from the Common Article 1 obligation 'to respect and to ensure respect' that no doubt also applies to Common Article 3. The first express mention in an international treaty of the duty to disseminate IHL relating to NIACs is contained in the very brief Article 19 AP II, which lays down this obligation in very general terms, without specifying what it entails. However, as AP II develops and supplements Common Article 3, 'dissemination of the one is inextricably bound up with dissemination of the other'.[117] There are also international 'soft law' documents confirming the need to spread knowledge of IHL and IHRL to all parties to an armed conflict (or to all armed groups), and to enhance such groups' practical understanding of the implications of these rules.[118] As there is no specific mechanism in NIACs established to ensure the application of IHL, dissemination becomes an essential measure for its application.

48   The rule on the obligation to disseminate Common Article 3 as widely as possible, both to armed forces and to the civilian population, is considered nowadays to be of

---

[111] See ICRC CIHL Study, at 3214, 3216, 3222, 3234, 3238, 3241; ICRC CIHL Database, Rule 142, Section A, IV and VI, Section B, III, and Rule 143, IV.
[112] ICRC CIHL Study, at 3265; ICRC CIHL Database, Rule 142, Section A, VI, and Section B, III.
[113] UNSC Res 1208 of 1998, Res 1265 of 1999; UNGA Res 58/122 of 2003, Res 59/197 and 59/211 of 2004, Res 61/30 of 2006; UN Human Rights Commission 2003/53, 2004/37, 2005/34, 2005/39, 2005/81.
[114] UNSC Res 1208 of 1998, 1265 of 1999, 1296 of 2000, 1674 of 2006, 1894 of 2009; *UN Secretary General Report* S/1999/957, above n 108.
[115] Muñoz-Rojas and Frésard, above n 93, at 15.   [116] Ibid, at 16.
[117] ICRC Commentary APs, at 1487.
[118] E.g., *UN Secretary-General Report on the Protection of Civilians in Armed Conflict*, S/2001/331, Recommendation 10, at 11; UNGA Res 3032 of 1972.

a customary character. 'The practice collected does not indicate that any distinction is made between instruction in IHL applicable in IAC or that applicable in NIAC.'[119] The importance of dissemination of IHL, 'no matter how the conflict may be characterized under international law', is expressed clearly in internal regulations of some states.[120] For example, the necessity to teach both IHL and IHRL to armed forces is explained by the fact that they may be 'required to deal with civilians in times of internal conflicts'.[121]

The obligation to disseminate the content of Common Article 3 is imposed on all the parties to an armed conflict—states and non-state actors. For states, it is valid both in time of peace and in time of an armed conflict; while for armed opposition groups, it applies in the event of an armed conflict. 49

With regard to states, the obligation to disseminate IHL relating to NIACs in peacetime should not be considered an additional burden. The principles, such as respect for and protection of enemies *hors de combat* and civilians, remain the same whatever the nature of the conflict. One cannot teach armed forces different types of behaviour with regard to IAC and NIAC. 'In practice, armed forces train their members in peacetime in view of [IACs]. If such training is properly accomplished, all soldiers will have the same reflexes in a [NIAC] [...] [A]t the lower levels of military hierarchy, the rules of behaviour are exactly the same.'[122] 50

With regard to armed opposition groups, they do not exist in peacetime, therefore there is no peacetime dissemination carried out by them and designed specifically for them. It is difficult to imagine an obligation for a future armed group to disseminate IHL before an armed conflict actually exists, because such a group is not yet an addressee of IHL. Nevertheless, it should have some knowledge of the Geneva Conventions, including Common Article 3, if the obligation to disseminate to the general public has been respected by the state before the outbreak of a NIAC.[123] In addition, armed opposition groups may be constituted by former members of a state's armed forces who received IHL instruction in the course of their military training. However, as the above cannot be taken for granted, they should undertake dissemination activities to their members in times of NIAC.[124] It is certainly a difficult task, but worthwhile for many reasons,[125] including a political one—'a reputation for being law abiding might help a party gain the "moral high ground" and might also lead to political gains [...] adherence to IHL will help facilitate post-conflict national reconciliation and a return to peace'.[126] 51

There are different tools that may be used in order to secure a commitment from an armed opposition group to disseminate knowledge of Common Article 3. Unilateral, bilateral, or multilateral methods may be applied in the context of a process of engagement and relationship with other parties to the conflict. The last two methods comprise, first and foremost, special agreements concluded between the parties, and providing for dissemination of the terms of such agreements, as well as of IHL, including Common 52

---

[119] ICRC CIHL Study, at 501 and 505.
[120] E.g., Philippines' AFP Standing Rules of Engagement of 2005, above n 92.
[121] ICRC CIHL Study, at 3233, 3238, 3241, 3245; and the ICRC CIHL Database, Rule 142, Section A, VI.
[122] Sassòli/Bouvier/Quintin, at 429.
[123] See MN 30–31.
[124] See ICRC CIHL Study, at 3214 (Colombia), 3259 (examples of reports of armed opposition groups).
[125] See MN 2 and 5.
[126] M. Mack, *Increasing Respect for International Humanitarian Law in Non-International Armed Conflicts* (Geneva: ICRC, 2008), at 31.

Article 3, to 'all units under their command, control and political influence', both to military personnel and civilians.[127] In some reported cases the parties also undertook to facilitate dissemination of ICRC appeals urging respect for IHL, and to distribute ICRC publications.[128]

53   Another tool that may serve the purpose of disseminating Common Article 3 to non-state armed groups is the adoption of a code of conduct by such groups. Such codes are usually simple, short texts, easy to understand in the process of instruction, and easily printed and distributed. Their preparation may be used to make the group's leadership aware of the importance of the Geneva Conventions.[129] However, sometimes codes of conduct are not compatible with IHL, hence one should be cautious about distributing them or disseminating their content.[130]

54   A commitment by an armed group to disseminate IHL may be also included in a unilateral declaration. Such a declaration serves as another form of express commitment to respect humanitarian rules if a group—not having the legal capacity to ratify international treaties—does not consider itself technically bound by the Geneva Conventions.[131]

55   Dissemination in NIACs should formally be directed not only at members of state armed forces and non-state armed groups, but also at the civilian population.[132] However, 'practice with respect to the obligation of armed opposition groups to encourage the teaching of [IHL] to the civilian population under their control is limited', though at least 'armed opposition groups have frequently allowed the ICRC to disseminate [IHL] to civilians living in areas they controlled'.[133] Hence the customary law indicates only states, and not all parties to the conflict, as responsible for encouraging the teaching of IHL to the civilian population.[134]

56   With regard to the methods and content of dissemination of Common Article 3, IHL does not lay down any requirements. The choice of means and ways to disseminate is left to the states (as in the case of IACs) or to the parties to the conflict. For reasons indicated above,[135] it is particularly relevant in NIACs to combine dissemination of IHL with dissemination of IHRL.

D. Legal Consequences of a Violation

57   The obligation to disseminate IHL is an obligation of due diligence and not an obligation of result. Due diligence means there is a need to adopt measures designed to ensure that

---

[127] Agreement concluded by parties to the conflict in Bosnia-Herzegovina of 22 May 1992, para 4, in Sassòli/Bouvier/Quintin, 1717, at 1720–1. See also Memorandum of Understanding of 27 November 1991 relating to the conflict between Croatia and Yugoslavia, para 13, ibid, 1713, at 1716; and Comprehensive Agreement on Respect for Human Rights and International Humanitarian Law Between the Government of the Republic of the Philippines and the National Democratic Front of the Philippines concluded in The Hague on 16 March 1998, Preamble, available at <http://www.theirwords.org>.

[128] See Ch 25, MN 14, of this volume.

[129] On the role of codes of conduct in dissemination of IHL, see 'A Collection of Codes of Conduct Issued by Armed Groups', 93 *IRRC* 882 (2011) 483, at 485–6; Mack, above n 126, at 22–3.

[130] Cf Islamic Emirate of Afghanistan, 'Code of Conduct for the Mujahideen', 9 May 2009, Sassòli/Bouvier/Quintin, at 2325.

[131] For more on unilateral declarations, see Mack, above n 126, at 19–21; and the database <http://www.theirwords.org>.

[132] ICRC Commentary APs, at 1488; and the Agreement of 22 May 1992 and Memorandum of 27 November 1991, above n 127.

[133] ICRC CIHL Study, at 508.   [134] Ibid, at 505, Rule 143.   [135] See MN 45 and 48.

legal obligations are met, but there are no criteria, indicators, or standards laid down in IHL to evaluate the adequacy of measures adopted by states, armed opposition groups, and others in the field of dissemination of the Geneva Conventions. In the case law of the European Court of Human Rights (ECtHR) this concept is developed in the context of state responsibility for preventing human rights violations by non-state entities, namely, states may be held responsible for a lack of due diligence in preventing the violation or in responding to it.[136] Such a standard does not easily translate into a concept of potential responsibility for the lack of dissemination by states' agents.

In one case before the ECtHR, the applicant claimed a violation of the right to life in a NIAC, and referred to the responsibility of officers for the violations committed by their subordinates because they had not adequately trained the latter in their legal obligations. The Court, applying human rights standards to the conduct of hostilities in a NIAC, did not directly address the question of adequate training, but stated 'that the Government's failure to invoke the provisions of any domestic legislation governing the use of force by the army or security forces in situations such as the present one, whilst not in itself sufficient to decide on a violation of the State's positive obligation to protect the right to life', was relevant for other reasons, namely with regard to respect for the principle of proportionality.[137] If the lack of legislation (or the refusal to disclose legal acts, except for one document) was not considered to be sufficient to decide on a violation of the right to life, the lack of dissemination of existing rules would be even less likely to lead to such a determination. However, there was a positive follow up—as this concrete judgment was widely transmitted to various departments of the state concerned, the IHRL and IHL issues were shortly mainstreamed into the training of security forces, judges, and prosecutors.[138] 58

In cases where IHL has been invoked during domestic proceedings, responsibility for the lack of dissemination was clearly vested with commanders. In Canada's commission of inquiry into the serious violations of IHL by its peacekeeping troops in Somalia, a number of officers were blamed for the violations committed by their subordinates because they had not trained their soldiers systematically to ensure they would have a comprehensive understanding of their legal obligations.[139] In an inquiry into crimes committed by the military personnel of another state against foreign detainees during an IAC, a few commanders were relieved from command or reprimanded for, inter alia, 'failing to ensure that soldiers [...] knew, understood and adhered to the protections afforded to detainees in the Geneva Convention III of 1949'.[140] 59

E. Critical Assessment

The obligation to disseminate the content of the Geneva Conventions is clear, and is one of the most important means for ensuring compliance with the Conventions. As a 60

---

[136] E.g. ECtHR, *Osman v United Kingdom*, Judgment, 28 October 1998, para 116; ECtHR, *A v United Kingdom*, Judgment, 23 September 1998, para 22; ECtHR, *Z and others v United Kingdom*, Judgment, 10 May 2001, para 73; ECtHR, *Okkali v Turkey*, Judgment, 17 October 2006, para 70.
[137] ECtHR, *Isayeva v Russia*, Judgment, 24 February 2005, para 199.
[138] Council of Europe, Committee of Ministers, Memorandum on the Violations of the ECHR in the Chechen Republic: Russia's Compliance with the European Court's Judgments—CM/Inf/DH(2006)32 revised 2 of 12 June 2007.
[139] Canada's Commission of Inquiry into the Serious Violations of IHL by Canadian Peacekeeping Troops in Somalia, ICRC CIHL Study, at 3265–6.
[140] United States, Taguba Report of 2004, ICRC CIHL Database, Rule 142, Section B, VI.

treaty obligation, accepted by all states in the world, it is much stronger than any other similar commitment contained in other branches of law, including the obligation under IHRL foreseen mainly in 'soft law' documents, to train police forces adequately in order to ensure the protection of IHRL.[141] The importance of dissemination is also formally recognized by states in their domestic legislation.[142]

61 In practice, however, such measures do not always work as well as they should.[143] There are even arguments that 'spreading knowledge of IHL may prove counterproductive where mechanisms of moral disengagement are present', because imparting knowledge of IHL 'may have a negative effect on combatants who [...] use it perversely or in bad faith to explain away the excesses committed'.[144] When the text of the present Article 84 AP I was discussed during the Diplomatic Conference 1974–7, it provided that states should communicate to one another their laws adopted to ensure the application of the AP I, but there was no support for the ICRC's proposal to include one more paragraph laying down explicitly that states were obliged to report particularly on measures taken with regard to dissemination.[145] Today some other international mechanisms motivate states to submit such reports internationally, for example biannual reports of the UN Secretary-General on the status of the Geneva Conventions and Additional Protocols, reports submitted at the International Red Cross and Red Crescent Conferences as follow-up to states' and National Red Cross and Red Crescent Societies' pledges undertaken during previous conferences, or reports submitted at international meetings of national inter-ministerial committees. However, all these mechanisms are based on 'soft law' documents and depend a lot on states' good will.

62 Dissemination work, even if done perfectly, cannot be seen as a universal remedy for all problems relating to compliance with the Geneva Conventions. Actually the argument about ignorance of IHL explaining the lack of respect for its rules[146] is relevant only with regard to provisions of an administrative character that are not necessarily known without proper instruction (for example on specific rights of POWs concerning their financial resources or relations with the exterior). The most important norms are obvious, they only confirm what every human being should know anyway. For example, a soldier is expected not to rape or to loot, even if he is not familiar with specific provisions of the Geneva Conventions prohibiting such acts. If people violate such non-administrative rules of IHL, it is not because of their ignorance in law but because of their bad faith.[147] Therefore it is necessary to use and combine all available measures, methods, and mechanisms ensuring better compliance with the Geneva Conventions, including dissemination of the Conventions in times of peace as well as in times of armed conflict.

ELŻBIETA MIKOS-SKUZA

---

[141] Cf above n 73.
[142] See the legislation as listed by the ICRC CIHL Study, above nn 5–6, 11–12, and 16.
[143] On the practical reasons for the lack of successful dissemination, see Sandoz, above n 48, at 31–5.
[144] Muñoz-Rojas and Frésard, above n 93, at 11.   [145] ICRC Commentary APs, at 963.
[146] See MN 2.   [147] See Hampson, above n 14, at 113–14.

Chapter 31. Grave Breaches of the Geneva Conventions

	MN
A. Introduction	1
B. Meaning and Application	10
I. The obligation to provide for effective penal sanctions	14
a. The content of the obligation	14
b. The question of the effectiveness of penal sanctions	19
c. The persons against whom effective penalties must be established	25
II. The obligation to search for persons who have allegedly committed, or have ordered to be committed, a grave breach	33
III. The obligation to bring to court persons allegedly responsible for a grave breach	41
IV. The obligation to hand over to another state persons suspected of a grave breach	49
V. The question of jurisdictional link, including universal jurisdiction	56
VI. Judicial guarantees and the question of the status of prisoners of war	62
C. Relevance in Non-International Armed Conflicts	66
D. Legal Consequences of a Violation	70
E. Critical Assessment	74

Select Bibliography

Condorelli, L., 'Il sistema della repressione dei crimini di guerra nelle Convenzioni di Ginevra del 1949 e nel primo Protocollo addizionale del 1977', in L. Lamberti Zanardi and G. Venturini (eds), *Crimini di guerra e competenza delle giurisdizioni nazionali* (Milan: Giuffrè, 1998) 23

Dautricourt, J.Y., 'La protection pénale des conventions internationales humanitaires—une conception de la loi-type', 34 *Revue de droit pénal et de criminologie* (1953) 191

Dörmann, K. / Geiβ, R., 'The Implementation of Grave Breaches into Domestic Legal Orders', 7 *JICJ* (2009) 703

Fleck, D., 'Shortcomings of the Grave Breaches Regime', 7 *JICJ* (2009) 833

W. Ferdinandusse, 'The Prosecution of Grave Breaches in National Courts', 7 *JICJ* (2009) 703

Henckaerts, J.-M., 'The Grave Breaches Regime as Customary International Law', 7 *JICJ* (2009) 683

Kreβ, C., 'Reflections on the Iudicare Limb of the Grave Breaches Regime', 7 *JICJ* (2009) 789

Moir, L., 'Grave Breaches and Internal Armed Conflicts', 7 *JICJ* (2009) 769

O'Keefe, R., 'The Grave Breaches Regime and Universal Jurisdiction', 7 *JICJ* (2009) 811

Pilloud, C., 'La protection pénale des Conventions internationales humanitaires', 35 *IRRC* 419 (1953) 842

Sandoz, Y., 'La répression pénale dans le cadre des efforts du Comité international de la Croix-Rouge pour mieux faire respecter le droit international humanitaire', in P.L. Lamberti Zanardi and G. Venturini (eds), *Crimini di guerra e competenza delle giurisdizioni nazionali* (Milano: Giuffrè, 1998) 75

Sandoz, Y., 'The History of the Grave Breaches Regime', 7 *JICJ* (2009) 657

Stewart, J., 'The Future of the Grave Breaches Regime: Segregate, Assimilate or Abandon?', 7 *JICJ* (2009) 855

A. Introduction

At the time of their adoption, the idea of introducing in the new Geneva Conventions provisions concerning the prosecution and punishment of individuals who violate the

Conventions was controversial. In particular, the International Committee of the Red Cross (ICRC) did not consider the question of criminal punishment of alleged war criminals as a priority.[1] Arguably, this was because the ICRC had proved ineffective in prompting the enforcement of the laws of war during the periods between wars,[2] and on account of the traditional preference of the organization for private diplomacy as a means to induce belligerents to respect the rules of warfare.[3] In addition, the ICRC had serious reservations about the war crimes trials that were spreading all over Europe at the end of the Second World War. For the ICRC, other objectives ought to predominate: the appeasement of the conflict between the Allied and the Axis Powers,[4] humane treatment and fair trials for the Axis prisoners of war (POWs) accused of war crimes,[5] and the protection of the German Red Cross and some of its top officials from the de-Nazification process.[6]

2   The insistence on the punishment of those responsible for war crimes by the Red Cross and Red Crescent Movement (as opposed to the ICRC at the time),[7] and the increasing and unprecedented reality of prosecution of war criminals before national courts,[8] pushed the ICRC to reconsider its stand. In a commentary presented to government experts in the summer of 1946, the then chief of the ICRC's Legal Division, Claude Pilloud, noted that punishment for violations of the Conventions was 'an extremely interesting idea'. He also added that

---

[1] The Pictet Commentary GC I, at 358, refers to the ICRC as 'naturally reluctant to propose punitive measures'. See also M. Lewis, *The Birth of the New Justice* (Oxford: OUP, 2014), at 238–9. A chapter of Lewis's book is dedicated to the historical analysis of the provisions criminalizing grave breaches in the GCs. As explained by the author, this analysis differs from previous studies in so far as it focuses on the diplomatic intervention of the ICRC for the protection of the accused war criminals, and uses the ICRC archives and other material not available to or consulted by previous scholars (at 231–2). In the following pages, the present author relies heavily on the Lewis study and the sources quoted by him.

[2] One such example was the failure by the ICRC to confront the Italian regime in connection with the bombing of Red Cross hospitals and the use of poison gas during Italy's invasion of Ethiopia. See Lewis, above n 1, at 237.

[3] Ibid, at 237–8.

[4] Ibid, at 238, quoting the position taken by the ICRC legal analyst Beck within the ICRC's legal commission (transcript of the meeting of 17 April 1945, 9 am, No 6: AICRC, A PV Jur 1, CR. 211).

[5] For the ICRC, war crimes trials raised issues relating to the denial of POW status to those accused of war crimes and the inadequate fair trial guarantees in special tribunals that were established to try such crimes, rather than questions respecting the enforcement of international humanitarian law through criminal punishment. Ibid, at 239.

[6] Ibid, at 239–40. Quoting the relevant transcripts and documents of the meetings of the ICRC's legal commission, Lewis underlines that the ICRC feared the dismantling of the German Red Cross, which had been completely Nazified in 1933, and criminal prosecution of its top officials, such as W.G. Hartmann, head of the Foreign Bureau of the German Red Cross, who acted as the main point of contact with the ICRC during the war. Apparently, Mr Hartmann and the German Red Cross did not defend the interests and principles of the Red Cross and Red Crescent Movement with respect to Jews and other non-Aryans deported by the Nazis to the Reich or detained in concentration camps. Mr Hartmann and other members of the German Red Cross were interned by the Allies in August 1945 and subsequently charged as 'delinquents of less importance' (ibid, at 240).

[7] Ibid, at 241. According to the *Report on the Work of the Preliminary Conference of National Red Cross Societies for the Studies of the Conventions and of Various Problems Relative to the Red Cross, Geneva July 26–August 3, 1946* (Geneva, 1947), the Commission entrusted with the study of the revision of the Convention relative to the Treatment of Prisoners of War and the drafting of a Convention relative to civilians, 'endorsed the principle embodied in Art 26 of the Draft of the Belgian Red Cross and Art 8 of the proposals of the Jugoslav Red Cross' on the question of sanctions, 'to the effect that violations of the treaty provisions should be considered as a "war crime" and be liable to the consequent penalties' (at 93–4). The position of the ICRC delegation on this point was that the 'principle ha[d] already been introduced in [the ICRC] preliminary Draft Prisoner of War Convention in 1921, but had unfortunately not been approved by experts and Governments' (ibid, at 94).

[8] As Draper aptly noted, '[a]t no other time in history have such a large number of enemy personnel been brought to trial and punishment for acts of war criminality' (G.I.A.D. Draper, 'The Implementation and Enforcement of Geneva Conventions and the Two Additional Protocols of 1977', 164 *RCADI* (1979-III) 1, at 36).

this was a solution that 'would very likely not only have the Convention relative to the treatment of prisoners of war as its object but also those concerning the treatment of the wounded and sick in armies in the field, as well as the Tenth and the Fourth Hague Conventions'.[9] Under Pilloud, the Legal Division of the ICRC thus became more open to the idea of including provisions on criminal punishment in the yet to be adopted new Conventions, although within the Division disagreement persisted on which violations had to be criminalized, and which judicial fora should deal with them.[10]

The process that finally led to the inclusion in the new Geneva Conventions of a set of crimes known as grave breaches (further complemented in 1977 by Additional Protocol (AP) I) was shaped by the respective agendas of the various actors involved.

After the Second World War the victorious states were mainly keen to maintain unfettered their sovereignty over the punishment of enemy war criminals. The United States (US) and the United Kingdom (UK) were therefore not at all enthusiastic with regard to the prospect of adding criminal provisions to the Conventions. They also disliked the idea of envisaging a system of repression based on the exercise of universal criminal jurisdiction by domestic courts, and they disliked even more the idea of a permanent international criminal court that could in future sit in judgment over their own nationals. Briefly, these Powers wanted to keep exclusive criminal jurisdiction over individuals accused of having committed war crimes against their own nationals (or the nationals of their allies), since they considered that the most appropriate forum to deal with this form of criminality was the one of the victim state.[11] After all, war crimes trials that were unfolding at the time were proving to be 'effective', both in terms of knowledge by the judges of the applicable substantive and procedural rules, and in terms of the articulation of favourable political and historical narratives of the war by the victorious states.

On the other hand, the liberated countries presumably were driven by the desire to ensure the *legitimacy* of the prosecution and punishment of war crimes committed in their territories during occupation.[12] Given the lack of any applicable national criminal legislation on war crimes, they had passed ad hoc rules.[13] The trials were therefore criticized for

---

[9] See Lewis, above n 1, at 241, quoting a note by Pilloud, July 1946, AICRC, CR. 240-6, at 9 (translation from French by Lewis). This interesting idea, however, should not have been developed up to a point where potential signatory states would consider ratification of the Conventions no longer acceptable. In the introduction to the materials sent to the government experts in preparation for the Conference of 14–26 April 1947, Pilloud thus insisted on the need to take the military requirements and the interests of the states into account. Ibid, at 241–2, quoting the introduction by Pilloud, 13 November 1946, AICRC, CR. 240-5. Lewis, however, reports that Ms Marguerite Frick-Cramer (who at that time had already left the ICRC) was originally supportive of the idea of criminal punishment for those who violate the laws of war, but then reversed her position.

[10] The ICRC Legal Division therefore approached a Swiss criminal lawyer Ernst Hafter, who raised two very interesting questions. First, which court (military or ordinary) should have competence to prosecute a POW who was accused of having committed crimes before his capture. Secondly, what punishment should be imposed on a convicted POW for crimes committed against the Detaining Power. Ibid, at 242–3.

[11] See, e.g., the positions expressed by the US and the UK delegations in the first Commission of the Conference of Government Experts held in Geneva in 1947: ICRC, *Conférence d'Experts Gouvernementaux pour l'étude des Conventions protégeant les victimes de la guerre. Genève, 14–16 avril 1947. Procès-verbaux de la Commission I. Révision de la Convention de Genève de 1929 pour l'amélioration du sort des blessés dans les armées en campagne et les dispositions connexes* (1947), vol II (2).

[12] For an analysis of the trials conducted in the European 'liberated' countries, see J. Elster, *Closing the Books: Transitional Justice in Historical Perspective* (New York: CUP, 2004), at 57–60.

[13] See, e.g., the French Order of 28 August 1944 (*Ordonnance du 28 août relative à la répression des crimes de guerre, Journal Officiel de la République Française*, 30 August 1944, at 780, also available at <http://www.legifrance.gouv.fr/>); the Norwegian Law of 13 December 1946 (No 14) on the Punishment of Foreign

relying upon retroactive criminal legislation, in contradiction to the principle of strict legality in criminal matters prescribed in their constitutions.[14] In addition, defences such as obedience to superior orders, although available to their own nationals accused of having collaborated with the Occupying Power, were expressly ruled out in the war crimes trials against enemy nationals.[15] Arguably, the 'liberated' countries therefore believed that the inclusion in the new Conventions of criminal provisions for the punishment of war crimes constituted a 'recognition' that they were in fact acting at least in conformity with international law.

6 Against this background, prominent international lawyers involved in the drafting process of the grave breaches provisions instead favoured a strong internationalist approach. The four experts invited by the ICRC to prepare the text of the common provisions of the Geneva Conventions for the final Diplomatic Conference agreed on a scheme that reflected their international approach.[16] First, they agreed upon a list of offences that contracting states would have the obligation to criminalize in their national legal orders, and required states to report within a given time frame to the Swiss Federal Government on the measures adopted. Secondly, they framed the obligation for each contracting state to repress these offences, and envisaged the possibility for an international criminal tribunal to exercise jurisdiction. Their draft also included an obligation for the contracting parties to establish the necessary rules for extraditing the persons accused of a grave breach in cases where they would not be brought before their national courts. In addition, the draft ruled out the defence of obedience to superior orders (but the prosecution would be required to prove that the accused could reasonably have realized that he was participating in the commission of a violation of the Conventions). At the same time, the draft clearly proclaimed the responsibility of those who had given the illegal orders, even if they were acting in the exercise of an official state function. Lastly, the draft included an obligation for the contracting states not to bring those accused of grave breaches before any special jurisdiction, and to ensure the application of procedures and rules that were neither less favourable than those applied to their own nationals, nor contrary to general principles of law or humanity. In particular, contracting states were obliged to ensure to the accused the right to all ordinary means of defence.

7 The ICRC, after its initial scepticism, turned to supporting the idea of including in the Conventions a set of provisions on criminal punishment for those responsible for violations of the Conventions. It was Jean Pictet, Director-Delegate of the ICRC, who apparently gave the decisive push in this direction. In a note to the Legal Division, he expressed his views on the need to include the obligation for each contracting state to punish, or surrender to another contracting party, individuals responsible for those violations of the

---

War Criminals, in *Law Reports of Trials of War Criminals* (London: HMSO, 1948), vol III, at 81; the Dutch Extraordinary Penal Law Decree of 22 December 1943, ibid, at 100.

[14] In this respect, the Pictet Commentary, in the introductory remarks to the comments on the grave breaches provisions, laconically observes: 'Whatever one's views may be on the repressive action taken after the Second World War, it will be agreed that it would have been more satisfactory, had it been possible to base it on existing rules without being obliged to have recourse to ad hoc measures' (Pictet Commentary GC I, at 353).

[15] See, e.g., the analysis of the ICRC Delegate Pierre Boissier, written in 1948, on the possible legal basis for future war crimes trials, where he noted that while French collaborators could avail themselves of the defence of obedience to superior orders, the same defence was not available to Germans based on Art 3 of the French Order of 28 August 1944. (See P. Boissier, 'La répression conventionnelle des crimes de guerre', 23 March 1948, AICRC, G.7 IX-2, quoted by Lewis, above n 1, at 250, fn 87.)

[16] For the draft provisions of the Committee of Experts, see Pictet Commentary GC I, at 358, fn 8.

Conventions which were to be considered war crimes.[17] As stated earlier, however, the crucial matter for the ICRC was the treatment of POWs accused of war crimes. Indeed, the US was implementing a policy in occupied Germany that created serious concerns at the ICRC. For the US, German POWs accused of war crimes and crimes against humanity were ordinary criminals. Apparently, the US was releasing some POWs, only to immediately re-arrest them as 'civilians' on the basis of war crimes and crimes against humanity charges. Other countries considered that the captured combatants accused of war crimes and crimes against humanity were not entitled to POW status. During the entire drafting process of the criminal provisions in the Geneva Conventions, the ICRC was therefore adamant in maintaining that in no circumstance whatsoever should criminal prosecution for war crimes constitute an 'excuse' for stripping away the accused's protection concomitant to their status as POWs, or for denying those persons fair trial guarantees.[18] As for the possibility of a future international criminal court, the ICRC was more inclined to think of such a court as a 'court of appeals' to which persons condemned at the national level might resort.[19] In no way did the ICRC advocate that it should be involved in criminal prosecutions, since it considered the need to protect its image of impartiality as the overriding concern.[20]

The provisions on criminal punishment for certain violations of the Conventions adopted by the Diplomatic Conference in 1949 reflect a compromise between these different goals and agendas. On the one hand, their revolutionary character is apparent. Contracting states obligated themselves to adopt 'any legislation necessary to provide effective penal sanctions'[21] for those responsible for committing, or ordering to be committed, any of the grave breaches listed. In addition, for the first time, the obligation to search for, bring before their own courts, or surrender to another contracting party those allegedly responsible for a grave breach was inserted in a treaty concerning the laws of warfare.[22] This represented a clear success for all those advocating a strong commitment in the fight against impunity of future war criminals, as well as an implicit recognition of the legitimacy of prosecutions before national courts carried out thus far. In addition, the obligation to ensure to the accused persons all the 'safeguards of proper trial and defence' (at the very least those prescribed in the Conventions themselves) was clearly spelt out. This was to reassure the ICRC that, in the future, war crimes trials would not cast any doubt on the fairness of the proceedings. For POWs, other provisions of the

---

[17] See J. Pictet, 'Note à Mlles et MM. les membres du Bureau et de la Commission juridique', 23 October 1947, Art 33, at 5, AICRC, CR. 240-4, quoted by Lewis, above n 1, at 249, fn 86.

[18] See in this respect Lewis, above n 1, at 246. It is telling that at the Government Experts Conference, the ICRC stated that although it condemned unequivocally 'crimes against principles it is in itself anxious to safeguard', '[it] has been taught by experience that the facts constituting war crimes can be more easily circumscribed than exactly defined'. It therefore observed that 'there is a certain risk of arbitrary action, especially in cases where to be accused of such a crime is sufficient to deprive a man of [prisoner of war] status'. See ICRC, *Report of the Conference of Government Experts for the Study of the Conventions for the Protection of War Victims (Geneva, April 14–26, 1947)*, at 205–6.

[19] This was the proposal advanced by Pierre Boissier, above n 15, and supported by the ICRC: see *Repression des violations des Conventions humanitaires, Rapport du Comité international*, No 20, 5 June 1948, AICRC, CRI 25.10.

[20] Ibid, where the ICRC states that 'the principal goal of the ICRC is to come to the aid of the war victims and ensure full application of the humanitarian conventions, but it's not for it to intervene in any way whatsoever so that the guilty will be punished'. (Quoted by Lewis, above n 1, at 252.)

[21] Art 49 GC I; Art 50 GC II; Art 129 GC III; Art 146 GC IV.

[22] See Art 50 GC I; Art 51 GC II; Art 130 GC III; and Art 147 GC IV. Previous agreements did not provide a similar obligation. See Pictet Commentary GC I, at 351–8.

relevant Convention complemented this obligation. In particular, to avoid the 'use' of war crimes trials to deny the status of POW to captured enemy combatants, a specific provision (Article 85) was inserted in Geneva Convention (GC) III, providing that POWs prosecuted by the Detaining Power for acts committed before capture, retain, even if convicted, all the benefits of the Convention.

9   This 'revolution', however, did not override all the concerns relating to the protection of state sovereignty. The attempt to incorporate a reference to the exercise of criminal jurisdiction by an international criminal court failed. In the Geneva Conventions, criminal repression for breaches rests in the hands of national jurisdictions. In addition, the obligation to surrender to another contracting party persons accused of having committed, or having ordered to be committed, a grave breach was subject to the provisions of national legislation, and to the existence of a prima facie case being made by the requesting party. The Geneva Conventions therefore do not constitute in and of themselves a basis for extradition procedures or other forms of surrender. At the same time, assessing whether the requesting High Contracting Party has made a prima facie case is a task left to the competent authorities of the custodial state. Finally, the proposals to rule out the defence of acting on superior orders, and to spell out that those giving illegal orders were criminally responsible even though acting in the exercise of an official function, did not find their place in the provisions on grave breaches.[23] Similarly, the proposal to oblige contracting states to report to the Swiss Government on the measures adopted to criminalize the grave breaches as offences in national legislation was ultimately defeated.[24]

B. Meaning and Application

10   Before examining in more detail the scope and content of the provisions of the Geneva Conventions on grave breaches, it is fitting to summarize them briefly.

11   The provisions in question are common to the four Geneva Conventions. They are mainly identical in content, the only difference being the list of acts amounting to grave breaches (Article 50 GC I; Article 51 GC II; Article 130 GC III; Article 147 GC IV). Each Convention proclaims that grave breaches are 'those involving any of the following

---

[23] See Final Record, vol II-B, Fourth Report drawn up by the Special Committee of the Joint Committee, 12 July 1949, at 115, where it is reported—without further information—that it was not possible to reach general agreement 'regarding the notions of complicity, attempted violation, duress or legitimate defence or the plea "by orders of a superior"' and that 'these notions should [have been] left to the judges who [would have applied] the national laws'. The failure to include in the GCs a provision ruling out—at least, in certain circumstances—the defence of superior orders for charges of grave breaches, is often referred to as an argument to prove the lack of sufficient *opinio juris* to support the existence of a customary rule precluding the availability of this defence. On the question of superior orders as a possible defence to charges of war crimes, see Y. Dinstein, *The Defence of 'Obedience to Superior Orders' in International Law* (Leiden: Sijthoff, 1965), in particular at 223 ff, where the author discusses the issue in light of the preparatory work of the GCs. The attempt to include such a provision failed again at the time of the adoption of AP I. The present author argues instead that there are sufficient grounds to assert the existence of a rule of customary international law (CIL) proscribing the acceptance by a court of a defence of having obeyed an order to commit an act that constitutes a war crime. In the ICC Statute, obedience to superior orders may constitute a defence to a charge of a war crime in specific circumstances (Art 33 ICC Statute) (but not to a charge of crimes against humanity or genocide). See P. Gaeta, 'The Defence of Obedience to Superior Orders: The Statute of the International Criminal Court *versus* Customary International Law', 10 *EJIL* (1999) 172. *Contra*, C. Garraway, 'Superior Orders and the International Criminal Court: Justice Delivered or Justice Denied', 81 *IRRC* 836 (1999) 785. On the availability of the defence of having acted in official capacity, see MN 43–48.

[24] Final Record, vol II-B, at 116.

acts, if committed against persons or objects protected' by the relevant Convention, namely: 'wilful killing', 'torture or inhuman treatment, including biological experiments', 'wilfully causing great suffering or serious injury to body or health'. To this common list, each Convention adds other acts. Geneva Conventions I, II, and IV also list 'extensive destruction and appropriation of property, not justified by military necessity and carried out unlawfully and wantonly'. Geneva Conventions III and IV also include 'compelling' a protected person 'to serve in the forces of the hostile Power', and 'wilfully depriving' a protected person 'of the rights of fair and regular trial prescribed' in the relevant Convention. The acts of 'unlawful deportation or transfer or unlawful confinement of a protected person' and 'taking of hostages' appear only in the list set out in GC IV.

The obligations undertaken by contracting parties in respect of the aforementioned grave breaches are the same in each Convention (Article 49 GC I; Article 50 GC II; Article 129 GC III; Article 146 GC IV).[25] First, there is the obligation 'to enact any legislation necessary to provide effective penal sanctions for persons committing, or ordering to be committed, any of the grave breaches'. Secondly, there is the obligation 'to search for persons alleged to have committed, or to have ordered to be committed, such grave breaches', and '[to] bring such persons, regardless of their nationality, before [their] own courts'. A contracting party has the possibility, 'if it prefers, and in accordance with the provisions of its own legislation, [to] hand such persons over for trial to another High Contracting Party concerned, provided such High Contracting Party has made out a *prima facie* case'. However, the Conventions also specify that '[i]n all circumstances, the accused persons shall benefit by safeguards of proper trial and defence', and set as a minimum the guarantees 'provided by Article 105 and those following of the [Third] Geneva Convention'.

Each of these obligations will now be examined in turn.

I. The obligation to provide for effective penal sanctions

a. *The content of the obligation*

On a literal interpretation, states parties to the Geneva Conventions are not obliged to criminalize acts amounting to grave breaches as such. The Conventions merely require them 'to enact any legislation necessary to provide for effective penal sanctions' for persons responsible for a grave breach. In other words, to the extent that 'effective penal sanctions' are envisaged, the obligation is complied with, regardless of the characterization in the internal legal order of the offence as 'a grave breach of the Geneva Convention'.[26] This might help to explain why the majority of states have not yet criminalized acts amounting

---

[25] This list is complemented by the grave breaches mentioned in Arts 11 and 85 AP I, and the latter Article expressly declares that grave breaches are to be regarded as 'war crimes'. This addition finally clarified the confusion that existed for some time after the adoption of the GCs between grave breaches and war crimes: see M.D. Öberg, 'The Absorption of Grave Breaches into War Crimes Law', 91 *IRRC* 873 (2009) 163, at 167.

[26] See G.I.A.D. Draper, 'The Geneva Conventions of 1949', 114 *RCADI* (1965-I) 63, at 156, who notes that '[i]f the acts called "grave breaches" are already subject to effective penal sanctions under the existing penal law of the State concerned its obligation under this article will have been discharged'. He also adds, however, that '[s]uch is not likely to be the case when one considers the wide nature of the acts prohibited and the class of persons, namely "protected persons", who are the potential victims of such acts'. See also, more recently, C. Kreβ, 'Reflections on the *Iudicare* Limb of the Grave Breaches Regime', 7 *JICJ* (2009) 789, at 795, who also observes that the practice of states does not reveal an *opinio juris communis* to this effect; and W. Ferdinandusse, 'The Prosecution of Grave Breaches in National Courts', 7 *JICJ* (2009) 723, at 729.

to grave breaches expressly,[27] and why some states maintain that ordinary offences in their criminal codes are applicable to the acts described in the Conventions as grave breaches.[28]

15   Following the Pictet Commentary,[29] not all commentators are comfortable with this position.[30] For instance, some authors have argued that—whatever the intention of the parties at the time of its adoption—it is doubtful that the aforementioned obligation 'could (still) be interpreted in a way as to leave states [a] far-ranging discretion'. According to these authors, a strict interpretation—whereby when effective penal sanctions are already provided for in the existing domestic criminal legislation, there is no obligation to adopt specific criminal rules on grave breaches—would ultimately 'defy the very object and purpose' of the provisions on grave breaches.[31] The reason being that contracting parties are clearly obligated to ensure punishment of grave breaches under universal criminal jurisdiction, which in turn requires states to 'implement legislation that is universal'.[32] Moreover, the authors in question argue that some grave breaches are so specific to situations occurring in warfare that it is unlikely that ordinary criminal legislation would be applicable to them. One example is that of the grave breach of 'unlawful transfer' of a protected person under Article 147 GC IV, which would require, in most cases, specific criminal legislation as a means to ensure an 'effective penal sanction'.[33] Lastly, and more generally, they argue that ordinary criminal offences 'do not reflect the particular war nexus that is inherent in the grave breaches'.[34] Other commentators propound a similar argument. In particular, they underline that grave breaches are crimes under international law: recourse to charging ordinary offences in order to repress grave breaches might have adverse effects when one has to consider certain defences (for instance acting on superior orders).[35]

16   These arguments, however, are not entirely convincing. First, one may note that national criminal law might already provide for universal criminal jurisdiction over ordinary criminal offences, including those applicable to acts amounting to grave breaches. Admittedly, when this is not the case, it would prove more expedient to enact legislation criminalizing grave breaches as such and providing for universal criminal jurisdiction over them. Theoretically, however, it is possible for a state to opt for a different course of action, namely to extend the territorial reach of ordinary offences relevant to grave breaches without creating new criminal offences under the title of 'grave breaches'. The present author is therefore not convinced that the 'the very object and purpose' of the grave

---

[27] According to a study based on the information of the Advisory Service of the ICRC, only 35 states have penalized all grave breaches as such, while additional 38 states have penalized most or some grave breaches as such. See R. van Elst, 'Implementing Universal Jurisdiction over Grave Breaches of the Geneva Conventions', 13 *LJIL* (2000) 815, at 825.

[28] For a reference to these countries, see van Elst, above n 27, at 825; and K. Dörmann and R. Geiß, 'The Implementation of Grave Breaches into Domestic Legal Orders', 7 *JICJ* (2009) 703, at 713–14, with relevant references.

[29] Pictet Commentary GC I, at 363.

[30] See Dörmann and Geiß, above n 28, at 706–10; van Elst, above n 27, at 828.

[31] Dörmann and Geiß, above n 28, at 708.

[32] Ibid, at 709. See also van Elst, above n 27, at 828.

[33] Dörmann and Geiß, above n 28, at 709. Another example is that of the wilful deprivation of the rights of fair and regular trial to a protected person under the terms of Art 130 GC III and Art 147 GC IV: see van Elst, above n 27, at 828.

[34] Dörmann and Geiß, above n 28, at 710; see also at 713–15, where the authors argue that ordinary criminal provisions are intrinsically unable to reflect the 'specific injustice' of the grave breaches.

[35] See van Elst, above n 27, at 828, and additional reference provided by that author in fn 58.

breaches provisions in the Geneva Conventions would be defeated by leaving contracting states a wider margin of discretion in this respect.

Secondly, it is true that ordinary criminal law may not cover all of the acts amounting to grave breaches of the Geneva Conventions; such acts, however, are very few. In any case, it would be only with respect to these acts that the need for an ad hoc criminalization would arise, so the obligation to provide for an effective penalty does not really imply an obligation to pass ad hoc criminal legislation for *all* acts amounting to grave breaches.

The third argument, namely that ordinary criminal offences fail to capture the 'international nature' of the crime (with the ensuing consequences[36]), raises a more general issue, which is related to what has to be described as a subjective belief concerning what the function and purpose are of the rules of international law comprising so-called international criminal law (ICL). For those who conceive of ICL as a *jus commune* to all states (meaning that individuals responsible for given acts shall be subject to the same criminal law, irrespective of the court before which they stand trial), the fragmentation of ICL through the application of domestic criminal offences will certainly appear inadequate or disturbing. This vision does not reflect—at least as of today—the reality of international society, whose primary subjects exhibit as their main distinguishing trait jurisdictional power over individuals, including in criminal matters. International criminal law has already achieved important objectives, such as imposing on states, through treaties, the obligation to punish certain acts which are illegal under international law. It has also gone so far as to make some acts 'directly' criminalized under international law, thus there is no breach of the principle of legality as laid down in human rights treaties when national courts punish such crimes, even in the absence of applicable domestic legislation at the time of the commission of the act.[37] To contend that ICL also imposes on states the duty to adopt at the national level an ad hoc set of identical criminal offences with the same *nomen juris* and legal ingredients as those found in the treaty, in the absence of an express treaty obligation in this regard, seems, at present, unwarranted.[38] Plainly, the enactment by states of ad hoc provisions on grave breaches would be preferable in order to enhance

---

[36] See P. Gaeta, 'International Criminalization of Prohibited Conduct', in A. Cassese (ed), *The Oxford Companion to International Criminal Justice* (Oxford: OUP, 2009) 63, at 70–3.

[37] In fact, the so-called principle of legality, which provides that an individual cannot be punished for conduct that was not criminal under the legal system of the forum state when it was carried out, is fully satisfied if the criminality of such conduct was instead provided for by a principle or rule of international law. See Art 15(2) ICCPR. See also Art 7(2) ECHR, as well as Art 10 of the Draft Code of Crimes against the Peace and Security of Mankind, adopted by the ILC, reprinted in report of the ILC on the work of its 43rd session, 29 April–19 July 1991, UN Doc A/46/10, 1991. Furthermore, international criminal courts and tribunals have consistently held that a court may enter convictions for a crime where it is satisfied that the offence (or the relevant mode of liability) was proscribed under CIL at the time of its commission. See, e.g., ICTY, *The Prosecutor v Tihomir Blaškić*, Appeals Chamber Judgment, IT-95-14-A, 29 July 2004, para 85 (holding same with respect to failure to punish subordinates); ICTY, *The Prosecutor v Milan Milutinović Ojdanić et al*, Appeals Chamber Decision on Dragoljub Ojdanic's Motion Challenging Jurisdiction, IT-99-37-AR72, 21 May 2003, para 30 (same with respect to the joint criminal enterprise mode of individual criminal responsibility); SCSL, *The Prosecutor v Sam Hinga Norman*, Appeals Chamber Decision on Preliminary Motion based on Lack of Jurisdiction, SCSL-2004-14-AR72(E), 31 May 2004, paras 38, 53 (same with respect to the war crime of child recruitment).

[38] Arguably, an example of an express treaty provision imposing on contracting states the obligation to criminalize and punish a crime as defined in the relevant treaty is Art 5 of the Genocide Convention, according to which '[t]he Contracting Parties undertake to enact, in accordance with their respective Constitutions, the necessary legislation to give effect to the provisions of the present Convention and, in particular, to provide effective penalties for persons *guilty of genocide* or any of the other acts enumerated in Article 3' (emphasis added).

b. *The question of the effectiveness of penal sanctions*

19 Regardless of whether contracting states decide to pass ad hoc criminal legislation on grave breaches or to rely on their ordinary criminal law, the Geneva Conventions expressly establish that national law shall provide 'effective penal sanctions' for persons allegedly responsible for a grave breach. At first sight, this wording might be read as requiring that persons found responsible for having committed a grave breach actually have a real penalty inflicted on them. The French text, however, states that contracting parties shall enact national legislation necessary 'pour fixer les sanctions pénales adéquates à appliquer' to persons responsible for a grave breach. The clear meaning here is that the penalty must be that 'most appropriate' for the illegal act. Arguably, this interpretation is the one that best reconciles the two texts. It seems also to be the one suggested in the Pictet Commentary, which explains that 'the legislation enacted on the basis of this paragraph should […] specify the nature and extent of the penalty for each infraction, taking into account the principle of due proportion between the severity of the punishment and the gravity of the offence'.[39]

20 In light of the great variation of legislative policy with regard to criminal sanctions, the penalty which an individual offender will actually face for a grave breach will depend on the state that tries him or her after capture. This outcome might again appear disturbing to those who would wish to see a system of international criminal justice for war crimes and other crimes under international law that relies upon a body of identical applicable domestic criminal rules. Nonetheless, disparity in applicable criminal penalties is the unavoidable consequence of a system of criminal repression founded on concurrent national criminal jurisdictions, as each state has its own system and policies for criminal punishment.

21 Difficulties arise when it comes to assessing whether the penalty is 'effective' with respect to the criminal act. Generally, this assessment depends on the weight one puts on one or the other traditional functions assigned to the punishment of crimes, namely retribution, protection, incapacitation, deterrence (general and special), and rehabilitation. Domestic legal systems might be more inclined to consider one of these objectives as predominant, which in turn will lead to ranges of 'effective' penalties that could vary remarkably with respect to comparable criminal offences in other states. Suffice it to refer here to the divide between the US, where retribution has a prominent place, and European countries, where instead there is greater concern for rehabilitation.[40] Looking for an objective yardstick against which to evaluate the 'effectiveness' of a criminal sanction will thus be a difficult, if not an impossible, mission.

---

[39] Pictet Commentary GC I, at 363. At the 1947 Government Experts Conference, the Commission dealing with the revision of the Wounded and Sick Convention proposed a definition of war crimes as violations of the Convention for which '[t]he responsible person shall be liable to *appropriate* penalties' (Art 33 (new)) (emphasis added), in ICRC, *Report of the Work of the Conference of Government Expert for the Study of the Conventions for the Protection of War Victims (Geneva, April 14–26, 1947)*, at 63.

[40] See J.D. Ohlin, 'Towards a Unique Theory of International Criminal Sentencing', *Cornell Law Faculty Publications, Paper 23* (2009) 373, at 376–82, also for additional references.

22 As for grave breaches, and more generally crimes in violation of international law, the lack of clarity as to the specific functions and purposes of ICL further complicates the matter. For instance, there are those who argue that the significance of repression of international crimes lies more in the narrative of holding the trial than in the punishment of the offender.[41] Others think otherwise, and contend that the primary purpose of criminal punishment for international crimes must be retribution and deterrence,[42] which in turn calls for greater punishment in light of the particular gravity of such crimes.[43]

23 Unfortunately, even the creation and practice of the modern international criminal courts do not help to shed much light on the matter. Their constitutive instruments concerning penalties and sentencing contain only very generic guidelines;[44] this is combined with the absence of a robust and coherent vision from the judges as to what sort of system of penalties and sentencing policy ought to be adopted.[45]

24 As things stand, one has to accept some degree of flexibility in assessing whether a penal sanction is 'effective' with respect to an act amounting to a grave breach. This flexibility, however, does not allow for any lapses of good faith by relevant state authorities in the selection of domestic charges against persons responsible for grave breaches, or for choosing an appropriate penalty in the sentencing phase. Practices that reveal a lenient attitude by the judicial authorities vis-à-vis their own nationals responsible for grave breaches (often members of the military)—both in terms of charging and sentencing—do not in fact fulfil the obligation to provide for effective penal sanctions clearly spelt out in the relevant provisions of the Geneva Conventions.[46]

c. *The persons against whom effective penalties must be established*

25 Effective penal sanctions must be directed against 'persons committing' or those 'ordering to be committed' a grave breach. The exact scope and content of these expressions is again left to the determination of national jurisdictions, which may therefore turn to their own

---

[41] See in this respect D. Luban, 'Fairness to Rightness: Jurisdiction, Legality, and the Legitimacy of International Criminal Law', in S. Besson and J. Tasioulas (eds), *The Philosophy of International Law* (Oxford: OUP, 2010) 569, at 574–7. On the so-called expressive function of international criminal law, see M. Drumbl, 'Collective Violence and Individual Punishment: The Criminality of Mass Atrocity', 99 *Northwestern University Law Review* (2005) 539.

[42] Ohlin, above n 40, at 382–92.

[43] According to Harmon and Gaynor, in the context of international crimes, '[e]xtremely lenient sentences should, in general, be avoided; a slap on the wrist of the offender, is a slap in the face of victims': see M.B. Harmon and F. Gaynor, 'Ordinary Sentences for Extraordinary Crimes', 5 *JICJ* (2007) 683, at 711. For strong arguments in support of retribution as the primary purpose of international criminal punishment, see Ohlin, above n 40, at 382–8.

[44] The drafters of statutes of various international criminal courts created so far could not agree upon a scale of penalties for the crimes under the jurisdiction of those courts, due to the widely divergent views on the matter. The judges of international criminal courts therefore enjoy great discretion in the sentencing phase, subject only to specific express limitations. For instance, Art 24(1) of the Statute of the ICTY provides that penalties must be limited to imprisonment and that, in determining the terms of imprisonment, the Tribunal shall have recourse to the 'general practice regarding prison sentences in the courts of the former Yugoslavia'. This last provision, however, was held to be non-mandatory by the Tribunal in several cases (see A. Cassese and P. Gaeta, *Cassese's International Criminal Law* (3rd edn, Oxford: OUP, 2013), at 36). See also, though referring to prison sentences in Rwanda, Art 23 ICTR Statute. As for the Statute of the ICC, Art 77 merely envisages the harshest penalty of imprisonment for a maximum of 30 years, while also providing for the possibility of life imprisonment 'when justified by the extreme gravity of the crime and the individual circumstances of the convicted person'.

[45] Ohlin, above n 40, at 392 ff. On the sentencing practice of the ICTY and ICTR, see D. Scalia, *Du principe de légalité des peines en droit international pénal* (Brussels: Bruylant, 2011), esp at 185–224, as well as S. D'Ascoli, *Sentencing in International Criminal Law* (Oxford: Hart Publishing, 2011), esp at 109–262.

[46] Ferdinandusse, above n 26, at 730–2.

principles and rules on individual criminal responsibility. The main significance of this specification in the common provisions on grave breaches lies, as the Pictet Commentary aptly points out, in the assertion that '[t]he joint responsibility of the author of an act and of the person ordering its commission is [...] established'.[47]

26   Analysing the case law of the ad hoc international criminal tribunals for the former Yugoslavia and Rwanda, one might contend that customary international law (CIL) contains rules on 'commission' and 'ordering' as modes of international criminal liability applicable to international crimes, including grave breaches of the Geneva Conventions. For instance, the International Criminal Tribunal for the former Yugoslavia (ICTY) has asserted that, under CIL, commission can also comprise a 'joint criminal enterprise' in three different forms.[48] The International Criminal Court (ICC) has instead developed the theory of co-perpetratorship, when interpreting Article 25(3)(a) of the ICC Statute referring to the commission of a crime jointly with another person.[49] The ICTY and the International Criminal Tribunal for Rwanda (ICTR) have also spelt out the legal requirements of 'ordering' as a mode of criminal liability.[50] One might wonder to what extent these alleged rules of CIL on commission and ordering are binding upon states and must therefore be applied by national courts exercising their criminal jurisdiction over acts constituting grave breaches of the Geneva Conventions.[51]

27   In this regard, the better view appears to be the one that advocates that these modes of liability are not a 'constitutive' component of international criminalization, and that national legal systems therefore do not have to implement them.[52] In practice, this means that, although one can find a customary definition, states are at liberty to continue to apply their own rules and principles on commission and ordering. Here again, it is clear that we are confronted with the idea that ICL is based upon the pluralism of domestic criminal systems,[53] although the latter are at liberty to rely on rules formed at the international level should they consider this necessary or desirable.

28   If one shares the view set out above (MN 18), and since contracting states are not obliged to apply the customary rules on the forms of criminal liability expressly mentioned in the grave breaches provisions of the Geneva Conventions (namely, according to Articles 49/50/129/146, committing and ordering the commission of a grave breach), they are *a fortiori* at liberty to rely on their domestic legal rules for other modes of liability, such as aiding and abetting, instigation, and so on. These modes of liability have a purely 'internal' pedigree, and it is therefore unlikely that a lacuna with respect to rules on principals and accessories in criminal offences will exist in domestic legal orders.

---

[47] Pictet Commentary GC I, at 363.
[48] See, e.g., ICTY, *The Prosecutor v Duško Tadić*, Appeals Chamber Judgment, IT-94-1-A, 15 July 1999, para 220.
[49] See, e.g., ICC, *The Prosecutor v Thomas Lubanga*, Decision on the confirmation of charges, ICC-01/04-01/06, 29 January 2007, paras 330–40.
[50] See, e.g., ICTR, *The Prosecutor v Laurent Semanza*, Appeals Chamber Judgment, ICTR-97-20-A, 20 May 2005, paras 360–1; ICTY, *The Prosecutor v Dario Kordić and Mario Čerkez*, Appeals Chamber Judgment, IT-95-14/2-A, 17 December 2004, paras 28–30.
[51] On the modes of criminal liability at the international criminal courts, see generally Cassese and Gaeta, above n 44, at 161–206.
[52] E. van Sliedregt, *Individual Criminal Responsibility in International Law* (Oxford: OUP, 2012), at 11–12.
[53] See *amplius* A.K.A. Greenwald, 'The Pluralism of International Criminal Law', 86 *Indiana Law Journal* (2011) 1063.

29 Criminal liability in the form of 'commission by omission' (or 'indirect omission') deserves a particular mention, since it is a mode of liability which is not accepted by all domestic legal systems (see Chapter 36 of this volume, MN 25–27 and 30). In this regard, the Pictet Commentary notes that in the common provisions on grave breaches, 'there is no reference to the responsibility of those who fail to intervene, in order to prevent or suppress an infraction', although '[i]n a number of such cases sentences of "guilty" have been passed by Allied courts'. It considers, however, that '[i]n view of the silence of the Convention it must be assumed that the matter is one which must be settled by national legislation, either by express provision or by applying the general provisions contained in the country's penal code'.[54]

30 Two developments might have affected the conclusion put forward in the Pictet Commentary. The first is the express reference in Article 86 AP I to the obligation of the High Contracting Parties and the Parties to the conflict to 'repress grave breaches [...] of the Conventions and of [the] Protocol which result from a failure to act when under a duty to do so'. The second is the assertion in the case law of international criminal courts, most notably that of the ICTY, of the existence of CIL on 'commission by omission'.[55] One might therefore argue that this form of responsibility for the repression of grave breaches is 'imposed' on states that are parties to the Geneva Conventions and AP I. However, one might note that Article 86 AP I does not expressly require the criminalization 'of the failure to act when under a duty to do so'.[56] In addition, as for the alleged development of a rule of CIL on commission by omission, one could again argue that it is available to states that wish to apply or implement it, but they are free to do otherwise.

31 Criminal responsibility for international crimes in the form of command/superior responsibility also warrants specific attention. This doctrine—which originates from the non-criminal rules of responsible military command—was relevant in some (controversial) leading cases after the Second World War.[57] However, it was only with the establishment of the first 'modern' international criminal tribunals (the ICTY and the ICTR) that this doctrine developed significantly, eventually finding its way into the ICC Statute.[58] In other words, here we face a theory of criminal liability that seems to have a purely 'international' origin.[59]

---

[54] Pictet Commentary GC I, at 364.

[55] See, e.g., ICTY, *Tadić*, above n 48, para 188; ICTR, *The Prosecutor v André Ntagerura et al*, Trial Chamber Judgment, ICTR-99-46-T, 25 February 2004, para 659; *The Prosecutor v André Ntagerura et al*, Appeals Chamber Judgment, ICTR-99-46-T, 7 July 2006, paras 334, 370.

[56] The ICRC Commentary APs for Art 86 AP I is ambiguous as regards the obligation to criminalize omission liability. It recognizes that it is for contracting states to establish under their domestic legal orders who has to carry out the duties established in the rules of IHL. It adds (at 1010, para 3538), 'It is self-evident, when a Detaining Power tries a prisoner belonging to the adverse Party, that the "duty to act" of the accused must be interpreted in the light of the powers and duties attributed to him under his own national legislation.' At the same time, it seems to consider that this provision implies the obligation to enact legislation to provide for effective penal sanctions (because of the reference to the obligation to repress but not the obligation to search for, bring to courts, or surrender persons as specified in the system of grave breaches of the Geneva Conventions).

[57] Among these cases, the most well-known is *Yamashita*, US Supreme Court, 327 US 1, 4 February 1946. See generally Cassese and Gaeta, above n 44, at 182–4. See also G. Mettraux, *The Law of Command Responsibility* (Oxford: OUP, 2009), at 3–21.

[58] See, e.g., ICTY, *The Prosecutor v Enver Hadžihasanović et al*, Appeals Chamber Decision on Interlocutory Appeal Challenging Jurisdiction in Relation to Command Responsibility, IT-01-47-AR72, 16 July 2003, para 17; Art 28 ICC Statute.

[59] See G. Werle, *Principles of International Criminal Law*, para 368, at 128, who describes superior responsibility for international crimes as 'an original creation of international criminal law'.

32   As is well known, under this doctrine, a person who wields hierarchical authority over a group of persons and exercises effective control over them, could, in certain circumstances, be held criminally responsible for failing to prevent and/or punish crimes committed by those subordinates. Controversy surrounds the question of whether superior responsibility is a form of vicarious liability for crimes committed by subordinates, or a separate offence committed by the superior who is derelict in his or her supervisory duties, or both (Chapter 36, MN 31, of this volume). Be that as it may, it is a fact that—as envisaged at the international level—superior responsibility is almost unknown to domestic criminal systems. It is only in the wake of the adoption of the ICC Statute that some state parties have felt it necessary to adopt rules to incorporate this type of responsibility at the national level, although in some cases they have expressly construed it as a separate offence of negligence. It seems premature to contend that states have the *obligation* (rather than the mere right) under CIL to provide for national rules incorporating the doctrine of superior responsibility for international crimes.[60] The national legislation enacted so far appears more as a choice by states parties to implement the ICC Statute in their domestic systems, rather than the expression of an *opinio juris* relevant to the existence of a rule of CIL obliging them to do so.

II. The obligation to search for persons who have allegedly committed, or have ordered to be committed, a grave breach

33   Unlike other treaty provisions relevant to the exercise of criminal jurisdiction, those contained in the Geneva Conventions oblige contracting parties 'to search for' persons who have allegedly committed, or have ordered to be committed, a grave breach. The provision thus imposes an obligation to carry out an activity (to search for) that implicitly secures the arrest of these persons in order to 'bring them before their own courts', as further required by the same provision.[61]

34   Questions arise as to which authorities of the state should carry out this activity. On a strict literal reading, the obligation is imposed on the 'High Contracting Parties', which have to bring suspects (once found) before their own courts; this requirement appears to put the burden on the executive authorities and would exclude the intervention of the judiciary.[62] However, this reading unduly restricts the scope of the provision, since this interpretation starts from the (wrong) assumption that the bearer of duties and obligations in international law is the executive branch of the state. More convincing is the thesis according to which, as is the case with international law in general, the obligation is incumbent on states as such, which will then have to discharge it on the basis of their respective legal orders. Therefore, if a domestic legal system provides that the judicial

---

[60] The principle of command and superior responsibility for international crimes (and above all war crimes) is, however, said to be clearly established in CIL: see ICRC CIHL Study, Rule 153. Importantly, as mentioned in Ch 36, MN 31–32, of this volume, Art 87 AP I does not expressly require contracting states to provide for the criminal liability of military commanders in the form of command responsibility but merely provides a right for them to do so.

[61] Pictet Commentary GC I states (at 365): 'The obligation imposed on the Contracting Parties to search for persons accused of grave breaches of the Conventions implies activity on their part.'

[62] See R. Maison, 'Les premiers cas d'application des dispositions pénales des Conventions de Genève par les juridictions internes', 6 *EJIL* (1995) 260, at 266–8, who stresses that this interpretation must be rejected on the basis of a correct understanding of the system of criminal repression of grave breaches enshrined in the Geneva Conventions.

authorities are competent to start investigations to identify and bring to justice persons allegedly responsible for a crime, nothing in the Geneva Conventions justifies stripping away their competence.[63]

Another question is whether a state should start the activity of 'searching for' someone only once it has information concerning the presence of the suspect on its territory. In this respect, the Pictet Commentary reads 'as soon as [a contracting party] is aware that a person on its territory has committed [a grave breach], it is its duty to see that such person is arrested and prosecuted without delay'.[64] If one follows this view, contracting states are not obliged to carry out any search if the suspected person is not allegedly on the territory of the state. In practice, this means that those (including the victims) who turn to the relevant state authorities to report the commission of a grave breach will at the same time have to present credible information that the alleged perpetrator can be found on the territory of the state. However, nothing in the wording of the provision allows for such a restriction. On the contrary, the obligation is framed in very broad terms and appears not to be subject to any restriction or condition.[65]

This question arose in the context of the proceedings brought by five Bosnian citizens, all residing in France, before the French judicial authorities, against unknown persons for acts amounting to, inter alia, grave breaches of the Geneva Conventions and allegedly committed against them in 1992 during the armed conflict in Bosnia-Herzegovina (the *Javor et al* case). While the investigating judge (*juge d'instruction*) found the Court was entitled to exercise its jurisdiction over such a case,[66] the Criminal Chamber of the Paris Court of Appeal reversed the decision, arguing that the grave breaches provisions were not self-executing in the French legal system.[67] The Court of Cassation confirmed this view.[68] It clarified that although the legislation implementing the Statute of the ICTY (adopted after the decision of the Court of Appeal)[69] was applicable, as there was no information regarding the presence of the suspects on French territory (required by the legislation in question), the French judicial authorities lacked jurisdiction over the case.[70]

The French Court of Cassation based its decision, inter alia, on the jurisdictional requirement of the presence of suspected persons on French territory, expressly set out in Article 1 of the applicable national legislation. Interestingly, the reference to the alleged non self-executing character of the obligation 'to search for' under the grave breaches provisions, in the decisions denying jurisdiction in *Javor*, implies that for the French courts this obligation—as set out in the grave breaches provisions—does not require the alleged

---

[63] Ibid, at 266–8.   [64] Pictet Commentary GC I, at 366–7.

[65] This is the view advocated by B. Stern, 'A propos de la competence universelle', in E. Yakpo and T. Boumedra (eds), *Liber Amicorum Judge Mohammed Bedjaoui* (The Hague: Kluwer, 1999) 735, at 747–8. See also Maison, above n 62, at 268–73; M. Henzelin, *Le principe de l'universalité en droit pénal international* (Basel/Brussels: Helbing & Lichtenhahn/Bruylant, 2000), at 354, para 1113.

[66] The text of the decision is available (in French) at <http://competenceuniverselle.files.wordpress.com/2011/07/jugement-tgi-6-mai-1994-javor.pdf>.

[67] The text of the decision is available (in French) at <http://competenceuniverselle.files.wordpress.com/2011/07/arret-ca-24-novembre-1994-javor.pdf>.

[68] Court of Cassation, Criminal Chamber, decision 26 March 1996. The decision is available (in French) at <http://competenceuniverselle.files.wordpress.com/2011/07/cass-26-mars-1996-javor1.pdf>.

[69] Law 2 January 1995, available (in French) at <http://legifrance.gouv.fr/affichTexte.do?cidTexte=JORFTEXT000000532676>.

[70] See decision of the Court of Cassation, above n 68.

presence of the suspect on national territory.[71] Simply put, this obligation was deemed incapable of having direct effect in the French legal system so as to establish jurisdiction over the alleged offences that had been committed against the Bosnian victims.

38 Arguably, the non self-executing character of the obligation to search for persons suspected of grave breaches stemmed—in the case at issue—from the fact that the crimes were committed abroad by foreigners and against foreigners. Had the allegations of grave breaches been brought against French nationals, or had they been related to facts occurring on French territory, one might wonder what the conclusions of the French courts would have been. In other words, one should distinguish between, on the one hand, the obligation to search for those suspected of grave breaches, and, on the other hand, the jurisdictional competence that may be necessary to prosecute any such suspect. We shall discuss in greater detail below (MN 56–61) the issue of the various grounds for jurisdiction with respect to grave breaches. Suffice it here to note that states that assert jurisdiction based on the principles of territoriality or active nationality do not usually request the presence of the alleged offender on the territory of the state for the purposes of judicial investigation and prosecution. The presence requirement is instead often demanded by states in order to acquire jurisdiction where the allegation is that offences have been committed abroad by foreigners and against foreigners. Such states are looking for a jurisdictional link in order to allow them to exercise criminal jurisdiction based on the principle of universality.

39 The obligation to search for persons allegedly responsible for grave breaches is also not limited 'geographically'. This clearly does not mean that in order to comply with such an obligation, the state can exercise jurisdictional acts in the territory of other states without their consent.[72] However, if a state has sufficient information to believe that a person has committed a grave breach and has grounds to believe that this person is under the jurisdiction of another state, it can submit to the latter a request for surrender or extradition.

40 Arguably, the 'obligation to search for' alleged violators, enshrined in the grave breaches provision, does not imply an obligation for contracting parties to carry out investigations to uncover the commission of a grave breach.[73] In other words, it is necessary that an allegation is made that a grave breach has been committed in order to trigger this obligation, even if the identity of the person responsible is unknown. This obligation is supplemented by other provisions of AP I, however, which reasserts the obligation of contracting parties to investigate (all) breaches of the Conventions as well as those listed in the Protocol.[74]

---

[71] In the words of the Criminal Chamber of the Paris Court of Appeal, the provisions on grave breaches 'revêtent un caractère trop général pour créer directement des règles de compétence extraterritoriale en matière pénale, lesquelles doivent nécessairement être rédigées de manière détaillée et précise'. (See above n 67.)

[72] A state is, however, also obligated to search for persons responsible for grave breaches in the territories where it is exercising its jurisdiction in conformity with international law (see in this regard L. Condorelli, 'Il sistema della repressione dei crimini di guerra nelle Convenzioni di Ginevra del 1949 e nel primo Protocollo addizionale del 1977', in L. Lamberti Zanardi and G. Venturini (eds), *Crimini di guerra e competenza delle giurisdizioni nazionali* (Milan: Giuffrè, 1998) 23, at 33–4).

[73] See in this vein M.N. Schmitt, 'Investigating Violations of International Law in Armed Conflict', 2 *Harvard National Security Journal* (2011) 31, at 39.

[74] Ibid, esp 40–3. In particular, one should mention Art 87(1) AP I, whereby military commanders must 'report to competent authorities breaches of the Conventions and of [the] Protocol' by 'members of the armed forces under their command and other persons under their control'. See also Art 87(3) AP I, that establishes the obligation of the High Contracting Parties and parties to the conflict to 'require any commander who is aware that subordinates or other persons under his control are going to commit or have committed a breach of the Conventions or of [the] Protocol, to initiate such steps as are necessary to prevent such violations of the Conventions or [the] Protocol, and, where appropriate, to initiate disciplinary or penal action against violators thereof'. Art 90 AP I also establishes the 'International Fact-Finding Commission'. Unfortunately,

III. The obligation to bring to court persons allegedly responsible for a grave breach

Contracting parties to the Geneva Conventions are obliged to exercise their adjudicatory jurisdiction in respect to persons allegedly responsible for a grave breach. The wording of the relevant provision could not be clearer, since it provides that they have to bring those persons before their own courts. In this respect, the grave breaches provisions differ from other treaties containing provisions for the repression of international crimes. For instance, under the terms of the 1984 UN Convention against Torture, a state party on whose territory an alleged torturer is found must, if it does not extradite that person, 'submit the case to its competent authorities for the purpose of prosecution' (Article 7(1)). This is the so-called 'Hague formula', enshrined in Article 7 of the Hague Convention for the Suppression of Unlawful Seizure of Aircraft. This formula does not imply an obligation to prosecute but leaves room for the exercise of prosecutorial discretion, if this is possible under the domestic legal system.[75] For grave breaches, this option seems to be unavailable.[76] To put it differently, the obligation under the grave breaches regime, to bring persons suspected of grave breaches before the courts of the state, means that these persons must stand trial if the prosecutorial authorities have collected sufficient evidence to bring a criminal charge. If sufficient evidence is gathered, the prosecutor cannot rely on the national rules on prosecutorial discretion and must prosecute the case.[77] It will then be for the courts to assess the criminal responsibility of the accused, in accordance with the minimum procedural guarantees provided for in GC III (and supplemented by Article 75(4) AP I)). On the other hand, contrary to what the Pictet Commentary seems to suggest,[78] the obligation of the High Contracting Parties to bring persons allegedly responsible for a grave breach before their own courts does not involve a duty to arrest the person suspected or accused of having committed a grave breach. The custodial state will thus have to follow its national rules on pre-trial detention and detention during trial.[79]

41

---

the Commission has so far remained a 'paper entity' (the expression is used by O. Ben Naftali and R. Peled, 'How Much Secrecy Does Warfare Need', in A. Bianchi and A. Peters (eds), *Transparency in International Law* (Cambridge: CUP, 2013) 321, at 354. According to some commentators, an obligation to investigate serious violations of IHL is included in the obligation to ensure respect for IHL, contained in CA 1. According to the same commentators, other norms of IHL and IHRL would constitute the legal basis for the obligation to investigate violations of IHL. (See A. Cohen and Y. Shani, 'Beyond the Grave Breaches Regime: The Duty to Investigate Alleged Violations of International Law Governing Armed Conflicts', *The Hebrew University of Jerusalem—International Law Forum, Research Paper N 02-12*, January 2011.) For the obligation to suppress all the breaches of the GCs not listed as grave breaches, see Ch 36 of this volume, MN 10–12.

[75] See G. Guillaume, 'La Convention de la Haye du 16 décembre 1970 pour la répression de la capture illicite d'aéronefs', 16 *AFDI* (1970) 35, at 50. See also, in respect to the 1984 Convention against Torture, the Judgment of the ICJ issued on 20 July 2012 in the *Questions Relating to the Obligation to Prosecute or Extradite case (Belgium v Senegal)*, para 90. Under the Hague formula, the prosecuting authorities should take their decision in the same manner as 'in the case of any ordinary offence of serious nature under the law of that State'.

[76] See Kreβ, above n 26, at 802–3.

[77] According to Kreβ, above n 26, at 802–3, prosecutorial discretion is allowed concerning the decision whether to take investigative steps as regards an alleged grave breach in the absence of the suspected offender. He argues that these measures 'fall outside the grave breaches regime and states are thus under no obligation to take such measures'. He seems therefore to take the view that under the GCs, it is a jurisdictional requirement that there be allegations concerning a person suspected of a grave breach who is actually present in the territory of the state. See, however, the discussion above, at MN 35–38. See also further MN 56–61. One might note that prosecutorial discretion over allegations of grave breaches is possible at the ICC (see Art 53 ICC Statute, regulating its exercise by the ICC Prosecutor).

[78] MN 35.   [79] See Kreβ, above n 26, at 800–1.

42   Arguably, the obligation at stake affects the freedom of states to enact national measures of amnesty or other measures of pardon covering acts involving grave breaches. These measures, if actually applied by the state concerned,[80] are unlikely to square with the duty to implement, in good faith, the said obligation.[81] The same might be said for provisions on amnesties eventually included in peace treaties, to the extent that such provisions cover and are actually applied to acts involving grave breaches.[82] Neither national measures on amnesty or pardon, nor provisions on amnesty in agreements concluded by belligerents, can bind third states;[83] in neither case can third states rely on such agreements to claim that they obviate the need for compliance with the obligation to search for and bring to court persons responsible for grave breaches.

43   More difficult is the question of the relationship between the obligation under discussion and the rules of CIL on immunities shielding some classes of state officials, or those who act on behalf of the state, from foreign criminal jurisdiction (respectively, so-called immunities *ratione personae* and immunities *ratione materiae*). The Geneva Conventions do not contain express provisions on the matter. One might therefore be tempted to contend that the obligation to punish persons responsible for grave breaches necessarily implies a derogation from the rules of CIL on immunities from foreign criminal jurisdiction. The International Court of Justice (ICJ) has taken a different stand, however. In the *Arrest Warrant* case, the Court noted that the obligation of prosecution or extradition contained in various international conventions for the prevention and punishment of certain serious crimes, 'in no way affects immunities under customary international law, including those of Ministers for Foreign Affairs'. According to the Court, '[t]hese remain opposable before the courts of a foreign State, even where those courts exercise such a jurisdiction under these conventions'.[84]

---

[80] If the measures of amnesty or pardon eventually issued in a country remain a dead letter or are disregarded by the competent authorities, the existence of such measures could not be considered an act contrary to the grave breaches provisions.

[81] See R. Kolb, 'The Exercise of Criminal Jurisdiction over International Terrorists', in A. Bianchi (ed), *Enforcing International Law Norms against Terrorism* (Oxford: Hart Publishing, 2004) 227, at 264. In discussing the scope of the obligation to repress the acts described in the so-called anti-terrorism conventions, he argues that it would run contrary to the obligation to implement a treaty in good faith to enact amnesty laws or to grant pardon for such acts. Only in limited and exceptional circumstances would such measures be admissible. His argument is applicable, *a fortiori*, to the grave breaches provisions, given the even broader content of the obligation to repress these breaches. For a critical discussion of the wider debate on the 'legality' under CIL of amnesty laws covering acts amounting to international crimes, see W.A. Schabas, *Unimaginable Atrocities* (Oxford: OUP, 2012), at 173–98.

[82] According to P. D'Argent, Arts 51/52/131/148, providing that '[n]o High Contracting Party shall be allowed to absolve itself or any other High Contracting Party of any liability incurred by itself or by another High Contracting Party in respect of [grave breaches]', implies that the High Contracting Parties cannot enter agreements providing for an amnesty. See P. D'Argent, 'Réconciliation, impunité, amnistie: quel droit pour quels mots?', 11 *La Revue Nouvelle* (2003) 30, at 33–4. See also P. D'Argent, *Les réparations de guerre en droit international public* (Brussels: Bruylant, 2003), at 771–4, with references to the *travaux préparatoires*.

[83] On the irrelevance of amnesty laws of a foreign state for national prosecution, see, e.g., the decision of the ECtHR in *Ely Ould Dah v France*, Decision on admissibility, 17 March 2009, at 18.

[84] ICJ, *Case concerning the Arrest Warrant of 11 April 2000 (Democratic Republic of Congo v Belgium)*, Judgment 14 February 2002, para 59. Interestingly, the case involved the arrest warrant issued by the Belgian competent authorities against the then acting Minister of Foreign Affairs of the Democratic Republic of Congo, inter alia, for charges that the Belgian Law applicable at the time considered to be 'grave breaches of the Geneva Conventions'. It is regrettable that the ICJ did not clarify the matter further, and failed to explain what would be the effective scope of the obligation to punish grave breaches should the rules on international immunities before foreign courts apply without exceptions in relation to persons suspected of committing or ordering the commission of a grave breach.

44 Since the case before the Court concerned immunities *ratione personae*, one might contend that this statement does not concern the other category of international immunities, namely those that protect an individual from foreign criminal jurisdiction for acts performed in an official capacity (immunities *ratione materiae*).[85] Nonetheless, the matter seems far from being settled. In the context of his work on the 'Immunity of State officials from foreign criminal jurisdiction', the then Special Rapporteur of the International Law Commission (ILC), Roman Kolodkin, argued that there are no sufficient elements in international practice to identify an exception to the rule on immunities *rationae materiae* in relation to international crimes.[86] With respect to the punishment of war crimes, in his view, the war crimes trials that took place after the Second World War were specific to the historical situation and do not constitute evidence of an exception to the rule on immunities in other contexts.[87] At the same time, he asserted that—regardless of the nature of the crime—these immunities do not apply in relation to offences perpetrated in the territory of the state exercising jurisdiction and in connection with activities performed in that state without its consent.[88] He also noted, however, that 'the issue of criminal prosecution and immunity of military personnel for crimes perpetrated during military conflict in the territory of a State exercising jurisdiction would seem to be governed primarily by humanitarian law'. Therefore, being a special case, the issue 'should not be considered within the framework of this topic'.[89] The stand taken by the Special Rapporteur sparked a lively debate within the ILC, with some members taking the view that one cannot interpret silence on the question of immunities in treaties concerning repression of international crimes as an implicit recognition that immunity applies in all cases involving the crimes that these treaties cover. Such an interpretation would render these treaties meaningless.[90]

---

[85] However, in a subsequent paragraph of the Judgment, the ICJ seems to consider that the international rules on immunities *ratione materiae* would also remain applicable in the case of charges of international crimes: ibid, para 61. In this paragraph, the Court clarified that 'the immunities enjoyed under international law by an incumbent or former Minister for Foreign Affairs do not represent a bar to criminal prosecution in certain circumstances'. Among these circumstances, the Court mentioned the case when 'a person ceases to hold the office of Minister for Foreign Affairs', since in this case 'he or she will no longer enjoy all of the immunities accorded by international law in other States'. According to the Court, 'Provided that it has jurisdiction under international law, a court of one State may try a former Minister for Foreign Affairs of another State in respect of acts committed prior or subsequent to his or her period of office, *as well as in respect of acts committed during that period of office in a private capacity*' (emphasis added). In this way the Court seems to imply that acts amounting to international crimes, if committed in 'an official capacity', would still be covered by the international rules on immunities *ratione materiae* before national jurisdictions (unless one considers that international crimes can never be considered acts committed in an official capacity). For a critical analysis of this obiter dictum of the Court, see A. Cassese, 'When May Senior State Officials Be Tried for International Crimes? Some Comments on the *Congo v. Belgium* Case', 13 *EJIL* (2002) 853. The view according to which immunities *ratione materiae* are not applicable in cases concerning international crimes is advocated, inter alia, in Art III of the *Resolution on the Immunity from Jurisdiction of the State and of Persons Who Act on Behalf of the State in case of International Crime*, adopted by the *Institut de droit international* at the Naples Session (2009), which provides that 'No immunity from jurisdiction other than personal immunity in accordance with international law applies with regard to international crimes.'

[86] Second report on immunity of State officials from foreign criminal jurisdiction, 10 June 2010, A/CN.4/631.

[87] Ibid, para 69.   [88] Ibid, paras 84–5   [89] Ibid, para 86.

[90] For a summary, see *Report of the International Law Commission*, General Assembly Official Records, 66th session, Supplement No 10 (A/66/10), at 222–4, § 121–31. One might argue the same with respect to the so-called immunities *ratione personae*. However, immunities *ratione personae* are 'temporary', protecting the person from foreign jurisdiction only until such time as that person holds a particular post (e.g., head of state or government, minister for foreign affairs, head of diplomatic mission), and in addition are limited to

45 Admittedly, it is unfortunate that the formula adopted in the Charter of the Nuremberg Tribunal, which highlights the 'irrelevance of the official capacity' of the defendant, is absent from the Geneva Conventions.[91] The draft of the Expert Committee convened by the ICRC for the drafting of the common provisions did contain such a rule.[92] It is unclear why the Final Diplomatic Conference dropped it. The matter must therefore be regulated in light of the content of the rules of CIL, and it is to be hoped that the work of the ILC will shed some light on this question.

46 The present author is convinced that the doctrine of immunities *ratione materiae* is profoundly at odds with the notion that individuals are directly responsible under international law for a certain class of international crimes, a class which certainly includes grave breaches of the Geneva Conventions. Asserting the applicability of the rules on immunities *ratione materiae* for grave breaches and other international crimes would mean shielding from criminal responsibility those who have abused their official capacity and committed acts that the international community considers criminal in nature, and therefore as deserving no protection under international law.[93] It would also mean that only those who had acted in a private capacity could be held accountable before the courts of a foreign state, although when it comes to grave breaches, and other war crimes, the great majority of these offences are committed by members of the belligerent armed forces and other state officials.

47 The alleged applicability of the doctrine of immunities *ratione materiae* for international crimes under CIL will also have an impact on the jurisdiction of the ICC. It would mean that Article 27 of the ICC Statute, which enshrines the principle of the irrelevance of official capacity for the purpose of criminal responsibility under the ICC Statute, and the inapplicability of immunities under international law before the Court, derogates from CIL and has legal force only on the basis of the treaty. As such, it would therefore be opposable only to states that are parties to the ICC Statute. The result would be that states

---

a specific class of state officials. The risk of impunity connected to the applicability of these immunities in respect of the crimes at stake is therefore not as great as in the case of the applicability, without exceptions, of immunities *ratione materiae*. These latter immunities do not come to an end (at least not until the state on behalf of which the individual has acted continues to exist). Should they apply to shield from foreign jurisdictions the individuals accused of an international crime, it would never be possible for a foreign court to exercise jurisdiction over such individuals, unless the state for which they have acted waives the immunity. On the question of the applicability of the international rules on personal immunities with respect to the exercise of national jurisdiction over international crimes, and the possible exceptions that might be envisaged *de lege ferenda*, see P. Gaeta, 'Immunity of States and State Officials: A Major Stumbling Block to Judicial Scrutiny?', in A. Cassese (ed), *Realizing Utopia. The Future of International Law* (Oxford: OUP, 2012) 227, at 233–5.

[91] See Art 7 of the Charter of the Nuremberg Tribunal.

[92] See Art III para 2 of the draft common articles prepared by the ICRC Expert Committee, reported in Pictet Commentary GC I, at 359, fn 1, whereby 'Full responsibility shall attach to the person giving the order, even if in giving it he was acting in his official capacity as a servant of the State.'

[93] See in this regard the stand taken by the Swiss Federal Tribunal in *A v Ministère Public de la Confédération*, Decision of 25 July 2012, BB.2011.140, concerning the alleged immunities *ratione materiae* of the former Algerian Minister of Defence, Khaled Nezzar, in respect of charges concerning war crimes and crimes against humanity, where it noted (at 5.4.3): '[I]l serait à la fois contradictoire et vain si, d'un côté, on affirmait vouloir lutter contre ces violations graves aux valeurs fondamentales de l'humanité, et, d'un autre côté, l'on admettait une interprétation large des règles de l'immunité fonctionnelle (*ratione materiae*) pouvant bénéficier aux anciens potentats ou officiels dont le résultat concret empêcherait, *ab initio*, toute ouverture d'enquête. S'il en était ainsi, il deviendrait difficile d'admettre qu'une conduite qui lèse les valeurs fondamentales de l'ordre juridique international puisse être protégée par des règles de ce même ordre juridique.' The text of the decision is available (in French) at <http://bstger.weblaw.ch/cache/pub/cache.faces?file=20120725_BB_2011_140.htm&ul=fr>.

not parties to the ICC could invoke before the Court the immunity *ratione materiae* of individuals (usually their own nationals) accused of grave breaches (and eventually other crimes under the jurisdiction of the Court).[94]

The present author is also convinced, however, that the issue of the applicability of immunities *ratione materiae* in relation to international crimes is inextricably linked with the issue of the exercise of criminal jurisdiction based on the universality principle. As the Kolodkin report indicates, there is less resistance to accepting the idea of the unavailability of these immunities when crimes have been committed in the territory of the state exercising jurisdiction (and when the territorial state has not consented to the exercise of official functions by the foreign state officials on its territory).[95] The concern is that those who have acted in an official capacity must be protected against the risks of abuse in the exercise of universal jurisdiction. According to the present author, these risks are exaggerated and are put forward precisely to shield from liability those who, while performing official functions, have committed crimes under international law. Ultimately, to take these concerns about abuse into account would mean seriously undermining the system of repression of international crimes, the development of which has benefitted immensely from the adoption of the grave breaches provisions.

IV. The obligation to hand over to another state persons suspected of a grave breach

A High Contracting Party, 'in accordance with the provisions of its own legislation', can opt to hand over for trial to another High Contracting Party persons allegedly responsible for a grave breach, if that other High Contracting Party 'has made out a prima facie case'. The system of repression of grave breaches thus relies upon the so-called principle of *aut dedere aut judicare* (one must either surrender or judge the individual) to ensure that those responsible will not escape criminal responsibility.

Among the different ways in which international provisions have incorporated the principle *aut dedere aut judicare*, the one envisaged for the repression of grave breaches makes the surrender (*dedere*) limb an option that will relieve the state that has custody of the suspect from the obligation to judge (*judicare*) him or her.[96] This also implies that the existence of a request to surrender has no bearing on the scope of the obligation of the state that receives an allegation of a grave breach. In other words, the obligation to search for and to bring before the national courts persons allegedly responsible for a grave breach must be complied with, even in the absence of a request for surrender by another contracting party. It is only in the case of surrender to another contracting party that the custodial state is relieved of its obligation to bring that person before its own national courts for trial.[97]

---

[94] See P. Gaeta, '*Ratione Materiae* Immunities of Former Heads of State and International Crimes: The Hissène Habré Case', 1 *JICJ* (2003) 186, at 192–4.

[95] See also para 61 of the ICJ Judgment in the *Arrest Warrant* case, above n 84, and quoted above n 85.

[96] See Henzelin, above n 65, at 353. In this sense, see also the Joint Separate Opinion of Judges Higgins, Kooijmans, and Buergenthal appended to the Judgment of the ICJ in the *Arrest Warrant* case (above n 84), para 30. This is the interpretation propounded by the ICJ in relation to the *aut dedere aut judicare* rule enshrined in Art 7 CAT, the wording of which reproduces the Hague Formula, which, to a greater extent than the grave breaches provisions, may be more susceptible to the interpretation requiring the treatment of the *dedere* and the *judicare* limbs as alternative obligations. See ICJ, *Questions Relating to the Obligation to Prosecute or Extradite (Belgium v Senegal)*, Judgment, 20 July 2012, paras 94–5.

[97] See Henzelin, above n 65, at 353. See also the ICJ in *Belgium v Senegal*, above n 96, para 94.

51   That surrender to another state is conditional upon the two requirements mentioned above—that the requesting state has a prima facie case and that the surrender is based on national legislation—clearly weakens the system of repression. As one commentator has aptly pointed out, a contracting state may well 'decline to try a person for lack of evidence in its possession', and at the same time decline 'to hand over the accused to a state which has such evidence'.[98] The national legislation may in fact consider the offence in question a political offence, which is usually an exception to extradition in relevant treaties.[99] In addition, it may lay down other obstacles to extradition, such as a ban on the extradition of nationals. The Geneva Conventions do not oblige the High Contracting Parties to amend their legislation on extradition. Article 88 AP I, which complements the system of repression of grave breaches of the Geneva Conventions, does not redress this situation. Although it requires contracting parties 'to afford one another the greatest measure of assistance' and to 'cooperate in the matter of extradition', this is to be in accordance with the system originally envisaged in the Conventions which subjects surrender to any restrictions that might apply in the national legislation of the requested state.[100]

52   As in the case of the express reference to the irrelevance of official capacity for the purposes of prosecution, the original draft by the Expert Committee convened by the ICRC before the Diplomatic Conference was more demanding than the eventual Conventions with respect to requiring extradition. The draft contained the obligation for contracting parties to 'enact suitable provisions for the extradition of any person accused of a grave breach' and made no mention of requests for extradition being handled in accordance with national law.[101] Arguably, here again we are confronted with an eventual compromise, reached at the Diplomatic Conference, to design grave breaches provisions that would be more acceptable to the powerful states.

53   One might wonder whether the state, having the custody of a person allegedly responsible for a grave breach, could be relieved from its obligation to bring this person before its own courts if it opted to surrender the suspect to a competent international criminal court. The Pictet Commentary envisages this possibility, where it asserts that the 'handing over of the accused to an international penal tribunal, the competence of which is recognized by the Contracting Parties', is not excluded by the provision at stake.[102] Similarly, and more recently, in the context of its work on the *Obligation to Extradite or Prosecute*, the ILC has referred to this alternative as a means to comply with its *aut dedere aut judicare* obligation.[103] However, it has pointed out that this would be possible unless 'a different

---

[98] See Draper, above n 26, at 159.

[99] It should be noted that the Genocide Convention rules out the possibility for contracting states to consider acts of genocide as 'political crimes' for the purpose of extradition. See on this issue R. Roth, 'The Extradition of *Genocidaires*', in P. Gaeta (ed) *The UN Genocide Convention. A Commentary* (Oxford: OUP, 2009) 278, at 282–6. In an *obiter dictum*, the ICTY Trial Chamber in *Furundžija* asserted that, considering the *jus cogens* status of the prohibition of torture, it cannot be considered as a political offence in the context of extradition (*The Prosecutor v Anto Furundžija*, Trial Chamber Judgment, IT-95-17/1-T, 10 December 1998, para 157). To the extent that the prohibition of grave breaches has a *jus cogens* character and one accepts this view, one could argue that the political offence clause should not bar the extradition of persons suspected of a grave breach.

[100] See ICRC Commentary APs, Art 88 AP I, at 1027, para 3568.

[101] Art II para 2 of the Articles proposed by the Expert Committee, reported in Pictet Commentary GC I, at 359, in the text of fn 1.

[102] Ibid, at 366.

[103] ILC, *Report of the Working Group on the Obligation to Extradite or Prosecute (Aut Dedere Aut Judicare)*, 22 July 2013, A/CN.4/L. 829, at 15, paras 33–4.

intention appears from the treaty or is otherwise established', as provided for in Article 28 of the Vienna Convention on the Law of Treaties.[104]

Does a state party to the Geneva Conventions fulfil its obligation to judge, or hand over the accused, if it surrenders a person allegedly responsible for a grave breach to the ICC? Answering this question in the affirmative is not as simple as it may appear at first sight. Setting aside the preliminary question of whether the correct application of the complementarity principle allows a contracting state not to discharge its primary duty to prosecute the crimes listed in the ICC Statute by surrendering the accused to the ICC,[105] one should take into account the following issues. First, the possibility of introducing into the system of repression of grave breaches a clause similar to the one provided in Article VI of the Genocide Convention, concerning trial by an international penal tribunal of competent jurisdiction, was discussed at the Final Diplomatic Conference but was in the end rejected.[106] This was another 'concession' to those states calling for more consideration to be given to state sovereignty in the approach to the punishment of individuals responsible for violations of the Geneva Conventions. Secondly, as the Pictet Commentary also underlines, and following the example of the Genocide Convention, an international criminal tribunal to which the suspect is surrendered 'shall be competent with respect to those Contracting Parties which shall have accepted its jurisdiction'. This requirement may thus bind parties to the Geneva Conventions that are also parties to the ICC Statute. When this is not the case, and the person suspected of a grave breach is a national of a state not party to the ICC Statute but a party to the Geneva Conventions, the alternative of surrendering this person to the ICC may not be available to the custodial state without implying a breach of its obligations under the Geneva Conventions. The state of nationality of the alleged offender might indeed claim that it has not accepted the jurisdiction of the ICC, and request the custodial state to comply strictly with its obligations under the Geneva Conventions. Things may be different if the jurisdiction of the ICC is triggered by the Security Council acting under Chapter VII of the United Nations Charter. According to one commentator, in cases of referrals by the Security Council, the jurisdiction of the ICC would stem from the resolution of the Security Council—binding on all members of the United Nations—and not from the ICC Statute.[107] The present author, however, does not share this view. The ICC Statute establishes an international organization governed—as all international organizations—by the so-called principle of speciality. The ICC can therefore exercise only the powers and competences that its states parties have delegated to it, expressly or implicitly. In addition, the relevant provisions of the ICC Statute clearly provide that the referral of a situation to the Court by the Security Council constitutes one of the conditions for the *exercise* of the Court's criminal jurisdiction, but it does not constitute the *source* of its jurisdiction. The referral by the Security Council of a situation in which crimes are committed on the territory or by a national of a state not party to the ICC Statute is no exception.[108]

---

[104] Ibid, at 34.

[105] See para 6 of the Preamble to the ICC Statute, whereby 'it is the duty of every State to exercise its criminal jurisdiction over those responsible for international crimes'.

[106] See Final Record, vol II-B, at 132.

[107] D. Akande, 'The Legal Nature of Security Council Referrals to the ICC and its Impact on Al Bashir's Immunities', 7 *JICJ* (2009) 333, esp at 341.

[108] Art 1 ICC Statute clearly states that the Court 'shall have the power to exercise its jurisdiction over persons for the most serious crimes of international concern, as referred to in this Statute', and that the 'jurisdiction and functioning of the Court shall be governed by the provisions of this Statute'. Arts 5 to 8

55 Be that as it may, the issue can certainly be framed differently for cases of surrender to the ICTY. The latter is an ad hoc judicial body created by the Security Council and endowed with authority which stems from binding decisions of the Security Council. All members of the UN are expected to accept the jurisdiction of this Tribunal and to comply with its requests for surrender that, under Article 103 of the UN Charter, prevail over any other international obligations of UN member states, including the obligation to judge or surrender as stipulated in the grave breaches provision.[109] Arguably, therefore, states that have surrendered persons suspected of a grave breach to the ICTY cannot be considered responsible for a violation of the *aut dedere aut judicare* principle as framed in the Geneva Conventions.

V. The question of jurisdictional link, including universal jurisdiction

56 Carrying out the obligations to search for, bring to court, or hand over, necessarily requires that the relevant state has criminal jurisdiction over grave breaches. The scope of the jurisdictional authority of contracting states over grave breaches is therefore crucial, and yet the Geneva Conventions do not expressly regulate the matter. The conventional wisdom, however, is that the Geneva Conventions establish a system of 'mandatory universal jurisdiction' over grave breaches. This expression is used to state two things at the same time: that contracting states are obliged to establish criminal jurisdiction based on the so-called universality principle; and, secondly, that they are obliged to exercise such jurisdiction to comply with the obligations to search for, bring to court, or hand over the suspect to another contracting state.

57 The grave breaches provisions do not define the universality principle in clear-cut terms. If one takes into account the *incipit* of the provisions ('*Each High Contracting Party* shall be under the obligation to search for') as well as the preparatory works as a supplementary means of interpretation, the logical conclusion is that the aforementioned obligations must be complied with regardless of the existence of any link with the crime or the alleged

---

define the crimes over which the Court 'shall have jurisdiction', while Art 12 sets forth the 'pre-conditions to the exercise of the jurisdiction of the Court'. The latter provision establishes that the Court 'may exercise its jurisdiction'—in the case of a referral by a state party or by virtue of a *proprio motu* investigation by the Office of the Prosecutor—if crimes are committed in the territory or by a national of a state party, or of a state that has accepted the ad hoc jurisdiction of the Court. Thus, this provision sets out a requirement for the Court to exercise its jurisdiction and not a requirement for the Court *to acquire* jurisdiction. This distinction is crucial. According to the first reading, the jurisdiction of the Court exists independently of where or by whom crimes are committed, and in that sense it is 'universal'. Such 'universal' jurisdiction cannot be exercised so long as the state has not accepted the jurisdiction of the Court either by becoming a party to the ICC Statute or on an ad hoc basis. However, this impediment disappears when the Security Council refers a situation to the Court. Thus, the 'universal' jurisdiction of the Court may be exercised by virtue of a Security Council referral, which operates to 'remove' a condition on the exercise—but is not the source—of the ICC's jurisdiction. On the 'universal' jurisdiction of the ICC, see, e.g., L.N. Sadat and R. Carden, 'The New International Court: An Uneasy Revolution', 88 *Georgetown Law Journal* (1999-2000) 381, at 407.

[109] Interestingly, in finding that Serbia had violated its obligation under Art VI of the Genocide Convention in the *Bosnian Genocide* case because it failed to surrender General Mladić to the ICTY, the ICTY relied on the fact that Serbia had signed the Dayton Agreement—and was therefore obliged to cooperate with the Tribunal—rather than on the binding nature of requests by the ICTY under the UN Charter (see Judgment, *Application of the Convention on the Prevention and Punishment of the Crime of Genocide (Bosnia and Herzegovina v Yugoslavia (Serbia and Montenegro)*, 26 February 2007, paras 439–50. The Court might have done so because of the uncertainty over several questions surrounding the UN membership status of the former Federal Republic of Yugoslavia.

offender.[110] Necessarily, therefore, contracting states are obliged to vest their competent authorities with such broad jurisdictional criminal reach.[111]

The main bone of contention is how broad universal criminal jurisdiction should be under the grave breaches system.[112] According to one view, once there is an allegation of a grave breach, the relevant contracting state should take the necessary steps to identify and locate the alleged offender, regardless of whether there is credible information that he or she is present on the territory under its jurisdiction. This interpretation is supported by the textual interpretation of the grave breaches provisions that 'do not logically presuppose the presence of the offender'.[113] Universal criminal jurisdiction will therefore be mandatory in what has been referred to as its 'pure' form. Under another view, the mandatory universal jurisdiction over grave breaches will be triggered only by the presence of the suspect on the territory of the state. This view is supported by reference to the Pictet Commentary[114] and finds some support in international case law.[115] In addition, the presence of the suspect on the territory of the state would be a necessary precondition for the meaningful exercise of the obligation to search for the suspect, as well as for the obligation to bring the suspect before the courts of the state or, in the alternative, to hand him or her over to another contracting state.[116]

Both views are partially correct. As already observed above (MN 35), the grave breaches provisions do not subject the obligation 'to search for' the suspect to the precondition that the suspect is present on the territory of the state. At the same time, to conceive of there being a mandatory obligation to exercise universal criminal jurisdiction without the suspect's ever having entered the territory of the state seems to be not only excessive,[117] but also contrary to the practice of states, which tend to establish some form of a 'link' with the crime (including the presence of the suspect on the territory) in order to acquire or trigger universal criminal jurisdiction, including over grave breaches.[118]

To resolve this apparent contradiction, we should observe that the grave breaches provisions cannot be interpreted as merely imposing a system of mandatory universal jurisdiction. On the contrary, they establish a system of mandatory exercise of criminal jurisdiction not only for states with no direct connection to the grave breach (neutral states), but also for the belligerents. Compliance with the mandatory exercise of criminal

---

[110] In this regard and for the necessary references to the preparatory works, see also R. O'Keefe, 'The Grave Breaches Regime and Universal Jurisdiction', 7 *JICJ* (2009) 811, at 813–15.

[111] Yet some judges of the ICJ have contested this view, and have denied that the grave breaches provisions have any impact whatsoever on the jurisdictional reach of contracting states, without, however, adducing any convincing arguments in support (ibid, at 817).

[112] For a discussion of this issue, see ibid, at 825–30.

[113] See the Dissenting Opinion of Judge van den Wyngaert in the *Arrest Warrant* case, above n 84, para 54.

[114] Above n 64 and relevant accompanying text.

[115] See Separate Opinion of Judge Guillaume in the *Arrest Warrant* case, above n 84, who considers that the 1949 GCs do not expressly regulate questions concerning the scope of national jurisdiction over grave breaches (Separate Opinion, at 39) and asserts (ibid, at 40) that 'Universal jurisdiction *in absentia* is unknown to international conventional law.'

[116] The present author has already put forward these arguments elsewhere: see P. Gaeta, 'National Prosecution of International Crimes: International Rules on Ground of Jurisdiction', in *Studi in onore di Gaetano Arangio-Ruiz* (Naples: Editoriale Scientifica, 2004) 1923, at 1936–7.

[117] See Cassese and Gaeta, above n 44, at 279–80.

[118] An overview of the national legislation on universal jurisdiction is available in a study prepared by Amnesty International, *Universal Jurisdiction: A Preliminary Survey of the Legislation around the World*, available at <http://www.amnesty.org/fr/library/asset/IOR53/004/2011/en/d997366e-65bf-4d80-9022-fcb8fe284c9d/ior530042011en.pdf>.

jurisdiction requires neutral states to act on the basis of the universality principle, while belligerent states will likely possess criminal jurisdiction for the violations of the laws of warfare under the principles of the territoriality of the offence and/or the nationality of the perpetrators or of the victim (i.e., respectively, the so-called active and passive personality principles).[119]

61 Seen from this perspective, it is therefore not surprising that the presence of the accused on the territory of the forum state is not mentioned in the grave breaches provision as a condition for the exercise of criminal jurisdiction. To include this would have meant providing a requirement, which is usually absent in national legislation, for criminal jurisdiction based on the territoriality and the active and passive nationality principles. This would have run counter to the main objective pursued by the adoption of the grave breaches provisions, namely to ensure the punishment of those responsible for violations of the Conventions. At the same time, the silence on the presence requirement does not necessarily mean that the drafters of the Conventions were envisaging a mandatory system of universal jurisdiction in its pure form. After all, such a system had never been envisaged in any prior treaty, neither is it found in any subsequent treaty dealing with criminal matters. On the contrary, states have shown a clear preference for the adoption of the principle of universal jurisdiction in the form of the *forum deprehensionis*. This does not mean that the 'voluntary' exercise of universal jurisdiction in its pure form is necessarily 'illegal' under CIL, including with respect to allegations of grave breaches. It is doubtful, however, that such exercise is mandatory under the terms of the Geneva Conventions.

VI. Judicial guarantees and the question of the status of prisoners of war

62 Ensuring due process to persons accused of grave breaches was the predominant concern of the ICRC during the whole process of preparation and drafting of the grave breaches provisions. It was a concern dictated by irregularities in the war crimes trials conducted by the courts of the victor states against enemy nationals after the Second World War,[120] and by the fear of political use being made of criminal proceedings.[121] Apparently, as long

---

[119] Common law countries usually consider that the so-called principle of passive personality, which justifies the assertion and exercise of criminal jurisdiction by the state of nationality of the victim of a crime committed abroad by a foreigner, is not admissible under CIL. The well-known case in the US is *Cutting* (see J.B. Moore, *A Digest of International Law* (Washington, DC: Government Printing Office, 1906), at 232–40). For a thorough analysis of the controversy surrounding this principle of jurisdiction, see G.R. Watson, 'The Passive Personality Principle', 28 *Texas International Law Journal* (1993) 14. However, with respect to the repression of war crimes, acts of terrorism and, more generally, crimes committed because of the specific nationality of the victim, the assertion of criminal jurisdiction based on the passive personality principle is uncontested (and has been progressively accepted in national legislations) even by those countries traditionally opposed to it. See *amplius*, also for the necessary reference, P. Gaeta, 'Il principio di nazionalità passiva nella repressione dei crimini internazionali da parte delle giurisdizioni interne', in G. Venturini and S. Bariatti (eds), *Studi in onore di Fausto Pocar* (Milan: Giuffrè, 2009), vol I, at 325.

[120] The trial of Japanese General Yamashita (above n 57) is a case in point; he sparked a lively debate—in the US and elsewhere—concerning respect for due process by the US military court which tried him in the Philippines. See Pictet Commentary GC III, at 413, also for the reference to other cases. On the wider debate concerning the use of military commissions by the US for the trial of 'unprivileged enemy belligerents', see, inter alia, D. Weissbrodt, 'International Fair Trial Guarantees', in A. Clapham and P. Gaeta (eds), *The Oxford Handbook of International Law in Armed Conflict* (Oxford: OUP, 2013) 410, at 428–39.

[121] See Lewis, above n 1.

as the grave breaches provisions obliged the forum state to comply with fair trial guarantees for the defendant, the ICRC was ready to make concessions at the Final Diplomatic Conference on other aspects contained in the draft of the Expert Committee.[122]

The Expert Committee had drafted a specific provision listing the safeguards that contracting states had to guarantee to 'any person accused of a breach' of the Conventions, including where that person was charged before an international jurisdiction.[123] It was not easy to have this proposal accepted by the Diplomatic Conference, in particular because some delegations (such as those of the Soviet Union and Hungary) considered that persons accused of war crimes had to be treated as normal criminal suspects.[124] A proposal by the French delegation was eventually adopted,[125] and became the current provision on judicial guarantees for those persons accused of any breach of the Conventions and not only grave breaches.[126] These guarantees are indicated to be, as a minimum, those enshrined in Articles 105 to 108 GC III, namely: the rights and means of defence; 'the right of appeal or petition from any sentence' pronounced upon the accused; the right to receive 'notification of findings and sentence', in a language the accused understands, if the sentence was not pronounced in his or her presence; and a series of rights connected to the execution of the sentence (for instance, the right to serve the sentence in the same establishments and under the same conditions as in the case of members of the armed forces of the Detaining Power, and in any case in conditions that 'shall in all cases conform to the requirements of health and humanity').[127] The Diplomatic Conference therefore did not include the other safeguards included in the draft of the Expert Committee, such as the prohibition against subjecting an accused person to 'any tribunal of extraordinary jurisdiction', or against imposing penalties or repressive measures more severe than those applied to the contracting states' own nationals or contrary 'to the general principles of law and humanity'. Nonetheless, the list of guarantees that shall be afforded to persons accused of a grave breach of the Geneva Conventions and AP I has been expanded by virtue of Article 75 AP I.[128] In addition, the guarantees that are expressly indicated by the relevant provisions to the benefit of persons accused of grave breaches constitute only a 'minimum standard' of treatment. As the ICRC correctly emphasizes, they 'do not in any way prevent more favourable treatment from being granted in accordance with other provisions of the Geneva Conventions and Additional Protocol I'.[129]

63

One specific aspect concerns the applicability of the status of POWs to those accused and convicted of a grave breach. Article 85 GC III expressly states that POWs 'prosecuted under the laws of the Detaining Power for acts committed prior to capture, shall retain, even if convicted, the benefits' of the Convention. The question whether this provision applies to captured enemy combatants who are accused of war crimes is of course crucial. One author

64

---

[122] Ibid, at 263, quoting a statement by Pilloud, who told Graven that '[the ICRC] vigorously desire[s] that the four elaborated articles will be accepted without change by the Diplomatic Conference, but it may be necessary *jeter du lest* [i.e. to throw out the ballast]'.

[123] Pictet Commentary GC I, at 359, in the text of fn 1.

[124] See Lewis, above n 1, at 265, also for the necessary reference.

[125] Pictet Commentary GC I, at 369.

[126] The GCs also provide that the contracting parties shall 'take measures necessary for the suppression of all acts' contrary to the Conventions 'other than the grave breaches'. See Ch 36 of this volume, MN 10.

[127] For a more detailed discussion of these guarantees, see Ch 59 of this volume.

[128] See Ch 59 of this volume.

[129] See ICRC, Advisory Service on International Humanitarian Law, 'Judicial Guarantees and Safeguards', available at <https://www.icrc.org/en/download/file/1089/judicial-garantee-icrc-eng.pdf>.

has forcefully argued that it does not.[130] In addition, some states have entered reservations to this provision for the purpose of denying the status of POW to persons accused or convicted of war crimes. These reservations (known as the 'communist reservations' since they were first formulated—although with different wording[131]—by the Soviet Union and other states of the Communist Bloc) caused great concern at the ICRC,[132] and sparked lively debate when they were actually invoked in relation to some armed conflicts.[133]

65   Arguably, these reservations are contrary to the object and purpose of the Convention.[134] It is also clear that—at least as regards those formulated also to cover persons *accused* of war crimes—their application could be considered incompatible with Article 5 paragraph 2 GC III, which provides that in case of doubt as to whether a person is entitled to the status of POW, he or she must enjoy the protection of the Convention until his or her status is determined by a competent tribunal.

C. Relevance in Non-International Armed Conflicts

66   As one commentator has pointed out, one of 'the most important shortcomings of the grave breaches regime is that its rules have been designed for international armed conflicts only'.[135] This does not mean that violations of the rules of IHL applicable to non-international armed conflict (NIAC), including violations of Common Article 3, do not entail individual criminal responsibility under international law. On the contrary, after the landmark ICTY decision in *Tadić*, this is now widely accepted. From a substantive point of view, therefore, most of the acts that constitute grave breaches of the Geneva Conventions would likewise be punishable in the context of NIAC as serious violations of Common Article 3, or as other war crimes. (See Chapter 36 of this volume, MN 22.)

67   The inapplicability of the grave breaches provisions means instead that the obligations of contracting states examined so far are confined to international armed conflicts (IACs). In the matter of criminal repression, contracting states would thus retain more freedom of action with regard to violations of rules of IHL committed in NIACs.

---

[130] See S. Glaser, 'La protection internationale des prisonniers de guerre et la responsabilité pour les crimes de guerre', 8 *Revue de droit pénal et de criminologie* (1950–51) 897, who considers that the status of POW cannot be invoked either during the criminal proceedings or after conviction (at 903).

[131] While the Soviet Union and other communist countries referred, in their reservation, to POWs who had been *convicted* (the Soviet Union gave assurances that the reservation would therefore not alter the effect of Art 85 GC III until 'the sentence has become legally enforceable'; see Pictet Commentary GC III, at 424), other countries formulated their reservation differently. For instance, the reservation formulated by the Democratic Republic of Vietnam reads: 'The Democratic Republic of Vietnam declares that prisoners of war *tried and convicted* of war crimes or crimes against humanity, in accordance with the principles laid down by the Nuremberg Judicial Tribunal, shall not benefit from the provisions of the present Convention as is specified in Article 85' (emphasis added). The same reservation was entered by the Provisional Revolutionary Government of the Republic of South Viet-Nam. As has been noted, if the word 'and' is read disjunctively then the reserving countries could 'circumvent' the obligations of GC III 'simply by indicting a prisoner of war for war crimes': see 'The Geneva Convention and the Treatment of Prisoners of War in Vietnam', 80 *Harvard Law Review* (1967) 851, at 862.

[132] See Pictet Commentary GC III, at 423–7.

[133] This was the case in the context of the Vietnam War; for reference, 'The Geneva Convention and the Treatment of Prisoners of War in Vietnam', above n 131.

[134] The issue would then arise of the consequences of the invalidity of the reservation, if this is considered contrary to the object and purpose of GC III.

[135] D. Fleck, 'Shortcomings of the Grave Breaches Regime', 7 *JICJ* (2009) 833, at 837.

The contention that the system of grave breaches of the Geneva Conventions is applicable only to breaches of the Conventions committed in IAC is mainly based on a textual interpretation of the relevant provisions.[136] In defining grave breaches, each Convention does in fact expressly require that such breaches involve any of the listed acts 'if committed against persons or property protected by the Conventions'. This wording certainly covers 'protected persons and objects', as defined by each Convention to identify those for whose sake the rules of the Geneva Conventions were adopted and who are therefore eligible, under the Conventions themselves, for a particular legal status.[137] However, it does not seem possible to argue that the notion of 'persons or property protected by the Conventions' also covers the beneficiaries of the protection afforded by Common Article 3, at least not if this provision is applied in the context of a NIAC—as its express wording requires. The traditional wisdom, at the time of the adoption of the Conventions and for a long time thereafter, was that war crimes were only a matter for IACs.[138] In addition, should the expression 'protected persons' also be used to refer to the categories of persons mentioned in Common Article 3 in the context of NIACs, the result would necessarily be that all other provisions of the Conventions that refer to 'protected persons' would likewise need to be deemed applicable to the persons protected by Common Article 3 in NIACs. Certainly, it would not be logical to contend that, in relation to the provisions on grave breaches alone, the expression 'protected persons' acquires a wider meaning that is precluded for all the other provisions of the Conventions using the same expression. The Geneva Conventions themselves clarify what is meant by 'protected persons or property' within each Convention.[139] The traditional reading of these provisions is that they refer only to persons and property in the context of IACs, and not also to persons protected by Common Article 3 in the context of NIACs. Lastly, while AP I has expanded the categories of persons and property to be protected by the Geneva Conventions, as well as the types of conduct that can constitute a grave breach, there is no reference to 'grave breaches' in AP II, applicable to certain categories of NIACs.[140] This is an additional element that points at the 'exclusive' nature of the grave breaches regime for war crimes committed against protected persons and objects in IACs, and as defined by the Geneva Conventions and AP I.

It would be also unconvincing to argue that since grave breaches are war crimes under CIL,[141] the provisions on grave breaches of the Geneva Conventions are applicable both to IAC and NIAC. The existence of rules of CIL that criminalize acts corresponding to grave breaches does not imply that the requirement that these acts are committed against

---

[136] See, in this respect, the stand taken by the ICTY, *The Prosecutor v Duško Tadić*, Appeals Chamber Decision on the Defence Motion for Interlocutory Appeal on Jurisdiction, IT-94-1-A, 2 October 1995, para 83. See, however, the Separate Opinion of Judge Abi-Saab, asserting the applicability of the grave breaches provisions to NIACs under CIL. On this point, also for additional reference to ICTY case law, see L. Moir, 'Grave Breaches and Internal Armed Conflicts', 7 *JICJ* (2009) 763, at 769–75.

[137] Art 13 GC I; Art 13 GC II; Art 4 GC III; Art 4 GC IV. The notion of 'protected persons and property' has been expanded by Arts 8, 44, and 45 AP I.

[138] See D. Plattner 'The Penal Repression of Violations of International Humanitarian Law Applicable in Non International Armed Conflicts', 30 *IRRC* 278 (1990) 409. This was also the position of the ICRC at least until 1993: *Final Report of the Commission of Experts Established Pursuant to Security Council Resolution 780*, UN Doc S/1994/674, 27 May 1992, para 52.

[139] Above n 137.

[140] See in this respect Y. Sandoz, 'The History of Grave Breaches Regime', 7 *IJICJ* (2009) 657, at 676–7.

[141] On criminalization of acts amounting to grave breaches under CIL, see J.-M. Henckaerts, 'The Grave Breaches Regime as Customary International Law', 7 *JICJ* (2009) 683, at 685–92.

protected persons or property is no longer in force. Similarly, the criminalization of grave breaches under CIL does not perforce imply that the obligations that states have crafted in the Geneva Conventions for the repression and punishment of grave breaches in the context of an IAC give rise to corresponding rules under CIL.[142]

D. Legal Consequences of a Violation

70 Every violation of a rule of international law entails the international responsibility of the state that has committed it. Violations of obligations incumbent upon parties to the Geneva Conventions under the grave breaches system are no exception. The ordinary consequences of an internationally wrongful act, as codified by the ILC in the Articles on State Responsibility, will therefore follow violations of such obligations.

71 The obligations forming the system of repression of grave breaches, however, belong to a specific category of international rules. Constituting a means of enforcement in the form of positive actions that contracting states must take 'to ensure respect for' the Conventions 'in all circumstances', it is unlikely that their infringement will injure another state, in particular neutral states. Although this does not preclude the latter from invoking the responsibility of another state party for a violation of its obligations under the grave breaches regime, the lack of a material interest in claiming such a responsibility will make such a possibility an infrequent occurrence in practice.

72 In abstract terms, things are different for belligerent parties. Lack of compliance with the system of criminal repression of grave breaches—at least by the enemy—may well directly affect their interests and push them to claim a violation of the pertinent rules of the Geneva Conventions. However, these are also infrequent occurrences in international practice. Even in the context of the *Armed Activity* case before the ICJ, the Democratic Republic of Congo—while claiming the failure by Uganda to comply, inter alia, with its obligations under Article 146 GC IV—did not request the Court to pronounce upon the violations by Uganda of its obligation to prosecute persons responsible for a grave breach.[143]

73 Clearly, the above remarks do not apply to violations of the obligation to ensure to those accused of breaches of the Conventions the minimum guarantees set forth in Article 105 GC III and the Articles that follow. When available and applicable, belligerents will also be bound by the various guarantees that human rights treaties provide in order to ensure respect for the right to fair trial for persons charged with a breach of the Geneva Conventions.

E. Critical Assessment

74 The compromise reached at the Diplomatic Conference with regard to grave breaches did not ensure great success for the system of their criminal repression. In the course of more than 60 years since their adoption, the Geneva Conventions have reached universality of ratification, but only a small percentage of contracting states have implemented the

---

[142] For a discussion of the matter, ibid, at 693–700.

[143] For the necessary reference, see T. Ingadottir, 'The ICJ *Armed Activity* Case—Reflections on States' Obligation to Investigate and Prosecute Individuals for Serious Human Rights Violations and Grave Breaches of the Geneva Conventions', 78 *NJIL* (2010) 581.

obligation to criminalize grave breaches and to adopt the principle of universal criminal jurisdiction for their repression.¹⁴⁴ This explains, at least in part, why the system has lain dormant for decades and remains so today.¹⁴⁵

At the same time, states not involved in armed conflicts where grave breaches are committed do not seem to take seriously into account their obligations to search for, prosecute, or surrender to another contracting party those suspected of being responsible for these breaches. For instance, some states prefer to expel persons suspected of being criminally responsible for a grave breach (and more generally a war crime) rather than bring them before their own courts.¹⁴⁶ As for the belligerents themselves, when they opt for prosecution, which is not always the case, they may be inclined to bring charges of ordinary criminal offences, even when there is the potential for prosecution of a grave breach. This might not be a concern in and of itself, at least not if one takes the view that the Geneva Conventions do not impose the duty to prosecute on the basis of a formal 'grave breach' charge. Concern arises, however, if a national prosecution under an 'ordinary' criminal charge does not entail an 'effective penal sanction' as expressly required by the relevant provisions of the Conventions. Concerns also arise when a criminal charge is formally one of a grave breach, but the penalty imposed on those found guilty does not reflect the seriousness of the crime.¹⁴⁷

When the UN Security Council established the first 'modern' international criminal tribunal, the ICTY, one might have hoped that it would inject fresh blood into the system of repression of grave breaches, since the ICTY's material jurisdiction expressly covered this class of offence.¹⁴⁸ Unfortunately, the contribution of the ICTY to the grave breaches regime has focused mainly on its general elements. For instance, the ICTY has pronounced on whether the support of a third state to an armed group turns a prima facie NIAC into an IAC, thus clarifying an aspect of the contextual element of grave breaches. In addition, for 'inter-ethnic' IAC it has relied on 'allegiance' (rather than nationality) for the identification of protected persons, and therefore expanded the category of potential victims of a grave breach.

But when it comes to the particular legal ingredients of offences amounting to grave breaches, the ICTY case law has been scant. This is certainly due to the fact that the Prosecutor has brought comparatively fewer charges of grave breaches than other charges. If the data collected by the present author are correct, of the 161 indictees, the Prosecutor charged only 31 with a grave breach (namely, less than 20 per cent of the total number). Of those, only 23 were tried (less than 15 per cent); while as regards the remaining indictees, they either died while being held in custody or before being transferred to the Tribunal, or the indictment was withdrawn. These figures do not necessarily mean that the Prosecutor had no evidence that acts amounting to grave breaches had actually been

---

¹⁴⁴ See van Elst, above n 27.

¹⁴⁵ The first criminal prosecution by a national jurisdiction on a charge of a grave breach under universal jurisdiction dates back to 1994, over 40 years after the adoption of the GCs: see *The Prosecutor v Refik Sarić*, Eastern Division of the Danish High Court, Decision, 25 November 1994, English version available at <http://tinyurl.com/p9qokr3>.

¹⁴⁶ See, e.g., the statement by the Director General of the Department of Citizenship and Immigration, B. Sheppit, before a Parliamentary Committee of Canada, who declared: '[W]e don't really care how we go about it [...] [I]f, for example, we can remove somebody because they don't have a visa, we don't really care that we don't class them as a war criminal.' (Quote in van Elst, above n 27, at 843 and accompanying reference in fn 103).

¹⁴⁷ See Ferdinandusse, above n 26.   ¹⁴⁸ See Art 2 ICTY Statute.

committed during the armed conflict. However, a successful charge of a grave breach requires—among other things—proof of the existence of an IAC and the protected status of the victim. By contrast, these two criteria are not necessary for charges of war crimes under another provision of the ICTY Statute, namely Article 3, concerning 'violations of the laws and customs of war' other than grave breaches. Since in the *Tadić* decision on jurisdiction the Appeals Chamber asserted that these violations also comprise serious violations of Common Article 3 of the Geneva Conventions and of customary IHL applicable both to NIACs and IACs,[149] the Prosecutor has shown a preference for relying on this provision for charges of war crimes rather than on charges of grave breaches.[150] Arguably, since charges under Article 3 of the ICTY Statute apply to any type of armed conflict, and regardless of the 'protected status' of the victim under the relevant Geneva Conventions, reliance on this provision was the easiest way for the Prosecutor to cover the brutality of acts committed by belligerents during the armed conflict.

78   The classification of the armed conflict as international in some areas of the former Yugoslavia by the ICTY, on the basis of the so-called 'overall control' test by a third state over the armed groups fighting a prima facie internal armed conflict, therefore made little difference when it came to drawing up the charges. Ironically, although the ICTY 'expanded' the notion of IAC, the category of war crimes that can be committed only in IACs was under-used by the Prosecutor, who preferred the more all-embracing category of war crimes.

79   It remains to be seen whether war crimes cases at the ICC will reverse the pattern followed by the ICTY and bring new life, at least at the international level, to the system of repression of grave breaches.

PAOLA GAETA

---

[149] ICTY, *Tadić*, above n 136, paras 128–36.

[150] On the 'disincentives' for the Prosecutor to rely upon Art 2 ICTY Statute (concerning grave breaches) rather than on Art 3 (concerning the broader category of violations of the laws and customs of war), see J. Stewart, 'The Future of the Grave Breaches Regime: Segregate, Assimilate or Abandon?', 7 *JICJ* (2009) 855, at 860–3.

Chapter 32. Domestic Implementation

	MN
A. Introduction	1
B. Specific Infrastructure and Administrative Preparation	8
I. National Information Bureaux	8
II. Separation of medical units and establishments	10
C. Adoption of Legislation in General	15
I. General observations	15
II. National Humanitarian Law Committees	18
III. Translation and communication	19
IV. Dissemination and training	20
V. Detailed execution and unforeseen cases	23
D. Adoption of Sanctions	25
I. Obligation to adopt sanctions	25
II. Type of measures	29
III. Legality	36
IV. Degree of detail	41
E. Enforcement of Sanctions	44

Select Bibliography

European Commission, *Law in Humanitarian Crises—How Can International Humanitarian Law Be Made Effective in Armed Conflicts* (Luxembourg: Office for the Official Publications of the European Communities, 1995) vol I

International Committee of the Red Cross, *The Domestic Implementation of International Humanitarian Law: A Manual* (Geneva: ICRC, 2011)

Kalshoven, F./Sandoz, Y. (eds), *Implementation of International Humanitarian Law* (Dordrecht: Martinus Nijhoff Publishers, 1989)

Pfanner, T., 'Various Mechanisms and Approaches for Implementing International Humanitarian Law and Protecting and Assisting War Victims', 91 *IRRC* 874 (2009) 279

La Rosa, A.-M./Wuerzner, C., 'Armed Groups, Sanctions and the Implementation of International Humanitarian Law', 90 *IRRC* 870 (2008) 327

Sassòli, M., 'The Implementation of International Humanitarian Law', 10 *YIHL* (2009) 45

Schmitt, M.N. (ed), *The Implementation and Enforcement of International Humanitarian Law* (Farnham: Ashgate, 2012)

Société internationale de droit militaire et droit de la guerre, *La mise en œuvre du droit international humanitaire au niveau national, spécialement eu égard au développement de la guerre moderne* (Brussels: Société internationale de droit militaire et droit de la guerre, 1989)

Ziegler, A.R., 'The Domestic Prosecution of International War Crimes and the Co-operation with International Tribunals', 7 *Swiss Review for International and European Law* (1997) 561

Ziegler, A.R., 'La mise en œuvre du droit international humanitaire (DIH) par la Suisse', 36 *Revue internationale du droit militaire et du droit de la guerre* (1997) 245

A. Introduction

1. The Geneva Conventions (GCs) explicitly underline that the state parties undertake not only to respect, but also to ensure respect for the Conventions in all circumstances.[1] This is not only a specific concretization of the general principle *pacta sunt servanda*, as restated, for example, in the Vienna Convention on the Law of Treaties of 1969; it must be interpreted as a specific obligation to implement the rules contained in these treaties at the domestic and international level.[2]

2. A (relatively small) number of concrete indications can be found in the Conventions as to how exactly implementation should be undertaken at the domestic level, as is typical in most international treaties. At the same time, most of the rules contained in these Conventions, and in modern international humanitarian law (IHL) in general, refer to very precise obligations during armed conflict.

3. Nevertheless, to achieve the protection sought by IHL, concrete preparatory measures have to be taken before and during an armed conflict.[3] Such measures may have to be taken at different levels, i.e. by various parts of the executive power, such as ministries and specific offices or administrative units, but also by the legislature, the judiciary, and other bodies, in particular of course by the armed forces.[4]

4. These measures are meant to ensure that the rules of IHL are fully and effectively respected. Into this category belongs, for example, the planning and construction of specific buildings that play an important role for protected persons during armed conflicts (like hospitals), or from which emanate specific dangers during armed conflicts (like works or installations containing dangerous forces).[5]

5. Similarly, when developing new weapons or adopting new means or methods of warfare, states have the obligation to review their compatibility with IHL or international law more generally.[6] While this obligation applies at all times, it is of course especially relevant before the outbreak of an armed conflict.

6. In addition, despite their concrete character, observance of the rules contained in the Geneva Conventions can hardly be expected without their prior dissemination, including (but not limited to) instruction of members of the armed forces. This includes—obviously, for internationally negotiated texts like the Geneva Conventions—their translation into a language that can easily be understood by anybody who might have obligations and

---

[1] CA 1. On the general obligations of states in this respect, see, in particular, Ch 6 of this volume.

[2] Domestic implementation forms the main core of this chapter. At the same time, a more comprehensive approach should include international mechanisms and non-legal approaches to ensuring respect for IHL; see, e.g., T. Pfanner, 'Various Mechanisms and Approaches for Implementing International Humanitarian Law and Protecting and Assisting War Victims', 91 *IRRC* 874 (2009) 279.

[3] On the general obligations of parties in this respect, see in particular Ch 6 of this volume.

[4] See, for a case study in this respect, A.R. Ziegler, 'La mise en oeuvre du droit international humanitaire (DIH) par la Suisse', 36 *Revue internationale du droit militaire et du droit de la guerre* (1997) 245; U.C. Jha, 'Implementation of International Humanitarian Law in the South Asian Countries', 9 *Indian Society of International Law Yearbook of International Humanitarian and Refugee Law* (2009) 151; and F. Kalshoven and Y. Sandoz (eds), *Implementation of International Humanitarian Law—Mise en œuvre du droit international humanitaire* (Dordrecht: Martinus Nijhoff Publishers, 1989).

[5] Section B.II of this chapter.

[6] Art 36 AP I; see, e.g., W. Heintschel v. Heinegg and G.L. Beruto (eds), *International Humanitarian Law and New Weapon Technologies—34th Round Table on Current Issues of International Humanitarian Law (San Remo, 8th–10th September 2011)* (Milan: International Institute of Humanitarian Law, 2012), and K. Lawand, 'Reviewing the Legality of New Weapons, Means and Methods of Warfare', 88 *IRRC* 864 (2006) 925.

rights under the Conventions, as well as control mechanisms to ensure that parties to the Conventions take their obligations seriously. It is thus only natural that states parties are regularly recommended to publish the text of the Geneva Conventions in their instruments of national publication.[7]

Similarly, the enforcement of such rules must be made clear. Traditional means to improve observance of legal rules are (criminal or administrative) sanctions that are applicable in the event that the desired behaviour does not take place. This *ex post* enforcement is usually imperfect, but is recognized as a relatively effective (though second best) means to improve the achievement of the desired behaviour and outcomes. Here it is not only the existence of sanctions, for example the punishment as such, but also the enforcement, i.e. the effective application of existing sanctions, that is necessary to improve general observance of the rules. Especially in recent years, the problem of impunity for internationally outlawed behaviour (in particular in the area of the protection of internationally guaranteed human rights and IHL)[8] has led to increased attempts to create institutions at the domestic and international levels that at least potentially can sanction violations of existing obligations. It has thus also led to an increased expectation that these institutions will investigate and sanction alleged violations, and that domestic and international actors will cooperate to achieve the goals of IHL.[9]

B. Specific Infrastructure and Administrative Preparation

I. National Information Bureaux

Certain administrative arrangements must be made and structures created before an armed conflict breaks out, in order to ensure that during the conflict the law will truly be respected.[10] Article 122 GC III and Article 136 GC IV oblige parties to provide for the establishment of so-called National Information Bureaux[11] that will be responsible for receiving and transmitting information to each other in respect of those protected persons (prisoners of war (POWs), civilians deprived of their liberty, etc) who are respectively in their power.[12] Although this duty is triggered only upon the outbreak of a conflict and in all cases of occupation, the fact that these provisions require the activation of such National Information Bureaux within the shortest possible time has led to an understanding that this implies a sufficient degree of preparation for their establishment during peacetime. Therefore, the 25th International Conference of the Red Cross, held in Geneva from 23 to 31 October 1986, in its Resolution 14 called upon states parties to consider taking such measures as might be necessary to institute their National Information Bureaux in peacetime, in order for them to be able to fulfil their tasks as soon as possible on the outbreak of an armed conflict.[13]

---

[7] Section C.I of this chapter.   [8] See also Ch 35 of this volume.

[9] Sections D and E of this chapter.

[10] See, for administrative measures to be taken, e.g., V. Nathanson, 'Preventing and Limiting Suffering Should Conflict Break Out: The Role of the Medical Profession', 82 *IRRC* 839 (2000) 601.

[11] See, e.g., M. Sassòli, 'The National Information Bureau in Aid of the Victims of Armed Conflicts', 27 *IRRC* 256 (1987) 6.

[12] See also Chs 49 and 53 of this volume.

[13] See, for a concrete recommendation to establish such a Bureau in the Summary of the conclusions and recommendations adopted by the participants in a workshop held in Namibia from 21–3 February 1996 with regard to Namibia, ICRC, 'National Workshop on the Implementation of International Humanitarian Law in Namibia', 36 *IRRC* 312 (1996) 348. See also in this respect Dansk Røde Kors/International Law

9   One might also mention here the other organizations that states are (sometimes implicitly) invited to create or to plan far ahead of an armed conflict in order to fulfil their obligations as regards respect for IHL, namely, national Red Cross and Red Crescent Societies, other voluntary societies (Article 26 GC I; Article 81 AP I; Article 18 AP II), and civil defence organizations (Article 63 GC IV; Articles 61–67 AP I). Even the use of the emblem foresees the involvement of local authorities regarding its proper use and control thereof. These authorities obviously must be designated ahead of time (Articles 42, 44, 53, and 54 GC I; Articles 44–45 GC II).[14]

II. Separation of medical units and establishments

10   The Geneva Conventions contain a plethora of obligations and very concrete measures to be taken to safeguard respect for and the protection of health care in armed conflicts in general.[15] In particular, several Articles explicitly require the separation of (potential or actual) military objectives and (medical) civilian objects.[16] The term 'medical units (and establishments)' in the relevant provisions refers to establishments and other units, whether military or civilian, organized for medical purposes, be they fixed or mobile, permanent or temporary. It includes, for example, hospitals and other similar units, blood transfusion centres, preventive medicine centres and institutes, medical depots, and the medical and pharmaceutical stores of such units.[17]

11   This principle applies not only during armed conflicts when certain structures are assigned specific uses or established for acute needs, but also during peacetime when such establishments and units are being planned and erected. Article 19 paragraph 2 GC I establishes the clear responsibility of the authorities to ensure that fixed medical establishments (and mobile units) are, as far as possible, situated in such a manner that attacks against military objectives cannot imperil their safety. Somewhat more vaguely, Article 18 paragraph 5 GC IV merely recommends that (civilian) hospitals[18] be situated as far as possible from military objectives in view of the dangers to which hospitals may be exposed by being close to military objectives. This is a corollary not only to the obligation that such establishments and units not be attacked, and at all times be respected and protected by the parties to a conflict (Article 19 paragraph 1 GC I and Article 18 paragraph 1 GC IV), but also to the parties' obligation to take precautionary measures against the effects of attacks (Article 58 AP I).

12   Obviously, the separation of medical units and establishments should be seen in connection with the obligation to ensure the distinction between such establishments and (potential or actual) military objectives through appropriate marking with the emblem.[19] In a similar vein, states have the possibility to establish, both in peacetime and upon

---

Committee, *Voluntary Review Procedure on National Implementation of International Humanitarian Law* (Copenhagen: International Law Committee of the Danish Red Cross, 1998).

[14] See Ch 43 of this volume for details.

[15] See ICRC Advisory Service on International Humanitarian Law, *Respecting and Protecting Health Care in Armed Conflicts and in Situations Not Covered by International Humanitarian Law (Factsheet)* (Geneva: ICRC, 2012).

[16] See also Ch 41 of this volume.

[17] See Art 19 GC I, Art 18 GC IV, and Art 8(e) AP I; and ICRC Commentary APs, paras 4711–12.

[18] See also Ch 11 of this volume.

[19] Arts 42–44 GC I, Arts 43–44 GC II, Art 18 GC IV, Art 18 AP I, Art 12 AP II; G.C. Cauderay, 'Visibilité du signe distinctif des établissements, des formations et des transports sanitaires', 72 *IRRC* 784 (1990) 319; see also Ch 43 of this volume. Such obligations for persons, property, and places to be properly identified, marked, and thus protected apply of course to other areas too, like cultural property or the preparation of

the outbreak of hostilities in their own territory—and, if the need arises, in occupied areas—hospital zones and localities so organized as to protect the wounded and sick from the effects of war, as well as personnel entrusted with the organization and administration of these zones and localities, and with the care of the persons therein assembled. Upon the outbreak and during the course of hostilities, the parties concerned may conclude agreements on mutual recognition of the hospital zones and localities they have created.[20] In practice, however, this seems to have happened only rarely so far (indeed, in Bosnia they were established by the Security Council, not by an agreement among the parties to the conflict).[21]

A similar obligation with regard to the planning and locating of works and installations (even during peacetime) may be found in Article 56(5) of Additional Protocol (AP) I with regard to such objectives containing dangerous forces (e.g. dams, dykes, and nuclear electrical generating stations).[22] Here, however, it has been clearly added that

13

> installations erected for the sole purpose of defending the protected works or installations from attack are permissible and shall not themselves be made the object of attack, provided that they are not used in hostilities except for defensive actions necessary to respond to attacks against the protected works or installations and that their armament is limited to weapons capable only of repelling hostile action against the protected works or installations.

In general terms, Article 58(a) and (b) AP I oblige parties to remove the civilian population, individual civilians, and civilian objects under their control from the vicinity of military objectives, and to avoid locating military objectives within or near densely populated areas as part of precautionary measures.

While the general obligation to avoid locating medical establishments (including civilian hospitals) close to military objectives applies during peacetime, it becomes particularly important during an armed conflict that mobile units are not located close to such objectives. Therefore, Article 19(2) GC I makes clear reference to mobile units too—a concept that is taken up in more detail by Article 12(1) AP I, referring to the duty to separate medical units to protect them from attacks against military objectives. In particular, Article 12(4) AP I sets out the prohibition against using medical units in an attempt to shield military objectives from attack.

14

C. Adoption of Legislation in General

I. General observations

As stated in the introduction to this chapter, states must normally enact national legislation and take practical measures in order for international rules to be applied domestically and be

15

---

specific identity cards, e.g., for journalists, see ICRC, Advisory Service on International Humanitarian Law, *The Domestic Implementation of International Humanitarian Law—A Manual* (Geneva: ICRC, 2011), Chapters 4 and 5.

[20] Arts 23 GC I, Arts 14 and 15 GC IV; see, e.g., A. Bouvier, 'Zones protégées, zones de sécurité et protection de la population civile', in K. Boustany and D. Dormoy (eds), *Perspectives humanitaires entre conflits, droit(s) et action* (Bruxelles: Bruylant, 2002), 251; on the establishment of safety zones during UN peace operations, see B. Oswald, 'The Creation and Control of Places of Protection during United Nations Peace Operations', 83 *IRRC* 844 (2001) 1013; see also Ch 18 of this volume.

[21] See, e.g., Sassòli/Bouvier/Quintin, at 1651 (Case No 194 on Sri Lanka).

[22] See, e.g., the recommendation that 'steps should be taken to provide special protection for dams and dykes' in the summary of the conclusions and recommendations adopted by the participants in a workshop held in Namibia from 21–3 February 1996 with regard to Namibia, in ICRC, above n 13; ICRC, *Domestic Implementation*, above n 19, Chapter 4.

fully effective. While in many instances the absence of domestic implementing legislation may not make the observance of the obligations under IHL impossible, generally speaking, national implementation substantially increases the likelihood of achieving the desired goals. In certain areas, the absence of national implementation rules not only may lead to limited effectiveness of the internationally agreed rules, but may also make it factually or legally difficult, if not impossible, to comply with the rules.[23] This idea is enshrined in the four Geneva Conventions and their Additional Protocols (Articles 47–48 GC I; Articles 48–49 GC II; Articles 127–128 GC III; Article 144–145 GC IV; Articles 83–84 AP I; Article 19 AP II; Article 7 AP III), and influences the policies and strategies of many actors in this field. Therefore, states are obliged to spread knowledge of the Conventions as widely as possible.

16   Implementation normally requires states to adopt a number of internal laws and regulations which may be achieved through the normal law-making process, although this does not exclude the adoption of such rules at a technical level (e.g. as internal regulations for the armed forces),[24] nor even the establishment of such rules in a more informal way (such as Codes of Conduct) in situations where an armed group is not officially entitled to adopt laws.[25] States must nevertheless establish rules on the punishment of violations, the use and protection of the emblems and protected signs, and the fundamental rights of protected persons.

17   The Advisory Service of the International Committee of the Red Cross (ICRC) offers technical assistance and documentation in order to improve the implementation of the obligations contained in the Geneva Conventions. Although promoting and implementing IHL is (still) considered to be primarily the responsibility of states (and possibly other armed groups, i.e. certain non-state actors), the ICRC has always had a policy to press potential belligerents for effective implementation of the internationally agreed norms. To this end, it created an Advisory Service on IHL to assist states to fulfil their obligations. Such advice may be of particular value where only limited governmental resources are available or internal opposition to implementation exists, as these responsibilities, owing to the broad range of issues associated with comprehensive implementation of the rules of IHL, require enhanced coordination and support from all the government departments and other entities concerned.

II. National Humanitarian Law Committees

18   To facilitate the process of effective implementation and enforcement, some states have created specific bodies within their administration either in the form of 'National

---

[23] See also P. Rowe, 'Implementation of International Humanitarian Law at the National Level with Special Reference to Developments of Modern Warfare', 28 *Revue de droit militaire et de droit de la guerre* 1/2 (1989) 187; and L. Hannikainen, R. Hanski, and A. Rosas (eds), *Implementing Humanitarian Law Applicable in Armed Conflicts: The Case of Finland* (Leiden: Martinus Nijhoff Publishers, 1992).

[24] See, e.g., the recommendation to the Namibian Government that the Ministry of Defence regulate protective use of the emblem within the framework of the regulations governing the armed forces in addition to the more technical provisions in this respect in the Namibia Red Cross Act of 1991, in the summary of the conclusions and recommendations adopted by the participants in a workshop held in Namibia from 21–3 February 1996 with regard to Namibia, see ICRC, above n 13. See also Pfanner, above n 2, at 283.

[25] In particular, the question of non-state actors' being bound by human rights treaties is controversial: see, e.g., Ch 20 of this volume; L. Zegveld, *The Accountability of Armed Opposition Groups in International Law* (Cambridge: CUP, 2002); A. Clapham, 'Human Rights Obligations of Non-State Actors in Conflict Situations', 88 *IRRC* 863 (2006) 491; and M. Mack, *Increasing Respect for International Humanitarian Law in Non-international Armed Conflicts* (Geneva: ICRC, 2008).

Interministerial Working Groups', often called 'Committees or Commissions for the Implementation of IHL', or in the form of 'National Humanitarian Law Committees or Commissions'.[26] Their purpose is normally to advise and assist the central government in its obligation of implementing and disseminating IHL. While the Geneva Conventions do not contain an explicit legal obligation to set up such bodies, it is recognized as an important step in ensuring the effective application of IHL, and has been advocated by the ICRC, the Intergovernmental Group of Experts for the Protection of War Victims, and the 26th International Conference of the Red Cross and Red Crescent held in Geneva in 1995.[27] As of 31 October 2011, the ICRC counted 101 such committees established by governments around the world.[28] These bodies normally bring together concerned government ministries, national civil organizations (like the national Red Cross and Red Crescent Societies), professional bodies (e.g. in the area of health or culture), and other groups having specific knowledge or expertise regarding the objectives protected by IHL (e.g. civil engineering).

III. Translation and communication

19 All the Geneva Conventions set out a duty of the parties to communicate to one another the official translations of the text of the Conventions, as well as the laws and regulations that they may adopt to ensure the application thereof. This must normally be done through the Swiss Federal Council and, during hostilities, through the Protecting Powers.[29] This obligation is provided for in identical manner in Article 48 GC I, Article 49 GC II, Articles 41 and 128 GC III, and Articles 99 and 145 GC IV.[30] These provisions should be read in conjunction with Article 55 GC I, Article 54 GC II, Article 133 GC III, and Article 150 GC IV, which provide that in addition to the authentic versions of the Conventions in English and French (as they resulted from the negotiations), the Swiss Federal Council shall arrange for official translations of the Conventions to be made into the Russian and Spanish languages.[31] Parties to the Conventions should automatically proceed to translate the texts into the languages used by them, at the latest upon ratification of the Conventions.[32]

IV. Dissemination and training

20 The Geneva Conventions (Article 47 GC I; Article 48 GC II; Articles 41 and 127 GC III; Articles 99 and 144 GC IV), as well as the Additional Protocols (Articles 80, 82–83,

---

[26] See I. Küntziger, 'Le droit international humanitaire au plan national: impact et rôle des Commissions nationale', 84 *IRRC* 846 (2002) 489.

[27] See Advisory Service on International Humanitarian Law, *National Committees for the Implementation of International Humanitarian Law (Factsheet)* (Geneva: ICRC, 2003).

[28] See Advisory Service on International Humanitarian Law, *Table of National Committees of International Humanitarian Law* (Geneva: ICRC, 2011).

[29] See also Ch 27 of this volume.

[30] See also Art 84 AP I, Art 26 of the 1954 Hague Convention on Cultural Property, and Art 37 of the 1999 Second Protocol to the 1954 Hague Convention on Cultural Property.

[31] See, on the obligations of Switzerland as a Depositary, the Report established by the Swiss Federal Council, 'Le rôle de la Suisse en tant que dépositaire des Conventions de Genève', *Swiss Official Journal, French Version (FF)* (2007) 5291. See also S. Wehrenberg, 'Die Schweiz als Depositarstaat der Genfer Abkommen', *Allgemeine Schweizerische Militärzeitschrift* (2006), at 7–8.

[32] See, e.g., the respective recommendation contained in the Summary of the conclusions and recommendations adopted by the participants in a workshop held in Namibia from 21–3 February 1996 with regard to Namibia, ICRC, above n 13. On the role of the ICRC with regard to implementation, see also Chs 24 and 26 of this volume.

and 87 AP I; Article 19 AP II) and many other treaties[33] in the area of IHL, contain an obligation for the states parties to take appropriate measures to disseminate the text of the respective treaties.[34] This means first and foremost that members of the armed forces need to be instructed as to the basic principles underlying IHL and the concrete behaviour that is expected or prohibited at their level in the command structure.[35] This rule has acquired customary character.[36] Normally, it also means an increased level of instruction for higher officials and the designation of specialists (legal advisers) at the various levels in the command structure. State practice establishes this rule as a norm of customary international law for state armed forces. The practice of states does not indicate that any distinction is made between advice on IHL applicable in international armed conflicts (IACs) and that applicable in non-international armed conflicts (NIACs). Armed opposition groups are not (yet) under a strict obligation to have legal advisers, but this does not mean that they could justify any violations of IHL by the absence of such specialists.[37] In principle, civilians should also be informed of the content of IHL.[38]

21 Military manuals are an additional tool used for the dissemination of IHL, although they may contain specific interpretations of the international rules.[39]

22 Besides instruction at the national level, various joint initiatives exist to foster the dissemination of IHL among military commanders and specialists worldwide.[40] The importance of teaching IHL at university level to all law students should also be mentioned, including the possibility of their participation in specific moot courts, in particular the Jean Pictet Competition.[41]

V. Detailed execution and unforeseen cases

23 Despite the detailed character of many rules and the obligation to translate and disseminate the texts, the general objectives and the spirit of the Conventions require more than strict obedience and respect for these rules in the specific situations covered. Article 45 GC I and Article 46 GC II largely take up a provision already contained in the earlier

---

[33] See in particular Arts 7 and 25 of the 1954 Convention on Cultural Property, and Art 37 of the Second Protocol of 1999 to that Convention.

[34] See the respective recommendation of ICRC experts regarding Namibia in 1996, in ICRC, above n 13: 'With the assistance of the Namibia Red Cross and the ICRC, efforts in the field of dissemination of and instruction in IHL, [...] should be stepped up. Not only should such instruction be part of the regular training programme of the armed forces; it should also be included in the training programmes of the Ministries of Health and of Home Affairs and in the curriculum of the Law Faculty of the University of Namibia.'

[35] The Swiss Government adopted at the very technical level a number of regulations and directives that are distributed to all members of the armed forces, referring to the behaviour necessary in order to fulfil the obligation under IHL, such as a 'Règlement de service', a Regulation entitled 'Bases légales du comportement à l'engagement', and an 'Aide-mémoire: les dix règles de base du droit international des conflits armés'. See Ziegler, above n 4.

[36] See ICRC CIHL Database, 2. Practice, Rule 142.

[37] Ibid, Rule 141.   [38] Ibid, Rule 143.

[39] The ICRC maintains a comprehensive list of such manuals. To what extent military manuals reflect state practice and *opinio juris* is a complex question; see J.-M. Henckaerts, 'Customary International Humanitarian Law: A Response to US Comments', 89 *IRRC* 866 (2007) 473, at 483.

[40] E.g., Central Role of the Commander: Accomplish the Mission Respecting the Law—CENTROC; LOAC–ICMM International Course on Law of Armed Conflict (LOAC) under the auspices of the International Committee of Military Medicine (ICMM); Senior Officers' Security and Rule of Law Conference; Senior Workshop on International Rules Governing Military Operations (SWIRMO), International Institute of Humanitarian Law (IIHL–San Remo).

[41] For details see Ch 30 of this volume, esp MN 36.

Geneva Conventions of 1929, 1906, and even, in part, 1864.[42] Despite the fact that the 1949 Conventions have reached a high degree of detail in some areas, the drafters were not willing to give up more generic provisions that would capture situations not otherwise described in detail. Therefore, this provision contains the specific reminder that even in cases where no previous implementation has taken place (including cases where a specific situation was never foreseen), the contracting parties, acting through their commanders-in-chief, are obliged to ensure full compliance with the Conventions (so-called 'detailed execution'). Failure to respect this provision leads, of course, to parallel responsibilities under international law for both the state (state responsibility) and individual commanders-in-chief (individual criminal responsibility)—a situation that was less clear under the 1929 text, where it appeared that a commander-in-chief might bear full responsibility, thereby possibly absolving the state entirely of its international responsibility.[43]

24 It is suggested that the states parties will have to take a plethora of detailed decisions both before and during an armed conflict that are of relevance as regards respect for the principles contained in the Geneva Conventions. Examples of such detailed (and sometimes rather technical) decisions that may or may not be taken in advance of a concrete situation include fixing the number of medical personnel and the amount of equipment to be left with any wounded who have to be abandoned (Article 12 paragraph 5 GC I), organizing a search for the wounded and making local arrangements for their collection and evacuation (Article 15 GC I), appealing to the charitable zeal of the local inhabitants (Article 18 GC I), determining the percentage of medical personnel to be retained (Article 31 GC I), and so on. Normally, even if general implementation rules should have been adopted beforehand, it is assumed that specific ad hoc instructions will have to be given and additional practical steps taken in execution of such general (written) rules.

D. Adoption of Sanctions

I. Obligation to adopt sanctions

25 While many of the implementation measures referred to so far may be characterized as having a preventive character, the nature of (criminal or administrative) sanctions imposed on individuals for violating specific rules contained in the Geneva Conventions may be mixed. Like (criminal) sanctions in general, they have a preventive character when it comes to dissuading persons in general from committing certain acts (deterrence or negative general prevention).[44] This is particularly true as regards the drafting and existence of laws, and the dissemination of their content among individuals who are likely to be involved in situations in which violations of IHL may occur. In addition, it is usually claimed that the certainty created by the existence of sanctions and their proper enforcement contributes to positive prevention in general, as they create a sense of security and confidence among the

---

[42] Convention for the Amelioration of the Wounded and Sick in Armies in the Field, 27 July 1929; Convention for the Amelioration of the Wounded and Sick in Armies in the Field, 6 July 1906; Convention for the Amelioration of the Condition of the Wounded in Armies in the Field, 22 August 1864.

[43] See Pictet Commentary GC I, 340–1.

[44] See, e.g., on these theories (developed primarily by German criminologists and criminal lawyers), in English, J. Gardner, 'The Functions and Justifications of Criminal Law and Punishment', in J. Gardner, *Offences and Defences: Selected Essays in the Philosophy of Criminal Law* (Oxford: OUP, 2007) 201.

population that justice will be done.⁴⁵ Maybe this aspect, as described by criminologists and certain domestic (mostly German) criminal lawyers, approaches the discussion on the fight against impunity in contemporary international law and politics. At the same time, the investigation of violations and the application of sanctions in individual cases can have a preventive effect when it comes to stopping a specific individual from committing other violations (special prevention).⁴⁶ But on the whole, sanctions are rather perceived as a measure to restore justice by punishing illegal behaviour and thus restoring the legal order (*ex post*), without, however, being able to restore the situation to what it was before (*ex ante*); they are a kind of a virtual reparation, in particular if combined with a duty to pay (civil) damages or a fine (pecuniary reparation).

26   The Geneva Conventions establish a legal obligation for the states parties to take measures necessary for the suppression of all acts contrary to the provisions of the Convention in question (Article 49 paragraph 3 GC I; Article 50 paragraph 3 GC II; Article 129 paragraph 3 GC III; and Article 146 paragraph 3 GC IV). This general obligation is specified and reinforced for a particular category of violations, called 'grave breaches', in all Conventions with the more concrete obligation to undertake to enact any legislation necessary to provide effective penal sanctions for persons committing, or ordering to be committed, any of the grave breaches of the Geneva Conventions as defined in Conventions.⁴⁷ Only with regard to the commission of grave breaches do the Conventions explicitly mention the obligation for a state party to search actively for alleged perpetrators and to bring such persons, regardless of their nationality, before its own courts. Additionally, for this category of violations, the Conventions explicitly mention the option of handing such persons over for trial to another state party.⁴⁸ In all circumstances, the accused persons shall benefit from safeguards of proper trial and defence, which shall not be less favourable than those provided for similar cases in the Geneva Conventions themselves for protected persons and POWs.⁴⁹

27   Although grave breaches of the Geneva Conventions and the international legal obligations contained therein are the provisions most discussed in legal writing,⁵⁰ and have led to the most concrete steps by governments and the international community to penalize them in specific treaties and domestic laws, this does not imply that states would be barred from taking similar measures with regard to other violations of the Geneva Conventions and IHL in general.⁵¹ This is particularly important with regard to Common Article 3 of the Geneva Conventions and violations of AP II when it comes to NIACs. These violations have been made subject to criminal sanctions not only in the Statute of the International Criminal Court (ICC Statute) (Article 8 relating to the definition of war crimes), but also

---

⁴⁵ See M.P. José, 'Positive General Prevention as a Respect for Legal Order', 2 *InDret* (2008), available at <http://ssrn.com/abstract=1416626>.

⁴⁶ See, e.g., J.J.M. van Dijk, *Criminal Law in Action: An Overview of Current Issues in Western Societies* (Leiden: Martinus Nijhoff Publishers, 1988) 331.

⁴⁷ Art 50 GC I; Art 51 GC II; Art 130 GC III; Art 147 GC IV; Arts 11, 85 AP I: for details see Ch 31 of this volume. See also, on the relationship between grave breaches and war crimes, M.D. Öberg, 'The Absorption of Grave Breaches into War Crimes Law', 91 *IRRC* 873 (2009) 163.

⁴⁸ Art 49 para 2 GC I; Art 50 para 2 GC II; Art 129 para 2 GC III; Art 146 para 2 GC IV; Art 88(2) AP I.

⁴⁹ Art 49 para 4 GC I; Art 50 para 4 GC II; Art 129 para 4 GC III; Art 146 para 4 GC IV.

⁵⁰ See also Chs 31 and 36 of this volume.

⁵¹ See, for case studies with regard to a particular domestic system, A.R. Ziegler, 'The Domestic Prosecution of International War Crimes and the Co-operation with International Tribunals', 7 *Swiss Review for International and European Law* (1997) 561; and A.R. Ziegler, 'Die Kooperation der Schweiz mit den internationalen Strafgerichten der UNO', 115 *Schweizerische Zeitschrift für Strafrecht* (1997) 382.

under the law of many states parties to the Geneva Conventions. It is generally considered that customary international law authorizes states to do so, even extending their competence based on the principle of universal jurisdiction in these cases.[52]

In recent years, following the adoption of the ICC Statute, more and more states have thoroughly analysed their obligations with regard to cooperation with the ICC (Article 86 of the ICC Statute) and the adoption of domestic sanctions regarding violations of the international law applicable in armed conflict. These endeavours have often led to the modification of existing legislation, or to the introduction of new legislation. 28

II. Type of measures

Neither the more general obligation to take measures for the suppression of acts contrary to the Geneva Conventions, nor the more precise obligation to enact any legislation necessary to provide effective penal sanctions for grave breaches of the Geneva Conventions, explicitly compels states to adopt specific legislation. This is true even for the suppression of grave breaches, as it only requires states to enact measures 'necessary to provide effective penal sanctions'. In both cases, it is thus imaginable that a state already has the necessary domestic legislation in place (and thus needs no further legislation),[53] or that the mere existence of the Geneva Conventions is considered sufficient to provide for penal sanctions for grave breaches or to suppress all acts contrary to the provisions of the Conventions.[54] 29

The latter situation, i.e. where the Conventions themselves are considered sufficient for a state to take domestic measures for the suppression of acts contrary to their provisions, is more complex. It relates to the question whether a legal system allows a treaty (or more generally any source of international law) to have such legal effects domestically. This issue was a major topic for writers at the end of the nineteenth century, when more and more treaties started to regulate issues having potential effects on the laws and obligations of individuals. The theoretical debate is known as the divide between monist and dualist thinkers, and has subsequently influenced the approach adopted in various states. 30

From a true dualist perspective, a source of international law can never have any direct application within a domestic legal order. For countries following a dualist approach, this is certainly true with regard to treaties, while the same systems often are more open to customary international law and accept it as part of the sources of law applicable before domestic courts. With regard to the treaty law of the Geneva Conventions, parties that follow a dualist approach will thus always have to adopt domestic (implementing) laws and regulations to suppress acts contrary to the Conventions. A typical example of a state 31

---

[52] Although this is usually disputed by the accused and their counsel in the respective trials. See, with regard to the first trials before the ICTY e.g., ICTY, *The Prosecutor v Duško Tadić*, Appeals Chamber Judgment, IT-94-1-A, 15 July 1999, paras 225 ff, and the comments by M. Sassòli and L.M. Olson, 'The Judgment of the ICTY Appeals Chamber on the Merits in the *Tadić* Case', 82 *IRRC* 839 (2000) 733; and with regard to Switzerland, the decision of the Military Tribunal at Lausanne, *Prosecutor v G*, Judgment of 18 April 1997, published in 92 *AJIL* (1998) 78 with comments by A.R. Ziegler.

[53] As a matter of fact, when the GCs were negotiated in 1949, some parties already had specific domestic (penal) legislation in place to punish violations of the laws and customs of war (as these rules had been known at least since 1899 in many states due to the Conventions with Respect to the Laws and Customs of War on Land of 29 July 1899). Examples are the provisions introduced in 1927 by Switzerland in its military penal code (as published in the *Swiss Official Journal* (BBl) 1927, 761 ff and the explanations by the Government of 26 November 1918 as published in BBl 1918, 469ff).

[54] The ICRC maintains a comprehensive database regarding the implementation of the GCs by the states parties, available at <https://www.icrc.org/ihl-nat>.

having to implement the Geneva Conventions into domestic law by a specific domestic act is the United Kingdom. The Geneva Conventions have thus been implemented by adopting the Geneva Conventions Act 1957,[55] but also by specific provisions in various other Acts (including the Army Act 1955[56] and the Air Force Act 1955).[57] Similarly, Australia has implemented the Geneva Conventions in its own Geneva Conventions Act 1957,[58] and several other states have adopted such Acts, most of the time combined with a number of more specialized Acts and specific modifications in other Acts of more general application.

32   Other states, however, allow treaties to take effect at the domestic level by following a more monist approach. But even in these states, the language and the character of some of the provisions used in international treaties may not be considered as having the necessary quality so as to allow for their direct application by judges or other competent authorities.[59] Many provisions of international treaties are therefore considered to have no direct effect in the national legal system and thus require measures of implementation. This issue is also known in some states, for example in the United States (US),[60] as the question of the self-executing or non self-executing character of specific rules of international law, and today many other countries having at least a partly monist tradition have also adopted this terminology.[61]

33   The decision whether a provision is self-executing is often left to the authorities that are applying the international norms, but sometimes there are clear indications in this respect by the executive or (rather rarely) in the text of a treaty itself. It remains for the domestic legal system to decide which state organ has the power to decide the issue, and whether, for example, judges are bound by statements made by the executive or in parliament. The specific criteria used to decide whether a norm is self-executing

---

[55] 'An Act to enable effect to be given to certain international conventions done at Geneva on the twelfth day of August, nineteen hundred and forty-nine, and for purposes connected therewith'. The original Act of Parliament has been modified since then, in particular by the Geneva Conventions (Amendment) Act 1995. See M.R. Eaton, 'National Implementation of International Humanitarian Law in the United Kingdom', in *ICRC Committees or Other National Bodies for International Humanitarian Law—Meeting of Experts* (Geneva, 1997); and P. Rowe and A. Meyer, 'The Geneva Conventions (Amendment) Act 1995: A Generally Minimalist Approach', 45 *ICLQ* (1996) 476.

[56] Here it is, e.g., s 30 that penalizes 'looting from persons killed, injured or captured in the course of hostilities'.

[57] See the overview provided by the ICRC in its respective database available at <https://www.icrc.org/ihl-nat>.

[58] Enacted 18 September 1957, amended by the Geneva Conventions Amendment Act 1991, enacted 4 March 1991. See G. Triggs, 'Australia's War Crimes Trials: All Pity Choked', in T.L.H. McCormack and G.J. Simpson (eds), *The Law of War Crimes: National and International Approaches* (Alphen aan den Rijn: Kluwer Law International, 1997) 123; and A.D. Mitchell, 'Is Genocide a Crime Unknown to Australian Law? *Nulyarimma v Thompson*', 3 *YIHL* (2000) 362.

[59] As an example, one might quote the finding by specialists from the ICRC, above n 13, regarding the situation in Namibia in 1996, that '[a]lthough Namibian courts can apply the provisions of the IHL treaties directly, it was considered necessary and useful that a specific act of Parliament be adopted to create a legal basis for the arrest of suspected war criminals, to specify the offences that constitute war crimes, to provide adequate sanctions for the latter and to define the procedure applicable to such offences and the jurisdiction of the courts'.

[60] For the US Supreme Court, it means 'to determine whether the President who negotiated it and the Senate that ratified it intended for the treaty to automatically create domestically enforceable federal law' (*Medellín v Texas*, 552 US 491 (2008)).

[61] E.g. Switzerland (as expressed by the Federal Supreme Court in ATF 124 III 90 or AFT 129 II 249, 257) or the Netherlands (see, e.g., H.G. Schermers, 'Some Recent Cases Delaying the Direct Effect of International Treaties in Dutch Law', 10 *MJIL* (1989) 266).

may differ, but the result is that a non self-executing norm cannot be applied by the authorities or enforced in the courts without prior legislative implementation.[62] For the Geneva Conventions, it has in recent years been held in most states that at least some of their provisions can be self-executing, while others may need domestic implementation measures.[63]

Three models of implementation can generally be found with regard to criminal measures: 34

— some states use their normal criminal law (military and civil) without introducing specific crimes relating to violations of IHL;
— some states adopt highly specific provisions in their law subjecting specific violations of IHL to sanctions; and
— a generic provision is used to subject violation of IHL obligations on the state to sanctions.

Of course these models may be combined, and implementation may be undertaken by adopting a separate specialized Act, or simply by modifying existing (criminal) laws.[64]

In addition, one should not forget that administrative and civil sanctions may be available in addition to, or as an alternative to, criminal sanctions where the latter are not compulsory under the Geneva Conventions. These can target the state and its entities,[65] as well as individuals. 35

III. Legality

The question of the method of implementation of IHL becomes particularly important when the taking of sanctions against individuals is at stake, as is the case with regard to the provisions of the Geneva Conventions obliging states to suppress acts contrary to the Conventions or to provide effective penal sanctions for grave breaches of the Conventions.[66] Most writers claim that these norms only instruct the states parties to adopt sanctions, leaving it to each state to decide on the exact type and intensity of specific sanctions for the various possible violations of the Geneva Conventions.[67] In addition, many domestic legal systems require enhanced legal certainty and specific procedural guarantees when it comes to the application of such sanctions, perhaps best expressed by the maxims *nullum crimen sine lege* (no crime without law) and *nulla poena sine lege* (no punishment without law). Sometimes it is also required that such a law must be written 36

---

[62] See, for the US, C.M. Vazquez, 'The Four Doctrines of Self-Executing Treaties', 89 *AJIL* (1995) 695.

[63] See, e.g., S.I. Vladeck, 'Non-Self-Executing Treaties and the Suspension Clause after *St Cyr*', 113 *YLJ* (2004) 2007; and for the practice of US courts, *United States v Lindh*, 212 F Supp 2d 541, 553–4 (ED Va 2002) (suggesting that numerous provisions of the GCs are self-executing); and *United States v Noriega*, 808 F Supp 791, 797–9 (SD Fla 1992).

[64] For practical advice regarding the various types of implementation, see ICRC Advisory Service on International Humanitarian Law, *Methods of Incorporating Punishment into Criminal Law* (Geneva: ICRC, 2003).

[65] See also Art 91 AP I.

[66] See G.P. Fletcher and J.D. Ohlin, 'Reclaiming Fundamental Principles of Criminal Law in the Darfur Case', 3 *JICJ* (2005) 539, at 557, who state: 'By its very nature, criminal law does not conform to those fields where customary law is possible.'

[67] See M. Bothe, 'Conclusions by the Chairman: National Implementation of International Humanitarian Law—Basic Issues', in M. Bothe, P. Macalister-Smith, and T. Kurzidem (eds), *National Implementation of International Humanitarian Law: Proceedings of an International Colloquium Held at Bad Homburg, June 17–19, 1988* (Leiden: Brill, 1990) 261, at 264.

(*lex scripta*) and must have been in force at the time when the acts were committed (*lex praevia*). Under many domestic criminal laws, the respective rules must also be sufficiently precise and clear (*lex stricta et certa*). These principles, sometimes simply referred to as the 'principle of legality' or 'rule of law' with regard to criminal offences and penalties,[68] are normally also considered part of basic human rights, such as expressed by Article 15 of the International Covenant on Civil and Political Rights (ICCPR).

37   In view of this tension, the critical question for legal systems that allow for international treaties to have direct effect becomes whether direct effect is achieved when the basis for the sanction is 'only' a provision of the Geneva Conventions without further implementing measures under domestic law—be they criminal law or any other type of law allowing for sanctions (such as administrative or disciplinary measures in many states). This particular problem had already been foreseen when the specific guarantees regarding *nullum crimen sine lege* were adopted in the major international human rights instruments. For example, Article 15(2) ICCPR provides that nothing in that Article shall 'prejudice the trial and punishment of any person for any act or omission which, at the time when it was committed, was criminal according to the general principles of law recognized by the community of nations', thereby stating explicitly that a crime may also be defined under international law.

38   An exception to the pure principle that any crime needs to be provided for in a (written) law was relied on during the war crimes trials at Nuremberg after the Second World War by the Control Council in its Law No 10 (Punishment of Persons Guilty of War Crimes, Crimes against Peace and against Humanity), in order to justify the recognition of the acts recognized as crimes under Article II. Therefore, this type of human rights provision is also known as a 'Nuremberg Clause'. It led to considerable debate when it was discussed and later inserted for the first time during the drafting of the 1948 Universal Declaration of Human Rights,[69] leading to reservations when subsequently included in the respective international treaties.[70] Nevertheless, today it remains a standard clause in human rights treaties, and was recently also used in the Charter of Fundamental Rights of the European Union.[71]

39   Despite the fact that the Nuremberg and Tokyo trials were based on the assumption that (customary) international law could constitute a sufficient basis for sanctions relating to violations of IHL, and that the 'Nuremberg Clause' later found its way into modern human rights treaties, this idea often met with resistance when it came to the application

---

[68] See in general P. Hauck, 'The Challenge of Customary International Crimes to the Principle of Nullum Crimen Sine Lege', 21 *Journal of International Law of Peace and Armed Conflict* (2008) 58; A. Ashworth, *Principles of Criminal Law* (5th edn, Oxford: OUP, 2006) 68; M. Catenacci, 'Nullum Crimen Sine Lege', in F. Lattanzi (ed), *The International Criminal Court. Comments on the Draft Statute* (Napoli: Editoriale Scientifica, 1998) 159; R. Haveman, 'The Principle of Legality', in R. Haveman, O. Kavran, and J. Nicholls (eds), *Supranational Criminal Law: A System Sui Generis* (Antwerp: Intersentia, 2003) 39.

[69] See J. Morsink, *The Universal Declaration of Human Rights: Origins, Drafting, and Intent* (Philadelphia, Pa: University of Pennsylvania Press, 1999) 55.

[70] See the reservation made by Germany with regard to Art 7(2) ECHR, published in the *German Official Journal* (BGBl) 1954 II, 14. See also H. Kelsen, 'Will the Judgment in the Nuremberg Trial Constitute a Precedent in International Law?', 1 *International Law Quarterly* (1947) 153, at 165; and K. Ambos, 'General Principles of Criminal Law in the Rome Statute', 10 *Criminal Law Forum* (1999) 1, at 5.

[71] Art 49(2): 'This Article shall not prejudice the trial and punishment of any person for any act or omission which, at the time when it was committed, was criminal according to the general principles recognised by the community of nations.'

of (criminal) sanctions at the domestic level in countries allowing for self-executing provisions of international treaties. This was particularly so with regard to violations other than grave breaches of the Geneva Conventions. Therefore, even a number of those states with a rather monist tradition have opted for written domestic law (or amendment of an existing law), satisfying the traditional requirements regarding the character of a norm leading to sanctions under domestic criminal law and procedure. Exceptionally some states, such as the US, opted originally for the self-executing character of the Geneva Conventions, even for those provisions leading to sanctions against individuals.[72]

In particular, domestic legal norms will have to establish the various elements of a crime necessary under national law, including the variations of these crimes, such as aiding and abetting or instigation. The same is true for possible defences or mitigating and aggravating factors which have an impact on the penalty or punishment. Furthermore, the competence of the respective tribunals and bodies needs to be established. 40

IV. Degree of detail

A particular problem has been the complexity of the norms to be sanctioned. Therefore, especially in the early years after ratification of the Geneva Conventions, many states did not adopt such laws at all, or used very basic provisions referring to international treaties (and sometimes customary international law) binding on a state.[73] This often led to criticism by criminal lawyers, who invoked the principle that rules leading to (criminal) sanctions must be sufficiently precise and clear (*lex stricta et certa*),[74] and stated that the norms did not provide the necessary degree of detail.[75] Only in the last 20 years, after the establishment of international criminal tribunals, and in particular the ICC, have a number of states adopted new provisions that are more detailed and precise with regard to the acts that are sanctioned under domestic law.[76] Even in this situation, it is not uncommon 41

---

[72] See *Hearing Before the Committee on Foreign Relations, United States Senate, Eighty-fourth Congress, First Session: on Executives D, E, F, and G, 82nd Congress, 1st Session, the Geneva Conventions for the Protection of War Victims, Opened for Signature at Geneva on August 12, 1949 [...]* (Washington, DC: US Government Printing Office, 1955) 58; but see also, regarding more recent cases law in US courts, C.A. Bradley, 'The Military Commissions Act, Habeas Corpus, and the Geneva Conventions', 101 *AJIL* (2007) 322, at 337–8, and C.M. Vázquez, 'Treaties as Law of the Land: The Supremacy Clause and the Judicial Enforcement of Treaties', 122 *HLR* (2008) 599, at 600 ff.

[73] A typical example was Art 109 of the Swiss Military Criminal Code, as introduced in 1950 to guarantee compliance with the 1949 GCs. It stated in a rather vague way that 'whoever acts contrary to the provisions of international agreements on the conduct of hostilities and for the protection of victims of war shall be punished'. See on Switzerland, in particular, D. Wüger, *Anwendbarkeit und Justiziabilität völkerrechtlicher Normen im schweizerischen Recht: Grundlagen, Methoden und Kriterien* (Bern: Stämpfli, 2005); or H. Vest, 'Zum Handlungsbedarf auf dem Gebiet des Völkerstrafrechts', 121 *Zeitschrift für Strafrecht* (2003) 46.

[74] See Hauck, above n 68.

[75] See on this problem in general G. Tullock, 'On the Desirable Degree of Detail in the Law', 2 *European Journal of Law and Economics* (1995) 199.

[76] A typical example in this respect is Germany. For many years, the German Criminal Code did not refer explicitly to the laws of war; war crimes were dealt with by the general rules contained in criminal law. On 26 June 2002, a 'Code of Crimes against International Law' (*Völkerstrafgesetzbuch*) was adopted concerning specific crimes described in the GCs of 1949, the APs of 1977, and in particular the ICC Statute of 1998 which initiated this process. Germany incorporated the crimes set out in the ICC Statute into its own law by passing specific legislation in addition to general criminal law in the form of a specific Code, which entered into force on 30 June 2002 (*Official Journal [BGBl]* I page 2254). See A. Eser and H. Kreicker (eds), *Nationale Strafverfolgung völkerrechtlicher Verbrechen, Bd. 1: Deutschland (von Helmut Gropengießer und Helmut Kreicker)* (Freiburg: Schriftenreihe des Max-Planck-Instituts für ausländisches und internationales Strafrecht, 2003); and J. Hartmann, 'Das deutsche Völkerstrafgesetzbuch', in H.-H. Kühne, R. Esser, and M. Gerding (eds),

to find rather detailed provisions (often more or less[77] copying the provisions of the ICC) with regard to grave breaches and certain other violations of the Geneva Conventions (such as misuse of the emblems) and other IHL treaties,[78] combined with generic provisions that make all other violations of the IHL obligations of a state subject to sanctions without stating them in detail.[79]

42 In states applying a rather high threshold with regard to the concreteness and degree of detail of the provisions instituting criminal sanctions, the main problem remains whether the international obligations referred to in such general clauses are self-executing. This has been discussed in detail for grave breaches, and has led in recent years in many states to the adoption of very concrete provisions incorporating the definition of war crimes as used in the ICC Statute. However, with regard to many other obligations under IHL (including aspects of the violation of the Geneva Conventions not considered to be grave breaches, or violations of Common Article 3) the problems remain. In these situations, many states rely on generic provisions containing sanctions referring to violations of the international obligations of the state in armed conflicts. Here, the question whether the international obligations are self-executing normally remains. An example of a provision that would seem sufficiently precise and foreseeable, and thus self-executing, might be Article 33 GC IV with regard to the prohibition of 'collective penalties', while the rather general reference in the same sentence to measures of 'terrorism' might arguably be too vague in view of the lack of a generally recognized definition of 'terrorism'.[80] Another example among the provisions of the Geneva Conventions that would seem too vague to justify the taking of concrete sanctions against individuals without further domestic implementing measures, is Article 38 GC III, which requires that 'the Detaining Power shall encourage the practice of intellectual, educational, and recreational pursuits, sports and games amongst prisoners, and shall take the measures necessary to ensure the exercise thereof by providing them with adequate premises and necessary equipment'.[81]

43 In addition to addressing the grave breaches of the Geneva Conventions, states are required to introduce specific provisions providing for sanctions relating to the abuse of the emblem.[82] This was sometimes done through highly technical acts relating to signs and trademarks in general (sometimes nevertheless combined with provisions in criminal laws). From a practical point of view, such provisions often lack visibility and

Völkerstrafrecht—12 Beiträge zum internationalen Strafrecht und Völkerstrafrecht (Osnabruck: Julius Jonscher Verlag, 2007) 121.

[77] Many countries adapt the structure and definition of the crimes contained in the ICC Statute and the relevant IHL treaties to their domestic criminal law system. This is particularly so in countries wanting to achieve a sufficient level of precision in the definition of the crimes. E.g., the new German Code of Crimes against International Law of 2002, above n 76, reformulates some of the wording of the relevant provisions of the GCs, the APs, and the ICC Statute in order to bring it into line with the domestic approach. The same is true for Switzerland's new provisions in this respect as adopted in 2010—see *Loi fédérale du 18 juin 2010 portant modification de lois fédérales en vue de la mise en oeuvre du Statut de Rome de la Cour pénale internationale* (in force since 1 January 2011), *Swiss Official Journal* (FF) 2008 3461ff; see H. Vest et al (eds), *Kommentar zum Völkerstrafrecht der Schweiz* (Zurich: Dike, 2014).

[78] See also Ch 43 of this volume.

[79] See, e.g., Art 264j ('Other violations of international humanitarian law') of the Swiss Criminal Code, introduced on the occasion of a general revision of the civil and military criminal codes following the implementation of the ICC Statute into domestic law (entered into force in 2011), above n 77.

[80] See J. Pejic, 'Terrorist Acts and Groups: A Role for International Law?', 75 *BYBIL* (2004) 71, at 72; and J. Baumgartner and A.R. Ziegler, 'Article 264j', in Vest et al (eds), above n 77, para 21.

[81] Baumgartner and Ziegler, above n 80, para 24.

[82] Arts 53, 54 GC I; Art 6(1) AP III. For details regarding the use of the emblem, see Ch 43 of this volume.

undermine the likelihood that they will be respected or that the authorities will enforce these rules.[83]

E. Enforcement of Sanctions

Apart from making it theoretically possible for domestic authorities and, in particular, judges to investigate and enforce respect for the Geneva Conventions, it is particularly important to ensure the application of such norms in practice, in order to fulfil the obligation to suppress all acts contrary to the provisions of the Conventions as well as similar obligations contained in other sources of international law.

While after the Second World War a number of trials took place in various countries around the world, and in particular before the International Military Tribunals (IMTs) of Nuremberg and Tokyo, the enforcement of respect for IHL by domestic authorities and tribunals was, generally speaking, deplorably weak. In this regard, the creation of various international criminal tribunals, starting in the 1990s, and most importantly the creation of the ICC in 1998, has certainly led to new developments, including at the domestic level. In particular with regard to the armed conflicts in the former Yugoslavia and Rwanda, the investigations and trials undertaken by the respective ad hoc international tribunals led not only to the improvement of domestic implementing legislation, but also (at least sometimes and in some places) to a change in mentality.[84] Yet this change has not been omnipresent, and major differences exist with regard to the resources available and states' capability and willingness to enforce IHL (the same applies to sanctions in response to gross violations of human rights).

Apart from this lack of willingness and capability, a number of problems should be mentioned relating to the prosecution of violations of IHL (and other rules of international law) in times of armed conflict. One is the question as to whether punishing perpetrators is desirable in view of an ongoing conflict, or whether reconciliation should be prioritized in the wake of an armed conflict.[85] This is a traditional problem relating to the peace-building process, and here the tensions between fighting impunity and allowing for reconciliation and integration between various actors continue to be hotly debated. In particular, the granting of amnesties and immunities from (criminal) jurisdiction present difficult issues under domestic and international law, even more so when they concern several states and/or international organizations and tribunals. While

---

[83] See, e.g., the recommendation by experts in an analysis of the domestic law of Namibia in 1996, in ICRC, above n 13: 'The provisions relating to use of the emblem contained in the Namibia Red Cross Act of 1991 were considered insufficient if not confusing. It was suggested that regulations be adopted to complete and clarify Section 3 of the Act and to provide for more appropriate sanctions for misuse of the emblem. Furthermore, an authority responsible for monitoring use of the emblem should be designated. [...] It was suggested that the Ministry of Defence regulate protective use of the emblem within the framework of the regulations governing the armed forces.'

[84] See the comprehensive database administered by the ICRC regarding cases before domestic tribunals with respect to violations of IHL (including the cooperation with the international criminal tribunals), available at <https://www.icrc.org/ihl-nat>.

[85] See, e.g., C. Rudolph, 'Constructing an Atrocities Regime: The Politics of War Crimes Tribunals', 55 *International Organization* (2001) 655; J. Sarkin, 'The Tension between Justice and Reconciliation in Rwanda: Politics, Human Rights, Due Process and the Role of the Gacaca Courts in Dealing with the Genocide', 45 *Journal of African Law* (2001) 143; and P. Akhavan, 'Justice and Reconciliation in the Great Lakes Region of Africa: The Contribution of the International Criminal Tribunal for Rwanda', 7 *Duke Journal of Comparative & International Law* (1996–7) 325.

it has become a standard feature of international tribunals that they deny effect to domestic amnesty laws or immunities, such situations continue to raise difficult questions regarding relations between states and cooperation with international tribunals. Recent proceedings before the International Court of Justice (ICJ),[86] and proceedings before international criminal courts[87] against former high-ranking officials (including heads of state), are telling examples of the problems that the enforcement of IHL may pose through the application of sanctions. Thus, the questions regarding the legitimacy of adjudication over individuals by foreign states and international tribunals can create tensions among states and have important repercussions for the regions where the conflict arose. States may be reluctant to start proceedings that risk tarnishing their relations with other specific states, or that may even lead to their violating general international law (with regard to immunities and treatment of witnesses, victims, and alleged perpetrators).

47   Lastly, one should not underestimate the practical problems and cost of investigating and adjudicating (alleged) crimes that have taken place during armed conflict.[88] Due to the conflict itself and the lapse of time that normally occurs before any proper investigation is possible, the evidence may be rather weak and difficult to obtain. This is even more likely if the investigation and adjudication take place far away from where the events happened. The absence of written documents and other factual evidence makes witness testimonies (including hearsay) particularly important. Furthermore, the protection of witnesses and the victims of such crimes may be difficult and risky.[89] The fact that the investigation, the trial, the protection of the witnesses, and the punishment of the perpetrator may involve high costs can lead to financial and political problems. This holds true for the international criminal tribunals (including the ICC) created in recent years, but even more so for domestic courts, especially when adjudicating crimes committed outside their territory and without the cooperation of the authorities in the state where the alleged crimes were committed. This situation may be further exacerbated by the need for the victims (and the accused) to get financial support[90] or apply for political asylum.[91] This

---

[86] In particular the cases 'Questions Relating to the Obligation to Prosecute or Extradite' (*Belgium v Senegal*) of 2012, 'Certain Questions of Mutual Assistance in Criminal Matters' (*Djibouti v France*) of 2006, 'Certain Criminal Proceedings in France' (*Republic of the Congo v France*) of 2003, and 'Arrest Warrant of 11 April 2000' (*Democratic Republic of the Congo v Belgium*) of 2000.

[87] In particular the proceedings in *The Prosecutor v Omar Hassan Ahmad Al Bashir* ICC-02/05-01/09 and *The Prosecutor v Charles Ghankay Taylor* (SCSL-03-01).

[88] A.R. Ziegler, S. Wehrenberg, and R. Weber (eds), *Kriegsverbrecherprozesse in der Schweiz/Procès de criminels de guerre en Suisse, Praktische Erfahrungen mit der Verfolgung und Beurteilung von Kriegsverbrechen aus Ex-Jugoslawien und Ruanda* (Zurich: Schulthess, 2009).

[89] See M. Othman, 'The "Protection" of Refugee Witnesses by the International Criminal Tribunal for Rwanda', 14 *IJRL* (2002) 495; and S. Wehrenberg, 'Art 98a–98d MStP (Zeugenschutz [Witness Protection])', in S. Wehrenberg et al (eds), *Kommentar zum Militärstrafprozess* (Zurich: Schulthess, 2008).

[90] See S. Wehrenberg, 'Ansprüche von ausländischen Opfern in schweizerischen Kriegsverbrecherprozessen', in Ziegler, Wehrenberg, and Weber (eds), above n 88, 143; S. Wehrenberg and D.V. Jabornigg, 'Art 84a–84k MStP (Opferhilfe)' and 'Art 163–165 MStP (Zivilrechtliche Ansprüche von Geschädigten [Civil Claims by Victims])', in Wehrenberg et al (eds), above n 89.

[91] In May 2011, four ICC witnesses filed applications for asylum in the Netherlands. See G. Sluiter, 'Shared Responsibility in International Criminal Justice: The ICC and Asylum', 10 *JICJ* (2012) 661. Another issue is the fact that certain persons may try to enhance the likelihood of their remaining in a foreign country by claiming that they have committed violations of IHL or human rights, contesting a possible extradition by contending that they would risk experiencing violation(s) of certain fundamental rights arising from an unfair trial if sent back (principle of non-refoulement); see A. Rasulov, 'Criminals as Refugees: The "Balancing Exercise" and Article 1F(B) of the Refugee Convention', 16 *Georgetown Immigration Law Journal* (2001–2)

problem exists before international courts too, but may be dealt with in a joint effort by the global community (or an important part of it). A number of non-governmental organizations have become very active in recent years, to ensure that such political and financial problems do not hamper the fight against impunity relating to violations of IHL and gross violations of human rights.[92]

ANDREAS R. ZIEGLER   STEFAN WEHRENBERG

815; J. Heller, 'What Happens to the Acquitted?' 21 *LJIL* (2008) 663; E. van Sliedrecht, 'International Crimes before Dutch Courts: Recent Developments', 20 *LJIL* (2007) 895; and E. van der Borght, 'Prosecution of International Crimes in the Netherlands: An Analysis of Recent Case Law', 18 *Criminal Law Forum* (2007) 87.

[92] In particular, one might mention the Geneva-based Swiss Association against Impunity (TRIAL), Geneva Call, or World Organization against Torture (OMCT), as well as traditional associations like Amnesty International or Human Rights Watch.

D. THE GENEVA CONVENTIONS IN CONTEXT

II. THE GENEVA CONVENTIONS IN CONTEXT

Chapter 33. The Universality of the Geneva Conventions

	MN
A. Introduction	1
B. 'Broad' Universality: The Rules of the Geneva Conventions as Part of Customary International Law	6
I. The significance of the claim to customary status	8
II. Custom as universality	13
III. Custom: between practice and *opinio juris*	17
C. 'Thick' Universality: The Trans-Civilizational Question	26
I. International humanitarian law and the Geneva Conventions: the importance of the exclusionary bent	29
II. The dominant consensus	33
III. A critique of the consensus	39
D. 'Deep' Universality: The Cosmopolitan Ambition	44
I. The Geneva Conventions' statism	46
II. The universalization of implementation	50
III. Individuals and rebel movements: evolutions in accountability	53
E. Critical Assessment	57

Select Bibliography

Bernard, V., 'Editorial: Engaging Armed Groups', 93 *IRRC* 883 (2011) 581

Boll, A.M., 'The Asian Values Debate and its Relevance to International Humanitarian Law', 83 *IRRC* 841 (2001) 45

Cockayne, J., 'Islam and International Humanitarian Law: From a Clash to a Conversation between Civilizations', 84 *IRRC* 847 (2002) 597, at 623–4

Condorelli, L., S. Scherrer/La Rosa, A.M. (eds), *Les Nations Unies et le droit international humanitaire/The United Nations and International Humanitarian Law, Actes du Colloque international à l'occasion du cinquantième anniversaire de l'ONU (Genève, 19, 20 et 21 octobre 1995)* (Paris: Pedone, 1998)

Danner, A.M., 'When Courts Make Law: How the International Criminal Tribunals Recast the Laws of War', 59 *Vanderbilt Law Review* (2006) 1

Dudai, R., 'Closing The Gap: Symbolic Reparations and Armed Groups', 93 *IRRC* 883 (2011) 783

Hofmann, C., 'Engaging Non-State Armed Groups in Humanitarian Action', 13 *International Peacekeeping* (2006) 396

Lafrance, L., *Droit humanitaire et guerres déstrucurées: l'exemple africain* (Montreal: Liber, 2006)

Mani, V.S., 'International Humanitarian Law: An Indo-Asian Perspective', 83 *IRRC* 841 (2001) 59

Mégret, F., 'From "Savages" to "Unlawful Combatants": A Postcolonial Look at International Humanitarian Law's "Other"', in A. Orford (ed), *International Law and its Others* (Cambridge: CUP, 2006), at 15–16

Meron, T., 'The Humanization of Humanitarian Law', 94 *AJIL* (2000) 239

Provost, R., 'The International Committee of the Red Widget: The Diversity Debate and International Humanitarian Law', 40 *Israel Law Review* (2007) 614

Sassóli, M./Shany, Y., 'Should the Obligations of States and Armed Groups under International Humanitarian Law Really Be Equal?', 93 *IRRC* 882 (2011) 426

A. Introduction

1   The Geneva Conventions are periodically hailed as having been ratified by every state in the international community.[1] This universal ratification is widely touted as one of the best guarantees of their implementation. Closely linked to that universality is a more technical claim, also broadly shared, about their customary character. Universalism also stands for the idea that international humanitarian law (IHL) is consonant with every culture and belief system. The moral authority of the Conventions is presented as no doubt enhanced by this largely shared sentiment about their universal character. Nonetheless, universality is a complex claim that requires some careful unpacking. It may be that it is occasionally brandished a little too easily when its reality is subtle.

2   The *claim* to universality is, to begin with, a particular claim that is itself historically and geographically situated, one whose very existence (as a claim) is not universal. In other words, one thing we can be sure of is that the claim to the universality of the Geneva Conventions is one that is itself part of a largely Western history of *universalism*. Universalism, paradoxically, is hardly universal. It therefore behoves scholars of the Geneva Conventions to better understand and explain what their relationship is to the idea of universals. What role does that claim serve in sustaining the normative aspirations of IHL? What is the history of the claim?

3   Moreover, there is a constant ambiguity to universality that will be a recurring motif of this chapter. Universality can refer to the *a priori* philosophical judgement, particularly concerning ethical statements, that something is true everywhere and anywhere, for example because it can be proved to flow from certain characteristics of human nature that are immutable ('universality'); or it can be a more sociological concept that refers to the degree to which something is effectively accepted by all relevant actors (however defined) as appropriate ('universal acceptance'). In that respect, there is something counterintuitive about a series of somewhat idiosyncratic treaties adopted late in human history incarnating the first pure form of universalism. In fact, most defences of the Geneva Conventions' universality are of the second, softer kind, although as we shall see, it is not evident that they can do away entirely with the first kind to explain why they are universally accepted.

4   Still, in practice, broad assertions as to the Geneva Conventions' universality often coexist with persistent doubts and questions about the means and ends of IHL. Even agreement that universality is a shared sociological quality of a norm rather than a metaphysical claim does require one to determine what the appropriate level of acceptability is. It is here that there has arguably been a perennial ambiguity about universality that has fed into the politics of the claim. For some, universality is primarily a function of state practice, at least after the adoption of the Conventions, and is best exemplified by massive ratification.[2] For others, universalism means that the Conventions embody some prior, or at least parallel, deeper consensus about the values underlying them. Such a claim may help minimize the lack of actual practice.[3] For yet others, universality refers to the constitutional or quasi-constitutional authority of the Conventions above and beyond

---

[1] With the emergence of new states that judgement may need to be regularly updated. See K. Thynne, 'The Universality of IHL: Surmounting the Last Bastion of the Pacific', 41 *Victoria University of Wellington Law Review* (2010) 135.

[2] In effect, universalism and universal ratification are equated. Ibid.

[3] Y. Dinstein, 'Humanitarian Law on the Conflict in Afghanistan', 96 *ASIL Proceedings* (2002) 23.

(although no doubt partly as a result of) their universal ratification, as a form of 'humanitarian common law'.[4] Lastly, for others universality in this day and age should be sought in the degree to which not only states or civilizations accept the Geneva Conventions, but individuals and non-state actors as well.

This chapter will accordingly envisage universality as referring specifically to:

— the degree to which particular norms of the Geneva Conventions have acquired customary international status (section B);
— the degree to which the Geneva Conventions reflect values and standards that are present in all cultures and civilizations (section C); and
— the degree to which the norms underlying the Geneva Conventions are considered universal and applicable by a range of non-state actors (section D).

B. 'Broad' Universality: The Rules of the Geneva Conventions as Part of Customary International Law

The word 'custom' can be somewhat ambiguous, as it refers both to, most classically, the material and psychological basis of a norm's being considered customary, and to the particular status that results from a norm's being considered custom. As the International Court of Justice (ICJ) put it, the fundamental rules of IHL, which the Geneva Conventions embody, constitute 'intransgressible principles of international customary law'.[5] Both are linked: a norm that is complied with by many states on the basis of its binding character will thus be considered binding on all. It is in these respects that norms' customary status and their universality are considerably intertwined.

Although there may have been more doubts about this in their early decades, most of the Geneva Convention's provisions are quite widely considered to have acquired customary status. For example, the ICJ held early on in the *Nicaragua v United States* case, against the scepticism of a minority of judges,[6] that the Conventions including Common Article 3 were customary,[7] a statement it subsequently reinforced in its Advisory Opinion on *Nuclear Weapons*.[8] This is perhaps in contrast to continuing debates about the exact customary status of Additional Protocols (APs) I and II. In practice, it seems that initial judgments to the effect that the bulk of the rules of the Geneva Conventions had customary status emboldened subsequent judgments to find the same, often gradually eliding some of the doubts that had been expressed early on. For example, the Secretary-General of the United Nations (UN), in the report that led to the creation of the International Criminal Tribunal for the former Yugoslavia (ICTY), indicated that '[t]he part of conventional international humanitarian law which has beyond doubt become part of international customary law is the law applicable in armed conflict as embodied in: the Geneva Conventions of 12 August 1949'.[9] According to the International Committee of the Red

---

[4] L. Joinet, 'The Universal Dimensions of Humanitarian Law in Armed Conflicts: An Arena for Action by Non-Governmental Organizations?', 16 *Social Justice* (1989) 26.
[5] ICJ, *Legality of the Threat or Use of Nuclear Weapons (Nuclear Weapons)*, Advisory Opinion, 8 July 1996, para 79.
[6] ICJ, *Case concerning Military and Paramilitary Activities in and against Nicaragua (Nicaragua v United States)*, Dissenting Opinion Jennings, 27 June 1986, at 537.
[7] Ibid, Merits, para 218.   [8] ICJ, *Nuclear Weapons*, above n 5, at 257–8.
[9] Report of the Secretary-General, S/25704, 3 May 1993, para 35.

Cross (ICRC) Study on Customary International Humanitarian Law (CIHL), 'the great majority of the provisions of the Geneva Conventions of 1949, including common Article 3, are considered to be customary law'.[10]

I. The significance of the claim to customary status

8 The question of the customary character of the Geneva Conventions is of general relevance to their application. Perhaps a significant aspect of that character is that it makes the Conventions binding even on states that have not ratified them. The importance of this was not lost on various tribunals prosecuting war crimes in the aftermath of the Second World War, which found that the 1907 Hague Regulations and the 1929 Geneva Conventions had acquired customary status regardless of ratification. Of course, because most states have ratified the 1949 Geneva Conventions, the prospect of binding states outside that circle is less relevant. Yet custom can still help bind states to treaty-originating customary developments which they might not have treated as law. In at least one case (*Nicaragua v United States*), the customary nature of the Geneva Conventions allowed the ICJ to bypass the fact that it did not have jurisdiction to adjudicate upon the Conventions per se.

9 At any rate, the Conventions' customary character is something to which international lawyers remain committed. There are several reasons for this. One is that the Geneva Conventions form the basis for further custom through a continuous and dynamic process, so that establishing their initial customary character is a necessary step to establishing their evolving customary development. Customary international law (CIL) may develop more dynamically than treaty regimes, based on a large amount of decentralized practice. There have been several occasions historically when treaty-originating custom seemed to overtake the treaty in ways that allowed for the significant development of the law. For example, the ICTY has found that customary rules have evolved that govern the regulation of non-international armed conflict (NIAC) beyond Common Article 3.

10 Another reason why arguments about the Geneva Conventions' customary character continue to be attractive, despite their limited practical implications, is a more general notion that the customary character of any norm reinforces the sense of its social groundedness. A treaty is not just the expression of a collection of voluntary individual commitments but stands a better chance of being seen as the expression of fundamental society norms. This is not irrelevant for a body of laws such as the Geneva Conventions that do claim to synthesize a more fundamental international community aspiration. There is a sense in which the Geneva Conventions today constitute the deep customary sediment of a multi-layered regime of humanitarian norms, the applicability of which beyond international conflicts has increasingly been recognized.

11 One could say that the customary argument is, as we shall see in section C, one argument in favour of their inter-civilizational universality. It upgrades international law of a contractual nature to general international law, and may even get us a step closer towards the coveted (however symbolic) *jus cogens* status. Of course, the customary character of international norms also means that states cannot opt out of them, except

---

[10] ICRC CIHL Study, vol I, at xxxvi.

through the quite onerous demands of the persistent objector doctrine. Even if a state withdrew from the Geneva Conventions, it would in effect remain bound by the vast majority of the Conventions' norms that have been found to have customary status. At any rate, even this looks somewhat improbable, since states in practice would much rather claim that they did not violate the Geneva Conventions than actually signal any intent to withdraw.

Lastly, even where a state has ratified the Conventions, establishing their customary character reinforces the sense of the legitimacy of international interventions, whether through universal jurisdiction or international criminal tribunals, to prosecute crimes committed on its territory, by or against its nationals. This explains why the ICTY and the International Criminal Tribunal for Rwanda were keen to emphasize the customary character of the Geneva Conventions, despite the former Yugoslavia and Rwanda having been party to them, which theoretically should have sufficed. Such efforts are understandable only if one sees them not as legitimizing the application of the Geneva Conventions *to* the interested states, but as legitimizing their application *by* all other members of the international community as a basis for the punishment of war crimes. Indeed, the increasing resort to international criminal law (ICL) makes it all the more necessary to anchor grave breaches and war crimes in deep common social standards (there is, at a certain level, a tension between a vision of IHL as a pure conventional commitment between equals, and resort to ICL as a mode of enforcement).

II. Custom as universality

When it comes to establishing the customary character of the provisions of the Geneva Conventions, there has long been a tradition that, despite the rise of international legal positivism, follows (to use the language of Martti Koskenniemi)[11] a 'descending' pattern of justification, from the 'conscience of mankind' or the 'needs of mankind',[12] to actual law. In the spirit of this school of thought, there is little doubt that 'humanity' is both immanent and universal. The Geneva Conventions are deeply embedded in a strong pre-existing social interest in the laws of war, that manifests itself quite clearly in the Conventions themselves, whether it be in the unorthodox Common Article 1 obligation to 'respect *and ensure respect*' (emphasis added) or in the unusual attribution of *universal* jurisdiction for grave breaches which is premised on the idea that certain war crimes are of universal concern. It is also evident in the continuing influence of the Martens Clause in the interpretation of the Conventions, as an exercise of codification of the laws of war that does not exhaust 'the usages established between civilized nations [...] the laws of humanity and the requirements of public conscience'.[13]

Accession to the Conventions, then, is construed more as recognition of the self-evidence of these beliefs than as a truly law-creating act—a concession to highly positivistic times rather than an abdication to them. For example, the ICJ has pointed out that 'it is undoubtedly because a great many rules of humanitarian law applicable in armed conflict are so fundamental to the respect of the human person and "elementary considerations of humanity" [...] that the Hague and Geneva Conventions have enjoyed

---

[11] M Koskenniemi, *From Apology to Utopia: The Structure of International Legal Argument* (Cambridge: CUP, 2006).
[12] J.S. Pictet, 'The New Geneva Conventions for the Protection of War Victims', 45 *AJIL* (1951) 462, at 462.
[13] Preamble, Hague Convention II on the Law and Customs of War on Land, 1899. See Ch 9 of this volume.

a broad accession'[14] (and not the opposite way round). Another way of looking at this is that the Geneva Conventions manifest deep community standards, as exemplified by the fact that 'the denunciation clauses that existed in the codification instruments have never been used'.[15] This idealistic tradition retains an appeal, and there is some work in moral theory that attempts to establish how something like the Geneva Conventions might be reconstructed from first principles.[16]

15   But it is also a tradition that remains vulnerable to the critique that it is abstract, vague, and highly contentious, especially when confronted with challenges of imperfect implementation. Indeed, the adoption of the Geneva Conventions themselves seems to contradict the suggestion that they embody principles that are already universal, and to make the case that a treaty was needed (if the principles were that universal in the first place then what need was there for a treaty?). An argument might be made that the Conventions are customary because they are universal, but this merely invites the question of what universality means. Universality in the sense of widespread recognition of or agreement about a norm's validity is not the same thing as saying a norm is customary law. That type of universality could go at least some way towards establishing *opinio juris* (as one of the key components of custom) in relation to that norm, but it cannot really be a substitute for practice. Certainly, few would argue that states 'universally' apply the Geneva Conventions. The question of practice is very difficult to ignore if one takes seriously the idea of custom, of norms following an at least partly ascending pattern from state consent.

16   A similar claim, in this context, is that the Geneva Conventions were in a sense customary before they even, as it were, became conventional. They merely synthesized existing CIL that was itself the expression of their social rootedness. The ICJ in *Nicaragua v United States* found that the Convention in some crucial respects only gave expression to existing laws of war. For example, there was an obligation for the United States to 'respect and ensure respect' for the Geneva Conventions, 'since such an obligation does not derive only from the Conventions themselves, but from the general principles of humanitarian law to which the Conventions merely give specific expression'.[17] According to the Pictet Commentary, Common Article 3 merely demands respect for rules 'already recognized as essential in all civilized countries, and embodied in the national legislation of the States in question, long before the Convention was signed'.[18] This argument pushes back the question of when that customary status was acquired, but then often locates that shift in a tradition from time immemorial that is never really proved, and of which one would have reason to be sceptical. In fact, in the context of the operation of the international criminal tribunals, there has been an even greater suspicion that 'custom' is heavily driven by policy and moral considerations articulated by judges on the basis of questionable teleological interpretations.[19]

---

[14] ICJ, *Corfu Channel case (UK v Albania)*, Judgment, 9 April 1949, para 79.
[15] ICJ, *Nuclear Weapons*, above n 5, para 81.
[16] E.g., the work of Walzer on the laws of war may be seen as an attempt to rationalize the existing content of the laws on the basis of moral theory. M. Walzer, *Just and Unjust Wars: A Moral Argument with Historical Illustrations* (4th edn, New York: Basic Books, 2006).
[17] ICJ, *Nicaragua v United States*, Merits, above n 6, para 220.   [18] Pictet Commentary GC IV, at 36.
[19] A.M. Danner, 'When Courts Make Law: How the International Criminal Tribunals Recast the Laws of War', 59 *Vanderbilt Law Review* (2006) 1.

III. Custom: between practice and *opinio juris*

17 The reality of competing cultural claims and nationalist passions means that it will be tempting to prove customary status by adopting a more 'ascending' pattern of thought, and grounding that status in something more incontrovertible, such as actual practice backed by *opinio juris*. The cardinal card in the stack when it comes to proving the practice element to ascertain the Conventions' customary status is, in fact, the very existence of the Conventions and their wide ratification. Wide ratification serves both to consolidate the Geneva Conventions' conventional authority *and* evidence their customary status. However, as Baxter once pointed out, wide ratification also makes it hard to know the content of a putative customary norm because the pool of states outside the treaty diminishes, and with it the opportunities to ascertain what states do outside a conventional obligation (this is what is often known as the 'Baxter paradox', and it is fully in evidence in relation to the Geneva Conventions).[20] As was already mentioned, the Geneva Conventions have been ratified by all states in the international community, making them arguably the only treaties ever to have reached that status. Moreover, it is often as if new states were eager to ratify them immediately upon becoming independent, as occurred most recently, for example, with South Sudan, in a sign that ratification is seen almost as an obligation for newcomers. This extremely broad ratification is, in fact, what most frequently earns the Geneva Conventions the label of being 'universal'.

18 Yet the truth is that mere ratification of a treaty, however significant it may be at the treaty level, cannot entirely exhaust international law's appetite for actual practice to establish custom. States could very much fail to abide by their Geneva Conventions' obligations despite being parties to them, and it is hard to see how that failure should not be treated in terms of both practice and *opinio juris* as at least as relevant as mere ratification. In that regard, although it may be tempting to think that a treaty norm that is universally binding conventionally must also be binding under customary law, in fact a universally binding conventional norm *qua* conventional norm could fail to qualify for customary status if a significant number of states failed to abide by it,[21] or abided by it only for reasons that clearly related to their conventional commitments. In other words, a treaty would remain a treaty under treaty law even if it was dead letter in practice (except through the quite radical scenario of desuetude),[22] whereas a custom can materialize only on the basis of concordant practice.

19 There is thus more to a norm's becoming customary than the fact that many states have signed on to its conventional avatar. This explains the attention to a certain *depth* of state practice when inquiring about custom, that also ties up with the notion of universality as a form of deep social acceptability. The CIHL Study, for example, went far beyond the identification of state consent to be bound by the Conventions and made it clear that its understanding of practice was very broad:

Both physical and verbal acts of States constitute practice that contributes to the creation of customary international law. Physical acts include, for example, battlefield behaviour, the use of certain weapons and the treatment provided to different categories of persons. Verbal acts include military manuals, national legislation, national case-law, instructions to armed and security

---

[20] R.R. Baxter, 'Treaties and Custom', 129 *RCADI* (1970) 25.
[21] Incidentally, this is a conclusion which tribunals have been prompt to reach when dealing with certain norms of IHL that were arguably no longer in tune with the times, such as the *si omnes* clause.
[22] R. Kolb, 'La désuétude en droit international public', 111 *RGDIP* (2007) 577.

forces, military communiqués during war, diplomatic protests, opinions of official legal advisers, comments by governments on draft treaties, executive decisions and regulations, pleadings before international tribunals, statements in international organizations and at international conferences and government positions taken with respect to resolutions of international organizations.[23]

20   This impressive list is so broad and non-hierarchic that it probably considerably extends the chances that some practice will be found. However, it is also true that there is much practice available anyhow, especially in international armed conflicts (IACs), where states have no doubt occasionally considered that adherence to the Conventions aligned substantially with their national interest. The CIHL Study is in itself testimony to the fact that a wide range of sources evidence some form of practice. Moreover, the one signal achievement of the Conventions is to have accumulated the sort of authority that would make it very unlikely, as a matter of *opinio juris*, for a state blatantly to claim that it was not bound by them; a state is much more likely to claim that, as a matter of fact, it did not violate them.

21   This is not to say, however, that there is no ambiguity in the attempt at grounding the Geneva Conventions in the canon of CIL. Noticeably, international tribunals have typically been much more cursory in their analysis of practice, especially when it comes to a number of more contentious developments beyond the text of the Conventions. This tendency was already apparent at Nuremberg and Tokyo and subsequent proceedings, where tribunals assumed a rough general homology between then existing conventional and customary law, often without bothering to identify by what process they came to that deduction or pinpointing what rules specifically had become customary. It continued with the ICJ's rather 'matter of course' treatment of the question of custom in the *Nicaragua v United States* case. It has been particularly notable with the extension of the regime applicable in IACs to NIACs, a quite contentious migration that the ICTY argued had occurred entirely customarily, despite the rather random examples of practice quoted.

22   Behind this tendency arguably lie some of the very ambiguities of the concept of custom, ambiguities only magnified by the existence of treaties that make it easier to confuse practice and *opinio juris*, and redefine each in terms of the other. If the Geneva Conventions had not existed at all, would it not have been considerably harder to establish that corresponding norms existed customarily without state practice? The existence of the Conventions, conversely, has made it easier to find a degree of pseudo-practice revolving around them. The Geneva Conventions provided significant impetus for domestic implementation, for example, which could substitute to a degree for actual practice in peacetime, which is all the more relevant since most states are not involved in warfare most of the time. Treaties also create a more stable basis from which expectations of conformity may emerge.

23   The multilateralization of humanitarian diplomacy has also offered a much greater reservoir of statements as to why and when states respect certain restraints in warfare than would have been available in a highly decentralized system deprived of treaty guidance and states' constant aspiration to be seen as complying with it (even when they are not). In fact, international bodies, which are often by nature much more committed to the goal of implementing the Geneva Conventions, and which sometimes structurally require that implementation (the International Criminal Court comes to mind), have become a

---

[23] ICRC CIHL Study, vol I, at xxxviii.

recognized if somewhat novel source of international practice. In short, the existence of instruments such as the Geneva Conventions made it easier to treat what might traditionally only have counted as *opinio juris* (statements, declarations) as practice.

This all made it easier and more tempting for the ICTY, for example, to dismiss 'the actual behaviour of the troops in the field' as too difficult to establish.[24] Instead, that tribunal redefined practice in terms of a number of acts or statements more characteristic of *opinio juris*, or which at the very least constituted only a resolutely 'soft' form of practice. What states *say* they do has arguably become more important than *what* they do, as if customary law was less about adherence to a certain behaviour than being held to one's own and repeated commitments. This prioritizing of the declaratory over the factual also underlined the evolving basis of respect for humanitarian norms as anchored in community expectations and 'good citizenship' rather than a preponderance of precedent. But it did also do away with what might arguably have been the hardest element to prove, namely that states ordinarily and generally respect the Geneva Conventions. The ICTY at times behaved as if it was in denial about the relative paucity of practice in conformity with the treaties, especially in NIAC.

Yet one cannot help considering that behind some of these complex manoeuvres to reinvest custom with a universalizing meaning, lies something more fundamental in the form of a reluctance to confront in full the consequences of what might well turn out to be radically contrary practice. What should one do if the Geneva Conventions do turn out to be routinely violated on battlefields? Should such violations be allowed to undermine the sense of an emerging, nay established, custom? Could international law rigidly adhere to an epistemology of sovereignty that ends up clashing with some of international lawyers' most cherished beliefs and sense of professional self? In reality, the belief that the Geneva Conventions *ought to be* treated as customary is likely to trump a significant degree of practice invalidating that belief. Hence the affirmation of the customary character of the Geneva Conventions reflects not only the fundamental evolution of what counts as custom, but also an inevitable return, for all the apparent detour through practice, to a certain irreducible belief, both moral and social, that the international community's best attempt at equipping itself with a humanitarian regime in war is valid in and by itself, a sort of quasi-legislative process that has become significantly decoupled from whether its subjects abide by it or not. In other words, the custom question ends up being significantly redefined as one of universality, understood at least as the quasi-universality of lip service.

C. 'Thick' Universality: The Trans-Civilizational Question

The difficulty is, of course, that if lawyers rely on the Geneva Conventions' universal status to establish their customary nature, they must then face up to that issue of universality. Meron has argued that 'consensus that the Geneva Conventions are declaratory of customary international law would strengthen the moral claim of the international community for their observance because it would emphasize their humanitarian underpinnings and deep roots in tradition and community values'.[25] But in a context where custom is itself derived from the Conventions' aura of universal authority, establishing

---

[24] ICTY, *The Prosecutor v Duško Tadić*, Appeals Chamber Decision on the Defence Motion for Interlocutory Appeal on Jurisdiction, IT-94-AR72, 2 October 1995, para 99.
[25] T. Meron, 'The Geneva Conventions as Customary Law', 81 *AJIL* (1987) 348, at 350.

the customary character of the Geneva Conventions cannot symmetrically do all the work to highlight their universality, or risk circularity. At best, the customary character of the Geneva Conventions establishes a particular kind of universality—that operating between states.

27 There remains a dimension that is not attested purely by international law's imprimatur and that is, in a sense, beyond it. The Conventions could have customary character on purely legal grounds yet nonetheless run against, or at least be in tension with, the significant culturally held views of a range of groups. The Conventions may be widely ratified, but that may not necessarily denote their universality, understood here as 'broad' universality, i.e. an understanding that they reflect a large consensus between civilizations or cultures about fundamental common humanitarian values. The question, as one author put it, is whether we are facing 'a body of law which is universal in scope, but also in moral or societal terms, in relation to the law's claim to reflect common interests and ideas'.[26]

28 In fact one might argue that, in a paradoxical way, the anxious and incantatory insistence on the Conventions' customary status is all the more indulged in that there are, simultaneously, doubts about their true universality. Let us not forget that the Geneva Conventions and IHL generally emerged historically precisely to remedy a breakdown in the universality of the values characteristic of the European Middle Ages that had produced the tradition of restraint in warfare. Europe, from the Napoleonic Wars to Hiroshima, had shown ample propensity to turn even against norms that were supposed to go to its very identity. Modernity had shredded the last remains of naturalist restraint in war. What was no longer morally obvious to all, therefore, would henceforth be imposed by law. The Geneva Conventions then emerged as the heroic but ambiguous standard-bearers for the moral standards that gave them their legitimacy, even as they had tragically ceased to be adhered to merely as moral standards. Customary law's inability entirely to hide the breakdown of that 'other' universality is of course revealed in some of the intellectual games it plays with the very notion of custom. But what of this civilizational universality beyond Europe and the Western world?

I. International humanitarian law and the Geneva Conventions: the importance of the exclusionary bent

29 International humanitarian law has had a history that was for a long time quite explicitly based on a vision of the antagonism of civilizations.[27] It has thus periodically been challenged as representing only a particular civilizational approach to the regulation of warfare. On one reading, the Geneva Conventions certainly represent an improvement from these origins. By the time of their adoption, the laws of war had been put on a more secular footing and embedded in a public international legal framework that was increasingly destined to make way for a variety of states. The international legal order's apparent neutrality and agnosticism about ends could not be particularly suspected of imposing anything more than very superficial common humanitarian standards (unlike, for

---

[26] A.M. Boll, 'The Asian Values Debate and its Relevance to International Humanitarian Law', 83 *IRRC* 841 (2001) 45.

[27] R. Provost, 'The International Committee of the Red Widget: The Diversity Debate and International Humanitarian Law', 40 *Israel Law Review* (2007) 614; F. Mégret, 'From "Savages" to Unlawful Combatants': A Postcolonial Look at International Humanitarian Law's "Other"', in A. Orford (ed), *International Law and its Others* (Cambridge: CUP, 2006), at 15–16.

example, human rights). In treating an increasing number of international participants as if they naturally could only embrace those standards, the Geneva Conventions also seemed to treat them as mature and responsible members in making of the international community. In fact, it is beyond doubt that the adoption and, more importantly, the implementation of the Geneva Conventions has, over the last decades, provided countless opportunities, frequently mediated by the ICRC, for international socialization into the language of respectable statehood.

Nonetheless, a case for the relative Western-centrism of the Geneva Conventions could still be made, from the outset. The ICRC, which convened the Geneva Conference, is a Swiss organization, its board composed exclusively of Swiss citizens. Although this Swiss-focused membership was justified by the need for the organization to be neutral, neutrality is hardly the same thing as universality. The Western focus of the Conventions may have been reinforced by the fact that the experience of the Second World War very much provided the background for the drafting exercise. Of the only 63 states that participated in the drafting effort (four of which attended as observers, and only a minority of which were highly active), only three African states took part (Ethiopia, Liberia, and Egypt). In fact, the absence of what was not quite yet the Third World was barely noticed, a sign perhaps of how disconnected the 1949 exercise was from some of the passions that had long begun brewing on the periphery of the Second World War's theatre.

Retrospectively, the absence of a great number of regions from the negotiating table would come to be viewed more harshly. The fact that the Geneva Conventions had not attracted greater participation from the outset may have been a factor in the emergence of problems that led to the need for and adoption of the Protocols to the Conventions. Limited universalism would subsequently help frame the Conventions, despite strenuous denials, as the project of one particular civilization, heavily centred on Europe. Although newly independent states ratified the Conventions relatively quickly upon acceding to independence, the perceived exclusion of wars of national liberation from the core of the Conventions made them an object of scepticism.

That this was the prevalent feeling between 1974 and 1977, as the Protocols were negotiated, was made clear by a number of delegations. Egypt, Burundi, Nigeria, and Uganda, for example, deplored the weak African participation in 1949.[28] Those sitting at the negotiating table in 1949 represented a strikingly homogeneous, relatively small proportion of humanity, at least in terms of diversity of cultures, religious influences, or even colour of skin. In some respects, the Conventions were negotiated a decade or two too early to have the sort of broad representation that would become a hallmark of diplomatic conferences in the 1960s and 1970s. It is not too much to claim that this would have tainted the Conventions' universality, even though it is of course possible that the states present in Geneva spoke for others, or that their experience was not that different from that of the states that would emerge from decolonization.

II. The dominant consensus

Yet it is also true that the Geneva Conventions, unlike international human rights law (IHRL), have largely escaped the cultural relativist debate. The strength of that challenge

---

[28] Official Records of the Diplomatic Conference on the Reaffirmation and Development of International Humanitarian Law applicable in Armed Conflicts (Geneva, 1974–7), vol V, 92, 118, 127.

has been far greater in relation to international human rights, particularly the Geneva Conventions' great contemporary, the Universal Declaration of Human Rights, which was also tainted by less than universal beginnings. The negotiations of the Human Rights Covenants adopted in 1966 seemed to re-open debates that had been temporarily bracketed in the brief euphoria of the after war. After the Cold War, a powerful second wave of cultural criticism challenged the universality of the notion of rights, particularly on the basis of supposedly distinct Asian values. By contrast, there has been no charismatic spokesperson for 'Asian values' when it comes to IHL of the sort that Lee Kuan Yew or Mahathir, however briefly, incarnated.

34 One might speculate, following René Provost's landmark analysis of the matter,[29] that there are several reasons why the Geneva Conventions have escaped the more potent forms of that critique. International human rights law, for example, is extremely demanding normatively in terms of states' preferences, and involves what were once thought to be inherently domestic matters. The same is arguably not true when it comes to IHL, which, although it may make heavy demands on the state in times of war, might certainly be thought to be less intrusive in terms of cultural preferences. Indeed, there is a case that war, unlike the domestic organization of societies, is a matter that is inherently international, and therefore one on which states may be more naturally predisposed to agree to common standards that transcend cultural and civilizational biases. Moreover, humanitarian law's globally pragmatic outlook avoids the pitfalls of contentious claims about rights. The claim, then, is one about the special status of IHL as uniquely *common*, in contradistinction to human rights' supposed divisiveness.

35 This does not mean that there has been no scholarship defending the Geneva Conventions' universality, particularly in the context of decolonization and occasional hostility to the project,[30] but that this scholarship has almost been pre-emptive in nature, strangely tackling a challenge that was not really made. Perhaps because of a lack of real contradiction, it is also a scholarship that has exhibited a relatively high degree of conformism in its stark reluctance to concede that the Geneva Conventions might do anything less than express a universal aspiration. It is worth emphasizing that those who have taken position in favour of the Geneva Conventions' universality have hardly been consigned to the West. In fact, many have come from the Global South, in the form of actors adamant not only that IHL applied to their countries, but that the West had in a sense not 'discovered' anything that other cultures had not known much earlier, sometimes by a few millennia.[31]

36 Scholars have pointed out that many cultures or civilizations, such as those of India, or Islam, or Africa, have produced rules concerning the regulation of warfare which, although they may differ in their particulars from those of the Geneva Conventions, by and large converge with those norms. Alfred Boll has argued that 'the principles which led to the establishment of these laws emanate from a perception of warfare which has been common to mankind through the ages'.[32] In fact, there is even an element of pride that regulation of warfare emerged in the East long before it did in the West. From this

---

[29] Provost, above n 27, at 627–46.
[30] M. Mubiala, 'African States and the Promotion of Humanitarian Principles', 29 *IRRC* 269 (1989) 93; A.T. Ariyaratne, 'Buddhism and International Humanitarian Law', 15 *Sri Lanka Journal of International Law* (2003) 11; M.K. Sinha, 'Hinduism and International Humanitarian Law', 87 *IRRC* 858 (2005) 285.
[31] V.S. Mani, 'International Humanitarian Law: An Indo-Asian Perspective', 83 *IRRC* 841 (2001) 59.
[32] Boll, above n 26, at 55.

perspective, civilizations or cultures are both precursors to modern IHL and the best embodiment of its newfound universal promise, since in the Geneva Conventions they recognize what they have always carried in themselves.

At a certain level it becomes tempting for those arguing actual universality to explain it as a function of the *necessary* universality of certain practices or emotions in war such as compassion, pity, or fear. The expression of these basic emotional impulses may vary according to culture and be tainted by a degree of idiosyncrasy, but all ultimately and inevitably converge to create the need for some form of restraint that respects, say, the fundamental dignity of human beings, or at least the sacredness of life. It is certainly quite remarkable that many cultures, many of which grew up significantly apart and sometimes with very little interaction, have come up with indigenous traditions of limitations in war relating to the means and methods of war, of persons *hors de combat*, or the treatment of civilians. The Geneva Conventions hardly invented things that had not existed, in some fashion or form, in other eras. One might even speculate that the inherently dialogical structure of war means that the laws of war have, in fact, been a tool of inter-civilizational dialogue, however precarious. It is trite to say that one does not wage war alone, so that the regulation of war is by necessity and despite enmity an exercise in mutual norm construction.

To sum up, the argument is something to the effect that the Geneva Conventions merely codified an aspiration or a set of rules common to all civilizations. Even though these cultures were not actually represented in Geneva, it would not have made much of a difference if they had been, given the extent to which the Conference's broad orientations were *a priori* universal. Much scholarship in this vein has, paradoxically, had the merit of helping the field rediscover a variety of indigenous humanitarian traditions, even if only for the rather self-serving purpose of showing how fundamentally compatible and conducive they were to the universal project.

III. A critique of the consensus

Despite this apparent consensus, there is no reason to think that IHL can avoid a deeper engagement with the cultural critique. René Provost, highlighting a 'lively non-debate', has argued that the idea of historical precursors to the laws of war in various cultures and civilizations hardly in and of itself makes the case for their universalism today. The increasing 'shift toward a more atomistic construction of the individual in humanitarian law'[33] and the 'humanization of humanitarian law'[34] may be factors forcing the laws of war to face up to the challenges of cultural specificities. Indeed, whilst many spokespersons for cultures and civilizations are willing to more or less subsume them under the broad mantle of IHL, there have at least been attempts to highlight the distinctness and continued existence of parallel traditions of restraint in war. The notion of an Islamic laws of war, in particular, as something more than one among many distant antecedents of the same global project, has gained some traction, perhaps because it is the most doctrinally unified and developed.[35] Some of the more fundamentalist strands of Islam give a reading of Islamic

---

[33] Provost, above n 27, at 634.
[34] T. Meron, 'The Humanization of Humanitarian Law', 94 *AJIL* (2000) 239.
[35] See, e.g., R. Murphy and M.M. El Zeidy, 'Prisoners of War: A Comparative Study of the Principles of International Humanitarian Law and the Islamic Law of War', 9 *International Criminal Law Review* (2009) 623.

laws of war that makes them appear less as a complement than as a radical antagonist of the laws of war, although of course such readings need to be critically analysed from the point of view of Islamic jurisprudence.[36] The whole debate occurs against a background where the problematic notion of a potential 'clash of civilizations'[37] seems destined to push the boundaries of what qualifies as universal. The periodic collapse of respect for IHL, especially in NIAC even when it comes to a provision as basic as Common Article 3, may be a sign that, aside from all the other pressures that threaten their implementation, persistent doubts about how the laws of war are understood and apprehended culturally may be part of the problem. Indeed, the ICRC has at least nodded in that direction by engaging in a range of more culturally sensitive projects, even if more at the level of the message than the content.

40   The strength of the cultural relativist challenge lies in its ability to show how worldwide state ratification is not the last word on universality, and how significantly different models of the laws of war might have emerged with greater participation. Wide ratification by newly independent countries in and by itself shows only that governments have over time found it in their interest to ratify, not necessarily that they entirely identify with the norms adopted in the Conventions, that the Conventions closely match national or infra-national understandings of war, or that somewhat different Conventions might not have been adopted had different states been present from the beginning. For many states, arriving, as it were, on the scene a decade or two after the Conventions were adopted, these were very much a 'take it or leave it' proposition given the vested interest already existing among states parties and the sheer unlikelihood of re-opening negotiations. No doubt becoming a party to the Geneva Conventions was part of the bundle of newfound respectability as a state, and at any rate, countries going through decolonization had more experience with domestic struggle than with the IACs primarily anticipated by the Geneva Conventions.

41   In this context, several general points deserve mention. First, there are some methodological biases in various readings of IHL's universality. There is a strong tendency to re-explore cultures of the past retrospectively, by trying to fit some of their normative productions into a contemporary grid heavily indebted to the Geneva Conventions. There is a temptation in many accounts to start from the premise that they are aiming to prove, and to make little effort at problematizing universality. The tone is 'developmentalist', with local cultures seen as essentially stepping-stones to the universal variant of IHL, perhaps shedding their idiosyncrasy in order to embrace the common language of modernity. Conveniently, the Geneva Conventions often appear as the logical concluding stage of efforts at regulating warfare. There is a danger 'in trying to compare and connect norms from vastly different moments in human evolution, thus overlooking centuries of change in moral, social and political thought'.[38]

42   Secondly, as Cockayne and Glenn have emphasized, there is a tendency to reduce traditions to 'static, monolithic constructs' when '[traditions] are in fact complex [...], both dynamic (varying over time) and plural (made up of varying sub-traditions)'.[39] Terms

---

[36] B.K. Freamon, 'Martyrdom, Suicide, and the Islamic Law of War: A Short Legal History', 27 *Fordham ILJ* (2003) 299.

[37] S.P. Huntington, *The Clash of Civilizations and the Remaking of World Order* (New Delhi: Penguin Books India, 1996).

[38] Provost, above n 27, at 626.

[39] J. Cockayne, 'Islam and International Humanitarian Law: From a Clash to a Conversation between Civilizations', 84 *IRRC* 847 (2002) 597; H.P. Glenn, *Legal Traditions of the World* (New York: OUP, 2014).

such as 'culture' or 'civilization' are notably difficult to pin down, and can give rise to a great deal of approximation, as when one speaks of 'Christian' or 'Christian majority' or 'Muslim' states, often forgetting that religion is only one among many factors shaping understandings about war. Indeed, claims of universality may underestimate the degree to which IHL has been a contested terrain even within every culture or civilization. For example, it may overshadow the extent to which a number of cultures have produced vigorous pacifist traditions that, for various reasons, are reluctant to engage in or accept as normatively desirable the regulation of warfare (Buddhism comes to mind). Conversely, the universality thesis might also underestimate the extent to which certain cultures (including Western culture) have produced norms that militate in favour of the harshest possible form of warfare.

Thirdly, the devil is in the detail, and whilst a broad historical brush may depict all societies as having had some sort of notion of restraint in warfare, it is also clear that not all have emphasized the same ideas or adopted the same institutions. For example, most cultures may have some sense of certain weapons or methods of combat being beyond the pale, but they may vary considerably as to what those are, based on quite distinct traditions. When it comes to the protection of victims of war, some of the very structural assumptions of the Geneva Conventions may be at odds with certain beliefs, just as contemporary IHL has been with some of the Western tradition's own complex ruminations on the matter. For example, the very rigid separation of the *jus in bello* from the *jus ad bellum*—a process that took several centuries to be effected in the West, and that betrays a rather stark and characteristically modern distinction between the launching and the waging of war—may well be incompatible with more holistic approaches to war. Moreover, the Geneva Conventions, as paragons of the modern project of regulation of warfare, fundamentally shift the basis for restraint in warfare to an obligation that lies in positive international law as a result of state consent. This is in contrast to many cultures' and the West's own traditional emphasis on honour and chivalry, or some mystical or religious basis. In doing this, the Conventions place much of the onus on respecting IHL on states, even as statehood, or at least a certain European understanding of it, may not be the most widely shared form internationally.

D. 'Deep' Universality: The Cosmopolitan Ambition

Beyond universality as a customary and civilizational issue lies another dimension, perhaps the least explored. Speaking of states and civilizations may be more than a little abstract, in a world where the fate of the Geneva Conventions (and particularly Common Article 3) increasingly relies on how a range of non-state actors feel they apply. Again, this is a scenario where state ratification or state practice may be relatively meaningless because it points to something alien to such actors. Many of them will be locked in struggles with the sovereign and, when they are not frankly revisionist in relation to the Geneva Conventions, often need to find reasons of their own to abide by the Conventions other than those that are directly linked to the state's own laws.

Rather, universality should increasingly be understood as a function of the extent to which IHL has penetrated individual consciences or the modus operandi of non-state actors. The universality of the Geneva Conventions might mean something closer to what is understood by universality in the human rights context, namely, something that points to an extremely widespread recognition of the inherent validity of its claims. There is much anecdotal evidence that this is universality's new frontier and that the concept now includes what one might call an effort at 'cosmopolitanization', i.e. at ensuring that all of the world's human beings and groups acknowledge the relevance of the Geneva Conventions.

I. The Geneva Conventions' statism

46   In fact, the 'statism' of the Geneva Conventions may discredit them in the eyes of certain non-state actors that will not be formally party to them, will not have participated in their adoption, and may even think that the Conventions, steeped as they are in inter-state reality, do not reflect their peculiar needs and constraints in warfare. This will be the case particularly when, in addition to not identifying with their state, armed groups mount a cultural or civilizational challenge against the dominance of modern IHL. In that respect, the case for the Geneva Conventions' civilizational universality, even if it is broadly credible, will be of little use when confronted with reticent actors whose understanding of their own culture may well be that it is irreducible and not simply a variant on a universal theme.

47   It has not helped that even non-state actors that have occasionally been willing to be bound by the Geneva Conventions have received a very lukewarm welcome. This was the case for the Palestine Liberation Organization, which entered into communication with the Swiss Federal Council in order to accede to the Conventions in 1989, only to find that the Government refused to confirm that the accession was valid, based on uncertainty about Palestine's status as a state. The bottom line seems to be that the Geneva Conventions were conceived to apply only to states, and that only such a status will allow one to accede to them. The Palestinian Authority's accession to the Conventions in April 2014 could be seen as a welcome extension of the applicability of the Geneva Conventions to a not-full-state actor, but it could also be seen as conferring that benefit on an entity that is the closest thing there is to a state.

48   It is worth noting that the Geneva Conventions' very internationalism arguably and paradoxically created conditions for a diminished cosmopolitan universality. The Geneva Conventions were part of a movement that contributed to make IHL, from rules about state responsibility to the choice of implementation mechanisms, above all a *states'* issue. Of course states were to implement the Conventions through domestic law in ways that impacted on individuals (criminal repression being the most obvious), and no effort was spared to encourage them to do so; but ultimately it was states that would make individuals accountable, and that eventually were made to be accountable themselves for actually abiding by the Conventions. In addition, states have been particularly jealous of their monopoly over implementation of the laws of war, a monopoly that is closely related to their monopoly over the pursuit of war *tout court*. The typical refusal to grant belligerent status or to recognize armed movements as parties to a conflict because this might symbolically enhance their status, which was particularly acute at the time of the adoption of the Geneva Conventions, also laid the ground for the laws of wars' subsequent unravelling in a variety of conflicts. Having been shunned, non-state actors were less likely to identify with the Conventions.

49   The Geneva Conventions were therefore part of a movement, begun in the late nineteenth century, that extracted the laws of war from the ambit of particular groups (notably the warrior class) and harnessed them to the power of the emerging international

society of states. One of the assumptions of that model was the understanding that it would be soldiers operating in regular armies who would wage war. The reality of many conflicts, both international and non-international, however, has been (and in a sense, that was true from the start) that they are not always, or even most often, waged by those who had been expected. Yet the state system has made it difficult to engage in a dialogue directly with these new actors, partly out of fear of conferring upon them an excessive degree of symbolic recognition. Indeed, a number of states have gone as far as to criminalize provision of any support—even training in the Geneva Conventions—to certain armed groups.[40]

II. The universalization of implementation

International organizations, whilst not quite non-state actors, have become significant participants in the global implementation of IHL. This is nowhere more clear than with the role of the UN generally and the Security Council specifically. This supranational governance of the humanitarian regime clearly points to its existence as a collective interest of the international system, and as one that expresses a universal concern. It was manifested most spectacularly in the launching of Chapter VII operations based in part on the existence of systematic violations of the laws of war, and the creation of ad hoc international criminal tribunals by the Council.

Non-governmental organizations (NGOs) and civil society actors have increasingly had a role in the implementation of the Geneva Conventions, as part of a larger phenomenon of co-governance of international law with states. Indeed, an interesting indicator of the evolving universality of the Geneva Conventions is the way, despite the quasi-total absence of non-state actors at their adoption, their implementation is seen less and less as the sole prerogative of states or of state-derived actors. For example, whereas implementation of the Conventions was traditionally seen as a 'High Contracting Party' responsibility with the assistance of a relatively state-orientated organization such as the ICRC, respect for the Geneva Conventions is increasingly something that has been taken up by a range of civil society actors. These thereby manifest the sort of universal esteem in which they hold the Geneva Conventions, and the way in which they see themselves as having a role in their implementation.

Moreover, today, not only strictly humanitarian organizations, but also many human rights organizations coming from a background that emphasizes the universality of rights rather than the universality of state obligations, are investing resources in the humanitarian project (Amnesty International and Human Rights Watch's turn to IHL is a case in point). The strategies used by civil society actors to encourage respect for the Geneva Conventions are many, but NGOs have tended to be behind every significant development of the laws of war in the last 10 years. Transnational civil society's commitment to the idea of universal jurisdiction for war crimes and to the proper functioning of international criminal tribunals is undoubted. Non-governmental organizations were very active in lobbying states to ask for Advisory Opinions from the ICJ in both the *Nuclear Weapons* and *Wall* Advisory Opinions.[41]

---

[40] *Holder, Attorney General et al v Humanitarian Law Project et al*, 561 US 25, 21 June 2010, 1.

[41] ICJ, *Nuclear Weapons*, above n 5. See also R. Falk, 'Nuclear Weapons Advisory Opinion and the New Jurisprudence of Global Civil Society', 7 *Transnational Law & Contemporary Problems* (1997) 333; ICJ, *Legal Consequences of the Construction of a Wall in the Occupied Palestinian Territory*, Advisory Opinion, 9 July 2004.

III. Individuals and rebel movements: evolutions in accountability

53   In reaction to some of the limitations of the Geneva Conventions, humanitarian interveners have also increasingly sought ways to treat non-state actors as participants in armed conflict. If anything the rise of international criminal justice and the fact that individuals can now answer for war crimes directly before the international community have not only practically increased the chances that they will be called to account, but also symbolically emphasized that individuals are ultimately answerable to the entire international community and the repositories of universal obligations. The Nuremberg Tribunal made the point forcefully that individuals could not 'hide' behind orders received or the law of their state, or argue that IHL's universality stopped at the door of sovereign national law.[42] Perhaps no phenomenon has done more to make the point that the Geneva Conventions apply potentially to all than the idea that, although it is primarily the state that has the broad obligation to implement them, individuals must uphold the Conventions and will be held to account.

54   Just as crucially, the case is frequently made that non-state actors other than individuals (i.e. armed groups) are bound by the laws of war, regardless of their lack of formal participation in the Conventions, either through the application of domestic law of a state party, or directly under international law, notably as a result of the growing body of Geneva Conventions-related CIL. Even before the adoption of the Protocols, the case had been made that whilst national liberation movements might not be in a position to adhere to the Geneva Conventions, they could be bound through special agreements. At any rate, the gradual assimilation of wars of national liberation to IAC starting in the 1960s, paved the way for the application of the Conventions to a broader set of actors beyond the state. Additional Protocol I has since allowed national liberation movements to deposit a 'unilateral declaration' with the Swiss Federal Council, indicating a willingness to apply both that Protocol and the Conventions,[43] a major if limited first step in applying the conventional laws of war to non-state actors.

55   Irrespective of the legal issue, significant efforts have been engaged in order to encourage non-state actors actually to feel bound by the Conventions. For example, the ICRC, under the broad dissemination heading, has gone beyond the traditional constituency that is the military, by training rebel movements in IHL. Moreover, since the 2000s, a number of highly innovative initiatives have been undertaken that seek to obtain more formal commitments by armed groups to respect basic obligations. Geneva Call in particular is an NGO that works directly with such groups in an effort to get them to sign a unilateral commitment, inter alia, not to use landmines; similarly, the UN's Special Representative on children in armed conflicts and the Coalition to Stop the Use of Child Soldiers have sought to obtain pledges that children will not be recruited. Although the Geneva Conventions as such are not what is at stake, there is little doubt that these efforts represent an attempt to further the broad legacy of the Conventions. There is even talk of armed groups owing reparations to persons who suffer violations of IHL at their hands.[44]

---

[42] *Judgment of the Nuremberg International Military Tribunal*, 41 *AJIL* (1947) 172, at 221.
[43] Art 96(3) AP I.
[44] See, e.g., R. Dudai, 'Closing the Gap: Symbolic Reparations and Armed Groups', 93 *IRRC* 883 (2011) 783; M. Sassóli and Y. Shany, 'Should the Obligations of States and Armed Groups under International Humanitarian Law Really Be Equal?', 93 *IRRC* 882 (2011) 426.

What is interesting in this novel process is the idea of taking instruments that derive 56
their authority from states and strictly bind only states, and bringing them down from
their formal Olympus to a range of actors. It is also telling that these efforts have run into
resistance from states that occasionally see them as bypassing their sovereign monopoly on
Geneva adherence; yet it is these same states that occasionally justify their own lack of diligence in implementing their obligations by the fact that they are facing non-state actors
who do not. Ultimately, recalcitrant states whose hostility to non-state actors paradoxically extends to preventing efforts at getting them to respect the Geneva Conventions, risk
being bypassed entirely by civil society efforts to connect directly with armed groups. It is
particularly interesting that the whole Geneva Call model involves a non-state actor talking directly to other non-state actors, and bypassing states and state actors in the process.
Such a model strongly underlines how universality manifests itself both at the source and,
potentially, at the receiving end.

E. Critical Assessment

The Geneva Conventions thus emerge as significantly universal, if that is understood as 57
referring to their customary character; problematically so if one understands universality
as referring to their acceptability across cultures and civilizations; and imperfectly so if
one sees universality as a function of their cosmopolitan acceptance. Part of the effort at
understanding the universality of the Geneva Conventions may, paradoxically, consist in
understanding the cultural specificity of the Conventions themselves, including in their
claim to universality. It is quite characteristic of the 'West' that, in producing universals,
it often seems unable to acknowledge its own peculiarism, as in the oft-repeated denial,
for example, that the red cross has any Christian origin when, plainly, it either does or is
quite reasonably perceived as such. In this concluding section I want to reflect briefly on
the tension between claims about universality and the reality of that universality, by suggesting three hypotheses.

First, it may be interesting to see IHL less as the product of some antecedent universal- 58
ity than as a *producer* of its own universality. For many states, the experience of IHL has
meant shunning, at least in international interactions, whatever indigenous vocabulary
of restraint in warfare they may have possessed, in favour of the somewhat impersonal
and interchangeable logos of the Geneva Conventions; it has meant, for example, speaking the language of Humanity, positivism, and sovereignty, rather than that of Divine
command, chivalry, or ritual. What was lost in terms of genuineness of the appeal was no
doubt gained in the ability to deploy a platform that transcended value systems. It may
be that in some cases the universal has started displacing the local—such is arguably the
power of norms backed by formidable symbolic power. Yet this does not put in question
the Conventions' universality, as much as it makes that universality appear as more of a
contradictory and dialectic process than the conventional account.

Secondly, the Geneva Conventions might be thought of as providing a platform pre- 59
cisely for engagement about diversity in approaches to war. In other words, even as the
Conventions have historically stood for a certain common model of restraint in warfare, their content might be more continuously renegotiated as a result of the normative encounter that they render possible. Provost, for example, has argued that Geneva
rules might be seen 'as common starting points for continuous and competing processes
of legal interpretation which will open spaces in which cultural particularism can be

accommodated'.[45] In this context, talk of 'regionalization' of the laws of war has occasionally emerged, perhaps as an implicit recognition that many conflicts are fought within regional contexts, and that IHRL has shown the way in terms of significant continental variations. It is also possible that the Geneva Conventions would provide the basis for a sophisticated 'overlapping consensus', one which betrays the fact that, as Cockayne has argued, each remains free to understand why *they* respect restraint in warfare.[46]

60   Thirdly, it may be that the Geneva Conventions do in the end express a particular universality, but that this is neither a thick nor a deep universality, and that this superficiality is not fundamentally detrimental to the project in the way that it would be with international human rights. In fact, one might argue that adherence to the laws of war as incarnated by the Geneva Conventions is ultimately more a manifestation of accession to a historically located grammar of statehood than the manifestation of an intemporal and truly universal aspiration. As states emerge and engage in the practice of sovereignty, they are inevitably drawn to appreciate some of the benefits of the laws of war in terms of their national interest, or are constrained to do so by structural factors, quite irrespective of prior cultural predispositions. This idea of IHL as a conventional and customary by-product of state interaction, potentially disconnected from or at least in tension with underlying cultural values, suggests a universality that is tremendously effective precisely because it is superficial and self-referential in its focus. In the analysis, the universality of the Geneva Conventions may be nothing else than the universality of war, suffering, and humanity in a world of states.

FRÉDÉRIC MÉGRET

---

[45] See Provost, above n 27.   [46] Cockayne, above n 39, at 623–4.

Chapter 34. Relationship with Prior and Subsequent Treaties and Conventions

	MN
A. Introduction	1
B. Applicable Rules and Principles	6
I. Interpretation of treaties	6
II. Applicability of treaties relating over time to the same subject matter	10
C. The Relationship with Previous International Humanitarian Law Treaties	16
I. The relationship with the older Geneva Conventions	16
II. The relationship with the Hague Conventions	23
D. The Relationship with Subsequent International Humanitarian Law Treaties	26
I. The Additional Protocols	26
a. Additional Protocol I	26
b. Additional Protocol II	32
c. Additional Protocol III	33
II. Other subsequent international humanitarian law treaties	34

Select Bibliography

Bothe/Partsch/Solf, at 32 f; 39 f; 44 f; 54 f
ICRC Commentary APs, paras 22–6; 57; 3740–75
Nolte, G., *Subsequent Agreements and Subsequent Practice of States outside of Judicial or Quasi-Judicial Proceedings*, Third Report for the ILC Study Group on Treaties over Time, 2012
Pictet Commentary GC I, at 407 f; GC II, at 277 f; GC III, at 635–40; GC IV, at 613–21

A. Introduction

International humanitarian law (IHL) is nowadays a complex legal system made up of a conspicuous number of treaties and customary rules, as well as instruments characterized by their non-binding character.

As the International Court of Justice (ICJ) observed, in making reference to the law of armed conflicts,

a large number of customary rules have been developed by the practice of States and are an integral part of the international law [...] The 'laws and customs of war'—as they were traditionally called—were the subject of efforts at codification undertaken in The Hague (including the Conventions of 1899 and 1907), and were based partly upon the St Petersburg Declaration of 1868 as well as the results of the Brussels Conference of 1874. This 'Hague Law' and, more particularly, the Regulations Respecting the Laws and Customs of War on Land, fixed the rights and duties of belligerents in their conduct of operations and limited the choice of methods and means of injuring the enemy in an international armed conflict. One should add to this the 'Geneva Law' (the Conventions of 1864, 1906, 1929 and 1949), which protects the victims of war and aims to provide safeguards for disabled armed forces personnel and persons not taking part in the hostilities. These two branches of the law applicable in armed conflict have become so closely interrelated that they are considered to have gradually formed *one single complex system*, known today as international humanitarian law. The provisions of the Additional Protocols of 1977 give expression and attest to *the unity and complexity of that law*.[1]

As the ICJ correctly pointed out, today IHL appears to be one single system which is characterized by the complexity of the many coexisting instruments and, at the same time, by its unity. 'Unity' means that IHL aims to avoid contradictions among its different legal sources: among customary rules and IHL treaties, and among IHL treaties *inter se*. Therefore, in applying customary law and in interpreting IHL treaties, bearing such unity in mind, a special effort to achieve a coherent reading and to avoid any inconsistencies is necessary.

3   Moreover, IHL (with the Geneva Conventions that stand as a cornerstone of the system), while characterized by unity, cannot be considered as a self-contained legal regime operating in a vacuum and indifferent to the entire system of international law surrounding it. Therefore, the rules that IHL contains have to be harmonized with other branches of international law, some of which appear to be of specific interest in relation to IHL, i.e. international human rights law as well as international criminal law which, not coincidentally, are the object of the following two chapters—Chapters 35 and 36.

4   This chapter is intentionally limited to the relationship with the main IHL treaties prior and subsequent to the Geneva Conventions.

5   In approaching the aspect of coordinating the 1949 Geneva Conventions with prior and subsequent treaties, one has to point out further, as a preliminary remark, that the Geneva Conventions do not contain a procedure for their own amendment or revision. Over time, starting in the mid-nineteenth century, the Geneva Law (like Hague Law) was supplemented and further developed through so-called 'self-standing' later treaties.[2] Only in 1977, on the occasion of the development of the 1949 Geneva Conventions through Additional Protocols (APs) I and II, did these two new IHL instruments insert a specific rule (respectively Article 97 AP I and Article 24 AP II) providing a procedure for amendment:

1. Any High Contracting Party may propose amendments to this Protocol. The text of any proposed amendment shall be communicated to the depositary, which shall decide, after consultation with all the High Contracting Parties and the International Committee of the Red Cross, whether a conference should be convened to consider the proposed amendment.
2. The depositary shall invite to that conference all the High Contracting Parties as well as the Parties to the Conventions, whether or not they are signatories of this Protocol.[3]

Additional Protocol III, relating to the adoption of an additional distinctive emblem, adopted in 2005, contains, at Article 13, a similar procedure for amendment. The above-mentioned Articles of the Additional Protocols appear to be consistent with Article 40 of the Vienna Convention on the Law of Treaties (VCLT) codifying the

---

[1] ICJ, *Legality of the Threat or Use of Nuclear Weapons*, Advisory Opinion, 8 July 1996, para 75 (emphasis added).
[2] See G. Nolte, *Subsequent Agreements and Subsequent Practice of States outside of Judicial or Quasi-Judicial Proceedings*, Third Report for the ILC Study Group on Treaties over Time, 2012, at 8.
[3] On the procedure of amendments to APs, see Bothe/Partsch/Solf, at 575; and ICRC Commentary APs, paras 3776–90.

B. Applicable Rules and Principles

I. Interpretation of treaties

The definition of the relationship of the Geneva Conventions with prior and subsequent 6
treaties may first be considered to some extent, and in broader terms, as a problem of specific application of the general criteria of interpretation of treaties. One may observe that the general law of treaties governs the conclusion, entry into force, application, interpretation, amendment, modification, and reservations of IHL treaties. Therefore, the rule for the interpretation of treaties as codified by the VCLT must be resorted to: moreover, it has been considered of general applicability by the case law of the international courts and tribunals.[4]

Article 31(1) VCLT ('General rule of interpretation') reads, 'A treaty shall be inter- 7
preted in good faith in accordance with the *ordinary meaning to be given to the terms* of the treaty *in their context* and *in the light of its object and purpose*' (emphasis added). In other words, textual, systematic, and teleological elements are the three criteria singled out by the general rule of interpretation in order to identify the meaning and the scope of the treaty provisions.

As to the systematic approach to interpretation, Article 31(2) VCLT explains the mean- 8
ing of the word 'context', specifying that the context of a treaty shall comprise, in addition to the text, including its preamble and annexes:

(a) [a]ny agreement relating to the treaty which was made between all the parties in connection with the conclusion of the treaty;
(b) [a]ny instrument which was made by one or more parties in connection with the conclusion of the treaty and accepted by the other parties as an instrument related to the treaty.

The notion of 'context' may, in a wide sense, correctly be applied to the relationship 9
between the Geneva Conventions and the previous and subsequent IHL treaties which may be considered instruments related to the Geneva Conventions. The negotiating states, in 1949, 'in connection with the conclusion' of the Geneva Conventions, refer to specific Articles in the previous Geneva Conventions,[5] as well as the Hague Conventions,[6] as related instruments in order to create a link and harmonization as to their reciprocal scope of application. Moreover, the Geneva Conventions, in turn, are specifically recalled by the subsequent three Additional Protocols[7] so as to create an overall legal consonance. Therefore, one can correctly affirm the existence of a 'legal context' created by the above-mentioned treaties, or even a legal system characterized by 'unity and complexity' (notwithstanding the 'self-standing' character of its components), as affirmed by the ICJ in the Advisory Opinion of July 1996 on the *Legality of the Threat or Use of Nuclear*

---

[4] See *Affaire de la délimitation de la frontière maritime entre la Guinée et la Guinée-Bissau*, Decision of 14 February 1985, in *Reports of International Arbitral Awards/Recueil de sentences arbitrales*, vol XIX, United Nations, 2006, at 165.
[5] See MN 16–22.   [6] See MN 24–25.   [7] See MN 26–33.

Weapons. The first step for the interpreter therefore is simply to be aware that each IHL treaty works in an overall IHL legal context, which requires adoption of the correct mental approach to finding the appropriate solution in solving any problems regarding the relationship of the Geneva Conventions with prior and subsequent IHL treaties,[8] looking at the terms of the treaty and to its object and purpose.

II. Applicability of treaties relating over time to the same subject matter

10 The interpreter, in deciding on the applicability of the Geneva Conventions provisions, will also take into account the general rules of the law of treaties on the application of two or more treaties adopted over time and relating to the same subject matter. Of course, this is an aspect of the relationship among treaties which the VCLT does not neglect in its general terms. In this regard, we should focus on Article 59 VCLT, covering the extinction of the operation of treaties implied by the conclusion of a later treaty, and on Article 30 VCLT, covering the application of successive treaties relating to the same subject matter.

11 As to Article 59(1) VCLT, a treaty shall be considered as terminated if all the parties to it conclude a later treaty relating to the same subject matter and:

(a) [i]t appears from the later treaty or is otherwise established that the parties intended that the matter should be governed by that treaty; or
(b) [t]he provisions of the later treaty are so far incompatible with those of the earlier one that the two treaties are not capable of being applied at the same time.

12 As to Article 30 VCLT, it opens with a savings clause regarding the applicability of Article 103 of the Charter of the United Nations (UN).[9] After that, Article 30 states that the rights and the obligations of the states parties to successive treaties relating to the same subject matter shall be determined in accordance with the following two criteria:

— When a treaty specifies that it is subject to, or that it is not to be considered as incompatible with, an earlier or later treaty, the provisions of that other treaty prevail (Article 30(2)).
— When all the parties to the earlier treaty are parties also to the later treaty but the earlier treaty is not terminated or suspended in operation under Article 59 mentioned above, the earlier treaty applies only to the extent that its provisions are compatible with those of the later treaty (Article 30(3)).

---

[8] The aforementioned Art 31(1) and (2) VCLT contain basic criteria for the interpretation of treaties. However we may consider relevant for our purpose Art 31(3) too, according to which the interpreter shall take into account, together with the context, '(a) [a]ny subsequent agreement between the parties regarding the interpretation of the treaty or the application of its provisions; (b) [a]ny subsequent practice in the application of the treaty which establishes the agreement of the parties regarding its interpretation; (c) [a]ny relevant rules of international law applicable in the relations between the parties'.

[9] Art 103 UN Charter: 'In the event of a conflict between the obligations of the Members of the United Nations under the present Charter and their obligations under any other international agreement, their obligations under the present Charter shall prevail.' It is evident that the priority of the Charter cannot operate in all those situations where the obligations contained in IHL treaties have a peremptory character.

Moreover, Article 30(4) VCLT describes the legal regime applicable when the parties to   13
the later treaty do not include all the parties to the earlier one. In such a case:

— as between states parties to both treaties, the later treaty applies; while
— as between a state party to both treaties and a state party to only one of the treaties, the treaty to which both states are parties governs their mutual rights and obligations.

This solution, applied to any type of treaty, IHL treaties included, is necessitated by the fundamental rules of the law of treaties regarding the relationship between the state parties to the treaty *inter se*, and between the state parties to the treaty and third states: 'Every treaty in force is binding upon the parties to it and must be performed by them in good faith' (Article 26 VCLT); and 'A treaty does not create either obligations or rights for a third State without its consent' (Article 34 VCLT).[10]

Moreover, Article 30(5)—having regard to the case considered above in which the   14
parties to the later treaty do not include all the parties to the earlier one—specifies that such a legal solution is without prejudice to Article 41 ('Agreements to modify multilateral treaties between certain of the parties only'), according to which:

Two or more of the parties to a multilateral treaty may conclude an agreement to modify the treaty as between themselves alone if:
(a) The possibility of such a modification is provided for by the treaty; or
(b) The modification in question is not prohibited by the treaty and:
   (i) Does not affect the enjoyment by the other parties of their rights under the treaty or the performance of their obligations;
   (ii) Does not relate to a provision, derogation from which is incompatible with the effective execution of the object and purpose of the treaty as a whole. (Article 41(1) VCLT)

Article 30(5) contains a savings clause as to any question of the termination or suspen-   15
sion of the operation of a treaty as a consequence of its breach,[11] or to any question of responsibility which might arise for a state from the conclusion or application of a treaty, the provisions of which are incompatible with its obligations towards another state under another treaty. Thus, the general law of treaties solves the legal relationship between the Geneva Conventions and prior and subsequent IHL treaties. These solutions are to some extent facilitated by the fact that the approach of states in negotiating treaties in the field of IHL has been to look for a codification of customary international law. To provide a codification means to work in the direction of an overall systematic rationalization of the rules. In the field of IHL,

most often a new set of treaties supplemented or replaced less detailed, earlier conventions in the wake of major wars, taking into account new technological or military developments [...] Today, IHL is not only one of the most codified branches of international law, but its relatively few instruments are also well coordinated with each other. Generally the more recent treaty expressly states that it either supplements or replaces the earlier treaty (among the States parties).[12]

Good coordination is also favoured by the fact that the codification of IHL instruments (usually involving years of preliminary works) is traditionally accompanied by the careful,

---

[10] On the topic of treaties and third states, see M. Fitzmaurice, 'Third Parties and the Law of Treaties', 6 *Max Planck Yearbook of United Nations Law* (2002) 37, esp at 44–66.
[11] This aspect is covered by Art 60 VCLT.   [12] Sassòli/Bouvier/Quintin, at 149.

694 *The Geneva Conventions in Context*

patient, and clever role of the International Committee of the Red Cross (ICRC), universally recognized as the discreet guardian of IHL.[13]

C. The Relationship with Previous International Humanitarian Law Treaties

I. The relationship with the older Geneva Conventions

16   The relationship between the Geneva Conventions and the older 'Geneva Law' is dealt with consciously by GC I,[14] by GC II,[15] and by GC III.[16] In contrast, GC IV does not contain any reference to previous Geneva Conventions because, during the codification undertaken in 1929 in Geneva, the states participating in the Conference did not conclude a specific instrument on the protection of civilians in armed conflict, notwithstanding the efforts made at that time by the ICRC in that direction.[17] Actually, GC IV is the first IHL instrument specifically devoted to the protection of civilians and the civilian population, especially with regard to the situation of military occupation: therefore, GC IV poses problems of coordination (tackled by GC IV itself in a specific Article of the final provisions) only with regard to the Hague Conventions, which, to some extent, cover the same subject matter (see section C.II of this chapter).

17   Geneva Conventions I, II, and III, while declaring in their respective Preambles their purpose of revising the previous instruments of 'Geneva Law' on the subject matter with which each of them deals, contain at the same time specific Articles regulating the relationship with the older Geneva treaties.

18   With respect to GC I, its Article 59, recalling the previous three conventional stages in the development of the regime for the protection of the wounded and sick in armed forces in the field, reads: 'The present Convention *replaces* the Conventions of 22 August 1864, 6 July 1906, and 27 July 1929, in relations between the High Contracting Parties' (emphasis added). It is a matter of fact that among the 196 states now parties to GC I, we find all the states parties or states which are successors of the states parties to the 1864 GC, to the 1906 GC, and to the 1929 GC I on the same subject matter. In other words, the three older Geneva Conventions have been replaced, for all states parties, by GC I: they are no longer in force, precisely because they are replaced by the subsequent Convention.[18] This is the typical situation provided by the customary international rules

---

[13]   See F. Bugnion, *Le Comité international de la Croix Rouge et la protection des victimes de la guerre* (Geneva: Comité international de la Croix Rouge, 1994), esp at 351–91.

[14]   The Preamble to GC I specifies that the Plenipotentiaries of the Governments met at the Diplomatic Conference in Geneva, in August 1949, for the purpose of revising the Geneva Convention for the Relief of the Wounded and Sick in Armies in the Field of 27 July 1929.

[15]   The Preamble to GC II specifies that the Plenipotentiaries of the Governments met at the Diplomatic Conference in Geneva, in August 1949, for the purpose of revising the Xth Hague Convention of 18 October 1907 for the Adaptation to Maritime Warfare of the Principles of the Geneva Convention of 1906. As I shall clarify later, in fact the Xth Hague Convention is, in substance, 'Geneva Law'.

[16]   The Preamble to GC III specifies that the Plenipotentiaries of the Governments met at the Diplomatic Conference in Geneva, in August 1949, for the purpose of revising the Geneva Convention concluded in Geneva on 27 July 1929, Relative to the Treatment of Prisoners of War.

[17]   See Bugnion, above n 13, at 140–5.

[18]   Pictet Commentary GC I observes that even supposing a time came [actually that later time has arrived] when the earlier Conventions no longer bound any state at all, they would still preserve a latent existence, so

on the law of treaties, as codified in Article 59 VCLT, according to which a treaty shall be considered as terminated if all the parties to it conclude a later treaty relating to the same subject matter, and it appears from the later treaty that the matter should be governed by that treaty.[19]

As to GC II, its relationship with 'Geneva Law' passes through the mediation of Hague Convention X of 18 October 1907, which adapted to maritime warfare the Geneva Convention of 1906 for the Amelioration of Wounded and Sick in Armies in the Field (in other words, Hague Convention X was utilized on the occasion of the Second Hague Peace Conference in 1907 to cover a subject traditionally proper to 'Geneva Law'[20]). Geneva Convention II, therefore, according to its Article 58, '*replaces* Hague Convention X of October 18, 1907, for the adaptation to maritime warfare of the principles of the Geneva Convention of 1906, in relations between the High Contracting Parties' (emphasis added).[21] As to current legal status of Hague Convention X in relation to the subsequent GC II, the same reasons explained above in discussing GC I and prior treaties on the same subject matter bring us to a similar conclusion: Hague Convention X is no longer in force because it was later replaced, for all states having ratified it, with GC II.

Regarding GC III, Article 134 provides for its relation to the 1929 Geneva Convention Relative to the Treatment of Prisoners of War (1929 GC II), while Article 135 provides for its relation to the Hague Convention on the Laws and Customs of War on Land, whether that of 1899 or that of 1907.[22]

As to the connection with 1929 GC II, the solution given by Article 134 GC III is to replace it ('The present Convention *replaces* [...]') in relations between the contracting parties. Even in this case we might conclude that 1929 GC II is no longer in force because all existing states that were once parties to that Convention are now parties to GC III.

Affirming that the older Geneva Conventions are no longer in force does not mean belittling their relevance and importance: first, they maintain a basic role in explaining the historical perspective, illuminating the conventional discipline now in force; secondly, the older Geneva Conventions remain as a factual element demonstrating, over a long period of time, the *opinio juris* of states in considering the soundness and paramount importance of the rules now captured in the Geneva Conventions, and their unquestionable nature as customary law,[23] a number of obligations being hallmarked as imperative.

---

that in the improbable event of a state's denouncing GC I, the earlier Conventions would become operative once more, and again would bind the denouncing power in its relations with other states (at 407). However, this solution seems quite theoretical.

[19] I note that Fiji and Papua New Guinea nominated the same day to ratify both GC I and 1929 GC I on the amelioration of the condition of the wounded and sick in armies in the field (respectively on 9 August 1971 and on 26 May 1976); and they did the same as regards GC III and 1929 GC II on the treatment of prisoners of war. It is evident that in this case too, where Fiji and Papua New Guinea ratified previous and subsequent conventions on the same day, the GCs replace the 1929 Conventions.

[20] This appears to be an element demonstrating that the traditional boundary between the law of The Hague and the law of Geneva never has been impermeable.

[21] See Pictet Commentary GC II, at 277. It should be noted that Hague Convention X of 1907 replaced in its turn Hague Convention III of 1899 for the adaptation to maritime warfare of the principles of the Geneva Convention of 22 August 1864. Art 25 reads: 'The present Convention, duly ratified, shall replace as between Contracting Powers, the Convention of 29 July 1899, for the adaptation to maritime warfare of the principles of the Geneva Convention. The Convention of 1899 remains in force as between the Powers which signed it but which do not also ratify the present Convention.'

[22] See Pictet Commentary GC III, at 635–9.

[23] One can find such use of the older GCs substantiated in the ICRC CIHL Study.

II. The relationship with the Hague Conventions

23   The relationship between the Hague Conventions 1899 and 1907 and Regulations, and GCs III and IV acquires a specific importance when one considers the complexity of the connection.

24   Article 135 GC III provides that in the relations between the Powers which are bound by the Hague Convention, whether that of 1899 or that of 1907, and which are also parties to GC III, 'this last Convention shall be *complementary* to Chapter II of the Regulations annexed to the above-mentioned Conventions of the Hague' (emphasis added). The aforementioned Chapter II of Section I (Articles 4 to 20), headed 'Prisoners of war', contains rules governing respect for and protection of prisoners of war (POWs). Therefore, looking at the letter of Article 135 GC III, it is evident that the goal of the parties was not to replace the Hague Conventions as such, but to intervene with an advanced regulation as to the specific subject matter of POWs, and such an advanced regulation has to be considered as complementary to the earlier rules.[24] Therefore, the two Hague Conventions must be deemed still to apply along with Chapter II of the annexed Regulations. In so far as coordination is concerned, having in mind the concept of complementarity, it does mean that the GC III regime is applicable between the contracting parties and its advanced standards prevail, while leaving in force the rules of Chapter II of the Regulations annexed to the Hague Conventions in so far as they do not contradict GC III itself.[25]

25   Concerning GC IV, Article 154 provides for the relationship with the Hague Conventions of 1899 and 1907, affirming that GC IV 'shall be *supplementary* to Sections II and III of the Regulations annexed to the above-mentioned Conventions of The Hague' (emphasis added). The notion of GC IV's being *supplementary* (not far from the notion of *complementary* used by GC III) is related to the fact that—as Pictet correctly notes—while 'the Hague Regulations codify the laws and customs of war and are intended above all to serve as a guide to armed forces', GC IV 'aims principally at the protection of civilians'.[26] Therefore, we may observe the absence of a complete superposition as between the two legal instruments. In fact, in Sections II and III of the Regulations we find a number of rules not related to the protection of civilians and civilian population, and therefore they remain in force because they are extraneous to the field of interest of GC IV: an example is the inviolability of *parlementaires* ('flags of truce', Articles 32 to 34) or, again, the rules on armistices (Articles 36 to 41). Moreover, GC IV is mainly focused on the protection of civilians in occupied territories, and therefore those rules of the Hague Regulations aiming at the protection of civilians in more general terms—in respect also to conduct not carried out by the Occupying Power in

---

[24] The rule contained in Art 135 GC III was inspired by the solution adopted by the previous 1929 GC II at Art 89: 'In the relations between the Powers who are bound either by The Hague Convention concerning the Laws and Customs of War on Land of 29 July 1899, or that of 18 October 1907, and are parties to the present Convention, the latter shall be complementary to Ch. 2 of the Regulations annexed to the above-mentioned Conventions of The Hague.'

[25] Pictet Commentary GC III provides a specific comparison between the provisions of the Hague Regulations and the corresponding Articles of GC III (at 637–40). He gives just two examples of the Hague Regulations remaining relevant: they are contained in Art 6 para 2, according to which 'prisoners may be authorized to work for public service, for private persons, or on their account'; and in Art 12, according to which 'prisoners of war liberated on parole and recaptured bearing arms against the Government to whom they had pledged their honour, or against the allies of that Government, forfeit their right to be treated as prisoners of war, and can be brought before the courts' (at 640, fn 1).

[26] Pictet Commentary GC IV, at 613 f.

an occupied territory—remain valid (for example, Article 23 according to which it is forbidden 'to destroy or seize the enemy's property, unless such destruction or seizure be imperatively demanded by the necessities of war'). We might add also that while GC IV is mainly focused, as already seen, on the protection of civilians in occupied territories, it gives no definition of 'occupied territory'. Therefore, we may affirm that such a definition is to be drawn from the Regulations (as an element of the 'legal context' including the Geneva Conventions), at least in its basic terms,[27] because the same notion of occupied territory has certainly acquired a new dimension looking at the scope of application of GC IV and at its substantive rules aiming at protection of civilians:[28] so, GC IV appears in this regard again as supplementary to the Hague Regulations.

D. The Relationship with Subsequent International Humanitarian Law Treaties

I. The Additional Protocols

a. Additional Protocol I

As to the relation of the Geneva Conventions to subsequent IHL treaties, the essential aspect to be considered is the link with the three Additional Protocols. In all such situations, the relationship is governed, as is usual in international law, by the later treaty, in so far as the Geneva Conventions: 26

— do not contain rules providing for a procedure of amendment or revision; and, moreover,
— do not prohibit modification of their content by subsequent treaties.

As to the Additional Protocols' approach to the Geneva Conventions, the purpose appears quite clear merely from their headings: the Additional Protocols propose themselves as 'additional', that is to say as supplementing the Geneva Conventions, as to substantive rules and to means of ensuring observance. Such additional character is underlined by the fact that a state cannot become party to the Protocols without being at the same time party to the Geneva Conventions.[29] 27

In this vein, AP I explains in general terms, in the Preamble, third paragraph, its aim 'to reaffirm and develop the provisions protecting the victims of armed conflicts and to supplement measures intended to reinforce their application'. Indeed, the wording of the paragraph is so wide as to cover, in an ideal trend of development over time, the *single complex system* of IHL made up both by The Hague and the Geneva instruments. In fact, AP I contains rules appertaining to what traditionally is referred to as Hague Law (rules on the conduct of hostilities), and rules appertaining to what is referred to as Geneva Law (rules aimed at protection and relief regarding the victims of armed conflicts). 28

---

[27] On the contrary, Pictet Commentary GC IV (at 617) affirms that GC IV is a complete document containing its own rules of application, and therefore the definition of 'occupied territory' contained in Art 42 of the Hague Regulations has no direct influence on the application of GC IV to civilian populations protected by its terms. See, for a detailed discussion, Ch 67 MN 8, 43–46, and 48, of this volume.

[28] On this aspect, see R. Kolb and S. Vité, *Le droit de l'occupation militaire* (Brussels: Bruylant, 2009), at 62 ff.

[29] Arts 92 and 94 AP I; Arts 20 and 22 AP II; Arts 8 and 10 AP III.

29 Moreover, AP I, while determining its scope of application in Article 1(3), defines at the same time its relationship with the Geneva Conventions, and confirms its additional and supplementary nature in respect to them. As has been observed, the relationship, in terms of 'supplementing', reveals that the Diplomatic Conference had a task not to revise, but to reaffirm and to develop the pre-existing law, avoiding the endangerment of existing obligations of states.[30]

30 In relation to such a general approach to the relationship between the Geneva Conventions and AP I, one may observe that a specific regulation is contained in Article 96 AP I. The solution in Article 96(1) may be defined as traditional according to the law of treaties dealing with the application of successive treaties relating to the same subject matter (Article 39 VCLT): in the event that the parties to the Geneva Conventions are also parties to AP I, the Geneva Conventions shall apply as supplemented by AP I. In other words, on the one hand, all states parties to the Geneva Conventions (at present 196 states) remain obliged by such basic instruments *inter se* (the Geneva Conventions are not replaced); but on the other hand, among the states parties to AP I (at present 174 states) the regime contained in the Geneva Conventions and obligatory for them is supplemented by AP I. So, as we have seen already, two treaty communities may be identified, which are to some extent overlapping: the larger, if not universal, community made up by all states parties to the Geneva Conventions; and the smaller community of states parties to AP I.[31] The two communities are not in mutual contradiction because the 1977 rules do not affect the enjoyment by the parties to the Geneva Conventions of their rights or the performance of their obligations: a correct solution according to the general international law of treaties.

31 Lastly, it is worth noting that Article 96 confirms the rejection of the clause of universal participation (*si omnes*) in applying Geneva instruments: in the event that one of the parties to the conflict is not bound by AP I, the parties to AP I shall remain bound by AP I in their mutual relations. However, they shall furthermore be bound by AP I in relation to each of the parties to the conflict which are not bound by it, if the latter accept and apply the provisions thereof. This is a further aspect as to the relationship between the Geneva Conventions and the subsequent Additional Protocols.[32]

b. *Additional Protocol II*

32 Additional Protocol II, relating to the protection of the victims of non-international armed conflicts (NIACs), has an approach similar to that of AP I: according to its Article 1(1), AP II aims to develop and supplement Common Article 3 to the Geneva Conventions without modifying its existing conditions of application, so as to ensure better protection for the victims of such armed conflicts. However, the enhanced regime contained in AP II does not apply in all situations of NIAC as covered by the wide scope of Common Article 3, but only to limited situations of armed conflict characterized by special intensity (conflicts 'which take place in the territory of a High Contracting Party between its

---

[30] ICRC Commentary APs, para 57.
[31] ICRC Commentary APs, para 3746.
[32] AP I, at Art 96 para 3, provides that the authority representing a movement of national liberation engaged in an armed conflict against a contracting party may undertake to apply the GCs and AP I in relation to that armed conflict by means of a unilateral declaration addressed to the depositary: the GCs and AP I are brought into force for the said authority as a party to the conflict with immediate effect, the authority assumes the same rights and obligations as those assumed by the contracting parties, and the GCs and AP I are equally binding upon all parties to the conflict.

armed forces and dissident armed forces or other organized armed groups which, under responsible command, exercise such control over a part of its territory as to enable them to carry out sustained and concerted military operations and to implement' the Protocol itself). This means that Common Article 3 continues to be applied by all states parties to the Geneva Conventions in situations of armed conflicts within the broad meaning given by Common Article 3, while AP II with its enhanced discipline applies (in addition to Common Article 3) to states having ratified it (at present 167 State) when involved in a NIAC having the intensity described in Article 1(1) AP II itself.[33]

c. *Additional Protocol III*

Additional Protocol III reaffirms and supplements the provisions of the Geneva Conventions and of the Additional Protocols as regards those rules concerning the use of distinctive emblems, so as to enhance their protective value and universal character. The Protocol recognizes an additional distinctive emblem, consisting of a red frame in the shape of a square on edge on a white background, enjoying equal status with the other historical red cross and red crescent emblems[34] (the 'third protocol emblem', usually known as the 'Red Crystal') (Article 2(1) and (2)). The treaty relation of AP III to the Geneva Conventions is specifically explained in Article 12 in the same way as the relationship of AP I and the Geneva Conventions. When the parties to the Geneva Conventions are also parties to AP III (at present 67 states), the Geneva Conventions shall apply as supplemented by AP III. When one of the parties to the conflict is not bound by AP III, the parties to AP III shall remain bound by AP III in relation to each of the parties to the conflict which is not bound by it, if the latter accept and apply the provisions thereof.

II. Other subsequent international humanitarian law treaties

As to the relationship between the Geneva Conventions and subsequent Conventions, we should also mention the 1980 Convention on Prohibition or Restriction on the Use of Certain Conventional Weapons Which May be Deemed to be Excessively Injurious or to Have Indiscriminate Effects, Article 1 of which was amended in December 2001. In order to define its scope of application, the Convention, in its amended Article 1, provides that it and its annexed Protocols shall apply not only in the situations referred to in Common Article 2 of the Geneva Conventions, including any situation described in Article 1(4) AP I, but also in situations referred to in Common Article 3 of the Geneva Conventions. Here, the relationship of a provision of a subsequent IHL treaty with the Geneva Conventions acquires a much more specific significance: it does not deal with developing, supplementing, or revising previous Geneva treaties; it is limited to circumscribing, by reference to the Geneva Conventions themselves, the scope of application (of the 1980 Convention), in situations of both IACs and NIACs, and thereby to creating a better harmonized overall IHL system.

A further and different kind of relationship between the Geneva Conventions and subsequent treaties may be found by looking at the Statute of the International Criminal Court (ICC Statute). In fact, the ICC Statute appears, to some extent, to be a means of implementation of the Geneva Conventions as regards the prosecution of grave/serious

---

[33] In this regard, see ICRC Commentary APs, paras 4446–57.
[34] The Red Lion and Sun is also a recognized emblem, but is no longer in use.

breaches. The ICC Statute, in extending its competence to war crimes, includes in 'war crimes' (Article 8(2)(a)) 'grave breaches of the Geneva Conventions [...], namely, any of the following acts against persons or property protected under the provisions of the relevant Geneva Convention [...] [the list of these grave breaches follows]'; moreover, with specific reference to armed conflicts not of an international character, the Statute includes in war crimes (Article 8(2)(c)):

> serious violations of Article 3 common to the [...] Geneva Conventions [...], namely, any of the following acts committed against persons taking no active part in the hostilities, including members of armed forces who have laid down their arms and those placed *hors de combat* by sickness, wounds, detention or any other cause: [...] [the list of these serious violations follows]

Similarly, the Arms Trade Treaty (2013) explicitly refers to grave breaches of the Geneva Conventions of 1949 in its Article 6(3), which prohibits any transfer of arms or items which would be used in the commission of such grave breaches.

36 We might close by observing that there may be some kind of relationship between the Geneva Conventions and subsequent treaties less connected (i.e. not containing specific reference) to the Geneva Conventions themselves: for example, the Convention for the Protection of Cultural Property (1954), the Convention on the Prohibition of Anti-personnel Mines (1997), and the Convention on Cluster Munitions (2008). It may be stated that in so far as these Conventions also relate to 'one single and complex system, known today as international humanitarian law' (as the ICJ affirmed in the *Nuclear Weapons Case*[35]), their reading may owe a debt to various aspects of the Geneva Conventions. For example, one might state that the notion of 'conflict not of an international character' contained in the Convention for the Protection of Cultural Property is derived from the meaning of 'conflict not of an international character' embodied in Common Article 3 of the Geneva Conventions.

PAOLO BENVENUTI

---

[35] Above n 1.

Chapter 35. The Complex Relationship Between the Geneva Conventions and International Human Rights Law

	MN
A. Introduction	1
B. Treaties that Explicitly Regulate their Relationship to the Geneva Conventions	11
I. The International Convention against the Taking of Hostages (1979)	12
II. The Inter-American Convention on Forced Disappearance of Persons (1994)	17
III. The International Convention for the Protection of All Persons from Enforced Disappearance (2006)	20
C. Explicit and Implied References to Situations of Armed Conflict in Human Rights Treaties which Do Not Provide for Specific Rules to Regulate the Relationship between the Two Regimes	23
I. Human rights treaties referring to their applicability in situations of armed conflict	24
a. The Convention on the Rights of the Child (1989) and its Protocol (2000)	24
b. The Convention on the Rights of Persons with Disabilities (2006)	25
c. The European Convention on Human Rights (1950)	26
d. The African Union Convention for the Protection and Assistance of Internally Displaced Persons in Africa (2009) and other African treaties	42
II. Implied references to the 1949 Geneva Conventions in human rights treaties	46
a. The *nullum crimen sine lege* rule in human rights law	46
b. Derogation clauses for times of emergency	49
c. The interpretation of the concept of arbitrary in the International Covenant on Civil and Political Rights	51
III. Treaties referring to other international instruments	56
a. The American Convention on Human Rights and its Articles 25 and 29	56
b. The African Charter on Human and Peoples' Rights (1981)	69
D. The General Articulation of the Relationship between Human Rights Rules and the Rules Contained in the Geneva Conventions	73
E. Critical Assessment	85

Select Bibliography

Arnold, R./Quénivet, N. (eds), *International Humanitarian Law and Human Rights Law: Towards a New Merger in International Law* (Leiden: Nijhoff, 2008)

Ben-Naftali, O. (ed), *International Humanitarian Law and International Human Rights Law* (Oxford: OUP, 2011)

Bethlehem, D., 'The Relationship between International Humanitarian Law and International Human Rights Law and the Application of International Human Rights Law in Armed Conflict', 2 *Cambridge Journal of International and Comparative Law* (2013) 180

Cerna, C., 'The History of the Inter-American System's Jurisprudence as Regards Situations of Armed Conflict', 2 *International Humanitarian Legal Studies* (2011) 1

Doswald-Beck, L., *Human Rights in Times of Conflict and Terrorism* (Oxford: OUP, 2011)

Gaggioli, G., *L'influence mutuelle entre les droits de l'homme et le droit international humanitaire à la lumière du droit à la vie* (Paris: Pedone, 2013)

Hill-Cawthorne, L., 'Humanitarian Law, Human Rights Law and the Bifurcation of Armed Conflict', *ICLQ* (forthcoming 2015)

Duffy, H., 'Harmony or conflict? The interplay between human rights and humanitarian law in the fight against terrorism', in L. Van Den Herik and N. Schrijver (eds), *Counter-Terrorism Strategies in a Fragmented International Legal Order* (Cambridge: CUP, 2013) 482

Jinks, D., 'Human Rights in Time of Armed Conflict', in A. Clapham and P. Gaeta (eds), *The Oxford Handbook of International Law in Armed Conflict* (Oxford: OUP, 2014) 656

Kolb, R./Gaggioli, G. (eds), *Research Handbook on Human Rights and Humanitarian Law* (Cheltenham: Edward Elgar, 2013)

Oberleitner, G., *Human Rights in Armed Conflict Law, Practice, Policy* (Cambridge: CUP, 2015)

OHCHR, *International Legal Protection of Human Rights in Armed Conflict* (2011)

Rowe, P., *The Impact of Human Rights Law on Armed Forces* (Cambridge: CUP, 2006)

Sassòli, M., 'The Role of Human Rights and International Humanitarian Law in New Types of Armed Conflicts', in O. Ben-Naftali (ed), *International Humanitarian Law and International Human Rights Law* (Oxford: OUP, 2011) 34

UN International Law Commission 'Conclusions of the Work of the Study Group on the Fragmentation of International Law: Difficulties arising from the Diversification and Expansion of International Law', UN Doc A/61/10 (2006 Report of the ILC), at 400–23

A. Introduction

1   The 1949 Geneva Conventions and the 1948 Universal Declaration of Human Rights were drafted around the same time, with much of the drafting taking place in the same city—Geneva. One might expect, therefore, that the two branches of law (international humanitarian law (IHL) and international human rights law (IHRL)) would sit comfortably together under the umbrella of the international legal system. But these two branches have different histories, and their relationship is quite complicated. While there is every reason to believe that we can articulate a coherent approach to the interplay between these two branches, we must first overcome a number of obstacles.

2   First, from the start there was mutual suspicion between those engaged in these two separate exercises. The founding members of the United Nations (UN) had just agreed that wars should be a thing of the past and that it would be illegal for one state to have recourse to force against another state. Embarking on a new codification of the laws of war seemed to contradict the new commitment to peace and the fresh arrangements for collective security to be ensured by the Security Council. On the other hand, those concerned with fashioning the new Geneva Conventions were legislating for the horrors of the Second World War, and were realistic and impatient about the need to codify protection for the victims of war. At the same time they were keen to insulate humanitarian law, and the work of the International Committee of the Red Cross (ICRC), from intergovernmental organizations and the politics that was seen to accompany the work of the UN.[1] Even

---

[1] See R. Kolb, 'The Relationship between International Humanitarian Law and Human Rights Law: A Brief History of the 1948 Universal Declaration of Human Rights and the 1949 Geneva Conventions', 38 *IRRC* 324 (1998) 409 (English online version). For a discussion of the 1968 Tehran Conference and the subsequent studies on human rights in armed conflict by the UN Secretary-General as well as the UNGA Res 2444 (XXIII) and 2675 (XXV), see S. Sivakumaran, *The Law of Non-International Armed Conflict*

many years later, after the entry into force of the human rights Covenants,[2] human rights were still not seen as ideologically neutral, and the ICRC remained cautious with regard to human rights campaigning by its National Societies. A long report, finalized in 1982, entitled 'The Red Cross and Human Rights', concluded that the ICRC is a 'movement of action rather than promotion, it devotes itself to practical tasks and generally refrains from taking a stand on controversial matters or in debates which divide society'.[3]

Secondly, even today, the two branches tend to operate within different 'interpretive' or 'epistemic' communities. International humanitarian law meetings tend to be dominated by specialists from the ICRC and governmental legal advisers who are part of the armed forces of the state. These meetings are seen by the participants as 'scientific', compared to the meetings in human rights fora which tend to be driven by civil society organizations and diplomats charged with promoting human rights as foreign policy at the international level. While, inevitably, human rights promotion by governments at the international level involves the pursuit of multiple foreign policies, it is nevertheless misleading to suggest that intergovernmental meetings on IHL are devoid of foreign policy agendas, or that they take place in an apolitical environment. The result of this cleavage between the communities is that not only have these worlds grown apart, but they have developed rather different approaches to the question of how the two branches of law should apply to the same situation.

Thirdly, there are very few international or national bodies that can actually exercise jurisdiction over a combination of both branches of law. This means that the case law on the interplay between these branches is often dependent on the jurisdictional limits imposed on the particular body entitled to exercise jurisdiction. On the one hand, this means that much of the case law is focused on applying regional human rights treaty regimes in the light of the Geneva Conventions, rather than the other way around; regional human rights courts have jurisdiction over violations of human rights treaties and do not have jurisdiction to apply the Geneva Conventions in the light of human rights law. This is obviously the case for the regional human rights courts and commissions in Europe, the Americas, and Africa. It also applies to the work of the UN treaty bodies and the Committee for the Arab Charter. On the other hand, international criminal tribunals may be empowered to apply provisions from the Geneva Conventions directly in the light of IHRL; certain provisions of the Geneva Conventions are applied directly as criminal law in these trials. Lastly in this context, we should nevertheless highlight that there are a few instances where international courts of general jurisdiction, such as the International Court of Justice (ICJ), find themselves able to apply both branches of international law simultaneously to the same facts.[4] At this point, despite three rulings from the ICJ, we find ourselves in territory where experts remain sharply divided.

(Oxford: OUP, 2012), at 44–7, and OHCHR, *International Legal Protection of Human Rights in Armed Conflict* (2011), esp at 94–106.

[2] The ICESCR (1966) entered into force 3 January 1976, and the ICCPR (1966) entered into force 23 March 1976.

[3] Working Document prepared for the Council of Delegates by the ICRC in collaboration with the Secretariat of the League of Red Cross Societies, at 92–3. The report goes on: 'This being so, when it undertakes to promote human rights, it does so with great discernment. While some National Societies have campaigned against torture or for better protection for children and handicapped persons, none, to our knowledge, has published arguments in favour of the holding of elections in the country or of trade union freedom. This does not in any way prejudice the importance of such rights, but proves how reserved are the National Societies with regard to any initiative which might be considered as impairing their neutrality.' See now S. Sayapin, 'The International Committee of the Red Cross and International Human Rights Law', 9 *Human Rights Law Review* (2009) 95.

[4] As pointed out by one experienced advocate and legal adviser, '[b]efore a court of general jurisdiction, it would be unlikely to be persuasive to contend that only one strand of law relevant to an issue should be

5   Part of the controversy relates to the rejection by some states, primarily the United States (US) and Israel, of the application of certain human rights treaties, in particular the International Covenant on Civil and Political Rights (ICCPR), extraterritorially.[5] This rejection is based in part on a particular reading of the wording of Article 2(1) ICCPR. The UN Human Rights Committee has nevertheless stated that the treaty does indeed apply when a state party acts in certain ways outside its territory.[6] There is less ambiguity with regard to other human rights treaties, and yet, as we shall see, controversy still surrounds the extent of a state's obligations when acting abroad or with extraterritorial effects.

6   To some extent, the sting may have recently gone out of this US rejection of the extraterritorial applicability of human rights treaty obligations. Not only has there been less insistence on this point in the more recent US reports to the UN Human Rights Committee,[7] but there is movement toward accepting the application of rules of *customary international law* protecting certain human rights when US officials act abroad. According to the *Operational Law Handbook* (2012) of the International and Operational Law Department of the Judge Advocate General's Legal Center and School of the US Army:

> For official US personnel (i.e., 'State actors' in the language of IHRL) dealing with civilians outside the territory of the United States, it is CIL [customary international law] that establishes the human rights considered fundamental, and therefore obligatory. Unfortunately, however, there exists no authoritative source that articulates which human rights the United States considers to be CIL.[8]

addressed': D. Bethlehem, 'The Relationship between International Humanitarian Law and International Human Rights Law and the Application of International Human Rights Law in Armed Conflict', 2 *Cambridge Journal of International and Comparative Law* (2013) 180, at 194.

[5] See N. Rodley, 'The Extraterritorial Reach and Applicability in Armed Conflict of the International Covenant on Civil and Political Rights: A Rejoinder to Dennis and Surena', 5 *EHRLR* (2009) 628; M.J. Dennis and A.M. Surena, 'Application of the International Covenant on Civil and Political Rights in Times of Armed Conflict and Military Occupation: The Gap Between Legal Theory and State Practice', 6 *EHRLR* (2008) 714; M. Milanovic, *Extraterritorial Application of Human Rights Treaties: Law, Principles and Policy* (Oxford: OUP, 2011); M. Gibney and S. Skogly (eds), *Universal Human Rights and Extraterritorial Obligations* (University of Pennsylvania Press: Philadelphia, Pa, 2010); F. Coomans and M.T. Kamminga (eds), *Extraterritorial Application of Human Rights Treaties* (Antwerp: Intersentia, 2004); K. da Costa, *The Extraterritorial Application of Selected Human Rights Treaties* (Leiden: Brill, 2012).

[6] General Comment 31, 26 May 2004, para 10, where the HRCttee states that the enjoyment of Covenant rights 'also applies to those within the power or effective control of the forces of a State Party acting outside its territory, regardless of the circumstances in which such power or effective control was obtained, such as forces constituting a national contingent of a State Party assigned to an international peace-keeping or peace-enforcement operation'.

[7] For the recent discussion of the legal opinions with regard to ICCPR and the UN Convention against Torture produced by H.Hongju Koh while he was the legal adviser at the US Department of State, see P. Margulies, 'Extraterritoriality and Human Rights: Time for a Change in the U.S. View?', Lawfare Blog (8 March 2014), available at <http://www.lawfareblog.com/extraterritoriality-and-human-rights-time-change-us-view>; the detailed legal memoranda by Koh are available at <http://justsecurity.org/wp-content/uploads/2014/03/state-department-iccpr-memo.pdf> and <http://justsecurity.org/wp-content/uploads/2014/03/state-department- cat-memo.pdf>. Note the latest written position of the US with regard to the interaction between IHL and human rights, as well as the extraterritorial application of the ICCPR: CCPR/C/USA/4, 30 December 2011, paras 504–9. Most recently, see Concluding Observations of the HRCttee with regard to the US: CCPR/C/USA/CO/4, 23 April 2014, para 4.

[8] *Operational Law Handbook* (2012), Chapter 3, 'Human Rights', at 45. Note that the Preface states that the *Handbook* 'is not intended to represent official US policy regarding the binding application of varied sources of law'. See also Watkin, who notes that 'even if it were determined that a human rights system of accountability did not apply as a matter of law to occupied territory, it would ordinarily be logical as a matter of policy to apply human rights norms to an occupier's policing function': K. Watkin, 'Controlling the Use of Force: A Role for Human Rights Norms in Contemporary Armed Conflict', 98 *AJIL* (2004) 1, at 27. Watkin has also made this point more recently, stating: 'The reliance on human rights "norms" often arises

The other part of the controversy relates to the relationship between these two branches of law (or more concretely, the relationship between some of the apparently conflicting norms within each branch). Different schools have claimed that these two branches of law are: congruent, concurrent, convergent, confluent, complementary, contradictory, in competition, or even in conflict. In turn it is said that one branch can cross-fertilize, reinforce, mutually influence, interpret, and bolster the other; or alternatively that one norm is said to displace, replace, supplant, curtail, or disapply the other. Without wishing to overemphasize the point, each group of scholars and governmental experts brings to this debate a set of assumptions about each branch of law and what should be its primary purposes, in theory and in practice. The policy arguments behind the different interpretations are never far below the surface. It is even said that application of human rights in certain circumstances would prevent fighters from carrying out their primary purposes; that humanitarian law contains too many opportunities for states to plead military necessity; and that human rights law offers terrorists too much protection and endangers innocent lives. Precisely because each branch has become quite specialized, lawyers from each branch tend to see outsiders as ill-equipped to offer a meaningful interpretation of the relevant rules.

This said, the present chapter will offer an explanation of the relationship between these two branches of law, relying in part on the multiple decisions of international bodies that have applied one, the other, or both branches of the law to a specific situation in a particular context. It is suggested that studying these findings is important, not because they necessarily have resolved the conundrum of the relationship between these branches, but rather because their developing doctrine will continue to influence this field for many years to come. As explained above, nearly every fact-finding or decision-making instance will be limited in one way or another as to what law it is empowered to apply. This makes it all the more relevant to understand how the one branch at the heart of the investigation is impacted by the other branch, rather than looking for a theory of everything. In essence this means that we shall often be using the rule on treaty interpretation to interpret the treaty over which the judges have jurisdiction in the light of another obligation binding on the parties. Of course no one will believe that the debate over the interplay between these branches can be simply resolved by resorting to formal rules of treaty interpretation. There will always remain a tension between a human rights approach focused on protecting the individual from abuse of power, and the approach taken by some specialists on the laws of war, which factors in a conception of military necessity and what can reasonably be expected of fighting forces. As already stated, these approaches are not necessarily hard-wired into the make-up of the branch of law, but in reality they may reflect the personal preferences and experience of the protagonists.

Judge Greenwood from the ICJ, speaking extrajudicially, captures the clash of cultures rather accurately:

To one group, human rights law is simply unsuited to the waging of warfare in any age but, particularly, the one that we have today. To them human rights law is designed for the quite different

in situations of governance (i.e. occupation, insurgency) where there is considerable strategic advantage in avoiding the alienation of the local population. Capture missions not only facilitate that goal, they also lead to more effective intelligence led operations. While a policy based approach may not fully embrace human rights standards, and is subject to rapid change, human rights based norms are having an impact on the conduct [of] contemporary operations.' See K. Watkin, 'Where IHL and IHRL Intersect—Part II', at <http://intercrossblog.icrc.org/blog/joint-series-where-ihl-and-ihrl-intersect-part-ii-of-ken-watkins-guest-post>.

environment of a normal state in the condition of peace and [is] therefore hopelessly unsuited to regulating conditions on or near a battlefield. To another group, human rights are the jewel in the crown of modern international law and the laws of war are being invoked by governments as an excuse to do things that they are not allowed to do at home.[9]

10   This is not the place to analyse in detail the vast array of literature engaged in this doctrinal debate. Much of it can indeed be explained by a culture clash, and much of the suspicion of human rights can still be traced, first, to a fear that human rights norms are less universal than the Geneva Conventions and, secondly, to an appreciation that the institutions and traditions that surround human rights accountability are very different from the discrete interventions associated with promoting compliance with IHL. We shall return to some of these issues later. For the moment, first we concentrate on how certain relevant treaties explicitly deal with their relationship with the Geneva Conventions; secondly, we explore how one set of treaties has been interpreted in the light of the treaties from the other branch; and, thirdly, we eventually tackle the perception that, in some circumstances, decision-makers may be left with an apparent choice as to which regime should prevail. All these analyses point to the fact that there is no one-size-fits-all approach to the relationship between human rights and the Geneva Conventions. One needs first to identify the particular treaty and see whether it contains a provision which regulates its relationship with the Geneva Conventions or IHL more generally. Then one needs to see which particular provision in the human rights treaty or the Geneva Conventions needs to be seen in the light of the other regime. Lastly, one needs to consider the contemporary context and the relevant case law. We shall finish by looking in some detail at the recent controversy over detention by states in non-international armed conflict (NIAC), and whether we should assume that IHL provides a legal basis for prolonged detention, or whether such an issue is dependent on human rights law, which may demand that a legal basis for detention be explicitly provided for in law, and that all detainees have the right to challenge the lawfulness of their detention before a judge. It is perhaps here that we find the sharpest divergence. The ways in which judges resolve this dilemma will, it is suggested, determine the more general articulation of the relationship between human rights and humanitarian law.

B. Treaties that Explicitly Regulate their Relationship to the Geneva Conventions

11   A number of relevant treaties contain clauses referring directly or indirectly to the Geneva Conventions. We shall consider here:

— the International Convention against the Taking of Hostages (1979);
— the Inter-American Convention on Forced Disappearance of Persons (1994); and
— the International Convention for the Protection of All Persons from Enforced Disappearance (2006).

These treaties refer to the Geneva Conventions in ways which will help us to build up a contemporary picture of the relationship between human rights treaty law and the

---

[9] C. Greenwood, 'Human Rights and Humanitarian Law: Conflict or Convergence', 43 *Case Western Reserve JIL* (2010) 491, at 494–5.

Geneva Conventions. We examine them in chronological order, because one can discern a slight shift over time in the technique used to articulate the relationship between treaties that may overlap and be equally applicable in a particular situation. We start early on with certain acts in international armed conflict (IAC) being exclusively covered by the Geneva Conventions, and we finish with some acts being covered concurrently by both the human rights treaty and the Geneva Conventions. A larger point now to be borne in mind is that states used explicitly to exclude the application of new treaties to situations which were already dealt with by the Geneva Conventions, but more recently the articulation allows for both regimes to apply. The argument can therefore be made that where a treaty is silent on this issue, it is fair to assume that both the new treaty and the relevant Geneva Convention are applicable to the facts.[10]

I. The International Convention against the Taking of Hostages (1979)

12 This treaty ('the Hostages Convention') is often ignored in the discussion concerning human rights and IHL, and yet its operation may have concrete effect before national and international courts, and its provision on the Geneva Conventions is very detailed. Although some may prefer to see this as an international criminal law treaty, rather than a human rights treaty, as we shall see, human rights law has now embraced international criminal law, so that human rights organizations will often craft their complaints in terms of offences being committed under these treaties (examples include torture, human trafficking, and enforced disappearances). Returning to the Hostages Convention, we see in the second preambular paragraph that the drafters recognized 'in particular that everyone has the right to life, liberty and security of person, as set out in the Universal Declaration of Human Rights and the International Covenant on Civil and Political Rights'. For human rights lawyers, the Convention took on a special life when Spain requested the extradition of Senator Pinochet and the arrest warrant in England included the offence of hostage-taking, an offence incorporated from the treaty into English law through the Taking of Hostages Act 1982. As is well known, the House of Lords eventually rejected the claim that Pinochet enjoyed immunity with regard to the proceedings relating to torture.[11]

13 The Convention contains a detailed provision articulating the relationship between this treaty and the Geneva Conventions. Article 12 reads:

In so far as the Geneva Conventions of 1949 for the protection of war victims or the Additional Protocols to those Conventions are applicable to a particular act of hostage-taking, and in so far

---

[10] We might recall here the distinction between two separate norms that are valid and two norms that are applicable. See further the ILC's 'Conclusions of the Work of the Study Group on the Fragmentation of International Law: Difficulties arising from the Diversification and Expansion of International Law', UN Doc A/61/10 (2006 Report of the ILC), para 251 (conclusion number 2). The clauses in the treaties we shall examine assume that both treaties are valid in that they cover the facts to which the situation relates. Some of the clauses provide that some norms in the treaties are not applicable to the parties, and the parties are only bound by their obligations under the GCs. Note also the ILC's 'Draft articles on the effect of armed conflicts on treaties' (2011), which include human rights treaties among the indicative list of treaties that are unaffected by armed conflict.

[11] The hostage-taking charges were in the end not considered relevant due to lack of evidence of that crime. See *R v Bartle and the Commissioner of Police for the Metropolis and others, ex parte Pinochet* [1999] UKHL 17. Lord Nichols considered there could be no immunity for state officials accused of hostage-taking; see the first *Pinochet* judgment which was later set aside, [1998] UKHL 41.

as States Parties to this Convention are bound under those conventions to prosecute or hand over the hostage-taker, the present Convention shall not apply to an act of hostage-taking committed in the course of armed conflicts as defined in the Geneva Conventions of 1949 and the Protocols thereto, including armed conflicts mentioned in article 1, paragraph 4, of Additional Protocol I of 1977, in which peoples are fighting against colonial domination and alien occupation and against racist regimes in the exercise of their right of self-determination, as enshrined in the Charter of the United Nations and the Declaration on Principles of International Law concerning Friendly Relations and Co-operation among States in accordance with the Charter of the United Nations.

14   This provision is sometimes interpreted as suggesting that the Hostages Convention does not apply in times of armed conflict. In fact the provision does no such thing. It states that where the grave breaches Articles of the Geneva Conventions oblige a state party to hand over or prosecute an individual accused of the crime of hostage-taking, the Hostages Convention does not apply. The logic is that the new 'extradite or prosecute' regime will not interfere with any pre-exiting similar regime which would have exactly the same effect. This provision nevertheless allows for the simultaneous application of the Hostages Convention with the Geneva Conventions where this particular obligation under the grave breaches provision is not applicable, or where the facts trigger the application of the Geneva Conventions' other Articles. Most importantly, because the Geneva Conventions do not foresee that hostage-taking in violation of Common Article 3 will give rise to an obligation for the states parties to prosecute or hand over an individual, this means the Hostages Convention, alongside Common Article 3, will apply to any acts committed in times of NIAC, including the war crime of hostage-taking.[12]

15   This was confirmed in a criminal case before the English courts, the *Zardad* case, where an Afghan warlord was prosecuted, tried, and sentenced for hostage-taking. The defence argued that under Article 12, the Hostages Convention excluded acts committed in times of internal armed conflict covered by the Geneva Conventions of 1949. The judge considered that the Convention was relevant for the interpretation of the implementing legislation, and went on to rule that the grave breaches regime of the Geneva Conventions did not bind parties to hand over or prosecute for acts committed in times of internal armed conflict.[13] The application of the Geneva Conventions to the same facts did not preclude Zardad from being prosecuted for hostage-taking. We might note that, even if the Geneva Conventions do not specify a duty to prosecute or extradite for such a violation of Common Article 3, it is now accepted that the same hostage-taking would also constitute a war crime. The regimes are in this way separate and concurrent in internal armed conflict, but in IAC only the Geneva Conventions' regime for extradition and prosecution applies, to the exclusion of the Hostages Convention.

16   This formula, which prevents the concurrent application of two competing 'extradite or prosecute' treaty regimes, is clear and uncontroversial. It is not replicated in the other later treaties which have employed different formulae.

---

[12] Art 12 would exclude the application of the Hostages Convention where the act took place in an armed conflict which triggered the application of the GCs due to the recognition of a self-determination struggle under the terms of Art 1(4) AP I. See further J.J. Lambert, *Terrorism and Hostages in International Law: A Commentary of the Hostages Convention 1979* (Cambridge: Grotius, 1990).

[13] R. Cryer, 'Zardad', in A. Cassese (ed), *Oxford Companion to International Criminal Justice* (Oxford: OUP, 2009) 979; see *R v Zardad (Ruling on the Taking of Hostages Act)*, Judgment and rulings pursuant to second preparatory hearing, Case No T2203 7676; ILDC 264 (UK 2004), 5 October 2004, Treacy J, paras 9–15.

II. The Inter-American Convention on Forced Disappearance of Persons (1994)

This human rights treaty ('the Forced Disappearance Convention') contains the following Article:

17

Article XV None of the provisions of this Convention shall be interpreted as limiting other bilateral or multilateral treaties or other agreements signed by the Parties.

This Convention shall not apply to the international armed conflicts governed by the 1949 Geneva Conventions and its Protocol concerning protection of wounded, sick, and shipwrecked members of the armed forces; and prisoners of war and civilians in time of war.

Again, one should notice that the provision does not actually exclude the continuing application of the human rights treaty in parallel with the Geneva Conventions; it only provides for the inapplicability of the human rights treaty to situations of IAC. Common Article 3 of the Geneva Conventions governing NIAC and the provisions of the Disappearances Convention therefore continue to apply simultaneously. Although at the time of writing several of the online versions of the Convention were using the expression 'the 1949 Geneva Conventions and their Protocols', the authentic version of the treaty refers to a single Protocol. There is therefore no doubt that this Article covers only IACs. Common Article 3 and the Forced Disappearance Convention therefore continue to apply at the same time and in parallel.

18

In 2010 the Inter-American Commission on Human Rights found a violation of this Forced Disappearance Convention with regard to facts that occurred during the internal armed conflict in Guatemala.[14] The Commission also found violations in connection with this armed conflict with regard to three other human rights treaties (that are all silent on their relationship to the application of the Geneva Conventions).[15] This case and other similar ones mean that, in practice, the Forced Disappearance Convention applies in times of NIAC, while it would not apply to an IAC.

19

III. The International Convention for the Protection of All Persons from Enforced Disappearance (2006)

This more recent UN treaty ('the Convention on Enforced Disappearance'), unlike the earlier Forced Disappearance Convention just discussed, does not preclude the application of the treaty in times of IAC. Article 43 of the Convention on Enforced Disappearance reads:

20

This Convention is without prejudice to the provisions of international humanitarian law, including the obligations of the High Contracting Parties to the four Geneva Conventions of 12 August 1949 and the two Additional Protocols thereto of 8 June 1977, or to the opportunity available to

---

[14] Report No 116/10, Case 12.590, Admissibility and Merits (36.3), *José Miguel Gudiel Álvarez and others ('Diario Militar') v Guatemala*, 22 October 2010, available at <http://www.oas.org/en/iachr/decisions/court/12.590Eng.pdf>.

[15] 'Guatemala violated Articles 3, 4, 5, 7, 8, 11, 13, 16, 17, 19, 22, 23 and 25 of the American Convention [on Human Rights], in conjunction with Articles 1.1 and 2 thereof, as well as Article 1 of the Inter-American Convention on Forced Disappearance of Persons, Articles 1, 6, and 8 of the Inter-American Convention to Prevent and Punish Torture, and Article 7 of the Convention of Belém do Pará [Inter-American Convention on the Prevention, Punishment and Eradication of Violence against Women], with respect to the victims and their next-of-kin.' Ibid, para 7.

any State Party to authorize the International Committee of the Red Cross to visit places of detention in situations not covered by international humanitarian law.

21 While the definition of 'enforced disappearance' is confined by Article 2 to acts committed 'with the authorization, support or acquiescence of the State', the treaty foresees an obligation on states parties to investigate and prosecute the same acts by non-state actors. The provision reads:

> Each State Party shall take appropriate measures to investigate acts defined in article 2 committed by persons or groups of persons acting without the authorization, support or acquiescence of the State and to bring those responsible to justice.[16]

This provision does not exclude situations of internal armed conflict. Such groups could be fighting the state either at the level of an internal disturbance which does not trigger the application of the Geneva Conventions, or in the context of an internal armed conflict covered by Common Article 3 of the Geneva Conventions. In addition, we can see that, based on the reference in Article 16 to situations of 'serious violations of humanitarian law', the treaty applies not only to situations of armed conflict affecting the state party, but also to issues of *non-refoulement* to both IACs and NIACs.[17]

22 In sum, obligations under the Convention on Enforced Disappearance are applicable to the states parties in times of armed conflict. The Geneva Conventions continue to apply concurrently in parallel. This more recent human rights treaty therefore presents a very different model from the exclusionary approach found in the other treaties discussed above.

C. Explicit and Implied References to Situations of Armed Conflict in Human Rights Treaties which Do Not Provide for Specific Rules to Regulate the Relationship between the Two Regimes

23 There is a second series of treaties that are explicitly stated as applying in times of armed conflict but which, by contrast with the treaties just examined, do not articulate their relationship with the Geneva Conventions or, more generally, with IHL. This section is divided into three parts:

— human rights treaties with an explicit reference to armed conflicts;
— human rights treaty provisions that imply a determination of the law of armed conflict in order to determine compliance with human rights law;
— human rights treaties that include the laws of armed conflict and empower the relevant jurisdiction to determine a violation of the laws of armed conflict (including the Geneva Conventions).

---

[16] Art 3 Convention on Enforced Disappearance.
[17] Art 16 Convention on Enforced Disappearance reads: '1. No State Party shall expel, return ("refouler"), surrender or extradite a person to another State where there are substantial grounds for believing that he or she would be in danger of being subjected to enforced disappearance. 2. For the purpose of determining whether there are such grounds, the competent authorities shall take into account all relevant considerations, including, where applicable, the existence in the State concerned of a consistent pattern of gross, flagrant or mass violations of human rights or of serious violations of international humanitarian law.'

I. Human rights treaties referring to their applicability in situations of armed conflict

a. *The Convention on the Rights of the Child (1989) and its Protocol (2000)*

24 The Convention on the Rights of the Child (1989) (CRC) includes provisions on direct participation in hostilities under the age of 15, on recruitment into the armed forces, and on measures 'to ensure protection and care of children who are affected by an armed conflict'.[18] The 2000 Optional Protocol on the Involvement of Children in Armed Conflict (CRC-OPAC) includes obligations on states parties to take similar measures with regard to direct participation in hostilities and recruitment with regard to those aged under 18, and, in contrast to the Convention, also addresses armed groups in its Article 4:

1. Armed groups that are distinct from the armed forces of a State, should not, under any circumstances, recruit or use in hostilities persons under the age of 18 years.
2. States Parties shall take all feasible measures to prevent such recruitment and use, including the adoption of legal measures necessary to prohibit and criminalize such practices.
3. The application of the present article under this Protocol shall not affect the legal status of any party to an armed conflict.

The ICRC Manual entitled *Domestic Implementation of International Humanitarian Law* seems to suggest that this treaty provision gives rise to binding obligations on the armed non-state actor. The ICRC enumerates a number of guiding principles with regard to the protection of children, and states that the 'Guiding Principles emphasize the *obligations of the States party to international treaties*, but that in no way alters the fact that these obligations also apply to armed groups involved in armed conflicts'.[19] The footnote reference is then to Article 4(1) CRC-OPAC. The UN Commission of Inquiry on Syria concluded in 2013 that 'Anti-Government armed groups are also responsible for using children under the age of 18 in hostilities in violation of the CRC-OPAC, which by its terms applies to non-State actors'. The summary also makes the same point: 'Both Government-affiliated militia and anti-Government armed groups were found to have violated the Optional Protocol to the Convention on the Rights of the Child on the involvement of children in armed conflict, to which the Syrian Arab Republic is a party.'[20] There is no question that both the Convention and its Protocol apply in times of armed conflict.[21] There is a good case that part of the Optional Protocol applies to all parties to a NIAC.

b. *The Convention on the Rights of Persons with Disabilities (2006)*

25 Article 11 of the Convention on the Rights of Persons with Disabilities is headed 'Situations of risk and humanitarian emergencies', and reads as follows:

States Parties shall take, in accordance with their obligations under international law, including international humanitarian law and international human rights law, all necessary measures to

---

[18] Art 38 CRC. Note that Art 38(1) also contains a general undertaking to respect and ensure respect for relevant rules of IHL.

[19] ICRC, 'Guiding Principles for the Domestic Implementation of a Comprehensive System of Protection for Children Associated with Armed Forces or Armed Groups', in *The Domestic Implementation of International Humanitarian Law: A Manual* (Geneva: ICRC, 2011), at 371.

[20] A/HRC/22/59, 5 February 2013, at 2 and para 4.

[21] The ICJ in the Advisory Opinion of 9 July 2004 on the *Legal Consequences of the Construction of a Wall in Occupied Palestinian Territory*, para 113, determined that the Convention was applicable in the Occupied Territory, and at para 131 considered relevant Arts 16, 24, 27, and 28.

ensure the protection and safety of persons with disabilities in situations of risk, including situations of armed conflict, humanitarian emergencies and the occurrence of natural disasters.

As the UN Committee develops its approach to the requirements of the Convention, we are likely to see terms in the Geneva Conventions being complemented or interpreted in the light of the developing law in this area. States must take measures under this treaty against the background of any obligations they have under the Geneva Conventions. Any measures are circumscribed by existing obligations under IHL. What is clear, in any event, is that the obligations in this treaty apply both in times of IAC and NIAC.

c. *The European Convention on Human Rights (1950)*

26   The European Convention on Human Rights (ECHR) states in its Article 15:

   1. In time of war or other public emergency threatening the life of the nation any High Contracting Party may take measures derogating from its obligations under this Convention to the extent strictly required by the exigencies of the situation, provided that such measures are not inconsistent with its other obligations under international law.
   2. No derogation from Article 2, except in respect of deaths resulting from lawful acts of war, or from Articles 3, 4 (paragraph 1) and 7 shall be made under this provision.

27   Three points can quickly be noted. First, the ECHR is stated to apply in times of war;[22] secondly, derogations from the right to life provision (Article 2) are allowed where these involve lawful acts of war; thirdly, derogations must be consistent with a state's other obligations under international law, and this would include obligations under the Geneva Conventions (we deal with this last point in more detail in section C.II.b of this chapter as it relates to several human rights treaties that allow for derogations).

28   Interestingly, no state party to the ECHR has ever derogated from its obligations under the right to life, and so the European Court of Human Rights (ECtHR) has not had the opportunity to apply the provision on the 'lawful acts of war' in the context of a specific derogation. Nevertheless, the Court seems to have noted this possibility and assumed that, during an actual armed conflict, IHL would provide an appropriate framework for assisting in determining violations of the right to life, even in the absence of a derogation. Even if the Court has not explicitly explained its use of IHL, it has resorted to the terminology of 'incidental loss of civilian life' in cases concerned with internal armed conflict.[23] But even where the Court refers to an 'illegal armed insurgency',[24] 'a very large group of armed fighters',[25] the 'evacuation of civilians',[26] and the use of 'indiscriminate weapons',[27] in the absence of a clear war footing relied on by the state, it nevertheless holds the authorities to the standards applicable to a law enforcement operation:

> The Court considers that using this kind of weapon in a populated area, outside wartime and without prior evacuation of the civilians, is impossible to reconcile with the degree of caution expected from a law-enforcement body in a democratic society. No martial law and no state of emergency has been declared in Chechnya, and no derogation has been made under Article 15 of

---

[22] Art 30 of the European Social Charter has a similar reference to derogations in times of war.
[23] See, e.g., ECtHR, *Ergi v Turkey*, Judgment, 28 July 1998, para 79; ECtHR, *Isayeva v Russia*, Judgment, 24 February 2005, para 176.
[24] ECtHR, *Isayeva v Russia*, above n 23, para 176.
[25] Ibid.   [26] Ibid, para 191.   [27] Ibid.

the Convention (see § 133). The operation in question therefore has to be judged against a normal legal background.[28]

In one case, concerning an IAC, the Strasbourg Court referred to 'rules of international humanitarian law' relating to obligations to protect the lives of those no longer 'engaged in hostilities'.[29] It explained with regard to the right to life:

> Article 2 must be interpreted in so far as possible in light of the general principles of international law, including the rules of international humanitarian law which play an indispensable and universally-accepted role in mitigating the savagery and inhumanity of armed conflict […][30]

It then referenced the four Geneva Conventions of 1949 and their Protocols.

In this way certain IHL principles have been indirectly applied through the prism of Article 2 ECHR. But, by declining to apply humanitarian law rules explicitly as the applicable law, the Court has left open the possibility that the Convention offers protection with regard to the right to life which goes beyond what is demanded by the laws of armed conflict. This point is perceptively made by Abresch, who picks up that the Court found a violation of the right to life based not so much on a violation of the laws of armed conflict, but on the fact that the taking of life was not justified in a democratic society as one of the aims listed in Article 2—viz the protection of life.[31] The key passage from the ECtHR reads:

> Even when faced with a situation where, as the Government submit, the population of the village had been held hostage by a large group of well-equipped and well-trained fighters, the primary aim of the operation should be to protect lives from unlawful violence. The massive use of indiscriminate weapons stands in flagrant contrast with this aim and cannot be considered compatible with the standard of care prerequisite to an operation of this kind involving the use of lethal force by State agents.[32]

Reference to the laws of war might have suggested that the aim to be taken into consideration would be the 'concrete and direct military advantage anticipated'.[33]

In a separate case, concerned with the situation in occupied Iraq in 2003, the Court again had to apply the right to life provision in Article 2 ECHR, which it did in terms which went beyond what would have been required by the law of armed conflict. In *Al-Skeini v United Kingdom*, the key issue was whether the acts of British soldiers in Occupied Iraq in the Basrah area brought the victims within the jurisdiction of the United Kingdom (UK) for the purposes of the ECHR. The Court held that the UK had assumed certain public powers, and that the soldiers had brought the individuals within the UK's jurisdiction through their actions.[34] The Court had no occasion to determine the legality of the killings, either under human rights law or under IHL, the sole issue being the UK's failure to conduct an investigation into the killings which would satisfy Article 2 ECHR.

---

[28] Ibid.   [29] ECtHR, *Varnava and others v Turkey*, Judgment, 18 September 2009, para 185.
[30] Ibid.
[31] W. Abresch, 'A Human Rights Law of Internal Armed Conflict: The European Court of Human Rights in Chechnya', 16 *EJIL* (2005) 741, at 765.
[32] ECtHR, *Isayeva v Russia*, above n 23, para 191.   [33] See Rule 14 of the ICRC CIHL Study.
[34] 'It can be seen, therefore, that following the removal from power of the Ba'ath regime and until the accession of the Interim Government, the United Kingdom (together with the United States) assumed in Iraq the exercise of some of the public powers normally to be exercised by a sovereign government. In particular, the United Kingdom assumed authority and responsibility for the maintenance of security in South East Iraq. In these exceptional circumstances, the Court considers that the United Kingdom, through its soldiers engaged in security operations in Basrah during the period in question, exercised authority and control over individuals killed in the course of such security operations, so as to establish a jurisdictional link between the deceased and

The Court referenced several relevant Articles of the Geneva Conventions,[35] and went on to apply the ECHR to the situation of an Occupying Power, demanding an independent investigation into the deaths. The Court recognized the difficulties presented by the context of occupation, but insisted on the procedural requirements entailed in its reading of Article 2 ECHR, and did not defer to the rather weaker regime for investigation foreseen by the Geneva Conventions of 1949. The Court took

> as its starting point the practical problems caused to the investigatory authorities by the fact that the United Kingdom was an Occupying Power in a foreign and hostile region in the immediate aftermath of invasion and war. These practical problems included the breakdown in the civil infrastructure, leading *inter alia* to shortages of local pathologists and facilities for autopsies; the scope for linguistic and cultural misunderstandings between the occupiers and the local population; and the danger inherent in any activity in Iraq at that time.[36]

33   In *Al-Jedda v United Kingdom* the Court referred explicitly to Geneva Convention (GC) IV and concluded that the regime for the internment of civilians should be considered a regime of 'last resort',[37] and that, in the absence of Security Council authorization or a valid derogation under the ECHR, there was no justification for such a detention under the ECHR. The Court examined whether 'there was any other legal basis for the applicant's detention which could operate to disapply the requirements of Article 5 §1',[38] and concluded there was not. To be clear, it was considered that the occupation of Iraq had ended three months before the three-year internment of the applicant. The UK Government therefore was not applying GC IV as such, but rather detaining the applicant 'under a legal regime derived from the law of belligerent occupation, as modified by the Security Council in Resolutions 1483 and 1511'.[39]

34   Nevertheless the judgment has been criticized by Pejic, and is seen by her as rejecting the proposition that 'IHL constitutes a valid legal basis for detention in international armed conflict, based on its conclusion that the Fourth Geneva Convention does not impose an obligation of internment on parties to such conflicts'.[40] She and others see GC IV as providing the requisite authorization through an application of a version of the *lex specialis* principle.[41] We return to the *lex specialis* debate below at MN 51–55 and 75–84. For the moment it suffices to stress that the Court was not, in fact, dealing with an IAC, nor was it claimed that GC IV applied *de jure* to the situation. In such circumstances it seems inappropriate to conclude that the GC IV displaces human rights law, or provides an implied legal basis for detention under human rights law. Importing bits and pieces of the Geneva Conventions by analogy, or in a derived way, into human rights law may not always be helpful and can be inappropriate. The present author can nevertheless foresee future situations where the full application of the Third Geneva Convention for the

the United Kingdom for the purposes of Article 1 of the Convention.' ECtHR, *Al-Skeini v United Kingdom*, Judgment, 7 July 2011, para 149.

[35] Art 121 GC III, Art 131 GC IV (on the duty to investigate deaths); and (with regard to grave breaches) Arts 49 and 50 GC I, Arts 50 and 51 GC II, Arts 129 and 130 GC III, and Arts 146 and 147 GC IV.

[36] ECtHR, *Al-Skeini v United Kingdom*, above n 34, para 168.

[37] ECtHR, *Al-Jedda v United Kingdom*, Judgment, 7 July 2011, para 107.   [38] Ibid.

[39] Ibid, para 87.

[40] See, e.g., J. Pejic, 'The European Court of Human Rights' *Al-Jedda* Judgment: The Oversight of International Humanitarian Law', 93 *IRRC* 883 (2011) 837, at 851.

[41] See also V. Gowlland-Debbas and G. Gaggioli, 'The Relationship between International Human Rights and Humanitarian Law: An Overview', in R. Kolb and G. Gaggioli (eds), *Research Handbook on Human Rights and Humanitarian Law* (Cheltenham: Edward Elgar, 2013) 77, at 93.

Protection of Prisoners of War could be considered to provide a legal basis for detention, and be considered a more appropriate regime than that provided by the human rights treaties. The key point is that the whole Geneva Convention regime applies *de jure*, with all that implies in terms of the application of the grave breaches provisions and access by the ICRC. The European Commission of Human Rights has in the past refused to consider that detention of certain prisoners of war (POWs) constituted a violation of their rights to liberty under the ECHR, where it was satisfied that the regime was operating correctly with full access by the ICRC.[42]

In the case of *Hassan v UK*, the ECtHR built on this approach. One issue in the case was the legality of the detention of Tarek Hassan during the armed conflict with Iraq in April 2003. The Court rejected the argument by the UK Government that capture during 'the active hostilities phase of an international armed conflict' fell to be determined exclusively under the Geneva Conventions and therefore fell outside the jurisdiction of the ECtHR.[43] The Court also rejected the argument, based in part on Article 12 GC III, that the transfer of custody to the US had removed Tarek Hassan from the jurisdiction of the UK, as the UK 'retained authority and control over all apects of detention relevant to the applicant's complaints under Article 5 [ECHR]'.[44] The Court was therefore faced with a real dilemma. On the one hand the text of Article 5 was seen by the Court as containing no room for detention on the grounds foreseen in GC III and GC IV; on the other hand the Government was arguing that the idea of a right to allege a breach of Article 5 ECHR would be 'inconsistent with the practical realities of conduct of active hostilities in an international armed conflict'.[45] The Court chose not to follow the argument that 'Article 5 was displaced by international humanitarian law as *lex specialis*'.[46] Instead it decided to treat this conundrum as a question of treaty interpretation in the light of subsequent practice and other international obligations.

35

---

[42] See *Cyprus v Turkey*, Report of the Commission, 10 July 1976, para 313, footnotes omitted: 'The Commission has taken account of the fact that both Cyprus and Turkey are Parties to the (Third) Geneva Convention of 12 August 1949, relative to the treatment of prisoners-of-war, and that, in connection with the events in the summer of 1974, Turkey in particular assured the International Committee of the Red Cross (ICRC) of its intention to apply the Geneva Conventions and its willingness to grant all necessary facilities for humanitarian action. In fact, ICRC delegates made regular visits to soldiers and civilians who had been granted prisoner-of-war status by the authorities on either side. They included, before the resumption of hostilities on 14 August 1974, 385 Greek Cypriots in Adana, who were visited by two ICRC delegates, one of them a doctor, 63 Greek Cypriots in Saray prison in the Turkish part of Nicosia and 3,268 Turkish Cypriots in camps in Cyprus. After fighting in August had come to an end the ICRC obtained permission to visit Greek Cypriot prisoners first in transit camps in Cyprus and then in three camps in Turkey, and several thousand Turkish Cypriot prisoners in four camps in the south of Cyprus. Having regard to the above, the Commission has not found it necessary to examine the question of a breach of Art 5 of the European Convention on Human Rights with regard to persons accorded the status of prisoners of war.' See also the Dissenting Opinion of Mr G. Sperduti, joined by Mr S. Trechsel, on Art 15 of the Convention: 'It can be said, in accordance with the above approach, that measures which are in themselves contrary to a provision of the European Convention but which are taken legitimately under the international law applicable to an armed conflict, are to be considered as legitimate measures of derogation from the obligations flowing from the Convention.'

[43] ECtHR, *Hassan v UK*, Judgment, 16 September 2014, para 76: 'The Government, in their observations, acknowledged that where State agents operating extra-territorially take an individual into custody, this is a ground of extra-territorial jurisdiction which has been recognised by the Court. However, they submitted that this basis of jurisdiction should not apply in the active hostilities phase of an international armed conflict, where the agents of the Contracting State are operating in territory of which they are not the occupying power, and where the conduct of the State will instead be subject to the requirements of international humanitarian law.'

[44] Ibid, para 78.   [45] Ibid, para 86.   [46] Ibid, para 88.

36   Citing Article 31(3)(b) of the Vienna Convention on the Law of Treaties (VCLT), the Court suggested that subsequent consistent practice by the High Contracting Parties to the ECHR could be taken 'as establishing their agreement not only as regards interpretation but even to modify the text of the Convention'.[47] The Court then took into account the absence of derogations under the ECHR (and ICCPR) when interning persons under GC III and GC IV. Turning to Article 31(3)(c) VCLT, the Court emphasized that 'the Convention must be interpreted in harmony with other rules of international law of which it forms part'.[48] The Court's interpretation nevertheless then established an implied ground for detention under Article 5 (lawful internment under GC III or GC IV) and went on to delimit the sort of review that would be required to satisfy Article 5(4) in this context. In short, the human rights Convention continues to apply, but detention in IAC is permitted where it is authorized under the Geneva Conventions, and the review of that detention has now to conform to the principles helpfully set out in the judgment in order to be compliant with the human right to challenge the legality of one's detention under Article 5(4) ECHR. The detail of the Court's reasoning at this point is so central to the core of this chapter that it deserves to be quoted at length:

> By reason of the co-existence of the safeguards provided by international humanitarian law and by the Convention in time of armed conflict, the grounds of permitted deprivation of liberty set out in subparagraphs (a) to (f) of that provision should be accommodated, as far as possible, with the taking of prisoners of war and the detention of civilians who pose a risk to security under the Third and Fourth Geneva Conventions. [...] It can only be in cases of international armed conflict, where the taking of prisoners of war and the detention of civilians who pose a threat to security are accepted features of international humanitarian law, that Article 5 could be interpreted as permitting the exercise of such broad powers.
>
> As with the grounds of permitted detention already set out in those subparagraphs, deprivation of liberty pursuant to powers under international humanitarian law must be 'lawful' to preclude a violation of Article 5 §1. This means that the detention must comply with the rules of international humanitarian law and, most importantly, that it should be in keeping with the fundamental purpose of Article 5 §1, which is to protect the individual from arbitrariness [...]
>
> As regards procedural safeguards, the Court considers that, in relation to detention taking place during an international armed conflict, Article 5 §§2 and 4 must also be interpreted in a manner which takes into account the context and the applicable rules of international humanitarian law. Articles 43 and 78 of the Fourth Geneva Convention provide that internment 'shall be subject to periodical review, if possible every six months, by a competent body'. Whilst it might not be practicable, in the course of an international armed conflict, for the legality of detention to be determined by an independent 'court' in the sense generally required by Article 5 §4 [...], nonetheless, if the Contracting State is to comply with its obligations under Article 5 §4 in this context, the 'competent body' should provide sufficient guarantees of impartiality and fair procedure to protect against arbitrariness. Moreover, the first review should take place shortly after the person is taken into detention, with subsequent reviews at frequent intervals, to ensure that any person who does not fall into one of the categories subject to internment under international humanitarian law is released without undue delay.[49]

37   The Court then concluded that at the time of Tarek Hassan's capture, the UK authorities had reason to believe that he could be detained as a POW, or as a person whose internment was necessary for imperative reasons of security (citing Articles 4A and 21

---

[47] Ibid, para 101.   [48] Ibid, para 102.   [49] Ibid, paras 104–6.

GC III and Articles 42 and 78 GC IV). As this was consistent with the UK's powers under the Geneva Conventions, it was not considered by the Court to be 'arbitrary'. In the light of the clearance for release and actual release of Hassan, the Court did not examine whether the actual screening process constituted 'an adequate safeguard to protect against arbitrary detention'.[50] Two last points bear emphasizing about this development: the Court explained, first, that the ECHR will be interpreted in this way only where the the relevant provisions of the Geneva Conventions are 'specifically pleaded by the respondent state' and, secondly, that the judgment relates only to detention in international armed conflict.

In non-international armed conflict the IHL regime is less developed, and the Geneva Conventions contain no explicit authorization to detain, nor any procedures for challenging any such detention. They do of course prescribe the treatment that must be accorded to detainees. Human rights law, on the other hand, demands that detention may not be arbitrary and must be for lawful purposes with a legal basis. The clash between those who claim that IHL contains an inherent right to detain in times of internal armed conflict, and those who claim that such detainees must be detained in accordance with a legal basis and have the right to challenge their detention under the ECHR, came to a head in the 2014 British High Court judgment delivered in *Serdar Mohammed v Ministry of Defence*.[51]

In *Serdar Mohammed* the plaintiff had been detained by the UK armed forces in Afghanistan for 110 days. The judgment found that in these circumstances, the Human Rights Act 1998 and the ECHR applied extraterritorially, the acts were attributable to the UK rather than to the North Atlantic Treaty Organization (NATO) or the UN, Article 5 ECHR was not qualified or displaced by the UN Security Council Resolutions, and neither was this human rights provision qualified or displaced by IHL.

As we just saw, Article 5 ECHR sets out grounds for detention and the rights of a detainee to challenge the lawfulness of a detention. The judgment rejects the idea that the Geneva Conventions, Additional Protocol (AP) II, or customary IHL provide a legal basis for detention in a NIAC. In the words of the judgment, 'Rather, their purpose is simply to guarantee a minimum level of humanitarian treatment for people who are in fact detained during a non-international armed conflict.'[52] The judgment also considered the argument 'that those engaged in a military operation must be able to accept the surrender of somebody who poses a threat to them and their mission and must be able to engage an adversary without necessarily having to use lethal force'.[53] It concluded, 'This argument justifies the capture of a person who may lawfully be killed. But it does not go further than that.[54] It therefore does not begin to justify the detention policy operated by the UK in Afghanistan.'[55]

In the background one can discern doubts that even if one could show that IHL provided a basis to detain people in NIAC for long periods, this without more would be

---

[50] Ibid, para 110.
[51] *Serdar Mohammed v Ministry of Defence* [2014] EWHC 1369 (QB); and see now [2015] EWCA Civ 843, the case will likely be appealed to the Supreme Court.
[52] Ibid, [251].   [53] Ibid, [252].
[54] Footnote in the original reads: 'See e.g. Debuf, *Captured in War: Lawful Internment in Armed Conflict* (2013) p. 389.'
[55] *Serdar Mohammed v Ministry of Defence*, above n 51, [253].

unworkable in the contemporary world. First, NIACs may revolve around many different types of armed groups, with uncertain distinctions between 'parties to an armed conflict and ordinary criminals';[56] secondly, there may be no identifiable point at which hostilities have ended, and so 'a power to detain until the end of hostilities would be particularly problematic';[57] and, thirdly, that even if one were to accept a future approach which would justify detention for 'imperative reasons of security', 'it would still be necessary to identify procedures by which such determinations are to be made'.[58] This question is set to remain divisive, and will most likely be resolved on a case-by-case basis, with each judgment gradually elaborating what are the combined constraints imposed by IHRL and IHL in the given circumstances. Much may depend on the quality of the relevant national law in the place of detention.

d. *The African Union Convention for the Protection and Assistance of Internally Displaced Persons in Africa (2009) and other African treaties*

42   The African Union Convention for the Protection and Assistance of Internally Displaced Persons in Africa (Kampala Convention) (2009) defines 'internally displaced persons' as those who have been forced to leave their homes, in particular 'as a result of or in order to avoid the effects of armed conflict'.[59] It applies in armed conflict and recognizes that some displacements may be justified under IHL.[60] Other African treaties that clearly apply in times of armed conflict include the African Charter on the Rights and Welfare of the Child (1990), the Protocol to the African Charter on Human and Peoples' Rights on the Rights of Women in Africa (2003), and the Protocol adopted by the Conference of the Great Lakes Region on the Prevention and Suppression of Sexual Violence against Women and Children (2006).

43   The Kampala Convention is perhaps the most explicit human rights treaty to date with regard to what is expected of armed non-state actors. The first point to note is that two different types of actors are included in its scope. According to Article 1(d), ' "Armed Groups" means dissident armed forces or other organized armed groups that are distinct from the armed forces of the state'; and under Article 1(n), ' "Non-state actors" means private actors who are not public officials of the State, including other armed groups not referred to in article 1(d) above, and whose acts cannot be officially attributed to the State.' The obligations for the members of the *armed groups* and the *non-state actors* are distinguished. By including references to the obligations of these groups, this treaty therefore unambiguously covers acts committed during armed conflict.

44   The terms are not dependent on the relatively demanding criteria set out in IHL. There is no suggestion that the group needs to be particularly organized, or be engaged in a certain level of violence, so that it would normally be considered a 'Party to the conflict' under IHL. The Kampala Convention is careful to include references to avoid the treaty ever being used as proof of legitimacy for the groups addressed:

> The provisions of this Article shall not, in any way whatsoever, be construed as affording legal status or legitimizing or recognizing armed groups and are without prejudice to the individual criminal responsibility of the members of such groups under domestic or international criminal law.[61]

---

[56] Ibid, [248]. [57] Ibid. [58] Ibid, [249]. [59] Art 1(k) Kampala Convention.
[60] Art 4(4)(h) Kampala Convention. [61] Art 7(1) Kampala Convention.

Interestingly, the Convention demands in its operative part that the states parties 45 '[r]espect and ensure respect for international humanitarian law regarding the protection of internally displaced persons'.[62] And there is an exception for states where displacement is justified under IHL.[63] Of course states are already obliged to respect and ensure respect for IHL; the importance of the inclusion of this obligation here is that it means these obligations can be reviewed by the Conference of States Parties, and inter-state cases could come before the African Court of Justice and Human Rights.[64] We might mention that the 2014 Protocol which would amend the Statute for the African Court, and which would add criminal jurisdiction over war crimes, refers to competence and experience in IHL as one of the relevant fields of expertise for judges in the new Court.[65]

II. Implied references to the 1949 Geneva Conventions in human rights treaties

a. *The* nullum crimen sine lege *rule in human rights law*

The ICCPR contains a guarantee in Article 15: 46

No one shall be held guilty of any criminal offence on account of any act or omission which did not constitute a criminal offence, under national or international law, at the time when it was committed.

And, for the avoidance of doubt, there follows a second clause, stating:

Nothing in this article shall prejudice the trial and punishment of any person for any act or omission which, at the time when it was committed, was criminal according to the general principles of law recognized by the community of nations.

Other human rights treaties and Declarations contain similar provisions.[66]

In determining whether an act was criminal under national or international law, a 47 decision-making body may have to refer to the provisions of the Geneva Conventions. In this way human rights courts have had to apply the provisions of the Geneva Conventions indirectly in response to the human rights claim that a certain act was not criminal at the time it was committed. So the ECtHR referred in particular to Article 18 GC IV to bolster the argument that the execution of a pregnant woman *hors de combat* in occupied territory constituted a war crime in Latvia in 1944.[67] Even more directly, the same Court came to analyse Common Article 3 to determine whether the shooting of a certain Tamás Kaszás by the applicant Korbely constituted an international crime in Hungary in 1956:

However there is no element in the findings of fact established by the domestic courts which could lead to the conclusion that Tamás Kaszás expressed in such a manner any intention to surrender. Instead, he embarked on an animated quarrel with the applicant, at the end of which he drew his gun with unknown intentions. It was precisely in the course of this act that he was shot. In these circumstances the Court is not convinced that in the light of the commonly accepted international

---

[62] Art 3(1)(e) Kampala Convention; see also Art 4(1) and the savings clause which specifically refers to instruments of IHL (Art 20(2)).
[63] Art 4(4)(h) Kampala Convention. [64] Art 22 Kampala Convention. See also Art 38(1) CRC.
[65] STC/Legal/Min/7(I) Rev 1, new Arts 4 and 6.
[66] See Art 15 ICCPR. See also Art 11(2) UDHR; Art 7 ECHR; Art 9 ACHR; Art 7(2) ACHPR; Art 15 Arab Charter of Human Rights; Art 49 Charter of Fundamental Rights of the European Union.
[67] ECtHR, *Kononov v Latvia*, Judgment, 17 May 2010, para 218.

law standards applicable at the time, Tamás Kaszás could be said to have laid down his arms within the meaning of common Article 3.[68]

The ECtHR went on to find that Korbely's conviction therefore constituted a violation of his human rights under the Convention.

48   Although the facts and law in these cases are more complex than presented here, the larger point is that a human rights body may have to determine whether or not the Geneva Conventions have been violated (in a way that amounts to an international crime) in order to determine whether there has been a violation of the right not be tried for a crime that did not exist at the time of its commission.

b. Derogation clauses for times of emergency

49   As we saw above, several human rights treaties allow states to derogate from certain rights in times of emergency, as long as these are 'not inconsistent with their other obligations under international law'.[69] The UN Human Rights Committee has stated that this covers 'particularly the rules of international humanitarian law'.[70]

50   Interestingly, the Committee has looked to the fair trial guarantees in IHL and concluded: 'As certain elements of the right to a fair trial are explicitly guaranteed under international humanitarian law during armed conflict, the Committee finds no justification for derogation from these guarantees during other emergency situations.'[71] This represents an interesting development in the relationship between the Geneva Conventions and human rights law. The fair trial guarantees found in IHL have been used to help define the outer limits of what constitutes a permissible derogation not only in times of armed conflict, but also in times of emergency falling short of armed conflict.[72]

c. The interpretation of the concept of arbitrary in the International Covenant on Civil and Political Rights

51   As we saw in section C.I.c of this chapter, the ECHR includes fixed lists of justifications for interfering with the right to life and the right to liberty. This meant that in the absence of a derogation, Russia was held not to have had a legitimate justification for the loss of life in the Chechnya operation, and the UK could not rely on an implied right to detain in an internal armed conflict in Afghanistan. The reasoning might have been different had these cases arisen under the ICCPR. The Covenant does not provide for the possibility of a derogation from the right to life in times of war; on the other hand, it does not exclusively list the possible justifications for interfering with the right to life or liberty.

52   With regard to the right to life, the Covenant provides that 'No one shall be arbitrarily deprived of his life.'[73] This has led to the argument that in appropriate circumstances, there will be no arbitrary deprivation of life if the acts are in conformity with the

---

[68] ECtHR, *Korbely v Hungary*, Judgment, 19 September 2008, para 91.
[69] Art 4(1) ICCPR. See also Art 15 ECHR; Art 30 European Social Charter (1961); Art 27 ACHR (1969); Art 4 Arab Charter on Human Rights (2004).
[70] General Comment 29 (States of emergency: Art 4), 24 July 2001, para 9; see also para 11.
[71] Ibid, para 16. See also Ch 68 of this volume for the influence of human rights law on occupation courts and judicial guarantees in GC IV.
[72] Relevant articles of the GCs include CA 3, and Art 105 GC III and Arts 64–78 GC IV. For completeness we should mention Arts 75, 85(4)(e) AP I, and Art 6 AP II.
[73] Art 6(1) ICCPR.

so-called *lex specialis* of IHL. In an oft-quoted passage, the ICJ explained the relationship as follows:

The Court observes that the protection of the International Covenant of Civil and Political Rights does not cease in times of war, except by operation of Article 4 of the Covenant whereby certain provisions may be derogated from in a time of national emergency. Respect for the right to life is not, however, such a provision. In principle, the right not arbitrarily to be deprived of one's life applies also in hostilities. The test of what is an arbitrary deprivation of life, however, then falls to be determined by the applicable *lex specialis*, namely, the law applicable in armed conflict which is designed to regulate the conduct of hostilities. Thus whether a particular loss of life, through the use of a certain weapon in warfare, is to be considered an arbitrary deprivation of life contrary to Article 6 of the Covenant, can only be decided by reference to the law applicable in armed conflict and not deduced from the terms of the Covenant itself.[74]

The Court uses the specificity of the law of armed conflict to determine the scope of the meaning of 'arbitrarily' in the Covenant in the context of the legality of the use of a certain weapon. One could imagine that a similar approach might be taken to the thorny issue of the legal basis for detention in times of IAC (following the judgment in *Hassan*), due again to the wording of the treaty which provides a sort of 'gateway' to IHL through the use of the word 'arbitrary'. Article 9(1) ICCPR states in part that 'No one shall be subjected to arbitrary arrest or detention. No one shall be deprived of his liberty except on such grounds and in accordance with such procedure as are established by law.'

The UN Human Rights Committee's developing approach to this issue may be gleaned from its recent 2014 General Comment on Article 9. In a crucial passage, and after considered discussion of whether IAC should be distinguished from NIAC for these purposes, it separated out IACs (with the attendant protection offered by the Geneva Conventions) from other situations:[75]

During international armed conflict, substantive and procedural rules of international humanitarian law remain applicable and limit the ability to derogate, thereby helping to mitigate the risk of arbitrary detention. Outside that context, the requirements of strict necessity and proportionality constrain any derogating measures involving security detention, which must be limited in duration and accompanied by procedures to prevent arbitrary application, as explained in paragraph 15 above, including review by a court within the meaning of paragraph 45 above.

The crucial passage from paragraph 15 reads:

If, under the most exceptional circumstances, a present, direct and imperative threat is invoked to justify the detention of persons considered to present such a threat, the burden of proof lies on States parties to show that the individual poses such a threat and that it cannot be addressed by alternative measures, and that burden increases with the length of the detention. States parties also need to show that detention does not last longer than absolutely necessary, that the overall length of possible detention is limited and that they fully respect the guarantees provided for by article 9 in all cases. Prompt and regular review by a court or other tribunal possessing the same attributes of independence and impartiality as the judiciary is a necessary guarantee for these conditions, as is access to independent legal advice, preferably selected by the detainee, and disclosure to the detainee of, at least, the essence of the evidence on which the decision is taken.[76]

---

[74] ICJ, *Legality of the Threat or Use of Nuclear Weapons*, Advisory Opinion, 8 July 1996, para 25.
[75] HRCttee, General Comment 35, 16 December 2014, para 66, footnotes omitted.
[76] Footnote in the original reads: 'On the relationship of article 9 to article 4 of the Covenant and international humanitarian law, see paragraphs 64 to 67 below.'

This suggests that a security detainee or internee in a NIAC enjoys the human right to an independent review of the necessity for the ongoing detention. More generally the Committee restated in paragraph 64 how the Covenant continues to apply in times of armed conflict: 'While rules of international humanitarian law may be relevant for the purposes of the interpretation of article 9, both spheres of law are complementary, not mutually exclusive.' It concludes, however, that '[s]ecurity detention authorized and regulated by and complying with international humanitarian law in principle is not arbitrary'.

55   As we have seen, the ICJ is clear that this type of human rights treaty 'does not cease to apply', it is not displaced (unlike some of the treaties discussed at MN 12–19). Its terms are simply interpreted by reference to the detailed rules of IHL. The continuing application of the human rights treaty is significant, as this means that complaints can continue to be brought before the relevant bodies and jurisdictions. If the human rights treaty were simply 'displaced', as is sometimes suggested, there could be no complaint that the human rights treaty had been violated. So we can conclude that, according to the ICJ's approach, a violation of the IHL on the conduct of hostilities may therefore constitute a violation of the prohibition on arbitrary deprivation of life under the ICCPR, and an internment in IAC that is not authorized by IHL could similarly be an arbitrary detention and a violation of ICCPR. But the human rights in the treaty may grant additional protection and procedural rights beyond what was offered by the Geneva Conventions.

III. Treaties referring to other international instruments

a. *The American Convention on Human Rights and its Articles 25 and 29*

56   In *Abella v Argentina*, the Inter-American Commission of Human Rights drew a number of conclusions about the relationship between the Convention and the law of armed conflict. According to the Report:

> On January 23, 1989, 42 armed persons launched an attack on the aforementioned barracks. The attack precipitated a combat of approximately 30 hours duration between the attackers and Argentine military personnel which resulted in the deaths of 29 of the attackers and several State agents.[77]

The Commission directly applied Common Article 3 of the Geneva Conventions. This has proven controversial, and the Inter-American Court has taken a different approach, ruling that the issue should be seen as a question of interpretation of the American Convention on Human Rights (ACHR) rather than the application of the rules in the

---

[77] IACommHR, *Abella v Argentina*, Case 11.137, Rep 55/97, OEA/Ser.L/V/II.95 Doc 7 rev at 271 (1997), para 1. Other petitions heard by the Commission relate to the American Declaration of the Rights and Duties of Man, considered binding on OAS member states via the OAS Charter. See IACommHR, *Coard et al v United States*, Case 10.951, Rep 109/99, September 1999 (relating to the US intervention in Grenada); IACommHR, *Salas and others v United States*, Case 10.573, Rep 31/93 of 14 October 1993 (concerning US intervention in Panama) (still pending); IACommHR, *Disabled Peoples' International et al v United States*, App No 9213, decision of 22 September 1987 (relating to UN bombing of asylum in Grenada in 1983, discontinued due to friendly settlement). Notably, in these cases against the US, the US argued that the cases should not be resolved by the Commission as they fell to be determined solely on the basis of the law of armed conflict. On 12 March 2002 the Commission authorized precautionary measures in favour of detainees being held by the US at Guantánamo Bay, Cuba (259/02). See the response of the US denying the jurisdiction of the Commission with regard to precautionary measures and the laws of armed conflict relating to the situation in Guantánamo, at <http://www.state.gov/s/l/38642.htm>; in another decision the Commission granted the request of a Guantánamo detainee, Mr Djamel Ameziane, for precautionary measures (211/08) on 20 August 2008.

Geneva Conventions. Nevertheless, we should examine the Commission's reasoning, as it explains again how terms such as 'arbitrary' are being interpreted by reference to the norms in IHL. The Commission stated as follows:

> The American Convention, as well as other universal and regional human rights instruments, and the 1949 Geneva Conventions share a common nucleus of non-derogable rights and a common purpose of protecting human life and dignity. These human rights treaties apply both in peacetime, and during situations of armed conflict. Although one of their purposes is to prevent warfare, none of these human rights instruments was designed to regulate such situations and, thus, they contain no rules governing the means and methods of warfare.[78]

The report later outlines how the Commission sees IHL providing the special rules to be used in order to apply the right to life in a human rights treaty:

> For example, both Common Article 3 and Article 4 of the American Convention protect the right to life and, thus, prohibit, *inter alia*, summary executions in all circumstances. Claims alleging arbitrary deprivations of the right to life attributable to State agents are clearly within the Commission's jurisdiction. But the Commission's ability to resolve claimed violations of this non-derogable right arising out of an armed conflict may not be possible in many cases by reference to Article 4 of the American Convention alone. This is because the American Convention contains no rules that either define or distinguish civilians from combatants and other military targets, much less, specify when a civilian can be lawfully attacked or when civilian casualties are a lawful consequence of military operations. Therefore, the Commission must necessarily look to and apply definitional standards and relevant rules of humanitarian law as sources of authoritative guidance in its resolution of this and other kinds of claims alleging violations of the American Convention in combat situations. To do otherwise would mean that the Commission would have to decline to exercise its jurisdiction in many cases involving indiscriminate attacks by State agents resulting in a considerable number of civilian casualties. Such a result would be manifestly absurd in light of the underlying object and purposes of both the American Convention and humanitarian law treaties.[79]

Furthermore, the Commission invoked the particular wording of Article 25 ACHR to bolster its case that it could apply the Geneva Conventions:

> 163. In addition, as States Parties to the American Convention, these same states are also expressly required under Article 25 of the American Convention to provide an internal legal remedy to persons for violations by State agents of their fundamental rights 'recognized by *the constitution or laws* of the state concerned or by this Convention' (emphasis supplied). Thus, when the claimed violation is not redressed on the domestic level and the source of the right is a guarantee set forth in the Geneva Conventions, which the State Party concerned has made operative as domestic law, a complaint asserting such a violation, can be lodged with and decided by the Commission under Article 44 of the American Convention. Thus, the American Convention itself authorizes the Commission to address questions of humanitarian law in cases involving alleged violations of Article 25.

The Commission then invoked another Article in the Convention to reinforce its application of humanitarian law:

> The Commission believes that in those situations where the American Convention and humanitarian law instruments apply concurrently, Article 29(b) of the American Convention necessarily require[s] the Commission to take due notice of and, where appropriate, give legal effect to applicable humanitarian law rules. Article 29(b)—the so-called 'most-favorable-to-the-individual-clause'—

---

[78] *Abella v Argentina*, above n 77, para 158.   [79] Ibid, para 161.

provides that no provision of the American Convention shall be interpreted as 'restricting the enforcement or exercise of any right or freedom recognized by virtue of the laws of any State Party [or by virtue] of another convention [to] which one of the said states is a party.'

The purpose of this Article is to prevent States Parties from relying on the American Convention as a ground for limiting more favorable or less restrictive rights to which an individual is otherwise entitled under either national or international law. Thus, where there are differences between legal standards governing the same or comparable rights in the American Convention and a humanitarian law instrument, the Commission is duty bound to give legal effect to the provision(s) of that treaty with the higher standard(s) applicable to the right(s) or freedom(s) in question. If that higher standard is a rule of humanitarian law, the Commission should apply it.[80]

60   Article 29 ACHR is entitled 'Restrictions Regarding Interpretation', and the relevant text reads:

No provision of this Convention shall be interpreted as:
[...]
b. restricting the enjoyment or exercise of any right or freedom recognized by virtue of the laws of any State Party or by virtue of another convention to which one of the said states is a party [...]

61   Paradoxically, despite the Commission's desire to offer the highest possible level of protection, its use of IHL has been criticized by Louise Doswald-Beck for presupposing that

an armed conflict can only be analysed within the parameters of an IHL mentality, which tends towards a *lex specialis* approach that in effect marginalizes human rights law [...] [T]he notion of 'combatants' and 'civilians' does not strictly speaking belong to human rights law, although treaty bodies do cede to the temptation to refer to 'civilians' when referring to individuals not themselves involved in hostilities. Rather the test of whether the right to life has been violated is whether the persons attacked were threats to life and whether the use of force against them was necessary and proportionate to protect life.[81]

62   Unless one accepts that the human right to life is only as protective as the applicable IHL, the point being made by Doswald-Beck is that human rights law continues to apply and allows for the intentional use of lethal force only where this is necessary to protect life. The Commission's reading of the law of armed conflict is that those attacking the barracks may be targeted with lethal force, and the Commission draws the conclusion that there was therefore no violation of the right to life under human rights law. An alternative approach would demand that the killing also be justified under human rights law, and if there was no immediate threat to human life, then those killed would have been the victims of a human rights violation. Many would argue that in this case, whichever reasoning is deployed, one comes to the same result, especially if one considers that the law of armed conflict actually includes proportionality and necessity requirements even when targeting those taking a direct part in hostilities.[82] But this is to duck the hard questions. There will be situations where there will be no imminent threat to human life from a fighter in an internal armed conflict, or from a civilian deemed directly participating in hostilities, and the basic rules of armed conflict would

---

[80] Ibid, paras 164–5. The author has corrected the misquotation from the Convention. The orginal Spanish report quotes the provision correctly.

[81] L. Doswald-Beck, *Human Rights in Times of Conflict and Terrorism* (Oxford: OUP, 2011), at 112.

[82] See generally N. Melzer, *Targeted Killing in International Law* (Oxford: OUP, 2008); N. Melzer, 'Keeping the Balance between Military Necessity and Humanity: A Response to Four Critiques of the ICRC's Interpretive Guidance on the Notion of Direct Participation in Hostilities', 42 *New York University Journal of International Law and Politics* (2010) 831.

suggest to many that it is not forbidden to target that individual. On the other hand, it is argued that human rights law demands that intentional lethal force is to be used only to protect another life. In a careful analysis of the *Chechnya case* (referred to at MN 28), Abresch concludes that:

> The case law is best interpreted as providing the same rule for battles as for arrests, and for civil wars as for riots. This does not mean that the intensity of conflict is legally immaterial. Resort to lethal force is more likely to be lawful if the insurgent is actively participating in battle, because then he poses an actual or imminent threat to others and capturing him would more likely unreasonably endanger government soldiers. But there is no *per se* rule that insurgents may be targeted with lethal force. [83]

It is suggested that the way to understand this dilemma is to admit that, although in IAC members of the armed forces enjoy combatant immunity (or the combatant's privilege) for certain killings directed at combatants from the armed forces of another state, in internal armed conflict no such privilege exists.[84] States have refused to extend this rule explicitly to internal armed conflict, for the very simple reason that this could imply a right to kill fighters not only for their own forces, but also for the insurgents.[85] States do not accept equality of arms in this context, and will be wary of any international rule relating to combatant immunity in NIAC in case it should become something turned against them, legitimizing the killing of members of the state's armed forces by those fighting for the rebel groups. This means that although one could argue that a member of the government armed forces who targets a fighter from the non-governmental side has not violated IHL, there may still have to be a separate inquiry into whether these actions were in conformity with human rights law. The ICRC Interpretive Guidance on the Notion of Direct Participation in Hostilities has been careful to state that 'its conclusions remain without prejudice to an analysis of questions related to direct participation in hostilities under other applicable branches of international law, such as human rights law'.[86]

63

The Inter-American Court of Human Rights has taken the application of the Convention in a different direction. In a first case, the Court was asked by the Commission to '[c]onclude and declare that the State of Colombia has violated the right to life, embodied in Article 4 of the Convention, and Article 3, common to all the 1949 Geneva Conventions'.[87]

64

---

[83] See Abresch, above n 31, at 759.

[84] For a recent discussion, see *R v Gul* [2012] EWCA Crim 280, [28]–[31], where it was accepted that there was no combatant immunity for the non-state armed groups fighting the UK in Iraq and Afghanistan; the Crown contended that the UK armed forces enjoyed combatant immunity in such a situation, but the Court did not rule on this point. Compare the situation in IAC and Art 43(2) AP I.

[85] See the fascinating account of the trial of Plenty Horses for the murder of Lieutenant Casey in 1891 by G. Solis, *International Humanitarian Law in War* (New York: CUP, 2010), at 30–4; see also the trial and execution of Captain Jack and three other Motoc Indians in 1873, ibid, at 425–6. However, with regard to CA 3 conflict, Solis states (ibid, at 212) that 'Taliban fighters are terrorists in violation of domestic law [...] They have no combatant immunity.' See further ibid, at 41–2, on 'combatant's privilege'.

[86] 'Interpretive Guidance on the Notion of Direct Participation in Hostilities under International Humanitarian Law Adopted by the Assembly of the International Committee of the Red Cross on 26 February 2009', 90 *IRRC* 872 (2008), at 993. Principle IX reads: 'IX. Restraints on the use of force in direct attack: In addition to the restraints imposed by international humanitarian law on specific means and methods of warfare, and *without prejudice to further restrictions that may arise under other applicable branches of international law*, the kind and degree of force which is permissible against persons not entitled to protection against direct attack must not exceed what is actually necessary to accomplish a legitimate military purpose in the prevailing circumstances' (emphasis added).

[87] IACtHR, *Las Palmeras Case*, Judgment on Preliminary Objections of February 4, 2000, (Ser C) No 67 (2000), para 12.

65 Colombia filed a number of preliminary objections, inter alia objecting that the Commission and the Court were 'not competent to apply international humanitarian law and other international treaties'. The Court admitted the objections with regard to both bodies, stating that the American Convention 'has only given the Court competence to determine whether the acts or the norms of the States are compatible with the Convention itself, and not with the 1949 Geneva Conventions'.[88] It is worth noting that the Court recalled that '[a]t the public hearing, the State indicated that it agreed that the Convention should be interpreted in harmony with other treaties, but it did not accept that the common Article 3 could be applied as a norm infringed by Colombia in an individual case'.[89] In the judgment on the merits the Court made no reference to Common Article 3, and went on to find violations of the right to life, and violations of the right to judicial remedies and guarantees for the next of kin.[90] On the facts there was no reason to revert to IHL to complement or interpret the right to life and the judicial guarantees protected by the Convention.

66 Two further cases, however, offer a few more clues as to the Court's approach. In the *Bámaca Velásquez Case*, the defendant state of Guatemala was reported to have indicated in oral argument that since the Court had 'extensive faculties of interpretation of international law, it could [apply] any other provision that it deemed appropriate':[91]

Although the Court lacks competence to declare that a State is internationally responsible for the violation of international treaties that do not grant it such competence, it can observe that certain acts or omissions that violate human rights, pursuant to the treaties that they do have competence to apply, also violate other international instruments for the protection of the individual, such as the 1949 Geneva Conventions and, in particular, common Article 3.

Indeed, there is a similarity between the content of Article 3, common to the 1949 Geneva Conventions, and the provisions of the American Convention and other international instruments regarding non-derogable human rights (such as the right to life and the right not to be submitted to torture or cruel, inhuman or degrading treatment). This Court has already indicated in the *Las Palmeras Case* (2000), that the relevant provisions of the Geneva Conventions may be taken into consideration as elements for the interpretation of the American Convention.[92]

67 In a second case against Colombia, the Inter-American Court of Human Rights recalled Article 29 ACHR and relied on Articles from AP II to interpret and apply Article 21 ACHR on the right to property and Article 22 ACHR on freedom of movement.[93] The Court's judgment also demands permanent training in humanitarian law for the Colombian armed forces.[94]

---

[88] Ibid, para 33.   [89] Ibid, para 34.
[90] IACtHR, *Las Palmeras Case*, Judgment, 6 December 2001.
[91] IACtHR, *Bámaca Velásquez Case*, Judgment, 25 November 2000, para 204.
[92] Ibid, paras 208–9. See further the Separate Concurring Opinion of Judge Sergio García Ramírez, para 24 (footnote omitted): 'It is not an issue of directly applying Article 3 common to the Geneva Conventions in the case, but of admitting the facts provided by the whole system of laws—to which this principle belongs—in order to interpret the meaning of a norm that the Court must apply directly.' See also Separate Opinion of Judge De Roux Rengifo, at 3–4, who regretted that 'that the issue of humanitarian laws was not introduced in relation to Article 2 of the American Convention. In a country undergoing an internal armed conflict, such as that experienced by Guatemala when the facts of the case occurred, the "legislative or other measures" that are needed in order to make the rights established in the Convention effective, undoubtedly include those that consist in assuming, disseminating and fulfilling the rules of humanitarian law applicable to that type of conflict and in investigating and punishing violations against them.'
[93] IACtHR, *Case of the Ituango Massacres v Colombia*, Judgment, 1 July 2006, esp paras 179–83 and 206–15.
[94] Ibid, para 426, operative para 21.

68 Most recently, in *Ecuador v Colombia*, the conduct of the Colombian armed forces was held by the Commission to fall within the jurisdiction of Colombia when they were operating in Ecuador. The Commission rejected the arguments of the respondent state that the issues were to be dealt with solely under IHL. It explained the interaction between the two regimes and the competence of the Commission *ratione materiae* in very clear terms:

> Due to their similarity and the fact that both norms are based on the same principles and values, international human rights law and IHL may influence and reinforce each other, following as a interpretative method that enshrined in Article 31.3.c of the Vienna Convention on the Law of Treaties, which establishes that in interpreting a norm 'any relevant rules of international law applicable in the relations between the parties' may be considered. The foregoing shows that international human rights law may be interpreted in the light of IHL and the latter may be interpreted in the light of international human rights law, as required.[95]

b. *The African Charter on Human and Peoples' Rights (1981)*

69 The African Charter, under the heading 'Applicable Principles', contains two Articles that authorize the African Commission on Human and Peoples' Rights to 'draw inspiration from international law on human and peoples' rights, [...] [including] instruments adopted by [...] African countries',[96] and

> take into consideration, as subsidiary measures to determine the principles of law, other general or special international conventions, laying down rules expressly recognized by member states of the Organization of African Unity [...] [and] general principles of law recognized by African states [...][97]

The Commission invoked these two Articles in an inter-state case and held that it would take the Geneva Conventions into consideration in the determination of the case as

> the Four Geneva Conventions and the two Additional Protocols covering armed conflicts, fall on all fours with the category of special international conventions, laying down rules recognised by Member States of the OAU and also constitute part of the general principles recognised by African States [...][98]

70 We might note the following paragraph:

> The besieg[ing] of the hydroelectric dam may also be brought within the prohibition contained in The Hague Convention (II) with Respect to the Laws and Customs of War on Land which provides in Article 23 that 'Besides the prohibitions provided by special Conventions, it is especially prohibited [...] to destroy the enemy's property, unless such destruction or seizure be imperatively demanded by the necessities of war'. By parity of reason, and bearing in mind Articles 60 and 61 of the [African] Charter, the Respondent States are in violation of the said Charter with regard to the just noted Article 23.[99]

71 Doswald-Beck has highlighted that the Commission might here have referred to Articles 53 and 56 paragraph 1 GC IV, but that it did not really look at questions of military necessity, going on to find, inter alia, violations of the right to property under the Charter (Article 14).[100] With regard to the exploitation of natural resources, Doswald-Beck's

---

[95] IACommHR, Case IP-02, Rep No 112/10, Inter-Am CHR, OEA/Ser.L/V/II.140 Doc 10 (2010), decision of 21 October 2010 (footnotes omitted), para 121.
[96] Art 60 African Charter.   [97] Art 61 African Charter.
[98] ACommHPR, *DRC v Burundi, Rwanda and Uganda*, Comm No 227/99 (2003), para 78.
[99] Ibid, para 84.   [100] Ibid, para 88; see Doswald-Beck, above n 81, at 109–10.

helpful analysis notes that 'in general occupation law does give some rights regarding State property to an occupying power, whereas the terms of the Charter are quite clear and without limitation'.[101] Similarly, mass transfers of persons were dealt under the Charter without reference to Article 49 GC IV. In sum, the Commission does not engage in any sort of *renvoi* to the Geneva Conventions, even when dealing with quite detailed questions relating to occupation. On the other hand, reading the whole decision, we see that IHL is invariably invoked to bolster the conclusions regarding human rights law. The Commission found, for example

> the killings, massacres, rapes, mutilations and other grave human rights abuses committed while the Respondent States' armed forces were still in effective occupation of the eastern provinces of the Complainant State reprehensible and also inconsistent with their obligations under Part III of the *Geneva Convention Relative to the Protection of Civilian Persons in Time of War* of 1949 and *Protocol 1 of the Geneva Convention.*

> They also constitute flagrant violations of Article 2 of the African Charter, such acts being directed against the victims by virtue of their national origin; and Article 4, which guarantees respect for life and the integrity of one's person and prohibits the arbitrary deprivation [of] rights.[102]

72   The African Court on Human and Peoples' Rights issued an order for provisional measures against Libya in March 2011. Part of the allegations against Libya before the Court were 'that Libyan security forces engaged in excessive use of heavy weapons and machine guns against the population, including targeted aerial bombardment and all types of attacks'.[103] The Commission was said to have found violations of the right to life under the Charter. The Court did not specifically cite any rules of IHL but ordered that

> [t]he Great Socialist People's Libyan Arab Jamahiriya must immediately refrain from any action that would result in loss of life or violation of physical integrity of persons, which could be a breach of the provisions of the Charter or of other international human rights instruments to which it is a party.[104]

D. The General Articulation of the Relationship between Human Rights Rules and the Rules Contained in the Geneva Conventions

73   As already mentioned, the large variety of international human rights monitoring bodies and jurisdictions, and the relative ease with which individuals and states can complain under human rights treaties, mean that the victims of armed conflict are likely to continue to frame their complaints in terms of human rights violations. In practice, tension or conflict between human rights law and IHL may be avoided by the relevant human rights body's simply determining that it has no jurisdiction over the application of IHL. Human rights law is then applied and interpreted in the light of the state's international obligations under humanitarian law,[105] or even without direct reference to that branch of

---

[101] Doswald-Beck, above n 81, at 110.
[102] ACommHPR, *DRC v Burundi et al*, above n 98, paras 79–80; see also para 89 referring to Art 27 GC IV.
[103] *African Commission on Human and Peoples' Rights v Great Socialist People's Libyan Arab Janiahiriya*, App No 00412011, Order for Provisional Measures, 11 March 2011.
[104] Ibid, para 25, operative para 1.
[105] More subtle is the influence that human rights law has played in the development of international criminal law when faced with violations of IHL. In *The Prosecutor v Duško Tadić*, IT-94-1-AR72, 2 October 1995,

law at all. Failing to refer to specific provisions of humanitarian law is obviously attractive where the very applicability of that law to the situation is contested. This is most likely to be the case in the context of a NIAC occurring on the territory of the state concerned. In such cases governments often prefer to deny the existence of an armed conflict and frame the issue as one of criminality or terrorism. But where the NIAC is taking place extraterritorially, for example during the the conflict between the Taliban and the Western Allies of the Afghan Government, the states concerned have recognized that there is a NIAC and have gone on to argue that human rights law is not meant to apply in such situations. As we have seen, this assertion has so far been rejected by one judgment in the UK, and it is difficult to see how it would be accepted by any of the regional human rights bodies, or the ICJ, in the light of their case law.

Before we embark on an attempt to discern the articulation between the competing norms of these two branches of law, we need to remind ourselves of the context. Some well-informed commentators have pointed out that the issues unfold against a background of increasing threats to security from armed groups and terrorists, and that 'the application of human rights law may result in problematic normative overreaching [...] lead[ing] to a law application exercise divorced from the actual conditions and needs of warfare and is likely to attract limited support from important constituencies'.[106] In the same vein, it has been suggested that the debate has been characterized by 'overly expansive claims on the part of non-governmental commentators, and anxiety on the part of the military that these developments are hampering the flexibility to act effectively to keep society safe'.[107] Of course much human rights law has been fashioned precisely because the non-governmental sector has made moral demands on the authorities to do things that the security services consider undermine their effectiveness. Whether or not powerful states refuse to accept this argumentation may be relevant, but it is unlikely to put off those advocating what has become known (in Meron's phrase) as the 'humanization of humanitarian law'.[108] Nevertheless, we shall endeavour 'to avoid the impression of a fluffy, utopian human-rightist disregard for the realities of international relations'.[109]

There is an abiding notion that the relationship between human rights law and IHL can be resolved through an application of the *lex specialis* maxim. As we shall see, this maxim is not as helpful as it might seem. It has been introduced into the discussion through two Advisory Opinions of the ICJ.[110] Since then, the ICJ has returned to this

paras 97 ff, the Appeals Chamber of the ICTY used human rights logic to suggest that the protection afforded to individuals in IAC ought to be extended to NIACs, so human rights may also be used to interpret the GCs, for example outlining the guarantees of fair trial, nevertheless in some circumstances the GCs may offer greater protection than the equivalent human rights rule: see the judgment of the Court of Appeal in the UK in *R (Haidar Ali Hussein) v Secretary of State for Defence* [2014] EWCA Civ 1087, at [45], 'As elaborated in the case law Article 3 ECHR employs a high threshold test of a minimum level of severity which it would not be appropriate to employ in the case of Common Article 3.'

[106] Y. Shany, 'Human Rights and Humanitarian Law as Competing Legal Paradigms for Fighting Terror', in O. Ben-Naftali (ed), *International Humanitarian Law and International Human Rights Law* (Oxford: OUP, 2011) 13, at 29.

[107] Bethlehem, above n 4, at 195.

[108] T. Meron, 'The Humanization of Humanitarian Law', 94 *AJIL* 2(2000) 239; and T. Meron, 'The Humanization of the Law of War', in *The Making of International Justice: A View from the Bench* (Oxford: OUP, 2011) 42.

[109] M. Milanović, 'Norm Conflicts, International Humanitarian Law, and Human Rights', in Ben-Naftali (ed), above n 106, 95, at 97.

[110] *Legality of the Threat or Use of Nuclear Weapons*, 8 July 1996, para 25; the *Legal Consequences of the Construction of a Wall in Occupied Palestinian Territory*, 9 July 2004, para 106.

topic in the context of the armed conflict between the Democratic Republic of Congo (DRC) and Uganda. The Court treated the law of occupation and the law of human rights together, and declined to suggest that one or other branch or norm should be displaced. It concluded that Uganda was responsible for violations of both human rights law and IHL in the DRC and in Occupied Ituri.[111] This is not the place to embark on a detailed dissertation on the scholarship which has been published in the wake of the ICJ's pronouncements.[112] What we might do, however, is make a few preliminary points about the doctrine.

76 First, it is increasingly recognized that human rights law applies in times of armed conflict alongside IHL.[113] Secondly, where the *lex specialis* maxim applies, it is with regard to a particular rule or norm, and it is not a principle to articulate a general relationship between the two branches of international law.[114] So, as we saw when we examined the ICCPR in section C.II.c of this chapter, the ICJ referred to the *lex specialis* of the specific rules in the law on the conduct of hostilities applicable in armed conflict, in order to see if there could be a violation of the prohibition on arbitrary deprivation of life under human rights law.[115]

---

[111] ICJ, *Armed Activities on the Territory of the Congo (Democratic Republic of the Congo v Uganda)*, Judgment, 19 December 2005, para 220.

[112] G. Gaggioli, *L'influence mutuelle entre les droits de l'homme et le droit international humanitaire à la lumière du droit à la vie* (Paris: Pedone, 2013); Doswald-Beck, above n 81, Chapter IV and 385–98; N. Melzer, 'Bolstering the Protection of Civilians in Armed Conflict', in A. Cassese (ed), *Realizing Utopia: The Future of International Law* (Oxford: OUP, 2012) 508; Y. Dinstein, *The Conduct of Hostilities under the Law of International Armed Conflict* (2nd edn, Cambridge: CUP, 2010) 19; Y. Dinstein, *The International Law of Belligerent Occupation* (Cambridge: CUP, 2009), at 81–8; R. Arnold and N. Quénivet (eds), *International Humanitarian Law and Human Rights Law: Towards a New Merger in International Law* (Leiden: Nijhoff, 2008); D. Thürer, 'International Humanitarian Law: Theory, Practice, Context', 338 *RCADI* (2008) 9, at 107–35; C. McCarthy, 'Human Rights and the Laws of War under the American Convention on Human Rights', 6 *EHRLR* (2008) 762; F.J. Hampson, 'The Relationship between International Humanitarian Law and Human Rights Law from the Perspective of a Human Rights Treaty Body', 90 *IRRC* 871 (2008) 549; M. Sassòli and L. Olson, 'The Relationship between International Humanitarian Law and Human Rights Law Where it Matters: Admissible Killing and Internment of Fighters in Non-International Armed Conflicts', 90 *IRRC* 871 (2008) 599; C. Droege, 'Elective Affinities? Human Rights and Humanitarian Law', 90 *IRRC* 871 (2008) 501; C. Droege, 'The Interplay between International Humanitarian Law and International Human Rights Law in Situations of Armed Conflict', 40 *Israel Law Review* (2007) 310; G. Gaggioli and R. Kolb, 'A Right to Life in Armed Conflicts? The Contribution of the European Court', 37 *IsrYBHR* (2007) 115; T. Meron, 'International Law in the Age of Human Rights: General Course on Public International Law', 301 *RCADI* (2004) 9, at 68–86; A. Orakhelashvili, 'The Interaction between Human Rights and Humanitarian Law: Fragmentation, Conflict, Parallelism, or Convergence?', 19 *EJIL* (2008) 161; W.A. Schabas, '*Lex Specialis?* Belt and Suspenders? The Parallel Operation of Human Rights Law and the Law of Armed Conflict, and the Conundrum of *Jus ad Bellum*', 40 *Israel Law Review* (2007) 592; H.-J. Heintze, 'On the Relationship between Human Rights Law and International Humanitarian Law', 86 *IRRC* 856 (2004) 789; R. Provost, *International Human Rights and Humanitarian Law* (Cambridge: CUP, 2002).

[113] See C. Greenwood, 'Scope of Application of Humanitarian Law', in D. Fleck (ed), *The Handbook of Humanitarian Law in Armed Conflict* (2nd edn, Oxford: OUP, 2007) 45, at 74: '[Some have argued] that human rights law is only intended to be applicable in time of peace. This view is not generally accepted and the better view is that human rights treaties are, in principle, capable of application in armed conflict.' See also the ILC's 'Draft articles on the effect of armed conflicts on treaties' (2011), which include in the indicative list of treaties that continue to apply in times of armed conflict, 'Treaties for the international protection of human rights'.

[114] Greenwood, above n 113, at 75; OHCHR, above n 1, at 58–68; and see further D. Jinks, 'Human Rights in Time of Armed Conflict', in A. Clapham and P. Gaeta (eds), *The Oxford Handbook of International Law in Armed Conflict* (Oxford: OUP, 2014) 656; J. d'Aspremont and E. Tranchez, 'The Quest for a Non-Conflictual Coexistance of International Human Rights Law and Humanitarian Law: Which Role for the *Lex Specialis* Principle?', in Kolb and Gaggioli (eds), above n 41, at 223–50.

[115] See ICJ, *Nuclear Weapons*, Advisory Opinion, above n 74, paras 25 ff.

In this way human rights law is seen as the general law, with certain provisions, for example relating to arbitrary deprivation of the right to life or arbitrary detention, providing *portals, gateways,* or *windows* to the detailed, more specific or specialized rules of IHL. Thirdly, some emphasize that the relationship is a two-way street, with human rights law in turn providing the detail for the application of IHL. For this school the emphasis should be on the rules of interpretation, in order to make sense of the articulation between two regimes which are not only converging but cross-fertilizing and mutually reinforcing.[116] Lastly, one category of writing has tended to emphasize the tension, or even contradiction, between a simultaneous application of both branches, and continues to ask difficult questions about the choices being made.[117] This has led at least one commentator to call for greater transparency in admitting that choices between conflicting norms are being made for policy reasons, or according to personal morality, and that such choices should be made in the political sphere rather than by courts presuming to apply the law.[118]

Space does not permit a detailed examination of the various areas where choices present themselves. We have seen that the regional bodies have simply applied human rights law with regard to detention, even where the Geneva Conventions were said to displace this with regard to so called 'security detainees' held under a regime 'derived from' that applicable to occupied territory (*Al Jedda*, at MN 33–34). *Lex specialis* has not operated as a simple maxim to displace human rights law. We have seen the African Commission apply human rights provisions to destruction of property and forced movement of people in an IAC, even where IHL rules which allow for military necessity might have provided a justification (*DRC v Burundi et al*, at MN 69–71). Even in the context of a court of general jurisdiction, the judges of the ICJ have declined to disapply one regime in favour of another (*DRC v Uganda*, at MN 75). Israel has claimed that the International Covenant on Economic Social and Cultural Rights is inapplicable to it with regard to occupied territory, and that the issues fall solely under IHL. The ICJ has disagreed and observed that

> the territories occupied by Israel have for over 37 years been subject to its territorial jurisdiction as the occupying Power. In the exercise of the powers available to it on this basis, Israel is bound by the provisions of the International Covenant on Economic, Social and Cultural Rights.[119]

We can conclude that perceived clashes between rules are most likely to be resolved by applying both regimes simultaneously. On the rare occasions when this would seem to authorize and prohibit detention simultaneously (POWs deprived of their liberty in a situation where the ECHR applies without derogation), it is unlikely that a court would

---

[116] See, e.g., Meron, Droege, Melzer, Orakhelashvili, Thürer, Heintze, and Gaggioli and Kolb, above n 112. And more recently, see M. Sassòli, 'The Role of Human Rights and International Humanitarian Law in New Types of Armed Conflicts', in Ben-Naftali (ed), above n 106, 34. See also n 105 above and Chs 53 and 68 of this volume.

[117] See esp Pejic, above n 40, Hampson, McCarthy, Sassòli and Olson, Abresch, and Doswald-Beck, above n 112. See also Bethlehem, above n 4, who suggests (at 187) that 'a helpful initial enquiry is simply whether particular HRL [human rights law] provisions are in common sense terms amenable to reasonable application in armed conflict'.

[118] See Milanović, above n 109.

[119] ICJ, *Legal Consequences of the Construction of a Wall*, Advisory Opinion, above n 21, para 112. Israel omits any reference to the occupied territories when reporting to the Committee on Economic Social and Cultural Rights on the grounds not only that the matter should be dealt with, if at all, by IHL, but also because, she says, 'the Convention, which is a territorially bound Convention, does not apply, nor was it intended to apply, to areas outside its national territory': Response to the list of issues on the third periodic report, dated September 2011, at 4–5. The Committee has regretted this absence of reporting and urged the inclusion of such information, UN Doc E/C.12/ISR/CO/3, 16 December 2011, para 8.

order that each POW had the right to a *habeas corpus* hearing to determine the legality of his continued detention. But we should not rule this out. One could imagine a situation where, strictly speaking, the application of the Geneva Conventions entitled a state to continue to hold POWs, and yet where no practical purpose was served by holding them because they were too old to return to the hostilities. In such circumstances, or other similar situations, one could imagine an enforceable human right to contest the continuing basis of the POWs' deprivation of liberty.[120]

79 Rather than articulating a hierarchy of regimes, it perhaps makes more sense to consider what Hampson and Lubbell call a 'blending' on a 'contextual spectrum'. They suggest, in the context of detention, that

> [t]he degree to which a departure from human rights law would be regarded as acceptable would depend on where the issue was located on the contextual spectrum. For example, the composition of the review mechanism would be toward the LOAC/IHL prism end of the spectrum. Periodicity of review, procedural rights, rights to information and to legal advice and rights of communication would probably be in the middle of the spectrum. Physical and psychological conditions of detention, including safeguards, and release/transfer in safe conditions would be at the human rights end of the spectrum.[121]

80 In the context of threats to the right to life, others have strenuously sought to show that in this context both branches of law reach the same conclusion. Melzer suggests that 'in identical circumstances, the standard of "military necessity" under IHL corresponds to the standard of "absolute necessity" under human rights law'.[122] Such a conclusion holds up only with a very humanitarian reading of military necessity, a reading which states that shooting a fighter is justified by military necessity only where the fighter poses an immediate threat to life. Sassòli and Olson, by contrast, admit that there are occasions where the two branches contradict each other, and they appeal to *lex specialis* to determine the more appropriate rule:

> The quintessential example of such a contradiction is that of a guerrilla leader shopping in a supermarket in the government-controlled capital of the country. Many interpret humanitarian law as permitting authorities to shoot to kill, since he is a fighter, but this is controversial. Human rights law would clearly say that he must be arrested and a graduated use of force must be employed, but this conclusion is based on precedents which arose in peacetime and human rights are always more flexible according to the situation.[123]

81 Their solution is a 'sliding scale', whereby extensive government control over the place 'points to human rights as the *lex specialis*', and if a government could carry out an arrest without danger then it has sufficient control for human rights law to apply. On the other hand, in areas which are beyond government control where there is an immediacy in the danger, arrest is too risky, and there is a degree of certainty that the target is a fighter, they suggest that targeting such fighters may be appropriate in reliance on IHL, while the

---

[120] Cf the suggestion by Sassòli in Ch 51 of this volume, at MN 30 ff, that human rights law has affected the rules on repatriation of POWs; see also the discussion of habeas corpus challenges for those wishing to contest their POW status in Ch 46 of this volume, at MN 61–64, and 68.
[121] *Amicus Curiae* brief submitted to the ECtHR in *Hassan v United Kingdom*, App No 29750/09, para 54.
[122] Melzer, *Targeted Killing in International Law*, above n 82, at 393.
[123] Sassòli and Olson, above n 112, at 613.

rules of law enforcement and human rights would still apply with regard to those who are merely suspects.¹²⁴

The context here is not: war or peace? Nor is it: territorial or extraterritorial? The question is which rules provide the better fit in this particular context. The answer may involve a degree of subjectivity from the decision-maker, but at least one can see what is going on.

States have so far rarely taken the opportunity to articulate their view on the relationship between the two regimes. The 'Updated European Union Guidelines on Promoting Compliance with International Humanitarian Law' of 2009 hardly advance our understanding: '[W]hile distinct, the two sets of rules may both be applicable to a particular situation and it is therefore sometimes necessary to consider the relationship between them.'¹²⁵ There are nevertheless multiple writings which compare and contrast the two regimes in contexts such as occupation, detention, targeted killings, the death penalty, investigations into deaths, and deprivation of the right to property.¹²⁶ Furthermore, there is an abiding sense in the doctrine that the two branches not only have different historical origins, but also have different purposes and addressees. Despite numerous suggestions that armed non-state actors have human rights obligations,¹²⁷ some traditional scholarship insists that only IHL is capable of binding the non-state party to an armed conflict. This is said to demonstrate that human rights law is therefore problematic in times of armed conflict, as it would upset the principle of equality between the parties.¹²⁸ While such argumentation may make perfect sense to those from the laws of war tradition, it makes no sense to many human rights lawyers. Human rights obligations are often calculated with regard to the capacity of the duty holder and what the victim might reasonably expect; human rights do not follow the logic of a 'level playing field'.

While the doctrinal debate on whether provisions of human rights treaties are binding on non-state actors is likely to rumble on for some time, the practice of UN Commissions of Inquiry (for example with regard to Syria) and the Special Rapporteurs of the UN Human Rights Council is, nevertheless, to detail violations of human rights by named

---

¹²⁴ Ibid, at 613–15; see also the UN OHCHR Report, 'Outcome of the Expert Consultation on the Issue of Protecting the Human Rights of Civilians in Armed Conflict', UN Doc A/HRC/11/31, 4 June 2009, para 14: 'As a way to inform the lex specialis principle in the context of armed conflict, it was suggested that, the more stable the situation, the more the human rights paradigm would be applicable; the less stability and effective control, the more the international humanitarian law paradigm would be applicable to supplement human rights law.' See also OHCHR, above n 1, at 67–8.
¹²⁵ 2009/C 303/06, para 13.
¹²⁶ A. Roberts, 'Transformative Military Occupation: Applying the Laws of War and Human Rights', 100 *AJIL* (2006) 580; D. Kretzmer, 'Targeted Killing of Suspected Terrorists: Extrajudicial Executions or Legitimate Means of Defence', 16 *EJIL* (2005) 171; Gaggioli and Kolb, above n 112, Sassòli and Olson, above n 112; Schabas, above n 112; Pejic, above n 40; J. Pejic, 'Procedural principles and safeguards for internment/administrative detention in armed conflict and other situations of violence', 87 *IRRC* 858 (2005); O. Ben-Naftali, 'PathoLAWgical Occupation: Normalizing the Exceptional Case of the Occupied Palestinian Territory and Other Legal Pathologies', in Ben-Naftali (ed), above n 106, 129; and on the duty to investigate killings, see generally ECtHR, *Al-Skeini v United Kingdom*, above n 34.
¹²⁷ C. Tomuschat, 'The Applicability of Human Rights Law to Insurgent Movements', in H. Fischer et al (eds), *Krisensicherung und Humanitärer Schutz—Crisis Management and Humanitarian Protection: Festschrift für Dieter Fleck* (Berlin: Berliner Wissenschafts-Verlag, 2004) 573; D. Fleck, 'Humanitarian Protection against Non-State Actors', in J.A. Frowein et al (eds), *Verhandeln für den Frieden—Negotiating for Peace: Liber Amicorum Tono Eitel* (Berlin: Springer, 2003) 69.
¹²⁸ Sivakumaran, above n 1, at 96–9.

armed groups and to use IHRL as the framework.[129] Dieter Fleck's most recent entry in his *Handbook of International Humanitarian Law* now demonstrates a degree of impatience with those who insist on repeating the 'myth' that armed groups are not bound by human rights law:

> Whereas the binding effect of international humanitarian law on non-state actors was never seriously disputed, the extent to which this would also apply to underlying human rights norms was shadowed by a widely believed myth according to which human rights could be claimed against the state, but not against individuals. That myth may have been supported by a limited textual understanding of human rights conventions, but it was never in keeping with custom, neither with practice, and cannot be upheld.[130]

E. Critical Assessment

85   The present chapter has sought to go into some detail to describe the articulation between the Geneva Conventions and certain human rights treaties and norms. We have seen that some treaties are explicit that their provisions do not apply where the laws of IAC apply. Other treaties are circumscribed by IHL, in that derogations cannot dilute individual protection below what is demanded by IHL. In some cases human rights treaty terms, such as 'arbitrarily', have been interpreted by reference to the specialized rules found in the law of armed conflict. Rather than providing a general theory, we have sought to disaggregate the treaties, the norms, and the bodies that apply and interpret them.

86   This explains, however, only the relationship between the provisions of certain human rights treaties and the Geneva Conventions. The more general articulation between human rights law and IHL has been properly and variously described as 'unsettled' or 'uncertain';[131] we prefer the label 'under construction'. Even if one separates out the discrete norms, it is hard simply to state that a targeted killing or a detention should be covered by one or the other regime. The target might be shopping or fighting; arrest might be feasible or impossible; detainees might be fully protected and able to challenge their detention under the provisions and institutions of the laws of occupation, or languishing in a long-term situation not properly foreseen or regulated by the laws of war.

87   An assessment of the jurisprudence from international human rights bodies suggests that they are at pains not to be seen to overstep their jurisdiction. We should therefore not be surprised that they have not articulated a general theory of the relationship between these two branches of law. The ICJ has so far avoided weighing in on the debate, and has upheld a simultaneous application of both branches of law. For the most part, states have come to accept that they have human rights obligations in times of armed conflict, although some will argue that certain human rights provisions, especially with regard to the right to life or the right to challenge detention, make sense only in times of armed conflict if they are applied in ways which reflect the rights of states under the laws of war.

---

[129] For the details, see A. Clapham 'Focusing on Armed Non-State Actors', in Clapham and Gaeta (eds), above n 114, at 766.

[130] D. Fleck, 'The Law of Non-International Armed Conflict', in D. Fleck (ed), *Handbook of International Humanitarian Law* (3rd edn, Oxford: OUP, 2013) 580, at 598.

[131] See, respectively, Sivakumaran, above n 1, at 87; and R. Cryer, 'The Interplay of Human Rights and Humanitarian Law: The Approach of the ICTY', 14 *Journal of Conflict and Security Law* (2010) 511, at 511.

It is here where opinions are sharply divided, and prioritizing humanitarian law through resort to the maxim *lex specialis derogat legi generali* fails to take into consideration the progressive protection offered by human rights law. A critical assessment would suggest a return to thinking about the purpose of these branches of law. Both seek to impose limits on violence and protect the vulnerable. If rules found in the Geneva Conventions of 1949 were designed to protect better the victims of war, it seems reasonable that the huge progress that has been made in developing the international legal framework for the protection of human rights should further enhance that protection. Those who are suspicious of such an approach, which stresses mutual reinforcement of the two branches, may, on closer inspection, be more concerned about how human rights law ushers in extra avenues for redress, accountability, and 'politicized' debate.[132]

In any one situation, a serious consideration of the relationship between these two branches of law will have to first answer the following questions:

— Are we in an IAC or a NIAC?
— Which norm are we considering (the right to life, freedom from detention, freedom of movement, the right to property, the right to education, etc)?
— Which type of actor is involved (a state, an armed group, an international organization, an individual, a corporate entity, etc)?
— Which regional human rights treaties might apply? (The African, American, and European systems all offer different options for the application of human rights in armed conflict.)
— What is the context? Is the individual an immediate threat? How much control does the party to the conflict enjoy? Is there an effective right to challenge detention etc?

There is no 'one-size-fits-all' answer to questions about the relationship between these branches.

This chapter has highlighted how one might characterize the two branches as concurrent, coexisting, consistent, convergent, coterminous, congruent, confluent, corresponding, cumulative, complementary, compatible, cross-fertilizing, contradictory, competitive, or even in conflict. Our contribution to the debate is best summarized as follows: 'It's contextual and it's complicated.'

ANDREW CLAPHAM

---

[132] There were serious misgivings about 'politicization' in the negotiations which led to the new Universal Periodic Review of the UN Human Rights Council, which now states that 'given the complementary and mutually interrelated nature of international human rights law and international humanitarian law, the review shall take into account applicable international humanitarian law': para A.2 of the annex to HRC Res 5/1, 18 June 2007.

Chapter 36. The Interplay Between the Geneva Conventions and International Criminal Law

	MN
A. The Progressive 'Individualization' of International Humanitarian Law through International Criminal Law	1
B. Violations of the Geneva Conventions other than Grave Breaches as War Crimes	10
I. The seriousness of the violation	13
II. The criminalization of the illegal conduct	19
C. The Geneva Conventions and Modes of Criminal Liability by Omission	25
D. Critical Assessment	33

Select Bibliography

Bantekas, I., 'Reflections on Some Sources and Methods of International Criminal and Humanitarian Law', 6 *International Criminal Law Review* (2006) 121

Danner, A.M., 'When Courts Make Law: How the International Criminal Tribunals Recast the Laws of War', 59 *Vanderbilt Law Review* (2006) 1

Darcy, S., 'Bridging the Gaps in the Laws of Armed Conflict? International Criminal Tribunals and the Development of Humanitarian Law', in N. Quénivet and S. Shah-Davis (eds), *International Law and Armed Conflict: Challenges in the 21st Century* (The Hague: T.M.C. Asser Press, 2010) 319

Meron, T., 'International Criminalization of Internal Atrocities', 89 *AJIL* (1995) 554

Sandoz, Y., 'The Dynamic but Complex Relationship between International Penal Law and International Humanitarian Law', in J. Doria, H-P Gasser, and M.C. Bassiouni (eds), *The Legal Regime of the International Criminal Court: Essays in Honour of Professor Igor Blishchenko* (Leiden/Dordrecht/Boston: Martinus Nijhoff, 2009) 1049

Sassòli, M., 'Humanitarian Law and International Criminal Law', in A. Cassese (ed), *The Oxford Companion to International Criminal Justice* (Oxford: OUP, 2009) 111

Sassòli, M./Grignon, J., 'Les limites du droit international pénal et de la justice pénale international dans la mise en oeuvre du droit international humanitaire', in A. Biad and P. Tavernier (eds), *Le droit international humanitaire face aux défis du XXIe siècle* (Brussels: Bruylant, 2012) 133

A. The Progressive 'Individualization' of International Humanitarian Law through International Criminal Law

Criminal punishment of those who violate the laws of warfare is among the traditional means to ensure compliance with the rules of international humanitarian law (IHL) and redress their violations.[1] As is well known, the 1949 Geneva Conventions gave a

---

[1] The principle that the individual soldier who violates the laws of war and commits at the same time a criminal offence, is liable to punishment before the courts of the enemy belligerents, is firmly embedded in international law. For an early doctrinal analysis of the principle, see J.W. Garner, 'Punishment of Offenders against the Laws and Customs of War', 14 *AJIL* (1920) 70. This principle has considerably evolved to include

tremendous impulse to the development of a system of enforcement of the rules of IHL through the introduction of criminal sanctions. The provisions included in the Geneva Conventions forming the so-called system of grave breaches (complemented by those of Additional Protocol (AP) I) are in fact among the early treaty provisions establishing mandatory prosecution under the principle *aut dedere aut judicare* (see *amplius*, Chapter 31 of this volume).

2   At the same time, although disagreement persists on the definition of international crimes[2] and the class of crimes regulated by international criminal law (ICL),[3] violations of the laws of war amounting to war crimes are invariably included in the list. This is not surprising, since war crimes are at the core of the birth and development of ICL, as any textbook on this subject explains,[4] and along with other crimes have prompted the creation of international criminal courts for their repression.[5]

3   The breadth of the interplay between the Geneva Conventions and ICL is thus apparent. The Geneva Conventions (and more generally IHL) enact rules the violation of which

---

both the criminal responsibility of private individuals for violations of the laws of war and, arguably, the right (and for grave breaches of the GCs, the obligation) for third states to call to account those responsible for such violations before their courts. For a brief overview of the history and development of the law of war crimes, and for further reference, see R. Cryer et al, *An Introduction to International Criminal Law and Procedure* (2nd edn, Cambridge: CUP, 2010), at 273–9.

[2] The concept of an international crime is nevertheless of considerable antiquity: see N. Politis, 'Y-a-t-il lieu d'instituer une juridiction criminelle internationale et, dans la supposition d'une réponse affirmative, comment l'organiser?', in *Premier Congrès International de Droit Pénal: Actes du Congrès 1926* (Paris: Libraire des Juris-Classeur-Editions Godde, 1927), at 409. According to some authors, international crimes might be said to encompass crimes the criminalization of which at the domestic level is mandated by international treaty law (see Y. Dinstein, 'International Criminal Law', 5 *IsrYBHR* (1975) 55, at 67). Arguably, however, international crimes proper are those the criminalization of which is directly provided for in international law, so that the alleged offender might be tried and punished by a competent tribunal, even in the absence of a municipal criminal law applicable to him, if the crime was proscribed by a rule of international law at the time of its commission. In this sense, international crimes include piracy, war crimes, crimes against humanity, genocide, and aggression. It is disputable whether they also include other crimes, such as torture as a discrete crime or terrorism. See, on the issue, Cryer et al, above n 1, at 8, also for the necessary references. See also P. Gaeta, 'International Criminalization of Prohibited Conduct', in A. Cassese (ed), *The Oxford Companion to International Criminal Justice* (Oxford: OUP, 2009) 63.

[3] ICL is usually defined as the body of rules of public international law concerning criminal responsibility of individuals for acts or omissions contrary to the laws of nations that amount to international crimes. It encompasses both substantive rules, namely those providing for the criminal responsibility of individuals who carry out the prohibited conduct, including the rules on defences and excuses and modes of criminal liability, and procedural rules regulating criminal proceedings before international criminal courts and tribunals. In addition, it includes rules relating to the establishment and exercise of criminal jurisdiction over international crimes by states and international criminal courts and tribunals, as well as the relationship between national and international criminal courts and tribunals in the event of concurrent jurisdiction. Issues relating to judicial cooperation among states and between states and international criminal courts and tribunals for the repression and punishment of international crimes, are also governed by ICL. See A. Cassese and P. Gaeta, *Cassese's International Criminal Law* (3rd edn, Oxford: OUP, 2013), at 3. On other broader definitions of ICL, see D. Luban, 'Fairness to Rightness: Jurisdiction, Legality, and the Legitimacy of International Criminal Law', in S. Besson et al (eds), *The Philosophy of International Law* (Oxford: OUP, 2010) 569, at 569–73. But see also G. Schwarzenberger, 'The Problem of an International Criminal Law', 3 *Current Legal Problems* (1950) 263, who propounded various definitions of ICL but considered that an international body of rules directly addressing criminal prohibitions on individuals did not exist (at least not at the time he was writing).

[4] See, e.g., Cassese and Gaeta, above n 3, at 4; R. Kolb, *Droit international pénal* (Basel/Brussels: Helbing Lichtenhahn/Bruylant, 2008), at 28.

[5] See Cassese and Gaeta, above n 3, at 253–70.

could give rise to individual criminal responsibility for war crimes,[6] and thus constitute the necessary point of departure for any judge who sits in a case concerning this class of international crimes. On the other hand, international criminal courts established to adjudicate international crimes, including war crimes, have provided new avenues for the enforcement of the rules of IHL and have partially redressed the weaknesses of pre-existing mechanisms. Any discourse on the interplay between the 1949 Geneva Conventions and ICL is therefore necessarily part of the broader picture concerning the enforcement of the rules of IHL.[7]

This cross-fertilization produced and continues to produce at least two main outcomes. First, courts dealing with war crimes need to embark upon the interpretation of rules of IHL, including key rules of the Geneva Conventions, independently of their strict criminal law content.[8] This is unavoidable, since a war crime charge necessarily calls for the determination of issues that go beyond the purely criminal aspect of the case. For instance, a court adjudicating war crime charges relating to the violation of a rule of the Geneva Conventions has to establish whether the relevant rule was applicable to the facts at issue. In particular, it has to determine whether the requirements set forth by Common Article 2 for the applicability of the Geneva Conventions are met at all. In respect to grave breaches, it has to verify that the proscribed conduct was committed against 'persons or property protected by the Convention'.[9] In turn, this requires the court to construe the exact meaning and purport of the key provisions of the Geneva Conventions concerning the requirements and conditions for persons or property to be considered protected by the Conventions.

The case law of national and international criminal courts shows how much the interpretation of the non-criminal aspects of the Geneva Conventions' provisions is crucial in a war crime case.[10] It is therefore not surprising that chapters in this volume refer abundantly to this case law, irrespective of whether they are dealing with the criminal aspect of a violation of the rules under discussion. The readers can therefore peruse the relevant chapters to discern the influence of ICL instruments and case law on the interpretation and application of the pertinent Geneva Conventions rules. Suffice it here to observe that the interpretation of rules of IHL by international criminal courts has necessarily greater resonance than the one emanating from national cases decided by national judges. The former may even influence the latter, and in any case is more susceptible to spark debate among commentators and practitioners than constructions set forth in purely national case law on war crimes.

---

[6] War crimes are usually defined as violations of the laws and customs of war that give rise to criminal responsibility of the individuals under international law. Therefore, the rules of IHL are, at least 'indirectly', a source of ICL. There are, however, rules of IHL, such as those describing the so-called grave breaches of the GCs and AP I, that are 'substantively part of ICL—even if they are contained in treaties of IHL *latu sensu*' (see M. Sassòli, 'Humanitarian Law and International Criminal Law', in Cassese (ed), above n 2, 111, at 112).

[7] See generally R. Kolb, *Ius in Bello. Le droit international des conflits armés* (2nd edn, Basel/Brussels: Helbing Lichtenhahn/Bruylant, 2009), at 470–96. See also the relevant chapters in Part II, Section C of this volume.

[8] On the contribution of the case law of international criminal courts to the interpretation and development of the rules of IHL, see Sassòli, above n 6, at 114–17.

[9] See Art 50 GC I, Art 51 GC II, Art 130 GC III, and Art 147 GC IV.

[10] In this respect see again Sassòli, above n 6, at 114–17. See also S. Darcy, 'Bridging the Gaps in the Laws of Armed Conflict? International Criminal Law and the Development of Humanitarian Law', in N. Quénivet and S. Shah-Davis (eds), *International Law and Armed Conflict* (The Hague: T.M.C. Asser Press, 2010) 319.

6   The second outcome of this process of cross-fertilization is the clearly discernible trend toward the 'individualization' of the rules of IHL through the broadening of the scope of application of the rules of ICL in the matter of war crimes. By 'individualization', the present author means the process through which international rules formed to regulate the behaviour of states and other collective entities recognized as subjects of international law are applied directly to individuals. This process, which most likely started to develop over the last half century, also affects other areas of international law.[11] In the field of IHL, it prompted the adoption of arguably loose criteria for discerning whether a rule addressing the parties to the armed conflict has in fact been criminalized so as to give rise to the international responsibility of the individual who infringed the rule. In this regard, commentators have argued that both the ad hoc International Criminal Tribunal for the former Yugoslavia (ICTY) and the International Criminal Tribunal for Rwanda (ICTR) have tended to conflate illegality of conduct under IHL with its criminality under ICL.[12] As a corollary, the concern is that the two ad hoc Tribunals might have unreflectively transplanted concepts and jurisprudence from IHL rules, 'without awareness that they may be novel to criminal law and hence without scrutiny as to whether they comply with the fundamental principles peculiar to criminal law'.[13] Considering the impact that the ICTY and ICTR case law has had in the drafting of the criminal law provisions in the International Criminal Court (ICC) Statute, the concerns above extend, therefore, to the statutory rules that the ICC has to apply.

7   The 'individualization' of the rules of IHL through the development of ICL is remarkable, particularly with respect to the Geneva Conventions. The rules of the Geneva Conventions have formed the basis for the identification of illegal acts amounting to war crimes beyond those constituting grave breaches. In addition, the provisions of the Geneva Conventions have grounded the expansion of modes of criminal liability, in particular those on 'commission by omission' and 'command responsibility'. There is perhaps a 'structural' reason for this trend. More than other instruments of IHL, the Geneva Conventions (together with AP I) impinge upon a scheme based on 'humanization and individualization of inter-belligerent enforcement'.[14] The Geneva Conventions are the first IHL instruments expressly dealing with the criminal responsibility of breaches of the rules contained therein. In addition, they also ban reprisals against protected persons and property—a ban that is 'one of the great civilizing achievements of the laws of armed conflict since World War II'.[15] Arguably, however, the prohibition of reprisals as a means to enforce the rules of the Geneva Conventions has raised expectations in the system of criminal repressions of the breaches of the Conventions. The tendency in the rules and practice of ICL to individualize the provisions contained in

---

[11] See the remarks by A-M. Slaughter, 'Rogue Regimes and the Individualization of International Law', 36 *New England Law Review* (2002) 815.

[12] B. van Schaack, 'Crimen Sine Lege: Judicial Lawmaking at the Intersection of Law and Morals', 97 *Georgetown Law Journal* (2008) 119, at 149–55.

[13] D. Robinson, 'The Identity Crisis of International Criminal Law', 21 *LJIL* (2008) 925, at 946–55, esp at 946.

[14] See D. Jinks, 'Humanization and Individualization in the Enforcement of International Humanitarian Law', paper submitted at a Colloquium on *Virtues, Vices and Human Behavior and Democracy in International Law*, organized by the Institute for International Law and Justice of the NYU Law School in Spring 2009, available at <http://iilj.org/courses/documents/2009Colloquium.Session1.Jinks.pdf>, at 9.

[15] K. Anderson, 'The Rise of International Criminal Law: Intended and Unintended Consequences', 20 *EJIL* (2009) 331, at 340.

the Geneva Conventions, and more generally the rules of IHL, is perhaps a response to these great expectations.

As for the trend (especially in the ICTY case law) to rely upon the provisions of the Geneva Conventions to identify modes of criminal liability by omission, another 'structural' reason might be discerned. Criminal liability by omission, as we shall see below (MN 30), necessarily presupposes that the individual fails to discharge a legal duty to act. The Geneva Conventions, aimed as they are at the protection of the victims of war, are replete with provisions that establish on belligerents a duty to protect identified groups of people (the 'protected persons'). The Geneva Conventions thus offered to the ICL judge a golden opportunity to argue that, since belligerents cannot but act through individuals, the ultimate bearers of the duties of protection established by the Geneva Conventions are the individuals acting on behalf of the parties to the conflict. From here the step to assert and develop theories of criminal liability by omission was thus an easy (although not an uncontroversial) one. 8

This chapter will focus on the two aspects of the process of 'individualization' of the rules of the Geneva Conventions mentioned above. First, it will examine to what extent the rules of the Geneva Conventions may constitute, and in fact have constituted, the basis for the identification of war crimes other than the grave breaches of the Geneva Conventions (MN 10–24). Secondly, it will analyse the application of modes of criminal liability for omission grounded on the violations of pertinent rules of the Geneva Conventions (MN 25–32). This will lead to a discussion on the possible 'side effects' of the expansion of the enforcement of the Geneva Conventions through ICL (MN 33–40). 9

B. Violations of the Geneva Conventions other than Grave Breaches as War Crimes

As Theodor Meron aptly noted, the inclusion in the Geneva Conventions of provisions requiring the criminalization of acts constituting grave breaches had the disadvantage of 'the creation of a category of other breaches, involving the violation of all remaining provisions of the Conventions, which are arguably less categorically penal'.[16] This is, however, not tantamount to saying that other violations of the Geneva Conventions do not warrant criminal punishment. The Geneva Conventions themselves implicitly recognize this state of affairs, as they provide that the High Contracting Parties 'shall take measures necessary for the suppression of all acts contrary to the provisions of the [Conventions] other than grave breaches'.[17] The Pictet Commentary explains that although 'the wording is not very precise', 'there is no doubt that what is primarily meant is the *repression* of infractions other than "grave breaches"'.[18] However, similar to the Geneva Conventions' provisions on grave breaches, the obligation to suppress is incumbent upon the High Contracting Parties. This primarily means that, at least prima facie, the obligation to suppress all acts contrary to the Geneva Conventions requires the enactment of municipal legislation. Again, as in the case of grave breaches, the Geneva Conventions do not constitute per 10

---

[16] T. Meron, 'International Criminalization of Internal Atrocities', 89 *AJIL* (1995) 554, at 564.
[17] Art 49 para 3 GC I; Art 50 para 3 GC II; Art 129 para 3 GC III; Art 146 para 3 GC IV.
[18] Pictet Commentary GC I, at 367.

se the legal basis for the direct criminalization of those violations as war crimes under international law.

11   To establish whether a violation of the Geneva Conventions other than a grave breach is a war crime, one might refer to the definition of war crime set forth by the ICTY Appeals Chamber in *Tadić*, according to which,

> the conditions for criminal responsibility for war crimes are: i) the individual conduct constitutes a 'serious infringement' of a rule of IHL […] ii) the rule violated must have a customary international law origin or be provided in an applicable treaty; and iii) the violation must entail, under customary or conventional law, the individual criminal responsibility of the person breaching the rule.[19]

12   In accordance with this definition, the violation of a rule enshrined in the Geneva Conventions amounts to a war crime if it is 'serious' and is criminalized under international law. These two requirements will now be briefly discussed in turn.

I. The seriousness of the violation

13   In the words of the ICTY Appeals Chamber in *Tadić*, a violation of a rule of IHL is serious when: (i) the conduct violates a rule protecting important values, and (ii) the breach involves grave consequences for the victim.[20] The International Committee of the Red Cross (ICRC) adopts instead a different definition of seriousness. In an Explanatory Note on the issue, it contends that 'violations are serious, and are war crimes if they *endanger protected persons* (e.g. civilians, prisoners of war, the wounded and sick) or *objects* (e.g. civilian objects or infrastructure) or if they *breach important values*'.[21] While one of the two ICTY facets of seriousness (that linked to the importance of the value of the rule breached) is maintained, the other requires only that the violation *endangers* protected persons or objects, short of involving *grave consequences* for the victim. In addition, in the ICRC definition, a violation is serious if only one of the two facets is fulfilled, as evidenced by the use of the disjunctive formula. In the ICTY definition, the two facets of seriousness are instead cumulative, i.e. they must be both fulfilled.

14   Establishing which rules of the Geneva Conventions 'protect important values', and could therefore amount to a war crime if violated, may be not an easy undertaking. The ICRC, for instance, did not attempt to provide a yardstick, and confined itself to referring to cases of abuses of dead bodies or recruiting children under 15 years old into the armed forces as examples of violations of IHL rules protecting 'important universal values'.[22] Arguably, this facet of the seriousness requirement is satisfied in these and similar violations of the Geneva Conventions rules protecting the physical and mental integrity of

---

[19] See ICTY, *The Prosecutor v Duško Tadić*, Appeals Chamber Decision on Jurisdiction, IT-94-1-A, 2 October 1995, para 94.

[20] Ibid. The ICTY Appeals Chamber gave the following example of a non-serious violation: '[T]he fact of a combatant simply appropriating a loaf of bread in an occupied village' would not amount to such a breach, 'although it may be regarded as falling foul of the basic principle laid down in Article 46(1) of the [1907] Hague Regulations [on Land Warfare] (and the corresponding rule of customary international law) whereby "private property must be respected" by any army occupying an enemy territory'.

[21] ICRC, Explanatory Note, 'What Are "Serious Violations of International Humanitarian Law"?', available at <http://www.icrc.org/eng/assets/files/2012/att-what-are-serious-violations-of-ihl-icrc.pdf> (emphasis added).

[22] Ibid.

protected persons. However, in practice, the dividing line between rules of the Geneva Conventions that protect important values and those which do not might be difficult to draw.

The second facet of the seriousness requirement set forth by the ICTY, i.e. that the breach involves grave consequences for the victim, operates to exclude from the international law of war crimes trivial violations of rules of IHL, regardless of whether they protect 'important values'. The assessment here is necessarily made on a case-by-case basis. Thus, for instance, in *Delalić*, the ICTY considered that while the rule prohibiting unjustified appropriation of private or public property protects an important value, in the case at stake the actual violation did not involve grave consequences for the victims and therefore fell outside the jurisdiction *ratione materiae* of the Tribunal.[23]

Importantly, if one applies the ICTY definition of seriousness, this second facet implies that war crimes are *crimes of result*, i.e. crimes are committed when harmful consequences stem from the illegal conduct, and not *crimes of conduct*, which are punishable simply on account of the illegality of the behaviour. Thus, an attack from land on a hospital ship protected by Geneva Convention (GC) II, and prohibited, inter alia, under Article 20 GC I, would not constitute a war crime unless the ship were actually hit and casualties were caused (although those carrying out an attack that, for various reasons, does not hit the target may be responsible for an attempt to commit a war crime).[24]

Things are different if one refers to the ICRC definition, which considers that violations of rules of IHL are serious, and are war crimes, if *they endanger* protected persons (e.g. civilians, prisoners of war (POWs), the wounded and sick) or objects (e.g. civilian objects or infrastructure). Under this definition, war crimes may thus be committed simply by carrying out illegal conduct that puts in danger protected persons or objects, without necessarily causing them harm. Also, the fact that violations can be considered serious solely on account of the values protected by the rule breached warrants the conclusion that, for the ICRC, war crimes can be committed simply by carrying out the prohibited conduct.

Some of the war crimes listed in the ICC Statute as serious violations of the laws and customs applicable in international armed conflicts (IACs) (Article 8(2)(b)) and non-international armed conflicts (NIACs) (Article 8(2)(e)) are crimes of conduct. The notion of seriousness in the ICC Statute appears therefore to be in conformity with the ICRC definition. However, one cannot fail to notice that some of the war crimes defined in the ICC Statute in terms of crimes of conduct are at odds with the seemingly corresponding war crimes listed in the grave breaches provisions of AP I. For instance, in AP I, the war crime of attacking civilians and civilian objects is clearly a crime of result, since it

---

[23] ICTY, *The Prosecutor v Zejnil Delalić et al*, Trial Chamber Judgment, IT-96-21-T, 16 November 1998, para 1154.

[24] It is doubtful whether attempt to commit a war crime is proscribed by customary international law. For those who argue that this is the case, see A. Cassese, 'Black Letter Lawyering v Constructive Interpretation', 2 *JICJ* (2004) 265. See *contra* G. Mettraux, *International Crimes and the Ad Hoc Tribunals* (Oxford: OUP, 2005), at 293–5. The latter author points out that the charging policy of the Prosecution at the ICTY is 'an indication that attempted war crimes [...] might be beyond the Tribunal's jurisdiction' (at 294). The ICC Statute, however, contains a general provision on attempt (Art 25(3)(f)), which also applies to war crimes.

is required that the illegal conduct causes 'death or serious injury to body or health', while in the ICC Statute this war crime is described as a crime of conduct.[25]

II. The criminalization of the illegal conduct

19   Establishing whether conduct that violates rules of IHL is criminal under international law is likewise not an easy undertaking. According to Meron, various factors are relevant, namely, 'whether the prohibitory norm in question, which may be conventional or customary, is directed to individuals, whether the prohibition is unequivocal in character, the gravity of the act, and the interests of the international community'.[26] Nevertheless, he also points out that 'the legal criteria for judging criminality in this area are still far from clear'.[27]

20   A useful point of departure is whether criminal or military courts have in fact consistently adjudicated breaches of IHL as war crimes, or whether the statute of an international criminal tribunal having jurisdiction over war crimes includes the breach in the list of punishable offences. In addition, the usual elements taken into account to discern the existence of a rule of customary international law (CIL) will come into play. [28]

21   As for the criminalization of violations of the Geneva Conventions other than grave breaches, the ICTY has for instance asserted the existence of a war crime by referring to, inter alia, Article 27 GC IV (for the war crime of rape against persons protected by GC IV),[29] and Articles 49, 50, 51, and 52 GC III (for unlawful labour).[30] In some other cases, the ICTY has referred to a provision of the Geneva Conventions as an element to prove the criminalization of the violation of a rule of IHL or the customary nature of such a rule, as in the case of the war crime of terror against the civilian population[31] and of plunder.[32]

22   In the ICTY case law, however, Common Article 3 is the most emblematic example of a provision of the Geneva Conventions the violation of which, although not listed as a grave breach, was considered to give rise to individual criminal responsibility for war

---

[25] See P. Gaeta, 'Serious Violations of the Law on the Conduct of Hostilities: A Neglected Class of War Crimes?', in F. Pocar, M. Pedrazzi, and M. Frulli (eds), *War Crimes and the Conduct of Hostilities: Challenges to Adjudication and Investigation* (Cheltenham: Edward Elgar, 2013) 20, at 33–4.

[26] T. Meron, 'Is International Law Moving towards Criminalization?', 9 *EJIL* (1998) 18, at 24.

[27] Ibid.   [28] See on this point Cassese and Gaeta, above n 3, at 68.

[29] See, e.g., ICTY, *The Prosecutor v Anto Furundžija*, Trial Chamber Judgment, IT-95-17/1-T, 10 December 1998, paras 165–9, 175.

[30] See, e.g., ICTY, *The Prosecutor v Blagoje Simić et al*, Trial Chamber Judgment, IT-95-9-T, 17 October 2002, para 86; ICTY, *The Prosecutor v Mladen Naletilić and Vinko Martinović*, IT-98-34-T, 31 March 2003, para 250.

[31] See ICTY, *The Prosecutor v Stanislav Galić*, Trial Chamber Judgment, IT-98-29-T, 5 December 2003; confirmed by the Appeals Chamber. In the relevant discussion, the *Galić* Trial Chamber addressed the *Tadić* criteria on the existence of a war crime. With respect to the prohibited conduct, the Trial Chamber convicted the accused of acts of violence the primary purpose of which was to spread terror among the civilian population, a violation of the laws or customs of war as set forth in Art 51 AP I. With respect to the fourth *Tadić* condition, namely whether the prohibition against terrorizing the civilian population entails, under customary or conventional law, the individual criminal responsibility of the person breaching the rule, the Chamber also referred to Art 33 GC IV as evidence of the criminalization of the prohibition (Trial Chamber Judgment, paras 113–37, at para 119). By contrast, the Appeals Chamber referred to Art 33 GC IV as evidence of the customary nature of the prohibition also enshrined in Art 51 AP I and Art 13 AP II (Appeals Chamber Judgment, para 88).

[32] In *Delalić et al*, above n 23, the Trial Chamber determined that plunder is firmly established in CIL and relied, inter alia, on Art 15 GC I, Art 18 GC II and GC III, and Art 33 GC IV to ground this assertion (para 315, fn 329).

crimes.³³ The ICTY Appeals Chamber took this stand with its very first decision on the appeal brought by the defence of Duško Tadić concerning, amongst other things, the scope of the jurisdiction *ratione materiae* of the ICTY. The question in dispute was whether the accused could be held responsible for war crimes perpetrated in the context of an armed conflict of a non-international character (as at that time the conflict in Bosnia-Herzegovina was considered). The Appeals Chamber answered in the affirmative. It did so by adopting an extensive interpretation of Article 3 of the Statute of the ICTY, which confers on the Tribunal jurisdiction over 'persons violating the laws or customs of war' without referring to the international and non-international nature of the armed conflict where such violations occur. This opened the door to the assertion by the Appeals Chamber that there were rules of CIL governing NIACs and that Common Article 3 (*rectius*: the rule of CIL originated by Common Article 3) was one of them; and to the assertion that under CIL serious violations of Common Article 3 gave rise to individual criminal responsibility for war crimes, including in NIACs. This was a revolutionary stand, since at that time (the beginning of the 1990s) the traditional wisdom was that individual criminal responsibility for war crimes was a matter 'confined' to war proper, namely, IACs. As the late Antonio Cassese (who participated, as President of the ICTY and of the Appeals Chamber, in the drafting of the decision) put it, it seemed 'crazy' to 'stick to the traditional concept that war crimes can only be committed in international armed conflict [...] A rape is a rape; a murder is a murder, whether it is committed within the framework of an international armed conflict [...] or a civil war.'³⁴ As aptly noted by a commentator, regardless of whether the ICTY Appeals Chamber was right that at the time of the commission of the acts attributed to the accused, serious violations of Common Article 3 (and the corresponding rule of CIL) could entail criminal responsibility for war crimes in NIACs, 'the subsequent evolution proved [Cassese] right'³⁵ (and the ICTY Appeals Chamber with him). In fact the ICTY's 1995 decision in *Tadić* authoritatively contributed to the recognition that serious violations of the rules of IHL applicable to NIACs give rise to individual criminal responsibility for war crimes (see Chapter 20 of this volume, section D), and undoubtedly constitutes a landmark decision in the field of IHL and the international law of war crimes.

The list of war crimes in Article 8 of the ICC Statute also includes violations of the Geneva Conventions other than grave breaches. In particular, this list includes the war crime of '[i]ntentionally directing attacks against buildings, material, medical units and transport, and personnel using the distinctive emblems of the Geneva Conventions in conformity with international law' (Article 8(2)(b)(xxiv)), which is based on corresponding prohibitions in the Geneva Conventions and other relevant IHL instruments.³⁶ Similarly,

---

³³ See ICTY, *Tadić*, above n 19, para 134.
³⁴ See J. Weiler, 'Nino In His Own Words', 22 *EJIL* (2001) 931, at 942.
³⁵ J-M Henckaerts, 'Civil War, Custom and Cassese', 10 *JICJ* (2012) 1095, at 1101.
³⁶ See ICRC, Advisory Service, War Crimes under the Rome Statute of the International Criminal Court and their source in International Humanitarian Law. Comparative Table, available at <http://www.icrc.org/eng/assets/files/other/en_-_war_crimes_comparative_table.pdf>. For this war crime, the table refers to the following provisions of the GCs: (i) for military and civilian medical units, including medical and religious personnel, Arts 19 para 1 and 24 GC I, Arts 23 and 36 GC II; (ii) for hospital ships, Art 20 GC I and Arts 22 para 1, 24 para 1, and 27 para 1 GC II; (iii) for medical transports, Art 35 para 1 GC I and Art 21 GC IV; (iv) for medical aircraft, Art 36 para 1 GC I and Art 22 paras 1 and 2 GC IV; (v) for civilian hospitals, Art 18 paras 1 and 3 GC IV; and (vi) for persons regularly and solely engaged in the operation and administration of civilian hospitals, Art 20 paras 1–2 GC IV.

the list contains the war crime of '[i]ntentionally using starvation of civilians as a method of warfare by depriving them of objects indispensable to their survival, including wilfully impeding relief supplies as provided for under the Geneva Conventions' (Article 8(2)(b) (xxv)), which is also based on provisions enshrined in the Geneva Conventions.[37] Acts amounting to serious violations of Common Article 3 of the Geneva Conventions are also included in the list (Article 8(2)(c)).

24   Theoretically, it is possible that in its findings on the criminal nature of some of the violations of the Geneva Conventions, the ICTY has 'created' new crimes. Indeed, a commentator has argued that in establishing the international criminalization of rules of IHL, the ICTY has embarked upon 'judicial creativity' and exercised a quasi-legislative function.[38] In addition, the inclusion of an offence in the list of war crimes of the ICC Statute does not per se guarantee that an act is actually a war crime under CIL.[39] At the same time, it is also theoretically possible that violations of other rules of the Geneva Conventions in addition to those mentioned above are criminal under international law. The point is that the criminalization of an illegal conduct under international law—if not directly provided for in a treaty[40]—must perforce be established by a rule of CIL. Given the specificities of this process of formation of international rules, [41] uncertainties therefore abound.[42]

C. The Geneva Conventions and Modes of Criminal Liability by Omission

25   As is well known, the illegal conduct constituting a criminal offence may consist of either an action or an omission. This may also be the case for international crimes, including war

---

[37] Ibid. For this war crime, the table refers, inter alia, to the following provisions: Arts 23 para 1, 55 para 1, and 59 para 1 GC IV.

[38] D. Mundis, 'The Legal Character and Status of the Rules of Procedure and Evidence of the ad hoc International Criminal Tribunals', 1 *International Criminal Law Review* (2001) 191.

[39] Art 10 ICC Statute states expressly that nothing in Part 1, which contains, amongst others, the provisions on the jurisdiction *ratione materiae* of the ICC, 'shall be interpreted as limiting or prejudicing in any way existing or developing rules of international law for purposes other than this Statute'. However, it has been contended that when the list of crimes to be submitted to the jurisdiction of the ICC was negotiated, the general understanding was that these had to reflect existing CIL. See J.M. Henckaerts, 'The Grave Breaches Regime as Customary International Law', 7 *JICJ* (2009) 683, at 691, also for the necessary reference.

[40] At the same time, a criminal offence which is only treaty-based (i.e., does not reflect CIL) raises the issue of its applicability vis-à-vis individuals who are not nationals of a state party and perform the conduct in the territory of a non-state party. This question is different from the one concerning the applicability of treaty-based universal criminal jurisdiction over nationals of non-party states. For a discussion of this issue, see M. Scharf, 'Application of Treaty-based Universal Jurisdiction to Nationals of Non-Party States', 35 *New England Law Review* (2001) 363. The question of the applicability of the provisions on universal criminal jurisdiction enshrined in the UN Torture Convention over nationals of non-party states was brought, amongst other things, by the Republic of the Congo against France in the case of *Certain Criminal Proceedings in France (Republic of the Congo v France)*. On 17 November 2010, the case was, however, removed from the Court's list at the request of the parties.

[41] The formation of international rules through custom is considered as 'the most difficult of all problems of international law' in G. Tunkin, 'Coexistence and International Law', 95 *RCADI* (1958) 9; even as a 'theoretical mine field' by M. Koskenniemi, 'The Pull of the Mainstream (reviewing Human Rights and Humanitarian Norms as Customary Law by Theodor Meron)', 88 *Mich LR* (1990) 1946, at 1947.

[42] On the difficult undertaking of the identification of rules of CIL in criminal matters, see Cassese and Gaeta, above n 3, at 13–14.

crimes. For instance, while 'taking of hostages' is a war crime that usually implies that an illegal action is accomplished, the *actus reus* of other war crimes may consist of the failure to take a required action, such as for the war crime of wilfully depriving a POW or other protected person of the rights of a fair and regular trial.[43]

When the *actus reus* of a criminal offence consists of the failure to take an action, one speaks of the crime of omission 'proper', or of 'genuine omission'. Crimes of omissions 'proper' must be distinguished from omission liability or 'indirect omission', which is a mode of criminal liability. The latter provides that a crime may also be committed by refraining from doing something, i.e. committing homicide by failing to prevent a person from drowning. In this hypothesis, one speaks of 'improper crimes of omission', or 'commission by omission'.[44] In most domestic criminal systems, criminal liability by omission is considered implicit in criminal prohibitions, unless the latter are formulated in a manner that unequivocally requires action by the perpetrator.[45]

In the post-Second World War case law, one finds examples of war crimes trials based upon commission by omission.[46] For instance, cases have been heard concerning ill-treatment of POWs through omission to provide medical care to a wounded member of the enemy armed forces[47] or to POWs;[48] killing by failure to care actively for children who were forcibly separated from their mothers;[49] omission to provide POWs with sufficient food, clothing, and medical care, which resulted in the death of some of the prisoners;[50] failure to prevent bodily and mental harm to POWs;[51] failure to undertake a rescue operation for shipwrecked civilians;[52] and so on.[53]

In addition, the ICTY and ICTR have held that this mode of liability is encompassed (although not expressly) in their respective Statutes (i.e. Article 7(1) and Article 6(1), respectively).[54] The ICTY has thus considered that 'inhuman treatment' as a grave breach

---

[43] See Art 130 GC III and Art 147 GC IV. See also Art 85(4) AP I. The denial of the right to a fair trial is listed as a war crime in the ICC Statute (Art 8(2)(a)(vi) and (c)(iv)); the ICTY Statute (Art 2(f)); the ICTR Statute (Art 4(g)); the SCSL Statute (Art 3(g)).

[44] See M. Duttwiler, 'Liability for Omission in International Criminal Law', in 6 *International Criminal Law Review* (2006) 1, at 4, also for additional reference.

[45] See E. van Sliedregt, *Individual Criminal Responsibility in International Law* (Oxford: OUP, 2012), at 54.

[46] For a review of these cases, see Duttwiler, above n 44, at 17–26.

[47] See *Alois Grisl*, tried on 24–6 June 1946 before a US Military Court in Salzburg. The accused was found guilty of having participated in the denial of proper medical attention to a wounded American airman. Review of Proceedings of a Military Commission in the case of the United States versus Alois Grisl, case 5-88, 24 February 1947, scanned pdf version available at <http://www.jewishvirtuallibrary.org/jsource/Holocaust/dachautrial/fs4.pdf>. See also Duttwiler, above n 44, at 17.

[48] See *Killinger and others (Dulag Luft Case)*, British Military Court, Wupperthal, 3 December 1945, UNWCC Law Reports, vol III, at 67. The refusal to provide satisfactory medical attention was among the forms of ill-treatment of the POWs in the charge against the accused. See also *Hiroshi Fujii*, United States Military Commission at Yokohama, mentioned by Duttwiler, above n 44, at 19.

[49] *Heinrich Gerike and seven others (The Velpke Children's Home Trial)*, British Military Court, Brunswick, 20 March–3 April 1946, UNWCC Law Reports, vol VII, at 76. The accused were charged with killing by wilful neglect a number of children in the Children's Home erected to house a number of Polish infants in Germany.

[50] See, e.g., *Sone Kenitji*, Netherlands East Indies, Temporary Court Martial, Batavia, 14 August 1946, 13 *International Law Reports* (1994) 299.

[51] See *Eric Heyer and six others (Essen Lynching* case), British Military Court, Essen, 22 December 1945, UNWCC Law Reports, vol I, at 88.

[52] *Helmuth von Ruchteschell*, British Military Court, Hamburg, 21 May 1947, UNWCC Law Reports, vol IX, at 82.

[53] See Duttwiler, above n 44. See also Cassese and Gaeta, above n 3, at 180, fn 2.

[54] ICTY, *The Prosecutor v Duško Tadić*, Appeals Chamber Judgment, IT-94-1-A, 15 July 1999, para 188.

of the Geneva Conventions and 'cruel treatment' (as a serious violation of Common Article 3) could be committed both by action and omission.[55] The ICC has also recognized that criminal liability for some crimes listed in Article 8 of the ICC Statute may arise out of an omission,[56] although the ICC Statute does not expressly make reference to a general mode of omission liability.[57]

29   The ICTY and ICTR have further held that failure to act may constitute the *actus reus* of participation in a joint criminal enterprise or other modes of criminal liability, such as aiding and abetting or instigation.[58] By contrast, ordering or planning seems necessarily to require a positive act by the perpetrator, thereby excluding criminal liability by omission.[59]

30   Controversy exists over whether criminal liability in the form of commission by omission is recognized by a rule of customary international criminal law.[60] There is general agreement, however, that criminal liability by omission necessarily requires that the individual fails to discharge a legal duty to act. For ICTY and ICTR, in the matter of war crimes the duty to act must be a legal duty,[61] and its source is (amongst others) the laws and customs of war.[62] The two ad hoc Tribunals have thus opened the way to a further

---

[55] ICTY, *Delalić et al*, above n 23, paras 543 and 552; ICTY, *The Prosecutor v Tihomir Blaškić*, Trial Chamber Judgment, IT-95-14-T, 3 March 2000, paras 154 and 186.

[56] See, e.g., ICC, *Katanga and Chui (Confirmation Decision)*, Pre-Trial Chamber, ICC-01/04-01/07, 30 September 2008, concerning the war crime of wilful killing under Art 8(2)(a)(i) (para 287); destruction of enemy's property under Art 8(2)(b)(xiii) (paras 310 and 315); inhuman treatment under Art 8(2)(a)(ii) (para 357); and committing outrages upon personal dignity, in particular humiliating and degrading treatment under Art 8(2)(b)(xxi) (paras 368–9).

[57] On the attempt to include a general definition on omission liability in the ICC Statute, see van Sliedregt, above n 45, at 55–7.

[58] See Cassese and Gaeta, above n 3, at 181–2, also for the necessary reference to the case law of the ICTY and the ICTR.

[59] Ibid.

[60] See L.C. Berster, '"Duty to Act" and "Commission by Omission" in International Criminal Law', 10 *International Criminal Law Review* (2010) 619, also for further reference (at 620, fnn 4 and 5).

[61] For the ICTY, see *The Prosecutor v Naser Orić*, Appeals Chamber Judgment, IT-03-68-A, 3 July 2008, para 43; *The Prosecutor v Radoslav Brđanin*, Appeals Chamber Judgment, IT-99-36-A, 3 April 2007, para 274; *The Prosecutor v Stanislav Galić*, Appeals Chamber Judgment, IT-98-29-A, 30 November 2006, para 175; *The Prosecutor v Blagoje Simić et al*, Appeals Chamber Judgment, IT-95-9-A, 28 November 2006, para 188; *The Prosecutor v Tihomir Blaškić*, Appeals Chamber Judgment, IT-95-14-A, 29 July 2004, paras 47–8 and 663; *Tadić*, above n 54, para 188. For the ICTR, see *The Prosecutor v André Ntagerura et al*, Appeals Chamber Judgment, ICTR-99-46-A, 7 July 2006, paras 334 and 370. In domestic criminal systems, the duty to act is not necessarily established by law, but can also result from contract, balance of power, agency or previous conduct (see van Sliedregt, above n 45, at 55). In English law, aiding and abetting by omission can stem from the failure to exercise the duty of supervision or control (ibid, at 117–18). The duty to act may also be the result of the duty to act in light of previous behaviour (ibid, at 118).

[62] See, e.g., ICTY, *The Prosecutor v Blaškić*, above n 61, para 663, fn 1384. See also ICTY, *The Prosecutor v Mile Mrkšić and Veselin Šljivančanin*, Appeals Chamber Judgment, IT-95-13/1-A, 5 May 2009, para 151. There is, however, uncertainty as to whether IHL is the source of the legal duty to act. According to the Appeals Chamber in *Tadić*, the duty to act must be 'mandated by a rule of criminal law' (para 188). This assertion was reaffirmed in subsequent case law of the ICTY, such as *The Prosecutor v Milorad Krnojelac*, Appeals Chamber Judgment, IT-97-25-A, 17 September 2003, para 188. Before the ICTY Appeals Chamber, defendant Šljivančanin challenged the Trial Chamber's decision to rely upon the rules of the GCs to identify the legal duty to act, arguing that it contradicted the Appeals Chamber's previous case law. However, the Appeals Chamber did not really address the issue and confined itself to stating that 'it [had] previously recognized that the breach of a duty to act imposed by the laws and customs of war gives rise to individual criminal responsibility'; but, in this respect, it just quoted the *Blaškić* Appeal Judgment (above

interplay between the Geneva Conventions and ICL. Regardless of the fact that the provisions of the Geneva Conventions are only binding upon the High Contracting Parties *qua* treaty law (and eventually, as far as Common Article 3 is concerned, the non-state actor groups in the context of NIACs: see Chapter 20 of this volume), they have relied upon these provisions to identify the legal duty that the accused was alleged to have failed to fulfil. For instance, in *Mrkšić and Šljivančanin*, the Appeals Chamber of the ICTY found that the accused Šljivančanin was duty bound to protect the POWs under Article 13 GC III, and that the violation of this duty had given rise to his individual criminal liability for aiding and abetting, by omission, the killing of the POWs.[63] The ICTR has even been explicit in this respect, and has stated that since a state exercises its international obligations through its organs, the latter are therefore under a legal duty to ensure that these obligations are complied with.[64]

Arguably, the conflation between the requirements set forth in rules of IHL addressing High Contracting Parties and/or parties to an armed conflict and individual criminal liability has occurred also in relation to so-called 'command responsibility'.[65] Regardless of whether command responsibility is in all instances a mode of criminal liability by omission, or what might better be described in some scenarios as a crime of omission per se,[66] it seems uncontroversial that it presupposes a pre-existing duty on the commander that he fails to discharge. In ICL instruments, this duty seems to be a formal legal duty to take all the necessary and reasonable measures to prevent the crimes that the subordinates are about to commit, and to punish them in case of commission.[67] In addition, the case law of the ICTY and ICTR has treated this duty

n 61, para 663, fn 1384). The Trial Chambers of the ICTY and ICTR have also referred to other potential sources of the duty to act, such as domestic laws, the position of the authority eventually held, or antecedent conduct. See also, for reference to the case law, Berster, above n 60, at 621–3. For reference to the scholarly debate, ibid, at 624–5.

[63] ICTY, *Mrkšić and Šljivančanin*, Appeals Chamber Judgment, above n 62, para 151. According to the Appeals Chamber, Arts 5, 12, and 13 GC III imposed on the accused Šljivančanin an 'ongoing duty to protect the prisoners of war' in the matter of treatment and transfer of POWs, since the accused was an agent of the Detaining Power (paras 71–2). In the opinion of the Appeals Chamber, the duty of the accused under IHL encompassed the obligation to treat POWs humanely, and not to transfer of custody of the POWs to anyone without being first assured that they would not be harmed (para 74).

[64] In *The Prosecutor v Vincent Rutaganira*, Trial Chamber Judgment, ICTR-95-1-C-T, 14 March 2005, a Trial Chamber of the ICTR held, '*ad abundantiam*', that 'international law also places upon a person vested with public authority a duty to act in order to protect human life. Indeed, the State to which it falls to carry out international obligations, can only act through all its representatives, be they in the upper reaches or at lower levels of Government. The State itself can fulfil its international obligations and not incur any responsibility not only because of its representatives' respect for human rights, but also by reason of actions taken, in the performance of their duties, to prevent any violation of the said rights'. In the opinion of the Trial Chamber, 'as any person, all public authorities have a duty not only to comply with the basic rights of the human person, but also to ensure that these are complied with, which implies a duty to act in order to prevent any violation of such rights' (paras 78–9).

[65] See generally B. Bonafé, 'Finding a Proper Role for Command Responsibility', 5 *JICJ* (2007) 599. See also the seminal study of M. Damaška, 'The Shadow Side of Command Responsibility', 49 *American Journal of Comparative Law* (2001) 455.

[66] See Bonafé, above n 65; see also Cassese and Gaeta, above n 3, at 191–2.

[67] See S. Sivakumaran, 'Command Responsibility in Irregular Troops', 10 *JICJ* (2012) 1129, at 1131, also for reference to international case law. Less clear is the source of this legal duty, an issue which is usually not discussed by commentators or in case law. According to Sivakumaran, this legal duty is inherent in the principle of responsible command (which applies equally to military commanders of state and non-state armed forces). Consequently, the same commentators consider that Arts 86(2) and 87 AP I (which are the pertinent rules of IHL on the responsibility and duties of commanders) merely establish the conventional framework for such a duty. Ibid, at 1131–37.

as giving rise to two separate legal obligations on the commanders,[68] which raised the issue of whether the duty to punish also applies to commanders who learn of the crimes only after their commission.[69]

32 However, this certainly has no express basis in the rules of IHL on command responsibility. As Darryl Robinson has aptly noted, Article 86(2) AP I clearly refers to the potential disciplinary or penal responsibility of commanders with respect to *ongoing or imminent* breaches of the Geneva Conventions or the Protocols by the subordinates, if they fail to 'take all the feasible measures' to prevent or repress the breaches.[70] On the other hand, Article 87 AP I imposes on the 'High Contracting Parties and the Parties to the conflict' the requirement, as a matter of humanitarian law, that commanders exercise the general (procedural) duty to prevent and, where appropriate, to repress violations of the Geneva Conventions or the Protocol. According to Robinson, these two provisions clearly reflect the structural differences between criminal law and humanitarian law. Article 87 AP I intends

> to promote compliance of subordinates with humanitarian law by requiring [from the High Contracting Parties or the Parties to the conflict] a system of prevention and repression. If a commander fails to punish past crimes, his government may be held liable for his breach of the rule. However, this is not the same as asserting that the commander is personally guilty of the subordinate's crime […][71]

The expansion in ICL of the scope of application of the rules of IHL on the responsibility and duties of military commanders constitutes therefore another instance of the tendency in ICL to assume 'the coextensiveness of the humanitarian law norm and the criminal law norm, without reflecting on the different structures and consequences and hence the different principles in play'.[72]

D. Critical Assessment

33 The trend towards the 'individualization' through criminal law of the rules of the Geneva Conventions sketched above presents remarkable advantages. The most evident is that ICL reveals to public opinion and the people of the parties to an armed conflict that responsibility for the horrendous crimes committed in conflict ultimately rests with individual offenders. Shifting the focus onto the individuals may thus have a cathartic or healing effect: it helps the victims of the atrocities committed in wartime to understand that 'the enemy' as an abstract and collective entity did not commit them. The additional seeds of hatred against the enemy group or nation that the notion of 'collective' guilt may

---

[68] See, e.g., ICTY, *Blaškić*, above n 61, para 83; ICTY, *The Prosecutor v Enver Hadžihasanović and Amir Kabura*, Appeals Chamber Judgment, IT-01-47-A, 22 April 2008, para 260.

[69] This is the so-called issue of the 'successor commander', which has been highly controversial at the ICTY: see, in particular, ICTY, *The Prosecutor v Enver Hadžihasanović et al*, Appeals Chamber Decision on Interlocutory Appeal Challenging Jurisdiction in Relation to Command Responsibility, IT-01-47-AR72, 16 July 2003. The applicability of the doctrine of command responsibility to the successor commander seems not to exist at the ICC. The ICC Statute provides that the criminal responsibility for failure to prevent and punish arises only when the superior has actual or constructive knowledge of the crimes of the subordinate before or during their commission (Art 28 ICC Statute). On the issue, see generally Cassese and Gaeta, above n 3, at 191–2.

[70] Robinson, above n 13, at 953–4.   [71] Ibid, at 954.   [72] Ibid.

plant may thus have no reason to grow. This in turn may facilitate reconciliation and longer-lasting peace among the groups or nations once at war.⁷³

In addition, holding criminally accountable those who violate IHL helps to restore confidence in the rule of law. As Röling noted, '[t]he legal order is the positive inner relation of the people to the recognized values of the community, which relation is disturbed by the commission of the crimes'.⁷⁴ Naturally, therefore, '[i]f crimes are not punished, the confidence in the validity of the values of the community is undermined and shaken'.⁷⁵ 34

One might consider that making individual offenders responsible before a court of law for violations of the rules of IHL they have committed is a more 'just' means of enforcement than resorting to reprisals. Only the alleged culprit will suffer the negative consequences of his illegal behaviour (while in the case of reprisals, and in most cases of collective sanctions, the entire group to which the individual offender belongs will be affected). The individualization of the rules of IHL through criminal law is therefore more consonant with the notion of 'responsibility' developed in modern domestic legal systems, which is a notion of 'individual' rather than 'collective' responsibility. In this sense, since arguably collective responsibility is typical of rudimentary legal systems, ICL contributes to the sophistication of the international legal system in line with the developments in national legal orders.⁷⁶ 35

The individualization of the rules of IHL through criminal law is not short of flaws. Leaving aside the concerns that have arisen from the point of view of ensuring respect for the principle of legality in criminal matters,⁷⁷ commentators have already identified some prominent shortcomings.⁷⁸ Above all, there is the risk that this process reduces attention to the rules of IHL that have no criminal law dimension at all. A great part of the rules of IHL (including those of the Geneva Conventions) covers issues violations of which are certainly not susceptible to nor warrant a criminal sanction. In this respect, one might think of rules contained in GC III devoted to POW camps. These rules are certainly important for the organization of the camps and the everyday life of POWs, but it is hard to discern from them any content that might potentially be a matter of concern for criminal law.⁷⁹ 36

The reduced attention to the non-criminal or non-criminalizable rules of IHL risks in turn generating the belief in public opinion, and even among international humanitarian lawyers, that 'all behaviour in armed conflict is either a war crime or lawful'.⁸⁰ The potential risk is that the criminal law of war swallows the rest of the laws of war, carrying with it the loss of the idea that compliance with IHL is not really about individual liability but 37

---

⁷³ See, e.g., Sassòli, above n 6, who underlines that when 'responsibility was attributed to states and nations or groups (and guilt was collectivized), each violation carried the seeds of the next war and its concomitant atrocities', and '[t]herein lies the civilizing and peace-seeking mission of ICL' (at 113).

⁷⁴ B.V.A. Röling, 'Criminal Responsibility for Violations of the Laws of War', 12 *revue belge de droit international* (1976) 8, at 22.

⁷⁵ Ibid.

⁷⁶ See on this point A. Cassese, *International Law* (2nd edn, Oxford: OUP, 2005), at 6–9.

⁷⁷ See MN 6. See also, e.g., J. Powderly, 'Judicial Interpretation at the Ad Hoc Tribunals: Method from Chaos?', in S. Darcy and J. Powderly, *Judicial Creativity at the International Criminal Tribunals* (Oxford: OUP, 2010) 17; A.M. Danner, 'When Courts Make Law: How the International Criminal Tribunals Recast the Law of War', 59 *Vanderbilt Law Review* (2006) 1.

⁷⁸ See in particular Sassòli, above n 6, at 117–19; and Anderson, above n 15, esp at 340–53.

⁷⁹ Anderson, above n 15, at 347.   ⁸⁰ Sassòli, above n 6, at 118

rather about the legitimacy built around shared values and rules for 'the social organization of conflict'.[81]

38   Lastly, one has to consider that criminal punishment of violations of the rules of IHL, although it may increase the perception of the effectiveness of this body of law and produce some deterrent effect, is often confined to dispensing post-conflict justice. Investigations and prosecutions during the armed conflict may face hurdles, in terms of collection of evidence, that might discourage even the most willing and able prosecutors. This is true also for international criminal courts, which might have to face the additional hurdle of uncooperative states or armed groups. It is therefore not surprising that the successful stories of repression of international crimes by international courts mainly concern those that took place when the armed conflict was over or that were achieved through foreign military intervention. Moreover, insistence on criminal justice might lead to undermining the importance of preventative means to achieve adherence to IHL rules.[82] It might even have led to increasing the reluctance of states to activate existing non-judicial procedures to establish violations of the rules of IHL, such as the International Fact-Finding Commission.[83]

39   Ultimately, one should not underestimate the importance of what might appear, from the point of view of ICL, an old-fashioned concept: that of the international responsibility of states. The Geneva Conventions themselves insist in a common provision that the High Contracting Parties are not allowed to absolve themselves of any liability incurred in respect of violations of the Geneva Conventions.[84] Although this common provision refers expressly to the grave breaches of the Geneva Conventions, it enshrines a principle—better enunciated in Article 3 of the Fourth Hague Convention and Article 91 AP I—that a High Contracting Party is responsible for the violations of the rules of IHL that are attributable to it. This responsibility remains even in cases where the individual authors have been punished. In practice, this means that breaches of the Geneva Conventions and of IHL in general may give rise to a dual responsibility under international law: of the High Contracting Party under the rules of international responsibility of states; and of the individual offenders under ICL.[85]

40   However, the potential responsibility of a High Contracting Party under the Geneva Conventions is wider than the international criminal responsibility of individuals. Indeed, it could arise from violations of *any* of the rules enshrined in the Geneva Conventions, not only those that are criminalized under international law. This in turn means that the state party to the Geneva Conventions is liable to provide for reparation, which includes financial compensation, for the damage caused by any violation of the Geneva Conventions or IHL in general. Traditionally, this has been interpreted as allowing only inter-state claims under international law, thus excluding the entitlement of individual victims to claim reparation vis-à-vis the responsible state.[86] This traditional interpretation is controversial, and individual victims have challenged it in a string of cases before domestic courts, with

---

[81] Anderson, above n 15, at 346–9.   [82] In this sense, see Sassòli, above n 6, at 117.
[83] Ibid.   [84] Art 49 para 3 GC I; Art 50 para 3 GC II; Art 129 para 3 GC III; Art 146 para 3 GC IV.
[85] See generally on this issue B. Bonafé, *The Relationship between State Responsibility and Individual Responsibility for International Crimes* (Leiden/Boston, Mass: Martinus Nijhoff, 2009).
[86] See N. Ronzitti, 'Compensation for Violations of the Law of War and Individual Claims', 12 *Italian Yearbook of International Law* (2002) 39.

contradictory outcomes.⁸⁷ The matter is thus far from being settled. Arguably, however, the recognition under international law of an individual claim to compensation for a violation of the rules of IHL would conform with the significant 'humanization' of the laws of war achieved since the adoption of the Geneva Conventions, and the pervasive effect that IHRL is playing while evolving in the same direction.⁸⁸

PAOLA GAETA

---

⁸⁷ See also, for the necessary reference to case law, C. Tomuschat, 'State Responsibility and the Individual Right to Compensation before National Courts', in A. Clapham and P. Gaeta (eds), *The Oxford Handbook of International Law in Armed Conflict* (Oxford: OUP, 2014) 811.

⁸⁸ See in this regard P. Gaeta, 'Are Victims of Serious Violations of International Humanitarian Law Entitled to Compensation?', in O. Ben-Naftali (ed), *International Humanitarian Law and International Human Rights Law* (Oxford: OUP, 2011) 305–27. See also, as regards the rules of IHL on the conduct of hostilities, G. Pinzauti, 'Good Time for a Change? Recognizing Individuals' Rights under the Rules of International Humanitarian Law on the Conduct of Hostilities', in A. Cassese (ed), *Realizing Utopia. The Future of International Law* (Oxford: OUP, 2012) 571. It should be noted that the Advisory Opinion of the ICJ in *Legal Consequences of the Construction of a Wall in the Occupied Palestinian Territory* seems to support the view that individual victims of violations of rules of IHL are entitled to reparation from the responsible state. The Court held that Israel was obliged 'to make reparation for all damage caused by the construction of the wall in the Occupied Palestinian Territory, including in and around East Jerusalem' (Advisory Opinion, 9 July 2004, para 163, 3, C, of the operative part) as a result of the violation of international law established by the Court. In its reasoning, the Court identified the beneficiaries of the obligation, namely, 'all the natural or legal persons concerned' (ibid, para 152). Admittedly, the Court did not identify which rules of international law entailed violations that led to the obligation to repair. The failure by the Court to clarify this point, however, might be interpreted as an indication that the issue was for the Court irrelevant, namely, that the obligation to repair followed naturally from the illegality of the Israeli conduct under the relevant rules of international law, including those on military occupation. See *amplius* P. D'Argent, 'Compliance, Cessation, Reparation and Restitution in the Wall Advisory Opinion', in P.-M. Dupuy et al (eds), *Völkerrecht als Wertordnung—Common Values in International Law, Festschrift für/ Essays in Honour of Christian Tomuschat* (Kehl: N.P. Engel Verlag, 2006) 463.

PART II

SPECIFIC ISSUES AND REGIMES

—

A. GENEVA CONVENTIONS I AND II

Chapter 37. Who Is Wounded and Sick?

	MN
A. Introduction	1
I. Establishment of the core protections	1
II. The progressive evolution of the protection of the wounded and sick	8
B. Meaning and Application	10
I. The protection of the wounded and sick members of the armed forces	10
II. The protection of wounded and sick civilians	17
III. The issue of rape	20
IV. The definition of the wounded and sick in Additional Protocol I	27
C. Relevance in Non-International Armed Conflicts	29
D. Critical Assessment	32

Select Bibliography

Bothe, M./Janssen, K., 'Issues in the Protection of the Wounded and Sick', 26 *IRRC* 253 (1986) 189
Dunant, H., *A Memory of Solferino* (Geneva: ICRC, 1986)
Kleffner, J.K., 'Protection of the Wounded, Sick, and Shipwrecked', in D. Fleck (ed), *The Handbook of International Humanitarian Law* (2nd edn, Oxford: OUP, 2008) 325
Sassòli/Bouvier/Quintin, at 195–7
Solf, W., 'Development of the Protection of the Wounded, Sick and Shipwrecked under the Protocols Additional to the 1949 Geneva Conventions', in Mélanges Pictet 237

A. Introduction

I. Establishment of the core protections

It is difficult to imagine how an ordinary businessman felt, witnessing the carnage that took place in what is now northern Italy on 24 June 1859, save for the powerful words that this man wrote after the battle:

> When the sun came up on the twenty-fifth, it disclosed the most dreadful sights imaginable. Bodies of men and horses covered the battlefield; corpses were strewn over roads, ditches, ravines, thickets and fields; the approaches of Solferino were literally thick with dead.[1]

The battle of Solferino is said to have been the deadliest battle to have taken place in nineteenth-century Europe since the battle of Waterloo on 18 June 1815. Six thousand dead and 40,000 wounded from the Austrian, Sardinian, and French armies were strewn across the open battlefield.[2] Dunant recalls that 'men of all nations lay side by side on the flagstone floors of the churches of Castiglione—Frenchmen and Arabs, German

---

[1] H. Dunant, *A Memory of Solferino* (Geneva: ICRC, 1986) (1862), at 41, available at <https://www.icrc.org/eng/assets/files/publications/icrc-002-0361.pdf>.
[2] The Battle of Solferino (24 June 1859), ICRC Resource Centre, available at <http://www.icrc.org/eng/resources/documents/misc/57jnvr.htm>.

and Slavs'.³ Faced with the mass of wounded soldiers, it did not matter to him to which army they belonged, nor which army doctors were to care for them. In fact, according to Dunant, 'three Austrian doctors came to help a young Corsican military surgeon',⁴ and 'a German surgeon, who had deliberately remained on the battlefield to bandage his compatriots, devoted himself to the wounded of both armies'.⁵

3   It took this horrific historical event and the trauma it entailed for Henry Dunant to ensure that basic principles of human ethics and morality be finally laid down in positive law, according to which, '[w]ounded or sick combatants, to whatever nation they may belong, shall be collected and cared for.'⁶ To that effect, the inviolability of ambulances and medical personnel who brought help to the wounded and sick had to be established, notably through the creation of an emblem (a red cross on a white background) that would recall their neutrality in the conflict and protect their humanitarian role.⁷

4   The legal protection of the wounded and sick in armed conflict situations is certainly at the core of modern international humanitarian law (IHL). In fact, and quite symbolically, the Geneva Conventions of 1864, 1904, and 1929, as well as the first two Geneva Conventions of 1949, focus precisely on this category of persons who suffer most directly from the consequences of war.

5   'Who is wounded and sick',⁸ or in other words who are the beneficiaries of the legal protection afforded by the 1949 Geneva Conventions and their Additional Protocols, is a question of fundamental importance, not only from a basic humanitarian perspective, but also because of the obligations it entails for the parties to the conflict: evacuation, care, and arguably also allowing humanitarian access to those in need of such care.⁹ Furthermore, the wounded and sick cannot be the object of an attack, provided that they do not participate in a hostile act themselves.¹⁰ Attacking the wounded and sick can constitute, as a matter of fact, a grave breach of the Geneva Conventions.¹¹

6   Until Additional Protocol (AP) I was adopted, in the early Conventions, protection was afforded to wounded and sick *combatants*, albeit that some provisions protecting wounded and sick *civilians* were present in Geneva Convention (GC) IV. In 1977, states, through the adoption of AP I, confirmed the protection of *all* wounded and sick, including civilians, the shipwrecked, and combatants of certain non-state armed groups. Common Article 3 and AP II, as well as customary international law, establish that these obligations also apply in situations of non-international armed conflicts (NIACs).

---

³ Dunant, above n 1, at 61.   ⁴ Ibid, at 65.   ⁵ Ibid.
⁶ Art 6 of the Convention for the Amelioration of the Condition of the Wounded in Armies in the Field of 1864.
⁷ See Arts 1, 2, and 7 of the 1864 Convention for the Amelioration of the Condition of the Wounded in Armies in the Field.
⁸ The issue of 'who is shipwrecked' is dealt with in Ch 38 of this volume.
⁹ See, e.g., R. Barber, 'Facilitating humanitarian assistance in international humanitarian and human rights law', 91 *IRRC* 874 (2009) 371; Swiss Federal Department of Foreign Affairs, *Humanitarian Access, Handbook on the Normative Framework*, Version 1.0 2011; Y. Naqvi and A. Pabst, *Humanitarian Assistance in Armed Conflict*, Conference of the Luxemburg Group, 24–5 May 2004, Graduate Institute of International Studies, Geneva.
¹⁰ See further Ch 42 of this volume.
¹¹ Art 50 GC I: 'Grave breaches to which the preceding Article relates shall be those involving any of the following acts, if committed against persons or property protected by the Convention: wilful killing, torture or inhuman treatment, including biological experiments, wilfully causing great suffering or serious injury to body or health, and extensive destruction and appropriation of property, not justified by military necessity and carried out unlawfully and wantonly.' Art 51 GC II has the same content.

Another matter of concern is 'what' constitutes a 'wound', or what type of 'sickness' is legally protected under the Geneva Conventions. The difficulty lies in the fact that 'there is no treaty definition of the sick or wounded, these terms being left to common sense and general usage'.[12] Rape as a weapon of war has been a characteristic of more recent armed conflicts, notably internal ones. But are victims of rape in armed conflict situations 'wounded' in the sense of the Geneva Conventions, and does the care to which they are entitled include abortion? To what extent the 1949 Geneva Conventions are able to answer these questions thus requires a contemporary interpretation of the relevant provisions on the 'wounded and sick' in those treaties.

II. The progressive evolution of the protection of the wounded and sick

The Convention for the Amelioration of the Condition of the Wounded in Armies in the Field of 1864 started by requiring the neutrality of ambulances and military hospitals and their personnel to be respected. Article 6 of the Convention then succinctly underlined that '[w]ounded or sick combatants, to whatever nation they may belong, shall be collected and cared for'. Thus, under this treaty, only wounded and sick *combatants* of armies in the *field* were covered. The Additional Articles relating to the Condition of the Wounded in War of 20 October 1868, which were drafted in order to adapt the 1864 Convention to seafaring,[13] did not bring more clarity to the issue of who exactly was to be considered the wounded and sick. Article 11 merely underlined that sailors, as well as soldiers, 'to whatever nation they may belong, shall be protected and taken care of by their captors'. More concrete was the 1906 Convention for the Amelioration of the Condition of the Wounded and Sick in Armies in the Field, which in Article 1 stated that the sick and wounded were '[o]fficers, soldiers, and other persons officially attached to armies, [...], without distinction of nationality'. It added that such wounded and sick persons who fell into the hands of the other belligerent, would be protected by prisoner of war (POW) status. The 1929 Convention, the purpose of which was 'to perfect and complete the provisions agreed to at Geneva on 22 August 1864, and 6 July 1906, for the amelioration of the condition of the wounded and sick in armies in the field', did not adopt new wording with regard to the definition of the wounded and sick.

In 1949, the regime elaborated by states, superseding the 1929 Convention,[14] maintained the distinction between wounded and sick combatants of armies in the field and those wounded at sea by adopting two distinct, although very similar, treaties: the Convention for the Amelioration of the Condition of the Wounded and Sick in Armed Forces in the Field (GC I) and the Convention for the Amelioration of the Condition of Wounded, Sick and Shipwrecked Members of Armed Forces at Sea (GC II). However, as from 1977, AP I no longer distinguished between the wounded and sick and the shipwrecked; instead it included *all* different categories of wounded and sick combatants, shipwrecked, and civilians under the same protection clauses.[15]

---

[12] L. Green, *The Contemporary Law of Armed Conflict* (New York: Manchester University Press, 1993), at 208; Pictet Commentary GC I, Art 12, at 136.
[13] J.K. Kleffner, 'Protection of the Wounded, Sick, and Shipwrecked', in D. Fleck (ed), *The Handbook of International Humanitarian Law* (2nd edn, Oxford: OUP, 2008) 325, at 326.
[14] Ibid, at 327.   [15] See also Green, above n 12, at 207.

B. Meaning and Application

I. The protection of the wounded and sick members of the armed forces

10   Geneva Conventions I and II of 1949 did not depart from the classic category of the 'wounded and sick' as being those persons belonging to the armed forces (the protection of wounded and sick *civilians* is covered by GC IV). Article 12 paragraph 1 GC I simply reads:

> Members of the armed forces and other persons mentioned in the following Article, who are wounded or sick, shall be respected and protected in all circumstances.

11   The fact that the two first Conventions apply to members of the armed forces is further confirmed by the links established with GC III. Article 13 of both GC I and GC II signals indeed that the 'wounded and sick' and the 'shipwrecked' are those belonging to the same category of persons that benefit from POW status, as set out in Article 4 GC III.[16] Thus, 'who is wounded and sick' under Articles 12 and 13 GC I and GC II strictly comprises not only combatants, but also persons who accompany the armed forces, such as war correspondents or supply contractors, members of crews, including crews of civil aircraft, and those taking part in a *levée en masse*.

12   Article 14 GC I adds that 'the wounded and sick of a belligerent who fall into enemy hands shall be prisoners of war, and the provisions of international law concerning prisoners of war shall apply to them'.[17] That said, the purpose of the two first Conventions and GC III is different. The provisions of GC I and GC II do not imply that in order to be protected, wounded and sick combatants must be in the power of the enemy, or that their status should be determined before they can be cared for.[18] They merely remind that, should wounded and sick combatants fall into the hands of the adverse party, GC III will also regulate their status and treatment.

13   An interesting question that arises in this context is whether the Conventions apply only to the wounded and sick belonging to the adverse party. In 1950, the Holland Special Court of Cassation denied that the 1929 Convention protected the wounded and sick of the same armed forces, in the case of a refusal by a German army doctor to provide care to a wounded Dutch soldier who had joined the German Army and had attempted to flee.[19]

14   A literal reading of GC I and GC II does not give a clear answer to that question. Unlike the preceding treaties, the words 'to whatever nation they may belong' (as in the 1864 Geneva Convention) or 'without distinction of nationality' (as in the 1929 Geneva Convention) do not appear in GC I and GC II of 1949. Article 12 of both GC I and GC

---

[16] See further Ch 44 of this volume.

[17] Art 16 GC II provides: 'Subject to the provisions of Article 12, the wounded, sick and shipwrecked of a belligerent who fall into enemy hands shall be prisoners of war, and the provisions of international law concerning prisoners of war shall apply to them. The captor may decide, according to circumstances, whether it is expedient to hold them, or to convey them to a port in the captor's own country, to a neutral port or even to a port in enemy territory. In the last case, prisoners of war thus returned to their home country may not serve for the duration of the war.'

[18] See in that sense Pictet Commentary GC II, Art 13, at 145: 'Article 13 cannot therefore in any way entitle a belligerent to refrain from respecting a wounded person, or to deny him the requisite treatment, even where he does not belong to one of the categories specified in the Article.'

[19] *In re PILZ, Holland*, Special Court of Cassation, 5 July 1950, in Sassòli/Bouvier/Quintin, vol II, Case No 104.

II refers to '[m]embers of the armed forces and other persons mentioned in the following Article'.

Furthermore, the established link with GC III and POW status makes the issue rather more confusing. Persons falling within the categories mentioned in the treaties (Article 13 GC I and GC II; Article 4 GC III) belong indeed to the adverse party. Unlike Article 4 GC III, however, Article 13 GC I does not require that the 'wounded and sick' be in the power of the enemy in order to benefit from the protection afforded by the Convention. This status appears only in Article 14 GC I, which confirms *a contrario*, that there is no requirement that one needs to be in the hands of the enemy in order to benefit from the protection afforded by Article 13 GC I.

In addition, in his Commentary to Article 13, Pictet notes that by 'virtue of a humanitarian principle, universally recognized in international law, of which the Geneva Conventions are merely the practical expression, any wounded or sick person whatever, even a "*franc-tireur*" or a criminal, is entitled to respect and humane treatment and the care which his condition requires'.[20] The principle of humanity, mentioned by Pictet, as well as the spirit of the Conventions, which *ratio legis* stem from the previous Conventions that provide for the protection of the 'wounded and sick' to 'whatever nation they may belong', warrants the interpretation that the provision applies to persons belonging to the same armed forces and not only to enemy nationals. This is confirmed when one looks at Rule 109 of the International Committee of the Red Cross (ICRC) Customary International Humanitarian Law Study.[21] The Rule reads: 'Whenever circumstances permit, and particularly after an engagement, each party to the conflict must, without delay, take all possible measures to search for, collect and evacuate the wounded, sick and shipwrecked without adverse distinction.' And the commentary to Rule 109 adds, '[this] rule applies to all wounded, sick and shipwrecked, without adverse distinction [...] This means that it applies to the wounded, sick and shipwrecked *regardless to which party they belong*'.[22] In addition, one ought to remember that human rights law, which applies in armed conflict situations, imposes a duty on states to respect the right to life and health of persons subject to their jurisdiction. That certainly is a binding obligation upon members of the armed forces with regard to the wounded and sick soldiers within their own ranks.

II. The protection of wounded and sick civilians

Article 16 paragraph 1 GC IV provides for the protection of the wounded and sick civilians:

The wounded and sick, as well as the infirm, and expectant mothers, shall be the object of particular protection and respect.

As in the provisions of GC I and GC II, no definition of the notion of 'wounded and sick' is given in GC IV.[23] As one can observe, Article 16 GC IV highlights the need for the protection of the infirm and of expectant mothers (who are neither wounded nor sick). The justification for their protection lies in the fact that, like the wounded and sick, the infirm and expectant mothers do not, nor can they, take part in hostilities.[24]

---

[20] Pictet Commentary GC I, at 145. [21] ICRC CIHL Study, vol I, Rule 109.
[22] Ibid, at 399 (emphasis added).
[23] As we shall see below, such a definition is, however, contained in Art 8(a) AP I.
[24] Pictet Commentary GC IV, Art 16, at 135; see further Ch 39 of this volume.

19   The *cause* of the illness or of the wound, or in other words whether the person has been wounded because of an armed attack or is ill for any other reason, is not to be taken into consideration. Even though the text of the Convention does not elaborate on this point, it may be argued that the principle of humanity does not allow for such distinctions. In addition, since one *ratio legis* of the protection of wounded and sick persons under IHL is the fact that they do not participate in hostilities, the origin of the wound or sickness is therefore irrelevant. That said, it is worth recalling here that the Geneva Conventions address acts and omissions, including with regard to the wounded and sick, only where there is a nexus with the conflict.

III. The issue of rape

20   As mentioned above (MN 7), one particular issue that has arisen since the drafting of the 1949 Geneva Conventions is the massive resort to rape as a weapon of war. Here, what is at stake is whether rape falls within the category of a 'wound' or a 'sickness' to be protected by the Geneva Conventions, as well as whether this entails an obligation to provide abortion services to rape victims.[25] Rape as a weapon of war and committed against members of the armed forces, thus falling within the scope of Article 12 GC I and GC II, is perfectly foreseeable. Rape, however, has tended to be a feature of contemporary NIACs, and the debate surrounding the issue has been addressed mainly within the 'wounded and sick' provision of Common Article 3.[26]

21   Nothing seems to prevent interpreting the Conventions as including rape victims in the category of the wounded and sick. As already mentioned, the Conventions do not provide for any definition of these notions. The reason for this was to allow the broadest possible protection. As Pictet pointed out, '[a]ny definition would necessarily be restrictive in character and would thereby open the door to every kind of misinterpretation and abuse. The meaning of the words "wounded and sick" is a matter of common sense and good faith.'[27]

22   Questions concerning this precise issue have been raised in the United Kingdom (UK) Parliament since 2010. In the House of Lords, the question from Lord Lester of Herne Hill was:

To ask Her Majesty's Government what is their strategy for ensuring that United Kingdom government-funded medical care for women and girls impregnated by rape in armed conflict is

---

[25] The US does not allow abortion for rape victims in armed conflict in its medical protocols. This has an impact on the ability of humanitarian agencies, including the ICRC, which are recipients of US aid, to offer the possibility to rape victims to have recourse to abortion, as a result of the application of the Helms Amendment of 1973, which provides that 'No foreign assistance funds may be used to pay for the performance of abortion as a method of family planning or to motivate or coerce any person to practice abortions' (§ 104(f) of the Foreign Assistance Act of 1961, as amended; Annual Foreign Operations Appropriations Acts), available at <http://transition.usaid.gov/our_work/global_health/pop/restrictions.html>.

[26] Global Justice Centre, *The Right to an Abortion for Girls and Women Raped in Armed Conflict, States' positive obligations to provide non-discriminatory medical care under the Geneva Conventions*, available at <http://www.globaljusticecenter.net>. Rape has been massively committed in the DRC throughout the conflict (see J. Adetunji, 'Forty-eight Women Raped Every Hour in Congo, Study Finds', *Guardian*, 12 May 2011, available at <http://www.guardian.co.uk/world/2011/may/12/48-women-raped-hour-congo>) and also in Kosovo in the late 1990s (see HRW Report, 'Serb Gang-Rapes in Kosovo Exposed', 21 March 2000, available at <http://www.hrw.org/news/2000/03/20/serb-gang-rapes-kosovo-exposed>). One should note that rape in armed conflict situations is not limited to women and girls. For instance, recent reports suggested that rape against boys was used in the Syrian conflict in 2011. See UN Human Rights Council, *Report of the Independent International Commission of Inquiry on the Syrian Arab Republic*, A/HRC/S17/2/Add.1, 23 November 2011, paras 69 ff.

[27] Pictet Commentary GC IV, Art 16, at 134.

non-discriminatory and includes abortion services where they are medically necessary in compliance with international humanitarian law.[28]

In that context, Lord Lester noted that the 'right at stake is not a right to abortion; it is the right of everyone "wounded and sick" in armed conflicts, including women, to appropriate and necessary life and health-saving medical care'.[29] Thus, the core of this debate was not whether or not rape victims could be considered as 'wounded and sick', but whether the UK was in violation of its IHL obligations by refusing to provide for abortions to rape victims. Indeed, in Lord Lester's view, the denial of provision for abortion in itself could constitute a form of torture, or inhuman and degrading treatment, prohibited by the Geneva Conventions.[30]

The UK has recognized that its policy would permit the provision of abortion services in line with international humanitarian law:

> It is the UK's view that in situations of armed conflict or occupation where denial of abortion threatens the woman's or girl's life or causes unbearable suffering, international humanitarian law principles may justify offering a safe abortion rather than perpetuating what amounts to inhumane treatment in the form of an act of cruel treatment or torture.[31]

This policy was first announced in the January 9, 2013 House of Lords debate led by Lord Lester. During that debate Baroness Northover, representing the Government, underlined that:

> As the [UK military] manual notes, and as my noble friend Lord Lester pointed out, where there is a direct conflict between national law and the fundamental obligation on parties to a conflict under Common Article 3 of the Geneva Conventions, the obligation is to comply with Common Article 3 . . . The denial of abortion in a situation that is life threatening or causing unbearable suffering to a victim of armed conflict may therefore contravene Common Article 3. Therefore, an abortion may be offered despite being in breach of national law by parties to the conflict or humanitarian organisations providing medical care and assistance.[32]

---

[28] The published version of the exchange of 9 January 2013 is found in *Hansard*, available at <http://www.publications.parliament.uk/pa/ld201213/ldhansrd/text/130109-0002.htm#13010975000294>, col 197.

[29] Ibid, 9 January 2013, col 198.

[30] In that sense, Lord Lester asked, 'can the Minister confirm that excluding access to abortions for women raped in war where such medical treatment is appropriate and necessary is discriminatory and likely to breach the Geneva Conventions and, most important, that international humanitarian law takes precedence over conflicting national laws which authorise torture or serious ill treatment by banning medically necessary abortions for the victims of rape in armed conflict?', ibid, col 200. Similar concerns were raised by Baroness Gould of Potternewton, in a question on 'Violence against women' in the House of Lords in December 2013. Lady Gould asked 'Her Majesty's Government what steps they are taking to address violence against women in countries experiencing conflict?' More specifically, she noted that 'girls and women raped in situations of armed conflict are considered the wounded and sick. That means that they have absolute rights to non-discriminatory medical care and attention under Common Article 3 of the Geneva Conventions, which states that no adverse distinction should be made on any grounds other than medical ones. However, because of the restrictions placed on the use of aid for the purpose of abortion, non-discrimination might signify that the outcome for each gender must be the same, but the treatment is not and should not be identical. Consequences—most notably pregnancy—necessitate distinct medical care, including the option of abortion. Denying abortion to female victims of war rape who are forced to bear the children of their rapists violates Common Article 3, the prohibition against torture and cruel treatment.' See at <http://www.publications.parliament.uk/pa/ld201314/ldhansard/text/131209-gc0001.htm#13120911000076>, col GC124.

[31] UK's June 2014 Practice Paper 'Safe and unsafe abortion: The UK's policy position on safe and unsafe abortion in developing countries', available at <https://www.gov.uk/government/publications/safe-and-unsafe-abortion-uks-policy-position-on-safe-and-unsafe-abortion-in-developing-countries>.

[32] See <http://www.publications.parliament.uk/pa/ld201213/ldhansrd/text/130109-0002.htm#13010975000273>, statement by Baroness Northover, 9 January 2013, col 209:

25 On 18 October 2013, the UN Security Council adopted Resolution 2122 (2013) which recognized 'the importance of Member States and United Nations entities seeking to ensure humanitarian aid and funding includes provision for the full range of medical, legal, psychosocial and livelihood services to women affected by armed conflict and post-conflict situations, and noting the need for access to the full range of sexual and reproductive health services, including regarding pregnancies resulting from rape, without discrimination'.[33] Subsequently, the EU, aligned with the United Kingdom, France and the Netherlands, recognized the right to abortion for victims of rape in armed conflicts under international humanitarian law.[34]

26 It is not possible, within the framework of this chapter, to comment further on this issue. Let us simply note that rape victims can be qualified as 'wounded and sick' within the meaning of the Geneva Conventions.

IV. The definition of the wounded and sick in Additional Protocol I

27 The purpose of this contribution is to focus on the relevant provisions on the wounded and sick in the 1949 Geneva Conventions. Nevertheless, reference to Article 8 AP I is necessary as, unlike the Geneva Conventions, it provides a more comprehensive definition of the notion of 'wounded and sick':

(a) 'wounded' and 'sick' mean persons, whether military or civilian, who, because of trauma, disease or other physical or mental disorder or disability, are in need of medical assistance or care and who refrain from any act of hostility. These terms also cover maternity cases, new-born babies and other persons who may be in need of immediate medical assistance or care, such as the infirm or expectant mothers, and who refrain from any act of hostility [...]

28 As one may note, the distinction between 'military' or 'civilian' wounded and sick is abandoned. In addition, the Article is more specific with regard to the cause of the wounds and sickness (disease, or other physical or mental disorder or disability). It also includes pregnant women, as well as new-born babies, and the infirm who are neither wounded nor sick in the usual sense of the terms. All these persons have in common a need for medical assistance, and in order to receive it, it is required that they refrain from participation in any hostilities. It is interesting to note that the condition to 'refrain from any act of hostility' is specified only in AP I and not in the Geneva Conventions. However, that does not in itself constitute a modification of the Conventions. Indeed, the 1949 Geneva Conventions' protection of the wounded and sick is entirely based on the idea that they cannot participate in hostilities or have laid down their arms, precisely because they are wounded or sick. In that sense, Article 8 AP I is a useful specification, but it does not modify the provisions contained in the Geneva Conventions. This also holds true with regard to the inclusion, within Article 8, of combatants as well as civilians in one single category of 'wounded and sick'. This again does not expand the span of protection of the 1949 Geneva Conventions but merely clarifies it, by concentrating in one provision what the 1949 Geneva Convention protection regime does in all four treaties. In other words, interpreted *in toto*, the interaction of the provisions of the Geneva Conventions would result in the same protection, i.e. the protection of all wounded and sick, be they members of the armed forces, civilians, or combatants of a non-state armed group.

---

[33] UNSC Res 2122 (2013).
[34] See <http://www.sophieintveld.eu/eu-recognises-the-right-to-abortion-for-war-rape-victims/> 1 October 2015.

C. Relevance in Non-International Armed Conflicts

The protection of the wounded and sick in the context of a NIAC is provided in paragraph 1(2) of Common Article 3 to all four Geneva Conventions, which simply reads: 'The wounded and sick shall be collected and cared for.' 29

Common Article 3 is applicable 'in the case of armed conflict not of an international character', and the obligation to collect the wounded and sick is incumbent on all parties, including armed non-state actors. The beneficiaries of the obligation may be inferred from paragraph 1(1) of Common Article 3 i.e. '[p]ersons taking no active part in the hostilities, including members of armed forces who have laid down their arms and those placed *hors de combat* by sickness, wounds, detention, or any other cause'. 30

The protection of the wounded and sick during NIAC has been further established through the elaboration of AP II[35] and is part of customary international law.[36] Hence, taken all together, the Geneva Conventions protect *all* wounded and sick, be they members of the armed forces or civilians, but also combatants from a non-state armed group who are *hors de combat*. 31

D. Critical Assessment

The protection of the wounded and sick lies at the very heart of IHL. Who should be regarded as 'wounded and sick' is of paramount importance in this regard, as the parties to the conflict will incur consequent legal obligations, such as searching for the wounded and sick, their evacuation and care. The principle of humanity has entirely permeated the provisions regarding the wounded and sick. Its application requires that *all* persons who have laid down their arms and are in need of medical assistance, be they civilians or members of the armed forces, be protected by the four Geneva Conventions 1949. In that sense AP I, even if it provides for a more precise definition of the wounded and sick, is a direct confirmation of the rules of the Geneva Conventions rather than an innovation. 32

The widespread use of rape as a weapon of war in contemporary armed conflicts has raised some challenges of interpretation with regard to the treatment and medical care to be provided to the victims of rape, in particular with regard to abortion. Nothing in the texts of the Conventions prevents one from interpreting the notion of 'medical care' as including abortion. In addition, the prohibition of discriminatory treatment obliges states at a minimum to ensure that all victims have access to the full range of health services, and to refer them to alternative health providers if those services refuse, for moral or legal reasons, to provide for abortion. 33

ANNYSSA BELLAL

---

[35] See Art 7 AP II: '1. All the wounded, sick and shipwrecked, whether or not they have taken part in the armed conflict, shall be respected and protected. 2. In all circumstances they shall be treated humanely and shall receive, to the fullest extent practicable and with the least possible delay, the medical care and attention required by their condition. There shall be no distinction among them founded on any grounds other than medical ones.'

[36] See ICRC CIHL Study, Rule 109. The customary law character of certain obligations linked to the wounded and sick in IACs as well as in NIACs has not been met with unanimous agreement within the scholarship: see J.P. Benoit, 'Mistreatment of the Wounded, Sick and Shipwrecked by the ICRC Study on Customary International Humanitarian Law', 11 *YIHL* (2008) 175.

Chapter 38. Who Is Shipwrecked?

	MN
A. Introduction	1
I. Towards The Hague	13
II. From 1907 Hague Convention X to 1949 Geneva Convention II	16
B. Meaning and Application	26
I. State practice since 1949	30
II. Developments in international shipping since 1949	34
III. When and for how long is a person shipwrecked?	39
C. Relevance in Non-International Armed Conflicts	45
D. Legal Consequences of a Violation	46
E. Critical Assessment	47

Select Bibliography

Doswald-Beck, L., *The San Remo Manual on the Law of Armed Conflict Applicable at Sea* (Cambridge: CUP, 1995)
Hore, P. (ed), *Dreadnought to Daring: 100 Years of Comment, Controversy and Debate in the Naval Review* (Barnsley: Seaforth Publishing, 2012)
Naval Staff, *British Maritime Doctrine (BR1806)* (2nd edn, London: The Stationery Office, 1999)
Pictet Commentary GC II
Roberts, A./Guelff, R. (eds), *Documents on the Laws of War* (3rd edn, Oxford: OUP, 2000)
Ronzitti, N. (ed), *The Law of Naval Warfare: A Collection of Agreements and Documents with Commentaries* (Dordrecht, Boston, London: Martinus Nijhoff, 1988)
Thomas, A./Duncan, J. (eds), *Annotated Supplement to the Commander's Handbook on the Law of Naval Operations* (Newport, RI: Naval War College, 1999)
Till, G., *Seapower: A Guide for the Twenty-First Century* (2nd edn, London: Routledge, 2009)
Tucker, R., *The Law of War and Neutrality at Sea* (Washington, DC: Naval War College, 1957)

A. Introduction

This chapter is notable for being concerned exclusively with the humanitarian consequences of war/armed conflict at sea. Naval operations are not generally as well understood as other aspects of armed conflict and, before examining the humanitarian law relating to those who are entitled to shipwrecked status, it will be useful to say something about the context in which it is applied. What is it that navies do, and what are their war-fighting roles? These questions are worth addressing immediately, before we move on to the substance of the chapter.

Naval doctrine recognizes three traditional fighting roles for navies: the conduct of sea control and sea denial operations; power projection; and economic warfare.[1] We shall be necessarily brief in describing each of these roles in turn.

---

[1] See, e.g., G. Till, *Seapower: A Guide for the Twentieth Century* (2nd edn, London/New York: Routledge, 2009), in particular Chapters 6 and 8 dealing with 'Command of the Sea and Sea Control' and 'Exploiting

3   *Sea control and sea denial operations* are conducted by navies to ensure they have sufficient control of the seas to project power ashore or conduct economic warfare. Sea denial operations are mounted to prevent an adversary achieving sea control. Through a mix of sea control and sea denial operations, each side in naval war will be trying to control the sea for its own use while denying its use to its opponent. Operations consist of naval forces (including, since the mid-twentieth century, maritime air forces) engaging in combat with opposing naval and air forces.

4   *Power projection* involves a naval force projecting power ashore to initiate or affect a land campaign. Given that we are discussing who is shipwrecked and when, the most relevant form of power projection is the mounting of amphibious landing operations, during which soldiers or marines land ashore from a naval force to engage in combat with shore-based defenders. Once amphibious forces reach shore, their welfare as potential victims of conflict would be covered by the rules relating to land warfare. In the process of mounting a landing, however, members of a landing force may find themselves in the sea following a successful attack on their landing craft.

5   *Economic warfare* is about the interference with or the protection of maritime trade. Offensive economic warfare involves naval forces interdicting both belligerent and neutral merchant shipping, to prevent contraband and other goods reaching the opposing belligerent's territory. It consists of both high seas interdiction operations and belligerent blockade. Warships order enemy and neutral merchant ships to stop, then exercise legitimate belligerent rights of visit and search, and, if necessary, capture or sink those ships if they are carrying contraband or attempting to run a blockade.[2] Defensive economic warfare is about protecting trade and the ships carrying it, including through escorting or convoying. It may also involve the deliberate routeing of shipping, including by the laying of minefields. While most naval warfare does not directly involve or affect civilians, economic warfare certainly does.

6   All three of these roles clearly have the potential to leave persons shipwrecked. The understandable assumption prior to the First World War was that the majority of those would be naval combatants, shipwrecked as a result of naval forces engaging each other in sea control/sea denial operations, with unarmed sailors abandoning their ships and taking to lifeboats/life-rafts, or floating in the sea with no immediate prospect of reaching the safety of land. Economic warfare was not considered the most likely cause of individuals finding themselves shipwrecked and entitled to protection, because only those vessels resisting visit and search would be subject to lawful attack and, given the risks of opposing a warship, it was not thought likely that many merchant ships would defy legitimate requests for them to stop and allow visit and search. That assumption proved erroneous, however. During the two World Wars, economic warfare proved to be a major cause of persons finding themselves shipwrecked, many of whom were civilians, not naval combatants. This experience led to 'shipwrecked' status achieving the significance it has in 1949 Geneva Convention (GC) II for the Amelioration of the Condition of Wounded, Sick and Shipwrecked Members of Armed forces at Sea.

Command of the Sea' respectively. For a doctrinal statement of one of the major maritime powers, see *British Maritime Doctrine (BR1806)* (2nd edn, London: The Stationery Office, 1999).

[2]   The conduct of economic warfare evolved over many years but, for convenience, need be traced back no further than the 1856 Paris Declaration.

7 The standard collective phrase employed in GC II to describe the victims of naval warfare entitled to protection is 'wounded, sick or shipwrecked'.[3] The wounded and sick, and the protections they are afforded, are dealt with in Chapters 37 and 39 of this volume, which leaves something to be said about those who are shipwrecked, hence this separate chapter.

8 The shipwrecked may also be wounded and sick as a consequence of either the circumstances that resulted in the loss of their ship, or the effects of extended periods awaiting rescue. Exposure is a particular risk, for example, even after only short periods in the sea. While this chapter is about who is shipwrecked, the scope for their also being in one or both of the other conditions should be borne in mind. Importantly, however, if individuals who are shipwrecked are also either wounded or sick (or, indeed, both), their shipwrecked status will not grant them any rights, protections, or advantages additional to those to which they would be entitled by virtue of their injuries or illness.

9 Who is shipwrecked? When does someone become shipwrecked, and at what point do they cease being so? These are important questions, because shipwrecked status extends protection to combatants even though they may be neither injured nor sick. Being deprived of the relative safety and security of their ship leaves many in distress. It is an understandable humanitarian measure to grant protection to them, because they will almost certainly no longer be either equipped for or physically capable of engaging in combat or supporting those who are. They will, indeed, be defenceless in the face of attack and be, quite literally, *hors de combat*—out of combat.

10 Importantly, this chapter discusses the shipwrecked in the context of GC II. The literal meaning of 'shipwrecked' is to suffer the destruction of one's ship at sea 'by sinking or breaking up'.[4] We need to extend this dictionary definition a little by including ships that have suffered catastrophic power failure to the extent that they are incapable of movement or of operating their equipment (including, in the case of warships, their weaponry), but which, nevertheless, remain seaworthy in other respects. Clearly, any individual at sea in a vessel of any sort is capable of becoming shipwrecked in the literal sense. Those individuals capable of being shipwrecked under the terms of GC II are differently defined, however.

11 Article 16 of the Convention states that those who are shipwrecked are to be granted prisoner of war (POW) status on capture. If one were to read Article 16 GC II in isolation, an understandable conclusion would be that anyone found in a shipwrecked condition at sea should be accorded POW status. This is not, of course, the case. Articles 12 and 13 GC II together define which persons are entitled to protection under the Convention if they are shipwrecked. Article 16 invariably needs to be read in conjunction with these two provisions, in particular the latter, which states that GC II applies only to certain categories of person to be found at sea. It is quite possible, therefore, for a person to be literally shipwrecked but not covered by the protections granted to the shipwrecked as defined by GC II. As we shall see, some of those who are literally shipwrecked may be civilians not granted protection under GC II. That is not to say that they are not protected. They will, of course, be entitled to protection under GC IV, concerning the protection of civilian persons in time of war. Their shipwrecked condition, while of humanitarian concern, will have no legal significance and grant them no

---

[3] As in GC II.
[4] Entry for 'shipwreck' in J. Pearsall (ed), *Concise Oxford English Dictionary* (10th edn, Oxford: OUP, 2002), at 1323.

additional rights of protection. Significantly, they will not be entitled to POW status on capture, unlike other civilians who are eligible to be regarded as shipwrecked under Article 13 GC II.

12   What follows starts with an account of the historical background to GC II. This is important in relation to merchant vessels being targeted as part of an economic warfare campaign. They are manned by civilians, might be thought of as civilian objects immune from attack, but in certain circumstances can be lawfully targeted. It is the status of sea-going civilians, whose ships become legitimate targets and who themselves become the victims of war at sea, that is an important rationale for the GC II provisions dealing with the shipwrecked. Although this chapter is commenting principally on GC II, it will also consider 1977 Additional Protocol (AP) I, in particular Article 8(b).

I. Towards The Hague

13   When the modern *jus in bello* first developed conventional substance in the middle of the nineteenth century, its focus was principally on the protection of the victims of warfare on land. The 1864 Geneva Convention was about the 'wounded of the armies in the field'; it did not mention victims at sea at all.[5] This was not altogether surprising. War at sea was not as visible as war on land, and did not have as great an impact on civilians.[6]

14   In 1868, Additional Articles were promulgated that were intended to extend the application of the 1864 Geneva Convention to war at sea.[7] Unfortunately, they failed to attract ratification and never entered into force (although during both the Franco-Prussian War of 1870–1 and the Spanish-American War of 1898 the parties agreed that they would be applied).[8] Preparations did commence towards the end of the nineteenth century to update the 1864 Geneva Convention, but those were overtaken by 1899 Hague Convention III, which was drawn up to adapt the 1864 Geneva Convention for use at sea. When the Geneva Convention itself was revised, in 1906, 1899 Hague Convention III rendered it unnecessary to extend it to naval warfare and it remained restricted to the protection of the victims of land warfare.

15   By the time of the Hague Conferences, general war at sea was being seriously contemplated once again. In 1905, the battle of Tsushima, during the Russo-Japanese War, became the most significant naval battle since Trafalgar, exactly a century before. The statesmen gathered in The Hague in 1907 focused particular attention on developing regulations for the conduct of naval war. One outcome was 1907 Hague Convention X, which replaced 1899 Hague Convention III, updating it to take account of the re-drafted Geneva Convention of 1906.

---

[5] The 1864 Convention's full title was Convention for the Amelioration of the Condition of the Wounded in Armies in the Field. The 1906 and 1929 Conventions added, after 'Wounded', the two words 'and Sick'. All three Conventions were applicable to land warfare alone.

[6] For a detailed account of the development of conventions dealing with naval war, see Pictet Commentary GC II, at 3–15.

[7] See Arts 6–14 of the 1868 Additional Articles Relating to the Condition of the Wounded in War, at <http://www.icrc.org/ihl.nsf/intro/125>.

[8] L. Penna, 'Commentary to the 1949 Geneva Convention II', in N. Ronzitti (ed), *The Law of Naval Warfare: A Collection of Agreements and Documents with Commentaries* (Dordrecht/Boston/London: Martinus Nijhoff, 1988) 534, at 534.

II. From 1907 Hague Convention X to 1949 Geneva Convention II

It was formally acknowledged at The Hague in 1907 that the process of losing their ship to enemy action could render individuals *hors de combat* without their suffering any physical injury.[9] Sailors are usually engaged in operating a complex weapons platform that needs a large crew working together as a team to be effective; they are not ordinarily equipped with personal weapons, and without the warship itself, they would be incapable of continuing to fight. If their ship is lost, they are also likely to be in distress, even if they have managed to get into lifeboats.

While 1907 Hague Convention X acknowledged shipwrecked status, it did not define it, nor did it stipulate who would qualify for it, in what circumstances, and for how long. Importantly, in relation to land operations, Article 1 of the 1906 Geneva Convention referred to 'officers, soldiers and *other persons officially attached to armies*',[10] with Article 2 stating that such persons, if captured, would be POWs. Entitlement to POW status was not reserved for those who were formally combatants, therefore, even though the majority would be. Both 1899 Hague Convention III and 1907 Hague Convention X stated that 'the shipwrecked, wounded or sick' would be entitled to POW status (Articles 9 and 14 respectively). By analogy, those legally classified as shipwrecked (and entitled to be regarded as POWs) included not only naval personnel (combatants), but also other persons officially present within a naval force, embarked in warships or in other vessels forming a part of that force (naval supply vessels, for example).[11] Those who did not qualify by this reasoning, however, included the civilian crews of merchant ships attacked and sunk during an economic warfare campaign.

There are three possible situations in which a merchant ship might lawfully be targeted or destroyed during an economic warfare campaign:

— while steaming independently but opposing the belligerent right of visit and search (for example by refusing to stop, or by physically preventing a boarding party visiting);
— while in convoy under naval operational control;[12] and
— if discovered during visit and search to be carrying contraband, and therefore subject to the law of prize (if the warship could not take the vessel as prize, it could destroy it after first removing its crew to safety).

Prior to 1914, of these three reasons for attack, that thought most likely to render civilians shipwrecked was the second. It was always reasonable (albeit not a legal obligation) to regard merchant ship crew members shipwrecked in those circumstances as victims of combat deserving of protection. Merchant ships in convoys protected by warships formed part of a naval force, their presence in a convoy almost certainly ordered by the authorities

---

[9] While 1899 was the first occasion on which the 'shipwrecked' were recognized in conventional law, there was evidence in practice dating back to the Revolutionary and Napoleonic Wars of a humanitarian need to rescue those enemy sailors whose ships were lost (Pictet Commentary GC II, at 85).

[10] Emphasis added.

[11] Art 11, 1907 Hague X refers to '[s]ailors and soldiers onboard, when sick or wounded, as well as other persons officially attached to fleets or armies'. Art 62 of the 1913 *Oxford Manual on Naval War* refers to individuals who follow a naval force without belonging to it, such as contractors, newspaper correspondents, etc, also stating they 'are entitled to be treated as prisoners of war'.

[12] By Art 63 of the 1909 London Declaration, a merchant vessel in convoy was deemed forcibly to be resisting the legitimate right of visit, search, and capture (while the London Declaration never entered into force, it represented the view prevailing at the time). This is reflected in L. Doswald-Beck (ed), *San Remo Manual on International Law Applicable to Armed Conflicts at Sea* (Cambridge: CUP, 1995), para 120.3, at 198.

in the vessels' flag state. Since convoying became general practice amongst the naval powers, the granting of potential shipwrecked status to civilian crews manning convoyed merchant ships was not a source of great controversy. A practice had already emerged of civilian crew members declaring an intention not to serve in similar circumstances in return for their release and repatriation.[13] While not granted POW status or detained until the end of hostilities, their declarations had a similar effect by ending their contribution to the flag state's war effort.

20   While civilians manning merchant ships in convoy might be accorded some protection if shipwrecked through enemy action, the status of all other merchant ships' crews who became actual victims of war was limited to that of civilian. Those who were crew members of merchant ships resisting visit and search were civilians participating in hostilities; their actions were arguably unlawful, they were certainly not entitled to POW status, and their legal position was therefore weak.

21   Also, before 1914, the extent to which convoying would become a significant feature of naval warfare was not generally appreciated. In theory, the law protected merchant ships as long as they submitted to visit and search (which convoying prevented). If merchant ships were sailing independently, carrying no contraband cargo and willing to submit to visit and search, they should have been safe. Unfortunately, policy based on that assumption failed to take adequate account of the impact of submarines on war at sea.

22   While the war at sea from 1914–18 had features of all three forms of naval warfare outlined at MN 2–5, it was the profound strategic importance and conduct of economic warfare that generated the most legal controversy. An unprecedented number of merchant vessels were targeted, with submarines playing an increasingly important role. This was surprising, as submarines were unsuitable for legitimate 'commerce raiding'. The conduct of visit and search and the capture as prize of vessels carrying contraband were virtually impossible activities for submarines to undertake.

23   Some assumed the law would restrict submarine operations and prevent their playing a significant role in economic warfare; they were proved utterly wrong. Submarines were used, and targeted merchant ships without warning, whether or not they were sailing under naval escort in convoy. Unrestricted submarine warfare became a major feature of naval war between 1914 and 1918. Hundreds of thousands of tons of independently sailing merchant ships were sunk unlawfully each month, and the vulnerability of shipping to attack eventually forced the British to introduce convoying in 1917 (which meant that British merchant ships could then be lawfully targeted without warning).[14] The use of submarines in this way was at the heart of the principal legal controversy in relation to war at sea during the First World War.

24   In the inter-war years an attempt was made to apply previously established rules to submarines. The resultant 1936 London Protocol stated very clearly that submarines conducting economic warfare operations were to comply with the same rules as surface warships. The unrestricted submarine warfare of the First World War was therefore confirmed as unlawful by the beginning of the Second World War. Unfortunately, this had little, if any, effect once war broke out in 1939. While the *Graf Spee*, the commerce raiding German

---

[13] Pictet Commentary GC III, at 65.
[14] See P. Padfield, 'The Submarine as Commerce Raider', in P. Hore (ed), *Dreadnought to Daring: 100 Years of Comment, Controversy and Debate in the Naval Review* (Barnsley: Seaforth Publishing, 2012) 95 and S. Haines, 'Law, War and the Conduct of Operations', in Hore (ed), 299.

pocket-battleship that cruised the southern Atlantic and Indian Oceans from September to December 1939, complied strictly with the law, by the end of that year the German High Command had instructed U-boat commanders to commence unannounced attacks on merchant vessels. In both the Atlantic and Pacific theatres of naval war, submarines (both Allied and Axis) launched attacks without warning, and convoying was resorted to in order to protect shipping.

The victims of the war at sea, in both World Wars, consequently included large numbers of civilians who were either members of merchant ships' crews or passengers in them. While, under the Hague rules, the crews of merchant ships attacked at sea would not be entitled to protection or be accorded POW status when captured, they were certainly shipwrecked and in very real distress. The numbers so affected, especially during the Second World War, pointed up the inadequacy of the conventional law dealing with victims of war at sea. By the end of the Second World War, merchant ship crews were strong candidates to be included in the list of persons entitled to both shipwrecked and POW status. This position was effectively reinforced by arguments articulated at Nuremberg in 1946, when the German fleet commander, Admiral Dönitz, stated that his ordering of unrestricted submarine attacks on merchant ships was a reprisal, that Britain had integrated its merchant ships into its naval effort by convoying, and that the distinction between combatant and non-combatant ships and crews had broken down as a consequence. He also famously pointed to similar orders issued by Admiral Nimitz to United States (US) Pacific Fleet submarine commanders. He contended that the actual practice of states in the use of unrestricted submarine warfare was reflecting a new customary norm that recognized different rules for surface warships and submarines.[15] One can contest Dönitz's argument but not the outcome of the orders he gave—large numbers of shipwrecked civilians required protection, whether the orders that gave rise to their condition were lawful or otherwise. Practice in the two World Wars and the arguments deployed by Dönitz at Nuremberg provided essential background to the negotiations leading to the incorporation of Article 13(5) into GC II.

B. Meaning and Application

Chapter II of GC II (consisting of Articles 12–21) deals with the 'wounded, sick and shipwrecked'. The two key provisions for determining who is shipwrecked are Articles 12 and 13. Article 12 merely states that '"shipwreck" means shipwreck from any cause and includes forced landings at sea by or from aircraft'. Article 13 goes on to define which categories of persons are eligible to be described as (wounded, sick and) shipwrecked, listing these under six subparagraphs. Those are identical to the subparagraphs contained in Article 13 GC I dealing with land warfare, and Article 4(A) GC III on POWs.[16] The categories of person listed in those common subparagraphs of GC I, GC II, and GC III are excluded from the definition of 'protected person' contained in Article 4 GC IV.

---

[15] D. Luban, 'The Legacies of Nuremberg', in G. Mettraux, *Perspectives on the Nuremberg Trial* (Oxford: OUP, 2008) 638.

[16] The explanation of why the three Articles from the first three GCs are identical is to be found in Pictet Commentary GC II, at 95. The Diplomatic Conference found that the list of those entitled to protection was precisely what they had already concluded was the list of those entitled to POW status.

27   It does not necessarily follow, however, that any person who is *de facto* shipwrecked but who is not protected under GC II, will be protected as a matter of course under GC IV. Article 4 GC IV excludes the nationals of neutral states from entitlement to protection when they are within the territory of a party to the conflict and their own state continues to maintain diplomatic relations with that party. It is possible for crew members of belligerent merchant vessels to be nationals of neutral states; indeed, today this would almost certainly be the norm rather than the exception. If a belligerent merchant vessel was, for some reason, lost within the territorial waters of the opposing belligerent, or if survivors of a lost ship managed to swim or row their life-raft into the territorial waters of the opposing belligerent, any crew members who were nationals of a neutral state could find themselves in that situation—theoretically unprotected. While such a situation may be imagined, as Pictet noted, 'any wounded, sick or shipwrecked person whatever—even a *franc-tireur* or a criminal—is entitled to respect and humane treatment and the care which his condition requires'.[17]

28   Article 13 GC II contains the list of categories of person to which the Convention applies. Since a purpose of that list was to define who would be entitled to POW status on capture, the bulk of Pictet's comments on it appeared in Pictet Commentary GC III. His comments on Article 13(5) were, however, very brief indeed, and he included the bulk of his comments on that paragraph alone in Pictet Commentary GC II. This should not be regarded as implying in any way that those persons listed under Article 13(1)–(4) and (6) are not protected persons under GC II; they most certainly are. It is even possible to conjure up possibilities for those categorized under paragraph (6) to have the potential for shipwrecked status (inhabitants of a non-occupied territory taking to boats to offer some measure of resistance to an invading force, would have this potential). Nevertheless, it is paragraph (5) that is rightly the principal focus of our comments here. Protection is extended to 'members of crews, including masters, pilots and apprentices of the merchant marine[18] and the crews of civil aircraft of the Parties to the conflict'.[19]

29   Any commentary on GC II today must take account of the potential situations in which the current law would need to be applied. Two factors need to be considered, therefore: first, any evidence of state practice since GC II was agreed that might have led to a change in the customary law relating to shipwrecked status; and, secondly, the modern circumstances in which the law would need to be applied.

I. State practice since 1949

30   There is a dearth of relevant practice and jurisprudence relating to conflict at sea since 1949. The relatively few naval wars have not been sustained over lengthy periods, and they have not featured situations in which the protection of the shipwrecked has been either a major or a contentious issue. Since the Second World War, conflicts with notable naval dimensions have included: the Korean War in the early 1950s; Suez in 1956; the war in Vietnam in the 1960s; the Indo-Pakistan War of 1971; the Battle of the Paracels between

---

[17] Pictet Commentary GC II, at 96.
[18] Passengers embarked in merchant vessels are excluded from the definition. In most cases they would be civilians protected by GC IV.
[19] The additional mention of the crews of civil aircraft, while appropriate, does not reflect a need to accommodate them in the Conventions as a consequence of substantial supportive evidence from the two World Wars. Survivors of an attack on a civil aircraft are somewhat less likely to survive and qualify as 'shipwrecked' than those surviving an attack on a ship. They are not commented upon further here.

the Chinese and Vietnamese navies in 1974; the Iran-Iraq War 1980–8; the Falklands/Malvinas War of 1982; and the two Gulf Wars of 1991 and 2003.

31 The most prominent naval war was that between the United Kingdom (UK) and Argentina, following the latter's invasion of the Falkland/Malvinas Islands in 1982. It was a predominantly maritime conflict and involved both sea control/denial operations and power projection. It did not, however, feature the conduct of economic warfare. Several warships were attacked and severely damaged or sunk, with significant numbers of naval personnel wounded and shipwrecked. A notably serious casualty was the Argentine cruiser, the *General Belgrano*, sunk by torpedoes fired from the British submarine *Conqueror*. Large numbers of Argentine naval personnel were shipwrecked as a result. None of those were recovered by British naval forces, however. They were all naval combatants and their legal status was never in doubt. Merchant ships and civilian manned vessels were also targeted and sunk, but they were British vessels that were either government-owned naval auxiliaries or commercial ships taken up from trade for use as support ships or troop transports. All their wounded and shipwrecked were recovered by other British vessels and legal status was not an issue. There was no instance of shipwrecked personnel on either side being targeted in breach of the protected status they enjoyed under GC II.[20]

32 The Iran-Iraq War lasted from 1980 to 1988, although the maritime aspects of it were largely concentrated in the years 1984–8, the period of the so-called 'Tanker War'. Large numbers of crude oil tankers were targeted by both Iran and Iraq. None of the attacks on merchant shipping was in accordance with the rules governing economic warfare at sea. In 1987, the worst year of the five, a total of 179 vessels were targeted (88 by Iraq and 91 by Iran), 125 of which were tankers. Apart from 34 Iranian-flagged vessels (all targeted by Iraq), the rest were of neutral flag. None was requested to submit to visit and search. All were attacked without warning, the majority with missiles, rockets, and grenades, with eight damaged by contact with free-floating mines. Only six of the vessels were actually sunk. A total of 41 civilian crew members were killed, 87 were injured, and over 15 were registered as missing. None of the small number of civilian crew members who might have been classed as shipwrecked was picked up by either Iranian or Iraqi naval vessels. The status of the survivors as legally shipwrecked and their entitlement to POW status were not issues during the conflict.[21] There is no record of shipwrecked persons being targeted, but if they had been, it would clearly have been in breach of GC IV rather than GC II in the majority of cases, as the vessels affected would have been of neutral flag—although the crews of belligerent flag vessels (Iranian vessels targeted by Iraq) may have been less easily categorized.

33 Given the paucity of naval war since 1949, and the lack of relevant practice in the most prominent conflicts, there is nothing to challenge the interpretation of 'shipwrecked' as it appears in Pictet Commentary GC II. The most significant attempt to review the law governing warfare at sea since 1949 has been the project that resulted in the *San Remo Manual on the Law of Armed Conflict Applicable at Sea*, published in 1995. Although that was not simply a review of the customary law on the subject, its publication was a key

---

[20] The facts of this conflict and the events during it are well publicized. The closest to a definitive account is the British official history of the conflict: L. Freedman, *The Official History of the Falklands Campaign* (2 vols) (Abingdon: Routledge, 2005).

[21] For the statistics quoted, see R. O'Rourke, 'The Tanker War', 114(5) *United States Naval Institute Proceedings* (May 1988), at 1023.

reason why the International Committee of the Red Cross (ICRC) Study on Customary International Humanitarian Law did not look into naval warfare.[22] In any case, it added nothing to what had been said in the Pictet Commentary GC II. Nevertheless, Pictet is not necessarily the last word on the matter. While there has been no evidence to support a shift in custom, the context within which the law has to be applied has changed over the last half century in ways that may have a profound influence on the law's application.

II. Developments in international shipping since 1949

34   Since 1949, the shipping industry has undergone very substantial change. Given the link between Article 13(5) GC II and entitlement to POW status on capture, its current characteristics are important. It is arguably the case that economic warfare of the intensity and purpose experienced during both the First and the Second World Wars is unlikely to be repeated. It certainly will not be unless another general great power war breaks out, with its effects being felt at sea. In that unlikely event, however, the law would have to cope with a truly international shipping industry and a set of circumstances for which it was never intended.

35   While merchant vessels still require a formal port of registry and flag, the bulk of the world's tonnage (almost 60 per cent) is now registered in the major open registries (or 'flags of convenience'). The top three flags globally are Panama, Liberia, and the Marshall Islands. Only one of the world's major powers is in the top 10 states of registry (China is in ninth place), while the UK is in seventeenth, the US is in twenty-first, and Russia is in twenty-seventh position. Unlike the situation experienced during the First and Second World Wars, when a major maritime power like the UK not only owned but also registered its merchant fleet, and could exercise control of its shipping in time of war, the control of shipping is now widely spread, with owners of ships, owners of cargoes, and flag states all having an input to the operation of a vessel. It can no longer be assumed that a state could control its shipping and establish convoys in the comprehensive manner in which they were established in the past. In addition, the crews of merchant vessels are these days genuinely multinational, with a great many ships having no nationals of the flag state embarked. The potential for neutral vessels and crew members from neutral states being affected by an economic warfare campaign is considerable.

36   A further problem of a very practical nature is that warships no longer have the wherewithal to search the majority of vessels on the high seas effectively to determine the nature of their cargoes. Most dry and general cargo is now containerized, containers having been first introduced at sea in 1956. Container ships are impossible to check outside a container port. One Danish-based but international company (Maersk) currently operates a class of eight vessels, each with a displacement of over 150,000 tons and capable of carrying over 15,000 containers when fully loaded. It is quite simply impossible to check the cargoes of these vessels at sea—and it is these vessels that would need to be the focus of an economic warfare campaign if it were to stand any chance of putting economic pressure on an opposing great power belligerent. Diverting ships to a port for checking would require a convenient and an adequate container port, and would cost the ship owners millions of dollars in lost revenue. To express it in stark terms, the standard manner in which economic warfare was conducted in the twentieth century is likely to prove quite inadequate in the twenty-first.

---

[22] ICRC CIHL Study, vol I, at xxxvi.

What does all this have to do with providing a definition of who is shipwrecked and when? Its relevance is to do with the likelihood of a situation arising today that would be similar to that which gave rise to Article 13(5) being included in GC II. That Article reflected the circumstances immediately preceding its drafting. The persons who were in the minds of those drafting it were members of the crews of vessels registered in a particular belligerent state, an understandable assumption being that, if not all, certainly a significant proportion would be nationals of the flag state. This is no longer likely to be the case. Finding a British-flagged ocean-going merchant vessel manned exclusively by British nationals would, for example, probably be very difficult. Indeed, on the outbreak of a general war of the sort likely to prompt an economic warfare campaign, it would not be surprising if merchant vessels flagged in the major belligerents had crews that included nationals of the opposing belligerents (something that would raise some doubts about the application of Article 16 GC II, which states that all who are shipwrecked are eligible for POW status[23]).

While this does not necessarily render Article 13(5) GC II moribund, it is important to understand the changing environment in which the law has to apply. The law has not changed as a result of this new reality (there has been no development in conventional law—notwithstanding Article 8(b) AP I—and no practice to affect customary law), but one needs to be aware of the challenges likely to be encountered in applying it in new circumstances. Since the absence of relevant practice also means we have nothing on which to base a firm prediction as to effect, we certainly cannot argue that this aspect of GC II no longer applies. It clearly would still apply, but would be likely to prove less than ideal for current circumstances.

III. When and for how long is a person shipwrecked?

The Commentary to AP I provides useful examples of situations in which shipwrecked status would apply, together with comment on the period of application. These are not repeated here, but what follows adds further amplification.[24] For the crew of a warship we can link it to their physical separation from their ship or, if they are still on board, to the inability of the vessel to continue its combat function. A ship badly damaged as a result of missile attack, for example, may be unable to continue to engage the enemy due to a catastrophic power failure. It may not be in any immediate danger of sinking and the captain of the vessel may have decided not to abandon ship. In these circumstances, the ship and its crew are incapable of fighting, are defenceless, and are extremely vulnerable to attack. In the heat of battle, their precise condition may not be altogether obvious to the enemy forces, who may continue to attack the vessel. This is the sort of ambiguous situation in which shipwrecked status may emerge.

It is entirely appropriate in the context of naval warfare to regard a totally disabled warship as 'lost' from the battle, its crew having been transformed by the condition of their ship into shipwrecked sailors entitled to protection. It may also be equally reasonable to suspect that the vessel will recover its fighting capacity. Once a vessel's totally disabled condition becomes obvious to the enemy, it should not continue to be targeted (indeed, attacking it would be a waste of time and resources, and, importantly, would result in no

---

[23] On the issue of nationality and POW status, see further Ch 44, MN 58, of this volume.
[24] See ICRC Commentary APs, at 308–45, paras 118–24.

discernible military advantage). If the vessel was taken under tow by another warship, however, the intention being to tow it back to port and repair the damage, it would remain a legitimate military objective and the crew would not be categorized as shipwrecked.

41   Clearly, reasonable judgement has to be applied to each set of circumstances. In the heat of battle, a decision may produce a different result from that arrived at in a considered post-conflict analysis. Once a ship is abandoned, of course, we can be reasonably certain that the crew who have taken to lifeboats or life-rafts, or who are swimming in the water, will qualify as shipwrecked. If another warship from their side in the conflict goes to their rescue, that vessel will continue to be a legitimate target (unless it is a hospital ship, of course) even while the shipwrecked sailors it is trying to rescue are not. Once those sailors have been taken on board the rescuing warship (and if they are neither wounded nor sick) they will lose their protected status as they will simply be re-joining the fighting forces of their state. If the rescuing vessel is an enemy vessel, the shipwrecked will lose that status once safely on board, but will then be eligible for protection under GC III as POWs following effective capture.

42   The termination of shipwrecked status actually points us to its humanitarian value. A man in the sea or on board a totally disabled vessel, is shipwrecked and protected. As soon as he is relieved from that situation he ceases being a protected person under GC II. If he is rescued by his own side, his status will be determined by his precise employment subsequent to rescue. As a naval combatant, he will revert to being a legitimate target. If he was a merchant ship crew member, he would cease being shipwrecked and become protected as a civilian, unless he was incorporated into the crew of another merchant ship. As a passenger in a rescuing ship, he will be protected under GC IV as a civilian if this places him in enemy hands. If he is a civilian falling into any of the GC II Article 13 categories and he is rescued by the enemy, he becomes captured and entitled to POW status (and will then be protected under GC III). Clearly, what is not permissible is for him to be attacked while he is shipwrecked. It is this protection that will guard him in law, for example, from a decision by an enemy commander to order the killing of the survivors of a destroyed warship (an act that was sadly not unknown during the two World Wars). This situation highlights why shipwrecked status is so fundamentally important, and why this situation at sea is different from a similar situation in land warfare. A soldier on a battlefield who has mislaid his weapon remains a legitimate target, unless he surrenders. A sailor in a similar situation (he has lost his weapon through the loss of his ship) becomes protected simply because he is shipwrecked in law. He does not need to surrender formally to achieve protected status, although he may well do so.

43   A shipwrecked sailor on reaching shore (be it a friendly, a neutral, or a belligerent shore) ceases to be entitled to protection as shipwrecked under GC II. The rules of land warfare will ordinarily apply to him from the point he steps on firm ground. No longer shipwrecked, if he is neither injured nor ill, and he finds himself ashore on enemy territory or on land under enemy control, if he is a naval combatant he will need to surrender to achieve protection as a POW under GC III. If, however, he is a former member of the crew of a lost merchant vessel, on reaching land he could become either a civilian entitled to protection under GC IV, or potentially a POW entitled to protection under GC III. Essentially, one can only be shipwrecked at sea, not when one is ashore. The 'sea' in this context is not restricted to the high seas, or to the waters beyond the territorial sea baseline. It can include internal waters (even to the extent of including the waters of an inland lake—common sense being applied to the circumstances). The 'sea' might also include a

small island, islet, or rock, especially if that area of 'dry land' is not capable of sustaining a person for any extended period. So an individual who has managed to swim to a rock for immediate safety may still be regarded, exceptionally, as shipwrecked; clearly, a reasonable degree of pragmatism honed by humanitarian concern needs to be applied in such circumstances.

Others who may find themselves shipwrecked include combatants conducting an amphibious assault, in which soldiers or marines land ashore from the naval force to engage in combat with shore-based defenders. Once amphibious forces are ashore, their welfare, if they become victims of conflict, is covered by the rules relating to land warfare. In the process of mounting an amphibious landing, especially one that is directly opposed, members of the landing force may find themselves in the sea as a result of a successful attack on their landing craft. Unlike those shipwrecked on the high seas, combatants in these circumstances are likely to be within a short distance of the shore, and may be armed with personal weapons and still capable of continuing with the fight. While the loss of their landing craft may have been an uncomfortable experience, they will not necessarily be vulnerable or in distress, and indeed may be determined to carry on fighting. Men in the water in these circumstances are perhaps the most difficult to categorize as shipwrecked and entitled to protection. Some may well be strictly speaking in that condition, but others will not be. It may in practice be impossible for a defending force that is opposing an amphibious landing to distinguish between those who are and those who are not legally shipwrecked. Importantly, to be entitled to protection as shipwrecked, those finding themselves in that physical condition will need to refrain from any act of hostility to be entitled to the protections afforded the shipwrecked.[25] While they will not be required to indicate their intention to surrender, they would need to avoid any action consistent with remaining hostile. For the opposing belligerent, reasonable judgement will need to be applied in a potentially ambiguous set of circumstances.

C. Relevance in Non-International Armed Conflicts

Combat operations at sea are not a common feature of non-international armed conflicts (NIACs), although it would certainly be wrong to dismiss their relevance altogether. Clearly, both the American and Spanish civil wars are two striking historical examples of NIACs during which naval operations played an important part, with blockade in particular being a notable feature in each. In relation to the treatment of victims, however, the categorization of individuals as shipwrecked, and their consequential entitlement to protection under GC II, is a feature of international armed conflict (IAC) and not NIAC. Those entitled to such in IAC are defined as being those who would be entitled to POW status on capture. Prisoner of war status does not exist in the context of NIAC; nor does combatant status. As we have demonstrated already, in defining those who are shipwrecked under GC II, there is significant linkage between the shipwrecked and the subsequent entitlement to POW status in IACs. The fact that nobody is entitled to POW status in NIACs does not mean, however, that shipwrecked status cannot apply in NIACs. Indeed, this status is specifically acknowledged in Article 3 paragraph 1(2) GC II, which states that the 'shipwrecked shall be collected and cared for'.

---

[25] Art 8(b) AP I.

D. Legal Consequences of a Violation

46 The protected status of those who are shipwrecked obliges all concerned to respect their condition. Under Article 51 GC II, it would be a grave breach wilfully to kill shipwrecked persons, to torture or subject them to inhuman treatment, or wilfully to cause great suffering or serious injury to their body or health. There has been no jurisprudence in relation to Article 51 GC II. Nevertheless, there will be appropriate lessons to be drawn from prosecutions brought to tribunals concerning such offences committed against other protected persons under relevant provisions of the other three Geneva Conventions.

E. Critical Assessment

47 The reason for the original grant of protected status to those who became shipwrecked was the fact that a shipwrecked naval combatant without his ship would be incapable of continuing to engage the enemy. He would be *hors de combat*, even if uninjured. He would be defenceless, whether in the water or in a lifeboat—and even while still on board his ship, if it were heavily damaged with no functioning weaponry. The extension of shipwrecked status to the crews of merchant ships in 1949 was a response to the substantial increase in the scope and intensity of economic warfare activity against merchant vessels, especially attacks on them mounted by submarines. The extension of shipwrecked status to those listed in Article 13(5) GC II was accompanied by the granting to them of POW status if captured.

48 The creation of protected status for those shipwrecked as a result of naval combat remains entirely understandable and necessary today. What is not so clear is the practicality of or necessity for the application of protected status under GC II to the crews of merchant ships, since they are civilians and, as such, covered by GC IV. By including them in GC II and granting them the possibility of shipwrecked status, the additional possibility of POW status under GC III is raised. It is worth asking if this remains appropriate.

49 In the years since Article 13(5) was included in GC II, the characteristics of the international shipping industry have altered to such a degree that it can by no means be assumed that the type of economic warfare experienced during both the First and Second World Wars would be conducted in future. Given the absence of general great power war and changes to the character of the international shipping industry, it is difficult to predict the extent to which the granting of shipwrecked status to merchant ship crews will be necessary. It might be, but it equally might not. It is important in this commentary to point up this uncertainty.

50 The law remains as it is, but could be inconsistent with what is likely to occur if conflict breaks out between major maritime powers. In those unfortunate circumstances, belligerent practice is likely to evolve rapidly to cope with the realities of twenty-first-century war at sea. This is especially the case in the context of economic warfare. We have pointed to the possible shortcomings of the law relative to the realities of the modern shipping environment, and by doing so have at least given warning to those providing legal advice to naval commanders about the uncertain characteristics of what they will face.

STEVEN HAINES

Chapter 39. The Obligations to Respect, Protect, Collect, and Care for the Wounded, Sick, and Shipwrecked

	MN
A. Introduction	1
B. Meaning and Application	6
I. The scope of the protective regime	6
II. The obligation to respect and protect	9
a. The notion	9
b. In all circumstances	16
III. The obligation to search for, collect, and evacuate	21
a. The notion	21
b. Nature of the obligation	27
c. Recording and forwarding of information	31
IV. The obligation to care for	32
a. The notion	32
b. Nature of the obligation	42
c. Obligation when compelled to abandon the wounded and sick	47
V. The distinction between combatants and civilians in international armed conflict	48
VI. Involvement of local inhabitants and relief societies: assistance in collecting and caring for the wounded, sick, and shipwrecked	55
a. Duties	55
b. Confidentiality and prohibition of penalties	61
C. Relevance in Non-International Armed Conflicts	65
I. The protective regime	65
a. Humane treatment and medical care	65
b. An obligation to search for and evacuate?	72
II. Security measures and counter-terrorism legislation	75
III. Application to non-state armed groups	81
D. Legal Consequences of a Violation	83
E. Critical Assessment	91

Select Bibliography

Benoit, J.P., 'Mistreatment of the Wounded, Sick and Shipwrecked by the ICRC Study on Customary International Humanitarian Law', 11 *YIHL* (2008) 175

Bothe, M./Janssen, K., 'Issues in the Protection of the Wounded and Sick', 26 *IRRC* 253 (1986) 189

Giacca, G., *Economic, Social and Cultural Rights in Armed Conflict* (Oxford: OUP, 2014)

Kleffner, J.K., 'Protection of the Wounded, Sick, and Shipwrecked', in D. Fleck (ed), *The Handbook of International Humanitarian Law* (3rd edn, Oxford: OUP, 2013) 321

McCoubrey, H., 'The Wounded and Sick', in P. Rowe (ed), *The Gulf War 1990–91 in International and English Law* (New York: Routledge, 1993) 171

Mehring, S., 'The Rights and Duties of Physicians in Armed Conflict', 103 *Militair-rechtelijk tijdschrift* (2010) 205

Pictet, J., 'The Medical Profession and International Humanitarian Law', 25 *IRRC* 247 (1985) 191

Rezek, J.F., 'Wounded, Sick and Shipwrecked Persons', in *International Dimensions of Humanitarian Law* (Paris: UNESCO, 1988) 153

Solf, W., 'Development of the Protection of the Wounded, Sick and Shipwrecked under the Protocols Additional to the 1949 Geneva Conventions', in Mélanges Pictet 237
Sassòli/Bouvier/Quintin, at 195–209.

A. Introduction

I don't care, they were only two and we left them to die. We had no possibility to take them, and they killed others so they deserve to die.[1]

1   The protection of the wounded, sick, or shipwrecked in armed conflict was the founding principle of the First Geneva Convention for the Amelioration of the Condition of the Wounded in Armies in the Field adopted in 1864. It was the sight of dying and wounded soldiers from the Battle of Solferino that led Henry Dunant to push for the creation of a neutral and impartial organization to protect and assist the war-wounded.[2]

2   The 1864 Convention sets out the fundamental obligation of states parties to collect and care for wounded and sick combatants without distinction as to nationality; the neutrality and inviolability of medical personnel and inhabitants of the country who bring help to the wounded; and the use of the distinctive sign of the red cross on a white background to identify hospitals, ambulances, and evacuation parties, as well as medical personnel.[3]

3   Since then, these principles have been sustained throughout all conventions and protocols dealing with the wounded and sick, including the 1949 Geneva Conventions, notably the Geneva Convention (GC) I for the Amelioration of the Condition of the Wounded and Sick in Armed Forces in the Field and GC II for the Amelioration of the Condition of Wounded, Sick and Shipwrecked Members of Armed Forces at Sea.[4] The latter essentially extended the protective regime from the wounded and sick on the battlefield to include certain victims of naval warfare, thereby encompassing shipwrecked members of the armed forces at sea.

4   Geneva Convention IV relative to the Protection of Civilian Persons in Time of War introduced a number of rules to ameliorate the condition of wounded and sick civilians,[5] although these provisions are markedly less detailed than those of GC I and GC II. Many of the provisions laid down in Additional Protocol (AP) I of 1977 ensure that the legal protection of civilians is equal to that provided for members of the armed forces, regardless of their status.

---

[1] Report of the Independent International Commission of Inquiry on the Syrian Arab Republic, 5 February 2013, UN Doc A/HRC/22/59, para 29. This Syrian interviewee, who supposedly joined an anti-Government armed group, describes how two government soldiers wounded in the overrunning of an army checkpoint in a hospital in Homs were left to die without the medical care and attention required by their condition.

[2] H. Dunant, *A Memory of Solferino* (Geneva: ICRC, 1986).

[3] Arts 1–7 of the 1864 Geneva Convention.

[4] GC II was applied for the first time during the Falkland Islands/Malvinas conflict between Argentina and the UK. See S.-S. Junod, *Protection of the Victims of Armed Conflict Falkland-Malvinas Islands (1982): International Humanitarian Law and Humanitarian Action* (2nd edn, Geneva: ICRC, December 1985), at 23–6.

[5] See Ch 37 of this volume.

This chapter analyses the provisions under the Geneva Conventions to understand 5
the set of obligations owed to wounded, sick, and shipwrecked combatants and civilians alike. The main legal issues to be discussed are whether wounded, sick, and shipwrecked civilians are entitled to the same protection as combatants in international armed conflict (IAC); whether the required treatment of the shipwrecked differs from that afforded to the wounded and sick; whether the civilian population has any rights and obligations towards combatant or civilian wounded, sick, and shipwrecked; whether Common Article 3 provides comparable standards of protection to those detailed in IAC; whether civilians and relief societies in non-international armed conflicts (NIACs) are protected against penalties for offering assistance, similar to the way in which they are protected in IAC; and whether/how these obligations to respect, protect, collect, and care for apply to armed groups in NIAC.

B. Meaning and Application

I. The scope of the protective regime

The protective regime of the wounded, sick, and shipwrecked differs depending on 6
whether the individuals are military or civilian. Geneva Conventions I and II provide a quasi-identical regime of protection for wounded, sick, and shipwrecked members of the armed forces, as well as for limited categories of civilians associated with the armed forces, while a more general and weaker/elementary system of protection for civilians is laid down in GC IV, regardless of their nationality.[6]

The Geneva Conventions distinguish between land and sea warfare, addressing the 7
wounded and sick as two separate categories, although the protection *ratione materiae* they receive under both Conventions is essentially identical.[7] The responsibilities of a party to the conflict towards the wounded, sick, and shipwrecked members of the armed forces arise independently of whether those wounded or sick members of armed forces are in enemy hands. Geneva Convention III on prisoners of war (POWs) comes into operation in line with its Article 4 when wounded or sick members of the armed forces fall into the power of the enemy.[8] In cases where the wounded, sick, and shipwrecked fall into the hands of a neutral Power, the latter shall apply, by analogy, the provisions of the Conventions.[9]

The protection afforded by the various provisions applies to a wide definition of 8
wounded, sick, and shipwrecked as long as they refrain from any hostile act.[10] Thus, as soon as a person in need of medical assistance or in peril at sea ceases to commit a hostile act, he or she is entitled to protection as being wounded, sick, and shipwrecked. Wounded or ill combatants who continue to engage in combat, evade capture, or perform their military duties will not be granted (or will lose) the protection and corresponding obligations of care: the person has to be effectively *hors de combat*, either because he or she has

---

[6] Arts 14–22 GC IV apply in general to wounded and sick civilians, as well as to other civilians in need of medical attention (e.g. the infirm and expectant mothers). GC IV further regulates certain aspects of protection of specific categories of civilians, namely the wounded and sick in occupied territory, and those who are interned. See Arts 57, 76, 81, 91, 106, 127, 132 GC IV.

[7] The interplay of the two Conventions is stipulated in Art 4 GC II, which provides that in cases of hostilities between land and naval forces, GC II shall apply only to forces on board ship. Forces that are put ashore would immediately become subject to the provisions of GC I.

[8] Art 14 GC I; Art 16 GC II.   [9] Art 4 GC I; Art 5 GC II.   [10] Art 8(a) AP I.

surrendered or due to incapacitation.[11] The same holds true for a wounded or sick civilian who participated directly in hostilities.

II. The obligation to respect and protect

a. The notion

9 The general obligation to respect and protect is a fundamental principle of international humanitarian law (IHL) with general scope. It may be understood as the foundation of the regime of protection of the wounded, sick, and shipwrecked.[12] The protection afforded to those who fall within the scope of a series of rules is broad: they 'shall be respected and protected in all circumstances',[13] in accordance with Article 12 GC I and Article 12 GC II. Correlative duties arise for every party to the conflict to respect, protect, and care for the wounded, sick, and shipwrecked. It does not matter to which party to a conflict the wounded, sick, and shipwrecked belong.

10 The general obligation to respect and protect requires that the wounded, sick, and shipwrecked must be treated humanely and cared for in any event, without distinction founded on sex, race, nationality, religion, political opinions, or any other similar grounds.[14] The obligation to respect imposes an obligation not to attack or harm them, while at the same time the obligation to protect demands that proactive measures be taken for their protection against various dangers arising in armed conflict situations (to provide the aid and care the person needs).

11 Although not stipulated, the duties of respect and protection primarily place obligations on the parties to the conflict, the military being the primary duty bearer. In addition, the obligation is extended to civilians, deriving both from general IHL and from Article 18 GC I, which states, 'The civilian population shall respect these wounded and sick, and in particular abstain from offering them violence.'[15]

12 Conceptually, the *obligation to respect* requires parties to an armed conflict to abstain from engaging in hostile acts against the wounded, sick, and shipwrecked. It is framed in terms of a negative obligation. The term 'respect' refers to an obligation to refrain from any attempts upon their lives or violence to their persons.[16] Under the law regulating the conduct of hostilities, the wounded and sick must never be considered lawful targets. Under the obligation to respect, it is unlawful directly or indiscriminately to attack them.

13 The obligation extends to other types of harmful conduct outside the conduct of hostilities. Article 12 paragraph 2 GC I prescribes that the wounded and sick shall be treated humanely, and provides a non-exhaustive catalogue of prohibited behaviour.[17] They shall not be murdered or exterminated, nor subjected to torture or to biological experiments; they shall not wilfully be left without medical assistance and care, nor shall conditions exposing them to contagion or infection be created.[18] Any form of attack on or harassment

---

[11] *UK Manual of the Law of Armed Conflict* (Oxford: OUP, 2005), para 5.6.1, at 58.

[12] The expression used has been accepted since the 1929 GC I. This principle was repeated in the APs to emphasize its importance: Art 10 AP I. See J.K. Kleffner, 'Protection of the Wounded, Sick, and Shipwrecked', in D. Fleck (ed), *The Handbook of International Humanitarian Law* (2nd edn, Oxford: OUP, 2008) 325, at 330.

[13] Art 12 para 1 GC I and GC II; Art 16 GC IV. See also Art 10(1) AP I; Art 7(1) AP II. Similar language is used in provisions relating, e.g., to the protection of medical transports (Art 35 para 1 GC I).

[14] Art 12 GC I and GC II.   [15] See also Art 17 AP I.

[16] Reference is made 'to spare, not to attack', Pictet Commentary GC I, Art 12, at 134–5.

[17] This is shown by the word 'in particular' in the second sentence.   [18] Art 12 GC I.

of those granted protection is therefore unlawful. Other forms of prohibited conduct are listed as grave breaches in Article 50 of the Convention, including 'inhuman treatment' and 'wilfully causing great suffering or serious injury to body or health'.[19] Furthermore, any form of belligerent reprisals against wounded, sick, and shipwrecked combatants, and all other persons covered by GC I and GC II, is strictly prohibited.[20]

To respect a wounded or sick soldier is not enough—this must be complemented by proactive measures, through the exercise of due diligence, to protect the wounded and sick from harm irrespective of its source. The obligation to protect connotes an active preservation and safeguarding of the wounded, sick, and shipwrecked, which relates to their specific vulnerability. The word 'protect' has been referred to in this context as meaning 'to come to someone's defence, to lend help and support' ('*prendre la défense de quelqu'un, prêter secours et appui*').[21] It involves a positive obligation to take appropriate measures to protect such persons against harm posed by soldiers and civilians, to safeguard them from any other dangers arising from the battlefield inherent in armed conflict (for example ongoing hostilities, explosive remnants of war) or those that may derive from other external elements (such as illness, natural hazards). The general obligation laid out in Article 12 paragraph 1 GC I is further specified by the obligation to care for the wounded and sick (Article 12 paragraph 2 GC I), to search for and collect them (Article 15 GC I), and to protect them against pillage and ill-treatment.[22]   14

The obligations to respect and protect are complementary concepts, and it may be argued that all other obligations in GC I and GC II derive from them, including provisions concerning the recording and forwarding of information (Article 16 GC I); as well as the protection of medical units and establishments (Article 19); and other related protection for medical personnel (Article 24).   15

b. In all circumstances

The words 'in all circumstances' make it clear that military wounded, sick, and shipwrecked are to be respected and protected at all times and in all places. They have to be respected and protected when 'they are with their own army or in no man's land as when they have fallen into the hands of the enemy'.[23] However, this requirement should already be taken into account during hostilities. In this sense, the requirement of humane treatment and care should be triggered as and when possible.   16

The duty to respect and protect the wounded, sick, and shipwrecked in all circumstances is considered to be part of customary IHL applicable in NIAC as well as in IAC.[24] It should be reiterated that the obligation is also extended to civilians.[25]   17

---

[19] See also Art 8(2)(a) ICC Statute.
[20] Art 46 GC I; Art 47 GC II. As for civilians, they are protected when in the hands of the adverse party, e.g., during internment or in occupied territory (Art 33 para 3 GC IV), as well as in the context of attack and targeting during hostilities (Art 52(1) AP I). The wounded and sick or shipwrecked military or civilians are covered by Part II of AP I, including Art 20.
[21] Pictet Commentary GC I, Art 12, at 134–5.
[22] Art 15 GC I; Art 18 GC II. ICRC CIHL Study, Rules 52 and 87. See also Art 8(2)(b)(xvi) ICC Statute. The prohibition of pillage was first incorporated in Art 47 of the Hague Regulations of both 1899 and 1907 pertaining to occupied territory, and then in Art 16 of the Hague Convention (X) with regard to the wounded, sick and shipwrecked, which was subsequently included in Art 3 of the 1929 GCs.
[23] Pictet Commentary GC I, Art 12, at 135.   [24] ICRC CIHL Study, Rules 109–11.
[25] Art 16 para 1 GC IV reads as follows: 'The wounded and sick, as well as the infirm, and expectant mothers, shall be the object of particular protection and respect.' See also Art 7(1) AP II. See further section C.I.a of this chapter.

18   The formulation emphasizes the *non-reciprocal nature* of the obligations of the Geneva Conventions.[26] This means that in situations where the enemy fails to respect its obligations, a party's own obligations pertaining to the wounded, sick, and shipwrecked will continue to remain applicable.

19   In addition, this terminology makes it clear that belligerents are not entitled to invoke military necessity as a ground for non-compliance, unless expressly provided for in the relevant rule. However, it should be noted that with regard to certain obligations, considerations of military necessity are integrated in certain rules pertaining to the protection of the wounded, sick, and shipwrecked. For instance, Article 12 GC I requires that the parties to the conflict, if compelled to abandon them to the enemy, must, 'as far as military considerations permit', leave part of their medical personnel and material to care for them. Moreover, the duty actively to search for, collect, and evacuate is incumbent upon parties to the conflict, especially 'after an engagement', or 'whenever circumstances permit'.[27] In addition, military practicability is also found explicitly in Article 16 paragraph 2 GC IV, which requires, 'as far as military considerations allow', that each belligerent facilitate the steps taken to search for the dead and wounded, and to assist the shipwrecked.

20   During the conduct of hostilities, the existing law can prove unsatisfactory for the protection of civilians or medical personnel rescuing injured individuals, or providing medical assistance, or removing the dead. Certain types of attack can have a detrimental effect on the relevant regime of protection; these include 'follow-up attacks' (also known as 'double-tap attacks' or 'secondary strikes'), which may infringe the specific rules relating to the protection of the wounded civilians and combatants. This practice of hitting a targeted strike site multiple times in a very short period of time can potentially be in contradiction to the duty to respect the wounded. It has been used by certain states and non-state armed groups, and may impact on the willingness of the rescuers to act.[28] Under existing law, the lawfulness of such practice will depend on who the rescuers are and whether the wounded refrain from any hostile act. If the rescuers are neither medical personnel, nor civilians not directly participating in hostilities, they remain legitimate targets, even while they rescue the wounded. The wounded being rescued would be incidental victims of such an attack, protected only by the proportionality principle and, arguably, precaution obligations.

III. The obligation to search for, collect, and evacuate

a. The notion

21   Not only must wounded, sick, or shipwrecked members of the armed forces who have fallen wounded or sick in the actual area where combat takes place be respected and protected, they must also be searched for, collected, and cared for in order to protect them

---

[26] See, by analogy, the interpretation of CA 1. See, e.g., ICRC Commentary APs, Art 1 AP I, para 51; Resolution 3 of the 30th International Conference of the Red Cross and Red Crescent, Geneva, 2007, preambular para 12.

[27] Art 15 GC I; Art 18 GC II.

[28] An explosive device is set off, and when first responders arrive a second one is exploded to cause more casualties and to inflict terror. Homeland Security Institute, *Underlying Reasons for Success and Failure of Terrorist Attacks: Selected Case Studies*, 4 June 2007, at 28. See also Report of the Independent International Commission of Inquiry on the Syrian Arab Republic, 2013, para 62. Such practice has also been used through unmanned aerial vehicles. C. Woods and C. Lamb, 'Obama Terror Drones: CIA Tactics in Pakistan Include Targeting Rescuers and Funerals', *The Bureau of Investigative Journalism*, 4 February 2012.

against dangers arising from the battlefield. Thus a number of rules lay down the actual steps to be taken by all parties to the conflict for the protection of the wounded, sick, and shipwrecked from the moment they fall in battle. This means that the obligations apply almost exclusively to operations which take place on the frontline.

Parties must 'without delay' take all possible measures to search for and collect any of the wounded, sick, or shipwrecked, as well as the dead.[29] As to the temporal scope of the obligation, a distinction is made between land and sea warfare. Whereas in a land engagement, this obligation exists 'at all times' from the moment the wounded and sick fall on the battlefield, and especially after an engagement, at sea the obligation exists only after an engagement.

Whenever circumstances permit, agreements between the parties, whether by armistice or ceasefire, may be made for the exchange, removal, and transport of the wounded left on the battlefield in both land and sea engagements.[30] Whenever possible, analogous arrangements should be made for the removal of the wounded and sick by land and sea from any besieged or encircled area, and for the passage of medical personnel or chaplains on their way to such an area.[31] At sea, belligerent warships can demand the handing over of the wounded, sick, and shipwrecked, whether they are on board hospital ships (civilian or military) or other vessels, private or neutral, provided they are in a fit state to be moved and that the warship involved has sufficient means to provide for their care and treatment.[32]

The obligation to search requires generally the belligerent to make a thorough search in the captured area so as to collect the wounded, sick, shipwrecked, and the dead.[33] Depending on the various constraints in the field, the obligation should not prove unduly onerous.

The obligation to collect entails a number of practical requirements vis-à-vis the potential victims. The parties to a conflict are required to take the necessary measures to ensure that the wounded, sick, and shipwrecked are protected from pillage and ill-treatment, and to ensure their adequate care, especially in situations where it might not be possible to evacuate them.[34]

The conditions for evacuation are spelled out in Articles 19 and 20 GC III, where POWs are to be evacuated humanely, safely, and as soon as possible from combat zones.[35] Only if there is a greater risk in evacuation may the wounded or sick be kept temporarily in the combat zone; however, they must not unnecessarily be exposed to danger.[36]

b. Nature of the obligation

The obligation to search for, collect, and evacuate the fallen is an obligation of means. As Pictet noted, 'the obligation to act without delay is strict; but the action to be taken

---

[29] Art 15 para 1 GC I and Art 18 para 1 GC II; see also Art 8 AP II.
[30] Art 15 para 2 GC I; Art 18 GC II.
[31] Art 15 para 3 GC I; Art 18 para 2 GC II; and Art 17 GC IV. Although the dead are not explicitly included, in practice the dead are collected simultaneously. See the interpretation by the ICRC on Rule 112.
[32] Art 14 GC II.
[33] The belligerent must also search for the dead and prevent their remains from being despoiled: Art 15 para 1 GC I and Art 18 para 1 GC II.
[34] Art 15 GC I; Art 18 GC II. ICRC CIHL Study, Rules 52 and 87. See also Art 8(2)(b)(xvi) ICC Statute. See further n 22 for the prohibition of pillage.
[35] As provided in Art 20 GC III, the measure of a humane evacuation requires POWs to be evacuated 'in conditions similar to those for the forces of the Detaining Power'.
[36] Art 19 para 2 GC III.

is limited to what is possible'.[37] The nature and extent of the assistance will depend upon two elements, as is clear from the wording of Article 15 GC I and Article 18 GC II: the capacities of the parties to the conflict ('take all possible measures') and the practicalities of the situation at hand ('whenever circumstances permit').

28   This set of rules creates a positive obligation to take appropriate action so as to create the circumstances that can facilitate search and collection. The term to 'take all possible measures' specifies that the obligation imposed on the parties to the conflict relates to the material possibilities existing *in the place* and *at the time* that the wounded and sick fall on the battlefield.[38] On the parallel issue of evacuating POWs, during the Eritrea–Ethiopia War (1998–2000), Eritrea described extremely difficult evacuation conditions for its POWs (to which Ethiopia offered rebuttal evidence that its soldiers faced similar and unavoidable difficult conditions): 'POWs were forced to walk from the front for hours or days over rough terrain, often in pain from their own wounds, often carrying wounded comrades, often in harsh weather, and often with little or no food and water'.[39] In light of these considerations, the Eritrea–Ethiopia Claims Commission (EECC) held that the Ethiopian troops 'satisfied the legal requirements for evacuations from the battlefield under the harsh geographic, military and logistical circumstances'.[40]

29   This obligation necessarily implies that in situations where the parties to the conflict are not able to search for, collect, and evacuate (and then ensuring adequate assistance), they have to do all they can to create the conditions so as to allow relief action, including the duty not arbitrarily to impede it. In light of these considerations, the parties to the conflict must do everything possible, subject to the state of combat, to allow the evacuation of the wounded and sick during combat activities.[41] For instance, the rationale of a duty to evacuate becomes apparent in cases where the requisite care to the wounded and sick cannot be afforded by the relevant party to the conflict. The duty to evacuate encompasses both a positive and a negative component: a duty to evacuate, and a duty not to obstruct any attempt to evacuate persons in need by relief societies or the civilian population.

30   As already mentioned, although belligerents are not entitled to invoke military necessity for not complying with their obligations, military considerations can impact on the *capacity* of the belligerents to uphold their obligations towards the wounded and sick.[42] Take, for instance, the Falkland/Malvinas armed conflict. It is reported that the small number of medical helicopters available, compared to the number of attack helicopters, was not sufficient to transport and evacuate the wounded from the war zone.[43] In fact, combat helicopters had to be used in order to help transport and evacuate the wounded and shipwrecked, with the risk of their being targeted since they were not under any special protection.[44]

c. Recording and forwarding of information

31   Once the wounded, sick, shipwrecked, or dead are collected by the competent medical personnel of the parties to the conflict, the parties must 'as soon as possible' gather the

---

[37] Pictet Commentary GC I, Art 15, at 151.
[38] This expression is found in ICRC Commentary APs, para 451.
[39] EECC, *Prisoners of War—Eritrea's Claim 17 between The State of Eritrea and The Federal Democratic Republic of Ethiopia*, Partial Award, 1 July 2003, para 67.
[40] Ibid, paras 67 and 68.
[41] Israel's High Court of Justice, *Physicians for Human Rights v Commander of IDF Forces in the Gaza Strip in 2004*, Judgment, 30 May 2004, para 23.
[42] See above, MN 19.   [43] Junod, above n 4, at 26–7.   [44] Ibid.

relevant information and keep detailed records in respect of any member of the adverse party who falls into their hands.[45] These records should, if possible, include: designation of the Power on which he or she depends; army, regimental, personal, or serial number; surname; first name or names; date of birth; any other particulars shown on his or her identity card or disc; date and place of capture or death; particulars concerning wounds or illness, or cause of death.[46] That list is indicative and non-exhaustive, and it is worth noting that other relevant information may be added to complement the particulars indicated, or to replace any of the aforementioned information.[47] Information shall be forwarded to the National Information Bureau that must be established in every country to receive and transmit information relating to the dead, the wounded and sick, POWs, and internees.[48]

IV. The obligation to care for

a. The notion

The duty to care for the wounded, sick, and shipwrecked, and its related requirements, derives from the general obligation to protect. The term to 'care for' means the provision of what is necessary for the health, welfare, maintenance, and protection of someone. As laid down in Article 12 GC I and Article 12 GC II, the duty to care for should be read broadly so as to include the principle of non-discrimination as well as humane treatment, thus involving a set of negative and positive obligations. For practical reasons, this requirement of care should apply from the time when it is possible to collect the fallen combatant. 32

Parties to the conflict and individual combatants are required to provide medical care and attention, based on the condition of the person concerned. Although IHL does not purport to define what the obligation of care entails, it should be understood broadly to include a wide range of activities, depending on the needs of the wounded and sick, that are not limited to treatment but may also include diagnosis, vaccination, or giving advice (depending on the availability of resources). To care for victims also requires a set of activities depending on the circumstances, for instance the transfer of seriously sick or wounded persons to hospitals and specialized institutions. Furthermore, the obligation to care for includes other essential forms of care of a non-medical nature, such as the provision of water, food, shelter, clothing, and hygiene, that are simultaneously required to ameliorate the condition of the person concerned.[49] 33

The fundamental duties for medical personnel are to provide care and treatment of the wounded or sick in strict accordance with generally accepted standards of medical ethics. Although the concept of medical ethics was not included *stricto sensu* in the Geneva Conventions, some activities that contradict medical ethics are specifically referred to.[50] The Geneva Conventions prohibit biological experiments, and the creation of conditions 34

---

[45] Arts 17, 120, and 122 GC III will apply to the wounded and sick when they are in a condition to assume the status of POW.
[46] Art 16 para 2(a)–(h) GC I; Art 19 para 2(a)–(h) GC II.
[47] Pictet Commentary GC I, Art 16, at 162.
[48] Art 16 GC I; Arts 122 and 123 GC III; Art 137 GC IV.
[49] See section B.V of this chapter for references to the wounded and sick who fall into enemy hands and are granted POW status (Art 14 GC I and Art 16 GC II). The wounded and sick in the power of one's own state should also enjoy similar standards in addition to those applicable under IHRL.
[50] Medical ethics here means anything related to the moral duties incumbent upon the medical profession.

exposing the wounded and sick to any contagion or infection.[51] Medical and scientific experiments that are not justified by the state of health of the protected person are also prohibited.[52]

35 The medical profession has adopted a number of codes, guidelines, and regulations. For instance, the World Medical Association (WMA) has adopted a code of ethics, as well as 'Regulations in Times of Armed Conflict and Other Situations of Violence',[53] which provide that in emergencies, physicians are required to render immediate attention to the best of their ability to civilians or combatants, and that 'no distinction shall be made between patients except those based upon clinical need'.[54]

36 The fundamental rule governing the obligation to respect, protect, and care for the wounded and sick is that of non-discrimination, which underlies IHL as a whole. Any adverse distinction based on sex, race, nationality, religion, political opinion, or similar criteria is prohibited.[55] The underlying idea is clearly that any victim—friend or foe—receives the same level of protection, respect, and care, based on need.[56]

37 Therefore, heavily injured or seriously ill persons should be treated in priority to those with wounds or sickness that are not life-threatening.[57] Similarly, the distribution of food and medicaments should follow this logic, based on the relative needs of each individual.[58] The only relevant criterion is therefore the degree of medical urgency. In accordance with this cardinal principle of equality, a party may therefore in some circumstances have to give priority to an adverse combatant before treating its own sick and wounded.

38 Medical personnel members of the armed forces may face a number of dilemmas and have to make difficult choices in armed conflicts relating to the triage of the wounded, when working with limited resources as well as poor security situations.[59] International humanitarian law does not define 'medical grounds' as criteria justifying any priority in treatment. Additional distinctions in treatment and attention may be permitted on the basis of the physical attributes of the protected persons. Thus, treating women 'with all consideration due to

---

[51] Art 12 para 2 GC I and GC II.   [52] Art 13 para 1 GC III; Art 32 GC IV.
[53] WMA Regulations in Times of Armed Conflict and Other Situations of Violence, Adopted by the 10th World Medical Assembly, Havana, Cuba, October 1956, and edited by the 11th World Medical Assembly, Istanbul, Turkey, October 1957, revised by the 35th World Medical Assembly, Venice, Italy, October 1983, the 55th WMA General Assembly, Tokyo, Japan, October 2004, editorially revised by the 173rd WMA Council Session, Divonne-les-Bains, France, May 2006, and revised by the 63rd WMA General Assembly, Bangkok, Thailand, October 2012. The WMA was created to promote the highest possible standards of medical ethics, medical education, and human rights.
[54] Ibid. Although those regulations are not binding under international law, they constitute a valuable reference. ICRC Commentary APs, Art 16 AP I, para 656; and AP II Art 10, para 4688. See also S. Mehring, 'The Rights and Duties of Physicians in Armed Conflict', 103(5) *Militair-rechtelijk tijdschrift* (2010) 205.
[55] Art 12 GC I and GC II. See also Arts 9 and 10 AP I. The 1929 GC II prohibited only distinction based on nationality.
[56] However, the equality-of-treatment standard is not always understood by all. In a NIAC, such as the one in Afghanistan, some wounded British soldiers complained in 2009 about sharing the same hospital wards with Taliban fighters at Camp Bastion in Helmand Province. The Ministry of Defence correctly replied that it is a well-established practice for casualties from both sides to be treated in the same hospitals in order to afford all patients the necessary level of care, protection, and dignity. In addition, Afghan civilians who suffer serious injuries are also treated at the field hospital as part of the coalition's 'hearts and minds' efforts. 'Troops Protest at Taliban Wounded Treatment', *Daily Telegraph*, 22 January 2009.
[57] It is spelled out that 'only urgent medical reasons will authorise priority in the order of treatment to be administered' (Art 12 para 3 GC I and GC II).
[58] J. Pictet, 'The Medical Profession and International Humanitarian Law', 25 *IRRC* 247 (1985) 191, at 197.
[59] 'Triage' is generally defined as 'the assignment of degrees of urgency to wounds or illnesses to decide the order of treatment of a large number of patients or casualties', see at <http://www.oxforddictionaries.com/definition/english/triage>.

their sex' is considered a favourable distinction, which is made compulsory under the Geneva Conventions, in addition to the general safeguards and benefits to which the wounded, sick, and shipwrecked are entitled.[60] It may be common sense to give special attention to wounded child combatants, or in relation to infirm civilians, and to expectant mothers, as stated in Article 16 GC IV.

The requirement of humane treatment is a fundamental principle that informs IHL with regard to the treatment of civilians, members of the armed forces, or those otherwise entitled to POW status. The requirement, that imposes an obligation of result, is set forth in specific provisions of all four Conventions, thus Article 12 paragraph 2 GC I and GC II provides that wounded, sick, and shipwrecked persons 'shall be treated humanely and cared for'.[61]

The scope of humane treatment is very broad, and in general terms it may prohibit any acts or omissions which cause mental or physical suffering, or represent attacks on bodily or mental integrity, or on human dignity.[62] The essential criterion is that of the preservation of human dignity. The Geneva Conventions do not provide exhaustive examples of what humane treatment involves. To decide what humane treatment comprises is 'a matter of common sense and good faith' according to Pictet, and it would be dangerous to provide a detailed definition, because it might limit the reach of the protection.[63] Obligations to the wounded and sick laid out in GC III may illustrate the scope of the obligation to treat the wounded and sick who are in enemy hands. They must be provided, inter alia, with sufficient food and water;[64] clothing appropriate to the climate;[65] with accommodation that affords sufficient standards of health and hygiene;[66] freedom in the exercise of religious practices;[67] and protection from insults and public curiosity.[68] As such, humane treatment is considered to go beyond medical treatment to cover 'all aspects of a man's existence'.[69] There is also a range of IHRL norms of particular relevance in this context. This includes not only the prohibition of inhuman treatment, but also the right to the highest attainable standard of physical and mental health.[70]

Reference to 'mercy killing' or 'battlefield euthanasia' has recently been used to characterize certain killings by the military where soldiers, basing themselves on a set of personal values, believe they are helping the mortally wounded.[71] Undoubtedly, there are cases where military medical care may be unable to save all seriously wounded combatants, or sufficiently relieve their suffering. However, there is no concept in IHL of mercy killing:[72] no military personnel are legally authorized to intentionally kill a gravely wounded combatant

---

[60] Art 12 para 4, GC I and GC II.
[61] See CA 3 para 1(1); Art 13 GC III, Art 27 GC IV. See also Art 75(1) AP I and Art 4(1) AP II. See further ICRC CIHL Study, Rule 87.
[62] See Arts 10 and 11 AP I. For the qualification of any acts or omissions as war crimes, the harm has to be 'serious'. See ICTY, *The Prosecutor v Dario Kordić and Mario Čerkez*, Appeals Chamber Judgment, IT-95-14/2-A, 17 December 2004, para 39: 'The Appeals Chamber recalls that inhuman treatment under Article 2 of the Statute is an intentional act or omission committed against a protected person, causing serious mental harm, physical suffering, injury or constitutes a serious attack on human dignity.'
[63] Pictet nonetheless defines it as 'the minimum treatment which must be accorded to the individual to enable him to lead an acceptable life': Pictet, above n 58, at 194.
[64] Art 26 GC III; Art 89 GC IV.   [65] Art 27 GC III; Art 90 GC IV.
[66] Arts 22 and 29 GC III; and Art 85 GC IV.   [67] Art 34 GC III; and Arts 86 and 93 GC IV.
[68] Art 13 para 2 GC III; Art 27 para 4 GC IV.   [69] Pictet Commentary GC I, Art 12, at 137.
[70] Art 7 ICCPR; Art 12 ICESCR. See generally G. Giacca, *Economic, Social and Cultural Rights in Armed Conflict* (Oxford: OUP, 2014).
[71] See, e.g., Canada, Court Martial Proceedings, *R v Semrau* [2010] *CM* 4010, 14 *YIHL* (2011) 8.
[72] Alston qualifies this practice as a 'dehumanization of the enemy'. Report of the Special Rapporteur on extrajudicial, summary, or arbitrary executions (A/HRC/4/20, 29 January 2007), paras 32 and 37.

in their own army, or any enemies who no longer pose an immediate threat to them, irrespective of whether it might be considered morally justifiable to do so.[73] Such action is incompatible with the obligation to treat injured combatants 'humanely', and with the obligation to 'respect and protect' them in all circumstances. This nonetheless indicates just how important ethics education is, for the military to tackle these ethical dilemmas.

b. Nature of the obligation

42   While the obligation to treat the wounded, sick, and shipwrecked humanely imposes an obligation of result, the obligation to care for the sick and wounded is an obligation of means, particularly in terms of medical care. The duty is couched in language that reflects the constraints of the situation, both temporal and practical. As with regard to the obligation to search for and collect (section B.III of this chapter), two elements inform the obligation to care for the sick and wounded: the capacities of the parties to the conflict; and the practicalities of the situation at hand.[74]

43   The obligation to care for not only includes the kind of care to be provided, but also the provision of sufficient medical infrastructure (structure, equipment, and staff) to ensure that the obligation to provide medical care is effectively fulfilled.

44   In assessing whether the parties have fulfilled their obligations, one would need to take into account the means and personnel available, bearing in mind the saying, 'no one is expected to do the impossible'. The EECC held that the requirement of medical care must be assessed in light of the harsh conditions in the combat zone, and of the limited range of medical training and equipment available to front-line troops.[75] Consequently, it seems important to draw a distinction between the legal obligation binding on parties governing their conduct in terms of obligations of means, and the actual material and financial capacity allocated by the parties to their medical services.

45   The requirement imposed here under IHL does not seem to factor in the economic capacity to allocate such resources, where not all states might have the same resources and capacities, but relates to the material possibilities limited to the actual situation in which the wounded person is cared for.[76] This was further articulated in Article 10(2) AP I, which provides that care must be administered 'to the fullest extent practicable and with the least possible delay', and recognizes that it might not be possible for a state to give the protected persons the medical care and attention required by their condition.

46   A duty to allocate means and personnel to the maximum extent of available resources could be drawn from IHRL. Under this regime, even in a prevailing security situation, where available resources are limited, the obligation remains for a state to strive to ensure the widest possible enjoyment of the relevant rights.[77]

---

[73] Ibid, paras 29–38.

[74] Art 10(2) AP I qualifies the compliance with this obligation to the material possibility to do so, where such care is to be provided 'to the fullest extent practicable and with the least possible delay'.

[75] EECC, Prisoners of War: Partial Award 17, above n 39, paras 64–5.

[76] The EECC held that 'Eritrea and Ethiopia cannot, at least at present, be required to have the same standards for medical treatment as developed countries. However, scarcity of finances and infrastructure cannot excuse a failure to grant the minimum standard of medical care required by international humanitarian law. The cost of such care is not, in any event, substantial in comparison with the other costs imposed by the armed conflict.' EECC, Prisoners of War: Partial Award 17, above n 39, para 138.

[77] Giacca, above n 70, Chapter 1.

c. Obligation when compelled to abandon the wounded and sick

In land warfare, a belligerent compelled to abandon its wounded and sick is obliged, so far 47
as military considerations (in French '*exigences*') permit, to leave medical personnel and
equipment to care for them.[78] The obligation is not absolute; reference is made by the Pictet
Commentary to a 'recommendation, but an urgent and forcible one'.[79] The commanders
are left a margin of appreciation based, on the one hand, on the medical personnel and
equipment available to be allocated to the wounded and sick, and, on the other hand, on
what would be needed for the remaining operational troops.[80] Thus, should they fall into
the hands of the enemy, military medical personnel remain protected[81] and must be free to
pursue their duties without hindrance, as long as the Detaining Power has not itself ensured
the care of the wounded and sick consistent with its obligations under GC I. Their presence does not, however, relieve the capturing armed forces from providing any additional
assistance that may be required under Article 12 GC I, which is an absolute obligation.

V. The distinction between combatants and civilians in international armed conflict

Under the Geneva Conventions, wounded, sick, and shipwrecked civilians do not seem 48
to be entitled to the same protection as combatants in IAC. A distinction is made between
the obligations in GC I and GC II to search for, collect, evacuate, and care for wounded
and sick combatants, and the obligations owed to their civilian counterparts in GC IV.

The practice of distinguishing combatant and civilian wounded and sick resulted in the 49
adoption of distinct Conventions in 1949, although the subsequent Protocols of 1977 deal
with the wounded, sick, and shipwrecked collectively. This distinction in the Conventions
may be explained by the fact that GC I and GC II indirectly establish which persons are
entitled to POW status.[82] The obligations under GC IV are specifically limited to searching for the killed and the wounded, assisting the shipwrecked (equating to 'collecting'),
and removing the wounded and sick (including the infirm, aged persons, children, and
maternity cases) from besieged or encircled areas.[83] Thus, there are a number of gaps in the
duties to search for, collect, evacuate, and care for civilian wounded and sick.

As Table 39.1 illustrates, in GC IV there is no explicit duty to collect and care for 50
wounded civilians, nor is there a duty to search for, collect, and care for sick civilians. This
fragmentation was remedied by the adoption of Article 8 AP I, stating that the rules for
the wounded, sick, and shipwrecked apply to all civilians. The International Committee
of the Red Cross (ICRC) Customary International Humanitarian Law (CIHL) Study
considered that the obligation has passed into customary law.[84] In addition, an obligation
to care for civilians was included under Article 10(2) AP I, as well as under Article 7(2) AP
II, and is also professed by the ICRC to constitute a norm of customary law.[85]

---

[78] Art 12 para 5 GC I.   [79] Pictet Commentary GC I, Art 12 para 5, at 141–2.
[80] If conditions permit, the military commander may appeal to the charity of the inhabitants on the basis of Art 18 GC I.
[81] Arts 24–32 GC I.
[82] Arts 14 GC I and Art 16 GC II respectively. This means that a wounded or sick combatant who has fallen into the hands of the enemy is at the same time a person who must be treated and assisted, and a captured combatant, who becomes a POW. Thus, the combatant is simultaneously protected by GC I and GC III, the first taking precedence in case of overlap. Once recovered, the combatant is protected by GC III, which provides equivalent guarantees relating to medical care. Pictet, above n 58, at 196.
[83] Arts 16 and 17 GC IV.   [84] ICRC CIHL Study, Rule 109.
[85] Art 10(2) AP I; Art 7 AP II. ICRC CIHL Study, Rule 110.

Table 39.1 The distinction between combatants and civilians in IAC

	Combatants				Civilians			
	Wounded	Sick	Shipwrecked	Dead (land warfare)	Wounded	Sick	Shipwrecked	Dead
Respect and protect	Art 12 GC I and GC II	Art 12 GC I and GC II	Art 12 GC II	Art 15 GC I	Art 16 GC IV	Art 16 GC IV		Art 16 GC IV
Search for	Art 15 GC I	Art 15 GC I	Art 18 GC II	Art 15 GC I	Art 16 GC IV			Art 16 GC IV
Collect	Art 15 GC I	Art 15 GC I	Art 18 GC II	Art 15 GC I			Art 16 GC IV	Art 16 GC IV
Evacuate	Art 15 GC I	Art 15 GC I	Art 18 GC II		Art 17 GC IV	Art 17 GC IV		Art 17 GC IV

51 However, this distinction in Geneva Convention treaty law between protections afforded to combatants versus those given to civilians should not be overstated, despite views occasionally expressed that the distinction is significant.[86] First, such protection may be derived from the general obligation of 'protection' under Article 16 GC IV, which is broad in scope so as to mean 'coming to their defence, lending help and support'.[87] The impersonal formulation used in this provision, that the wounded and sick 'shall be the object of particular protection and respect', may suggest that some form of obligation to act is binding on the parties to the conflict. There is clearly an obligation to come to the rescue of the civilians in need, which could, to a limited extent, be interpreted so as to encompass a duty to search for and collect.

52 Secondly, reference may be made to the actual practice in light of the fundamental principle of humanity, in virtue of which a wounded combatant and a wounded civilian are entitled to identical protection. The fact is that in practical terms, the parties to the conflict cannot ignore civilians in need of assistance, as they are entitled to the same protection as any wounded combatants.[88] This could imply the provision of first aid treatment and their safe evacuation to the hospitals facilities.

53 Thirdly, there is a clear interpenetration of the different protective regimes where, on the one hand, civilian hospitals are authorized to treat sick or wounded members of the armed forces, as provided for in Article 19 paragraph 2 GC IV, and, on the other hand, GC I and GC II (Article 22 paragraph 5 and Article 34 paragraph 4, respectively) allow the military medical service to extend the humanitarian activities to wounded and sick civilians. The three Conventions thus overlap, which demonstrates that the protection of the human person takes precedence over the distinction normally drawn between members of the armed forces and civilians.[89]

---

[86] J.P. Benoit, 'Mistreatment of the Wounded, Sick and Shipwrecked by the ICRC Study on Customary International Humanitarian Law', 11 *YIHL* (2008) 175, at 195 and 207–8.
[87] Pictet Commentary GC IV, Art 16 GC IV, at 134.
[88] Ibid, at 135–6. See also the practice relating to Rule 109 in the ICRC CIHL Study.
[89] Pictet Commentary GC IV, Art 16 GC IV, at 136.

In light of these considerations, to claim categorically that civilians would be afforded 54
less protection is somewhat misleading; however, perhaps the argument should be nuanced.
The question is not so much whether civilians are afforded the same level of protection as
their military counterparts, but rather on whom the duty is imposed. As noted earlier, the
primary responsibility under GC I and GC II falls on the parties to the conflict, who are the
direct addressees of the provisions. It is a matter of common sense that on the battlefield this
responsibility inevitably falls on the shoulders of military with regard to the fallen combatant, as codified in Article 12 GC I and GC II ('Parties to the conflict shall, without delay
[…] take all possible measures […]'). The corresponding provision in GC IV differs slightly,
in that Article 16 requires that 'each Party to the conflict shall facilitate the steps'. Thus,
the armed forces, in addition to their general obligation to protect, which incurs a positive
obligation to act, have an obligation to create the circumstances for facilitating the work of
civilians and relief organizations responsible for searching for, collecting, and bringing in
civilian casualties resulting from land and naval action.[90] As such, cooperation should be
established between the military authorities (including their medical personnel) and civilian authorities for any searches for civilian wounded, sick, and shipwrecked.

VI. Involvement of local inhabitants and relief societies: assistance in collecting and caring for the wounded, sick, and shipwrecked

a. Duties

Military commanders are authorized under Article 18 GC I to appeal to the inhabitants 55
(including inhabitants of invaded or occupied areas) to collect and care for the wounded
and sick, of whatever nationality. In naval warfare, the situation differs, as there are no
inhabitants to whom appeals may be made. However, the belligerent may appeal to commanders and captains of neutral vessels to fulfil this task, which they may also perform
'of their own accord'.[91]

This is the only provision of the Convention that is addressed specifically to the civilian 56
population, and it seeks to supplement the resources of medical services that may be insufficient or inadequate. It lays down the principle that the protection of the wounded and
sick is grounded in the ideal of universality, from which three principles may be derived
(adapting the Pictet Commentary):

— The protection and facilities accorded to the inhabitants by a belligerent party must be
   accorded to them by the adverse party.
— The inhabitants must be authorized spontaneously to collect and care for the wounded
   and sick.
— The fact of assisting the wounded and sick can never be subjected to penalties.[92]

The text of the Conventions does not impose a duty upon the civilian population towards 57
the victims of armed conflict. Civilians and the civilian population as such have no direct

---

[90] Ibid, at 135. The High Court of Justice of Israel generally emphasized that 'combat forces are required to abide by the rules of humanitarian law regarding the care of the wounded, the ill, and bodies of the deceased': *Physicians for Human Rights v The Commander of the Israeli Defense Forces*, HCJ 2941/02 HCJ 2936/02, 8 April 2002.
[91] Art 21 para 2 GC II. Necessary protection shall be accorded to such vessels by all the belligerents. Pictet Commentary GC II, Art 21, at 151.
[92] Pictet Commentary GC I, Art 18, at 185.

obligation to protect and care for others, just as they do not have an obligation to search for and collect enemy combatants or civilians in need of assistance. While there is an explicit obligation on the civilian population to respect these wounded and sick,[93] it is not stipulated that the inhabitants have in certain circumstances an obligation to collect and care for them. (This does not pre-empt the possibility of imposing positive obligations on individuals in domestic law to act and to render assistance to persons who are in danger, subject to penal sanctions.[94]) Similarly, in naval warfare, neutral vessels are not bound to fulfil this task and therefore cannot be obliged to act.[95]

58   There are no obligations to respond to an appeal from the military authorities, but in the event that the civilian population do, they will be granted the necessary protection. As such, persons engaged in such activities do not fall within the IHL definition of medical personnel; they would, however, still benefit from the protection afforded to civilians generally.[96] Moreover, the civilian population are entitled to assist the wounded, sick, and shipwrecked if they wish to do so.[97] This includes the right to receive the wounded into one's home, or to take them to a medical establishment. This entitlement is recognized as belonging to individuals, as well as to legal persons such as relief societies or national Red Cross Societies.[98]

59   It should be noted that although the wounded and sick are entrusted to inhabitants, they remain under the control of the military authorities who are responsible for their condition and medical treatment. This implies that military authorities should specify the degree of control intended to be exercised over the wounded and sick. It will rest with the military authorities to collect the identities of the wounded and sick, to inform the relevant Power of origin, and to ensure that they receive appropriate care and are treated humanely.

60   In light of these considerations, there is a clear connection between the obligation in Article 18 GC I and the one found in Article 12 GC I and Article 12 GC II concerning the general obligation to respect and protect. In addition to the obligation falling on private persons to respect the well-being of combatants who do not or no longer participate in hostilities, states must ensure that this obligation is respected by those private individuals.

b. *Confidentiality and prohibition of penalties*

61   Other key issues with regard to this rule appear to be the question of confidentiality and the prohibition of penalization, which will be discussed in turn below.

62   During the Second World War, authorities ordered civilians, including doctors, under threat of punishment for failure to do so, to report the presence of any suspected enemy, which discouraged persons in need from seeking care from a doctor.[99] It should be stated that it was not so much about confidentiality or medical secrecy, but about the

---

[93] Art 18 para 2 GC I. See also Art 17(1) AP I.
[94] It is an offence under the domestic legislation of several states to abandon the wounded and sick. See ICRC CIHL Study, vol I, Rule 109, at 397.
[95] In addition, vessels may not be captured for such transport, although they remain liable for any violations of neutrality they may commit. Art 21 para 3 GC II.
[96] See Pictet Commentary GC I, Art 18, at 188.
[97] Art 18 para 2 GC I provides: 'The military authorities shall permit the inhabitants and relief societies, even in invaded or occupied areas, spontaneously to collect and care for wounded or sick of whatever nationality.'
[98] Art 18 para 2 GC I; Art 17(1) AP I.
[99] ICRC Commentary APs, Art 16 AP I, para 671; Pictet, above n 58, at 201.

principle that the wounded and sick should not be denounced.[100] In this regard, the WMA International Code of Medical Ethics stated that physicians shall

respect a patient's right to confidentiality. It is ethical to disclose confidential information when the patient consents to it or when there is a real and imminent threat of harm to the patient or to others and this threat can be only removed by a breach of confidentiality.[101]

The protection of medical duties was not incorporated in any specific provision of the Conventions, as the representatives could not agree on the principle.[102] This question was raised again during the drafting of the Additional Protocols, where the representatives attempted to take a step forward. This led to the inclusion of the principle, under Article 16(3) AP I, that no person engaged in medical activities shall be compelled to provide information concerning the wounded or sick if it is believed that such information would be harmful to those persons and their families.[103] The rule was qualified, however, by two exceptions, one of them being rather problematic. The first exception relates to the compulsory notification of communicable diseases, while the second requires that the persons engaged in medical activities would have to disclose such information if required by a national law of their own party.[104] To subordinate such a norm of international law to national law deprives part of the norm of its substance. The general clause remains fully effective, however, in relation to the adverse Party and an Occupying Power.[105] In any event, the national law or its application could be challenged for compatibility with human rights law.[106] 63

Another question relates to the protection of persons against any form of harassment or ill-treatment for giving care to sick or wounded persons. Geneva Convention I states that 'no one may ever be molested or convicted for having nursed the wounded or sick',[107] which means that medical personnel, military or civilian, shall not be punished for having carried out a medical activity in conformity with medical ethics, whatever the circumstances or beneficiaries of this activity. This clause establishes a fundamental principle in rather clear terms, that those performing medical activities cannot be regarded as engaging in a hostile act or interference in the conflict, while reaffirming that all wounded and sick persons are to be assisted without distinction based on nationality or allegiance. The reference to penalties in this context covers any form of sanction, including both penal and administrative measures, such as, for example, dismissing an employee or expelling a medical student from university. 64

---

[100] ICRC Commentary APs, Art 16 AP I, para 670.
[101] Adopted by the 3rd General Assembly of the World Medical Association, London, England, October 1949 and amended by the 22nd World Medical Assembly, Sydney, Australia, August 1968 and the 35th World Medical Assembly, Venice, Italy, October 1983, and the 57th WMA General Assembly, Pilanesberg, South Africa, October 2006.
[102] ICRC Commentary APs, Art 16 AP I, paras 671–4.
[103] Art 16(3) AP I. See also Art 10(3) AP II. Information is understood here as any relating to activities, connections, position, or simply the existence of the wounded itself. ICRC Commentary APs, Art 16 AP I, para 682.
[104] Art 16(3) AP I.
[105] With regard to AP II, protection from compulsion and the prohibition against penalization for refusing or failing to provide the relevant information are 'subject to national law': Art 10(3) and (4) AP II.
[106] See further ECtHR, *Z v Finland*, Judgment, 5 February 1997; see also ECtHR, *I v Finland*, Judgment, 17 July 2008.
[107] See also Art 17(1) AP I, addressing the whole population, which states that '[n]o one shall be harmed, prosecuted, convicted or punished for such humanitarian acts'. This provision was adopted by consensus and no reservations to it have been made.

C. Relevance in Non-International Armed Conflicts

I. The protective regime

a. Humane treatment and medical care

65　The substantive rules applicable in NIAC relating to the protection of the wounded, sick, and shipwrecked are drafted in a succinct and less detailed form compared to the series of norms contained in the Geneva Conventions applicable to IAC. The protection is provided for in paragraph 1(2) of Common Article 3, which simply reads in absolute and unconditional terms: 'The wounded and sick shall be collected and cared for.'[108] The protective regime is reduced to the minimum core that confines itself to stating the principle, without further developing the protection of those in need or the safeguards for those who administer such protection.

66　The absence of any reference here to the obligation to 'respect and protect' within the meaning of Article 12 GC II is notable. This is explained by the fact that in order to be acceptable to all the negotiating states, any language that might have been seen as encouraging rebels to rise up and enjoy subsequent 'protection' under the Conventions needed to be avoided.[109] This being said, Common Article 3 does provide the wounded and sick with 'respect and protection' within the meaning discussed in detail throughout this chapter, especially in light of the general requirement of humane treatment.

67　As mentioned earlier, the requirement of humane treatment is a key principle informing the whole system of protection under IHL.[110] Its purpose is to uphold and protect the inherent human dignity of the individual, which provides that persons who do not take an active part in hostilities 'shall in all circumstances be treated humanely'.[111] This includes 'members of armed forces who have laid down their arms and those placed *hors de combat* by sickness, wounds, detention, or any other cause'.[112]

68　The scope and meaning of this principle was not elaborated further in treaty text,[113] the focus being instead on the four subparagraphs which specify the absolute prohibitions that result from the principle of humane treatment itself, including violence to life and person, in particular murder of all kinds, mutilation, cruel treatment, and torture; the taking of hostages; or outrages upon personal dignity, in particular humiliating and degrading treatment. This reveals that instead of defining humane treatment, the states parties chose to elaborate on the prohibited acts that are incompatible with humane treatment. The wording 'To this end' suggests that humane treatment remains the primary obligation, of which the stated prohibited acts are a concrete manifestation. Therefore this

---

[108] 'Shipwrecked' is referred to in GC II, Art 3. The wording expresses a 'categorical imperative which cannot be restricted and needs no explanation': Pictet Commentary GC I, Art 3, at 56. It is not stipulated who shall collect and care for, although the parties to the conflict remain the primary addressees.

[109] Pictet Commentary GC I, Art 3, at 57.

[110] The humane treatment principle features in all four Conventions: Art 12 GC I; Art 12 GC II; Arts 13, 20, 46 GC III; Arts 27, 37, 127 GC IV.

[111] See also the entire part dedicated to humane treatment in AP II.

[112] CA 3; Art 8(2)(c) ICC Statute.

[113] Pictet argued that it would not serve its purpose to provide a clear, detailed exposition of the principle of humane treatment which could lead to the imposition of certain limitations. The delegations to the Diplomatic Conference sought a certain flexibility in adopting the wording of the provision, without going into too much detail. Pictet Commentary GC I, CA 3, at 53–4. For an opposite view, see D.A. Elder, 'The Historical Background of Common Article 3 of the Geneva Convention of 1949', 37 *Case Western Reserve JIL* (1979) 37, at 61.

does not exclude any other prohibitions deriving from the principle of humane treatment, such as scientific experiments or wilfully leaving the wounded or sick without medical assistance.[114]

69   The need for further codification resulted in the adoption of AP II, which developed the content of Common Article 3. The protection of the wounded and sick has been further developed through the elaboration of AP II, and is considered, by some, to be part of international customary law.[115] According to Article 7(1) and (2) AP II, the wounded, sick, and shipwrecked 'shall be respected and protected', and '[i]n all circumstances they shall be treated humanely and shall receive to the fullest extent practicable and with the least possible delay, the medical care and attention required by their condition'. It would be difficult to contest that these obligations to provide protection and to ensure medical care made explicit in AP II, could not be considered an authoritative interpretation of the general requirement laid down in Common Article 3, deriving from the duty to collect and care for, as well as the requirement of humane treatment.

70   In addition, one ought to remember that human rights law, which applies in armed conflict situations, imposes a number of negative and positive obligations on states to respect, protect, and fulfil the right to life[116] and health[117] subject to their jurisdiction. Those are certainly binding obligations upon the states parties to the conflict with regard to the wounded and sick soldiers and civilians. If, and the extent to which, those same obligations equally bind armed groups remains contested.

71   Arguably, the protection of the right to health could be part of the normative content of the prohibition of torture, or inhuman or degrading treatment or punishment,[118] as much as withholding necessary medical treatment could amount to 'inhuman treatment'.[119]

b. *An obligation to search for and evacuate?*

72   Compared to treaty law relating to IAC, no duty to search and evacuate was included by the drafters in Common Article 3. The duty to search for and evacuate could be derived implicitly from the general obligation to collect the wounded and sick, as well as from the general requirement of humane treatment. However, it would stretch Common Article 3 too far to read in these obligations, especially with regard to a purposed duty to search,

---

[114] Art 12 GC I and GC II. It follows that obligations under IHL may be considered broader than under international criminal law, which is limited to the listed prohibitions. Therefore, even though certain acts prohibited in IAC, such as medical or scientific experiments, or wilfully leaving the wounded or sick without medical assistance, are absent from the treaty lists, they can be considered additional manifestations of the prohibited behaviour. See, e.g., International Institute of Humanitarian Law, *The Manual on the Law of Non-International Armed Conflict with Commentary* (San Remo: IIHL, 2006), at 14.

[115] Art 7 AP II; see also ICRC CIHL Study, Rule 109. The customary law character of certain obligations linked to the wounded and sick in IAC as well as in NIACs has not met with unanimous agreement within the scholarship, see Benoit, above n 86, at 175–219.

[116] Human rights treaty bodies and courts have interpreted the right to life as including such positive measures. With regard to treating the wounded during armed conflict, see, e.g., ECtHR, *Ahmed Özkan and others v Turkey*, Judgment, 6 April 2004, paras 307–8; ECtHR, *Varnava and others v Turkey*, Judgment, 18 September 2009, para 185; IACtHR, *Neira Alegria et al v Peru*, Judgment, 19 January 1995, para 74.

[117] Art 12 ICESCR. Withholding medical treatment from particular individuals or groups is an egregious violation of the duty to respect this right: CESCR, General Comment 14, 11 August 2000, UN Doc E/C.12/2000/4, para 50.

[118] ECtHR, *Poltoratskiy v Ukraine*, Judgment, 23 April 2003; ECtHR, *Kalashnikov v Russia*, Judgment, 15 July 2002.

[119] AComHPR, *Huri-Laws v Nigeria*, Comm 225/98, Decision, 6 November 2000, para 41; ECtHR, *Istratii and others v Moldova*, Judgment, 27 March 2007, paras 46–58; IACtHR, *Montero-Aranguran et al (Detention Center of Catia) v Venezuela*, Judgment, 5 July 2006, paras 101–3.

since the provisions afford protection only to persons falling *under the direct control* of a party to the conflict. Therefore such a duty may not have direct relevance for Common Article 3. An argument could be made that there is at least a negative component of the obligation not to arbitrarily obstruct any search or evacuation by other entities, such as relief societies or private individuals, if this would lead to a deprivation/denial of care.[120]

73 According to Article 8 AP II, which develops and reaffirms the obligation to collect the wounded and sick contained in Common Article 3,

> [w]henever circumstances permit and particularly after an engagement, all possible measures shall be taken, without delay, to search for and collect the wounded, sick and shipwrecked, to protect them against pillage and ill-treatment, to ensure their adequate care, and to search for the dead, prevent their being despoiled, and decently dispose of them.[121]

74 As seen in the extract from Article 8 above, the beneficiaries of the legal protection afforded by the duty to search for and collect the wounded, sick, and shipwrecked are extended to include the dead in AP II.[122] Under customary law, the CIHL Study suggests that the obligation to search 'without delay' applies equally to NIACs, however this is not without criticism as to an alleged lack of practice.[123] In addition, the CIHL Study enhances the rule by adding the obligation to take all possible measures to evacuate the wounded, sick, and shipwrecked without adverse distinction.

II. Security measures and counter-terrorism legislation

75 Security measures and counter-terrorism legislation have had a serious impact on the protection of the wounded and sick. The problem is that during NIAC and other situations of violence, private doctors, first-aid workers, or even ordinary civilians have been punished for assisting or treating the wounded and sick.[124] Indeed, reference should be made to the private persons who act, or the improvised groups of volunteers that come into existence, during the conflict as a matter of urgency. Relying on the civilian population's assistance often remains the last bastion of humanity in the scourge of war, where civilian medical services or humanitarian assistance are disrupted by reason of hostilities and/or lack of resources.

76 Within the complex array of domestic, regional, and international legislation and policy addressing specific questions of terrorism, the issue is that the laws, policies, practice, and regulations of governments may contradict the provisions of IHL. The scope of the criminal category of terrorism in certain counter-terrorism legislation has made it possible to criminalize medical activities.[125] For instance, domestic legislation prohibiting

---

[120] The principle of humane treatment includes the obligation to ensure that civilian populations deprived of essential supplies have access to humanitarian relief. This obligation is confirmed under CIHL, and binds both governmental and non-governmental parties to NIACs.

[121] Art 8 AP II.

[122] Ibid, however missing persons are not included. Part II, Section III, Arts 32–33 AP I.

[123] Benoit, above n 86, at 175–219.

[124] This can have a serious impact on the victims and casualties in NIAC, who often rely on spontaneous civilian aid. See Art 14(1) and (2) Turku Declaration of Minimum Humanitarian Standards, adopted by an expert meeting convened by the Institute for Human Rights of Åbo Akademi University in Turku/Åbo, Finland, in 1990.

[125] In its Country Report on Human Rights Practices for 1996, the US Department of State noted, with regard to the provisions of the Turkish Penal Code and Anti-Terror Law prohibiting assistance to illegal organizations or armed groups, that '[d]uring internal armed conflict, medical personnel should not be punished solely for treating the wounded' (Washington, DC: US Government Printing Office, 1997), at 1163.

'assistance' to illegal organizations or armed groups may be used extensively, or be interpreted broadly, so as to prosecute health professionals who administer care to persons suspected of being members of, or having been involved in activities of, these groups or organizations.[126] In the 2004 case of *De La Cruz Flores v Peru,* the Inter-American Court of Human Rights (IACtHR) reiterated the prohibition on criminalizing medical acts. In that case the defendant was detained and criminally convicted in Peru for allegedly rendering support to the Peruvian Maoist armed group Sendero Luminoso, by administering necessary medical treatment.[127] After having cited a number of international norms, including Article 12 GC I and AP II, the IACtHR held that Peru had violated the principle of legality under the American Convention,

> for penalizing a medical activity, which is not only an essential lawful act, but which it is also the physician's obligation to provide; and for imposing on physicians the obligation to report the possible criminal behavior of their patients, based on information obtained in the exercise of their profession.[128]

The main point here is that this can have serious consequences for persons in need of medical care and treatment, civilians and combatants alike. On the one hand, injured or ill persons will be prevented or discouraged from seeking medical assistance for fear of being denounced, arbitrarily arrested, or ill-treated, as was the case in the Libyan or the Syrian armed conflicts.[129] On the other hand, civilians as well as medical staff may refuse to provide medical assistance to the wounded or sick for fear of retaliation from security forces or armed groups.[130]

See also Report of the Independent International Commission of Inquiry on the Syrian Arab Republic, 5 February 2013, para 18.

[126] See, e.g., the US legislation, 18 USC 2339A (b) (1). See also 2339B (g) (4) and 2339C (e) (13). 'Material support or resources' have been described as comprising 'any property [...] or service, [...] lodging, training, expert advice or assistance, [...] communications equipment, facilities, [...] and transportation, except medicine or religious materials'. Only medicine, and not medical assistance, is excluded.

[127] IACtHR, *Case of De La Cruz-Flores v Peru*, Judgment, 18 November 2004 (Merits, Reparations, and Costs). See also another case dealt by the HRCttee concerning a doctor accused of having treated and supplied medicines to 'terrorists' and their family members—HRCttee, *Marlem Carranza Alegre v Peru*, CCPR/C/85/D/1126/2002, 17 November 2005, Comm No 1126/2002. The Working Group on Arbitrary Detention held that 'it is common for sick or injured persons engaged in clandestine activities to seek the assistance of professionals who can provide effective treatment and will observe the rules of confidentiality of the medical profession. Providing such assistance does not, however, constitute militant activism. In such cases, at most, the physician can be accused of not reporting to the appropriate authorities a matter that was possibly associated with a crime, but that would not necessarily constitute collaborating with someone to commit a crime.' Working Group on Arbitrary Detention, 27 February 2012, A/HRC/WGAD/2010/32, Opinions adopted by the Working Group on Arbitrary Detention at its fifty-ninth session, 18–26 November 2010, No 32/2010 (Peru), para 27.

[128] IACtHR, *Case of De La Cruz-Flores v Peru*, above n 127, para 102.

[129] International Commission of Inquiry to investigate all alleged violations of international human rights law in the Libyan Arab Jamahiriya, Report, UN Doc A/HRC/17/44, 1 June 2011, paras 130–9. In the Syrian conflict, there have been documented instances of 'doctors, Government forces and snipers interfering with or blocking timely access to medical treatment, compounded by a general climate of fear that prevents civilians from accessing state hospitals, [which] has meant that those wounded in hostilities have languished without assistance, prevented from accessing basic emergency medical care. Government forces have violated the Common Article 3 provision to the Geneva Conventions that "the wounded and sick shall be collected and cared for."' Report of the Independent International Commission of Inquiry on the Syrian Arab Republic, 5 February 2013, para 40.

[130] Report of the Independent International Commission of Inquiry on the Syrian Arab Republic, 5 February 2013, paras 40 and 144. In Syria, many injured persons were prevented from receiving treatment in both public and private hospitals. Medical staff were allegedly warned not to treat or provide any assistance to the victims, and those who set up alternative medical facilities or provided medical treatment were persecuted (ibid, paras 80–2).

77 For reasons that are self-evident, in order that the wounded, sick, and shipwrecked may be afforded assistance and medical care, it follows that those providing the assistance and care should themselves be respected and protected. If the intention is to protect the wounded and sick, it is important that the persons caring for them, as well as medical buildings and facilities, remain fully protected. On this point, the ICRC has argued that the clause on the wounded and sick in Common Article 3 implies that 'medical personnel' be protected as 'a subsidiary form of protection granted to ensure that the wounded and sick receive medical care'.[131]

78 Common Article 3 makes it clear that the wounded and sick shall be cared for, and this is so notwithstanding the characteristics, activities, and beliefs of the persons concerned, or the origin of their injuries or illnesses. A clear boundary should thus be established between punishable conduct under the rule of law and those acts that are performed exclusively within the framework of medical care. Common Article 3 offers the protection to any person performing medical activities, as long as they are 'taking no active part in the hostilities'.[132]

79 Significant progress was made with AP II under Article 10(1), which codified the rule that no one shall be punished for having carried out medical activity in conformity with medical ethics. In addition, domestic norms that are contrary to the principles of medical ethics cannot be imposed on persons engaged in medical activity. They shall 'neither be compelled to perform acts or to carry out work contrary to, nor be compelled to refrain from acts required by, the rules of medical ethics or other rules designed for the benefit of the wounded and sick, or this Protocol' (Article 10(2) AP II).

80 International human rights law will also be relevant through a number of norms relating to humane treatment, liberty and security, fair trial, or the right to work, though some of these norms may be subject to limitations and open to derogations. It follows that any ill-treatment or violence against civilians or against any health professionals seeking to care for the wounded or sick, or any arbitrary effort to prevent medical care being provided to those in need, would be equally prohibited.

III. Application to non-state armed groups

81 Since Common Article 3 is applicable 'in the case of armed conflict not of an international character', the obligation to collect and care for the wounded and sick is incumbent on all parties, including armed non-state actors. However, this is not without difficulty. The nature and extent of the care would depend upon the capabilities of the armed group, as well as on the situation at the time of the action. These obligations have been followed by a number of armed groups through bilateral agreements concluded between parties to the conflict and through internal instructions (for example codes of conduct).[133] The obligations are explained in a realistic fashion in Article 7 AP II, which calls for medical care and attention to be provided 'to the fullest extent practical and with the least possible

---

[131] ICRC CIHL Study, Rule 25.
[132] Persons subject to criminal process have a number of important safeguards of a dual treaty-based nature, i.e. CA 3, para 1(d), as well as IHRL norms.
[133] See S. Sivakumaran, *The Law of Non-International Armed Conflict* (Oxford: OUP, 2012), at 275. E.g., with respect to the practice and commitments of armed groups, the National Liberation Army of Libya issued a set of guidelines: 'Give immediate medical treatment/first aid to anyone who needs it. There is a duty to

delay'; and with regard to the obligation to search for and collect, Article 8 demands that 'all possible measures' are taken 'whenever circumstances permit'.

Of course, one might ask whether the non-state armed group has the capacity to uphold 82 certain obligations, since what an armed group can actually deliver is context-dependent and capacity-related. But this is a practical matter and not a legal requirement. Providing medical care ranges from basic first aid treatment to more complex types of care. It is common practice that the ICRC teaches members of the armed groups the basics of first aid and gives them medical materials, equipment, and supplies, so that civilians and combatants who are *hors de combat* and in need of medical assistance may be treated in the field. The general principle is that IHL requires the wounded and sick to be cared for, to the best of the ability of both state and non-state parties, under the prevailing adverse conditions of armed violence.

D. Legal Consequences of a Violation

In accordance with Article 50 GC I and Article 51 GC II, any wilful killing, torture or 83 inhuman treatment, including biological experiments, wilfully causing great suffering or serious injury to the body or health of the sick, wounded, and shipwrecked, are characterized as grave breaches and engage in consequence the criminal responsibility of the individuals who commit them. In accordance with Article 147 GC IV, any wilful killing, torture or inhuman treatment, including biological experiments, wilfully causing great suffering or serious injury to the body or health of wounded and sick civilians protected by GC IV, constitute grave breaches of the Convention.

The 'grave breaches' regime applicable to these offences also imposes procedural obliga- 84 tions upon Contracting Parties, which are provided for in Common Articles 49, 50, and 146 of GC I, GC II, and GC IV respectively (see Chapter 31 of this volume). This provision common to all Geneva Conventions imposes on the High Contracting Parties two types of obligations:

— a duty to criminalize these acts in domestic legislation; and
— a duty to search for persons alleged to have committed such grave breaches, who happen to be in their territory, and to bring them before their own courts.[134]

A state party may also choose to extradite the alleged perpetrators to another state that also seeks their prosecution for the same crimes. The regime, Abi-Saab writes,

purports to be water-tight against impunity, by imposing on States parties the alternative obligation to prosecute or extradite, [...] a principle [which] is more stringent than that of 'universal jurisdiction' largely recognized as applicable to war crimes in general, which is merely permissive.[135]

search for, collect, and aid the injured and wounded from the battlefield of both sides. The dead must also be collected, treated with respect, and buried.' O. Bangerter, 'A Collection of Codes of Conduct Issued by Armed Groups', 93 *IRRC* 882 (2011), at 499.

[134] For a state party also party to AP I, this list is extended by Art 85(2) of that Protocol, which reads: 'Acts described as grave breaches in the Conventions are grave breaches of this Protocol if committed against persons in the power of an adverse Party protected by Articles 44, 45 and 73 of this Protocol, or against the wounded, sick and shipwrecked of the adverse Party who are protected by this Protocol, or against those medical or religious personnel, medical units or medical transports which are under the control of the adverse Party and are protected by this Protocol.'

[135] G. Abi-Saab, 'The Concept of "War Crimes"', in Sienho Yee and Wang Tieya (eds), *International Law in the Post-Cold War World* (London: Routledge, 2001) 99, at 112.

85 The Statute of the International Criminal Court (ICC) incorporates these 'grave breaches' into Article 8(2)(a) as a category of war crimes, viz in Article 8(2)(a) from (i) to (iii). For NIACs, the relevant provision is to be found in Article 8(2)(c)(i), which is taken from Common Article 3.

86 Additionally, an intentional attack against places where the sick and wounded are collected, provided they are not military objectives, is a war crime under Article 8(2)(b)(ix) of the ICC Statute. The question arises as to whether attacks on hospital and humanitarian objects give rise to a violation of the duty to 'provide care for the sick and the wounded' as enunciated by Common Article 3. The answer is to be found in Article 8(2)(e)(iv) of the ICC Statute, according to which the same act committed in armed conflicts not of an international character is also an offence identified in the Statute under the heading 'other serious violations of the laws and customs' applicable in NIAC.

87 Among the scant case law on the protection of wounded and sick, it is worth noting that depriving wounded and sick civilians, who were detained alongside combatants by Yugoslav military personnel, of medical care, was considered to constitute cruel treatment under Article 3 of the Statute of the International Criminal Tribunal for the former Yugoslavia (ICTY).[136]

88 Questions arise as to whether the obligation to collect and care for, being a positive obligation, can give rise to omission liability for war crimes in the event of a violation of this obligation. Assuming that the obligation also applies vis-à-vis the belligerents' own combatants, whether this can amount to a war crime per se, and thereby entail individual criminal responsibility, is debatable. While the failure to search for, collect, and care for the wounded and sick could certainly meet the threshold of having serious consequences for the victims, it is not clear whether or not individual criminal responsibility for the violation of this exists under customary law. In any event, the omission could *constitute* the *basis* of several crimes under international law, including wilful killing or murder, torture, inhuman treatment, and wilfully causing great suffering or serious injury to body or health (see further Chapter 36, MN 25–30, of this volume).

89 Another aspect of the topic involves the question of whether engagement of civilians leading to serious violations of the rules of IHL may be subject to war crimes proceedings. In the present context, participation of a civilian directly and/or indirectly in the mistreatment of the wounded or sick would, for example, amount to a war crime.[137] The general answer is that civilians may indeed be liable for war crimes under certain conditions. One approach is that the responsibility of civilians for the commission of war crimes is supported where there is a link between the accused civilian and a 'Party to the conflict'. The jurisprudence confirms this. At the international level, the issue has been dealt with

---

[136] ICTY, *The Prosecutor v Mile Mrkšić et al*, Trial Chamber Judgment, IT-95-13/1-T, 27 September 2007, paras 516–17. Cruel treatment is therein defined as an intentional act or omission causing serious mental or physical suffering or injury to, or constituting a serious attack on human dignity upon, a person taking no active part in the hostilities. The Trial Chamber concluded that 'while many prisoners received serious injuries [...], in such cases the infliction of injuries and the failure to provide treatment for the injuries caused, is in reality the same behaviour. The deprivation of medical care in such cases is subsumed in the acts of mistreatment themselves.' Ibid, para 528.

[137] On the violations of the Geneva Conventions as war crimes, see Ch 36, MN 10–24, of this volume.

by the International Criminal Tribunal for Rwanda (ICTR) in several cases, including in *Akayesu*.[138] The view of the ICTR in *Musema* was:

So it is well-established that the post-World War II Trials unequivocally support the imposition of individual criminal liability for war crimes on civilians where they have a link or connection with a Party to the conflict.[139]

A similar position was taken by the ICTY in the *Kunarac* case.[140] In the *Akayesu* Appeal Judgment the ICTR reversed its view taken in *Musema*, stating that

common Article 3 requires a close nexus between violations and the armed conflict. This nexus [...] implies that, in most cases, the perpetrator of the crime will probably have a special relationship with one party to the conflict. However, such a special relationship is not a condition precedent to the application of common Article 3 and, hence of Article 4 of the Statute.[141]

Judgments of national courts have also applied the laws of warfare to the conduct of civilians.[142] The Elements of Crimes for Article 8 under the ICC Statute (which are designed to assist the ICC in the interpretation and application of Articles 6, 7, and 8) equally require that offences be connected to the *conflict*, omitting any reference to the need for a link with a party to the conflict.[143]

E. Critical Assessment

The rules relating to the obligations owed to the wounded, sick, and shipwrecked were primarily drafted against the backdrop of traditional IACs between the regular armed forces of states, IHL needing mainly to protect these persons against the enemy and to ensure their adequate treatment under GC I and GC II. Unfortunately, not only combatant casualties of armed conflict, but also civilian casualties are caused in modern warfare, where armed hostilities occur in or near urban densely populated areas as a result of air bombardment, artillery, or mortar strikes. In this regard, GC IV provides protection to non-combatants (i.e. civilians), but the regime is clearly different from those afforded in the other Geneva Conventions.

---

[138] ICTR, *The Prosecutor v Jean-Paul Akayesu*, Trial Chamber Judgment, ICTR-96-4, 2 September 1998, para 631.

[139] ICTR, *The Prosecutor v Alfred Musema*, Trial Chamber Judgment and Sentence, ICTR-96-13-T, 27 January 2000, para 274.

[140] In particular it held: 'It would appear to the Trial Chamber that common Art. 3 may also require some relationship to exist between a perpetrator and a party to the conflict. Since, in the present case, the three accused fought on behalf of one of the parties to the conflict, the Trial Chamber does not need to determine whether such a relationship is required, and if so, what the required relationship should be.' ICTY, *The Prosecutor v Dragoljub Kunarac, Radomir Kovač and Zoran Vuković (Foča)*, Trial Chamber Judgment, IT-96-23 and IT-96-23/1, 22 February 2001, para 407.

[141] ICTR, *Akayesu*, above n 138, paras 444–5.

[142] See, e.g., *Niyonteze v Public Prosecutor*, Tribunal Militaire de Cassation, 27 April 2001, at 40–1.

[143] The ICC Elements of Crimes, Article 8. The ICRC CIHL Study summarizes the state of practice on the issue as following: 'Practice in the form of legislation, military manuals and case-law shows that war crimes are violations committed either by members of the armed forces or by civilians against members of the armed forces, civilians or protected objects of the adverse party. National legislation typically does not limit the commission of war crimes to members of the armed forces, but rather indicates the acts that are criminal when committed by any person. Several military manuals contain the same approach. A number of military manuals, as well as some legislation, expressly include the term "civilians" among the persons that can commit war crimes.' See ICRC CIHL Study, Rule 156 (Definition of War Crimes).

92   The provisions concerning relief for civilians are generally weak, but this has been redressed by the terms of the Additional Protocols, which contain provisions amplifying the obligation to care for persons protected by GC I and GC II. They are innovative in this respect, extending the scope of the earlier Conventions so that civilians, as well as military personnel, are entitled to protection.

93   Beyond that, it must be admitted, however, that the regime of protection regarding the sick and wounded is not fully adequate in situations of NIAC, the regime remaining rather generic and lacking in detail. We have seen that even under customary humanitarian law certain lacunae remain, such as the delicate issue of the extent to which the civilian population and health professionals are protected against harassment or conviction, and for refusing to disclose to the authorities information relating to the wounded and sick in their care. In this context, as suggested in this chapter, the protection regime and related obligations may be interpreted and modified by IHRL and state practice, thereby providing the best protection possible to individuals in need.

GILLES GIACCA*

---

* Gilles Giacca has written this chapter in an entirely personal capacity. The opinions expressed herein are his own and do not necessarily correspond to those held by the ICRC or its legal division.

Chapter 40. The Status, Rights, and Obligations of Medical and Religious Personnel

	MN
A. Introduction	1
B. Meaning and Application	6
I. The scope and nature of protection	6
a. The scope of medical personnel protected	6
b. The nature of protection	7
c. Similar protection for related personnel	10
d. Spontaneous medical care by the civilian population	16
e. Civilian hospital personnel	20
f. Protection for religious personnel	22
g. Identification of medical and religious personnel	25
h. Protection of military medical and religious personnel at sea	30
i. Loss of protection for religious and medical personnel	32
j. Duties of medical personnel in international armed conflict	35
II. Treatment upon capture of medical and religious personnel and repatriation	36
C. Relevance in Non-International Armed Conflicts	40
D. Legal Consequences of a Violation	46
E. Critical Assessment	52

Select Bibliography

Baccino-Astrada, A., *Manual on the Rights and Duties of Medical Personnel in Armed Conflicts* (Geneva: ICRC/League, 1982)

De Waard, P./Tarrant, J., 'Protection of Military Medical Personnel in Armed Conflicts', 35 *UWA Law Review* (2010) 157

Hiebel, J.-L., 'Human Rights Relating to Spiritual Assistance as Embodied in the Geneva Conventions of 1949', 20 *IRRC* 214 (1980) 3

Lunze, S., 'Serving God and Caesar: Religious Personnel and their Protection in Armed Conflict', 86 *IRRC* 853 (2004) 69

O'Brien, R., *A Manual of International Humanitarian Law for Religious Personnel* (Adelaide: Australian Red Cross, 1993)

Pictet, J., 'The Medical Profession and International Humanitarian Law', 85 *IRRC* 247 (1985) 191

A. Introduction

The protection of the wounded, and later the medical personnel caring for them, can be traced back to the middle of the sixteenth century.[1] A humanitarian desire to care for

---

[1] P. De Waard and J. Tarrant, 'Protection of Military Medical Personnel in Armed Conflicts', 35 *UWA Law Review* (2010) 157, at 160, citing L.C. Green, 'The Relations between Human Rights Law and International Humanitarian Law: A Historical Overview', in S.C. Breau and A. Jachec-Neale (eds), *Testing the Boundaries of International Humanitarian Law* (London: British Institute of International and Comparative Law, 2006) 49, at 65; and G. Butler and S. Maccoby, *The Development of International Law* (London: Longmans Green, 1928), at 149.

war-wounded was one of the primary motivations for the elaboration of the first Geneva Convention in 1864, and indeed the foundation of the Red Cross Movement. In 1859, Henry Dunant, a citizen of Geneva, witnessed the battle of Solferino in northern Italy at which thousands of wounded soldiers died, whose lives could have been saved with adequate medical care. In 1862, Dunant published his famous book *A Memory of Solferino*, in which he proposed to set up relief societies in each nation to care for the wounded in time of war. He also proposed the adoption of an international agreement to protect medical staff and the injured.[2]

2   On 9 February 1863, the Geneva Society of Public Welfare, under the presidency of Gustave Moynier, appointed a Committee to consider the idea of recruiting voluntary male nurses to serve the armed forces in the field. Initially naming itself the 'International Relief Committee for Injured Combatants', in 1875 the Committee adopted the name the 'International Committee of the Red Cross' (ICRC). It convened an International Conference in Geneva on 26 October 1863 that adopted proposals to create national Red Cross societies and decided that a red cross on a white background should be the distinctive sign of the medical personnel (the inversion of the Swiss flag, as 'a compliment to Switzerland').[3] The following year, the Diplomatic Conference held on 8–22 August 1864 adopted the Geneva Convention for the Amelioration of the Condition of the Wounded in Armies in the Field. The main principles laid down in that Convention and maintained by the 1949 Geneva Conventions are: care for the wounded without adverse distinction; neutrality of medical personnel; and use of the Red Cross emblem to identify relief services.[4]

3   Thus, whenever possible, and particularly after hostilities occur, each party to a conflict must do all it can to find and evacuate the wounded and sick as quickly as possible, regardless of the party to which they belong and of whether or not these victims of conflict have taken direct part in hostilities.[5] They must then, as far as practicable, be given the necessary medical care. In providing assistance, the only lawful distinction that may be made is on medical grounds.[6] In accordance with their neutral role, medical personnel must be respected and protected, losing this protection only if they commit acts harmful to the enemy.[7] Attacks against medical and religious personnel and objects displaying the distinctive emblems of the Geneva Conventions (the red cross, the red crescent,[8] and, since 2005, the red crystal)[9] are prohibited.[10] These fundamental rules for the protection of the victims of conflict are the mainstay of 'Geneva law'.

4   The core provision of the 1949 Geneva Conventions with respect to medical and religious personnel is set out in Article 24 of the 1949 Geneva Convention (GC) I for the Amelioration of the Condition of the Wounded and Sick in Armed Forces in the Field:

Medical personnel exclusively engaged in the search for, or the collection, transport or treatment of the wounded or sick, or in the prevention of disease, staff exclusively engaged in the administration

---

[2] See, e.g., D. Schindler and J. Toman, *The Laws of Armed Conflicts* (3rd rev edn, Dordrecht: Martinus Nijhoff, 1988), at 230–1.
[3] See Art 53 GC I; and Pictet Commentary GC I, at 298.   [4] Ibid.
[5] See ICRC CIHL Study, Rule 109.   [6] See ibid, Rule 110.   [7] See ibid, Rule 25.
[8] During the 1876–8 war between Russia and Turkey, the Ottoman Empire declared that it would use the red crescent on a white background in place of the red cross. While respecting the red cross symbol, the Ottoman authorities believed the red cross was, by its nature, offensive to Muslim soldiers. In the 1929 GC, both the red cross and red crescent were recognized emblems. The red lion and sun also became a recognized emblem, though is no longer in use. See ICRC, 'The History of the Emblems', 14 January 2007, at <http://www.icrc.org/eng/resources/documents/misc/emblem-history.htm>.
[9] AP III.   [10] See ICRC CIHL Study, Rule 30.

of medical units and establishments, as well as chaplains attached to the armed forces, shall be respected and protected in all circumstances.

The protection granted by GC I is limited to army medical personnel and army chaplains in a situation of international armed conflict (IAC), though in the view of the ICRC Customary International Humanitarian Law (CIHL) Study, state practice has resulted in the broader rule that 'medical personnel exclusively assigned to medical duties must be respected and protected in all circumstances', attaining the status of a customary international humanitarian law (IHL) rule applicable both in IAC and in armed conflict of a non-international character (NIAC).[11] State practice and *opinio juris* for the rule are stronger with respect to IAC than NIAC, though the rule can also be seen as deriving from the customary international law obligation in Common Article 3 to the 1949 Geneva Conventions, whereby the wounded and sick 'shall be collected and cared for'.

B. Meaning and Application

I. The scope and nature of protection

a. *The scope of medical personnel protected*

Under GC I, the term 'medical personnel' is broad in scope, encompassing 'doctors, surgeons, dentists, chemists, orderlies, nurses, stretcher-bearers, etc, who give direct care to the wounded and sick',[12] as long as they are members of the armed forces.[13] The only qualifying condition is that they be 'exclusively engaged' in looking for, transporting, treating, or caring for the wounded or sick, or in preventing disease,[14] or a combination of such tasks. The words 'exclusively engaged' require that the assignment be permanent, which is not the case in the provision addressing auxiliary medical personnel (discussed at MN 11).[15]

b. *The nature of protection*

The protection afforded to those who fall within the scope of the various provisions is broad: they 'shall be respected and protected in all circumstances'. In accordance with the meaning accorded to the terms 'respected and protected' elsewhere in GC I, murder and physical violence are strictly prohibited, as is medical experimentation. Such persons must not 'wilfully' be left without medical assistance and care, nor exposed to contagion or infection.[16]

The notion of 'respect' refers to an obligation to refrain from any acts of violence against those covered by the provisions. Any form of attack by enemy forces on those granted protection is thus unlawful. The duty to 'protect' imposes an additional obligation to ensure that others do not interfere with the work of medical personnel, let alone allow them to be harmed in any way. Thus, should they fall into the hands of the enemy,[17] military medical

---

[11] ICRC CIHL Study, Rule 25.   [12] Pictet Commentary GC I, at 218.
[13] See also Art 15 AP I, which extends protection afforded by the GCs to civilian medical and religious personnel. The issue of such civilian personnel is discussed further below in MN 16–21.
[14] In 'modern armies, hygienic and prophylactic measures for the prevention of disease—inoculation, delousing, disinfection of water supply, and so on—form an important part of the work of the medical staff': Pictet Commentary GC I, at 219.
[15] Ibid.   [16] Art 12 GC I.
[17] A party to a conflict that 'is compelled to abandon wounded or sick to the enemy shall, as far as military considerations permit, leave with them a part of its medical personnel and material to assist in their care': Art 12 GC I.

personnel on land must be free to pursue their duties without hindrance, as long as the capturing armed force has not itself ensured the care of the wounded and sick consonant with its obligations under GC I.[18] In any event, these medical personnel must be treated humanely, without any distinction founded on sex, race, nationality, religion, political opinion, or other similar criteria.

9   The words 'in all circumstances' make it clear that medical personnel 'are to be respected and protected at all times and in all places, both on the battlefield and behind the lines, and whether retained only temporarily by the enemy or for a lengthy period'.[19] In accordance with Article 7 GC I, military medical personnel and chaplains 'may in no circumstances renounce in part or in entirety the rights secured to them' by the Convention. Further, no special agreement shall adversely affect the situation of medical personnel or chaplains, 'nor restrict the rights which it confers upon them'.[20]

c. Similar protection for related personnel

10   Similar protection to medical personnel is also afforded under Article 24 to administrative staff of medical units and establishments, again on condition that they be exclusively engaged in administrative tasks related to medical care and assistance. Such personnel include not only office staff, but also ambulance drivers, cooks, and cleaners.[21]

11   Under Article 25 GC I, temporally limited protection but to the same standard is afforded to 'auxiliary medical personnel', namely members of the armed forces 'specially trained' for use as hospital orderlies, nurses, or auxiliary stretcher-bearers, who look for, transport, treat, or care for the wounded or sick. They must 'likewise' be respected and protected in all circumstances 'if they are carrying out these duties at the time when they come into contact with the enemy or fall into his hands'.[22] It has been argued that this provision 'must not be interpreted too literally. A bandsman detailed for medical duties, but waiting his turn and not actually engaged in treating the wounded at the moment when his unit is captured, must nevertheless be respected and protected. At that moment he is no longer a combatant or even a bandsman, but a part of the Medical Service.'[23]

12   Further, under Article 26 GC I, the staff of national Red Cross (and Red Crescent) societies and that of 'other Voluntary Aid Societies',[24] as long as they are 'duly recognized and authorized by their Governments' to act as medical personnel of their armed forces, are afforded the same protection as military medical personnel under Article 24. This applies in so far as they are carrying out the same duties as that personnel, and provided that 'the staff of such societies are subject to military laws and regulations'. It is, however, incumbent on each state party engaged in an IAC to notify the enemy, either in peacetime or when hostilities break out, of the names of the societies 'which it has authorized, under its responsibility, to render assistance to the regular medical

---

[18] In particular, in accordance with Arts 12–17.
[19] Pictet Commentary GC I, at 220.   [20] Art 6 GC I.
[21] Pictet Commentary GC I, at 219.
[22] For the remainder of their time such personnel will be assigned to other military duties. There is said to be no reason why the personnel protected by this provision 'should not also include military personnel who are combatants in the true sense of the word': Pictet Commentary GC I, at 222.
[23] Ibid, at 223.
[24] The ICRC observes that the term 'voluntary aid societies' does not mean that staff of such societies are necessarily unpaid. It means that their work is not based on any obligation to the state, but on an undertaking of their own free will. Pictet Commentary GC I, at 225.

service of its armed forces'. This notification must occur 'in any case' before the societies are actually employed.[25]

Article 27 expressly allows a 'recognized Society of a neutral country' to 'lend' its medical personnel and units to a party to the conflict, but only with 'the previous consent of its own Government and the authorization of the Party to the conflict concerned'. All such personnel and units must be placed under the control of that party to the conflict. The 'neutral' government must also notify its consent to the enemy of the state that has accepted its offer of assistance, while the party to the conflict that accepts such assistance is required to notify its enemy before any use is made of such medical personnel and units. Should they be captured by the enemy, they may not be detained.[26] Article 27 further provides that in no circumstances shall the medical assistance provided by the third (neutral) state be considered as interference in the armed conflict.[27] 13

Of further note is the provision in 1977 Additional Protocol (AP) I whereby the relevant provisions of Articles 27 and 32 GC I are applied to permanent medical units and transports (other than hospital ships, to which Article 25 GC II applies), and their personnel made available to a party to the conflict for humanitarian purposes by either a neutral or another state not party to the conflict; by a recognized and authorized aid society of such a state; or by an impartial international humanitarian organization.[28] 14

According to GC I, recognized organizations of neutral states can make their medical personnel and units available to the parties to the conflict in accordance with the procedure and rules laid down in Article 27. The aim of Article 9(2) AP I is thus to extend this possibility to two other categories: a recognized and authorized aid society of a neutral state, and an 'impartial international humanitarian organization'. Already under Article 9 GC I it was stipulated that the provisions of the Convention 15

constitute no obstacle to the humanitarian activities which the International Committee of the Red Cross or any other impartial humanitarian organization may, subject to the consent of the Parties to the conflict concerned, undertake for the protection of wounded and sick, medical personnel and chaplains, and for their relief.[29]

d. *Spontaneous medical care by the civilian population*

Without prejudice to the obligations upon an Occupying Power to give 'both physical and moral care to the wounded and sick',[30] it is specifically foreseen under GC I that military authorities 'may appeal to the charity of the inhabitants voluntarily to collect and care 16

---

[25] Art 26 GC I.

[26] Art 32 GC I. Unless otherwise agreed, they are allowed to return to their country, or 'if this is not possible, to the territory of the Party to the conflict in whose service they were, as soon as a route for their return is open and military considerations permit'. Pending release, they are required to continue their work under the direction of the adverse party 'preferably [...] in the care of the wounded and sick of the Party to the conflict in whose service they were'. On departure, they are required to take their personal effects and any instruments, arms, and, if possible, the means of transport that belong to them. They must receive the same food, lodging, allowances, and pay as are granted to the corresponding personnel of the armed forces by whom they are held.

[27] According to Art 4 GC I, neutral Powers are required to apply 'by analogy' the provisions of the Convention to 'members of the medical personnel and to chaplains of the armed forces of the Parties to the conflict, received or interned in their territory, as well as to dead persons found'.

[28] Art 9(2) AP I.

[29] See, e.g., 'Technical Note: The Red Cross and its Role as an Auxiliary to Military Medical Services', 23 *IRRC* 234 (1983) 139, at 139–41.

[30] Art 18 para 4 GC I.

for, under their direction, the wounded and sick'. The Pictet Commentary asserts that the obligation to treat a wounded soldier without delay, regardless of his nationality, is of such urgency that, if the relevant army medical service cannot cope, civilians in the state in which fighting is taking place 'must be asked to help'. With all due respect, this appears to be somewhat overstated. The provision in Article 18 is permissive, not obligatory. There is thus no requirement that the party to the conflict engage civilians in care of the wounded or sick (nor is there any corresponding obligation on civilians to respond positively to any request; they may not be compelled to assist).[31]

17   However, any individuals who do respond to this appeal must certainly be granted 'the necessary protection and facilities'.[32] Furthermore, should the enemy take or retake control of the area where such medical care is being provided, these individuals must be granted the same protection and the same facilities.[33] 'The principle according to which a fallen combatant is entitled to respect and care thus becomes universal.'[34]

18   The military authorities are also obliged to permit the civilian population and relief societies, 'even in invaded or occupied areas, spontaneously to collect and care for wounded or sick of whatever nationality'. In any event, it is prohibited either to 'molest' (i.e. harass or ill-treat) or to convict anyone for having cared for the wounded or sick.[35] Analogous provisions are set out in Article 21 GC II for care by civilians of military wounded at sea or shipwrecked.

19   Under GC I, the civilian population as a whole is required to 'respect' the (military) wounded and sick, and must not, 'in particular', carry out acts of violence against them.[36] The duty imposed is thus not to 'protect' them. Of note, this is the only provision in the 1949 Geneva Conventions where a rule is explicitly addressed to the civilian population. With respect to a similar provision in AP I,[37] the ICRC Commentary argues that 'as with any rule in the Protocol, it is appropriate to recall that it is up to the High Contracting Parties to respect and to ensure respect for it in all circumstances, [...] and therefore to instruct the civilian population accordingly'.[38] While this assertion is not generally questioned, arguably these provisions also impose a substantive obligation upon civilians. A civilian who kills or harms a wounded soldier surely commits a criminal offence under national law, but is also seemingly a direct addressee of IHL.

e. Civilian hospital personnel

20   According to Article 20 of GC IV Relative to the Protection of Civilian Persons in Time of War, those persons who are 'regularly and solely engaged in the operation and administration of civilian hospitals', including personnel engaged in searching for, removing, and transporting, and caring for wounded and sick civilians, the infirm,

---

[31] Again, the Pictet Commentary asserts that '[a]nyone who finds a fallen combatant can, and must, pick him up and give him help': Pictet Commentary GC I, at 184. Cf Ch 39, section B, of this volume, where it is highlighted that there may nonetheless be obligations under domestic law to search and care for the wounded and sick.
[32] Art 18 GC I.   [33] Ibid.   [34] Pictet Commentary GC I, at 184.
[35] Art 18 GC I. See further section C of this chapter and Ch 39, section C, of this volume, for a discussion of counter-terrorism measures taken against those providing medical assistance in a NIAC.
[36] Art 18 GC I.
[37] Art 17(1) AP I: 'The civilian population shall respect the wounded, sick and shipwrecked, even if they belong to the adverse Party, and shall commit no act of violence against them.'
[38] ICRC Commentary APs, at 211–12.

and maternity cases, must be respected and protected. Other personnel engaged in operating and administrating civilian hospitals are entitled to respect and protection under the Article while they are employed on such duties.

Thus, to fall within the definition of those entitled to respect and protection, staff must be regularly and solely engaged in the operation or administration of a civilian hospital as defined in Article 18 of the Convention.[39] The term 'regularly' excludes temporary staff, while the word 'solely' bars them from doing any other work. These two conditions are cumulative.[40]

f. Protection for religious personnel

According to Article 24 GC I, the same level of protection granted to military medical personnel—'shall be respected and protected in all circumstances'—is also accorded to 'chaplains attached to the armed forces'.[41] The attachment of religious personnel may be either permanent or temporary, 'unless otherwise specified', according to Article 8(k) AP I, but as with medical personnel, only religious personnel exclusively assigned by the state to religious duties are protected.

A chaplain is not defined in the 1949 Geneva Conventions, but was ordinarily understood at the time of their adoption as being a member of the clergy of the Christian Church.[42] Such a denominational limitation is anachronistic, and thus AP I included a more general definition of 'religious personnel' as meaning 'military or civilian persons, such as chaplains, who are exclusively engaged in the work of their ministry' and who are attached to the armed forces, medical units, medical transports, or civil defence organizations of a party to an IAC.[43] Indeed, to accept otherwise would be to discriminate between religions, itself a violation of a fundamental principle underlying both the Geneva Conventions and human rights law.[44]

---

[39] Under Art 18, civilian hospitals are those organized to give care to the wounded and sick, the infirm, and maternity cases. A state that is party to a conflict is required to provide all civilian hospitals with certificates of their status, confirming that the buildings they occupy are not used for any purpose which would deprive these hospitals of protection, namely acts harmful to the enemy. The fact that sick or wounded members of the armed forces are nursed in these hospitals, or the presence of small arms and ammunition taken from such combatants and not yet handed to the proper service, shall not be considered to be acts harmful to the enemy. Moreover, protection may cease only after due warning has been given. (See Art 19.)

[40] Pictet Commentary GC I, at 159.

[41] Under Art 36 GC II, similar protection is afforded to the religious personnel of hospital ships and their crews.

[42] According to Lunze, '[b]efore the separation of Church and State, the legal protection of life and limb of these clergy was a matter for religious law. In Europe, the norms of the Catholic Church established two related prohibitions: clergy were not to be targeted in military campaigns, and they were not allowed to actively engage in warfare.' S. Lunze, 'Serving God and Caesar: Religious Personnel and their Protection in Armed Conflict', 86 *IRRC* 853 (2004) 69, at 70.

[43] Art 8(d)(i), (ii), and (iv) AP I. The ICRC Commentary on the Protocol observes that the definition of the term 'religious personnel' was inserted in Art 8 on the initiative of the Holy See, which presented an amendment to the draft text under consideration at the 1974–7 Diplomatic Conference, remarking that 'religious personnel and medical personnel were mentioned together in a number of articles in the Geneva Conventions of 1949', and that 'it was desirable that the former should be defined in order to avoid any misunderstanding'. ICRC Commentary APs, at 115–16.

[44] See, e.g., Art 12 para 2 GC I for the wounded and sick, and in IHRL, Art 2(1) ICCPR, under which '[e]ach State Party [...] undertakes to respect and to ensure to all individuals within its territory and subject to its jurisdiction the rights recognized in the present Covenant, without distinction of any kind, such as [...] religion'. Under Art 2(2) ICESCR, states parties 'undertake to guarantee that the rights enunciated in the [...] Covenant will be exercised without discrimination of any kind as to [...] religion'.

24   The CIHL Study concluded that state practice has established that the rule whereby religious personnel shall be respected and protected in all circumstances is a customary rule applicable in both IAC and NIAC.[45]

g. Identification of medical and religious personnel

25   Under Article 38 GC I, the red cross on a white background is designated as the 'emblem and distinctive sign' of the medical service of armed forces. For states whose armed forces' medical services were 'already' using as their emblem the red crescent (or the red lion and sun) on a white background, the Convention also recognized such emblems. According to Article 40, medical personnel are required to wear, on their left arm, a 'water-resistant armlet' bearing the relevant emblem that has been 'issued and stamped by the military authority'.[46] This obligation encompasses the following: medical personnel who are members of the armed forces; administrative staff of medical units and establishments; staff of national Red Cross and Red Crescent societies, and other voluntary aid societies duly recognized and authorized by their governments; and medical personnel and units lent by the recognized society of a neutral state to a party to the conflict. In accordance with Article 40, all religious personnel falling within the ambit of Article 24 shall also bear the red cross emblem in the same manner as medical personnel covered by this provision.

26   Such personnel, in addition to wearing an identity disc, shall also carry a special identity card bearing the distinctive emblem. The card must be water-resistant and of such size that it can be carried in the pocket. It must be worded in the national language; include the surname and first names, date of birth, rank, and service number of the bearer; and state in what capacity the bearer is entitled to the protection of GC I. The card must carry the photograph of the owner and also either his signature, or his finger-prints or both. Lastly, it must be embossed with the stamp of the military authority.[47]

27   Controversially, a 2013 decision by the United States (US) Court of Appeals for the District of Columbia held that an identity card was constitutive for medical personnel status.[48] The Court held that

> the Convention speaks in mandatory terms. [...] The commentary to the Convention expressly provides for the identification elements we set forth above. It does so in mandatory terms. [...] Neither the Convention nor the commentary provide [sic] for any other means of establishing that status.[49]

This holding was the subject of an appeal to the US Supreme Court in December 2013. The petition for a writ of certiorari asserted:

> Article 24 by its terms [...] protects all medical workers who are exclusively engaged in medical activities. Nothing in Article 24 suggests that its protections disappear if a medical worker does

---

[45] ICRC CIHL Study, Rule 27.
[46] Not using the emblem is, however, not a violation of IHL.
[47] Art 40 GC I. An example of an identity card for medical and religious personnel attached to the armed forces is set out in Annex II of GC I.
[48] US Court of Appeals (District of Columbia), *Mukhtar Yahia Naki Al Warafi v Barack Obama et al*, No 11-5276, May 2013, at 4–7, available at <http://www.cadc.uscourts.gov/internet/opinions.nsf/7D20723558 D7132685257B75004E3CBE/$file/11-5276-1437798.pdf>.
[49] Ibid, at 6.

not have an identity card and an armlet. There also is no other provision in the Convention that purports to place such a precondition on the protections afforded by Article 24.[50]

The petition further argued that

Article 40 identification is not the only way to be in such a position. Al Warafi [the petitioner] has successfully demonstrated that he was exclusively engaged in medical work, despite having neither a card nor an armlet. In any event, nothing in Article 40 or the Commentary provides that the penalty for failing to have an identity card and an armlet is outright denial of all Article 24 protections.[51]

In its responding brief on behalf of the US President, the US Department of Justice claimed that the identity card was a prerequisite for recognition as medical personnel, and stated that '[i]n any event, petitioner does not challenge in his certiorari petition the district court's factual findings demonstrating that he was not exclusively employed as a medic'.[52] On 5 May 2014, the Supreme Court denied Al Warafi's petition.[53]

In no circumstances, however, may the relevant personnel be deprived of their identity cards, nor of the right to wear the armlet. In case of loss, they are entitled to receive duplicates of the cards and to have the insignia replaced.[54] In the specific case of medical personnel and units lent from a neutral state, such personnel must be provided with the requisite identity cards prior to leaving the state to which they belong.[55]

Under Article 41, auxiliary medical personnel are required to wear, 'but only while carrying out medical duties, a white armlet bearing in its centre the distinctive sign in miniature; the armlet shall be issued and stamped by the military authority'. Such personnel must carry military identity documents that specify any special training they have received, the temporary character of their medical duties, and their authority to wear the armlet.[56]

h. Protection of military medical and religious personnel at sea

Under Article 36 GC II, similar protection to that granted to military medical personnel on land is afforded to medical and hospital personnel of hospital ships and their crews. Further, 'they may not be captured during the time they are in the service of the hospital ship, whether or not there are wounded and sick on board'.[57] As the Pictet Commentary observes, however, this protection is not extended to coastal lifeboats and their shore installations when the personnel is in service in these boats and at these installations: 'This is one more humanitarian problem in urgent need of solution since the Second Convention does not settle all its various aspects—and indeed it is not within the scope of that instrument to do so.'[58] The problem was partially addressed in Article 23 AP I, which provides that other medical ships and craft

shall, whether at sea or in other waters, be respected and protected in the same way as mobile medical units under the Conventions and this Protocol. Since this protection can only be effective if they

---

[50] *Mukhtar Yahia Naki Al Warafi v Barack Obama et al*, Petition for a Writ of Certiorari to the US Court of Appeals for the District of Columbia Circuit, 23 December 2013, at 17.
[51] Ibid, at 18.
[52] *Mukhtar Yahia Naki Al Warafi v Barack Obama et al*, Brief for the Respondent in Opposition, 28 March 2014, at 10, available at <http://www.justice.gov/osg/briefs/2013/0responses/2013-0768.resp.pdf>.
[53] US Supreme Court, *Mukhtar Yahia Naki Al Warafi v Barack Obama et al*, Denial of Petition for Writ of Certiorari, 13-768, 5 May 2014.
[54] Art 40 GC I.   [55] Art 27 GC I.   [56] Art 41 GC I.   [57] Art 36 GC II.
[58] Pictet Commentary GC II, at 206.

can be identified and recognized as medical ships or craft, such vessels should be marked with the distinctive emblem and as far as possible comply [with Article 43(2) GC II].

In 1984, the National Lifeboat Societies and state-maintained rescue services, as members of the International Lifeboat Conference, unanimously adopted a report on the protection of rescue craft in situations of armed conflict, calling for improved protection of rescue craft and their crews, and of fixed coastal installations and staff of lifeboat institutions in periods of armed conflict.[59] Specifically, they recommended that a simplified manual be drawn up for all coxswains or those in command on, inter alia, use of radio and radar transponders, and proposed an interpretation of the relevant texts of GC II whereby the crews of rescue craft and personnel in fixed coastal installations should enjoy the same protection as that accorded by Articles 36 and 37 of the Convention to crews of hospital ships and to religious and medical personnel.[60]

31   Religious, medical, and hospital personnel assigned to the medical or spiritual care of members of the armed forces at sea must, if they fall into the hands of the enemy, be respected and protected; they may continue to carry out their duties as long as this is necessary for the care of the wounded and sick.[61]

i. Loss of protection for religious and medical personnel[62]

32   Article 21 provides that protection of 'fixed establishments and mobile medical units of the Medical Service' ceases only where they are used 'to commit, outside their humanitarian duties, acts harmful to the enemy'. This applies *mutatis mutandis* to military medical personnel and religious personnel. Although the term 'acts harmful to the enemy' is not defined in the 1949 Geneva Conventions, it seems clear that military medical personnel may not participate in hostilities; nor, according to one military manual, may they seek to shield military objectives from attack.[63] The notion of acts harmful to the enemy, despite the plural form, presumably applies to a singular act. It also appears to be a broader concept than taking active (or direct) part in hostilities. Indeed, the ICRC argued at the 1949 Diplomatic Conference that it encompassed any acts the purpose or effect of which is to harm the adverse party by facilitating or impeding military operations.[64] The Pictet Commentary suggests for medical units that 'use of a hospital as a shelter for able-bodied combatants or fugitives, as an arms or ammunition dump, or as a military observation post', or 'deliberate siting of a medical unit in a position where it would impede an enemy attack', would similarly be acts harmful to the enemy.[65] For individuals, acts leading to loss of protection would presumably include acts amounting to indirect participation in hostilities, such as engaging in manufacture or transportation of munitions for one party to the conflict other than to the front line or for a specific military operation. Akin to direct participation in hostilities, however, loss of protection would arguably be temporally limited to the duration of harmful acts.[66]

---

[59] See, e.g., P. Eberlin, 'The Protection of Rescue Craft in Periods of Armed Conflict', 25 *IRRC* 246 (1985) 140.
[60] Ibid, at 140.   [61] Art 37 GC II.
[62] On loss of protection more generally beyond the medical context, see Ch 42 of this volume.
[63] Australia, *The Manual of the Law of Armed Conflict*, Australian Defence Doctrine Publication, 2006, para 9.11, cited in ICRC CIHL Study, 'Practice Relating to Rule 25. Medical Personnel'.
[64] Final Record, vol II-A, at 59. See also R.W. Gehring, 'Protection of Civilian Infrastructures', 42(2) *Law and Contemporary Problems* (1978) 86.
[65] Pictet Commentary GC I, at 200–1.
[66] According to the ICRC, '[w]here IHL provides persons other than civilians with immunity from direct attack, the loss and restoration of protection is governed by criteria similar to, but not necessarily identical with,

Military medical or religious personnel may, however, be armed with light weapons,[67] which they may use for their own defence or for the defence of the wounded and sick in their care without losing protection. Thus, under Article 22(1) GC I, the fact that personnel of a medical unit or establishment are armed, and even that they use the arms in their own defence or in defence of wounded and sick in their charge, shall not deprive a medical unit or establishment of the protection guaranteed by Article 19.[68] As the ICRC has observed, 'neither the mere caring for enemy wounded and sick military personnel nor the sole wearing of enemy military uniforms or bearing of its insignia can be considered a hostile act'.[69]

The loss of protection otherwise afforded to medical personnel where they commit acts harmful to the enemy applies *mutatis mutandis* to religious personnel.[70] The ICRC notes that this is explicitly recognized by Germany's Military Manual, even though the Manual also observes that chaplains in the German army are not armed.[71] In contrast, the *Manual on the Law of Armed Conflict* of the United Kingdom (UK) affirms that the Geneva Conventions are silent on whether chaplains may be armed, although the *Manual* points out that it is UK policy that chaplains should be unarmed.[72] Lunze argues that the provisions applicable to medical personnel 'cannot simply be applied to religious personnel as well'. Indeed, they cannot protect those in his spiritual care, because they are not protected from attack by IHL. He justly affirms, though, that medical personnel should be permitted to use weapons in self-defence, while acknowledging that 'many countries have chosen not to equip their religious personnel with arms'.[73]

j. Duties of medical personnel in international armed conflict

The fundamental duties upon medical personnel are to provide care and treatment of the wounded or sick in strict accordance with generally accepted medical ethics,[74]

---

direct participation in hostilities.' See ICRC, 'Interpretive Guidance on the Notion of Direct Participation in Hostilities under International Humanitarian Law', 90 *IRRC* 872 (2008) 991, at 997.

[67] This may extend beyond revolvers or other side-arms to encompass even assault rifles, but is limited to weapons intended for transport and use by one person. Light weapons should thus not be confused with those defined in the International Small Arms Control Standards ('any man-portable lethal weapon designed for use by two or three persons serving as a crew'). ISACS 01.20: Glossary of terms, definitions and abbreviations, 17 June 2014, available at <http://www.smallarmsstandards.org/isacs/0120-en.pdf>.

[68] De Waard and Tarrant, above n 1, at 168, observe: 'In many modern armed conflicts, a state of internal disorder may exist, which, apart from the conflict itself, may engender acts of violence. It is therefore essential to defend the wounded and sick against such acts. Also, although wounded soldiers are considered *hors de combat*, they may not necessarily be totally incapacitated and it is important to maintain order within medical facilities.'

[69] ICRC CIHL Study, Rule 25.

[70] ICRC CIHL Study, Rule 27. See Ch 42 of this volume for further details of when protection afforded by the 1949 GCs is lost.

[71] See German Military Manual, 1992, paras 817–20.

[72] UK Ministry of Defence, *Manual on the Law of Armed Conflict* (Oxford: OUP, 2004), para 7.30. An earlier UK LOAC Pamphlet from 1981 provided: 'Chaplains attached to the armed forces have protected status and may not be attacked [...] They may not be armed.' Cited in ICRC CIHL Study, 'Practice Relating to Rule 27. Religious Personnel'.

[73] Lunze, above n 42, at 76; see also Ch 42 of this volume.

[74] Furthermore, according to Art 16(1) AP I, 'Under no circumstances shall any person be punished for carrying out medical activities compatible with medical ethics, regardless of the person benefiting therefrom.' Under para 2 of the same provision it is further prohibited to compel anyone 'to perform acts or to carry out work contrary to the rules of medical ethics or to other medical rules designed for the benefit of the wounded and sick or to the provisions of the Conventions or of this Protocol, or to refrain from performing acts or from carrying out work required by those rules and provisions'.

including the principle of triage[75] and the general duty of medical confidentiality.[76] Under Article 12 GC I, '[o]nly urgent medical reasons will authorize priority in the order of treatment to be administered.' Medical personnel are thus required to care for the wounded and sick without any distinction founded on sex, race, nationality, religion, political opinions, or any other similar criteria.

II. Treatment upon capture of medical and religious personnel and repatriation

36 The conditions for the treatment of medical and religious personnel and their repatriation are set out in Articles 28–32 GC I. Any permanent medical or religious personnel who are members of the armed forces and who fall into the hands of the enemy must be held 'only in so far as the state of health, the spiritual needs and the number of prisoners of war require'.[77] Under Article 30, all other permanent personnel must be returned to the party to the conflict to which they belong, 'as soon as a road is open for their return and military requirements permit'. On departure, they must take with them all personal effects, as well as all instruments belonging to them.[78]

37 Personnel who are retained are not prisoners of war (POWs).[79] Nevertheless, they must at least benefit from all the provisions of GC III Relative to the Treatment of Prisoners of War. They are required to carry out, in accordance with professional ethics, their respective medical and spiritual duties on behalf of POWs, 'preferably those of the armed forces to which they themselves belong'.[80] Although retained personnel in a camp are subject to its internal discipline, they must not be required to perform any work outside their medical or religious duties.[81]

38 In contrast, auxiliary medical personnel (as defined under Article 25 GC I) shall, upon capture, be POWs, but they must be employed on their medical duties 'in so far as the need arises'.[82] This difference in approach is explained by the fact that auxiliary personnel

---

[75] Triage is generally defined as 'the sorting of and allocation of treatment to patients and especially battle and disaster victims according to a system of priorities designed to maximize the number of survivors': Merriam-Webster online dictionary, 'Triage', at <http://www.merriam-webster.com/dictionary/triage>. See, e.g., C. Enemark, 'Triage, Treatment and Torture: Ethical Challenges for US Military Medicine in Iraq', 7 *Journal of Military Ethics* (2008) 186.

[76] Under Art 16(3) AP I, 'No person engaged in medical activities shall be compelled to give to anyone belonging either to an adverse Party, or to his own Party except as required by the law of the latter Party, any information concerning the wounded and sick who are, or who have been, under his care, if such information would, in his opinion, prove harmful to the patients concerned or to their families. Regulations for the compulsory notification of communicable diseases shall, however, be respected.' In NIACs falling within the scope of AP II, the corresponding provision in Art 10(3) is more problematic, as it makes the duty of confidentiality 'subject to national law'.

[77] Art 28 GC I. The same provisions apply to administrative staff of medical units and establishments, staff of national Red Cross and Red Crescent societies, and other voluntary aid societies duly recognized and authorized by their governments, and medical personnel and units lent by the recognized society of a neutral state to a party to the conflict.

[78] Art 30 GC I. By virtue of Art 31, the selection of personnel for return must be made 'irrespective of any consideration of race, religion or political opinion, but preferably according to the chronological order of their capture and their state of health'.

[79] Art 4(C) GC III.

[80] These activities are to be carried out within 'the framework of the military laws and regulations of the Detaining Power, and under the authority of its competent service'.

[81] Art 28(2)(c) GC I. These provisions do not relieve the Detaining Power of its obligations with regard to the medical and spiritual welfare of the POWs it holds.

[82] Art 29 GC I.

'are as much "combatant" as medical, and their repatriation would help to increase the military potential of the home country'.[83]

Religious, medical, and hospital personnel assigned to the medical or spiritual care of members of the armed forces at sea who fall into the hands of the enemy must be sent back 'as soon as the Commander-in-Chief, under whose authority they are, considers it practicable'.[84] On leaving the ship they are permitted to take with them their personal property. It is permitted to a party to the conflict to retain some personnel, where necessary 'owing to the medical or spiritual needs of prisoners of war'. In this event, they must be brought to land as soon as possible. Upon landing they become subject to the provisions of GC I, as described above.[85] 39

C. Relevance in Non-International Armed Conflicts

Common Article 3 would offer the same protection to medical and religious personnel as it would to others 'taking no active part in the hostilities'.[86] Committing acts harmful to the enemy clearly constitutes taking active part in the hostilities, and any such personnel doing so will be open to lawful attack for such time as this may occur: 'They lose their protection if they commit, outside their humanitarian function, acts harmful to the enemy.'[87] The ICRC has argued: 40

It is clear that in practice protection of medical personnel against violence will be as important in situations of non-international armed conflict as in those of international armed conflict. In addition, at the Diplomatic Conference leading to the adoption of the Additional Protocols, the USSR [former Soviet Union] stated that this rule was necessary, even in non-international armed conflicts, for medical personnel who disarmed a wounded soldier would otherwise forfeit their right to protection, unless they threw away the weapon.[88]

As noted above, the ICRC believes that the customary rules whereby medical personnel exclusively assigned to medical duties, and religious personnel exclusively assigned to religious duties, 'must be respected and protected in all circumstances' are also applicable in NIACs.[89] Moreover, the ICRC has argued that Common Article 3, which requires that the wounded and sick be collected and cared for, implies that medical personnel be protected as 'a subsidiary form of protection granted to ensure that the wounded and sick receive medical care'.[90] The specific obligation to respect and protect medical and religious personnel is set forth in Article 9 AP II, to which no reservations have been made.[91] In the *Al Warafi* case cited above, the US Court of Appeals accepted that a Talib could benefit from the obligation if he was exclusively medical personnel, even though, as noted, it denied Al Warafi medical personnel status, inter alia because he had no identity card.[92] 41

---

[83] Pictet Commentary GC I, at 258.   [84] Art 37 GC II.   [85] Ibid.
[86] See Ch 21 of this volume.   [87] ICRC CIHL Study, Rules 25 and 27.   [88] Ibid, Rule 25.
[89] Ibid, Rules 25 and 27.   [90] Ibid, Rule 25.
[91] According to Art 9(1) AP II, '[m]edical and religious personnel shall be respected and protected and shall be granted all available help for the performance of their duties. They shall not be compelled to carry out tasks which are not compatible with their humanitarian mission.' Art 11(f) of the draft of AP II submitted by the ICRC to the 1974–7 Diplomatic Conference offered a definition of medical personnel, but the proposal was not accepted. See, e.g., ICRC CIHL Study, 'Practice Relating to Rule 25. Medical Personnel'.
[92] US Court of Appeals (District of Columbia), *Mukhtar Yahia Naki Al Warafi v Barack Obama et al*, above n 48.

42   There are, however, particular risks for medical personnel providing care and treatment to wounded fighters in a NIAC, as they may be accused of providing support to terrorists. Thus, Sassòli and Bouvier cite the example of Peru, where a Peruvian Medical Association reported in 1994 that doctors

> are caught in crossfire—on the one hand coercion by terrorist threats, and on the other punitive action by the government, which considers them as collaborators with terrorism without taking into account the circumstances in which medical care is given, an indispensable factor in distinguishing between a criminal act and normal conduct [...] Unfortunately in Peru it seems that we are reaching the point where even the right of the wounded or sick terrorist to have medical attention is denied, and where the physician who attends him is considered a criminal.[93]

43   A more recent example comes from Afghanistan. In May 2010, it was reported that the ICRC had been teaching Taliban fighters basic first aid and giving them medical equipment, so that fighters wounded during battles with the North Atlantic Treaty Organization and Afghan government forces could be treated in the field. In a newspaper article, a 'leading figure in Kandahar's local government' was quoted anonymously as saying that the Taliban did 'not deserve to be treated like humans. [...] They are like animals, and they treat the people they capture worse than animals [...] These people don't deserve this help.'[94] In contrast, a Fox News reporter noted on air that US marines interviewed on a base in Afghanistan were not shocked or upset by the news, because they routinely treated wounded Taliban members when they captured them in combat.[95]

44   In contrast, in the 2013 trial of three UK Royal Marines accused of murdering a wounded Talib in Afghanistan, one of the accused, Sergeant Alexander Blackman (subsequently convicted of murder), is heard on a video camera-recording of the incident asking his two co-accused (both acquitted of the charge of murder) whether either 'want[s] to do first aid on this idiot'. One of the co-accused replies 'No', while the other says, 'I'll put one in his head if you want.'[96] Common Article 3 requires that the wounded and sick be collected and cared for, although failure to do so is not a war crime under customary IHL, at least according to the CIHL Study, and is not a war crime falling within the jurisdiction of the International Criminal Court (ICC).[97]

45   As Lunze argues, while Common Article 3 'cannot serve as a basis to claim active support for religious activities, its humane treatment requirement may also be deemed to result in some safeguards for religious freedom'.[98] Human rights law will also be potentially relevant. In accordance with Article 18 of the 1966 International Covenant on Civil and Political Rights (ICCPR), the right to freedom of religion is non-derogable.[99] Thus,

---

[93] Federación Medica Peruana, 'Medical Practice in the Context of Internal Armed Conflict', Peru, August 1994, cited by M. Sassòli and A.A. Bouvier, *How Does Law Protect in War?* (Geneva: ICRC, 1999), at 1376.

[94] J. Boone, 'Red Cross Gives First Aid Lessons to Taliban', *Guardian*, 25 May 2010, available at <http://www.guardian.co.uk/world/2010/may/25/red-cross-first-aid-taliban>.

[95] Fox News, 'Red Cross Teaching Taliban First Aid', 26 May 2010, available at <http://video.foxnews.com/v/4214695/red-cross-teaching-taliban-first-aid/>, cited in B.A. Gutierrez, S. DeCristofaro, and M. Woods, 'What Americans Think of International Humanitarian Law', 93 *IRRC* 884 (2011) 1009, at 1026.

[96] 'Marines Accused in Court Martial of Executing Afghan Insurgent after Clash', *Guardian*, 23 October 2013, available at <http://www.theguardian.com/uk-news/2013/oct/23/marines-accused-court-martial-execution-afghan-insurgent>.

[97] See Art 8(2)(c) ICC Statute.   [98] Lunze, above n 42, at 78.   [99] See Art 4(2) ICCPR.

D. Legal Consequences of a Violation

In accordance with Articles 49 and 50 GC I, wilful killing, torture, or inhuman treatment, or wilfully causing great suffering or serious injury to body or health of any military medical or religious personnel of a party to an IAC, constitute a grave breach of the Convention. The only exception to this would be killing medical personnel by an attack while such personnel were engaged in acts harmful to the enemy, otherwise such acts shall lead to the consequences foreseen in the provisions on grave breaches.[101]

46

The ICC Statute makes it an offence under the jurisdiction of the ICC, both in IACs and in NIACs, intentionally to direct attacks against medical personnel 'using the distinctive emblems of the Geneva Conventions in conformity with international law'.[102]

47

There is little international jurisprudence relating to the protection of medical or religious personnel. In the so-called *Vukovar Hospital* case[103] before the International Criminal Tribunal for the former Yugoslavia (ICTY), the Trial Chamber discussed whether the deprivation of medical care from 'women, elderly men and wounded and sick patients' of Vukovar hospital, who were among those detained by Yugoslav military personnel, constituted cruel treatment as defined under Article 3 of the ICTY Statute.[104] It observed:

48

> Whether particular conduct amounts to cruel treatment is a question of fact to be determined on a case by case basis. In the Chamber's view, the failure to provide adequate medicine or medical treatment would constitute the offence of 'cruel treatment' if, in the specific circumstances, it causes serious mental or physical suffering or injury, or constitutes a serious attack on human dignity and if it is carried out with the requisite *mens rea*.[105]

Somewhat surprisingly, the Trial Chamber declared itself 'not persuaded that the acts of deprivation of medical care of those who had been previously injured, in and of themselves, were of the nature to cause severe, serious pain or suffering to amount to torture or cruel treatment'. Since physical injuries were inflicted on the detainees, and on the basis that 'the more seriously injured patients at Vukovar hospital were not included in this group of prisoners', and further that 'they were not held for any extended time', the Trial Chamber took the view that

> while many prisoners received serious injuries [...], in such cases the infliction of injuries and the failure to provide treatment for the injuries caused, is in reality the same behaviour. The deprivation of medical care in such cases is subsumed in the acts of mistreatment themselves.[106]

---

[100] US, Fourth periodic report to the Human Rights Committee in accordance with the ICCPR, 30 December 2011, para 506.
[101] For further details, see Ch 42, MN 40–47, of this volume. On grave breaches, see Ch 31 of this volume.
[102] See, respectively, Art 8(2)(b)(xxiv) and Art 8(2)(e)(ii) ICC Statute.
[103] ICTY, *The Prosecutor v Mile Mrkšić, Miroslav Radić & Veselin Šljivančanin*, IT-95-13/1-T, 27 September 2007.
[104] Ibid, paras 516–17. Cruel treatment is therein defined as an intentional act or omission causing serious mental or physical suffering or injury to, or constituting a serious attack on human dignity upon, a person taking no active part in the hostilities.
[105] Ibid, para 517. Thus, the perpetrator must have acted with a direct intent to commit cruel treatment, or with indirect intent, i.e. in the knowledge that cruel treatment was a probable consequence of his act or omission.
[106] Ibid, para 528.

49 There is also relevant jurisprudence from the International Criminal Tribunal for Rwanda (ICTR). According to the indictment against André Rwamakuba:

> Between 18 and 25 April 1994, at Butare University Hospital, André RWAMAKUBA, often accompanied by Dr Geoffroy Gatera, soldiers, militiamen and armed civilians, ordered, instigated, committed, or otherwise aided and abetted killings of Tutsi patients and displaced persons seeking refuge at Butare University Hospital with intent to destroy, in whole or in part, the Tutsi ethnic group. Thus, during an official delegation's visit to the Hospital, he asked a woman unknown but identified as the head of Doctors Without Borders not to treat Tutsi casualties, to get rid of them and not to admit any others. During the above-mentioned period, Andre RWAMAKUBA, armed with a small axe hung on his belt, and often accompanied by Dr Gatera, armed soldiers, Interahamwe militiamen and civilians armed with machetes, axes and clubs, went around the hospital wards checking identity cards and identifying Tutsi refugees and patients, selecting them and putting them on board a vehicle manned by Interahamwe armed with clubs and machetes. The persons taken away were never seen again. During this period, in the morning or afternoon, during his rounds, Andre RWAMAKUBA regularly removed drips from patients, in particular, in a ward where unidentified sick Tutsi women were admitted.[107]

50 In its judgment, however, the Tribunal's Trial Chamber found that the prosecution had failed to prove at all or beyond a reasonable doubt the allegations against the accused at the Butare University Hospital.[108]

51   Medical personnel have also been convicted of war crimes. In 1949, a German medical officer who refused to allow medical personnel to care for a wounded deserter and who ordered (or at least permitted) a subordinate to shoot the person, was convicted of war crimes by a Dutch district court; the conviction was upheld in 1950 by a special court of appeal.[109] The *Peleus* case concerned a German U-boat on patrol which, on 13 March 1944, came across the Greek steamer *SS Peleus*. It sank the *Peleus* with two torpedoes; but then to conceal the submarine's presence, the U-boat commander decided to sink the wreckage, even though several survivors were clinging to the hull and to the *Peleus*' rafts. One of those who opened fire into the wreckage in an effort to sink it was the U-boat's doctor, Walter Weisspfennig, who was subsequently convicted of war crimes at the Hamburg war trials and executed by firing squad.[110] This was the only case in which U-boat personnel were convicted of war crimes committed during the Second World War.

E. Critical Assessment

52 The duty to respect and protect both military and civilian medical and religious personnel in all circumstances is part of customary IHL applicable in NIAC as well as in IAC. The protection applies 'at all times and in all places, both on the battlefield and behind the lines', and whether such personnel are retained 'only temporarily by the enemy or for

---

[107] ICTR, *The Prosecutor v André Rwamakuba*, Indictment, ICTR-98-44C-I, 9 June 2005, para 15.

[108] ICTR, *The Prosecutor v André Rwamakuba*, Trial Chamber Judgment, ICTR-98-44C-I, 20 September 2006, para 205.

[109] District Court of The Hague (Special Criminal Chamber), *In re Pilz*, Judgment, 21 December 1949; Special Court of Cassation, *In re Pilz*, Judgment, 5 July 1950, Annual Digest, 17 (1950), at 391–2; original report in 681 *Nederlandse Jurisprudentie* (1950).

[110] *Trial of Kapitänleutnant Heinz Eck and four others for the Killing of Members of the Crew of the Greek Steamship Peleus, Sunk on the High Seas*, British Military Court, Hamburg, 17–20 October 1945, UNWCC Law Reports, vol I (1947), at 1–21.

a lengthy period'. Deliberate killing or wounding of military and civilian medical and religious personnel entitled to protection under IHL (i.e. not committing acts harmful to the enemy) would amount to a war crime.

In the ongoing Syrian conflicts, medical personnel have frequently been attacked, and many have been killed. On 2 July 2012, the Syrian Government passed counter-terrorism legislation that effectively made it a crime to provide medical care to anyone suspected of belonging to the opposition.[111] In September 2013, the Independent International Commission of Inquiry on the Syrian Arab Republic (Syria Commission of Inquiry) issued a special report to the UN Human Rights Council entitled 'Assault on medical care in Syria', stating that targeting of medical personnel was one of the most 'insidious trends' of the conflict, with ambulance drivers, nurses, doctors, and medical volunteers attacked, arrested, unlawfully detained, and disappeared.[112] From April to June 2011, government forces 'carried out a wave of arrests against medical professionals in Damascus'.[113] Furthermore, according to one journalist writing in November 2013:

> At the beginning of 2011, there were more than 30,000 doctors practicing in Syria. Now, more than 16,000 doctors have fled, and many of those left are in hiding. Of the more than 160 doctors killed since the conflict began, more than ninety have been assassinated for doing their jobs; some had been placed on 'wanted' lists. At least thirty-six paramedics, in uniform on authorized missions, have been killed by Syrian military snipers or shot dead at checkpoints. In areas contested or controlled by rebels, such as Homs and Aleppo, branches of the Syrian Arab Red Crescent have been shelled. When government forces stormed the city of Deir Ezzor in June 2012, they informed Dr Ghassam Shoubet at the Deir Ezzor branch of the Red Crescent, 'It is forbidden to carry out any first aid activities.' Emergency medical squads are routinely prevented from evacuating not only wounded rebel fighters but also injured children and other civilians from rebel-held territory.[114]

According to the Syria Commission of Inquiry's report, 'The clearly established pattern indicates that Government forces deliberately target medical personnel to gain military advantage by depriving the opposition and those perceived to support them of medical assistance for injuries sustained.'[115] The situation was said to be so dire that the general populace often elects not to seek help for 'fear of arrest, detention, torture or death'.[116] The Commission of Inquiry reaffirmed earlier recommendations on the need to ensure the protection of civilians and compliance with IHL, and concluded that the parties to the conflict 'must respect the special protection afforded to medical facilities and personnel'.[117] The Commission entreated the Syrian Government to fulfil 'its obligations under international human rights law to ensure the right to health, a right that is closely and inextricably linked to the rights to life, human dignity, non-discrimination, equality and the prohibition against torture and ill-treatment'.[118]

Aside from the widespread, deliberate targeting of medical personnel seen in Syria, the general principles applicable to medical and religious personnel are also potentially subject to certain caveats. As we have seen, the origin of the protection was firmly rooted in

---

[111] Independent International Commission of Inquiry on the Syrian Arab Republic, 'Assault on Medical Care in Syria', UN Doc A/HRC/24/CRP.2, 13 September 2013, para 21; and see A. Sparrow, 'Syria's Assault on Doctors', *New York Review of Books*, 3 November 2013, available at <http://www.nybooks.com/blogs/nyrblog/2013/nov/03/syria-assault-doctors/>.
[112] Syria Commission of Inquiry, 'Assault on Medical Care in Syria', above n 111, para 21.
[113] Ibid, para 22.   [114] Sparrow, above n 111.
[115] Syria Commission of Inquiry, 'Assault on Medical Care in Syria', above n 111, para 29.
[116] Ibid, para 32.   [117] Ibid, para 42.   [118] Ibid.

the need to protect medical and religious personnel *belonging to the armed forces of states*: to allow them to care for, physically or spiritually, the sick, wounded, and shipwrecked, as well as those whose lives could not be saved. While the customary norm offers similar protection to civilian medical and religious personnel too, it is assumed that any such civilians will not actively participate in hostilities at any time; such is not necessarily the case with all military medical personnel.

56   Moreover, caring for wounded enemy combatants is not always well perceived by fellow members of an armed force (or fellow nationals). For this reason, military medical personnel (and arguably also religious personnel) are allowed to carry with them a small firearm (e.g. a pistol or revolver), both to protect themselves and to protect those for whom they are caring. This scenario cannot, though, be easily transposed to a NIAC, at least as far as a non-state party to the conflict is concerned. Thus, in a NIAC, while the duty to respect and protect medical personnel caring for a sick or injured rebel fighter certainly persists, it is assumed that such medical personnel will be both civilian and unarmed. There is no equivalent status for medical or religious personnel attached to a non-state armed group as for military medical or religious personnel attached to a state armed force.

57   Lastly, while spontaneous efforts by the civilian population to care for the wounded and sick must be both protected and respected, the obligation upon the civilian population as a whole is only to 'respect' the (military) wounded and sick. There is thus no positive obligation to assist a wounded person. Arguably, however, this obligation to refrain from acts of violence against the sick or wounded has gone beyond the realm of IAC whence it originated. Where violence amounted to torture or even murder, it could even be seen as reflecting one aspect of a more general, peremptory norm of international human rights law.

STUART CASEY-MASLEN

Chapter 41. Buildings, Material, and Transports

	MN
A. Introduction	1
B. Meaning and Application	5
I. Medical buildings	7
II. Medical material	8
III. Medical transports	12
a. Medical vehicles	13
b. Medical aircraft	16
c. Medical vessels	22
C. Relevance in Non-International Armed Conflicts	30
D. Legal Consequences of a Violation	34
E. Critical Assessment	37

Select Bibliography

ICRC, 'Violence against Health Care, Part I: The Problem and the Law', 95 *IRRC* 889 (2013)
ICRC, 'Violence against Health Care, Part II: The Way Forward', 95 *IRRC* 890 (2013)
International Institute of Humanitarian Law, *San Remo Manual on International Law Applicable to Armed Conflicts at Sea* (Cambridge: CUP, 1995)
Kleffner, J./Heintschel von Heinegg, W., 'Protection of the Wounded, Sick and Shipwrecked', in D. Fleck (ed), *The Handbook of International Humanitarian Law* (3rd edn, Oxford: OUP, 2013) 321
Program on Humanitarian Policy and Conflict Research, *Manual on International Law applicable to Air and Missile Warfare* (Bern: HPCR, 2009)
Program on Humanitarian Policy and Conflict Research, *Commentary on the HPCR Manual on International Law Applicable to Air and Missile Warfare* (Harvard: HPCR, 2010)
Spieker, H., 'Medical Transportation', in MPEPIL

A. Introduction

Since its beginnings, international humanitarian law (IHL) has protected not only the wounded and sick, but also the medical buildings, material, and transports required for their care. The 1864 Geneva Convention thus provided for the protection of military hospitals, ambulances, and their material. Its rules were revised multiple times to reflect changes in warfare and medical treatment. The Convention was therefore adapted to cover naval warfare, supplemented with rules dealing with medical aircraft, and aligned towards the protection of wounded and sick civilians.

Consequently, the 1949 Geneva Conventions (GCs) contain a detailed regime of protection. For the care of wounded and sick members of armed forces on land, GC I protects fixed medical establishments, including buildings, against attack[1] and, to a certain extent, if they fall into enemy hands.[2] It further protects medical material under

---

[1] Arts 19, 21, and 22 GC I.   [2] Arts 19 para 1 and 33 para 2 GC I.

enemy control,[3] and governs the protection of medical transports,[4] including medical aircraft,[5] both during the conduct of hostilities and when in the power of the enemy. It thereby addresses the treatment of medical buildings, material, and transports of both armed forces' medical services and aid societies entitled to the privileges of the Convention.[6]

3   Extending protection to shipwrecked members of the armed forces at sea, GC II supplements the rules on medical transports by protecting medical vessels[7] and aircraft.[8] Medical buildings on land are protected against attack from the sea.[9] Medical material is protected in cases either of fighting on board a warship,[10] or of boarding vessels transporting medical equipment.[11]

4   Within its provisions on general protections for civilian populations against certain consequences of war, GC IV protects civilian hospitals against attack[12] and governs the protection of medical transports,[13] including medical aircraft.[14] It contains additional rules on the maintenance of medical services[15] and the protection of property[16] in occupied territories.

B. Meaning and Application

5   The protection of medical buildings, material, and transports is derived from the protection of medical units. Enshrined in Article 19 GC I, the concept of a 'medical unit' is today defined in Article 8(e) of Additional Protocol (AP) I, and considered to have a corresponding customary international law content.[17] The term 'medical unit' thus comprises all fixed establishments or mobile units, whether military or civilian, permanent or temporary, organized for medical purposes, namely the search for, collection, transportation, or treatment of the wounded, sick, and shipwrecked, or for the prevention of disease. It includes, for example, hospitals, medical depots, and pharmaceutical stores.

6   Unlike property belonging to the armed forces' medical services or civilian medical units, real and personal property of aid societies duly recognized and authorized within the meaning of Article 26 GC I is always regarded as private property. Article 34 GC I thus governs the protection of buildings, material, and transports of recognized aid societies[18] engaged in caring for the wounded and sick of the armed forces.[19] Given this preferential treatment, which ultimately prohibits the taking of war booty and confiscation of all property of such aid societies,[20] and allows for its requisition only under strict conditions,[21] concerns were expressed prior to the adoption of Article 34 GC I that this could 'induce the State to turn its hospitals into Red Cross establishments, to prevent their material from being captured'.[22] The decision to treat the property of aid societies independently from the property of armed forces'

---

[3] Art 33 GC I.   [4] Arts 19, 21, 22, and 35 GC I.   [5] Arts 36 and 37 GC I.
[6] Art 34 GC I.   [7] Arts 22, 24–27, 29–35, and 38 GC II.   [8] Arts 39 and 40 GC II.
[9] Art 23 GC II.   [10] Art 28 GC II.   [11] Art 38 GC II.
[12] Arts 18 and 19 GC IV. See Ch 11 of this volume.   [13] Art 21 GC IV.   [14] Art 22 GC IV.
[15] Arts 56 and 57 GC IV.   [16] Art 53 GC IV. See Chs 71 and 72 of this volume.
[17] ICRC CIHL Study, Rule 28.   [18] Pictet Commentary GC I, at 271.   [19] Ibid, at 277.
[20] Ibid.   [21] Art 34 para 2 GC I.   [22] Pictet Commentary GC I, at 278.

medical units for 'humanitarian considerations', in order not to hinder the development of such societies,[23] remains relevant—not least because of a general reluctance in practice to integrate aid societies into the armed forces' medical services as provided for in Article 26 GC I.[24]

I. Medical buildings

Bearing in mind that mobile medical units typically do not comprise buildings,[25] medical buildings are protected only with regard to fixed medical establishments. In addition to being protected against attack during the conduct of hostilities, buildings of fixed medical establishments are, to a certain degree, protected if under enemy control. According to Article 33 paragraph 2 GC I, the buildings (and material and stores) of fixed military medical establishments remain subject to the laws of war, but may not be diverted from their purpose as long as they are required for the care of the wounded and sick. An exception is permissible only if a commander of forces in the field makes use of them in the case of urgent military necessity, provided previous arrangements have been made for the welfare of the wounded and sick nursed in them. However, the diversion of such establishments' purposes due to urgent military necessity is deemed an 'extreme measure'.[26] Recourse to a reference to 'the laws of war' was considered justified at the time of adoption, partly because 'a gradual change for the better which would automatically benefit medical buildings and material' was thought possible.[27] Consequently, the protection of medical buildings under enemy control remains dependent on the currently applicable laws of war, most relevantly those on the destruction, seizure, and pillaging of property. Given that customary international law today prohibits the destruction or seizure of enemy property unless required by imperative military necessity,[28] without making any exceptions for medical buildings, 'a gradual change for the better' cannot yet be observed. The pillaging of property, however, remains prohibited under the laws of war.[29] In the case of occupation, an occupying state is regarded only as the administrator of public buildings belonging to the hostile state and must safeguard the capital of such properties in accordance with Article 55 of the Hague Regulations.

7

II. Medical material

The material of medical units having fallen into enemy hands is treated differently, depending on whether it is part of a mobile medical unit (Article 33 paragraph 1 GC I) or a fixed medical establishment (Article 33 paragraph 2 GC I). While this distinction was debated during the drafting of Article 33 GC I, it is in line with previous legal regimes, and leads to improved protection of mobile medical units,

8

---

[23] Ibid.
[24] For an overview of National Red Cross and Red Crescent Societies' practice, see International Federation of Red Cross and Red Crescent Societies, *National Red Cross and Red Crescent Societies as Auxiliaries to the Public Authorities in the Humanitarian Field* (Geneva: IFRC, 2003), at 18.
[25] Pictet Commentary GC I, at 272.
[26] Ibid, at 275.   [27] Ibid, at 274.   [28] ICRC CIHL Study, Rule 50.   [29] Ibid, Rule 52.

9   which would otherwise be subject to the more permissive rules on fixed medical establishments.[30]

9   In the case of fixed medical establishments, medical material and stores remain subject to the laws of war, with the rules on seizure of property,[31] including war booty[32] and confiscation of movable property,[33] being most relevant to their treatment following capture. Parties to the conflict may seize enemy military equipment, including medical material and stores, as war booty[34]—as long as the safeguards contained in Article 33 paragraph 2 GC I do not apply.

10   If part of a mobile medical unit, medical material falling into the power of the enemy shall be reserved for the care of the wounded and sick. Contrary to previous legal regimes, Article 33 GC I no longer requires the restitution of a medical unit as a whole to its country of origin. Instead, GC I allows for the retention of its medical material, partly because of the 'practical obstacles to the restoring of equipment under modern war conditions'.[35] Hence, if it falls into enemy hands, material of mobile medical units should be used for the care of those being looked after in the captured unit, or subsidiarily for the treatment of others if no patients within the units require care.[36]

11   Medical stores of fixed establishments, and medical material of both fixed establishments and mobile units, are explicitly protected against intentional destruction within Article 33 paragraph 3 GC I. Considered a 'remarkable step forward in humanitarian legislation', GC I is not confined to the protection of medical material against destruction by the enemy, but also protects it against destruction by forces seeking to prevent it from falling into enemy hands.[37]

III. Medical transports

12   The protection of medical units extends to all means of medical transportation, i.e. medical transports.[38] While all forms of medical transports must be respected and protected,[39] the legal regimes governing their protection differ. Whereas the provisions contained in GC I and GC II protect medical transports assisting wounded, sick, and shipwrecked members of the armed forces, GC IV protects medical transports coming to the aid of wounded and sick civilians.[40]

a. Medical vehicles

13   Medical vehicles are protected under GC I and GC IV, GC II being restricted to the protection of medical transportation by water and air. Within GC I medical vehicles are covered as mobile medical units (Article 19 GC I) and medical transports (Article 35 GC I), but not explicitly referred to or defined.

14   Article 8(h) AP I contains a definition of 'medical vehicles' which is also applicable to GC I and GC IV.[41] Medical vehicles are defined as 'any medical transports by land', considered to include motor cars and railway vehicles such as trains.[42] Inland water transports (in contrast to sea-going craft),[43] as well as amphibious medical transports

---

[30] Pictet Commentary GC I, at 273.   [31] ICRC CIHL Study, Rule 50.   [32] Ibid, Rule 49.
[33] Ibid, Rule 51.   [34] Ibid, Rule 49.
[35] Pictet Commentary GC I, at 273.   [36] Ibid, at 274.   [37] Ibid, at 276.
[38] Art 8(g) AP I.   [39] Art 35 para 1 GC I. See Ch 39 of this volume.
[40] See Chs 37 and 38.   [41] Pictet Commentary GC I, at 280.
[42] ICRC Commentary APs, at 131, para 387.   [43] Pictet Commentary GC I, at 281.

when used on land,[44] are also protected as medical vehicles. Contrary to Article 21 GC IV, which requires medical vehicles to move in convoy in order to be protected, Article 35 GC I protects both convoys and isolated vehicles.[45] Following the definition's extension to all medical transports, whether military or civilian, within Article 8(g) AP I, considered to reflect customary international law,[46] the restriction contained in Article 21 GC IV is today seen as obsolete, and civilian medical transports are considered protected even when not in convoy.

The protection of medical vehicles under enemy control is governed by Article 35 paragraph 2 GC I and Article 21 AP I. Although generally protected as 'mobile medical units',[47] medical vehicles are not treated as such in case of capture due to 'the military importance of transport vehicles in modern warfare'.[48] In accordance with Article 35 paragraph 2 GC I, medical vehicles remain subject to the laws of war, on condition that the party to the conflict that captures them shall in all cases ensure the care of the wounded and sick within the vehicle. Unlike 'mobile medical units', the vehicles do not have to be reserved for the care of wounded and sick but may be disposed of (e.g., taken as war booty). They may even be used for military transportation if the distinctive emblem has been removed.[49]   15

b. Medical aircraft

Medical aircraft are protected within Articles 36 and 37 GC I, Articles 39 and 40 GC II, and Article 22 GC IV. The Geneva Conventions regime has been developed around the protections contained in GC I. Articles 39 and 40 GC II may thus be considered 'merely a repetition of the corresponding provisions of [...] [GC I], with the addition of references to the shipwrecked and to alighting on water'.[50]   16

Neither of the provisions contains a definition of the term 'medical aircraft'. Subsequent codification and clarification processes, however, have established a consolidated understanding of the term which is in line with an interpretation already embedded in the Pictet Commentary. Accordingly, the term 'aircraft' covers not only airplanes, helicopters, and 'any new type of flying machine',[51] but also any vehicle deriving support in the atmosphere from reactions of the air.[52] Such vehicles are considered 'medical aircraft' when fulfilling several conditions regarding their use, functions, and control. They must be used exclusively for medical functions, which are limited to the removal or conveyance of the wounded and sick, and the transport of personnel and equipment. Search and rescue operations are excluded from protection for reasons of military security.[53] It may be argued, however, that the definition contained in Article 36 GC I should today be interpreted to include the provision of medical care en route (MedEvac), given the modern capability of armed forces not only to evacuate the wounded, but also to treat them during transportation.[54]   17

---

[44] ICRC Commentary APs, at 249, para 839.   [45] Pictet Commentary GC I, at 280.
[46] ICRC CIHL Study, Rule 29.   [47] Art 35 para 1 GC I.
[48] Pictet Commentary GC I, at 282.
[49] Ibid.   [50] Pictet Commentary GC II, at 215.   [51] Pictet Commentary GC I, at 289.
[52] Harvard Program on Humanitarian Policy and Conflict Research (HPCR), *Manual on International Law Applicable to Air and Missile Warfare* (Bern: HPCR, 2009), Rule 1(d).
[53] Pictet Commentary GC I, at 288; Art 28(4) AP I; and Rule 86(b) HPCR *Manual*, above n 52.
[54] HPCR, *Commentary on the HPCR Manual on International Law Applicable to Air and Missile Warfare* (Harvard: HPCR, 2010), at 42, para 3.

18 The rules on the marking of medical aircraft differ between GCs I/II and GC IV.[55] In any case, protection based on markings alone was considered insufficient in 1949, given that the conditions of modern warfare make it possible to fire at an aircraft before its markings become visible.[56] While additional markings and means of identification were recommended in Article 36 paragraph 2 GC I and Article 39 paragraph 2 GC II (later formalized through the adoption of Annex I to AP I), it was hoped that introducing a legal regime requiring agreements for all forms of medical aviation would enhance their protection.

19 Under the GC regime, medical aircraft may not be attacked and must be respected as long as they operate in accordance with an agreement concluded between the parties to the conflict. Unlike Article 18 of the 1929 GC I, according to which agreements were mandatory only for flying over the firing line and over the zone situated in front of clearing or dressing stations, as well as over all enemy or enemy-occupied territory, the Geneva Conventions subject all operations to the conclusion of agreements. Moreover, medical aircraft are expressly prohibited from flying over enemy or enemy-occupied territory unless agreed otherwise,[57] for example to bring medical assistance to the wounded in a besieged zone.[58] Aircraft operating without or in violation of an agreement do so 'at their own risk and peril'[59]—which arguably refers to a factual risk rather than a loss of immunity in law. If a medical aircraft is obliged to land in enemy or enemy-occupied territory due to weather conditions, engine trouble, or similar causes, the adverse party has the right under Article 36 paragraph 5 GC I to take the wounded, sick, or shipwrecked, as well as the aircraft's crew, as POWs, and to treat medical personnel and material according to the Convention (e.g., take the aircraft as war booty if belonging to the armed forces of the adverse party).[60] Given that flight over territory controlled by an adverse party is no longer prohibited under AP I, Article 30(2) AP I provides for different possibilities for the treatment of a medical aircraft and its occupants depending on the outcome of inspection, but ultimately foresees the same result as in the case of a medical aircraft having violated an agreement,[61] i.e. the seizure of the aircraft and treatment of its occupants depending on their status. It adds that medical aircraft having been permanently assigned to such functions may be used thereafter only as medical aircraft—an important difference if compared to the changeable use of medical vehicles which fall into enemy hands. Furthermore, Article 36 paragraph 4 GC I requires medical aircraft to obey every summons to land. Addressed to aircraft operating over enemy or enemy-controlled territory and own territory close to enemy lines, its scope of application was largely maintained in Article 30(1) AP I. The right of neutral states to summon medical aircraft to land is governed in Article 37 paragraph 1 GC I and Article 31(1) AP I.[62] In either case, medical aircraft may be inspected,[63] with AP I setting out not only the conditions of inspection safeguarding the interests of the wounded,[64] but also the consequences of its result.[65] Lastly, Article 37 GC I governs the rights of neutral states, balancing their sovereign rights with considerations of humanity. Medical aircraft may therefore fly over neutral territory, land on it, and use it as a port of call if complying with a number of conditions.[66] Having previously informed the neutral power, they are immune from attack only when respecting

---

[55] Art 22 GC IV makes their marking optional; Pictet Commentary GC IV, at 174.
[56] Pictet Commentary GC I, at 288.
[57] Art 36 para 3 GC I and Art 39 para 3 GC II.   [58] Pictet Commentary GC I, at 291.
[59] Ibid, at 288 and 291.   [60] Ibid, at 293.   [61] Art 30(4) AP I.
[62] See Ch 5, section D.I.f, of this volume.
[63] Art 36 para 4 GC I; Art 30(1) AP I; Art 37 para 1 GC I; and Art 31(3) AP I.
[64] Arts 30(2) and 31(3) AP I.   [65] Arts 30(3) and (4), and 31(3) AP I.   [66] Art 31(1) AP I.

the agreement bilaterally entered into with the neutral power,[67] including any possible conditions and restrictions imposed by the neutral power equally on all parties to the conflict.[68] The situation of the wounded and sick permanently disembarked after the landing on neutral territory is also governed by Article 37 paragraph 3 GC I and Article 31(4) AP I. While a medical aircraft may normally continue its flight after an inspection following a summons to land,[69] an officer in charge may decide, with the consent of the local authorities, that the wounded and sick should remain permanently on neutral territory. In this case, they shall be detained where required by international law, and the costs of their detention borne by the power on which they depend.

Following the adoption of the Geneva Conventions, it was noted that the Diplomatic Conference of 1949 'virtually paralyzed medical aviation' by requiring an agreement for all activity of medical aircraft.[70] The rules of AP I were thus adopted in the hope of 'giv[ing] new life to medical aviation'.[71] By introducing a regime based on different zones of operation, the Protocol is in conflict with some of the rules of the Conventions and must be considered to replace them among parties to the Protocol. Additional Protocol I no longer requires an agreement for the operation of medical aircraft in all circumstances. According to Article 25 AP I, in and over land areas physically controlled by friendly forces, or in and over sea areas not physically controlled by an adverse party, respect for and protection of medical aircraft is not dependent on any agreement with the adverse party. A party to the conflict may, for greater safety, notify the adverse party in accordance with the rules of Article 29 AP I, especially when operating within the range of surface-to-air weapons systems, but it is not required to do so. According to Article 26 AP I, in and over those parts of the contact zone (where forward elements of opposing forces are in contact) which are physically controlled by friendly forces, and in and over areas the physical control of which is not clearly established, agreement is furthermore not legally required but only recommended.[72] In such areas, the protection of medical aircraft is considered to be fully effective only by prior agreement between the parties to the conflict. However, a medical aircraft must be protected as soon as it is recognized as such, regardless of any agreement. Prior agreement continues to be a legal requisite in areas controlled by an adverse party, including occupied territories and parts of the contact zone physically controlled by the adversary, according to Article 27(1) AP I. Contrary to Article 36 paragraph 3 GC I, flights over enemy or enemy-occupied territory are, as such, not prohibited. The wording of Article 27(1) AP I further suggests that parties to the conflict should consent, and should refuse to give their agreement only in the event of imperative reasons.[73]

20

To date, it remains unclear to what extent the rules contained in AP I reflect customary international law. The Customary International Humanitarian Law Study, while concluding that '[m]edical transports assigned exclusively to medical transportation must be respected and protected in all circumstances',[74] merely recalls the rules of the Conventions and AP I without drawing conclusions about the customary international law nature of either one. The Commentary to the Elements of War Crimes under the Statute of the International Criminal Court (ICC Statute) notes with respect to Article 36 GC I and Article 22 GC IV that 'these rules on medical aircraft are outdated' and that 'the present

21

---

[67] Ibid. [68] Art 31(5) AP I. [69] Art 31(3) AP I.
[70] ICRC Commentary APs, at 27, para 967.
[71] Ibid, at 281, para 974. [72] Ibid, at 290, para 1009. [73] Ibid, at 294, para 1020.
[74] ICRC CIHL Study, Rule 29.

law is reflected in the provisions of AP I'.[75] The HPCR *Manual on International Law Applicable to Air and Missile Warfare*,[76] being the most current restatement of existing international law relating to medical aviation, largely reflects the rules of AP I. Similar to Article 25 AP I, Rule 77 provides that in and over areas controlled by friendly forces (and sea areas not controlled by the adverse party),[77] the specific protection of medical aircraft of a belligerent party is not dependent on the consent of the enemy. Unlike AP I, and not without controversy,[78] the *Manual* does not distinguish between areas controlled by the enemy and those parts of the contact zone controlled by friendly or own forces, or areas where physical control is not clearly established. According to Rule 78, protection of medical aircraft in all of these areas can be fully effective only by virtue of prior consent, given that the distinction between areas controlled by the enemy and the contact zone may be blurred.[79]

c. Medical vessels

22   Geneva Convention II contains a detailed regime protecting hospital ships, craft (Article 22–35 GC II), and ships chartered for the transport of medical equipment (Article 38 GC II). It also protects sick-bays on board a warship in case of fighting, as well as sick-bays and their equipment under the control of the enemy (Article 28 GC II). Medical material in sick-bays remains subject to the laws of war, i.e. may be seized, as long as it is not required for the care of the wounded and sick or applied to other purposes, pursuant to the commander's decision after ensuring the proper care of the wounded and sick accommodated in the sick-bays. While the boarding of enemy warships is rare in modern warfare, sick-bays may fall under enemy control following the capture of a vessel.[80]

23   Hospital ships are defined within Article 22 GC II as ships built or equipped specially and solely to assist the wounded, sick, and shipwrecked members of the armed forces. The definition has been enlarged with the adoption of Article 22(1) AP I, according to which provisions relating to hospital ships also apply where vessels carry wounded, sick, and shipwrecked civilians. The restriction contained in Article 21 GC IV, according to which vessels specially provided for the conveyance of wounded and sick civilians are protected only if they form a convoy, is hence also considered obsolete with respect to medical vessels. The protections apply to hospital ships wherever they are operating and whatever tonnage they possess. Article 26 GC II nevertheless encourages the use of ships of over 2,000 tons gross for the transport of the wounded, sick, and shipwrecked over long distances and on the high seas, to ensure maximum comfort and security. While lifeboats (Article 26 GC II) and coastal rescue craft (Article 27 GC II) employed for the rescue and transport of the wounded, sick, and shipwrecked may be of significantly lower tonnage, hospital ships must indeed have the necessary capacities (for example space and equipment) in order not only to transport, but also to treat and assist the wounded, sick, and shipwrecked in all circumstances. To be protected, hospital ships must be notified to the conflict parties no later than 10 days prior to their use. While Article 22 GC II only requires the notification of their name, registered gross tonnage, length from stem to stern, and number of masts and funnels, it is today suggested that notification should include all available information

---

[75] K. Dörmann, *Elements of War Crimes under the Rome Statute of the International Criminal Court: Sources and Commentary* (Cambridge/Geneva: CUP/ICRC, 2003), at 352 and 357.
[76] HPCR *Manual*, above n 52.   [77] HPCR *Commentary*, above n 54, at 188, para 5.
[78] Ibid, at 189, para 1.   [79] Ibid.   [80] Pictet Commentary GC II, at 176.

whereby the ship may be identified (such as its call sign or radio frequencies).[81] It is further recommended that notification is made in the form of a general notification in advance.[82] Hospital ships utilized by National Red Cross or Red Crescent Societies, officially recognized relief societies, or private persons, are equally protected according to Article 24 GC II, but must be notified, officially commissioned, and certified by one of the conflict parties. If belonging to a neutral country, such hospital ships must be placed under the control of one of the parties to the conflict with the previous consent of the neutral country's own government and the authorization of the conflict party concerned.[83] Article 22(2) AP I extends this protection to hospital ships made available to a conflict party by any neutral state or impartial international humanitarian organization.

24   Hospital ships must in no circumstances be attacked or captured, and must be respected and protected (Article 22 GC II). The scope of this obligation is partially laid out within GC II itself, with Article 29 GC II requiring a hospital ship to be able to leave a port which has fallen into enemy hands, and Article 32 GC II demanding that a hospital ship not be classed as a warship as regards its stay in a neutral port.

25   Article 34 paragraph 2 GC II prohibits hospital ships from possessing or using secret code for their wireless or other means of communication. According to the Pictet Commentary, it requires hospital ships to communicate in clear terms, or at least in a universally known code.[84] Article 34 paragraph 2 GC II is today largely seen as outdated, detrimental to the humanitarian mission, and in need of revision. For one thing, most radio, computer, and satellite communications are today routinely encrypted. The prohibition of the use of secret code is furthermore considered a hindrance to direct communication between a warship and a hospital ship, since non-coded communication risks giving away the warship's position to the adversary. Hospital ships thus cannot be directly informed about the numbers of casualties, the fleet's movement, or designated casualty pickup points. Indirect communication via naval bases on shore can cause delays and be detrimental to rapid medical assistance.[85] Rule 171 of the *San Remo Manual on International Law Applicable to Armed Conflicts at Sea* therefore notes that '[i]n order to fulfil most effectively their humanitarian mission, hospital ships should be permitted to use cryptographic equipment. The equipment shall not be used in any circumstances to transmit intelligence data nor in any other way to acquire any military advantage.' Given modern communications technology, hospital ships could be equipped with at least a decoder-receiver, allowing them to receive coded messages and decipher them without transmitting coded messages themselves—a possibility widely considered to be at odds with the Article 34 GC II prohibition on both the use and possession of a secret code for sending and receiving encrypted communications.[86]

26   Article 35 paragraph 1 GC II is also considered inadequate for modern-day conflicts by many. While it allows for the crew's armament for their own defence or that of the sick and wounded, it does not provide for the armament of the ship itself for self-defence purposes.

---

[81] International Institute of Humanitarian Law (IIHL), *San Remo Manual on International Law Applicable to Armed Conflicts at Sea* (Cambridge: CUP, 1995), Rule 169 and Commentary.
[82] Ibid.   [83] Art 25 GC II.
[84] Pictet Commentary GC II, at 193.
[85] For an account of the difficulties encountered regarding communication during the 1982 conflict between the UK and Argentina in the South Atlantic, see P. Eberlin, 'Identification of Hospital Ships and Ships Protected by the Geneva Conventions of 12 August 1949', 22 *IRRC* 231 (1982) 315, at 324.
[86] See *contra* J. Roach, 'The Law of Naval Warfare at the Turn of Two Centuries', 94 *AJIL* (2000) 64, at 75.

27 Today the argument is made that hospital ships may be equipped with purely deflective means of defence, such as chaff and flares, although the presence of such equipment should be notified.[87] The armament of hospital ships may in no circumstances serve to prevent a lawful search of the vessel. According to Article 31 GC II, parties to the conflict have the right to take a number of control measures, such as searching hospital ships, controlling the use of their means of communication, making hospital ships take a certain course, and even detaining them for up to seven days.

27 In addition to hospital ships, GC II protects small craft employed by the state or an officially recognized lifeboat institution for coastal rescue operations, so far as operational requirements permit, if such craft have been notified like hospital ships.[88] Considered 'excessively formal to make the notification of such craft a condition of their protection',[89] Article 22(3) AP I now only recommends their notification, rather than legally requiring it.

28 Article 38 GC II adds one final category of vessels to the protections of the Convention. Considered 'truly humanitarian in scope',[90] it grants safe conduct for carrier ships. Accordingly, ships chartered for the purpose of transporting equipment exclusively intended for the treatment of the wounded and sick, or the prevention of disease, are protected if notified to the adverse power, which must approve the particulars regarding the voyage of such ships, such as course, date, and speed.[91] The adverse party may board these ships, but not capture or seize their equipment. While the inclusion of pharmaceutical products intended for the prevention of disease was considered a 'very liberal provision',[92] given that able-bodied combatants would benefit from them too, and doubts were expressed whether the plenipotentiaries were fully aware of the scope of Article 38 GC II,[93] the provision today seems in line with the approach taken in the definition of 'medical units' contained in Article 8(e) AP I, which comprises preventive medicine centres and institutes.

29 Other ships and craft are not covered by GC II. Article 23 AP I, however, extends a certain degree of protection to all ships and craft fulfilling the definition in Article 8(i) AP I. A fishing boat requisitioned exclusively for the transport of medicines to a hospital situated on an island,[94] while being neither a hospital ship, nor a craft or carrier ship protected under GC II, is therefore to be respected and protected—albeit to a lesser degree. Since the conditions for according protection to hospital ships, craft, and carriers are more strict, the provisions offering protection are more extensive. Consequently, in addition to being subject to certain control measures,[95] other medical ships and craft remain subject to the laws of war, meaning that their equipment may be seized.

C. Relevance in Non-International Armed Conflicts

30 Common Article 3 requires that in case of non-international armed conflict (NIAC), the wounded and sick shall be collected and cared for.[96] In order to avoid any form of

---

[87] *San Remo Manual*, above n 81, Rule 170. For an overview of recent practice, see R. Grunawalt, 'Hospital Ships in the War on Terror: Sanctuaries or Targets?', 58 *Naval War College Review* (2006) 89, at 105–7.
[88] Art 27 GC II.
[89] ICRC Commentary APs, at 259, para 881.   [90] Pictet Commentary GC II, at 213.
[91] Ibid, at 214.   [92] Ibid, at 213.   [93] Ibid.
[94] ICRC Commentary APs, at 262, para 886.   [95] Art 23(2) AP I.   [96] CA 3 para 1(2).

recognition of non-state armed groups, states nevertheless chose not to refer to 'respect' for or the 'protection' of the wounded and sick.[97] Additional Protocol II thus substantially developed the rules on the protection of the wounded, sick, and shipwrecked, including of medical units, in Articles 7–12 AP II. This was, however, done in the belief that the newly adopted rules of AP II would merely make explicit what was already implicitly contained in Common Article 3.[98]

According to Article 11(1) AP II, medical units and transports shall be respected and protected at all times and shall not be the object of attack. However, AP II does not contain any definitions. Given that the terminology used is identical to that of AP I, it is today not only interpreted by analogy to AP I,[99] but considered to have a corresponding customary international law content.[100]

Whereas Article 11 AP II conjunctively refers to both 'medical units' and 'transports', medical transports must be considered a part of the definition of medical units. Referring to the definition of medical transports under AP I, all forms of medical transportation (i.e. by land, air, or water) are covered within the customary obligation to respect and protect medical transports.[101] However, no specific treaty or customary international rules can be identified regarding the protection of medical vehicles, aircraft, and vessels in NIACs. The *San Remo Manual on International Law Applicable to Armed Conflicts at Sea* has refrained from formally pronouncing on the application of the rules protecting medical aircraft and vessels during NIACs. It limits itself to noting that its scope is intentionally not explicitly limited to international armed conflicts (IACs) in order to not 'dissuade the implementation of these rules in non-international armed conflicts regarding naval operations'.[102] The HPCR *Manual on International Law Applicable to Air and Missile Warfare* expressly states that the objective of the *Manual* is to produce a restatement of existing law applicable in IACs, but adds that this is done without prejudice to the possible application of some of the rules to NIACs.[103] Its Commentary therefore indicates on a case-by-case basis whether the same or a similar rule is applicable in NIACs. With respect to the protection of medical aircraft, the Commentary considers the various rules differentiating between certain areas of operation to be applicable in NIACs.[104] An exception is made for rules relating to neutral territory, as the law of neutrality applies only in IACs.[105] Furthermore, any rules entailing a possible seizure of medical aircraft are not considered applicable in NIACs.[106]

Rules relating to the protection of medical buildings and material are subject to the same limitation. While their general protection may be inferred from the obligation to care for the wounded and sick, their treatment, especially if they fall into enemy hands, is not conclusively governed under IHL applicable in NIACs. While customary international law provides for rules regarding pillage[107] and destruction of property,[108] no rules allowing or prohibiting the taking of war booty have so far been identified.[109] The

---

[97] Pictet Commentary GC I, at 57.   [98] ICRC Commentary APs, at 1403, para 4627.
[99] Ibid, at 1403, para 4631.   [100] ICRC CIHL Study, Rule 28.
[101] Ibid, Rule 29. See MN 12.
[102] *San Remo Manual*, above n 81, Rule 1 and Commentary. For an overview of issues relating to naval operations and NIACs, see N. Ronzitti, 'Naval Warfare', in MPEPIL.
[103] HPCR *Manual*, above n 52, Rule 2(a).
[104] HPCR *Manual*, above n 52, and *Commentary*, above n 54, Rules 75, 77, 78, and 79.
[105] HPCR *Manual*, above n 52, and *Commentary*, above n 54, Rules 84 and 85.
[106] HPCR *Manual*, above n 52, and *Commentary*, above n 54, Rule 80(c) and (d).
[107] ICRC CIHL Study, Rule 52.   [108] Ibid, Rule 50.   [109] Ibid, Rule 49.

D. Legal Consequences of a Violation

34 In IACs, the 'extensive destruction and appropriation of property, not justified by military necessity and carried out unlawfully and wantonly', if committed against protected property, constitutes a grave breach under GCs I, II, and IV.[110] While the concept of protected property, unlike protected persons, is not generally defined within the Conventions, and consists more of a 'description of what cannot be attacked, destroyed or appropriated',[111] medical units are considered protected under all the Conventions.[112] The Pictet Commentary further adds that this category of grave breaches covers in particular cases of destruction of buildings or material belonging to enemy medical units, in violation, for example, of Article 33 paragraph 3 GC I, or seizures of medical material or transports without the prescribed conditions being respected.[113] The requirement for extensiveness is generally interpreted to exclude isolated acts of destruction or appropriation.[114] Article 85(2) AP I extends the definition of protected persons against whom and property against which a grave breach may be committed to all medical or religious personnel, medical units, or medical transports as defined in Article 8(e) AP I, most importantly all civilian medical units. It limits protection to those under the control of the adverse party and protected by the Protocol.[115]

35   The extensive destruction and appropriation of property, not justified by military necessity and carried out unlawfully and wantonly if committed against protected property, is today listed as a grave breach of the Conventions within the ICC Statute's definition of war crimes in IACs.[116] As in the case of the grave breaches provisions themselves, the material elements of the crime differ depending on the underlying rules establishing different levels of protection for distinct categories of property.[117] Given the limited case law on the protection of property,[118] the findings of the International Criminal Tribunal for the former Yugoslavia (ICTY) in the *Blaškić* case are considered instructive by many—including its interpretation of the notion of 'extensive'. Concerning the destruction of property in occupied territory by the occupying power, the ICTY held that

> an occupying power is prohibited from destroying movable and non-movable property except where such destruction is made absolutely necessary by military operations. To constitute a grave breach, the destruction unjustified by military necessity must be extensive, unlawful and wanton. The notion of 'extensive' is evaluated according to the facts of the case—a single act, such as the destruction of a hospital, may suffice to characterise an offence under this count.[119]

Additionally, the ICC Statute defines a number of acts committed in the conduct of hostilities against medical units as other serious violations of the laws and customs applicable

---

[110] See Ch 31 of this volume.   [111] Dörmann, above n 75, at 33.
[112] Pictet Commentary GC I, at 371.
[113] Ibid, at 372.   [114] Pictet Commentary GC IV, at 601.
[115] ICRC Commentary APs, at 992, para 3468. The ICRC Commentary notes that 'the expression "under the control of the adverse Party" is justified by the fact that such persons and objects may come, for example, from a non-belligerent State, an aid society recognized and authorized by such a State or even an impartial international humanitarian organization which makes them available to a Party to the conflict'.
[116] Art 8(2)(a)(iv) ICC Statute.   [117] Dörmann, above n 75, at 81.   [118] Ibid, at 33.
[119] ICTY, *The Prosecutor v Tihomir Blaškić*, Trial Chamber Judgment, IT-95-14-T, 3 March 2000, para 157.

in IACs. These acts include the intentional direction of attacks against hospitals and places where the sick and wounded are collected, provided they are not military objectives, the destruction and seizure of enemy property unless imperatively demanded by the necessities of war, and the intentional direction of attacks against buildings, material, medical units and transports, as well as against personnel using the distinctive emblems in conformity with international law.[120]

In NIACs, war crimes as defined in the ICC Statute cover both serious violations of Common Article 3,[121] and other serious violations of the laws and customs applicable in armed conflicts not of an international character.[122] While Common Article 3 paragraph 1(2) requires that the wounded and sick be collected and cared for (an obligation from which the protection of medical units may be deduced), serious violations of Common Article 3 within Article 8(2)(c) of the ICC Statute are limited to acts committed against persons taking no active part in hostilities referred to in Common Article 3 paragraph 1. Acts committed against medical units are thus criminalized as serious violations of Common Article 3 only in so far as they fall within one of the categories of Article 8(2)(c)(i) of the ICC Statute, e.g. violence to life and person, or murder. Article 8(2)(e) of the ICC Statute, however, defines other serious violations of the laws and customs applicable in NIACs, and explicitly criminalizes certain acts committed against medical units in the conduct of hostilities.[123] Further, acts committed against medical units can be prosecuted under the charges of pillage,[124] or destruction or seizure of property not imperatively demanded by the necessities of the conflict.[125] When determining the lawfulness of destruction or seizures, the underlying rules applicable in NIACs must be kept in mind[126]—as well as the lack of specific provisions on requisitions, contributions, seizures, or the taking of war booty.[127]

E. Critical Assessment

The protection of the wounded, sick, and shipwrecked remains as relevant now as in the early days of IHL. Therefore, medical buildings, material, and transports required for their care are equally in continued need of protection.[128] Since their adoption in 1949, the rules contained in GCs I, II, and IV have most certainly contributed to their protection. By merging the rules applicable to medical units of the armed forces' medical services and civilian medical units, AP I has had an important impact on the protection of civilians factually, as well as on the application of the rules of the Geneva Conventions legally. While the relationship between legal rules contained in AP I and GC I, II, or IV has to be determined on a case-by-case-basis, it may be noted that, in general, many rules of AP I extending protection to civilian medical units are today considered reflective of customary international law. While the rules of GCs I, II, and IV can, as a matter of treaty law, be replaced by the rules of AP I only among the parties to the Protocol, they should be interpreted with due regard for applicable customary international rules.

---

[120] Art 8(2)(b)(ix), (xiii), and (xxiv) ICC Statute.   [121] Art 8(2)(c) ICC Statute.
[122] Art 8(2)(e) ICC Statute.
[123] Art 8(2)(e), esp (ii) and (iv), ICC Statute.   [124] Art 8(2)(e)(v) ICC Statute.
[125] Art 8(2)(e)(xii) ICC Statute.   [126] Dörmann, above n 75, at 486.   [127] Ibid, at 465.
[128] ICRC, *Health Care in Danger: A Sixteen-Country Study* (Geneva: ICRC, 2011) and ICRC, *Health Care in Danger: Violent Incidents Affecting Health Care, January 2012–December 2013* (Geneva: ICRC, 2014).

38 Regarding medical buildings, material, and transports, the Geneva Conventions themselves make several references to 'the laws of war' in force. The destruction and seizure of buildings of fixed medical establishments, the material of fixed medical establishments, medical vehicles, and equipment of sick-bays which have fallen into enemy hands, all remain subject to the laws of war. While in each case certain safeguards are applicable, protecting the wounded and sick affected, it may nevertheless be questioned if this approach is still adequate—also taking into account states' positive obligation to take all feasible measures to ensure access to healthcare under international human rights law.[129]

39 The appropriateness of the rules in the Geneva Conventions can certainly be challenged regarding their provisions on medical aviation and hospital ships. In both cases, the view is broadly shared that the rules are detrimental to effective medical assistance. Subjecting all medical aviation to the conclusion of agreements had already been criticized as a hindrance at the time of the adoption of AP I. With the required amount of state practice and *opinio juris*, it can therefore be argued that customary international law (as reflected in AP I or the HPCR *Manual*) differs from the rules contained in Articles 36 and 37 GC I. The lack of regulation concerning the armament of hospital ships for purposes of self-defence within GC II can be seen as a danger for their safety; the prohibition on the use of encrypted communications technology as prejudicial to the care of the wounded, sick, and shipwrecked. While so far the argument has not been made that this prohibition is obsolete under customary international law, mainly because contrary state practice and *opinio juris* are not considered sufficiently 'dense'[130] to have led to a *desuetudo*, the appropriateness of the rules of GC II has nevertheless been questioned both in theory and practice. It thus remains to be seen how the rules on medical aviation and hospital ships are addressed, and what significance is accorded to the rules of GCs I, II, and IV, should a formal treaty process be undertaken in the future transforming non-binding restatements of international law, such as the *San Remo Manual* or HPCR *Manual*, into binding, new treaty law.[131]

KATJA SCHÖBERL

---

[129] CESCR, General Comment 14 (2000), E/C.12/2000/4. See generally, G. Giacca, *Economic, Social and Cultural Rights in Armed Conflict* (Oxford: OUP, 2014).

[130] H. Waldock, 'General Course on Public International Law', in The Hague Academy of International Law, *Collected Courses of the Hague Academy of International Law* (Leiden: A.W. Sijthoff, 1962), vol 106, 1, at 44.

[131] For a discussion of the prospects of the adoption of new treaty law regarding naval warfare, see Roach, above n 86, at 76.

Chapter 42. Loss of Protection

	MN
A. Introduction	1
B. Meaning and Application	9
I. Acts harmful to the enemy	9
II. Acts not causing loss of protection	14
a. General	14
b. Armed personnel	15
c. Presence of arms and ammunition taken from the wounded	19
d. Care for civilian wounded and sick	21
e. Specific rules on land	23
f. Specific rules at sea	27
III. Consequences of loss of protection	30
a. General	30
b. Unheeded warning and time limit	32
c. Status and treatment of medical personnel after capture	34
C. Relevance in Non-International Armed Conflicts	37
D. Legal Consequences of a Violation	40
E. Critical Assessment	48

Select Bibliography

The number of sources in the doctrine specifically dealing with the loss of protection is limited, but mention thereof is made in the more general works on IHL, or in specific articles about the protection of medical units, transports, or personnel

Cassese, A., 'Under What Conditions May Belligerents Be Acquitted of the Crime of Attacking an Ambulance?', 6 *JICJ* (2008) 385

ICRC CIHL Study, Rules 25, 27, 28, 29, and 30

Kleffner, J., 'Protection of the Wounded, Sick and Shipwrecked', in D. Fleck (ed), *The Handbook of International Humanitarian Law* (2nd edn, Oxford: OUP, 2008) 325

Pictet, J., 'La profession médicale et le droit international humanitaire', 67 *IRRC* 754 (1985) 191

Pictet Commentary GC I, at 200–5 and 218–21

Pictet Commentary GC II, at 190–206

Rubenstein, L./Bittle, M., 'Responsibility for Protection of Medical Workers and Facilities in Armed Conflict', 375 *The Lancet* (2010) 329

Sassòli/Bouvier/Quintin, at 197–202

Schoenholzer, J.P., 'The Doctor in the Geneva Conventions of 1949', 6 *IRRC* 1 (1953), supplement

De Waard, P./Tarrant, J., 'Protection of Military Medical Personnel in Armed Conflicts', 35 *UWA Law Review* (2010) 157

A. Introduction

As is well known, it was the suffering of the numerous wounded soldiers after the battle of Solferino in 1859 that motivated the Swiss businessman Henry Dunant to start lobbying for the creation of a set of conventions to govern the behaviour of states during armed conflicts, to prevent or at least alleviate this suffering.[1] Since the creation of the first Geneva Convention, the body of international humanitarian law (IHL) has evolved in a substantial and impressive way. The logic during the negotiations that led to the different conventions has always aimed at keeping a balance between the protection of humanity and military necessity.

2   In this way, states realized that protection and respect for their wounded soldiers not only was a positive way to safeguard the soldiers' lives, but also made sense from a military point of view. Such protection would allow the armies to recover their soldiers when hostilities came to an end, while reducing the number of casualties, which in turn helped to moderate the complaints of local public opinion about the human cost of war.

3   However, in order to protect and respect the lives of the wounded and sick, the actors responsible for providing this protection must be able to fulfil their functions in the best possible conditions.[2] Also, the support provided to the wounded and sick should be considered as a lawful and not a hostile act, even when the wounded and sick belong to the 'enemy'.[3] This care provided to the wounded and sick should in principle never be seen as interference in the war effort of either party. Medical and religious personnel are endowed with a neutral position, which places them outside the hostilities and the theatre of war.[4] Thus, to protect the wounded and sick meant that those responsible for providing this protection were also entitled to respect, which led to numerous provisions in the Geneva Conventions dedicated thereto.

4   This logic led to the inclusion of detailed rules in the 1949 Geneva Conventions regarding the protection of the wounded, sick, and shipwrecked;[5] medical and religious personnel;[6] medical buildings, material, and transports;[7] hospitals;[8] hospital ships and sick-bays;[9] and about the use and protection of the emblem.[10]

5   The same *ratio legis* which led to the rules on the protection of these different categories also has a corollary: if the protection has to be provided and respected because it does not interfere with military necessity or affect military advantage, this protection should thus also cease as soon as the protection provided affects the military advantage of the adversary.

6   Concretely, as is discussed in detail elsewhere,[11] the protection of medical and religious personnel, both on land and at sea, is granted and guaranteed as long as those personnel are 'exclusively engaged' in the functions which they are allowed and supposed to fulfil in the context of the Conventions.[12] If they exceed those functions, they lose their protection. It has to be mentioned here, though, that other than hospital staff, who have their own specific protection in Article 20 GC IV, the personnel concerned in the Geneva

---

[1] H. Dunant, *A Memory of Solferino* (Geneva: ICRC, 1959), at 8.
[2] See in this way also J.P. Schoenholzer, 'The Doctor in the Geneva Conventions of 1949', 6 *IRRC* 1 (1953), supplement, at 12.
[3] See J. Pictet, 'La profession médicale et le droit international humanitaire', 67 *IRRC* 754 (1985) 191, at 199.
[4] Ibid. [5] See Chs 37, 38, and 39 of this volume. [6] See Ch 40 of this volume.
[7] See Ch 41 of this volume. [8] See Ch 11 of this volume. [9] See Chs 11 and 38 of this volume.
[10] See Ch 43 of this volume. [11] See Ch 40 of this volume.
[12] See Art 24 GC I and Art 36 GC II.

Conventions are *military* personnel.[13] However, Article 12 of Additional Protocol (AP) I, which is considered to be a reflection of customary law,[14] expands the protection and the rules related thereto to *civilian* personnel under certain conditions.

The Geneva Conventions include specific rules governing loss of protection of medical units and establishments,[15] hospital ships and sick-bays,[16] hospitals,[17] and land and sea transports.[18] The wording and logic of these provisions is similar, stating that the protection of the different categories of units and establishments 'shall not cease, unless they are used to commit, outside their humanitarian duties, acts harmful to the enemy'. The Conventions add, however, that this protection may cease only 'after due warning has been given, naming, in all appropriate cases, a reasonable time limit, and after such warning has remained unheeded'. While this rule is similar for all the different categories, the Conventions explicitly spell out some examples of certain acts that do not lead to the discontinuance of protection. The examples mentioned for the different units or establishments differ,[19] but in general the situations listed are acts or circumstances which might be deemed normal or necessary in order to fulfil their purpose and functions in an effective and satisfactory way.

Medical aircraft and air transports, the use of which was not as widespread during the negotiations of the Geneva Conventions as it is now, have their own provisions governing their protection.[20] The Conventions do not include specific rules governing the loss of protection of these units, but do include provisions stating that this protection is subject to the consent of the adversary or to an agreement between the parties to the conflict.[21] One might thus assume that under the regime of the Geneva Conventions, this protection will cease if an aircraft is deployed and used without clear agreement about the conditions and specificities of its actions. However, the *Manual on International Law Applicable to Air and Missile Warfare*[22] specifies the rules for medical aircraft in these types of situations, stating that 'in areas controlled by friendly forces, the specific protection of medical aircraft of a Belligerent Party is not dependent on the consent of the enemy'.[23] The *Manual* suggests that consent should still be sought if the aircraft is deployed over areas physically controlled by the enemy and in the contact zones, and specifies that '[a]lthough in the absence of such consent, medical aircraft in the contact zone operate at their own risk, they must nevertheless be respected once they have been identified as such'.[24]

---

[13] For a detailed analysis of what 'military' as opposed to 'civilian' personnel means, see Ch 40 of this volume.
[14] ICRC CIHL Study, Rule 25.   [15] Arts 21–22 GC I.   [16] Arts 34–35 GC II.
[17] Art 19 GC IV.   [18] Art 21 GC IV.
[19] For medical units and establishments, see Art 22 GC I; for hospital ships and sick-bays, see Art 35 GC II; for hospitals, see Art 19 GC IV.
[20] Arts 36–37 GC I; Arts 39–40 GC II; Art 22 GC IV. For a detailed analysis of the rules governing medical aircraft, see Ch 41 of this volume.
[21] E.g., in Art 39 GC II, it is stated that '[m]edical aircraft [...] shall be respected by the Parties to the conflict, while flying at heights, at times and on routes specifically agreed upon between the Parties to the conflict concerned'. While this does not explicitly state that the protection will cease if the aircraft fly at heights, at times, or on routes not agreed by the parties, an *a contrario* reasoning could lead to this conclusion. The same might be said, e.g., for the rules about the summons to land, etc.
[22] Harvard Program on Humanitarian Policy and Conflict Research (HPCR), *Manual on International Law Applicable to Air and Missile Warfare* (Cambridge, Mass: HPCR, 2009). The rules regarding military aircrafts are stipulated in Rules 75–87.
[23] Ibid, Rule 77, at 29.   [24] Ibid, Rule 78(a), at 29.

B. Meaning and Application

I. Acts harmful to the enemy

9   Some of the treaty provisions providing protection to medical units, establishments, and transports, and to medical and religious personnel, specify that this protection ceases if the units or establishments are 'used to commit, outside their humanitarian duties, acts harmful to the enemy'.[25] As far as the exact meaning of the words 'acts harmful to the enemy' is concerned, Pictet notes in his Commentaries that the delegates at the Diplomatic Conference in 1949 deemed that it was unnecessary to define this term, as its meaning was self-evident and must remain quite general.[26] However, in preparation for the Diplomatic Conference, the International Committee of the Red Cross (ICRC) drafted the following alternative wording, in case the delegates preferred it to be more explicit, 'acts the purpose of which or effect of which is to harm the adverse Party, by facilitating or impeding military operations'.[27]

10   In general, the use of medical units, personnel, or establishments in a way that means they take a direct part in hostilities or contribute to military action beyond their humanitarian function, would be considered as constituting an act harmful to the enemy, as they must respect the neutrality they claim for themselves, which requires them to refrain from all interference, be it direct or indirect, in military operations.[28] It is outside the scope of this chapter to discuss the detailed meaning of the expression '[taking] a direct part in hostilities', but one might refer to the series of expert meetings organized by the ICRC, the outcome document of which stated that in order to qualify as direct participation in hostilities, a specific act must meet a set of cumulative criteria:

the act must be likely to adversely affect the military operations or military capacity of a party to an armed conflict, or alternatively, to inflict death, injury or destruction of persons or objects protected against direct attack (threshold of harm) and

there must be a direct causal link between the act and the harm likely to result either from that act, or from a coordinated military operation of which that act constitutes an integral part (direct causation) and

the act must be specifically designed to directly cause the required threshold of harm in support of a party to the conflict and to the detriment of another (belligerent nexus).[29]

11   However, these cumulative criteria and the Interpretive Guidance as such were conceptualized in light of direct participation of civilians for targeting purposes, and the concept of 'acts harmful to the enemy' could include acts that arguably do not strictly fulfil all these requirements.[30]

---

[25] See Art 21 GC I; Art 34 GC II; Art 19 GC IV.   [26] Pictet Commentary GC I, at 200.
[27] Ibid.
[28] See in this regard also ICRC CIHL Study, Rule 25.
[29] N. Melzer, *Interpretive Guidance on the Notion of Direct Participation in Hostilities under International Humanitarian Law* (Geneva: ICRC, 2009), at 46. It should be mentioned here that the experts present at the meetings did not unanimously agree with the outcome document and formulation, and the issue has sparked some debate in the doctrine. For a detailed analysis of this debate, reference may be made to the Spring 2010 issue of the *Journal of International Law and Politics*, where various participants to the expert meetings discuss the Interpretive Guidance in detail: 42 *Journal of International Law and Politics* (2010) 637.
[30] See in this regard, e.g., the comments made in Bothe/Partsch/Solf, at 411; R.W. Gehring, 'Loss of Civilian Protections under the Fourth Geneva Convention and Protocol I', 90 *Military Law Review* (1980)

Examples of 'acts harmful to the enemy' which are often cited by the doctrine are sheltering able-bodied combatants in a medical unit or transport, using medical units as an arms or ammunitions dump or transport, the installation of an observation post or firing position on a hospital, the deliberate siting of a medical unit in a position where it would impede an enemy attack, etc.

The provisions regulating the loss of protection add that in order for the protection to cease, the acts harmful to the enemy must be committed 'outside [the unit's or establishment's] humanitarian duties'. The requirement as such is interesting, as it may help in distinguishing between acts committed without the intention of causing harm but which might have a harmful effect on the enemy, and acts which are committed with the intention of harming the enemy.[31] This gives rise to the question whether there are acts which are harmful to the enemy but are committed to fulfil humanitarian duties, and which thus do not lead to the loss of protection. Examples of these kind of acts include the waves given off by an x-ray apparatus in a hospital which might interfere with the transmission or reception of wireless messages or radar, interference in tactical operations by lights used by a medical establishment, or the case where a mobile medical unit accidentally breaks down while being moved in accordance with its humanitarian function, thereby obstructing a crossroads of military importance.[32] The assessment of the difference between acts which purposely harm the enemy and those which could harm the enemy but are related to the 'fulfilment of the humanitarian duties' is difficult to make, but it is important that this assessment is always made in good faith in order to safeguard the protection of these cardinal rules of IHL. When the assessment is difficult, or if it could lead to confusion, the medical units, establishments, and personnel should be given the benefit of the doubt.

II. Acts not causing loss of protection

a. General

The provisions governing the loss of protection actually spell out some examples of acts or conditions which should not be considered as depriving medical units, establishments, transports, or personnel of their protection.[33] Some rules are similar for all of the protected categories, but differences or specifics relating to the nature or functions of the units or establishments are mentioned for (civilian) hospitals,[34] hospital ships, sick-bays of vessels,[35] and medical units and establishments.[36] This summary of conditions and situations is not exhaustive,[37] and these may be interpreted as examples of conditions which might be or seem harmful to the enemy, or as being not in accordance with the neutrality of the units, establishments, or personnel, but which are necessary in order to assure satisfactory functioning and which are thus not 'outside their humanitarian duties'.

49; N. Melzer, *Targeted Killing in International Law* (Oxford: OUP, 2008), at 329. These authors argue that the concept of 'acts harmful to the enemy' is much wider than the concept of 'direct participation in hostilities'.

[31] See in this regard also P. De Waard and J. Tarrant, 'Protection of Military Medical Personnel in Armed Conflicts', 35 *UWA Law Review* (2010) 157, at 175.

[32] ICRC Commentary APs, at 175.   [33] See Art 22 GC I; Art 35 GC II; Art 19 GC IV.

[34] Art 19 GC IV.   [35] Art 35 GC II.   [36] Art 22 GC I.

[37] See also Pictet Commentary GC I, at 203.

b. Armed personnel

15   The fact that the personnel of the medical units or establishments are armed, and that they use arms in their own defence or in the defence of the wounded and sick in their charge, should not be considered as depriving them of the protection guaranteed by the Conventions.[38] The purpose of this provision is to allow medical personnel to ensure the maintenance of order and discipline in the units or establishments, and to protect them against individual hostile acts by pillagers or irresponsible members of the armed forces.[39] It would be illogical to prevent the medical personnel from defending themselves and their patients when they are faced with an unlawful substantial threat to their patients or themselves.[40] The wording of Article 22(1) GC I is slightly different from the wording of Article 35(1) GC II, which states explicitly that the weapons can be used for the maintenance of order. Even though this possibility has not been included specifically in Article 22(1) GC I, it may be argued that the maintenance of order is required not only in hospital ships or sick-bays, but also in hospitals on land.[41]

16   The meaning of 'maintenance of order' is quite uncontroversial in this regard, and examples include denying unauthorized persons access to the hospital and preventing patients from leaving the premises without permission,[42] but one might also refer to the need to prevent patients or others from engaging in criminal acts which might put the general discipline and order of the hospital, sick-bay, or hospital ship at risk, such as a situation where a patient or a common criminal enters the medical unit or establishment and tries to sexually assault a patient. In this case a light weapon might be used by medical personnel in order to compel the attacker to stop.

17   As far as the meaning of 'unlawful attack' is concerned, its concrete definition is more debatable and may give rise to confusion. Undoubtedly, the medical personnel would be allowed to use their weapons in order to defend themselves or their patients against enemy soldiers who commit grave breaches of the Geneva Conventions,[43] such as the torturing or wilful killing of the wounded and sick. On the other side of the equation, it is also clear that medical personnel may not use their weapons to prevent (lawful) capture of the unit by the enemy.[44] However, everything in between these two extremes is open to debate, and could lead to legal and operational confusion. What is clear is that in theory, when using their weapons and countering these unlawful attacks, the personnel will remain bound by national criminal law on the use of force, and this may demand proportionality and necessity. However, given the fact that the weapons can be used only in the defence of the personnel or their patients, and assuming that the unlawful attack is directed at them by the enemy, virtually all acts in such defence should fall within these principles.

18   This raises the question what kind of weapons medical personnel are allowed to carry. Given the fact that the purpose of these weapons is to defend medical personnel and their patients, their nature should also be purely defensive.[45] It may be argued that, in theory, light individual portable weapons such as side-arms, revolvers, or rifles should suffice for the given purpose.[46] This has been confirmed in the military manuals of various

---

[38] Art 22(1) GC I; Art 35(1) GC II.
[39] Pictet Commentary GC II, at 194.   [40] See in this regard also Pictet, above n 3, at 209.
[41] See also Pictet Commentary GC II, at 194.   [42] Ibid.
[43] Art 50 GC I; Art 51 GC II; Art 130 GC III; and Art 147 GC IV. See also Ch 31 of this volume.
[44] See Pictet Commentary GC I, at 203.   [45] See in this regard also Pictet, above n 3, at 209.
[46] See Pictet Commentary GC II, at 194.

states, and weapons such as machine guns, weapons that have to be handled by more than one person, or weapons intended for use against objects (such as missile launchers and anti-tank weapons) have been explicitly excluded.[47]

c. Presence of arms and ammunition taken from the wounded

Both Article 22(3) GC I and Article 35(3) GC II stipulate that the presence in the units or establishments of small arms and ammunition which have been taken from the wounded and sick but not yet handed to the proper service, shall not lead to a loss of protection.[48]

The presence of arms or ammunition in a medical unit or establishment might, at first glance, give the impression to an adversary that the unit or establishment was being used in a way which might cause a loss of protection. For example, the presence of weapons might be interpreted by the enemy as a sign that the unit or establishment was, or is, used by soldiers as a weapons storage facility, operational headquarters, or hide-out. These examples could in theory lead to the loss of protection for the unit or establishment concerned, but the provision was added explicitly to reconfirm that the mere presence of arms or ammunition taken from the wounded and sick, but not yet handed to the proper service, should *not* lead to a loss of protection. In the operational reality of a situation of armed conflict, medical establishments or units often have a large inflow of wounded and sick, who are often carrying weapons. The transfer of these weapons to the proper unit which will take care of them might take a long time, or might not necessarily be a priority. However, this should not be a reason to lift the protection of the unit or establishment provided by the Conventions.

d. Care for civilian wounded and sick

In the Articles regulating the loss of protection for medical units, medical establishments, hospital ships, and sick-bays of vessels, it is stipulated that the fact that their humanitarian activities extend to the care of wounded or sick (or shipwrecked) civilians shall not deprive them of their protection.[49] These rules have their counterpart in Article 19 paragraph 2 GC IV, which authorizes civilian hospitals to shelter and treat military wounded and sick.

The provisions confirm that the protection of the wounded and sick should continue without any form of discrimination and regardless of the military or civilian character of the patient.[50] While this is in line with the prohibition of discrimination in international human rights law (IHRL), it is also perfectly in line with the Hippocratic Oath of the medical personnel. Moreover, the character of modern warfare has moved the battlefield from the historical battlegrounds outside populated areas to more metropolitan or residential areas. This leads to the fact that one single act of war (especially in air warfare) can easily impact both civilians and soldiers. The victims of these acts of war should then also be able to be treated in the same buildings by the same medical personnel.[51]

---

[47] See ICRC CIHL Study, Rule 25.
[48] Art 35(3) uses 'portable' arms instead of 'small' arms, but the expressions basically cover the same concept.
[49] Art 22(5) GC I; Art 35(4) GC II.   [50] Pictet Commentary GC IV, at 156.
[51] See also Pictet Commentary GC I, at 204.

e. Specific rules on land

23 Article 22 GC I, which governs the rules relating to the loss of protection of medical units and establishments on land, mentions two additional specific examples of acts or conditions which do not cause a loss of protection.

24 The first one, in Article 22(2), specifies that in the absence of armed orderlies, if the unit or establishment is protected by a picket, by sentries, or by an escort, this does not deprive it of its protection provided by the Conventions.

25 The purpose of this rule is, as was the case with the rules relating to the use of arms by medical personnel, to protect the medical unit or establishment so that it can fulfil its humanitarian function in a satisfactory way. It has already been pointed out by Pictet in his Commentary to this Article that the reference to the 'absence of armed orderlies' should be interpreted as 'in the absence of armed orderlies in sufficient numbers to ensure the protection of a medical unit in any given case'.[52] Medical units and establishments are usually protected by armed orderlies, but the fact that pickets, sentries, or an escort—which are usually made up of soldiers—are present does not mean that the protection is lost. This extra protection, as is the case with the orderlies, has a purely defensive nature, and the use of their weapons is subject to the same conditions as apply to the use of arms by medical personnel (MN 15–18).[53] As is the case with the medical personnel, this means, for example, that the soldiers who might be present may not oppose the occupation or control of the unit by the enemy.

26 Article 22(4) GC I specifies that the fact that personnel and material of the veterinary service are found in the unit or establishment, without forming an integral part thereof, should not lead to the loss of protection. Given the current mechanized nature of armed conflict, animals are used very rarely, and this provision—while still forming a part of the positive law of the Geneva Conventions—appears to have lost some of its importance.

f. Specific rules at sea

27 The Geneva Conventions also include some specific examples of situations in the context of naval warfare which might seem harmful to the enemy but which are not to be considered as leading to the loss of protection as they are an inherent part of the normal functioning of the humanitarian units in question.

28 In this way, Article 35 GC II mentions that the presence on board hospital ships of transport apparatus exclusively intended to facilitate navigation or communication should not lead to loss of protection. In theory these materials could be used to communicate important military information to other members of the armed forces, but their mere presence should not lead to loss of protection as such. The use of this equipment could give rise to some debate, but in case of doubt it should be assumed that the materials are used in good faith.

29 The last paragraph of Article 35 GC II states that the protection of a hospital ship will not be lost if the unit is used for the transport of equipment and of personnel intended exclusively for medical duties, over and above the normal requirements. This provision was included to clarify that hospital ships may in exceptional circumstances be used to transport medical personnel and equipment over and above their normal capacity. It is not the intention of this provision to allow hospital ships to be used as a means of transport for large quantities of material that could contribute to the war effort.[54]

---

[52] Ibid. [53] See also ICRC Commentary APs, at 179.
[54] See also Pictet Commentary GC II, at 197.

III. Consequences of loss of protection

a. General

In general, the loss of protection for medical units, establishments, or transports, or for medical or religious personnel in one of the above-mentioned situations (MN 9–13), does not change their basic nature as providers of protection for the wounded and sick. The Geneva Conventions acknowledge, however, that the protection afforded may sometimes be misused, which would or could cause harm to the war effort or the military interests of the opposing party. This is why in certain instances protection may be lost. However, the special nature of these units, establishments, transports, or personnel does not change, and the Conventions spell out some specific rules which enhance the respect for these different categories, even if their protection is temporarily removed.[55]

More specifically, when acts harmful to the enemy are undertaken and protection is lost, the unit, establishment, or personnel responsible for those acts can in theory become a legitimate military target, and thus may be directly attacked and even destroyed by the enemy. When engaging in acts or activities that might cause loss of protection, medical or religious personnel should act with caution, as their loss of protection could endanger the entire establishment or unit which might also be perceived as engaging in this behaviour.[56] However, even if some of the personnel or units are perceived to be engaging in acts harmful to the enemy, 'there is no justification for the damage and destruction of medical equipment, furniture, official documents or patient files, each of them being purely civilian objects'.[57] In addition, after the attack has been launched, and the enemy's military disadvantage has been removed, the units, establishments, or personnel should continue to be respected, and should be allowed to continue their medical duties.[58] The previously protected unit, establishment, or personnel loses its protection and remains a legitimate target only as long as it is reasonably necessary for the opposing side to respond to the military activity.[59] However, for persons, one might also argue that, as they are members of the armed forces and lost protection as medical personnel, they permanently turn into combatants and may thus be targeted at any time. Furthermore, the basic rules of IHL relating to precaution and proportionality still have to be respected when the decision to launch the attack is made.[60] These basic rules will often lead *de facto* to the situation that the unit will not be directly attacked, as the destruction of these entities, especially when they are treating various wounded and sick, would often probably be excessive in relation to the concrete and direct military advantage anticipated, and thus not proportionate. However, this may be more an operational than a legal matter, and history has shown various examples where the military advantage apparently was deemed sufficient to launch an attack.[61] In

---

[55] Cf section B.II.a of this chapter.
[56] See also De Waard and Tarrant, above n 31, at 171.
[57] Report of the Commission of Inquiry on Lebanon pursuant to Human Rights Council Resolution S-2/1, 23 November 2006, A/HRC/3/2, at 43, para 167, available at <http://www.securitycouncilreport.org/atf/cf/%7B65BFCF9B-6D27-4E9C-8CD3-CF6E4FF96FF9%7D/Lebanon%20A%20HRC%203%202.pdf>.
[58] See also section B.III.c of this chapter.
[59] See also in this regard ICTY, *The Prosecutor v Stanislav Galić*, Appeals Chamber Judgment, IT-98-29-A, 30 November 2006, para 346. In its judgment, the Appeals Chamber used similar wording in order to discuss the temporal aspect of this loss of protection.
[60] See also J. Kleffner, 'Protection of the Wounded, Sick and Shipwrecked', in D. Fleck (ed), *The Handbook of International Humanitarian Law* (2nd edn, Oxford: OUP, 2008) 325, at 344.
[61] For a contemporary overview, see L. Rubenstein and M. Bittle, 'Responsibility for Protection of Medical Workers and Facilities in Armed Conflict', 375 *The Lancet* (2010) 329. In this article, the authors present the

this regard, reference might be made, for example, to the war between Israel and Lebanon in August 2006,[62] the non-international armed conflict (NIAC) in Sri-Lanka,[63] or to the NIAC in Syria in 2012.[64]

b. Unheeded warning and time limit

32   The Conventions add that, even in situations where certain acts may lead to a loss of protection, the protection may cease only 'after a due warning has been given, naming in all appropriate cases, a reasonable time limit and after such warning has remained unheeded'.[65] This extra requirement was added to avoid the principle of loss of protection being interpreted too strictly, leading to reduced protection for the units, establishments, personnel, or patients concerned.[66]

33   In concrete terms, this means that the enemy has to warn the unit, establishment, or personnel concerned to put an end to the harmful acts. This warning should be clear and specific, and it should mention the harmful act in which the unit, establishment, or personnel is engaged.[67] It must then give a 'reasonable' time limit before launching the attack. This time limit will vary according to the particular case, but must be long enough in order to allow the acts to be stopped, or to allow the formulation of a response in situations where an incorrect accusation has been made.[68] If this warning remains unheeded, the time limit has passed, and the act harmful to the enemy remains in place, the attack may thus be launched if the principles relating to proportionality and precautions are respected. The provisions also add, however, that the time limit need only be provided 'in all appropriate cases'. This means that there might be cases in which no time limit would be required, for example if a body of troops approaching a hospital were to be met by weapons fire from all the windows of the hospital. In this situation, fire would obviously be returned without delay.[69]

c. Status and treatment of medical personnel after capture

34   As mentioned above,[70] personnel who lose their protection can become a military target if they engage in acts harmful to the enemy, and they thus may be directly attacked in certain circumstances.

---

results of their research, which analysed information from various sources about the attacks on wounded and sick individuals, medical personnel, medical facilities, or medical transport, and about the improper use of medical facilities or emblems. The research covered the period 1980–2009 and includes conflicts such as those in El Salvador, the Philippines, the former Yugoslavia, Nepal, and East-Timor amongst others.

[62] Report of the Commission of Inquiry on Lebanon, above n 57, at 42–7, para 161–87.

[63] See, e.g., HRW, 'Sri Lanka: Repeated Shelling of Hospitals Evidence of War Crimes', Press Release, 8 May 2009, in which HRW documented at least 30 attacks on hospitals and other medical establishments in the period between December 2008 and May 2009.

[64] See, e.g., HRW, 'Syria: Fighter Planes Strike Aleppo Hospital', Press Release, 15 August 2012.

[65] See Art 21 GC I; Art 34 GC II; and Art 19 GC IV.

[66] See also Pictet Commentary GC I, at 201; and Pictet Commentary GC II, at 191–2.

[67] In this regard, reference might be made to the conflict in Gaza in December 2008 and January 2009, where a Fact-Finding Mission mandated by the UN Human Rights Council referred to the attack on the Al-Quds and Al-Wafa hospital without a concrete warning, and concluded that this was a clear violation of (inter alia) Art 19 GC IV. The mission also stated that the general warning given to the population in Gaza was not sufficient, and that the warning must be detailed and effective, taking the specifics and functions of hospitals into account. See Report of the United Nations Fact-Finding Mission on the Gaza Conflict, 25 September 2009, A/HRC/12/48, at 141–9, paras 596–652.

[68] See also Pictet Commentary GC II, at 192.   [69] See also Pictet Commentary GC I, at 202.

[70] See section B.III of this chapter.

However, the fact that medical or religious personnel lose their protection does not mean 35
that their status changes.[71] The general rule that provides for protection is temporarily (or arguably permanently—see MN 31) suspended while the personnel in question participate in the war effort and engage in those acts harmful to the enemy. However, the particularities of their status and the respect which is provided throughout the Conventions for their profession and functions do not cease. This is also reflected in the rules relating to the status and treatment of medical personnel after they have been captured.[72] In theory, medical and religious personnel captured by the enemy should be repatriated immediately, unless their services are needed to secure the state of health and the spiritual needs of prisoners of war (POWs).[73] During this captivity, they do not receive POW status, but they are to receive 'as a minimum the benefits and protection of the present Convention, and shall also be granted all facilities necessary to provide for the medical care of, and religious ministration to prisoners of war'.[74] This means that the Detaining Power can 'apply to retained medical personnel only those provisions of the Prisoners of War Convention that are manifestly to their advantage'.[75] If the personnel engaged in an act harmful to the enemy, it is possible that they have violated rules of national criminal law, for which they may be punished given the fact that they do not have combatant status if they retain their capacity as medical or religious personnel. If one were to argue that the personnel engaged in acts harmful to the enemy permanently become combatants, it would imply that they cannot be punished for their acts harmful to the enemy as they acquire combatant privilege. However, this would also imply that they could be interned as POWs until the end of active hostilities. Alternatively, one might also argue that personnel who engage in acts harmful to the enemy permanently lose their status and become civilians, in which case there would be no protection gap as they would fall under the protection of the other relevant Geneva Conventions.

In the opinion of this author, the first option, in which the personnel lose their 36
protection only temporarily but retain their status, is preferable, as it coincides with the necessity to provide protection to those fulfilling certain fundamental functions in armed forces who should not generally be considered or treated as combatants, not just because of their different training and expertise, but especially because of the contribution they make to alleviating the suffering and human impact of the conduct of hostilities.

C. Relevance in Non-International Armed Conflicts

The *ratio legis* supporting the protection offered by the Conventions in international 37
armed conflict (IAC),[76] also applies in NIACs: as the wounded and sick are explicitly protected in Common Article 3, one might argue that the medical and religious personnel, the establishments, and the units providing this protection should also be protected and

---

[71] In theory, the status of the medical or religious personnel could change if the party to which they belonged explicitly changed their status to (say) that of combatants. This would mean of course that the protection would be lost, and this could in theory happen in extreme situations where the party concerned suffered from an unprecedented lack of combatants, but in practice these kinds of situations will seldom occur. For a detailed analysis, see De Waard and Tarrant, above n 31, at 175–82.
[72] For a detailed analysis of the rules governing this situation, see Ch 40 of this volume.
[73] See also Art 28 GC I.   [74] Art 33 GC III.   [75] Pictet Commentary GC I, at 243.
[76] See section A of this chapter.

respected.⁷⁷ However, this reasoning is not entirely uncontested,⁷⁸ and if a similar parallel reasoning were to be made for the rest of the rules, arguably most of the body of law applicable in IACs would also apply in NIACs.

38 Nonetheless, the protection of medical units, transports, and establishments, and of medical and religious personnel in NIACs has been stipulated in Additional Protocol (AP) II.⁷⁹ Also, this protection is arguably a part of customary international humanitarian law.⁸⁰ In this way, reference might also be made to the fact that the Statute of the International Criminal Court (ICC) penalizes the attacking of medical units, transports, or establishments, or of medical or religious personnel in NIACs.⁸¹

39 Assuming that the rules relating to protection apply in NIAC, one might argue that the rules concerning loss of protection apply too. In Article 11(2) AP II it is provided that '[t]he protection to which medical units and transports are entitled shall not cease unless they are used to commit hostile acts, outside their humanitarian function'. The paragraph also restates the rules about the obligation for the attacking party to issue a warning with a reasonable time limit where appropriate (see MN 7 and 32). However, the wording of the Article in AP II is slightly different from that in the Geneva Conventions: AP II mentions 'hostile acts', while the Conventions use the term 'acts harmful to the enemy'. Nevertheless, as has been argued before, the meaning of both terms is the same.⁸² While this rule about the loss of protection has specifically been included in AP II only as regards the protection of medical units and transports, it may be applied by analogy to medical and religious personnel.⁸³

D. Legal Consequences of a Violation

40 A violation of the rules under scrutiny in this chapter may lead to the criminal responsibility of the person(s) who attacked the protected unit, transports, establishment, or personnel, as it might constitute a war crime for the reasons stated below. However, in some cases certain acts which might lead to the loss of protection for these protected subjects might also entail criminal responsibility under national law for the individuals engaged in these acts.

41 An attack directed against a medical unit or establishment, or against medical or religious personnel, can lead to a number of criminal consequences for the person ordering or executing the action.⁸⁴

---

⁷⁷ See also ICRC Commentary APs, at 124. For a more detailed analysis of the applicability of the rules regarding the protection of medical and religious personnel, medical units, and medical establishments in NIACs, see Chs 40 and 41 of this volume.

⁷⁸ See, e.g., S. Sivakumaran, *The Law of Non-International Armed Conflicts* (Oxford: OUP, 2012), at 278.

⁷⁹ Arts 9 and 11 AP II.

⁸⁰ See ICRC CIHL Study, Rules 25, 27, and 28. See also the various examples of national legislation, military manuals, and other documents and statements which might be regarded as state practice confirming the customary nature of these rules, in the ICRC's CIHL Database. See also Sivakumaran, above n 78, at 280. See further the view of the Colombian Constitutional Case in this regard, which argued that the obligation in AP II to respect and protect medical and religious personnel and medical units has attained customary status: Colombian Constitutional Court, Constitutional Case No C-291/07, Judgment of 25 April 2007, at 69.

⁸¹ ICC Statute, Art 8(2)(e)(ii) and (iv). See also section D of this chapter.

⁸² See ICRC Commentary APs, at 1435.

⁸³ See also ICRC CIHL Study, Rules 25, 27, and 28.

⁸⁴ For an analysis of the different modes of criminal responsibility, command responsibility, universal jurisdiction, grave breaches, etc, see, e.g., A. Cassese, *International Criminal Law* (Oxford: OUP, 2003); E. van

First, under the grave breaches regime, certain violations of the Geneva Conventions 42
may lead to criminal responsibility before the court of the country to which the perpetrator of the violation belongs, and to universal jurisdiction in every state in which the national system and legislation can provide a head of jurisdiction.[85] The relevant Articles of the Geneva Conventions[86] state that a grave breach includes 'any of the following acts, if committed against persons or property protected by the Conventions: wilful killing, [...] and extensive destruction and appropriation of property, not justified by military necessity and carried out unlawfully and wantonly'. Thus, an attack which is wilfully and purposely directed against medical or religious personnel may lead to the criminal responsibility of the person executing or ordering the act. Similarly, an act directed against a medical unit or establishment which causes the extensive destruction thereof, and which is 'not justified by military necessity and carried out unlawfully and wantonly', may also be a grave breach of the Conventions and lead to criminal responsibility. One of the questions that arises in this regard is that of the *mens rea* of the perpetrator of the violation. In theory, as the text of the provision states, in the case of 'wilful killing' the perpetrator should arguably have directed the attack against the protected person, knowing that that person was protected and effectively wanting to cause his or her death. As far as the destruction of the units or establishments is concerned, the fact that the destruction has to be 'not justified by military necessity' and 'carried out unlawfully or wantonly' could lead to a similar conclusion. However, the destruction or wilful killing may also be a response to an act which might be perceived as an 'act harmful to the enemy'. The assessment of *mens rea* has to be made at the moment the act in question was perpetrated. If the conduct of the protected person, unit, or establishment was lawful, but was perceived as unlawful at the time, in theory the accused might resort to the defence of 'military necessity', or even that of 'self-defence'. In this regard, reference might be made to a case before an Italian military court which had to judge the situation where Italian troops, who were defending a strategic position on the crossing of a bridge, fired on an ambulance which was crossing the bridge because they were under the impression that it was a car-bomb.[87] In this case, the court held that the action was covered by the defence of putative 'special military necessity' and acquitted the two defendants.[88]

Secondly, in addition to possible criminal responsibility for grave breaches, perpetrators 43
may fall under the jurisdiction of the ICC.[89] Grave breaches of the Geneva Conventions can come within the jurisdiction of the Court, and Article 8(2)(a)(i) and (iv) of the ICC Statute define as war crimes the '[w]ilful killing' of persons protected by the Geneva

---

Sliedregt, *The Criminal Responsibility of Individuals for Violations of International Humanitarian Law* (The Hague: Asser Press, 2003); R. Cryer et al, *International Criminal Law and Procedure* (Cambridge: CUP, 2007).

[85] For a detailed analysis of the system of repression of grave breaches under the GCs, see Ch 31 of this volume.

[86] Art 50 GC I; Art 51 GC II; Art 130 GC III; and Art 147 GC IV.

[87] For an analysis of this case and the concepts of military necessity, see A. Cassese, 'Under What Conditions May Belligerents Be Acquitted of the Crime of Attacking an Ambulance?', 6 *JICJ* (2008) 385.

[88] Ibid, at 386–90. The author, however, argues that the excuse of putative self-defence could have been the accurate basis to exclude the criminal responsibility both under international law and under Italian criminal law. Here a parallel could also be made with the *McCann* case, ECtHR, *McCann and others v United Kingdom*, Judgment, 27 September 1995. Both the soldiers in the *McCann* case, like the soldiers in this Italian case, acted on (incorrect) assumptions. These assumptions are relevant not just for the determination of a violation of a specific rule of IHL or IHRL, but also for the determination of the *mens rea* of the perpetrators, and may have an effect on the criminal consequences of their actions.

[89] Arts 5–21 ICC Statute.

Conventions, or the '[e]xtensive destruction and appropriation of property [protected by the Geneva Conventions], not justified by military necessity and carried out unlawfully or wantonly'. Attacks which are thus incorrectly directed against medical units, establishments, or transports, or against medical or religious personnel, could fall under these general provisions.[90] However, Article 8(2)(b),(ii), (ix), and (xxiv) of the ICC Statute also define as war crimes other 'serious violations of the laws and customs applicable in international armed conflict', namely: '[i]ntentionally directing attacks against civilian objects, that is, objects which are not military objectives';[91] 'intentionally directing attacks against buildings dedicated to religion, [...] hospitals and places where the wounded and sick are collected, provided they are not military objectives';[92] and '[i]ntentionally directing attacks against buildings, material, medical units and transport, and personnel using the distinctive emblems of the Geneva Conventions in conformity with international law'. Attacks directed against the categories under scrutiny in this chapter could thus fall under these provisions in situations of IAC.

44   Similar provisions are provided with regard to NIACs, which could be seen as reconfirmation of the applicability of the rules on protection and the loss thereof in these types of conflicts. In this regard, in addition to the war crimes which stem from violations of Common Article 3 (and which would cover medical personnel who were taking no active part in hostilities), Article 8(2)(e) of the ICC Statute provides that in 'armed conflicts not of an international character' the following acts may be considered as war crimes: '[i]ntentionally directing attacks against buildings, material, medical units and transport, and personnel using the distinctive emblems of the Geneva Conventions in conformity with international law';[93] and 'intentionally directing attacks against building dedicated to religion, [...] hospitals and places where the sick and wounded are collected, provided they are not military objectives'.[94] The perpetrator of any of these acts in NIACs may thus also be subject to international criminal responsibility.[95]

45   It should be mentioned here that certain acts which might lead to the loss of protection, could also entail criminal responsibility under national law for the actors involved. In this regard, reference might be made to the situation where medical or religious personnel engage in acts harmful to the enemy by directly participating in hostilities. Combatants—as opposed to medical and religious personnel—enjoy the 'combatant immunity' or 'combatant privilege', which gives them the right to participate in hostilities.[96] As mentioned above,[97] personnel who directly participate in the hostilities lose their protection, but this does not change their status, and they do not become combatants.[98] This also means that they may be held criminally liable under national law for the acts they commit during such participation, in circumstances in which combatants might escape this liability because of the privilege that comes with their status.

---

[90] See further K. Dörmann, *Elements of War Crimes under the Rome Statute of the International Criminal Court* (Cambridge: CUP, 2003), at 29–33.

[91] Art 8(2)(b)(ii) ICC Statute.   [92] Art 8(2)(b)(ix) ICC Statute.

[93] Art 8(2)(e)(ii) ICC Statute.

[94] Art 8(2)(e)(iv) ICC Statute.

[95] For a detailed analysis of war crimes in NIACs, see E. La Haye, *War Crimes in Internal Armed Conflicts* (Cambridge: CUP, 2008).

[96] See also Art 43(1) AP I.   [97] See also section B.III.a of this chapter.

[98] See, however, the various possibilities mentioned in MN 30. If one considers the possibility that the personnel engaged in acts harmful to the enemy permanently become combatants, they would be exempt from national criminal prosecution as they benefit from the combatant's privilege.

In addition, one could imagine a situation where particular medical units, establishments, or transports are used to render certain points, areas, or military forces immune from military operations. These acts will not only result in the loss of protection of the establishments, units, or transports concerned, but could also lead to criminal consequences.[99] Similarly, the improper use of the distinctive emblems of the Geneva Conventions—which is explicitly prohibited[100]—resulting in death or serious personal injury, can also lead to criminal responsibility in IAC.[101]

Further, the perpetrator of perfidious or treacherous wounding or killing of individuals belonging to the hostile nation or army, may be prosecuted for war crimes through the use of the mechanisms available for the repression of grave breaches,[102] or through the ICC Statute, which has criminalized such acts in both IACs[103] and NIACs.[104] While the text of the ICC Statute uses the wording 'treacherously', the Articles 'must be understood as criminalizing perfidy or at least as criminalizing certain forms of perfidy'.[105] For the meaning of this prohibition of perfidy, reference may be made to the definition of 'perfidy' under Article 37 AP I,[106] which states that '[a]cts inviting the confidence of an adversary to lead him to believe that he is entitled to, or is obliged to accord, protection under the rules of international law applicable in armed conflict, with intent to betray the confidence, shall constitute perfidy'. Obviously, when an actor undertakes an act which might be classified as perfidy, that person will lose the protection he or she enjoys under the Geneva Conventions, and will also become a legitimate military target.

E. Critical Assessment

The rules governing the protection and loss of protection of religious and medical units, transports, and personnel, are in line with and inspired by the general spirit of IHL which constantly tries to uphold a balance between the principle of humanity and military necessity. While rules stipulating protection for the providers of care to the wounded and sick are undoubtedly needed, specific provisions and rules which take the realities and logic of an armed conflict into account are also of prime importance. If the implementation of the rules is deemed too unrealistic or too damaging to the war effort by any of the actors involved, these rules might lose their effectiveness and their protective nature.

In operational terms, it is often very difficult to determine whether an act which might seem in accordance—or not—with the humanitarian function of the actor concerned, is harmful to the enemy and could lead to a loss of protection. In case of doubt, caution should be the main principle guiding the acts of both the providers of care and the actors responding to the perceived harmful acts. The risk of an incorrect assessment is just too great, and it might have terrible consequences for a large number of vulnerable people.

---

[99] Art 8(2)(b)(xxiii) ICC Statute. [100] Art 53 GC I and Arts 44–45 GC II.
[101] Art 8(2)(b)(vii). There is, however, no equivalent provision for NIACs. See also W. Schabas, *The International Criminal Court: A Commentary on the Rome Statute* (Oxford: OUP, 2010), at 233.
[102] Art 85(3)(f) AP I, which lists the perfidious use of the protective emblems of the GCs as a grave breach.
[103] Art 8(2)(b)(xi) ICC Statute. [104] Art 8(2)(e)(ix) ICC Statute.
[105] O. Triffterer, *Commentary in the Rome Statute of the International Criminal Court: Observer's Notes, Article by Article* (2nd edn, Munchen/Oxford/Baden-Baden: C.H. Beck/Hart Publishing/Nomos, 2008), at 384. For more information on the prohibition and meaning of perfidy, see Ch 43 of this volume.
[106] Ibid. The author notes that at the negotiations of the Preparatory Commission regarding the elements of crimes, delegates agreed that this should be the case. To support this argument, he refers to proposals by some delegations which were all wholly or partly based on the definition in Art 37 AP I.

50 Even though the principles relating to the (loss of) protection of medical establishments, units, or personnel are generally respected and incorporated by the parties to the conflict, there are too many examples of violations, which have often had dire consequences. Also, it sometimes might seem operationally interesting to walk the fine line that separates legitimate acts from illegal or harmful ones, and there might be considerable temptation to use an ambulance to transport guerilla fighters or to use a helicopter carrying the emblem to rescue a hostage.[107]

51 However, the rules regulating the protection of the wounded and sick, and thus also relevant for the actors providing this protection and care, are the basis for the creation of the entire body of IHL. While the rules on loss of protection are necessary, and not every attack against a protected actor must be punished, the international community as a whole should do everything in its power to respect the rules which protect medical personnel, to ensure respect for these rules, and to condemn violations with a clear and unequivocal voice.

TOM HAECK

---

[107] E.g., the case of the Colombian authorities who used a helicopter marked with the protective emblem of the ICRC to rescue the hostage Ingrid Betancourt from the Revolutionary Armed Forces of Colombia (FARC). See BBC, 'Red Cross Emblem Misuse', 6 August 2008, available at <http://news.bbc.co.uk/1/hi/world/americas/7545519.stm>. See also Ch 43 of this volume.

Chapter 43. The Use of the Emblem

	MN
A. Introduction	1
B. Complex Set of Provisions	5
I. International humanitarian law	6
a. Treaty provisions	6
b. Customary rules	10
II. Miscellaneous provisions referring to the emblem	11
C. Different Uses	15
I. Terminology	15
II. Two different uses	16
a. Protective use	18
b. Indicative use	20
c. Use of the emblem for fundraising	21
III. Size and dimensions	22
IV. No double emblem	25
V. Temporary use	26
D. Multiple Users	27
I. Use of the emblem as a protective device	28
a. In times of armed conflict	28
b. In peacetime	29
II. Use of the emblem as an indicative device	30
a. In times of armed conflict	30
b. In peacetime	31
III. The special case of the ICRC and the International Federation	33
IV. Use by medical services of armed groups engaged in NIAC	34
V. Use by multinational forces	35
VI. Use by private military and security companies	37
VII. Use by non-Red Cross/Red Crescent organizations	38
E. Temporal Scope of Application	39
I. In peacetime	40
II. In times of internal tensions and disturbances	42
III. In times of armed conflicts	43
F. The Conditions for Use	45
I. Authorization	46
II. Control	49
III. Medical activities	51
G. The Prevention and Repression of Misuse	52
I. A responsibility that covers all situations	52
II. The types of misuse	54
a. Imitation	57
b. Improper use	58
c. Perfidious use	59
III. Misuse as a war crime under international criminal law	60
IV. The role of the state	61
a. Domestic legislation	63
b. The model laws	69

V. The role of the National Societies		70
VI. The role of the International Committee of the Red Cross		72
H. Unity and Plurality		76
I. The short era of unity		77
II. The loss of unity		78
III. Plurality		79
I. Current Challenges		82
I. The emblem as a target		83
II. The lack of visibility of protected personnel and installations		84
III. Misuse on the Internet		85
IV. The rare use of the red crystal		86
V. Displaying or not displaying?		88
J. Critical Assessment		92

Select Bibliography

Bouchet-Saulnier, F., *Dictionnaire pratique du droit humanitaire* (Paris: La Découverte, 1998)

Bouvier, A., 'Special Aspects of the Use of the Red Cross or Red Crescent Emblem', 29 *IRRC* 272 (2004) 438

Bugnion, F., *The Emblem of the Red Cross: A Brief History* (Geneva: ICRC, 1977)

Bugnion, F., *Red Cross, Red Crescent, Red Crystal* (Geneva: ICRC, 2007)

Cauderay, G.C., 'Visibility of the Distinctive Emblem on Medical Establishments, Units, and Transports', 30 *IRRC* 277 (1990) 295

Cauderay, G.C./Bouvier, A., *Manual for the Use of Technical Means of Identifications by Hospital Ships, Coastal Rescue Craft, Other Protected Craft and Medical Aircraft* (Geneva: ICRC, 1995)

Eberlin, P., *Protective Signs* (Geneva: ICRC, 1983)

ICRC, *Study on the Use of the Emblems, Operational and Commercial and Other Non-Operational Issues* (Geneva: ICRC, 2011)

Meyer, M., 'Protecting the Emblems in Peacetime: The Experiences of the British Red Cross', 29 *IRRC* 272 (1989) 459

Pictet, J., 'The Sign of the Red Cross', 2(4) *IRRC Supplement* (1949) 143

Quéguiner, J.F., 'Commentary on the Protocol Additional to the Geneva Conventions of 12 August 1949 and Relating to the Adoption of an Additional Distinctive Emblem (Protocol III)', 89 *IRRC* 865 (2007) 175

Sandoz, Y., 'The Red Cross and Red Crescent Emblems: What is at Stake?', 29 *IRRC* 272 (1989) 405

Slim, H., 'Protection of the Red Cross and Red Crescent Emblems and the Repression of Misuse', 29 *IRRC* 272 (1989) 420

Sommaruga, C., 'Unity and Plurality of the Emblems', 32 *IRRC* 289 (1992) 333

A. Introduction

1 Almost one century after Jean-Jacques Rousseau set down 'clearly and for all time, the fundamental rule of the modern law of war [...] [that] soldiers who are hors de combat [...] must be preserved and their suffering must be relieved', the fate of military victims of armed

conflicts remained miserable.[1] The spectacular development of new weapons, in particular artillery and the deployment of massive conscription armies, which marked the nineteenth century, drastically modified the conditions of warfare. Huge numbers of casualties began to overwhelm what were once rather well-organized and efficient military medical services, and the wounded were left unattended on the battlefield. Doctors and medical orderlies were fired upon, taken away from their patients, and routinely captured and kept as prisoners.

It was in this context that the idea of 'neutralization' (a term later replaced by 'respect' and 'protection') of the wounded and of those in charge of their care gradually emerged.[2] Early proposals aimed at giving a permanent protected status to the wounded and to medical personnel were often accompanied by the following suggestion: identify *all* military medical services with a unique and specific emblem. The idea behind this suggestion was to replace the traditional practice where military medical services used to opt for individual signs of identification, usually flags of different colours (a rather ineffective system, since in many cases enemy forces would simply not be cognizant of these emblems and even less ready to respect them). This idea was clearly developed in 1857 by Lucien Baudens, Inspector of the French Army Medical Services, in the context of an analysis of the then recent conflict in Crimea. Reporting on a dramatic incident during which Russian batteries covering the retreat of their troops fired on doctors who had come to collect and care for the wounded left on the battlefield, he suggested that

[s]uch mistakes would be impossible if by agreements between nations, doctors and hospital staff wore a distinctive sign, the same in all armies and all countries, by which they would be easily recognized by both sides.[3]

In this regard, Henry Dunant came to play a decisive role. Reflecting upon the disastrous battle of Solferino (24 June 1859), of which he had been a direct witness, and the ineffectiveness of the military medical services he had observed—in particular because of their poor organization and their lack of status—he proposed two solutions to this issue in *A Memory of Solferino*.[4] First, voluntary relief societies should be formed in all countries and would back up the military medical services (as 'auxiliaries'), preparing themselves to do so in peacetime. Secondly, to enable them to act effectively, the military medical services and the voluntary relief societies would be recognized as neutral following the adoption of 'some international principle sanctioned by a Convention inviolate in character which, once agreed upon and ratified, might constitute the basis'[5] for the establishment of a protected status for those taking care of the wounded on the battlefield.

---

[1] J. Pictet, *Development and Principles of International Humanitarian Law* (Dordrecht/Boston/Lancaster: Martinus Nijhoff Publishers, 1985), at 23.

[2] For an analysis of the proposals made by precursors (very often distinguished members of military medical services), see J. Guillermand, 'The Contribution of Army Medical Officers to the Emergence of Humanitarian Law', 29 *IRRC* 271 (1989) 306.

[3] Ibid.   [4] H. Dunant, *A Memory of Solferino* (Geneva: ICRC, 1986 [1862]), at 147.

[5] Ibid.

3   In just a few lines, Dunant laid the foundations of both modern international humanitarian law (IHL) (the Law of War) and of what would eventually materialize as the International Red Cross and Red Crescent Movement. His proposals were examined and developed during an International Conference in 1863 and endorsed by the Diplomatic Conference, which led to the adoption of the first *Geneva Convention for the Amelioration of the Condition of the Wounded in Armies in the Field* of 22 August 1864.

4   Quite naturally, the idea of 'neutralization' of the military medical services and their auxiliaries led directly to the idea of making them visible by a distinctive sign that would be the same in all countries, that would be internationally recognized by treaty, and the violation of which would be punishable by law.[6] In particular, both the 1863 International Conference[7] and the 1864 Convention led to the creation of clear and simple provisions regulating the use of the emblem. The question was addressed in Article 7 of the Convention:

> A distinctive and uniform flag shall be adopted for hospitals, ambulances and evacuation parties. It should in all circumstances be accompanied by the national flag.
>
> An armlet may also be worn by personnel enjoying neutrality but its issue shall be left to the military authorities.
>
> Both flag and armlet shall bear a red cross on a white ground.[8]

In the decades that followed the adoption of this provision and through successive revisions of the treaties, history, wars, and politics conspired to complicate an initially rather straightforward idea, namely, the effective protection of military wounded on the battlefield and those entrusted with their care through a protected status and a uniform sign of identification. The rules regulating the use of the emblem were also considerably expanded and complicated into a number of 'hard law' provisions, both treaty law and customary provisions, complemented by 'soft law' instruments that address specific types of use or specific categories of users. Most of these provisions have been developed in the field of IHL, while others belong to international criminal law or other branches of public international law. For example, the categories of legitimate users of the emblem were consistently expanded;[9] new signs and signals were created;[10] new uses were accepted;[11] and the use of the emblem was authorized in new types of situations.[12]

B. Complex Set of Provisions

5   In this section, we shall mention briefly the main provisions and instruments which touch on the emblem. A detailed analysis of the most essential rules which stem from the Geneva Conventions (GCs) will be developed in subsequent sections of this chapter.

---

[6] This idea was not formulated in Dunant, above n 4.

[7] See Resolution 8: 'They [voluntary medical personnel] shall wear in all countries, as a uniform distinctive sign, a white armlet with a red cross.'; and Recommendation c: 'that a uniform distinctive sign be recognized for the Medical Corps of all armies, or at least for all persons of the same army belonging to this Service; and, that a uniform flag also be adopted in all countries for ambulances and hospitals'.

[8] For the reasons that led to the adoption of this particular emblem, see MN 77 and n 174.

[9] See MN 27 ff.   [10] See MN 79.   [11] See MN 16.   [12] See MN 42.

I. International humanitarian law

a. Treaty provisions

The majority of IHL treaty provisions were, at least initially, designed to apply only to international armed conflicts (IACs). Today, however, it is generally admitted that, *mutatis mutandis*, the rules regulating the use of the emblems should apply to both IACs and non-international armed conflicts (NIACs).[13] A number of military manuals also provide for similar conditions of use in both types of conflict.[14]

At this juncture, we should briefly comment on two separate issues. The first relates to the links between the rules spelled out in the four 1949 Conventions, and the second relates to the links between the rules adopted in 1949 and those adopted in the 1977 and 2005 Additional Protocols. The first issue was clearly and convincingly addressed in Pictet Commentary GC II, where it is stated that '[f]or all general information regarding the distinctive emblem the reader should refer to Chapter VII of the Commentary on the First Convention [...] [I]n this regard, the First Convention constitutes *sedes materiae*.'[15] Therefore, in case of doubt as to the exact meaning of the rules of GC II and GC IV on the use of the emblem, reference should be made to the more detailed rules developed in GC I.

As for the second issue, it has often been argued that the rules relating to the wounded and sick adopted in 1977 (by a conference on the Reaffirmation and Development of IHL) were intended to clarify some issues rather than develop completely new norms.[16] To give only one example, although Common Article 3 of the Geneva Conventions does not mention the use of the emblem, its use during NIACs had never been seriously questioned, and Article 12 of Additional Protocol (AP) II only clarified some aspects of this use. For these reasons, although this commentary focuses on the rules adopted in 1949, it would be absurd not to interpret the 1949 rules on the emblem without taking into account the rules adopted in 1977 (and those in the 2005 AP). It must be conceded[17] that the scope and exact meaning of many rules adopted in 1949 have been changed by more recent provisions.[18]

---

[13] This view was in particular followed in ICRC, *Study on the Use of the Emblems, Operational and Commercial and Other Non-Operational Issues* (Geneva: ICRC, 2011) (Emblem Study), available at <http://www.icrc.org/eng/resources/documents/publication/p4057.htm>. In this comprehensive study, which 'benefited from the feedback on various aspects received from states' (at 20), a distinction is made only between 'In peacetime' and 'In times of armed conflicts'. See also the ICRC CIHL Study.

[14] ICRC CIHL Study, at 208, fn 34. [15] Pictet Commentary GC II, at 226.

[16] See, e.g., W. Solf, 'Development of the Protection of the Wounded, Sick and Shipwrecked under the Protocols Additional to the 1949 Geneva Conventions', in Mélanges Pictet 237, at 237–8: 'Part II of *Protocol I* [...] was intended to remedy deficiencies [...] relevant to the protection of wounded [...] It thus supplements the relevant provisions of the four *1949 Geneva Conventions* which must be considered together with the new provisions.' A similar view was also developed in J.-P. Lavoyer, 'National Legislation on the Use and Protection of the Emblem of the Red Cross or Red Crescent', 36 *IRRC* 313 (1996) 482: 'As regards the use of the emblem, it should be noted that the Protocols reinforce the rules contained in the Geneva Conventions [...].'

[17] This is also illustrated by the customary rules, which do not distinguish between IACs and NIACs, see MN 10.

[18] See, e.g., Art 38 GC I. The purpose of this provision was to limit the use of the crescent and of the lion and sun to the states that *already* used them. In spite of this attempt, many states eventually decided to adopt the crescent rather than the cross. This was never contested by other states parties. It must therefore be admitted that well before the adoption of AP III, which clearly put the four emblems on a par, the content of Art 38 had been modified by state practice. See also International Law Commission (ILC), *Subsequent Agreements and Subsequent Practice of States outside Judicial or Quasi-Judicial Proceedings* (19 April 2012) (ILC Report), ILC(LXIV)/SG/TOT/INFORMAL/1, at 43.

9   The relevant treaty provisions are as follows:

GC I: Articles	36	Medical Aircraft
	38	Emblem of the Convention
	39	Use of the Emblem
	40	Identification of Medical and Religious Personnel
	41	Identification of Auxiliary Personnel
	42	Marking of Medical Units and Establishments
	43	Marking of Units of Neutral Countries
	44	Restrictions in the Use of the Emblem. Exceptions
	53	Misuse of the Emblem
	54	Prevention of Misuse
GC II: Articles	41	Use of the Emblem
	42	Identification of Medical and Religious Personnel
	43	Marking of Hospital Ships and Small Crafts
	44	Limitations in the Use of Markings
	45	Prevention of Misuse
GC IV: Articles	18	Protection of Hospitals
	19	Discontinuance of Protections of Hospitals
	20	Hospital Staff
	21	Land and Sea Transport
	22	Air Transport
AP I: Articles	8	Terminology
	18	Identification
	38	Recognized Emblems
	85	Repression of Breaches of this Protocol
	Annex 1	Regulations Concerning Identification
AP II: Article	12	The Distinctive Emblem
AP III: Articles	1	Respect for and Scope of Application of this Protocol
	2	Distinctive Emblems
	3	Indicative Use of the third Protocol Emblem
	4	International Committee of the Red Cross and International Federation of Red Cross and Red Crescent Societies
	5	Missions under United Nations Auspices
	6	Prevention and Repression of Misuse
	7	Dissemination

b. Customary rules

10 The use of the emblem is mentioned in two rules of the International Committee of the Red Cross (ICRC) Customary International Humanitarian Law Study:

Rule 30. Attacks directed against medical and religious personnel and objects displaying the distinctive emblems of the Geneva Conventions in conformity with international law are prohibited.[19]

Rule 59. The improper use of the distinctive emblems of the Geneva Conventions is prohibited.

Both rules are applicable in IACs and NIACs.

---

[19] But the display of the emblem is not a condition for protection. See MN 19, 88, and 91.

II. Miscellaneous provisions referring to the emblem

The United Nations (UN) Secretary-General's Bulletin, *Observance by the United Nations Forces of International Humanitarian Law*, includes the following provision: 11

9.7 The United Nations force shall in all circumstances respect the Red Cross and Red Crescent emblems. These emblems may not be employed except to indicate or to protect medical units and medical establishments, personnel and material. Any misuse of the Red Cross or Red Crescent emblems is prohibited.[20]

The Regulations on the Use of the Emblem of the Red Cross or the Red Crescent by the National Societies, adopted by the 20th Red Cross and Red Crescent International Conference (Vienna, 1965) and revised by the Council of Delegates (Budapest, 1991),[21] address in minute detail the use of the emblem by National Red Cross/Red Crescent Societies. They cover both peacetime and armed conflict situations. Although these Regulations are, strictly speaking, binding only upon National Societies, the ICRC and the International Federation pledged to apply them to the fullest possible extent. 12

The UN Convention of 8 November 1968 on Road Signs and Signals provides that two road signs may be used to indicate the direction of civilian hospitals.[22] The same Convention also provides for a choice of three different signs for first-aid stations. According to the Preamble to the 1968 Convention, these signs have been chosen 'to facilitate international road traffic and to increase road safety'. The objective is thus very different from making hospitals identifiable in times of armed conflict, which is the aim of the other provisions discussed above. It has been argued, however, that these signs 'are not in conformity with the rules on the use of the emblem'.[23] 13

In concluding this section, it should be mentioned that not only *distinctive signs* (the cross, the crescent, the red lion and sun, the red crystal)[24] and *distinctive signals*[25] are protected by the rules mentioned above, but also *names*[26] and *logos*.[27] 14

C. Different Uses

I. Terminology

Before examining the different types of use of the emblem envisaged in the treaties, some clarification of the terminology used in this chapter is necessary: 15

— Following the rule proposed in the Commentary to Article 38 GC I,[28] the words 'red cross/crescent/lion and sun' are printed in lower case when they refer to the emblem, upper-case letters (capitals) being reserved for the Red Cross/Red Crescent institutions.

---

[20] UN Secretary General, *Secretary-General's Bulletin on Observance by the United Nations Forces of International Humanitarian Law*, UN Doc. ST/SGB/1999/13, 6 August 1999.

[21] 'Regulations on the Use of the Emblem of the Red Cross or Red Crescent by the National Societies', 32 *IRRC* 289 (1992) 339, available at <http://www.icrc.org/eng/resources/documents/misc/57jmbg.htm>.

[22] UN Economic Commission for Europe, Inland Transportation Committee, 'Convention on Road Signs and Signals' (8 November 1968), E/CONF.56/17/Rev.1/Amend.1.

[23] See Emblem Study, above n 13, at 195. For a detailed analysis of the 1968 Convention, see ibid, at 72 and 195–202.

[24] Art 8(l) AP I.

[25] See Art 8(m) and Annex I AP I, which provide for a number of technical means of identification.

[26] See, e.g., Arts 44 para 1 and 53 GC I. [27] See Emblem Study, above n 13, at 29, 155, and 199.

[28] See Pictet Commentary GC I, at 297.

— As there is no clear rule on whether the singular or plural should be used when referring to the emblem,[29] we shall use 'emblem' when discussing general issues and 'emblems' when discussing points relating to the four different signs defined in the relevant treaties and their designation.

— The notion of 'Distinctive Emblem(s)' is not clearly defined. In Chapter VII of GC I, it covers both indicative and protective uses.[30] In Article 8(l) AP I and in AP III, this notion seems to be restricted to the protective use. Following a rule clearly spelled out in the *Study on the Use of the Emblems*,[31] we shall emphasize the distinction between the two different uses of the emblem by referring either to the 'protective emblem' ('emblem used as a protective device', or 'emblem used for protective purposes'), or to the 'indicative emblem' ('emblem used as an indicative device', 'emblem used for indicative purposes', or 'logo').

II. Two different uses

16 Before the adoption of Article 44 GC I, only one use of the emblem was defined in the Geneva Conventions. The only function of the emblem was to identify installations and personnel protected by the Convention in times of armed conflicts. As auxiliaries to the military medical services, National Societies were entitled to use the emblem only for those of their members who, in times of conflict, would serve under the authority of the military medical services. However, with the massive development of their peacetime activities that followed the First World War, National Societies began to feel it was necessary to display the emblem in such peacetime situations and activities to identify themselves as National Societies. Their wish to have such use of the emblem recognized as lawful in the IHL treaties was not met during the 1929 Diplomatic Conference.[32] This meant that, in theory and under a strict interpretation of the text of the 1929 Convention, National Societies could use the emblem only for those of their activities relating to the support of military medical services in peacetime, and should renounce its use should an armed conflict occur. For rather obvious reasons, 'this stipulation remained a dead letter'.[33]

17 Article 44 GC I has addressed this problem. It draws a clear distinction between two possible uses of the emblem, and 'successfully reconciles the two needs that had become apparent'.[34] Though a positive development offering an adequate response to a legitimate expectation of the National Societies, the solution adopted in Article 44 has also complicated the understanding and the application of the rules on the emblem. The emblem is now used for very different types of purposes by very different actors.[35] It is, however, much too late to wonder whether 'at the outset it would not have been better to adopt two distinct emblems'.[36]

a. Protective use

18 When used as a *protective* device, the emblem is the visible sign of the special protection under IHL (mainly the Geneva Conventions and their Additional Protocols) for certain

---

[29] Compare, e.g., the Regulations on the Use of the Emblem, above n 21, and Art 2 AP III ('Distinctive Emblems').

[30] When used as a protective device, the emblem is the visible manifestation of the protection provided by the GCs to specific persons and objects. When used as an indicative device, the emblem only marks a link with the Red Cross/Red Crescent institutions. See MN 18 and 20.

[31] See Emblem Study, above n 13, at 25.

[32] See Pictet Commentary GC I, at 325.   [33] Ibid.   [34] Ibid.   [35] See MN 27.

[36] A sensible question raised in the Commentary. See Pictet Commentary GC I, at 330.

categories of persons, units, and transports (in particular medical personnel, facilities, and means of transport).[37] It is of course in this case that the emblem has its essential significance. Strictly speaking, the protective use is possible only in times of armed conflict, when IHL becomes applicable.

The protective sign has been qualified as a 'virtually constitutive element of protection'.[38] This rather obscure formula refers to the fact that the protective marking is *not compulsory*,[39] a fact that is often ignored and which has led to serious controversies. Legally speaking, a medical unit that does not display the emblem remains protected; however, the risk of inadvertent attack as a result is significantly higher. In reality, some armed forces choose not to identify their medical installations, on the basis that a clear marking of all protected installations might provide too much tactical information to the enemy, or in situations where the emblem is the object of disrespect or even of deliberate attacks.[40]

b. Indicative use

When used as an *indicative* device, the emblem illustrates the link between the person or object displaying it and a component of the International Movement of the Red Cross and the Red Crescent (the Movement). Its only purpose is to demonstrate this link, without implying the protection of the Convention. Indicative use is not restricted to any specific situation, but the categories of authorized users will vary depending on the type of situations.[41]

c. Use of the emblem for fundraising

Considering the prestige and renown of the emblems, the temptation to use them for fundraising purposes has always been high within the Movement. Attempts to regulate this use have proved rather painful, the Movement being caught between the necessity to generate resources for its humanitarian activities and concern over decreased respect for the emblem. From an initially very restrictive position,[42] the approach has been gradually relaxed, but it remains fairly restrictive and cautious.[43] As such, the Movement, National Societies, and the ICRC have adopted separate guidelines and rules on this question. In this respect, the following instruments should be mentioned in particular:[44]

— *Rules applicable to the Movement.* Resolution 10 on Movement Policy for Corporate Sector Partnerships, Council of Delegates, 2005, Annex on Substantive Provisions of

---

[37] For a comprehensive list of persons, units, and transports entitled to use the protective emblem, see MN 27 ff.

[38] See Pictet Commentary GC I, at 324.

[39] This is in fact clearly affirmed in Art 42 para 4 GC I: 'Parties to a conflict shall take the necessary steps, *in so far as military considerations permit*, to make the distinctive emblems indicating military units and establishments clearly visible [...]' (emphasis added).

[40] This question will be discussed in more detail in MN 88–91.   [41] See MN 30.

[42] Expressed, e.g, in the Commentary to Art 44 GC I: 'The emblem must retain its high significance and prestige in all circumstances, and any practice likely to lower it in the eyes of the public must be scrupulously avoided [...] Red Cross organizations, to raise funds, have sometimes sold objects bearing the red cross. Such practices are likely to lessen [...] the standing of the emblem and are therefore prejudicial to the good name of the Red Cross as a whole.' See Pictet Commentary GC I, Art 44, at 335.

[43] See, e.g., Art 23 of the Regulations on the Use of the Emblem, above n 21, which prohibits inter alia the display of the emblem or of a National Society logo on items for sale by partner commercial companies of the National Society.

[44] For a complete analysis, see Emblem Study, above n 13, at 203–33 (for the rules applicable to National Societies) and 244–53 (for the rules applicable to the ICRC).

the International Red Cross and Red Crescent Movement Policy for Corporate Sector Partnerships.[45]

— *Rules applicable to National Societies*. Regulations on the Use of the Emblem of the Red Cross or Red Crescent by the National Societies.[46] Article 23 ('Campaigns and events organized by the National Society') defines in significant detail the conditions and limits of cooperation projects between National Societies and commercial partners.

— *Rules applicable to the ICRC*. The ICRC has accepted to respect 'to the fullest possible extent'[47] the 1991 Regulations on the Use of the Emblem by the National Societies. Additionally it has adopted the following instruments:
  (a) the Guidelines on the Use of the Name and Image of the ICRC by Providers of Goods and Services;[48] and
  (b) the Guidelines on the Use of the Red Cross Emblem and the Name and Logo of the ICRC for Fundraising Purposes.[49]

III. Size and dimensions

22 The emblem must be visible and easy to identify.[50] When used as a protective device, the emblem should be as large and visible as possible. It 'should always retain its original form, i.e. nothing shall be added to the [emblem] [...] or the white ground'.[51] To enhance its visibility a distinctive signal may be used.[52] The exact shape of the cross, the crescent, or the crystal[53] has not been precisely established. The justifications for this flexibility in the design have been convincingly explained in the Commentary to Article 38 GC I:

> The Proceedings of the Diplomatic Conference of 1906 are, moreover, explicit: the Conference deliberately refrained from defining the form of the cross, since definition might have led to dangerous abuses. The reasons are clear. If the form of the cross had been rigidly defined, attempts might have been made to justify attacks on installations protected by the Convention, on the pretext that the emblems displayed were not of the prescribed dimensions. Similarly, unscrupulous persons could have taken advantage of a rigid definition to use a slightly larger or slightly smaller red cross for commercial purposes.[54]

These considerations remain perfectly valid today, and have been reiterated in Article 5 of the Regulations on the Use of the Emblem, which states that 'A cross formed with two cross-pieces, one vertical and the other horizontal crossing in the middle, shall be used.

---

[45] Council of Delegates of the International Red Cross and Red Crescent Movement, Seoul, 16–18 November 2005, 87 *IRRC* 860 (2005) 814.
[46] Regulations on the Use of the Emblem, above n 21.
[47] See Emblem Study, above n 13, at 23.
[48] ICRC, 'Guidelines on the Use of the Red Cross Emblem and the Name and Logo of the ICRC for Fundraising Purposes' (2006), available online at <http://www.icrc.org/eng/resources/documents/misc/5a6j7j.htm>.
[49] ICRC, 'Guidelines on the Use of the Red Cross Emblem and the Name and Logo of the ICRC for Fundraising Purposes', (2006), available online at <http://www.icrc.org/eng/resources/documents/misc/5a6j7j.htm>.
[50] See F. Bugnion, *L'emblème de la Croix-Rouge* (Geneva: IHD, 1977).
[51] Regulations on the Use of the Emblem, above n 21, Art 5.
[52] See Annex I AP I; and Regulations on the Use of the Emblem, above n 21, Art 6.
[53] For additional information on the adoption of the red crystal, see MN 86.
[54] Pictet Commentary GC I, at 305.

The shape and direction of the crescent are not regulated.'[55] For similar reasons, neither the shape of the white background, nor the exact shade of red has been fixed.[56]

To avoid any confusion between protective and indicative uses in time of armed conflict, Article 44 GC I provides that, when used in time of armed conflict as an indicative device, the emblem should be 'comparatively small in size'. The indicative emblem should also 'be accompanied by the name or initials of the National Society'.[57] The same principle is repeated in Article 4 of the Regulations: 23

> Any confusion between the protective use and the indicative use of the emblem must be avoided. In armed conflicts, the National Society which continues its peacetime activities shall take all the necessary measures to ensure that the emblem used indicatively, displayed on persons or objects, is seen only as marking their connection with the National Society and not as conferring the right to protection under international humanitarian law. In particular, the emblem shall be relatively small and shall not be placed on armlets or roofs. The National Society shall endeavour to follow the latter rule in peacetime so as to avoid from the very beginning of a conflict any confusion with the emblem used as a protective device.[58]

This limitation is not absolute, as was explained in the Commentary to Article 44 GC I:

> For practical reasons, the Conference rejected a proposal that it should lay down the maximum dimensions of the indicatory sign. It merely stipulated that it should be comparatively small in size—that is, small in proportion to the protective sign used for any given category of persons or objects. Common sense must decide the actual size.[59]

Today it is generally accepted that in specific situations, National Societies have the right to use a large size for the indicative emblems, for example in situations of internal disturbances and tensions, of natural catastrophes, or during leisure events where they must be very visible.[60] 24

IV. No double emblem

Article 38 GC I makes it clear that states parties must choose one of the three emblems.[61] The question of the use of the double emblem by the military medical services has been debated for decades.[62] Legal analysis clearly proves that such use, especially when the emblem is used as a protective device, should not be permitted.[63] Further, the ICRC has consistently objected to this practice. It was on this basis that it refused the recognition of National Societies using the double emblem.[64] 25

V. Temporary use

Under AP III, military medical services have the option of changing their protective emblem: 26

> The medical services and the religious personnel of armed forces of High Contracting Parties may, without prejudice to their current emblems, make temporary use of any distinctive emblem referred to in paragraph 1 of this Article where this may enhance protection.[65]

---

[55] See Regulations on the Use of the Emblem, above n 21.
[56] The same applies to the design of the red crystal.
[57] See Regulations on the Use of the Emblem, above n 21, Art 5.   [58] Ibid, Art 4.
[59] Pictet Commentary GC I, at 311.   [60] See Emblem Study, above n 13, at 117–21.
[61] An obligation reaffirmed in Art 2(1) AP III.
[62] For a detailed analysis and example of countries that have attempted to use the double emblem, see F. Bugnion, *Red Cross, Red Crescent, Red Crystal* (Geneva: ICRC, 2011), at 18–21.
[63] As for the indicative use, a more flexible approach might be tolerated. See Bugnion, above n 50, at 113.
[64] Ibid; Bugnion, above n 62, at 18–21.   [65] Art 2(4) AP III.

This provision has been adopted with a primary view to reinforcing the prohibition of the use of the double emblem. It should also help in solving the sometimes delicate question posed by the use of different emblems within military coalitions.[66] Article 2(4) AP III also offers state parties the possibility of using *any* (i.e. not only the red crystal) distinctive emblem on a *temporary* basis. Such a temporary use is possible only 'where this may enhance protection',[67] and this provision does not permit the substitution of the usual emblem by a combination of several emblems.

D. Multiple Users

27 Initially restricted to use by the personnel in charge of the military wounded of the armies in the field, the use of the emblem gradually has been extended to a large number of other users. This section outlines the persons or objects entitled to display the emblem, depending on its use as a protective or indicative device, as well as on the situations in which it is used.

I. Use of the emblem as a protective device

a. In times of armed conflict

28 In times of armed conflict the emblem may be used as a protective device for:

— medical services (personnel and units, such as hospitals, means of transport, etc) and religious personnel of states' armed forces;[68]
— medical personnel units and transports of National Societies that have been duly recognized and authorized by their governments to assist the medical services of the armed forces, when they are employed exclusively for the same purposes as the latter and are subject to military laws and regulations;[69]
— other recognized and authorized voluntary aid societies, subject to the same conditions as those defined above for National Societies;[70]
— civilian hospitals (public or private) that are recognized as such by the state authorities and authorized to display the emblem;[71] and, in occupied territory and in zones of military operations, persons engaged in the operation and administration of such civilian hospitals (and also in the search for, removal and transport of and provision of care for wounded and sick civilians, the infirm and maternity cases);[72]

---

[66] For a practical example of such situations, see Sassòli/Bouvier/Quintin, 'Case 176, Saudi Arabia, Use of the Red Cross Emblem by US Forces'.

[67] For a more detailed analysis of the scope of this provision, see Emblem Study, above n 13, at 42–3 and 189–90.

[68] See Arts 39–44 GC I; Arts 22–23, 26–28, 34–37, 39, and 41–44 GC II; Art 18(1) and (4) AP I; and Art 12 AP II. The protected medical services and religious personnel of states' armed forces are defined under Arts 19–25 and 35–36 GC I; Arts 22–23, 26–28, 34–37, and 39 GC II; Arts 8(c)–(m), 9(2), 12, 13, 15, and 21–31 AP I; and Arts 9 and 11 AP II.

[69] See Arts 40 and 42–44 GC I. Protected National Society medical personnel, units, and transports are defined under Arts 24, 26–27, and 34 GC I; Arts 24–25 and 27 GC II; and Arts 8(c), (e), and (g)–(j), and 9(2) AP I.

[70] Art 44 para 1 GC I. Voluntary aid societies are defined under Arts 26–27 GC I and Art 9(2)(b) AP I.

[71] Art 18 para 3 GC IV. GC IV extends the right to use the emblem to land, sea, and air transports as defined under its Arts 21 and 22. Annex I, Art 6 GC IV also provides that 'zones reserved exclusively for the wounded and sick may be marked by means of the Red Cross (Red Crescent, Red Lion and Sun) emblem on a white ground'.

[72] Art 20 paras 1, 2, and 3 GC IV.

— all civilian medical and religious personnel in occupied territory and in areas where fighting is taking place or is likely to take place;[73]
— all civilian medical units and transports, as defined under AP I, recognized by the competent authorities and authorized by them to display the emblem.[74]

b. In peacetime

In peacetime the emblem may be used as a protective device for: 29

— medical services and religious personnel of states' armed forces;[75]
— National Societies' medical units and transports, whose assignment to medical duties in the event of an armed conflict has already been determined, and who may display the emblem as a protective device in peacetime, with the authorities' consent.[76]

II. Use of the emblem as an indicative device

a. In times of armed conflict

In times of armed conflict the emblem may be used as an indicative device for: 30

— National Societies;[77]
— the International Federation;
— the ICRC.[78]

b. In peacetime

In peacetime the emblem may be used as an indicative device for: 31

— National Societies;[79]
— the International Federation;
— the ICRC;
— ambulances and first-aid stations operated by third parties, when exclusively assigned to provide free treatment to the wounded and sick, as an exceptional measure, on condition that the emblem is used in conformity with national legislation and that the National Society has expressly authorized such use.[80]

In addition to the long lists of authorized users set out in this section and in section D.I of this chapter, five other uses should be addressed briefly at this juncture: 32

— the special case of the ICRC and the International Federation;
— the use of the emblem by medical services of armed groups engaged in a NIAC;
— the use by multinational forces;

---

[73] Art 18(3) AP I. Protected civilian medical and religious personnel are defined in Arts 8(c)–(d) and 15(1) AP I. This category may include the medical personnel of National Societies, provided that they correspond to the definition of AP I.

[74] Art 18(4) AP I. Protected civilian medical units and transports are defined in Arts 8(e) and (g), 12, and 13 AP I. These categories may include medical units and transports of National Societies, provided that they correspond to the definitions of AP I.

[75] Art 44 para 1 GC I.

[76] Art 13 of the 1991 Regulations, above n 21. See also Emblem Study, above n 13, at 71–9.

[77] Art 44 para 2 GC I.   [78] Emblem Study, above n 13, at 28 and 151.

[79] Art 44 para 2 GC I.

[80] Art 44 para 4 GC I. For greater convenience, the use of the emblem by third parties' ambulances and first-aid stations authorized by a National Society is included under 'indicative device'. However, the link between those users and the Movement is tenuous, since it merely consists in the authorization given by the National Society. This authorization is permissible only in peacetime. See Emblem Study, above n 13, at 186–91.

— the use by private military and security companies; and
— the use by non-Red Cross/Red Crescent organizations.

III. The special case of the ICRC and the International Federation

33 The ICRC and the International Federation of Red Cross and Red Crescent Societies may use the emblem at all times (in peacetime as well as in times of armed conflict) without restriction.[81] Depending on the context (conflictual or non-conflictual situations), the use of the emblem by the ICRC is either protective or indicative, and covers both medical and non-medical activities. In particular,

> [the Geneva Conventions] recognize the work which the [ICRC] does, outside their actual provisions, for the protection of the victims of war. Most of these activities are not, strictly speaking, 'protected' by the Geneva Conventions, in the way that those of the Medical Service of the armed forces are. But the extension of the use of the protective sign to cover them is fully justified; such activities largely result from mandates given to the Committee under the terms of the Conventions themselves, and there is a major humanitarian interest in facilitating them. [...] Wherever circumstances do not demand the use of the protective sign—that is in the majority of cases—the sign will be purely indicatory.[82]

IV. Use by medical services of armed groups engaged in NIAC

34 Although they are not expressly mentioned in the list of users set out at MN 28, medical services of armed groups party to a NIAC are entitled to use the emblem as a protective device. This use is justified by both treaty provisions[83] and customary law.[84] The use of the emblem by such medical services is subjected *mutatis mutandis* to the same conditions as are applicable to government armed forces medical services.[85]

V. Use by multinational forces

35 A first distinction should be made between collective security operations carried out by individual member states acting with the authorization of the Security Council or by the competent organs of regional organizations, and operations carried out under the command and control of the international organizations concerned. In the former case, the conventional rights and obligations of the national armed forces engaged in these operations remain applicable. The situation is more controversial in the latter situation. International organizations are not party to the relevant treaties and 'are not entitled as such to use the emblem'.[86] However, the general view is that multinational forces are authorized to use the emblem. In particular, this view was held by the expert commentator on AP III, who said:

> However, when the Organization acts through the national armed forces of its member states, there is no doubt that the medical services and religious personnel of those forces have the right to use the distinctive emblems—and also the obligation to respect them.[87]

---

[81] Art 44 para 3 GC I. The ICRC and the International Federation have, however, accepted to observe the principles of the Regulations on the Use of the Emblem by the National Societies. Additionally, the ICRC has adopted rather strict rules regulating the use of its name and logo in fundraising. See MN 21 and 54.
[82] Pictet Commentary GC I, at 336.   [83] See Art 12 AP II.   [84] MN 10.
[85] See also Emblem Study, above n 13, at 38 and 167–9.
[86] See Emblem Study, above n 13, at 161.
[87] See J.F. Quéguiner, 'Commentary on the Protocol Additional to the Geneva Conventions of 12 August 1949, and relating to the Adoption of an Additional Distinctive Emblem (Protocol III)', 89 *IRRC* 865 (2007) 175, at 195.

Two specific instruments also support this view: the UN Secretary-General's Bulletin of 1999[88] and Article 5 AP III, which authorizes the use of the emblems by 'Missions under the United Nations auspices'.[89]

VI. Use by private military and security companies

The question of the emblem's use by private military and security companies is even more controversial than the previous one (MN 35), considering the very different types of activities carried out by such companies, the great diversity of situations in which they are involved, and their often very poor record when it comes to observance of international rules. The use of the emblem by private military and security companies is not expressly addressed in any treaty. As such, the general view is that they are not entitled to use the emblem.[90]

VII. Use by non-Red Cross/Red Crescent organizations

In the early 1970s, a number of private or non-governmental non-Red Cross/Red Crescent organizations (in particular medical organizations of a new kind, acting with full independence) were formed. Many of them unilaterally decided to use the emblem or imitations thereof,[91] in most cases without any authorization or control. Initially they were a serious source of dispute and gave rise to numerous controversies with Red Cross or Red Crescent organizations (in particular with the ICRC, which feared that a general decline of the protection conferred by the emblem would result). The question has gradually lost much of its substance, since in the meantime, most non-governmental organizations have adopted and made widely known their own logos. Although theoretically such organizations could qualify as 'voluntary aid societies' under Article 26 GC I, this has not happened, since these organizations are reluctant to be restricted by the conditions of state control outlined in that provision.[92]

E. Temporal Scope of Application

The many provisions discussed in section B of this chapter apply separately or cumulatively in a number of situations, from peacetime to situations of armed conflict.

I. In peacetime

In peacetime the emblem may be used only in its indicative function. In this context, the main users of the emblem will be the National Red Cross or Red Crescent Societies. As already mentioned, this use is strictly outlined in the Regulations on the Use of the Emblem by the National Societies[93] and is, in most cases, regulated under domestic

---

[88] UN Secretary-General, n 20.
[89] 'The medical services and religious personnel participating in operations under the auspices of the United Nations may, with the agreement of participating states, use one of the distinctive emblems mentioned in Articles 1 and 2.'
[90] See Emblem Study, above n 13, at 179–85.   [91] MN 57.
[92] MN 49. For a detailed analysis of this question, see Emblem Study, above n 13, at 170–8; and A. Bouvier, 'Special Aspects of the Use of the Red Cross or Red Crescent Emblem', 29 *IRRC* 272 (1989) 438.
[93] MN 12.

legislation.[94] It should also be restricted to the activities carried out by the National Society, 'in conformity with the principles laid down by the International Red Cross Conference'.[95] In conformity with the national legislation and with the express permission of the National Society, the emblem may be used in time of peace to identify non-Red Cross/Red Crescent ambulances and first-aid posts exclusively assigned for the purpose of giving free treatment to the wounded and sick.[96] However, this last authorization should be strictly limited to peacetime and remain an exceptional measure.

41   Lastly, as a measure of preparation for wartime, the marking in peacetime of civilian hospitals and medical units which, in time of armed conflict, would be entitled to display the emblem as a protective device is acceptable.[97] Of course, the requirements of authorization and control by the competent authorities remain applicable to these cases.[98]

II. In times of internal tensions and disturbances

42   In situations of internal tensions and disturbances, the applicable provisions remain essentially the same as in peacetime. The only possible use of the emblem is thus, in principle, for an indicative purpose, and in this case the size of the emblem should usually be small.[99] However, this principle is not absolute. The Commentary to Article 4 of the Regulations (which appear to have relaxed the conditions spelled out in Article 44 GC I[100]) stipulates, 'however the use of large-size emblem [by the National Society] is not excluded in certain cases, such as events where it is important for first-aid workers to be easily identifiable'. Such use of the large-size emblem must be authorized, or at least not forbidden, by domestic legislation.[101] It is noted that the practice of National Societies has sometimes been to display a large-size emblem or logo to enhance their security and safe access.

III. In times of armed conflicts

43   In situations of armed conflicts, it should first of all be recalled that, as far as the use of the emblem is concerned, very similar rules and principles apply in IACs and in NIACs.[102] It is of course in these situations that most of the rules regulating the use of the emblem will apply, and its use will depend on the context, either as an indicative device (in particular for the peacetime activities that the National Society will continue during an armed conflict) or as a protective one.

44   In occupied territories, the military medical services of the Occupying Power must display their own emblem. Officially authorized civilian hospitals must display the emblem of their own state. The control of the correct use of the emblem by civilian hospitals remains under the responsibility of the occupied state. However, if it is no longer functioning, the Occupying Power has to substitute itself for the authority of the occupied state.[103]

---

[94] See ICRC, 'Model Law on the Emblems' (Model Law), Art 6, available at <http://www.icrc.org/ara/assets/files/model-law-emblem-0708-eng.pdf>.
[95] See Art 44 para 3 GC I.   [96] See Art 44 para 4 GC I.
[97] See Emblem Study, above n 13, at 71–9.   [98] MN 49.
[99] See Art 44 para 2 GC I; and Art 16 Regulations on the Use of the Emblem, above n 21.
[100] See Bouvier, above n 92.
[101] Ibid, at 450.   [102] See MN 10 and Bouvier, above n 92, at 454.
[103] See Emblem Study, above n 13, at 65–70.

F. The Conditions for Use

As mentioned previously,[104] in spite of many different users and several possible uses of the emblem, all relevant rules have a common denominator. This conditions the use of the emblem on three basic requirements:

— the use must be *authorized* (no 'autonomous' use);
— it must be *controlled*; and
— generally, in its protective function, display of the emblem must be limited to *medical activities*.[105]

I. Authorization

The principle that only *authorized* entities may use the emblem is clearly spelled out in the treaties.[106] Although the formulation of this condition may differ ('under the direction of the competent military authority'; 'only if so authorized by the state'; 'with the consent of the competent authority'; 'under the direction of the competent authority'; 'in conformity with national legislation'), the principle remains the same. Authorization should prevent misuse of the emblem by limiting the circle of users.

The competent authority with the power to authorize the use of the emblem depends on the nature of the intended user. Use by military entities must in principle be authorized by a military authority.[107] The exact nature of the 'competent military authority' has not been fixed in the treaties, and a certain amount of flexibility is left to the state parties. In most cases[108] the responsibility to authorize is delegated to the Ministry of Defence. As for the civilian entities, the authorization may be given either to a military or to a civilian authority, and can exceptionally be delegated to the National Society, in its capacity as auxiliary to the public authorities.[109] In NIACs,[110] the use of the emblem is also subject to authorization. Governmental authorities (civilian and/or military) and *de facto* authorities[111] of the rebel forces must discharge this responsibility.

It has been argued that in exceptional circumstances, a National Society may use the emblem without authorization from the competent authorities.[112] Such circumstances would include situations where the government can no longer exercise its normal prerogatives and cases of acute NIACs where the government has practically disintegrated. As soon as the competent authorities have recovered their normal functions, 'the situation should be rectified i.e. the [National Society] should obtain the authorization to use the emblem'.[113]

---

[104] MN 4.
[105] Notwithstanding the right of the ICRC and of the International Federation to use the emblem at all times (either as a protective or as an indicative device) for all their activities, including non-medical ones. See in particular Art 7 of the Model Law, above n 94.
[106] See, in particular, Art 39 GC I; Art 18 GC IV; Art 18 AP I; and Art 12 AP II.
[107] MN 28.
[108] This is the approach recommended in Art 3 of the Model Law, above n 94, and followed in many national laws.
[109] See Emblem Study, above n 13, at 60–4. The Model Law, above n 94, mentions the Ministry of Health as the competent authority, but does not rule out a possible role for the Ministry of Defence.
[110] See Art 12 AP II.
[111] See Emblem Study, above n 13, at 64; and ICRC Commentary APs, para 4746.
[112] See Emblem Study, above n 13, at 107–8; and Bouvier, above n 92, at 443–7.
[113] See Emblem Study, above n 13, at 107.

II. Control

49 The requirement for control of use of the emblem seems to be even more important than the principle regarding its authorization.[114] Only tight control will prevent misuse of the emblem and allow for the prosecution of those who have committed serious violations. In addition to the criminalization of misuse of the emblem in national law, we should recall the provisions of the Statute of the International Criminal Court (ICC) referred to below (MN 60), which include misuse of the emblem as one of the war crimes within the jurisdiction of that court.[115]

50 In practice, the authorities in charge of such control should be the same as those entitled to grant authorization for the use of the emblem. This is the approach followed in Articles 2 and 4 of the ICRC Model Law on the Emblems.[116]

III. Medical activities

51 As a protective device, the emblem may in principle be used only for medical activities. This limitation is clearly mentioned in a number of provisions regulating the use of the emblem,[117] which refer specifically to *medical* personnel, *medical* transports, *medical* units, and *medical* establishments or *hospitals*.[118]

G. The Prevention and Repression of Misuse

I. A responsibility that covers all situations

52 As mentioned previously,[119] the use of the emblems is subject to very strict conditions that aim both at maximizing their protective value and at preventing *misuse*[120] that would inexorably jeopardize their essential functions. As such, states parties to the treaties have accepted a comprehensive obligation, and enjoy a primary responsibility that includes both preventive and repressive measures. This obligation was clearly reaffirmed in AP III, which invites states to

> take measures necessary for the prevention and repression, at all times, of any misuse of the distinctive emblems mentioned [...] and their designations, including the perfidious use and the use of any sign or designation constituting an imitation thereof.[121]

The use of the emblem is regulated at all times, both in times of armed conflict and in peacetime.[122]

---

[114] See Pictet Commentary GC I, at 308: 'What is essential is that all armed forces should exercise official control of every use of the emblem.'

[115] With regard to the individual criminal responsibility of commanders and other superiors, see Art 28 of the ICC Statute.

[116] Model Law, above n 94.

[117] See, e.g., Art 44 GC I; Art 18 GC IV; Art 18 AP I; Art 12 AP II; Art 1 of the Regulations on the Use of the Emblem, above n 21; or Arts 2–5 of the Model Law, above n 94.

[118] As mentioned in MN 28, National Societies may use the emblem for non-medical activities, but only in its indicative function. The ICRC also enjoys specific conditions for use (MN 33).

[119] See in particular MN 45.

[120] In this section, the term 'misuse' should be understood as encompassing all violations of the rules regulating the use of the emblems. A similar definition appears in the Emblem Study, above n 13, at 30.

[121] Art 6 AP III.   [122] See Emblem Study, above n 13, at 294.

53 Without entering into minute detail, *preventive* measures include in particular: the adoption of national legislation and regulations;[123] the obligation to disseminate the rules[124] on the use of the emblem as widely as possible;[125] the prohibition of registering trademarks that constitute imitations of the protected emblems and denominations; the establishment of mechanisms to ensure compliance; the training of legal advisers for the armed forces;[126] and the adoption of preparatory measures for identification and signalization in peacetime.[127] *Repressive* measures will generally include criminal prosecution and fines, imprisonment, disciplinary measures, and correctional labour. Both preventive and repressive measures may be found in legislative and regulatory/administrative acts. The most serious misuses are qualified as war crimes.[128]

II. The types of misuse

54 The general principle regulating this matter is that 'any use not expressly authorized by international humanitarian law is considered a misuse of the emblem'.[129] Misuses can range from mere carelessness, to intentional and at times perfidious misuse: 'Between these extremes one can conceive of abuses of every possible degree of gravity.'[130]

55 A distinction should be made between misuse of the protective emblem and misuse of the indicative emblem.[131] The former type of misuse, committed by definition in times of armed conflict, is of course 'infinitely more serious, because it may endanger human lives'.[132] Misuse of the indicative emblem (often for commercial purposes), even if it does not have such immediate consequences, should also be firmly repressed because it is detrimental to the credibility of the emblem in general.

56 The rules regulating the use of the emblem prohibit three different types of misuse: imitation; improper use (including 'usurpation'); and perfidious use (a type of misuse restricted to armed conflict situations).

a. Imitation

57 Article 53 GC I and Article 6 AP III prohibit the use of signs or designations that, owing to their shape and/or colour or title, may be confused with the emblems or their names. State parties have the responsibility to decide whether a given mark (many imitations are created by commercial companies) constitutes an imitation. The criterion to be used should be 'whether there is a risk of confusion in the public mind between the sign or designation and the emblem or its name'.[133] Similarly, and due to the confusion which may arise with the

---

[123] See Art 54 GC I; Art 45 GC IV; Art 6 AP III; and MN 64.
[124] For a full list of relevant provisions, see MN 5 and Lavoyer, above n 16.
[125] Arts 47/48/127/144 GCs I–IV; Arts 80 and 87 AP I; Art 19 AP II; Art 7 AP III. Armed and security forces should be the prime addressees of dissemination programs, but other groups (medical circles, youth, civil society as a whole) should also be targeted. For a detailed presentation of this preventive obligation, see Emblem Study, above n 13, at 282–5.
[126] See Art 82 AP I.   [127] MN 40.   [128] MN 60.
[129] See Quéguiner, above n 87, at 197. See also Pictet Commentary GC I, at 386: 'Use of the emblem is forbidden to everyone not expressly authorized by the Convention. [...] Use of the emblem [...] is forbidden "whatever the object of such use".'
[130] Ibid, at 381.
[131] A distinction clearly spelled out in Arts 9 and 10 of the Model Law, above n 94. See also Pictet Commentary GC I, at 380.
[132] Pictet Commentary GC I, at 381.   [133] Ibid, at 385.

distinctive emblem of the red cross, the Swiss flag (or imitations thereof) is also protected, and instances of misuse are prohibited in Article 53 GC I.[134]

b. *Improper use*[135]

58 The concept of improper use includes two separate types of misuse. It is defined as the use of protected emblems, signs, or signals by

> entities or persons that are not entitled to do so (commercial enterprises, pharmacists, private doctors, non-governmental organizations, ordinary individuals etc) or, in the case of persons normally authorized to use the emblem, of their doing so without respecting the rules of the Conventions and their Protocols [...][136]

c. *Perfidious use*

59 Codified in Article 37 AP I,[137] perfidy is defined as '[a]cts inviting the confidence of an adversary to lead him to believe that he is entitled, or is obliged to accord protection [...] with intent to betray that confidence'. Perfidious uses of the emblem include cases where, during armed conflict, it is used for non-authorized activities such as the transport of ammunition or the camouflage of military installations with the intention of deceiving the adversary. The most serious example of perfidious use of the emblem, i.e. 'the perfidious use of emblems [...] referred to in articles 37 (*Prohibition of perfidy*) and 38 (*Recognized emblems*) of the Protocol [I], for the purpose of killing, injuring or capturing an adversary, constitutes a grave breach under [Article 85.3(f) AP I] if it leads to death or serious injury to body or health'[138] and will qualify as a war crime.

III. Misuse as a war crime under international criminal law

60 Misuse of the emblem or attacks against persons and objects protected by the emblem are defined as war crimes under the ICC Statute, as follows:

> Making improper use of a flag of truce, of the flag or of the military insignia and uniform of the enemy or of the United Nations, as well as of the distinctive emblems of the Geneva Conventions, resulting in death or serious personal injury [...] (Article 8(2)(b)(vii), IACs)

> Intentionally directing attacks against buildings, material, medical units and transport, and personnel using the distinctive emblems of the Geneva Conventions in conformity with international law [...] (Article 8.2(b)(xxiv), IACs)

> Intentionally directing attacks against buildings, material, medical units and transport, and personnel using the distinctive emblems of the Geneva Conventions in conformity with international law [...] (Article 8(2)(e)(ii), NIACs)

IV. The role of the state

61 As parties to the treaties and as direct addressees of most of their rules, states have a primary role to play and a clear responsibility in the implementation of the rules regulating

---

[134] For an analysis of the use of national armorials, see ibid, at 388. See also Emblem Study, above n 13, at 309–12, where graphic examples of imitations are provided.

[135] See Arts 53 and 54 GC I; Art 6 AP III.

[136] See Quéguiner, above n 87, at 197. See also Emblem Study, above n 13, at 30; and ICRC CIHL Study, at 209, where examples of improper uses are provided.

[137] For a more detailed analysis of the notion of perfidy, see ICRC CIHL Study, at 223–5; and E. David, *Principes de droit des conflits armés* (4th edn, Brussels: Bruylant, 2008), at 1177, paras 2.253–56.

[138] See ICRC Commentary APs, para 3499; ICRC CIHL Study, at 568, 566–603 (Rule 156 on war crimes); and David, above n 137, para 4.188.

the use of the emblem. In particular, they must adopt legal,[139] regulatory, administrative, and practical measures. Through these measures states should, for example:[140]

— define which emblem(s), sign(s), and signals are recognized and protected by the state;
— define the authorized uses of the emblems;
— define those entitled to use the emblem;
— establish which authorities are in charge of authorizing, monitoring, and controlling the use of the emblem;
— regulate the means and mechanisms by which those authorized to do so can identify themselves; and
— implement the obligation to disseminate the relevant rules as widely as possible.[141]

In order to take into account the differences in their structures, legal systems, and organizations, some flexibility is left to states in carrying out these obligations. For example, they often benefit from the support provided by their National Societies, acting as their auxiliaries in the humanitarian field,[142] or by the ICRC.[143] In countries that have established National IHL Committees,[144] these inter-ministerial bodies are in most cases directly involved in the prevention and repression of misuse of the emblem.

a. Domestic legislation

In spite of their fairly detailed wording, many conventional rules regulating the use of the emblem are not self-executing. Without clear identification of the authorities in charge of authorizing and controlling the use of the emblem,[145] without precise and dissuasive penalties for those committing misuse, without strict definitions of those entitled to use the emblem, the adequate implementation of the legal regime will prove almost impossible.

It was precisely to these ends that Article 54 GC I[146] was adopted:

The High Contracting Parties shall, if their legislation is not already adequate, take measures necessary for the prevention and repression, at all times, of the abuses referred to under Article 53.

The domestic legislation should apply to all forms of individual and collective misuse. It should address in particular the following issues:

— the distinction between the different possible uses;
— the definition of the scope of the protection (which emblems and signals are protected);
— the definition of the distinctive emblem and designation of its use by the state;
— the designation of those entitled to use the emblem as a protective device;
— the conditions for its use by the National Society and the international organization of the Movement;
— the definition of appropriate sanctions in cases of misuse;
— the obligation of dissemination of the applicable rules; and
— the designation of the authorities in charge of authorizing and controlling the use of the emblem.[147]

---

[139] MN 66. [140] For a detailed analysis of these obligations see Emblem Study, above n 13, at 275–81.
[141] MN 53. [142] MN 70. [143] MN 72.
[144] More than 100 such bodies have been established. For an updated list, see ICRC, 'Table of National Committees and other national bodies on international humanitarian law' (31 August 2014), available at <http://www.icrc.org/eng/resources/documents/misc/table-national-committees.htm>.
[145] MN 46 ff. [146] See also Art 45 GC II.
[147] For a more complete analysis, see Emblem Study, above n 13, at 275–81.

66 As regards the *form of domestic legislation* to be adopted, a certain amount of flexibility is left to state parties. Different types of legislation are resorted to, from stand-alone acts to specific provisions inserted in general laws. Rules on the use of the emblem may thus be found in 'Geneva Conventions Acts'; 'Red Cross or Red Crescent Society Recognition Laws'; 'Laws on the Use of the Emblems'; 'Laws on War Crimes'; 'Emergency Acts'; 'Trade-Marks Laws'; or in specific parts of Penal Codes, Codes of Military Justice, or Civil Codes. No general rules (based, for example, on monist/dualist traditions or common/civil law systems) can be drawn from current practice. However, it might be said that in common law countries the rules on the emblem are usually part of Geneva Conventions Acts, and in civil law countries they will usually appear either in ad hoc acts or in provisions in the criminal code.

67 In terms of *penalties,* the most common practice consists in sentencing violators to imprisonment and/or a fine. Many national laws provide for a minimum and maximum penalty, without much precision as to the criteria to be observed when determining the level of severity. Many laws regard the fact that misuse is committed by civil servants or during armed conflict as aggravating factors. As already mentioned, the most serious misuses (perfidious use—MN 60) constitute war crimes,[148] and violators must face individual criminal responsibility.[149]

68 In 1952, Jean Pictet wrote rather bluntly that 'in most cases […] national legislation is still most inadequate'.[150] The situation has now clearly improved. More than 120 state parties have adopted national laws of implementation.[151] Although some of them are adequate,[152] many remain incomplete[153] or outdated. With the passage of time, the penalties established (in particular the fines) have often lost most of their dissuasive potential. Obviously, much work remains to be done in this field; however, a more comprehensive analysis and assessment of the domestic legislation regulating the use of the emblem would go beyond the objectives of this chapter.

b. *The model laws*

69 As already mentioned, states parties to GC I and GC II, as well as to AP III, have the obligation[154] to enact domestic legislation for the prevention and repression of misuses of the emblem. In spite of the mandatory character of this duty, states have often neglected to adopt appropriate legislation. 'To make this important and complicated task easier for the authorities',[155] the ICRC has regularly[156] drafted model laws for the protection of

---

[148] See the references to the ICC Statute, MN 60; to the ICRC Commentary APs, para 3499; and to the ICRC CIHL Study, at 575.
[149] For a complete analysis of the concept of 'war crime', see Ch 31 of this volume.
[150] See Pictet Commentary GC I, at 393.
[151] Most are available at <https://www.icrc.org/applic/ihl/ihl-nat.nsf/vwLawsByCountry.xsp?xp_topicSelected=GVAL-992BU8>.
[152] See, e.g., the law adopted in 1997 by Cameroon, Law No 97-2 of 10 January 1997 on the Protection of the Red Cross Emblem and Name, available at <http://www.icrc.org/applic/ihl/ihl-nat.nsf/implementingLaws.xsp?documentId=3F10A3CE5F9EE6D6C1256A32002569D8&action=openDocument&xp_country Selected=CM&xp_topicSelected=GVAL-992BU8&from=state>.
[153] E.g., very few states have integrated the new emblem established by AP III, Switzerland being one of the few exceptions.
[154] See Art 54 GC I (a similar provision, Art 28, was spelled out in the 1929 GC I) and Art 45 GC II.
[155] See Pictet Commentary GC I, at 394.
[156] The first attempt was made in 1932, in connection with the 1929 GCs.

the emblem upon which national legislation might be based.¹⁵⁷ Regularly updated, the model laws are widely used and have clearly contributed to the improvement of domestic legislation. The latest (2008) version of the 'Model law on the emblems'[158] contains, inter alia, basic definitions; rules on both the protective and indicative uses; rules on use by hospitals, by medical units, by the National Society, the ICRC, and the International Federation; measures of control and penalties in case of misuse.[159] While the model laws can rarely be used in and of themselves, they may still constitute a useful 'checklist' for those states willing to legislate in this domain.

V. The role of the National Societies[160]

National authorities should have a natural ally in the National Societies in their efforts to ensure respect for the emblem, since the latter share a direct interest in and responsibility for enforcement along with the states. The National Societies should be on the watch for misuse of the emblem and should approach those responsible for violations. More specifically, National Societies should first of all make sure that their own activities are carried out in conformity with the rules regulating the use of the emblem.[161] The very high renown and reputation of the emblem is one of the greatest assets of the National Societies. Considering their ever-increasing need for additional resources, National Societies are often tempted to 'use' the emblem in their fundraising programs at the serious risk of loss of prestige.[162] 70

As already mentioned, National Societies support the efforts made by states in the prevention of misuse of the emblem, in particular through their programmes of dissemination of IHL.[163] Some National Societies have been given by their national authorities, either expressly or tacitly, specific responsibilities in approaching violators of the rules, an arduous, thankless, but indispensable task.[164] It should further be mentioned that some National Societies have been assigned, through domestic legislation, specific responsibilities in times of internal tensions or NIACs.[165] 71

---

[157] This approach has been followed in several other treaties. The ICRC Advisory Service on IHL has gradually developed a number of model laws. For a full list, see ICRC, 'National implementation of IHL: model laws' (29 September 2009), available at <http://www.icrc.org/eng/resources/documents/legal-fact-sheet/national-implementation-model-laws.htm>.

[158] ICRC, 'Model Law on the Emblems' (15 July 2008), available at <http://www.icrc.org/eng/resources/documents/misc/emblem-model-law-150708.htm>.

[159] The 2008 Model Law was drafted primarily for civil law systems (as indicated in note 1 of the Law). For states with a common law system, the ICRC Advisory Service has drafted a 'Model Law Geneva Conventions [Consolidation] Act', available at <https://www.icrc.org/eng/resources/documents/misc/geneva-conventions-protocols-model-law-310808.htm>.

[160] For a more detailed analysis, see Emblem Study, above n 13, at 287–96. The specific role of the National Societies has been reaffirmed and developed in preambular para 7 of Resolution 2 and in preambular para 15 of Resolution 3, adopted by the 2007 International Conference, available at <https://www.icrc.org/eng/resources/documents/resolution/30-international-conference-resolution-2-2007.htm>.

[161] MN 23.

[162] Arts 7 ('Internal regulations') and 23 ('Campaigns and events organized by the National Society') of the Regulations on the Use of the Emblem, above n 21, are good examples of the difficulty in striking an appropriate balance between conflicting interests.

[163] For examples of the sometimes very determined approaches of National Societies, see Sassòli/Bouvier/Quintin, at 854 and 1737 (UK).

[164] For a thorough analysis of this function, see M. Meyer, 'Protecting the Emblems in Peacetime: The Role of the British Red Cross Society', 29 *IRRC* 272 (1989) 459. The author mentions that in 35 years, the 'Society has taken up approximately 900 actual cases of unauthorized use or misuse of the emblem' (ibid, at 460, fn 1).

[165] See, e.g., Art 9 of the Georgian 'Law on the emblem and designation of the red cross and red crescent, 1997', available at <http://www.icrc.org/applic/ihl/ihl-nat.nsf/implementingLaws.xsp?documentId=

VI. The role of the International Committee of the Red Cross

72　Under Article 5 of the Statutes of the Movement, the ICRC has the responsibility 'to undertake the tasks incumbent upon it under the Geneva Conventions, to work for the faithful application of international humanitarian law applicable in armed conflicts and to take cognizance of any complaints based on alleged breaches of that law' (Article 5(2)(c)), and, further, 'to work for the understanding and dissemination of knowledge of international humanitarian law applicable in armed conflicts and to prepare any development thereof' (Article 5(2)(g)). It is on these bases, and acting in its role of 'guardian', that the ICRC has for decades been involved in the prevention of misuse of the emblem.[166]

73　In addition to the role it played in the drafting of model legislation,[167] the tasks and responsibilities of the ICRC in this regard include the following aspects:[168]

— the ICRC first takes all measures to make sure that it acts in conformity with existing rules;
— it actively promotes the universal ratification and proper implementation of the applicable rules and treaties;
— it contributes to the dissemination of the rules;
— it advises belligerents and parties to armed conflicts on measures required to prevent or stop misuse of the emblem; and
— it assists the National Societies in their efforts to prevent and denounce misuse.[169]

74　The ICRC has repeatedly voiced its concern about disrespect for the emblem, in a variety of conflicts, both international and non-international.[170]

75　In its confidential approaches (direct negotiations or *rappels du droit* sent as *note verbale*) the ICRC systematically reminds the parties to conflicts of their responsibility in terms of prevention and repression of misuse of the emblem.[171]

H. Unity and Plurality

76　I hope that [...] we shall bear in mind the fact that the emblem worn by each of us is not the privilege of any one state, people or religion, but a sign of respect for wounded and defenceless victims and a token of solidarity with human beings in distress.[172]

37C7164B2D3656CCC32566190040C848&action=openDocument&xp_countrySelected=GE&xp_topicSelected=GVAL-992BU8&from=state>: 'In case of internal conflict in the country, the Society of the Georgian Red Cross has the right to independently decide, with the consent of the parties to the conflict, by whom and how the protective emblem shall be used.' A similar mandate is given in Law No 97-2, s 12 of Cameroon, above n 152.

[166] For a comprehensive analysis of this role, see Y. Sandoz, 'The International Committee of the Red Cross as Guardian of International Humanitarian Law' (31 December 1998), available at <http://www.icrc.org/eng/resources/documents/misc/about-the-icrc-311298.htm>.

[167] MN 69.　　[168] For a complete presentation, see Emblem Study, above n 13, at 297–303.

[169] For a detailed analysis of the activities carried out by the ICRC, see H. Slim, 'Protection of the Red Cross and Red Crescent Emblems and the Repression of Misuse', 29 *IRRC* 272 (1989) 420, at 433–7.

[170] For a list of public appeals and denunciations by the ICRC, see ICRC CIHL Study, at 209, in particular fns 39–41.

[171] For practical examples of such approaches, see Sassòli/Bouvier/Quintin, at 1651 (Sri Lanka) and 1720 (former Yugoslavia).

[172] Declaration made by Alexandre Hay, President of the ICRC, before the International Conference in Manila in 1981, quoted in Quéguiner, above n 87, at 175.

I. The short era of unity

The adoption of the red cross as the unique sign of identification of the military medical services and their auxiliaries has always been considered as one of the major achievements of the 1864 Geneva Convention.[173] The reasons why this very emblem—a red cross on a white background—was proposed in 1863 and endorsed in the 1864 Convention have never been completely elucidated.[174] The main concern was to adopt 'a single emblem that [was] identifiable from a great distance and easy to recognize and reproduce'.[175] The sign was supposed to be devoid of any political, religious, or cultural dimension. However, Henry Dunant and the other members of the Geneva Committee were all devout Calvinists, and the participants in the 1863 and 1864 Conferences emanated mainly from Christian countries, so none of these protagonists probably realized that the choice of such an emblem might eventually be considered as problematic (if not contentious) by followers of other faiths.

II. The loss of unity

The unity of the distinctive sign did not last long. As early as 1876, a new sign appeared on the battlefield. Involved in an armed conflict against Russia, the Ottoman Empire unilaterally decided that it would use a new sign, the red crescent on a white background, but would nonetheless respect the sign displayed by its adversaries. The reason given for this change was that the 1864 emblem 'gave offence to Muslim soldiers'.[176] Other states parties to the Convention temporarily accepted this, for the duration of the conflict. This event marked the end of the unity of the emblem, and the beginning of long and bitter controversies.

III. Plurality

In 1929, the wounded and sick Convention was revised. The red crescent and the red lion and sun (an emblem used only by Persia, which considered it could use neither the cross, nor the crescent) were recognized along with the red cross, with only one restriction: only the states that *already* used them before the adoption of the 1929 Convention could continue to do so. Then, in 1949, three options were proposed to the plenipotentiaries:

— the adoption of a completely new emblem, supposed to replace the existing ones;
— the return to the cross as the sole emblem of the Convention; and
— an Israeli proposal to adopt a fourth emblem: the red shield of David.

The first two proposals were immediately rejected. The third was hotly debated, but finally rejected by a one-vote majority.[177] The Diplomatic Conference had to recognize the deadlock and reverted to the compromise reached in 1929, reaffirmed in almost the same wording in Article 38 GC I. Finally, during the 1974–7 Conference that led to the adoption of the two Additional Protocols, the status quo was maintained and a new Israeli proposal to have the red shield of David recognized as an additional emblem was withdrawn.[178]

---

[173] MN 4.
[174] In spite of very minute analysis. See Quéguiner, above n 87, at 176, fn 5: 'Conference documents [...] shed no light on the reasons for the choice. We are therefore reduced to conjecture.'
[175] Ibid, at 176.
[176] See ibid, fn 6.
[177] See Bugnion, above n 50, at 52 and 57.
[178] See Quéguiner, above n 87, at 177 and Bugnion, above n 62, at 16.

80   The absence of any progress on the issue of the plurality of emblems has progressively led to rather serious problems.[179] First, the coexistence of two signs easily associated with two monotheist religions can lead and has led people to conclude that the signs have a religious dimension.[180] Obviously, this is a very dangerous perception in the case of conflicts involving opposing adversaries identified by different emblems and followers of different faiths. Secondly, the religious dimension that became inevitably (though erroneously) associated with the red cross and the red crescent prevented certain National Societies from adopting these emblems at all, which is an imperative condition to be recognized as a member of the Movement.[181] Thirdly, the Article 38 GC I 'solution' poses an additional risk: the proliferation of non-recognized emblems by states and National Societies that are not ready to adopt the cross or the crescent.[182] Though accurate in certain regards (states that are not predominantly Muslim do not use the red crescent), the religious perception of the emblems is far from universal. Many states that are officially atheist (the Soviet Union National Society displayed both the cross and the crescent) or predominantly Hindu, Shinto, or Buddhist use the cross, together with a number of states with mixed but predominantly Muslim populations.[183]

81   The problems caused by the plurality of emblems should not be underestimated: they have led to very bitter controversies, have sometimes prevented National Societies from deploying activities on some parts of their national territory, and they have jeopardized the universality of the Movement. Yet it should be recognized that, at least during IACs, very few instances of misuse of the emblem can be attributed to a deliberate intention to target the 'other' emblem used by the adversary.

I. Current Challenges

82   In previous sections of this chapter, a number of obstacles to respect for the use of the emblem and challenges to full implementation of the rules regulating its use have been identified. Some of the factors contributing to the unsatisfactory level of protection supposedly granted by the emblem in today's armed conflicts include: the plurality of emblems; the complexity of the applicable rules; the weaknesses of some of the implementation mechanisms; and the sometimes very serious cases of misuse (the list of problems is unfortunately longer). In addition to these 'traditional' obstacles, new challenges have emerged in recent years. Some of them will be briefly addressed in this section.

---

[179] A risk clearly identified by the President of the ICRC in 1992: 'Yet the coexistence of the two emblems has had the effect of accentuating their religious connotation in public opinion, for there can be no doubt that this identification with a religious group has to some extent affected the victims of conflicts in which each of the adversaries uses a different emblem. As we have already said, "the emblem derives its protective value from the fact that the same sign is used by friend and foe" and if the emblem loses its neutrality, there is a great danger of its becoming a target.' See C. Sommaruga, 'Unity and Plurality of the Emblem', 32 *IRRC* 289 (1992) 333.

[180] The Islamic Republic of Iran renounced the use of the red lion and sun in 1980.

[181] See Statutes of the Movement, Art 4(5).

[182] For a list of non-recognized emblems, see Bugnion, above n 62, at 65–74; and for an analysis of the risks, see Sommaruga, above n 179.

[183] Niger, Nigeria, Chad, Senegal, Lebanon, Indonesia (the largest Muslim country in the world), or Mali, to name but a few.

I. The emblem as a target

It has been argued that in some new forms of armed conflict, in particular in *asymmetric conflicts* where completely different types of armed forces are fighting each other, the weakest party might 'knowingly target the "soft spots" of its adversary',[184] including medical installations and personnel identified by the emblem. It is on this basis that in some recent conflicts, and in particular in Afghanistan, several armed forces have decided not to display the emblem. If proved right,[185] this line of argument would constitute a serious challenge to the effectiveness of the emblem, and increase the risks faced by medical personnel and war wounded. A shift from (mostly) inadvertent attacks on protected persons to intentional and systematic targeting would put into question fundamental aspects of IHL.

II. The lack of visibility of protected personnel and installations

The increasing widespread use of long-range means of combat (hardly compensated by progress made in their accuracy) clearly increases the risks of damage to protected personnel and installations. Although in many cases damage is inadvertently caused as a result of individual mistakes,[186] such damage nonetheless constitutes a serious threat to the continuation of humanitarian activities. The applicable provisions of IHL (especially those adopted in 1949, but even the 1977 rules) are sometimes outdated and prove clearly insufficient,[187] and as a result, pragmatic approaches have to be crafted by humanitarian actors. For example, the ICRC has decided to provide the GPS coordinates of its health facilities systematically to all parties to a conflict.[188]

III. Misuse on the Internet

Although less life-threatening than the challenges mentioned above, misuse of the emblem and of the designations of the emblems on the Internet can have devastating effects and lead to serious loss of prestige and respect of the emblem. The global and transnational nature of the Internet renders many of the traditional mechanisms of implementation (e.g., adoption of domestic national legislation) impracticable or simply irrelevant. The Movement has started addressing these issues, and recommendations have been issued,[189] but the problem is far from being solved as instances of misuse of the emblems and of the designations, sometimes for fraudulent purposes, remain a frequent occurrence in practice, and in particular in internationally publicized humanitarian crises.

---

[184] See, e.g., Leon de Winter, 'The Red Cross as a Target', available at <http://www.mci-forum.com/the-red-cross-as-a-target/>.

[185] But there are good reasons to challenge this theory. See MN 88. As for the ICRC (which has maintained a permanent operational presence in Afghanistan since 1992), it has never renounced using its logo on vehicles, offices, and residences.

[186] See the rather embarrassed apologies offered by the US Central Command to the ICRC following the bombing of ICRC warehouses, in Sassòli/Bouvier/Quintin, Case 253 (Afghanistan), at B3.

[187] Some progress was made in the 1999 Second Protocol to the Hague Convention on Cultural Property (see in particular para 56 of the *Guidelines for the Implementation of the 1999 Second Protocol Cultural Property*), but much remains to be done in this field.

[188] ICRC, *Health Care in Danger: Making the Case* (Geneva: ICRC, 2011), at 20.

[189] See Emblem Study, above n 13, at 314–19.

IV. The rare use of the red crystal

86   As already mentioned,[190] the adoption of AP III was the result of a long and in many respects very controversial process. Almost six years after its entry into force (on 14 January 2007) only 62 states[191] have ratified AP III, and even fewer have taken appropriate measures of national implementation. In spite of the many advantages it offers as a sign devoid of any religious or political connotations, the red crystal has not (yet?) made its way to the battlefield, even on a temporary basis.[192] The only actual use of the red crystal of which this author is aware is the indicative use made by the Israeli Magen David Adom team deployed in Haiti after the January 2010 earthquake.[193]

87   Generating the same worldwide recognition of and respect for the red crystal as is widely afforded to the red cross and red crescent remains a huge challenge. All efforts should be made to dismiss both the perception that the red crystal was 'invented' for the sole purpose of serving Israeli interests and concerns, and to convince those states experiencing problems with the cross or the crescent that they can find a viable alternative in resorting to the crystal.

V. Displaying or not displaying?

88   Following several incidents of targeting medical personnel, transports, and infrastructures, some states with armed forces deployed in international operations (mostly in Iraq and Afghanistan) have renounced displaying the emblem to identify their medical personnel and installations. This decision, if generalized, could have significant effects on the protection of victims of armed conflicts. However, before examining the extent of this practice and its potential effects, one should first of all recall that displaying the emblem is not (and has never been) compulsory.[194] In a recent report to the ILC by one of its members,[195] it has been clearly reaffirmed that states have a 'scope of discretion' and that, in spite of the rather strong wording of Article 12 AP II ('the distinctive emblem […] shall be displayed'),[196] they can actually decide not to display the emblem.

89   Some of the reasons explaining why a state would decide not to display the emblem have been clearly spelled out by the German Federal Government in response to a parliamentary question:

> The Federal Armed Forces are confronted in Afghanistan with enemy forces who do not respect this form of international protection. As other providers of ISAF [International Security Assistance Force] contingents, the Federal Armed Forces have experienced that marked vehicles have been targeted. Partly, these medical units and vehicles, clearly distinguished as such by their protective emblem, have even been preferred as targets. The Federal Armed Forces have thus, alongside with Belgium, France, the UK, Canada and the US, decided within ISAF to disguise the protective emblem on medical vehicles. This occurs in the case of the German ISAF contingent by painting over the protective emblem.[197]

---

[190] MN 79.
[191] Mostly Western states, virtually no predominantly Muslim countries; for a list of state parties, see <http://www.icrc.org/ihl.nsf/WebSign?ReadForm&id=615&ps=P>.
[192] As permitted under Art 2(4) AP III.
[193] For a description of these activities, see Shira Katiy, 'MDA activities in Haiti', *Maged David Adom in Israel*, available at <http://www.mdais.com/344/315.htm>.
[194] See Pictet Commentary GC I, at 307, 'there is no obligation on a belligerent to mark its units with the emblem'; see also David, above n 137, para 2.70, and MN 19.
[195] See ILC Report, above n 18, at 36.
[196] Very similar wording is used in Art 42 GC I and in Art 18 AP I.
[197] Quoted in the ILC Report, above n 18, at 36, fn 181.

The 'scope of discretion' left to states in this field also appears very clearly in military manuals and in the rules of engagement of military alliances.[198] The US Manual (which reproduces the North Atlantic Treaty Organization (NATO) Standard Agreement (STANAG) almost *verbatim*) provides a good example of such discretion:

A-5. Camouflage of the Geneva Emblem

The NATO STANAG 2931 provides for camouflage of the Geneva emblem on medical facilities where the lack of camouflage might compromise tactical operations. Medical facilities on land, supporting forces of other nations, will display or camouflage the Geneva emblem in accordance with national regulations and procedures. When failure to camouflage would endanger or compromise tactical operations, the camouflage of medical facilities may be ordered by a NATO commander of at least brigade level or equivalent. Such an order is to be temporary and local in nature and countermanded as soon as the circumstances permit. It is not envisaged that large, fixed medical facilities would be camouflaged. The STANAG defines medical facilities as medical units, medical vehicles, and medical aircraft on the ground.

NOTE Under tactical conditions, the need for concealment may outweigh the needs for recognition (AR 750-1).[199]

Although perfectly legal, the optional use of the emblem has of course a reverse side that was clearly identified by Pictet when he pointed out that 'as the enemy can respect a medical unit only if he knows of its presence, respect for the camouflaged unit will be purely theoretical'.[200] Nevertheless, this reverse side may not be so clearly recognized by the proponents of the new restrictive approach to the use of the emblem. Indeed, if the recent practice developed in Iraq and Afghanistan were to become systematic, the situation could become fairly problematic. It is also very possible, however, that this change of practice is the result of the very confusing (in particular for the 'enemy') combination of military and humanitarian operations carried out by the very same forces, a feature rather specific to the two conflicts mentioned.[201]

J. Critical Assessment

At the end of these detailed comments on the use of the emblem, the time has come to reach some conclusions.

To begin with, it is necessary to acknowledge that—in spite of the vital contribution that the emblem can bring, and has brought, to the protection of victims of armed conflicts and other dangerous situations—many rules regulating its use are now showing their age. This is of course particularly true for the ones adopted in 1949, which still constitute the bulk of the applicable provisions.

Quite naturally, these rules were developed to address specific problems that had occurred during the Second World War. Designed to apply to large-scale conflicts in

---

[198] See, e.g., NATO Standard Agreement ('STANAG') 2931 of 1998: 'Orders for the Camouflage of the Red Cross and Red Crescent on Land in Tactical Operations' (on file with the author).
[199] See Field Manual FM 4-02.4 'Appendix A: The Geneva Conventions', available at <http://www.globalsecurity.org/military/library/policy/army/fm/4-02-4/appa.pdf>.
[200] See Pictet Commentary GC I, at 307.
[201] For a very critical but in our view fully relevant assessment of such combined operations, see J. Williamson, 'Using Humanitarian Aid to "Win Hearts and Minds": A Costly Failure?', 93 *IRRC* 884 (2011) 1035.

which relatively organized armies were fighting each other, their implementation in today's conflicts is sometimes problematic, but certainly not impossible.

95   In parallel, the rules adopted in 1977 were marked by important developments, notably the extension of the protection of the emblem both to military and civilian victims, and the clarification of the rules regulating the use of the emblem in NIACs.

96   In most cases, these modifications have occurred for very good reasons, although sometimes with questionable motivation. The results have been very positive in many respects—more people are protected effectively; more activities can be carried out on behalf of victims of armed conflicts or other emergencies; new rules have facilitated the universal acceptance of the emblem[202]—but these developments have also led to more problematic consequences that may be witnessed in today's conflicts.[203]

97   The dilemmas that result from these developments have been clearly identified. For example, discussing the respective advantages and disadvantages of allowing the use of the emblem by civilian medical personnel, the ICRC expressed the following views:

> Any widening of the applicability of the red cross emblem will inevitably entail a far greater risk of misuse and violation; this in turn might compromise the repute attaching to the emblem and undermine its very great significance and good name. Hitherto, the use of the emblem has been confined to a clearly defined category of persons who are subject to military discipline. Even in these circumstances, the prevention of misuse has met with no small difficulties. If, therefore, the use of the emblem is extended to ill-defined categories of civilians, scattered over the country, who are not subject to discipline, proper registration or strict supervision, the combating of abuse would become impracticable, and the consequences would be borne by those who are legally entitled to the protection of the emblem […][204]

98   The ICRC again expressed a very similar concern during the negotiation of the 1977 Additional Protocols:

> Extending the use of the emblem to all doctors without distinction […] would hardly be possible nor would it be desirable. In fact, if the value of this emblem is to be retained, it is important to limit its use to those who are entitled to use it under the Conventions; moreover, its widespread use would make any control impossible.[205]

Therefore, expanding the number of users also means multiplying the risks of misuse.[206] New signs and new signals might decrease the distinction of the emblem and increase its disrespect. Also, the variety of possible uses of the same or similar emblems could well lead to confusion and lack of observance. For this author, these concerns remain valid and should carefully be kept in mind should future developments of the rules regulating the use of the emblem be envisaged. This being said, in spite of their apparent complexity, the rules remain realistic and adequate, especially when one considers their rationale, essential components, and common denominator: only *medical activities* carried out with the *authorization* and under the *control* of the competent authorities can enjoy the protection of the emblem.[207]

99   In addition, and more surprisingly, the rules adopted in 1977, in spite of their modernization, have shown some sign of obsolescence. The role of new humanitarian actors has not been properly addressed, and new forms of warfare and technological developments, in particular in the field of information technologies, are *de facto* ignored. These loopholes certainly decrease the level of protection that should be given to the victims of armed

---

[202] MN 80.   [203] MN 83.   [204] Pictet Commentary GC IV, at 158.
[205] ICRC Commentary APs, para 740.   [206] MN 27 ff.   [207] MN 51.

conflicts and to those in charge of assisting them. More specifically, one can only regret that so little attention has been paid to improving the technical means of identification provided for in Annex I to AP I.[208] Further, Internet tools, GPS systems, and many other recent technological instruments that are widely available could significantly improve the level of protection of medical installations. Some of these instruments are used pragmatically and on an ad hoc basis, but no serious efforts have been made lately in terms of codification.

100 In the absence of significant developments in treaty law, customary law has—to some extent and with all the uncertainties attached to custom—addressed some of the most urgent needs, like the absence of any reference to the use of the emblem in Common Article 3. In the same vein, belligerents' practice has also led to the 'simplification' of some rules that had become difficult to implement (such as the distinction between large dimensions/relatively small size of the emblem, categories of medical personnel, etc).

101 In spite of many shortcomings, the emblem remains an essential tool of protection, and it still works. Therefore, no effort should be spared in the ongoing attempts to prevent violations, to improve the control of its use and the repression of violations. In this respect, the many developments that have occurred in the field of international criminal law should be seen as very positive steps.

102 Paradoxically, even the ever-increasing number of imitations of the emblem, the controversies and public uproar raised by the most blatant misuse, and the sometimes very determined efforts made by alleged violators to deny the occurrence of misuse, should all be seen as signs that the value attached to the emblem is still high. After all, if a head of state feels obliged to offer public and official apologies following a clear misuse of the emblem by his troops,[209] or when dozens of furious 'Letters to the Editor' immediately follow the publication of an article mentioning the support given by a tobacco manufacturer to an institution associated with the Red Cross/Red Cross Movement,[210] one should assume that the emblem continues to have value, and that efforts in preventing its misuse are paying off.

103 Despite misuses, occasional loss of prestige, and legal and technological challenges, the emblem deserves to be supported and the rules regulating its use better implemented. Parties to all armed conflicts should keep in mind the words of one of the best-known experts on this question, 'l'emblème est tabou!'[211] The survival of innumerable victims of present and future conflicts does indeed depend on full respect of the emblem.

ANTOINE A. BOUVIER*

[208] In spite of a clear mechanism of revision provided for in Art 98 AP I. This author was involved in the latest (in 1993) process of revision of Annex I. The debate was still almost entirely focused on mechanisms and systems (radio signals, radar identification) that had been developed during the Second World War or during the Cold War.

[209] President Uribe of Colombia, after Betancourt rescuers illegally used the emblem in 2008, see Sassòli/Bouvier/Quintin, Case 247 (Colombia).

[210] 'L'industrie du tabac finance la Croix-Rouge genevoise', *La Tribune de Genève* (9 September 2012), available at <http://www.tdg.ch/geneve/actu-genevoise/industrie-tabac-finance-croixrouge-genevoise/story/11271180>.

[211] Y. Sandoz, 'L'emblème est tabou/the stakes are high', 141 *ICRC Bulletin* (October 1987), at 2.

* This chapter reflects the author's personal views and does not engage the responsibility of the ICRC. The author wishes to thank very warmly Ms Lindsey Cameron, Ms Miriam Mc Leod, Mr Stéphane Hankins, Mr Yves Sandoz, and Ms Anaïs Tobalagba for their careful reading of the manuscript and their extremely useful comments and suggestions. The author takes full and exclusive responsibility for any mistakes or inaccuracies, and for any opinion expressed.

B. GENEVA CONVENTION III

Chapter 44. Who Is a Prisoner of War?

	MN
A. Introduction	1
B. Meaning and Application	6
I. Article 4(A)	7
a. 'fallen into the power of the enemy'	8
b. 'members of the armed forces'	11
c. 'militias or volunteer corps forming part of'	22
d. 'militias […] volunteer corps […] organized resistance movements'	24
e. 'belonging to a Party to the conflict'	26
f. 'commanded by a person responsible'	32
g. 'fixed distinctive sign'	36
h. 'carrying arms openly'	44
i. 'conducting operations in accordance with the laws and customs of war'	47
j. General application of the Article 4(A)(2) criteria	53
k. 'government not recognized'	60
l. 'persons who accompany the armed forces'	65
m. 'members of crews […] of the merchant marine and […] civil aircraft'	70
n. 'inhabitants of non-occupied territory, who […] spontaneously take up arms'	72
II. Article 4(B)	77
C. Critical Assessment	79

Select Bibliography

Canada, Chief of Defence Staff, *Law of Armed Conflict at the Operational and Tactical Levels* (Ottawa, 13 August 2001)

Dinstein, Y., *The Conduct of Hostilities under the Law of International Armed Conflict* (2nd edn, Cambridge: CUP, 2010)

Esgain, A./Solf, W., 'The 1949 Geneva Conventions Relating to the Treatment of Prisoners of War: Its Principles, Innovations, and Deficiencies', 41 *North Carolina Law Review* (1963) 537

Germany, Ministry of Defence, *Humanitarian Law in Armed Conflicts Manual* (Bonn, 1992)

Israel, Military Court at Ramallah, *Military Prosecutor v Kassem and others*, 13 April 1969

Levie, H., *Prisoners of War in International Armed Conflict* (Newport, RI: Naval War College Press, 1978) vol 59

Pictet Commentary GC III

UK, House of Lords Privy Council, *Osman Bin Haji Mohamed Ali v Public Prosecutor*, 29 July 1969, Law Reports, vol I, 430

UK, Ministry of Defence, *The Manual of the Law of Armed Conflict* (Oxford: OUP, 2004)

US, Dept of the Army, *Field Manual 27-10 The Law of Land Warfare* (18 July 1956)

US, Dept of the Army, *Army Regulation 190-8, Enemy Prisoners of War, Retained Personnel, Civilian Internees and Other Detainees* (1 October 1997)

A. Introduction

1 It is difficult to overstate the importance of prisoner of war (POW) status to international humanitarian law (IHL). Far more than a mere administrative label or legal moniker, POW status is the most important IHL instrument for addressing the inherent conflict of interest of wartime detention. During armed conflict, states are frequently faced with the competing goals of, on the one hand, reducing enemy capacity and will to fight through destructive means, and, on the other hand, being entirely responsible for the health, welfare, and life-sustaining functions of captured and surrendered enemies. History has shown states are often unable to strike a principled humanitarian balance between these competing concerns, especially under the strain of armed conflict. Historically, dismal POW detention conditions and low survival rates have been a testament to the wisdom of committing POW treatment standards to international law. The elaborate, and frankly onerous, treatment standards developed by states for Geneva Convention (GC) III have made great strides in humanizing wartime detention on a number of fronts. In addition to ensuring humane and respectful conditions of detention, GC III has made the prospect of surrender less daunting in some cases, speeding the termination of hostilities that might otherwise persist as unnecessary and protracted fights to the death.

2 Historically, qualifications for POW status were quite simple. States typically reserved POW status as a matter of custom, and later treaty law, for members of the opposing state's regular armed forces. Late nineteenth- and early twentieth-century codifications, however, expanded the POW class to include other groups, including certain militias and other persons who routinely accompanied armed forces in battle. The 1929 Geneva Convention Relative to the Treatment of Prisoners of War (1929 GC II) consciously omitted a definition of 'prisoner of war', opting to rely instead on the Hague tradition's conception of belligerent groups.[1] The result has been perceived as a merger of sorts between conditions for POW status and conditions expected of combatants generally. Generous treatment obligations notwithstanding, many regard combatant immunity—insulation from prosecution for warlike acts that do not violate IHL—as the most significant by-product of POW status for the majority of subcategories of POW. This widely held view persists despite the fact that not one of GC III's 143 Articles mentions combatant immunity.[2] Understanding the relationship between POW status and combatant immunity is thus an important aspect of GC III. This commentary will advocate an understanding of Article 4 GC III that is limited to determining POW status independently from controversial questions of combatant or unlawful combatant status. The primary benefits of this approach are to identify areas of interpretive consensus and to apply the remarkably humanitarian internment regime of GC III as widely as intended by the Convention's drafters.

3 The GC III provisions on POW qualification appear as Articles 4 and 5. Article 4, the longest of the GC III articles, identifies six groups whose members qualify for POW status. The primary legal significance of POW status is to activate the remaining Parts and Sections of GC III that outline POW treatment standards and obligations. Article 5

---

[1] Pictet Commentary GC III, at 13.
[2] The Geneva Conventions did not address combatant immunity. It is only since 1977 that Art 43 AP I states: 'Members of the armed forces [...] are combatants, that is to say, they have the right to participate directly in hostilities.'

represents the Conventions' effort to guarantee regularity in the procedures Detaining Powers use to evaluate POW status and will be discussed in Chapter 46 of this volume.

While the POW qualification provisions of GC III present a contrast in length and detail, they share the characteristic of vexing interpretive ambiguity. Immediately after the Conventions entered into force, states' armed forces and legal representatives struggled to operationalize the GC III POW qualification provisions through practice. Each provision reflects simultaneously the Conventions' important goal of preserving humanity in armed conflict while securing broad substantive legal consensus among states. While each serves as a critical gateway to important protections for victims of war, these Articles also reflect the regulatory limits of international consensus and compromise.

There is no small irony that the drafters' effort to clarify entitlement to POW status provokes an extensive interpretive commentary such as that offered by this chapter and by previous commentators. Yet 50 years after entering into force, the qualification conditions for POW status remain contested in many respects. The language of Article 4 often permits both sides of debates on POW classification issues to claim victory. In addition to commenting on and, it is hoped, clarifying the GC III POW qualification provisions, this chapter offers brief observations on present and future interpretive issues relating to the important function of detainee status determinations.

B. Meaning and Application

Article 4(A) GC III enumerates six groups whose members are eligible for POW status. Although qualification criteria vary between groups, once members of a qualifying group have fallen into the power of an enemy, they qualify unequivocally for POW status. That is, GC III makes no further distinctions between the six groups. For instance, although distinctions may be made or even required between officers and enlisted POWs, the fact that a detained enemy qualifies by virtue of membership in the regular armed forces rather than by virtue of participation in a *levée en masse* (see MN 72–76), is not itself a basis for further distinction under the Convention. Additionally, Article 4(B) describes circumstances in which certain persons under the power of an enemy party are to be treated consistent with POWs, though not necessarily accorded *de jure* POW status.

I. Article 4(A)

The six groups enumerated in Article 4(A) often seem to run together or bleed over, particularly with regard to use of military terms of art such as 'armed forces' and 'militia'. The greatest interpretive challenge of Article 4 has been to develop a distinct meaning and identity for each of the six groups. The following sections evaluate and distinguish each of the Article 4(A) groups in turn.

a. *'fallen into the power of the enemy'*

Drafters of Article 4(A) adopted the phrase 'fallen into the power of the enemy' to replace the term 'capture' which had appeared in previous instruments regulating treatment of POWs.[3] Armed conflicts preceding GC III had seen various efforts by states to reclassify or alter the status of POWs. For instance, military personnel captured following political

---

[3] Art 1(1) 1929 GC II.

capitulation, but not conflict termination, were widely denied POW status in the Second World War.[4] Detaining Powers also withdrew or denied POW status to captured military personnel accused of war crimes or who had attempted to escape internment.[5] Use of the phrase 'fallen into the power of the enemy' in GC III, however, does not appear intended to operate particularly exclusively. Instead, 'fallen into the power of' includes detention, captivity, or enemy control, regardless of the circumstances that gave rise to these conditions. Whether by surrender, surprise capture, desertion,[6] or having been overcome by active force, members of Article 4 qualifying groups are POWs once under the power of enemy forces.[7]

9   Some measure of ongoing physical control or restraint on personal liberty seems required by Article 4. Typically such control takes the form of either internment or parole. Indeed, nearly every protective provision of GC III that follows from Article 4 classification anticipates some restraint on liberty.[8] In this respect the term 'fallen into the power of' differs somewhat from GC IV treatment of civilians. Article 4 GC IV uses the term 'in the hands of a Party to the conflict' to identify civilians eligible for GC IV protected person status.[9] Where mere presence in territory controlled by foreign, enemy forces is sufficient to establish protected person status under GC IV, a measure of personal control or captivity is clearly foreseen by GC III POW status. Thus it is clear that GC III obligations would not attach to Article 4 GC III groups merely operating or residing in occupied or enemy-controlled territory.

10 Generally, Detaining Powers make determinations of entitlement to POW status at or near the beginning of detention. The general rule, confirmed by Article 5 GC III, is that such determinations persist for the duration of detention. That is, once a Detaining Power determines an individual is entitled to POW status under Article 4(A), nothing short of repatriation can divest POW status. Changes neither in the nature of the armed conflict nor in the nature of the parties to the conflict can divest a POW of the protections of GC III. For instance, consider the case of an international armed conflict (IAC) that has been converted into a non-international armed conflict (NIAC) by virtue of a change in the nature of the parties involved. Although the non-international character of the converted conflict would generally excuse Detaining Powers from classifying captured fighters as POWs, POWs captured prior to conversion of the armed conflict's character would undoubtedly retain their protected status under GC III for the duration of their detention. The question of NIACs that have been converted to IACs by virtue of involvement of an opposing state party to the Conventions has surfaced recently, and is treated in Chapters 1 and 2 of this volume. Whether such transformations in the nature of armed conflicts can

---

[4] Pictet Commentary GC III, at 75 (citing *Report of the International Committee of the Red Cross on its activities during the Second World War*).

[5] Ibid, at 76.

[6] The 1990–1 Gulf War featured widespread desertions by Iraqi armed forces, all of whom were treated as POWs by UK forces. P. Rowe, 'Prisoners of War in the Gulf Area', in P. Rowe (ed), *The Gulf War 1990–91 in International and English Law* (London: Sweet & Maxwell, 1993) 188, at 191. The question of the status and treatment of deserters remains somewhat unsettled in scholarly circles. In particular, concern for the safety of deserters exists in light of the requirement that POWs be detained collectively with other POWs. M. Sassòli, 'The Status, Treatment and Repatriation of Deserters under International Humanitarian Law', *International Institute of Humanitarian Law, Yearbook* (1985) 9.

[7] Following Germany's surrender in the Second World War, France maintained that hundreds of thousands of members of the German armed forces who had surrendered rather than having been 'captured' were not POWs but rather 'Surrendered Enemy Personnel'. H. Levie, *Prisoners of War in International Armed Conflict* (Newport, RI: Naval War College Press, 1978), vol 59, at 35, fn 136.

[8] Part III, GC III.   [9] Art 4 GC IV and see Ch 55 of this volume.

affect POW status of detained persons is worthy of brief consideration. No provision of Article 4 explicitly addresses the possibility of a change in the character of a conflict affecting the status of detained persons. That is, GC III does not appear to anticipate that detained members of a non-state, organized armed group formerly fighting a NIAC would become POWs simply by virtue of their organization later affiliating itself with state's armed forces sufficient to convert the armed conflict into one of an international character. While considerable humanitarian and equitable considerations might counsel according POW status to such detainees *ex post* detention and classification, it cannot be said that GC III compels such an outcome. According such detainees POW status as a matter of practice or policy might be commendable and/or even achieved by agreement of the parties to the conflict. But as a general matter, permitting post-capture events to alter determinations of status appears a dangerous course of action, too susceptible to manipulation by Detaining Powers, and therefore deliberately rejected by the drafters of the GC III.

b. 'members of the armed forces'

In terms of coverage, Article 4(A)(1) reflects the longest-established and, historically, the least-controversial subcategory of POW. Members of states' regular armed forces were the prototypical POW class long before GC III.[10] Numerically, members of regular armed forces of states have also comprised the vast majority of POWs.[11] The exact composition of, and prerequisites for, membership in states' armed forces have not been matters committed to international law.[12] The prevalent practice has been for states to organize and define membership in their armed forces through domestic legislation.[13]

Whether mere membership in the armed forces is alone sufficient to establish Article 4(A)(1) status is unclear. Some commentators identify additional criteria, found in earlier Hague Regulations Articles 1, 2, and 3, as implied requirements of POW status under Article 4(A)(1), especially as a matter of customary international law.[14] The Privy Council adopted such a view of Article 4(A)(1) in the *Mohamed Ali* case.[15] The Privy Council gave especially strong weight to the 1958 British *Manual of Military Law*, which stated, 'Should *regular* combatants fail to comply with these four conditions, they may in certain cases become unprivileged belligerents. This would mean that they would not be entitled to the status of prisoners of war upon their capture'.[16]

The Privy Council's inclusive view of Article 4(A)(1) with respect to the Article 4(A)(2) conditions is further supported by the Conventions' relationship to the Hague Regulations. The 1949 Geneva Conventions are not typically understood to displace the Hague Tradition;[17] instead, the Conventions supplement the Hague Regulations. In this

---

[10] Lieber Code, Art 49.
[11] In the 1991 Gulf War, the overwhelming majority of approximately 86,000 Iraqi POWs were members of the Iraqi armed forces under the power of coalition forces. Rowe, above n 6, at 188.
[12] L. Oppenheim, *International Law: War and Neutrality* (London: Longmans, Green and Co, 1912), vol II, at 94.
[13] Levie, above n 7, at 36.
[14] Y. Dinstein, *The Conduct of Hostilities under the Law of International Armed Conflict* (2nd edn, New York: CUP, 2010), at 42–4; Pictet Commentary GC III, 62–3.
[15] UK, House of Lords Privy Council, *Osman Bin Haji Mohamed Ali v Public Prosecutor*, 29 July 1969, Law Reports, vol I, 430.
[16] Ibid, citing UK *Manual of Military Law* (London: HMSO, 1958) Part III, para 96.
[17] Art 135 GC III.

respect, one might reasonably expect states to require that detained persons claiming POW status pursuant to Article 4(A)(1) have complied with the four criteria enumerated in Article 4(A)(2) and earlier in the Hague Regulations.[18]

14   Still, the textual case for non-applicability of the Article 4(A)(2) and Hague conditions to Article 4(A)(1) groups is compelling. First, ordinary canons of statutory interpretation counsel that the four Hague criteria's enumeration in a subsequent, though separate, POW qualification provision of GC III indicates the criteria do not operate with respect to regular armed forces described in Article 4(A)(1). Incorporating by inference, and without reference, the Article 4(A)(2) conditions into Article 4(A)(1) violates a fundamental canon of interpretation and does violence to what appears to have been a deliberate drafting decision.[19]

15   Secondly, the historical use of the Hague conditions does not support their use against regular armed forces and armies. The Hague Regulations themselves employ the four conditions appearing later in Article 4(A)(2) GC III only to identify *militias and volunteer corps* qualifying for the rights and duties of war. Like GC III, the Hague Regulations' use of the criteria does not appear in proximity to an enumeration of *'armies'*.

16   Moreover, the clause immediately following the Hague Regulations' four conditions describes the possibility of militia and volunteer corps constituting a state's 'army'. The Article instructs states to consider such forces under the Regulations' denomination of 'army', rather than as militia or volunteer corps. It is likely that states regarded integration of a militia into regular armed forces as a sufficient guarantee that the concerns addressed by the four conditions would be met by co-location or incorporation, or would be otherwise unnecessary. States appear to have thought that, like the armed forces of which they would form part, integrated militia and volunteer corps would exhibit the traditional aspects of military organization and appearance so important to the ordered and disciplined conduct of hostilities. The most immediately relevant legal result seems to be that militia and volunteer corps comprising a state's 'army' should not in a *de jure* sense be subject to the four conditions applicable to militia and volunteer corps generally.

17   Thirdly, current military manuals do not lend significant support to the inclusive view of Article 4(A)(1) GC III regular armed forces with respect to the Article 4(A)(2) conditions. In fact, the 2004 UK *Manual of the Law of Armed Conflict*, which replaced the 1958 *Manual of Military Law* relied upon by the Privy Council in the *Mohamed Ali* case (see MN 12), does not include the passage incorporating Article 4(A)(2) criteria to regular armed forces at all.

18   It is true, the current UK *Manual* requires that organized armed forces of a party serve 'under a command responsible […] for the conduct of its subordinates' and be 'subject to an internal disciplinary system'.[20] Yet inclusion of these two conditions on regular armed forces' POW status seems derived from Additional Protocol I (AP I), to which the UK is party, rather than from Article 4(A)(2) GC III. Additional Protocol I employs both of the conditions included in the current UK *Manual* in its definition of 'armed forces'.[21] Had the UK derived from Article 4(A)(2) GC III any conditions on regular armed forces POW

---

[18] In fact, the four criteria are of earlier vintage than the Hague Conventions, appearing initially in the 1874 Brussels Declaration, which never entered into force.
[19] Final Record, vol II-A, at 466.
[20] UK, Ministry of Defence, *The Manual of the Law of Armed Conflict* (Oxford: OUP, 2004), para 8.3.1.
[21] Art 43(1) AP I.

status other than mere membership, one would have expected enumeration of all four Article 4(A)(2) GC III criteria.

Military manuals of other states party to AP I instruct their armed forces similarly. The Canadian *Law of Armed Conflict* manual describes regular armed forces entitled to POW status only with respect to the two Article 43 AP I criteria.[22] And the German manual *Humanitarian Law in Armed Conflicts* merely mentions the two AP I criteria for regular armed forces as well.[23]

The work of respected IHL commentators supports the non-inclusive view as well. Contrasting members of armed forces with independently operating volunteer and militia corps, Draper observed, 'Members of the armed forces who persistently violate the Law of War do not lose their POW status upon capture. The effect of Articles 4, 5 and 85 of the Geneva POW Convention, 1949, makes this clear.'[24] Other commentators have shared this view.[25] Lastly, states have not publicly cited failure to comply with the Article 4(A)(2) criteria by members of armed forces as a basis for denying POW status during modern armed conflicts. Although records of POW classification tribunals conducted under Article 5 vary in detail and completeness, the author is aware of no clear-cut POW status denials that were based on an individual member of the armed forces' (or the entire force's) failure to adhere to the Article 4(A)(2) criteria in any recent IAC.

Therefore, the plainest reading of Article 4(A)(1) is the soundest. Members of regular armed forces qualify for POW status under GC III simply by virtue of their membership in such organizations. Determinations of status under Article 4(A)(1) should require only reliable indicia of status, such as an identification card, leave and earnings statement, or similar documentary, physical, or testimonial evidence indicating membership in a state party's regular armed forces as determined by domestic law. Failure to observe the four Hague criteria seems irrelevant for POW status determinations under Article 4(A)(1) and better left to the separate matter of identifying individual misconduct or war crimes. To be sure, state determinations of POW status by virtue of membership in armed forces under AP I or customary law may take into account an individual's battlefield conduct and appearance. This is especially true with respect to combatants' obligations to distinguish themselves from civilians and to carry arms openly during attack, both of which are mentioned explicitly as prerequisites to POW status in AP I.[26]

c. *'militias or volunteer corps forming part of '*

Previous law-of-war instruments employed the term 'form part of' with a literal or physical connotation.[27] It seems members of irregular armed groups or militias could be accorded POW status only by physically accompanying, integrating into, or attaching to formations of regular armed forces in combat or manoeuvres.

---

[22] Canada, Chief of Defence Staff, *Law of Armed Conflict at the Operational and Tactical Levels* (Ottawa, 13 August 2001), paras 304, 1006.1.a.
[23] Germany, Ministry of Defence, *Humanitarian Law in Armed Conflicts Manual* (Bonn, 1992), paras 304, 705.
[24] G. Draper, 'The Present Law as to Combatancy', in M. Meyer and H. McCoubrey (eds), *Reflections on Law and Armed Conflicts: The Selected Works on the Laws of War by the Late Professor Colonel G.I.A.D. Draper, OBE* (The Hague: Kluwer Law, 1998) 197, at 197.
[25] Sassòli/Bouvier/Quintin, at 178.   [26] Art 44(3)–(4) AP I.
[27] Art 1 Hague Regulations; Art 21, Institute of International Law, *Oxford Manual on the Laws of War on Land* (9 September 1880).

23   Use of the term by Article 4(A)(1) GC III, however, seems to intend a less physical or literally corporeal meaning. Under GC III, militia or volunteer corps may be said to form part of a state's armed forces, and therefore qualify for POW status under Article 4(A)(1), merely by bureaucratic measures of organization. Attachment orders, designations of command authority, orders confirming operational or administrative control, or other military bureaucratic measures are common means to accomplish the sort of integration likely anticipated by Article 4(A)(1). Thus members of militias and volunteer corps might qualify for POW status under Article 4(A)(1) regardless of failure physically to co-locate or operate alongside regular armed forces. Such an understanding is consistent with expressions at the Conventions' Diplomatic Conference in favour of acknowledging the wide variety in tables of organization of modern armed forces.[28]

d. 'militias [...] volunteer corps [...] organized resistance movements'

24   Article 4(A)(2) reflects a perennial debate in the codification of POW qualification criteria. The topic provoked significant deliberation and dispute at the Conventions' 1949 Diplomatic Conference, as it had at nearly every preceding conference that addressed the status of captured irregular fighters.[29] The first interpretive task of Article 4(A)(2) is to identify a class of organization distinct from the regular, conventional armed groups and militia groups forming part thereof described in Article 4(A)(1). The task is not easy, as both provisions employ the phrase 'militia or volunteer corps', with Article 4(A)(2) simply adding reference to 'organized resistance movements'.

25   The soundest approach likely appreciates Article 4(A)(2) groups as operating entirely independently from the formations and tables of organization of regular armed forces. The record of the Diplomatic Conference indicates that states supporting the inclusion of such groups envisioned that partisans and guerillas would be included in this description in particular.[30] Whereas militias and volunteer corps described in Article 4(A)(1) evince indicia of integration into (hence 'forming part of') regular armed forces, the organizations enumerated in Article 4(A)(2) should be understood to operate without such connections to regular armed forces or other Article 4(A)(1) groups. Independent command, separate lines of authority, and other aspects of autonomous operations may be indicative of the militias and volunteer corps described by Article 4(A)(2). While not dispositive, peculiarities of states' domestic organizing legislation may also assist efforts to distinguish Article 4(A)(2) militia from those of Article 4(A)(1).[31] In sum, Article 4(A)(2) militia are distinct from those of Article 4(A)(1) by virtue of action, operation, and regulation independent from a state's regular armed forces.

e. 'belonging to a Party to the conflict'

26   '[B]elonging to a Party to the conflict' is perhaps the least appreciated condition of Article 4(A)(2) POW status.[32] In some sense the term expresses the fundamental requirement

---

[28] Final Record, vol II-A, at 237–8.   [29] Ibid, at 238–42.
[30] Ibid, at 561.
[31] Ibid, at 237. British representatives at the Diplomatic Conference described such militia as part of their general organization of defences.
[32] Israel, Military Court at Ramallah, *Military Prosecutor v Kassem and others*, 13 April 1969. The *Kassem* court observed, 'the literature on the subject overlooks the most basic condition of the right of combatants to be considered as prisoners of war, namely, the condition that the irregular forces must belong to a belligerent party'. Ibid.

that those participating in armed conflict be part of a collective effort. War has always been distinguished as a collective endeavour, distinct from acts of individual violence. So the GC III requirement of belonging to a state was not novel, and indeed is not unique to the POW qualifications of the 1949 Conventions. For instance, Article 2 of each Geneva Convention limits material applicability to armed conflict between states parties.[33] Thus armed conflict, no matter its intensity or duration, between groups not belonging to states parties to the Conventions can never implicate the POW status provisions of GC III.

Sound interpretation counsels that the 'belonging to' requirement not merely duplicate the later, Article 4(A)(2) criterion of being subject to command or other authority. Thus the requirement of 'belonging to a Party' is best understood as a comment on the nature of the authority the militia or volunteer corps in question answers to overall. That is, the relevant inquiry examines the group's relationship, if any, with a sponsoring state rather than the internal aspects and organization of the group itself. The 'belonging to' provision clearly anticipates that Article 4(A)(2) militias and volunteer corps belong to a state—a legal entity capable of ratifying or acceding to the Conventions as a 'Party'. Therefore only militia, volunteer corps, and organized resistance movements that enjoy the sanction or imprimatur of a state may legitimately claim POW status under Article 4(A)(2). 27

It seems that acceptable indicia or evidence of 'belonging' might take any number of forms. As a general matter, Article 4 does not offer examples or details concerning evidentiary burdens or requisite proof. Like questions with respect to the organization and composition of regular armed forces, particulars of how a state indicates belonging, possession, or sanction of an Article 4(A)(2) group are better regarded as aspects of domestic rather than international law. The most obvious and reliable means of indicating belonging, however, would be domestic legislation or some other form of codified municipal law such as an executive order. 28

Pictet's Commentary observes that no express indication or authorization is necessary to establish belonging. In fact, the Commentary's understanding of Article 4(A)(2) abandons all requirements of formality, accepting *de facto* relationships as sufficient to indicate belonging.[34] For example, Pictet argues that aspects of a group's operations, such as 'deliveries of equipment and supplies', might indicate that a group belongs to a state.[35] 29

Although not addressed specifically to POW status determinations, later legal developments call the Commentary's operational view of 'belonging' into question. Evaluating relationships between irregular armed groups and states for purposes of state responsibility and conflict classification, international tribunals have generally not regarded mere logistical support as sufficient to attribute to or associate such groups with a state.[36] Instead, current doctrine appears to recognize *de facto* relationships more commonly in conditions where the state in question controls or directs operations.[37] 30

---

[33] See Ch 1 of this volume.
[34] Pictet Commentary GC III, at 57. For the view that *de facto* arrangements cannot be accepted as evidence of belonging, see Levie, above n 7, at 43.
[35] Pictet Commentary GC III, at 57.
[36] ICTY, *The Prosecutor v Duško Tadić*, Appeals Chamber Judgment, IT-94-1-A, 15 July 1999, paras 92, 131–40, 145, 162; ICJ, *Military and Paramilitary Activities in and against Nicaragua (Nicaragua v United States)*, Judgment, 27 June 1986, para 115.
[37] K. Del Mar, 'The Requirement of "Belonging" under International Humanitarian Law', 21 *EJIL* (2010) 105, at 110–13.

Thus a situation that satisfies requirements of control, for purposes of conflict classification for instance, might conceivably also satisfy the requirement of 'belonging to a Party' for purposes of Article 4(A)(2) POW classification. Still, as some authors conclude, the 'belonging to' requirement likely carries a meaning distinct from the doctrines used for attribution of acts of an armed group to a state or for purposes of conflict classification.[38] Merely providing supplies or other logistical support does not seem sufficient to establish that an organized group belongs to a state for purposes of Article 4(A)(2) POW classification. The rationale of the 'belonging to' requirement seems logically related to the goal of guaranteeing state responsibility for the conduct of the organized group in question. Where formal sanction and imprimatur, or even operational control and direction, might assure responsibility, mere logistical support offers no guarantee that the state in question actually influences the operations of the organization under consideration, or is willing to accept responsibility for its operations. Thus it seems the soundest understanding admits *de facto* evidence of belonging but calls for something more than mere logistical support.

31 Early drafts of GC III required that Article 4(A)(2) groups or their sponsoring states provide enemy state parties notice of participation in hostilities and therefore the fact of their 'belonging'.[39] A further proposal was more specific, envisioning a bilateral exchange on the subject between warring powers. The latter proposal required notice of irregular groups' participation in hostilities 'through a means by which they are able to make and reply to communications' as a prerequisite to conferring POW status on members of such groups.[40] Governments in exile during the Second World War made such declarations with respect to resistance forces.[41] Ultimately, however, states abandoned any reference to notice in favour of the requirement simply of 'belonging' to a party. Although the practice of providing notice of belonging might prove wise or facilitate Article 4(A)(2) determinations by Detaining Powers, there is presently no affirmative requirement to communicate that an armed group or militia belongs to a state party.

f. 'commanded by a person responsible'

32 The fact of command is sufficient to satisfy the first of the four, alpha-numerically enumerated conditions for Article 4(A)(2) groups' POW status. As is true of the four conditions generally, indications of command can be borrowed from the traditional characteristics of regular armed forces. Regularly issuing orders, planning and leading operations, disseminating instructions, conducting training, and supervising activities are common indications of command presence.[42]

33 There are no suggestions that formal indicia of command, such as appointment orders, tables of organization, orders of battle, or other military formalities, are required of Article 4(A)(2) groups. Nor is there any indication that an Article 4(A)(2) group's commander or

---

[38] Ibid.
[39] International Conference of the Red Cross, *Report of the XVIIth International Conference of the Red Cross, Draft Revised or New Conventions for the Protection of War Victims*, 1948, at 53.
[40] Final Record, vol III, at 58 and 62.
[41] K. Marek, *Identity and Continuity of States in Public International Law* (2nd edn, Geneva: Librairie Droz SA, 1968), at 441, fn 8. The Dutch Royal Emergency Decree of September 1944 incorporated the Netherlands Forces of the Interior into the Dutch Army: ibid.
[42] US, Dept of the Army, *Regulation 600-20, Army Command Policy* (20 September 2012), para 1-5.

other leaders must hold a military position, rank, or affiliation other than *de facto* leader of the organization in question.

Although no particular standard is indicated, it is reasonable to conclude that some level of compliance by subordinates or effectiveness is required. A showing that the commander regularly influences the actions and activities of the group's members seems sufficient to establish command for purposes of POW classification. Effectiveness of command to the degree required to establish superior responsibility under international criminal law does not seem to be called for under Article 4(A)(2)(a). For instance, when enemy operations prevent the exercise of command and control, a commander may be said no longer to exercise effective command and may therefore no longer be held personally liable for his subordinates' actions.[43] The same should not be said for Article 4(A)(2)(a) analysis of groups. That is, disruptions of command owing to enemy operations should not prevent an organization that previously or ordinarily enjoyed an effective command structure from qualifying under Article 4(A)(2)(a).

The rationale for the command requirement is not related exclusively to identifying groups appropriate for POW status. The command requirement also bolsters broader goals of battlefield discipline and order, comprising an incentive to irregular armed groups to organize themselves and account for their operations. Additionally, the command criterion strengthens the enforcement of IHL generally, serving as support for the operation of command or superior responsibility as a theory of vicarious liability in military justice and international criminal law.

g. 'fixed distinctive sign'

The display of uniforms and insignia has long been regarded as a prima facie indication of combatancy and therefore of entitlement to POW status. In fact, the treatment provisions of GC III envision POWs maintaining military insignia and uniforms even while in captivity.[44] It is therefore unsurprising that Article 4(A)(2) requires that irregular fighting groups display a fixed distinctive sign to qualify for POW status.

Distinctive signs need not amount to a full military uniform to satisfy Article 4(A)(2)(b). The requirement appears instead to envision a functional approach. Badges, patches, flashes, and other standardized apparel may satisfy the requirement.[45] The essential minimums appear to be a degree of uniformity within the group in question, some measure of consistency over time, and, of course, visible distinction from the appearance of the civilian population. Pictet in particular emphasizes the importance of groups maintaining a single, unvarying emblem.[46] Pictet also emphasizes exclusivity, suggesting a distinctive sign 'must be used only by that organization'. Examples of recognized signs might also include hats, scarves, and armbands.[47]

---

[43] ICTY, *The Prosecutor v Zejnil Delalić et al*, Appeals Chamber Judgment, IT-96-21-A, 20 February 2001, para 197 (quoting ICTY, *The Prosecutor v Zejnil Delalić*, Trial Chamber Judgment, IT-96-21-T, 16 November 1998); ICTY, *The Prosecutor v Timohir Blaškić*, Appeals Chamber Judgment, IT-14-A, 19 July 2004, para 67; ICTY, *The Prosecutor v Enver Hadžihasanović*, Decision on Joint Defence Interlocutory Appeal of Trial Chamber Decision on Rule 98*bis* Motions for Acquittal, IT-01-47-T, 11 March 2005, para 164.
[44] Art 40 GC III.   [45] *Kassem and others*, above n 32.
[46] Pictet Commentary GC III, at 60.
[47] H. Parks, 'Special Forces' Wear of Non-Standard Uniforms', 4 *Chicago JIL* (2003) 493–560, at 517, 542; J. Spaight, *War Rights on Land* (London: MacMillan and Co, 1911), at 57. Levie argues that such removable articles violate the requirement that signs be 'fixed': Levie, above n 7, at 48.

38   While persuasive sources suggest that display should be constant, practice and practical considerations suggest that something less than literally constant display satisfies the requirement.[48] For example, failure by a group to display its distinctive sign while not engaged in military operations or while truly disengaged from military service should not disqualify that organization under Article 4(A)(2)(b). Groups' practices such as authorizing the wear of civilian attire in some circumstances should not disqualify a group from POW status. The essential consideration seems to be that failures to display distinctive signs be unrelated to operational concerns and not deliberately result in military advantage. Thus, failure to display distinctive insignia or uniforms while conducting personal hygiene or physical fitness training, should not compromise groups' technical adherence to the Article 4(A)(2)(b) condition.

39   The rationale for the distinctive sign requirement is not only to facilitate identification and therefore classification of group members upon capture. The distinctive sign requirement serves broader humanitarian ideals as well. Uniforms and other visual indications of combatant status are essential to successful observance of the principle of distinction in attacks. In fact, the requirement that attackers limit the effects of military operations to combatants to the greatest extent feasible, relies extensively on defenders' prominent and regular display of distinctively military insignia and apparel.[49] Accordingly, perceived relaxation of this requirement by AP I provoked sharp criticism and legal consternation.[50]

40   The logic of the distinctive sign requirement seems to extend to vehicles and other means used by groups claiming POW status under Article 4(A)(2). It is possible that failure by an organization regularly to mark its vehicles may disqualify members from POW status under the provision. Pictet is unequivocal in stating that an organization's distinctive sign must be displayed by its vehicles.

41   Modern practice with respect to land vehicles in particular calls the marking requirement into question, especially for purposes of POW status determinations. While marking of ships and aircraft seems to be an absolute requirement,[51] marking of ground transport seems less consistent.[52] Modern practice seems to rely on the inherent or visibly military character of land vehicles, such as tanks or mobile artillery, to satisfy the marking requirement rather than markings and insignia. It is likely the marking requirement is reserved to vehicles lacking a distinctively military appearance. Overall, vehicle marking seems less relevant to determining POW status under Article 4(A)(2) than to issues concerning the principle of distinction for purposes of targeting.

42   The question of recognizable signs has been raised recently. Especially in conflicts between dissimilar cultures, confusion and difficulties may arise with respect to recognition of distinctive signs. In 2002, a US Government memorandum analysing the status of captured fighters noted that the Afghan Taliban wore clothing indistinguishable from that of local civilians.[53] Although reports also indicated that Taliban members regularly

---

[48] Pictet Commentary GC III, at 59–60.   [49] Arts 44(3) and 58(c) AP I.   [50] Art 44(3) AP I.

[51] Harvard Program on Humanitarian Policy and Conflict Research, *Manual on International Law Applicable to Air and Missile Warfare* (March 2010), Rule 1(x); Institute of International Humanitarian Law, *San Remo Manual on International Law Applicable to Armed Conflicts at Sea* (12 June 1994), para 13(g).

[52] M. Matheson, 'The United States Position on the Relation of Customary International Law to the 1977 Protocols Additional to the 1949 Geneva Conventions', 2 *American University Journal of International Law and Policy* (1987) 415, at 419.

[53] US Dept of Justice, Office of Legal Counsel, 'Status of Taliban Forces Under Article 4 of the Third Geneva Convention', in J. Dratel and K. Greeberg (eds), *The Torture Memos* (New York: CUP, 2005) 136, at 138.

wore black turbans, the memorandum concluded they were worn by coincidence rather than by design. One memorandum observed, 'there is no indication that black turbans were systematically worn to serve as an identifying feature of the armed group'.[54]

43 There is no apparent requirement that militia or volunteer corps, or the state to which they belong for that matter, register or provide notice of the sign or emblem they will use. Instead, GC III appears to rely on repeated exposure, consistency, and the inherent military character of signs to establish their being interpreted as qualifying distinctive insignia of a fighting organization.

h. 'carrying arms openly'

44 Of the four criteria, Article 4(A)(2)(c) presents perhaps the least textual ambiguity.[55] The 'carrying arms openly' requirement seems concerned primarily with communicating the military character of a group. Persons carrying weapons, particularly weapons of a peculiarly military character, such as crew-served weapons or rockets, make clear their battlefield role and, in some cases by weapon type, their affiliation. Groups that permit members to carry weapons in holsters or protective cases should not be precluded from Article 4(A)(2) status. Like the requirement for distinctive insignia, a functional analysis seems appropriate. The 'carrying arms openly' condition of Article 4(A)(2)(c) should disqualify only groups that routinely encourage members to hide weapons in order to mask their members' military character or to gain a tactical advantage from enemy forbearance.

45 Like the requirement of displaying distinctive insignia, in addition to informing POW status determinations, Article 4(A)(2)(c) vindicates important humanitarian concerns related to the principle of distinction. At least at the time of the Conventions' drafting, open display of means of war was usually a reliable indication of intent to participate in hostilities, and often an indication of membership in an organized armed group. Recent analysis emphasizes that carrying weapons openly might not always serve to distinguish militias from civilians, especially in areas where the general population carries weapons regularly.[56]

46 Modern operations, for instance cyber operations during armed conflict, might call into question the nature and exact parameters of the term 'arms'. A recent manual on the subject of IHL and cyber warfare retained the requirement, though noted that display of the arms of cyber warfare (laptops, servers, etc) seem ill-suited to vindicating the rationale of the 'carrying arms openly' requirement.[57]

i. 'conducting operations in accordance with the laws and customs of war'

47 The condition that states' militia and volunteer corps that do not form part of the regular armed forces conduct their operations according to 'the laws and customs of war' seems never to have been in doubt for inclusion in Article 4(A)(2). The requirement is entirely in keeping with the 1949 Conventions' effort to emphasize implementation and enforcement to a greater degree than their IHL predecessors. As effectively as any other criterion, the IHL compliance criterion sorts out honourable fighting organizations from brigands and opportunists who leverage the chaos of the battlefield to personal advantage. Article 4(A)(2)(d) also ensures a degree of reciprocal observance of the Conventions to the

---

[54] Ibid. [55] Levie, above n 7, at 50. [56] Ibid.
[57] M.N. Schmitt et al (eds), *Tallinn Manual on International Law Applicable to Cyber Warfare* (Cambridge: CUP, 2013), Rule 26, para 13.

extent one envisions reciprocity as having continued relevance in IHL.[58] In addition to supporting the POW classification function, Article 4(A)(2)(d) also supports the important goal of inducing and reinforcing IHL compliance.

48   The relative indeterminacy of IHL is by now notorious. Differences of opinion concerning its content and meaning have been manifest not only between adversaries, but even within established military alliances and on eminent panels of international tribunals.[59] Accordingly, questions may arise as to what rules and norms are included in the 'laws and customs of war'. As a pragmatic tool for classification, it seems best to envision Article 4(A)(2)(d) as concerning violations of only an indisputable nature or universal rules and customs of war. Close legal interpretive calls, cutting-edge legal debates, and controversial rules do not seem the appropriate focus of Article 4(A)(2)(d). Only laws and customs on which widespread agreement and support is evident should be considered in Article 4(A)(2)(d) inquiries.

49   Still, evaluating the scope of rules and customs at issue, it seems one must envision an evolving body of law. Any question of freezing the corpus of law to the period when the Conventions were drafted seems neither textually compelled nor consistent with the historical roots of the condition of IHL compliance itself. Thus, application of Article 4(A)(2)(d) seems to require a contemporaneous snapshot of applicable law and norms rather than a retrospective analysis. Furthermore, armed groups clearly cannot be held to standards drawn from instruments not ratified by the party to which they belong. The *corpus juris* for Article 4(A)(2)(d) inquiries, then, should comprise only *applicable* treaty law and, of course, customary rules.

50   In a similar vein, and recalling the Martens Clause (see also Chapter 9 of this volume) as a critical and persistent feature of the regulation of armed conflict, one might well ask whether violations of norms recognized as operating during armed conflict, yet not technically forming part of the 'laws and customs of war' or IHL, are relevant to Article 4(A)(2)(d) determinations. One might colourably assert that the Martens Clause incorporates by reference outside humanitarian norms, such as human rights law, into IHL. No authoritative or persuasive source seems to have addressed the question specifically. At present, the argument of Martens incorporation appears to be in the nature of *lex ferenda* rather than *lex lata*. The soundest approach to Article 4(A)(2)(d), therefore, limits inquiries to norms drawn exclusively from law-of-war instruments and sources.

51   Beyond questions as to the type of norms relevant to Article 4(A)(2)(d), there may be room for debate as to what sort of violations or breaches are relevant. Certainly, wide-scale and systematic law-of-war violations by an organization preclude that group and its members from qualification for POW status under Article 4(A)(2).

52   Whether isolated or 'one-off' incidents, however, can disqualify a group from Article 4(A)(2) is less clear. Rather than frequency or scale of violation, the issue of systematic endorsement or neglect may prove more useful. If an organization orders or approves of violations of the laws and customs of war by its members, disqualification from Article 4(A)(2) status may be appropriate. If, however, members of the organization conduct operations inconsistent with the law of war without the imprimatur or even knowledge of

---

[58] S. Watts, 'Reciprocity and the Law of War', 50 *Harvard International Law Journal* (2009) 365.

[59] See ICTY, *The Prosecutor v Ante Gotovina et al*, Appeals Chamber Judgment, IT-06-90-A, 16 November 2012. The Appeals Chamber split on the nature of the principle of discriminate attack, perhaps the most fundamental aspect of IHL.

the organization, the possibility of the organization still qualifying under Article 4(A)(2) seems feasible and consistent with general tenor of the Article. Similarly, rare or merely episodic neglect of discipline leading to IHL violations should not disqualify a group under Article 4(A)(2)(d).[60] However, routine or systematic neglect of discipline, or failure to prevent or punish IHL breaches, clearly disqualifies an organization from meeting the important requirement of 'conducting operations in accordance with the laws and customs of war'.

j. General application of the Article 4(A)(2) criteria

Aside from the exact meaning of each Article 4(A)2 criterion, there is the question of the level of application of the conditions as a whole. In particular there is some question whether the Article 4(A)(2) conditions are to be applied to groups, or on an individual basis to persons claiming POW status. Textual clues from the Article itself are most persuasive. Like other Articles of GC III, Article 4(A)(2) is structured as a 'Convention in miniature', with a preamble and subsequent enumerated sub-articles.[61] The preamble to Article 4(A)(2) concludes by prefacing the four enumerated conditions with the following phrase, 'provided that *such militias or volunteer corps* [...] fulfil the following conditions' (emphasis added). The only condition the Article 4(A)(2) preamble directs toward individual members is that of membership itself.

Brief consideration of the Article 4(A)(2) conditions themselves reinforces the conclusion that they are to be applied to groups rather than individuals. First, the Article 4(A)(2)(a) requirement of a command hierarchy seems far better suited to evaluating a group or organization than an individual.[62] Although an individual might be subject to command authority in a personal capacity, applying the command condition in this way merely re-examines the issue of membership raised previously in the Article's preamble. Furthermore, a full understanding of whether an individual is actually subject to command necessarily requires analysis of the relevant group's command hierarchy, requiring a group-level analysis all the same.

Secondly, the Article 4(A)(2)(b) condition of displaying distinctive insignia is similarly group-focused by nature. Although an individual might attempt to design, acquire, and regularly display an insignia, badge, or other article suggesting a military character, such a sign would become distinctive only through its adoption by and association with a group. While the fact of whether a detainee displayed a sign or not could often be determined by a Detaining Power, analysis of whether the sign was distinct would require considerations of a collective nature. In particular, the Detaining Power would have to determine whether the sign in question was displayed with sufficient regularity, uniformity, and consistency to serve as a reliable visual indication of belligerent status.

Rejection of a fifth Article 4(A)(2) criterion by states may further indicate the nature of the criteria overall. At the Conference of Government Experts that produced the initial draft GC III, representatives of major powers proposed the requirement of controlling territory or a region as a prerequisite to a group's eligibility for POW status.[63]

---

[60] US, Dept of the Army, *Field Manual 27-10 The Law of Land Warfare* (18 July 1956), para 64.d.
[61] Art 3 GC III; Pictet Commentary GC III, at 34.
[62] Levie, a proponent of individual application of the Art 4(A)(2) criteria, recognized the impossibility of applying the command requirement to individuals. See Levie, above n 7, at 46.
[63] Pictet Commentary GC III, at 45.

Although ultimately rejected as too difficult to administer, the requirement of territorial control does clearly represent a criterion that in practice could only be met by a group.

57   Last with respect to level of application, individual application of the Article 4(A)(2) conditions would place the status of detainees in jeopardy of manipulation by the Detaining Power. Mischaracterizations or falsifications of individual battlefield conduct are a simple matter for a Detaining Power seeking to disqualify persons from POW status. In particular, the motive for an individual or small-unit captor to do so may be strong immediately following a violent engagement with the detainee. A trumped up IHL breach or allegation that a detainee had removed distinctive insignia could have the grave consequence of disqualification from the elaborate GC III protective regime. By comparison, the motives and opportunities to fabricate failure to meet the Article 4(A)(2) conditions at a group or organizational level are greatly reduced.

58   An influential commentator has suggested that foreign nationality is an implied condition of combatancy as a matter of customary international law.[64] That is, persons who share the nationality of the Detaining Power are ineligible for combatant status and therefore POW status.[65] Although the suggestion is made with respect to Article 4(A)(2) conditions, the logic of this implied condition applies to all six categories of Article 4 POWs. While there is a compelling logic to the condition of foreign nationality, it is difficult to say GC III compels it. Given the scale and nature of the Second World War, it is unlikely the drafters of GC III were unaware of the likelihood that a Detaining Power would find its own nationals among detained enemy forces. The drafters certainly had ample opportunity to include foreign nationality as a condition of POW status. Secondly, and on a similar note, nationality figures significantly in the classification system of GC IV. The Conventions' drafters explicitly excluded states' own nationals from protected person status under GC IV.[66] Failure to address POW nationality by GC III is thus all the more conspicuous considering the deliberate attention the issue receives in GC IV. Lastly, states' military legal manuals do not widely include foreign nationality as a prerequisite to POW status. It is possible the foreign nationality requirement is best understood as a condition only of lawful combatancy and not of POW status, to the extent one is willing to regard these inquiries as legally distinct.[67]

59   Lastly, there is the question of what degree of compliance is required with respect to each Article 4(A)(2) condition. A commentator observed, 'most Capturing Powers will deny the benefits and safeguards of the Convention to any [...] individual who is in any manner delinquent in compliance'.[68] The Article 4(A)(2) criteria cannot reasonably be understood to be strict or absolute. For instance, occasional disobedience of orders by subordinates of a group should not ordinarily disqualify its members from POW status on the basis of failure to meet the command criterion. Similarly, the failure of some members to wear uniforms on a particular operation would not disqualify the group from POW status on the basis of the requirement to display a fixed distinctive sign. Application of

---

[64] Dinstein, above n 14, at 46.

[65] Sassòli/Bouvier/Quintin, at 177; H. Lauterpacht, *Oppenheim's International Law* (7th edn, London: Longmans, 1952), vol II, at 268; Levie, above n 7, at 81; R. Hingorani, *Prisoners of War* (2nd edn, New York: Oceana, 1982), at 31–2; Art 103 of UK, *The Law of War on Land, being Part III of the Manual of Military Law* (London: HMSO, 1958).

[66] Art 4 GC IV.

[67] Thus also R.-J. Wilhelm, 'Peut-on modifier le statut des prisonniers de guerre?', 35 *IRRC* 417 (1953) 681, at 682.

[68] Levie, above n 7, at 45.

k. 'government not recognized'

Article 4(A)(3) is undoubtedly a provision that reflects the great improvement GC III offers over previous POW instruments. Experience had shown that states at war frequently raised objections to the political legitimacy of their enemies. Therefore tying POW status to diplomatic recognition proved flawed. Additionally, political regimes displaced or vanquished by combat raised the question whether fighting forces belonging to the formerly effective regime could continue to claim POW status. Article 4(A)(3) adroitly divorces POW status entirely from political legitimacy or diplomatic recognition between enemies.

The primary historical examples that appear to have inspired Article 4(A)(3) are Second World War French forces loyal to the French National Liberation Committee led by General Charles De Gaulle, and Italian forces who resisted German and allied Italian forces after the last two united.[69] Following International Committee of the Red Cross (ICRC) consultations, Germany accorded POW status to captured French forces belonging to the Liberation Committee, despite Germany's refusal to recognize the Committee's international legal personality or authority.[70]

Pictet observes that apart from recognition of their sponsoring regime, the persons described in Article 4(A)(3) should be regarded as identical to those in Article 4(A)(1). This view would seemingly include irregular militias 'forming part of armed forces' of a government not recognized by the Detaining Power. This view, however, fails to account for significant textual differences between Articles 4(A)(1) and (3). Where Article 4(A)(1) mentions 'armed forces', Article 4(A)(3) refers to 'regular armed forces'. Furthermore, while Article 4(A)(1) explicitly includes 'members of militias or volunteer corps forming part of such armed forces', Article 4(A)(3) includes no such reference.

Still, textual considerations notwithstanding, formalistic adherence would undermine the provision's effectiveness as a response to the scenarios that inspired Article 4(A)(3). For example, confining Article 4(A)(3) POW status to regular armed forces would exclude from POW status Article 4(A)(2) fighters who belonged to an authority or government the Detaining Power did not recognize.

No authoritative source elaborates the condition that Article 4(A)(3) POWs 'profess allegiance to a Government or authority'. Although allegiance is often expressed by pledges, oaths, or contracts, formalities do not seem the focus of Article 4(A)(3). Accordingly, a reasonable interpretation would merely require indicia of a *de facto* connection, either operational or administrative. Likewise, no authoritative source elaborates the nature of authority to whom allegiance must be professed. The clearest case seems to be that of a regime or government that constitutes an admitted state party to the Conventions that merely lacks enemy diplomatic recognition. Similarly, an authority that formerly constituted a party to the Conventions but has been displaced or deposed by armed conflict would likely qualify. Indeed governments in exile seem to be the Article 4(A)(3) paragon. The text of Article 4(A)(3) may permit still broader application, especially if legal effect is given to the use of the term 'authority' in addition to that of 'government'. In this vein, a colourable case could be made for an 'authority' that never held *de jure* governmental

---

[69] Pictet Commentary GC III, at 61–2.   [70] Ibid.

power yet exhibited effective governmental attributes, or that formerly carried out effective governmental functions. It seems reasonable in such a situation to require, as does Pictet, that the authority in question express an acceptance of the Conventions.[71] Such a case, however, may still be in the nature of application as a matter of policy or of *lex ferenda*. It should be emphasized that Article 4(A)(3) does not include armed forces of regimes representing states whose very existence is in question. At a minimum, the regime in question must claim to represent an entity accepted as a state party to the Conventions. The conflict classification regime of Common Article 2 reinforces this interpretation.[72]

l. 'persons who accompany the armed forces'

65   While states have recently deployed private contractors to theatres of conflict, and delegated to them military functions with greater frequency, the phenomenon of contractors on the battlefield is not a new one. Neither is the question of their status upon capture new. Both the Hague Regulations and the 1929 GC II include provisions according POW status to persons who 'follow an army without being part of it'. Each treaty enumerated 'correspondents, newspaper reporters, sutlers, or contractors' as examples of persons who would enjoy POW status if detained.

66   Article 4(A)(4) GC III retains the theme of its predecessors while enumerating a more complete and contemporary list of examples. The question of unlawful participation in hostilities by military contractors has been hotly debated. It is difficult to find agreement on the range of permissible functions for Article 4(A)(4) groups. Still, the debate over unlawful combatancy, or whether international law recognizes such an offence, should not cloud POW classification under Article 4. Lawfulness of the participation in, and the consequences of, any range of functions performed by Article 4(A)(4) groups are better appreciated as a matter for criminal prosecution than as issues for disqualification from POW status. The soundest approach, like that with respect to other categories of POW, is to leave issues of individual pre-capture conduct to the GC III provisions on criminal prosecution, rather than to regard them as part of the POW classification process.

67   As with determinations of POW status under Article 4 generally, *de facto* affiliation appears to be sufficient to establish status. In fact, where Hague and preceding Geneva instruments required possession of an identification card, GC III does not. Thus, in addition to possession of a card, co-location, shared logistical arrangements, contractual arrangements, and apparel might each indicate qualification under Article 4(A)(4). As Pictet suggests, it is the capacity of service to armed forces rather than the peculiarities of affiliation that support Article 4(A)(4) POW status.[73]

68   Despite a relaxation of formal indicia of affiliation, it is clear that the person in question under Article 4(A)(4) must have been authorized to accompany the armed forces. Stragglers and others persons merely following formations of armed forces are not envisioned under Article 4(A)(4). Even apparent tolerance of such persons' presence seems inadequate to give rise to POW status. Instead, Article 4(A)(4) seems to describe persons who perform official or sanctioned functions for the armed forces or the party to whom they belong.

69   The view advocated in this section has the advantage of simplifying the controversial issue of the status of captured private military security contractors (PMSCs).[74] While the

---

[71] Pictet Commentary GC III, at 63.   [72] See Ch 1 of this volume.
[73] Pictet Commentary GC III, at 65.
[74] L. Cameron, 'Private Military Companies: Their Status under International Humanitarian Law and its Impact on their Regulation', 88 *IRRC* 863 (2006) 573.

legitimacy of assigning combat functions to PMSCs is contested, and their entitlement to combatant immunity is even more contentious, a clear case can be made for according POW status to PMSCs under Article 4(A)(4). Members or employees of PMSCs that enjoy *de facto* affiliation with a state party and authority to accompany the latter's armed forces, should upon capture enjoy status as POWs under Article 4(A)(4) at a minimum. The consequences of their participation in hostilities or other actions in connection with the armed conflict in question should be considered separately by the Detaining Power. Although some might advocate such status, it is unlikely that PMSCs would qualify as POWs under Article 4(A)(2). Most importantly, the *private* nature of PMSCs would seem to prevent their ever satisfying the 'belonging to' requirement of Article 4(A)(2). Excluding PMSCs from consideration under Article 4(A)(2) offers the further advantage of avoiding consideration of the issue of combatant immunity which many, but not this author, associate with Article 4(A)(2) status.

m. 'members of crews [...] of the merchant marine and [...] civil aircraft'

More so than provisions concerning other categories of POW status, provisions addressing the status of merchant crew have been interpreted as a commentary on the range of persons parties may lawfully detain during armed conflict. Authority to capture members of the merchant marine seems to have changed frequently in the early twentieth century. With GC III, authority to detain such persons is made clear, although delineation of such authority is not the purpose of Article 4(A)(5).

The purpose of Article 4(A)(5), of course, is to identify members of merchant marine and their airborne counterparts as eligible for POW status when detained by enemy forces. While not typically expected to take direct part in the conduct of hostilities, merchant seamen and aircrew often find themselves integrated into military, even offensive, operations. The rationale for their detention, as with all POWs, is to prevent them from rejoining and contributing to the success of enemy military operations.

n. 'inhabitants of non-occupied territory, who [...] spontaneously take up arms'

The sixth enumerated class of GC III POW status is commonly equated with historical conceptions of the *levée en masse*. Recognized at least since the 1899 Hague Regulations, substantively speaking the *levée en masse* category of POW was little affected by GC III. Despite proposals to broaden the class, states appeared determined to preserve the bounds of the *levée en masse* as they stood under pre-existing instruments and practice.

The critical concept of the *levée en masse*, and therefore of Article 4(A)(6), is spontaneity. In this regard, the *levée en masse* POW class is a temporally restricted status. Only inhabitants of unoccupied territory who respond to invasion without the opportunity or time to organize themselves as another class of POW may avail themselves of Article 4(A)(6). The *levée en masse* provision anticipates that conditions of invasion may preclude a national of invaded territory from joining the armed forces or qualifying militia of his state. Similarly, conditions of invasion may preclude a group of nationals who have formed a militia from establishing a command hierarchy, from developing distinctive signs, or from affiliating with a party to the conflict either formally or functionally. Although failure to distinguish themselves from the civilian population may form the basis of war crimes prosecutions, for the *levée en masse*, failure to display a distinctive emblem visible at a distance will, for a limited time, not ordinarily preclude POW status.

74 Spontaneity does not appear to refer to the invasion itself. The members of a *levée en masse* need not be individually surprised by the invasion that provokes them. Accordingly, members may respond to an immediate call to arms from either government or fellow citizens, and still qualify under Article 4(A)(6).[75]

75 It has been emphasized that open display of arms is a particularly important criterion of *levée en masse* POW status.[76] The requirement is both reasonable and textually compelled. Especially where conditions prevent selection and dissemination of uniforms or other distinctive emblems, carrying arms openly is the sole visible signal of members' intent to separate themselves from the civilian population as combatants.

76 However, as soon as the members of a *levée en masse* have the opportunity to organize, establish state affiliation, or meet the other Article 4(A)(2) criteria—that is, as soon as their resistance is no longer spontaneous—they may no longer resort to Article 4(A)(6) for POW status. It is chiefly in this respect that Article 4(A)(6) describes a temporally restricted class.

II. Article 4(B)

77 Article 4(B)(1) is consistent with logic of internment and detention of POWs generally. The records of the Diplomatic Conference indicate that states added the Article to prevent POWs from losing their status if released by a Detaining Power into enemy-occupied territory.[77] Article 4(B)(1) makes clear that should a Detaining Power find it necessary to re-intern released POWs owing to hostilities outside occupied territory, such POWs would retain the benefit of all GC III treatment provisions, though perhaps not *de jure* POW status. While the text of Article 4(B)(1) is limited to armed forces, its logic seems appropriate to two additional combatant classes of POW status as well, namely, those described in Article 4(A)(2) and (3). The conditions described seem to preclude members of the *levée en masse* described in Article 4(A)(6). Thus members of militia, volunteer corps forming part of armed forces, and militia, volunteer corps, and organized resistance movements meeting the relevant and respective conditions should enjoy the benefits of GC III if detained by an Occupying Power.

78 Finally, Article 4(B)(2) proceeds from a long-standing obligation of the law of neutrality. Applicable during international armed conflict, Article 11 of Hague Convention V respecting the rights and duties of neutral powers and persons in case of war on land of 18 October 1907 requires that neutral powers intern 'troops belonging to belligerent armies' they receive on their territory (see also Chapter 5, MN 38, of this volume), including POWs interned in a neutral state based upon an agreement between the parties to an IAC (see Chapter 51, MN 17, of this volume). Article 4(B)(2) GC III refers to 'persons belonging to one of the categories enumerated by the present Article'. It is reasonable to equate these terms with the categories of GC III, Article 4(A)(1), (2), and (3). It is unclear, however, whether the obligation to intern extends to prisoners described in GC III, Article 4(A)(4), (5), and (6). The former two categories, persons accompanying armed forces and certain air crews, are an uncomfortable fit with the term 'troops' (in Article 11 of the Hague Convention), while the latter category, the *levée en masse*, seems to strain the notion of 'belonging to the belligerent armies' (in the same Article).

---

[75] Pictet Commentary GC III, at 67. Levie offers an opposing view, grounded in a passage of the records of the Diplomatic Conference. See Levie, above n 7, at 65 (citing Final Record, vol II-A, at 420–1).
[76] Pictet Commentary GC III, at 67.   [77] Final Record, vol II-A, at 432.

C. Critical Assessment

Strictly speaking, Article 4 GC III does not identify general requirements for individual belligerent conduct, or for armies and armed groups generally. Nor, strictly speaking, does Article 4 constitute a code of conduct or enumeration of criminal offences. Article 4 merely identifies groups whose members are entitled to POW status and enumerates *conditions* for other groups whose members are entitled to POW status. The only consequence of failing to meet the descriptions and conditions of Article 4 per se is denial of POW status to persons who have fallen into the power of the enemy. And purely by the terms of GC III, the only consequence of failing to qualify for POW status is denial of the Convention's intricate system of humanitarian treatment obligations.

Yet historically, failure to attain POW status has meant significantly more. There has long been an historic linkage between POW status and combatant immunity. Combatant immunity, more so than POW treatment conditions, constitutes perhaps the most desirable customary benefit of POW status. Indeed, combatant immunity is often a matter of life and death. But if combatant immunity is currently the most attractive aspect of POW status, it is simultaneously the aspect that most tempts states to deny POW status to captives. To be sure, the Conventions' surpassingly humane POW treatment regime represents a significant administrative and logistical burden to Detaining Powers. Yet whether states can actually economize from the standpoint of detention operations, either administratively or logistically, by denying POW status is increasingly unlikely as the international legal system moves toward detention treatment parity.[78] The incentive to deny POW status in order to evade the obligations attendant on establishing POW camps is becoming progressively minimal. By comparison, the prospect of holding detainees criminally responsible for their belligerent acts is the far greater incentive for Detaining Powers to deny POW status. Criminal prosecution for belligerency represents not only an opportunity for severe justice, but also a potentially powerful physical and political deterrent to further enemy belligerency.

While resorting to traditional criteria of combatancy to define the POW class initially achieved a degree of regulatory efficiency, it seems now that pairing POW status and combatant immunity may have been more harmful than helpful. In particular, the conceptual coupling of combatant status with POW status seems to have unnecessarily narrowed the operation of the core function of GC III, namely, its protective internment regime. Coupling POW status and combatant immunity has likely induced states to deprive detainees of mutually beneficial and humane treatment conditions as a collateral consequence of their desire to deny combatant immunity to certain groups of fighters. An understanding of GC III that decouples combatant immunity from POW status would go a long way towards reducing unnecessary and overbroad deprival of the GC III internment regime. In fact, GC III itself began the process by including two subcategories of POW not entitled to combatant immunity. Neither Article 4(A)(4) persons accompanying the force, nor Article 4(A)(5) crews are understood to be combatants under existing IHL.[79]

Lastly, greater doctrinal clarity from states would be especially useful on POW classification subjects such as the level of application of Article 4(A)(2) conditions, the relevance

---

[78] D. Jinks, 'The Declining Significance of POW Status', 45 *Harvard International Law Journal* (2003) 301.
[79] Art 50 AP I identifies both POW subcategories as civilians.

of those conditions to members of regular armed forces, as well as other issues of interpretation addressed above. Through military legal manuals and regulations, states could easily alleviate much of the doctrinal indeterminacy that has surrounded the GC III POW classification regime for over 50 years. As both the benefactors of potential detainees and as potential Detaining Powers, states would profit clearly and directly from such interpretive efforts. As the ultimate authorities on the meaning of the Conventions, states are uniquely positioned to clarify and advance understanding of these critical instruments for injecting a degree of humanity into armed conflict. Even if this commentary has missed the mark in its elaboration or interpretation of the GC III classification regime, it will have been worthwhile if it provokes from states clarifications or corrections of any of these persistent and troublesome ambiguities.

SEAN WATTS*

---

* The views in this commentary are produced in the author's personal capacity. I am grateful to Ms Kristin Kooima and Mr Steven Rupert for valuable research assistance.

Chapter 45. Status and Treatment of Those Who Do Not Fulfil the Conditions for Status as Prisoners of War

	MN
A. Introduction	1
B. Meaning and Application	4
I. Consequences of not respecting conditions in Article 4(A) GC III	4
II. Relationship between Article 44 AP I and the Geneva Conventions	17
a. Article 44(3), (4), (5) AP I	18
b. Meaning of Article 44(6) and (7) AP I	24
III. The 'unlawful combatant' debate: various positions on status, treatment, and consequences	26
IV. Residual protection under GC IV	32
a. Why and where this matters	32
b. Protected civilians initially treated as prisoners of war: aspects of internment, transfer, and deportation lawful for prisoners of war but not for protected civilians	42
V. Minimum treatment standards: Common Article 3 and Article 75 AP I	47
VI. International human rights law protection when conditions of prisoner of war status are not fulfilled	51
VII. (Irregular) Renditions for persons who are not protected civilians	54
VIII. Recent examples: Israel and the United States	58
C. Relevance in Non-International Armed Conflicts	71
D. Legal Consequences of a Violation	78
E. Critical Assessment	82

Select Bibliography

Baxter, R.R., 'So-Called "Unprivileged Belligerency": Spies, Guerillas, and Saboteurs', 28 *BYBIL* (1951) 323

Chesney, R.M., 'Prisoners of War', in MPEPIL

Debuf, E., *Captured in War: Lawful Internment in Armed Conflict* (Oxford: Hart Publishing, 2013)

Dinstein, Y., 'Unlawful Combatancy', in F.L. Borch and P.S. Wilson (eds), *International Law and the War on Terror* (Newport, RI: Naval War College Press, 2003), vol 79

Dörmann, K., 'The Legal Situation of "Unlawful/Unprivileged Combatants"', 85 *IRRC* 849 (2003) 45

Dörmann, K., 'Unlawful Combatants', in MPEPIL

ICRC CIHL Study, Rule 106 (vols I–II)

ICRC Commentary APs, at 519–42, 861–90

Levie, H.S., *Prisoners of War in International Armed Conflict* (Newport, RI: Naval War College Press, 1978) vol 59

Pictet Commentary GC III, at 44–73

Pictet Commentary GC IV, at 45–51, 52–8

Sassòli, M., 'Combatants', in MPEPIL

Sassòli, M./Olson, L.M., 'The Relationship between International Humanitarian and Human Rights Law Where It Matters: Admissible Killing and Internment of Fighters in Non-International Armed Conflict', 90 *IRRC* 871 (2008) 599

Watkin, K., 'Warriors without Rights? Combatants, Unprivileged Belligerents, and the Struggle over Legitimacy', HPCR Occasional Paper (Winter 2005), available at <http://www.hpcrresearch.org/sites/default/files/publications/OccasionalPaper2.pdf>

A. Introduction

1 Throughout its development, international humanitarian law (IHL) has sought to regulate who may directly participate in hostilities, i.e. be considered a 'combatant' with immunity from punishment under domestic law for such participation.[1] Persons participating in hostilities *without* meeting the requirements of IHL, namely the 1907 Hague Regulations,[2] or, later, Geneva Convention (GC) III[3] or Additional Protocol (AP) I,[4] have been called many names, including 'unlawful combatants' or 'unprivileged belligerents/combatants', despite such terms not appearing in IHL treaties. While generally these terms have been used to indicate that such individuals do not have the combatant privilege to wound or kill enemy combatants and destroy enemy military objectives, the terms' meanings and the consequences for individuals when the terms are applied to them have varied.[5] Whatever the label given to such individuals, when GC III provides no protection, GC IV has been considered—although also not without controversy—to provide residual protection to them, as GC IV was designed to protect persons in the hands of the enemy, namely enemy nationals living in the territory of the belligerent state and inhabitants of occupied territories.[6]

2 Additional IHL rules also safeguard captured individuals lacking combatant status: Article 3 common to the four Geneva Conventions and Article 75 AP I. Common Article 3 has been described as a 'convention in miniature' and 'ensures the application of the rules of humanity which are recognized as essential by civilized nations'.[7] Article 75 AP I provides minimum, fundamental guarantees to 'persons who are in the power of a Party to the conflict and who do not benefit from more favourable treatment'.[8]

3 The fight against terrorism in the early twenty-first century again brought to the fore the debate on 'belligerent status'[9] and, in particular, the meaning of the conditions for prisoner of war (POW) status laid down in Article 4(A) GC III and the consequences for failing to meet them. Chapter 44 of this volume explains Article 4(A) GC III, so this chapter focuses on the status and treatment of individuals who do not fulfil the conditions for POW status.

---

[1] See, e.g., Arts 9–11 Brussels Declaration 1874; Arts 1–3 Hague Regulations; Art 4 GC III; Arts 43–44 AP I.

[2] Art 1 Hague Regulations.   [3] Art 4 GC III.   [4] Art 44 AP I.

[5] K. Dörmann, 'The Legal Situation of "Unlawful/Unprivileged Combatants"', 85 *IRRC* 849 (2003) 45, at 45–6.

[6] Art 4 GC IV defines the persons protected as civilians under that Convention. Art 5 GC IV, which provides for limited derogations from the protections in GC IV, assists with understanding the scope of Art 4 GC IV.

[7] Pictet Commentary GC III, at 34.   [8] Art 75(1) AP I.

[9] Pictet Commentary GC III, at 45–7.

B. Meaning and Application

I. Consequences of not respecting conditions in Article 4(A) GC III

While the drafters of GC III tried to fill gaps in protection, they failed to define many of the key terms of the conditions for personal application of GC III. Yet for appropriate application of GC III, it is critical to understand the meaning and scope of these conditions. Lack of precision regarding these conditions is of concern, since status determinations are almost always made by the Detaining Power and only rarely by an independent court,[10] although Article 5 GC III requires that a tribunal determines the status of persons who committed belligerent acts and whose status is in doubt.

As discussed in detail in Chapter 44 of this volume, the armed force/group to which the individual belongs must fulfil certain conditions in order for a person who has fallen into the hands of the enemy to be accorded POW status. These conditions are provided for in Article 4(A) GC III, which lists the six categories to which a person may belong in order to be eligible for POW status.

One condition stipulated in Article 4(A) GC III is that the armed force/group must belong to a party to the conflict. If an individual participates in hostilities without belonging to a group, which belongs to a party to the conflict, he or she does not violate IHL for that mere participation, despite some disagreement on that point.[11] Rather, by such participation in hostilities, the individual attains no privileged status as a combatant or, upon capture, as a POW.

One of the six categories listed in Article 4(A) GC III is members of militias or other volunteer corps, including organized resistance movements. Such militias and volunteer corps must—in addition to 'belonging' to a party to the conflict—fulfil the following four conditions found in Article 4(A)(2)(a)–(d) GC III for their members to qualify as POWs:

— operate under a responsible command;
— have a fixed distinctive sign recognizable at a distance;
— carry arms openly; and
— conduct operations in accordance with the laws and customs of war.[12]

Given the explicit reference in Article 4(A)(2), it is generally agreed—although not without some debate[13]—that the conditions listed in Article 4(A)(2) are collective, i.e., required to

---

[10] A few rare examples of such status determinations having been made by a court include *Ex parte Quirin*, 317 US 1, 63 SCt 2 (1942) and *Military Prosecutor v Omar Mahmud Kassem and others*, Israel Military Court sitting in Ramallah (1969), in Sassòli/Bouvier/Quintin, at 1070; see also Ch 46, MN 42–55, of this volume.

[11] See, e.g., US Military Commissions Act of 2006, 10 USC §950v(b) (13) & (15) (hereinafter MCA 2006); US Military Commissions Act of 2009, 10 USC §950t (13) & (15) (hereinafter MCA 2009); the Military Manual of the Netherlands, *Humanitair Oorlogsrecht: Handleiding*, Voorschrift No 27-412, Koninklijke Landmacht, Militair Juridische Dienst, 2005, §0308, (stating that '[t]hose who engage in acts of war without being entitled to do so (known as "unlawful combatants") thereby commit a war crime for which they can be prosecuted'), cited in ICRC CIHL Database, Rule 156; Italian Wartime Military Penal Code (entered into force in 1941 as amended in 2002), Art 167; Italian Court of Cassation, *Bouyahia Maher Ben Abdelaziz et al*, Judgment No 1072 of 17 January 2007, para 2.1; *Ex parte Quirin*, above n 10, at 317 US 31. See also the discussion at MN 13–16.

[12] The challenges for irregular forces always to fulfil these conditions led to the legal developments found in AP I discussed at MN 17–25.

[13] See, e.g., *Kassem*, above n 10, at 1072 (stating that 'a member of an underground organization [...] must clearly fulfill all the four [...] conditions and that the absence of any of them is sufficient to attach to him the character of a combatant not entitled to be regarded as a prisoner of war'); H.S. Levie, *Prisoners of War in International Armed Conflict* (Newport, RI: Naval War College Press, 1978), vol 59, at 44–5.

be fulfilled by the group, rather than by the individual.[14] Without belonging to a group that fulfils these conditions, an individual would not be entitled to POW status upon capture.

8   Given the significant consequences for failing to meet the conditions laid down in Article 4(A)(2)(a)–(d), it is important that those conditions should not be interpreted too strictly: '[I]t should be sufficient if such forces are under instruction to comply with those conditions and that most of their members actually do not commit obvious violations of those rules.'[15] Or, as another expert suggests, the determination may be made based on the 'general policy of the organization as this is evidenced by its activities, or on the consistent practice of a significant part of its members'.[16]

9   The United States (US) Government's conclusion in 2002[17] that the Taliban, as a group, failed to meet three of the four Article 4(A)(2) conditions, and hence that its members were not legally entitled to POW status, caused significant controversy. This was largely due to the fact that the Government's analysis required that *regular* armed forces comply with the conditions of Article 4(A)(2).[18] This is an issue elaborated upon in Chapter 44, MN 12–21, of this volume, but suffice it to say here that neither Article 4(A)(1) nor (3) expressly lists the Article 4(A)(2) conditions for members of the armed forces of a party to the conflict and militias or volunteer corps forming part of such armed forces. This was intentional on the part of the drafters of GC III, who strove to make clear that the conditions did not attach to members of the armed forces:[19] 'The idea underlying these definitions is that the regular armed forces fulfil these conditions per se and, as a result, they are not explicitly enumerated with respect to them.'[20]

---

[14] See ICRC Commentary APs, at 551 (stating that a person's POW status 'depends on the possible disqualification of the armed forces to which he belongs. This point has never been doubted, even if individually the member of the said organization or armed force complies with the conditions which he is capable of fulfilling'). For the view that all six conditions are group attributes but the individual must also wear the distinctive sign, carry weapons openly, and comply with IHL, see G.I.A.D. Draper, 'The Status of Combatants and the Question of Guerilla Warfare', 45 *BYBIL* 73, 195–9 (1971); and W.T. Mallison and S.V. Mallison, 'The Juridical Status of Irregular Combatants under the International Humanitarian Law of Armed Conflict', 9 *Case Western Reserve JIL* (1977) 39, at 62.

[15] M. Sassòli, 'Combatants', in MPEPIL, para 12.

[16] F. Kalshoven, 'The Position of Guerrilla Fighters under the Law of War', 11 *The Military Law and Law of War Review* (1972) 55, at 87.

[17] Memorandum Opinion from J. Bybee, Assistant Attorney-General, for the Counsel to the President, Status of Taliban forces under Article 4 of the Third Geneva Convention of 1949 (7 February 2002), at 2 (hereinafter Bybee Memo).

[18] Ibid, at 4–7.

[19] Final Record vol II-A, at 413–14, 466–7, 477–80, and vol III, at 61. But see Bybee Memo, above n 17, at 5 (stating that interpreting the conditions of Art 4(A)(2) as applying only to the groups listed, could lead to the conclusion that regular armies could evade their obligations under IHL); Y. Dinstein, 'Unlawful Combatancy', in F.L. Borch and P.S. Wilson (eds), *International Law and the War on Terror* (Newport, RI: Naval War College Press, 2003), vol 79, at 159 (arguing that '[t]here is merely a presumption that regular armed forces would naturally meet those conditions. But the presumption can definitely be rebutted'); *Ex parte Quirin*, above n 10, at 35–6 (pre-dating the 1949 GCs and concerning German members of the armed forces who took off their uniforms when on a sabotage mission in the US); *Mohammed Ali and another v Public Prosecutor* [1969] AC 430, at 449–50 (holding that 'it is not enough to establish that a person belongs to the regular armed forces to guarantee to him the status of a prisoner of war but that even members of the armed forces must observe the cumulative conditions imposed on irregular forces, although this is not stated *expressis verbis* in the Geneva Conventions or in the Hague Regulations').

[20] ICRC CIHL Study, vol I, Rule 4, at 15. See Pictet Commentary GC III, at 63 (indicating, in reference to Art 4(A)(3), that '[t]hese "regular armed forces" have all the material characteristics and all the attributes of armed forces in the sense of sub-paragraph (1): they wear uniform, they have an organized hierarchy and they know and respect the laws and customs of war. The delegates to the 1949 Diplomatic Conference were therefore fully justified in considering that there was no need to specify for such armed forces the requirements stated in sub-paragraph (2)(a), (b), (c) and (d)').

Another condition that must be fulfilled to attain POW status is the individual requirement to distinguish oneself from the civilian population. It is generally considered that customary IHL establishes that an individual member of the armed forces of a party to an international armed conflict (IAC), and of other armed groups belonging to a party to such a conflict, who fails, at the time of capture, to distinguish himself or herself from the civilian population, loses his or her combatant status and thus forfeits POW status.[21] If this lack of distinction from the civilian population does not amount to perfidy, it is not a violation of IHL.[22]

Lastly, combatants must respect IHL. 'If they violate IHL they must be punished, however, they do not lose their combatant status and, if captured by the enemy, remain entitled to prisoner-of-war status, except if they have violated their obligation to distinguish themselves.'[23] 'Only failure to distinguish oneself from the civilian population [...] or being caught as a spy [...] or a mercenary warrant forfeiture of prisoner-of-war status.'[24]

In sum, the consequences for not fulfilling the conditions of Article 4(A) GC III and customary law are twofold. First, the person does not qualify for POW status upon capture and, therefore, does not receive the protections found in GC III for persons with that status. And, secondly, since 'unlawful combatants' have no combatant privilege of immunity from domestic prosecution for acts that, while in compliance with IHL, may be crimes under domestic law, they may be held criminally liable for their actions.

With regard to criminal accountability, 'unlawful combatants' may be prosecuted for their mere participation in hostilities even if they respect IHL rules, so long as domestic law provides for this (including as a war crime if so titled under domestic law). Domestic law must so provide because their participation in hostilities is not a violation of IHL:[25]

> The absence in IHL of an express right for civilians to directly participate in hostilities does not necessarily imply an international prohibition of such participation. Indeed, as such, civilian direct participation in hostilities is neither prohibited by IHL nor criminalized under the statutes of any prior or current international tribunal or court.[26]

That said, there is not absolute agreement that participation in hostilities by 'unlawful combatants' is not an IHL violation.[27] An example of such disagreement that has received significant attention because, inter alia, it concerns detainees held at the Guantánamo Bay detention facility, is the US treatment, through the Guantánamo military commissions, of direct participation in hostilities as a war crime.[28] The US success in this regard

---

[21] ICRC CIHL Study, vol I, Rule 106, at 384–9; Sassòli, above n 15, para 6. See also Art 44 para 4 AP I (specifically regarding the distinction requirement applicable in exceptional circumstances).

[22] Regarding disagreement on whether individual participation in hostilities constitutes a violation of IHL, see the examples provided above n 11, and the discussion at MN 13–16.

[23] Sassòli/Bouvier/Quintin, at 177.   [24] ICRC CIHL Study, vol I, Rule 4, at 16.

[25] See, e.g., Dörmann, above n 5, at 70–1 (citing Y. Dinstein, 'The Distinction between Unlawful Combatants and War Criminals', in Y. Dinstein (ed), *International Law at a Time of Perplexity* (Dordrecht: Martinus Nijhoff Publishers, 1989) 103, at 114; Kalshoven, above n 16, at 73); M. Schmitt, 'Humanitarian Law and Direct Participation in Hostilities by Private Contractors or Civilian Employees', 5 *Chicago JIL* (2005) 511, 520; Y. Dinstein, *The Conduct of Hostilities under the Law of International Armed Conflict* (Cambridge: CUP, 2004) 234; G.P. Fletcher, 'The Law of War and its Pathologies', 38 *Columbia Human Rights Review* (2007) 517, at 541; D.J.R. Frakt, 'Direct Participation in Hostilities as a War Crime: America's Failed Efforts to Change the Law of War', 46 *Valparaiso University Law Review* (2012) 729.

[26] N. Melzer, *Interpretive Guidance on the Notion of Direct Participation in Hostilities under International Humanitarian Law* (Geneva: ICRC, 2009), at 83–4 (footnotes omitted).

[27] See examples provided above n 11.

[28] MCA 2009, above n 11, § 950t (13) & (15) (replacing MCA 2006, above n 11).

remains to be seen.[29] However, at the time of writing, it is noteworthy that—since the first version of these military commissions was authorized in 2001[30]—only one detainee, Omar Khadr, has been convicted (through a guilty plea) based on *direct attack* on US soldiers (not protected civilians).[31] In late 2013, Khadr moved to appeal his conviction,[32] arguing he was wrongfully convicted for acts that were not war crimes under international or US law at the time committed. Central to his argument on appeal is the Court's determination in *Hamdan II*[33] that the Military Commissions Act (MCA) of 2006 does not authorize retroactive prosecution of crimes that were not prohibited as war crimes triable by military commission under US law at the time the conduct occurred. In determining which war crimes were triable under US law, the Court looked at the US statute[34] in force at the time of the alleged crime, which gave the military commissions the power to try violations of the law of war, and held that the use of 'law of war' in that statute referred to the *international* law of war.[35] Thus, if the act at the time committed was not considered a crime under the international law of war, it was not covered by the US statute and, thus, could not be tried by the military commissions.

15   While *Hamdan II* found specifically that the crime of material support for terrorism was not an international war crime pre-2006, its reasoning could have far-reaching effects on the ongoing military commissions at Guantánamo Bay. Another Guantánamo detainee, Ali Hamza Ahmad Suliman Al-Bahlul, successfully attained a reversal of his conviction on conspiracy on the basis of *Hamdan II*.[36] However, whether Khadr or others may continue to rely on *Hamdan II* remains unclear, since the Court's rehearing *en banc* of Al-Bahlul's case.[37] The *en banc* Court, under 'plain error' review, vacated Al-Bahlul's military commission convictions for material support for terrorism and solicitation of others to commit war crimes but affirmed his conviction for conspiracy (yet leaving the possibility that it too could be overturned).[38] The *en banc* Court's decision raised, but did not expressly answer, the question regarding how much remains of the panel opinion in *Hamdan II* that 'had rejected—on statutory grounds—the ability of the military

---

[29] Frakt, above n 25 (arguing that the US has failed in its attempt to treat direct participation in hostilities as a war crime).

[30] 'Military Order—Detention, Treatment and Trial of Certain Non-Citizens in the War against Terrorism', 13 November 2001, 66 Fed Reg 57833 (16 November 2001). In response to the invalidation of these military commissions by the Supreme Court in *Hamdan v Rumsfeld*, 548 US 557 (2006), Congress passed MCA 2006, above n 11; MCA 2006 was subsequently replaced with MCA 2009, above n 11.

[31] Frakt, above n 25, at 762. Khadr pleaded guilty in 2010 to murder in violation of the law of war, attempted murder in violation of the law of war, spying, conspiracy, and providing material support for terrorism; the pre-trial agreement is available at <http://www.defense.gov/news/Khadr%20Convening%20Authority%20Pretrial%20Agreement%20AE%20341%2013%20Oct%202010%20(redacted).pdf>. Majid Khan's conviction (through a guilty plea) in 2012 of the attempted murder in March 2002 of President Musharraf would constitute a similar example, if one considers Musharraf not to have been a person protected under IHL from direct attack at that time (when he had not yet left the Office of the Army Staff to take the oath for his second term as a civilian president). See *US v Khan*, Stipulation of Fact, Prosecution Exhibit 001 (Khan) (13 Feb 2012), paras 28–41, 109, available at <http://www.mc.mil/Portals/0/pdfs/Khan/Khan%20(PE001)%20-%20Stipulation%20of%20Fact.pdf>.

[32] Brief on behalf of appellant is available at <http://justsecurity.org/wp-content/uploads/2013/11/khadr.cmcr_.brief_.pdf>.

[33] *Hamdan v United States*, 696 F3d 1238 (DC Cir 2012) (addressing the crime of material support for terrorism) (hereinafter *Hamdan II*).

[34] 10 USC § 821.   [35] *Hamdan II*, above n 33.

[36] *Al-Bahlul v United States*, Case No 11-1324, Doc No 1417123 (DC Cir, 25 January 2013).

[37] *Al-Bahlul v United States*, Case No 11-1324, Doc No 1502277 (DC Cir, 14 July 2014).

[38] Ibid.

commissions to try any pre-MCA offenses not recognized as international war crimes at the time of the relevant conduct'.[39] This question, among others, has been remanded to the original three-judge panel.[40] Of course, it should be mentioned that these developments do not address post-2006 conduct.

In conclusion on the point regarding 'unlawful combatants'' direct participation in hostilities not constituting an IHL violation, it bears repeating that 'unlawful combatants' may be prosecuted under domestic law that criminalizes their specific acts, such as murder of 'lawful combatants', committed during their participation in hostilities. And if they seriously infringed rules of IHL, they may be prosecuted for war crimes, as may POWs.

II. Relationship between Article 44 AP I and the Geneva Conventions

Additional Protocol I was drafted to supplement the four Geneva Conventions.[41] However, unlike the four Conventions, AP I is not universally ratified, thus its provisions, unless they are found already in the Geneva Conventions or are customary, are not binding on non-party states. One of the most controversial aspects of AP I is Article 44, which expands POW status by relaxing combatancy requirements in certain circumstances for individuals using methods of guerilla warfare.[42] This Article was hotly debated during its drafting, and its customary status continues to be disputed. Although still highly controversial, understanding its relationship to the Geneva Conventions is particularly important for the debate on 'unlawful combatants'.

a. Article 44(3), (4), (5) AP I

According to AP I, a member of an organized armed group, who is under a command responsible to a party to the IAC and subject to internal discipline, is entitled to POW status upon capture,[43] so long as the member of the armed group individually, at the time of capture,[44] respects the obligation to distinguish himself or herself from the civilian population.[45] The member must distinguish himself or herself while engaged in an attack or a military operation preparatory to an attack; *or, in exceptional situations*[46] *when he or she cannot distinguish himself or herself*, he or she shall retain his or her status as a combatant, provided that, in such situations, he or she carries arms openly during each military engagement and when he or she is visible to the adversary while engaged in a military deployment preceding the launching of an attack in which he or she is to participate.[47]

The express requirement in Article 44(3) AP I that all members of armed forces, whether regular or irregular, must distinguish themselves from the civilian population is not new. While it was not expressly stated in the Hague Regulations or in GC III, it was clear that regular armed forces (not just irregular armed forces) had to distinguish themselves.[48] However, the relaxation of the requirements for distinguishing oneself in

---

[39] S.I. Vladeck, 'What's Left of Hamdan II? Quite a Lot, Actually…', Just Security (17 July 2014), available at <http://justsecurity.org/12989/left-hamdan-ii-lot-actually/>.
[40] *Al-Bahlul*, above n 37.
[41] Art 1 para 3 AP I.
[42] ICRC Commentary APs, at 520.   [43] Art 43 AP I.   [44] Art 44(5) AP I.
[45] Art 44(3) AP I.
[46] Many states have limited these situations to occupied territories and conflicts covered by Art 1(4) AP I (wars of national liberation). See ICRC CIHL Study, vol I, Rule 106, at 388.
[47] Sassòli/Bouvier/Quintin, at 179.   [48] ICRC CIHL Study, vol I, Rule 106, at 385.

exceptional circumstances in Article 44(3) was highly controversial during its drafting[49] and remains so.

20   The Article 44(3) exceptional circumstances exception to the requirement to distinguish oneself was developed to address the concern that guerillas could not realistically fulfil all four conditions set out in Article 4(A)(2) GC III, and thus to ensure compliance with IHL.[50] However, some states criticize this exception as dangerously eroding the principle of distinction, placing the civilian population at risk.[51] At the time of writing, 173 states have ratified AP I, but among those that have not are several key states, such as the US and Israel, expressing opposition to this provision.[52] In particular, a significant number of reservations and understandings indicate a lack of agreement on the meaning of this Article.[53] Thus, the second sentence of Article 44(3) AP I—the relaxed requirement for combatants to distinguish themselves—cannot be considered customary law.[54] And, the rule remains—unless a state is party to AP I—that '[c]ombatants must distinguish themselves from the civilian population while they are engaged in an attack or in a military operation preparatory to an attack. If they fail to do so, they do not have the right to prisoner-of-war status.'[55]

21   Article 44(4) AP I clarifies that the rule on forfeiture of status also pertains to the distinction requirements applicable in exceptional circumstances in Article 44(3). While it is customary law that an individual combatant retains POW status only if he or she individually respects the obligation to distinguish himself or herself at the time of capture,[56] Article 44(4)'s extension of this to the new distinction requirements applicable in exceptional circumstances is not.

22   The rule found in Article 44(5) AP I makes explicit that status forfeiture applies only to combatants captured in the act.[57] That assessment of whether the individual properly distinguished himself or herself occurs at the time of capture, however, is not new to IHL:

> There is no doubt that this is, 'mutatis mutandis', analogous to the situation of the spy, and consequently there is some relationship with the concept of unprivileged belligerent. Like a spy, the combatant who does not carry his arms openly must be caught in the act for the sanction to be applicable to him. Similarly, like him, a combatant who is captured while he is not committing this breach, does not incur any responsibility for acts which he committed previously.[58]

---

[49] Art 44(3) was 'one of the most bitterly disputed articles' during the drafting of AP I. ICRC Commentary APs, at 521. Art 44 was adopted by 73 votes in favour, 1 against, and 21 abstentions. Official Records of the Diplomatic Conference on the Reaffirmation and Development of International Humanitarian Law applicable in Armed Conflict, vol VI, at 121–39.

[50] Supporters of the expansion of POW status reasoned that 'guerilla fighters will not simply disappear by putting them outside the law applicable in armed conflict, on the basis that they are incapable of complying with the traditional rules of such law. Neither would this encourage them to at least comply with those rules which they are in a position to comply with, as this would not benefit them in any way.' ICRC Commentary APs, at 520.

[51] ICRC CIHL Study, vol I, Rule 106, at 387, fn 22.

[52] See, e.g., Israel, Statement at the Diplomatic Conference on the Reaffirmation and Development of International Humanitarian Law applicable in Armed Conflict, Official Records, above n 49, vol VI, at 121–2, ss 17 and 19; 'Message from the US President to the Senate Transmitting Protocol II Additional to the 1949 Geneva Conventions', 29 July 1987, at 4.

[53] Examples come from Australia, Canada, France, Germany, and the UK.

[54] ICRC CIHL Study, vol I, Rule 106, at 387–9; J.M. Henckaerts, 'Customary International Humanitarian Law: A Response to US Comments', 89 *IRRC* 866 (2007) 473, at 481.

[55] ICRC CIHL Study, vol I, Rule 106, at 384.   [56] Ibid, at 384–9. Sassòli, above n 15, para 6.

[57] 'The link in time between violation and capture must be so close as to permit those making the capture to take note of it themselves. Thus this is a case of "flagrante delicto".' ICRC Commentary APs, at 540 (footnotes omitted).

[58] Ibid (footnotes omitted).

Such a rule ensures a combatant retains his or her status whether or not he or she may have violated his or her obligation to distinguish himself or herself in the past. 'This rule should, in many cases, cover the great majority of prisoners and will protect them from any efforts to find or to fabricate past histories to deprive them of their protection.'[59]

Article 44(4) AP I further provides POW treatment for those who fail to meet the conditions for POW status,[60] including the application of the procedural and judicial guarantees found in GC III and AP I.[61] While this provision is unique to AP I, Common Article 3 and Article 75 AP I are generally agreed to apply as customary IHL,[62] as does international human rights law (IHRL) in some cases, providing minimum protections with similar effect, particularly regarding judicial guarantees. These minimum standards are discussed in more detail below.

b. Meaning of Article 44(6) and (7) AP I

Article 44(6) AP I, adding that no one who is a combatant under GC III may be denied status under AP I, 'is a savings clause designed to make clear that article [44] is not intended to supplant Article 4 of the third Geneva Convention of 1949 in cases where the latter would entitle a prisoner to prisoner-of-war status'.[63] This provision reinforces the coexistence of Article 4 GC III (and thus the Hague Regulations) and Article 44 AP I.[64]

Article 44(7) AP I addresses the concern that, with AP I's expansion of POW status, the general practice of states' regular armed forces wearing uniforms might be questioned.[65] The International Committee of the Red Cross (ICRC) Commentary clarifies that Article 44(3) 'does not mean that a combatant of a regular army can never dispense with wearing a uniform while he is engaged in hostile acts. However, this possibility is open to him [...] only in the same situations and under the same exceptional conditions as those which apply to members of guerilla forces.'[66]

III. The 'unlawful combatant' debate: various positions on status, treatment, and consequences

The debate surrounding who are 'unlawful combatants' and the protection regime applicable to them is not new.[67] However, it revived in intensity with the 2001 conflict in

---

[59] Ibid, at 539, citing Official Records, above n 49, vol XV, at 403, para 91.
[60] ICRC Commentary APs, at 537–8; Official Records, above n 49, vol XV, at 403, para 90.
[61] ICRC Commentary APs, at 538.
[62] Dörmann, above n 5, at 70. See also M. Matheson, Remarks, 'Session One—The United States Position on the Relation of Customary International Law to the 1977 Protocols Additional to the 1949 Geneva Conventions', in M.P. Dupuis et al, 'The Sixth Annual American Red Cross–Washington College of Law Conference on International Humanitarian Law: A Workshop on Customary International Law and the 1977 Protocols Additional to the 1949 Geneva Conventions', 2 *American University International Law Review* (1987) 415, at 427–8; Office of the Press Secretary, The White House, *Fact Sheet: New Actions on Guantánamo and Detainee Policy*, 7 March 2011 (regarding Executive Order 13567, Periodic Review of Individuals Detained at Guantánamo Bay Naval Station Pursuant to the Authorization for Use of Military Force, 7 March 2011), available at <http://www.whitehouse.gov/the-press-office/2011/03/07/fact-sheet-new-actions-guant-namo-and-detainee-policy>.
[63] Official Records, above n 49, vol XV, at 403, para 92.
[64] ICRC Commentary APs, at 541.   [65] Ibid, at 542.   [66] Ibid.
[67] Dörmann, above n 5, at 46.

Afghanistan involving US and other coalition forces.[68] The main positions on the status and treatment of, and the consequences for, 'unlawful combatants' are described below.

27   If an individual does not fulfil the conditions in Article 4 GC III, i.e., is an 'unlawful combatant', he or she is not provided POW status under GC III. Whether GC IV protects this 'unlawful combatant' is debated. Some consider that due to their 'unlawful' participation in hostilities, such individuals cannot qualify as civilians as defined by Article 4 GC IV and, thus, are not protected by that Convention.[69] In part, it is argued that such 'unlawful' participation violated IHL and, thus, the individual deserves no protection from it, and certainly not the same protection due to peaceful civilians. The (domestic) case law often referenced to support this view is *Ex parte Quirin*,[70] a decision that pre-dates GC IV.

28   A second position considers GC IV to apply to 'unlawful combatants' if the nationality criteria (found in Article 4) are met, but with certain territorial limitations for application of specific protections[71] under GC IV. The territorial limitations are that GC IV would apply only to 'unlawful combatants' operating in occupied territory or if the 'unlawful combatants' are aliens on enemy territory. These limitations exclude persons fighting in their own territory against an advancing enemy that has not yet attained control over the territory (so-called 'battlefield unlawful combatants').[72] Thus, this position hinges on a narrow definition of occupied territory, i.e., that the law of occupation does not apply until the armed forces invading a foreign territory have established actual control over it. However, the Pictet Commentary provides a different understanding of Article 6 GC IV that is more in line with the Convention drafters' objectives:

> So far as individuals are concerned, the application of the Fourth Geneva Convention does not depend upon the existence of a state of occupation within the meaning of [...] Article 42 [of the Hague Regulations] [...] The relations between the civilian population of a territory and troops advancing into that territory, whether fighting or not, are governed by the present Convention. There is no intermediate period between what might be termed the invasion phase and the inauguration of a stable regime of occupation. Even a patrol which penetrates into enemy territory without any intention of staying there must respect the Conventions in dealing with the civilians it meets. [...] The Convention is quite definite on this point: all persons who find themselves in the hands of a Party to the conflict or an Occupying Power of which they are not nationals are protected persons. No loophole is left.[73]

Furthermore, the conclusion that protection does not extend 'to unlawful combatants operating in the territories of the parties to a conflict (Part III, Section 1) and in enemy

---

[68] Ibid, at 45.

[69] See, e.g., R.K. Goldman and B.D. Tittemore, 'Unprivileged Combatants and the Hostilities in Afghanistan: Their Status and Rights under International Humanitarian and Human Rights Law', *ASIL Task Force Papers* (2002), at 38, available at <http://www.pegc.us/archive/Journals/goldman.pdf>.

[70] *Ex parte Quirin*, above n 10.

[71] They would not be covered by provisions in Part III, Sections III and IV, however, they would be protected by the general provisions found in Part II and also Part III, Section I. Dörmann, above n 5, at 62–3. See generally Ch 52, MN 44–48, of this volume.

[72] K. Dörmann, 'Unlawful Combatants', in MPEPIL, para 10. Supporters of this position point to the reference in Art 5 'in the territory of a Party of the conflict' and the fact that Part III, Section I GC IV refers to 'the territories of the parties to the conflict' for their conclusion that 'only the home territory of an enemy country is covered by these terms, thus [GC IV] only [applies to] aliens in enemy territory' (ibid, para 10). See, e.g., R.R. Baxter, 'So-Called "Unprivileged Belligerency": Spies, Guerrillas, and Saboteurs', 28 *BYBIL* (1951) 323, at 328.

[73] Pictet Commentary GC IV, at 60. See generally Ch 67, MN 41–51, of this volume.

territory (Part III, Section 2) is not consistent, given that the definition of protected persons is the same'[74] for all parts of the Convention.

Yet another view considers GC IV to cover 'unlawful combatants' if they fulfil the nationality criteria found in Article 4, without creating a 'no-man's land' through a territorial limitation.[75] The International Criminal Tribunal for the former Yugoslavia (ICTY) found, in the *Delalić* case, that '[i]f an individual is not entitled to the protections of the Third Convention as a prisoner of war (or of the First or Second Conventions) he or she necessarily falls within the ambit of Convention IV, provided that its article 4 requirements are satisfied'.[76] The next section in this chapter further elaborates why this is the correct understanding of GC IV's personal scope of application. 29

Regardless of the position one holds on the applicability of GC IV to 'unlawful combatants', generally all consider them protected by the Martens Clause (see Chapter 9, MN 72–92, of this volume) and/or by customary law, in particular the minimum protections found in Common Article 3 and in Article 75 AP I: 30

The protective rules apply regardless of the way in which such persons have participated in hostilities (e.g. in accordance with IHL or not; in accordance with national law or not; etc.). Nor does it matter whether the person was a member of an armed rebel group, a member of the armed forces of a State or a civilian who (temporarily) took a direct/active part in hostilities.[77]

Lastly, within the 'unlawful combat' debate, disagreement exists as to whether an 'unlawful combatant's' participation in hostilities is a violation of IHL. As has been already stated in this chapter and although some disagree,[78] such participation is not a violation of international law but rather of domestic law, and thus may be penalized if the state has enacted the appropriate domestic legislation.[79] Also, it should be recalled that even '[a]s "civilians", unprivileged combatants may be attacked while they unlawfully directly participate in hostilities. If they fall into the power of the enemy, Convention IV [...] permits administrative detention for imperative security reasons.'[80] 31

IV. Residual protection under GC IV

a. Why and where this matters

Before 1949, no treaty specifically protected civilians in the hands of the enemy. An important safety net is provided by GC IV to ensure that individuals, when in enemy hands, do not lack protection. Many of the provisions of GC IV attempt to ensure that the human suffering of the First World War and, particularly, the Second World War does not reoccur. 32

In order to achieve this, the definition of persons protected by GC IV, found in Article 4, is quite broad, with the key criteria being nationality.[81] As the Geneva Conventions are universally ratified, GC IV protects—during IAC—all persons who are not nationals 33

---

[74] Dörmann, above n 5, at 59.
[75] See, e.g., ibid, at 59–60. See also Bothe/Partsch/Solf, at 261 ff; E. David, *Principes de droit des conflits armes* (2nd edn, Brussels: Bruylant, 1999), at 397 ff.
[76] ICTY, *The Prosecutor v Zejnil Delalić et al*, Judgment, IT-96-21-T, 16 November 1998, para 271.
[77] Dörmann, above n 5, at 48.
[78] See examples provided, above n 11 and discussion at MN 13–16.
[79] Baxter, above n 72, at 338–9.   [80] Sassòli/Bouvier/Quintin, at 178.
[81] For a full discussion of Art 4 GC IV, see Ch 55 of this volume.

of the party to the conflict or Occupying Power in whose hands they are,[82] *unless* they enjoy protection under one of the other three Geneva Conventions, or are nationals of a co-belligerent state in the territory of the belligerent state or occupying state or are nationals of a neutral state in the territory of the belligerent state and their state of nationality has normal diplomatic representation in that state. In *Tadić*, the ICTY 'abandon[ed] this literal interpretation of the definition of protected person [...] and replace[d] the factor of nationality by the factors of allegiance and effective protection'.[83] While this approach sought to adapt the definition of protected persons 'to the principal challenges of contemporary conflicts',[84] it has met with criticism.[85]

34   Persons protected by GC IV are not limited to civilians but include members of armed forces.[86] The protected person category of GC IV

> includes members of the armed forces—fit for service, wounded, sick or shipwrecked—who fall into enemy hands. The treatment such persons are to receive is laid down in special Conventions to which the provision refers. They must be treated as prescribed in the texts which concern them. But if, for some reason, prisoner of war status—to take one example—were denied them, they would become protected persons under the [Fourth] Convention.[87]

35   This safety net is crucial for 'unlawful combatants', including individuals who fail to fulfil the requisite conditions of Article 4(A)(2),[88] as well as spies and mercenaries: '[T]he terms espionage, sabotage, terrorism, banditry and intelligence with the enemy, have so often been used lightly, and applied to trivial offenses, that it was not advisable to leave the accused to the mercy of those detaining them.'[89] This safety net, however, can be just as important—when doubts arise about status—for members of merchant navy and civil aircraft crew, demobilized members of the armed forces of an occupied territory, and diplomats in enemy territory.[90]

36   Individuals who do not qualify for POW status are protected persons under GC IV if they meet the nationality criteria in Article 4.[91] As discussed previously, this position is not held universally:[92] some argue that 'unlawful combatants' belong to a third, different category outside the protection of the Geneva Conventions, because they should not be privileged compared to those who comply with the conditions for POW status.[93] However, it must be recalled that GC IV permits internment of individuals who pose an imperative threat to security and does not shield them from prosecution for crimes

---

[82] For exceptions, see Art 70 GC IV, regarding nationals of the Occupying Power who sought refuge in that territory before occupation, and Art 44 GC IV, applicable to the territory of a party to the conflict, regarding not treating refugees as enemy aliens 'exclusively on the basis of their nationality de jure of an enemy State' (which does not mean that they are not protected by GC IV).

[83] M. Sassòli and L.M. Olson, 'The Judgment of the ICTY Appeals Chamber on the Merits in the Tadić Case', 82 *IRRC* 839 (2000) 733, at 743. ICTY, *The Prosecutor v Duško Tadić*, Appeals Chamber Judgment, IT-94-1-A, 15 July 1999, paras 163–9.

[84] See T. Meron, 'Classification of Armed Conflict in the Former Yugoslavia: Nicaragua's Fallout', 92 *AJIL* (1998) 236, at 238–42; C. Greenwood, 'International Humanitarian Law and the Tadić Case', 7 *EJIL* (1996) 265, at 273–4; W. Fenrick, 'The Development of the Law of Armed Conflict through the Jurisprudence of the International Tribunal for the Fomer Yugoslavia', in M.N. Schmitt and L.C. Green (eds), *The Law of Armed Conflict: Into the Next Millennium* (Newport, RI: Naval War College Press, 1998), vol 71, 77, at 91–2; and ICTY, *The Prosecutor v Zejnil Delalić et al*, above n 76, paras 245–66.

[85] See, e.g., Sassòli and Olson, above n 83, at 743–7.
[86] Pictet Commentary GC IV, at 46.   [87] Ibid, at 50. See also Art 4 para 3 GC IV.
[88] Pictet Commentary GC IV, at 50.   [89] Ibid, at 53 (footnote omitted).   [90] Ibid, at 50–1.
[91] Ibid, at 30.   [92] See discussion at MN 27–30.
[93] See, e.g., discussion at MN 27; Goldman and Tittemore, above n 69, at 38. See also Final Record, vol II-A, at 621.

committed, including their participation in hostilities. And while civilians enjoy the general protections from dangers caused by hostilities, they do so only when not directly participating in hostilities.

The diplomatic discussions surrounding this issue during the drafting of what ultimately became Articles 4 GC III and GC IV were not without debate.[94] In the negotiations on GC III, '[i]t was an open question whether it was desirable to give protection to persons who did not conform to the laws and customs of war'.[95] For example, the Union of Soviet Socialist Republics (USSR) argued, but the Netherlands disagreed, that GC IV applies if the conditions for being a POW found in Article 4 GC III are not met.[96] During the discussions on GC IV, 'two schools of thought had become evident [...] that of those delegations which wished for a broad and "elastic" Convention, and that of those which wanted a restricted Convention'.[97] As a compromise for Article 4 GC IV protecting 'unprivileged combatants' (who meet the nationality criteria), Article 5, which provides certain limitations to the rights and privileges, was included in GC IV.[98]

Article 5 GC IV permits derogation in application of certain GC IV protections to individuals who are 'definitely suspected of or engaged in activities hostile to the enemy state'[99] or Occupying Power, e.g. spies and saboteurs;[100] it can only do so if the Convention applied to them as protected persons. The derogations are essentially limited to the relations of the person with the outside world.[101] This includes the right to correspond and to receive relief, spiritual assistance, or visits from the Protecting Power or the ICRC,[102] although one might argue that the visits by the ICRC and the Protecting Power are not rights of the detainee but control mechanisms of GC IV.[103] The derogations end 'at the earliest date consistent with the security of the State or Occupying Power'.[104] Article 5 clearly states that the rights to humane treatment and fair trial may not be derogated.[105]

The Pictet Commentary summarizes well the general principle embodied in the four Geneva Conventions:

> Every person in enemy hands must have some status under international law: he is either a prisoner of war and, as such, covered by the Third Convention, a civilian covered by the Fourth Convention, or again, a member of the medical personnel of the armed forces who is covered by the First Convention.[106]

---

[94] For a summary, see Dörmann, above n 5, at 55–8. [95] Final Record, vol II-A, at 433.
[96] Final Record, vol II-B, at 271 ff.
[97] Final Record, vol II-A, at 622. See generally ibid, at 620 ff; Pictet Commentary GC IV, at 52.
[98] For Art 4 GC IV, there were 31 votes in favour, 9 abstentions: Final Record, vol II-B, at 377. For Art 5 GC IV, there were 29 votes in favour, 8 against, and 4 abstentions: ibid, at 384.
[99] Art 5 para 1 GC IV. [100] Art 5 para 2 GC IV. See Final Record, vol II-A, at 796, 814–15.
[101] This limitation is explicit with regard to occupied territories: Art 5 para 2 GC IV. However, for enemy aliens held on the territory of a Party to the conflict, it results from the argument that the exercise of rights other than communication rights cannot possibly be 'prejudicial to the security of such State' under the text of Art 5 para 2: Pictet Commentary GC IV, at 56.
[102] Pictet Commentary GC IV, at 56.
[103] It should also be noted that the Detaining Power 'remains fully bound by the obligation [...] to transmit to the official Information Bureau particulars of any protected person who is kept in custody for more than two weeks. This is not, in fact, a right or privilege of the protected person, but an obligation of the Detaining Power.' Ibid.
[104] Art 5 para 3 GC IV. [105] Ibid. [106] Pictet Commentary GC IV, at 51.

40 In addition to state practice supporting this view of GC IV's personal scope of application,[107] the ICTY, not only in *Delalić* referenced above but also in *Blaškić*, made clear that civilians are 'persons who are not, or no longer, members of the armed forces'.[108] The Israeli High Court of Justice provides another example of practice; it concluded, in 2005, that it was

> difficult [...] to see how a third category can be recognized in the framework of the Hague and Geneva Conventions. It does not appear to us that we were presented with data sufficient to allow us to say, at the present time, that such a third category has been recognized in customary international law.[109]

41 Article 45(3) AP I, adopted by consensus in 1977,[110] supports this understanding of the personal scope of application of GC IV. If GC IV did not protect 'unlawful combatants', the phrase in that Article referring to a person who took part in hostilities but 'does not benefit from more favourable treatment in accordance with the Fourth Convention'[111] would be meaningless.[112]

b. *Protected civilians initially treated as prisoners of war: aspects of internment, transfer, and deportation lawful for prisoners of war but not for protected civilians*

42 The procedural rules for interning civilians differ from those for POWs.[113] Civilians are also protected from deportation out of occupied territory. Challenges to upholding these IHL protections for civilians arose, for example, for the UK in the *Rahmatullah case*,[114] discussed below (MN 45).

43 With respect to civilian internment, there must be a review of the reasons for interning a civilian, as civilians—unlike combatants who are captured and become POWs[115]—may be interned only if and as long as they pose an imperative threat to security.[116] Articles 43 and 78 GC IV provide internment review procedures applicable to civilian internees on the territory of a party to the conflict and in occupied territory respectively, giving some detail regarding the type of review body and the timing of review. So an individual who was first treated as a POW, not previously having had a review of his or her internment based on whether he or she posed an imperative threat to security, must have such a review. If the individual does not pose such a threat, he or she must be released.[117] If his or her internment is maintained, the Detaining Power must periodically review the internment decision with a view

---

[107] See, e.g., US Military Manual FM 27-10, *The Law of Land Warfare* (Washington, DC: US Department of the Army, 1956), at 31, 98 ff (contrasting with the US position taken post-2001 in relation to what it formerly called the 'war on terror'); United Kingdom, War Office, *Manual of Military Law, Part III, The Law of War on Land* (London: HMSO, 1958), s 96.

[108] ICTY, *The Prosecutor v Blaškić*, Judgment, IT-95-14-T, 3 March 2000, para 180.

[109] Israeli Supreme Court sitting as the High Court of Justice, *Public Committee against Torture in Israel v Government of Israel et al (Targeted Killings case)*, HCJ 769/02, 11 December 2005, para 28.

[110] Official Records, above n 49, vol VI, 155.

[111] Art 45 para 3 AP I.   [112] Dörmann, above n 5, at 51.

[113] For further elaboration, see Ch 64, MN 37–56, of this volume.

[114] *Yunus Rahmatullah v Secretary of State for Foreign and Commonwealth Affairs and Secretary of State for Defence* [2011] EWCA Civ 1540. See also subsequent appeals *Rahmatullah II* [2012] EWCA Civ 182 and *Rahmatullah III* [2012] UKSC 48.

[115] But see Arts 109–117 GC III (referring to repatriation of POWs during the conflict for medical reasons).

[116] Arts 132 and 133 GC IV.   [117] Art 132 GC IV.

to amending it favourably, if circumstances permit.[118] Under GC IV, it is required that—at the latest—internment must cease 'as soon as possible after the close of hostilities'.[119]

Article 45 GC IV permits, under certain conditions, the transfer of civilian internees to another power.[120] These conditions include that the Transferee Power must be party to the Geneva Convention and that the Detaining Power must be assured that the Transferee Power will apply the Convention; if the Transferee Power fails to apply the Convention, the original Detaining Power must take effective measures to correct the situation or request the return of the internees, the Transferee Power being required to comply with such a request.[121] However, Article 49(1) GC IV prohibits '[i]ndividual or mass forcible transfers, as well as deportations of protected persons from occupied territory [...], regardless of their motive'.[122] Persons in occupied territory protected by GC IV 'cannot be deported; they can therefore only be interned, or placed in assigned residence, within the frontiers of the occupied country itself'.[123] '[U]nlawful deportation or transfer or unlawful confinement of a protected person'[124] constitute grave breaches of GC IV.

The UK was confronted with the issues of the timely release of a civilian and the appropriateness of his deportation out of occupied territory. In *Rahmatullah*,[125] the Court of Appeal directed the issue of a writ of habeas corpus in respect of Yunus Rahmatullah. Rahmatullah, a citizen of Pakistan, was taken into custody by British forces in Iraq in February 2004 and then handed over to US forces, which transferred him to Afghanistan and, in June 2004, detained him in Bagram.[126] In 2011, the Court of Appeal indicated

[n]ow that the US Detainee Review Board has made its determination [that Rahmatullah was 'not an enduring security threat'[127]] and now that the Iraq conflict is ended it seems [...] at least strongly arguable (and, at least on the evidence [...] which we have heard, correct) that [Rahmatullah] should have been released by virtue of the provisions of Articles 49, 132, and 133 of Geneva IV.[128]

Further, the Court found that 'the UK Government is [...] strongly arguably [...] entitled either to demand his release or to demand his return to UK custody under Article 45 [of GC IV]'.[129] Thus, the Court of Appeal directed the issue of a writ of habeas corpus against the Secretaries of State for Foreign Affairs and for Defence in respect of Yunus Rahmatullah.[130] The UK requested Rahmatullah's release to British authorities;[131] the US did not grant the request.[132]

The situation, where an individual initially classified as a POW and removed from occupied territory subsequently is determined to be a civilian, constitutes a violation of Article 49 of GC IV. To remedy the situation, the individual should be returned to that territory.

---

[118] Arts 43 and 78 GC IV.
[119] Art 133 GC IV.   [120] This provision is similar to Art 12 GC III relative to POWs.
[121] Art 45 GC IV.   [122] Art 49 para 1 GC IV.   [123] Pictet Commentary GC IV, at 368.
[124] Art 147 GC IV.
[125] *Rahmatullah*, above n 114. See also subsequent appeals, *Rahmatullah II*, above n 114, and *Rahmatullah III*, above n 114.
[126] *Rahmatullah*, above n 114, para 3.   [127] Ibid, para 10.
[128] Ibid, para 33. See also *Rahmatullah III*, above n 114, para 36.
[129] *Rahmatullah*, above n 114, para 34. See also *Rahmatullah III*, above n 114, paras 37–9. *Rahmatullah III*, above n 114, para 18: 'Quite independently of the 2003 MoU, the UK remained under a continuing obligation, by virtue of GC4, to take such steps as were available to it to ensure that Mr Rahmatullah was treated in accordance with the conventions' requirements and, if necessary, to demand his return.'
[130] *Rahmatullah*, above n 114, para 54; see also *Rahmatullah II*, above n 114, para 1.
[131] *Rahmatullah II*, above n 114, para 2.
[132] Ibid, paras 4, 10. See also *Rahmatullah III*, above n 114, para 78 (reproducing the relevant passages from the US written response to the UK's request).

V. Minimum treatment standards: Common Article 3 and Article 75 AP I

47 As discussed above,[133] GC IV has a gap in its personal scope of application, namely the nationality criteria (as modified by the *Tadić* allegiance exception). However, individuals falling in that gap are not left without protection under IHL. Minimum protections were provided in 1899 through the Martens Clause[134] and then, in 1949, through Common Article 3, which provides more detailed protection than the Martens Clause. And while both recognized the right to minimum standards, neither provides the specific provisions established in 1977 through Article 75 AP I. All these minimum standards, as well as those crystallized in customary law,[135] also supplement the protections to individuals covered by GC IV.[136]

48 Article 75 AP I 'envisaged covering above all the grey area which would always exist whatever might be done, between combatants in the strict sense, as defined in Article 4 of the third Geneva Convention [...] and [...] draft Protocol I, and the peaceful civilian population',[137] whether that be due to, say, adversaries having the same nationality or fluidity of the concept of occupation.[138] Article 45(3) AP I indicates that Article 75 is also to protect 'unlawful combatants'. By defining minimum guarantees, Article 75 AP I—applicable in all conflicts as a matter of customary law—provides the minimum treatment standards and supplements existing protection, for example for those individuals affected by Article 5 GC IV.[139]

49 Specifically, Article 75 supplements GC IV protections for those held by the enemy on enemy territory by ensuring respect for certain judicial guarantees,[140] and it provides additional protections relating to treatment and deprivation of liberty, increasing in some instances the protections contained in Part III, Sections I, II, and IV GC IV.[141] Article 75 also supplements GC IV protections for those held by the enemy in occupied territory by providing additional judicial guarantees, for example the presumption of innocence and other protections relating to treatment and deprivation of liberty.[142]

50 Recognizing the development of IHRL since 1949, many protections in Article 75 mirror certain IHRL provisions. Article 75 also makes clear that '[n]o provision of this Article may be construed as limiting or infringing any other more favourable provision granting greater protection, *under any applicable rules of international law,* to persons covered by

---

[133] See discussion at MN 33.

[134] In 1899, the Martens Clause was 'inserted in the preamble to the Hague Convention on Land Warfare, precisely in an attempt to forestall the conclusion that the treatment of captured resistance fighters, as an "unforeseen case" on which a "written undertaking" had not been achieved, was therefore "left to the arbitrary judgment of military commanders"': F. Kalshoven and L. Zegveld, *Constraints on the Waging of War* (3rd edn, Geneva: ICRC, 2001), at 41. See also Pictet Commentary GC III, at 49.

[135] See, e.g., ICRC CIHL Study, vol I, Rules 87–105 (fundamental guarantees) and Rules 118–28 (persons deprived of liberty), at 306–83, 428–56.

[136] 'The provisions of this Section [Treatment of Persons in the Power of a Party to the Conflict] are *additional* to the rules concerning humanitarian protection of civilians and civilian objects in the power of a Party to the conflict contained in the Fourth Convention, particularly Parts I and III thereof [...]'(Art 72 AP I, emphasis added).

[137] Mr Surbeck, ICRC, in: Official Records, above n 49, Vol XV, at 25.

[138] ICRC Commentary APs, at 558. See also ibid, at 870–1.   [139] Dörmann, above n 5, at 67.

[140] Art 75 para 4 AP I.   [141] Art 75 paras 1–3 AP I. See Dörmann above n 72, para 33.

[142] See Dörmann, above n 72, para 33.

paragraph 1'.¹⁴³ Additional Protocol I clearly recognizes that IHRL provides and supplements protections during armed conflict:

> The provisions of this Section [Treatment of Persons in the Power of a Party to the Conflict] are additional to the rules concerning humanitarian protection of civilians and civilian objects in the power of a Party to the conflict contained in the Fourth Convention [...], *as well as to other applicable rules of international law relating to the protection of fundamental human rights during international armed conflict.*¹⁴⁴

VI. International human rights law protection when conditions of prisoner of war status are not fulfilled

As '[h]uman rights continue to apply concurrently in time of armed conflict',¹⁴⁵ IHRL can provide protections to individuals who do not fulfil the conditions for POW status. If an individual is not protected by GC III but rather protected by GC IV, IHRL may still supplement GC IV protections. When comparing the treaty provisions regulating internment in the two branches of law, however, IHL applicable to civilians in IAC is more specific than IHRL.¹⁴⁶ That said, 51

> both branches [of law] mostly lead to the same results. The treatment of persons detained or otherwise in the power of a state is prescribed in a very similar way. The judicial guarantees for persons undergoing trial are likewise very similar, but they are better developed in human rights. The jurisprudence of the European Court of Human Rights [...] which never explicitly refers to humanitarian law—concerning deliberate or indiscriminate attacks against civilians in Chechnya and eastern Turkey shows that even on such a typical humanitarian law subject as precautionary measures, which have to be taken for the benefit of the civilian population when attacking military objectives, human rights can lead to the same result as humanitarian law.¹⁴⁷

Protections under IHRL become more relevant when neither GC III nor GC IV applies. Common Article 3 and Article 75 AP I serve as an initial safety net, but the protections of IHRL then supplement these minimum IHL rules, for example through the principle of *non-refoulement* discussed in more detail in MN 54–57, below. 52

Yet even with IHRL concurrently applicable in armed conflicts, relying on human rights to provide protection may offer only a minimal solution in certain contexts. In some situations, IHRL may face limitations to its application, for example due to a treaty's formal scope of application or perhaps due to a state's availing itself of a treaty's derogation clause.¹⁴⁸ 53

---

¹⁴³ Art 75 para 8 AP I (emphasis added). ¹⁴⁴ Art 72 AP I (emphasis added).
¹⁴⁵ ICRC Commentary APs, at 1340. See also ICRC Commentary APs, at 843. For further discussion on the relationship between IHRL and IHL and the application generally of IHRL in armed conflict, see Ch 35 of this volume.
¹⁴⁶ The principal difference between IHL and IHRL with regard, say, to procedural regulation of internment, is that the IHL approach is satisfied by an administrative review (Arts 42 and 78 GC IV), while the human rights approach calls for judicial review (e.g., Art 9(4) ICCPR). In this instance, however, IHL in IAC should be seen as *lex specialis* with regard to the type of reviewing body. See also ECtHR, *Hassan v UK*, Judgment, 16 September 2014, paras 104, 109, and 110.
¹⁴⁷ M. Sassòli and L.M. Olson, 'The Relationship between International Humanitarian and Human Rights Law Where It Matters: Admissible Killing and Internment of Fighters in Non-International Armed Conflict', 90 *IRRC* 871 (2008) 599, at 600–1 (footnote omitted).
¹⁴⁸ Ibid, at 626. See also Ch 35, MN 26–31 and 49–50, of this volume.

VII. (Irregular) Renditions for persons who are not protected civilians

54 Another concern is the transfer of 'unlawful combatants' (and others) from one state to another, generally for the purpose of arrest, detention, and/or interrogation by the receiving state. Sometimes these transfers occur secretly, and some have resulted in the transferee's mistreatment.[149] These extrajudicial transfers from one state to another have been referred to as irregular or extraordinary rendition. Whether the person is rendered from the territory of the rendering state or the territory of another state, protections apply to safeguard the individual.

55 If the individual is not a protected person under GC III or GC IV, neither Article 12 GC III nor Article 45 GC IV, which place limitations on the transfer of internees, applies to protect the individual from or upon transfer. These individuals, however, remain protected by the principle of *non-refoulement*, which prohibits the 'transfer of persons from one state to another if they face a risk of violations of certain fundamental rights',[150] found in other provisions of international law.[151]

56 The principle of *non-refoulement* is explicitly provided for in several IHRL instruments, including the Convention against Torture (CAT),[152] the American Convention on Human Rights (ACHR),[153] the International Convention for the Protection of All Persons from Enforced Disappearance,[154] and the Charter of Fundamental Rights of the European Union.[155] However, given the potential limitations to IHRL mentioned above,[156] conventional IHRL may not provide protection in all circumstances. For example, with respect to transfers of detainees held at the Guantánamo Bay detention facility to other countries, the US has indicated that it applies the principle of *non-refoulement* under the CAT as a matter of policy, not as a legal obligation,[157] seemingly based on the determination that at least that CAT provision does not apply extraterritorially.

57 Nevertheless, customary international law fills any gap in conventional protection. While the minimum IHL protections found in Common Article 3 and Article 75 AP

---

[149] C. Droege, 'Transfer of Detainees: Legal Framework, *Non-Refoulement*, and Contemporary Challenges', 90 *IRRC* 871 (2008) 669, at 669. See also M.J. Garcia, 'Renditions: Constraints Imposed by Laws on Torture' (Congressional Research Service RL32890, 8 September 2009), at 5.

[150] Droege, above n 149, at 670.

[151] The principle of *non-refoulement* 'is found—with some variations as to the persons it protects and the risks it protects from—in refugee law, extradition treaties, international humanitarian law and international human rights law.' Ibid. See generally Ch 58, MN 62–71, of this volume.

[152] Art 3 CAT.   [153] Art 22(8) ACHR.   [154] Art 16 ICED.

[155] Art 19(2) Charter of Fundamental Rights of the European Union.

[156] See discussion at MN 53; see also Ch 35 of this volume.

[157] In response to the issue raised by the UN Committee against Torture on application of the *non-refoulement* guarantee to all detainees, including those detained outside US territory, the US stated: 'Noting paragraph 6 of this Report[, which indicates that the report does not address the geographic scope of the Convention as a legal matter], United States *policy* is not to transfer any person to a country where it is more likely than not the person will be tortured or, in appropriate cases, where the person has a well-founded fear of persecution based on a protected ground and would not be disqualified from persecution protection on criminal or security-related grounds.' Periodic Report of the United States of America to the UN Committee against Torture (12 August 2013), CAT/C/USA/3-5, 4 December 2013, para 66 (emphasis added). See also Fourth Periodic Report of the United States of America to the UN Committee on Human Rights Concerning the International Covenant on Civil and Political Rights, 30 December 2011, CCPR/C/USA/4, 22 May 2012, para 560 (referring to transfers from the Guantánamo Bay detention facility and the US *policy* not to transfer individuals to countries where it has been determined that they are more likely than not to be tortured).

I do not specifically address the transfer of detainees, they both prohibit torture and other forms of ill-treatment, as does customary IHL.[158] These provisions

should be interpreted in the light of the interpretation given to the parallel provisions in human rights law. If the absolute human rights law prohibition of torture and other forms of ill-treatment precludes the transfer of a person at risk of such treatment, there is no reason why the absolute prohibition in humanitarian law should not be interpreted in the same way.[159]

Thus, even minimum IHL safeguards should protect an individual held in relation to an armed conflict from the transfer to a third state where a real risk of his or her ill-treatment exists.

VIII. Recent examples: Israel and the United States

Israeli and US measures taken with respect to 'unlawful combatants' deserve examination. Israel adopted a specific law on the detention of 'unlawful combatants' in order to '[aid and advance] the state's battle against terrorist bodies that have declared total war against it. As such, it is itself intended to prevent the return of activists in these organizations, and of those who take part in terrorist attacks against the state, to the cycle of hostilities.'[160] The Incarceration of Unlawful Combatants Law,[161] passed by the Knesset in 2002, defines an 'unlawful combatant' as

a person who has participated, directly or indirectly, in hostilities against the State of Israel, or was a member of a force conducting hostilities against the State of Israel, and in respect of whom the conditions granting prisoner of war status under international humanitarian law, as specified in article 4 of the Third Geneva Convention of 12 August 1949 relative to the Treatment of Prisoners of War, do not apply.[162]

This Law also introduced broad grounds for interning members of groups ('unlawful combatants') who were not entitled to POW status.[163] In 2008, an Israeli district court, in interpreting this Law, adopted an expansive understanding of 'unlawful combatant', particularly regarding membership.[164] Upon appeal, in 2008, however, the Supreme Court disagreed, stating that it could not accept a holding 'whereby the family cell [...] can be deemed a hostile force, so as to satisfy the requirements'[165] of the Law.

---

[158] ICRC CIHL Study, vol I, Rule 90, at 315. See also ibid, vol I, Rule 87, at 306 ('civilians and persons *hors de combat* must be treated humanely').

[159] Droege, above n 149, at 675. See also ibid, at 676. E. Gillard, 'There's No Place like Home: States' Obligations in Relation to Transfers of Persons', 90 *IRRC* 871 (2008) 703, at 727: 'The prohibition on torture and other forms of ill-treatment under international humanitarian law applies to all persons in the effective control of a party to a conflict. Consequently, to the extent that the interpretation of the prohibition of torture and other forms of ill-treatment in international humanitarian law is to be guided by the jurisprudence of the human rights monitoring bodies, *all* such persons are protected from transfers that may put them at risk of such treatment.'

[160] Supreme Court of Israel, *A v State of Israel*, Adm Det App 7750/08, 23 November 2008, para 15 (unofficial translation provided in Sassòli/Bouvier/Quintin, at 1193). Ibid: 'Conversely the purpose of the Administrative Detention Law is to prevent danger to state security by individual persons and for specific reasons.'

[161] Incarceration of Unlawful Combatants Law 5762-2002. This Law was amended in 2008.

[162] Ibid, s 2.

[163] Ibid, ss 2 and 7. See Ch 64 of this volume for a more detailed discussion of internment.

[164] *A v State of Israel*, above n 160, para 3 (unofficial translation provided in Sassòli/Bouvier/Quintin, at 1191).

[165] Ibid, para 11 (unofficial translation provided in Sassòli/Bouvier/Quintin, at 1192).

59   In 2005, the Israeli Supreme Court, in the *Targeted Killings case*, had concluded that no room for a third category of persons existed at that time under international law.[166] And, in 2008, the Israeli Supreme Court clarified that the definition of 'unlawful combatant' under the Incarceration of Unlawful Combatants Law 'does not create a separate category of treatment from the viewpoint of international humanitarian law, but constitutes a sub-group of the category of "civilians" '.[167]

60   Another set of issues relates to US practice since 2001, following the onset of hostilities in Afghanistan.[168] One example, concerning 'unlawful combatants', is the US position taken in 2002 that the Taliban and Al-Qaeda were not protected by GC III or GC IV and were entitled to humane treatment only as a matter of policy.[169] Other examples are the US positions on its detention authority and the definitions of 'enemy combatant' employed by the executive, legislative, and judicial branches that have evolved over time.

61   For example, in *Hamdi*, the US Government offered a definition of 'enemy combatant' that more closely tracked a 'direct participation in hostilities' standard than would subsequent definitions. The definition offered was 'an individual who [...] was "part of or supporting forces hostile to the United States and its coalition partners" in Afghanistan *and who* "engaged in an armed conflict against the United States" there'.[170]

62   After *Hamdi*, the Order Establishing the Combatant Status Review Tribunals (CSRTs) broadened the definition of 'enemy combatant'. The Order provided that an 'enemy combatant' is

> an individual who was part of or supporting Taliban or al Qaeda forces, or associated forces that are engaged in hostilities against the United States or its coalition partners. This includes any person who has committed a belligerent act or has directly supported hostilities in aid of enemy armed forces.[171]

63   According to this definition, anyone who merely supports the Taliban or Al-Qaeda is deemed a 'combatant'. However, mere support of the war effort does not constitute combatancy.[172] The concern with this standard is that it establishes 'guilt' by association, that is, simply being a group member—regardless of one's contribution—would make one an 'enemy combatant' under this US definition.

64   Through the MCA 2006, Congress endorsed the Administration's CSRT definition[173] and added a definition of '*unlawful* enemy combatant'.[174] Like the CSRT definition, the MCA definition includes as 'combatants' persons who have only supported, but not directly participated in, hostilities. However, the MCA definition of 'unlawful enemy

---

[166] *Targeted Killings case*, above n 109, para 28.
[167] Supreme Court of Israel, *Iyad v State of Israel*, CrimA 6659/06, 11 June 2008, para 12.
[168] Material in this section has been drawn from L. Olson, 'Guantánamo *Habeas* Review: Are the D.C. District Court's Decisions Consistent with IHL Internment Standards?', 42 *Case Western Reserve JIL* (2009) 197, at 214–18.
[169] Memorandum from President George W. Bush to National Security Advisors, 'Humane Treatment of Taliban and al Qaeda Detainees', 7 February 2002, para 3, available at <http://www.pegc.us/archive/White_House/bush_memo_20020207_ed.pdf>.
[170] *Hamdi v Rumsfeld*, 542 US 507, 516 (2004) (citing Brief for the Respondents, at 3) (emphasis added).
[171] Memorandum from the Deputy Secretary of Defense to the Secretary of the Navy, Order Establishing Combatant Status Review Tribunal, 7 July 2004, at 1, available at <http://www.defenselink.mil/news/Jul2004/d20040707review.pdf>.
[172] See, e.g., Melzer, above n 26, at 51–2.   [173] MCA 2006, above n 11, § 948a(1)(ii).
[174] Ibid, § 948a(1)(i).

combatant' may be somewhat narrower than the CSRT definition of 'enemy combatant'. For example, the US Government had acknowledged that the CSRT definition of 'enemy combatant' might include a 'little old lady in Switzerland' sending money to support a charity which, unbeknownst to her, turned out to be a front for Al-Qaeda.[175] Such a person would appear to fall outside the MCA definition, under which the person must have '*purposefully* and materially supported hostilities'.[176] Nevertheless, even the inclusion of 'hostilities' in relation to 'support' does not prevent this definition from being applied over-broadly—possibly extending outside the scope of armed conflict.

Employment of this 'category' of persons also affects their treatment upon capture. For example, the US incorporated the notion of 'unlawful enemy combatant' in the revised Army Field Manual on Human Intelligence Collector Operations, which confusingly overlaps with the protected person categories found in IHL.[177] According to the Field Manual, 'unlawful enemy combatants' may be subjected to the restricted interrogation technique called 'separation'[178] to prevent them from communicating with other detainees by keeping them physically isolated. 'Separation' may be combined with other interrogation techniques.

The Supreme Court's determination in 2006 in *Hamdan*[179] that at least Common Article 3 applied to the conflict between the US and Al-Qaeda was largely understood as a determination that this conflict was indeed not of an international character. This raised the concern of transplanting IAC concepts and terminology such as 'combatants' into the non-international armed conflict (NIAC) context.

In 2009, the Obama Administration abandoned the term 'enemy combatant' (for 'unprivileged enemy belligerent').[180] And despite the Administration's explicitly indicating that its authority to detain those persons held at Guantánamo Bay was based on the Authorization for Use of Military Force (AUMF) that is 'necessarily informed *by the principles of the law of war*',[181] critics were not so certain that the new standard provided by the Obama Administration substantially changed the US position on whom it could detain: 'The Obama Administration's definition of its scope of detention authority is similar to the Bush Administration's definition describing who could be treated as an

---

[175] See *In re Guantánamo Detainee Cases*, 355 F Supp 2d 443, 475 (DDC 2005). The Government backed off from this extreme view. See *Al Marri v Pucciarelli*, 534 F 3d 213, 226 (4th Cir 2008) (Motz, J, concurring).

[176] See MCA 2006, above n 11, § 948a(1)(i) (emphasis added).

[177] The Army Field Manual states: 'Unlawful enemy combatants: Unlawful enemy combatants are persons not entitled to combatant immunity, who engage in acts against the United States or its coalition partners in violation of the laws and customs of war during an armed conflict. For purposes of the war on terrorism, the term "unlawful enemy combatant" is defined to include, but is not limited to, an individual who is or was part of or supporting Taliban or al Qaida forces, or associated forces that are engaged in hostilities against the United States or its coalition partners.' Department of the Army, Human Intelligence Collector Operations, Field Manual 2-22.3 (FM 34-52) (2006), paras 6–18, available at <https://www.fas.org/irp/doddir/army/fm2-22-3.pdf>. See also ibid, paras 6–19 (making a further distinction between an 'unlawful enemy combatant' or an individual 'associated with or supporting the unlawful enemy combatants'). This Field Manual on interrogation replaces the 1992 Field Manual, and this revised version was publicly released on 6 September 2006.

[178] See ibid, Appendix M.

[179] *Hamdan*, above n 30, at 628–31 (concluding that, at the very least, CA 3 applies to the US conflict with Al-Qaeda because it is a 'conflict *not* of an international character').

[180] The US Congress similarly changed terminology to 'alien unprivileged enemy belligerent'; see, e.g., MCA 2009, above n 11, § 948(c).

[181] Respondents' Memorandum Regarding the Government's Detention Authority Relative to Detainees Held at Guantánamo Bay, *In re* Guantánamo Bay Detainee Litigation, Misc No 08-442 (TFH) (DC Cir March 13, 2009), at 1 (March 13 Memo), available at <http://www.justice.gov/opa/documents/memo-re-det-auth.pdf> (emphasis added).

"enemy combatant," differing only in that it requires "substantial support," rather than "support".[182]

68   The Obama Administration's clarification in 2009 of its standard for detention of persons held at Guantánamo Bay, however, did not 'define the contours of authority for military operations generally, or detention in other contexts'.[183] Then, in the National Defense Authorization Act for Fiscal Year 2012, Congress confirmed that the AUMF includes the authority to detain non-citizens captured outside the US, who 'planned, authorized, committed or aided' the attacks of 11 September 2001, or harboured persons responsible for those attacks[184] or persons who were

> part of or substantially supported al-Qaeda, the Taliban, or associated forces that are engaged with hostilities against the United States or its coalition partners, including any person who has committed a belligerent act or has directly supported such hostilities in aid of such enemy forces.[185]

Nevertheless,

> [w]hile there are serious questions concerning the scope and viability of the 'substantial support' prong for detention, all of the cases to arise thus far have turned on the membership prong—with the government arguing that the detainee in question was 'part of' al Qaeda or the Taliban.[186]

Uncertainty remains regarding whether the scope of detention authority conferred by the AUMF applies to US citizens, lawful residents, or to non-citizens captured within US territory.[187]

69   While particularly affecting, but not limited to, the detainees held at the US Naval Station at Guantánamo Bay, Cuba, the US executive,[188] legislative,[189] and judicial[190] branches continue to refine—not without controversy—'the scope of the government's authority to detain these, and other, detainees pursuant to the [AUMF] [...] as informed by the law of war'.[191] Even though this refinement focuses on US domestic law (namely, the AUMF), interpretations of the traditional protected person categories found in IAC are being impacted. The search for clarity on internment in NIAC is thus, in some instances, spilling over and affecting—not always positively—the rules applicable in IAC.

70   From an IHL perspective, the main concern with the various versions of the US category of 'unlawful combatant' (whether so-called or not) is that they inappropriately

---

[182] J.K. Elsea and M.J. Garcia, 'Wartime Detention Provisions in Recent Defense Authorization Legislation' (Congressional Research Service R42143, 23 June 2014), at 8 (citation omitted), available at <http://fas.org/sgp/crs/natsec/R42143.pdf>.

[183] March 13 Memo, above n 181, at 2.

[184] National Defense Authorization Act for FY2012 (P.L. 112- 81), § 1021(b)(1) (authorizing detention of certain categories of persons) (2012 NDAA).

[185] Ibid, § 1021(b)(2).

[186] S.I. Vladeck, 'Detention after the AUMF', 82 *Fordham Law Review* (2014) 2189, at 2194 (footnote omitted).

[187] 2012 NDAA, above n 184, § 1021(e).

[188] See, e.g., March 13 Memo, above n 181; Executive Order 13567, Periodic Review of Individuals Detained at Guantánamo Bay Naval Station Pursuant to the Authorization for Use of Military Force, 7 March 2011.

[189] See, e.g., MCA 2009, above n 11, § 948(c); 2012 NDAA, above n 184, §§ 1021–4 (authorizing detention of certain categories of persons).

[190] Particularly pertinent are the DC Circuit Courts, as they are hearing the Guantánamo *habeas* cases. See, e.g., B. Wittes, R.M. Chesney, and L. Reynolds, 'The emerging law of detention 2.0: The Guantánamo *habeas* cases as lawmaking' (Harvard Law School and Brookings, April 2012), available at <http://www.brookings.edu/research/reports/2011/05/guantanamo-wittes>; R.M. Chesney, 'Who May Be Held? Military Detention through the *Habeas* Lens', 52 *Boston College Law Review* (2011) 769; Olson, above n 168, at 197.

[191] *Hamlily v Obama*, 616 F Supp 2d 63, 66 (DDC 2009).

merge the concept of 'combatants' and civilians who pose an imperative threat to security, because the definition of 'enemy combatant' is broader than the corresponding POW definition found in GC III.[192] The US 'enemy combatant' category adds elements of the 'imperative-reasons-of-security' standard for interning civilians during IAC, with some elements possibly even sweeping broader than that standard.[193] This 'enemy combatant' standard for detention purposes is also particularly dangerous for the protection of persons in armed conflict because, if someone is detainable as a 'combatant', he or she may arguably, according to the logic to which the term 'combatant' refers, also be attacked when not *hors de combat*.

C. Relevance in Non-International Armed Conflicts

The debate of the early twenty-first century regarding 'unlawful combatants', in contrast to that of the drafters of the four Geneva Conventions, is further complicated by the fact that most conflicts today are NIACs, not IACs. Unlike in IAC, the IHL provisions of NIAC protecting persons in the hands of the enemy are *not* set out according to protected person categories, such as POWs or civilians. Furthermore, IHL of NIACs 'foresees no combatant status, does not define combatants and does not prescribe specific obligations for them',[194] as states did not wish to confer the right to participate in hostilities and its ensuing combatant immunity on non-state actors in NIACs.[195]

71

Thus, to speak of persons not qualifying for POW status or as being 'unlawful *combatants*' is misplaced in the context of a NIAC. However, in NIACs, it still, as in IACs, remains essential for the protection of persons to know when someone may be detained. Unfortunately, neither IHL nor IHRL provides clear answers in NIAC.[196] For example, while the US position since 2001 continues to be refined, it has generally considered that it may detain enemy fighters in NIACs similarly to combatants in IACs.[197] This position has caused significant controversy, with critics asserting that IHRL regulates if, and when, persons may be detained in NIACs.[198]

72

Whether 'unlawful combatants' may be detained in NIACs and, more generally, what, if any, legal basis exists under IHL to detain persons in relation to a NIAC[199] are fundamental questions. Responses to these questions are critical to providing satisfactory protection to persons detained in relation to a NIAC.

73

While IHL of NIAC recognizes that internment occurs in NIACs,[200] it contains no indication of the grounds for or procedures by which a person may be detained. This

74

---

[192] See Art 4 GC III. Art 44 AP I is not referenced here as the US is not a party to that treaty and that Article's content is not generally considered customary. ICRC CIHL Study, vol I, Rule 106, at 387–9; Henckaerts, above n 54, at 481.

[193] Its application also potentially extends beyond association with any armed conflict to law enforcement operations.

[194] Sassòli/Bouvier/Quintin, at 343.

[195] The issue of the illegality of non-state actors taking up arms against the state—that is, engaging in armed conflict—is a matter regulated not by IHL but by domestic law.

[196] Sassòli and Olson, above n 147, at 601.   [197] Ibid. See also Olson, above n 168, at 216–24.

[198] Sassòli and Olson, above n 147, at 601.

[199] See, e.g., *Serdar Mohammed and Minstry of Defence* [2014] EWHC 1369 (QB). For further discussion, see E. Debuf, *Captured in War: Lawful Internment in Armed Conflict* (Oxford: Hart Publishing, 2013), at 464–88.

[200] See, e.g., CA 3 para 1, and Arts 5 and 6 AP II. See Debuf, above n 199, at 465–9 (discussing why the mention of internment in CA 3 and AP II provides no implicit basis for internment in NIAC, namely that the purpose of these provisions is to regulate treatment and conditions of internment rather than provide a legal basis for it).

stands in contrast to GC III concerning POWs and GC IV concerning civilians, applicable in IACs:[201]

> Where international humanitarian law for non-international armed conflict fundamentally differs from that regulating international armed conflict and occupation is in the fact that it does not prescribe either the grounds for security internment, or the essential procedural safeguards that must accompany such deprivation of liberty, and therefore, '[i]n non-international armed conflicts, IHL cannot possibly be seen as a sufficient legal basis for detaining anyone.'[202]

In addition, no legal basis for internment in NIAC currently exists in customary IHL.[203]

75   Yet as in IAC, military necessity exists in NIAC to detain members of the armed forces of the parties to the conflict. Until IHL of NIAC is developed to include a direct legal basis to detain, the main option available for states to legally detain in NIAC is to adopt domestic law providing the legal basis.[204] If the state is involved in a NIAC abroad, it could seek to conclude an agreement with the host state, granting such authority based on that state's domestic law.[205] Both of these options, however, are asymmetric, providing no legal option for the non-state actor to detain in the NIAC.

76   The conclusion of special agreements between the parties to the conflict, as encouraged by Common Article 3, to extend application of the Geneva Conventions to the conflict could be a solution for state and non-state actors.[206] A second option, discussed in Chapter 64, MN 64–70, of this volume is the analogous application of IHL of IACs to NIACs;[207] however, it is argued that '[t]he principle of legality opposes any deprivation of liberty by analogy on a legal basis designed to deprive a person of his or her liberty in circumstances that do not apply to the specific internee or detainee concerned'.[208] Another option for state and non-state actors could be recourse to a United Nations (UN) Security Council resolution adopted under Chapter VII of the UN Charter providing a legal basis for detention; however, whether the Security Council has the legal capacity to do this remains debated, as does the specificity of the language required in such a resolution.[209]

77   Lastly, it should be noted that, while it is beyond the scope of this commentary to address the conduct of hostilities, the debate regarding 'unlawful combatants' in NIACs has consequences for targeting. As mentioned above,[210] if 'unlawful combatants' are detained analogously to 'combatants', they may arguably also be attacked when not *hors de combat*. This possible consequence cannot be ignored when answering the question of who may be detained in relation to a NIAC. To do so, risks undermining protections existing for persons from the effects of hostilities.

D. Legal Consequences of a Violation

78   A state is responsible for internationally wrongful acts committed by its organs, including armed forces.[211] Thus, a state is responsible for violations of IHL[212] and IHRL attributable

---

[201] See Chs 46 and 64 of this volume.
[202] Debuf, above n 199, at 487–8 (citing M. Sassòli, 'The Status of Persons Held in Guantánamo under International Humanitarian Law', 2 *JICJ* (2004) 96, at 105).
[203] See, e.g., *Serdar* above n 199, paras 254–67. See also Debuf, above n 199, at 469–73.
[204] Debuf, above n 199, at 488.   [205] Ibid, at 489.
[206] Ibid.   [207] Sassòli and Olson, above n 147, at 623–5.
[208] Debuf, above n 199, at 473.   [209] Ibid, at 490–5.   [210] See discussion at MN 70.
[211] Art 4 ILC Articles on State Responsibility.
[212] ICRC CIHL Study, vol I, Rule 149, at 530–6. See Art 3 Hague Convention IV and Art 91 AP I. See also Art 51 GC I; Art 52 GC II; Art 131 GC III; Art 148 GC IV.

to it, and 'measures to stop and repress them [...] must be directed against the state responsible for the violation[s]'.²¹³ Serious violations of IHL also give rise to individual criminal responsibility.²¹⁴ Specifically, state parties must 'provide effective penal sanctions for persons committing, or ordering to be committed, any of the grave breaches'²¹⁵ of the four Geneva Conventions.

International humanitarian customary law prohibits the arbitrary deprivation of liberty.²¹⁶ What constitutes the arbitrary deprivation of liberty of protected persons in an IAC depends upon the substantive rules of IHL discussed in this commentary. Particularly relevant for persons labelled 'unlawful combatants' are those rules concerning POWs and civilians found in Chapters 47–51 and 64–66 of this volume, respectively. Additionally, Article 130 GC III makes it a grave breach to deprive a POW of the rights of fair and regular trial prescribed by GC III.²¹⁷ And while Chapter 64 elaborates upon the consequences of depriving a person, which includes an 'unlawful combatant', of the protection he or she deserves as a *civilian*,²¹⁸ two brief comments will be made here. 79

First, it must be borne in mind that 'unlawful confinement' of a protected civilian is a serious violation of IHL, constituting a grave breach of GC IV.²¹⁹ Further, it is criminalized under other treaties and international instruments, including the International Criminal Court Statute, the ICTY Statute, the UN–Cambodia Agreement Concerning the Prosecution under Cambodian Law of Crimes Committed during the Period of Democratic Kampuchea, and the UN Transitional Administration in East Timor Regulation 2000/15 for East Timor.²²⁰ It is also a crime under the domestic law of several states.²²¹ 80

Secondly, in addition to the decisions of judicial and quasi-judicial bodies discussed in Chapter 64 of this volume, that have addressed the regulation of internment in relation to armed conflict, mention should be made of the precautionary measures issued by the Inter-American Commission on Human Rights (IACHR) regarding detention at Guantánamo Bay, because the measures address the situation of individuals labelled 'unlawful combatants'. In 2002, the IACHR adopted—in the context of the US considering 'itself to be at war with an international network of terrorists'—precautionary measures, requesting that the US 'take urgent measures necessary to have the legal status of the detainees at Guantánamo Bay determined by a competent tribunal'²²² rather than 81

---

²¹³ Sassòli/Bouvier/Quintin, at 386.
²¹⁴ See, e.g., Lieber Code; Art 50 GC I; Art 51 GC II; Art 130 GC III; Art 147 GC IV; Art 85 AP I. See also Art 1 of the London Agreement for the Prosecution and Punishment of the Major War Criminals of the European Axis, 8 August 1945 (establishing 'an International Military Tribunal for the trial of war criminals whose offenses have no particular geographical location whether they be accused individually or in their capacity as members of the organizations or groups or in both capacities'). See, generally, ICRC CIHL Study, vol I, Rules 151–5, at 551–67.
²¹⁵ Art 49 GC I; Art 50 GC II; Art 129 GC III; Art 146 GC IV.
²¹⁶ ICRC CIHL Study, vol I, Rule 99, at 344–52.
²¹⁷ See also Art 8(2)(a)(vi) of the ICC Statute.   ²¹⁸ Ch 64, MN 71–76, of this volume.
²¹⁹ Art 147 GC IV.
²²⁰ Art 8(2)(a)(vii) ICC Statute; Art 2(g) ICTY Statute; Art 9 of the 2003 UN–Cambodia Agreement Concerning the Prosecution under Cambodian Law of Crimes Committed during the Period of Democratic Kampuchea; UNTAET Regulation 2000/15, s 6(1)(a)(vii).
²²¹ See ICRC CIHL Database, Rule 99.
²²² IACommHR, Precautionary Measures 259/02, Persons detained by the United States in Guantánamo Bay, Cuba, 12 March 2002, available at <https://www.oas.org/en/iachr/pdl/decisions/GuantanamoMC.asp#MC25902>.

a political authority, in order to ensure that the detainees 'would be afforded the legal protections commensurate with that status'.[223] The US responded that it considers, inter alia, the IACHR to lack 'the jurisdictional competence to request precautionary measures dealing with the law of armed conflict' and 'the authority to request precautionary measures of States that are not parties to the American Convention'.[224] Nevertheless, the IACHR extended these precautionary measures in 2005 and 2013.[225]

E. Critical Assessment

82 As IHL only permits weakening the military potential of the enemy,[226] the principle of distinction is key to the effective functioning of IHL. Therefore, IHL defines who may and may not be attacked, and requires those individuals who can be attacked in the armed conflict to distinguish themselves from those who cannot be attacked. One of the reasons members of armed forces/groups have been labelled 'unlawful combatants' is that they failed on this point, i.e., to distinguish themselves from the civilian population. While distinguishing oneself is an IHL requirement for POW status (and concomitantly to be a combatant), the use of this new, third category of persons—'unlawful combatants'—in recent years has actually blurred the distinction between civilians and combatants, and risks undermining the protection of civilians from hostilities as well as the protections established in 1949 by GC III and GC IV for persons in enemy hands. Appropriate application of IHL is needed to reduce these risks, but clarity in various areas of IHL would help as well.

83 Essential protection in IACs is provided by GC III and GC IV. And while the denial to 'unlawful combatants' of protection under one or both of these treaties in the early twenty-first century often has been due to a misunderstanding of various treaty provisions, the protection provided in IACs is not complete. Due to limitations in the personal scope of application of GC IV, gaps remain in coverage, in particular with regard to the state's nationals, as the Convention does not apply to them.[227] Regarding GC III, greater clarity is necessary on the meaning of the conditions, in particular of Article 4(A)(2) GC III, for POW status of other armed groups not part of the armed forces of the party to the conflict; having the Detaining Power apply imprecise criteria increases the risk of abuse.

84 Since the adoption of GC III and GC IV, IHRL has developed significantly and may be turned to for protection. However, the extent of IHRL's application in IACs and in NIACs not only may vary with each context, but also may not always be clear.[228] In addition, a mechanical application of IHRL may not always be realistic, in particular for persons captured on the battlefield.[229] Guidance in this area would help ensure the necessary protection.

85 Many conflicts are no longer IACs but rather NIACs and involve persons other than members of regular armed forces. In practice, even if members of an armed group serving

---

[223] Ibid.
[224] 'Additional Response of the United States to request for precautionary measures, *Detainees in Guantánamo Bay, Cuba*, IACHR, 15 July 2002, available at <http://www.state.gov/s/l/38642.htm>. See also 'Response of the United States to Request for Precautionary Measures: Detainees in Guantánamo Bay, Cuba', 41 *ILM* (2002) 1015.
[225] IACommHR, Extensions of Precautionary Measures 259/02, Persons detained by the United States in Guantánamo Bay, Cuba, 20 October 2005 and 23 July 2103, available at <https://www.oas.org/en/iachr/pdl/decisions/GuantanamoMC.asp#28oct>.
[226] See, e.g., St Petersburg Declaration of 1868 and Art 46 Hague Regulations.
[227] Pictet Commentary GC IV, at 372–3. But see the *Tadić* allegiance exception, discussed at MN 33.
[228] See Ch 35 of this volume.   [229] See, e.g., Ch 64 of this volume, MN 43.

a continuous combatant function are not civilians, it is often difficult to distinguish them from the civilian population. In addition, the 'unlawful combatant' category has been used in NIACs. This use has contributed to a worrisome blurring of the distinction between civilians and combatants. Clarity on who may be attacked—and thus killed—in NIACs would greatly increase protection. In this area, clarity on the meaning of 'direct participation in hostilities' is crucial and, while extensive efforts have been made in recent years,[230] this concept remains unsettled. In addition, clarity regarding the scope of admissible internment and the required procedures to be followed when a state or non-state actor captures and interns someone in relation to the NIAC is necessary to ensure protection.

These concerns grow with the increasing 'civilianization'[231] of armed conflicts. For example, as seen in the Iraq and Afghanistan armed conflicts, more and more 'private military and security companies, whose members are usually not combatants, are […] present in conflict areas'.[232] In addition, civilians are increasingly undertaking integral support functions and are even part of frontline military operations (in large part due to technological developments), which has 'prompted some legal scholars to indicate 21st century armed forces may be in danger of employing civilians in combat roles'.[233]

State forces carrying out UN operations also pose a challenge to proper application of IHL. The 1994 Convention on the Safety of United Nations and Associated Personnel protects from attack military and police personnel on a UN operation.[234] While the Convention does not apply to 'an enforcement action under Chapter VII of the Charter of the United Nations in which any of the personnel are engaged as combatants against organized armed forces and to which the law of international armed conflict applies',[235] IHL should apply whenever UN forces resort to force in an armed conflict.[236] Even with the UN Secretary-General's Bulletin, 'Observation by United Nations Forces of International Humanitarian Law',[237] it remains controversial whether IHL applies (and, if so, which provisions) to peace support operations carried out by states' forces deployed under the auspices of the UN.[238]

If various IHL provisions may be criticized for lacking clarity or not protecting all persons at risk in armed conflicts once captured by the enemy, the foundational protections provided in IHL remain strong and effective overall. With the technological development of new forms of warfare, these fundamental principles of IHL must be affirmed and continue to be applied in good faith.

LAURA M. OLSON*

---

[230] See, e.g., Melzer, above n 26.   [231] Sassòli/Bouvier/Quintin, at 163.
[232] Ibid, at 164.
[233] K. Watkin, 'Combatants, Unprivileged Belligerents and Conflicts in the 21st Century', Background paper prepared for the Informal High-Level Expert Meeting on the Reaffirmation and Development of IHL, Cambridge, 27–9 January 2003 (HPCR), at 16, available at <http://www.hpcrresearch.org/sites/default/files/publications/Session2.pdf>.
[234] Arts 1 and 7 Convention on the Safety of United Nations and Associated Personnel.
[235] Ibid, Art 2.
[236] See, e.g., ibid, Art 20 (leaving room for conjecture whether IHL may be applicable when the Convention itself applies or only in situations not covered by the Convention).
[237] UN Secretary-General's Bulletin, 'Observation by United Nations Forces of International Humanitarian Law', 6 August 1999, UN Doc ST/SGB/1999/13, Section 8.
[238] M. Sassòli, 'Internment', in MPEPIL, para 15.

* The views expressed in this chapter are made in the author's personal capacity and do not represent the position or views of the US Department of Homeland Security or the US Government.

Chapter 46. Determination of Prisoner of War Status

	MN
A. Introduction	1
B. Meaning and Application	12
I. Reasons for presumption of prisoner of war status	12
II. Who benefits from the presumption in the Third Geneva Convention?	15
III. When is there a doubt and whose doubt is relevant?	19
IV. To what does the doubt refer?	26
a. Whether the group of which the individual is a member belongs to a party to the international armed conflict or fulfils the four conditions listed in Article 4(A)(2)	27
b. Nationals of the Detaining Power	41
V. 'Competent tribunal' standards to determine status	42
VI. Procedural guarantees before an Article 5 tribunal, including the influence of international human rights law	56
VII. Options for a person the Detaining Power wants to consider as having POW status but who does not want POW status	61
C. Relevance in Non-International Armed Conflicts	65
D. Critical Assessment	66

Select Bibliography

Bogar, T.J., 'Unlawful Combatant or Innocent Civilian? A Call to Change the Current Means for Determining Status of Prisoners in the Global War on Terror', 21 *Florida JIL* (2009) 29

Jinks, D., 'The Declining Significance of POW Status', 45 *Harvard International Law Journal* (2004) 367

Kastenberg, J., 'The Customary International Law of War and Combatant Status: Does the Current Executive Branch Policy Determination on Unlawful Combatant Status for Terrorists Run Afoul of International Law, or Is It Just Poor Public Relations?', 36 *Gonzaga Law Review* (2003–4) 495

Levie, H.S., 'Prisoners of War in International Armed Conflict', 59 *International Law Studies* (1977) 1

Naqvi, Y., 'Doubtful Prisoner-of-War Status', 84 *IRRC* 847 (2002) 571

Rosas, A., *The Legal Status of Prisoners of War: A Study in International Humanitarian Law Applicable in Armed Conflicts* (Helsinki: Suomalainen Tiedeaktemia, 1976)

Sassòli, M., 'La "guerre contre le terrorisme", le droit international humanitaire et le statut de prisonnier de guerre', 39 *CanYIL* (2001) 211

Vierucci, L., 'Prisoners of War or Protected Persons qua Unlawful Combatants? The Judicial Safeguards to which Guantánamo Bay Detainees are Entitled?', 1 *JICJ* (2003) 284

A. Introduction

Prisoner of war (POW) status is of importance in international humanitarian law (IHL). Combatants taken by the enemy are in a critical position of vulnerability, and history has shown the importance of enacting binding rules to safeguard standards of treatment

1

during detention, in order to ensure their survival. In this respect, the Third Geneva Convention (GC III) is a great achievement in the quest for *humanizing* detention in situations of armed conflict. Even so, and despite an effort to clarify the captured combatants' status, with a detailed Article on categories of people entitled to POW status and conditions that must be fulfilled, doubt may arise from confusion on the battlefield, from political changes in governments and authorities inherent to armed conflicts, and from divergent interpretations of IHL.

2   To avoid the possibility that Detaining Powers might easily deny POW status to enemy combatants who have fallen into their power, and to guarantee regularity in the procedures to determine a POW's status, the drafters of the Convention introduced a provision for the benefit of those who have fallen into the power of an enemy. According to Article 5 paragraph 2 GC III, if any doubt exists as to whether persons having committed a belligerent act and finding themselves in the power of the enemy are entitled to POW status, those persons shall benefit from the protection of GC III until the question is settled by a competent tribunal.

3   This provision was included following a suggestion by the International Committee of the Red Cross (ICRC), and was meant to ensure that persons belonging to regular armed forces and whose status was unclear would benefit from some protection upon capture.

4   The first version of this provision was less precise.[1] After discussion, it was suggested that it should apply in case of doubt, i.e. when it is uncertain if someone *having committed belligerent acts and having fallen into the hands of the enemy* belongs to one of the categories enumerated in Article 4 GC III.

5   In its initial version, the text referred to those '*captured*' by the enemy. After proposals made during the Stockholm Conference and the 1947 Diplomatic Conference, the word '*capture*' was replaced with the expression '*fallen into the power of the enemy*'. This was deemed necessary to ensure that all combatants held by the enemy would be granted the protective status of a POW, including, for instance, those who voluntarily surrender, like the German soldiers who in May 1945 voluntarily passed into the Allied Powers' custody but were denied POW status and treated as 'Surrendered Enemy Personnel'.

6   The term 'responsible authority' appearing in the first version was also changed to 'competent tribunal', after the proposal to use the term 'military tribunal' was rejected. The choice of 'competent tribunal' was meant to ensure respect for some form of basic judicial guarantees.

7   Nearly 30 years later, Article 45 of Additional Protocol (AP) I was adopted, with the intention to reaffirm and further develop Article 5 GC III. In the light of developments in armed conflicts since the Second World War, in particular those brought about by guerrilla warfare, a development was deemed necessary to establish a procedure that would guarantee that those entitled to the POW status would benefit from it. Indeed, as the risk of severe punishment faced by someone having taken part in hostilities and fallen into the power of the enemy is quite high, specific procedures to protect such a person further were agreed upon by delegations to the Diplomatic Conference in 1974–7. Article 45 lists cases where a person must be presumed to have POW status.

---

[1] 'Should any doubt arise whether any of the aforesaid persons belongs to any of the categories named in the said Article, the said person shall have the benefit of the present Convention until his or her status has been determined by some responsible authority', ICRC, Revised and New Draft Conventions for the Protection of War Victims, texts approved by the XVIIth International Red Cross Conference, Stockholm, 1948, at 53–4.

Indeed, in the light of Articles 43 and 44 AP I, and as a consequence of the recognition   8
of irregular armed forces, a member of the armed forces of a party to the conflict may be
captured while not engaged in military operations and while carrying on daily personal
activities. In this context, it may be difficult for the captor to know whether the person is
entitled to POW status or not. Article 45 establishes in certain circumstances a legal presumption in favour of granting POW status to that person. In addition, if the prisoner is
to be tried for acts relating to the hostilities, his or her status should be determined before
the trial, as this may not only give him or her the benefit of the procedural guarantees
prescribed by GC III, but may also affect the substantive accusation; for instance if the
person is being prosecuted for mere participation in hostilities.

More than half a century after the adoption of GC III, and despite all the efforts made   9
in the drafting of its 143 Articles, controversies about who is entitled to POW status
remain. The obligation set forth in Article 5 GC III, namely for the Detaining Power to
treat combatants detained in accordance with GC III until their status has been determined by a competent tribunal, and the presumption established by Article 45 AP I,
represent important mechanisms in the protection of this vulnerable category of persons.

As POW status implies not only that someone engaged in belligerent acts may not be   10
punished for merely participating in hostility, but also that the POW's may be legally
detained until the end of active hostilities without any individual determination, the mirror problem equally arises and is discussed in this chapter: that someone given POW
status by the Detaining Power denies that he or she is combatant and therefore a POW.
Doubts may therefore be raised by the individuals concerned who may not be facing (or
deny and want to be acquitted of) any charge that they participated in hostilities. Any
finding that they are not entitled to POW status would require a new legal basis for detention or internment.

This chapter aims to shed light on the interpretation and meaning of the POW status   11
determination process. When possible, it will refer to past and recent state practice.

B. Meaning and Application

I. Reasons for presumption of prisoner of war status

After the Second World War and the denial of POW status to many prisoners by Germany,   12
granting additional protection to those who have fallen into the power of the enemy was
deemed necessary to avoid a situation in which Detaining Powers could easily refuse that
status to detainees or withdraw it from them. To prevent this and to provide additional
protection to combatants who have fallen into the power of an enemy, Article 5 GC III
establishes an obligation for the Detaining Power to treat those who have committed a
belligerent act and have fallen into its power in accordance with GC III, until a competent
tribunal has determined their status.

Article 45 AP I aims at supplementing Article 5 paragraph 2 in establishing a presump-   13
tion of POW status in favour of a combatant who has fallen into the power of an enemy,
'if he claims the status of prisoner of war, or if he appears to be entitled to such status, or if
the Party on which he depends claims such status on his behalf'. Indeed, the drafters of the
Protocol understood that it could be difficult, and even unrealistic, especially in the case
of members of resistance movements, to put the burden of proving entitlement to POW

status on the shoulders of the detainees, requiring them to give information such as the names and ranks of individuals within their military hierarchy.

14 According to the Commentary,

> it is obvious that in the [first] paragraph [of Article 45] the authors of the Protocol intended to reduce to a minimum those cases in which a captor could arbitrarily deny the status of prisoner of war to a person who had been apprehended. To this purpose they introduced a complete set of legal presumptions which automatically operate in favour of persons who have been captured.[2]

II. Who benefits from the presumption in the Third Geneva Convention?

15 Article 5 paragraph 2 GC III serves an important purpose. It seeks to ensure that combatants who find themselves in the power of an enemy will benefit from protection from the very beginning of their detention, asserting a presumption that they are protected by GC III until the contrary has been established.[3]

16 The presumptive benefit of GC III applies to anyone who has committed a belligerent act and fallen into the power of the enemy, and whose entitlement to POW status is in doubt. Article 45 AP I establishes a presumption of POW status in favour of persons who have taken part in hostilities and fallen into the power of the enemy. This presumption applies in three cases: (i) the detainee claims such status; (ii) the detainee appears to be entitled to such status; and (iii) the party on which this person depends claims such status on his or her behalf.

17 Therefore, a combatant having committed a belligerent act and captured while openly carrying arms during hostilities, or wearing a visible distinctive sign, shall be presumed entitled to the POW status. The same goes for someone carrying an identification document giving information on his or her belonging to armed forces. Circumstantial evidence, such as being captured near a military objective, or carrying a military document, etc, should lead to the same conclusion. As the POW status is a protective one, and because the person captured is in a vulnerable position, the legal presumption established by IHL should not be interpreted restrictively.

18 If the person has not committed a belligerent act, the presumption does not apply. If it appears that the person is in fact a civilian having participated in hostilities, this person shall benefit from the protection of GC IV or of Article 75 AP I.

III. When is there a doubt and whose doubt is relevant?

19 The Convention does not define nor give an indication as to what exactly can constitute a doubt under Article 5, and the Commentary is rather brief on this issue as well, mentioning only the case of deserters and persons who accompany the armed forces and have lost their identification card.[4] The term 'doubt' is generally defined as a feeling of uncertainty, or as the absence of a settled conviction.

---

[2] ICRC Commentary APs, para 1746.
[3] H.S. Levie, 'Prisoners of War in International Armed Conflict', 59 *International Law Studies* (1977) 1, at 56.
[4] Pictet Commentary GC III, at 77.

20 However, the term 'any doubt' in Article 5 GC III should not be limited to uncertainties in the mind of the Detaining Power.[5] This reading is reinforced by Article 45 AP I. The Detaining Power has the obligation to interpret GC III and AP I in good faith.[6] Nevertheless, the position of the Detaining Power entails a risk of abuse due to its *position dominante* in the interpretation and application of the rule.[7] Article 45 AP I (when applicable), establishes a presumption of POW status, and puts the burden of reversing this presumption, before a competent tribunal, on the Detaining Power: 'Indeed, under paragraph 1 the decision as to the status of the captured person no longer lay with the captor alone: that paragraph thereby widened the scope of Article 5 of the third Geneva Convention of 1949.'[8] Moreover, the presumption must be rebutted in a proceeding before a competent tribunal. Therefore the burden of convincing the competent tribunal of entitlement to POW status does not lie on the shoulders of the detainees under Article 5 GC III. This would entail the risk of undermining the protection this Article aims to provide them.

21 Generally, a doubt regarding a person's status will arise at the moment when he or she falls into the power of the enemy. However, the question of whether someone is entitled to POW status may also arise during a judicial trial. This was the case, for instance, during the trials of members of Indonesian armed forces in Malaysia (see MN 41), trials of members of a Palestinian organization (see MN 31), and during the trial of the Panamanian General Noriega in the United States (US).[9] Despite the fact that Article 45 AP I was not applicable to these cases, the judges involved deemed it necessary to adjudicate on the status of the accused, and declared themselves competent to do so.

22 More often, a doubt arises when a combatant falls into the power of the enemy and does not, at first sight, fall into one of the categories listed in Article 4 GC III, or if he or she fails to fulfil the conditions of a specific category. Unsurprisingly, it is those persons who might be covered by Article 4(A)(2) GC III that generate the most doubt.

23 The fact that a person claims to be entitled to POW status—when not being given such a status from the beginning by the Detaining Power—should also raise a doubt within the meaning of Article 5 GC III, as well as when such a claim is made by the party to which he or she belongs. This is also consistent with Article 45 AP I, which was designed to clarify and supplement Article 5 paragraph 2 GC III—especially in respect to guerrilla warfare combatants—which, according to the Commentary, remained 'rather imprecise and at an embryonic stage'.[10]

24 The wording of Article 5 prescribes an assessment of each individual situation by a competent tribunal for every prisoner with respect to whom a doubt exists, and not a collective determination applicable to all members of a specific group.

25 Where the judicial tribunal concludes that the accused is a POW, subsequent procedures shall be conducted in accordance with the requirements of GC III.

---

[5] See Amnesty International, Memorandum to the US Government on the Rights of People in US Custody in Afghanistan and Guantánamo Bay, April 2002, Doc AI AMR 51/053/2002, at 34.
[6] Art 26 VCLT.
[7] See E. David, *Principes de droit des conflits armés* (5th edn, Brussels: Bruylant, 2012), at 513.
[8] Official Records of the Diplomatic Conference on the Reaffirmation and Development of International Humanitarian Law applicable in Armed Conflicts (Geneva, 1974–7), vol XV, at 433.
[9] See *Military Prosecution v Omar Mahmud Kassem and others*, Israel Military Court sitting in Ramallah, 13 April 1969, reproduced in 42 *ILR* 470; *United States v Noriega*, District Court for the Southern District of Florida, 8 December 1992, 808 F Supp 791 (1992).
[10] ICRC Commentary APs, para 1726.

IV. To what does the doubt refer?

26 Doubts as to whether an individual who has fallen into the power of the enemy is entitled to POW status may pertain to different issues and be diverse in nature. As Article 5 paragraph 2 GC III refers to *any* doubt, this includes, for instance, factual, legal, and circumstantial doubts, as well as doubts pertaining to the individual concerned or to the group to which he or she belongs.

a. *Whether the group of which the individual is a member belongs to a party to the international armed conflict or fulfils the four conditions listed in Article 4(A)(2)*

27 Article 5 GC III stipulates that the protections afforded by the Convention apply '[s]hould any doubt arise as to whether persons, having committed a belligerent act and having fallen into the hands of the enemy, belong to any of the categories enumerated in Article 4'. The doubt thus refers to elements of Article 4 GC III. How does someone prove that the constitutive elements of entitlement to POW status are or are not fulfilled by a combatant who has fallen into the power of the enemy? International humanitarian law does not prescribe specific rules of procedure or a precise formula in this respect.

28 With regard to a combatant falling into the category of Article 4(A)(2) GC III—as already stated, possibly the one most susceptible of raising doubts—all constitutive elements could raise a doubt. For details of the constitutive elements of this Article, please refer to Chapter 44, MN 24–59, of this volume.

29 Changes in the classification of a conflict may also arise. Due to the fact that GC III does not address this issue, and because, generally, allowing *ex post facto* events to affect the status of detainees is problematic and subject to manipulation, changes in the nature of the conflict arising after the status determination process should not raise doubts (see Chapter 44, MN 10, of this volume). However, the nature of the conflict can still be contested at the moment a combatant falls into the power of the enemy.

30 The question of whether an armed group belongs to a party to the conflict—to a government in exile, for instance, or to a government not acknowledging a resistance movement fighting on its behalf, or a government denying such an affiliation[11]—may also raise a doubt in respect to the entitlement of its members to POW status. Unlike the requirement of being under a responsible command, which refers to internal factors such as the structure, the chain of command, and the organization of the group, belonging to a party to the conflict refers to external factors such as the relationship of the group with an entity and the nature of this entity (see Chapter 44, MN 26–31, of this volume). In the context of international armed conflict (IAC—the only context of POW status determination), a 'Party to the Conflict' must be a state (or under Article 1(4) AP I, a people exercising its rights to self-determination under the terms of that Article), represented by a government (or an authority representing a people). The recognition of the government does not need to be universal or uncontested, as specified in Article 4(A)(3) GC III, but the fact that a state party to the conflict takes responsibility for the irregular armed forces is important. Although the relationship of the group with a state may be officially expressed in domestic legislation or order, this is not a requirement of Article 4(A)(2) GC III. Indeed, '[s]ince the Hague Conferences […] this condition is no longer considered essential'.[12] However, a *de facto* relationship between the group and a state party to the

---

[11] Levie, above n 3, at 40–3.   [12] Pictet Commentary GC III, at 57.

conflict must exist. Therefore, in the absence of express evidence of belonging, a doubt may be raised as to whether there is tacit agreement regarding such a relationship, and whether this agreement does in fact indicate with sufficient clarity for which party the group is fighting.[13]

31 For instance, in the case of *Kassem*, the Israeli Military Court sitting in Ramallah had to determine whether members of the Popular Front for the Liberation of Palestine were entitled to POW status. In the course of its analysis, the Military Court looked at the question of whether this organization belonged to a party to an armed conflict with Israel, in this case Jordan. It concluded that this was not the case because no government accepted responsibility for that organization. In reaching its conclusion, the Military Court referred to criteria such as the fact that the organization was illegal in Jordan and that the Jordanian authorities had taken measures against it, including the use of firearms.[14]

32 According to the wording of Article 4(A)(2) GC III, the obligation to meet the four conditions listed appears to apply to the group rather than to each of its individual members.[15]

33 It may be very difficult for detainees to demonstrate that they fulfil the condition according to which they must be 'commanded by a person responsible for his subordinates', without compromising future operations of the group. Indeed, presenting evidence asserting that the resistance movement is being 'commanded by a person responsible for his subordinates', without revealing critical information concerning the identity of the leaders of the group, could prove to be nearly impossible.[16]

34 The requirement of wearing a distinctive sign visible at a distance is a crucial one, as the absence of such a sign on the uniform of an individual will, of course, not only raise doubts as to his or her entitlement to POW status, but might also serve as a basis for denying such status to that person. This requirement should be interpreted broadly so as to include badges, hats, scarves, armbands, etc,[17] but no matter what the distinctive sign is, it should be worn in a consistent manner by all members of the group.

35 Members of an armed group who have fallen into the power of the enemy while not wearing a distinctive sign should not automatically be denied POW status, but, depending on the circumstances, their situation could raise some form of doubt. In such a case, they should have their status determined pursuant to Article 5 GC III and/or Article 45 AP I procedures. For instance, the failure to wear a distinctive sign while not engaging in hostilities and carrying out personal activities should not deprive the person of POW status. Indeed, as stated by the Privy Council in *Ali and another v The Public Prosecutor*:

In neither the Hague Regulations nor in the Geneva Convention is it expressly stated that a member of the armed forces has to be wearing uniform when captured to be entitled to be so treated.[18]

36 The case of spies and saboteurs may also require the intervention of an Article 5 determination tribunal to clarify their status. For instance, the fact that someone claims to be a member of the armed forces of a party to a conflict upon arrest while wearing civilian clothes, has been deemed to raise a doubt that should be adjudicated by a competent tribunal.[19]

---

[13] Ibid.
[14] *Military Prosecution v Omar Mahmud Kassem and others*, above n 9, at 477–8.
[15] See Ch 44 of this volume, at MN 53–59.
[16] On this issue, see Levie, above n 3, at 46.
[17] Pictet Commentary GC III, at 59–60.
[18] UK, House of Lords Privy Council, *Osman Bin Haji Mohamed Ali v Public Prosecutor* [1969] 1 AC 430, at 449.
[19] Ibid.

37 In the context of cyber warfare, doubts may arise as to whether a combatant using a laptop, a cell phone, or another electronic device is fulfilling the requirement of carrying arms openly and is thus entitled to POW status.[20]

38 The obligation to conduct operations in accordance with the laws and customs of war, in order to fulfil another requirement for POW status, is a strong incentive for members of armed groups to comply with IHL. The exact content of the expression 'laws and customs of war', contained in Article 4(A)(2) GC III, and whether or not specific military operations are conducted in accordance with these rules, leaves room for interpretation and different opinions. The question of to what extent or from which point violations of IHL by a group or its members are sufficient to disqualify all of its members from POW status, could constitute a doubt within the meaning of the Article 5 GC III POW determination process. Of course, general and widespread disregard of IHL by an armed group would preclude its members from POW status, but conduct inconsistent with IHL by some members of the group, without the agreement or even the knowledge of the organization, should not. According to the Pictet Commentary, Article 4(A)(2)(d) GC III requires that members of the armed group 'respect the Geneva Conventions to the fullest extent possible'.[21]

39 With regard to the criterion that the group conducts its operations in accordance with laws and customs of war, the Netherlands' delegation was of the opinion that, to conclude that this criterion was not fulfilled, it should

> become clear from declarations or instructions emanating from responsible command of the irregular forces or from declarations of its members, that the force is not willing or able to respect [...] the rules and principles of international law applicable in armed conflict. The actual behaviour of some of its members could thus never serve as a presumption to that effect.[22]

40 The case of private contractors may also raise doubts in respect of their entitlement to POW status upon capture. Under Article 4(A)(4) GC III, some of them could be entitled to POW status, *provided that they have received authorization and an identity card from the armed forces which they accompany*. However, the absence of such a card should not automatically preclude someone from being granted POW status. Considering the increase in the use of private contractors, as well as the various functions they carry out and the different contractual relations they may have with a party to the conflict, the question of whether they are, in each specific case, entitled to POW status may raise doubts and require determination by an Article 5 GC III tribunal. The question of whether someone may be considered to be a mercenary, and therefore not be entitled to POW status according to Article 47 AP I, would also most probably require determination by such a tribunal, considering the numerous cumulative criteria prescribed by this Article and the complexity of assessing them.

b. *Nationals of the Detaining Power*

41 The nationality of the detainee could cast a doubt on his or her entitlement to POW status. Indeed, in contradistinction to Article 4 GC IV, Article 4 GC III is silent on nationality. The question of whether or not possessing a foreign nationality is a condition to POW

---

[20] According to the *Tallinn Manual*, even if computers and software 'qualify as weapons, the requirement to carry arms openly has little application in the cyber context'. M.N. Schmitt (ed), *Tallinn Manual on International Law Applicable to Cyber Warfare* (Cambridge: CUP, 2013), at 87.

[21] Pictet Commentary GC III, at 61.   [22] Official Records, above n 8, vol XIV, at 473.

status may raise sufficient doubt, requiring that a determination be made by a competent tribunal. This was the case in *Public Prosecutor v Oie Hee Koi*,[23] brought before the United Kingdom Privy Council on appeal from Malaysia. This case concerned Chinese Malays belonging to the Indonesian armed forces and captured in Malaysia during the armed conflict between Malaysia and Indonesia. The Privy Council 'reached the conclusion that the Convention does not extend the protection given to prisoners of war to nationals of the detaining power'.[24] This decision has been criticized[25] and was in contradiction with other decisions. For instance, in the case of *In re Territo*,[26] involving an individual serving as a private in the Italian Army Engineers Corps, captured in Italy by US Forces in 1943 and detained as a POW in the United States, the detainee claimed that his detention as a POW was illegal because he was born in the United States and was a citizen of that country. The Ninth Circuit Court of Appeals judges stated:

We have reviewed the authorities with care and we have found none supporting the contention of petitioner that citizenship in the country of either army in collision necessarily affects the status of one captured on the field of battle.[27]

Therefore, the question cannot be regarded as completely settled, and opinion remains divided.[28] Thus, before denying POW status to a person who appears to meet the requirements of Article 4 GC III on the basis of nationality, the Detaining Power should allow the issue to be settled by a competent tribunal in conformity with Article 5 paragraph 2 GC III.

V. 'Competent tribunal' standards to determine status

During the Diplomatic Conference of 1974–7, the 'competent tribunal' was dubbed 'the finger of destiny',[29] since it has the power to grant POW status, and consequently combatant immunity, to someone who has taken part in hostilities; or it can state that the person is a civilian—protected by GC IV—liable for any acts of hostility and who could be sentenced to death.

International humanitarian law does not provide a definition of what constitutes a competent tribunal, neither does it prescribe a specific form for it. Given that such a tribunal must be established in good time and that prisoners are often held near front lines, the competent tribunal may take different forms and be, for instance, of an administrative nature, including a military commission. It must nevertheless provide some guarantees regarding its competence, composition, impartiality, and effectiveness. In this sense, and to ensure a meaningful reading of the term 'competent tribunal', it should be distinct and independent from those involved in the first screening of detainees.

---

[23] *Public Prosecutor v Oie Hee Koi and connected appeal* [1967] UKPC 21 (4 December 1967).
[24] Ibid, at 8.
[25] See R. Baxter, 'The Privy Council on Qualification of Belligerent', 63 *AJIL* (1969) 290.
[26] *In re Territo* (9th Cir) 156 F 2d 142 (1946).
[27] Ibid, at 145. See also *Ex parte Quirin*, 317 US 1 (1942), at 38.
[28] See Ch 44, MN 58, of this volume. For opinions that possessing foreign nationality is an implied condition to POW status, see, in particular, H. Lauterpacht (ed), *Openheim's International Law, Disputes, War and Neutrality* (7th edn, London: Longmans, 1952), vol II, at 268; Y. Dinstein, *The Conduct of Hostilities under the Law of International Armed Conflict* (2nd edn, New York: CUP, 2004), at 40–1. For opinions to the contrary, see, e.g., R.-J. Wilhelm, 'Peut-on modifier le statut des prisonniers de guerre?' 35 *IRRC* 415 (1953) 516; Levie, above n 3, at 75–6; K.H. Tse, 'The Relevancy of Nationality to the Right of Prisoner of War Status', 8 *Chinese JIL* (2009) 395.
[29] See intervention of Mr de Breucker (Belgium), Official Records, above n 8, vol XIV, at 336.

44　As previously mentioned (at MN 6), during the drafting process of Article 5 GC III, a proposal to amend the first version by replacing the term 'responsible authority' with 'military tribunal', was considered in order to ensure that the decision to classify someone as a POW would not be left to a single individual, and to avoid arbitrary decisions by a local commander who might be of a very low rank. After discussion, the term 'competent tribunal' was preferred instead, because it provides for the settlement of the question by a civil court when so provided by the laws of the Detaining Power.[30] As already noted, the aim of this Article is to prevent the Detaining Power from arbitrarily denying POW status to combatants who have fallen into its hands. Drafters of the Convention were in particular seeking to prevent a situation whereby a field commander could, without any other formality, determine that someone was not a POW and execute him or her on the spot.[31]

45　State practice in this respect shows that tribunals under Article 5 paragraph 2 GC III vary as to their forms. For instance, one military manual provides for the tribunal to comprise a single officer of the legal branch of the army, appointed by a competent authority and in concurrence with the Judge Advocate General;[32] another envisions a single judge of the Supreme Court of the state or territory in which the person is detained;[33] and yet another calls for a panel of three commissioned officers.[34]

46　Case law has also recognized judicial civilian and military tribunals as meeting the requirement for a 'competent tribunal' under Article 5 paragraph 2 GC III. For instance, in the trial of *Kassem and others*, the Military Court of Israel, sitting in Ramallah, considered itself competent to determine the status of the accused. A US District Court judge did the same in the case of General Manuel Antonio Noriega, arrested by the US in the context of its invasion of Panama in 1989, and granted Noriega POW status despite the earlier contrary decision of the Government.[35]

47　As a competent tribunal in the sense of Article 5 GC III is not a judicial or disciplinary tribunal, the requirements in Articles 82–108 GC III are not applicable to the POW status determination procedure.

48　The *competent tribunal* of Article 5 paragraph 2 GC III, which may be of an administrative nature, is to be distinguished from the *judicial tribunal* of Article 45(2) AP I. Drafters of the Convention and of AP I were aware that such a competent tribunal would likely be settled near front lines in a short period of time, and that some flexibility would thus be required in its formation.

49　Article 45(2) AP I brings an additional right and a procedural safeguard for persons not considered POWs who are tried for criminal offences. These persons have the right to assert entitlement to POW status, and to have that question adjudicated *de novo* by a judicial tribunal, notwithstanding previous decisions made pursuant to Article 45(1) AP I or Article 5 paragraph 2 GC III.[36] According to the Commentary, during the Diplomatic

---

[30] See Final Record, vol II-B, at 270.
[31] See ibid, at 270–1; see also *Military Prosecution v Omar Mahmud Kassem and others*, above n 9, at 472.
[32] Canada, Prisoner-of-War Status Determination Regulations, 25 January 1991, SOR/91-134, Art 4.
[33] Australia, Geneva Convention Act 1957, as amended, Part III, s 10(A).
[34] US, Enemy Prisoner-of-War, Civilian Internees and Other Detainees, US Army Regulation 190-8, 1 October 1997, at 1-6(c) ('US AR 190-8').
[35] *United States v Noriega*, above n 9. No status determination tribunals were constituted during the US operation in Panama. See Ltc W. Johnson, Lcdr D. Lee, *Operational Law Handbook*, JA 422, International and Operational Law Department, The Judge Advocate General's Legal Center and School (Charlottesville: 2014), at 19, fn 69.
[36] See Official Records, above n 8, vol XIV, at 433.

Conference it was noted that requiring the status determination tribunal to provide guarantees in respect to its competence, composition, and procedures was 'a great deal to ask, so close to the frontline'.[37] Therefore, it was agreed that, 'each time a prisoner who is not detained as a prisoner of war is to be judged for an offence related to hostilities, the intervention of a judiciary tribunal is required, even for deciding the status of the person concerned'.[38]

In view of the great differences in national judicial procedures, it was not thought possible to establish a firm rule that this question must be decided before the trial for the offence, but it should be so decided if at all possible, because on it depends the whole array of procedural protections accorded to prisoners of war by the Third Convention, and the issue may go to the jurisdiction of the tribunal. The judicial tribunal may either be the same one that tries the offence or another one. It may be either a civilian or a military tribunal, the term 'judicial' meaning merely a criminal tribunal offering the normal guarantees of judicial procedure.[39]

That is to say, a plea made by the accused that he or she is entitled to POW status 'must be examined in accordance with judicial, not administrative, procedure, and, if possible, on a preliminary basis'.[40]

50 The following are examples from US practice, focusing particularly on questions raised by the status of those detained in the context of the 'War on Terror'. Indeed, the majority of the examples the author has been able to find come from the practice of the United States.

51 One of the first cases of a Detaining Power passing regulations to establish a tribunal in compliance with Article 5 GC III is the US in the context of the Vietnam War, where the US Army issued a directive to that effect.[41] According to that directive, the Article 5 tribunal had to consist of three or more officers, at least one of whom would be a judge advocate or other military lawyer familiar with the Geneva Conventions.[42]

52 The US also conducted status determination tribunals during *Operation Desert Storm* in the context of the 1991 Gulf War. In that case, after interrogation, it appeared that a large number of detainees were in fact displaced civilians who had not taken part in hostilities. Despite the fact that they had not committed a belligerent act, Article 5 tribunals were nevertheless conducted to verify their status.[43]

53 At the beginning of US intervention in Afghanistan, in October 2001, in the context of the 'War on Terror', the military authority was of the opinion that GC III was applicable to all persons captured, and that, in case of doubt as to their entitlement to POW status, the question would be determined in accordance with Article 5 GC III.[44] After intense internal debates on the issue, on 7 February 2002, President Bush stated that GC III was applicable to members of the Taliban who had fallen into the power of the US, but not to members of Al-Qaeda, as that group was not a state party to the Conventions but an

---

[37] ICRC Commentary APs, para 1745.   [38] Ibid.
[39] See Official Records, above n 8, vol XIV, at 443.   [40] Ibid.
[41] See US Military Assistance Command, Vietnam, Directive No 20-5, Inspections and Investigations: Prisoners of War Determination of Eligibility (15 March 1968), reprinted in 768 *AJIL* (1968); see also US Military Assistance Command, Vietnam, Directive No 138-46, Military Intelligence: Combined Screening of Detainees (27 December 1967); and Levie, above n 3, at 57.
[42] Art 6(e)(1), US Military Assistance Command, Vietnam, Directive No 20-5, above n 41.
[43] See *Operational Law Handbook*, JA 422, above n 35, at 19, fn 69.
[44] See 'Report of Independent Panel to Review Department of Defense Detention Operations', August 2004 (Schlesinger Report), at 80, available at <http://www.defense.gov/news/aug2004/d20040824finalreport.pdf>.

international terrorist group. As for the Taliban, President Bush stated that they were not entitled to POW status because they failed to meet the requirements of Article 4 GC III, and that both the Taliban and Al-Qaeda members were 'unlawful combatants'.[45] As the US Government was of the opinion that members of neither Al-Qaeda nor the Taliban were entitled to POW status, US authorities contended that no doubt existed concerning their status.[46] Therefore, no status determination or hearing process was undertaken with respect to them. However, according to many, including the ICRC, there was a sufficient doubt to trigger the application of Article 5 GC III.[47] This was also the view of the Inter-American Commission of Human Rights, which authorized precautionary measures in this respect:

> [T]he Commission decided to request that the United States take the urgent measures necessary to have the legal status of the detainees at Guantanamo Bay determined by a competent tribunal. [...] [T]he Commission's decision was based upon, inter alia, its finding that doubts existed as to the legal status of the detainees, including the question of whether and to what extent the Third Geneva Convention or other provisions of international humanitarian law applied to some or all of the detainees and what implications this may have for their international human rights protections [...][48]

54 The determination of the status of those detained at Guantánamo by a competent tribunal pursuant to Article 5 GC III never happened, as it was clear for the US that Guantánamo detainees did not fall into any of the Article 4 GC III categories. However, this did not mean that these persons were not entitled to any mechanism of judicial review of the legality of their detention. In 2004, after the *Rasul v Bush*[49] Supreme Court decision, in which it was ruled that an alien detained at Guantánamo might present a statutory habeas corpus writ before a Federal District Court, the US established the Combatant Status Review Tribunals (CSRT) for those detained at Guantánamo. Proponents of the CSRT asserted that as the Geneva Conventions were not applicable to the 'War on Terror', and consequently no Article 5 status determination tribunal was required, these tribunals provided an acceptable due process alternative. Combatant Status Review Tribunals were criticized by those asserting that there was an IAC between the US-led coalition and Afghanistan from October 2001 to June 2002,[50] to which IHL applied.[51] For opponents,

---

[45] See Memorandum from the President of the United States for the Vice President et al, 'Subject: Humane Treatment of al Qaeda and Taliban Detainees' (7 February 2002), reproduced in Schlesinger Report, Appendix C.

[46] See, e.g., declaration of State Department Spokesman Richard Boucher, noon briefing, 8 February 2002.

[47] See, in particular, ICRC News Release of 9 February 2002; Amnesty International, Memorandum to the US Government on the Rights of People in US Custody in Afghanistan and Guantánamo Bay, April 2002, Doc AI AMR 51/053/2002, at 32–4.

[48] OAS, IACommHR, Precautionary measures, PM-259/02 'Persons Detained by the United States in Guantánamo Bay' (12 March 2002), available at <http://www.oas.org/en/iachr/pdl/decisions/Guantanamo MC.asp#MC25902>. See also Detainees in Guantánamo Bay, Cuba; Request for Precautionary Measures, IACommHR (13 March 2002), available at <http://www1.umn.edu/humanrts/cases/guantanamo-2003.html>.

[49] *Rasul v Bush*, 542 US 466 (2004). See also *Hamdi v Rumsfeld*, 542 US 507 (2004), issued the same day on which the US Supreme Court held (at 509) that 'due process demands that a citizen held in the United States as an enemy combatant be given a meaningful opportunity to contest the factual basis for that detention before a neutral decision maker'.

[50] In June 2002, a transitional government was formed led by Hamid Karzai, after he was appointed by the Loya Jirga.

[51] On this issue, see, e.g., M. Sassòli, 'La "guerre contre le terrorisme", le droit international humanitaire et le statut de prisonnier de guerre', 39 *CanYIL* (2001) 211.

CSRT did not meet the standards of an Article 5 tribunal, in particular because they did not offer sufficient due process guarantees,[52] and because their function was to classify 'enemy combatants' and not to determine the status of detainees held at Guantánamo.[53]

In *Hamdan v Rumsfeld*, the case of a Yemeni national captured in Afghanistan in 2001 and transferred to Guantánamo in 2002, the US Supreme Court, after having established that, as a minimum, Common Article 3 was applicable to the conflict between the US and Al-Qaeda, held that this 'requires that Hamdan be tried by a regularly constituted court affording all the judicial guarantees which are recognized as indispensable by civilised peoples'.[54] The term 'regularly constituted', although not defined in the Geneva Conventions, is generally understood as meaning 'established and organized in accordance with the laws and procedures already in force in a country'.[55] It that sense, it includes military courts, but definitively excludes special tribunals. As for the requirement 'all the judicial guarantees which are recognized as indispensable by civilized peoples', which is not defined by the Conventions, the Court was of the opinion that 'it must be understood to incorporate at least the barest of those trial protections that have been recognized by customary international law. Many of these are described in Article 75 of Protocol I to the Geneva Conventions of 1949, adopted in 1977 (Protocol I).'[56] The military commission established to prosecute Hamdan did not meet these requirements. The question of whether or not a 'competent tribunal' must determine his status in accordance with Article 5 GC III was reserved by the Court.

VI. Procedural guarantees before an Article 5 tribunal, including the influence of international human rights law

International humanitarian law is silent on the procedural guarantees applicable to the POW status determination process. Although not a criminal procedure, considering the importance of the question at stake before a status determination tribunal, examples from specific national regulations adopted to implement Article 5 GC III tribunals show an intention to provide for procedural guarantees that may be similar to those required by criminal proceedings. For instance, the right to be present during the hearing and to be assisted by counsel,[57] the right not to testify against oneself,[58] the right to an interpreter,[59] and the right to present evidence.[60] The tribunal should have the power to appoint

---

[52] See Memorandum for Secretaries of the Military Departments et al, 'Subject: Implementation of Combatant Status Review Tribunal Procedures for Enemy Combatants Detainees at US Naval Base, Guatanamo, Cuba' (14 July 2006), available at <http://www.defense.gov/news/aug2006/d20060809csrtprocedures.pdf>.

[53] For an analysis of CSRT, see T.J. Bogar, 'Unlawful Combatant or Innocent Civilian? A Call to Change the Current Means for Determining Status of Prisoners in the Global War on Terror', 21 *Florida JIL* (2009) 29.

[54] *Hamdan v Rumsfeld*, 548 US 557 (2006), at 631–2 (references omitted).

[55] Ibid. The US Supreme Court is referring to the Pictet Commentary GC IV and the ICRC CIHL Study.

[56] *Hamdan v Rumsfeld*, above n 54, at 633.

[57] See, e.g., Canada, Prisoner-of-War Status Determination Regulations, above n 32, Art 10; US AR 190-8, above n 34, at 1-6(e)(5)—right to be present, but does not mention the right to a counsel; Arts 7(c) and 8, US Military Assistance Command, Vietnam, Directive No 20-5, above n 41; *Military Prosecution v Omar Mahmud Kassem and others*, above n 9, during which trial defendants were assisted by counsel.

[58] See, e.g., Art 10, US Military Assistance Command, Vietnam, Directive No 20-5, above n 41; US AR 190-8, above n 34, at 1-6(e) (8),

[59] See, Canada, Prisoner-of-War Status Determination Regulations, above n 32, Art 11; US AR 190-8, above n 34, at 1-6(e)(5); Art 7(b) and 12, US Military Assistance Command, Vietnam, Directive no 20-5, above n 41.

[60] See, e.g., US AR 190-8, above n 34, at 1-6(e)(5); Art 7(a), US Military Assistance Command, Vietnam, Directive No 20-5, above n 41.

witnesses and to require the production of evidence.[61] The decision of the tribunal should be recorded[62] and be subject to some form of revision.[63]

57 International human rights law (IHRL), which remains applicable in times of armed conflict (see Chapter 35 of this volume), should also supplement IHL in determining those procedural guarantees that must be respected by the competent tribunal under Article 5 GC III. However, the fact that the status determination process is not of a criminal nature and may be undertaken by an administrative tribunal, or even by an administrative board, and near the front lines must be kept in mind.

58 Regarding the standard of proof, although IHL does not provide any indication in this respect, and despite the fact that status determination tribunal may be of an administrative nature, it should at least consider the preponderance standard.[64] The Canadian Regulations specify that for denying a detainee POW status, the competent tribunal should be satisfied that on the balance of probabilities the detainee is not entitled to POW status.[65]

59 Article 5 GC III and Article 45 AP I are also silent on the question of on which of the parties the burden of establishing the status of a detainee lies. However, the 'general spirit'[66] of these Articles, as well as the limited possibilities and resources of the detained person, should lead to the conclusion that the burden should be placed on the Detaining Power, or, as a minimum, not on the detainee alone.

60 When Article 45 AP I is applicable, as it establishes a presumption in favour of the detainee, the burden of reversing the presumptive status established by IHL should lie on the Detaining Power. Indeed, as the Commentary on this Article indicates:

> By means of this system [the set of rules established by Article 45 AP I] they [the authors of the Protocol] have therefore reversed the burden of proof by putting it on a 'competent tribunal', in contrast with Article 5 of the Third Convention. It is up to this tribunal to furnish proof to the contrary every time that the presumption exists and it wishes to contest it. This will often be difficult, not least when it is a question of proving that the person who has been apprehended does not belong to the armed forces on which he is deemed to depend.[67]

VII. Options for a person the Detaining Power wants to consider as having POW status but who does not want POW status

61 Some persons, despite falling into one of the categories enumerated in Article 4 GC III and therefore being entitled to POW status, may prefer not to be granted this protection but, for instance, to be accorded another protective status, such as that of a refugee. This might be the case, in particular, for deserters. Indeed, if treated as POWs, they will be

---

[61] See, e.g., Art 13, US Military Assistance Command, Vietnam, Directive No 20-5, above n 41.

[62] See, e.g., Canada, Prisoner-of-war Status Determination Regulations, above n 32, Art 16; US AR 190-8, above n 34, at 1-6(e)(10); Art 6(f)(3), US Military Assistance Command, Vietnam, Directive No 20-5, above n 41.

[63] See, e.g., Canada, Prisoner-of-War Status Determination Regulations, above n 32, Art 17, Art 6(g)(1), US Military Assistance Command, Vietnam, Directive No 20-5, above n 41, providing that decisions made by Status Determination Tribunals would be revised by the MACV Staff Judge Advocate.

[64] See Canada, Prisoner-of-War Status Determination Regulations, above n 32, Art 13(g); US AR 190-8, above n 34, at 6(e)(9).

[65] Canada, Prisoner-of-War Status Determination Regulations, above n 32, Art 13(g).

[66] See A. Rosas, *The Legal Status of Prisoners of War: A Study in International Humanitarian Law Applicable in Armed Conflicts* (Helsinki: Suomalainen Tiedeaktemia, 1976), at 410.

[67] ICRC Commentary APs, para 1746.

interned with their former fellow army members. The Detaining Power will be under the obligation to notify their capture to the Power on which they depend but with which they broke their allegiance, and to return them to that Power at the end of active hostilities. All these POW protective rights may put the security of a deserter and his or her family at risk. International humanitarian law does not address the issue of deserters, or that of any other person who is entitled to POW status but who, for any reason, does not want the benefit of it.

The right to POW status is inalienable according to Article 7 GC III. As a result, a prisoner cannot renounce it and a Detaining Power cannot change the status of POW once it has been granted. Therefore, a deserter should declare his or her situation at the earliest opportunity.[68] Because the difference between a combatant who surrenders and a deserter might not be evident at first sight, for instance in the context of a spontaneous mass surrender, the question of whether that person is a deserter in need of a different treatment may be brought before a status determination tribunal. Indeed, as the protection granted by Article 5 GC III is *presumptive*, it can be reversed by a competent tribunal. The same goes for the *presumptive* status of Article 45 AP I. However, after a decision has been made, or if the detainee does not mention at the earliest opportunity that he or she is a deserter so that the Detaining Power has no doubt about his or her POW status, it will not be possible to change it later and, despite being a deserter, that person will be treated as a POW.[69] Nevertheless, IHL does not prevent the Detaining Power from granting POW status to deserters. However, the principle of *non-refoulement* should be kept in mind, and might well prevent repatriation at the end of hostilities (see Chapter 51, MN 42, of this volume). Deserters not granted POW status will be civilians protected under GC IV.

Prisoners of war who wish to sever their allegiance while in captivity can do so, but they will remain POWs. As mentioned, this status is inalienable and cannot be changed once granted. This important rule protects POWs from pressure and measures of indoctrination utilized by the Detaining Power. However, the Detaining Power should take specific steps to ensure the protection of their lives, dignity, and health, including, for instance, by providing them with separate quarters.[70]

Another important question, not covered by GC III, is what procedure applies to an individual whom a Detaining Power wants to treat as a POW but who seeks to challenge such a classification. At the time of drafting GC III, POW status and treatment was considered the best protection an individual could get. However, it implies detention until the end of active hostilities, without any judicial or even administrative control. A Detaining Power may consider an individual as a member of the armed forces of the enemy even if that individual has not committed any belligerent act. This question is not dealt with by IHL, but one might consider that someone who wants to challenge his or her classification as a POW should be able to challenge the legality of his or her detention under GC III in habeas corpus or similar proceedings under IHRL, which remains applicable in armed conflict.[71] While GC III constitutes for POWs the *lex specialis* on the question of the legal

---

[68] See M. Sassòli, 'The Status, Treatment and Repatriation of Deserters under International Humanitarian Law', *IIHL Yearbook* (1985) 9, at 15.
[69] Ibid; R.-J. Wilhelm, 'Peut-on modifier le statut des prisonniers de guerre?', 35 *IRRC* 417 (1953) 681, at 681.
[70] See Sassòli, above n 68, at 25.
[71] On this issue, see F. Hampson, 'The Geneva Convention and the Detention of Civilians and Alleged Prisoners of War', *Public Law* (1991) 507. See also, ICTY, *The Prosecutor v Milorad Krnojelac*, Trial Chamber

basis for detention and the right to personal freedom, one has to determine whether GC III is actually applicable in law to the particular individual, or if, for instance, this person is not rather a civilian protected by GC IV. Another possibility would be to consider that despite its wording and the historical purpose mentioned above, the Article 5 tribunal should also decide the status issue when this 'mirror' problem arises, i.e. when it is not the state but the individual concerned who denies that he or she has POW status. The disadvantage of this solution is that Article 5 tribunal may not offer the full guarantees of a habeas corpus procedure. The advantage is that Article 5 paragraph 2 certainly applies extraterritorially, while there is some controversy over the extraterritorial application of IHRL.[72]

C. Relevance in Non-International Armed Conflicts

65 In situations of non-international armed conflict (NIAC), IHL does not provide for combatant status, nor for the status of POW. Combatant immunity therefore is foreign to situations of NIAC, and the question of status determination for POWs does not arise. However, some provisions provide for minimum standards of treatment and procedural guarantees in NIAC. At a minimum, Common Article 3 prohibits 'the passing of sentences and the carrying out of executions without previous judgment pronounced by a regularly constituted court, affording all the judicial guarantees which are recognized as indispensable by civilized peoples' against any person '*hors de combat*'. What constitutes a 'regularly constituted court' is not defined by the Geneva Conventions, and it should be understood as meaning 'established and organized in accordance with the laws and procedures already in force in a country'.[73] For instance, it was considered that sentencing a detainee for an act that does not constitute an offence under the laws of armed conflict before a military commission, such as a charge of conspiracy, was not in compliance with the requirements of Common Article 3.[74] As stated previously, the terms 'all the judicial guarantees which are recognized as indispensable by civilized peoples' are also not defined by the Geneva Conventions. The provision has to be understood as including at least minimum standards recognized under international customary law. For instance, the right of an accused to be present at his or her trial, and the right to be informed of the evidence against him or her.[75] There is controversy over the legal basis and grounds which would justify a person's being interned without trial in a NIAC. There is further disagreement over which procedural guarantees would apply to such a person.[76] If internment of members of an armed group (with a continuing combat function) is considered to be an inherent right for parties in NIACs, the question concerning the procedure which would allow an individual to contest his or her internment bears some similarities with that discussed in MN 64 above.

Judgment, IT-97-25-T, 15 March 2002, paras 116–24; *The Prosecutor v Blagoje Simić et al*, Trial Chamber Judgment, IT-95-9-T, 17 October 2003, para 659.

[72] See Ch 35 of this volume, at MN 5, 6, 35, 39, and 73.
[73] ICRC CIHL Study, Rule 100 and related commentary. [74] *Hamdan v Rumsfeld*, above n 54.
[75] See further Ch 23 of this volume, at MN 1–76.
[76] See Ch 35, MN 38–41, Ch 45, MN 73–76, and Ch 64, MN 64–70, of this volume.

D. Critical Assessment

66 The incorporation of the protective safeguard established by Article 5 GC III in favour of those who have committed belligerent acts and have fallen into the power of an enemy, and whose status may be unclear, was a necessary addition to the legal rules provided by IHL to protect those who have fallen into the power of an enemy. In stating that they shall benefit from the protection of GC III and be treated as if they were POWs until their status has been determined by a competent tribunal, this Article had the goal of reducing arbitrary denial of POW status in the midst of battlefield action. Despite the fact that examples from state practice in establishing status determination tribunals seem rather sparse, the obligation to treat doubtful cases of POW status in accordance with Article 5 is agreed.

67 However, when a case does not raise a doubt in the assessment of the Detaining Power, but does so in the view of one of the other entities or persons concerned, the situation is more problematic. There seems to be a lack of clarity about what should constitute sufficient doubt under Article 5, or the consequences of the existence of such a doubt in the mind of persons or entities other than the Detaining Power. In this respect, the content of Article 45 AP I reduces uncertainties to a minimum by establishing a presumption of POW status in any of three situations: (i) when the person raises a doubt; (ii) when factual or circumstantial elements could lead to the conclusion that this person is entitled to POW status; or (iii) when the Power on which the person depends claims such status. When Article 45 AP I is not applicable, the three situations of presumptive POW status should serve as guidance, and a case falling into one of these categories should be considered as raising sufficient doubt to warrant submission of the issue to a competent tribunal under Article 5 GC III.

68 As for the mirror problem that someone given POW status by the Detaining Power denies that he or she is a combatant and therefore a POW, it is suggested that this person should be able to challenge the issue before a tribunal. This could be done either through habeas corpus, or via similar proceedings under IHRL, or by recognizing that the Article 5 tribunal is competent to address this issue and should do so in such a case.

MARIE-LOUISE TOUGAS

Chapter 47. Evacuation and Transfer of Prisoners of War

	MN
A. Introduction	1
B. Meaning and Application	4
I. Evacuation from the combat zone	6
a. Obligations prior to evacuation	7
b. Obligations during evacuation	15
II. Transfer from one camp to another	26
a. Obligations prior to transfer	28
b. Obligations during transfer	37
III. Transfer from one Detaining Power to another	41
a. Drafting history	41
b. 'Reservations' to Article 12 and objections thereto	46
c. Types of transfers covered	49
d. Specific requirements before and during the transfer	53
e. Specific requirements after the transfer	58
IV. Transfer from a camp to penitentiary establishments	68
C. Relevance in Non-International Armed Conflicts	69
D. Legal Consequences of a Violation	75
E. Critical Assessment	79

Select Bibliography

Levie, H., *Prisoners of War in International Armed Conflict* (Newport, RI: Naval War College Press, 1978), at 98–106, 187–94

Pictet Commentary GC III, at 128–39, 171–6, 253–8, 462–3

Pinzauti, G., 'Protecting Prisoners of War: The *Mrkšić et al.* Appeal Judgment', 8 *JICJ* (2010) 199

Sassòli, M./Tougas, M.-L., 'International Law Issues Raised by the Transfer of Detainees by Canadian Forces in Afghanistan', 54 *McGill Law Journal* (2011) 959

A. Introduction

Prior to the 1929 Geneva Convention Relative to the Treatment of Prisoners of War (1929 GC II), the transfer of prisoners of war (POWs) was virtually unregulated in international humanitarian law (IHL) instruments. The 1880 *Manual of the Laws of War on Land* drafted by the Institute of International Law, which contained rules on the treatment of POWs, was silent on their transfer. Article 14 of the 1899 and 1907 Hague Regulations merely provided that the bureau of information relative to POWs established by the belligerent states should receive full information on transfers of POWs from the various services concerned. 1

The 1929 GC II laid the foundation for most rules relating to the evacuation and transfer of POWs.[1] Those rules are now found in Articles 19, 47, 48, and 97 GC III. However, GC 2

---

[1] See Arts 7, 25, 26, and 56 of the 1929 GC II. The 1929 GC II is no longer in force as it was replaced by GC III. See Art 134 GC III.

III significantly added new provisions, Articles 20 and 46, which obliged the Detaining Power to ensure adequate material conditions during evacuation or transfer. This filled the gap in the 1929 GC II.

3   While the above-mentioned provisions of the 1899 and 1907 Hague Regulations, 1929 GC II, and GC III apply to evacuation and transfers in general, a notable point of GC III is that Article 12 paragraphs 2 and 3 provide specific rules on transfer of POWs from one Detaining Power to another.[2]

B. Meaning and Application

4   Life as a POW begins for a combatant when he or she falls into the power of the enemy. The circumstances in which this occurs may vary from one case to another. Prisoners of war may be captured during active combat, or in a relatively calm area where heavy fighting is not taking place. Captured POWs may number only one, a few, a few hundred, or a few thousand. There may be wounded and sick POWs among those captured. The military unit concerned may or may not have the adequate means to transport the POWs. Prisoner of war camps may not exist, or even if they do, they might be distant from the place of capture. The terrain might be rough, the climate could be harsh, and the only method of transfer might be by sea, which could render the journey to the POW camp hazardous. Whatever the circumstances, the military unit concerned is bound to move captured POWs from one place to another, unless it decides to release them on the spot. However, each case of capture of POWs presents different challenges for the Detaining Power, depending on the circumstances.

5   The aim of GC III is to minimize the risk to POWs while they are being moved from one place to another. It makes a distinction between, on the one hand, the movement of POWs from the place of capture to a camp (section B.I of this chapter) and, on the other hand, the movement of POWs from one camp to another (section B.II). The former is dealt with in Articles 19 and 20 GC III, and the latter in Articles 46 to 48. The special case of transfers from one Detaining Power to another, provided for in Article 12, is discussed in section B.III. The question of transfers of POWs to penitentiary establishments is considered in section B.IV.

I. Evacuation from the combat zone

6   The Final Record of the Diplomatic Conference indicates that the draft Articles which later became Articles 19 and 20 GC III did not attract much controversy and were adopted without objection.[3] These articles are located in Part III, Section I, entitled 'Beginning of Captivity', and specifically envisage the removal of POWs from the combat zone (or 'danger zone' or 'fighting zone', which terms are used interchangeably in Article 19) to a camp. Therefore, the movement of POWs at this phase is characterized as an 'evacuation' rather than a 'transfer' as in Articles 46 to 48.[4] While Articles 19 and 20 specifically deal with evacuation from the combat zone, even when POWs are not being evacuated from

---

[2] For other types of transfers under GCs, see Chs 51, 58 and 66 of this volume.
[3] See the references in the Final Record, vol III, at 219.
[4] ICRC, *Report on the Work of the Conference of Government Experts for the Study of the Conventions for the Protection of War Victims (Geneva, April 14–26, 1947)*, at 128.

such zone, those Articles should be observed when removing POWs from the place of capture to a camp.

a. Obligations prior to evacuation

The Detaining Power is obliged to take various precautions before evacuating POWs. Article 19 paragraph 3 GC III requires that POWs should not be exposed to danger until such time as the Detaining Power begins their evacuation from the fighting zone. For example, an incident in which a wounded POW was allegedly forced to spend a night on top of a trench while artillery exchanges occurred, would not be consistent with this provision.[5]

The precaution in Article 19 paragraph 3 does not entitle the Detaining Power to leave POWs in the fighting zone as long as it wishes. Thus, Article 19 paragraph 1 provides that '[p]risoners of war shall be evacuated, as soon as possible after their capture, to camps situated in an area far enough from the combat zone for them to be out of danger.'[6] Prompt evacuation may not always be possible, for example when there is a large number of POWs,[7] but the Detaining Power should seize every opportunity to remove POWs as far as possible from the combat zone.

The Detaining Power should identify which camps meet the criteria in Article 19 paragraph 1 GC III at the relevant time. In identifying such camps, the Detaining Power should take into account Articles 13 and 23 GC III, and ensure that POWs, at the time of arrival at the relevant camps, are not exposed to the fire of the combat zone. If the POWs continue to face the danger of the combat zone at the time of arrival to the relevant camps, the evacuation cannot be considered complete. Therefore, the Detaining Power would have to search for other camps that meet the criteria set out in Articles 13, 19 paragraph 1, and 23. For example, during the 1991 Gulf War, the United States (US) moved Iraqi POWs through at least three transit camps until they reached the final destination, the camps in Saudi Arabia,[8] which seemed to be, as required by Article 19 paragraph 1 GC III, 'far enough from the combat zone for them to be out of danger'.

After being evacuated to safe camps, further movements of POWs due to the approach of the combat zone are characterized as 'transfers' in GC III, and are regulated by Articles 46 to 48, in the section entitled 'Transfer of Prisoners of War after Their Arrival in Camp'. Such transfers are distinct from evacuation.

The exceptions to the requirement in Article 19 paragraph 1 (see MN 8) are wounded and sick POWs. Article 19 paragraph 2 requires the Detaining Power to weigh the risk of evacuating such POWs and that of leaving them in the danger zone. If the former risk outweighs the latter, wounded and sick POWs may 'temporarily' be kept back in the danger zone. In this regard, the forced evacuation of the wounded and sick during the Second World War, and the deaths of many of them in consequence, would clearly have fallen short of the requirements set out in Article 19 GC III, had that provision existed at the time.[9] The risks to health as a result of evacuating wounded and sick POWs should, as

---

[5] EECC, *Prisoners of War—Ethiopia's Claim 4*, Partial Award, 1 July 2003, para 72.
[6] See, e.g., ibid for a case in which it was concluded that the Detaining Power generally took the necessary measures to evacuate its POWs promptly.
[7] See, e.g., US, *Conduct of the Persian Gulf War: Final Report to the Congress* (Washington DC: US Department of Defense, 1992), at L-13 and L-18.
[8] Ibid, at L-14.
[9] See, e.g., Judgment, International Military Tribunal for the Far East (IMTFE), in B.V.A. Röling and C.F. Rüter (eds), *The Tokyo Judgment* (Amsterdam: University Press Amsterdam, 1977), vol I, at 401–3.

far as possible, be assessed by medical personnel. The presumption derived from the word 'temporarily' is that, as soon as the situation allows, the Detaining Power should evacuate POWs without further delay.[10] Therefore, the changing situation should be monitored constantly for this purpose. However, whether evacuated or not, wounded and sick POWs are also protected by GC I and GC II,[11] and the obligations to protect and care for the wounded and sick therein apply.

12 When persons entitled to protection as POWs have fallen into the power of an adverse party under unusual conditions of combat which prevent their evacuation as provided for in Articles 19 and 20, they shall be released and all feasible precautions shall be taken to ensure their safety.[12] This general rule envisages a situation where a military unit can neither keep POWs out of danger before evacuation, nor evacuate them in humane conditions, in which case they should be released even if it means that they might rejoin their own armed forces. Holding POWs for certain death is therefore prohibited. In the event that wounded and sick POWs must be released, the military unit concerned should, as far as military considerations permit, leave with them a part of its medical personnel and material to assist in their care, in accordance with Article 12 paragraph 5 GC I.

13 Article 19 GC III applies in the case of evacuation of POWs on land as well as at sea. However, Article 16 GC II constitutes *lex specialis* in case of evacuation at sea. Captured wounded, sick, and shipwrecked persons at sea are considered POWs.[13] Article 16 provides four options after their capture: hold them; convey them to a port in the Detaining Power's territory; convey them to a neutral port; or convey them to a port in the enemy territory. Therefore, persons captured at sea should be evacuated just like any other POWs, but the destination does not have to be a POW camp of the Detaining Power.

14 The Detaining Power should decide, as soon as possible after the capture of POWs at sea, the destination of such prisoners. In the event that a port of the Detaining Power is chosen, the obligation to evacuate does not cease at that port but continues until the POWs reach safe camps as required by Article 19 paragraph 1 GC III. If a neutral port is chosen, this would constitute the special case of transfer of POWs from one Detaining Power to another, which is regulated by Article 12 paragraphs 2 and 3 (section B.III of this chapter), as well as by Articles 109 to 117 GC III (see Chapter 51, MN 13–17, of this volume). Where a port in the enemy territory is selected, this could amount either to repatriation or a transfer from one Detaining Power to another, depending on whether the 'enemy' is the home country of the POWs or its co-belligerent state.

b. Obligations during evacuation

15 As soon as the evacuation of POWs commences, the obligations in Article 20 GC III to ensure humane conditions of evacuation apply. Such obligations apply to any kind of evacuation, such as by land or sea, and to any kind of POWs, such as the wounded and sick or able-bodied. The Detaining Power must be prepared for the logistical challenges which may arise in the most difficult scenarios, such as the capture of large numbers of POWs who need to be moved to a camp situated far away, through harsh terrain and climate.[14] In practical terms, the Detaining Power would need trucks, ships, airplanes, food, water,

---

[10] For examples of evacuation of the wounded and sick POWs, see, e.g., EECC, *Prisoners of War—Eritrea's Claim 17*, Partial Award, 1 July 2003, para 69; *Conduct of the Persian Gulf War*, above n 7, at L-13.
[11] Art 14 GC I and Art 16 GC II.   [12] Art 41(3) AP I.   [13] Art 16 GC II.
[14] Röling and Rüter (eds), above n 9, at 402–3.

appropriate clothing, medical services, and adequate numbers of troops to carry out the whole evacuation operation. These may or may not be sufficiently available, depending on the financial and material resources of the state concerned. Lack of resources does not release the Detaining Power from its obligations under Article 20,[15] but at the same time the resources available to the armed forces of developed countries cannot be expected to be the same as those of developing countries.

To evacuate POWs, some means of transportation is required, but Articles 19 and 20 do not prescribe any specific type of transportation, such as by land, sea, or air. Evacuation carried out by transportation has caused much difficulty, even for the most resourceful armed forces, particularly in cases where the number of POWs was large.[16] Therefore, in many instances, POWs had to evacuate on foot.

Evacuation on foot is not prohibited per se by Article 20. Article 7 of the 1929 GC II limited such evacuation to not more than 20 kilometres per day. This limitation was initially included in a draft GC III[17] but was later deleted, since a new article containing detailed requirements to ensure humane conditions of evacuation, which later became Article 20, was intended to cover such a limitation.[18]

Long-distance evacuations on foot in harsh conditions, as seen during the Second World War, are clearly prohibited.[19] At the same time, the Detaining Power cannot wait in the combat zone for hours and days until all the POWs have been shuttled to safe camps, which would be inconsistent with the requirement to evacuate POWs 'as soon as possible after their capture' in Article 19 paragraph 1. Therefore, the Eritrea–Ethiopia Claims Commission (EECC) concluded that the evacuation on foot in the instant case did not violate Articles 19 and 20 in spite of the harsh terrain and climate.[20] However, the Commission found Eritrea and Ethiopia liable for inhumane treatment as a result of forcing Ethiopian and Eritrean POWs respectively to evacuate without footwear.[21]

Whatever the method of evacuation, the Detaining Power shall take all suitable precautions to ensure the safety of POWs during evacuation as required by Article 20 paragraph 2. For example, the Detaining Power should be aware of minefields, approaching enemy warships,[22] or even armed groups which are parties to an ongoing non-international armed conflict (NIAC) and which may pose danger to POWs. The danger may not always be related to military operations: harsh terrain, such as steep valleys, deep rivers, and rapid river flow, as well as hostile civilians[23] may also present a danger to POWs. In all these cases, the Detaining Power should choose an alternative route or immediately evacuate the POWs to a safer place.

As the evacuation proceeds, POWs will start requiring their basic needs, namely food and water. Such needs become particularly acute in case of long-distance evacuation on foot through harsh geographical and climatic conditions. The quantity of food needs to be sufficient for the POWs to continue with the journey and not to fall prey to malnutrition.[24]

---

[15] EECC, *Prisoners of War—Ethiopia's Claim 4*, above n 5, para 89 and *Prisoners of War—Eritrea's Claim 17*, above n 10, para 89.
[16] *Conduct of the Persian Gulf War*, above n 7, at L-18.
[17] ICRC, *Report*, above n 4, at 127.   [18] Ibid, at 128.
[19] See, e.g., Röling and Rüter (eds), above n 9, at 401–3; *Trial of Arno Heering* and *Trial of Willi Mackensen*, British Military Court, Hanover, 1946, UNWCC Law Reports, vol XI, at 79 and 81 respectively.
[20] EECC, *Prisoners of War—Ethiopia's Claim 4*, above n 5, para 74; *Prisoners of War—Eritrea's Claim 17*, above n 10, para 68.
[21] EECC, *Prisoners of War—Ethiopia's Claim 4*, above n 5, para 74; EECC, *Prisoners of War—Eritrea's Claim 17*, above n 10, para 68.
[22] See, e.g., Röling and Rüter (eds), above n 9, at 410–12.
[23] Pictet Commentary GC III, at 175.   [24] See, e.g., Röling and Rüter (eds), above n 9, at 402.

The water needs to be potable and should not affect the health of POWs, for example by leading to dysentery.

21   Clothing and medical attention should also be provided where necessary. Particularly in harsh climate conditions, such as low temperatures or heavy snow, clothing suitable for such conditions should be provided. In addition, wounded and sick POWs should be given necessary medical attention, regardless of whether they became wounded or sick before or after their capture.

22   Article 20 paragraph 1 provides that the evacuation of POWs shall always be effected humanely, but also 'in conditions similar to those for the forces of the Detaining Power in their changes of station'. Therefore, where food, water, clothing, and medical attention are limited for the military units, they may also be limited for POWs. However, POWs may be in a situation different from that of troops of the Detaining Power, since they may not be accustomed to the specific climate and terrain, and may be physically and psychologically weakened by combat, capture, and evacuation.[25] Therefore, Article 20 paragraph 1 does not require the 'same' treatment as the forces of the Detaining Power but only 'similar' treatment. The special circumstances of POWs should be taken into account when interpreting Article 20.

23   When the evacuation is over a long distance, POWs may have to stop at transit camps before continuing their journey to their final destination. The Pictet Commentary to GC III characterizes 'transit camps' as 'those which the military authorities may have to establish in a combat zone in order to house prisoners captured during military operations in that particular zone', and further notes that 'it is not always possible to require that such camps should fulfil all the material conditions specified in the Convention'.[26] Such camps are to be distinguished from transit camps of a permanent kind envisaged in Article 24 GC III. Article 20 paragraph 4 requires that if POWs must pass through transit camps not of a permanent kind, their stay in such camps shall be as brief as possible. In the case of the 1991 Gulf War, the US set up three types of transit camps ('division collection points', 'corps holding facilities', and 'theatre camps') to house POWs before they were moved to the permanent camps in Saudi Arabia.[27] The first two were closer to the frontline and could be considered as transit camps, whereas the third could be considered to fall within the category of 'transit or screening camps of a permanent kind' within the meaning of Article 24.[28]

24   The bulk of Article 20 deals with the material conditions of evacuation but the obligation in Article 20 paragraph 1 always to carry out evacuation humanely extends to the troops' behaviour. Article 13 GC III already requires humane treatment of POWs, but Article 20 paragraph 1 confirms that such obligation should also be observed during their evacuation. An illustrative case is the ill-treatment which led to the deaths of at least 30 POWs during a forced march in the course of the Second World War, which was considered a war crime.[29]

25   The final requirement set out in Article 20 is to establish, as soon as possible, a list of POWs who are being evacuated. Once POWs are in the hands of the enemy Power, that Power is responsible for ensuring that the whereabouts of those POWs are accounted for

---

[25] Pictet Commentary GC III, at 173–4. [26] Ibid, at 176.
[27] *Conduct of the Persian Gulf War*, above n 7, at L-13 to L-14. [28] Ibid, at L-13 to L-16.
[29] See, e.g., *Mackensen*, above n 19, at 81. See also Röling and Rüter (eds), above n 9, at 401–3, 411.

at all times (see Chapter 49 of this volume). For this purpose, the first step is to establish a list of POWs who are evacuated. While it may not be feasible to establish such a list while combat is ongoing, it should be established as soon as the circumstances allow. As the Pictet Commentary to Article 20 provides, at least the information specified in Article 17 paragraph 1—namely the POW's surname, first names and rank, date of birth, and army, regimental, or serial number, or equivalent information—should be registered.[30] The list should also mention changes in the status of POWs, such as deaths and escapes, and should be updated whenever there are further changes.

II. Transfer from one camp to another

After POWs are evacuated to camps situated outside of the combat zone, they may be transferred to other camps for various reasons, such as overcrowding or the approach of the combat zone. Articles 46 to 48 GC III, located under the heading 'Transfer of Prisoners of War after Their Arrival in Camp', regulate such transfers. 26

The basic principles are the same as those in Articles 19 and 20 concerning evacuation of POWs, and most of the commentary set out in section B.I of this chapter also applies to transfers between camps. However, since transfers of POWs often take place in more predictable situations, the obligations of the Detaining Power are more detailed, and merit additional discussion. 27

a. Obligations prior to transfer

Article 46 GC III begins by requiring the Detaining Power to take into account the interests of the POWs when transferring them. This provision was proposed by Italy during the Diplomatic Conference with a view to avoiding transfer of POWs unless it was absolutely necessary and to preventing any delay in repatriation.[31] Examples cited during the Diplomatic Conference were the transfers of POWs from the United Kingdom (UK) and North Africa to the US, and from Egypt to New Zealand during the Second World War.[32] 28

Even with rapid techonogical developments in the means of transportation since the adoption of GC III, particularly those by air, the transfer of POWs to a distant camp would still present difficulties in meeting the range of obligations under Articles 118 and 119 GC III, in particular the obligations to release and repatriate without delay after the cessation of active hostilities, to bear the cost of repatriation, and to ensure conditions of transfer similar to those stipulated in Articles 46 to 48 GC III. The difficulties would be especially acute in the case of a long-distance repatriation of hundreds and thousands of POWs. Therefore, if there are options, the camp which would render the repatriation least difficult should be chosen. 29

When the decision not to transfer POWs is based on their interests, particularly the possibility of delay in repatriation, it must be consistent with the other provisions of GC III. For example, POWs may not be left in the camp if they are exposed to the fire of the combat zone contrary to Article 23. The interests of POWs or the potential difficulty of the eventual repatriation cannot serve as justifications in such a situation. 30

---

[30] Pictet Commentary GC III, at 175. [31] Final Record, vol II-B, at 290.
[32] Final Record, vol II-A, at 268.

31　If the transfer of sick or wounded POWs is contemplated, Article 47 paragraph 1 requires the same considerations as those set out in Article 19 paragraph 2.[33] Therefore, if the wounded and sick cannot be transferred without endangering their recovery, they should be left at the present camp, even if it means that they may rejoin their own armed forces and potentially return to combat in the future.[34]

32　Article 47 paragraph 2 envisages a specific situation: approach of the combat zone to the camp. In such a case, the Detaining Power can transfer POWs only in one of the following two situations:

— when the transfer can be carried out in adequate conditions of safety; or
— when the POWs are exposed to greater risks by remaining on the spot than by being transferred.

In relation to the first situation, there was a case during the Second World War where more than one-third of over 2,000 POWs died during a transfer lasting 160 kilometres in harsh conditions in order to escape the approaching enemy forces.[35] Such a case, if it were to take place today, would clearly be contrary to the requirements for transfer set out in Article 47 paragraph 2. On the other hand, the Detaining Power may have reasons to believe that its forces could resist the approaching enemy forces and that the transfer of POWs would merely put them in the midst of the combat zones. In any case, if it is reasonably clear that the safety of POWs in the camp can no longer be ensured, the transfer should commence immediately. If adequate conditions of safety cannot be guaranteed for a planned transfer, the prisoners should be released, even if this means that they may rejoin their own armed forces.[36] The execution of POWs simply because the Detaining Power cannot transfer them in adequate conditions is prohibited and would constitute a grave breach of GC III.[37] If transfers of POWs are carried out in harsh conditions with intent to cause a number of deaths, or if such transfers result in a number of deaths due to recklessness, they would also be tantamount to wilful killing, which is also a grave breach of GC III.[38]

33　In terms of keeping track of the POWs being transferred, Article 46 paragraph 3 specifically requires the Detaining Power to draw up a complete list of all transferred prisoners 'before their departure', which is in marked contrast to Article 20 paragraph 2 which requires establishing such a list 'as soon as possible' without specifying the exact time limit.

34　In addition, Article 48 provides detailed rules relating to the arrangements to be made before the transfer of POWs which find their origin in Article 26 of the 1929 GC II. According to Article 48 paragraph 1, POWs shall be informed of their departure and of their new postal address so that they can inform their next of kin. However, the responsibility to notify the Information Bureau of transfers of POWs and to advise the next of kin concerned lies with the Detaining Power pursuant to Article 122 GC III. Article 48 paragraph 1 does not in any way replace the Detaining Power's obligation under Article 122.

---

[33] See MN 11, above.
[34] ICRC, *Report*, above n 4, at 165.
[35] See Röling and Rüter (eds), above n 9, at 402–3.
[36] *The Ministries Case*, US Military Tribunal IV, Nuremberg, 1947, *Trials of War Criminals before the Nuremberg Military Tribunals under Control Council Law No 10*, vol XIV, at 444.
[37] See Art 130 GC III and Art 40 AP I.
[38] See Ch 31 of this volume for more detail on the grave breaches of the Geneva Conventions.

With a view to facilitating continued communication between POWs and their next of kin, Article 48 paragraph 3 requires the Detaining Power to make arrangements so that mail and parcels will be forwarded to the destination camp. Clearly, when the former camp is captured or destroyed by the enemy forces, the Detaining Power would not be able to fulfil this obligation. In such a case, the information transmitted to the Information Bureau pursuant to Article 122 becomes all the more important in order that the next of kin are able to find out the location of POWs.

According to Article 48 paragraphs 2 and 3, POWs may take with them their personal belongings up to a maximum of 25 kilograms as well as communal property. Such allowance is particularly important when the detention is prolonged, since POWs may wish to keep objects that would sustain their mental well-being, such as letters from their families. However, the Detaining Power may limit the weight of such objects depending on the conditions of transfer.

b. Obligations during transfer

Similar to Article 20, Article 46 paragraphs 2 and 3 prescribe the conditions in which transfers of POWs should be carried out.[39] However, the more predictable nature of transfers of POWs between camps requires the Detaining Power to take additional precautions. Article 20 paragraph 1 requires transfer conditions 'similar' to those of the forces of the Detaining Power, whereas Article 46 paragraph 2 requires conditions 'not less favourable' than those applicable to such forces, thereby establishing the minimum standard of transfer conditions.

Similar to Article 20 paragraph 2, Article 46 paragraph 3 requires the Detaining Power to take precautions to ensure the safety of POWs during transfer. However, Article 46 paragraph 3 requires 'adequate' precautions, including taking into account the type of climatic conditions which the POWs are used to and not endangering their health during transfer, thereby imposing stricter obligations than the 'suitable' precautions in Article 20.

In addition, Article 46 paragraph 3 specifically deals with transfers by sea or by air. During the preparatory work of GC III, the International Committee of the Red Cross (ICRC) stressed the particular danger of transfers of POWs by sea.[40] Indeed, the Judgment of the International Military Tribunal for the Far East (IMTFE) reported incidents where 'prison ships were often attacked in the same manner as other Japanese ships by the Allied forces who could not distinguish them from other ships.'[41] For this reason, the ICRC proposed to include various safeguards in the relevant draft provision, such as equipping vessels with life-boats and life belts, attaching special markings to the vessels, requiring the presence of a representative of the Protecting Power, and using neutral vessels as opposed to the vessels of the parties to the conflict.[42] Although these proposals were not included in the end, nothing prevents states from adopting one or more of these measures proposed by the ICRC to enhance the protection of POWs transferred by sea.

---

[39] See MN 15–25, above. For relevant cases, see Röling and Rüter (eds), above n 9, at 402–3 and 411–12; *High Command Case*, US Military Tribunal V, Nuremberg, 1947, *Trial of War Criminals*, above n 36, vol XI, at 638, vol XII, at 37, and vol XIV, at 443–7; *Heering* and *Mackensen*, above n 19.

[40] ICRC, *Revised and New Draft Conventions for the Protection of War Victims: Remarks and Proposals Submitted by the International Committee of the Red Cross* (Geneva: ICRC, 1949), at 49.

[41] See Röling and Rüter (eds), above n 9, at 411.   [42] ICRC, *Revised*, above n 40, at 50.

40 The obligation in Article 46 paragraph 3 to provide food, drinking water, and the necessary clothing and medical attention, is identical to that in Article 20 paragraph 2. However, Article 46 paragraph 3 provides 'shelter' as an additional requirement, which was proposed by the UK during the Diplomatic Conference since 'no shelter was provided during overnight halts' in cases which had occurred during the Second World War.[43]

III. Transfer from one Detaining Power to another

a. Drafting history

41 Prior to GC III, only two types of movement of POWs were regulated in international law, particularly in the 1929 GC II:

— transfers between camps belonging to a single Detaining Power; and
— transfers from a Detaining Power to the Power to which the POWs originally belonged ('repatriation').

42 However, during the Second World War, transfers which fell into neither of the two types were often carried out: transfers from one Detaining Power (transferring Power) to a Power to which the POWs did not belong (receiving Power). If the receiving Power was not a party to the 1929 GC II, POWs lost the protection under the Convention to which they were entitled when they were detained by the transferring Power. If the receiving Power was a party to the 1929 GC II, the POWs still benefited from its protection, but whether the receiving Power alone or both the transferring and receiving Powers were responsible for applying the 1929 GC II was not clear.[44]

43 At the Conference of Government Experts held in 1947, the ICRC proposed a provision prohibiting transfer of POWs from a state party to the proposed Convention to a non-state party, which was approved without substantial discussion. However, with respect to transfers between parties to the proposed Convention, views were divided as to whether the transferring and receiving Powers would both be responsible for implementing the Convention or only the receiving state.[45] On this question, the drafts of the proposed Convention on POWs submitted by the ICRC adopted joint responsibility of the transferring and receiving Powers for implementing the Convention.[46]

44 However, the debate over joint responsibility and sole responsibility of the receiving Power was revived at the Diplomatic Conference.[47] States that supported sole responsibility mentioned, inter alia, the following shortcomings of joint responsibility: the risk in case of disagreement between the transferring and receiving Powers over the interpretation of the proposed Convention; difficulty in identifying the responsible authority in case of failure to carry out the Convention; and the potential of providing an excuse for either of the Powers to interfere in the affairs of the other. States in favour of joint responsibility highlighted the advantages of joint responsibility, such as the possibility of providing

---

[43] Final Record, vol II-A, at 269.
[44] For an indication of the latter position, see para 2(J) of the Memorandum of Understanding between the United States of America and France on Repatriation and Liberation of Prisoners of War, 11 and 13 March 1947.
[45] ICRC, Report, above n 4, at 116–17.
[46] ICRC, Draft Revised or New Conventions for the Protection of War Victims (Geneva: ICRC, 1948), at 56; Final Record, vol I, at 75.
[47] For references to the relevant parts, see Final Record, vol III, at 218.

adequate material conditions by the wealthier Power. The UK later proposed a compromise draft, which subsequently became Article 12 paragraphs 2 and 3. However, the draft of this Article was adopted with a substantial number of votes against, thus reflecting its controversial nature.[48]

The adopted Article combined both positions mentioned above. The bottom line of Article 12 paragraph 2 is that, once POWs are transferred to another Power, the responsibility to apply GC III rests with the receiving Power and not with the transferring Power. The responsibility of the transferring Power is engaged only when the receiving Power fails to carry out GC III 'in any important respect'. Therefore, the responsibility of the transferring Power is engaged only on an ad hoc basis.

b. 'Reservations' to Article 12 and objections thereto

The statements made by states with regard to Article 12 paragraphs 2 and 3, and the objections to them at the time of signature or ratification of, or accession to GC III, also reflected the controversial nature of this Article. Many states made statements to the effect that the transferring Power retained the obligation to implement GC III vis-à-vis the transferred POWs,[49] which clearly went beyond the requirements of Article 12 paragraphs 2 and 3. Other states expressly objected to these statements and stated that their application constituted a violation of GC III.[50] What are the legal consequences of the above-mentioned statements and objections?

Information from the depositary of GC III, the Swiss Federal Council, indicates that the statements mentioned above were formulated as 'reservations'.[51] 'Reservation' is defined in Article 2(1)(d) of the 1969 Vienna Convention on the Law of Treaties as 'a unilateral statement [...] whereby it purports to exclude or to modify the legal effect of certain provisions of the treaty in their application to that State'. However, the statements referred to above add obligations to the transferring Power beyond what is required by Article 12 paragraphs 2 and 3. Adding obligations does not 'exclude or modify the legal effect' of Article 12 paragraphs 2 and 3, hence the statements are not reservations.[52] This conclusion is in line with the 2013 *Guide to Practice on Reservations* prepared by the UN International Law Commission (ILC).[53]

Since the above-mentioned statements are merely unilateral declarations, only those states that made the declarations are obliged to apply GC III even after those states have transferred POWs to another state. Other states parties to GC III are not bound to apply it to POWs transferred to another state, except in the case envisaged in Article 12 paragraph 3. These conclusions are in line with the ILC's 2006 *Guiding Principles Applicable to Unilateral Declarations of States Capable of Creating Legal Obligations*.[54] In addition, the general rules on the legal effects of reservations and of objections to reservations in Article 21 of the Vienna Convention on the Law of Treaties do not apply to these statements.

---

[48] Committee II of the Diplomatic Conference, at which GC III was negotiated, adopted the draft article by 14 votes to 10, with 1 abstention (Final Record, vol II-A, at 350), and at the plenary by 29 votes to 8 (Final Record, vol II-B, at 276).

[49] Final Record, vol I, at 342, 343, 345, 347, 350, 352, 353, 354, 355, and 356.

[50] See, e.g., 314 UNTS 334–5.   [51] Final Record, vol I, at 342.

[52] C. Pilloud, 'Reservations to the 1949 Geneva Conventions', 5 *IRRC* 52 (1965) 343, at 344.

[53] UN Doc A/66/10/Add.1, at 90–2. The General Assembly took note of the *Guide* by Res 68/111 of 16 December 2013 and attached the text of the *Guide* to that resolution.

[54] UN Doc A/61/10, at 368–9, paras 7 and 9. The General Assembly took note of the *Guiding Principles* by Res 61/34 of 4 December 2006.

c. Types of transfers covered

49 Article 12 paragraphs 2 and 3 only cover transfers of POWs from one Detaining Power to another. They exclude transfers to non-state actors, such as armed groups and private military and security companies, unless they belong to the Detaining Power.[55] Transfers within different military units of the Detaining Power and cases of repatriation of POWs are also not covered.

50 Transfers of POWs between different Powers may take place in a variety of ways. The most straightforward method is a transfer from one Detaining Power to a co-belligerent state, such as the transfer of POWs from the US to the Republic of Vietnam during the Vietnam War.[56] The transfer may also be to a neutral or non-belligerent Power, as envisaged in Article 4(B)(2) and Articles 109 to 111 GC III (see Chapter 51, MN 13–19, of this volume). The transfer of members of the Union of Soviet Socialist Republics (USSR) armed forces captured by armed groups to Switzerland in 1982, for internment during the conflict in Afghanistan, is an analogous example.[57]

51 Article 12 paragraph 2 covers not only a single transfer between two Detaining Powers, but also transfers through more than two Detaining Powers. For example, during the 1991 Gulf War, Iraqi POWs captured by the UK and France were first transferred to their own transit camps. They were then transferred to transit camps belonging to the US, which in turn transferred the POWs to permanent camps belonging to Saudi Arabia.[58]

52 Such transfers between Detaining Powers might occur in various situations, such as an evacuation from the combat zone, or a transfer between camps, as discussed above. For example, during the 1991 Gulf War, Iraqi POWs captured by the UK were evacuated by US transport to the transit camps belonging to the US.[59] On the other hand, General Noriega was captured by the US in 1989 during the international armed conflict (IAC) with Panama and was subsequently transferred from the US to France 21 years after his capture.[60] Therefore, transfers may occur instantly at the time of capture of POWs, or days, months, or even years after the capture.

d. Specific requirements before and during the transfer

53 Article 12 paragraph 2 first requires that the receiving Power must be a party to GC III. However, since virtually all states are now parties to the Geneva Conventions, including GC III, this requirement will invariably be met. This first requirement nevertheless indicates that transfers to entities that are not states, such as non-state actors and international organizations, are excluded.

54 The transferring Power should then be satisfied that the receiving Power is willing and able to apply GC III. Article 12 paragraph 1 does not specify the means by which the willingness

---

[55] Art 4(A)(2) GC III; Art 43(1) AP I. See also Ch 44, MN 26–31, of this volume, and K. Okimoto, 'The Relationship between a State and an Organized Armed Group and Its Impact on the Classification of Armed Conflict', 5–3 *Amsterdam Law Forum* (2013) 33.

[56] H. Levie, 'Procedures for the Protection of Prisoners of War in Viet-Nam: A Four-Way Problem', 65 *ASIL Proceedings* (1971) 209, at 211–12.

[57] ICRC, 'Afghanistan', 22 *IRRC* 229 (1982) 234, and 22 *IRRC* 230 (1982) 290, at 291. See Ch 51, MN 18 and 19, of this volume.

[58] *Conduct of the Persian Gulf War*, above n 7, L-13 to L-14.

[59] P. Rowe, 'Prisoners of War in the Gulf Area', in P. Rowe (ed), *The Gulf War 1990–91 in International and English Law* (London: Routledge, 1993) 188, at 198.

[60] G. Corn and S. Finegan, 'America's Longest Held Prisoner of War: Lessons Learned from the Capture, Prosecution, and Extradition of General Manuel Noriega', 71 *Louisiana Law Review* (2011) 1, at 35.

and the ability should be ascertained. A state may have an excellent record in the treatment of POWs, but the transferring Power should not presume the willingness of this state on that basis. The transferring Power should obtain some form of confirmation from the receiving Power which leaves no doubt that it is willing to apply GC III. The clearest expression is by way of a written agreement between the transferring and receiving Powers. For example, the Republic of Korea and the US concluded a memorandum of agreement in 1982, which provided that '[t]he armed forces of both parties undertake to treat all enemy prisoners of war […] in accordance with the provisions of the Geneva Conventions of 1949' and that '[t]he armed forces of the ROK [Republic of Korea] will accept and will be responsible for maintaining and safeguarding EPW/CI [enemy prisoners of war/civilian internees] whose custody has been transferred to them by the armed forces of the USA.'[61] Similar agreements were concluded between the UK and US during the 1991 Gulf War,[62] and among Australia, the UK, and the US during the 2003 Gulf War.[63] Such special agreements are authorized under Article 6 GC III, provided they do not fall short of the provisions of GC III.

On the other hand, the ability of the receiving Power to apply GC III cannot be ascertained by simple confirmation from that Power. The transferring Power, by directly visiting the camps, should obtain specific information, such as that concerning the location, size, and layout of the camps, as well as the quantity and quality of food and water, and the quality of medical services. If the receiving Power lacks the ability to apply GC III, the transferring Power could provide assistance to the receiving Power before the POWs are transferred.[64]

Pursuant to developments in international human rights law (IHRL) and its practice and jurisprudence, the transferring Power would have to ensure a number of additional procedural safeguards, namely:

— to inform the person concerned in a timely manner of the intended transfer;
— to provide an opportunity to make representations to an appropriate body in order that that person might express any fears regarding his or her transfer to the receiving Power;
— to permit access to legal assistance; and
— to allow the person concerned to challenge the decision to transfer before an independent and impartial body.[65]

Due to the individual nature of the risk assessment, the Detaining Power should assess the willingness and ability of the receiving Power to apply GC III with respect to each POW to be transferred, in addition to the general assessment of its willingness and ability discussed above in MN 54 and 55.

Transfers effected under Article 12 paragraph 2 must also meet the obligations during evacuation from the combat zone or transfer between camps discussed in sections B.I and B.II of this chapter.

---

[61] Paras 1 and 2 of the Memorandum of Agreement on the Transfer of Prisoners of War/Civilian Internees (United States of America and Republic of Korea), 12 February 1982.
[62] Arrangement for the Transfer of Enemy Prisoners of War and Civilian Internees from the Custody of the British Forces to the Custody of the American Forces, 31 January 1991, reproduced in Rowe (ed), above n 59, at 348–9.
[63] Arrangement for the Transfer of Prisoners of War, Civilian Internees and Civilian Detainees between the Forces of the United Kingdom of Great Britain and Northern Ireland, the United States of America and Australia, 23 March 2003, reproduced in S. Talmon, *The Occupation of Iraq* (Oxford: Hart Publishing, 2013), vol II, at 588.
[64] See, e.g., *Conduct of the Persian Gulf War*, above n 7, at L-4.
[65] For an in-depth analysis, see C. Droege, 'Transfers of Detainees: Legal Framework, Non-Refoulement and Contemporary Challenges', 90 *IRRC* 871 (2008) 669, at 679–80.

e. Specific requirements after the transfer

58 Once POWs are transferred, the receiving Power is responsible for the application of GC III while the POWs are in its custody. However, pursuant to Article 12 paragraph 3, the obligation of the transferring Power is revived where the receiving Power fails to carry out the provisions of GC III in any important respect. In such a case, the transferring Power should, depending on the situation:

— take effective measures to correct the situation;
— request the return of the POWs; or
— implement both measures.

If a request to return the POWs is made, the receiving Power has no choice but to return the POWs as required by Article 12 paragraph 3. Some controversial questions regarding Article 12 paragraph 3 will be discussed below.

59 First, may the receiving Power review the status of POWs and remove such status if necessary? Some bilateral agreements specifically provide that only the transferring Power can classify the status of POWs,[66] which is an interpretation in line with Article 12 paragraph 3. The willingness and ability of the receiving Power to apply GC III while POWs are in its custody are a clear expression that the receiving Power accepted the transferring Power's classification of the captured persons as POWs.[67] The receiving Power may suggest that the transferring Power reconsider the classification, but the receiving Power may not reclassify the status of POWs while they are in its custody. Reclassification by the receiving Power and the denial of the applicability of GC III constitute a failure to 'carry out the provisions of the Convention in any important respect' within the meaning of Article 12 paragraph 3, and the transferring Power should take effective corrective measures or request the return of POWs.

60 The obligation of the receiving state to apply GC III continues until the final release and repatriation of the POWs pursuant to Article 5 paragraph 1 GC III.[68] Therefore, even when an IAC between state A and state B has ended, state C, which holds POWs transferred by state A or B, must apply GC III until their final release and repatriation. Likewise, state A or B continues to bear the obligation to take action in case state C fails to carry out GC III in any important respect, even if the IAC no longer exists. For example, General Noriega was captured by the US in 1989 during the IAC with Panama, classified as a POW, and extradited to France in 2010 and then to Panama in 2011.[69] France was, therefore, under the obligation to apply GC III, and the US was under the obligation to take action in case of any failure by France to comply with GC III, even when the IAC between the US and Panama had ended. Such obligations continued until General Noriega was repatriated to Panama.

61 When POWs are transferred through multiple Powers, a question arises as to whether all the previous transferring Powers are responsible for taking action in case the last

---

[66] Memorandum of Agreement, above n 61; Arrangement for the Transfer of Enemy Prisoners of War, above n 62; and Arrangement for the Transfer of Prisoners of War, above n 63.

[67] However, see *United States v Noriega*, 808 F Supp 791 (SD Fla 1992) (No 88-91-Cr), reproduced in Sassòli/ Bouvier/Quintin, vol II, at 1369.

[68] For the status of POWs who refused to be repatriated, see Ch 51, MN 49–50, of this volume.

[69] See generally J. Crook (ed), 'Eleventh Circuit Approves General Noriega's Extradition to France', 103 *AJIL* (2009) 590.

receiving Power 'fails to carry out the Convention in any important respect'. Article 12 paragraph 3 provides that 'if *that Power* [the receiving Power] fails to carry out the provisions of the Convention [...] *the Power by whom the prisoners of war were transferred*' (emphasis added) shall take action. Therefore, Article 12 paragraph 3 governs the relation between the transferring Power and the Power which received POWs directly from the former. Hence, if state A transferred POWs to state B, which in turn transferred them to state C, state A should take action against state B for the latter's non-compliance with GC III, and not against state C for its non-compliance. For example, if state B transfers the POWs to state C without fulfilling the requirements in Article 12 paragraph 2, state A should request state B to have the POWs returned to the custody of state B, and then, if necessary, to state A, since such transfer by state B would constitute a failure 'to carry out the Convention in any important respect'.

What constitutes a failure 'to carry out the Convention in any important respect'? As the Pictet Commentary to GC III states, grave breaches of GC III as set forth in Article 130 clearly constitute such failure.[70] However, other violations of GC III could also be considered as such failure, such as the deaths of many POWs caused by the inability of the receiving Power to provide food due to inadequate financial resources.

How can such failure be established? Some bilateral agreements specifically allow the transferring Power to have access to transferred POWs in order to verify their treatment.[71] According to Article 12 paragraph 3, the Protecting Power may also notify the transferring Power of such failure. The Protecting Power could provide credible information on the treatment of POWs since it has the right to visit them pursuant to Article 126 GC III, a right also accorded to the ICRC. However, in the case of the ICRC, the findings of its visits are normally shared only with the Power actually detaining the POWs, which would be a bar to sharing the findings with the transferring Power. Therefore, it is all the more important for the transferring Power to make arrangements that would ensure its access to the transferred POWs in the hands of the receiving Power. The modalities of visits to POW camps by the transferring Power should be akin to those followed by the Protecting Power and the ICRC stipulated in Article 126 GC III, in order for the visits to be meaningful.

What is meant by 'effective measures to correct the situation'? The UK highlighted the difficulty of this question by asking as follows in the Diplomatic Conference: 'Would the first country be prepared to go to war with its ally in order to enforce implementation of the Convention, or to invade the territory of its ally in order to recover the prisoners?'[72] In case of failure to ensure adequate material conditions of internment, such as overcrowding and lack of food, water, and medical care, the transferring Power could assist in constructing additional camps and providing additional supplies.[73] Difficulties arise when the problems are related to the behaviour of the camp staff, such as ill-treatment of POWs. In such a case, the transferring Power may assist the receiving Power in the management and training of the camp staff, but if such measures prove to be inadequate, the transferring Power must request the return of the POWs. For example, during the Vietnam War, when the US became aware that a number of POWs had gone missing after it transferred

---

[70] Pictet Commentary GC III, at 137–8.
[71] Memorandum of Agreement, above n 61; Arrangement for the Transfer of Enemy Prisoners of War, above n 62; and Arrangement for the Transfer of Prisoners of War, above n 63.
[72] Final Record, vol II-A, at 246.   [73] Ibid, at 438.

them to the Republic of Vietnam at the frontline, the US decided to conduct the transfers at the camps of the Republic of Vietnam instead of at the frontline.[74]

65 When POWs are returned to the Power requesting the return (requesting Power) pursuant to Article 12 paragraph 3, the transfer should be conducted in accordance with Articles 46 to 48 GC III. In this connection, the Power returning the POWs (returning Power) may not invoke the interests of POWs mentioned in Article 46 paragraph 1 to refuse their return. In addition, the returning Power may not invoke Article 12 paragraph 3 and request the return of the POWs who had already been returned to the requesting Power. The only Power that can request the return of the POWs from the requesting Power under Article 12 paragraph 3 is the Power that had their custody immediately prior to that requesting Power.

66 What if the requesting Power is not willing or able to apply GC III? The returning Power would be confronted with two competing obligations: the obligation to return the POWs pursuant to Article 12 paragraph 3, and the principle of *non-refoulement*. In such a case, the returning Power should either put an end to the situation which initially led the transferring Power to request the return of POWs, or should identify another receiving Power, such as a neutral Power, which is prepared to receive the POWs under the terms of Article 12 paragraphs 2 and 3.

67 Due to the various procedural safeguards for transfers of POWs stipulated in Article 12 paragraphs 2 and 3, this is often referred to as one form of the principle of *'non-refoulement'*.[75] However, it is more advanced than its counterparts in international refugee and human rights law since:

— the pre-transfer assessment covers the willingness and ability to apply all the provisions of GC III, and not only specific risks such as torture and enforced disappearances, as in the case of 1984 Convention against Torture (CAT) and the 2006 International Convention for the Protection of All Persons from Enforced Disappearance;
— Article 12 applies to transfers from one Detaining Power to another regardless of the location, whereas the application of the principle of *non-refoulement* founded on IHRL may be controversial in cases where the transfer takes place outside the territory of the Detaining Power; and
— Article 12 paragraph 3 requires the transferring Power to take action in case of non-compliance with GC III by the receiving Power, whereas the relevant treaties of international refugee and human rights law do not explicitly require this.

IV. Transfer from a camp to penitentiary establishments

68 Article 22 paragraph 1 GC III prohibits internment of POWs in penitentiaries, and Article 97 paragraph 1 further prohibit transfers of POWs from a camp to penitentiary establishments, such as prisons for convicted criminals, to undergo disciplinary punishment.[76] Since the nature of disciplinary sanctions for violations of internal regulations of the camp, such as attempts to escape from the camp, is different from punishment for a criminal offence, penitentiary establishments are not considered suitable for POWs undergoing disciplinary

---

[74] Levie, above n 56, at 212.
[75] See, e.g., Droege, above n 65, at 674–5. See also, UN, 'Note to the Under-Secretary for Special Political Affairs and the Under-Secretary for General Assembly Affairs', *UN Juridical Yearbook* (1962) 241, at 244.
[76] See also Art 56 1929 GC II.

punishment. However, the drafters had a more basic consideration in mind: military dignity and honour.[77] Since POWs were detained during their normal course of duty and not as a result of a criminal conviction, treating POWs in the same way as criminal convicts was considered 'an affront to military dignity'.[78] Article 108 paragraph 1 does not exclude transfers of POWs to penitentiary establishments in the event that they are convicted of criminal offences,[79] but POWs should be separated from other convicts and their detention should conform to the provisions of GC III.

C. Relevance in Non-International Armed Conflicts

The evacuation of detainees from a place of detention exposed to danger arising out of a NIAC is specifically regulated in Article 5(2)(c) of Additional Protocol (AP) II. However, a similar provision cannot be found in Common Article 3. Neither AP II nor Common Article 3 contains specific provisions expressly regulating evacuation from the combat zone, the conditions of evacuation,[80] or the transfer from one party to a NIAC to another.[81] Therefore, significant gaps exist in IHL in the regulation of evacuation and transfer of detainees in NIAC.

So far as GC III is concerned, it applies to an IAC in accordance with its Article 2, and therefore the provisions relating to the evacuation and transfer of POWs discussed above do not apply automatically to NIACs. However, those provisions could apply to NIACs in at least three situations:

— when the parties to the conflict conclude special agreements;
— when allies conclude special agreements; or
— when a party to the conflict makes a unilateral declaration.

Article 3 paragraph 3 GC III envisages special agreements between the opposing parties to a NIAC in order to bring all or part of the provisions of GC III into force. For example, an agreement based on Article 111 GC III was concluded between the USSR and armed groups in Afghanistan in 1982 to transfer captured members of the USSR armed forces to Switzerland.[82]

In addition, two or more states cooperating to fight an armed group in a NIAC may conclude special agreements to apply the provisions of GC III on evacuation and transfer to captured members of armed groups. For example, Afghanistan and Canada concluded an agreement by which the parties agreed to treat detainees captured by the Canadian armed forces in accordance with GC III.[83] Although captured members of armed groups in Afghanistan do not qualify as POWs, GC III is made applicable to them when they are transferred from Canada to Afghanistan. The Convention ceases to apply to the captured

---

[77] ICRC, *Report*, above n 4, at 218.   [78] Pictet Commentary GC III, at 462.
[79] See, e.g., *Noriega*, above n 67, at 1361. See, however, Pictet Commentary GC III, at 463.
[80] Note, however, that CA 3 and Arts 4 and 5 AP II do provide general obligations to treat humanely persons who do not take a direct part or who have ceased to take part in hostilities.
[81] However, the principle of *non-refoulement* founded on IHRL continues to regulate transfers of detainees in NIAC.
[82] ICRC, 'Afghanistan', above n 57.
[83] Arrangement for the Transfer of Detainees between the Canadian Forces and the Ministry of Defence of the Islamic Republic of Afghanistan, 18 December 2005, reproduced in Sassòli/Bouvier/Quintin, vol III, at 2305–6.

persons when they have been returned to the armed groups on which they depend, which is analogous to repatriation within the meaning of Article 118 GC III.[84] It may also cease to apply if such persons object to their return to the armed groups due to serious reasons for fearing that, after their return, they may be the subject of measures affecting their life or liberty.

73 A unilateral declaration by a party to a NIAC could also bring GC III into force. Principle 1 of the 2006 ILC *Guiding Principles Applicable to Unilateral Declarations of States Capable of Creating Legal Obligations* provides that '[d]eclarations publicly made and manifesting the will to be bound may have the effect of creating legal obligations.'[85] For example, the International Criminal Tribunal for the former Yugoslavia (ICTY) concluded in the *Mrkšić et al* case that the Yugoslav People's Army (JNA) made a unilateral declaration to apply GC III. Therefore it was required to fulfil the conditions in Article 12 paragraph 2 when it abandoned Croatian POWs who subsequently were held by the Territorial Defence (TO), another entity of the armed forces of the former Yugoslavia.[86]

74 What happens when POWs already interned by a state are subsequently captured by an armed group? For example, state A may be engaged in an armed conflict concurrently against state B and an armed group in the territory of state B. If some members of state A armed forces are captured by state B, they would be classified as POWs, but would their status change if the armed group subsequently takes over their custody? Two situations might be envisaged:

— when state B transfers the POWs to the armed group; and
— when the armed group overruns the camp of state B and captures the POWs.

The first scenario is a violation of Article 12 paragraph 2 since state B may transfer POWs only to another state party to GC III. Therefore, state B should cease such transfer and have the POWs returned to its custody. In the second scenario, state B is not transferring the POWs of its own will. Instead, they are taken by the armed group by force. In such a case, those POWs would be considered released from state B's custody and therefore cease to be POWs. They are now in the exclusive custody of the armed group, hence the IHL rules applicable to NIAC provide protection instead of GC III.

D. Legal Consequences of a Violation

75 Violations of the provisions of GC III relating to the evacuation and transfer of POWs have not been prominent in cases before international and national courts compared to those relating to their treatment during detention. However, past cases demonstrate that violations of the provisions in GC III relating to evacuation and transfer could entail both individual criminal responsibility and state responsibility.

76 Inhumane treatment during the evacuation and transfer of POWs has been considered a war crime in several past cases. The most prominent example is the Judgment of the IMTFE in which a former Prime Minister of Japan was found guilty of violations

---

[84] M. Sassòli and M.-L. Tougas, 'International Law Issues Raised by the Transfer of Detainees by Canadian Forces in Afghanistan', 54 *McGill Law Journal* (2011) 959, at 979.
[85] Above n 54, at 368.
[86] ICTY, *The Prosecutor v Mile Mrkšić et al*, Appeals Chamber Judgment, IT-95-13/1-A, 5 May 2009, paras 69 and 71.

of the laws or customs of war for, inter alia, not taking action against an evacuation of POWs in the Philippines in 1942 which resulted in many deaths.[87] Several military courts established after the Second World War also found military officers guilty of war crimes for ill-treating POWs and failing to ensure humane conditions during the transfer of POWs.[88] Today, such treatment of POWs would amount to grave breaches under Article 130 GC III, namely wilful killing, torture or inhuman treatment, or wilfully causing great suffering or serious injury to body or health.

The *Prisoners of War* cases before the EECC were rare instances where Articles 19, 20, 46, and 47 of GC III were explicitly applied to the evacuation and transfer of POWs. The Commission found that Eritrea and Ethiopia were liable for inhumane treatment when Ethiopian and Eritrean POWs respectively were forced to march without footwear during evacuation,[89] and that Eritrea was liable for inhumane treatment during transfers between camps due to physical abuse by Eritrean guards.[90] The Commission awarded US$4,000,000 to Eritrea[91] and US$7,500,000 to Ethiopia[92] for the unlawful treatment of Eritrean and Ethiopian POWs respectively, including for inhumane treatment during their evacuation and transfer. Such awards were in line with the general rule to pay compensation for violations of IHL as reflected in Article 3 of 1907 Hague Convention IV and Article 91 AP I.

77

The *Mrkšić et al* case mentioned in MN 73 was a rare instance in which the ICTY specifically applied Article 12 GC III. In this case, the ICTY considered whether the JNA fulfilled the requirements in Article 12 paragraph 2 when it abandoned Croatian POWs who were subsequently held and murdered by the TO, another entity of the Yugoslav armed forces. The Tribunal concluded that the JNA officer concerned had failed to comply with the requirements in Article 12 paragraph 2 GC III.[93] The ICTY also concluded that an accused, a JNA commander, rendered substantial practical assistance to the TO to murder Croatian POWs, by deciding to abandon them and allowing the TO to take over their custody and to murder them, while being aware that such murder would occur as a result of abandoning them.[94] He was found guilty of aiding and abetting murder, and was sentenced to 20 years' imprisonment.[95] This case provided an indication of the legal consequences of omissions when transferring POWs to another Detaining Power.

78

E. Critical Assessment

Geneva Convention III inherited the provisions on evacuation and transfer of POWs in the 1929 GC II, but was also a leap forward from the 1929 GC II in the sense that GC III specifically required the Detaining Power to carry out evacuations and transfers of POWs

79

---

[87] Röling and Rüter (eds), above n 9, at 462–3.
[88] *Heering* and *Mackensen*, above n 19, and *Yamamoto* and *Uchiyama and Fukuda Trials*, Australian Military Courts, Rabaul and Singapore, 1946 and 1947, both referred to in *Heering* and *Mackensen*, at 80, fn 1.
[89] EECC, *Prisoners of War—Ethiopia's Claim 4*, above n 5, para 74; *Prisoners of War—Eritrea's Claim 17*, above n 10, para 68.
[90] EECC, *Prisoners of War—Ethiopia's Claim 4*, above n 5, para 137.
[91] EECC, *Eritrea's Damages Claims*, Final Award, 17 August 2009, para 233.
[92] EECC, *Ethiopia's Damages Claims*, Final Award, 17 August 2009, para 213.
[93] ICTY, *Mrkšić et al*, above n 86, para 103.
[94] ICTY, *The Prosecutor v Mile Mrkšić et al*, Trial Chamber Judgment, IT-95-13/1-T, 27 September 2007, paras 621–2.
[95] Ibid, paras 712–13.

in humane conditions in Articles 20 and 46. The conditions of evacuation and transfer of detainees in NIAC cannot be radically different from those in IAC. Hence, the obligations contained in Articles 19, 20, 46, and 47 GC III should be applicable to NIAC as a matter of customary international law.

80   Article 12 paragraphs 2 and 3 GC III on transfers between Detaining Powers were also a major achievement of the 1949 Diplomatic Conference. However, some important aspects were not dealt with, namely the possibility of the receiving Power to review the status of transferred POWs, the obligations of the previous Detaining Powers in relation to the current Detaining Power in case of transfers through multiple Detaining Powers, and the methods of monitoring the treatment of POWs by the transferring Power once they are transferred to the receiving Power. Such aspects could be regulated by ad hoc bilateral agreements among the Detaining Powers, but such agreements are not always guaranteed. Therefore, until such time as the opportunity arises to codify the modern practice of transfers of POWs between Detaining Powers under Article 12 paragraphs 2 and 3, it is hoped that this commentary will provide useful guidance.

KEIICHIRO OKIMOTO*

---

* The views expressed herein are those of the author and do not necessarily reflect the views of the United Nations.

Chapter 48. Treatment of Prisoners of War

	MN
A. Introduction	1
B. Meaning and Application	8
I. Temporal applicability of the Convention's safeguards	8
II. Responsibility of the Detaining Power	12
III. Fundamental rules for the treatment of prisoners of war	17
a. Humane treatment and prohibition of reprisals	17
b. Prohibition of physical maltreatment, mutilations, and medical experiments	20
c. Protection against public curiosity	23
d. Retention of civil capacity	25
e. Free maintenance	28
f. Non-discrimination and placement in camps	30
g. Protection of women	35
IV. Beginning of captivity	38
a. Conditions for evacuation	38
b. Release on the spot	42
c. Transfer during evacuation and after arrival in camp	44
d. Location of camps	48
e. Identification and interrogation	52
f. Property of prisoners	59
V. Conditions of captivity	66
a. Internment or release on parole	66
b. Places of internment	71
c. Quarters	73
d. Food, clothing, and canteens	76
e. Hygiene and medical care	80
f. Prerogatives of medical and religious personnel	84
g. Religious, intellectual, and physical activities	87
VI. Relations with the detaining authorities	90
a. Camp command structure, discipline, and ranks of prisoners of war	90
b. Prisoners' representatives and complaints against the authorities	94
VII. Labour and financial resources	97
a. Obligation and right to work	97
b. Conditions of labour and remuneration	100
c. Finances of prisoners of war	103
d. Management of prisoners' finances	105
VIII. Relations with the exterior	110
C. Relevance in Non-International Armed Conflicts	112
D. Legal Consequences of a Violation	117
E. Critical Assessment	122

Select Bibliography

Crawford, E., *The Treatment of Combatants and Insurgents under the Law of Armed Conflict* (Oxford: OUP, 2010)

Fischer, H., 'Protection of Prisoners of War', in D. Fleck (ed), *Handbook of International Humanitarian Law* (2nd edn, Oxford: OUP, 2008) 367

Hingorani, R.C., *Prisoners of War* (2nd edn, New York: Oceana Publications, 1982)

Levie, H.S. (ed), *Prisoners of War in International Armed Conflict* (Newport, RI: Naval War College Press, 1978) vol 59, at 185–7
Pictet Commentary GC III, at 139–405
Rosas, A., *The Legal Status of Prisoners of War: A Study of International Humanitarian Law Applicable in Armed Conflicts* (Helsinki: Suomalainen Tiedeakatemia, 1976)
Rowe, P., 'Prisoners of War in the Gulf Area', in P. Rowe (ed), *The Gulf War 1990–91 in International and English Law* (London/New York: Sweet & Maxwell/Routledge, 1992) 188

A. Introduction

1 Prisoners of war (POWs) may be interned in international armed conflicts (IACs) in order to preclude their further involvement in hostilities. As long as the conflict is ongoing, belligerents may restrict the liberty of a POW without any particular procedure and for no individual reason. Anyone qualifying as a POW (see Chapter 44 of this volume) may be held in custody by virtue of his or her legal status, even without having actively participated in fighting. As any other person *hors de combat*, POWs may not be attacked during internment and must be humanely treated.[1] Moreover, they deserve special protection because of their status as defeated enemies, and are immune from prosecution for lawful acts of war.

2 Prisoners of war are therefore among the most vulnerable victims of war, since they are at the mercy of the enemy and are more likely to suffer ill-treatment by enemy military forces and even the civilian population (see MN 15). In the past, they became the chattel of their captors and could be arbitrary imprisoned, enslaved, held for ransom, or summarily executed. It was not until the end of the nineteenth century that the status of POWs and their corresponding treatment were defined in international treaties. In the Regulations, annexed to Hague Convention II of 1899, respecting the laws and customs of war on land, states agreed for the first time to limit their respective sovereign rights on POWs, granting them special protection and humane treatment, without ignoring the need for balance between the conflicting interests of the Detaining Power and those of the prisoners' home country. The Hague Regulations of 1907 reproduced the provisions of 1899, with minimal further details. However, the First World War proved that those rules were still too vague, so belligerents were compelled to sign special agreements to overcome deficiencies on disputed points. The adoption of the 1929 Geneva Convention Relative to the Treatment of Prisoners of War (1929 GC II) expanded safeguards for POWs. Nevertheless, at the outbreak of the Second World War, not only had the 1929 Convention not been ratified by two of the major belligerents (the Soviet Union and Japan), but even its application by the adhering parties often proved unsatisfactory due to a lack of precision in its provisions or to a restrictive interpretation of their scope. Hence, the Convention was replaced by Geneva Convention (GC) III, which defined more precisely the conditions of captivity in the light of the main difficulties encountered during the previous conflict.

3 Such a detailed regime for POW treatment has been established by GC III that no further codification has been deemed necessary, except for a few clarifications included in Additional Protocol (AP) I, mainly dealing with the attribution of POW status to

---

[1] ICRC CIHL Study, vol I, at 164; Art 41 AP I.

certain kinds of fighters (e.g. guerrillas).[2] Nowadays, all United Nations (UN) member states have ratified GC III, and it is generally agreed that its fundamental provisions correspond to international customary law, as has been recognized by the Eritrea–Ethiopia Claims Commission (EECC) in its partial awards on the treatment of POWs during the 1998–2000 conflict between the countries concerned.[3]

The development of international human rights law (IHRL) has contributed to strengthening the protection of people in detention, either in peacetime or in war situations. However, the defence of POWs is left primarily to international humanitarian law (IHL), as *lex specialis*, whereas IHRL safeguards are mainly relevant for detainees deprived of their liberty, for reasons related to a conflict, who are not otherwise entitled to POW treatment.

The guarantees laid down in GC III apply from the moment POWs fall into the hands of the enemy until their release and repatriation, according to Article 5. The rules concerning the handling of POWs during captivity are organized in two main Parts: Part II (Articles 12–16), providing for the general protection of POWs; and Part III (Articles 17–108), thoroughly regulating the rights and duties of the prisoners, the Detaining Power, and the Power on which the prisoners depend, with regard to almost all aspects of internment. The division into these two Parts may suggest the existence of a distinction between two sets of provisions, the first concerning fundamental and intangible principles, always and immediately applicable, and the second relating to more technical norms to be implemented only when POWs are definitely transferred into permanent camps. This view, discussed at length during the preparatory Conference of 1947, was not embraced by the majority of the Government Experts, who agreed about the immediate application of each Part of the Convention from the moment the beneficiaries are captured or have otherwise fallen into the power of the enemy (see MN 8).[4]

Part III is in turn divided into six sections. Section I (Articles 17–20) relates to issues usually arising upon capture, such as the identification and interrogation of the prisoners, the handling of their property, and evacuation from the battlefield. Section II is devoted to the detailed conditions of internment and is organized into eight chapters. Chapter I (Articles 21–24) concerns the establishment of camps. Chapter II (Articles 25–28) deals with accommodation, food, and clothing of POWs, whereas sanitary measures are the object of Chapter III (Articles 29–32). Chapter IV is made up of Article 33, a single provision on retained medical and religious personnel. The activities of POWs are dealt with in Chapter V (Articles 34–38), while Chapters VI (Articles 39–42) and VII (Articles 43–45) set out the rules governing discipline in camps and the rank of POWs, respectively. Chapter VIII (Articles 46–48) regulates the transfer of prisoners.

Section III (Articles 49–57) is devoted to POWs' labour, while Section IV (Articles 58–68) relates to their finances. Section V (Articles 69–77) deals with POWs' contacts with the outside. Lastly, Section VI concerns relations with the authorities and is divided into three chapters: the first is made up of Article 78, a single provision concerning complaints against the conditions of captivity; the second (Articles 79–81) concerns

---

[2] Arts 43–45 AP I.
[3] EECC, *Prisoners of War—Ethiopia's Claim 4*, Partial Award, 1 July 2003, paras 30–2; EECC, *Prisoners of War—Eritrea's Claim 4*, Partial Award, 1 July 2003, paras 39–41.
[4] Pictet Commentary GC III, at 74.

B. Meaning and Application

I. Temporal applicability of the Convention's safeguards

8   As stated in Article 5 paragraph 1, GC III applies from the moment those who are entitled to POW treatment 'fall into the power' of the adversary. This wording aims to extend the scope of the previous 1929 Convention whose guarantees were claimed to benefit only prisoners 'captured' in the course of combat operations, whereas those who had voluntary surrendered were sometimes argued to be deprived of any protection. The more inclusive expression is meant to avoid practices of undue 'transformation' of POWs upon the final capitulation of their parent state, as occurred in 1945 when the Allied Powers denied POW status to enemy personnel who fell into their hands following the collapse of Germany and Japan, because they had not technically been captured but voluntary submitted themselves to Allied custody.[5]

9   According to the present provision, the exact time of the initial applicability of GC III corresponds not only to the moment prisoners are taken during the course of fighting, but also to the moment when they fall into the power of the enemy following mass capitulation or surrender to the enemy.[6] Thanks to the new wording, no misinterpretation about the initial time of application of GC III would occur, even with respect to those who are entitled to POW treatment although they do not directly participate in hostilities by definition (e.g. retained medical and religious personnel).[7]

10 The same extensive meaning is to be given to the clauses of GC III where the word 'capture' is still used (e.g. Articles 14 paragraph 3, or 22). Nonetheless, the term 'capture' has not lost its relevance in determining the temporal application of GC III. Prior to capture, in fact, persons entitled to POW treatment who no longer have the means to defend themselves or who have surrendered, may be *hors de combat* although they have not yet fallen into the power of the enemy. In this case they remain protected by the general rules in favour of persons *hors de combat*, but do not benefit from GC III until they are physically in the power of the adversary.[8] It follows that any dispute concerning the exact time when someone is *hors de combat*, or how surrender can be accomplished, has no influence on the initial application of GC III, because this dispute rather concerns the temporal application of the rule protecting persons *hors de combat* from attacks.[9]

11 The beginning of the application of GC III does not change even if doubt exists as to whether a captured person is entitled to POW treatment. In fact, Article 5 paragraph 2

---

[5] Ibid, at 75–7.

[6] In truth, a different attitude towards the encouragement of surrender or desertion, and the consequent recognition of POW status of the enemy forces, clearly emerged as a military strategy in the Falklands War or the 1991 Gulf War. See P. Rowe, 'Prisoners of War in the Gulf Area', in P. Rowe (ed), *The Gulf War 1990–91 in International and English Law* (London/New York: Sweet & Maxwell/Routledge, 1992) 188, at 188 and 191.

[7] ICRC Commentary APs, para 1614.

[8] Ibid, paras 1601–2 and 1611–13. See also H. Fischer, 'Protection of Prisoners of War', in D. Fleck (ed), *Handbook of International Humanitarian Law* (2nd edn, Oxford: OUP, 2008) 367, at 384, who underlines that '[c]ustody of a prisoner of war only commences with an act by a competent state organ'.

[9] ICRC CIHL Study, at 962–3 (United States); ICRC CIHL Database, Rule 47, Section B, VI (United Kingdom).

extends protection to doubtful cases, at least until the status of persons in custody is determined by a competent tribunal of the Detaining Power (see Chapter 46 of this volume). Whenever it is ascertained that a person does not enjoy POW treatment, his or her detention is not regulated by GC III, unless the captor voluntarily applies it. On the other hand, the Convention's safeguards must be granted to anyone qualifying as a POW for the entire duration of internment until its definite termination, even if a prisoner is recaptured after an attempted escape.

II. Responsibility of the Detaining Power

States are responsible for the correct application of IHL and are liable for all wrongful acts committed by their armed forces.[10] Article 12 paragraph 1 GC III reasserts the responsibility of the Detaining Power for the treatment of POWs, and clarifies that prisoners are not in the power of the individuals who captured them but are in the hands of the state of which the captors are the agents. Hence, a Detaining Power is responsible for the wrongful acts of all its organs, be they military or civilian, as well as for the unlawful behaviour of any person or entity formally empowered to exercise elements of governmental authority, or acting *de facto* on the instructions of, or under the direction or control of, the state, or even for violations committed by private persons or groups that the captor acknowledges and adopts as its own conduct.[11]

The scope of the responsibility of the Detaining Power is apparent in Article 57 paragraph 1 GC III, which concerns prisoners working for private employers. Although control and protection over working POWs may be delegated to private persons, within certain limits,[12] the provision underlines that the Detaining Power, the military authorities, and the commander of the camp to which such prisoners belong remain entirely and directly responsible for any aspect of their treatment (see MN 90). The same may be said whenever a state relies, as is often the case in contemporary conflicts, on private contractors for carrying out functions or tasks on its behalf, such as the interrogation or guarding of persons deprived of their liberty.[13]

The principle of responsibility implies not only that the Detaining Power must desist from any act or omission contrary to the rules of GC III, but also that it has a positive duty

---

[10] This is a long-standing rule of customary IHL codified by Art 3 of the 1907 Hague Convention IV and Art 91 AP I. See ICRC CIHL Study, vol I, at 530. Such a fundamental rule seems to have been contradicted by the EECC when it decided to limit its own task to the assessment of the responsibility of the parties only when it could find proof of frequent or recurring violations, avoiding having to deal with each individual incident of illegality suggested by the evidence: EECC, *POWs—Ethiopia*, above n 3, para 54; EECC, *POWs—Eritrea*, above n 3, para 56. The approach of the Commission has been strongly criticized, but it should be viewed as a regrettable isolated position, mainly dictated by the limited availability of time and resources, that does not disprove the well-established principle mentioned above. See G. Venturini, 'International Law and the Conduct of Military Operations', in A. de Guttry, H.H.G. Post, and G. Venturini (eds), *The 1998–2000 War between Eritrea and Ethiopia* (The Hague: T.M.C. Asser Press, 2009) 279, at 291; M. Sassòli, 'The Approach of the Eritrea–Ethiopia Claims Commission towards the Treatment of Protected Persons in International Humanitarian Law', ibid, 341, at 347–49.

[11] See Arts 4, 8 and 9 ILC Articles on State Responsibility and ICRC CIHL Study, vol I, at 530–6.

[12] Civilian employers may not order disciplinary punishment, nor use weapons against POWs, except in legitimate self-defence. The treatment afforded to the prisoners must not be inferior to that established by the Convention. Pictet Commentary GC III, at 296.

[13] K. Dörmann and L. Colassis, 'International Humanitarian Law in the Iraq Conflict', 47 *GYIL* (2004) 293, at 333. See also L. Cameron and V. Chetail, *Privatizing War: Private Military and Security Companies under Public International Law* (Cambridge: CUP, 2013), at 86–7, who observe that 'if PMSCs act as guards, they may not shoot or use weapons against POWs who attempt to escape'.

to prevent violations of the Convention by its organs or any other agent. For example, with respect to incidents of beatings and abuse of Eritrean POWs, the EECC has noted that 'the evidence fell short of showing that such unlawful abuse was permitted by Ethiopia, but Ethiopia was held liable for failing to take effective measures to prevent it'.[14]

15 Furthermore, a Detaining Power may incur responsibility when it fails to act with due diligence to prevent and punish any violation committed by private persons or entities against POWs. The duty to protect people in custody from mistreatment by civilians has been clearly affirmed by a United Kingdom (UK) Military Court, which convicted a soldier of the German Army for failing to prevent the assault and killing by a hostile crowd of civilians of three British airmen whom he was responsible for escorting to a special unit for interrogation. The escort's individual responsibility was assessed on the basis that he, 'as the representative of the Power which had taken the airmen prisoners, had the duty to prevent them from escaping but also of seeing that they were not molested'.[15]

16 Even if the above judgment refers to a case of individual responsibility for war crimes, the duty of protection of POWs from mistreatment by private persons equally applies to the state, since the responsibility of the Detaining Power for the treatment of POWs exists irrespective of the responsibility attributable to individuals for any violation of the Convention, as specified in the second sentence of Article 12 paragraph 1 GC III.

III. Fundamental rules for the treatment of prisoners of war

a. Humane treatment and prohibition of reprisals

17 Article 13 GC III provides for the absolute obligation of the Detaining Power to afford humane treatment to POWs with respect to any aspect of their life during the entire period of internment. The same provision emphasizes the temporal scope of this principle which applies 'at all times', so that no violation may be justified by reference to the circumstances of the hostilities or any other security need of the Detaining Power.

18 The absolute character of the fundamental right to humane treatment is reaffirmed by Article 14 paragraph 1 GC III, under which POWs are entitled, 'in all circumstances', to respect for their persons and honour. Prisoners deserve protection not only from physical violence, which certainly has degrading effects on their mental health, but also from any act or omission specifically meant to impair their morale and their sense of honour. Their moral independence must be preserved against any act of intimidation, and they are to be treated with due consideration of their role as combatants who suffered the misfortune of being defeated by the enemy (see also MN 89 on respect for their allegiance to the Power on which they depend).

19 Detailed guidance on what constitutes humane behaviour protecting the physical and moral integrity of POWs is given by additional GC III provisions. Among them, Article 13 paragraph 3, prohibiting reprisals against POWs, confirms the absolute nature of the guarantee of humane treatment, from which no derogation is permitted (see Chapter 29 of this volume). Hence, a belligerent may not suspend the operation of GC III rules even if the enemy violates the same obligations.

---

[14] EECC, *Final Award, Eritrea's Damages Claims*, 17 August 2009, para 230.
[15] British Military Court at Essen, *The Essen Lynching Case. Trial of Eric Heyer and six others*, 18–19 and 21–2 December 1945, *Law Reports of Trials of War Criminals*, vol I, 1947, at 90.

b. Prohibition of physical maltreatment, mutilations, and medical experiments

20 The second sentence of Article 13 paragraph 1 prohibits any unlawful act or omission causing death or seriously endangering the health of POWs, and condemns them as serious breaches of GC III. In truth, most of the grave breaches listed in Article 130 GC III are concrete examples of behaviour contrary to the previous ban, such as wilful killing,[16] torture, or inhuman treatment, as well as any action or omission wilfully causing great suffering or serious injury to body or health (e.g. unwarranted shooting, summary execution, beating, cruelty). The ban on physical violence against POWs is reconfirmed by Article 42, which qualifies the use of weapons as an extreme measure to keep discipline inside the camps or to oppose escape, which must be preceded by warnings.[17]

21 Furthermore, the third sentence of Article 13 paragraph 1 forbids mutilations and medical or scientific experiments, while Article 130 includes biological experiments among the grave breaches. Unless they are justified by the medical, dental, or hospital treatment of the POW concerned, and are carried out in his or her interest, such practices are never allowed, even if prisoners consent.[18] This was not the view of the United States (US) military tribunal at Nuremberg, when it maintained that, in order to conduct lawful human experiments, anyone participating had to give voluntary consent after having been informed of the risks involved.[19] However, since it is disputable how much informed consent a person may genuinely give while under the control of the enemy, evaluation based only on the prisoner's need is certainly preferable.[20]

22 In addition to the above-mentioned provision, Article 11 AP I explicitly includes, among the prohibited practices against protected persons, the removal of tissues or organs for transplantation. Exceptions are allowed for donations of blood for transfusions or of skin for grafting, provided that they are given voluntarily and for therapeutic purposes. The same provision reaffirms that the only permitted justification for any medical procedure is the objective therapeutic need for the benefit of the person concerned, though it expressly recognizes the right of persons deprived of their liberty to refuse any surgical operation.[21] It is further required that medical procedures be 'consistent with generally accepted medical standards which would be applied under similar circumstances to persons who are nationals of the Party conducting the procedure and are in no way deprived of liberty'. This criterion may prevent the risk of arbitrary evaluation of the appropriate treatment, as well as the consequent discrimination between captives and the population of the detaining state. Moreover, it allows for the possibility for each belligerent to apply different medical standards, due to the available economic and sanitary means (see MN 29).

---

[16] Except for death penalties pronounced and executed in accordance with Arts 100 and 101 GC III.

[17] The rule corresponds to and should be interpreted in light of Art 3 of the Code of Conduct for Law Enforcement Officials, UNGA Res 34/169, 17 December 1979, as well as Arts 9 and 10 of the Basic Principles on the Use of Force and Firearms by Law Enforcement Officials, adopted by the 8th UN Congress on the Prevention of Crime and the Treatment of Offenders, Havana, Cuba, 27 August to 7 September 1990.

[18] The same conditions have been applied by the SCSL when it condemned widespread mutilations against civilians. See SCSL, *The Prosecutor v Alex Tamba Brima, Ibrahim Brazzy Kamara and Santigie Borbor Kanu*, Trial Chamber Judgment, SCSL-04-16-T, 20 June 2007, para 724.

[19] United States, Military Tribunal at Nuremberg, *Brandt case (The Medical Trial)*, Judgment, 20 August 1947.

[20] The UN Human Rights Committee, in its General Comment 20 concerning Art 7 ICCPR, which prohibits torture and cruel, inhuman, or degrading treatment, has underlined that special protection against medical or scientific experiments is necessary in the case of persons not capable of giving valid consent, in particular those under any form of detention or imprisonment.

[21] In this event medical personnel should try to obtain written agreement from the patient.

c. Protection against public curiosity

23   Under Article 13 paragraph 2 GC III, the moral integrity of POWs must be assured by preventing their exposure to insults and public curiosity. No libel, slander, or offence against POWs is allowed, and their privacy must be respected. Moreover, prisoners may not be exposed to humiliation and violence by putting them on display in the streets, or parading them before enemy armed forces or civilians. Furthermore, not only is any use of public statements and appearances of prisoners for the purpose of propaganda contrary to the Convention, but even pictures and videos of POWs published or broadcast in newspapers and magazines, on television, or on the Internet may be prohibited, even if they do not depict acts or violence or intimidation against the captives. All states must apply this rule, irrespective of their participation in a conflict, because the retransmission of prohibited images is not permitted either.[22] However, whether showing images of POWs is contrary to the Convention may depend on the purpose for which the images are made and the use to which they are put.[23] Although the very act of taking pictures of a POW must be allowed for legitimate official purposes, such as the registration and documentation of prisoners, as well as the collection of proof of their proper treatment or relevant evidence for their prosecution, the way in which images are taken and their publication may constitute a breach of Article 13.[24]

24   According to the US Court of Appeals, which dealt with a case concerning the disclosure of photographs depicting abusive treatment of detainees by US soldiers in Iraq and Afghanistan,[25] the release of images of POWs may be consistent with the Convention when two specific conditions are fulfilled: first, the pictures displayed must not enable the identification of individual prisoners; secondly, their dissemination is not to be aimed in itself at humiliating the internees or exploiting them for ideological purposes, but only at genuinely heightening public awareness of their treatment during internment. Provided that these conditions are met, the dissemination of documentation showing captives subject to ill-treatment may contribute to applying IHL correctly by deterring future violations. However, it has been held that the 'humiliation' test is a subjective one and cannot guarantee a uniform interpretation of the norm in every circumstance, therefore the sole and most appropriate test for assessing whether the release of pictures or videos of POWs is lawful would depend on the condition that the prisoners' features cannot be recognized.[26]

d. Retention of civil capacity

25   The full civil capacity of POWs must be preserved, at least in so far as it is allowed by the restrictions necessarily imposed by captivity. Article 14 paragraph 3 GC III provides that POWs shall retain their civil capacity enjoyed at the time of their capture, which is usually regulated by the law of the country of origin, or of domicile, of a prisoner, or even by

---

[22] Dörmann and Colassis, above n 13, at 298–301.

[23] G.D. Solis, *The Law of Armed Conflict: International Humanitarian Law in War* (New York: CUP, 2010), at 324.

[24] On the illegitimacy of the broadcast of Saddam Hussein's images after his capture, see ibid, at 325; B. Dougherty, 'Saddam Hussein Is a Prisoner of War', 264E *Bofaxe*, 2003, available at <http://www.ifhv.de/documents/bofaxe/bofaxe2003-2004/x264e.pdf>.

[25] US Court of Appeals for the Second Circuit, *American Civil Liberties Union v Department of Defense*, No 06-3140-cv, 22 September 2008, at 50–1. On videos and pictures showed for propaganda reasons during the 1991 Gulf War, see Rowe, above n 6, at 194–5.

[26] The issue is dealt with extensively in G. Risius and M.A. Meyer, 'The Protection of Prisoners of War against Insults and Public Curiosity', 295 *IRRC* (1993) 288, at 294–5.

the legislation of other countries where, for instance, the prisoner holds property rights.[27] The reference to the time of capture is merely aimed at determining the applicable legislation governing a POW's civil status, but it is not to be interpreted as restricting the civil rights granted to a prisoner by the competent country to those in existence at the date of his capture.[28]

On the other hand, the present provision is not meant to secure full civil rights for POWs in the country holding them in custody. Moreover, according to the second sentence of Article 14 paragraph 3, the captor has the power to limit the exercise of civil rights by POWs not only within, but even outside its territory. Since the evaluation of the reasons which justify a restriction required by captivity is completely left to the Detaining Power itself, the exercise of POWs' civil rights may easily be subjected to arbitrary limitations.[29]

Besides the allowable restrictions, the retention of civil capacity by POWs imposes an obligation on the Detaining Power to create the most favourable conditions to enable prisoners to exercise their civil rights in foreign countries as well as in its territory. Appropriate procedures and facilities must be adopted to allow POWs to safeguard their interests abroad by proxy or by correspondence. Article 77 GC III requires the Detaining Power to facilitate the preparation and the authentication of any legal documents which the prisoners might find it necessary to execute. Prisoners must be allowed to consult a lawyer in order to be informed and assisted in drafting their documents correctly, including wills (see Chapter 49 of this volume), according to the applicable legislation. The transmission of all papers intended for POWs or despatched by them should occur without undue delay. In practice, the International Committee of the Red Cross (ICRC) Central Tracing Agency is usually called upon to ensure the delivery of the relevant documents to POWs or to their families.[30]

e. Free maintenance

The Detaining Power must guarantee the maintenance and medical care of POWs, supplying them with what is necessary to satisfy their basic needs and to preserve their health, as required by Article 15 GC III. Prisoners' maintenance must be provided free of charge, so the related expenses may neither be deducted from the prisoners' wages, nor may they be replaced, in whole or in part, by any relief supplies sent from the countries of origin or from humanitarian organizations. This does not mean that the Detaining Power may arbitrarily refuse to admit supplies from the outside, since POWs enjoy a right to receive individual or collective relief (see MN 111). Moreover, the Detaining Power must permit and facilitate access to humanitarian relief and medical assistance, if it cannot provide for the basic needs of POWs on its own.[31]

Meeting the essential needs of POWs free of charge is an absolute duty. There is no general clause in GC III allowing exceptions for economic constraints, even when the Detaining Power does not have the necessary resources to maintain its own troops adequately. However, the means concretely available, the local conditions, as well as the economic resources of belligerents must be taken into account in practice when assessing

---

[27] Final Record, vol II-A, at 400. [28] Ibid, at 404.
[29] H.S. Levie (ed), *Prisoners of War in International Armed Conflict* (Newport, RI: Naval War College Press, 1978), vol 59, at 185–7.
[30] ICRC, 'War and Family Links: Relevant Legal Texts', 27 November 2000, available at <http://www.icrc.org/eng/resources/documents/misc/57jmgm.htm>.
[31] ICRC CIHL Study, vol I, at 431.

whether the captor has fulfilled its obligation.[32] The EECC has recognized, with reference to the requirements of medical care in POW camps, that poor countries are not expected to have the same standards as developed countries. Nevertheless, economic difficulties may not excuse a failure to grant at least the minimum standards required by IHL.[33] In the end, notwithstanding the availability of external humanitarian assistance, when the Detaining Power proves unable or unwilling to fulfil the minimum requirements of GC III, it should be ready to give up direct control over the POWs.[34]

f. Non-discrimination and placement in camps

30 The principle of equal treatment of POWs is stated in Article 16 GC III, which prohibits any discrimination among captives based on race, nationality, religious belief, political opinions, or any other similar grounds.[35] The general rule allows for certain exceptions founded on special personal characteristics of each prisoner, such as rank, sex, age, state of health, or aptitude for work.

31 Though it may appear to be in contrast with the principle set out above, Article 22 paragraph 3, concerning places and conditions of internment, requires that POWs are grouped together on the basis of their nationality, language, and customs in order to enable the better administration of the camps and favour good relationships among prisoners. Captives belonging to the same armed forces must be placed together, except if they consent to be separated. This rule, which is meant to prevent the separation of the forces of the country in the mere interest of the Detaining Power, was reaffirmed by the EECC when it found Ethiopia liable for having segregated Eritrean POWs without their consent in order to promote defections and to break down internal discipline and cohesion among them.[36]

32 The assembling of POWs on the basis of the above criteria is consistent with the principle of non-discrimination, provided that, after being interned in different camps or compounds, captives are not subject to unlawful differentiation. In practice, however, discrimination against POWs on illicit grounds is frequent, since the Detaining Power tends to afford better treatment to more pliant prisoners, or to those expected to be more sympathetic to the captor's ideological perspectives and hostile to the Power on which they depend. By contrast, less favourable conditions are reserved for more aggressive or

---

[32] In a case concerning individual responsibility for detention conditions of protected persons, the ICTY found the accused not culpable, since the lack of food and insufficient medical care were caused by the war not by a deliberate intention to starve the detainees or deprive them of the necessary assistance: see ICTY, *The Prosecutor v Zlatko Aleksovski*, Trial Chamber Judgment, IT-95-14/1-T, 25 June 1999, paras 173 and 182.

[33] EECC, *POWs—Ethiopia*, above n 3, para 125; EECC, *POWs—Eritrea*, above n 3, para 138. It is worth noting that this position clearly mirrors the approach usually adopted to clarify the nature of states' obligations in respect of economic, social, and cultural rights that are binding in times both of peace and war. The Committee on Economic, Social and Cultural Rights, in particular, has observed, with reference to the International Covenant on Economic, Social and Cultural Rights provisions, that 'any assessment as to whether a State has discharged its minimum core obligations must also take account of resource constraints applying within the country concerned. Article 2(1) obligates each State party to take the necessary steps to "the maximum of its available resources". In order for a State party to be able to attribute its failure to meet at least its minimum core obligations to a lack of available resources it must demonstrate that every effort has been made to use all resources that are at its disposition in an effort to satisfy, as a matter of priority, those minimum obligations': CESCR, *General Comment 3, The Nature of State Parties Obligations (Art 2, para 1)*, 14 December 1990, at 10.

[34] Fischer, above n 8, at 400. [35] See Ch 10 of this volume.

[36] EECC, *POWs—Eritrea*, above n 3, para 84.

antagonistic POWs. The illegitimacy of this tendency was reaffirmed when Eritrea was condemned for discriminatory treatment of POWs, especially those coming from the Tigray region, who were treated worse than others, while those considered as deserters were given favourable treatment.[37]

In practice, when ideological or religious disputes arise between prisoners grouped together, segregation on the basis of personal opinions is permitted to ensure the safety of the POWs themselves, provided that the disputes do not depend on any incitement by the Detaining Power. Any decision of this kind, however, would be consistent with GC III only as long as separated captives were subject to no further unlawful discrimination.[38]

Frequent incidents resulting in the killing or wounding of POWs, due to ideological disputes between 'believers' and 'loyalists', occurred among Iraqi detainees in Iranian camps. The UN monitoring mission pointed out that the separation of groups of prisoners was not only a legitimate and necessary security measure, but also a suitable preventive instrument, together with a more balanced attitude of Iranian authorities towards all prisoners.[39]

g. Protection of women

Article 14 paragraph 2 GC III establishes that female POWs must be treated in a manner equivalent to male captives, except for in circumstances where due regard for their sex is required. The Convention lays down specific obligations in situations considered to be particularly sensitive, including possible exposure to sexual violence and maternity needs. According to Article 25 paragraph 4 and Article 29 paragraph 2, dormitories and sanitary installations used by male and female prisoners must be separated, and men must not have access to female facilities, even if women consent, in order to reduce the risk of rape, forced prostitution, or any other form of sexual assault against women in camps.[40] Article 75(5) AP I further requires that in all circumstances women detainees must be under the direct supervision of women.

Article 49 paragraph 1 GC III permits the Detaining Power to take gender into account in the utilization of the labour of POWs, so allowance must be made for the physical capabilities of each woman in the designation of work duties.

In addition to these provisions, the principle requiring adequate consideration for the needs of women covers any provision relating to POW treatment, even if it is not always explicitly mentioned. Although women POWs are usually few in number, the application of GC III provisions will adequately fulfil their specific needs only if attention is paid to their gender-specific needs (e.g. food, hygiene, health care).[41]

---

[37] EECC, *POWs—Ethiopia*, above n 3, para 83.
[38] On the issue, see also A. Rosas, *The Legal Status of Prisoners of War: A Study of International Humanitarian Law Applicable in Armed Conflicts* (Helsinki: Suomalainen Tiedeakatemia, 1976), at 436–7.
[39] UN Doc S/16962, 22 February 1985, at 10–17, 43–4. See also Memorandum from the ICRC to the States Parties to the Geneva Conventions of 12 August 1949 concerning the conflict between Islamic Republic of Iran and Republic of Iraq, Geneva, 7 May 1983, and Second Memorandum from the ICRC to the States Parties to the Geneva Conventions of 12 August 1949 concerning the conflict between Islamic Republic of Iran and Republic of Iraq, Geneva, 10 February 1984, in Sassoli/Bouvier/Quintin, at 1493 and 1498.
[40] On sexual abuses, see Ch 17 of this volume.
[41] For a comprehensive analysis of the matter, although not limited to the treatment of women as POWs, see J. Ashdown and M. James, 'Women in Detention', 92 *IRRC* (2010) 123; J. Gardam and M. Jarvis, *Women, Armed Conflict and International Law* (The Hague: Kluwer Law International, 2001).

IV. Beginning of captivity

a. Conditions for evacuation

38 Under Article 19 paragraph 1 GC III, the captor has the duty to transfer prisoners to permanent camps as soon as possible, though the temporal requirement is not defined more specifically, since it depends on the circumstances. In practice, the front-line unit which has taken the prisoners may not have the means to evacuate them, or the necessary arrangements may take longer due to the needs of those fighting. Moreover, POWs who are unfit for evacuation for health reasons may be temporarily kept to the rear of the conflict zone if any move is hazardous to their lives.[42]

39 From the time of capture until complete evacuation, the Detaining Power has a general duty to treat POWs humanely, adopt all suitable precautions to ensure their safety, protect them against unnecessary danger, and provide them with shelter if possible.[43] In order to allow them to seek cover from dangers on the battlefield, they should not be tied up, unless this measure is absolutely necessary to prevent escape or the destruction of military information.[44] Article 20 paragraph 2 GC III requires that POWs are supplied with sufficient food and water, clothing, and medical attention, while Article 20 paragraph 1 specifies that they must be afforded 'conditions similar to those for the forces of the Detaining Power in their changes of station'. The provision is to be understood as requiring that POWs be evacuated in conditions at least similar to those experienced by the forces of the Detaining Power. This view was adopted by the EECC to assess whether the parties complied with the applicable law when evacuating POWs from the battlefield. Although prisoners suffered extremely harsh treatment, both parties claimed that their 'soldiers faced nearly the same unavoidably difficult conditions'. The Commission found that, in the light of the 'harsh geographic, military and logistical circumstances', the belligerents had overall satisfied the legal requirements.[45]

40 In certain circumstances, however, mere comparison with the conditions experienced by the forces of the Detaining Power may not be adequate if it is not borne in mind that prisoners' state of health, training, and habits may differ widely from those of their captors. Conditions that might be endurable by the latter, might not be bearable for the former. As a consequence, even though the handling of POWs during evacuation is similar to the treatment of the capturing forces, the manner in which the evacuation is performed may violate the requirements of IHL if the personal conditions of prisoners are not duly taken into account in order to minimize the dangers to their life and health.[46]

41 One of the main threats to the safety and humane treatment of POWs during evacuation is inadequate transport conditions (see Ch 47, MN 15–24, of this volume). Nevertheless, GC III does not provide for specific guidance on this matter, so the correct behaviour of the Detaining Power depends on the circumstances of the conflict and the resources available. Transferring POWs using vehicles with insufficient capacity to hold them, or forcing them into excessively long daily marches, are practices deemed to be inconsistent with IHL, because they either cause a high number of deaths, or subject prisoners to unbearable

---

[42] Art 19 para 2 GC III. Levie (ed), above n 29, at 99–100.
[43] Art 19 para 3 GC III. Pictet Commentary GC III, at 172. Practices of deliberate killing and abusive treatment at capture or its immediate aftermath against Ethiopian prisoners by Eritrean forces have been condemned as blatant violations of the obligation to ensure humane treatment and evacuation: EECC, *POWs—Ethiopia*, above n 3, paras 63–8.
[44] Fischer, above n 8, at 385–6.
[45] EECC, *POWs—Ethiopia*, above n 3, paras 71–4; EECC, *POWs—Eritrea*, above n 3, paras 66–9.
[46] Fischer, above n 8, at 392; Pictet Commentary GC III, at 174.

hardship. The Convention does not specify a maximum distance that prisoners can walk each day,[47] so the required length of the march must be determined in the light of the personal conditions of the individuals concerned, as well as of climate and geographical factors, provided that the bounds of humane treatment are not overstepped. Forcing POWs to walk without footwear during evacuation under extremely harsh conditions was condemned by the EECC as inhuman treatment because it unnecessarily compounded the suffering of prisoners.[48]

b. Release on the spot

Whenever the requirements for evacuation cannot be fulfilled, the Detaining Power has the duty either to suspend the process, resuming it only if the prisoners would run greater risks by remaining where they are, or to release the POWs according to the rule codified in Article 41 paragraph 3 AP I, which is recognized as a general norm of customary international law.[49] In particular, when capture occurs in unusual circumstances of combat, making it difficult to keep or evacuate prisoners in a timely way, their release on the spot is required, provided that all feasible precautions are taken to ensure their safety. The situations envisaged by this provision refer, for instance, to the enemy's capture by a small or a long-distance patrol not equipped to detain and evacuate prisoners, or by commandos operating behind enemy lines or even during air operations. Nevertheless, its scope is not limited to this kind of event but covers any battle situation where circumstances render the care and evacuation of POWs impossible.[50] 42

The main purpose of this obligation is to counter the practice of getting rid of prisoners whenever the strict application of IHL rules proves too hard and conflicts with military necessity.[51] This is why the provision requires the releasing party to take 'all feasible precautions' in order to ensure the enemy's survival, for example by supplying the released prisoners with food, water, and means to signal their location.[52] In any case, the provision cannot be interpreted as demanding that the capturing forces deprive themselves of the resources necessary to complete their mission.[53] 43

c. Transfer during evacuation and after arrival in camp

If evacuation takes place over a relatively long period of time, POWs may be held temporarily in transit camps set up near the area of combat operations (see Ch 47, MN 23, of this volume). Due to their location, those camps would not fulfil all the material requirements for permanent camps. Therefore, Article 20 paragraph 3 GC III requires that prisoners' stay in such camps shall be 'as brief as possible'.[54] 44

No rule of IHL provides for an explicit obligation to set up transit camps on land as is categorically required for permanent internment camps. Therefore, in certain 45

---

[47] Art 7 1929 GC II limited foot marches to 20 kilometres a day, except in certain specified situations.
[48] EECC, *POWs—Ethiopia*, above n 3, para 74; EECC, *POWs—Eritrea*, above n 3, para 68.
[49] ICRC CIHL Study, vol I, at 169.
[50] Fischer, above n 8, at 394.
[51] The execution of a Vietnamese prisoner because his being held in custody would have threatened the security of the platoon which captured him, was condemned by the US Army Board of Review in *United States v Staff Sergeant Walter Griffen*, Judgment, 2 July 1968, 39 CMR 586 (1968); pet. rev. den.18 USCMA 622, 39 CMR 293 (1968); H.S. Levie (ed), *Documents on Prisoners of War* (Newport, RI: Naval War College Press, 1979), vol 60, at 752–6.
[52] ICRC CIHL Study, at 973 (Canada) and 974 (Kenya, UK).
[53] ICRC CIHL Database, Rule 47, Section C, VI.   [54] Fischer, above n 8, at 393.

circumstances, even warships may be assimilated to use as transit camps, temporarily holding POWs before moving them to another transit camp or permanent land-based installation. The lawfulness of detention aboard ships will depend on the specific circumstances of the conflict, as well as the interests of the POWs. Whenever a ship offers the only or the most appropriate accommodation to protect prisoners, its temporary use is consistent with IHL. During the 1982 Falklands conflict, for instance, most Argentine prisoners were held aboard British warships before their repatriation, because the particular circumstances of the operations rendered the setting up of long-term land-based camps a less convenient solution for the well-being of the prisoners themselves.

46 During Operation Enduring Freedom (OEF) and Operation Iraqi Freedom (OIF), it was reported that a large number of POWs were taken into custody on board US amphibious assault ships in the Arabian Sea or the Indian Ocean, where their treatment seemed to meet the essential standards required by IHL.[55] Although today's military ships may offer more comfortable accommodation and care to POWs than could be envisaged at the time of the drafting of GC III, it cannot be denied that their use may still expose prisoners to concrete risks of attacks, since the vessels lose neither their qualification as legitimate military objectives, nor their right to engage the enemy. Similarly to what occurs in transit camps on land, safeguards for POWs held at sea are diminished by definition, which is why their presence on warships must be strictly as brief as possible. Permanent internment on naval vessels would otherwise result in an ostensible violation of the obligations to keep POWs far from the combat zone and to avoid using them to shield sensitive military objectives (see MN 49).

47 Transit camps used during evacuation are not to be confused with the 'transit or screening camps of a permanent kind' mentioned in Article 24 GC III, which are installations, remote from the danger zone, used for inter-camp transfers, that shall meet the standards required for all permanent camps.[56] Whenever the Detaining Power finds it necessary to transfer POWs from the permanent camp to which they were originally assigned, the conditions set out in Articles 46–48 GC III, essentially mirroring those required during initial evacuation, must be observed (see Chapter 47, MN 26–40, of this volume).

d. Location of camps

48 Article 19 paragraph 1 GC III requires that POWs are accommodated in permanent internment camps 'far enough' from the combat zone. In modern conflicts, however, very few places are completely out of danger, due to air warfare and the use of long-range weapons. The wording of the Convention should be understood in a flexible manner, taking into account the specific circumstances of the conflict, the stability of the front line, and military developments.[57] While in the past the combat zone was defined only by reference to the range of land- and sea-launched weapons, nowadays it would correspond to the 'area of military ground operations and tactical measures supporting them from air or sea'.[58]

49 The same interpretation should be given to the meaning of Article 23 paragraph 1, which reasserts that POWs must be located where they may not be exposed to the fire of the combat zone, and adds a prohibition on intentionally using prisoners to shield certain military targets from attacks. In spite of the ban, the habit of using POWs as

---

[55] W.G. McMillan, 'Something More than a Three-Hour Tour: Rules for Detention and Treatment of Persons at Sea on US Naval Warships', *The Army Lawyer* (2011) 31, at 33–4 and 36–7; P. Noone et al, 'Prisoners of War in the 21st Century: Issues in Modern Warfare', 50 *Naval Law Review* (2004) 1, at 19–38.
[56] Pictet Commentary GC III, at 176.   [57] Ibid, at 172.   [58] Fischer, above n 8, at 391.

human shields has been reported in most IACs since the Second World War.[59] Thanks to the development of international criminal law, however, such a practice is strongly condemned and explicitly considered as a war crime.[60]

Even if located far from military objectives or outside the fighting zone, internment camps may nevertheless be exposed to the dangers of the active hostilities. As a consequence, certain requirements specifically meant to protect POWs against air bombardment or other hazards of warfare operations should be applied scrupulously. In particular, Article 23 paragraph 2 GC III provides that POWs must be supplied with air raid shelters and other protective facilities, such as gas masks or antiradiation garments.[61] The obligation is not an absolute one, so the Detaining Power has the duty to furnish protective tools only in so far as they are provided to civilians living in proximity to the camps. If shelters, either separate from the civilian ones or shared with them, are available to POWs, the latter must be free to enter them as quickly as possible upon the sounding of an alarm, with the exception of those prisoners assigned to specific duties relating to the protection of their quarters, who may be required to take the same action as is demanded from the Detaining Power's armed forces in similar circumstances.[62]

In order to further protect POWs against unwitting attacks by belligerents, Article 23 paragraph 3 GC III requires the captor to notify the adversaries of all useful information concerning the geographical location of camps, which should be marked with the special letters 'PW' or 'PG', or any other system agreed upon, to facilitate their aerial identification in daytime. Such marking systems must be used for no other purpose, but must be applied only 'when the military situation permits', as stated by Article 23 paragraph 4. Such wording should not be understood, however, as giving the Detaining Power excessive discretion in determining the criteria of applicability of the rule, therefore 'whenever circumstances permit, camps must be marked'.[63]

e. Identification and interrogation

As soon as possible after their capture, prisoners must be identified and their personal data included in a list drawn up before evacuation, in order both to establish the accountability of the Detaining Power for the individuals taken into its custody and to avoid unascertainable disappearances. The identification of captured persons serves other practical and humanitarian purposes, such as the establishment of their status under IHL and the consequent enjoyment of their rights, as well as the transmission of information concerning their fate to the power on which they depend and to their relatives.

---

[59] During the 1990–1 Gulf War, for instance, such treatment had been threatened against Coalition prisoners. See 'Putting Noncombatants at Risk: Saddam's Use of "Human Shields"', January 2003, available at <https://www.cia.gov/library/reports/general-reports-1/iraq_human_shields/iraq_human_shields.pdf>, at 3. In truth the death of at least one allied pilot used as human shield to protect Iraqi installations has been reported by Rowe, above n 6, at 196. More extensively on the issue, see M.N. Schmitt, 'Human Shields in International Humanitarian Law', 38 *IsrYBHR* (2008) 17.

[60] See Art 8(2)(b)(xxiii) ICC Statute; ICRC CIHL Study, at 337; M. Pedrazzi, 'Using Human Shields as a War Crime', in F. Pocar, M. Pedrazzi, and M. Frulli (eds), *War Crimes and the Conduct of Hostilities: Challenges to Adjudication and Investigation* (Cheltenham/Northampton: Edward Elgar, 2013) 98, esp at 109.

[61] On the need to provide Iraqi POWs with gas masks against the permanent threat of chemical attacks by Iraq during the 1990–1 Gulf War, see Rowe, above n 6, at 198.

[62] Pictet Commentary GC III, at 189.

[63] Ibid, at 190. On reported violations of these rules by Korea and North Vietnam, see Fischer, above n 8, at 399.

53   Article 20 paragraph 2 GC III requires lists of POWs to be drawn up in several copies in order to facilitate checking their identity upon arrival at camps, and such lists must at least include the details that prisoners are bound to give in compliance with Article 17 paragraph 1, i.e.: surname and first names; rank; date of birth; army, regimental, personal, or serial number; or equivalent information.[64] The same data are to be found on the identity card that each belligerent must supply, in duplicate, to every person who might become a POW. The Power of origin may add further details on its personnel, such as the signature, the fingerprints, the photograph, the blood group, or even the religious denomination of the card's owner. Prisoners are bound to show the document on demand, unless they have lost it. In no case may they be left without identity documents, so the Detaining Power can never take them away, and it is required to issue a new card to those who possess none.[65]

54   Whenever prisoners are unable to give the required data due to their state of health, they are to be handed over to medical service and the Detaining Power shall have recourse to all possible alternative means to establish their identity, provided that it does not inflict any form of coercion or inhuman treatment on POWs. Methods serving this purpose would include recourse to identification cards or identification tags, if available, interrogation of other prisoners captured at the same time and place, transmission of photographs, and fingerprinting. Nowadays, thanks to modern technology, identification can be done through blood and DNA tests, although their possible use solely for intelligence purposes may be controversial.[66]

55   If a prisoner is capable of identifying himself or herself but wilfully refuses to furnish the required information, or gives incorrect indications, Article 17 paragraph 2 GC III allows the captor lawfully to restrict the special privileges accorded to that prisoner's rank or status under the Convention, although in no case may the fundamental guarantees granted to all POWs be withdrawn.[67]

56   Although POWs' obligation to supply information is limited to the requirements set out above, no provision prohibits their interrogation on further issues. In truth, it would be unrealistic to expect that the Detaining Power would not try to take advantage of its control of prisoners to discover details regarding the military planning of the enemy, as well as any other useful information. Nevertheless, the way to conduct questioning is limited by the Convention: first, interrogations must be carried out in a language that POWs understand; secondly, but no less important, prisoners may not be subject to any form of coercion, neither to compel them to give the information requested, nor to sanction them for their possible refusal. In particular, Article 17 paragraph 4 GC III expressly forbids physical or mental torture, threats or insults, and unpleasant or disadvantageous treatment of POWs.[68] Other forms of pressure on prisoners are permitted, provided that they do not result in inhuman treatment or in conduct forbidden by the Convention. Thus, the captor may have recourse to psychological tricks, such as the promise of preferential

---

[64] Any information concerning a POW must be forwarded by the most rapid means to the Power on which the prisoner depends, in accordance with Art 122 GC III (see Ch 49, MN 10–12, of this volume).

[65] Art 17 para 3 and Art 18 para 2 GC III.

[66] Noone et al, above n 55, at 56–68.   [67] Pictet Commentary GC III, at 159–60.

[68] Frequent violations of the prohibition on subjecting POWs to inhuman treatment during interrogation have been ascertained by the EECC, *POWs—Ethiopia*, above n 3, paras 75–6, which found Eritrea liable for permitting coercive interrogation. Practices of torture and abusive treatment against POWs and other detainees, although occurring in almost every armed conflict, are systematically condemned by international or national monitoring bodies, as well as criminal courts. See, e.g., the first judgment of the Extraordinary Chambers in the Courts of Cambodia (ECCC), which found the accused responsible for torture against

treatment (e.g. better accommodation, rations, or pay), although the real concession of any privilege would appear unlawful if contrary to the principle of non-discrimination between prisoners.[69] Nevertheless, it is worth remembering that the non-discrimination provision should be understood as excluding differentiation only when it is disadvantageous for the moral and material well-being of POWs.[70]

The Convention does not establish specific temporal conditions for interrogation: it may be held any time the Detaining Power deems it convenient, though it will mostly occur as soon as possible after capture, to exploit the more fragile psychological situation of the prisoner in an attempt to get all possible information. However, when POWs need medical care immediately upon capture, any delay of the necessary treatment for purposes of interrogation would be inconsistent with the Convention.[71] Frequency and duration of questioning are not specifically limited, in so far as they do not turn out to be inhumane. 57

With regard to the site of interrogation, no particular rules are set forth by GC III, although the recourse to secret detention centres is certainly inadmissible, as it is inconsistent with the duty to notify the opposing party and the ICRC about the location of every POW and every internment camp.[72] The legitimacy of questioning in protected sites like medical units may be a matter of debate when the gathering of information is not limited to what is strictly necessary to identify and treat the patient but covers issues that may be harmful to the enemy. During OIF it was reported that some Iraqi prisoners, in need of immediate medical care after capture, were transferred to a US hospital ship in the North Arabian Sea where they were identified and registered as required by GC III, but they were not interrogated further to avoid the risk that the ship would lose its protected status.[73] 58

f. Property of prisoners

The Detaining Power has the right to search POWs and to confiscate, as war booty, military equipment belonging to the opposing state, which becomes property of the captor state, not of the individual who seized it. By contrast, none of the prisoners' property and nothing that is necessary for their personal use and protection may be seized.[74] Therefore, certain articles of POWs' equipment may not be taken, even if they are the property of the state on which the prisoners depend, since they are necessary to preserve either the safety of the prisoners (e.g. helmets, gas masks, bulletproof vests, and similar items) or their personal dignity. Hence, according to Article 18 paragraphs 1 and 3 GC III, POWs shall retain any article used for clothing or feeding, their marks of rank and decorations,[75] as well as further items of sentimental value. 59

Vietnamese POWs during the conflict between Cambodia and Vietnam from 1975 to 1979: ECCC, *Prosecutors v Kaing Guek Eav alias Duch*, Trial Chamber, 001/18-07-2007/ECCC/TC, 26 July 2010, paras 446–8. For a deeper analysis of the issue, see Ch 16 of this volume.

[69] Noone et al, above n 55, at 45; Fischer, above n 8, at 395.
[70] Pictet Commentary GC III, at 154.
[71] Noone et al, above n 55, at 42–3; for a contrary position, see Levie (ed), above n 29, at 109.
[72] During the Iran–Iraq War, the parties did not register the totality of POWs and accused each other of keeping them in secret camps. While the UN mission sent to investigate the situation of prisoners was not able to verify the latter allegations (UN Doc S/16962, at 10–17, 25–6, 30–1, 43–4, 45–50; and UN Doc S/20147, 24 August 1988, at 17–18, 22, 26–8, 32), the ICRC denounced both sides for not regularly registering POWs as required by the Convention and holding them in detention centres to which it did not have access (ICRC, Iran/Iraq Memoranda, in Sassòli/Bouvier/Quintin, at 1492, 1497, and 1499).
[73] Noone et al, above n 55, at 38–56.   [74] ICRC CIHL Study, vol I, at 173–5 and 437–9.
[75] The right to keep and wear badges of rank and nationality, as well as decorations, is further supported by Art 40 GC III, since it contributes to ensuring respect for POWs' honour.

60   Nevertheless, arms, military equipment, military documents, means of transport, and other objects which could be used for escape or other dangerous purposes may be seized for security reasons, regardless of whether these items are owned by the POWs or their parent state.[76] It follows that even those articles which prisoners are in principle allowed to retain may be taken away, provided that certain conditions are met. For instance, uniforms or other clothing resembling apparel used by civilians may be confiscated if they are seen as essential tools facilitating escape, but in this event the Detaining Power must replace them with similar articles that are more difficult to convert into civilian clothes, although prison uniforms should be avoided.[77]

61   When articles of significant commercial value, such as jewels, are taken from POWs for security reasons, i.e. to preclude any attempt at bribery, the same safeguards as are provided for money shall apply, as specified by Article 18 paragraph 5 GC III. Sums of money carried by POWs are to be considered as their personal property, not as war booty; however, such sums may be withheld by the Detaining Power if they exceed the maximum amount that prisoners may keep (see MN 105). According to Article 18 paragraph 4 GC III, the impounding of prisoners' money and other articles of value must be ordered by an officer as soon as possible after capture, but not before the actual amount, details of valuable objects, and the particulars of the owner have been recorded in a special register, and a corresponding itemized receipt, on which the name, rank, and unit of the person issuing it have been legibly inscribed, has been given to each prisoner concerned. At the end of their captivity POWs have the right to get back their property in its initial condition, as affirmed by Article 18 paragraph 6 GC III.

62   In compliance with Articles 58 paragraph 1 and 59 GC III, money properly possessed by POWs, both in the currency of the Detaining Power and in any other currency, must be deposited in the POWs' accounts, and may be converted into a different currency only with the consent of the prisoner concerned. The Detaining Power may confiscate money only when there is clear proof that it has been obtained illegally.[78]

63   The EECC has maintained that the obligations set forth in Article 18 GC III correspond to customary international law, and that whenever POWs' personal property is taken, there must be a corresponding receipt and the property must be held safely until its return. On this basis it found both Eritrea and Ethiopia liable for losses suffered by POWs, for not having complied with such requirements adequately.[79]

64   According to Article 68 paragraph 2 GC III, POWs are entitled to claim for compensation from their Power of origin with respect to personal effects, monies, or valuables impounded by the Detaining Power and not returned on prisoners' repatriation, or with respect to those personal items to be used during captivity which have been lost by the prisoners, allegedly due to the fault of the Detaining Power, without having been replaced. To this end, each prisoner concerned must receive a statement, signed by the captor's

---

[76] Iraqi prisoners held in the UK during the Gulf War were not allowed to use personal computers in order to continue their studies in the camp: G. Risius, 'Prisoners of War in the United Kingdom', in Rowe (ed), above n 6, at 300. On the difficulty of establishing the ownership of the items carried by POWs, see R.C. Hingorani, *Prisoners of War* (2nd edn, New York: Oceana Publications, 1982), at 135–6. For examples of items that may or may not be seized, see Pictet Commentary GC III, at 166.
[77] Fischer, above n 8, at 387; Levie (ed), above n 29, at 112–13.
[78] Fischer, above n 8, at 389.
[79] EECC, *POWs—Ethiopia*, above n 3, paras 77–80; EECC, *POWs—Eritrea*, above n 3, paras 72–7.

responsible officer, showing all available information on the reasons why the prisoner's property has not been returned (see MN 109).

In the end, refund to the victims will depend solely on the will and the economic resources of their parent state, as well as on compensation agreements between the parties at the end of the conflict. The absence of a right to claim compensation directly from the Detaining Power significantly impairs the interests of the prisoners, unless the captor voluntarily sets up special mechanisms to make good those damages complained about.[80]

V. Conditions of captivity

a. Internment or release on parole

The Detaining Power may exercise control over POWs through internment in special camps, whether or not they are fenced in. Prisoners are usually forbidden to leave the camp and their freedom of movement inside the camp may be further restricted, provided that specific regulations are made known to the internees. Prisoners may not be tied up in camps, nor may they be held in solitary confinement or in penitentiaries, unless such measures are imposed in execution of penal or disciplinary sanctions, or for health reasons in the interest of the POW concerned.[81]

The captor might decide partially or wholly to release prisoners on parole or promise, in accordance with Article 21 paragraph 2 GC III, especially when this choice may 'contribute to the improvement of their state of health'. An offer of release on parole may grant prisoners the privilege of freely leaving the camp temporarily, in exchange for a promise that they will not escape. When the release on parole is permanent, prisoners may be allowed to return home or to rejoin their military units, provided that they do not engage in hostilities against the enemy for the duration of the conflict.

Release on parole is not only a practice beneficial to the prisoners, it may also be advantageous to the captor, since it may prevent POWs from further participating in hostilities, while reducing the burdens of maintaining them. However, since the Second World War the use of parole has been limited, mainly because parent states usually prevent POWs from accepting such offers.[82]

In practice, the concession of parole is not the completely autonomous decision of the captor, since the latter must respect the regulations of the country on which each prisoner depends, which may prohibit its soldiers from accepting, in whole or in part, such proposals. In this regard, Article 21 paragraph 3 GC III establishes that belligerents must notify

---

[80] Allegations of unlawful seizure and confiscation of private belongings of arrested persons are addressed by the leaked ICRC, 'Report on the Treatment by the Coalition Forces of Prisoners of War and Other Protected Persons by the Geneva Conventions in Iraq during Arrest, Internment and Interrogation', February 2004, available at <http://www.globalsecurity.org/military/library/report/2004/icrc_report_iraq_feb2004.htm>, at 21–2, which recounts, however, that systems of registration of detainees' belongings and systems of compensation were gradually set up.

[81] Art 21 para 1 and Art 22 para 1 GC III.

[82] Hingorani, above n 76, at 121–2; G.D. Brown, 'Prisoner of War Parole: Ancient Concept, Modern Utility', 156 *Military Law Review* (1998) 200. In May 2003, a US decision on the release of Iraqi POWs on parole was reported (J. Mintz and V. Loeb, 'Americans Release 3500 Prisoners of War on Parole', 10 May 2003, at <http://www.smh.com.au/articles/2003/05/09/1052280441727.html>). The request to sign a 'parole' document, in which prisoners swore not to engage in hostile actions against Coalition soldiers, might be consistent with the Convention, assuming that active hostilities were not yet at an end; if they were at an end, POWs would anyway have to be released (see Ch 51 of this volume).

each other of their rules regarding parole. Nevertheless, if allowed to accept it under the laws of their country of origin, prisoners are free to accept any offer of parole.

70   When given in conformity with the above-mentioned conditions, parole involves a personal undertaking, on the prisoner's honour, that he or she will scrupulously respect the engagements agreed with the captor. Similarly, the Power on which the prisoner depends must abstain from requiring or accepting any service, information, or behaviour from the parolee which is contrary to the promise given. In the event that POWs, after breaching their parole, rejoin their parent state, the latter is bound neither to subject them to penal or disciplinary sanctions, nor to send the parolees back to the captor. On the other hand, if POWs breach their parole but are recaptured by the same belligerent, they may legitimately be tried and sentenced by the Detaining Power, provided that the guarantees for a fair trial are applied.[83]

b. Places of internment

71   Article 22 paragraph 1 GC III provides that POWs must be accommodated in areas 'affording every guarantee of hygiene and healthfulness'. The requirement refers to the geographical position of the camps rather than to the health conditions within them. As a consequence, they should not be located in the vicinity of dangerous areas or installations, such as atomic energy sites, nor should they be placed in regions where essential resources, like water, are not available or cannot be easily supplied. The same provision sets forth an outright obligation to locate POW premises on land, in order to avoid the permanent off-shore confinement of prisoners in warships which do not guarantee appropriate conditions of treatment and control over the correct application of IHL.[84]

72   The minimum standards of hygiene and healthfulness in zones of internment of POWs should be at least equal to those foreseen for the local population.[85] However, when the elements of climate are different from those to which a prisoner is accustomed and produce injurious effects, Article 22 paragraph 2 GC III requires the captor to remove the prisoner concerned from the dangerous site as soon as possible.

c. Quarters

73   As a general rule, the housing of POWs should conform at least to the accommodation provided to the captor's national troops billeted in the same area. Nevertheless, although the use of tents to house POWs is thus not in itself contrary to the Convention provided they fulfil the conditions relating to quarters, it appears to be a violation of Article 25 paragraph 1 to house the personnel of the Detaining Power in concrete buildings while prisoners are sheltered in tents, including without adequate protection against shelling.[86]

74   Article 25 paragraph 2 further specifies that the treatment of POWs must be as favourable as that furnished to the Detaining Power's own troops with regard to the dimensions of dormitories (total surface and minimum cubic space), the presence of general installations such as sanitary facilities, and the provision of bedding and blankets. In addition, quarters used by POWs, individually or collectively, as well as sanitary conveniences, must

---

[83] Pictet Commentary GC III, at 181–2.
[84] See C.W. Ling, 'Post-World War II British "Hell-Ship" Trials in Singapore', 8 *JICJ* (2010) 1035, on the trials of Japanese war criminals responsible for the indefinite detention of thousands of POWs held by the Japanese in the so-called 'Hell Ships' in extremely harsh conditions and subject to attacks by unwitting Allied submarines.
[85] Pictet Commentary GC III, at 183.   [86] ICRC Report, above n 80, at 23.

be protected from damp and must be adequately lighted and heated, particularly between dusk and lights-out, which is usually leisure time for the prisoners. Since lighting is an essential instrument to prevent escape, the Detaining Power is at liberty to illuminate all space deemed necessary. However, during sleeping hours, prisoners are not to be exposed to excessive light to avoid disturbing their rest. Additionally, the necessary precautions against the risk of fire, such as fire-extinguishers, water tanks, or fire-alarm systems, must be taken.[87] According to Article 26 paragraph 5 GC III, relating to food supplies, camps must be provided with adequate premises for messes, protected from the sun and the elements, and consistent with the safety requirements already mentioned.

The adoption of the standard of conditions afforded to forces of the Detaining Power as the basic criterion in setting up POW camps may not be adequate to guarantee the prisoners' safety during captivity, if allowance is not made for the habits and customs of the prisoners, as required by the second sentence of Article 25 paragraph 1 GC III. The latter provision does not mean that a Detaining Power must systematically accord more favourable treatment to POWs if they are accustomed to higher standards, although it would be appropriate to adopt equitable solutions to balance the conditions afforded to the captor's forces with the possible specific needs of the prisoners, provided that in no case are the latter subject to treatment detrimental to their state of health. Hence, the living conditions of POWs must be assessed by qualified medical personnel on an individual basis and in light of the concrete circumstances (see MN 83).[88]

d. Food, clothing, and canteens

Prisoners of war have the right to a basic daily ration of food and to drinking water sufficient to keep them in good health, according to Article 26 paragraphs 1 and 3 GC III. In particular, food and water supplies are adequate only if loss of weight and the development of nutritional deficiencies are prevented in respect of each individual prisoner. As a consequence, the quantity, quality, and variety of food rations must be determined by the actual needs of the prisoners, taking into account the climate conditions where they are interned as well as their dietary habits. To this end, Article 26 paragraph 4 recommends that POWs be allowed, as far as possible, to take part in the preparation of their own meals, including any additional food which they may have in their possession.

Correct maintenance under GC III requires the captor to supply adequate and appropriate clothing to POWs, including underwear, footwear, and captured enemy uniforms, provided that those articles are suitable to safeguard the health of prisoners, particularly in areas with harsh climatic conditions. Respect for the dignity and honour of POWs implies that they may not be forced to wear uniforms of the captor, unless they have been appropriately altered. The obligation to supply clothing in sufficient quantity is a continuing one, hence the Detaining Power shall provide for the regular replacement and repair of POWs' garments.[89]

Under Article 28 GC III, each camp must be provided with a canteen where POWs may purchase articles of daily use at price levels not in excess of the locally prevailing market rate.[90] The presence of canteens and the availability of a variety of items, especially

---

[87] Art 25 para 3 GC III; Pictet Commentary GC III, at 194–5.
[88] Pictet Commentary GC III, at 193.
[89] Art 27 GC III; Pictet Commentary GC III, at 200–2.
[90] For details of the items that should be available at canteens, see Pictet Commentary GC III, at 203.

tobacco, may have a positive effect on the morale of prisoners. According to Article 26 paragraph 3, second sentence, the use of tobacco must be permitted, but the same duty does not extend to either alcoholic drinks or addictive drugs. In light of the development of medical opinion on the dangers of smoking, the obligation is to be interpreted as allowing, or even requiring, the restriction of smoking in enclosed and public places within the camps.

79 When actually installed, canteens are not always operated in the interests of POWs, due to a lack of control over the prices charged, which are frequently much higher than the market rates, and to a shortage of available items, usually resultant upon the scarce availability of canteen-type articles in the territory of the captor. The Convention does not specifically address these inconveniences, therefore it has been maintained that additional and more detailed prescriptions, even through special agreements, are desirable.[91] Nonetheless, Article 28 paragraphs 2 and 3 lays down rules on the use of profits made from sales at the canteens, aimed at improving the benefits to the prisoners themselves and at limiting possible abuse.

e. Hygiene and medical care

80 Under Article 29 GC III, sanitary conditions must ensure the cleanliness and healthfulness of camps. Therefore, the Detaining Power has a duty to provide prisoners with clean and hygienic toilet facilities, which are sufficiently numerous and accessible during the day and at night. Prisoners must be furnished with water, soap, installations, instruments, and the time necessary for their personal hygiene and laundry, as well as to keep their quarters clean. Each prisoner should be able to take a hot bath or shower at least once a week, although complete body washing with cold water is not contrary to GC III if the climate permits. Baths or showers may be made compulsory for POWs, unless their health is not impaired. Indeed, washing must be compulsory, if necessary to prevent epidemics in the camps.

81 Prisoners should be thoroughly examined and disinfected upon entry into the camp, and those suffering from contagious diseases must be placed in quarantine. In addition, they must be inoculated with all necessary vaccines as required by their health, taking into account their constitution and the risks to which they are exposed. The administration of vaccines may vary according to the climate and the actual threats of epidemic diseases, or even biological attacks, with respect to each POW camp.[92] Restrictions on medical treatments provided for by Article 13 GC III would not apply to inoculations of vaccines regularly approved by the sanitary authorities of the Detaining Power, in conformity with international standards. By contrast, the inoculation of experimental vaccines, still not officially approved, may be controversial in light of the prohibition on the carrying out of medical experiments on POWs. In this case, the choice of the Detaining Power may be reasonably justified if the same vaccine is administered to its own troops. Moreover, a rigorous assessment must be made of the concrete risk of an outbreak either of a deadly epidemic, or of a biological or chemical attack to which the prisoners would be exposed, otherwise the Detaining Power and the individuals responsible for the administration of the vaccine would commit a violation of GC III.[93]

---

[91] Hingorani, above n 76, at 123–4.
[92] Pictet Commentary GC III, at 206–7.
[93] See Noone et al, above n 55, at 60–6.

Article 30 paragraph 1 GC III requires that each camp has an infirmary at least for 82
minor first aid, including, where necessary, isolation wards for the treatment of contagious
or mental illnesses. Prisoners must be allowed to seek medical examination on their own
initiative, and must obtain, upon request, a certificate of medical treatment indicating
the nature of their ailment and the care received. In cases of serious diseases, requiring
surgery or hospital care, POWs must be admitted to any suitable military or civilian medical unit, should the camp medical installations not be equipped to provide the necessary
treatment. Moreover, special and rehabilitative facilities must be made available to the
disabled.[94] In accordance with the general principle of free maintenance of POWs, the cost
of all treatment, including the supply of dentures and other appliances, must be borne by
the Detaining Power.

Article 31 GC III introduces a procedure whereby qualified doctors must conduct med- 83
ical inspections once a month to assess the state of health of prisoners, as well as to detect
contagious diseases. During inspections the most efficient available methods of diagnosis
should be used, and the weight of each prisoner must be checked and recorded in order to
assess his level of nutrition. Regular visits offer an opportunity to verify the general standards of hygiene in the camp and the adequate conditions of quarters.

f. Prerogatives of medical and religious personnel

Article 30 paragraph 3 GC III provides that POWs shall preferably receive attention from 84
medical personnel of their parent state and, if possible, of their same nationality. This provision must be read in conjunction with Article 32, which authorizes the Detaining Power
to require prisoners who have been medically trained, but who are not attached to their
armed forces medical service, to exercise their skills in favour of captives dependent upon
the same Power. An analogous provision is found in Article 36, concerning POWs who are
ministers of religion without having officiated as chaplains to their own forces: they shall
be at liberty, whatever their denomination, to exercise their ministry in favour of prisoners
of the same faith. Prisoners who exercise medical and religious activities must be paid for
their work and may not be compelled to carry out any other job.[95] They may be granted the
same treatment as that enjoyed by retained personnel, which is regulated by Article 33 GC
III. Nevertheless, they are not eligible to be relieved under special agreements between the
parties, since their internment is uniquely based on their POW status.

On the other hand, medical personnel of a belligerent army, as well as chaplains, who 85
have fallen into the hands of the enemy, may not be interned as combatants. In principle
they should not be deprived of their liberty and should be repatriated, unless the adversary
decides to retain them for the purpose of assisting POWs.[96] In this event, they must receive
at least the same treatment afforded to POWs. Moreover, they shall be granted all facilities to exercise their medical or spiritual functions for the benefit of prisoners, in accordance with their professional etiquette. Yet their activities shall be carried out under the

---

[94] The obligation to take all necessary measures to ensure the protection and safety of persons with disabilities in situations of risk, including armed conflicts, humanitarian emergencies, and the occurrence of natural disasters, in accordance with international law, especially IHL and IHRL, has been reaffirmed by Art 11 of the UN Convention on the Rights of Persons with Disabilities (UNGA Res A/RES/61/106), 16 December 2006, in force since 3 May 2008, ratified by 141 states as of 7 March 2014.

[95] Art 62 para 2 GC III. Pictet Commentary GC III, at 233–4.

[96] H. McCoubrey, 'The Protection of Creed and Opinion in the Laws of Armed Conflict', *Journal of Conflict and Security Law* (2000) 135, esp para 5.

supervision of the competent authorities of the Detaining Power, in conformity with its military laws and regulations,[97] and in accordance with the internal discipline of the camp in which the personnel are retained. According to IHL fundamental principles, 'religious personnel must refrain from preaching hatred against other religions and against the adversary'.[98] Special privileges accorded to retained personnel are set forth in Article 33 paragraph 2, and are reproduced, with a few further details, in Article 35 concerning chaplains.

86   In the end, Article 33 paragraph 1 GC III underlines that the Detaining Power remains fully responsible for the medical and spiritual care of POWs, regardless of the availability of retained personnel. In this respect, Article 37 explicitly provides that, in the absence of religious personnel of their faith, POWs may require that an appropriate minister be appointed.

g. Religious, intellectual, and physical activities

87   Articles 34 and 38 GC III concern the organization of leisure time to maintain the physical and mental well-being of POWs during captivity. Complete liberty in the exercise of religious rituals must be ensured, in so far as the disciplinary routine of the Detaining Power is observed, provided that the latter does not substantially impede the practice of religion. Intellectual, educational, recreational, and physical activities, including sports and games, are to be encouraged, as long as each individual preference is respected. Appropriate premises and equipment, including sufficiently large, clean, and covered areas for religious services, as well as suitable open space for general outdoor recreation, must be made available.

88   Religious freedom must be –read as covering the observance of any creed, even if prohibited under the laws of the Detaining Power, or the right to not believe. Prisoners of war must not be subjected to ideological pressure adversely affecting their freedom of thought and their honour, neither by the captor nor by other inmates.[99] Therefore, the Detaining Power must both permit the prisoners to organize their own intellectual pursuits and promote analogous activities, such as lectures, study courses, or radio broadcasts, provided that they are not compulsory for captives.

89   In armed conflicts characterized by a strong ideological nature, propaganda activities are usually used by the Detaining Power to induce POWs to change their allegiance towards the Power of origin, as occurred in Iran, when Iraqi POWs were systematically subjected to various forms of ideological and political pressure, including intimidation, forced participation in mass demonstrations decrying their government, and programmes of re-education. Such practices were denounced by the ICRC as serious attacks on the honour and dignity of prisoners, contrary to the Convention.[100] Similar forms of indoctrination and discrimination based on political grounds, attributed to both parties, had been reported even in the Korean and the Vietnam Wars.[101] Nevertheless, political propaganda or religious proselytism are not forbidden by definition, provided that they rely on voluntary attendance and are not used as grounds for discriminatory treatment among

---

[97] Pictet Commentary GC III, at 219.
[98] N. Kumar, 'Religious Personnel', in Fleck (ed), above n 8, 419, at 420.
[99] McCoubrey, above n 96, para 4.
[100] ICRC, Iran/Iraq Memoranda, in Sassòli/Bouvier/Quintin, at 1493 and 1498.
[101] Rosas, above n 38, at 438.

POWs (see MN 34).¹⁰² Moreover, it has been held that a POW may not be subjected to propaganda contrary to the spirit of GC III, whereas any dissemination of information reaffirming the rights of the individual in accordance with the Geneva Conventions is permissible.¹⁰³ Therefore, assuming that the permissible activities are not limited merely to informing POWs of the content of the Geneva Conventions, any measure aimed at genuinely informing them about the practices of their government and the violations of basic rules of IHL and HRL may be deemed compatible with the Convention. In this light, even recourse to forms of political pressure may be justified, if exercised with the same aims as specific programmes for dismantling particularly odious regimes responsible for the most serious violations of international law, such as the de-Nazification process carried out by the Allied Forces at the end of the Second World War, or the de-Baathification of Iraq launched by the Coalition during the occupation of the country.¹⁰⁴

VI. Relations with the detaining authorities

a. Camp command structure, discipline, and ranks of prisoners of war

The organization and management of every POW camp, and all its labour and outlying units, are under the responsibility of a commissioned officer belonging to the regular armed forces of the Detaining Power. Thus the delegation of the command of POW camps to private actors is not allowed, though the latter may perform various tasks relating to the installation and the maintenance of a camp (see also MN 13).¹⁰⁵ According to Article 39 paragraph 1 GC III, the camp commander must be in possession of a copy of the Convention and must ensure its knowledge and its correct application by the camp staff and guards, in order to prevent any violation which would also be attributable to the commander. Article 39 paragraphs 2 and 3 regulates the obligation imposed on POWs to salute the camp commander and the enemy forces, depending on their respective ranks. Members of the captor's army are not required to salute POWs, even if the latter are of superior rank. Nevertheless, they should return the salute of a prisoner as a matter of military courtesy. 90

Full information about the treatment of POWs during captivity, and about the regulations or any other disciplinary rule they must observe, is to be disseminated in the camp by publicly posting the text of GC III and any other relevant document in places visible to prisoners, as required by Article 41. Information must additionally be handed to the prisoners' representatives, and POWs who do not have access to the text of the Convention are to be supplied with a copy upon request. The Convention should be disseminated in the prisoners' own language, while general regulations of the Detaining Power as well as individual commands must be given in a language that prisoners can understand. This obligation would entail the use of interpreters, or a requirement that guards learn essential orders in the prisoners' language.¹⁰⁶ 91

Articles 44 and 45 GC III prescribe that prisoners, officers, and non-commissioned officers must always be treated with the regard due to their rank and age, which entails that 92

---

¹⁰² Ibid, at 435–7.   ¹⁰³ Pictet Commentary GC III, at 145.
¹⁰⁴ On the compatibility of those practices with the law of occupation, see R. Kolb, 'Occupation in Iraq since 2003 and the Powers of the UN Security Council', 90 *IRRC* (2008) 29, at 48; M. Sassòli, Legislation and Maintenance of Public Order and Civil Life by Occupying Powers', 16 *EJIL* (2005) 661, at 671–2.
¹⁰⁵ Cameron and Chetail, above n 13, at 83–6.
¹⁰⁶ Pictet Commentary GC III, at 245. The obligations set forth in Art 41 correspond to customary law in the view of the EECC, *POWs—Ethiopia*, above n 3, para 144.

different treatment may be accorded to officers and others. To this end, Article 43 GC III requires the belligerents to communicate to each other, immediately upon the outbreak of hostilities, the titles and ranks of all persons entitled to POW status or treatment, as well as the information about any titles and ranks that are subsequently created. The Detaining Power is obliged to recognize promotions in rank duly notified by the home state, unless they are manifestly made after the capture in order to remove POWs from forced labour.

93   The privileged condition of officers is particularly evident with respect to work: unlike enlisted soldiers, commissioned officers may only volunteer for work, but may not be compelled to perform any labour, whereas non-commissioned officers may be required to perform only supervisory work, as specified in Article 49 paragraphs 2 and 3 GC III. Moreover, private soldiers of the same armed forces are to be assigned as orderlies in officers' special camps or compounds. In this case, those prisoners would not be required to perform other work.

b. Prisoners' representatives and complaints against the authorities

94   In every camp there must be POW representatives, whose main task is to defend prisoners' interests before the detaining authorities, the Protecting Powers, the ICRC, or any other assisting organization. They must contribute to the well-being of POWs and are responsible for any system of mutual assistance organized amongst them, although they may not be held responsible, simply by virtue of their role, for any offences committed by prisoners.[107] Representatives must share the nationality, language, and customs of the prisoners whom they represent. In camps where POWs of mixed nationality or culture are accommodated, it is necessary to appoint as many representatives as the number of the different groups of prisoners living there.

95   Detailed rules for the selection of representatives are laid down in Article 79 GC III, while Article 81 lists a gamut of privileges accorded to them, similar to those enjoyed by medical or religious personnel assisting POWs. In addition, Article 78 paragraph 4 allows representatives to send periodic reports on the situation in the camps and the needs of the prisoners to the Protecting Power or other competent external authority.

96   According to Article 78 GC III, representatives may receive complaints from POWs regarding their conditions of captivity and related requests addressed to the detaining authorities. Complaints must be communicated to the Protecting Powers or the relevant assisting actors by the prisoners' representatives, or even directly by the prisoners themselves. Through this procedure, POWs are allowed to make their complaints known to the Detaining Power at any time they find it necessary. Their right may never be limited, nor may prisoners be punished, even if their complaints turn out to be unfounded, as has been confirmed by the EECC, which found Eritrea liable for a lack of complaints procedures in its camps, and for unlawfully punishing complaining prisoners by beating them and segregating them from the rest of camp.[108]

VII. Labour and financial resources

a. Obligation and right to work

97   According to Article 49 paragraph 1 GC III, the Detaining Power is entitled to compel POWs to work, provided that they are physically fit and their personal features, such as

---

[107] Arts 79 para 1 and 80 GC III.   [108] EECC, *POWs—Ethiopia*, above n 3, paras 147–50.

age, sex, rank, and physical aptitude, are duly taken into account. Although it cannot be denied that the right to utilize the labour of prisoners primarily serves the economic and military interests of the Detaining Power, the same provision underlines that a special purpose of work should be to maintain the physical and mental health of captives. This wording does not involve an absolute right to work in favour of POWs and a corresponding duty for the Detaining Power to provide work. The principle can, however, be relevant whenever the health of prisoners is likely to suffer if they do not work and the Detaining Power deliberately ignores their need.[109]

98 Article 50 GC III specifies that POWs may be employed not only in any work connected with camp administration, installation, or maintenance, but also in almost every productive sector except for metallurgical, machinery, and chemical industries, or for any labour having a military character or purpose. The principle manifestly responds to the interest of the Power of origin to reduce to a minimum the exploitation of POWs for purposes contributing to the war effort of the enemy.[110] Such a criterion was applied by the EECC to conclude that by using POWs to work on roads of public utility, Eritrea did not violate GC III.[111]

99 Although POWs may not be compelled to perform work of a military character, a literal interpretation of the provision does not exclude the possibility that prisoners might volunteer for labour of this kind, as might occur with regard to unhealthy or dangerous work, including the removal of mines or similar devices, as envisaged by Article 52 GC III. Before accepting, prisoners must be informed by the Detaining Power of the risks involved, and in no circumstances may they give up further guarantees secured by the Convention. They also cannot validly consent to any work that would be looked upon as humiliating for the Detaining Power's forces.

b. Conditions of labour and remuneration

100 In compliance with Article 51 GC III, worker POWs must be granted suitable and safe conditions, not inferior to those enjoyed by the nationals of the Detaining Power under the relevant domestic legislation. Furthermore, they must receive appropriate training and means of protection to avoid risks exceeding those normally run by civilian workers. Article 53 lays down detailed rules with regard to working time, while Article 55 requires POWs to be visited regularly by medical personnel, at least once a month, to verify if they are fit for work, especially for the specific tasks assigned to them. Prisoners themselves are entitled to ask for examination. Whenever a prisoner is judged unfit for work, the competent medical personnel may recommend that he or she be exempted therefrom.

101 According to Article 54 paragraph 2 GC III, the necessary medical care must be supplied to any prisoner who is a victim of an accident at work, or who has contracted an illness in the course of, or in consequence of, work. Hence, every labour detachment needs to be equipped with the essential means for first aid in case of emergency. Disabled POWs are entitled to medical assistance in conformity with the requirements established by Articles 15 and 30 GC III, as well as with the national legislation of the Detaining Power concerning the protection of labour.[112] Furthermore, the captor must issue a document certifying the injury or disability of the prisoner concerned, the circumstances in which

---

[109] Fischer, above n 8, at 403.
[110] It is worth remembering here that forcing POWs to serve in the enemy armed forces constitutes a grave breach of the Convention, according to Art 130 GC III.
[111] EECC, *POWs—Ethiopia*, above n 3, para 133.   [112] Pictet Commentary GC III, at 284–5.

it arose, and the treatment supplied, in order to allow the captive to submit claims to the Power of origin as envisaged by Article 68 paragraph 1 (see MN 109).

102   Under Articles 54 paragraph 1 and 62 GC III, all working POWs have the right to fair pay, fixed by the detaining authorities. The Convention contemplates a single basic rate of pay, although nothing precludes a Detaining Power from granting higher rates to prisoners engaged in more dangerous activities, or for jobs requiring greater skills, or even as a production incentive, provided that different treatment does not result in discrimination among prisoners for the same kind of work. Remuneration may legitimately be lower than civilian workers' wages, since POWs are maintained at the expense of the captor. The Convention establishes that the rate of payment may not be less than the minimum of one-fourth of a Swiss Franc, which is now ostensibly anachronistic in most world economies. So it would be desirable to update the amount through a revision of the clause, or at least by special agreements among belligerents. Prisoners' representatives, their advisers, and assistants also have a right to a wage taken out of the canteen profits, if any, otherwise the wage must be directly paid by the Detaining Power at a fair rate, fixed on the basis of the average amount given to other POWs.

c. Finances of prisoners of war

103   Prisoners of war are entitled to monthly advances of pay, paid by the Detaining Power on behalf of the parent state and deposited, together with further financial sources, to the special account that must be held for every prisoner.[113] Article 60 GC III lays down a scale of pay for each rank, from private to general, which is to be used until belligerents conclude special agreements on the matter. Pending the reaching of such agreements, Article 60 paragraph 3 allows the Detaining Power to adopt temporary and reasonable limitations on the amount of pay for each POW, whenever the sums established by the Convention would appear excessively higher than the remuneration of its own armed forces, or when some other reasons 'seriously embarrass' the captor itself (e.g. financial difficulties or economic crisis). In such an event the amounts made available to 'Prisoners ranking below sergeants' should not be less than those given to corresponding ranks of the Detaining Power. The minimum monthly rate fixed by the Convention, on the basis of 1949 rates of pay, is the equivalent of eight Swiss Francs. It is consequently unlikely that the above-mentioned circumstances would occur, other than when very poor countries take part in a conflict. However, with regard to most belligerents, the figures set forth in Article 60 certainly need to be updated.[114]

104   Article 61 GC III envisages another source of money, that is 'supplementary pay' from the state of origin, which cannot, however, relieve the Detaining Power from the obligation to make advances of pay. The captor is thus required to accept sums forwarded by the enemy for distribution to POWs depending on it, provided that all prisoners of the same category receive the same amount and all belonging to that category are paid. The supplementary pay is to be credited to each individual account as soon as possible, as should occur with remittances of money addressed individually or collectively to prisoners by their families or humanitarian organizations, in compliance with Article 63 paragraph 1 GC III.

---

[113] Art 64 GC III.
[114] Iraqi prisoners held by British forces during the Gulf War were supposed to be given £3 per day, although payment did not occur before the termination of internment. See Rowe, above n 6, at 198.

d. Management of prisoners' finances

105 For minimum expenses within the camp, POWs must have access to cash or other forms of payment, like scrip money or coupons. The corresponding amount must be debited from their individual accounts and must not exceed the maximum level fixed by the captor according to Article 58 paragraph 1 GC III. If purchases outside the camp are permitted and require cash payment, they may be made either by the prisoners on their own, or by the camp administration on their behalf, and must be charged to their individual accounts, in compliance with the rules for such transactions established by the Detaining Power.[115]

106 Article 63 paragraph 2 GC III reiterates the basic principle under which each prisoner has the right to use the credit balance of his or her account within the limits fixed by the captor. The latter shall make the payments on behalf of the POWs as they request, including payments made abroad, among which remittances to dependants must be given priority. Transfers of money outside the territory of the Detaining Power, however, are subject to the financial or monetary restrictions that the captor regards as essential. In practice, this can cause severe limitations on transfers of funds abroad, unless the procedure set forth in Article 63 paragraph 3 GC III is followed, with the agreement of the Power of origin of the prisoner concerned. In this case, all necessary details are notified to the home state, which will make the payment to the beneficiaries. The prisoner's account will be debited by a corresponding amount, while the sums so deducted are placed to the credit of the Power of origin, so that the final settlement of each transaction will occur at the end of hostilities under the framework of the compensation arrangements between the belligerents.[116]

107 In order to ensure that the captor correctly applies its obligations concerning POWs' financial resources, Article 65 paragraph 1 GC III requires that every entry in a prisoner's account must be certified by the signature or the initials of the prisoner concerned, or of the representative acting on his or her behalf. According to paragraph 2, prisoners are entitled to check their accounts and obtain a copy of them, which may also be inspected by the representatives of the Protecting Power during their visits. The last paragraph of Article 65 provides for the exchange of information between belligerents regarding the amount of the accounts of the POWs, subject to special agreements between the parties.

108 Article 66 GC III provides that at the end of captivity, absent any different agreement between the parties, the Detaining Power must provide each prisoner with a statement of his or her account, showing the credit balance due at that time. In addition, the captor is required to send detailed lists showing the amount of their credit balances to the government of origin of the POWs whose captivity has been terminated. Such provisions are aimed at enabling POWs to prove their entitlement to the sums certified by the Detaining Power, and to ensure the correct application of the principle set forth in the last paragraph of Article 66, which places upon the Power of origin the responsibility for actually settling the account with the prisoners.

109 Although the entire credit balance of each POW whose captivity is terminated is due by his or her parent state, it cannot be overlooked that the final amount may be derived from different sources, partly imputable to the Detaining Power and partly to the Power of

---

[115] Art 58 para 2 GC III.
[116] As specified in Art 63 para 4 GC III, the Detaining Power may apply the procedure on the basis of Model Regulations in Annex V GC III.

origin. Therefore, an adjustment between the sums to be debited from the prisoners' state of origin and its credits shall be reached through a special compensation agreement between the parties at the close of the conflict. To this end, allowance must also be made for credits arising out of the transfer of funds in accordance with Article 63 paragraph 3 and payments made by the prisoners' parent state in compliance with Article 68, which entitles POWs to submit, to their Power of origin, claims for compensation with respect to occupational accidents and the loss of personal property imputable to the Detaining Power.[117]

VIII. Relations with the exterior

110 Essential to the morale of POWs is the possibility to contact the outside world through regular correspondence with their relatives (see Chapter 49, MN 22–27, of this volume). Article 70 GC III sets forth the right of POWs to send, immediately upon capture, or not later than one week after their arrival at a camp, as well as upon any further transit, a special card directed to their relatives and to the Central Tracing Agency, with details about their location and health. Thereafter, POWs are permitted to send not less than two letters and four postcards every month, according to Article 71 GC III. Correspondence must be forwarded without delay, and it cannot be retained for disciplinary reasons. Censorship is allowed, but must be done as quickly as possible and only once by either the despatching state or the receiving state.[118] Numerical restrictions may be imposed only in the interest of the POWs, if the difficulties of the captor in carrying out the necessary censorship causes excessive delay. Correspondence addressed to POWs may be limited only by their home state, possibly at the request of the Detaining Power. In cases of an urgent need to communicate, POWs must be permitted to send telegrams at their own expense. A complete ban on correspondence may be imposed for military or political reasons, provided that such a ban is temporary and as short as possible.[119]

111 The Convention regulates the shipment of individual or collective relief supplies of various kinds, which may not be subject to restrictions unless they are proposed by the Protecting Power, the ICRC, or other humanitarian organizations on account of exceptional transportation problems. Shipments and correspondence are exempt from postal dues, as well as from import, customs, and other duties.[120] In compliance with Article 69 GC III, the Detaining Power is required to keep the prisoners and their home state informed of any measure adopted concerning POWs' contacts with the exterior.

C. Relevance in Non-International Armed Conflicts

112 When captured by the enemy, neither members of state armed forces, nor members of non-state armed groups participating in a non-international armed conflict (NIAC) enjoy

---

[117] An accurate presentation of state practices concerning compensation for POWs of their nationality, may be found in the judgments relating to claims by former POWs, detained in Siberia during the Second World War, against Japan, for settlement of the credit balances, as well as for compensation for damages suffered during internment. See Tokyo District Court, *Kamibayashi et al v Japan*, 4 April 1989, paras 3–5. The Court, however, dismissed the claims on the grounds that at the time there was no customary law requiring a state to compensate POWs depending upon it for credit balances or accidents at work attributable to a Detaining Power. Ibid, paras 6, 7.

[118] Art 76 para 1 GC III. When censorship is carried out on goods, it must not be injurious to them, and the addressee or a delegate must be present. Ibid, para 2.

[119] Ibid, para 3.   [120] Arts 72–75 GC III.

POW status. Nevertheless, IHL does not prevent their internment, although it does not clearly allow detention of enemy fighters only to hinder their further participation in the conflict.

Aside from any debate concerning the status of captured persons as well as the legality of their detention,[121] each party to a NIAC must respect the principles of humane treatment and non-discrimination in favour of detained persons, laid down by Common Article 3. When AP II is applicable, the parties are also obliged to observe the protections in favour of individuals deprived of their liberty for reasons related to the hostilities, set forth in Articles 4 and 5.

Although the above-mentioned provisions are not comparable to the articulated and detailed rules of GC III, the analogy with the principles on POW treatment is undeniable.[122] Hence, the Convention has a relevant role in the definition and development of the scope of the law applicable in NIACs regarding material conditions of detention. In practice, parties fighting in NIACs often announce their intention to respect IAC standards, or even to undertake legal obligations to observe them, usually abiding by such engagements.[123] Moreover, customary IHL on the handling of persons *hors de combat* during NIACs is deemed essentially similar to the customary rules on POW treatment, which in turn correspond to the content of GC III.[124] Thus, practice and legal interpretation prove that persons who have taken active part in hostilities and have been deprived of their liberty for reasons related to a NIAC, enjoy treatment largely equivalent to that afforded to POWs under GC III,[125] the sole difference being the denial of combatant immunity to members of non-state armed groups,[126] who are more likely to be tried as traitors or terrorists.[127]

---

[121] For an accurate analysis of the issue, see D. Casalin, 'Taking Prisoners: Reviewing the International Humanitarian Law Grounds for Deprivation of Liberty by Armed Opposition Groups', 93 *IRRC* (2011) 743; and M. Sassòli and L.M. Olson, 'The Relationship between International Humanitarian and Human Rights Law Where It Matters: Admissible Killing and Internment of Fighters in Non-International Armed Conflicts', 90 *IRRC* (2008) 599.

[122] In this respect the ICTY has significantly held that 'Common Article 3 of the Geneva Conventions reflects the same spirit of the duty to protect members of armed forces who have laid down their arms and are detained as the specific protections afforded to prisoners of war in Geneva Convention III as a whole, particularly in its Article 13': ICTY, *The Prosecutor v Mile Mrkšić and Veselin Šljivančanin*, Appeals Chamber Judgment, IT-95-13/1-A, 5 May 2009, para 70.

[123] See S. Sivakumaran, 'Lessons for the Law of Armed Conflict from Commitments of Armed Groups: Identification of Legitimate Targets and Prisoners of War', in 93 *IRRC* (2011) 463, at 478–81.

[124] ICRC CIHL Study, vol I, at 428–51.

[125] This is proved even by the fact that ICRC delegates are usually allowed to visit and register conflict-related detainees, either by the government or the armed groups, as was reported in 1995 during the conflict in Somalia between the government forces of President Egal and the armed militia of the Idegale. 'Somaliland: ICRC Action in a Complex Patchwork of Clans', ICRC News Release 8, 22 May 1995, available at <http://www.icrc.org/eng/resources/documents/news-release/2009-and-earlier /57jly6.htm>. See also 'Democratic Republic of the Congo: Visiting Conflict-Related Detainees', 31 August 2012, available at <http://www.icrc.org/eng/resources/documents/interview/2012/congo-kinshasa-interview-2012-08-30.htm>, reporting that the ICRC visited for the first time the detainees held by the March 23 Movement (M23).

[126] E. Crawford, *The Treatment of Combatants and Insurgents under the Law of Armed Conflict* (Oxford: OUP, 2010), at 78–141; D. Jinks, 'The Declining Significance of POW Status', 45 *Harvard International Law Journal* (2004) 367, at 422–40.

[127] See, e.g., the trial of Abdullah Öcalan, leader of the PKK, the armed group responsible for violent attacks and terrorist activities, fighting against Turkey for the independence of the Kurdish population, which is referred to in the judgment of the ECtHR (Grand Chamber), *Öcalan v Turkey*, Judgment, 12 May 2005.

115   In principle, dealing with members of non-state armed groups captured by governmental authorities would not entail any particular difference with respect to the handling of POWs, apart from a few norms concerning aspects strictly inherent to the status of a POW as a member of a state army (e.g. rules on ranks and related differential treatment), as well as those observance of which presupposes, in whole or in part, that prisoners are backed by a state-like apparatus (e.g. certain provisions on identification and notification, on financial resources, and on complaints over loss of personal property).[128]

116   By contrast, the level of organization of a non-state armed group, as well as its methods of conducting hostilities, its effective territorial control, and its relations with external actors, may truly give rise to practical difficulties in applying to enemy fighters all the detailed obligations concerning the treatment of POWs, be those fighters governmental forces or individuals belonging to other entities.[129] Furthermore, it cannot be overlooked that the proper conduct of detention operations depends, above all, on the availability of those resources necessary to fulfil prisoners' minimal needs, and such needs should be assessed in light of the same criteria applied when taking into account the limited economic means of a country. Due to the great diversity characterizing armed groups, the application by analogy of POW treatment may be effective only if the norms requiring duties beyond the actual capabilities of non-state actors are identified on a case-by-case basis, and interpreted in a flexible manner in light of the circumstances, provided that their essence and fundamental objectives are not impaired.

D. Legal Consequences of a Violation

117   When a Detaining Power is responsible for an infringement of GC III, it has a duty of reparation, which may take the form of restitution, compensation, and satisfaction, either singly or in combination.[130] The punishment of the offenders does not relieve the state of its obligation to make good the damages caused, nonetheless the investigation to establish the facts resulting in harm or injury, and the prosecution of the perpetrators, may be part of the whole reparation process as a possible form of satisfaction.[131] With respect to mistreatment of POWs, reparation is due to their parent state, but prisoners themselves may not claim for restitution or compensation vis-à-vis the Detaining Power, unless the latter agrees to provide reparation directly to individuals on the basis of special agreements or unilateral actions, through legislative means and even court decisions.[132]

---

[128] On the treatment of detainees by government forces during the conflict in Sri Lanka, see Report of the Commission of Inquiry on Lessons Learnt and Reconciliation, November 2011, at 166–71, available at <http://www.llrcaction.gov.lk/llrc-report.html>.

[129] E.g., it may be difficult for armed groups to provide specialist medical treatment to wounded enemy fighters, as occurred in Sri Lanka, where the ICRC reported that the Liberation Tigers of Tamil Eelam (LTTE) facilitated the handover of wounded soldiers of the Sri Lanka Army, who required specialist care available only in government-controlled areas. See *Sri Lanka: ICRC facilitates handover of wounded soldier to authorities*, ICRC News Release 09/189, 22 January 2009, available at <http://www.icrc.org/eng/resources/documents/news-release/2009-and-earlier/sri-lanka-news-220108.htm>.

[130] This is a customary rule of IHL consistent with the general norms on state responsibility for internationally wrongful acts. See Art 34 ILC Articles on State Responsibility and ICRC CIHL Study, vol I, at 537–50.

[131] Pictet Commentary GC III, at 129–30; ICRC CIHL Study, vol I, at 540.

[132] ICRC CIHL Study, vol I, at 541–5.

118 Reparation is due for any breach of GC III irrespective of the specific rules infringed. Nevertheless, the position maintained by the EECC may be acceptable in this context. The EECC took into account the seriousness of the violations, the number of ascertained or probable victims, and the extent of the injury or damage caused to calculate the amount of the compensation owed by a Detaining Power.[133] In such cases, the EECC drew a distinction between more severe and less serious breaches, on the basis of the importance of the obligations infringed for POWs' survival and well-being, for the sole purpose of assessing the damages. In particular, the following acts or omissions have been qualified as less serious violations: depriving POWs of footwear during evacuation and permitting unnecessary suffering during transfer between camps; failing to protect or confiscating prisoners' personal properties; subjecting prisoners to unlawful conditions of labour; preventing POWs from complaining about their treatment and seeking redress, as well as punishing those who attempted to complain. On the other hand, the most serious violations, which, in the view of the EECC, required heavier damages were: failing to protect POWs from being killed, beaten, or physically and mentally abused; failing to provide adequate maintenance and medical care; and refusing relief packages and permission for ICRC personnel visits.[134]

119 The criterion adopted by the EECC is certainly useful to assess damages in light of the circumstances of a specific conflict and the evidence available. However, it cannot result in a classification of GC III rules into more or less serious obligations, which would appear at odds with the spirit of the Convention that does not contemplate any hierarchy between the obligations imposed on the parties. It follows that, as already noted, no distinction based on the relevance of GC III rules with respect to POWs' survival and well-being may exclude the Detaining Power's responsibility for every violation imputable to it. The same may be said regarding the responsibility of those individuals acting on behalf of the state or in their private capacity, who are to be punished for any behaviour contrary to IHL, as part of the Detaining Power's positive obligation to enforce IHL.

120 A difference based on the gravity of the violation is adopted, however, to establish the individual penal responsibility for war crimes against POWs which consist of grave breaches of the Convention according to Article 130 GC III. The development of international criminal law and the jurisprudence of international, mixed, and national courts, since the Second World War, have contributed to identifying which specific acts or omissions contrary to the provisions of GC III may amount to war crimes against POWs.[135] Nonetheless, a breach of any of the rules of the Convention may entail individual penal responsibility if it involves serious consequences for the victims that may be qualified as a war crime (i.e. torture or inhuman treatment, great suffering, or serious injury to body or health), provided that the deliberate intent of the actor to mistreat the prisoners is proved. It is worth recalling that in a case concerning the handling of prisoners detained in the Bosnian Čelebići camp, the ICTY gave a comprehensive definition of the notion of inhuman treatment as 'an intentional act or omission, that is an act which, judged objectively, is deliberate and not accidental, which causes serious mental

---

[133] EECC, *Final Award, Ethiopia's Damages Claims*, 17 August 2009, para 209; EECC, *Eritrea's Damages*, above n 14, para 229.
[134] EECC, *Ethiopia's Damages*, above n 133, para 210; EECC, *Eritrea's Damages*, above n 14, para 230.
[135] See, e.g., the practices listed in Art 8 ICC Statute.

or physical suffering or injury or constitutes a serious attack on human dignity'.[136] The Tribunal has also underlined that whether any particular act is inconsistent with the principle of humane treatment is a question of fact to be judged in all the circumstances of a particular case.[137]

121 The treatment of protected persons during armed conflicts may also be evaluated according to IHRL standards, usually interpreted in the light of the relevant IHL provisions.[138] The responsibilities of a state violating pertinent IHRL rules binding upon it may then be assessed by IHRL supervisory bodies.[139] This has been done by the Inter-American Court of Human Rights (IACtHR) and the Inter-American Commission on Human Rights (IACommHR), which have regularly condemned states under their jurisdiction for arbitrary killing and mistreatment of civilians and detainees during armed conflicts.[140] The ECtHR has also dealt with claims concerning the application of provisions of the European Convention on Human Rights (ECHR) to situations of armed conflicts, although it has been reluctant to invoke IHL explicitly or use it as a tool of interpretation.[141] No case has yet specifically addressed the treatment of POWs during an IAC.[142] Nevertheless, it may be said that there is substantial correspondence between the fundamental rules of IHRL and IHL on the handling of POWs, so the development of IHRL jurisprudence on the issue would certainly contribute to enhancing the protection of POWs.[143]

E. Critical Assessment

122 The body of rules for POW treatment enshrined in GC III consists of an extremely detailed regime, the correct and good faith application of which may genuinely contribute towards mitigating the suffering of the victims experiencing prolonged internment during armed conflicts, without overlooking the need to balance the interests and the real capabilities of the belligerent parties. The application of GC III by analogy to NIACs, and the correspondence of its fundamental principles with the essential rules of IHRL on the treatment of detained persons, prove that the system is, on the whole, still up-to-date

---

[136] ICTY, *The Prosecutor v Zejnil Delalić et al*, Trial Chamber Judgment, IT-96-21-T, 16 November 1998, para 543.

[137] Ibid, para 544.

[138] C. Droege, 'The Interplay between International Humanitarian Law and International Human Rights Law in Situations of Armed Conflict', 40 *Israel Law Review* (2007) 310.

[139] On the difficulties that an IHRL monitoring body may face in assessing the conduct of a state during armed conflicts in the light of IHRL obligations, see F.J. Hampson, 'The Relationship between International Humanitarian Law and Human Rights Law from the Perspective of a Human Rights Treaty Body', 90 *IRRC* (2008) 549.

[140] E.J. Buis, 'The Implementation of International Humanitarian Law by Human Rights Courts: The Example of the Inter-American Human Rights System', in R. Arnold and N. Quénivet (eds), *International Humanitarian Law and Human Rights Law: Towards a New Merger in International Law* (Leiden: Koninklijke Brill NV, 2008) 269.

[141] A. Reidy, 'The Approach of the European Commission and Court of Human Rights to International Humanitarian Law', 80 *IRRC* (1998) 513, at 551. See, however, most recently, ECtHR, *Hassan v UK*, Judgment, 16 September 2014, para 104.

[142] With reference to the conflict between Turkey and Cyprus, the European Commission of Human Rights did not find it necessary to examine whether the detention of persons accorded the status of POWs violated Art 5 ECHR. European Commission of Human Rights Report, *Cyprus against Turkey*, 10 July 1976, para 313.

[143] H.-J. Heintze, 'On the Relationship between Human Rights Law Protection and International Humanitarian Law', 86 *IRRC* (2004) 789.

and flexible enough to adapt to the reality of modern armed conflicts.[144] Nevertheless, the effectiveness of POW protection is highly dependent on the level of the ideological struggle between belligerent parties. Since POWs are *de facto* tools in the hands of the captor, their treatment, as well as the interpretation of relevant IHL provisions, will unavoidably be tailored to serve its political and military purposes. Independent mechanisms to assess state and individual responsibility are, then, essential instruments to clarify the scope of the norms and the limits to belligerent conduct, in order to avoid arbitrary application of the Convention.

SILVIA SANNA

---

[144] As has been previously noted, certain provisions concerning the finances of POWs and their management would need to be updated or adapted to the reality of NIACs. However, the practice of armed conflicts that have followed the entry into force of the Convention has not showed a systematic application of such rules, therefore it might be inferred that they have fallen into desuetude.

Chapter 49. Relations with the Outside World

	MN
A. Introduction	1
B. Meaning and Application	4
I. The main information agencies	4
a. The National Information Bureau	5
b. The ICRC Central Tracing Agency	6
c. Facilitating the work of the NIB and CTA	7
II. Notification and record of capture	8
a. Capture cards	8
b. Notification by the NIB and the CTA	10
c. State practice	13
III. Specific notifications	14
a. Judicial proceedings	14
b. Death: Notification, recording, and burial instruction	15
c. Reply to enquiries	17
d. State practice	20
IV. The creation of official documents by prisoners of war and their transmission	21
V. Communication with the outside world	22
a. Red Cross messages and 'anxious for news' messages	23
b. Modern communication facilities	24
c. Limitations	25
VI. Relief	28
C. Relevance in Non-International Armed Conflicts	29
D. Legal Consequences of a Violation	30
E. Critical Assessment	31

Select Bibliography

Djurovic, G., *Central Tracing Agency of the International Committee of the Red Cross* (Geneva: Henry-Dunant Institute, 1986)

ICRC, *The International Prisoner of War Agency: The ICRC in World War One* (Geneva: ICRC, 2007)

ICRC, 'The Role of the Central Tracing Agency of the ICRC in Restoring and Maintaining Family Links in Times of Armed Conflicts', the Winton M. Blount History Symposium (2008), available at <http://postalmuseum.si.edu/symposium2008/Mehler-Central_Tracing_Agency_of_the_ICRC.pdf>

ICRC Central Tracing Agency, 'Family links network', available at <http://familylinks.icrc.org/en/Pages/home.aspx>

Pictet Commentary GC III, at 340–50 and 572–90

Sassòli, M., 'The National Information Bureau in Aid of the Victims of Armed Conflicts', 27 *IRRC* 256 (1987) 6

Sassòli/Bouvier/Quintin, at 224–5

A. Introduction

1   One of the most distressing effects of armed conflicts is remaining without information on the fate of family members who have become separated. The lack of such knowledge causes mental anguish, which has been described as 'inhuman treatment of both the detainee and the family concerned'.[1] The Convention Relative to the Treatment of Prisoners of War of 12 August 1949 (GC III) provides very detailed instructions for ensuring the contact of prisoners of war (POWs) with the outside world, precisely to prevent such a situation. These include the obligations to register and transmit information with respect to POWs, their right to communicate with the outside world, and their right to receive relief.

2   This chapter discusses these rights and their procedural requirements. Section B.I outlines the main institutions and information agencies entrusted with implementing them—the National Information Bureau and the Central Tracing Agency—and the obligations of states to facilitate their work (Articles 74–75, 122–124 GC III). Section B.II outlines the obligation of states to register POWs and to transmit notification of their capture to their families and to the special agencies (Articles 69, 70, 77, 94, 122 GC III). Section B.III deals with specific notifications—judicial proceedings (Articles 79, 80, 102, 104, 107 GC III), death (Articles 120–122 GC III), and enquiries to determine the location of POWs or enquiries regarding a death (Articles 120–122 GC III). Section B.IV outlines the instructions applicable to the creation of official documents and their transmission (Articles 77, 120 GC IV). Section B.V deals with POWs' communication with the outside world through either Red Cross messages or modern communication facilities, and discusses the possible limitations (Articles 71, 76 GC III). Lastly, section B.VI deals with POWs' right to receive relief supplies (Articles 72–75 GC III).

3   Section C of this chapter examines the relevance of those obligations in non-international armed conflicts (NIACs); section D examines responsibility in the event of violations; and section E provides an overall evaluation.

B. Meaning and Application

I. The main information agencies

4   Geneva Convention III provides that there should be two information bodies: the National Information Bureau (NIB),[2] and the Central Tracing Agency (CTA).[3] The Convention defines in detail their organization and tasks, which include the collection, recording, and

---

[1] ACommHPR, *Amnesty International and others v Sudan*, Comm No 48/90, 50/91, 52/91, 89/93 (1999), para 54. See also the 21th International Conference of the Red Cross, Res XI, Istanbul, 6–13 September 1969: 'The international community has consistently demanded humane treatment for prisoners of war, including identification and accounting for all prisoners [...], authorisation for prisoners to communicate with each other and with the exterior.'

[2] Art 122 para 1 GC III uses the term 'official Information Bureau', even though the title of the Article is 'National Bureaux'. I shall refer to this entity as the National Information Bureau, as the relevant academic literature tends to do. See, e.g., M. Sassòli, 'The National Information Bureau in Aid of the Victims of Armed Conflicts', 27 *IRRC* 256 (1987) 6, at 14.

[3] The Convention uses the term 'Central Prisoners of War Information Agency'. Yet in practice, the task of this agency has always been entrusted to the ICRC Agency, which, since July 1960, has been called the 'Central Tracing Agency'.

transmission of information concerning each POW, and the facilitation of POWs' right to communicate with the outside world.

a. The National Information Bureau

Article 122 GC III imposes an obligation on the belligerents (and neutral states who have received POWs) to establish an official NIB as soon as hostilities and/or occupation start. States are under an obligation to ensure its effectiveness and to provide it with information on POWs, including their identity, location, and state of health. The NIB has to transmit this information to the party concerned through the Protecting Power and the CTA, and must reply to enquiries regarding POWs. As the NIB needs to be operational from the first days of the conflict, the International Committee of the Red Cross (ICRC), in a resolution from the 25th International Conference of the Red Cross, urged States Parties to consider making the necessary preparations for its establishment during peacetime.[4] It had been further recommended that the NIB should not be too independent from the state in order to facilitate the flow of information (as it is the state's responsibility to make sure that the NIB functions properly).[5]

b. The ICRC Central Tracing Agency

Article 123 GC III provides that a 'Central Prisoners of War Information Agency shall be created in a neutral country'. The Agency is entrusted with ensuring the exchange of information between the NIBs and transmitting the information to the families of POWs. The origin of the Agency, known then as the Basel Agency, goes back to the Franco-Prussian War in 1870. During the First World War, when it was named the 'International Prisoners-of-War Agency', and the Second World War, when it became the 'Central Agency for Prisoners of War', the Agency fulfilled its crucial role of collecting and transmitting information, and restoring contact between people separated by war, including POWs. The Diplomatic Conference of Geneva of 1949 did not interfere with the existing structure and legal basis of the Agency. Although during the Diplomatic Conference it was proposed that the Agency be placed under the permanent responsibility of the ICRC, it was decided to retain a certain flexibility, and thus Article 123 GC III stipulates that the ICRC shall, when 'it deems necessary', propose its services for the creation of such an Agency. Yet in practice, in all post-1949 armed conflicts, it has been the ICRC's agency that has fulfilled this role. It has become a permanent department of the ICRC, at the disposal of the belligerents. In 1960, the Agency's name was changed to the 'Central Tracing Agency', as the Agency had evolved to deal with not only international armed conflicts (IACs), but also NIACs, as well as internal unrest. The most important activities of the CTA concerning POWs are the recording, centralizing, and transmission of information regarding their identity and location, and, where relevant, concerning any escapes, hospitalization, or death. In practice, the ICRC actively collects and transmits, through its CTA, such information.

c. Facilitating the work of the NIB and CTA

A number of provisions govern the work of the NIB and the CTA. States must grant them free postage for mail and provide security for the means of transportation, such

---

[4] The 25th International Conference of the Red Cross, Res XVI, Geneva, 23–31 October 1986.
[5] Sassòli, above n 2, at 8.

as railways, wagons, or airplanes, to facilitate the requisite exchange of information.[6] Where an NIB is created, the parties have an obligation to cooperate in good faith with each other, as that cooperation is essential as regards their respect for GC III's obligations, and all parties to an IAC are obliged to collect and forward information on POWs. The United Nations (UN) Secretary-General's Bulletin on observance by UN forces of international humanitarian law states that the UN forces shall facilitate the work of the ICRC's CTA.[7] National and other international rules on data collection and protection shall be interpreted in a way that will facilitate the obligations set out in GC III, and ensure the collection and transmission of information. At the same time, limitations set out in more recent human rights instruments relating to privacy and data protection, which are more up-to-date and detailed, shall also be taken into account. As in this case international humanitarian law (IHL) and international human rights law (IHRL) are two branches of law that have a common objective of protecting persons, they should be harmonized and interpreted in a way that they complement and reinforce each other. The principle *lex specialis derogat legi general* suggests that the branch of law which is more detailed and adapted to the situation will prevail.[8]

II. Notification and record of capture

a. Capture cards

8 Immediately upon capture, POWs must be able to write directly to their relatives and to the CTA informing them of their capture.[9] The 'capture card' has to be filled in not later than a week from the date of capture. The Convention provides a model of a capture card that should be issued by the Detaining Power. This enables the Detaining Power to prepare a stock of cards at the beginning of hostilities, so that they may be filled in within the required time frame (Annex IV (b)). The Detaining Power is obliged to provide each POW with the opportunity to fill in a capture card, yet POWs are free to choose not to do so. Moreover, while filling in a capture card, a POW may restrict the information provided to that referred to in Article 17 GC III, according to which POWs are bound to provide only their surname, first names, date of birth, rank, and any army, regimental, personal, or serial number; and POWs cannot be coerced into providing any information in the event that they refuse to do so.

9 The capture card must be transmitted directly to the POW's family and to the CTA. This, in practice, has enabled the CTA to be informed of the capture faster than through a notification by the NIB, and it provides an additional channel, making sure that POWs do not remain unaccounted for, thus allowing the CTA to cross-check information. It also makes it possible for the families to have access to information in those cases where they were evacuated as a result of the armed conflict (which would make it very unlikely

---

[6] See Arts 74–75 and 124 GC III.

[7] UN Secretary-General's Bulletin, Observance by United Nations Forces of International Humanitarian Law, UN Doc ST/SGB/1999/13, 6 August 1999, para 9.8.

[8] M. Sassòli and L.M. Olson, 'The Relationship between International Humanitarian Law and Human Rights Law Where It Matters: Admissible Killing and Internment of Fighters in Non-International Armed Conflict', 90 *IRRC* 871 (2008) 599; M. Sassòli, 'Le DIH, une *lex specialis* par rapport aux droit humains?', in A. Auer, A. Fluckiger, and M. Hottelier (eds), *Les droits de l'homme et la constitution: Etudes en l'honneur du Professeur Giorgio Malinverni* (Zurich: Schulthess, 2007) 375.

[9] Art 70 GC III.

that they would receive the POW's capture card directly by mail). Article 70 GC III indicates that the cards shall be sent to the family/relatives of POWs. Yet it seems that these terms should be interpreted broadly, as POWs may have no family but there may be other persons they would like to inform of their situation. This is supported by Article 122 paragraph 4 GC III, which states that the NIB has to transmit (to the Power concerned through the Protecting Power and the CTA) the 'name and address of the person to be informed'.

b. Notification by the NIB and the CTA

As noted by Pictet, 'the system of capture cards does not in any way diminish the role of the Information Bureaux provided for in Article 122'.[10] Each State Party must provide its NIB with information on any POWs it holds.[11] Similarly, the NIB must receive the name and address of the person to be informed, and the address to which correspondence for the prisoner may be sent. Generally, information relating to their capture, location (including transfer, release, hospitalization, escape, or recapture), and health (or death) should be available from the Detaining Power. Any additional information depends on the willingness of the individual POW to provide it.

The CTA, for its part, has to collect all the information it can 'through official or private channels'. In practice it gets notification from capture cards, the states, ICRC delegates who have visited the POWs, and the families themselves, who may contact the CTA directly.

Transmission of the information must be by 'the most rapid means', which today includes all electronic means. The NIB has to transmit the information to the enemy state through the intermediary of the Protecting Power and the CTA.[12] What happens in cases where a POW does not want the information to be transmitted? As matter of policy, the CTA does not transmit the information if it is believed that this could cause prejudice either to the POW, or to his or her family.[13] Coupled with the provision according to which the POW may not be coerced into supplying any information (Article 17 paragraph 4 GC III), it seems that in cases where this is the will of the POW, for whose benefit these rules were drafted, the information must not be transmitted. For example, Belgian regulations provides that if Belgian POWs have not expressed their refusal to have their families informed of their situation, a letter will be sent to the address of the person recorded as 'to be informed'.[14]

c. State practice

Many military manuals mention the obligation to provide a capture card, and the duty to record and notify personal details of a POW, which suggests that at least the obligation to

---

[10] Pictet Commentary GC III, at 342. [11] Art 122 paras 4, 5, and 6, and Art 94 GC III.
[12] According to Art 123 para 2 GC III, the CTA must transmit that information to the country of origin of the POW or the state on which the POW depends.
[13] GC IV provides for such an explicit exception for civilian detainees in Art 140 para 2. Sassòli notes that if the POW's country of origin is different from the state for which he or she has enlisted, the CTA will notify his or her country of origin only if the POW agrees that the country of origin will know that the POW was enlisted in the armed forces of another country. See Sassòli, above n 2, fn 26; G. Djurovic, *Central Tracing Agency of the International Committee of the Red Cross* (Geneva: Henry-Dunant Institute, 1986), at 247.
[14] Belgique, *Structure et fonctionnement du Bureau de Renseignements sur les prisonniers de guerre*, Procédure spécifique, Ministère de la Défense, 2007, at 11, para 12(c)(1).

record and notify information is of a customary nature.[15] In 2003, the United Kingdom (UK) Minister of State for the Armed Forces, stated:

> Upon being taken prisoner, Iraqi combatants are evacuated to a safe location [...] They are held initially at collection points by the unit taking them prisoner, where their identity is established and recorded [...] In accordance with Article 70 of the Geneva Convention relative to the treatment of prisoners of war, upon capture, and subsequently following any change in location, every prisoner of war is given the opportunity to write direct to his or her family [...] Prisoner of war details are given to the ICRC who has the responsibility for the distribution of letters, parcels and Capture Cards.[16]

The requirement to establish an NIB also appears in numerous military manuals.[17] Belgium's Specific Procedure on the Prisoners of War Information Bureau (2007) states that its tasks include 'collecting and registering the following information concerning each prisoner of war in the power of the Belgian armed forces'.[18] And Australia's Official Committee with regard to the armed conflict in Iraq stated in 2003:

> [Australia] did develop all the national structures required to deal with prisoners, including a national information bureau which we established in conjunction with the Department of Foreign Affairs and Trade. Had we taken prisoners and been formally responsible for them, they would have been given identities and numbers and we would then have had to activate the international regimes back through Australia for the central tracing agency which goes back through Geneva to inform that organisation of the people we had identified and for whom we were responsible.[19]

Yet in most post-Second World War IACs, states have not established a NIB. They have simply transmitted the required information to the CTA, and the work of the NIB has *de facto* been done by ICRC delegates or through the assistance of national Red Cross societies.[20] For example, during the Iran–Iraq war, the ICRC offered its services to both countries, and throughout the eight years of conflict the ICRC registered POWs on both sides.[21]

III. Specific notifications

a. *Judicial proceedings*

14 The Protecting Power and the prisoners' representative shall be informed by the Detaining Power of any judicial proceedings against POWs.[22] In the absence of a Protecting Power, the ICRC shall be notified.[23] Such notification shall include the identity of the POW, his

---

[15] Rule 123 ICRC CIHL Study, and ICRC Database, practice on Rule 123.

[16] UK, House of Commons, Written Answer by the Minister of State for the Armed Forces, Ministry of Defence, *Hansard*, 14 April 2003, vol 403, Written Answers, col 572W.

[17] See the military manuals cited in the ICRC CIHL Database under the practice on Rules 123 and 116.

[18] Belgique, above n 14, at 6–7, para 7(a)(1).

[19] Australia, Senate, Foreign Affairs, Defence and Trade Legislation Committee, Estimates (Consideration of Budget Estimates), Official Committee, *Hansard*, 4 June 2003, at 388.

[20] See Djurovic, above n 13, at 199; Sassòli, above n 2, at 14.

[21] 'ICRC activities in favour of prisoners of war during the Iraq–Iran war and the Gulf war', ICRC Resource Centre, 11 March 2003, available at <http://www.icrc.org/eng/resources/documents/misc/5kjjva.htm>.

[22] Prisoners' representatives are elected by the POWs and represent their fellow prisoners before the military authorities, the Protecting Powers, and the ICRC. See Arts 79 and 80 para 1 GC III and Ch 48, MN 94–96, of this volume. The Convention does not specify whether the Detaining Power shall also notify the NIB or CTA.

[23] H.-P. Gasser, 'Respect for Fundamental Judicial Guarantees in Time of Armed Conflict: The Part Played by ICRC Delegates', 32 *IRRC* 287 (1992) 121, at 133.

or her place of confinement, the accusations, the identity of the court which will try the case, and the date and place fixed for the opening of the trial.[24] Without proof that notification was received at least three weeks before the opening of the trial, the trial has to be postponed.[25] A summary notification of the first instance judgment is required, and it shall be sent immediately, indicating whether there is a right of appeal and whether it is to be exercised. A more detailed notification is required for final convictions, or in the event of the imposition of the death penalty by a court of first instance,[26] which shall include the court's decision, a summary report of the investigation and the trial, and the location at which the sentence will be served. If the sentence was not pronounced before them, POWs shall be notified in a language they understand.[27]

b. Death: Notification, recording, and burial instruction

The death of POWs and the location of their graves shall be notified as rapidly as possible to the NIB, which is entrusted with forwarding the information to the Protecting Power and CTA.[28] Lists of graves, recorded by a Graves Registration Service—which must be established by the Detaining Power—shall be transmitted to the Power on which the POW depends.[29] Death certificates, a proposed model for which is provided in Annex IV (d), shall include the identity of the POW, the date and place of death, the cause of death, and the date and place of burial.

The Convention specifies the conditions of burial to ensure respect for the dead, which include burial in individual graves, a prohibition on collective graves without prior identification, and, if possible, burial according to religious rites.[30] The NIB shall be responsible for collecting valuable items left by POWs and transmitting them to the Power concerned.[31]

c. Reply to enquiries

It is useful to distinguish between three kinds of enquiries: enquiries to determine the location of POWs, enquiries in the event of death, and criminal enquiries in light of commission of a war crime. Enquiries to determine the fate and whereabouts of the POW are covered by Article 122 GC III, which entrusts the NIB with responsibility for replying to all enquiries sent to it[32] (see Chapter 13 of this volume).

The obligation to open enquiries about the cause of a death is set out under Article 121 GC III, and may be expanded by the obligation to enquire into alleged war crimes laid down in Articles 129–130 GC III (see Chapter 31 of this volume). In the case of death from suspicious or unknown causes, an enquiry shall be opened. This shall be notified to the Protecting Power, and anyone criminally responsible should be prosecuted.[33] Moreover, family members or other interested individuals and organizations may address their enquiries on the death to the NIB. In cases where the NIB does not

---

[24] Arts 104 and 107 GC III. See also Art 102 GC III, which requires that the judicial authority pronouncing sentence on a POW must be the same as in the case of members of the armed forces of the Detaining Power.
[25] Art 104 para 4 GC III.   [26] Art 107 para 2 GC III.
[27] This does not imply that the accused may be tried in absentia. It refers to the pronouncement of the sentence. See Final Record, vol II-A, at 512.
[28] Art 120 paras 2 and 3 GC III; and Art 122 paras 3 and 5 GC III.   [29] Art 120 para 6 GC III.
[30] Art 120 paras 4 and 5 GC III. See Ch 14, MN 30–33, of this volume.
[31] Art 122 para 3 GC III. This shall also be done in cases where POWs were released or escaped.
[32] Art 122 para 7 GC III.   [33] Art 121 paras 1 and 3 GC III.

possess the information required, it must 'make any enquiries necessary to obtain the information which is asked for'.[34]

19   If there is the suspicion of the commission of a crime or a war crime, such as a death resulting from torture, relatives, and other official and non-official organizations related to the POW, may ask for more details on the causes and circumstances of the death, and what judicial steps have been taken in the search for and prosecution of those responsible. This is in accordance with the right of the families to know the truth about the fate of their relatives, and more generally with the need to ensure accountability for commission of crimes.

d. State practice

20   Rule 116 of the Customary International Humanitarian Law Study states that 'with a view to the identification of the dead, each party to the conflict must record all available information prior to disposal and mark the location of the graves'.[35] In a resolution adopted in 1974 on assistance and cooperation in accounting for persons who are missing or dead in armed conflicts, the UN General Assembly called upon parties to armed conflicts to 'take such action as may be within their power to help locate and mark the graves of the dead' and 'to cooperate, in accordance with the Geneva Conventions of 1949, with Protecting Powers or their substitutes and with the ICRC in providing information on the […] dead in armed conflicts'.[36] This obligation is also found in IHRL. Article 17(3)(g) of the 2006 UN Convention on Enforced Disappearance imposes the duty of recording, 'in the event of death during the deprivation of liberty, the circumstances and cause of death and the destination of the remains'.

IV. The creation of official documents by prisoners of war and their transmission

21   According to Article 14 paragraph 3 GC III, POWs retain the civil capacity they enjoyed at the time of their capture, i.e. they are able to draw up and execute legal documents such as powers of attorney. Moreover, the Detaining Power is required to grant each POW the necessary facilities for the preparation, execution, and transmission of such documents, including the right to consult a lawyer for this purpose.[37] The validity of legal documents drawn up by a POW depends on the national legislation of his or her own state. In the case of wills, the state of origin has to inform the Detaining Power about its national requirements.[38] The transmission of all necessary documents (for and from the POW) shall be facilitated through the Protecting Power or the CTA without undue delay. In the case of wills, a certified copy of the will shall be sent to the CTA.[39]

---

[34] Art 122 para 7 GC III. See also Ch 14 of this volume. The right to present an enquiry to the NIB is not restricted to deaths.

[35] On the practice, see ICRC CIHL Database on Rule 116, including, inter alia, Azerbaijan's Law concerning the Protection of Civilian Persons and the Rights of Prisoners of War (1995), which provides, '[e]ach party buries [the dead] after they take all the measures for their identification'; military manuals, such as those of Canada, Cameroon, and the Netherlands, also include these obligations (ibid).

[36] 'Assistance and Cooperation in Accounting for Persons Who are Missing or Dead in Armed Conflicts', UNGA, A/RES/3220 (XXIX) (6 November 1974).

[37] Art 77 GC III.   [38] See Art 120 para 1 GC III.   [39] Ibid.

V. Communication with the outside world

Prisoners of war have the right to maintain contact with the outside world.[40] They must be allowed to send and receive letters and cards free of postage in their own language.[41] Such letters may not be delayed or retained for disciplinary reasons. Model cards and letters are provided in Annex IV (c). The 20th International Conference of the Red Cross in 1965 adopted a resolution on the treatment of POWs in which it recognized that 'the international community has consistently demanded [...] the facilitation of communication between prisoners of war and the exterior'. Article 8 of the 1973 Protocol to the Agreement on Ending the War and Restoring Peace in Vietnam states that all captured military personnel and captured civilians 'shall be allowed to exchange post cards and letters with their families'. In 1992, in its final report to the United States (US) Congress on the conduct of the Gulf War, the US Department of Defense stated that no POW in the hands of Iraq 'was permitted the rights otherwise afforded them by [the 1949 Geneva Convention III], such as the right of correspondence authorized by Article 70'.[42]

a. Red Cross messages and 'anxious for news' messages

Red Cross messages are open letters, comprising one part on which the sender may write a message and one part on which the relative may reply.[43] Each part contains the name and full address of the sender and the addressee. The message may only contain family or private news. The ICRC and National Societies have been facilitating the transmission of 'Red Cross messages' by various means—electronically, by mail, telephone or personal delivery—until normal means of communication are restored. In specific situations, pre-printed Red Cross messages are used which contain the standard text 'Anxious for news' or 'Safe and well/I am alive'. 'Anxious for news' messages may be used by relatives in emergency situations, and are useful in circumstance in which there are security constraints, because they do not need to be censored. They are published on the ICRC family links website, and in other media.[44] For example, during the Iraq–Iran conflict, the ICRC reported that concerning 50,000 Iraqi POWs, it could not 'maintain effective surveillance of the flow of Red Cross messages between the prisoners and their families'. In contrast, with respect to the 7,300 Iranian POWs, the ICRC declared that '[o]n the whole, the exchange of Red Cross messages between the prisoners and their families works well'.[45] All in all, 13 million Red Cross messages were exchanged between Iraqi and Iranian POWs and their families.[46] In the armed

---

[40] See also Rule 125 ICRC CIHL Study.   [41] Art 71 GC III.
[42] US Department of Defense, Final Report to Congress on the Conduct of the Persian Gulf War, Appendix O, 'The Role of the Law of War', 10 April 1992, 31 *ILM* (1992), at 630.
[43] See ICRC, *Restoration of Family Links: Waiting for News* (Geneva: ICRC, 2002).
[44] The ICRC website allows families to have access to information on how to search for their relatives. For example, for relatives who are still looking for persons who went missing during the Iraq–Iran war, see 'Restoring Family Links in the Islamic Republic of Iran', available at <http://familylinks.icrc.org/en/Pages/Countries/Iran.aspx>. Moreover, there is an 'online tracing service' relating to a number of specific conflicts, at <http://familylinks.icrc.org/en/Pages/online-tracing.aspx>.
[45] *Second Memorandum from the International Committee of the Red Cross to the States Parties to the Geneva Conventions of August 12, 1949 Concerning the Conflict between Islamic Republic of Iran and Republic of Iraq*, Geneva, 10 February 1984. See also ICRC, 'Conflict between Iraq and Iran: ICRC Appeal', 23 *IRRC* 235 (1983) 221.
[46] 'Spotlight: Decades of Helping in Iraq, Operational Update', ICRC Resource Centre, 14 February 2003, available at <http://www.icrc.org/eng/resources/documents/misc/5jrl27.htm>.

conflict between Eritrea and Ethiopia, the ICRC noted in 1998 that it visited the 163 POWs being held in Fiche camp:

> All of these prisoners have now been registered. [...] Prisoners of war who had not yet been in contact with their families wrote Red Cross messages which will be distributed via the Ethiopian Red Cross Society, the Red Cross Society of Eritrea and other National Societies.[47]

More recently, and without prejudice to the classification of the conflict and of the persons concerned, in Afghanistan, since 2005, the ICRC has collected and transmitted about 59,000 Red Cross messages to and from detainees by the Afghan authorities, US forces, the NATO-led International Security Assistance Force, and armed groups.[48] Between 2002 and 2008, around 40,000 Red Cross messages were exchanged between those held captive in Guantánamo Bay, Cuba, and their families.[49]

b. Modern communication facilities

24 Prisoners of war who have been without news for a long period, and those who are 'at a great distance from their homes', shall be allowed to send telegrams.[50] However, as means of communication have evolved greatly since 1949, the provision of GC III that establishes the right of the POW to maintain relations with the external world, to send and receive messages, should be facilitated through modern means of communication such as the Internet, cellular phone, or video-link, using texts, e-mails, or Skype, in order to make their right as effective as possible in the twenty-first century. For example, and again without prejudice to the classification of the conflict and of the persons concerned, in January 2008 the ICRC set up a video conferencing programme in their office in Kabul, that allowed 1,500 calls in eight months between detainees at US detention facilities in Bagram with their families in Afghanistan who came to ICRC offices in Kabul. In Iraq, since 2003 over 30,000 satellite phone calls have been made, and more than 8,000 names of detainees may be found on ICRC's family link website.[51]

c. Limitations

25 Certain limitations on the right to communicate and correspond may be introduced when the Detaining Power 'deems it necessary'. This may be for technical reasons (transportation, means of finance of translation) or for security reasons (censorship[52]). However, Article 70 GC III prescribes that a minimum of two letters and four cards per month must be allowed. It further instructs that a complete prohibition of correspondence for military or political reasons 'shall be only temporary and its duration shall be as short as possible', and that it may be invoked only as an exceptional measure.[53]

---

[47] 'Ethiopia/Eritrea: ICRC Delegates Visit Prisoners of War in Ethiopia and Provide Medical Assistance for Conflict Victims', ICRC News Release 98/27, 9 July 1998, available at <http://www.icrc.org/eng/resources/documents/misc/57jp7w.htm>.

[48] *Restoring Links between Dispersed Family Members*, ICRC, May 2011, at 5, available at <http://www.icrc.org/eng/assets/files/other/icrc-002-0592.pdf>.

[49] ICRC, 'The Role of the Central Tracing Agency of the ICRC in Restoring and Maintaining Family Links in Times of Armed Conflicts', the Winton M. Blount History Symposium (2008), at 5, available at <http://postalmuseum.si.edu/symposium2008/Mehler-Central_Tracing_Agency_of_the_ICRC.pdf>.

[50] Art 71 para 2 GC III.

[51] ICRC, above n 49, at 5. See also 'Guantánamo Internee Speaks by Telephone with Family in Sudan', ICRC News Release 08/104, 19 June 2008, at <http://www.icrc.org/eng/resources/documents/news-release/2009-and-earlier/sudan-news-190608.htm>.

[52] Art 76 GC III.   [53] See Art 76 para 3 GC III.

The Detaining Power and the Power on which the POWs depend may censor correspondence sent by and to POWs, but such censoring must be done as quickly as possible.[54] No censorship should be carried out in countries of transit.

In 1983, the ICRC noted in a memorandum that '[a]lthough thousands of messages are sent each month by Iraqi families through the ICRC and hence to the Iranian military authorities for censorship and distribution, a great many prisoners of war complain they have received no mail for many months';[55] and concerning the Iraqi authorities it noted, in relation to the Iranian detainees, that 'the exchange of Red Cross messages between the prisoners and their families works well, though delays which may sometimes be quite long are still caused by the Iraqi censorship procedure'.[56]

VI. Relief

Prisoners of war have the right to receive relief supplies, and this has been incorporated in many military manuals.[57] This is a fundamental right—'one of the inalienable rights established by the Prisoners of War Convention'.[58] Relief may include food, clothing, books, musical instruments, scientific equipment, or sports gear, allowing POWs 'to pursue their studies or their cultural activities'.[59] Relief parcels, which shall be exempted from any import, customs, and other dues, may be individual or collective. Limitations may be proposed only by the Protecting Power for the benefit of the POW, or by the ICRC (or other humanitarian organization) regarding their own shipment due to exceptional impediments. The Detaining Power may not delay the delivery to the POW. In the case of collective relief,[60] POW representatives may organize the distribution of POW relief material.

C. Relevance in Non-International Armed Conflicts

While POW status is explicitly defined only for combatants in IACs, the core obligations should also be applied in NIACs—for both state and non-state actors. These include the obligation of notification, and the obligation to facilitate the detainees' rights to communication with the outside world[61] and to receive relief. Preventing these communications may lead to the commission of war crimes (see section D of this chapter). As non-state actors cannot create a national agency, their efforts to allow detainees to communicate with their families should be facilitated by the ICRC.

D. Legal Consequences of a Violation

Violations of the Articles under review in this chapter would lead to state responsibility of the High Contracting Party for breaching its international obligations set out in

---

[54] Art 76 para 1 GC III.

[55] *Memorandum from the International Committee of the Red Cross to the States Parties to the Geneva Conventions of August 12, 1949 Concerning the Conflict between Islamic Republic of Iran and Republic of Iraq*, Geneva, 7 May 1983.

[56] Second Iran/Iraq Memorandum (1984), above n 45.

[57] See, Arts 72, 73, and 76 GC III; see also practice referred to in ICRC CIHL Study and Database for Rule 118.

[58] Pictet Commentary GC III, at 342.   [59] Art 72 para 1 GC III.

[60] See Ch 12 of this volume.   [61] See Rule 125 ICRC CIHL Study.

GC III. Some of these obligations overlap with the obligation to account for persons reported missing.[62] In addition, while examining the broader consequences of certain violations (such as not providing information on captured POWs, or not allowing POWs to communicate with the outside world), they may also contribute to the establishment of individual criminal responsibility for acts of inhuman treatment (Article 130 GC III) or even enforced disappearance.[63] The European Court of Human Rights has found that preventing the transmission of information for the benefit of the families of persons missing during armed conflict amounted to inhuman treatment.[64] Resolution II of the 24th International Conference of the Red Cross in 1981 considered that enforced disappearances 'imply violations of fundamental human rights such as the right to life, freedom and personal safety, the right not to be subjected to torture or cruel, inhuman or degrading treatment'.

E. Critical Assessment

31 The Articles under review in this chapter are very detailed and somewhat technical. Their interpretation would merit adaptation to new technologies and to the contemporary context of armed conflicts. However, the fundamental nature of these obligations should not be underestimated. These obligations not only guarantee a minimum standard of communication for the benefit of the well-being of the POW and his or her next of kin; they are a part of a broader logic, which aims at preventing war crimes such as extra-judicial executions, enforced disappearances, and inhuman treatment or torture. They also prevent POWs becoming listed as missing persons, and implement the right of families to know the fate of their relatives.[65]

SHARON WEILL

---

[62] See Ch 13 of this volume.

[63] The systematic practice of enforced disappearance constitutes a crime against humanity. Art 7(2)(i) ICC Statute defines enforced disappearance as 'the arrest, detention or abduction of persons by, or with the authorization, support or acquiescence of, a State or a political organization, followed by a refusal to acknowledge that deprivation of freedom or to give information on the fate or whereabouts of those persons, with the intention of removing them from the protection of the law for a prolonged period of time'. See also Art 17(3) ICED.

[64] See, e.g., ECtHR, *Kurt v Turkey*, Judgment, 25 May 1998, para 188, and ECtHR, *Cyprus v Turkey*, Judgment, 10 May 2001, para 189.

[65] All these rules are of a customary nature; see Rules 98, 105, and 117 of the ICRC CIHL Study.

Chapter 50. Penal or Disciplinary Proceedings Brought against a Prisoner of War

	MN
A. Introduction	1
B. Meaning and Application	7
I. Prisoners of war are subject to the laws, regulations, and orders in force for the armed forces of the Detaining Power	7
a. The principle	7
b. Implementation of this principle	8
II. Preference for disciplinary over judicial measures wherever possible	13
III. Prisoners of war normally to be tried by military courts	16
IV. Proceedings for acts committed prior to capture	20
a. Retention of benefits of GC III if convicted	23
b. No punishment for mere participation in hostilities	24
V. Rules on penalties	25
a. General principles	25
b. Disciplinary sanctions	28
c. Judicial proceedings	29
d. The death penalty	30
e. Unsuccessful escape attempts and connected offences	31
f. Prohibitions against transfer to penitentiary establishments	33
VI. Fair trial and procedural rights for prisoners of war	34
C. Relevance in Non-International Armed Conflicts	42
D. Legal Consequences of a Violation	43
E. Critical Assessment	44

Select Bibliography

Gasser, H.-P., 'Respect for Fundamental Judicial Guarantees in Time of Armed Conflict: The Part Played by ICRC Delegates', 32 *IRRC* 287 (1992) 121

Meyer, M.A., 'Liability of POWs for Offences Committed Prior to Capture: The Astiz Affair', 32 *ICLQ* (1983) 948

Reichstein, M., 'The Extradition of General Manuel Noriega: An Application of International Criminal and Humanitarian Law to Answer the Question, "If So, Where Should He Go?"', 22 *Emory International Law Review* (2008) 857

A. Introduction

The armed forces of a state not subject to a strict disciplinary code are unworthy of their description as the armed forces of a state. It is therefore a fundamental principle of international humanitarian law (IHL) that those who are entitled to prisoner of war (POW) status should remain subject to some form of military discipline despite the fact they are held in captivity by a state with which their own state is engaged in an international armed conflict (IAC).

2   Geneva Convention (GC) III applies only where an IAC is taking place. What follows in this chapter refers to this type of conflict, although it is possible that the parties to the conflict may have agreed between or among themselves to enter into a special agreement by which some or all parts of GC III will apply to captured 'fighters'.[1]

3   Articles 82 to 108 GC III inclusive refer to judicial and disciplinary sanctions. This distinction will be understood in the armed forces of many, but not all, states. In some, military courts will have jurisdiction to try members of the armed forces for what could be described as criminal offences, along with breaches of the military code. In other states the armed forces may have legal power to deal only with disciplinary breaches, with jurisdiction over criminal offences resting with the civilian judicial system. In captivity, however, all POWs must be treated equally, so a uniform system is adopted by GC III,[2] where POWS may be of different nationalities and thus depend upon a number of separate states.

4   Since this chapter deals with penal and disciplinary sanctions, it must take into account the standards which various human rights treaties and bodies have imposed upon such proceedings since 1949. In turn, these standards will inform the question of what is a 'fair trial', since wilfully depriving a POW of the rights of a fair and regular trial is a grave breach of GC III.[3]

5   It should be borne in mind that whilst the greatest proportion of POWs held by the Detaining Power will be members of the armed forces of a party to the IAC, the definition of 'prisoner of war' in Article 4 GC III can encompass others who are civilians. In so far as they are not released and repatriated, they will be subject to the same obligations and entitlements as other POWs, including trial by a military court.

6   This chapter will consider the meaning and effect of Articles 82 to 108 GC III in the light of modern conditions where states are involved in an IAC. The effective working of the safeguards for POWs set out in these Articles will be realized only if they are implemented (in some form) in the national law of the detaining state.

B. Meaning and Application

I. Prisoners of war are subject to the laws, regulations, and orders in force for the armed forces of the Detaining Power

a. *The principle*

7   The principle that POWs are to be treated in the same way as the detaining state would treat its own armed forces pervades GC III. It could hardly be otherwise when it is often the case that POWs, as a group, will comprise the armed forces of more than one state, and the obligations for their well-being and safety are placed on the Detaining Power. That state must possess the legal power to maintain discipline, in effect, over members of the armed forces of another state who are detained by it as POWs.

---

[1] Arts 3 penultimate paragraph, 6, and 7 GC III. See Ch 25 of this volume. The term 'fighters' is used here in a descriptive rather than in a legal sense, since members of a non-state armed group are not 'combatants' within the terminology of IHL.

[2] Art 16 GC III, although differences in rank, sex, age, health, or professional qualifications are recognized.

[3] Art 130 GC III. It cannot be assumed that a 'trial' in this context refers only to judicial proceedings brought against a POW. The ECtHR has been willing to treat disciplinary hearings by a military court or by a

b. Implementation of this principle

For some states an obligation imposed in a treaty, such as in Article 82 GC III, to subject 8
POWs to its laws, regulations, and orders will not be sufficient to give it legal authority to do so unless this has been implemented into its national law. Whether some form of implementation of Article 82 is required or not will depend upon how the detaining state generally treats the relationship between international and national law. For some the presence of Article 82 will be sufficient, but for others some form of legislation will be required. This is particularly significant with the development of human rights principles relating to fair trial procedures and the obligation on a state to show that the tribunal concerned has been 'established by law'.[4]

For those states requiring some form of implementation of Article 82 there would 9
appear to be two choices as to how to achieve this. The first, and perhaps the simplest, is to provide in the disciplinary code applying to the state's armed forces that those subject to its military disciplinary law will include POWs. The second is to provide a separate code of discipline to apply only to POWs, but which would use the courts, either civilian or military, or other processes applicable where a similar breach of this code has been alleged against a member of the state's own armed forces. The advantage of the second approach is that a state can provide a tailor-made POW disciplinary system, to be brought into effect should it subsequently become a Detaining Power. Whichever format is adopted, it will be essential that the disciplinary system that becomes applicable to POWs is consistent with both GC III and the Detaining Power's international human rights obligations.[5] A system of military justice which is inconsistent with the state's international human rights obligations in respect of its own armed forces will not be cured by applying that same system for POWs should the state become a Detaining Power.

Where some form of implementation of a treaty obligation is required by a state, it 10
is likely to prove to be a much more difficult exercise to ensure that a POW is not to be subject to judicial proceedings where, during an escape attempt, he commits an offence against the territorial law, 'with the sole intention of facilitating [his] escape and which [does] not entail any violence against life or limb, such as offences against public property [or] theft without intention of self-enrichment'.[6]

It may also prove difficult for a state to try a POW for an offence committed prior 11
to capture unless it has criminalized the necessary range of offences—from genocide, to crimes against humanity, to war crimes—in its domestic law. If it wishes to give itself the power to try a POW for an offence unrelated to the armed conflict, the state will have to ensure that its civilian or military courts possess jurisdiction to try such offences committed outside its territory. The practical problems of attempting to try

---

commander as involving 'criminal penalties' if the punishment involves, e.g., a loss of liberty, thereby bringing into play Art 6 of the Convention. See ECtHR, *Engel v The Netherlands*, Judgment, 8 June 1976, para 81. For further discussion of this issue, see MN 25.

[4] Art 14(1) ICCPR; Art 6 ECHR. The term, 'regularly constituted court' appears in CA 3 to the 1949 GCs and in Art 75(4) AP I, and it must by now reflect a principle of customary IHL.

[5] The situation may, however, be posed where the Detaining Power is not a party to any human rights treaty or where it has entered into reservations concerning the discipline of its armed forces. Many of the obligations, however, contained in Arts 82–108 reflect international human rights obligations and will be binding on the state as such.

[6] Art 93 GC III and see below MN 32.

a POW for such acts committed prior to capture are discussed in section B.IV of this chapter.

12 The essential point from the foregoing is that it may not be sufficient for a state merely to become a party to the Geneva Conventions. To ensure practical compliance with the international obligations under Articles 82 to 108, those states which must implement international law into their national law must do so to ensure that POWs are subject to the same law as members of the armed forces of the Detaining Power.

II. Preference for disciplinary over judicial measures wherever possible

13 This expressed preference for disciplinary measures rather than judicial measures is to be found in Article 83 GC III, but it can also be seen at work in other Articles.[7] It is necessary for two reasons. First, a sound system of military discipline requires members of armed forces to exercise a standard of conduct more tightly controlled by military superiors and with more severe penalties than would be expected in civilian employment. Secondly, the dividing line in the armed forces of some states between invoking judicial or disciplinary proceedings is not entirely clear, but the leniency required by Article 83 is directed towards a choice of disciplinary proceedings. Thus, striking a guard in a POW camp could be charged as a criminal offence such as assault, and so be dealt with by way of judicial proceedings, or, alternatively, it could be dealt with as a disciplinary offence. Whilst the limits on punishments to be imposed by disciplinary proceedings are set out in Article 89 GC III, no such limitations may be imposed on penalties following judicial proceedings, simply because crimes range widely in their seriousness and thus may call for severe punishment.[8]

14 The justifications for this preference are that POWs owe no allegiance to the Detaining Power[9] and that the principal function of the POW regime, in this regard, should merely be to maintain discipline, both amongst the POWs themselves and in relation to the Detaining Power itself.

15 In practice it may be that these disciplinary punishments are imposed by the military authorities of the Detaining Power, in much the same way as they could be imposed, *mutatis mutandis*, by a commander over his subordinates in the armed forces of many states.

III. Prisoners of war normally to be tried by military courts

16 Article 84 GC III embraces the principle that POWs remain members of the armed forces of their own state.[10] It is entirely appropriate that they should be tried by the same military court (or civilian court[11]) as employed by the Detaining Power in respect of members of its

---

[7] Arts 82 para 2, and 93 GC III.

[8] There are, however, provisions in Arts 100 and 101 relating to the death penalty.

[9] Arts 87 and 100 direct that this principle must be taken into account by the military authorities, or be drawn to the attention of a court trying a POW. The obligation of a POW to obey the laws, regulations, and orders of the Detaining Power is clearly based on some principle other than that of allegiance to the Detaining Power. It seems clear that it cannot derive from the military law of the state on which he depends, since his obligations from that source may be in direct conflict with the laws, regulations, or orders of the Detaining Power. It can only derive from GC III as the *quid pro quo* for the obligations assumed by the Detaining Power for the POW's benefit and protection under that Convention.

[10] See also Arts 60 and 62 relating to advances of pay. It should be borne in mind, however, that certain civilians can also become POWs; see Art 4(A)(4)–(6) GC III. See also MN 19.

[11] The national law of the detaining state may require members of the armed forces to be tried by a civilian court for some (or all) criminal offences, and all civilians to be tried only by a civilian court.

own armed forces, since the POWs cannot be tried by the state upon which they depend. This Article fits alongside the obligation of the Detaining Power in Article 82 to subject POWs to the laws, regulations, and orders in force applying to its own armed forces.

In reality, POWs would receive little protection if the military court by which they were to be tried was a court in name only. Article 84 GC III stresses that a military court must be able to offer the essential guarantees of independence and impartiality which are generally recognized. In addition, the guarantees offered by Article 105 GC III applicable to judicial proceedings are to apply to it. It may be, however, that all the requirements of this latter Article do not apply to the military courts of the Detaining Power. In order to comply with this Article, the state concerned may need to implement the Article's requirements by some form of domestic legal power, whether by primary legislation or otherwise. The essentials of a fair trial in this context are discussed in section B.VI of this chapter.

Article 84 GC III does not mean that a POW can be dealt with only by a military court for a breach of the laws, regulations, or orders in force of the Detaining Power. It is recognized in the armed forces of many states that lesser penalties than those available before a military court may be imposed by a commander. Assuming that this is also recognized by the Detaining Power, the camp commander (as compared with a military court) may impose disciplinary sanctions on POWs.[12]

Should civilians, such as individuals representing authorized defence contractors or war correspondents, be held as POWs, they will be subject to the same military courts or form of disciplinary processes as their fellow detainees from the armed forces. They cannot expect any separate form of treatment, although their status may cause the Detaining Power problems, especially if its own military courts would have no jurisdiction to try civilians at all. It is likely to be the case that the range of activities carried out by defence contractors, in or around combat areas, is much greater in modern armed conflicts than it was when GC III was drafted, and hence the potential number of POWs who fall into this class will have increased proportionally. An issue that might arise in this case is the suitability of trying a civilian in a military court.[13]

IV. Proceedings for acts committed prior to capture

Article 85 has proved to be the most contentious Article of GC III. Initially, this was not because of any doubt that the Detaining Power could prosecute POWs under its law for crimes committed prior to capture, but because the Article goes on to provide that, if convicted, such individuals will retain the benefits of GC III (see MN 23).[14] A small number of states entered a reservation to Article 85 in respect of POWs convicted by the Detaining Power of war crimes or crimes against humanity, as those concepts were then understood following the Nuremberg and Tokyo trials.[15]

---

[12] Arts 87 and 96 GC III.
[13] The trial of a civilian POW (e.g. a defence contractor) by a military court is not *ipso facto* a breach of the ECHR, see ECtHR, *Martin v United Kingdom*, Judgment, 24 October 2006.
[14] For an example, see US District Court SD Florida, *United States v Noriega*, 746 F Supp 1506 (1990); 808 F Supp 792 (1992). Art 85 should be read in conjunction with Art 5 (first paragraph).
[15] The reservations were not set out in identical terms but they are still in force for Albania, Angola, China, Democratic Peoples Republic of Korea, Russian Federation, and Vietnam. Australia, Barbados, the UK, and the US objected to these reservations. Were the reservations to be invoked, the convicted individual would become a person protected by GC IV. The effect would be that Art 4 para 4 GC IV would not preclude that Convention from applying.

21   It is possible that a person otherwise entitled to POW status may forfeit it in two situations:

— where a member of the armed forces has engaged in espionage;[16] or
— where he has failed to distinguish himself sufficiently from the civilian population.[17]

These are not examples of a POW being denied the benefit of Article 85, but of situations where that Article does not apply since the person will no longer be entitled to the status of a POW.[18] He will, however, be a protected person under GC IV.

22   Article 85 GC III does not make it clear whether 'acts committed prior to capture' means crimes related to the IAC, or whether it might encompass any crime committed in any place by someone who subsequently becomes a POW. It is likely that Article 85 bears the wider meaning.[19] In any event, it would be necessary for the Detaining Power to possess jurisdiction under its law in respect of such a crime and over the individual concerned.[20] It should also be borne in mind that POWs are required to answer questions only in respect of their 'surname, first names and rank, date of birth, and army, regimental, personal or serial number',[21] so questioning relating to any other matter may fall upon

---

[16] Art 30 of the Hague Regulations requires an alleged spy to be placed on trial before any punishment. Although Art 46 AP I does not specifically require a trial, it is suggested that the loss of POW status should not take place without a determination by a competent tribunal envisaged by Art 5 para 2 GC III. See also, below n 17.

[17] Should a member of the armed forces make no effort to distinguish himself from the civilian population, it is likely that he will forfeit his POW status. For an example, see Judicial Committee of the Privy Council (UK), *Osman bin Mohamed v Public Prosecutor* [1969] 1 AC 430, at 452; Israeli Military Court, *the Swarka Case*, 1974, cited in ICRC CIHL Study, vol II, Chapter 33, para 35. *Quaere* whether he can take the benefit of Art 44(4) AP I if his acts occurred otherwise in a situation 'where, owing to the nature of the hostilities an armed combatant cannot so distinguish himself [from the civilian population]'. ICRC CIHL Study, Rule 106 does not impose any such limitation.

[18] This conclusion follows from a combination of Arts 5, 82, and 85 GC III. Examples include Judicial Committee of the Privy Council (UK), *Osman bin Mohamed v Public Prosecutor* [1969] 1 AC 430 (where Art 85 GC III is not referred to); Judicial Committee of the Privy Council (UK), *Public Prosecutor v Oie Hee Koi et al* [1968] AC 829. Compare G. Nolte, *Third Report for the ILC Study Group on Treaties over Time: Subsequent Agreements and Subsequent Practice of States outside Judicial or Quasi-Judicial Proceedings*, ILC (LXIV) SG/TOT/INFORMAL/1, 19 April 2012, who argues (at 54) that the failure of a combatant to distinguish himself from a civilian is 'an exception' to Art 85 GC III; and G. Solis, *The Law of Armed Conflict* (Cambridge: CUP, 2010), at 223, who argues that there is no conflict with Art 85, 'because the captured soldier, due to his lack of uniform or distinguishing sign, never achieved a POW status to retain'. It is suggested that the danger of creating exceptions to Art 85 are obvious, whilst to accept the argument advanced by Solis would create a real risk to members of the enemy armed forces at the moment of capture, whose lack of POW status at that moment would avoid the rigorous approach envisaged by Art 5 GC III. The view of the author is supported by the Israeli Military Court, *Military Prosecutor v Kassem et al* (1969) 42 ILR 470, at 481, which concerned an Israeli military court's acting as an Art 5 GC III competent tribunal to determine whether a member of the PLO was entitled to POW status on capture. It held he was not. As he did not act on behalf of a state, he could never have acquired POW status and thus benefit from Art 85, even if he distinguished himself from civilians. It was necessary, however, to make a formal determination of this by a competent tribunal under Art 5, since a doubt had arisen as to his status.

[19] See, e.g., US District Court SD Florida, *United States v Noriega* 746 F Supp 1506 (1990), which concluded, at 1529, that 'the Geneva Convention was never intended, and should not be construed, to provide immunity against prosecution for common crimes committed against the detaining power before the outbreak of hostilities'; M. Meyer, 'Liability of Prisoners of War for Offences Committed Prior to Capture: The Astiz Affair' 32 *ICLQ* (1983) 948.

[20] Although the Pictet Commentary on GC III took the view, at 419, that '[a]n act in respect of which there could be no extradition should not be punished by the Detaining Power', the court in *United States v Noriega*, 746 F Supp 1506, at 1528, rejected this proposition, on the basis that the 'Commentary was not part of the treaty', although it did go on to find that the offences alleged against Noriega were actually extraditable as being offences under the law of Panama and the US.

[21] Art 17 GC III. Nor may any moral or physical inducement be made to him to secure a confession (Art 99). Recognizing that an alleged confession has been a major source of miscarriages of justice in normal

deaf ears. In practical terms, it is very unlikely that a detaining state could achieve a fair trial of a POW for any type of crime committed prior to capture, unless the evidence was such that a case beyond reasonable doubt could be made out through evidence gathered independently of the accused. Even then, and even in a case which involved an allegation of criminal activity related to the armed conflict, such a prosecution would give rise to the difficulty that an accused POW would be very unlikely to be able to call defence witnesses, particularly members of his own armed forces who have not themselves become POWs.

a. Retention of benefits of GC III if convicted

The basic principle is that a POW convicted for a crime committed prior to capture is to be treated in the same way as a member of the armed forces of the detaining state in terms of trial and any sentence which would otherwise amount to imprisonment.[22] Once subjected to judicial proceedings, a POW is in a position no different from that of any other POW who is subjected to such proceedings for a crime committed after capture. A POW ceases to be a POW only upon release and repatriation by the Detaining Power.[23]

b. No punishment for mere participation in hostilities

During an IAC, IHL does not consider as unlawful under that body of law acts, ranging from killing to destruction of property, which in virtually all systems of national law would amount to criminal offences. If committed by those entitled to do so,[24] and within the limits of IHL, those who are entitled to POW status as combatants will, if captured, be entitled to immunity under national law in respect of those acts. This is sometimes spoken of as 'the combatant's immunity' or 'privilege', and it applies to the courts of the detaining state, party to GC III.[25]

V. Rules on penalties

a. General principles

Military discipline cannot be enforced by the POWs' own commanders[26] (assuming they have also become POWs); the camp commandant must therefore perform this

---

criminal cases, it is possible that the law of the detaining state may have in place greater safeguards to prevent the admissibility of unreliable confessions.

[22] Arts 82 and 87 GC III. A member of the armed forces of the detaining state may be subject to trial before a civilian court and be required to serve any period of imprisonment in a civilian prison. The POW has the additional benefits that the Protecting Power must be informed if the detaining state has decided to institute judicial proceedings (Art 104), or if conviction for the offence might involve the death penalty (Art 100; see MN 30), which cannot be carried out for six months (Art 101). In addition, the standards of treatment of a POW must comply with GC III, even if these are not matched for members of the armed forces of the detaining state.

[23] Arts 5 para 1, 109–119 GC III. See Ch 51 of this volume.

[24] In Art 43(2) AP I such individuals are styled as 'combatants'. A civilian who takes an active part in hostilities is not entitled to commit such acts. If he is subsequently captured, he is not a POW protected by GC III unless he comes within Art 4 GC III. He could be tried merely for the acts of participation by any state which had jurisdiction over him or over his acts.

[25] See, e.g., *Military Prosecutor v Kassem et al*, above n 18, at 472; *Public Prosecutor v Oie Hee Koi*, above n 18, at 860–1, and compare the dissenting view at 867–8. In assessing whether this 'combatant immunity' applies, the courts of the detaining state may have to determine whether the alleged acts committed by a POW prior to capture were, or were not, contrary to IHL. In practical terms it is a means of reconciling a conflict of laws. The principle can have little relevance before an international criminal tribunal, since the acts which come within it will not be unlawful under (or will be permitted by) IHL.

[26] Art 96 para 3 GC III.

hierarchical role.[27] He can do so effectively only if he is able to operate the disciplinary system of his own state, with which he should be familiar.

26 Were GC III to impose a limit on the severity of any penalties[28] to be imposed when judicial proceedings have been taken, it would interfere with the independence of the judiciary (whether the court is a military or a civilian one). There is no such limitation, nor, for the same reason, are there any provisions requiring the severity of the penalty to be the same as (or similar to) that which would apply to a member of the armed forces of the detaining state convicted of the same offence. It is possible, therefore, that a POW convicted of, say, assaulting a camp guard would receive a more severe penalty than that imposed on a member of the armed forces of the detaining state who has been convicted of assaulting a military superior.

27 The fact that the POW owes no allegiance to the Detaining Power must, however, be taken into consideration by the court, or the authorities, before whom a POW may receive a disciplinary or judicial penalty.[29]

b. Disciplinary sanctions

28 Disciplinary sanctions are set out in Article 89 GC III. They include a fine, which is to be no greater in amount than 50 per cent of the advances of pay and working pay over a period of 30 days,[30] discontinuance of privileges,[31] fatigue duties not exceeding two hours daily,[32] and confinement.[33] The last three penalties may be awarded for a maximum each

---

[27] Art 39 GC III. The regulations applying to POWs must be issued to them in a language they understand (Art 41). *Quaere* whether the commander's responsibility for discipline and order within the POW camp could compromise his impartiality when making a decision on pre-trial confinement. For an analogy, see ECtHR, *Hood v United Kingdom*, Judgment, 18 February 1999, para 58; ECtHR, *Boyle v United Kingdom*, Judgment, 8 January 2008, para 36. These cases were, however, based upon Art 5(3) ECHR, which required such decisions to be made by a person 'authorised by law to exercise judicial power'.

[28] The only limitation is that the penalty, as a type, must be one to which members of the detaining state could also be subject (Art 87). The conditions under which the penalty is served by POWs, however, must not be contrary to the provisions of Ch III (Arts 82–108), as to which see, in particular, Arts 87–90, 97, 98, 108.

[29] Art 87 GC III. See also the discussion above n 9.

[30] Art 89 GC III. Advances of pay and working pay are set out in Arts 60 and 62 GC III (see Ch 48, MN 103, of this volume). For an account of the interpretation of advances of pay, see G. Risius, 'Prisoners of War in the United Kingdom', in P. Rowe (ed), *The Gulf War 1990–91 in International and National Law* (London: Routledge/Sweet & Maxwell, 1993) 289, at 300. Since the amount of advances in pay will vary with the rank of the POW, the limit as to the amount of the fine will also vary as between different ranks of POW. This difference in treatment is permitted by Art 16 GC III.

[31] In peacetime it is a common practice for commanders to be able to grant privileges to their subordinates, which, not being based upon a legal entitlement, can be withdrawn relatively informally. Similar principles apply to a POW camp commander, which gives him considerable leeway to grant or to withhold privileges, depending on the circumstances he faces in maintaining order and security amongst POWs. It may be that the loss of privileges will be seen by a POW to be harsher than a fine or a requirement to undertake fatigue duties.

[32] Commissioned officers cannot receive a penalty of fatigue duties (Art 89). This reflects the principle that officers cannot be compelled to work (Art 49). The different treatment of one group of POWs (officers) is permitted by Art 16 GC III since it depends on their rank. It is also common in the armed forces of states for officers to be exempt from some, but not all, disciplinary penalties which may be imposed on other ranks.

[33] Confinement refers to a place within the POW camp where the loss of liberty is over and above that involved in being a POW. It must meet the conditions set out in Arts 97 and 98. Confinement is likely to involve the loss of some, or all, privileges and of working pay. In principle there is no reason why it should involve the loss of advances of pay. Even though an officer is awarded a penalty of confinement, the spirit of Art 89(3) suggests that he should not be required to perform fatigue duties.

of 30 days.[34] There are no limitations imposed by GC III on any combination of these penalties. Thus, a POW could be sanctioned by a fine and confinement. It might be argued that these sanctions are not of such a nature as to act as a deterrent to POWs set on breaching the rules and orders laid down by the camp authorities.[35]

c. Judicial proceedings

Judicial proceedings may be brought in relation to the same criminal offences and before the same courts as would normally have jurisdiction over a member of the armed forces of the detaining state.[36] Given the potential risk to the life, liberty,[37] or treatment of a POW following conviction by a court of the detaining state, it is not surprising to see in GC III a number of fair trial safeguards,[38] discussed in detail in section B.VI of this chapter and in Chapter 59, MN 9–58, of this volume. These safeguards would have a more limited practical effect were the Protecting Power not to be informed before the trial has commenced. Article 104 GC III requires the detaining state to notify the Protecting Power at least three weeks before the opening of the trial, failing which the trial cannot take place until adequate notice has been given.[39] 29

d. The death penalty

The death penalty may be imposed on a POW only in judicial proceedings and subject to the limitations discussed in MN 26–27 and 29. In addition, POWs and the Protecting Power must be informed as to which offences might attract the death penalty.[40] If imposed, this penalty must not be carried out until at least six months have elapsed from the time the Protecting Power has been informed in accordance with Article 107. The possibility of the death penalty being imposed on a POW is discussed further at MN 40. 30

e. Unsuccessful escape attempts and connected offences

In some armed forces a strong obligation is placed upon members who have become POWs, to attempt to escape in order to rejoin their own forces.[41] There is, perhaps, as 31

---

[34] Art 90 GC III, which also deals with successive penalties.

[35] See H. Fischer, 'Protection of Prisoners of War', in D. Fleck (ed), *The Handbook of International Humanitarian Law* (2nd edn, Oxford: OUP, 2008) 367, at 410. If disciplinary sanctions would be inadequate in a particular case, judicial procedures could be invoked. In an extreme case, serious disorder within a POW camp could be met with the use of firearms, subject to warnings (Art 42). It should not be overlooked that such action would have serious consequences for the guards (see Arts 121 (inquiry), 130 (grave breach), and their criminal law) and for the state under a human rights treaty to which it is a party. As to the latter, see ECtHR, *K.-H. W. v Germany*, Judgment, 22 March 2001.

[36] Arts 82 and 87 GC III, although see Art 83 GC III. See also Arts 102 and 108 GC III.

[37] A POW sentenced by a court of the detaining state to a period of imprisonment will be required to serve that sentence before repatriation (Art 119).

[38] See Arts 99, 103–107 GC III.

[39] E.g. see *Public Prosecutor v Oie Hee Koi*, above n 18, at 855. In the absence of a Protecting Power, the detaining state is required to 'request or [...] accept [...] the offer of the services of a humanitarian organization, such as the [ICRC] to assume the humanitarian functions performed by Protecting Powers' (Art 10 GC III). See generally, H.-P. Gasser, 'Respect for Fundamental Judicial Guarantees in Time of Armed Conflict: The Part Played by ICRC Delegates', 32 *IRRC* 287 (1992) 121, at 131.

[40] Should the detaining state wish subsequently to add to this range of offences, it must have the concurrence of the state upon which the POWs depend (Art 100). This is unlikely to be acceded to unless the latter state wishes to act in a similar way.

[41] A successful escape attempt is defined in Art 91 GC III. If a POW succeeds in his escape attempt and is subsequently captured again whilst serving with his own armed forces, he cannot be subsequently punished for his successful attempt (Art 91).

strong an obligation on the part of the POW camp authorities to prevent them from doing so. Any attempt to escape is likely to infringe the discipline regulations imposed by the military authorities, and may possibly involve the commission of criminal offences. The mere fact of attempting to escape, followed by re-capture, is to attract disciplinary sanctions only, even if it is a repeated offence.[42] This is a significant safeguard for POWs, since it prevents the detaining state from classifying escape attempts as a separate type of offence, attracting a harsher penalty than that which might be imposed for any other breach of discipline.[43]

32 In practical terms, the commission by a POW of a criminal offence during an escape attempt is a real possibility. Such offences might range from damaging property belonging to the military authorities, to travelling on public transport with forged documents. Were a detaining state able to take judicial proceedings against a failed escape, it would be able to impose punishments more severe than those which could be imposed for disciplinary breaches only. To prevent this, Article 93 GC III provides that these activities, although normally criminal offences, should be dealt with by way of disciplinary sanctions only.[44]

f. Prohibitions against transfer to penitentiary establishments

33 Since military discipline, imposed by the military authorities of the detaining state, is to apply to all POWs, it is prohibited to transfer a POW to a civilian prison or penitentiary in order to undergo a period of confinement imposed by way of a disciplinary sanction.[45] If a POW is, however, sentenced by a court for a criminal offence, he will serve this period of imprisonment in the same establishment as would a member of the armed forces of the detaining state for a similar offence.[46] The POW will be required to complete his sentence prior to repatriation.[47]

VI. Fair trial and procedural rights for prisoners of war

34 Article 84 GC III requires the court before which a POW is to be tried to offer 'the essential guarantees of independence and impartiality as generally recognised'.[48] This court is likely to be a military one, unless, for the offence charged, a member of the armed forces of

---

[42] Art 92 GC III. Those who 'aid or abet' an escape will also be liable to disciplinary sanctions. This formulation is not sufficiently wide to cover those who assist an escape attempt without aiding and abetting it (Art 93 GC III).

[43] This protection is also coupled with the requirement that a POW who has made good his escape from the POW camp but has not yet re-joined his own forces, is, if recaptured, to be handed over to the military authorities (Art 92 GC III).

[44] This supports the principle set out in Art 83 GC III. These two Articles in combination are an example of where a POW is being treated differently from (and more leniently than) members of the armed forces who commit a criminal offence in similar circumstances in trying to desert from their military barracks. For this principle to have any practical effect it must be part of the national law of the detaining state, by implementation or otherwise. This is important, since the effect of the Article is to exempt a group of individuals (POWs who have failed to make good their escape) from certain offences contrary to the criminal law of that state.

[45] Art 97 GC III. He cannot be detained in a civilian prison merely by the fact that he is a POW—see Art 39.

[46] Art 108 GC III. The establishment could be a civilian prison or a military detention centre. See, e.g., *United States v Noriega*, above n 14.

[47] Art 119 GC III.

[48] This Article should be read together with Art 130. Thus, a 'fair and regular trial' in Art 130 must encompass a court which is independent and impartial. See also Ch 59, MN 11, of this volume.

the detaining state could be tried by a civilian court. It may be difficult for a military court to provide the necessary independence and impartiality required of it.

It is likely that the guidelines set out by a human rights body will be extremely important, or persuasive, in understanding the requirement in GC III that a military court must be independent and impartial when it is to try a POW. In a number of decisions, beginning in 1997,[49] the European Court of Human Rights (ECtHR) analysed the perceived procedural flaws of certain military courts in this regard.[50] All these cases, however, involved members of the armed forces being tried for criminal offences before a military court of their own state. Prisoners of war would, of course, be tried by a military court consisting of members of the armed forces of the detaining state, but the problems of establishing independence, although different, will remain considerable. As a minimum, the members of the court, and those who appoint them, must be independent of the chain of command involved with the running of the POW camp. They must also be free to make an independent judgment, unfettered by any appraisal of their individual decision-making, promotion prospects, or levels of pay. It will be easier to show independence if the judge in the military court (as distinct from the other members of the court) is a civilian judicial official, rather than a military officer.[51] Moreover, the decision to charge a POW and the prior investigation must all be independent of this chain of command. These will, in practical terms, be difficult standards for a detaining state to establish, particularly if they do not exist, in whole or in part, for members of its own armed forces being tried before a military court.[52]

Although the Protecting Power must be notified by the detaining state of a decision to institute judicial proceedings against a POW,[53] and be given the opportunity to attend the trial,[54] it is taken for granted that the Protecting Power will try to ensure that the basic procedural standards required of any fair trial are met. This must involve an obligation to ensure itself that the trial of a POW is before a military (or civilian) court which is independent and impartial.[55]

Should he be convicted, a POW can appeal his conviction or sentence only if,[56] in similar circumstances, a member of the armed forces of the detaining state would have a

---

[49] See also the ACommHPR, *Constitutional Rights Project v Nigeria*, Case No 60/91 (1995), para 14; *Centre for Free Speech v Nigeria*, Case No 206/97 (1999), para 15. See also L. Burgorgue-Larsen and A. Ubede De Torres, *The Inter-American Court of Human Rights, Case Law and* Commentary (Oxford: OUP, 2011), paras 25.15–25.22. See also Rule 100 of the ICRC CIHL Study, vol I, at 356.

[50] ECtHR, *Findlay v United Kingdom*, Judgment, 25 February 1997. Further examples include ECtHR, *Grieves v United Kingdom*, Judgment, 16 December 2003; ECtHR, *Cooper v United Kingdom*, Judgment, 16 December 2003; ECtHR, *Gurkan v Turkey*, Judgment, 3 July 2012.

[51] It is, of course, possible that a military officer with legal qualifications and with sufficient experience may be able to fulfil, and be perceived to fulfil, the same role in the military court as a civilian judge. As a minimum, he must be independent of the chain of command—*Grieves v United Kingdom*, above n 50. A judge with no legal qualifications may be a member of a military court, but he must also be independent of the military chain of command—*Gurkan v Turkey*, above n 50, para 19.

[52] Although Art 102 GC III does not refer to the independence of courts, it does require the courts to be the same.

[53] Art 104 GC III.   [54] Art 105 GC III; and to be informed of the sentence (Art 107 GC III).

[55] The duty of Protecting Powers is stated in very general terms in Art 8 to be to 'safeguard the interests of the Parties to the conflict', although they are 'not in any case to exceed their mission under the present Convention'.

[56] It is suggested that the words in Art 106 which refer to 'the reopening of the trial' should be interpreted as meaning the opening of a new trial where the conviction appealed from is quashed. It would appear that GC III does not impose an obligation on the detaining state to provide machinery for the quashing of a conviction without holding a new trial. It may be, however, that the national law of that state so provides for members of its armed forces. Prisoners of war should be able to take advantage of this.

right to appeal or to petition.[57] A problem here is that there may be no appeal provided in the national law of the Detaining Power for a member of its armed forces convicted by a military court. In 1949 some states did not provide for a right of appeal from a military court, on the basis that military discipline must be enforced speedily and only by the military authorities, who alone understand the need for discipline. In these circumstances a POW would not be entitled under GC III to appeal his conviction.[58] Such a position would run counter to Article 14(5) of the International Covenant on Civil and Political Rights (ICCPR). For the role of human rights treaties in the trial of POWs, see MN 39.

38 The taking of disciplinary sanctions against POWs can give rise to some of the issues discussed above. Although styled as 'disciplinary', the punishment imposed by a commander might, in reality, be criminal in nature, requiring the same degree of independence and impartiality as that applicable to a court. This requirement could clearly not be met by a commander acting alone. Even if a POW waived his right to an independent and impartial court, and accepted the punishment of the camp commander under Article 96 GC III, there might be no breach of his rights under a human rights treaty but a POW cannot renounce any rights under GC III.[59] Indeed, a denial of the rights to a POW of a fair and regular trial prescribed in the Convention is a grave breach of GC III.

39 The basic ingredients of fair disciplinary[60] and trial[61] hearings, along with the proper treatment of POWs subjected to these procedures, are contained in GC III.[62] These can only be said to be supplemented as a means of interpretation by equivalent procedures in human rights treaties. These treaties will continue to apply during armed conflict, except in so far as there is any derogation notice issued in respect of those rights from which a state party is permitted to derogate. A relevant treaty will apply on the territory of the detaining state and, if that state detains POWs during the course of military operations abroad, there too.[63]

40 A human rights treaty may go so far as to amount to the *lex specialis* on a specific point. Thus, the prohibition of the use of the death penalty accepted by the detaining state may, in effect, mean that Articles 100 and 101 GC III will have no significance.

41 Although a detaining state is permitted to transfer a POW to another state which is a party to GC III,[64] it will be unable to do so if there is a real risk that the fair trial provisions

---

[57] Art 106 GC III. See also Ch 59, MN 54–58, of this volume. In Pictet Commentary GC III, the term 'petition' was used to take into account the fact that, at the time, there was no appeal under 'Anglo-Saxon legislation' from the decision of a court-martial and that a convicted person could only petition higher command to reconsider the decision of that court. The term 'petition' could now mean a petition for clemency from the head of state, or (under its earlier meaning) a petition which is in reality an appeal to higher military authorities. In the case of the latter interpretation, the ECtHR would be likely to take the view that any non-judicial alteration of a decision of a judicial body would indicate a lack of independence of that judicial body.

[58] Art 75(4)(j) AP I does not give a right to appeal unless such a right exists within the law of the state concerned. The ICRC CIHL Study does not go further than Art 75 AP I.

[59] Art 7 GC III.   [60] Art 96 GC III.   [61] Arts 99, 102, 103, 105 GC III.

[62] See Ch 59, MN 23–52, of this volume, and Art 75 AP I.

[63] Although the ECtHR, in *Al-Skeini v United Kingdom*, Judgment, 7 July 2011, was concerned with the position in occupied territory, it is likely that the authority and control over individuals would be sufficient to bring POWs within the jurisdiction of the Detaining Power for the purposes of fair trial rights. A similar position is likely to be taken by the HRCttee under the ICCPR. Where the obligations under a human rights treaty conflict with GC III, it must have been intended by states party to both treaties in relation to Art 5 ECHR (permissible grounds for deprivation of liberty) that GC III will prevail; ECtHR, *Hassan v United Kingdom*, Judgment, 16 September 2014, paras 109–111.

[64] Art 12 GC III (see Ch 47, MN 41–67 of this volume). The detaining state must be satisfied as to the willingness and ability of the receiving state to comply with GC III. In *United States v Noriega*, 694 F Supp 2d 1268 (2007); 695 F Supp 2d 1358 (2007), the court concluded that Art 12 did not prevent extradition of Noriega

of GC III will not, or cannot, be applied should the transfer take place. The trial of a POW could be conducted by the detaining state for a crime committed whilst he was a POW, or for a crime committed prior to capture. A number of different states may also wish to try that same individual for a crime committed prior to capture. The detaining state will be unable to transfer him if it considers that there is a real risk that any trial in the receiving state would be before a court (whether military or not) lacking the necessary independence and impartiality, or where the treatment of the POW would infringe GC III and/or its human rights obligations.

C. Relevance in Non-International Armed Conflicts

Geneva Convention III applies only during an IAC. The effect of this is that an individual captured by opposing forces during a non-international armed conflict (NIAC) is not entitled to POW status under that Convention, although one or all parties to the conflict may treat individuals in a similar way.[65]   42

D. Legal Consequences of a Violation

Those who have wilfully deprived a POW of the 'rights of fair and regular trial prescribed in [GC III]' will have committed a grave breach of that Convention.[66] As with all grave breaches of GC III, states are required to enact any legislation necessary to provide effective penal sanctions, so as to enable a defendant, whatever his nationality, to be tried under its law.[67] In addition, any denial of a POW's right to a fair trial granted by a human rights treaty could result in the relevant human rights body holding the detaining state responsible for a violation of human rights law.[68]   43

---

to France, and that it was sufficient for the US (as the Detaining Power) to satisfy itself that Noriega would receive in France 'the same benefits he has enjoyed during his confinement in the United States' (695 F Supp 2d 1358, 1360). Although the court relied upon a declaration made by the US State Department that these rights were those 'to which Noriega was entitled under this Court's ruling *and* as specified in Geneva III' (ibid), it did not require the US Government to obtain an undertaking from France that Noriega would be accorded the status of a POW. It is suggested that the court's reasoning is not consistent with Art 12. A prerequisite of the obligation of the transferring state to satisfy 'itself of the willingness and ability of [the receiving state] to apply the Convention' must be that the receiving state will accord any transferee the status of a POW, since it is only such a person who is entitled as of right to the protections of GC III. An obligation on the receiving state merely to provide 'the same benefits' to a transferee as he enjoyed in the transferring state is not only difficult to assess, but also fails to recognize that a POW is entitled to all the rights given by GC III, whether they are reflected in those 'benefits' or not. *Quaere* whether Saddam Hussein was entitled to POW status when captured by US forces in December 2003. If so, the US, as a detaining state, would have had to consider whether by handing him over to the Iraqi authorities in 2004, he would be denied his rights under GC III, or whether this constituted a case of repatriation. In ECtHR, *Saddam Hussein v Albania et al*, Admissibility Decision, 14 March 2006, the Court decided only that he was not within the jurisdiction of a state party to the ECHR. It did not consider any issue under GC III. It would appear that the detaining state could not transfer a POW to the ICC, since that court is not a party to the GCs.

[65] See generally Ch 25 and 48, MN 114–116, of this volume.
[66] Art 130 GC III and, for those states party to it, the ICC Statute, Art 8(2)(a)(vi). In an attempt to prevent a grave breach of this nature, a POW could invoke Art 78 GC III, or, where this is permitted by the law of the detaining state, bring an action in its courts; *United States v Noriega*, 808 F Supp 791, 797.
[67] Art 129 GC III.
[68] It is likely that the ECtHR would decide that a state party to the ECHR will owe obligations to a POW under Art 6 of that Convention; ECtHR, *Al-Skeini v United Kingdom*, above n 63. The fair trial rights granted

E. Critical Assessment

44 The system of disciplinary sanctions and judicial procedures envisaged by GC III is based upon military disciplinary systems as they existed in 1949, and upon the assumption that a detaining state will have a military legal system in place which will guarantee fair disciplinary hearings or military court trials for POWs. To ensure protection of POWs, GC III sets out minimum safeguards—that the court should be independent and impartial, along with some basic trial rights—which we would now describe as human rights standards. It is for states to ensure that their military courts[69] (in particular) can fulfil the obligations in Article 82 to 108 GC III. In practice, some governments will be unwilling to consider a change to their military legal systems in the face of opposition from their senior military commanders, who are often considered to be the best individuals to judge the needs of military discipline. The effect of this will be that POWs may be faced with a military court which will fail the test of objective independence and impartiality, and which cannot therefore comply with the requirements of GC III.

45 The relationship between the obligations contained in GC III and national law has been referred to above. This will be a particularly important issue if the national law and procedure of the military court system of the detaining state, applicable to members of its armed forces, fails to comply with the obligations of that state under GC III. There is a very real possibility that this will be the case, since a state is unlikely to change its military court system in the event that it becomes a Detaining Power and is required to try a POW before those same courts.

PETER ROWE

---

by a human rights treaty may not be identical with the prohibition on the denial of a fair and regular trial under Art 130 GC III, since the latter refers to the rights 'prescribed in this Convention'.

[69] A 'military' court may take a variety of forms, depending upon its type of membership.

Chapter 51. Release, Accommodation in Neutral Countries, and Repatriation of Prisoners of War

Marco Sassòli

	MN
A. Introduction	1
B. Meaning and Application	7
I. Repatriation and accommodation in neutral countries during hostilities	7
a. Repatriation of wounded and sick prisoners of war	7
b. Unilateral repatriation and exchanges of able-bodied prisoners of war	10
c. Rules common to all cases of repatriation during hostilities	11
d. Accommodation in a neutral country	13
II. Repatriation at the end of active hostilities	20
a. Determination of the end of active hostilities	20
b. International armed conflicts turning into non-international armed conflicts	24
c. Unilateral and unconditional character of the obligation	25
d. The non-refoulement principle and relevance of the refusal of the prisoner of war to be repatriated	30
e. Obligations of the Power on which the prisoner of war depends?	43
f. Destination of the prisoners of war	44
g. Practical arrangements and modalities	45
III. Cases where repatriation at the end of active hostilities is not required	48
IV. Status and treatment of prisoners of war who are not repatriated	49
C. Relevance in Non-International Armed Conflicts	51
D. Legal Consequences of a Violation	56
E. Critical Assessment	64

Select Bibliography

Dinstein, Y., 'The Release of Prisoners of War', in Mélanges Pictet 37

Fischer, H., 'Protection of Prisoners of War', in D. Fleck (ed), *Handbook on International Humanitarian Law* (2nd edn, Oxford: OUP, 2008) 367

Pictet Commentary GC III, at 506–57

C. Maia, R. Kolb and D. Scalia, *La protection des prisonniers de guerre en droit international humanitaire* (Brussels: Bruylant, 2015), at 447–554.

Sassòli, M., 'The Status, Treatment and Repatriation of Deserters under International Humanitarian Law', *Yearbook of the International Institute of Humanitarian Law* (1985) 9

Shields Delessert, C., *Release and Repatriation of Prisoners of War at the End of Active Hostilities: A Study of Article 118, Paragraph 1, of the Third Geneva Convention Relative to the Treatment of Prisoners of War* (Zurich: Schulthess, 1977)

de Zayas, A., 'Repatriation', in MPEPIL

A. Introduction

Under international humanitarian law (IHL), and independently of any *jus ad bellum* considerations, the only legitimate aim which may be pursued in armed conflict is to

1

weaken the military potential of the adversary. The obligation to respect enemy combatants who surrender or are otherwise *hors de combat* would not be realistic if prisoners of war (POWs) could not be deprived of their freedom, in order to hinder them from participating in hostilities. This purpose of internment indicates when it must end: when POWs could not participate anyway, either because hostilities have ended or when they are, for the foreseeable duration of the hostilities, individually unable to participate therein. From this purpose, it also follows that a Detaining Power may release POWs earlier: when they promise not to return, for the duration of the hostilities, to the power for which they had fought (release on parole, see Chapter 48 of this volume, MN 66–70). In addition, the aim of hindering their participation in hostilities can be achieved by interning them in a neutral country. Such accommodation in a neutral country is encouraged by Geneva Convention (GC) III. As it involves an end of captivity by the enemy, it is discussed in this chapter. Lastly, a Detaining Power may unilaterally or in an exchange agree to the earlier repatriation of POWs, and in some circumstances it is even encouraged to do so.

2   The main legal issues arising in relation to the repatriation of POWs that frequently led to controversies and human suffering in the past, are:

— exactly when the obligation to repatriate all POWs arises;
— whether this obligation is unilateral and independent of the repatriation by the adversary of POWs belonging to the Detaining Power;
— whether and when an objection by POWs to being repatriated may authorize or oblige the Detaining Power not to repatriate them, and what their protection will be after such a refusal.

3   In history, delayed repatriation of some or all POWs frequently led to unnecessary suffering and additional obstacles to peace once active hostilities had ended. The Hague Regulations did not fix an exact time for repatriation; they stipulated only that it be '[a]fter the conclusion of peace […] as quickly as possible'. The 1929 Geneva Convention Relative to the Treatment of Prisoners of War required belligerents to agree on the issue, in particular 'normally [to] include' stipulations on the issue in a ceasefire agreement. Even in recent conflicts, reciprocity considerations caused years of delay in the repatriation of all POWs. More than 1,000 Moroccan POWs remained detained for up to 15 years after the end of active hostilities.[1] Conversely, at the end of the Second World War, millions of POWs were forcibly repatriated to the Soviet Union where many of them were executed or sent to labour camps, some simply because the Soviet Union considered that these prisoners should not have surrendered to Nazi Germany.[2] In many contemporary conflicts, POWs still fear repatriation, inter alia because they are considered as traitors by their own states.

4   Release means the end of a deprivation of freedom, while repatriation in the context of POWs means return to the Power on which they depend, i.e. in whose armed forces they served before falling into the hands of the enemy. (This will be discussed further below in MN 44.) The provisions of GC III on the release and repatriation of POWs are organized

---

[1] See UN Doc S/2001/398 of 24 April 2001, para 9; and E. David, *Principes de droit des conflits armés* (4th edn, Brussels: Bruylant, 2008), at 596.
[2] C. Shields Delessert, *Release and Repatriation of Prisoners of War at the End of Active Hostilities: A Study of Article 118, Paragraph 1, of the Third Geneva Convention Relative to the Treatment of Prisoners of War* (Zurich: Schulthess, 1977), at 154–6.

as follows: section I of Part IV (Articles 109–117) deals with the termination of captivity during hostilities; and section II of Part IV (Articles 118 and 119) with release and repatriation at the end of hostilities. (Section III on the termination of captivity by death has been discussed in Chapter 14 of this volume.)

During hostilities, Article 109 sets out the principle that some categories of wounded or sick POWs (and, under Article 114, those who suffered from accidents) must be directly repatriated (except if they object). It also encourages accommodation in neutral countries of other categories of wounded and sick POWs, and agreements for the repatriation or internment in neutral countries of able-bodied POWs who were interned for a long time. Article 110 and Annex I to the Convention—the Model Agreement Concerning Direct Repatriation and Accommodation in Neutral Countries of Wounded and Sick Prisoners of War—detail who should be repatriated and who should be interned in a neutral country. Articles 112 and 113, as well as Annex II to the Convention—the Regulations Concerning Mixed Medical Commissions—deal with the establishment and functioning of Mixed Medical Commissions, which determine who benefits from the preceding rules. Article 111 encourages agreements allowing the internment of able-bodied POWs in a neutral country. Article 115 deals with the special case of POWs undergoing sentences; Article 116 with the costs of repatriation; and Article 117 prohibits the employment of repatriated POWs on active military service.

At the end of hostilities, the key provision of Part IV is Article 118 paragraph 1, which prescribes that POWs must be 'released and repatriated without delay after the cessation of active hostilities', except, under Article 119 paragraph 5, if they are indicted or sentenced. The remaining paragraphs of Articles 118 and 119 deal with the repatriation procedure, its costs, the treatment of POWs and their belongings during repatriation, and with the search for dispersed POWs.

B. Meaning and Application

I. Repatriation and accommodation in neutral countries during hostilities

a. Repatriation of wounded and sick prisoners of war

Prisoners of war who are seriously wounded or sick, including those who suffered from non-self-inflicted accidents during internment,[3] must be repatriated during hostilities, as their internment is no longer needed to prevent them from participating in hostilities. Article 110 paragraph 1(1)–(3) GC III defines what constitutes being 'seriously wounded or sick' for the purposes of benefiting from the right to direct repatriation. Under Article 110 paragraph 1(2), this includes POWs who are unlikely to recover within one year. While this period may have been appropriate in contexts such as the Second World War, which was still fresh in the minds of the drafters of the 1949 Diplomatic Conference, considering the brevity of most contemporary armed conflicts and the progress made by medical science, the period of one year should arguably be reduced. In the opinion of the present author, this necessitates a revision of the Convention, or it may—and should—be stipulated in a special agreement between the parties to the conflict. A special agreement concluded between the belligerents to define the categories and modalities of prisoners to be repatriated is given preference by

---

[3] Art 114 GC III.

GC III. A Model Agreement annexed to the Convention lists typical examples of medical diagnoses which must lead to direct repatriation. These examples are not exhaustive and do not preclude the obligation to repatriate similar cases.[4] It has been suggested that this Model Agreement should be revised and completed according to the development of medical science,[5] but this has never been done. Belligerents are not obliged to conclude an agreement based on the model, but any other agreement may not adversely affect POWs by depriving those defined in Article 110 paragraph 1 of their right to be directly repatriated.[6] In the absence of an agreement, the Detaining Power must nevertheless repatriate such persons, and bear the costs of such repatriation up to its frontiers. The principles of the Model Agreement and of the Regulations Concerning Mixed Medical Commissions apply in this case.[7]

8 Generally, Mixed Medical Commissions must determine who must be repatriated under Article 110 paragraph 1 and the criteria established in a special agreement and the Model Agreement. Such Commissions must be set up upon the outbreak of hostilities and function in accordance with regulations outlined in Annex II to GC III.[8] Decisions of Mixed Medical Commissions must be communicated to the Detaining Power, the International Committee of the Red Cross (ICRC), the Protecting Power, and the POW; and the POW must receive, in the event that repatriation is proposed, a repatriation certificate.[9] Article 113 clarifies who is entitled to an examination and how such an examination must proceed. A Mixed Medical Commission consists of three members: one appointed by the Detaining Power and two neutral nationals, a surgeon and a physician, appointed by the ICRC acting in agreement with the Protecting Power (if such a Power exists). Under the regulations annexed to GC III, the neutral members must be approved by the parties to the conflict concerned, i.e. equally by the Power upon which the POWs depend. If the ICRC is unable to appoint such neutral members, perhaps because the parties concerned do not agree, the Protecting Power must appoint them. In this case, no approval by the parties is needed. In most recent conflicts, no Protecting Power was appointed. Nevertheless, Mixed Medical Commissions established in conformity with GC III functioned in the Vietnam War,[10] and in the conflict between Iran and Iraq.[11]

9 If no Mixed Medical Commissions exist, or, if they do exist, before they decide on an individual case, the Detaining Power may—and in the author's view must—spontaneously repatriate POWs who fall, in its view, under Article 110 paragraph 1.[12] Indeed, the obligation under Article 109 paragraph 1 is not dependent upon a decision by a Mixed Medical Commission. Repatriation constitutes a unilateral obligation, 'regardless of number or rank';[13] 'man for man exchanges are therefore expressly prohibited'.[14] Seriously wounded POWs were repatriated during several recent international armed conflicts (IACs) in which no Mixed Medical Commissions functioned,[15] but this was often done within the

---

[4] Pictet Commentary GC III, at 650.
[5] J.-M. Rubli, 'Repatriation and Accommodation in Neutral Countries of Wounded and Sick Prisoners of War', 5 *IRRC* 57 (1965) 623, at 629.
[6] Art 6 para 1 GC III.   [7] Art 110 para 4 GC III.
[8] See for details Rubli, above n 5, at 625–8.
[9] See Art 11, Regulations concerning Mixed Medical Commissions, Annex II to GC III, and Repatriation Certificate, Annex IV E to GC III.
[10] *ICRC Annual Reports* 1967, at 25; 1968, at 30; 1969, at 34; 1970, at 37.
[11] *ICRC Annual Reports* 1982, at 64–5; 1983, at 57–9; 1984, at 62; 1985, at 67–9; 1986, at 66–7; 1987, at 77.
[12] Art 112 para 2 GC III; and Pictet Commentary GC III, at 509 and 528.
[13] Art 109 para 1 GC III.   [14] Pictet Commentary GC III, at 509.
[15] See *ICRC Annual Reports* 1956, at 30 (Suez War); 1962, at 23 (Indian POWs held in China); 1967, at 6–7 (Arab–Israeli conflict); 12 *IRRC* 132 (1972), at 138–43 and 12 *IRRC* 133 (1972), at 199–203 (India and

framework of an exchange. If such exchanges implied that POWs who were entitled to repatriation under GC III were not repatriated, then those agreements violated IHL. In all cases, the ICRC arranged and organized the repatriations.

b. Unilateral repatriation and exchanges of able-bodied prisoners of war

Although frequent in practice, exchanges of able-bodied POWs are not favoured by GC III because they can be considered to be an exercise in trading human beings, and always risk leaving some POWs behind, as adversaries never detain exactly the same number of POWs. The term 'exchange' appears in GC III only for correspondence (between POWs and their families). The non-repatriation of POWs who must be repatriated under IHL, because they cannot be exchanged, would be a violation of IHL. However, during hostilities, whenever repatriation is optional and subject to the agreement of the parties, exchange agreements do not violate IHL.[16] It is however preferable to link repatriation not to numbers but to objective criteria such as length of captivity,[17] age, or sex, or to repatriate 'all for all'.[18] From a humanitarian point of view, unilateral repatriations of POWs are the best solution[19] and may initiate a cycle of repatriations in a spirit of positive reciprocity. 10

c. Rules common to all cases of repatriation during hostilities

Some rules are common to all cases of repatriation during hostilities. First, 'no sick or injured prisoner of war [...] may be repatriated against his will during hostilities'.[20] Even though this prohibition was opposed by many delegations during the 1949 Diplomatic Conference,[21] the Pictet Commentary considers that it should apply, by analogy, to all repatriations during hostilities.[22] Indeed, POWs themselves are best qualified to judge, in the necessarily volatile situation reigning during hostilities, whether a repatriation, which the Convention presumes to be in their interest, is indeed preferable to continued internment. In all cases mentioned above—MN 9 and 10—the ICRC visited POWs before their repatriation and checked to see if they wished to be repatriated; where they did not, this wish was respected. 11

Secondly, no person repatriated during hostilities 'may be employed on active military service' during the hostilities in the course of which the POW was captured.[23] This applies to all cases of repatriation during hostilities and is a consequence of the principle which underpins GC III, namely, that the internment of POWs is justified by the 12

Pakistan); UN Docs S/16963 of 19 February 1985, S/17216 of 24 May 1985, and S/17258 of 12 June 1985 (Iran and Iraq); *ICRC News Release* 00/01 of 20 January 2000 (Zimbabwean and Rwandan POWs in the conflict in the Democratic Republic of Congo).

[16] UK Ministry of Defence, *The Manual of the Law of Armed Conflict* (Oxford: OUP, 2004), para 8.146.1; ICRC CIHL Database, Canada, Rule 128, Section C, III; ICRC CIHL Study, at 2886 (Israel), at 2886 (The Netherlands), at 2886 (United States). See, for practice between Angola, Cuba, and South Africa in the conflict in Angola and Namibia, *ICRC Annual Reports* 1984, at 10, and 1989, at 13.

[17] A criterion explicitly mentioned in Art 109 para 3 GC III. A period of 18 months to two years of captivity has been suggested by Shields Delessert, above n 2, at 117–18.

[18] ICRC CIHL Study, at 2885 (Croatia/Socialist Federative Republic of Yugoslavia).

[19] North Vietnam periodically released US POWs (see *ICRC Annual Report* 1969, at 37); in 1982, the UK repatriated 190 able-bodied Argentinean POWs during the Falklands/Malvinas conflict (see A. de Zayas, 'Repatriation', in MPEPIL (2011), para 3); Chad released Libyan POWs (see *ICRC Annual Report* 1983, at 21).

[20] Art 109 para 3 GC III.

[21] Canada, UK, Belgium, New Zealand, Final Record, vol II-A, at 291; A. Rosas, *The Legal Status of Prisoners of War: A Study of International Humanitarian Law Applicable in Armed Conflicts* (Helsinki: Suomalainen Tiedeakatemia, 1976), at 476–7.

[22] Pictet Commentary GC III, at 512–13.   [23] Art 117 GC III.

purpose of preventing them from participating in hostilities. According to Article 6 GC III, even an agreement on the repatriation of POWs could not authorize such employment. Furthermore, a POW cannot waive the prohibition by voluntarily enrolling for active military service. Article 7 GC III bars such waiver, and the prohibition is clearly equally established in favour of the Detaining Power, which has a right not to see POWs it repatriated during hostilities again engaged in active military service against it. It remains to be clarified how broadly the term 'employed on active military service' must be understood. The Pictet Commentary suggests that it covers 'any participation, whether direct or indirect, in armed operations against the [former] detaining power or its allies [...] but does not prevent their enrolment in unarmed military units engaged solely in auxiliary, complementary or similar work'.[24] 'Active military service' is certainly broader than 'direct participation in hostilities'.[25] However, the 1949 Diplomatic Conference rejected the proposal to include within it every form of military service, i.e. every case of integration into the military hierarchy.[26] In any case, even former POWs recaptured as combatants while engaged in active military service would benefit from POW status and should be eligible for repatriation during hostilities, if they fulfil the medical requirements making such repatriation compulsory.[27] The phrase 'may be employed' in Article 117 GC III indicates that the prohibition is not addressed to the individual but to the state. Therefore, a violation of the prohibition by the state should not deprive members of its armed forces of their POW status.

d. Accommodation in a neutral country

13 The objective of preventing POWs from participating further in hostilities can be achieved just as easily by internment in neutral hands. From a humanitarian point of view, this has the advantage of the POWs not being in the power of hostile forces but rather in a country which is often able and willing to offer better medical treatment, accommodation, and services than belligerents. In the First World War this system produced excellent results.[28]

14 Three cases of internment in neutral countries must be distinguished. First, the less seriously wounded and sick, who fulfil the conditions of Article 110 paragraph 2 detailed in the list appearing in section I.B of the Model Agreement (see above, MN 5), may be interned in a neutral country if such internment increases their prospects of recovery. Detaining Powers have an obligation to endeavour to reach such an agreement.[29] In this case, Mixed Medical Commissions fulfil the same role as for direct repatriations (see MN 8). Secondly, for able-bodied POWs who have undergone a long period of captivity, states are entitled to conclude such agreements, although this remains an option rather than an obligation.[30] In both cases, there is no legal requirement to have the agreement of the Power on which the POWs depend.[31] While it may be difficult to imagine a neutral country interning soldiers of a belligerent country without the latter's agreement, under the

---

[24] Pictet Commentary GC III, at 539.
[25] See ICRC, 'Interpretive Guidance on the Notion of Direct Participation in Hostilities under International Humanitarian Law', 90 *IRRC* 872 (2008) 991.
[26] Final Record, vol II-A, at 374–5. See, for a US undertaking during the Vietnam War going even further, R. Falk, 'International Law Aspects of Repatriation of Prisoners of War during Hostilities', 67 *AJIL* (1973) 465, at 470.
[27] Pictet Commentary GC III, at 516–17.   [28] Ibid, at 511.   [29] Art 109 para 2 GC III.
[30] Art 109 para 3 GC III.
[31] Pictet Commentary GC III, at 521. See, however, the opposing view of the Netherlands: ICRC CIHL Database, The Netherlands, Rule 128, Section A, III.

law of neutrality, the neutral country would anyway be obliged to guard such persons and ensure they do not take part again in military operations.[32] The third case, encouraged by Article 111—internment of other able-bodied POWs in a neutral country—requires the agreement of the Detaining Power, the Power on which the POWs depend, and the neutral country.

Any transfer of POWs to neutral countries is subject to Article 12 GC III, requiring that before a transfer takes place, a Detaining Power has to satisfy itself of the willingness and ability of the Receiving Power to apply the Convention. Moreover Article 12 states that the Detaining Power retains a residual responsibility and that it must, if necessary, request the return of the POWs.

The duration of the internment in a neutral country is fixed in the special agreement. This notwithstanding, POWs must[33] be repatriated when they fulfil the conditions laid out in the provisions for the direct repatriation of seriously wounded and sick POWs, or when their mental or physical powers remain, even after treatment, considerably impaired.[34] In the case of seriously wounded and sick POWs, arguably, no agreement by the former Detaining Power is necessary, as direct repatriation is an obligation of the Detaining Power and of the transferee neutral country.[35] In any case, POWs must be repatriated at the end of active hostilities.[36]

As required by Article 4(B)(2) GC III,[37] as a minimum (with the exception of some provisions mentioned in that Article), any transferred POWs continue to benefit from the provisions relating to the treatment of POWs under GC III. The parties may not derogate from these provisions to the detriment of POWs in any transfer agreement.[38] Furthermore, every transferred POW benefits from the treatment agreed upon by the parties to the transfer agreement.

Since the First World War, the only context in which POWs have been interned in neutral countries has arguably been a non-international armed conflict (NIAC)—the armed conflict in Afghanistan between 1979 and 1989.[39] However, the Union of Soviet Socialist Republics (USSR) had a massive troop presence in Afghanistan. Many Soviet soldiers fell into the power of Afghan resistance movements. To alleviate their fate, the ICRC successfully negotiated an agreement with the USSR, the Afghan opposition movements, Pakistan, and Switzerland, under which Soviet soldiers detained by the Afghan opposition movements could be transferred to and interned in Switzerland for two years, by application of GC III *by analogy*. Eleven Soviet soldiers visited by the ICRC accepted this offer. Those who still wished to be repatriated after the two-year period of internment

---

[32] Art 14 para 2 of [Hague] Convention V respecting the rights and duties of neutral powers and persons in case of war on land of 18 October 1907.

[33] The French text stipulates '*seront rapatriés*', which corresponds to an obligation that should have been translated as 'shall be repatriated' (Pictet Commentary GC III, at 519).

[34] Art 110 para 3 GC III.

[35] Art 12 para 2, and see Pictet Commentary GC III, at 519–20. Anyway, Art 4(B)(2) GC III guarantees them POW treatment, which includes the repatriation obligations discussed in this chapter.

[36] Arts 111 and 118 para 1 GC III.

[37] Art 4(B)(2) GC III applies to persons whom neutral countries 'are required to intern under international law', and Art 14 para 2 of Hague Convention V (above n 32) requires that wounded and sick POWs interned in a neutral country be guarded by that country, as it must ensure their not taking part again in military operations.

[38] Art 6 GC III.

[39] It should be noted, however, that many saw this conflict as an IAC, starting with the Soviet invasion of Afghanistan, followed by the installation, by the USSR, of an Afghan Government friendly to the USSR,

were repatriated to the Soviet Union.⁴⁰ The absence of other examples of internment in a neutral country may be due to the short duration of most recent IACs, the difficulty of finding countries which consider themselves, and are considered by the parties, as neutral and which are willing to accept POWs, and to disagreements between belligerents about their respective status and how to classify the conflict.

19   The precedent of Afghanistan equally demonstrates that in state practice, the wishes of the individual POWs were ascertained and respected before they were accommodated in a neutral country. It is not certain that Article 109 paragraph 3 also applies to internment in neutral countries. However, a Detaining Power transferring such POWs against their will to a neutral country should at least take steps to ensure that that country will respect any wishes the POWs might have not to be repatriated at the end of active hostilities. In addition, the arguments mentioned below (MN 30–42) for respecting the wish of a POW not to be repatriated at the end of active hostilities, should be even more persuasive as regards a transfer to a neutral country during hostilities.

II. Repatriation at the end of active hostilities

a. Determination of the end of active hostilities

20   In view of the problems, delays, and resulting suffering linked with repatriation at the end of past conflicts (see MN 3), GC III links the point in time when repatriation must begin to the facts on the ground and not to a legal situation, nor to agreements between the parties.⁴¹ Under Article 118 GC III, repatriations must begin 'without delay after the cessation of active hostilities'. The meaning of 'without delay' will be discussed below (MN 45–46). The crucial question is when active hostilities actually *end*. A mere suspension of hostilities is not sufficient;⁴² but even when there is an apparent end to hostilities, the future cannot be predicted and resumption is always possible.⁴³ In an international society where the use of force is outlawed, IACs seldom end with the *debellatio* (total defeat) of one side or a genuine peace. Most frequently, they result in unstable ceasefires, often imposed by the United Nations (UN) or third states, they continue at a lower intensity, or they are frozen. Acts of violence often break out again later. Moreover, declarations by states in international *fora* and the actual behaviour of their forces do not always coincide.

21   The concept of 'active hostilities' is more restrictive than that of 'military operations',⁴⁴ because the former necessarily consist of acts of violence while the latter need not. The concept of hostilities has been defined in another context as 'the (collective) resort by the parties to the conflict to means and methods of injuring the enemy'.⁴⁵ Ongoing troop

---

and years of fighting between that Government, supported by the USSR, and Afghan resistance movements harboured in Pakistan and supported by the United States.

⁴⁰ See, for this precedent, 24 *IRRC* 241 (1984) 230, at 239–40.
⁴¹ See the German Military Manual ZDv 15/2, *Humanitäres Völkerrecht in bewaffneten Konflikten, ein Handbuch* (August 1992), para 731. The position taken by India in 1972, that it would repatriate Pakistani POWs only once a peace treaty was signed and Pakistan recognized Bangladesh, therefore clearly violated GC III (see P. Bretton, 'De quelques problèmes du droit de la guerre dans le conflit indo-pakistanais', 18 *AFDI* (1972) 201, at 218–21).
⁴² H. Lauterpacht (ed), *Oppenheim's International Law* (7th edn, London: Longmans, 1952), vol II, at 613.
⁴³ India mentioned in 1971 the mere possibility that hostilities might resume as one of the reasons for not repatriating Pakistani POWs, see H. Levie, 'Legal Aspects of the Continued Detention of the Pakistani Prisoners of War by India', 67 *AJIL* (1973) 512, at 513.
⁴⁴ Used in Art 6 GC IV (see Ch 3 of this volume, MN 17).
⁴⁵ Interpretive guidance, above n 25, at 1013.

movements do not preclude there being an end to active hostilities. Further, and contrary to the justification given by Iran for not repatriating Iraqi POWs after the end of active hostilities in 1987,[46] the mere fact that the adversary continues to occupy part of the territory of the Detaining Power constitutes an even weaker justification for not repatriating POWs. Even if resistance fighters in an occupied territory are interned under Article 4(A)(2) GC III, they must, in the author's view, be released once violent resistance against the Occupying Power and possible hostilities outside the occupied territory have ceased. The same must be true for former members of the armed forces of the Occupied Power re-interned by the Occupying Power under Article 4(B)(1) GC III. Under this provision, they may be re-interned even if they were in the first place liberated 'while hostilities were going on outside the territory it occupies'. Once active hostilities end, within and outside the occupied territory, they must however be released, like all other POWs, under the general rule.

On the one hand, mere absence of fighting is certainly not sufficient. On the other hand, it is too much to require that the conditions must 'render it out of the question for the defeated party to resume hostilities',[47] since this would not be the case even when a peace treaty has been concluded.[48] There must be a reasonable expectation that hostilities will not resume.[49] The complete defeat and occupation of one party satisfies this condition. In other cases, the determination of whether a risk of resumption exists must take agreements (such as a ceasefire which is unlimited in duration) into account. If agreements actually end hostilities, the repatriation process must start, even if sporadic ceasefire violations and military casualties continue to occur.[50] If an armistice is monitored by peacekeeping forces, this is generally a good indication of a lasting cessation of hostilities.[51] The same applies to a United Nations Security Council (UNSC) Resolution calling for an end of hostilities if it is respected on the ground, as well as to unilateral declarations by both belligerents that they will stop the fighting. In the absence of an agreement or unilateral declarations, it is reasonable to wait for a certain period to determine whether active hostilities have actually ended.[52] A determination then equally depends on what parties are saying. In the reverse situation, when there is continuing fighting on

---

[46] See J. Quigley, 'Iran and Iraq and the Obligations to Release and Repatriate Prisoners of War after the Close of Hostilities', 5 *American University Journal of International Law and Policy* (1989) 73, at 75; and, e.g., UN Doc S/21104 of 24 January 1990.

[47] Lauterpacht (ed), above n 42, at 613.

[48] Y. Dinstein, 'The Release of Prisoners of War', in Mélanges Pictet 37, at 44.

[49] Shields Delessert, above n 2, at 97–105; G. Schwarzenberger and E.D. Brown, *A Manual of International Law* (6th edn, Abingdon: Professional Books, 1976), at 175, write 'when, in good faith, neither side expects a resumption of hostilities'. Dinstein, above n 48, at 44; R. Murphy and M. El Zeidy, 'Prisoner of War: A Comparative Study of the Principles of Humanitarian Law and Islamic Law of War', 9 *International Criminal Law Review* (2009) 623, at 636; H. Fischer, 'Protection of Prisoners of War', in D. Fleck (ed), *Handbook on International Humanitarian Law* (2nd edn, Oxford: OUP, 2008) 367, at 414–15 (the criterion must be an objective estimation).

[50] See *ICRC Annual Report* 2007, at 243 and 247 (Armenia and Azerbaijan).

[51] Fischer, above n 49, at 415.

[52] Rowe reports that after the surrender of Argentinean forces on the Falkland/Malvinas Islands, '[m]ost Argentinian prisoners of war were released nine days after the surrender [of 14 June but that] pending indications that hostilities had definitely ceased, we retained 593 selected prisoners until 14 July [...], [who] because of their specialist skills or their seniority [would] have greatly enhanced [Argentina's] ability to conduct further military operations against us': P. Rowe, 'Prisoners of War in the Gulf Area', in P. Rowe (ed), *The Gulf War 1990–91 in International and English Law* (London/New York: Sweet & Maxwell/Routledge, 1992) 188, at 202. The six-month period suggested by Shields Delessert, above n 2, at 105, is certainly too long under contemporary conditions.

the ground (despite an agreement or unilateral declarations), it is decisive whether this fighting corresponds with the will of the parties. A declaration by a party that it will not resume hostilities, responding to a similar declaration by the adverse party, must be presumed to be genuine, except where the facts on the ground clearly contradict it, or where the declaring authority has lost control over the state it represented. Indeed, a party that resumes hostilities it has declared to have ended will inevitably meet the opprobrium of the UN and third states. On the other hand, there could be a situation where a NIAC erupts involving forces that are not (or no longer) under the control of the state having declared the end of hostilities and its (former) adversary (a situation discussed below, MN 24).

23   The question of when the obligation to repatriate POWs becomes operative was adjudicated by the Eritrea–Ethiopia Claims Commission. While its decision was not very well defended, it is compatible with the position suggested here. On 18 June 2000, Ethiopia and Eritrea concluded an Agreement on the Cessation of Hostilities. The Commission did not consider that date as the starting point of the repatriation obligation, mentioning that it 'received no evidence regarding implementation of that agreement'.[53] Therefore, a subsequent Agreement of 12 December 2000 was considered as the starting point of the repatriation obligation, as it was to 'permanently terminate military hostilities', though the Commission failed to explain that this agreement had actually been implemented on the ground.[54]

b. *International armed conflicts turning into non-international armed conflicts*

24   Sometimes an armed conflict continues even though its character changes from an IAC to a NIAC. This could trigger the obligation to repatriate POWs, as only a minority opinion argues that in a NIAC the members of adverse armed forces or groups may be detained until the end of active hostilities without further procedures (see MN 53). When the conflict in Afghanistan, which started as an IAC, was considered to have turned into a NIAC with the election of the Karzai Government in 2002, the United States (US) arguably lost detention authority under GC III.[55] The US understandably objected that continuing hostilities in Afghanistan (and elsewhere) against the Taliban and Al-Qaeda made continued detention of Taliban and Al-Qaeda operatives necessary.[56] The US Supreme Court held that since active hostilities did not end in such a case, POWs need not be repatriated yet.[57] In the author's view, the fact that active hostilities had not ended as of 2014 did not justify automatic internment as for POWs, but necessitated, as soon as the IAC was over, individualized determination of the risk of participation in the NIAC. The US in fact undertook such determinations despite its stated position.[58] In addition, we should recall

---

[53] EECC, *Prisoners of War—Eritrea's Claim 17*, Partial Award, 1 July 2003, para 145.
[54] Ibid, para 146.
[55] See, for this discussion and references for the different positions, J. Bellinger and V. Padmanabhan, 'Detention Operations in Contemporary Conflicts: Four Challenges for the Geneva Conventions and Other Existing Law', 105 *AJIL* (2011) 201, at 230, in particular fn 158.
[56] *Maqaleh v Gates*, US Court of Appeals for the District Court of Columbia, 21 May 2010, 605 F 3d, at 4.
[57] *Hamdi v Rumsfeld*, 542 US 507 (2004), at 520–2.
[58] Information on the Combatant Status Review Tribunals/Administrative Review Boards can be found on US Department of Defense, *Combatant Status Review Tribunal* (17 October 2007), available at <http://www.defense.gov/news/combatant_Tribunals.html>. For an overview of the process of review in Afghanistan, see J.A. Bovarnick, 'Detainee Review Boards in Afghanistan: From Strategic Liability to Legitimacy', *The Army Lawyer* (June 2010) 8.

c. Unilateral and unconditional character of the obligation

Under Article 118 paragraph 1 GC III, the obligation to repatriate POWs does not depend upon an agreement between the parties. The Conference of Government Experts drafting the Geneva Conventions intended it to be unilateral.[60] Paragraphs 2 and 4 of the Article are careful in laying down rules on repatriation modalities and the costs of repatriations in the absence of an agreement between the parties. Paragraph 4(b) explicitly states that when an agreement on sharing the costs of repatriations is inevitable, '[t]he conclusion of this agreement shall in no circumstances justify any delay in the repatriation of the prisoners of war'. Each co-belligerent is bound individually for all POWs that it holds,[61] but if it has previously transferred POWs to a co-belligerent, it also remains jointly responsible for their release and repatriation.[62] Under Islamic law,[63] POWs 'may' be released against ransom or subject to reciprocity (two possibilities incompatible with GC III), or as a gracious act. It even recommends release when active hostilities have ceased. Strict respect for GC III is therefore not contrary to Islamic law.

While the obligation to repatriate is unilateral and unconditional, reciprocity considerations have frequently delayed the repatriation of all POWs. After the conflict in Cyprus, Turkey tried to establish a link between repatriation of POWs and the release of civilian detainees.[64] In the conflict between Iran and Iraq, tens of thousands of POWs were not repatriated until two years after the end of active hostilities,[65] and thousands of them were not repatriated until 12 years had passed.[66]

The issue of delay was also adjudicated by the Eritrea–Ethiopia Claims Commission, but in an unfortunate way. After the end of the conflict, Ethiopia repatriated more than a thousand POWs only 23 months after the end of active hostilities. Twenty months of the delay were found to be justified by the Commission for reasons of reciprocity,[67] although the parties had agreed 'to release and repatriate without delay all prisoners of war'.[68] The Commission admitted:

> The language of Article 118 is absolute. Nevertheless, as a practical matter, and as indicated by state practice, any state that has not been totally defeated is unlikely to release all the POWs it holds without assurance that its own personnel held by its enemy will also be released, and it is unreasonable to expect otherwise.[69]

---

[59] Art 5 para 1 GC III.
[60] Report on the Work of the Conference of Government Experts, at 243–4.
[61] See for India and Bangladesh, *ICRC Annual Reports* 1971, at 50 and 1974, at 20; and for the Indian argument that the agreement of both was necessary, Levie, above n 43, at 514. After the Second Gulf War the US and Saudi Arabia agreed that 'release and repatriation of prisoners of war would be a matter for joint approval of the two governments' (Rowe, above n 52, at 200).
[62] Art 12 para 3 GC III.   [63] Murphy and El Zeidy, above n 49, at 645–7.
[64] *ICRC Annual Report* 1974, at 11. See also the Indian argument that Pakistan should first have allowed the emigration of Bengalis, in Levie, above n 43, at 514.
[65] See, for the reciprocity argument made by Iraq, UN Doc S/21104 of 24 January 1990; and Quigley, above n 46, at 77 and 79.
[66] See, for a detailed account, David, above n 1, at 595; UN Doc S/RES/0598 of 20 July 1987; *ICRC Bulletin*, No 177, October 1990, at 1; *ICRC News Release* 00/06 of 12 April 2000.
[67] EECC, *POWs—Eritrea's Claim 17*, above n 53, paras 144–63.
[68] Peace Agreement between Ethiopia and Eritrea (Algiers, 2000), at 2(1) and (2).
[69] EECC, *POWs—Eritrea's Claim 17*, above n 53, para 148.

This is not only a sad finding about a frequent violation of IHL, but also an attempt by the Commission to justify it in law. The Commission noted that 'Eritrea suggested that the obligation to repatriate should be seen as unconditional but acknowledged the difficulty of the question and the contrary arguments under general law.'[70] Yet, under Article 60(5) of the Vienna Convention on the Law of Treaties (VCLT), the possibility for a state injured by a violation of a treaty to suspend its operation as a consequence of a breach does not apply 'to provisions relating to the protection of the human person contained in treaties of a humanitarian character, in particular to provisions prohibiting any form of reprisals against persons protected by such treaties'. Similarly, under the law of state responsibility, countermeasures are not permitted where they affect obligations of a 'humanitarian character prohibiting reprisals'.[71] Article 13 paragraph 3 GC III prohibits reprisals against POWs. Not repatriating POWs at the end of active hostilities in order to induce the power on which they depend to repatriate POWs clearly constitutes a measure of reprisal against POWs. It is therefore impossible to understand what 'arguments under general law' could have justified the conduct of Ethiopia. Nevertheless, the Commission found that 'given the character of the repatriation obligation and state practice, it is appropriate to consider the behavior of both Parties in assessing whether or when Ethiopia failed to meet its obligations under Article 118'.[72]

28   The reference by the Commission to 'state practice' in the author's view cannot be seen as a reference to subsequent practice which has to be taken into account in the interpretation of a treaty. The wording of Article 118 is clear, when considered in context and against the object and purpose of GC III, its unilateral (non-reciprocal) character is confirmed by rules of the law of treaties and of state responsibility. It might be argued that even such a rule could fall into desuetude and be replaced by a new rule of customary international law; however, first, the obligation to repatriate POWs (who do not object to being repatriated) might be a peremptory rule of international law (*jus cogens*), and could therefore be replaced only by another rule of *jus cogens* (which the alleged rule allowing repatriation to be subject to reciprocity is clearly not). Secondly, while repatriations of POWs were clearly often delayed for reciprocity reasons after GC III entered into force, such delays were criticized by other states, by the UN,[73] and by the ICRC.[74] Nor did the delaying states justify their delay by reference to a new rule of customary international law. There have also been other instances when states have repatriated POWs unilaterally,[75] or expressed the view that POWs must be repatriated unconditionally and unilaterally.[76] The alleged practice is therefore not general and it is not accompanied by an *opinio juris*. In short, state practice has not introduced a rule for reciprocity in the application of Article 118.

---

[70] Ibid, para 148.   [71] ILC Articles on State Responsibility, Art 50(1)(c).
[72] EECC, *POWs—Eritrea's Claim 17*, above n 53, para 149.
[73] See UN Doc S/RES/1369 of 14 September 2001, para 5(f) (concerning Eritrea and Ethiopia).
[74] See *ICRC Annual Reports* 2001, at 87 (Eritrea and Ethiopia); 2003, at 127 (Chad and Central African Republic); 2009, at 188; and 2010, at 212 (Eritrea and Djibouti).
[75] See *ICRC Annual Reports* 1971, at 41 (1967 Arab–Israeli conflict); 1988, at 36; and 1989, at 32 (unilateral repatriation by Libya despite Chad's refusal). See also ICRC CIHL Study, at 2863 (Bosnia/Serbia/Croatia); ICRC CIHL Study, at 2880 (ICRC); ICRC CIHL Study, at 2882 (Croatia/Federal Republic of Yugoslavia; Bosnia-Herzegovina/Serbia/Croatia; UN).
[76] See ICJ, *Case concerning Trial of Pakistani Prisoners of War (Pakistan v India)*, Pleadings of Pakistan, at 5 and 6; UK Ministry of Defence, above n 16, para 8.168; UN Doc S/PRST/1996/15 of 4 April 1996, at 2.

After the armed conflicts between Iran and Iraq,[77] in Bosnia-Herzegovina,[78] and 29
between Eritrea and Ethiopia,[79] Detaining Powers also tried to justify their refusal to
repatriate POWs without delay by the fact that the adverse party had not clarified the fate
of their missing servicemen. If reciprocity concerning repatriation of POWs were acceptable, such an extension would be understandable. Indeed, the repatriation obligation
extends not only to POWs registered by the ICRC, but to all POWs, including those who
are secretly detained in violation of GC III. The Eritrea–Ethiopia Claims Commission
was 'not prepared to conclude that Ethiopia violated its obligation [...] by suspending
temporarily further repatriations pending a response to a seemingly reasonable request
for clarification of the fate of a number of missing combatants it believed captured by
Eritrea who were not listed as POWs'.[80] Such a link is even less acceptable than subjecting the repatriation of POWs to reciprocity in general.[81] First, it is problematic to link
an obligation of result of one side (the obligation to release and repatriate POWs) with
an obligation of means of the other side (the obligation to clarify the fate of missing
persons). Secondly, and more importantly, the approach of the Commission would in
practice sound the death knell for the repatriation of POWs. Unfortunately, after every
armed conflict, the fate of many combatants, civilians, and POWs remains unclear, and
former belligerents do not undertake everything in their power to clarify the fate of such
persons.[82] Even today, there are still missing servicemen from the Second World War,
from the Korean War, the Vietnam War, the Arab–Israeli Wars, the conflict in Cyprus,
from the Iraq–Kuwait conflict in 1991, and from the conflicts in the former Yugoslavia.
Under the Commission's approach, hundreds of thousands of POWs from those wars
would have risked being retained until today. Fortunately, state practice, to which the
Commission refers without analysis, is more humane.

d. *The non-refoulement principle and relevance of the refusal of the prisoner of war to be repatriated*

Since the adoption of GC III, an increasing number of POWs have expressed a wish not 30
to be repatriated at the end of active hostilities. The controversy over whether such a wish
existed, how it could be validly established, and whether it allowed a Detaining Power
not to repatriate POWs expressing such a wish, gave rise to a major international dispute at the end of the Korean conflict. The starting point must be the wording of Article
118: 'Prisoners of war shall be released and repatriated without delay after the cessation
of active hostilities.' One might contend that the terms 'release' and 'repatriation' imply
two distinct operations, and that it is impossible to repatriate someone who has been
'released'.[83] But the wording might also imply that release and repatriation are two simultaneous and indissociable operations.[84]

The *travaux préparatoires* confirm the absolute character of the obligation. Austrian 31
proposals that POWs should be entitled to apply for their transfer to any other country

---

[77] *ICRC Annual Reports* 2004, at 278; 2005, at 304; 2007, at 334.
[78] C. Girod, 'Bosnia and Herzegovina: Tracing Missing Persons', 36 *IRRC* 312 (1996) 387, at 388.
[79] EECC, *POWs—Eritrea's Claim 17*, above n 53, para 153.
[80] Ibid, para 160.   [81] Equally critical David, above n 1, at 597.
[82] See M. Sassòli and M.-L. Tougas, 'The ICRC and the Missing', 84 *IRRC* 848 (2002) 727.
[83] B. Schapiro, 'Repatriation of Deserters', 29 *BYBIL* (1952) 310, at 323; M. Flory, 'Vers une nouvelle conception du prisonnier de guerre', 58 *RGDIP* (1954) 53, at 72.
[84] Shields Delessert, above n 2, at 175–84; Fischer, above n 49, at 412 and 414.

which is ready to accept them,[85] or that they must at least have the option of not returning to their country if they so desire,[86] were almost unanimously rejected. Reasons adduced for this rejection were strict immigration laws[87] and concerns that POWs would not be able to express their choice in complete freedom because the Detaining Power could exercise some pressure or influence. It has therefore been argued that this rejection ought not to be construed as prescribing forcible repatriation;[88] it was merely intended to prevent POWs from having the *right* to be sent at great expense 'to the other side of the world',[89] and to avoid introducing an escape clause that Detaining Powers might use as a pretext not to repatriate all other POWs.[90] At the time, some 2 million Second World War POWs who had served in the forces of the Axis Powers were still detained in the USSR.[91]

32 Even an interpretation of Article 118 in the light of IHL as a whole and of its humanitarian object and purpose does not provide a clear answer to the question of whether POWs who object to their repatriation may or must not be repatriated. On the one hand, IHL's main concern is the protection of POWs, and it should therefore not require actions against their will, and even less repatriation of such prisoners to a country where they might be persecuted.[92] The POWs themselves are best qualified to evaluate such risks of persecution. To rely on their evaluation instead of an appraisal of the risks by the Detaining Power avoids abuses by the latter, additional disagreements between the parties, and unlawful retention of POWs by the enemy by way of reciprocity. On the other hand, only repatriation returns POWs to the situation in which they found themselves before falling into the power of the enemy: GC III deals only with the exceptional situation—that of being in the power of the enemy—not with the normal situation—that of POWs being under the control of their own armed forces. An exception relating to the readiness of an individual to return might eliminate the right of POWs to be repatriated;[93] IHL is essentially a regulatory system applied, interpreted, and enforced by the belligerent parties. The alleged wish of the POWs not to be repatriated would give the Detaining Power an easy way of escaping its obligations. In addition, Article 7 GC III bars POWs from renouncing, while in captivity, their rights under GC III. Lastly, it could be argued that the express prohibition against repatriating POWs against their will during hostilities (see MN 11) may indicate *e contrario* that such a prohibition does not exist at the end of active hostilities.

33 However, a further element to be taken into account in interpreting Article 118 paragraph 1 is the other obligations of the parties to the treaty,[94] in this case under international human rights law (IHRL) and international refugee law in particular. Both those other branches of international law prohibit the transfer of persons to a state, including their own, where they risk being tortured or ill-treated. The prohibition against expelling, extraditing, or otherwise

---

[85] Final Record, vol II-A, at 324. The US, the Soviet Union, and the UK opposed the Austrian proposal.
[86] Cf Final Record, vol II-A, at 462.
[87] Report on the Work of the Conference of Government Experts, at 245.
[88] M. Garcia-Mora, *International Law and Asylum as a Human Right* (Washington, DC: Public Affairs Press, 1956), at 114.
[89] The representative of the UK in Final Record, vol II-A, at 324.
[90] Shields Delessert, above n 2, at 168–72; Rosas, above n 21, at 482; Final Record, vol II-A, at 324.
[91] Pictet Commentary GC III, at 543; Shields Delessert, above n 2, at 171.
[92] Flory, above n 83, at 74.
[93] Shields Delessert, above n 2, at 191–4; J. Stone, *Legal Controls of International Conflicts: A Treatise on the Dynamic of Disputes and War-Law* (New York: Rinehart, 1973), at 681–2; J. Pictet, *Development and Principles of International Humanitarian Law* (Dordrecht/Geneva: M. Nijhoff/Henry Dunant Institute, 1985), at 39.
[94] Art 31(3)(c) VCLT.

forcibly removing persons to a territory where their life or freedom might be threatened on account of their race, religion, nationality, membership of a particular social group, or political opinion, referred to as the *'non-refoulement* principle',[95] first appeared in Article 33 of the Convention Relating to the Status of Refugees of 1951.[96] The same principle extends under IHRL to cases in which there is no discrimination, but there it is limited to a threat of torture, or inhuman or degrading treatment or punishment—and for European states to the risk of the death penalty[97] or of a flagrant denial of justice.[98] It was recognized by the Human Rights Committee (HRCttee)[99] and was considerably developed in the jurisprudence of the European Court of Human Rights (ECtHR).[100] The United Nations High Commissioner for Refugees (UNHCR) considers that this prohibition, 'as codified in universal as well as regional human rights treaties is in the process of becoming customary international law, at the very least at regional level'.[101]

The jurisprudence of human rights bodies offers indications regarding the degree of assurance a Detaining Power would need before POWs are repatriated and the probability of ill-treatment that would bar repatriation. On the former issue, domestic laws and diplomatic assurances alone are not sufficient; rather, all circumstances and sources of information must be taken into account.[102] In relation to the probability that ill-treatment will occur, the ECtHR, the UN Committee against Torture, and the HRCttee have developed different, though not incompatible, criteria. Ultimately, however, all available facts and the circumstances of the specific case at hand must be assessed.[103]

34

---

[95] See, for a definition, E. Lauterpacht and D. Bethlehem, *The Scope and Content of the Principle of Non-Refoulement: Opinion* (UNHCR, Legal Publications, 2003), para 252; and for a detailed study under different human rights instruments, K. Wouters, *International Legal Standards for the Protection from Refoulement* (Antwerp: Intersentia, 2009), at 187–423.

[96] See also Art II para 3 AU Convention Governing the Specific Aspects of Refugees Problems in Africa (1969); and Art 19(2) Charter of Fundamental Rights of the European Union (2000).

[97] ECtHR, *Al-Saadoon v UK* (just satisfaction), 2 March 2010, para 144.

[98] ECtHR, *Othman v UK*, 17 January 2012, paras 258–87 (admission of evidence obtained by torture).

[99] HRCttee, *General Comment 20*, para 9. Later it broadened the risk which triggers the application of the principle to 'irreparable harm' (see HRCttee, *General Comment 3*, para 12). That the ICCPR covers *non-refoulement* has been contested by the US (see UN Doc CCPR/C/USA/CO/3/Rev1 of 18 December 2006, para 16). As a state party to the CAT, the US nevertheless admits that it is bound by that treaty's *non-refoulement* provision, but it argues that it is limited, in conformity with the wording of that treaty, to cases of risk of torture, and only to cases in which it is 'more likely than not that [the person] would be tortured' (UN Doc CCPR/C/USA/CO/3/Rev1/Add1 of 12 February 2008, at 9).

[100] See already the ECommHR in *X v The Netherlands* (1965), Decision, No 1983/63, and *X v Germany* (1967), Decision, No 3040/67. See also the ECtHR in *Soering v United Kingdom*, Judgment, 7 July 1989, paras 88 and 90–91; *Saadi v Italy* (Grand Chamber), Judgment, 28 February 2008, para 126; *Vilvarajah and others v United Kingdom*, Judgment, 30 October 1991, para 103; *Ahmed v Austria*, Judgment, 17 December 1996, para 39; *H.L.R. v France*, Judgment, 29 April 1997, para 34; *Jabari v Turkey*, Judgment, 11 July 2000, para 38; *Salah Sheekh v The Netherlands*, Judgment, 11 January 2007, para 135.

[101] UNHCR, *Advisory Opinion on the Extraterritorial Application of Non-Refoulement Obligations under the 1951 Convention relating to the Status of Refugees and its 1967 Protocol* (2007), para 21.

[102] See the ECtHR, *Saadi v Italy*, above n 100, paras 147 and 148; HRCttee, *Alzery v Sweden*, No 1416/2005, CCPR/C/88/D/1416/2005, 25 October 2006, paras 11.4 and 11.5; and Concluding Observations on Sweden, CCPR/CO/74/SWE, 24 April 2002, para 12(b). Even the US, which has a very restrictive interpretation of the *non-refoulement* principle, declares that '[d]iplomatic assurances are not used as a substitute for a case-specific assessment' (UN Doc CCPR/C/USA/CO/3/Rev1/Add1, above n 99, at 10).

[103] See, for an overview, Wouters, above n 95, at 246–64, 391–5, 458–75, and the criteria he suggests at 542–8.

35   This principle of *non-refoulement* has been recognized as a peremptory rule,[104] and as such it would prevail over Article 118 GC III in the event that there was a conflict between the Article and the principle.[105] The principle has been recognized by the United Nations General Assembly (UNGA) to apply to POWs.[106] For protected civilians, the principle is explicitly anchored in Article 45 paragraph 4 GC IV. The Pictet Commentary, which was written before most of the aforementioned developments in IHRL, admits an exception to the principle of Article 118 when a POW has serious reasons for fearing 'unjust measures affecting his life or liberty, especially on grounds of race, social class, religion or political views, and that consequently repatriation would be contrary to the general principles of international law for the protection of the human being'.[107]

36   In the author's view, a prohibition against forcible return must equally apply in the case of threats of punishment for the mere fact of having been captured and interned as a POW. Allowing such a punishment would render GC III meaningless and is therefore implicitly prohibited by the Convention itself: it is hardly conceivable that 196 states could be party to a Convention the very purpose of which is to protect POWs in the power of the enemy, if they considered that the mere fact of having been made a prisoner by the enemy could entail legitimate punishment after repatriation.

37   Respecting the *non-refoulement* principle does not actually solve the problem of POWs objecting to their repatriation. It may be diplomatically sensitive for a Detaining Power, a Protecting Power, or the ICRC to decide whether a refusal is based upon substantial reasons and whether there is indeed a risk of persecution. In addition, POWs may object to their repatriation based on the risk of human rights violations other than persecution, torture, cruel, inhuman, or degrading treatment, or arbitrary deprivation of life. In the end, it is difficult to claim that an IHL treaty such as GC III, which aims at protecting POWs from abuses by their Detaining Power, obliges the latter to repatriate them forcibly and not to respect their will.

38   The Pictet Commentary stresses that (except when the *non-refoulement principle* applies) repatriation must be the rule,[108] and that GC III has 'certainly not established a system under which repatriation depends solely on the wishes of the prisoner of war concerned'.[109] However, the Commentary reserves the possibility that the Detaining Power and the Power on which the POWs depend may conclude an agreement under Article 6 GC III, to respect the wishes of POWs.[110] Except in case of special agreement, the Commentary combines respect for the individual POW's will and objective reasons, but extends the latter beyond the *non-refoulement* principle to 'unjust measures affecting [...] life or liberty'.[111] It adds that each case must be examined individually,[112] and that 'supervisory bodies must be able to satisfy themselves without any hindrance that the requests have been made absolutely freely and in all sincerity, and to give prisoners of war any information which may set at rest groundless fears'.[113] The Commentary therefore links the substantive rule with an implementation and supervision mechanism, which

---

[104] See J. Allain, 'The *Jus Cogens* Nature of *Non-Refoulement*', 13 *IJRL* (2001) 533; and Cartagena Declaration on Refugees (adopted at a colloquium held in Cartagena, Colombia, 19–22 November 1984), Section III, para 5.
[105] Even the Pictet Commentary GC III, at 549, admits that parties may derogate from the obligation to repatriate POWs to take their wishes into account, which suggests that the obligation to repatriate POWs against their will does not belong to *jus cogens*.
[106] UNGA Res 610 (VII), 3 December 1952 (on the Korean War).
[107] Pictet Commentary GC III, at 547.   [108] Ibid, at 546–7.   [109] Ibid, at 548.
[110] Ibid, at 549.   [111] Ibid, at 547.   [112] Ibid.   [113] Ibid, at 548.

is justified in practice but very difficult to justify in law (and which would lead to the absurd result that a Detaining Power preventing the ICRC from visiting POWs must forcibly repatriate all POWs). Many scholars are extremely reluctant to admit,[114] or are even opposed to, an exception to the general rule of repatriation of all prisoners, before a mechanism is established that guarantees that POWs may express their will freely and that their wishes will be respected.[115] Lastly, the Commentary stresses that its entire interpretation presupposes that 'the Convention as a whole has been applied to the letter and in spirit by the belligerents, particularly as regards the co-operation of the Protecting Powers and scrutiny by them',[116] which is nearly never the case in contemporary armed conflicts. The Commentary does not provide for an interpretation in cases where this presupposition is not applicable.

Today, '[t]he ICRC would not in principle lend its services to facilitate the return of people against their will',[117] but ICRC lawyers still consider that the mere wishes of POWs could not be a bar to repatriation.[118] Might this lead to the pharisaic result that a Detaining Power has to repatriate POWs against their will without ICRC involvement?

In this author's view, state practice has developed since the Pictet Commentary was published in 1960, and it must be taken into account when interpreting Article 118, paragraph 1 today.[119] While a review of state practice before the conclusion of GC III does not provide a definitive answer,[120] state practice in all IACs since 1953 has uniformly been to respect the wish of the POW not to be repatriated.[121] The Republic of Korea even made a declaration when ratifying Additional Protocol (AP) I: 'A party detaining prisoners of war may not repatriate its prisoners [against] their openly and freely expressed will.'[122] Several

---

[114] Rosas, above n 21, at 483–4.

[115] A. Esgain and W.A. Solf, 'The 1949 Geneva Conventions Relating to the Treatment of Prisoners of War: Its Principles, Innovations and Deficiencies', 41 *North Carolina Law Review* (1963) 537, at 593–4; Shields Delessert, above n 2, at 174–5, 191–203; Y. Dinstein, 'Refugees and the Law of Armed Conflicts', 12 *IsrYBHR* (1982) 94, at 102; in Korea, although the system of supervision had been discussed at length, it proved inadequate (cf R.R. Baxter, 'Asylum to Prisoners of War', 30 *BYBIL* (1953) 489, at 490–5).

[116] Pictet Commentary GC III, at 546.

[117] C. Droege, 'Transfers of Detainees: Legal Framework, Non-Refoulement and Contemporary Challenges', 90 *IRRC* 871 (2008) 669, at 681. See, for the ICRC position concerning Morocco and Western Sahara, ICRC CIHL Study, at 2895; ICRC, *Communication to the Press* No 00/46, 14 December 2000; ICRC, *Communication to the Press* No 02/38, 7 July 2002.

[118] Droege, above n 117, at 674.

[119] Art 31(3)(b) VCLT. As here, T. Meron, 'The Humanization of International Humanitarian Law', 94 *AJIL* (2000), at 256. Slightly more nuanced than hereafter, G. Nolte, 'Third Report for the ILC Study Group on Treaties over Time, Subsequent Agreements and Subsequent Practice of States outside of Judicial or Quasi-judicial Proceedings', 19 April 2012, UN Doc ILC(LXIV)/SG/TOT/INFORMAL/1, at 21–3.

[120] For a detailed historical review of state practice, see Schapiro, above n 83, at 312–22.

[121] See ICRC CIHL Study, at 2891 and 2892 (UN/Democratic People's Republic of Korea/China in two instances); ICRC Annual Report 1988, at 25 (Somalia and Ethiopia); US, *Conduct of the Persian Gulf War, Final Report to Congress* (April 1992) Appendix 0-20, available at <http://www.dtic.mil/cgi-bin/GetTRDoc?Location=U2&doc=GetTRDoc.pdf&AD=ADA249390>, and Rowe, above n 52, at 203 (US and Saudi practice at the end of the Second Gulf War in 1991); Art IX(1)(e) of Annex 1A to the *Peace Agreement for Bosnia and Herzegovina, Agreement on the Military Aspects of the Peace Settlement*, reproduced in Sassòli/Bouvier/Quintin, at 1730; ICRC CIHL Study, at 2892 (Croatia/Socialist Federal Republic of Yugoslavia); ICRC CIHL Study, at 2892 (Bosnia-Herzegovina/Serbia/Croatia); *ICRC Annual Report* 1988, at 25–6 (Ethiopia/Somalia). For the end of hostilities in the Vietnam conflict, see de Zayas, above n 19, para 13. See in scholarly writings Y. Dinstein, 'Prisoners of War', in R. Bernhardt (ed), *Encyclopedia of Public International Law* (Amsterdam: North Holland Publishing Company, 1982), vol IV, at 151. De Zayas, above n 19, para 10, and Fischer, above n 49, at 416, remain more reluctant.

[122] Declaration/Reservation of the Republic of Korea to Art 85(4)(b) AP I.

states so provide in their military manuals.¹²³ The Eritrea–Ethiopia Claims Commission held that 'there must be adequate procedures to ensure that individuals are not repatriated against their will'.¹²⁴

41   In practice, such a wish not to be repatriated was always expressed to the ICRC,¹²⁵ which reduced the risk of manipulation. Maintaining as the controlling factor the informed, freely expressed will of the POW is also preferable for policy reasons to relying on mere respect for the *non-refoulement* principle. In the absence of third-party adjudication, it would be up to the Detaining Power to determine whether the fear of persecution of the POW refusing to be repatriated was justified. However, the Detaining Power is in a particularly uncomfortable position as regards taking such a decision. At a delicate moment such as the end of active hostilities, the Detaining Power may be fearful of refuelling the conflict by accusing the adverse party of persecuting its own soldiers. The ICRC, acting as 'a screening mechanism', would obviously not agree to offer an opinion on whether a POW was justified in fearing persecution, as such a determination would not be appreciated by the Power of origin of the POWs, and in addition would violate the Committee's working principle of confidentiality, as it would inevitably be based on information the ICRC gathers when fulfilling its mandate on the adverse side. Therefore, all concerned prefer to let the will of the POW be determinative, and it would be formalistic to take this into account only if the POW claims that this unwillingness is related to a fear of persecution. This result is not at variance with Article 7 GC III, stipulating that POWs cannot renounce their rights, since it would be impossible to interpret that provision as 'prohibiting a prisoner of war from renouncing his "right" of being forcibly repatriated'.¹²⁶ Nevertheless, the rule suggested here does not imply that the Detaining Power or any third state has an obligation to grant POWs asylum. As discussed below (MN 50), this may lead to the continued internment of those former POWs well beyond the end of active hostilities.

42   The Pictet Commentary provides for two exceptional cases: POWs who had been illegally conscripted into the armed forces of the Detaining Power (e.g. as an Occupying Power), and deserters who have gone over to the Detaining Power (to be distinguished from those who sever their allegiance while in captivity).¹²⁷ It considers that they are not POWs and that the Detaining Power has no obligation to repatriate them. Indeed, in this case, under Article 4 GC IV, such persons would be civilians.¹²⁸ As such, the *non-refoulement* principle applies to them,¹²⁹ and if they have fallen into the power of the Detaining Power in an occupied territory, any forcible transfer is prohibited.¹³⁰ If they wish, they must nevertheless be repatriated.¹³¹

---

¹²³ ICRC CIHL Database, Canada, Rule 128, Section D, III; ICRC CIHL Study, at 2893 (Israel); ICRC CIHL Database, Israel, Rule 128, Section D, III; ICRC CIHL Database, United Kingdom, Rule 128, Section D, III.
¹²⁴ EECC, *POWs—Eritrea's Claim 17*, above n 53, para 147.
¹²⁵ See ICRC CIHL Study, vol I, at 455, with references to practice in the former Yugoslavia, and below n 145.
¹²⁶ Schapiro, above n 83, at 323; Flory, above n 83, at 72; R.C. Hingorani, *Prisoners of War* (2nd edn, New York: Oceana Publications, 1982), at 183–4.
¹²⁷ Pictet Commentary GC III, at 549. In the 2nd Gulf War, even such deserters were treated as POWs (Rowe, above n 52, at 191).
¹²⁸ See, for deserters, M. Sassòli, 'The Status, Treatment and Repatriation of Deserters under International Humanitarian Law', *Yearbook of the International Institute of International Humanitarian Law* (1985) 9, at 19–22 and 35–6.
¹²⁹ Art 45 para 4 GC IV.   ¹³⁰ Art 49 para 1 GC IV.
¹³¹ Arts 35 and 133 GC IV; and Chs 57, 58, and 66 of this volume.

e. Obligations of the Power on which the prisoner of war depends?

The unilateral obligation of the Detaining Power to repatriate POWs may be seen as implying the obligation of the Power on which they depend to accept them.[132] If POWs are directly transferred from internment by the Detaining Power to detention by the Power on which they depend, they continue to benefit from the minimum guarantees of Article 75 AP I which are considered to reflect customary international law, even beyond the general close of military operations, as they have never been released.[133] Some even argue that POWs transferred to the Power on which they depend should continue to benefit from POW status if they continue to be detained as enemies, as GC III applies until their 'final release and repatriation'.[134] In this author's view, such an interpretation is dangerous, as it might be understood as depriving such detainees of an individual determination of the legality of their detention under IHRL along with the procedural guarantees associated with that branch of law.

43

f. Destination of the prisoners of war

Prisoners of war must be repatriated to the Power on which they depend, i.e. the state in whose armed forces they served. This may not necessarily be their home country, but the assumption of the Convention is that they should be returned to the situation they were in before captivity. In some cases, this assumption is not justified. First, at the moment of repatriation, some POWs may express their wish to be repatriated to their country of nationality, rather than to the Power on which they depend.[135] Secondly, the Power on which the POWs depended may have ceased to exist, may have disintegrated, or parts of it may have successfully established a new state. In such cases POWs should be released according to their wishes. Thirdly, if POWs are interned on the territory of their own country which has been occupied, they must be released on the spot.[136] The principle of *non-refoulement* nevertheless applies equally in this case.[137] In case of partial occupation, and subject to the respect for their wishes discussed above, POWs should be repatriated to the non-occupied part of their country.[138] Fourthly, in the case of the end of active hostilities in a war of national liberation (to which GC III would apply via Article 1(4) AP I), should a new state be established on a territory which was subject to foreign occupation or colonial domination, the normal rules apply. In the case where a racist regime is defeated, and in the case where the national liberation movement is unsuccessful, all POWs must be released on the spot.

44

---

[132] Shields Delessert, above n 2, at 204.   [133] Art 3(b) AP I.

[134] Art 5 para 1 GC III; and F. Gouin, 'Prisonniers de guerre aux mains de leur puissance d'origine: pour une application des Conventions de Genève jusqu'à leur "libération et rapatriement définitifs"', 27 *Windsor Yearbook of Access to Justice* (2009) 321, at 321–45.

[135] In 1958, members of the French Foreign Legion were repatriated from Vietnam to their countries of origin (see *ICRC Annual Report* 1958, at 23).

[136] Pictet Commentary GC III, at 547.

[137] See, for the extraterritorial application of the *non-refoulement* principle, including if the person to be transferred is already present on the territory of the transferee state, ECtHR, *Al-Saadoon v United Kingdom*, above n 97, para 144; UN Doc CCPR/C/USA/CO/3/Rev of 18 December 2006, above n 99, para 16; UNHCR, Advisory Opinion, above n 101, paras 24, 26, and 43; Lauterpacht and Bethlehem, above n 95, paras 114 and 241; Droege, above n 117, at 682–3; E.-C. Gillard, 'There's No Place Like Home: States' Obligations in Relation to Transfers of Persons', 90 *IRRC* 871 (2008) 703, at 715. The US denies that the *non-refoulement* principle applies extraterritorially: *United States (Immigration and Naturalization Service) v Haitian Centers Council Inc*, 509 US 155 (1993) and UN Doc CCPR/C/USA/CO/3/Rev of 18 December 2006, above n 99, para 10.

[138] Shields Delessert, above n 2, at 178.

g. Practical arrangements and modalities

45 Although Article 118 requires repatriation 'without delay' after cessation of active hostilities, the Eritrea–Ethiopia Claims Commission acknowledged that 'repatriation cannot be instantaneous. Preparing and coordinating adequate arrangements for safe and orderly movement and reception, especially of sick or wounded prisoners, may be time-consuming'.[139] In most cases agreements are concluded after lengthy negotiations.[140] Seriously wounded, ill, or aged POWs, or those who have undergone a long internment, are often prioritized.[141] The actual repatriation may take place at the ceasefire line, by air-lift, or through a third country.[142]

46 As belligerents who have just ended hostilities may not easily come to an agreement on details, GC III formulates with great care and detail, but not entirely successfully, rules to ensure that POWs can be repatriated without agreement. Each Detaining Power must establish and execute unilaterally without delay a repatriation plan. Prisoners of war may not simply be released without arrangements for their repatriation.[143] In practice such plans are most often suggested and largely executed by the ICRC.[144] It is at this stage that ICRC delegates verify in an interview without witnesses the wish to be repatriated of every individual POW.[145] The repatriation plan must obviously also cover POWs who were released (on parole or unilaterally) by the Detaining Power on its territory during the

---

[139] EECC, *POWs—Eritrea's Claim 17*, above n 53, para 147.

[140] See *ICRC Annual Reports* 1964, at 19 (Algeria and Morocco); 1966, at 12 (India and Pakistan); 1967, at 8 and 1968, at 33 (1967 Arab–Israeli conflict); 1970, at 71 (Saudi Arabia and Yemen); 1973, at 12 (1973 Arab–Israeli conflict); 1973, at 26, and 1974, at 35 (India and Pakistan); 1979, at 39 (China and Vietnam); 1989, at 16 (Angola, Cuba, and South Africa); 2000, at 78 (Ethiopia and Eritrea). See also *ICRC News Release* 00/21, 17 June 2000 (Democratic Republic of the Congo, Rwanda, Zimbabwe, and Namibia) and Art IX of Annex 1A to *the Peace Agreement for Bosnia and Herzegovina, Agreement on the Military Aspects of the Peace Settlement*, reproduced in Sassòli/Bouvier/Quintin, at 1730.

[141] See *ICRC Annual Reports* 1966, at 12 (India and Pakistan); 1971, at 42 (1967 Arab–Israeli conflict); 1974, at 20 (Bangladesh, India and Pakistan); 1987, at 27, and 1988, at 25 (Ethiopia and Somalia); 1989, at 86 (Iran and Iraq); 2000, at 209 (Western Sahara).

[142] F. Bugnion, *The International Committee of the Red Cross and the Protection of War Victims* (Geneva/Oxford: ICRC/Macmillan, 2003), at 699.

[143] Fischer, above n 49, at 414, referring to an Iraqi violation of this obligation when it simply sent Kuwaiti POWs back through the desert at the end of the 1991 conflict.

[144] See *ICRC Annual Reports* 1957, at 21 (Suez conflict); 1970, at 71 (Saudi Arabia and Yemen); 1969, at 47 (1967 Arab–Israeli war); 1973, at 12 and 15 (1973 Arab–Israeli conflict); 1974, at 11 (Cyprus); 1974, at 35 (Bangladesh, India, and Pakistan); 1979, at 39 (China and Vietnam); 1989, at 16 (Angola, Cuba, and South Africa); 1991, at 101 (2nd Gulf War); 2000, at 73 (Zimbabwean, Namibian, and Rwandan POWs); 2000, at 62 (Sudanese POWs released by Uganda); 2000, at 209 (Western Sahara); 2003, at 266 (Iran and Iraq). See, for the conflict between Cameroon and Nigeria, *ICRC News Release* 98/39 of 24 November 1998; ICRC CIHL Study, at 2862 (Ethiopia/Eritrea); ICRC CIHL Study, at 2863 and 2901 (Final Act of the Paris Conference on Cambodia); ICRC CIHL Study, at 2901 and 2902 (Croatia/Socialist Federative Republic of Yugoslavia); ICRC CIHL Study, at 2901 (Bosnia-Herzegovina/Serbia/Croatia); UN Doc E/CN.4/1993/50 of 10 February 1993 in ICRC CIHL Study, at 2901 (UN in Bosnia-Herzegovina); ICRC CIHL Study, at 2902 (Bosnia-Herzegovina); ICRC CIHL Database, Rule 128, Section G, III (Cameroon); UNSC Res 1284, 17 December 1999 (UN in Iraq/Kuwait); UN Commission on Human Rights Res 1996/71, 23 April 1996, § 12 (UN on Bosnia-Herzegovina/Croatia/Federal Republic of Yugoslavia). See also above n 140.

[145] The right of the ICRC to interview POWs without witnesses is granted by Art 126 GC III. See for state practice *ICRC Annual Reports* 1988, at 25 (Somalia and Ethiopia); 1998, at 62 and 68 (Cameroon and Nigeria); 2003, at 266 (Iran and Iraq); *ICRC News Releases* 00/07 of 2 March 2000, 03/62 of 1 September 2003, and 03/72 of 8 November 2003 (Western Sahara); *ICRC Annual Report* 2005, at 220, and *ICRC News Releases* 01/44 of 8 November 2001, 06/01 of 8 January 2006, and 08/71 of 23 April 2008 (Armenia and Azerbaijan).

conflict, and allow the ICRC to establish their wish to be (or not to be) repatriated.¹⁴⁶ The plans and modalities for repatriation must be communicated to the POWs. The involvement of the ICRC reduces the practical importance of Article 118 paragraph 4 on the apportionment of cost, which again attempts to ensure that repatriation is not delayed by disagreements over finances.

Article 119 GC III prescribes that the repatriation itself must be conducted under conditions similar to those of transfers of POWs during the period they were interned,¹⁴⁷ and what must be done with the POWs' valuables and personal effects. Finally, as the end of active hostilities is often accompanied by revolutionary changes or chaos in one or more of the states involved, POWs in camps which are no longer guarded sometimes simply flee in an unorganized way and thus become dispersed or go missing. As long as they find themselves on the territory of the Detaining Power not occupied by the Power on which they depend (or on another territory occupied by the Detaining Power), they remain POWs, benefiting from GC III. Article 119 paragraph 7 prescribes the establishment of commissions to search for and ensure the repatriation of such dispersed POWs. However, such commissions have never been established. The ICRC has tried to solve such cases in cooperation with the former belligerents. Moreover, since dispersed POWs are often considered 'missing', several mechanisms including former belligerents and the ICRC, set up to clarify the fate of missing persons, equally fulfilled the tasks of the commissions foreseen in Article 119 paragraph 7.¹⁴⁸

III. Cases where repatriation at the end of active hostilities is not required

Prisoners of war who are or were subject to judicial proceedings 'for an indictable offence'¹⁴⁹ may be retained beyond the end of active hostilities until such proceedings have ended and they have, if convicted, served their sentence.¹⁵⁰ The criminal proceedings must at least have started when the repatriation obligation would otherwise exist. Prisoners of war may not be retained on mere suspicion, with a view to possible future judicial proceedings.¹⁵¹ For such time, retained POWs continue to benefit from POW status and treatment.¹⁵² They may equally be extradited to another state wishing to prosecute them for an extraditable offence, but only if the latter is able and willing to comply with GC III.¹⁵³

---

¹⁴⁶ See, for the controversies on and solutions for this issue years after the conflict between Iran and Iraq had ended, *ICRC Annual Report* 2004, at 278.
¹⁴⁷ See Ch 47 of this volume, MN 26–40.
¹⁴⁸ See Sassòli and Tougas, above n 82, at 746–8.
¹⁴⁹ This term is meant to exclude civil proceedings (see Final Record, vol II-A, at 455–6, and vol II-B, at 318).
¹⁵⁰ Art 119 para 5 GC III.
¹⁵¹ Fischer, above n 49, at 417. India's refusal in 1972 to repatriate Pakistani POWs because Bangladesh envisaged prosecuting some of them for genocide was not acceptable (see Bretton, above n 41, at 218 and 221–4; and Levie, above n 43, at 514).
¹⁵² Art 5 para 1 GC III. See the different US Decisions concerning Manuel Antonio Noriega, reproduced in Sassòli/Bouvier/Quintin at 1344–73.
¹⁵³ Art 12 para 3 GC III. See, for the extradition of Noriega to France, Sassòli/Bouvier/Quintin, at 1367–70, and G. Corn and S. Finegan, 'America's Longest Held Prisoner of War: Lessons Learned from the Capture, Prosecution and Extradition of General Manuel Noriega', 71 *Louisiana Law Review* (2011) 1112, at 1143–4. In the case of the Argentinean Captain Astiz, the UK chose not to extradite POWs even for extraditable offences (M. Meyer, 'Liability of POWs for Offences Committed prior to Capture: The Astiz Affair', 32 *ICLQ* (1983) 948, at 954).

IV. Status and treatment of prisoners of war who are not repatriated

49 Prisoners of war who are, for whatever reason, unlawfully not repatriated when they should have been, remain protected by GC III until they are effectively repatriated.[154] The status of those who were (in the present author's view lawfully) not repatriated at the end of active hostilities because they objected to their repatriation is less clear. If they are released on the spot and given asylum by the (former) Detaining Power, they lose POW status and protection under IHL. If they are released into a territory occupied by the Detaining Power, they are protected by GC IV as enemy nationals no longer protected by GC III.[155]

50 A Detaining Power that does not repatriate POWs because of their refusal is not obliged to grant them asylum, and the possibility of continuing to detain such persons who have no right to be present on its territory cannot be excluded under IHRL. Under IHL, it would, in this author's view, be inappropriate to continue to provide such persons POW status and treatment.[156] The Detaining Power has done what the GC III requires in order to end their status, and detention continues only because they do not wish to benefit from the right offered by the Convention. With their refusal to be repatriated at the time of final repatriation,[157] such persons sever their link of allegiance with the Power on which they depended. A continued application of GC III would be inappropriate, as many of its provisions presuppose soldiers, subject to military hierarchy, whose allegiance is with the power on which they depend. Therefore, as GC III ceases to apply, but the former POW remains an enemy national who fell into the power of the adverse party before the general close of military operations, and who is not yet finally released, repatriated, or re-established, such a person remains protected by GC IV.[158] This interpretation, suggested by the ICRC, was accepted in 1991 by Saudi Arabia for Iraqi POWs who refused repatriation. Indeed, Saudi Arabia did not agree to the release of these POWs on its own territory, and at that time no third country had yet agreed to accept them.[159] Those former POWs were therefore not yet 're-established' in the sense of Article 6 paragraph 4 GC IV and remained protected by GC IV. This is without prejudice to the application of IHRL and international refugee law (if the POWs refusing to be repatriated had to fear persecution)[160] to such persons. On many issues these branches of law will constitute the *lex specialis* prevailing over the less specific rules of GC IV.

C. Relevance in Non-International Armed Conflicts

51 Traditionally, the absence of combatant and POW status constitutes one of the main differences between the IHL of NIACs and the IHL of IACs, and this has not changed in the

---

[154] Art 5 para 1 GC III. [155] Arts 4 and 6 para 3 GC IV.

[156] This has, however, apparently been the approach of the ICRC in Eritrea and Ethiopia, *ICRC Annual Reports* 2003, at 66, and 2004, at 71 and 72. Later Annual Reports are vague, referring to the 'relevant provisions of the 1949 Geneva Conventions' (*ICRC Annual Reports* 2007, at 103; 2005, at 86; and 2006, at 99).

[157] Until the 'last call', i.e. the time of the final repatriation, POWs who earlier (during or after the end of hostilities) refused repatriation remain POWs (*ICRC Annual Report* 1991, at 112).

[158] See, for the definition of protected persons under GC IV, Art 4 GC IV; and for its temporal scope of application, see Art 6 GC IV.

[159] *ICRC Annual Report* 1991, at 102.

[160] S. Jaquemet, 'The Cross-Fertilization of International Humanitarian Law and International Refugee Law', 83 *IRRC* 843 (2001) 651, at 663–4; and de Zayas, above n 19, para 11 ('especially if motivated by fears of political persecution').

light of the recent tendency to bring the two regimes closer to each other. The traditional understanding is therefore that in NIACs, members of insurgent armed groups may not be detained for the mere purpose of preventing them from further participation in hostilities. They must benefit either from judicial or procedural guarantees prescribed by IHRL in case of detention, or, according to some, from at least an individual administrative decision and procedure analogous to that which GC IV prescribes for the internment of protected civilians for imperative security reasons.[161] For members of governmental armed forces captured by armed groups, the legal regime is even less clear. On the one hand, armed groups are traditionally seen as not being bound by IHRL, and one may cast doubt on their practical capacity to provide for procedural guarantees. On the other hand, IHL cannot deny such groups the option of detaining government soldiers to prevent them from fighting against the group. In any case, rebel fighters and government soldiers must be released when the individual reason for their detention ceases. If this reason was the risk they constitute for the state (or the armed group) because they might participate in hostilities, then there should be a decision to release them following an end of hostilities which can be expected to be permanent.[162] To determine when this moment arrives, the interpretation of the term 'end of active hostilities' mentioned above in MN 20–23 may be applied by analogy. In practice, exchanges are nevertheless frequent.[163] Although the conflict in Afghanistan was not explicitly classified as non-international by the US Supreme Court, the Court recognized the general principle that internment may not last longer than active hostilities, but added that '[i]f the practical circumstances of a given conflict are entirely unlike those of the conflicts that informed the development of the laws of war, that understanding may unravel'.[164]

If fighters in a NIAC are tried and sentenced for having used force against the state, they must be released after having served their sentence, and the end of active hostilities is immaterial. It is much more controversial whether rebel armed groups may try government soldiers for having used force against them, and whether they are at all able to offer a fair trial. However, in both cases, Article 6(5) AP II encourages the authorities in power at the end of hostilities 'to grant the broadest possible amnesty to persons who have participated in the armed conflict, or those deprived of their liberty for reasons related to the armed conflict, whether they are interned or detained'. This provision explicitly refers equally to interned persons, although they do not receive a sentence which would allow them to benefit from an amnesty. To determine when such an amnesty should be granted, an application by analogy of the understanding of the term 'end of active hostilities' discussed above is appropriate.

As mentioned elsewhere in the present volume, some states and some authors want to apply certain rules on combatants and POWs to persons they label as 'unlawful combatants' by analogy in NIACs.[165] The starting point of such an analogy is the idea that members of rebel armed groups (and, the present author would add, members of government

---

[161] See, for a discussion and references, M. Sassòli and L. Olson, 'The Relationship between International Humanitarian Law and Human Rights Law Where It Matters: Admissible Killing and Internment of Fighters in Non-International Armed Conflict', 90 *IRRC* 871 (2008) 599, at 618–27.
[162] By analogy with Arts 132 and 133 GC IV. See ICRC CIHL Study, at 2873–4 (United States). Of the same opinion, David, above n 1, at 594.
[163] UNSC Res 999 (1995), 16 June 1995, para 8 (concerning Tajikistan).
[164] *Hamdi v Rumsfeld*, above n 57, at 521.
[165] See Ch 45, MN 76, and Ch 64, MN 64 and 65, of this volume.

armed forces) may be detained by the adversary, like POWs, for the mere purpose of hindering them from further participation in hostilities. Usually such an analogy is only invoked for the benefit of the state, allowing it to detain members of an insurgent armed group (who had a continuous fighting function) without an individual procedure for the duration of the conflict. If the 'war on terror' is seen as a transnational NIAC, this would lead to indefinite detention, as it is impossible to determine when such a 'war on terror' ends (which in the view of the present author is one of the reasons why it is inappropriate to classify the 'war on terror' as an armed conflict under IHL, and particularly inappropriate to apply by analogy some rules on POWs).[166] Nevertheless, following the reasoning in favour of the analogy, such detention would no longer be justified after the end of active hostilities. The main criterion remains, however, whether the continued detention is necessary for state security.[167]

54   As the termination of captivity during an IAC depends upon the individual situation of the POW—no longer being able to participate in hostilities—or an agreement between the parties, these rules may be applied quite easily by analogy in NIACs, in which the same conditions may be fulfilled.

55   Analogy with GC III is more difficult to apply to the repatriation aspect than to the release aspect. First, any 'repatriation' or return, distinct from release, is conceivable only in a NIAC in which a rebel armed group controls territory, and which is covered by AP II. Secondly, in NIACs, government soldiers would have to be returned to the governmental forces and rebel fighters to the armed group for which they were fighting. However, the IHL of NIACs neither protects nor respects the allegiance of a member of an insurgent armed group. In any case, the *non-refoulement* principle applies to IACs and NIACs equally, and it is widely recognized that non-state actor persecution is equally relevant. As no obligation to 'repatriate' exists (but only, at best, an obligation to end captivity by analogy to the IHL of IACs), the thorny question of whether the will of the POW not to be repatriated is determinant is less relevant in NIACs. A detaining party may certainly respect the will of a detainee. A government handing detainees over to a non-state armed group against their will would violate its IHRL obligation to protect those persons' human rights, since such persons would, in most cases, remain on the territory of the state but the latter could no longer guarantee their rights. As for a non-state armed group, it may be expected to respect the wish of a detained government soldier not to be returned (even absent any risk of persecution) and to remain with the insurgent group, but it would be difficult to argue that the group has such an obligation. The practice of the ICRC appears to be that in NIACs too, it does not become involved in the repatriation of persons against their will.[168]

D. Legal Consequences of a Violation

56   As mentioned above (MN 27), neither reprisals involving protected persons nor reciprocity are legally available as means to induce compliance with the repatriation obligation.

---

[166] Critical N. McDonald and S. Sullivan, 'Rational Interpretation in Irrational Times: The Third Geneva Convention and the "War on Terror"', 44 *Harvard International Law Journal* (2003) 301, at 312–15.

[167] D. Jinks, 'The Declining Significance of POW Status', 45 *Harvard International Law Journal* (2004) 367, at 419.

[168] See, e.g., ICRC CIHL Study, at 2901 and 2902 (Croatia/Socialist Federative Republic of Yugoslavia); ICRC CIHL Study, at 2901 (Bosnia-Herzegovina/Serbia/Croatia).

United Nations Security Council resolutions demanding an end to hostilities have often urged belligerents to repatriate POWs,[169] and should do so systematically.

An 'unjustifiable delay in the repatriation of prisoners of war' constitutes a grave breach under AP I[170] and is a crime under the domestic law of several states.[171] The unjustifiable character of the delay depends of the substantive rules of IHL discussed in this chapter. The crime covers repatriations both during and after the end of active hostilities (i.e. violations of Article 109 paragraph 1 and Article 118 paragraph 1 GC III),[172] but, in this author's view, there is no grave breach where there is a failure to conclude an agreement with a neutral country under Article 109 paragraph 3, nor is there such a breach with regard to non-repatriation by a neutral country in violation of Article 110 paragraph 3. In the first case no repatriation is concerned, and in both cases the substantive obligation presupposes an agreement between the parties concerned. An official of a neutral country who does not repatriate despite the belligerents' agreement in a situation where the conditions of Article 110 paragraph 3 are fulfilled could nevertheless be considered to have committed a grave breach.

It is interesting to note that an unjustifiable delay in the repatriation of POWs is not a war crime under the International Criminal Court (ICC) Statute, although it appeared as an 'exceptionally serious war crime' in the 1991 International Law Commission (ILC) Draft Code of Crimes against Peace and Security of Mankind,[173] and later as a war crime in the 1996 Draft Code.[174] The reasons for this omission from the ICC Statute remain unclear. Some claim that the violation was not considered to be sufficiently serious,[175] others that there were doubts about whether its criminalization has attained customary law status.[176] No published records of the Rome Conference exist. The rest of the *travaux préparatoires* contain no evidence for those claims.[177] Although this may not be the reason for the omission from the Rome Statute, in this author's view, it is particularly difficult to establish individual responsibility for the crime under discussion. How can a mere soldier or officer commit this war crime? Both during and after the end of hostilities, repatriation presupposes arrangements by the authorities at the highest level. Except at the top level of government, an individual will rarely have the necessary knowledge (much less the required intent) concerning the unjustifiable nature of any delay. Members of a Mixed

---

[169] See UNSC Res 598 (1987) (Iran and Iraq). [170] Art 85(4)(b) AP I.
[171] ICRC CIHL Study, at 2868–71 (Argentina, Armenia, Australia, Azerbaijan, Bangladesh, Belarus, Bosnia-Herzegovina, Canada, Cook Islands, Croatia, Cyprus, Czech Republic, Denmark, El Salvador, Estonia, Georgia, Germany, Hungary, Ireland, Jordan, Lebanon, Lithuania, Netherlands, New Zealand, Nicaragua, Niger, Norway, Philippines, Moldova, Slovakia, Slovenia, Spain, Tajikistan, United Kingdom, Socialist Federative Republic of Yugoslavia, Zimbabwe); ICRC CIHL Database, Rule 128, Section A, IV (Australia, Democratic Republic of the Congo, Jordan, Rwanda).
[172] ICRC Commentary APs, para 1000.
[173] Art 22(2)(a), ILC, Draft Code of Crimes against the Peace and Security of Mankind in *YILC* (1991), vol II, part II, at 97.
[174] Art 20(c)(2), ILC, Draft Code of Crimes against the Peace and Security of Mankind, adopted by the ILC at its 48th session in *YILC* (1996), vol II, part II at 53.
[175] H. von Hebel and D. Robinson, 'Crimes within the Jurisdiction of the Court', in R.S. Lee (ed), *The International Criminal Court: The Making of the Rome Statute: Issues, Negotiations and Results* (The Hague/London: Kluwer Law International, 1999), at 104.
[176] R. Cryer et al, *An Introduction to International Criminal Law and Procedure* (2nd edn, Cambridge: CUP, 2010), at 294.
[177] *Report of the* Ad Hoc *Committee on the Establishment of an International Criminal Court*, UNGA Official Records, Supplement No 22, A/50/22 (1995), para 72; *Report of the Preparatory Committee on the Establishment of an International Criminal Court*, vol I (1996), para 74.

Medical Commission who reject direct repatriation of POWs clearly fulfilling the criteria of Article 110 paragraph 1 may be an exception. Even at the highest level of government, the criteria to determine when a delay is unjustifiable are, as we have seen above, subject to multiple controversies and include numerous grey zones. Although it has been suggested above that solutions exist for those controversies, and although uncertainties and controversies exist for many other rules of IHL underlying war crimes, it would seem to this author inappropriate to label as war criminals those government leaders who follow the 'jurisprudence' of the Eritrea–Ethiopia Claims Commission and retain POWs for reasons of reciprocity (see MN 27), or who follow Hersch Lauterpacht and repatriate POWs only once conditions 'render it out of the question for the defeated party to resume hostilities' (see MN 22).

59   Conversely, forced repatriation may also constitute an international crime, which is more easily attributable to even low-level individuals, for example as aiding and abetting, than an omission to repatriate. As soon as the *non-refoulement* principle discussed above is violated, forced repatriation could be an act of aiding and abetting the crime of torture by the officials of the Power on which the POW depends.

60   The notion of aiding and abetting has been interpreted broadly in international jurisprudence.[178] Ad hoc tribunals consider that a knowledge-based *mens rea* is sufficient.[179] The accused does not need to be present at the place and moment where the crime is committed.[180] The assistance can be given before the commission of the unlawful act,[181] but it needs to have a substantial effect on the commission of the unlawful act.[182] It is obvious that a Power on which a POW depends could not have tortured or ill-treated a former POW if that person had not been repatriated.

61   In the *Vukovar Hospital* case,[183] the International Criminal Tribunal for the former Yugoslavia (ICTY) convicted an officer of the Yugoslav People's Army (JNA) for war crimes in connection with the transfer of Croat men, held under the custody of the JNA, from the Vukovar hospital to a hangar in Ovčara, where they were left in the hands of irregular Serb forces who killed them after the JNA withdrew. The ICTY convicted the officer, inter alia, because his failure to protect his prisoners, after he had transferred the detainees to the local Serb forces and left Ovčara, contributed to the murders, while he had a duty under Article 12 GC III to protect the POWs even after the order to withdraw, and this duty 'included the obligation not to allow the transfer of custody of the prisoners of war to anyone without first assuring himself that they would not be harmed'.[184]

62   This case concerned transfers, not repatriations. Furthermore, unlike the POWs transferred in that case, repatriated POWs are no longer POWs once repatriated, and their

---

[178] See, e.g., ICTY, *The Prosecutor v Anto Furundžija*, Trial Chamber Judgment, IT-95-17/1-T, 10 December 1998, para 235, and ICTR, *The Prosecutor v Nahimana, Barayagwiza et Ngeze*, Appeals Chamber Judgment, ICTR-99-52-A, 28 November 2007, para 482.

[179] See F. Lafontaine, 'Parties to Offences under the Canadian Crimes against Humanity and War Crimes Act: An Analysis of Principal Liability and Complicity', 50 *Les Cahiers de droit* (2009) 967.

[180] ICTY, *The Prosecutor v Duško Tadić*, Trial Chamber Judgment, IT-94-1-T, 7 May 1997, para 687.

[181] See, e.g., ICTY, *The Prosecutor v Mitar Vasiljević*, IT-98-32-T, Judgment, 29 November 2002, para 70; and ICTY, *The Prosecutor v Tihomir Blaškić*, IT-95-14-T, Judgment, 3 March 2000, para 285.

[182] See, e.g., *Furundžija*, above n 178, paras 234–35 (confirmed on Appeal).

[183] ICTY, *The Prosecutor v Mile Mrkšić (Vukovar Hospital Case)*, Appeals Chamber Judgment, IT-95-13/1-A, 5 May 2009, para 69. See also G. Pinzauti, 'Protecting Prisoners of War: The *Mrkšić et al*, Appeal Judgement', 8 *JICJ* (2010) 199.

[184] ICTY, *Mrkšić*, above n 183, para 74.

torture or ill-treatment cannot constitute a war crime. Nevertheless, the case shows that criminal responsibility for repatriation in violation of the *non-refoulement* principle may arise, and that it may arise even in a NIAC.[185] However, in the case of repatriation, a court would have to evaluate the duty of care of a transferring suspect, taking into account that while Article 12 presents transfer only as an option, Article 118 foresees the obligation to repatriate (the violation of which could equally have criminal consequences).

In addition, at least the ECtHR has considered the mere fact of transferring detainees 63 to a state where they will be sentenced to death or tortured as constituting an instance of inhuman treatment.[186] Thus, if international criminal law is interpreted in light of IHRL as the *lex specialis* in this respect, such a transfer could constitute inhuman treatment of a POW, a grave breach under Article 130 GC III, and a war crime under Article 8(2)(a)(ii) of the ICC Statute. Indeed, when POWs begin their transfer, they are still POWs, and therefore are persons protected under GC III against whom grave breaches may be committed.

E. Critical Assessment

Even more than other rules of GC III, the rules on the release and repatriation of POWs 64 were drafted against the backdrop of traditional IACs between regular armed forces of states towards which those POWs keep their allegiance, IHL needing only to protect them against the enemy and to ensure that they may return as soon as possible to their previous situation. Such conflicts still exist, and for such conflicts the rules of GC III remain a realistic regime, though perhaps not the most humanitarian regime one could wish for (because the rules allow the deprivation of the liberty of innocent people for an unknown duration). The case of individuals who do not fit the stereotype of a patriotic soldier wishing to be repatriated as soon as possible can be easily addressed if one takes into account the development of the rest of international law and subsequent practice. However, allowing increased flexibility in interpreting the rules opens the door to abuses by Detaining Powers, at least in the absence of an efficient screening and enforcement mechanism.

Beyond that, it must, however, be admitted that the regime is no longer fully adequate 65 when faced with many modern armed conflicts. Many such conflicts are not of an international character and/or involve persons other than members of regular armed forces. Many of those actively involved in such conflicts do not wish to be repatriated, or risk continuing to constitute a threat to the Detaining Power even after the end of open fighting between the parties. In conformity with the growing tendency in international law to take the circumstances of each individual case fully into account, the time may have come in many conflicts not to determine collectively the time when a fighter must be released and/or repatriated, but to determine this through individual decisions. One might thus imagine that even during an armed conflict, periodic individual determinations would need to be made to balance that individual's right to freedom against the legitimate security interests of the Detaining Power, i.e. the probability that this individual will again participate in hostilities and the extent of the threat this individual represents when doing so. Conversely, at the end of organized hostilities, some POWs may still constitute a threat sufficient to justify their continued detention. It had already been suggested by some

---

[185] Ibid, paras 70–1.
[186] See ECtHR, *Soering*, above n 100, para 88; and ECtHR, *Al-Saadoon*, above n 97, para 144.

authors a long time ago that the end of active hostilities should be interpreted in a flexible and individualized manner.[187] Such full individualization can be realized only by changing the existing law. It remains to be seen whether this is realistic, and even if it is, whether it will be accepted by states. In this author's view, it should be envisaged only once sufficient safeguards against abuses are accepted. Recent experience with claims by democratic states that enemies may be detained indefinitely, without any procedural safeguards, call for caution in this respect. Despite the progress of the international criminal justice system, IHL remains, essentially, a system that depends on self-application. Given the rarity of third-party adjudication and enforcement, the advantages of the schematic solutions of GC III, which refer to points in time that are more easily established objectively, should not be underestimated, at least for the great majority of POWs. One might even wonder whether fully individualized solutions are compatible with the essence of armed conflicts, which are a collective phenomenon. Fully individualized solutions may therefore be conceivable only when the IHL of IACs is no longer needed because the phenomenon it regulates—IACs—no longer exists. Until that day, the regime of GC III, interpreted and modified by IHRL and state practice, as suggested in this chapter, may remain the best protection genuine POWs may obtain. However, this regime, with all its schematic solutions, should not be extended by analogy to other people and NIACs.

MARCO SASSÒLI*

---

[187] Shields Delessert, above n 2, at 106–10.

* I would like to thank Ms Nishat Nishat, LLM for her thorough preparatory research and for the revision of this chapter, and I am grateful to the co-editors for their useful comments and suggestions.

C. GENEVA CONVENTION IV

---

1. GENERAL

Chapter 52. The Structure of Geneva Convention IV and the Resulting Gaps in that Convention

	MN
A. Introduction	1
B. Meaning and Application	3
I. The importance of the different sorts of territory referred to in GC IV	3
a. Parts of the Convention	3
b. Protected persons	6
c. Article 5	7
II. Own and occupied territory	9
a. 'In the territory of a Party to the conflict'	9
b. Occupied territory	17
III. Territory that is neither own nor occupied	18
a. Exercise of control over territory unrelated to the conflict	19
b. Exercise of control related to the conflict	36
C. Resulting Gaps and Possible Solutions	38
I. Resulting gaps—civilians in neither own nor occupied territory with protection needs resembling those of protected civilians	39
a. Ill-treatment	39
b. Forcible deportation	40
c. Deprivation of liberty—internment or detention with a view to criminal proceedings	41
II. Possible solutions—their merits and their inadequacies	44
a. Applying Section I of Part III to the invasion phase	44
b. Using an expanded understanding of 'in the territory of a Party to the conflict'	49
c. Using an expanded understanding of 'occupied territory'	62
d. Common Article 3 and Article 75 AP I	72
D. Relevance in Non-International Armed Conflicts	74
E. Critical Assessment	75

Select Bibliography

Debuf, E., *Captured in War: Lawful Internment in Armed Conflict* (Oxford: Hart Publishing, 2013)

Gasser, H., 'Protection of the Civilian Population', in D. Fleck (ed), *The Handbook of Humanitarian Law in Armed Conflict* (2nd edn, Oxford: OUP, 2008) 237

Kalshoven, F./Zegveld, L., *Constraints on the Waging of War: An Introduction to International Humanitarian Law* (4th edn, Geneva: ICRC, 2011) 58

Siegrist, M., 'The Functional Beginning of Belligerent Occupation' (LLM Thesis, Geneva: The Graduate Institute, 2009; eCahiers, No 7, April 2011, at 35–77, available at <http://iheid.revues.org/75?lang=en>)

Zwanenburg, M., Bothe, M./Sassòli, M., 'Is the Law of Occupation Applicable to the Invasion Phase?', 94 *IRRC* 885 (2012) 29

A. Introduction

1 While the protection offered by international humanitarian law (IHL) to the wounded, sick,[1] and prisoners of war (POWs)[2] applies regardless of where those protected persons are, as long as they 'have fallen into the power' of the enemy,[3] the protection regime for civilians is more nuanced. The impetus behind the rules remains that those who find themselves in the hands of the enemy ought to be protected.[4] However, since the specific circumstances in which a civilian may find himself or herself in the hands of a party to the conflict are various, the protection is dependent on this. While POWs, for example, are to be protected while they are physically in the power of the enemy, civilians may be 'in the hands' of the enemy merely by virtue of being in territory which is controlled by a party to the conflict.[5]

2 The traditional division in the protection regime for civilians contains three categories:

— protection for civilians against the hostilities;
— protection for civilians in the national territory of a party to the conflict; and
— protection for those civilians in occupied territory.

Under the pre-Geneva Conventions law, the first and last of these categories were thought to exist on a temporal continuum.[6] The assumption animating the legal framework was that as a party is invading the territory of its adversary, the civilians in that territory require protection against the effects of the hostilities. However, once the invading party has replaced the local authorities, the civilian population is protected by the law of occupation. Therefore, the type of protection extended to those on territory that is being invaded differs from protection for the population of the occupied territory. On the other hand, the situation of alien civilians in the hands of a party to the conflict by virtue of being in that party's national territory is arguably significantly different from that of those civilians who find themselves in invaded or occupied territory. This difference may be due to the fact that while both these types of civilians might find themselves in need of protection, in occupied territory there is no existing legal framework to govern the interaction between the Occupying Power and the civilians. In a state's own territory, on the other hand, domestic law already governs the relationship between that party and civilians. Thus, while some protection is still necessary for enemy civilians, an entire framework is not required in the latter case.[7] Therefore, there emerge three distinct

---

[1] Mostly contained in GC I and GC II.   [2] Mostly contained in GC III.
[3] Art 5 GC I; Art 4 GC III.
[4] J.S. Pictet, 'The New Geneva Conventions for the Protection of War Victims', 45 *AJIL* (1951) 462, at 473.
[5] Pictet Commentary GC IV, at 47.
[6] E.g., Art 41 of the *Oxford Manual* of 1880 reads: 'Territory is regarded as occupied when, as the consequence of invasion of hostile forces, the state to which it belongs has ceased, in fact, to exercise its ordinary authority therein, and the invading state is alone in a position to maintain order there.' *Oxford Manual of the Laws of War on Land*, 9 September 1880, reproduced in D. Schindler and J. Toman (eds), *The Laws of Armed Conflicts: A Collection of Conventions, Resolutions and Other Documents* (3rd edn, Dordrecht/Geneva: Nijhoff/Henry Dunant Institute, 1988), at 38. This reasoning is also seen in the decision of the American Military Tribunal in the *Hostages Trial*. In determining whether the situation before it constituted occupation under the Hague Regulations, the Tribunal drew a distinction between invasion and occupation: *The Hostages Trial, Trial of Wilhelm List and others*, US Military Tribunal, Nuremberg, UNWCC Law Reports, vol VIII, at 55–6.
[7] This is evident in Art 38 GC IV.

ways to classify the protection of civilians according to the territory in which they find themselves:

— protection granted to civilians in the territory of the enemy party to the conflict;
— protection granted to civilians in invaded territory (where 'invaded' is short for all military operations carried out on the adversary's territory in the absence of a state of occupation); and
— protection granted to civilians in occupied territory.

Each of these involves a slightly different set of rules.

B. Meaning and Application

I. The importance of the different sorts of territory referred to in GC IV

a. Parts of the Convention

The distinction between protection of civilians in the course of hostilities, in the national territory of the enemy party, and in occupied territory is reflected in the very structure of Geneva Convention (GC) IV. The Convention is divided into four Parts. Part I contains general provisions, several of which are common to the four Conventions, and Part IV contains common provisions concerning the execution of the Convention. Part II contains 14 provisions and is concerned with providing general protection to the civilian populations affected by the conflict. Most of these relate to the establishment of special zones and the protection of medical objects and personnel. The brevity of Part II is a result of a conscious decision of the Drafting Committee to remove the bulk of such protection from the final draft.[8] Part III, where most of the substance of the Convention lies, provides detailed guarantees on the status and treatment of protected persons.

Part III is in turn divided into four Sections. At the outset, the title of Section I introduces one of the crucial structural elements of the Convention. The Section is entitled 'Provisions Common to the Territories of the Parties to the Conflict and to Occupied Territories'. Thus, it sets up the dichotomy between 'Territories of the Parties'[9] and 'Occupied Territories'. This division is further cemented by the distinction between Section II, dealing with rules concerning 'Aliens in the Territory of a Party to the Conflict', and Section III, which regulates 'Occupied Territories'. Section IV regulates the treatment of internees without specifying to which territory it applies. However, since the Convention provides for internment only in own or occupied territory,[10] Part IV can apply to internees only in own or occupied territories. Thus, with the exception of the (mostly) conduct of hostilities rules contained in Part II, determining which rules protect a particular civilian will depend on first determining whether the civilian is in a party's own territory or occupied territory.

In sum, the structure of the Convention reflects the regime of differentiated protection depending on the classification of territory. Where a party wishes to take an action

---

[8] Pictet Commentary GC IV, at 10. It is mainly AP I that seeks to provide civilians protection from the conduct of hostilities.
[9] For the purposes of this chapter, I shall refer to this as 'own territory'.   [10] Art 79 GC IV.

on its own territory, it must comply with Sections I, II, and IV of Part III. Where territory is in an 'invasion stage', i.e. where hostilities continue, both parties are bound by Part II. Lastly, where a party has occupied a territory, it is bound by Sections I, III, and IV of Part III.

b. Protected persons

6   While the question of who is a protected civilian is dealt with in detail in Chapter 55 of this volume, for present purposes it is nevertheless vital to refer to this issue, since the division between territory as own or occupied is also contained in Article 4 GC IV. In identifying the criteria to be fulfilled for a person to be protected by GC IV, the Article makes reference to a 'belligerent State' and 'Occupying Power' in a way that implies that these are mutually exclusive. Article 4 begins with the general rule that all persons who find themselves in the hands of a party to the conflict or Occupying Power of which they are not a national are protected. The rest of the Article details exceptions to this general rule. The division between own and occupied territory is most clearly implied by the exception that relates to nationals of neutral states in contrast to nationals of a co-belligerent state. The Article provides that '[n]ationals of a neutral State who find themselves *in the territory of a belligerent State*, and nationals of a co-belligerent State, shall not be regarded as protected persons while the State of which they are nationals has normal diplomatic representation in the State in whose hands they are'.[11] The exception relating to neutral state nationals is qualified by their location—that they must be in the 'territory of a belligerent State'—whereas the location of nationals of a co-belligerent state is not qualified in this way. This suggests that protection, or rather protected person status, is limited for neutral state nationals on the territory of a belligerent state. This issue is addressed in the Pictet Commentary to GC IV, which clearly differentiates between those who are protected 'in the territory of belligerent States' and 'in occupied territories', and excludes nationals of a neutral state from protected person status only in the territory of a belligerent state and not in occupied territories.[12]

c. Article 5

7   If any doubt remained about the importance of the classification of territory for the purposes of GC IV protection, this can be dispelled by the text of Article 5 GC IV on derogations.[13] The first paragraph of the Article outlines the case of a protected person in 'the territory of a Party to the conflict'. The second paragraph does the same for protected persons in 'occupied territory'. No other scenario is referred to. This further supports the position that the treatment of persons protected by GC IV is intertwined with the territory in which those persons are. It also cements the 'own'/'occupied' distinction in GC IV.

8   Classification of the territory (as either own or occupied), together with nationality, is of the utmost importance in order to ascertain the protection to which a civilian is entitled. Such a classification is crucial to determine who enjoys protected person status in the first place. Further, precisely what protections are enjoyed by the person is also linked to whether he or she is a protected person in a party's own territory, or a protected person in occupied territory.

---

[11] Emphasis added.   [12] Pictet Commentary GC IV, at 46.
[13] See also Ch 54 of this volume, section B.I.b.

II. Own and occupied territory

a. 'In the territory of a Party to the conflict'

As discussed above (MN 6), Article 4 paragraph 2 GC IV introduces the phrase 'in the territory of a belligerent State'. Further, Part III of GC IV is divided into four Sections, each with its own scope of applicability. Section I contains 'Provisions Common to the Territories of the Parties to the Conflict and Occupied Territories'; Section II applies to 'Aliens in the Territory of a Party to the Conflict'; and Section III applies to 'Occupied Territory'.[14] Thus, the 'territory of a belligerent' or 'territory of a Party to the conflict' emerge in contrast to 'occupied territory', and are phrases that have a crucial bearing on determining the applicability of Section II of Part III.

At first glance, the reference in GC IV to 'territory of a belligerent' seems to be capable of being understood as the territory of either party of the conflict—a belligerent's own territory or its opponent's. However, the situation of protected persons 'in the territory of a belligerent State' is generally understood to relate to the situation where enemy nationals (and other protected persons) are on a belligerent state's own territory,[15] and therefore the corresponding provisions contained in Section II of Part III apply to such territory. While this is generally uncontroversial, there are at least five arguments which may nevertheless be presented to support this interpretation.

First, the drafting history of GC IV indicates that the Section containing rules for such territory was intended for the protection of enemy civilians in the territory of a party who were interned *en masse* during the Second World War. The seeds of GC IV were sown in 1923 when the XIth International Conference called for a Conference to supplement the Hague Regulations. In response to this, the XIIth Conference drafted regulations that aimed to protect civilians in the territory of an enemy state.[16] The protection of such civilians was also in the minds of those at the 1929 Diplomatic Conference, who unanimously recommended a study that would lead to the conclusion of 'an international Convention on the conditions and protections of civilians of enemy nationality on the territory of a belligerent'.[17] Such recommendations led to the 'Tokyo Draft'.[18] In Article 1, the Tokyo Draft sets out whom it aims to protect. In paragraph (b) it clearly explicates that apart from enemy nationals in occupied territory, an enemy civilian is a 'national of an enemy country in the territory of a belligerent'. This was the historical context of the regime of protection in GC IV. Therefore, it is reasonable to interpret this section as seeking to provide protection to the group of people that its predecessor(s) sought to protect—enemy nationals in the territory of a party to the conflict.

Secondly, in order to be a protected person under GC IV, a person needs to be 'in the hands' of a party to the conflict of which he or she is not a national (Article 4 paragraph 1 GC IV). If 'in the hands' is understood to mean 'subject to the jurisdictional authority of' then, according to the traditional philosophy that animates international law, a civilian would be in the hands of a party either when he or she is in the party's own territory or

---

[14] For completeness, Section IV contains provisions which are 'Regulations for the Treatment of Internees'.
[15] E.g., see D. Fleck (ed), *The Handbook of International Humanitarian Law* (2nd edn, Oxford: OUP, 2008), at 311.
[16] ICRC, *The Geneva Conventions of August 12, 1949*, Preliminary Remarks (Geneva: ICRC, 2008), at 17.
[17] Ibid.
[18] Draft International Convention on the Condition and Protection of Civilians of enemy nationality who are on territory belonging to or occupied by a belligerent, Tokyo (1934).

when he or she is in occupied territory.[19] Therefore, if not in occupied territory, protected persons 'in the territory of a belligerent' are protected vis-à-vis the territorial state.

13 Thirdly, the rules relating to the treatment of protected persons 'in the territory of a belligerent' are contained in a Section entitled 'Aliens in the Territory of a Party to the Conflict', which implies that protected persons are non-nationals in that territory. Part III of GC IV, which contains special rules for protected persons only, is divided into four Sections. The title of Section I distinguishes between 'Territories of the Parties to the Conflict' and 'Occupied Territories', but contains provisions that apply to both. However, while the rules that apply only to occupied territories are contained in Section III, 'Occupied Territories', the corresponding provisions that apply only to the territories of the parties to the conflict are contained in Section II, 'Aliens in the Territory of a Party to the Conflict'. If 'Aliens' is read as a description of the relationship between the protected persons and the territory in which they find themselves, this indicates that this Section applies to the Party in relation to its own territory. Applying this Section to aliens in the territory of the other party would leave enemy nationals unprotected, and would be applicable only to nationals of neutral states without diplomatic relations with the non-territorial belligerent.

14 Fourthly, and perhaps most crucially, are considerations deriving from the protection granted by the provisions themselves. Drafted before the era when international human rights law (IHRL) had come into its own, the Geneva Conventions sought to provide maximum humanitarian protection while respecting the principle of territorial sovereignty. Section II of Part III of GC IV is rather bare and covers only the most basic matters, such as the right to leave (Article 35 GC IV), humane treatment and timely repatriation for those in confinement (Article 37 GC IV), the minimum standard of treatment for non-repatriated persons (Article 38 GC IV), provisions on means of existence (Article 39 GC IV) and employment (Article 40 GC IV), internment (Article 42 GC IV), treatment of refugees (Article 44 GC IV), and transfers to another power (Article 45 GC IV). If this section were to apply only to a party's own territory then this minimalism seems more reasonable, since it represents the compromise between assuring humanitarian treatment and respecting territorial sovereignty. Further, the particular deference in Article 38 to provisions concerning aliens in time of peace to regulate the situation of protected persons, also implies that this section is intended to regulate the relationship between a party and protected aliens in its own territory.

15 Lastly, and related to the previous point, the substance of certain articles of Section II of Part III implies a fairly high degree of control, such as would be fulfilled only in situations of occupation (as traditionally understood under Article 42 of the Hague Regulations) or on a party's national territory. For instance, in order to abide by Articles 39 and 40, which deal with granting protected persons the opportunities to find paid employment and the conditions on compelling protected persons to work, a belligerent must either be an Occupying Power or on its own territory. Since this section does not cover occupied territory, it necessarily applies to a party's own territory. The traditional understanding of 'the territory of a belligerent' is the belligerent's own national territory. This interpretation is based on the above arguments and is generally uncontroversial.

16 This territory includes overseas territory, such as Anguilla, Bermuda, British Antarctic territory, British Indian Ocean territory, British Virgin Islands, Cayman Islands, Gibraltar, Montserrat, Pitcairn Islands, Saint Helena, Ascension and Tristan da Cunha,

---

[19] See also Pictet Commentary GC IV, at 47.

South Georgia and the South Sandwich Island, and Turks and Caicos Islands, all of which are the United Kingdom's (UK's) overseas territories.[20] Overseas territory is territory which is a part of the principal state's national territory but which is physically not located in the same geographical area, but the sovereignty of the state over the territory is not controversial.

b. Occupied territory

Occupied territory is discussed in detail in Chapter 67 of this volume. However, without prejudicing the discussion in that chapter, it might be said that there are two possible understandings of occupied territory for the purposes of GC IV. The first is by application of the Hague Regulations' definition of occupation requiring actual control in the form of an administration, or at least the capacity for such administration. Control in this sense would be such that it would allow the Occupying Power to discharge all the duties incumbent on it. The second understanding of occupation is more flexible, allowing for a power to be bound under provisions of GC IV incrementally as it acquires the requisite amount of control to discharge particular duties. Thus, occupation begins as soon as there is control, but not all provisions of GC IV come into effect immediately.

III. Territory that is neither own nor occupied

Article 4 GC IV begins with a very broad definition of protected persons, i.e. all persons who find themselves in the power of a party to the conflict but who are not the nationals of that party. The structure of GC IV then betrays the assumption that in reality all persons requiring the protection of the Convention will be either in a party's own territory, or in enemy territory which has been occupied. This raises the question of whether it is possible to be in the power of a party to the conflict without being in either of these territories. Or alternatively to be in a territory over which a state exercises some form of control but which is neither its own nor occupied. There are various degrees of control a state may exercise over territory short of such territory being straightforwardly the state's own or occupied. Such control may either be related to the conflict or not.

a. Exercise of control over territory unrelated to the conflict

A state may exercise control over territory which is not straightforwardly its national territory for reasons that are unrelated to the conflict. Further, it may either have consent to exercise such control, or it may not. Two cases where a state might have consent either from the sovereign or from the population to control the territory are leasehold territories and dependent territories. Two cases where a state exercises control without consent are territories which it has previously occupied and colonies.

A leasehold territory is a territory that is legally a part of state A but which has been put at the disposal of state B through an agreement between the states. While not part of the sovereign territory of a state, lease territories in most instances are under the effective control of the leasing or administering state. Taking the examples of Hong Kong between 1898 and 1997, and Guantánamo Bay after 1934, there seems little doubt that the UK and the United States (US) respectively exercised effective control in a way which is not very different from

---

[20] These territories are considered as such by the UK. The status of the Falkland Islands is more controversial. See UK Government, *Types of British Nationality—British Overseas Territories Citizens*, available at <https://www.gov.uk/types-of-british-nationality/british-overseas-territories-citizen>.

military occupation. While the two cases are different because the latter is purely a military base, nevertheless, the control exerted over this territory still involved, in the case of Hong Kong, and involves, in the case of Guantánamo Bay, the capacity of the leasing state to impose its will on all those within the territory. Thus, persons in these places were (Hong Kong) and are (Guantánamo Bay) in the power of the UK and the US respectively.

21   The alternative to treating lease/concession territory as not being part of a party's own territory for the purposes of GC IV leads to unacceptable results. Given that the substantive rules of GC IV apply only to a party's own territory or occupied territory, this would mean that in a hypothetical conflict between China and the UK in 1984, Chinese nationals in Hong Kong, who would be subject to both the physical and legal control of the UK, would not enjoy any of the protections of GC IV.

22   However, it might be possible to make an argument on the basis of the conditions and implementation of the specific lease agreements that the leasing party does not have effective control or jurisdiction over the territory. In this case, it might be possible to claim that these should not be treated in the same way as 'the territory of a party to the conflict'.

23   Therefore, for the purposes of GC IV, 'the territory of a party to the conflict' ought to be understood more broadly to include leasehold territory, without prejudice to general international law claims to territory.

24   Dependent territories are those territories which enjoy a great degree of autonomy in internal affairs but depend on the principal or metropolitan state for international representation. While historically, dependent territories have included colonies, today they would also include territories which are in a consensual relationship of dependence with the metropolitan state. This includes entities such as the Crown Dependencies of the UK (The Isle of Man and Channel Islands), Greenland and the Faroe Islands, which are dependent on Denmark, and Aruba, Curaçao, and Sint Maarten, which are dependent on The Netherlands.

25   It is not immediately obvious that the relationship between the metropolitan state and dependent or administered territories is identical to the relationship between that state and its national territory. Metropolitan states tend not to exercise physical control over dependent territory.

26   Nevertheless, there are at least five arguments which may be advanced to support the position that the sort of control exercised by the metropolitan state over such territory ought to be regarded as equivalent to that exercised over its national territory.

27   First, a person in a dependent territory is in the power of the principal state since, for the purposes of international law, these territories are usually represented by the principal state. For instance, the UK has signed the Geneva Conventions on behalf of the Channel Islands. There is no practice of any dependent territory becoming signatory to the Geneva Conventions. Nor are these territories recognized as states by the United Nations (UN). Therefore, it would seem that either international law as such does not apply to these territories, or that the treaty obligations of the principal state are also applicable on dependent or administered territory. Thus, at least for the purposes of international obligations, this territory is under the jurisdiction of the principal state, and therefore the people on this territory are in the power of the principal state.

28   Secondly, the inhabitants of most of these territories have the nationality of the principal state. This seems to be indicative of the sort of relationship between the principal state and the territory which warrants protection for enemy nationals in the territory. Even if nationality is not equated to allegiance, not treating dependent territory as the principal

state's territory would mean that should the principal state be involved in an international armed conflict (IAC) and inhabitants of a dependent territory find themselves in the territory of the enemy state, they would be protected enemy nationals. Nationals of the state opposing the principal state, however, would not. This seems odd for 'enemy nationals'.

It could be argued that the situation discussed above is precisely the situation pertaining to neutral nationals in a party's national territory if the neutral state does not have normal diplomatic representation. The neutral national would be a protected person under GC IV, while a national of the state party to the conflict would not be protected by the Geneva Conventions when in the territory of the neutral state.

Nevertheless, it is difficult to accept that territory which is so closely aligned to the principal state that its inhabitants share the nationality of the principal state ought to be treated as neutral. And to the extent that territory may only be a state's own, its enemy's, or a neutral state's, it seems much more intuitive to treat this territory as the state's own.

Further, to the extent the Geneva Conventions seem to rely on normal diplomatic relations as an indicator of protection needs, dependent territories should be regarded as a party's national territory, since neutral nationals on dependent territory would carry out their diplomatic relations through the principal state. Thus, if diplomatic relations between a neutral state and the principal state are ruptured and the principal state is involved in an IAC, the neutral state's national does not have diplomatic relations with any entity that represents the territory.

While none of the above arguments is convincing on its own, it seems that the Geneva Conventions look to three elements in order to consider whether persons should be protected persons under GC IV:

— the territory in which those persons find themselves;
— their nationality; and
— in the case of non-enemy nationals not in occupied territory, whether normal diplomatic representation continues.

Therefore, in light of these three factors, a strong case can be made that territory which is administered by a party to the conflict, whose inhabitants have the nationality of that party, and whose diplomatic relations are carried out by that party, ought to be considered to be sufficiently under the control of that party to the conflict to attract the application of the parts of GC IV applicable in that party's territory.

The last argument which may be made in favour of treating dependent and administered territory as part of the principal state's territory is based on Article 35 GC IV. Given the high degree of internal control of the independent government of such territories, it is difficult to see how much of Sections I and II of Part III might be relevant. However, to the extent that the principal state is responsible for the movement of persons in and out of the territory, Article 35 GC IV might well be relevant.

In contrast to leasehold territories and dependent territories, a state may also exercise effective control over a territory without the consent of the sovereign or the population. One such instance is where a state is an Occupying Power over a third state in the context of a separate conflict. However, provided that relationships are viewed through the lens of protected persons, this scenario does not pose great difficulties, since all persons except co-belligerent nationals (provided their state has normal diplomatic relations) present on this territory are protected persons in relation to the occupying state in any event. Thus, while the question of how to classify this territory in the context of the new conflict might be an interesting one from a purely technical perspective, for the purposes of determining the legal regime applicable to the territory and the persons on it, this question has little bearing.

35   Curiously, the same does not seem to be true for colonies. Though the concept of 'colonies' is not straightforward for international law, and the classification of territories as 'Non-Self-Governing Territories' by the UN Special Committee on Decolonization attracts much controversy in contemporary times,[21] if the matter is examined from the perspective of the pre-UN era, it seems that in the First World War and the Second World War, colonies of belligerents were treated as part of the colonial power. Indeed, when the colonial power became party to the conflict, its colonies did too. Thus, colonies were treated as a party's national territory. This implies that the regime for a party's national territory provided by GC IV would be applicable in colonies. If regarded in isolation from general international law questions about the right to self-determination, this seems appropriate, since the sort of control that a colonial state would exercise over its colony would be akin to that which it exercises over its own territory.

b. Exercise of control related to the conflict

i. Operations conducted on neutral states

36   A state may conduct operations in the territory of a neutral state with that state's consent, in the course of which civilians may fall into its power. In this case, it is unclear whether IHL applies to this situation at all. Arguably, such an operation ought to be governed by human rights law and the domestic law of the neutral state. This question is explored thoroughly in Chapter 4 of this volume, section B.I.b. The consequences of insisting on the applicability of GC IV to such a situation would in any event mean that no substantive rule of GC IV would protect civilians in the hands of party, and the relationship between the two would be governed by other bodies of law.

ii. Invaded territory

37   Assuming that the Geneva Conventions are applicable in the territory (including on flagged ships on the high seas) (see Chapter 4, section B.I.b of this volume), the most obvious candidate for territory that is neither own nor occupied is 'invaded' territory, which has not yet been placed under the authority of the invading force and in which hostilities continue to occur. Under a Hague Regulations' understanding of occupation, this territory is not occupied[22] (and is clearly not the invading forces' own territory). Under the more flexible approach to occupation (Chapter 67, section B.V.d of this volume), this territory would attract the application of some parts of the law of occupation but not others. Thus, in some ways and for certain purposes, this territory is neither own nor occupied even under a flexible definition of occupation.

C. Resulting Gaps and Possible Solutions

38   If it is accepted that the main aim of GC IV is to protect civilians (which is fairly uncontroversial), it seems that, when coupled with the Hague Regulations' definition of

---

[21] For instance, Gibraltar remains on the list despite having had two referendums on its sovereignty, one in 1967 and one in 2002. Though it must be noted that these referendums gave the people of Gibraltar the choice between British or Spanish sovereignty over the island. See Government of Gibraltar, *Information Services: Political Development*, available at <https://www.gibraltar.gov.gi/political-development>.

[22] See Ch 67 of this volume, at MN 41.

occupation, the structure of the Convention betrays the assumption that in the invasion phase, the protection needs of civilians can adequately be met by rules on the conduct of hostilities and those contained in Part II. This creates a very serious lacuna in protection for those civilians who find themselves personally (i.e. not merely by virtue of being in the realm of administrative influence) in the power of the enemy during the invasion phase. It is likely that such civilians will have pressing protection needs, many of which resemble those of protected civilians in the custody of an enemy belligerent. Such needs may include protection from ill-treatment, forcible deportation, and arbitrary deprivation of liberty.

I. Resulting gaps—civilians in neither own nor occupied territory with protection needs resembling those of protected civilians

a. Ill-treatment

In the first instance, the most urgent protection need of civilians who come into contact with an invading force is protection against ill-treatment. This ill-treatment is distinct from being the object of attack in a conduct of hostilities sense, from which they are protected by virtue of the rule that an attacking party may direct its attacks only against military objectives.[23] Ill-treatment here refers to the kind of ill-treatment which requires a higher degree of control over the individual, such as subjection to biological experiments, wilful causation of a high degree of suffering, or serious injury to body or health, including sexual violence.

b. Forcible deportation

Just as in the case of an occupation, civilians may be forcibly deported or removed from invaded territory, either individually or *en masse*, as an invading force advances.

c. Deprivation of liberty—internment or detention with a view to criminal proceedings

An invading force may wish to take civilians into its custody for a number of reasons ('battlefield detainees'). One likely scenario is where a civilian is directly participating in hostilities. An invading force may wish to hold such a civilian in its power, at least until the end of the operation in which it is engaged, but perhaps even beyond that, until the end of the conflict. While there are good reasons to allow an invading power to hold in its custody such civilians who pose a threat to its security, the situation also creates a need to protect the civilian against arbitrary and/or indefinite deprivation of his or her liberty. Generally, protection against arbitrary deprivation of liberty includes having a legal basis for such deprivation, informing the person of the reasons for deprivation of his or her liberty, and regular review of those reasons, which results in release in cases where the reasons are no longer relevant (see Chapter 64 of this volume, section B.III and IV for further details).

Further, an invading power may wish to try a civilian for the acts he or she has committed against its forces, or for war crimes even if not committed against its forces. In this case, the protection needs of the civilian would include judicial guarantees and safeguards, including a legal basis that complies with the principle of legality, an impartial

---

[23] Art 52(2) AP I, which reflects customary law.

43 Thus, there are clearly situations in which civilians will fall into the hands of an invading force which is not carrying out operations on its own territory, or which has not consolidated its control sufficiently to be regarded as an Occupying Power under the Hague Regulations. So, while they are protected persons under Article 4 paragraph 1 GC IV, they do not benefit from any of the substantive provisions in Part III. Nevertheless, the enemy state may exercise sufficient control over these individual civilians so as to give rise to protection needs that cannot be addressed by the rules in Part II of GC IV. This could be seen as a problem, and some solutions are canvassed in the next section.

II. Possible solutions—their merits and their inadequacies

a. Applying Section I of Part III to the invasion phase

44 One possible solution might be to apply Section I of Part III to the invasion phase, and thus to the invading Power's treatment of civilians it encounters. The title of Part III of GC IV is 'Status and Treatment of Protected Persons'. Therefore, in order to fit within the rules of treaty interpretation, it would need to be shown that the civilians in question meet the definition of 'protected persons'. Under the traditional understanding of the term, determining whether someone falls within the category of 'protected person' in GC IV involves first determining the territory that person is in (Article 4 paragraph 2 GC IV). However, it could be argued that the text of Article 4 in fact allows for another reading, under which the protection of the Convention is not contingent on the person's being in either own or occupied territory. The first paragraph of the Article reads:

> Persons protected by the Convention are those who at a given moment and in any manner whatsoever, find themselves, in case of a conflict or occupation, in the hands of a Party to the conflict or Occupying Power of which they are not nationals.

The civilians under discussion fulfil this condition unless they are nationals of the invading Power.[24] Thus, it might be argued that these civilians are protected persons under GC IV.

45 The title of Section I of Part III is 'Provisions Common to the Territories of the Parties to the Conflict and to Occupied Territories'. Once again, this title is capable of accommodating a reading which could justify applying this section to the invasion phase. After all, invaded territory is a territory of a party to the conflict. Further, no rule in this Section would make such an interpretation absurd.

46 Applying this Section to the invasion phase would fill the most pressing of the protection gaps created by the structure of GC IV. It contains general prohibitions against ill-treatment (Article 27), as well as specifically prohibiting using civilians as human shields (Article 28), coercion, corporal punishment (Article 31), torture, murder and other brutality (Article 32), collective punishment, pillage and reprisals (Article 33), and taking hostages (Article 34).

47 However, unless an argument could be made that forced transfer or arbitrary detention is a form of ill-treatment covered by the general guarantee of 'respect for their person' or

---

[24] M. Sassòli, 'A Plea in Defence of Pictet and the Inhabitants of Territories under Invasion: The Case for the Applicability of Convention IV during the Invasion Phase', 94 *IRRC* 885 (2012) 42, at 43.

humane treatment, nothing in this Section gives sufficient guidance on these matters. Further, even if it were argued that arbitrary detention is prohibited, Article 27 clarifies that the parties to the conflict may intern civilians (to the extent it is a 'measur[e] of control and security [...] necessary as a result of the war'). What this Section does not provide, however, is the procedure to do so lawfully.

48 Therefore, a strong argument may be made that the Convention should be interpreted in such a way that Section I of Part III is applied to the invasion phase. While this is desirable because it provides civilians in invaded areas with basic guarantees against ill-treatment, the gaps in the Convention concerning the transfer of such civilians and the deprivation of their liberty remain.

b. Using an expanded understanding of 'in the territory of a Party to the conflict'

49 As explained above (MN 11–15), five arguments may be advanced for interpreting 'in the territory of a Party to the conflict' as limited to aliens in a party's own territory, i.e.:

— that this seems to have been the intention of the drafters;
— that such an interpretation is a consequence of the requirement that the persons to be protected find themselves in the hands of the enemy;
— that the subtitle of Section II of Part III refers to 'Aliens';
— that such an interpretation makes coherent the rules of Section II of Part III; and
— that such an interpretation fits with the traditional classification of territory as either own, invaded, or occupied.

50 Even if most of these arguments could successfully be countered,[25] it is difficult to deny that the actual rules relating to protected civilians in the territory 'of a Party to the conflict' seem, by their nature, to indicate that they should be applicable to protected civilians in a party's own territory. For example, as discussed above (MN 15), it would be strange to hold a belligerent not in its own territory to the obligation of providing protected persons the opportunity to find paid employment (under Article 39 GC IV) without considering the presence of such a belligerent as occupation.

51 Nevertheless, let us assume that the arguments for an expanded reading of what can be considered as falling under 'territory of a Party to the conflict' are defensible. The next question is whether such a reading assists in finding rules in GC IV which may be applied

---

[25] E.g., with regard to the first of these arguments, it might be countered that under Art 32 VCLT, the *travaux préparatoires* may act only as a secondary means of interpretation in the event the meaning of the provisions remains unclear despite recourse to the ordinary meaning of the words in light of the object and purpose of the treaty. This argument might be developed by pointing out that 'territory of a Party to the conflict', according to the ordinary meaning of the words, does not seem obviously to exclude the territory of the opponent. Further, since the object and purpose of GC IV is to provide protection for civilians persons in the event of armed conflict, if an expansive meaning assists in protecting another category of civilians without requiring an unreasonable stretch of the ordinary meaning of the words, then such an expansive meaning is a legitimate reading. In relation to the second argument, it could be pointed out that while presence on own and occupied territory are two examples of what 'in the hands of the enemy' could mean, being detained by a party to the conflict is uncontroversially to be in the hands of that Power regardless of where such detention is. In relation to the third argument, it could be pointed out that 'alien' could equally refer to the relationship between the person in question and the party in whose power that person finds himself or herself. There are no compelling reasons to think of this merely as a relationship that concerns territory. With regard to the fourth argument, one could attempt to advance the view that while reading Section II or Part III makes most sense if 'in the territory of a Party to the conflict' is taken to mean a party's national territory, reading 'in the territory of a Party to the conflict' more broadly also makes sense. Lastly, the traditional distinction between the three types of territory could be challenged in light of the context of modern conflicts.

in situations where a state is conducting military operations against another state extraterritorially without occupying it.

52   Section I of Part III provides for minimum standards of humane treatment. Section II of this Part contains provisions on the procedure for the deprivation of liberty of protected persons. However, since the underlying assumption in the Pictet Commentary to GC IV is that rules relating to civilians in the territory of a belligerent are for 'enemy nationals retained on the territory of one of the Parties to the conflict',[26] a 'new' reading of the applicability of relevant provisions is required so that Section II of Part III would apply to invaded (but not occupied) territory.

i. Legal basis for internment or detention with a view to criminal proceedings

53   Article 41 GC IV authorizes the internment of protected civilians, with Article 42 specifying that the reason for such internment must be that it is necessary for the security of the Detaining Power, and with Article 43 setting up the review procedure. What is not clear, however, is whether Article 42 can itself be the legal ground for internment. For dualist systems, a legal basis in domestic law must always be established in any event.[27] In the context of monist systems, we need to enquire into whether the provision is intended to be self-executing, and whether it is clear and precise enough to be able to be so.[28] The Pictet Commentary to Article 42 points out that since

> [i]t did not seem possible to define the expression 'security of the State' in a more concrete fashion [i]t is [...] left very largely to Governments to decide the measure of activity prejudicial to the internal or external security of the State which justifies internment or assigned residence.[29]

Arguably, however, such a decision would have to be made in a way that conforms to the principle of legality, which requires that the detention be 'undertaken in accordance with procedures, laid out in both domestic and international law'[30] so that it is foreseeable. Therefore it must be embodied in a clear and precise domestic law as such.[31]

54   In the case of detention for criminal proceedings, GC IV does not provide guidance regarding what kind of crimes may be tried. However, as with internment, in order to conform to the principle of legality as defined by international law, including IHRL, the applicable law must be previously established, such that the person charged could have foreseen that his or her act might have led to such proceedings (see Chapter 59, section B.II.d, of this volume).

55   Participation in hostilities by civilians is one act for which an invading state is likely to want to detain civilians. Participation in hostilities by civilians is not generally accepted as a war crime,[32] and is thus not a ground for an exercise of universal jurisdiction. Further, an invading state which is not yet an Occupying Power would not apply the law of the

---

[26] Pictet Commentary GC IV, at 244.
[27] P. Malanczuk, *Akehurst's Modern Introduction to International Law* (7th edn, New York: Routledge, 1997), at 65.
[28] C.M. Vázquez, 'The Four Doctrines of Self-Executing Treaties', 89 *AJIL* (1995) 695, at 710–15.
[29] Pictet Commentary GC IV, at 257.
[30] T. Davidson and K. Gibson, 'Experts Meeting on Security Detention Report', 40 *Case Western Reserve JIL* (2009) 323, at 341.
[31] For the contrary position, that Art 42 may itself be the legal basis for detention, see J. Pejic, 'Procedural Principles and Safeguards for Internment/Administrative Detention in Armed Conflict and Other Situations of Violence', 87 *IRRC* 858 (2005) 375, at 383.
[32] N. Melzer, *Interpretive Guidance on the Notion of Direct Participation in Hostilities under International Humanitarian Law* (Geneva: ICRC, 2009), at 85.

territorial state (i.e. it does not exercise territorial jurisdiction). Therefore, it is most likely that if an invading state wishes to prosecute a civilian for acts such as participation in hostilities in the invasion phase, it will be forced to rely on its own domestic legislation which is applicable extraterritorially, even to non-nationals.

As the criminal codes of many states tend to apply either on their territory or to their nationals, it is unlikely that an invading state will be able to apply its criminal code to civilians it encounters as it invades enemy territory. However, an invading state might have legislation which applies to acts that affect its nationals, that is, legislation which relies on the passive personality principle of jurisdiction. Domestic anti-terrorism legislation might be such a legal basis. While in some cases, this sort of legislation might be both appropriate and precise enough to serve as a legal basis, in other cases it may not be either of these.

In addition to this, it is not clear what the basis would be for enforcing the invading state's domestic legislation in the territory of the invaded state. While such enforcement jurisdiction may be granted extraterritorially where a state acts either with the consent of the territorial state or explicitly in the framework of the law of occupation, both these situations are precluded here.

Therefore, while in some cases an invading state may be able to rely on its domestic law as the legal basis for detention, there will be other cases where this will be insufficient. In those cases, there may not be a legal basis which meets the requirements of the principle of legality. Further, enforcement jurisdiction, even where the legislative jurisdiction can be established, remains problematic to assert in the invasion phase. Applying Section II of Part III to invaded territory does not provide adequate answers to these problems.

ii. Judicial guarantees, humane treatment, review of detention, and release

In the event that persons find themselves in detention or facing trial, their treatment will be regulated by Articles 37 and 38 GC IV, and therefore they will be entitled to humane treatment and essential judicial safeguards as outlined by IHRL. Further, in the case of security detention, such persons will be entitled to have their continued detention reviewed at least twice yearly in conformity with Article 43 GC IV. Further, they must be released as soon as the reasons for their internment cease (Article 46 GC IV).

iii. Transfer

The matter of transfer from invaded territory is not addressed in Section II of Part III. Article 45 GC IV covers transfer to another power, and deals with the transfer of custody rather than physical deportation. Though this may be relevant in some cases, it is not intended to address deportation as such. Thus, applying the expanded interpretation of 'in the territory of a belligerent' does not provide any additional guidance as to the rule covering deportation from invaded territory.

iv. Merits and inadequacies of using an expanded understanding of 'in the territory of a Party to the conflict' in Section II of Part III

From the above exercise, it may be concluded that applying the parts of GC IV that relate to protected persons in the territory of a party to the conflict to those civilians who are neither aliens in a belligerent state nor in occupied territory (i.e. in territory undergoing invasion), does not provide sufficient guidance regarding the legal basis for three of the areas examined: detention, criminal prosecution, or deportation. However, it does provide for some minimum standards for treatment and guarantees in case of trial.

c. Using an expanded understanding of 'occupied territory'

62 Another option is to use an expanded understanding of 'occupied territory', known as 'functional theory of occupation', such that it would allow at least some provisions of Section III of Part III to be applied to the civilians in a territory being invaded. Arguments to support such an understanding of the notion of occupation are laid out in Chapter 67, section B.V.d, of this volume, so here we need only examine whether this would be an adequate solution to fill the gap identified.

63 Since detention necessarily involves being in the power of a party, under this broader view of occupation, persons detained in the course of an invasion would benefit from the provisions that attach to their treatment, provided they meet the nationality criteria of Article 4 GC IV. However, for each relevant provision, a corresponding level of control will be required, and then one would have to determine whether the state or its agents actually exercised this level of control.

i. Legal basis for detention

64 While GC IV provides for the possibility to intern protected civilians in occupied territory, Article 78 cannot itself serve as a legal basis for internment by the invading party in an invaded territory (rather than an occupied territory) since it clearly speaks of internment being in accordance with a procedure previously established by the Occupying Power.[33] Further, in relation to applicable criminal law, the inhabitants of an occupied territory may be tried for offences under the existing law of the occupied territories, or under new legislation passed by the Occupying Power which has been published. In this way, the rules of GC IV would satisfy the principle of legality in the case of a traditional occupation. However, in the case of invasion, the state wishing to detain a civilian does not exercise the requisite control over governmental functions in order to be entitled to enforce the existing laws of the invaded state. Absent this control, general international law would preclude the extraterritorial exercise of jurisdiction. Further, any new laws that might be adopted by the military commander will meet the same challenges with regard to the extraterritorial application of the principle of legality and enforcement jurisdiction that we found when considering applying to this situation the rules for the territory of a party to the conflict (see MN 53–58).

ii. Criminal trials—acts for which a person may be tried

65 Under Article 70 GC IV, the Occupying Power shall not convict protected civilians for acts committed before the occupation. This provision does not seem to require a minimum level of authority as such, it is merely a prohibition. If a broad definition of occupation is used, however, this would mean that a person cannot be tried for an act he committed before he was arrested or captured, since under an expanded notion of occupation, the rule applies here as soon as the person is arrested or captured. The Pictet Commentary to this Article states that in this instance, 'laws and customs of war' are war crimes over which the Occupying Power would exercise universal jurisdiction.[34] Since IHL neither prohibits nor privileges civilian participation in hostilities, participation alone is generally not a war crime.[35] Therefore, one way to view the combination of the

---

[33] This was also the view of the IACommHR in *Coard et al v United States*, Rep No 109/99, 29 September 1999, para 53.
[34] Pictet Commentary GC IV, at 349–50.   [35] Melzer, above n 32.

theory of functional occupation and Article 70 is to assert that in the course of an invasion, a person cannot be tried by a Detaining Power for an act committed before capture unless it is a war crime. However, it is unrealistic to bar a state from prosecuting civilians who have attacked its forces. This would confer upon such civilians a privilege similar to combatant immunity.

It could be argued that the act of hostilities or the attack that the civilian has engaged in is not an act that occurred 'before' the invasion or occupation but rather during it. And that therefore it is not excluded by Article 70 GC IV. This argument would be successful where the act and the capture or arrest of the civilian occur in close temporal proximity. It seems reasonable to see the two as part of the same event if the capture or arrest takes place in the moments after an attack or engagement. However, it is more difficult to maintain this position if a civilian is captured or arrested after the end of an operation or engagement. So while this solution to reconcile functional occupation theory and Article 70 GC IV may work in some cases, in others the problem remains.

iii. Criminal trials—courts

The rules in GC IV regarding which courts may apply laws in occupied territory also assume that the Occupying Power will have more control over the governmental functions than a state does in the invasion phase. Under GC IV, the two types of courts functioning in occupied territory are the existing courts of the occupied territories and regularly constituted non-political military courts formed by the Occupying Power. This means that all offences must be tried by one of these courts, physically within the occupied territory. Article 66 GC IV implies that courts of appeal may sit outside the occupied country. In the course of invasion, the state does not exercise enough control to oversee the acts of existing courts of the occupied territory. With regard to establishing its own courts, this will have to be evaluated in light of what law is being enforced, the concerns regarding jurisdiction in a situation short of occupation, and IHRL concerns regarding military courts. It is unlikely that in the invasion stage, a state will have the sufficient *de facto* control over territory to establish such courts.

Moreover, if these provisions on courts are put together with the above interpretation of Article 70 regarding acts committed before capture, it would mean that even if the Detaining Power is able to establish non-political military courts, these courts would not always be able to try protected civilians for acts committed prior to capture. This would leave the existing courts of the occupied territory as the only authority able to try protected civilians. The Detaining Power, not having established governmental control, may not be in a position to do so without relying on the existing courts of the territorial state to prosecute its civilians. This might prove to be unrealistic for mere direct participation in hostilities.

iv. Transfers for the purposes of trial

Another factor which may have a bearing on the ability of a state to try civilians encountered during invasion is Article 49 GC IV, relating to transfers and deportations. Under this provision, an Occupying Power may not deport inhabitants of an occupied territory to its own territory or any other state. This Article does not seem to require a very high degree of control for a state to be bound by the obligation as it is a negative obligation. Indeed, the International Criminal Tribunal for the former Yugoslavia (ICTY) has accepted that civilians are protected from deportation from the moment they fall into the hands of the enemy.[36] The first matter to be determined here is what constitutes 'occupied territory' in such cases, and whether this would indeed be the very spot of soil on which the person happens to be (see Chapter 67, section B.V.b). Nevertheless, regardless of how this question is answered, Article 49 GC IV would forbid the transfer of a protected civilian outside the state in which the person is captured or arrested. This is a further indirect restriction on the jurisdiction in which that person may be tried, as the provision prevents the capturing state from transferring him or her to the courts in its own territory, reinforcing the rule that that any trials will have to take place within the state where the person was captured.

v. Humane treatment and judicial guarantees

70   Nevertheless, regardless of the problems outlined above, it is clear that should protected persons find themselves in detention, they are entitled to be treated humanely. Should they find themselves facing trial, they are entitled to certain minimum judicial guarantees reflected in the substance of Article 75 of Additional Protocol (AP) I, which is considered customary law in any event (see MN 72). However, on account of having the invasion phase classified as occupation, they also benefit from the rule on humane treatment as outlined in Article 76 GC IV, and from the procedural guarantees outlined in Articles 71–76 GC IV.

vi. Merits and inadequacies of using an expanded understanding of 'occupied territory'

71   It seems that during the invasion phase, in order to establish legal bases both for detention and for courts to try and hear appeals, the degree of control required resembles that which is required for occupation in the traditional sense. Applying a functional theory of occupation to the invasion phase, and thereby placing the detention of persons within the scope of the law of occupation, does not dispense with the very real problem that these provisions inherently require an occupation in the more traditional sense. If they are applied to the invading state in the absence of such an occupation, they could lead to situations where unrealistic limitations are placed on the ability of the invading state to detain and try civilians.

d. *Common Article 3 and Article 75 AP I*

72   Common Article 3 and Article 75 AP I lay out fundamental guarantees for persons not, or no longer, participating in hostilities. Both of these provisions are generally accepted as a reflection of customary international law, thus binding even those states which are not party to AP I.[37] Further, the substance of Common Article 3 has been accepted as applicable in both types of armed conflicts.[38] These guarantees go a long way towards filling the gap created by the structure of GC IV, without requiring the kind of reinterpretation

---

[36] ICTY, *The Prosecutor v Mladen Naletilić and Vinko Martinović*, Trial Chamber Judgment, IT-98-34-T, 31 March 2003, paras 222 and 517.

[37] For CA 3, see ICJ, *Case concerning Military and Paramilitary Activities in and against Nicaragua (Nicaragua v United States of America)*, Judgment of 27 June 1986, Merits, para 218. See ICRC CIHL Database, Rules 87, 89, 90, 91, 92, 93, 96, 99, 100, 101, 102, 103. See also Office of the Press Secretary, The White House, 'Fact Sheet: New Actions on Guantánamo and Detainee Policy', 7 March 2011, available at <http://www.whitehouse.gov/the-press-office/2011/03/07/fact-sheet-new-actions-guant-namo-and-detainee-policy>. The final paragraph of this Fact Sheet states that 'The U.S. Government [which is not party to AP I] will [...] choose out of a sense of legal obligation to treat the principles set forth in Article 75 as applicable to any individual it detains in an international armed conflict, and expects all other nations to adhere to these principles as well.'

[38] *Nicaragua v United States of America*, above n 37.

suggested above. These basic guarantees apply to all persons, regardless of the territory in which they find themselves, and include humane treatment, safeguards in cases of internment or detention with a view to a fair trial, and judicial guarantees in the event that these individuals face criminal proceedings. All of these are spelt out in great detail.

Nevertheless, while Article 75 AP I obliterates the need to perform semantic gymnastics over whether one is a 'protected person' in 'belligerent' or 'occupied' territory, it brings us to the same point as the application of the relevant rules of occupied territory. Questions remain regarding the establishment of the legal basis and the practicalities relating to the court.

D. Relevance in Non-International Armed Conflicts

The classification of territory is important in IACs in order to determine which rules of GC IV are applicable. Relatedly, since some acts, such as unlawful deportation and unlawful confinement, are grave breaches when committed against protected persons,[39] it is also crucial to know what sorts of deportations or confinement would be considered unlawful. By contrast, Common Article 3 does not require such a classification of territory, since it relies on control over persons as the determinant of applicability. In any event, it would be difficult to apply these concepts in a non-international armed conflict, since the involvement of a maximum of one state means that a state is only ever acting on its own territory or with the consent of the territorial state, and so the idea of an enemy state's territory is not applicable.[40]

E. Critical Assessment

The structure of GC IV is based on a particular typology for the classification of territory. In order to determine if and which parts of GC IV are relevant to a particular civilian, it must first be determined how the territory that person is in is classified. On a traditional reading of the Conventions, there are only two types of territory: a belligerent party's own territory, or occupied territory. This binary classification of territory, and its consequences for the way in which GC IV protection is applied, creates a lacuna in protection for civilians who fall into the power of an invading force before the territory is considered occupied. Fortunately, the most pressing protection need of such civilians—that they are treated humanely—is uncontroversially addressed by Article 75 AP I, which is now generally accepted as reflecting customary law.[41] However, problems remain concerning the legal framework for the basis of the deprivation of liberty of 'battlefield detainees' who are not POWs. With increasing acceptance that IHRL applies extraterritorially and in parallel to IHL, even in IAC, the need to provide lawful ways of conducting battlefield detention before the establishment of an administration as an Occupying Power will become more urgent.

NISHAT NISHAT

---

[39] Art 147 GC IV.
[40] If the NIAC takes place on the territory of a third state then it is either also an IAC, or the state is acting with the consent, perhaps even in support, of the territorial state.
[41] See above n 37.

Chapter 53. Maintenance and Re-establishment of Family Links and Transmission of Information

	MN
A. Introduction	1
B. Meaning and Application	8
I. Notion of 'family'	8
II. Privacy of information and data protection	15
III. Communication of family news and facilitation of family enquiries	23
a. Family news	24
b. Family enquiries	30
c. Obligation to encourage the work of organizations	33
IV. Maintenance and re-establishment of family links; transmission of information	35
a. Protection of the civilian population as such	36
b. Protection of 'protected persons' in general	37
c. Protection of aliens in the territory of a party to the conflict	38
d. Protection of civilians in occupied territory	39
e. Protection of interned persons	41
V. Tracing services and transmission of information	57
a. Official Information Bureau	58
b. Central Tracing Agency	68
C. Relevance in Non-International Armed Conflicts	75
D. Legal Consequences of a Violation	79
E. Critical Assessment	85

Select Bibliography

Boutruche, T., 'Missing and Dead Persons', in MPEPIL

Council of Delegates, Resolution 4, 'Restoring Family Links Strategy (and Implementation Plan) for the International Red Cross and Red Crescent Movement (2008–2018)', 23–4 November 2007.

Djurovic, G., *The Central Tracing Agency of the International Committee of the Red Cross: Activities of the ICRC for the Alleviation of the Mental Suffering of War Victims* (Geneva: ICRC, 1986), at 259 ff.

Draper, G.I.A.D., 'The Reunion of Families in Time of Armed Conflict', 17 *IRRC* 191 (1977) 57.

Egger, D./Toman, J., *Family Reunification: Collection of Documents* (Geneva: Henry-Dunant Institute, 1997), at 184 ff.

Sassòli, M., 'The National Information Bureau in Aid of the Victims of Armed Conflicts', 27 *IRRC* 256 (1987) 6.

A. Introduction

Regulation of the maintenance and re-establishment of family links and transmission of information in the context of protected civilians is based on two concerns: first, to prevent protected persons from going missing; and, secondly, where a person is missing, to re-establish links through information, in particular to protect the family as a unit. Legal regulation addresses the situation of protected persons and that of their families, the latter, as expressed in Article 32 of Additional Protocol (AP) I, having the 'right to know the fate of their relatives'. Both concerns form the object and purpose of the Geneva Convention (GC) IV provisions on the maintenance and re-establishment of family links and transmission of information, as distinct but not mutually exclusive obligations.

2   Protecting the link between a person and his or her family first became an issue in international humanitarian law (IHL) in the context of the legal regime protecting prisoners of war (POWs). Article 8 paragraph 2 of the 1929 Convention Relative to the Treatment of Prisoners of War (1929 GC II) provided that every POW should, as soon as possible, be enabled to correspond with his family. Not later than one week after his arrival in camp, and similarly in the case of sickness, each prisoner was expected to be enabled to send a postcard to his family informing them of his capture and/or the state of his health (Article 36 paragraph 2). Parties to the armed conflict were obliged to inform as soon as possible a so-called 'Information Bureau' of all captures of prisoners effected by their armed forces, providing all available particulars of identity to enable the families concerned to be notified quickly, and stating the official addresses via which families might write to the prisoners (Article 77).[1] The GC IV regime on the maintenance and re-establishment of family links and transmission of information relating to civilians is shaped by the legal obligations of the parties to the armed conflict in general, and of Detaining Powers in particular. The occupation regime contains complementary duties of an Occupying Power, both in terms of restoring family links and of transmitting information. Facilitating and supporting obligations are incumbent on all parties to GC IV.

3   Armed conflicts almost inevitably separate families and disrupt family relations, affecting among the civilian population both civilian persons in general and civilians 'specially' protected under GC IV. Families as such are prone to being disrupted and dispersed due to an armed conflict; this applies to families in the power of their 'own' party to the conflict, as well as to families of aliens in the territory of a party to the conflict and families in occupied territory. The basic legal obligation of parties to the armed conflict is the duty to enable civilians, including but not limited to protected persons under GC IV, to give news of a strictly personal nature to members of their families and to receive news from them (Article 25 paragraph 1). They are further required to forward such correspondence (Article 25 paragraph 1) and to facilitate enquiries by members of a family disrupted due to hostilities (Article 26). Parties are also obliged to establish an 'official Information Bureau', responsible for receiving and transmitting information in respect of protected persons who are in the power of a party to the conflict, and to provide the Bureau with information (Article 136). Lastly, the parties must facilitate the transmission of information by a so-called 'Central Information Agency' (Article 140 paragraph 2 GC IV).

4   The legal obligations of Detaining Powers under GC IV with regard to maintaining and re-establishing family links concentrate on accommodating members of the same family together during internment, especially parents and children (Article 82 paragraph 2), and allowing internees to receive visitors, especially close relatives (Article 116). Obligations regarding the transmission of information comprise, in particular, the duties to allow the sending and receiving of letters and cards (Article 107), to enable detainees to send internment cards (Article 106), to allow the receipt of individual parcels or collective shipments

---

[1] On the GC III regime, see Ch 49 of this volume.

(Article 108), and the duty to inform protected persons, the Power to which they owe allegiance, and, as the case may be, their Protecting Power of measures taken as regards detainees' relations with the exterior in general (Article 105). Additional legal obligations of a Detaining Power address, for example, the duties to censor correspondence as quickly as possible (Article 112) and to facilitate certain legal acts (Article 113).

Occupying Powers are obliged, for example, to ensure that members of the same family are not separated when protected persons are forcibly transferred or evacuated from occupied territory (Article 49 paragraph 3). In addition, they have to facilitate the identification of children, as well as registration of their parentage (Article 50 paragraph 2). In the context of an Occupying Power's legal obligation to provide or allow humanitarian assistance to be delivered to an inadequately supplied civilian population, it has the duty to permit receipt of individual relief consignments.[2]

The duty to create the so-called Central Information Agency (now Central Tracing Agency[3]) is incumbent on all High Contracting Parties to GC IV in order to collect and transmit information in respect of protected persons who are in the power of a party to the conflict (Article 140 paragraphs 1 and 2). Further, all states parties have to reduce, as far as possible, charges for telegrams sent by or to internees (Article 110 paragraph 5), to eventually supply Protecting Powers, the International Committee of the Red Cross (ICRC), or other duly approved organizations with suitable means of transport for mail and relief shipments (Article 111 paragraph 1), and to give requisite financial aid to the CTA (Article 140 paragraph 3).

Tracing services have been at the heart of the International Red Cross and Red Crescent Movement from its beginning. On the basis of the 'Agenda for Humanitarian Action' adopted in Resolution 1 of the 28th International Red Cross and Red Crescent Conference, and its General Objective 1 on respecting and restoring the dignity of missing persons and their families, in 2007 the Council of Delegates of the Movement adopted a 'Restoring Family Links Strategy' and Implementation Plan for the years 2008–18 in order to strengthen the capacity of the network composed of the CTA, tracing agencies in ICRC delegations, and the National Societies' tracing services. 'Restoring family links' (RFL) is the generic term used for a variety of activities with a view to preventing separation and disappearance, restoring and maintaining contact between family members, and clarifying the fate of persons reported missing. Apart from armed conflicts and situations of violence falling below the threshold of the Geneva Conventions' Common Article 3, the 2007 RFL strategy and implementation plan covers natural and 'man-made' disasters, management of human remains, and information on the dead and international migration.

B. Meaning and Application

I. Notion of 'family'

Provisions on the maintenance and re-establishment of family links and transmission of information are based on the 'right of families to know'. However, neither the notion of 'family'—'family group'[4] or 'relatives'—nor that of 'next of kin'[5] is defined further in

---

[2] Art 62 GC IV.
[3] In 1960 the name was changed to 'Central Tracing Agency' (CTA), see further MN 68.
[4] Pictet Commentary GC IV, at 196.   [5] Art 138 para 1 GC IV.

IHL. The Pictet Commentary on GC IV defines the term 'family' as 'people who are related or connected by marriage'.[6] Clarification provided by this definition is limited given that, as far the term 'family' is perceived as a natural notion, it is exclusively subjective, since it depends on who and what is subjectively perceived as 'belonging to one family'. Perceptions are moulded, in particular, by a person's emotional setting and subjective evaluation, as well as by social, cultural, religious, traditional, and contextual determinations, and consequently vary. A more objective terminology is provided by legal definitions in national systems. These offer a whole variety of definitions, all resulting from and designed for accommodating the differing cultural, sociological, and legal traditions. The definition and determination of, for instance, which persons are related in a legal sense, are in essence discretionary.

9   The family as a fundamental social and humanitarian value is the underlying concept of the provisions on family news in GC IV. This is incorporated not only in IHL, but also in international human rights law (IHRL).[7] In particular, Article 23(1) of the International Covenant on Civil and Political Rights (ICCPR) provides that the 'family is the natural and fundamental group unit of society and is entitled to protection by society and the State'. Article 17(1) ICCPR specifies that '[n]o one shall be subjected to arbitrary or unlawful interference with his [...] family, home or correspondence', and Article 17(2) that '[e]veryone has the right to protection of the law against such interference or attacks'. In Article 10(1), the International Covenant on Economic, Social and Cultural Rights (ICESCR) recognizes that the 'widest possible protection and assistance should be accorded to the family, which is the natural and fundamental group unit of society, particularly for its establishment', while Article 10(3) states that '[s]pecial measures of protection and assistance should be taken on behalf of all children and young persons'. Article 8 of the European Convention on Human Rights (ECHR) provides:

1. Everyone has the right to respect for his private and family life, his home and his correspondence.
2. There shall be no interference by a public authority with the exercise of this right except such as is in accordance with the law and is [...] for the protection of [...] the rights [...] of others.

Likewise Article 7 of the European Union (EU) Charter of Fundamental Rights states that '[e]veryone has the right to respect for his or her private and family life, home and communications'. While Article 17(1) of the American Convention on Human Rights (ACHR) confirms the family to be 'the natural and fundamental group unit of society and is entitled to protection by society and the state', Article 18(1) of the African Charter on Human and Peoples' Rights (ACHPR) recognizes the family as 'the natural unit and basis of society' which is to be 'protected by the State'.[8] Article 18(1) of the African Charter on the Rights and Welfare of the Child looks at the family as 'the natural unit and basis of society' which 'shall enjoy the protection and support of the State for its establishment

---

[6] Pictet Commentary GC IV, at 192.
[7] Irrespective of details of the specific relationship between IHL and IHRL (see Ch 35 of this volume), IHRL does not cease to be applicable in situations of armed conflict. It is recognized that IHRL could complement IHL.
[8] According to Art 18(2) the state has 'the duty to assist the family which is the custodian of morals and traditional values recognized by the community'.

and development'. Article 12 of the Universal Declaration of Human Rights (UDHR) provides:

> No one shall be subjected to arbitrary interference with his privacy, family, home or correspondence, nor to attacks upon his honour and reputation. Everyone has the right to the protection of the law against such interference or attacks.

The question remains whether IHRL is able to elucidate the meaning of the term 'family'. The United Nations Human Rights Committee (HRCttee) found that 'the concept of the family may differ in some respects from State to State, and even from region to region within a State, and that it is therefore not possible to give the concept a standard definition'. On the other hand, 'when a group of persons is regarded as a family under the legislation and practice of a State, it must be given the protection' under the ICCPR.[9] In its General Comment on Article 17 ICCPR, the HRCttee stated that, for the purposes of the Article, the term 'family' should be interpreted as including 'all those comprising the family as understood in the society of the State party concerned'.[10] The Executive Committee of the United Nations High Commissioner for Refugees distinguishes a 'nuclear family' from 'family', and refers to the 'nuclear family' as consisting of a husband, wife, and their minor children, while at the same time acknowledging that many societies understand 'family' as including dependent unmarried children, minor siblings, and dependent elderly parents.[11] The EU's Directive on the right to family reunification refers to third country nationals, and allows states to provide for reunification of unmarried partners, as well as dependent adult children.[12] Several states earlier implicitly recognized same-sex partners as eventually forming a family.[13] The European Court of Human Rights (ECtHR) has specifically referred to the relationship between husband and wife and children dependent on them within the notion of family,[14] as well as—depending on the circumstances, and especially in relation to children—brothers and sisters, persons living together outside marriage, and grandparents.[15] The Inter-American Commission on Human Rights (IACommHR) has recommended to various states the establishment of central records 'to account for all persons who have been detained, so that their relatives and other interested persons may promptly learn of any arrests'.[16]

10

---

[9] HRCttee, General Comment 19, para 2.   [10] HRCttee, General Comment 16, para 5.

[11] Executive Committee of the High Commissioner's Programme, EC/49/SC/CPR.14, 4 July 1999.

[12] European Union, Council Directive 2003/86/EC, 22 September 2003.

[13] I.e., by recognizing a right of reunification for same-sex partners; see, e.g., W. Kälin et al (eds), *Incorporating the Guiding Principles on Internal Displacement into Domestic Law: Issues and Challenges*, Studies in Transnational Legal Policy No 41 (Washington, DC: American Society of International Law, 2010), at 296, available at <http://www.brookings.edu/~/media/research/files/papers/2010/1/19%20internal%20displacement/0119_internal_displacement_complete.pdf>.

[14] ECtHR, *B v United Kingdom*, Judgment, 8 July 1987, 'the mutual enjoyment by parent and child of each other's company constitutes a fundamental element of family life'.

[15] ECtHR, *Johnston and others v Ireland*, Judgment (Merits and just satisfaction), 18 December 1986; ECtHR, *Moustaquim v Belgium*, Judgment (Merits and just satisfaction), 18 February 1991; ECtHR, *Vermeire v Belgium*, Judgment (Merits), 29 November 1991.

[16] IACommHR, *Annual Report 1980–1981*, Doc OEA/Ser.L/V/II.54 Doc 9 rev 1, 16 October 1981, at 113, 129; IACommHR, *Report on the situation of human rights in Argentina*, Doc OEA/Ser.L/V/II.49, Doc 19, 11 April 1980, at 264; IACommHR, *Report on the situation of human rights in Chile*, Doc OEA/Ser.L/V/II.66 Doc 17, 9 September 1985, at 72; IACommHR, *Report on the situation of human rights in Peru*, Doc OEA/Ser.L/V/II.83 Doc 31, 12 March 1993, at 60.

11   The ICRC and National Red Cross/Red Crescent Society tracing services use the terms 'relatives' and 'loved ones' as synonyms,[17] and understand and use the term 'family' in a similar broad sense, 'to include all those who consider themselves and are considered by each other to be part of the family'.[18] 'Family' thus encompasses

> relatives in a direct line—whether their relationship is legal or natural—spouses, brothers and sisters, uncles, aunts, nephews and nieces, but also less closely related relatives, or even unrelated persons, belonging to it because of a shared life or emotional ties (cohabitation, engaged couples etc). In short, all those who consider themselves and are considered by each other, to be part of a family, and who wish to live together, are deemed to belong to that family.[19]

Such broad understanding and use of the term 'family' entails that, for example, several national tracing services exercise a relatively wide discretion in determining who is entitled to use their services.[20] States tend to accept and support a generally broad use of the term 'family' in this respect.[21]

12   The notion of family on the one hand is to be distinguished from the right to family reunification on the other. In particular, in cases outside the context of GC IV, where family reunification entails the admission of a person to a foreign country, 'countries often only consider family reunification for first degree family members, such as parents and their children, and direct siblings',[22] i.e. the 'core' or 'nuclear' family. A social relatedness and even 'growing up like a child of the family' is—as a rule—not sufficient in order to be granted an entry permit.[23] International human rights law reflects this differentiation, as only some instruments elaborate on both the notion of family and a possibly ensuing right to family (re)unification. Article 10(1) of the Convention on the Rights of the Child (CRC) provides that 'applications by a child or his or her parents to enter or leave a State Party for the purpose of family reunification shall be dealt with by States Parties in a positive, humane and expeditious manner'. Article 19(1) of the African Charter on the Rights and Welfare of the Child specifically addresses family unity in pronouncing that

> [e]very child shall be entitled to the enjoyment of parental care and protection and shall, whenever possible, have the right to reside with his or her parents. No child shall be separated from his parents against

---

[17] Res 4, 'Restoring Family Links Strategy (and Implementation Plan) for the International Red Cross and Red Crescent Movement (2008–2018)'; Council of Delegates, 23–24 November 2007.

[18] Restoring Family Links, 'Our Beneficiaries', available at <http://familylinks.icrc.org/en/Pages/HowWeWork/How-we-work.aspx>.

[19] ICRC Commentary APs, para 2997.

[20] E.g., the German Red Cross Tracing Service takes a broad approach with regard to the questions of whose tracing requests to accept and pursue, e.g. accepting the request of a German godmother to search for her godchild in Pakistan, as well as of in which contexts.

[21] See, e.g., § 2(1)(4)(a) of the German Tracing Services Data Protection Act (*Suchdienstedatenschutzgesetz*) of 2 April 2009, available at <http://www.gesetze-im-internet.de/bundesrecht/sddsg/gesamt.pdf>.

[22] Restoring Family Links, 'Reuniting Families', available at <http://familylinks.icrc.org/en/Pages/HowWeWork/reuniting-families.aspx>.

[23] In practice, this policy approach is often coupled with the impossibility of providing the required documentation regarding relatedness. This has led a number of states to demand DNA tests for those seeking to exercise the right to family reunification. Notwithstanding the obvious benefits, such practice entails disadvantages in cases where, e.g., the biological relatedness does not coincide with the legal one. Quite often the requirement of a biological link is in contradiction to family recognition policies in home and receiving countries—as the case may be—of persons applying for family reunification. See T. Heinemann and T. Lemke, 'Biological Citizenship Reconsidered: The Use of DNA Analysis by Immigration Authorities in Germany', 39(4) *Science, Technology and Human Values* (2014) 488. See also M.G. Weiss, 'Strange DNA: The Rise of DNA Analysis for Family Reunification and its Ethical Implications', 7 *Genomics, Society and Policy* (2011) 1, at 8–13; and T. Heinemann and T. Lemke, 'Suspect Families: DNA Kinship Testing in German Immigration Policy', *Sociology* (2012) 1, at 7–10.

his will, except when a judicial authority determines in accordance with the appropriate law, that such separation is in the best interest of the child.[24]

Article 19(2) gives 'every child who is separated from one or both parents' the 'right to maintain personal relations and direct contact with both parents on a regular basis',[25] and Article 19(3) provides for a right to know.[26] The 2003 EU Council Directive on the right to family reunification[27] and its 2014 guidance[28] show a relatively broad understanding of the term 'family'. With regard to the right to family reunification, the guidance retains the rather strict conditions for family reunification of the Directive, though leaving room for the discretion ('appreciation') of the EU member states to consider the sociological and/or emotional environment and questions of dependency.[29]

To sum up, IHRL instruments recognize the family as a good and as a value. They provide for protection of the family, and in doing so base themselves on a rather broad understanding of the term 'family'. Although approaches to recognizing 'all interested persons' as family have not generally crystallized as legally binding IHRL, it is clear that 'family' comprises persons beyond the 'nuclear family', including, but not limited to, in particular close relatives and those forming part of the perceived family on the basis of the respective sociological background of the persons concerned. When it comes to questions of family reunification, and possibly entailing issues of entry permits, IHRL instruments explicitly provide for limitations to the rights of families and family members, implementing considerations, appreciations, and a balance of differing and possibly conflicting interests.[30] 13

In situations regulated by IHL—armed conflicts—the law does recognize the family as something to be protected, and the right of families to know the whereabouts of family members who have gone missing due to the armed conflict. International humanitarian law takes note of the fact that for protected persons, only the authority within whose hands or under whose control these protected persons find themselves is able to provide information and/or maintain or re-establish family links. With regard to the question of definition and issues of the 'right to know', IHRL and the *ratio* of IHL call for a broad 14

---

[24] See also Art 9(1) CRC: right of a child not to be separated from his or her parents.

[25] Addressing the issue of separation from parents, Art 25(1) of the Charter provides: 'Any child who is permanently or temporarily deprived of his family environment for any reason shall be entitled to special protection and assistance.'

[26] Art 19(3): 'Where separation results from the action of a State Party, the State Party shall provide the child, or if appropriate, another member of the family with essential information concerning the whereabouts of the absent member or members of the family. States Parties shall also ensure that the submission of such a request shall not entail any adverse consequences for the person or persons in whose respect it is made.'

[27] EU Council Directive, 2003/86/EC of 22 September 2003 on the right to family reunification; see recitals 10 and 13 of the Directive, respectively. It takes explicit note of the different legal systems and domestic practices in EU member states, as well as of various procedures for examination of applications.

[28] Communication from the Commission to the European Parliament and the Council on guidance for application of Directive 2003/86/EC on the right to family reunification of 3 April 2014, COM(2014) 210 final.

[29] Art 4 of the Directive and point 2.2 of the guidance document.

[30] The ICCPR, ECHR, and the UDHR take a defensive approach and guarantee protection against arbitrary and unlawful interference or attack, but allow justified and lawful interference; HRCttee, General Comment 16, para 1: 'The obligations imposed by this article require the State to adopt legislative and other measures to give effect to the prohibition against such interferences and attacks as well as to the protection of this right.' The ICESCR takes a more humanitarian approach, granting the '*widest possible* protection and assistance' to the family (Art 10(1), emphasis added). Hence, IHRL leaves space for the discretion of states and their legal systems to determine the material, and also personal, scope of protection of the family, especially with regard to family reunification.

understanding of the term 'family'. A narrow understanding and application run counter to the goals to prevent persons from going missing and to protect the family as a unit, which are the basis of IHL regulation of the maintenance and re-establishment of family links. A narrow understanding and application as preconditions to the right to family communication and enquiries do not reflect the reality of life in all parts of the world. They do not respond to humanitarian needs in contexts where the functioning of communities and the well-being of individuals depend on social, cultural, religious, and/or traditional structures beyond the nuclear family or even extended nuclear family. With regard to the question of family reunification entailing the granting of entry permits, neither IHRL nor state practice demands a generally broad approach. In the framework of situations of armed conflict states are, however, encouraged to be as flexible as possible, and to take into consideration social, cultural, religious, and traditional aspects as comprehensively as they are able, in order to respond to the existing humanitarian concerns of persons not necessarily reflecting the narrow conception of a nuclear family.

II. Privacy of information and data protection

15 The right of families to know the fate of their relatives and the attempt to prevent protected persons from going missing, being the motivation for regulation of the maintenance and re-establishment of family links and transmission of information, reflect an automatic concurrence of different interests, in particular the right of families and family members to know the fate of their relatives, the interest of the individual protected civilian to retain his or her autonomy as regards personal data, the interests of the authority exercising control over the person in question, the Protecting Power/CTA as an actor collecting information, and the state of the person's origin and/or residence.

16 Information privacy is the relationship between the collection and dissemination of data, technology, the public expectation of privacy, and the legal and political issues surrounding them. Apart from indications with a view to specific situations (Article 43 paragraph 2, Article 137 paragraph 2, Article 140 paragraph 2 GC IV), the rules of the Geneva Conventions do not contain a general rule on the consideration, appreciation, and balancing of the different interests at stake in an armed conflict. In IHRL, Article 17 ICCPR, based on Article 12 UDHR, guarantees freedom from 'arbitrary or unlawful interference with [a person's] privacy'. While 'unlawful interference' means that 'no interference can take place except in cases envisaged by the law', and the law itself 'must comply with the provisions, aims and objectives of the Covenant',[31] 'arbitrary interference' may also extend to interference provided for by law, in so far as such law may not be in accordance with the provisions, aims, and objectives of the Covenant, or may not be reasonable in the particular circumstances.[32] Hence, General Comment 16 to Article 17 ICCPR indicates that the unlawfulness and arbitrariness of an interference may be assessed only by a proportionality test—i.e. balancing the object and purpose of the different interests of the individual involved or the group concerned on the one hand, and those of the interfering actor on the other—and reiterates the need for such a balancing exercise in stating that 'the protection of privacy is necessarily relative'.[33]

---

[31] HRCttee, General Comment 16, para 3.   [32] Ibid, para 4.
[33] Ibid, para 7. See also Privacy Rights in the Digital Age, A Proposal for a New General Comment on the Right to Privacy under Article 17 of the International Covenant on Civil and Political Rights, March 2014, at 3, available at <https://www.aclu.org/sites/default/files/assets/jus14-report-iccpr-web-rel1.pdf>.

17 In the context of the maintenance and re-establishment of family links and transmission of information, the protection of privacy and privacy of data[34] focus mainly on both (i) the relationship between the protected person and the agency collecting and processing information (e.g., the Detaining Power/official Information Bureau; CTA; Protecting Power), and (ii) the relationship between the protected person and his or her family or home state or state of residence. The former relationship involves the issue of censorship. The latter raises questions of whose interests prevail in situations where the protected person objects to the transmission of information because he or she does not want his or her family to be informed about his or her whereabouts or physical condition, while either the family or home state/state of residence seeks to maintain or re-establish such links.

18 Censorship in the context of transmission of information is provided for by GC IV, both implicitly and explicitly. Article 25 paragraph 1 contains an implicit reference and a legal obligation with regard to censorship, in that parties to an armed conflict have the duty to forward family news 'speedily and without undue delay'. This requirement contains the obligation to ensure that, for example, censorship is to be carried out promptly and must give priority to examining family news. Within the legal regime on internment, explicit reference is made in Article 107 paragraph 1 and Article 112 paragraph 1, according to which the number of letters and cards addressed to/'received by' internees may be limited, inter alia, on the basis of practicability concerns with regard to transport or censorship. Article 112 paragraph 1 provides for the censorship of correspondence of internees to be done as quickly as possible; the delivery of relief consignments may not be delayed under the pretext of difficulties of censorship (Article 112 paragraph 2). With regard to customary law in this context, censorship is confirmed with regard to persons deprived of their liberty, who must be allowed to correspond with their families 'subject to reasonable conditions relating to frequency and the need for censorship by the authorities' (Customary International Humanitarian Law (CIHL) Study, Rule 125).

19 Censorship in the context of transmission of information is a somewhat 'natural' phenomenon in the practice of parties. The interests of the individual protected person with regard to data privacy and freedom of thought, conscience, religion or belief, opinion, and expression have to be weighed against the interests of the parties to the armed conflict with respect to safety, military effectiveness, and national security. Censorship executed within the framework of the safeguards provided by GC IV does balance these conflicting interests proportionally.

20 The protection of privacy and privacy of data may be infringed in situations where the protected person objects to the transmission of information because he or she does not wish information on his or her whereabouts or condition to be released, or in situations where provision of information may be dangerous for the protected person or family members. The question is whether the interests of the individual prevail over those of the authority which has the person under its control (i.e. the Detaining Power), those of the actor collecting the information (i.e. the Protecting Power/CTA), or those of the actor seeking the information (i.e. the family or the home state/state of residence). International humanitarian law answers this question only partly. For instance, according to Article 43 paragraph 2, the duty to provide the names of persons who have been interned or

---

[34] In addition, the rights to freedom of thought, conscience, religion or belief (Art 18 ICCPR), opinion, and expression (Art 19 ICCPR) are relevant.

placed under assigned residence, as well as decisions on reconsideration of such measures or eventual releases to the Protecting Power/CTA, applies only under the precondition that the protected person concerned does not object. Here the interests of the protected person prevail. For the situation of internment, Article 106 explicitly states that it is the Detaining Power's duty to 'enable' the internee to send an internment card, thus leaving it to the protected individual to decide whether to provide information or not.

21   International human rights law is expansive, in that the HRCttee has recognized the right to privacy protecting the right to freely express one's identity.[35] Both the ECtHR[36] and the IACtHR[37] have recognized the 'right to identity and personal development, and the right to establish and develop relationships with human beings and the outside world'. Such a right to establish and develop relationships almost inevitably encompasses the right not to establish and develop such relationships. Further, the right to privacy has evolved to include specific rights to access and control of one's personal data.[38] The ECtHR found that 'protection of personal data is of fundamental importance to a person's enjoyment of his or her right to respect for private and family life'.[39] In doing so it has taken a broad view of what personal data constitute.[40] Even public information can fall within the scope of private life when it is systematically collected and stored in files held by the authorities.[41] As a consequence, a protected person generally has the right not to disclose information, and to object to the collection or transmission of information.

22   As with other human rights, the 'right to protection of data' is qualified. The provisions of GC IV on the transmission of information constitute the legal basis authorizing restrictions on the right to protection of data. However, the question remains whether there are any limits to such restrictions; in other words, whose interests prevail in terms of protecting data or of disclosing data? Both interests have to be balanced against each other. As for the protected person concerned, protection of his or her data has a high but not absolute priority, as indicated by, inter alia, Article 43 paragraph 2 and Article 137 paragraph 2 GC IV.[42] As for family members, their right to be informed has neither a higher nor a lower priority. In cases where, for example, protection/transmission has an impact on the security of either the protected person or the family, these interests prevail, as stated by Article 137 paragraph 2 GC IV. In family reunification scenarios, where information

---

[35] HRCttee, *Coeriel et al v The Netherlands*, Comm No 453/1991, UN Doc CCPR/C/52/D/453/1991 (1994), 31 October 1994, para 102; see also ECtHR, *Botta v Italy*, Judgment, 24 February 1998, para 34.

[36] ECtHR, *Peck v United Kingdom*, Judgment, 28 January 2003, para 57: 'The protection of private life encompasses a series of factors associated with the dignity of the individual, including, for example, the ability to develop his or her own personality and aspirations, to determine his or her own identity and to define his or her own personal relationships. The concept of private life encompasses aspects of physical and social identity, including the right to personal autonomy, personal development and the right to establish and develop relationships with other human beings and with the outside world.'

[37] IACtHR, *Murillo v Costa Rica*, Judgment, 28 November 2012, para 143.

[38] Already in this direction, HRCttee, General Comment 16, para 10; M. Nowak, *UN Covenant on Civil and Political Rights: CCPR Commentary* (2nd edn, Kehl: Engel, 2005), at 388.

[39] ECtHR, *MK v France*, Judgment, 18 April 2013, para 32.

[40] E.g., ECtHR, *Botta v Italy*, Judgment, 24 February 1998, para 34; ECtHR (Grand Chamber), *S and Marper v United Kingdom*, Judgment, 4 December 2008, paras 66–7.

[41] ECtHR (Grand Chamber), *Rotaru v Romania*, Judgment, 4 May 2000, para 43. E.g., certain information on a protected person is openly available to an official Information Bureau (Arts 136 ff), so that the question will have to be answered whether the individual protected person has the right to object to the collection, collation, and transmission of such publicly available information (see MN 63).

[42] Art 137 para 2 addresses the case where transmission of information by an official Information Bureau is dangerous ('detrimental') for a protected person or for his or her relatives.

requests, among others, are linked to, for instance, claims to maintenance or proof of blood relationship (as this occurs quite often in practice), not only do the concurrent unilateral interests of the protected person and individual family members compete, but they have to be weighed against each other. Rights and interests of third persons, for example descendants, must be taken into account too. In such situations, it is not one or the other conflicting interest or right which generally prevails. Solutions will have to be orientated along the lines of the object and purpose of the respective guarantees, and will have to be weighed and balanced. The same applies as regards the home state/state of residence: the protected person's interests and rights have to be weighed, especially against the interest of preventing persons from going missing and the right and duty to exercise (diplomatic) protection. In cases where the Detaining Power is involved in such a balancing exercise, its presumed interest in fulfilling legal obligations, its general expectation of reciprocity, and its presumed aim to prevent protected persons from going missing have to be taken into account. However, in all situations where processing of information would be detrimental to the protected person and/or his or her family, the interest in preventing such damage must prevail (see Article 137 paragraph 2).

III. Communication of family news and facilitation of family enquiries

In situations of armed conflict, family unity may not be touched except within the strict limits of military necessity.[43] Rules protecting family rights in armed conflict aim at protecting the unity of the family. Means to achieve this are the protection of family communication, as well as the maintenance and re-establishment of family links.[44]

a. Family news

One of the core provisions of GC IV on the maintenance and re-establishment of family links and transmission of information is contained in Article 25 paragraph 1 GC IV. The underlying idea is to mitigate adverse effects on the civilian population of 'the outbreak of hostilities immediately result[ing] in the severance of postal communications'.[45] The provision spells out the obligations, first, to enable all persons in the territory of a party to the conflict, or in a territory occupied by it, to give news of a strictly personal nature to members of their families and to receive news from them, as well as, secondly, to forward this correspondence 'speedily and without undue delay'. The provision is intended to safeguard the family unit. The notion of 'news to and from family members'—often referred to as 'family news'—extends to 'all particulars, news, questions, information, etc concerning the personal and family life of a person'.[46] The words 'strictly personal nature' exclude any information of a type which is not personal and not humanitarian in character from the guarantee in Article 25 paragraph 1.

The words 'shall be enabled' in Article 25 paragraph 1 indicate that the guarantee of family news is the responsibility and legal obligation of the parties to the conflict.[47] It

---

[43] 'Protection of the Civilian Population in Periods of Armed Conflict', Report to the 26th International Conference of the Red Cross and Red Crescent, 15 September 1995, available at <http://www.icrc.org/eng/resources/documents/report/26th-conference-report-150995-c.htm>, 'Reunification of Families Dispersed by War', point 2.4.
[44] See also ibid, point 2.2.   [45] Pictet Commentary GC IV, at 191.   [46] Ibid, at 192.
[47] This aspect of the guarantee provided by Art 25 para 1 GC IV is not addressed, e.g., by the official German translation of the provision; BGBl 1954 II at 917, BGBl 1956 II at 1586.

results from the existence of the armed conflict alone, is part of a general protection of the civilian population as such against certain consequences of war, and extends to 'all persons in the territory of a Party to the conflict, or in a territory occupied by it'. It is thus applicable to the civilian population as a whole, including but not limited to 'protected persons' according to GC IV, as well as including a party's own civilian population.[48] The guarantee of family news is independent from potential additional specific circumstances such as detention, internment, assigned residence, or the like. Specific conditions for family correspondence in situations of internment are regulated in Articles 105–116 GC IV. The geographical location of the family member sending or receiving the news is irrelevant ('wherever they may be').

26   Parties to the armed conflict further have the duty to forward such family news 'speedily and without undue delay' (Article 25 paragraph 1). This obligation prevents parties from hampering transmission (negatively) and (positively) requires them to ensure that no obstacles and delays are in the way other than those caused by the fact of the existence of an armed conflict as such. As a consequence, for example, censorship is to be carried out promptly and has to give priority to examining family news. However, the wording of Article 25 paragraph 1 does not require parties to the conflict to ensure the speediest means of forwarding the news, for example to ensure the availability of air mail.[49]

27   The words 'shall be enabled' in Article 25 paragraph 1 indicate not only a legal obligation of the parties to the conflict, but also a corresponding right of the civilian person concerned.[50] This dimension has been enshrined in the provision from its very beginning:

> The right to give his family news of a personal nature and to receive personal news from them is one of the inalienable rights of man [...] That is why the Diplomatic Conference of 1949 proclaiming this right rejected proposals that the Article should be placed in Part III, Section I [i.e. Articles 27 et seq on Status and Treatment of Protected Persons—Provisions Common to the Territories of the Parties to the Conflict and to Occupied Territories], where its field of application would have been less wide.[51]

However, as for rights and privileges under GC IV in general (for Article 5 paragraph 1, see Chapter 54 of this volume), Article 5 paragraph 2 specifies that a protected person in occupied territory who is detained as a spy or saboteur, or as a person 'under definite suspicion of activity hostile to the security of the Occupying Power', is 'regarded as having forfeited rights of communication' under GC IV only,[52] thus possibly affecting transmission of information.[53] A precondition for such forfeit is that 'absolute military security so requires', and the full rights and privileges of a protected person shall resume as soon as the security of the Occupying Power so permits (Article 5 paragraph 3).

28   Whereas the first sentence in Article 25 paragraph 1 refers to 'news'—thus leaving space for a variety of media carrying such news to be covered—the second sentence refers to 'this correspondence', i.e. news to be conveyed by postal mail. This understanding is confirmed by Article 25 paragraph 2, which requires parties to the armed conflict to consult with a 'neutral intermediary, such as the Central Agency provided for in Article 140 [GC IV]', on how to ensure observance of their obligations under paragraph 1 in cases where it

---

[48] See Pictet Commentary GC IV, at 192.   [49] Ibid, at 192.
[50] This is the approach taken, e.g., by the official German translation of Art 25(1) GC IV.
[51] Pictet Commentary GC IV, at 192.
[52] On differences between the authentic English and French texts, see ibid, at 57.
[53] For details see Ch 54 of this volume.

'becomes difficult or impossible to exchange family correspondence by the ordinary post'. Article 25 paragraph 2 is the legal basis for the so-called Red Cross/Red Crescent Messages (RC Messages)—open letters containing family news. In situations when family news may not be exchanged by ordinary means like telephone or postal mail, National Red Cross/Red Crescent Societies provide a specific form for such family news. A completed form is transferred to the family member via the CTA and the International Red Cross and Red Crescent tracing network. Article 25 paragraph 3 specifies that 'the compulsory use of standard forms containing twenty-five freely chosen words' and 'the limitation of the number of these forms despatched to one each month' are the only lawful restrictions on family correspondence imposable by the parties to the armed conflict. This further confirms such literal interpretation, as does the historical context of the provision in Article 25 GC IV.

Although family correspondence in the strict sense and the RC Messages are still an important practical means to maintain and re-establish family links, the guarantees provided by Article 25 also apply to new means of communication, in particular to fax, telephone, mobile phone, Internet phone (Skype), or e-mail services and the like. When these are available and their use is feasible, duties and rights contained in Article 25 extend to these media. Whether such use is actually feasible depends, inter alia, on whether parties to an armed conflict deem it necessary to conduct censorship and, if so, whether it is practically possible to censor family correspondence or RC Messages in a specific situation. As a rule, written messages, such as fax and e-mail, are easier to censor in practice than oral ones. Oral messages are often required to reflect written ones, the latter having been censored prior to the oral contact. 29

b. Family enquiries

Another core provision of GC IV on the maintenance and re-establishment of family links and transmission of information is contained in Article 26 GC IV. The Article recognizes a right of members of a family which is dispersed due to an armed conflict to enquire about other family members, in that it establishes a legal obligation of parties to an armed conflict to facilitate such enquiries. The regulation provided for in Article 26 GC IV is based on the experience of the Second World War.[54] With a view to the fact that hostilities in armed conflict almost inevitably lead to families being disrupted and dispersed, it is a humanitarian concern to re-establish family links and, if possible, reunite the family members. Both Article 26 and Article 25 are intended to safeguard the family unit, and both Articles apply to all civilians in an international armed conflict (IAC). However, in the same way as Article 25 does not focus on news of any kind but only on family news, Article 26 does not address restoring links between all displaced persons, but solely on those between displaced family members. 30

The wording of Article 26 does not go into much detail as to how enquiries are to be facilitated. Practical examples include 31

> the organization of official information bureaux and centres; notification by postal authorities of changes of address and possible places of evacuation; the arranging of broadcasts; the granting of facilities for forwarding requests for information and the replies; and, as a precautionary measure, the provision of identity discs for children under twelve years of age, as provided in Article 24, paragraph 3, of the Convention [...].[55]

---

[54] See the extensive description in Pictet Commentary GC IV, at 195 ff.
[55] Pictet Commentary GC IV, at 196 ff. See also Ch 62, MN 12–18, of this volume.

The objective of any facilitation effort is to renew contact between members of dispersed families and to facilitate meeting, 'if possible'. Mandatory measures to be taken by parties to an armed conflict with a view both to facilitating family enquiries and to preventing civilians from going missing, are the establishment of an official Information Bureau and the encouragement of the work of organizations engaged in the task of renewing family contacts and reuniting dispersed families.

32   The provision's wording—'if possible'—already emphasizes that the duty to facilitate does not as such result in an obligation to grant an entry permit with the purpose of family reunification. State practice shows that states tend to insist on retaining their respective legal policies on entry, even with regard to entry requests emanating from contexts of armed conflicts, and on a case-by-case approach, whether in terms of individual or group requests (for example, when a state decides to grant entry permits for a certain number of persons from a specific conflict situation). The practical result is quite often that all states concerned understand that their respective counterpart is the one on whom the obligation to facilitate reunification is incumbent. In such situations, the clause 'if possible' may be informed by IHRL provisions. The fact that human rights protect the family alone is not conclusive, as states have the authority to weigh the unity of the family against other interests and values.[56] Provisions giving special emphasis to specific aspects of the family (for example children, Article 10(3) ICESCR), or pronouncing on the right of a child not to be separated from his or her parents (for example Article 9 CRC, Article 19 of the African Charter on the Rights and Welfare of the Child) lead to an obligation on all states concerned not to deny their mutual responsibilities, and to work towards a practical and pragmatic solution.

c. Obligation to encourage the work of organizations

33   In addition to the obligation to (directly) facilitate family enquiries, provided for in the first sentence of Article 26 GC IV, the second sentence sets out a mandatory measure to be taken by a party to a conflict in order to facilitate family enquiries, which is the duty to encourage the work of organizations engaged in the task of renewing family contacts and reuniting dispersed families. Whereas the establishment of an official Information Bureau is a measure directly imposed on a party to an armed conflict, the obligatory encouragement of specified organizations is an indirect means of facilitating family enquiries. In a number of states, organizations of different kinds are active in the field of tracing services, both as regards situations of armed conflict or internal violence, and following natural or technological disasters, or similar crisis situations. In particular, the majority of National Red Cross and Red Crescent Societies provide tracing services, both internationally and domestically. Whereas in armed conflicts, prior to the adoption of the Geneva Conventions of 1949, National Societies generally focused on the transmission of the so-called RC messages[57] (see MN 28), their mandate has been broadened, and today comprises active tracing services and the restoration of family links. In various cases, their activity is additionally mandated by their governments.[58] Article 140 paragraph

---

[56] E.g., Art 17(1) ICCPR protects against 'arbitrary and unlawful interference', and Art 10(1) ICESCR provides for the 'widest possible protection'.
[57] Pictet Commentary GC IV, at 198.
[58] E.g., the German Red Cross has been commissioned to effect the tracing service according to Art 26 GC IV and Arts 33(3) and 74 AP I, in addition to the tasks of the official Information Bureau according to Art 136

4 emphasizes that provisions on the Information Bureau and the CTA do not restrict the variety of activities of the ICRC and 'relief societies'. Such 'relief societies' include[59] National Red Cross/Red Crescent Societies.[60]

The duty to 'encourage' encompasses in particular the creation of such organizations, as well as support for their work. In order to benefit from the responsibilities provided for in Article 26, organizations need explicitly to fulfil two conditions: they have to be 'acceptable' to the party to the conflict—which in practice means they have to be accepted by it—and they must comply with its security regulations. Additional requirements are possible, especially under domestic law, provided these are not employed to prevent a tracing organization from being created. In this respect, the duty to encourage amounts to an obligation to refrain from using domestic law in order to hamper the creation of such an organization.[61] Hence, the duty to 'encourage' goes beyond merely tolerating the activities of a tracing organization, and amounts to an obligation actively to facilitate, foster, and support its work.

IV. Maintenance and re-establishment of family links; transmission of information

Beyond the obligations to enable persons in their territory to communicate and enquire about family news, parties to an IAC have a number of responsibilities with a view to achieving two goals: maintaining family links in armed conflict, and preventing a person from going missing.

a. Protection of the civilian population as such

In relation to the civilian population as such and as a whole, Article 24 paragraph 3 GC IV requires parties to an IAC to 'endeavour' to make sure that children under the age of 12 wear identity discs or similar identifying items. The purpose of this measure is to facilitate recognition of children, in order to ensure that they are not separated from their families; and in the event of separation, to facilitate reunification with their families. The age limit is set at 12 years, as older children are considered to be able to identify themselves sufficiently without the assistance of such means.[62] However, the use of identity discs is merely a recommendation ('or by some other means'), and parties to a conflict are free to use different methods and systems of identification.[63] This is underlined by the fact that during the drafting of this provision, it was feared that children's identity discs would be used to discriminate against or persecute them.[64] Nevertheless, lacking an alternative, the recommendation to use identity discs was included in the text, albeit that tracing practice is scarce.

GC IV, as well as conveyance of correspondence under Art 25 para 2 GC IV, by the German Act on the German Red Cross and other voluntary aid societies (as defined in the Geneva Conventions) of 5 December 2008.

[59] Pictet Commentary GC IV, at 560.
[60] For a description of 'relief societies', see Art 142 GC IV. National Red Cross/Red Crescent Societies already assist protected persons according to the GCs and their APs, as well as according to the Statutes of the International Red Cross and Red Crescent Movement, in particular Arts 3 and 5 of the Statutes of the International Red Cross and Red Crescent Movement; see in this context the so-called RFL Strategy of the Movement, at MN 7.
[61] Slightly differently, Pictet Commentary GC IV, at 198, 'Any organization which satisfies these two conditions must, as a rule, be allowed to carry on its work in connection with the reuniting of dispersed families.'
[62] See Final Record, vol II-A, at 637.   [63] Pictet Commentary GC IV, at 189.
[64] See Final Record, vol II-A, at 637–38.

b. Protection of 'protected persons' in general

37 According to Article 27 paragraph 1 GC IV, all protected persons in the sense of Article 4 GC IV are entitled to respect for their family rights 'in all circumstances' (Chapters 55 and 60 of this volume). The regimes protecting both aliens in the territory of a party to the conflict and civilians in occupied territory contain a number of references to 'the Protecting Power' (Chapter 27 of this volume). In situations where parties to an IAC renounce their right to designate Protecting Powers—as seems to be common practice since the Falkland Islands/Islas Malvinas conflict[65]—the ICRC or the CTA may exercise this function.

c. Protection of aliens in the territory of a party to the conflict

38 With a view to preventing aliens in the territory of a party to the conflict from going missing in the event of internment or assigned residence, Article 43 paragraph 2 requires the Detaining Power to inform the Protecting Power/CTA of the names of those persons, as well as of decisions regarding reconsideration of such measures or eventual release. In addition, this duty may benefit family members of those protected persons when they get access to such information. The wording 'unless the protected persons concerned object' allows for individual concerns to be taken into account. Hence this is a case where IHL provides that the right of an individual protected person to protection of his or her data is given priority in the case of a conflict of interests with the rights of other persons or institutions (see MN 63).

d. Protection of civilians in occupied territory

39 In the framework of the legal regime in occupied territories, and in the case of evacuations of civilians within or from occupied territory and of transfers back to their homes, the Occupying Power has the duty, according to Article 49 paragraph 3 GC IV, to ensure[66] that 'members of the same family are not separated' from one another. However, the provision limits this obligation by adding the words 'to the greatest practicable extent'. It encompasses the ensuing duty to reunite family members when the family becomes separated.[67] The obligation to inform the Protecting Power/CTA of evacuations and transfers (Article 49 paragraph 4) complements the objective of keeping the family united or, alternatively, of reuniting it. At the same time, it fosters the goal of preventing civilians in occupied territory from going missing. The Occupying Power is further obliged to take 'all necessary steps to facilitate the identification of children and the registration of their parentage', according to Article 50 paragraph 2, which enhances the requirement set out in Article 24 paragraph 3. Whereas Article 24 paragraph 3 generally obliges parties to a conflict 'to endeavour' to provide for the identification of children under 12 (see MN 36), Article 50 paragraph 2 imposes a somewhat stronger duty on Occupying Powers. Although it does not require the establishment of a comprehensive identification system, Occupying Powers are prohibited from, among other things, impeding systems already working in the occupied territory.[68] In addition, the Occupying Power is prevented from

---

[65] See H.-J. Heintze, 'Protecting Power', in MPEPIL, para 13.
[66] Somewhat differently, Pictet Commentary GC IV, at 281, 'very strong recommendation'.
[67] Ibid, at 281.
[68] Art 50 para 2 GC IV calls on the Occupying Power to take measures to facilitate the identification of children and to register their parentage. Depending on whether the state concerned has already established a system for the identification of children or not, the Occupying Power is thus asked to retain such identification systems, or at least to keep existing administrative services in place, and support them. Pictet Commentary GC IV,

changing children's family or personal status, or their nationality, thus protecting both the children and their parents.[69]

As supplementary measures, Article 71 paragraph 2 requires Occupying Powers to inform the Protecting Power/CTA of proceedings instituted by them against protected civilians in occupied territory, in respect of charges involving the death penalty or imprisonment for a term of two years or more. In addition, the Protecting Power/CTA has the right to obtain information on any other proceedings against protected persons.[70] A judgment involving such a sentence is to be communicated 'as rapidly as possible' and with the relevant grounds to the Protecting Power/CTA[71] (Article 74 paragraph 2). An Occupying Power is prevented from executing a death sentence for six months following receipt of notification by the Protecting Power/CTA of the final judgment or order denying a pardon or reprieve (Article 75 paragraph 2).[72]

40

e. *Protection of interned persons*

Regulations on keeping families together and attempting to prevent protected persons from going missing are of specific relevance in the context of internment of protected persons. Geneva Convention IV provides for, for example, rules on protecting family relations at the beginning (accommodation) and end of internment, as well as during internment (relations with the exterior, in particular internment cards, correspondence in general, effecting legal acts, and receiving visitors and humanitarian assistance).

41

i. Accommodation

In situations where protected persons are interned, Article 82 paragraph 2 GC IV obliges the Detaining Power to accommodate members of the same family, in particular parents and their children, together in the same place of internment. This duty applies during the entire internment, except where separation is only temporary and results from the employment of internees, medical/health reasons, or from the need to enforce penal and disciplinary sanctions on internees according to Chapter IX GC IV. Provided that (both) parents are interned and their children left at liberty, and without the care of one of the parents, the internees have the option to demand that their children be interned with them. The Detaining Power is required to decide such requests on an individual basis, taking into account in particular and among other criteria the age of the child(ren) in question.[73] Article 82 paragraph 3 requires the Detaining Power to set up family camps housing interned members of the same family in the same premises, and accommodating them separately from other internees 'wherever possible'. Under the same provision the Detaining Power is required to provide facilities for leading a proper family life.

42

As soon as reasons for the internment no longer exist (Chapter 66 of this volume), the Detaining Power has the obligation to release interned civilians (Article 132 paragraph 1 GC IV). Even while hostilities are ongoing, parties to the armed conflict are encouraged to conclude agreements for the release, repatriation, return, or settlement in a neutral country of certain classes of internees, in particular children, pregnant women, and mothers with infants and young children (Article 132 paragraph 2). This regulation is motivated by the protection of children as such—according to Article 37, states parties

43

---

at 287, 'the extreme importance of having a system for identifying children, especially very young children, must be emphasized'.

[69] Pictet Commentary GC IV, at 288.   [70] On details see ibid, at 354 ff.
[71] On details see ibid, at 360 ff.   [72] On details see ibid, at 362.   [73] See ibid, at 381.

are bound to ensure that a child deprived of liberty has the 'right to maintain contact with his or her family through correspondence and visits, save in exceptional circumstances'[74]—but it has at least secondary protective effects for the maintenance of family links. Although Article 132 paragraph 2 does not explicitly mention this as an option, parties to the conflict are not prevented from taking note of the needs and wishes of families to be reunited, as the provision refers 'in particular' to children and mothers with infants and young children.

ii. Relations with the exterior

44   The second strand of safeguards for the maintenance and re-establishment of family links in the context of internment regulations, comprises rules on relations with the exterior during internment, in particular on sending an internment card and postal mail in general, on effecting legal acts, and on receiving visitors.

45   In general, the Detaining Power has the underlying duty to inform internees, the state of origin, and, respectively, the state of residence as well as the Protecting Power/CTA on measures taken with regard to internees' relations with the exterior (Article 105 GC IV). This obligation applies 'immediately upon' internment, and in the event of subsequent changes in such measures.

46   The most specific obligation of a Detaining Power is contained in Article 106 GC IV, which provides that internees are entitled to send a so-called 'internment card' in order to inform both their families and the CTA of their situation.[75] The obligation falls due at the moment of internment, 'at the latest not more than one week after the internee's arrival in a place of internment'. The Detaining Power is obliged to forward the internment card 'as rapidly as possible', and to refrain from 'delaying it in any way'. Apart from communicating the internee's arrival at a site, internment cards may also be used to inform of sickness, or of transfer to a hospital or to another internment site. Annex III of GC IV sets out a model internment card, providing for information on personal data, as well as on the time and place of detention, and the internee's address and state of health. The purpose of the internment card is to facilitate tracing of interned protected civilians in contrast to delivering internees' messages (see MN 28). Sickness therefore triggers the right to an internment card, where such sickness will result in a change of address.[76] It is the decision of the internee whether or not to complete the card, as reflected in the language 'shall be enabled to send'.

47   According to Article 107 paragraph 1, Detaining Powers have the obligation to allow internees to send and receive letters and cards.[77] Unlike Article 106 on internment cards, Article 107 does not limit the addressees of such correspondence to family and the CTA. The amount of correspondence which internees are allowed to send may be restricted by Detaining Powers on the basis of, inter alia, military, security, and practicability considerations. The minimum number prescribed is two letters and four cards per month. It is the object of the provisions of Chapter VIII GC IV to secure that correspondence actually reaches its destination.[78] Therefore, 'the minimum of two letters and four cards per month […] seems to be best suited to the possibilities of rapid censorship'.[79] Censorship of correspondence is lawful according to Article 112 paragraph 1, but has to be done as quickly as possible. Annex III to GC IV provides for a model internee correspondence card.

---

[74] See ibid, at 513, 'because of what children represent for the future of humanity'.
[75] Ibid, at 446. [76] Ibid, at 447.
[77] On the question of postal charges on correspondence, see ibid, at 460 ff. [78] Ibid, at 449.
[79] Ibid.

The number of letters and cards addressed to/'received by' internees may also be limited, 48
for example, on the basis of practicability concerns with regard to transport or censorship.
Such limitation is to be effected by the internee's state of origin or the state of residence,
'possibly at the request of the Detaining Power' (Article 107 paragraph 1). Correspondence
must be transmitted 'with reasonable despatch' and not be delayed. Retention of correspondence for disciplinary reasons is prohibited without exception. Article 125 paragraph
4 explicitly provides that internees undergoing disciplinary punishment and serving their
sentence may not be deprived of their right to correspondence.[80]

According to Article 113 paragraph 1, the detaining state has the obligation to provide 49
'all reasonable facilities' for the transmission of legal documents sent by or to be received
by internees. The provision mentions wills, powers of attorney, letters of authority, 'or any
other documents', and is based on the recognition that internees retain their full civil law
personality, as explicitly stated in Article 80. Context as well as the object and purpose of
the provision clarify that it covers all documents which are 'essential for [internees'] family relationships or for the conduct of their affairs'.[81] The wording foresees transmission of
such documents by the Detaining Power itself, or by the CTA or a Protecting Power. The
criterion of 'all *reasonable* [...] facilities' is intended to avoid misuse of the provision by
internees.[82] Since the internment system does not create a 'one-for-all' civil law applicable
to all internees for the entirety of their affairs, a whole variety of different domestic laws
might be applicable. Article 113 paragraph 2 therefore grants internees access to a lawyer,
and generally obliges the Detaining Power to facilitate the execution and authentication
of documents in due legal form. Article 114 deals with the management of property, and
requires the Detaining Power to afford internees 'all facilities to enable them to manage
their property', including, in very exceptional circumstances, leaving the internment site.
The precondition is that 'this is not incompatible with the condition of internment' and
applicable law. In the event that an internee is involved in court proceedings, Article 115
provides for the Detaining Power, at the request of the internee, to ensure both that the
court is informed of the fact of the internee's detention, and that all necessary steps are
taken to prevent any prejudice, by reason of his or her internment, to the internee's rights
and interests as a party to court proceedings and as regards the decision of the court.[83]

In exceptional circumstances, a party to the conflict may decide on the prohibition 50
of correspondence, 'either for military or political reasons'. According to Article 112
paragraph 3 GC IV, such prohibition shall be only temporary and its duration shall be as
short as possible.

In case use of postal mail by internees is not practically feasible or sufficient, or where 51
the matter is urgent, Detaining Powers must allow internees to use telegrams (Article 107
paragraph 2). The same applies to modern means of communication, including e-mail
or Skype, provided such services exist. However, this requirement applies only to correspondence with an internee's relatives, or in cases where the internee has been a long time
without news. Charges have to be borne by the internees, but may be paid in the currency
at their disposal. Article 110 paragraph 5 requires states parties to GC IV to endeavour to
reduce 'so far as possible' the charges for messages sent by internees or addressed to them.[84]

---

[80] See ibid, at 450 ff. [81] Ibid, at 471. [82] Ibid, at 472. Emphasis added.
[83] Art 115 does not provide for a moratorium on behalf of the internee and/or his or her family members.
[84] Equivalent regulation for the official Information Bureau and the Central Information Agency in Art
141 GC IV.

52 'In no case may the Parties to a conflict impose on internees for their correspondence any language other than their mother tongue.'[85] However, according to Article 107 paragraph 3, parties to the conflict are called upon to authorize the use of other languages in situations where this is necessary.[86]

53 Internees are to be allowed to receive visitors, especially—but not only—close relatives, according to Article 116 GC IV.[87] The Detaining Power is required to permit visits 'at regular intervals and as frequently as possible', but has otherwise discretion to determine the frequency.[88] Article 116 goes on to provide that in urgent cases, '[a]s far as is possible, […] particularly in cases of death or serious illness of relatives', an internee may be allowed to leave the internment site (see also MN 49).

iii. Humanitarian assistance

54 The third strand of safeguards for the maintenance of family links and the transmission of information in the framework of internment regulations, secures the provision of humanitarian assistance. Detaining Powers must permit internees not only to send and receive correspondence, but also to receive humanitarian assistance, according to Article 108 paragraph 1 GC IV. This provision contains the obligation of the Detaining Power to allow internees to receive individual parcels or collective shipments of relief goods. Although delivering relief goods to individuals is not free from ambiguities,[89] the Article again takes note of the two aims of the legal regime under GC IV, namely, to maintain family links and to prevent persons from going missing. However, the guarantee as regards the receipt of humanitarian assistance does not affect the obligation of a Detaining Power to provide adequate supplies for civilian internees. As far as internees in occupied territories are concerned, the general provision of Article 62 GC IV—being part of the legal regime on humanitarian assistance provided in occupied territory in general, and not in the specific situation of internment—obliges the Occupying Power to allow for relief goods to be sent to individual protected persons, though unlike an Occupying Power's legal obligations in relation to collective relief, 'subject to imperative reasons of security'. 'Thus the fact that an Occupying Power agrees to the relief schemes referred to in Article 59 [GC IV] does not mean that it need not allow into its territory relief consignments addressed to individuals.'[90] As a rule,[91] relief goods are exempted from import, customs, and other dues (Article 110 paragraph 1), as well as from postal dues, provided they are sent by postal mail, according to Article 110 paragraph 2 and the Universal Postal Convention of 1947.[92]

55 Military necessity is the only criterion on the basis of which the quantity of relief goods for civilian internees may be restricted (Article 108 paragraph 2). In such a case, the Detaining Power has to notify the organization which is providing the assistance, as well as the Protecting Power/CTA, of such restrictions in order to enable them to regulate and adapt quantity standards and procedures.[93] The Detaining Power has the right to control

---

[85] Pictet Commentary GC IV, at 452. [86] See ibid.
[87] On differences in state practice during the Second World War, see ibid, at 475.
[88] On practicalities and different practice, see ibid.
[89] See the extensive explanation ibid, at 453–4. [90] Ibid, at 329.
[91] Exceptions are regulated in Art 110 paras 3 and 4.
[92] The last sentence of Art 110 para 2 extends the legally binding force of the Universal Postal Convention of 1947 to states not being parties to the latter convention.
[93] Pictet Commentary GC IV, at 455, holds that restrictions must only be temporary.

relief consignments (Article 112 paragraph 2). In doing so, the Detaining Power has to make sure that goods are not exposed to deterioration. In order to prevent misappropriation, the actual examination is executed in the presence of either the addressee, or a duly delegated fellow internee, or the Internee Committee mentioned in Article 109. It is prohibited to delay the delivery of consignments under the pretext of difficulties of censorship (Article 112 paragraph 2).

56 In cases where it is impossible for, in particular, the Detaining Power—due to military operations in a broad sense[94]—to secure that internees send and receive correspondence in general (Article 107), send an internment card in particular (Article 106), and receive humanitarian relief goods (Article 108), or where it is impossible to facilitate legal acts according to Article 113, so-called special transport[95] may be organized. In other words, these obligations may be met by the ICRC/CTA, 'any other organization duly approved by the Parties to the conflict'—namely National Red Cross and Red Crescent Societies[96]—or a Protecting Power (Article 111 paragraph 1):

> [Detaining] Powers concerned are not released from their obligation to ensure that these transport operations can take place, but when they find it impossible to fulfil that obligation satisfactorily, they are in duty bound to assist possible action [...] with a view to remedying the situation.[97]

Such support may consist, as the case may be, of supplying transport, allowing transport circulation, and granting safe conducts.[98] Where special transport is organized, it may also be used to transport documents addressed to the official Information Bureau according to Article 136, or to the Central Information Agency according to Article 140, as well as documents of the ICRC, 'other organizations', or the Protecting Power/CTA (Article 111 paragraph 2). Article 111 paragraph 3 confirms that parties to the conflict remain free to agree on different transport options. Unless the parties concerned agree otherwise,[99] the costs of the use[100] of such special transport are to be apportioned between the states whose nationals benefit from it and on the basis of its size (Article 111 paragraph 4).

V. Tracing services and transmission of information

57 Another set of rules aimed at preventing persons from going missing, and at the same time supporting the maintenance and re-establishment of family links, are the provisions on tracing services in a broad sense and the transmission of information. These rules focus on establishing an official Information Bureau and the CTA.

a. Official Information Bureau

58 The first mandatory measure to support tracing services is the establishment of an 'official Information Bureau' according to Article 136 paragraph 1 GC IV. The official Information Bureau is an authority of each party to an armed conflict, and its establishment is obligatory. It is thus not any form of 'superior body' but a national Bureau and national authority. The obligation pursuant to Article 136 comprises the establishment of this national agency and its utilization in a certain way. It requires certain information to be communicated, and to be communicated in a specific form.

---

[94] Ibid, at 465. [95] Ibid, at 467. [96] Ibid, at 464. [97] Ibid, at 466.
[98] See also ibid, at 467. [99] Ibid, at 468.
[100] On costs for the setting-up of special transport, see ibid, at 468.

59 According to the wording of the provision, the legal obligation is imposed on 'each of the Parties to the conflict', and '[u]pon the outbreak of a conflict and in all cases of occupation'.[101] The *ratio* of the regime is to enhance tracing services in order to prevent protected persons from going missing, and, as the case may be, to support the re-establishment of family links. State practice has shown that for functional reasons, many states parties have already established an official Information Bureau in times of peace, before the outbreak of an armed conflict.

60 The Convention creates the legal obligation to establish the official Information Bureau without stipulating details for its creation, leaving, in particular, its legal quality and position under domestic law, as well as its composition and working methods, to the discretion of the states parties. The only exception is that a 'special section' of the Bureau is to be made responsible for taking all necessary steps to identify children whose identity is in doubt, including, in particular, recording details of their parents or other close relatives, if available (Article 50 paragraph 4). It is up to the states parties to decide whether or not, and eventually in which form, to merge the official Information Bureau with the Bureau to be established for prisoners of war (POWs) under GC III.

61 The official Information Bureau has three major tasks:

— to receive and to transmit information in respect of protected persons (Article 4) 'who are in its power' (Articles 137 paragraph 1 and 138);
— to reply to enquiries addressed to it concerning protected persons (Article 137 paragraph 1); and
— to collect and forward personal valuables left by protected persons (Article 139).

62 The official National Information Bureau receives and transmits information in respect of protected persons, but as the Bureau is not a general information-collecting agency, only a certain type of information as regards specific protected persons is collected and transmitted (Article 136 paragraph 2): that information must refer to measures taken by the party to the conflict in whose power the protected persons are. This is information the party necessarily has in its possession. The party is therefore obliged to provide information to its national Bureau 'within the shortest possible period', and has the duty to ensure that the information is communicated to the Bureau by all its national agencies 'promptly' (Article 136 paragraph 2). Information is collected and transmitted on protected persons 'who are kept in custody for more than two weeks, who are subjected to assigned residence or who are interned'. Collected information is to be transmitted to the state of origin of the protected person or, respectively, to the state in whose territory the person resided. Unlike with regard to the obligations flowing from Articles 25 and 26, where the need to become active is triggered either by the protected person or by members of his family, the collection and transmission of information by the official Information Bureau according to Article 137 paragraph 2 must be implemented by the party to the conflict on its own initiative, and almost 'automatically' once the armed conflict has started. The obligation is not dependent on enquiries by, say, a family member or the state of origin of the protected person. Any written communications made by the Bureau must be authenticated by signature or a seal (Article 137 paragraph 3).

---

[101] On the mandatory immediacy, see ibid, at 524.

63 The objectives of the obligation to collect and communicate information are to prevent any protected person from going missing in the context of armed conflicts and to facilitate supporting family links.¹⁰² The motivation behind the regulation is to secure information which enables both the precise identification of the protected person and the rapid notification of his or her state of origin/residence and family. Where a protected person objects to information on his or her identity being collected or collated and transmitted, or if he or she does not reveal information, the interests and rights of the individual have to be weighed against the interests, rights, and obligations of both the Detaining Power and the state of origin/residence (see MN 38). Where the Detaining Power possesses the information, or has to retrieve it from the protected person, the rights of the individual are given high priority.¹⁰³ However, in those cases where individuals strive to take advantage of the fact of their internment in order to, for example, obscure or commit criminal offences or avoid prosecution,¹⁰⁴ the rights of the individual protected person will necessarily be given lower priority. In such situations additional circumstances will have to apply in order for the individual rights to take precedence. Article 137 paragraph 2 explicitly provides for such a case, stating that information is to be forwarded, 'unless its transmission might be detrimental to the person concerned or to his or her relatives'. Such a balancing of conflicting rights does not relieve the Detaining Power from having to do everything possible to fulfil its obligation to collect and transmit information. In this way, the Information Bureau has to make efforts towards the individual concerned, to clarify the meaning as well as the object and purpose of the legal framework, the status and function of the Information Bureau, as well as its working methods and procedures. If the protected person concerned 'legitimately' refuses to reveal information even on this basis, the Information Bureau has to communicate the objection to the state of origin or to the state in whose territory the person resided.¹⁰⁵

64 The information has to relate to those protected persons who are kept in custody for more than two weeks, who are subjected to assigned residence, or who are interned. Article 136 paragraph 2 lists transfers, releases, repatriations, escapes, admittances to hospitals, births, and deaths as examples of information to be provided to the Information Bureau, and Article 138 paragraph 1 adds to this list the date, place, and nature of the action taken with regard to the individual, and the address at which correspondence may be sent to the person, while Article 138 paragraph 2 requires communication of the state of health of internees who are seriously ill or seriously wounded.¹⁰⁶ The mandatory list of protected persons with respect to whom information is to be transmitted to the Bureau is not exhaustive, and does not exclude the collection and transmission of information on protected persons in additional circumstances relating to practical humanitarian concerns.

65 Regarding the timeline, Article 136 paragraph 2 provides that the Information Bureau is to be given the information 'within the shortest possible period', and agencies have to

---

¹⁰² Ibid, at 537, 'to avoid persons disappearing without trace and all links between them and their families being cut'. See also Ch 13, section A.II., of this volume.
¹⁰³ Ibid, at 535, '[w]hile the detaining power is under an obligation to try to obtain information by interrogating the protected person, that person is not bound to supply such information'.
¹⁰⁴ Cases of withholding information and deliberately becoming untraceable occur quite frequently in the practice of tracing services.
¹⁰⁵ Pictet Commentary GC IV, at 527 and 535.
¹⁰⁶ For further details on information which is to be communicated, including specification of health status, issuing death certificates, and lists of graves, see Arts 138 para 2, 129 paras 2 and 3, and 130 para 3, as well as Pictet Commentary GC IV, at 527 and Ch 65, MN 57, of this volume.

process information 'promptly' to the Bureau. The state of health of internees who are seriously ill or seriously wounded (i.e. at least those sick or wounded internees whose life is in danger[107]) is to be communicated 'regularly and if possible every week'. A decisive criterion for determining whether any provision of information meets these requirements is that the Bureau must be enabled to comply with the mandatory provisions of Article 137.[108] Article 137 specifies that the Bureau shall transmit information through the CTA/Protecting Power (Chapter 27 of this volume). It is obliged to communicate information 'immediately' and 'by the most rapid means', and the equivalent obligation is imposed on the CTA/Protecting Power. The actual 'most rapid means' are subject to technical developments and the circumstances prevailing at the time.

66   The second task of the official Information Bureau, according to Article 137 paragraph 1, is to reply to enquiries addressed to it concerning protected persons. The provision does not specify who is entitled to make such enquiries, nor which information may be required. Apart from the CTA and other official or unofficial bodies,[109] in practice often family members of a protected person require information. The Bureau is obliged to reply to all requests (Article 137 paragraph 1), unless transmission of information 'might be detrimental to the person concerned or to his or her relatives' (Article 137 paragraph 2), and provided the protected person concerned has not objected to information being forwarded (see MN 38 and 63). In such situations information would be communicated to the CTA only. Hence, in the case of an enquiry from a private individual—possibly a family member—the Information Bureau has to seek authorization from the protected person before transmitting information.[110]

67   In the framework of the obligation of the parties to the conflict to establish an official Information Bureau, and in this way to facilitate family enquiries, Article 139 governs the third task of the Bureau, that is, the responsibility to collect and forward all personal valuables which have been left by protected persons mentioned in Article 136, in particular for those who have been repatriated or released, or who have escaped or died.[111] The Bureau forwards the personal valuables 'to those concerned', i.e. to the protected person in situations of repatriation or release, or to family members, heirs, loved-ones, etc, as the case may be, and provided that persons 'concerned' beyond family members are known to the Bureau. It is to forward the objects directly or, 'if necessary', through the CTA. The second sentence of Article 139 details requirements for the sending of articles.[112] As far as Internet services are available, costs incurred by the Agency do not present a relevant issue. With regard to postal mail and telegraph services, Articles 141 and 110 GC IV provide for free postage of all mail and, as far as possible, partial or total exemption from telegraph charges.[113]

b. Central Tracing Agency

68   In addition to establishing an official Information Bureau, the second mandatory measure with a view to enabling and facilitating tracing services is the creation of a 'Central Information Agency' in accordance with Article 140 paragraph 1 GC IV. The Agency has two major tasks under Article 140 paragraph 2, which are similar to those of the official

---

[107] Pictet Commentary GC IV, at 536.   [108] Ibid, at 527.
[109] Ibid, at 531.   [110] Ibid, at 531.   [111] For details see ibid, at 538.
[112] For details see ibid, at 539.
[113] For details on agreement on costs in case of voluminous/costly sending, see ibid, at 540.

Information Bureau: information is to be collected concerning protected persons in a specific situation; and that information is to be transmitted to certain addressees. However, the Agency's set-up and purpose are different, as it is designed as a 'purely humanitarian body concerned exclusively with the fate of war victims',[114] functioning in a neutral and impartial way. The establishment of this Agency is a legal obligation incumbent not only on the parties to an armed conflict, but on all parties to GC IV, and it is left open in the text whether the Agency is established by the parties to the conflict, by the ICRC, or, upon its proposal, by a National Red Cross/Red Crescent Society or any other body. What Article 140 does require, though, is that the Agency is 'created in a neutral country', in order to secure the neutrality and impartiality of the Agency itself.[115] Today the Agency is called the 'Central Tracing Agency' (CTA) and is an institution at and of the ICRC in Switzerland, integrated into the latter's organizational structure (for instance, Article 78 paragraph 3 of Additional Protocol I (AP I) refers to 'the Central Tracing Agency of the International Committee of the Red Cross'). Its name was changed to 'Central *Tracing* Agency' in 1960[116] in order to reflect, in particular, its focus on the fate of POWs and civilians alike.[117] Its predecessors were an agency created by the ICRC without clear legal basis[118] during the First World War, and a new 'Central Prisoners of War Agency' founded in 1939, on the basis of Article 79 of the 1929 Convention Relative to the Treatment of Prisoners of War, which, during and after the Second World War, expanded its scope to civilians. The Agency fulfils the functions of both the Central Prisoners of War Information Agency according to Article 123 GC III and the Central Information Agency according to Article 140 GC IV.[119]

The first task of the CTA is to collect information on protected persons who are kept in custody for more than two weeks, who are subjected to assigned residence, or who are interned (Article 136 paragraph 2). This is done either through 'official' channels—in particular through the national official Information Bureau according to Article 137 GC IV (see MN 58–67)—or through 'private' channels (Article 140 paragraph 2). Such 'private' channels are not further specified but comprise methods of information gathering which enable the Agency 'to obtain the greatest possible amount of information concerning persons sought by their family' and to approach 'all those who might be of assistance, whether public authorities, institutions, or private persons'.[120] ICRC delegations often include a 'CTA' section staffed with delegates, sometimes seconded by the National Red Cross or Red Crescent Societies.[121] Just as the national Information Bureau is not prevented from collecting and transmitting information on additional categories of persons, the CTA may extend its functions to additional *protected* persons.[122] Like the official Information Bureau, and again unlike the obligations flowing from Articles 25 and 26, the CTA collects the information on its own initiative and not following a request from either side.

---

[114] Ibid, at 532. [115] See ibid, at 543. See also Ch 26, MN 29–32, of this volume.
[116] 'Annual Report of the International Committee', 1 *IRRC* 8 (1961) 433, at 433–34 (emphasis added).
[117] Restoring Family Links, 'Glossary of Restoring Family Links terms', available at <http://familylinks.icrc.org/en/Pages/NewsAndResources/Glossary.aspx>; Hong Kong Red Cross, 'History', available at <http://www.redcross.org.hk/rcmovement/history.html>.
[118] ICRC Commentary APs, para 3241.
[119] GC III and GC IV allow for the establishment of either separate agencies or a joint institution.
[120] Pictet Commentary GC IV, at 543. [121] ICRC Commentary APs, para 4553.
[122] Pictet Commentary GC IV, at 544.

70 The second task of the CTA is to transmit the collected information to the country of origin or residence of the persons concerned (Article 140 paragraph 2) 'as rapidly as possible'. It is left to the states to determine whether the information communicated by the Agency is to be received by the national Information Bureau of the country of origin or residence, any other agency of that country, or directly by the persons concerned.[123] In situations where the protected person concerned does not agree to information to be collected and transmitted, his or her rights and interests have to be balanced against those of the other actors concerned, along the same lines as described in the context of official Information Bureaux (see MN 38, 63, and 66). Article 140 paragraph 2 reiterates the approach taken in Article 137 paragraph 2, in that where transmission 'might be detrimental to the persons whom the said information concerns, or to their relatives' (Article 140 paragraph 2), that information is not to be transmitted. In those cases where a national Information Bureau has been involved and where such an issue has occurred, the Bureau has the responsibility to alert the Agency which will take the 'necessary precautions' in accordance with Article 137 paragraph 2. The Agency has full discretion as to whether and, if so, to whom to forward the information.[124]

71 As far as Internet services are available, potential costs incurred by the CTA are not an issue. With regard to postal mail, telegraph services, transport charges and customs dues, Articles 141 and 110 provide for free postage of all mail and, as far as possible, partial or total exemption from telegraph charges.[125] In addition, and according to Article 140 paragraph 2 second sentence, parties to the conflict are obliged to provide the CTA with 'all reasonable facilities for effecting' transmissions. This provision encompasses broader material support and extends to, say, prioritizing communications of the CTA or the provision of broadcasting opportunities.[126] An additional facility in this sense is addressed in Article 111 paragraph 1, providing for the supply ('shall endeavour to supply') of means of transport in order to ensure the forwarding of correspondence, lists, and reports being exchanged between the Agency and national Information Bureaux.[127] Article 140 paragraph 3 requires states parties to GC IV, 'and in particular those whose nationals benefit by the services of the Central Agency', to give the Agency 'the financial aid it may require'.[128]

72 In addition to transmitting the information which has been collected by the Agency itself, the CTA has the task of transmitting the information and objects which the parties to the conflict are obliged to send to the Agency according to several provisions of GC IV. Thus:

— the CTA assists in the exchange of family correspondence according to Article 25 paragraph 2;
— it receives duplicates of medical certificates issued to civilian internees by the medical authorities of the Detaining Power according to Article 91 paragraph 4;
— it receives and files internment cards and transmits the information contained therein according to Article 106;
— it transmits wills, powers of attorney, letters of authority, or any other documents intended for internees or despatched by them according to Article 113;

---

[123] Ibid, at 546. [124] On details see ibid. [125] See comprehensively ibid, at 552–5.
[126] For details, in particular examples from the Second World War, see ibid, at 547.
[127] See ibid, at 547–8. [128] See ibid, at 548–9, on the question of apportionment of costs.

— it receives duly certified copies of official records of death according to Article 129; and
— it collects and forwards personal valuables belonging to persons who, in particular, have been repatriated or have died, according to Article 139 (see MN 67).

It is inherent in the institution of the CTA that it is responsible for replying to enquiries from all parties and persons concerned, and for investigations triggered by these enquiries.[129] In general, the Agency may take over 'a number of other activities in accordance with circumstances and requirements'.[130]

The obligation of a state party to an armed conflict to transmit information on those protected persons named in Article 136 paragraph 2 (see MN 62–65) to the CTA/Protecting Power is intended to prevent mistakes or loss of information, and to centralize the variety of information and information sources, 'thus giving the Agency a general view of the situation of protected persons in the hands of all the belligerents'.[131] On the basis of its mandate, the CTA itself evaluates each and every document it receives with a view to assisting protected persons.[132] In situations where the Agency deems it appropriate to communicate information to persons concerned without informing state authorities, it does so provided it is detrimental neither to the protected person nor to his or her family members.[133] As a consequence, the Agency is authorized to request and receive 'all information, even of confidential nature, for its own files'.[134] However, it has to take individuals' rights in terms of data protection into account, and, as the case may be, balance these against the object and purpose pursued by the legal regulation under GC IV (see MN 38, 63, and 66).

C. Relevance in Non-International Armed Conflicts

Rules in GC IV providing for the maintenance and re-establishment of family links and the transmission of information are applicable in IACs only, and the regime of Common Article 3 does not contain any equivalent regulation. It is AP II which—in terms of maintenance of family links—indirectly requests the men and women of a family to be accommodated together in internment or detention (Article 5(2)(a)). Additional Protocol II also provides that persons deprived of their liberty for reasons related to the conflict are to be 'allowed to send and receive letters and cards, the number of which may be limited' by the state or non-state authority which is responsible for internment or detention 'if it deems necessary' (Article 5(2)(b)). The ICRC organizes a mail service in NIACs.[135] With a view to the goal of re-establishing family links, Article 4(3)(b) obliges parties to a NIAC to take 'all appropriate steps […] to facilitate the reunion of families temporarily separated'.

International human rights law covers some of the aspects of the maintenance and re-establishment of family links and the transmission of information that are prescribed in GC IV for IACs (see MN 13–22). It complements IHL in NIACs (see Chapter 35 of

---

[129] Ibid, at 544. [130] See examples from the Second World War ibid, at 545.
[131] Ibid, at 530.
[132] Ibid, at 532: 'Absolutely independent of States, it is free, if it considers it expedient, not to inform States of facts known to it, if such information might place in danger the very persons it has the duty of assisting. This policy […] has procured […] the absolute confidence of war victims and of the governments themselves.'
[133] Ibid, at 533. [134] Ibid, at 531.
[135] *Protection of the civilian population in periods of armed conflict*, Report to the 26th International Conference of the Red Cross and Red Crescent, 15 September 1995, point 4.

this volume) and confirms the crucial role of the family. Whereas the ACHPR and the African Charter on the Rights and Welfare of the Child state a right of the family to protection 'by the State' (both Article 18(1)), and the ECHR protects against 'interference by a public authority' (Article 8), the ACHR broadens the state-focused perspective and provides for 'protection by society and the state' (Article 17(1)). Article 17(1) ICCPR has already explicitly introduced the notion of 'protection by society and the state', and Article 10(1) generally refers to the 'widest possible protection and assistance' without specifying the addressee of this right. The HRCttee has specified that protection is required against attacks and interferences, 'whether they emanate from State authorities or from natural or legal persons'.[136] The more specific human rights regime implies the 'possibility to live together', which requires measures 'to ensure the unity or reunification of families, particularly when their members are separated for political, economic or similar reasons'.[137] It also implies a right of a child not to be separated from his or her parents,[138] a duty to protect the family from interference by third parties,[139] and a request for protection 'against all such interferences and attacks whether they emanate from State authorities or from natural or legal persons'.[140] The ECtHR[141] and the HRCttee[142] have held that the suffering of family members caused by a state's failure to investigate the fate of missing persons may constitute inhuman treatment, which may arguably result in a duty of the state to investigate the fate of the missing.[143]

77 Hence, IHRL confirms state obligations with regard to the maintenance and re-establishment of family links for situations of NIAC. While the content with regard to the respective duties of non-state actors in NIAC is less specific, non-state actors are not free from obligations (see Chapter 35 of this volume). Guarantees with regard to protection of the family are not restricted to states as addressees, and thus generally apply to non-state actors too. There is no *carte blanche* for non-state actors to disrupt and disperse family units. The practical implications of such a finding are more complex, however; that is, legal regulation may be effective only provided it has a chance of being observed, which presumes, first of all and apart from political will, knowledge of the rules. Actual capacity to implement applicable provisions usually is an additional issue. As a result, non-state actors' human rights obligations with regard to the maintenance and re-establishment of family links will probably have a stronger chance of application in the form of refraining from hampering maintenance and re-establishment than in the form of positive action.

78 Customary international law for NIACs today addresses both the maintenance and the re-establishment of family links.[144] According to Rule 105 of the CIHL Study, family life 'must be respected as far as possible'. Members of the same family are to be

---

[136] HRCttee, General Comment 16, para 1.   [137] HRCttee, General Comment 19, para 5.
[138] Art 9(1) CRC; Art 19(1) African Charter on the Rights and Welfare of the Child.
[139] HRCttee, General Comment 16, para 1.
[140] Ibid.   [141] ECtHR, *Cyprus v Turkey*, Judgment, 10 May 2001, para 157.
[142] HRCttee, *Concluding Observations on Bosnia and Herzegovina*, 22 November 2006, UN Doc CCPR/C/BIH/CO/1, para 14.
[143] E.g., K. Gulick, 'Protection of Family Life', in Kälin et al (eds), above n 13, at 309–10.
[144] On the underlying state practice and *opinio juris*, see ICRC CIHL Study on Rules 105, 117, 119, 120, 123, 125, and 126.

accommodated together during any deprivation of liberty (Rules 119[145] and 120[146]). The personal details of persons deprived of their liberty must be recorded (Rule 123), and those persons must be allowed to correspond with their families, 'subject to reasonable conditions relating to frequency and the need for censorship by the authorities' (Rule 125). Correspondence is to be of a strictly personal nature.[147] Rule 126 requires that persons deprived of their liberty must be allowed to receive visitors 'to the degree practicable'. According to Rule 117, parties to the conflict must take 'all feasible measures to account for persons reported missing as a result of armed conflict and must provide their family members with any information [they have] on their fate'. This customary obligation is based on the practice of states and international organizations in a number of cases, including regarding persons missing as a result of the armed conflicts in Bosnia-Herzegovina, East Timor, Guatemala, Kosovo, and the former Yugoslavia.[148] The Plan of Action for the years 2000–3, being adopted by consensus by the 27th International Conference of the Red Cross and Red Crescent, including by states parties to the Geneva Conventions, requires that all parties to an armed conflict ensure that 'every effort is made to clarify the fate of all persons unaccounted for and to inform the families accordingly'.[149]

D. Legal Consequences of a Violation

A violation of a rule in the Geneva Conventions might constitute a crime under international criminal law and under national criminal legislation. Hence, a perpetrator might be held responsible individually, as the case may be, and in addition to any potential responsibility of the state on whose behalf the individual is acting. A potentially relevant crime is the enforced disappearance of persons. The International Convention for the Protection of All Persons from Enforced Disappearance (ICED) provides in Article 1:

1. No one shall be subjected to enforced disappearance.
2. No exceptional circumstances whatsoever, whether a state of war or a threat of war, internal political instability or any other public emergency, may be invoked as a justification for enforced disappearance.

Article 2 defines 'enforced disappearance' as

the arrest, detention, abduction or any other form of deprivation of liberty by agents of the State or by persons or groups of persons acting with the authorization, support or acquiescence of the State, followed by a refusal to acknowledge the deprivation of liberty or by concealment of the fate or whereabouts of the disappeared person, which place such a person outside the protection of the law.

---

[145] Rule 119 ICRC CIHL Study: 'Women who are deprived of their liberty must be held in quarters separate from those of men, except where families are accommodated as family units, and must be under the immediate supervision of women.'
[146] Rule 120 ICRC CIHL Study: 'Children who are deprived of their liberty must be held in quarters separate from those of adults, except where families are accommodated as family units.'
[147] ICRC CIHL Study on Rule 125. In addition, the ICRC requires the exchange of so-called RC Messages (see MN 28) as one of the conditions of its visits, irrespective of the nature of the armed conflict.
[148] ICRC CIHL Study on Rule 117, including notes 10, 12–14.
[149] 27th International Conference of the Red Cross and Red Crescent, Res 1.

Article 5 provides that

[t]he widespread or systematic practice of enforced disappearance constitutes a crime against humanity as defined in applicable international law and shall attract the consequences provided for under such applicable international law.

States parties to the Convention are obliged to 'take the necessary measures to hold [perpetrators] criminally responsible' (Article 6) and to 'make the offence of enforced disappearance punishable by appropriate penalties' (Article 7). Violations of GC IV's provisions on the maintenance and re-establishment of family links and transmission of information constitute acts prohibited under the Convention, provided such violations qualify as, in particular, 'concealment of the fate or whereabouts' of the person who has been deprived of liberty in the context of armed conflict. This will typically be the case, for example, when a detention is not notified or a Detaining Power does not react to a family enquiry.

80   Enforced disappearance of persons is also one of the possible classes of conduct comprising crimes against humanity under the Statute of the International Criminal Court (ICC Statute).[150] In particular, since the *Nacht und Nebel Erlass* (Night and Fog Decree) issued on 7 December 1941 by Hitler, this crime has been committed in order to make people vanish without a trace.[151] According to Article 7(1)(i) of the ICC Statute, the enforced disappearance of persons constitutes a crime against humanity when committed as part of a widespread or systematic attack directed against any civilian population. This includes the arrest, detention, or abduction of persons by, or with the authorization, support, or acquiescence of, a state or a political organization, followed by a refusal to acknowledge that deprivation of freedom, or to give information on the fate or whereabouts of those persons, with the intention of removing them from the protection of the law for a prolonged period of time.[152] With regard to the obligations of states addressed in this chapter, the deprivation of liberty, including the maintenance of an existing detention which may also have been lawful, and the refusal to acknowledge such a deprivation of liberty or to give information on a detained person, thus constitutes a relevant *actus reus*. However, the simple failure to provide information even without a request is not enough. Also, the perpetrator of the deprivation of liberty is not necessarily the same person as the one who withholds information.[153]

81   Hence, violations of obligations under IHL rules addressed in this chapter which might in fact meet the above-mentioned criteria of Article 7(1)(i) of the ICC Statute, and thus constitute crimes against humanity, comprise the following:

— If a person is not released by a Detaining Power as soon as the reasons which necessitated his or her internment no longer exist,[154] and the Detaining Power refuses to give

---

[150] Article 7(1)(i) ICC Statute. No equivalent alternative can be found in Art 8 ICC Statute concerning war crimes.

[151] For more detailed information on this alternative of the crimes against humanity, see O. Triffterer (ed), *Commentary on the Rome Statute of the International Criminal Court* (2nd edn, Munich: Beck, 2008) Art 7, paras 73–4.

[152] Art 7(2)(i) ICC Statute. For more detailed information on the types of conduct covered by Art 7(1)(i) ICC Statute, see G. Werle, *Principles of International Criminal Law* (2nd edn, The Hague: T.M.C. Asser, 2009), paras 908 et seq.

[153] For more detailed information concerning the elements of crime, see Werle, above n 152, para 909.

[154] See relevant obligations contained in Art 132 para 1 GC IV.

information concerning this person on request, Article 7(1)(i) of the ICC Statute is applicable.
— Also, if a party to the conflict does not facilitate enquiries, made by members of families dispersed owing to the armed conflict with the object of renewing contact with one another,[155] or does not enable persons in its territory, or in a territory occupied by it, to give news of a strictly personal nature to members of their families, wherever they may be, and to receive news from them, or delays and does not forward correspondence,[156] this amounts to a refusal to give information on the fate or whereabouts of persons deprived of their liberty in the sense of Article 7(2)(i) of the ICC Statute. More specific rules expressly relate to interned persons.[157]
— Likewise, if a Detaining Power fails to provide the relevant Protecting Power, as rapidly as possible, with the names of any protected persons who have been interned or subjected to assigned residence, or who have been released from these situations, this violation of Article 43 paragraph 2 GC IV might constitute a crime against humanity.

The information on the fate or whereabouts of persons deprived of their liberty mentioned in Article 7(2)(i) of the ICC Statute includes, inter alia, official records of a death.[158] Furthermore, any measure taken by a party to the conflict concerning any protected persons who are kept in custody for more than two weeks, who are subjected to assigned residence, or who are interned,[159] as well as information regarding the state of health of internees who are seriously ill or seriously wounded,[160] falls into this category. 82

Rather explicit is also the obligation that the adverse party to the conflict shall transmit all relevant information concerning persons who have been reported missing in order to facilitate searches.[161] A violation of this rule might constitute a war crime if the person reported missing is in fact deprived of his or her liberty. 83

Violations of provisions on the maintenance and re-establishment of family links and the transmission of information entail not only individual criminal responsibility, but also state responsibility under international law, in particular under the Draft Articles on State Responsibility. Even a single enforced disappearance—irrespective of the circumstances[162]—is a violation of IHRL and is an offence which states parties to the UN Convention on Enforced Disappearances are obliged to criminalize under their domestic law.[163] According to Article 18 of the Convention, each state party shall guarantee to 84

---

[155] Art 26 GC IV.

[156] Art 25 para 1 GC IV. The correspondence may be restricted (Art 25 para 3 GC IV) but not prohibited. Those who are responsible for the internment or detention of the persons deprived of their liberty for reasons related to the armed conflict shall respect that these persons shall be allowed to send and receive letters and cards (Art 5(2)(b) AP II).

[157] The right for an interned person to correspond with his or her family is enshrined in particular in Art 106 GC IV. Mail may not be delayed or retained. Regarding internees subject to disciplinary punishment, see Art 125 para 3 GC IV.

[158] See relevant obligations contained in Art 129 para 3 GC IV.

[159] See relevant obligations contained in Art 136 para 2 GC IV.

[160] See relevant obligations contained in Art 138 para 2 GC IV.

[161] Art 33(1) AP I. Each party to the conflict shall ensure that such information is supplied to the CTA (Art 33(3) AP I).

[162] Art 1(2) ICED.

[163] Art 4 of the Convention. See Ch 35, section B.III, of this volume for a more thorough discussion of the relationship between the GCs and the ICED as well as with the Inter-American Convention on Forced Disappearance of Persons.

any person with a legitimate interest in this information, such as relatives of the person deprived of liberty, his or her representatives, or his or her counsel, access to at least some basic information listed in this provision.

E. Critical Assessment

85 Regulations on the maintenance and re-establishment of family links and the transmission of information in GC IV are characterized by a remarkable degree of detail. This is explained and motivated by experiences in the context of family links with respect to civilians during the Second World War, and today GC IV still sets out the general framework of obligations and rights of all parties concerned. This degree of detail is somewhat disproportionate to the fact that the legal regime with regard to clarification of the fate of missing persons and family reunification is left with certain lacunae in GC IV.

86 Rights and obligations in the context of accounting for missing persons are based on the right of families to know the fate of their missing relatives in armed conflict. This right underlies the regulation in Article 26 GC IV, but only Article 32 AP I states this right explicitly.[164] The duty to account for persons reported missing has crystallized into customary law (see MN 78) and is an 'obligation of means'.[165] Accordingly, each party to the conflict must use its best efforts. This comprises searching for and facilitating the search for persons reported missing as a result of conflict, as well as keeping records of deceased persons and of persons deprived of their liberty. Appropriate methods of establishing the fate of missing persons include exhumation and tracing mechanisms, such as the setting up of special commissions.[166] Where such commissions are created, states have an obligation to cooperate with each other and with the commissions. This obligation is based on a simple practical necessity, since one (eventually former) party to the armed conflict will possess or may have access to the *ante mortem* data, while the other party holds the *post mortem* information. Cooperation between both parties is the only way to implement the right of families to know the fate of their missing relatives in armed conflict, and the obligation to cooperate thus is an inevitable consequence. Practice indicates that the obligation to account for missing persons arises at the latest after an adverse party provides notification of those who are missing.[167] However, the obligation to provide available information is an 'obligation of result'.[168] Available information is to be provided. Although the obligation to search for persons who have been reported missing according to Article 33(1) AP I has crystallized into the customary duty to take all feasible measures to account for persons reported missing as a result of armed conflict,[169] the scope of the obligation is limited to parties to an IAC. It is not incumbent on states not parties to a conflict. This constitutes one of the most important deficiencies of the law governing the maintenance and re-establishment of family links.

87 Whereas Article 26 GC IV directs the duty to facilitate family enquiries at the parties to the conflict, Article 74 AP I expands the obligation to all states parties. This duty to

---

[164] See ICRC Commentary APs, paras 1217–18 on an already pre-existing right.
[165] ICRC CIHL Study, interpretation of Rule 117.
[166] See ibid, including notes 37–40.   [167] Ibid.   [168] Ibid.
[169] ICRC CIHL Study, Rule 117.

facilitate family reunification is applicable to all civilians in the territory of a state party, including its own nationals. However, in particular in situations where part of the family is not located in the territory of a state party, the duty to facilitate does not necessarily result in a duty to grant an entry permit for the purpose of family reunification. For NIACs, Article 4(3)(b) AP II does not provide for an obligation to facilitate family reunification for states party to the Protocol, nor does customary law close this gap.

HEIKE SPIEKER

Chapter 54. The Derogation Clause

	MN
A. Introduction	1
B. Meaning and Application	5
I. The scope of application of Article 5	5
a. An individual protected person	5
b. Geographical scope of application	7
c. Definite suspicion	10
d. Activity hostile to the security of the state/Occupying Power	13
II. The *ratione materiae* scope of the derogations	19
a. Rights and privileges that, if exercised, would be prejudicial to the security of the state (home territory of party to the conflict)	19
b. Rights of communication (occupied territory)	23
III. The extent of the derogations	25
a. Necessity and proportionality	25
b. Safeguards	26
C. Relevance in Non-International Armed Conflicts	31
D. Legal Consequences of a Violation	33
E. Critical Assessment	36

Select Bibliography

Baxter, R., 'So-Called "Unprivileged Belligerency": Spies, Guerillas, and Saboteurs', 28 *BYBIL* (1951) 323

Callen, J., 'Unlawful Combatants and the Geneva Conventions', 44 *Virg JIL* (2004) 1025

Dinstein, Y., *The International Law of Belligerent Occupation* (Cambridge: CUP, 2009)

Dinstein, Y., *The Conduct of Hostilities under the Law of International Armed Conflict* (2nd edn, Cambridge: CUP, 2010)

Dörmann, K., 'The Legal Situation of "Unlawful/Unprivileged Combatants"', 85 *IRRC* 849 (2003) 45

Gehring, R., 'Loss of Civilian Protections under the Fourth Geneva Convention and Protocol I', 90 *Military Law Review* (1980) 49

Gill, T./Van Sliedregt, E., 'Guantánamo Bay: A Reflection on the Status and Rights of "Unlawful Enemy Combatants"', 1 *Utrecht Law Review* (2005) 28

Goodman, R., 'The Detention of Civilians in Armed Conflict', 103 *AJIL* (2009) 48

A. Introduction

Captioned 'derogations', Article 5 of Geneva Convention (GC) IV allows a party to a conflict or an Occupying Power to derogate to a certain extent from the rights afforded by the Convention to the 'protected persons' as defined in Article 4. Article 5 applies when in occupied territory, or in the territory of a party to the conflict, an Occupying Power or a party to the conflict is satisfied that an *individual* protected person is definitely suspected of being engaged in acts hostile to the security of the Occupying Power or party. Although Article 5 shares some common features with the derogations clauses enshrined in human rights treaties,[1] it is not applicable to a *situation*. By contrast, a derogation under international human rights law (IHRL) entails consequences for every person subject to the jurisdiction of the state availing itself of the derogation.

2   Current Article 5 was absent from the 1948 draft adopted in Stockholm at the XVIIth International Red Cross Conference. States may have thought it unnecessary to include a special provision on spies and saboteurs because states have a right to defend themselves from espionage.[2] In the same vein, Article 5 might have been motivated by the imperative to set limits to this right of states more than by the need to permit derogations.[3]

3   Nevertheless, many delegates at the Diplomatic Conference feared that rights provided to civilians would be subject to abuses by spies and saboteurs. Derogations were deemed necessary in view of 'the very great difficulty in tracking down these underground activities'.[4] The threat to internal security was considered as 'one of the main preoccupations of national leaders in time of war'.[5]

4   Saboteurs of yesterday are the terrorists of today.[6] Even though the United States (US) Administration does not explicitly rely on Article 5 GC IV as regards the legal framework applicable to Al-Qaeda detainees in Guantánamo,[7] the past and contemporary debate over Article 5 focuses on the notion of 'unlawful combatant' which lies at the very heart of the US's legal doctrine concerning the 'war' on terrorism.

B. Meaning and Application

I. The scope of application of Article 5

a. An individual protected person

5   The words 'individual protected person' used in respect to those suspected of or engaged in activities hostile to the security of the state, reflect the intent of the drafters to ensure that the measures taken in derogation from GC IV would be based on grounds specific to each individual.[8] This imperative goes with the requirement of a 'definite suspicion' in Article 5 paragraph 2, that the individual person is engaged in hostile acts.

6   The words 'protected person' make clear and confirm that spies, saboteurs, and other persons suspected of or engaged in hostile acts are and remain 'protected' by GC IV (on condition that they meet the nationality—or arguably the allegiance—criterion). Indeed, these persons do not benefit from the prisoner of war (POW) status if they fall into the hands of the enemy, mainly because they act clandestinely without wearing the uniform of their armed forces.[9] If they were to fall outside GC IV because of the hostile nature of their acts, Article 5 would be devoid of any effect.[10] For this reason, Article 5 is

---

[1] Art 15 ECHR, Art 4 ICCPR, and Art 27 ACHR.
[2] ICRC, *The Geneva Conventions of August 12, 1949: Analysis for the Use of National Red Cross Societies* (Geneva: ICRC, 1950) vol II, at 88.
[3] Ibid.
[4] Final Record, vol II-A, at 814.   [5] Ibid, at 796.
[6] Y. Dinstein, *The International Law of Belligerent Occupation* (Cambridge: CUP, 2009), at 63.
[7] This is mainly due to the US Administration's contention that the GCs do not directly apply to the conflict between the US and Al-Qaeda (with the notable exception of CA 3 since the ruling of the Supreme Court in the case *Hamdan v Rumsfeld*, 548 US 557, 29 June 2006).
[8] Final Record, vol II-A, at 796.   [9] Art 46 AP I; *Ex parte Quirin*, 317 US 1, 31 July 1942.
[10] The Chamber Judgment of the ECtHR in the case of *Kononov v Latvia* of 24 July 2008 (overruled by the Grand Chamber's Judgment of 17 May 2010) is an example of a divergent reading of Art 5 in this respect: at para 131.

relied upon in legal literature as a justification that 'unlawful combatants' (i.e. civilians participating in hostilities without entitlement, or combatants having failed to distinguish themselves) are protected by GC IV.[11] If there is a controversy on the application of Article 5 (and hence of GC IV) to 'unlawful combatants', it does not lie therein. Even the US Administration relies upon Article 5 to acknowledge that some 'unlawful belligerents' fall within the scope of GC IV.[12] The controversy pertains to the geographical scope of Article 5.

b. Geographical scope of application

According to some authors, 'unlawful combatants' captured on the battlefield do not fall under the terms of Article 5, which according to the main view strictly applies to the home territory of a party to the conflict and to occupied territory,[13] and are hence excluded from the scope of GC IV. This view is based on a narrow reading of what is an occupied territory and, more generally, that none of the provisions in Part III of GC IV applies in the battlefield or in the invaded territory. Even if one takes this view and considers that Article 5 does not apply to 'hostile civilians' captured on the battlefield (i.e. neither on the home territory of a party to the conflict nor in occupied territory), the minimum of protection provided by Article 75 of Additional Protocol (AP) I would apply by virtue of Article 45(3) AP I[14] (by virtue of the customary nature of Article 75 AP I for the non-contracting parties to AP I).[15]

As a minimum, the 'hostile civilian' captured in a supposedly legal 'no man's land' from the point of view of GC IV must be granted humane treatment and a fair trial if prosecuted on the same scheme as clearly provided by Article 5 paragraph 3 GC IV. The controversy on the geographical scope of Article 5 has therefore no impact on the treatment that must be granted 'at any time and in any place whatsoever'[16] to the 'hostile civilian'.

The common standard of treatment (paragraph 3) for situations contemplated in paragraph 1 (home territory of a party to the conflict) and paragraph 2 (occupied territory) does not mean that there is no need to distinguish between them. Their legal regimes differ in respect of the nature of the rights and the extent to which they may be derogated from.

c. Definite suspicion

Article 5 concerns offenders as much as suspects of hostile acts towards state security. It was pointed out by delegates at the Diplomatic Conference that action against spies and saboteurs had to be taken long before they were convicted.[17] The proposed Soviet amendment which restricted the scope of Article 5 to 'persons convicted'[18] was thus rejected.

---

[11] K. Dörmann, 'The Legal Situation of "Unlawful/Unprivileged Combatants"', 85 *IRRC* 849 (2003) 45, at 50.

[12] Opinion of the Office of Legal Counsel, '"Protected Person" Status in Occupied Iraq under the Fourth Geneva Convention', 18 March 2004, at 12–13.

[13] J. Callen, 'Unlawful Combatants and the Geneva Conventions', 44 *VirgJIL* (2004) 1025, at 1039–40; R. Baxter, 'So-Called "Unprivileged Belligerency": Spies, Guerrillas, and Saboteurs', 28 *BYBIL* (1951) 323, at 328.

[14] 'Any person who has taken part in hostilities, who is not entitled to prisoner-of-war status and who does not benefit from more favourable treatment in accordance with the Fourth Convention shall have the right at all times to the protection of Article 75 of this Protocol [...]'

[15] See notably ICRC CIHL Study, Rule 87 ('Civilians and persons hors de combat must be treated humanely') and Rule 100 ('No one may be convicted or sentenced, except pursuant to a fair trial affording all essential judicial guarantees').

[16] Art 75(2) AP I.   [17] Final Record, vol II-A, at 798.   [18] Ibid, at 797.

11 As a counterbalance to this prerogative of the state, both in paragraphs 1 and 2 Article 5 requires a *definite* suspicion that someone is engaged in acts hostile to the security of the state/Occupying Power. This word may be the most important one in Article 5, in so far as it sets the burden of proof in order to proceed to derogations. Many delegations at the Diplomatic Conference insisted upon this standard of proof to ensure 'a fair balance between the rights of the State and those of protected persons'.[19] According to the rationale behind Article 5, this provision can 'never be applied as a result of a mere suspicion'.[20]

12 The notion of '*suspicion légitime*', used in the French wording of Article 5, is known in Continental law as the procedure whereby a court may be asked by a superior court to withdraw when there is a *suspicion légitime* over its impartiality. The requesting party must rely on objective and well-founded facts that constitute legitimate reasons to believe that the court suffers from partiality (this is the case when a judge has expressed personal opinions on the case).[21] Turning back to the 'definite suspicion' of Article 5, this notion could then be construed as requiring a similarly high standard of proof as for Article 42, which allows a party to the conflict to intern civilians for security reasons, that is to say '*serious and legitimate reasons to think* that [people] may seriously prejudice [the state's] security by means such as sabotage or espionage'.[22] Nevertheless, the requirement of a *definite* suspicion does not protect individuals from abuses by states as long as suspicion rests upon charges that remain to be proven.[23] Fair trial guarantees (Article 5 paragraph 3) are, in this regard, of paramount importance if the individual is to be tried.

d. Activity hostile to the security of the state/Occupying Power

13 The generic terms 'activity hostile to the security of the [state/Occupying Power]', used in paragraphs 1 and 2 of Article 5, are not defined, nor are espionage and sabotage in GC IV (even though Article 68 refers to espionage and 'serious acts of sabotage against the military installations of the Occupying Power').

14 Other texts of international humanitarian law (IHL) (Article 88 of the Lieber Code, Article 29 of the Hague Regulations, and Article 46 AP I) allow one to identify the key elements of a definition of espionage in wartime:

— *espionage can only be committed in an area controlled by the enemy* (Article 29 of the Hague Regulations, which restricts the definition of espionage to an activity committed 'in the zone of operations of a belligerent', is too restrictive in this respect);[24]

— *espionage consists of gathering information on behalf of a hostile party* (importantly, Article 46(3) AP I adds that in occupied territory, the information gathered or attempted to be gathered must be of 'military value');

— *a spy acts clandestinely or on false pretences* (*a contrario*, anyone who gathers or attempts to gather information while dressed in the uniform of his or her armed forces is not

---

[19] Ibid, at 796 and 815.   [20] Pictet Commentary GC IV, at 58.
[21] G. Cornu (ed), *Vocabulaire juridique* (Paris: Presses Universitaires de France, 2001), at 850.
[22] ICTY, *The Prosecutor v Zejnil Delalić et al (Čelebići Camp)*, Trial Chamber Judgment, IT-96-21-T, 16 November 1998, para 576. See also Pictet Commentary GC IV, at 258; EECC, *Civilians Claims—Ethiopia's Claim 5*, Partial Award, 17 December 2004, para 104. This assertion does not mean that any protected person interned on the basis of Art 42 would be deprived of his or her rights afforded to the protected interned civilians by GC IV (Section IV): Art 5 strictly limits derogations, in the territory of a party to the conflict, to the rights that would 'if exercised in the favour of such individual person, be prejudicial to the security of the state'.
[23] Final Record, vol II-A, at 798.
[24] Y. Dinstein, *The Conduct of Hostilities under the Law of International Armed Conflict* (2nd edn, Cambridge: CUP, 2010), at 241–2.

considered as a spy) and is therefore not entitled to POW status (the consequence of which is that he or she may be punished for his or her acts of espionage) if he or she is taken in the act.

Concerning the second component of the definition, it was rightly pointed out at the expert meeting on the supervision of the lawfulness of detention during armed conflict, organized by the University Centre for IHL in 2004, that today spies help to ensure the correct application of the principle of distinction by gathering information on the military nature of an objective.[25]

15 Sabotage is not defined elsewhere in IHL (Article 68 GC IV mentions only the 'serious acts of sabotage'—understood as destruction—'against the military installations')[26] and is rarely defined as such in military manuals. When a definition of sabotage is given, it is kept in very broad terms, such as those of Australia's *Manual of the Law of Armed Conflict* (2006), which states that '[g]enerally speaking, saboteurs are persons operating behind the lines of the enemy to commit acts of destruction'.[27] Military manuals rather insist upon the fact that a saboteur not in uniform runs the risk of being treated as a spy, which means no entitlement to POW status and punishment for espionage if taken in the act.

16 Yet if acts of sabotage can be carried out in uniform, what distinguishes acts of lawful belligerency from acts of unlawful belligerency such as sabotage? The question is even more difficult if one considers, as the Pictet Commentary GC IV to Article 5 does, that sabotage 'should be understood to mean acts whose object or effect is to damage or destroy material belonging to the army of occupation or utilized by it'. What then is the difference between an attack on a military objective and sabotage? For the purpose of Article 5, the hypothesis of a saboteur in uniform is not directly relevant, because GC IV does not cover protected persons under GC III (POWs). Sabotage nonetheless suffers from a lack of a clear and comprehensive definition in IHL.

17 The words 'activities hostile to the security' of the state/Occupying Power vest the latter with a far broader margin of appreciation than the notions of espionage and sabotage do (even taking into account the lack of a comprehensive definition of sabotage in IHL). Article 42 GC IV also leaves to the state 'substantial discretion' in determining that a protected person poses a threat to its security.[28] Similarly, the European Court of Human Rights (ECtHR) considers, with respect to Article 15 of the European Convention on Human Rights (ECHR), that 'it falls to each Contracting State, with its responsibility for "the life of [its] nation", to determine whether that life is threatened by a "public emergency"' because of the 'direct and continuous contact [of the authorities] with the pressing needs of the moment'.[29] The wide margin of appreciation given to states to make the initial determination appears to be a common feature of the derogation power in IHL and IHRL.

---

[25] University Centre for International Humanitarian Law, 'Expert Meeting on the Right to Life in Armed Conflict and Situations of Occupation' (September 2005), available at <http://www.geneva-academy.ch/docs/expert-meetings/2005/3rapport_droit_vie.pdf>, at 17.

[26] See, for examples (and counter-examples) of 'serious acts of sabotage', Pictet Commentary GC IV, at 344.

[27] Art 7.19, quoted by the ICRC CIHL Database, Practice Relating to Rule 107; in *Ex parte Quirin*, above n 9, the saboteur was defined as 'an enemy combatant who without uniform comes secretly through the lines for the purpose of waging war by destruction of life or property'.

[28] IACommHR, *Coard et al v United States*, Report no 109/99, 29 September 1999, para 53; ICTY, *Čelebići Camp*, Trial Judgment, above n 22, paras 574 and 583.

[29] ECtHR, *Brannigan and McBride v United Kingdom*, Judgment, 25 May 1993, para 43.

18   Nevertheless, this margin of appreciation is not unlimited.[30] The International Criminal Tribunal for the former Yugoslavia (ICTY) contended that although 'the language of Article 5 is very broad and its provisions may be applicable in a wide variety of situations', 'espionage, sabotage and intelligence activities for the enemy forces or enemy nationals' seem 'above all' to be included and a mere 'individual's political attitude towards the State' excluded.[31] The ICTY moreover observed that some clear-cut examples of acts hostile to state security in the sense of Article 5 (a civilian shooting an enemy soldier or secreting a bomb in the enemy encampment) involve 'direct harm to the adversary, rather than merely granting support to the forces of the party with which the civilian is aligned'.[32] In like manner, the Pictet Commentary GC IV to Article 42 considers that subversive activities which are of 'direct assistance to an enemy Power' threaten the security of the state. These expressions of 'direct harm' and 'direct assistance' remind one of 'direct participation in hostilities'. Indeed, as highlighted above, the idea that Article 5 applies to 'unlawful belligerency', that is direct participation (without entitlement) in hostilities, is widely accepted in legal literature as well as in practice.

II. The *ratione materiae* scope of the derogations

a. Rights and privileges that, if exercised, would be prejudicial to the security of the state (home territory of party to the conflict)

19   As noticed by the Pictet Commentary GC IV, Article 5 is the only Article in GC IV which speaks of the rights *and privileges* of protected persons. According to the Commentary, the rights of protected persons are 'privileges' compared to the persons who do not enjoy protection under GC IV.[33] From a natural law perspective, one distinguishes the 'right', which is a legal entitlement of a human being, and the 'privilege', which is granted by a legal authority to specific classes of individuals. 'Privileges' can be taken away—in contrast to 'rights'.[34] Within the frame of GC IV, this distinction would be relevant to the extent that some rights of the protected person cannot be taken away by the state, even in time of war. These rights, which are to be respected in all circumstances, are set forth in Article 5 paragraph 3. But obviously, 'rights' in Article 5 paragraph 1 are not equivalent to 'rights' in the natural law theory because derogations from some of them are permitted. As for the 'privileges', if the expression refers to some advantages to which civilian internees are entitled 'for their comfort' (such as allowances for buying tobacco and toilet requisites),[35] they can hardly be deemed to be, if exercised, prejudicial to state security.

20   Indeed, the rights referred to by Article 5 paragraph 1 are strictly those which, 'if exercised in the favour of such individual person', would 'be prejudicial to the security of' the state. Moreover, according to paragraph 3 of Article 5, these rights cannot be

---

[30] Ibid; HRCttee, General Comment 29, *States of Emergency (Article 4)*, 24 July 2001, para 3.
[31] ICTY, *Čelebići Camp*, Trial Judgment, above n 22, para 567; ICTY, *The Prosecutor v Dario Kordić and Mario Čerkez (Lašva Valley)*, Trial Chamber Judgment, IT-95-14/2-T, 26 February 2001, para 280.
[32] ICTY, *Čelebići Camp*, Trial Judgment, above n 22, para 568.
[33] Pictet Commentary GC IV, at 56.
[34] This is in this sense that the ECtHR has stated in the case *Hirst v United Kingdom (No 2)*, Judgment (Grand Chamber), 6 October 2005, para 59, that 'the right to vote is not a privilege'; this is not to say that the right to vote is absolute, but rather that it cannot be unduly denied to some sections of the population (*in casu* convicted persons who are detained) at the risk of undermining the principle of universal suffrage and the democratic validity of the legislature thus elected (para 62).
[35] Art 98 GC IV.

those to humane treatment and to fair trial if prosecuted. In light of the drafting history of Article 5,[36] the rights that can be derogated from are, above all, the rights of communication with the outside world (Chapter VIII, captioned 'relations with the exterior').

It may be put forward, though, that the rights of protected persons to correspond with and to receive visits or shipments from the exterior are prejudicial to state security only when the hostile activity is that of espionage. There is a real risk that information gathered by espionage will be conveyed to the enemy. But for all other 'hostile civilians', having, for example, taken up arms without being entitled to do so, there is no apparent reason for detaining them *incommunicado*.[37] Derogations are not designed for the punishment of 'unlawful combatants'. They are, strictly, means for states to protect themselves against subversive activities. This is the reason why state security cannot be a valid reason for depriving 'hostile civilians' of the benefit of humane treatment. 21

As for the right of periodical reassessment by an independent and impartial body of the decision of internment or placing in assigned residence (Article 43 GC IV), it might be discussed whether this right would be non-derogable under IHL or IHRL. If it is non-derogable, it is not by virtue of Article 5 paragraph 3, which restricts the 'rights of fair and regular trial' to the 'case of trial', whereas Article 43 contemplates the case of *internment* of protected persons, i.e. without being prosecuted under criminal law. As pointed out at MN 30, the right to *habeas corpus* belongs to the non-derogable rights under IHRL. Thus, according to the simultaneous application of IHL and IHRL in time of war, the right under Article 43 GC IV to have a decision periodically reassessed by an independent and impartial body (be it a court or an administrative board) on the lawfulness of its internment, cannot be subject to derogations. This has been confirmed in the practice of the ICTY.[38] In similar vein, the US Supreme Court held that even 'enemy combatants' must, at least when they are US citizens or are held at Guantánamo Bay, be given, on constitutional grounds, a meaningful opportunity to contest the factual basis for their detention before a neutral decision maker.[39] 22

b. *Rights of communication (occupied territory)*

In occupied territory, the scope of derogations is far more limited. For contracting parties to AP I, there are no derogations possible except for spies. Article 45(3) AP I is the *lex specialis* to Article 5 paragraph 2 in this respect. 23

For non-contracting parties to AP I, derogations in occupied territory are expressly limited to the rights of communication of the detained protected person. Even if the rights that can be derogated from in the territory of a party to a conflict are first and foremost (if not only) the rights of communication, paragraph 2 has been formulated on purpose in a more restrictive way than paragraph 1. Indeed, a certain resistance is tolerated inasmuch as residents of the occupied territory have no duty of allegiance to the Occupying Power. 24

---

[36] Final Record, vol II-A, at 814.
[37] R. Gehring, 'Loss of Civilian Protections under the Fourth Geneva Convention and Protocol I', 90 *Military Law Review* (1980) 49, at 82 (the assessment whether a protected person is engaged in activity hostile to security must be made on a case-by-case basis).
[38] ICTY, *Čelebići Camp*, Trial Judgment, above n 22, paras 579–83; and ICTY, *Lašva Valley*, Trial Chamber Judgment, above n 31, para 286.
[39] *Hamdi v Rumsfeld*, 542 US 507, 28 June 2004 (US citizen detained on US soil); *Rasul v Bush*, 542 US 466, 28 June 2004 (as regards foreign nationals detained at Guantánamo).

III. The extent of the derogations

a. Necessity and proportionality

25 As for any derogation power, derogations must be necessary and strictly proportionate to the exigencies of the situation. The yardstick in the home territory of a party to the conflict (rights, if exercised, that would be prejudicial to state security) is lower than the 'absolute military security' required for derogations in occupied territory. This much more restrained criterion has been justified by the understanding that in occupied territory, 'the population could naturally be expected to do everything in its power to embarrass the invading forces'.[40] As with derogation clauses in human rights treaties,[41] derogations are of a temporary nature and must be terminated as soon as the danger ceases to exist (Article 5 paragraph 3 *in fine*).

b. Safeguards

26 With respect to occupied territory, some authors have questioned the relevance of the safeguards set forth in Article 5 paragraph 3: 'If only provisions relating to communication can be derogated from, why is there a need to indicate as minimum protections humane treatment and fair trial?'[42] The fair trial guarantees are, as specified by Article 5 paragraph 3, 'in case of trial'. Even if espionage is not forbidden as such by IHL, spies and saboteurs can be prosecuted according to domestic law.[43] As for the imperative of humane treatment, it is an important criterion to determine the rights that can be derogated from. With regard to occupied territory, the derogation from the right to receive spiritual assistance for a dying believer might be considered as inhuman treatment,[44] despite the fact that it belongs to the rights of communication with the outside world.

i. Humane treatment

27 The imperative to treat humanely any person, be it a spy or a saboteur, in all circumstances was recalled by the Eritrea–Ethiopia Claims Commission with regard to civilians who were notably 'detained on suspicion of espionage or other offenses against Ethiopian state security'.[45] It found Ethiopia responsible for a breach of IHL, 'for holding Eritrean civilians on security related charges in prisons and jails under harsh and unsanitary conditions and with insufficient food, and for subjecting them to beatings and other abuse'.[46] The imperative of humane treatment forbids the use of any physical or moral coercion to obtain information, contrary to what might have been stated by some authors[47] and an Israeli enquiry commission.[48]

ii. Fair trial (and other procedural) safeguards

28 The right to a fair trial is particularly important in criminal proceedings against 'hostile civilians', because spies and persons guilty of 'serious acts of sabotage' may be subjected to

---

[40] Final Record, vol II-A, at 797. [41] HCRttee, above n 30, para 4.
[42] Dörmann, above n 11, at 66; see also A. Rosas, *The Legal Status of Prisoners of War* (Helsinki: Suomalainen Tiedeakatemia, 1976), at 412.
[43] Dinstein, above n 24, at 242–3. [44] Pictet Commentary GC IV, at 56.
[45] EECC, *Civilians Claims—Eritrea's Claims 15, 16, 23, and 27–32*, Partial Award, 17 December 2004, para 111.
[46] Ibid, Finding 9.
[47] J. Yoo, 'Terrorists Have No Geneva Rights', *Wall Street Journal*, 26 May 2004; Gehring, above n 37, at 83.
[48] See extracts of the Report of the Landau Enquiry Commission of 1987, in Sassòli/Bouvier/Quintin, at 1094–5.

the death penalty.⁴⁹ More than a mere 'right to a trial' provided by Article 30 of the Hague Regulations, Article 5 paragraph 3 GC IV ensures a right to a *fair and regular* trial.

The procedural guarantees of a 'regular trial' are spelt out in Articles 64 to 76 GC IV (with regard to occupied territory), notably the right of the accused persons to be promptly informed in a language which they understand of the charges brought against them, the right to present evidence, to call witnesses, to be assisted by a counsel and aided by an interpreter, as well as the right of appeal if convicted. The 'generally recognized principles of regular judicial procedure' of Article 75(4) AP I add non-derogable rights to this list, such as the presumption of innocence and the principle of retroactivity *in mitius* (originally stemming from IHRL).⁵⁰ As long as these rights are guaranteed, proceedings before military tribunals would not be contrary to Article 5 GC IV,⁵¹ and are foreseen by Article 66 of GC IV.

As mentioned at MN 22, the right to *habeas corpus* belongs to the rights that cannot be derogated from under IHRL. While the right to *habeas corpus* is not listed among the non-derogable rights in Article 4(2) of the International Covenant on Civil and Political Rights (ICCPR), it was considered as non-derogable by the Human Rights Committee in order to secure (as a procedural safeguard) the non-derogability of rights such as the right to life or the prohibition of torture and cruel or inhuman punishment.⁵² Nevertheless, the right to *habeas corpus* under IHRL cannot be considered as requiring that in time of war the lawfulness of the detention must be reviewed *by a court*. Article 43 GC IV leaves, for example, the choice between a court and an administrative board (as long as the latter is an independent and impartial body).

C. Relevance in Non-International Armed Conflicts

There is no provision equivalent to Article 5 GC IV in IHL treaty law applicable to non-international armed conflicts (NIACs) (Common Article 3 and AP II). The question may be asked whether there is a right under IHL customary law for parties to NIACs to derogate (to certain extent) from some of the rights afforded to civilians. While AP II does not provide legal basis for deprivations of liberty, it clearly contemplates the case of internments (notably for security reasons) by laying down minimum conditions of detention in Article 5. These conditions were conceived as the *minima* ('shall be respected as a minimum') that have to be afforded to persons deprived of their liberty in NIACs. Accordingly, the possibility to derogate from some of these provisions would be excluded. At the same time, Article 5 AP II contains some rights of communication that could be prejudicial to the state or insurgents if exercised, notably the right to correspond. Nevertheless, the right to correspond is not absolute according to paragraph 2 of Article 5 ('within the limits of their capabilities') and subparagraph b ('may be limited by competent authority if it deems necessary'). The right to correspond could be diminished so as to accommodate state or insurgents' security without resorting to derogations.

---

⁴⁹ Art 68 para 2 GC IV.
⁵⁰ The principle of retroactivity *in mitius* (Art 15 ICCPR) is non-derogable by virtue of Art 4(2) ICCPR; see HRCttee, above n 30, paras 11 and 16 concerning the non-derogable character of the principle of the presumption of innocence.
⁵¹ R. Goodman, 'The Detention of Civilians in Armed Conflict', 103 *AJIL* (2009) 48, at 58; *Hamdan v Rumsfeld*, above n 7.
⁵² HRCttee, above n 30, paras 15–16.

32   In any case, the non-derogable rights under IHRL (that merge with and go beyond the safeguards laid down in Article 5 paragraph 3) remain in force in NIACs in so far as IHRL makes no distinction between international armed conflicts (IACs) and NIACs.

D. Legal Consequences of a Violation

33   Contrary to the regime of derogations in human rights treaties, there is no requirement under Article 5 GC IV to notify the other state parties of the derogation, nor is there a treaty monitory body which can assess whether the derogation is strictly required by the exigencies of the situation. From a criminal law perspective, the question may be asked, nevertheless, whether and to what extent disrespect for the provisions of Article 5 may constitute war crimes in IACs and NIACs.

34   According to Article 147 GC IV, disrespect for the safeguards of humane treatment and fair trial protections (which are guaranteed by Article 5, paragraph 3) may give rise to grave breaches of GC IV,[53] taking into consideration that the person subject to the derogations of Article 5 is and remains a *protected person* (fulfilling, then, the condition expressed by Article 147). Similarly, in NIACs, these actions are serious violations of Common Article 3.[54]

35   As regards the unlawful confinement of a protected person, listed in the grave breaches of Article 147 GC IV, Article 5 GC IV has been correctly referred to, in the practice of the ICTY, as a means of interpretation of Articles 42 and 43 GC IV on the issue of the legality of confinement of 'enemy' civilians in a given case, and not, in and of itself, as a basis for a finding of a grave breach for unlawful detention.[55]

E. Critical Assessment

36   It may be asked whether Article 5 GC IV is (still) relevant. In the home territory of a party to a conflict, the rights that can be derogated from because they would, if exercised, be prejudicial to state security are not extensive (if the criterion of 'prejudicial to the security of state' is narrowly construed and applied on a case-by-case basis) and could be diminished by virtue of the limitation power inherent to GC IV in place of derogations. In occupied territory, Article 45(3) AP I has deprived Article 5 GC IV of any effect except for spies.

37   Article 5 nevertheless still bears relevance, as it constitutes the best evidence that 'unlawful combatants' (notably in the US's doctrine on the 'war' on terror) are and remain protected by GC IV, provided that they meet the nationality criterion.

ANNE-LAURENCE GRAF-BRUGÈRE

---

[53] Grave breaches of GC IV are war crimes according to Art 8(2)(a) ICC Statute.
[54] Serious violations of CA 3 are war crimes according to Art 8(2)(c) ICC Statute.
[55] ICTY, *Čelebići Camp*, Trial Judgment, above n 22, paras 564–83; ICTY, *Lašva Valley*, Trial Chamber Judgment, above n 31, paras 280–91. See also ICTY, *The Prosecutor v Zejnil Delalić et al (Čelebići Camp)*, Appeals Chamber Judgment, IT-96-21-A, 20 February 2001, para 328 (reading of the requirement of 'as soon as possible' of Art 43 GC IV in light of the notion of 'definite suspicion' of Art 5).

2. CIVILIANS IN THE HANDS OF THE ENEMY: GENERAL PROTECTION

Chapter 55. Who Is a Protected Civilian?

	MN
A. Introduction	1
B. Meaning and Application	8
I. Protection of civilians in the Hague Regulations	8
II. The regime of protected persons within the Fourth Geneva Convention	10
a. Cases of application of GC IV	17
b. 'In the hands of a Party to the conflict'	25
c. Protected persons must not have the nationality of the party in whose hands they are	27
III. Neutrality, co-belligerence, and diplomatic representation, and their use with respect to protected persons	35
IV. The broader protection of the civilian population in Part II GC IV	43
V. The distinctions between prisoners of war, unlawful combatants, and protected civilians	47
C. Relevance in Non-International Armed Conflicts	54
D. Legal Consequences of a Violation	58
E. Critical Assessment	62

Select Bibliography

Arai, Y., *The Law of Occupation: Continuity and Change of International Humanitarian Law, and its Interaction with International Human Rights Law* (Leiden: Martinus Nijhoff Publishers, 2009)
Benvenisti, E., *The International Law of Occupation* (2nd edn, Oxford: OUP, 2012)
Dinstein, Y., *The International Law of Belligerent Occupation* (Cambridge: CUP, 2009)
Draper, G.I.A.D., 'The Protected Person in Occupied Territory', 114 *RCADI* (1965) 59
ICRC, *Occupation and Other Forms of Administration of Foreign Territory* (Geneva: ICRC, 2012)
ICRC, *The Use of Force in Armed Conflicts: Interplay between the Conduct of Hostilities and Law Enforcement Paradigms* (Geneva: ICRC, 2013)
Kolb, R./Vité, S., *Le droit de l'occupation militaire. Perspectives historiques et enjeux juridiques actuels* (Brussels: Bruylant, 2009)
Melzer, N., *Targeted Killings in International Law* (Oxford: OUP, 2008)
Pictet Commentary GC IV, 45–51
Sassòli, M., 'The Status of Persons Held in Guantánamo under International Humanitarian Law', 2 *JICJ* (2004) 96

A. Introduction

The definition of 'civilian' represents a crucial topic in international humanitarian law (IHL) and is essential for the application of the distinction between combatants and civilians, a cardinal principle of IHL, as the International Court of Justice (ICJ) called it in the *Nuclear Weapons* Advisory Opinion.[1] This fundamental legal distinction aims to respond to another principle of IHL, namely that of military necessity ('the only legitimate object which States should endeavour to accomplish during war is to weaken the military forces of the enemy'[2]), and to the vulnerability of civilians in contemporary conflicts.

2   Hence, it is important to define who is considered a civilian under IHL. According to Geneva Convention (GC) III and Additional Protocol (AP) I, a civilian in an international armed conflict (IAC) is any person who is not a member of the armed forces of a party to a conflict. Consequently, civilians may not be attacked except if they participate directly in hostilities.

3   Whereas the Saint Petersburg Declaration implicitly formulated the principle of distinction between combatants and civilians, the Hague Regulations did not specifically repeat this fundamental distinction. There were, however, several rules that benefited civilians in certain circumstances during an armed conflict (Article 25—prohibition of attacks on non-defended cities, prohibition of pillage, etc). Only in 1977 did AP I codify and spell out the principles in Article 48.

4   While earlier inter-state wars mainly affected opposing armed forces, the Second World War affected more civilians than members of the military; civilians became the subject of deliberate and indiscriminate attacks, and suffered in occupied territories and concentration camps. The events of the Second World War, including the persecution of Jews, prompted a drastic alteration in international law. Differently from the past, international law now shows greater concern for human beings in the context of armed violence. To avoid the horrors of the World Wars, the United Nations (UN) Charter went so far as to even outlaw the threat and use of force through Article 2(4). At the same time, states adopted the Geneva Conventions and adopted a specific convention solely concerned with civilians, so as to guarantee their minimum protection in the event of an armed conflict.

5   Geneva Convention IV is thus the first comprehensive treaty dealing with the protection of civilians during IACs. As the fundamental Article 27 paragraph 1 states, civilians are entitled

> in all circumstances, to respect for their persons, their honour, their family rights, their religious convictions and practices, and their manners and customs. They shall at all times be humanely treated, and shall be protected especially against all acts of violence or threats thereof and against insults and public curiosity.

Geneva Convention IV further provides a series of rules in favour of protecting civilians, even though some of them may incidentally be involved in hostilities.

6   This Convention contains two parallel regimes of protection. On one hand, there are general rules for the protection of the civilian population set forth in Part II GC IV, such as respect for protected zones and hospitals, the protection of children under the age of 15, the provision of humanitarian assistance for certain beneficiaries, and facilitating family reunifications. These issues are discussed in the relevant chapters of this volume. On the other hand, the Convention establishes a much more detailed and

---

[1] ICJ, *Legality of the Threat or Use of Nuclear Weapons*, Advisory Opinion, 8 July 1996.
[2] Saint Petersburg Declaration, preambular para 2.

protective regime in favour of certain human groups, called 'protected persons', set forth in Part III GC IV.

At first glance, this double regime of protection may present itself as archaic and far removed from the reality of contemporary armed conflicts where the whole civilian population is directly or indirectly involved. However, the practice of international institutions and the interpretation of the provisions by international human rights monitoring bodies, as well as by international criminal tribunals, have managed to maintain the usefulness of these rules through a committed reading of the specific purposes of IHL, addressing contemporary forms of occupation, inter-state violence, transnational terrorism, one-sided violence, and the privatization of violence. Despite this, the limits of IHL and the response of other international regimes regarding its legal loopholes should be recognized.

B. Meaning and Application

I. Protection of civilians in the Hague Regulations

The situation of civilians caught up in armed violence was already considered, albeit not expressly, in the Hague Regulations.[3] Draper explains that the lack of direct references to civilians within the Hague Regulations is because, as a rule, civilians were absent during military operations, so it was not necessary to regulate their fate. However, references to civilians in the Hague Regulations of 1907 take into account the extension of military operations into inhabited territories. In this context, the protection in favour of their inhabitants is justified.[4] Thus, although the Hague Regulations of 1907 are focused more on the fate of the goods and resources controlled by the Occupying Power than on the treatment of people, the Regulations considered a number of safeguards in favour of persons during occupation.[5]

The few references in the Hague Regulations regarding the civilian population affected by armed violence include various terms such as 'individuals', 'private persons', 'inhabitants', 'family', and 'population'.[6] This complex landscape generates various difficulties when determining whether the benefits of belonging to any of these categories might be extended to the others. In addition, a critical problem is that the Hague Regulations do not settle the issues of whether rules in favour of 'inhabitants' apply by analogy to 'private persons' or are excluded for certain sectors of a 'population'. Attempts to regulate, at least partially, the fate of civilians failed before the outbreak of the Second World War.[7]

---

[3] Arts 4, 46, 52 para 1, 52 para 2 Hague Regulations; G.I.A.D. Draper, 'The Protected Person in Occupied Territory', 114 *RCADI* (1965), at 119.
[4] Draper, above n 3, at 119–21.
[5] R. Kolb and S. Vité, *Le droit de l'occupation militaire. Perspectives historiques et enjeux juridiques actuels* (Brussels: Bruylant, 2009), at 116–17; and see Ch 69 of this volume.
[6] Kolb and Vité, above n 5, at 116.
[7] E.g., Protection of Civilian Populations against Bombing from the Air in Case of War, League of Nations, Unanimous Resolution of the League of Nations Assembly, 30 September 1938. See also Draft Convention for the Protection of Civilian Populations against New Engines of War (1938).

II. The regime of protected persons within the Fourth Geneva Convention

10   Geneva Convention IV is based on the above-mentioned regime but recognizes new rules for military conduct. As a consequence, GC IV institutes a dual regime of protection: on the one hand, it establishes protections for the civilian population as a whole; and on the other hand, it qualifies certain foreigners and inhabitants of occupied territories as protected persons.

11   The interaction between the Hague Regulations and GC IV is regulated through the legal concept of protected persons,[8] as seen in Article 4 GC IV[9] which addresses the heterogeneous regime of the Hague Regulations without repealing it (outlined in Article 154 GC IV). In defining (negatively) civilians as all persons not belonging to the armed forces, it bases itself on the definition given in the Hague Regulations on belligerents (Article 1). Lastly, GC IV maintains the rules on civilian property during occupation and IACs included in the Hague Regulations; however, it links its protection to the civilian population and the protected persons who interact with this property (see Chapter 71, MN 5–6, of this volume).

12   As mentioned, GC IV employs negative definitions for both the civilian population and protected persons. Article 4 therefore excludes persons from its scope, rather than listing those protected by it. On the one hand, the concept of 'civilian population' excludes combatants who are beneficiaries of GC I, GC II, or GC III (such as the armed forces, military or paramilitary groups comparable to these, members of armed groups, circumstantial *levée-en-masse* combatants, etc), pursuant to the enumeration of combatants according to Article 4 GC III. When AP I entered into force, the 'civilian population' also excluded the participants in hostilities set forth in Articles 43 and 44 (regular armed forces and identifiable combatants).

13   On the other hand, protected persons under GC IV are those who are not protected by GC I, GC II, or GC III, and who are not considered as nationals of the party to the conflict or of the Occupying Power in whose hands they are. There are criteria, however, that determine which persons GC IV can protect.

14   Unlike the Hague Regulations, the category of protected persons within GC IV also excludes legal persons from its protection and focuses on the protection of individuals.[10] This is an adequate exclusion, since it is problematic for the parties to the conflict or the Occupying Power to establish the nationality of legal persons. Nationality can, however, be determined by using the theory of the place of incorporation of the legal person, or the nationality of shareholders that control it.[11] The anthropocentric spirit of several provisions of GC IV on protected persons is nevertheless incompatible with legal persons, which cannot be illegally confined or forced to participate in hostilities. For instance, during the occupation of Lebanon by Israel, in operational terms it would have been difficult for the Occupying Power to differentiate Lebanese legal persons from those legal persons established by Israeli shareholders in the occupied territory or other multinational companies. In any case, the damages that legal persons

---

[8] S. Hobe and O. Kimminich, *Einführung in das Völkerrecht* (Tübingen: UTB Verlag, 2008), at 510.
[9] Art 3 of the Draft Convention for the Protection of Civilian Persons of Time of War defined the term 'protected persons'; currently this definition is to be found in Art 4 GC IV. See Final Record, vol I, at 114.
[10] Kolb and Vité, above n 5, at 121. See, however, MN 8.
[11] ICJ, *Barcelona Traction, Light and Power Company, Limited (Belgium v Spain)*, Judgment, 5 February 1970, paras 35–7; ICJ, *Ahmadou Sadio Diallo (Republic of Guinea v Democratic Republic of Congo)*, Judgment, 30 November 2010, paras 156–7.

suffer (whether public or private, for-profit or welfare) due to armed violence are covered by the rules of IHL regarding civilian populations and individuals included in GC IV. Moreover, appropriation of property of a legal person could be classified as pillage, pursuant to Article 33 GC IV.

Nonetheless, the exclusion of legal persons in GC IV is not absolute, since Article 53 includes an element of the Hague Regulations concerning legal persons. This provision protects civilian property against destruction, pointing out that the protection is extended to individuals' personal property, collective groups, state patrimony, other public authorities, or social or cooperative organizations. Thus, their protection is linked to that granted to civilian property and individuals by the Geneva Conventions and, indeed, by the Hague Regulations.

The fact that legal persons are not considered as protected persons and not protected by that regime does not mean they may not be bound by IHL and international law.[12] Particularly in the case of armed conflicts, the state in which a company carries out its activities, as well as the state in which it has been incorporated, should respect and ensure that multinational enterprises respect international humanitarian standards.[13]

a. Cases of application of GC IV

The legal regime covering protected persons, as well as the one established in Part III GC IV, applies regardless of the legality of the use of armed violence under international law. The rules of IHL do not evaluate the legality of an occupation or of the outbreak of hostilities in an IAC, an area regulated by *jus ad bellum*. For instance, the Supreme Court of India made the injudicious decision to exclude a Portuguese man, the Reverend Monsignor Sebastião Francisco Xavier dos Remedios Monteiro, from the protected persons regime. The Court justified this decision by arguing that the Indian annexation of Goa was legal.

Through Operation Vijay, India did away with its Portuguese enclaves and declared the annexation of Goa by controlling the territory. In application of the Goa, Daman and Diu (Citizenship) Order 1962, the Reverend Monteiro kept his Portuguese nationality, receiving a temporary residence permit. In the absence of a new residence permit, he was deported. He claimed before Indian courts that he was entitled to the protection of GC IV because, under that regime, he could not have been deported from the territory of Goa, as set out in Article 49 GC IV. However, the Supreme Court of India held that the recovery of Goa was legal; therefore, in view of the Court, since 20 December 1961, the date of annexation of the Portuguese enclave, the regime of protected persons set forth in GC IV did not apply to the Reverend Monteiro.[14]

In addition, according to Article 2, GC IV applies, on the one hand, to an armed conflict that arises between two or more of the High Contracting Parties and, on the other hand, to a situation of total or partial occupation of a High Contracting Party on the territory of another party, even if it meets with no armed resistance.[15] In both cases,

---

[12] ICRC, *Business and International Humanitarian Law: An introduction to the Rights and Obligations of Business Enterprises under International Humanitarian Law* (Geneva: ICRC, 2006), at 14–21; O. Martin-Ortega, 'Business and Human Rights in Conflict', 22 *Ethics & International Affairs* (2008), 273, at 281–2.

[13] CA 1.

[14] Supreme Court of India, *Rev Mons Sebastião Francisco Xavier dos Remedios Monteiro v The State of Goa*, 26 March 1969.

[15] M. Bothe, 'Occupation', in R. Bernhardt (ed), *Encyclopedia of Public International Law* (Amsterdam: Elsevier Science Publishers, 1992–2003), vol III, 763, at 763. The author defines 'Occupation' as 'the holding of possession in the sense of actual control of the territory of another state (or of parts of it)'.

the common provisions apply to territories of the parties to the conflict and to occupied territories (Part III Section I, GC IV), or specifically to occupied territories (Section III, GC IV). International criminal courts, such as the International Criminal Tribunal for the former Yugoslavia (ICTY), have understood that the provisions on IAC in the Geneva Conventions also apply to prima facie non-international armed conflicts, that are, however, to be considered international, resulting from the 'overall control' by a second state over a non-state armed group involved in such a conflict.[16]

20   Section I of Part III GC IV lays down general principles in favour of protected persons, regulating the possible scenarios that may arise during armed violence. Furthermore, this regime is subdivided according to the various degrees of vulnerability of the protected persons. As a result, GC IV establishes special safeguards for the inhabitants of occupied territories, aliens in the territory of a party to the conflict, and for persons deprived of their liberty for imperative security reasons. Further, the law on belligerent occupation contained in the rules of the Hague Regulations, which already reflected customary international law before the adoption of the 1949 Convention, interacts with the rules on occupation enshrined in the latter. Additionally, the IHL rules on occupation have been accompanied by a growing interaction with the rules of international human rights law (IHRL).

21   While not specified in Article 4 GC IV (but only in the titles of Sections II and III of Part III GC IV), the drafters of the Convention understood that the category of *protected persons* includes both inhabitants of occupied territories and persons of enemy nationality who find themselves in the territory of the other party to the conflict. This was something that the Tokyo Draft tried to cover before the Second World War.[17] This assertion has merit, since GC IV regulates safeguards aimed at protecting both situations of vulnerability. The common element in both cases is that *protected persons* must not have the nationality of either the party to the conflict or the Occupying Power in whose hands they are. Therefore, the law applicable to *protected persons* during IACs does not regulate the treatment by the states parties with regard to their *own nationals*, leaving this aspect to be governed by IHRL, national law, and the general regime for the protection of the civilian population.[18]

22   Why was the category of protected person established in IHL? This category responds to the inter-state vision based on IHL's mutual reciprocity.[19] Each state pledged to treat nationals of the other party properly, with the legitimate expectation that opponents would give their nationals the same adequate treatment. For this reason, GC IV provisions for protected persons apply only to states parties, since they undertake to provide

---

[16] See Ch 1, section B.VI, and Ch 2, section C, of this volume; ICTY, *The Prosecutor v Ivica Rajić*, Trial Chamber Decision Review of the Indictment Pursuant to Rule 61 of the Rules of Procedure and Evidence, IT-95-12-R61, 13 September 1996, paras 32 and 35; ICTY, *The Prosecutor v Duško Tadić*, Appeals Chamber Judgment, IT-94-1-A, 15 July 1999, para 137; ICTY, *The Prosecutor v Tihomir Blaškić*, Trial Chamber Judgment, IT-95-14-T, 3 March 2000, para 123; ICTY, *The Prosecutor v Zejnil Delalić et al (Čelebići Camp)*, Appeals Chamber Judgment, IT-96-21-A, 20 February 2001, paras 14, 26, and 234; ICTY, *The Prosecutor v Radoslav Brdanin*, Trial Chamber Judgment, IT-99-36-T, 1 September 2004, para 124; ICTY, *The Prosecutor v Mladen Naletilić and Vinko Martinović (Tuto and Štela)*, Trial Chamber Judgment, IT-98-34-T, 31 March 2003, para 183. See also ICC, *The Prosecutor v Thomas Lubanga Dyllo*, Pre-Trial Chamber, Decision on the confirmation of charges, ICC-01/04-01/06, 29 January 2007, para 211.

[17] Pictet Commentary GC IV, at 45; and see Kolb and Vité, above n 5, at 20.

[18] Pictet Commentary GC IV, at 46.

[19] T. Meron, 'International Law in the Age of Human Rights: General Course on Public International Law', 301 *RCADI* (2003) 9, at 54.

protection to those who are not their nationals due to reciprocity.[20] Applicable in various scenarios, GC IV has global reach because almost all states have ratified it. In addition, its application is being discussed in certain occupied territories where the situation has not been internationally defined, such as in Western Sahara.[21] Despite the underlying expectation of reciprocity, Article 33 GC IV prohibits resorting to reprisals against protected persons and their property in the event that the other party to the conflict fails to comply with this regime of protection,[22] and Article 60(5) of the Vienna Convention on the Law of Treaties (VCLT) excludes the possibility of extinction or suspension of the operation of GC IV as a consequence of its breach.

The protected persons regime also applies to people who do not have the nationality of the other party to the conflict. In addition, GC IV deploys its effects with regard to refugees persecuted before the outbreak of hostilities (due to their situation of vulnerability in relation to the state of which they are or were nationals and which they fled) in two respects. First, under Article 44, protected persons who are refugees should not be treated as enemy nationals merely based on their nationality of the enemy state (which persecuted them). Secondly, under Article 70 paragraph 2, refugees who are not protected persons because they are nationals of the Occupying Power, benefit from certain protection against unfair criminal prosecutions and deportations. It is only under Article 73 AP I that refugees become protected persons regardless of their nationality. As for stateless persons, they benefit from the status of protected persons under Article 4 GC IV, which excludes certain persons from such protection based upon their nationality while stateless persons have no nationality.[23]

If certain nationals of the Occupying Power or party to the conflict do not benefit from the status of protected persons, they nevertheless cannot be returned, extradited, or deported to the state of which they are nationals due to the principle of *non-refoulement* outlined in international law.[24] In addition, for protected persons, the principle of *non-refoulement* limits the derogations of Article 5 under GC IV, even when the safety of the state is threatened by the protected persons' direct participation in hostilities.[25]

b. 'In the hands of a Party to the conflict'

This requirement refers to the protected person's legal (under the jurisdiction of) or physical (detention or control) subjection to one party to the conflict. The typical example of protected persons being in the power of a party to the conflict occurs when they are physically under the permanent control of an Occupying Power or a party to the conflict. For instance, in 2003, two Sunni Muslim Iraqi detainees in Basra who were set to be handed over to the Iraqi High Tribunal by the British military contingent from the Multi-National Force in the context of Operation Iraqi Freedom, qualified as protected persons under

---

[20] Pictet Commentary GC IV, at 48. [21] Ibid.
[22] Art 50 Hague Regulations; Art 33 GC IV. See further Ch 29 of this volume.
[23] See *amplius* Ch 63 of this volume. During the Diplomatic Conference of Geneva, the International Refugee Organization (IRO) argued that the definition of Art 4 should extend to stateless persons since they lack per se the nationality of the Occupying Power or of the party to the conflict (Pictet Commentary GC IV, at 20).
[24] Art 33 Refugee Convention 1951; ECtHR, *Soering v United Kingdom*, Judgment, 7 July 1989, para 91; ECtHR, *Mamatkulov and Askarov v Turkey*, Judgment, 4 February 2005, para 67; ECtHR, *Iskandarov v Russia*, 23 September 2010, Judgment, para 125; ECtHR, *Saadi v Italy*, Judgment, 28 February 2008, para 138.
[25] F.M. Váldez, *La ampliación del concepto de refugiado en el derecho internacional contemporáneo* (Lima: Pucp, 2004), at 160–1.

the terms of GC IV.[26] Other similar examples are found in the case of the Bosnian Serbs detained by Bosnian Muslims and Bosnian Croats in the Čelebići camp, which was under the jurisdiction of Bosnia-Herzegovina; or in the case of the Vietnamese prisoners held at the Tuol Sleng prison by the Khmer Rouge. However, the status of protected persons also extends to those individuals who have not been retained or physically seized. The Pictet Commentary points to the fact that being under the power of a party to the conflict transcends physical control and comprises persons who are in territory under the control of the party.[27] The ICTY held in *The Prosecutor v Rajić* that the Bosnian population that lived in the village of Stupni Do (in the Vareš area), 'could be treated as being constructively "in the hands of" Croatia, although they were not directly or physically "in the hands of" Croatia'.[28] The Tribunal reached this conclusion merely because the forces of the Croatian Defence Council (HVO), which were under control of Croatia, controlled the village.[29] This position has remained the same in subsequent findings.[30] One Trial Chamber held, however, that in such circumstances, the foreign state must have a further degree of control over the armed group to become an Occupying Power.[31] Furthermore, it must be noted that the interpretation of the phrase in Article 4 paragraph 1 GC IV 'find themselves', as applied to those who come to be in the hands of the party to the conflict or Occupying Power at the material time, should not be a narrow one. According to the United Kingdom (UK) Supreme Court, '[t]o make a happenstance or coincidence a prerequisite of protection seems to introduce a wholly artificial and unwarranted restriction on its availability under the convention'.[32] Lastly, one should remember that the rules on the conduct of hostilities do not differentiate between protected persons and other civilians.

26   Regarding the spatial application of the rules throughout the territory of a party to the conflict or occupied territories, it is necessary to determine whether protected persons are all persons fulfilling the nationality requirements and finding themselves in the occupied territory or on the own territory of a party to the conflict. Since this is not specified in GC IV, the ICTY has considered that the spatial application of the rule depends on the content thereof. Thus, its application might be linked directly to the geographic area where hostilities take place, but it might also refer to the entire territory of the party to the conflict.[33] On this basis, it may be said that the regime for the protection of the civilian population and protected civilians in enemy hands, extends to the entire territory of the parties to the conflict.

c. Protected persons must not have the nationality of the party in whose hands they are

27   Article 45 of the Hague Regulations establishes that the inhabitants of the occupied territory should not have to swear 'allegiance' to the Occupying Power, and therefore it

---

[26] ECtHR, *Al-Saadoon and Mufdhi v United Kingdom*, Admissibility Decision, 30 June 2009, paras 39–48.
[27] Pictet Commentary GC IV, at 47.
[28] ICTY, *Rajić*, above n 16, paras 36–7.   [29] Ibid.
[30] ICTY, *The Prosecutor v Duško Tadić*, Trial Chamber Judgment, IT-94-1-T, 7 May 1997, para 579; ICTY, *The Prosecutor v Zejnil Delalić et al* (*Čelebići Camp*), Trial Chamber Judgment, IT-96-21, 16 November 1998, para 246; ICC, *The Prosecutor v Germain Katanga & Mathieu Ngudjolo Chui*, Pre-Trial Chamber, Decision on the confirmation of charges, ICC-01/04-01/07, 30 September 2008, para 268.
[31] ICTY, *Naletilić and Martinović*, above n 16, para 214.
[32] *Secretary of State for Foreign and Commonwealth Affairs and another v Rahmatullah* [2012] UKSC 48, [33]–[34].
[33] ICTY, *The Prosecutor v Duško Tadić*, Decision on the Defence Motion for Interlocutory Appeal on Jurisdiction, IT-94-1-T, 2 October 1995, para 67.

prohibits acts of coercion against them.³⁴ Thus, the Hague Regulations opt not to legitimize the occupying administration with respect to the population under its control. In addition, the Hague Regulations recognize the obligations of nationals in their states based on the personal jurisdiction of the occupied state.

Geneva Convention IV reiterates these ideas with regard to nationals of the occupied territories and aliens of enemy nationality, indicating that 'allegiance' is not owed with respect to the other party—in an IAC—nor with respect to the Occupying Power—in occupied territories.³⁵ It also stresses the importance of 'allegiance' and nationality in order to identify who is a protected person.³⁶ Hence, in GC IV, there are several rules of conduct pertaining to protected persons that are based on the criteria of nationality and 'allegiance'. The reason for IHL's focus on these two criteria is based on the fact that the relation of the state to its own nationals is regulated by domestic law and other international regimes. Therefore, relations between the state and its nationals are excluded from the scope of the provisions relating to protected persons in GC IV.³⁷

Article 4 GC IV provides that protected persons are those who are not nationals of the party to the conflict or of the Occupying Power. A literal interpretation of Article 4 paragraph 1 would thus lead one to conclude that a national is someone who holds a legal link with the state according to its citizenship laws. It would be within the purview of the state to determine who is a national and who is not a national, as pointed out in the ICJ *Nottebohm* case, although nationality at the international level for some purposes may be limited to effective nationality.³⁸

The ICTY, however, interpreted Article 4 GC IV as also referring to individuals who owe allegiance to the opposing party to the conflict, although they might possess the same nationality as those into whose hands they had fallen. As the Appeals Chamber put it:

> Article 4 of GC IV, if interpreted in the light of its object and purpose, is directed to the protection of civilians to the maximum extent possible. It therefore does not make its applicability dependent on formal bonds and purely legal relations. Its primary purpose is to ensure the safeguards afforded by the Convention to those civilians who do not enjoy the diplomatic protection, and correlatively are not subject to the allegiance and control, of the State in whose hands they may find themselves. In granting its protection, Article 4 intends to look to the substance of relations, not to their legal characterization as such.³⁹

The ICTY considered this broad interpretation to be pursuant to the preparatory work of GC IV and as conforming to other rules of GC IV, such as the rules on the expansion of the category of protected persons. This interpretation also includes persons who are formally nationals of the party to the conflict or of the Occupying Power, as is the case of refugees.⁴⁰ As a result, the test to determine who is or is not a national (and, therefore, a protected

---

³⁴ Draper, above n 3, at 121.   ³⁵ Art 68 GC IV.   ³⁶ Arts 68, 98, 105, 107, and 135 GC IV.
³⁷ Pictet Commentary GC IV, at 46.
³⁸ ICJ, *Nottebohm (Liechtenstein v Guatemala)*, Judgment, 6 April 1955, at 23; IACtHR, *Niñas Yean y Bosico v República Dominicana*, Judgment, 8 September 2005, para 136. However, the ILC Draft Articles on Diplomatic Protection establish that in cases of multiple nationality and a claim against a third state, '[a]ny State of which a dual or multiple national is a national may exercise diplomatic protection in respect of that national against a State of which that person is not a national'. This would mean that, according to ILC, the theory of effective nationality is no longer in force.
³⁹ ICTY, *Tadić*, above n 16, para 166. See also ICTY, *The Prosecutor v Zlatko Aleksovski*, Appeals Chamber Judgment, IT-95-14/1-A, 24 March 2000, para 146.
⁴⁰ Final Record, vol II-A, at 561–2, 793–6, 813–14; ICTY, *Tadić*, above n 16, paras 165–8.

person) is not limited to the assessment of formal ties of nationality. The 'allegiance' of certain individuals to the party of the conflict should be analysed. This approach broadens the concept of 'protected persons' by including other ties such as ethnicity.[41] As explained by the Appeals Chamber in the so-called *Čelebići* case,

> [t]he nationality requirement in Article 4 of Geneva Convention IV should therefore be ascertained within the context of the object and purpose of humanitarian law, which 'is directed to the protection of civilians to the maximum extent possible'. This in turn must be done within the context of the changing nature of the armed conflicts since 1945, and in particular of the development of conflicts based on ethnic or religious grounds.[42]

31   Thus, for instance, the ICTY Appeals Chamber, in dealing with NIACs that have been classified as international due to the overall control of one armed group by a second state, considered that inhabitants of Prijedor, under the power of Bosnian-Serb forces, were protected persons, despite the fact that those who engaged in the violence and the victims held the same nationality.[43] Likewise, in the Lašva Valley area, the Appeals Chamber considered that the Bosnian Muslims were in the power of Croatia while there were ethnic differences between the perpetrators and the victims, despite the identity of nationalities among them, as has been stated in various cases.[44] These results could have been reached merely by considering that those persons were in the hands of a state of which they were not nationals, who controlled those persons (of the same nationality as the victims). However, in the case of the Čelebići camp, the Appeals Chamber went further and considered that Bosnian Serbs who were subjugated to Bosnian forces were protected persons since they were arrested because of their Serbian identity, meaning that they were considered to be subjects of Serbia and, therefore, a threat to the newly constituted Bosnia-Herzegovina.[45]

32   In the confirmation of charges of Thomas Lubanga for enlisting and conscripting children under 15 years old, the International Criminal Court (ICC) Pre-Trial Chamber adopted the same approach to ethnicity previously proclaimed by the ICTY.[46] Therefore, the Pre-Trial Chamber considered that during the trial, the Trial Chamber could evaluate whether war crimes were committed against protected persons in the context of the inter-ethnic conflict between the Hema and the Lendu (funded by the exploitation of natural resources and by the incursion from Uganda into Congolese territory until 2 June 2003). Eventually, the Trial Chamber found that the Ugandan military occupation of Bunia airport did not change the legal nature of the conflict, which was of a non-international character.[47] For its part, the comprehensive interpretation of the term 'national' has been also used by the Extraordinary Chambers in the Courts of Cambodia (ECCC), pointing out that some Cambodians, coming from the East and detained in the S-21 prison, were protected persons since

---

[41] ICTY, *Tadić*, above n 16, para 166; *Aleksovski*, above n 39, paras 150–2; ICTY, *Delalić et al*, above n 16, para 84.

[42] ICTY, *Delalić et al*, above n 16, para 73.   [43] ICTY, *Tadić*, above n 16, para 168.

[44] ICTY, *Tadić*, above n 16, paras 166 and 168; ICTY, *Delalić et al*, above n 30, para 247; ICTY, *Aleksovski*, above n 39, paras 150–2; ICTY, *Delalić et al*, above n 16, para 84; ICTY, *The Prosecutor v Dario Kordić and Mario Čerkez*, Trial Chamber Judgment, IT-95-14/2, 26 February 2001, para 152.

[45] ICTY, *Aleksovski*, above n 39, paras 147–52.

[46] ICC, *Lubanga*, above n 16, paras 277–80; ICC, *Katanga and Ngudjolo Chui*, above n 30, paras 289–92.

[47] ICC, *The Prosecutor v Thomas Lubanga*, Judgment pursuant to Article 74 of the Statute, ICC-01/04-01/06, 14 March 2012, para 564.

the Khmer Rouge considered them to be sympathizers of Vietnam and enemies of the Democratic Republic of Kampuchea.[48]

Despite the extensive interpretation of Article 4 GC IV, it is important to mention that parties to the conflict face difficulties in implementing the criteria of nationality and allegiance/ethnicity. To identify the protected persons, the Occupying Power must not only demand their identity documents, in which the nationality of the occupied state is indicated, but must also ask about their allegiance to the state, something that it is virtually impossible to verify. Additionally, the fact that the Occupying Power has to ask about allegiance introduces subjectivity that could hamper the implementation of IHL in contexts that, by contrast, require simple and clear rules.

Furthermore, it is necessary to determine the full extent of the adoption of the criterion of allegiance/ethnicity in interpreting Article 4 paragraph 1 GC IV. In other words, whether the criterion of nationality is applicable to inter-ethnic conflicts and whether the criterion of allegiance/ethnicity is applicable to other conflicts that are devoid of an ethnic component. In this regard, it should be noted that the criterion of nationality remains sufficient to obtain protected person status under Article 4 GC IV, but in the absence of a separate nationality, the ethnicity/allegiance test has been used, as seen in international jurisprudence, to confer protected person status upon additional persons.

III. Neutrality, co-belligerence, and diplomatic representation, and their use with respect to protected persons

As has previously been noted, some individuals, such as nationals of a party to the conflict who are on a territory controlled by their own party, are excluded from the scope of Article 4 GC IV. In addition, Article 4 paragraph 2 states that '[n]ationals of a neutral State who find themselves in the territory of a belligerent State, […] shall not be regarded as protected persons while the State of which they are nationals has normal diplomatic representation in the State in whose hands they are.' It should be pointed out that when it mentions persons in 'the territory of a belligerent state', the provision is referring to citizens of neutral states who are in the territory of a belligerent state rather than an occupied territory.[49] Indeed, the exclusion of neutral nationals from protected person status does not apply in occupied territories. Giving that phrase a different interpretation, so that nationals of neutral states would be excluded not only from a state's own unoccupied territory but also from protection in occupied territory, would, as has been asserted by the UK Supreme Court, 'arbitrarily—and for no comprehensible reason—remove from the protection of the convention an entire swathe of persons who would be entirely deserving of and who naturally ought to be entitled to that protection'.[50]

In addition, Article 4 paragraph 2 GC IV states that certain third party nationals (neutral nationals on the unoccupied territory of a belligerent, and co-belligerent nationals in an occupied territory) should not benefit from protected person status where there is 'normal diplomatic representation'.[51] There is nothing in customary international law, or in pertinent subsequent instruments such as the Vienna Convention of 1961 on Diplomatic Relations, that deals with the meaning of the term 'normal diplomatic representation'. The phrase implies that 'representations made by the diplomatic representative will be

---

[48] ECCC, *The Prosecutor v Duch*, No 001/18-07-2007/ECCC/TC, Judgment, 26 July 2010, paras 425–6.
[49] *Rahmatullah*, above n 32, [30]. [50] Ibid, [32]. [51] ICTY, *Blaškić*, above n 16, paras 144–6.

followed by results and that satisfactory replies will be given to him'.[52] Thus normality is equated, first, with the development of activities that the diplomatic representative has in the territory of the belligerent state. However, it is not the diplomatic representative's own work that defines what 'normal diplomatic representation' means, but the effective response of the state in whose territory the representative is. Therefore, normal diplomatic representation would be identified by the 'effectiveness' of the diplomatic protection operating between two states.

37   The configuration of 'normal diplomatic representation' fulfils a specific role in GC IV. Its existence implies the exclusion from the regime governing protected persons of persons holding the nationality of a co-belligerent state and finding themselves in the territory of a belligerent state, but not of persons holding the nationality of a neutral state in an occupied territory.

38   For its part, co-belligerence refers to the participation in hostilities of two or more states as allies. The reason for the exclusion of nationals of a co-belligerent state from the category of protected persons is that they may request assistance from the party to the conflict, with the mediation of normal diplomatic representation, resorting to diplomatic protection. The exclusion of nationals of co-belligerent states from the protected persons regime shows, once again, the inter-state rationale of the protection afforded by GC IV: if a remedy is available in international law, it is unnecessary for the parties to deploy the obligations under IHL. However, this exclusion should be approached from the framework of Article 4 GC IV, and therefore the concept of normal diplomatic representation cannot be detached from the ultimate purpose of the Convention, that is, the protection of civilians. The strict standard to determine whether the state is a co-belligerent affects the scope of protection of civilians, since those who are nationals of the co-belligerent state would not be included in Article 4. In other words, if the co-belligerence configuration is drawn broadly, a greater number of persons would be excluded from GC IV. Therefore, as the ICTY has stated, co-belligerence must be understood from a material point of view, that is, from effectiveness: 'it is important not to limit oneself to the formal or superficial elements but also to examine the current relations between the two countries at the relevant time and region'.[53]

39   Such a relation is reflected between two or more states in the specific case of an IAC. For the ICTY Trial Chamber in the *Blaškić* case, it was necessary to delve beyond the mere absence of a declaration of war, the existence of diplomatic relations, or of a number of treaties signed between states in order to determine if the states were co-belligerents.[54]

40   The Appeals Chamber confirmed this interpretation, stating that it must be demonstrated, first, that the states were allies and, secondly, that they enjoyed effective and satisfactory diplomatic representation with each other. The fact that HVO and the armed forces of Bosnia-Herzegovina fought each other at times cannot be ignored simply because the states had formal diplomatic relations. According to the Appeals Chamber, the Trial Chamber's analysis of the true situation was consonant both with the pragmatic considerations suggested by the Commentary to the GC IV and with the object and purpose of Article 4 GC IV.[55] In this case, the states were Bosnia-Herzegovina and Croatia,

---

[52] Pictet Commentary GC IV, at 49. See also Final Record, vol II-A, at 814.
[53] ICTY, *Blaškić*, above n 16, para 137.   [54] Ibid, paras 139–43.
[55] ICTY, *The Prosecutor v Tihomir Blaškić*, Appeals Chamber Judgment, IT-95-14-A, 29 July 2004, paras 186–9.

which achieved independence from the Federal Republic of Yugoslavia (FRY) and shared secessionist interests. Thus, it is important to discard the co-belligerence in cases where the behaviour of the state in the development of a conflict is ambivalent. For example, diplomatic alliances between the Republic of Bosnia-Herzegovina and the Republic of Croatia against Serbia, coupled in parallel with clashes between the two, did not generate co-belligerence between the two states with respect to internationalized internal armed conflicts in the Lašva Valley area.

Neutrality is the legal status, permanent or not, of a state that abstains from participating in an IAC.[56] As a general rule, a neutral state should avoid getting involved in an armed conflict; however, this does not mean that the state cannot assist civilians who are affected by the conflict.

Geneva Convention IV, when referring to a neutral state, interacts with the rules of customary international law on neutrality, especially those reflected in Hague Convention V on Rights and Duties of Neutral Powers, and establishes the relationship with protected persons. Article 4 paragraph 2 GC IV points out that '[n]ationals of a neutral State who find themselves in the territory of a belligerent State [...], shall not be regarded as protected persons while the state of which they are nationals has normal diplomatic representation in the state in whose hands they are.' From the reading of the aforementioned article, the permanence of normal diplomatic representation of the neutral state, accredited to the Occupying Power, does not prejudice the protected person status of nationals of such a neutral state in an occupied territory.[57]

IV. The broader protection of the civilian population in Part II GC IV

The main victims of an armed conflict today, whether international or non-international, are civilians. As has already been stated, the horrors of the Second World War led to the creation of GC IV, and although it has been enforced for over six decades, the suffering of civilian populations has continued. While the first three Geneva Conventions were designed to regulate the plight of participants in hostilities, GC IV is the instrument designed to regulate the protection of civilians. Overall, the protection afforded by the Convention is subdivided into one part aimed at protected persons and one aimed at the civilian population. The latter type of protection is general and can be found in Part II.

The regime in Part II GC IV establishes some general rules on aid and relief for all civilians that become independent from the reciprocity scheme implicit in Article 4. This interpretation emerges from a literal reading of Article 13 GC IV:

> The provisions of Part II cover the whole of the populations of the countries in conflict, without any adverse distinction based, in particular, on race, nationality, religion or political opinion, and are intended to alleviate the sufferings caused by war.

If nationality (or ethnicity/allegiance) is the criterion that differentiates a protected person from another who is not a protected person, in Part II the protection cannot be conditioned on nationality or allegiance. This is protection that cannot be denied to any human

---

[56] See for more details Ch 5 of this volume; R.L. Bindschedler, 'Neutrality', in Bernhardt (ed), above n 15, 548.
[57] Y. Arai, *The Law of Occupation* (Boston, Mass: Martinus Nijhoff, 2009), at 305.

being. In this regard, it must be understood that the list of grounds prohibited by Article 13 GC IV is not limited by the text of the Convention.[58]

45 In Part II, GC IV introduces safeguards that guarantee some protections to civilians, irrespective of their nationality.[59] It should not be forgotten that civilians who directly participate in hostilities lose their protection against attacks and the effects of hostilities for such time as they take a direct part in hostilities, but they do not lose their civilian status. Therefore, Part II extends to both protected persons and the civilian population in general, the first category being included in the second. In this way, protected persons enjoy a privileged status of protection, while civilians who do not qualify as protected persons are secured with safeguards contained in Part II GC IV.

46 Although its provisions do not offer minimum guarantees of humane treatment but deal with other matters, the *raison d'être* of Part II is based on elementary considerations of humanity—protection against certain effects of barbarism resulting from armed conflicts.[60]

V. The distinctions between prisoners of war, unlawful combatants, and protected civilians

47 In the context of an IAC there are two regimes governing protected persons, one according to GC III and another according to GC IV. These regimes are applicable in circumstances when a person falls into enemy hands: combatants who become prisoners of war (POWs) being protected by GC III, and civilians being protected by GC IV.[61]

48 Unlike combatants, civilians cannot be the targets of a lawful armed attack. From the *ratione personae* stance, differentiating between a combatant and civilian becomes relevant to the application of GC III and GC IV because, as we have just said, combatants benefit from the status of POW while civilians do not.

49 There is a difference, in *ratione loci* terms, between the rules which apply to protected persons under the GC IV regime and POWs. While combatants who become POWs can be moved elsewhere, civilians protected by GC IV cannot be transferred or deported from an occupied territory.[62] This prohibition has been commented on by Pictet and used in 2002 by the Supreme Court of Israel in the case of *Kipah Mahmad Ahmed Ajuri and others*, in which the petitioners were going to be transferred from the West Bank to the Gaza Strip.[63] Recently, the ECCC also took Article 49 GC IV into consideration when they sentenced Khmer Rouge leaders Nuon and Khieu for forced transfer of the civilian population.[64]

50 Regarding detention, POWs may be interned because of the simple risk that they will participate in hostilities, while protected civilians may be detained for two specific reasons only: (i) under national law (or the security law introduced by the Occupying Power); and

---

[58] Pictet Commentary GC IV, at 128. [59] Draper, above n 3, at 124.
[60] Pictet Commentary GC IV, at 127.
[61] M. Sassòli, 'The Status of Persons Held in Guantánamo under International Humanitarian Law', 2 *JICJ* (2004) 96, at 101.
[62] Art 49 GC IV; see further Chs 47 and 58 of this volume; and Sassòli, above n 61, at 106.
[63] Supreme Court of Israel, *Kipah Mahmad Ahmed Ajuri et al v IDF Commander in West Bank et al*, HCJ 7015/02, 3 September 2002, para 20.
[64] ECCC, *Prosecutors v Nuon Chea and Khieu Samphan*, No 002/19-09-2007/ECCC/TC, 4 August 2014, Judgment, para 450.

(ii) for imperative security reasons.[65] Concerning the above-mentioned analysis, it may be maintained that GC IV protects those whom GC III does not protect. This rule is derived from the content of Article 4 GC IV.[66]

Turning to the subject of civilians and unlawful combatants, it must be noted that the term 'unlawful combatant' is included neither in GC IV nor in customary international law. It is mentioned here to address the unfortunate tendency to see unlawful combatants as outside the regime of protected persons. In the context of the so-called 'war on terror', the then administration of the United States of America at the time considered that persons held in Guantánamo were neither combatants nor civilians; they were categorized as 'unlawful combatants',[67] stripping them of the protection of both GC III and GC IV and creating a legal black hole. The Obama Administration subsequently decided not to use the terms 'war on terror' and 'unlawful combatant'. Nevertheless, it still considered the 'armed conflict against the Taliban, Al Qaeda and their associates' to be an armed conflict to which GC III applied by analogy, but which does not protect captured enemies, because although they are enemy belligerents, they are not lawful combatants, and therefore they are covered only by Common Article 3.[68]

While in some ways, the terms 'civilians', 'combatants' and 'prisoners of war' are defined in IHL treaties, the expression 'unlawful combatant' does not specifically appear in any Article. According to Dörmann, an 'unlawful combatant' could be defined as a person who, in the context of an IAC, takes a direct part in hostilities without any right to do so, and who is not classified as a POW when he or she falls into the hands of the enemy.[69] This definition coincides with the report of the Inter-American Commission on Human Rights on terrorism and human rights, which states in paragraph 69:

> In converse to this is the status in international armed conflicts of the 'unprivileged' combatant, sometimes referred to as an 'unlawful combatant', namely a person who does not have the combatant's privilege but directly participates in hostilities. Such unlawful belligerents include irregular or part-time combatants, such as guerrillas, partisans, and members of resistance movements, who either fail to distinguish themselves from the civilian population at all times while on active duty or otherwise do not fulfil the requirements for privileged combatant status, as well as those privileged combatants who violate the requirements regarding mode of dress, such as regular military personnel who are caught spying while out of uniform. Others falling within the category of unprivileged combatants are civilians, non-combatant personnel in the armed forces, as well as non-combatant members of the armed forces who, in violation of their protected status, actively engage in hostilities.[70]

Thus, GC III would not apply to unlawful combatants. However, being an unlawful combatant does not deprive the individual of the application of GC IV.[71] That said, it is important to recognize that protection is differentiated from that applicable to protected persons: as long as a civilian participates directly in hostilities, he or she is not protected against being the target of attack. This rule has been reaffirmed by the Supreme Court of Israel in *The Public Committee against Torture in Israel et al v Government of Israel et al*.[72]

---

[65] Sassòli, above n 61, at 103–4.   [66] Ibid, at 101.   [67] Ibid, at 100.
[68] M. Sassòli, 'The International Legal Framework for Fighting Terrorists According to the Bush and Obama Administrations: Same or Different, Correct or Incorrect', 104 *Proceedings of the 104th Annual Meeting of the ASIL* (2011) 277, at 277–80.
[69] K. Dörmann, 'The Legal Situation of "Unlawful/Unprivileged Combatants"', 85 *IRRC* 849 (2003) 45, at 46.
[70] Ibid.   [71] Ibid, at 50.   [72] Supreme Court of Israel, HCJ 769/02, at 30.

53   But with regard to the protected person regime in GC IV, this treaty excludes only nationals from a state not a party to GC IV, nationals of the Occupying Power, and nationals of a neutral or co-belligerent state with normal diplomatic representation. Therefore unlawful combatants who are not excluded from the regime by these nationality restrictions could benefit from the protection offered by the GC IV regime for protected persons.[73]

C. Relevance in Non-International Armed Conflicts

54   With regard to NIACs, two important points must be discussed: (i) the legal threshold for the application of the rules on the protection of civilians; and (ii) the interaction with other regimes.

55   In connection with the first issue, it should be mentioned that the regime established in GC IV does not apply in the context of a NIAC. In this case, the protection of 'persons taking no active part in the hostilities' derives from Common Article 3 to the Geneva Conventions. Moreover, AP II establishes a similar feature. However, there is a tendency today to consider members of an armed group not to be civilians and to apply, by analogy, a status-based approach similar to that applicable to combatants in IACs. For targeting purposes, the International Committee of the Red Cross (ICRC) is of the view that they are not to be considered civilians (if they have a continuous fighting function).[74] There is also a different approach which argues that the fact that the person is a fighter is only one element in favour of applying the conduct of hostilities paradigm, and that other factors should also be taken into consideration. As for the question whether and under what procedure such members of armed groups may be detained, the US considers that they may lawfully be detained, like POWs in IACs, until the end of active hostilities. Others suggest applying by analogy the regime covering civilian internees under GC IV (allowing internment for imperative security reasons, but requiring an individual determination of such reasons and a right of appeal), while still others suggest applying IHRL in the absence of IHL rules on this issue.[75] In our view, IHL proposes a unified regime that contains rules of conduct that analogously recognize in NIACs the protections provided to civilians by GC IV and AP I. However, this analogous regime remains incomplete. For this reason, in the absence of a specific regime covering protected persons in NIACs, other international law regimes (such as human rights law) provide protection.[76]

56   Hence, in IHRL, there is a process of specification that identifies groups needing special protection due to their identity or their vulnerability. International human rights law has established specific rules protecting persons against violence that expressly include persons with disabilities, children, women, internally displaced persons, refugees, victims of enforced disappearance, older adults, indigenous peoples, and relatives who have suffered from serious violations of human rights. The obligations set forth in IHRL are frequently applied with the rules of IHL. These rules are also applicable in IACs, but the

---

[73] See further Ch 45 of this volume; Dörmann, above n 69, at 49.
[74] ICRC, *Interpretive Guidance on the Notion of Direct Participation in Hostilities in International Humanitarian Law* (Geneva: ICRC, 2010), at 27, 31–6.
[75] See, for this debate and references, Ch 35, MN 20–24, of this volume.
[76] See Ch 35 of this volume.

importance of their applicability is crucial in the context of a NIAC, given the lack of a comprehensive set of rules of IHL applicable to these conflicts.[77]

Within the framework of international law to counter terrorism, developed during the 1960s, various conventions for the repression of different terrorist acts, such as the taking of hostages or attacks against internationally protected persons (including diplomatic agents), have been adopted. Some of these conventions exclude their application during armed conflicts, others exclude conduct of armed forces, yet other conventions allow for their application concurrently with IHL.[78] Depending on their characteristics, the above-mentioned conventions may be applicable during all armed conflicts, including NIACs, prohibiting practices that may affect the civilian population or protected persons. In addition, this regime addresses the conduct of members of the civilian population and protected persons who participate in hostilities, with ancillary consequences that should not affect the safeguards set forth in IHL for the said situations. These provisions have particular relevance, since they justify repressive policies in the framework of the global fight against terrorism.[79]

D. Legal Consequences of a Violation

Section I, Part IV, GC IV establishes measures aimed at ensuring compliance with obligations in favour of protected persons. It is important to emphasize the uniformity of the term 'protected person' to describe those who may be victims of a 'grave breach' of the Geneva Conventions.[80] Article 146 GC IV lays down the obligation to undertake legislative measures regarding the commission of grave breaches set forth in Article 147 and other acts contrary to GC IV. To consider an act as a grave breach, it is necessary to determine the status of 'protected person' for the persons affected, in so far as GC IV only criminalizes actions committed against protected persons and not those against the civilian population in general. With this regulatory framework, the ICTY, to date, has convicted 17 persons for the commission of grave breaches. In addition, the ECCC, in the case against Kaing Guek Eav, condemned Comrade 'Duch', the director of Tuol Sleng (S-21) prison camp, for committing grave breaches under GC IV.[81]

---

[77] IACtHR, *Masacre de Mapiripán v Colombia*, Judgment, 15 September 2005, paras 111 and 113; IACtHR, *Anzualdo Castro v Perú*, Judgment, 22 September 2009, para 37. Along the same lines, see IACtHR, *Gelman v Uruguay*, Judgment, 24 February 2011, para 76; IACtHR, *Uzcátegui et al v Venezuela*, Judgment, 3 September 2012, paras 190 and 204; IACtHR, *Vélez Restrepo and family v Colombia*, Judgment, 3 September 2012; IACtHR, *Río Negro Massacres v Guatemala*, Judgment, 4 September 2012, paras 120, 142, and 174; IACtHR, *Nadege Dorzema et al v Dominican Republic*, Judgment, 24 October 2012, paras 152–4 and 164. See also Art 10 UN Convention on the Rights of Persons with Disabilities (2008).
[78] See further Ch 35 of this volume.
[79] M. Bedjaoui, 'L'humanité en quête de paix et de développement', 324 *RCADI* (2006), 59, at 170–2.
[80] G. Werle, *Tratado de Derecho Penal Internacional* (Valencia: Tirant Lo Blanch, 2011), at 595.
[81] ICTY, *Tadić*, above n 16; *Delalić et al (Čelebići Camp)*, above n 16; ICTY, *The Prosecutor v Stevan Todorović*, Trial Chamber Judgment, IT-95-9/1, 31 July 2001; ICTY, *Blaškić*, above n 55; ICTY, *The Prosecutor v Dario Kordić and Mario Čerkez*, Appeals Chamber Judgment, IT-95-14/2-A, 17 December 2004; ICTY, *The Prosecutor v Ivica Rajić*, Trial Chamber Judgment, IT-95-12, 8 May 2006; ICTY, *The Prosecutor v Mladen Naletilić & Vinko Martinović*, Appeals Chamber Judgment, IT-98-34, 3 May 2006; ICTY, *The Prosecutor v Miroslav Bralo*, Appeals Chamber Judgment, IT-95-17-A, 2 April 2007; ICTY, *The Prosecutor v Radoslav Brđanin*, Appeals Chamber Judgment, IT-99-36, 3 April 2007; ICTY, *Jadranko Prlić et al*, Trial Chamber Judgment, IT-04-74-T, 29 May 2013; ECCC, *The Prosecutor v Duch*, Appeals Chamber Judgment, No 001/18-07 2007-ECCC/SC, 3 February 2012.

59 In contemporary international criminal law, beyond the grave breaches listed in Article 8(2)(a) of the Statute of the International Criminal Court (ICC), 26 war crimes have been introduced in Article 8(2)(b) for IAC. War crimes in NIACs are listed in Article 8(2)(c) and (e). However, the victims of such crimes do not necessarily have to be protected persons.

60 Furthermore, acts committed as part of a widespread or systematic attack directed against the civilian population, whether or not they are protected persons, may be covered by the concept of crimes against humanity included in Article 7 of the ICC Statute. Even though the ICC has not issued a decision on crimes against humanity, it has interpreted the elements of such a crime. In the case of crimes against humanity committed in armed conflicts, the ICC has understood the notion of 'civilian population' by reference to the IHL framework. Likewise, the ICC has understood that this category is not affected by the presence of combatants or persons participating in hostilities.[82]

61 The practice of the ICC has also determined a definition of 'civilian population' which is independent from the qualification within the framework of IHL. This happened in the confirmation of charges against Jean-Pierre Bemba Gombo, in the situation of the Central African Republic, and Joshua Arap Sang, Kirimi Muthaura, William Samoei Ruto, and Uhuru Muigai Kenyatta, in the case of Kenya. The ICC has affirmed that the civilian population victim of a crime against humanity comprises groups of people that may be identified by their nationality, ethnicity, or other characteristics, such as their apparent political affiliation.[83]

E. Critical Assessment

62 The rules of IHL are not static in time but are subject to progressive development, which leads to a deepening of their content;[84] otherwise, the regulatory system designed for the restriction of violence would be outdated in relation to contemporary conflicts. The very purpose of protecting civilians and combatants means that the interpretation of GC IV, in particular with regard to understanding who constitute protected persons and a civilian population, is undertaken in accordance with developments in other branches of international law, as well as against the background of the jurisprudence of international criminal tribunals. Thus, the oversight of international law bodies in other branches may lead to a reading of humanitarian treaties conditioned by the other applicable rules which aim to restrict violence.

---

[82] ICC, *Katanga and Ngudjolo Chui*, above n 30, para 276.

[83] E.g., ICC, *The Prosecutor v Francis Kirimi Muthaura and Uhuru Muigai Kenyatta*, Pre-Trial Chamber, Decision on the Confirmation of Charges Pursuant to Article 61(7)(a) and (b) of the Rome Statute, ICC-01/09-02/11, 24 May 2012, paras 108–10; ICC, *The Prosecutor v William Samoei Ruto, Henry Kiprono Kosgey and Joshua Arap Sang*, Pre-Trial Chamber, Decision on the Confirmation of Charges Pursuant to Article 61(7)(a) and (b) of the Rome Statute, ICC-01/09-01/11, 23 January 2012, para 172; ICC, Pre-Trial Chamber, Decision Pursuant to Article 15 of the Rome Statute on the Authorization of an Investigation into the Situation in the Republic of Kenya, ICC-01/09-19-Corr, 31 March 2010, para 81; ICC, Decision Pursuant to Article 61(7)(a) and (b) of the Rome Statute on the Charges of the Prosecutor against Jean-Pierre Bemba Gombo, Pre-Trial Chamber, ICC-01/05-01/08-424, 15 June 2009, para 76; ICC, *Katanga and Ngudjolo Chui*, above n 30, para 399.

[84] Supreme Court of Israel, *Kipah Mahmad Ahmed Ajuri et al v IDF Commander in West Bank et al*, HCJ 7015/02, para 40.

It is true that the category of protected person originates in classical IHL. It has been inherited from the Hague Regulations, following a scheme of reciprocity that is currently being questioned. Because the individual should be seen as the main beneficiary of international law, that law must be updated in order to comply with this objective. However, it must be understood that humanitarian rules are limited in their interpretation, inasmuch as they are pragmatic rules that also respond to the need to find a balance between military necessity and the principle of humanity.

This dual tension influences the analysis of the law and will determine a reading more or less inclined to greater protection of the civilian population. The value of humanity takes on real meaning when called upon to help those civilians who are caught in an armed conflict or in an occupied territory.

ELIZABETH SALMÓN

Chapter 56. The Prohibition of Collective Punishment

	MN
A. Introduction	1
B. Meaning and Application	4
I. Legislative history	7
II. Subsequent developments	10
III. Collective punishment and related acts	13
C. Relevance in Non-International Armed Conflicts	20
D. Legal Consequences of a Violation	26
I. Criminal responsibility	26
II. State responsibility	32
E. Critical Assessment	34

Select Bibliography

Darcy, S., *Collective Responsibility and Accountability under International Law* (Ardsley, NY: Transnational, 2007), at 7–80

Darcy, S., 'Prosecuting the War Crime of Collective Punishment; Is it Time to Amend the Rome Statute?', 8 *JICJ* (2010) 29

Garner, J.W., 'Community Fines and Collective Responsibility', 11 *AJIL* (1917) 511

Kalshoven, F., *Belligerent Reprisals* (2nd edn reprint, Leiden/Boston, Mass: Martinus Nijhoff, 2005)

Kretzmer, D., *The Occupation of Justice* (Albany, NY: State University of New York Press, 2002)

Sivakumaran, S., 'War Crimes before the Special Court for Sierra Leone: Child Soldiers, Hostages, Peacekeepers and Collective Punishments', 8 *JICJ* (2010) 1009

A. Introduction

A fundamental precept of both law and justice requires that individuals be held responsible only for their own wrongful conduct, and that punishment should be directed in such a manner that it distinguishes between the guilty and the innocent. Collective punishment disregards such basic principles, yet has remained a common feature of armed conflict. Plato wrote that warring parties in Ancient Greece should 'carry on the conflict only to the point of compelling the guilty to do justice by the pressure of the suffering of the innocent'.[1] Grotius considered that 'no one who is innocent of wrong may be punished for the wrong done by another',[2] yet invading and occupying armies have resorted to collective punishment as a means of suppressing resistance, maintaining order, and subjugating local populations. The historical record shows numerous examples of collective penalties being imposed in response to

---

[1] *Republic*, Book V, 471b, in E. Hamilton and H. Cairns (eds), *The Collected Dialogues of Plato* (Princeton, NJ: Princeton University Press, 1989), at 710.

[2] H. Grotius, *De Jure Belli ac Pacis Libri Tres* (Amsterdam: Johan Blaeu, 1646), Book II, Chapters XXI, IX, XII, trans F.W. Kelsey (Washington, DC: Carnegie Endowment for International Peace, Division of International Law, 1925), vol II, at 537, 539.

individual acts, most notably during the two World Wars and in the context of colonial insurgencies.[3] The Nuremberg judgment provides an example of a particularly extreme Nazi Germany collective punishment policy, whereby 'the responsibility for all acts of sabotage is attributed not only to individual perpetrators but to the entire Czech population'.[4]

2   International humanitarian law (IHL) prohibits wartime collective punishment, with rules contained in many of the regime's major treaties outlawing the practice. The main provision protecting civilians from collective punishment is Article 33 of Geneva Convention (GC) IV, which expressly prohibits collective penalties and states that '[n]o protected person may be punished for an offence he or she has not personally committed'. These treaty stipulations ended the degree of uncertainty that had surrounded the ambiguous rule in Article 50 of the Hague Regulations. That Article provided that '[n]o general penalty, pecuniary or otherwise, can be inflicted upon the population on account of the acts of individuals for which they cannot be regarded as jointly and severally responsible'; as was observed during the 1949 Diplomatic Conference, Article 50 'did not exclude the possibility of collective sanctions for individual acts for which populations might be considered collectively responsible'.[5] The prohibition of collective punishment is also found in GC III with respect to prisoners of war (POWs) (Articles 26 paragraph 6 and 87 paragraph 3), and in Additional Protocol (AP) I (Article 75(2)(d) and (4)(b)) and AP II (Articles 4(2)(b) and 6(2)(b)). The Additional Protocols treat the rule against collective punishment as a fundamental guarantee, and highlight the importance of the rule on individual responsibility in the context of penal proceedings. Imposition of collective punishment is listed as a war crime in the International Criminal Tribunal for Rwanda (ICTR) (Article 4(b)) and Special Court for Sierra Leone (SCSL) (Article 3(b)) statutes, although it is omitted from the International Criminal Court (ICC) Statute.

3   The rule against collective punishment, according to the International Committee of the Red Cross (ICRC) Customary International Humanitarian Law (CIHL) Study, has attained a customary international law status for both international armed conflicts (IACs) and non-international armed conflicts (NIACs).[6] Nevertheless, a survey of the more recent practice of armed conflicts reveals a continuing tendency of some parties to impose measures of collective punishment in violation of the laws of armed conflict. For example, collective punishment has been a feature of the recent conflicts in the Democratic Republic of Congo,[7] Pakistan,[8] Ethiopia,[9] Indonesia,[10] Iraq, and, most prominently,

---

[3] See generally S. Darcy, *Collective Responsibility and Accountability under International Law* (Ardsley, NY: Transnational, 2007), at 7–80.

[4] International Military Tribunal (Nuremberg), *Judgment and Sentences*, 1 October 1946, reprinted in 41 *AJIL* 1 (1947) 172, at 325.

[5] Final Record, vol II-A, at 648–9.   [6] ICRC CIHL Study, at 374–5.

[7] Human Rights Watch, *'You Will be Punished': Attacks on Civilians in Eastern Congo* (New York: Human Rights Watch, 2009), at 93.

[8] A. Liptak, 'My Brother's Keeper; Is the Group Responsible for the Individual's Crime?', *New York Times*, 8 February 2004, Section 4, at 5; Human Rights Watch, 'Pakistan: End Collective Punishment in Swat', 22 July 2010, available at <http://www.hrw.org/news/2010/07/21/pakistan-end-collective-punishment-swat>.

[9] Human Rights Watch, *Collective Punishment: War Crimes and Crimes against Humanity in the Ogaden area of Ethiopia's Somali Regional State* (New York: Human Rights Watch, 2008).

[10] A. Marshall, 'The Widow's Battalion', *New York Times Magazine*, 20 January 2002, at 30.

Israel and Palestine. In 2004, the United Nations (UN) envoy in Iraq, Lakhdar Brahimi, labelled the United States (US) assault on Fallujah as collective punishment.[11] The ICRC has stated in the context of the Israel/Palestine conflict that '[t]he whole of Gaza's civilian population is being punished for acts for which they bear no responsibility. The closure therefore constitutes a collective punishment imposed in clear violation of Israel's obligations under international humanitarian law'.[12] The prohibition of collective punishment accordingly remains a vital rule of IHL.

B. Meaning and Application

4 The prohibition of collective punishment under IHL is encapsulated in two interrelated norms. The first is that an individual may be punished for acts or omissions only where there is personal wrongdoing on that person's part; that is to say, one person cannot generally be punished for the acts of another. The second is that mass or collective punishments or penalties are prohibited. Collective punishment is defined as 'a form of sanction imposed on persons or a group of persons in response to a crime committed by one of them or a member of the group'.[13] The two basic propositions are set out in Article 33 paragraph 1 GC IV: 'No protected person may be punished for an offence he or she has not personally committed. Collective penalties and likewise all measures of intimidation or of terrorism are prohibited.' As will be seen, the language of Article 33 is no longer a precise reflection of contemporary understandings of the prohibition of collective punishment. The CIHL Study sets out more accurately the two components of the rule against collective punishment:

Rule 102. No one may be convicted of an offence except on the basis of individual criminal responsibility.

Rule 103. Collective punishments are prohibited.

5 This formulation draws on the relevant provisions found in the two Additional Protocols, discussed in section B.II of this chapter, where the emphasis moves from personal commission to personal responsibility, and from collective penalties to collective punishments. The Pictet Commentary GC IV presaged these changes with its broadened interpretation of Article 33 paragraph 1:

The first paragraph embodies in international law one of the general principles of domestic law, i.e. that penal liability is personal in character. This paragraph then lays a prohibition on collective penalties. This does not refer to punishments inflicted under penal law, i.e. sentences pronounced by a court after due process of law, but penalties of any kind inflicted on persons or entire groups of persons, in defiance of the most elementary principles of humanity, for acts that these persons have not committed.[14]

6 It is useful for understanding the content of the prohibition of collective punishment to consider the legislative history of Article 33 paragraph 1 GC IV and the rule against collective punishment during armed conflict.

---

[11] T. Cambanis. 'UN Envoy Offers Plan for Interim Government', *Boston Globe*, 15 April 2004.
[12] 'Gaza Closure: Not Another Year!', ICRC News Release 10/103, Geneva/Jerusalem, 14 June 2010.
[13] P. Rabbat and S. Mehring, 'Collective Punishment', in MPEPIL, para 1.
[14] Pictet Commentary GC IV, at 225–6.

I. Legislative history

7 The preparatory work to the Geneva Conventions reveals strong support for the inclusion of a rule against collective punishment in the proposed civilians' convention. There was unanimous support, for example, in Committee II of the 1946 Preliminary Conference of National Red Cross Societies, that 'all collective penalties exercised against the civilian population following acts imputed to nationals of the occupied State, must be formally prohibited'.[15] Article 30 of the ICRC's influential Draft Convention for the Protection of Civilian Persons in Times of War, submitted to the XVIIth International Red Cross Conference in Stockholm in 1948, proposed:

> No protected person may be punished for an offence he has not himself committed. Collective penalties are forbidden.
>
> Measures of reprisal against protected persons or their property are forbidden. The destruction of movable property or real estate, which military operations do not make absolutely necessary, is forbidden, as are all measures of intimidation, or of terrorism.[16]

The ICRC was motivated to include these rules because it felt that the principle of individual responsibility is 'one of the most important in law'.[17]

8 At the 1949 Diplomatic Conference itself, the rules on individual responsibility and collective punishment proved uncontroversial and elicited little by way of comment from the delegates. The Italian delegate welcomed this 'new principle of international law', given the more limited protection against collective sanctions provided by Article 50 of the 1907 Hague Regulations.[18] The delegates at the 1899 Hague Peace Conference had been more permissive, having felt that collective punishment should be allowed against a population, 'as a consequence of reprehensible or hostile acts committed by it as a whole or at least permitted by it to be committed'.[19] It was considered that 'passive responsibility' was a sufficient basis for the imposition of collective penalties, such as 'extraordinary contributions'.[20] Article 33 GC IV removed this concept of collective responsibility as a basis for punishment, and, as the Pictet Commentary affirms, 'it will no longer be possible to inflict penalties on persons who have themselves not committed the acts complained of'.[21] The prohibition of reprisals against civilians and their property in Article 33 copper-fastens the prohibition of collective punishment, and protects civilians from being the target of reprisal action in response to breaches of the laws of war.[22]

---

[15] CICR, *Conférence préliminaire des sociétés nationales de la Croix-Rouge pour l'étude des conventions et de divers problèmes ayant trait à la Croix-Rouge, Genève, 26 Juillet–3 août 1946: procès-verbaux* (Séance plénière du samedi 3 août 1946), vol VII, at 32. See also ibid, at 37; ICRC, *Commission of Government Experts for the Sstudy of Conventions for the Protection of War Victims*, Geneva, 14–26 April 1947; *Preliminary Documents Submitted by the International Committee of the Red Cross*, III, *Condition and Protection of Civilians in Time of War* (translation), at 16–17; ICRC, *Report on the Work of the Conference of Government Experts for the Study of the Conventions for the Protection of War Victims, Geneva, April 14–26, 1947* (Geneva: ICRC, 1947), at 285, Art 23.

[16] ICRC, *Draft Revised or New Conventions for the Protection of War Victims* (Geneva: ICRC, May 1948), at 166.

[17] Ibid, at 167.   [18] Final Record, vol II-A, at 648–9.

[19] *The Proceedings of the Hague Peace Conferences, Translation of the Official Texts: The Conference of 1899*, Prepared in the Division of International Law of the Carnegie Endowment for International Peace under the supervision of J. Brown Scott (New York: OUP, 1920); *Report to the Conference*, by Edouard Rolin, Annex 1 to the Minutes of the Fifth Meeting, 5 July 1899, at 65. See further *In re Kappler*, Italy, Military Tribunal of Rome, 20 July 1948, Case No 151, 15 *Annual Digest and Reports of Public International Law Cases* (1948) 471.

[20] *The Proceedings of the Hague Peace Conferences*, above n 19, at 65.

[21] Pictet Commentary GC IV, at 225.   [22] See further Ch 29 of this volume.

The rule protecting civilians from acts of collective punishment has counterparts in the IHL rules aimed at the protection of POWs.[23] Wartime practices, particularly during the two World Wars, demonstrated the vulnerability of POWs to collective punishments, and provided the impetus for a legislative response.[24] The ICRC proposal to prohibit collective disciplinary measures against POWs affecting food was accepted during the 1929 Diplomatic Conference,[25] as, more importantly, was the broader German suggestion that 'collective disciplinary penalties are forbidden for individual offences'.[26] Both of these are reflected in the 1929 Convention Relative to the Treatment of the Prisoners of War.[27] The general rule was 'intended to avoid that which occurs, in accordance with the law of least effort, whereby camp commanders punish prisoners collectively instead of searching for the authors of individual acts'.[28] This first unambiguous international treaty rule addressing collective punishment was unquestionably violated during the Second World War. The International Military Tribunal for the Far East noted that mass beatings, torture, imprisonment, or killings were a common response of the Japanese authorities to individual acts by POWs, particularly where the actual offender could not be found.[29] The existing rules were reaffirmed in GC III,[30] but the more general prohibition was changed from one of '[c]ollective penalties for individual acts' to that of '[c]ollective punishment for individual acts'. This revised provision was adopted after little comment by delegates at the 1949 Diplomatic Conference.[31]

II. Subsequent developments

The prohibition of collective punishment in the Geneva Conventions is supplemented by the rules in the Additional Protocols, and may also be interpreted in light of relevant international human rights law (IHRL) and international criminal law (ICL). It bears noting that the relevant rules in the Geneva Conventions are limited to POWs and to civilians in occupied territory or otherwise in the hands of party of which they are not nationals. The Additional Protocols both contain rules against collective punishment and affirm that any punishment must be based on individual responsibility.[32] During the drafting of the Additional Protocols, it was suggested that the words 'for which he or she

---

[23] See generally Ch 48 of this volume.
[24] See, e.g., Art 12, ILA, 'Proposed International Regulations for the Treatment of Prisoners of War' (1921), *Report of the 30th Conference of the International Law Association*, The Hague, 1921, at 236–46; 'Projet de Code des prisonniers de guerre, déportés, évacués et réfugiés', 5 *Revue internationale de la Croix-Rouge* (1923) 771, at 786–814.
[25] *Actes de la Conférence Diplomatique convoquée par le Conseil Fédéral Suisse pour la revision de la Convention du 6 Juillet 1906 pour l'amélioration du sort des blessés et malades dans les armées en campagne et pour l'élaboration d'une convention relative au traitement des prisonniers de guerre et réunie à Genève du 1er au 27 juillet 1929* (Genève: Imprimerie du Journal de Genève, 1930), at 23, Art 14(3).
[26] 'Des peines disciplinaires collectives sont défendues pour les délits individuels', *Ière Sous-commission (juridique et diplomatique) de la II ème Commission, séance du vendredi 5 juillet à 3h. 30*, at 2 (available at the library of the ICRC, Geneva, reference no 345.21/14-1 B).
[27] Art 11 para 4 and Art 46 para 4.
[28] 'Cette disposition correspond à la proposition très judicieuse de l'Allemagne, qui est destinée à éviter, qu'en vertu de la loi du moindre effort, les commandants des camps ne se laissent aller à punir collectivement les prisonniers au lieu de rechercher les auteurs d'actes individuels', *Actes de la Conférence Diplomatique*, above n 25, at 488 [author's translation].
[29] N. Boister and R. Cryer (eds), *Documents on the Tokyo International Military Tribunal* (Oxford/New York: OUP, 2008), at 545, 571–3.
[30] Art 87 para 3 and Art 26 para 6 GC III.   [31] Final Record, vol II-A, at 501–2.
[32] Art 75(2)(d) and (4)(b) AP I; Art 4(2)(b) and Art 6(2)(b) AP II.

is not personally responsible' replace 'which he or she has not personally committed'. This new formulation would also, for example, 'cover cases of complicity resulting from higher orders'.[33] Article 75(4)(b) AP I sets out as a fundamental guarantee that 'no one shall be convicted of an offence except on the basis of individual penal responsibility'. This is also expressed in human rights law; Article 7 of the African Charter on Human and Peoples' Rights, for example, provides that '[p]unishment is personal and can be imposed only on the offender'.[34] The Inter-American Commission on Human Rights has commented on the scope of the principle of individual responsibility thus:

[C]riminal prosecutions must comply with the fundamental requirement that no one should be convicted of an offense except on the basis of individual penal responsibility, and the corollary to this principle that there can be no collective criminal responsibility. [...] This restriction does not, however, preclude the prosecution of persons on such established grounds of individual criminal responsibility such as complicity, incitement, or participation in a common criminal enterprise, nor does it prevent individual accountability on the basis of the well-established superior responsibility doctrine.[35]

11 Additional Protocol I brings the non-individual punishment aspect of the prohibition of collective punishment into line with basic principles of penal law. Article 75(2)(d) AP I also prohibits collective punishments 'at any time and in any place whatsoever', a slightly more expansive rule than the outlawing of 'collective penalties' in Article 33 paragraph 1 GC IV. Collective punishment is to be understood in a broad sense, outlawing 'not only penalties imposed in the normal judicial process, but also any other kind of sanction'.[36] It bears noting that the equally authentic French language versions of the Additional Protocols retain the phrase *peines collectives* from GC IV, although it is apparent from the drafting history of the Protocols that the delegates did not intend for the prohibition to be limited to punishments solely handed down under penal law.[37]

12 Although the scope of application of AP I is broader than that of the Geneva Conventions, the rules on collective punishment are to be found amongst the fundamental guarantees of Article 75, and accordingly apply to persons 'who are in the hands of a party to the conflict'.[38] Acts amounting to collective punishment directed against civilians in the hands of an adverse party could be seen to run counter to the 'principles of humanity and the dictates of the public conscience',[39] as well perhaps as the rules protecting civilians from the conduct of hostilities.[40] It is clear, however, that no IHL treaty rule exists specifically prohibiting a belligerent from resorting to collective punishment against an enemy population that is not in that belligerent's power, although ICL treats collective punishment as a war crime, as discussed below in section D. It bears noting that the Human Rights Council's Commission of Inquiry on Lebanon 'formed a clear view that, cumulatively, the deliberate and lethal attacks by the IDF [Israel Defense Forces] on civilians and civilian objects amounted to collective punishment'.[41]

---

[33] *Official Records of the Diplomatic Conference on the Reaffirmation and Development of International Humanitarian Law applicable in Armed Conflicts* (Geneva, 1974–7), vol VIII, at 348.

[34] See also Art 5(3) ACHR.

[35] IACommHR, *Report on Terrorism and Human Rights*, OEA/Ser.L/V/II.116, 22 October 2002, para 227.

[36] ICRC Commentary APs, at 1374.   [37] *Official Records*, above n 33, vol VII, at 87–90.

[38] Art 75(1) AP I, and see further, by analogy, Ch 55, MN 25 and 26, of this volume.

[39] Art 1(2) AP I.   [40] Arts 48–56 AP I.

[41] *Report of the Commission of Inquiry on Lebanon pursuant to Human Rights Council Resolution S-2/1*, 23 November 2006, para 25.

III. Collective punishment and related acts

As with many of the acts the treaties seek to prohibit, the Geneva Conventions neither define nor provide examples of collective punishment. The absence of a definition may be felt more acutely in the context of collective punishment given the range of forms that such actions might take, and because the underlying act might itself already be subject to an IHL prohibition. Guidance may be found in the *travaux préparatoires* of the relevant treaties, in case law, and in practice that has been condemned by international organizations as amounting to unlawful collective punishment. The interpretation of the rules in question is to be done in good faith, giving the terms their ordinary meaning in the context of the Geneva Conventions and in light of the treaties' object and purpose.[42] This section seeks to delimit the concept of collective punishment by distinguishing it from related and occasionally overlapping acts, and by providing a number of illustrative examples.

In the context of IACs, numerous examples of collective punishment can be found from the World Wars, as well as from more recent conflicts. During the Second World War, the German army conducted a 'punitive expedition in continuous operation' against the Russian population, involving mass executions of civilians and destruction of property.[43] The levying of collective fines also occurred,[44] a practice which the drafters of the Hague Regulations clearly had in mind when adopting Article 50. Colonial-era conflicts also often featured collective punitive measures, ostensibly taken in response to acts of resistance. The British had legislated for the power of colonial authorities to impose collective punishments, such as in the Emergency Powers (Collective Punishment) Regulations (1955) in Cyprus, the Defence (Emergency) Regulations (1945) in Palestine, and various Collective Punishment Ordinances in Nigeria, Kenya, Northern Rhodesia, Nyasaland, and Somaliland.[45] British practice in Malaya, where 'food was withheld from villages judged guilty of sheltering insurgents',[46] is similar to instances of practice of the US army following the 2003 invasion of Iraq, where the military was 'imprisoning the relatives of suspected guerrillas, in hopes of pressing the insurgents to turn themselves in'.[47] This strategy sought to 'punish not only the guerrillas but also make it clear to ordinary Iraqis the cost of not cooperating'.[48] Examples of Israeli practices in the Occupied Palestinian Territories that have been described as collective punishment include house demolitions, prolonged curfews, closures of towns and villages, transfer of relatives, and restrictions on electricity and water supplies.[49]

---

[42] Art 31(1) VCLT.
[43] R. Lemkin, *Axis Rule in Occupied Europe* (Washington, DC: Carnegie Endowment for International Peace, Division of International Law, 1944), at 236–7.
[44] *In re Rauter*, The Netherlands, Special Criminal Court, 4 May 1948, Special Court of Cassation, 12 January 1949, Case No 193, 16 *Annual Digest and Reports of Public International Law Cases* (1949) 526.
[45] See A.W.B. Simpson, *Human Rights and the End of Empire; Britain and the Genesis of the European Convention* (Oxford/New York: OUP, 2001), at 955, 1062–4.
[46] J. Pilger, *Hidden Agendas* (London: Vintage, 1999), at 24.
[47] D. Filkins, 'A Region Inflamed: Strategy; Tough New Tactics by US Tighten Grip on Iraq Towns', *New York Times*, 7 December 2003, at 1.
[48] Ibid.
[49] See, e.g., C. Shalev, *Collective Punishment in the West Bank and the Gaza Strip* (Jerusalem: B'tselem—The Israeli Information Center for Human Rights in the Occupied Territories, 1990); Al-Haq, 'Collective Punishment in 'Awarta; Israel's Response to the Killing in Itamar Settlement', 156/2011, 22 April 2011, at 18–19; HRComm Res 2003/6, 15 April 2003, para 12; UNGA Res 58/99, 9 December 2003, UNGA

Large-scale military operations have also been viewed as themselves amounting to collective punishment.[50]

15   The lawfulness of several of these collectively punitive measures may be challenged on grounds other than the rule against collective punishment, especially those involving serious consequences for victims. That being said, the norm against collective punishment does not serve merely to capture those actions not addressed elsewhere by the Geneva Conventions. While it may be seen to address such lesser acts, the prohibition of collective punishment also serves to remind parties to an armed conflict that protected persons are not objects to be used in the pursuance of military or security aims. The Supreme Court of Israel, for example, sought to justify house demolitions on the basis of deterrence:

> [The aim is] to achieve a deterrent effect, and such an effect should naturally apply not only to the terrorist himself, but to those surrounding him, and certainly to family members living with him. He should know that his criminal acts will not only hurt him but also are apt to cause great suffering to his family.[51]

Such a justification runs counter to the rule in Article 33 paragraph 1 GC IV, yet the Israeli authorities have at various times pursued policies of expressly punitive house demolitions.[52]

16   The formulation of Article 33 paragraph 1 of GC IV is particularly relevant to an understanding of the rule against collective punishment, in that it outlaws '[c]ollective penalties and *likewise* all measures of intimidation or of terrorism' (emphasis added). Collective punitive measures can thus be seen as belonging to a category of prohibited actions that are aimed at coercing or threatening protected persons through the commission of one or more of a variety of acts. A distinguishing feature of collective punishment is that it comprises a course of action taken in response to a prior act, whereas measures of intimidation or terrorism are not understood in this manner. Where the prior act amounted to a violation of IHL, a justification for collective punishment might be sought under the increasingly circumscribed doctrine of belligerent reprisals, discussed further below in this section, although collective punishment violating Article 33 paragraph 1 might also have been resorted to following lawful acts.

17   Economic sanctions undertaken by a party to an armed conflict may violate the prohibition of collective punishment if directed at protected persons and carried out in response to particular acts, either lawful or unlawful. The comprehensive blockade of the Gaza Strip

---

Res 59/124, 10 December 2004; UNGA Res 60/107, 8 December 2005; UNGA Res 61/119, 14 December 2006; UNGA Res 62/109, 17 December 2007; UNGA Res 63/98, 8 December 2008; UNGA Res 64/94, 19 January 2010; UNGA Res 65/105, 20 January 2011; UNGA Res 66/79, 12 January 2012.

[50] See, e.g., *Report of the United Nations Fact-Finding Mission on the Gaza Conflict*, A/HRC/12/48, 25 September 2009, paras 60, 74, 91, 1171, 1320, 1457, 1494; *Report of the Independent Fact-Finding Committee on Gaza: No Safe Place*, Presented to the League of Arab States, 30 April 2009, at 6, 112, 13; Amnesty International, 'Israel/Gaza: Operation "Cast Lead": 22 Days of Death and Destruction', 2 July 2009, at 1; HRCouncil Res S-3/1, 15 November 2006.

[51] HC 698/85, *Daghlas v The Military Commander of the Judea and Samaria Region*, 40(2) PD 42. See further M. Shamgar, 'The Observance of International Law in the Administered Territories', 1 *Israel Yearbook on Human Rights* (1971) 262, at 276; D. Kretzmer, *The Occupation of Justice* (Albany, NY: State University of New York Press, 2002) at 163.

[52] See C. Levinson, 'Chronicle of a West Bank Murder', *Haaretz*, 15 June 2012; 'B'Tselem to Attorney General: Do Not Allow Home Demolition of Relatives of the Murderers of Fogel Family', B'Tselem Press Release, 10 May 2012; C. Levinson, 'IDF Planning to Demolish Homes of Dozens of Palestinian Militants in West Bank', *Haaretz*, 4 July 2014.

by Israel has been viewed as a measure of collective punishment by various international and non-governmental organizations,[53] and a UN fact-finding mission concluded that 'one of the principle motives behind the imposition of the blockade was a desire to punish the people of the Gaza Strip for having elected Hamas'.[54] In the *Gaza Fuel and Electricity case*, petitioners argued unsuccessfully before the Israeli courts that the restrictions on electricity and fuel supplies to the Gaza Strip amounted to collective punishment.[55] It was concluded elsewhere, however, that these actions evidenced 'an intent to subject the Gaza population to conditions such that they would be induced into withdrawing their support from Hamas'.[56] It is apposite that the prohibitions of collective punishment, intimidation, and terrorism are grouped together in GC IV, given that a particular course of action may have several overlapping rationales, such as deterrence, punishment, or intimidation. The SCSL, as discussed in section D, considers that an element of the war crime of collective punishment is the specific intent to punish collectively.

The prohibition of collective punishment is closely related to the prohibition of reprisals, with both included in Article 33 GC IV. A belligerent reprisal is a deliberate violation of the laws of armed conflict taken in response to an enemy's prior breach and for the purpose of seeking a return to observance of the law.[57] The two concepts are technically distinct, because reprisals are directed at the armed forces, property, or civilians of a belligerent party that violated IHL (although under the Geneva Conventions and AP I they may no longer be directed at persons and property protected under these treaties[58]), while collective punishments are directed at innocent individuals because of the acts of other individuals. Nevertheless, a belligerent reprisal nearly inevitably involves collective measures that strike in fact at innocent persons, and accordingly they are often considered by public opinion and in international statements as acts of collective punishment in such instances. A Chamber of the International Criminal Tribunal for the Former Yugoslavia (ICTY) has used the term 'reprisals' in this non-technical sense, and explained how reprisals may amount to collective punishment:

Reprisals typically are taken in situations where the individuals personally responsible for the breach are either unknown or out of reach. These retaliatory measures are aimed instead at other more vulnerable individuals or groups. They are individuals or groups who may not even have any

---

[53] 'Gaza Closure: Not Another Year!', above n 12; Amnesty International, above n 50, at 51; Palestinian Centre for Human Rights, 'The Illegal Closure of the Gaza Strip: Collective Punishment of the Civilian Population', 10 December 2010; OHCHR, 'How Can Israel's Blockade Be Legal?—UN Independent Experts on the "Palmer Report"', Geneva, 13 September 2011.

[54] UN HRCouncil, *Report of the International Fact-Finding Mission to Investigate Violations of International Law, Including International Humanitarian Law and Human Rights Law, Resulting from the Israeli Attacks on the Flotilla of Ships Carrying Humanitarian Assistance*, 27 September 2010, para 54. See, however, *Report of the Secretary-General's Panel of Inquiry on the 31 May 2010 Flotilla Incident*, September 2011, para 77; A. Bell, 'A Critique of the Goldstone Report and its Treatment of International Humanitarian Law', 104 *ASIL Proceedings* (2010) 79, at 80–1. See also A. Cohen, 'Economic Sanctions in IHL: Suggested Principles', 42 *Israel Law Review* (2009) 117, at 128–32.

[55] *Petition for an Order Nisi and an Urgent Request for Injunction, Jaber al Bassiouni Ahmed et al v The Prime Minister and Minister of Defence*, HCJ 9132/07, 28 October 2007. English translation available at <http://www.adalah.org/eng/features/opts/petition%20-%20english.doc>.

[56] *Report of the United Nations Fact-Finding Mission on the Gaza Conflict*, A/HRC/12/48, 25 September 2009, para 1329.

[57] See further F. Kalshoven, *Belligerent Reprisals* (2nd edn reprint, Leiden/Boston, Mass: Martinus Nijhoff, 2005); see further Ch 29 of this volume.

[58] Art 46 GC I; Art 47 GC II; Art 13 para 3 GC III; Art 33 para 3 GC IV; Art 20 AP I.

19 This feature precisely leads to outlawing reprisals against protected persons. In the past, reprisals were typically directed at civilians or POWs. Not all belligerent reprisals are to be considered as acts of collective punishment in a large understanding of the term, however, given that the law of belligerent reprisals does not prescribe the form such an action might take, merely those protected persons or objects against whom or which reprisals are unlawful. Under IHL, reprisals against persons and property protected by the Geneva Conventions are now unlawful,[60] as are those outlawed under the Hague Convention for the Protection of Cultural Property and, with some controversy, by AP I.[61]

C. Relevance in Non-International Armed Conflicts

20 Collective punishment is not listed amongst the prohibited acts of Common Article 3 applicable in NIACs, although collective punitive measures involving violence to life and person, the taking of hostages, outrages on personal dignity, or the denial of fair trial rights would obviously be covered by the Article. The prohibition of collective punishment in Article 33 GC IV is addressed to civilians in the hands of the enemy, both in occupied territories and in the territories of the parties to an IAC. Protected persons are defined by GC IV as those 'who, at a given moment and in any manner whatsoever, find themselves, in case of a conflict or occupation, in the hands of a Party to the conflict or Occupying Power of which they are not nationals'.[62] Additional Protocol II extends the prohibition of collective punishment under IHL to NIACs. Using language identical to that used in AP I, Article 4(2)(b) AP II categorically prohibits collective punishments, while Article 6 on 'Penal Prosecutions' states that 'no one shall be convicted of an offence except on the basis of individual penal responsibility'.[63] The ease of inclusion of these rules in a treaty applying to situations of NIAC affirms the fundamental nature of the prohibition of collective punishment.

21 The lacuna regarding collective punishment in NIACs was obvious soon after the adoption of the Geneva Conventions. A Commission of Experts meeting in Geneva in 1955 to examine 'the Application of Humanitarian Principles in the Event of Internal Disturbances', suggested that in addition to the minimum standards of Common Article 3, the rules in Articles 33 and 34 GC IV should also be respected by all parties during 'internal disturbances'.[64] The Experts' Report stated that:

With regard to the clause often referred to as 'collective responsibility', the Commission was unanimous in disapproving the conception of the possible responsibility of an individual, due uniquely to the fact that he or she was a member of a given group, independently of criminal acts committed by him or her. The incarceration and the punishment of members of the families of

---

[59] ICTY, *The Prosecutor v Zoran Kupreškić et al*, Case No IT-95-16-T, Trial Chamber, Judgment, 14 January 2000, para 528.

[60] Art 46 GC I; Art 47 GC II; Art 13 para 3 GC III; Art 33 para 3 GC IV.

[61] Art 4(4) Hague Convention for the Protection of Cultural Property (1954); Arts 20, 51(6), 52(1), 53(c), 54(4), 55(2), and 56 (1) and (4) AP I. On the reprisal prohibitions in AP I see, e.g., A.D. Sofaer, 'The Rationale for the United States Decision', 82 *AJIL* 4 (1988) 784, at 785; Darcy, above n 3, at 148–66.

[62] Art 4 para 1 GC IV. See Ch 55 of this volume.   [63] Art 6(2)(b) AP II.

[64] 'Report of the Commission of Experts for the Study of the Question of the Application of Humanitarian Principles in the Event of Internal Disturbances', 9(1) *Revue internationale de la Croix-Rouge* (1956), Supplement, 11, at 17.

persons implicated in 'internal disturbances', and more especially of their children, should be strictly condemned.[65]

During the work on the 'reaffirmation and development of international humanitarian law applicable in armed conflicts' in the 1970s, Canada submitted to the 1971 Conference of Government Experts a draft protocol to the Geneva Conventions which proposed extending GC IV's provisions on individual responsibility and collective penalties to NIAC.[66] During the drafting of AP II, one conference delegate commented that 'the concept of collective penalties was outmoded',[67] while another considered that the prohibition of collective punishment was 'already accepted not only in various domestic legislations but also in customary international law'.[68] The fundamental guarantee in Article 4 AP II that forbids collective punishment applies to civilians and to other persons who are *hors de combat*.[69]

Applying AP II's prohibition of collective punishment requires the existence of an armed conflict 'in the territory of a High Contracting Party between its armed forces and dissident armed forces or other organized armed groups which, under responsible command, exercise such control over a part of its territory as to enable them to carry out sustained and concerted military operations and to implement this Protocol'.[70] There are over 165 High Contracting Parties to AP II, numbering among which are four of the permanent United Nations Security Council (UNSC) members, and states not parties have not expressed any disagreement with the rules on collective punishment. The United States of America, a state not party, has stated that '[i]t is the opinio juris of the US that persons detained in connection with an internal armed conflict are entitled to humane treatment as specified in Articles 4, 5 and 6' AP II.[71] It is widely accepted that the prohibition of collective punishment is a rule of customary IHL applicable in NIACs.[72] According to the UN Secretary-General, '[v]iolations of common article 3 of the Geneva Conventions and of Article 4 of Additional Protocol II thereto committed in an armed conflict not of an international character have long been considered customary international law'.[73] Human rights norms and domestic law may also be of relevance should collective punishment be resorted to by parties during an internal conflict. Amnesty International has described collective punishment as 'inherently unlawful',[74] and UN human rights bodies have condemned collective punishment, including outside the context of armed conflict.[75]

The practice of NIACs reveals instances of collective punishment in violation of IHL. In the Democratic Republic of Congo, for example, the Democratic Forces for the Liberation of Rwanda have pursued a policy of collective punishment and threatened the civilian population:

You, the population of Mihanda, be on guard. We are going to kill the pregnant women and open their stomachs and we are even going to kill the young girls. The men will be decapitated

---

[65] Ibid.
[66] ICRC, *Report on the Work of the Conference of Government Experts on the Reaffirmation and Development of International Humanitarian Law Applicable in Armed Conflicts, Geneva, May 24–June 12, 1971* (Geneva: ICRC, 1971), at 57–9.
[67] *Official Records*, above n 33, vol IX, at 427.   [68] Ibid, at 455.   [69] Art 4(1).
[70] Art 1(1) AP II. See Ch 19, MN 5, of this volume.
[71] Report on US Practice, 1997, Chapter 5.3, ICRC CIHL Database, Practice Relating to Rule 103.
[72] ICRC CIHL Study, at 374–5.
[73] *Report of the Secretary-General on the Establishment of a Special Court for Sierra Leone*, UN Doc S/2000/915, 14 October 2000, para 14.
[74] Amnesty International, above n 50, at 65.
[75] See *Concluding Observations of the Human Rights Committee: Libyan Arab Jamahiriya*, 6 November 1998, UN Doc CCPR/C/79/Add.101, para 12.

like the salted fish. Since they are trying to force us out of Congo, we will punish the population of Ziralo.[76]

25 The UN Secretary-General considered that federal and Serbian Government forces in Kosovo used disproportionate force to terrorize and subjugate the local population, as 'collective punishment to teach them that the price of supporting the Kosovo Albanian paramilitary units is too high'.[77] Human Rights Watch considers that forced relocation of civilians by the Ethiopian Government in the conflict areas of the Somali Region 'amounts to the unlawful transfer of the population and collective punishment of Ogaadeeni communities perceived to be supporting the Ogaden National Liberation Front'.[78] Family members have also been detained or killed by Ethiopian forces for failing to produce wanted fighters,[79] while the Pakistani military has engaged in forced evictions or demolition of the homes of relatives of suspected militants.[80] The Sierra Leone Truth and Reconciliation Commission reported that all armed groups participating in the civil war 'pursued a strategy of detaining women and girls whom they believed to be relatives and supporters of the opposing forces with the intention of violating them and punishing them for the perceived association with enemy forces'.[81] Indictments before the SCSL alleged, for example, that armed groups committed numerous crimes, 'to punish the civilian population for allegedly supporting the elected government'.[82] The Special Court has convicted several individuals for the war crime of collective punishment committed in a NIAC, as the next section demonstrates.

D. Legal Consequences of a Violation

I. Criminal responsibility

26 International criminal law treats collective punishment as a war crime for which individual criminal responsibility arises. Two ad hoc international criminal tribunals, the ICTR and SCSL, have jurisdiction over the war crime of collective punishment expressly set out in their Statutes.[83] The Statutes address war crimes in NIAC, and list collective punishment as a violation of Common Article 3 and AP II. According to the UN Secretary-General, the international crimes in the SCSL Statute are 'considered to have the character of customary international law at the time of the commission of the crime'.[84] In relation to IAC, no international treaty has to date designated collective punishment as a war crime. It was not included as a grave breach of the Geneva Conventions or in the ICC Statute,

---

[76] Human Rights Watch, above n 7, at 54.
[77] *Report of the Secretary-General Prepared Pursuant to Resolutions 1160 (1998) and 1199 (1998) of the Security Council*, UN Doc S/1998/912 (1998), para 7.
[78] Human Rights Watch, above n 9, at 34.   [79] Ibid, at 49.
[80] Human Rights Watch, above n 8.
[81] *Report of the Sierra Leone Truth and Reconciliation Commission* (2004), vol II, Chapter 2: Findings, at 72.
[82] See, e.g., *The Prosecutor v Brima, Kamara and Kanu*, Further Amended Consolidated Indictment, SCSL-2004-16-PT, 13 May 2004, para 41.
[83] Art 4(b) ICTR Statute, UNSC Res 955 (1994) 955, and Art 3(b), Statute of the SCSL, having been established by an Agreement between the UN and the Government of Sierra Leone pursuant to UNSC Res 1315 (2000) of 14 August 2000.
[84] Report of the Secretary-General on the establishment of a SCSL, UN Doc S/2000/915, 14 October 2000, para 12.

although a strong argument may be made for the existence of such a crime in customary international law.

The 1919 Commission on the Responsibility of the Authors of the War and on Enforcement of Penalties included collective penalties in the list of violations of the laws and customs of war for which prosecution was recommended, giving the example of Belgian families punished for the escape of their relatives who were liable for military service.[85] Violations of Article 50 of the Hague Regulations were considered as war crimes during the post-Second World War trials, although no prosecutions arose specifically for collective punishment.[86] The Nuremberg Tribunal considered that breaches of provisions of the Hague Regulations, including Article 50, 'were already recognised as war crimes under international law', a proposition that 'is too well settled to admit of argument'.[87] The UNGA affirmed the principles of international law set out in the Nuremberg Charter and Judgment,[88] although an attempt to include collective penalties as a grave breach of the Geneva Conventions failed on the basis that offences 'of varying degrees of gravity' should not be treated as grave breaches, given that some acts of collective punishment could be 'less serious' than others.[89] Nevertheless, the International Law Commission's 1991 Draft Code of Crimes against the Peace and Security of Mankind treated collective punishment as 'an exceptionally serious war crime',[90] and the Commission felt by 1996 that such a war crime also applied in NIAC.[91] A 1974 UN General Assembly Declaration stated that collective punishment is a form of repression that 'shall be considered criminal'.[92]

Proposals of the Preparatory Committee for the Establishment of an International Criminal Court had favoured the inclusion of collective punishment as a war crime in the Statute,[93] although it was excluded from both the draft submitted to the 1998 Rome Conference[94] and Article 8 of the final ICC Statute. Adriaan Bos, a chair of the Preparatory Committee, attributed the omission to states 'involved in annexation or occupation of "foreign" territory'.[95] Although Article 8 of the Statute is exhaustive in terms of war crimes over which the ICC has jurisdiction, the Statute cannot be interpreted as 'limiting or prejudicing in any way existing or developing rules of international law for purposes other than this Statute'.[96] The adoption of an amendment to include war crimes concerning the

---

[85] *Violations of the Laws and Customs of War: Reports of the Majority and Dissenting Reports of American and Japanese Members of the Commission of Responsibilities, Conference of Paris, 1919*, at 16–19, 44.

[86] See *In re Kappler*, above n 19; *In re Rauter*, above n 44; *United States of America v Wilhelm List et al*, Judgment, 19 February 1948, Case No 7, XI *Trials of War Criminals before the Nuremberg Military Tribunals under Control Council Law No 10*, at 757.

[87] Nuremberg judgment, above n 4, at 248. See also *United States of America v Wilhelm List*, above n 86, at 1239.

[88] UNGA Res 95(I), 11 December 1946.   [89] Final Record, vol II-B, at 118.

[90] Art 22(2)(a) Draft Code of Crimes against the Peace and Security of Mankind, *Report of the Commission to the General Assembly on the Work of its Forty-third Session* (1991), vol II, Part 2, *Yearbook of the International Law Commission*, UN Doc A/CN.4/SER.A/1991/Add.1 (Part 2), at 104–5.

[91] Art 20(f)(ii) *Report of the Commission on the Work of its Forty-eighth Session* (1996), vol II, Part 2, *Yearbook of the International Law Commission*, UN Doc. A/CN.4/SER.A/1996/Add.1 (Part 2), at 53–4.

[92] UNGA Res 3318 (XXIX), *Declaration on the Protection of Women and Children in Emergency and Armed Conflict*, 14 December 1974.

[93] See, e.g., *Report of the Preparatory Committee on the Establishment of an International Criminal Court*, UN Doc A/51/22, vol II, (1996), at 61, 63.

[94] Draft Statute for the International Criminal Court, Art 5, *Report of the Preparatory Committee on the Establishment of an International Criminal Court, Addendum*, UN Doc A/CONF.183/2/Add.1, 14 April 1998.

[95] In conversation with the author, July 2004.   [96] Art 10 ICC Statute.

use of certain prohibited weapons in NIAC at the 2010 Kampala Review Conference[97] demonstrates that the enumeration of war crimes in Article 8 is not unalterable. A number of states provide for the war crime of collective punishment in national legislation or military manuals.[98] Acts amounting to collective punishment may be punishable in and of themselves as war crimes, or possibly even as crimes against humanity. Djamchid Momtaz considers that a non-individual punitive sanction 'incontestably violates the provisions of common Article 3', violations of which are treated as war crimes by the ICC Statute.[99] Amnesty International considers that practices of collective punishment can amount to crimes against humanity.[100] That being said, there may be instances where the underlying acts may not be criminal,[101] and accordingly such collective punishment would fall outside the jurisdiction of the ICC.

29   Contemporary ICL jurisprudence on collective punishment comes primarily from the prosecutions of the war crime before the SCSL, which was primarily focused on crimes occurring in a NIAC. The SCSL Statute does not define the war crime of collective punishment, nor is it accompanied by 'Elements of Crimes' as is the ICC Statute, and one commentator has stated that '[n]owhere is there greater silence than on the definition of collective punishments'.[102] The SCSL Appeals Chamber put forward its own elements of the war crime of collective punishment:

> the indiscriminate punishment imposed collectively on persons for omissions or acts for which some or none of them may or may not have been responsible;
>
> the specific intent of the perpetrator to punish collectively.[103]

30   The SCSL Appeals Chamber also sought to distinguish collective punishments from attacks on civilians:

> The targeting of protected persons as objects of war crimes and crimes against humanity may not necessarily be predicated upon a perceived transgression by such persons and therefore does not constitute collective punishments. Thus, the mens rea element of collective punishments represents the critical difference between this crime and the act of targeting. While targeting takes place on account of who the victims are, or are perceived to be, the crime of collective punishments occurs in response to the acts or omissions of protected persons, whether real or perceived. The targeting of protected persons who are residents of a particular village, for instance, is therefore distinct from the collective punishment of protected persons in a given village who are perceived to have committed a particular act, such as providing rebel forces with shelter.[104]

31   In defining the elements of the war crime of collective punishments, several Chambers of the SCSL cited with approval the view of the ICRC, as expressed in various commentaries,

---

[97] Resolution RC/Res.5, 10 June 2010.
[98] See ICRC CIHL Database, Practice Relating to Rule 103.
[99] D. Momtaz, 'War Crimes in Non-International Armed Conflict under the Statute of the International Criminal Court', 2 *YIHL* (1999) 177, at 183.
[100] Amnesty International, above n 50, at 89.
[101] W.A. Schabas, *The UN International Criminal Tribunals* (Cambridge: CUP 2006), at 279.
[102] S. Sivakumaran, 'War Crimes before the Special Court for Sierra Leone: Child Soldiers, Hostages, Peacekeepers and Collective Punishments', 8(4) *JICJ* (2010) 1009, at 1021.
[103] SCSL, *The Prosecutor v Moinina Fofana and Allieu Kondewa*, Appeals Chamber Judgment, SCSL-04-14-A 28 May 2008, para 224. See, however, Partially Dissenting Opinion of Honourable Justice Renate Winter, ibid, paras 44–63.
[104] SCSL, *Fofana and Kondewa*, above n 103, para 223.

that the prohibition of collective punishment should be interpreted broadly and that it extends beyond judicially sanctioned penalties.[105] This broad interpretation is important under IHL, but in the context of ICL an excessively loose definition of collective punishment could run up against the requirement under the principle of legality that penal statutes be interpreted strictly.[106]

II. State responsibility

Legal consequences for a violation of the prohibition of collective punishment include state responsibility, as well that of individual perpetrators. Such a violation was argued before the International Court of Justice (ICJ) in hearings for the *Legal Consequences of the Construction of a Wall in the Occupied Palestinian Territories Advisory Opinion*,[107] although the Court did not find a breach of Article 33 GC IV. The Hague Regulations, the Geneva Conventions, and AP I provide that High Contracting Parties are liable for reparations in the event of breaches of those treaties.[108] Individuals or states may make complaints before certain human rights bodies alleging that acts of collective punishment violate human rights norms, notwithstanding questions of the applicability of IHRL during situations of armed conflict.[109] The UN Human Rights Commission (HRComm) 'affirmed' that

> the punitive measures imposed by Israel, the occupying Power, on the Palestinian civil population, including collective punishment, border closures and severe restrictions on the movement of people and goods, arbitrary arrests and detentions, destruction of homes and vital infrastructure, including religious, educational, cultural and historical sites, led to a steep deterioration in the socio-economic conditions, perpetuating a dire humanitarian crisis throughout the Occupied Palestinian Territory, including East Jerusalem, and affirming that these punitive measures violate the International Covenant on Civil and Political Rights and the International Covenant on Economic, Social and Cultural Rights.[110]

The UN Human Rights Committee (HRCttee) considered that Israel, as a state party to the International Covenant on Civil and Political Rights, should 'cease its practice of collective punitive home and property demolitions'.[111] British practices of collective punishment in Cyprus have been scrutinized under the European Convention on Human Rights,[112] while violations of the right to private and family life have been found and reparations ordered by the European Court of Human Rights in relation to property destruction by the Turkish military.[113] In condemning practices of collective punishment in the Occupied Palestinian Territories, the UNGA has reaffirmed the obligations of High Contracting Parties to the Geneva Conventions, including in relation to penal sanctions, and demanded 'that Israel, the occupying Power, comply fully with the provisions of

---

[105] See SCSL, *The Prosecutor v Norman, Fofana and Kondewa*, Trial Chamber Decision on Motion for Judgment of Acquittal pursuant to Art 98, SCSL-04-14-T, 21 October 2005, para 117; SCSL, *The Prosecutor v Brima, Kamara and Kanu* Trial Chamber Judgment, SCSL-2004-16-T, 20 June 2007, paras 680–81.
[106] See S. Darcy, 'Prosecuting the War Crime of Collective Punishment; Is it Time to Amend the Rome Statute?', 8 *JICJ* (2010) 29, at 40–6.
[107] ICJ, Public Sitting, 23 February 2004, Verbatim Record, CR 2004/1, at 51.
[108] Art 3 Hague Regulations; Art 91 AP I.   [109] See Ch 35 of this volume.
[110] HRComm Res 2005/7, 14 April 2005, Preamble.
[111] HRCttee, *Concluding Observations of the Human Rights Committee: Israel*, CCPR/C/ISR/CO/3, 3 September 2010, para 17.
[112] For an account, see Simpson, above n 45, at 931–1019.
[113] See, e.g., ECtHR, *Akdivar and others v Turkey*, App No 21893/93, Judgment, 16 September 1996.

the Fourth Geneva Convention of 1949 and cease immediately all measures and actions taken in violation and in breach of the Convention'.[114]

E. Critical Assessment

34 The prohibition of collective punishment remains an important IHL rule, applicable to all armed conflicts as a matter of both treaty and customary international law. The relevant provisions of Article 33 GC IV were included without hesitancy in the treaty, demonstrating a decisive negation by the drafters of the Geneva Conventions of any perceived lawfulness or legitimacy of wartime practices of collective punishment. Both civilians and POWs are protected from collective punishment, and subsequent legal developments have seen the prohibition extended to NIAC and designated as a punishable war crime under ICL. The wording of Article 33 paragraph 1 GC IV is to be read in light of the slight revisions to the formulation of the prohibition of collective punishment in the Additional Protocols, and can also be supplemented by both IHRL and ICL. The ICRC has consistently advocated that an overly restrictive reading of the prohibition of collective punishment be avoided, correctly insisting that it extends beyond official sanctions or judicially approved punishments. To distinguish collective punishments from other collective measures, such as attacks on civilians or mass expulsions, the element of punishment is key, and it implies that the measures taken are in response to a prior unlawful or hostile act, and for the purpose of punishing a group from within which such an act was committed. This interpretation can be accommodated within the broad reading favoured by the ICRC and should limit any tendency to categorize any unlawful collective measure against protected persons as collective punishment. It bears repeating that the prohibition of collective penalties in Article 33 paragraph 1 GC IV is one of three prohibitions in the provision, the other two being 'measures of intimidation or terrorism'.

35 The range of measures comprising collective punishments is considerable, with practice revealing property destruction, murder of civilians, detention, prolonged curfews, and inhuman treatment amongst others. The use of economic sanctions by states or international organizations can have an adverse impact on the rights or welfare of the general population,[115] and if undertaken by a party to an armed conflict, the prohibition of collective punishment may come into play. Economic sanctions specifically aimed at a civilian population in response to the commission of hostile acts may amount to acts of collective punishment.[116] If such measures are imposed by an Occupying Power, this might also contravene other obligations under IHL, such as the prohibition of measures of intimidation, the rule against starvation, and the duty of 'ensuring the food and medical supplies of the population'.[117]

---

[114] UNGA Res 66/79, 12 January 2012, para 3.

[115] See, e.g., D. Peksen, 'Better or Worse? The Effect of Economic Sanctions on Human Rights', 46 *Journal of Peace Research* (2009) 59–77; J. Matam Farrell, *United Nations Sanctions and the Rule of Law* (Cambridge: CUP, 2007).

[116] See, however, A. Bell, 'A Critique of the Goldstone Report and its Treatment of International Humanitarian Law', 104 *ASIL Proceedings* (2010) 79, at 80–1. See also A. Cohen, 'Economic Sanctions in IHL: Suggested Principles', 42 *Israel Law Review* (2009) 117, at 128–32.

[117] Art 33 para 1 GC IV; Art 54 AP I; Art 55 GC IV.

36 The classification of collective punishment as a war crime in the ICTR and SCSL Statutes represents an important development from the perspective of the enforcement of IHL rules. The SCSL jurisprudence is a useful source for determining the contours of the war crime of collective punishment. It is regrettable that such a war crime has not been included in the ICC Statute, particularly in light of the permanent nature of the institution when compared with its temporary counterparts. War crimes in the ICC Statute also tend to be defined with suitable precision so as to avoid any conflict with the principle of legality. This is clearly desirable in the case of collective punishment, given the various forms that the breaches of this prohibition in IHL have taken.

SHANE DARCY

Chapter 57. The Right to Leave

	MN
A. Introduction	1
B. Meaning and Application	6
I. Historical overview and rationale of the right to leave	6
II. Denial of the right to leave	8
a. The scope and meaning of 'national interest'	8
b. Enforcing the denial of applications to leave	13
III. Procedural aspects of decisions regarding applications to leave	16
IV. Conditions and costs of departure	19
V. Special cases of repatriation in occupied territory	23
VI. The relevance of other international legal regimes	26
a. The right to leave of persons falling outside the scope of international humanitarian law	26
b. International refugee law	30
C. Relevance in Non-International Armed Conflicts	31
D. Legal Consequences of a Violation	34
E. Critical Assessment	39

Select Bibliography

Gowlland-Debbas, V. (ed), *The Problem of Refugees in the Light of Contemporary International Law Issues* (The Hague: Martinus Nijhoff Publishers, 1994)

Juss, S., 'Free Movement and the World Order', 16 *IJRL* (2004) 289

Kochenov, D., 'The Right to Leave Any Country Including Your Own in International Law', 28 *Connecticut JIL* (2012–13) 43

Murphy, S.D./Kidane, W./Snider, T.R., *Litigating War: Mass Civil Injury and the Eritrea–Ethiopia Claims Commission* (New York: OUP, 2013)

Pictet Commentary GC IV, at 234–76

Sassòli, M., 'The Approach of the Eritrea–Ethiopia Claims Commission towards the Treatment of Protected Persons in International Humanitarian Law', in A. de Guttry, H.G. Post, and G. Venturini (eds), *The 1998–2000 War between Eritrea and Ethiopia* (The Hague: T.M.C. Asser Press, 2009) 341

A. Introduction

Freedom of movement is one of the cornerstones of human liberty and a condition for the free development of a person; other fundamental rights depend on it.[1] Denying civilians the right to move freely within and outside the borders of belligerent territory has become a significant issue during war. Particularly, the right of civilians to leave the territory is a

---

[1] S. Juss, 'Free Movement and the World Order', 16 *IJRL* (2004) 289, at 291; HRCttee, General Comment 27, Freedom of Movement (Art 12), 2 November 1999, para 1; D. Kochenov, 'The Right to Leave Any Country Including Your Own in International Law', 28 *Connecticut JIL* (2012–13) 43.

central component of their liberty and freedom of movement, and is the primary focus of this chapter.

2   The right to leave is firmly entrenched in international law.[2] The right is also enshrined in Geneva Convention (GC) IV, the applicable rules of which depend on a number of factors, including the classification of the conflict and whether the territory is occupied or not. In an international armed conflict (IAC), Articles 35–37 and 48 GC IV establish when protected persons, as defined in Article 4, may avail themselves of the right to leave. Articles 35–37 apply to foreigners on a party's own non-occupied territory or to civilians on enemy territory, and Article 48 applies to civilians whose territory is occupied. Conversely, the international humanitarian law (IHL) rules on non-international armed conflict (NIAC) say very little about the right of civilians to leave the territory where a NIAC is taking place. Yet such civilians may be protected by international human rights law (IHRL).

3   The right to leave is not an absolute right; it is restricted in the case of convicted criminals and those attempting to evade prosecution or other civil duties.[3] In armed conflicts, further limitations apply. Under Article 35 GC IV, all protected persons are entitled to leave the territory at the outset of or during a conflict, unless their departure is 'contrary to the national interests of the State'. Article 35 also establishes the procedures for deciding on applications to leave the territory, and Articles 36 and 37 set out the conditions for and details of departures. In occupied territory, protected persons who are not nationals of the Power whose territory is occupied may avail themselves of the right to leave under Article 48, subject to the conditions in Article 35.

4   State practice demonstrates broader limitations on the right to leave, which arguably go beyond the circumstances envisioned in GC IV: as a matter of national sovereignty, states are adamant about maintaining control over the entry, exit, and free movement of people within their borders, as 'no state will accept another's dictate as to what constitutes national interest, especially in time of war'.[4] For instance, restrictions are applied to civilians in possession of military secrets who have nearly, but not yet, reached military age, who do not possess a visa to enter another state, and who are financially indebted to the state.[5] As a result, some question whether the right to leave is really a 'right' and, if so, whether it may be realized in an international law context, outside of a state's domestic constitutional domain.[6] Conversely, since the Cold War and collapse of the Soviet Union, the right to leave is increasingly recognized in the national legislation of states, in countless international legal instruments, and a growing body of state practice defines in more detail when the right may be realized during armed conflict.[7]

5   Since the drafting of the Geneva Conventions, this tension has led to a number of contemporary and contentious legal issues under IHL, discussed in this chapter. Such issues include: reasons for denying the right to leave; enforcing denial of the right to leave; the

---

[2] See, e.g., Art 12 ICCPR, Art 10 CRC (1989); Art 13 UDHR (1948); Art 5 CERD (1965).
[3] G. Goodwin-Gill, 'The Right to Leave, the Right to Return and the Question of a Right to Remain', in V. Gowlland-Debbas (ed), *The Problem of Refugees in the Light of Contemporary International Law Issues* (The Hague: Martinus Nijhoff Publishers, 1994) 93, at 96.
[4] R.W. Gehring, 'Loss of Civilian Protections under the Fourth Geneva Convention and Protocol I', 90 *Military Law Review* (1980) 49, at 84.
[5] Goodwin-Gill, above n 3, at 96.   [6] Ibid, at 98.
[7] K. Hailbronner, 'Comments On: The Right to Leave, the Right to Return and the Question of a Right to Remain', in Gowlland-Debbas (ed), above n 3, 109.

procedural aspects of decisions regarding applications to leave; the conditions and costs of departure for persons permitted to leave; and the applicability of other international legal regimes, specifically for persons who are not protected persons under Article 4, or, who, under Article 48, are nationals of the Power whose territory is occupied.

B. Meaning and Application

I. Historical overview and rationale of the right to leave

6 During the Second World War, civilians were repatriated reciprocally through diplomatic channels or with the assistance of Protecting Powers.[8] For example, in 1942, more than 2,000 civilians—of British, French, and German nationality—were permitted to return home through exchanges.[9] Others, including 28,000 Italians, were permitted (by Great Britain) to return home without any condition of reciprocity.[10] The Articles in GC IV on the right to leave were drafted in light of such practices.

7 According to the Pictet Commentary, Article 35 enables the departure of protected persons 'who may desire to leave the territory', but does not stipulate their destination.[11] Thus, such persons may return to their home or a third country. Importantly, the phrase, 'desire to leave', implies that protected persons may not be repatriated against their will, nor may they be forcefully expelled to a country where they risk persecution.[12] The latter principle is non-derogable and a cornerstone of international refugee law, which may provide complementary protection.[13] In light of this, it is shocking that the Eritrea–Ethiopia Claims Commission (EECC) found that belligerents are granted broad powers to expel enemy nationals during an IAC,[14] and that Eritrea was within its right as a belligerent to enforce the departure of thousands of Ethiopian civilians.[15]

II. Denial of the right to leave

a. *The scope and meaning of 'national interest'*

8 As the right to leave is not unconditional, Article 35 GC IV allows a state to deny the right to an individual who is neither involved in nor suspected of hostile activity, if that person's departure is contrary to the state's 'national interest'.[16] According to the Pictet Commentary, this is a reflection of states typically refusing to repatriate certain classes of civilians, including those of an age to bear arms (from 16 to 60 years old) and those whose departure would threaten the security of the state.[17]

9 The term 'national interest', adopted in the Convention, is broader than 'security considerations', which was included in the Tokyo and Stockholm Drafts and rejected at the Diplomatic Conference.[18] Thus, belligerents are entitled to object to a protected person's

---

[8] Pictet Commentary GC IV, at 234.
[9] Ibid. [10] Ibid.
[11] This principle applies to all protected persons under Art 4 GC IV, except for civilian internees covered by Art 132 GC IV.
[12] Pictet Commentary GC IV, at 235. See also in this volume Ch 58 and Ch 51, section B.II.d, for the refusal to be repatriated.
[13] See below section B.VI.b and Ch 58 of this volume.
[14] EECC, *Civilian Claims—Eritrea's Claims 15, 16, 23, and 27–32*, Partial Award, 17 December 2004, Part VIII; Ch 58, MN 103–108, of this volume.
[15] EECC, *Civilian Claims—Ethiopia's Claim 5*, Partial Award, 17 December 2004, para 121.
[16] Gehring, above n 4, at 84. [17] Pictet Commentary GC IV, at 236. [18] Ibid.

departure in quite broad and discretionary terms, not only for security reasons, but also, for example, if the national economy would suffer.[19] Consequently, 'national interest' may include virtually any sphere that increases a belligerent's own state power or compromises that of its enemy.[20] Further, in light of the 'war on terror', 'national interest' is increasingly invoked to restrict individual rights.[21] Thus, according to the Commentary, states must 'safeguard the basic principle by showing moderation and only invoking these reservations when reasons of the utmost urgency so demand'.[22]

10 Denying the departure of a protected person must therefore occur in only the most extreme circumstances, as an exception to the rule. The interpretation of the EECC of the meaning and scope of 'national interest' is therefore controversial.[23] The Commission referred to legal scholarship to interpret the term as preventing the departure of residents suitable for military service or who might assist the adverse party's war efforts.[24] Ethiopia's internment of 85 Eritrean students was therefore justified under Article 35, as the students were of military age and Ethiopia could reasonably have feared that they would return to Eritrea to join the armed forces.[25]

11 The Commission's decision is problematic for numerous reasons. First, belligerents may intern civilians only as one of the most severe measures of control.[26] Internment is not justified merely because a person is of enemy nationality or of military age.[27] Such an interpretation could result in the internment of most adults of enemy nationality, which runs contrary to the object and purpose of GC IV.[28] Although Article 35 permits a state to deny the right to leave in the 'national interest', it does not justify internment on the same grounds.[29] The legal basis of internment must be justified under Article 42 GC IV, and only if 'the security of the Detaining Power makes it absolutely necessary'.[30] Further, IHL expressly prohibits the deprivation of liberty on a collective basis.[31] The security reasons justifying internment must be connected to the individual.[32]

12 Any limitations of GC IV must be interpreted in good faith and in light of its object and purpose.[33] While denying applications to leave may restrict the rights of certain groups (including those of military age or who may join enemy forces), if 'national interest' is interpreted broadly, virtually all adults of enemy nationality could be denied the right to leave. This again runs contrary to the purpose of the Convention, which is to protect

---

[19] Ibid. The Commentary uses the example of countries of immigration, where the departure of a large number of aliens might cause economic hardships; other examples include highly skilled workers engaged in vital national defence projects, such as weapons research: Gehring, above n 4, at 85.
[20] Gehring, above n 4, at 85.
[21] Kochenov uses Guantánamo Bay as an extreme but important example to illuminate the fundamental issues that correspond to and are often infringed simultaneously with the right to leave and freedom of movement. British Control Orders have also been invoked to curtail the freedom of suspected terrorists (placing a number of conditions on the suspected person) without any evidence to prosecute them: Kochenov, above n 1, at 69–70.
[22] Pictet Commentary GC IV, at 236.   [23] EECC, *Eritrea's Claims 15, 16, 23, and 27–32*, above n 14.
[24] Ibid, para 116.   [25] Ibid, para 117.   [26] Pictet Commentary GC IV, at 257.
[27] Pictet Commentary GC IV, at 258 and fn 1; M. Sassòli, 'The Approach of the Eritrea–Ethiopia Claims Commission towards the Treatment of Protected Persons in International Humanitarian Law', in A. de Guttry, H.G. Post, and G. Venturini (eds), *The 1998–2000 War Between Eritrea and Ethiopia* (The Hague: T.M.C. Asser Press, 2009) 341, at 345.
[28] Sassòli, above n 27.   [29] Ibid.   [30] See Ch 64, section B.I.a, of this volume.
[31] Art 33 GC IV; Art 75(2)(d) AP I; Ch 64 of this volume, at MN 26: ICTY, *The Prosecutor v Zejnil Delalić et al*, Trial Chamber Judgment, IT-96-21-T, 16 November 1998, at 583.
[32] Sassòli, above n 27, at 345.   [33] Kochenov, above n 1, at 64; Art 31 VCLT.

b. Enforcing the denial of applications to leave

Protected persons denied permission to leave under Article 35 (or Article 48) GC IV may be left at liberty within the territory of the state.[35] However, to enforce denial of the right to leave, GC IV permits confinement as an alternative,[36] but in only two circumstances and as an extreme measure. First, under Article 37, on a belligerent's own, non-occupied territory, protected persons may be prosecuted for violating the laws of the belligerent state and 'confined pending proceedings or serving a sentence involving loss of liberty'. Under Article 76, protected persons convicted of crimes may be detained and serve out their sentences on occupied territory. Secondly, Article 42 permits belligerents to intern or place protected persons in assigned residence for security reasons if 'absolutely necessary'. Similarly, in occupied territory and for 'imperative reasons of security', belligerents may intern protected persons under Article 78.

Importantly, Article 37 provides that protected persons must be humanely treated during their confinement, and upon their release they may apply to leave the territory. Article 76 provides for similar protections for protected persons detained in occupied territories, where 'treatment [...] must take into account the principles of humanity and respect for human dignity'. Neither Article defines what humane treatment is, yet Article 27 GC IV, Article 75 of Additional Protocol (AP) I, and Common Article 3 provide minimum guarantees. Further, the treatment of internees must be interpreted in light of IHRL, which provides important details on the standards of treatment for internees during armed conflict.[37]

The foregoing Articles were violated during the Ethiopian–Eritrean war when Eritrea allegedly detained Ethiopian civilians in extremely poor conditions. Ethiopian civilians were held in police stations, jails, and prisons, and were subjected to physical and psychological abuse, and to substandard living, sanitary, and health conditions.[38] Prisoners were beaten, and some reports indicated the intentional killings of prisoners by Eritrean guards.[39] The Commission found that such inhumane conditions were contrary to Articles 27 and 37 GC IV.[40]

III. Procedural aspects of decisions regarding applications to leave

Applications to leave must be decided in accordance with 'regularly established procedures', whereby a number of safeguards must be established to prevent arbitrary decisions under Article 35 GC IV. First, the conditions of departure must be transparent.[41] States are given discretion to appoint a responsible authority, so long as decisions are objective, thorough, and made as rapidly as possible.[42] Such decisions must ensure that protected persons

---

[34] Kochenov, above n 1, at 69; Gehring, above n 4, at 86; see also Ch 64 of this volume.
[35] S.D. Murphy, W. Kidane, and T.R. Snider, *Litigating War: Mass Civil Injury and the Eritrea–Ethiopia Claims Commission* (New York: OUP, 2013).
[36] Ibid.
[37] See Ch 65 of this volume; ICRC CIHL Database, Rule 87.
[38] EECC, *Ethiopia's Claim 5*, above n 15, paras 79 and 81.   [39] Ibid, para 78.
[40] Ibid, paras 77–82, Findings of Liability for Violation of International Law, paras 5–6.
[41] Pictet Commentary GC IV, at 236.   [42] Ibid.

are given an opportunity to submit their application and the grounds on which they wish to leave, which must be weighed fairly against the legitimate interests of the state.[43]

17   Article 35 paragraph 2 contains a right of appeal for persons refused permission to leave the territory. Either an appropriate court or an administrative board must reconsider the refusal as soon as possible. While some countries during the Second World War set up administrative procedures, others set up special courts for aliens.[44] The system therefore offers states a choice between administrative or judicial procedures to accommodate what is already in place.[45] Rules of procedure are left to the government's discretion, and may be oral or written.[46] In essence, protected persons must have the widest possible facilities to plead their case.[47] Accordingly, as adopted by various states during the Second World War, governments may extend their facilities beyond the minimum requirements in Article 35 GC IV.[48]

18   Article 35 paragraph 3 provides safeguards for protected persons denied permission to leave, where, upon request, the Protecting Power may receive reasons for a negative decision and the names of all persons denied permission to leave. This safeguard makes it possible for such persons to provide information to their families and the authorities in their home country, ultimately preventing arbitrary treatment by the Detaining Power.[49] The obligation to provide the Protecting Power with such information is limited in two ways. The Detaining Power may withhold information, first, if protected persons do not want the authorities in their home country to know their whereabouts and, secondly, if the Detaining Power has legitimate state interests and security reasons against providing such information.

IV. Conditions and costs of departure

19   For civilians granted permission to leave, Article 36 GC IV includes a number of safeguards applicable to individual and group departures, which must be carried out under satisfactory conditions regarding safety, hygiene, sanitation, and food. According to the Commentary, at the outbreak of or during war, conditions of departure will vary depending on the means of transport and the economic situation of a country.[50] In any case, states are to 'take all necessary precautions to avoid endangering the life and health of the protected persons and to ensure their journey takes place under satisfactory conditions'.[51]

20   Despite economic hardship and devastation due to war, the EECC found both Eritrea and Ethiopia liable for failing to meet the minimum humanitarian standards under Articles 35 and 36 GC IV. Ethiopia failed to ensure the humane and safe treatment of Eritreans during their departure, as civilians were exposed to extreme heat, overcrowding, food and water shortages, and other physically inhumane conditions.[52] Eritrea was similarly held liable for failing to provide humane conditions of transport for Ethiopians, as deportees were transported under harsh, hazardous, and sometimes fatal conditions.[53]

21   Under Article 35 paragraph 1, civilians entitled to leave may take the 'necessary funds for their journey' and a 'reasonable amount of their effects and articles of personal use'. What is 'reasonable' includes the personal effects and articles those persons can carry during their journey.[54] This provision was put in place to ensure that protected persons are

---

[43] Ibid, at 237.   [44] Ibid.   [45] Ibid.   [46] Ibid, at 238.   [47] Ibid.
[48] Ibid.   [49] Ibid.   [50] Ibid, at 239.   [51] Ibid, at 240.
[52] EECC, *Eritrea's Claims 15, 16, 23, and 27–32*, above n 14, paras 99–106.
[53] EECC, *Ethiopia's Claim 5*, above n 15, paras 130–1.   [54] Pictet Commentary GC IV, at 237.

not prevented from making use of the right to leave by being denied adequate resources.[55] Such was the case when Ethiopians were expelled from Eritrea without an opportunity to collect their property or arrange their affairs, which was a violation of Article 35.[56] Although short notice to collect property or arrange affairs, or even instances of interference by officials, will not be sufficient to violate Article 35,[57] the Commission found that Eritrean officials wrongfully seized and interfered with Ethiopians attempting to leave in cases of 'forcible evictions from homes that were thereafter sealed or looted, blocked bank accounts, forced closure of businesses followed by confiscation, and outright seizure of personal property by the police'.[58]

Normally, the cost of transportation is the responsibility of the individual concerned. However, historically, financial difficulties during wartime have delayed or prevented protected persons from leaving, depriving them of the right entirely.[59] In such cases, all costs of travel are to be borne by the country of destination or the country of nationality.[60] The cost of travel to the frontier of the Detaining Power is the responsibility of protected persons, or, if circumstances demand, of the country of residence.[61] In times of war, civilians may be required to go through a number of bureaucratic processes, including clearances before obtaining exit permits, fees, and taxes, before being permitted to leave.[62]

V. Special cases of repatriation in occupied territory

Under Article 48 GC IV, protected persons who are not nationals of the Power whose territory is occupied may have a right to leave. In accordance with Article 4, Article 48 applies to aliens in occupied territory, including nationals of belligerent and neutral countries (without normal diplomatic relations), and stateless persons or those whose nationality is doubtful.[63] Conversely, nationals of the occupied country or of the Occupying Power and its allies are not covered.[64] Those entitled to leave under Article 48 are subject to the conditions of Article 35, including the procedures and limitations for reasons of 'national interest'.

In contrast to the courts appointed to consider applications to leave under Article 35 GC IV, such courts do not already exist in occupied territory and must be set up by the Occupying Power. This difference is important, as deportation of protected persons from occupied territory is forbidden under Article 49. The Occupying Power cannot use courts already established on its own territory but must institute a procedure in the occupied territory for applications to leave.

Under legislation adopted by Israel as an Occupying Power, departure from occupied territories is restricted and there is no general right to exit.[65] Exit permits have been granted to residents of the territories to go to Israel, but not necessarily beyond the borders to other countries.[66] In practice, if such civilians are granted permission to leave the territories, their freedom of movement is restricted to within Israel's borders. However, Article 48 does not say otherwise; any national of the Power whose territory is occupied

---

[55] Ibid. [56] EECC, *Ethiopia's Claim 5*, above n 15, paras 133–4. [57] Ibid, para 134.
[58] Ibid, para 135. [59] Pictet Commentary GC IV, at 240. [60] Ibid. [61] Ibid.
[62] EECC, *Ethiopia's Claim 5*, above n 15, paras 67–8.
[63] Pictet Commentary GC IV, at 276. [64] Ibid.
[65] This is discussed extensively in Y. Zilbershats, 'The Right to Leave Israel and its Restriction on Security Grounds', 28 *Israel Law Review* (1994) 626.
[66] Ibid, at 674–9.

is not permitted to leave under IHL. According to Zilbershats, 'this situation is unacceptable, particularly since belligerent occupation has lasted for a long period of time'.[67] This circumstance highlights the importance of applying IHRL,[68] discussed in the following section, as 'there is nothing to prevent also granting the right to leave to residents of the territories who are citizens of the power from which the territory was taken [...] such an approach would not involve any harm to state security'.[69]

VI. The relevance of other international legal regimes

a. The right to leave of persons falling outside the scope of international humanitarian law

26 As the provisions in the Geneva Conventions do not exist in a vacuum, an important consideration in interpreting the right to leave under IHL is the other obligations of the parties to the treaty.[70] Several IHRL instruments provide for the freedom of movement or the right to leave.[71] Most importantly, the right to leave under IHRL, namely Article 12 of the International Covenant on Civil and Political Rights (ICCPR), applies to everyone, including citizens and illegal aliens, and is a right to leave any country, including one's own.[72]

27 Article 12 ICCPR continues to apply during wartime and in occupied territories,[73] although it may be derogated from during public emergencies that threaten the life of a nation (Article 4)[74] and is limited by Article 12(3), which permits states to restrict the right to leave in exceptional circumstances.[75] Thus, for civilians who are not protected persons or not protected by Article 48 GC IV, as they are nationals of a party whose territory is occupied, IHRL may apply.[76] According to the United Nations (UN) Human Rights Committee (HRCttee), it would be a clear violation of the Covenant if the rights enshrined in Article 12 were restricted by distinctions of any kind, including national origin.[77] Thus, unlike IHL, which limits the right to leave on the basis of nationality to protected persons, the Covenant applies to every person.

28 According to the HRCttee, the limitations under the ICCPR on the right to leave must not nullify the principle of the liberty of movement and are governed by strict

---

[67] Ibid, at 679.

[68] As noted by the EECC, 'customary law concerning the protection of human rights remains in force during armed conflicts, enjoying particular relevance in any situations involving persons who may not be protected fully by international humanitarian law, as with a Party's acts affecting its own nationals': *Ethiopia's Claim 5*, above n 15, para 28.

[69] Zilbershats, above n 65, at 679.

[70] Ch 51, MN 33, of this volume; Art 31(3)(c) VCLT.

[71] For more on regional and international instruments on the right to leave, see C. Harvey and R.P. Barnidge, 'Right to Leave in International Law', 19 *IJRL* (2007) 1; Kochenov, above n 1.

[72] HRCttee, above n 1, para 8.

[73] See in general ICJ, *Legal Consequences of the Construction of a Wall in the Occupied Palestinian Territories*, Advisory Opinion, 9 July 2004.

[74] For a thorough discussion of how the right to leave may be restricted in occupied territories, see Zilbershats, above n 65.

[75] Ibid, at 661.

[76] For a nuanced analysis of the interplay between IHRL and IHL, see M. Sassòli and L. Olson, 'The Relationship between International Humanitarian Law and Human Rights Law Where it Matters: Admissible Killing and Internment of Fighters in Non-International Armed Conflict', 90 *IRRC* 871 (2008) 599; see also Ch 35 of this volume.

[77] HRCttee, above n 1, para 18.

requirements, including for reasons of national security, public order, public health or morals, and the rights and freedoms of others.[78] Restrictions must be based on clear legal grounds, precise criteria, and may not confer unfettered discretion on those charged with their execution.[79] Restrictions must also meet the test of necessity and requirements of proportionality,[80] and must be the 'least intrusive instrument amongst those which might achieve the desired result'.[81]

Protected persons covered by IHL, but denied the right to leave for reasons of 'national interest', may also be covered by IHRL. Restrictions under IHRL for reasons of 'national security' are narrower than those of 'national interest' under Article 35 GC IV. According to Kiss, the former includes two elements, 'national' and 'security'. The element of 'national' requires the interest of the whole nation to be at stake, which excludes interests of governments, regimes, or power groups.[82] The term 'security' may be understood in reference to its meaning under Article 2(4) of the UN Charter.[83] Thus, only if the right to leave would undermine the territorial integrity or political independence of an entire nation, may it be restricted by 'national security'.[84] However, certain acts falling outside the scope of 'national security' under IHRL may fall within other permissible restrictions under Article 12 ICCPR, such as 'public order'.[85]

b. International refugee law

Civilians caught up in armed conflict may desire to leave a country to seek asylum. Thus, during an armed conflict, restricting the refugees' right to leave must incorporate the relevant rules of IHRL and refugee law. The right to leave under international law includes the right to seek, but not to obtain, asylum or to enter another state.[86] However, arguably, if individuals are exposed to persecution or a violation of their human rights in the country of residence, there may be a duty on that state not to deny the right to leave, and on the state of asylum not to restrict admission.[87] In essence, states

> ought not to exercise their own rights to control the movement of persons, including the admission of individuals to their territory, in an 'abusive' manner, that is […] with a view to ensuring that potential refugees remain in their own country and do not find protection.[88]

This proposition is supported by the principle of non-rejection at the frontier and the prohibition on torture and cruel, inhuman and degrading treatment or punishment. Both principles are widely recognized under international refugee law, the former establishing that no person shall be subjected to rejection at the frontier (or to expulsion) if that person may be subjected to persecution or ill-treatment.[89] Both principles limit a state's ability to

---

[78] Ibid, para 11. [79] Ibid, para 13. [80] Ibid, paras 11, 15, 16. [81] Ibid, para 14.
[82] A.C. Kiss, 'Permissible Limitations on Rights', in L. Henkin (ed), *The International Bill of Rights: The Covenant on Civil and Political Rights* (New York: Columbia University Press, 1981) 290, at 290; Zilbershats, above n 65, at 628.
[83] Kiss, above n 82, at 296; Zilbershats, above n 65, at 629.
[84] Kiss, above n 82, at 296; Zilbershats, above n 65, at 629.
[85] For more on the HRCttee's examination of the scope of permissible restrictions on the right to leave, see Harvey and Barnidge, above n 71.
[86] Goodwin-Gill, above n 3, at 99; Harvey and Barnidge, above n 71.
[87] Goodwin-Gill, above n 3, at 99. [88] Ibid.
[89] UN Declaration on Territorial Asylum (1967), Art 3(1); UNHCR EXCOM, Conclusion No 6 (XXVIII), Non-refoulement, 1977, (c); ECtHR, *Chahal v United Kingdom*, Judgment, 15 November 1996, para 80.

control the entry and removal of civilians, and must be incorporated alongside IHL rules on the right to leave.[90]

C. Relevance in Non-International Armed Conflicts

31   International humanitarian law says very little on the freedom of movement of civilians within and outside the territory where a NIAC is taking place. Common Article 3 is silent on the question of movement, but does prohibit humiliating and degrading treatment, which may arguably be violated if civilians are prevented from leaving a territory where they may face ill-treatment. Article 17 of AP II prohibits compelling civilians to leave the territory for reasons connected to the conflict, and forbids the forceful displacement of civilians except for their security or imperative military reasons.[91] According to the International Committee of the Red Cross (ICRC) Commentary, the Article 'covers forced movement and does not [...] restrict the right of civilians to move about freely within the country [...] or to go abroad'.[92] Thus, it appears implicit that civilians have a general right to leave the territory; yet the scope of this right is not delineated.

32   The IHL rules applicable in NIACs do not protect civilians based on their nationality; the status of protected person and the corresponding protection regime in IACs represent a significant difference between the two regimes. The relevant IHL rules applicable in IAC provide that the right for civilians to leave is linked to nationality; thus, applying these rules by analogy to NIACs is difficult, if not counterproductive, as persons in NIACs are covered regardless of their status or nationality, the only condition being that they do not participate in hostilities. Accordingly, in the case of civilians wishing to leave the territory of a state where a NIAC is taking place, of which they are nationals, and where IHL is silent, it may be more pragmatic to apply the rules under IHRL or international refugee law (in the case of asylum seekers), which apply regardless of nationality and may provide wider protection.

33   Since IHL is virtually silent on the right of asylum seekers to leave the territory of a state where a NIAC is taking place, international refugee law provides essential protection. In particular, under international refugee law, the same rules on the right to leave apply to asylum seekers regardless of their nationality or whether the country of residence is caught up in an armed conflict (IAC or NIAC) or not. Accordingly, asylum seekers exposed to persecution or human rights violations on the territory of a state where a NIAC is taking place must not be denied the right to leave that territory, nor may they be rejected at the frontier of the country of asylum.[93]

D. Legal Consequences of a Violation

34   A state is responsible for a wrongful act or omission if it is attributable to the state under international law and it constitutes a breach of an international obligation of the state.[94] Thus, a violation of the right to leave under IHL (and IHRL), if breached by an organ of a state, is attributable to that state.[95] In interpreting a statement by Judge Roberto

---

[90] Goodwin-Gill, above n 3.
[91] See Ch 58 of this volume.   [92] ICRC Commentary APs, para 4851.
[93] See MN 30; Goodwin-Gill, above n 3.   [94] Art 2 ILC Articles on State Responsibility.
[95] Ibid, Art 4.

Ago, former International Law Commission (ILC) Rapporteur on State Responsibility, Goodwin-Gill claims

a 'primary' rule of international law, perhaps, forbids the 'abusive' exercise of rights of control over the movement of persons, rights which will be violated if certain limits are exceeded in the course of their exercise, or if they are exercised with the (sole) intention of harming others.[96]

Importantly, the EECC found both states internationally responsible for violating a number of provisions relating to the right to leave under GC IV, and ordered compensation for damages by each side in instances of violations of the law. The Commission found that both expelled persons and those who left voluntarily were entitled to compensation, as the latter did not waive their right to humane and safe treatment.[97]

The UN Compensation Commission (UNCC) was established to deal with more than 1.7 million claims resulting from the 1990–1 Iraqi invasion and occupation of Kuwait. Although the UNCC was not formally established to judge violations of IHL, it ordered monetary compensation for instances of Iraq's violation of the international law on the use of force.[98] The UNCC Governing Council gave fixed sums to hundreds of thousands of individuals who were displaced or injured,[99] including any person who, as a result of Iraq's unlawful invasion and occupation of Kuwait, departed from Iraq or Kuwait during the period 2 August 1990 to 2 March 1991.[100] Importantly, the UNCC Governing Council held Iraq liable for direct loss to foreign nationals, including individual loss resulting from the departure from or inability to leave Iraq or Kuwait.[101]

Individual criminal responsibility may flow from serious violations of IHL and grave breaches of the Geneva Conventions and AP I.[102] A direct violation of the right to leave under IHL does not necessarily give rise to individual criminal responsibility, but violations of other fundamental rights related to the right to leave may do so. For example, if, as in the case of Eritrea–Ethiopia, individuals are confined unlawfully to prevent them from leaving, this may give rise to a grave breach of GC IV.[103] Similarly, if the departure of protected persons takes place under substandard conditions, this may give rise to a grave breach of GC IV if such conditions are inhuman.[104]

According to the International Court of Justice (ICJ), if a state violates its IHRL obligations (notably Article 12 ICCPR), the responsibility of that state is engaged under international law.[105] In its Advisory Opinion on the *Legal Consequences of the Construction of a Wall in the Occupied Palestinian Territories*, the ICJ found that Israel's construction of the wall impeded the liberty of movement of the inhabitants in the Occupied Palestinian Territories, thus violating Article 12 ICCPR.[106] Consequently, Israel was legally obligated

---

[96] See R. Ago, 'Second Report on State Responsibility', UN Doc A/CN.4/233 (1970) 191, at 193, in Goodwin-Gill, above n 3, at 99.
[97] EECC, *Eritrea's Damages Claims*, Final Award, 17 August 2009, para 313.
[98] UNCC, Criteria for Expedited Processing of Urgent Claims, S/AC.26/1991/1, Decision 1, 2 August 1991, para 10; M.J. Matheson, 'The Damage Awards of Eritrea–Ethiopia Claims Commission', 9 *The Law and Practice of International Courts and Tribunals* (2010) 1, at 5.
[99] Matheson, above n 98, at 6. [100] UNCC Decision 1, above n 98, para 10.
[101] Ibid, para 18(e); UNSC Res 687 (1991).
[102] According to the ICTY Appeals Chamber, for a violation to be serious, 'it must constitute a breach of a rule protecting important values, and the breach must involve grave consequences for the victim': ICTY, *The Prosecutor v Duško Tadić*, Appeals Chamber, Decision on the Defence Motion for Interlocutory Appeal on Jurisdiction, 2 October 1995, para 94(iii).
[103] See, e.g., ICTY, *Delalić et al*, above n 31; Ch 64 of this volume. [104] Art 147 GC IV.
[105] ICJ, *Wall* Advisory Opinion, above n 73, para 147; see also Ch 58 of this volume.
[106] ICJ, *Wall* Advisory Opinion, above n 73, para 134.

to make reparations in the form of restitution to all natural and legal persons who suffered material damage as a result of the construction of the wall.[107]

E. Critical Assessment

39 The purpose of GC IV is the protection of civilians during armed conflict. Accordingly, at the time of drafting, GC IV envisioned restricting the right to leave in exceptional circumstances. Recent armed conflicts and instances of occupation, however, illuminate the questionable relevance and pragmatism of the IHL rules on the right to leave. This is particularly so in the many cases when IHL is silent on the right of civilians to leave—in NIACs, cases of occupation when a civilian is a national of the occupied Power, and in IACs when civilians are not protected persons. In such cases, it seems unjustifiable to deny individuals the right to move freely or to leave merely on the basis of their nationality; it is therefore essential to apply IHRL and international refugee law (in the case of asylum seekers) alongside IHL, which provide protection to individuals regardless of nationality.

40 States have increasingly and illegally circumvented the rights of individuals and groups to move freely and to leave belligerent territory during war. Such is the case when states interpret 'national interest' too broadly and create undue hardship for individuals to make use of the right to leave. In practice, states obstruct enjoyment of the right to leave by instigating a number of blanket prohibitions on grounds related to 'national interest' or security.[108] According to the HRCttee, such grounds include access to classified information, terrorism, and 'brain drain'—when well-trained specialists attempt to leave the territory.[109] Particularly frightening is that states increasingly invoke the 'war on terror' in order to restrict the right to leave, in turn infringing other fundamental rights and possibly committing grave breaches, such as unlawful confinement, denial of procedural safeguards, and collective punishment.[110] In light of this, suspending the right to leave must take place in only the most narrowly defined circumstances, with the minimum procedural safeguards, and only on a case-by-case basis. The right to leave is of indispensable importance; it goes to the heart of liberty and democracy, 'and should be regarded in a much broader context than the limited and practically weak reflection which it receives in international [humanitarian] law'.[111]

PAMELA ANNE HYLTON

---

[107] Ibid, paras 147–57.
[108] Kochenov, above n 1, at 69.
[109] HRCttee, above n 1, para 17; Kochenov, above n 1, at 69.
[110] Kochenov, above n 1, at 69.
[111] Ibid, at 71.

Chapter 58. The Transfer and Deportation of Civilians

	MN
A. Introduction	1
B. Meaning and Application	8
I. The prohibition of transfer and deportation in occupied territory	8
a. Rationale and key characteristics of Article 49 GC IV	8
b. The notion of forcible transfer and deportation under Article 49	12
c. The forcible character of transfer and deportation	16
d. Evacuation	20
e. The prohibition of transfer and deportation under international human rights law	26
f. The prohibition of transfer and deportation under customary international law	32
II. The prohibition of transfer in international armed conflict	36
a. Rationale and key characteristics of Article 45 GC IV	36
b. Transfer, expulsion, and extradition	41
c. The prohibition of transfer to a state not respecting the Geneva Convention	47
d. Prohibition of transfer to a state of persecution	55
e. The prohibition of transfer under international refugee law	62
f. The prohibition of transfer under international human rights law	68
C. Forced Displacement in Non-International Armed Conflict	75
I. The prohibition of forced displacement within the territory	76
II. The prohibition of forced departure outside the territory	87
D. Legal Consequences of a Violation	93
E. Critical Assessment	99

Select Bibliography

Chetail, V., 'Armed Conflict and Forced Migration: A Systemic Approach to International Humanitarian Law, Refugee Law and Human Rights Law', in A. Clapham and P. Gaeta (eds), *The Oxford Handbook of International Law in Armed Conflict* (Oxford: OUP, 2014) 700

Henckaerts, J.-M., 'Deportation and Transfer of Civilians in Time of War', 26 *Van JTL* (1993) 469

Hulme, K., 'Armed Conflict and the Displaced', 17(1) *IJRL* (2005) 91

Jacques, M., *Armed Conflict and Displacement: The Protection of Refugees and Displaced Persons under International Humanitarian Law* (Cambridge: CUP, 2012)

Meindersma, C., 'Legal Issues Surrounding Population Transfers in Conflict Situations', 41 *NILR* (1994) 31

Piotrowicz, R., 'Displacement and Displaced Persons', in E. Wilmshurst and S. Breau (eds), *Perspectives on the ICRC Study on Customary International Humanitarian Law* (Cambridge: CUP, 2007) 337

A. Introduction

The forcible transfer and deportation of civilians raise complex and ambiguous issues of international humanitarian law (IHL). Indeed, forced displacement in times of armed conflict is traversed by two contradictory driving forces. On the one hand, no one contests the fundamental value behind the right to be protected against forced transfer. As restated by the International Criminal Tribunal for the former Yugoslavia (ICTY), '[t]he prohibition against forcible displacements aims at safeguarding the right and aspiration of individuals to live in their communities and homes without outside interference'.[1] From this angle, the very term '"transfer" is a euphemism to hide the trauma of the forced separation from one's homeland and the consequent dislocation of one's identity and traditions'.[2]

2   On the other hand, forcible displacement is frequently perceived as an unfortunate, if not ineluctable, consequence of armed conflicts. The Eritrea–Ethiopia Claims Commission (EECC) even affirmed that '[t]he flight of civilians from the perceived danger of hostilities is a common, and often tragic, occurrence in warfare, but it does not, as such, give rise to liability under international humanitarian law'.[3] This assertion is doubtful, as will be demonstrated by the present chapter.

3   It is however true that IHL approaches forced displacement in a piecemeal fashion: three main sets of norms are applicable in different contexts with specific objectives. Following the typical categorization scheme of IHL, the content of each applicable rule depends on whether forced movement of civilians takes place in an occupied territory, in an international armed conflict (IAC), or in a non-international armed conflict (NIAC).

4   First, in times of occupation, Article 49 paragraph 1 of Geneva Convention (GC) IV prohibits any types of forcible transfer and deportation. This general prohibition is the logical corollary of the law of occupation which is primarily aimed at maintaining the status quo of the occupied territory. Its *raison d'être* is to make sure the Occupying Power will not change the demographic composition of the occupied territory for the purpose of colonizing it. In parallel to this general prohibition, Article 49 paragraph 6 further proscribes any transfer of its own population into the territory it occupies.[4] The duties of the Occupying Power are thus straightforward, and they operate in a two-way direction.

5   Secondly, the reach of IHL is more limited in IAC. Article 45 GC IV does not enshrine a general prohibition but a specific one, determined by reference to the state of destination: it prohibits any transfer to a state which does not respect GC IV or may persecute protected persons.

6   Thirdly, in NIACs, the protection granted by the Geneva Conventions is arguably non-existent, since Common Article 3 does not prohibit forced displacement. However, the minimum standards endorsed in Common Article 3 would likely be violated by the collective deportation of civilians.[5] In any event, its silence has been subsequently filled in by Article 17 of Additional Protocol (AP) II, which has largely been inspired by Article 49 GC IV.

---

[1] ICTY, *The Prosecutor v Milorad Krnojelac*, Appeals Chamber Judgment, IT-97-25-A, 17 September 2003, para 218.

[2] A. de Zayas, 'Forced Population Transfer', in MPEPIL.

[3] EECC, *Central Front—Ethiopia's Claim 5 between the Federal Democratic Republic of Ethiopia and the State of Eritrea*, Partial Award, Central Front, 17 December 2004, para 53.

[4] This provision is not developed in this chapter. For further discussion, see Ch 73 of this volume.

[5] See also in this sense M. Jacques, *Armed Conflict and Displacement: The Protection of Refugees and Displaced Persons under International Humanitarian Law* (Cambridge: CUP, 2012), at 51, fn 13; A.M. de Zayas, 'International Law and Mass Population Transfers', 26 *Harvard International Law Journal* (1975) 207, at 221.

Furthermore, whether forced displacement takes place in an occupied territory or within the territory of a state party to an IAC or a NIAC, GC IV and AP II are not the only source of protection for displaced persons. While analysing each of these three different scenarios, the present chapter demonstrates that, in this field as in many others, IHL has been considerably enriched and reinforced by international human rights law (IHRL), international refugee law (IRL), and international criminal law (ICL).[6]

B. Meaning and Application

I. The prohibition of transfer and deportation in occupied territory

a. Rationale and key characteristics of Article 49 GC IV

The prohibition enshrined in Article 49 paragraph 1 GC IV is clear and categorical:

> Individual or mass forcible transfers, as well as deportations of protected persons from occupied territory to the territory of the Occupying Power or to that of any other country, occupied or not, are prohibited, regardless of their motive.

This broad and inclusive prohibition entails four main characteristics: all kinds of transfer and deportation are proscribed in times of occupation irrespective of their destination, their purpose, the number of displaced persons, or even the crimes and other hostile acts they may have committed.

The destination of transfer and deportation is indeed immaterial. In contrast to Article 45 GC IV, which allows the transfer of protected persons to a party to the Convention in certain circumstances, forcible displacement is proscribed in categorical terms without regard to the location to which protected persons are actually removed. Presumably, this broad geographical scope also covers forcible transfer of civilians *within* the occupied territory. While the wording of Article 49 paragraph 1 GC IV is not crystal clear and the International Committee of the Red Cross (ICRC) Commentary is silent on this issue,[7] this interpretation is confirmed by AP I. Its Article 85(4)(a) lists among other grave breaches, 'the deportation or transfer of all or parts of the population of the occupied territory within or outside this territory, in violation of Article 49 of the Fourth Convention'. Contrary to the position of the Israeli Supreme Court,[8] the ICRC Commentary on AP I underlined that 'by using the word "nevertheless", paragraph 2 [of Article 49 which deals with evacuation] clearly shows that paragraph 1 also prohibits forcible transfers within occupied territory'.[9] This question of interpretation is thus now settled, and has been further confirmed by the Statute of the International Criminal Court (ICC).[10]

---

[6] For a similar exercise focusing on refugee protection, see V. Chetail, 'Armed Conflict and Forced Migration: A Systemic Approach to International Humanitarian Law, Refugee Law and Human Rights Law', in A. Clapham and P. Gaeta (eds), *The Oxford Handbook of International Law in Armed Conflict* (Oxford: OUP, 2014) 700.

[7] One should add that, other than recalling the historical context of its adoption, the ICRC Commentary is not particularly instructive on Art 49.

[8] See especially HC *302172, Sheikh Suleiman Abu Hilu et al v State of Israel et al*, 27(2) *Piskei Din* 169, quoted in 5 *IsrYBHR* (1975) 384, at 387.

[9] ICRC Commentary APs, at 1000, fn 28.

[10] Art 8(2)(b)(viii) ICC Statute. See also ICTY, *Krnojelac*, above n 1, para 220.

10 Among the other key characteristics of the prohibition of forcible transfer and deportation, Article 49 paragraph 1 explicitly restates that the motive is irrelevant. An illegal purpose for displacement is thus not required.[11] The general nature of the prohibition entails another substantial feature: it applies without regard to the fact that protected persons have committed crimes, sabotage, or any other activities that may represent a threat to public order or national security.[12]

11 Lastly, as underlined by the text of Article 49 paragraph 1, no distinction is made between individual or collective deportation and forcible transfer. Both are prohibited, irrespective of the number of protected persons who are forcibly transferred or deported. This specification would not have raised further comments had the Israeli Supreme Court not developed a very peculiar interpretation. According to the Court, Article 49 paragraph 1 would be limited only to mass deportations of the kind carried out by the Nazis, and would not prohibit individual deportation for reasons of public order and security.[13] Such a reading is patently biased and, as underlined by the great majority of the doctrine,[14] does not conform to the ordinary reading of Article 49 paragraph 1 in due accordance with its object and purpose.

b. The notion of forcible transfer and deportation under Article 49

12 Given the broad and inclusive scope of Article 49 paragraph 1 GC IV, the decisive factor triggering the applicability of the prohibition contained therein relies on the very notions of forcible transfer and deportation. However, their respective meanings have raised considerable and longstanding debates. There are two different interpretations: for some, forcible transfer and deportation are two distinctive notions,[15] whereas others consider that they are largely the same.[16] In fact, each interpretation may invoke some valid arguments. On the one hand, by referring explicitly and distinctively to 'forcible transfers, as well as

---

[11] Y. Arai-Takahashi, *The Law of Occupation. Continuity and Change of International Humanitarian Law, and its Interaction with International Human Rights Law* (Leiden/Boston, Mass: Martinus Nijhoff Publishers, 2009), at 329.

[12] It is however sometimes argued that Art 49 does not apply to the expulsion of infiltrators who are non-citizens of the occupied territory and endanger public security in the territory: Y. Dinstein, 'The Israeli Supreme Court and the Law of Belligerent Occupation: Deportation', 23 *IsrYBHR* (1993) 1, at 18; HC 454/85 etc, *Gtwarawi et al v Minister of Defence et al*, 39(3) *Piskei Din* 401, at 410 and 412, 16 *IsrYBHR* (1986) 332, at 334, paras (f) and (h). This interpretation has been rightly criticized and dismissed by Arai-Takahashi, above n 11, at 331.

[13] *Abu Awad v The Military Commander* [1979] HCJ 97/79, para 11; *Afu v IDF Commander in the West Bank* [1988] HCJ 785/87, PD 42(2) 4.

[14] See, among many others, Jacques, above n 5, at 28; A. Margalit and S. Hibbin, 'Unlawful Presence of Protected Persons in Occupied Territory? An Analysis of Israel's Permit Regime and Expulsions from the West Bank under the Law of Occupation', 13 *YIHL* (2010) 245, at 256–60; Arai-Takahashi, above n 11, at 338; T. Meron, *Human Rights and Humanitarian Norms as Customary Law* (Oxford: Clarendon Press, 1989), at 49; Dinstein, above n 12, at 15; D. Kretzmer, *The Occupation of Justice: The Supreme Court of Israel and the Occupied Territories* (New York: State University New York Press, 2002), at 48–51; B. Dayanim, 'The Israeli Supreme Court and the Deportations of Palestinians: The Interaction of Law and Legitimacy', 30 *Stanford Journal of International Law* (1994) 115, at 157–66; J.-M. Henckaerts, 'Deportation and Transfer of Civilians in Time of War', 26 *Van JTL* (1993) 469, at 471.

[15] See, e.g., C. Bassiouni, *Crimes against Humanity in International Law* (Cambridge: CUP, 2011), at 381; C. Hall, 'Crimes against Humanity, par. 1(d)', in O. Triffterer (ed), *Commentary on the Rome Statute of the International Criminal Court* (Baden-Baden: Nomos, 1999) 136, at 136; G. Werle, *Principles of International Criminal Law* (The Hague: T.M.C. Asser Press, 2005), at 240; Henckaerts, above n 14, at 472.

[16] See notably C. Meindersma, 'Legal Issues Surrounding Population Transfers in Conflict Situations', 41 *NILR* (1994) 31, at 33; de Zayas, above n 5, at 208; M. Stavropoulou, 'The Right Not to Be Displaced', 9 *American University Journal of International Law and Policy* (1994) 689, at 690.

deportations', Article 49 paragraph 1 suggests that there are two notions with different scope and meaning. Following such a stance, the cross-border element can represent the distinguishing feature between the two notions: transfers take place within the territory of a state, whereas deportations presuppose the crossing of an international border from one state to another. On the other hand, both forcible transfer and deportation refer to the same reality: a forcible displacement. In this regard, Article 49 paragraph 1 makes no difference regarding the destination to which protected persons are forcibly transferred or deported.

The actual practice is not very clear, as exemplified by the ICTY case law. Several judgments have considered that both terms may be read as covering forcible movements within and outside the territory.[17] Nevertheless, the prevailing understanding of the ICTY is to presume that they have an autonomous meaning:

> Deportation may be defined as the forced displacement of persons by expulsion or other coercive acts from the area in which they are lawfully present, without grounds permitted under international law. Deportation requires the displacement of persons across a national border, to be distinguished from forcible transfer which may take place within national boundaries.[18]

However, in stark contrast with this stance, the ICC Statute encapsulates the two terms within one single definition, without reference to any particular destination.[19] The *Elements of Crimes* further confirm that '"[d]eported or forcibly transferred" is interchangeable with "forcibly displaced"'.

It is true that the notion of forcible transfer under general international law is all but clear.[20] This is notably reflected by the definition elaborated by the International Law Commission (ILC) in its commentary to the Draft Code of Crimes against the Peace and Security of Mankind: '[T]he forcible transfer of population could occur wholly within the frontiers of one and the same State.'[21] If transfer *could* occur within the territory, nothing precludes that it *could* also happen outside the territory. Two years later, this interpretation was retained by the Draft Declaration on Population Transfer and the Implantation of Settlers, which defines unlawful population transfer as

> a practice or policy having the purpose or effect of moving persons into or out of an area, *either within or across an international border, or within, into or out of an occupied territory*, without the free and informed consent of the transferred population and any receiving population.[22]

---

[17] See, in particular, ICTY, *The Prosecutor v Dragan Nikolić*, Review of Indictment Pursuant to Rule 61, IT-94-2-R61, 20 October 1995, para 23; ICTY, *The Prosecutor v Tihomir Blaškić*, Trial Chamber Judgment, IT-95-14-T, 3 March 2000, para 234; ICTY, *The Prosecutor v Milomir Stakić*, Trial Chamber Judgment, IT-97-24-T, Trial Judgment, 31 July 2003, para 679.

[18] ICTY, *The Prosecutor v Milorad Krnojelac*, Trial Chamber Judgment, IT-97-25-T, 15 March 2002, para 474. See also ICTY, *The Prosecutor v Radislav Krstić*, Trial Chamber Judgment, IT-98-3, 2 August 2001, paras 521, 531–2; ICTY, *The Prosecutor v Radoslav Brđanin*, Trial Chamber Judgment, IT-99-36, 1 September 2004, para 540. This understanding was further endorsed by the ICTY Appeals Chamber in *The Prosecutor v Milomir Stakić*, Appeals Chamber Judgment, IT-97-24-A, 22 March 2006, para 300.

[19] See Art 7(2)(d).

[20] See the diverging views expressed within the Institute of International Law about the notion of transfer: *Annuaire de l'Institut du droit international*, Session de Sienne, 1952 (44, II), at 138–69.

[21] ILC, *Report of the International Law Commission on the Work of its 48th Session, 6 May–26 July 1996*, Official Documents of the United Nations General Assembly's 51st session, Supplement no 10 (A/51/10), Art 18, at 122.

[22] UN Sub-Commission on the Promotion and Protection of Human Rights, the Population Transfer Declaration, E/CN.4/Sub.2/1997/23, 27 June 1997, Art 3 (emphasis added).

15   From the more specific angle of Article 49 GC IV, the considerable energy devoted by scholars and tribunals to identify the respective meaning of transfer and deportation is largely disproportionate and arguably useless. Both transfer and deportation are prohibited by Article 49 paragraph 1 in the same terms. This categorical prohibition applies equally to forced displacement within and outside the occupied territory, without regard to the putative differences between the two terms. Clearly, the distinction between the two 'has no bearing on the condemnation of such practices in international humanitarian law'.[23]

c. *The forcible character of transfer and deportation*

16   The legal nature of the removal is irrelevant. What matters is the forcible character of the displacement (whether labelled deportation or transfer). This common feature constitutes the central element for identifying the measures prohibited by Article 49 paragraph 1 GC IV. While implicit in the notion of deportation, the compulsory nature of displacement has been explicitly re-emphasized by Article 49 paragraph 1 with the adjective 'forcible' before the term 'transfer'. The ICRC Commentary has deduced from such a specification that 'the Conference decided to authorize voluntary transfers by implication, and only to prohibit "forcible" transfer'.[24]

17   Following this interpretation *a contrario*, the key issue for triggering the prohibition under Article 49 paragraph 1 is no longer to assess whether there is a transfer or a deportation but instead whether the displacement is forced or voluntary. Thus, the borderline between lawful and unlawful displacement relies on the distinction between voluntary and involuntary movement of persons. As restated by the ICTY in numerous judgments, 'the essential element is that the displacement be involuntary in nature'.[25] In other words, 'the displacement of persons is only illegal where it is forced, i.e. not voluntary'.[26]

18   In contrast to the endless discussions raised by the alleged divergences between transfer and deportation, the forcible nature of the displacement benefits from a consensual definition. Both the ICTY case law and the ICC *Elements of Crimes* concur in providing a broad definition which covers both physical and psychological force:

> The term 'forcibly' is not restricted to physical force, but may include threat of force or coercion, such as that caused by fear of violence, duress, detention, psychological oppression or abuse of power against such person or persons or another person, or by taking advantage of a coercive environment.[27]

---

[23] ICTY, *Krstić*, above n 18, para 522. It is ironic that this acknowledgement is made by the ICTY in *Krstić* just after alleging, in the previous sentence, that there is a distinction under CIL: ibid, para 521. The irrelevance of such distinction is further confirmed by Art 147 GC IV, which considers both unlawful deportation and transfer as grave breaches.

[24] Pictet Commentary GC IV, at 279. Though Pictet primarily justified his interpretation *a contrario* on the basis of the drafting history, the *travaux préparatoires* are much less obvious than he suggested. Some states, including the USSR, were concerned by the risk of abuse which might result from the idea of a voluntary transfer: Final Record, vol II-A, at 664 and 759. In fact, Art 49 para 1 could be construed in a way different from the one suggested by the ICRC: a transfer is by definition compulsory, and the term 'forcible' was restated to avoid any ambiguity on this point and to underline its common feature with deportation.

[25] ICTY, *The Prosecutor v Blagoje Simić, Miroslav Tadić and Simo Zarić*, Trial Chamber Judgment, IT-95-9-T, 17 October 2003, para 125. Among many other similar restatements see *Stakić*, above n 18, para 279.

[26] ICTY, *Simić et al*, above n 25, para 125.

[27] Report of the Preparatory Commission for the ICC, Finalized Draft Text of the Elements of the Crimes, PCNICC/2000/INF/3/Add.2, 6 July 2000, at 11. See also ICTY, *Krstić*, above n 18, para 529; ICTY, *Krnojelac*, above n 18, para 475; and ICTY, *Stakić*, above n 18, para 281. Though this interpretation has been made in the context of the crime against humanity, it remains relevant for assessing by analogy the forcible character of displacement under Art 49 GC IV.

Following this inclusive approach, the ICTY has constantly underlined the paramount importance of the genuine consent of the persons concerned for distinguishing lawful from unlawful displacement.[28] This assessment should be carried out with due regard to all the circumstances prevailing at the time.[29] The fact that the person has expressed his or her consent does not obviate the need for inquiring into the truly voluntary nature of such a consent: '[W]hile persons may consent to (or even request) their removal, that consent must be real in the sense that it is given voluntarily and as a result of the individual's free will, assessed in the light of the surrounding circumstances.'[30] In sum, 'what matters is the *personal* consent or wish of an individual, as opposed to collective consent as a group, or a consent expressed by official authorities, in relation to an individual person, or a group of persons'.[31]

d. Evacuation

Despite the broad and categorical prohibition of transfer and deportation, the second paragraph of Article 49 GC IV still permits the Occupying Power to 'undertake total or partial evacuation of a given area if the security of the population or imperative military reasons so demand'. According to the ICRC Commentary, '[u]nlike deportation and forcible transfers, evacuation is a provisional measure […] often taken in the interests of the protected persons themselves'.[32] The security of the population indeed constitutes the first ground of evacuation under Article 49 paragraph 2 GC IV,[33] but it is not the only one. The second ground is more problematic, as it justifies evacuation for 'imperative military reasons' on their own, without any specific consideration for the displaced persons.

Allowing evacuation on the mere ground of military necessity has been considered incoherent with the absolute prohibition of transfer endorsed in the previous paragraph: 'Article 49, on this point at least, codifies a circular reasoning: a forced transfer of the population is prohibited regardless of its motive, unless that motive is the necessity of subduing the enemy.'[34] Though the Occupying Power retains a substantial margin of appreciation, not all military objectives can justify evacuation.[35] The wording of Article 49 paragraph 2 qualifies evacuation on such a ground by requiring military reasons to be 'imperative'. As observed by the ICRC Commentary to AP II, '[t]he situation should be

---

[28] ICTY, *Krnojelac*, above n 1, para 229.
[29] ICTY, *Stakić*, above n 18, para 282. See also ICTY, *The Prosecutor v Vidoje Blagojević and Dragan Jokić*, Trial Chamber Judgment, IT-02-60-T, 17 January 2005, para 596.
[30] ICTY, *Stakić*, above n 18, para 279. See also ICTY, *Blagojević and Jokić*, above n 29, para 596; ICTY, *The Prosecutor v Dragoljub Kunarac, Radomir Kovac and Zoran Vukovic*, Trial Chamber Judgment, IT-96-23-7 and IT-96-23/1-T, 22 February 2001, para 460, cited with approval in ICTY, *The Prosecutor v Dragoljub Kunarac, Radomir Kovac and Zoran Vukovic*, Appeals Chamber Judgment, IT-96-23 and IT-96-23/1-A. 12 June 2002, paras 127–8; ICTY, *Simić et al*, above n 25, para 125.
[31] ICTY, *Simić et al*, above n 25, para 128.   [32] Pictet Commentary GC IV, at 280.
[33] This is obviously the case for separating civilians from military objectives, as notably restated by Art 58 AP I: 'The Parties to the conflict shall, to the maximum extent feasible: a) without prejudice to Article 49 of the Fourth Convention, endeavour to remove the civilian population, individual civilians and civilian objects under their control from the vicinity of military objectives.' Art 49 para 5 GC IV also restates: 'The Occupying Power shall not detain protected persons in an area particularly exposed to the dangers of war unless the security of the population or imperative military reasons so demand.' One should add that the term 'detain' is clearly not appropriate and must be understood as 'retain', in line with the French version of the Convention which uses the term *retenir* (and not *détenir*).
[34] T.A. van Baarda, 'Seeing through the Fog: Distinguishing between Evacuation and Deportation', 18 *Humanitarian Exchanges* (2001) 15, at 15.
[35] Meindersma, above n 16, at 49.

22 scrutinized most carefully as the adjective "imperative" reduces to a minimum cases in which displacement may be ordered'.[36] The plural of the 'military reasons' at stake arguably reinforces this understanding. Hence, only several and imperative military reasons can trigger evacuation.

22 Furthermore, military reasons should not be confused with political objectives. In response to the phenomenon of ethnic cleansing, the ICRC further underlines that, '[c]learly, imperative military reasons cannot be justified by political motives. For example, it would be prohibited to move a population in order to exercise more effective control over a dissident ethnic group.'[37] This interpretation was endorsed by the ICTY when it observed, with regard to Srebrenica, that '[t]he evacuation was itself the goal and neither the protection of the civilians nor imperative military necessity justified the action'.[38] More generally, the ICTY has also recalled that '[e]vacuation is by definition a temporary and provisional measure'.[39] It has further insisted on its exceptional character, in underlining that 'recourse to such measures would only be lawful in the gravest of circumstances and only as measures of last resort'.[40]

23 In parallel to the relatively limited set of circumstances justifying evacuation, Article 49 GC IV also regulates the implementation phase of evacuation. It sets out four requirements regarding the destination of the evacuation, its duration, the treatment of displaced persons, and notification of the Protecting Power. First, as far as the destination of evacuation is concerned, Article 49 paragraph 2 proscribes displacement 'outside the bounds of the occupied territory except when for material reasons it is impossible to avoid such displacement'. As a result, displacement must not take place too far from the habitual residence of protected persons. This is reinforced by the second requirement limiting the evacuation's time frame: protected persons 'shall be transferred back to their homes as soon as hostilities in the area in question have ceased'. Evacuation must thus be temporary—i.e. for the duration of hostilities in the area concerned—and cannot compromise the return of protected persons to their habitual place of residence.

24 The third requirement details the treatment of displaced persons during the evacuation process. According to Article 49 paragraph 3, the Occupying Power shall ensure a minimum standard of living (including 'proper accommodation' and 'satisfactory conditions of hygiene, health, safety and nutrition'), as well as the family unity of displaced persons. These obligations are nevertheless not absolute, for they are required 'to the greatest practicable extent'. This qualification is bound to take into account the practical contingencies inherent in any evacuation process organized in a situation of emergency.[41]

25 The last requirement is more formal: according to Article 49 paragraph 4, '[t]he Protecting Power shall be informed of any transfers and evacuations as soon as they have taken place'. Notification thus does not have to be given before the evacuation. This was justified by the drafters 'in light of the necessity for secrecy in regard to military operations'.[42] The ICRC Commentary admits *a posteriori* notification.[43] Though procedural in

---

[36] ICRC Commentary APs, para 4853.   [37] Ibid.
[38] ICTY, *Krstić*, above n 18, para 527.   [39] ICTY, *Blagojević and Jokić*, above n 29, para 597.
[40] ICTY, *Simić et al*, above n 25, para 125, fn 218.
[41] According to the UK, which requested its insertion during the *travaux préparatoires*, this would also be required in the interests of the displaced persons themselves: Final Record, vol II-B, at 416.
[42] Final Record, vol II-A, at 759.
[43] Pictet Commentary GC IV, at 282. This interpretation is probably influenced by the French version of the Geneva Convention, which supposed that evacuation had already been carried out before: '*La Puissance*

nature, this obligation of information has a much more substantial effect: it plays a role in order to ensure due respect for the basic rules enshrined in Article 49. According to the ICRC, this notification enables the Protecting Power to monitor the implementation of evacuation.⁴⁴

e. *The prohibition of transfer and deportation under international human rights law*

The prohibition of transfer and deportation under IHL is substantially reinforced by IHRL. Despite the absence of any explicit equivalent to Article 49 GC IV, protection against forced displacement is inferred from a wide range of basic rights (including protection from interference with one's home and the right to adequate housing).⁴⁵ The most emblematic right is clearly the right to freedom of movement and choice of residence, as endorsed in Article 12 paragraph 1 of the International Covenant on Civil and Political Rights (ICCPR), as well as by all its regional counterparts.⁴⁶

As restated by the Human Rights Committee (HRCttee), 'the right to reside in a place of one's choice within the territory includes protection against all forms of forced internal displacement'.⁴⁷ Its applicability in times of armed conflict is beyond doubt. It has notably been endorsed by the United Nations (UN) Guiding Principles on Internal Displacement in the following terms:

1. Every human being shall have the right to be protected against being arbitrarily displaced from his or her home or place of habitual residence.
2. The prohibition of arbitrary displacement includes displacement: […] [i]n situations of armed conflict, unless the security of the civilians involved or imperative military reasons so demand.⁴⁸

The parallel between this last paragraph and Article 49 paragraph 1 GC IV is striking, and likely intended. Following a similar stance, the HRCttee has inferred from the inclusion of deportation and forcible transfer within the notion of 'crimes against humanity' under the ICC Statute that '[t]he legitimate right to derogate from article 12 of the Covenant during a state of emergency can never be accepted as justifying such measures'.⁴⁹ More generally, the Committee recalls that

---

protectrice sera informée des transferts et évacuations dès qu'ils auront eu lieu' (emphasis added). The English version appears more demanding as it suggests that notification should be done at the very beginning of evacuation, 'as soon as' it is carried out.

⁴⁴ Pictet Commentary GC IV, at 282.

⁴⁵ See, e.g., CESCR, General Comment 7: The Right to Adequate Housing (Art 11(1) of the Covenant): Forced Evictions, 20 May 1997, in HRI/GEN/1/Rev.9, vol I, 27 May 2008, 38–43, para 3, 5, and 12.

⁴⁶ Art 26(1) Arab Charter of Human Rights; Art 22(1) ACHR; Art 2(1) ECHR; and Art 12(1) ACHPR.

⁴⁷ HRCttee, General Comment 27: Freedom of Movement (Art 12), 2 November 1999, para 7. Among other similar restatements, see Sub-Commission Resolution 1997/29 (Freedom of movement and population transfer), PP 2 and OP 3, as well as Art 4 of the Draft Declaration on Population Transfer and the Implantation of Settlers. See also Art 16 of ILO Convention No 169 concerning Indigenous and Tribal Peoples in Independent Countries (1989), and Art 10 of Declaration on the Rights of Indigenous Peoples, annexed to UNGA Res 61/295, 13 September 2007.

⁴⁸ Principle 6 of the UN Guiding Principle on Internal Displacement, E/CN.4/1998/53/Add.2, 1998. See also Art 4(4) of the African Union Convention for the Protection and Assistance of Internally Displaced Persons (2009).

⁴⁹ HRCttee, General Comment 29: States of Emergency (Art 4), 31 August 2001, para 13(d).

the possibility of restricting certain Covenant rights under the terms of, for instance, freedom of movement (article 12) or freedom of assembly (article 21) is generally sufficient during such situations and no derogation from the provisions in question would be justified by the exigencies of the situation.[50]

28   In its well-known Advisory Opinion of 9 July 2004, the International Court of Justice (ICJ) acknowledges that the construction of a wall in the occupied Palestinian territory is a violation of Article 12 ICCPR. It first observes that, as the derogation notified by Israel was limited to Article 9 of the Covenant, Israel is bound to respect all the other provisions, including freedom of movement. It then concludes on the basis of the information available to it that the construction of the wall does not come within the restrictions provided for under Article 12(3) ICCPR.[51] As underlined by the Court, 'it is not sufficient that such restrictions be directed to the ends authorized; they must also be necessary for the attainment of those ends'.[52] It thus endorses the interpretation of the HRCttee, according to which, as an exception to the right of freedom of movement, restrictions 'must conform to the principle of proportionality' and 'be the least intrusive instrument amongst those which might achieve the desired result'.[53]

29   While the right to freedom of movement is limited to forced displacement within the territory of a state, IHRL is not indifferent to deportation and transfer outside the state's territory. Expulsion of nationals is even explicitly prohibited by several regional treaties, including Protocol No 4 to the European Convention on Human Rights (ECHR) (Article 3), the American Convention on Human Rights (ACHR) (Article 22(5)), and the Arab Charter of Human Rights (Article 27(2)).

30   Though there is no similar prohibition in the African Charter on Human and Peoples' Rights (ACHPR), it is arguably implicit in the right to return to one's country as acknowledged by Article 12(2) ACHPR. This interpretation has been notably endorsed by the HRCttee with regard to Article 12(4) ICCPR. As restated in its General Comment 27, the right of a person to enter his or her own country 'also implies prohibition of enforced population transfers or mass expulsions to other countries'.[54]

31   While nationals of an occupied state cannot be transferred or deported to other countries under IHRL, the situation is different with regard to non-nationals. On the one hand, collective expulsion of aliens is prohibited by a significant number of human rights treaties.[55] On the other hand, under IHRL, individual expulsion of non-nationals

---

[50] Ibid, para 5. One should add that the ICCPR is the only core human rights treaty of the UN which contains a derogation clause. The CERD, the CEDAW, the International Convention on the Protection of the Rights of All Migrant Workers and Members of Their Families (ICRMW), and the Convention on the Rights of Persons with Disabilities (CRPD) do not have a derogation mechanism, and they all enshrine the right to freedom of movement and choice of residence. See Art 5(d)(i) CERD; Art 15(4) CEDAW; Art 39 ICRMW; Art 18(1) CRPD.

[51] ICJ, *Legal Consequences of the Construction of a Wall in the Occupied Palestinian Territory*, Advisory Opinion, 9 July 2004, para 137.

[52] Ibid.   [53] Ibid.   [54] HRCttee, General Comment 27, above n 47, para 19.

[55] Art 22(9) ACHR; Art 12(5) ACHPR; Art 4 of Protocol No 4 ECHR; Art 26(2) Arab Charter of Human Rights; Art 25(4) CIS Convention on Human Rights and Fundamental Freedoms; Art 19(1) Charter of Fundamental Rights of the European Union. See also at the universal level, Art 22(1) ICRMW. Furthermore, though not explicitly mentioned in the ICCPR, the HRCttee considers that such prohibition is implicit in Art 13: HRCttee, General Comment 15: The Position of Aliens under the Covenant, 11 April 1986, para 10.

remains possible. This represents *a contrario* the main added value of IHL. Nevertheless, even in such instances, IHRL still prohibits any expulsion to a state where there is a real risk of torture, or of degrading or inhuman treatment.[56] Apart from the specific case of individual expulsion of non-nationals from an occupied territory to a safe third country, IHL and IHRL coincide in substance and are thus mutually supportive.

f. The prohibition of transfer and deportation under customary international law

The question whether Article 49 GC IV codifies customary international law (CIL) has given rise to longstanding debates. Dinstein asserts that the prohibition enshrined in this provision 'incontrovertibly goes beyond customary international law',[57] whereas others consider, in line with the ICRC Commentary,[58] that Article 49 restates a pre-existing custom.[59] Between these two opposing views, a middle position argues that it is a partial codification. But here again, there is a wide range of variations for determining which exact part of Article 49 is declarative of such custom. For Meron, 'at least, the central elements of Article 49 [...] are declaratory of customary law', except the prohibition of individual deportations.[60] By contrast, according to Bassiouni, only transfers for the purposes of extermination and slavery were prohibited by general international law before the adoption of the Geneva Conventions.[61]

Whatever their respective merits, these longstanding discussions have lost their relevance today, and their interest is mainly historical; for the prohibition of mass and individual transfer or deportation is nowadays clearly part of CIL. This has been most notably confirmed by the ICRC Study on Customary International Humanitarian Law (CIHL). According to its Rule 129A, '[p]arties to an international armed conflict may not deport or forcibly transfer the civilian population of an occupied territory, in whole or in part, unless the security of the civilians involved or imperative military reasons so demand'.

Although the customary law nature of this prohibition is as such not seriously contested,[62] the ICRC Study has been the subject of criticism. In particular, the wording of Rule 129A has been held 'unfortunate'[63] because it does not specifically mention evacuation as a notion on its own. Following the previous writings of its main editor,[64] the ICRC Study equates evacuation with the exception to the rule. This has been criticized as blurring, if not negating, the very specificity of evacuation.[65] Though unfortunate from a

---

[56] See section B.II.f of this chapter.
[57] Dinstein, above n 12, at 13.   [58] Pictet Commentary GC IV, at 279.
[59] See, e.g., de Zayas, above n 5, at 212–13; Henckaerts, above n 14, at 481–2; Jacques, above n 5, at 22–5.
[60] Meron, above n 14, at 48–9.   [61] Bassiouni, above n 15, at 384.
[62] See, however, HC 698/80, *Kawasme et al v Minister of Defence et al*, 35(1) *Piskei Din* 617, 11 *IsrYBHR* (1981) 349, at 350.
[63] R. Piotrowicz, 'Displacement and Displaced Persons', in E. Wilmshurst and S. Breau (eds), *Perspectives on the ICRC Study on Customary International Humanitarian Law* (Cambridge: CUP, 2007) 337, at 342. See also J.L. Greer, 'A Critique of the ICRC's Customary Rules Concerning Displaced Persons: General Accuracy, Conflation, and a Missed Opportunity', 192 *Military Law Review* (2007) 116.
[64] Henckaerts, above n 14, at 473.
[65] Piotrowicz, above n 63, at 342: 'The notion of evacuation is different from deportation; it is intended to protect the population being evacuated rather than to allow removal as such. Deportations and forced transfers are always unlawful; evacuations may be permissible. In this respect the wording of the Rule is unfortunate because it suggests that *deportations or forcible transfers* may in fact be lawful if they can be justified by the need to ensure the security of those affected, or else due to imperative military reasons.' For a similar account, see Jacques, above n 5, at 29–30; S. Sivakumaran, *The Law of Non-International Armed Conflict* (Oxford: OUP, 2012), at 287–8; Arai-Takahashi, above n 11, at 344.

purely humanitarian perspective, such understanding of the rule seems to be more consonant with the actual practice. Whether labelled as 'evacuation', 'deportation', or 'transfer', the core content of the norm prohibits any forced displacement, except when duly justified by the security of the civilian population or imperative military reasons.[66]

35   The wording of Rule 129A is unfortunate for another reason, which is rarely mentioned. The reference to the 'civilian population of an occupied territory, in whole or in part' establishes a dangerous and disputable threshold. It suggests, in blatant contradiction with the text of Article 49 GC IV, that *individual* deportations or transfers are still permissible, because CIL would prohibit only *collective* forcible displacements when the 'civilian population' *as a group of persons* is transferred or deported 'in whole or in part'. The risk of such misinterpretation is all but hypothetical, and could even be invoked in support of the highly controversial interpretation of Article 49 paragraph 1 carried out by the Israel Supreme Court.[67]

II. The prohibition of transfer in international armed conflict

a. Rationale and key characteristics of Article 45 GC IV

36   The scope and content of Article 45 GC IV diverge from those of Article 49 in four significant ways. The first and most obvious difference concerns their territorial scope: Article 49 applies to an occupied territory, whereas Article 45 concerns the territory of a state party to an IAC which is not occupied. Secondly, whereas Article 49 proscribes any transfer and deportation in general terms without regard to the destination, the prohibition contained in Article 45 is precisely defined by reference to the state of destination. Transfer is prohibited in three specific circumstances: the destination state is not party to the Geneva Convention; it is not willing or able to apply the Convention; or it persecutes protected persons. The primary rationale of Article 45 is thus to prevent a state party from evading its own obligations by transferring a protected person to another state which does not respect the basic standards endorsed in GC IV.

37   Thirdly, in contrast to Article 49, there is no explicit restatement regarding the forcible nature of the transfer. During the drafting history, the initial version of Article 45 referred to the involuntary nature of the transfer.[68] This precision was subsequently deleted on a proposal made by the Canadian Delegation, in order 'to ensure more effective protection'.[69] The absence of any reference to the forcible nature of the transfer was thus motivated by the need to provide protected persons with 'a better safeguard in view of the pressure which might be brought to bear on them by the Occupying Power in order to obtain their consent to their transfer to a Power which was not a party to the Convention'.[70]

---

[66] Although this chapter is not the place to develop this issue further, one might argue that Rule 129A is not specific to IHL; it reflects instead a broader customary norm prohibiting forced displacement unless it is necessary to protect national security, public order, and the rights and freedoms of others.

[67] As mentioned at MN 11, the Israeli Supreme Court has wrongly construed Art 49 para 1 as excluding individual deportation from its scope. Going one step further, it even held that deportation of more than 400 persons was not contrary to Art 49, on the fallacious argument that 'deportation orders under discussion [...] were essentially individual in nature, not collective, the 415 orders being a collection of personal orders': HC 5973192 etc, *The Association of Civil Rights in Israel et al v The Minister of Defence et al*, 47(1) Piskei Din 267, 23 IsrYBHR (1993) 353, at 356.

[68] Final Record, vol I, at 120.   [69] Ibid, vol II-A, at 826.   [70] Ibid, at 764.

Fourthly, the prohibition contained in Article 45 GC IV is limited to transfers only. 38
The ICRC Commentary proposes a generic and factual definition encompassing '[a]ny movement of protected persons to another State, carried out by the Detaining Power on an individual or collective basis'.[71] This inclusive definition is grounded on the assumption that 'Article 45 uses the word "transfer" in a very broad sense.'[72] However, the definition proposed by the ICRC presumes that transfer is limited to inter-state displacements, unlike Article 49 which applies equally to internal and external ones.

In fact, though this may be surprising, there is no unified concept of transfer in IHL. 39
When they drafted GC IV, state delegates did not have a very clear idea about this notion. As acknowledged during the *travaux préparatoires*, 'there was some hesitation as to what was really meant by transfer'.[73] As a result, the same term, 'transfer', may have different meanings from one provision to another in GC IV. Transfers under Article 49 have been construed by some as referring to forced displacement within the territory, whereas the opposite interpretation has been maintained for transfers under Article 45. Adding to the confusion, transfer of internees under Article 127 GC IV has been interpreted as covering both external and internal displacements.[74]

For the purposes of Article 45, the ICRC Commentary gives the following possible 40
examples of transfer: 'internment in the territory of another Power, repatriation, the returning of protected persons to their country of residence or their extradition'.[75] Though not mentioned in this illustrative list, the term 'transfer' also clearly includes 'rendition'. In fact, the two notions significantly overlap, for rendition is generally defined as 'the involuntary transfer of an individual across borders without recourse to extradition or deportation proceedings'.[76] Transfer and rendition share an additional common feature: both are distinct from expulsion and extradition.

b. *Transfer, expulsion, and extradition*

In contrast to Article 49 GC IV, deportation is not explicitly mentioned in the prohibition 41
expressed in Article 45. The ICRC Commentary considers that 'In the absence of any clause stating that deportation is to be regarded as a form of transfer, this Article would not appear to raise any obstacle to the right of Parties to the conflict to deport aliens in individual cases when State security demands such action.'[77] Excluding expulsion from the notion of transfer is not only astonishing but even counterproductive: a state can simply evade its obligation by deporting protected persons to states to which transfer is specifically prohibited by Article 45.

Although highly disputable in terms of protection, the ICRC's interpretation echoes 42
the concern of several states expressed during the drafting history. Some delegations considered 'inadmissible for a State to be unable to expel a dangerous individual, particularly in war time', while others 'feared that [...] the provisions of the Convention might be evaded, "transfers" taking place under the guise of "deportations"'.[78] A majority of

---

[71] Pictet Commentary GC IV, at 266.   [72] Ibid, at 267.
[73] Final Record, vol II-A, at 826.   [74] Pictet Commentary GC IV, at 498.   [75] Ibid, at 266.
[76] M.L. Satterthwaite, *The Legal Regime Governing Transfer of Persons in the Fight against Terrorism* (Public Law & Legal Theory Research Paper Series, Working Paper No 10-27, New York University School of Law, May 2010), at 2.
[77] Pictet Commentary GC IV, at 266.   [78] Final Record, vol II-A, at 809.

delegations nevertheless considered that deportation and transfer should be treated on an equal footing.[79]

43   It remains the case that the absence of an explicit reference to deportation has justified a very restrictive interpretation in contradiction to the object and purpose of Article 45. This drawback of GC IV has nonetheless been neutralized by the subsequent evolution of international law. As will be developed in section B.II.e and f of this chapter, both IRL and IHRL clearly include expulsion among the measures covered by the principle of *non-refoulement*.

44   Another important distinctive characteristic of transfer under Article 45 GC IV concerns its interaction with extradition. Unlike expulsion, a specific provision is devoted to extradition in the fifth and final paragraph: 'The provisions of this Article do not constitute an obstacle to the extradition, in pursuance of extradition treaties concluded before the outbreak of hostilities, of protected persons accused of offences against ordinary criminal law.' The rationale of this provision is twofold. As underlined by the ICRC Commentary, 'it was [...] important to preserve the existing character of extradition as an act of penal procedure and to prevent it serving as a pretext for persecution'.[80]

45   In order to achieve these dual objectives, two cumulative conditions must be fulfilled: the applicable treaty of extradition has to have been adopted before the beginning of hostilities; and extradition may be requested only for offences against ordinary criminal law. If one of these requirements is lacking, the prohibition of transfer under Article 45 remains plainly applicable to extradition. The first condition is aimed at avoiding the conclusion of a treaty for the purpose of circumventing the prohibition of transfer.[81] This might happen during the hostilities at the request of an ally state, or after the cessation of hostilities under pressure from the victorious Power. The second requirement follows the same objective of preventing abusive requests for extradition: a protected person has to be accused of an offence against ordinary criminal law, as opposed to a political offence. The traditional distinction between ordinary and political offences constitutes a well-known feature of extradition law and IRL, which has since been taken up by IHL.[82]

46   The wording of Article 45 paragraph 5 is nevertheless unfortunate: a protected person may be accused of an offence against ordinary criminal law, even when the ordinary law offence has been committed for a political purpose or when the extradition request itself has been submitted with a political purpose. In these cases, the risk of persecution is thus not totally prevented. Nevertheless, the relevant treaty of extradition would probably mitigate such a risk, as this kind of treaty generally includes a clause prohibiting extradition for political and/or discriminatory purposes. In any event, similarly to expulsion, the principle of *non-refoulement* under both IRL and IHRL covers extradition, and thus compensates for the ambiguities of IHL.

c. The prohibition of transfer to a state not respecting the Geneva Convention

47   Article 45 GC IV is a safeguard clause aimed at preserving the full benefit of the Convention. Its first paragraph requires states parties to abstain from transferring protected persons to a Power which is not a party to the Geneva Convention. Needless to say,

---

[79] Ibid, at 809 and 827.   [80] Pictet Commentary GC IV, at 270.

[81] This also excludes *a fortiori* a request for extradition which is not grounded on a treaty.

[82] For further discussion about the historical origins of this distinction in the law of extradition and refugee law, see V. Chetail, 'Théorie et pratique de l'asile en droit international classique: étude sur les origines conceptuelles et normatives du droit international des réfugiés', 115 *RGDIP* (2011) 625.

this provision has now lost its *raison d'être* with the virtual universal ratification of GC IV. Mere ratification of the Geneva Convention is not sufficient in itself, however, to permit transfer to another state party.

According to Article 45 paragraph 3, '[p]rotected persons may be transferred by the Detaining Power only to a Power which is a party to the present Convention and after the Detaining Power has satisfied itself of the willingness and ability of such transferee Power to apply the present Convention'.[83] Any transfer is thus subordinated to effective respect for the Convention by the state to which the protected person would be transferred. Two conditions are required by Article 45 paragraph 3: prior to any transfer, the Detaining Power has to assess whether the other state party is (i) willing and (ii) able to apply GC IV. As highlighted by the ICRC, willingness is a subjective criterion and ability an objective one.[84] As a possible instance of the former, the Commentary mentions the case when 'the Detaining Power has reason to fear that certain categories among the persons transferred may be subjected to discriminatory treatment by the authorities of the country receiving them'.[85]

Regarding the second criterion based on inability to apply the Convention, the ICRC Commentary refers to the situation where protected persons cannot be transferred because 'economic difficulties will prevent the receiving Power from providing for their maintenance, as required by the Convention'.[86] Nevertheless, this inability may also derive from many other circumstances, such as political instability, internal disturbances, breakdown of law and order in the whole or parts of the territory, and any other situations where the state of destination may not exercise sufficient control to ensure effective respect for GC IV.

In any event, the two criteria required by Article 45 paragraph 3 are cumulative: a state may be willing to apply the Convention without being able to do so, and vice versa. Hence, an ability to apply the Convention cannot be presumed from willingness to do so: the two conditions are distinct and require a specific inquiry. In view of this, both criteria have to be assessed with due regard to all relevant circumstances of each case, including the general situation in the destination state and the personal circumstances of the person concerned (such as his or her individual and family background, origin, race, religion, political opinion, past activities, etc). Past violations of the Geneva Convention, as well as a real risk of future violations, are clearly relevant for assessing a state's willingness and ability to apply the Convention.[87]

Similarly, the lack of will or the inability to apply the Convention should be presumed from massive and systematic violations. Whether systematic or not, the violations in question might concern virtually any provision of the Geneva Convention. They may include—but are not limited to—Article 45, prohibiting any secondary transfer carried out by the destination state to a third state in contravention of the Convention. The most relevant provisions are those applicable to civilian internees, including the conditions of internment (Articles 84–131) and its location (which cannot be situated in areas particularly exposed to the dangers of war, in accordance with Article 83).

---

[83] The same rule does apply to prisoners of war, as restated in Art 12 para 2 GC III.
[84] Pictet Commentary GC IV, at 268.   [85] Ibid, at 268.   [86] Ibid.
[87] Violations do not have to be necessarily committed by the state and its authorities. Those committed by non-state actors also have to be taken into account when the state is unable or unwilling to prevent them.

52 Indeed, in contrast to the other paragraphs, the personal scope of Article 45 paragraph 3 is most likely to be limited to civilian internees.[88] This is apparent from the wording of this provision: the transferring state is referred to as 'the Detaining Power' and, when it comes to the state of destination, the text of the Article underlines that '[civilians] are in its custody'. Moreover, the *travaux préparatoires* confirm that state delegates clearly had civilian internees in mind when they drafted Article 45 paragraph 3,[89] and by doing so, they further referred to the analogy with prisoners of war.[90]

53 In any case, the willingness and ability of the receiving state does not absolve the transferring state from responsibility vis-à-vis the protected person when the transfer is completed. Article 45 paragraph 3 specifies that once the person has been transferred to the receiving Power,

> if that Power fails to carry out the provisions of the present Convention in any important respect, the Power by which the protected persons were transferred shall, upon being so notified by the Protecting Power, take effective measures to correct the situation or shall request the return of the protected persons. Such request must be complied with.

As underlined during its drafting, this provision 'was intended to prevent […] the danger of the transferring Power ceasing to take any further interest in the interned'.[91]

54 Article 45 paragraph 3 establishes a dual regime of responsibility: the primary responsibility rests on the receiving Power to which the person has been transferred; the sending Power which transferred the protected person retains a subsidiary responsibility.[92] The sending state remains responsible towards the transferred persons when the receiving Power fails to fulfil its obligation under the Convention 'in any important respect' and after it has been notified of such a failure by the Protecting Power. In such a case, the sending state may even request the return of the protected person in order to prevent any future violations.

d. Prohibition of transfer to a state of persecution

55 The already substantial protection of Article 45 paragraph 3 GC IV is complemented by an additional safeguard prohibiting any transfer to a state where the protected person may be persecuted for political or religious reasons. According to Article 45 paragraph 4, '[i]n no circumstances shall a protected person be transferred to a country where he or she may have reason to fear persecution for his or her political opinions or religious beliefs'. The rationale of this prohibition is slightly different from and more specific than the previous one: whereas the other prohibitions of transfer contained in Article 45 are aimed at ensuring due respect for GC IV, the prohibition set out in its fourth paragraph pursues a separate—albeit complementary—purpose of preventing persecution.

56 Article 45 paragraph 4 gave rise to no discussion during the drafting of GC IV, probably because the rule laid down therein was self-evident. Underlining the importance of this provision, the Chinese delegate simply declared that 'the granting of asylum to political refugees was in accordance with international usage and was one of the governing

---

[88] See in this sense Pictet Commentary GC IV, at 269.
[89] Final Record, vol II-A, at 661 and 827.
[90] Ibid, at 661 and 765; Final Record, vol II-B, at 414.
[91] Final Record, vol II-A, at 828.
[92] The drafting of this original regime nevertheless gave rise to lively debate, and its final version is clearly the result of a compromise. See in particular the discussions between state delegates, Final Record, vol II-A, at 661–2 and 827; and Final Record, vol II-B, at 413–14.

principles of the International Refugee Organization'.⁹³ Legally speaking, the prohibition of transfer is nonetheless different from the granting of asylum. The former is a negative notion (prohibiting states from transferring protected persons to a country of persecution), whereas the latter is a positive concept (which entails admission to residence and lasting protection).

Although the two notions are clearly interrelated and in fact mutually supportive, Article 45 paragraph 4 does not guarantee asylum as such. It ensures instead that protected persons who are in the territory of a state party to an IAC will not be transferred to a state of persecution. This may imply asylum, but not necessarily nor automatically: the sending state retains the possibility of transferring the protected person to another safe third state (and if the protected person is a civilian internee, provided that this state party is further willing and able to apply the Geneva Convention as required by the preceding paragraph).

Compared to Article 45 paragraph 3, paragraph 4's personal scope is larger as it covers any protected persons (and not only civilian internees—see MN 52 above). However, the prohibition of transfer applies only in the case of certain specific types of persecution, namely, those based on the political opinions or religious beliefs of the protected persons. The reason for this particular focus is both pragmatic and historical. In practice, political and religious persecutions were—and are still today—the most common forms of persecution. Moreover, when GC IV was drafted, there was no universally binding definition of the term 'refugee'. That term was defined in broader terms two years later by the Convention relating to the Status of Refugees (the Refugee Convention). In parallel to political opinion and religious belief, three other grounds of persecution have been added in the refugee definition: race, nationality, and membership of a particular social group.⁹⁴

Nonetheless, the prohibition of transfer under IHL may be broader than the refugee definition under the 1951 Convention, the latter excluding persons who have committed particularly serious crimes (crimes against peace, war crimes, crimes against humanity, serious non-political crimes, and acts contrary to the purposes and principles of the UN).⁹⁵ By contrast, by using the term 'in no circumstances', Article 45 paragraph 4 presumes the absolute character of the prohibition of transfer to a state of persecution.

However, the absolute character of this prohibition is not as clear as it might appear. The interaction between Article 45 paragraph 4 and paragraph 5 devoted to extradition is complex and ambiguous. Indeed, the wording of the fourth and fifth paragraphs is contradictory: Article 45 paragraph 4 prohibits any transfer in categorical terms; whereas Article 45 paragraph 5 specifically permits extradition of protected persons by stating that 'the provisions of this Article [including thus the previous paragraph] […] do not constitute an obstacle to […] extradition'.

As mentioned at MN 45, it is true that Article 45 paragraph 5 requires fulfilment of two conditions allegedly aimed at avoiding extradition as a pretext for persecution. These conditions nevertheless remain insufficient for achieving this purpose, because a person may be persecuted even when the requesting state meets the rather formal requirements that his or her extradition has been requested for an offence against ordinary criminal law and carried out on the basis of a treaty concluded before the outbreak of hostilities. This

---

⁹³ Final Record, vol II-A, at 662.
⁹⁴ Art 1(A)(2) Refugee Convention. ⁹⁵ Art 1(F) Refugee Convention.

hiatus in protection is nonetheless highly hypothetical, thanks to the concurrent applicability of IRL and IHRL.

e. *The prohibition of transfer under international refugee law*

62   Both in pith and substance, the prohibition of transfer under Article 45 GC IV echoes the principle of *non-refoulement* enshrined in IRL and IHRL. While their respective content significantly overlaps, the prohibition of *refoulement* presents some key characteristics which highlight the added value of IRL and IHRL for regulating the transfer of protected persons.

63   The principle of *non-refoulement* has been most notably laid down in Article 33(1) of the Refugee Convention, according to which:

> No Contracting State shall expel or return ('refouler') a refugee in any manner whatsoever to the frontiers of territories where his life or freedom would be threatened on account of his race, religion, nationality, membership of a particular social group or political opinion.

As mentioned at MN 58, the personal scope of refugee protection is broader than that of Article 45 paragraph 4, as the former includes three additional grounds of persecution.

64   The most important added value of the refugee law principle of *non-refoulement* lies in its material scope. The inclusive wording of Article 33 of the Refugee Convention—through the generic expression 'in any manner whatsoever'—encompasses any act of forcible removal or rejection that puts the person concerned at risk of persecution; the decisive consideration is the consequence of this act, namely, whether one's life or liberty would be threatened on account of a Convention reason. While embracing transfer, rendition, and extradition,[96] the material scope of the prohibition contained in IRL is broader than its IHL counterpart for, in contrast to the latter, Article 33 explicitly includes expulsion. Furthermore, Article 32 of the Refugee Convention requires some procedural guarantees governing the deportation process.[97]

65   Although the material scope of Article 33 of the Refugee Convention is broader than that of Article 45 GC IV, it suffers from two substantial drawbacks. First, the refugee law principle of *non-refoulement* could be derogated from by states 'in time of war or other grave and exceptional circumstances'. Indeed, Article 9 of the Refugee Convention contains a broad derogation clause which can apply to virtually any of its provisions.[98] Though this may surprise some, in practice Article 9 has nonetheless rarely been invoked by states parties. If the derogation clause is not applied, the principle of *non-refoulement* accordingly remains applicable in times of armed conflicts.

66   Secondly, even in such a case, there remain limitations inherent to Article 33. In parallel to the exclusion clauses of the refugee definition mentioned at MN 59, the principle of

---

[96] On the applicability of Art 33 to extradition, see W. Kälin, M. Caroni, and L. Heim, 'Article 33, para. 1', in A. Zimmermann (ed), *The 1951 Convention Relating to the Status of Refugees and its 1967 Protocol: A Commentary* (Oxford: OUP, 2011) 1327, at 1364–7; G.S. Goodwin-Gill and J. McAdam, *The Refugee in International Law* (3rd edn, Oxford: OUP, 2007), at 257–62; V. Chetail, 'Le principe de non refoulement et le statut de réfugié en droit international', in V. Chetail and J.-F. Flauss (eds), *La Convention de Genève du 28 juillet 1951 relative au statut des réfugiés—50 ans après: bilan et perspectives* (Brussels: Bruylant, 2001) 3, at 50–5.

[97] The additional protection provided by this provision is nevertheless limited to 'refugees lawfully in [the] territory' of state parties, and the procedural guarantees contained in Art 32 may be suspended for 'compelling reasons of national security'.

[98] For further discussions, see U. Davy, 'Article 9', in Zimmerman (ed), above n 96, 781.

non-refoulement enshrined in the 1951 Convention is not absolute. Article 33(2) provides that the benefit of *non-refoulement* cannot be claimed by a refugee 'whom there are reasonable grounds for regarding as a danger to the security of the country in which he is, or who, having been convicted by a final judgment of a particularly serious crime, constitutes a danger to the community of that country'. These two exceptions constitute a noticeable difference from Article 45 GC IV. This difference still remains relative since, as mentioned at MN 60–61, Article 45 paragraph 5 permits extradition for ordinary offences, without any specific requirement regarding the seriousness of the crime and the existence of a previous final conviction.

In sum, the prohibition of *refoulement* under IRL offers broader protection than the prohibition of transfer under IHL with regard to its personal and material scope. By contrast, Article 45 GC IV retains its relevance when a state party to an IAC has decided to derogate from the Refugee Convention under its Article 9, or when it applies the two exceptions in Article 33(2). This minimal protection offered by IHL is nonetheless considerably enhanced by IHRL. 67

f. *The prohibition of transfer under international human rights law*

In parallel to IHL and IRL, the principle of *non-refoulement* is firmly anchored in IHRL. It has been endorsed in an impressive range of human rights treaties at both universal and regional levels.[99] In addition to these explicit endorsements, treaty bodies have inferred from the general prohibition of torture, inhuman and degrading treatment an implicit duty of *non-refoulement*.[100] 68

Besides its multiple legal bases, the human rights principle of *non-refoulement* represents a substantial added value to both IHL and IRL; it even compensates for and obviates the limits of its two counterparts. Unlike Article 45 GC IV, the prohibition of *refoulement* under IHRL encompasses both expulsion and extradition. It thus reinforces the prohibition contained in IRL, while confirming that extradition is included by explicitly mentioning it among other possible measures of compulsory return.[101] In any event, both IRL and IHRL follow the same inclusive approach, encompassing any act of forcible removal (whether transfer, rendition, expulsion, extradition, or interception). 69

Thus, the decisive factor relies on the risk to be faced in the country of destination. In contrast to IRL and IHL, the nature of the risk is not persecution but principally torture or inhuman and degrading treatment. This divergence is less significant than it might appear, since persecution may be considered a form of degrading treatment.[102] Thanks to a broad interpretation of the interdiction of torture and other ill-treatment, the European 70

---

[99] See Art 3 CAT, Art 16 ICED; and at the regional level Art 22(8) ACHR, Art 13(4) of the 1985 Inter-American Convention to Prevent and Punish Torture, Art 19(2) of the 2000 Charter of Fundamental Rights of the European Union, and Art 28 of the 2004 Arab Charter on Human Rights.

[100] ECtHR, *Soering v United Kingdom*, Judgment, ECHR (1989) Series A, No 161, paras 87–8; HRCttee, General Comment 20: Replaces General Comment 7 Concerning Prohibition of Torture and Cruel Treatment or Punishment (Art 7), para 9. See also more generally Committee on the Rights of the Child, General Comment 6: Treatment of Unaccompanied and Separated Children Outside their Country of Origin, CRC/GC/2005/6, 2005, para 27.

[101] Among the explicit restatements of *non-refoulement* duty in the six treaties mentioned above n 99, only one of them—the ACHR—does not refer to extradition *expressis verbis*, although this was later clarified by the Inter-American Convention to Prevent and Punish Torture.

[102] For further discussions, see notably V. Chetail, 'Are Refugee Rights Human Rights? An Unorthodox Questioning of the Relations between Refugee Law and Human Rights Law', in R. Rubio Marin (ed), *Human Rights and Immigration* (Oxford: OUP, 2014) 19, at 35–7.

Court of Human Rights has most notably extended the prohibition of *refoulement* to risks of the death penalty[103] and of indiscriminate violence of a particularly high intensity, as in situations of armed conflict.[104] Treaty bodies have further confirmed that the willingness of the receiving states to duly respect human rights treaties is not sufficient in itself to obviate any risk of ill-treatment. Hence the so-called diplomatic assurances endorsing this kind of undertaking do not release sending states from their obligations under the principle of *non-refoulement*.[105]

71 More generally, IHRL presents two distinctive features. First, the notion of torture, inhuman or degrading treatment is not subordinated to any specific ground as required by IHL and IRL. Secondly, contrary to the Refugee Convention, the human rights principle of *non-refoulement* is absolute and cannot be derogated from in times of armed conflict.[106] The protection against *refoulement* provided by IHRL is thus definitively broader than that under Article 33 of the Refugee Convention and Article 45 paragraph 4 GC IV.

72 The picture may be different with regard to the prohibition of transfer to a state which is unwilling or unable to apply GC IV, contained in the third paragraph of Article 45. Some ICRC experts have inferred from this last provision that IHL 'affords [...] a greater protection than that normally granted by the principle of *non-refoulement*',[107] because the nature of the risk covered by Article 45 paragraph 3 encompasses any of the rights and protections of GC IV. This is perhaps true, but it is uniquely within the specific scope of Article 45 paragraph 3, namely, for civilian internees in an IAC and provided that they are not instead subjected to a measure of expulsion or extradition. One might further argue that serious violations of GC IV triggering the prohibition of transfer under Article 45 paragraph 3 also constitute inhuman or degrading treatment prohibiting *refoulement* under IHRL.

73 Quite significantly, the ICRC Study contains no rule equivalent to Article 45 GC IV, nor does it contain any parallel duty of *non-refoulement*. The 'complete omission of a Rule on *non[-]refoulement*' has been criticized as an 'error [...] truly unfortunate' and 'a missed opportunity to affirm the robust rights of refugees in the context of conflict'.[108] The reasons for such omission are difficult to know. This could be attributed to some lack of interest in IRL on the part of the ICRC, or to an attempt to equalize protection of internally displaced persons with that of refugees by neglecting their specificities.[109]

---

[103] See ECtHR, *Al-Saadoon v United Kingdom*, Judgment, 2 March 2010, para 144, where the Court held that the transfer carried out by the UK forces to the Iraqi police within the territory of Iraq was a violation of Art 3 ECHR because of the risk of the death penalty. Other rights may be involved, such as freedom from arbitrary detention and the right to a fair trial: ECtHR, *Z and T v United Kingdom*, 28 February 2006; ECtHR, *Tomic v United Kingdom*, 14 October 2003.

[104] ECtHR, *Sufi and Elmi v United Kingdom*, Judgment, 28 June 2011, para 250.

[105] ECtHR, *Othman (Abu Qatada) v United Kingdom*, 17 January 2012, paras 187–9; CtteeAT, *Agiza v Sweden*, Comm No 233/2003 (2005), CAT/C/34/D/233/2003, para 13.4; HRCttee, *El Alzery v Sweden*, Comm No 1416/2005 (2006), CCPR/C/88/D/1416/2005, para 11.5.

[106] ECtHR, *Chahal v United Kingdom*, Judgment, 15 November 1996, para 80; CtteeAT, *Tapia Paez v Sweden*, Comm No 39/1996 (1996), CAT/C/18/D/39/1996, para 14.5.

[107] E.C. Gillard, 'There's No Place Like Home: States' Obligations in Relation to Transfers of Persons', 90 *IRRC* 871 (2008) 703, at 710. See also C. Droege, 'Transfers of Detainees: Legal Framework, Non-Refoulement and Contemporary Challenges', 90 *IRRC* 871 (2008) 669, at 674–5.

[108] Greer, above n 63, at 126. See also Piotrowicz, above n 63, at 345–6, who further notes the inconsistent reference to Art 3 CAT in the practice quoted by the ICRC CIHL Study in support of the more general and distinctive prohibition of transfers in occupied territory under Rule 129A.

[109] Greer, above n 63, at 124.

Whatever the exact motivations are, the absence of any specific rule on *non-refoulement* in the ICRC Study is not so surprising after all. It fairly reflects the current state of the law: the relatively dated and limited rule of Article 45 paragraph 4 GC IV has been absorbed within the human rights principle of *non-refoulement* which is both broader and more protective. One can still regret that while using—and even abusing—human rights law materials in substantiating its own argumentation, the ICRC Study failed to restate one of the most obvious norms of CIL: the absolute right not to be transferred or returned to a state where there is a real risk of torture, inhuman or degrading treatment.[110]

C. Forced Displacement in Non-International Armed Conflict

Common Article 3 is silent on forced displacement. The indifference of IHL persisted until 1977 when Article 17 AP II was adopted. Unlike Article 49 GC IV, which prohibits any forced displacement within and outside the occupied territory, Article 17 AP II establishes a distinction between internal and external displacement. Its first paragraph governs displacement of civilians within the territory, while the second deals with displacement outside the territory of a state. Besides this primary distinction, the differences between the law of occupation and the law of NIAC are noticeable and have to be examined further.

I. The prohibition of forced displacement within the territory

Article 17 (1) AP II provides:

The displacement of the civilian population shall not be ordered for reasons related to the conflict unless the security of the civilians involved or imperative military reasons so demand. Should such displacements have to be carried out, all possible measures shall be taken in order that the civilian population may be received under satisfactory conditions of shelter, hygiene, health, safety and nutrition.

This provision broadly corresponds to Article 49 GC IV concerning the prohibition of forced displacement and its exceptions, as well as the conditions governing the implementation of evacuations. There are, however, several differences between the two provisions. Some are mainly formal, whereas others are much more substantial.

Among the semantic differences between the two provisions, the notion of 'protected persons' in GC IV is substituted by the term 'civilian population' in AP II, the latter term, according to the ICRC, including 'individuals or groups within the territory'.[111] Furthermore, the notions of transfer and deportation referred to in Article 49 paragraph 1 GC IV are encapsulated in Article 17(1) AP II within the generic term 'displacement'. Quite oddly, there is no explicit mention of the forcible character of displacement in the text of Article 17(1). Its forced nature is nevertheless presumed from the fact that

---

[110] For further discussions about its customary law nature, see notably E. Lauterpacht and D. Bethlehem, 'The Scope and Content of the Principle of *Non-Refoulement*: Opinion', in E. Feller, V. Türk, and F. Nicholson (eds), *Refugee Protection in International Law* (Cambridge: CUP, 2003) 87, at 149 ff; Goodwin-Gill and McAdam, above n 96, at 345–54; V. Chetail, 'The Transnational Movement of Persons under General International Law: An Inquiry into the Customary Law Foundations of International Migration Law', in V. Chetail and C. Bauloz (eds), *Research Handbook on Migration and International Law* (Cheltenham: Edward Elgar Publishing, 2014) 1, at 35–41.
[111] ICRC Commentary APs, at 1472, para 4852.

displacement has to be 'ordered', and from the general heading of the Article, i.e. the 'prohibition of forced movement of civilians'.

78   Compared to Article 49 GC IV, Article 17(1) AP II presents two important specificities which substantially restrict its scope and in turn highlight the limits of the protection granted by AP II in the field of forced displacement. First, contrary to the general prohibition of any types of forcible transfer and deportation enshrined in GC IV, Article 17(1) does not prohibit forced displacement as such. The prohibition is more subtly limited to the *order* to displace. As rightly underlined by Piotrowicz, 'the prohibition, on the face of it, is on the "ordering" of displacement rather than the displacement itself. These are clearly different things'.[112]

79   More generous interpretations are always possible, and even recommended by the object and purpose of IHL.[113] It nevertheless remains the case that the text of Article 17(1) AP II specifically requires an order to fall within the scope of its prohibition. The term 'order' entails something more than the forcible nature of the displacement, even if the two largely overlap both in practice and in principle.[114] During the drafting of AP II, an early version proposed more inclusive terms by prohibiting displacement to 'be ordered or compelled'.[115] Though the *travaux préparatoires* are not crystal clear about the exact reasons behind the deletion of the term 'compelled', the final version of Article 17(1) restricts the scope of the prohibition rather than the contrary.[116] The specific requirement for such an order has been restated in the subsequent practice, and notably endorsed in the ICC Statute[117] as well as in the ICRC Study.[118]

80   The second key characteristic of Article 17(1) relies on the reasons for the displacement so ordered. Whereas Article 49 paragraph 1 GC IV explicitly prohibits any transfers 'regardless of their motive', Article 17(1) AP II limits its prohibition to a displacement 'ordered for reasons related to the conflict'. According to the ICRC Commentary (and in line with the drafting history), this additional requirement is supposed to take into account the fact that displacement may be necessary in certain cases of epidemics or natural disasters. This explanation is not convincing, however, for in such cases the exception based on the security of civilians is plainly applicable without the need to qualify the scope of the prohibition further.

81   Furthermore, the phrase 'reasons related to the conflict' is more vague and more open to abuse than the exceptions expressed in Article 17(1). Clearly, the risk inherent in this specific requirement is the by-passing of the two legitimate exceptions by arguing that the displacement is not related to the conflict but justified by other reasons, whether political, economic, or demographic ones, or any other motivations.[119] Though vague

---

[112] Piotrowicz, above n 63, at 347.
[113] See J. Willms, 'Without Order, Anything Goes? The Prohibition of Forced Displacement in Non-International Armed Conflict', 91 *IRRC* 875 (2009) 547, at 547–65; Jacques, above n 5, at 58–61.
[114] See nevertheless Sivakumaran, above n 65, at 285.
[115] Conference of Government Experts 1972, Report, vol I, para 2503, vol II CE/COM II/85, at 50.
[116] See also in this sense the statements of the state delegates from Canada, Romania, and Iran, Meeting of Committee III, 4 April 1975 (CDDH/III/SR. 37; XIV, 387), reprinted in H. Levie (ed), *The Law of Non-International Armed Conflict: Protocol II to the 1949 Geneva Conventions* (Dordrecht: Martinus Nijhoff Publishers, 1987) at 531, 537–8.
[117] Art 8(2)(e)(viii) ICC Statute.   [118] ICRC CIHL Study, Rule 129B.
[119] See K. Hulme, 'Armed Conflict and the Displaced', 17 *IJRL* (2005) 91, at 103: '[W]hat may be of concern [...] is whether the forced removal or displacement of civilians based on illegal tactics falls within the phrase "reasons connected with the conflict". For example, displacement of civilians from areas rich in

and disputable, it has ultimately been retained in the ICC Statute[120] and the ICRC Study.[121]

82 In any event, IHRL remains applicable, whether or not the displacement is justified by a reason related to the armed conflict. It is further noticeable that the prohibition of arbitrary displacement expressed in the UN Guiding Principles does not retain the two above-mentioned requirements of Article 17(1) AP II, while endorsing the exceptions based on the security of the civilian population and imperative military reasons.[122]

83 The prohibition endorsed in the Guiding Principles is more consonant with IHRL, and in particular with the right to freedom of movement. Even if some treaties permit a state to derogate from this right, this is not the case for all human rights treaties.[123] Furthermore, when such a possibility is explicitly provided by the relevant convention, the state party can derogate from the right to free movement only to the extent that the other requirements for triggering the derogation mechanism are duly respected (including most notably the principle of proportionality, compatibility with the other obligations under international law, and the prohibition of any discrimination based on race, colour, sex, language, religion, or social origin).

84 The practice of treaty bodies provides some interesting guidance about the possibility to derogate from the right to free movement in times of armed conflict. In particular, the Inter-American Commission has held that the evacuation of the Miskito population in a zone of combat was justified under the derogation mechanism of the American Convention on Human Rights. Three main principles may be drawn from the findings of the Commission. First, evacuation should be strictly proportionate to the military danger against the security of the state and its population. Thus, 'even granting the Government of Nicaragua a margin of discretion, since it was a military decision applied to a military emergency', the Commission makes clear that 'the Government's argument that this planned relocation was [...] a result of a military emergency requires careful examination to determine whether it was in proportion to the nature of the emergency'.[124] It further insists that 'the forced evacuation [...] is only justifiable in the absence of any other alternative to meet a serious emergency'.[125]

---

minerals or oil, or tactics of "ethnic cleansing" (not necessarily involving acts or threats of violence), may not have any connection with the conflict.'

[120] Art 8(2)(e)(viii) ICC Statute.   [121] ICRC CIHL Study, Rule 129B.

[122] A similar provision may be found in the African Union Convention for the Protection and Assistance of Internally Displaced Persons in Africa (Kampala Convention) (2009). Its Art 4(4)(b) nevertheless qualifies it by using the phrase 'in accordance with international humanitarian law'. This reference proves to be unfortunate, as it may suggest that the higher threshold of Art 17 AP II should be transposed *mutatis mutandis* into the broader prohibition endorsed in the Kampala Convention. In any event, its Art 4(4)(d) recalls that prohibited displacement also includes, without any particular exception or qualification, 'displacement caused by generalized violence or violations of human rights'.

[123] Besides the UN treaties already mentioned, the Arab Charter includes, among underogable rights, Art 27(1), according to which 'no one shall be [...] prohibited from residing, or compelled to reside, in any part of his country'.

[124] IACommHR, *Report on the Situation of Human Rights of a Segment of the Nicaraguan Population of Miskito Origin*, OEA/Ser.L./V.II.62 doc 10 rev 3, 29 November 1983, paras 19–20.

[125] Ibid, para 20. It concluded that evacuation was proportionate in the particular circumstances of the case, because 'the prevailing situation in the zone at the time of the move was in fact very tense, and created both a danger to the lives of the Miskitos and a threat to the Nicaraguan Government': ibid, para 19.

85   Secondly, evacuation must remain temporary: '[T]he measure should not outlast the emergency, and termination of the emergency should allow the return of the civilian populace to their original region, if they so desire.'[126]

86   Thirdly, forced evacuation must not be decided or carried out on a discriminatory ground. In particular, it must not constitute 'a form of punishment applied to what may have been considered a disloyal ethnic group'.[127] This is particularly important, in order to avoid a scenario where an evacuation allegedly justified by the security of the population or military reasons is in truth a disguised measure of ethnic cleansing.

II. The prohibition of forced departure outside the territory

87   The prohibition of internal displacement under AP II is complemented by a specific provision governing forced movement outside the territory. According to Article 17(2) AP II, '[c]ivilians shall not be compelled to leave their own territory for reasons connected with the conflict'. Contrary to the prohibition of internal displacement expressed in the previous paragraph, the one contained in Article 17(2) is not mentioned among the norms of CIL proposed by the ICRC.

88   Although inspired by Article 49 GC IV, the exact content of Article 17(2) is not entirely clear; it raises two main questions regarding its geographical scope and the type of prohibited measures. First, this provision raises the question whether the term 'their own territory' refers to the territory of the state or that under the control of belligerents. The ICRC Commentary has advocated a broad meaning in line with this second interpretation:

> In fact, this formula [own territory] appears to be better suited to all the possible cases which might arise in a situation covered by Protocol II, and to take into account, in particular, situation where the insurgent party is in control of an extensive part of the territory. In this case the insurgents, too, should respect the obligation laid down here, and not compel civilians to leave the area under their authority.[128]

This interpretation is disputable for one simple reason: if Article 17(2) covers forced departure outside the territory under the control of insurgents, this provision would be a curious redundancy given that Article 17(1) AP II already prohibits displacement within the state's territory as a whole. The circularity of the ICRC interpretation would further lead to an absurd result: while addressing both state agents and insurgents, the prohibition of displacement under the first paragraph of Article 17 would be subjected to two exceptions, whereas the one established in the second paragraph would be absolute. Thus, the first paragraph should rather be understood as dealing with displacement within the territory, and the second with displacement outside the territory of a state.

89   The second question about the scope of Article 17(2) AP II relates to the type of displacements prohibited. The provision bans forced departure from the territory, without referring to transfer and deportation as in Article 49 GC IV. However, the difference between the two provisions is negligible. Sivakumaran has rightly observed:

> Practice has also shown that cross-border transfers may take place in non-international armed conflicts. Although Additional Protocol II does not use the term 'deportation', the prohibition on compelling civilians 'to leave their own territory for reasons connected with the conflict' is precisely that.[129]

---

[126] Ibid, para 21.   [127] Ibid, para 30.
[128] ICRC Commentary APs, at 1474, para 4859.   [129] Sivakumaran, above n 65, at 286.

Similarly to Article 49 paragraph 1 GC IV, the legal nature of the removal is thus irrelevant; what matters is the forcible character of the displacement, be it physical (as apparent from an act of deportation) or psychological (including threat of coercion and similar pressure to leave the country).

Furthermore, although Article 17(2) AP II is not as explicit as Article 49 paragraph 1 GC IV, the general prohibition includes both individual and collective forced departures.[130] Nonetheless, the type of prohibited displacement is circumscribed in AP II by a significant restriction which is not required under Article 49 paragraph 1 GC IV. Similarly to Article 17(1), the second paragraph subordinates the prohibition of forced departure to 'reasons connected with the conflict'. As already underlined, such an elusive notion raises more questions than answers. The drafting history does not provide a working definition of these reasons triggering the prohibition of forced displacement. State delegates were primarily concerned that Article 17(2) should not interfere with normal extradition proceedings and with domestic judicial systems still using exile as a penalty.[131] Though the ultimate rationale is unclear, explicit reference to these exceptional cases has been deleted in the final version in favour of a broader reference to 'reasons connected with the conflict'.[132]

The main example mentioned by the ICRC Commentary is as vague as the wording of Article 17(2). It envisages the 'expulsion of groups of civilians across the boundaries by armed forces or armed groups *because of military operations*'.[133] The ICRC continues, without further specification, 'basically these are the kind of cases that the Conference intended to cover'.[134] When discussing the case of individual deportations, it restates that 'if such a measure arises from the situation of conflict, it constitutes forced movement within the meaning of this article'.[135] The ICRC Commentary continues with a circular reasoning underlying that *a contrario*, 'a sentence following conviction giving the option to leave the territory, might not be considered as such. If the conviction is not related to the conflict, it is clear that that measure is not covered by the article under consideration here.'[136]

In any event, one cannot conclude, as has sometimes been argued, that 'if the deportation follows a conviction with no relation to the conflict, it falls outside the ambit of the article and remains within the realm of a state's exclusive jurisdiction on domestic matters'.[137] International human rights law is still relevant for circumscribing the competence of the state through, most notably, the prohibition of collective expulsion, the principle of *non-refoulement*, and due process guarantees governing deportation. More generally, and as also mentioned before, expulsion of nationals is further prohibited by IHRL.

D. Legal Consequences of a Violation

As with many other breaches of international law, forced displacement decided and/or carried out in contravention of IHL and IHRL entails two types of legal consequences. First, at the state level, such a violation engages the international responsibility of the

---

[130] ICRC Commentary APs, at 1474, para 4860.
[131] Bothe/Partsch/Solf, at 693; and CDDH/215/Rev.l, para 150.
[132] Bothe/Partsch/Solf, at 693; and CDDH/215/Rev.l, para 150.
[133] ICRC Commentary APs, at 1474, para 4861 (emphasis added). [134] Ibid.
[135] Ibid, para 4864. [136] Ibid, paras 4864–5. [137] Jacques, above n 5, at 65.

state. This has most notably been reaffirmed by the ICJ in its Advisory Opinion on the *Wall in the Occupied Palestinian Territories*[138] with regard to the violations of Article 49 GC IV and of the right to freedom of movement under Article 12 ICCPR. As a result, the ICJ recalled that Israel was internationally bound to put an end to its violations and to make reparation. Given the character and the importance of the rights and obligations involved in this particular case, the Court has further concluded that all states are under the twofold obligation not to recognize the illegal situation resulting from the construction of the wall, and not to render aid or assistance in maintaining the situation created by such construction. It has also restated, in accordance with Common Article 1 of the four Geneva Conventions, that all states parties to GC IV are under the obligation to ensure the compliance of Israel with IHL.

94 At the individual level, the prohibition of forced displacement has also been a well-established feature of ICL since the Nuremberg trials.[139] Article 147 GC IV includes 'unlawful deportation or transfer […] of a protected person' among the grave breaches of the Convention. This has been reaffirmed by Article 85(4)(a) AP I. Although the notion of grave breaches is confined to IAC, the ICC Statute acknowledges that unlawful deportation or transfer can also constitute a war crime in NIAC. Its Article 8(2)(e)(viii) qualifies as a war crime in NIAC the fact of 'ordering the displacement of the civilian population for reasons related to the conflict, unless the security of the civilians involved or imperative military reasons so demand'.

95 This reproduces Article 17(1) AP II, and accordingly suffers from the same restrictions (see section C.I of this chapter). It is true that in practice the requirement of an order is primarily a question of fact which is closely linked with the individual responsibility of the perpetrator. This is, however, the only crime in the entire ICC Statute that specifically requires such an order.[140] Thus, while excluding those who only carry out the order, this war crime is limited to the persons who have *de jure* or *de facto* authority to give such an order.[141]

96 Besides the order, the requirement of reasons related to the conflict is equally problematic. Most of the difficulties associated with this elusive notion could be avoided if it were construed by reference to the general purposes of the armed conflict. Indeed the reasons related to the conflict are broader than the military reasons. They include other typical reasons for an armed conflict, whether political, economic, territorial, national, religious, or ethnic. Such an interpretation would thus neutralize the risk of abuses identified earlier and be consonant with the evolution of international law as notably acknowledged in IHRL.

---

[138] ICJ, *Legal Consequences of the Construction of a Wall in the Occupied Palestinian Territories*, above n 51.
[139] Art 6(c) Nuremberg Charter; Art 11(1)(c) Control Council Law No 10; Art V(c) Tokyo Charter.
[140] The *Elements of Crimes* are particularly insistent on this requirement: after mentioning it twice, they further underline that '[t]he perpetrator was in a position to effect such displacement by giving such order'.
[141] See also in this sense Willms, above n 113, at 561–2; A. Zimmermann, 'Article 8, Paragraph 2', in Triffterer (ed), above n 15, at 281. The requirement of an order may have further implications with regard to the very nature of the prohibited forced displacement. Indeed, it has been argued that '[t]he use of the term "ordering" makes it clear that only acts which are directly aimed at removing the respective civilian population from a given area are prohibited. Thus, other acts which do not possess such a character but which lead to the same result, such as the intentional starvation of the civilian population in order to force them to leave a certain area, are not prohibited by article 8 para. 2(e)(viii) of the Statute.': Zimmermann, 'Article 8', ibid, at 281. See also Werle, above n 15, at 329.

The ICC Statute also presents one potentially important characteristic. The broad wording of Article 8(2)(e)(viii) and the absence of any indication to the contrary suggest that prohibited displacement can take place within and outside the territory, thereby including deportation and other related measures of transfer to another state.[142] This interpretation would align this criminal act with war crimes in IAC.

In IAC, Article 8 of the ICC Statute refers to the prohibition of deportation and transfer twice: Article 8(2)(a)(vii) restates 'unlawful deportation and transfer' as a grave breach of GC IV; Article 8(2)(b)(viii) then reproduces Article 85(4)(a) AP I and refers to 'the deportation or transfer of all or parts of the population of the occupied territory within or outside this territory'. Although the latter is already encompassed by the former, there remains one difference worth mentioning. Unlawful deportation and transfer of one single protected person can be a grave breach of GC IV. By contrast, the term 'all or parts of the population' under Article 85(4)(a) AP I requires the forced displacement of more than one civilian. The *Elements of Crimes* of Article 8(2)(a)(vii) further confirm that 'the perpetrator deported or transferred one or more persons to another State or to another location'. This accordingly includes forced displacement within and outside the territory of the state.

E. Critical Assessment

As amply exemplified in this chapter, IHL cannot operate in splendid isolation from the other branches of public international law. International criminal law, IRL, and IHRL play a critical role, not only by reinforcing IHL but, more importantly, by filing its gaps and compensating for its limits. This holds true with regard to forced displacement, as well as for many other key issues related to the law of armed conflict, though this is perhaps more obvious in this specific domain than in others.

Indeed IHL was not conceived to provide a comprehensive and coherent regime of protection against forcible displacement in armed conflicts. Thus one should not be surprised that its impact is fairly limited. The few provisions contained in GC IV and AP II are insufficient on their own; they make sense only when taken together with other applicable rules of IHRL and IRL.

The incomplete reach of IHL is further exacerbated by its complex normative structure anchored on a traditional triptych: occupation, IAC, and NIAC. Among these three scenarios, the one applicable in occupied territory represents the most accomplished set of international humanitarian norms devoted to forced displacement. Nonetheless, the norms enshrined in GC IV still coexist with those of IHRL, while ICL ensures that their violations are duly sanctioned.

The normative parallelism between IHL and IHRL is more striking in NIAC, even if this issue has only lately come onto the agenda of the former with the adoption of AP II. These two branches of international law largely coincide in substance, and thus are mutually supportive. Nevertheless IHRL offers broader protection than IHL in NIACs. As mentioned above, the requirement of an order to displace combined with a specific reason related to the conflict represents a relatively high threshold for triggering the prohibition of forcible displacement expressed in AP II. This mitigates the impact of Article 17(1)

---

[142] For a similar account, see Werle, above n 15, at 328–9; Zimmermann, above n 141, at 281.

AP II and its customary law twin to such an extent that IHL can hardly be considered as the legal frame of reference governing forced displacement in NIACs.

103 Although IHL is commonly presumed as the most detailed branch of law in times of IACs, it is ironically the less substantial one when it comes to forcible displacement. There is indeed no general prohibition, but only a specific one limited to transfers to those states unable or unwilling to apply GC IV. This weakness has been considered 'a legal gap in the existing protection regime, as international humanitarian law does not regulate the forced displacement of civilians in unoccupied territory during an international armed conflict'.[143]

104 The absence of any general prohibition does not necessarily mean that forced displacement is permitted in IACs. This was, however, the simplistic conclusion of the EECC, when it assumed that '[i]nternational humanitarian law gives belligerents broad powers to expel nationals of the enemy State from their territory during a conflict'.[144] It then asserted on this basis that 'Ethiopia could lawfully expel […] nationals of an enemy belligerent, although it was bound to ensure them the protections required by Geneva Convention IV and other applicable international humanitarian law.'[145]

105 The ILC Special Rapporteur on Expulsion rightly observed that this assertion 'has no clear support in customary international law'.[146] According to him, 'it is evident that the practice in the matter is rather different. Nor is there any basis for this thinking, whatever may have been implied, in international humanitarian law'.[147] He proposed instead an extremely nuanced state of the law grounded on the three following assumptions:

(a) there is no rule of international law that requires a belligerent State to allow nationals of an enemy State to remain in its territory, but there is also no rule that requires such State to expel them; (b) the collective expulsion of foreign nationals of an enemy State is practised by some States, to varying degrees, and finds support in most of the literature, both historically and in modern times; (c) this State practice and the literature seem to consider that such expulsion must be allowed only in the case of aliens who are hostile to a receiving State at war with their country.[148]

106 With due respect, the current state of international law is even more straightforward than this sophisticated understatement. The silence of IHL means nothing else than that the solution must be found elsewhere, that is, in other applicable branches of international law, thereby including IHRL and IRL. Following such a stance, collective expulsion is prohibited in absolute terms by IHRL and applies to any aliens, irrespective of their nationality. Individual expulsions are still possible when enemy nationals represent a danger to the public order and national security, unless there is a risk of torture, or inhuman or degrading treatment in the state of destination.[149]

107 This line of reasoning even finds an additional support in IHL itself. Article 38 GC IV stipulates:

---

[143] Jacques, above n 5, at 22.
[144] EECC, *Civilian Claims—Eritrea's Claims 15, 16, 23, and 27–32*, Partial Award, 25 *Reports of International Arbitral Awards* (2004), para 81.
[145] Ibid, para 82.
[146] ILC, *Third Report on the Expulsion of Aliens*, M. Kamto, Special Rapporteur, A/CN.4/581, 19 April 2007, at 41, para 126.
[147] Ibid.   [148] Ibid, at 42, para 134.
[149] This arguably reflects CIL. For further discussions about expulsion in CIL, see Chetail, above n 110, at 35–41 and 54–8.

With the exception of special measures authorized by the present Convention, in particular by Articles 27 and 41 thereof, the situation of protected persons shall continue to be regulated, in principle, by the provisions concerning aliens in time of peace.

Though neglected by commentators, Article 38 GC IV is bound to play a crucial role for the purpose of articulating IHL with IHRL. This provision not only restates the continuing applicability of the latter as a complement to the former, it also underlines that, except for the special measures permitted by IHL (such as internment), the legal regime applicable to non-citizens in time of peace shall remain the rule. In other words, Article 38 GC IV establishes a presumption that the ordinary rules of IHRL and IRL continue to be applicable to non-citizens. Of course states can still reverse this presumption by resorting to the derogation mechanism under the relevant treaties. However, such a clause is not provided by all human rights treaties, and even where it is, the use of the derogation mechanism is subordinated to several requirements. According to these conditions, and in particular the necessity test, it is doubtful whether the expulsion of enemy nationals would be strictly required by the exigencies of the situation on grounds only of their nationality, without any other particular danger to public order or national security.

As exemplified by the expulsion of enemy nationals, IHRL opens up new perspectives for understanding traditional issues of armed conflicts. The minimum, if not minimalist, protection granted by IHL is upgraded by the cumulative application of the other applicable branches of international law. Though every specialist is naturally inclined to see armed conflict through the myopic lens of his or her own discipline, no single branch offers a definitive answer. The multifaceted challenges of armed conflicts can be apprehended only through a systemic approach of the applicable branches of international law. From this broader perspective, the law of armed conflict resembles a legal puzzle comprising several pieces which make sense only when put together. Such a systemic approach not only provides the global picture; it also ensures that IHL, ICL, IRL, and IHRL are no longer competitors but brothers in arms. **108**

VINCENT CHETAIL

Chapter 59. Judicial Guarantees

	MN
A. Introduction	1
B. Meaning and Application	5
I. The relationship between international humanitarian law and international human rights law	5
II. Elements of judicial guarantees	9
a. Requirement of an 'impartial' and 'regularly constituted court'	10
b. The right to be informed without delay of the particulars of the offence and to have all necessary rights and means of defence	22
c. The requirement of individual criminal responsibility	28
d. The principle of *nullum crimen, nulla poena sine lege*	31
e. The presumption of innocence	35
f. The right of the accused 'to be tried in his presence'	36
g. The right against self-incrimination	39
h. The principle of 'equality of arms'	41
i. The principle of *ne bis in idem*	45
j. The right to a public trial	51
k. Notification of Protecting Power	53
l. The right to appeal	54
C. Relevance in Non-International Armed Conflicts	59
D. Legal Consequences of a Violation	60
E. Critical Assessment	61

Select Bibliography

Amnesty International, *Fair Trial Manual* (2nd edn, London: Amnesty International, 2014)

Doswald-Beck, L., *Human Rights in Times of Conflict and Terrorism* (Oxford: OUP, 2011)

Gasser, H.-P., 'Respect for Fundamental Judicial Guarantees in Time of Armed Conflict: The Part Played by ICRC Delegates', 32 *IRRC* 287 (1992) 121

Lubell, N., 'Human Rights Obligations in Military Occupation', 94 *IRRC* 885 (2012) 317

Pejic, J., 'Procedural Principles and Safeguards for Internment/Administrative Detention in Armed Conflict and Other Situations of Violence', 87 *IRRC* 858 (2005) 375

Pejic, J., 'The Protective Scope of Common Article 3: More than Meets the Eye', 93 *IRRC* 881 (2011) 189

Somer, J., 'Jungle Justice: Passing Sentence on the Equality of Belligerents in Non-International Armed Conflict', 89 *IRRC* 867 (2007) 655

UN Office of the High Commissioner for Human Rights, *International Legal Protection of Human Rights in Armed Conflict* (New York/Geneva: United Nations, 2011)

Weissbrodt, D., 'International Fair Trial Guarantees', in A. Clapham and P. Gaeta (eds), *The Oxford Handbook of International Law in Armed Conflict* (Oxford: OUP, 2014) 410

A. Introduction

1 Judicial guarantees in international humanitarian law (IHL) refer broadly to 'guarantees that must be afforded to anyone suspected of having committed a criminal offence'.[1] Criminal punishment is a significant exception to the temporary detention or internment of protected persons during armed conflict. Deprivation of liberty based on a penal process does not necessarily cease upon the 'general close of military operations'.[2] It may even result in the imposition of the death penalty.[3] Judicial guarantees are thus among the fundamental obligations incorporated in Common Article 3 paragraph 1(1)(d) as part of the 'minimum yardstick' reflecting 'elementary considerations of humanity'.[4] These rules are also considered part of customary international law (CIL) applicable in all armed conflicts.[5]

2 The emergence and expansion of international human rights law (IHRL) has profoundly shaped judicial guarantees in contemporary IHL. The Geneva Diplomatic Conference deliberated from 21 April to 12 August 1949 before adopting the four Conventions. The United Nations (UN) in Paris had adopted the Universal Declaration of Human Rights (UDHR) just a few months earlier, on 10 December 1948.[6] Articles 10 and 11 of the Declaration contained only basic hortatory provisions on the right to 'a fair and public hearing by an independent and impartial tribunal'. Although the rules enshrined in the Declaration are now recognized as customary international rules, such status was far from established at that time.[7] Judicial guarantees were thus rather basic in both IHL and IHRL in 1949. For instance, Common Article 3 paragraph 1(1)(d) simply prohibits 'the passing of sentences and carrying out of executions without previous judgment pronounced by a regularly constituted court, affording all the judicial guarantees which are recognized as indispensable by civilized peoples'.

3 The provisions applicable to international armed conflicts (IACs) are somewhat more elaborate. In particular, the relevant provisions of Geneva Convention (GC) IV include Article 5 ('rights of fair and regular trial' for spies or saboteurs), Articles 67 to 78 (judicial guarantees in penal procedures in occupied territories),[8] Article 123 (disciplinary punishment in place of internment), and Article 126 (application of right to a 'regular trial' to internees). Article 146 paragraph 4 GC IV provides 'safeguards of proper trial and defence' for persons accused of grave breaches, and corresponds to Articles 49, 50, and 129

---

[1] See J. Pejic, 'The Protective Scope of Common Article 3: More than Meets the Eye', 93 *IRRC* 881 (2011) 189, at 211.
[2] See, e.g., Art 6 GC IV.
[3] See, e.g., Art 100 GC III; Art 68 GC IV.
[4] ICJ, *Case concerning Military and Paramilitary Activities in and against Nicaragua (Nicaragua v United States)*, Judgment, 27 June 1986, para 218.
[5] See ICRC CIHL Study, vol I, Rules, at 352. Rule 100 reads: 'No one may be convicted or sentenced, except pursuant to a fair trial affording all essential judicial guarantees.'
[6] UNGA Res 217A(III), UN Doc A/810 (1948).
[7] See, e.g., T. Meron, *Human Rights and Humanitarian Norms as Customary Law* (Oxford: Clarendon Press, 1989); H. Hannum, 'The Status of the Universal Declaration of Human Rights in National and International Law', 25 *Georgia Journal of International and Comparative Law* (1995–6) 317. The ICJ has made reference to the UDHR on numerous occasions in its judgments. See, e.g., ICJ, *United States Diplomatic and Consular Staff in Tehran*, Judgment, 24 May 1980, para 91: 'Wrongfully to deprive human beings of their freedom and to subject them to physical constraint in conditions of hardship is in itself manifestly incompatible with the principles of the Charter of the United Nations, as well as with the fundamental principles enunciated in the Universal Declaration of Human Rights.'
[8] For a detailed discussion of judicial guarantees in occupied territories, see Ch 68, MN 52–80, of this volume.

of GCs I, II, and III respectively. Geneva Convention III also includes judicial guarantees specifically for prisoners of war (POWs) in Articles 99 to 108.[9]

The essence of these provisions was largely subsumed by the adoption of the more elaborate judicial guarantee provisions in Article 75(4) of Additional Protocol I (AP I) and the corresponding, though less elaborate, provision in Article 6 of Protocol II (AP II) relevant to non-international armed conflicts (NIACs). The Protocols were elaborated between 1974 and 1977 in the Diplomatic Conference on the Reaffirmation and Development of International Humanitarian Law Applicable in Armed Conflicts. Prior to that period, on 16 December 1966, the UN had adopted the International Covenant on Civil and Political Rights (ICCPR), which entered into force on 23 March 1976.[10] The Covenant contained relatively elaborate provisions on judicial guarantees in its Articles 14 and 15. The *travaux préparatoires* of AP I and AP II indicate that IHL judicial guarantees were based on the ICCPR. Indeed, the International Committee of the Red Cross (ICRC) Commentary observes that Article 75(4) AP I 'reproduces, in some cases word for word, the corresponding provisions of the Covenant on Civil and Political Rights'.[11] Furthermore, the subsequent jurisprudence on judicial guarantees—whether before jurisdictions such as the European Court of Human Rights (ECtHR) or the International Criminal Tribunal for former Yugoslavia (ICTY)—has significantly elaborated the definition and scope of such IHRL provisions, and by extension the corresponding IHL provisions. To the extent that, first, Article 75 AP I is an explicit treaty rule of IHL (and therefore specifically applicable in times of armed conflict), secondly, it can be considered today a customary rule applicable in both IACs and NIACs,[12] and, thirdly, it represents a minimum contemporary yardstick for judicial guarantees in times of armed conflict,[13] it is also helpful to consider it when looking at some of the specific rules of the Geneva Conventions (or when interpreting the content of Common Article 3 applicable to NIACs).[14]

B. Meaning and Application

I. The relationship between international humanitarian law and international human rights law

Since both IHL and IHRL regulate judicial guarantees, it is important to consider their interrelationship before considering the specific provisions of the Geneva Conventions.

---

[9] See Ch 50 of this volume.   [10] Adopted by UNGA Res 2200A (XXI), 16 December 1966.
[11] ICRC Commentary APs, para 3005.
[12] The judicial guarantees set forth under Art 75(4) are considered in the ICRC CIHL Study as CIL applicable in both IAC and NIAC. See ICRC CIHL Study, Rule 100.
[13] Unlike the multiple dispersed provisions in the 1949 GCs, Art 75(4) AP I sets forth judicial guarantees in a single consolidated provision. It thus constitutes 'a sort of "summary of the law"'. See Commentary APs, para 3007. Art 75(1) AP I further specifies that it applies to persons who 'do not benefit from more favourable treatment under the Conventions or under this Protocol'. Apparently, this qualification was intended as a residual clause: 'When it presented the draft article, the ICRC expressed its concern that a minimum of protection should be granted in time of armed conflict to any person who was, for one reason or another, unable to claim a particular status, such as that of prisoner of war, civilian internee in accordance with the fourth Convention, wounded, sick or shipwrecked' (ICRC Commentary APs, para 3001).
[14] The ICRC Commentary to the APs emphasizes that while CA 3—also part of CIL—refers to the 'judicial guarantees which are recognized as indispensable by civilized peoples', Art 75(4) 'rightly spells out these guarantees'. Thus 'this article, and to an even greater extent, Article 6 of Protocol II (Penal prosecutions), gives valuable indications to help explain the terms of Article 3 on guarantees' (see ICRC Commentary APs, para 3084).

It is now commonly accepted that IHL and IHRL are complementary and not mutually exclusive.[15] The object and purpose of both bodies of law is the protection of human dignity. Nonetheless, these bodies of law are distinct, have developed separately, and differ in their scope of application.[16]

6   Considering the common objectives but different scopes of application of IHRL and IHL, what is the applicable body of law with respect to judicial guarantees in armed conflict? In its Advisory Opinion on the *Legal Consequences of the Construction of a Wall*, the International Court of Justice (ICJ) explained that some rights are protected only by human rights law, while others are protected by humanitarian law, and 'yet others may be matters of both these branches of international law'.[17] It has been argued that judicial guarantees fall within this third category of 'matters of both branches of international law'.[18] In that regard, the Customary International Humanitarian Law (CIHL) Study affirms that

> international humanitarian law contains concepts the interpretation of which needs to include a reference to human rights law, for example, the provision that no one may be convicted of a crime other than by a 'regularly constituted court affording all the judicial guarantees which are recognized as indispensable'.[19]

It has also been reasonably asserted that

> a closer examination of the respective [IHL and IHRL] provisions—particularly of Article 75 of Additional Protocol I and of Article 14 of the ICCPR—demonstrates that the specific guarantees listed are nearly identical. Based on the overlapping nature of the fair trial standards applicable both in situations of armed conflict and in peacetime and the common aim of the respective

---

[15] See, e.g., W.A. Solf, 'Problems with the Application of Norms Governing Interstate Armed Conflict to Non-International Armed Conflict', 13 *Georgia Journal of International and Comparative Law* (1983) 291, at 295: 'Human rights law and humanitarian law operate concurrently, complementing and reinforcing each other'; H.-P. Gasser, 'International Humanitarian Law and Human Rights Law in Non-International Armed Conflict: Joint Venture or Mutual Exclusion?', 45 *GYIL* (2002) 149. See also HRCttee, General Comment 29, para 3: 'During armed conflict, whether international or non-international, rules of international humanitarian law become applicable and help, *in addition to the provisions in article 4 and article 5, paragraph 1*, of the Covenant, to prevent the abuse of a State's emergency powers' (emphasis added). See further HRCttee, General Comment 31, para 11: 'The Covenant applies *also in situations of armed conflict* to which the rules of international humanitarian law are applicable. While, in respect of certain Covenant rights, more specific rules of international humanitarian law may be specially relevant for the purposes of the interpretation of Covenant rights, both spheres of law are complementary, not mutually exclusive' (emphasis added). Those who argue for complementarity between the two bodies of law (see, e.g., J. Pejic, 'Procedural Principles and Safeguards for Internment/Administrative Detention in Armed Conflict and Other Situations of Violence', 87 *IRRC* 858 (2005) 378) often refer to the wording of Arts 72 and 75(1) AP I and the preambular paragraph 2 of AP II. Art 72 reads: 'The provisions of this Section are additional to the rules concerning humanitarian protection of civilians and civilian objects in the power of a Party to the conflict contained in the Fourth Convention, particularly Parts I and III thereof, as well as to *other applicable rules of international law relating to the protection of fundamental human rights during international armed conflict*' (emphasis added). Art 75(1) AP I reads in its relevant part 'persons who are in the power of a Party to the conflict and who do not benefit from more favourable treatment under the Conventions or under this Protocol shall be treated humanely in all circumstances and shall enjoy, *as a minimum*, the protection provided by this Article without any adverse distinction' (emphasis added). The preambular paragraph 2 of AP II reads, 'international instruments relating to human rights offer a basic protection to the human person'. The ICRC Commentary to AP II specifies that the reference to international instruments includes treaties adopted by the UN, such as the ICCPR and the CAT, as well as the regional human rights treaties (see Commentary APs, paras 4428–30). See further Ch 35 of this volume.
[16] See Ch 35, MN 1–7, of this volume.
[17] ICJ, *Legal Consequences of the Construction of a Wall in the Occupied Palestinian Territory*, Advisory Opinion, 9 July 2004, para 106.
[18] Pejic, above n 1, at 213, fn 69.   [19] ICRC CIHL Study, at xxxvii.

provisions, it is possible to identify a list of judicial guarantees that are binding in armed conflict (as well as outside of it).[20]

On the other hand, if the meaning of judicial guarantees under IHL were defined by strict reference to IHRL, this would raise serious practical challenges. Armed conflict can often severely disrupt the justice system, and the administration of justice in itself is closely linked to state functions and organs. Bearing this in mind, the case for a more nuanced application of IHRL in interpreting IHL may be persuasive. It may be that, in some instances (for example military occupation, or NIACs), IHL rules *limit/restrict* the full exercise of human rights. Such a contextualized approach would recognize the possible impediments to complete fulfilment of all human rights in certain situations, respect the principle of equality of belligerents, and reconcile a 'humanitarian minimum' with obligations that are reasonable and realistic for *all* parties to the conflict, and thus respectful of the delicate balance IHL seeks to strike between pragmatism and idealism in regulating war.

A final noteworthy point is that, in at least one respect, IHL may be more exacting than IHRL. Judicial guarantees under IHL are non-derogable. This contrasts with the regime under IHRL, which contains clauses permitting derogations in time of war.[21] Since judicial guarantees are provided for under IHL (both in treaty and in custom), it may be concluded that a state cannot completely dispense with judicial guarantees during armed conflict, because that would be 'inconsistent' with its IHL obligations.

II. Elements of judicial guarantees

The Geneva Conventions do not contain a single consolidated provision listing all judicial guarantees applicable in armed conflict. Rather, they set out an elaborate system of guarantees, with rules applicable to various categories of protected persons, and further distinguish between IAC and NIAC. Thus, IHL contains distinct provisions regulating penal proceedings as they relate to: POWs, civilians, civilian internees, and parties to the conflict in NIAC. For ease of reference, the table reproduced in the Annex to this chapter sets out all the relevant provisions and rules based on the category of protected persons and the applicable legal regime (i.e. IAC or NIAC). The sections that follow elaborate specific elements of these rules, to the extent that the provisions dealing with specific categories of protected persons are not addressed in more detail elsewhere in this volume.

a. Requirement of an 'impartial' and 'regularly constituted court'

Before addressing the specific judicial guarantees, it is necessary to consider the general requirement of 'an impartial and regularly constituted court',[22] which aims to ensure that no person is ever punished outside of the justice system, be it in times of peace or war.

---

[20] Pejic, above n 1, at 213.
[21] This refers in particular to Art 4 ICCPR, which allows a state party to derogate from its obligations regarding judicial guarantees under limited conditions, such as a public emergency threatening the life of the nation, where the measures for derogation do not contravene other obligations under international law.
[22] The term 'regularly constituted court' is used in CA 3 para 1(1)(d), and the term 'impartial' is used, in conjunction with 'regularly constituted court', in Art 75(4) AP I. Art 66 GC IV uses the term 'properly constituted', when referring to non-political military courts of the Occupying Power that can try protected persons. Courts would be properly constituted when they are able to provide a 'regular trial' in accordance with Art 71 GC IV.

i. International armed conflicts

11 In IAC, the requirement of impartiality and independence of courts is found both in the POW regime (see Chapter 50 of this volume) and in the set of rules on civilians. With respect to POWs, Article 102 GC III expresses the broad understanding of what a 'regularly constituted' court is under the POW regime (namely, the same military courts and procedures under which members of the armed forces of the Detaining Power are tried). There is an additional safeguard built into Article 84 GC III (to be read in conjunction with Article 105 GC III), which requires that whatever court is ultimately used (anticipating the eventuality, for instance, that the Detaining Power might use its civilian courts to try POWs), it conforms to the guarantees of 'independence and impartiality as generally recognized'. The exact meaning of this phrase may be understood only by reference to Article 105 GC III, which lists the exact rights and means to be afforded to a POW during trial. This was an intentional referral by the drafters, meant to indicate the precise list of guarantees that an 'independent' and 'impartial' court should afford to POWs.[23]

12 Regarding civilians, GC IV provides that protected persons in occupied territory (and internees who are in the national territory of the Detaining Power, by analogy)[24] may be tried only by 'properly constituted, non-political military courts, on condition that the said courts sit in the occupied country'.[25] The meaning of 'properly constituted' can be gleaned both from the wording of Article 71 (as being able to conduct a 'regular trial') and from the Pictet Commentary to Article 66:

> This wording definitely *excludes* all special tribunals. It is the *ordinary military courts* of the Occupying Power which will be competent. Such courts will, of course, be set up *in accordance with the recognized principles governing the administration of justice*.
>
> It will be seen later (Article 71 and following) that the proceedings in such courts are governed by a set of extremely detailed provisions, providing protected persons with *every guarantee of respect for the human person*.[26]

ii. Non-international armed conflicts

13 In NIACs, the applicable provisions are to be found in Common Article 3 to the Geneva Conventions and AP II. Common Article 3 paragraph 1(1)(d) refers to a 'regularly constituted court', and Article 6(2) AP II refers to a court 'offering the essential guarantees of independence and impartiality.'

14 As regards Common Article 3, the Pictet Commentary provides no clarification as to the meaning of the term 'regularly constituted', and contemporary jurisprudence has interpreted this requirement in the light of IHRL. A notable instance is the 2006 United States (US) Supreme Court Judgment in *Hamdan*, holding that the military commissions established by the Bush Administration to prosecute 'enemy combatants' captured in the Afghanistan conflict were not regularly constituted.[27] The majority opinion held that 'regularly constituted' means 'established and organized in accordance with the laws and procedures already in force'.[28] In his Concurring Opinion, Justice Kennedy also held that a court is regularly established when it 'relies upon […] standards deliberated upon and chosen in advance'.[29] This interpretation has been criticized by some for being too

---

[23] Pictet Commentary GC III, at 412.
[24] Art 126 GC IV. GC IV did not include any judicial guarantee provisions specifically addressing non-internee civilians in national territory. AP I closed this gap by providing the legal guarantees listed in its Art 75.
[25] Art 66 GC IV.   [26] Pictet Commentary GC IV, at 340 (emphasis added).
[27] *Hamdan v Rumsfeld*, 548 US 577 (2006).   [28] Ibid, at 632.   [29] Ibid, at 637.

state-centric, in disregard of the equal obligation of non-state actors to comply with this requirement of Common Article 3.[30]

15 In substance, the US Supreme Court interpreted this basic judicial guarantee in the light of IHRL. This relates in particular to the requirement under Article 14(1) ICCPR and other human rights instruments that a tribunal be 'competent' and 'established by law'.[31] The CIHL Study states that 'a court is regularly constituted if it has been established and organized in accordance with the laws and procedures already in force in a country'.[32] It also points to a number of states that have incorporated this requirement in national legislation or in military manuals.[33]

16 The jurisprudence of the ICTY has adopted a more flexible approach in so far as it was an ad hoc tribunal established by the UN Security Council in view of exigent circumstances and thus ostensibly not 'regularly constituted'. In the *Tadić* case, the Appeals Chamber held that the criterion 'established by law' means established 'in accordance with the rule of law', and that its jurisdiction was lawfully established in so far as it (i) was established by a competent organ (i.e. the UN Security Council), and (ii) observed the minimum requirements of procedural fairness.[34] The Special Court for Sierra Leone (SCSL) has further clarified that

> to be 'established by law', [a tribunal's] establishment must accord with the rule of law. This means that it must be established according to proper international criteria; it must have the mechanisms and facilities to dispense even-handed justice, providing at the same time all the guarantees of fairness and it must be in tune with international human rights instruments.[35]

17 It is paradoxical that in certain respects, the jurisprudence of the UN tribunals legitimizing the establishment of ad hoc international criminal jurisdictions demonstrates the flexibility that some would argue should apply to non-state actors with respect to judicial guarantees in armed conflict. Neither the UN Security Council nor non-state actors possess the state institutions required for the 'regular' constitution of courts *stricto sensu*. Perhaps there is greater faith that, in contrast with states and non-state actors, the UN will be less inclined to abuse the looser concept of a jurisdiction that merely accords with the 'rule of law' rather than strict compliance with previously established procedures.

18 As regards AP II, one may similarly seek guidance in IHRL to further specify the meaning of 'independence' and 'impartiality' in the context of criminal proceedings in NIACs.[36] The UN Human Rights Committee (HRCttee) has held that the right to an independent

---

[30] See, e.g., K. Anderson, 'Hamdan and Common Article Three's Obligations upon Non-State Actors', *Kenneth Anderson's Law of War and Just War Theory Blog*, 13 July 2006, available at <http://kennethandersonlawofwar.blogspot.nl/2006/07/hamdan-and-common-article-threes.html>.

[31] The requirement under IHRL is found in Art 14(1) ICCPR and Art 6(1) ECHR. For human rights jurisprudence on this notion, see, e.g., ECtHR, *Fatullayev v Azerbaijan*, Judgment, 20 April 2010, para 144: 'The Court reiterates that the object of the term "established by law" in Article 6 of the Convention is to ensure "that the judicial organization in a democratic society does not depend on the discretion of the executive, but that it is regulated by law emanating from Parliament"' (citing ECtHR, *Gurov v Moldova*, Judgment, 11 July 2006, para 34; ECtHR, *Coëme and others v Belgium*, 22 June 2000, para 99).

[32] ICRC CIHL Study, at 355.   [33] See ICRC CIHL Database, Rule 100.

[34] ICTY, *The Prosecutor v Duško Tadić*, Appeals Chamber Decision on the Defence Motion for Interlocutory Appeal on Jurisdiction, IT-94-1-AR72, 2 October 1995, para 45.

[35] SCSL, *The Prosecutor v Morris Kallon, Sam Hinga Norman and Brima Bazzy Kamara*, Appeals Chamber Decision on Constitutionality and Lack of Jurisdiction, SCSL-2004-14-PT, SCSL-2004-15-PT, and SCSL-2004-16-PT, 13 March 2004, para 55.

[36] See Art 14(1) ICCPR; Art 6(1) ECHR; Art 8(1) ACHR; Arts 7(1)(d) and 26 ACHPR.

and impartial tribunal is absolute and admits of no exception or qualification.[37] The requirement of 'impartiality' is understood to consist of two sub-requirements: subjective and objective impartiality.[38] The HRCttee has clarified that

> a situation where the functions and competences of the judiciary and the executive are not clearly distinguishable or where the latter is able to control or direct the former is incompatible with the notion of an independent and impartial tribunal within the meaning of Article 14, paragraph 1, of the Covenant.[39]

Regarding objective impartiality, the HRCttee has pointed out that 'a tribunal must also *appear to a reasonable observer* to be impartial'.[40] Subjective impartiality therefore refers to the actual state of mind of the judge or jury, and is generally presumed.[41] Thus, judges must

> not allow their judgment to be influenced by personal bias or prejudice, nor harbour preconceptions about the particular case before them, nor act in ways that improperly promote the interests of one of the parties to the detriment of the other.[42]

19   The jurisprudence of international criminal tribunals has also affirmed the requirement for an 'independent' tribunal. Articles 12 and 13 of the ICTY Statute require that all judges must be independent, and persons of high integrity and impartiality. The Statutes of the International Criminal Court (ICC), International Criminal Tribunal for Rwanda (ICTR), SCSL, and the Special Tribunal for Lebanon (STL) contain similar provisions.[43] The Appeals Chambers of both the ICTY and the ICTR have held that 'the fundamental human right of an accused to be tried before an independent and impartial tribunal is generally recognized as being an integral component of the requirement that an accused should have a fair trial'.[44] The ICTY Appeals Chamber has also held that, in principle, a tribunal and its judges benefit from a presumption of impartiality.[45] Therefore, the burden is on the defendant to establish that a court is not impartial in a given case.[46] However, this presumption of impartiality 'should not be construed as relieving an individual Judge of his or her duty to withdraw from a particular case if he or she believes that his or her impartiality is in question'.[47]

---

[37] See, e.g., HRCttee, *Gonzalez del Rio v Peru*, Comm No 263/1987, UN Doc CCPR/C/46/D/263/1987 (1992), para 5.1: 'The Committee recalls that the right to be tried by an independent and impartial tribunal is an absolute right that may suffer no exception.'

[38] ECtHR, *Findlay v United Kingdom*, Judgment, 25 February 1997, para 73.

[39] HRCttee, *Bahamonde v Equatorial Guinea*, 20 October 1993, Comm No 468/1991, para 9.4.

[40] HRCttee, General Comment 32, para 21 (emphasis added).

[41] See L. Doswald-Beck, *Human Rights in Times of Conflict and Terrorism* (Oxford: OUP, 2011), at 337.

[42] See HRCttee, General Comment 32, para 21. See also HRCttee, *Karttunen v Finland*, Comm No 387/1989, UN Doc CCPR/C/46/D/387/1989 (1992), para 7.2; and Arts 40 and 45 ICC Statute.

[43] Art 67(1) ICC Statute referring to the impartiality of proceedings, and Art 8(2)(c)(iv) ICC Elements of Crimes outlining the contours of the 'war crime of sentencing or execution without due process'; Art 12 ICTR Statute; Art 13 SCSL Statute; Art 9(1) STL Statute, all referring to the impartiality of the appointed judges.

[44] ICTY, *The Prosecutor v Anto Furundžija*, Appeals Chamber Judgment, IT-95-17/1-A, 21 July 2000, para 177; ICTR, *Ferdinand Nahimana et al v The Prosecutor*, Appeals Chamber Judgment, ICTR-99-52-A, 28 November 2007, para 28; ICTR, *The Prosecutor v Clément Kayishema and Obed Ruzindana*, Appeals Chamber Judgment, ICTR-95-1-A, 1 June 2001, paras 51 and 55.

[45] ICTY, *Furundžija*, above n 44, paras 182, 196, and 197.

[46] See, e.g., ICTY, *The Prosecutor v Prlić et al*, Decision of the President on Jadranko Prlić's Motion to Disqualify Judge Arpad Prandler, IT-04-74-T, 4 October 2010, para 7 and references cited.

[47] See ICTY, *Furundžija*, above n 44, para 175.

In light of the above developments in IHRL and international criminal law (ICL), two interesting questions arise that may require reconciliation between IHL and IHRL requirements:

— To what extent can the meaning of 'regularly constituted' court in NIAC (as per Common Article 3) fully subscribe to or deviate from the IHRL requirement of a court 'established by law'?
— To what extent can the use of military courts to try civilians in times of military occupation be in direct contradiction to the IHRL requirement of independence and impartiality?

As far as the first question is concerned, in the ordinary course of events, non-state armed groups will not have the benefit of a formal legislature or judicial system, and will therefore be unable to establish 'regularly constituted courts' within the meaning of IHRL. The solution may simply be to apply minimum standards contextually and flexibly in making particular determinations. For instance, if one shifts the focus onto the requirement under AP II that a court 'offers the essential guarantees of independence and impartiality', rather than on the formalistic requirement of a court 'established by law', non-state armed groups would appear not to be precluded from setting up courts.[48] It would be the *guarantees* that such courts can provide that would be the yardstick of their compliance with IHL. It is understood that overly flexible interpretations of the law carry their risks. On the one hand, the inordinate dilution of judicial guarantees will undermine humanitarian protection. On the other hand, however, impossible standards may render IHL unrealistic and irrelevant in extreme contexts, even to non-state belligerents acting in good faith, and thus ultimately erode the protection that IHL seeks to provide in the first place.

With regard to the second question, the CIHL Study points out that military tribunals and special security courts must respect the same requirements of independence and impartiality as civilian tribunals.[49] Article 66 GC IV provides in relevant part that 'the Occupying Power may hand over the accused to its properly constituted, non-political military courts'; Article 71 further provides that '[n]o sentence shall be pronounced by the competent courts of the Occupying Power except after a regular trial'. (For a more detailed analysis of Article 71 guarantees, see Chapter 68 of this volume.) The HRCttee, however, urges caution with respect to such jurisdictions:

This could present serious problems as far as the equitable, impartial and independent administration of justice is concerned. Quite often the reason for the establishment of such courts is to enable exceptional procedures to be applied which do not comply with normal standards of justice. While the Covenant does not prohibit such categories of courts, nevertheless the conditions which it lays down clearly indicate that the trying of civilians by such courts should be very exceptional and take place under conditions which genuinely afford the full guarantees stipulated in article 14.[50]

---

[48] For an in-depth discussion of this question, see J. Somer, 'Jungle Justice: Passing Sentence on the Equality of Belligerents in Non-International Armed Conflict', 89 *IRRC* 867 (2007) 655; M. Sassòli, 'Taking Armed Groups Seriously: Ways to Improve their Compliance with International Humanitarian Law', 1 *International Humanitarian Legal Studies* (2010) 5; M. Sassòli and Y. Shany, 'Debate: Should the Obligations of States and Armed Groups under International Humanitarian Law Really Be Equal?', 95 *IRRC* 882 (2011) 425.

[49] See ICRC CIHL Study, at 356.   [50] See HRCttee, General Comment 13, para 4.

In this regard, regional human rights bodies have held that trials of civilians by military courts constitute a violation of the right to be tried by an independent and impartial tribunal.[51] The HRCttee does recognize, however, that in exceptional circumstances, such trials are not necessarily inconsistent with IHRL:

> Trials of civilians by military or special courts should be exceptional, i.e. limited to cases where the State party can show that resorting to such trials is necessary and justified by objective and serious reasons, and where with regard to the specific class of individuals and offences at issue the regular civilian courts are unable to undertake the trials.[52]

Thus, trials of civilians by military courts are arguably justified in the exceptional circumstances of occupation by a foreign power where the ordinary state institutions, including civilian courts, are temporarily displaced. This is true at least with respect to crimes introduced by the Occupying Power, and where the Occupying Power is barred by IHL from giving its civilian courts jurisdiction because to do so would amount to annexation.

b. *The right to be informed without delay of the particulars of the offence and to have all necessary rights and means of defence*

22 The right to 'be informed without delay of the particulars of the offence' is specified in GC III and GC IV. Article 96 GC III reads in its relevant part, '[b]efore any disciplinary award is pronounced, the accused shall be *given precise information regarding the offences of which he is accused*'.[53] Similarly, Article 105, paragraph 4 reads:

> Particulars of the charge or charges on which the prisoner of war is to be arraigned, as well as the documents which are generally communicated to the accused by virtue of the laws in force in the armed forces of the Detaining Power, shall be communicated to the accused prisoner of war in a language which he understands, and in good time before the opening of the trial. The same communication in the same circumstances shall be made to the advocate or counsel conducting the defence on behalf of the prisoner of war.

23 Article 71 paragraph 2 GC IV reads:[54]

> Accused persons who are prosecuted by the Occupying Power shall be *promptly informed, in writing, in a language which they understand*, of the particulars of the charges preferred against them, and shall be brought to trial as rapidly as possible.

---

[51] See also ACommHPR, *Media Rights Agenda v Nigeria* (224/98), para 64: 'The Commission also finds the trial in contravention of the basic principle of fair hearing contained in Principle 5 of the United Nations Basic Principles on the Independence of the Judiciary (The UN Basic Principles) and article 7 (1) (d) of the African Charter.' Also see *Civil Liberties Organization and others v Nigeria* (2001) AHRLR 75, para 44: 'It has been stated elsewhere in this decision, that a military tribunal per se is not offensive to the rights in the Charter, nor does it imply an unfair or unjust process. We make the point that military tribunals must be subject to the same requirements of fairness, openness, justice, independence and due process as any other process. What causes offence is failure to observe basic or fundamental standards that would ensure fairness. As that matter has been dealt with above, it is not necessary to find that a tribunal presided over by a military officer is a violation of the Charter. It has already been pointed out that the military tribunal fails the independence test.' ECtHR, *Cyprus v Turkey*, Judgment 10 May 2001, para 358: '[T]here is no reason to doubt that these courts suffer from the same defects of independence and impartiality which were highlighted in its *Incal v Turkey* judgment in respect of the system of National Security Courts established in Turkey by the respondent State, in particular the close structural links between the executive power and the military officers serving on the "TRNC" military courts. In the Court's view, civilians in the "TRNC" accused of acts characterized as military offences before such courts could legitimately fear that they lacked independence and impartiality.' The ECtHR has made the same determination with respect to occupied territories. See *Cyprus v Turkey*, para 359.

[52] HRCttee, General Comment 32, para 22.   [53] Emphasis added.   [54] Emphasis added.

And Article 123 paragraph 2 GC IV reads:⁵⁵

Before any disciplinary punishment is awarded, the accused internee *shall be given precise information regarding the offences of which he is accused*, and given an opportunity of explaining his conduct and of defending himself.

In IHRL, this judicial guarantee is included in the ICCPR, European Convention on Human Rights (ECHR), and several other instruments.⁵⁶ The ICCPR and ECHR require that the accused be provided with such information 'promptly' or 'without delay', and in a language which the accused understands.⁵⁷ The Statutes of the ICC, ICTY, ICTR, and SCSL also recognize this judicial guarantee.⁵⁸

The right of the accused to benefit from the 'safeguards of proper trial and defence' is provided for under all four Geneva Conventions.⁵⁹ A reference to 'all necessary rights and means of defence' is also included in the Additional Protocols,⁶⁰ as well as in the ICCPR, regional human rights conventions, and other international instruments.⁶¹ The CIHL Study has elaborated several subcategories of this guarantee, including: (i) the right to defend oneself or to be assisted by a lawyer of one's choice; (ii) the right to free legal assistance if the interests of justice so require; (iii) the right to sufficient time and facilities to prepare the defence; and (iv) the right of the accused to communicate freely with counsel.

The Commentary to AP I further clarifies that the requirement to have all necessary rights and means of defence is an umbrella requirement, comprising various other guarantees:

[I]t is therefore clear that a defendant who does not understand the language used by the judicial authorities must be provided with an interpreter. By the same token, he must be able to understand the assistance given by a qualified defence lawyer. If these conditions were not fulfilled, the defendant would not have the benefit of all necessary rights and means of defence.⁶²

The underlying rationale of this judicial guarantee is the principle of 'equality of arms'. For example, with respect to POWs under GC III, the accused has the right to 'a qualified advocate or counsel of his own choice, to the calling of witnesses and, if he deems necessary, to the services of a competent interpreter'.⁶³ If the accused fails to appoint counsel, 'the Detaining Power shall appoint a competent advocate or counsel to conduct the defence'.⁶⁴ The counsel is entitled to a minimum two-week period of pre-trial preparation

---

⁵⁵ Emphasis added.
⁵⁶ Art 14(3)(a) ICCPR; Art 40(2)(b)(ii) CRC; Art 6(3)(a) ECHR; Art 8(2) ACHR; Principles 10–14 of the Body of Principles for the Protection of All Persons under Any Form of Detention or Imprisonment.
⁵⁷ With regard to 'promptly', the ICRC Commentary to AP I specifies that 'it is difficult to determine a precise time limit, but ten days would seem the maximum period' (ICRC Commentary APs, para 3072). The Commentary does not specify where the 10 days maximum requirement is derived from, but the presumption is that it is from the prevailing IHRL standard at the time (given that the preceding paragraph refers to ICCPR). With respect to the formulation, 'in a language in which he understands', the ICRC Commentary explains that 'this is a formula which has been used since 1929 in the Geneva Conventions, and covers both written and verbal communications' (ICRC Commentary APs, para 3071).
⁵⁸ Art 67(1)(a) ICC Statute; Art 21(4)(a) ICTY Statute; Art 20(4)(a) ICTR Statute; Art 17(4)(a) SCSL Statute; Art 15 (regarding suspects in a criminal trial) and Art 16(4)(a) STL Statute (regarding accused).
⁵⁹ See Art 49 para 4 GC I; Art 50 para 4 GC II; Art 129 para 4 and Arts 105–108 GC III; Art 146 para 4 GC IV.
⁶⁰ See Art 75(4)(a) AP I; Art 6(2)(a) AP II.
⁶¹ See Art 14(3) ICCPR; Art 6(3) ECHR; Art 8(2) ACHR; Art 7(1) ACHPR; Art 11 UDHR; Art 19(e) Cairo Declaration on Human Rights in Islam; Art 48(2) EU Charter of Fundamental Rights.
⁶² ICRC Commentary APs, para 3096.   ⁶³ Art 105 para 1 GC III.   ⁶⁴ Ibid, para 2.

and 'the necessary facilities to prepare the defence of the accused', which may include conferring 'with any witnesses for the defence, including prisoners of war'.[65] Similarly, GC IV reiterates the right of accused persons to be assisted by a qualified counsel of their own choice, 'who shall be able to visit them freely and shall enjoy the necessary facilities for preparing the defence',[66] the right to 'present evidence necessary to their defence, and [...] in particular, call witnesses',[67] and the right to 'be aided by an interpreter, both during preliminary investigation and during the hearing in court'.[68] If an accused does not choose counsel, the Protecting Power may provide him or her with one (and if the accused 'has to meet a serious charge and the Protecting Power is not functioning, the Occupying Power, subject to the consent of the accused, shall provide an advocate or counsel').[69]

27 The rights and 'necessary facilities for preparing the defence' find their IHRL equivalent in the right to 'adequate time and facilities for the preparation of his defence'.[70] 'Facilities' means access to documents, records, and other evidence that the accused or his or her defence counsel need to prepare the case. The defendant need not personally consult the file.[71] However, he or she must be able to communicate freely with counsel.[72] Such communication, according to IHRL, should benefit from conditions of full respect for its confidentiality.[73]

c. The requirement of individual criminal responsibility

28 This judicial guarantee figures in GC IV and in the Hague Regulations, and represents in effect a prohibition against collective punishments and reprisals, which were common in armed conflicts prior to the adoption of the Geneva Conventions.[74] Article 33 GC IV explicitly provides that 'no protected person may be punished for an offence he or she has not personally committed'.[75] The CIHL Study indicates that the principle of individual criminal responsibility is a rule of customary law in both IACs and NIACs.[76] It notes that the principle was already recognized in the Lieber Code, and has been repeated in many humanitarian law treaties since then.[77]

29 While not expressly stated in all human rights instruments,[78] it is self-evident that the elaborate list of fair trial guarantees would be rendered moot if there were no antecedent principle of individual criminal responsibility. The HRCttee has held that imposing collective punishments would amount to a violation of 'peremptory norms of international law'.[79]

---

[65] Ibid, para 3.   [66] Art 72 para 1 GC IV.   [67] Ibid.
[68] This includes the right 'to object to the interpreter and to ask for his replacement'. Ibid, para 3.
[69] Ibid, para 2.
[70] Art 14(3)(b) ICCPR; Art 6(3)(b) and (c) ECHR; Art 8(2)(c) and (d) ACHR; and Art 7(1)(c) ACHPR.
[71] ECtHR, *Kamasinski v Austria*, Judgment, 19 December 1989, paras 87–88; HRCttee, *O.F. Norway*, UN Doc CCPR/C/OP/2, 26 October 1984, para 5.5. See also HRCttee, General Comment 32, para 32.
[72] HRCttee, General Comment 32, paras 32–3.   [73] Ibid, para 34.
[74] See Pictet Commentary GC IV, which clarifies (at 225) that the Article seeks to limit 'penalties of any kind inflicted on persons or entire groups of persons, in defiance of the most elementary principles of humanity, for acts that these persons have not committed'.
[75] Also see Art 75(4)(b) AP I for the more recent formulation of this principle, 'no one shall be convicted of an offence except on the basis of individual penal responsibility'.
[76] See ICRC CIHL Study, Rules 102 and 151.
[77] See Arts 44 and 47 Lieber Code; Art 84 Oxford Manual; Art 49 GC I/Art 50 GC II/Art 129 GC III/Art 146 GC IV; Art 28 Hague Convention for the Protection of Cultural Property; Art 15 Second Protocol to the Hague Convention for the Protection of Cultural Property; Art 85 AP I; Art 14 Amended Protocol II to the Convention on Certain Conventional Weapons; Art 9 Ottawa Convention; Art 4 CRC-OPAC.
[78] See Art 5(3) ACHR: 'Punishment shall not be extended to any person other than the criminal'; and Art 7(2) ACHPR: 'Punishment is personal and can be imposed only on the offenders.'
[79] HRCttee, General Comment 29, para 11.

The principle of individual criminal responsibility is also the fundamental principle 30
underlying ICL.[80] It is a general principle of international law, recognized in the domestic
legal systems of the world. The international tribunals' case law and the ICC Statute indicate that beyond actually committing a crime, the scope of 'individual responsibility' as a
general principle includes several forms of participation, such as attempting to commit a
crime, assisting in it, facilitating, aiding, or abetting it, or planning or instigating it, and
also extends to the doctrine of command responsibility.[81]

d. *The principle of* nullum crimen, nulla poena sine lege

This fundamental judicial guarantee is contained in Article 99 GC III, Article 67 GC IV, 31
Article 75 AP I, and Article 6 AP II.[82] It refers to the principle of legality, or *nullum crimen, nulla poena sine lege*, and is also among the rules identified in the CIHL Study as a norm of
customary IHL in both IACs and NIACs.[83] This principle covers both prohibited criminal
conduct and the corresponding punishment. It encompasses the following distinct elements:

— the principle of non-retroactivity (*nullum crimen, nulla poena sine lege praevia*);
— the prohibition against analogy (*nullum crimen, nulla poena sine lege stricta*);
— the principle of certainty (*nullum crimen, nulla poena sine lege certa*); and
— the prohibition against uncodified (i.e. unwritten) or judge-made criminal provisions (*nullum crimen, nulla poena sine lege scripta*).[84] This last principle presumably applies to national law, since Article 15 of ICCPR clarifies that the principle of legality may also be satisfied by international law, which necessarily includes 'unwritten' customary law as well as general principles of law.

Consistent with Article 15 ICCPR, the ICRC Commentary to AP I explains that 32

> although the principle of legality (*nullum crimen, nulla poena sine lege*) is a pillar of domestic criminal law, the lex should be understood in the international context as comprising not only written law, but also unwritten law, since international law is in part customary law.[85]

The principle of *nullum crimen* is found in all the general human rights instruments,[86] 33
and is considered to be non-derogable.[87] It requires that a conviction be based on a
crime that is expressly legislated or codified, is sufficiently precise in definition of both
the prohibited conduct and corresponding punishment, and the prosecution of which
is foreseeable.[88] In this last respect, the ECtHR held in *Jorgic v Germany*[89] that the

---

[80] See Art 7(1) ICTY Statute; Art 6(1) ICTR Statute; Art 6 SCSL Statute; Art 25 ICC Statute; Art 3 STL Statute.
[81] See, e.g., Art 25 ICC Statute. Also see Art 28 ICC Statute on command responsibility.
[82] Art 99 GC III reads in its relevant passage: 'No prisoner of war may be tried or sentenced for an act which is not forbidden by the law of the Detaining Power or by international law, in force at the time the said act was committed.' Art 6(2)(c) AP II is more extensive and reads as follows: '[N]o one shall be held guilty of any criminal offence on account of any act or omission which did not constitute a criminal offence, under the law, at the time when it was committed; nor shall a heavier penalty be imposed than that which was applicable at the time when the criminal offence was committed; if, after the commission of the offence, provision is made by law for the imposition of a lighter penalty, the offender shall benefit thereby [...]'
[83] See ICRC CIHL Study, Rule 101.
[84] C. Kreß, '*Nulla poena nullum crimen sine lege*', in MPEPIL.
[85] ICRC Commentary APs, para 3104.
[86] Art 15 ICCPR; Art 7 ECHR; Art 9 ACHR; Art 7(2) ACHPR.
[87] See Art 4(2) ICCPR; Art 15(2) ECHR; Art 27(2) ACHR.
[88] See Doswald-Beck, above n 41, at 302–6, and jurisprudence cited therein.
[89] ECtHR, *Jorgic v Germany*, Judgment, 12 July 2007, para 93.

requirement of foreseeability with respect to whether 'ethnic cleansing' constituted genocide was satisfied so long as the accused, 'if need be with the assistance of a lawyer, could reasonably have foreseen that he risked being charged with and convicted of genocide for the acts [of considerable severity and duration] he had committed in 1992' in the former Yugoslavia.[90]

34 The evolution of this principle in ICL is instructive. The introduction of crimes against humanity in the 1945 Nuremberg and Tokyo Charters without a basis in treaty or customary law was the subject of considerable debate, and vague recourse to general principles of law prevailed over strict adherence to the principle of legality in order to ensure that mass atrocities falling outside the purview of war crimes did not go unpunished.[91] With respect to the 1993 ICTY Statute, however, the UN Secretary General's Report to the Security Council noted that

the application of the principle *nullum crimen sine lege* requires that the international tribunal should apply rules of international humanitarian law which are beyond any doubt part of customary law so that the problem of adherence of some but not all states to specific conventions does not arise.[92]

Thus, where there was uncertainty, ICTY jurisprudence defined international crimes under customary IHL based on illustrative provisions on the 'laws or customs of war'.[93] With the shift from an ad hoc to a permanent jurisdiction—and with the benefit of ICTY–ICTR jurisprudence—the 1998 ICC Statute adopted a stricter codification of international crimes (and corresponding Elements of Crimes) in contrast to the more flexible ICTY approach.[94] Furthermore, the ICC Statute now contains provisions that *expressly* prohibit retroactive criminalization[95] or criminalization by analogy,[96] and also recognize the *favor rei* principle requiring ambiguities to be interpreted in favour of the accused.[97] Thus, the principle of *nullum crimen sine lege* is now more firmly entrenched in international criminal law.[98]

e. *The presumption of innocence*

35 This right is not explicitly mentioned in the Geneva Conventions but figures in both Article 75 AP I and Article 6 AP II. The presumption of innocence means that the burden is on the prosecution to prove guilt ('beyond a reasonable doubt' in common law jurisdictions, or 'to the intimate conviction of the trier of fact' in civil law jurisdictions). In IHRL, this requirement is set forth in Article 14(2) ICCPR and other instruments.[99]

---

[90] Ibid, para 113.
[91] See Kreß, above n 84, para 16.
[92] UNSC Report of the Secretary-General pursuant to Paragraph 2 of Security Council Resolution 808 [1993], UN Doc S/25704, 3 May 1993, para 34.
[93] Art 3 ICTY Statute. See also ICTY, *Tadić*, above n 34, paras 94–127.
[94] See Arts 6, 7, and 8 ICC Statute.   [95] Art 11 ICC Statute.
[96] Art 24 ICC Statute. But see Art 7(1)(k), including within the definition of 'crimes against humanity', '[o]ther inhumane acts *of a similar character* intentionally causing great suffering, or serious injury to body or to mental or physical health' (emphasis added).
[97] Art 22 ICC Statute. These principles were also applied by the ad hoc tribunals in their practice, but they had not been expressly formulated in their respective Statutes. For a discussion of the principle *in dubio pro reo* before the ICTY, e.g., see ICTY, *The Prosecutor v Fatmir Limaj et al*, Appeals Chamber Judgment, IT-03-66-A, 27 September 2007, para 21.
[98] See A. Cassese, 'Nullum crimen sine lege', in A. Cassese (ed), *The Oxford Companion to International Criminal Justice* (Oxford: OUP, 2009) 438, at 439.
[99] Art 40(2)(b)(i) CRC; Art 6(2) ECHR; Art 8(2) ACHR; Art 7(1) ACHPR; Art 11 UDHR; Art XXVI American Declaration on the Rights and Duties of Man; Principle 36 of the Body of Principles for

The HRCttee and the Inter-American Commission on Human Rights have held that the presumption of innocence is a non-derogable right.[100] This right is also codified in the Statutes of the ICC, ICTY, ICTR, SCSL, and the STL.[101] Today it remains as relevant as before to recall that this guarantee, together with the principle of individual criminal responsibility (discussed in section B.II.c of this chapter), 'may play an important role when criminal prosecutions are brought against persons on the basis of their membership of a group'.[102]

f. The right of the accused 'to be tried in his presence'

This right is not explicitly mentioned in the Geneva Conventions but figures clearly in Article 75(4)(e) AP I, which reads, 'anyone charged with an offence shall have the right to be tried in his presence'. As the AP I Commentary explains, this right would be a necessary guarantee for the effective exercise of other rights:

[T]he defendant is present at the sessions where the prosecution puts its case, when oral arguments are heard, etc. In addition, the defendant must be able to hear the witnesses and experts, to ask questions himself and to make his objections or propose corrections.[103]

Several countries made reservations to this provision in AP I upon ratification, contemplating exceptional situations where disruptive behaviour would require removal of an accused from the trial.[104] This is consistent with the US Supreme Court dictum in *Hamdan v Rumsfeld* that 'an accused must, absent disruptive conduct or consent, be present for his trial and must be privy to the evidence against him'.[105]

Under IHRL, the ICCPR and other human rights instruments recognize the right to be present,[106] although recent international jurisprudence and practice in some domestic jurisdictions, as well as the STL, allow for trials in *absentia* under strict legal conditions.[107] The ECtHR has held, for example, that an accused may waive his or her right

---

the Protection of All Persons under Any Form of Detention or Imprisonment; Art 48(1) EU Charter of Fundamental Rights.

[100] See HRCttee, General Comment 29, para 11: 'States parties may in no circumstances invoke article 4 of the Covenant as justification for acting in violation of humanitarian law or peremptory norms of international law, for instance by taking hostages, by imposing collective punishments, through arbitrary deprivations of liberty or by deviating from fundamental principles of fair trial, including the presumption of innocence.'

[101] Art 66 ICC Statute; Art 21(3) ICTY Statute; Art 20(3) ICTR Statute; Art 17(3) SCSL Statute; Art 16(3)(a) STL Statute.

[102] See ICRC Commentary APs, at 882, para 3108.

[103] Ibid, para 3110.

[104] See the reservations made upon ratification of the APs by Austria, Germany, Ireland, Liechtenstein, and Malta, which noted that in some exceptional situations, a judge could order the removal of the accused where his or her behaviour causes a disturbance in the trial.

[105] *Hamdan v Rumsfeld*, above n 27, per Stevens J, at 71.

[106] See Art 14(3)(d) ICCPR; Art 6(3)(c) ECHR; Art 8(2)(d) ACHR. The last two Articles provide for the right to defend oneself, thus making the right to be present at the trial implicit in these guarantees, according to the recent jurisprudence of the regional human rights bodies (see, e.g., ECtHR, *Sejdovic v Italy*, Judgment, 1 March 2006, para 81).

[107] For the general rule under IHRL, see Art 14(3)(d) ICCPR; Art 6(3)(c) ECHR; Art 8(2)(d) ACHR. See Art 22 STL Statute providing for trials *in absentia*. Also see General Comment 32, para 36: 'Proceedings in the absence of the accused may in some circumstances be permissible in the interest of the proper administration of justice, i.e. when accused persons, although informed of the proceedings sufficiently in advance, decline to exercise their right to be present.' *In absentia* trials will be compatible with Art 14(3)(d) ICCPR 'if the necessary steps are taken to summon accused persons in a timely manner and to inform them beforehand about the date and place of their trial and to request their attendance' (ibid). See further HRCttee, *Daniel*

to be present, given that he or she makes the waiver 'of his [or her] own free will, either expressly or tacitly', and that the waiver 'be established in an unequivocal manner, be attended by minimum safeguards commensurate with its importance, and [should] not run counter to any important public interest'.[108] In those limited circumstances, however, the accused retains the right to counsel, even if he or she has chosen not to attend the trial.[109]

g. *The right against self-incrimination*

39   This prohibition is set forth in GC III and GC IV,[110] as well as in AP I and AP II.[111] It is also recognized in military manuals and other state practice.[112] The 'right to remain silent' is a fundamental judicial guarantee, not least because its violation is often linked to coercion and mistreatment. In this regard, a US court held *In re Guantánamo Detainee cases* that one of the reasons why Combatant Status Review Tribunals were unconstitutional was their reliance on forced confessions: 'The Supreme Court has long held that due process prohibits the government's use of involuntary statements obtained through torture or other mistreatment.'[113]

40   This judicial guarantee is also found in the main international human rights treaties and instruments.[114] The HRCttee has stated that 'the law should require that evidence provided by means of such methods or any other form of compulsion is wholly unacceptable'.[115] The UN Convention against Torture provides that statements made as a result of torture may not be invoked as evidence in any proceedings.[116] The HRCttee has also stated that domestic law must 'prohibit the use or admissibility in judicial proceedings of statements or confessions obtained through torture or other prohibited treatment'.[117] The ECtHR has held that

[a]lthough not specifically mentioned in Article 6 of the Convention, there can be no doubt that the right to remain silent under police questioning and the privilege against self-incrimination are

---

Monguya Mbenge v Zaire, UN Doc CCPR/C/OP/2, 8 September 1977, para 14.1: 'This provision and other requirements of due process enshrined in article 14 cannot be construed as invariably rendering proceedings *in absentia* inadmissible irrespective of the reasons for the accused person's absence. Indeed, proceedings *in absentia* are in some circumstances (for instance, when the accused person, although informed of the proceedings sufficiently in advance, declines to exercise his right to be present) permissible in the interest of the proper administration of justice. Nevertheless, the effective exercise of the rights under article 14 presupposes that the necessary steps should be taken to inform the accused beforehand about the proceedings against him (Art 14 (3)(a)). Judgement *in absentia* requires that, notwithstanding the absence of the accused, all due notification has been made to inform him [or her] of the date and place of his trial and to request his [or her] attendance'; ECtHR, *Colozza v Italy*, Judgment, 12 February 1985, paras 27–30. Cf Art 63(1) and Art 67(1)(d) ICC Statute; Art 21(4)(d) ICTY Statute; Art 20(4)(d) ICTR Statute; Art 17(4)(d) SCSL Statute.

[108] ECtHR, *Borisov v Russia*, Judgment, 13 March 2012, para 34 (citing ECtHR, *Jones v United Kingdom*, App No 30900/02, 9 September 2003, and ECtHR, *Sejdovic v Italy*, above n 106).

[109] ECtHR, *Poitrimol v France*, Judgment, 23 November 1993, para 34: 'A person charged with a criminal offence does not lose the benefit of this right merely on account of not being present at the trial.'

[110] Art 99 GC III: 'No moral or physical coercion may be exerted on a prisoner of war in order to induce him to admit himself guilty of the act of which he is accused.' Art 31 GC IV: 'No physical or moral coercion shall be exercised against protected persons, in particular to obtain information from them or from third parties.'

[111] Art 75(4)(f) AP I and Art 6(2)(f) AP II, 'no one shall be compelled to testify against himself or to confess guilt'

[112] See ICRC CIHL Database, Rule 100.

[113] *In re Guantánamo Detainee cases*, District Court for the District of Columbia, Judgment, 31 January 2005.

[114] Art 14(3)(g) ICCPR; Art 40(2)(b)(iv) CRC; Art 8(2)(g) ACHR; Principle 21 of the Body of Principles for the Protection of All Persons under Any Form of Detention or Imprisonment.

[115] HRCttee, General Comment 13, para 14.   [116] Art 15 CAT.

[117] HRCttee, General Comment 20, para 12.

generally recognized international standards which lie at the heart of the notion of a fair procedure under Article 6 [ECHR].[118]

The ICC, ICTY, ICTR, SCSL, and STL Statutes also provide for this guarantee.[119]

h. *The principle of 'equality of arms'*

This right is recognized both in GC III and GC IV,[120] as well as in AP I. The principle applies to domestic legal systems, irrespective of their differing criminal procedures. In this regard, the Commentary to AP I is instructive: '[T]his provision was worded so as to be compatible with both the system of cross-examination of witnesses and with the inquisitorial system in which the judge himself conducts the interrogation.'[121] 41

The principle of equality of arms is equally recognized in IHRL.[122] The ECtHR has clarified, however, that this right to 'adversarial argument' does not mean procedurally 42

> that in order to be used as evidence statements of witnesses should always be made at a public hearing in court: to use as evidence such statements obtained at the pre-trial stage is not in itself inconsistent with [this requirement] provided the rights of the defence have been respected.[123]

The general principle is that

> an accused should be given an adequate and proper opportunity to challenge and question a witness against him, either at the time the witness was making his statement or at some later stage of the proceedings.[124]

The right 'to obtain the attendance and examination of witnesses' under IHRL has been interpreted to include the right of an accused to have the court summon relevant witnesses on his or her behalf.[125] The ECtHR has found a violation of the right to a fair trial where a defendant was arbitrarily denied the opportunity to hear an essential witness.[126] 43

The Statutes of the ICC, ICTY, ICTR, SCSL, and STL all provide for this right.[127] According to the jurisprudence of the ICTY and the ICTR, the obligation to ensure equality of arms 'obliges the judicial body to ensure that neither party is put at a disadvantage'[128] when presenting its case, but does not 'necessarily amount to the material equality of possessing the same financial and/or personal resources'.[129] 44

i. *The principle of* ne bis in idem

The principle of *ne bis in idem* (or the 'double jeopardy' rule) is intended to uphold the finality of criminal proceedings by prohibiting multiple trials for the same offence, at least 45

---

[118] ECtHR, *Murray v United Kingdom*, Judgment, 8 February 1996, para 45.
[119] Arts 55(1)(a) and 67(1)(g) ICC Statute; Art 21(4)(g) ICTY Statute; Art 20(4)(g) ICTR Statute; Art 17(4)(g) SCSL Statute; Arts 15 and 16 STL Statute.
[120] Art 96 para 4 and Art 105 para 1 GC III; Art 72 para 1 and Art 123 para 2 GC IV.
[121] ICRC Commentary APs, para 3114.
[122] Art 14(3)(e) ICCPR; Art 6(3)(d) ECHR; Art 8(2)(f) ACHR.
[123] ECtHR, *Kostovski v The Netherlands*, Judgment, 20 November 1989, para 41.   [124] Ibid.
[125] HRCttee, General Comment 32, para 39.
[126] ECtHR, *Vidal v Belgium*, Judgment, 22 April 1992, paras 34–35. The principle does not traditionally apply to judgments of foreign courts.
[127] Art 67(1) ICC Statute; Art 21(4)(e) ICTY Statute; Art 20(4)(e) ICTR Statute; Art 17(4)(e) SCSL Statute; Art 16(4)(e) STL Statute.
[128] ICTY, *The Prosecutor v Duško Tadić*, Appeals Chamber Judgment, IT-94-1-A, 15 July 1999, para 48.
[129] ICTR, *Kayishema & Ruzindana*, above n 44, para 69.

within the same jurisdiction.[130] It is explicitly contained in Article 86 GC III: 'No prisoner of war may be punished more than once for the same act, or on the same charge.'

46 Similarly, under Article 117 GC IV: 'No internee may be punished more than once for the same act, or on the same count.'[131]

47 Furthermore, the *ne bis in idem* guarantee can be implicitly read in Common Article 3 paragraph 1(1)(d) (see Chapter 23 of this volume, MN 16).

48 This is a firmly recognized principle of IHRL.[132] *Ne bis in idem* is also contained in the Statutes of the ICC and other international criminal tribunals (both within the ICC and tribunals themselves, and before national jurisdictions).[133]

49 With respect to the application of the principle between the jurisdiction of the tribunals and domestic jurisdictions, the ICTY and ICTR Statutes are based on primacy over domestic jurisdictions, meaning that while national courts cannot re-try cases already tried by the international tribunals, the converse does not apply, but only if the offences for which the accused was charged were characterized as ordinary, or if the domestic proceedings were not impartial or independent, or were designed to shield the accused from international criminal responsibility, or the case was not diligently prosecuted.[134]

50 The situation is somewhat more complex under the ICC Statute, since unlike the ICTY and ICTR, the ICC has complementary jurisdiction—it may exercise jurisdiction only if national courts either have not initiated proceedings with respect to the same conduct, or if such proceedings are not 'genuine' because, inter alia, they are for the purpose of shielding the person concerned from criminal responsibility, or otherwise were not conducted independently or impartially, and were conducted in a manner which, in the circumstances, was inconsistent with an intent to bring the person concerned to justice.[135] Although only states or defendants may challenge admissibility under the ICC Statute, it is not clear whether the same rules with respect to genuine national proceedings would apply to the informal courts of non-state actors.

j. *The right to a public trial*

51 This judicial guarantee is implicit in the Geneva Conventions,[136] and is made explicit in AP I. It is recognized in IHRL[137] and aims to ensure the transparency of the proceedings.[138]

---

[130] HRCttee, General Comment 32, para 55. See also HRCttee, *AP v Italy*, UN Doc CCPR/C/OP/2, para 67: 'The Committee observes that this provision prohibits double jeopardy only with regard to an offence adjudicated in a given State.'

[131] See also Art 75 AP I. The Commentary to AP I specifically notes that 'the drafters of the article have tried to stay as close as possible to the Covenant [i.e. ICCPR] (Article 14, paragraph 7). The Rapporteur expressed himself as follows about it: "the provision on ne bis in idem [...] is drawn from the United Nations Covenant on Civil and Political Rights [...] and is so drafted as to pose the minimum difficulties to States in an area where practice varies widely."'

[132] Art 14(7) ICCPR; Art 4(1) Protocol No 7 to the ECHR; Art 8(4) ACHR.

[133] Art 20 ICC Statute; Art 10 ICTY Statute; Art 9 ICTR Statute; Art 9 SCSL Statute; Art 5 STL Statute.

[134] See Art 8(2) ICTY Statute; Art 9(2) ICTR Statute.   [135] Arts 17(2) and 20 ICC Statute.

[136] See Art 74 GC IV: 'Representatives of the Protecting Power shall have *the right to attend the trial of any protected person, unless the hearing has, as an exceptional measure, to be held held in camera* in the interests of the security of the Occupying Power, which shall then notify the Protecting Power. A notification in respect of the date and place of trial shall be sent to the Protecting Power' (emphasis added); see also Art 104 GC III, which requires the Detaining Authority to inform the Protecting Power of the details of any impending trial against a POW.

[137] Art 14(1) ICCPR; Art 6(1) ECHR; Art 8(5) ACHR; Section A(3)(f) of the African Commission's *Fair Trial Principles*; Art 47 of the EU Charter of Fundamental Rights. See also HRCttee, General Comment 32, para 29.

[138] See HRCttee, General Comment 32, para 28: 'The publicity of hearings ensures the transparency of proceedings and thus provides an important safeguard for the interest of the individual and of society at large.' See also ECtHR, *Stefanelli v San Marino*, Judgment, 8 February 2000, para 19: 'The Court reiterates that it is

Only exceptional circumstances justify proceedings held in camera. There is a distinction, however, between the proceedings and the judgment. The Commentary to AP I clarifies:

> It may be *necessary because of the circumstances and the nature of the case to hold the proceedings in camera*, but the judgment itself must be made in public, unless, as the Rapporteur pointed out, this is prejudicial to the defendant himself; this could be the case for a juvenile offender.[139]

It further points to Article 14(1) ICCPR for direction as to the situations in which public proceedings are not appropriate:

> As regards holding oral proceedings *in camera*, Article 14, paragraph 1, of the Covenant gives some clear indications: 'The Press and the public may be excluded from all or part of a trial for reasons of morals, public order "(*ordre public*)" or national security in a democratic society, or when the interest of the private lives of the parties so requires, or to the extent strictly necessary in the opinion of the court in special circumstances where publicity would prejudice the interests of justice.'[140]

International criminal law also requires that a defendant have a public hearing, subject to certain strictly defined limitations.[141]   52

k. *Notification of Protecting Power*

If a Protecting Power is appointed, protected persons stand to benefit from numerous notification requirements contained in GC IV in connection with penal proceedings. In addition to the right of the protected persons to be promptly informed of the charges against them, Article 71 GC IV also requires the Occupying Power to inform the Protecting Power of all proceedings instituted against protected persons involving the death penalty or imprisonment for two years or more. The provision includes a non-exhaustive list of particulars to be included in the notification.[142] Article 74 GC IV further requires the Occupying Power to notify the Protecting Power of the date and place of trial, and of a judgment involving a death sentence or imprisonment for two years or more.[143] If no such Protecting Power exists, one view is that the Occupying Power is relieved of the Protecting Power notification requirements. However, the Occupying Power should notify the ICRC if the latter has assumed humanitarian functions normally performed by Protecting Powers during occupation pursuant to Article 11 GC IV. Even in the absence of such a substitution, however, it might be argued that the notification of the ICRC is nevertheless necessary in order to allow the ICRC to fulfil its right of visitation under Articles 76 and 143 GC IV.   53

---

a fundamental principle enshrined in Art 6 §1 that court hearings should be held in public. This public character protects litigants against the administration of justice without public scrutiny; it is also one of the means whereby people's confidence in the courts can be maintained. By rendering the administration of justice transparent, publicity contributes to the achievement of the aim of Art 6 §1, namely a fair trial, the guarantee of which is one of the principles of any democratic society.'

[139] ICRC Commentary APs, para 3118 (emphasis added). See a similar formulation in HRCttee, General Comment 32, para 29: 'Even in cases in which the public is excluded from the trial, the judgment, including the essential findings, evidence and legal reasoning must be made public, except where the interest of juvenile persons otherwise requires, or the proceedings concern matrimonial disputes or the guardianship of children.'

[140] ICRC Commentary APs, para 3119 (emphasis added).

[141] Art 21(2) ICTY Statute; Art 20(2) ICTR Statute; Art 17(2) SCSL Statute; Art 13 UN–Cambodia Agreement Concerning the Prosecution under Cambodian Law of Crimes Committed during the Period of Democratic Kampuchea; Art 17 STL Statute. See also Art 8(a), ILC Draft Code of Crimes against the Peace and Security of Mankind (1991).

[142] Pictet Commentary GC IV, at 355.

[143] Notably, under Art 74 para 2 GC IV the appeal period in case of death sentences 'shall not run until notification of judgment has been received by the Protecting Power'.

l. The right to appeal

54 This right is contained in GC III[144] and GC IV, as well as in AP I. Article 106 GC III provides:

> Every prisoner of war shall have, in the same manner as the members of the armed forces of the Detaining Power, the right of appeal or petition from any sentence pronounced upon him, with a view to the quashing or revising of the sentence or the reopening of the trial. He shall be fully informed of his right to appeal or petition and of the time limit within which he may do so.

Article 73 GC IV is more specific as to the legal basis of the appeal:

> A convicted person shall have the right of appeal *provided for by the laws applied by the court*. He shall be fully informed of his right to appeal or petition and of the time limit within which he may do so.
>
> The penal procedure provided in the present Section shall apply, as far as it is applicable, to appeals. *Where the laws applied by the Court make no provision for appeals, the convicted person shall have the right to petition against the finding and sentence to the competent authority of the Occupying Power*.[145]

The Commentary to Article 73 GC IV explains:

> In countries where the law makes no provision for appeal either in or outside the Courts, an extra-judicial appeal procedure should be instituted. It should be added that this right to petition an executive authority *with certain jurisdictional functions* must be distinguished sharply from the right to petition for pardon under Article 75 of the Convention.[146]

55 In relation to Article 106 GC III, the Commentary explains that the English and French texts deliberately diverge:

> Whereas the former refers to '[…] the right of appeal or petition […] with a view to the quashing or revising of the sentence or the reopening of the trial', the latter uses the wording '[…] le droit […] de recourir en appel, en cassation ou en revision […]' The reason is that under Anglo-Saxon legislation there is no judicial procedure for appeal in penal matters, but before becoming final the sentence must be confirmed by the military high command. The phrase 'right of petition' refers to this.[147]

Furthermore, the Commentary clarifies that although POWs have the right to appeal or petition 'in the same manner as the members of the armed forces of the Detaining Power', '[i]t would not seem […] that the drafters of the Convention intended by this wording to give prisoners of war access to certain means of appeal which are available only to nationals of the country concerned'.[148] It is also noteworthy that this provision makes no reference to appeals for pardon or reprieve:

> This does not mean that convicted prisoners of war, their defending advocates or even the Protecting Power may not submit an appeal for mercy to the authority which under the national legislation is empowered to grant a pardon or reprieve. The Convention deals only with the legal procedure for appeal.[149]

56 It appears, therefore, that the drafters of the Conventions were aware that given the multiplicity of legal systems, some jurisdictions would not provide a judicial procedure for appeals, and that POWs might also be denied the appeal procedures available to nationals of the Detaining Power. The CIHL Study notes, however, that both national and

---

[144] Art 106 GC III.
[145] Emphasis added.
[146] Pictet Commentary GC IV, at 359 (emphasis added).
[147] Pictet Commentary GC III, at 493.
[148] Ibid.
[149] Ibid.

international law have developed significantly since 1949, referring again to the influence of IHRL on IHL:

> The majority of States now have constitutions or legislation providing for the right to appeal, especially those adopted or amended since the adoption of the Additional Protocols. In addition, the International Covenant on Civil and Political Rights, the Convention on the Rights of the Child and the regional human rights conventions all provide for the right to appeal to a higher tribunal. The Inter-American Commission on Human Rights has stated that the right of appeal can never be dispensed with and must be provided in situations of non-international armed conflict. In conclusion, the influence of human rights law on this issue is such that it can be argued that the right of appeal proper—and not only the right to be informed whether appeal is available—has become a basic component of fair trial rights in the context of armed conflict.[150]

57 In the contemporary world, the right of appeal is accepted by all major legal traditions as an important judicial guarantee for the proper administration of justice.[151] Furthermore, Article 14(5) ICCPR expressly recognizes that '[e]veryone convicted of a crime shall have the right to his conviction and sentence being reviewed by a higher tribunal according to law'.

58 In view of the interrelationship between IHRL and IHL, and the influence of the ICCPR on Article 75(4) AP I in particular, it would be sound to conclude that subparagraph (j) includes a right of appeal, even if the particular procedure is left to be determined by domestic law.

C. Relevance in Non-International Armed Conflicts

59 For the applicability of judicial guarantees in NIAC, please see Chapter 23 of this volume.

D. Legal Consequences of a Violation

60 Depriving a protected person of the 'rights of fair and regular trial prescribed in [GC IV]' could entail both individual criminal responsibility and state responsibility. On the individual level, a person who wilfully denies a protected person judicial guarantees will have committed a grave breach of the Convention.[152] Indeed, the ICC Elements of Crimes state that one of the elements under Article 8(2)(a)(vi) of the ICC Statute on 'War crimes' is that '[t]he perpetrator deprived one or more persons of a fair and regular trial by denying judicial guarantees as defined, in particular, in the third and the fourth Geneva Conventions of 1949'. With respect to NIACs, non-state armed groups often do not possess sufficient resources or trained personnel to institute fully-fledged court proceedings with all the attendant judicial guarantees. Nevertheless, the act of individual members of non-state armed groups divesting the accused of judicial guarantees may constitute a war crime under Article 8(2)(c)(iv) of the ICC Statute.[153] With respect to states, violations of the right to fair and regular trial encompassed by the Geneva Conventions could be challenged before a number of international human rights bodies.

---

[150] ICRC CIHL Study, Rule 100.
[151] See the legislation from Argentina, Canada, New Zealand, Spain, Democratic Republic of the Congo, and the United Kingdom cited in the ICRC CIHL Study online database, available at <http://www.icrc.org/customary-ihl/eng/docs/v2_rul_rule100_sectionl>.
[152] Art 147 GC IV.   [153] Ch 23 of this volume, MN 77–99.

E. Critical Assessment

61 Judicial guarantees are one of the core principles of IHL. Their violation may amount to a grave breach of the Geneva Conventions.[154] They were incorporated in the Geneva Conventions in 1949 as minimum standards applicable to different categories of persons against whom penal proceedings might be instituted. Article 75 AP I and Article 6 AP II reflect a more condensed and elaborate list of judicial guarantees based largely on Article 14 ICCPR. This is a measure of the significant progress of IHL and the expanding ambit of its protection. There are practical limits, however, to the application of these standards, especially in the context of NIACs where non-state actors invariably do not benefit from formal legislatures and judicial systems. Thus, IHL must simultaneously uphold the highest standards, whilst also applying them reasonably and realistically in widely divergent contexts. The acute controversy surrounding the prosecution of 'enemy combatants' before US military commissions in the 'war on terror' demonstrates the continuing relevance and centrality of judicial guarantees to the future development of IHL.

PAYAM AKHAVAN[*]

Annex

Judicial Guarantees under the Geneva Conventions

Category of protected persons	Applicable legal regime (IAC or NIAC)	Rules contained in the GCs, APs, or CIHL	Details of Rules
Prisoners of war	IAC	Art 99 GC III	- *Nullum crimen* principle - Prohibition against self-incrimination - Right to defend oneself or through counsel
		Art 100 GC III Art 101 GC III	- Restrictions on the death penalty
		Art 102 GC III	- Rightly constituted independent and impartial tribunal
		Art 103 GC III	- Right to be tried without undue delay - No prolonged confinement while awaiting trial
		Art 104 GC III	- Notification of proceedings to the Protecting Power

---

[154] See Art 130 GC III ('wilfully depriving a prisoner of war of the rights of fair and regular trial prescribed in this Convention') and Art 147 GC IV ('wilfully depriving a protected person of the rights of fair and regular trial prescribed in the present Convention'). In NIAC, CA 3 para 1(1)(d) prohibits 'the passing of sentences and the carrying out of executions without previous judgment pronounced by a regularly constituted court, affording all the judicial guarantees which are recognized as indispensable by civilized peoples'.

[*] The author gratefully acknowledges the valuable research assistance of Mariya Nikolova in the preparation of this chapter.

Category of protected persons	Applicable legal regime (IAC or NIAC)	Rules contained in the GCs, APs, or CIHL	Details of Rules
		Art 105 GC III	- Right to be informed of the charges in a language which the accused understands - Right to an interpreter - Right to counsel - Right to adequate time and facilities for the preparation of defence (at least 2 weeks before opening of trial) + possibility for counsel to visit accused and interview him or her in private, and confer with any witnesses accused wishes to call - Right to be tried in one's presence - Right to a public judgment (unless specific reasons for in camera proceedings)
		Art 106 GC III	- Right to appeal - Right to be informed of the possibility to appeal
		Art 107 GC III	- Notification of findings and sentence - In case of death sentence, a specific regime of notification
		Art 108 GC III	- Serving of sentence on a par with members of the armed forces of the Detaining Power
		Art 129 para 2 GC III	- Grave breaches provisions (persons alleged to have committed or to have ordered to be committed grave breaches, shall be brought, regardless of their nationality, before the courts of the High Contracting Party)
		Art 129 para 3 GC III	- Penal prosecutions for *other* acts contrary to the GC provisions (i.e. *other violations of IHL*)
Civilians a) Aliens on the territory of a Party to the conflict	IAC	Art 38 GC IV Art 75 AP I	- Previously primarily regulated by domestic law (aliens are covered by the same regime as enemy nationals); now explicitly regulated by AP I, Art 75
Civilians b) In Occupied Territory	IAC	Art 64 GC IV	- Penal legislation in Occupied Territories
		Art 65 GC IV	- Right to know in their own language the penal provisions enacted by the Occupying Power
		Art 66 GC IV	- Accused may be handed over to properly constituted courts in the occupied country.
		Art 67 GC IV	- The principles of non-retroactivity and that the penalty should be proportionate to the offence. - The requirement that courts take into account that the accused is not a national of the Occupying Power.
		Art 68 GC IV	- Limitations to penalties for minor offences. - Death penalty provisions and limitations.
		Art 69 GC IV	- Right to have period spent under arrest deducted from the period of imprisonment.

Category of protected persons	Applicable legal regime (IAC or NIAC)	Rules contained in the GCs, APs, or CIHL	Details of Rules
		Art 70 GC IV	- Non-retroactivity of legislation existing at the time of the crime for offences committed before the occupation.
		Art 71 GC IV	- Right to be promptly informed, in a language which they understand, of the particulars of the charges - Right to be brought to trial as rapidly as possible - Notification of the Protecting Power regarding any charges involving imprisonment for 2+ years and death penalty - Protecting Power can receive the particulars of the proceedings - Right to adequate time (see last paragraph of Art 71, which is particularly strict as to the start date of trial)
		Art 72 GC IV	- Right to present evidence - Right to call witnesses - Right to a defence counsel - Right to an interpreter - Right to object to an interpreter
		Art 73 GC IV	- Right to appeal - Same procedural guarantees shall apply to the appeals proceedings
		Art 74 GC IV	- Right to a public trial (or at least one which the Protecting Power can attend), unless for security reasons in camera proceedings are necessary - Very strict rules again on the opening of the appeals phase (in particular as regards death penalty and sentences of imprisonment of 2 years or more). - Occupying Power must inform the Protecting Power of the date and place of trial and of judgment involving the death sentence.
		Art 75 GC IV	- Death sentence (allow for pardon/reprieve). Prohibition on execution until 6 months after receipt of notification to Protecting Power.
Civilian internees	IAC	Art 117 GC IV	- Penal sanctions for internees having committed an offence *during* internment - *Ne bis in idem*
		Art 118 GC IV	- Courts should take into account the fact that the internee is not a national of the Detaining Power - Prohibits mistreatment while serving disciplinary or judicial sentences
		Art 121 GC IV	- Escape shall not be deemed an aggravating circumstance in a case where an internee is prosecuted for an offence committed during his or her escape

Category of protected persons	Applicable legal regime (IAC or NIAC)	Rules contained in the GCs, APs, or CIHL	Details of Rules
All parties to NIAC (in particular, persons accused of criminal offences relating to the armed conflict)	NIAC	CA 3, Art 6 AP II, and CIHL (incl Art 75 AP I as a customary rule)	- Technically all judicial guarantees are covered in the law of NIAC as well. The discussion here is on feasibility of the obligation of non-state armed groups to fulfil all requirements of judicial guarantees.

Chapter 60. Other Issues Relating to the Treatment of Civilians in Enemy Hands

	MN
A. Introduction	1
B. Meaning and Application	5
I. Section I: Provisions common to the territories of the parties to the conflict and to occupied territories	5
a. Treatment of protected persons in general: Article 27	5
b. Danger zones: Article 28	26
c. Responsibilities: Article 29	34
d. Application to Protecting Powers and relief organizations: Articles 30, 142, and 143	40
e. Prohibition of coercion: Article 31	45
f. Prohibition of physical suffering: Article 32	48
II. Section II: Aliens in the territory of a party to the conflict	54
a. Persons in confinement: Article 37	54
b. Non-repatriated persons: Article 38	58
c. Means of existence: Article 39	64
d. Employment: Article 40	68
e. Cancellation of restrictive measures: Article 46	72
III. Section III: Inviolability of rights in occupied territories	77
C. Relevance in Non-International Armed Conflicts	80
D. Legal Consequences of a Violation	88
I. State responsibility	88
II. Individual criminal responsibility	89
E. Critical Assessment	92

Select Bibliography

Dederer, H.G., 'Enemy Property', in MPEPIL

Fleck, D. (ed), *The Handbook of International Humanitarian Law* (2nd edn, Oxford: OUP, 2008)

Johannot Gradis, C., *Le patrimoine culturel matériel et immatériel: quelle protection en cas de conflit armé?* (Zürich: Schulthess, 2013)

Kolb, R., 'Etude sur l'occupation et sur l'article 47 de la Convention de Genève IV de 1949 relative à la protection des personnes civiles en temps de guerre: le degré de l'intangibilité des droits en territoire occupé', 10 *Annuaire Africain de Droit International* (2002) 267

Melzer, N., *Targeted Killing in International Law* (Oxford: OUP, 2008), at 158–67

Sassòli, M., 'State Responsibility for Violations of International Humanitarian Law', 84 *IRRC* 846 (2002) 401

Sassòli, M., 'Human Shields and International Humanitarian Law', in A. Fischer-Lescano et al (eds), *Paix en liberté: Festschrift für Michael Bothe zum 70. Geburtstag* (Baden-Baden: Nomos, 2008) 567.

Stewart, J.G., *Prosecuting the Pillage of Natural Resources* (New York: Open Society Institute, 2011)

A. Introduction

1   This chapter discusses certain issues relating to the treatment of civilians in enemy hands. The fundamental guarantees for civilians protected by the Fourth Geneva Convention (GC IV) underlie these issues, whilst many of the thematic chapters in this volume have touched on these values this chapter will provide an Article by Article analysis of the key provisions containing these guarantees.

2   Geneva Convention IV is concerned with the protection of civilians, and states have to apply it in situations of international armed conflict (IAC) and occupation.[1] The Tokyo Draft, aimed at protecting civilians, served as inspiration for GC IV.[2] The Draft was designed to protect two categories: the first, which was an entirely new idea, consisted of 'enemy civilians on the territory of a belligerent'; the second, complementing the Hague Regulations, consisted of 'civilians in the power of the enemy in occupied territories'. Although the Tokyo Draft was never put into effect, it was used as a basis for GC IV: Part II of GC IV covers the 'whole of the populations of the countries in conflict', i.e. all civilians;[3] and Part III of GC IV, entitled 'Status and Treatment of Protected Persons', is divided into five sections, of which the first four cover specific categories of protected persons.[4]

3   The main issues in GC IV discussed in this chapter relate to the treatment of civilians in enemy hands, namely: fundamental guarantees (Article 27); human shields (Article 28); responsibilities (Article 29); application to Protecting Powers and relief organizations (Articles 30, 142, and 143); prohibition of coercion (Article 31); prohibition of physical suffering (Article 32); persons in confinement (Article 37); non-repatriated persons (Articles 38–40); restrictive measures (Article 46); and the inviolability of rights (Article 47). These issues are laid down in Part III of GC IV and spread out over three sections, all of them covering 'protected persons'. At the same time, the category of civilians falling within the scope of 'protected persons' differs in each section.[5]

4   In general, for each Article discussed in this chapter, an analysis of its meaning and application will be given, taking into account other relevant fields of law. Furthermore, section C briefly discusses the relevance in non-international armed conflicts (NIACs) and section D touches upon the legal consequences of a violation of the aforementioned provisions.

B. Meaning and Application

I. Section I: Provisions common to the territories of the parties to the conflict and to occupied territories

a. *Treatment of protected persons in general: Article 27*

i. Preliminary remarks on Article 27

5   Article 27 is considered the basis of GC IV, reflecting the spirit of international humanitarian law (IHL), proclaiming 'the principle of respect for the human person and the inviolable character of the basic rights of individual men and women'.[6] This Article codifies

---

[1] CA 2; see further Chs 1, 2, 3, and 4 of this volume.
[2] Draft International Convention on the Condition and Protection of Civilians of enemy nationality who are on territory belonging to or occupied by a belligerent, adopted at the 15th International Conference of the Red Cross in 1934.
[3] Arts 4 para 3 and 13 GC IV.   [4] See further Chs 52 and 55 of this volume.
[5] See further Chs 52, 55, and 67 of this volume.   [6] Pictet Commentary GC IV, at 200.

the intrinsic rights and freedoms of the human being in IAC. The purpose of Article 27 GC IV is clearly to protect the fundamental human rights of civilians. Being the core provision of GC IV, all the other provisions have to be interpreted in line with this Article. Notwithstanding the focus on individual rights, paragraph 4, stating that 'the Parties to the conflict may take such measures of control and security in regard to protected persons as may be necessary as a result of the war', allows the balancing of individual rights with the interests of the belligerents. Considering that Article 27 is seen as reflecting the intrinsic rights and freedoms of the human being, international human rights law (IHRL) can and should be used to a certain extent as a means to interpret the provisions contained in this Article.

Part III, Section I, and thus Article 27, applies to protected persons both in territories of the parties to the conflict and in occupied territories. The first paragraph of Article 27 provides that protected persons are entitled to respect, in all circumstances, as regards several 'fundamental' rights. The 'right to respect' means that a state should 'refrain from interfering directly or indirectly with the enjoyment of the right'.[7] Thus, states should refrain from interfering with the protected person's person, honour, family rights, religious convictions and practices, and manners and customs. Moreover, not only should High Contracting Parties refrain from interfering with these rights, but they should also protect persons against abuses of these rights, as mentioned in the second sentence of paragraph 1.[8]

ii. Respect for one's person

The Pictet Commentary states that the right to respect for one's person has to be understood in its widest sense. Accordingly, 'it covers all the rights of the individual, that is, the rights and qualities which are inseparable from the human being by the very fact of his existence and his mental and physical powers'.[9] It then goes on to mention some rights which are included, namely the right to physical, moral, and intellectual integrity, and argues that the right to life, although not mentioned explicitly in the Article, may be implied.[10] Another right discussed in the Pictet Commentary in relation to the right to respect for one's person, is the 'right to personal liberty, and in particular, the rights to move about freely'. This right is said to be different from the absolute rights mentioned in the Convention but is nevertheless applicable. As Pictet explains, this right

> can naturally be made subject in war time to certain restrictions made necessary by circumstances. So far as the local population is concerned, the freedom of movement of civilians of enemy nationality may certainly be restricted, or even temporarily suppressed, if circumstances so require. That right is not, therefore, included among the other absolute rights laid down in the Convention, but that in no wise means that it is suspended in a general manner. Quite the contrary: the regulations concerning occupation and those concerning civilian aliens in the territory of a Party to the conflict are based on the idea of the personal freedom of civilians remaining in general unimpaired. The right in question is therefore a relative one which the Party to the conflict or the occupying power may restrict or even suspend within the limits laid down by the Convention.[11]

Pictet also states that the right to life is implied, 'for without it there would be no reason for the other rights mentioned'.[12] We might also mention that the prohibition of slavery, the prohibition of torture or inhuman or degrading treatment or punishment, and the

---

[7] See CESCR, General Comment 14 (E/C.12/2000/4), para 33. See Ch 6, MN 42–43, of this volume for the interpretation of the wording 'in all circumstances'.
[8] See MN 10 and Ch 6 of this volume.   [9] Pictet Commentary GC IV, at 201.   [10] Ibid.
[11] Ibid, at 201–2.   [12] Ibid, at 201.

prohibition of the retroactivity of penal measures are all non-derogable in time of armed conflict.[13] Thus, with regard to the interpretation of the right to respect for one's person, it may be asserted that the above-mentioned rights are included in its ambit. Furthermore, if this right is to be interpreted in its widest sense, it might be argued that other key rights, such as the right not to be taken hostage, the right not to be abducted, and the right not to be detained without acknowledgement, would come within its scope as well.[14]

iii. Respect for honour

8   The right of respect for honour is described by Pictet as a right 'invested in man because he is endowed with a reason and a conscience', and the fact that a civilian has the enemy nationality does not justify any interference with that person's honour or reputation. In IHRL instruments, 'honour' and 'reputation' are either mentioned alongside or are included in the rights to privacy, family, and home.[15] The discrepancy here is that the Universal Declaration of Human Rights (UDHR), the International Covenant on Civil and Political Rights (ICCPR), and the American Convention on Human Rights (ACHR) seem to cover 'honour' in private and public life, while the European Convention on Human Rights (ECHR) seems to cover a person's honour only in his or her private life. In order to see if IHL covers both private and public life or only private life, we might take a look at the Hague Regulations, where it is provided that 'family honour and rights […] must be respected', which might be understood as meaning honour in private life given that it refers to 'family honour'.[16] Violating family honour was considered to encompass sexual assault, but this was not mentioned explicitly due to the conventions of that time.[17] Article 27 GC IV, by stating 'their honour, their family rights', makes a distinction between these two concepts. Therefore, it might be argued that this distinction has been made deliberately in order to include honour in public life within the notion of 'honour' as set out in this Article. Another reason could be that the terms have been separated in order to give more attention to violations of honour, following the meaning of the Hague Regulations, namely refraining from acts of sexual assault. The term 'honour' is quite vague, and it is not clear precisely what is included. However, it might be asserted that in IHL, respect for honour includes at least that members of states' armed forces should refrain from sexual assault. This is also reinforced by the due diligence obligation in the second paragraph of Article 27 GC IV, where it is mentioned that '[w]omen shall be especially protected against any attack on their honour, in particular against rape, enforced prostitution or any form of indecent assault', stressing several forms of sexual assault in the context of honour.[18] The kind of violation mentioned above will mainly involve a physical attack. It is not clear if respect for honour could also encompass a moral violation, for example when a person is being humiliated or his or her reputation is being damaged. If this is the case, a certain level of seriousness is probably necessary, as has been reasoned under some of the IHRL instruments.[19]

---

[13] See HRCttee, General Comment 29, para 13; ECtHR, *Saadi v Italy*, Grand Chamber Judgment, 28 February 2008, paras 127, 138, and 140.

[14] HRCttee, above n 13, para 13.

[15] The word 'honour' is expressly mentioned in Art 12 UDHR, Art 17 ICCPR, and Art 11 ACHR, while it is deliberately omitted from Art 8 ECHR which nevertheless protects it under the notion of 'private life'.

[16] Hague Convention (IV) on War on Land and its Annexed Regulations (1907), Art 46.

[17] C. Arrabal Ward, 'Significance of Wartime Rape', in M. Texler Segal and V. Demos (eds), *Gendered Perspectives on Conflict and Violence* (Bingley: Emerald Group Publishing Ltd, 2013), vol 18, 189.

[18] See Chs 17, MN 7–42, and 61, MN 12–13, of this volume.

[19] ECtHR, *A v Norway*, Judgment, 9 April 2009, paras 63, 64.

iv. Respect for family rights

As mentioned at MN 8, the right to respect for family rights stems from the Hague   9
Regulations that address the Occupying Power. Article 27 GC IV extends the scope
to all protected persons. Pictet explains that this right implies that family ties must be
maintained, as well as restored if necessary.[20] The right of respect for family rights is
also considered as customary law,[21] as shown, inter alia, by many military manuals and
IHRL instruments that contain provisions prohibiting arbitrary interference with family
life.[22] The International Committee of the Red Cross (ICRC) Customary International
Humanitarian Law Study (CIHL Study) identified that 'respect for family life requires, to
the degree possible, the maintenance of [the] family unit, contact between family members and the provision of information on the whereabouts of family members'.[23]

These three aspects of the right to respect for family life identified in the CIHL Study are   10
reflected in several Articles of GC IV.[24] Note, however, that those Articles are more concerned with protecting than with respecting family rights. Considering that those Articles
are based on Article 27 GC IV, it seems that the notion 'shall be protected' in the second sentence of Article 27 paragraph 1 also applies to all the rights mentioned in the first sentence.
The word 'especially' seems to reinforce this assertion: not only shall their rights as protected
persons as mentioned in the first sentence be protected, but they shall also 'especially' be protected 'against all acts of violence [etc]'.[25] It might thus be argued that a High Contracting
Party has a positive obligation to undertake action to protect persons from rights abuses.[26]

In order to interpret the notion of 'family', recourse may be had to IHRL instruments.   11
The ICCPR's notion of family has been interpreted 'to include all those comprising the
family as understood in the society of the state party', which seems logical considering
that the inclusion criteria for 'family' differ as between states.[27] The European Court of
Human Rights (ECtHR) has a similar understanding of family life, stating that it 'is not
confined solely to families based on marriage and may encompass other *de facto* relationships, taking into account a number of factors'.[28]

It seems that for IHL a similar interpretation may be used. Whether a (protected) person is a member of a 'family' or not is of importance for a state, in order for it to comply   12
with the IHL obligations imposed upon it concerning the treatment of family (members).
In order to determine whether a person may be considered a 'family member', the parties
to the conflict have to comply with their own domestic law and, if applicable, private international law, whereas Occupying Powers have to respect and apply the domestic law of the
occupied territory.[29] Furthermore, it needs to be mentioned that the absolute protection
of family rights cannot be guaranteed in an armed conflict situation.[30]

---

[20] Pictet Commentary GC IV, at 202.   [21] ICRC CIHL Study, vol I, at 379, Rule 105.
[22] See, e.g., Art 23(1) ICCPR, Art 10 ICESCR, Art 17(1) ACHR, and Art 15(1) ACHPR.
[23] ICRC CIHL Study, vol I, at 380–2. See also Ch 53.   [24] See, e.g., Arts 25, 26, 39, 40, and 50 GC IV.
[25] However, the customary rule and AP I only mention 'respect'.
[26] While 'respecting' means that a state should refrain from interfering with a right, 'protecting' implies action on the part of the state to ensure that individuals' rights are not abused (CESCR, General Comment 14, E/C.12/2000/4, para 33).
[27] HRCttee, General Comment 16, para 5.
[28] ECtHR, *X, Y, and Z v UK*, Grand Chamber Judgment, 22 April 1997, para 36, recalling several cases where this has been said by the Court; I. Roagna, *Protecting the Right to Respect for Private and Family Life under the European Convention on Human Rights* (Strasbourg: Council of Europe, 2012).
[29] Art 43 Hague Regulations and Art 64 GC IV.
[30] EECC, *Civilians Claims—Eritrea's Claims 15, 16, 23 & 27–32*, Partial Award, 17 December 2004, para 154.

v. Respect for religious convictions and practices

13 Article 46 of the Hague Regulations provides that religious convictions and practice have to be respected by the Occupying Power. Article 27 GC IV reaffirms this, extends it to all protected persons, and adds that this right should be protected as well. At the same time, neither the customary rule nor Additional Protocol (AP) I mentions that this right should be protected but only demands explicitly that it be respected.[31]

14 Geneva Convention IV specifies explicitly in several Articles how the religious convictions and practice of protected persons must be respected and protected.[32] With regard to the interpretation of religious convictions and practices, the Pictet Commentary, reiterated in the Commentary to Article 75 AP I, notes that the notion of religious convictions and practices should be understood in a broad sense, covering all philosophical and ethical convictions.[33] Some examples of what comes within the scope of this concept may be found in the earlier-mentioned Articles of GC IV.[34] In addition, IHRL instruments, such as the ICCPR, determine that the right to freedom of religion 'cannot be derogated from, even in time of public emergency'.[35] According to the Human Rights Committee's General Comment, the freedom to *have or adopt* a religion 'does not permit any limitations whatsoever', but the freedom to *manifest* one's religion may be limited.[36] Furthermore, states parties to the ICCPR are required to prohibit propaganda for war and the incitement of religious hatred.[37] International humanitarian law does not seem to limit the right to have a religion either, considering that specific Articles underline the importance of religion for persons in the most vulnerable situation, namely when interned.[38] However, paragraph 4 of Article 27 GC IV provides a basis for the parties to the conflict to limit these rights by taking measures of security and control with regard to protected persons.[39]

vi. Respect for manners and customs

15 Article 27 paragraph 1 also mentions respect for manners and customs. The Pictet Commentary identifies 'manners' as 'individual behaviour' or 'constant personal habits', whereas 'customs' refers to the 'usages of a particular society'.[40] It further explains that respect for manners and customs is especially of importance during occupation, and is meant to protect persons and communities against 'cultural genocide'.[41] Under IHL, culture is protected in several Articles, such as the maintenance and education of children,[42] the prohibition of forcible transfer of protected persons,[43] and by the protection of cultural property as mentioned in Article 27 of the Hague Regulations and the Convention for the Protection of Cultural Property in the Event of Armed Conflict.[44] The Additional Protocols similarly reiterate the other rights mentioned in the Articles concerning fundamental guarantees, but not manners and customs or culture.[45] In the field of IHRL,

---

[31] ICRC CIHL Study, vol I, at 375, Rule 104 and Art 75 AP I. Note, however, that the scope of these rules is broader, applying to all persons not profiting from a more favourable treatment.
[32] Arts 30 para 3, 38 para 3, 50 para 3, 76 para 3, 86, 93, and 130 GC IV.
[33] ICRC Commentary APs, para 3034.   [34] Above n 32.
[35] Art 4(2) ICCPR; HRCttee, General Comment 22, para 1.
[36] Art 18 ICCPR; HRCttee, General Comment 22, paras 3 and 8.
[37] Art 20 ICCPR; HRCttee, General Comment 11, para 2.
[38] See, e.g., Arts 30 para 3 and 93 GC IV.   [39] See MN 24–25.
[40] Pictet Commentary GC IV, at 203.   [41] Ibid.   [42] Art 50 GC IV.
[43] Art 49 para 1 GC IV.
[44] Convention for the Protection of Cultural Property in the Event of Armed Conflict (1954).
[45] Art 75 AP I; Art 4 AP II.

some instruments mention the right to cultural life[46] and aim at safeguarding intangible cultural heritage, which does include the manners and customs of communities, groups, and individuals.[47] It can thus be argued that cultural heritage, and therefore manners and customs, are protected during armed conflict through IHL, IHRL, and the UNESCO Convention.[48]

vii. Humane treatment

16 The principle of humane treatment is incorporated in Article 27 paragraph 1 GC IV. This principle underlies all the Geneva Conventions (for all protected persons) as well as Common Article 3 (in NIAC); it is recognized by the Additional Protocols as being a fundamental guarantee (in IAC under Article 75 AP I, persons not benefiting from a more favourable treatment, and in NIAC under Article 4 AP II, persons not, or no longer, taking direct part in hostilities); and it is identified as customary law (for civilians and persons *hors de combat*).[49] This principle is especially important with regard to people who find themselves in a most vulnerable position, namely when interned.

17 As Pictet had already stated and as repeated in the CIHL Study, it is unnecessary and even useless to define precisely which acts would fall within the notion of humane treatment.[50] Instead, the question might be reversed to consider what inhuman treatment is, or, as mentioned in the Pictet Commentary under Article 147 on inhuman treatment as a grave breach, defining inhuman treatment as 'the sort of treatment which [has] ceased to be humane'.[51] Geneva Convention IV contains provisions in which examples of inhuman treatment may be found, among which the provision on grave breaches, which includes several acts in the notion of inhuman treatment.[52] The Pictet Commentary explains that the meaning of inhuman treatment goes beyond physical injury or injury to health, and that '[c]ertain measures, for example, which might cut the civilian internees off completely from the outside world and in particular from their families, or which caused grave injury to their human dignity, could conceivably be considered as inhuman treatment'.[53] The principle of humane treatment applies 'at all times', meaning that, for example, the ongoing hostilities cannot be used to justify any violation of the principle of humane treatment whatsoever.[54]

18 In international criminal law (ICL) the International Criminal Tribunal for the former Yugoslavia (ICTY), in the *Čelebići Camp* case, found that

inhuman treatment is an intentional act or omission, that is an act which, judged objectively, is deliberate and not accidental, which causes serious mental or physical suffering or injury or constitutes a serious attack on human dignity.

---

[46] See, e.g., Art 27 ICCPR; Art 27 UDHR; and Arts 13, 14, 15 ICESCR.
[47] UNESCO Convention for the Safeguarding of Intangible Cultural Heritage (2003), Art 2.
[48] Ibid; C. Johannot Gradis, *Le patrimoine culturel matériel et immatériel: quelle protection en cas de conflit armé?* (Zürich: Schulthess, 2013), at 149–87, 497–701, 709–13.
[49] ICRC CIHL Study, vol I, at 306, Rule 87. [50] Pictet Commentary GC IV, at 204.
[51] Pictet Commentary GC IV, at 598.
[52] E.g., Art 27 para 1 second sentence (emphasis added): 'They shall at all times be humanely treated, and shall be protected *especially* against all acts of violence or threats thereof and against insults and public curiosity.' This would mean that, e.g., violation of the protection against public curiosity could amount to inhuman treatment. Furthermore, Art 32 gives examples of inhuman treatment that may be considered to form a non-exhaustive list. See also the provision on grave breaches, Art 147 GC IV, which includes in the notion of inhumane treatment 'biological experiments, wilfully causing great suffering or serious injury to body or health'.
[53] Pictet Commentary GC IV, at 598.
[54] H. Fischer, 'Protection of Prisoners of War', in D. Fleck (ed), *The Handbook of International Humanitarian Law* (2nd edn, Oxford: OUP, 2008) 367, at 378.

The Tribunal continued:

[I]nhuman treatment is intentional treatment which does not conform with the fundamental principle of humanity, and forms the umbrella under which the remainder of the listed 'grave breaches' in the Conventions fall. Hence, acts characterised in the Conventions and Commentaries as inhuman, or which are inconsistent with the principle of humanity, constitute examples of actions that can be characterised as inhuman treatment.[55]

It then stated that

[u]ltimately, the question of whether any particular act which does not fall within the categories of the core group is inconsistent with the principle of humane treatment, and thus constitutes inhuman(e) treatment, is a question of fact to be judged in all the circumstances of the particular case.[56]

19 Several international and regional human rights instruments contain a prohibition of inhuman treatment.[57] The European Commission on Human Rights (ECommHR) defined the notion of 'torture or inhuman or degrading treatment or punishment' on the basis of the degree of severity of ill-treatment, distinguishing three levels: torture, inhuman treatment or punishment, and degrading treatment or punishment. It defined inhuman treatment as covering 'at least such treatment as deliberately causing severe suffering, mental or physical, which in the particular situation is unjustifiable'.[58] The assessment of the minimum level of severity 'depends on all the circumstances of the case, such as the duration of the treatment, its physical or mental effects and, in some cases, the sex, age and state of health of the victim'.[59] It can thus be seen that the assessment of the case depends on the facts. The same approach is taken by the Human Rights Committee (HRCttee) with regard to Article 7 ICCPR, in that the distinction between the terms depends on the 'nature, purpose and severity of the treatment applied'.[60]

20 As already stated at MN 17, defining humane treatment under IHL may be done by asking what inhuman treatment comprises. Assessing whether an act would amount to inhuman treatment depends on the facts of the case, and ICL and IHRL could complement IHL in this determination. Nevertheless, it should be mentioned here that if the concept of humane treatment under IHL is analysed by instead asking what inhuman treatment is, while also taking into account the analysis under IHRL, the Geneva Conventions would seem to skip over the possibility of a category of degrading treatment which, as can be seen under IHRL, requires a lesser degree of severity than inhuman treatment.[61] However, when looking at Common Article 3, the substance of which is said to apply to IACs as well,[62] it requires that persons taking no active part in hostilities shall

---

[55] ICTY, *The Prosecutor v Zejnil Delalić et al (Čelebići Camp)*, Trial Chamber Judgment, IT-96-21-T, 16 November 1998, paras 512–44, esp para 543.

[56] Ibid, para 544; See also the ICC Elements of Crimes, 'Definition of Inhuman Treatment as a War Crime' (ICC Statute, Art 8(2)(a)(ii)-2), at 14. For a further discussion on the threshold of severity and intent, see Ch 16, MN 42–46, of this volume.

[57] E.g. Art 7 ICCPR, Art 5 UDHR, Art 3 ECHR, Art 5(2) ACHR, and Art 5 ACHPR.

[58] ECommHR, *The Greek case*, 5 November 1969, 12-II *YECHR* (1969), at 186.

[59] ECtHR, *Ireland v UK*, Judgment, 18 January 1978, para 162.

[60] HRCttee, General Comment 20, para 4.

[61] See, e.g., ECtHR, in the *Greek Case*, above n 58, where it defined degrading treatment as treatment or punishment that 'grossly humiliates the victim before others or drives the detainee to act against his/her will or conscience'.

[62] Pictet Commentary GC IV, at 38; ICJ, *Military and Paramilitary Activities in and against Nicaragua (Nicaragua v United States of America)*, Merits, Judgment, 27 June 1986, at 114, para 218.

be treated humanely, and to that end it prohibits 'outrages upon personal dignity, in particular humiliating and degrading treatment'.[63] It therefore might be argued that if a protected person were to suffer degrading treatment or punishment, this would also violate the requirement for humane treatment under Article 27 GC IV. It might then be argued that the notion of inhuman treatment under Article 147 GC IV includes outrages upon personal dignity, including humiliating and degrading treatment, and thus the threshold of the degree of severity for inhuman treatment under the Geneva Conventions would be lower than in IHRL.[64]

The ICTY Statute does not make any explicit reference to outrages upon personal dignity, or degrading or humiliating treatment. It considers inhuman any 'acts characterised in the Conventions and Commentaries as inhuman, or which are inconsistent with the principle of humanity',[65] which would mean that outrages upon personal dignity would possibly come within its ambit. The Statute of the International Criminal Court (ICC) includes in the list of war crimes in IAC, 'Torture or inhuman treatment, including biological experiments', 'Wilfully causing great suffering or serious injury to body or health', and 'Outrages upon personal dignity, and in particular humiliating and degrading treatment'.[66] But the ICC Statute includes outrages upon personal dignity in a separate provision (thus the notion does not appear in the paragraph listing inhuman treatment), and inhuman treatment is considered as a grave breach by the ICC Statute whereas outrages upon personal dignity are listed under 'other serious violations' (even though AP I considers outrages upon personal dignity to constitute a grave breach).[67]

viii. All acts of violence or threats thereof

Under Article 27 GC IV, states must provide protection against all acts of violence or threats thereof. It may thus be asserted that a High Contracting Party has to ensure the safety of protected civilians in the face of acts of violence, regardless of whether such an act is committed by military forces or not, or whether the act can be attributed to the state or not. Note that Article 13 GC III sets out a similar provision, including protection of prisoners of war (POWs) against 'acts of intimidation'. Pictet's Commentary explains there that the protection extends to moral values, such as the moral independence of a POW.[68] For the purposes of Article 27 GC IV, the 'threat' to commit a physical act of violence may be considered the same as an 'act of intimidation'. Protected persons also need to be protected against insults and public curiosity, which may be said to fall within the notion of honour, as found in the first sentence of paragraph 1 of Article 27. In an ICRC-sponsored plenary debate in 2006, the British Red Cross Society proposed guidelines for a contemporary interpretation to protect civilian security internees (and POWs) from public curiosity, proposing to 'interpret the existing prohibition against insults and public curiosity […] as normally prohibiting the public transmission of images of prisoners of war as identifiable individuals, and in all cases, as forbidding the public transmission

---

[63] CA 3 para 1(1)(c).
[64] Note that Art 85(4)(c) AP I has added to the list of grave breaches 'other inhuman and degrading practices involving outrages upon personal dignity, based on racial discrimination'.
[65] See MN 18. [66] Art 8(2)(a)(ii) and (b)(xxi) ICC Statute.
[67] Art 85(4)(c) AP I. See also Ch 16 of this volume, esp MN 28, 38–57, and M. Nowak, 'Torture and Other Cruel, Inhuman or Degrading Treatment or Punishment', in A. Clapham and P. Gaeta (eds), *The Oxford Handbook of International Law in Armed Conflict* (Oxford: OUP, 2014) 387, esp at 399–401.
[68] Pictet Commentary GC III, at 141.

of images of prisoners of war which undermine their personal dignity', and calling upon states and others to apply this to civilian security internees too.[69]

23   Paragraph 2 of Article 27 concerns the special protection of women. Here again, honour is discussed in the light of sexual assault. For more discussion of the special protection of women, see Chapters 17 and 61 of this volume. Paragraph 3 of Article 27 concerns discrimination, which is discussed in Chapter 10.

ix. Measures of control and security

24   Paragraph 4 of Article 27 reserves the right for the parties to the conflict to take 'measures of control and security'. Whereas the first three paragraphs of Article 27 concern individuals, paragraph 4 takes into account the interest of the state. This provision seems to provide a broad general basis for law enforcement measures. The Pictet Commentary and the *travaux préparatoires*, however, explain clearly that paragraph 4 is not meant to serve as a derogation from the fundamental rights of the protected civilians, mentioned in paragraph 1.[70] No derogation is thus allowed, unless explicitly provided for under other provisions of IHL.[71]

25   To understand what is actually provided for under IHL, the notion in Article 27 paragraph 4 of 'such measures of control and security in regard to protected persons as may be necessary as a result of the war' needs to be elaborated upon. Examples of such measures may be found in GC IV,[72] and it is clearly specified that these measures have a defined limit, to be found in Articles 41 and 78 GC IV, where it is stated that no recourse may be had to 'any other measure of control more severe than that of assigned residence or internment'[73] or 'at the most, [subjection of the protected persons] to assigned residence or to internment'.[74] Article 27 paragraph 4 GC IV serves as the general basis for internment of civilian detainees as set out in Articles 41–43, 68, and 78 GC IV.[75] Article 42 allows internment of protected persons (aliens in territory of a party to the conflict) 'if the security of the Detaining Power makes it absolutely necessary'. Article 68 requires states to ensure that 'the duration of such internment [replacing imprisonment after conviction] or imprisonment is proportionate to the offence committed' and 'the only measure adopted for depriving protected persons of their liberty'. Furthermore, Article 78 allows internment of protected persons (civilians in occupied territory) 'for imperative reasons of security', making it clear that an assessment of necessity and proportionality is required.[76] It can thus be concluded that the structure of GC IV (allowing for measures of security and control in Article 27 paragraph 4) is a closed system, under which deprivation of life or liberty is completely prohibited,[77] except in the cases mentioned above.[78] Measures of control and security which are less invasive than assigned residence and internment in

---

[69] M. Meyer and K. Studds, *Upholding Human Dignity and the Geneva Conventions: The Role of the Media in Protecting Prisoners of War and Civilian Security Internees against Insults and Public Curiosity*, Draft Resolution, 5th draft of 1 September 2005, 14 July 2006, available at <http://www.icrc.org/eng/assets/files/other/amic_kevin_studds_final.pdf>.
[70] Pictet Commentary GC IV, at 207.   [71] E.g., Arts 5 or 53 GC IV.
[72] Arts 64 and 66 GC IV.   [73] Art 41 GC IV.   [74] Art 78 GC IV.   [75] Art 79 GC IV.
[76] ICTY, *Čelebići Camp*, above n 55, para 576.
[77] See, e.g., Art 32 GC IV, where murder or any other measure of brutality by civilian or military agents is prohibited.
[78] Art 79 GC IV: no internment of protected persons except in accordance with Arts 41–43, 68 (where the death penalty is allowed only if 'such offences were punishable by death under the law of the occupied territory in force before the occupation began'), and 78 GC IV.

occupied territories are regulated by Article 43 of the Hague Regulations and Article 64 GC IV which, save for some exceptions, explain that the local laws remain in force.

b. Danger zones: Article 28

26 The Pictet Commentary points out that putting persons in places of strategic importance to render a point or area immune from military operations (danger zones) cannot be considered a permissible ruse of war. It goes on to explain how the notion of 'military operations' should be interpreted, namely, as any act of warfare conducted by enemy forces or groups that can be placed under the same umbrella as regular armed forces.[79]

27 The concept of the prohibition of 'human shields' has developed over the years due to, among other reasons, the increase of armed conflict in urban areas. International humanitarian law has paid attention to this trend. Additional Protocol I extends the prohibition against using persons to render objectives immune from military operations to the (own) civilian population of a party to the conflict.[80] The CIHL Study identifies that 'the use of human shields is prohibited' in IAC and NIAC.[81] In addition, a positive obligation is also placed upon states to endeavour to remove the civilian population from the vicinity of military objectives.[82]

28 In order to see which acts come within the scope of Article 28 GC IV, the elements of the Article need to be assessed. The term 'military operations' has been explained above, and it seems that this interpretation remains valid.[83] Thus, we shall continue with the notion 'presence of a protected person', which includes 'movements' of protected persons, as can be seen from Article 51 paragraph 7 AP I, which specifies 'movements' explicitly. With regard to the location or, in other words, the 'points and areas', the Pictet Commentary explains that 'the prohibition is expressed in an absolute form and applies to the belligerents' own territory as well as to occupied territory, to small sites as well as to wide areas'.[84]

29 The wording 'may not' in Article 28 should be interpreted narrowly. At the same time, the words 'be used' may be interpreted broadly, covering: putting a person near an object, allowing a person to place himself or herself next to an object, forces or groups moving themselves or placing a military object in an area where many protected persons are situated, and so on.[85]

30 The meaning of 'to render […] immune' has been further explained in AP I, where it is defined to include at the least '[to] shield, favour or impede military operations (or military objectives)'.[86] Although we are not discussing Article 51(7) AP I here, the explanation given there may be used in the interpretation of Article 28 GC IV. That a certain point or area will be actually rendered immune from military operations is not necessary for the provision to be violated, because this depends on the assessment of proportionality. The adversary might not necessarily be violating IHL, even though it attacks the military objective while there is a protected person present.

---

[79] Pictet Commentary GC IV, at 208; to identify regular armed forces, Art 4 GC III and Art 43 AP I (which is considered to be customary law in the ICRC CIHL Study, vol I, at 12) may be consulted.
[80] Art 51(7) AP I.   [81] ICRC CIHL Study, vol I, at 337, Rule 97.   [82] Art 58(a) AP I.
[83] At MN 26.   [84] Pictet Commentary GC IV, at 209.
[85] E.g., the 'Early Warning Procedure' conducted by the IDF. See, for an assessment, R. Otto, 'Neighbours as Human Shields? The Israel Defense Forces' "Early Warning Procedure" and International Humanitarian Law', 86 IRRC 856 (2004) 771.
[86] AP I is used to interpret Art 28 GC IV.

31   Article 28 GC IV does not require states to remove protected civilians from the vicinity of military objectives (as long as the intention behind leaving them there is not to shield a military objective). However, Article 38 paragraph 4 GC IV guarantees the right of protected persons to move from an area that is particularly exposed to the dangers of war. This is subject to authorization of the state, which has to provide such authorization without any discrimination between protected persons and nationals of the state. It may thus be considered that states have a positive obligation here to protect the lives of these protected persons.

32   Article 28 GC IV is written in such a way that it does not matter if the protected person chose to be present in order to render a certain point or area immune from military operations (also known as a voluntary human shield). Therefore, for the purpose of the Geneva Conventions, there is no need to make a distinction between voluntary human shields or persons who are present without their consent.

33   In the legal literature, it is sometimes argued that a distinction should be made between persons who are voluntary human shields and those who are not, because those who are voluntary could be said to be taking direct part in hostilities and would thus be targetable.[87] However, in practice it is almost impossible to judge or analyse whether a person shielding a military objective is doing this of his or her own free will.[88]

c. *Responsibilities: Article 29*

34   Article 3 of Hague Convention IV already provided that a belligerent party 'shall be responsible for all acts committed by persons forming part of its armed forces'. Article 29 GC IV elaborates upon this provision by expanding the category of those committing the acts to include 'agents' of the state, while limiting its scope in line with the goal of the given Convention, applying only to the treatment accorded to protected persons by its agents. Pictet explained in his Commentary that the application of the principle of state responsibility is determined by the relevant rules of international law. He went on to say that the 'responsibility principle' entails certain obligations upon states, namely an implied obligation to 'instruct their agents on their rights and duties' and an obligation to make reparation in the event that an agent of the state has committed an act in violation of the Convention.[89] A similar provision with regard to POWs may be found in Article 12 GC III. Article 29 GC IV should be read in conjunction with Article 148 GC IV concerning the prohibition on a High Contracting Party absolving itself from any liability incurred in respect of grave breaches as listed under Article 147 GC IV.

35   With regard to the first part of Article 29 GC IV, which refers to 'the Party to the conflict in whose hands protected persons may be', it might be argued that explicit reference is made to 'the Party to the conflict' in order to exclude the application of the provision to the Occupying Power, because states wanted to avoid direct responsibility for acts of local authorities in cases of occupation.[90] However, it might also be argued that it is phrased as such to clarify that the 'party' responsible is the one in whose hands the protected person is.[91] This seems more logical, especially in light of the current law of state

---

[87] Y. Dinstein, *The International Law of Belligerent Occupation* (Cambridge: CUP, 2009), at 105.
[88] M. Sassòli, 'Human Shields and International Humanitarian Law', in A. Fischer-Lescano et al (eds), *Paix en liberté: Festschrift für Michael Bothe zum 70. Geburtstag* (Baden-Baden: Nomos, 2008) 567.
[89] Coming from Art 3 Hague Regulations already.   [90] Final Record, vol II-A, at 713.
[91] See Ch 52 of this volume: to be a protected person, you have to be 'in the hands of a Party to the conflict' (Art 4 GC IV).

responsibility⁹² and the location of the Article in Section I which is applicable to both situations, i.e. protecting both enemy civilians in the territory of a party to a conflict and civilians in an occupied territory. Thus, when the protected person is in the party's hands, the party is responsible for the treatment accorded to that person.

Whereas Article 3 of Hague Convention IV and Article 91 AP I refer to 'armed forces', Article 29 GC IV specifies that state responsibility is incurred for the treatment accorded to protected persons 'by its [state] agents'. The Commentary to the ILC Articles on State Responsibility explains, based on several sources of law, that 'the general rule is that the only conduct attributed to the state at the international level is that of its organs of government, or of others who have acted under the direction, instigation or control of those organs, i.e. as agents of the state', but not limited to those who have some kind of allegiance towards the state.[93]

In order to discover whether a state is responsible for the treatment accorded to protected persons, reference may be made to the ILC Articles on State Responsibility, as well as to the case law of the ICJ and ICTY, where discussion is still ongoing as regards the degree of control necessary for attribution to a state of the acts and omissions of individuals not having the formal status of an organ of the state.[94] A possible solution might be to argue that the test of control applies differently in each situation. The test for the degree of control by a state over an individual who is not a *de jure* organ of the state might then differ, so that one would apply the overall control test for the classification of the conflict, whereas the effective control test would apply as regards the attribution of acts for the purposes of state responsibility.

Article 29 concerns responsibility for the 'treatment' of protected persons. In simple terms, it may be understood that the conduct of a state consists of acts and omissions.[95] It may thus be argued that the treatment referred to in Article 29 includes omissions as well. This reaffirms the due diligence obligation of the state and implies that a state may be held responsible if it did not act in order to prevent or stop treatment to a protected person that

---

[92] E.g., GC IV imposes obligations on the Occupying Power which may be responsible for acts attributable to it under the law of state responsibility, which includes local authorities. See the Report of the ILC Commission on the work of its 53rd session, Draft Articles on Responsibility of States for Internationally Wrongful Acts with commentaries, II(2) *YILC* (2001), at 68.

[93] Ibid, at 38.

[94] In short, the ICJ in the *Nicaragua* case concluded that although the US was responsible for the 'planning, direction and support', there was 'no clear evidence of the United States having actually exercised such a degree of control in all fields as to justify treating the *contras* as acting on its behalf'. The ICTY Appeals Chamber rejected the position of the ICJ as applied by the Trial Chamber and decided that 'the requirement of international law for the attribution to States of acts performed by private individuals is that the State exercises control over the individuals. The degree of control may, however, vary according to the factual circumstances of each case. The Appeals Chamber fails to see why in each and every circumstance international law should require a high threshold for the test of control'. It thus applied the 'overall control' test. In the later *Genocide* case, the ICJ did not subscribe to the view of the ICTY Appeals Chamber. It argued that the Appeals Chamber was not called to rule on questions of state responsibility, while the overall control test may be applicable and suitable to determine the nature of an armed conflict. ICJ, *Nicaragua v United States of America*, above n 62, at 51, para 86, and at 62, para 109; ICTY, *The Prosecutor v Duško Tadić*, Appeals Chamber Judgment, IT-94-1-A (1999), at 1518, 1541, para 117, and at 167, paras 396–407; ICJ, *Case concerning Application of the Convention on the Prevention and Punishment of the Crime of Genocide (Bosnia and Herzegovina v Serbia and Montenegro)*, Judgment, 26 February 2007, at 204–6, paras 391–5, see also ibid, Dissenting Opinion of Judge Al-Khasawneh, at 241.

[95] Art 2 ILC Articles on State Responsibility.

would amount to a violation of IHL, or if it did not make full reparations for the loss or injury caused.[96]

39   As a last point, the Article clarifies that state responsibility is to be viewed separately from 'any individual responsibility which may be incurred'.[97] Pictet explains:

> The Convention thus shows clearly that two distinct responsibilities [state responsibility and individual responsibility] co-exist and emphasizes that they are not alternatives but supplementary to one other. The fact that the State has made good the damage caused in no way diminishes the responsibility of the author of the offence and vice versa. [...] [T]he two forms of punishment for violations of the convention thus run parallel to each other.[98]

d. Application to Protecting Powers and relief organizations: Articles 30, 142, and 143

40   Article 30 GC IV, providing a way for protected persons to ask for assistance, was new in the field of IHL. The importance of this Article has to be stressed here, in that it provides the possibility for individuals, as protected persons, to be heard. The Article should be read in conjunction with Articles 142 and 143 GC IV, which cover the special roles of relief societies and other organizations.

41   To understand what is included in Article 30 GC IV, we need to start with its wording that protected persons

> shall have every facility for making application to the Protecting Powers, the International Committee of the Red Cross, the National Red Cross (Red Crescent, Red Lion and Sun) Society of the country where they may be, as well as to any organization that might assist them.

The words 'shall have' entitle protected persons to use this right, while placing an obligation on the High Contracting Parties to facilitate applications to the organizations listed in the Article. As explained by the Pictet Commentary, this right is absolute, meaning that all protected persons, as defined by Article 4 GC IV, are entitled to it. According to Pictet, 'every facility for making application to' is understood as 'a right of communication which may be exercised under all circumstances' but 'may be suspended if the seriousness of the circumstances so demands'.[99] It may thus be concluded that this phrase should be interpreted broadly, and that the right to communicate, based on the need for assistance of protected persons, may be executed in many different ways for many different reasons. It is not specified precisely what is understood by the right to communicate, nor the facility for making application.

42   The application may be made to the Protecting Powers and the ICRC, or to the National Red Cross Society of the country where the protected person may be. Pictet has already highlighted the difficult position of the National Red Cross Societies with regard to protected persons in states party to the conflict, or in occupied territory, due to their affiliations with the nationals of the country in which they work.[100] Therefore, it might be helpful to apply to National Red Cross Societies of other states that are not parties to the conflict and might have

---

[96] ICJ, *Corfu Channel*, Merits, Judgment, 9 April 1949, at 22–3; ICJ, *United States Diplomatic and Consular Staff in Tehran (United States of America v Iran)*, Judgment, 24 May 1980, at 31–2, paras 63 and 67. See further Ch 6 of this volume on due diligence.

[97] See Ch 36 of this volume.

[98] Pictet Commentary GC IV, at 210.   [99] Pictet Commentary GC IV, at 214–15.

[100] Ibid, at 216.

more independence in their way of working.[101] This is possible because Article 30 also includes a further body to which protected persons must be able to apply, that is, 'any organization that might assist them'. There is no definition or exhaustive list of which other organizations would come within the scope of this term, but some indications are given in other provisions of IHL treaties, namely organizations whose object is to give spiritual aid or material relief,[102] as well as relief societies[103] and humanitarian organizations.[104] Furthermore, Article 142, addressed to the Detaining Power, demands that, with regard to protected persons who are interned, the facilitation of visits by 'such societies or organizations [as the ones stated above] may be constituted in the territory of the Detaining Power, or in any other country, or they may have an international character'. This would mean that those organizations, as long as they have been lawfully constituted under the law of any country in the world, would have the right to provide their assistance and receive all facilities from the parties to the conflict or Occupying Power, as long as their aim is in compliance with the activities mentioned in paragraph 1 of Article 142 GC IV and they are capable of executing these activities. It should be noted that the granting of facilities to assist organizations may be restricted or limited due to military or security considerations.[105] Furthermore, Article 5 paragraph 2 GC IV provides for derogation from the right to communicate as well.[106]

Article 30 paragraph 2 GC IV stresses that the authorities must grant all facilities in order to enable protected persons to make an application to those organizations. This means not only that the making of an application should not be hindered, but that the Article also contains a positive obligation requiring the states parties to undertake action in order to facilitate applications by protected persons to the relevant organizations. In addition to some examples of what actions parties should undertake as mentioned by the Pictet Commentary, one could today consider the provision of (limited) access to the Internet and social media in order to enable communication by protected persons with the said organizations.

The first phrase of Article 30 paragraph 3 emphasizes the right of the Protecting Power and the ICRC to visit protected persons as provided for in Article 143.[107] The paragraph then stresses that, in addition to facilitating the right to visit for the above-mentioned organizations, other organizations providing spiritual aid or material relief should also have their visits to protected persons facilitated. While the right for the Protecting Powers and the ICRC to visit protected persons is almost absolute, and the Detaining Power and Occupying Power do not have much discretion to prohibit or restrict those visits, it seems that they have more discretion as regards the facilitation of visits by other organizations due to the use of the wording 'shall facilitate as much as possible'.

e. Prohibition of coercion: Article 31

This Article is very general in that it prohibits the exercise of physical or moral coercion against protected persons. Article 31 GC IV represented an enormous step forward in the protection of civilians as it expands significantly the scope of the prohibition of one

---

[101] It should be noted that such National Societies are then coordinated by the ICRC as a lead agency, according to Art 5.3.1 of the Seville Agreement on the organization of the international activities of the components of the International Red Cross and Red Crescent Movement (1997).
[102] Art 30 para 3 GC IV.
[103] Arts 30 and 142 para 1 GC IV.   [104] Art 81 para 4 AP I.
[105] Arts 30 para 2 and 142 para 1 GC IV   [106] Art 5 para 2 GC IV and Ch 54 of this volume.
[107] See also Ch 26, MN 25–26, of this volume.

type of coercion, namely the compelling of inhabitants of an occupied territory to provide information, as laid down in Article 44 of the Hague Regulations. Pictet explains in his Commentary that this prohibition is not absolute but 'applies in so far as the other provisions of the Convention do not implicitly or explicitly authorize a resort to coercion'.[108] An example of such an authorization to coerce is Article 40 GC IV, which provides a basis to compel protected persons to work. What will not be discussed here is coercion as a means and method of warfare;[109] neither will we look at coercion as a defence under criminal law, or at economic coercion by states, which could affect protected persons.[110]

46 'Coercion' may be understood as '[t]he action of persuading someone to do something by using force or threats'.[111] International human rights law may also be used to interpret the notion. There are many kinds of coercion. The ECtHR, in the case of *MC v Bulgaria*, explained the kinds of circumstances that can create a coercive environment.[112] A report by Amnesty International listed several of these forms of coercive circumstances in the context of sexual violence, namely fear of violence, duress, detention, psychological oppression, and abuse of power.[113] These forms of circumstances relate to both physical and mental or moral coercion. The prohibition in Article 31 GC IV goes beyond these forms of coercion, but includes those of torture and inhuman or degrading treatment.[114]

47 International humanitarian law implicitly and explicitly allows certain coercive measures. In some cases, such as in the case of compelled labour as provided for under Article 40 GC IV, the state is specifically allowed to exercise some form of coercion.[115] The prohibition of coercion as laid down in Article 31 is not absolute but needs to be read together with those Articles that allow for the limitation of the prohibition. Especially of importance are the measures of control and security that parties may take as provided for in Article 27 paragraph 4 GC IV, as regards which parties have a broad discretion.

f. *Prohibition of physical suffering: Article 32*

48 The purpose of the prohibition of physical suffering in Article 32, even though it might be said that this prohibition is already encompassed by Article 27 GC IV (see section B.I.a of this chapter), is to emphasize expressly absolute respect for the human person.[116] It addresses the 'High Contracting Parties' instead of the parties to the conflict or Occupying Powers, in order to emphasize the importance of the prohibition. At the same time the Article is concerned mostly with parties to the conflict and the Occupying Powers because it refers to the fact that the parties should have 'protected persons in their hands'.[117] The High Contracting Parties are thus 'prohibited from taking any measure of such a character as to cause the physical suffering or extermination' of such protected persons.

---

[108] Pictet Commentary GC IV, at 220.
[109] See D.L. Byman and M.C. Waxman, 'Kosovo and the Great Air Power Debate', 24 *International Security* (2000) 5.
[110] See G.J. Knoops, *Defenses in Contemporary International Criminal Law* (2nd edn, Leiden: Nijhoff, 2008).
[111] Oxford Dictionaries, 'coercion', available at <http://www.oxforddictionaries.com/definition/english/coercion?>.
[112] ECtHR, *MC v Bulgaria*, Judgment, 4 December 2003, at 180.
[113] Amnesty International, *Rape and Sexual Violence: Human Rights Law and Standards in the International Criminal Court* (London: Amnesty International Publications, 2011), at 19.
[114] See Ch 16 of this volume.   [115] See further section B.II.d of this chapter.
[116] Pictet Commentary GC IV, at 221.   [117] Art 4 GC IV and Ch 55 of this volume.

49 As mentioned in the Pictet Commentary, the initial draft prohibited acts or omissions that are 'likely to cause' physical suffering was changed at the Diplomatic Conference into 'of such a character as to cause'.[118] This may be interpreted as covering not only any measures directly causing, but also any measure indirectly causing the physical suffering of a protected person in the hands of a High Contracting Party.[119] An example of a measure with direct effect would be a measure requiring the killing of a protected person, while the Article also seems to cover indirect measures, such as denying a protected person water to drink, which indirectly would lead to his or her death. Such an act can also be defined as murder. Another example that might be mentioned here is the use of forced labour as a method of indirect extermination of POWs during the Second World War.[120] In the criminalization of extermination, this 'indirectness' has been taken into account as well. While the notion of 'physical suffering', as set out in Article 32 GC IV, may be interpreted as comprising any bodily harm, 'extermination' has a different connotation, namely 'murder on a large scale—mass murder',[121] including indirect means of causing death.[122] The former notion is understood as covering measures directed at individuals, while the latter is understood to cover measures addressing groups.

50 Article 32 then sets out the acts to which the prohibition applies. The notion of murder does not need much explanation. Murder refers to 'any form of homicide not resulting from a capital sentence by a court of law in conformity with the provisions of the Convention'.[123] What needs to be mentioned here is that murder committed without a causal connection to the armed conflict is not covered by this Article but would be covered by the domestic law of the state that has jurisdiction over the crime.[124] This can also be seen from the possible authors of the prohibited acts, namely, civilian or military agents.[125] But any such act committed by a non-agent with a nexus to the conflict would nevertheless violate IHL, as they are all prohibited by the first sentence of Article 32 and other provisions of IHL.

51 Corporal punishment had already been prohibited under the 1929 Convention with regard to POWs.[126] Furthermore, its prohibition is identified as a customary rule by the CIHL Study.[127] Article 75(2)(a)(iii) AP I also repeats the prohibition, while extending its scope. Corporal punishment may be interpreted as 'any punishment in which physical force is used and intended to cause some degree of discomfort, however light'.[128] The prohibition is absolute, and in Articles 118 and 119 GC IV specific provisions are set out with regard to penalties and punishment for internees. Human rights law may also be used to interpret the prohibition of corporal punishment.[129] Corporal punishment would amount to a grave breach if it

---

[118] Pictet Commentary GC IV, at 222.
[119] Note that this is an interpretation different from the one given in the Pictet Commentary.
[120] See, e.g., IMT, *Trial of the Major War Criminals before the International Military Tribunal* (Nuremberg: IMT, 1948), vol XX, at 1.
[121] UNWCC, *1948 History of the United Nations War Crimes Commission and the Developments of the Laws of War* (London: HMSO, 1948), at 194.
[122] ICTR, *The Prosecutor v Clément Kayishema and Obed Ruzindana*, Trial Chamber Judgment, ICTR-95-1-T, 21 May 1999, para 146, 'extermination includes [...] the creation of conditions of life that leads to mass killing'.
[123] Pictet Commentary GC IV, at 222.
[124] See ICRC CIHL Study, vol I, at 311, and vol II, at 2061.
[125] See, for the meaning of 'agents', MN 36.   [126] Art 46 para 3 1929 GC II.
[127] ICRC CIHL Study, vol I, at 3.
[128] UN Committee on the Rights of the Child (2001), General Comment 1, para 11.
[129] See, e.g., ECtHR, *A v UK*, Judgment, 23 September 1998; ECtHR, *Tyrer v UK*, Judgment, 25 April 1978; see also HRC, *Osbourne v Jamaica*, Communication 759/1997, 13 April 2000, UN Doc

were to amount to torture or inhuman treatment, or if it would cause great suffering or serious injury to body and health.[130] According to the HRCttee, the prohibition on torture, cruel, inhuman, or degrading treatment or punishment 'must extend to corporal punishment'.[131]

52   The Commentary on Article 11 AP I, which repeats the prohibition of mutilation, states that 'physical mutilation' refers 'particularly [to] amputations and injury to limbs'. Furthermore, ICL may be consulted to see how the term 'mutilation' is interpreted. In the *Tadić* case before the ICTY, reference is made to sexual mutilation in the finding of the facts.[132] Under the ICC Statute, mutilation is defined as a war crime.[133] In the Elements of Crimes it is stated that for this crime, '[t]he perpetrator subjected one or more persons to mutilation, in particular by permanently disfiguring the persons or persons, or by permanently disabling or removing an organ or appendage', which leaves room for other acts to fall within the notion of 'mutilation'.[134] These acts do not appear to be prohibited as such under IHRL, but would fall under the prohibition of torture and inhuman or degrading treatment or punishment. Rule 92 of the CIHL Study also asserts that the prohibition of mutilation, as well as the prohibition of medical or scientific experiments, is customary law. Non-consensual medical or scientific experimentation is expressly prohibited under Article 7 ICCPR. International humanitarian law repeats the prohibition of medical and scientific experiments in Article 11 AP I, and provides more guidance on how to interpret this notion.

53   As can be seen in the last part of Article 32 GC IV, the list is made non-exhaustive through the wording 'any other measures of brutality'. According to the Pictet Commentary, this wording is similar to the reference to 'acts of violence' in Article 27 GC IV.[135] Furthermore, reference is made to the possible authors of such acts, namely civilian or military agents, in order to address the responsibility of both the individual perpetrators and the state.[136]

II. Section II: Aliens in the territory of a party to the conflict

a. Persons in confinement: Article 37

54   The purpose of Article 37 GC IV is to protect persons with enemy nationality on the territory of a party to the conflict from arbitrary treatment by the authorities during their confinement. This Article covers protected persons confined pending criminal proceedings or serving a sentence, but is not concerned with persons detained for security purposes which is dealt with in Articles 41 to 43 GC IV.[137] The confinement pending proceedings or the serving of a sentence is regulated by domestic penal law. Furthermore, IHRL provides for extensive procedural and substantive law regarding persons in confinement. Therefore, IHRL should be consulted in order to understand the notions 'confined pending proceedings' and 'serving a sentence involving loss of liberty'.[138]

CCPR/C/68/D/759/1997, para 9.1; IACtHR, *Caesar v Trinidad and Tobago*, Judgment, 11 March 2005, paras 67–89.

[130] Art 147 GC IV.   [131] HCRttee, General Comment 20, 10 March 1992, para 5.
[132] ICTY, *The Prosecutor v Duško Tadić*, Trial Chamber Judgment, IT-94-1-T, paras 193, 237, 726–30.
[133] Arts 8(2)(b)(x)-1 and 8(2)(c)(i)-2, 8(2)(e)(xi)-1 ICC Statute.
[134] ICC Elements of Crimes, War Crime of Mutilation (ICC Statute, Article 8(2)(b)(x)-1).
[135] At first sight 'acts' seem to exclude conduct through omission; it is however also possible to contend that the word is used here also to encompass omission.
[136] See MN 34.   [137] See Ch 64 of this volume.
[138] See Ch 23 of this volume, although concerned with the context of a NIAC, and Ch 59 of this volume, written in the context of protected civilians, can be consulted for the discussion of judicial guarantees deriving from IHRL. Also, the ICRC CIHL Study, vol II, at 2328–492 provides a clear overview.

The CIHL Study identifies a customary rule prohibiting arbitrary deprivation of liberty, applying to both IAC and NIAC situations.[139] Arbitrary deprivation of liberty may amount to inhuman treatment which would violate Article 37 paragraph 1 GC IV and Article 27 GC IV, and in a NIAC situation it would violate Common Article 3. Furthermore, if applicable, it would amount to a violation of Article 75 AP I (considered to reflect customary law) and Article 5(3) AP II. According to Article 147 GC IV, inhuman treatment and unlawful confinement are considered to be grave breaches of the Geneva Conventions, and are criminalized by several statutes of international criminal courts and tribunals.[140] Examples of inhuman treatment (relating to deprivation of liberty) include poor conditions of detention, cases of solitary confinement, and lack of adequate food, water, and medical treatment.[141]

Article 37 paragraph 2 starts with the words 'As soon as they are released', which is an interesting phrase. The question is what is meant by 'release' today: does this comprise, for example, home arrest, detention at home, release on temporary licence, or release on conditions? This is of relevance with regard to the moment that protected persons who were in confinement may ask to leave the territory. Especially in the case of release after being confined pending proceedings, it could be that the final verdict has not been given yet but a protected person suspected of a crime is released on conditions (awaiting trial). What likely will happen then is that a protected person will file a demand to leave, which will often be refused on grounds that it is 'contrary to the national interests of the state'.[142]

It should be noted that both Articles 37 and 38 GC IV may be said to contain an implicit obligation on the party to the conflict to provide judicial guarantees for protected persons. Under Article 37, it might be argued that if there were insufficient judicial guarantees, that could amount to inhuman treatment, which assertion could be backed up by the vulnerable situation of persons in confinement needing all the safeguards they can get. Under Article 38, it might be argued that protected persons should have at least the right to fair trial, which could be added to the non-exhaustive list of minimum guarantees seen below.

b. Non-repatriated persons: Article 38

As the Hague Regulations dealt only with the situation of protected persons in occupied territory, GC IV complements them with further provisions regarding protected persons in the territory of the party to the conflict.

Article 38 regulates the minimum standards applicable with regard to those protected civilians who are not willing or able to make use of the right to leave the territory of a party to the conflict.[143] Persons who are likely to benefit from this provision include 'enemy aliens' and refugees in the territory of a party to the conflict (note that Section II concerns only the territory of a party to the conflict and not occupied territory).[144] The

---

[139] ICRC CIHL Study, vol I, at 344 and 352.
[140] See Art 8(2)(a)(ii) and (vii) ICC Statute; and Art 2(b) and (g) ICTY Statute.
[141] ICRC CIHL Study, at 318, 319. [142] Pictet Commentary, at 235, 236; Ch 57 of this volume.
[143] See Art 35 GC IV and Ch 57 of this volume.
[144] See also Art 73 AP I, 'refugee' can be interpreted broadly: a person who does not in fact enjoy the protection of a government. Several instruments provide for a definition of 'refugee', such as the Convention Relating to the Status of Refugees of 28 July 1951 (and its Protocol of 1967), the Statute of the Office of the United Nations High Commissioner for Refugees (UNHCR) of 14 December 1950, and the Organization of African Unity Convention Governing the Specific Aspects of Refugee Problems in Africa of 10 September 1969. Under Art 38 GC IV only refugees with 'enemy' nationality were covered by GC IV, while Art 73 AP I extends this to all refugees who are on the territory of a party to the Conflict.

chapeau of Article 38 explains that, in principle, the domestic law, complemented by the relevant international law concerning aliens, will continue to apply to the situation of protected persons (law applicable to aliens during peacetime). The exception to this rule is the restrictive measures or 'special measures' as authorized by GC IV, 'particularly by Articles 27 and 41'. As discussed, the system of measures of control and security is a closed system under GC IV. Although states parties have considerable discretion in implementing those measures, they cannot be more strict or more severe than assigned residence or internment.[145] Thus, domestic and international law, such as IHRL, refugee law, and private international law, as well as treaties and custom between states regarding residence and diplomatic protection, regulate the situation of protected persons, unless IHL has provided for regulation, as can be understood by the wording 'in principle', which leaves room for exceptions under IHL. Furthermore, Pictet refers to the growing tendency in national and international law to protect the principle of equal treatment between a state's own nationals and aliens, which is also reflected in some of the rights mentioned in Article 38 GC IV. Under IHRL, aliens are supposed to have the same rights as nationals, except for political rights and the right to enter the country.[146] It is not clear to what extent limitations are allowed under IHRL with regard to enemy aliens. This has to be assessed according to the situation in the light of applicable domestic and international law.[147]

60 Article 38 GC IV continues with a non-exhaustive list of the rights granted to protected persons in any case. The first right entitles protected persons to be enabled to receive individual and collective relief, meaning that the party in whose hands the protected person is, is not allowed to prohibit this.[148] The second right listed is the entitlement to receive medical attention and hospital treatment. Here the principle of equal treatment (or non-discrimination on the basis of nationality) is explicitly added.[149] This does not, however, preclude the possibility of discriminatory treatment based on medical urgency.[150] The third right entitles protected persons to practise their religion. This can be interpreted in the same way as has been explained above.[151]

61 The fourth right aims at preventing a situation where only protected persons are left in a danger zone while the nationals of the territory are authorized to move away from it. The wording of this Article leaves it to the party to the conflict concerned to decide whether civilians are authorized to move or not. Again, the equal treatment principle is used as the

---

[145] Art 41 GC IV.
[146] Pictet Commentary GC IV, at 245; and IHRL instruments, such as ICCPR, ICESCR, ECHR, ACHR, ACHPR.
[147] See, e.g., Arts 1(3), 55, and 56 UN Charter (1945); Art 14 and Protocol 12 ECHR; Art 24 ACHPR; Art 2 ACHPR; ICJ, *Barcelona Traction, Light and Power Company Limited (Belgium v Spain)*, Judgment, 5 February 1970, para 34; Germany's Administrative Court of Berlin, *Serbian Prisoners of War case*, 11 April 2006, para 33; H. Lambert, *The Position of Aliens in Relation to the European Convention on Human Rights* (Strasbourg: Council of Europe Publishing, 2007).
[148] See also Ch 12 of this volume; Arts 58–62 GC IV regarding occupied territory (by analogy); Part IV Section II AP I; Rule 55 ICRC CIHL Study.
[149] If this right is elaborated upon, it may be argued that IHRL should be used for the interpretation of the right to health. An example is General Comment 14 to the ICESCR, explaining that states have a several obligations deriving from this right, namely to respect, protect, and fulfil (CESCR, General Comment 14, E/C.12/2000/4, para 33).
[150] Note that the principle of equal treatment is not precisely the same as the principle of non-discrimination. Equal treatment can still be discriminatory. See also Ch 10 of this volume.
[151] MN 14 and 42.

means to protect the protected persons. Thus, if the party decides that its nationals should move, it must so authorize the protected persons too. Article 38 paragraph 4 is closely linked to Article 28 GC IV. If a state would authorize the departure of its nationals but not enemy aliens or refugees residing in such a danger zone, not only would this right have been breached but it could also amount to a violation of Article 28 which prohibits the use of protected persons as human shields.[152] Furthermore, according to Article 27 GC IV, the parties have a positive obligation to protect protected persons against all acts of violence or threats thereof. If nothing is done to protect them from the dangers of war, this might amount to a violation of Article 27 GC IV.

The last right in the list provides special protection for three categories of persons who are more vulnerable: children under the age of 15, pregnant women, and mothers of children under 7 years of age. Not only should they benefit from the same treatment as the nationals of the territory, they should as much as possible benefit from preferential treatment.[153] Preferential treatment covers 'the whole body of provisions, normally promulgated in countries at war, for the benefit of persons whose weakness in one respect or another warrants special care. Measures granting preferential treatment may be most varied in scope and application'.[154]

A right which is not listed but is of crucial importance is the right to judicial guarantees, especially the right to a fair trial. As scholars have pointed out, 'Aliens accused of having committed a criminal offence in connection with the conflict are entitled to a trial in accordance with the international obligations of the state, in particular with the human rights conventions.'[155] Furthermore, the minimum guarantees, including judicial guarantees, as listed under Article 75 AP I are considered to be customary law, so it can be asserted that the 'minimum' guarantees listed under that Article are likely the same guarantees that should be granted to the protected persons 'in any case' under Article 38 GC IV.[156]

c. Means of existence: Article 39

Although states had been making efforts to support enemy civilians in their means of existence, because they were suffering from difficult living conditions as a result of war, the experiences in the Second World War showed that these measures were not sufficient. Therefore, Article 39 was drafted in order to address these issues.[157]

The Article provides the opportunity to find paid employment to protected persons who have become jobless as a result of the war. This implies that there must be a causal connection between the armed conflict and the reason why a person lost his or her job, and it seems that the Article does not apply to protected persons who had already lost their jobs before the beginning of the armed conflict. Note that Article 39 refers to an 'opportunity' and not to a 'right'.[158] Granting an opportunity is not the same as granting

---

[152] MN 26–33.
[153] IHRL instruments with regard to protection of children are: the CRC (1989), the CRC-OPAC (2000), the ILO Convention No 182 on the Elimination of the Worst Forms of Child Labour (1999), the ICC Statute, as well as Security Council Resolutions 1261 (1999), 1314 (2000), 1379 (2001), and 1460 (2003). See also Chs 61 and 62 of this volume.
[154] Pictet Commentary GC IV, at 248, 249.
[155] H.P. Gasser, 'Protection of the Civilian Population', in Fleck (ed), above n 54, 237, at 315.
[156] See further Ch 59 of this volume.
[157] Final Record, vol I, at 119; vol II-A, at 656, 740, 824–5.
[158] Nevertheless, the Pictet Commentary GC IV refers, at 250, to the 'right to work'.

a right.[159] The ordinary meaning of 'opportunity' is 'a time or set of circumstances that makes it possible to do something'.[160] It can thus be asserted that the party to the conflict has to create equal opportunities for both its own nationals and for protected persons in its hands, who have lost their jobs due to the armed conflict, to find paid employment without discrimination on the basis of nationality.

66   The creation of such an opportunity may be limited in two ways, namely, by security considerations and by compelled labour. The former limitation may endanger any opportunity to find paid employment, because parties have a lot of discretion in deciding upon measures of control and security. The latter limitation is discussed in section B.II.d of this chapter. If measures of control are applied, for example assigned residence or internment, which result in the protected person's being unable to support himself or herself, Article 39 paragraph 2 provides that 'the said Party shall ensure his support and that of his dependents', where 'shall ensure' may be interpreted in the light of IHRL 'to guarantee that the holder of the right is able to gain access to the enjoyment of the right when he or she is unable to do it for him or herself'.[161] It is not clear precisely what is meant by 'especially if such a person is prevented for reasons of security from finding paid employment on reasonable conditions'. It could mean that the party to the conflict has to support such persons (and their dependants) because they are not able to find jobs at all due to the measures applied to them; because they did find jobs but they bear no relation to what those persons are qualified to do, leaving them with insufficient income for their dependants (e.g. a lawyer working on a conveyor belt in a shoe factory); or because they are not able to negotiate reasonable conditions for their employment due to the fact that they are enemy aliens. No clarity is provided, and it is left to the authorities to apply this phrase in a reasonable manner.

67   The Pictet Commentary seems to interpret the 'support' mentioned in Article 39 as referring to an allowance, i.e. financial support, and gives some indicators as to the amount to be given. There seems to be room to argue that 'support' may be interpreted in a broader manner, allowing for support in the form of food, clothes, shelter, and so on. Allowances are explicitly mentioned in Article 39 paragraph 3, where it is stated that protected persons may receive them from the providers listed in the Article. (It should be recalled that Article 38 GC IV already provides for the right of protected persons to receive individual or collective relief sent to them by whomever.) As a last point it should be explained that 'dependents' in paragraph 2 of the Article should be interpreted according to the domestic law of the state. Note, however, that Article 39 itself does not require that a dependant must be a relative of a protected person referred to in paragraph 2.

d. Employment: Article 40

68   The Hague Regulations prohibit a state 'to compel the nationals of the hostile party to take part in the operations of war directed against their own country', while the 1929 GC II allowed forced labour for POWs but restricted it to 'work having no direct connection

---

[159] See, e.g., R.M. Veatch, 'Justice and the Right to Health Care: An Egalitarian Account', in T.J. Bole and W.B. Bondeson (eds), *Rights to Health Care* (Dordrecht: Kluwer, 1991) 83, at 91, 92.

[160] Oxford Dictionaries, 'opportunity', available at <http://www.oxforddictionaries.com/definition/english/opportunity>.

[161] V. Abramovich and C. Courtis, 'Apuntes sobre la exiligibilidad judicial de los derechos sociales', in C. Courtis and R.A. Santamaría (eds), *La protección judicial de los derechos sociales* (Quito: Ministerio de Justicia y Derechos Humanos, 2009) 3, at 8.

with the operations of the war'.¹⁶² The Geneva Conventions contain several Articles regulating forced labour with regard to POWs,¹⁶³ protected persons in the territory of a party to the conflict and occupied territory, and protected persons who have been interned.¹⁶⁴ Furthermore, according to the CIHL Study, 'uncompensated or abusive forced labour is prohibited'.¹⁶⁵

The purpose of Article 40 GC IV was not to prevent or prohibit forced labour but, according to Pictet, 'to prevent enemy aliens from being employed for purposes which conflict with the interests of their home country'. The first paragraph of the provision spells out the requirement for equal treatment between nationals and protected persons, namely that if nationals are not compelled to work, protected persons should not be either. It is important to understand what is meant by 'compelled to work'. The notion 'compelled to work' is similar to 'forced labour'. Forced labour is defined by the International Labour Organization (ILO) as 'all work or service which is exacted from any person under the menace of any penalty and for which the said person has not offered himself voluntarily'.¹⁶⁶ The ILO also explains what is not included under 'forced labour' for the purposes of its Convention.¹⁶⁷ Most of the IHRL instruments have similar provisions on forced labour.¹⁶⁸ Articles 40 and 51 GC IV allow the party to the conflict and the Occupying Power to compel protected persons to work, whereas this would only be acceptable under ILO Convention 29, which excludes from the scope of forced labour 'cases of emergency', or circumstances that would 'endanger the existence or the well-being of the whole or part of the population'.¹⁶⁹ If the facts of the case do not comply with this ground of exception, then the activities would seem to fall under the 'forced labour' definition and thus amount to a violation of this Convention. The question is consequently which law takes precedence, which normally is solved by taking into account the *lex specialis* rule or the *lex posteriori* rule. It seems, however, that Article 40 GC IV itself already contains the solution. As the first paragraph requires that protected persons may be compelled to work only to the same extent as nationals, we should first take a look at the nationals. The civilian nationals of a party to the conflict are not covered by GC IV but by domestic law (and relevant ILO Conventions). Thus, this means that the prohibition of forced labour applies to them, unless the activities would fall under one of the exceptions already mentioned above. If the nationals are prohibited from being compelled to work, protected persons cannot be compelled to work either. This construction could render Article 40 moot.

In the event that the exception applies, nationals as well as protected persons could be compelled to work. Paragraph 2 of Article 40 GC IV explains that persons of enemy nationality may only be compelled to do work which is not directly related to the conduct of military operations, preventing their waging war against their own country. The list of permitted activities in paragraph 2 nevertheless leaves a broad margin for interpretation, and the question is to what extent enemy aliens would be prevented from contributing to the war effort against their own state.

The third paragraph of Article 40 requires that protected persons should benefit from equality of treatment with nationals concerning working conditions and safeguards. This means that, in general, domestic law should be consulted to see what the applicable law

---

[162] Art 23 Hague Regulations; and Arts 27–34 of 1929 GC II.   [163] Arts 49–57 GC III.
[164] Arts 40, 51, and 95 GC IV.   [165] Rule 95 ICRC CIHL Study.
[166] Art 2(1) Forced Labour Convention No 29 (1930).   [167] Art 2(2).
[168] Art 8(3) ICCPR; Art 6 ICESCR; Art 6 ACHR; Art 4 ECHR.   [169] Art 2(2)(d).

is. The fourth paragraph provides protected persons compelled to work with the right to complain by making an application to the Protecting Powers, the ICRC, the National Red Cross Society, or any other organization assisting them.[170]

e. Cancellation of restrictive measures: Article 46

72 Article 46 GC IV regulates the cancellation of restrictive measures regarding protected persons. All the measures that are still in place after the close of hostilities, i.e. 'in so far as they have not been previously withdrawn', shall be cancelled as soon as possible after the close of hostilities. This implies that if a measure could have been withdrawn before the close of hostilities, this should have happened already.

73 Restrictive measures may be understood as measures of control and security. As mentioned, states have a considerable margin of appreciation in taking such measures.[171] This may be seen, for example, in Article 39 paragraph 2 GC IV, which is aimed at persons who are in assigned residence or forbidden to work in certain areas due to measures of security or control. Other examples are internment as in Article 41 GC IV, or the restriction of movement. Article 64 GC IV, which applies to a situation of occupation, may be used for the interpretation of measures of security.[172]

74 As mentioned in numerous documents, restrictive measures should not result in increased suffering for the most vulnerable population groups.[173] In addition, for Article 46 to apply, the states concerned must be parties to the conflict, and it would concern only those measures aimed at, or affecting, protected persons.

75 The interpretation of the notion 'as soon as possible after the close of hostilities' has been discussed elsewhere in this Commentary.[174] It suffices to say here that the close of hostilities is not the same as the conclusion of a peace agreement. As stated in Article 6 paragraph 4 GC IV, protected persons shall continue to benefit from GC IV when their release, repatriation, or re-establishment takes place after the general close of military operations.

76 As already mentioned by Pictet, the second paragraph of Article 46 GC IV seems rather out of place because it concerns property and not persons. The paragraph concerns 'their property', where 'their' seems to refer to all protected persons as in the first paragraph. It then states that the cancellation has to be in accordance with the law of the 'Detaining Power', which seems to limit the scope of application of this paragraph to protected persons who are/were detained. However, GC IV apparently uses the term 'Detaining Power' in a wider sense as the power (other than an Occupying Power) in whose hands a protected person is, even if that person is not deprived of his or her liberty. Restrictive measures affecting property include, for example, the freezing of bank accounts.[175] To get a clearer understanding of enemy property law, national law and IHRL should therefore be consulted.[176]

---

[170] See Art 30 GC IV. [171] ICTY, Čelebići Camp, above n 55, paras 574–76; MN 24–25.
[172] N. Melzer, Targeted Killing in International Law (Oxford: OUP, 2008), at 162–5.
[173] See, e.g., 'Consistent policy towards regimes against which the EU applies restrictive measures', 20 August 2013, (2013/C 239 E/02), available at <http://eur-lex.europa.eu/LexUriServ/LexUriServ.do?uri=OJ:C:2013:239E:0011:0018:EN:PDF>, which is a recommendation from the European Parliament to the Council stating, under general observation 'R', that 'all restrictive measures must comply with human rights, international humanitarian law, due process, proportionality and the right to effective redress, and must on no account penalise the most vulnerable population groups in countries affected by these measures'.
[174] Ch 66, MN 15–18, of this volume.
[175] EECC, Eritrea's Claims 15, 16, 23 & 27–32, above n 30, at 32, 33, para 145, 146.
[176] For a concise overview on enemy property, see H.G. Dederer, 'Enemy Property', in MPEPIL, at 430.

III. Section III: Inviolability of rights in occupied territories

Article 47 GC IV applies only to occupied territories.[177] In an occupied territory, almost everyone may be considered to be a protected person.[178] The purpose of this provision, which is at the beginning of Section III, is to provide protection through the law of occupation with regard to persons in the hands of the Occupying Power.[179] It should be read in conjunction with Articles 7 and 8 GC IV, which prohibit or render ineffective (see Chapters 7 and 8 of this volume respectively), first, special agreements that 'adversely affect the situation of protected persons' or 'restrict the rights which [the Convention] confers upon them' and, secondly, the renunciation by protected persons of any of the rights conferred upon them or granted to them through special agreements.[180]

Article 47 GC IV provides the guarantees for protected persons in occupied territory, which in no way may be affected by any new or modified institutions or government, or by any other agreements concluded between the authorities of the occupied territory and the Occupying Power, or by a unilateral statement of annexation.[181] In short, the guarantees for protected persons in occupied territory are protected through Article 47 GC IV and cannot drop below the level guaranteed by GC IV in any way.[182] However, there may be agreements that provide more rights and guarantees.

If occupation continues after the general close of military operations, Article 47 remains applicable until the end of occupation.[183]

C. Relevance in Non-International Armed Conflicts

In a NIAC situation, Common Article 3 provides for minimum guarantees, requiring, like Article 27 GC IV in an IAC situation (MN 16–21), that '[p]ersons taking no active part in the hostilities [...] shall in all circumstances be treated humanely'. To that end, Common Article 3 prohibits several acts, such as violence to life and person,[184] the taking of hostages,[185] and outrages upon personal dignity, and it requires judicial guarantees.[186]

There is no explicit prohibition against using 'human shields' in NIACs, as is found in Article 28 GC IV. However, the use of human shields in NIACs is considered a violation of a customary rule of IHL.[187] Furthermore, it may sometimes constitute the taking of hostages, and will always be considered an outrage upon personal dignity, in particular as humiliating and degrading treatment as prohibited by Common Article 3.

State responsibility may arise in situations of NIAC for the treatment of persons as defined under Common Article 3, namely, persons taking no active part in hostilities and those placed *hors de combat*. This has been discussed in Chapter 20 of this volume at MN 55–60.[188]

---

[177] See Chs 67–74 of this volume. [178] See Ch 55 of this volume.
[179] Pictet Commentary GC IV.
[180] Arts 7 and 8 GC IV.
[181] See further Ch 69 of this volume, at MN 18–29.
[182] R. Kolb, 'Etude sur l'occupation et sur l'article 47 de la Convention de Genève IV de 1949 relative à la protection des personnes civiles en temps de guerre: le degré de l'intangibilité des droits en territoire occupé', 10 *Annuaire Africain de Droit International* (2002) 267, at 300.
[183] Art 6 para 3 GC IV. [184] See further Ch 22 of this volume.
[185] See further Ch 15 of this volume. [186] See further Ch 23 of this volume.
[187] ICRC CIHL Study, vol I, at 337, Rule 97. [188] See also Ch 16, MN 71–77, of this volume.

83   Common Article 3 does not provide an explicit right to make application to the Protecting Powers or the ICRC, but it allows 'an impartial humanitarian body, such as the International Committee of the Red Cross', to offer its services to the parties to the conflict.[189] There is no explicit reference to a Protecting Power.[190]

84   In situations of NIAC, coercion is not explicitly prohibited. However, Common Article 3 paragraph 1(1) requires humane treatment, and prohibits violence to life and person, including torture. If the act of coercion would amount to any such acts, it is certainly prohibited under Common Article 3.

85   Common Article 3 paragraph 1(1)(a) protects the fundamental guarantees of persons taking no active part in hostilities and persons placed *hors de combat* in a similar manner to Article 32 GC IV, prohibiting acts such as murder, mutilation, and torture.[191] This has been reaffirmed in the CIHL Study, which shows state practice and *opinio juris* in NIAC situations prohibiting the same acts as listed in Article 32 GC IV.[192]

86   As already mentioned above,[193] if arbitrary deprivation of liberty would amount to inhuman treatment, this would violate Common Article 3. Furthermore, Common Article 3 provides for judicial guarantees.[194]

87   Articles 38 to 40 GC IV provide for minimum guarantees with regard to non-repatriated persons. In Common Article 3 there are no specific regulations for non-repatriated persons because its minimum guarantees apply to all persons taking no active part in hostilities or *hors de combat*, without making a distinction based on nationality.[195] Neither is there a provision similar to Article 46 GC IV in Common Article 3. However, there remains the possibility to agree upon similar guarantees under a special agreement. The same applies to the inviolability of rights in occupied territory as provided for under Article 47 GC IV, considering that the concept of occupied territories is not provided for under the law of NIAC.

D. Legal Consequences of a Violation

I. State responsibility

88 Violations of the provisions discussed in this chapter will give rise to state responsibility with all the usual consequences. Aspects of attribution are discussed at MN 34–39. Chapter 20 of this volume (at MN 55–60) explains issues of state responsibility in NIACs, while Chapter 6 covers issues regarding the due diligence obligations of states.

II. Individual criminal responsibility

89 With regard to a violation of Articles 27, 31, 32, or 37 GC IV, Article 147 GC IV classifies torture and inhuman treatment as grave breaches. For discussion of individual criminal responsibility for these acts, see Chapter 16 of this volume, at MN 78–90.

---

[189] CA 3 para 2.   [190] See further Ch 27 of this volume, at MN 27.
[191] See further Ch 22 of this volume.
[192] Inter alia, ICRC CIHL Study, Rules 87–93.   [193] MN 55.
[194] See further Ch 23 of this volume.
[195] Note, however, Art 5 AP II, concerning persons whose liberty has been restricted, which provides for similar guarantees.

Furthermore, the prohibition of the use of human shields has been addressed at the 90
international level by military tribunals,[196] the ICTY,[197] and the ICC.[198] In some cases,
the use of human shields may amount to the taking of hostages, which explicitly qualifies
as a grave breach under Article 147 GC IV, while the use of human shields is not listed
explicitly as a grave breach but could qualify as such when it amounts to inhuman treatment. The same may be seen in the ICC Statute, where the taking of hostages is a grave
breach under Article 8(2)(a)(viii) and the use of human shields is considered a war crime
under Article 8(2)(b)(xxiii).[199] In many countries domestic legislation is in place criminalizing the use of human shields.[200] Their use in NIACs has been identified as a violation
of a customary rule of IHL.[201] Furthermore, it may sometimes constitute the taking of
hostages, and will always be considered as an outrage upon personal dignity, in particular
humiliating and degrading treatment as prohibited by Common Article 3.

Other violations of the Geneva Conventions, such as violations of the right to make 91
application to the ICRC or of the provisions concerning non-repatriated persons,[202] are
not considered war crimes as such.

E. Critical Assessment

Over the last few decades some fields of international law, in particular IHRL and ICL, 92
have evolved extensively, influencing in turn the interpretation of some of the notions used
in IHL, in particular those relating to the fundamental guarantees of protected civilians
(Articles 27, 31–34, 37, 38 GC IV).

Some of the Articles discussed in this chapter have become the subject of intense legal 93
debate, such as the those on human shields (Articles 28 and 38 paragraph 4) or state
responsibility (Article 29), triggering many discussions among the judiciary and scholars,
while other topics seem to have received a clear and straightforward interpretation, such as
the facilitation of applications (Article 30), which has not been influenced by other fields
of law in any significant way.

---

[196] *Trial of Kurt Student*, British Military Court, Lüneberg, 1948, UNWCC Law Reports, vol IV, at 118; *The United States of America v Wilhelm von Leeb et al*, US Military Tribunal, Nuremberg, Judgment, 27 October 1948.

[197] ICTY, *The Prosecutor v Radovan Karadžić and Ratko Mladić*, Initial Indictment, IT-95-5-I, 24 July 1995, paras 46–8. The use of human shields is not criminalized as such in the Statute of the ICTY, but if it can be considered as, e.g., inhuman or cruel treatment, it comes within the scope of a grave breach as defined in Art 2(b) of the Statute. Other possibilities could be Art 2(c) and/or a violation of the laws or customs of war as in Art 3 of the Statute.

[198] Art 8(2)(b)(xxiii) ICC Statute, with regard to IAC.

[199] See Ch 15 of this volume and the ICC Elements of Crimes describing the elements of hostage-taking, namely: '1. The perpetrator seized, detained or otherwise held hostage one or more persons. 2. The perpetrator threatened to kill, injure or continue to detain such person or persons. 3. The perpetrator intended to compel a State, an international organization, a natural or legal person or a group of persons to act or refrain from acting as an explicit or implicit condition for the safety or the release of such person or persons.' Taking a protected person as to serve as a human shield in order to prevent an attack from the belligerent is likely to comply with these elements, and could thus amount to the taking of hostages.

[200] See, for an overview, the practice found by the ICRC CIHL Study, vol II, at 2285.

[201] ICRC CIHL Study, vol I, at 337, Rule 97.

[202] See further Ch 10 of this volume regarding non-discrimination (based on nationality): discrimination as such is not a war crime but can be considered an element of certain war crimes, crimes against humanity, and genocide.

94   At the same time, there are also some rights which raise the question whether they are still of relevance today or whether they require clarification, such as the regulation of forced labour (Article 40) and the cancellation of restrictive measures affecting property in accordance with the law of the Detaining Power (Article 46 paragraph 2).

95   It remains to be seen how the influence of other fields of law will impact the interpretation and development of IHL in the future. In all likelihood, as may be seen from the foregoing analysis, the influence of other fields of international law will reinforce and strengthen the protection of civilians even further.

IRIS VAN DER HEIJDEN

3. SPECIFIC PROTECTION

Chapter 61. Special Rules on Women

	MN
A. Introduction	1
B. Meaning and Application	6
I. Protection of women	6
II. Protection of specific categories of women	17
a. Grounds for preferential treatment	18
b. Personal safety and shelter	20
c. Health, food, and household items	22
III. Protection of women detainees	29
a. Quarters	30
b. Sanitation	33
c. Health and medical care	37
d. Food and work	39
e. Execution of penalties	42
f. Release	43
C. Relevance in Non-International Armed Conflicts	44
D. Legal Consequences of a Violation	49
I. State responsibility	50
II. Criminal responsibility	55
III. The Security Council	58
E. Critical Assessment	59

Select Bibliography

Barrow, A., 'UN Security Council Resolutions 1325 and 1820: Constructing Gender in Armed Conflict and International Humanitarian Law', 92 *IRRC* 877 (2010) 221

Gardam, J., 'Women, Human Rights and International Humanitarian Law', 38 *IRRC* 324 (1998) 421

Gardam, J., 'The Neglected Aspect of Women and Armed Conflict: Progressive Development of the Law', 52 *NILR* (2005) 197

Gardam, J./Jarvis, M., 'Women and Armed Conflict: The International Response to the Beijing Platform for Action', 32 *Columbia Human Rights Law Review* (2000) 1

Gardam, J./Jarvis, M., *Women, Armed Conflict and International Law* (The Hague: Kluwer, 2001)

Krill, F., 'The Protection of Women in International Humanitarian Law', 25 *IRRC* 249 (1985) 337

Lindsey, C., 'Women and War: An Overview', 82 *IRRC* 839 (2000) 561

A. Introduction

International humanitarian law (IHL) does not distinguish between individuals on the basis of sex. Women are afforded the same protection as is given to men and may not be discriminated against.[1] Consequently, women benefit from the general protections

---

[1] CEDAW Committee, General Recommendation No 30 on Women in Conflict Prevention, Conflict and Post-Conflict Situations, UN Doc CEDAW/C/GC/30, 18 October 2013, para 20.

offered by the Geneva Conventions (GCs), including those relating to combatants (Articles 14 and 16 GC III), the wounded, sick, and shipwrecked (Articles 12 GC I and GC II), and civilians and persons detained in connection with an armed conflict (Articles 13 and 27 paragraph 3 GC IV). Whilst the inclusion of the principle of non-adverse distinction was an achievement at the time of the writing of the Conventions, it is now considered an essential norm in treaty IHL,[2] and is accepted, though under the principle of non-discrimination (Chapter 10 of this volume), in customary IHL[3] and international human rights law (IHRL).[4] In relation to women more specifically, this principle is enshrined in Article 2 of the Convention on the Elimination of Discrimination against Women (1979) (CEDAW).

2   Yet whilst the Geneva Conventions stress that no adverse distinction based on sex should be made, women also benefit from specific protection enshrined in these Conventions.[5] Differentiation on the basis of sex is allowed, is even compulsory, provided its impact is favourable.[6] Formal equality, if applied in situations where individuals are essentially unequal, does not automatically lead to real equality. Given women's lack of full participation in many societies, as well as their gender and biological roles, armed conflicts reinforce inequalities in society and increase women's vulnerability.[7] Therefore IHL provides for special rules on women,[8] an approach adopted by IHRL which encourages positive measures to fill in the discrimination gap.[9]

3   The majority of these provisions relate to women's status as civilians, as traditionally women rarely fall within the category of combatants. The United Nations (UN) Security Council aptly summarizes the situation: '[I]nternational humanitarian law affords general protection to women [...] as part of the civilian population during armed conflicts and special protection due to the fact that they can be placed particularly at risk.'[10] States involved in armed conflicts are urged to make all efforts 'to spare women [...] from the ravages of war'.[11]

4   The common meaning of those provisions of the Geneva Conventions that mention women, is that women are viewed as being at greater risk of suffering from the conflict. In IHL, women are protected due to their vulnerability in relation to sexual assault, or in their roles as mothers or expectant mothers. Moreover, falling into one of certain specified categories (pregnant women, maternity cases, and mothers of children under 7 years of age) means heightened protection. In contrast, IHRL, which views women as a vulnerable group in times of armed conflict, does not distinguish between these categories of women.[12] Whilst an in-depth discussion of why women civilians are particularly affected

---

[2] Arts 9 (wounded, sick, shipwrecked persons) and 75 (general application) AP I.
[3] See ICRC CIHL Study, Rule 88 on Non-Discrimination.
[4] See, e.g., Art 2 paras 2 and 3 ICESCR; Art 2 para 1 ICCPR; Art 1 para 3 UN Charter (1945).
[5] CEDAW Committee, General Recommendation No 30, above n 1, para 20.
[6] See, e.g., Arts 12 para 4 GC I and GC II.
[7] See UN, *Women, Peace and Security* (United Nations, 2002), at 14–5; CEDAW Committee, General Recommendation No 30, above n 1, para 34.
[8] Pictet Commentary GC IV, at 205.   [9] See, e.g., CEDAW.
[10] UNSC Res 1960, 16 December 2010, Preamble; UNSC Res 1888, 30 September 2009; UNSC Res 1894, 11 November 2009, para 21; 27th International Conference of the Red Cross and Red Crescent, Plan of Action for the Years 2000–2003 (1999).
[11] UNGA Res 3318 (XXI), 14 December 1974, Declaration on the Protection of Women and Children in Emergency and Armed Conflict, para 4.
[12] See, e.g., UNGA Res 48/104, Declaration on the Elimination of Violence against Women, 20 December 1993, Preamble (DEVAW); HRCouncil, Follow-up to Resolution 4/8 of 30 March 2007

by violence in armed conflict is beyond the remit of this Commentary, we might recall, in the words of the Beijing Platform for Action, that this is tied to 'their status in society and their sex',[13] and that women are viewed as inferior.[14] This link between peacetime discrimination against women and abuse of women in armed conflict has been stressed by the Special Rapporteur on Violence against Women.[15]

The protection offered to women in armed conflict may be divided into two main categories, that is their protection as 'free individuals' and their protection as detainees, the former category being further divided into the protection offered to all women and the protection offered to women who fulfil certain requirements. As 'civilians, particularly women [...], account for the vast majority of those adversely affected by armed conflict [...], and increasingly are targeted by combatants and armed elements',[16] ensuring their personal safety is fundamental (section B.I of this chapter). Additional protection from the consequences of war is offered to mothers, whether expectant, having given birth, or of a child under 7 years of age (section B.II of this chapter). Last but not least, the Geneva Conventions offer protection to women who are detained either as civilians or as prisoners of war (POWs) (section B.III of this chapter).

B. Meaning and Application

I. Protection of women

Articles 12 GC I/GC II offer 'respect, protection, humane treatment and care'[17] to the wounded, sick, and shipwrecked. Likewise, Article 14 GC III is central to its Convention, since it calls for respect for POWs, which involves respect for the physical and moral person of the POW, as well as respect for the POW's honour.[18] All three Articles refer to women,[19] requiring women to be treated with all consideration/regard due to their sex. As central as Articles 12 GC I/GC II and Article 14 GC III are to their respective Conventions, Article 27 GC IV,[20] which refers to the protection of women, is the cornerstone of GC IV.[21] It

---

Adopted by the Human Rights Council at its Fourth Session Entitled 'Follow-up to Decision S-4/101 of 13 December 2006, adopted by the Council at its Fourth Special Session Entitled "Situation of Human Rights in Darfur"', 20 June 2007; HRCouncil Group of Experts on the Situation of Human Rights in Darfur, Res 6/35, 14 December 2007.

[13] Beijing Declaration and Platform for Action, Fourth World Conference on Women, A/CONF.177/20 (1995) and A/CONF.177/20/Add.1 (1995), 15 September 1995, para 135.

[14] See also DEVAW, above n 12, Preamble.

[15] *Report of the Special Rapporteur on Violence against Women, its Causes and Consequences*, UN Doc A/66/215, 1 August 2011, para 40; *Report of the Special Rapporteur on Violence against Women, its Causes and Consequences* UN Doc A/HRC/4/34, 17 January 2007, para 63; *Report of the Special Rapporteur on Violence against Women, its Causes and Consequences*, UN Doc A/HRC/11/6/Add.5, 27 May 2009, para 44 (*2009 Report of Special Rapporteur*); *Report of the Special Rapporteur on Violence against Women, its Causes and Consequences*, UN Doc A/HRC/7/6/Add.4, 28 February 2008, para 101 (*2008 Report of Special Rapporteur*).

[16] UNSC Res 1325, 31 October 2000, Preamble. See also CEDAW Committee, General Recommendation No 30, above n 1, para 35.

[17] Pictet Commentary GC I, at 135.   [18] Ibid, at 143–6.

[19] For Arts 12 para 4 GC I/GC II and Art 14 GC III to apply, the woman must fall within one of the categories enumerated in Arts 13 GC I/GC II and Art 4 GC III respectively.

[20] It must be noted that Art 27 GC IV does not protect women from the activities of the state of which they are a national.

[21] Pictet Commentary GC IV, at 199–200.

7   Articles 12 paragraph 4 GC I/GC II stipulate that 'women shall be treated with all consideration due to their sex'. The original Commentary explained the expression 'consideration due to their sex' by referring to women as 'beings who are weaker than oneself and whose honour and modesty call for respect'. Remarkably, though without implications,[22] Article 14 GC III uses 'regard due to their sex' rather than 'consideration due to their sex'. The original Commentary explains that the three factors that must be taken into account are: (i) weakness; (ii) honour and modesty, which covers rape, forced prostitution, and any form of indecent assault,[23] as well as humiliating treatment; and (iii) pregnancy and child-birth.[24] These three elements have been used in the International Committee of the Red Cross (ICRC) *Model Manual on the Law of Armed Conflict for Armed Forces*, which states that 'due regard must be paid to [women's] physical strength, the need to protect their honour and modesty and to the special demands of biological factors such as menstruation, pregnancy and childbirth'.[25]

8   These protective measures base the status of women on biological factors, a literal interpretation of 'sex' referring to the biological difference between men and women. However, today, the difference between men and women is often construed in terms of gender, whereby social, economic, and cultural factors are taken into consideration. In this new light, 'consideration/regard due to their sex' now refers to biological (e.g. menstrual cycle and reproductive function, menopause), socio-economic (e.g. power relationships between women and men, cultural and traditional practices), and psychosocial factors (depression, eating disorders, etc) that may affect and determine women's status.[26] Furthermore, a contextual reading (the other paragraphs in Articles 12 GC I/GC II and Article 14 GC III relate to humane treatment) of the expression 'consideration due to their sex' links to the overarching concept of human dignity that is central to understanding which measures need to be adopted to offer appropriate respect, protection, treatment, and care to women.

9   Article 27 GC IV proclaims the basic principle of protection for human beings and the right to humane treatment, thereby stating the core principles upon which the entire law of the Geneva Conventions is founded. The state is obliged not only to respect civilians, but also to protect them, i.e. to take all the precautions and measures in its power to prevent the proscribed acts and help victims. Of particular importance is that these standards must be observed in 'all circumstances' and at 'all times'. Article 27 paragraph 2 is devoted to the protection of women.

10   Unlike Articles 12 GC I/GC II and Article 14 GC III, Article 27 GC IV does not use the expression 'consideration due to their sex' to refer to the protection of women. Instead, it clarifies that women need to be especially protected from attacks on their honour, and contains a list of three acts from which women must be protected in particular—rape, enforced prostitution, and any form of indecent assault—which are recurrent crimes against women in armed conflict.[27]

---

[22] See Commentary on Rule 134 ICRC CIHL Study.
[23] See section B.I of this chapter, at MN 12–13.   [24] Pictet Commentary GC III, at 147.
[25] ICRC, *Model Manual on the Law of Armed Conflict for Armed Forces* (Geneva: ICRC, 1999), para 1405.6.
[26] These three factors are particularly important in relation to women's health. See, e.g., CEDAW Committee, General Recommendation No 24 on Article 12: Women and Health, UN Doc A/54/38/Rev.1, 5 February 1999, para 12(a), (b), and (c).
[27] See, e.g., Commission on Human Rights, UN Doc E/CN.4/RES/2003/45, 23 April 2003; Commission on Human Rights, UN Doc E/CN.4/RES/2004/46, 20 April 2004; Commission on Human Rights, UN Doc E/CN.4/RES/2005/41, 19 April 2005.

The second paragraph of Article 27 is the subject of two different, albeit complementary, interpretations. First, it offers additional protection, for the word 'especially' is used. This means that women benefit from the general protections and respect stated in paragraph 1 *and* those listed in paragraph 2. Secondly, the provision lists acts that *particularly* affect women, and thus it may be seen only as an illustration of the types of violations of the principles spelled out in paragraph 1.

The concept of honour is key to understanding Article 27 paragraph 2 GC IV. Honour is understood as a moral and social quality given to human beings because they are endowed with reason and a conscience.[28] Literally, honour relates to reputation and, to some extent, to humility and modesty. The word might be better understood with reference to Article 14 GC III, although it concerns POWs, which refers to the 'honour' of predominantly male POWs. Moreover, as 'honour' is also used in Article 27 paragraph 1, which covers *all* protected persons (men included), literally, it should not be interpreted in any different manner. Nonetheless, the application of the concept of honour in relation to POWs is associated with preserving their moral integrity and avoiding shame and humiliation, rather than physical harm. Applied to women in relation to acts such as rape, enforced prostitution, and any form of indecent assault, this understanding of the concept of honour, which is socially constructed and often sustained by male ideas about women's chastity, modesty, and associated frailty and dependence, appears inappropriate.[29] Moreover, as women 'are often portrayed as symbolic bearers of their cultural and ethnic identity, and as producers of future generations',[30] the word 'honour' resonates as referring to the honour of the community rather than that of the women themselves.

Influenced by IHRL, a more contemporary reading of the notion of 'honour' integrates the key concept of human dignity.[31] International criminal tribunals[32] and human rights bodies[33] construe rape, enforced prostitution, and indecent assault as physical, rather than reputational, attacks upon a woman. Further, inasmuch as Additional Protocol (AP) I supplements the Geneva Conventions,[34] it is important to note that Article 75(2)(b) AP I understands these acts as comprising outrages upon personal dignity, while Article 76 AP I fails to mention 'honour' and lists the prohibited acts only after declaring that women 'shall be the object of special respect'. Likewise Section 7 paragraph 3 of the 1999 UN Secretary-General's Bulletin removes the reference to honour and provides that '[w]omen shall be especially protected against any attack'.[35] International humanitarian law has thus distanced itself from a concept of honour that used to be defined not by the

---

[28] Pictet Commentary GC IV, at 202.

[29] *Report of the Special Rapporteur on Violence against Women, its Causes and Consequences* UN Doc E/CN.4/1998/54, 26 January 1998, para 11.

[30] ICRC, *Addressing the Needs of Women Affected by Armed Conflict*, (Geneva: ICRC, 2004), at 10 (Addressing the Needs of Women).

[31] ICTY, *The Prosecutor v Anto Furundžija*, Trial Chamber Judgment, IT-95-17/1-T, 10 December 1998, para 183.

[32] ICTR, *The Prosecutor v Jean Paul Akayesu*, Trial Chamber Judgment, ICTR-96-4, 2 September 1998; ICTY, *Furundžija*, above n 31, para 183; ICTY, *The Prosecutor v Zejnil Delalić et al*, Trial Chamber Judgment, IT-96-21-A, 16 November 1998, para 475.

[33] See ECtHR, *Aydin v Turkey*, Judgment, 25 September 1997; IACommHR, *Raquel Martín de Mejía*, 10.970 (Peru), Rep no 5/96, 1 March 1996.

[34] See Art 1 para 3 AP I.

[35] United Nations Secretariat, Observance by United Nations Forces of International Humanitarian Law, UN Doc ST/SGB/1999/13, 6 August 1999 (Bulletin).

nature of the act but rather by the wider community, and now tends to view these acts as violent attacks upon women's physical integrity. That being said, not all such acts have a physical element; Article 27 paragraph 2 GC IV covers a wide spectrum of acts affecting a woman's physical and mental integrity.[36] In this light the word 'honour' may have to be re-evaluated when interpreting Article 27 paragraph 2 GC IV.

14   The three attacks from which women shall be protected 'in particular' in accordance with Article 27 paragraph 2 GC IV are rape, enforced prostitution, and any form of indecent assault.[37] None of these acts was defined in the Conventions (maybe because the Geneva Conventions were not meant to constitute a criminal code) or in the original commentary (perhaps because of the rather Victorian attitude displayed towards women and an unwillingness to explain such concepts in mechanical terms). Drawing upon the definitions of rape found in states' domestic laws, the International Criminal Tribunal for the former Yugoslavia (ICTY) provided a definition of 'rape' in the *Furundžija* case,[38] which was based on the *Akayesu* Judgment[39] and subsequently developed in the *Kunarac* case before the ICTY.[40] This definition of 'rape' now forms the core of the definitions used by other international criminal tribunals.[41] It covers more than just penetration, thus moving away from 'the historic focus on the act of penetration [which] largely derives from a male preoccupation with assuring women's chastity and ascertaining paternity of children'.[42] Rape and other acts of a sexual nature are thus uncoupled from the idea of a woman's reputation and honour.[43]

15   The second category of violation is 'enforced prostitution', which is used interchangeably with 'forced prostitution' in Article 76(1) AP I.[44] The second category appeared in the GC IV in order to reflect specifically the abuse suffered by women who were forced to provide sexual services in brothels during the Second World War.[45] The Special Rapporteur on Systematic Rape, Sexual Slavery, and Slavery-like Practices during Armed Conflict has defined 'forced prostitution' as 'conditions of control over a person who is coerced by another to engage in sexual activity',[46] clearly refuting the idea that such an act should be understood as violating a woman's honour. Although sexual slavery and forced prostitution may overlap,[47] they are distinct crimes to be prosecuted separately. Whilst sexual slavery refers to the condition whereby a person exercises ownership-like rights over a person, enforced prostitution denotes the situation whereby an individual

---

[36] See ICTR, *Akayesu*, above n 32, para 688.

[37] An in-depth discussion on these terms is provided in Ch 17 of this volume, section B.I.

[38] ICTY, *Furundžija*, above n 31, para 185.   [39] ICTR, *Akayesu*, above n 32, paras 597–8.

[40] ICTY, *The Prosecutor v Dragoljub Kunarac, Radomir Kovač and Zoran Vuković*, Appeals Chamber Judgment, IT-96-23 & IT-96-23/1-A, 12 June 2002, para 127.

[41] See, e.g., the crime of rape as defined in the Elements of Crimes of the ICC Statute (Art 7(1)(g)(1) and Art 8(2)(b)(xxii)(1), with regard to rape as a crime against humanity and rape as a war crime respectively): 'The perpetrator invaded the body of a person by conduct resulting in penetration, however slight, of any part of the body of the victim or of the perpetrator with a sexual organ, or of the anal or genital opening of the victim with any object or any other part of the body.'

[42] *Final Report of Special Rapporteur on Systematic Rape, Sexual Slavery and Slavery-like Practices during Armed Conflict*, UN Doc E/CN.4/Sub.2/1998/13, 22 June 1998, para 24 *(Final Report of Special Rapporteur)*.

[43] *Report of the Special Rapporteur on Violence against Women, its Causes and Consequences*, UN Doc E/CN.4/2001/73, 23 January 2001, para 38.

[44] See, e.g., *Final Report of Special Rapporteur*, above n 42, para 31.

[45] Pictet Commentary GC IV, at 205. 'Enforced prostitution' was prohibited prior to the Second World War under the laws prohibiting the mistreatment of women (see *Final Report of Special Rapporteur*, above n 42, para 17).

[46] *Final Report of Special Rapporteur*, above n 42, para 42.   [47] Ibid, para 33.

forces a person to engage in an act of sexual nature, expecting to obtain some pecuniary advantage.[48]

Thirdly, 'any form of indecent assault', understood as an assault of a sexual nature short of rape,[49] such as groping or fondling a woman's breast, is prohibited. This specific terminology does not appear in any other international *corpus juris*. In IHRL and international criminal law (ICL) reference is made to sexual violence, which covers rape and acts of similar gravity.[50] Whilst these acts are 'intended to inflict severe humiliation on the victims',[51] they are also violent acts and thus fall within the prohibition of cruel, inhuman, or degrading treatment or punishment, as the International Criminal Tribunal of Rwanda (ICTR) observed in the *Akayesu* case.[52] Yet indecent assault in the sense used by the Geneva Conventions does not necessarily meet these thresholds; rather, indecent assault extends to a wider range of acts of a sexual nature.

II. Protection of specific categories of women

The Geneva Conventions proceed from the premise that whilst the men are fighting, women are in charge of the children and the household.[53] Therefore, an array of provisions intended to alleviate the sufferings caused by war directly refer to women. Yet, according to the Geneva Conventions, not all women are to be afforded particular treatment in terms of personal safety, shelter, health, food, water, etc. This stands in contrast to Rule 134 in the Customary International Humanitarian Law (CIHL) Study of the ICRC, which offers such protection to all women. Despite the general applicability spelled out in Rule 134, and in Resolution 2 of the 26th International Conference of the Red Cross and Red Crescent,[54] it is not feasible to expand the application of the rules spelled out below to all women, as Rule 134 specifically refers to specific categories of women in a separate section in the explanation of the rule.

a. *Grounds for preferential treatment*

The categories of women who are marked for preferential treatment are pregnant women, maternity cases, and mothers of children under 7 years of age. Whilst in the Geneva Conventions expectant mothers and maternity cases often feature alongside the wounded and sick, and are thus assimilated to these groups,[55] these categories of women are expressly covered under 'wounded' and 'sick' in AP I.[56]

---

[48] This reflects the definitions of 'sexual slavery' and 'enforced prostitution' in the ICC Elements of Crimes. With regard to sexual slavery, see Art 7(1)(g)-2 (crime against humanity) and Art 8(2)(b)(xxii)(2) (war crime); and with regard to enforced prostitution, see Art 7(1)(g)-3 (crime against humanity) and Art 8(2)(b)(xxii)(3) (war crime).

[49] In *Furundžija* the ICTY stated that rape was the most serious manifestation of sexual assault: ICTY, *Furundžija*, above n 31, para 175.

[50] *Report of the Secretary General on Conflict-related Sexual Violence*, UN Doc A/66/657–S/2012/33, 13 January 2012, para 3. Sexual violence is defined in the ICC Elements of Crimes in Art 7(1)(g)-6 (crime against humanity), and in Art 8(2)(b)(xxii)(6) and Art 8(2)(e)(vi)(6) (war crime).

[51] *Final Report of Special Rapporteur*, above n 42, at para 22.

[52] ICTR, *Akayesu*, above n 32, para 688.

[53] UNGA, 66th Session, Third Committee, Items 28 of the Agenda, Statement by the International Committee of the Red Cross (ICRC), New York, 13 October 2011 (ICRC Statement 2011).

[54] 26th Conference of the Red Cross and Red Crescent, 7 December 1995, Resolution 2.

[55] F. Krill, 'The Protection of Women in International Humanitarian Law', 25 *IRRC* 249 (1985) 337, 348. Generally, women are associated with the wounded and sick, see Arts 12 GC I/GC II.

[56] Art 8 AP I.

19   Although it is acknowledged that there is some arbitrariness in choosing the age of the children in the third category (7 years old) and in selecting the other categories (pregnant/expectant mothers and maternity cases), these parameters were deemed by the drafters as appropriate, reasonable, and generally in accord with the requirements of the physical and mental development of children.[57] Whilst pregnant or expectant women refers to women's condition prior to childbirth, the concept of 'maternity cases' covers labour and a short period after childbirth,[58] and implies that such women are in need of medical assistance. Indeed, Article 8 AP I refers to maternity cases as women 'who may be in need of immediate medical assistance and care'. In contradistinction, 'nursing mothers', in Article 70 AP I, refers to mothers of babies, the stress being on the protection and care of the child.[59] That it was deemed necessary to add 'nursing mothers' shows that the concept of 'maternity cases' relates to birthing. Moreover, the term 'nursing mothers', rather than 'maternity cases', appears only once in the Geneva Conventions (Article 89 GC IV), alongside references to pregnant women and children under 15 years of age.

b. *Personal safety and shelter*

20   In view of the vulnerability of some categories of women, ensuring their personal safety is fundamental.[60] Article 14 GC IV provides for the creation of hospital and safety zones and localities so as to protect certain categories of civilians from the effects of war. The common denominator between all those listed in Article 14 GC IV is that such individuals are deemed to not take part in the hostilities, and to suffer a weakness that makes them incapable of contributing to the conflict. Expectant mothers and mothers of children under 7 years of age are seen as one such group of individuals who can seek refuge in these hospital and safety zones and localities. Article 14 GC IV may be considered as customary.[61] It is noteworthy that Rule 35 in the CIHL Study[62] does not specifically refer to these categories but applies to 'civilians', which means that any woman is to be protected in these locations. Yet Article 14 GC IV goes a step further than Rule 35, inasmuch as it offers protection from both the indirect and direct effects of war.[63] Direct effects include bombardment, aerial attacks, etc, whilst indirect effects cover issues that are of particular relevance to these two categories of women: health, sanitation, housing, shelter, heating, etc. This means that these women's personal safety is assured, whilst they are also able to find shelter in a broader sense.

21   The personal safety of specific groups of women is also found in Articles 16 paragraph 1 and 17 GC IV. Article 16 GC IV provides that expectant mothers, along with the wounded, sick, and infirm who are deemed not to take part in hostilities and to be in a state of weakness, shall be the object of particular protection and respect. This means that such women are not only to be spared and not attacked, but should also be assisted and supported,[64] obligations that are moreover applicable to female detainees.[65] This dual

---

[57] Pictet Commentary GC IV, at 126.
[58] The expression '*femmes en couche*' in the French version of the GCs confirms this interpretation.
[59] ICRC Commentary APs, Art 70 AP I.
[60] 'Personal safety' is defined as 'safety from dangers, acts of violence of threats thereof against members of the civilian population not or no longer taking a direct part in hostilities'. ICRC, *Addressing the Needs of Women*, above n 30, at 17.
[61] See examples provided in the practice relating to Rule 35 ICRC CIHL Study.
[62] Rule 35 ICRC CIHL Study.   [63] Pictet Commentary GC IV, at 127.
[64] Ibid; Art 16 para 1 GC IV.   [65] Pictet Commentary GC IV, at 127; Art 76 para 2 GC IV.

obligation is absolute, no derogations being permitted: the safety of expectant mothers is to be assured.

c. Health, food, and household items

Besides ensuring that the physical integrity of certain categories of women is protected, the Geneva Conventions offer women a range of benefits regarding health, food, and household items. Although health might be considered as part of personal safety (and thus to some extent subsumed under the category 'Personal safety and shelter' examined in section B.II.b. of this chapter), the special protection relating to food and household items is warranted because of women's reproductive and caretaking functions. These special protections are additional to the protection granted to the general civilian population.

Two provisions mentioned earlier, Articles 14 and 16 paragraph 1 GC IV (MN 20–21), offer general protection to certain categories of women. Article 14 GC IV protects expectant mothers and mothers of children aged under 7 from the effects of war, by allowing their admission to hospital and safety zones and localities, which must, however, first be established by agreement between the parties to the conflict. It implies shielding women from the negative impact of the war on health, sanitation, housing, etc, and providing women with life-saving services such as maternal programmes.[66] In relation to expectant mothers, Article 16 paragraph 1 GC IV demands particular protection and respect, by including them in the category of the wounded and sick, which undoubtedly allows them to benefit from medical assistance, and arguably food and other essentials.

Moreover, Article 23 GC IV, a provision designed to save the most vulnerable and most worthy of protection and assistance from the impact of war,[67] specifically requires all belligerents to allow the free and unlimited passage of medical supplies, food, and clothing intended for expectant mothers and maternity cases, whether these women are nationals of an enemy, allied, associated, or neutral state.[68] Article 23 GC IV is, however, subject to the proviso that there be no military advantage gained from the provision of such materials. Yet it is highly unlikely that consignments for these women, which are often barely sufficient to meet their basic needs,[69] will increase the military and economic capacity of a belligerent.[70] The provision was intended to refer to situations of blockade, and has subsequently been interpreted in this sense.[71] Article 23 GC IV was later complemented by Article 70 AP I, extending the circle of beneficiaries to nursing mothers and affirming that in the distribution of these consignments, priority should be given to these categories of women.

In occupation, Article 50 paragraph 5 GC IV requires the Occupying Power not to impede the application of preferential measures that were in effect prior to the occupation in regard to food, medical care, and protection against the effects of war in relation to expectant mothers and mothers of children under 7 years of age. Article 38 GC IV, which refers to specific categories of women who are aliens in the territory of a party to the conflict, stipulates that

---

[66] ICRC Statement 2011, above n 53.   [67] Pictet Commentary GC IV, at 179.
[68] Ibid, Art 23 GC IV.
[69] See, e.g., ICRC Annual Report 2011, *ICRC's Operational Approach to Women and Girls*, Annex 2, at 31, for the kind of items given to women.
[70] Pictet Commentary GC IV, at 182.
[71] See, e.g., Israeli Ministry of Foreign Affairs, *The Operation in Gaza, Factual and Legal Aspects*, July 2009, para 1300; Israeli Supreme Court, *Jaber Al-Bassiouni Ahmed and others v Prime Minister and Minister of Defence*, HCJ 9132/07, Judgment, 30 January 2008, para 13.

all such protected persons must be regulated by peacetime provisions. Reference is made to a series of provisions to protect individuals who are deemed weak and thus warrant special care.[72] Pregnant women and mothers of children under 7 years shall benefit from this preferential treatment, similar to that provided to nationals in a similar situation.

26   Although 'war may compromise women's access to healthcare',[73] the Geneva Conventions deem only specific categories of women to warrant protection. In contrast, General Recommendation No 24 of CEDAW, which expands on Article 12 on women and health, asserts that states 'should ensure that adequate protection and health services [...] are provided for women in especially difficult circumstances, such as those trapped in situations of armed conflict',[74] thereby offering protection to all women.[75] Similarly, Resolution 2 of the 26th Conference of the Red Cross and Red Crescent calls for measures 'to ensure that women victims of conflict receive medical, psychological and social assistance', dropping the reference to specific categories of women.[76]

27   The Geneva Conventions specifically provide for the medical protection of maternity cases, for these women are considered to be in a vulnerable position owing to childbirth and to the fact that their health and life, as well as those of the child, might be at risk. This fits with Rule 134 in the CIHL Study, which, like Article 8 AP I, views these women as being entitled to the same rights as those who are sick and wounded; and it fits with Article 10(2) ICESCR, which states that 'special protection should be accorded to mothers during a reasonable period before and after childbirth'.[77] For these women, medical care is essential,[78] and they are to be provided with ante-natal, obstetric, and postnatal care, or be brought to a place where such care is available.

28   Maternity cases are protected in a number of provisions in GC IV. Article 18 GC IV stresses that civilian hospitals, which gain their protected status because they treat, inter alia, maternity cases, must be protected and respected. Further, the Geneva Conventions explicitly safeguard the free movement of women who are about to give birth. This is of vital importance, as checkpoints, closures, and curfews often imperil the lives of pregnant women who are unable to reach a hospital in time for a safe delivery.[79] The United Nations Commission on Human Rights has further linked the personal safety and health of maternity cases to human dignity, in a resolution condemning the denial of access to hospitals to pregnant women who are 'force[d] [...] to give birth at checkpoints under hostile, inhumane and humiliating conditions'.[80] In this vein, Article 17 GC IV offers protection to maternity cases in relation to evacuation from besieged or encircled areas. Although evacuation is not compulsory, since the words 'shall endeavour' are used, it is strongly recommended to proceed to an evacuation after local agreements have been made.[81] Article 21 GC IV stipulates that maternity cases may be brought to safety by land

---

[72] E.g., see Pictet Commentary GC IV, at 290.
[73] UNGA, 64th session, Third Committee, item 28 of the agenda, statement by the ICRC, New York, 14 October 2010.
[74] CEDAW Committee, General Recommendation No 24, above n 26, para 16.
[75] See also CEDAW Committee, General Recommendation No 19 on Violence against Women, UN Doc A/47/38, 29 January 1992, para 19.
[76] 26th Conference of the Red Cross and Red Crescent, above n 54, Res 2.
[77] Art 10 para 2 ICESCR.
[78] See *Report of the Special Rapporteur on the Right of Everyone to the Enjoyment of the Highest Attainable Standard of Physical and Mental Health*, UN Doc A/68/297, 9 August 2013, para 43.
[79] ICRC, *Addressing the Needs of Women*, above n 30, at 44.
[80] HRComm, Res 2005/7, 14 April 2005.   [81] Pictet Commentary GC IV, at 139.

and sea transport, provided these comprise convoys, i.e. groups of vehicles. The convoy is allowed to use the emblem. Such a convoy must be respected and protected, thus not only it is prohibited to attack or harm a convoy, but the state must also ensure that the convoy and those who are operating it are indeed respected and protected.[82] Article 22 GC IV further protects medical aircraft (both in convoys and flying singly) carrying, inter alia, maternity cases. In this instance marking is not compulsory. The conditions of the flight need to be agreed upon by the belligerents.[83]

III. Protection of women detainees

Although there are fewer women than men detained as either civilians or POWs,[84] the Geneva Conventions contain a corpus of rules concerning women in detention, most of which are derived from the provisions and principles discussed in sections B.I. and B.II of this chapter. These provisions seek to protect women's physical (especially sexual) integrity and to ensure that due consideration is paid to maternity cases. Concurrently, the Geneva Conventions reiterate states' obligations not to discriminate against women belonging to the enemy party.

a. Quarters

Specific accommodation arrangements must be made for women. To avoid women being subjected to indecent assault, and to ensure that they are treated with all the regard due to their sex, the Geneva Conventions oblige states where possible to separate men and women when deprived of liberty.[85] This preventive stance is adopted in Articles 25, 29, and 97 GC III, and in Articles 76 paragraph 4, 85, and 124 GC IV, which must be interpreted in the light of Article 14 paragraph 2 GC III and Article 27 GC IV respectively. Rule 119 in the CIHL Study, which deals with accommodation for women deprived of their liberty, also links this physical separation of men and women to the requirement to take into account women's needs and to prevent women from becoming victims of sexual violence.[86]

Yet GC IV does not specify that women must be separated from men in all circumstances; Article 82 GC IV encourages the Detaining Power to lodge members of the same family together. In contrast, Article 124 paragraph 3 GC IV, relating to the premises for disciplinary punishments of female civilian internees held for imperative security reasons, requires the Detaining Power to arrange for women internees to undergo their punishment in separate quarters, and under the immediate supervision of women. Also, Article 76 paragraph 4 GC IV stipulates that women in pre-trial detention or serving a sentence should be kept in separate quarters and under the direct supervision of women. Read in conjunction with Article 27 paragraph 2, this allows for women to be free from the threat of assault from strangers. As a further safeguard against potential violations of women's dignity, Article 97 paragraph 4 GC IV requires that female internees be searched only by women.

In contrast, the protection offered to female POWs is less extensive. Article 25 GC III only requires men and women to have separate dormitories and not separate quarters.

---

[82] Ibid, at 171. [83] Ibid, at 174.
[84] ICRC, *Women and War* (ICRC, 2008), at 22.
[85] The *Kunarac* case, above n 40, para 132, shows that the lack of separation of quarters may lead to sexual attacks.
[86] Rule 119 ICRC CIHL Study refers to Rule 134 (specific needs of women) and to Rule 93 (victims of sexual violence).

Supervision by female staff is not obligatory, and the rule that searches be carried out only by female staff does not feature in GC III. This might be explained by the fact that POWs are predominantly male, and it might have been difficult for a Detaining Power to find female guards to supervise and search women. That being said, it is possible to interpret this provision in such a way that female POWs have separate quarters, are supervised by women, and are searched only by women. Indeed, in the case of disciplinary punishment by confinement, or punishment following a judicial sentence, the Detaining Power is, in accordance with Article 97 paragraph 4 GC III and Article 108 GC III respectively, required to provide separate quarters (i.e. sleeping quarters and conveniences), as well as to ensure that female POWs are under the supervision of female staff. Moreover subsequent rules, such as Article 75 paragraph 5 AP I and Rule 119 in the CIHL Study,[87] spell out a general obligation to provide such treatment to all women deprived of their liberty for reasons related to the armed conflict. The Standard Minimum Rules for the Treatment of Prisoners also confirm that women should be kept in separate quarters[88] and be under the immediate supervision of women.[89] Therefore the relevant provisions of GC III may be interpreted so as to include separate quarters, rather than only dormitories and conveniences, and to oblige the Detaining Power to ensure that women detainees are under the authority of a woman. As for body searches of female POWs, they must be conducted in a manner consistent with human dignity,[90] which means that 'persons subjected to body searches should be examined only by persons of the same sex'.[91]

b. Sanitation

33   The Geneva Conventions enjoin states to provide prisoners with adequate sanitation facilities. From a human rights perspective, the right to adequate sanitation, which is based on Articles 11 and 12 ICESCR, is considered fundamental to human dignity[92] and privacy,[93] and is considered 'a human right that is essential for the full enjoyment of life and all human rights'.[94]

34   Article 29 paragraph 2 GC III requires states to ensure that sanitary measures are taken to keep the camps in a clean and healthy state. Prisoners of war are to be provided with water and soap for their personal hygiene, with facilities and installations for that purpose (e.g. baths and showers), and with enough time to wash (Article 29 paragraph 3 GC III). Moreover, conveniences are to comply with the rules of hygiene and to be kept clean. In situations where POWs are undergoing punishment, Article 97 paragraph 2 calls upon the Detaining Power to ensure that the same standards of sanitation are maintained. Whilst Article 29 paragraphs 1 and 3 and Article 97 paragraph 2 do not specifically refer to women, it is nonetheless possible to interpret them so as to require the Detaining Power to attend to women's special health and sanitary needs (e.g., relating to menstruation). Read in light of Article 14 paragraph 2 GC III ('with all the regard due to their sex'), facilities

---

[87] Rule 119 ICRC CIHL Study.
[88] Economic and Social Council (ECOSOC), Standard Minimum Rules for the Treatment of Prisoners, Res 663 C (XXIV) and 2076 (LXII), 31 July 1957 and 13 May 1977 respectively, Rule 8.
[89] Ibid, Rule 53.
[90] See, e.g., ECtHR, *Valasinas v Lithuania*, Judgment, 27 July 2001, para 117.
[91] ICRC, *Addressing the Needs of Women*, above n 30, at 128.
[92] HRCouncil, *Human Rights and Access to Safe Drinking Water and Sanitation*, UN Doc A/HRC/RES/15/9, 6 October 2010, para 3.
[93] CESCR, General Comment 15 on the Right to Water (Articles 11 and 12 ICESCR) (2002), UN Doc E/C.12/2002/11, 20 January 2003, para 29.
[94] UNGA Res 64/292, 3 August 2010, para 1.

need to be set up so as to cater for women's privacy, safety, and needs, and arranged so as to grant them appropriate time to wash and clean, especially during menstruation.[95]

Concerning civilian internees, Article 85 paragraph 1 GC IV obliges the Detaining Power to provide accommodation that fulfils certain minimum standards with regard to hygiene and health, standards which are also applicable to premises for disciplinary punishments (Article 124 paragraph 2 GC IV). According to Article 85 paragraph 3 GC IV, sanitary conveniences are to be maintained in a clean state, and baths and showers are to be available for the internees. The internees must be provided with sufficient water and soap for their daily personal hygiene, and be given enough time for washing and cleaning. According to the original Commentary, these sanitary facilities 'must be so constructed as to preserve decency and cleanliness'.[96] As most articles relating to civilian detainees are based on those enshrined in GC III, which deals with POWs, an analogy may be drawn with regard to the state's duties to pay particular attention to women's sanitary and health needs. 35

Article 29 paragraph 2 GC III and Article 85 paragraph 4 GC IV oblige the Detaining Power to provide women with sanitary conveniences separate from those of men. The original Commentary explained that this separation was necessitated by 'the most elementary rules of decency'.[97] However, this is not provided for women who, either as civilians or as POWs, are undergoing disciplinary punishment. Article 124 paragraph 3 GC IV does not specifically refer to sanitary conveniences, though the term 'quarters', in contradistinction to 'sleeping quarters' mentioned in Article 85 paragraph 4 GC IV, could also cover sanitary conveniences. Article 97 paragraph 4 GC III, which covers the premises for female POWs undergoing punishment, does not specify that sanitary conveniences must be separate. Moreover, the term 'quarters' can be widely interpreted to include such facilities. This interpretation is supported by Rule 8 of the Standard Minimum Rules for the Treatment of Prisoners, which stipulates that 'the whole of the premises allocated to women shall be entirely separate'.[98] 36

c. Health and medical care

The Detaining Power is under the obligation to provide free medical care and medicines to all detainees. As women's health issues are different from those of men, the Detaining Power needs to provide specific services that include screening for cervical and breast cancer,[99] medical check-ups assessing the risk of anaemia and mineral deficiencies,[100] and so on. 37

According to Article 91 GC IV, maternity cases among civilian internees must be transferred to institutions where adequate medical assistance can be provided. This is a rule that is also enshrined, for both POWs and all civilians deprived of their liberty, in the Standard Minimum Rules for the Treatment of Prisoners.[101] Moreover, the standard of care these cases receive should not be less than that applied to the general population. The inclusion of maternity cases in Article 91 GC IV reflects the desire to ensure that women are given proper medical attention when giving birth and shortly thereafter, as internment camps are unsuitable places for giving birth. After all, internment is not a punishment, 38

---

[95] ICRC, *Addressing the Needs of Women*, above n 30, at 135–56.
[96] Pictet Commentary GC IV, at 387 and 494.   [97] Pictet Commentary GC III, at 207.
[98] ECOSOC, above n 88, Rule 8.
[99] ICRC, *Addressing the Needs of Women*, above n 30, at 115 and 132.
[100] Ibid, at 131.   [101] ECOSOC, above n 88, Rule 23(1).

and thus when women give birth they are entitled to receive the care they need. Also to this effect, Article 127 GC IV stipulates that these women should not be transferred if the journey would be detrimental to them, unless their safety imperatively so demands. The women's state of health and physical fitness must be determined individually if they are to be transferred.

d. Food and work

39 The quality, quantity, and variety of the daily food ration distributed in civilian internment, as well as in POW camps, depend on the particular characteristics of the individuals and the context (e.g. climate, amount of work).[102] Nevertheless, Article 89 paragraph 1 GC IV and Article 26 paragraph 1 GC III, which use similar language, oblige the Detaining Power to ensure that internees are in a good state of health to prevent the development of nutritional deficiencies. This certainly calls for an individual appraisal, where the sex of the person is likely to be taken into account.

40 Moreover, according to Article 89 paragraph 5 GC IV, expectant and nursing mothers are to be given supplementary provisions of food (e.g. specific vitamin and mineral supplements, as well as a diet containing sufficient calories and protein)[103] to cater for their physiological needs. This Article sits alongside the principle that certain categories of women are to be given preferential treatment.

41 The Detaining Power has the right to compel POWs to work. Yet, as Article 49 GC III explains, the type and amount of work to be carried out by POWs depends on a variety of factors, including sex. Interpreted in the light of Article 16 GC III, this means that women's physical strength and specificities must be taken into account when assigning work to them. Given a broad interpretation, it would also mean that pregnant women, maternity cases, and women with young children should be exempted from mandatory work.[104]

e. Execution of penalties

42 Article 88 GC III reiterates in strong language the principle of non-adverse discrimination in relation to penal and disciplinary sanctions, i.e. in relation to the rules on sentencing and the treatment of women whilst undergoing punishment. The comparators are women (Article 88 paragraph 2 GC III) and men (Article 88 paragraph 3 GC III) in the armed forces of the Detaining Power. Such an Article might now be seen as redundant in the light of the principle of non-discrimination enshrined in IHRL.

f. Release

43 Article 132 GC IV encourages states to conclude agreements with neutral parties in regard to releasing, repatriating, and returning certain categories of individuals to these states. Among the categories listed are pregnant women, and mothers with infants and young children. No equivalent provision exists in GC III. However, it might be possible to interpret Article 14 GC III, which contains the 'regard due to their sex' clause, as encouraging the Detaining Power to grant early repatriation of female POWs who are pregnant and those who are mothers of young children. Such a reading is confirmed by Annex I, which reproduces the Model Agreement Concerning Direct Repatriation and Accommodation in Neutral Countries of Wounded and Sick Prisoners of War that relates to Article 110 GC

---

[102] Pictet Commentary GC IV, at 393; Pictet Commentary GC III, at 197.
[103] ICRC, *Addressing the Needs of Women*, above n 30, at 121.   [104] Ibid, at 148.

III, and lists 'women prisoners of war who are pregnant or mothers with infants and small children' among the individuals to be given priority in the repatriation. These women benefit from special protection, along with the sick and wounded and children, as they are deemed to be at higher risk in internment and POW camps.

C. Relevance in Non-International Armed Conflicts

Undoubtedly the gist of the main provisions concerning women applies in non-international armed conflict (NIAC). The principle of non-adverse discrimination spelled out in Articles 12 GC I/GC II and Article 27 paragraph 3 GC IV applies in NIAC. Common Article 3 of the Geneva Conventions and Article 2(1) and (4) AP II reiterate the principle. Further, Rule 88 (on Non-Discrimination) in the CIHL Study stipulates that this norm applies in NIAC too. In addition, the principle of non-discrimination, which is enshrined in a variety of IHRL instruments, applies at all times, as derogations from the principle of non-discrimination based on sex are not permitted.[105] Women should not be discriminated against in NIAC. 44

Article 12 paragraph 4 GC I/GC II obligates states to treat wounded, sick, and shipwrecked women with the regard due to their sex. There is no corresponding provision in IHL instruments regulating NIAC. The legal support for asserting that this rule also applies in NIAC is mainly found in a range of UN resolutions that do not characterize the nature of the armed conflict when exhorting parties to the conflict to respect and protect women.[106] Likewise, Resolution 2 of the 26th Conference of the Red Cross and Red Crescent does not differentiate between the types of conflict when it encourages states to set up programmes, 'to ensure that women victims of conflict receive medical, psychological and social assistance'.[107] 45

Article 27 paragraph 2 GC IV, which protects women from attacks on their honour, features in IHL instruments relating to NIAC in a modified form. Reference to the concept of 'honour' is dropped and replaced by 'outrages upon personal dignity' in Common Article 3 paragraph 1(c), and in Article 4(2)(e) AP II. Article 4(2)(e) AP II almost mirrors Article 27 paragraph 2 GC IV, with the addition of 'humiliating and degrading treatment' to the list of acts that fall within the definition of 'outrages upon personal dignity'. In contrast, Common Article 3 does not expressly refer to rape and sexual violence (short of rape), which may nevertheless be subsumed under 'cruel treatment and torture' (Common Article 3 paragraph 1(a)) and 'humiliating and degrading treatment' (Common Article 3 paragraph 1(c)) respectively. Indeed, in *Furundžija* the ICTY explained that rape was implicitly prohibited under Common Article 3.[108] The protection offered to women in NIAC with respect to freedom from sexual violence is phrased in terms of physical harm and harm to human dignity rather than to honour.[109] Moreover, a range of instruments that condemn sexual violence do not make a distinction on the basis of the nature of the 46

---

[105] See, e.g., Art 4 para 1 ICCPR, which specifies that derogations may not involve 'discrimination solely on the basis of […] sex'.
[106] UNSC Res 1325, above n 16; UNSC Res 1820, 19 June 2009; UNSC Res 1889, 5 October 2009; UNSC Res 1960, above n 10.
[107] 26th Conference of the Red Cross and Red Crescent, above n 54, Res 2.
[108] ICTY, *Furundžija*, above n 31, paras 166–8. See also *Final Report of Special Rapporteur*, above n 42, para 69.
[109] See ICTR, *The Prosecutor v Pauline Nyiramasuhuko*, Trial Chamber Judgment and Sentence, ICTR-98-42-T, 24 June 2011, paras 6178–9.

armed conflict, e.g. Section 7.3 of the 1999 UN Secretary-General's Bulletin,[110] reports by the Secretary-General,[111] CEDAW General Recommendation No 19 on Violence against Women,[112] etc. The International Criminal Court (ICC) Statute (Article 8(2)(e)(vi)) also confirms that rape and other forms of sexual violence, such as sexual slavery, enforced prostitution, and sexual violence, are prohibited in NIAC.[113] No doubt, women must be protected from sexual violence in NIAC.

47   Whilst the Geneva Conventions protect specific categories of women—pregnant women, maternity cases, and mothers with children under the age of 7—neither AP II nor Common Article 3 refers to these categories. Likewise, the section on the protection offered to women in NIAC in Rule 134 in the CIHL Study does not explicitly mention these categories, although the general rule demanding respect for the 'specific protection, health and assistance needs of women affected by armed conflict' is stated to apply in NIAC.[114] Maternity cases are often subsumed under the 'sick, wounded and shipwrecked' category in IAC, and one might contend that NIAC provisions relating to the 'sick, wounded and shipwrecked' also apply to maternity cases. In NIAC the wounded and sick must be protected and respected: Common Article 3 paragraph 2, and Article 7 AP II and Rule 110 in the CIHL Study (treatment and care of the wounded, sick, and shipwrecked) apply irrespective of the nature of the conflict.

48   In NIAC, detained women are to be treated humanely, for the general principle of humane treatment is applicable irrespective of the nature of the conflict. Moreover, detained women also enjoy the benefit of quarters separate from those of men and are to be kept under the immediate supervision of women. Article 5 paragraph 2(a) AP II thus reflects many aspects of the key provisions found in GC III and GC IV, though one should recall that the concept of POWs does not exist in NIAC. Rule 119 in the CIHL Study and Section 8(e) of the Secretary-General's Bulletin[115] confirm the application of this norm in NIAC. While no reference is made to maternity cases in detention centres, the rules relating to the sick and wounded, as discussed above, are to apply to these women too.

D. Legal Consequences of a Violation

49   Violations of the special rules concerning women in the Geneva Conventions may be divided into grave breaches, specifically enumerated in Article 50 GC I, Article 51 GC II, Article 130 GC III, and Article 147 GC IV, and other acts contrary to the provisions of the Conventions. Whilst the violations of all rules contained in the Geneva Conventions entail state responsibility, only violations of those rules that are considered as grave breaches entail criminal responsibility. Furthermore, different international criminal tribunals, as well as the Statute of the ICC, provide for the criminalization of certain acts prohibited in the Geneva Conventions.

---

[110] Bulletin, above n 35.
[111] See, e.g., *Report of the Secretary-General on Conflict-related Sexual Violence*, above n 50, para 3.
[112] CEDAW Committee, General Recommendation No 19, above n 75.
[113] Statute of the International Criminal Court (1988).
[114] ICRC CIHL Study. See summary by J.M. Henckaerts in 87 *IRRC* 857 (2005) 175, at 210.
[115] Bulletin, above n 35.

I. State responsibility

If the armed forces of a state violate any of the provisions discussed in section B of this chapter, the state incurs responsibility for their acts.[116] United Nations bodies have in past decades taken a lead role in reminding states of their obligations towards women in armed conflict,[117] and in condemning violence, especially sexual violence, against women.[118] The first legal consequence of the violation of international legal treaty obligations is the duty to cease the act, and to offer appropriate assurances and guarantees of non-repetition. In relation to gender-based violence in armed conflict, the Security Council has '*demand[ed]* that all parties put an end to such practices'.[119]

The second legal consequence is to offer reparation for violations of IHL.[120] However, under the classic law of state responsibility, compensation is not offered to individuals but to the state. A rare example of compensation being directly awarded to women having suffered sexual assault is the awards made by the United Nations Compensation Commission, established by the Security Council to deal with claims arising from the Gulf conflict of 1990–1.[121] The Basic Principles and Guidelines on the Right to a Remedy and Reparation for Victims of Gross Violations of International Human Rights Law and Serious Violations of International Humanitarian Law explain that states are to adopt a range of reparation measures,[122] and that a victim's right to a remedy cannot be discriminatory towards women.[123] The Declaration on the Elimination of Violence against Women,[124] the Inter-American Convention on the Prevention, Punishment and Eradication of Violence against Women,[125] the Protocol of the African Charter on Human and Peoples' Rights on the Rights of Women in Africa,[126] and the Council of Europe Convention on Preventing and Combating Violence against Women and Domestic Violence,[127] all expressly grant women access to reparations. The Special Rapporteur on Violence against Women has noted that '[t]here are signs that the traditional neglect of women in the reparations domain […] is ending'.[128]

The Geneva Conventions are peculiar inasmuch as they compel states to penalize a number of violations of the treaties.[129] The Security Council has reiterated states' obligations to prosecute those responsible for war crimes perpetrated against civilians, and more

---

[116] Art 4 ILC Articles on State Responsibility.
[117] UNGA Res 59/141, 25 February 2005; UNGA Res 59/171, 24 February 2005; UNGA Res 62/94, 25 January 2008.
[118] UNSC Res 1674, 28 April 2006, para 5; UNSC Res 1325, above n 16; UNSC Res 1820, above n 106; Vienna Declaration and Programme of Action, UN Doc A/CONF.157/24 (part 1), 13 October 1993, para 28; Beijing Declaration and Platform for Action, above n 13, para 33.
[119] UNSC Res 1674, above n 118, para 5.   [120] See, e.g., UNSC Res 1894, above n 10.
[121] United Nations Compensation Commission, Determination of Ceilings for Compensation for Mental Pain and Anguish, S/AC.26/1992/8, 27 January 1992, at Category C.
[122] UNGA Res 60/147, 16 December 2005, para 7.
[123] Ibid, paras 11–12. In relation to compensation to women victims of violence, see *2008 Report of Special Rapporteur*, above n 15, para 86.
[124] Art 4(d) DEVAW, above n 12.
[125] Art 7(f) and (g) Inter-American Convention on the Prevention, Punishment and Eradication of Violence against Women (1994).
[126] Arts 4 and 10 Protocol of the African Charter on Human and Peoples' Rights on the Rights of Women in Africa (2003).
[127] Arts 5(2) and 30 Council of Europe Convention on Preventing and Combating Violence against Women and Domestic Violence (2011).
[128] *Report of the Special Rapporteur on Violence* UN Doc A/HRC/14/22, 23 April 2010, para 25. See, e.g., ECommHR, *Cyprus v Turkey*, App Nos 6780/74 and 6950/75, 10 July 1976.
[129] Art 49 GC I; Art 50 GC II; Art 129 GC III; Art 146 GC IV.

53   particularly perpetrators of sexual violence.[130] Moreover, states are obliged, if requested by another state or an international criminal tribunal, to surrender alleged war criminals.

Further, under the principle of due diligence, states are obliged to train troops to abide by the Geneva Conventions, put domestic measures into place to investigate alleged violations of the Conventions, and provide redress for individuals. These obligations to prevent, investigate, protect, prosecute, redress, adequately punish, and compensate for wrongs committed by the state and its agents through the principle of due diligence, are of particular relevance to women[131] as they obligate the state 'not merely to protect against violence, but rather to eliminate its "causes"—that is, gender discrimination at structural, ideological and operational levels'.[132] However, such a wide interpretation cannot be given to the provisions of the Geneva Conventions themselves, as they aim at protecting women from the effects of armed conflict and not at eliminating discrimination.

54   Human rights instruments, which offer complaint mechanisms that are more accessible to individuals alleging a violation of a human right, have been used to deal with violations of the aforementioned rules. Most claims made to these bodies tend to focus on sexual violence.[133] Rape and sexual violence violate the prohibition on torture and cruel, inhuman, or degrading treatment,[134] and also impair other human rights, including the right to the highest attainable standard of physical and mental health under the ICESCR.

II. Criminal responsibility

55   Although there is no explicit reference to acts against women in the list of grave breaches in the Geneva Conventions, some of the acts enumerated in the relevant Articles may be interpreted so as to cover violence against women. This is particularly important inasmuch as acts that fall within the definition of a grave breach must be criminalized in national law, and alleged culprits must be brought to justice in accordance with the grave breaches system of repression. Only acts of sexual violence, including rape and enforced prostitution, are indirectly covered by the grave breaches provisions[135] and are now widely viewed as war crimes under customary international law (see Chapter 17 of this volume, section D.I).

56   Other violations of the protection to which women are entitled in armed conflict are not explicitly referred to by the Geneva Conventions as offences to be criminalized under national law, and do not fall into any of the categories mentioned in the grave breaches provisions. However some acts, such as outrages upon personal dignity (not all rising to the level of inhuman treatment), are now seen as constituting serious violations of IHL and are thus defined as war crimes (under, for example, Article 8(2)(b)(xxi) of the ICC Statute). That being said, a range of other violations of the Geneva Conventions (e.g., denying free passage to maternity cases, or failing to provide sanitary conveniences separate from those provided to men) fail to meet the *Tadić* requirements,[136] and cannot thus

---

[130] See, e.g., UNSC Res 1325, above n 16, para 11; UNSC Res 1888, above n 10, Preamble and para 7. See also G8, Declaration on Preventing Sexual Violence in Conflict, 11 April 2013.

[131] *2009 Report of Special Rapporteur*, above n 15, para 64; *2008 Report of Special Rapporteur*, above n 15, para 65.

[132] *2009 Report of Special Rapporteur*, above n 15, para 87.

[133] The author of this commentary is unaware of cases that examine violations of women's rights in armed conflict other than relating to sexual offences.

[134] See, e.g., ECtHR, *Aydin*, above n 33, paras 83–4; and IACommHR, *Mejía*, above n 33, paras 182–8.

[135] See discussion in Rule 156 ICRC CIHL Study.

[136] ICTY, *The Prosecutor v Duško Tadić*, Appeals Chamber Decision on the Defence Motion for Interlocutory Appeal on Jurisdiction, IT-94-1, 2 October 1995, para 94.

be considered as war crimes under customary international law. Still, states are allowed, should they so wish, to criminalize under national law violations of IHL that are not listed in the grave breaches provisions of the Geneva Conventions or as war crimes in the ICC Statute.[137]

Sexual violence is also a serious violation of IHL in NIAC, as the crime can be subsumed under Article 8(2)(c)(i) and (ii) of the ICC Statute. Further, rape and acts of a similar nature are specifically referred to in Article 8(2)(e)(vi) of the ICC Statute, and are listed as serious violations of IHL in Rule 156 in the CIHL Study.

III. The Security Council

The Security Council has also acted to facilitate respect for and enforcement of the IHL rules relating to women in a number of ways. First, the Security Council has condemned sexual violence when used as a tactic of war to target civilians deliberately, or as part of a widespread or systematic attack against civilian populations.[138] Secondly, pursuant to Article 13(b) of the ICC Statute, the Security Council is able to refer situations to the ICC. It has 'recall[ed] the inclusion of a range of sexual violence offences in the Rome Statute of the International Criminal Court and the statutes of the ad hoc international criminal tribunals',[139] and situations referred to the ICC by the Security Council have led to arrest warrants' including sexual violence as a war crime.[140] Thirdly, the Security Council has established a range of mechanisms, the purpose of which is to monitor, analyse, and report on conflict-related sexual violence so as to provide the Security Council with timely, accurate, and reliable information in order to take action to prevent and respond to conflict-related sexual violence.[141] Three UN posts have been created—the Special Rapporteur on Violence against Women (1994), the Special Rapporteur on the Situation of Systematic Rape, Sexual Slavery, and Slavery-like Practices (1995), and the Special Representative on Sexual Violence in Conflict (2009)—to monitor violations perpetrated against women, notably in armed conflict. The Secretary-General also reports on the subject.[142] Fourthly, the Security Council has enjoined the Secretary-General of the UN to mainstream sexual violence in armed conflict in all UN reports to the Security Council,[143] and has requested the Secretary-General to monitor the implementation of pledges on the prevention, prohibition, and investigation of sexual violence made by parties to armed conflict on the Security Council's agenda.[144] This policy of 'naming and shaming' has now been broadened to encompass 'parties suspected of committing or being responsible for patterns of rape and other forms of sexual violence'.[145] Yet again, the focus is on sexual violence rather than on the protection of women more generally.

---

[137] See discussion in Rule 156 ICRC CIHL Study.
[138] See, e.g., UNSC Res 1888, above n 10, para 1; UNSC Res 2106, 24 June 2013, para 2.
[139] See, e.g., UNSC Res 1888, above n 10, Preamble.
[140] See, e.g., ICC, *The Prosecutor v Ahmad Muhammad Harun and Ali Muhammad Ali Abd-Al-Rahman*, Pre-Trial Chamber I, ICC-02/05-01/07, 27 April 2007, at Counts 14 and 43.
[141] *Report of the Secretary-General on Conflict-related Sexual Violence*, above n 50, para 7.
[142] UNSC Res 1820, above n 106, para 15.   [143] See, e.g., UNSC Res 1888, above n 10, para 24.
[144] UNSC Res 1960, above n 10, para 6; UNSC Res 2106, above n 138, paras 5–8.
[145] See, e.g., *Report of the Secretary-General on Conflict-related Sexual Violence*, above n 50, Annex. However, it should be noted that most parties listed are non-state actors.

E. Critical Assessment

59 Overall the Geneva Conventions provide special protection for pregnant women, maternity cases, and mothers of children aged under 7, and address the vulnerability of women to sexual violence in armed conflict. These provisions have been criticized for perpetuating stereotypical ideas of women as weak individuals whose 'honour' is defined by reference to male views on women, associating women with children, and failing to consider gender rather than sex as the distinguishing factor.

60 It is claimed that IHL rules are archaic and reflect the very stereotypical ideas about women (honour is likened to virtue)[146] that perpetuate discrimination and violence against women, and lead to the stigmatization and rejection of victims of sexual violence.[147] That being said, a modern interpretation of IHL confirms the view that sexual violence is a violation of a woman's physical and mental integrity. Although violence against women in armed conflict is the manifestation of unequal power relations between men and women, it is not the aim of the Geneva Conventions to tackle the roots of discrimination based on sex and address social, economic, and structural inequalities.[148] Nonetheless the Geneva Conventions can be used to debunk the idea that women are property, spoils of war. Likewise, in some cultures the rape of women is viewed as a violation of the honour of the community, rather than of the individual herself.[149] Yet again, IHL is not meant to alter cultural traditions and perceptions, but to ensure that certain standards of treatment towards women are being respected. Feminists also argue that IHL is old-fashioned, in that it considers women as civilian victims (of sexual violence) and men as combatants.[150] Whilst this might have been the case when the Geneva Conventions were drafted, the fact that many women are now in the armed forces or armed opposition group challenges this view.[151] It is thus not possible to apply a historical interpretation anymore. The ICRC has recognized that 'the relevant question is not who is more vulnerable but rather who is vulnerable to what particular risks', and 'it is an oversimplification to see one gender as active (male combatants) and the other as passive (female victims)'.[152] The absence of rape in the list of grave breaches also suggested that states were not under the duty to criminalize and prosecute rape (and sexual violence more generally). Nevertheless, in the 1990s, when feminists claimed that 'rape ought to be a war crime', rape was already a war crime under customary law, albeit rarely prosecuted,[153] and this was confirmed by the subsequent progressive case law and statutes of the international criminal tribunals (see Chapter 17 of this volume, section D.I).

61 Another criticism levelled at the Geneva Conventions is that the rationale for protecting women is their nurturing and caring roles as regards children: the majority of provisions

---

[146] The notion of attack upon a woman's honour 'reinforces the notion of rape as a social stigma rather than an attack against a woman's personal and psychological well-being': J. Gardam and M. Jarvis, 'Women and Armed Conflict: The International Response to the Beijing Platform for Action', 32 *Columbia Human Rights Law Review* (2000) 1, at 56.

[147] *Final Report of Special Rapporteur*, above n 42, para 16.

[148] ICRC Annual Report 2011, Annex 2, above n 69, at 30: '[T]he ICRC does not claim to reform gender relations.'

[149] A. Barrow, 'UN Security Council Resolutions 1325 and 1820: Constructing Gender in Armed Conflict and International Humanitarian Law', 92 *IRRC* 877 (2010) 221, at 224.

[150] See discussion in *2009 Report of Special Rapporteur*, above n 15, para 43.

[151] ICRC, *Women and War*, above n 84, at 18.

[152] ICRC Annual Report 2011, Annex 2, above n 69, at 30.

[153] *Final Report of Special Rapporteur*, above n 42, para 69.

protecting women view them in this capacity. The commingling of the specific concerns of women with those of children tends to prove that women are viewed only in their reproductive roles. The original Commentary to Article 132 GC III explains that pregnant women and mothers of infants and young children were included in the provision 'because of what children represent for the future of humanity'.[154] Additional Protocol I does little to dispel this, as the expression 'nursing mothers' was introduced to protect future generations. This association with children serves to highlight the reproductive functions of women to the exclusion of their other, non-reproductive related needs. Whilst it is logistically coherent to regroup women and children, it instrumentalizes women's bodies and minds as vehicles to care for children. This exposes a feminine model of a woman whose aim is to give birth to and care for children. Yet it is not only in their role as carers of the disabled, children, or the elderly that women ought to be protected: women perform a variety of roles, often acting as the backbone of society. Today, women's participation is visible in a number of fields previously thought to be the exclusive preserve of men.

A further criticism is that the association with children gives the impression that women, like children, are powerless and in need, thereby infantilizing women.[155] Lumped together with children in the same category of vulnerability, women's needs, experiences, and roles in armed conflict are often overlooked. The protection rather than prohibition language found in the Geneva Conventions buttresses this viewpoint, for it addresses women's needs within a welfare paradigm. What is more, this normative recognition aligns women with victimhood, denying them any individual and/or collective agency as active participants in armed conflict. Having said that, the focus may slowly be shifting from a victimization-oriented approach to one of empowerment. The resilience shown by women is a testimony to their real power in armed conflict, a fact acknowledged by Security Council Resolution 1325, which views women not simply as vulnerable individuals, or as victims, but rather as a driving force for change and peace.[156]

Since the drafting of the Geneva Conventions, the concept of 'gender' has emerged in a number of legal instruments[157] and through the cases.[158] Whilst 'sex' refers to the biological features of a person, 'gender' 'denotes the culturally expected behaviour of men and women based on roles, attitudes and values ascribed to them on the basis of their sex'.[159] Whilst the concept of 'gender' could be used to apply to both men and women, gender is often understood as relating to women only.[160] Indeed sexual violence against men is framed in terms of violation of personal integrity. This is, however, changing. Recently a proper application of the concept of gender in IHL has reinforced that sexual violence, whether perpetrated against a man or a woman, is an act against a person's physical integrity.[161] Further, the application of the concept of 'gender' rather than 'sex'

---

[154] Pictet Commentary GC IV, at 513.
[155] Report of Special Rapporteur on Violence against Women, its Causes and Consequences, UN Doc E/CN.4/2001/73/Add.2, 6 February 2001, para 25.
[156] See also CEDAW Committee, General Recommendation No 30, above n 1, para 6.
[157] See, e.g., Art 7(1)(h) ICC Statute.   [158] Delalić et al, above n 32, para 493.
[159] ICRC, *Addressing the Needs of Women*, above n 30, at 7.
[160] See, e.g., CEDAW Committee, General Recommendation No 19, above n 75; UNSC Res 1674, above n 118; UNGA Res 60/1, 24 October 2005, para 116.
[161] See, e.g., the commentary on Rule 134 ICRC CIHL Study that specifies that 'the prohibition of sexual violence applies equally to men and women', and so does Rule 93 on rape and other forms of sexual violence of the ICRC CIHL Study; UNSC Res 1960, above n 10. See also the gender-neutral definition of 'rape' in *Final Report of Special Rapporteur*, above n 42, para 24, and ICC Statute, fn 15 (relating to Art 7 para 1(g)(1)) and fn 50 (relating to Art 8(2)(b)(xxii)(1)).

could shift the focus away from sexual violence to other human activities prohibited by the Geneva Conventions. It would help in understanding male and female roles in armed conflict, and thus offer better-tailored protection to such individuals. After all, the ICRC admits that '[g]ender analysis is [...] used to better appreciate the respective sociocultural roles attributed to men and women when it comes to the division of labour, productive and reproductive activities, and access to and control over resources and benefits'.[162] Better protection for women can be achieved by espousing a holistic approach to women's and men's roles, responsibilities, and experiences.

NOËLLE QUÉNIVET*

---

[162] ICRC, *Women and War*, above n 84, at 3.
* I would like to thank Richard A. Edwards for proofreading this chapter.

Chapter 62. Special Rules on Children

	MN
A. Introduction	1
B. Meaning and Application	4
I. Legal definition of a child	5
II. Protection of the child in armed conflict under international humanitarian law	11
a. Status and ties	12
b. Education	19
c. Assistance and care	24
d. Special zones	29
e. Arrest	33
f. Death penalty	35
g. Participation of children in hostilities in international armed conflict	36
C. Relevance in Non-International Armed Conflicts	45
D. Legal Consequences of a Violation	51
I. Incidents and modalities of state and non-state actor accountability	52
II. Criminal responsibility	59
E. Critical Assessment	63

Select Bibliography

Bald, S.H., 'Searching for a Lost Childhood: Will the Special Court of Sierra Leone Find Justice for its Children?', 18 *American University International Law Review* (2002) 537

Coomaraswamy, R., 'The Optional Protocol to the Convention on the Rights of the Child on the Involvement of Children in Armed Conflict: Towards Universal Ratification', 18 *International Journal of Children's Rights* (2010) 535

Dennis, M.J., 'Current Development: Newly Adopted Protocols to the CRC', 94 *AJIL* (2000) 789

Drumbl, M.A., *Reimagining Child Soldiers in International Law and Policy* (Oxford: OUP, 2012)

Dupuy, K.E./Peters, K., *War and Children: A Reference Handbook* (Santa Barbara, Cal: Praeger Security International, 2010)

Grover, S.C., *Prosecuting International Crimes and Human Rights Abuses Committed against Children* (Berlin: Springer-Verlag, 2010)

Happold, M., 'The Optional Protocol to the CRC on the Involvement of Children in Armed Conflict', 3 *YIHL* (2000) 226

Happold, M., 'International Humanitarian Law, War Criminality and Child Recruitment: The Special Court for Sierra Leone's Decision in Prosecutor v Samuel Hinga Norman', 18 *LJIL* (2005) 283

Kuper, J., *Military Training and Children in Armed Conflict: Law, Policy, and Practice* (Leiden: Martinus Nijhoff, 2005)

Mendez, P.K., 'Moving from Words to Action in the Modern "Era of Application": A New Approach to Realizing Children's Rights in Armed Conflicts', 15 *International Journal of Children's Rights* (2007) 219

Vandenhole, W./Parmentier, S./Derluyn, I. (eds), *International Law on Children and Armed Conflict* (Antwerp: Intersentia, 2011)

A. Introduction

1 Within the last few decades, civilians have become increasingly affected by the waging of wars, with battlefields located in urban areas or through the involvement of non-state actors and new means of warfare. For children in particular, armed conflicts are without question one of the most dangerous threats to life, health, and development: '[T]he child, by reason of his physical and mental immaturity, needs special safeguards and care, including appropriate legal protection, before as well as after birth.'[1] The twentieth century gave rise to a constantly growing legal corpus devoted to the protection of children. The existing special rules are the result of an extensive process of codification, not in one single field of international law but in different fields of law influencing each other. The fate of children is addressed in such areas as family law, labour law, refugee law, international human rights law (IHRL) and international criminal law (ICL), among others. For the protection of children in armed conflicts, international humanitarian law (IHL) articulates international standards for children, both as victims and as participants in the hostilities.

2 In 1939, the International Committee of the Red Cross (ICRC) and the International Union for Child Welfare (IUCW) had already prepared a draft agreement dealing exclusively with the protection of children's rights. With the advent of the Second World War, however, the process was temporarily set aside. During the War, the ICRC was able to implement special treatment for children, for example, placing children aged under 18 in special camps and supporting family reunification by organizing radio broadcasts, but its work was at that time not legally anchored nor based on an international agreement. In 1946, the Bolivian Red Cross submitted a draft version of a specific Convention on the Protection of Children in the Event of International Conflict or Civil War to the Preliminary Conference of the National Red Cross Societies, representing the joint effort of the ICRC and the IUCW to strengthen the specific protection for the most vulnerable in one single treaty.[2] Although the draft Convention was put aside, special provisions concerning children were incorporated into the comprehensive body of law now comprising the cornerstone of the laws of armed conflict, the Geneva Conventions of 1949. Regulations concerning the special protection of children, as drafted by the ICRC, were adopted as such by the Diplomatic Conference in 1949 and came into force on 21 October 1950. While the Geneva Conventions have acquired the status of customary international law (CIL), they have a number of weaknesses concerning the protection of children in terms of modern-day conflicts.[3]

3 As an inherent part of the group of civilians protected by GC IV in times of war, children benefit from a general protection, that is, the humane treatment of civilians in times of armed conflicts. This protection is granted with respect to their physical well-being, but also as regards their psychological integrity, by prohibiting certain conduct, torture, coercion, or reprisals. As civilians, children are at all times to be distinguished from combatants and must not be the target of a direct attack.[4] As a distinct protected group of

---

[1] Para 9 of the Preamble to the Convention on the Rights of the Child (CRC).
[2] Report on the Work of the Preliminary Conference of National Red Cross Societies for the study of the Conventions and of various Problems relative to the Red Cross, Geneva, July 26–August 3, 1946, available at <http://www.loc.gov/rr/frd/Military_Law/pdf/RC_report-1946.pdf>, at 101 ff.
[3] C. Hamilton, 'Children Protection in Complex Emergencies', in C.W. Greenbaum et al (eds), *Protection of Children During Armed Political Conflict* (Antwerp: Intersentia, 2006), at 27.
[4] D. Plattner, 'Protection of Children in International Humanitarian Law', 24 *IRRC* 240 (1984) 140.

vulnerable people, they are furthermore addressed by specific Articles within GC IV, which will be discussed in detail in this chapter, and interpreted in light of current challenges and legal developments following the events of 1949, the adoption of the Additional Protocols (APs) and recent legal initiatives. To draw a comprehensive picture of the special rules on children and to establish the broadest possible system of protection, the influence of neighbouring fields of international law on IHL must be considered, and overlaps taken into consideration.[5]

B. Meaning and Application

The rules of GC IV that provide for special protection addressed explicitly and exclusively to children, raise the question of the identification of the notion of children as a group distinguishable from the general group of civilians or other groups of protected persons.

I. Legal definition of a child

Age limits and defining characteristics of childhood, adolescence, and adulthood vary from country to country and culture to culture; the age of puberty fluctuates, depending on climate, race, and the individual.[6] Marrying, driving, or voting, as legally enshrined rights, are not bound to one universal age limit but depend on the domestic civil law of the respective country. Consequently, a precise and universally applicable definition of 'children' does not exist: international law does not define a fixed age limit for children or a definition of the 'child', and neither does IHL or IHRL.[7] Nonetheless, one of the core issues as regards protection of children is the question of the lower and upper age limits. Lacking a comprehensive approach, the different legal instruments contain different upper age limits and incorporate numerous provisions applicable to children of different ages.

The Geneva Convention of most interest here, GC IV, refers to children in different circumstances and different roles, but does not offer any common definition of the child.

Children under the age of 7 are mentioned not as exclusive bearers of certain rights, but only in relation to the rights of their mothers. Reference to this age limit is made mostly in Articles concerning access to welfare or preferential treatment, in conjunction with maternity cases or nursing women (Articles 14, 38, 50 GC IV). The necessity for special

---

[5] UN Doc A/Res 54/263.

[6] A.F. Vrdoljak, 'Cultural Heritage in Human Rights and Humanitarian Law', in O. Ben-Naftali (ed), *International Humanitarian Law and International Human Rights Law* (Oxford: OUP, 2011) 250, at 259.

[7] There is also no common approach within human rights instruments concerning the upper age limit of children. E.g., the 1965 UN General Assembly recommendation relating to the minimum age for marriage determines a minimum lower limit of 15 years (UN Doc A/Res 2018 (XX)). Under the 1989 CRC, a child, however, is every human being below the age of 18 years, unless, under the law applicable to the child, majority is attained earlier (Art 1 CRC). The combination of a relatively high limit of 18 years of age with reference to the earlier majority under national law quickly found favour during the codification, because it allows some flexibility (R. Brett, 'Rights of the Child', in C. Krause and M. Scheinin (eds), *International Protection of Human Rights: A Textbook* (Turku: Abo Akademi Institute for Human Rights, 2009) 227, at 235). The Optional Protocol to the CRC and the African Charter on the Rights and Welfare of the Child share this approach, and consider any person who has not attained the age of 18 years to be a child. The UN Standard Minimum Rules of the Administration of Juvenile Justice determine that 'in those legal systems recognizing the concept of the age of criminal responsibility for juveniles, the beginning of that age shall not be fixed at too low an age level, bearing in mind the facts of emotional, mental and intellectual maturity' (Rule 4, UN Doc A/Res 40/53 Annex).

protection and care of children of a very young age is mirrored in the provisions concerning the identification of children, which is of utmost importance if they are separated from their parents or orphaned. Twelve years of age applies as the upper limit for children in the provisions on identification measures through, for instance, identity discs, as laid down in Article 24 GC IV. The regulations entailing the age limit of 15 years reflect the importance of this stage of the physical and psychological development of children, who are extremely affected and often severely hampered by the waging of war. Children up to 15 years are beneficiaries of provisions relating to safety zones (Article 14 GC IV), provisions enshrining the obligations of an Occupying Power to maintain welfare measures and institutions (Article 50 GC IV), or granting additional food relative to their physiological needs in times of detention and providing for special accommodation and education during that time (Article 89 GC IV). The highest upper age limit, 18 years, is set with respect to sentencing for criminal offences, such as in Article 68 paragraph 4 GC IV, which prohibits the infliction of the death penalty against a protected person who was at the time of the commission of the offence below that upper age limit. The same highest upper age limit is set by Article 51 paragraph 2, allowing the Occupying Power to compel protected persons to work—if they are over 18 years of age. The distinction made between teenagers and adults with regard to their abilities to balance conduct and consequences, or to avoid being manipulated, is considered in these provisions.

8   The definition of a 'child' and the respective age limits have also become a major point of discussion in the legal developments following the Geneva Conventions of 1949. Neither AP I nor AP II contains a fixed age limit for a person to be considered a child, as the majority of states argued against the background of their traditional national approach without finding a mutual consensus.

9   Of special importance in this regard, and reflected in the drafting process of the respective Articles, is the question of the participation of children in hostilities. Their active involvement in armed conflict, not solely as victims but also as participants, has possibly the most drastic effects on their childhood and development. At the Diplomatic Conference of 1977, the drafters of AP I were not able to identify a generally accepted rule, and the proposal of Brazil to prohibit the recruitment of persons below 18 years of age was rejected.[8] The outcome of the Conference (Article 77(2) AP I) was a compromise. It required states that recruit from among persons who have attained the age of 15 years but not yet 18 years to give priority to those who are oldest. Thus, after the adoption of the Additional Protocols there was a strong tendency to consider the limit of 15 years of age a reasonable basis for a definition: 'It is possible to understand the point of view adopted by the Diplomatic Conference without fully agreeing with it.'[9] The commentators on the text argued that the age of 15 at this time most often corresponded to state practice. However, there was also consent among them that some flexibility was appropriate, for those who remained children, both physically and mentally, after the age of 15.

10 Criminal prosecutorial aspects of the participation of children in armed conflict are expressly addressed in the Statute of the International Criminal Court (ICC Statute) and the Statute of the Special Court for Sierra Leone (SCSL Statute). According to Article 8(2)(b)(xxvi) and (e)(vii) of the ICC Statute, conscripting or enlisting children under the

---

[8] *Official Records of the Diplomatic Conference on the Reaffirmation and Development of International Humanitarian Law applicable in Armed Conflicts* (Geneva, 1974–7), vol XIV, at 301.

[9] ICRC Commentary APs, para 3185.

age of 15 is considered a war crime. However, the Court has no jurisdiction over persons who have not reached the age of 18 at the time of the commission of the offence, as laid down by Article 26 of the Statute. The prosecution of so-called 'child soldiers' falls under the jurisdiction of the state parties or another international tribunal with jurisdiction over children, but not the ICC itself. The SCSL Statute offers a solution for this complicated relationship between the avoidance of impunity on the one hand, and respect for mental and intellectual maturity on the other. The SCSL Statute provides the Court with competence to try child or juvenile soldiers between 15–18 years of age. However, it is envisaged in Article 15(5) that such cases will be referred to the truth and reconciliation mechanism.

II. Protection of the child in armed conflict under international humanitarian law

In AP I, special protection of children is explicitly laid down in Article 77: 11

Children shall be the object of special respect and shall be protected against any form of indecent assault. The parties to the conflict shall provide them with the care and aid they require, whether because of their age or for any other reason.

Within the Geneva Conventions this is not explicitly addressed. A reference to age is given in Article 16 GC III and Article 27 paragraph 3 GC IV regarding privileged treatment due to health, sex, and age. Special reference to age, however, is rather brought to light if one combines the several specific provisions on the protection of children and the benefits they enjoy according to their particular needs and vulnerabilities.

a. Status and ties

The protection of a child's welfare is highly dependent on his or her family ties. The Second 12
World War, with its aerial bombardments, mass deportations, flights, and migration, led to the separation of thousands of families. Young children, some of them maybe too young to be aware of their own identity, were (and still are) especially in need of means of identification so that they might be found.

The respective provisions covering protection would be rendered much less effective 13
if the parties to the conflict were not obliged to keep track of children and enable them to reunite with their families.[10] Children under 12 must be made identifiable by wearing identity discs or other means of identification, as laid down in Article 24 paragraph 3 GC IV. Although the identity disc was controversially debated due to the lack of standardization at that time, it was incorporated as the sole example of a means of identification. It should state its bearer's surname, date of birth, address, the father's first name, and, if possible, other information, such as a photograph of the wearer or his or her blood type. Interestingly, the provisions in paragraphs 2 and 3 of Article 24 apply to children below the age of 15, but with regard to the issue of identification, the age limit was lowered, based upon the recommendation of the ICRC. Children over the age of 12 were thought able to clarify their identity themselves.

In cases of occupation, the Occupying Power is required to facilitate the identification 14
of children and the registration of their parentage. Article 50 GC IV does not imply an obligation for the Occupying Power to set up necessary institutions itself, but it may not

---

[10] S. Singer, 'The Protection of Children during Armed Conflict Situations', 26 *IRRC* 252 (1986) 133, at 155.

hinder the regular working of existing institutions. It may not, in any circumstances, change children's personal status, birth certificates, or names, nor enrol them in any type of organizations under its authority. These provisions must be interpreted in the light of historical incidents that happened during the Second World War, when compulsory mass enrolments into, for instance, political movements took place.[11] Enlistment in official or semi-official armed forces of parties to the conflict is governed by Article 51 GC IV.

15   An official Information Bureau is to be set up to cooperate with the Occupying Power in identifying children who are orphaned or separated from their families, and for recording the relevant information. Information sharing should be institutionalized for the whole territory of the armed conflict, and not only in the occupied area. Article 136 GC IV as a counterpart lays down the obligation of the various departments of the state to cooperate promptly with the Bureau. The parties to the conflict shall take the necessary measures to ensure that children who are orphaned or separated from their families as a result of the war, are not left to their own resources (Article 24 GC IV).

16   The Occupying Power must not hinder the application of any preferential measures which may have been adopted prior to the occupation in favour of children under 15 years of age, expectant mothers, and mothers of children aged under 7 years. Preferential measures are, inter alia, food, medical care, and protection against the effects of war (Article 50 paragraph 5 GC IV).

17   Special importance is given to the value of the family, enshrined in a general obligation on all parties to the conflict to facilitate the reunification of families, as discussed in detail in Chapter 53 of this volume. Family members have a right to news and are permitted to give news to family members, by virtue of Article 25 GC IV, even in times of occupation by the hostile party. The right to family news as specified in paragraph 1 is twofold, and comprises the right to give and receive personal news between people who are related or married. As a necessary enabler to reunite families, the importance of this right was underlined in 1949 at the Diplomatic Conference, integrating it into the provisions addressing the civilian population as a whole, without any reservation as to territory or nationality.[12] This right of family members is mirrored in the obligation of the parties to the conflict not to impede contacts but to forward news without delay, as explicitly stated by the Article. In cases of disrupted means of official communication, Article 25 paragraph 2 addresses the assignment of these tasks to such neutral intermediary authorities as, for instance, the central agency provided for in Article 140 GC IV and the institutions of the Red Cross Movement, particularly the National Societies. Notably, the empowerment of a neutral intermediary has provided a valuable and practically importance resource, as closed borders and blocked communications, have sometimes made communication at least difficult, if not impossible, in the present century characterized by electronic means of contact. Article 25 itself leaves the organization and work of the neutral intermediary open to agreement between the states concerned. The specific reference to the Red Cross bodies, however, presents a very explicit and strong legal basis for their involvement and intervention to protect family ties.

18   The importance of the Red Cross and its experience in this field of work is also stressed in Article 26 GC IV. During the Second World War mass separations were caused by bombardment, deportations, or evacuations. People separated from their relatives were in need of reunification, and therefore enquiry cards were distributed and the Dispersed

---

[11] Plattner, above n 4, at 145.   [12] Final Record, vol II-A, at 710 f.

Families Section in Geneva was established. A legal basis for current mechanisms to ensure reunification through different channels was enshrined in sentences 1 and 2 of Article 26 GC IV. Family members must be allowed to make enquiries, even helped to do so, by referring them to an information bureau, or other types of organizations working in that field—with the consent of the parties to the conflict and in accordance with security regulations—and the Red Cross institutions.

b. Education

Not only the protection of a family life, but also the broad cultural environment in which the child grows up is emphasized by the Geneva Conventions, including moral, religious and traditional values. Children are therefore entitled to practise their religion and continue their education. Article 24 GC IV enshrines broad protection for the maintenance of children, with regard both to beneficiaries of the provision and its substance. Being incorporated into Part II on the general protection of populations against certain consequences of war, the Article applies to children regardless of their nationality; both foreigners and nationals of the conflict party in control of a respective territory are within the ambit of the provision. The parties to the conflict must facilitate this in all circumstances and make sure, as far as possible, that they entrust persons of the similar cultural tradition with these tasks (Article 24 paragraph 1 GC IV), an obligation also set out in AP I for times of evacuation (Article 78 AP I). Stemming from past experiences of war, with the powers of propaganda machinery still in mind, to entrust a child's intellectual development to a person close to his or her origin is one way to prevent the separation of that child from his or her roots. However, although great emphasis is placed on the maintenance of the child's environment and educational development, Article 24 GC IV does not give detailed instructions on how to implement the obligation. It is left to the discretion of the state to choose the appropriate means.

The general obligation is renewed by Article 50 GC IV regarding occupied territories, in which the Occupying Power must ensure maintenance and education, if the existing institutions cannot provide for this. In conjunction with Article 43 of the Hague Regulations concerning the Laws and Customs of War on Land, the Occupying Power must take all measures to restore and ensure public order and safety, while at the same time respecting the existing laws of the country. Interestingly, and although other Articles of the Geneva Conventions specify a certain age limit, Article 50 does not make explicit reference to the age of the bearer of the right. Pictet, in his Commentary to the Geneva Conventions, refers to the purpose of the institutions mentioned in paragraph 1 as an indicator that those protected are reasonably those up to 15 years of age.[13] The institutions indicated in the Article may, however, be of various natures and are not narrowed down, although several Articles also refer to specific institutions involved in child maintenance, as, for instance, the medical facilities mentioned in Articles 56 and 57.

Not only in times of occupation but even more so during detention, Article 94 GC IV enshrines concrete provisions for internees with regard to religious, intellectual, and physical activities, concentrating on the needs of children in paragraphs 2 and 3. The positive effects of physical and intellectual activities for the well-being of internees were already recognized and then realized through Article 17 of the the 1929 Convention on Prisoners of War. The 1949 Convention strengthens this approach to engage the Detaining Power

---

[13] ICRC Commentary GC IV, at 285 f.

more actively in its responsibilities towards internees. Practical measures range from providing libraries and facilities to read and study, to setting up playgrounds and sport facilities.[14]

22 The attendance of schools outside of the place of internment must also be ensured, and special playgrounds shall be placed at the disposal of children and young people so that they can engage in physical exercise, sports, and outdoor games, an obligation that was later renewed in Article 78(2) AP I and Article 4(3)(a) AP II.

23 Disciplinary punishment must take age into account, as well as sex and conditions of health, and may never be inhuman, brutal, or dangerous, in accordance with Article 119 GC IV and Article 89 GC III.

c. Assistance and care

24 Children are entitled to assistance and care, medicine, food, and clothing. Several Articles within different parts of GC IV consider these rights in greater detail. Article 23 lays down the general obligation of the High Contracting Parties to grant free passage of those goods necessary for medical and religious care. Specifically mentioned within this Article is the free passage of essential goods, food, clothing, and tonics for children aged under 15, reflecting the special needs of their physical development. To ensure that only materials of a non-military nature are distributed, and not those that might be used to enhance the economic strength of a party to the conflict, several preconditions are enshrined in the Article, for instance by distinguishing categories of recipients and establishing supervision.[15]

25 As noted above (MN 19), Article 24 GC IV focuses on psychological development, addressing the needs of children to be able to practise their religion and to continue education. If possible, this is to be entrusted to persons from a similar cultural background. This Article highlights the obligation of the parties to the conflict to take over the efforts necessary to a child's development, specifically in cases of orphaned children or those separated from their families.

26 Non-discrimination with regard to nationals of the state on whose territory enemy aliens find themselves is furthermore granted, by Article 38 paragraph 5 GC IV, to children under 15, pregnant women, and mothers of children under 7, as regards preferential treatment, special welfare, and access to medical facilities and additional food. In the case of child internment, and to guarantee the appropriate and necessary provision for their physical development, additional food is given to children, as to pregnant and nursing women, as laid down by Article 89 paragraph 5. Within Part IV, Section II of AP I (Relief in favour of the civilian population) Article 70(1) mirrors the priority given to the needs of children, mothers of young children, or pregnant women.

27 When undertaking transfers or evacuations from occupied territories, it must be ensured that members of the same family are not separated, by virtue of Article 49 GC IV, and the proper working of all institutions devoted to the care and education of children must be facilitated (Article 50 GC IV).

28 Very young children are protected mainly through the obligations owed to their mothers. Interned maternity cases shall be admitted to any institution where adequate

---

[14] Similarly and in support, Art 38 GC III.
[15] H. Spieker, 'The Right to Give and Receive Humanitarian Assistance', in H.-J. Heintze and A. Zwitter (eds), *International Law and Humanitarian Assistance* (Berlin: Springer-Verlag, 2011) 7, at 17.

treatment can be given, and must receive care not inferior to that provided for the general population (Article 91 GC IV). Expectant mothers shall not be transferred to places where staying may be detrimental to their health (Article 127 GC IV). Interned expectant and nursing mothers must be given additional food by virtue of Article 89 GC IV, in proportion to their physiological needs. Pregnant women and mothers having dependent infants who are arrested, detained, or interned for reasons related to the armed conflict must have their cases considered with the utmost priority, as laid down in Article 76 AP I.

d. Special zones

As part of the general protection of the population against certain consequences of war, the High Contracting Parties to GC IV may 'establish in their own territory and, if the need arises, in occupied areas, hospital and safety zones and localities so organized as to protect from the effects of war children under fifteen, expectant mothers and mothers of children under seven' (Article 14 paragraph 1). These zones may be established in times of peace and after the outbreak of hostilities. This possibility takes into consideration the special vulnerability of children, who require special protection from long-range weapons, especially against aerial bombardment. The conflicting parties are specifically advised by GC IV to reach limited agreements for the transfer of protected persons from given areas for their protection, listing children along with maternity cases, the wounded or sick, and other groups of people. They shall endeavour to conclude agreements for the passage of religious personnel, medical personnel, and medical equipment to such areas (Articles 15–17 GC IV). 29

Article 24 paragraph 2 GC IV further approves the transfer of children far away from the hostilities, if necessary even to a neutral country that need not be a High Contracting Party. Article 24 paragraph 2 led to discussion during the drafting process of the prejudicial psychological and physical effects of removal or evacuation of children, with the ICRC and the IUCW pressing for a very narrow interpretation of when such removal might be necessary.[16] In light of the importance of family ties, evacuations are to be made only under the strict conditions included in the final document, not present in prior drafts. The Protecting Powers system should be activated in this context, giving consent to the transfer. The consent of the Protecting Powers applies in cases where the children being evacuated are nationals of the enemy party to the conflict. With regard to children of other nationalities, the consent of a representative of the child's country of origin, for instance an embassy, must be obtained. The second condition in Article 24 paragraph 2 refers back to paragraph 1, stating that evacuations may be conducted only if the maintenance of children, as laid down in Article 24 paragraph 1, is guaranteed in the country of reception. 30

If transfers or evacuations have taken place, Article 49 GC IV sets out conditions in relation to families too, as their members shall not be separated. In addition, during the hostilities, the release and repatriation of certain classes of internees, in particular children, mothers, or the wounded and sick, shall be agreed upon by the parties to the conflict, in accordance with Article 132 paragraph 2 GC IV. 31

Similar provision on safety areas and conditions for the transfer of children were negotiated at the 1974–7 Diplomatic Conference, and were enshrined in detail in Article 78 AP I. Compelling reasons of a medical nature, for instance, have been listed as a precondition to 32

---

[16] See further debated in Bothe/Partsch/Solf, at 482 f.

evacuating children of the opposing party to a conflict. If possible, the written consent of the persons responsible for the children shall be given, and the supervision of a Protecting Power arranged.

e. Arrest

33 Children under the age of 15 who are directly participating in the hostilities, despite the prohibition of recruitment, and who have fallen into the power of the adverse party, shall continue to benefit from special protection. That special protection is granted whether or not they are prisoners of war (POWs), under the conditions set out in Article 77 AP I. If children are arrested, detained, or interned for reasons related to the armed conflict, they shall be held in quarters separate from those of adults (Article 77(4) AP I). According to Article 76 GC IV, proper regard must be paid to child detainees in occupied territories. Furthermore, and in light of the special value of family ties, interned members of the same family shall be lodged together to ensure a family life (Article 82 GC IV). If adult internees have children who are not under arrest, they may ask for all of them to be interned together.[17]

34 During detention, children may not be compelled to work, as provided in Article 51 paragraph 2 GC IV. The parties to conflicts shall endeavour, during the course of hostilities, to conclude agreements for the release, repatriation, return to places of residence, or accommodation in a neutral country of children in particular (Article 132 GC IV).

f. Death penalty

35 Article 68 paragraph 4 GC IV was based on a proposal made by the ICRC and the IUCW, and states that an Occupying Power may not impose the death penalty on a child who was under 18 years of age at the time of the offence. In this respect the age limit mirrors comparable provisions in domestic criminal laws. With Article 68 paragraph 4, GC IV paved the way to a prohibition on the imposition of the death penalty on children, one that has been strengthened by IHL, with Article 77(5) AP I and Article 6 AP II. This prohibition is complemented by IHRL, as, for instance, by Article 6(5) of the International Covenant on Civil and Political Rights 1966, Article 4(5) of the American Convention on Human Rights 1969, or Article 37(a) CRC.

g. Participation of children in hostilities in international armed conflict

36 As mentioned above (MN 9), the Additional Protocols were the first international treaties to cover the participation of children in armed conflicts. Article 77 paragraph 2 AP I provides that the parties to the conflict shall take all feasible measures to ensure that children who have not attained the age of 15 years do not take direct part in hostilities, and in particular, the parties shall refrain from recruiting them into their armed forces. This norm does not prohibit forms of indirect participation such as support activities. However, children may be involved in transporting of weapons and munitions, as well as in the collection of information by reconnaissance missions, and these actions are not covered by the Additional Protocols. Such participation includes hostile acts harmful to the enemy without using a weapon, which raises the question of whether it might constitute

---

[17] M.T. Dutli, 'Captured Child Combatants', 30 *IRRC* 278 (1990) 421, at 423.

direct participation in the hostilities.[18] Whatever the answer is, if the children are captured, they must receive the special treatment appropriate to their age.[19]

The provisions of IHL on child recruitment must be read in conjunction with IHRL. In accordance with Article 45(c) CRC, the Committee requested the United Nations (UN) Secretary-General to undertake a study. This 1990 UN Study on the Impact of Armed Conflict on Children[20] led to the establishment of the post of the Special Representative of the UN Secretary-General on Children in Armed Conflict, and to subsequent resolutions of the Security Council. Although mostly of a political nature, Security Council Resolutions may entail some form of legal obligation, and further the application and dissemination of the provisions of IHL.

According to IHRL, the forced or compulsory recruitment of children constitutes a form of slavery under Article 3 of the International Labour Organization's (ILO's) Convention on the Worst Forms of Child Labour.[21] Children in armed conflict are also particularly protected by the CRC, which marks a significant change in the conceptual approach to child protection, from welfare to rights. The CRC is a unique human rights treaty because it deals comprehensively with the rights of children, and its standard of protection for children in armed conflict is largely based on the ideas and regulations first codified by the Geneva Conventions.

The link to situations of armed conflict is established in Article 38 CRC. States are to respect and ensure respect for the specific rules applicable to children in IHL. The provision specifically addresses the state's duty to ensure that children under 15 do not participate directly in hostilities. One major part of the obligation is the prohibition on the recruitment of children under 15 years into the state's armed forces. Prioritizing the oldest of those aged between 15 and 18 during recruitment is another aspect of the obligation. With reference to their general obligation under IHL to protect civilians from the effects of war, the state parties shall take all feasible measures to protect children from the effects of armed conflicts. This wording mirrors Article 77 AP I and reflects the standard of protection laid down in 1977. According to its nature as a human rights treaty, the CRC addresses states parties, whereas IHL deals with the parties to the conflict. However, the identical wording of Article 38 CRC and Article 77 AP I meant that it was not possible for drafters to effect any improvement, which was disappointing for many human rights activists. The undoubtedly unsatisfying standard, although being the lowest common denominator, runs counter both to the progressive codification of international law and to the goal of the CRC, which, according to Article 3 CRC, is to ensure that the 'best interests' of the child are protected. It is highly unlikely that it is in the best interests of a child aged 15 to be recruited and to take direct part in the hostilities.

Particularly problematic was the question why the 1989 CRC, which was drawn up more than a decade after the adoption of AP I and marks considerable progress in the general protection of the child, contains no protection exceeding that of Article 77 AP I.[22]

---

[18] O.M. Uhler and H. Coursier, *Geneva Convention Relative to the Protection of Civilian Persons in Time of War: Commentary* (Geneva: ICRC, 1958), at 154.

[19] N.J. Udombana, 'War Is Not Child's Play! International Law and the Prohibition of Children's Involvement in Armed Conflicts', 20 *Temple International and Comparative Law Journal* (2006) 57, at 75.

[20] UN Doc A/51/306.

[21] ILO Convention Concerning the Prohibition and Immediate Elimination of the Worst Forms of Child Labour (1999).

[22] H.-J. Heintze, 'Children Need More Protection under International Humanitarian Law', 4 *HuV-Informationsschriften* (1995) 200, at 200.

This failure was all the more regrettable because, when the CRC was being negotiated, the opponents of the relevant improvement in child protection (in particular the United States, Iran, and Iraq) did not put forward a particularly strong legal argument. As a matter of fact, the United States was of the opinion that neither the General Assembly nor the Human Rights Commission was a suitable forum for the revision of existing IHL.[23] Many states and non-governmental organizations took up the issue to raise the level of protection beyond that provided by IHL, especially concerning the recruitment and participation of children in armed conflicts. The ICRC argued that it had repeatedly expressed its support to call for the minimum age of combatants to be raised from 15 to 18 years of age. Article 38 is an exception in the CRC, because all other provisions protect children until they have reached the age of 18. The second criticism was even more severe, because the Article undermines existing standards of IHL. Whereas Article 38 CRC, like AP I, prohibits only direct participation, AP II also prohibits indirect participation. The ICRC also objected to the wording 'all feasible measures' in Article 38(4) CRC, because of a serious risk of weakening IHL standards. Many provisions in the CRC were designed as absolute obligations, and thus provided more effective protection than anything covered by the words 'feasible measures'. The recommendation of the ICRC to confine the Article to paragraph 1 was not followed.

41   In parallel, a Working Group of the UN Human Rights Commission drafted the Optional Protocol on Involvement of Children in Armed Conflict. Due to continued controversial opinions, the process was not completed until 2000. The end result was an improvement in comparison with Article 38 CRC. The Preamble to the Optional Protocol underlines that this document is in line with the main objective of the CRC. It states that an optional protocol to the Convention, raising the age of possible recruitment of persons into armed forces and their participation in hostilities, will contribute effectively to the implementation of the principle that the best interests of the child are to be a primary consideration in all actions concerning children. Article 2 of the Optional Protocol to the CRC prohibits compulsory recruitment under the age of 18 into a state's armed forces. According to Article 4(1), non-state actors are also bound. Armed groups, distinct from the armed forces, should not in any circumstances recruit persons under the age of 18 years. Against the background of the misuse of child soldiers by armed groups in many modern armed conflicts, the inclusion of non-state actors is to be welcomed. The state parties are also obliged to provide for criminalization of child recruitment under domestic law. However, in the literature some authors argue that this may be problematic in many cases:

[I]t is likely to be of limited effect because those who take up arms against the lawful government of a country already expose themselves to the most severe penalties under domestic law, and because the capacity of a government to enforce its laws is often very limited in situations of non-international armed conflicts.[24]

42   Voluntary recruitment of those under the age of 18 into the national armed forces is allowed in cultural systems in which children aged 16 are deemed capable of sustaining their families by serving in the armed forces as soldiers. As this prohibition does not

---

[23] UN Doc E/CN.4/1989, SR. 55, Add.1, at 6, para 25.
[24] R. Arnold, 'Children and Armed Conflict', in MPEPIL, para 15.

apply to military schools, it opens a possibility for circumventing the age limits set for recruitment.

Article 3 of the Optional Protocol reflects a compromise between legal cultures, because it permits voluntary recruitment below 18 years. However, state parties to the Optional Protocol are required to deposit a binding declaration of their minimum voluntary recruitment age, and the Article stipulates (in paragraphs a–d) safeguards to ensure voluntariness, consent of parents or legal guardians, information on duties, and proof of age prior to acceptance into military service. The declaration of age can only be withdrawn in favour of a higher age. This happened, for example, in the case of Paraguay, which had originally declared an age of 16 years but raised it in light of international pressure in 2006 to 18 years. Around 25 per cent of more than 100 state parties to the Optional Protocol have indicated a minimum voluntary recruitment age below the age of 18. Article 4 prohibits the direct participation of children below the age of 18 years in hostilities. However, this prohibition does not cover indirect participation, which may often be equally dangerous for children. In the light of the general prohibition of any participation in hostilities by children below the age of 15 years, it is quite contradictory that the Optional Protocol prohibits only direct participation. This has to be considered a weakening of existing standards. This is even more regrettable because, while children may be recruited into the armed groups to be used as cooks, porters, spies, and sexual slaves, due to their desire to act as 'adults' and a general higher fear threshold than that of their elders, they are quite efficient fighters.[25]

Despite existing prohibitions, there are many examples of the actual involvement of children as combatants in national armed forces and other armed groups (child soldiers). However, in the event of their capture, even if under 15 years of age, they are entitled to be treated as POWs if they meet the necessary criteria. Thus, a precondition is the recruitment into the armed forces of one of the parties to the conflict, which nevertheless is unlawful for children under 15 years of age, as enshrined in Article 77 AP I. If not unlawfully recruited into the official armed forces of a conflict party, but nonetheless directly participating in the hostilities, the child temporarily, for the duration of his or her direct participation, loses protection from attack, but not the special protection granted to him or her as a child in the event of capture.[26]

C. Relevance in Non-International Armed Conflicts

Over the last few decades we have seen an increase in non-international armed conflicts (NIACs). Therefore, one has to ask how much of the established legal framework on the protection of children is applicable to these conflicts.

Customary IHL certainly applies to conflicts of a non-international character. State practice establishes the rule that children affected by armed conflict are entitled to special respect and protection. This rule constitutes a norm of CIL, applicable to both types of conflict, international and non-international.[27] It is, furthermore, supported by

---

[25] S. Sayapin, 'The International Committee of the Red Cross and International Human Rights Law', 9 *Human Rights Law Review* (2009) 95, at 113.
[26] N. Melzer, 'Interpretive Guidance on the Notion of Direct Participation in Hostilities under International Humanitarian Law', 90 *IRRC* 872 (2008) 991, at 1027.
[27] ICRC CIHL Study, at 479.

47 To identify written obligations and rights, treaty law applicable to NIAC must be analysed as a major source. Common Article 3 does not entail a specific reference to the rights of children, but sets forth fundamental guarantees relating to the treatment of persons taking no active part in the hostilities. Under this Article, civilians, including children, have at least the basic right to be treated humanely. There should not be any violence to their lives and persons or their dignity.

48 Nonetheless, children as a distinct group are not without specific protection during NIACs. Additional Protocol II mirrors some of the provisions of GC IV discussed above and lays down a protective standard in those conflicts governed by the Protocol. Article 4, entitled 'Fundamental guarantees', includes paragraph 3, which is devoted exclusively to children. It stipulates that '[c]hildren shall be provided with the care and aid they require'. This Article then enumerates special measures relating to children, giving substance to the general rule stated above. The structure of Article 4 shows how important the authors of AP II considered the protection of children during NIACs, and it thereby enables us to maintain that the principle of special protection of children during these conflicts is affirmed.

49 Of most importance—and here reflecting the protective standard of GC IV—are family ties, and the maintenance of a child's positive physical and mental development against the effects of hostilities. Children's education, not only academic but also religious and moral, is protected and shall continue even if they are separated from their families (Article 4(3)(a) AP II, comparable to Article 24 GC IV). If families are separated, family reunion is of utmost importance, and Article 4(3)(b) binds the parties to the conflict to take all appropriate steps to facilitate that reunion, although without going into more detail, as is done by its counterparts, Articles 24–26, 50, and 136 GC IV.

50 Additional Protocol II also deals with the involvement of children in the hostilities, and interestingly, on this point, goes further than the provisions laid down by AP I. Article 77 paragraph 2 AP I provides that the parties to the conflict shall take all feasible measures to ensure that children who have not attained the age of 15 years do not take direct part in hostilities and, in particular, the parties shall refrain from recruiting them into their armed forces. This norm does not prohibit forms of indirect participation such as support activities. In contrast, AP II strengthens the protective standard, because it prohibits both direct and indirect participation in hostilities by children below 15 years of age (Article 4(3)(c)). In addition, Article 4(3)(d) AP II provides that children under 15 years of age who, despite the prohibition, directly participate in the hostilities, enjoy the special protection afforded by AP II if captured. Lastly, according to Article 6(4) AP II, the death penalty shall not be pronounced on those who were below 18 years of age at the time of the commission of the offence.

D. Legal Consequences of a Violation

51 As the Security Council has stressed, governments have the primary role in providing protection and relief to all children affected by armed conflict, and 'all actions undertaken by United Nations entities within the framework of the monitoring and reporting mechanism must be designed to support and supplement the protection and rehabilitation

roles of national Governments'.[28] However, as we see every day, parties to conflicts fail to respect and protect individuals in times of armed conflict, and therefore mechanisms on the international level must be considered. To provide an overview of the legal consequences of violations of the Geneva Convention rules on child protection, it is necessary to discuss two further approaches: on the one hand, the responsibility of parties to the conflict; and on the other hand, the criminal responsibility of individuals committing crimes under IHL, in this regard against children.

I. Incidents and modalities of state and non-state actor accountability

For IACs, Article 3 of Hague Convention IV provides that states are liable to pay compensation for violations of IHL. The International Law Commission (ILC) Draft Articles on State Responsibility confirm this obligation, and have had a considerable influence on jurisprudence and legal literature in past years.[29] Nevertheless, while all states may be held to have a legal interest in the protection of children, the enforcement mechanism definitely needs further improvement and support by other mechanisms. International law, including the rules concerning children, cannot be enforced by a central body in the way that domestic law can. This weakness is often exploited.

Compliance by non-state parties to the conflict with IHL provisions is even more difficult to achieve due to the contested standing of non-state armed groups in international law. Outside the classical mechanisms of IHL itself, a new inclusive approach has been developed by the Swiss-based organization Geneva Call, to strengthen compliance and the commitment of non-state armed groups. By signing the so-called Deed of Commitment, non-state armed groups publicly commit to respecting the IHL provisions, and by doing so take ownership of these norms.[30] This general approach is paralleled by a specific focus by the organization on the protection of children in armed conflict. As listed by the 2013 Report of the UN Secretary-General on children and armed conflict, 46 armed non-state groups were named as perpetrators of grave violations against children. The Deed of Commitment for the Protection of Children from the Effects of Armed Conflict was developed specifically to address the obligation of non-state conflict parties, not only to adhere to protective norms, but also, and even more so, to address positive obligations for the groups to provide aid and care. To date, 10 non-state armed groups have signed the Deed of Commitment for the Protection of Children, and Geneva Call is involved with twice that number in order to negotiate further signatures.[31]

The activities of the UN confirm significant steps in the direction of holding parties to armed conflicts accountable. The Security Council is entitled to employ coercive measures to deal with a threat to or breach of the peace. The violation of children's rights in armed conflicts has been considered to constitute a threat to peace. In Resolution 1612 (2005), the Security Council emphasized 'its primary responsibility for the maintenance of international peace and security and, *in this connection*, its commitment to address the widespread impact of armed conflict on children'.[32] The Security Council condemns all violations of

---

[28] UN Doc S/Res/2068 (2012).
[29] R. Wolfrum and D. Fleck, 'Enforcement of International Humanitarian Law', in D. Fleck (ed), *The Handbook of International Humanitarian Law* (2nd edn, Oxford: OUP, 2008) 675, at 678.
[30] Available at <http://www.genevacall.org/>.
[31] For more information, see <http://www.genevacall.org/what-we-do/child-protection/>.
[32] Emphasis added.

international law, including IHL, IHRL, and refugee law, committed against children in situations of armed conflict. It demands that all relevant parties immediately put an end to such practices and take special measures to protect children. Furthermore, the Security Council notes that reference to a situation concerning children and armed conflict is not a legal determination, within the context of the Geneva Conventions and the Additional Protocols thereto, and that reference to a non-state party does not affect its legal status.[33] In accordance with Resolution 1539, the Secretary-General submitted a report in 2005 on the promotion and protection of the rights of children in armed conflict, mentioning the 2003 Children and Armed Conflict Report of the Secretary-General. The report covers six grave violations and abuses (the killing and maiming of children; recruitment of child soldiers; attacks on schools and hospitals; rape or other grave sexual violations; abduction of children; and denial of humanitarian access of children); the action plan for a systematic and comprehensive monitoring and reporting mechanism; incorporation of best practices for disarmament, demobilization, and reintegration programmes; and measures to control illicit sub-regional and cross-border activities that are harmful to children. These measures are supported by other activities of the Security Council.

55 One mechanism of accountability is the reporting mechanism pursuant to Security Council Resolution 1998 (2011), covering the situation in 23 countries. The UN Secretary-General strongly urges states involved in armed conflicts to initiate investigations and prosecutions in order to address the question of impunity of perpetrators of grave violations committed against children.[34] Parties (including non-state armed groups) responsible for the recruitment and use of children, the killing and maiming of children, sexual violence against children, and/or attacks on schools and hospitals have to conclude action plans in accordance with UN Security Council Resolutions 1539 (2004), 1612 (2005), 1882 (2009), and 1998 (2011), in conjunction with the respective country task forces on monitoring and reporting. By Resolution 1998 (2011) the Security Council requested the Secretary-General to designate those parties to conflicts that engage in recurrent attacks on schools and/or hospitals, and/or recurrent attacks or threats of attacks against protected persons in relation to schools and/or hospitals in situations of armed conflict, and to bear in mind all other violations and abuses against children. In the understanding of the UN, schools and hospitals include all educational and medical facilities, determined by the local context, as well as informal facilities provided for education and health care. An attack on a school or hospital constitutes a violation of IHL. Even in cases where attacks on schools and/or hospitals may not result in child casualties, they may affect children through the disruption of educational and/or medical services.[35] The states concerned should allow independent access to the UN for the purpose of monitoring and reporting on grave violations against children. The Security Council calls for increased pressure on those parties who are persistent perpetrators of grave violations against children, and may apply targeted measures.

56 Other UN activities further contribute to the improvement of the protection of children. The 2012 Report of the Special Representative of the Secretary-General for Children and Armed Conflict concludes that since the General Assembly's call to relevant parties in conflicts to take time-bound and effective measures to end grave violations against children, considerable progress has been made in eliciting commitments from armed forces

---

[33] UN Doc S/PRST/2013/8.   [34] UN Doc S/2012/261, para 237.   [35] Ibid, para 226.

and groups to end the recruitment and use of children. To date six government forces, as well as 14 non-state armed groups, have signed action plans with the United Nations to halt child soldiering.[36] The action plans set out a comprehensive process by which the party to a conflict will cease the recruitment and involvement of children in a durable manner. The process broadly involves four main stages: the verification and identification of children in the ranks of the armed forces or group; the separation of children from the armed forces or group; the establishment of prevention mechanisms, including the strengthening of the domestic legal framework prohibiting child recruitment, the issuance of directives to uniformed personnel, and the establishment of punitive measures for offenders; and the socioeconomic and psychosocial reintegration of children into civilian life. The action plans also serve as key documents to monitor commitments by armed forces and groups to end grave violations against children.

57 The 2013 Report of the Secretary-General on children and armed conflict, submitted pursuant to Security Council Resolution 2068 (2012), deals again with the implementation of the Security Council resolutions and presidential statements on children and armed conflict, in particular by strengthening the monitoring and reporting of all grave violations against children.[37] The Report describes a number of emerging challenges regarding the impact of the evolving nature of armed conflict. It also explores tools to enforce compliance by armed forces and armed groups with child rights obligations. Compliance by parties with their international obligations on child rights should be effected by increased political pressure by the Council through full use of the 'toolkit' of the Working Group on Children and Armed Conflict,[38] by strengthening the sanctions regime expanding the criteria of sanctions committees and establishing a thematic or ad hoc sanctions committee for violations against children, as well as by closer cooperation between the Council and the ICC in relation to crimes committed against children. In 2013, Liechtenstein and a non-governmental organization published recommendations for addressing the issue of persistent perpetrators, focusing on the need for enhanced Security Council action and the efficient use of targeted measures.[39]

58 The UN Secretary-General has received an increasingly worrisome number of reports of child casualties in the course of military operations using weaponized unmanned aerial vehicles, or armed drones. He calls upon relevant states to take all measures necessary to ensure that attacks involving drones comply with the principles of precaution, distinction, and proportionality, and to conduct transparent, prompt, and effective investigations when casualties may have occurred. In addition, the mixed use of armed and surveillance drones has resulted in permanent fear in some communities, affecting the psychosocial well-being of children and hindering the ability of such communities to protect their children. Reports further indicate that the use of drones has a wider impact on children, especially their access to education. For example, in some situations, both boys and girls have ceased attending school owing to the fear of drone strikes.[40] In February 2014 the Security Council reiterated its concern about the situation of vulnerable groups affected by armed conflict, among them children. The Council expressed particular concern about

---

[36] Action Plans with Armed Forces and Armed Groups, Office of the Special Representative of the Secretary-General for Children and Armed Conflict, available at <http://childrenandarmedconflict.un.org/our-work/action-plans/>.
[37] UN Doc S/2013/245.   [38] UN Doc S/2006/724.
[39] UN Doc S/2013/158.   [40] UN Doc S/2013/245, para 11.

sexual and gender-based violence, and violations and abuses against children in situations of armed conflict. The Council recognized the importance of ending impunity for such acts through strengthened police, justice, and corrections capacity, and the incorporation of child protection perspectives in all rule-of-law programmes, including through justice sector reform, child protection, and gender-based violence training. Furthermore, the Council underlined its intention, when establishing and renewing the mandates of UN missions, to include provisions for the protection of children in conflict and post-conflict situations, including through the appointment of child protection and gender advisers, and provisions to protect children's rights, and to facilitate women's full participation and access to justice through legal, judicial, and security sector reforms, and wider post-conflict reconstruction processes.[41]

II. Criminal responsibility

59 Children may be the victims of a grave breach under Article 50 GC I, Article 51 GC II, Article 130 GC III, or Article 147 GC IV, or of other war crimes under CIL.[42]

60 Under the ICC Statute, 'conscripting or enlisting children under the age of 15 years into armed forces or groups or using them to participate actively in hostilities is a war crime, both in international and internal armed conflict' (Article 8). Charges under this provision were brought against Thomas Lubanga Dyilo, the President of the '*Union des Patriotes Congolais*', who was convicted of violating Article 8(2)(e)(vii) by committing the crimes of conscripting and enlisting children under the age of 15 years into his armed group.[43]

61 The Special Court for Sierra Leone (SCSL) was, however, the first international court to determine that the recruitment and use of children under 15 years constitutes a war crime not only under Article 4(c) of its Statute, but also under CIL. Consequently, for the first time in history, a small number of children also testified as witnesses before the Court.[44] In addition, in view of the large number of children who participated in the civil war in Sierra Leone, the Court was given jurisdiction over alleged crimes committed by any person of 15 years of age or older who was associated with armed actors at the time of the alleged commission of the crimes (Article 7 of the Statute of the SCSL). With regard to persons aged between 15 and 18, the Statute provides for re-adaptation and reintegration measures. These should be taken into consideration and be preferred to repressive measures, independent of the fact that the SCSL is competent to try persons under the age of 18. However, this competence has not been exercised because the Tribunal limits its prosecutions, in accordance with Article 1(1) of its Statute, to persons who bear the greatest responsibility for the crimes committed in Sierra Leone since 30 November 1996. Early in his tenure, the first Chief Prosecutor of the Court stated that, as a matter of policy, he did not intend to indict persons for crimes that they had committed when they were children, but instead meant to prosecute those who bore the greatest responsibility for those crimes, interpreted as the adult recruiters and commanders.[45]

62 On 26 April 2012, the SCSL found the former President of Liberia, Charles Taylor, guilty of aiding and abetting war crimes committed by the Revolutionary United Front

---

[41] UN Doc S/PRST/2014/5.
[42] A.S.J. Park, 'Child Soldiers and Distributive Justice: Addressing the Limits of Law?', 53 *Crime, Law and Social Change* (2010) 329, at 330 f.
[43] ICC, *The Prosecutor v Thomas Lubanga Dyilo*, Judgment, 14 March 2012, ICC-01/04-01/06, paras 1358 et seq; and UN Doc A/67/256, para 2.
[44] UN Doc A/67/256, para 4.   [45] Ibid, para 5.

(RUF) during the 1991–2002 civil war in Sierra Leone. The Court's judgment against Charles Taylor marks the first time that a former head of state has been convicted of war crimes against children committed by an armed group that was found not to be under his direct command and control.[46] The verdicts passed in 2012 by international courts against the Congolese warlord Thomas Lubanga and the former President of Liberia, Charles Taylor, in addition to the recent transfer of Bosco Ntaganda, represent significant progress, and send a clear signal that child recruitment is a war crime and that perpetrators of violations against children will be held accountable. International justice complements national accountability mechanisms in cases where national authorities are unwilling or unable to bring alleged perpetrators to justice. While a key challenge in conflict areas is weak political will, often a lack of capacity and resources severely cripples the ability of national authorities to prosecute child rights violations. In this context, the provision of capacity-building support by the United Nations to governments may assist in reducing the accountability gap.[47]

E. Critical Assessment

63 Children are entitled to the general protection afforded to civilians during times of armed conflict. In addition, the Geneva Conventions include detailed obligations towards children as victims of the conflict. Such children are widely covered by these provisions. The recruitment and participation of children in hostilities, and the problem of children as perpetrators of IHL violations, however, are not addressed by the Geneva Conventions. In this regard, the provisions of the Conventions were improved by APs I and II. Standing alone, GC IV cannot provide a sufficient framework but must be applied in conjunction with subsequent texts, as well as other sources of international law. The establishment of a body of CIL applicable in armed conflicts is another important pillar, as is the influence of IHRL. In the 1980s, the overlap between both fields of international law, IHRL on the one hand and IHL on the other, became more and more obvious.[48] A landmark concerning the protection of the child is represented by the codification of the CRC in 1989. It was the first human rights treaty containing IHL obligations, and was therefore a breakthrough. Article 38 CRC raises the question of the relationship between IHRL and IHL. It is doubtless an interesting development, that a human rights body—the Committee on the Rights of the Child—deals with the implementation of obligations which mirror those in Article 77 AP I. This points towards strong support for the weak mechanisms of IHL implementation. The practice of the Committee reflects its willingness to incorporate and synthesize IHL; however, it cannot take binding decisions, and thus it seeks compliance rather than apportioning blame. Ultimately, it contributes to the solidification of CIL.[49] In its most direct reference to Article 38 CRC, the Committee recommended, for example, that Israel should:

---

[46] SCSL, *The Prosecutor v Charles Taylor*, Appeals Chamber Judgment, SCSL-03-01-A, 26 September 2013; UN Doc A/67/265, para 2.

[47] UN Doc S/2013/245, para 14.

[48] H.-J. Heintze, 'On the Relationship between Human Rights Law Protection and International Humanitarian Law', 86 *IRRC* 856 (2004) 789, at 793.

[49] D. Weissbrodt, J.C. Hansen, and N.H. Nebitt, 'The Role of the Committee on the Rights of the Child in Interpreting and Developing International Humanitarian Law', 24 *Harv HRJ* (2011) 115, at 153.

(a) Establish and strictly enforce rules of engagement for military and other personnel which fully respect the rights of children as contained in the Convention and protected under IHL; (b) Refrain from using and/or targeting children in armed conflict and comply fully with article 38 of the Convention, and as much as possible with the Optional Protocol on the involvement of children in armed conflict.[50]

64   A growing concern is the number of persistent perpetrators of grave violations against children. The 12th Secretary-General's Report listed 29 parties to conflicts as violators.[51] Therefore, the Office of the Special Representative continues to encourage parties who have not yet entered into dialogue with the United Nations, or signed an action plan, to do so.

65   In sum, the development, implementation, and enforcement of the protection of children involved in armed conflicts has been improved in the last years. The current mechanisms are much stronger than those of 1977. However, against the background of the huge number of children who are involved and used in armed hostilities, the topic is still on—and must stay on—the agenda.

HANS-JOACHIM HEINTZE   CHARLOTTE LÜLF

---

[50] UN Doc CRC/15/Add.195, para 59.   [51] UN Doc A/67/845–S/2013/245, 15 May 2013.

Chapter 63. Special Rules on Refugees

	MN
A. Introduction	1
B. Meaning and Application	10
C. Relevance in Non-International Armed Conflicts	18
I. Refugees and the application of international humanitarian law in non-international armed conflict	19
II. Internally displaced persons as an analogous group to refugees in non-international armed conflict	23
D. Legal Consequences of a Violation	26
E. Critical Assessment	31

Select Bibliography

Cohen, R./Deng, F.M., *Masses in Flight: The Global Crisis of Internal Displacement* (Washington, DC: Brookings, 1998)

Goodwin-Gill, G.S./McAdam, J., *The Refugee in International Law* (3rd edn, Oxford: OUP, 2007)

Jaquemet, S., 'The Cross-Fertilization of International Humanitarian Law and International Refugee Law', 83 *IRRC* (2001) 651

Kälin, W., 'Flight in Times of War', 83 *IRRC* (2001) 629

Lambert, H./Farrell, T., 'The Changing Character of Armed Conflict and the Implications for Refugee Protection Jurisprudence', 22 *IJRL* (2010) 237

Sassòli/Bouvier/Quintin, at 226–30, with references to cases in vols II and III

Wouters, K., *International Legal Standards for the Protection from Refoulement* (Oxford: Hart Publishing Ltd, 2009)

A. Introduction

Since the Second World War, international law has seen a proliferation of treaties and other instruments governing refugees. The 1949 Geneva Convention (GC) IV laid down the first rules concerning refugees, though these were quickly eclipsed by the 1951 Convention Relating to the Status of Refugees (Refugee Convention). As such, while the special rules regarding refugees in GC IV remain applicable in the context of armed conflict, it is the Refugee Convention which largely develops and implements rules concerning the protection of refugees in the modern era, under the supervision of the United Nations (UN) High Commissioner for Refugees.   1

Refugees are, by definition, individuals who cross international borders to seek protection and refuge in another state. Refugees who flee their country are protected under international humanitarian law (IHL) as civilians affected by an armed conflict where their host state takes part in an international armed conflict (IAC), or is beset by   2 non-international armed conflict (NIAC).¹ The special rules regarding refugees developed under GC IV seek to provide additional protection to refugees based on their unique status, by ensuring that refugees are not treated unfavourably because of their nationality, and that refugees are specifically protected when the host state becomes occupied by the state of their nationality.² Further, the Convention codifies the principle of protection against refoulement.³

3 The special rules governing refugees in GC IV were created in response to the situation of refugees during the Second World War, and in part codified operational rules and laws developed during the War concerning the treatment of refugees.⁴ The Geneva Conventions, coupled with the 1948 Universal Declaration on Human Rights, were thus seen 'as the response of the world community to massive violations of the elementary principles of humane treatment of individuals in times of crisis'.⁵ During the Second World War, various belligerent countries made special allowances, exempting refugees from measures taken against enemy aliens by setting up special tribunals to distinguish between enemy aliens ('real enemies') and refugees who originally came from an enemy country ('friendly enemies').⁶ Those identified as refugees enjoyed a more favourable status than enemy aliens.⁷

4 Article 44 GC IV codifies the underlying purpose of such rules aimed at distinguishing—and affording more favourable treatment to—refugees, by requiring a Detaining Power not to 'treat as enemy aliens exclusively on the basis of their nationality "de jure" of an enemy State, refugees who do not, in fact, enjoy the protection of any government'. This Article aims to protect, during hostilities, refugees against treatment as enemy aliens based solely on nationality, which prior to 1949 would have been the norm.

5 Article 70 paragraph 2 GC IV provides complementary protection to refugees by prohibiting an Occupying Power from arresting, prosecuting, convicting, or deporting nationals of the Occupying Power—who are therefore not protected persons under the text of Article 4—if they sought refuge in the occupied state for offences committed before the outbreak of hostilities, and which would not, during peacetime, justify extradition. Thus, while Article 44 addresses the refugees' relations with the authorities of the country which receives them, Article 70 governs their position vis-à-vis their country of origin when that country becomes the Occupying Power.⁸

6 Refugees in some circumstances may be considered within the class of 'protected persons' by virtue of Article 4 GC IV, which defines 'protected persons' as 'those who, at a given moment and in any manner whatsoever, find themselves, in case of a conflict or occupation, in the hands of a Party to the conflict or Occupying Power of which they are not nationals'.⁹ Article 70 paragraph 2, applicable to occupied territories, is complemented for enemy aliens who find themselves on a state's own territory by Article 45 paragraph 4

---

¹ Sassòli/Bouvier/Quintin, at 226–30, with further references.
² Arts 44 and 70 para 2 GC IV.   ³ Art 45 GC IV.   ⁴ Pictet Commentary GC IV, at 263.
⁵ S.R. Chowdhury, 'A Response to the Refugee Programs in Post Cold War Era: Some Existing and Emerging Norms of International Law', 7(1) *IJRL* (1995) 100, at 106.
⁶ Pictet Commentary GC IV, at 263.   ⁷ Ibid.   ⁸ Pictet Commentary GC IV, at 350.
⁹ Although the interpretation of Art 4 has been subject to controversy in the *Tadić* case (ICTY, *The Prosecutor v Duško Tadić*, Appeals Chamber Judgment, IT-94-1-A, 15 July 1999), a conservative approach to its application is taken here.

GC IV, which prevents the transfer of protected persons to a state where they fear persecution based on religious or political opinion.

In addition to Article 45 paragraph 4, Article 49 paragraph 1 GC IV generally prohibits forcible transfers of protected persons out of occupied territories, 'regardless of their motive'. Thus, together, Article 70 paragraph 2, Article 45 paragraph 4, and Article 49 paragraph 1 provide effective protection, based on the principle of non-refoulement which has subsequently been fully developed under international refugee law.

Additional Protocol (AP) I extended further protection to refugees by including them within the general category of 'protected persons', having recognized problematic gaps existing in the regime created by the Geneva Conventions. Article 73 AP I specifically incorporates refugees and stateless persons into the definition of 'protected persons' for the purposes of Parts I and III GC IV, 'in all circumstances and without any adverse distinction'.[10] Under GC IV, the category of persons protected (as defined in Article 4 paragraphs 1 and 2) is based on nationality, and therefore did not account for the situation of refugees in all circumstances.[11] This left refugees at the mercy of the belligerent state, to determine whether or not they should be considered 'protected persons'.[12] Thus, Article 73 AP I remedies this situation by expressly including refugees within the class of 'protected persons' as regards more general rules outlined in the Convention. Consequently, for those states that are party to AP I, refugees would now be fully entitled to the benefits granted to 'protected persons', including protection against refoulement found under Article 45 paragraph 4 GC IV.

As already noted above, shortly after the introduction of the Geneva Conventions, the Refugee Convention was introduced, providing much more detailed rules governing this group of individuals. The rules set out in the Refugee Convention provide a much narrower definition of refugees than found in GC IV, and operate to manage state obligations towards refugees in any circumstances, regardless of the existence of conflict. The creation of the UN High Commissioner for Refugees (UNHCR) in 1950 and the adoption of the 1951 Refugee Convention have led to the development of a distinct body of international refugee law, which is now the primary body of law addressing refugee and refugee-like situations. Thus, the special rules regarding refugees under GC IV operate to enforce rules which are now well established within international refugee law, but do so in the specific context of armed conflict and hostilities.

B. Meaning and Application

Refugees are recognized as a distinct category of persons whose status warrants special consideration in a conflict. The GC IV special rules on refugees were primarily concerned with the situation that arose when refugees, who fled their state of nationality and sought asylum in another country, found the country of refuge engaged in war with their country of origin, such that the refugees would—but for their special recognition—be considered enemy aliens by the authorities of the host state during the conflict. However, as exiles, refugees no longer have any connection with or protection from their state of nationality; they also have not established any permanent connection (such as acquiring a new

---

[10] Part II GC IV already applies to refugees as part of the collective 'civilian population'.
[11] ICRC Commentary APs, at 846.   [12] Ibid.

11   For the purposes of the Geneva Conventions, the definition of 'refugee' as developed under the Refugee Convention has been found to be too technical and restrictive;[13] thus, the Commentary to the Conventions recommends a broad interpretation of the term 'refugee' which is capable of including any person who does not 'enjoy the protection of any government' and is, in law, a national of an enemy state party to the conflict. For the purposes of the Geneva Conventions, refugees may therefore essentially be characterized as people who have fled their home country to seek refuge on alien soil as a result of political events or a threat of persecution, and who thus find themselves without the protection normally afforded by the state to which they belonged, but who are not yet entitled to the legal protection of the state which has given them refuge.[14]

nationality) with the country of refuge. Thus refugees, in this situation, effectively do not enjoy the *de facto* protection of any government.

12   Article 44 GC IV seeks to clarify that 'the status of a refugee as an alien is largely artificial and should not lead to automatic curtailment of his or her rights'.[15] Essentially, this Article attempts to ensure that the designation of 'enemy' status does not rest solely on the formal criterion of nationality, rather adjusting the test to ensure that a wider variety of considerations are taken into account which can reveal the 'spiritual affinity' or 'ideological allegiance' of the individual.[16] This is particularly important for refugees who find themselves in the territory of a state engaged in an IAC with the refugees' state of origin, as the refugees will likely be formally recognized as 'nationals' of the state of origin, but would be unlikely to hold an 'ideological alliance' to that state from which they fled. While nationals who enjoy the protection of their government and sympathize with the cause of their country may represent a danger to the safety of the country in which they are residing, the opposite is to be presumed in the case of refugees.[17] As such, the term 'refugee' in this context implies that the persons concerned are opposed to the political system in force in their home country.[18] However, the status of 'refugee' in this context does not, in and of itself, give a person complete immunity from security measures, nor does it prevent the adoption of security measures such as internment.[19]

13   Article 44 GC IV is also complemented by the inclusion of a similar provision in Article 8 of the subsequent Refugee Convention, which states that exceptional measures—'which may be taken against the person, property or interests of nationals of a foreign State'— shall not be applied to a refugee who is formally a national of the said state, solely on account of such nationality.[20] This provision of the Refugee Convention clearly reflects Article 44 GC IV and establishes a link between the two regimes.[21]

14   Article 70 paragraph 2 GC IV seeks to elaborate on the protection intended to be afforded to refugees in occupied territories who are not protected persons in a situation of conflict, by prohibiting their arrest, prosecution, conviction, or deportation from the occupied territory. This prohibition is 'derived from the idea that the right to asylum enjoyed [...] before the occupation began must continue to be respected by their home

---

[13] Pictet Commentary GC IV, at 264.
[14] Ibid, at 264.
[15] S. Jaquemet, 'The Cross-Fertilization of International Humanitarian Law and International Refugee Law', 83 *IRRC* (2001) 651, at 655.
[16] Pictet Commentary GC IV, at 264.   [17] Ibid.   [18] Ibid.   [19] Ibid, at 264–5.
[20] Art 8 Convention Relating to the Status of Refugees (1951).
[21] Jaquemet, above n 15, at 655; see also W. Kälin, 'Flight in Times of War', 83 *IRRC* (2011) 629, at 633.

country when it takes over control as Occupying Power in the territory of the country of asylum'.[22] There are, however, two exceptions to this general rule:

— where offences are committed after the outbreak of hostilities; and
— where a national of an Occupying Power committed offences under common law 'before the outbreak of hostilities which, according to the law of the occupied state, would have justified extradition in time of peace'.[23]

The latter exception corresponds with the laws that would operate during peacetime, under which extradition of refugees or asylum claimants would ordinarily be authorized for ordinary criminal offences, as distinct from offences of a political, religious, or military character.[24] Article 70 paragraph 2 further specifies that offences must be such in the 'law of the occupied state', ensuring that occupation authorities do not arrest and deport refugees for arbitrary offences, but only where such offences are commonly recognized as being criminal offences. This 'double incrimination' criterion is a standard feature of domestic and international treaties dealing with extradition. In order for an offence to be determined as warranting extradition under the law of the occupied state, the law of the occupied state would thus implicitly have to recognize the alleged offence as one of a 'common' nature (as opposed to, for example, one of a political nature warranting protection).[25] Further, occupying authorities must 'produce proof that the charges are sufficient to warrant such action', thus providing a safeguard against arbitrary arrest and deportation.[26]

Article 49 paragraph 1 GC IV expressly prohibits forcible transfers and deportations of protected persons from an occupied territory, regardless of their motive. Article 49 paragraph 2 also provides a very narrow and limited exception to the prohibition, allowing for evacuation outside of the occupied territory only 'when for material reasons it is impossible to avoid such displacement', and on condition that '[p]ersons thus evacuated shall be transferred back to their homes as soon as hostilities in the area in question have ceased'. Article 49 paragraph 1 is also bolstered by Article 70 paragraph 2 in relation to refugees.[27]

On a belligerent's own territory, Article 70 paragraph 2 and Article 49 paragraph 1 are complemented by Article 45 paragraph 4 GC IV, which prevents the transfer of protected persons to a state where they fear religious or political persecution. The class of 'protected persons' under GC IV includes both 'persons of enemy nationality living in the territory of a belligerent State' and individuals who have no nationality.[28] Thus, refugees who find their state of refuge engaged in conflict with their state of nationality may be included in the category of 'protected persons' for the purposes of Article 45 paragraph 4 GC IV, in the limited circumstances available.[29] Further, for those states that have ratified AP I, the obligation under Article 45 paragraph 4 will now expressly include refugees.

Under the Geneva Conventions, many provisions relevant for civilians were developed within the context of IACs and designed for non-nationals of the state holding power over the respective territory.[30] Many provisions of the Geneva Conventions therefore may not be applicable to persons displaced in an area controlled by their own government.[31]

---

[22] Pictet Commentary GC IV, at 351.   [23] Ibid, at 351–2.
[24] Ibid.   [25] Ibid.   [26] Ibid, at 352.   [27] Ibid, at 279.   [28] Ibid, at 46–7.
[29] E.g., this protection would not be available if the state of nationality was an Occupying Power of the state of refuge; however, in this case, Art 70 para 2 would provide protection against refoulement.
[30] R. Cohen and F.M. Deng, *Masses in Flight: The Global Crisis of Internal Displacement* (Washington, DC: Brookings, 1998), at 84.
[31] Ibid.

While Article 49 GC IV prohibits the forcible transfer of protected persons out of an occupied territory, it does provide, to a limited extent, for the displacement of protected persons within an occupied territory. However, some provisions contained in Part II of GC IV, which 'cover the whole of the populations of the countries in conflict', have general application to displaced persons; further, as AP I does not distinguish between civilians on the basis of nationality, much of the protection set out in Part IV of AP I also applies to displaced persons.[32]

C. Relevance in Non-International Armed Conflicts

18 The Geneva Conventions and AP I apply specifically to IACs. Common Article 3 and the subsequent AP II apply to NIACs.

I. Refugees and the application of international humanitarian law in non-international armed conflict

19 As noted in section B of this chapter, refugees are protected by the pertinent rules of GC IV, generally when the state in which they are located is involved in an IAC or beset by internal armed conflict.[33] However, refugees who flee to a state not taking part in an armed conflict are not protected by IHL. In such cases, they receive protection from international refugee law, as well as through the activities of the UNHCR.[34]

20 Much of the development as concerns treatment and protection of refugees has been formulated under international human rights law (IHRL) and international refugee law. While there is a voluminous database of information and cases regarding the acceptance and treatment of refugee claimants related to NIAC, these cases pertain almost exclusively to refugees who have fled the conflict and sought refuge in a state not party to the conflict. The discussion turns on determining *who* is a refugee under the Refugee Convention when the claimant has fled a civil war or NIAC situation, and particularly on the interpretation and application of the rules covering exclusion.[35]

21 Refugees who find themselves in a state beset by NIAC will have access to protection by virtue of Common Article 3 and AP II, and as part of the civilian population under those provisions where they take no active part in hostilities. Further, refugees in such a context will have the continued benefit of application of specific provisions of international refugee law, such as the protection against refoulement to a state where they fear persecution.

22 However, other international aspects of the law of armed conflict do apply to refugees—as members of the 'civilian population'—during internal armed conflict. As

---

[32] Ibid, at 84–5.

[33] J.-Ph. Lavoyer, 'Refugees and Internally Displaced Persons: International Humanitarian Law and the Role of the ICRC', 305 *IRRC* (1995) 162, at 168; Sassòli/Bouvier/Quintin, at 226–30.

[34] Lavoyer, above n 33, at 169.

[35] For examination of these issues, see, e.g., G.S. Goodwin-Gill and J. McAdam, *The Refugee in International Law* (3rd edn, Oxford: OUP, 2007); K. Woulters, *International Legal Standards for the Protection from Refoulement* (Oxford: Hart Publishing Ltd, 2009); H. Lambert and T. Farrell, 'The Changing Character of Armed Conflict and the Implications for Refugee Protection Jurisprudence', 22(2) *IJRL* (2010) 237; M.R. von Sternberg, 'The Plight of the Non-Combatant in Civil War and the New Criteria for Refugee Status', 9 *IJRL* 2 (1997) 169; M.R. von Sternberg, 'Political Asylum and the Law of Internal Armed Conflict: Refugee Status, Human Rights and Humanitarian Law Concerns', 5 *IJRL* 2 (1993) 153.

discussed in the *Tadić* case, this means: fundamental rights continue to apply in civil wars; a distinction must be maintained between civilian populations and military operations at all times; civilian populations should not be made the object of attack; dwellings and other installations used only for civilian purposes should not be the object of a military attack; military operations must not be conducted against places designed for the sole protection of civilians, including refugee centres; and the civilian population should not be subjected to reprisal, forcible transfer, or assault on their integrity.[36]

II. Internally displaced persons as an analogous group to refugees in non-international armed conflict

23 With the rise in internal armed conflict, citizens or nationals of a state affected and displaced by the hostilities within their territory have become known as 'internally displaced persons' or IDPs. '[D]isplacement is often a consequence of violations of humanitarian law during armed conflict, or failure to comply with other norms intended to protect people in situations of violence.'[37] 'When civilians flee a conflict zone, it is a good indication that the warring parties are indifferent to their rights under humanitarian law, or are deliberately ignoring their responsibilities.'[38] Legally binding on both state and non-state actors, IHL should adequately address, in general, many of the problems associated with internal displacement during armed conflict, through prohibitions on attacking civilians or civilian property, indiscriminate attacks, starving civilians as a method of warfare, and carrying out reprisals against civilians.[39] It is the violation of such rules which often cause civilians to flee. Internally displaced persons are, practically speaking, considered as the equivalent of refugees in the context of NIAC, as they do not effectively enjoy the protection of any government.

24 Internally displaced persons are internationally defined as

persons or groups of persons who have been forced or obliged to flee or to leave their homes or places of habitual residence, in particular as a result of or in order to avoid the effects of armed conflict, situations of generalized violence, violations of human rights or natural or human-made disasters, and who have not crossed an internationally recognized State border.[40]

From this definition, two primary elements emerge:

(1) the coercive or otherwise involuntary character of that person's movement, and
(2) the fact that such movement takes place within national borders.[41]

25 International humanitarian law is primarily aimed at addressing and protecting those displaced by an IAC; civilians displaced by internal armed conflict enjoy similar but less detailed protection.[42] As nationals of the state in which hostilities are occurring, IDPs are considered part of the civilian population and are intended to be afforded all of the protections available to that class of persons under relevant IHL. Specific protections to address internal conflict and displacement are set out under AP II, which, for example, expressly

---

[36] ICTY, *The Prosecutor v Duško Tadić*, Appeals Chamber Decision on the Defence Motion for Interlocutory Appeal on Jurisdiction, IT-94-1-AR72, 2 October 1995.
[37] J. Kellenberger, 'The ICRC's Response to Internal Displacement: Strengths, Challenges and Constraints', 91 *IRRC* (2009) 475, at 478–9.
[38] Ibid, at 479.   [39] Ibid, at 478–9.
[40] UN Guiding Principles on Internal Displacement, UN Doc E/CN.4/1998/53/Add. 2.
[41] Kälin, above n 21, at 644.   [42] Sassòli/Bouvier/Quintin, at 226–30.

prohibits any party to an armed conflict from compelling or intentionally inducing displacement of the civilian population.[43]

D. Legal Consequences of a Violation

26 Under IHL, the state with effective control over a territory is legally responsible for the human rights and protection of its inhabitants.[44] This includes a responsibility to uphold the obligations set out under the Geneva Conventions, including with respect to the special rules for refugees discussed in this chapter. Under general IHL, 'States have a collective responsibility for compliance by other States and armed opposition movements [...] They also have the obligation to bring persons accused of having committed grave breaches thereof before their own courts, and they may also hand such persons over to another State for trial.'[45]

27 Under the 1998 Rome Statute of the International Criminal Court (ICC), as well as under customary law, the deportation or transfer of all or parts of the population of an occupied territory constitutes a war crime during IAC.[46] Consequently, anyone who deports refugees in violation of the Geneva Conventions and the ICC Statute may be found to have carried out a war crime.[47] The same applies in NIAC. However, the extent to which war crimes exist for similar acts in NIAC under customary law remains debatable.[48] As concerns Article 44 GC IV, the legal consequences of a violation under international law are uncertain. This is particularly so since war-time measures such as internment remain available in limited circumstances for civilians who are nationals of an enemy state.

28 The forced displacement or transfer of civilians has also been found to constitute a crime against humanity when the requisite elements are met.[49] Refoulement to a country where persecution is feared is also recognized as a crime against humanity.[50] It is now settled that crimes against humanity do not require a connection to any armed conflict.[51]

29 At the international level, there are no individual complaints mechanisms available to the victims of violations of IHL.[52] Refugees may be able to resort to international human rights treaty bodies which allow for individual complaint processes and remedies, where

---

[43] Kellenberger, above n 37, at 479; Art 17 AP II.
[44] Woulters, above n 35, at 19, citing D. Fleck (ed), *The Handbook of Humanitarian Law in Armed Conflicts* (Oxford: OUP, 1999), at 242; T. Meron, 'Applicability of Multilateral Conventions to Occupied Territories', 72 *AJIL* (1978) 542, at 543.
[45] Lavoyer, above n 33, at 164.
[46] Art 8(2)(e)(viii) ICC Statute.   [47] See ICRC CIHL Study, vol I, at 460.
[48] J. Willms, 'Without Order, Anything Goes? The Prohibition of Forced Displacement in Non-International Armed Conflict', 91 *IRRC* (2009) 547, at 549.
[49] See ICTY, *The Prosecutor v Ante Gotovina et al*, Trial Chamber Decision, IT-06-90-PT, 19 March 2007, paras 24–8; ICTY, *The Prosecutor v Vidoje Blagojević and Dragan Jokić*, Trial Chamber Judgment, IT-02-60-T, 17 January 2005; Art 7 ICC Statute, 'where the deportation is carried out as part of a widespread or systematic attack on any civilian population'; Jaquemet, above n 15, at 670.
[50] Woulters, above n 35, at 67; see also ICTY, *The Prosecutor v Tihomir Blaškić*, Appeals Chamber Judgment, IT-95-14-A, 29 July 2004.
[51] ICTY, *Tadić*, above n 36, para 141.
[52] H.-J. Heintze, 'On the Relationship between Human Rights Law Protection and International Humanitarian Law', 86 *IRRC* (2004) 789, at 800. See also C. Droege, 'Elective Affinities? Human Rights and Humanitarian Law', 90 *IRRC* (2008) 501, at 543.

the state has consented to such individual communications. However, international jurisdiction is available only 'when all national remedies have been exhausted and only for the reparation of violations of individual human rights'.[53] This has tremendous implications for refugees, who may not have the ability—practical or legal—to access remedies through the domestic or national judicial systems. Like everyone else, refugees may also contact special bodies established by the Human Rights Council—such as the Special Rapporteur on the Human Rights of Migrants, or the Working Group on Arbitrary Detention—in order to ask them to exert pressure on state authorities.

For IDPs, resort may be had to the domestic legal system for violations under AP II in the context of NIACs. For example, the Colombian Constitutional Court condemned the forced displacement of Colombian civilians during an internal armed conflict, which it found to have been caused by violence and violations of IHL.[54] However, as concerns the use of national or domestic legal remedies, '[n]ational courts have a poor record when it comes to the prosecution of war crimes and other international crimes arising out of armed conflicts'.[55] This is typically attributed to political motivations and a strong trend towards favouring peace over justice, that is, reconciliation with former political foes, including through amnesty, rather than their prosecution, as the latter may be construed as retaliation or even continuation of the conflict.[56] As such, both refugees and IDPs may find it difficult, in practice, to pursue legal remedies for breaches of their rights during armed conflict.

E. Critical Assessment

The special rules for refugees developed under Article 44 and Article 70 paragraph 2 GC IV, along with complementary rules under Article 45 paragraph 4 GC IV, and AP I and AP II, seek to provide refugees with protection based on their unique status, as well as their status as protected persons and civilians in general, during armed conflict. Given the specific international refugee law regime developed shortly after the creation of the Geneva Conventions, a significant portion of any critical assessment has to focus on the way in which these two systems work together. International humanitarian law and international refugee law can apply concurrently during armed conflict, and also successively as concerns refugees who flee to a safe third state.[57]

International humanitarian law and refugee law 'come into contact quite naturally' when refugees are produced by, or caught in, an armed conflict.[58] In this context, individuals are both refugees and victims of conflict, and ought to find themselves concurrently under the protection of both humanitarian and refugee law.[59] Where the state in which the conflict is occurring is a party to the Refugee Convention, particularly affected individuals should have access to protection under both international refugee law and IHL. Article 5 of the Refugee Convention expressly contemplates the concurrent application of its protections with other instruments that confer 'rights and benefits' on refugees.[60]

---

[53] Heintze, above n 52.
[54] Constitutional Court of Columbia, Constitution revision of Additional Protocol II and the Law 171 of 16 December 1994, implementing this Protocol, Judgment, Constitutional Case No C-225/95, 18 May 1995, para 33, cited in Willms, above n 48, at 556.
[55] J. Dugard, 'Bridging the Gap between Human Rights and Humanitarian Law: The Punishment of Offenders', 324 *IRRC* (1998) 445, at 453.
[56] Ibid.   [57] Jaquemet, above n 15, at 652.   [58] Ibid.   [59] Ibid.   [60] Ibid, at 653.

In addition, where an individual refugee is inside a conflict zone, the benefits and protections afforded under IHL and international refugee law are quite complementary, thus producing little tension or conflict between the regimes and the specific provisions for the protection of refugees.

33   The special rules regarding refugees under the GC IV are extended to refugees during IAC by virtue of IHL, even where international refugee law will not apply. The Refugee Convention has also been criticized for its specific allowance for deviation from protections and rules regarding refugees during conflict, and its lack of any core, non-derogable rights, including the principle of non-refoulement, although IHRL—applicable to everyone, including refugees—has largely filled those gaps.[61]

34   A significant proportion of international displacement, particularly in the latter half of the twentieth century, has resulted from armed conflict, both international and internal. Individuals often flee conflict zones as the result of breaches of IHL and gross violations of human rights committed against civilians during the conflict.[62] For refugees inside a conflict zone, the wide application of IHL serves as an important protection mechanism. Unlike international refugee law, IHL binds all parties to a conflict, including dissident groups and non-state actors. This is crucial for refugees, who may find themselves under the territorial control of a non-governmental entity.[63]

35   In practice, it appears that IHL offers greater protection for refugees and IDPs who remain inside the conflict zone. However, armed conflict often produces refugees who flee to safe third states as a result of violations of IHL.[64] Thus, where IHL effectively fails to protect, the successive application of refugee law becomes increasingly important as a mechanism of redress and protection for refugees who suffered violations of IHL or human rights during the conflict.

36   International humanitarian law, which provides a much broader definition for refugees, protects only those who are in a territory in which armed conflict is taking place. 'This limitation has resulted in considerable challenges to the refugee protection regime',[65] as refugees often flee conflict zones to safe states not party to the conflict, and these persons will not necessarily fit within the much stricter definition of 'refugee' under the Refugee Convention in such circumstances.[66] This common phenomenon both illustrates the interrelated causal factors which give rise to the operation of IHL and refugee law, and identifies one of the significant gaps which exists between these two legal regimes in addressing the situation of refugees in conflict.

37   To the extent that individuals are both nationals of an enemy or neutral state *and* considered as refugees under the Refugee Convention, IHL and refugee law complement each other well.[67] However, the narrow and complex definition of 'refugee' under the Refugee Convention has been criticized for its lack of effective protection for individuals fleeing armed conflict: '[C]ourts in many countries held for a long time that refugee status could not be granted to those fleeing armed conflict.'[68] Subsequent developments at the regional and national level concerning refugees have to a certain extent sought to rectify this gap in legal protection. For example, the 1969 Organization of African Unity (OAU) Convention Governing Specific Aspects of the Refugee Problem in Africa broadened the definition of 'refugee' to include 'every person who, owing to external aggression, occupation, foreign

---

[61] See Art 9 of the 1951 Convention concerning derogation during conflict. Jaquemet, above n 15, at 654.
[62] Jaquemet, above n 15, at 652.   [63] Ibid, at 657.   [64] Ibid, at 665.
[65] Kälin, above n 21, at 630.   [66] Ibid.   [67] Ibid, at 632.   [68] Ibid, at 635.

domination or events seriously disrupting public order in either part or the whole of his country of origin or nationality, is compelled to leave his place of residence in order to seek refuge in another place outside his country of origin or nationality'.[69] Similarly, Central American countries enlarged the refugee definition, based on the OAU model, under the 1984 Cartagena Declaration on Refugees.[70] At the national level, some individual states have utilized legal tools, such as 'complementary grounds' and 'humanitarian and compassionate grounds', to enable refugee protection for individuals fleeing conflicts who would otherwise fall outside the narrow definition of 'refugee' in limited contexts.

BETHANY HASTIE   FRANÇOIS CRÉPEAU

---

[69] Art I OAU Convention Governing Specific Aspects of the Refugee Problem in Africa 1969; see also Kälin, above n 21, at 637–8.

[70] Kälin, above n 21, at 638.

4. INTERNMENT

Chapter 64. Admissibility of and Procedures for Internment

	MN
A. Introduction	1
B. Meaning and Application	9
I. Meaning of assigned residence, internment, and voluntary internment	9
II. Grounds for internment/assigned residence	12
a. 'Only if the security of the Detaining Power makes it absolutely necessary'/'imperative reasons of security'	12
b. Relationship between Articles 78 and 49 paragraph 1 GC IV	28
c. Distinguishing internment and hostage-taking	30
d. 'Incarceration of Unlawful Combatants Law'	32
III. Procedural requirements	37
a. Nature of deciding body: 'court or administrative board'	38
b. Are IHL rules *lex specialis* vis-à-vis the IHRL right to *habeas corpus*?	40
c. Reconsideration of internment	48
d. According to a 'regular procedure'	51
IV. Geneva Convention IV as the legal basis for internment	57
C. Relevance in Non-International Armed Conflicts	63
D. Legal Consequences of a Violation	71
E. Critical Assessment	77

Select Bibliography

Bellinger III, J.B./Padmanabhan, V.M., 'Detention Operations in Contemporary Conflicts: Four Challenges for the Geneva Conventions and Other Existing Law', 105 *AJIL* (2011) 201
ICRC CIHL Study and Database, Rule 99
ICRC Guidelines, 'International Humanitarian Law and the Challenges of Contemporary Armed Conflicts', 30IC/07/8.4 (October 2007), Annex 1 (originally published as J. Pejic, 'Procedural Principles and Safeguards for Internment/Administrative Detention in Armed Conflict and Other Situations of Violence', 87 *IRRC* 858 (2005) 375)
Pictet Commentary GC IV, at 255–62, 343–7, 367–9
Sassòli, M., 'Internment', in MPEPIL
Sassòli, M./Olson, L.M., 'The Relationship between International Humanitarian and Human Rights Law Where It Matters: Admissible Killing and Internment of Fighters in Non-International Armed Conflict', 90 *IRRC* 871 (2008) 599
Shany, Y., 'The Israeli Unlawful Combatants Law: Old Wine in a New Bottle?', Research Paper No 03-12, The International Law Forum of the Hebrew University of Jerusalem Law Faculty, 15 January 2012

A. Introduction

Under international humanitarian law (IHL), civilians are protected, in particular from direct attack so long as they are not participating in hostilities, because the only legitimate aim that may be pursued in armed conflict is to weaken the military potential of the adversary.¹ Despite the civilian population's entitlement to general immunity, there may arise situations where a party to an armed conflict considers a civilian to be an imperative threat to security. Geneva Convention (GC) IV provides that, if absolutely necessary to neutralize this threat and in accordance with proper procedures, a party to a conflict may take safety measures, which at most may be to intern or place in assigned residence aliens in the territory of a party to the conflict or persons in occupied territory. The Convention also provides for voluntary internment or placement in assigned residence, in situations rendering it necessary for the protected person.

2   While previous attempts had been made to create a treaty dedicated to protecting civilians during armed conflict—similar to those protecting the sick and wounded on the battlefield and prisoners of war (POWs)—none was successful until after the Second World War, with the adoption of GC IV. Many of the provisions of GC IV, including those authorizing and regulating internment, attempted to ensure that the human suffering caused by civilian internment during the First World War and, particularly, the Second World War would not reoccur. For example, GC IV is designed to protect enemy civilians on the territory of a party to the conflict *and* persons in occupied territory. While authorizing internment or assigned residence,² GC IV recognized that such deprivation of liberty without criminal charge as a preventive security measure is extreme, even in armed conflict, and thus set limits on its use, delimiting when it is admissible and requiring that certain procedures be followed. '[I]nternment both in the territory of the parties to the conflict and in occupied territory is subject to rules which would have provided millions of human beings with protection if they could have been applied during the Second World War.'³

3   Unfortunately, however, universal ratification of GC IV did not put an end to human suffering and controversies related to the internment and placing of civilians in assigned residence. The legal issues frequently causing such controversies—even today, say, in response to terrorism—focus on the fundamental usage limits provided in GC IV: the scope of admissible internment, i.e. what constitutes an imperative threat to the security of the detaining power, and the required review procedures.

4   The GC IV provisions on the admissibility of and procedures for internment are organized as follows:

— Section II of Part III (Articles 41–43) concerns aliens in the territory of a party to the conflict;
— Section III of Part III (Articles 68, 78) deals with occupied territory; and
— Section IV of Part III (Article 79) reaffirms that protected persons shall not be interned except in accordance with Articles 41–43, 68, and 78.

5   For aliens in the territory of a party to the conflict, Article 41 provides that the Power in whose hands they find themselves may not have recourse to any other control measure more severe than that of assigned residence or internment. Article 42 stipulates that '[t]he internment or placing in assigned residence of protected persons may

---

¹ F. Bugnion, *The International Committee of the Red Cross and the Protection of War Victims* (Geneva: ICRC, 2003), 195. See, e.g., St Petersburg Declaration of 1868 and Art 46 Hague Regulations.
² The term 'internment' will generally be used in this chapter to refer to internment and assigned residence, unless otherwise specified, in order to avoid unnecessary repetition of terms.
³ Pictet Commentary GC IV, at 372.

be ordered only if the *security* of the Detaining Power makes it *absolutely necessary*;[4] and that if a person's situation so requires, she or he may voluntarily demand internment. In occupied territory, Article 78 states that '[i]f the Occupying Power considers it necessary, for *imperative reasons of security*, to take safety measures concerning protected persons, it may, at the most subject them to assigned residence or to internment'.[5]

Article 68 paragraph 1, applicable in occupied territory, provides that persons who committed minor offences solely intended to harm the Occupying Power may also be interned, and in fact may only be punished by 'simple' imprisonment or internment for a duration proportionate to the offence committed.

Review must be made of the reasons for interning a civilian, as civilians—unlike combatants who are captured and become POWs[6]—may be interned only if and for the length of time that they pose an imperative security threat.[7] Articles 43 and 78 GC IV provide internment review procedures applicable to civilian internees on the territory of a party to the conflict and in occupied territory respectively, giving some detail regarding the type of body and timing of review.[8]

In addition to addressing the admissibility of and procedures for internment, both Article 41 paragraph 2 and Article 78 paragraph 3, in referring to Article 39, touch upon the welfare (accommodation, food, clothes, hygiene, medical care, and financial resources) of people forced to leave their homes due to assigned residence, without internee status, ensuring that they have some means of existence.[9] Article 41 paragraph 2 goes further by explicitly indicating that Part III, Section IV GC IV on the treatment of internees shall serve as a guide for the treatment of persons placed in assigned residence, dispelling fears that 'an unscrupulous government might prefer to resort to this measure in order to avoid the obligations imposed upon it by internment'.[10] In addition, Article 43 requires the Protecting Power (usually replaced by the International Committee of the Red Cross (ICRC)) to be informed of the names of any protected persons interned or subject to assigned residence or of those released and decisions of the review courts/boards. This is to help ensure the internees' safety by preventing ill-treatment, disappearances, and arbitrary detention. While Article 43 applies only to aliens on the territory of a party to the conflict—not occupied territory—other provisions in the treaty ensure that all internees are so protected.[11]

B. Meaning and Application

I. Meaning of assigned residence, internment, and voluntary internment

Assigned residence and internment are forms of deprivation of liberty, imposed on persons not for violating any criminal law of the party on whose territory they find themselves or of the Occupying Power, but rather because that party or Power 'may, for reasons of its

---

[4] Art 42 GC IV (emphasis added).
[5] Art 78 GC IV (emphasis added).
[6] But see Arts 109–117 GC III (referring to repatriation of POWs during the conflict for medical reasons).
[7] Arts 132 and 133 GC IV.   [8] Arts 43 and 78 para 2 GC IV.
[9] Pictet Commentary GC IV, at 257, 369.
[10] Pictet Commentary GC IV, at 257. See Final Record, vol III, at 126.
[11] Arts 105, 136–137 GC IV.

own, consider them dangerous to its security and is consequently entitled to restrict their freedom of action'[12] as a preventive security measure. Assigned residence and internment constitute the most severe 'measures of control'[13] to which a state may resort.

10   Assigned residence 'move[s] certain people from their domicile and force[s] them to live […] in a locality which is generally out of the way and where supervision is more easily exercised'.[14] Assigned residence is not the same as being placed under surveillance; surveillance is a form of supervision that 'allows the person concerned to remain in his usual place of residence'.[15] Internment constitutes a form of assigned residence, 'since internees are detained in a place other than their normal place of residence',[16] but is generally more severe because it 'implies an obligation to live in a camp with other internees'.[17] States' laws may, however, interpret assigned residence and internment differently.

11   Internment may also be voluntary, that is at the person's request, because it is in his or her, rather than the state's, interests. Under Article 42 GC IV this possibility exists only for aliens in a party's own territory, not in an occupied territory. This difference may be justified by the fact that enemy aliens may more likely fear hostility from the local population surrounding them than the local inhabitants of an occupied territory. 'Voluntary internment is subject to three conditions: it must be requested by the protected person concerned, his request must be made through the representatives of the Protecting Powers and it must be warranted by the situation of the applicant.'[18] The lack of a Protecting Power should not be considered as hindering a party to a conflict from accepting such a request, which may then be presented through the ICRC or directly by the person concerned.[19] The first two conditions 'prevent requests for internment being made lightly and ensure that internment is not ordered on the false pretext that it was asked by those concerned'.[20] As situations and individual circumstances vary, the responsible authorities assess fulfilment of the third condition regarding whether internment is justified. Most cases concern those who cannot earn their living,[21] but there may also be 'cases where a person's security may be threatened by hostile actions committed by the general public'.[22] State authorities must give favourable consideration to an internment request that satisfies these conditions; '[t]he protected persons have then an absolute right to be interned'.[23] If, however, no request was made or internment fails to be justified by the concerned person's circumstances, the state may not grant the request.[24]

II. Grounds for internment/assigned residence

a. 'Only if the security of the Detaining Power makes it absolutely necessary'/'imperative reasons of security'

12   The texts of Article 42—'only if the security of the Detaining Power makes it absolutely necessary'—and of Article 78—'imperative reasons of security'—make clear that security grounds must absolutely necessitate the individual's internment or assigned residence;

---

[12] Pictet Commentary GC IV, at 368.   [13] Art 41 para 1 GC IV. See also Art 27 para 4 GC IV.
[14] Pictet Commentary GC IV, at 256.
[15] Ibid.   [16] Ibid.
[17] Pictet Commentary GC IV, at 256. See also Final Record, vol II-A, at 808.
[18] Pictet Commentary GC IV, at 258.
[19] See by analogy for the transmission of information on POWs, Bugnion, above n 1, at 551, fn 11.
[20] Pictet Commentary GC IV, at 259.   [21] Ibid.   [22] Ibid.
[23] Ibid. See Final Record, vol II-A, at 826.   [24] Pictet Commentary GC IV, at 258–9.

no other reasons justify these forms of deprivation of liberty, as Article 79 GC IV expressly states.[25] For appropriate application, it is thus critical to understand the meaning and scope of these grounds for internment, which are not defined in GC IV.

As the Pictet Commentary explains, 13

[i]t did not seem possible to define the expression 'security of the State' in a more concrete fashion [in the Convention]. It is thus left very largely to Governments to decide the measure of activity prejudicial to the internal or external security of the State which justifies internment or assigned residence.[26]

The International Criminal Tribunal for the former Yugoslavia (ICTY) agrees that 'the decision of whether a civilian constitutes a threat to the security of the State is largely left to its discretion',[27] but this does not mean that no parameters exist to this discretion.

In finding the accused guilty of unlawful confinement of civilians,[28] the ICTY 'interpreted Article 42 [GC IV] as permitting internment only if there are "serious and legitimate reasons" to think that the interned persons may seriously prejudice the security of the detaining power by means such as sabotage or espionage'.[29] 14

Thus, '[s]ubversive activity carried on inside the territory of a Party to the conflict or actions which are of direct assistance to an enemy Power'[30] may meet the threshold of an imperative threat to security. Providing logistical support, analogous to that described in GC III[31] for persons 'accompanying' the armed forces rather than being part of them, can be considered direct assistance. However, as the ICTY Trial Chamber held, 'the mere fact that a person is a national of, or aligned with, an enemy party cannot be considered as threatening the security of the opposing party where he is living and is not, therefore, a valid reason for interning him or placing him in assigned residence'.[32] 15

As indicated by the ICTY, for purposes of internment, persons by their 'activities, knowledge or qualifications [must represent] a *real* threat' to [the state's] *present or future* security'.[33] This is the logical corollary to the fact 'no civilian should be kept in assigned residence or in an internment camp for a longer time than the security of the detaining party absolutely demands'.[34] 16

As an individual's internment can only be based on his or her constituting an imperative threat to security, this form of deprivation of liberty cannot be employed out of mere 17

---

[25] Art 79 GC IV: 'The Parties to the conflict shall not intern protected persons, except in accordance with the provisions of Articles 41, 42, 43, 68 and 78.' ICTY, *The Prosecutor v Zejnil Delalić and others*, Trial Chamber Judgment, IT-96-21-T, 16 November 1998, para 581 (hereinafter *Čelebići Camp*): '[S]uch measures of detention should only be taken if absolutely necessary for reasons of security. Thus, if these measures were inspired by other considerations, the reviewing body would be bound to vacate them.'

[26] Pictet Commentary GC IV, at 257. See also ibid, at 368 (reiterating that '[i]n any case such measures can only be ordered for real and imperative reasons of security; their exceptional character must be preserved').

[27] ICTY, *Čelebići Camp*, above n 25, paras 574, 583. See also ICTY, *The Prosecutor v Dario Kordić & Mario Čerkez*, Trial Chamber Judgment, IT-95-14/2-T, 26 February 2001, paras 282–5.

[28] ICTY, *Čelebići Camp*, above n 25, paras 1143, 1145.

[29] ICTY, *Čelebići Camp*, above n 25, paras 576–7. See also ibid, para 582 (referencing Art 78 GC IV, applicable to occupied territory, as also safeguarding the rights of interned persons).

[30] Pictet Commentary GC IV, at 258. [31] Art 4(A)(4) GC III.

[32] ICTY, *Čelebići Camp*, above n 25, para 577. [33] Ibid (emphasis added).

[34] Ibid, para 581 (footnote omitted).

usefulness to the Detaining Power, such as solely for the purposes of intelligence gathering. As the ICRC explains, 'internment [...] for the sole purpose of intelligence gathering, without the person involved otherwise presenting a real threat to State security, cannot be justified'.[35] The United States (US) Supreme Court, for example, recently concurred; the Court interpreted the 2001 Authorization for Use of Military Force as including implicitly the power to detain 'enemy combatants', but it noted that 'that indefinite detention for the purpose of interrogation is not authorized'.[36]

i. (In)significance of past acts

18   As internment is based on the threat posed by an individual, that individual's past activities may be an important factor in assessing whether he or she constitutes a significant threat to the state's security such as to justify internment.[37] However, since this form of deprivation of liberty is a preventive measure to protect the state now and in the future, it may be not be used to punish a person for prior acts.

19   Given that internment cannot be used for punishment, note must be made of Article 68 GC IV, which addresses criminal penalties, including the death penalty, and references internment. Article 68 paragraph 1 does not provide an additional basis to intern, nor does it indicate that internment can be used as a criminal sanction,[38] or justify internment in order to avoid providing the full protections available in a criminal process. Rather, Article 68 paragraph 1 urges the Occupying Power to intern rather than imprison for certain less serious acts,

> because the authors of the Convention wished to make it possible for the military courts of the Occupying Power to give persons guilty of minor offences the benefit of the conditions of internment provided for in Articles 79 et seq. The provision was a humane one and was intended to draw a distinction between such offenders and common criminals.[39]

It should be noted that '[i]nternment and imprisonment are only mentioned as maximum penalties, and less severe penalties still, such as placing under arrest or fines, may be applied in the case of persons accused of minor offences'.[40]

20   In describing minor offences, Article 68 paragraph 1 indicates that these offences must not have serious consequences for the Occupying Power, that is, no attempt on the life of the members of occupying forces, nor cause grave collective danger or serious damage to the Occupying Power's property or the property it uses.[41] Article 68 paragraph 1 also stipulates that the offences 'must have been "solely" intended to harm the Occupying Power. The inclusion of the word "solely" excludes acts which harm the Occupying Power indirectly.'[42] Given that an occupied population holds no allegiance to an Occupying Power, GC IV recognizes that minor offences directed only at harming the Occupying Power may occur and should not be treated like common criminality, which may indirectly harm not only the occupier but others as well.

---

[35] ICRC Guidelines, 'International Humanitarian Law and the Challenges of Contemporary Armed Conflicts' 11, 30IC/07/8.4 (October 2007), Annex 1 (originally published as J. Pejic, 'Procedural Principles and Safeguards for Internment/Administrative Detention in Armed Conflict and Other Situations of Violence', 87 *IRRC* 858 (2005) 375), at 380 (hereinafter ICRC Guidelines).

[36] *Hamdi v Rumsfeld*, 542 US 507, at 521 (2004).

[37] Report on the ICRC-Chatham House expert meeting on procedural safeguards for security detention in non-international armed conflict, London, 22–3 September 2008, at 5 (footnote omitted), available at <http://www.icrc.org/eng/resources/documents/report/security-detention-report-091209.htm>.

[38] 'Internment is a preventive administrative measure and cannot be considered a penal sanction.' Pictet Commentary GC IV, at 343.

[39] Ibid, at 343–4.   [40] Ibid.   [41] Art 68 para 1 GC IV.

[42] Pictet Commentary GC IV, at 343. See also Final Record, vol II-A, at 765.

ii. Internment versus criminal proceedings

21 In relation to past acts that were criminal in nature, it 'is of crucial importance that internment not be used as an (disguised) alternative to criminal proceedings'.[43] A person may not be interned solely based on suspicion of criminal activity that no longer constitutes, or never did constitute, an imperative threat to state security; in such cases the person may be held only in accordance with the applicable criminal law.

22 That said, an apprehended individual who has allegedly committed criminal acts subjecting him or her to criminal proceedings, may—based on additional facts—simultaneously be an imperative threat to the state's security. As mentioned above, past criminal acts may be a factor in assessing the threat that the individual poses now or in the future. Thus, while admissible internment and detention based on criminal proceedings have distinct, separate bases for the deprivation of liberty, the surface area covered by them may overlap.

23 When overlap occurs because each regime provides an applicable legal basis, the state is not required to prioritize one type of deprivation of liberty over the other, for example, to pursue criminal proceedings instead of administrative proceedings. However, this has raised concern that internment might be used to avoid providing the fuller panoply of rights available to the individual in criminal proceedings. In such circumstances, opting for internment—an administrative measure that provides fewer protections than a criminal proceeding and that results in a deprivation of liberty that can last the duration of the conflict—may be seen as inappropriately circumventing the criminal process and thus an individual's rights. It must be noted, however, that practice in armed conflict demonstrates that internment is generally preferable to criminal prosecution:

> In the vast majority of cases, and unless they are tried for war crimes, internees are spared prosecution under domestic law in international armed conflict and are simply released when they no longer pose a security threat, and in any case must be released when hostilities cease. In this context, strange as it may sound internment can actually be preferable to criminal trial from the internee's standpoint. It is likely to last for a shorter time than if the activity that led to internment was the subject of domestic proceedings.[44]

24 The key remains, however, that the internment must be valid, that is, undertaken on an admissible basis and according to required procedures; internment cannot be a ruse to avoid applying the appropriate legal regime. This concern, for example, was raised with regard to US internment in relation to the formerly titled 'war on terror', mainly because of disagreement regarding the existence of an armed conflict or the classification of the armed conflict, and thus whether IHL provides the basis to intern. If IHL is not applicable then IHL-based internment cannot be a valid alternative to criminal proceedings.

iii. Individualized reasons

25 No explicit provision in GC IV requires that the decisions to assign residence or intern be taken individually, because

> there might be situations—a threat of invasion for example—which would force a government to act without delay to prevent hostile acts, and to take measures against certain categories without always finding it possible to consider individual cases. The safeguards provided in Article 43 seem adequate to reduce the risk of arbitrary decisions.[45]

---

[43] Report on the ICRC-Chatham House expert meeting, above n 37, at 5 (footnote omitted).
[44] J. Pejic, 'The European Court of Human Rights' *Al-Jedda* Judgment: The Oversight of International Humanitarian Law', 93 *IRRC* 883 (2011) 1, at 12–13.
[45] Pictet Commentary GC IV, at 256. See Final Record, vol III, at 126.

26   However, as the ICTY has clarified, 'it must be borne in mind that the measure of internment for reasons of security is an exceptional one and can never be taken on a collective basis',[46] that is, there must be an individual nexus.[47] For example, as mentioned previously, the mere fact that a person is an enemy national or aligned with the enemy party cannot justify internment.[48] This, however, does not exclude nationality as *a* factor to be considered. Pictet highlights this when contrasting occupied territory with the territory of a party to the conflict: 'In occupied territories the internment of protected persons should be even more exceptional than it is inside the territory of the Parties to the conflict; for in the former case the question of nationality does not arise.'[49]

27   Also, '[t]he fact that an individual is male and of military age should not necessarily be considered as justifying the application of these measures'.[50] At most, this fact may be a reason, under Article 35 GC IV, to prohibit those individuals from leaving the country. It is quite startling, then, that the Eritrea–Ethiopia Claims Commission upheld Ethiopia's internment of 85 Eritrean university students of military age under Article 35 GC IV because they 'might have returned to Eritrea and joined the Eritrean forces if left at large'.[51]

b. Relationship between Articles 78 and 49 paragraph 1 GC IV

28   The scope of Article 78's authorization of an Occupying Power to assign place of residence or intern remains delimited by Article 49 paragraph 1, which prohibits '[i]ndividual or mass forcible transfers, as well as deportations of protected persons from occupied territory [...], regardless of their motive'.[52] Protected persons in occupied territory 'cannot be deported; they can therefore only be interned, or placed in assigned residence, within the frontiers of the occupied country itself'.[53]

29   The relationship between Articles 78 and 49 paragraph 1 was at issue in *Ajuri v IDF Commander*,[54] where the Israeli Supreme Court sitting as the High Court of Justice reviewed the legality of the orders of the Israeli Defense Force Commander in Judea and Samaria, that required three residents of that area (the West Bank) to live for the next two years in the Gaza Strip. The question presented to the Court was whether the orders amounted to a deportation from one territory to another in violation of Article 49 paragraph 1 of GC IV. Should Judea and Samaria be considered an occupation different from the one in the Gaza Strip, or did the orders merely constitute an assignment of residence permissible under Article 78 GC IV? The Court held that 'Judea and Samaria and the Gaza Strip are effectively one territory subject to one belligerent occupation by one occupying power',[55] thus concluding that no deportation forbidden under Article 49 paragraph 1 had occurred.

---

[46] ICTY, *Čelebići Camp*, above n 25, para 583. See also ICTY, *Kordić and Čerkez*, above n 27, para 285; Art 75(2)(d) AP I (prohibiting collective punishments).
[47] See also Pictet Commentary GC IV, at 367 (stating in the context of Art 78 GC IV that 'there can be no question of taking collective measures: each case must be decided separately').
[48] ICTY, *Čelebići Camp*, above n 25, para 577.   [49] Pictet Commentary GC IV, at 367.
[50] ICTY, *Čelebići Camp*, above n 25, para 577.
[51] EECC, *Civilians Claims–Eritrea's Claims 15, 16, 23, and 27–32*, Partial Award, 17 December 2004, para 117. See M. Sassòli, 'Internment', in MPEPIL, para 9.
[52] Art 49 para 1 GC IV. Unlawful deportation or transfer of a protected person is a grave breach of GC IV: Art 147 GC IV.
[53] Pictet Commentary GC IV, at 368.
[54] *Ajuri v IDF Commander in West Bank*, Case No HCJ 7015/02 [2002] *Israeli Law Reports* 1.
[55] Ibid, at 2.

c. Distinguishing internment and hostage-taking

Another limitation on admissible internment is that it cannot amount to hostage-taking, which is prohibited by and constitutes a grave breach of GC IV.[56] Hostage-taking is the 'seizure or detention of a person (the hostage), combined with threatening to kill, to injure or to continue to detain the hostage, in order to compel a third party to do or to abstain from doing any act as an explicit or implicit condition for the release of the hostage'.[57]

The specific intent characterizing hostage-taking distinguishes it from internment (or criminal detention).[58] Such intent is distinguishable from and does not constitute permissible grounds for internment laid out in Articles 42 and 78 GC IV, that is, the individual must pose a present or future, imperative threat to security. Internment thus may not be for the sole purpose of exchanging the internee for other persons in enemy hands, or for using the internee as a 'bargaining chip' in negotiations.[59] For example, in relation to the administrative detention of several Lebanese citizens, the Israeli Supreme Court in 2000[60] reversed a previous decision[61] and held that

> a person could not be held in administrative detention [under the Emergency Powers (Detention) Law] where he does not constitute a threat to state security, when the purpose of detention is that the person serve as a 'bargaining chip' in negotiations over the release of security forces held captive or missing.[62]

d. 'Incarceration of Unlawful Combatants Law'

The Knesset passed the Incarceration of Unlawful Combatants Law in 2002[63] to counter the Israeli Supreme Court's 2000 decision mentioned in MN 31, prohibiting the internment of an individual for sole use as a 'bargaining chip'.[64] This Law introduced broader grounds for interning members of groups ('unlawful combatants') who were not entitled to POW status:

> [T]he principal purpose of the Unlawful Combatants Law relates to aiding and advancing the state's battle against terrorist bodies that have declared total war against it. As such, it is itself intended to prevent the return of activists in these organizations, and of those who take part in terrorist attacks against the state, to the cycle of hostilities. Conversely the purpose of the Administrative Detention Law is to prevent danger to state security by individual persons and for specific reasons.[65]

---

[56] Arts 34 and 147 GC IV.

[57] ICRC CIHL Study, vol I, at 336 (referencing Art 1 of the International Convention against the Taking of Hostages); see also ICC Elements of Crimes, Art 8(2)(a)(viii) and (c)(iii). ICTY, *Kordić and Čerkez*, above n 27, para 314: '[A]n individual commits the offence of taking civilians as hostages when he threatens to subject civilians, who are unlawfully detained, to inhuman treatment or death as a means of achieving the fulfilment of a condition.' See more generally Ch 15 of this volume.

[58] ICRC CIHL Study, vol I, at 336.   [59] See also ICRC Guidelines, above n 35, note 20.

[60] *Anonymous (Lebanese citizens) v Minister of Defense*, FCrA 7048/97, Judgment, 12 April 2000, ILDC (IL 2000).

[61] A.D.A. 10/94, *Anonymous Persons v Minister of Defense*, 13 November 1997. For a discussion of the 1997 case, see O. Ben-Naftali and S.S. Gleichgevitch, 'Missing in legal action: Lebanese hostages in Israel', 41 *Harvard International Law Journal* (2000) 185, at 187–99.

[62] *Fawzi Muhammad Mustafa Ayub v State of Israel*, 23 Nissan 5768 (2 May 2005), para 1 (referencing Crim Reh 7048/97, *Flunis v Minister of Defense*, PD 54(1) 721).

[63] Incarceration of Unlawful Combatants Law 5762-2002. This Law was amended in 2008.

[64] Y. Shany, 'The Israeli Unlawful Combatants Law: Old Wine in a New Bottle?', Research Paper No 03-12, The International Law Forum of the Hebrew University of Jerusalem Law Faculty, 15 January 2012, at 1.

[65] Supreme Court of Israel, *A v State of Israel*, Adm Det App 7750/08, 23 November 2008, para 15 (unofficial translation in Sassòli/Bouvier/Quintin, at 1193).

33   The Incarceration of Unlawful Combatants Law states that it regulates such deprivation of liberty in conformity with IHL.[66] Several concerns with regard to the Law's consistency with IHL arise; however, the one concern that will be addressed here is whether the Law's threshold establishing an individualized threat, and thus permitting internment, equates with that required by GC IV.

34   The Israeli Supreme Court first addressed this issue in 2008.[67] The dispute generally concerned reliance on the combination of the Law's sections 2 and 7:

> [T]he state argued that it is sufficient to prove that a person is a member of a terrorist organization in order to prove his individual danger to the security of the state […] By contrast, the appellants' approach was that relying upon abstract 'membership' in an organization that perpetrates hostile acts against the State of Israel […] renders meaningless the requirement of proving an individual threat, contrary to constitutional principles and international humanitarian law.[68]

> The lower court had adopted a broad understanding of 'unlawful combatant', particularly regarding membership, and found that the individual who belonged to a family involved in arms smuggling was an unlawful combatant because the family cell was engaged in acts hostile to Israel.[69]

35   The Supreme Court disagreed, stating that it could not accept a holding 'whereby the family cell […] can be deemed a hostile force, so as to satisfy the requirements'[70] of the Law. The Court held that 'it is not sufficient that the person be in the ranks of some entity that is hostile to the state and whose existence endangers its security, but it must be an entity that carries out, in an active and organized manner, hostile terrorist activity against the State of Israel'.[71]

36   This result reinforces that '[e]ven under such extreme conditions, restricting liberty should be based on some degree of individual risk assessment, established on the basis of a meaningful body of evidence'.[72] It also demonstrated the importance of procedural safeguards: 'The initial and periodical judicial review[s] under the 2002 Law appear to be a critical bulwark against abuses and excesses.'[73]

III. Procedural requirements

37   For aliens on the territory of a party to the conflict, Article 43 GC IV provides that '[a]ny protected person interned or placed in assigned residence shall be entitled to have such action reconsidered as soon as possible by an appropriate court or administrative board'[74] and, if the decision is maintained, to have it reviewed periodically, at least twice yearly.[75] In occupied territory, Article 78 provides that decisions regarding assigned residence or internment must be made 'according to regular procedure to be prescribed by the Occupying Power in accordance with the provisions'[76] of GC IV. Article 78 also provides that this procedure includes the right to appeal and that such appeals shall be decided with

---

[66] Incarceration of Unlawful Combatants Law 5762-2002, s 1.
[67] Supreme Court of Israel, *Iyad v State of Israel*, CrimA 6659/06, 11 June 2008. See also *A v State of Israel*, above n 65.
[68] *Iyad v State of Israel*, above n 67, para 20.
[69] *A v State of Israel*, above n 65, para 3 (unofficial translation in Sassòli/Bouvier/Quintin, at 1191).
[70] Ibid, para 11 (unofficial translation in Sassòli/Bouvier/Quintin, at 1192).   [71] Ibid.
[72] Shany, above n 64, at 23.   [73] Ibid.   [74] Art 43 para 1 GC IV.   [75] Ibid.
[76] Art 78 para 2 GC IV.

the 'least possible delay';[77] if the appeal is upheld, it must be 'subject to periodical review, if possible every six months, by a competent body'[78] set up by the Occupying Power.

a. Nature of deciding body: 'court or administrative board'

Under GC IV, either a court or an administrative board may make the decision regarding the internment of an alien on the territory of a party to the conflict.[79] These alternatives were to '[provide] sufficient flexibility to take into account the usage in different States'.[80] In occupied territory, GC IV does not specify the reviewing body, indicating only that review must be 'by a competent body'.[81] The Pictet Commentary explains, however, that the Occupying Power 'must observe the stipulations in Article 43',[82] and it is left 'to the Occupying Power to entrust the consideration of appeals either to a "court" or a "board"'.[83]

Article 78 paragraph 2 states that the body must be *competent* (emphasis added). Article 43 paragraph 1 indicates that the court or administrative board must be *appropriate* (emphasis added). For internment, the review body is deemed competent/appropriate where the administrative review decision is made by a board (not one official) with the authority to make a final decision regarding release.[84] Such 'joint decision[s] [...] [offer] the protected persons a better guarantee of fair treatment'.[85] It must be recalled that given that review of internment 'is not a criminal trial and does not lead to the conviction of internees, but is an administrative procedure, human rights law requirements concerning an independent and impartial tribunal and a fair trial do not apply to such board'.[86] Whether on the territory of a party to the conflict or in occupied territory, '[t]he essential point is [...] that the authorities should examine [the appeal] with absolute objectivity and impartiality'.[87]

b. Are IHL rules lex specialis *vis-à-vis the IHRL right to* habeas corpus?[88]

The development of international human rights law (IHRL) since the adoption of the 1949 Geneva Conventions necessitates addressing whether the IHL rules applicable in international armed conflict (IAC) are *lex specialis* in respect to IHRL. Focus here is placed on the right to *habeas corpus* since, in practice, the principal difference between IHL and IHRL, with regard to procedural regulation of internment, is that the IHL approach is satisfied by an administrative review,[89] while the human rights approach calls for judicial review.[90]

When comparing the treaty provisions regulating internment in the two branches of law, IHL applicable to civilians in IAC is more specific than IHRL. The former explicitly guarantees, for civilian internees, a right to appeal and a time frame for periodic review

---

[77] Ibid. [78] Ibid. [79] Art 43 GC IV. [80] Pictet Commentary GC IV, at 260.
[81] Art 78 para 2 GC IV. [82] Pictet Commentary GC IV, at 368. [83] Ibid, at 368–9.
[84] Sassòli, above n 51, para 10. Pictet Commentary GC IV, at 260. ICTY, *Čelebići Camp*, above n 25, para 1137. IACommHR, *Coard et al v US*, Case No 10.951, Report No 109/99, 9 BHRC 150 (29 September 1999), OEA/Ser.L/V/11.106 doc 6 [1999], para 60.
[85] Pictet Commentary GC IV, at 369. [86] Sassòli, above n 51, para 10.
[87] Pictet Commentary GC IV, at 260.
[88] Material in this section has been substantially based on text written by this author in M. Sassòli and L.M. Olson, 'The Relationship between International Humanitarian and Human Rights Law Where It Matters: Admissible Killing and Internment of Fighters in Non-International Armed Conflict', 90 *IRRC* 871 (2008) 599, at 618–27; L.M. Olson, 'Practical Challenges of Implementing the Complementarity between International Humanitarian and Human Rights Law: Demonstrated by the Procedural Regulation of Internment in Non-International Armed Conflict', 40 *Case Western Reserve JIL* (2009) 437, at 450–6.
[89] Arts 42 and 78 GC IV. [90] See, e.g., Art 9(4) ICCPR.

if not released; treaty-based human rights do not indicate this with regard to security detention. International humanitarian law explicitly permits review by an administrative board *or* a court. Given the specificity of IHL on the review process and, importantly, that IHL was precisely designed to regulate the extreme situations of armed conflict, IHL in IAC should be seen as *lex specialis* with regard to the type of reviewing body. Additionally, the ICRC Customary International Humanitarian Law Study found no requirement for judicial review of internment in IACs.[91]

42   It must, however, be recalled that *lex specialis* is only one of several interpretive tools to resolve conflict between rules:

> [I]n a given situation one answer to a conflict between norms may be suggested by *lex specialis* but another by the later-in-time principle [...], and there is no overriding rule that determines which must prevail. Rather decision makers or adjudicators must consider all aspects of the context of the specific situation, including the apparent intent of the parties and the overall object and purpose of the regimes in question.[92]

Most IHRL 'treaties entered into force after many of the IHL treaties. Thus, the maxim of *lex posterior* must be considered when evaluating'[93] the IHL–IHRL relationship.[94]

43   There is also appeal in applying IHRL and mandating judicial review in all cases of civilian internment/assigned residence due to the presumption that judicial review is more likely to be independent and impartial.[95] Yet it may not be feasible for states, possibly interning thousands of people (such as the nearly 30,000 held by the US in Iraq in 2007[96]), to bring all internees before a judge without delay during armed conflict. While it may be argued that development of IHRL should (and has) constrain(ed) IHL pragmatism[97] that strikes a balance between military necessity and humanity in the extreme context of armed conflict, an infeasible obligation risks severely hampering the effective conduct of war and could thus lead to less compliance with the rules in the long term—for example, summary executions disguised as battlefield killings. Furthermore, relying on human rights to require judicial review may not offer a fully satisfactory solution in all contexts; in certain circumstances, IHRL may face limitations to its application, for example, due to a treaty's formal scope of application or perhaps due to a state's availing itself of a treaty's derogation clause.[98]

44   Human rights bodies have elaborated upon the content of IHRL through their jurisprudence, which does not exist to the same extent for IHL as there are fewer expert bodies mandated to apply it. Thus, recourse to IHRL is appealing when interpreting IHL, but precedents of human rights bodies specifically addressing procedural regulation of security detention in relation to armed conflict are rare.

45   One such case is *Coard v United States*,[99] which concerned the detention by US forces in 1983 of members of the previous Government of Grenada for a total of nine to 12 days

---

[91] ICRC CIHL Study, Rule 99, vol I, at 345–6.
[92] M.J. Matheson, 'The Fifty-Eighth Session of the International Law Commission', 101 *AJIL* (2007) 407, at 427.
[93] Olson, above n 88, at 448.
[94] See Ch 35 of this volume for a full discussion of the IHL–IHRL relationship.
[95] ICRC Guidelines, above n 35, at 387.
[96] G. Lubold, 'Do US Prisons in Iraq Breed Insurgents?', *The Christian Science Monitor*, 20 December 2007, available at <http://www.csmonitor.com/2007/1220/p01s01-woiq.htm>.
[97] See Ch 35, MN 54–55, 73–89, of this volume.
[98] See Ch 35, MN 26–31, 49–50, of this volume.
[99] IACommHR, *Coard*, above n 84. The most recent decision of the ECtHR, *Hassan v UK*, Judgment of 16 September 2014, goes into the same direction.

(six to nine of which were after the cessation of hostilities) with no review of their detention. The Inter-American Commission on Human Rights (IACommHR) reviewed this in light of Articles I and XXV of the American Declaration—together providing that no one may be deprived of the right to liberty, except in accordance with norms and procedures established by pre-existing law. Article XXV, paragraph 3 provides for the remedy of *habeas corpus* for all persons detained. The Commission, however, indicated that review through the American Declaration 'does not mean [...] that the Commission may not make reference to other sources of law in effectuating its mandate, including international humanitarian law'.[100] The Commission stated that 'the standard to be applied must be deduced by reference to the applicable *lex specialis*',[101] explaining that 'the standards of humanitarian law help to define whether the detention of the petitioners was "arbitrary" or not under the terms of Articles I and XXV of the American Declaration'.[102]

46 The IACommHR found detention without any review 'incompatible with the terms of the [American] Declaration as understood with reference to [Article] 78 of Geneva Convention IV'.[103] The Commission determined that,

> pursuant to the terms of Geneva Convention IV and the Declaration, [the necessary review of detention] could have been accomplished through the establishment of an expeditious judicial or board (quasi-judicial) review process carried out by US agents with the power to order the production of the person concerned, and release in event the detention contravened applicable norms or was otherwise unjustified. What is required when an armed force detains civilians is the establishment of a procedure to ensure that the legality of detention can be reviewed without delay and is subject to supervisory control.[104]

47 The case makes several important points. The Commission identified IHL as *lex specialis*. It recognized that during active hostilities it may be impossible to provide for a *habeas corpus* review.[105] It further indicated that while review must be with the least possible delay and with a certain level of oversight,[106] review requirements may be satisfied by a quasi-judicial board consisting of reviewing personnel with the authority to order the production of the detainees and their release (if warranted), such that 'the decision to maintain detention does not rest with the agents who effectuated the deprivation of liberty'.[107] While at least one expert disagrees,[108] the Commission does not appear to require that review personnel be independent of the executive.

c. *Reconsideration of internment*

48 The initial reconsideration of the decision to intern or place in assigned residence does not occur automatically; the person must request such review.[109] However, once requested, the review must take place as soon as possible.[110] If an initial review results in continued internment, the court or administrative board must reconsider the case periodically, 'with a view to favourably amending the initial decision if circumstances permit'.[111] Through periodical review, 'the responsible authorities will be bound to take into account the

---

[100] Ibid, para 38. [101] Ibid, para 42. [102] Ibid. [103] Ibid, para 57.
[104] Ibid, para 58.
[105] L. Doswald-Beck, *Human Rights in Times of Conflict and Terrorism* (New York: OUP, 2011), at 278.
[106] IACommHR, *Coard*, above n 84, paras 58 and 60.
[107] Ibid, para 60. See also ibid, paras 55 and 58. Doswald-Beck above n 105, at 278.
[108] See, e.g., Doswald-Beck, above n 105, at 278. [109] Pictet Commentary GC IV, at 260.
[110] Art 43 para 1 GC IV; Pictet Commentary GC IV, at 260, 368.
[111] Pictet Commentary GC IV, at 261. See Final Record, vol II-A, at 826.

49 The same review process is provided by GC IV for persons in occupied territory as for aliens in the territory of a party to the conflict. The only difference is the requirement for regular reconsideration of the decision to intern: '[T]he six-monthly review of decisions [...], which is compulsory in the case of internees in the actual territory of a belligerent, is optional[, albeit recommended,] in occupied territory.'[113] This flexibility was provided for out of the concern that '[c]onditions in occupied territory vary from place to place and time to time, and to lay down a rigid rule [...] might cause an Occupying Power to be put in a position where it would be unable to comply with the rule'.[114]

50 '[I]t might be argued that the six-monthly review requirement is outdated and must be replaced by the much shorter delays that have developed in international human rights law',[115] in particular due to the human right to have prompt access to *habeas corpus*. However, current practice does not support such a requirement for internment in IAC. That said, as no one may be interned any longer than imperative security needs demand,[116] '[i]t will be an advantage, therefore, if States Party to the Convention afford better safeguards (examination of cases at more frequent intervals, or the setting up of a higher appeal court)'[117] than the minimum laid down in GC IV.

d. According to a 'regular procedure'

51 Article 78 paragraph 2 GC IV indicates that decisions regarding internment 'shall be made according to a *regular procedure* to be prescribed by the Occupying Power in accordance with the provisions of [...] [GC IV]'.[118] 'It is for the Occupying Power to decide on the procedure to be adopted; but it is not entirely free to do as it likes; it must observe the stipulations in Article 43 [...]'[119]

52 Thus, while the interning authority maintains considerable discretion, the procedural requirements stipulated in Article 43 GC IV provide a minimum baseline. Many procedural guarantees found in IHRL for *habeas corpus* proceedings are not provided for in GC IV with respect to internment, nor have they crystallized into customary requirements for internment in relation to IAC. For example, there exists no right for the interned individual in an IAC to present evidence or to access all evidence against him. '[T]he decision of the board may be based upon secret evidence that is not available to the person to be interned.'[120] Likewise, no provision grants a right to be present at proceedings. Further, GC IV does not provide for the right of legal representation or assistance, but neither does it prohibit it.

53 The Convention implicitly requires that the person interned 'be informed promptly, in a language he understands, of the reasons why these measures were taken',[121] so that the internee may meaningfully exercise his or her right to appeal provided for in GC IV.[122] It was not until the adoption of Additional Protocol (AP) I in 1977 that an IHL treaty

---

[112] Pictet Commentary GC IV, at 261. [113] Pictet Commentary GC IV, at 371. See ibid, at 368.
[114] Final Record, vol II-B, at 440. [115] Sassòli, above n 51, para 10.
[116] Pictet Commentary GC IV, at 261. [117] Ibid.
[118] Art 78 para 2 GC IV (emphasis added).
[119] Pictet Commentary GC IV, at 368. See Final Record, vol II-B, at 440–1.
[120] Sassòli, above n 51, para 10. [121] Art 75(3) AP I. [122] Art 78 para 2 GC IV.

explicitly articulated the safeguard. Article 75 is generally considered customary law, thus making this a requirement for all interning authorities.

54   With regard to being informed of the reasons for internment, the ICRC Commentary APs explains that

> [w]ithin a period which should not exceed, say, ten days, any one deprived of liberty for actions related to the armed conflict must be informed of the reasons for this measure unless he is released. [...] [I]f he is to be interned, a decision should duly and properly be taken and communicated to the person concerned.[123]

55   Furthermore, '[t]he right of a person to know why he or she has been deprived of liberty may be said to constitute an element of the obligation of human treatment, as a person's uncertainty about the reasons for his or her detention is known in practice to constitute a source of acute psychological stress'.[124] This is particularly so because '[u]ncertainty about one's legal situation is often compounded by prohibitions or restrictions on contact with the outside world, including families'.[125]

56   Nothing prevents the interning Power from providing procedural guarantees additional to those specified in GC IV: 'The procedure provided for in the Convention is a minimum. It will be an advantage, therefore, if States Party to the Convention afford better safeguards [...]'[126]

IV. Geneva Convention IV as the legal basis for internment

57   In order not to be deemed arbitrary and thus unlawful, internment must have a basis in law, that is, sufficiently precise substantive and procedural provisions that are accessible to the individual: 'Case law of competent courts, international treaties or a custom with sufficient stability and legal force may fulfill this requirement.'[127]

58   Specifically with regard to internment under IHL—whether for POWs or civilians— 'it is almost uniformly recognized and accepted in state practice that IHL governing international armed conflict provides a sufficient legal basis'.[128] For example, in *Coard v United States*[129] and in the Decision on Request for Precautionary Measures (*Detainees at Guantánamo Bay, Cuba*),[130] the IACommHR 'has held that in the case of an international armed conflict, the internment of POWs or civilian internees is not arbitrary, if it complies with the requirements laid down in the Geneva Conventions III and IV of 1949'.[131] And while *Coard* did not answer the question of 'what the situation would be if an international treaty [...] allow[s] for detention, but national law provides differently',[132] for example, in

---

[123] ICRC Commentary APs, at 877 (paras 3079–80).
[124] ICRC Guidelines, above n 35, at 384.
[125] Dr J. Kellenberger, ICRC President, ASIL Annual Meeting Grotius Lecture, *Confronting Complexity through Law: The Case for Reason, Vision and Humanity*, 28 March 2012, at 9, available at <http://intercrossblog.icrc.org/blog/kellenberger-grotius-lecture-asil-the-case-for-reason-vision-and-humanity>. See also C. Droege, '"In Truth the Leitmotiv": The Prohibition of Torture and Other Forms of Ill-treatment in International Humanitarian Law', 89 *IRRC* 867 (2007) 515, at 533 and fn 112.
[126] Pictet Commentary GC IV, at 261.   [127] Sassòli, above n 51, para 32.
[128] Pejic, above n 44, at 11. See now HCtHR, *Hassan v UK*, above n 99, paras 104, 109 and 110. But see Doswald-Beck, above n 105, at 124 (questioning whether the ECtHR would agree that GC III provides a lawful grounds for interning combatants, since Art 5(1) ECHR does not list such grounds), 257.
[129] IACommHR, *Coard*, above n 84.
[130] IACommHR, *Detainees at Guantánamo Bay, Cuba* (Decision on Request for Precautionary Measures), 12 March 2002, reprinted in 41 *ILM* 532 (2002).
[131] Sassòli, above n 51, para 32.   [132] Doswald-Beck, above n 105, at 257.

59 Thus, what seemed to be an implicit finding by the ECtHR in *Al-Jedda v United Kingdom*[134]—that GC IV provides no independent basis for internment—astonished.[135] In finding that Mr Al-Jedda's internment by British troops in Iraq breached Article 5(1) of the European Convention for the Protection of Human Rights and Fundamental Freedoms (ECHR), the Court addressed whether a United Nations (UN) Security Council Resolution could displace human rights treaties, in this case the ECHR, by virtue of Article 103 of the UN Charter, and thereby authorize such internment. The Court framed the key question as 'whether Resolution 1546 placed the United Kingdom under an obligation to hold the applicant',[136] determining that if there is no clear obligation, it must be 'presum[ed] that the Security Council does not intend to impose any obligation on Member States to breach fundamental principles of human rights'.[137]

60 In turning to IHL, the Court assessed—per its key question—whether IHL 'places an obligation on an Occupying Power to use indefinite internment without trial'.[138] The Court determined 'from the provisions of the Fourth Geneva Convention that under international humanitarian law internment is to be viewed not as an obligation on the Occupying Power but as a measure of last resort',[139] and thus does not displace United Kingdom (UK) obligations under the ECHR. The ECtHR's determination that GC IV could not operate to disapply the ECHR requirements,[140] leads to the conclusion that the ECtHR dismissed GC IV as a legal basis for internment.[141]

61 While the Court is correct that IHL does not require internment, the Court's apparent resulting conclusion that IHL therefore provides no legal basis to intern runs counter to the requirements of the principle of legality. As discussed above, GC IV (and GC III) meets the principle's requirements by providing detailed grounds and procedures for internment; there is no requirement that the internment must be mandated, rather than permissive.

62 Furthermore, if IHL were interpreted to require (rather than authorize) internment, this would be detrimental in practical terms both to those conducting the hostilities and those affected by them. Requiring internment of everyone who poses an imperative threat to security could create significant operational challenges and in particular leads to un-humanitarian results for those interned solely due to that mandate.[142]

C. Relevance in Non-International Armed Conflicts[143]

63 International humanitarian law of non-international armed conflict (NIAC) indicates that internment occurs in NIACs, but it contains no indication of the grounds on which or the procedures by which a person may be interned:[144]

---

[133] Ibid (footnote omitted).   [134] *Al-Jedda v United Kingdom* [2011] ECHR 1092 (7 July 2011).
[135] Pejic, above n 44, at 2. After this manuscript has been completed, the ECtHR has clarified in *Hassan v UK*, above n 99, paras 104, 109 and 110, that a state may prevail itself of Art 78 GC IV as a legal basis for interning civilians in an IAC.
[136] *Al-Jedda*, above n 134, para 101.   [137] Ibid, para 102.   [138] Ibid, para 107
[139] Ibid, para 108   [140] Ibid para 107.   [141] Pejic, above n 44, at 7.   [142] Ibid, at 11.
[143] Material in this section has been substantially based on text written by this author in Sassòli and Olson, above n 88, at 623–5.
[144] See, e.g., CA 3 para 1; Arts 5 and 6 AP II. See also *Serdar Mohammed v Minstry of Defence* [2014] EWHC 1369 (QB), at [239]–[251].

A particular humanitarian concern related to detention in non-international armed conflict is the lack of procedural safeguards for persons subject to internment [...] In the absence of IHL norms, states often resort to policy directives or apply domestic law, neither of which has proven to be satisfactory from a protection standpoint.[145]

This section discusses a possible solution—the analogous application of IHL of IACs to NIACs. The positive and negative implications of doing so are also highlighted.

64   Applied by analogy, IHL of IAC would provide bases for internment. The standards of GC IV could be applied to civilians, and those of GC III to fighters designated as 'combatants'.[146] The question arises, however, as to whether the analogous application of the law of IAC sufficiently considers the fundamental distinction between that law and the law of NIAC—that is, that the rules applicable to IAC generally apply only to protected person categories, such as POWs or enemy civilians, and that no such categories exist in NIAC.[147] Even if the distinction in NIAC could be made by function rather than status, on which criteria should the assessment of a civilian or 'combatant' be based? Should 'combatants' be measured against the criteria in Article 4 GC III or Article 44 AP I, or perhaps through the 'membership approach' used to interpret 'direct participation in hostilities' in NIACs?[148] Would Article 5-type tribunals[149] need to be instituted in NIACs to make the determination?

65   If GC III is applied by analogy, a participant in hostilities could be detained without any individual periodic review for the whole duration of the conflict. However, it is much more difficult in NIACs than in IACs to determine who is actually a fighter.[150] Such a determination must therefore be made on an individual basis. It is also much harder to determine the actual end of hostilities than in an IAC between states, where hostilities may conclude with a ceasefire or surrender.

66   All this may support application, if at all, of the law of IAC to NIAC by analogy to GC IV alone, as there are no combatants and hence no concomitant POW status in NIAC. In NIAC, this would avoid internment of persons without review or possible release[151] for the duration of the conflict. Application of GC IV, however, brings with it an internment standard—imperative threat to security—that is broader in scope than that for determining combatancy.[152]

67   However, it should also be considered whether analogy legally can be made to IHL applicable to IAC, when doing so displaces specific human rights rules, overriding the formal *lex specialis* maxim. Unlike in IAC, IHL of NIAC does not have explicit rules providing for or procedurally regulating internment.[153] As human rights rules exist that address security detention, applying IHL of IAC by analogy to NIACs on this issue may be unlike analogies made, for example, to the definition of military objectives, a term unique to IHL.[154] International human rights law, therefore, would logically constitute

---

[145] Kellenberger, above n 125.   [146] ICRC CIHL Study, vol I, at 352.
[147] Sassòli and Olson, above n 88, at 607–8. See also N. Melzer, *Interpretive Guidance on the Notion of Direct Participation in Hostilities under International Humanitarian Law* (Geneva: ICRC, 2009), at 27–30 (hereinafter DPH Guidance).
[148] DPH Guidance, above n 147, at 25.
[149] Art 5 GC III. See Ch 46 of this volume. In IACs, such tribunals are under the text of the provision only supposed to adjudicate the status if a Detaining Power wants to deny a person POW status (ibid, MN 64).
[150] See Sassòli and Olson, above n 88, at 607–8, 613–16.
[151] But see Arts 109–117 GC III (referring to repatriation of POWs *during* the conflict for medical reasons).
[152] Art 4 GC III, or Art 44 AP I, or the 'membership approach' (using direct participation in hostilities); DPH Guidance, above n 147, at 70.
[153] *Serdar Mohammed v Minstry of Defence*, above n 144, at [291]–[293].
[154] Sassòli/Bouvier/Quintin, at 343. It is argued that '[t]he principle of legality opposes any deprivation of liberty by analogy on a legal basis designed to deprive a person of his or her liberty in circumstances that do not

the *lex specialis*, except if the reasoning by analogy created an IHL rule that then again constitutes *lex specialis* compared with the IHRL rule.

68   Yet analogy to IHL of IAC need not exclude application of IHRL. For example, if procedural IHL rules applicable to IAC regulating civilian internment are found inadequate for NIAC, human rights could fill the gap.[155] However, given the potential limitations of IHRL—for example, non-universality, dispute regarding extraterritorial application, and limitation and derogation clauses[156]—it may provide no regulation of state internment in many cases. As for the non-state actors—*if* they are bound at all by IHRL—they will face conceptual difficulties in complying with it.[157]

69   Thus, given the recognized relationship between the two branches of law, the objectives of both branches, and the differences between states and non-state actors, the solution may be to harmonize appropriately application of both bodies of law. Application to NIACs of the IHL rules of IACs pertaining to civilians provides procedures for internment binding both the state and the non-state actor, as well as places a constraint upon the basis for internment. These obligations apply equally to all parties to the conflict. Such application does not preclude corresponding parallel application of IHRL. Thus, if application of IHRL is required to provide further detail with regard to the regulation of civilian internment,[158] consistent with the maxim of *lex specialis*, IHRL may step in, clarifying state obligations. While derogation from IHRL may still occur, analogous application of IHL of IACs—as it cannot be derogated[159]—would set a minimum baseline.

70   This complementary approach would ensure procedural protection for interned non-state actors, and it would bring much needed clarity to the non-state actor's obligations, thus procedurally protecting members of the state's armed forces captured in NIAC. Also, the concern of impracticable obligations arising, for example, from judicial review of internment without delay in all cases, remains limited as human rights treaties include derogation clauses providing states a regulated 'out' in such situations.[160] The practicality of this approach, however, does not make it legally binding, and the concerns mentioned above, particularly regarding the appropriateness of analogy to IHL of IAC—and within this law of GC IV rather than GC III—remain.

D. Legal Consequences of a Violation

71   A state is responsible for internationally wrongful acts when committed by its organs, including armed forces.[161] Thus, a state is responsible for violations of IHL[162] and IHRL attributable to it, and 'measures to stop and repress them [...] must be directed against the state responsible for the violation[s]'.[163] Serious violations of IHL also give rise to individual

---

apply to the specific internee or detainee concerned'. E. Debuf, *Captured in War: Lawful Internment in Armed Conflict* (Oxford: Hart Publishing, 2013), at 473. See also Ch 45, section C, of this volume.

[155] ICRC Guidelines, above n 35, at 377–8.   [156] See Ch 35 of this volume, at MN 5–6, 49–50.
[157] See Olson, above n 88, at 452–6; Sassòli and Olson, above n 88, at 622–3.
[158] ICRC Guidelines, above n 35, at 377.   [159] But see Art 5 GC IV.
[160] However, for a list of practice pointing to the non-derogability of *habeas corpus*, see ICRC CIHL Study, at 350–1 and accompanying footnotes; see also ICRC Guidelines, above n 35, at 387.
[161] Art 4, Draft Articles on State Responsibility, adopted by the International Law Commission at its 53rd session, in 2001, and submitted to the General Assembly (A/56/10).
[162] ICRC CIHL Study, vol I, Rule 149, at 530–6. See Art 3 Hague Convention IV; Art 91 AP I. See also Art 51 GC I; Art 52 GC II; Art 131 GC III; Art 148 GC IV.
[163] Sassòli/Bouvier/Quintin, at 386.

criminal responsibility.¹⁶⁴ Specifically, states parties must 'provide effective penal sanction for persons committing, or ordering to be committed, any of the grave breaches'¹⁶⁵ of the four Geneva Conventions.

'Unlawful confinement' of civilians is a grave breach of GC IV¹⁶⁶ and is criminalized under other treaties and international instruments, including the ICC Statute, the ICTY Statute, the UN–Cambodia Agreement Concerning the Prosecution under Cambodian Law of Crimes Committed During the Period of Democratic Kampuchea, and the UN Transitional Administration in East Timor Regulation 2000/15 for East Timor.¹⁶⁷ It is also a crime under the domestic law of several states.¹⁶⁸

The unlawful character of the confinement depends on the substantive rules of IHL discussed in this chapter. Whether in occupied territory¹⁶⁹ or on the territory of a party to the conflict, the confinement will be unlawful in the following two circumstances:

(i) when a civilian or civilians have been detained in contravention of Article 42 of Geneva Convention IV, i.e. they are detained without reasonable grounds to believe that the security of the Detaining Power makes it absolutely necessary; and
(ii) where the procedural safeguards required by Article 43 of Geneva Convention IV are not complied with in respect of detained civilians, even where their initial detention may have been justified.¹⁷⁰

Thus, '[a]n initially lawful internment clearly becomes unlawful if the detaining party does not respect the basic procedural rights of the detained persons and does not establish an appropriate court or administrative board as prescribed by article 43 of GC IV'¹⁷¹ or, in occupied territory, Article 78 GC IV.¹⁷²

For example, in the *Čelebići Camp* case, the ICTY found the accused guilty of unlawful confinement of civilians—grave breaches of GC IV.¹⁷³ The Tribunal held that the 'confinement of civilians in the Čelebići prison camp was a collective measure aimed at a specific group of persons, based mainly on their ethnic background, and not a legitimate security measure',¹⁷⁴ and that the internees were not granted the procedural rights

---

¹⁶⁴ See, e.g., Lieber Code, Arts 44 and 47; Art 49 GC I; Art 50 GC II; Art 129 GC III; Art 146 GC IV; Art 85(1) AP I. See also Art 1 of the London Agreement for the Prosecution and Punishment of the Major War Criminals of the European Axis, 8 August 1945 (establishing 'an International Military Tribunal for the trial of war criminals whose offenses have no particular geographical location whether they be accused individually or in their capacity as members of the organizations or groups or in both capacities'). See generally ICRC CIHL Study, vol I, Rules 51 and 56.
¹⁶⁵ Art 49 GC I; Art 50 GC II; Art 129 GC III; Art 146 GC IV.   ¹⁶⁶ Art 147 GC IV.
¹⁶⁷ Art 8(2)(a)(vii) ICC Statute; Art 2(g) ICTY Statute; Art 9 of the 2003 UN–Cambodia Agreement Concerning the Prosecution under Cambodian Law of Crimes Committed During the Period of Democratic Kampuchea; UNTAET Regulation 2000/15, s 6(1)(a)(vii).
¹⁶⁸ See ICRC, Customary IHL Database, 2. Practice, Rule 99.
¹⁶⁹ In referring to Art 78 of GC IV, the ICTY found that 'respect for these procedural rights is a fundamental principle of the convention as a whole': ICTY, *Čelebići Camp*, above n 25, para 581.
¹⁷⁰ ICTY, *The Prosecutor v Zejnil Delalić and others*, Appeals Chamber Judgment, IT-96-21-A, 21 February 2001, para 322.
¹⁷¹ ICTY, *Čelebići Camp*, above n 25, para 583. See also ICTY, *Delalić et al*, above n 170, para 322 (affirming the Trial Chamber's view).
¹⁷² K. Dörmann, *Elements of War Crimes under the Rome Statute of the International Criminal Court* (Cambridge: CUP, 2003), at 117–18.
¹⁷³ ICTY, *Čelebići Camp*, above n 25, paras 1143, 1145.   ¹⁷⁴ Ibid, para 1134.

required by Article 43 GC IV[175] as no appropriate body reviewed their internment.[176] Another example may be found in *Kordić*, where the ICTY also convicted the accused for, inter alia, unlawful confinement of civilians.[177]

76 Few other judicial or quasi-judicial bodies have specifically addressed the regulation of internment in relation to armed conflict. In relation to Guantánamo Bay, the Human Rights Chamber for Bosnia-Herzegovina found that the state had breached the ECHR 'by handing over [persons] into illegal detention by US forces', as information on the basis for their detention was neither sought nor received.[178] The ECtHR, in the *Al-Jedda* case discussed above, found that Mr Al-Jedda's internment between 2004 and 2007 in Iraq by the UK violated his rights under the ECHR.[179] The *Coard* case, also discussed above, provides another example; the IACommHR found detention without any review, during an IAC, 'incompatible with the terms of the [American] Declaration as understood with reference to art. 78 of Geneva Convention IV'.[180]

E. Critical Assessment

77 The parameters that GC IV established in 1949 regarding the admissibility of and procedures for internment and assigned residence, would have protected many people during the two World Wars. They continue to provide essential protection in today's IACs. While the authorization of deprivation of liberty based on security reasons for an unknown duration may not seem humanitarian, history has shown that, if not permitted so as also to be regulated to prevent abuse, much worse occurs.

78 Yet the protection provided in IACs is not complete. Due to limitations in the personal scope of application of GC IV, gaps remain in coverage, in particular with regard to the state's nationals, as the Convention does not apply to them.[181] Since the adoption of GC IV, IHRL has significantly developed and can be turned to for protection. However, as touched upon above, the extent of IHRL's application in IACs, as well as in NIACs, remains unclear. Guidance in this area would help ensure the necessary protection.

79 Many of today's conflicts are not IACs but rather NIACs, and they involve persons other than members of regular armed forces. This has contributed to a worrisome blurring of the distinction between civilians and combatants in IACs. Clarity is necessary—regarding the scope of admissible internment and the required procedures to be followed when a state or non-state actor captures someone in relation to the NIAC—to ensure protection. One need not look far for examples of where this clarity would be helpful.

80 The member states of the multi-national coalitions faced this challenge when the Iraq and Afghan conflicts transitioned from IACs to NIACs.[182] While particularly affecting, but not limited to, the detainees held at the US Naval Station at Guantánamo Bay, Cuba,

---

[175] Ibid, para 1135. [176] Ibid, paras 1135–41.
[177] ICTY, *Kordić and Čerkez*, above n 27, paras 834, 836.
[178] Human Rights Chamber for Bosnia and Herzegovina, *Boudellaa and others v Bosnia and Herzegovina and the Federation of Bosnia and Herzegovina* (Case Nos CH/02/8679, CH/02/8689, CH/02/8690, CH/02/8691), 13 *Bosnian Human Rights Chamber* 297 (2002), paras 233 and 237.
[179] *Al-Jedda*, above n 134. In *Hassan v UK*, above n 99, paras 104, 109, and 110, the ECtHR decided that internment in conformity with Art 78 GC IV did not violate the ECHR.
[180] *Coard*, above n 84, para 57.
[181] Pictet Commentary GC IV, at 372–3.
[182] See generally J.B. Bellinger III and V.M. Padmanabhan, 'Detention Operations in Contemporary Conflicts: Four Challenges for the Geneva Conventions and Other Existing Law', 105 *AJIL* (2011) 201.

the US executive,[183] legislative,[184] and judicial[185] branches continue to refine—not without controversy—'the scope of the government's authority to detain these, and other, detainees pursuant to the Authorization for Use of Military Force [AUMF] [...], as informed by the law of war'.[186] Even though this refinement focuses on US domestic law (the AUMF), interpretations of the traditional protected person categories found in IAC are being impacted. The search for clarity on internment in NIAC is thus in some instances spilling over and affecting—not always positively—the rules applicable in IAC.[187]

81. The armed conflicts in Afghanistan and Iraq can also demonstrate other unique challenges faced at the time of writing—those posed by multi-national coalitions. Multinational coalitions can take various forms, and 'the distinct nature of each such operation has legal implications for a number of issues, such as the mandate and basis for detention'.[188] It also remains controversial whether IHL applies (and, if so, which provisions) to peace support operations carried out by states' forces deployed under the auspices of the UN.[189] The UN Secretary-General's Bulletin, 'Observation by United Nations forces of international humanitarian law', provides some clarity when it indicates that persons detained by UN forces must be treated '[w]ithout prejudice to their legal status [...] in accordance with the relevant provisions of the Third Geneva Convention of 1949, as may be applicable to them *mutatis mutandis*'.[190] 'The latter reservation may take into account the fact that some of those persons are civilians who would be more appropriately treated under the provisions of Convention IV applicable to civilian internees.'[191]

82. If GC IV's restrictions on and procedural requirements for internment can be criticized as insufficient, particularly for not mandating judicial review, they nevertheless provide an essential, minimum threshold below which protections cannot fall in IAC. Of course, nothing in IHL prohibits states from providing greater protection, including judicial review. Unfortunately, today's conflicts still demonstrate that most people would already greatly appreciate having even these rules respected.[192]

LAURA M. OLSON*

---

[183] See, e.g., Respondents' Memorandum Regarding the Government's Detention Authority Relative to Detainees Held at Guantánamo Bay, *In re Guantánamo Bay Detainee Litigation*, Misc No 08-442 (TFH) (DC Cir March 13, 2009), available at <http://www.justice.gov/opa/documents/memo-re-det-auth.pdf>; Executive Order 13567, Periodic Review of Individuals Detained at Guantánamo Bay Naval Station Pursuant to the Authorization for Use of Military Force, 7 March 2011.

[184] See, e.g., National Defense Authorization Act for FY2012 (2012 NDAA, PL 112-81), Sections 1021–4.

[185] See, e.g., L.M. Olson, 'Guantánamo *Habeas* Review: Are the D.C. District Court's Decisions Consistent with IHL Internment Standards?', 42 *Case Western Reserve JIL* (2009) 197; R.M. Chesney, 'Who May Be Held? Military Detention through the *Habeas* Lens', 52 *Boston College Law Review* (2011) 769; B. Wittes, R.M. Chesney, and L. Reynolds, *The Emerging Law of Detention 2.0: The Guantánamo Habeas Cases as Lawmaking* (Harvard Law School and Brookings, April 2012), available at <http://www.brookings.edu/~/media/research/files/reports/2011/5/guantanamo%20wittes/05_guantanamo_wittes.pdf>.

[186] *Hamlily v Obama*, 616 F Supp 2d 63, 66 (DDC 2009).   [187] See, e.g., Olson, above n 185.

[188] C. Droege, 'Transfers of Detainees: Legal Framework, *Non-Refoulement* and Contemporary Challenges', 90 *IRRC* 871 (2008) 669, at 681.

[189] Sassòli, above n 51, para 15.

[190] UN Secretary General's Bulletin, 'Observation by United Nations Forces of International Humanitarian Law', 6 August 1999 UN Doc ST/SGB/1999/13, s 8.

[191] Sassòli, above n 51, para 15.   [192] Sassòli and Olson, above n 88, at 627.

* The views expressed in this chapter are made in the author's personal capacity and do not represent the position or views of the US Department of Homeland Security or the US Government.

Chapter 65. Treatment of Internees

	MN
A. Introduction	1
B. Meaning and Application	10
I. General concerns	10
a. Equality before the law	10
b. Maintenance of internees and their dependants	12
c. Accommodation and groupings of internees	16
II. Places of internment	17
III. Food and clothing	18
IV. Hygiene and medical attention	21
V. Religious, intellectual, and physical activities	23
a. Religious duties	23
b. Recreation, study, and sports	24
c. Working conditions	25
VI. Personal property and financial resources	26
a. Valuables and personal effects	26
b. Financial resources and individual accounts	27
VII. Administration and discipline	28
a. Camp administration	28
b. General discipline, complaints, and petitions	30
VIII. Relations with the exterior	34
a. Internment card	35
b. Correspondence	37
c. Relief shipments	38
d. Visits	39
IX. Penal and disciplinary sanctions	40
a. General provisions—applicable legislation	40
b. Penalties	44
c. Disciplinary punishments	48
d. Escapes	52
e. Investigations, confinements awaiting hearing	53
f. Procedures for disciplinary offences	54
X. Transfers of internees	56
XI. Deaths	57
C. Relevance in Non-International Armed Conflicts	64
D. Legal Consequences of a Violation	67
E. Critical Assessment	76

Select Bibliography

Bellinger III, J.B./Padmanabhan, V.M., 'Detention Operations in Contemporary Conflicts: Four Challenges for the Geneva Conventions and Other Existing Law', 105 *AJIL* (2011) 201

Chesney, R.M., 'Iraq and the Military Detention Debate: Firsthand Perspectives from the Other War, 2003–2010', 51 *Virg JIL* (2011) 549

Deeks, A.S., 'Administrative Detention in Armed Conflict', 40 *Case Western Reserve JIL* (2009) 403

Goodman, R., 'The Detention of Civilians in Armed Conflict', 103 *AJIL* (2009) 48

Kleffner, J.K., 'Operational Detention and the Treatment of Detainees', in T. Gill and D. Fleck (eds), *Handbook of the International Law of Military Operations* (Oxford: OUP, 2010) 465

Oswald, B. and Winkler, T., 'The Copenhagen Process: Principles and Guidelines on the Handling of Detainees in International Military Operations', 83 *NJIL* (2004) 128

Pejic, J., 'Procedural Principles and Safeguards for Internment/Administrative Detention in Armed Conflict and Other Situations of Violence', 87 *IRRC* 858 (2005) 375

Pictet Commentary GC III, at 370–510

UK Ministry of Defence, *The Manual of the Law of Armed Conflict* (Oxford: OUP, 2004), at 232–51

A. Introduction

1   The law concerning the treatment of internees has a relatively brief history.[1] Internees were not provided with effective protection under international law by any convention or treaty prior to the Second World War. This is not to say, however, that the international community did not recognize the need to have rules concerning the treatment of internees. Lessons learned from the large number of civilians interned by belligerents during the First World War led to a proposition by the International Committee of the Red Cross (ICRC) in 1921 that the protection of civilians should be studied. A *Draft International Convention on the Condition and Protection of Civilians of Enemy Nationality Who Are on Territory Belonging to or Occupied by a Belligerent* was adopted by the 1934 International Conference of the Red Cross in Tokyo (Tokyo Draft).[2] That Tokyo Draft was not adopted by states, as the Second World War interrupted plans to hold an international conference.[3]

2   With the outbreak of the Second World War the ICRC proposed that belligerent states should give effect to the Tokyo Draft, but this was not accepted. Instead, belligerent states accepted a subsequent proposal by the ICRC that the 1929 Convention Relative to the Treatment of Prisoners of War (1929 Convention) 'be applied by analogy to any such civilian who had been or would be interned'.[4] The key problem with belligerent states accepting the analogous application of the 1929 Convention to civilians is that there were no legal protections afforded to civilians held in occupied territory.[5] This lacuna in the law had a devastating impact: 'As many countries were occupied, millions of civilians were left without protection at the mercy of the enemy Power and were liable to be deported, taken as hostages, or interned in concentration camps'.[6]

3   Based on the experiences of the Second World War, the ICRC drew up a complete text of rules concerning the protection of civilians, including the treatment of internees. The text was introduced to states by way of the 1948 Red Cross Conference in Stockholm (Stockholm Conference). The Stockholm Conference created a set of rules that 'provide the protection to which every human being is entitled'.[7] The draft document of the

---

[1] For a more detailed account of the development of GC IV, see the Introduction to the Pictet Commentary GC IV, at 1–9.

[2] The Tokyo Draft dealt with issues such as the internment of civilians in 'fenced-in camps' (Art 15); separate camps and health conditions (Art 16); and the application of the Convention Relative to the Treatment of Prisoners of War (1929) applying by analogy (Art 17).

[3] For a more detailed account, see Pictet Commentary GC IV, at 3–4.   [4] Ibid, at 4–5.

[5] Ibid, at 5.   [6] Ibid, at 5.   [7] Ibid, at 9.

Stockholm Conference was debated during the 1949 Diplomatic Conference in Geneva (1949 Diplomatic Conference). By the end of the 1949 Diplomatic Conference, states had reaffirmed and ensured 'by a series of detailed provisions, the general acceptance of the principle of respect for the human person in the very midst of war'.[8]

4 The provisions for the treatment of internees that were settled on during the 1949 Diplomatic Conference in Geneva are found in Geneva Convention (GC) IV Section IV. That Section consists of Articles 79–131, which are contained in 11 chapters that regulate:

— general concerns about internees
— places of internment
— food and clothing
— hygiene and medical attention
— religious, intellectual, and physical activities
— personal property and financial resources
— administration and discipline
— relations with the exterior
— plenary and disciplinary sanctions
— transfers of internees, and
— deaths.

The Articles concerning treatment of internees comprise about one-third of GC IV. They cover all classes or categories of internees—security, criminal, and voluntary—and apply to both international armed conflict (IAC) and occupation. The provisions in Section IV, however, deal only with protected persons. Even then, those in pre-trial detention or completing sentences are not covered—except in the special case foreseen in Article 68 paragraph 1 GC IV, where internment replaces simple imprisonment in the case of non-serious offences in occupied territories.

5 Internees who are aliens within the territory of a party to the conflict also benefit from the treatment provisions in Part III, Section II of GC IV; and those who are in occupied territories benefit from the treatment provisions in Part III, Section III of GC IV.

6 While Section IV is clearly inspired by the regulations relating to the treatment of prisoners of war (POWs) found in GC III[9]—internees should not be treated less favourably than POWs[10]—there are several Articles that reflect the specific needs of interned civilians. These Articles include the support of dependants of internees (Article 81); payment for work (Article 94); management of property (Article 114); and dealing with (civilian) court cases (Article 115).

7 The notion of respect for the human person through humane treatment is at the heart of all treatment provisions in GC IV.[11] There are two other principles that also provide a

---

[8] Ibid.   [9] See GC III, Part III, Sections II–IV.   [10] Pictet Commentary GC IV, at 479.
[11] This notion is consistent with the universal human rights principle that '[a]ll persons deprived of their liberty shall be treated with humanity and with respect for the inherent dignity of the human person' (see Art 10 ICCPR). See also Basic Principles for the Treatment of Prisoners (1990) Principle 1; and Body of Principles for the Protection of All Persons under Any Form of Detention or Imprisonment (1988) Principle 1. See also J. Pejic, 'The Protective Scope of Common Article 3: More than Meets the Eye', 93 *IRRC* 881 (2011) 1, at 27.

foundation for the provisions: the principle that internment is not a punishment but acts as a precautionary measure to protect the Detaining Power from potential hostile acts or attitudes that might be committed by protected persons;[12] and the understanding that the needs of internees are often balanced against the security concerns and resource limitations faced by the Detaining Power.

8   The treatment of internees must now be interpreted in accordance with other areas of international law—including international human rights law (IHRL) and international criminal law (ICL). For example, IHRL prescribes protections for persons deprived of their liberty,[13] including prohibitions against torture, cruel, and inhuman treatment,[14] and enforced disappearances.[15]

9   There have also been many developments in IHRL jurisprudence,[16] and significant engagements by United Nations (UN) organizations[17] that, while not always specifically directed to internment, are still important for contextualizing how those deprived of their liberty should be treated so as to comply with extant generally accepted standards. The ICRC has also developed institutional guidelines reflecting its official position concerning some key aspects of the treatment of internees and detainees.[18]

---

[12] See Ch 55 of this volume for the definition of protected civilians.

[13] See, e.g., the UDHR, ICCPR, CRC, Standard Minimum Rules for the Treatment of Prisoners (1955), Body of Principles for the Protection of All Persons under Any Form of Detention or Imprisonment (1988), Basic Principles for the Treatment of Prisoners (1990), Declaration of Basic Principles of Justice for Victims of Crime and Abuse of Power (1985), Basic Principles and Guidelines on the Right to a Remedy and Reparation for Victims of Gross Violations of International Human Rights Law and Serious Violations of International Humanitarian Law (2005). See also regional agreements, such as, e.g., the ACHR; Inter-American Convention to Prevent and Punish Torture (1985); Inter-American Convention on Forced Disappearance of Persons (1994); ECHR; European Convention for the Prevention of Torture and Inhuman or Degrading Treatment or Punishment (1987); Convention on Action against Trafficking in Human Beings (2005); Charter of Fundamental Rights of the European Union; ACHPR; African Charter on the Rights and Welfare of the Child (1990).

[14] CAT. [15] ICED.

[16] E.g., in relation to the condition of detention, human rights bodies have found violations of the prohibition of inhuman treatment not only in cases of active maltreatment, but also in cases of very poor conditions of detention and lack of adequate food, water, or medical treatment, as well as in cases of solitary confinement. See HRComm, *Amendola Massiotti and Baritussio v Uruguay*, Views, 26 July 1982, at 10–13; *Deidrick v Jamaica*, Views, 9 April 1998, at 9.3; *Marais v Madagascar*, Views, 24 March 1983, at 17(4); *Larrosa Bequio v Uruguay*, Views, 29 March 1983, at 10(3); *Gomez de Voituret v Uruguay*, Views, 10 April 1984, at 12(2); *Espinoza de Polay v Peru*, Views, 6 November 1997, at 8(6); ACommHPR, *Civil Liberties Organisations v Nigeria (151/96)*, Decision, 15 November 1999, at 25–7; ECommHR, *Greek case*, Report, 5 November 1969, at 186; ECtHR, *Keenan v United Kingdom*, Judgment, 3 April 2001, at 115; IACtHR, *Velásquez Rodríguez case*, Judgment, 29 July 1988, at 156; IACtHR, *Castillo Petruzzi et al case*, Judgment, 30 May 1999, at 194. In relation to the protection of women from sexual violence in armed conflict, human rights bodies have held that rape can constitute torture; see ECtHR, *Aydin v Turkey*, Judgment, 25 September 1997, at 83–6; IACommHR, Case 10.970 (Peru), Report, 1 March 1996, at V(A)(3)(a).

[17] In relation to the protection of women from sexual violence in armed conflict see, e.g., UNSC Res 1325 (2000) OP 10; UNSC Res 1820 (2008) OP 3; UNSC Res 1888 (2009) OP 7; UNSC Res 1889 (2009) OP 12; UNSC Res 1960 (2010); UN SC Res 2106 (2013); and UNSC Res 2122 (2013). For the protection of children affected by armed conflict, see UNSC Res 1882 (2009) OP 1. For the protection of civilians in armed conflict, see UNSC Res 1674 (2006) OP 5. See also the Secretary-General's Bulletin entitled 'Observance by United Nations Forces of International Humanitarian Law' (1999), Section 8.

[18] Report prepared by the ICRC, *International Humanitarian Law and the Challenges of Contemporary Armed Conflict* (30IC/07.8.4), Annex 1, prepared for the 30th International Conference of the Red Cross and Red Crescent 2007.

B. Meaning and Application

I. General concerns

a. Equality before the law

Article 80 GC IV, in keeping with the principle that internment is not a punishment but a precautionary measure, provides that internees retain their civil capacity in accordance with their status.[19] There are at least three effects that arise from this provision. First, internees have the right to be recognized before the law. Secondly, the impact of the caveat, 'compatible with their status', reflects the fact that the very nature of internment will restrict some of the legal rights of internees. For example, national laws might limit the rights of individuals, even those not interned, on the basis of nationality or age. Furthermore, 'war legislation, especially so far as enemy property is concerned',[20] may limit the extent to which internees are able to access all their property. Thirdly, if the rights of internees are restricted, they must be restricted in accordance with the law.

The notion of equality before the law is compatible with provisions found in both the Universal Declaration of Human Rights (UDHR) and the International Covenant on Civil and Political Rights (ICCPR). Both the UDHR and the ICCPR provide that '[e]veryone has the right to recognition everywhere as a person before the law'.[21] The need for restrictions on internees to be in accordance with the law raises two issues. First, any limitation as to the rights of internees must not be based solely on distinctions such as 'race, colour, sex, language, religion, or social origin'.[22] Secondly, any legislative measures taken to limit the rights of internees must at the very least be in accordance with generally accepted notions of the rule of law laid down in IHRL.

b. Maintenance of internees and their dependants

Article 81 GC IV creates obligations for the Detaining Power to maintain the internee, and to support the internee's dependants where dependants are unable to support themselves. Maintenance is to be taken in the broadest sense—the provision of everything necessary for the life and health of the internee, including medical attention.

The standard used to judge the level of maintenance may be controversial. Controversy is likely to arise in relation to the extent to which the limited resources of the Detaining Power might justify a lower standard of maintenance of internees. It is not possible to provide a definitive statement of what constitutes the minimum standard of maintenance, as that standard will vary according to context. Important considerations may include the culture of the Detaining Power, shortages caused by the conflict, and whether such shortages affected the general population as well as the internees.[23] However, it is reasonable to expect that the standard of care provided to the internee by the Detaining Power must be greater than that available to the general non-interned population, because the restriction of liberty means that those interned cannot fend for themselves.

The requirement to provide medical attention should be interpreted in accordance with Article 12 of the International Covenant on Economic Social and Cultural Rights

---

[19] See also MN 26–27 and MN 34–39, below, for more detail concerning specific aspects of internees retaining their civil capacity.
[20] Pictet Commentary GC IV, at 376.
[21] Art 6 UDHR; Art 16 ICCPR.
[22] Art 4(1) ICCPR.
[23] ICTY, *The Prosecutor v Zlatko Aleksovski*, Trial Chamber Judgment, IT-95-14/1-T, 25 June 1999, at 173.

(ICESCR),[24] which provides for the 'highest attainable standard of physical and mental health [including] the creation of conditions which would assure to all medical service and medical attention in the event of sickness'.[25] The provision of medical attention would also require the Detaining Power to be proactive, in the sense of conducting health checks so as to ensure the prevention and control of diseases.[26]

15 The requirement that the Detaining Power support the dependants of internees gives effect to the reality that internment will have adverse effects on the internee's family. While not expressly provided for by Article 81 paragraph 3 GC IV, it may be assumed that decisions concerning the requirement to support an internee's dependant may be based on submissions made to the Detaining Power by internees, their dependants, or organizations such as the ICRC and UN agencies such as the High Commissioner for Human Rights. The interpretation of who constitutes a dependant may also give rise to differing interpretations. Accepting that resources might be limited because of wartime constraints, it would be appropriate to interpret 'dependants' to include any persons who are considered by the internee's general community to rely on the internee for their day-to-day well-being.

c. Accommodation and groupings of internees

16 Article 82 paragraph 1 GC IV privileges the accommodation of internees according to nationality, language, and custom, but emphasizes that separation of internees of the same nationality should not be based solely on language. The general thrust of the Article is to reinforce that whatever grouping is selected, it should where possible privilege the needs of the internee rather than those of the Detaining Power.

II. Places of internment

17 Chapter II of Section IV GC IV includes self-explanatory and detailed provisions on the places in which internees may be interned, such as their location, marking, and the need to locate them away from hazards such as shelling[27] (Article 83); the need to intern them separately from POWs and criminals (Article 84); accommodation and hygiene (Article 85); premises for religious services (Article 86), which may certainly also be multidenominational; and canteens (Article 87). Air raid shelters must be provided (Article 88). It is reasonable to assume that the reference to 'shelters […] adequate in structure' in that Article means that structures must be suitable to withstand potential hazards. So, for example, if the only threat is from small arms and not from artillery attacks, the structures need be built to withstand only small arms fire.

III. Food and clothing

18 While Article 90 GC IV regulates clothing of internees (see MN 19), Article 89 deals with the quality, quantity, and variety of food and drinking water, and with customary dietary requirements. The implication is that the actual needs of the internee must be taken into account, rather than some other standard such as that achieved by the local population. The requirements, say, of expectant mothers, children, and internees in ill health, might

---

[24] Art 12(1) and (2)(d) ICESCR. [25] Art 12. [26] Art 12(2)(c).
[27] See, e.g., ICRC, *Report of the ICRC on the Treatment of Coalition Forces of Prisoners of War and Other Protected Persons by the Geneva Conventions in Iraq during Arrest, Internment and Interrogation* (February 2004), para 57(2).

be quite different from those of the general population or even other internees. However, it was recognized by the International Criminal Tribunal for the former Yugoslavia (ICTY) in the *Aleksovski* case that, when determining food rationing for internees, the Detaining Power should consider the impact of food shortages caused by the conflict and whether those shortages should affect internees and non-internees, including the internment camp authorities, equally.[28] Useful guidance concerning appropriate nutritional standards could be obtained from relevant health experts and the World Health Organization, particularly in relation to children and young adult internees.[29] Detaining Powers also need to consider how best to meet the religious and cultural requirements of internees; for example, internees who require *halal* or vegetarian food will need to be catered for. Food and water rations cannot be reduced as forms of punishment.[30]

Article 90 GC IV concerns clothing and starts with the presumption that internees will provide their own. This presumption is based on the requirement contained in Article 90 that at the time of being taken into custody, internees will be given 'all facilities to provide themselves with necessary clothing, footwear and change of underwear'.[31] The Article also requires the Detaining Power to permit internees to procure sufficient clothing. Recognizing, however, that internees might not have the opportunity to do so, Article 90 paragraph 1 stipulates that the Detaining Power must provide them with clothing free of charge. In certain circumstances it might be the case that the clothing that the internee has is too soiled or in very poor condition; or that the internee's clothing or footwear is inadequate for the conditions in which the internee is held. In such cases it is clear that the Detaining Power will have to provide adequate clothing or footwear for the internee. Where the Detaining Power does not have access to appropriate civilian clothing, because, for example, it cannot source such clothing locally, it should seek the assistance of the ICRC or a philanthropic organization to provide the appropriate clothing. Article 90 paragraph 2 GC IV reinforces the general principle that internees should not be exposed to ridicule. Paragraph 3 of Article 90 GC IV aims to ensure that the Detaining Power maintains a safe place of work by providing internees with clothing suitable for the tasks they are carrying out. Thus, where an internee volunteered to work in the rain, the Detaining Power would be required to provide adequate waterproof clothing to protect that internee's health. Arguably, the requirement for protective clothing would extend to providing appropriate protective gear, such as a hat, glasses, gloves, and shoes, in situations where an internee is undertaking hazardous work or working in a hazardous place.

The obligation to permit internees to use tobacco[32] needs to be interpreted in light of concerns relating to the health effects of tobacco for those who use the product, and also in relation to others who might be affected by it. States that are party to the World Health Organization Framework Convention on Tobacco Control will have to adjust how they sell or distribute tobacco to internees.[33] Furthermore, Detaining Powers will also need to

---

[28] See ICTY, *Aleksovski*, above n 23, at 173.
[29] See, e.g., World Health Organization nutrition publications, available at <http://www.who.int/nutrition/topics/nutrecomm/en/index.html>.
[30] Art 100 para 2 GC IV prohibits reductions in food rations. See also MN 48–51, below, for the types of punishments that might be imposed on internees.
[31] Art 90 para 1 GC IV.   [32] Art 89 para 3 GC IV.
[33] World Health Organization Framework Convention on Tobacco Control (2005). E.g., see Art 5 para 2(b) concerning 'preventing and reducing tobacco consumption, nicotine addiction and exposure to tobacco smoke'.

comply with obligations concerning 'protection from exposure to tobacco smoke in indoor workplaces, public transport, indoor public places and, as appropriate, other public places'.[34]

IV. Hygiene and medical attention

21   Articles 91 and 92 GC IV deal with the right of internees to be medically assessed[35] and, if necessary, treated. The requirement that internees 'shall, for preference, have the attention of medical personnel of their own nationality' should not be interpreted to mean that local standards of medical care are in all cases appropriate. For example, it would not be appropriate to provide an internee with only a local healer or community health care practitioner, if the standard of care that they provide does not meet generally accepted health care standards. The obligation under Article 91 paragraph 4 to provide those who have undergone treatment with an official certificate is important from at least three perspectives. First, it provides an accountability mechanism to ensure that medical treatment was provided, and that the medical treatment was appropriate. Secondly, the certificate allows other health experts to facilitate ongoing medical attention should such attention be required. Thirdly, should there be insurance issues concerning the medical treatment received, the certificate provides evidence of the treatment.

22   While it may not always be possible to provide internees with the best health services, the authorities must not 'demonstrate a deliberate resolve to cause [...] [detainees] great suffering or serious injury to body or health'.[36] At least one investigation into the treatment of internees has recommended that internees be examined by a qualified doctor as soon as reasonably possible, and that 'an electronic or written record of examination of all [...] [detainees] should be made at the time of the examination and preserved'.[37] The provision of medical assistance to internees will also be interpreted pursuant to generally accepted international principles concerning medical ethics. For example, the involvement of health personnel in 'any professional relationship with [...] detainees the purpose of which is not solely to evaluate, protect or improve their physical and mental health'[38] is restricted. The United States (US) military has also developed extensive guidance concerning the treatment of internees. For example, the US Department of Defense Instruction, *Medical Program Support for Detainee Operations*, sets standards concerning the treatment that health care and medical personnel are permitted to undertake in relation to internees, the keeping of internees' medical records, the release of internees' medical information, and the requirement to obtain consent for medical treatment and intervention.[39]

V. Religious, intellectual, and physical activities

a. Religious duties

23   Article 93 GC IV creates a broad obligation for the Detaining Power to allow internees to practise their religion and 'enjoy complete latitude in the exercise of their religious

---

[34] World Health Organization Framework Convention on Tobacco Control (2005), Art 8.
[35] See also Art 125 para 2 GC IV.
[36] See ICTY, *Aleksovski*, above n 23, at 82.
[37] See the *Report of the Baha Mousa Inquiry*, The Right Honourable Sir William Gage (Chairman) (2011), vols I–III (2011), Recommendation 30.
[38] Principles of Medical Ethics relevant to the Role of Health Personnel, Particularly Physicians, in the Protection of Prisoners and Detainees against Torture and Other Cruel, Inhuman or Degrading Treatment or Punishment (1982), Principle 3.
[39] DODI2310.08E, 6 June 2006. For a detailed criticism of US practices concerning the provision of medical attention to detainees, *Situation of Detainees at Guantánamo Bay*, UN Doc E/CN.4/2006/120, 15 February 2006, at 72–82.

duties',[40] subject to the disciplinary routine of the camp. The right to practise one's religion may also be limited by law, in order to protect 'public safety, order, health or morals or the fundamental rights and freedoms of others'.[41]

b. Recreation, study, and sports

Article 94 GC IV creates *a broad* obligation on the Detaining Power to 'encourage intellectual, educational and recreational pursuits, sports and games amongst internees'. Internees are not required to participate in such activities,[42] thus ensuring that the Detaining Power cannot be seen to 'punish' internees, for example by forcing them to exercise. Internees may undertake studies and continue their education. This is particularly important for children. In this respect, the Convention on the Rights of the Child[43] provides further guidance. Any action concerning a person under 18 years old shall be taken with the best interests of the child as the primary consideration,[44] and the right to education is one that is achieved on the basis of equal opportunity.[45]

c. Working conditions

Recognizing that work is important for an internee's well-being,[46] Article 95 GC IV permits either voluntary or non-voluntary work to be undertaken by the internee during internment.[47] This provision and Article 96 foresee, however, many safeguards for voluntary and non-voluntary work. Internees may resign from the work that they are doing—but only after a working period of six weeks, and subject to eight days' notice. It may be assumed that if the work the internee is undertaking is essential for the well-being of other internees, the Detaining Power may not accept the resignation. Article 96 deals with the particular risks resulting from the placement of internees in labour detachments, ensuring accountability even when internees work outside the internment camp, possibly for private employers.

VI. Personal property and financial resources

a. Valuables and personal effects

Article 97 GC IV concerns the valuables and personal effects of internees. Items with personal or sentimental value may not be taken away. This will involve a cultural perspective. For example, some cultures place a very high value on amulets and talismans, which if removed from the internee might create a great deal of stress for that person. While not expressly stated in Article 97, the Detaining Power would have the authority to remove items, even if they are valuable or of sentimental value, if those items might threaten

---

[40] Violation of the right to respect for religious practices is a punishable offence under the legislation of several states; see ICRC CIHL Database, 2. Practice, Rule 104—Respect for Convictions and Religious Practices, and Rule 127—Respect for Convictions and Religious Practices of Persons Deprived of their Liberty.
[41] Art 18(3) ICCPR.
[42] Art 94 para 1 GCIV.
[43] CRC.
[44] Ibid, Art 3 para 1.
[45] Ibid, Art 28 para 1.
[46] During the negotiations of this Article, the delegate from the UK argued that '[g]enerally speaking, work helped internees to maintain their morale. That was an important consideration from a humanitarian point of view, and it was therefore desirable to provide all facilities to enable internees to do some form of work [...] even though this might not be an economic proposition' (see statement from Mr Speake (United Kingdom), Final Record, vol II-A, at 680).
[47] See also Art 40 and 51 GC IV.

either the safety of others or good order in the camp. Of course, pillage is prohibited.[48] As for medicines or drugs, it would be reasonable to permit a medical practitioner or other appropriate health practitioner, such as a nurse or pharmacist, to decide whether those medicines or drugs should remain with the internee.[49]

b. Financial resources and individual accounts

27 Article 98 GC IV deals with the allowances internees must receive from the Detaining Power and may receive from other sources. The account into which the allowances are to be paid 'is a regular account'. The meaning of 'regular account' is not clear. It would be reasonable to assume that such accounts must be held with institutions that are governed by law and have properly managed corporate governance structures.

VII. Administration and discipline

a. Camp administration

28 Article 99 GC IV captures two notions of accountability, each of which ensures that places of internment are administered appropriately. The first is command and control. Every internment camp must be under the authority of a responsible person—chosen from the Detaining Power's military or civilian administration. This excludes private military and security companies. The officer in charge must ensure that his or her staff are instructed in the relevant provisions of GC IV, have been carefully selected, have adequate standards of education and intelligence,[50] and have the required training in matters such as the application of the Convention against Torture (CAT).[51] In addition, Internee Committees, dealt with by Articles 102, 103, and 104, play an important role in the administration of a camp, and as regards communication between the internees and those in charge of the camp.

29 The text of GC IV and the special agreements concluded under it must be posted, or copies of the same must be in the possession of the Internee Committee.[52] Regulations, orders, or notices must equally be posted inside places of internment.[53] All documents and orders and commands must be given in a language that the internee understands. Linguistic difficulties in understanding can lead to frustrations, which might escalate to violence. For example, the ICRC noted that it 'occasionally observed persons deprived of their liberty being slapped, roughed up, pushed around or pushed to the ground […] because of poor communication skills (a failure to understand or a misunderstanding of orders given in English was construed by guards as resistance or disobedience)'.[54]

b. General discipline, complaints, and petitions

30 Article 100 GC IV sets the general principle concerning the disciplinary regime in places of internment, and must be read alongside the general prohibitions contained in GC IV, including those whose violation constitutes a grave breach under Article 147 (see MN 67–75, below). Article 101 regulates petitions and complaints brought forward by

---

[48] Art 33 GC IV. See also practice relating to Rule 122—Pillage of Personal Belongings of Persons Deprived of their Liberty, ICRC CIHL Database, for a list of national legislation specifically prohibiting pillage.
[49] See The Standard Minimum Rules for the Treatment of Prisoners (1955), Rule 43 (4).
[50] See, e.g, ibid, Rule 46.   [51] Art 10 CAT.   [52] Art 99 para 2 GC IV.
[53] Art 99 para 3 GC IV; see Ch 9, MN 16, of this volume.
[54] ICRC, *Report of the ICRC on the Treatment of Coalition Forces of Prisoners of War and Other Protected Persons by the Geneva Conventions in Iraq during Arrest, Internment and Interrogation* (February 2004), at 40.

internees. The Commentary to Article 101 paragraph 1 explains that 'the procedure for submitting petitions […] must be compatible with the normal requirements of discipline and the administration of the place of internment and petitions must not be used for purposes other than those arising under the Convention'.[55] Complaints must also 'be strictly concerned with conditions of internment, failing which they would not be accepted'.[56] However, today, the right to petition and complain is interpreted more widely, so as to cover violations against human right provisions that impact on internment.

There are at least three global human rights treaty bodies that may consider communications from internees: the Human Rights Committee (HRCttee),[57] the Committee against Torture (CtteeAT),[58] and the Committee on Enforced Disappearances (CtteeED).[59] In relation to the CAT, states parties also undertake to ensure that 'any individual who alleges he has been subjected to torture in any territory under his jurisdiction has the right to complain to, and to have his case promptly and impartially examined by, its competent authorities'.[60] As the ICRC has a right to visit internees and to interview them in private,[61] petitions and complaints may equally be addressed to the ICRC. When regional human rights treaty obligations apply, internees may also have a right to petition or complain.

The petition and complaints mechanism in GC IV does not address procedures for making complaints. Consistent with the communication system that exits in human rights treaties, it is reasonable to expect that any petition or complaint by individual internees or the Internee Committee will meet the following requirements: (i) it must not be anonymous; and (ii) it must relate to a matter that is within the Detaining Power's ability to deal with. Each petition or complaint to the Detaining Power will need to be investigated by a competent and independent body so as to ascertain the facts and identify what remedial steps need to be taken. Such steps, particularly if there have been gross violations of human rights, must include considerations of reparations.[62]

The requirement for periodic reports by the Internees Committee to the Protecting Power detailing the situation in places of internment in Article 101 paragraph 4 GC IV, must be distinguished from possible obligations of the Detaining Power to report to the relevant human rights treaty bodies and, under the Universal Periodic Review, to the UN Human Rights Council.[63]

---

[55] Pictet Commentary GC IV, at 434.   [56] Ibid, at 435.

[57] The HRCttee may consider individual petitions and complaints relating to states parties pursuant to the First Optional Protocol to the ICCPR Art 1. The right to complain and the HRCttee's consideration of complaints are subject to Arts 2, 3, and 5 of the Optional Protocol.

[58] The CtteeAT may consider individual petitions and complaints relating to states parties who have made the necessary declaration pursuant to Art 22 CAT. For further details of the procedures and role of the CtteeAT, see M. Nowak and E. McArthur, *The United Nations Convention against Torture: A Commentary* (New York: OUP, 2008), at 719–97.

[59] The CtteeED may consider individual petitions and complaints pursuant to Arts 31 and 30 ICED.

[60] Art 13 CAT. For further details of the individual complaints mechanism, see Nowak and McArthur, above n 58, at 439–51.

[61] See Ch 26 of this volume; Art 142 para 3 and Art 143 para 5 GC IV.

[62] See Art 14 CAT; Art 24 ICED; and the Guidelines on the Right to a Remedy and Reparation for Victims of Gross Violations on International Human Rights and Serious Violations of International Humanitarian Law (2005).

[63] See, e.g., Arts 41–42 ICCPR; for the UN Human Rights Council, see UN Doc A/RES/65/281, 17 June 2011.

VIII. Relations with the exterior

34 Article 105 GC IV sets the tone concerning accountability by requiring the Detaining Power to notify internees, the Power to which internees owe allegiance, and their Protecting Power of both the measures and modifications taken to give effect to Articles 106–116. Those Articles ensure that internees can maintain relations with the exterior, transmit and execute legal documents, and manage their property and legal proceedings; but they also deal with the possibility of censorship (Article 112) and special means of transport if a Detaining Power is unable to fulfil its duties because of military operations (Article 111). The rules cited in MN 35–39 deserve specific discussion.

a. *Internment card*

35 A key aspect of relations with the exterior is the opportunity for internees to communicate with the exterior. Article 106 GC IV provides details on the right of internees to inform family members and the Central Tracing Agency (CTA)[64] about their detention, address, and state of health.[65] This information may be conveyed on a card—an internment card—a template of which is found in Annex III of GC IV. The ICRC has highlighted the need to fill out internment cards accurately, because failure to do has led to 'unnecessary delays of several weeks or months before families were notified, […] sometimes resulting in no notifications at all'.[66] While internees have a right to notify others of their internment, there is no obligation to do so.

36 The principle in Article 106 is reinforced by the ICED, which provides that no one shall be held in secret detention and that state parties to that Convention '[g]uarantee that any person deprived of liberty shall be authorised to communicate with […] his or her family, counsel or any other person of his or her choice, subject only to the conditions established by law, or if he or she is a foreigner, to communicate with his or her consular authorities, in accordance with applicable international law'.[67]

b. *Correspondence*

37 Internees may also send and receive letters in accordance with the provisions spelt out in Article 107 GC IV. Advances in communication, such as the use of computers and mobile phones, mean that the intention behind Article 107 must be extended to other forms of communication not considered at the time of drafting.[68] In other words, all forms of communication with the exterior should be facilitated. If forms of communication are restricted, the restrictions must be related to resource issues (such as limited bandwidths for the Internet) or military necessity (such as when military forces impose communication blackouts on their own personnel), and not be used as a means of punishing internees. Of course, Detaining Powers are able to call on other organizations, such as the ICRC, to

---

[64] See Art 140 GC IV.

[65] This right is also recognized in the legislation of several states; see practice relating to Rule 125—Correspondence of Persons Deprived of their Liberty, ICRC CIHL Database.

[66] ICRC, *Report of the ICRC on the Treatment of Coalition Forces of Prisoners of War and Other Protected Persons by the Geneva Conventions in Iraq during Arrest, Internment and Interrogation* (February 2004), para 11.

[67] Art 17(2)(d) ICED. The Vienna Convention on Consular Relations (1963) also creates a similar requirement of notification to consular officials—see Art 36(1)(b).

[68] The ICRC has stated that it has assisted internees to communicate with their families by means of telephone and video calls in both Iraq and Afghanistan. See ICRC, *Persons Detained by the US in Relation to Armed Conflict and the Fight against Terrorism: The Role of the ICRC* (Geneva: ICRC, 2012), at 5–6.

assist them with helping internees to communicate with family members and those who might assist the internee.[69]

c. Relief shipments

Articles 108–110 GC IV deal with the receipt of individual parcels or collective relief by internees. Special agreements might also be entered into between relevant organizations to facilitate shipments. If special agreements are not adopted then the draft regulations located in Annex II of GC IV are to be applied. The matter of postal dues for letters, parcels, and financial services in the context of internees is specifically dealt with by the Universal Postal Convention.[70]

d. Visits

Article 116 paragraph 1 GC IV raises three matters of importance. First, internees are allowed visitors. Secondly, near relatives are especially privileged as a category of visitors. Thirdly, visits should occur at regular intervals and as frequently as possible. Article 116 paragraph 2 allows internees to visit their homes in urgent cases, such as the death of or serious injury to relatives. The ICED echoes GC IV, obliging a state party to '[g]uarantee that any person deprived of their liberty shall be authorised to […] be visited by his or her family, counsel or any other person of his or her choice subject only to the conditions established by law'.[71] Notwithstanding the broad terms in which Article 116 paragraph 1 is expressed, it is reasonable for the Detaining Power to restrict who may visit the internee, and when they might visit. For example, it would be reasonable for the Detaining Power to prohibit an internee from receiving visits from persons who might jeopardize the security and good order of the internment camp. Similarly, it would be reasonable for the Detaining Power to restrict visits to particular hours so as better to manage the security and daily routine of the camp. What is clearly not acceptable is prohibiting an internee from receiving visitors. In other words, in certain circumstances access to, and frequency of, visits may be restricted, but they must never be prohibited.

IX. Penal and disciplinary sanctions

a. General provisions—applicable legislation

Article 117 GC IV recognizes that the laws in force in the territory in which internment takes place continue to apply to internees. However, the application of these laws must be consistent with the international law obligations of the Detaining Power and, more specifically, subject to the provisions in Articles 117–126. Furthermore, Article 117 implies that the Detaining Power must apply those laws to internees, and any breaches of those laws must be dealt with in accordance with national laws and procedures.

Another provision which deserves special mention is Article 126 GC IV, which makes the judicial guarantees foreseen in Articles 71–76 (relating to criminal proceedings brought by an Occupying Power) applicable 'by analogy, to proceedings against internees who are in the national territory of the Detaining Power'. This provision may seem surprising, as it means that if the Detaining Power would have immediately arrested such persons in view of a criminal prosecution, instead of first interning them, that Detaining Power

---

[69] Art 111 GC IV; see also Art 43 ICED.
[70] Art 7 para 3 Universal Postal Convention (1994).
[71] Art 17(2)(d) ICED.

42   would not have been bound by such guarantees but only by its domestic legislation and IHRL.[72] Article 126 ensures the same treatment for those interned during occupation and those interned in the national territory of the Detaining Power.

42   A further important issue is that Article 117 paragraph 2 accepts that there might be reasons to create offences that apply only to internees. Such offences—referred to as disciplinary offences—are those which are not dealt with by the general laws, regulations, or orders that are applicable to non-internees. Typical disciplinary offences include not obeying lawful orders or directions of the staff running the internment facility, or failing to return to a place of accommodation when required to do so. Article 117 paragraph 2 also limits punishments for disciplinary offences to 'disciplinary punishments'. Disciplinary punishments are dealt with in Article 119 GC IV. As stated in the Commentary to GC IV, disciplinary punishments 'are not those authorised under ordinary law, but those inflicted for infractions of the internment regulations'.[73] Further detail concerning disciplinary punishments is also found in Articles 119–125.

43   Regardless of whether the offence is criminal or disciplinary, '[n]o internee may be punished more than once for the same act, or on the same count'.[74] The principle that internees should not be punished more than once for the same act is also found in international criminal statutes[75] and in human rights treaties, such as the ICCPR,[76] Protocol 7 to the ECHR,[77] and the ACHR.[78]

b. Penalties

44   Article 118 GC IV deals with penalties and moderates the application of extant laws in the territory in which internment takes place. Article 118 paragraph 1 seeks to ensure that the relevant authorities take into account as far as possible the special circumstances of non-nationals of the Detaining Power.

45   Imprisoned internees must be placed in premises that have daylight and must not be subject to any form of cruelty. Penitentiary premises, by virtue of Article 124 GC IV, cannot be used for disciplinary punishment.

46   Under Article 118 paragraph 3, '[i]nternees who have served disciplinary or judicial sentences shall not be treated differently from other internees'. This rule is subject to at least two caveats. The first is that Article 120 paragraph 2, which concerns internees who are recaptured after having escaped or attempted to escape, permits internees to be placed under surveillance, and in that context, it expressly provides that Article 118 paragraph 3 does not apply in such circumstances. The second caveat allows for the separation of internees after they have served their sentence, for their own safety or the safety of other internees.

47   Article 118 paragraph 5 provides an accountability measure by requiring the Detaining Power to inform the relevant Internee Committee of 'all judicial proceedings instituted against internees whom they represent, and of their result'. This measure permits internees a level of comfort, knowing that judicial proceedings against them are monitored by an independent entity. The measure also allows an internee to complain about the judicial process or finding through the office of the Internee Committee pursuant to Article 101 paragraph 2 GC IV.[79]

---

[72] See Art 38 GC IV. [73] Pictet Commentary GC IV, at 477. [74] Art 117 para 3 GC IV.
[75] See Art 20 ICC Statute. [76] Art 14(7) ICCPR. [77] Art 4 Protocol 7 to the ECHR.
[78] Art 8(4) ACHR.
[79] See MN 28–33, above, for the representational role played by internee committees.

c. Disciplinary punishments

48 Moving away from penal offences and punishments, Article 119 GC IV provides an exhaustive list of the disciplinary punishments that the Detaining Power may impose on internees. The punishments include: a fine, restriction of privileges, fatigue or extra duties, and confinement. The punishments are listed in a manner that suggests that the fine is the least severe form of punishment and confinement the most severe. Consequently, when punishing an internee, the sentencing authorities would need to justify the punishment based on generally accepted sentencing principles.

49 Fines would not be a sentencing option where the internee does not have an income, and in that instance the sentencing authority would need to turn to other available punishments. In relation to privileges, a privilege may be restricted only if it is one which is not guaranteed or provided for by GC IV.[80] In other words, the right to have food or water, or the right to receive visitors, cannot be removed, but the privilege of watching TV or listening to the radio may be denied. Fatigue or extra duties might be imposed, but only if they do not last longer than two hours, and provided there is a nexus between the duty and the maintenance of the place of internment.[81] Fatigue or extra duties cannot be imposed, for example, where the duty requires the internee to undertake a service that is in the personal interest of an internment camp guard. Confinement 'must be understood [...] as the loss of liberty for disciplinary reasons as opposed to deprival of liberty as a statutory punishment'.[82] Pre-trial confinement for discipline offences is dealt with by Article 122 paragraphs 2 and 3. Furthermore, the form of confinement for disciplinary reasons is subject to the application of both Article 124 and Article 125.[83] Cumulative punishments are limited to a maximum of 30 days.[84] Punishments, in other words, must be measured against the standard of humane treatment.

50 The disciplinary punishment regime is subject to a chapeau: 'In no case shall disciplinary penalties be inhuman, brutal or dangerous for the health of internees. Account shall be taken of the internee's age, sex and state of health.'[85] Therefore, the punishments identified in Article 119 must all comply with the fundamental principle prohibiting inhuman treatment; and in deciding what is inhuman, the authorities must also consider the internee's health, age, and sex. In interpreting the prohibition against inhuman treatment during internment, Detaining Powers will also need to comply with their obligations under other international regimes. For example, the provisions concerning the prohibition of torture, cruel, inhuman, and degrading treatment or punishment which are dealt with in the CAT would also apply to the treatment of internees.[86] Similarly, the prohibition against inhuman and degrading treatment found in general IHRL conventions such as the ICCPR would also apply.[87] Furthermore, collective punishments are prohibited.[88]

---

[80] Ibid.   [81] Art 119 para 1(3).   [82] Pictet Commentary GC IV, at 483.
[83] See MN 51, below.   [84] Art 119 para 3.
[85] Art 119 para 2. Similar provisions exist in Arts 27 and 32 GC IV. For an indicative list of ill-treatment punishments, see the ICRC, *Report of the ICRC on the Treatment of Coalition Forces of Prisoners of War and Other Protected Persons by the Geneva Conventions in Iraq during Arrest, Internment and Interrogation* (February 2004), para 25.
[86] See Art 1 CAT, which defines torture, and Art 16 CAT, which defines cruel, inhuman, and degrading treatment or punishment. For more details concerning the interpretation of torture and cruel, inhuman, and degrading treatment, see Nowak and McArthur, above n 58, at 27–86 and 503–37 respectively.
[87] See Art 7 ICCPR.   [88] See Art 33 GC IV and Ch 56 of this volume.

51 Articles 124 and 125 provide further guarantees for those undergoing disciplinary punishment. Article 125 paragraph 4 prescribes that internees cannot be deprived of the 'benefit of the provisions of Articles 107 and 143' of the Convention. It appears that the reference to Article 107 is a typographical error—the reference should be to Article 101 which concerns the right to petition. On that basis, internees undergoing disciplinary punishments may petition or complain about their treatment, including their punishment. The reference to Article 143 means that internees undergoing disciplinary punishments must not be denied the same levels of supervision from the Protecting Power and the ICRC to which other internees are entitled.

d. Escapes

52 Internees who are recaptured after having escaped or attempting to escape are not subject to criminal punishment. Pursuant to Article 120 paragraph 1 GC IV, they are subject to disciplinary punishments only.[89] The rationale for treating acts of escape or attempted escapes as disciplinary offences is founded on the fact that such acts are 'patriotic gestures [...] and quite understandable'.[90] Article 121 GC IV deals with offences connected with escapes.

e. Investigations, confinements awaiting hearing

53 Under Article 122 GC IV, allegations of disciplinary offences must be investigated immediately. The Article is silent as to what constitutes an investigation, but one assumes that the Detaining Power must appoint a person with the appropriate knowledge and skills to carry out the investigation, and the investigator must carry it out impartially and independently. Where a Detaining Power holds an internee in pre-trial confinement in view of disciplinary punishment, the duration of that custody must be kept to a minimum and must never be more than 14 days. Investigators will need to ensure that they can comply with the 14-day limit or the internee will have to be released. In recognition of general sentencing principles, any time spent in pre-trial custody is to be deducted from the sentence of confinement.

f. Procedures for disciplinary offences

54 The procedures for imposing disciplinary punishments are laid out in Article 123 GC IV. These procedural provisions are consistent with human rights arrangements, such as the ICCPR,[91] the ECHR,[92] and the ACHR.[93] The rights to examine witnesses and have recourse to a qualified interpreter are provisions which, consistent with general human standards, reinforce the 'principle of equality of arms [...] [thus] ensuring an effective defence by the accused and their counsel'.[94] Punishments may be imposed by courts or higher authorities, or by the commandant of a place of internment, the commandant's delegate, or the commandant's replacement. The list of persons who may order punishments is therefore divided between formal authorities outside the internment structure, and the commandant's authority within the internment structure. The

---

[89] Internees who aid and abet an escape or attempted escape are also subject to disciplinary punishments and the caveats articulated in Art 120 para 2.
[90] Pictet Commentary GC IV, at 485.   [91] Art 14(3)(e) and (f) ICCPR.
[92] Art 6(3)(d) and (e) ECHR.   [93] Art 2(a) and (f) ACHR.
[94] HRCttee, General Comment 32, Art 14: Right to equality before courts and tribunals to a fair trial, 23 August 2007, para 39.

reason for including the formal authorities is to reinforce accountability by ensuring that 'the competence of the responsible commandant, however extensive it may be, is neither universal nor without appeal'.[95]

Another matter dealt with by Article 123 is that of maintaining a register in the place of internment, so as to provide a record of the disciplinary punishments imposed on internees. The register must be open to inspection by relevant organizations such as the ICRC. Article 123 provides no detail of what must be recorded in the register. However, Pictet Commentary GC IV provides that the register should contain details concerning

> the exact names of those convicted, the nature and duration of the punishment, the date and place in which it was carried out, the motives for punishment, the name of the authority which took the decision, and the signature of the commandant, since it is his personal duty to keep the register. Furthermore, the register should include a reference to the enquiry file, to facilitate thorough study of any possible complaints.[96]

It is reasonable to expect that the register should also contain the details of the offence committed, whether there was an appeal against a conviction or punishment, and the results of the appeal. Information about the offence and appeal reduces the need to refer to another file, which in turn reduces the risk of losing information. Whether the register is in electronic or paper format, it is essential that the records cannot be tampered with by unauthorized users, and that they are kept in a safe and secure manner. One advantage of paper registers is that their pages can be numbered, which limits the risk of information about internees being removed from the register.

X. Transfers of internees

If the transfer is to another Power then the provisions in Article 45 GC IV would apply on a party's national territory, while transfers are outlawed altogether from occupied territories under Article 49 GC IV. Under Article 127 GC IV, all transfers are to be conducted humanely, and any decision to transfer must also be consistent with the best interests of the internee. The Detaining Power must compile a complete list of internees who are to be transferred.

XI. Deaths

While Article 130 GC IV deals with the burial and gravesites of internees, Article 129 focuses on wills, death certificates, and records of death. It therefore serves a dual purpose: (i) ensuring that the beneficiaries of the deceased internee are not disadvantaged; and (ii) ensuring that the Detaining Power keeps proper records for the purpose of accountability. These records are important evidence for the family and beneficiaries of the internee, particularly in relation to administrative matters such as insurance claims. The records are also fundamentally important for reasons of accountability. First, the certificate and record reinforce each other to the extent that each death is properly recorded, so that the family and other interested parties may know what happened to the deceased internee. Secondly, the records might form the basis of subsequent investigations or claims made against the Detaining Power. A further level of accountability is imposed by requiring a copy of the record of death to be transmitted without delay to the Protecting Power and the CTA.[97]

---

[95] Pictet Commentary GC IV, at 491. [96] Pictet Commentary GC IV, at 492–3.
[97] For a more detailed discussion of the CTA, see Art 140 GC IV and Ch 53 of this volume.

Where states have obligations under the ICED, they must be able to provide information about the cause of death of any person who has died during the deprivation of liberty.[98] Pursuant to Article 131 paragraph 3 GC IV, the Detaining Power must forward lists of graves of deceased internees, through the Information Bureau,[99] to the state on whom the deceased internee was dependent.

58   Continuing the theme of accountability, Article 131 obliges the Detaining Power to investigate the deaths of or serious injuries to internees in certain enumerated circumstances, and to inform the Protecting Power of the results of such investigations. In addition, investigations might also need to be carried out in situations where human rights provisions such as Article 6 ICCPR apply.[100]

59   Conducting official investigations in relation to deaths or serious injuries ensures that laws concerning the use of force are adhered to, that those accountable for the death or serious injury are brought to justice, and that systemic flaws in the handling of internees are identified.[101] Such investigations are also important in assessing whether victims or their beneficiaries are entitled to claim reparations.

60   While Article 131 paragraph 1 is silent as to what is meant by an 'official enquiry', it is clear that, as a minimum, such investigations must be independent and impartial, and must comply with procedural obligations. The High Court in the UK has stated that investigations relating to the death of a civilian at the hands of state agents must be

official, i.e. initiated by the state; timely, i.e. in both initiation and completion; independent i.e. both formally and practically, from those implicated in the events; open, i.e. to a sufficient element of public scrutiny as well as to the involvement of the next-of-kin; and effective, i.e. capable of achieving objective accountability of the state agents and thus of leading, as appropriate, to conclusions about all the circumstances, including the background issues […] as well as about responsibility […] and the identification and punishment of those responsible.[102]

61   The term 'serious injury' is not defined in Article 131 paragraph 1. The Commentary to Article 131 explains that in most cases serious injury should refer to cases where an internee requires in-patient treatment in a hospital or an infirmary.[103] That definition would encompass cases where an internee suffers a combination of injuries, including physical and psychological harm.

62   Article 131 paragraph 2 requires the Detaining Power to communicate with the Protecting Power about the investigation, including providing the Protecting Power with a report of results of the investigation.

[98] Art 7 para 3(g) ICED.
[99] For a more detailed discussion about the Information Bureau, see Art 136 GC IV and Ch 53 of this volume.
[100] See, e.g., the report by P. Alston, United Nations Special Rapporteur on Extrajudicial, Summary or Arbitrary Executions: 'It is undeniable that during armed conflicts circumstances will sometimes impede investigation. Such circumstances will never discharge the obligation to investigate […] but they may affect the modalities or particulars of the investigation' (Report E/CN.4/2006/53 (8 March 2006), at 36); with regard to Art 2 ECHR, see below n 101 and 102.
[101] See, e.g., the investigation concerning the death of Baha Mousa: *The Report of the Baha Mousa Inquiry, The Right Honourable Sir William Gage (Chairman)* (2011), vols I–III. See also ECtHR, *Al-Skeini and others v United Kingdom*, Judgment, 7 July 2011, at 163.
[102] *Al-Skeini v Secretary of State for Defence* [2004] EWHC 2911 (Admin), at [322]. See IACommHR, *Juan Carlos Abella v Argentina*, Case 11.137 Report No 55/97, 18 November 1997, particularly at 414, in which the Commission spells out the minimum steps that should be taken in investigating a death of a civilian at the hands of state agents. While the comments in *Abella* refer to executions by state agents, the points made by the Commission are relevant to investigating the abuse and mistreatment of internees. See also *Al-Skeini*, above n 101, para 167.
[103] Pictet Commentary GC IV, at 509.

A final aspect of accountability concerning deaths in internment is the Detaining Power's obligation to 'take all necessary steps to ensure the prosecution of the person or persons responsible'.[104] Under the ICC Statute this requirement is particularly important, because a failure to take such steps might be relevant under Article 17 of that Statute.[105]

63

C. Relevance in Non-International Armed Conflicts

Although internment may occur in non-international armed conflicts (NIACs),[106] the provisions regulating the treatment of internees in such conflicts are much less elaborate and detailed than those contained in GC IV. In addition to the minimum standards provided by Common Article 3 and the requirement of humane treatment,[107] certain specific provisions concerning treatment may be found in Articles 4 and 5 of Additional Protocol (AP) II. Notwithstanding the narrowness of Articles 4 and 5, it is clear that they were inspired by the provisions concerning internment in GC IV and human rights provisions contained in the ICCPR.[108] Another point to note in relation to treatment is that Article 5 AP II has a wider reach than GC IV's internee provisions, because AP II treatment standards extend to any person who has been deprived of his or her liberty for reasons related to the armed conflict.

64

Even though these provisions are clearly inspired by those contained in GC IV,[109] it is reasonable to assume that they have different degrees of force with regard to the standard of treatment to be achieved. While pursuant to the provisions of GC IV the standard provided by the Detaining Power must generally be greater than that available to the general non-interned population,[110] in situations of NIACs the detaining authority is required to provide internees with a standard of treatment equal to that of the local civil population. In fact, although the obligations contained in Article 5(1) AP II are absolute and unconditional, their content may vary depending on the living conditions within the local community. The minimum requirement remains to provide internees with the means necessary for survival, the necessities of life, and the benefit of relief actions.[111]

65

The principles and rules of GC IV may serve as a guideline in NIACs.[112] Accordingly, parties to a NIAC may decide to bring into force, by means of special agreements, all

66

---

[104] Art 131 para 3 GC IV.

[105] Art 17 ICC Statute provides that 'the Court shall determine that a case is inadmissible where: (a) the case is being [...] prosecuted by a State which has jurisdiction over it, unless the State is unwilling or unable to genuinely to carry out the [...] prosecution'.

[106] The possibility of internment in NIACs can be assumed from the specific references to internment in Art 5 and Art 6(5) AP II.

[107] See Chs 21, 22, and 23 of this volume.   [108] E.g., see ICRC Commentary APs, at 4509.

[109] Namely, Arts 85, 89, 90, 93, 95, and 108.   [110] See MN 13, above.

[111] As in situations of NIACs the living conditions of the local population are usually very poor, it would have been unrealistic to adopt norms requiring a greater standard of treatment of internees; see ICRC Commentary APs, at 4573. See also ICTY, *Aleksovski*, above n 23, at 169–82.

[112] See J. Pejic, 'Procedural Principles and Safeguards for Internment/Administrative Detention in Armed Conflict and Other Situations of Violence', 87 *IRRC* 858 (2005) 375, at 377; for a discussion, see L. Olson, 'Practical Challenges of Implementing the Complementarity between International Humanitarian and Human Rights Law: Demonstrated by the Procedural Regulation of Internment in Non-International Armed Conflict', 40 *Case Western Reserve JIL* (2009) 437, at 450 ff; M. Sassòli and L. Olson, 'The Relationship between International Humanitarian Law and Human Rights Law Where it Matters: Admissible Killing and Internment of Fighters in Non-International Armed Conflict', 90 *IRRC* 871 (2008) 599, at 623 ff; and

or part of the provisions of GC IV[113], or the regime and standards for civilians foreseen therein may be applied by analogy to NIACs.[114] For instance, even though there is no treaty provision requiring the detaining party to transfer the remains of the dead to their families, or to identify the dead prior to their disposal in the context of NIACs,[115] the provisions set forth in Articles 129–131 GC IV, nevertheless, have in some cases been applied to NIACs.[116]

D. Legal Consequences of a Violation

67 A number of violations constitute grave breaches under Article 147 GC IV. These violations include:

— wilful torture or inhuman treatment of internees;[117]
— wilfully causing great suffering or serious injury to the body or health of internees;
— wilfully depriving internees of the rights of fair and regular trial;[118] and
— compelling internees to serve in the forces of a hostile power.

68 Other serious violations might arise in relation to the treatment of internees, including enforced disappearance. Although GC IV does not expressly refer to enforced disappearance, the numerous provisions and extensive requirements concerning registration, visits, and transmission of information laid down therein,[119] are nonetheless aimed at preventing incommunicado detentions and enforced disappearances.[120] These actions are prohibited by international humanitarian law, the ICED, the Inter-American Convention on the Forced Disappearance of Persons, and the domestic legislation of numerous states.[121]

69 The systematic practice of enforced disappearance constitutes a crime against humanity under the ICC Statute.[122] Furthermore, although enforced disappearance is not listed

---

L. Lopez, 'Uncivil Wars: The Challenge of Applying International Humanitarian Law to Internal Armed Conflicts', 69 *New York University Law Review* (1994) 916, at 950 ff.

[113] See Ch 25 of this volume.
[114] See J.-M. Henckaerts, 'Study on Customary International Humanitarian Law: A Contribution to the Understanding and Respect for the Rule of Law in Armed Conflicts', 87 *IRRC* 857 (2005) 175, at 188–90.
[115] See Rule 114—Return of the Remains and personal Effects of the Dead, and Rule 116—Accounting for the Dead, ICRC CIHL Database.
[116] See 'Plan of Operation for the Joint Commission to Trace Missing Persons and Mortal Remains', Proposal 2.1, ICRC CIHL Study, at 252; and Comprehensive Agreement on Respect for Human Rights and International Humanitarian Law in the Philippines (1998), ICRC CIHL Study, Part IV, Art 3 para 4, at 253. See also UN Commission on the Truth for El Salvador, *Accountability and Human Rights* (1993), ICRC CIHL Study, at 573; and 22nd International Conference of the Red Cross (1973), Resolution V, ICRC CIHL Study, at 706.
[117] For instance, failure to comply with the obligations set forth in Arts 76, 85, 87, and 89–92 GC IV might amount to inhuman treatment of internees; see, by analogy, ICTY, *Aleksovski* case, above n 23.
[118] See Arts 66–75 GC IV, which apply by virtue of Art 126 GC IV.
[119] See, in particular, Arts 83, 105, 106, 107, and 116 GC IV; see also Arts 136–138 GC IV.
[120] Pejic, above n 112, at 384–5.
[121] See Practice Relating to Rule 98—Enforced Disappearance, ICRC CIHL Database, for an updated list of domestic legislation which specifically prohibits this practice. For the limits of the application of the Inter-American Convention, see Ch 35 section B.II., of this volume.
[122] Art 7(1)(i) ICC Statute.

as a crime against humanity in the ICTY Statute, in the *Kupreškić* case the Tribunal held that enforced disappearance may violate several human rights that would fall within the offence of inhumane acts dealt with in Article 5(i) of its Statute.[123]

In addition, similar provisions on the prohibition of unacknowledged detention are contained in the ICED and soft law instruments,[124] and are taken into account to assess violations of other fundamental rights by most human rights bodies, such as the HRCttee,[125] the European Court of Human Rights (ECtHR),[126] the Inter-American Commission on Human Rights (IACommHR),[127] and the Inter-American Court of Human Rights (IACtHR).[128]

Although the practice of enforced disappearance constitutes a crime against humanity only where it is widespread or systematic, the prohibition of unacknowledged detention is absolute and not subject to derogation.[129] Accordingly, a failure to comply with the provisions preventing enforced disappearances contained in GC IV might lead to a violation of IHL and IHRL, and be ground for complaints to be brought before bodies such as the HRCttee, the CtteeED, and competent regional human rights courts.[130]

Pillage is another offence that might arise in relation to the treatment of internees. It is listed as a war crime under the ICTY Statute,[131] the International Criminal Tribunal for Rwanda (ICTR) Statute,[132] and the Statute of the Special Court of Sierra Leone (SCSL).[133] It may be inferred from the ICTY case law that pillage will be considered a 'serious' violation of IHL only where the property taken is 'of sufficient monetary value for its unlawful appropriation to involve grave consequences for the victims'.[134]

Certain breaches of the provisions concerning the treatment of internees may amount to violations of IHRL, regardless of whether they constitute a war crime or a crime against humanity.[135] In particular, they may fall under the crime against humanity of

---

[123] ICTY, *The Prosecutor v Zoran Kupreškić*, Trial Chamber Judgment, IT-95-16-T, 14 January 2000, at 566.

[124] See UN Declaration on the Protection of All Persons from Enforced Disappearance, UNGA 47/133, 18 December 1992; HRCttee, General Comment 29 on Art 4 of the ICCPR; Body of Principles for the Protection of All Persons under Any Form of Detention or Imprisonment, Principles 12 and 16(1).

[125] HRCttee, *Quinteros v Uruguay*, Views, 21 July 1983, at 12.3–14; HRCttee, *Lyashkevich v Belarus*, Views, 3 April 2003, at 9.2.

[126] ECtHR, *Kurt v Turkey*, Judgment, 25 May 1998, at 133–4; ECtHR, *Timurtas v Turkey*, Judgment, 13 June 2000, at 96–8; ECtHR, *Cyprus case*, Judgment, 10 May 2001, at 156–8.

[127] See, inter alia, IACommHR, Case 9466 (Peru), Resolution, 30 June 1987, at 137-2; IACommHR, Case 9844 (El Salvador), Resolution, 13 September 1988, at 144-2; IACommHR, Case 9786 (Peru), Resolution, 14 September 1988, at 35-2.

[128] IACtHR, *Velásquez Rodríguez case*, above n 16, at 155–8.

[129] See Rule 98—Enforced Disappearance, ICRC CIHL Database; and HRCttee, General Comment 29 on Art 4 of the ICCPR.

[130] See Basic Principles and Guidelines on the Right to a Remedy and Reparation for Victims of Gross Violations of International Human Rights Law and Serious Violations of International Humanitarian Law (2005), Principle 26.

[131] Art 3(e) ICTY Statute. [132] Art 4(f) ICTR Statute. [133] Art 3(f) SCSL Statute.

[134] See ICTY, *The Prosecutor v Zejnil Delalić*, Initial Indictment, IT-96-21, 21 March 1996, at 37, and Trial Chamber Judgment, 16 November 1998, at 584–92 and 1154; see also ICTY, *The Prosecutor v Goran Jelisić*, Trial Chamber Judgment, IT-95-10-T, 14 December 1999, at 46–9, where the defendant pleaded guilty to the offence of having stolen money and other valuables from detainees upon their arrival at Luka camp in Bosnia-Herzegovina.

[135] See Chs 35 and 36 of this volume.

74 For instance, in the *Al-Skeini* and *Al-Jedda* cases,[137] the ECtHR found that the UK had obligations under the ECHR during the occupation of Iraq in 2003 to 2004.[138] In *Al-Skeini*, the ECtHR held that the failure to conduct an independent and effective investigation into a number of deaths of Iraqi civilians amounted to a violation of the right to life.[139] Likewise, the ECtHR determined in the *Al-Jedda* case that the internment of an Iraqi civilian in a UK-operated detention centre in Bashrah for over three years constituted a violation of the right to liberty and security.[140]

imprisonment in violation of fundamental rules of international law, which covers equally rules on the treatment of prisoners.[136]

75 However, certain IHRL provisions may be subject to derogation in cases of armed conflict. Accordingly, for example, breaches relating to the working conditions of internees would amount to violations of the prohibition of forced or compulsory labour contained in most IHRL treaties,[141] unless those provisions were subject to formal derogation.[142]

E. Critical Assessment

76 There is a general acceptance that the internment provisions in GC IV need to be reviewed from the perspective both of contemporary armed conflicts and the impact of IHRL obligations. For example, in 2005 Pejic wrote an influential article in which she argued that internment falls within both IHL and IHRL.[143] In 2007, the ICRC recognized that 'recent state practice—e.g. internment by States party to multinational coalitions—has been characterised by divergences in the interpretation and implementation of the relevant rules, which has given rise to serious concerns'.[144] The ICRC used Pejic's paper to develop consistency in approaches on the application of both IHL and IHRL to situations including internment.[145] The Copenhagen Process is an example of the concern some states have that extant standards of treatment of those deprived of their liberty in contemporary military operations are inadequate.[146] The concerns of both states and the Red Cross movement were also expressed in late 2011 when the ICRC was invited to 'pursue further research [...] to: i) to ensure that [IHL] remains practical and relevant in providing legal protections to all persons deprived of their liberty in relation to armed conflict'.[147]

---

[136] Art 7(1)(e) ICC Statute; and N.S. Rodley and M. Pollard, *The Treatment of Prisoners under International Law* (3rd edn, Oxford: OUP, 2009) at 422–3.

[137] See *Al-Skeini*, above n 101; and ECtHR, *Al-Jedda v United Kingdom*, Judgment, 7 July 2011.

[138] In both cases, the ECtHR overruled its previous case law on the territorial scope of the ECHR, see ECtHR, *Banković et al v Belgium et al*, Admissibility, 12 December 2001; ECtHR, *Behrami and Behrami v France, Saramati v France, Germany and Norway*, Admissibility Decision, 2 May 2007.

[139] Art 2 ECHR.

[140] Art 5(1) ECHR.

[141] See Art 1 Forced Labour Convention, C29 (1930); Arts 1 and 2 Convention concerning the Abolition of Forced Labour (1957); Art 8(3) ICCPR; Art 4(2) ECHR; Art 6(2) ACHR; Art 15 ACHPR.

[142] See, e.g., Arts 4(2) and 8(3) ICCPR and Arts 4(2) and 15(2) ECHR. See, however, ECtHR, *Hassan v UK*, Judgment, 16 September 2014, paras 99–103.

[143] See Pejic, above n 112.

[144] 30th International Conference of the Red Cross and the Red Crescent (2007), *International humanitarian law and the challenges of contemporary armed conflicts*, 30IC./07/8.4, at 11.

[145] Ibid.

[146] Note from the Permanent Mission of Denmark to the United Nations, *Information for the Secretary-General's Report on the Status of the Additional Protocols Relating to the Protection of Victims of Armed Conflicts and on Measures to Strengthen the Existing Body of International Humanitarian Law*, 1 July 2008.

[147] 31st International Conference of the Red Cross and Red Crescent 2011, Resolution 1—Strengthening legal protection for victims of armed conflicts, at 6.

Any study of the rules concerning the treatment of internees viewed through the lens of early twenty-first-century armed conflicts will raise at least three issues worthy of critical assessment. First, interning or detaining individuals in contemporary IACs, including situations of belligerent occupation, makes it difficult to separate treatment standards on the basis that internment is not punitive. Secondly, the increasing relevance of IHRL in establishing standards of treatment for those deprived of their liberty makes it difficult to claim that the GC IV treatment framework is the only legal framework that applies. Thirdly, because of the increasing relevance of IHRL, there is a corresponding demand that Detaining Powers develop better investigative and reparations legal frameworks and procedures for dealing with alleged abuses concerning treatment.

In contemporary IAC, Detaining Powers will not always be able to separate internees on the basis that they are either security or criminal internees. In many circumstances internees may be both. For example, an internee might be detained initially for a criminal offence, such as laying improvised explosive devices, but also be held because he or she is a security threat. In such cases it is difficult to apply non-punitive treatment provisions.[148]

International human rights law has an increasingly important role to play in relation to establishing principles, rules, and standards concerning the treatment of internees pursuant to GC IV. This role derives primarily from three developments. First, the development of specific treaty regimes, such the CAT and the ICED, makes it impossible for states party to those treaties to ignore legal obligations arising from them.[149] Secondly, the wide reach of some human rights bodies, such as the Working Group on Arbitrary Detention,[150] and human rights tribunals, such the ECtHR,[151] has led to a broader role for IHRL in all forms of deprivation of liberty. Thirdly, a number of provisions concerning treatment of internees have been developed in soft-law instruments that form the basis for discussions concerning any form of deprivation of liberty.[152]

Conducting investigations arising from allegations of disputes, in light of both IHL and IHRL obligations and standards, would require Detaining Powers to adopt three key practices. First, they must have a system permitting internees to submit a petition or make a complaint concerning their treatment.[153] Secondly, the Detaining Power has an obligation to investigate any serious allegation of abuse that comes to its notice.[154] Thirdly, the investigation must be effective in the sense of being both formally and practically independent and prompt, involving those affected (including the victim's next of kin) and being open to public scrutiny.[155] Lastly, the investigation must identify relevant perpetrators of the abuse[156] and provide appropriate reparations to the victim.[157]

BRUCE OSWALD   LUCREZIA IAPICHINO*

---

[148] See MN 10–11, above.   [149] See MN 7–9, above.

[150] E.g., see the opinion of the Working Group concerning the Treatment of Detainees in Guantànamo Bay in *Opinions adopted by the Working Group on Arbitrary Detention*, A/HRC/13/30/Add.1, 4 March 2010. See also the *Report of the Working Group on Arbitrary Detention*, A/HRC/16/47, 2010, at 37–51, where the Group explains why IHRL applies to situations of armed conflict.

[151] See *Al-Jedda*, above n 137.

[152] E.g., the Basic Principles for the Treatment of Prisoners (1990) and the Body of Principles for the Protection of All Persons under Any Form of Detention or Imprisonment (1988).

[153] See MN 30–31, above.   [154] See *Al-Skeini*, above n 101, para 165.   [155] Ibid, at para 167.

[156] Ibid, at para 166.   [157] Ibid.

* The present chapter is the result of the joint work of the authors and reflects their common opinion. Nevertheless, sections A, B, and E are attributed to Bruce Oswald, and sections C and D to Lucrezia Iapichino. Bruce and Lucrezia would like to express their thanks to Mr Tom Andrews, Ms Julia Wang, Ms Bethany Wellington, and Ms Natasha Robbins for their assistance with this chapter.

Chapter 66. End of Internment

	MN
A. Introduction	1
B. Meaning and Application of the Core Articles relating to Release, Repatriation, and Accommodation in Neutral Countries	8
I. Article 132: Release based on the reasons which necessitated internment	8
a. Release of interned person as 'soon as reasons which necessitated' internment no longer exist	8
b. Agreements for release, repatriation, and return to places of residence or accommodation in neutral countries	12
II. Article 133: Release after the close of hostilities	15
a. Internment shall cease as soon as possible after the close of hostilities	15
b. Limitation concerning those against whom penal proceedings are pending and those previously sentenced	20
c. Searching for dispersed internees	25
III. Article 134: Repatriation and return to the last place of residence	27
IV. Article 135: Costs of returning released or repatriated internees	32
a. Costs of returning internees	33
b. Costs of repatriation and transfers	34
c. Special agreements	37
C. Relevance in Non-International Armed Conflicts	38
D. Legal Consequences of a Violation	40
E. Critical Assessment	44

Select Bibliography

Debuf, E., *Captured in War: Lawful Internment in Armed Conflict* (Oxford: Hart Publishing, 2013)

Gasser, H.-P., 'Protection of the Civilian Population', in D. Fleck (ed), *Handbook of International Humanitarian Law* (2nd edn, Oxford: OUP, 2008) 237, at 322–3

Pictet Commentary GC IV at 510–20

UK Ministry of Defence, *The Manual of the Law of Armed Conflict* (Oxford: OUP, 2004), at 251–2

A. Introduction

There are at least two reasons why it is important to reflect on the principles guiding the 'end of internment' for internees being held during armed conflict. First, from the individual internee's perspective, the right to the 'end of internment' is an extension of the principle of humane treatment. The knowledge that internment is temporary and not indefinite provides internees and their relatives with a level of psychological comfort. Secondly, from a more strategic perspective, ensuring that internment ends is one aspect of establishing the conditions for the return to peace. Evidence of the strategic importance of the end of internment is amply exhibited in a number of peace treaties and ceasefire agreements that have provisions relating to the 'end of internment' as a component of establishing peace or a cessation of hostilities.

2   Provisions concerning the 'end of internment' are found in Geneva Convention (GC) IV, Part III, Section IV, Chapter XII, Articles 132–135.[1] These four Articles concern a number of issues of legal and practical significance, including determining when internment is to cease, establishing agreements concerning the release of certain classes of internees, repatriation and return to their last place of residence, and expenses relating to the release or repatriation of internees. The provisions cover all classes or categories of internees—security, criminal, and voluntary—and apply to both international armed conflict (IAC) and occupation. However, persons detained following a criminal conviction are covered only if they were sentenced to a period of internment under Article 68 GC IV. Chapter XII of GC IV is similar to Part IV, sections I and II of GC III, which deal with the termination of captivity of prisoners of war.

3   Pursuant to Chapter XII of GC IV, there are three ways in which internment may end:

— Internees must be released by the Detaining Power 'as soon as the reasons which necessitated [their] internment no longer exist'.[2]
— Alternatively, internment 'shall cease as soon as possible after the close of hostilities'.[3]
— In some circumstances, such as those concerning vulnerable classes of internees, special reasons may exist justifying their release.

4   Chapter XII also canvasses the use of agreements to facilitate the end of internment. Agreements may be entered into between relevant state powers and other organizations for a variety of reasons. These reasons may include the accommodation of internees in neutral countries, the establishment of committees after the close of hostilities or at the end of an occupation to enable states to search for dispersed internees, the allocation of costs for returning or repatriating internees, and the exchange and repatriation of a state's nationals in enemy hands. Obligations are also created for each state party to the Convention which require that, at the close of hostilities or occupation, states must endeavour to 'ensure the return of all internees to their last place of residence, or to facilitate their repatriation'.[4] Lastly, there is also provision in the Convention to create a regime concerning expenses incurred when returning or repatriating internees.

5   In the context of the Geneva Conventions, the notion of a requirement to ensure the 'end of internment' for civilians in conflict was first raised by way of a resolution at the 10th International Red Cross Conference held in 1921. That resolution reminded delegates of the need for 'humane treatment of all political prisoners, their exchange, and, so far as possible, their release'.[5] However, it was not until 1947 that the International Committee of the Red Cross (ICRC) genuinely considered the issue of release and repatriation of internees. In its *Report on the Work of the Government Experts for the Study of the Conventions for the Protection of War Victims*,[6] the Experts considered a range of provisions

---

[1] States have not recorded formal reservations concerning these provisions.
[2] Art 132 para 1 GC IV. Hereafter, any reference to an 'Art' relates to GC IV, unless stated otherwise.
[3] Art 133 para 1.   [4] Art 134.
[5] 10th International Conference of the Red Cross and Red Crescent held in Geneva from 30 March to 7 April 1921.
[6] *Report on the Work of the Government Experts for the Study of the Conventions for the Protection of War Victims* (1947).

to deal with release and accommodation of internees in neutral countries.[7] In 1948, the ICRC, relying on the *Report*, canvassed two Articles concerning internee release, repatriation, and accommodation in neutral countries. The first Article was intended to apply during hostilities and during occupation, and the second Article was intended to apply after the close of hostilities.[8] The final version of this document was distributed in August 1948 during the Seventeenth International Red Cross Conference, having been only slightly amended from the May 1948 draft prepared by the ICRC.[9]

Neither the term 'release' nor the term 'repatriation' is defined in the provisions governing the end of internment. It can safely be assumed that 'release' means the end of the internment and, therefore, an end to the internee's deprivation of liberty. 'Repatriation', based on the context in which that term is used in Articles 132 and 134 GC IV, is a 'special case of transfer',[10] in the sense that transfers of internees take into account the wishes of the internees and the Detaining Power. In contrast, repatriation 'also brings into consideration the wishes of the country of origin of the internee'.[11] Thus, repatriation involves the release of an internee in the internee's country of origin by way of transfer to that country.

When comparing repatriations and transfers, it is also worth noting that the transfer of an internee may facilitate ongoing detention in another state, whereas repatriation in the context of Chapter XII is intended to facilitate the permanent release of an internee. A transfer may be organized with or without the consent of the internee, whereas repatriation should be undertaken only where the internee is willing to be repatriated to his or her country of origin. The ICRC provisions are silent as to whether an internee may be sent to a country which is not his or her country of origin. As is briefly discussed below,[12] this silence is of limited significance when other treaty regimes, such as the 1951 Refugee Convention and the Convention against Torture (CAT), create obligations for the Detaining Power which address this issue.

B. Meaning and Application of the Core Articles relating to Release, Repatriation, and Accommodation in Neutral Countries

I. Article 132: Release based on the reasons which necessitated internment

a. *Release of interned person as 'soon as reasons which necessitated' internment no longer exist*

Article 132 paragraph 1 GC IV creates an obligation to release internees 'as soon as the reasons which necessitated' their internment no longer exist. This Article applies during

---

[7] Ibid, Arts 63–71.
[8] Draft Revised or New Conventions for the Protection of War Victims established by the International Committee of the Red Cross with the assistance of National Experts, National Red Cross Societies and other Humanitarian Organisations, 17th International Red Cross Conference (Stockholm, August 1948), Arts 121 and 122.
[9] Revised and New Draft Convention for the Protection of War Victims: Texts Approved and Amended by the XVII International Red Cross Conference (Geneva, 1948), Arts 121 and 122.
[10] Pictet Commentary GC IV, at 513.
[11] Ibid. For a more detailed discussion of transfers, see Ch 58 of this volume.
[12] See MN 29 and 42.

hostilities or occupation, and supports the rule under Article 42 GC IV that internment 'may be ordered only if the security of the Detaining Power makes it absolutely necessary' (see for occupied territories the only slightly different wording of Article 78 GC IV). The drafting records for this Article demonstrate that the obligation is intended to emphasize the importance of 'the exceptional and, in principle, temporary nature of internment'.[13] Furthermore, the obligation reinforces the fundamental rule of law that no one should be held in arbitrary or unlawful detention.

9   The test for determining the necessity of continuing internment appears to be either objective or subjective, or a combination of both. In some cases it might be objectively determined that, for reasons such as age or health, there is insufficient basis for justifying a person's internment. For example, a terminally ill person should be released or repatriated on the basis that he or she is no longer a security threat by virtue of his or her prognosis.[14] In contrast, a subjective determination relies on the Detaining Power's subjective view that there is no basis to hold an internee. Thus, the Detaining Power might conclude that even though there is sufficient evidence to intern a person for security reasons, it is in the Detaining Power's own interest to release that internee. Of course, it will sometimes be the case that both objective and subjective reasons will lead to an internee's release.

10   It also seems that an internee must be released where there is an abuse of the fundamental procedural elements of internment. For example, where the Detaining Power has not established appropriate review procedures for determining ongoing internment, the internee must be released. In such cases it could be argued that release must occur because the Detaining Power cannot demonstrate that there are reasons which necessitate ongoing detention.[15]

11   The so-called War on Terror has raised at least one major concern relating to the release of an internee: the creation of domestic law which prohibits or restricts the ability of the Detaining Power to release an internee on the territory of the Detaining Power.[16] If such a person cannot be repatriated because of the *non-refoulement* principle, the options for the Detaining Power in such cases are limited. It can either seek to transfer the person to another state willing to accept him or her, or hold the person indefinitely. Indefinite detention when there are no reasons necessitating detention clearly violates Article 132 paragraph 1 GC IV, and could be a grave breach pursuant to Article 147 GC IV.

b. *Agreements for release, repatriation, and return to places of residence or accommodation in neutral countries*

12   Article 132 paragraph 2 GC IV focuses on humanitarian concerns that arise when vulnerable individuals are interned. There are two dimensions at play in Article 132. The first is the need to ensure humane treatment of internees who, because they are vulnerable for reasons such as health or age, require special consideration when determining whether to release, repatriate, or return them to their places of residence or accommodation in neutral countries. The second is the need for states to enter into agreements to facilitate the release, repatriation, and return of vulnerable internees.

---

[13] See Draft Revised or New Conventions, above n 8, at 207.
[14] See also Pictet Commentary GC IV, at 511, for an age-related example.
[15] See ICTY, *The Prosecutor v Zejnil Delalić et al*, Appeals Chamber IT-96-21-A, 20 February 2001, paras 320–2.
[16] The US Congress has, for example, enacted funding measures which initially barred internees held in Guantánamo Bay from being released into the US. See J. Elsea and M. Garcia, *The National Defense Authorisation Act for FY2012: Detainee Matters*, Congressional Research Service Report for Congress (2012), available at <http://www.fas.org/sgp/crs/natsec/R42143.pdf>.

There are few examples of Detaining Powers entering into agreements for the purposes 13
of releasing, repatriating, or returning vulnerable detainees during hostilities. However,
there is at least one instance where an agreement to end hostilities has prioritized the
return of vulnerable internees. The 1973 Agreement between Vietnam and the United
States (US) provided:

Persons who are seriously ill, wounded or maimed, old persons and women shall be returned first.
The remainder shall be returned either by returning all from one detention place after another or in
order of their dates of capture, beginning with those who have been held the longest.[17]

More recently the United Nations Security Council (UNSC) has called on all those 14
involved in negotiating and implementing peace agreements to adopt a gender perspective in relation to, among other things, the special needs of women and girls during
repatriation.[18]

II. Article 133: Release after the close of hostilities

a. Internment shall cease as soon as possible after the close of hostilities

Article 133 paragraph 1 GC IV creates an obligation for the Detaining Power to cease 15
internment 'as soon as possible after the close of hostilities'. Unfortunately, the use of the
phrases 'as soon as possible' and 'close of hostilities' are both open to varying interpretations. Does 'as soon as possible' mean that internees must be released within a particular
time frame which is objectively determined, or is it the case that the time frame is a matter
for the Detaining Power to determine? The practice of states suggests that 'as soon as possible' is most often determined subjectively, after the parties have reached an agreement as
to when they will release internees. Previous agreements between states have, for example,
not stipulated a time period for release of internees,[19] required release of internees after a
particular event occurs,[20] or required release at the 'earliest possible date'.[21] However, there
are also some examples where Detaining Powers have had to release internees 'without
delay' or 'immediately'.[22]

A factor that might cause confusion is that the phrase 'close of hostilities' is differ- 16
ent from the phrase 'general close of military operations' used as the general test in
Article 6 for the application of GC IV.[23] The Pictet Commentary states that the phrase

---

[17] Protocol to the Agreement on Ending the War and Resorting Peace in Vietnam Concerning the Return of Captured Military Personnel and Foreign Civilians Captured and Detained (1973) Art 4(b), available at <http://www.cvce.eu/content/publication/2001/10/12/656ccc0d-31ef-42a6-a3e9-ce5ee7d4fc80/publishable_en.pdf>. There is also evidence that in 1997, during the conflict in Sudan, female detainees with children were released: see UNGA Res 51/112, 5 March 1997, para 11.

[18] UNSC Res 1325, of 31 October 2000, para 8(a).

[19] E.g., the Agreement between the Parties to the Conflict in Bosnia-Herzegovina on the Release and Transfer of Prisoners (1992) Art 3(1).

[20] E.g., the Bangladesh–India–Pakistan Agreement on the Repatriation of POWs and Civilian Internees, 9 April 1974 (para 10), which provided that release would occur after Kum Mela (an Indian religious festival); and the Dayton Accord Annex 1-A (1995) Art IX, 1(c), which provided that release would occur 30 days after a transfer of authority.

[21] E.g., the Agreement on a Comprehensive Political Settlement of the Cambodia Conflict (1991), Part VI, Art 21.

[22] E.g., Agreement between the Government of the Federal Democratic Republic of Ethiopia and the Government of the State of Eritrea (2000) Art 2(2); and UNSC Res 686 (1991) para 2(c). See also Ch 51 of this volume, at MN 26–29 and 45–46.

[23] See Ch 3 of this volume, at MN 17.

'close of hostilities' should be interpreted in the same sense as the wording used in a similar provision concerning prisoners of war (POWs) in GC III, 'the cessation of active hostilities'.[24] The qualitative difference between each of the phrases is clear. The phrase 'close of hostilities' suggests that hostilities have ended but that peace has not yet been established. 'Cessation of active hostilities', on the other hand, suggests either that some military operations are still being conducted, or that hostilities exist but are not 'active', and therefore armed conflict might break out sporadically and that military operations continue, albeit at a less intense level.[25] The phrase 'general close of military operations' has been interpreted to mean 'the final end of fighting between all those concerned'.[26]

17   While it is clear from Article 131 that internment shall cease as soon as possible after the close of hostilities, the practice of states suggests that where they have entered into peace or ceasefire agreements, the release of internees is usually dealt with in those agreements.[27] Thus in a number of cases internment has ceased only upon an agreement's entering into force. It is not always the Detaining Powers that determine when the release of internees is to occur. There has been at least one instance of the Security Council's calling for the release of internees.[28]

18   Notwithstanding that different approaches have been taken concerning the timing of the release of internees, it is clear that the paramount issue is ensuring that indefinite internment is avoided. An important aspect of the obligation to avoid indefinite internment is ensuring that the release of internees does not lead to a breakdown of law and order, and that the humanitarian needs of internees are met. Thus, Detaining Powers should interpret the temporal requirement of 'as soon as possible' in the context of 'what is reasonable and necessary in the circumstances', by considering factors such as the maintenance of law and order, and the resources available to ensure that released internees are not vulnerable.[29] In relation to whether the release should occur at the close of hostilities, the preferred test from a humanitarian perspective is to release internees at the 'cessation of active hostilities', because this is likely to occur sooner than 'the close of hostilities' or 'general close of military operations' standards, and therefore is of greater benefit to internees. Of course, it is also open to the Security Council to determine that the release of internees is to occur immediately even if a conflict is still underway.

19   The 'General Treatment' provisions found in Article 27 GC IV require among other things that protected persons 'shall be protected especially against all acts of violence or

---

[24] Pictet Commentary GC IV, at 514–15. See also Ch 51 of this volume, at MN 20–23.

[25] Note that the term 'end of active hostilities' is also used in Art 31(1) AP I, and it is suggested in the ICRC Commentary to that Article that the term does not suggest that a peace agreement or ceasefire must exist. See ICRC Commentary APs, at 253.

[26] Pictet Commentary GC IV at 62. See Ch 3, MN 17, of this volume.

[27] E.g., Agreement between Ethiopia and Eritrea, above n 22, Art 2(2); Dayton Accord Annex 1-A (1995) Art IX; and Protocol to the Agreement of Ending the War in Vietnam, above n 17, Art 7(b).

[28] See UNSC Res 686 (1991) [2(c)], concerning the 'immediate release of all Kuwaiti and third country nationals being detained in Iraq'.

[29] This is the approach taken by the US and Iraq pursuant to the Agreement between the United States of America and the Republic of Iraq on the Withdrawal of United States Forces from Iraq and the Organisation of their Activities during their Temporary Presence in Iraq (2008). Art 22(4) of that Agreement provides that the 'US shall release all remaining detainees in a safe and orderly manner, unless otherwise requested by Iraq'. In referring to the release of detainees pursuant to that Agreement, Brigadier General Quantock (US Army) stated, 'We are working very hard with the Iraqi government to ensure the releases are conducted in a safe and orderly manner to prevent disrupting the noticeable gains in security and stability enjoyed by Iraqi citizens.' US Department of Defense, 'Coalition Begins Releasing Detainees Under New Security Agreement', 3 February 2009, available at <http://www.defense.gov/news/newsarticle.aspx?id=52930>.

threats thereof and against insults and public curiosity'. One implied consequence of that provision is that internees must be released in a safe environment—in the sense that their release does not lead to violence or threats of violence against them.

b. Limitation concerning those against whom penal proceedings are pending and those previously sentenced

Article 133 paragraph 2 GC IV contains an important provision that concerns those internees who have criminal proceedings pending against them, or who are serving a sentence for criminal offences.[30] In both cases, internees may be held until close of proceedings, or until the sentence is completed. However, criminal proceedings must have commenced against the internees in order for their continued detention to be justified. The provision does not apply to disciplinary offences.

In cases where internees are accused of committing serious crimes, such as genocide, war crimes, or crimes against humanity, their release might be affected by claims relating to universal jurisdiction or other treaty obligations. For example, the obligation to search for, and bring to justice, individuals accused of committing grave breaches will limit the ability to release an internee at the end of hostilities. It is also relevant to note that where offences have allegedly been committed by an internee outside of the territory in which he or she is interned, the internee is 'liable to extradition in pursuance of extradition treaties concluded before the outbreak of the conflict'.[31] Extradition, however, is also governed by the obligations of states to ensure that a person is not extradited 'where there are substantial grounds for believing that he would be in danger of being subjected to torture'.[32] The principle of *non-refoulement*, which prohibits forcibly removing someone to a territory where his or her life or freedom could be threatened because of his or her race, religion, nationality, membership of a particular group, or political opinion, is also relevant to limiting the place to which a person could be returned.[33]

The exercise of the limitation in Article 133 is clearly discretionary, as evidenced by the words in the provision, 'if circumstances require'. When exercising this discretion, it is reasonable to expect that the Detaining Power will need to consider issues such as whether it is appropriate to grant early release of internees as a gesture of goodwill, whether the release is in the interests of justice, the applicable norms concerning the granting of amnesties, and the need to maintain law and order.

While not expressly mentioned in Article 133, it is reasonable to require that where internees are being held because they have committed criminal offences, the Detaining Power will maintain relevant documents and evidence that justify ongoing detention. Furthermore, the Detaining Power is required by Article 77 to ensure that relevant records of those protected persons accused or convicted of offences, who are held in custody, are handed over to the authorities of the liberated territory at the close of occupation. This requirement should also be applied when, at the close of hostilities, detainees are handed over to another state for prosecution.

There is some evidence of state practice regarding the release of internees who are accused of committing criminal offences or serving sentences. For example, Article 24

---

[30] Art 133(2).
[31] UK Ministry of Defence, *The Manual of the Law of Armed Conflict* (Oxford: OUP, 2004), at 231.
[32] CAT Art 3(1).
[33] See Ch 51, MN 33–37, and Ch 58, MN 55–74, of this volume for a detailed discussion concerning the principle of *non-refoulement*.

of the Agreement between the US and Iraq on the withdrawal of US Forces from Iraq provides that US Forces will 'turn over custody of wanted detainees to Iraqi authorities pursuant to a valid Iraqi arrest warrant'.[34] On the other hand, the General Framework Agreement for Peace in Bosnia-Herzegovina restricts the ability of the parties to that Agreement to release internees, by requiring each party to continue to detain individuals pursuant to an order or request by the International Criminal Tribunal for the former Yugoslavia (ICTY).[35] Further, some international agreements specifically provide that release provisions do not apply to ordinary criminals.[36]

c. *Searching for dispersed internees*

25   There is considerable benefit in establishing agreements to search for internees in situations where large numbers of people have been interned and records of internees have been poorly maintained. Such agreements assist in reminding the Detaining Power that the obligation to release internees as soon as possible after the close of hostilities requires the relevant Power to take proactive steps to ensure that it knows who is interned and where they are being held. Article 133 paragraph 3 GC IV should also serve to remind the Detaining Power of the value of keeping accurate registers and records of all internees who are held, released, transferred, or repatriated by the authorities.

26   At the end of some conflicts, the breakdown of law and order might be at a level where control over internees is lost and they therefore become dispersed. In such cases, accurate registers and records are important to allow organizations, such as the ICRC, to locate internees and provide them with assistance.

III. Article 134: Repatriation and return to the last place of residence

27   To give practical meaning to the obligation in Article 133 paragraph 1 concerning the cessation of internment (see MN 15), Article 134 encourages Detaining Powers to 'ensure the return of all internees to their last place of residence, or to facilitate their repatriation'. The *travaux préparatoires* confirm that this rule is intended to create a distinction between the Detaining Power's obligation to return internees to their domicile, and the obligation to facilitate repatriation. The Italian delegation offered a simple explanation for this distinction, that is, the Detaining Power, having taken such persons away from their domicile, is 'duty bound', 'when the protected person is released, to return him to the place at which he resided when interned'.[37] The obligation arising from a request to be repatriated is different, because that request emanates from the internee, and therefore the rule recognizes that the Detaining Power 'is not bound to ensure his repatriation, merely to facilitate it'.[38]

28   The limitations of Article 134 are obvious when considering obligations on Detaining Powers not to return an interned person to a place to which that person does not wish to be sent. The *travaux préparatoires* for Article 134 do not explain why the narrow approach in the obligation merely to *facilitate* repatriation was taken by the Drafting Committee, except to say that 'the Committee did not wish to create obligations for Detaining Powers that were outside the Convention'.[39]

---

[34] Agreement between the United States of America and the Republic of Iraq, see above n 29, Art 22(4).
[35] Dayton Accord Annex 1-A (1995) Art IX, 1(g).
[36] E.g., the General Peace Agreement for Mozambique (1992) Protocol VI, 8, III (1); and The Cotonou Agreement on Liberia (1993), Art 10.
[37] Final Record, vol II-B, at 465–6. Comments by the Italian Delegate, Mr Maresca.
[38] Ibid, at 466.   [39] Final Record, vol II-A, at 844.

Due to developments in relation to the right to claim asylum and the principle of *non-refoulement* (see Chapter 51 of this volume, MN 33–36), it is almost impossible for Detaining Powers to take a narrow approach to Article 134. The practical effect of these developments is that the intent of the 1948 Stockholm Conference Draft Article, which formed the basis for Article 134, is applied to Detaining Powers and obligates them, in certain circumstances, to take into account the wishes of a person as to where he or she would like to be sent. For example, where a person does not wish to be repatriated to his or her country of origin because he or she believes that he or she will be persecuted or ill-treated, the wishes of that person will be paramount because of obligations arising from the 1951 Refugee Convention or CAT. Detaining Powers will also be limited in releasing or repatriating persons in circumstances where those persons may be subject to the death penalty.[40] The ICRC assists Detaining Powers in assessing the concerns and needs of internees, by giving internees an opportunity to raise any fears they might have about repatriation.[41]

There might be situations where a Detaining Power may have no option but to repatriate a person to his or her country of origin because, for example, no other country is willing to accept that person. In such cases, a practice has developed of obtaining diplomatic assurances that the repatriated person will not be persecuted, mistreated, or subjected to the death penalty. Although diplomatic assurances do not override the legal obligations of the Detaining Power, they are generally accepted as a method to permit repatriation in circumstances where concerns for the well-being of the repatriated person might arise.[42]

An important issue for Detaining Powers is the prohibition on transferring or deporting individuals released from internment. For example, Article 49 GC IV prohibits the deportation of protected persons from occupied territory. While evacuation is permitted if imperative military reasons so demand, there are limits as to the permissible extent of displacement.[43] The issue of displacement during armed conflict is also dealt with in the *Guiding Principles on Internal Displacement*.[44] In relation to free and informed consent, under Article 8 GC IV a protected person cannot renounce the protections afforded to him or her pursuant to GC IV.

IV. Article 135: Costs of returning released or repatriated internees

Article 135 GC IV provides for the costs of returning or repatriating internees in the following situations:

— returning a person to his or her pre-internment home;
— returning a person taken into custody on the high seas;
— voluntary repatriation;
— forcible repatriation; and
— voluntary internment.

---

[40] Second Optional Protocol to the ICCPR (1989). See, e.g., Art 6 ICCPR; Art 2, Protocols 6 and 12 ECHR; Protocol to the ACHR to Abolish the Death Penalty (1990).

[41] E.g., the Dayton Accord, in which it was agreed that the ICRC would 'privately interview each prisoner at least forty-eight (48) hours prior to his or her release' (Annex 1A, Art IX, 1(c)). See also the ICRC official position on interviewing detainees, available at <https://www.icrc.org/eng/resources/documents/misc/detention-visits-010407.htm>.

[42] See Ch 51, MN 34, of this volume, concerning assurances.   [43] Art 49 paras 2–6.

[44] UN Doc E/CN.4/1998/53/Add.2, 10 May 1998.

a. Costs of returning internees

33 Article 135 paragraph 1 does not distinguish between classes of internees, and it therefore applies to criminal, security, and voluntary internees. Thus, where an internee is to be returned to his or her last place of domicile before he or she was interned, Article 135 paragraph 1 provides that the Detaining Power shall bear the cost incurred. Where, however, a person is taken into custody while in transit on the high seas, the Detaining Power is responsible for paying the cost of returning the internee to the point of departure, or the cost of completing the journey. It is reasonable to assume that where a person has been taken into custody while in transit by aeroplane, the obligation to pay for that person's return to his or her point of departure, or to complete the journey, would by analogy be the same as if the person was taken into custody on the high seas.

b. Costs of repatriation and transfers

34 There might also be situations where the Detaining Power refuses to permit a released internee to remain in that power's own territory where he or she previously resided. In such cases, the repatriation of the internee is founded on the wish of the Detaining Power, and therefore the cost of that repatriation is borne by the Detaining Power. Where, however, the internee elects to return to his or her country of origin, the cost-sharing is calculated on the basis that the Detaining Power pays for the internee's journey to the border of the Detaining Power's territory, and the internee, or the internee's government, pays the remainder of the cost of repatriation. It is reasonable to assume that this arrangement of cost-sharing would also apply to situations where an internee wishes to go to a country that is not his or her country of origin. Thus, if an internee is permitted to remain in the state in which he or she has been interned but the internee nonetheless wishes to leave that state, the Detaining Power will be responsible for paying the transport costs only up to the border of its state.

35 Where a person is categorized as a voluntary internee pursuant to Article 42 GC IV, the Detaining Power is not required to pay the cost of repatriation. This takes into account the fact that the reason for internment was the desire of the person to be interned, and therefore the person should bear any costs arising from being returned.[45]

36 Pursuant to Article 135 paragraph 3 and Article 45 GC IV, parties engaged in transfers are able to make arrangements as to the apportionment of costs between them.

c. Special agreements

37 Consistent with humanitarian principles, Article 135 paragraph 4 GC IV permits Detaining Powers to seek solutions to alleviate the suffering of internees by entering into special agreements concerning costs. Such agreements might cover, for example, the role of international organizations, such as the ICRC or the Office of the United Nations High Commissioner for Refugees, in paying certain repatriation costs or providing services in kind.

C. Relevance in Non-International Armed Conflicts

38 Internment in non-international armed conflicts (NIACs) is considered through the wider lens of the principles guiding the 'restriction of liberty'.[46] The circumstances surrounding the liberation of a person whose liberty has been restricted—in the sense of ending that person's

---

[45] See Pictet Commentary GC IV, at 519.

[46] The term 'restriction of liberty' as used in Art 5 AP II, 'covers all detainees and persons whose liberty has been restricted for reasons related to the conflict'. See ICRC Commentary APs, para 4564.

internment—are dealt with in three provisions: Common Article 3 and AP II, Articles 4 and 5. The first concerns the prohibition against taking hostages.[47] This prohibition stipulates that a detaining party cannot refuse to release a person from custody because it wishes to use that person for the purposes of bargaining. Secondly, a detaining party must take all necessary measures to ensure the safety of a person it has decided to release.[48] This requirement obligates the detaining party to consider issues such as where and when a person should be released. Thus, for example, if a detaining party has a reasonable belief that the release of a person from custody in a particular neighbourhood would jeopardize that person's safety, the detaining party must consider ways and means to ensure the person's safety. In such circumstances, one way to ensure the person's safety might be to arrange for the ICRC or another similar humanitarian organization to facilitate the logistics for the release of the person, thus avoiding the situation where a person walks out of the detention facility into a hostile community.[49]

Even though GC IV does not apply in NIACs as a matter of law, there are a number of examples where the release provisions found in Articles 133 and 134 have been applied by analogy by detaining parties in NIACs. For example, The Cotonou Agreement on Liberia in 1993 provided that all 'prisoners of war [sic]' and detainees should immediately be released, but also stipulated that ordinary criminals were not covered by that provision.[50] A subsequent peace agreement between the Government of Liberia, the Liberians United for Reconciliation and Democracy, and the Movement for Democracy in Liberia and Political Parties provided for the immediate and unconditional release of all 'prisoners, prisoners of war [sic], including non-combatants and abductees'.[51]

D. Legal Consequences of a Violation

The following violations could arise in relation to the release and repatriation of internees:

— hostage-taking and unlawful confinement;
— forcible repatriation of an internee; and
— refusal to pay costs.

---

[47] See Ch 15 of this volume, CA 3 para 1(1)(b) of the GCs, and Art 4(1)(c) AP II. The term 'hostages' here refers to 'persons who are in the power of a party to the conflict or its agent, willingly or unwillingly, and who answer with their freedom, their physical integrity or their life for the execution of orders given by those in whose hands they have fallen, or for any hostile acts committed against them' (ICRC Commentary APs, para 4537). The term 'hostage' has been defined more recently in the International Convention against the Taking of Hostages (1979) Art 1(1). The Elements of Crimes for the ICC Statute crime of hostage-taking extend the above International Convention against the Taking of Hostages by including 'safety of the person' as an additional factor in the condition of release (see Art 8(2)(a)(viii) and (c)(iii)).

[48] Art 5(4) AP II.

[49] E.g., the Agreement between Croatia and the Federal Republic of Yugoslavia on the Release and Repatriation of Prisoners (1992) Art 1(4), which provided for ICRC assistance in repatriating internees; Final Act of the Conference on Cambodia (1992) Part VI, Art 21, which provided that all POWs and civilian internees were to be released at the earliest possible date under the direction of the ICRC; and the Agreement on Permanent Ceasefire and Security Arrangements Implementation Modalities between the Government of Sudan and the SPLM/SPLA during the pre-interim and interim periods (2004), where release was to occur on the endorsement of the peace agreement and the ICRC was to be involved in the process of arranging the releases. See also the discussion in Ch 64, section C, of this volume, where the author argues that the provisions on internment could be applied by analogy to the detention of fighters in NIAC.

[50] Cotonou Agreement, above n 36, Art 10. See also the General Peace Agreement for Mozambique (1992) Protocol VI, para 8 III, which provided for the release of prisoners except for those being held for ordinary crimes.

[51] Comprehensive Peace Agreement Between the Government of Liberia and the Liberians United for Reconciliation and Democracy (LURD) and the Movement for Democracy in Liberia (MODEL) and Political Parties (2003) Art IX.

41 Failing to release internees at the close of hostilities would constitute a grave breach of Article 147 GC IV. First, it would constitute a breach on the basis that not releasing internees, or threatening not to release internees, might be considered to constitute hostage-taking if accompanied by the necessary intent (see Chapter 15 of this volume, at MN 49 and 71), in the sense that those persons would be deprived of their liberty by unnecessarily prolonged internment.[52] It might also meet the threshold for action that constitutes a war crime pursuant to the Statute of the International Criminal Court (ICC Statute).[53] Secondly, if the refusal to release internees does not amount to hostage-taking, the unlawful confinement of those persons would nevertheless be a grave breach where it could be shown that they were being held even though the reasons that necessitated their internment no longer existed.[54] Unlawful confinement is also an offence pursuant to the ICC Statute.[55] The elements of such an offence could be established quite easily where it could be shown, for example, that the commander of an internment facility was not releasing an internee even though there was no justification for internment. Unlawful confinement might also arise where the procedural requirements for interning a person have been breached and the person is not released.[56] A further example of an unlawful confinement of a civilian might also arise where the Detaining Power delays, without valid and lawful reason, the departure of a foreign national who wishes to leave the territory after he or she has been released from internment.[57] Both hostage-taking and unlawful confinement are also breaches of the domestic laws of most states.[58]

42 Repatriation could be a violation of the *non-refoulement* provisions found in customary international law and Article 33 of the 1951 Refugee Convention. Forcibly repatriating a person released from internment where there are substantial grounds for believing that the person would be in danger of being subjected to torture would violate Article 3(1) CAT and the prohibitions found in other human rights treaties. From an international criminal law (ICL) point of view, this may constitute aiding and abetting in torture.

43 Allegations that a Detaining Power breached its human rights obligations concerning end of internment by, for example, not releasing an internee after the close of hostilities, and therefore breaching the human rights obligation of a right to liberty, may be referred to a number of human rights bodies.[59]

E. Critical Assessment

44 There are at least five issues that arise at the end of internment that require critical assessment. The first relates to coalition operations; the second to the safety of persons released; the third is the practice of conditional release; the fourth is the role of an independent

---

[52] See Pictet Commentary GC IV, at 600–1.   [53] Arts 8(2)(a)(viii) and 8(2)(c)(iii) ICC Statute.
[54] Pictet Commentary GC IV, at 599.   [55] See Art 8(2)(a)(vii) ICC Statute.
[56] See ICTY, *The Prosecutor v Zejnil Delalić et al*, Trial Chamber Judgment, IT-96-21-T, 16 November 1998, para 583. See also, e.g, ICTY, *The Prosecutor v Dario Kordić and Mario Čerkez*, Trial Chamber Judgment, IT-95-14/2-T, 26 February 2001.
[57] ICRC Commentary APs, para 1001.
[58] According to the ICRC CIHL Database, 'Practice Relating to Rule 128—Release and Return of Persons Deprived of their Liberty', a number of countries have enacted the GC IV grave breaches provision into domestic law.
[59] See Ch 35 of this volume.

organization in overseeing release and repatriation; and the fifth is the role of the Security Council in determining the release and repatriation of internees.

One important matter that arises in coalition operations is determining the extent to which a Detaining Power retains ongoing control over an internee who has been handed over to another Detaining Power. For example, does the Detaining Power that initially interned the person have any legal basis for seeking the release of the internee whom it transferred or handed over? It seems that the answer is no.[60]

As mentioned above,[61] there is an obligation in armed conflicts where AP II applies to ensure the safety of those released from any form of detention.[62] It is reasonable that the obligation to ensure the safety of those released from detention, including internment, requires the Detaining Power to take into consideration such matters as whether the general environment into which the internee is to be released is safe, whether that particular internee will be safe if released in a particular place or at a particular time, and whether the means of release are safe. Apart from these general issues concerning release and safety, Detaining Powers party to the IECD also have obligations concerning release. Article 21 of that Convention requires a state party to take the appropriate steps to ensure that it can verify that an internee has actually been released, to ensure the physical integrity of internees who are released, and ensure that any internee who is released is able fully to exercise his or her rights at the time he or she is released.

Where, for example, a Detaining Power has held a large number of internees, and there are inadequate resources to provide for those internees, or where the goal of 'winning the hearts and minds' of the local community is important, there might be very good reasons to release internees on conditions. The provisions of Chapter XII of GC IV do not, however, envisage conditional release.[63] There is, though, some practice to suggest that such releases do take place. For example, during the International Force for East Timor (INTERFET) operations in East Timor in 1999, a number of detainees were conditionally released on the basis that they undertook to exhibit good behaviour, report regularly to United Nations Civilian Police (UNCIVPOL) and appear before a court to be tried, if and when required.[64] The conflict in Afghanistan has also provided a forum for conditional release of internees. In 2010 it was reported that internees were being released into their local communities, after representatives of the local communities signed a statement that they would monitor and supervise the internees' conduct, and support their reintegration into the community. Internees were also required to sign a pledge renouncing violence.[65]

One way of dealing with issues arising from the release or transfer of internees, is for states to enter into agreements in which they seek assurances from each other concerning matters such as the treatment of an internee, when an internee might be released, or the conditions for his or her transfer.[66] One contentious issue that arises from such agreements is whether the state that interned the individual in the first instance, but which then

---

[60] See Copenhagen Process: Principles and Guidelines, Principle 15 and accompanying commentary, available at: <http://um.dk/en/-/media/UM/English-site/Documents/Politics-and-diplomacy/Copenhangen%20Process%20Principles%20and%20Guidelines.pdf> See, however, for foreigners detained on a state's own territory, Art 45 para 2 GC IV; see also MN 48.

[61] See MN 38.   [62] See for IACs MN 19, and for NIACs MN 38.

[63] The notion of conditional release does exist in the context of POWs.

[64] See B. Oswald, 'The INTERFET Detainee Management Unit in East Timor', 3 *YIHL* (2000) 347.

[65] See, e.g., 'Khowst Governor Hosts Release Shura for Seven Former Detainees' (2010), available at <http://www.dvidshub.net/news/54262/khowst-governor-hosts-release-shura-seven-former-detainees>.

[66] Such agreements give effect to, e.g., Art 12 GC III and Art 45 GC IV.

transferred him or her to another state, can demand the release, or for that matter return, of the internee. Despite the clear wording of Article 45 paragraph 2 GC IV, it would seem that a state's ability to force another state to release a detainee who has been transferred is limited by the fact that the transferring state does not have control over the internee. Therefore, notwithstanding an agreement, the issue of who has control over the internee means that, pragmatically speaking, the second state can continue to hold the internee or even re-transfer him or her.[67]

49   There has been increasing involvement of international organizations, particularly the ICRC, in relation to the release and repatriation of internees. This is of fundamental importance, because it ensures greater transparency and accountability as regards the release and repatriation of interned persons, and therefore encourages their humane treatment. Having the ICRC present at the time of release of internees assists in ensuring that those persons are not released in a situation where they fear for their own safety, and that there is the means to track the well-being of those persons after release. Similarly, permitting the ICRC to interview internees prior to their release or repatriation assists in ensuring that their wishes concerning where they are released or repatriated are brought to the attention of the relevant authorities. Some of the functions that the ICRC has undertaken in relation to release and repatriation include: 'privately interviewing each prisoner' prior to his or her release;[68] arranging releases pursuant to peace agreements;[69] and directing the release of internees in coordination with other international organizations.[70] In at least one case, internees have been 'released to the Red Cross authority' in the area in which the detention occurred.[71] It should therefore be general practice in all situations of internment that, at the very least, the ICRC or another appropriate organization be invited to interview internees about to be released, and should be present at the time of release.

50   It is sometimes the case that the decision to release, repatriate, or return internees will rest with an entity other than the Detaining Power. For example, the Security Council, pursuant to its Chapter VII powers, might demand that a Detaining Power release, repatriate, or return internees.[72] Such an exercise of power by the Security Council would mean that a Detaining Power would, as a component of its obligations under the Charter of the United Nations, have to release or repatriate interned persons even if the Detaining Power could justify ongoing internment. When the Security Council exercises such powers, it must do so in a manner that is consistent with the provisions of Chapter XII of GC IV.

BRUCE OSWALD*

---

[67] See, e.g., *Secretary of State for Foreign and Commonwealth Affairs v Rahmattulah* [2012] UKSC 48.
[68] Dayton Accord, Annex IA, Art IX (1)(c). This right is based upon Art 143 para 5 GC IV.
[69] See, e.g., the Agreement on Permanent Ceasefire in Sudan, above n 49, at 1.9.
[70] See, e.g., the Agreement on the Cambodia Conflict, above n 49, Part VI, Art 21.
[71] The Comprehensive Peace Agreement in Liberia, above n 51, Art IX.
[72] See, e.g., UNSC Res 686 (1991), 2(c), in which the Security Council demanded that Iraq 'immediately release […] all Kuwaiti and third-State nationals detained by Iraq'.

* I would like to thank Ms Romy Faulkner, Ms Bethany Wellington, Mr Thomas Andrews and Ms Natasha Robbins for their assistance with this paper. I would also like to thank the co-editors of this volume for their helpful comments. As always, my thanks go to Ms Liz Saltnes for her support.

5. OCCUPIED TERRITORIES

Chapter 67. The Concept and the Beginning of Occupation

	MN
A. Introduction	1
B. Meaning and Application	8
I. Establishment of effective control by the Occupying Power	12
a. Necessary presence of armed forces?	12
b. Occupation of the air and the sea?	15
c. Occupation despite resistance?	16
d. The possibility of control is sufficient	18
e. Minimum duration?	20
f. Minimum extent of territory?	21
g. Indirect occupation through control by an armed group?	22
h. Joint control by a coalition	24
II. Loss of effective control by the adverse party	25
III. Lack of consent	28
IV. Irrelevance of other criteria	36
V. A distinction between invasion and occupation?	41
a. The systematic argument	43
b. Is it sufficient to exercise control over a person or over the piece of land on which that person is found?	45
c. A flexible understanding of the obligations of an Occupying Power?	46
d. A functional understanding of the concept of occupation itself?	47
VI. The special case of occupation without armed resistance	52
VII. Occupation in national liberation wars	55
C. Relevance in Non-International Armed Conflicts	57
D. Legal Consequences of a Violation	58
I. The consequences of occupation in international criminal law	59
II. Occupation and jurisdiction under international human rights law	60
III. Particular efforts to ensure respect by Israel for the rules on military occupation in Geneva Convention IV	61
E. Critical Assessment	62

Select Bibliography

Benvenisti, E., 'Occupation, Belligerent', in MPEPIL

Benvenisti, E., *The International Law of Occupation* (2nd edn, Oxford: OUP, 2012)

Dinstein, Y., *The International Law of Belligerent Occupation* (Cambridge: CUP, 2009)

Ferraro, T., 'Determining the Beginning and End of an Occupation under International Humanitarian Law', 94 *IRRC* 885 (2012) 133

von Glahn, G., *The Occupation of Enemy Territory: A Commentary on the Law and Practice of Belligerent Occupation* (Minneapolis, Minn: University of Minnesota Press, 1957)

Grignon, J., *L'applicabilité temporelle du droit international humanitaire* (Geneva: Schulthess, Collection genevoise, 2014)

ICRC, *Occupation and Other Forms of Administration of Foreign Territory, Expert Meeting* (Geneva: ICRC, 2012)

Kolb, R./Vité, S., *Le droit de l'occupation militaire: perspectives historiques et enjeux juridiques actuels* (Brussels: Bruylant, 2009)

Koutroulis, V., *Le début et la fin de l'application du droit de l'occupation* (Paris: Pedone, 2010)
Pictet Commentary GC IV, at 21–2, 59–61
Roberts, A., 'What Is a Military Occupation?', 55 *BYBIL* (1984) 261
Vité, S., 'L'applicabilité du droit international de l'occupation militaire aux activités des organisations internationales', 86 *IRRC* 853 (2004) 9
Zwanenburg, M., 'The Law of Occupation Revisited: The Beginning of an Occupation', 10 *YIHL* (2007) 99

A. Introduction

1 International humanitarian law (IHL) offers more detailed and far-reaching protection to protected civilians who find themselves in an occupied territory than to anyone else. Even states obsessed with their sovereignty admit that international law regulates their conduct when they act on the territory of another sovereign state which they have no title to rule. From a humanitarian point of view, civilians in occupied territories deserve and need particularly detailed protection; they are living on their own territory, and through no choice of their own come into contact with the enemy. This happens merely because the enemy has gained territorial control over the place where they live.

2 Because such a detailed and protective regime applies to occupied territories, it is crucial to determine what occupation is, and when the rules of Geneva Convention (GC) IV on occupied territories start to apply to a certain place or person during an armed conflict. Logically, occupation must first be defined before one can enquire when it begins, yet these two questions are so interlinked that they may be considered as two sides of the same coin. In recent history it is not surprising that belligerents have often denied, or were reluctant to admit, that a territory over which they gained control was an occupied territory. In part this is done in order to justify non-respect for the detailed rules of this regime. Other reasons are, however, perhaps even more important. In an international legal order prohibiting aggression and the acquisition of territory by force, military occupation is inevitably suspect; in public opinion it has a 'pejorative connotation',[1] even when the military force that leads to an occupation does not violate *jus ad bellum*. In addition, any occupation necessarily deprives the local population, if it constitutes a people, at least temporarily of its right to self-determination, and it is incompatible with the idea that the will of the population must be the basis of the authority of government.[2] Furthermore, when an armed conflict erupts due to a dispute over territory, the party gaining control over that territory will never treat it as an occupied territory. Lastly, we have to recognize that the very concept of military occupation is based upon territorial control and one state hindering another state's exercise of control over its own territory, but modern warfare is often not about territorial control. In addition, control may be exercised from a distance and the enemy may be more or less a failed state. However, as long as no specific rules are adopted to cover such new situations, there is no reason not to apply the law of occupation, even if the situation does not conform to the traditional pattern of military occupation.

---

[1] ICRC, *Occupation and Other Forms of Administration of Foreign Territory, Expert Meeting* (Geneva: ICRC, 2012), at 16.
[2] Cf Art 21(3) UDHR.

Deviation from the traditional stereotype of occupation is not a sufficient reason for the law not to apply.

The main legal issues arising in relation to the concept and beginning of military 3 occupation are how much control a state must exercise, and over what extent of territory, before it can be considered an Occupying Power. This also raises the controversy whether the rules of GC IV on military occupation already apply during the invasion of a territory. Furthermore, it must be clarified whether the rules of GC IV on military occupation become inapplicable by virtue of consent to or the legality of the foreign presence.

Whether a territory is or is not considered occupied under IHL has important practical 4 implications. The rules of IHL on military occupation, set out in the Geneva Conventions and discussed in this and the following chapters (and those foreseen in the Hague Regulations), protect a great variety of collective rights of the occupied population. The Hague Regulations include in particular the right not to be subject to changes affecting the laws in force in the country,[3] or rules on the use of private or public property for public or state interests.[4] Geneva Convention IV prohibits voluntary population movements (settlements) encouraged by the state.[5] Those rules cannot be found in IHL applicable outside occupied territories or in international human rights law (IHRL). Such conduct would be perfectly legitimate if adopted by a state in its own territory. Similarly, under GC IV, individual deportations are absolutely prohibited where these take place from occupied territories,[6] and a state has a clear treaty-based obligation to accept outside humanitarian assistance for the benefit of civilians in need in an occupied territory.[7] Such prohibition and obligations apply only where the territory is considered occupied. It is crucial, therefore, to know when a territory is occupied.

Historically, before the First World War, debates about the definition of occupation 5 took place in a different policy context. Typical Occupying Powers at that time, such as Germany and Russia, favoured a low threshold of territorial control for the law of occupation to apply, because at the time the law of military occupation was mainly seen as giving the occupant powers under international law. Conversely, those states which feared being occupied, such as Belgium, The Netherlands, Switzerland, and France, insisted on a high threshold of territorial control, making the applicability of the law of occupation more difficult and distinguishing occupation from invasion: 'No one doubted that an invading army would seek to attain [...] effective control over the occupied populations.'[8] The Hague Regulations attempted to reconcile these two interests with their definition of occupation,[9] which failed to clarify the issue. Today, in particular after the experience of the Second World War and the creation of detailed protection for civilians in GC IV, the interests at stake are inverted. The humanitarians and prospective occupied countries aim to apply the international rules on occupation as soon as possible, while prospective or actual Occupying Powers seek to avoid their application. Occupation has thus become a burden rather than a source of rights for the Occupying Powers. Humanitarians fear

---

[3] Cf Art 43 Hague Regulations.   [4] Cf Arts 46–56 Hague Regulations.
[5] Cf Art 49 para 6 GC IV.   [6] Cf Art 49 para 1 GC IV.   [7] Cf Art 59 GC IV.
[8] E. Benvenisti, *The International Law of Occupation* (2nd edn, Oxford: OUP, 2012), at 45.
[9] Cf Art 42 Hague Regulations.

that occupiers who control a territory will refrain from administering it, and fail to comply fully with the many obligations under GC IV and other applicable rules of IHL on military occupation.[10]

6   In the past 50 years, any discussion about the law of occupation, including its definition and constituent elements, has been overshadowed by one case in particular, the Palestinian territory occupied by Israel. Although atypical, this case has attracted the most international and domestic jurisprudence, scholarly writings, and practice of states and international organizations. For military occupation under GC IV, this case is anomalous because of its history, duration, and the desire of the Occupying Power to annex the occupied territory *de jure* or *de facto*. In addition, technically IHL of military occupation applies due to the 1967 armed conflict between Israel, Egypt, Jordan, and Syria, while the main issue today is the distinct concept of alien occupation, i.e. the right to self-determination of the Palestinian people. In this context, any discussion about the constitutive elements of an occupation and when it starts is influenced by the arguably distinct debate of whether Gaza and parts of the West Bank, from which Israeli forces have withdrawn, are still occupied territories. The case of the Palestinian territory, on which nearly all international attention has focused (with short interludes during the Iraqi occupation of Kuwait and the United States (US) occupation of Iraq), has completely overshadowed, if not led to a neglect of, other cases where the rules of IHL on military occupation arguably applied. These cases include the Indian intervention in East Pakistan, the Soviet presence in Afghanistan and Iraqi control over vast parts of Iranian territory in the 1980s, the Indonesian presence in East Timor, the Indian presence in Kashmir, the Moroccan presence in the Western Sahara, the US invasions of Grenada and Panama in the 1980s, control of the Eastern Congo by several neighbouring African states, the (direct and indirect) Armenian presence in Nagorno Karabach, the intermittent Turkish military operations in Northern Iraq, the Ethiopian presence in Somalia, the Russian presence in Abkhazia and South Ossetia, the presence of US and coalition forces in Afghanistan displacing the Taliban as the *de facto* government in 2001, or, most recently, the occupation of Crimea by Russia. At least some attention has been given to other cases of occupation: the mutual control by Eritrea and Ethiopia of small parts of each other's territory during the 1998–2000 war was covered by an international arbitration; the International Court of Justice (ICJ) dealt with the Ugandan occupation of the Congolese Ituri province; and the Turkish presence in Northern Cyprus has attracted the attention of the European Court of Human Rights (ECtHR), which implicitly classified it as an occupation, without directly applying the rules of IHL on military occupation. As for the question of whether and when the rules of IHL on military occupation apply to an international territorial administration or the presence of forces of an international organization, the cases of Kosovo, East Timor, and Somalia have led to intense scholarly debates.

7   The term 'occupation' appears in Common Article 2 paragraph 2 of the Geneva Conventions, which makes all of the Geneva Conventions (not only GC IV) applicable in 'cases of partial or total occupation of the territory of a High Contracting Party, even if the said occupation meets with no armed resistance'. Furthermore (and more importantly in practice), the most important and lengthy part of GC IV is Part III on protected persons, which contains an entire section (Section III) applicable to 'occupied territories'. Equally

---

[10] Benvenisti, above n 8, at 46.

applicable to occupied territories are Section I, containing, as its title indicates, 'provisions common to the territories of the parties to the conflict and to occupied territories', and Section IV, prescribing detailed rules protecting protected civilians interned for imperative security reasons. Lastly, under Article 4(B)(1) GC III, former members of the armed forces of the Occupied Power reinterned by an Occupying Power benefit from the treatment accorded to prisoners of war (POWs). Conversely, Article 4(A)(6) of GC III reserves POW status for participants in a *levée en masse* to '[i]nhabitants of a non-occupied territory'.

B. Meaning and Application

The Geneva Conventions do not define 'occupation'. Under the general rule on treaty interpretation,[11] and according to Article 154 GC IV, which states that GC IV is supplementary to Section III of the Hague Regulations on 'military authority over the territory of the hostile state', it seems appropriate to refer to the Hague Regulations for a definition, Article 42 of which states:

> Territory is considered occupied when it is actually placed under the authority of the hostile army. The occupation extends only to the territory where such authority has been established and can be exercised.

The only authentic version of the Hague Regulations is the French version, which indicates that the territory must be '*placé de fait sous l'autorité de l'armée ennemie*'. This is clearer than the English translation and means that occupation is exclusively a question of fact.[12] Most authors and the ICJ understand this definition rather restrictively, requiring a high degree of control and administration—and not mere presence—by the hostile army.[13] However, as will be discussed later (MN 48) in relation to the question whether the rules of IHL on military occupation already apply during an invasion, many argue that the concept of occupation in GC IV is broader than that found in the Hague Regulations.

The criteria which must be fulfilled for a territory to be considered occupied under the definition found in the Hague Regulations are generally summarized as requiring:

— effective control by one state engaged in an international armed conflict (IAC) against another state, over parts of the territory of the latter;
— loss of effective control by the latter over that part of its territory; and
— lack of consent by the latter.[14]

The first two criteria are explicitly mentioned by the 1880 *Oxford Manual*,[15] and they still appear in the 2004 UK *Manual of the Law of Armed Conflict* and the ICJ judgment in *DRC*

---

[11] Art 31(3)(c) VCLT.
[12] ICTY, *The Prosecutor v Mladen Naletilić and Vinko Martinović*, Trial Chamber Judgment, IT-98-34-T, 31 March 2003, para 211; V. Koutroulis, *Le début et la fin de l'application du droit de l'occupation* (Paris: Pedone, 2010), at 20–74 and 97–149; T. Ferraro, 'Determining the Beginning and End of an Occupation under International Humanitarian Law', 94 *IRRC* 885 (2012) 133, at 134–6.
[13] See MN 18.
[14] ICRC *Expert Meeting*, above n 1, at 17–23; Ferraro, above n 12, at 139–43; P. Spoerri, 'The Law of Occupation', in A. Clapham and P. Gaeta (eds), *The Oxford Handbook of International Law in Armed Conflict* (Oxford: OUP, 2014) 182, at 188–92.
[15] Art 41 of the *Oxford Manual of the Laws of War on Land*, adopted by the Institute of International Law, 1880, reproduced in D. Schindler and J. Toman, *The Laws of Armed Conflicts* (4th edn, Nijhoff: Leiden, 2004) 29, at 35.

v Uganda.¹⁶ The third criterion is inherent in the condition that the occupying army must be 'hostile'.¹⁷

10   The International Criminal Tribunal for the former Yugoslavia (ICTY) set out more detailed 'guidelines' in the *Naletilić* case, which do not contradict but rather detail the above-mentioned criteria:

- the occupying power must be in a position to substitute its own authority for that of the occupied authorities, which must have been rendered incapable of functioning publicly;
- the enemy's forces have surrendered, been defeated or withdrawn. In this respect, battle areas may not be considered as occupied territory. However, sporadic local resistance, even successful, does not affect the reality of occupation;
- the occupying power has a sufficient force present, or the capacity to send troops within a reasonable time to make the authority of the occupying power felt;
- a temporary administration has been established over the territory;
- the occupying power has issued and enforced directions to the civilian population.¹⁸

11   In the text that follows, the traditional criteria will be discussed first, followed by those criteria which are not relevant. Then the controversy of whether and to what extent the rules of IHL on military occupation already apply during an invasion will be addressed. Lastly, special cases will be dealt with, such as occupation without armed resistance and national liberation wars.

I. Establishment of effective control by the Occupying Power

a. *Necessary presence of armed forces?*

12   Most experts believe that an occupation can only begin with the presence of foreign armed forces on the ground.¹⁹ In contrast, some others consider that effective control may be exercised remotely, either through control of entry into the territory, the territorial airspace or sea, or through control over living conditions in a territory.²⁰ In reality, those taking the latter view focus on the issue of the end of occupation and want to argue that the Gaza Strip is still occupied by Israel, although Israeli forces withdrew from the Gaza Strip in 2005.²¹ Indeed, a majority of international institutions adopt this position regarding

---

¹⁶ UK Ministry of Defence, *The Manual of the Law of Armed Conflict* (Oxford: OUP, 2004), para 11.3; ICJ, *Armed Activities on the Territory of the Congo (DRC v Uganda)*, Judgment, 19 December 2005, para 173.

¹⁷ J. Grignon, *L'applicabilité temporelle du droit international humanitaire* (Geneva: Schulthess, Collection genevoise, 2014), at 119–22.

¹⁸ ICTY, *Naletilić*, above n 12, para 217 (footnotes omitted).

¹⁹ ICRC *Expert Meeting*, above n 1, at 17–19; Y. Dinstein, *The International Law of Belligerent Occupation* (Cambridge: CUP, 2009), at 44; Ferraro, above n 12, at 143–7; H.-P. Gasser, 'Protection of the Civilian Population', in D. Fleck (ed), *Handbook on International Humanitarian Law* (2nd edn, Oxford: OUP, 2008) 237, at 274; M. Zwanenburg, 'The Law of Occupation Revisited: The Beginning of an Occupation', 10 *YIHL* (2007) 99, at 126; M. Bothe, 'Beginning and End of Occupation', in *Actes du Colloque de Bruges, Les défis contemporains au droit de l'occupation, 20–21 octobre 2005*, Collège d'Europe, Comité international de la Croix-Rouge, Collegium, No 34, 2006, at 27; Spoerri, above n 14, at 189.

²⁰ See, at least for a territory of small dimensions and with the necessary technology, P. Spoerri, *Die Fortgeltung völkerrechtlichen Besatzungsrechts während der Interimsphase palästinensischer Selbstverwaltung in der West Bank und Gaza* (Frankfurt am Main: Europäische Hochschulschriften, 2001), at 237.

²¹ S. Solomon, 'Occupied or Not: The Question of Gaza's Legal Status after the Israeli Disengagement', 19 *Cardozo Journal of International and Comparative Law* (2011) 59, at 72–3; M. Mari, 'The Israeli Disengagement from the Gaza Strip: an End of the Occupation?', 8 *YIHL* (2005) 356, at 363 and 365; E. Benvenisti, 'The Law

the Gaza Strip.²² Whether a territory which was once occupied by ground forces may continue to be occupied by remote control is a question dealt with in Chapter 74, MN 39–40, of this volume.

From a strictly logical point of view, one might argue that the same criteria should be used to determine the beginning, the existence, and the end of an occupation.²³ However, many experts consider that on the question of whether foreign armed forces must be present on the ground, there is no congruence between the criteria for the beginning of occupation and those for its end.²⁴ Indeed, once ground forces establish sufficient control over territory (and over persons, so that they are considered to be in the hands of the Occupying Power), occupation may be maintained remotely. No one argues, however, that a besieged town, e.g. Leningrad in the Second World War, is an occupied territory before the besieged forces surrender, simply because the besieger controls the airspace and all entry to and exits from the territory, and therefore life in the besieged town. While resistance within an occupied territory does not necessarily end occupation, it is difficult to imagine that occupation being established over a place while the ground forces of the Occupied Power still resist and control that place. In addition, to maintain that occupation can be established remotely without the armed forces ever gaining control of the territory on the ground, would also deprive the civilian population of this territory of combatant and POW status if they engaged in *levée en masse*, as the latter is reserved to '[i]nhabitants of a non-occupied territory'.²⁵ A concept of occupation established through remote control is also incompatible with the actual obligations of an Occupying Power prescribed by the rules of IHL. Without ground control, an Occupying Power cannot respect the many rights it is required to protect and to fulfil, e.g. concerning public order and civil life, health or education, foreseen in the pertinent rules of IHL.²⁶ Therefore, it is only logical that some proponents of the concept of remote or virtual occupation derive from IHL a 'duty to occupy'²⁷ through ground forces.

However, it is not necessary for the occupying forces to be present on each square metre of a territory. According to the topographical features of the territory, the density of the population, and the degree of resistance (even passive or non-military), it is sufficient if occupying troops are positioned strategically on the ground and, if necessary, are then able to be dispatched fairly quickly to demonstrate and enforce their authority.²⁸

13

14

on Asymmetric Warfare', in M.H. Arsanjani et al (eds), *Looking to the Future: Essays on International Law in Honor of W. Michael Reisman* (Leiden, Boston: Martinus Nijhoff, 2011) 929, at 943; S. Darcy and J. Reynolds, 'An Enduring Occupation: The Status of the Gaza Strip from the Perspective of International Humanitarian Law', 15 *Journal of Conflict & Security Law* (2010) 211, at 220 and 226–7; S. Dikker Hupkes, *What Constitutes Occupation?* (Leiden: E.M. Meijers Instituut, 2008), at 22, 35, 51, 84–9; very nuanced: Benvenisti, above n 8, at 54. However, it must be mentioned that the Institut de droit international already envisaged in 1913, when drafting the *Oxford Manual of the Laws of Naval Warfare*, that a coastal area or island might be occupied by the mere presence of ships, which exercise actual authority over those land areas through their firepower (see *Annuaire de l'IDI*, Session de Christiania 1912–Session d'Oxford 1913 (Brussels: Lesigne, 1929), at 920). See, for further historical precedents and authors who could be considered to support a concept of remote occupation, Koutroulis, above n 12, at 40, fn 126.

²² See UN Doc A/HRC/12/48, 25 September 2009, paras 273–9; UN Doc A/HRC/15/21, 22 September 2010, paras 63–6. For an overview of these positions, see Grignon, above n 17, at 293–5.
²³ Ferraro, above n 12, at 156; with some hesitation, ICRC *Expert Meeting*, above n 1, at 11, mentioning that the *sui generis* character of some situations could alter the criteria.
²⁴ ICRC *Expert Meeting*, above n 1, at 17 and 19; Ferraro, above n 12, at 157–8. *Contra* Y. Shany, 'Faraway so Close: The Legal Status of Gaza after Israel's Disengagement', 8 *YIHL* (2005) 369, at 378.
²⁵ Art 4(A)(6) GC III; Art 2 Hague Regulations.   ²⁶ Ferraro, above n 12, at 147.
²⁷ Benvenisti, above n 8, at 54.
²⁸ ICRC *Expert Meeting*, above n 1, at 17; E. Benvenisti, 'Occupation, Belligerent', in MPEPIL (2009), para 8; US, *Department of the Army Field Manual FM 27-10, The Law of Land Warfare* (1956), para 356.

b. Occupation of the air and the sea?

15   Some scholars consider that not only land, but also the territorial sea and the airspace above the territory of another state may be occupied.[29] In the context of no-fly zones over Iraq, these scholars even consider that the air may be occupied when the underlying land is not. Although this may be desirable from a humanitarian perspective, as it may lead to obligations for states exercising such control, the result is absurd. Occupation is a concept of the law of land warfare.[30] Once land is occupied, the Occupying Power may equally have rights and obligations concerning the airspace over such territory and the territorial sea adjacent to such territory.[31] However, the territorial sea or the airspace cannot possibly be occupied alone. They follow, as on other issues, the territory which justifies the rights the territorial state exercises over them.

c. Occupation despite resistance?

16   As long as resistance continues in a given place, the occupation of that place cannot begin. However, once a place is occupied and the armed forces of the Occupied Power are no longer able to resist, periodic but temporary resistance in some areas of the occupied territory does not stop a territory from being considered occupied.[32] Article 4(A)(2) GC III indirectly confirms this by conferring (under certain conditions) POW status on '[m]embers of [...] organized resistance movements, belonging to a Party to the conflict, and operating in or outside their own territory, even if this territory is occupied', should they fall into the power of the Occupying Power. If any organized resistance barred occupation, such resistance fighters would by definition never find themselves in an occupied territory. Most experts add that even temporarily successful resistance does not bar occupation.[33] They usually refer to a decision of a US Military Tribunal after the Second World War, which held:

> It is clear that the German Armed Forces were able to maintain control of Greece and Yugoslavia until they evacuated them in the fall of 1944. While it is true that the partisans were able to control sections of these countries at various times, it is established that the Germans could at any time they desired assume physical control of any part of the country. The control of the resistance forces was temporary only and not such as would deprive the German Armed Forces of its status of an occupant.[34]

Such a theory may be practical for a criminal tribunal operating with hindsight. Disadvantages exist when the rules of IHL must be interpreted for those who fight during an armed conflict. For example, if resistance fighters succeed in liberating part of an occupied territory, neither they nor the Occupying Power will know whether the liberation is temporary or not.

17   In light of the foregoing, it is submitted that in conformity with the second sentence of Article 42 of the Hague Regulations ('The occupation extends only to the territory where

---

[29] Koutroulis, above n 12, at 35–41.

[30] Thus equally the position of the 'United States, Department of State Memorandum of Law on Israel's Right to Develop New Oil Fields in Sinai and the Gulf of Suez', 16 *ILM* (1977) 749.

[31] Benvenisti, above n 8, at 55; Dinstein, above n 19, at 47–8.

[32] ICRC *Expert Meeting*, above n 1, at 17; ICTY, *Naletilić*, above n 12, para 217; Benvenisti, above n 8, at 51; Dinstein, above n 19, at 45; K. Dörmann and L. Colassis, 'International Humanitarian Law in the Iraq Conflict', 47 *GYIL* (2004) 293, at 308.

[33] Dinstein, above n 19, at 45.

[34] *The Hostages Trial, Trial of Wilhelm List and others*, United States Military Tribunal, Nuremberg, 1947–8, UNWCC Law Reports, vol VIII, 34, at 56.

such authority has been established and can be exercised'), which was disregarded by the US tribunal (cited above),[35] any act of resistance which leads to a loss of territorial control over a part of a territory must end—possibly temporarily—the occupation in that part of the territory.[36] In any case, an Occupying Power would be materially unable to fulfil its obligations in a place controlled by resistance fighters.

d. *The possibility of control is sufficient*

A majority of experts consider that a *possibility* of exercising control over the territory or part of it is sufficient.[37] However, this possibility must be based on a ground presence in the territory. This idea may be expressed by requiring that the Occupying Power must control a territory but not necessarily its population.[38] This latter idea flows from the former, but, as already mentioned, control over territory vanishes where the population is able successfully to resist as part of an organized resistance. Conversely, the mere military capability of a belligerent to control a given territory at its will is not sufficient if that belligerent chooses not to invade it with ground forces. In addition, the ICJ seems to require that the authority *is actually* exercised.[39] In this writer's view, this does not mean that occupying forces need be present everywhere. However, it would mean that a foreign state is not an Occupying Power if it is present in enemy territory and chooses not to exercise authority. With all due respect for the ICJ, if it is established both that the territorial sovereign is hindered from exercising authority and that there is no consent, it is contrary to legal logic to deny that the occupying state has the manifold obligations under the IHL rules on military occupation to protect and fulfil (i.e. to exercise authority), simply because it chooses not to exercise authority.[40] Correctly, the UK *Manual* requires only that 'the occupying power is in a position to substitute its authority for that of the former government'.[41]

18

The concept of occupation may be interpreted by factoring in the obligations of an Occupying Power under the IHL rules of military occupation. A territory is then considered occupied only if the Occupying Power is able to comply with its obligations, in particular with Article 43 of the Hague Regulations, requiring it to maintain or restore public order and civil life.[42] As will be discussed below (MN 46) in relation to the allegedly

19

---

[35] Critical also Benvenisti, above n 8, at 47.

[36] Similarly ICRC Commentary APs, para 1700, which refers to *Case No 45 Trial of Carl Bauer, Ernst Schrameck and Herbert Falten*, Permanent Military Tribunal, Dijon, 1945, UNWCC Law Reports, vol VIII, 15, at 18, in which it was held: 'Any part of territory in which the occupant has been deprived of actual means for carrying out normal administration by the presence of opposing military forces would not have the status of "occupied" territory within the terms of Arts 2 and 42 of the Hague Regulations. The fact that other parts of the occupied country, as a whole, are under effective enemy occupation would not affect this situation.' As here also Ferraro, above n 12, at 151–2. Note that the House of Lords considered in *Al-Skeini* that the UK had lost jurisdiction over parts of Iraq it occupied because of the amount of resistance: *Al-Skeini and others v Secretary of State for Defence* [2007] UKHL 26, [83].

[37] ICRC *Expert Meeting*, above n 1, at 19; Dinstein, above n 19, at 44–5; Benvenisti, above n 8, at 49–50; Benvenisti, in MPEPIL, above n 28, para 5; M. Bothe, '"Effective Control": A Situation Triggering the Application of the Law of Belligerent Occupation, Background Document', in ICRC *Expert Meeting*, above n 1, at 39; M. Bothe, 'Effective Control During Invasion: A Practical View on the Application Threshold of the Law of Occupation' 94 *IRRC* 885 (2012) 37, at 39–40; G. von Glahn, *The Occupation of Enemy Territory: A Commentary on the Law and Practice of Belligerent Occupation* (Minneapolis, Minn: University of Minnesota Press, 1957), at 29; Shany, above n 24, at 375–8; Spoerri, above n 14, at 190; ICTY, *Naletilić*, above n 12, para 217.

[38] Benvenisti, above n 8, at 48. [39] ICJ, *DRC v Uganda*, above n 16, para 173.

[40] Bothe in ICRC *Expert Meeting*, above n 1, at 39. Critical also Ferraro, above n 12, at 150–1.

[41] UK *Manual*, above n 16, para 11.3. [42] ICRC *Expert Meeting*, above n 1, at 18.

distinct invasion phase, the obligations of an Occupying Power, including under Article 43 of the Hague Regulations, are nevertheless mainly obligations of means, and are therefore flexibly adapted to the amount of authority and factual possibilities of the occupying forces.

e. Minimum duration?

20 The Occupying Power need not control a part of a territory for a minimum duration. The Eritrea–Ethiopia Claims Commission (EECC) was satisfied with 'just a few days'.[43] A Swiss Military Manual envisages the control of an Occupying Power changing several times and remaining for a very short period.[44] The occupation may be instant or take time to consolidate to reach the necessary degree of control.[45] Furthermore, a standard requiring a certain duration would not be practicable for parties, fighters, victims, and humanitarian organizations, because they would be required to foresee how control over territory would develop before they could know whether they must comply with the pertinent rules of IHL, are protected by them, should have complied with them from the beginning, or may invoke them at all. Conversely, a concept of occupation without a minimum duration is practicable only if applied functionally, i.e. not all the rules of IHL on military occupation apply at once.[46]

f. Minimum extent of territory?

21 As for the minimum extent of territory a party must control, it is uncontroversial that a state may be occupied in part. Experts agree that a single village or a small island may be occupied.[47] Extreme adherents to the position that GC IV applies during the invasion phase, discussed below (MN 45), would argue that to torture, beat, arrest, detain, or deport a person, invading forces must necessarily control the spot on which that person is found.[48] That spot would then constitute an occupied territory; it is under their control and the territorial state is no longer able to exercise its authority over that spot. Neither GC IV nor the Hague Regulations clarify the minimum amount of territory that needs to be controlled for it to become an occupied territory. One might therefore consider the portion of land on which a single house is built as occupied if the enemy has control over that house but not over the neighbouring house, separated from the former through the 'frontline'. No one would deny that if such a situation arises after a ceasefire, the last house in the occupied territory before the ceasefire line and its inhabitants would benefit from the rules of IHL on military occupation. Admittedly, while a state may comply with all obligations of an Occupying Power in a village, a concept of occupation fragmenting single houses and the portion of land on which they are located will inevitably lead to a functional concept of occupation, under which the portion of land on which the house is built must be considered occupied for the purposes of the applicability of certain rules of IHL on occupation, but not for others (see MN 47–50). Conversely, even if one rejects

---

[43] EECC, *Central Front—Eritrea's Claims 2, 4, 6, 7, 8 & 22*, Partial Award, 28 April 2004, para 57.
[44] Switzerland, *Gesetze und Gebräuche des Krieges (Auszug und Kommentar), Reglement 51.7/IId* (16 January 1987), Art 152.
[45] Grignon, above n 17, at 114–15.
[46] ICRC *Expert Meeting*, above n 1, at 24. For a discussion of such a functional concept of occupation, see MN 47–51.
[47] ICRC *Expert Meeting*, above n 1, at 24.
[48] M. Sassòli, 'A Plea in Defence of Pictet and the Inhabitants of Territories under Invasion: The Case for the Applicability of Convention IV during the Invasion Phase', 94 *IRRC* 885 (2012) 42, at 45.

the concept of remote occupation, it is possible that armed forces may control a strip of land adjacent to their country's frontier while remaining physically on their side of the border. Thus, in the case of the Palestinian territory, even if Gaza were no longer considered occupied since 2012, the buffer zone officially declared by Israel around the Gaza Strip, consisting of a military no-go area, in which Israel hinders the entry of Palestinians by firing on them from Israeli territory, may still be considered as occupied, at least for the purpose of the applicability of those rules on occupation with which Israel is able to comply without entering the Gaza Strip.[49]

g. Indirect occupation through control by an armed group?

Normally, to qualify as an occupied territory, armed forces of the Occupying Power are required to exercise the necessary control over a territory. As this is a question of fact, other *de jure* or *de facto* agents (e.g. a private military company[50]) may equally contribute to such control or exercise it alone. What counts is that those who exercise control are acting on behalf of—or are controlled by—a foreign power. When a foreign state exercises control over an armed group, which in turn controls a territory during an armed conflict against the territorial state, the state controlling the group is constructively an Occupying Power.

To reach such a conclusion, one has to consider the controversial question of the necessary degree of control by the foreign state over the armed group. For purposes of attribution of state responsibility for illegal conduct to a state, the ICJ requires *effective* control over the conduct, or complete dependence of the armed group on the relevant state, while it has left open whether mere *overall* control by a foreign state over the armed group fighting a prima facie non-international armed conflict is sufficient to classify the conflict as international.[51] The ICTY considers that *overall* control over an armed group is sufficient both for purposes of attribution of conduct of the armed group to the controlling state and for the classification of the conflict as international if that state is a foreign state.[52] Logically, an ICTY Trial Chamber therefore considered *overall* control as sufficient to trigger an occupation by the state controlling an armed group,[53] which led to an absurd result: Croatia was legally an Occupying Power in parts of Bosnia where it never directed the armed group, the Croatian Defence Council (HVO) made up of Bosnian Croats, to be present. Thus, the HVO fighters had to comply with the restraints applicable to an Occupying Power while operating on territory inhabited by Bosnian Croats, including when carrying out activity on their own initiative while fighting against the Bosnian Government. Another ICTY Chamber applied the law of military occupation only if the foreign state, Croatia, had 'a further degree of control' than mere overall control (without clarifying whether effective control was required and, if so, whether the effective control must be exercised by the foreign state over the group, or alternatively by the group or the foreign state over the territory in question).[54] In this

---

[49] See, e.g., Al Haq, *Shifting Paradigms, Israel's Enforcement of the Buffer Zone in the Gaza Strip* (Ramallah, Al Haq, 2011).

[50] Benvenisti, above n 8, at 61.

[51] See ICJ, *Military and Paramilitary Activities in and against Nicaragua (Nicaragua v US)*, Merits, 27 June 1986, para 115; ICJ, *Case concerning Application of the Convention on the Prevention and Punishment of the Crime of Genocide (Bosnia and Herzegovina v Serbia and Montenegro)*, Merits, 26 February 2007, paras 396–407.

[52] ICTY, *The Prosecutor v Duško Tadić*, Appeals Chamber Judgment, IT-94-1-A, 15 July 1999, paras 116–44.

[53] ICTY, *The Prosecutor v Tihomir Blaškić*, Trial Chamber Judgment, IT-95-14, 3 March 2000, para 149. There was no appeal on this aspect of the finding.

[54] ICTY, *Naletilić*, above n 12, para 214. There was no appeal on this aspect of the finding.

author's view it is necessary that the foreign state has effective control over the conduct which in turn establishes the armed group's effective control of the territory in question.[55] Others object, saying that overall control by the foreign state makes IHL of IACs applicable, and once it is applicable, what has to be determined is only whether the armed group had effective control over the territory.[56] To justify their position, they could invoke the jurisprudence of the ECtHR which, in the *Loizidou* case, considered that Turkey's overall control over the authorities of the 'Turkish Republic of Northern Cyprus' was sufficient to find the former responsible for human rights violations committed by the latter. Indeed, the victims of those violations were considered as falling under Turkey's jurisdiction.[57] In this author's view, the difference between this and the question discussed here—whether IHL of military occupation applies—is that human rights obligations had to be complied with by the authorities of the 'Turkish Republic of Northern Cyprus' (assuming they are bound at all by them) on their own territory, while the IHL of military occupation must only be applied in a foreign territory. It is therefore entirely conceivable that it is sufficient that a state has overall control over unrecognized authorities in another state to make it responsible for their human rights violations, while to make IHL of military occupation applicable, it needs effective control over conduct triggering such applicability.

h. *Joint control by a coalition*

24 When an occupation is implemented by a coalition of states, which jointly exercise effective control over a territory as discussed above, but without any one of them individually exercising the necessary threshold of authority,[58] a mechanical application of the law designed for individual Occupying Powers would deprive the population of the territory of the benefit of the rules of IHL of military occupation—and indeed of all rules of GC IV on protected civilians (see MN 43 and 44). It is therefore suggested that we should aggregate the presence and actions of different coalition forces to determine whether the IHL of military occupation applies. If it does, each coalition member could be considered to be functionally bound by the obligations of an Occupying Power in its actions, where any of the following conditions are met:

— if these actions contribute to the necessary control of the coalition, or would typically be carried out by an Occupying Power; or
— if they are actions the coalition is required to take under positive obligations foreseen by IHL of military occupation.[59]

---

[55] That effective control is here the decisive test is also the opinion of the ICRC *Expert Meeting*, above n 1, at 23, and Benvenisti, above n 8, at 61, who justifies his position by the obligations to protect. In this author's view, the effective control test also applies to obligations to respect.

[56] Ferraro, above n 12, at 158–60.

[57] ECtHR, *Loizidou v Turkey*, Judgment, 18 December 1996, at 2235–6, para 56; and ECtHR, *Cyprus v Turkey*, Judgment, 10 May 2001, para 77.

[58] In the case of Iraq in 2003 and 2004, UNSC Res 1483 (2003) considered in preambular para 14 that the US and the UK were Occupying Powers, while other coalition members were explicitly mentioned in preambular para 15 as not being Occupying Powers. As the US and the UK had in their respective areas of occupation sufficient control through their forces to fulfil individually the criteria of an Occupying Power, this did not raise major problems, while it would if no coalition partner had on its own sufficient control to be an Occupying Power under IHL.

[59] Dörmann and Colassis, above n 32, at 302–4; Ferraro, above n 12, at 161–2; Spoerri, above n 14, at 190; L. Lijnzaad, 'How Not to Be an Occupying Power: Some Reflections on Security Council Resolution 1483

II. Loss of effective control by the adverse party

Most authors, manuals, and judicial decisions discuss loss of control or authority by the sovereign or previous administrator over the territory, or substitution by the Occupying Power, as a separate criterion.[60] One might doubt whether loss of effective control is not inherent in the first requirement, namely, acquisition of territorial control by the enemy. However, as it is sufficient under this first requirement that the Occupying Power is in a position to exercise control over the territory, followed by positive obligations to exercise such control, those obligations incumbent upon the enemy power would be neither justified nor necessary if the authorities previously in control could fulfil all governmental functions over such a territory.

The mere fact that the administration or local authorities of the territorial sovereign continue to exercise functions of government does not bar the existence of an occupation. On the contrary, the rules of IHL on military occupation largely require that local authorities be permitted to function.[61] Such possible power-sharing is generally qualified as vertical, whereby the Occupying Power maintains control over the local administration in the occupied territory and has the final say.[62] Horizontal power sharing (where the occupied authority and the occupier cooperate on an equal footing), on the other hand, would be incompatible with occupation, because it would cast doubt on the ability of the Occupying Power to impose its will.[63] The present writer objects to the view that occupation is simply a vertical relationship, as one has to recall that IHL requires local authorities have the final say in many fields (e.g. private law or education). In addition, the decisive distinction cannot be that between the ousted sovereign and local authorities. In a unitary state, primary education and sewage may depend upon the central government, while in a decentralized state these responsibilities may fall on municipalities. In both cases the Occupying Power has the same obligation to allow the existing system to function. Decisive for the existence of an occupation is the fact that the Occupying Power could, if it so wished, have the final say in all respects. If it is not IHL or its political decision but its factual inability which hinders it from having the final say, the territory is not occupied. This ability to have the final say in turn is based upon the presence of the occupying forces. The local sovereign or authorities have no control over the presence of the occupying forces, whose conduct is regulated by the Occupying Power and IHL, not by the authorities of the occupied state.

What does not exist cannot be replaced. The question therefore arises whether the rules of IHL on military occupation apply when 'the ousted sovereign' lacked control even before the Occupying Power established control. First, as discussed below in relation to the Israeli argument against the applicability of GC IV to the West Bank and Gaza (see MN 36), the local authorities that are replaced need not necessarily be those of the

---

and the Contemporary Law of Occupation', in L. Lijnzaad, J. van Sambeek, and B. Tahzib-Lie (eds), *Making the Voice of Humanity Heard* (Leiden: Nijhoff, 2004), at 298.

[60] *The Hostages Trial*, above n 34, at 55; Bothe in ICRC *Expert Meeting*, above n 1, at 38; R. Kolb and S. Vité, *Le droit de l'occupation militaire: perspectives historiques et enjeux juridiques actuels* (Brussels: Bruylant, 2009), at 139; Dinstein, above n 19, at 39.

[61] See Art 43 Hague Regulations and Ch 69 of this volume. See also Art 6 para 3 GC IV, which implies that an occupation may exist even when the Occupying Power does not exercise the function of government in a territory.

[62] Ferraro, above n 12, at 148–9.   [63] ICRC *Expert Meeting*, above n 1, at 20.

legitimate sovereign. They may be those of a third state, including a previous Occupying Power (except if the sovereign liberates its own territory), or of an armed group. It does not matter whether that group was fighting against the later Occupying Power independently of the occupied country, or alongside the Occupying Power.[64] What counts are the facts: (i) establishment of control, (ii) during an IAC, (iii) by a state over a territory which was not its own before the IAC. Indeed, conquest is no longer a title for acquisition of territory in international law.[65] Under this approach, establishing effective control over (parts of) the territory of a failed state constitutes military occupation.[66]

III. Lack of consent

28   Consent by a state to the presence of foreign troops on its territory and their exercise of control over that territory not only makes the rules of IHL on military occupation inapplicable,[67] but also hinders the applicability of all other rules of IHL of IACs. Even the applicability of IHL of IACs in the case of belligerent occupation without armed resistance, discussed below, presupposes lack of consent by the territorial state. The consent must obviously be given before the foreign military presence begins. Subsequent consent does not hinder the applicability of the rules of IHL on military occupation as soon as the condition of control is fulfilled.[68] Whether subsequent consent ends an occupation is dealt with in Chapter 74 of this volume. According to experts consulted by the International Committee of the Red Cross (ICRC), the consent must be genuine, valid, and explicit.[69] Some add that the consenting state must in addition have effective control over the territory.[70] It is argued that only an authority with *de facto* control over the territory just before the occupation can validly consent.[71] *De jure* authority without *de facto* control is not sufficient. In this author's view, mere consent by authorities with *de facto* control against the will of the *de jure* authority is equally insufficient.

29   To evaluate the validity of consent (for the purposes of determining whether IHL of military occupation applies), it is suggested that recourse should be made to the rules of the law of treaties on the validity of a state's consent to be bound by a treaty, as codified in the Vienna Convention on the Law of Treaties (VCLT). Indeed, if consent is valid for the purposes of the law of treaties, then it would be unimaginable that it would not be valid for the purpose of hindering the application of IHL of military occupation.[72] An alternative could be to refer to consent in the law of state responsibility as a circumstance precluding wrongfulness,[73] although occupation is not unlawful under IHL. However, the discussion of the International Law Commission (ILC) on when consent precludes

---

[64] See, for the case where an armed group which had effective control is ousted by foreign forces, Bothe, above n 19, at 30, fn 19, who considers that even if the territorial state consents, IHL of military occupation applies (provisionally) when the authority of the territorial government is not re-established.

[65] M.N. Shaw, *International Law* (6th edn, Cambridge: CUP, 2008), at 502.

[66] This approach is implicitly shared by those who consider that for the purposes of the IHL of military occupation, the absence of consent must be presumed in the case of a failed state (see below MN 31), and by Australia when it considered the IHL of military occupation to apply to its presence in Somalia (see below MN 54).

[67] ICRC *Expert Meeting*, above n 1, at 21; Benvenisti, in MPEPIL, above n 28, para 1; UK *Manual*, above n 16, para 11.1.2.

[68] See also Art 47 GC IV.

[69] ICRC *Expert Meeting*, above n 1, at 21; Spoerri, above n 14, at 190.

[70] Bothe, above n 19, at 30.   [71] Ferraro, above n 12, at 153–4.

[72] ICRC *Expert Meeting*, above n 1, at 21.   [73] ILC Articles on State Responsibility, Art 20.

wrongfulness insists that the validity of the consent is not a question of state responsibility but depends on the primary rules concerned,[74] or on 'the rules of international law relating to the expression of the will of the State'.[75] The ILC explicitly suggests that 'the principles concerning the validity of consent to treaties provide relevant guidance'.[76] Special Rapporteur Roberto Ago went even further, writing that 'the end-result of that consent is clearly the formation of an agreement'.[77]

To be valid, the consent must not be tainted by a reason of invalidity under the VCLT.[78] For the applicability of the law of occupation, it is particularly important to determine whether consent obtained by a foreign state by coercion hinders the application of IHL of military occupation. The law of treaties accepts that international relations continue to be based on power. Therefore, consent to a treaty and the treaty itself are invalid because of coercion only if the consent to be bound has been obtained through a threat or use of force, contrary to the United Nations (UN) Charter.[79] As for the state organ which must give consent, it must be able to bind the state under international law.[80] Whether it is competent under the constitutional law of the state concerned is irrelevant,[81] except in the case of a violation of a constitutional rule of fundamental importance which would be evident to any state.[82] In the discussion about the legality of military assistance on request, which parallels in many respects the question discussed here (although it concerns *jus ad bellum*), many nevertheless suggest a more restrictive approach, i.e. that only the highest authorities of a state can invite foreign armed forces onto its territory.[83] This would, however, once more imply that a treaty providing for such presence would be valid under the law of treaties, while the consent to the presence would not be valid for *jus ad bellum* or *jus in bello* purposes.

Furthermore, consent must be explicit, not presumed. Therefore, it cannot be given by a failed state lacking effective governmental authorities.[84] Some add that consent must be given by the recognized government of a recognized state.[85] As the determination of an occupation is a question of fact, the present writer would require consent by the *de facto* government of the state and would not consider consent by an ineffective *de jure* government, perhaps in exile, as sufficient.

Among scholars, there is a tendency to diminish the role of consent by the territorial state as barring the applicability of the IHL rules on military occupation.[86] They point out that the same conflict of interest, covered by these rules, exists when the territorial state consents to the military presence on its territory,[87] or that what counts today is the non-allegiance of the population.[88] However, it is not clear whether these remarks are made *de lege lata*. The present author would insist that the IHL rules on military

---

[74] Ibid, Commentary, paras 4 and 8 to Art 20. [75] Ibid, para 5. [76] Ibid, para 6.
[77] Eighth report on State responsibility by R. Ago, UN Doc A/CN.4/318, *YILC* (1979), vol II, part 1, para 57.
[78] ICRC *Expert Meeting*, above n 1, at 21. [79] Art 52 VCLT. [80] Art 7 VCLT.
[81] Art 27 VCLT. [82] Art 46 VCLT.
[83] See discussions of the Institute of International Law on Intervention by Invitation, G. Hafner Rapporteur, 74 *Yearbook of the Institute of International Law* (2011) 179, at 234, 235, 252, and 258–73. In the resolution finally adopted, the issue is not mentioned (ibid, at 360).
[84] ICRC *Expert Meeting*, above n 1, at 23. [85] Benvenisti, above n 8, at 67.
[86] ICRC *Expert Meeting*, above n 1, at 20–1.
[87] A. Roberts, 'What Is a Military Occupation?', 55 *BYBIL* (1984) 261, at 300; Bothe, in ICRC *Expert Meeting*, above n 1, at 37; Zwanenburg, above n 19, at 109 (without drawing the conclusion that IHL of military occupation applies).
[88] Benvenisti, above n 8, at 59–60.

occupation apply even if the local population (perhaps at a first stage) welcomes foreign troops, or if the latter argue that they are acting merely in the interests of the local population and of the adverse state.[89] Any other interpretation would lead to endless controversies over the applicability of IHL, based on subjective judgements and considerations of legitimacy. Conversely, it seems problematic to allow a criterion as difficult to establish as that of the allegiance of the population or a conflict of interest, to turn a foreign military presence to which the government of the territorial state has consented into a belligerent occupation. Does this imply mandatory periodical referendums regarding any foreign military presence? In any case, no precedent is known in which IHL rules on military occupation were applied (or claimed to apply *de jure*) after the host state had given its valid consent (see however MN 35 below).[90]

33   The conclusion of a ceasefire or armistice cannot imply consent precluding the applicability of the IHL rules on military occupation, even if such agreement specifically allows one belligerent to control territory of another which it did not control before the outbreak of hostilities.[91] Otherwise, the archetype of an occupied territory, the Israeli-occupied Palestinian territory, would not be occupied because the Israeli presence in the West Bank and the Gaza Strip is implicitly permitted by the 1967 ceasefire agreement.[92] Similarly, the fact that the 2008 ceasefire between Georgia and Russia brokered by France allowed a provisional Russian military presence on undisputed Georgian territory,[93] did not make the law of military occupation inapplicable to such territory. Some authors justify this result by reference to Articles 6/6/6/7 common to the Geneva Conventions (which state that agreements between belligerents cannot deprive protected persons of rights under the Geneva Conventions) and Article 47 GC IV (which states the same for agreements between an Occupying Power and local authorities).[94] In this author's view, this reasoning is not convincing (although the result is correct). Article 47 does not apply to agreements (e.g. a ceasefire, an armistice, or a peace treaty) between the Occupying and Occupied Powers. As for Article 6/6/6/7, it hinders the parties from modifying the rules of IHL on military occupation, but not from ending an occupation, e.g. by concluding a peace treaty which transfers sovereignty of the occupied territory to the former Occupying Power. A more convincing argument for the aforementioned conclusion is based on a systematic interpretation of the IHL rules on occupation read in conformity with subsequent practice. Under Article 6 GC IV, and even more under Article 3(b) Additional Protocol (AP) I, the rules of IHL on military occupation continue to apply beyond the general

---

[89] Kolb and Vité, above n 60, at 78–9.
[90] ICRC *Expert Meeting*, above n 1, at 21.
[91] Pictet Commentary GC IV, at 22; Roberts, above n 87, at 267; M. Bothe, 'Occupation after Armistice', in R. Bernhardt (ed), *Encyclopedia of Public International Law* (Amsterdam: Elsevier, 1993), vol III, 761, at 763. *Contra* Dinstein, above n 19, at 36. Bothe, above n 19, at 27, considers that IHL of military occupation applies only if the armistice refers to it.
[92] 'United States Department of State: Background on Israel', Bureau of Near Eastern Affairs (22 February 2010), available at <http://www.state.gov/r/pa/ei/bgn/3581.htm>. For an overview of the facts see ICJ, *Legal Consequences of the Construction of a Wall in the Occupied Palestinian Territory*, Advisory Opinion, 9 July 2004, paras 73–5; HRCouncil, Report of United Nations Fact-Finding Mission on the Gaza Conflict, 'Human Rights in Palestine and other Occupied Arab Territories' (25 September 2009) UN Doc A/HRC/12/48, para 177.
[93] Independent International Fact-Finding Mission on the Conflict in Georgia (IIFFMCG), *Report*, 30 September 2009, vol II, at 219; Human Rights Watch, 'Up in Flames: Humanitarian Law Violations and Civilian Victims in the Conflict over South Ossetia', *Report*, 23 January 2009, at 25.
[94] Kolb and Vité, above n 60, at 92.

close of military operations, which is most often based upon a ceasefire or an armistice. If ceasefires or armistices ended an occupation, the aforementioned provisions would largely lack their desired effect.

For similar reasons, surrender, which implicitly allows a belligerent to occupy the territory of the surrendering adversary, cannot count as consent barring the applicability of the rules of IHL on military occupation.[95] While the Hague Regulations were not considered to apply to the post-surrender occupation of Germany and Japan following the Second World War, the Geneva Conventions would now apply,[96] which results from the intention of the drafters.[97]

If a state withdraws its consent to a foreign military presence and the foreign troops nevertheless stay on, this not only constitutes an aggression under *jus ad bellum*,[98] but also turns the presence into an occupation,[99] provided that the foreign forces control the territory where they are present and hinder control of the territorial state under the criteria discussed above.[100] If the territorial state defends itself against this aggression, Article 2 paragraph 1 governs the occupation, otherwise Article 2 paragraph 2 GC IV applies.[101]

IV. Irrelevance of other criteria

At least for a belligerent occupation during, or resulting from, an armed conflict, in which territory which was not previously controlled by it fell under the control of a belligerent, it is equally irrelevant whether the enemy was sovereign over that territory.[102] Israel argues that the West Bank and Gaza, which it occupied in 1967, are not occupied territories because at the time of occupation they were not 'the territory of a High Contracting Party' as required by Common Article 2 for the applicability of the Geneva Conventions.[103] The ICJ rejected this argument (at least for an occupation occurring during an IAC under Common Article 2 paragraph 1), stating that it was sufficient that Jordan and Israel (the ICJ only had to deal with the West Bank) were parties to the Geneva Conventions and engaged in an IAC which led to the occupation of the West Bank.[104] The EECC correctly held that the ICJ's finding (that it is irrelevant whether the occupied territory belongs to another High Contracting Party) applies even where the occupied territory is subsequently found to have belonged to (but was not controlled before the conflict by) the belligerent who occupied it.[105] This author suggests an exception in the case where a state liberates its own territory, which was occupied by its adversary during a previous armed

---

[95] Pictet Commentary GC IV, at 22; Dinstein, above n 19, at 32–3.
[96] Kolb and Vité, above n 60, at 95–9; Roberts, above n 87, at 270–1; von Glahn, above n 37, at 281, 283.
[97] Final Record, vol II-A, at 623–4.
[98] See Definition of Aggression, UNGA Res 3314 (XXXIX), Art 3(e).
[99] Dinstein, above n 19, at 37, 42; Bothe, above n 19, at 32; Koutroulis, above n 12, at 87–8, who rightly mentions that this is one of the few situations in which *jus ad bellum* influences *jus in bello*.
[100] In *DRC v Uganda*, above n 16, after the ICJ found that Congo had withdrawn its consent to the presence of Ugandan troops (para 53), it started to analyse whether the Ugandan presence satisfied its requirements for effective control over the territory (paras 172–80).
[101] See for the latter case Kolb and Vité, above n 60, at 79–81, who mention Namibia as an example.
[102] In this respect the present author disagrees with ICRC Commentary APs, para 112, when it states that occupation of a territory which has not yet been formed as a state is covered by Art 1(4) AP I but not by Art 2 common to the GCs, although this interpretation appears (mistakenly) in the preparatory works of AP I.
[103] M. Shamgar, 'The Observance of International Law in the Administered Territories', 1 *IsrYBHR* (1971) 262–77.
[104] ICJ, *Legal Consequences of the Construction of a Wall*, above n 92, paras 90–101.
[105] EECC, *Central Front—Ethiopia's Claim 2*, Partial Award, 28 April 2004, paras 28 and 29.

conflict and remained occupied until the most recent armed conflict.¹⁰⁶ However, if the sovereignty over the territory is contested, the IHL rules on military occupation apply,¹⁰⁷ as they do in all cases in which a state invades territory it considers to be its own, e.g. when Argentina invaded the Falkland/Malvinas islands in 1982,¹⁰⁸ if such ownership is contested by the adversary.

37   As for every other rule or concept of IHL, any *jus ad bellum* consideration, such as whether the occupation is lawful or unlawful, is irrelevant for the determination of whether a territory is occupied.¹⁰⁹ Even territory coming under the control of a belligerent exercising its right to self-defence, or which is authorized by the UN Security Council to use force, is an occupied territory (the issues of a UN authorized occupation and occupation by UN forces will be discussed below at MN 38, 40, and 54). Additionally, Article 47 GC IV clarifies that no annexation by the Occupying Power, and no agreement concluded with the authorities of the occupied territory subsequent to the occupation (to be distinguished from consent by the Occupied Power, discussed above at MN 28–35), can alter the status of a territory as occupied.

38   While it is clear that UN Security Council authorization for the use of force does not make the rules of IHL on military occupation inapplicable,¹¹⁰ it is more controversial when the UN Security Council has authorized the very presence of the Occupying Power. Thus, it has been argued that in such cases this presence is not an occupation (but in the case of Iraq in 2003–4 the Council explicitly stated that at least the US and the United Kingdom (UK) were Occupying Powers). Some authors argue that the Security Council may end an occupation altogether, not by changing the facts on the ground but by requalifying a belligerent occupation as an international transitional administration.¹¹¹ Under Article 103 of the UN Charter, UN Security Council resolutions prevail over any other international obligation,¹¹² including the obligations that flow from military occupation under IHL. According to the letter of the Article, this is at least the case for treaty obligations.¹¹³ Obviously, one might argue that definitions are not an obligation and therefore cannot be overridden by the Security Council. However, the determination that a territory is occupied leads to certain IHL obligations, and the determination that the territory is not occupied would mean that such obligations no longer exist and thus would override them in substance. Many argue that the UN Security Council cannot derogate from *jus cogens*.¹¹⁴ However, there is no centralized organ that could determine that a resolution derogating from IHL is contrary to a norm of *jus cogens*. In addition, a norm of *jus cogens* is defined by Article 53 VCLT as 'accepted and recognized by the international community of States as a whole as a norm from which no derogation is permitted'. If a resolution was approved by at least nine members of the UN Security Council and not opposed by one

---

¹⁰⁶ Implicitly Benvenisti, above n 8, at 43, requiring that the Occupying Power 'has no title'.
¹⁰⁷ Ibid, at 59.   ¹⁰⁸ Roberts, above n 87, at 280.   ¹⁰⁹ *The Hostages Trial*, above n 34, at 59.
¹¹⁰ Dörmann and Colassis, above n 32, at 302.
¹¹¹ S. Vité, 'L'applicabilité du droit international de l'occupation militaire aux activités des organisations internationales', 86 *IRRC* 853 (2004) 9, at 28. See also M. Ottolenghi, 'The Stars and Stripes in Al-Fardos Square: The Implications for the International Law of Belligerent Occupation', 77 *Fordham Law Review* (2004) 2177.
¹¹² ICJ, *Questions of Interpretation and Application of the 1971 Montreal Convention arising from the Aerial Incident at Lockerbie (Libyan Arab Jamahiriya v US)*, Order, 14 April 1992, para 126.
¹¹³ For an opinion that this does not cover obligations under customary international law, see ibid, Dissenting Opinion of Judge Bedjaoui, para 29.
¹¹⁴ See extensively Koutroulis, above n 12, at 100–13.

permanent member (see Article 27(3) of the UN Charter), it could violate a norm of *jus cogens* as defined by the VCLT only if it was clearly established that before the resolution was adopted, the norm derogated from constituted *jus cogens*. Indeed, the states adopting the resolution apparently considered that derogation from the IHL norm *is* permitted, otherwise they would not have voted in favour of the resolution. This would cast serious doubts on whether the international community of states as a whole indeed considers that no derogation from the IHL norm is permitted. Lastly, the question arises whether the rule setting the definition of occupation belongs to *jus cogens*. Some answer affirmatively, because the definition of occupation is essential for the operation of the protective rules, some of which belong to *jus cogens*.[115]

Nevertheless, in this author's opinion, any derogation from the rules of IHL by the UN Security Council must be explicit, and its resolutions must be interpreted whenever possible in a manner compatible with IHL. The mandate of the Security Council to maintain international peace and security enforces *jus ad bellum*. Just as a state implementing *jus ad bellum* by using force in self-defence must comply with IHL, any measure authorized by the Council must be implemented in a manner that respects IHL.[116]

A distinct issue is whether the rules of IHL on military occupation apply at all to a UN-led territorial administration. Apart from the general controversies whether the UN or other international organizations are bound by IHL (see Chapter 1 of this volume, MN 16–19), some object to the mere possibility that UN peacekeeping forces could be subject to the obligations of an Occupying Power.[117] Significantly, the *UN Secretary-General's Bulletin on Observance by United Nations Forces of International Humanitarian Law*, which refers to many rules UN forces must respect under IHL while engaged as combatants in armed conflicts, does not mention one rule of IHL on belligerent occupation.[118] Opponents to the applicability of IHL in such a case argue that the rights and obligations accruing to Occupying Powers under IHL flow from the conflict inherent in the relationship between traditional Occupying Powers and the population under occupation. Therefore, it follows that the same rights and obligations are not relevant to the altruistic nature of a peacekeeping operation, which is deployed in conformity with the general interest.[119] They argue, as a protective force, peacekeepers are accepted—if not welcomed—by the local population, and thus do not require the strictures of IHL. This rather rosy view of the relationship between peacekeepers and the local population is not always borne out by reality. The level of altruism or good intentions may be difficult to measure, and will change according to one's perspective; it is not a sound basis for determining whether IHL applies to a given conflict. If this was decisive, why should operations carried out by individual states or regional organizations claiming their motives are purely altruistic be subject to IHL? In this writer's opinion, denying the applicability of IHL of military occupation to UN peacekeeping operations based on the alleged altruistic nature of the operation sometimes disregards reality and always mixes a *jus ad*

---

[115] Ibid, at 114.
[116] See T. Meron, 'Prisoners of War, Civilians and Diplomats in the Gulf Crisis', 85 *AJIL* (1991) 104, at 106, and, for the ECHR, ECtHR, *Al-Jedda v United Kingdom*, Judgment (Grand Chamber), 7 July 2011, para 102.
[117] Gasser, above n 19, at 272.   [118] UN Doc ST/SGB/1999/13, 6 August 1999.
[119] D. Shraga, 'The United Nations as an Actor Bound by International Humanitarian Law', in L. Condorelli, A-M. La Rosa, and S. Scherrer (eds), *Les Nations Unies et le droit international humanitaire, Actes du Colloque international à l'occasion du cinquantième anniversaire des Nations Unies, Genève, 19, 20 et 21 octobre 1995* (Paris: Pedone, 1996) 317, at 328; Vité, above n 111, at 19.

bellum argument into whether *jus in bello* applies.[120] Another line of argument holds that IHL of belligerent occupation cannot apply to transitional international civil administrations because, under their Security Council mandate and subsequent practice, such administrations make changes to local legislation and institutions which would not be permitted under the IHL of military occupation.[121] This argument however invites the question whether the territory over which the transitional civil administration is established is an occupied territory for which such changes are not admissible. Arguably, when the UN or a regional organization has effective control or power over a territory without the consent of the sovereign of that territory, it is an occupying force.[122] When the sovereign consents and allows a foreign power to administer its territory, the rules of IHL on military occupation do not apply. However, as long as rules of international law for international administration not qualifying as occupation are lacking and subsidiary to the UN Security Council resolution establishing the international administration, the latter should be guided, by analogy, by the rules of belligerent occupation, with which it shares a commonality.[123]

V. A distinction between invasion and occupation?

41 Many authors, military manuals, the ICJ, and the EECC distinguish between the invasion phase and the occupation phase.[124] The proponents of this distinction argue that the rules of GC IV pertaining to occupied territories apply only during the latter phase.[125] Their argument is based mainly on a certain understanding of Article 42 of the Hague Regulations and the argument that the concept of occupation under GC IV must necessarily be the same as under the Hague Regulations (see MN 8). In addition, as discussed above, occupation must involve some control, while mere presence does not imply control. Lastly, in other international instruments, occupation is explicitly dealt with as a consequence of an invasion, which suggests that the two phases cannot coexist.[126] To avoid

---

[120] Vité, above n 111, at 27, replies that the Security Council does not derogate from IHL but creates a situation to which IHL on its own terms does not apply.

[121] Ibid, at 24.

[122] Benvenisti, above n 8, at 63; M. Hoffman, 'Peace-Enforcement Actions and Humanitarian Law: Emerging Rules for "Interventional Armed Conflict"', 82 *IRRC* 837 (2000) 193, at 203 and 204; B. Levrat, 'Le droit international humanitaire au Timor oriental: entre théorie et pratique', 83 *IRRC* 841 (2001) 77, at 95–6; J. Cerone, 'Minding the Gap: Outlining KFOR Accountability in Post-Conflict Kosovo', 12 *EJIL* (2001) 469, at 483–5; Spoerri, above n 14, at 191. Roberts, above n 87, at 291 (citing D. Bowett, *United Nations Forces: A Legal Study of United Nations Practice* (1964)), writes that most or all customary or conventional laws of war would apply.

[123] M. Sassòli, 'Droit international pénal et droit pénal interne: le cas des territoires se trouvant sous administration internationale', in M. Henzelin and R. Roth (eds), *Le droit pénal à l'épreuve de l'internationalisation* (Paris/Geneva/Brussels: L.G.D.J./Georg/Bruylant, 2002) 119, at 141–9; Vité, above n 111, at 29–33; M. Kelly et al, 'Legal Aspects of Australia's Involvement in the International Force for East Timor', 83 *IRRC* 841 (2001) 101, at 115; Norwegian Institute of International Affairs and Lessons-Learned Unit of the Department of Peacekeeping Operations, *Comprehensive Report on Lessons-Learned From United Nations Operation in Somalia: April 1992–March 1995* (New York: Department of Peacekeeping Operations, 1995), para 57.

[124] US *Manual FM 27-10*, above n 28, para 352; Zwanenburg, above n 19, at 107–8; M. Zwanenburg, 'Challenging the Pictet Theory', 94 *IRRC* 885 (2012) 30; Bothe, *IRRC*, above n 37, at 37–9; Koutroulis, above n 12, at 47–69; G. Schwarzenberger, 'The Law of Belligerent Occupation: Basic Issues', 30 *NJIL* (1960) 10, at 18–21; ICJ, *DRC v Uganda*, above n 16, paras 172, 173, and 219; EECC, *Central Front—Eritrea's Claims*, above n 43, para 57.

[125] Dinstein, above n 19, at 41–2; Gasser, above n 19, at 276–7.

[126] Bothe, *IRRC*, above n 37, at 37–8. See also ICRC Commentary APs, para 1699.

unsatisfactory results, some of the proponents of the distinction nevertheless admit that occupation immediately follows the invasion phase.[127]

On the contrary, Jean S. Pictet, who is followed by many experts, the ICRC, and the ICTY, holds that the concept of occupation under GC IV is different from that of the Hague Regulations:

> There is no intermediate period between what might be termed the invasion phase and the inauguration of a stable regime of occupation. Even a patrol which penetrates into enemy territory without any intention of staying there must respect the Conventions in its dealings with the civilians it meets.[128]

This approach (hereafter referred to as 'the Pictet theory') may be justified by several, partly alternative, arguments. First, a systematic interpretation of GC IV, taking its object and purpose into account, leads to the conclusion that enemy control over a person in an invaded territory is sufficient to make this person protected by the rules of GC IV on occupied territories. Secondly, even if occupation is defined purely territorially, civilians falling into the power of the enemy during an invasion perforce find themselves on a piece of land controlled by that enemy. The main objection to the 'Pictet theory' is that it requires from invading forces what they cannot deliver. Followers of Pictet reply that the very wording of the provisions of GC IV (and arguably that of the Hague Regulations) is flexible enough not to require what is impossible in the invasion phase. Alternatively, the concept of control could be interpreted functionally, requiring a different threshold for different rules. Lastly, some rules of Section III of Part III of GC IV may be seen as conferring on invading forces certain rights, e.g. a legal basis for security measures, internment, or the requisition of labour, a point completely neglected by adherents and critics of the 'Pictet theory'. Arguably, otherwise, invading forces would have simply no legal basis to arrest and detain civilians who threaten their security.

a. *The systematic argument*

Most of the rules of GC IV, i.e. Articles 27–141, forming Part III of the Convention, benefit only 'protected civilians', as defined in Article 4. This provision reads:

> Persons protected by the Convention are those who, at a given moment and in any manner whatsoever, find themselves, in case of a conflict or occupation, in the hands of a Party to the conflict or Occupying Power of which they are not nationals.

To explain why inhabitants of invaded territories are protected civilians by arguing that they are in the hands of an Occupying Power is circular.[129] However, Article 4 equally covers persons who find themselves in the hands of a party 'to the conflict'. When inhabitants of an invaded territory fall under the control of invading forces, e.g. by arrest and detention, they are without a doubt in the hands of a party to the conflict of which they are not nationals, and are therefore protected persons. As such, they must benefit from

---

[127] EECC, *Central Front—Eritrea's Claims*, above n 43, para 57; Bothe, *IRRC*, above n 37, at 39–41.
[128] Pictet Commentary GC IV, at 60, followed by ICRC *Expert Meeting*, above n 1, at 24–6; ICRC, *Report to the 31st International Conference of the Red Cross and Red Crescent, International Humanitarian Law and the challenges of contemporary armed conflicts*, ICRC, Geneva, October 2011, available at <https://www.icrc.org/eng/assets/files/red-cross-crescent-movement/31st-international-conference/31-int-conference-ihl-challenges-report-11-5-1-2-en.pdf>; Kolb and Vité, above n 60, at 65–86; *Naletilić*, above n 12, at 219–22; Sassòli, *IRRC*, above n 48, at 42–50.
[129] Zwanenburg, *IRRC*, above n 124, at 32–3.

some rules of Part III of GC IV dealing with the 'status and treatment of protected persons'. Those rules are separated into rules applicable to aliens who find themselves on non-occupied territory of a state (Section II) and those applicable to occupied territories (Section III). The two categories are mutually exclusive, and must arguably cover all possible situations in which a civilian is in enemy hands. As for Section I, its title, referring to 'Provisions common to the territories of the parties to the conflict and to occupied territories', can be read as encompassing not only the invading state's own territory and any occupied territories, but also any other territory of a party to the conflict.[130] This issue is discussed in depth in Chapter 52 of this volume. According to the present author, under a systemic interpretation, the term 'common' in the title of Section I must be considered to refer to what appears in the following Sections II and III. Furthermore, the *travaux préparatoires* show that Part III was intended to cover (only) two categories of persons: aliens on the territory of a party to the conflict, and the population of occupied territories.[131]

44 Therefore, defenders of the 'Pictet theory' argue, if invaded territory was not considered occupied under the categories of GC IV, 'protected civilians' falling into the hands of the enemy on invaded territory would not be protected by any rule of Part III.[132] However, their argument continues, there is no possible reason why those persons need or deserve less protection than other civilians who are in the power of the enemy, and it is unimaginable that the Convention's drafters would have left such a gap between foreigners found in a party to the conflict's own non-occupied territory and persons found in the territory occupied by a party to the conflict.[133] To take an example mentioned by Pictet,[134] it seems absurd that the deportation of civilians would not be prohibited in the invasion phase by GC IV,[135] but would be absolutely prohibited once the invasion turned into an occupation. Inhabitants of a territory under invasion are enemy nationals encountering a belligerent on their own territory, independently of their will, which is precisely the situation for which the rules of IHL on military occupation were made.

---

[130] Many experts therefore suggest that Section I already applies during an invasion phase (ICRC *Expert Meeting*, above n 1, at 26, and Ch 52, MN 44–48, of this volume).

[131] Committee III, 'Report to the Plenary Assembly', Final Record, vol II-A, at 821: 'Part III constitutes the main portion of our Convention. Two situations presenting fundamental differences had to be dealt with: that of aliens in the territory of a belligerent State and that of the population—national or alien—resident in a country occupied by the enemy.' The ICRC's 'preliminary remarks' to the text of the GCs are even more explicit: '[Convention IV] distinguishes between foreign nationals on the territory of a party to the conflict, and the population of occupied territories. It is divided into five Sections. Section I contains provisions common to the above two categories of persons [...]' (*The Geneva Conventions of 12 August 1949* (Geneva: ICRC, 2010), at 32).

[132] Benvenisti, in MPEPIL, above n 28, para 6; Koutroulis, above n 12, at 63.

[133] Admittedly, as those who defend the distinction between invaded and occupied territory mention (see e.g. Zwanenburg, *IRRC*, above n 124, at 33–4), other distinctions found in IHL, e.g. between IACs and NIACs, or between protected and other civilians, equally lead to gaps in protection. However, those other distinctions may be explained from the perspective of states keen to protect their sovereignty and reluctant to accept international rules governing how they behave on their territory and/or towards their own nationals. Once they have accepted international rules protecting enemy nationals on their own and on occupied territory, a legal black hole between those two categories cannot be explained, even from the perspective of states keen to protect their sovereignty.

[134] Pictet Commentary GC IV, at 60.

[135] Art 49 para 1 GC IV applies only in occupied territories.

b. Is it sufficient to exercise control over a person or over the piece of land on which that person is found?

To avoid such a gap in protection, Pictet argues that to trigger the applicability of the provisions of GC IV on occupied territories and apply them to a particular person, control over that person (in a territory which is not the invader's own) must be sufficient.[136] Many object and claim that according to the ordinary meaning of the terms (and Article 42 of the Hague Regulations), occupation must include control over territory.[137] Indeed, a person may be arrested or detained but not 'occupied'. To consider this objection, one might suggest a functional approach to the amount of territory that can be occupied (see MN 21). The main objection against this interpretation is that many rules of GC IV, in particular those setting out positive obligations of an Occupying Power, cannot possibly be respected by invading forces, and unrealistic interpretations of IHL rules must be avoided.[138]

45

c. A flexible understanding of the obligations of an Occupying Power?

Followers of the 'Pictet theory' counter the criticism that it leads to unrealistic demands by replying that the rules of IHL of military occupation are not strict obligations of result.[139] To take one example, under Article 50 GC IV, a provision often mentioned by adherents of the distinction between invasion and occupation,[140] an Occupying Power has the obligation to facilitate, with the cooperation of the national and local authorities, the proper functioning of children's educational institutions. First and foremost this obligation prohibits interfering with the activities of those institutions.[141] Forces invading a village are perfectly capable of refraining from requisitioning the only school located in that village. Admittedly, supporting such institutions might require a certain degree of control and authority; yet support will depend upon the circumstances and the capabilities of the invading troops. According to the clear wording of Article 50 ('facilitate'), supporting these institutions is an obligation of means.

46

d. A functional understanding of the concept of occupation itself?

The concept of occupation itself can also be understood functionally. In this sense, a territory is considered occupied for the purpose of the applicability of certain rules of IHL of military occupation, but not for others (see for a critical analysis and some consequences Chapter 52, MN 63–72, of this volume). In particular, this approach may be defended on the arguably distinct issue of the end of an occupation, where the Occupying Power still retains some aspects of control after withdrawing, such as Israel after it withdrew from the Gaza Strip.[142]

47

The concept that only some rules of IHL apply during the invasion phase is not new. Many authors and the EECC, who distinguish occupation and invasion, nevertheless

48

---

[136] Pictet Commentary GC IV, at 60–1; ICTY, *Naletilić*, above n 12, para 221. For the distinct issue when a person is under the jurisdiction of a state, human rights bodies have considered that control over the person abroad is sufficient: see HRCttee, General Comment 31, 26 May 2004, para 10; ECtHR, *Al-Skeini and others v United Kingdom*, Judgment, 7 July 2011, paras 136–7; HRCttee, *Lopez Burgos v Uruguay* (Comm No 52/1979), 29 July 1981, UN Doc CCPR/C/13/D/52/1979.
[137] Zwanenburg, *IRRC*, above n 124, at 32 and 34; Bothe, *IRRC*, above n 37, at 39.
[138] Zwanenburg, *IRRC*, above n 124, at 35; Bothe, *IRRC*, above n 37, at 39 and 41.
[139] See, for a full discussion, M. Siegrist, *The Functional Beginning of Belligerent Occupation*, The Graduate Institute, Geneva, eCahiers, No 7, April 2011, at 35–77, available at <http://iheid.revues.org/75?lang=en>.
[140] Zwanenburg, *IRRC*, above n 124, at 35.   [141] Pictet Commentary GC IV, at 286.
[142] See Ch 74, MN 40, and ICRC *Expert Meeting*, above n 1, at 31–3.

admit that some rules of GC IV already apply during invasion.¹⁴³ Pictet himself distinguishes the Hague Regulations from GC IV, arguing that for the latter, 'the word "occupation" […] has a wider meaning than it has in Article 42 of the Hague Regulations',¹⁴⁴ which implies that his theory does not apply to the Hague Regulations. However, one might argue that an invader must already respect the prohibition in Article 44 of the Hague Regulations, which states that a belligerent is forbidden 'to force the inhabitants of territory occupied by it to furnish information about the army of the other belligerent'.¹⁴⁵

49 Others, including the ICTY,¹⁴⁶ want to distinguish between the rules protecting persons¹⁴⁷ and those protecting property, with only the former applying during the invasion phase. Pictet writes: 'So far as individuals are concerned, the application of the Fourth Geneva Convention does not depend upon the existence of a state of occupation within the meaning of the Article 42 [Hague Regulations].'¹⁴⁸ One might consider however, that property is protected because of the individuals who own it. In addition, why should, say, Article 57 GC IV, limiting the possibility to requisition hospitals, not yet apply during the invasion phase? This author suggests analysing which rules apply during the invasion phase not according to pre-established broad categories, but for every rule in every case, according to the degree of control the invader exercises in that given case. This also avoids the difficulty of determining when the invasion phase turns into the occupation phase.¹⁴⁹ For the beginning of occupation, such an understanding would parallel the functional concept of end of occupation, which is inherently adopted by all scholars,¹⁵⁰ UN Documents,¹⁵¹ and states that still consider Gaza to be occupied by Israel, but do not require Israel to re-enter the Gaza Strip to maintain law and order, or to ensure that detainees in Gaza are treated humanely by local authorities.¹⁵² Pictet's remarks point in the same direction, whereby 'Articles 52, 55, 56 and even some of the provisions of Articles 59 to 62 […] presuppose presence of the occupation authorities for a fairly long period'.¹⁵³ Under such a functional understanding of occupation, an invaded territory could at a certain point already be occupied for the purpose of the applicability of Article 49 (prohibiting deportations), but not yet occupied for the application of Article 55 (on food and medical supplies). On such a sliding scale of obligations, which apply according to the degree of control, obligations to abstain would be applicable as soon as the conduct they prohibit is materially possible (respectively, the person benefitting from the prohibition is in the hands of the invading forces), while obligations to provide and to guarantee would apply only at a later stage. This sliding scale would also be more adapted to the fluid realities of modern warfare and the absence of frontlines than the traditional 'all or nothing' approach.

---

¹⁴³ EECC, *Western Front—Aerial Bombardment and Related Claims, Eritrea's Claims 1, 3, 5, 9–13, 21, 25 and 26*, Partial Award, 19 December 2005, para 27; Dinstein, above n 19, at 40–2; Benvenisti, above n 8, at 51–3; Koutroulis, above n 12, at 69–71; Dörmann and Colassis, above n 32, at 301.

¹⁴⁴ Pictet Commentary GC IV, at 60. Critical Ferraro, above n 12, at 136–9.

¹⁴⁵ Siegrist, above n 139, at 66–7.

¹⁴⁶ ICTY, *Naletilić*, above n 12, paras 221 and 587. In *The Prosecutor v Ivica Rajić*, Review of the Indictment pursuant to Rule 61, 13 September 1996, paras 38–42, the ICTY applies, however, Art 53 of GC IV during the invasion phase.

¹⁴⁷ Benvenisti, above n 8, at 52.   ¹⁴⁸ Pictet Commentary GC IV, at 60.

¹⁴⁹ Bothe, *IRRC*, above n 37, at 39–40.

¹⁵⁰ See, e.g., Solomon, above n 21, 59; Darcy and Reynolds, above n 21, 211; and Mari, above n 21, 356.

¹⁵¹ See UN Doc A/HRC/12/48, 25 September 2009, paras 273–9, and UN Doc A/HRC/15/21, 22 September 2010, paras 63–6.

¹⁵² As it should under Art 43 Hague Regulations and Arts 27 and 76 GC IV, respectively.

¹⁵³ Pictet Commentary GC IV, at 60.

The main objections to the differentiated applicability of the rules of IHL on military 50 occupation are, first, that nothing in the text of GC IV suggests such an approach and, secondly, that the rules of IHL must be clear and foreseeable for those applying them in the field.[154] To counter the first point, applying the text (which does not clarify whether or not it applies during an invasion) without such a differentiation leads to absurd results, which are contrary to the object and purpose of GC IV, both when no rule of GC IV is applicable and when all rules of GC IV are considered to apply during the invasion phase. According to the weight one gives to the second point and the important consideration of practicability, it may be preferable not to apply a sliding scale according to the facts of each and every situation, but to determine *ex ante* which rules apply and which do not apply during an invasion. This approach was suggested by Pictet, referred to above. Others have suggested making a distinction between:

— those rules where a significant gap in protection would exist if they were not applicable during the invasion phase (Articles 49, 51 paragraphs 2–4, 52, 53, 57, and 63 GC IV);
— obligations to provide or respect which are triggered by activities of the Occupying Power and which therefore, in any event, apply during the invasion phase only if the Occupying Power is able and willing to undertake such activities (Articles 64–75, 54, 64 paragraph 1, 66, and 78 GC IV), e.g. to try or intern protected civilians; and
— the obligations to provide or respect due to the mere fact of occupation (Article 43 of the Hague Regulations and Articles 48, 50, 51 paragraph 1, 55, 56, 58, 59–61, and 62 GC IV), which would not yet apply during an invasion.[155]

After a detailed analysis, another commentator has suggested that Articles 47, 48, 49, 51 paragraph 1, 53, 58, 59, 61 (1st sentence), 63, 64–75, 76, and 78 GC IV apply during the invasion phase, while Articles 50, 51 paragraphs 2–4, 52, 54–7, 60, 61 (starting with the 2nd sentence), 62, and 77 GC IV do not yet apply during an invasion.[156]

Both a flexible interpretation of the obligations and a functional understanding of 51 occupation would generally solve all the examples mentioned by those who conclude that the 'Pictet theory' leads to unrealistic results.[157]

VI. The special case of occupation without armed resistance

Paragraph 2 of Article 2 common to the Geneva Conventions covers a situation not cov- 52 ered by paragraph 1: 'Despite its wording ["even" if the occupation meets with no armed resistance], paragraph 2 only addresses itself to cases of occupation with no a declaration of war and without hostilities.'[158] In particular, paragraph 2 was introduced following the experience of the German occupation of Bohemia and Moravia in March 1939 and of Denmark in April 1940, which was not resisted by the Czechoslovak and Danish armed forces because such resistance was considered useless.[159] However, it equally covers, first, the occupation of a country with no means to resist (for example, no armed forces), secondly, the continued presence of foreign armed forces once the consent of the sovereign is

---

[154] Zwanenburg, *IRRC*, above n 124, at 35.   [155] See Siegrist, above n 139, at 47–77.
[156] Grignon, above n 17, at 133–43.
[157] Zwanenburg, *IRRC*, above n 124, at 34–5; Bothe, *IRRC*, above n 37, at 39 and 41.
[158] ICRC Commentary APs, para 65; Pictet Commentary GC IV, at 21–2; ICJ, *Legal Consequences of the Construction of a Wall*, above n 92, para 95.
[159] Dinstein, above n 19, at 31–2; Kolb and Vité, above n 60, at 76.

withdrawn, thirdly, cases where such presence otherwise becomes unlawful and, fourthly, an occupation resisted by armed non-state actors not controlled by the state.[160] An example of the third case was the continued presence of South Africa in Namibia after the South African mandate terminated.[161] As for the fourth case, one might also consider that Article 2 paragraph 1 common to the Geneva Conventions applies each time a state uses force on the territory of another state, without the consent of that state.

53   The foreign presence must be belligerent, present on the ground, and satisfy all other conditions mentioned above (MN 12–35). The territory must be 'coercively' seized, which some consider as a 'state of war in the material sense',[162] while others call it 'pacific' coercive occupation but agree that IHL applies.[163] The requirement that the adverse party loses effective control must, as suggested above, be understood as referring to the final control over the presence of military forces (see MN 26). In this sense the mere presence of foreign forces without consent is sufficient.[164] Indeed, when there is no armed resistance, the invader has even less reason and justification to interfere with or to replace the existing administration of civil life. Arguably, contrary to paragraph 1, the wording of paragraph 2 requires that the territory occupied is that of another High Contracting Party. This would, however, introduce an important *jus ad bellum* and legitimacy issue into the determination of whether IHL is applicable. If all other conditions for the applicability of IHL of military occupation discussed above are fulfilled, in this writer's view, it must be sufficient if a state invades a territory which is not its own, even if it denies that the territory is that of another state. The reference in paragraph 2 to the 'territory of a High Contracting Party' may simply be understood as clarifying in 1949 that the Geneva Conventions apply only between parties, and that the state controlling the territory before the invasion must be a party to the Geneva Conventions.

54   Article 2 paragraph 2 should make IHL applicable to UN-authorized operations which do not meet armed resistance and which establish control over a territory without the consent of the territorial state. Australia, for example, considered that IHL of military occupation applied *de jure* to its UN operation in Somalia, which met with no armed resistance from the territorial sovereign.[165] More doubtful is whether the law of military occupation applies to UN-run peacekeeping forces deployed based upon Chapter VII of the UN Charter, meeting no armed resistance and effectively running a territory, when the territorial state does not consent. Paragraph 2 of Article 2 common to the Geneva Conventions suggests an affirmative answer. However, most would object that paragraph 2 is an exception clause applying IHL beyond armed conflicts, which must be limited to situations where the foreign military presence is that of another state. In any case, the IHL of military occupation would apply only if the international territorial administration is run or *de facto* controlled by military forces. Paragraph 2 does not cover every international presence not meeting the consent of the sovereign, but only belligerent, i.e. military, presences meeting no armed resistance, the difference being that a military occupier could overcome armed resistance if it existed, while a civilian presence could not have done so.

---

[160] Kolb and Vité, above n 60, at 76.
[161] Ibid, at 79–80. In UN Doc A/RES 2871 (XXVI), 20 December 1971, para 8, the UNGA explicitly calls upon South Africa to respect GC IV.
[162] Dinstein, above n 19, at 31–2.
[163] M. Bothe, 'Occupation, Pacific', in Bernhardt (ed), above n 91, at 766–7; Roberts, above n 87, at 274–6.
[164] Koutroulis, above n 12, at 27; Kolb and Vité, above n 60, at 76.
[165] M. Kelly, *Restoring and Maintaining Order in Complex Peace Operations* (Leiden: Nijhoff, 1999), at 178.

VII. Occupation in national liberation wars

Under Article 1(4) AP I, national liberation wars are subject to IHL of IACs, and both parties are then equally bound by the rules of IHL on military occupation. However, what territory can be considered as occupied in national liberation wars? In the first place, it is highly unrealistic to expect a state labelled as a racist regime, or as one engaged in colonial domination or alien occupation, to accept such classification in relation to itself, and such a state is consequently unlikely to accept that it has to comply with IHL of IACs in its entirety. Even less realistic would be to expect the national liberation movement to comply with the rules of belligerent occupation on any territory it seeks to liberate and therefore call its own territory. In theory, a racist regime would likely be considered as occupying the entire territory of the state it governs. In case of colonial domination, the entire territory of the colony would be occupied. As for alien occupation, this concept in Article 1(4) AP I is not the same as that of belligerent occupation in IHL[166] (since in the case of belligerent occupation, the rules of IHL of IACs on occupied territories would already be applicable, thus depriving the notion of alien occupation in Article 1(4) AP I of any scope and purport). Alien occupation therefore does not necessarily entail the applicability of the law of belligerent occupation.[167] However, it is to be expected that a territory controlled by an alien occupier and in which it deprives a distinct people of their right to self-determination, would be considered an occupied territory under IHL (at least if the alien occupier is present with its military forces).[168]

55

Conversely, a national liberation movement would have to comply with the rules of IHL on military occupation only in a territory other than that for which the people it represents has a right to self-determination, e.g. the territory of a state other than that against which the national liberation war is directed,[169] the metropolitan territory of a colonial dominator, or a territory within the state affected by the national liberation war on which another people has a right to self-determination, if it acquires control over that territory. Lastly, the case of belligerent occupation without armed resistance probably does not apply to national liberation wars, as Article 1(4) AP I explicitly covers only 'armed conflicts'.

56

C. Relevance in Non-International Armed Conflicts

Through the alleged existence of rules of customary international law common to non-international armed conflicts (NIACs) and IACs, the contemporary tendency is to bring the law of NIACs closer to the law of IACs; together with combatant and POW status, the legal regulation of military occupation constitutes one of the few sets of rules to escape such a tendency to merge the bodies of rules of IHL. Occupation presupposes an IAC.[170] Indeed, as occupation involves control over territory without the consent of the authority that had control prior to the armed conflict, any application by analogy of the rules of IHL of military occupation to a NIAC can only refer to territory controlled by the insurgents, but never to the territory under

57

---

[166] ICRC Commentary APs, para 112.   [167] *Contra* Bothe/Partsch/Solf, at 266–7.
[168] Although this is not entirely clear from what they write, this opinion is probably shared by Kolb and Vité, above n 60, at 86–7.
[169] Roberts, above n 87, at 292–3.
[170] Dinstein, above n 19, at 33–4; Gasser, above n 19, at 272; Kolb and Vité, above n 60, at 73.

governmental control.¹⁷¹ However, IHL must treat both parties to an armed conflict equally. It would be impossible to convince insurgents to treat territory they liberated as occupied. There are nevertheless suggestions to apply by analogy the rules of IHL on military occupation to the legislative powers and detention authority of an armed group.¹⁷² Some also suggest that if, in the course of a NIAC, a secessionist authority gains control of parts of metropolitan territory over which it has no claim of secession, it should apply IHL of military occupation. However, no legal basis is provided for such an obligation, and those suggesting it must admit that the metropolitan government taking control of secessionist territory cannot be required to apply IHL of military occupation.¹⁷³

D. Legal Consequences of a Violation

58 Clearly, the notion of occupation cannot be violated; only the rules that become applicable in the course of an occupation can be violated. For such violations to be committed, it is immaterial whether the state or the individual erroneously considers that that rules did not apply, as long as the facts making them applicable are known. Nevertheless, in this first chapter on occupation, it is necessary to discuss the conduct criminalized in occupied territories, to analyse the relationship between the concept of occupation in IHL and that of jurisdiction in IHRL, and to mention specific efforts to enforce GC IV on military occupation.

I. The consequences of occupation in international criminal law

59 Only one war crime expressly requires that the proscribed conduct takes place in an occupied territory: the deportation or transfer of protected persons within or out of an occupied territory in violation of Article 49 GC IV constitutes a grave breach under Article 147 GC IV. This is also a war crime under Article 8(2)(a)(vii) of the ICC Statute, which equally covers transfers of protected civilians out of a party's own territory in violation of Article 45 GC IV. The (even voluntary) transfer of a party's own population (which by definition does not consist of protected persons and is therefore not covered by Article 147 GC IV) is criminalized by Article 85(4)(a) AP I as a grave breach and under Article 8(2)(b)(viii) of the ICC Statute as a war crime if it is conducted by an Occupying Power and directed into an occupied territory. Pictet's Commentary considers that the extensive appropriation of property, covered by Article 147 GC IV, can only be committed in an occupied territory.¹⁷⁴ While this may be the most frequent situation, it is submitted that pillage of property of protected persons, prohibited by Article 33 paragraph 2 GC IV, equally applicable on a party's own territory, may also constitute a grave breach.

---

¹⁷¹ Spoerri, above n 14, at 185.
¹⁷² D. Casalin, 'Taking Prisoners: Reviewing the International Humanitarian Law Grounds for Deprivation of Liberty by Armed Opposition Groups', 93 *IRRC* 883 (2011) 743, at 756, and generally Ch 70, MN 71–76, of this volume.
¹⁷³ Benvenisti, above n 8, at 61; M. Bothe, 'Occupation, Belligerent', in Bernhardt (ed), above n 91, at 765.
¹⁷⁴ Pictet Commentary GC IV, at 601.

II. Occupation and jurisdiction under international human rights law

Only persons who find themselves under the jurisdiction of a state party benefit from the protection of IHRL treaties.[175] While the concept of jurisdiction is interpreted differently under various IHRL treaties, human rights courts and treaty bodies consider that an occupied territory is under the jurisdiction of the Occupying Power.[176] This is also the stand taken by the ICJ for, inter alia, the International Covenant on Civil and Political Rights and the International Covenant on Economic Social and Cultural Rights.[177] As soon as a territory is classified as occupied, a person on such territory may enforce through the available mechanisms and procedures of IHRL the rights protected by GC IV, if these rights find an equivalent in IHRL. This offers such persons an individual complaints mechanism not available under IHL.

60

III. Particular efforts to ensure respect by Israel for the rules on military occupation in Geneva Convention IV

Only as regards respect for GC IV, and in particular with regard to its rules applicable to occupied territories, and only with regard to Israel, has the UN called upon states parties to GC IV to meet and discuss their obligations under Article 1, to ensure respect for GC IV.[178] Switzerland, the depositary of GC IV, has convened such meetings when it has received sufficient support from states,[179] which was not the case for the last call by the UN General Assembly. Two Expert Meetings held in 1998,[180] and a Conference of the High Contracting Parties to GC IV held in 1999 and reconvened in 2001,[181] reiterated the applicability of GC IV to the Occupied Palestinian Territories and concern about lack of respect for that treaty by Israel. During these meetings, violations of GC IV were

61

---

[175] See Art 1 ECHR/ACHR. Formally, the ACHPR and the ICESCR do not foresee such a limitation. Under the wording of Art 1 ICCPR, a state must guarantee the rights it protects to 'all individuals within its territory and subject to its jurisdiction'. See generally M. Milanovic, *Extraterritorial Application of Human Rights Treaties* (Oxford: OUP, 2011).

[176] See, for the ECtHR, *Loizidou v Turkey*, above n 57, para 56; ECtHR, *Cyprus v Turkey*, above n 57, para 77; ECtHR, *Al-Jedda v United Kingdom*, above n 116, para 77; ECtHR, *Al-Skeini*, above n 136, para 142; and ECtHR, *Hassan v United Kingdom*, Judgment (Grand Chamber), 16 September 2014, paras 74–80. For the ICCPR, see HRCttee, Concluding Observations of the Human Rights Committee: Israel, 21 August 2003, UN Doc CCPR/CO/78/ISR, para 11; HRCttee, Concluding Observations of the Human Rights Committee: Israel, 18 August 1998, UN Doc CCPR/C/79/Add.93, para 10. For the ICESCR, see Concluding Observations of the Committee on Economic, Social and Cultural Rights: Israel, 23 May 2003, UN Doc E/C.12/1/Add.90, paras 15 and 31. For the Inter-American system, see IACommHR, *Coard et al v United States*, Case Report No 109/99, 1999, para 37; and for the African system, see ACommHPR, *Democratic Republic of Congo v Burundi, Rwanda and Uganda*, Com 227/1999, 25 May 2006.

[177] ICJ, *Legal Consequences of the Construction of a Wall*, above n 92, paras 107–12; ICJ, *DRC v Uganda*, above n 16, paras 216–17. See generally as here Milanovic, above n 175, at 144–7.

[178] See UN Docs S/RES/681 of 20 December 1990; A/RES/ES-10/2 of 5 May 1997; A/RES/ES-10/3 of 15 July 1997; A/RES/ES-10/4 of 19 November 1997; A/RES/ES-10/6 of 24 February 1999; A/RES/ES-10/10 of 7 May 2002; A/RES/ES-10/15 of 2 August 2004; A/RES 64/10 of 1 December 2009, para 5; A/RES 64/92 of 19 January 2010.

[179] P.-Y. Fux and M. Zambelli, 'Mise en oeuvre de la Quatrième Convention de Genève dans les territoires palestiniens occupés: historique d'un processus multilatéral (1997–2001)', 84 *IRRC* 847 (2002) 661.

[180] See Switzerland, Federal Department of Foreign Affairs, *Experts' Meeting on the Application of the Fourth Geneva Convention*, Press release, Geneva, 11 June 1998, and *Chairman's Report, Experts' Meeting on the Fourth Geneva Convention*, Geneva, 27–9 October 1998, both available at <http://www.eda.admin.ch>.

[181] *Declaration Adopted at the Conference of High Contracting Parties to the Fourth Geneva Convention*, 5 December 2001, 84 *IRRC* 847 (2002) 679.

identified in general terms, in particular in occupied territories, and suggestions were put forward on how future violations might be prevented and what measures third states might take to implement their obligation to ensure respect for GC IV. In addition, UN organs dealing with human rights have dispatched several fact-finding missions to the Occupied Palestinian Territories, which dealt extensively with GC IV.[182]

E. Critical Assessment

62 The best protection possible under IHL is provided by the rules on military occupation. However, most contemporary armed conflicts are not covered by those rules because they are NIACs. Even in IACs, the emphasis of the law on military occupation on territory, over which a belligerent gains control displacing 'the local sovereign', is very old-fashioned and not adapted to many modern armed conflicts without frontlines. In these contemporary conflicts, which are not about territory, and in which belligerents do not try to overcome the enemy by gaining control over its territory, air power, which is by definition not territorial, has an increasing role, and states often rely upon local insurgents in the enemy country, who reasonably cannot be expected to comply with the obligations of an occupier in their own country. The situations of military occupation that actually exist today are so few, disparate, and marked by historical and political specificities, that it is difficult to draw general conclusions from state practice, in particular on the concept and start of occupation.

63 If the protective effect of GC IV is insufficient in today's situations of occupation, this is mainly due to general reasons concerning lack of respect by states for IHL and not to reasons specific to the rules of GC IV on military occupation. In addition, most Occupying Powers try to escape the opprobrium inherent in any classification of a territory as occupied, and seek to avoid the ensuing far-reaching obligations by denying that their presence constitutes an occupation as defined in IHL. Such an avoidance strategy is facilitated by the absence of a definition of the concept of occupation in GC IV, on which the applicability of most of its provisions depends. The definition provided by the Hague Regulations is only slightly clearer. Neither clarifies how much control over how much territory is necessary for a foreign state to be an Occupying Power. As demonstrated in this contribution, IHL nevertheless excludes factors other than the facts—effective control on the ground—from the definition and therefore in the assessment of whether the IHL of military occupation applies.

64 Most bona fide controversies about the definition of occupation, which are general and abstract, i.e. not only due to whether a classifier wants to subject a certain situation to GC IV, turn on the dichotomy between clear-cut categories and a sliding scale. As shown throughout this contribution, this author favours a sliding scale, leading to a flexible interpretation of the amount of control and territory necessary to make the law of military occupation applicable—but therefore also a sliding scale of obligations, which increase according to the extent of control and of territory controlled. Such a sliding scale has many advantages. Specifically, it keeps GC IV realistic, adapting it to the infinite variety of real-life situations, makes the law applicable according to needs, and reduces the importance of theoretically thorny controversial binary categories such as existence versus

---

[182] See lastly UN Doc A/HRC/RES/S-21/1 of 24 July 2014, para 13.

absence of control, or invasion versus occupation. *De lege lata* such a sliding scale may be based upon the interpretation of treaty terms and what states actually do on the ground, while their statements admittedly do not always point in this direction. On the other hand, this commentator must admit that clear-cut categories have advantages. Human beings reflecting on reality and regulating it have always known clear-cut categories with fundamentally different real (and legal) consequences, arguably to avoid abuse. A child is born or not, and a human being is dead or alive. The advantage of clear-cut categories in a system depending on self-application, without centralized adjudication and enforcement, as is the case for GC IV, is to reduce possible controversies, abuse, and self-serving, subjective evaluation. Soldiers who must apply the law in the field can be trained to apply the entire regime of the IHL of military occupation in certain situations, while they—or their lawyers—would perforce position their situation on a sliding scale at the point most favourable to them, e.g. consider that they have little control and therefore few obligations. This author chooses to face such risks instead of accepting gaps in protection. The risk of subjective, self-serving interpretations cannot be avoided, even when adopting the clearest-cut category of occupation.

MARCO SASSÒLI[*]

---

[*] I thank Ms Nishat Nishat, LLM, for her thorough preparatory research when she was a doctoral student and research assistant at the University of Geneva, Ms Julia Grignon, professor at the University Laval, Canada, for the many ideas she gave me in her doctoral thesis on the temporal scope of application of IHL, which I supervised, and Ms Annie Hylton, LLM, and Ms Yvette Issar, LLM, research assistants at the Geneva Academy of International Humanitarian Law and Human Rights and the University of Geneva, respectively, for further research and the revision of this chapter. I am equally grateful to my co-editors for their useful and challenging comments and suggestions.

Chapter 68. Law-Making and the Judicial Guarantees in Occupied Territories

	MN
A. Introduction	1
B. Meaning and Application	5
I. The scope of the Occupying Power's legislative power under Article 64 GC IV	5
a. Overview	5
b. The necessity test based on security grounds	10
c. The necessity of maintaining public order and civil life	12
d. The necessity of fulfilling obligations under the Geneva Conventions	13
e. The necessity of fulfilling obligations under international human rights law	15
f. The exceptions based on Security Council Resolutions	16
II. Administrative structures in occupied territories	18
a. Overview	18
b. Modifications of administrative personnel	21
c. The prohibition of coercive or discriminatory measures against public officials or judges in occupied territory	23
III. The local judicial system and judges in occupied territory	24
a. The local judiciary	24
b. The protection of local judges	27
c. Jurisdiction of local tribunals	30
IV. Occupation courts	33
a. Overview	33
b. Composition and requirements of occupation courts	36
c. Relationship with local courts in occupied territories	40
d. Offences against the penal/security laws of Occupying Powers and the prohibition of double jeopardy	41
e. The jurisdiction of occupation courts over war crimes	42
f. Appeals	44
g. Petitions	46
V. The protection of refugees in occupied territories	47
VI. Judicial guarantees	52
a. Immunity from arrest, prosecution, and conviction for acts committed, or for opinions expressed, before the occupation	52
b. General remarks on fair trial guarantees in occupied territory	54
c. General principles of criminal law	59
d. The right to trial by an independent, impartial, and regularly constituted court	62
e. Fair trial guarantees under Article 71 GC IV	63
f. The rights relating to means of defence	68
g. The right of convicted persons to be informed of available remedies and of their time limits	75
h. The right to public proceedings and notification of the Protecting Power	77
i. The right to have time spent in custody and on trial deducted from the period of imprisonment	80
VII. Sanctions, penalties, humane treatment, and handover	81
a. Sanctions for minor offences	81
b. Death penalty	83
c. Humane treatment of the accused and the convicted	92
d. The duty to hand over accused or convicted persons	94

C. Relevance in Non-International Armed Conflicts	95
D. Legal Consequences of a Violation	98
I. Overview	98
II. Elements of the war crime of denying fair trial guarantees	100
E. Critical Assessment	103

Select Bibliography

Benvenisti, E., *The International Law of Occupation* (2nd edn, Oxford: OUP, 2012)

Dinstein, Y., *The International Law of Belligerent Occupation* (Cambridge: CUP, 2009)

von Glahn, G., *The Occupation of Enemy Territory: A Commentary on the Law and Practice of Belligerent Occupation* (Minneapolis, Minn: University of Minnesota Press, 1957)

Playfair, E. (ed), *International Law and the Administration of Occupied Territories: Two Decades of Israeli Occupation of the West Bank and Gaza Strip* (Oxford: Clarendon Press, 1992)

Roberts, A., 'Prolonged Military Occupation: The Israeli-Occupied Territories since 1967', 84 *AJIL* (1990) 44

Ronen, Y., 'Blind in their Own Cause: The Military Courts in the West Bank', 2 *Cambridge Journal of International and Comparative Law* (2013) 738

Sassòli, M., 'Legislation and Maintenance of Public Order and Civil Life by Occupying Powers', 16 *EJIL* (2005) 661

Schwenk, E. H., 'Legislative Power of the Military Occupant under Article 43, Hague Regulations', 54 *YLJ* (1945) 393

Shamgar, M. (ed), *Military Government in the Territories Administered by Israel 1967–1980* (Jerusalem: Alpha Press, 1982)

Shehadeh, R., *Occupier's Law: Israel and the West Bank* (rev edn, Washington, DC: Institute for Palestinian Studies, 1988)

Sivakumaran, S., 'Courts of Armed Opposition Groups: Fair Trials or Summary Justice?', 7 *JICJ* (2009) 489

Weill, S., 'The Judicial Arm of the Occupation: The Israeli Military Courts in the Occupied Territories', 89 *IRRC* 866 (2007) 395

A. Introduction

1 When compared with Article 43 of the Hague Regulations, Article 64 of Geneva Convention (GC) IV gives the Occupying Power a broader ambit of legislative authority in occupied territories.[1] Like its progenitor, Article 64 paragraph 1 GC IV sets out the general principle of preserving the local laws in force in occupied territories. As will be explained below, however, by comparison to Article 43 of the Hague Regulations, Article 64 GC IV expands the scope of exceptions to the general duty to preserve local laws. In exceptional circumstances, the Occupying Power is not only allowed to change the laws in force, but is even bound to enact laws pursuant to the objective of giving effect to the obligations under GC IV. As our analysis below will show, such prescriptive power is recognized especially for the benefit of the local civilian population.

2 Under Article 64 GC IV, such wide parameters of the Occupying Power's law-making capacity can be evidenced by the wording 'may, however, subject the population of the

---

[1] See Pictet Commentary GC IV, at 337. *Contra* G. Schwarzenberger, *International Law as Applied by International Courts and Tribunals*, II: *The Law of Armed Conflict* (London: Stevens & Sons, 1968), at 194.

occupied territory to provisions which are essential to enable the Occupying Power to fulfil its obligations under the present Convention'. This marks a contrast to the approach of subjecting the Occupying Power's prescriptive power to a stringent test of necessity as under Article 43 of the Hague Regulations, which reads, '[t]he authority of the legitimate power having in fact passed into the hands of the occupant, the latter shall take all the measures in his power to restore, and ensure, as far as possible, public order and safety, while respecting, unless absolutely prevented, the laws in force in the country'. The most salient explanations for such a 'paradigmatic shift' are that the welfare state concept has been ingrained in the normative structure of GC IV, and that the development of international human rights law (IHRL) has impacted upon the interpretation of its relevant provisions.[2] The Geneva law of occupation imposes a variety of positive duties on the Occupying Power in addressing social and economic affairs, such as child welfare, labour, food, hygiene, and public health.[3] The Occupying Power must modify and abrogate local laws that become incompatible with international humanitarian law (IHL) rules, or enact new laws to ensure effective guarantees of the rights of inhabitants under occupation.

The drafting records of GC IV suggest that at the Diplomatic Conference in Geneva (1949), there was a clear shift in the scope of the Occupying Power's law-making power with respect to the Hague Regulations. On the one hand, the first paragraph of the Stockholm draft text (1948) of Article 64 attached no exception to the general rule imposing on the Occupying Power the obligation to preserve local penal laws and tribunals. On the other hand, the second paragraph of this text, which addressed the Occupying Power's enactment of 'provisions', was subject to only one exception, the necessity of 'assur[ing] the security of the members and property of the forces or administration of the Occupying Power, and likewise of the establishments used by the said forces and administration'.[4] At the Diplomatic Conference,[5] the United States (US) Delegate submitted an amendment giving Occupying Powers extensive power to modify local laws and tribunals.[6] The first paragraph of this text read, '*Until changed by the Occupying Power* the penal laws of the occupied territory shall remain in force and the tribunals thereof shall continue to function in respect of all offences covered by the said laws.'[7] However, because this was considered a dilution of Article 43 of the Hague Regulations, there emerged a compromise text, based on a United Kingdom (UK) amendment,[8] which essentially became the current text of Article 64.[9] Its hallmark is that, while more grounds were introduced as exceptions to the ban on Occupying Powers' prescriptive power, they were at least made explicit in order to avoid any abuse.

In the following section, we shall start by analysing the extent to which Occupying Powers' invocation of exceptional grounds allows them to exercise prescriptive powers

---

[2] E. Benvenisti, *The International Law of Occupation* (2nd edn, Oxford: OUP, 2012), at 72–4.
[3] Final Record, vol II-A, at 672 and 833. See also A. Roberts, 'Prolonged Military Occupation: The Israeli-Occupied Territories since 1967', 84 *AJIL* (1990) 44, at 94.
[4] ICRC, *Revised and New Draft Conventions for the Protection of War Victims—Texts Approved and Amended by the XVIIth International Red Cross Conference* (revised translation) (1948), at 131; and Final Record, vol I, at 122.
[5] Final Record, vol II-A, at 669–71.
[6] Ibid, at 670. What the US delegate had in mind was the need to deal with Nazi laws in occupied Germany and Austria.
[7] Ibid, vol III, at 139, No 294 (emphasis added).
[8] Ibid, vol II-A, at 672; and vol III, Annexes, at 139–40, Nos 295 and 296.
[9] Ibid, vol II-A, at 771.

under Article 64 GC IV. Once the parameters of their law-making power are delineated, it becomes necessary to examine specific issues, such as local administrations and judiciary in occupied territories, occupation courts, and the protection of refugees. As is clear from the plethora of the pertinent rules under GC IV, issues of judicial guarantees and humane treatment for accused or convicted persons in occupied territories call for special inquiries. Judicial guarantees and rules on humane treatment are discussed elsewhere in this commentary.[10] In the present chapter particular attention will be paid to the situation of occupied territories. In sections C. and D. we shall assess, respectively, the implications of the relevant rules of occupation to non-international armed conflict (NIAC) and the legal consequences of violations of the rules of occupation.

B. Meaning and Application

I. The scope of the Occupying Power's legislative power under Article 64 GC IV

a. Overview

5   Article 64 paragraph 1 GC IV refers only to 'penal laws'. This raises the question whether the two exceptional grounds on which an Occupying Power may repeal or suspend laws (ensuring the application of GC IV; and the effective administration of justice) are irrelevant for law other than criminal law. Moreover, starting with the phrase '[t]he Occupying Power may [...] subject the population of the occupied territory to provisions', the second paragraph sets out the circumstances in which the Occupying Power can exercise prescriptive power, rather than repealing or suspending the penal laws contemplated in the first paragraph.[11]

6   As regards the Occupying Power's legislative initiatives, Article 64 paragraph 2 refers to three grounds of necessity:

— fulfilling obligations under GC IV;[12]
— maintaining the orderly government of the territory; and
— ensuring the security of the Occupying Power, of the members and property of the occupying forces or administration, as well as the establishments and lines of communications used by them.

On closer inspection, both the first and second paragraphs of Article 64 refer to the two grounds based on necessity for enacting new provisions: compliance with obligations under GC IV; and the security rationales. Yet the necessity of maintaining orderly government is missing from the first paragraph as a ground for repealing or suspending penal laws.

7   While the first paragraph's reference is confined to penal laws, the two paragraphs ought to be read together, so that all types of local laws may be contemplated as within the scope of application of the first paragraph.[13] Indeed, reference only to penal laws in the first paragraph reflects the drafters' intention to underscore the Occupying Power's modification of penal laws as the most serious scenario.[14] Similarly, articulating the

---

[10] See Chs 16, 17, 23, 59, and 60 of this volume.
[11] Final Record, vol II-A, at 833.   [12] Ibid.
[13] Y. Dinstein, *The International Law of Belligerent Occupation* (Cambridge: CUP, 2009), at 111.
[14] Pictet Commentary GC IV, at 335.

maintenance of orderly government within the second paragraph may be considered to underscore the need for new provisions to address situations such as the general collapse of the local government.

In short, Article 64 GC IV is understood as allowing the Occupying Power to repeal or suspend local laws, or to enact new laws, whether penal, administrative, or civil,[15] pursuant to any of the three grounds enumerated in the second paragraph and described above.[16] Some general remarks should be made, though, before we look at each of these grounds. Despite the permissive word 'may' employed in both the first and second paragraphs, the Occupying Power is considered not only entitled, but even bound to ensure civil life and to give effect to the obligations under Geneva Conventions. This salient feature should be compared to the more restrictive scope of the prescriptive power inherent in the text of Article 43 of the Hague Regulations. The latter does not allow the Occupying Power to modify local laws 'unless absolutely prevented' from respecting the laws in force in the country, and then only with special regard to the need 'to restore, and ensure, as far as possible, public order and safety'.

As regards the temporal scope of new legislation enacted by the Occupying Power, this is valid only for the duration of the occupation. The longer the period of occupation, the greater the need to undertake positive duties and promulgate new laws to cope with the evolving social and economic needs of the inhabitants. The formerly occupied sovereign Power may freely abolish and modify such laws. But it may instead leave them in force, if these laws are in the interests of the inhabitants.

b. *The necessity test based on security grounds*

The Occupying Power can amend existing laws or enact new provisions to counter any direct threat to its security, as understood in a broad sense (which includes the security of the personnel and property of the occupying forces or administration, and of lines of communication).[17] Penal provisions may be introduced to ban the possession of firearms, and to strengthen the punishment of acts of terrorism and sabotage.[18]

Unsurprisingly, national military manuals describe security interests as the most salient ground for derogating from existing laws, including those protecting fundamental rights in occupied territory.[19] The necessity of maintaining order and ensuring security entitles the Occupying Power to suspend constitutional safeguards for civil and political rights in occupied territory for the duration of the occupation.[20] However, to prevent abuse of security measures, the proportionality of such measures to the exigencies of the occupied territory should be stringently assessed.

c. *The necessity of maintaining public order and civil life*

The necessity of maintaining orderly government ought to be understood sufficiently broadly to encompass preservation of public order and civil life in general (the authentic

---

[15] The Drafting Committee No 2 could not agree on whether to qualify the term 'provisions' in the draft text of Art 64 para 2 with the adjective 'penal': Final Record, vol III, Annexes, at 139–40, No 296.
[16] M. Sassòli, 'Legislation and Maintenance of Public Order and Civil Life by Occupying Powers', 16 *EJIL* (2005) 661, at 670.
[17] Pictet Commentary GC IV, at 339.   [18] Dinstein, above n 13, at 112.
[19] UK Ministry of Defence, *Manual of the Law of Armed Conflict UK Manual* (Oxford: OUP, 2004), at 286–8. See also US, *Department of the Army Field Manual FM 27-10, The Law of Land Warfare* (1956), para 371.
[20] M. Greenspan, *The Modern Law of Land Warfare* (Berkeley, Ca: University of California Press, 1959), at 223.

French version of Article 43 of the Hague Regulations refers to '*l'ordre et la vie publics*'). It can cover the task of restoring, maintaining, or ensuring public order, or the security of the population under occupation. The Occupying Powers may impose longer prison sentences to deter looting or sabotage of infrastructure in occupied territory.[21] They may also embark on law reforms affecting economic and social life, such as the circulation of currency[22] and changes to a traffic code.[23] Clearly, abolishing discriminatory laws comes within the bounds of '*ordre public*'.[24] In occupied Iraq, many economic measures adopted by the Coalition Provisional Authority (CPA) along the lines of neo-liberal ideology, which simplified the procedure of concluding public contracts, amended Iraqi company law, and liberalized trade and foreign investment,[25] were controversial.[26] Furthermore, laws promulgated pursuant to Occupying Powers' moral standards may be perceived as enhancing their 'ethnocentric' cultural values in occupied territories.[27]

d. *The necessity of fulfilling obligations under the Geneva Conventions*

13 This ground of necessity ought to be widely interpreted in two respects. First, although Article 64 refers only to 'the present Convention' (GC IV), it may be considered as encompassing the four Geneva Conventions, or even the entirety of IHL, conventional or customary.[28] Secondly, notwithstanding the permissive word 'may' in Article 64, the effective interpretation in accordance with Common Article 1 of the Geneva Conventions ('to respect and to ensure respect for the present Convention in all circumstances') *obliges* the Occupying Power to fulfil a variety of duties under the Geneva Conventions. In the event that any legislation in force in occupied territory is incompatible with the requirements of the Geneva Conventions, the Occupying Power is bound to amend or repeal such legislation and, if necessary, enact new laws.

14 It should be noted that in the light of Article 27 of the Vienna Convention on the Law of Treaties, the Occupying Power cannot invoke laws of the occupied state to justify its failure to implement the Geneva Conventions. The obligations under the latter must prevail over any inconsistent legislation in the territory.[29]

e. *The necessity of fulfilling obligations under international human rights law*

15 It is not immediately clear whether the obligations under IHRL provide a separate ground for the necessity exception under Article 64 GC IV.[30] Yet fulfilling obligations under

---

[21] CPA, Order No 31, CPA/ORD/10 Sep 2003/31.
[22] CPA, Order No 43, CPA/ORD/14 October 2003/43.
[23] CPA, Order No 86, CPA/ORD/19 May 2004/86.
[24] Compare US Military Tribunal, Nuremberg, *Krupp Trial, Law Reports of Trials of War Criminals*, vol X, 69, at 135.
[25] See, e.g., CPA Order No 54, 2004 CPA/ORD/24 February 2004/54; Order No 87, CPA/ORD/14 May 2004/87; Order No 39, CPA/ORD/19 September 2003/39 and CPFR/ORD/20 December 2003/39; and Order No 64, CPA/ORD/29 February 2004/64.
[26] M. Zwanenburg, 'Existentialism in Iraq: Security Council Resolution 1483 and the Law of Occupation', 86 *IRRC* 856 (2004) 745, at 757–9.
[27] A. Pellet, 'The Destruction of Troy Will Not Take Place', in E. Playfair (ed), *International Law and the Administration of Occupied Territories: Two Decades of Israeli Occupation of the West Bank and Gaza Strip* (Oxford: Clarendon Press, 1992) 169, at 201–2. See also R. Shehadeh, *Occupier's Law: Israel and the West Bank* (rev edn, Washington, DC: Institute for Palestinian Studies, 1988), at 13.
[28] Dinstein, above n 13, at 113.   [29] Pictet Commentary GC IV, at 336.
[30] Sassòli, above n 16, at 676. For an affirmative view, see S. Wills, 'Occupation Law and Multinational Operations: Problems and Perspectives', 77 *BYBIL* (2006) 256, at 267.

IHRL in occupied territory may be encompassed within the two explicit grounds under Article 64 GC IV: (i) the necessity of maintaining public order; and (ii) the necessity of fulfilling the obligations under the GC IV.[31] From these grounds may be derived the Occupying Power's positive duties to give effect to IHRL in occupied territory.[32] In Iraq, the CPA carried out a sweeping reform of the Iraqi criminal and criminal procedural laws to make them compatible with the relevant standards of international IHRL.[33]

f. *The exceptions based on Security Council Resolutions*

Under Articles 25 and 103 of the United Nations (UN) Charter, decisions of the Council adopted under Chapter VII of the UN Charter are binding on all member states. The legal basis for their binding nature, which is evidenced in the mandatory language used in Chapter VII-based resolutions, may be found in Articles 24 and 25 of the UN Charter.[34] In this regard, the Security Council, acting under Chapter VII of the UN Charter, can abrogate the law of occupation, including Article 64 GC IV.[35] Further, some authors argue that the Council can authoritatively terminate or change the legal status of occupation by transforming it to that of an international transitional administration, even though the facts on the ground remain the same.[36]

However, even the mandatory resolution of the Security Council must take heed of the core principles of IHL and IHRL that are considered *jus cogens*.[37] In keeping with Article 47 GC IV, the Occupying Powers and the displaced sovereign are debarred from depriving protected persons of the benefits of this Convention. This principle is supplemented by two adjunct rules. Consonant with Article 7 paragraph 1 GC IV, the Occupying Power and other states parties are disqualified from concluding special agreements that would undermine the rights of protected persons.[38] Mindful of the coercive circumstances of war and occupation, the framers also introduced Article 8, preventing protected persons from renouncing any of their rights under this treaty.

---

[31] Pictet Commentary GC IV, at 335.

[32] ICJ, *Armed Activities on the Territory of the Congo (Democratic Republic of the Congo v Uganda)*, Judgment of 19 December 2005, paras 178–9.

[33] M.J. Kelly, 'Iraq and the Law of Occupation: New Tests for an Old Law', 6 *YIHL* (2003) 127, at 139.

[34] See ICJ, *Legal Consequences for States of the Continued Presence of South Africa in Namibia (South West Africa) Notwithstanding Security Council Resolution 276 (1970)*, Advisory Opinion, 21 June 1971, at 52–4, paras 112–16; ICJ *Case concerning Questions of Interpretation and Application of the 1971 Montreal Convention Arising from the Aerial Incident at Lockerbie (Libyan Arab Jamahiriya v United Kingdom)*, Request for the Indication of Provisional Measures, 14 April 1992, at 15, para 39. See also Art 103 of the UN Charter.

[35] T.H. Irmscher, 'The Legal Framework for the Activities of the United Nations Interim Administration Mission in Kosovo: The Charter, Human Rights, and the Law of Occupation', 44 *GYIL* (2001) 353, at 383.

[36] S. Vité, 'L'applicabilité du droit international de l'occupation militaire aux activités des organisations internationales', 86 *IRRC* 853 (2004) 9, at 28.

[37] E. de Wet, *The Chapter VII Powers of the United Nations Security Council* (Oxford: Hart Publishing, 2004), at 215; A. Tzanakopoulos, *Disobeying the Security Council: Countermeasures against Wrongful Sanctions* (Oxford: OUP, 2011). See the implications flowing from the relevant cases of the regional courts: ECtHR, *Al-Skeini v United Kingdom*, Judgment (Grand Chamber), 7 July 2011; ECtHR, *Al-Jedda v United Kingdom*, Judgment (Grand Chamber), 7 July 2011 (suggesting the presumption in interpretation that the Security Council should act in accordance with IHRL, while stating that 'clear and explicit language' would be needed for any possible departure from the obligations of IHRL); and ECJ, Joined Cases C-402/05 P and C-415/05 P, *Kadi & Al Barakaat v Council of the European Union* [2008] 3 CMLR 41 (annulling a Council regulation adopted pursuant to the sanctions imposed by UN Security Council resolutions, while holding carefully that it had no authority to question resolutions of the Security Council as such).

[38] In contrast, the contracting parties can enter into special agreements to create more rights for protected persons: R. Kolb, *Ius in bello: le droit international des conflits armés: précis* (2nd edn, Basel: Helbing Lichtenhahn, 2009), at 400.

II. Administrative structures in occupied territories

a. Overview

18 That the Occupying Power must not tamper with the basic structure and institutions of the government in occupied territory may be deduced from the general principle, laid down under Article 64 GC IV and Article 43 Hague Regulations, that it is a transitional authority without assuming sovereign power.[39] Any attempt to introduce *permanent* reform or alteration in the existing administrative structure is presumed to flout such a general principle[40] and the principle of self-determination of peoples. Further, under Article 47 GC IV, protected persons must not be divested of the benefits and rights derived from GC IV or IHL in general, either by virtue of any change introduced into the administrative institutions or government of the occupied territory, or on the basis of any agreement concluded between the Occupying Power and the authorities of the occupied territories. To prevent the welfare of the civilian population being detrimentally affected, under Article 54 paragraph 1 GC IV it is also forbidden to apply any coercive or discriminatory measures against the existing administration (and against judges). When confronted with the invading and occupying authorities, such officials' right to resign is clearly guaranteed.

19 It should be noted, however, that the rationale for this general principle is strictly humanitarian. Clearly, it is 'not to protect the political institutions and government machinery of the State as such'.[41] Accordingly, a converse measure may be justified, that is, for the purpose of improving the living conditions of the civilian population, it may exceptionally be permissible to make alterations to administrative institutions and personnel. It is possible to invoke any of the three general grounds under Article 64 GC IV in order to justify the introduction of changes in the administrative structure. To do so to meet the welfare needs of the local population, for instance, is not incompatible with Article 47 GC IV.[42]

20 Article 54 GC IV, not found in the Stockholm draft text, was inserted at the Diplomatic Conference.[43] Under the first paragraph of this provision, it is forbidden to change the status of public officials or judges in occupied territories and to apply to them sanctions, or coercive or discriminatory measures, if they abstain from duties for reasons of conscience.

b. Modifications of administrative personnel

21 The prohibition on altering the status of public officials stipulated in Article 54 paragraph 1 is subject to the exceptions in paragraph 2, which refers to two scenarios. The first sentence of Article 54 paragraph 2 refers to the case where the labour force of administrative personnel may be requisitioned under Article 51 paragraph 2 (see further at MN 22). Using words that seem to contradict the prohibition contained in paragraph 1, the second sentence of Article 54 paragraph 2 then sets out the 'right' of the Occupying Power to remove public officials. Clearly, civil servants must not be dismissed arbitrarily, for example for refusing to comply with orders inconsistent with international law.[44] Such a 'right to remove', although allegedly supported by long usage until the Second World

---

[39] P. Fauchille, *Traité de droit international public*, II: *Guerre et neutralité* (Paris: Librairie Arthur Rousseau, 1921), at 228.
[40] L. Oppenheim, *International Law: A Treatise*, II: *Disputes, War and Neutrality*, ed H. Lauterpacht (7th edn, London: Longmans, 1952), at 437.
[41] Pictet Commentary GC IV, at 274.   [42] Dinstein, above n 13, at 123–5.
[43] Final Record, vol II-A, at 774.
[44] UK *Manual*, above n 19, at 283. See also *Mr P (Batavia) v Mrs S (Bandoeng)* (1947) 14 *Annual Digest* 260.

War,[45] was criticized for undermining the first paragraph of Article 54 at the Diplomatic Conference.[46] In the end, however, the majority of the delegates agreed that the second paragraph containing the right of dismissal was essential to cope with the situation of occupation in which officials were systematically indoctrinated by the former authorities of the occupied state.[47]

As noted above, despite the right to resign of the local administrative officials or judges, 22 as derived from the ban on coercive measures against them under Article 54 paragraph 1 GC IV, the Occupying Power is allowed exceptionally to requisition their services under Article 51 paragraph 2 GC IV. However, the legality of such requisitions must be analysed only by reference to the three specific grounds of necessity contained under the latter provision:

— meeting the need of the occupying armed forces;
— ensuring the public utility services; and
— taking care of the feeding, sheltering, clothing, transportation, or health of the occupied civilian population.

As an interpretive methodology, these specific rules under Article 54 paragraph 2 and Article 51 paragraph 2 GC IV may be supplemented by the three grounds of necessity under the general clause in Article 64 GC IV.[48]

c. *The prohibition of coercive or discriminatory measures against public officials or judges in occupied territory*

As noted above at MN 20, under Article 54 paragraph 1 GC IV, it is forbidden to take any 23 detrimental measures (sanctions, or coercive or discriminatory measures) against public officials or judges in occupied territory. The Occupying Power cannot compel nationals of the occupied country to participate in military operations against their own country. As a corollary, the police, which the Occupying Power has maintained or created *de novo*, must not be compelled to act against lawful combatants, such as resistance movements that fulfil the criteria of distinction.[49] This holds true even if they were in the belligerent's service prior to the initiation of the armed conflict.[50]

III. The local judicial system and judges in occupied territory

a. *The local judiciary*

Under Article 54 paragraph 1 and the second sentence of Article 64 paragraph 1 GC IV, 24 the general rule is that the Occupying Power is bound to maintain local courts (dealing with both civil and criminal affairs) and to leave the status of judges intact.[51] Still, classic publicists maintained that in occupied territories, if the local judicial system became dysfunctional, as in case of the breakdown and disorganization of local administration of

---

[45] Pictet Commentary GC IV, 308; Oppenheim, above n 40, at 445.
[46] Final Record, vol II-A, at 774–5.   [47] Ibid, at 775, 809, and 829.
[48] C. Greenwood, 'The Administration of Occupied Territory in International Law', in Playfair (ed), above n 27, 241, at 256.
[49] UK *Manual*, above n 19, at 283.   [50] Art 23(2) Hague Regulations (1907).
[51] Compare M. Shamgar, 'The Observance of International Law in the Administered Territories', 1 *IsrYBHR* (1971) 262, at 269 (discussing the Golan Heights where, absent local judiciaries, the Occupying Power was considered authorized to set up its civil court).

justice, the Occupying Power was allowed to set up its own judiciary to exercise civil and criminal jurisdictions over the inhabitants.[52]

25   The draft records of Article 64 paragraph 1 second sentence presented two circumstances in which abolishing tribunals would exceptionally be justified:

— preventing 'corrupt or unfairly constituted' courts from applying inhumane or discriminatory laws, as in the case of Nazi laws on racial hierarchy and eugenics;[53] and
— 'the necessity for ensuring the effective administration of justice', which addresses the circumstances where judges have resigned pursuant to Article 54 paragraph 1, or where courts have crumbled during hostilities.[54]

26   This chapter agrees that the Occupying Power is allowed to modify the overall judicial system in accordance with any of the aforementioned three grounds under the general clause of Article 64.[55] However, when engaging in such a 'structural reform', the Occupying Power must give paramount importance to the independence of judges. Accordingly, any drastic alteration of the judiciary must be more stringently construed than that of the administrative structure in general.

b. The protection of local judges

27   In view of the prohibition of sanctions or any coercive or discriminatory measures against judges (and against the public officials in general) under Article 54 paragraph 1, if judges decide to remain in office during the occupation, their right to pass judgment must not be interfered with.[56] In particular, they must not be coerced into rendering judgments in the name of the Occupying Power.[57]

28   The second sentence of Article 54 paragraph 2, which exceptionally recognizes the Occupying Power's 'right' to remove public officials, does not speak of the dismissal of judges. Still, some authorities suggest the Occupying Power's competence to remove judges.[58] Contrariwise, others suggest that judges may never be dismissed, attaching cardinal importance to judicial independence. In their view, the framers could not have accidentally omitted any reference to 'judges' in the second paragraph (in contrast to the first paragraph which specifically refers to them).[59]

29   This chapter argues that with respect to the dismissal or suspension of individual judges, the three grounds of necessity under the general clause of Article 64 paragraph 1 may come into play. The necessity of 'ensuring the effective administration of justice' under the second sentence of Article 64 paragraph 1 may address the case of judges resigning on grounds of conscience or for fear of being perceived as collaborating with

---

[52] J.W. Garner, *International Law and the World War* (New York: Columbic University Press, 1949), vol II, at 91; Fauchille, above n 39, at 235–6.
[53] Final Record, vol II-A, at 670 and 833. See also US Military Tribunal, Nuremberg, *Krupp Trial*, above n 24, at 135.
[54] Final Record, vol II-A, at 672, 771, and 833.
[55] N. Bentwich, 'The Legal Administration of Palestine under the British Military Occupation', 1 *BYBIL* (1920-21) 139, at 141–3; Dinstein, above n 13, at 134.
[56] Oppenheim, above n 40, at 447.
[57] E.H. Schwenk, 'Legislative Power of the Military Occupant under Article 43, Hague Regulations', 54 *YLJ* (1945) 393, at 406.
[58] Pictet Commentary GC IV, at 308; Dinstein, above n 13, at 133.
[59] H.-P. Gasser, 'Protection of the Civilian Population', in D. Fleck (ed), *The Handbook of International Humanitarian Law* (2nd edn, Oxford: OUP, 2008) 237, at 290.

the Occupying Power,[60] or fleeing *en masse* in anticipation of the invading army.[61] In the event of prolonged occupation, the need inevitably arises to fill the vacancies left by retiring judges. It has been suggested that the Occupying Power may appoint judges not only from the ranks of local lawyers, but also from judges of its own nationality.[62] However, this chapter argues that in view of the need to maintain the integrity of the local judiciary, and of the right of self-determination of peoples, the Occupying Power may appoint its own nationals from its metropolitan territory only exceptionally. This is limited to the circumstances in which there is a lack of qualified lawyers among the local population in the occupied territories. Further, when confronted with judges who have formed the institutional devices for the egregious ideology of the overthrown regime, the Occupying Power is entitled, or even enjoined, to lay them off on security grounds. The Occupying Power might also argue that maintaining such judges would pose 'an obstacle to the application of the present Convention' within the meaning of Article 64 paragraph 1.[63]

c. Jurisdiction of local tribunals

Neither Article 64 GC IV, nor any treaty-based rule of IHL regulates civil and commercial courts in occupied territories.[64] Yet the Occupying Power is entitled to change or close such courts in so far as this is necessary on any of the three grounds under Article 64. One caveat is that inhabitants must not be hindered from accessing local courts. This is made clear by Article 23(1)(h) of the Hague Regulations, which prohibits any belligerent party from 'declar[ing] abolished, suspended, or inadmissible in a court of law the rights and actions of the nationals of the hostile party'. With respect to the jurisdictional scope of the local tribunals, this does not encompass civil or commercial proceedings filed by inhabitants against the occupying administration.[65]

As regards criminal jurisdiction, tribunals of the occupied territory must be maintained to deal with offences against the territorial sovereign's penal laws, namely crimes committed by the inhabitants against other civilians or their property. Given that Article 64 paragraph 1 expressly spells out the preservation of *penal* laws as a general rule, the Occupying Power's exceptional competence to transform local criminal tribunals must be more narrowly construed than in the case of civil courts.

Traditionally, local courts have been prevented from exercising any jurisdiction (either civil or criminal) over matters concerning the Occupying Power itself, its armed forces, or its allies, which arise during the period of occupation.[66] Notwithstanding such 'jurisdictional division', under IHL local courts are not prevented from undertaking judicial review of the Occupying Power's legislative acts (civil or criminal) in the light of the general

---

[60] A.V. Freeman, 'War Crimes by Enemy Nationals Administering Justice in Occupied territory', 41 *AJIL* (1947) 579, at 589.
[61] Final Record, vol II-A, at 672 and 771.   [62] Pictet Commentary GC IV, at 336.
[63] Final Record, vol II-A, at 670 and 833; US, *FM 27-10*, above n 19, para 373.
[64] G. von Glahn, *The Occupation of Enemy Territory: A Commentary on the Law and Practice of Belligerent Occupation* (Minneapolis, Minn: University of Minnesota Press, 1957), at 109.
[65] Ibid, at 108.
[66] Ibid, at 108 and 112; and A.G. Green, 'The Military Commission', 42 *AJIL* (1948) 832, at 833 and 842. See also US, *FM 27-10*, above n 19, para 374 (stipulating a separate structure within the judiciary for civil and disciplinary (criminal) affairs in relation to members of the occupying armed forces, or accompanying civilians).

clauses under Article 43 of the Hague Regulations and Article 64 GC IV.[67] Irrespective of the efficacy of such reviews, courts of some occupied states during the two World Wars showed boldness in challenging the Occupying Power's abusive laws under the Hague Regulations.[68] As a further step, in the event that members of the Occupying Power commit grave breaches of Geneva Conventions but are not prosecuted, local tribunals should not be debarred from trying them under Article 146 GC IV.[69]

IV. Occupation courts

a. Overview

33 Historically, the Occupying Power has been vested with the power to set up military tribunals of its own to try offences committed by the local population against members of occupation forces or the administration.[70] The occupation courts (including military commissions) set up by the Allies during and in the aftermath of the two World Wars provide an abundance of precedent.[71]

34 When Article 66 is read in conjunction with the prescriptive power under Article 64, it is clear that the Occupying Power is entitled to establish military courts[72] (namely, occupation courts) to try offences against its security/penal laws in occupied territories. Article 66 contemplates tribunals to deal with occupied inhabitants' violations of orders, proclamations, and other legislative acts issued by the Occupying Power. Evidently, such tribunals' jurisdiction encompasses offences committed by inhabitants against occupation personnel.[73] In the event that the Occupying Power's civilian nationals, such as settlers, who are not civilians accompanying its armed forces, have committed infractions of its security/penal laws in the occupied territory, they may be subject to the same military court as the one contemplated under Article 66.[74] As an alternative to occupation courts, the Occupying Power may assign jurisdiction to prosecute offenders to its own military tribunals.[75] All these possibilities do not prevent

---

[67] F. Morgenstern, 'Validity of the Acts of the Belligerent Occupant', 28 *BYBIL* (1951) 291, at 309.

[68] See, e.g., Court of Appeal of Liège (Belgium), 13 February 1917, (1917) 44 *Journal du Droit International (Clunet)* 1809, at 1813; Norway, District Court of Aker, *Øverland* case, 25 August 1943, (1943-5) 12 *Annual Digest* 446, at 447. See also other cases cited in Y. Arai-Takahashi, *The Law of Occupation: Continuity and Change of International Humanitarian Law, and its Interaction with International Human Rights Law* (Leiden: Martinus Nijhoff, 2009), at 147–57.

[69] *Contra*, G.A. Finch, 'Jurisdiction of Local Courts to Try Enemy Persons for War Crimes', 14 *AJIL* (1920) 218, at 223; and von Glahn, above n 64, at 112.

[70] See, e.g., C. Meurer, *Die Völkerrechtliche Stellung der vom Feind Besetzten Gebiete* (Tübingen: J.C.B. Mohr, 1915), at 27–8; C. Rousseau, *Le droit des conflits armés* (Paris: Pédone, 1983), at 150–1; and Y. Ronen, 'Blind in their Own Cause: The Military Courts in the West Bank', 2 *Cambridge Journal of International and Comparative Law* (2013) 738, at 744.

[71] See, e.g., E.E. Nobleman, 'American Military Government Courts in Germany', 40 *AJIL* (1946) 803, at 805; R.P. Masterton, 'Military Commissions and the War on Terrorism', 36 *International Lawyer* (2002) 1165.

[72] von Glahn, above n 64, at 115.   [73] Garner, above n 52, at 85; Fauchille, above n 39, at 237.

[74] Z. Hadar, 'The Military Courts', in M. Shamgar (ed), *Military Government in the Territories Administered by Israel 1967–1980* (Jerusalem: Alpha Press, 1982), at 171, 197–8. See, however, Ronen, above n 70, at 744 (explaining that since the early 1980s, the policy of the Israeli Attorney-General has changed from the earlier stance of allowing the military courts in the West Bank and the Gaza Strip to try Israeli nationals and residents when they were charged with offences in those occupied territories, to the position of prosecuting such Israeli nationals and residents in the occupied territories before Israeli courts).

[75] Gasser, above n 59, at 305.

the Occupying Power from allocating jurisdiction even over penal/security laws to local courts maintained in the territory.[76]

Another special tribunal that may be set up by the Occupying Power is one designed to try offences committed by members of its military forces.[77] In practice, such persons, and civilians accompanying armed forces (including civilian contractors) who are governed by Article 4A(4) GC III, are liable to face court-martial.[78] The legal basis for the creation and competence of such military tribunals is to be found in the Occupying Power's domestic statutes rather than in international law.[79]

b. Composition and requirements of occupation courts

Article 66 GC IV requires 'occupation courts' to be 'properly constituted, non-political military courts'.[80] This is in order to exclude summary trials by commanders in the field.[81] It excludes all types of special tribunals, when read in tandem with Common Article 3 Geneva Conventions, which requires a 'regularly constituted court, affording all the judicial guarantees which are recognized as indispensable by civilized peoples', and Article 75(4) Additional Protocol (AP) I, which demands 'an impartial and regularly constituted court respecting the generally recognized principles of regular judicial procedure'.[82] These terms suggest that the courts must be established in accordance with the laws and procedures already in force in the country concerned.[83]

The adjective 'non-political' was inserted to prevent the judiciary serving as a vehicle for 'political or racial persecution', as happened during the Axis occupation in Europe during the Second World War.[84] As will be seen in section D.II of this chapter, failure to provide fair trial guarantees may give rise to a grave breach and a war crime under Article 130 GC III and Article 8(2)(a)(vi) of the Statute of the International Criminal Court (ICC Statute). The term 'military courts' refers to 'courts whose members have military status and are subordinate to the military authorities'.[85] Civilians are not debarred from serving in occupation courts, but they must be subject to direct military control and authority.[86]

As will be examined in section B.VI.b of this chapter, the Occupying Power's authority to establish only military courts under Article 66 GC IV is qualified by the growing tendency of IHRL to rule out trials of civilians by military tribunals.[87] The doctrinal discourses provide two ways to overcome this difficulty. According to one school of thought, the requirements of IHRL should be considered *lex posterior*. As a corollary, on this interpretation, the Occupying Power would be forestalled from bringing civilians before the military tribunals within the meaning of Article 66 GC IV. It should be noted that in view of the permissive or elective connotation of the word 'may' in that provision, it is not necessary that civilians accused of offences stipulated in the occupation laws be handed over to the military courts. The second strand of argument, which this chapter endorses, is

---

[76] S. Weill, 'The Judicial Arm of the Occupation: The Israeli Military Courts in the Occupied Territories', 89 *IRRC* 866 (2007) 395, at 399. Such a possibility is not excluded, because Art 66 employs the permissive wording 'may' when discussing the handover of the accused.
[77] Schwenk, above n 57, at 405. [78] Greenspan, above n 20, at 255.
[79] von Glahn, above n 64, at 111. [80] Final Record, vol II-A, at 833.
[81] Dinstein, above n 13, at 137.
[82] Pictet Commentary GC IV, at 340. [83] ICRC CIHL Study, vol I, at 355.
[84] Pictet Commentary GC IV, at 340. [85] Ibid. [86] von Glahn, above n 64, at 116.
[87] See below nn 143 and 144, and ECtHR, *Cyprus v Turkey*, Judgment, 10 May 2001 (Grand Chamber), para 358.

that IHL on military justice in occupied territories is considered *lex specialis*.[88] Even then, given the growing influence of IHRL on the procedural requirements of military justice in occupied territories, it can be argued that the military courts which are not equipped with the degree of impartiality and independence required of civilian tribunals are no longer admissible.

39 Further, under the first sentence of Article 66 GC IV, such military courts must 'sit in the occupied country', in line with the principle of territoriality for criminal jurisdiction. This requirement corresponds to Article 76 paragraph 1 GC IV, which demands that persons accused or convicted of offences are detained in occupied territories. This also applies, whenever possible, to courts that hear appeals from occupation courts.[89]

c. Relationship with local courts in occupied territories

40 In essence, in the occupied territory there is a 'dual system' for the judiciary. On the one hand, local tribunals deal with offences committed by inhabitants against other inhabitants or their property in the occupied territory on the basis of the local laws and rules of procedure, in so far as this does not involve the occupying forces[90] or pose a serious security threat to occupying authorities.[91] This is explicitly recognized in the second sentence of Article 64 paragraph 1 GC IV. On the other hand, occupation courts address offences against the security of the occupation army or administration, including damage to its communications and property.[92] Moreover, the *a contrario* interpretation of the second sentence of Article 64 paragraph 1 GC IV suggests that in the absence of the effective function of the local judiciary, civilians accused of offences against local penal laws may be brought before the military courts set up by the Occupying Power. The effective administration of justice can be deemed lacking in cases where the local courts have collapsed, where the due process guarantees are seriously questioned, and where there is undue delay in the criminal proceedings. Further, both local tribunals and occupation courts are considered entitled to adjudicate upon violations of laws and customs of war, including war crimes, even though on this matter the exercise of the jurisdiction by the latter may obtain.[93]

d. Offences against the penal/security laws of Occupying Powers and the prohibition of double jeopardy

41 Clearly, in occupied territories the same act may give rise to different offences (security offences and ordinary criminal law offences), so that an offender may be tried by the Occupying Power's military court and by the local court. There is here neither a clash of jurisdiction nor the violation of the *ne bis in idem* principle,[94] in so far as the nature of such a 'mixed offence' tried by each court is different.[95] This can also be sustained by the

---

[88] See, e.g., M. Sassòli, 'La Cour européenne des droits de l'homme et les conflits armés', in S. Breitenmoser et al (eds), *Human Rights, Democracy and the Rule of Law: Liber Amicorum Luzius Wildhaber* (Zurich: Dike, 2007), 709, at 717–18.

[89] Art 66 second sentence GC IV.   [90] von Glahn, above n 64, at 108.

[91] Gasser, above n 59, at 305.

[92] von Glahn, above n 64, at 112.

[93] Ibid, for the competence of the occupation courts to exercise jurisdiction over violations of laws and customs of war.

[94] Though not recognized under GC IV (except for civilian internees under Art 117 para 3), this is embodied under Art 75(4)(h) AP I. See also Art 86 GC III for POWs.

[95] T.S. Kuttner, 'Israel and the West Bank: Aspects of the Law of Belligerent Occupation', 7 *IsrYBHR* (1977) 166, at 194.

plain language of Article 75(4)(h) AP I, which considers double jeopardy only in the case of penal proceedings instituted by the same state party.[96] Moreover, there may be circumstances in which the 'mixed offences' constitute war crimes (or other international crimes), but neither the military tribunal nor the local court examines them in that light. Such cases could be tried by the ICC under Article 17 of the ICC Statute, due to an 'unwillingness' genuinely to try and punish offenders.

e. The jurisdiction of occupation courts over war crimes

The Occupying Power is obligated to enact appropriate legislation to try and punish persons who have committed grave breaches of the Geneva Conventions.[97] Arguably, under customary international law, the Occupying Power may be considered even under an obligation to punish all war crimes.[98] The occupation courts can be given the jurisdiction for that purpose.[99] The prosecution and punishment of grave breaches and other war crimes are specifically recognized under Article 70 paragraph 1 GC IV as an exception to the general rule on prohibiting the arrest, prosecution, and conviction of protected persons for acts committed before the occupation. 42

One doctrinal question is whether the occupation courts can be accorded jurisdiction to prosecute past war crimes (and crimes against humanity) that were unconnected to the armed conflict immediately prior to the occupation. This chapter argues that the Occupying Power can promulgate its own laws criminalizing such international crimes (including crimes against humanity) perpetrated by the former regime of the occupied state,[100] even though this is not linked to the implementation of IHL. This chapter considers that, alternatively, the persons accused of such crimes may be brought before the local courts which may operate in parallel. The legal ground for the occupation courts, set up under Article 66 GC IV, to entertain jurisdiction over such past international crimes lies in the prescriptive power of the Occupying Power, as recognized in Article 64 paragraph 2 GC IV. Under the rule contained in the latter paragraph, one can appeal to the security ground and the necessity of implementing 'obligations under the present Convention' (which can be read in a broad manner to encompass the obligations of IHL in general, which are in turn influenced by IHRL) to justify such a move.[101] From the perspective of transitional justice, to leave unpunished past international crimes committed by the old regime may endanger *ordre public*, obstructing national reconciliation. This consideration holds true above all with respect to past war crimes (and crimes against humanity). It should be noted, however, that on this reading, those grounds can equally be relevant to other crimes perpetrated in the past, such as economic or financial crimes. In occupied Iraq, the CPA, through the medium of the Iraqi Governing Council, adopted the law penalizing international crimes which had been committed by the Baathist regime.[102] However, it is very doubtful that the Iraqi Special Tribunal was created in accordance with 43

---

[96] See also the Seventh Protocol to the ECHR, Art 4(1).   [97] Arts 146 and 147 GC IV.
[98] For such an affirmative view, see Sassòli, above n 16, at 675. While it is debatable whether an Occupying Power has an obligation under customary international law to prosecute all war crimes other than the grave breaches of the GCs, it has a right to do so.
[99] UK *Manual*, above n 19, at 294. See also M.J. Kelly, *Restoring and Maintaining Order in Complex Peace Operations: The Search for a Legal Framework* (The Hague: Kluwer, 1999), at 124.
[100] Sassòli recognizes this expressly: Sassòli, above n 16, at 675.   [101] Ibid.
[102] Governing Council, The Statute of the Iraqi Special Tribunal, 10 December 2003, 'Annex' to CPA Order No 48, 10 December 2003 CPA/ORD/9 Dec 2003/48.

the requirements under Article 66. Indeed, it was the Interim Government of Iraq that should have established it,[103] or endorsed it retroactively.

f. Appeals

44   With respect to appeals regarding judgments handed down by military courts in occupied territories, the second sentence of Article 66 GC IV speaks of a preference that an appellate system should be set up in occupied territory. Still, according to Article 73 paragraph 1, the Occupying Power is not necessarily enjoined to create a system of appeal within the framework of the occupation courts.[104] Yet, as will be discussed below,[105] this issue needs to be re-evaluated through the lens of IHRL. Where appeal procedures are available, an appeal may be lodged before the military appeal court in the occupied territory, akin to an ordinary appeal.[106] With respect to its occupied territories, following the *Arjov* case,[107] Israel set up the echelon of military courts of appeal in 1989.[108]

45   As noted in section B.III.c of this chapter, local tribunals in the occupied territory can assume jurisdiction over penal and civil laws that were in force before the occupation. In the event that their higher-instance courts are located in the unoccupied part of the sovereign state under occupation, the question arises whether litigants should be allowed to institute appellate proceedings outside the occupied zone. Does the Occupying Power have to respect 'the laws in force' of the occupied territory, which include civil and criminal procedural laws governing appeals? In reality, appeals to higher instances outside the occupied area have proven intractable or non-viable. Instead, the Occupying Powers may opt to confer the authority to hear appeals upon a newly created judicial body within the occupied territory.[109]

g. Petitions

46   Even where there is no possibility of appeal according to the relevant procedural laws, under Article 73 GC IV a convicted person has the right to petition the 'competent authority of the Occupying Power' to have the finding and sentence reviewed. This 'competent authority' can be the theatre commander of the Occupying Power or a military governor.[110] The obvious disadvantage is that neither of them constitutes a judicial organ.

V. The protection of refugees in occupied territories

47   Under Article 70 paragraph 2 GC IV, refugees who are received in the territory of the occupied state 'before the outbreak of hostilities' can claim immunity from arrest, prosecution, conviction, or deportation from the occupied territory, although it is only under Article 73 AP I that they are turned into protected persons, while they are not under GC IV. Clearly, this principle was inserted in reaction to the experience of Jewish refugees in Axis-occupied

---

[103] Sassòli, above n 16, at 675.   [104] von Glahn, above n 64, at 117.
[105] See section B.VI.g of this chapter.
[106] Pictet Commentary GC IV, at 358. Compare Art 106 GC III.
[107] HCJ 87/85 *Arjov et al v Commander of IDF in the Judea and Samaria Region et al*, 42(1) PD 353, at 375–9 (per President Shamgar) (English excerpt in 18 *IsrYBHR* (1988) 255).
[108] Dinstein, above n 13, at 139.
[109] C. Fairman, 'Asserted Jurisdiction of the Italian Court of Cassation over the Court of Appeal of the Free Territory of Trieste', 45 *AJIL* (1951) 541, at 543 and 548; M. Drori, 'The Legal System in Judea and Samaria: A Review of the Previous Decade with a Glance at the Future', 8 *IsrYBHR* (1978) 144, at 150.
[110] See von Glahn, above n 64, at 117.

European territories during the Second World War. Article 70 paragraph 2 is complementary to the rule embodied in Article 44 GC IV, which addresses refugees' relation with the authorities of the receiving state.

Exceptions to this right are allowed in respect of two offences only: (i) offences committed after the outbreak of hostilities; and (ii) offences under common law committed prior to the start of hostilities, which the law of the occupied state would have designated as extraditable in time of peace.[111] As regards the first exception, the Pictet Commentary to GC IV condones the otherwise prohibited measures of arrest, prosecution, conviction, or deportation of pre-war refugees, if these refugees have committed acts of treason against their state of origin (such as propaganda broadcasts) during hostilities.[112]

With respect to the second exception, this is intended to prevent fugitives benefiting from the protection given to refugees. Whether a specific ordinary crime falls within the range of 'offences under common law' which would justify extradition depends on the law of the occupied state, not on that of the Occupying Power.[113] One of the litmus tests for distinguishing such ordinary criminal offences is whether or not the alleged offences are of a political nature.[114] If they are, the refugees must not be extradited from the occupied state.[115] There must also be 'adequate proof' that the offence has been perpetrated by the person sought for extradition.[116]

Those suspected (or indicted by the authorities of their state of origin) of having committed political offences may also benefit from the *non-refoulement* principle under IHRL where they have reason to fear persecution on account of their political opinions or religious belief. This ought to be read with Article 33 of the 1951 Geneva Refugee Convention, which broadens the persecutory grounds, going beyond religious belief and political opinion and covering three other grounds: race, nationality, and membership of a social group. Admittedly, Article 33 of the Geneva Refugee Convention suffers from two defects: (i) the limited persecutory grounds that do not contain such obvious grounds as gender and sexual orientation;[117] and (ii) the inclusion of the exception (Article 33(2)) linked to national security. By comparison, with regard to this second aspect, the proscription under the *jus cogens non-refoulement* principle under IHRL is absolute.

On closer inspection, the parameters of the text of Article 70 paragraph 2 GC IV seem restricted in two respects. First, the principle of a special safeguard for refugees is confined to measures leading to deprivation of liberty and displacement. As such, freedom from measures that do not directly affect the physical integrity of refugees, such as denial or restriction of their rights to property and professional activity, is not encompassed within the scope of the safeguard.[118] Secondly, the category of refugees protected by Article 70 paragraph 2 (and under Article 44) is non-comprehensive, being confined to 'pre-war refugees', namely, those who have sought refuge in the occupied territory 'before the outbreak of hostilities'.[119] The protection does not cover persons who were accepted as

---

[111] Art 70 para 2 GC IV.   [112] Pictet Commentary GCIV, at 351.   [113] Ibid, at 351–2.
[114] Ibid.   [115] Dinstein, above n 13, at 181.   [116] Ibid.
[117] Note, however, that this provision has been construed to include such groups in some circumstances. Refugee claims based on sexual orientation and gender identity may be encompassed within the ground 'membership of a particular social group'. On this matter, see International Commission of Jurists, *Yogyakarta Principles—Principles on the Application of International Human Rights Law in Relation to Sexual Orientation and Gender Identity*, March 2007, Principle 23; and UNHCR, *Guidelines on International Protection No 9: Claims to Refugee Status based on Sexual Orientation and/or Gender Identity within the context of Article 1A(2) of the 1951 Convention and/or its 1967 Protocol relating to the Status of Refugees*, and the cases cited at 11–14.
[118] Dinstein, above n 13, at 181.   [119] Ibid.

asylum-seekers after the commencement of hostilities but before the territory of the host state was occupied.[120] This deficiency is unresolved under Article 73 AP I. The latter provision follows the 'pre-hostilities' definition, addressing the safeguarding of persons who have been recognized, prior to the initiation of hostilities, as stateless persons or refugees under the pertinent international law, or under the national law of the state of refuge or residence. Still, the text of Article 73 AP I has modified the scope of 'protected persons' within the meaning of Article 4 GC IV to cover refugees with the Occupying Power's nationality.[121]

VI. Judicial guarantees

a. *Immunity from arrest, prosecution, and conviction for acts committed, or for opinions expressed, before the occupation*

52 Under Article 70 paragraph 1 GC IV, protected persons must not be subject to arrest, prosecution, or conviction for acts committed, or for opinions expressed, prior to the occupation, or during a temporary interruption thereof. This principle provoked no controversy at the Diplomatic Conference.[122] What this provision contemplates in relation to acts done, or opinions voiced, 'prior to the occupation' is relatively clear. In contrast, what is meant by such acts or opinions 'during a temporary interruption' of the occupation seems ambiguous at first glance. As explained by Dinstein,[123] this aspect deals with the situation in which an inhabitant wrongly assumes the end of occupation and performs some action (such as forming a political association or holding an assembly) that threatens, or disseminates opinions that are at loggerheads with, the Occupying Power's security law. When the occupation resumes, such an individual person is protected from legal proceedings for what he or she has done or said. Above all, this text benefits local magistrates or officials, who may fear arrest or prosecution for legal action that they took before the occupation or during an interlude.[124]

53 The only exception to this principle is the case of 'breaches of the laws and customs of war', to which the immunity provided under Article 70 paragraph 1 does not apply.[125] This exception is corroborated by the universal duty to repress grave breaches of the Geneva Conventions, as envisaged under Article 146 GC IV[126] (and under Article 86 AP I).

b. *General remarks on fair trial guarantees in occupied territory*

54 The provisions under Section III of GC IV (Articles 64–77) deal with the requirements for fair trial guarantees for protected persons who are accused and held in detention on criminal charges, as well as for those who are convicted. Special note should also be taken of two provisions: Common Article 3 of the Geneva Conventions that recognizes fair trial guarantees; and Article 75(4) AP I, which, in its *chapeau*, requires 'an impartial and regularly constituted court respecting the generally recognized principles of regular judicial

---

[120] Bothe/Partsch/Solf, at 448.
[121] ICRC Commentary APs, at 854.   [122] Final Record, vol II-A, at 769, 790, and 834.
[123] Dinstein, above n 13, at 141.
[124] Pictet Commentary GC IV, at 349.
[125] Art 70 para 1 GC IV. Pictet defines this term as 'the whole of the rules relating to the conduct of hostilities and to the treatment of war victims, particularly under the Geneva Conventions, the Hague Regulations, and unwritten international law': Pictet Commentary GC IV, at 349.
[126] Pictet Commentary GC IV, at 350.

procedure'. Clearly, the rules enunciated under those provisions have long been embedded within the bedrock of general international law.[127]

Above all, invoking Article 75(4) AP I[128] and its customary law equivalent entails salient advantages. First, as will be examined in section D.II of this chapter on war crimes, *ratione materiae*, the categories of fair trial guarantees enumerated under Article 75(4) AP I are more detailed than those contained in GC IV. Secondly, unlike the rules embodied in Articles 65–77 GC IV, Article 75(4) AP I has a broader span of application *ratione personae* (as does Common Article 3), encompassing all persons, exceeding the definition of 'protected persons' under Article 4 GC IV.[129] Contrary to the view discernible in the *travaux préparatoires*,[130] the scope of application of Article 75(4) AP I is not limited to persons deprived of liberty[131] but extends to cover *all* persons,[132] including the Parties' own nationals.[133] After all, the customary norm distilled from the text furnishes minimum safeguards for all persons who do not benefit from more favourable treatment under the Geneva Conventions or AP I. Thirdly, the minimum guarantees derived from Article 75(4) AP I are of special relevance to persons tried by armed groups' courts in NIAC.[134]

While the practice of IHRL provides elaborate elements of judicial guarantees that must be accorded to all accused persons in occupied territory,[135] both the International Covenant on Civil and Political Rights (ICCPR) (Article 4) and regional human rights treaties do not ascribe non-derogability to any of the provisions on fair trial guarantees,[136] except for the principle of non-retroactivity of criminal law.[137] Nonetheless, the documents produced by the treaty-based bodies, such as the Human Rights Committee's (HRCttee) General Comment 29 and the Inter-American Commision on Human Rights' (IACommHR) *Report on Terrorism and Human Rights*, help ascertain the non-derogable and customary law elements of due process guarantees. Even so, IHRL lags behind IHL on this matter. Among those rights that are expressly contained in GC IV, only the right to be informed of the nature and cause of an accusation is classified as non-derogable, and this only under the IACommHR's *Report*.[138]

---

[127] ICRC CIHL Study, vol I, at 352–6; *US Army, Operational Law Handbook* (2002), Chapter 2, at 5.
[128] Cf Art 6(2) AP II and Art 67 ICC Statute.
[129] See C. Olivier, 'Revising General Comment No 29 of the United Nations Human Rights Committee: About Fair Trial Rights and Derogations in Times of Public Emergency', 17 *LJIL* (2004) 405, at 408.
[130] See *Official Records of the Diplomatic Conference on the Reaffirmation and Development of International Humanitarian Law Applicable in Armed Conflicts,* vol XV, (1978), at 460–1, CDDH/407Rev.1, paras 41–2 (Report of Committee III); ibid, vol III, at 292; and ibid, vol XV, at 40, CDDR/III/SR.43, para 80. Contrast these with ibid, vol XV, CDDH/III/SR. 43, para 74 (Italian Delegation).
[131] Bothe/Partsch/Solf, at 463.   [132] ICRC CIHL Study, vol I, at 352–74, Rules 100–2.
[133] See EECC, *Civilians Claims—Eritrea's Claims 15, 16, 23, and 27–32*, 17 December 2004, paras 30 and 97.
[134] Cf *Hamdan v Rumsfeld* (2006) 126 S Ct 2749, at 2797 (recognizing the methodology of using Art 75 AP I as an aid to interpreting CA 3).
[135] See L. Doswald-Beck and R. Kolb, *Judicial Process and Human Rights: Texts and Summaries of International Case-Law, International Commission of Jurists* (Kehl: N.P. Engels, 2004).
[136] The drafters of AP I articulated specific elements of fair trial under Art 75(4) AP I to forestall derogation under Art 4 ICCPR: *Official Records*, above n 130, at 28.
[137] The prohibition of retroactive application of criminal law is designated as non-derogable in the ICCPR (Art 4), ACHR (Art 27), and ECHR (Arts 7 and 15).
[138] IACommHR, *Report on Terrorism and Human Rights*, OEA/Ser.L/V/II.116, 22 October 2002, para 261(b).

57 The HRCttee's General Comment 29 affirms the applicability of 'fundamental requirements of fair trial' during armed conflict and in time of occupation.[139] Yet the rights recognized as non-derogable are limited to three rights (the right of access to a court in the case of criminal proceedings, the right to be presumed innocent, and the right to habeas corpus or *amparo*),[140] none of which is expressly contained in GC IV.

58 The practice of IHRL suggests that any security courts, which are types of military tribunals, must satisfy the same requirements (most notably, independence and impartiality) as civilian tribunals.[141] Restricting access of defendants only to such military courts has earned a stern rebuke from the African Commission on Human and Peoples' Rights (ACommHPR)[142] and the IACommHR.[143] There is even jurisprudence which excludes outright military tribunals from trying civilians.[144]

c. General principles of criminal law

59 Articles 65 and 67 GC IV embody general principles of criminal law that must be complied with in criminal proceedings in occupied territories, including the *nullum crimen sine lege* principle and the ban on collective punishment. The IACommHR's *Report on Terrorism and Human Rights* contains a detailed inventory of non-derogable rights. It vouchsafes 'the fundamental principles of criminal law' as non-derogable, referring to those principles, as well as the principle of *non bis in idem*, the *nulla ponea sine lege* principle, and the presumption of innocence.[145]

60 Undoubtedly, the principle of *nullum crimen sine lege* is the cardinal principle,[146] of which the ban on retroactive application of penal laws is a part.[147] To shore up this principle, the drafters of the Geneva Conventions inserted the requirement of public notification *in writing* under Article 65 GC IV.[148] Accordingly, the validity of penal provisions may be contested if they are not published and brought to the knowledge of the inhabitants in their own language.[149]

61 Under Article 67 GC IV, the penalty must be proportionate to the offence. The prohibition of collective punishment[150] is placed under Article 33 paragraph 2 in Part III, Section I of GC IV, so as to highlight its marked significance in occupied territories and in territories of parties to the conflict.[151] Further, to supplement the general principles of criminal law, the drafters have reiterated that the Occupying Power must take into account the fact that the accused lack allegiance to it.[152]

---

[139] HRCttee, General Comment 29, States of Emergency (Art 4), 31 August 2001, para 16.

[140] Ibid. There is, however, a reference to the prohibition of collective punishment.

[141] HRCttee, General Comment 32, (Art 14) Right to Equality Before Courts and Tribunals and to Fair Trial, 24 July 2007, para 22; IACommHR, *Salinas v Peru*, Case 11.084, Rep No 27/94, 30 November 1994, Section V(3); ECtHR, *Martin v UK*, Judgment, 24 October 2006, para 44.

[142] ACommHPR, *Civil Liberties Organisation and others v Nigeria*, No 151/96, Decision, 15 November 1999, para 23.

[143] IACommHR, *Report on Terrorism and Human Rights*, above n 138, paras 230 and 261.

[144] ACommHPR, *Media Rights Agenda v Nigeria*, Com 224/98, 6 November 2000, para 62; IACtHR, *Cantoral Benavides case*, Judgment, 18 August 2000, Series C, No 69, paras 112–13.

[145] IACommHR, *Report on Terrorism and Human Rights*, above n 138, para 261(a).

[146] Art 65 second sentence GC IV; Art 67 first sentence GC IV; Art 75(4)(c) AP I.

[147] Art 65 second sentence GC IV.   [148] Pictet Commentary GCIV, at 338.

[149] The requirement of 'publication' was introduced by the US proposal at the Geneva Diplomatic Conference: Final Record, vol II-A, at 765 and 833.

[150] HRCttee, General Comment 29, above n 139, para 11 (describing it as non-derogable).

[151] See also Art 50 Hague Regulations; Art 75(4)(b) AP I.

[152] Art 67 second sentence GC IV. Final Record, vol II-A, at 765 and 833.

d. The right to trial by an independent, impartial, and regularly constituted court

The right to trial by an independent, impartial, and regularly constituted court is not expressly recognized under Article 66 GC IV. While there is a specific provision for prisoners of war (POWs) under GC III,[153] the absence of any counterpart for civilian detainees under GC IV is an oversight. However, this gap is filled by the *chapeau* of Article 75(4) AP I.[154] As in the case of other fair trial guarantees, elaborate meanings regarding the notions of independence and impartiality are inferable from the practice of the treaty-based bodies of IHRL.

e. Fair trial guarantees under Article 71 GC IV

i. Overview

Article 71 GC IV embodies the fair trial guarantees for accused persons in the occupied territories. Some fair trial rights, including the right to be presumed innocent, which are not explicitly contained in GC IV, may be considered inherent in the notion of 'a regular trial' within the meaning of Article 71 paragraph 1 GC IV.[155]

ii. The right to be informed of the nature and the cause of accusation

In occupied territory, Article 71 paragraph 2 GC IV guarantees the right of the accused to be informed of particulars of the charges or accusation.[156] This ought to be read in tandem with Article 75(4)(a) AP I. Under Article 71 paragraph 2 GC IV, the accused must be made privy to the nature and cause of accusation 'promptly' (or 'without delay' under Article 75(4)(a) AP I) and in a language that he or she understands.[157] Further, in the case of any disciplinary punishment that may be pronounced by the commandant of the place of internment, Article 123 paragraph 2 GC IV affirms the right of the accused internee to be given 'precise information' about the offences which he or she is accused of having committed.

iii. Notifications to the Protecting Power

The Occupying Power must notify the Protecting Power of all proceedings against protected persons, charges against whom may lead to the death penalty or a sentence of imprisonment of two years or more.[158] This is an improvement upon the draft text originating from the Stockholm text,[159] which confined the requirement of notification to cases involving charges of a grave nature.[160] In addition, the Protecting Power may request information on 'any other proceedings' instituted against protected persons, namely, cases of a less grave nature.[161] Article 136 GC IV requires National Information Bureaux to be apprised of all those pertinent judgments. Under Articles 137 paragraph 1 and 140, they must transmit the information on accused persons to the state of which they are nationals,

---

[153] Art 84 para 2 GC III.
[154] Further, this right is considered customary law since the post-Second World War war crimes trials: K. Dörmann, *Elements of War Crimes under the Rome Statute of the International Criminal Court: Sources and Commentary* (Cambridge: CUP, 2003), at 104–5.
[155] Pictet Commentary GC IV, at 354.
[156] See US Military Tribunal, Nuremberg, *The Justice Trial*, 17 February–4 December 1947, *Law Reports of Trials of Major War Criminals*, vol VI, (1948), 1–110; 14 *Annual Digest* (1947) 278.
[157] Pictet Commentary GC IV, at 354.   [158] Art 71 para 2 second sentence GC IV.
[159] ICRC, above n 4, at 133.   [160] Final Record, vol II-A, at 770 and 790.
[161] Art 71 para 2 third sentence GC IV.

66 With respect to the notifications of serious cases to the Protecting Power, Article 71 paragraph 3 furnishes a minimum time span of three weeks before the first hearing.[162] This is in order to assist the Protecting Power to study the case before the court hearing, which it may attend under Article 74. Procedurally, the notifications must contain at least the following elements:

— a description of the accused;
— the place of residence or detention;
— specific details of the charge(s), including the penal provisions under which the charge is instituted;
— the designation of the court that will undertake the hearing; and
— the venue and date of the first hearing.[163]

The second element (the place of residence or detention) ensures detainees' right to be visited by delegates of the Protecting Power and of the ICRC under Article 76 paragraph 6 GC IV.[164] At the opening of the trial, evidence must be adduced to show compliance with the requirements under Article 71 paragraph 3, failing which the hearing must be adjourned.[165]

iv. The right to trial without undue delay

67 Article 71 paragraph 2 GC IV, unlike Article 75(4) AP I, specifically recognizes the right of the accused to be tried 'as rapidly as possible'. Generally, it may be suggested that reasonableness with regard to the length of time may be determined by reference to the practice of international IHRL.[166] It may be proposed that the duration should be calculated from the time of the charge up to the final judgment, including the appeal.[167] Its reasonableness may hinge upon: (i) the complexity of the case; (ii) the behaviour of the accused; and (iii) the diligence of the authorities.[168]

f. The rights relating to means of defence

i. Overview

68 Article 72 GC IV contains several specific rights derived from the principle of equality of arms, which is inherent in the notion of a 'fair trial'.[169] While the second sentence of

---

[162] Committee III initially set the time limit as eight days, but in line with the draft text of current Art 104 GC III, the proposal to follow the three-week rule was adopted without any dissention: Final Record, vol II-A, at 801.

[163] Art 71 para 3 third sentence GC IV.

[164] This must also be read together with Art 143 GC IV.

[165] Art 71 para 3 second sentence GC IV.

[166] On one hand, it seems to be widely accepted that this right has hardened into customary law since the post-Second World War war crimes trials: Dörmann, above n 154, at 104–5. On the other hand, the specific question of the minimum length of time within which the accused should be brought to trial may be contested. At least in literal sense, it is true that the standard contained in Art 71 GC IV ('as rapidly as possible') is more stringent than the equivalent standard under Art 9(3) ICCPR ('within a reasonable time'): Ronen, above n 70, at 757.

[167] HRCttee, General Comment 13, 13 April 1984.

[168] See, e.g., ECtHR, *Tomasi v France*, Judgment, 27 August 1992, A241-A, para 102; IACtHR, *Genie Lacayo Case*, Judgment, 29 January 1997, Series C, No 30, para 77.

[169] HRCttee, No 779/1997, *Äärelä and Näkkäläjärvi v Finland*, 24 October 2001, para 7.4; ACommHPR, *Avocats Sans Frontières v Burundi*, No 231/99(2000), paras 26–7.

Article 105 paragraph 1 GC III recognizes the right of a POW to be apprised of defence rights 'in due time before the trial', there is no explicit counterpart to this right under Article 72 or any other provision of GC IV.[170] Nevertheless, by way of analogous interpretation, this right is deemed implicit under Article 72 GC IV.[171]

69 The rights of defence of the accused persons, or of their advocate or counsel, enunciated under this provision are:

— the right to present evidence necessary for their defence;
— the right to call witnesses;
— the right to be assisted by a qualified advocate or counsel of their own choice;
— the rights of the advocate or the counsel to visit the accused freely, and to enjoy facilities necessary for preparing the defence; and
— the right to an interpreter during preliminary investigations and during hearings in court.

Under Article 123 GC IV, protected persons who are accused of a disciplinary offence while interned under Article 68 (and Article 78) are entitled to the following rights:

— the right to be given an opportunity to explain their conduct and to defend themselves;
— the right to call witnesses; and
— the right to have recourse to the services of a qualified interpreter.

70 The rights of defence safeguarded under Article 72 GC IV may be compared to Article 75(4) AP I. Its subheading (a) mentions 'all necessary rights and means of defence' in a general manner, allowing this term to be used as an interpretive device for accommodating detailed elements developed in the practice of IHRL. Among the rights of defence contained in GC IV, the right to examine and to have examined witnesses is the only one that features expressly under Article 75(4) AP I (subheading (g)). The following analyses will focus on three of the above rights of defence that need more detailed explication.

ii. The right to defend oneself in person, or to be assisted by a lawyer of one's own choice

71 Under Article 72 paragraph 1 GC IV, accused persons have the right to 'present evidence necessary to their defence and [...] to be assisted by a qualified advocate or counsel of their own choice'. This is supplemented by counsel's right to visit accused persons, a right that mirrors the right of the latter to communicate freely with their counsel.[172] Access to lawyers may be exercised both before and during the trial. The Occupying Powers should follow the liberal practice of IHRL in requiring access to lawyers at the interrogation phase.[173]

---

[170] Another omission is that, as compared to Art 105 para 3 GC III, Art 72 GC IV does not recognize the right of counsel to have at least two weeks to prepare the defence before the start of the trial.

[171] Pictet Commentary GC IV, at 357.

[172] See HRCttee, General Comment 13, 13 April 1984; the Body of Principles for the Protection of All Persons under any Form of Detention or Imprisonment, UNGA Res 43/173, 9 December 1988, Principle 18; ACommHPR, *Principles and Guidelines on the Right to a Fair Trial and Legal Assistance in Africa*, 15–29 May 2003, Sections G and N, para 2. See also Art 67(1)(b) ICC Statute; Art 21(4)(b) ICTY Statute; Art 20(4)(b) ICTR Statute; Art 17(4)(b) Statute of SCSL.

[173] See, e.g., HRCttee, *Little v Jamaica*, No 283/1988, View of 1 November 1991, paras 8.3–8.4; ACHPR, *Avocats Sans Frontières v Burundi*, No 231/99, Decision, 23 October–6 November 2000, para 30; ECtHR, *Averill v United Kingdom*, Judgment, 6 June 2000, paras 57–61.

72   Under Article 72 paragraph 2, where the accused fail to choose an advocate or counsel, the Protecting Power can make the necessary appointment. However, if the accused face serious charges but the Protecting Power is not operative, it is the Occupying Power's duty to provide an advocate or counsel, with their consent. Whenever feasible, *free* legal assistance should be proffered, as recognized under IHRL.[174] The need for legal services free of charge ought to be assessed by reference to such factors as the complexity of the case and the seriousness of the offence.[175]

iii. The right to sufficient time and facilities to prepare the defence

73   Article 72 paragraph 1 GC IV guarantees the right of the accused to the 'necessary facilities' for preparing the defence, without, however, adverting to 'sufficient time'. Nevertheless, the requirement for necessary facilities for the defence under Article 72 GC IV ought to be construed as entailing this temporal element. Indeed, such an interpretation conforms to the customary norm that has developed through interaction with the practice of IHRL[176] and international criminal law (ICL).[177] While bearing in mind that this right is among those the interpretation of which differs widely as between a time of armed conflict and peacetime,[178] one may rely on the criteria developed by the ACommHPR in order to assess the adequacy of the time available for preparing a defence:

— the complexity of the case;
— the defendant's access to evidence;
— the length of time prior to proceedings; and
— prejudice to the defence.[179]

iv. The right to assistance of an interpreter or a translator

74   Under Article 72 paragraph 3 GC IV, the right of the accused to be assisted by an interpreter must be guaranteed during preliminary investigations and the hearing. An accused can nonetheless object to the interpreter at any time and ask for his or her replacement. Again, for elaborate elements of the right to assistance of an interpreter, reliance should be placed on the practice of IHRL.[180] Article 72 GC IV fails, however, to mention the right to assistance in translating documents necessary for a defence. Whenever the interest of justice requires, the Occupying Power should afford linguistic assistance to effectuate the right to 'necessary facilities for preparing the defence'.[181]

---

[174] Art 14(3)(d) ICCPR; Art 6(3)(c) ECHR; Art 8(2)(e) ACHR. See also IACtHR, *Exceptions to the Exhaustion of Domestic Remedies case*, Advisory Opinion, OC-11/90, 10 August 1990, paras 25–7. See further Art 67(1)(d) ICC Statute; Art 21(4)(d) ICTY Statute; Art 20(4)(d) ICTR Statute; Art 17(4)(d) SCSL Statute.

[175] See, e.g., HRCttee, *Currie v Jamaica*, No 377/1989, View of 29 March 1994, CCPR/C/50/D/377/1989, paras 13.2–13.4; ECtHR, *RD v Poland*, 18 December 2001, paras 47–52.

[176] Art 14(3)(b) ICCPR; Art 6(3)(b) ECHR; Art 8(2)(c) ACHR.

[177] Art 67(1)(b) ICC Statute; Art 21(4)(b) ICTY Statute; Art 20(4)(b) ICTR Statute; Art 17(4)(b) SCSL Statute.

[178] S. Sivakumaran, 'Courts of Armed Opposition Groups: Fair Trials or Summary Justice?', 7 *JICJ* (2009) 489, at 505.

[179] ACommHPR, *Principles and Guidelines on the Right to a Fair Trial and Legal Assistance in Africa*, 15–29 May 2003, N, para 3(c).

[180] Art 14(3)(f) ICCPR; Art 8(2)(a) ACHR; and Art 6(3)(e) ECHR. See also ECtHR, *Kamasinski v Austria*, Judgment, 19 December 1989, A 168, para 74. See also Art 67(1)(f) ICC Statute; Art 21(4)(f) ICTY Statute; Art 20(4)(f) ICTR Statute; Art 17(4)(f) SCSL Statute.

[181] Admittedly, there remains a question whether to translate not just oral statements, but also all documents employed as evidence.

g. The right of convicted persons to be informed of available remedies and of their time limits

Under Article 73 paragraph 1 GC IV and Article 75(4)(j) AP I, convicted persons have the right to be informed about any appeal and the right to petition, and of their time limits.[182] It ought to be noted that Article 73 paragraph 1 GC IV does not recognize the right of appeal as such,[183] but only the right to be informed of available remedies and their time limit. This can be seen from the wording 'the right of appeal provided for by the laws applied by the court'.[184] Moreover, the second sentence of Article 66 GC IV, which provides that '[c]ourts of appeal shall preferably sit in the occupied territory', does not require a system of appeal from trial courts. Even Article 75(4)(j) AP I is confined to recognizing the right to be advised of judicial (appeal or petition) or other remedies (pardon or reprieve),[185] and of their time limits. As noted by the ICRC Commentary to AP I, when the Additional Protocols were adopted, the majority of states had yet to recognize a right of appeal in their laws.[186] By contrast, the ICRC Customary International Humanitarian Law Study considers that the normative influence of IHRL[187] is sufficiently abundant and solid that the right of appeal proper now forms part of customary IHL.[188]

The second paragraph of Article 73 GC IV, which did not exist in the original Stockholm text,[189] consists of two distinct rules. First, if the appeal procedure is available, the Occupying Power must comply with the penal procedural rules embodied in Part III, Section III of GC IV. There are special procedural safeguards in the case of judgments pronouncing the death penalty or a sentence of imprisonment of two years' duration or more. The time limit for appeals must not run until the Protecting Power receives the notification of the judgment.[190] Secondly, in the absence of appeal procedures, convicted persons must be notified of the right to petition against the finding and sentence to the 'competent authority' of the Occupying Power.[191] Still, the effectiveness of such a non-judicial procedure is questionable. This chapter suggests that convicted persons or petitioners in occupied territory be allowed access to the Occupying Power's administrative and constitutional procedures to file their grievances with regard to measures taken in occupied territories.[192]

h. The right to public proceedings and notification of the Protecting Power

Article 74 paragraph 1 GC IV recognizes the right of representatives of the Protecting Power to attend the trial of the accused in occupied territory.[193] In practice, however, absent the nomination of the Protecting Power, this role has been assumed by the ICRC representatives.[194] Clearly, the rule contained in Article 74 paragraph 1 GC IV is for the

---

[182] IACommHR, *Report on Terrorism and Human Rights*, above n 138, para 261(c)(v) (recognizing non-derogability of this right).
[183] See, e.g., UK *Manual*, above n 19, at 297; and Israel, *Arjov*, above n 107, at 259.
[184] See also Art 106 GC III.   [185] ICRC Commentary APs, at 885.   [186] Ibid.
[187] IACommHR, *Report on Terrorism and Human Rights*, above n 138, para 261(c)(v).
[188] ICRC CIHL Study, vol I, at 369–70.
[189] Final Record, vol II-A, at 770.   [190] Art 74 para 2 fourth sentence GC IV.
[191] Art 73 para 2 second sentence GC IV.
[192] The Supreme Court of Israel operates as the High Court of Justice to undertake administrative review of the discretion exercised by the military courts: HCJ 460/86 *Matar v The Military Court in Shechem et al*, 40(3) PD 817, at 818–19; as cited in Dinstein, above n 13, at 139; and Ronen, above n 70, at 745.
[193] For POWs tried in occupied territories (or elsewhere), see Art 105 para 5 GC III.
[194] In this regard, see H.-P. Gasser, 'Respect for Fundamental Judicial Guarantees in Time of Armed Conflict: The Part Played by ICRC Delegates', 32 *IRRC* 287 (1992) 121.

purpose of preventing arbitrary detention of protected persons.[195] The presence of the Protecting Power can be denied only in the case of *in camera* proceedings for reasons of security. If excluded, the representatives must be notified of such exclusion, and of the date and place of trial.[196]

78   Admittedly, Article 74 paragraph 1 GC IV stops short of acknowledging the right to public proceedings. Yet this provision must be read in conjunction with the customary norm that parallels Article 75(4)(i) AP I, which endorses the right of persons prosecuted for an offence to have the judgment pronounced publicly.

79   Under Article 74 paragraph 2 GC IV, judgments involving the death sentence or imprisonment for two years or more must be communicated to the Protecting Power 'as rapidly as possible'.[197] This rule complements the requirement of notification under Article 71 paragraph 2 second sentence.[198] This notification must be made irrespective of the presence of the Protecting Power's representatives at the hearings.[199] Such information on convicted persons, including the place where their sentences are to be served, is essential for the right to visit of the Protecting Power and the ICRC in accordance with Articles 76 paragraph 6 and 143 GC IV.[200] In the event that the sentences handed down are shorter than two years' imprisonment, records of such judgments must be kept by the court and be available for examination by representatives of the Protecting Power.[201]

i. *The right to have time spent in custody and on trial deducted from the period of imprisonment*

80   Under Article 69 GC IV, those convicted and sentenced to imprisonment are entitled to have time spent under arrest and on trial deducted from their final sentence. This provision did not appear in the Stockholm text. At the Diplomatic Conference, the text, which was initially attached as the last sentence of draft Article 74 paragraph 2,[202] was transformed into a separate provision.[203]

VII. Sanctions, penalties, humane treatment, and handover

a. *Sanctions for minor offences*

81   The first paragraph of Article 68 GC IV, which addresses offences that do not result in serious consequences for the Occupying Power, contemplates punishment based on 'simple' imprisonment or internment.[204] Those persons guilty of minor offences and sentenced to 'internment' can take advantage of Article 76 paragraph 1, under which such persons must be, 'if possible', kept separate from common criminals. In contrast, graver offences are punishable with harsher penalties. The offenders may be sentenced to long-term imprisonment, solitary confinement, 'penal servitude',[205] and even capital punishment, under the conditions stipulated in Article 68 paragraphs 2–4.

---

[195] ICRC CIHL Study, vol I, at 345–6.   [196] Art 74 para 1 GC IV.
[197] Art 74 para 2 first sentence GC IV.   [198] See Final Record, vol II-A, at 770.
[199] Pictet Commentary GC IV, at 360.   [200] Ibid.
[201] Art 74 para 2 third sentence GC IV.
[202] See Final Record, vol III, Annexes, at 144, para 309.   [203] Final Record, vol II-A, at 801.
[204] At the Diplomatic Conference, some delegates described the measure of 'simple' imprisonment as imprisonment 'of the least severe kind': Pictet Commentary GC IV, at 344.
[205] Ibid, at 346. This sanction excludes deportation, as Art 76 requires the convicted persons to serve in the occupied territory: ibid.

The nature of sanction envisaged by the first paragraph encompasses both imprisonment, which is a penal sanction, and internment, which, by contrast, is a preventive administrative measure akin to the regime envisaged under Article 78 GC IV. Occupation courts can subject persons guilty of minor offences to the internment regime governed by Part III Section IV of GC IV,[206] or convert a sentence of imprisonment to one of internment for the same duration.[207] Still, unlike internment as an administrative measure under Article 78, in cases where internment is used as a penalty for a minor offence, judges must intervene at the outset to determine its length.[208] Under the Stockholm text of Article 68(1), only internment was contemplated for minor offences. However, at the Diplomatic Conference, 'simple imprisonment' was added as an alternative,[209] because internment as an administrative sanction was considered inadequate by some Western delegates.[210]

b. Death penalty

i. General remarks

Article 68 paragraph 2 GC IV envisages the possibility that the military court in the occupied territory may impose a capital punishment on protected persons who are convicted of any of three serious offences:

— espionage;
— 'serious acts of sabotage against the military installations of the Occupying Power'; and
— 'intentional offences which have caused the death of one or more persons'.

Where the death penalty is yet to be abolished in the occupied territory, local courts (apart from occupation courts or other military tribunals) retain their competence to apply it to cases of felony which are based on local criminal laws and are unrelated to the security of the occupied territory.[211]

With respect to sabotage, the adjective 'serious' was added by the delegates at the Diplomatic Conference to forestall the abuse of capital punishment. Destroying an air base or a strategically important line of communication is 'serious'.[212] In contrast, such individual acts as refusal to work or obey orders is insufficient, whatever 'damage' this may cause.[213]

ii. Local law condition

The application of the death penalty is subject to the proviso that any of the three offences described above was punishable by death under the law of the occupied state before the beginning of the occupation. If the occupied state has left the occupied territory without any option of capital punishment, then the Occupying Power is disqualified from reintroducing it.[214]

This 'local law' qualification was, however, a bone of contention at the Diplomatic Conference. At Committee III, some Western delegations found it illogical to make the availability of the death penalty depend on the occupied state's legislation, rather than on the laws and customs of war.[215] There was also an objection that any state about to be occupied would abolish the death penalty just before its territory was

---

[206] Ibid, at 343. [207] Art 68 para 1 third sentence. [208] Gasser, above n 59, at 307–8.
[209] Final Record, vol II-A, at 765. [210] Ibid, at 674 (UK Delegation).
[211] Dinstein, above n 13, at 145. [212] Pictet Commentary GC IV, at 344. [213] Ibid.
[214] Dinstein, above n 13, at 144. [215] Final Record, vol II-A, at 834.

overrun, to prevent its nationals being sentenced to death.[216] The dissidents' main intention was to retain a broad possibility of applying capital punishment when confronted with security threats in occupied territory. Even at the subsequent Plenary Meeting, 'Anglo-Saxon' countries (Canada, New Zealand, the UK, and the US) unsuccessfully endeavoured to delete this local law condition,[217] prompting some of them eventually to attach reservations.[218] By contrast, most delegates regarded the local law condition essential for the protection of offenders who acted with patriotic motives.[219]

iii. Acknowledging the lack of a duty of allegiance

87 Under Article 68 paragraph 3 GC IV, local courts or occupation courts must refrain from pronouncing capital punishment unless they duly acknowledge that the accused, being non-nationals of the Occupying Power, are not bound by a duty of allegiance. The importance of this criterion is clear from its inclusion in Article 118,[220] and the comparable requirement under the second sentence of Article 67.[221]

iv. Non-application of capital punishment to special categories of offenders

88 Article 68 paragraph 4 GC IV makes it clear that the death penalty cannot be pronounced with regard to a person under the age of 18 years at the time of the offence. The delegates at the Diplomatic Conference were not unanimous, however, with the US delegation characterizing this condition as 'sweeping'.[222]

89 This condition is supplemented by Article 76(3) AP I, which prohibits the execution of pregnant women and mothers with infants, and calls on the Occupying Power not to pronounce the death penalty against such women.[223] The first sentence of this text, which deals with pronouncement of capital punishment against such women, mixes the recommendatory language 'To the maximum extent feasible' with the mandatory word 'shall'. It stops short of outright proscribing the execution of such women. This should not, however, be construed as allowing the Occupying Power merely to postpone the execution of expectant women or mothers with infants who have yet to be weaned. They must never be executed, even after their infant children are no longer dependent.[224]

v. Penal procedures for protected persons sentenced to death

90 Under Article 75 paragraph 1 GC IV, protected persons sentenced to death have the right to petition for a pardon or reprieve. According to Article 73, the right of petition must always be guaranteed, in contrast to a right of appeal that may be exercised only where available. While appeals for a pardon or reprieve may be made in respect of other sentences, such appeals are mandatory in the case of capital punishment. Petition procedures are left to the Occupying Power's discretion.[225] Under Article 75 paragraph 2, the death penalty

---

[216] Pictet Commentary GC IV, at 345.
[217] Final Record, vol III, Annexes, at 141, para 301. Another (unsuccessful) proposal was to cover 'attempted homicide resulting in grave injury' as an offence punishable by the death penalty.
[218] Ibid, vol I, at 346, 349, 352–3. The UK reservation to Art 68 GC IV was withdrawn on 15 December 1971. In contrast, the US reservation to Art 68 GC IV on 2 August 1955 is still maintained. See the ICRC website, available at <http://www.icrc.org/applic/ihl/ihl.nsf/States.xsp?xp_viewStates=XPages_NORMStatesParties&xp_treatySelected=380>.
[219] Pictet Commentary GC IV, at 345.   [220] See also Arts 87 and 100 GC III.
[221] Pictet Commentary GC IV, at 346.
[222] Final Record, vol II-A, at 673.
[223] See Art 6(5) ICCPR which contains the ban on carrying out the death penalty against pregnant women.
[224] ICRC Commentary APs, at 895.   [225] Pictet Commentary GC IV, at 362.

may be applied only after six months from the date of the Protecting Power's receiving notification either of the final judgment, or of an order denying a pardon or reprieve.[226]

91 The minimum six-month suspension rule is, however, subject to the exceptions under Article 75 paragraph 3, a clause introduced at the Diplomatic Conference.[227] Despite its potentially controversial nature, this paragraph did not attract much discussion.[228] Under this paragraph, the period of suspension may be reduced in cases of 'grave emergency involving an organized threat to the security of the Occupying Power or its forces'. Such 'grave emergency' must be 'particularly serious and critical'.[229] The application of capital punishment to a convicted person should be strictly proportionate ('really necessary') to the objective of repressing disturbances and preventing any further sacrifice.[230] The legality of such an exceptional measure ought to be assessed on an individual basis.[231] Article 75 paragraph 3 provides procedural safeguards, requiring the Protecting Powers to be informed of such a reduction, and accorded 'reasonable time and opportunity' to make representations to 'the competent occupying authorities'.

c. Humane treatment of the accused and the convicted

92 Article 76 GC IV is a compendium text governing the treatment of protected persons accused of offences, as well as of those who are convicted.[232] Due account should be taken of the relevant international rules for detained persons.[233] Under Article 76 paragraph 1, convicted persons must serve their sentences in the occupied territory. Moreover, any sentence of imprisonment imposed on them must be served there, as is implicit in the prohibition of deportation under Article 49.[234]

93 Under the second sentence of Article 76 paragraph 1, whenever feasible, protected persons convicted under the Occupying Power's penal law should be segregated from ordinary criminals, because their offences are considered to have been motivated by patriotism.[235] Detained persons must be guaranteed sufficient conditions of food and hygiene to sustain their good health. Their conditions must be equivalent to those obtaining in the occupied state's penitentiary systems.[236] As with female POWs regulated under Article 25 paragraph 4 GC III, Article 76 paragraph 4 GC IV demands that the place of confinement of women must be set apart from that of men and be under direct female supervision. Similarly, the Occupying Power must ensure that 'proper regard' is had to special need of minor detainees under Article 76 paragraph 5. Further, all those detainees have the right to receive appropriate spiritual assistance under Article 76 paragraph 3. To reinforce those safeguards, they have the right to be visited by delegates of the Protecting Power and the ICRC under Article 76 paragraph 6, who monitor their conditions under Article 143.

d. The duty to hand over accused or convicted persons

94 Under Article 77 GC IV, upon the close of occupation, protected persons accused of offences or convicted by the occupation courts must be handed over to the authorities of the liberated occupied state, with the pertinent records.[237] This obligation is not limited

---

[226] Final Record, vol II-A, at 835. [227] Ibid, vol III, Annexes, at 144–5, para 310.
[228] Ibid, vol II-A, at 771. [229] Pictet Commentary GC IV, at 362. [230] Ibid.
[231] Ibid, at 363. [232] Final Record, vol II-A, at 790.
[233] See, e.g., Body of Principles for the Protection of All Persons under any Form of Detention or Imprisonment, above n 172.
[234] Pictet Commentary GC IV, at 363. [235] Ibid, at 363–4.
[236] Art 76 para 1 second sentence GC IV. [237] Final Record, vol II-A, at 772 and 835.

to accused persons awaiting trial. It also covers those who are convicted and serving sentences.[238]

C. Relevance in Non-International Armed Conflicts

95   The analysis now turns to the question whether the IHL rules discussed above in relation to the legal regime of occupation may be applied by analogy to NIAC.[239] It should be noted that the Lieber Code (1863) was crafted for the purpose of application to the US Civil War. Armed opposition groups may modify the legal order[240] through the exercise of de facto legislative, administrative, and judicial functions within the segment of the territory they control.[241] In the case of prolonged territorial control, it becomes a practical necessity to enact their 'laws' regulating the social and economic affairs of the inhabitants, and to implement administrative and judicial measures.[242] This does not suggest that they have a right or duty to do so pursuant to the criteria under Article 64 GC IV.[243] At least we can say, however, that under IHL, they are not prohibited from doing so.[244] Even then, their capacity ought to be assessed in the specific context, taking into account the degree of territorial control and their available resources.[245]

96   Armed groups may take the initiative to establish courts that exercise civil and criminal jurisdiction, as well as courts which, akin to occupation courts, try offences of security/penal laws. The rationale for such initiatives may be found in the term 'regularly constituted court' under Common Article 3 of the Geneva Conventions. This term should be read sufficiently widely to embrace a court of an armed group established under its 'laws', going beyond a court grounded on national laws and procedures.[246]

97   Clearly, armed groups' courts must be equipped with fair trial guarantees.[247] They are bound by the customary rules derived not only from Common Article 3 of the Geneva Conventions (and Article 75 AP I), but also from Article 6(2) AP II which requires 'a court

---

[238] See also Pictet Commentary GC IV, at 366.

[239] At the Conference of Government Experts (1971), when ascertaining the scope of draft AP II, delegates expressly referred to the word 'occupation' with respect to the territory controlled by an armed group: ICRC, *Conference of Government Experts on the Reaffirmation and Development of International Humanitarian Law Applicable in Armed Conflicts*, Report on the Work of the Conference (Geneva: ICRC, 1971), at 63–4, CE/Com.II/13 rev 1.

[240] Bothe/Partsch/Solf, at 651.

[241] For legislation by armed opposition groups, see, e.g., Liberation Tigers of Tamil Eelam, 'Tamil Eelam Child Protection Act' (Act No 3 of 2006); and other examples cited in S. Sivakumaran, 'Lessons for the Law of Armed Conflict from Commitments of Armed Groups: Identification of Legitimate Targets and Prisoners of War', 93 *IRRC* 882 (2011) 463, at 467. For measures relating to detention and internment, see L. Zegveld, *Accountability of Armed Opposition Groups in International Law* (Cambridge: CUP, 2002), at 65–6; D. Fleck, 'The Law of Non-International Armed Conflict', in Fleck (ed), above n 59, 605, at 628.

[242] Sivakumaran, above n 178, at 494.   [243] Ibid, at 496 and 498.   [244] Ibid, at 498.

[245] A. Roberts and S. Sivakumaran, 'Lawmaking by Nonstate Actors: Engaging Armed Groups in the Creation of International Humanitarian Law', 37 *Yale JIL* (2012) 107, at 140.

[246] Sivakumaran, above n 178, at 499–500. *Contra*, ICRC CIHL Study, at 355; A.M. La Rosa and C. Wuerzner, 'Armed Groups, Sanctions and the Implementation of International Humanitarian Law', 90 *IRRC* 870 (2008) 327, at 340.

[247] Dörmann, above n 154, at 412.

offering the essential guarantees of independence and impartiality'.[248] The applicability of Article 6 AP II to courts of armed groups is borne out in the draft records of Article 6(2)(c),[249] with the terms 'national and international laws' in the draft text replaced by the words 'under the law'.[250] What components of fair trial guarantees are 'indispensable' within the meaning of Common Article 3 is ascertainable through a *renvoi* to Article 6(2) AP II and Article 75 AP I. Moreover, since Article 6 AP II is premised on Articles 14 and 15 ICCPR, the practice of IHRL can assist in identifying elements of due process rights.[251]

D. Legal Consequences of a Violation

I. Overview

Violations of the above-mentioned rules relating to legislative power and judicial guarantees in the occupied territories constitute internationally wrongful acts. The Occupying Power would be obliged, under the law on state responsibility, to cease and not to repeat such internationally wrongful acts, and where necessary to make reparations for any injury caused by those acts.[252] In this section, however, the discussion will focus on war crimes, as salient examples of the legal ramifications that would arise if those rules were breached. 98

Wilfully depriving protected persons of 'the rights of fair and regular trial' is a grave breach under Article 147 GC IV and Article 85(4)(e) AP I, and a war crime under Article 8(2)(a)(vi) of the ICC Statute. It may be argued that those war crimes are the serious breaches of obligations that arise under the peremptory norms of general international law. These obligations generate *erga omnes* effect on all states. Further, when civilians are denied access to local tribunals in occupied territories, there may arise the war crime of '[d]eclaring abolished, suspended or inadmissible in a court of law the rights and actions of the nationals of the hostile party' under Article 8(2)(b)(xiv) of the ICC Statute. 99

II. Elements of the war crime of denying fair trial guarantees

The ICC *Elements of Crimes* suggest that for the purpose of the war crime under Article 8(2)(a)(vi) of the ICC Statute, the fair trial rights laid down in GC IV (and GC III) are not exhaustive. Its first element reads, 'The perpetrator deprived one or more persons of a fair and regular trial by denying judicial guarantees as defined, *in particular*, in the third 100

---

[248] According to the *Elements of Crimes* concerning Art 8(2)(c)(iv) ICC Statute, that the court is not 'regularly constituted' means that it does not provide 'the essential guarantees of independence and impartiality' as provided in Art 6 AP II.
[249] See *Official Records of the Diplomatic Conference on the Reaffirmation and Development of International Humanitarian Law Applicable in Armed Conflicts*, vol IX, at 300–1, 314, CDDH/I/SR.63, paras 59–64 and SR.64, paras 54 and 79 (Committee I); *Official Records of the Diplomatic Conference on the Reaffirmation and Development of International Humanitarian Law Applicable in Armed Conflicts*, vol VII, at 92–4, CDDH/SR.50, paras 56–78 (Plenary); ICRC Commentary APs, at 1399, para 4605.
[250] This is so even though the French text, equally authentic, retains the original wording '*d'après le droit national ou international*'.
[251] Bothe/Partsch/Solf, at 650–1.
[252] See Arts 28, 30, and 31 of the Articles on Responsibility of States for Internationally Wrongful Acts adopted by the International Law Commission on 10 August 2001: *Report of the International Law Commission, Fifty-third Session*, A/56/10, Ch IV.

and the fourth Geneva Conventions of 1949'.²⁵³ Indeed, wilful deprivation of other essential components of due process rights, such as those enumerated in the 1977 Additional Protocols, suffices for the *actus reus* of this war crime.²⁵⁴

101   Drawing on Article 75(4) AP I to verify the contents of 'judicial guarantees' is all the more necessary because the list of such guarantees contained in GC IV is shorter even than the rights enumerated in GC III. Three rights are expressly safeguarded for POWs in GC III, but not in respect of civilians under occupation in GC IV:

— the right to be judged by an independent and impartial court;²⁵⁵
— the right to be informed of defence rights;²⁵⁶ and
— freedom from double jeopardy (*non bis in idem*).²⁵⁷

To these may be added the rights of the accused guaranteed in the Additional Protocols:

— the right to be presumed innocent;²⁵⁸
— the right to be present at one's trial;²⁵⁹
— the right not to testify against oneself or to confess guilt;²⁶⁰ and
— the right to have the judgment pronounced publicly.²⁶¹

This exemplary catalogue of the contents of judicial guarantees may be amplified through the evolution of IHRL.

102   In the case of courts of armed groups in NIAC, divesting the accused of fair trial guarantees may constitute a war crime under Article 8(2)(c)(iv) of the ICC Statute, the provision that essentially embodies Common Article 3 paragraph 1(1)(d) of the Geneva Conventions. The list of 'all judicial guarantees which are generally recognized as indispensable' under this provision is open-ended.²⁶² Ascertaining these elements may be facilitated by reference to the non-exhaustive minimum elements under Article 6(2) AP II, the customary law equivalents to Article 75(4) AP I, and the practice of IHRL.

E. Critical Assessment

103   Nowadays, the Occupying Powers find themselves to be in greater need than before of invoking the exceptional grounds for prescriptive power under Article 64 GC IV. This is partly because of welfare notions in cases of prolonged occupation, or partly due to the controversial scenario of 'transformative' occupation.²⁶³ The emergence of UN post-conflict administrations, whose laws are often modelled on the law of occupation, adds a new momentum to the dynamism of the law of occupation, marking a departure from the 'conservationist' premise²⁶⁴ under Article 43 of the Hague Regulations.

---

²⁵³ Emphasis added.   ²⁵⁴ Dörmann, above n 154, at 100.   ²⁵⁵ Art 84 para 2 GC III.
²⁵⁶ Art 105 para 1 GC III.
²⁵⁷ Art 86 GC III. See, however, Art 117 para 3 GC IV for interned civilians.
²⁵⁸ Art 75(4)(d) AP I; Art 6(2)(d) AP II.   ²⁵⁹ Art 75(4)(e) AP I; Art 6(2)(e) AP II.
²⁶⁰ Art 75(4)(f) AP I; Art 6(2)(f) AP II.   ²⁶¹ Art 75(4)(i) AP I.
²⁶² Dörmann, above n 154, at 409–10.
²⁶³ N. Bhuta, 'The Antinomies of Transformative Occupation', 16 *EJIL* (2005) 721.
²⁶⁴ As regards the critique of the application of the law of occupation by analogy to the post-conflict UN administration, see E. de Wett, 'The Direct Administration of Territories by the United Nations and its Member States in the Post Cold War Era: Legal Bases and Implications for National Laws', 8 *Max Planck United Nations Yearbook* (2004) 292. For the so-called 'conservationist' principle, see G. Fox, 'The Occupation of Iraq', 36 *Georgetown JIL* (2005) 195.

As discussed above, many detailed elements of fair trial guarantees, which are derived 104 from the 'practice' of the treaty-based bodies of IHRL, are recognized as customary IHL. In view of the *lex specialis* maxim, which necessitates a specific contextual analysis of the interaction between IHL and IHRL,[265] the fair trial guarantees under GC IV (and their customary concomitants) are considered as serving as a 'prism' for '*filtering*' (rather than funnelling) the components fleshed out in IHRL.[266] How such a process of filtering can be rationalized depends on the particular circumstances. For the issue of judicial guarantees, the fulcrum of their normative weight should rest on the generic term, 'the generally recognized principles of regular judicial procedure', under the *chapeau* of Article 75(4) AP I. Evidently, its non-exhaustive minimum safeguards leave potential for ongoing elaboration.

With respect to punishment imposed on offenders, one might recall that one of the 105 three categories of offences susceptible to capital punishment under Article 68 paragraph 2 GC IV is 'intentional offences which have caused the death of one or more persons'. Such offences, if carried out against other civilians or civilian members of the occupying administration, may constitute a war crime. Yet we should recall that capital punishment is excluded under the ICC Statute. With the abolitionist tendency preponderant in IHRL,[267] the Occupying Power should desist from capital punishment, even if this is a lawful option.

Turning to NIAC, it ought to be noted that armed groups are not *ipso facto* impeded 106 from enforcing disciplinary and criminal proceedings against offenders in accordance with IHL.[268] Such offenders may be captured soldiers of government forces, those of other armed groups, or members of their own forces. At least in the area where they exert a stable and sustained control, armed groups should be able to conduct trials, while affording due process guarantees. As a logical further step, armed groups should be able to prosecute war crimes.[269] The defensibility of such a proposal is reinforced with the line between war crimes committed in IAC and in NIAC becoming less marked under customary law. All these factors suggest that, as a policy, enabling armed groups to assume the role of 'stakeholders' in IHL is essential for bolstering their compliance with obligations.[270] The time may have come to allow them to enact and implement their 'laws' in conformity with IHL, and to ascertain what can be drawn from their 'practice' in shaping customary IHL.[271]

YUTAKA ARAI-TAKAHASHI

---

[265] A. Lindroos, 'Addressing Norm Conflicts in Fragmented Legal System: The Doctrines of *Lex Specialis*', 74 *NJIL* (2005) 27, at 42. See also ICTY, *The Prosecutor v Dragoljub Kunarac et al*, Trial Chamber Judgment, IT-96-23-T&IT-96-23/1-T, 22 February 2001, para 471.

[266] See Dinstein, above n 13, at 86 (emphasis added).

[267] See Second Optional Protocol to the ICCPR; Sixth Protocol to the ECHR; Thirteenth Protocol to the ECHR; and Protocol to the American Convention on Human Rights to Abolish the Death Penalty.

[268] Sivakumaran, above n 178, at 498.   [269] Ibid, 511.

[270] M. Sassòli, 'The Implementation of International Humanitarian Law: Current and Inherent Challenges', 10 *YIHL* (2007) 45, at 65.

[271] See G. de Beco, 'Compliance with International Humanitarian Law by Non-State Actors', 18 *JIL of Peace & Armed Conflict* (2005) 190, at 191–2.

Chapter 69. The Administration of Occupied Territory

	MN
A. Introduction	1
I. 'Administration' in the case of belligerent occupation	1
II. History and sources	3
III. The general principles of the law of occupation and their relevance for territorial administration	8
B. Meaning and Application	14
I. Occupation as a temporary situation	14
a. Respect for the legal and institutional status quo	14
b. Protection of the status quo: 'inviolability of rights' and respect for loyalty to the displaced government	18
II. The elements of the duty of good governance	33
a. Maintenance and development of an adequate normative order	38
b. An adequate administrative apparatus	42
c. A functioning court system ensuring respect for the rule of law	44
d. Respect for the fundamental rights of the population	46
e. Effective law enforcement respecting at the same time human rights	59
f. Adequate food and shelter for the population, adequate living conditions in general	65
g. Protection of private property	69
h. Health	71
i. Access to humanitarian assistance	73
j. Education	76
k. Protection of family rights	78
l. The possibility of religious life	79
m. Use of natural resources and protection of the environment	81
n. Cultural property	90
o. Public revenue	93
p. International relations	95
III. The protection of the interests of the Occupying Power	101
a. Security	101
b. The sustenance of the army of occupation	104
C. Legal Consequences of a Violation	106
D. Critical Assessment	111

Select Bibliography

Ben-Naftali, O./Shany, Y., 'Living in Denial: The Application of Human Rights in the Occupied Territories', 37 *Israel Law Review* (2003–4) 17

Benvenisti, E., *The International Law of Occupation* (2nd edn, Oxford: OUP 2012)

Boon, K.E., 'The Future of the Law of Occupation', 46 *CanYIL* (2008) 107

Dinstein, Y., *The International Law of Belligerent Occupation* (Cambridge: CUP, 2009)

Harpaz, G./Shany, Y., 'The Israeli Supreme Court and the Incremental Expansion of the Scope of Discretion under Belligerent Occupation Law', 43 *Israel Law Review* (2010) 514

Kolb, R./Vité, S., *Le droit de l'occupation militaire* (Brussels: Bruylant, 2009)

Parameswaran, K., *Besatzungsrecht im Wandel. Aktuelle Herausforderungen des Rechts der militärischen Besetzung* (Baden-Baden: Nomos, 2008)

Playfair, E. (ed), *International Law and the Administration of Occupied Territories: Two Decades of Israeli Occupation of the West Bank and the Gaza Strip* (Oxford: Clarendon Press, 1992)

Sassòli, M., 'Legislation and Maintenance of Public Order and Civil Life by Occupying Powers', 16 *EJIL* (2005) 661

Schmitt, M.N. (ed), *Detention and Occupation in International Humanitarian Law* (Farnham: Ashgate, 2012)

Spoerri, P., 'The Law of Occupation', in A. Clapham and P. Gaeta (eds), *The Oxford Handbook of International Law in Armed Conflict* (Oxford: OUP, 2014) 182

Talmon, S. (ed), *The Governance of Occupied Territory in Contemporary International Law* (Oxford: Hart Publishing, 2012)

Vité, S., 'L'articulation du droit international humanitaire et des droits économiques, sociaux et culturels en temps d'occupation', in M.D. Voyame et al (eds), *International Law, Conflict and Development: The Emergence of an Holistic Approach in International Affairs* (Leiden: Nijhoff, 2010) 19

A. Introduction

I. 'Administration' in the case of belligerent occupation

1   When territory of an enemy belligerent is invaded in the course of an armed conflict, the establishment of *de facto* control triggers the application of the law of occupation.[1] This means, inter alia, that the Occupying Power is responsible for 'public order and safety' in the territory.[2] This situation may be of a short duration, but there are also cases of long-term occupation. In order to fulfil this obligation, especially in the case of long-term occupation, the law of occupation, for practical reasons, requires the Occupying Power to establish some kind of permanent set-up for the administration of the occupied territory. To the extent that the Occupying Power cannot, or is not willing to, allow the pre-existing institutions of the occupied territory to continue to function, it will have to establish its own administration. The purpose of this chapter is to examine the legal issues involved in this type of territorial administration. International law must accommodate conflicting interests: the interests of the state whose territorial control has been displaced by a foreign army, at least for the time being, the interest of the Occupying Power, and the interests of the population which needs adequate living conditions and may be torn between the two states.

2   There are situations where similar conflicting interests are present, but which have to be distinguished because their legal basis is different. The first is the treaty-based presence of foreign forces, a 'pacific occupation'.[3] There is also a widespread practice to establish an international territorial administration as a measure to restore peace in a given area. The basis for the latter type of administration is usually a decision of an international organization, in most cases accepted by the state or states concerned.[4] Such

---

[1] E. Benvenisti, 'Occupation, Belligerent', in MPEPIL, para 4; Y. Dinstein, *The International Law of Belligerent Occupation* (Cambridge: CUP, 2009), at 42.

[2] Art 43 Hague Regulations.

[3] E. Benvenisti, 'Occupation, Pacific', in MPEPIL. For a basic categorization of various forms of military presence, see also M. Bothe, *Streitkräfte internationaler Organisationen* (Cologne/Berlin: Heymanns Verlag, 1968), at 88.

[4] M. Benzing, 'International Administration of Territories', in MPEPIL; on the question of the similarities or dissimilarities between these situations and belligerent occupation *stricto sensu*, see A. Roberts, 'What Is a Military Occupation?', 55 *BYBIL* (1984) 249, at 289 ff; R. Kolb, 'Etude sur l'occupation et sur l'article 47 de la IVème Convention de Genève du 12 août 1949 relative à la protection des personnes civiles en temps de

situations are outside the scope of the present chapter, but where appropriate, reference is made to similar problems arising in such cases. Examples of this type of foreign presence in a given territory are the administration of the territory of Kosovo after 1999[5] and the regime of public authority established in Iraq after October 2003.[6] Most cases of what is called transformative occupation fall within this category. Their legal regime is determined by the relevant decision of the organization. But lacunae in that regime may, if appropriate, be filled by reference to the law of occupation.[7]

II. History and sources

Belligerent occupation is a rather old phenomenon in armed conflict, yet its legal regime as we know it today developed during the nineteenth century.[8] The basic principles of the law of occupation were already formulated as customary law in the earlier restatements and codification of the law of armed conflict: in the Brussels Declaration of 1874,[9] in the Oxford Manual of the *Institut de droit international* 1880,[10] and then in the Hague Regulations on the Law of Land Warfare of 1899 and 1907 which formulate the fundamental principles of occupation law in a concise, even minimalist, way.[11]

Although large parts of Western Europe were occupied during the First World War, no attempt at a new formulation of the law of occupation was made between the two World Wars.[12] The painful experiences of the Second World War,[13] however, triggered the development of new rules additional to the Hague Regulations, which are found in Geneva Convention (GC) IV.[14] The general rules of the Hague Regulations nevertheless

---

guerre: le degré d'intangibilité des droits en territoire occupé', 10 *African Yearbook of International Law* (2002) 267, at 282 ff; M. Sassòli, 'Legislation and Maintenance of Public Order and Civil Life by Occupying Powers', 16 *EJIL* (2005) 661, at 686.

[5] UNSC Res 1244, 10 June 1999, paras 3–5.

[6] After the US–British invasion of Iraq, which started on 29 March 2003, the invading forces soon gained *de facto* control over Iraqi territory. This was a normal belligerent occupation. In this regard, UNSC Res 1483, 22 May 2003, recalled the obligations existing under the Hague Regulations and the GCs, expressly referring to the responsibilities of Occupying Powers. However, UNSC Res 1511 of 16 October 2003, para 13 then authorizes a multinational force, which gives a different basis to the foreign military presence in Iraq, thus putting into question the application of the law of occupation. The latter resolution is reaffirmed by UNSC Res 1546, 8 June 2004, para 9. See M.R. Hover, 'The Occupation of Iraq: A Military Perspective on Lessons Learned', 94 *IRRC* 885 (2012) 339; K. Watkin, 'Use of Force during Occupation: Law Enforcement and Conduct of Hostilities', 94 *IRRC* 885 (2012) 267, at 279.

[7] P. Spoerri, 'The Law of Occuption', in A. Clapham and P. Gaeta (eds), *The Oxford Handbook of International Law in Armed Conflict* (Oxford: OUP, 2014) 182, at 191.

[8] Benvenisti, above n 1, para 2; E. Benvenisti, *The International Law of Occupation* (2nd edn, Oxford: OUP, 2012), at 21; R. Kolb and S. Vité, *Le droit de l'occupation militaire* (Brussels: Bruylant, 2009), at 19 ff; Y. Arai-Takahashi, 'Preoccupied with Occupation: Critical Examinations of Historical Development of the Law of Occupation', 94 *IRRC* 885 (2012) 51, at 55; G.N. Barrie, 'The International Law Relating to Belligerent Occupation in the Advent of the Twenty-first Century', *Tydskrif vir die Suid-Afrikaanse reg* (2012) 433, at 435 ff.

[9] Arts 1–8, D. Schindler and J. Toman, *The Laws of Armed Conflicts, A Collection of Conventions, Resolutions and Other Documents* (4th edn, Boston, Mass: Martinus Nijhoff, 2004), at 21.

[10] Arts 41–60, ibid, at 29.   [11] Kolb and Vité, above n 8, at 31 ff.

[12] In contradistinction to the law relating to the fate of the wounded and sick and of prisoners of war which was the object of an update through the 1929 GCs. On the difference as to the development of the law relating to prisoners and wounded and sick on the one hand and the law of occupation on the other, see A. Becker, 'The Dilemmas of Protecting Civilians in Occupied Territory: The Precursory Example of World War I', 94 *IRRC* 885 (2012) 117; see also Arai-Takahashi, above n 8, at 63.

[13] See, e.g., US Military Tribunal, *US v Wilhelm List et al (Hostages Case)*, Judgment, 19 February 1948.

[14] Spoerri, above n 7, at 184.

remain relevant. Additional Protocol (AP) I adds only a few details to this body of law. These rules do not specifically address the 'administration' of the occupied territory. The regime of administration has to be derived from the said general rules of the Hague Regulations through their interpretation. Norms concerning some specific questions are found in GC IV.

5   The experience of brutal injustice committed in the first half of the twentieth century also triggered another relevant legal development, namely, the international protection of human rights.[15] The application of international human rights guarantees presupposes that the state[16] to be bound by these guarantees has jurisdiction, though not necessarily territorial jurisdiction, over the beneficiary of the guarantee. In situations of armed conflict, a party to a conflict exercises jurisdiction in cases of detention and of occupation, and in cases of non-international armed conflict (NIAC) the governmental party exercises as a matter of law territorial jurisdiction over the entire territory of the state. Thus, international human rights law (IHRL) has become relevant for the administration of occupied territory.[17] This has become an important component of the law of administration of occupied territory. It presupposes that human rights apply not only within the territory of the state in question, but also extraterritorially, i.e. where the state exercises some kind of jurisdiction outside its own territory. This principle has given rise to some controversy, but it is now well established by courts[18] and human rights bodies.[19]

6   The law of occupation, including the administration of occupied territory, has remained relevant in the practice of conflicts after the Second World War.[20] The most prominent example is the occupation of Palestinian territory by Israel. It is this long-term occupation which raises particular problems of territorial administration. But the development of the law of occupation should not be evaluated on the basis of this example alone. The following other examples of belligerent occupation should be mentioned:

— The occupation of Kuwait by Iraq in 1990 ended within a few months with the liberation of Kuwait.
— In the course of the dissolution of the Soviet Union, the ethnic division between Armenia and Azerbaijan led to an armed conflict concerning the area of Nagorno Karabakh, mainly populated by Armenians but situated within Azerbaijan. The armistice of 1994 resulted in a situation where Armenia occupies part of the territory of Azerbaijan even beyond the territory of the original Armenian enclave.[21]

---

[15] R. Kolb, 'Human Rights and Humanitarian Law', in MPEPIL; Benvenisti, above n 1, para 13.
[16] Non-state parties to an armed conflict will as a rule not be able to establish *de facto* control over foreign territory.
[17] Benvenisti, above n 1, para 7; see also MN 56–58.
[18] ICJ, *Legal Consequences of the Construction of a Wall in the Occupied Palestinian Territory*, Advisory Opinion, 9 July 2004, para 102.
[19] HRCttee, General Comment 31, The Nature of General Legal Obligations Imposed on States Parties to the Covenant, 26 May 2004, para 10; see also S. Vité, 'L'articulation du droit international humanitaire et des droits économiques, sociaux et culturels en temps d'occupation', in M.D. Voyame et al (eds), *International Law, Conflict and Development* (Leiden: Nijhoff, 2010) 19, at 26 ff; see further Ch 35 of this volume.
[20] Benvenisti, *International Law of Occupation*, above n 8, 167 ff; Barrie, above n 8, at 441 ff.
[21] See UNGA Res 60/285, 7 September 2006, and 62/243, 14 March 2008 ('The situation in the occupied territory of Azerbaijan') and Council of Europe, Parliamentary Assembly, Res 1416, 25 January 2005, OP 1; see also N. Ronzitti, *Il conflitto del Nagorno-Karabakh e il diritto internazionale* (Turin: Giappichelli, 2014), at 39 ff.

— The dissolution of Yugoslavia led to an armed conflict between the former members of the Federal Republic of Yugoslavia from 1991–5. During that conflict, situations of occupation of parts of the territory of the new states by other new states occurred.[22]
— Another example is the occupation of parts of the territory of Ethiopia by Eritrea,[23] as well as parts of Eritrean territory by Ethiopia,[24] in the Eritrea–Ethiopia War 1998–2000.
— Between 1999 and 2002, parts of the territory of the Democratic Republic of the Congo (DRC) were occupied by Uganda. This occupation has been the subject of a judgment of the International Court of Justice (ICJ), which has elucidated important legal questions concerning occupation.[25]
— The occupation of Iraq by the intervening forces in 2003[26] was soon replaced by a different regime on 1 July 2004.[27]
— Special problems arise where there is an attempt to change the territorial status of certain areas, where this change is not recognized by the international community at large and where, thus, this change, in the eyes of the international community, amounts to nothing more than establishing *de facto* control by a state over the area in question. Thus, most states regard the current situation in Northern Cyprus as a case of belligerent occupation of that territory by Turkey. This is the basis for the case law of the European Court of Human Rights (ECtHR), which treats acts of the authorities governing this territory as being attributable to Turkey.[28]
— The same holds probably true for the status of the former Spanish Sahara after Spain abandoned this colony in 1975 and Morocco invaded it. The international community has not recognized Moroccan sovereignty over that territory. Although the relevant resolutions of the Security Council are not explicit as to the status of the territory, the United Nations General Assembly (UNGA) uses the term 'occupation'.[29]
— Arguably, this is also the legal situation of Crimea after it was joined to the Russian Federation in 2014.

It must be added that at least in the cases of Northern Cyprus and the former Spanish Sahara, the legal discourse rather relates to the application of human rights than to that of the humanitarian law of occupation.[30]

---

[22] See, e.g., ICTY, *The Prosecutor v Mladen Naletilić and Vinko Martinović*, Trial Chamber Judgment, IT-98-34-T, 31 March 2003, paras 210 et seq, 583.
[23] See, e.g., EECC, *Central Front—Ethiopia's Claim 2*, Partial Award, 28 April 2004, paras 52, 70, 99.
[24] See, e.g., EECC, *Central Front—Eritrea's Claims 2, 4, 6, 7, 8, & 22*, Partial Award, 28 April 2004, paras 71, 74, 78; see on these cases A. Gioia, 'The Belligerent Occupation of Territory', in A. De Guttry (ed), *The 1998–2000 War between Eritrea and Ethiopia* (The Hague: T.M.C. Asser, 2009) 351, and T.D. Gill, 'The Law of Belligerent Occupation', ibid, 365.
[25] ICJ, *Case concerning Armed Activities on the Territory of the Congo (DRC v Uganda)*, 19 December 2005, at 168, paras 167 et seq.
[26] UNSC Res 1483, 22 May 2003.   [27] UNSC Res 1546, 8 June 2004; see also MN 22.
[28] ECtHR, *Loizidou v Turkey*, Judgment, 18 December 1996; *Cyprus v Turkey*, Judgment, 10 May 2001; *Xenides-Arestis v Turkey*, Judgment, 22 December 2005; *Solomou et al v Turkey*, Judgment, 24 June 2008.
[29] UNGA Res 34/37, 21 November 1979. See C. Chinkin, 'Laws of Occupation', in N. Botha (ed), *Conference on Multilateralism and International Law with Western Sahara as a Case Study* (Pretoria: Verloren van Themaat Center, 2010) 196.
[30] As to Northern Cyprus, see the case law quoted above n 28; as to the former Spanish Sahara, the *Report of the OHCHR Mission to Western Sahara and the Refugee Camps in Tindouf, 15/23 May and 19 June 2006*, not published as UN document, available at <http://www.arso.org/OHCHRrep2006en.pdf>.

7   International law governing belligerent occupation thus consists of three layers which evolved out of historically consecutive steps in the development of this body of law: (i) the traditional customary rules that had developed during the nineteenth century and were then codified in the Hague Regulations; (ii) the new rules contained in GC IV of 1949 and in AP I of 1977, with their clear emphasis on the protection of the civilian population; and (iii) international human rights rules. The earlier layers cannot remain unaffected by the new developments; they have to be interpreted taking these new developments into account.

III. The general principles of the law of occupation and their relevance for territorial administration

8   The law of occupation may be summarized in three principles which determine the rights and duties of an Occupying Power in establishing and operating the administration of an occupied territory:[31]

— Occupation is a temporary situation, not equivalent to annexation.
— The Occupying Power has a duty of good governance.
— The Occupying Power may take measures to ensure the safety and sustenance of its army and of the administration of an occupied territory.

The first principle protects the interest of the state whose territory is occupied and whose authority is displaced. It safeguards, as a matter of principle, the continuity of the pre-existing legal system (conservationist principle, *principe de stabilité juridique*).[32] The second principle safeguards the interests of the population. The third makes the necessary concessions to the interests of the Occupying Power. That specific need to balance state interests is not relevant for NIACs. Therefore, the law of occupation does not apply in the case of NIACs.[33]

9   There is a certain tension between these principles. None of them is absolute. The duty of good governance may entail the need to take measures displacing the pre-existing order to an extent hardly compatible with the temporary character of the occupation. The right of the Occupying Power to take measures for ensuring its safety may limit the duty of good governance. In the solution of concrete problems, these interests have to be accommodated and balanced against each other.[34] The idea of systemic integration, put forward by the International Law Commission (ILC) in a somewhat different context,[35] and the principle of proportionality[36] are used as guidelines for these purposes.

10   The regime of belligerent occupation is designed to protect the relevant interests of the parties to a conflict, and those of individuals affected by the conflict while the outcome of the conflict is not decided. It therefore prohibits the Occupying Power from taking measures that would demonstrate that it treats the situation as final and considers the territory and its inhabitants as its own territory or as its own nationals. An occupation may not

---

[31] For a similar way of summarizing the issues, see Benvenisti, above n 1, at para 24.
[32] Kolb and Vité, above n 8, at 187 et seq.   [33] Spoerri, above n 7, at 185.
[34] For examples, see Vité, above n 19, at 37 et seq.
[35] ILC, *Fragmentation of International Law: Difficulties Arising from the Diversification and Expansion of International Law*, Report of the Study Group of the International Law Commission. Finalized by M. Koskenniemi, UN Doc A/CN.4/L.682, paras 37 et seq, 410 et seq.
[36] Supreme Court of Israel, *Beit Sourik Village Council v Government of Israel*, 30 June 2004; see MN 102.

become, by *fait accompli*, an annexation. Several provisions of the Hague Regulations and GC IV serve this purpose (Article 45 of the Hague Regulations: prohibition to compel the population to take an oath of allegiance; Article 51 GC IV: prohibition to compel the population to serve in the army of the Occupying Power; also Article 47 GC IV: a change in the status of the territory may not affect the individual rights of protected persons). In its Advisory Opinion concerning the construction of the wall in the Occupied Palestinian Territory, the ICJ has stated that acts amounting to a *de facto* annexation are prohibited.[37]

The need for these protections is obvious during the 'hot' phase of an armed conflict. Yet these protections need to remain relevant even when this hot phase is over. This is expressly recognized by Article 6 paragraph 3 GC IV on the scope of application *ratione temporis*, which extends the scope of application of the provisions on occupation beyond 'the general close of military operations'.[38] This is particularly important for territorial administration in the case of a long-term occupation.

The obligation of good governance is the key element protecting the interests of the population of the occupied territory, and thus is of fundamental importance for territorial administration.[39] It is expressed in general terms in Article 43 of the Hague Regulations, supplemented by other provisions thereof, and is elaborated further in the relevant provisions of GC IV. In addition, this is the domain where international human rights are most relevant.

On the other hand, the law of occupation is no exception to the rule that international humanitarian law (IHL) has to accommodate diverging interests of different belligerents. Two essential interests of the Occupying Power are protected: its security, and the sustenance of its army. The latter interest is perhaps a little outdated, as the need for the army of occupation to live out of the resources of the territory has become less relevant in light of modern supply logistics. There are specific rules safeguarding the interests of the Occupying Power, but there is no general reservation of military necessity. Exceptions to the duties of the Occupying Power following from the principle of continuity or of good governance cannot be established by sweeping references to military necessity.[40]

B. Meaning and Application

I. Occupation as a temporary situation

a. *Respect for the legal and institutional status quo*

The rule that occupation is a temporary situation requires the Occupying Power to leave the pre-existing law and institutions of the occupied territory essentially unchanged. This principle of continuation of pre-existing law is expressly formulated in Article 43 of the Hague Regulations. The only expressly recognized exception is the situation where the Occupying Power is 'absolutely prevented' from doing so. The principle

---

[37] ICJ, *Wall*, Advisory Opinion, above n 18, in particular paras 121 et seq.
[38] See A. Roberts, 'Occupation, Termination of' in MPEPIL, esp paras 11 et seq; see also Ch 74 of this volume.
[39] C. Greenwood, 'The Administration of Occupied Territory in International Law', in E. Playfair (ed), *International Law and the Administration of Occupied Territories* (Oxford: Clarendon Press, 1992) 241, at 253.
[40] Kolb and Vité, above n 8, at 260 ff. The authors convincingly show that in the Hague Regulations and in the GCs, references to 'military necessity' are highly differentiated, which excludes any sweeping or catch-all use of that concept.

is repeated, as far as penal laws are concerned, by Article 64 GC IV, which contains exceptions formulated in broader terms. The texts therefore suggest that there is a strict rule of maintaining the status quo, with very limited exceptions. This seems to impose severe limitations on the other two principles governing the law of occupation, namely the duty of good governance and the right to ensure the security of the Occupying Power. Recent practice, however, seems to suggest that there are reasons to shift the emphasis from maintaining the status quo to the other two principles, especially the duty of good governance.[41]

15   An important reason for the Occupying Power not to maintain pre-existing law is a situation where that law contravenes international law, in particular IHRL. The duty to maintain the pre-existing law of the territory could not require the Occupying Power to violate human rights.[42] This is of particular importance where the conflict which had led to an occupation was triggered by a poor human rights situation, or even massive violations of human rights in the country in question. The issue arose in relation to occupations established by the victorious Powers after the Second World War; there, however, the authority assumed by the Allied Powers after the unconditional surrender of Germany went beyond those of an Occupying Power under the normal law of belligerent occupation. In recent practice, the problem has been argued in cases of so-called 'transformative' or 'humanitarian' occupation. Examples on point include the situations in Kosovo[43] and in East Timor,[44] which are comparable[45] in this respect, and the occupation of Iraq after 2003.[46] Nevertheless, the notion of transformative occupation must not be misunderstood as a *carte blanche* for the Occupying Power to disregard the law of the occupied territory. Unless there is a formal backing by competent international institutions (in particular the Security Council), the benign purpose of the occupation cannot serve as a justification for introducing changes otherwise not warranted under the law of occupation.[47] The notion of 'transformative occupation' has to be treated with caution. In the cases just mentioned, there was a Security Council resolution as the basis for the foreign presence in a given territory. In such situations, the principle that the local law of the occupied territory must be preserved is modified if and to the extent that the Security Council mandate so requires. Where there is no such United Nations (UN) mandate, the Occupying Power's positive duty to protect the fundamental rights of the inhabitants of the territory may also require some changes in the pre-existing law—if one accepts the proposition that this positive aspect of human rights duties for the Occupying Power must also be applied extraterritorially.

16   The balance of the three elements of the law of occupation is also affected by the duration of the occupation. In the case of a long-term occupation, which may last for decades,

---

[41] Benvenisti, above n 1, para 28; K. Parameswaran, *Besatzungsrecht im Wandel* (Baden-Baden: Nomos, 2008), at 177 et seq, expresses reservations concerning this trend.
[42] G.H. Fox, *Humanitarian Occupation* (Cambridge: CUP, 2008) 218 ff; G.H. Fox, 'Transformative Occupation and the Unilateralist Impulse', 94 *IRRC* 885 (2012) 237, at 257.
[43] See UNSC Res 1244, above n 5.
[44] UNSC Res 1272, 25 October 1999, Establishment of a United Nations Transitional Administration in East Timor (UNTAET).
[45] See MN 2.
[46] See above n 6; Fox, 'Transformative Occupation and the Unilateralist Impulse', above n 42, at 250.
[47] Fox, 'Transformative Occupation and the Unilateralist Impulse', above n 42, at 256 ff.

the duty of good governance incumbent upon the Occupying Power will often require changes in the pre-existing law in order to adapt it to new situations for the benefit of the population of the occupied territory.[48] This includes in particular the need to take measures for the protection of the environment and to facilitate appropriate land use by a growing population. In adopting such measures, the Occupying Power must of course take into account all elements of good governance, in particular the fundamental rights of the population of the occupied territory. The essential point is not that the maintenance of the status quo is automatically diluted as a consequence of the duration of the occupation, but that the interest of the population may require changes. The duration of the occupation must in no case serve as a pretext for avoiding the restraints imposed by the law of occupation. The Supreme Court of Israel proposes a balancing exercise, taking into account, on the one hand, the needs of current economic life, and on the other the principle of continuity.[49] This is plausible as a matter of principle, but much depends on the concrete balancing decision.

The principle of continuation also applies to the administration of the territory, in particular the justice system. The same exceptions apply.[50]

b. Protection of the status quo: 'inviolability of rights' and respect for loyalty to the displaced government

i. 'Inviolability of rights'

Geneva Convention IV adds an important protection to the principle of continuity as enshrined in the Hague Regulations: Article 47 GC IV deprives of legal effect measures which otherwise could result in a change of status of the occupied territory and thus give a free hand to the Occupying Power to deal with the population of the territory as it likes. The provision is a consequence of abuses that occurred during the Second World War and the conflicts preceding it, where a (provisionally) victorious belligerent had tried to eliminate the protections provided by the law of belligerent occupation for the population of territory occupied in the course of the conflict by changing its legal status.[51] Although based on historic experience, and thus addressing problems of the past, the provision continues to be of practical relevance. Three types of changes are envisaged: changes in the institutions of the occupied territory; agreements between the Occupying Power and the local or national authorities of the occupied territory; and annexation.

Article 47 formulates the legal effect of the provision in terms of the subjective rights of protected persons. These persons may not be deprived of the benefits of the Convention. But at least indirectly, the provision also objectively preserves the legal position of the displaced government.

In some cases,[52] a belligerent occupying a territory has established new institutions in the occupied territory. After its invasion of China in 1931, Japan established a new state

---

[48] Sassòli, above n 4, 679; Parameswaran, above n 41, at 190.
[49] Supreme Court of Israel, *Bassil Abu Aita et al v Commander of the Judea and Samaria Region and Officer-in-charge of Customs and Excise, Omar Abdu Kadar Kanzil v Officer-in-Charge of Customs, Gaza Strip Region and The Regional Commander of the Gaza Strip*, HC 69/81–HC 493/81, Judgment, 4 April 1983; see MN 94.
[50] Art 64 para 1 GC IV.
[51] Pictet Commentary GC IV, at 293 ff; Kolb, above n 4, at 298 ff.
[52] For a comprehensive review of cases, see Kolb, above n 4, 302 ff.

named Manchukuo, which was really a Japanese puppet regime. This territorial change was not recognized by the international community.[53]

21 In Northern Cyprus, a new state was installed, too, which has not been recognized as such by the international community. As a consequence, this territory is still considered as occupied territory.

22 In the case of the occupation of Iraq after 2003, a transition process took place that gradually terminated the legal situation of belligerent occupation and thus made Article 47 GC IV inapplicable, at a moment in time which is somewhat difficult to determine.[54] New Iraqi institutions were established under the direction of the Occupying Power.[55] This was expressly recognized by the Security Council; it 'determined that the (newly created) Governing Council and its ministers are the principal bodies of the Iraqi interim administration, which [...] embodies the sovereignty of the State of Iraq'.[56] Thus, a new representation of the people of the occupied territory was installed not only by the Occupying Power, but also by the competent organ of the UN. In this manner, a process of transition was initiated which was eventually to lead Iraq back to fully fledged self-government. Although the institution of the administration by the Occupying Power, namely the 'Authority', was not immediately dissolved, its military component, the army of occupation, received a new mandate from the Security Council which had as its main purpose to ensure the stability required for the transition process.[57] All this progressively modified the character and status of the foreign military presence from belligerent occupation to a kind of visiting force. In light of the fact that this process took place under the control and direction of the Security Council, the danger of abuse, which Article 47 GC IV tries to prevent, does not exist. Article 47 GC IV was not meant to prevent such a development.

23 As to the second type of change, the Occupying Power may set up puppet regimes ('Quisling' governments[58]), the likes of which then try to renounce, in the name of the population, the benefits of the law of occupation. This will have no legal effect. The prohibition does not exclude all types of arrangements between an Occupying Power and authorities representing the population of the occupied territory, but only those which have the effect of restricting the rights of the population.[59] In this respect, the question of the effect of the agreements between Israel and the Palestine Liberation Organization (PLO) concerning important modalities of the occupation regime (the so-called Oslo Agreements)[60] deserves a differentiated answer: the agreements were meant to prepare a peace arrangement, but they did not terminate the occupation.[61] Thus, they cannot

---

[53] T.D. Grant, 'Doctrines (Monroe, Hallstein, Brezhnev, Stimson)', in MPEPIL, paras 8 et seq.

[54] See Ch 74 of this volume.

[55] For a legal evaluation of this process, see Sassòli, above n 4, at 683 et seq; B. Reschke, *Post-Conflict: Wiederherstellung von Staatlichkeit. Völkerrechtliche Aspekte der Friedessicherung im Irak* (Cologne: Heymanns, 2008) 128 ff; for a careful look at the scope of the changes relating to the law of occupation, see also Kolb and Vité, above n 8, 293 ff, and Parameswaran, above n 41, at 204 ff.

[56] UNSC Res 1511, 16 October 2003, para 4.

[57] Ibid, para 13.

[58] This type of 'government' is named after the Prime Minister of Norway installed by Germany after the occupation of Norway during the Second World War.

[59] Kolb, above n 4, at 299.

[60] Interim Agreement on the West Bank and the Gaza Strip between the Government of Israel and the PLO, the representative of the Palestinian People, 28 September 1995. For an analysis, see Kolb, above n 4, at 305 ff.

[61] Benvenisti, above n 8, 115 ff.

deprive the population of any right its members may have under the law of occupation, and must not be interpreted in that way.

Geneva Convention IV expressly provides for cooperation between the Occupying Power and the authorities existing in the occupied territory for the benefit of the population.[62] This may also require some kind of arrangement between the Occupying Power and the local authorities of the occupied territory.

Annexation is a traditional means by which belligerent occupants have tried to get rid of the restraints of the law of occupation. Although the occupation of Manchuria by Japan rather belongs to the first category of changes just mentioned, as there was no attempted annexation, the reaction of the international community was based on the principle of non-recognition of territorial acquisitions achieved through an unlawful use of military force (Stimson doctrine).[63] The principle was reiterated by various UN Resolutions. According to the so-called Friendly Relations Declaration, 'No territorial acquisition resulting from the threat or use of force shall be recognized as legal.'[64]

The formulation of the General Assembly's definition of aggression[65] is a little broader still, 'No territorial acquisition or special advantage resulting from aggression is or shall be recognized as legal.'

These general principles are the basis for the non-recognition of the annexation of East Jerusalem and the Golan by Israel, which is regarded as being without legal effect by the UN[66] and by the ICJ.[67]

There remains, however, the question of whether and when there is a moment in time at which a change of status, or even annexation, will have come about and there can no longer be a question of occupation. The position of the parties over a period of time and the reaction of the international community matter in this respect. The international community apparently has not accepted the claim made by Argentina that the Falkland/Malvinas Islands constituted a territory occupied by Great Britain which it had a right to recover.[68] Despite the condemnation of Argentina's 1982 invasion, the territorial dispute is still open, but its solution is not at all sought through the application of the law of occupation. In the case of the occupation of Iraq after 2003, the international community effectively recognized the transition. In the case of the Occupied Palestinian Territory, there is no recognition of, but a general protest against, the annexation of parts of the territory declared by Israel. In the case of the annexation of Goa by India in 1961, the Supreme Court of India held that the annexation was valid and the law of occupation no longer applicable.[69] In 1974, Portugal recognized the Indian sovereignty over Goa by a treaty with retroactive effect.[70] Thus, the prohibition of territorial acquisition by unlawful use of force and the ensuing maintenance of the

---

[62] See MN 43; esp Arts 50 and 56 GC IV.
[63] Grant, above n 53.
[64] Declaration of Principles of International Law concerning Friendly Relations and Cooperation among States in accordance with the Charter of the United Nations, UNGA Res 2625 (XXV), 24 October 1970, Annex, Principle of the prohibition of the use of force.
[65] UNGA Res 3314 (XXIX), 14 December 1974, Annex, Art 5 para 3.
[66] See, in particular, UNSC Res 478, 20 August 1980.
[67] The ICJ *Wall* Advisory Opinion, above n 18, paras 96 and 98, refers to the relevant UN Resolutions.
[68] M. Waibel, 'Falkland Islands/Islas Malvinas', in MPEPIL, esp paras 12 et seq.
[69] Supreme Court of India, *Monteiro v State of Goa*, 26 March 1969, reported by Sassòli/Bouvier/Quintin, at 917.
[70] R.K. Dixit, 'Goa, Conflict', in MPEPIL, esp para 21.

29   The effects of non-recognition based on the prohibition of the use of force coincide with the rule enshrined in Article 47 GC IV: the population affected by the attempt of annexation or other modification of territorial status retains the benefits of the law of occupation. Whether this rule will deter the Occupying Power from pursuing and implementing the said status changes is another question. The main sanction following the non-recognition of these changes will lie in the reaction of third states and of the international community at large. On the other hand, Article 47 does not exclude arrangements between the Occupying Power and authorities representing the population of the occupied territory which effect an improvement of the situation of the population.

ii. Respect for loyalty to the displaced government

30   A related important guarantee against an Occupying Power's establishing itself as the new legitimate authority in an occupied territory is the prohibition, expressed in various provisions, to require acts or expressions of allegiance by members of the population. This is expressed in general terms in Article 45 of the Hague Regulations (prohibition to compel the inhabitants to swear allegiance). This is supplemented by Article 51 GC IV, which prohibits compulsion to serve in the armed forces of the Occupying Power or to become involved in its military operations. Compulsion to serve in the armed forces of the Occupying Power constitutes a grave breach in the sense of Article 147 GC IV, and thus a war crime (Article 8(2)(a)(v) of the Statute of the International Criminal Court (ICC)).

31   The loyalty of the population to the displaced government is also protected to a certain degree: inhabitants may not be forced to furnish information of military relevance to the Occupying Power (Article 44 of the Hague Regulations). Officials of the existing administration may not have sanctions applied to them if they cease to exercise their functions for reasons of loyalty to the displaced government ('for reasons of conscience', Article 54 GC IV).

iii. The prohibition on population transfers

32   Another very important guarantee of the temporary character of an occupation is the prohibition on transferring parts of the Occupying Power's own population into the occupied territory (Article 49 GC IV). The Occupying Power may not change the demographic structure of the occupied territory so as to create a *fait accompli* and a basis for annexation. This is the consistent interpretation upheld by the UN and confirmed by the ICJ in the *Wall* case.[72] This is also an issue in respect of Northern Cyprus.[73]

II. The elements of the duty of good governance

33   Article 43 of the Hague Regulations imposes on the Occupying Power the duty to restore and ensure 'public order and safety'. This, it is submitted, goes beyond a duty to prevent physical harm. The French version of the Regulations, the only authentic text, is indeed

---

[71] For a close analysis, see Kolb, above n 4, at 308 ff.
[72] Above ICJ, *Wall*, Advisory Opinion, n 18, for details see Chs 58 and 73 of this volume.
[73] A.M. de Zayas, 'The Illegal Implantation of Turkish Settlers in Northern Cyprus', in G.-H. Gornig et al (eds), *Iustitia et pax. Gedächtnisschrift für Dieter Blumenwitz* (Berlin: Duncker & Humblot, 2008) 721.

much broader. The Occupying Power is under a duty '*de rétablir et d'assurer [...] l'ordre et la vie publics*'. The notion of 'order' is there as well, but the French text refers to 'public life' instead of 'safety'. This broader concept of the duty of the Occupying Power also finds a basis in the negotiating history.[74] In its Resolution concerning the occupation of Iraq after 2003, the Security Council expressly called upon the Occupying Power to '*promote the welfare* of the Iraqi people though the effective administration of the territory'.[75] This duty is further specified by concrete duties contained in the Hague Regulations themselves and then in GC IV, addressing the issues of health, education, and the fulfilment of basic needs. If one takes all these elements together, there is indeed a duty to ensure the well-being of the population. This is, in modern parlance, the duty of good governance.[76]

What is implied in this duty of good governance depends on the circumstances. It is a contextual duty. This is of particular importance in the case of long-term occupation: the longer the occupation lasts, the more extensive are the duties of the Occupying Power to ensure the well-being of the population.

What are the elements of this duty of good governance? Generally speaking, the Occupying Power must conduct its administration of the occupied territory according to what is expected of the modern state, which is a welfare state with a broad range of regulatory responsibilities.[77] This brings into play, in addition to the law of occupation, other rules of international law applicable in relation to the occupied territory, to activities conducted on it or having an effect on the territory.

On the basis of the concretizations found in the various treaty texts, the duties of good governance may be listed as follows:

— the maintenance and, if necessary, the development of an adequate normative order;
— an adequate administrative apparatus;[78]
— a functioning court system ensuring respect for the rule of law;[79]
— respect for the fundamental rights of the population;
— effective law enforcement respecting at the same time human rights;
— adequate food and shelter for the population, adequate living conditions in general;
— the protection of private property;
— health care;
— acceptance of relief, if food, clothing, medical supplies, or shelter are not provided;
— education;
— protection of family interests;
— the possibility of religious life;
— sustainable use of natural resources and environmental conservation;
— protection of cultural property;
— an adequate system of public finance (raising revenue and spending); and
— an adequate conduct of international relations of the territory in accordance with international law.

---

[74] Sassòli, above n 4, at 663 et seq. [75] UNSC Res 1483, above n 6, para 4 (emphasis added).
[76] F.N. Botchway, 'Good Governance: The Old, the New, the Principle, and the Elements', 13 *Florida JIL* (2001) 159; S. Seppänen, 'Good Governance in International Law', The Erik Castrén Research Reports 13/2003; R. Dolzer, 'Good Governance: Neues transnationales Leitbild der Staatlichkeit?', 64 *Zeitschrift für ausländisches öffentliches Recht und Völkerrecht* (2004) 535.
[77] E. Benvenisti, 'Water Conflicts during the Occupation of Iraq', 97 *AJIL* (2003) 860, at 867.
[78] Greenwood, above n 39, 252 ff. [79] Ibid, 261 ff.

37 All these duties of good governance relate to what the Occupying Power must or must not do, not to what the Occupying Power must achieve. They are obligations of means, not obligations of result.[80] The Occupying Power must care for the well-being of the population. It is not a guarantor of that well-being.

a. Maintenance and development of an adequate normative order

38 Good governance presupposes an adequate legal order. The Hague Regulations assume that this order remains as it existed at the time the occupation began. But the same provision also presupposes that the Occupying Power has a (*de facto*) legislative power. If the provision requires the Occupying Power to respect the pre-existing order 'unless absolutely prevented', this implies a regulatory power of the Occupying Power if it is so prevented. This preference for the pre-existing order seems adequate in the case of a short-term occupation. But in the case of a territorial administration of a longer duration, good governance entails a duty of the Occupying Power to adapt the regulatory order to changing needs. This is necessary for the benefit of the population of the occupied territory.

39 This basic approach is detailed in GC IV.[81] As to penal law, Article 64 GC IV establishes the principle of continuity of the pre-existing law, but allows for an exception where this principle would be an 'obstacle to the application of the present Convention'. Therefore, the Occupying Power is not only allowed, but also obliged to adopt those legislative measures which are necessary to ensure all the protections which are granted by the general and specific provisions of GC IV, in particular Articles 27 and 50 to 61.

40 The complete picture of the normative order in the occupied territory does not only contain the pre-existing law, but may also comprise legislative acts executed by the 'national' or 'local' authorities of the territory under the control and supervision of the Occupying Power. This normative order is therefore a multilevel legal phenomenon. The distribution of legislative functions between the Occupying Power and national or local authorities varies from case to case. In the case of Northern Cyprus, because Turkey treats that territory as an independent state, the 'national' authorities have a complete legislative power. In the case of the Palestinian occupied territory, that division of powers varies, according to the so-called Oslo Agreements, between different types of areas (Areas A, B, and C) where the Palestinian Authority has different competences.[82]

41 Concrete issues of this normative order are treated below.

b. An adequate administrative apparatus

42 Good governance also means good administration. The *de facto* authority, which is the characteristic of occupation, implies that the Occupying Power has at least the ultimate control of that administration. The principle of continuation also applies to administration (Article 54 GC IV), but with certain modifications in the interest both of the Occupying Power and that of the officials concerned. On the one hand, the Occupying Power may remove public officials from their posts (Article 54 paragraph 2 *in fine*); on the other hand, it may not force officials to continue in service if they refuse to do so 'for reasons of conscience' (Article 54 paragraph 1 GC IV). In some cases, the pre-existing administration's personnel may simply have disappeared during the invasion phase. In these cases, the Occupying Power must take the administration into its own hands, at least in the beginning.

---

[80] Sassòli, above n 4, 664 ff.   [81] See MN 14; also Ch 68 of this volume.
[82] Interim Agreement, 28 September 1995, above n 60, Arts XI, XIII, and XVII.

Administration of Occupied Territory

An Occupying Power has a certain discretion as to the division of powers between the Occupying Power's own administration and the use of local administrative structures and personnel. Like law-making, administration under the Occupying Power is a multilevel phenomenon. The division of tasks will not necessarily be the same as in the field of law-making. Some provisions of GC IV expressly provide for cooperation between the Occupying Power and the national or local authorities for the benefit of the population.[83]

c. A functioning court system ensuring respect for the rule of law

The principle of continuation applies, *mutatis mutandis*, to the court system.[84] The local courts can continue to function (Article 54 GC IV), but the Occupying Power may also remove judges from their posts. In order to exercise effective control, the Occupying Power will at least establish its own court of last instance. Litigation between members of the population and the Occupying Power will take place only before the courts of the latter.

It is important that effective access to impartial justice is available to the entire population. A court established by the Occupying Power must provide the necessary guarantees of impartiality and independence from the administrative and/or military authorities of the Occupying Power.

d. Respect for the fundamental rights of the population

There are three different types of sources for the duty of the Occupying Power to respect the fundamental rights of the population: relevant provisions of the Hague Regulations; relevant provisions of GC IV; and the law of human rights (treaties and customary law).

A duty to respect fundamental rights is, as a matter of substance, already implicit in the general rule of Article 43 of the Hague Regulations. In modern understanding, 'public order and safety' means a guarantee of the rule of law, and therefore of human rights. In addition, there are a number of provisions in the Hague Regulations that contain substantive guarantees of human rights: Articles 44 and 45 protect the population against forcible compulsion to commit acts of what could be considered treason by their own country (furnishing information to the Occupying Power, swearing allegiance to the Occupying Power). Article 46 protects 'family honour and rights, the lives of persons, private property and religious beliefs and practices'. This is, in a nutshell, a basic catalogue of human rights. As to the protection of private property,[85] this protection goes further than that provided by the International Covenant on Civil and Political Rights (ICCPR).

Geneva Convention IV also guarantees fundamental rights to be respected with regard to 'protected persons'. These are, in particular, members of the population of an occupied territory (Article 4 paragraph 1 GC IV), with a few exceptions: nationals of co-belligerent states which have a 'normal diplomatic representation' with the Occupying Power (but not of neutral states), and persons protected by the other Geneva Conventions (wounded, sick, and shipwrecked persons, and prisoners of war (POWs)).[86] A core of human rights protections is formulated in Article 27 GC IV. It repeats, first, the guarantees of Article 46 of the Hague Regulations. Although it does not mention private property, it guarantees

---

[83] Arts 50, 56 GC IV; Greenwood, above n 39, 252 ff.
[84] For more details, see Ch 68 of this volume.
[85] See Ch 71 of this volume.   [86] Art 4 paras 2 and 4 GC IV.

49   This is supplemented by two specific guarantees: the first one relating to the protection of women (Article 27 paragraph 2); the second one relating to non-discrimination (Article 27 paragraph 3).[87] Women shall be protected 'against any attack on their honour, in particular against rape, enforced prostitution or any form of indecent assault'.

50   The non-discrimination clause in Article 27 paragraph 3 is of a general nature (all persons shall be treated 'with the same consideration'). It relates to all kinds of measures by the Occupying Power against members of the population. There is no exhaustive list of forbidden criteria of adverse distinction, the criteria mentioned (race, religion, political opinion) are only important examples.[88]

51   Violations of Article 27 paragraphs 1 and 2 (inhuman treatment, acts of violence) are grave breaches of GC IV (Article 147 GC IV), thus war crimes (Article 8(2)(a)(ii) and (iii) ICC Statute), and may also be crimes against humanity in the sense of Article 7(1)(f) ICC Statute. Violations of paragraph 2 are war crimes in the sense of Article 8(2)(b)(xxi) and (xxii), and crimes against humanity in the sense of Article 7(1)(g) ICC Statute.

52   This core of fundamental rights, which applies generally in favour of all protected persons, is supplemented by a number of guarantees that apply specifically in the case of occupation.

53   Article 51 GC IV provides a certain protection against forced labour. A duty to work (requisition of labour) may be imposed only upon inhabitants over the age of 18, only for certain purposes (needs of the army of occupation, public utility services, assistance to the population in need), and not outside the occupied territory. Persons thus forced to work may not be involved in military operations. Certain standards of working conditions must be respected.

54   The free exercise of religion, guaranteed by Article 46 of the Hague Regulations, is strengthened by a protection of the functions of ministers of religion (Article 58 GC IV). They are permitted to grant 'spiritual assistance' to the members of their religion.

55   Articles 66–77 GC IV provide substantial procedural guarantees in case of criminal prosecutions.[89]

56   In addition to, and in parallel with, these protections provided by IHL, IHRL, as it has developed during the decades after the Second World War, applies to the exercise of *de facto* power by the Occupying Power.[90] The essential conditions for the application of IHRL are fulfilled. This field of law protects persons who are subject to the 'jurisdiction' of a state against exercises of that jurisdiction. In the *Wall* case, the ICJ clearly stated that the *de facto* power of the Occupying Power is an exercise of jurisdiction in this sense.[91] Jurisdiction here is not limited to territorial jurisdiction, it may also be jurisdiction exercised outside of a state's territory. Although there are questions where IHL, as *lex specialis*, would take precedence over human rights, the law of belligerent occupation is not such a question, and parallel application of both fields of law is thus possible.[92] The Occupying

---

[87] See also Ch 10 of this volume.   [88] Pictet Commentary GC IV, at 222.

[89] For details see Ch 59 of this volume.

[90] For details see also MN 5 above and Ch 35 of this volume. See, in particular, J.A. Frowein, 'The Relationship between Human Rights Regimes and Regimes of Belligerent Occupation', 28 IsrYBHR(1998) 1; O. Ben-Naftali and Y. Shany, 'Living in Denial: The Application of Human Rights in the Occupied Territories', 37 *Israel Law Review* (2003/4) 17.

[91] See already ICJ, *Wall*, Advisory Opinion, above n 18. As to social rights, see Ch 70 of this volume.

[92] This is indeed the conclusion of the ICJ in the *Wall* case, despite the fact that the Court refers to the *lex specialis* rule. That conclusion is also *grosso modo* unanimously accepted by legal doctrine, albeit with

Power is therefore bound by universal and regional human rights conventions to which it is a party,[93] and by customary human rights law.

57 This implies a number of very important practical consequences. The population of the occupied territory possesses a whole range of rights guaranteed by the general human rights treaties as well as by specific treaties,[94] such as conventions for the prohibition of torture,[95] for the elimination of all kinds of discrimination against women,[96] and on the rights of the child.[97] These include rights which are politically important, such as the rights of freedom of expression and assembly, and the right to freedom of the press. The protections of human rights thus strengthen and expand the protections granted by the Hague Regulations and by GC IV, for instance the prohibition of forcible transfers according to Article 49 GC IV. On the other hand, the Occupying Power may avail itself of derogation clauses such as Article 4 ICCPR,[98] which would, however, not limit the application of any guarantee provided by IHL. For example, the procedural guarantees of Article 14 ICCPR may be suspended, but not those provided by Articles 71 and 72 GC IV. There is in principle a parallel application of IHL and IHRL, which means that the protection most favourable to the victim applies, it being understood, however, that specific limitations of human rights may result from the existence of an armed conflict.

58 The duty to respect human rights implies a duty to protect human rights. This entails, at least to a certain extent, a positive duty to take measures allowing the population to enjoy the protection of these rights,[99] which includes a duty to take measures to eliminate existing discrimination.[100] Specific positive duties derive from treaties on economic and social rights. In particular, each state party to the International Covenant on Economic, Social and Cultural Rights (ICESCR) 'undertakes to take steps […] with a view to achieving progressively the full realization of the rights recognized' by the Covenant. As a matter of principle, this duty is also incumbent upon an Occupying Power. But as this duty is anyway limited by the availability of adequate resources, and may be limited pursuant to Article 4 ICESCR, the context of an occupation may to a certain extent narrow the scope of these positive duties.[101]

---

various nuances: see Frowein, above n 90, at 10 ff; M. Bothe, 'Humanitäres Völkerrecht und Schutz der Menschenrechte: auf der Suche nach Synergien und Schutzlücken', in P.M. Dupuy et al (eds), *Common Values in International Law: Essays in Honour of Christian Tomuschat* (Kehl: Engel, 2006) 63, at 77 ff; Dinstein, above n 1, at 85 ff; Ben-Naftali and Shany, above n 90, at 56; Watkin, above n 6, at 301 ff.

[93] The application of the ECHR to cases of occupation by states parties to the Convention has become controversial due to a somewhat unfortunate formulation used by the ECtHR in the *Banković* case, see Bothe, above n 92, at 71. The question seems now to be settled in favour of the application of the Convention, in particular in the light of the *Al-Skeini* and *Hassan* judgments of the ECtHR: *Al-Skeini and others v United Kingdom*, Grand Chamber, 7 July 2011; *Hassan v United Kingdom*, Grand Chamber, 16 September 2014.

[94] The ICJ in the *Wall* case, quoted above n 18, para 103, singles out the two Covenants and the Convention on the Rights of the Child.

[95] Convention against Torture and other Cruel, Inhuman or Degrading Treatment or Punishment, 10 December 1984, currently (summer 2014) 155 parties.

[96] Convention on the Elimination of All Forms of Discrimination against Women, 18 December 1979, currently (summer 2014) 188 parties.

[97] Convention on the Rights of the Child, 20 November 1989, currently (summer 2014) 194 parties, i.e. all states except the US, Somalia, and South Sudan.

[98] On the derogation concerning the Occupied Palestinian Territory, see the Advisory Opinion in the *Wall* case, above n 18, para 127.

[99] On positive duties see HRCttee, General Comment 31, The Nature of the General Legal Obligation Imposed on States Parties to the Covenant, 26 May 2004, para 6.

[100] Pictet Commentary GC IV, at 222. [101] Vité, above n 19, at 28 ff.

e. Effective law enforcement respecting at the same time human rights

59 Law enforcement[102] is essential for the peaceful population. It protects civilians and enables them to pursue their normal life. Therefore, effective law enforcement is an essential ingredient of good governance. On the other hand, measures of law enforcement may limit freedom. In this relationship, human rights protect the interests of freedom. The principle of proportionality is an important restraint against excessive law enforcement measures.

60 This is of particular importance in the case of forcible measures for law enforcement. The Occupying Power must, as a rule, take those measures to ensure public safety that a state would take in a similar situation outside occupation, i.e. in a 'law enforcement mode'.[103] This may include the use of forcible measures, but these forcible measures are carefully limited by requirements of legality, necessity, and proportionality. Two issues are of particular practical relevance in this respect, namely, the destruction of property and deadly use of force ('targeted killings').

61 As to the destruction of property, the first question to be asked is whether Article 53 GC IV constitutes a *lex specialis*, which would prohibit any destruction of property for law enforcement purposes, as law enforcement does not fall within the scope of destruction that is permissible under that provision, namely, destruction 'rendered absolutely necessary by military operations'. In its Advisory Opinion on the construction of a wall in the Palestinian occupied territory,[104] the ICJ appears not to admit any other justification for destruction. However, at least in the case of a long-term occupation, it could be argued that there are other legitimate reasons for demolitions, for example demolitions to allow infrastructure developments for the benefit of the population. But this would be lawful only in extreme circumstances under limited conditions. Destruction could be lawful only if it is a necessary means to achieve a lawful end and after a full judicial review. The widespread practice of demolition orders concerning buildings allegedly erected without permit as a rule does not meet these requirements.[105] The demolition order would be legal only if the refusal of the permit were lawful. But if the prohibition of building is part of an unlawful practice of denying otherwise lawful uses of private property, it is unlawful under international law as violating the guarantee of property under Article 46 of the Hague Regulations. Enforcement of such unlawful restraints on the use of property is itself unlawful.

62 As to the so-called targeted killings, the rules for the use of firearms are the standards applicable to law enforcement agents in times of peace. The relevant human rights standard is the prohibition of 'arbitrary' killing according to Article 6 ICCPR. What this means for the use of firearms by the police is well formulated by the publication entitled 'Human Rights Standards and Practice for the Police', issued by the UN High Commissioner for Human Rights. The standard to be observed is formulated as follows:

Firearms are to be used only in extreme circumstances.

Firearms are to be used only in self-defence or defence of others against imminent threat of death or serious injury, or

---

[102] For more details see Ch 68 of this volume.   [103] See also MN 64 and 101.
[104] ICJ, *Wall*, Advisory Opinion, above n 18, para 135 *in fine*.
[105] As to recent developments, see the Report of the Special Rapporteur on the situation of human rights in the Palestinian territories occupied since 1967, R. Falk, UN Doc A/HRC/20/32, 25 May 2012, at 14; see also MN 69–70.

To prevent a particularly serious crime that involves a grave threat to life, or

To arrest and prevent the escape of a person posing such a threat and who is resisting efforts to stop the threat, and

In every case, only when less extreme measures are insufficient.

Intentionally lethal use of force and firearms shall be permitted only when strictly unavoidable in order to protect human life.[106]

The status of the person so targeted as combatant or civilian is irrelevant in this context of law enforcement. 63

However, situations may arise in the context of an occupation where resistance against the Occupying Power amounts to a situation of armed conflict, in the same way as it may happen within a state where it triggers a NIAC.[107] It is, however, difficult to determine when this threshold is reached.[108] Depending on the type of resistance, the legal situation may be somewhat different. If the resistance fighters are part of an armed group which legally speaking belongs to the other party to the conflict, i.e. the state to which the occupied territory belongs, the ensuing hostilities are part of the original IAC. If the resistance fighters cannot be attributed to that other party to the conflict, i.e. if they are non-state actors, the rules concerning fighting in a NIAC apply. In such a situation, the applicable legal standards of behaviour change. This does not mean that IHL displaces IHRL as *lex specialis*.[109] Yet the interplay between human rights and IHL is different. The Occupying Power may act in an 'armed conflict mode'. In this case, Article 53 GC IV, just quoted at MN 61, is the rule applicable to the destruction of property. The use of deadly force is inherent in the conduct of hostilities. This means that combatants belonging to the Occupied Power, including members of resistance movements, and the fighters, i.e. persons with a continuous combat function,[110] involved in an additional NIAC, may be targeted. Other persons, i.e. civilians, may be targeted only while they are directly participating in hostilities (Article 13 paragraph 3 AP II). But as IHRL, including the right to life, continues to apply, it means that this type of targeting is permissible only to the extent that there is a genuine conduct of hostilities scenario. In the case where belligerent occupation meets some resistance, as in the case of an insurgency within a state, that scenario does not exist as a continuum. Where this scenario has ceased and has been replaced, at least for the time being, by a more peaceful one, that type of use of deadly force remains 'arbitrary' in the sense of Article 6 ICCPR and therefore is unlawful.[111] 64

f. *Adequate food and shelter for the population, adequate living conditions in general*[112]

Adequate food and shelter constitute a basic need. The Occupying Power is under a duty to ensure that this need is satisfied. It must ensure, 'to the fullest extent of the means 65

---

[106] Professional Training Series No 5/Add. 3 (New York and Geneva, 2004) (emphasis added). In the same sense the 'Basic Principles on the use of Force and Firearms by Law enforcement Officials', adopted by the Eighth United Nations Congress on the Prevention of Crime and the Treatment of Offenders, 1990, available at <http://www2.ohchr.org/english/law/pdf/firearms.pdf>. See Watkin, above n 6, at 296 ff.

[107] Watkin, above n 6, at 268, 276 ff, 285 ff.   [108] See Spoerri, above n 7, at 200 ff.

[109] Watkin, above n 6, at 301 ff.

[110] N. Melzer, *Interpretive Guidance on the Notion of Direct Participation in Hostilities* (Geneva: ICRC, 2009), at 33.

[111] For a detailed discussion of practical cases, see Watkin, above n 6, at 310 ff.

[112] See Ch 70 of this volume, at MN 23–33.

available to it', the food supplies of the population (Article 55 paragraph 1 GC IV). Article 11 ICESCR is also relevant in this connection.

66 In particular, the Occupying Power must take into account the needs of the most vulnerable parts of the population. As formulated by the 31st International Conference of the Red Cross and Red Crescent:[113]

> Specific protection is due to certain categories of persons in recognition of factors such as age, gender or disabilities, which make such persons more vulnerable in times of armed conflict. To safeguard adequate protection for all victims of armed conflicts, including situations of occupation, without discrimination, such factors must be taken into account.

67 Article 50 paragraph 5 GC IV ensures the continuation of pre-existing measures relating to food and medical care taken for the purpose of giving preference to specific vulnerable groups, namely, children under the age of 15, expectant mothers, and mothers with children aged under 7.

68 The duty to ensure adequate living conditions means that the population may not be prevented from pursuing its usual gainful activities. This is one of the reasons why the construction of a wall or barrier in the Occupied Palestinian Territory has been criticized as unlawful.[114] As aptly formulated in a declaration of the International Committee of the Red Cross (ICRC), '[the Barrier] runs counter to Israel's obligation to ensure [...] the well-being of the civilian population living under its occupation'.[115]

g. Protection of private property

69 Private property is an essential element of adequate living conditions. According to Article 46 of the Hague Regulations, the Occupying Power must respect private property. Destruction of private property is severely restricted even if fighting occurs during an occupation (Article 53 GC IV). Nevertheless, destruction of private property for law enforcement purposes must also be possible as an element of good governance, i.e. to the extent this is normally permissible in the internal order of states, which means that it is subject to the rule of proportionality.

70 Respect for private property also implies the right to use this property. Yet all legal orders provide for limitations of the use of private property for the sake of protecting other relevant, in particular public, interests. An important example is restrictions on building which may be necessary to ensure orderly land use and development. This is of particular relevance in the case of a long-term occupation. The applicable rules on building and land use will be contained in the pre-existing law of the territory which the Occupying Power may, as a matter of principle, not change.[116] But changes may, or even must, be made where the interest of the population, in the light of changing circumstances, so requires.[117]

---

[113] See 31st International Conference of the Red Cross and Red Crescent, Resolution 2, Four-Year Action Plan for the Implementation of International Humanitarian Law, Doc 31/C/11/R2, Objective 2.

[114] See, inter alia, the statement by the representative of the League of Arab States before the ICJ, Public sitting, 25 February 2004, CR 2004/5, at 30–2.

[115] 'Israel/Occupied and Autonomous Palestinian Territories: West Bank Barrier causes serious humanitarian and legal problems', ICRC News release 04/12, 18 February 2004, available at <http://www.icrc.org/eng/resources/documents/misc/5wacnx.htm>.

[116] See MN 14–16.

[117] A. Cassese, 'Powers and Duties of an Occupant in Relation to Land and Natural Resources', in Playfair (ed), above n 39, 419, at 422.

However, the adoption of rules which practically render impossible a reasonable use of land, be it for building or agricultural purposes, is unlawful.[118]

h. Health[119]

Health care is also a basic need. This is in particular stressed by Articles 55–57 GC IV. According to Article 55 paragraph 1, the Occupying Power must ensure, 'to the fullest extent of the means available to it', the medical supplies of the population. Before requisitioning such supplies for the purposes of the occupation forces and administration personnel, the requirements of the civilian population must be taken into account. The Occupying Power must also, 'to the fullest extent of the means available to it', ensure the functioning of an adequate health care infrastructure (medical and hospital establishments and services, public health and hygiene, under Article 56 GC IV). The duty imposed on the Occupying Power to care for the health of the population involves taking effective measures against communicable diseases. The needs of the most vulnerable parts of the population must be taken into account. Article 12 ICESCR is also relevant in this connection. 71

Access to health care is one of the problems raised by the construction of the wall in the Occupied Palestinian Territory: in a number of situations, the wall prevents adequate and speedy access for parts of the population to medical establishments.[120] 72

i. Access to humanitarian assistance

If the aforementioned basic needs cannot be satisfied with the resources of the territory and those of the Occupying Power, the latter is under the duty to accept and facilitate relief actions organized by third parties (Article 59 GC IV; Article 69 AP I).[121] [122] That duty covers a broad range of commodities: food, medical supplies, clothing, bedding, means of shelter (which covers not only tents, but also building materials for civilian housing), other supplies for the survival of the civilian population, and objects necessary for religious worship. The only condition applicable to this duty to accept relief actions is the existence of a need: there is no provision for objections based on military considerations; there is only the possibility to 'divert' relief consignments in the case of 'urgent necessity', but only in the interest of the population of the territory. This means that the distribution of the relief may be modified to a certain extent in relation to the intent of the providers of such relief. But this does not open up the possibility of rejecting the relief altogether. 73

Such relief action may not relieve the Occupying Power of its responsibilities to ensure the fulfilment of the needs of the population (Article 60 GC IV). 74

Third states must grant free passage to such relief consignments. They have a certain right of control in order to verify that a consignment is used only for providing relief to the population of the occupied territory and not for the support of the Occupying Power. 75

---

[118] M. Rishmawi, 'The Administration of the West Bank under Israeli Rule', in Playfair (ed), above n 39, 267, at 288.
[119] See Ch 70, MN 34–40, of this volume.
[120] ICJ, *Wall*, Advisory Opinion, above n 18, para 133.
[121] See Ch 12 of this volume.
[122] H. Spieker, 'Humanitarian Assistance, Access in Armed Conflict and Occupation', in MPEPIL, esp paras 7 et seq.

j. Education

76 Education is also a basic need.[123] The Occupying Power has to ensure that this need is satisfied (Article 50 GC IV). Under Article 50 paragraph 1 GC IV it must ensure the proper workings of education institutions. In addition, the guarantees of the ICESCR (Article 13), of the Convention on the Elimination of All Forms of Discrimination against Women (CEDAW) (Article 10), and in particular of the Convention on the Rights of the Child (CRC) apply. Therefore, the Occupying Power has to take measures to ensure equal treatment of men and women in the field of education (Article 10 CEDAW). The right of the child to education (Articles 28 and 29 CRC) must be implemented by the Occupying Power through appropriate measures. This may include accepting relief actions providing education materials, or allowing outside organizations to build school facilities.

77 The duty of the Occupying Power to ensure education facilities may in many ways encounter obstacles which must be overcome. This is a thorny problem in the case of the Occupied Palestinian Territory. The construction of the wall and the establishment of settlements have created obstacles for children trying to reach their schools.[124] It is a duty of the Occupying Power to eliminate the negative impacts of such obstacles.

k. Protection of family rights

78 The protection of family rights is in a general way ensured by Article 46 of the Hague Regulations. The identification of children is facilitated by Article 50 GC IV. In addition, Article 23 ICCPR requires the state and society (the former includes the Occupying Power) to protect the family. Article 10 ICESCR is also relevant in this connection.

l. The possibility of religious life

79 The 'religious convictions and practices' of the population of the occupied territory have to be respected (Article 27 paragraph 1 GC IV). In addition, the Occupying Power 'shall permit ministers of religion to give spiritual assistance to the members of their religious communities'. The Occupying Power must also allow, and facilitate, the distribution of consignments of books and other articles required for religious needs (Article 58 GC IV).

80 Freedom of religion is also guaranteed by Article 18 ICCPR.

m. Use of natural resources and protection of the environment

81 Sustainable use of natural resources, careful environmental management, and preservation of the environment are essential elements of good governance. According to the Hague Regulations, a distinction must be drawn in this respect between resources which are private property and those which are public property.

82 The basic rule concerning resources which are private property is that they are not open to appropriation by the Occupying Power, except in the case of requisitions (see MN 86). They continue to be in the hands of their private owners, who may use them as they like. That right to use them, however, remains subject to legal limitations, in particular those serving environmental purposes, found in the pre-existing law which is maintained.[125] The duty of good governance also implies a duty to introduce such limitations as may be necessary in order to respect international legal standards concerning the protection of the environment, for instance the establishment and administration of protected areas. Yet

---

[123] See also Ch 70 of this volume at MN 48–55.
[124] ICJ, *Wall*, Advisory Opinion, above n 18, para 133.
[125] See MN 38–41 and 97.

such limitations must serve genuine environmental concerns. The establishment of large protected areas for the purpose of removing the population and having an empty space in the interest of military training and other security purposes is unlawful, subject to the possibility of requisitions.[126] This is, however, the situation in large parts of the Occupied Palestinian Territory in 'Area C'.[127]

In contradistinction to private property, the Hague Regulations allow a limited use of those natural resources that are public property (Article 55 of the Hague Regulations) ('real estate, forests, and agricultural estates') by the Occupying Power. What is public property is determined according to the law of the occupied territory as it existed at the time when the occupation started. In many countries, minerals in the ground are public property, not the property of the owners of the land under which they are situated. In such a case, the exploitation of such resources is governed by Article 55. If the state whose territory is occupied has granted concessions for the exploration and/or exploitation of such mineral resources, these concessions are private property which has to be protected under Article 46 of the Hague Regulations.[128] Living resources (game, fish) are as a rule not public property but subject to appropriation according to the law in force. 83

The essential limitation is that the Occupying Power is only the 'administrator and usufructuary'. In relation to renewable resources, this means that the Occupying Power can use their proceeds but must 'safeguard the capital' (Article 55 of the Hague Regulations, second sentence)[129]—in modern terms, a sustainable management of renewable resources. The yield of the resource must be maintained. 84

The meaning of Article 55 for the management of non-renewable resources such as oil is more difficult to ascertain. It could be argued that any exploitation of a non-renewable resource necessarily depletes the capital and is therefore unlawful. But it could also be argued that at least a reasonable exploitation is permissible if it takes place at a rate practised at the time when the occupation began. The opening of new extraction fields or areas, however, goes beyond what is admissible under Article 55.[130] 85

There is another limitation derived from a systematic interpretation of a number of provisions of the Hague Regulations relating to taxes, contributions, and requisitions (Articles 48, 49, 51, and 52). Their proceeds may only be used for the needs of the occupied territory, as well as for the needs of the army and administration of occupation. This principle also applies to the use of natural resources. They may not be used for the general profit of the Occupying Power.[131] The principles of good administration of public property and of the protection of private property also mean that the Occupying Power must use due diligence to protect natural resources against unlawful exploitation and pillage.[132] 86

---

[126] See MN 104–105.
[127] Map published by OCHA on access restrictions for the Palestinian population in the West Bank, available at <http://www.ochaopt.org/documents/ocha_opt_west_bank_access_restrictions_dec_2012_geopdf_mobile.pdf>. See above n 82 concerning the different areas in the Occupied Palestinian Territory.
[128] US Department of State Memorandum of Law on Israel's Right to Develop New Oil Fields in Sinai and the Gulf of Suez, 1 October 1976, 16 *ILM* (1977) 723, at 748 ff.
[129] Benvenisti, above n 77, at 869.
[130] US Department of State Memorandum, above n 128, at 736 ff; see also Cassese, above n 117, 428 ff. *Contra*, Reply by the Ministry of Foreign Affairs of Israel, 1 August 1977, 17 *ILM* (1978) 432.
[131] US Department of State Memorandum, above n 128, at 742 ff. See Spoerri, above n 7, at 186; Cassese, above n 177, at 430 ff.
[132] ICJ, *DRC v Uganda*, above n 25, paras 242 et seq.

87   In addition, the Occupying Power must respect customary international environmental law in relation to the occupied territory.[133] This means, inter alia, that the Occupying Power must use due diligence to avoid trans-frontier pollution,[134] which might cause damage to third states and areas beyond national jurisdiction. Thus, such acts as the destruction of oil wells during the occupation of Kuwait by Iraq, which caused heavy damage to the marine environment and the coastal environment of adjacent states, are prohibited.[135]

88   The Occupying Power must also respect the principle of equitable utilization in relation to water resources shared between the occupied territory and other states.[136] This is needed for the management and use of shared water resources, a question that was important for the occupation of Iraq after 2003 and which remains important for the Occupied Palestinian Territory.

89   The continuity of the legal system of the occupied territory[137] also means that environmental treaties applicable in relation to the occupied territory remain valid and must be respected.[138] An important example is the Convention on International Watercourses,[139] which enshrines and concretizes the principle of equitable utilization.

n. Cultural property

90   A basic protection of cultural property results from Article 56 of the Hague Regulations, which extends the protection of private property to what might be called cultural property. It also prohibits 'seizure of, destruction or wilful damage done to […] historic monuments [and] works of art and science'.

91   The newer rules on the protection of cultural property in occupied territory are treaty-based. There is, on the one hand, the specific Convention on the protection of cultural property in times of armed conflict,[140] and, on the other hand, the World Heritage Convention, further discussed below at MN 92, as it relates to cultural heritage. Article 5(1) of the Hague Convention of 1954 obligates the Occupying Power to support the national authorities of the occupied territory 'in safeguarding and protecting its cultural property'. This provision is premised on the assumption that these authorities continue to function, as provided by the principle of continuation of pre-existing institutions. Article 5(2) addresses the situation where these authorities are unable to fulfil their tasks. Then it is the Occupying Power itself which has to 'take the most necessary measures of preservation', 'as far as possible'. This is a duty of good governance that is somewhat watered down (only the most necessary measures, and only as far as possible). This realistic approach shows the contextual nature of good governance. Such measures include a protection against looting.

92   Another important case is the World Heritage Convention,[141] to which nearly all states (190) are parties. The United Nations Educational, Scientific and Cultural Organization (UNESCO) has been concerned about the cultural and natural heritage of Palestine since

---

[133] Benvenisti, above n 77, at 866.   [134] T. Koivurova, 'Due Diligence', in MPEPIL, esp para 19.

[135] UN Compensation Commission, 'F 4 claims', see T.A. Mensah, 'United Nations Compensation Commission (UNCC)', in MPEPIL, esp at para 46.

[136] L. del Castillo Laborde, 'Equitable Utilization of Shared Resources', in MPEPIL.

[137] See MN 38–41.   [138] Benvenisti, above n 77, 866 et seq.

[139] Convention on the Law of the Non-navigational Uses of International Watercourses, 21 May 1997; see Benvenisti, above n 77, at 866.

[140] Hague Convention of 14 May 1954, supplemented by the Second Protocol of 26 March 1999. See for details C. Johannot Gradis, *Le patrimoine culturel matériel et immatériel: quelle protection en cas de conflit armé* (Geneva: Schulthess, 2014), at 351–495.

[141] Convention Concerning the Protection of the World Cultural and Natural Heritage of 16 November 1972.

the establishment of a UNESCO office in Ramallah in 1998.[142] At that time, the practice meant that neither Israel (as Palestine was not Israeli territory) nor Palestine (not being a state party to the Convention) could officially ask for the designation of heritage sites. In 2011, Palestine ratified the Convention shortly after being admitted as a member of UNESCO.[143] Then Palestine designations were accepted, the first one being the Church of the Nativity in Bethlehem.

o. Public revenue

Maintenance of the local law as it exists means, inter alia, that applicable tax law is maintained 'as far as possible' and that the inhabitants of the territory continue to pay taxes or similar levies (Articles 48 and 51 of the Hague Regulations). This revenue must be used for the purpose of administering the territory, not for the profit of the Occupying Power. For the same purpose, the Occupying Power may also levy special contributions (Article 49 of the Hague Regulations).[144]

93

The principle of maintenance of existing tax legislation is not absolute. The Hague Regulations prescribe it 'as far as possible'. The principle of good governance, understood in the light of the current practice of the regulatory state, requires a system of taxation which corresponds to current needs. On that basis, the Supreme Court of Israel has held that the law of occupation allows the introduction of a new tax as required by the economic needs of the time.[145] Before the Court was a challenge to the introduction of a new excise duty that constituted a change in relation to the pre-existing law.[146] Concerning the legality of changing the existing law, the Court pointed to the fact that the formula 'as far as possible' in Article 48 is less strict than 'unless absolutely prevented' in Article 43.[147] The Court then relied, in order to justify its decision, in substance on the principle of good governance:

94

[F]reezing taxation activities in their general form and employed by the military government in the beginning of its rule may bring about over the years, particularly if a few decades are involved, a freezing of the economy.[148]

Later on, the Court expressly relied on Article 43 of the Hague Regulations:

[I]n the matter of the obligation to assure public life, a continuing obligation is involved [...] and it should accordingly be fulfilled, only in consideration of the circumstances, which change from time to time, and with due regard to the needs occasioned by the passage of time [...] The circumstances referred to are not simply those of security, but also relate to the economy, health, communications and the like.[149]

---

[142] Palestine and the World Heritage Convention, available at <http://whc.unesco.org/en/news/821/>.
[143] Date of ratification 8 December 2011.
[144] See G. von Glahn, 'Taxation under Belligerent Occupation', in Playfair (ed), above n 39, 341, at 342 ff.
[145] Supreme Court of Israel, above n 49. For an overview of Israeli practices concerning taxation, see H. Jabr, 'Financial Administration of the Israeli-Occupied West-Bank', in Playfair (ed), above n 39, 377.
[146] The Jordanian Excise Tax Law as regards the West Bank and the relevant British Ordinances for Palestine as regards the Gaza Strip.
[147] Supreme Court of Israel, *Bassil Abu Aita et al*, above n 49, at 77.
[148] Ibid, at 88. The Court then refers to a number of examples of Occupying Powers changing the existing system of taxation.
[149] Ibid, at 129. The economic reasoning which on that basis is used to justify the new tax cannot be discussed in the present framework.

p. *International relations*

95 There are different types of international legal norms applicable to an occupied territory which have to be distinguished: (i) international law (treaties and customary law) binding the Occupying Power in the exercise of its authority over the occupied territory; (ii) international law binding the state whose authority is *de facto* displaced in relation to the occupied territory at the beginning of the occupation; (iii) general rules of customary international law; and (iv) treaties concluded during the time of occupation.

96 As to the first type of norm it has been pointed out above that human rights treaties, as well as customary human rights law binding the state which is the Occupying Power, are also applicable to the authority that the state exercises over the occupied territory.[150] However, it should be asked whether this applies to measures of territorial control a state must take to respect the rights of third states.[151] If they treat the Occupying Power as the correct addressee of relevant norms, this may be practically convenient, but it might amount to recognizing a *de facto* situation as legally valid, which they are not obliged to recognize as such.

97 The situation is rather different where the problem is whether the Occupying Power has to comply with the international law applicable to the territory in question before the occupation began, which is the second type of legal norm to be distinguished. It has already been pointed out that the continuity of the legal system means that international obligations of the state whose territory is occupied must be respected by the Occupying Power in its activities relating to the occupied territory.[152] This is also a requirement of good governance. Relations between the outside world and the occupied territory and its inhabitants must continue and be developed, and these relations are to be governed, first, by the international law applicable at the beginning of the occupation.[153]

98 Good governance may, however, also require that this law is developed in light of the circumstances. This raises the question of to what extent the Occupying Power is entitled to conclude treaties with respect to the occupied territory and to enter into cooperative arrangements with other states. The principles already developed in respect of legislation[154] should apply *mutatis mutandis*. The Occupying Power is entitled to conclude such treaties to the extent that this is really required for the benefit of the population. The fact that occupation constitutes only a temporary authority, however, entails as a consequence that the Occupying Power, at least as a matter of principle, would have to conclude that treaty in its capacity as Occupying Power and not in the name of the Occupied Power, and would not be able to create obligations in relation to the territory beyond the duration of the occupation.[155]

99 The situation is different where the 'local' authorities of the occupied territory are themselves in a position to engage in international intercourse. This is a rather exceptional situation which may only occur in the case of a long-term occupation, as in the case of Palestine. Palestine, apparently with the acquiescence of Israel, concluded an Interim

---

[150] See MN 46–58.

[151] T. Meron, 'Applicability of Multilateral Conventions to Occupied Territories', 72 *AJIL* (1978) 542, esp the debate on the Chicago Convention on International Civil Aviation at 551 ff.

[152] As to treaties concerning the protection of the environment, see MN 82.

[153] For treaties concluded under the aegis of the ILO, see J. Quigley, 'The Right to Form Trade Unions under Military Occupation', in Playfair (ed), above n 39, 295, at 307 ff.

[154] See MN 38–41.   [155] Benvenisti, above n 77, at 871.

Association Agreement on Trade and Cooperation with the European Community (EC) in 1997.[156] An Agreement on the further liberalization of agricultural products entered into force in 2012. The European Union (EU) cooperates with the Palestinian Authority in a number of projects for assistance. But it appears that diplomatic and consular relations between the Palestinian Authority and third states are a difficult borderline exercise of diplomatic practice.

The conduct of foreign relations concerning the occupied territory thus is a complex question. The principle of good governance requires the Occupying Power to ensure normal life in the occupied territory also by engaging in international contacts and dealings necessary for that purpose. On the other hand, third states are not obliged to accept the occupation as legally valid and enter into negotiations or other contacts with the Occupying Power. In many cases, third states will continue to accept the displaced government as representing the population of the occupied territory, even if that government controls only a small part of its territory or is only a government in exile.[157]

III. The protection of the interests of the Occupying Power

a. Security

Normal law enforcement will also provide for the security of the Occupying Power. In other words, the security of the Occupying Power is a legitimate objective of law enforcement. The principle, explained above, remains that the Occupying Power must proceed in the law enforcement mode to satisfy its security interests, unless there is a situation of armed conflict.[158] As already pointed out, human rights limit the powers the Occupying Power possesses in this respect, but the security interests of the Occupying Power also limit the human rights of the population of the occupied territory.

The guiding principle for achieving this balance of interests is the principle of proportionality. In taking measures to satisfy its security interests, the Occupying Power may not restrict the rights of the population of the occupied territory to a degree disproportionate in relation to the security improvement achieved by the measure in question. This principle of proportionality has consistently been recognized in the case law of the Supreme Court of Israel in cases relating to the Occupied Palestinian Territory. In a case concerning the construction of the 'security barrier' in the Occupied Palestinian Territory, the Court held that the particular part of this edifice was unlawful, as the damage done to the property interest of the Palestinian villagers was disproportionate in relation to the security gains obtained through the construction.[159] The same considerations apply concerning the demolition of houses for security reasons.[160] Admittedly, proportionality is a difficult principle. The balancing process it implies involves uncertainties.

---

[156] 97/430/EC: Council Decision of 2 June 1997 concerning the conclusion of the Euro-Mediterranean Interim Association Agreement on trade and cooperation between the European Community, of the one part, and the PLO for the benefit of the Palestinian Authority of the West Bank and the Gaza Strip, [1997] OJ L187/1. Art 73 of the Agreement defines the territorial scope of application on the Palestinian side as 'the West Bank and the Gaza Strip'.

[157] K. Tiroch, 'Governments in Exile', in MPEPIL, esp paras 17 et seq.

[158] See MN 62–64.

[159] Supreme Court of Israel, *Beit Sourik*, above n 36. See N. Keidar, 'An Examination of the Authority of a Military Commander to Requisition Privately Owned Land for the Construction of the Separation Barrier', 38 *Israel Law Review* (2005) 247.

[160] See MN 59–64.

103 As to the restrictions on the personal freedom of movement for the sake of security, IHL provides for a specific type of deprivation of liberty, namely, internment (Articles 79–135 GC IV). The substantive guarantees involved in this regime are similar to those applying as regards POW status.[161]

b. The sustenance of the army of occupation

104 The Hague Regulations provide for two types of measures allowing an Occupying Power to ensure the sustenance of the army of occupation: requisitions in kind or services, as a matter of principle against compensation (Article 52); and, under certain conditions, money contributions (Article 49). This does not really correspond to modern conditions. An army of occupation is no longer required to live off the resources of the occupied territory. Nor are the measures described really adequate in the case of a long-term occupation. Yet Article 55 GC IV also provides for the requisition of foodstuffs, articles, or medical supplies by the Occupying Power.

105 The right of requisition is strictly limited to the needs of the army of occupation, which may include the needs of the occupation administration. Article 52 of the Hague Regulations allows requisitions only 'for the needs of the army of occupation'. Article 55 GC IV is somewhat clearer concerning the scope of the licence: requisitions are permissible 'for the use by the occupation forces and administration personnel'. Consequently, it is not allowed to requisition movable or real property simply in the interest of the state which is the Occupying Power. For example, when Israel reserves the use of certain areas in the Occupied Palestinian Territory as firing zones for training purposes of the Israel Defense Forces (IDF), and restricts the right of the persons habitually living in those areas to remain there and pursue gainful, in particular farming, activities, this is unlawful because it constitutes a requisition not for the needs of the army of occupation but for the general interest of the Israeli armed forces not specifically related to the occupation.[162]

C. Legal Consequences of a Violation

106 The violation of the norms described above by agents of the Occupying Power entails the international responsibility of the latter.[163] As most of these norms create *erga omnes* obligations, under Article 48 paragraph 1(b) of the ILC Articles on State Responsibility, this responsibility exists not only in relation to the state whose territory happens to be occupied (the injured state), but also in relation to all states. Third states may also invoke this responsibility, as provided in Article 48 paragraph 2.

107 In addition, under Article 8 of the ILC Articles on State Responsibility, the Occupying Power may be responsible for acts performed by local authorities of the occupied territory as they act 'under the direction or control' of the Occupying Power. This is the basis of

---

[161] See Ch 65 of this volume.

[162] The case is well documented by several Israeli (B'tselem, Association for Civil Rights in Israel) and international NGOs. See B'tselem, *Means of Expulsion: Violence, Law, and Lawlessness against Palestinians in the Southern Hebron Hills* (July 2005), available at <http://www.btselem.org/download/200507_south_mount_hebron_eng.pdf> and The Association for Civil Rights in Israel, 'Info-sheet: The 12 Villages of Firing Zone 918 in the South Hebron Hills', 7 November 2012, available at <http://www.acri.org.il/en/2012/07/firing-zone-918-infosheet>; also Michael Bothe, 'Limits of the right of expropriation (requisition) and of movement restrictions in occupied territory', Expert Opinion, 2 August 2012, available at <http://www.acri.org.il/en/wp-content/uploads/2013/01/Michael-Bothe-918-position.pdf>.

[163] ICJ, *Wall*, Advisory Opinion, above n 18, paras 147 et seq.

the judgments of the ECtHR relating to Northern Cyprus, which attribute the acts of the 'state' of Northern Cyprus to Turkey as an Occupying Power.[164]

The general rules relating to means to ensure compliance with IHL apply to the law of occupation as well. It should be noted that a number of recent court cases and arbitral awards relating to IHL deal with the law of occupation.[165] This is also the case with international criminal courts.[166] As has been shown above,[167] the violation of a number of obligations imposed upon an Occupying Power constitutes grave breaches of GC IV or AP I, and consequently war crimes.[168]

There are, however, some specific questions concerning the law of occupation. The most important one is the parallel application of IHRL and IHL. This means that not only the substantive human rights guarantees apply in case of an occupation, but also the remedies which exist under the law of human rights, e.g. the complaint or quasi-complaint procedures pursuant to the ECHR,[169] the ACHR, or the Optional Protocol to the ICCPR. Implementation procedures developed by the UN Human Rights Commission and now the UN Human Rights Council apply to situations of occupation, and are indeed used in this context, in particular the instrument of Special Rapporteurs.[170]

To the extent that courts of the Occupying Power possess jurisdiction in relation to an occupied territory,[171] their role as a means to ensure the Occupying Power's compliance with the law of occupation is essential.[172]

D. Critical Assessment

The law of belligerent occupation, as it has developed during the last 150 years, has proved to constitute a viable and appropriate balance of interests. That balancing of interests constitutes a daily challenge in the concrete practical application of that body of law. As in any balancing process, there are uncertainties and the danger of abuse. Therefore, there is a need to strengthen the procedures ensuring the correct implementation of the relevant law. The development of international criminal jurisdictions and the increased use of judicial settlement have shown their potential for that purpose. But these developments are far from covering every case of occupation.

Three traditional basic principles have withstood the pressures of changing political circumstances:

— Occupation is a temporary situation, not an equivalent to annexation. This implies, inter alia, a duty of the Occupying Power to respect, as a matter of principle, the pre-existing local law (principle of continuity) and to avoid measures amounting to a *de facto* annexation.

---

[164] See MN 6. For a differentiated analysis, see Frowein, above n 90, at 13 ff.
[165] ICJ, *DRC v Uganda*, above n 25; ICJ, *Wall*, Advisory Opinion, above n 18; EECC, *Central Front—Ethiopia's Claim 2*, above n 23, and also see above n 24.
[166] ICTY, *Naletilić and Martinović*, above n 22.   [167] See in particular at MN 46–58.
[168] See Ch 31 of this volume.   [169] ECtHR, *Loizidou*, above n 28; ECtHR, *Al-Skeini*, above n 93.
[170] As regards the Occupied Palestinian Territory, see, e.g., the report quoted above n 105.
[171] See MN 44–45.
[172] As regards the case law of the Israeli courts in relation to the Occupied Palestinian Territory, see, inter alia, the decisions quoted above nn 36 and 49; D. Kretzmer, 'The Law of Belligerent Occupation in the Supreme Court of Israel', 94 *IRRC* 885 (2012) 207.

— The Occupying Power has a duty of good governance in relation to the occupied territory.
— The Occupying Power may take measures to ensure the safety and sustenance of its army, and administration of the occupied territory.

A certain tension may exist between these three principles. They must be balanced in concrete circumstances.

113   While these principles have been preserved, the law of belligerent occupation has not been static. The interpretation of the law of belligerent occupation has proved to be flexible enough to adapt to new developments. Important developments have to be noted. But the said principles are not set aside by a sweeping reference to novel notions like the 'transformative occupation'.

114   In the case of a long-term occupation like that in Palestine, the duty of good governance may have a special weight in relation to the principle of continuity.

115   The two most important legal developments have been the emergence of international guarantees of human rights and the impact of the Charter of the United Nations.

116   The recognition of an extraterritorial application of human rights has considerably strengthened the legal protection of the inhabitants of an occupied territory. The law of belligerent occupation, being part of IHL, does not displace human rights as *lex specialis*. Both areas of international law can be applied in parallel and cumulatively provide protection, provided that limitations of human rights are recognized as respecting the principle of proportionality. On the other hand, respect for human rights may require some limitations to the principle of continuity.

117   The impact of the law of the Charter is mainly to be noted where a belligerent occupation occurs after an armed conflict and is the object of Security Council measures taken for restoring or maintaining international peace and security. This is the realm of what is called transformative occupation. A mandate given by a binding Security Council decision may indeed modify the legal regime applicable to a belligerent occupation, in particular by imposing measures which otherwise would be at odds with the principle of continuity.

MICHAEL BOTHE

Chapter 70. Economic, Social, and Cultural Rights in Occupied Territories

	MN
A. Introduction	1
B. Meaning and Application	7
I. Economic, social, and cultural rights embodied in the rules contained in the Geneva Conventions	7
II. The application of the international human rights law of economic, social, and cultural rights in occupied territories	13
a. International human rights law provisions relevant to socio-economic rights	13
b. The sources of conventional human rights obligations in occupied territories	16
III. The specific scope and nature of the obligations of the occupier	23
a. The obligation to provide food and medical supplies	23
b. The obligation to ensure and maintain public health and hygiene	34
c. Rules relating to labour and enlistment of protected persons	41
d. Rules on education for children	48
IV. The relationship between the rules contained in the Geneva Conventions and positive duties of protecting and fulfilling economic, social, and cultural rights	56
a. The scope of the occupier's legislative powers	56
b. The term 'to the fullest extent of the means available to it'	63
C. Relevance in Non-International Armed Conflicts	71
D. Legal Consequences of a Violation	77
I. Human rights mechanisms	77
II. United Nations Security Council	85
III. International criminal responsibility	87
E. Critical Assessment	92

Select Bibliography

Arai-Takahashi, Y., *The Law of Occupation: Continuity and Change of International Humanitarian Law, and its Interaction with International Human Rights Law* (Leiden: Martinus Nijhoff Publishers, 2009)

Benvenisti, E., *The International Law of Occupation* (2nd edn, Oxford: OUP, 2012)

Giacca, G., *Economic, Social and Cultural Rights in Armed Conflict* (Oxford: OUP, 2014)

Horowitz, J.T., 'Human Rights, Positive Obligations, and Armed Conflict: Implementing the Right to Education in Occupied Territories', 1(2) *Journal of International Humanitarian Legal Studies* (2010) 304

Kolb, R./Vité, S., *Le droit de l'occupation militaire. Perspectives historiques et enjeux juridiques actuels* (Brussels: Bruylant, 2009)

Lubell, N., 'Human Rights Obligations in Military Occupation', 94 *IRRC* 885 (2012) 317

Riedel, E., 'Economic, Social and Cultural Rights in Armed Conflict', in A. Clapham and P. Gaeta (eds), *Oxford Handbook of International Law in Armed Conflict* (Oxford: OUP, 2014) 441

Vité, S., 'The Interrelation of the Law of Occupation and Economic, Social and Cultural Rights: The Examples of Food, Health and Property', 90 *IRRC* 871 (2008) 629

A. Introduction

1   The international law on occupation (occupation law) regulates, through a wide range of governance-related rules, how an occupied territory and its population are to be administered.[1] These rules are contained in the provisions derived from the occupier's general duty, under the 1907 Hague Regulations, to take all feasible measures to restore and ensure adequate conditions of life for the civilian population (Article 43 of the Hague Regulations). The 1949 Geneva Convention (GC) IV imposes obligations on the occupier with regard to matters such as health, food, and relief assistance; work and employment; and education or cultural matters, although in a disparate manner and sometimes without elaborating the precise meaning of these obligations.

2   From the outset, it should be noted that the term 'economic, social, and cultural rights' (ESC rights) does not appear in any of the four Geneva Conventions, nor in any previous or subsequent international humanitarian law (IHL) treaties or documents. Economic, social, and cultural rights are derived from the international legal framework that is designed to promote and protect the human rights of all individuals.[2] Economic, social, and cultural rights have been recognized and included in various domestic laws and constitutions, as well as a range of international and regional treaties.[3] But while ESC rights are not specifically included as such, their protection is articulated in GC IV regulating relations between the occupier and the persons and objects in territory under its control. The specificity of occupation law is that, in addition to the 'ordinary' rules of IHL relating to the conduct of hostilities or that set standards for treatment of individuals in enemy hands, it encompasses rules that relate, principally, to the administration or governance of occupied territories, which include welfare provisions.

3   The obligations *ratione materiae* under GC IV are numerous and provide a set of rules that include, inter alia:

— the responsibility not to deprive inhabitants of any of the benefits of GC IV by any change introduced into the institutions or government of the occupied territory, or by any agreement between local authorities and the Occupying Power (Article 47);
— the duty not to engage in individual or mass forcible transfers (Article 49; see Chapter 58 of this volume);
— the requirement to facilitate the proper working of all institutions devoted to the care and education of children (Article 50);
— the ability to require work only under special conditions (Article 51);
— the prohibition on creating unemployment (Article 52), or on destroying real or personal property during military operations unless absolutely necessary (Article 53; see Chapters 71 and 72 of this volume); and

---

[1] The duties of an Occupying Power are to be found primarily in Arts 42–56 Hague Regulations and Arts 27–34 and 47–78 GC IV, as well as in certain provisions of AP I, when applicable, such as Arts 69–70.
[2] See generally E. Riedel, G. Giacca, and C. Golay (eds), *Economic, Social and Cultural Rights: Contemporary Issues and Challenges* (Oxford: OUP, 2014).
[3] Ibid. Of all the human rights treaties, particular mention should be made of the ICESCR (1966), as it remains the only treaty that expressly sets international standards pertaining to ESC rights that are of a global reach and potentially applicable in all situations (even though the Covenant's application in wartime and situations of occupation was not originally foreseen). As of June 2015, the ICESCR had been ratified by 164 states parties.

— the obligations to ensure food and medical supplies for the population (Article 55), to ensure and maintain medical and hospital establishments and services and public health and hygiene (Article 56), to agree to relief schemes on behalf of the population if they are inadequately supplied (Article 59), to ensure the rapid distribution of relief consignments (Article 61), or to ensure that protected persons receive the individual relief consignments sent to them (Article 62).

In addition, the rules relating to the consignment of medical supplies, food and clothing (Article 23), and child welfare (Article 24) also apply in occupied territory.

All these rules are evidently pertinent to the protection of ESC rights of the civilian population, for they address certain aspects or components of substantive ESC rights. Accordingly, this chapter analyses the relevant provisions not covered by other chapters, in order to understand how obligations owed under IHL to the civilian population in occupied territory pertain to ESC rights.

In particular, this chapter discusses the relationship between GC IV and human rights norms relating to ESC rights. The application of occupation law does not exclude human rights law from concurrent application,[4] but this demands a full appreciation of two topical and controversial issues: the application of certain human rights treaties extraterritorially; and the relationship between those treaties and IHL. But for the purpose of the present chapter, the complementary application of the Geneva Conventions and the international rules on ESC rights will be addressed to the extent that there are rules in areas common to both branches of law, and to the extent that international human rights law (IHRL) may inform the content of the relevant IHL rules.[5]

The main legal issues to be discussed are how GC IV's rules of a socio-economic nature operate; how ESC rights apply in occupied territories, and how they may affect the assessment of the content of the obligations derived under GC IV; to what extent the application of human rights obligations adds substantive duties to those set forth in GC IV; how human rights obligations—which may entail important legislative, administrative, financial, institutional, or social measures—are to be implemented within this legal framework; and whether, and if so to what extent, the prolonged character of an occupation influences or affects the interpretation and application of ESC rights.

B. Meaning and Application

I. Economic, social, and cultural rights embodied in the rules contained in the Geneva Conventions

It is important to understand what it means when we refer to 'ESC rights' when dealing with GC IV. The fact that many of the Geneva Conventions' rules aim to ensure that local inhabitants are not denied health care, food, water, shelter, or access to them, has prompted certain commentators to employ a language of 'rights' when considering those rules.[6] The idea has been advanced whereby the rights listed in the International Covenant

---

[4] See Ch 35 of this volume.
[5] This does not mean that there may not be opposite situations where IHL norms may be used to define the scope of ESC rights norms, but the aim of this chapter is to focus on the meaning and application of the GCs.
[6] L. Doswald-Beck, *Human Rights in Times of Conflict and Terrorism* (Oxford: OUP, 2011), at 473; Sassòli, Bouvier, and Quintin argue, for instance, that in contrast to four specific areas in which human rights law

on Economic Social and Cultural Rights (ICESCR) are 'included in one form or another' under IHL.[7] Reference has been made to 'ESC rights embodied in IHL treaty-based rules', 'types of economic and social rights addressed by IHL', 'protection of economic, social and cultural rights', or 'economic social and cultural rights in occupied territory'.[8]

8   One might question whether speaking of rights in this way is appropriate, not only because rules embodied under IHL refer to duties of Contracting Parties, rather than articulating rights of individuals, but also because most human rights law concerning ESC rights is simply not mirrored in IHL rules. Military occupation of foreign territories encompasses a larger range of problems than those foreseen by IHL, especially when occupation is prolonged. Suffice it to mention here that GC IV provides scant protection of the right to work beyond questions relating to compulsory labour, requisitioning services, and labour conditions of protected persons working at the request of the occupier.[9] Even though GC IV imposes certain obligations with regard to education, health, food, or labour, the meaning and content of these obligations cannot be equated to the IHRL of ESC rights, which is a distinct legal regime.

9   This general comment is warranted for a number of reasons, at least from the point of view of the civilian population under occupation. First, and undeniably, the protection afforded by the human rights law of ESC rights through its application may affect the assessment of the content of the obligations derived from GC IV. The IHRL of ESC rights can help to elucidate elements or aspects that are mentioned under IHL, but which may remain too vague and ambiguous to provide effective guarantees for individuals, especially during lengthy occupations. Economic, social, and cultural rights can inform the meaning of certain rules under the law of occupation on issues relating to food, health, or education, and as such broaden the scope of protection, which may be referred to as a *human rights-broadening phenomenon*. Certain substantive ESC rights provisions that appear to be of particular relevance in situations of prolonged occupation may be incorporated into terms such as '*civil life*',[10] 'the *proper working* of all institutions devoted to the care and *education* of children',[11] the 'duty of ensuring the *food and medical supplies* of the population',[12]

---

seems to provide more detail (procedural guarantees in case of detention, use of firearms by law enforcement officials, medical ethics, and the definition of torture), IHL provisions are better adapted to armed conflict with respect to: the right to life in the conduct of hostilities; the prohibition of inhuman and degrading treatment; the right to health; the right to food; and the right to individual freedom (in IACs). Sassòli/Bouvier/Quintin, at 455–7.

[7] Doswald-Beck, above n 6, at 473.

[8] Sassòli/Bouvier/Quintin, at 246. Arai-Takahashi argues that 'IHL contains detailed rules concerning economic, social, and cultural rights specifically tailored to occupation. The parties to an armed conflict must implement such rules *immediately*, rather than *progressively* as in relation to the rights embodied in the ICESCR': Y. Arai-Takahashi, *The Law of Occupation: Continuity and Change of International Humanitarian Law, and its Interaction with International Human Rights Law* (Leiden: Martinus Nijhoff Publishers, 2009), at 355–74 and 413.

[9] The ICJ appropriately relied on the negative obligation of the occupier not to interfere with the right to work of the occupied population, where the physical barriers created by the construction of the wall, as well as numerous other restrictions on movement, undermined their ability to earn their livelihood. ICJ, *Legal Consequences of the Construction of a Wall in the Occupied Palestinian Territory*, Advisory Opinion, 9 July 2004, paras 130, 133, and 134.

[10] In an occupied territory the rules relative to living conditions of civilians under occupation are derived from the occupier's general duty to take all feasible measures to restore and ensure 'civil life' (*vie public[que]*), as set forth under the authentic French version of Art 43 Hague Regulations. The term 'civil life' has therefore been reinterpreted on its assumed purpose, as referring to the general welfare of the local population as a whole. See further G. Giacca, *Economic, Social and Cultural Rights in Armed Conflict* (Oxford: OUP, 2014), Chapter IV.

[11] Art 50 para 1 GC IV (emphasis added).   [12] Art 55 para 1 GC IV (emphasis added).

or the phrase '*to the fullest extent of the means available to it*'.¹³ In this sense, human rights law can provide a normative clarification, with its extensive jurisprudence and practice and specific guidance on the interactions between the occupier's administration and the civilian population in the context of ordinary life.

Secondly, the application and implementation of IHRL is relevant to the extent that it adds substantive duties to those found in GC IV, where that Convention may be silent on a number of questions relating not only to ESC rights, but also to civil and political rights, such as freedom of opinion or of assembly, or the freedom of the press. For instance, there is virtually nothing in the Geneva Conventions on the right to housing (other than Article 53 GC IV prohibiting the destruction of real property), the right to water and sanitation, or the right to education.¹⁴ These rights, however, may be significantly affected during military operations in occupied territory, for practical and/or legal reasons. The fact that human rights law may provide detailed guidance to the occupier does not mean, though, that they cannot be lawfully restricted by limitations under IHRL or by the application of IHL rules.

Thirdly, the applicability of IHRL opens the door to human rights monitoring bodies and enforcement mechanisms. International human rights law provides procedures for individual complaints that do not exist under the Geneva Conventions. While IHL rules are not justiciable per se before human rights bodies, violations of ESC rights—whether or not regulated by the Geneva Conventions—of individuals living under occupation, and independently from their status under IHL, could fall under the scrutiny of judicial or quasi-judicial human rights bodies.¹⁵

Therefore, the reference to ESC rights in this context should be understood in a broad sense as referring to rules belonging to both legal regimes that can indeed be applied and interpreted in the light of each other, especially when they provide regulation in areas common to both.

II. The application of the international human rights law of economic, social, and cultural rights in occupied territories

a. *International human rights law provisions relevant to socio-economic rights*

Before addressing the relevant GC IV rules, a brief comment is in order on the IHRL of ESC rights. The widely ratified treaty text, the ICESCR, includes a number of provisions relevant to occupied territories.¹⁶ It should be noted, however, that a number of civil and political rights instruments incorporate socio-economic rights, or have been interpreted through the interrelated obligations of certain key rights, as encompassing certain aspects of ESC rights, such as the right to life, the right to freedom from torture and other cruel,

---

¹³ Arts 55 para 1 and 56 para 1 GC IV (emphasis added).
¹⁴ Although Art 43 Hague Regulations requires respect for local laws.
¹⁵ On the indirect protection of socio-economic rights through civil and political rights, see section B.II of this chapter.
¹⁶ Included are the right to self-determination (Art 1); the principle of non-discrimination (Art 2(2)); the right to work (Arts 6 and 7); the right to an adequate standard of living (Art 11), which includes adequate food, water and sanitation, or housing; the right to the highest attainable standard of health (Art 12); education (Arts 13 and 14); or the right of everyone to take part in cultural life and to benefit from scientific, literary, or artistic production (Art 15).

inhuman, or degrading treatment, the right to respect for private and family life, the right to property, or the right to freedom of movement.[17]

14 The application of ESC rights is a multifaceted, and at times complex, endeavour. Under the ICESCR, states parties have a continuous general obligation to realize ESC rights, which has to be discharged through a series of specific obligations that are of a varying nature. While the ICESCR generally allows for the progressive realization of rights taking into account the state's maximum available resources,[18] some minimum obligations are of immediate effect and continue to apply even in times of armed conflict and military occupation. A right can thus be translated into a series of obligations, some of which are of an immediate and others of a progressive nature.

15 While certain provisions have been identified as being of actual immediate application,[19] the obligation 'to take steps' (*s'engage à agir*) has been interpreted as imposing immediate obligations to take deliberate and targeted steps and use all appropriate means.[20] Another set of immediate obligations concerns the *minimum core content* of each of the rights protected under the ICESCR. This obligation creates fundamental minimum duties of both a negative and a positive nature. It has been pointed out in general terms that 'a minimum core obligation to ensure the satisfaction of, at the very least, minimum essential levels of each of the rights is incumbent upon every State party'.[21] Some of the minimum core obligations referred to by the ICESCR may be found in the Geneva Conventions' rules relating to the requirements for foodstuffs, basic health services, and medical supplies in accordance with the provisional nature of occupation, although the full ESC rights obligations may further require the state to implement long-term strategies, programmes, and other measures.

b. *The sources of conventional human rights obligations in occupied territories*

16 The question of whether conventional human rights law, and ESC rights more specifically, do in fact apply concurrently to IHL rules in occupied territories has proven controversial. The specific legal basis of such treaty obligations can be those binding on the occupier based on its own treaty ratifications, or those of the state that is occupied.[22]

17 One issue revolves around the extraterritorial application of human rights treaties of the occupier itself. The question of the extraterritorial application of human rights treaties when state agents or forces operate outside the national territory remains debated, and this is not the place to analyse in detail the vast array of case law and doctrinal literature.[23] Much of it can indeed be explained by the fact that situations of occupation may bring

---

[17] See, e.g., ECtHR, *Dogan and others v Turkey*, Judgment, 29 June 2004; ECtHR, *Akdivar and others v Turkey*, Judgment, 16 September 1996, paras 196 and 202; ACommHPR, *The Social and Economic Rights Action Center and the Center for Economic and Social Rights v Nigeria*, Comm No 155/96, 2001; HRCttee, General Comment 16, (Art 17) Right to Privacy, 8 April 1988, para 9.

[18] The general nature of state obligations in the realization of these rights is found in Art 2(1) ICESCR.

[19] Art 2(2) on non-discrimination; Art 3 on the principle of equality between women and men; Art 10(3) on the obligation to take special measures of protection and assistance on behalf of children and young persons; Art 7(a)(i) on equal pay; Art 8 on the right to form trade unions and to strike; Art 13(2)(a) on free and compulsory primary education to all; and Art 13(3) on freedom of parents to choose the type of education for their children.

[20] CESCR, General Comment 3, 14 December 1990, para 2.   [21] Ibid, para 10.

[22] As a matter of customary law, there are no such obstacles since the occupant is bound by all human rights obligations that form part of customary international law. See generally N. Lubell, 'Human Rights Obligations in Military Occupation', 94 *IRRC* 885 (2012) 317.

[23] See generally, Giacca, above n 10, Chapter II.

the local population under the jurisdiction of the Occupying Power, rendering applicable IHRL treaties to which it is a party.[24]

While this is the most common approach developed by the international case law and extensively discussed in the doctrine, it primarily takes the perspective of human rights bodies engaged in human rights accountability, dealing with the states parties under a specific treaty regime.[25] But as a matter of law, the human rights obligations of the occupied state itself may also have legal significance in occupied territories.

In fact, the territory might become the medium through which the applicable IHRL binds the occupier.[26] The application to the occupier of obligations accepted by the occupied state may derive from occupation law, by virtue of the ratification and domestic implementation of human rights treaties by the occupied state prior to occupation. This stems from a dynamic interpretation of Article 43 of the Hague Regulations relating to the requirement to uphold the domestic legislation of the occupied state (to respect 'unless absolutely prevented, the laws in force in the country'), as implied by the ICJ in the *DRC v Uganda* case.[27] The occupier is bound to respect the rights in the human rights treaties ratified by the occupied state by operation of the law of occupation. The 'laws in force in the country' under Article 43 of the Hague Regulations may be read so as to include all the norms in force in the occupied territory, including IHRL.[28] The ordinary meaning of the term offers no indication that it must be limited to domestic laws *stricto sensu*. It can be generally assumed that the duty to respect 'the laws in force' comprises primary and secondary legislation and domestic court precedents, but it could also include international obligations derived from human rights treaties.[29] It should be noted that such an interpretation would be limited to monist states, where national and international law

---

[24] ICJ, *Wall*, Advisory Opinion, above n 9; ICJ, *Case concerning Armed Activities on the Territory of The Congo (DRC v Uganda)*, Judgment, 19 December 2005; ICJ, *Application of the International Convention on the Elimination of All Forms of Racial Discrimination (Georgia v Russian Federation)*, Order, Request for the Indication of Provisional Measures, 15 October 2008. There has been an extensive debate in academic literature on the preliminary conditions for the extraterritorial application of human rights treaties, mainly in existing case law relating to civil and political rights. See M. Milanovic, *Extraterritorial Application of Human Rights Treaties: Law, Principles and Policy* (Oxford: OUP, 2011).

[25] As a procedural matter, it should be noted that the legal basis for the application of human rights treaties can be important in delimiting the competence of human rights bodies. Usually, their competence would be limited to states parties of the respective instruments as a matter of extraterritorial jurisdiction.

[26] R. Kolb and S. Vité, *Le droit de l'occupation militaire. Perspectives historiques et enjeux juridiques actuels* (Brussels: Bruylant, 2009), at 314.

[27] The Court took the law of occupation as the starting point of its legal reasoning, noting that: 'Uganda was the occupying Power in Ituri at the relevant time. As such it was under an obligation, according to Article 43 of the Hague Regulations of 1907, to take all the measures in its power to restore, and ensure, as far as possible, public order and safety in the occupied area, while respecting, unless absolutely prevented, the laws in force in the DRC. This obligation comprised the duty to secure respect for the applicable rules of international human rights law and international humanitarian law, to protect the inhabitants of the occupied territory against acts of violence, and not to tolerate such violence by any third party.' ICJ, *DRC v Uganda*, above n 24, para 178.

[28] This is supported by a number of commentators: Kolb and Vité, above n 26, at 189–96 and 314; C. McCarthy, 'Legal Reasoning and the Applicability of International Human Rights Standards during Military Occupation', in N. Quénivet and R. Arnold (eds), *International Humanitarian Law and Human Rights Law: Towards a New Merger in International Law* (Leiden: Martinus Nijhoff Publishers, 2008) 127; W. Kälin and J. Künzli, *The Law of International Human Rights Protection* (Oxford: OUP, 2009), at 154–5.

[29] E. Benvenisti, *The International Law of Occupation* (Princeton, NJ: Princeton University Press, 2004), at 17.

constitute a single, integrated order, or dualist states that had incorporated a version of the treaty obligations in their national law. In such cases, the human rights obligations contained in the treaties automatically acquire domestic validity, as 'laws in force' in the state concerned.[30]

20   This approach stems from a concern about divergence in operative human rights standards as between the occupying state and the occupied territory, if for instance both states involved are not bound by the same instruments. It is also an affirmation of the principle of continuity of obligations for those human rights that are vested in the population. The underlying idea is that human rights protection applicable in occupied territories should not depend on the identity of the occupier. Should not the occupier be bound by the treaties of the territorial state on whose territory it is operating? If not, this would be an important setback to the legal protection conferred on the civilian population living in the territory concerned.[31]

21   The Coalition Provisional Authority (CPA) in occupied Iraq justified a reform of the local labour code by noting that Iraq, as a state party to the International Labour Organization (ILO) Conventions 182 and 138, had the obligation 'to take affirmative steps towards eliminating child labour'.[32] Thus, the reform undertaken by those Occupying Powers prohibits child labour, and sets the minimum age for admission to employment and work.[33] Commentators seem generally to agree that the adoption of such laws that are genuinely necessary to protect human rights law are lawful under occupation law.[34] This of course invites the question whether this measure by the CPA was undertaken as matter of legal obligation, or whether it was just considered desirable as a matter of policy. Problems remain as to whether it can be assumed that the occupier may change the laws in force to give effect to the human rights treaties the previous government has ratified, an issue discussed further in section B.IV of this chapter.

22   In sum, in terms of the binding nature of human rights treaty obligations, there is an area of convergence between the legal basis derived from Article 43 of the Hague Regulations and the principle of extraterritoriality of human rights norms. The Occupying Power will thus be bound in theory by all the human rights instruments ratified by each of them. This would ensure the maximum level of protection for the civilian population under occupation.[35]

---

[30] In a dualist system an incorporation of international law is needed in order to be considered as binding domestic law.

[31] Of course, if both the occupier and the occupied state are party to the same relevant human rights instruments, this should not pose great difficulties, as in the *DRC v Uganda* case, above n 24.

[32] Order 89 recognizes the 'CPA's obligation to provide for the effective administration of Iraq, to ensure the wellbeing of the children and workers of Iraq and to enable the social and economic functions of everyday life'. CPA, Order No 89, Amendments to the Labour Code—Law No 71 of 1987 CPA/ORD/05 May 2004, preambular para 7.

[33] It is interesting to note that the US, as part of the CPA, implemented an international convention to which it is not party to (ILO Convention No 138). In this way, the occupier administers temporarily the obligations of the occupied state.

[34] M. Sassòli, 'Legislation and Maintenance of Public Order and Civil Life by Occupying Powers', 16(4) *EJIL* (2005) 661, at 676.

[35] Kolb and Vité refer to the highest common denominator, even though both the occupier and the occupied are not bound by the same instruments: Kolb and Vité, above n 26, at 331. This is what Eric David calls '*[une] interpénétration des sphères juridiques*': E. David, *Principes de droit des conflits armés* (4th edn, Brussels: Bruylant, 2008), at 565.

III. The specific scope and nature of the obligations of the occupier

a. *The obligation to provide food and medical supplies*

Under the law of occupation, there is a clear obligation on the occupier to ensure that the basic needs of the population under its control are fulfilled.[36] This mainly results from Article 55 paragraph 1 GC IV, where the Occupying Power has the duty, to the fullest extent of the means available to it, to ensure food, medical supplies, and 'other articles' to the civilian population.

The list of goods is not limited to the provision of necessary foodstuffs and medical stores, but would include, in the meaning of 'other articles', any supplies necessary to support the needs of the civilian population.[37] This is essentially a question of applying common sense in order to determine whether certain supplies are needed or not in a specific situation. This provision also derives from the general duty to take all feasible measures to restore and ensure adequate conditions of life for the civilian population (Article 43 of the Hague Regulations).

The obligation is further reinforced by the corresponding duty to bring in the necessary articles when 'the resources of the occupied territory are inadequate',[38] thus corroborating and incorporating the general obligation to allow the free passage of medical supplies, food, and clothing, as well as to facilitate relief schemes under Articles 23 and 59–62 GC IV. Thus, the Occupying Power must either ensure that the civilian population receives essential supplies, or allow relief actions to be undertaken.[39] It should be noted that the Convention does not stipulate the means and method by which the necessary goods are supplied or imported. Their origin has no bearing, i.e. whether they are imported from the occupier's own national territory or from any other country.[40]

Under GC IV this obligation must be read in conjunction with Article 56, which sets out the Occupying Power's duty to ensure and maintain 'the medical and hospital establishments and services, public health and hygiene in the occupied territory'. The list of essential supplies was extended with the adoption of Article 69 of the 1977 Additional Protocol (AP) I. This provision further stipulates that relevant goods must be provided 'without adverse distinction'.

There is a continuing obligation to ensure food and medical supplies, and the needs of the civilian population and the extent of the urgency of ensuring supplies must be carefully assessed on a case-by-case basis and in light of the local requirement.[41] Although no

---

[36] On the rules and activities relating to relief and humanitarian assistance, see Ch 12 of this volume.

[37] Art 55 para 1 GC IV. Included are clothing, bedding, tents, and suchlike, and anything that might alleviate the plight of a civilian population. See Pictet Commentary GC IV, at 310. Art 69(1) AP I supplements paragraph 1 of Art 55 GC IV, stipulating that the Occupying Power must also ensure the provision of clothing, bedding, means of shelter, other supplies essential to the survival of the civilian population, as well as objects necessary for religious worship. See ICRC Commentary APs, paras 2779–85.

[38] It remains unclear what the criteria are to assess whether the resources of the occupied territory are 'inadequate'. The expression is similar to the wording of Art 59 GC IV ('inadequately supplied') or Art 70 AP I ('not adequately provided'), and has been deliberately formulated in vague terms. The general idea is to maintain 'at a reasonable level the material conditions under which the population of the occupied territory lives'. Pictet Commentary GC IV, at 310.

[39] See Ch 12 of this volume.   [40] Pictet Commentary GC IV, at 310.

[41] The ICRC CIHL Study refers to 'civilians in need', its Rule 55 referring to access for humanitarian relief. It seems clear that need of the population operates as the trigger for the obligation to agree to and to facilitate relief schemes on behalf of the population in an occupied territory.

specific guidance is available in this regard, '[i]t is the "essential" character of such requirements that must be the determining factor'.[42]

28   Little indication as to the nature and quality of these prescriptions is provided, or as to how the 'extent of the means available to it' is to be assessed. The occupier enjoys broad discretionary powers on how such obligations should be implemented. The corresponding IHRL obligations regarding social rights could certainly bring further clarity to the meaning of what is adequate, in particular on the right to an adequate standard of living and the right to health. They establish a minimum entitlement to adequate food, clothing, water, housing, and health, as well as to the continuous improvement of living conditions. It is worth mentioning that during the drafting of Article 55 GC IV with regard to food and medical supplies, there was an attempt to include an explicit reference to 'international standards of nutrition' in the obligation to ensure a food supply to the civilian population. This proposal was unanimously rejected because delegations found it difficult to commit to standards which had not been approved and established.[43]

29   The minimum core content of the human right to adequate food seems to converge with IHL to ensure distribution of food to the civilian population or the acceptance and facilitation of external relief assistance. But the right to food is not limited to the fundamental right to freedom from hunger under Article 11(2) ICESCR. As the Committee on Economic, Social and Cultural Rights (CESCR) further notes, it shall therefore 'not be interpreted in a narrow or restrictive sense which equates it with a minimum package of calories, proteins and other specific nutrients'.[44] In this sense, the scope of obligation under IHRL goes beyond the minimum obligations defined by IHL. Although all steps cannot be taken at the same time for the full realization of the normative content, in situations of prolonged occupation the occupier may need to take positive measures to ensure the economic and physical accessibility of food. This may require positive responses, such as adopting appropriate legislative, administrative, budgetary, judicial, promotional, and other measures. It may include long-term strategies, programmes, and other 'measures in regard to *all* aspects of the food system, including the production, processing, distribution, marketing and consumption of safe food, as well as parallel measures in the fields of health, education, employment and social security'.[45] Particular attention should also be paid to ensure the most sustainable management and use of natural resources for food production.[46] Such proactive measures are more of a long-term character to achieve progressively the full realization of the right to an adequate standard of living as set forth in Article 11(1) ICESCR.

30   While imposing clear obligations in this regard, GC IV (as well as AP I) does not, however, disregard the material difficulties that the occupier may face in practice. The provisions stipulate that the occupier is bound '[t]o the fullest extent of the means available to it'.[47] Financial constraints or transport problems, for instance, may seriously affect the capacity of the authorities concerned to meet their obligations.[48] However, such limitations must not be used by these authorities to evade their responsibilities. They must be in a position to show they have exhausted all available means to meet the

---

[42] ICRC Commentary APs, para 2794.
[43] This shows that the delegates were not averse to integrating international standards *en devenir* to structure the responsibilities of the occupier. Final Record, vol II-A, at 745.
[44] CESCR, General Comment 12: The right to adequate food (Art 11), 12 May 1999, para 6.
[45] Ibid, para 25.   [46] Ibid, para 25.   [47] Art 55 GC IV; Art 69(1) AP I.
[48] Pictet Commentary GC IV, at 310.

essential needs of the population. This means that if the occupier is not in a position to fulfil its duty to provide the civilian population under its control with essential supplies, it must agree to relief schemes on behalf of that population (Article 59 paragraph 1 GC IV).[49]

As a general rule, the requisitioning of foodstuffs, medical supplies, and other articles available in the occupied territory is not permitted.[50] Exceptions to this rule are only allowed subject to three cumulative conditions: (i) the requirements (stipulated above) of the civilian population have first been taken into account;[51] (ii) requisitions must be intended for use by the occupation forces and administrative personnel only;[52] and (iii) it is required that fair value be paid for any requisitioned goods.[53] Reaffirming the principle expressed in Article 52 of the Hague Regulations, this means that requisitioned goods shall 'as far as possible, be paid for in ready money; if not, their receipt shall be acknowledged'.[54]

The last paragraph of Article 55 paragraph 3 GC IV stipulates the role of the Protecting Powers in verifying the state of food and medical supplies.[55] Such activities by the Protecting Powers may also include assistance to the occupier on the measures undertaken to ensure the food and medical supplies of the population, including lending their good offices for the importing of relevant goods within the parameters set out under Article 9 GC IV.[56] The activities of supervision and assistance must take account of the temporary restrictions of the imperative military requirements, and may therefore be suspended temporarily for a limited period of time.[57]

In addition, GC IV provides that an Occupying Power undertaking an evacuation for the security of the civilian population or for imperative military reasons,

shall ensure, to the greatest practicable extent, that proper accommodation is provided to receive the protected persons, that the removals are effected in satisfactory conditions of hygiene, health, safety and nutrition, and that members of the same family are not separated.[58]

b. The obligation to ensure and maintain public health and hygiene

In accordance with Article 56 paragraph 1 GC IV, the occupier is obliged to ensure and maintain the medical and hospital establishments and services, public health, and hygiene. Moreover, it is responsible for adopting and applying prophylactic and preventive measures necessary to combat the spread of contagious diseases and epidemics.[59]

Geneva Convention IV in this case takes into account both levels of administration in the occupied territory. The occupier has a shared responsibility to ensure these

---

[49] See Ch 12 of this volume.   [50] Art 55 GC IV.
[51] This is in line with the Hague Regulations rule that requisitions 'shall be in proportion to the resources of the country (Art 52 para 1). The qualifications applicable in occupied territories are somewhat restrictive when compared to Art 23(g) Hague Regulations, applicable during hostilities, that permits the seizure of the enemy's property if it is 'imperatively demanded by the necessities of war' without requiring a belligerent to consider the needs of the civilian population. The Lieber Code defined military necessity as 'the necessity of those measures which are indispensable for securing the ends of war, and which are lawful according to the modern law and usages of war' (Art 14). On the specific conditions in cases where civilian hospitals are requisitioned, see Art 57 GC IV.
[52] See the general rule on requisitions in kind and services laid down in Art 52 Hague Regulations.
[53] The 'extensive appropriation of property, not justified by military necessity', which includes requisitions, is considered be a grave breach under Art 147 GC IV.
[54] Art 52 para 3 Hague Regulations.   [55] See Ch 27 of this chapter.
[56] Pictet Commentary GC IV, at 312.   [57] Ibid. See also Art 9 para 3 GC IV.
[58] Art 49 para 3 GC IV. See also Rule 131 ICRC CIHL Study.   [59] See also Art 14 AP I.

prescriptions 'with the cooperation of national and local authorities' for the purpose of Article 56 paragraph 1. This shows clearly that the occupier should not bear the whole burden of organizing health services and taking measures to control epidemics.[60] The tasks fall above all on the competent services of the occupied country itself. This means that as long as those tasks are fulfilled, the occupier is merely required not to impede or interfere with those activities.[61] However, from the moment the local authorities fail, which is likely to happen, the occupier has a positive obligation to cooperate with the local authorities to ensure such services, on the basis of its available means.[62]

36   Measures necessary to combat the spread of contagious diseases and epidemics are diverse, and the Pictet Commentary refers to

> supervision of public health, education of the general public, the distribution of medicines, the organization of medical examinations and disinfection, the establishment of stocks of medical supplies, the despatch of medical teams to areas where epidemics are raging, the isolation and accommodation in hospital of people suffering from communicable diseases, and the opening of new hospitals and medical centres.[63]

37   It should be noted that the content of all those measures required to organize hospitals and health services and the taking of measures to control epidemics may be found in the complementary application of the right to health under IHRL. The right to the highest attainable standard of health, as defined by Article 12 ICESCR and further interpreted by the CESCR in General Comment No 14,[64] suggests respect for the following four inter-related and essential elements:

— *availability*, namely, functioning public health and health care facilities, goods and services, as well as programmes, have to be available in sufficient quantity, including underlying determinants, such as safe drinking water and adequate sanitation facilities;[65]
— *accessibility*, namely, health facilities, goods, and services must be accessible to everyone without discrimination, especially the most vulnerable or marginalized people;[66]
— *acceptability*, namely, health facilities, goods, and services must be respectful of medical ethics, sensitive to cultures, communities and gender, and must be provided in local languages;[67]
— *quality*, namely, health facilities, goods, and services must also be scientifically and medically appropriate and of good quality, which requires skilled medical personnel, scientifically approved and unexpired drugs and hospital equipment, safe and potable water, and adequate sanitation.[68]

---

[60] Pictet Commentary GC IV, at 313.   [61] Ibid.
[62] On the material difficulties that the occupier may encounter in practice, see the commentary on Art 55 GC IV at MN 28.
[63] Pictet Commentary GC IV, at 314.
[64] CESCR, General Comment 14: The Right to the Highest Attainable Standard of Health (Art 12), 11 August 2000, UN Doc E/C.12/2000/4.
[65] Ibid, para 12(a). The underlying determinants of health includes safe and potable drinking water and adequate sanitation facilities; hospitals, clinics, and other health-related buildings; trained medical and professional personnel receiving domestically competitive salaries; and essential drugs, as defined by the WHO Action Programme on Essential Drugs.
[66] Ibid, para 12(b).   [67] Ibid, para 12(c).   [68] Ibid, para 12(d).

The obligation under Article 56 to permit 'medical personnel of all categories […] to carry out their duties' is instrumental in fulfilling the general obligation of ensuring and maintaining the medical and hospital establishments and services, and public health and hygiene benefits. This involves measures to safeguard the activities of medical personnel, 'who must therefore be exempted from any measures (such as restrictions on movement, requisitioning of vehicles, supplies or equipment) liable to interfere with the performance of their duty'.[69] Article 56 paragraph 2 GC IV deals with the duty to grant to new hospitals that are set up in occupied territory the recognition provided for in Article 18 GC IV, including the right to display the red cross emblem, as well as the duty to grant recognition to hospital personnel, including the distribution of identity cards to its staff, and transport vehicles in conformity with Article 20 GC IV.

Article 56 paragraph 3 GC IV calls for respect for the moral and ethical susceptibilities of the civilian population where the occupier adopts health or hygiene measures. This is in conformity with the essential element of the right to health relating to acceptability, where health facilities, goods, and services must respect medical ethics, be sensitive to cultures, communities, and gender, and must be provided in local languages.[70]

As a general rule, under Article 57 GC IV, it is prohibited to requisition civilian hospitals, whether privately or publicly owned. Exceptions to this rule, which may interfere with the right to health of inhabitants, are that they can be requisitioned, first, only for a limited time and, secondly, only in cases of 'urgent necessity for the care of military wounded and sick'. This means that requisition is not permitted in situations where the occupier's own medical establishment is able to manage the care of the wounded and sick of its army. On the other hand, where the occupier is entitled to requisition, the Convention requires that the occupier restore the hospital to its normal use as soon as the urgent necessity ceases to exist.[71] Thirdly, the requisitioning of civilian hospitals requires that suitable arrangements are made 'in due time' for the care and treatment of the patients, and for the needs of the civilian population for hospital accommodation, in line with IHRL obligations. Further, the requisitioning of material and stores from civilian hospitals is prohibited so long as they are necessary for the needs of the civilian population, under Article 57 paragraph 2 GC IV. It follows that in the event of of requisitioning of material, the provision places the occupier under an obligation to replace the material used as soon as possible, in accordance with Article 55 GC IV.[72] It should be noted that Article 14(2) AP I, in this context, specifically prohibits the requisitioning of civilian medical units, their equipment, their *matériel*, or the services of their personnel, so long as these resources are necessary for the provision of adequate medical services for the civilian population, and for the continuing medical care of any wounded and sick already under treatment.[73]

---

[69] Pictet Commentary GC IV, at 314.
[70] General Comment 14, para 12(c). The medical profession has adopted a number of codes, guidelines, and regulations, e.g. the World Medical Association (WMA) has adopted an International Code of Medical Ethics, adopted by the 3rd General Assembly of the WMA, London, England, October 1949 and amended by the 22nd World Medical Assembly, Sydney, Australia, August 1968, the 35th World Medical Assembly, Venice, Italy, October 1983, and the 57th WMA General Assembly, Pilanesberg, South Africa, October 2006.
[71] Pictet Commentary GC IV, at 316.   [72] Pictet Commentary GC IV, at 318.
[73] The ICRC CIHL Study only refers, in its Rule 30, to attacks directed against medical objects displaying the distinctive emblems of the Geneva Conventions as a customary rule.

c. Rules relating to labour and enlistment of protected persons

41   On matters of work and employment, the Convention deals specifically with circumstances relating to forced labour and the requisitioning of services under Articles 51–52 GC IV.[74] First of all, as a general rule, the occupier may not compel protected persons to serve in its armed or auxiliary forces. It follows that neither pressure nor propaganda which aims at securing voluntary enlistment is permitted.

42   Article 51 GC IV sets limits on working conditions when regulating labour and the enlistment of protected persons. Article 51 paragraph 2 GC IV allows the occupier to compel protected persons who are over 18 years of age to carry out work necessary for any of three reasonable objectives: the needs of the army of occupation; or for the public utility services; or for the welfare of the occupied population (i.e. feeding, sheltering, clothing, transportation, or health). Moreover, the requisitioning services shall not involve any military operations or contribute to improving the state of military preparation of the occupier's forces, i.e. the war effort.[75] However, the clause 'work necessary for the needs of the army of occupation' involves a 'wide variety of services'.[76] The Pictet Commentary refers to fodder, transport services, the repairing of roads, bridges, ports, and railways, or the laying/repair of telecommunication networks.[77] These types of activities may be seen to a certain extent as contributing to the military preparation of the occupying forces.[78] There is indeed a certain level of overlap between the maintenance needs of the army of occupation and its strategic or tactical requirements referred to in this provision.[79] On the other hand, it is generally agreed that work such as the construction of fortifications, trenches, aerial bases, or in the armament industry could not be required.[80] It is also prohibited to compel protected persons to employ forcible means to ensure the security of the installations where they are performing compulsory labour.[81]

43   Irrespective of the three legitimate objectives which may justify compelling protected persons to carry out work, such work must always take place in the occupied territory,[82] and it is important to stress that the inhabitants compelled to work will always retain their civilian status. Further, it is prohibited to requisition labour where it would lead to mobilization of workers in an organization of a military or semi-military character.[83] This provision was designed to avoid this common practice witnessed during the Second World War, which can conflict with the civilian status of those workers.

44   Protected persons whose services have been requisitioned are entitled under Article 51 paragraph 2 GC IV to the continued application of local legislation concerning working conditions and safeguards, including, in particular, matters such as wages, hours of work,

---

[74] See Rule 95 on Forced Labour, ICRC CIHL Study.   [75] Art 51 para 2 GC IV.
[76] Pictet Commentary GC IV, at 294.
[77] Ibid. The UK Manual refers to the requisitioning services relating to the construction of the military defences or airfields, the production of munitions, the movement of military supplies, or the laying or lifting of minefields. UK Ministry of Defence, *The Manual of the Law of Armed Conflict* (Oxford: OUP, 2005), at para 11.53.1.
[78] As a matter of policy, Gasser and Dörmann suggest that it would be better to prohibit all work for the benefit of the occupying forces. See H.-P. Gasser and K. Dörmann, 'Protection of the Civilian Population', in D. Fleck (ed), *The Handbook of International Humanitarian Law* (3rd edn, Oxford: OUP, 2013) 231, at 288.
[79] Pictet Commentary GC IV, at 294.
[80] This is also intended to prevent assignment to locations that might be considered military objectives, which would expose the relevant inhabitants to the danger of becoming military targets. Gasser and Dörmann, above n 78, at 288.
[81] Art 51 para 2 GC IV, 3rd sentence.   [82] Art 51 para 3 GC IV.   [83] Art 51 para 4 GC IV.

equipment, preliminary training, and compensation for occupational accidents and diseases. Considering their benefit to the occupied population, the relevant human rights norms, including the ILO Conventions on the protection of workers, are considered to remain applicable. Although these labour issues are covered by the Geneva Conventions, they are also covered concurrently by these instruments.

A conflict of norms might arise in this case, as Article 8(3) of the International Covenant on Civil and Political Rights (ICCPR) and Article 6 ICESCR prohibit forced or compulsory labour.[84] Although Article 8(3) ICCPR provides for a number of exceptions, compelling protected persons to work for the needs of the occupying army, or for the sheltering and health of the local population, under Article 51 GC IV could be in contradiction to the Covenant, as it will not fall within any of the exceptions provided for. There is clearly a norm conflict arising out of this. International humanitarian law would need to be read down on the basis of the *lex posterior*, as human rights law has overtaken this aspect of IHL. It would not be reasonable for an Occupying Power to be allowed to require, in an occupied territory from enemy nationals, what it is today (unlike in 1949) not allowed to require on its own territory from its own nationals. As such, Article 51 paragraph 2 GC IV would be superseded or displaced by the relevant human rights norms on forced labour. 45

It is also prohibited under Article 52 GC IV to take any measures calculated to cause unemployment or restricting the opportunities offered to workers, so as to induce them to work for the Occupying Power.[85] The question arises as to whether this rule applies if the measures are undertaken for reasons other than inducing workers to work for the Occupying Power. That question was not addressed by the Pictet Commentary.[86] During the occupation of Iraq, the actions undertaken by the CPA to defeat the Ba'ath ideology embedded in the Iraqi police, security services, and the armed forces, by dissolving these entities, created unemployment on a massive scale.[87] Even though the occupiers were given a legal mandate for transformative change by the Security Council,[88] they were legally obligated to abide by the law of occupation. The purpose of dissolving these entities was clearly not to induce the Iraqi workers to work for the CPA, so it remains unclear, as the treaty is silent on this issue, to what extent this policy, which had such detrimental effects, is allowed under the Geneva Conventions or is lawful under international law.[89] From a human rights perspective, the question might be raised whether such a policy 46

---

[84] CESCR, General Comment 18, para 6. See also Art 4 UDHR and Art 5 Slavery, Servitude, Forced Labour and Similar Institutions and Practices Convention, 60 *LNTS* 253, 1926. The ILO defines forced labour as 'all work or service which is exacted from any person under the menace of any penalty and for which the said person has not offered himself voluntarily': Art 2(1) and (2), ILO Convention No 29 concerning Forced or Compulsory Labour, 1930. See also ILO Convention No 105 concerning the Abolition of Forced Labour, 1957. Art 4(2) ECHR further provides: 'No one shall be required to perform forced or compulsory labour.'

[85] This is in line with the requirement under Art 51 para 3 GC IV that any compulsory labour must be carried out inside the occupied territory. Pictet Commentary GC IV, at 300.

[86] It should be noted that the ICJ did refer to Art 52 GC IV, although Israel's policy clearly did not aim at inducing Palestinians to work for Israel. ICJ, *Wall*, Advisory Opinion, above n 9, para 126.

[87] CPA, Coalition Provisional Authority Order Number 2: Dissolution of Entities (23 May 2003), available at <http://www.iraqcoalition.org/regulations/20030823_CPAORD_2_Dissolution_of_Entities_with_Annex_A.pdf>.

[88] UNSC Res 1483, 22 May 2003.

[89] D.J. Scheffer, 'Future Implications of the Iraq Conflict: Beyond Occupation Law', 97 *AJIL* (2003) 842, at 855.

could comply with the legal regime of limitations under Article 4 ICESCR, which allows states parties to restrict ESC rights under certain conditions.[90]

47   Generally, it should be noted that the Geneva Conventions do not regulate work-related issues outside the aforementioned circumstances. The rules under the Geneva Conventions cannot be compared with the range of obligations relating to the right to work developed under the ICESCR and ILO Conventions, assuming they remain applicable in occupied territories. Take, for instance, the physical interference caused by the construction of the wall and other restrictions on movement in the Occupied Palestinian Territory, and the impact this has had on the livelihoods of Palestinians wishing to go to work or access education, as confirmed by the International Court of Justice (ICJ).[91] The Court relied on the ICESCR, and not on the Geneva Conventions or the Hague Regulations, when examining the negative obligations not to interfere with those rights. In light of this, it would seem reasonable to assert that ESC rights, and the right to work more specifically, are applicable and do substantively add protection in areas already governed and protected under IHL.

d. Rules on education for children

48   The question of education has to be read as part of the broader protection of children in occupied territories derived from IHL treaty-based rules.[92] Article 50 GC IV sets out the occupier's obligations in relation to the education of children.[93] With the cooperation of the national and local authorities—a formula similarly expressed in Article 56 in connection with hygiene and public health—the occupier has the shared responsibility to facilitate the proper working of all institutions devoted to the care and education of children.[94] Should the local institutions be inadequate, the occupier shall make arrangements for the maintenance of education, if possible by persons of the occupied population's own nationality, language, and religion, of children who are orphaned or separated from their parents as a result of the war and who cannot be adequately cared for by a near relative or friend.[95] The application of any preferential measures or treatment prior to the occupation in favour of children under 15 shall not be hindered (this also applies for pregnant women, and for mothers of children aged under 7).[96]

49   The obligations to facilitate the 'proper working' of institutions devoted to education are both negative and positive in nature. Under Article 50 GC IV, the occupier is bound generally not to interfere with educational activities established in occupied territory, and to support local authorities to fulfil their educational obligations, and to ensure such fulfilment itself where the responsible authorities are unable to do so. The

---

[90] Under Art 4 ICESCR, limitations are permissible only to the extent they are necessary to promote the general welfare in a democratic society, i.e. the limits or restrictions imposed must be proportionate to achieve the stated goal. The provision restricts both the reasons for which these rights may be limited, and the way in which such limits may be operated. It is submitted that the stated exception of 'general welfare' under Art 4 ICESCR should be read so as to include other possible grounds for restriction, such as 'national security' or 'public order'. See further in Giacca, above n 10, Chapter II.

[91] The *Wall* Opinion demonstrated, inter alia, that the construction of the wall interfered with the enjoyment by the Palestinians of their ESC rights (work, health, education, adequate standard of living including adequate food, clothing, and housing) found in Arts 6, 7, 10, 11, 12, 13, and 14 ICESCR, as well as in Arts 16, 24, 27, and 28 CRC. ICJ, *Wall*, Advisory Opinion, above n 9, paras 130–1.

[92] Arts 23–24, 38, 50, 76, and 89 GC IV. See also ICRC CIHL Study, Rule 135 on Children, which states that '[c]hildren affected by armed conflict are entitled to special respect and protection'.

[93] The term 'children' is not defined in Art 50 GC IV, or under IHL more generally. Pictet Commentary GC IV, at 285.

[94] Art 50 para 1 GC IV.   [95] Art 50 para 3 GC IV.   [96] Art 50 para 5 GC IV.

occupier remains internationally responsible to provide services to the local population under its effective control, as well as for local authorities providing services. The emphasis on the principle of non-interference with education is related to the fact that occupation is meant to be temporary. In situations where the occupation is short, the main responsibility of the occupier is to avoid measures that hinder or prevent the regular functioning of the education system as it was prior to occupation. This focuses on the negative duties of the occupier not to impede the normal functioning of educational institutions.

Part II of GC IV, providing special protection for children primarily in zones of combat, remains applicable in occupied territory. States parties must take the necessary measures to ensure that children under 15, who are orphaned or are separated from their families as a result of the war, are not left to fend for themselves.[97] The occupier has to ensure that their maintenance, the exercise of their religion, and their education are facilitated in all circumstances. Their education shall, as far as possible, be entrusted to persons of a similar cultural tradition.[98] In addition, the rules forbidding the enlistment of children in 'formations' or organizations subordinate to them can also indirectly ensure the education of children,[99] as well as any other complementary IHL or human rights treaty-based rules prohibiting the recruitment of children into armed forces.[100]

The question of the definition of the form and content of education, as well as the individuals to whom the Geneva Conventions refers, may have a bearing on the scope of protection. With regard to the meaning given to the term 'children', the Geneva Conventions use different age limits with respect to different measures of protection, although the category of children intended to be protected in the 1950s was generally those below 15 years of age.[101] Under human rights law and pursuant to the Convention on the Rights of the Child (CRC), the standard is different: '[A] child means every human being below the age of eighteen years unless, under the law applicable to the child, majority is attained earlier.'[102] Unlike other rules,[103] Article 50 GC IV does not set any upper limit for the children it refers to, except for the last paragraph relating to preferential measures in regard to food, medical care, and protection adopted prior to occupation. Therefore, it is arguable that, since the drafting of the Geneva Conventions, current international standards developed under human rights law should be taken into account so as to raise the age limit from 15 to 18 on this particular issue.[104]

There is no general definition of the word 'education'. It is defined neither in the Geneva Conventions nor in their two 1977 Additional Protocols. The Pictet Commentary refers

---

[97] Art 24 para 1 GC IV. [98] Ibid.
[99] Art 50 para 2 GC IV. The term 'formation' refers to organizations or movements that are devoted largely to political aims. See also Art 51 para 1 GC IV.
[100] Art 77 AP I; Art 38(4) CRC; CRC-OPAC. [101] Pictet Commentary GC IV, at 285.
[102] Art 1 CRC.
[103] 18 years of age: compulsion to work in occupied territory (Art 51 GC IV), pronouncement of the death penalty (Art 68 GC IV); 15 years of age: hospital and safety zones (Art 14 GC IV), consignment of relief supplies (Art 23 GC IV), measures relating to child welfare (Arts 24 and 38 para 5 GC IV), same preferential treatment for aliens as for nationals (Art 38 GC IV), preferential measures in regard to food, medical care, and protection adopted prior to occupation (Art 50 GC IV), additional food for interned children in proportion to their physiological needs (Art 89 GC IV); 12 years of age: arrangement for all children to be identified by the wearing of identity discs, or by some other means (Art 24 GC IV).
[104] See Ch 62, MN 5–10, of this volume.

to a wide variety of institutions and establishments devoted to the care and education of children, including 'child welfare centres, orphanages, children's camps, children's homes and day nurseries, "medico-social" reception centres, social welfare services, reception centres, canteens, etc'.[105] The emphasis of the Pictet Commentary is on the notion of child 'care', but obviously the list is not exhaustive, and it should be understood in its broadest sense so as to include first and foremost schools and other educational establishments. This would follow the approach taken in other international instruments, such as the CRC and the ICESCR, and subsequent interpretation by the United Nations (UN) treaty bodies.

53   The text of neither the CRC nor the ICESCR explicitly establishes such a definition of education. Hence, the form and content of 'education', very much like the notion of cultural rights, is open to debate and may be subject to definitional difficulties.[106] One definition provided by the United Nations Educational, Scientific and Cultural Organization (UNESCO) is very broad. It defines 'education' as

the entire process of social life by means of which individuals and social groups learn to develop consciously within, and for the benefit of, the national and international communities, the whole of their personal capacities, aptitudes and knowledge.[107]

In contrast, most international instruments, including those in the area of human rights, define education narrowly, confining it to formal instruction or teaching as the basis for what is protected by the right to education.[108] From a human rights law point of view, the case for a more expansive definition of forms of education protected by human rights treaties can certainly be made. More specifically, human rights treaties leave references to the aims and objectives of education fairly broad, and very much in line with the spirit of a comprehensive definition of education. Article 26(2) of the 1948 Universal Declaration of Human Rights (UDHR) and Article 13(1) of the ICESCR stipulate that 'education shall be directed to the full development of the human personality'. Article 29 CRC elaborates even further on the aims of education, i.e. the 'development of the child's personality, talents and mental and physical abilities to their fullest potential'. In addition, the CESCR and the CRC Committee have clarified in their practice that the right to education encompasses both pre-school and non-formal education.[109]

54   In light of the above, it becomes clear that there is little guidance under IHL concerning the nature and substance of educational provision. The type of education protected under the Geneva Conventions would cover formal and non-formal instruction at the

---

[105] Pictet Commentary GC IV, at 286.

[106] 'The right of everyone to take part in cultural life is also intrinsically linked to the right to education (Arts 13 and 14), through which individuals and communities pass on their values, religion, customs, language and other cultural references, and which helps to foster an atmosphere of mutual understanding and respect for cultural values.' CESCR, General Comment 21, 'The Right of Everyone to Take Part in Cultural Life (Art 15 of the ICESCR)', UN Doc E/C.12/GC/21, para 2.

[107] Art 1(a) UNESCO, Recommendation Concerning Education for International Understanding, Co-operation and Peace and Education Relating to Human Rights and Fundamental Freedoms, UNESCO General Conference, 18th Session, Paris, 1974.

[108] J. Bourke Martignoni, *Echoes from a Distant Shore: The Right to Education in International Development: With Special Reference to the Role of the World Bank* (Zurich: Schulthess Verlag, 2012), at 42. See also ECtHR, *Campbell and Cosans v UK*, Judgment (Merits), 25 February 1982, para 33.

[109] CESCR, Concluding Observations: United Kingdom of Great Britain and Northern Ireland, UN Doc E/1995/22, §276; CRC, General Comment 7, 'Implementing Child Rights in Early Childhood', UN Doc CRC/C/GC/7/Rev.1, 2005, para 30. See CRC, Day of General Discussion on the Right of the Child to Education in Emergency Situations: Recommendations, 49th Session, 19 September 2008, para 19.

primary, secondary, and vocational levels; however, it would exclude tertiary education, as well as adult education for individuals over 18. Thus, in comparison to these provisions on education, IHRL is far more detailed and provides a contemporary understanding of educational needs in a modern society, in terms of availability, accessibility, and quality.[110]

In state practice there exists little evidence of how occupiers have applied and interpreted their positive obligations under those relevant provisions with respect to the education of children. In occupied Iraq, the CPA, in collaboration with development agencies, the UN, and non-governmental organizations (NGOs), engaged in a vast programme of reconstruction of the Iraqi educational system, rebuilding and renovating school infrastructure, instituting training programmes for teachers and administrators, and elaborating a four-year strategic plan for reform of the education curriculum.[111] This benevolent consideration to education finds its roots in the political and strategic efforts of the coalition to move towards reconstruction of the country, but it is unclear whether this was done out of respect for legal obligations to ensure education to children, or if this should be understood only as a matter of policy.

IV. The relationship between the rules contained in the Geneva Conventions and positive duties of protecting and fulfilling economic, social, and cultural rights

a. The scope of the occupier's legislative powers

The occupier's entitlement to legislate, especially in situations of stable and prolonged occupation, has been subject to much debate, and it is uncertain whether the occupier can legislate with the aim of implementing human rights law in the area under its effective control.[112] Generally, legal impediments imposed by IHL are not absolute, and a number of changes may be allowed and even required in light of a complementary reading of obligations deriving from IHL and IHRL. Otherwise, the protective nature of the conservationist approach conceived in short-term occupation would transform itself into an instrument for legal and socio-economic stagnation in prolonged occupation.[113]

The elusive concept of the necessity to respect 'unless absolutely prevented, the laws in force in the country' under Article 43 of the Hague Regulations, appears to have a far broader and more humanitarian component that would justify expansion of the grounds permitting changes to local laws. This comprises three elements—military, legal, and material necessity—which may leave ample room to manoeuvre to regulate

---

[110] The right to education under human rights law serves two general purposes. It seeks on the one hand to give individuals an education, and it aims to ensure that education is provided in an adequate and appropriate manner on the other. Arts 13 and 14 ICESCR, and Arts 28 and 29 CRC. See generally, T. Karimova and G. Giacca, 'Education as a "Battleground" in Conflicts in 2012', in S. Casey-Maslen (ed), *War Report 2012* (Oxford: OUP, 2013) Chapter 6. It should be noted that an Occupying Power must respect local traditions and preferences under IHL.

[111] CPA, 'Iraqi Ministry of Education Enters Final Stage to Sovereignty', Press Release, 3 April 2004, available at <http://www.iraqcoalition.org/pressreleases/20040403_ed_PR.html>; UNICEF, *UNICEF Iraq Programme Update: 1–31 October 2003*, UNICEF Iraq Support Centre, Amman, Jordan, October 2003, available at <http://iraq.undg.org/uploads/doc/IraqOct.pdf>.

[112] Kolb and Vité, above n 26, at 189. See further Chs 67 and 68 of this volume.

[113] Tricky balancing remains necessary under occupation law between the interests of the occupier and those of the civilian population. On the one hand, over-restrictive rules on legislative and institutional changes may lead to stagnation, and hence be detrimental to the population, while on the other hand over-permissive rules would grant a wide margin to the occupier, for instance in the field of commercial legislation, to promote its own economic and political interests under the guise of benefitting the local population.

socio-economic issues and services.[114] The contribution of GC IV is significant in this regard. In accordance with the terms of Article 64 GC IV, conditions for legal change convey a more flexible approach to the occupier's legislative powers, which supplements the negative test proposed in Article 43 of the Hague Regulations.[115] Under Article 64 paragraph 2 GC IV, the occupier is entitled to modify existing laws when this is 'essential' to fulfil its obligations under the Convention (e.g. Articles 46, 49, or 50 GC IV), to maintain orderly government in occupied territory, or to ensure its own security. As such, IHL obligations should be understood in a broader normative context. Arguably, the necessity of fulfilling the obligations under the Geneva Conventions comprises not only all IHL obligations, but also the Occupying Power's obligations under public international law at large,[116] which could include its different legal regimes. There would be a process of assimilation through a broad reading of Article 43 of the Hague Regulations and Article 64 GC IV. So, it appears that the regime of occupation is not per se closed or resistant to the other international norms.[117]

58   In this context, how far can this regime accommodate the occupier's obligations to implement the IHRL of ESC rights, whether in the form of legislation, or administrative, budgetary, judicial, or other measures? Adopting certain positive measures to implement the minimum core obligations of ESC rights does not necessarily involve far-reaching reforms to the point of being in full contradiction with the basic foundational principle of occupation law. On the other hand, it is arguable that a bona fide implementation of the ICESCR may imply some radical changes. For instance, implementation of the right to work implies structural reforms to achieve steady socio-economic progress in the long term.[118] However, it is submitted that most ESC rights provisions do not automatically require fundamental changes to the system, at least from the basic normative threshold perspective. The Covenant is not about reforming the structure of the local society, introducing a new constitutional or political system, or modifying a taxation system or the political economy of the occupied territory. It is about implementing international standards.[119]

59   As regards health issues, it would be reasonable when the occupation lasts for a long time to adopt a legislative framework that seeks to improve all aspects of 'environmental and

---

[114] P. Spoerri, 'The Law of Occupation', in A. Clapham and P. Gaeta (eds), *Oxford Handbook of International Law in Armed Conflict* (Oxford: OUP, 2014) 182, at 194–5; Arai-Takahashi, above n 8, at 116; G. von Glahn, *The Occupation of Enemy Territory: A Commentary on the Law and Practice of Belligerent Occupation* (Minneapolis, MN: University of Minnesota Press, 1957), at 97.

[115] On the contention that Art 64 GC IV recognizes the authority of the occupier to modify all types of laws (and not only penal laws), beyond the limited scope of legislative authority recognized under Art 43 Hague Regulations, see Benvenisti, above n 29, at 100–5. UK Ministry of Defence, above n 77, para 11.25.1. For an opposite view contending that Art 64 GC IV is relevant only to penal legislation, while non-penal legislation is governed solely by Art 43 Hague Regulations, see J.A. Carballo Leyda, 'The Laws of Occupation and Commercial Law Reform in Occupied Territories: Clarifying a Widespread Misunderstanding', 23(1) *EJIL* (2012) 179.

[116] Spoerri, above n 114, at 195, fn 23.

[117] During the Diplomatic Conference the delegates were not averse to integrating international standards *en devenir* to structure the responsibilities of the occupier. During the negotiations, human rights law was still embryonic in character, which explains why a proposal by the Mexican delegation to give the occupier the right to modify local legislation which is contrary to the principles of the UDHR was defeated. Final Record, vol II-A, at 671.

[118] Art 6(2) ICESCR.

[119] As the CESCR asserted in relation to political and economic systems, 'the Covenant is neutral and its principles cannot accurately be described as being predicated exclusively upon the need for, or the desirability of a socialist or a capitalist system, or a mixed, centrally planned, or *laissez-faire* economy, or upon any other particular approach'. General Comment 3, para 8.

industrial hygiene', pursuant to Article 12(2)(b) ICESCR, or to take steps to reduce 'the stillbirth-rate and of infant mortality and for the healthy development of the child' (Article 12(2)(a)). Moreover, while it would be appropriate to enact regulations and other measures in order to 'improve methods of production, conservation and distribution of food by making full use of technical and scientific knowledge, by disseminating knowledge of the principles of nutrition' under Article 11(2)(a) ICESCR, it would clearly be questionable whether occupation law would allow reform of 'agrarian systems', which might amount to an agenda for societal reforms.[120] What about legislating to legalize workers' trade unions? Would the introduction of a system of social welfare that did not exist prior to occupation be prohibited? Would an occupier be permitted to raise taxes on corporations and the wealthy to sustain a viable welfare system or to guarantee a workable health care system? Such changes could go beyond a sustainable interpretation of the law of occupation, and would be at odds with the conservationist principle underlying this regime.

The right to education can also reveal a complex and sensitive debate. Involvement in educational programmes has not been uncommon in the past practices of various Occupying Powers, which often contravene occupation law and the right to education. For instance, indoctrination through education was used as a vehicle to maintain the hold of the Indonesian Army over East Timor. This was part of a broad policy of political, social, and economic integration of 'the province' with Indonesia.[121] Conscious of the difficulties encountered in prolonged occupation, it is nonetheless submitted that an occupier has the duty to ensure education, and any limitation has to be duly justified.

Having said this, the ICJ in the *Wall* Advisory Opinion stated as follows:

> The territories occupied by Israel have for over 37 years been subject to its territorial jurisdiction as the occupying Power. In the exercise of the powers available to it on this basis, Israel is bound by the provisions of the International Covenant on Economic, Social and Cultural Rights. Furthermore, it is under an obligation not to raise any obstacle to the exercise of such rights in those fields where competence has been transferred to Palestinian authorities.[122]

To a certain extent, this approach taken by the Court could nuance the extent to which an Occupying Power has to and may protect and fulfil ESC rights. Moreover, other arguments against extensive involvement of the occupier in the administration of the occupied territory relate to the fact that such an approach will perpetuate and solidify its presence. It reinforces the perception of a 'benign occupation' that seeks to protect human rights, and these above-mentioned examples illustrate this point. Of course, there will always be the risk that states use the human rights argument to interpret and transgress the law in a self-serving manner, in order to pursue their own political or economic interests, especially when they are afforded considerable latitude in discerning what measures to take to implement their obligations. It is clear that any fundamental changes to a territory's institutional structure should be made by the legitimate sovereign state in light of a participative decision-making processes at the local level, in accordance with the right to self-determination, and not by a foreign power. But it is submitted that in many respects the implementation of socio-economic rights drawn

---

[120] S. Vité, 'The Interrelation of the Law of Occupation and Economic, Social and Cultural Rights: The Examples of Food, Health and Property', 90 *IRRC* 871 (2008) 629, at 639.
[121] Benvenisti, above n 29, at 155.   [122] ICJ, *Wall*, Advisory Opinion, above n 9, para 112.

62 from internationally recognized standards does not overhaul the institutional structures of the occupied territory, or suppose any fundamental legal reforms that would be contrary to the law of occupation.

In any event, the latitude granted to the occupier should be limited to what is absolutely necessary under human rights law instruments applicable in the territory, and must stay as close as possible to local standards as well as to local cultural, legal, institutional, and economic traditions.[123] Efforts by scholars and existing case law to address the extent of the occupier's power and duty to modify the local legislation of the occupied territory may offer only general guidance.[124] As Benvenisti suggests, ultimately 'there is no general formula that could substitute for the process of analyzing each and every act, taking note of all the relevant interests at stake and the available alternatives'.[125] The ability of the occupier to legislate in the field of human rights needs therefore to be carefully assessed on a case-by-case basis and in light of the content of the norm.

b. The term 'to the fullest extent of the means available to it'

63 The law of occupation includes certain provisions that are context-dependent, similar to Article 2(1) ICESCR.[126] This is based on the qualifying term 'as far as possible' (*autant qu'il est possible*) contained in Article 43 of the Hague Regulations, which emphasizes the conduct-orientated feature of the duty to restore and ensure public order and civil life. As we have seen, under GC IV the occupier is obliged to ensure, 'to the fullest extent of the means available to it', the food and medical supplies of the population (Article 55), and hygiene and public health (Article 56) in the occupied territory.[127] This means that the obligations are to be assessed on the basis of available resources, the occupier being required to do the best it can.

64 When dealing with international obligations pertaining to ESC rights, inevitably there are questions as to the issue of resources and their allocation. Difficulties arise as to the methods by which the occupier is required to fund public services underlying many ESC rights. The evaluation of the available resources raises the fundamental question as to whether one should take into consideration all the resources of the Occupying Power(s), or only those available and generated in the occupied territory?

65 Under the Hague Regulations the occupier can collect taxes, dues, and tolls imposed for the benefit of the administration of the occupied territory, which may determine the capacity of the occupier to fulfil its obligations under GC IV.[128] But it may also happen that the socio-economic conditions existing in a territory before the occupation were deplorable. Therefore such resources may not be sufficient to ensure the minimum core of ESC rights. In this case, the occupier will not be able to rectify this situation materially in the short term, particularly if existing infrastructure is inadequate due to developmental problems or severe damage to socio-economic structures and services.

---

[123] M. Sassòli, 'Legislation and Maintenance of Public Order and Civil Life by Occupying Powers', 16 *EJIL* (2005) 661, at 677.

[124] See, e.g., D. Kretzmer, *The Occupation of Justice: The Supreme Court of Israel and the Occupied Territories* (New York: State University of New York Press, 2002).

[125] Benvenisti, above n 29, at 16.

[126] Usually under IHL there is no such margin of discretion, which is consonant with the non-derogable nature of many of its rules. States have a general obligation to respect IHL rules 'in all circumstances', regardless of the county's level of economic development.

[127] Arts 55 and 56 GC IV; Pictet Commentary GC IV, at 309. See also Art 69(1) AP I.

[128] See Arts 48 and 49, as well as Arts 51 and 52, Hague Regulations.

This is not without difficulties, because in the administration of the occupied territory, 66
tension would arise concerning the allocation of resources and prospective expenditure
between issues of security and economic and political interests on the side of the occupier, and the welfare of the civilian population living in those territories. It would in
fact be difficult to sustain an argument that, during long-term occupation, the occupier
has the duty to ensure and restore the civilian life that prevailed before the occupation
and that it would have no obligations to improve the standards of living.[129] It is unclear
whether the occupier is obligated to provide the occupied with the same level of social
services as is available within its own borders. In line with a contextual interpretation of
GC IV this does not seem to be the case, because equal treatment is made explicit only
in relation to protected aliens who are in the territory of a party to a conflict, who are
generally entitled to the same level of health care as is provided to nationals of the state.[130]
No analogous provisions exist in the sections of the Convention concerning protected
persons in an occupied territory. It would be of course unrealistic to expect the occupier,
who is entrusted with the discretion to balance conflicting interests, to apply the same
standards and obligations to the occupied territory as those expected with regard to ESC
rights in the state's own territory.

The occupier seems to be entitled to a wide discretion in ascertaining the allocation of 67
sufficient resources to discharge its obligations.[131] It is then challenging to delineate specific parameters, although it is conceivable that at the beginning of the occupation, when
the situation might remain unstable in localized geographical areas, priority should be
given to restoring security and public order within the territory, while assuring the minimum level of welfare to the inhabitants as prescribed by IHL and human rights. Over the
longer term, and in more peaceful and stable circumstances, it is reasonable to consider a
progressive shift in the allocation of resources towards civil life.

In this context, it should not be forgotten that the occupier would have to use its own 68
resources and, if necessary, seek assistance from the international community.[132] Long-term
occupation, such as East Timor which lasted for 24 years, shows the relevance of particular human rights for the well-being of the Timorese. When Indonesia invaded in 1975, it
undoubtedly encountered a population already facing serious developmental problems.
Moreover, it is not suggested that some of the violations of socio-economic rights that
occurred during the occupation period were not also commonplace in Indonesia itself, a
country that encountered economic development problems, but the context of military
occupation made these violations more severe in conjunction with the limited ability to
rectify them through seeking legal remedies.[133]

---

[129] Final Record vol II-A, at 774 and 827. Benvenisti noted that an American proposal, aiming at clarifying that occupiers were not obliged to set in the occupied territory 'higher standards of living than those prevailing before the occupation began', was opposed. E. Benvenisti, 'The Laws of Occupation and Commercial Law Reform in Occupied Territories: A Reply to Jose Alejandro Carballo Leyda', 23(1) *EJIL* (2012) 199, at 202.

[130] Art 38 para 2 GC IV. E.g., Art 38 para 5 GC IV states that 'children under fifteen years, pregnant women and mothers of children under seven years shall benefit by any preferential treatment to the same extent as the nationals of the State concerned'.

[131] O. Ben-Naftali and Y. Shany, 'Living in Denial: The Application of Human Rights in the Occupied Territories', 37 *Israel Law Review* (2003–4) 17, at 101.

[132] See generally Ch 12 of this volume.

[133] The Commission for Reception, Truth and Reconciliation (CAVR), *Chega! The Report of the Commission for Reception, Truth and Reconciliation*, Timor-Leste, Dili, 2006, para 136, available at <http://www.cavr-timorleste.org>.

69   With regard to the right to an adequate standard of living, investment in East Timor created economic growth, but it was geared toward the Indonesian Government's security concerns.[134] How can such a situation be assessed under international law? It is submitted that the principle of reasonableness could be a relevant yardstick against which to assess compliance by an occupier with its international law obligations. First, there was a contrast between investment and growth in sectors such as transport and communications and government administration (more than 50 per cent), and that of agriculture (less than 10 per cent). The authorities could not have been unaware that in this agrarian society more than 80 per cent of the population relied on agriculture for their livelihood, but only 10 per cent of cultivable land was used for such purposes, mainly because of security policies restricting movement of the population as well as conflicts over land ownership.[135] Poor investment in this sector would as a result equate to poverty, and evidence shows that at the end of occupation in 1999, East Timor ranked as one of the poorest countries in the world, with high levels of infant mortality and chronic malnutrition, far behind Indonesia in terms of development.[136]

70   There is a strong argument in favour of what can be reasonably expected from an occupier who takes on the responsibility of continuing occupation for decades. In order to implement human rights, policy choices are all the more important, and this case illustrates that the occupier's distorted priorities in terms of allocation of resources can lead to harmful effects on the civil life of the civilian population.

C. Relevance in Non-International Armed Conflicts

71   Formally, the law of occupation does not apply in non-international armed conflict (NIAC).[137] However, a number of authors argue that the law of occupation could be applied by analogy to territories administered by a non-state armed group in NIACs.[138]

72   This approach stems from practical reasons. Generally, the scope of application of IHL rules binding on armed non-state actors (ANSAs), when they are applicable, is limited, which may lead to a gap in protection for the civilian population.[139] On the one hand, there are situations where an armed conflict may fall below the required intensity, or may simply have ended, following, for instance, a peace agreement with an effective ceasefire;[140] and on the other hand, even when applicable, the relations between these actors and the persons in territory under their control may not materially be covered by these norms.

73   In prolonged situations of violence relating to separatist movements, when ANSAs have relatively stable control over the territory and population, IHL rules applicable in NIAC

---

[134] Ibid, para 137.   [135] Ibid, para 57.   [136] Ibid, para 26.
[137] See Ch 67, MN 57, of this volume.
[138] L. Zegveld, *Accountability of Armed Opposition Groups in International Law* (Cambridge: CUP 2002), at 65–6; D. Fleck, 'The Law of Non-International Armed Conflict', in D. Fleck (ed), *The Handbook of International Humanitarian Law* (3rd edn, Oxford: OUP, 2013) 581, at 605; D. Casalin, 'Taking Prisoners: Reviewing the International Humanitarian Law Grounds for Deprivation of Liberty by Armed Opposition Groups', 93 *IRRC* 883 (2011) 743, at 756; S. Sivakumaran, *The Law of Non-International Armed Conflict* (Oxford: OUP, 2012), at 529–32.
[139] Treaty-based humanitarian law of NIAC comprises two main regimes, one found in CA 3 and the other in AP II.
[140] Most IHL norms would no longer be applicable. See Art 2(2) AP II referring to the continued applicability of Arts 5 and 6.

have a limited reach in terms of protection, in particular when it comes to socio-economic rights. In this respect, the issue raises complex conceptual difficulties in situations where an ANSA controls part of a territory, and especially when it administers it by maintaining security and public order, and delivering basic services. Although treaty and customary rules potentially afford a significant level of protection, especially to civilians, many acts and omissions of ANSAs would not be governed by IHL.

Of course, a number of provisions regarding 'humane treatment' of persons not involved in the hostilities and who are under the control of belligerents remain relevant. They include requirements for the care of children, including socio-economic aspects such as education, and prohibit the recruitment or participation in hostilities of children under the age of 15. In addition, all of the rules regulating the conduct of hostilities applicable to NIACs, such as the principles of distinction, proportionality, or precaution in attack, protect civilians and civilian objects such as schools or hospitals.[141] However, IHL might not give all the necessary answers for the protection of the rights of people living under the control of ANSAs—in particular when it comes to issues relating to the daily life of the population, which goes on with or without the legitimacy or international recognition of the entity governing the territory in which they live.

Only the law of occupation provides specific rules that relate to the governance of a territory, but these rules are not transposable to internal armed conflict. In the absence of a humanitarian law of occupation for NIACs, commentators propose finding the solution within the operation of IHL itself. Even though IHRL may be applied to ANSAs with control over territory in order to fill the gap in protection, such an application remains controversial according to some.[142] It is argued that even though certain general protections and prohibitions contained in occupation law are already applicable to NIACs, through treaty or customary law,[143] the principles behind other rules could be applicable in the same way. Reference is made, for instance, to Article 43 of the Hague Regulations, to restore and ensure, as far as possible, public order and civil life.[144]

This could be a useful approach; however, as noted above, the notions of civil life or the welfare of the population remain rather vague, and it was suggested that we rely on human rights law to define these notions. In many ways, we have asserted that the legal regime of occupation encompasses a limited approach to the well-being of the civilian population that is geared toward a short-term perspective for occupation. As such, the law of occupation does not provide the necessary detail for understanding the content of the obligations, which should be read in light of ESC rights. Some of these limitations ultimately make a case for the argument of applying human rights law to non-state actors. It is submitted that ESC rights could add substantive and qualitative obligations to those rules of IHL as a complementary set of protection. But, in order to

---

[141] Rules 1, 2, 5–24 ICRC CIHL Study; A. Cassese, *International Law* (2nd edn, Oxford: OUP, 2005), at 415–20.
[142] S. Sivakumaran, above n 138, at 530.
[143] Included are the protection afforded to the wounded and sick; the protection of civilian objects such as hospitals; the principle of humane treatment; the prohibition of collective penalties, pillage, or reprisals; the taking of hostages; the prohibitions of deportation and forcible transfer; or the right to due process and judicial guarantees. Ibid, at 530.
[144] Ibid. The rules relating to occupation in the ICRC CIHL Study apply only to IACs. See Rules 41, 129A, and 130.

D. Legal Consequences of a Violation

I. Human rights mechanisms

77 Victims of breaches of IHL have no means of recourse either to the Fact-Finding Commission under Article 90 AP I (where applicable), or to another body for the determination of violations of IHL. However, in so far as violations of the relevant Geneva Conventions relating to ESC rights also entail violations of IHRL applicable to the occupied civilian population, recourse can be made to human rights treaty bodies.[146]

78 In terms of accountability, UN monitoring bodies, including commissions of inquiry and fact-finding missions, as well as regional commissions and courts, seem to provide a potentially valuable avenue to enhance the accountability of states occupying a foreign territory. They have jurisdiction over human rights norms that are related to, or overlap with, Geneva Convention rules applicable during military occupation. Obviously, here we shall not embark on an exhaustive catalogue of incidents of occupier-accountability regarding ESC rights, but we do offer examples of legal accountability before the European Court of Human Rights (ECtHR), as well as mechanisms for accountability derived from the UN Commission on Human Rights and its successor, the Human Rights Council.

79 At the regional level, in the case of *Cyprus v Turkey*, the ECtHR addressed, inter alia, restrictions on movement imposed on Greek Cypriots living in the northern part of Cyprus occupied by Turkish forces.[147] Although the ECtHR could not rule on socio-economic rights directly, nor on the right of freedom of movement, since Turkey was not party to Protocol 4 to the European Convention on Human Rights (ECHR), it did consider the fact that the movement of Greek Cypriots was subject to strict and invasive police control within their own villages, as well as with regard to neighbouring villages and towns.[148]

80 The Court agreed with the Commission's conclusions that restrictions which plagued the daily lives of the Greek Cypriots meant that they lived 'in a hostile environment in which it is hardly possible to lead a normal private and family life'.[149] Thus, the ECtHR found that these interferences amounted to a violation of private and family life, and respect for the home, in breach of Article 8(1) ECHR.[150] The Court noted in support of its findings that the adverse circumstances to which the Greek Cypriots were subjected should be considered as part of an overall analysis of the living conditions of the population concerned, such as the absence of normal means of communication, the unavailability in practice of the Greek-Cypriot press, the difficult choice with which parents and schoolchildren

---

[145] See Giacca, above n 10, Chapter V.

[146] Many human rights conventions offer the possibility of individual complaints.

[147] Violations of both the right to one's home and the right to enjoyment of one's possessions were found by the Court. ECtHR, *Cyprus v Turkey*, Judgment, 10 May 2001, paras 174 and 186.

[148] Ibid, para 287. The Commission noted that visitors to the homes of Greek Cypriots were physically accompanied by police officers, and in certain cases this even extended to the physical presence of state agents in the homes of Greek Cypriots.

[149] Ibid, para 300.

[150] Ibid, paras 294–5, 299–301. It should be noted that no legal basis for these restrictions, nor any justification such as security or public order, had been advanced that could have attracted the limitation clause of Art 8(2) ECHR.

were faced regarding secondary education, the restrictions on access to medical treatment, and the restrictions on, or the impossibility of preserving, property rights upon departure or on death.[151]

On education more specifically, the Court ruled that there had been a violation of Article 2 of Protocol 1 to the ECHR.[152] As noted above, changes in the educational system can have profound effects on the structure of life in an occupied territory and alter long-term behaviour. In this case, the Turkish authorities refused to allow the operation of secondary school facilities for Greek Cypriots that were once available to them.[153] Moreover, school-books destined for use in their primary schools were considered to be subject to excessive measures of censorship in light of Article 10(1) ECHR.[154] As for health care issues, the difficulties experienced in the area of health care under consideration essentially stemmed from the controls imposed on the Greek Cypriots' freedom of movement. The restrictions and formalities applied to freedom of movement (delays in the processing of requests of patients to receive medical treatment in the south, or denials of visits by Greek-Cypriot doctors of their choice) constituted impediments to access to medical treatment and hindrances to participation in inter-communal events (meetings and other gatherings).[155]

On the invasion of Kuwait by Iraq and subsequent Iraqi Occupation (1990–1), the UN Special Rapporteur stressed the importance of human rights law during military occupation. During that period the occupying forces committed grave violations of human rights, including the systematic destruction and pillaging of the economic infrastructure of Kuwait (banks, transport companies, industrial installations, schools, museums, libraries, religious and cultural institutions, hotels, private housing, etc), which was considered as having seriously undermined the enjoyment by the Kuwaiti people of their ESC rights.[156]

In the 2009 report of the UN Human Rights Council fact-finding mission on the Gaza conflict, various aspects of the ICESCR were included in the final report of the investigation, relating on the one hand to the actual military operations during the hostilities between Israel and Palestinian armed groups, and, on the other hand, to the effect of the blockade by Israel on the civilian population living in Gaza. The report criticized the overall objectives and strategy of the blockade of Gaza since 2006, and highlighted a wide range of adverse effects the blockade had on ESC rights, which are more easily identifiable. Although the current situation in Gaza could either be considered as an occupation, where Israel is able to exercise its power and influence over that territory, or as a situation of siege,[157] the report unequivocally favoured the former, and as a result

---

[151] Greek Cypriots who decided to resettle in the south were no longer considered legal owners of the property which they left behind, thus amounting to a violation of Art 1 of Protocol 1 to the ECHR. ECtHR, *Cyprus v Turkey*, above n 147, para 300.

[152] Ibid, paras 273–81.   [153] Ibid.

[154] The Court found a violation of Art 10(1) (freedom of expression), ibid, paras 248–55.

[155] In this connection, Cyprus observed that 'the requirement to obtain permission for medical treatment and the denial of visits by Greek-Cypriot doctors or Maronite doctors of their choice interfered with the right of Greek Cypriots in the north to respect for their private life'. Ibid, para 283.

[156] W. Kälin, *Human Rights in Times of Occupation: The Case of Kuwait* (Berne: LBE, 1994), at 1. For a full discussion on the case of Kuwait, see further in Giacca, above n 10, Chapter IV.

[157] Y. Shany, 'The Law Applicable to Non-Occupied Gaza: A Comment on *Bassiouni v. Prime Minister of Israel*', Hebrew University International Law Research Paper No 13-09, 27 February 2009, at 1–19. See also Milanovic, above n 24, at 142–4.

noted that Israel retains a number of positive obligations under IHL towards the civilian population to ensure its civil life and welfare, including the provision of food and medical supplies.[158]

84 The restriction on medical supplies, as well as power and fuel cuts, disrupted civil life over a broad range of activities, from business to education, health services, industry and agriculture, but in particular the functioning of hospitals, water, and sanitation, which was considered a violation both of the ICESCR and of IHL rules.[159] To give but two examples: restrictions on movement affected university students either planning to study or studying abroad, as well as impeding academics and scholars from travelling abroad on academic exchanges.[160] In addition, restrictions on goods resulted in a lack of educational material and equipment necessary for maintaining adequate teaching standards.[161]

II. United Nations Security Council

85 The protection of civilians in armed conflicts generally, as well as of women and children in particular, has been on the agenda of the UN Security Council since the end of the 1990s through a number of thematic resolutions. With respect to children, arguably the Council's most significant action was in adopting Resolution 1612 (2005), establishing a monitoring and reporting mechanism (MRM) at country level, and a Security Council Working Group on children and armed conflict.[162] The MRM addressed six 'grave violations' against children in situations of armed conflict, including attacks against schools and hospitals.[163]

86 One of the main concerns of this mechanism was to address the trend towards greater victimization of the civilian population, and to condemn the targeting of children and the objects that have a significant presence of children, such as schools. It is commonly acknowledged that children continue to account for the vast majority of victims of acts of violence, including as a result of deliberate targeting, indiscriminate, or excessive use of force.

III. International criminal responsibility

87 International criminal law (ICL) relates to 'the most serious crimes of international concern',[164] which give rise to individual international criminal responsibility. Violations of the rules of IHL relating to ESC rights can directly and indirectly overlap with international crimes.

---

[158] Report of the United Nations Fact Finding Mission on the Gaza Conflict, UN Doc A/HRC/12/48, 15 September 2009, paras 187 and 273–80. The relevant provisions relating to the duties of an Occupying Power under GC IV include the obligations contained in Arts 50 (duty to facilitate the working of care and education institutions), 55 (duty to ensure food and medical supplies to the population), 56 (duty to ensure and maintain medical and hospital establishments and services), 59 (duty to agree on relief schemes if the occupied territory is not well supplied), and 60 (duty to continue performing obligations even if third parties provide relief consignments). Ibid, para 1301.

[159] Ibid, paras 1311, 1315, and 1729.   [160] Ibid, para 1270.

[161] This situation caused allegedly a decline in attendance and performance at governmental schools. Ibid, para 1269.

[162] UNSC Res 1612, 26 July 2005, §3. See also Res 1882 (2009) and 1998 (2011). The MRM is established when parties in a conflict-affected state are listed in the annexes of the Secretary-General's annual report on children and armed conflict.

[163] These grave violations against children are: killing or maiming children; recruitment or use of children as soldiers; rape and other grave sexual abuse of children; abduction of children; attacks against schools or hospitals; and denial of humanitarian access for children. *Report of the Secretary-General, Children and Armed Conflict*, UN Doc A/59/695-S/2005/72, 9 February 2005, para 68; UNSC Res 1612, para 2.

[164] Art 1 ICC Statute.

Destroying homes, targeting hospitals, cutting off electricity or water sources leading to forced displacement, or excluding certain groups from education, health care, or cultural life systematically or on a broad scale, could in some cases be action serious enough to fall within the purview of ICL. In the field of health, for instance, some of these provisions of the Geneva Conventions have been criminalized and codified as international crimes in the Statute of the International Criminal Court (ICC). The Elements of Crimes explain that the word 'health' refers to physical and mental health or integrity.[165] Other provisions specifically protect buildings dedicated to public health from attack,[166] as well as objects and persons using the Geneva Conventions emblem.[167]

88 It should be noted that ICL has a very limited reach in the context of positive obligations relating to the socio-economic administration of an occupied territory that seek to ensure the welfare of the civilian population. In this respect the focus should be on the applicability of ESC rights and obligations, and relevant human rights law mechanisms, rather than on the possible criminalization of relevant IHL rules.[168]

89 This being said, violations of some of the relevant rules of the Geneva Conventions discussed in the present chapter may incur individual criminal responsibility. The unlawful deportation or transfer of a protected person, or compelling inhabitants in the occupied territory to serve in the occupier's armed forces, are deemed to be grave breaches of GC IV,[169] and are punishable as war crimes under the ICC Statute.[170] Although the list of grave breaches includes no specific violations of relief consignment rules, intentional and unlawful refusal of access to civilians (or attacks against humanitarian personnel, installations, material, or convoys) could be considered as falling under the grave breach of inhuman treatment of the victims, where their access to humanitarian assistance was impeded or obstructed.[171]

90 International humanitarian law strictly prohibits the starvation of civilians as a method of warfare in armed conflict.[172] Under the ICC Statute, the intentional use of starvation of civilians as a method of warfare is a war crime. This includes 'wilfully impeding relief supplies as provided for under the Geneva Conventions'.[173] The ICC Statute also defines the crime against humanity of 'extermination' as including 'the deprivation of access to food and medicine, calculated to bring about the destruction of part of a population'.[174]

---

[165] Elements of Crimes, Art 8(2)(a)(ii)-1, War Crime of Torture, para 1; Art 8(2)(a)(ii)-2, War Crime of Inhuman Treatment, para 1; Art 8(2)(b)(x)-1, War Crime of Mutilation, para 1; Art 8(2)(b)(x)-2, War Crime of Medical or Scientific Experiments, para 1; Art 8(2)(e)(xi)-1, War Crime of Mutilation, para 1; Art 8(2)(e)(xi)-2, War Crime of Medical or Scientific Experiments, para 1.

[166] Art 8(2)(b)(ix) and (2)(e)(iv).   [167] Art 8(2)(b)(xxv).

[168] See generally E. Schmid, *Taking Economic, Social and Cultural Rights Seriously in International Criminal Law* (Cambridge: CUP, 2014).

[169] Art 147 GC IV. The prohibition to compel civilians in occupied territory to serve in the armed forces of the occupier has been recognized since the post-Second World War war crimes trials. See, e.g., *Von Leeb and others*, US Military Tribunal, Nuremberg, 28 October 1948, 15 AD 376, at 394.

[170] Under Art 8(2)(a) ICC Statute, 'the deportation or transfer [by the Occupying Power] of all or parts of the population of the occupied territory within or outside [the territory it occupies]', constitutes a war crime in international armed conflicts.

[171] It should be noted that the ICC Statute criminalizes intentional attacks against personnel, installations, material, units, and vehicles involved in humanitarian assistance or peacekeeping missions as a war crime. Art 8(2)(b)(iii) ICC Statute.

[172] Art 54 AP I strictly prohibits starvation of civilians as a method of warfare.

[173] Art 8(2)(b)(xxv) ICC Statute.   [174] Art 7(1)(b) and (2)(b) ICC Statute.

Thus, the denial of humanitarian assistance to civilians may generally constitute the war crime of starvation under certain conditions.[175]

91 In the *Krstić* case, the Trial Chamber of the International Criminal Tribunal for the former Yugoslavia (ICTY) found that blocking aid convoys was part of the 'creation of a humanitarian crisis as a prelude to the forcible transfer of the Bosnian Muslim civilians'.[176] This incurred individual criminal responsibility for inhuman acts and persecution as crimes against humanity.[177] In other situations, the ICTY established that depriving detainees of food and other vital services in detention centres constitutes the basis for the charges of war crimes and crimes against humanity.[178]

E. Critical Assessment

92 The rules under GC IV encompass a number of obligations and legal safeguards for the civilian inhabitants under occupation; the subsequent elaboration and development of the IHRL framework has further enhanced that protection. Although the term 'ESC rights' does not appear as such in the Geneva Conventions, one can see how it has entered the IHL discourse due to the influence exercised by human rights law.

93 As we have seen, the specific effect deriving from the applicability of human rights law is that it may affect the assessment of the content of the obligations under GC IV, as well as providing additional obligations where GC IV is silent. In this context, human rights law may broaden the scope of protection, beyond mere basic humanitarian protection. The interrelationship between legal regimes remains complex, and each of the areas governed by these legal regimes in times of occupation would need to be examined contextually on a case-by-case basis.[179]

94 For stabilized and prolonged occupation, it is evident that the occupier through its administration cannot limit itself to the humanitarian baseline of protection: legal steps need to be undertaken on the whole area of ESC rights, involving, for instance, administrative and financial measures, strategies, programmes, and action plans in the fields of health, food, education, employment, and social security. However, the legal analysis should not portray a naive assumption that situations of military occupation can be assimilated to situations of peace. The occupier is generally an interested party, with specific objectives to achieve, and there is a clear tension or conflict of interests between pursuing its own policies and goals and those of the local civilian population, as well as the interests of the ousted government. Occupation is a state of exception and should be treated as such. The occupier does not derive public authority from the people it governs but from the fact of effective control. Although negative and positive human rights obligations binding on the occupier are relatively easily identifiable, the application of ESC rights makes the endeavour rather challenging.

GILLES GIACCA*

---

[175] See further Ch 12 of this volume.
[176] ICTY, *The Prosecutor v Radislav Krstić*, Trial Chamber Judgment, IT-98-33, 2 August 2001, para 615.
[177] Ibid, paras 618 and 653.
[178] ICTY, *The Prosecutor v Delalić et al*, Trial Chamber Judgment, IT-96-21-T, 16 November 1998, para 1119.
[179] A. Roberts, 'Transformative Military Occupation: Applying the Laws of War and Human Rights', 100 *AJIL* (2006) 580, at 599.

* Gilles Giacca has written this chapter in an entirely personal capacity. The opinions expressed herein are his own and do not necessarily correspond to those held by the ICRC or its legal division.

Chapter 71. Protection of Private Property

	MN
A. Introduction	1
B. Meaning and Application	5
I. Protection of property in occupied territories under Article 53 GC IV	5
II. Article 53 GC IV and military necessity as an exception	7
a. Overview	7
b. Military necessity under Article 53 GC IV and the applicability of Article 23(g) of the Hague Regulations to occupied territories	9
III. Pillage	14
IV. Respect for private property and the prohibition on confiscating private property	19
V. Requisition of private property	22
a. Requisition of private movable property (requisition in kind)	22
b. Requisition of private immovable property	25
VI. Seizure of movable private property and *munitions de guerre*	28
VII. Requisition of relief supplies and medical property	32
VIII. Expropriation	34
IX. Special rules concerning cultural property	37
a. Seizure, requisition, and destruction of cultural property	38
b. Pillage of cultural property	40
C. Relevance in Non-International Armed Conflicts	41
I. Destruction or seizure of property	41
II. Pillage	44
III. Cultural property	45
D. Legal Consequences of a Violation	46
I. Overview	46
II. Destruction and appropriation of property as a grave breach and a war crime	47
III. Destruction or seizure of property not justified by imperative military necessity as a war crime in international and non-international armed conflict	53
IV. War crimes of pillage	56
V. War crimes specifically relating to cultural property	58
E. Critical Assessment	60

Select Bibliography

Brilmayer, L./Chepiga, G., 'Ownership or Use? Civilian Property Interests in International Humanitarian Law', 49 *Harvard International Law Journal* (2008) 413

Lauterpacht, E., 'The Hague Regulations and the Seizure of Munitions de Guerre', 32 *BYBIL* (1955–6) 218

Lubell, N., 'The ICJ Advisory Opinion and the Separation Barrier: A Troublesome Route', 35 *IsrYBHR* (2005) 283, at 294–9

McNair, A.D./Watts, A.D., *The Legal Effects of War* (Cambridge: CUP, 1966)

O'Keefe, R., *The Protection of Cultural Property in Armed Conflict* (Cambridge: CUP, 2006)
Stewart, J.G., *Corporate War Crimes: Prosecuting the Pillage of Natural Resources* (New York: Open Society Foundations, 2010)

A. Introduction

1   Article 53 of Geneva Convention (GC) IV lays down the general rule on prohibiting the Occupying Power from destroying 'real or personal property' in occupied territories. The material scope of this prohibition covers both private and public property. This general rule is, however, subject to a limitation clause which provides an exception, 'where such destruction is rendered absolutely necessary by military operations'. It should be noted that the equivalent rules are found in the earlier instruments of the laws of war. Article 13(h) of the 1874 Project of an International Declaration Concerning the Laws and Customs of War (Brussels Declaration), albeit dealing with conduct of hostilities, has provided the basis for Article 23(g) of the Hague Regulations. The latter rule, emulating the text of the former, prohibits destruction and seizure of 'the enemy's property' during the conduct of hostilities.[1] Again, this general rule is subject to the special case where such destruction or seizure 'is imperatively demanded by the necessities of war'. This chapter will also dwell upon the specific rules concerning the prohibition of pillage, which are derived from Article 28 of the Hague Regulations (the ban on pillage as a forbidden method of warfare) and Article 33 GC IV (outlawing of pillage in the territories of the parties to the conflict and in occupied territories).

2   Article 53 GC IV, which did not feature in the 1934 Tokyo Draft Text of the Civilians Convention, first appeared as the second sentence of Article 30(2) of the 1948 Stockholm draft text (the current text of Article 33 paragraph 2 GC IV).[2] This second sentence provided that '[a]ny destruction of personal or real property which is not made absolutely necessary by military operations, is prohibited, as are likewise all measures of intimidation or terrorism'.[3] At the Geneva Diplomatic Conference (1949), because the second sentence of the draft text concerned a matter distinct from the issues addressed by the remaining part of the text (the prohibition of punishment of protected persons for offences they did not commit, the prohibition of collective penalties and of reprisals against protected persons and their property), the Delegates decided to turn it into a separate provision (Article 48A of the Geneva draft text),[4] which later became the current text of Article 53 GC IV. The Rapporteur justified this new provision, explaining that the rules under Section III of the Hague Regulations relating to occupation were unclear about the issue of destruction of property.[5]

---

[1] Albeit controversial, in the *Wall* Advisory Opinion, the ICJ held that '[o]nly Section III [of the Hague Regulations of 1907, which govern the issues of occupied territories,] is currently applicable in the West Bank and Article 23(g) of the Regulations in Section II [which deals with hostilities], is thus not pertinent': ICJ, *Legal Consequences of the Construction of a Wall in the Occupied Palestinian Territory*, Advisory Opinion, 9 July 2004, 136, at 185, para 124.

[2] The first paragraph of this provision addressed a different matter of individual responsibility and prohibition of collective penalties. See *Revised and New Draft Conventions for the Protection of War Victims: Texts Approved and Amended by the XVIIth International Red Cross Conference* (Revised Translation) (Geneva: ICRC, 1948), at 123.

[3] Ibid.   [4] Final Record, vol II-A, at 719–21.   [5] Ibid, at 721 and 829.

One of the contentious matters at the Diplomatic Conference was whether this protection should cover only property appertaining to private persons as envisaged by the 1948 Stockholm draft text, or should be expanded to encompass state and collective property as urged by the Soviet proposal.[6] Despite the hesitations voiced by some western delegates,[7] the United States (US) Delegation supported the broader concept of property to cover state and collective property.[8] It was explained that Article 23 of the Hague Regulations does not refer to the ban on destroying or seizing the property of enemy 'nationals' as such.[9] Accordingly, even this text of 1907 was interpreted as not excluding property owned by a state, or by social or cooperative organizations.[10]

This chapter analyses the protection of property in occupied territories under Article 53 GC IV, the prohibition of pillage under Article 33 paragraph 2, and the destruction and appropriation of property as a grave breach of GC IV under Article 147 GC IV. It first delineates the scope of application of the general rule under Article 53, examining how the concept of military necessity operates as an exception to this rule. The relatively sparse 'normative density' of the Geneva rules on the protection of property can be compared to the more elaborate Hague rules, which are largely left intact. Hence, it is necessary to examine those rules that regulate issues of confiscation, requisition, and seizure of private property. Appraising those Hague rules is of special importance, not least for the purpose of clarifying the notion of 'appropriation' under Article 147 GC IV. Moreover, brief inquiries will also be made into the special international humanitarian law (IHL) rules that address distinct categories of property, such as cultural property, relief supplies, and medical property. The relevant rules on such types of property constitute *lex specialis* in relation to the rules on protection of private property in occupied territories. In two final sections, the chapter will turn to two main questions: the extent to which those distinct rules analysed in international armed conflict (IAC) may be considered relevant in non-international armed conflict (NIAC); and the violations of those rules as grave breaches under Article 147 GC IV and other germane rules of international criminal law (ICL).

B. Meaning and Application

I. Protection of property in occupied territories under Article 53 GC IV

With regard to the ambit of the protected property, Article 53 refers to property 'belonging individually or collectively to private persons, or to the State, or to other public authorities, or to social or cooperative organizations'. Strictly construed, the text suggests that its protected legal interest is limited to the property *owned* by the persons or entities, but not extended to cover the property *used* by them.[11] This provision may be compared with Article 52 of Additional Protocol (AP) I, which proscribes any 'attack' against civilian objects, defined in a broad manner under that provision, irrespective of their ownership. Admittedly, however, the latter provision deals with

---

[6] Ibid, at 719–20. [7] Ibid, at 650 (Canadian and UK Delegations). [8] Ibid, at 720.
[9] This reasoning is owed to the Monaco proposal: ibid, at 650.
[10] Ibid, vol I, at118; vol II-A, at 719–21, 812, 829, and 856; vol II-B, at 417–18; vol III, at 134.
[11] Cf L. Brilmayer and G. Chepiga, 'Ownership or Use? Civilian Property Interests in International Humanitarian Law', 49 *Harvard International Law Journal* (2008) 413, at 423–5.

an attack against objects not under the control of the attacking party, hence not the property that is in the power of the Occupying Power as contemplated by Article 53 GC IV. In the case of private property, this chapter argues that it does not matter whether or not such property belongs to 'protected persons' within the meaning of Article 4 GC IV.

6   It should also be noted that with the welfare concept and humanitarian considerations shaping the normative underpinnings of GC IV, even the rules governing private property are not concerned with the value of economic assets as such, but are more concerned about property used as 'a means of livelihood' for vulnerable civilians.[12] This may explain why the text of Article 53 GC IV does not mention any requirement of compensation for the destroyed assets, leaving the matter to be resolved on the basis of the rules on state responsibility and human rights law.[13]

II. Article 53 GC IV and military necessity as an exception

a. Overview

7   The prohibition on destruction of property stipulated under Article 53 GC IV is subject to an exception based on military necessity ('except where such destruction is rendered absolutely necessary by military operations').[14] The text of Article 53 GC IV uses the words 'absolutely necessary by military operations', while Article 23(g) of the Hague Regulations uses 'imperatively demanded by the necessities of war'. The difference is often seen as semantic[15] or 'minimal'.[16] However, a closer look at the draft records reveals that at the Geneva Diplomatic Conference, the drafters deliberately narrowed the parameters of the generic notion 'necessities of war' to the notion 'the necessity of military operations'. The former notion appeared as essential part of the limitation clause in the Drafting Committee's proposed text. However, fearing that this would over-broaden the scope of exception, the Soviet Delegate submitted an amendment, proposing that the wording 'which is not absolutely required by the necessities of war' be replaced by the clause 'which is not made absolutely necessary by military operations'.[17] As we now see in Article 53, the Soviet amendment was decisively favoured in the vote.[18]

8   Since it is the Occupying Power that initially judges whether military necessity allows derogation from the general rule,[19] there is always a risk of abuse in this 'subjective' evaluation.[20] While providing such judicial avenues are not required under IHL, owners whose property has been destroyed may wish to turn to any administrative or constitutional procedures available in the territory of the Occupying Power. In addition,

---

[12] See, e.g., H. Lauterpacht, 'The Problem of the Revision of the Law of War', 29 *BYBIL* (1952) 360, at 363.
[13] On this matter, see HCJ 24/91, *Timraz et al v IDF Commander of the Gaza Strip*, 45(2) PD 325, 335, English excerpt in 23 *IsrYBHR* (1993) 337 (per Shamgar J).
[14] ICTY, *The Prosecutor v Tihomir Blaškić*, Trial Chamber Judgment, IT-95-14-T, 3 March 2000, para 157; *The Prosecutor v Mladen Naletilić and Vinko Martinović*, Trial Chamber Judgment, IT-98-34-T, 31 March 2003, para 577.
[15] Y. Dinstein, *The International Law of Belligerent Occupation* (Cambridge: CUP, 2009), at 196. See also K. Dörmann, *Elements of War Crimes under the Rome Statute of the International Criminal Court: Sources and Commentary* (Cambridge: CUP, 2003), at 83.
[16] H. McCoubrey, *International Humanitarian Law: Modern Developments in the Limitation of Warfare* (2nd edn, Dartmouth: Ashgate, 2000), at 200.
[17] Final Record, vol II-A, at 720.   [18] Ibid, at 721 (22 votes to 10).
[19] Pictet Commentary GC IV, at 302.
[20] *Corrie et al v Caterpillar*, 403 F Supp 2d 1019, at 1025 (2005).

the concept 'rendered absolutely necessary by military operations' under Article 53 GC IV should be interpreted strictly.[21] The Eritrea–Ethiopia Claims Commission (EECC), when analysing the destruction of civilian buildings such as bridges and railways by the Ethiopian troops who retreated from the occupied Eritrean territory, interpreted the concept narrowly, considering it should be linked to direct employability of the destroyed property for military operations.[22]

b. Military necessity under Article 53 GC IV and the applicability of Article 23(g) of the Hague Regulations to occupied territories

Where hostilities of short duration erupt in occupied territories riddled with insurgent activity, these are governed by the rules on conduct of hostilities, including Article 23(g) of the Hague Regulations.[23] That said, in such volatile occupied territories, it is very difficult to pinpoint the threshold of violence that would justify the shift in the applicable normative paradigm from the law enforcement procedures to IHL rules on conduct of hostilities.[24] In such situations, the concurrent applicability of those two paradigms may be contemplated.

In the Advisory Opinion on *the Legal Consequences of the Construction of a Wall in the Occupied Palestinian Territory*, the International Court of Justice (ICJ) was confronted with the issue, inter alia, of the Israeli destruction of private property in Palestinian occupied territories. When applying Article 53 GC IV, the Court dispensed with applying the rules governing the conduct of hostilities, including Article 23(g) of the Hague Regulations.[25] The ICJ's rationale was that because Article 23(g) of the Hague Regulations appears in a section on the conduct of warfare ('Section II—Hostilities'), rather than in the section on belligerent occupation ('Section III—Military Authority over the Territory of the Hostile State'), it was germane only in appraising the conduct of hostilities.[26] Assuming that this logic should be followed, the Court appears to be rather quick in finding that the destructions were not 'rendered absolutely necessary by military operations' under Article 53 GC IV.[27]

Notwithstanding the ICJ's textual construction, this chapter argues that the applicability of Article 23(g) of the Hague Regulations to occupied territories is not *ipso facto* excluded.[28] In the *Krupp* case, the US Military Tribunal at Nuremberg[29] recognized the applicability of Article 23(g) to occupied territories. It ruled that 'it is quite clear from

---

[21] R. Murphy and D. Gannon, 'Changing the Landscape: Israel's Gross Violations of International Law in the Occupied Syrian Golan', 11 *YIHL* (2008) 139, at 165.
[22] EECC, *Central Front—Eritrea's Claims 2, 4, 6, 7, 8, and 22*, Partial Award (2004), para 88.
[23] See N. Lubell, 'The ICJ Advisory Opinion and the Separation Barrier: A Troublesome Route', 35 *IsrYBHR* (2005) 283, at 294–9; Y. Arai-Takahashi, *The Law of Occupation: Continuity and Change of International Humanitarian Law, and its Interaction with International Human Rights Law* (Leiden: Martinus Nijhoff, 2009), at 296–301; HCJ 4219/02, *Gusin v IDF Commander of the Gaza Strip*, 56(4) PD 608, 610–11, English excerpt in 32 *IsrYBHR* (2002) 379, at 380; and *Mara'abe et al v Prime Minister of Israel et al* (*Alfei Menashe* case), HCJ 7957/04, 45 ILM 202 (2006), and English excerpt in 37 *IsrYBHR* (2007) 345, at 349, para 5.
[24] Lubell, above n 23, at 295–8.   [25] ICJ, *Wall* Advisory Opinion, above n 1, at 185, para 124.
[26] Ibid, at 189, para 132. See also the Separate Opinion of Judge Higgins, ibid, 207, at 213, para 24.
[27] ICJ, *Wall* Advisory Opinion, above n 1, at 192, para 135.
[28] *Report of the Special Rapporteur of the Commission on Human Rights, John Dugard, on the Situation of Human Rights in the Palestinian Territories Occupied by Israel Since 1967*, UN Doc E/CN.4/2004/6/Add.1, 27 February 2004, para 29; Lubell, above n 23, at 294; Dinstein, above n 15, at 53, 135, and 195–6. See also the Israeli case law: HCJ 2056/04, *Beit Surik Village Council v Government of Israel*, 30 June 2004, para 32.
[29] See *Krupp Trial*, US Military Tribunal, Nuremberg, 1947–8, UNWCC Law Reports, vol X, at 136.

the language and context of [Article] 23(g) [...] that it was never intended to authorize a military occupant to despoil on an extensive scale the industrial establishments of occupied territory'. The Tribunal added that '[w]hat was intended merely was to authorize the seizure or destruction of private property *only in exceptional cases when it was an imperative necessity for the conduct of military operations in the territory under occupation*'.[30] From this dictum, it is plain that the Tribunal did not exclude the destruction of property occurring as a necessary part of the conduct of hostilities in occupied territories.

12   The applicability of subparagraph (g) to occupied territories may be corroborated by the drafting history of subparagraph (h) of Article 23 of the Hague Regulations. The drafters at the Second Hague Peace Conference (1907) added this subparagraph to address affairs in the adversary's territories, including those relating to occupied inhabitants.[31] This train of thought was confirmed in the post-Second World War war crimes trials.[32]

13   At the Geneva Diplomatic Conference (1949), it was not the 'transplantation' of the concept 'necessities of war' from the text of Article 23(g) of the Hague Regulations into the draft text of Article 53 GC IV that was controversial. As discussed above, the issue was the wider ambit that the concept 'necessities of war' was considered to recognize in the exception. The Pictet Commentary GC IV, while not ruling out the applicability of Article 23(g) in occupied territories, appears to view Article 53 GC IV as a kind of *lex specialis* in relation to the general rule embodied in Article 23(g) of the Hague Regulations. This does not, however, suggest that Article 23(g) is debarred from application by virtue of Article 53 GC IV. The Pictet Commentary notes that

> since that rule [Article 23(g) of the Hague Regulations] is placed in the section entitled 'hostilities', it covers *all property in the territory involved in a war*; its scope is therefore much wider than that of the provision under discussion [Article 53 GC IV], which is only concerned with property situated in occupied territory.[33]

III. Pillage

14   Pillage, whether done in occupied territories or other territory, has been traditionally associated with looting, plunder, or sacking carried out by individual soldiers.[34] Individual theft and collective sacking have been considered contrary to military honour. Such unlawful appropriation of property must be distinguished from booty of war (*butin de guerre*),[35] which applies to the seizure of any movable state property on a battlefield (irrespective of its military character).[36]

15   Article 28 of the Hague Regulations proscribes pillage of a town or a place, even when taken by assault.[37] This rule is supplemented by the rules that specifically contemplate

---

[30] Ibid, emphasis added.
[31] T.E. Holland, 'Article 23(h)', 28 *LQR* (1912) 94, at 94.
[32] See, e.g., *The Justice Trial*, US Military Tribunal, Nuremberg, 17 February–4 December 1947, UNWCC Law Reports, vol VI, at 1–110 (examining Art 23(h), together with Arts 43 and 46 Hague Regulations).
[33] Pictet Commentary GC IV, at 301 (emphasis added). See also Lubell, above n 23, at 296.
[34] Dinstein, above n 15 at 207, para 491; Y Dinstein, *The Conduct of Hostilities under the Law of International Armed Conflict* (2nd edn, Cambridge: CUP, 2010), at 246.
[35] G. Carducci, 'Pillage', in MPEPIL, paras 1 and 3.
[36] W.G. Downey Jr, 'Captured Enemy Property: Booty of War and Seized Enemy Property', 44 *AJIL* (1950) 488, at 494–5; Dinstein (2010), above n 34, at 247.
[37] See also Art 3 para 1 1929 GC I; Art 15 para 1 GC I; Art 16 para 2 GC IV. See also Art 7 Hague Convention IX with respect to naval attacks; Arts 16, 21 para 1 Hague Convention X (Convention for the Adaptation to Maritime Warfare of the Principles of the Geneva Convention) (1907); and Art 18 para 1 GC II.

application in occupied territories: Article 47 of the Hague Regulations and Article 33 paragraph 2 GC IV, which embody the absolute ban on pillage of any property, private or public. The prohibition of pillage, as set forth under these provisions, is not subordinated to any exceptions based on military necessity.

Rather than confining the target of pillage to private property,[38] most publicists consider that the anti-pillage rules also safeguard public property, or the communal property jointly owned by local populations.[39] The gist of pillage is that its purpose is *essentially* 'for personal or private gain'.[40] This is corroborated by the Elements of Crimes of the International Criminal Court (ICC) Statute.[41] The 'private' character of the act is not affected even when the articles are taken for the purpose of transferring them to third parties, including, for instance, to a charitable institution.[42]

While noting that the purpose of pillage is *primarily* private, this chapter proposes that the prohibition against pillage should be understood even more broadly so as to encompass collective and organized pillage, and even officially sanctioned or ordered form of plundering.[43] In the *Delalić* case, the International Criminal Tribunal for the former Yugoslavia (ICTY) Trial Chamber held that the war crime of 'plunder of public or private property' under Article 3(e) of the ICTY Statute encapsulated the organized seizure of property carried out as a pattern of a systematic economic exploitation of occupied territories.[44] The wide parameters of pillage cover a wholesale deprivation of enemy property that would reduce the entirety of enemy property to war booty,[45] and the abuse of the rights to levy contributions and to carry out requisition.[46] The question of pillage may arise if the exploitation of natural resources carried out by Occupying Powers or corporations cannot be justified either as requisitions under Article 52, or as *munitions de guerre* under Article 53 paragraph 2 of the Hague Regulations. These issues will be examined below.

Pillage may be perpetrated by civilians,[47] who may be members of the occupying authorities' administration, or gangs of civilians in occupied territories, or corporations registered in a third state. Indeed, the nationality of the perpetrators of pillage does not matter.[48] The Occupying Power can be held responsible for failing to prevent the pillage and punishing offenders.[49] Such a positive obligation was confirmed by the ICJ in the *Armed Activities* (Democratic Republic of Congo (DRC)/Uganda) case. There, the Court

---

[38] C. Rousseau, *Le droit des conflits armes* (Paris: Pédone, 1983), at 164.
[39] E.H. Feilchenfeld, *The International Economic Law of Belligerent Occupation* (Carnegie Endowment for International Peace, 1942), at 31. See also Dinstein (2010), above n 34, at 246.
[40] A.V. Freeman, 'Responsibility of States for Unlawful Acts of their Armed Forces', 88 *RCADI* (1955) 267, at 327; Y. Dinstein, 'The International Law of Belligerent Occupation and Human Rights', 8 *IsrYBHR* (1978) 104, at 128; Dinstein (2010), above n 34, at 246.
[41] ICC Elements of Crimes, Pillage as a War Crime, Art 8(2)(b)(xvi) and (e)(v) ICC Statute.
[42] Feilchenfeld, above n 39, at 30, para 123.
[43] G. Schwarzenberger, *International Law as Applied by International Courts and Tribunals,* II: *The Law of Armed Conflict* (London: Stevens & Sons, 1968), at 244.
[44] ICTY, *The Prosecutor v Zejnil Delalić et al*, Trial Chamber Judgment, IT-96-21-T, 16 November 1998, para 590.
[45] Pictet Commentary GC IV, at 226. See Rousseau, above n 38, at 164–5.
[46] Feilchenfeld, above n 39, at 31.
[47] A. Zimmermann, 'Article 8(2)(b)(xvi)', in O. Triffterer (ed), *Commentary on the Rome Statute of the International Criminal Court* (2nd edn, Oxford: Hart Publishing, 2008), at 408, 410.
[48] Feilchenfeld, above n 39, at 30.
[49] Ibid. See also EECC, *Western Front, Aerial Bombardment and Related Claims—Eritrea's Claims 1, 3, 5, 9–13, 14, 21, 25, and 26*, Partial Award, 19 December 2005, para 36.

highlighted the occupier's affirmative duties to prevent looting, plundering, and exploitation of (including trafficking in) the natural resources of the DRC, which acts were committed not only by members of Uganda's military forces, but also by private persons.[50]

IV. Respect for private property and the prohibition on confiscating private property

19 Article 46 of the 1907 Hague Regulations lays down the general rule on inviolability of private property in occupied territory (first paragraph) and the prohibition on confiscating private property in occupied territory (second paragraph). Confiscation is a taking (seizure) of property without the need to pay compensation.[51] Under IHL, lawful confiscation is confined to appropriation of *public* movable property of the adverse party to the conflict.[52] There is a presumption that private property loses immunity from confiscation if it is in the actual service of the adversary when found or seized.[53]

20 Confiscation may be distinguished from booty of war,[54] which relates only to military equipment seized or found on the battlefield. If confiscated goods are treated as such, this would transfer the title to the captor, with no requirement of compensation for the appropriation.[55] Nevertheless, this distinction has become blurred in practice.[56] Some states treat confiscation and war booty as coming within a generic concept of 'spoils of war'.[57]

21 Despite the ban on confiscating private property, the Occupying Power may acquire *private* property in the occupied territory. Apart from the two exceptions expressly set forth in the Hague Regulations (requisitions under Article 52;[58] and seizure under Article 53 paragraph 2),[59] this chapter contemplates the case of expropriation.[60] Our examination will now turn to each of these exceptional cases.

V. Requisition of private property

a. Requisition of private movable property (requisition in kind)

22 Under Article 52 of the Hague Regulations, the Occupying Power may requisition private movable property.[61] Requisition in kind was developed as a means to fill the loss of resources

---

[50] ICJ, *Case concerning Armed Activities on the Territory of the Congo (DRC v Uganda)*, Judgment, 19 December 2005, paras 245–8.

[51] D. Kretzmer, 'The Advisory Opinion: The Light Treatment of International Humanitarian Law', 99 *AJIL* (2005) 88, at 96–7.

[52] Australia, Defence Force Manual, Canada, LOAC Manual, New Zealand, Military Manual, as cited in ICRC CIHL Study, vol I, at 178.

[53] Israel, High Court, *Al-Nawar* case, Judgment, 11 August 1985 (per Judge Shamgar); as cited in ICRC CIHL Study, vol II, Part 1, at 1066, para 414.

[54] This is often defined as 'enemy military objects (or equipment or property) captured or found on the battlefield': ICRC CIHL Study, vol I, at 174.

[55] A. McDonald and H. Brollowski, 'Requisitions', in MPEPIL, para 19.

[56] ICRC CIHL Study, vol I, at 178–9.

[57] Germany, Military Manual, as cited in ICRC CIHL Study, vol I, at 178–9.

[58] G. Schwarzenberger, 'The Protection of Private Property in the Law of Belligerent Occupation', 1 *Indian Journal of International Law* (1960/61) 193, at 212.

[59] On the battlefield, we might add another form of exception: the case of appropriating weapons and military equipment of enemy forces as booty of war: Dörmann, above n 15, at 277–8. See also L. Oppenheim, *International Law: A Treatise*, ed Hersch Lauterpacht (7th edn, London: Longman, 1952), vol II, at 401–2.

[60] Schwarzenberger, above n 43, at 266.

[61] Lauterpacht/Oppenheim defines requisition in kind as 'the demand for the supply of all kinds of articles necessary for an army, such as provisions for men and horses, clothing, or means of transport': above n 59, at 409.

available to the belligerent parties, as pillage was gradually forbidden. Procedurally, decisions on requisitioning must be made by a local commander.[62] Requisitioned assets must be paid for in cash, failing which a receipt must be provided with the requirement to redeem it as soon as possible.[63]

Requisition may be carried out only for the purpose of satisfying the needs of the occupying army.[64] As held in the *Krupp* case, requisitioned goods cannot be diverted to meet demands of the Occupying Power's industry or to feed its home population.[65] Requisitioning must be proportionate to the 'resources of the country'.[66] There is disagreement over whether the assessment of proportionality ought to be in relation to the resources of the entire occupied territory, or relative to the local area specifically affected by the requisitioning measure.[67] With the welfare concept preponderant under GC IV, the occupiers' right to requisition is subordinated to their duty to ensure the well-being of the civilians under occupation.[68]

The requisition of private movable property under Article 52 results in the transfer of its title (ownership) to the Occupying Power, albeit that the latter must defray compensation. With the transfer of the title, there is no obligation to return the requisitioned goods to the original owner.[69] This marks a contrast to the requisition of private *immovable* property, which, as will be explained at MN 25–27, does not give rise to the acquisition of the title.[70] Yet some authors argue that the passing of a title of the requisitioned chattels does not occur where the needs of the occupying army do not call for the Occupying Power's acquisition of that title.[71]

b. *Requisition of private immovable property*

There is no express legal basis for requisitioning immovable property for temporary use under GC IV and the 1907 Hague Regulations. In the *Wall* Advisory Opinion, with special regard to the question of Israel's (allegedly temporary) requisition of private real property in occupied territories, the ICJ highlighted that the prohibition under Article 46 paragraph 2 of the Hague Regulations is not accompanied by any exceptions, such as the qualifying phrase 'needs of the army of occupation' under Article 52 of the Hague Regulations.[72] The Court's presumed rationale was that *all* instances of the Israeli authorities taking property from inhabitants in the affected part of the occupied West Bank were not temporary requisitions but tantamount to confiscation

---

[62] Art 52 para 2 Hague Regulations.
[63] Art 52 para 3 Hague Regulations. This requirement to redeem the receipt was introduced in the text of the 1907 Hague Regulations, but not in its precursor of 1899: Dinstein, above n 15, at 231.
[64] Art 52 para 1, 1st sentence Hague Regulations.
[65] *Krupp Trial*, above n 29, at 135–7; *Weizsaecker et al (Ministries Trial)*, 14 April 1949, 16 *ILR* 344, at 360. See also Netherlands, Special Criminal Court, *In re Shipbuilding Yard 'Gusto'*, 2 September 1947, 14 *ILR* 309.
[66] Art 52 para 1, 2nd sentence Hague Regulations.
[67] Cf Feilchenfeld, above n 39, at 37 (proportionality assessed not in relation to a specific individual owner but in a holistic manner); and M.S. McDougal and F.P. Feliciano, *Law and Minimum World Public Order: Transnational Coercion and World Public Order* (New Haven, Conn: New Haven Press, 1961), at 820 (proportionality relative to a specific locality).
[68] McDonald and Brollowski, above n 55, para 23.
[69] Schwarzenberger (1968), above n 43, at 274–6.   [70] Ibid.
[71] A.D. McNair and A.D. Watts, *The Legal Effects of War* (Cambridge: CUP, 1966), at 394, and cases cited in fn 5.
[72] ICJ, *Wall* Advisory Opinion, above n 1, at 192, para 135. See also Schwarzenberger, above n 43, at 245.

within the meaning of Article 46 paragraph 2 of the Hague Regulations.[73] The Court thus dispensed with examining the needs of the occupation army or any other security considerations, as would otherwise be required under Articles 23(g) and 52 of the Hague Regulations.[74]

26 Many publicists have claimed that the Occupying Power has the right to requisition immovable property for temporary use.[75] Some argue that requisition in kind under Article 52 of the Hague Regulations should cover the requisition of immovable private property, including the temporary use of land[76] and 'possession in immovables'.[77] Admittedly, even according to this view, semi-permanent dispossession of the immovable property and de facto transfer of title to the Occupying Power amount to confiscation forbidden under Article 46 paragraph 2 of the Hague Regulations.[78] Nevertheless, the weakness of this approach is that the term 'in kind' is clearly confined to chattels.[79] The better view is to contend that the ban on confiscation under Article 46 paragraph 2 of the Hague Regulations does not apply to temporary use of private immovable property for purposes demanded by 'the necessities of war'.[80] To avoid abuse, this chapter proposes that the conditions contained under Article 52 of the Hague Regulations be applied by analogy. It suggests that the use of immovable private property be constrained by the requirement to pay cash or to issue a receipt,[81] or to defray 'compensation' for the use of the private immovable property.[82]

27 It ought to be noted that immovable private property may be appropriated only for a temporary period.[83] The Occupying Power acquires only possession, not the title to the private immovable property. The owner of the requisitioned property may claim compensation both for the use of the property[84] and for any damage done to it.[85]

VI. Seizure of movable private property and *munitions de guerre*

28 Under Article 53 paragraph 2 of the Hague Regulations,[86] the Occupying Power may seize three distinct categories of movable property, even of a private nature ('[a]ll appliances [...] adapted for the transmission of news, or for the transport of persons or things,

---

[73] See ICJ, *Wall* Advisory Opinion, above n 1, Separate Opinion of Judge Thomas Buergenthal, at 240–1, para 3 (criticizing the Court's failure to evaluate military necessity without sufficient evidence).

[74] See Kretzmer, above n 51, at 98 (rebuking the Court's omission to examine the distinction between confiscation prohibited under Art 46 Hague Regulations, and the temporary requisition of immovable property which may be justified under Art 52 Hague Regulations).

[75] E.g., see G. von Glahn, *The Occupation of Enemy Territory: A Commentary on the Law and Practice of Belligerent Occupation* (Minneapolis, MN: University of Minnesota Press, 1957), at 186; and *UK Manual of the Law of Armed Conflict* (Oxford: OUP, 2004), at 300. See also Pictet Commentary GC IV, at 301.

[76] Schwarzenberger (1968), above n 43, at 245–6 and 269.   [77] Ibid, at 288.
[78] Ibid, at 266.   [79] Dinstein, above n 15, at 228.   [80] Oppenheim, above n 59, at 403.
[81] Ibid, at 403–4 and 411–12.   [82] Ibid, at 411–12.   [83] von Glahn, above n 75, at 186.
[84] See, e.g., HCJ 401/88, *Abu Rian et al v IDF Commander of Judea and Samaria*, 42(2) PD 767, at 770, English excerpt in 23 *IsrYBHR* (1993) 296.

[85] Dinstein, above n 15, at 227. See HCJ 290/89, *Goha v Military Commander of Judea and Samaria*, 43(2) PD 116, at 120, English excerpt in (1993) 23 *IsrYBHR* 323–4 (per President Shamgar).

[86] The precursor to this text was Art VI of the 1874 Brussels Project, which nonetheless limited the special items that benefited from restoration and compensation to means of transport and communication, all of which were movable assets, as well as immovable property like a railway plant. It should be noted that despite the ambivalence of the text of the second paragraph of Art 53, which seems to contemplate its application not only to private but also to public movable property, the *travaux préparatoires* are considered to suggest that this paragraph applies only to private property: E. David, *Principes de droit des conflits armés* (5th edn, Brussels: Bruylant, 2012), at para 2.476.

exclusive of cases governed by naval law'; depots of arms; and, generally, all kinds of *munitions de guerre*). The only condition is that seized items need to be restored and compensation fixed when peace is made. The second paragraph, which is an amalgamation of two paragraphs of Article 6 of the 1874 Brussels Declaration, is distinctive in allowing seizure of even private movable property, if that property is of such special kind (munitions of war, depots of arms, means of transport, and means of transmission of news). Much of the controversy relating to Article 53 of the Hague Regulations surrounds the term of art '*munitions de guerre*/munitions of war'. This may aptly be defined as any movable goods that are military equipment, and those other movable items that may be employed in warfare.[87] That said, determining the parameters of its definition remains hotly disputed.[88] One of the continuing polemics relates to the question whether petroleum falls within the scope of this notion.[89] According to the earlier case law, Article 53 of the Hague Regulations does not contemplate *munitions de guerre* that are in 'actual hostile use' when seized. In such cases of war, the owner may be deprived of the right to claim return of the seized property and compensation for it.[90]

As compared with the requisition in kind governed under Article 52 of the Hague Regulations, there is no requirement of proportionality under Article 53 of the Hague Regulations. In addition, the purpose of the seizure of goods under this provision is not confined to the needs of the occupying army. A literal construction would suggest that the Occupying Powers may seize movable assets without regard to resources of the occupied country.[91] Even so, such a sweeping view must be constrained by the requirement to give primacy to the humanitarian need of the occupied population if, for example, petroleum is at all considered as falling within '*munitions de guerre*'. 29

While there is no duty to pay in cash immediately, the seized property must be returned and compensation paid when peace is made, save in cases governed by the law of prize. In theory, in view of the duty of restoration, the seizure transfers merely possession of the object, not its ownership.[92] The general rule that the ownership is preserved suggests that the Occupying Powers are debarred from selling it.[93] Admittedly, unlike appliances for transmitting news, rolling stock, or other vehicles, use of which by the Occupying Power may cause only wear, some personal items, such as ammunition or petroleum (if the latter is considered *munitions de guerre*), may be exhausted or depleted. It is perhaps because of the need to accommodate such circumstances that not only restoration but 30

---

[87] E. Lauterpacht, 'The Hague Regulations and the Seizure of Munitions de Guerre', 32 *BYBIL* (1955–6) 218, at 242. See Netherlands, Special Court of Cassation, in *Re Esau*, 21 February 1949, 16 *ILR* (1949) 482, at 483 (excluding boring machines, lathes, lamps, tubes, and gold from the definition of *munitions de guerre*).

[88] Cf C.A. Farleigh, 'The Validity of Acts of Enemy Occupation Authorities Affecting Property Rights', 35 *Cornell Law Quarterly* (1949–50) 89, at 107 (discussing bank accounts), with H.A. Smith, 'Booty of War', 23 *BYBIL* (1946) 227, at 228–9 (referring to 'all movable articles for which a modern army can find any normal use', including food, drink, and tobacco).

[89] For the classic case law, see Singapore, Court of Appeal, *NV de Bataafsche Petroleum Maatschappij and Others v The War Damage Commission*, 13 April 1956, 23 *ILR* (1956) 810. See also R.D. Langenkamp and R.J. Zedalis, 'What Happens to the Iraqi Oil?: Thoughts on Some Significant, Unexplained International Legal Questions Regarding Occupation of Oil Fields', 14 *EJIL* (2003) 417.

[90] See *Cession of Vessels and Tugs for Navigation on the Danube* case, 1 *RIAA* (1921) 97, at 105–6.

[91] Dinstein, above n 15, at 233.

[92] See Australia, Defence Force Manual (1994), paras 1225–31; as cited in ICRC CIHL Study, vol II, Part 1, at 1047–8.

[93] P.C. Jessup, 'A Belligerent Occupying Power's Power over Property', 38 *AJIL* (1944) 457, at 459; Dinstein, above n 15, at 234. See Austria, Supreme Court, 20 June 1951, *Requisitioned Property (No 2)* case, 18 *ILR* 696.

even compensation is stipulated upon the return of peace. This issue will be dealt with at MN 31 immediately below. Arguably, this understanding can be corroborated by the drafters' intention. At the First Hague Peace Conference (1899), the requirement of compensation was introduced because there was opposition to the initial suggestion that the conduct contemplated under Article 53 paragraph 2 of the Hague Regulations be treated as sequestration.[94]

31   In cases of seizure of means of transport and communication, the conjunctive obligation of restoration and compensation makes sense, because this seizure may result in loss of profit.[95] In contrast, with respect to seizure of *munitions de guerre*, which often involves movable goods that may be worn out or are perishable, it is more cogent to contemplate an alternative duty of either return, or compensation if the option of restitution is not viable.[96]

VII. Requisition of relief supplies and medical property

32   The general principle of respect for property under Article 53 GC IV ought to be read together with special rules constraining the Occupying Power's ability to requisition special categories of property: food and medical supplies (Article 55); civilian hospitals and their medical supplies (Article 18 and 57 GC IV); and relief consignments (Articles 60–62 GC IV). These rules are supplemented by other pertinent rules: Article 14 AP I (property of medical units); Article 21 AP I and Article 35 GC I (medical vehicles); and Article 23 AP I (medical ships).

33   Special regard should also be had to the rule of customary international law (CIL) derived from Article 54(2) AP I.[97] According to this paragraph, unless the third and fifth paragraphs of that provision apply and provide exceptions, inter alia, on grounds of imperative military necessity, it is forbidden to attack, destroy, remove, or render useless objects indispensable to the survival of the civilians. The non-exhaustive inventory of such objects includes movable items (such as foodstuffs, crops, and livestock) and immovable property (such as agricultural areas, drinking water installations and supplies, and irrigation works). Generally, in so far as the test of military necessity is met, the Occupying Power may resort to the so-called 'scorched earth' policy to bar the advance of enemy forces in the occupied territory. However, under Article 54 AP I, the Occupying Power is, unlike the territorial sovereign, forbidden from carrying out such a tactic against property, private or public, which constitutes 'objects indispensable to the survival of the civilian population'.[98]

VIII. Expropriation

34   Expropriation is defined as the compulsory acquisition of private property by the authorities against the payment of compensation.[99] The European Court of Human Rights (ECtHR) has broadly interpreted the notion of 'expropriation' to encompass not only 'formal' or 'direct' forms of expropriation, but also any 'indirect expropriation' that

---

[94] P. Bordwell, *The Law of War between Belligerents: A History and Commentary* (Chicago, Ill: Callaghan & Co, 1908), at 325–6.
[95] Ibid, at 326.   [96] Ibid. See also Dinstein, above n 15, at 235.
[97] See ICRC CIHL Study, Rule 54, at 189 et seq.   [98] See Art 54(2) AP I.
[99] Kretzmer, above n 51, at 97.

irreversibly and permanently deprives private property of its economic value,[100] the effect of which is so serious as to make the property of little meaningful use.[101]

Under IHL, it has been suggested that expropriation undertaken pursuant to the law in force of the occupied country is not forbidden.[102] One rationale for this is to argue that expropriation is implicitly recognized by way of an *a contrario* interpretation of Article 46 paragraph 2 of the Hague Regulations, the text that prohibits confiscation only. Still, to limit the possibility of abuse, the Occupying Power's authority of expropriation should be constrained by the grounds of necessity under Article 43 of the Hague Regulations and Article 64 GC IV. Any expropriating measures ought ultimately to be pursuant to the objective of enhancing the interest of either the population or the occupied state.[103]

Appropriate guidance for the legality of expropriation may be obtained from the practice established in international human rights law (IHRL). The point of departure is to demand if expropriation is pursuant to a public interest or objective, and if carried out in conformity with local procedural rules that must be non-discriminatory and conform to due process guarantees.[104] Administrative procedural rules should include the right to a hearing prior to the occurrence of the expropriation or seizure.[105] Public interest may be seen as shorthand for the well-being of the civilian population.[106] In occupied territories, the procedure for expropriation may exceptionally be the laws enacted by the occupation authorities.[107] Ideally, in case of prolonged occupation, the Occupying Power should interpret the test of lawfulness in a substantive sense, and ensure that such legal basis is 'sufficiently accessible, precise and foreseeable' to the civilian population.[108] The Occupying Powers should also integrate the test of proportionality (a reasonable balance to be struck between the social end and the adverse effect on the aggrieved persons) into the concept of military necessity under Article 43 of the Hague Regulations and Article 64 GC IV. For the appraisal of proportionality, it is strongly advised that the Occupying Power examine whether the complainants have suffered from any 'individual and excessive burden',[109] and whether there has been a sufficient amount of compensation, the two subtests enunciated in the ECtHR's case law.[110]

---

[100] U. Kriebaum and A. Reinisch, 'Property, Right to, International Protection', in MPEPIL, paras 39 and 51.
[101] ECtHR, *Pine Valley Developments Ltd and others v Ireland*, Judgment, 29 November 1991, para 56.
[102] Schwarzenberger, above n 43, at 266; and Dinstein, above n 15, at 225, para 533. See also Poland, Supreme Court, First Division, *Marjamoff and others v Włocławek (Communal District of)*, 5 December 1924, 2 *AD* (1923–4) 444, at 444–5. *Contra*, Oppenheim, above n 59, at 403.
[103] von Glahn, above n 75, at 186; and M.J. Kelly, 'Iraq and the Law of Occupation: New Tests for an Old Law', 6 *YIHL* (2003) 127, at 155. See also Feilchenfeld, above n 39, at 38 and 50;
[104] Kriebaum and Reinisch, above n 100, para 19.
[105] HCJ *393/82, A Cooperative Society Lawfully Registered in the Judea and Samaria Region v Commander of the IDF Forces in the Judea and Samaria region et al (A Teachers' Housing Cooperative Society v The Military Commander of the Judea and Samaria Region)*, (1983) 37(4) Piskei Din 785, English excerpt in 14 *IsrYBHR* (1984) 301, at 311–12 (per Barak J).
[106] Ibid. [107] *Marjamoff and others v Włocławek*, above n 102, at 445.
[108] See, e.g., ECtHR, *Carbonara and Ventura v Italy*, Judgment, 30 May 2000, paras 63–5.
[109] ECtHR, *James and others v UK*, Judgment, 21 February 1986, para 50.
[110] *Carbonara and Ventura v Italy*, above n 108, para 67. For the element of compensation, see also HCJ 202/81, *Tabib et al v Minister of Defence et al*, 36(2) PD 622, 632, excerpt in English in 13 *IsrYBHR* (1983) 364, at 368 (per I. Shilo J).

IX. Special rules concerning cultural property

37   Article 1 of the 1954 Hague Convention defines cultural property as all 'movable or immovable property of great importance to the cultural heritage of every people'. Under general IHL, Article 53 AP I and Article 16 AP II furnish supplementary rules, safeguarding cultural property that 'constitute[s] the cultural or spiritual heritage of peoples'.[111] As regards cultural property that does not fit the threshold set by Article 1 of the 1954 Convention and Article 53 AP I (or Article 16 AP II), the Occupying Power remains bound under Articles 27 and 56 of the 1907 Hague Regulations and Article 5 of the 1907 Hague Convention IX.[112] Indeed, Article 56 paragraph 1 of the Hague Regulations focuses specifically on cultural property in occupied territories. Under this provision, the property of institutions dedicated to religion, charity, education, the arts and sciences, whether it is immovable or movable, is fictitiously to be categorized as private property, even if it is owned by a state.

a. Seizure, requisition, and destruction of cultural property

38   Under Article 56 paragraph 2 of the Hague Regulations, the Occupying Powers are absolutely prohibited from seizing, destroying, or causing wilful damage to institutions dedicated to religion, the arts and sciences (and the institutions devoted to charity and education), historic monuments, and works of art and science.[113] No derogation is permissible from this rule of CIL.[114] Any infraction of this rule must be made the subject of legal proceedings.[115]

39   For the states parties to the 1954 Hague Cultural Property Convention, it is forbidden to requisition *movable* cultural property in occupied territories (or in any territories of the member states).[116] This interdiction applies to both private and state cultural property. It is a special rule that should be compared to the general rule on requisition set forth under Article 52 of the 1907 Hague Regulations.

b. Pillage of cultural property

40   Under the first sentence of Article 4(3) of the 1954 Hague Cultural Property Convention, pillaging is, together with theft, misappropriation, and vandalism, specifically singled out as among the proscribed acts that are directed against the cultural property defined in Article 1 of that Convention. This is an absolute obligation without any waiver based on imperative military necessity. The wording of Article 4(3), 'undertake to prohibit, prevent and [...] put a stop to any form of [...] pillage', suggests

---

[111] ICTY, *The Prosecutor v Dario Kordić and Mario Čerkez*, Trial Chamber Judgment, IT-95-14/2-T, 26 February 2001, para 361; and Appeals Chamber, IT-95-14/2-A, 17 December 2004, paras 89–90. For the argument that by reference to 'peoples' under the former, the drafters set the threshold of application of Art 53 AP I higher than that of Art 1 of the 1954 Convention, see *Official Record*, vol X, at 220, para 68; F. Kalshoven, *Reflections on the Laws of War: Collected Essays* (Leiden: Martinus Nijhoff, 2007), at 226; and ICRC CIHL, vol I, at 130 and 132. Contra *Kordić and Čerkez*, Appeals Chamber, para 91; ICRC Commentary APs, at 1469; R. O'Keefe, 'Protection of Cultural Property', in D. Fleck (ed), *The Handbook of International Humanitarian Law* (2nd edn, Oxford: OUP, 2008) 431, at 439–42.

[112] ICRC Commentary APs, at 645, para 2060.

[113] Oppenheim, above n 59, vol II, 404–5, para 142.

[114] Kalshoven, above n 111, at 226. See also the ICRC CIHL Study, vol I, at 132, Rule 40A.

[115] R. O'Keefe, *The Protection of Cultural Property in Armed Conflict* (Cambridge: CUP, 2006), at 31.

[116] The 1954 Hague Conventions for the Protection of Cultural Property in the Event of Armed Conflict, Art 4(3), 2nd sentence.

a positive obligation. The Occupying Power must ensure that no armed groups, mobs, or other individual persons are engaged in any of the prohibited acts in circumstances of civil disorder.[117]

C. Relevance in Non-International Armed Conflicts

I. Destruction or seizure of property

The prohibition on destroying or seizing an adversary's property not required by 'imperative military necessity', which derives from Article 23(g) of the Hague Regulations in the IAC context, is fully established as a rule of CIL in NIAC as well.[118] What should be highlighted is that in NIAC, there is no legal regime of 'occupation', so that this customary law applies to all property in the context of NIAC. This is corroborated by Article 8(2)(e)(xii) of the ICC Statute, which classifies this violation as a war crime in NIAC. 41

As regards the seizure of an adversary's military equipment, the Customary International Humanitarian Law Study suggests neither conventional nor customary rules that prohibit such an act in NIAC.[119] Similarly, according to this study, there is not enough empirical data to confirm the emergence of customary rules that cover the confiscation or requisitioning of private property in NIAC.[120] That said, some national military manuals prohibit not only destruction, but also seizure of private property in NIAC (save in case of imperative military necessity).[121] 42

We should also note the customary rule that is distilled from the second sentence of Article 14 AP II. According to this, it is forbidden to attack, destroy, remove, or render useless objects indispensable to the survival of the civilians in NIAC.[122] The open-ended list of such indispensable objects is the same as the counterpart applicable in IAC (Article 54(2) AP I). Yet unlike the latter rule governing IAC, the normative edge of the former rule is not blunted by the escape valve of military necessity.[123] 43

II. Pillage

In NIAC, the prohibition of pillage under Article 4(2)(g) AP II is recognized as a customary norm.[124] As seen below at MN 56–57, this is corroborated by the fact that flouting this rule gives rise to war crimes that come within the jurisdictions of the three United Nations (UN) ad hoc war crimes tribunals.[125] 44

III. Cultural property

According to Article 19 of the 1954 Hague Cultural Property Convention, the provisions relating to 'respect' for cultural property defined under Article 1 of that Convention 45

---

[117] This is part of the customary IHL: ICRC CIHL Study, vol I, at 134; US, *Annotated Supplement to the Commander's Handbook on the Law of Naval Operations* (1997), para 8.5.1.6, fn 122.
[118] ICRC CIHL Study, vol I, at 177. [119] Ibid, at 174. [120] Ibid, at 181–2.
[121] Ibid, at 181. [122] Ibid, at 189–91. [123] See Art 54(3) and (5) AP I.
[124] ICRC CIHL Study, vol I, at 182–5, Rule 52.
[125] Art 3(e) ICTY Statute; Art 4(f) ICTR Statute; and Art 3 SCSL Statute. See also Argentina, National Court of Appeals, *Military Junta* case, Judgment, 9 December 1985, as cited in ICRC CIHL Study, vol I, at 1098, para 666.

1530   *Geneva Convention IV*

must apply to NIAC as minimum rules.[126] Departing from such a timid approach, Articles 3 and 22(1) of the 1999 Second Protocol to the 1954 Convention make clear that the scope of application of this Protocol encompasses NIAC. Additional guarantees for cultural objects and places of worships in NIAC are specifically laid down in Article 16 AP II.

D. Legal Consequences of a Violation

I. Overview

46 Article 147 GC IV contemplates 'extensive destruction and appropriation' within the rubric of grave breaches.[127] As such, it is incorporated as a war crime under Article 8(2)(a)(iv) of the ICC Statute.[128] Moreover, of special relevance to the protection of property under the ICC Statute are the following offences: destruction or seizure of an adversary's property unless demanded by imperative military necessity; and pillage. They form a catalogue of war crimes that apply in both IAC and NIAC.

II. Destruction and appropriation of property as a grave breach and a war crime

47 Extensively destroying and appropriating property under Article 147 GC IV is one of the eight categories of the grave breaches of the Geneva Conventions that fall within the ICC's jurisdiction (Article 8(2)(a)(iv) of the ICC Statute). Clearly, synthesized in that text are two discrete offences against property: extensive destruction, and extensive appropriation.

48 Unlike the phrase 'destruction of property' that features in the 'substantive rules' found in IHL treaties, the notion of 'appropriation of property' appears only in the text on grave breaches of GC IV (see also Chapter 72, MN 43, of this volume). Unsurprisingly, this war crime has often been prosecuted in tandem with the offences of pillage or extensive destruction of property.[129] Moreover, determining the meaning of 'appropriation' depends upon the rules of the Hague Regulations concerning dispossession of property, the issue analysed above. In the *IG Farben* case, the accused was found guilty of the war crimes of plunder of public and private property, exploitation, spoliation, and 'other offences against property'. Although the discussion took place in the context of plunder, the US Military Tribunal found that the gist of such offences was that owners were deprived of their property involuntarily, against their will.[130]

49 This grave breach crime sets a higher threshold than the war crime of destroying or seizing the enemy's property, a crime that will be examined immediately below. This may be seen in the *actus reus* of this crime. First, under the former, a qualifying adjective 'extensive' is appended to the term 'destruction'. In the *Blaškić* case, the ICTY held that the extensive nature of destruction could be determined on the basis of specific facts of the case. According to the ICTY, a single act, such as the destruction of a hospital, may be

---

[126] There is controversy over whether this reference to 'respect' should be construed narrowly as indicating Art 4 alone, or widely as denoting other provisions concerning 'respect for cultural property': S. Sivakumaran, *The Law of Non-International Armed Conflict* (Oxford: OUP, 2012), at 376–7.
[127] See also Art 50 GC I.   [128] See also Art 8(2)(b)(xii) ICC Statute.
[129] However, see, inter alia, ICTY, *The Prosecutor v Jadranko Prlić et al*, 2nd Amended Indictment, IT-04-74-T, 11 June 2008, Count 22.
[130] *The IG Farben Trial*, US Military Tribunal, Nuremberg, 14 August 1947–29 July 1948, UNWCC Law Reports, vol X, at 42–7.

sufficient.¹³¹ At first glance, this interpretation seems different from the strict interpretation given by Pictet Commentary GC IV, which states that the qualifying word 'extensive' excludes an isolated incident of wrecking.¹³² Still, sharp-eyed observers note that a footnote is attached to the Pictet Commentary, specifically recognizing that a bombing of a single civilian hospital may suffice if done intentionally.¹³³

Secondly, destruction must be carried out 'unlawfully and wantonly'.¹³⁴ As for the qualifying adverb 'wantonly', this is transplanted from the text of Article 6(b) of the International Military Tribunal (IMT) Charter.¹³⁵ This should be considered close to the mental element of 'recklessness'.¹³⁶

The notion 'unlawfully' should be assessed in the light of the overarching concept of military necessity, or 'necessities of war' under Articles 53 (destruction of property), 57 (requisition of medical property), and 147 GC IV (extensive destruction and appropriation of property, as among the grave breaches). In other words, the war crimes of destruction or appropriation of property do not materialize if military necessity precludes their unlawfulness. That seems obvious but, as analysed above, the 'hard question' lies in determining the concept of military necessity. Clearly, the same consideration applies to the war crime under Article 8(2)(b)(xiii) and (e)(xii) of the ICC Statute of destroying or seizing property unless demanded by imperative military necessity. The crimes will be examined below at MN 53–55.

It is clear that, as is true of all war crimes, the contextual requirement must be met at the outset. This means that 'a sufficient link'¹³⁷ or 'an evident nexus' must be established between the criminal act and the armed conflict.¹³⁸ Generally, such a nexus can be proved when the alleged crimes are 'closely related to the hostilities'.¹³⁹ With regard to *mens rea*, the ICTY's case law indicates that 'the perpetrator must have acted with the intent to destroy the protected property or in reckless disregard of the likelihood of its destruction'.¹⁴⁰

III. Destruction or seizure of property not justified by imperative military necessity as a war crime in international and non-international armed conflict

Under the ICC Statute, destroying or seizing an adversary's property, unless demanded by imperative military necessity, is categorized as a war crime both for IAC (Article 8(2)(b)(xiii)) and NIAC (Article 8(2)(e)(xii)).

As discussed above, its ambit of application in an IAC context is broader than the grave breach form of property offences.¹⁴¹ Otherwise, there is no suggestion that the

---

¹³¹ ICTY, *Blaškić*, above n 14, para 157, referring explicitly to Pictet Commentary GC IV, at 601.
¹³² Pictet Commentary GC IV, at 601. ¹³³ Ibid. See also Ch 72, MN 44, of this volume.
¹³⁴ Dörmann, above n 15, at 83. ¹³⁵ Dinstein (2009), above n 15, at 197.
¹³⁶ ICTY, *Kordić and Čerkez*, Trial Chamber, above n 111, para 346 ('reckless disregard'). See also G. Werle, *Principles of International Criminal Law* (The Hague: T.M.C. Asser Press, 2005), at 110.
¹³⁷ Dörmann, above n 15, at 27.
¹³⁸ ICTY, *Blaškić*, above n 14, paras 69 et seq. See also ICTY, *The Prosecutor v Duško Tadić*, Trial Chamber Judgment, IT-94-1-T, 7 May 1997, para 573.
¹³⁹ ICTY, *Naletilić and Martinović*, above n 14, para 177.
¹⁴⁰ ICTY, *The Prosecutor v Radoslav Brdanin*, Trial Chamber, Judgment, IT-99-36-T, 1 September 2004, para 589.
¹⁴¹ Ibid, at 251.

constituent elements of 'destruction' in both genres of war crimes be understood differently.[142] Moreover, the keywords in the limitation clauses, 'rendered absolutely necessary by military operations' under Article 53 GC IV or 'necessities of war' under Article 8(2)(b)(xiii) of the ICC Statute, should be seen as reflecting the same idea.[143] The term 'necessities of the conflict' under Article 8(2)(e)(xii) of the ICC Statute may also be understood as indicating the cognate idea. In a nutshell, there is no difference in the constituent elements of this war crime in IAC or NIAC.[144]

55   With regard to the seizure of enemy property, the keyword 'seizure' ought to be examined like the term 'appropriation' as discussed above at MN 48. Determination of this term depends on the context in which the dispossession has taken place (occupation, military operation, prizes at sea) and on the category of property affected.[145]

IV. War crimes of pillage

56   The war crime of pillage has long been embedded in the bedrock of customary IHL since before the Second World War.[146] Article 6(b) of the IMT Charter[147] recognized 'plunder' of public or private property. It was applied to the systematic looting of art and other cultural objects in occupied territory.[148] Under the ICC Statute, pillaging of property of any genre in IAC, whether in occupied territories or otherwise, is criminalized under Article 8(2)(b)(xvi), while the equivalent rule appears under Article 8(2)(e)(v) for NIAC.[149]

57   In contrast to the International Criminal Tribunal for Rwanda (ICTR) Statute (Article 4(f)), the ICTY Statute does not refer explicitly to pillage as such. Nevertheless, this category of war crime is readily ascertainable under two headings: (i) a grave breach of the Geneva Conventions based on 'extensive destruction and appropriation of property, not justified by military necessity and carried out unlawfully and wantonly' (Article 2(d) of the ICTY Statute), the issue discussed above; and (ii) violations of laws and customs of war that consist of 'plunder of public or private property' (Article 3(e) of the ICTY Statute). Indeed, the ICTY has understood pillage as part of the notion of plunder. In *Prosecutor v Kordić*, the Appeals Chamber endorsed the Trial Chamber's decision that the essence of the war crime of plunder lay in 'all forms of unlawful appropriation of property in armed conflict for which individual criminal responsibility attaches under international criminal law, *including those acts traditionally described as "pillage"*'.[150]

V. War crimes specifically relating to cultural property

58   The crux of the rules under Articles 27 and 56 of the Hague Regulations is incorporated as a war crime under the ICC Statute. Intentionally directing attacks against buildings dedicated to religion, art, and science (as well as to education or to charitable purposes), and against

---

[142] Ibid, at 254.
[143] Ibid, at 249–50; and ICRC CIHL Study, at 575. For a different view, see, however, Ch 72, MN 47, of this volume.
[144] Dörmann, above n 15, at 486.
[145] Ibid, at 256–7, and the different meanings given in the literature cited in n 15.
[146] See the discussion in Feilchenfeld, above n 39, at 31.
[147] See also Art 2(1)(b) Control Council Law No 10.
[148] 'Judicial Decisions, International Military Tribunal (Nuremberg), Judgment and Sentences October 1, 1946', 41 *AJIL* (1947) 172, at 237. See also Oppenheim, above n 59, vol II, at 400–1.
[149] See Art 3(e) ICTY Statute; Art 4(f) ICTR Statute; and Art 3 SCSL Statute.
[150] ICTY, *Kordić and Čerkez*, Appeals Chamber, above n 111, para 79 (emphasis added); approving Trial Chamber, above n 111, para 352.

historical monuments, in so far as they are not military objectives, is classified as a war crime both in IAC (Article 8(2)(b)(ix)) and in NIAC (Article 8(2)(e)(iv)). This is a conduct-based offence, which does not require any deleterious result (damage or destruction) of such attacks.

Under Article 15(1) of the 1999 Second Protocol to the Hague Cultural Property Convention, it is a 'serious violation' of this Protocol to make cultural property (protected under the Convention and the Second Protocol) the object of attack (subparagraph (d)), or to commit 'theft, pillage, misappropriation or acts of vandalism' against the cultural property (subparagraph (e)).[151] Yet under Article 16(1) of the Second Protocol, those acts enumerated in subparagraphs (d) and (e) are not classified as the acts that require the states parties to establish jurisdiction when alleged offenders are present in their territories.

E. Critical Assessment

In the absence of a definition of the notion 'property' under IHL treaties, some crucial guidelines may be gleaned from the practice of IHRL. The ECtHR has interpreted the notion of 'possessions' under Article 1 of the First Protocol to the ECHR more broadly than that of 'ownership'. The former is considered to encompass pecuniary rights connected to shares, patents, arbitration awards, entitlements to pension or other social security benefits, as well as entitlements to a rent.[152] A more dynamic approach is discernible in the case law of the Inter-American Court of Human Rights. Through its autonomous and evolutive interpretation,[153] that Court has considered the right to property under Article 21 of the American Convention on Human Rights to cover indigenous peoples' communal property,[154] their right to own natural resources collectively in their traditionally occupied land,[155] and even 'incorporeal elements and any other intangible object capable of having value'.[156] In occupied territories, an occupier's exploitation of natural resources may clash with indigenous peoples' collective ownership of such resources, which they deem as essential for their ancestral heritage and cultural identity. As a policy issue, such communal concepts of property rights should be encompassed within the definition of cultural property under Article 1 of the 1954 Hague Convention.[157]

In NIAC, IHL proffers little guidance on rights and duties of armed opposition groups (or of the UN or multinational forces) that exert control over certain territories. There is a limit to the application of the law of occupation by analogy to issues such as the seizure and requisition of property.[158] As a policy argument, it is cogent to suggest that rebel

---

[151] Subparagraph (e) is derived from the first sentence of Art 4(3) of the 1954 Hague Cultural Property Convention.

[152] A. Grgic et al, *The Right to Property under the European Convention on Human Rights: A Guide to the Implementation of the European Convention on Human Rights and its Protocols* (Strasbourg: Council of Europe, 2007), at 7 and 9.

[153] IACtHR, *Mayagna (Sumo) Awas Tingni Community v Nicaragua*, Judgment, 31 August 2001, Series C, No 79 (2001), para 146.

[154] Ibid, para 148.

[155] IACtHR, *Case of the Sawhoyamaxa Indigenous Community v Paraguay*, Merits, Reparations, and Costs, Judgment, 29 March 2006, para 118. See also *Saramaka People v Suriname*, Interpretation of the Judgment on Preliminary Objections, Merits, Reparations, and Costs, Judgment, 12 August 2008, Series C, No 185, para 16.

[156] IACtHR, *Mayagna (Sumo) Awas Tingni Community v Nicaragua*, above n 153, para 144.

[157] See also Ch 72 of this volume.   [158] Sivakumaran, above n 126, at 531.

groups be allowed to seize or requisition some property as a way of giving them an incentive to abide by IHL.¹⁵⁹ Still, the time may have come for AP II to be amended to address issues of 'occupation' in NIAC.

62   As a final note, with the trajectory of IHRL steadily in progress, it is possible that war crimes impinging on property rights in occupied territories may supply an experimental ground for fleshing out corporate liability for war crimes.¹⁶⁰ Where multinational corporations are involved in extensive appropriation or pillage of natural resources in occupied territories, or in the parcel of territories controlled by insurgents in NIAC, the recognition of such new dimension of responsibility may provide a viable alternative for ensuring justice.

YUTAKA ARAI-TAKAHASHI

---

[159] J.G. Stewart, *Corporate War Crimes: Prosecuting the Pillage of Natural Resources* (New York: Open Society Foundations, 2010), at 21–2.

[160] See *Corrie et al v Caterpillar*, 403 F Supp 2d 1019 (2005); and 503 F 3d 974 (2007).

Chapter 72. Protection of Public Property

	MN
A. Introduction	1
B. Meaning and Application	6
I. The distinction between private and public property	6
a. Relevance of the distinction	6
b. The question of the qualification of common and indigenous lands	13
II. The distinction between movable and immovable state property	18
a. The distinction	18
b. Administrative duties of the Occupying Power with regard to immovable property	20
c. The use of movable property	29
III. The exception to the prohibition: unless 'rendered absolutely necessary by military operation'	35
C. Relevance in Non-International Armed Conflicts	41
D. Legal Consequences of a Violation	43
E. Critical Assessment	48

Select Bibliography

Arai-Takashi, Y., *The Law of Occupation: Continuity and Change of IHL: Continuity and Change of International Humanitarian Law, and its Interaction with International Human Rights Law* (Leiden: Martinus Nijhoff Publishers, 2009)

Cassese, A., 'Power and Duties of an Occupant in Relation to Land and Natural Resources', in E. Playfair (ed), *International Law and the Administration of Occupied Territories: Two Decades of Israeli Occupation of the West Bank and Gaza Strip* (New York: OUP, 1992) 419

Cummings, E.R., 'Oil Resources in Occupied Arab Territories', 9 *Journal of International Law and Economics* (1974) 533

Dinstein, Y., 'The International Law of Belligerent Occupation and Human Rights', 8 *IsrYBHR* (1978) 104

Dinstein, Y., *The International Law of Belligerent Occupation* (Cambridge/New York: CUP, 2009)

Duruigbo, E., 'Permanent Sovereignty and People's Ownership of Natural Resources in International Law', 38 *Georgetown International Law Review* (2006) 33

Feilchenfeld, E.H., *The International Economic Law of Occupation* (Washington, DC: Carnegie Endowment for International Peace, 1942), at 221–6

Scobbie, I., 'Natural Resources and Belligerent Occupation: perspectives from international humanitarian and human rights law', in S. Akram et al (eds), *International Law and the Israeli–Palestinian Conflict: A Rights-Based Approach to Middle East Peace* (Routledge: London, 2011) 229

Schrijver, N., *Sovereignty over Natural Resources: Balancing Rights and Duties* (Cambridge: CUP, 1997)

A. Introduction

1   While Cummings considers that property rights have been given less attention in international law during the twentieth century,[1] the prohibition on the destruction of public property during occupation has come under intense scrutiny from both scholars and practitioners. It is indeed a recurrent legal issue before international courts, and is also at the core of major developments affecting the laws of occupation, environmental law, and economic, social, and cultural rights.

2   The prohibition on destroying public property may be traced back to the Lieber Code.[2] The laws of occupation, and in particular Articles 53 and 55 of the Regulations annexed to Hague Convention IV, began the international codification of this prohibition, which was later complemented in 1949 with Article 53 of Geneva Convention (GC) IV and inserted in the list of grave breaches in Article 147 of the same Convention. Therefore, Articles 53 and 147 GC IV must be read in conjunction with the Hague Regulations, especially Article 23(g), Article 53, and Article 55. Article 53 GC IV reinforces Article 23(g) of the Hague Regulations by stating the clear prohibition on destruction, and narrows down the prohibition to the occupied territories.

3   Article 53 GC IV sets forth the general prohibition of destruction of property by the occupying authorities, unless this is made 'absolutely necessary by military operations'. The prohibition is thus mitigated in accordance with the purpose of international humanitarian law (IHL), which seeks 'to diminish the evils of war so far as military necessity permits'.[3] Article 53 GC IV is stricter and offers a more nuanced approach than the Hague Regulations.[4] In addition, Article 147 provides for the prosecution of the grave breach of 'extensive destruction and appropriation of property, not justified by military necessity and carried out unlawfully and wantonly'. A discrepancy exists between the content of the prohibition on the belligerents, set forth in Article 53 GC IV, and the conduct listed in the grave breach provision of GC IV: the latter includes not only destruction of property (that must qualify as 'extensive' to amount to a grave breach), but also 'appropriation of property', which is not expressly prohibited in Article 53. In addition, while Article 53 sets the exception of destruction which was made 'absolute necessary by military operations', Article 147 merely refers to the exception of military necessity (see MN 43).

4   Questions have arisen with regard to the distinction between private and public property; other issues relate to the distinction suggested by the Hague Regulations, which divides state properties between immovable and movable, categories which can be difficult to apply. There are also questions regarding the nature of duties devolved to occupying authorities (e.g. usufruct for non-renewable energy). The prohibition on the destruction

---

[1] E.R. Cummings, 'Oil Resources in Occupied Arab Territories', 9 *Journal of International Law and Economics* (1974) 533, at 552.

[2] Art 44 of the 1863 Lieber Code provides: '[A]ll destruction of property not commanded by the authorized officer [...] [is] prohibited under the penalty of death, or such other severe punishment as may seem adequate for the gravity of the offense.' Instructions for the Government of Armies of the United States in the Field, prepared by Francis Lieber, promulgated as General Order No 100 by President Abraham Lincoln, Washington, DC, 24 April 1863.

[3] Hague Convention Respecting the Laws and Customs of War on Land (IV), 18 October 1907, Preamble, para 5.

[4] H. Dichter, 'The Legal Status of Israel's Water Policies in the Occupied Territories', 35 *Harvard International Law Journal* (1994) 565, at 578.

of property in Article 53 GC IV also raises questions as to the definition of and threshold for its exception, namely situations where the destruction is made absolutely necessary by military operations. The laws of occupation do not provide a definition of the principle of absolute necessity or its threshold. This has caused concerns amongst scholars and practitioners; debates regarding the understanding of the derogation through practice and case law will be presented and analysed.

The prohibition of destruction of property remains crucial, especially in times of occupation: the temporary character of occupation means that the occupying authorities have a duty of care. It is important to clarify the limits placed on this duty, which include possibly allowing commercial exploitation of the usufruct (see MN 20–22) stemming from immovable property, and the possibility of selling the movable state property to private individuals.

B. Meaning and Application

I. The distinction between private and public property

a. Relevance of the distinction

Article 53 GC IV has a broad scope as it prohibits the destruction of 'real and personal property belonging individually or collectively to private persons, or to the State, or to other public authorities, or to social or cooperative organizations'. For the purpose of this provision, therefore, it is not necessary to identify to whom the 'real or personal property' belongs, since all the possible 'owners' are listed. Similarly, Article 33 paragraph 2 GC IV, in prohibiting pillage, does it in absolute terms and does not make any distinction based on ownership. The distinction between private and public property is instead relevant under the Hague Regulations.[5]

Originally, Article 53 GC IV had been designed to protect private property only. Yet the 1949 Diplomatic Conference's delegates stressed that Article 23(g) of the Hague Regulations did not make the distinction between private and public property when mentioning 'the enemy's property', and that new types of property had emerged since 1899. It was therefore decided that Article 53 would apply to both public and private property.[6] This gives Article 53 GC IV a specific feature which does not really fit with the rest of the scope of the Convention: the Convention aims at protecting civilians in times of war; prohibiting the destruction of public property is consequently an extension of the concept of this protection as granted to civilians.

The inclusion of public property in Article 53 GC IV is the result of the development of state intervention in the private sector and of state-owned property. Indeed, the law of occupation originally gave 'primacy to private over public property',[7] and the extension of protection to public property is considered to be the outcome of a policy of tolerance developed at the end of the nineteenth century.[8] The United States (US) Arbitrator W.D.

---

[5] See more specifically Arts 46 para 2, 53, and 55. [6] Pictet Commentary IV, at 300–1.
[7] Y. Arai-Takashi, *The Law of Occupation: Continuity and Change of IHL: Continuity and Change of International Humanitarian Law, and its Interaction with International Human Rights Law* (Leiden: Martinus Nijhoff Publishers, 2009), at 195.
[8] Ibid.

Hines provided another explanation: the purpose of this extension was to shift the burden of war from private individuals to the belligerent state.[9]

9   Nevertheless, the identification of what constitutes private property and what is public property is relevant only in the context of the Hague Regulations, as explained above. Modern laws and regulations have sometimes blurred the distinction between the two. When there is a doubt as to the nature of the property, it should be considered to be public until its private character is established.[10] This view has been challenged in its rationale, as it gives more opportunities for the occupying authorities to expand their power over state properties.[11] It has also been suggested that we look at the legislation of the occupied state to determine the status of the property.[12] Another technique to determine whether property is public or private would be to examine the nature of its owner. Yet another argument put forward has been to look at who would lose the most if the property was qualified as private or public, the state or private individuals:[13] the US *Manual* suggests that 'for the purpose of treatment of property under belligerent occupation, it is often necessary to look beyond strict legal title to ascertain the character of the property on the basis of the beneficial ownership thereof'.[14] Others have defined tests; there is, for example, one test which looks at the substantial identity of the owner, relying on categorization based on three parts (elements of state control, other elements of state interest, function of enterprise) to determine whether the property is public or not.[15]

10 Besides, the nature of the property might change: for example, a public property might be sold to become private before the beginning of an occupation in order to avoid any losses for the state. There are other complex situations, such as when a concession is given by the state to private entities.[16] Another example may be found in the participation of the state in private enterprise.[17] Other issues involve the fact that some occupation periods have gone on for some time, and as a result some occupants have become more interventionist in their administration of immovable property.[18] These debates about the distinction stem from legal and societal evolutions of the concept of property.

11 There is sometimes uncertainty with regard to the public or private nature of some natural resources: while natural resources are public, some scholars argue for exceptions. It has been said that although Kuwaiti oil and oil wells were state-owned and contributed

---

[9] UN, *Cession of Vessels and Tugs for Navigation on the Danube case (Allied Powers, Germany, Austria, Hungary and Bulgaria)*, Award 2 August 1921; G. Schwarzenberger, *International Law, as Applied by International Courts and Tribunals*, III: International Constitutional Law (London: Stevens & Sons, 1957), at 257.

[10] G. von Glahn, *The Occupation of Enemy Territory: A Commentary on the Law and Practice of Belligerent Occupation* (Minneapolis, Minn: University of Minnesota Press, 1957), at 179; UK Ministry of Defence, *Manual of the Law of Armed Conflict* (Oxford: OUP, 2004), at 304, para 11.90; Israel High Court, *Al-Nawar v The Minister of Defence et al*, HCJ 574/82, Judgment of 11 August 1985, 16 *IsrYBHR* (1986) 321.

[11] A. Cassese, 'Power and Duties of an Occupant in Relation to Land and Natural Resources', in E. Playfair (ed), *International Law and the Administration of Occupied Territories: Two Decades of Israeli Occupation of the West Bank and Gaza Strip* (New York: OUP, 1992) 419, at 438.

[12] B. Boczek, *International Law: A Dictionary* (Lanham, Md: Scarecrow Press, 2005), at 135; M. Tignino, 'Water, International peace and security', 92 *IRRC* 879 (2010) 647, at 663.

[13] M. Greenspan, *The Modern Law of Land Warfare* (Berkeley, Ca: University of California Press, 1959), at 292.

[14] US Department, *Army Field Manual of the Law of Land Warfare* (1956) § 394(a).

[15] E.H. Feilchenfeld, *The International Economic Law of Occupation* (Washington, DC: Carnegie Endowment for International Peace, 1942), at 57–61.

[16] Y. Dinstein, *The International Law of Belligerent Occupation* (Cambridge/New York: CUP, 2009), at 211; UN, *Affaire relative à la concession des phares de l'Empire ottoman (Greece, France)*, Award, 24–7 July 1956.

[17] See Feilchenfeld, above n 15, at 221–2.   [18] Cassese, above n 11, at 423.

to the war effort, the benefits of extraction of the oil were primarily for individuals or private companies. Therefore, the destruction of the oil wells would not fall under Article 53 GC IV.[19] This interpretation contradicts Pictet's Commentary on Article 53 and the ordinary reading of the provision.

Those discussions demonstrate that the distinction between private and public property, as well as what actually falls within the concept of public property, is sometimes unclear. The arguments for broadening the concept of public property may help the state, which then has more to lose in times of occupation; the argument seeking to present natural resources as private property would include arguments about compensation for private companies or individuals whose property has been destroyed or damaged. As developed below, the effort to perceive some natural resources as private might actually be for the benefit of local communities, and support them in an effort towards self-determination.

b. *The question of the qualification of common and indigenous lands*

Article 1(2) of the International Covenant on Economic, Social and Cultural Rights states that '[i]n no case may a people be deprived of its own means of subsistence'.[20] Furthermore, in accordance with Article 16 of the Charter of Economic Rights and Duties of States (1974), states are economically responsible for all the destruction done to 'countries, territories and peoples affected'. As a result, an Occupying Power must administer the territory in a way that would not be detrimental to the inhabitants, including indigenous people. It is a reminder that exploitation needs to be careful, and should not impede the right to development and self-determination. This protection, which stems from international human rights law, is compatible with the IHL approach to public and private property. This dual protection is certainly important, as it allows for respect for the principle of permanent sovereignty over natural resources and the principle of self-determination to be applicable during occupation.[21]

Yet the main issue lies in the qualification of common lands as public or private property.[22] Gasser refers to indigenous lands and common lands as public, and says they should be administered the same way as other immovable public property.[23] Yet indigenous lands are at the heart of conflicts over property: most property regimes were changed under colonization, to be later reclaimed by indigenous peoples who wished to apply their own qualification to the land. Consequently, there are tensions in different countries where the two norms sometimes coexist. Occupation adds another layer of complexity in terms of qualification. If the water is considered to be public under state domestic legislation, but is perceived as private under indigenous customary law, the occupant faces the difficult choice of categorizing the property. Besides, the qualification of public lands for most traditional forms of ownership does not necessarily reflect the complex nature of

---

[19] R. Zedalis, 'Burning of the Kuwaiti Oilfields and the Laws of War', 4 *Van JTL* (1991) 711, at 711–12.
[20] See further on economic, social and cultural rights in occupied territory, Ch 70 of this volume.
[21] N. Schrijver, *Sovereignty over Natural Resources: Balancing Rights and Duties* (Cambridge: CUP, 1997); I. Scobbie, 'The Wall and International Humanitarian Law', Speech at UN International Meeting on the Impact of the Construction of the Wall in the Occupied Territory, Geneva, 15–16 April 2004. See also UNGA Res 1803 (XVII), 14 December 1962, 'Permanent Sovereignty over Natural Resources'.
[22] See further for private property, Ch 71 of this volume.
[23] H.P. Gasser, 'Protection of the Civilian Population', in D. Fleck (ed), *Handbook of International Humanitarian Law* (2nd edn, Oxford/New York: OUP, 2008) 209, at 261.

indigenous ownership.[24] In some countries, land which is qualified as public, and which would fall under Article 53 GC IV, is quite extended, and would take up almost the entire territory, while some communities would contest those lands' being public or state-owned. State ownership over these territories is therefore an issue for discussion.

15   The main issue is to know whether permanent sovereignty over natural resources is vested in states or in peoples. Duruigbo has analysed most views on the issue and concludes that the land should belong to the people keeping control over natural resources, while the state might manage those resources.[25] Meanwhile, he suggests that the management of resources should undergo a 'de-concentration of the right to management'[26] to avoid the state taking control of those resources. He argues in favour of a private form of ownership based on the Texan model, in which indigenous people would keep ownership of natural resources while the state manages them at a federal level.[27] This is a new approach to natural resources which, instead of approaching such resources as immovable public property, looks at them as falling into the category of private property.

16   An illustration of this argument is to be found in the administration of the regimes of *mulk* and *mubah* in the Palestinian Occupied Territories: those categories do not match the division between public and private property under the laws of occupation; trying to match the concepts involves fitting the square peg of Ottoman law-based property classifications into the round hole of civil and Roman legal categories.[28] One approach is to have those common lands protected during occupation by analogy: an important part of the West Bank and Gaza water falling under the *mulk* regime (which means 'captured') is private. Most of that water is owned by local water authorities, making it private. The most important uncaptured (and therefore associated with 'public') water reserve located in the Mountain Aquifer and the Jordan River falls under the *mubah* regime. It is considered that once private individual needs have been met, the remaining water will also be captured by individuals or companies. Therefore, the *mubah* water is a form of private property, except for the quantity of water used by the Jordanian state.[29] This means that water usage must be determined carefully so that it may be known how much is captured/private and how much is uncaptured/public. If we follow the rule that domestic law, or indigenous customary law, applies to the natural resources of the occupied territories, then the Palestinian water should mainly be considered as private, and therefore should fall under another regime than the one contained in Article 53 GC IV, a regime which would be more protective of the inhabitants. This means that Israeli occupying authorities should not be using the usufruct of the water as if it were immovable public property. This example demonstrates the importance of taking local norms into account. The issue is, however, that IHL claims to be universal and the enforcement of the law of occupation must be done in a neutral way. Trying to work by analogy might, however, be the best way to accommodate both international law and local laws.

---

[24] L. Alden Wily, *Land Rights Reform and Governance in Africa: How to Make it Work in the 21st Century?* (New York: Drylands Development Centre and Oslo Governance Centre, UNDP, 2006).

[25] E. Duruigbo, 'Permanent Sovereignty and People's Ownership of Natural Resources in International Law', 38 *Georgetown International Law Review* (2006) 33, at 34.

[26] E. Duruigbo, 'Realizing the People's Rights to Natural Resources', 12 *The Whitehead Journal of Diplomacy and International Relations* (2001) 111, at 112.

[27] Ibid, at 118.

[28] G. Abouali, 'Continued Control: Israel, Palestinian Water and the Interim Agreement', 9 *The Palestine Yearbook of International Law* (1996/97) 63, at 85.

[29] Ibid, at 86.

The area of state property has therefore known several important developments over 17
time, due to the change of the nature of occupation (the development of a longer-term
occupation), the development of environmental law, or the changes inherent in property types. Scholars disagree on the way forward, with some seeking to extend the
boundaries of IHL so as to encompass more commercial elements that would be beneficial to the Occupying Power but also to the populations of the occupied territories,
while others prefer the status quo, focusing mainly on protecting the population and
property in the occupied territory. The prohibition of destruction of state property is
never questioned though. The only limit to that principle is the exception of military
necessity.

II. The distinction between movable and immovable state property

a. *The distinction*

Hague law has drawn a distinction between movable and immovable property. Article 18
53 of the Hague Regulations refers to movable property (*propriété mobilière de l'Etat*) and
Article 55 of the Hague Regulations refers to real property (*immeuble*); Article 53 GC IV
refers to real or personal property (*biens immobiliers* and *mobiliers*). While it is difficult
to conceive of 'personal property' of a state, the rest of Article 53 GC IV and the French
version suggest that the movable property of a state is equally covered by this provision.
In accordance with Article 53 of the Hague Regulations, the occupying forces can take
possession of movable public property belonging to the state which 'may be used for military operations'. The Article looks at two categories of movable property: cash, funds, and
realizable securities on the one hand; and depots of arms, means of transport, stores, and
supplies on the other hand. The list is not exhaustive. Movable property might be derived
from immovable property, such as bottled water from an underground spring, or coal
extracted from a mine.

Article 55 of the Hague Regulations deals with immovable property belonging to the 19
hostile state: occupying authorities can act only as an administrator and usufructuary of
that property; ownership is never transferred. Immovable state property includes public
hospitals (which are also protected by Article 18 GC IV, which protects all hospitals,
public and private), underground water resources, dams, dykes, lines of communication,
and railways.[30]

b. *Administrative duties of the Occupying Power with regard to immovable property*

i. The rules on usufruct

Article 55 of the Hague Regulations deals with the duties of the occupying authorities. 20
The basic rule is that the Occupying Power must administer immovable state property
like a good *pater familias*, benefiting from the usufruct of the property. One cannot
neglect, abandon, waste, or over-exploit property, as summarized by Dinstein when he
states that mining 'must not exceed average production levels previously established'.[31]
The Occupying Power must therefore 'maintain the integrity of the corpus of the property

---

[30] US Military Tribunal, Nuremberg, *United States of America v Wilhelm List et al (Hostages Trial)*, Judgment 29 February 1948, UNWCC Law Reports, vol VIII.

[31] Dinstein, above n 16, at 215.

to ensure its continued existence'.[32] For example, Uganda could exploit the immovable public property in Congo, but was expected to ensure that the substance of the usufruct would not be damaged.[33] An illustration of careless exploitation may be found in the argument that despite being non-renewable, the quantity of oil in Iraq would replenish the wells and would therefore justify intense usage; it was defeated on the basis that the quantity of oil did not justify excessive usage.[34] The purpose of the law is to avoid an occupation that would be 'ruthless, without consideration of the local economy'.[35] An example of a problematic exploitation has been given by Scobbie with regard to some agricultural lands in the Palestinian Occupied Territories which can no longer be utilized, destroying them de facto.[36] The *Guano* case confirmed the Occupying Power's status as usufructuary for immovable state property.[37]

21 The concept of usufruct stems from Roman law. The reliance on this civil law concept has been criticized due to some uncertainties: which legal system should be referred to when defining usufruct and its legal consequences, that of the Occupying Power or that of the occupied territory? The case law does not provide guidelines on the matter. Meanwhile, Hampson finds the idea of applying the Roman concept of usufruct to IHL useful where it is the nature of the immovable property in question to produce a repeated yield. It is slightly more complex when the state property is a non-renewable resource.[38] There is no guidance provided by the law on usufruct in such cases, as the Romans thought natural resources would always renew.[39] Due to their nature, the Occupying Power would have to limit or minimize exploitation of non-renewable resources to ensure the continuity of the corpus without extinguishing it. Yet this is open to debate, as in civil law a usufructuary may continue the exploitation of non-renewable resources in the same way as an owner would.[40]

22 The concept of usufruct, although useful in determining the use the occupying authorities can make of immovable state property, therefore recognizes the inherent limits attached to the nature of the immovable property.

ii. Limits to usufruct

23 Can the usufruct of state property be used 'for any purpose whatsoever'?[41] There are limits to the benefit of the usufruct; yet some scholars believe that it includes a commercial use.[42] This is the outcome of an extended reading of Article 55 of the Hague Regulations,

---

[32] J. Stone, *Legal Controls of International Conflict: A Treatise on the Dynamics of Disputes and War-Law*, (New York: Rinehart, 1954), at 714.
[33] ICJ, *Armed Activities on the Territory of the Congo (DRC v Uganda)*, Judgment, 19 December 2005.
[34] J.J. Paust, 'The United States as Occupying Power over Portions of Iraq and Special Responsibilities under the Laws of War', 27(1) *Suffolk Transnational Law Review* (2003) 1, at 12–13.
[35] IMT, *Trial of German Major War Criminals*, Judgment, 30 September 1946.
[36] Scobbie, above n 21.
[37] Franco-Chilean Arbitral Tribunal, Affaire du Guano (Chili, France), Award, 5 July 1901.
[38] F. Hampson, *Property Rights and the Law of War: The Devastation of Kuwait* (unpublished, 1991), at 8–9, cited in I. Scobbie, 'Natural Resources and Belligerent Occupation: Mutation through Permanent Sovereignty', in S. Bowen (ed), *Human Rights, Self-Determination and Political Change in the Occupied Territories* (The Hague/Boston/London: Martinus Nijhoff Publishers, 1997) 221, at 227.
[39] Scobbie, above n 38, at 238.
[40] B.M. Claggett and O.T. Johnson, 'May Israel as Belligerent Occupant Lawfully Exploit Previously Unexploited Oil Resources of the Gulf of Suez?', 72(3) *AJIL* (1978) 558, at 568.
[41] Cassese, above n 11, at 428.
[42] von Glahn, above n 10, at 177; Y. Dinstein, 'The International Law of Belligerent Occupation and Human Rights', 8 *IsrYBHR* (1978) 104, at 129–30; A. Gerson, 'Off-shore Oil Exploitation by a Belligerent

which perceives an implicit prohibition of sale limited to the immovable property itself, but not to its fruits. Looking at the implementation of the principle in domestic law sheds light on the understanding of the principle at stake. In connection with this very matter, limits may be found in Israeli domestic case law: the Occupying Power can use the public railways, but it cannot remove them and transplant them elsewhere to construct a new railway for its military operation.[43] Guidance is also provided by the International Military Tribunal at Nuremberg: one cannot transgress 'the outside limits of permissible economic exploitation',[44] as reinforced by the International Court of Justice (ICJ).[45] The purpose of the duties is to ensure that the economy is maintained during occupation, but not exploited negatively: the economy, the owners of the property, and the population should not be deprived of assets; the war effort should not be reinforced unfairly by using property that does not belong to the occupying authorities; the products from any such property should be used in a way that does not negatively affect people and property.[46] Therefore, how can usufruct be used commercially, and to what purpose is its use limited? The commercial use of immovable state property must support the costs of the occupation, or protect the interests and meet the needs of populations of the occupied territory.[47] It cannot be used to further the economic interests of the Occupying Power by, for example, harvesting fruit in the territory to feed its population in the home state, or by promoting or furthering a policy, a strategy, or an agenda. However, Dinstein argues in favour of relaxing some rules in order to cater for the economic and social needs of the population living in the occupied territory when the occupation is of long duration.[48] The limits on financial exploitation of usufruct are explained by the purpose of IHL, which is to protect the population during occupation and not to empower the occupying authorities and extend prerogatives.[49]

Examples of the limits on the right to usufruct include the construction of a canal between the Mediterranean and the Dead Sea, which was rejected by the international community due to the fact that the Occupying Power has a temporary administrative right which encompasses the duties of protecting and respecting the territory. This means that the occupying belligerent cannot erect new constructions that would damage the landscape, or that would not be profitable for the inhabitants of the occupied territory. Another example is the argument put forward regarding the creation of a permanent structure which does not benefit the local population, such as the Jerusalem light rail.[50]

Occupant; the Gulf of Suez Dispute', 71(4) *AJIL* (1977) 725, at 725; M.S. McDougal and F.P. Feliciano, *Law and Minimum World Public Order: The Legal Regulation and International Coercion* (New Haven, Conn.: Yale University Press, 1961), at 812–13.

[43] M.P. Reynolds, 'The Jaffa Jerusalem Railway Company Arbitration 1922', 6(2) *Arab Law Quarterly* (1991) 215.

[44] Schwarzenberger, above n 9, at 250.

[45] ICJ, *Armed Activities on the Territory of the Congo (DRC v Uganda)*, above n 33.

[46] *The United States of America v Alfried Krupp et al*, United States Military Tribunal, Nuremberg, 31 July 1948, UNWCC Law Reports, vol X.

[47] Cassese, above n 11, at 422; Israel High Court, *Mustafa Dweikat v Government of Israel et al (Elon Moreh Case)*, Judgment, 22 October 1979, HCJ 390/79; Israel High Court of Justice; *Jami'at Iscan Al-Ma'almun, Communal Society Registered at the Judea and Samaria Area Headquarters v Commander of IDF Forces in the Judea and Samaria Region*, Judgment, 28 December 1983, HCJ 393/82.

[48] Dinstein, above n 42, at 112; Israel Supreme Court, *The Christian Society for the Holy Places v Minister of Defence et al*, Judgment 1971, HCJ 337/71.

[49] Cummings, above n 1, at 582.

[50] D. Kretzmer, 'The Law of Belligerent Occupation in the Supreme Court of Israel', 94 *IRRC* 885 (2012) 207, at 223.

25   The construction of a new oil well in the West Bank post-1967 raised questions. If oil is to be considered as immovable property, the creation of such wells would have been contrary to IHL as it would go beyond the concept of usufruct. Yet Dinstein is of the opinion that constructing new oil wells or operating new mines should be acceptable, to match the needs of the local population which are increasing.[51] However, a close reading of Article 55 of the Hague Regulations clearly demonstrates that duties as an usufructuary would include avoiding the creation of wells, since 'creating' is not part of usufruct,[52] as demonstrated by Cummings, who uses a comparative analysis of Roman law, civil law, and common law on the matter.[53]

26   The commercial use of usufruct is consequently framed for specific purposes and is subject to strict conditions. This debate demonstrates again the flexibility of IHL when it comes to adapting to modern challenges under occupation. The suggestion that conditions need to be relaxed in order to meet the growing needs of the occupied population also demonstrates that the field of IHL is under constant pressure and must evolve, while keeping its purpose and its principles intact.

iii. Natural resources

27   While there is some controversy concerning non-renewable natural resources (see MN 15), natural resources are in general immovable public property under domestic law, falling within the ambit of Article 53, to which the rule of usufruct applies.[54] Consequently, the Occupying Power can benefit from the usufruct in a reasonable way, but not in a way that would destroy the resource. The idea that there is a positive duty to respect natural resources is clear in the work of several scholars.[55] They cite the ICJ's decision in the *DRC v Uganda* case, which states that the occupying authorities 'must take appropriate measures to prevent the looting, plundering and exploitation of natural resources in occupied territories'.[56] The occupation by the Israeli authorities has raised questions regarding natural resources, and the risk of depletion has been raised.[57]

28   Qualifying natural resources as a movable or immovable property can be sometimes difficult. Dinstein considers oil to be movable state property, based on the fact that there is no clear difference between crude underground oil and drilled oil.[58] Coal, on the other hand, looks different once carved out and extracted from the mine. Dinstein concludes that the lack of difference with regard to oil therefore means that oil is movable public property. The United Kingdom (UK) *Manual* does not make this distinction but nevertheless considers oil to be movable public property.[59] This argument might also be applied to water, yet water is considered to be immovable property. Arai-Takashi refines the argument by

---

[51] Dinstein, above n 16, at 216.
[52] Cour de Cassation, *Administration des eaux et forêts v Falck*, Judgment, 1927.
[53] Cummings, above n 1, at 561.
[54] The question whether non-renewable natural resources are subject to usufruct is controversial in the context of possible pillage of natural resources. See J.G. Stewart, *Corporate War Crimes: Prosecuting the Pillage of Natural Resources* (New York: The Open Society Institute, 2010), at 58–62.
[55] E. Benvenisti, *The International Law of Occupation* (Princeton, N.J.: Princeton University Press, 1993), at 81; I. Scobbie, 'Natural Resources and Belligerent Occupation: Perspectives from International Humanitarian and Human Rights Law', in S. Akram et al (eds), *International Law and the Israeli–Palestinian Conflict: A Rights-Based Approach to Middle East Peace* (Routledge: London, 2011) 229, at 229.
[56] ICJ, *Armed Activities on the Territory of the Congo (DRC v Uganda)*, above n 33, at 244–8.
[57] Scobbie, above n 55, at 229.   [58] Dinstein, above n 42, at 130.
[59] UK, *Manual of the Law of Armed Conflict* (London: UK Ministry of Defence, 2005), para 11.81.1.

suggesting that to be movable, property has to be severed from the land[60] (which could be problematic if severing it harmed the property[61]). However, most academics and courts have declared oil to be immovable.[62]

c. The use of movable property

Movable property may be seized and may be used for military purposes. Examples of movable public property would include packs of bottled water and weapons, but also means of transport. Movable property also includes financial assets, cash, and funds (as per Article 53(1) of the Hague Regulations) which belong to the state.

i. The purposive interpretation of the use

The wording of Article 53 of the Hague Regulations, which states that movable public property which *may* be used for military purposes may be seized by the Occupying Power, has been debated: must these purposes be only military? The Italian Court of Cassation decided that 'objects may be seized in so far as they serve, or are intended for, the purpose of warfare or of belligerent operations'.[63] The Singapore Court has also put forward the concept of 'direct military' use, which would suggest a purposive idea.[64]

There is, however, a trend that broadens the list of state movable property which may be used: Zedalis includes 'property capable of assisting the advancement of military operations',[65] therefore expanding the list of state movable property that might be used. Dinstein has a rather broad understanding of 'military' and includes, for example, a tractor as having a military use.[66] His purpose in expanding the concept is to generate money used to support the costs of occupation.[67] This is an attempt to broaden the category which has important effects in practice, as it leads to very little property having no military purpose, such as non-military books. The list of movable property is non-exhaustive, and there is indeed the possibility of an extended understanding as to what falls under 'military purpose'. Indeed, Dinstein's example could very well come within 'military purpose', as he would consider selling movable property to support the costs of occupation, which could be perceived as a military purpose.

ii. Commercial use of public movable property

Some scholars consider that the legal effect of Article 53 of the Hague Regulations is to regard state movable property as part of the Occupying Power's war booty,[68] except for cultural property which would be 'immune from capture'.[69] Once seized by the Occupying Power, it becomes its property without the need to pay compensation, as illustrated by the *Al Nawar* case, in which it was decided that 'all movable properties seized on the battlefield might be regarded as part of the war booty'.[70] Dinstein underlines that there is in theory

---

[60] Arai-Takashi, above n 7, at 212.   [61] Cummings, above n 1, at 558–9.
[62] Ibid, at 557–8; M. Leigh, 'Department of State Memorandum of Law on Israel's Right to Develop New Oil Fields in Sinai and the Gulf of Suez', 16(3) *International Legal Material* (1977) 733, at 735; Singapore Court of Appeal, *N.W. de Bataafsche Petroleum Maatschapij and others v The War Damage Commission*, Judgment, 13 April 1956.
[63] Corte Suprema di Cassazione, *Colorni v Ministry of War*, Italy, Judgment 1950, 17 *International Law Reports* (22 March 1950), Case no 138, at 419–20.
[64] Singapore CA, *N.W. de Bataafsche Petroleum Maatschapij*, above n 62.   [65] Zedalis, above n 19, at 724.
[66] Dinstein, above n 16, at 219; W.G. Downey, 'Captured Enemy Property: Booty of War and Seized Enemy Property', 44 *AJIL* (1950) 488, at 499.
[67] Dinstein, above n 42, at 131.   [68] Gasser, above n 23, at 292.
[69] Dinstein, above n 42, at 130.   [70] Israel High Court, *Al-Nawar*, above n 10.

a difference between state movables and war booty: Article 53 of the Hague Regulations is addressed only to state movables which 'may be used for military operations', which is different from the concept of 'booty' which is applicable to all movables. Yet in practice, Dinstein says that what falls under Article 53 as movable is so broad that the distinction hardly applies,[71] relying on the *Monmousseau* case to make his point.[72] Gerstenblith considers that movable property can be part of the war booty, based on an analysis of sections 31, 34, and 35 of the Lieber Code.[73] Gasser suggests that movable state property which may be used for military purposes is indeed part of the booty, but he places a restriction on it: it cannot be requisitioned until the needs of the population have been met.[74] There would therefore be no restriction on a commercial use of movable public property that has been seized.

33 The issue concerns whether ownership of title to movable property is transferred, and whether commercial use is acceptable. While some believe that the use made of movable property can only be military,[75] others think that it may be sold to support the costs of occupation or to meet the needs of the local population.[76] It seems that Article 53 of the Hague Regulations indeed transfers ownership of title to the occupying authorities. Yet again, domestic courts provide an interesting approach: the Dutch Supreme Court has another reading and believes that 'the occupant does not become the owner of those means of conveyance by the sole fact of occupying the area concerned, but is only entitled to appropriate them by taking possession of them'.[77] Such an interpretation would prevent the occupying authorities from using those movables after the end of the occupation, and it would also limit any commercial use.

34 The stakes are again high, as it is the very purpose of IHL that is in question; in that light, occupation laws are protective and do not empower the occupying authorities, unless it is for well-being of the local population or to protect its security. Yet it is a reality of occupation that costs need to be met and the population need to be taken care of.

III. The exception to the prohibition: unless 'rendered absolutely necessary by military operation'

35 The other controversial element within Article 53 GC IV is the exception to the prohibition on destruction of property, dictated by the absolute necessity for military operations. This exception may refer to situations during which 'there are no other means to secure military safety'.[78] For Werle and Jessberger, the exception to destruction implies that destruction is not permitted if there exists an alternative to achieve a military goal.[79] It has also been defined as 'an urgent need, admitting of no delay, for the taking by a commander of measures, which are indispensable for forcing as quickly as

---

[71] Dinstein, above n 16, at 218.
[72] Cour d'Appel d'Orléans, *L'Etat français v Etablissements Monmousseau*, Judgment, 1948.
[73] P. Gerstenblith, 'The Obligations Contained in International Treaties of Armed Forces to Protect Cultural Heritage in Times of Armed Conflicts', in L. Rush (ed), *Archaeology, Cultural Property, and the Military* (Woodbridge: Boydell Press, 2010) 4, at 6.
[74] Gasser, above n 23, at 292.   [75] Cummings, above n 1, at 576–7.
[76] Dinstein, above n 42, at 131.
[77] Supreme Court of The Netherlands, *Public Prosecutor v N*, Judgment, 26 May 1941.
[78] A. Zimmermann, 'Article 8(2)(b)(viii)', in O. Triffterer (ed), *Commentary of the Rome Statute of the International Criminal Court: Observer's Notes, Article by Article* (Baden-Baden: Nomos, 1999) 227, at 232.
[79] G. Werle and F. Jessberger, *Principles of International Criminal Law* (The Hague/New York: T.M.C. Asser Press/West Nyack, 2005), at 339–40.

possible the complete surrender of the enemy'.⁸⁰ In the pre-Geneva Conventions case law the concept was considered as requiring urgency, and 'a reasonable connection between the destruction and the overcoming of the enemy forces'.⁸¹ The Lieber Code also states that 'military necessity, as understood by modern civilized nations, consists in the necessity of those measures which are indispensable for securing the ends of war, and which are lawful according to the modern law and usages of war'.⁸² This variety of approach and definition demonstrates the level of subjectivity inherent in the exception to the prohibition.

There have been criticisms of the inclusion of the exception to the prohibition in Article 53 GC IV. For some scholars, integrating the principle could be perceived as a surrender to war, defeating the ultimate purpose of mitigating the impact of war.⁸³ They fear the return of the *Kriegraison*, which justifies using all means to win a war.⁸⁴ For others, the inclusion of the principle of military necessity in Article 53 GC IV is actually a sign of the compromise IHL seeks to reach between humanitarian requirements and the reality of war, a balance which is necessary.⁸⁵ It is the demonstration of the awareness of IHL that military considerations must be taken into account.⁸⁶ One should not understand from this exception that destruction is accepted: as stated in the *Hostages Trial*, destruction is not 'an end in itself'. The aim of IHL is indeed not to prevent war but to mitigate its impact: taking into account the principle of military necessity does not weaken Article 53 GC IV but is a way of considering the reality of war. The issue is to know when it is acceptable to fall back on the exception.

While Article 53 GC IV appears to restrict reliance on the principle of necessity to justify destruction, there is no clear yardstick provided as to when the exception might be used: when is it acceptable to derogate from Article 53 GC IV and rely on the exception, when 'destruction is rendered absolutely necessary by military operations'?

It is left to the Occupying Power to decide when military necessity is 'absolute'. For some, this could be understood as carte blanche to rely on and use, or abuse, the principle of military necessity, since there is no clear definition of what it comprises. This exception could be interpreted extensively, which would be contrary to the spirit of the Convention since it leaves it to the Occupying Power to decide whether destruction is necessary or not.⁸⁷ The occupier becomes the judge and party. Yet military necessity is not an unlimited justification, and it must be explained.

In the Eritrea–Ethiopia Claims Commission (EECC), the argument that the destruction of the Ethiopian town of Zalambessa could have been justified on the ground of military necessity was rejected: there was no evidence that its destruction had been rendered necessary.⁸⁸ The EECC did not set out a clear threshold as to what constituted a necessary

---

⁸⁰ W.G. Downey, 'The Law of War and Military Necessity' 47 *AJIL* (1953) 251, at 254.
⁸¹ *Hostages Trial*, above n 30, at 66.   ⁸² Lieber Code, above n 2, para14.
⁸³ H. Shue and D. Wippman, 'Limiting Attacks on Dual-Use Facilities Performing Indispensable Civilian Functions', 35 *Cornell International Law Journal* (2002) 559, at 559.
⁸⁴ M.N. Hayashi, 'The Martens Clause and Military Necessity', in H.M. Mensel (ed), *The Legitimate Use of Military Force: The Just War Tradition and the Customary Law of Armed Conflict* (London: Ashgate, 2008) 135, at 137.
⁸⁵ M. Schmitt, 'Military necessity and Humanity in International Humanitarian Law: Preserving the Delicate Balance', 50(4) *VirgJIL* (2010) 795.
⁸⁶ C. Greenwood, 'Historical Development and Legal Basis', in Fleck (ed), above n 23, 1; D. Kretzmer, 'The Advisory Opinion: The Light Treatment of International Humanitarian Law', 99(1) *AJIL* (2005) 88, at 98–9.
⁸⁷ Hayashi, above n 84, at 138.
⁸⁸ EECC, *Central Front—Ethiopia's Claim 2*, Partial Award, 28 April 2004, para 71.4.

destruction; this might be explained by the fact that the parties did not directly challenge the destruction as a main argument. In the *Wall* Advisory Opinion,[89] the ICJ considered that the erection of constructions had violated Article 53; it was 'not convinced that the destructions carried out contrary to the prohibition of Article 53 of GC IV were rendered absolutely necessary by military operations',[90] but the ICJ did not explain what *would* render them absolutely necessary. The lack of criteria to define absolute military necessity is not remedied in the *DRC v Uganda* case,[91] although there the Court found a violation of Article 53.

40   The stakes consequent upon the interpretation of Article 53 GC IV have an impact in other branches of international law: some have questioned whether military necessity would outweigh environmental concerns. This would mean, for example, the construction of new buildings or the destruction of state property on occupied land in the name of military necessity. Any urban settlement which affects the landscape is prohibited unless there is military necessity for it. For example, it has been argued that the construction of urban settlements and a wall in the Palestinian Occupied Territories has changed the landscape and the traditional environment, with no clear purpose of military necessity, therefore violating Article 53 GC IV and Article 55 of the Hague Regulations.[92] For the wall to be erected, olive and fruit trees had to be uprooted, and Palestinians have to negotiate a labyrinth to circulate and access different services (schools, hospitals, and others). Besides, Israel could have built the wall on its side of the border without destroying Palestinian agricultural lands.[93] The structure was built on the basis of the principle of military necessity, yet it violated the prohibition of the destruction of property.

C. Relevance in Non-International Armed Conflicts

41   During non-international armed conflicts (NIACs), the destruction and seizure of public property is prohibited, unless required by military necessity.[94] This rule is to be found in Article 8(2)(e)(xii) of the Statute of the International Criminal Court (ICC) and in domestic military manuals too. Pillage is also prohibited during NIAC, in accordance with Article 4(2)(g) of Additional Protocol II (AP) II and Rule 52 of the Customary International Humanitarian Law Study, the prohibition being found in the ICC Statute (Article 8(2)(e)(v)), domestic military manuals, and national case law as well. With regard to private property, the same rules applies; however, there is no specific rule that allows or prohibits the confiscation of private property during NIACs—this would be a matter for domestic courts to regulate.[95]

42   It is clear that most rules relating to public property are to be found in the law on military occupation, which is generally considered not to be susceptible to application by analogy in NIACs (Chapter 67 of this volume, at MN 57). However, some suggest an analogy between a non-state armed group exploiting natural resources, and the rule of

---

[89] ICJ, *Legal Consequences of the Construction of a Wall in the Occupied Palestinian Territory*, Advisory Opinion, 9 July 2004.
[90] Ibid, para 135.   [91] ICJ, *DRC v Uganda*, above n 33.   [92] Scobbie, above n 21, at 24.
[93] Ibid.   [94] ICRC CIHL Study, Rule 50.   [95] Ibid, Rule 51.

IHL of military occupation allowing an Occupying Power to extract such resources as a usufructuary.[96] This would inevitably lead to unequal treatment in the application of an IHL rule as between the governmental side and the insurgent side, and will be difficult to accept for many armed groups, in particular those fighting for secession and representing a distinct ethnic group to which they consider the natural resources to belong.

D. Legal Consequences of a Violation

Article 147 GC IV states that 'extensive destruction and appropriation of property, not justified by military necessity and carried out unlawfully and wantonly', constitutes a grave breach. At first sight, since the Convention does not impose an express prohibition of appropriation of property on the Occupying Power, one might be tempted to argue that this is an illegal act entailing only individual criminal responsibility. However, appropriation of property as a grave breach certainly applies to the requisition of civilian hospitals and their materials, and of foodstuffs, which are covered by substantive provisions of GC IV, as the Pictet Commentary suggests.[97] Also, appropriation in the context of grave breaches finds its corresponding substantive prohibition on the belligerents in Article 33 paragraph 2 GC IV, concerning the prohibition of pillage,[98] and also 'outside' GC IV, namely in the illegal appropriations of property in occupied territories under the Hague Regulations. 43

To qualify as grave breaches, the destruction and appropriation of property must be extensive. The Pictet Commentary suggests that this means that an isolated instance of destruction or appropriation 'won't be enough' to qualify as a grave breach. However, it is argued that if the act were 'intentional', it would be inadmissible to draw the conclusion that it does not constitute a grave breach. [99] 44

The question therefore arises of when an act of destruction or appropriation of property is extensive (see also Chapter 71 of this volume, MN 49). The International Criminal Tribunal for the former Yugoslavia (ICTY) case law clarified that this is a threshold that must be evaluated 'according to the facts of the case', since 'a single act, such as the destruction of a hospital, may suffice to characterise an offence under this count'.[100] In subsequent case law, however, the ICTY seems to consider that to be 'extensive', the destruction of property (and therefore also the appropriation) must be carried out on a large scale.[101] 45

According to one commentator, destruction of property is extensive if it affects objects necessary for the survival of civilians, such as food, agriculture, drinking water, irrigation, and supplies, as listed in Article 54 AP I.[102] 46

Both extensive destruction and appropriation of property constitute a grave breach only if they are 'not justified by military necessity'. Another discrepancy exists here with respect to destruction of property in Article 53 GC IV, which makes the destruction 47

---

[96] Stewart, above n 54.   [97] Pictet Commentary GC IV, at 601.   [98] Ibid.
[99] Ibid, fn 1, where the example is given of the bombing of a single civilian hospital.
[100] ICTY, *The Prosecutor v Tihomir Blaškić*, Trial Chamber Judgment, IT-95-14-T, 3 March 2000, para 157.
[101] See ICTY, *The Prosecutor v Mladen Naletilić & Vinko Martinović*, Trial Chamber Judgment, IT-98-34-T, 31 March 2003, para 179. See also ICTY, *The Prosecutor v Dario Kordić and Mario Čerkez*, Trial Chamber Judgment, IT-95-14/2-T, 26 February 2001, para 341; ICTY, *The Prosecutor v Milan Martić*, Trial Chamber Judgment, IT-95-11-T, 12 June 2007, para 90; ICTY, *The Prosecutor v Ante Gotovina et al*, Trial Chamber Judgment, IT-06-90-T, 15 April 2011, para 1765.
[102] Arai-Takashi, above n 7, at 191.

lawful only 'where such destruction is rendered absolutely necessary by military operations'. The wording of Article 53 is thus stricter than in the corresponding grave breach, leaving less room to individuals charged with destruction of property to rely on military necessity to escape criminal responsibility (see, however, Chapter 71, MN 54, of this volume).

E. Critical Assessment

48 Most of the modern issues that occupation law faces in terms of the public/private divide, the distinction between movable and immovable, natural resources and the environment, the role of human rights, the issue of threshold for military necessity, or the definition of destruction, can be solved by an 'evolutive interpretation':[103] for example, the Supreme Court of Israel has adopted an evolutive approach to the Hague Regulations in order to adapt them to present-day circumstances. This would allow for some flexibility as long as the very spirit of the laws of occupation, and in particular the Geneva Conventions, is respected. This would mean, for example, that selling movable property would be acceptable if and only for the benefit of the population, but not for the enrichment of the Occuying Power.

49 Over time, as stressed by Scobbie,[104] the nature of occupation has changed, especially in connection with Iraq.[105] It might be that the law will also have to evolve to adapt to a new genre of occupation, which will also have an impact on property. This is relevant for scholars who believe that it is becoming difficult to enforce the laws of occupation, illustrated by the shortcomings of the concept of usufruct when it comes to non-renewable resources.

ANICÉE VAN ENGELAND

---

[103] Cassese, above n 11, at 424; Israel High Court of Justice, *Abu Aita et al v The Military Commander of the Judea and Samaria Region*, HCJ 69/81, Judgment, 5 April 1983; *A Teacher's Housing Cooperative Society v The Military Commander of the Judea and Samaria Region et al*, HCJ 393/82, Judgment, 1982.
[104] Scobbie, above n 55, at 234.   [105] See Ch 67 of this volume.

Chapter 73. Prohibition of Settlements

	MN
A. Introduction	1
I. Regulation in the Hague Regulations	1
II. The occurrences of the Second World War	2
a. Nazi Germany's expansion plans in Eastern Europe	3
b. Settlement in German territories east of the Oder-Neisse Line	4
c. Soviet transfer operations in the Baltic States	5
III. The aftermath of the Second World War and later developments	6
IV. The current conflict zones	10
a. The occupied Palestinian territories	11
b. Northern Cyprus	17
c. The former Yugoslavia	19
B. Meaning and Application	20
I. The meaning and scope of the prohibition	21
a. The rationale	21
b. The territorial scope	23
c. The scope *ratione personae*	28
d. The prohibited activities: deportation and transfer	31
e. Non-state actors	35
f. Duty of prevention?	38
II. Restriction and/or justification	40
a. Security	40
b. Military necessity	42
c. National emergency	43
III. The ban on settlements as customary law	44
C. Relevance in Non-International Armed Conflicts	47
D. Breaches of Other Norms of International Law	48
I. Self-determination—right to the homeland	48
II. Land rights	50
III. Other rights	54
E. Remedies	55
I. Procedural remedies	55
a. Remedies under international humanitarian law	55
b. Application to the International Court of Justice	56
c. Recourse to the courts of the Occupying Power	57
d. Recourse to the courts of third states	59
e. Remedies under human rights instruments	64
II. Substantive remedies	65
F. Critical Assessment	67

Select Bibliography

Arai-Takahashi, Y., *The Law of Occupation: Continuity and Change of International Humanitarian Law, and its Interaction with International Human Rights Law* (Leiden/Boston, Mass: Martinus Nijhoff, 2009)

Ben-Naftali, O./Gross, A.M./Michaeli, K., 'Illegal Occupation: Framing the Occupied Palestinian Territory', 23 *Berkeley JIL* (2005) 551

Benvenisti, E., *The International Law of Occupation* (Princeton, NJ: Princeton University Press, 1993)

Dinstein, Y., *The International Law of Belligerent Occupation* (Cambridge: CUP, 2009)
Falk, R.A., Report on the Situation of Human Rights in the Palestinian Territories Occupied since 1967, UN Doc A/HRC/20/32, 25 May 2012
Falk, R.A./Weston, B.H., 'The Relevance of International Law to Palestinian Rights in the West Bank and Gaza: In Legal Defense of the Intifada', 32 *Harvard International Law Journal* (1991) 129
Kretzmer, D., *The Occupation of Justice: The Supreme Court of Israel and the Occupied Territories* (Albany, NY: State University of New York Press, 2002)
Mallison, W.T./Mallison, S.V., *The Palestine Problem in International Law and World Order* (Harlow: Longman, 1986)
Playfair, E. (ed), *International Law and the Administration of Occupied Territories: Two Decades of Israeli Occupation of the West Bank and the Gaza Strip* (Oxford: Clarendon Press, 1992)
Quigley J., 'Living in Legal Limbo: Israel's Settlers in Occupied Palestinian Territory', 10 *Pace International Law Review* (1998) 1
Roberts, A., 'Prolonged Military Occupation: The Israeli-Occupied Territories since 1967', 84 *AJIL* (1990) 44
Ronen, Y., 'Status of Settlers Implanted by Illegal Territorial Regime', 79 *BYBIL* (2008) 194
Stone, J., *Israel and Palestine: Assault on the Law of Nations* (Baltimore, Md./London: The Johns Hopkins University Press, 1981)
Williams, R.C./Gürel, A., *The European Court of Human Rights and the Cyprus Property Issue: Charting a Way Forward* (Oslo: Peace Research Institute–Cyprus Centre, 2011)
de Zayas, A., 'Ethnic Cleansing: Applicable Norms, Emerging Jurisprudence, Implementable Remedies', in J. Carey, W.V. Dunlop, and R.J. Pritchard (eds), *International Humanitarian Law: Origins* (Ardsley, NY: Transnational Publishers, 2003) 283
Report of the independent international fact-finding mission to investigate the implications of the Israeli settlements on the civil, political, economic, social and cultural rights of the Palestinian people throughout the Occupied Palestinian Territory, including East Jerusalem, UN Doc A/HRC/22/63, 7 February 2013

A. Introduction

I. Regulation in the Hague Regulations

1 The Hague Regulations of 1907 did not encompass an explicit prohibition of implantation of settlers in occupied territory. Nonetheless, two provisions had some relevance on the issue. Article 43 enjoined the Occupying Power to respect the laws in force in the country. Additionally, Article 46 stated that private property must be respected and could not be confiscated. Through these two provisions any governmental programmes of an Occupying Power designed to introduce settlers forcibly into occupied territory were implicitly ruled out. The fact that in 1907 no explicit ban on transfer of settlers was laid down is easily explainable. Generally, the Hague Regulations are fairly brief and succinct. On the other hand, it seemed inconceivable at the beginning of the twentieth century that massive population transfers could be caused by armed conflict. Although the Hague Regulations have not been widely ratified by the states which came into existence in the process of decolonization after 1945, they are generally recognized as propositions under international customary law.[1]

---

[1] International Military Tribunal of Nuremberg, Judgment, 30 September and 1 October 1946, 65; ICJ, *Legality of the Threat or Use of Nuclear Weapons*, Advisory Opinion, 8 July 1996, 226, at 256 para 75; *Legal*

II. The occurrences of the Second World War

The Second World War brought about colossal plans for population transfers and the establishment of settlers in land occupied after hostilities. Little consideration was given to the plight of the populations concerned. Strategic thinking prevailed. Many of the measures taken were motivated by racial prejudices and hatred. These population transfers, amounting more often than not to ethnic cleansing in modern terminology, involved mass violations of human rights, with huge loss of human life.

a. *Nazi Germany's expansion plans in Eastern Europe*

Nazi Germany went ahead with settlement plans for Poland, and even parts of Ukraine and Belarus, then constituent elements of the Union of Soviet Socialist Republics (USSR or Soviet Union). The German Government determined that large parts of the Polish population should be expelled further to the east, and that German settlers should take over the land thus deprived of its inhabitants. Only a fraction of that utopian project could be realized, the German military-industrial complex lacking the requisite capacity to bring about such profound changes while waging war at the same time. The Polish population lived in a state of absolute insecurity and lawlessness. No remedies were at their disposal.[2] Those affected by the official plans simply had to leave their homes and plots of land to the newcomers who, for the most part, had no say in the allocations granted to them.[3]

b. *Settlement in German territories east of the Oder-Neisse Line*

After the unconditional surrender of Germany on 8 May 1945, the German population living in the German territories east of the Oder-Neisse line was almost completely expelled. The Soviet Union and Poland acted with reference to the Potsdam Agreement of the victorious Allied Powers.[4] Section XIII of that Agreement provided that the 'transfer to Germany' of German populations remaining in Poland, Czechoslovakia, and Hungary 'will have to be undertaken'. The three Governments agreed that 'any transfers […] should be effected in an orderly and humane manner'. No mention was made of the Germans living in the eastern parts of Germany. However, almost immediately, the Soviet Union and Poland started sending settlers to those territories provisionally assigned to them, which at the same time were purposefully emptied of their original populations. At that time, the borders of Germany as of 31 December 1937 had not yet been modified. The eastern provinces of Germany were still German territory, as explicitly stipulated in the Agreement itself, according to which final determinations on territorial questions were to be made through a peace settlement with regard both to the city of Königsberg and the adjacent territory (now oblast Kaliningrad) (Section VI), and to the territories provisionally to be placed under Polish administration (Section IX (b)). Legal justification was sought in accordance with the assumption that through its defeat

---

Consequences of the Construction of a Wall in the Occupied Palestinian Territory, Advisory Opinion, 9 July 2004, 136, at 172, para 89.

[2] See, e.g., M. Broszat, *Nationalsozialistische Polenpolitik 1939–1945* (Stuttgart: Deutsche Verlagsanstalt, 1961), at 85–102; C. Madajczyk, *Die Okkupationspolitik Nazideutschlands in Polen 1939–1945* (Köln: Pahl-Rugenstein, 1988), at 163–384.

[3] See Madajczyk, above n 2, at 441–53, on the establishment of German settlers.

[4] Of 2 August 1945, reprinted in I. von Münch (ed), *Dokumente des geteilten Deutschland* (Stuttgart: Alfred Kröner, 1968), at 32.

Germany had ceased to exist as a state,[5] and that therefore the rules of humanitarian law were not applicable.[6] It cannot be denied that the operation, in modern terminology, amounted to ethnic cleansing. Because of the egregious atrocities committed beforehand at the hands of the Nazi Government, doubts as to the lawfulness of the policy of expulsion and resettlement were not publicly articulated. The immediate transformation of the provisional status of occupation to a nearly definitive status of annexation, providing unlimited room for the establishment of Russian and Polish settlers, was generally accepted. In the circumstances prevailing at the collapse of the Third Reich, on obvious moral grounds, Germany and its nationals lacked any support for their legal interests from any third power.[7]

c. Soviet transfer operations in the Baltic States

5   During the Second World War (1940), the Soviet Union annexed the three Baltic states—Estonia, Latvia, and Lithuania. Hundreds of thousands of persons resisting the incorporation of their home countries into the USSR were deported to the eastern parts of the Soviet Union. Subsequently, during the decades until the re-emergence of these states as sovereign nations, Soviet nationals moved in great numbers to those states.[8] The Soviet Union did not consider itself an Occupying Power. From its perspective, incorporation into the Soviet Union was definitive. Therefore, the legal regime of occupation was not deemed to be applicable. After the three states had regained their independence, they opted for a policy of eradication of what they considered illegal occupation by the Soviet Union, aiming to send back at least those persons of Russian origin who had some nexus with the former Soviet authorities. In a leading decision, the European Court of Human Rights (ECtHR) found that in view of Article 8 of the European Convention on Human Rights (ECHR, right to respect for one's home), a balancing of interests had to take into account the closeness of the relationship with the country concerned.[9] However, that decision deliberately refrained from assessing the legal position under the auspices of international humanitarian law (IHL).

III. The aftermath of the Second World War and later developments

6   At the Nuremberg trial against the major war criminals of Nazi Germany, the accused were charged, inter alia, with war crimes under Article 6(b) of the Charter of the International Military Tribunal (Count 3). Under section E—Plunder of Public and Private Property—the indictment listed activities which foreshadowed the prohibition later established in Article 49 paragraph 6 of Geneva Convention (GC) IV, namely,

---

[5] Concept conceived by H. Kelsen, 'The International Legal Status of Germany to be established immediately upon Termination of the War', 38 *AJIL* (1944) 689, at 692; H. Kelsen, 'The Legal Status of Germany according to the Declaration of Berlin', 39 *AJIL* (1945) 518, at 519.

[6] See E. Benvenisti, *The International Law of Occupation* (Princeton, NJ: Princeton University Press, 1993), at 91–2; Y. Blum, 'The Missing Reversioner: Reflections on the Status of Judea and Samaria', 3 *Israel Law Review* (1968) 279, at 293.

[7] But see Benvenisti, above n 6, at 94–6, who argues that the doctrine of *debellatio* cannot be reconciled with the modern concept of international law.

[8] See Y. Ronen, 'Status of Settlers Implanted by Illegal Territorial Regimes', 79 *BYBIL* (2008) 194, at 211; A. de Zayas, 'Ethnic Cleansing: Applicable Norms, Emerging Jurisprudence, Implementable Remedies', in J. Carey et al (eds), *International Humanitarian Law: Origins* (Ardsley, NY: Transnational Publishers, 2003) 283, at 294.

[9] ECtHR, *Slivenko v Latvia*, Judgment, 9 October 2003.

confiscation of businesses, plants, and other property (paragraph 3). It was specifically mentioned that the defendants (paragraph 7)

abrogated the rights of the local populations in the occupied portions of the USSR and in Poland and in other countries to develop or manage agricultural and industrial properties, and reserved this area for exclusive settlement, development, and ownership by Germans and their so-called racial brethren.

The charge was enunciated in similar terms under section J (Germanization of Occupied Territories):

In certain occupied territories purportedly annexed to Germany the defendants methodically and pursuant to plan endeavored to assimilate those territories politically, culturally, socially, and economically into the German Reich. The defendants endeavored to obliterate the former national character of these territories. In pursuance of these plans and endeavors, the defendants forcibly deported inhabitants who were predominantly non-German and introduced thousands of German colonists.

The judgment itself addressed these charges only incidentally.

Article 49 GC IV was elaborated by the 1949 Diplomatic Conference against the background of the traumatizing experiences of the Second World War. Attention was focused mainly on the criminal excesses of the German Nazi regime in Eastern Europe. Officially, no attention was given to the resettlement of the German territories to the east of the Oder-Neisse line by nationals of the victorious Powers and their allies, at a time when those territories were still placed under a regime of occupation.

At the Diplomatic Conference on the Reaffirmation and Development of International Humanitarian Law applicable in Armed Conflicts (1974–7), the breach of Article 49 paragraph 6 was included in Additional Protocol (AP) I as a new item in the list of grave breaches (Article 85(4)(a)). While GC IV has been universally ratified, AP I has not received acceptance by all states (in May 2015 the number of states parties was 174). Among the states still absent are Israel, Turkey, and the United States. The rule which qualifies Article 49 paragraph 6 as a grave breach could therefore apply to those states solely *qua* customary law.[10]

The Draft Code of Crimes against the Peace and Security of Mankind, adopted by the International Law Commission (ILC) in 1996[11] but not acted upon by the General Assembly, listed as a war crime the 'transfer by the Occupying Power of parts of its own civilian population into the territory it occupies' (Article 20(c)(i)). Thereafter, the Diplomatic Conference on the Establishment of an International Criminal Court (ICC) also agreed on including this offence in the Rome Statute of that Court adopted by the Conference (Article 8(2)(b)(viii)).

IV. The current conflict zones

Currently, there are mainly two conflict zones where allegations have been raised that Article 49 paragraph 6 GC IV has been continuously violated over many years. It is above all with regard to these zones that practice has emerged that sheds a light on the meaning and the scope of the ban on the transfer of populations into occupied territory.

---

[10] See MN 44. [11] *YILC* 1996, vol II, Part 2, 17, at 53.

a. The occupied Palestinian territories

11   Soon after the Six-Day War between Israel and its neighbours, Israel began constructing settlements in the occupied Palestinian territories, in Gaza, in the West Bank, including East Jerusalem, and on the Golan Heights. Notwithstanding numerous, almost permanent appeals to Israel to refrain from its settlement policy, the Israeli Government has not generally put a halt to such activities.

12   The Security Council addressed the issue of Israeli settlements for the first time in respect of the City of Jerusalem. By Resolution 298 (1971) of 25 September 1971 it confirmed, 'in the clearest possible terms', that all actions taken to change the status of the City, 'including expropriation of land and properties, transfer of populations and legislation aimed at the incorporation the occupied section are totally invalid'. In 1979 it extended its criticism of the Israeli policy to the entire occupied territory, 'determin[ing] that the policy and practices of Israel in establishing settlements in the Palestinian and other Arab territories occupied since 1967 have no legal validity'.[12] The only weak point of that Resolution was the fact that three states abstained (Norway, the United Kingdom (UK), and the United States (US)). In 1980, the issue was taken up again. This time, the Security Council 'determine[d]', by unanimity in an operative paragraph of the relevant Resolution,

> that all measures taken by Israel to change the physical character, demographic composition, institutional structure or status of the Palestinian and other Arab territories occupied since 1967, including Jerusalem, or any part thereof have no legal validity and that Israel's policy and practice of settling parts of its population and new immigrants in those territories constitute a flagrant violation of the Geneva Convention relative to the Protection of Civilian Persons in Time of War [...][13]

Since that time, no other Resolutions have been adopted by the Security Council. All attempts to confirm the earlier condemnations have failed because the US has made regularly use of its veto power. However, US delegates in the Security Council have explained that their rejection of the relevant draft proposals should not be interpreted as approval of the Israeli policy.[14]

13   In 1976 the United Nations General Assembly (UNGA) adopted for the first time a Resolution[15] by which it '[s]trongly deplore[d] the measures taken by Israel' in the occupied Palestinian territories 'that alter their demographic composition or geographical nature, and particularly the establishment of settlements', declaring additionally that such measures 'have no legal validity'. From there on, similar Resolutions have been adopted year after year with overwhelming majorities. In the Resolution of 26 November 2013,[16] the UNGA reaffirmed again the illegality of the Israeli settlements in the Palestinian territory occupied since 1967, including East Jerusalem.

---

[12] UNSC Res 446 (1979), 22 March 1979, op para 1. See also the subsequent Resolution 452 (1979), 20 July 1979, Preamble, para 3.

[13] UNSC Res 465 (1980), 1 March 1980, op para 5.

[14] Thus, US Ambassador Rice said in the meeting of the SC on 18 February 2011: '[W]e reject in the strongest terms the legitimacy of continued Israeli settlement activity [...] Continued settlement activity violates Israel's international commitments, devastates trust between the parties, and threatens the prospects for peace', S/PV.6484, 4.

[15] UNGA Res 31/106 A, 16 December 1976, adopted by 129 to 3 votes with 4 abstentions.

[16] UNGA Res 68/15, adopted by 165 votes against 6 (Canada, Israel, Marshall Islands, Micronesia, Palau, USA) with 6 abstentions (Australia, Cameroon, Papua New Guinea, Paraguay, South Sudan, Tonga).

In its Advisory Opinion on the building of a wall (according to Israeli terminology, 'security fence') in the occupied Palestinian territory, the International Court of Justice (ICJ) also addressed the settlement policy of the Israeli Government. Without any hesitation, the ICJ concluded that Article 49 paragraph 6 GC IV was applicable, and that accordingly the Israeli settlements were established 'in breach of international law'.[17] De facto as a partial response to the Advisory Opinion, but formally in execution of a unilateral Disengagement Plan adopted by its Cabinet in June 2004, Israel withdrew its troops and all the settlers from the Gaza strip in August 2005. On the other hand, settlement activities in the West Bank and in East Jerusalem continue unabated. According to recent estimates, 450,000 to 500,000 Israeli settlers live in the West Bank,[18] and the number of Jewish inhabitants of East Jerusalem has risen to roughly 190,000 persons.[19]

On the part of the main organs of the International Red Cross Movement, which is the guardian of the integrity of IHL, the Israeli settlement policy has been condemned in clear and unambiguous terms. A statement of the International Committee of the Red Cross (ICRC) of 5 December 2001[20] was echoed on the same day by the conference of High Contracting Parties to the Fourth Geneva Convention (paragraph 12).[21] The President of the ICRC has added that Israel's systematic support of the settlements has led to a 'profound alteration of the economic and social landscape of the West Bank'.[22]

Negotiations in different frameworks seeking a peaceful solution to the conflict have been going on for decades. At the time of writing, the prospect that a solution could one day be found seems rather unrealistic. On the Palestinian side, the whole of the West Bank, according to the boundary line as it existed in 1967, is considered occupied territory to which the ban on settlements applies. As far as the Israeli side is concerned, only one thing is clear, namely, that the settlement policy has been implemented, with differing degrees of intensity, for almost half a century.[23] On the other hand, no reliable statement can be made as to the ultimate objective of the Israeli Government. It has never openly accepted the two-state option, according to which a Jewish state and a Palestinian state should eventually exist side by side.[24] It stands to reason that regarding the settlement issue, Article 49 paragraph 6 GC IV plays a pivotal role.

---

[17] ICJ, *Wall* Advisory Opinion, above n 1, at 184, para 120, 192, para 134.

[18] Report of Special Rapporteur Richard Falk on the situation of human rights in the Palestinian territories occupied since 1967, A/HRC/20/32, at 12, para 25: 450,000. B'Tselem indicates a figure of 500,000: see 'Statistics on Settlements and Settler Population' (last updated 11 May 2015), available at <http://www.btselem.org/settlements/statistics>.

[19] According to B'Tselem's calculation, above n 18.

[20] ICRC, 'Conference of High Contracting Parties to the Fourth Geneva Convention', Statement, 5 December 2001, available at <http://www.icrc.org/eng/resources/documents/misc/57jrgw.htm>.

[21] *Conference of High Contracting Parties to the Fourth Geneva Convention: Declaration*, 5 December 2001, available at <http://unispal.un.org/UNISPAL.NSF/0/8FC4f064B9BE5BAD85256C1400722951>.

[22] 'Challenges to International Humanitarian Law: Israel's Occupation Policy', 94 *IRRC* 888 (2012) 1503, at 1507.

[23] See, e.g., D. Kretzmer, 'The Advisory Opinion: The Light Treatment of International Humanitarian Law', 99 *AJIL* (2005) 88, at 89. For a detailed description of the different governmental plans, see the report of the NGO B'Tselem, *Land Grab: Israel's Settlement Policy in the West Bank*, (May 2002), at 11–20, available at <http://www.btselem.org/download/200205_land_grab_eng.pdf>.

[24] But see the official statement, 'The State of Israel's policy towards the Palestinian government', 18 March 2007, available at <http://www.mfa.gov.il/mfa/pressroom/2007/pages/the state of israels policy towards the palestinian government 18-mar-2007.aspx>: 'Israel stands for a two state solution.' A fact sheet issued by the Institute for Middle East Understanding, 'The Israeli Government & The Two-State Solution', 15 July 2013, available at <http://imeu.net/news/article0024179.shtml>, shows that the sympathy shown by Prime Minister Netanyahu for a two-state solution in an address at Bar Ilan University on 14 June 2009, was only a 'tactical speech for the rest of the world' (Deputy Minister of Transportation Tzipi Hotovely).

b. Northern Cyprus

17 The second of the prominent conflict zones is Northern Cyprus. In 1974, the ethnic conflict between Greek and Turkish Cypriots, the two main population groups living on the island, reached dramatic dimensions. Activist elements from the Greek population attempted a coup against Archbishop Makarios, the President of the Republic of Cyprus, in order to reach enosis, the incorporation of the island into Greece. The Turkish Government, viewing this development as a vital threat against the security and the interests of the Turkish Cypriot population, invaded the island by its military forces. In so doing, it invoked the Treaty of Guarantee of 16 August 1960,[25] by virtue of which Greece, Turkey, and the UK had been recognized as guarantee Powers. The armed forces of Cyprus, acting for the defence of the Greek Cypriot community, could not resist the invasion forces. They had to withdraw to the south, and almost the entire population of Greek ethnicity also fled, or was expelled, to the south; and vice versa, the members of the Turkish Cypriot community moved to the northern part of the island. Through an exchange of population, those Turkish Cypriots living in the south of the island could later move to the north. Hence, de facto, the invasion led to partition of the island. Thirty-five per cent of the territory is under Turkish control, while the greater part (60 per cent) is controlled by the Greek-dominated Government of Cyprus.[26]

18 On 15 November 1983, the 'Turkish Republic of Northern Cyprus' (TRNC) was proclaimed in the northern part of the island. To date, this entity has not been recognized by the international community as a state, with the sole exception of Turkey. The Security Council declared that the declaration was legally invalid.[27] Until 1999, it affirmed in its annual resolutions the 'territorial integrity' of the Republic of Cyprus.[28] This position has not been abandoned, but it is no longer explicitly reiterated each time. Still, the international community, in particular the United Nations (UN), regards Cyprus as an undivided legal entity for which only the Greek-orientated Government in Nicosia is entitled to speak. Notwithstanding this legal premise, the authorities in control of the territory, in close cooperation with the Turkish armed forces deployed there, progressively operated a programme of settlements. Turkish settlers were brought in large numbers from the Turkish mainland territory to the island. On a massive scale, land owned by Greek Cypriots was distributed to the newcomers, a process that was facilitated by Article 159 of the Constitution of the TRNC, according to which that original ownership was no longer recognized by the TRNC. As a consequence, the legality of any interference was unassailable before the TRNC courts. With a view eventually to reaching a settlement of the property issue, the TRNC established in 2005 an Immovable Property Commission (IPC), empowered to order, if requested, restitution, exchange of properties, or compensation. These modalities of settlement were approved by the ECtHR in light of the requirements of the ECHR.[29] According to recent estimates, the number of Turkish settlers seems to have achieved parity with the indigenous Turkish Cypriot population of the island.[30]

---

[25] 382 UNTS 3.
[26] Roughly 2.7 per cent are controlled by the UN force UNFICYP, while another 2.7 per cent form part of the British bases still present on the island.
[27] UNSC Res 541 (1983), 18 November 1983, op para 2.
[28] UNSC Res 1251 (1999), 29 June 1999, Preamble, para 4.
[29] ECtHR, *Demopoulos and others v Turkey*, Decision, 1 March 2010.
[30] Parliamentary Assembly of the Council of Europe, Doc 9799, 2 May 2003, Summary, para 1.

Some voices even contend that they exceed the indigenous Turkish population, many elements of which have left the island. Precise figures are not available.[31]

c. *The former Yugoslavia*

During the wars in the former Yugoslavia, millions of people were uprooted. While on account of their ethnicity some people were driven out from their ancestral homes, others were established there. Generally, the periods of occupation were relatively short. The Dayton Peace Agreement of 14 December 1995 traced new boundaries between Croatia, Bosnia-Herzegovina, and Serbia-Montenegro. As from that time, the legal debate shifted from the regime of belligerent occupation to the field of criminal law, with its sanctions against ethnic cleansing as rules of *jus cogens*.

B. Meaning and Application

Article 49 paragraph 6 GC IV is a succinct provision, drafted in clear and unambiguous language. The sentence that the Occupying Power 'shall not deport or transfer parts of its own civilian population into the territory it occupies' leaves little room for interpretive exercises. In particular, it can be perceived at first glance that the prohibition is not restricted by any clause permitting exceptions in specific circumstances. Obviously, the drafters wanted Article 49 paragraph 6 to be observed rigidly and scrupulously. It will be seen that no discussion took place on the provision at the 1949 Geneva Conference. Thus, recourse to the *travaux préparatoires* can be of no avail for the purposes of departing from, circumventing, or relativizing the prohibition on the introduction of settlers into occupied territory.

I. The meaning and scope of the prohibition

a. *The rationale*

It is not difficult to find the *raison d'être* of Article 49 paragraph 6. Occupation is, by its very essence as a legal concept, a temporary situation. The Occupying Power holds certain powers and responsibilities during the time it controls foreign territory as a consequence of armed conflict. This temporary situation should not be susceptible to being changed unilaterally through the exercise of military might. If the Occupying Power introduces parts of its own population into the territory it factually controls, this may directly amount to, or can easily be converted into, a progressive process of annexation eroding the sovereign powers of the nation concerned. Yet in the world of today, shaped by the principle of non-use of force under the UN Charter (Article 2(4)), acquisition of foreign territory by force is unlawful. Conquest does not confer title.[32] Humanitarian law does not interfere with this basic principle of modern international law. Changes of territorial sovereignty must be brought about by mutual consent through international

---

[31] See assessment by Ronen, above n 8, at 219–22; A. de Zayas, 'The Illegal Implantation of Turkish Settlers in Occupied Northern Cyprus', in G.H. Gornig et al (eds), *Justitia et Pax. Gedächtnisschrift für Dieter Blumenwitz* (Berlin: Duncker & Humblot, 2008) 721.

[32] See O. Ben-Naftali et al, 'Illegal Occupation: Framing the Occupied Palestinian Territory', 23 *Berkeley JIL* (2005) 551, at 570–2; A. Pellet, 'The Destruction of Troy Will Not Take Place', in E. Playfair (ed), *International Law and the Administration of Occupied Territories: Two Decades of Israeli Occupation of the West Bank and the Gaza Strip* (Oxford: Clarendon Press, 1992) 169, at 174–80.

treaty. Yet the implantation of settlers is one of the strategies that may undermine the prohibition of acquisition of territory by resort to use of force, as well as the fundamental principle of self-determination with its inherent territorial component.

22   At the Geneva Diplomatic Conference of 1949, where Article 49 received its final shape, no discussion took place about the rationale lying behind the proposed draft provision. The substance of the text prepared by the XVIIth International Red Cross Conference in Stockholm (August 1948)[33] was accepted *telle quelle* with only a small drafting change. Given the excesses that had been witnessed during the Second World War, in particular the attempts by Nazi Germany to colonize large parts of Polish territory, it apparently seemed obvious to every delegation that a provision of that type was needed. Not even the reasons that were in the minds of everyone present needed to be explained. Article 49 paragraph 6 was absolutely uncontroversial. The amputation of German territory and the settlement of the Polish citizens in land that formally still belonged to Germany were not mentioned, nor what had happened in the Baltic states.

b. *The territorial scope*

23   The territorial scope of Article 49 paragraph 6 is clearly defined. The provision is intended to protect, on the one hand, the state which has lost control of parts of its territory, but primarily, on the other hand, the population in such territories.

24   Article 49 paragraph 6 does not introduce a specific and novel standard of occupation. It relies on Article 42 of the Hague Regulations, which provides that a territory is considered occupied 'when it is actually placed under the authority of the hostile army'.[34] It stands to reason that policies of transfer of population presuppose a certain stabilization of the situation.[35] Only after territorial control has been consolidated can an Occupying Power seriously think of establishing persons of its own nationality in the land occupied by it.

25   There can be no doubt that as of April 2014, Gaza and the West Bank must still be considered occupied territory. Although the Israeli Defense Forces left Gaza in August 2005, the strip of land is still under Israeli control. All of Gaza's borders, with the exception of the southern border with Egypt at the crossing of Rafah, are monitored and supervised by Israel. Even the maritime border is closed. Since 2005, however, Israel has renounced establishing Jewish colonies in Gaza.

26   Similar considerations apply to the West Bank. Although, according to the complex network of agreements between Israel and the Palestinian Authority, the population in the occupied territory has certain rights of self-government in one of the three zones (Zone A), Israel has maintained tight powers of control concerning the other two zones (Zones B and C). Even in Zone A, the overall responsibility for all issues relating to public security remains in the hands of Israel. Access to the West Bank is dependent on access to Israel, i.e. on authorization by the Israeli Government. This regime of closure applies to foreigners as well. No one can freely pay a visit to the West Bank, and persons whose presence the Israeli Government considers inconvenient are routinely denied entry into the Palestinian territory. In its Advisory Opinion of July 2004, the ICJ stated unambiguously that all

---

[33] Final Record, vol I, 113, at 121 (Art 45(5)).   [34] ICJ, *Wall* Advisory Opinion, above n 1, 167, para 78.
[35] For detailed discussion of the concept and end of occupations, see Chs 67 and 74 of this volume.

the territories behind the armistice line of 1967 ('green line') have the status of occupied land.³⁶ This is not contested by the Israeli Government.³⁷

Pursuant to the view of the international community, the northern part of Cyprus, where the TRNC was proclaimed on 15 November 1983, must be deemed to have the legal status of Cypriot territory occupied by Turkey. As already observed, the UN has never recognized the TRNC as a new sovereign state. According to its viewpoint, Cyprus is still one state where, because of the presence of Turkish armed forces in the north, the legitimate Government is prevented from exercising its authority. This appraisal of the legal position is generally shared in the international community. The ECtHR observed in a number of decisions that Turkey is responsible for the human rights violations occurring there at the hands of the local authorities because these authorities are controlled by the Turkish armed forces.³⁸ Although the invasion took place in 1974, more than 40 years ago, the ECtHR has not departed from its assessment of the legal position.³⁹ Obviously, however, the ECtHR did not apply IHL since its jurisdiction is confined to the ECHR.

c. *The scope* ratione personae

The text of Article 49 paragraph 6 specifies that the prohibition is directed only against the 'civilian population' of the Occupying Power. Thereby, it implicitly acknowledges that an Occupying Power must be able to send into an occupied territory governmental agents who are required for the fulfilment of the functions incumbent upon it, pursuant to the Hague Regulations and the relevant provisions of GC IV. All of these persons discharge temporary tasks, related to the limited period of occupation. In this regard, no formalistic distinctions should be drawn between civil or military servants proper, employed by the Occupying Power itself, and other persons working in the service of other entities. Since the Occupying Power is obligated, under Article 43 of the Hague Regulations, to restore and ensure 'public order and safety', it may be necessary, in particular, to operate public services like power grids, communication networks, or public transport. While even 50 years ago all such services were organized under the auspices of the state as public authorities, privatization has committed them mostly into the hands of private entities. The persons entrusted with public service responsibilities must be provided with suitable accommodation in the territory where they exercise their functions. Hence, the Occupying Power cannot be prevented from sending them to those places. They are not meant to stay for good in the area under occupation. As soon as the occupation comes to its end, the functional necessity of their stay ends simultaneously.

Primarily, the prohibition focuses on persons having the nationality of the Occupying Power. In light of the intention of the prohibition, however, it would not seem appropriate to embrace a narrow formalistic construction of the text. One might think of an armed conflict where two Powers, A and B, acting as allies, have defeated a third state. In such instances, it

---

³⁶ ICJ, *Wall* Advisory Opinion, above n 1, 167, para 78.
³⁷ See, e.g., A. Margalit and S. Hibbin, 'Unlawful Presence of Protected Persons in Occupied Territory?', 13 *YIHL* (2010) 245, at 251.
³⁸ ECtHR, *Loizidou v Turkey*, Judgment (Preliminary Objections), 23 March 1993, paras 62–4; Judgment (Merits), 18 December 1996, paras 52–6.
³⁹ ECtHR, *Cyprus v Turkey*, Judgment, 10 May 2001, para 77; *Xenides-Arestis v Turkey*, Judgment, 22 December 2005, para 27; *Demopoulos*, above n 29, para 95; *Lordos and others v Turkey*, Judgment, 2 November 2010, para 31.

would amount to an obvious circumvention of the ban if state A transferred nationals of state B to the occupied territory, while state B did the same with regard to nationals of state A. In such circumstances, too, the occupied country would be in need of protection against the introduction of persons who are alien to the territory concerned.[40]

30   A similar situation could arise if a state made use, for the purpose of implementing a settlement policy, of foreigners living in its territory who, although totally socialized as inhabitants of their country of abode, have not yet been naturalized. Indeed, quite a number of European countries have large contingents of aliens living within their borders who have still kept their original nationality notwithstanding their intimate involvement with their host nations. Introducing such 'auxiliaries' instead of relying on nationals proper would also have to be considered unlawful under the terms of Article 49 paragraph 6.[41] It would be futile to speculate on other instances where the nationality of the settlers and their ties of allegiance differ.

d. *The prohibited activities: deportation and transfer*

31   The operations prohibited are the deportation or transfer of a population. The two terms were chosen concomitantly in order to keep some harmony within the provision, the first paragraphs of which (paragraphs 1–5) deal with 'mass forcible transfers' and 'deportations' of protected persons from an occupied territory to the territory of an Occupying Power. Visibly, the main emphasis of Article 49 GC IV is placed on securing members of the local population against forcible removal from their places of residence. When an Occupying Power wishes to remove those people, it has to do so by forcible measures that may properly be called 'deportation'. However, it rarely, if ever happens in practice that a government deports elements of its own population into an occupied territory. It will confine itself to organizing such a movement, to inducing its own nationals to benefit from the opportunities open to them in a foreign land. Accordingly, the term 'deportation' will generally remain moot within the framework of Article 49 paragraph 6.[42] Given the disparity between the two windows of Article 49, it would have been more logical to establish Article 49 paragraph 6 as an independent provision.[43]

32   Transfer is therefore the key concept characterizing the forbidden operation. It should be noted that, in contrast to Article 49 paragraph 1, the text omits the word 'forcible'. Quite understandably, the drafters proceeded from the assumption that settlement activities unfold in a manner which is essentially different from measures of removal taken to the detriment of the population in an occupied territory. Few states, if any, could ever order persons of their own nationality to establish themselves outside the national boundaries. Forcible measures could hardly attain the aim pursued; they would deter rather than attract the potential addressees. In any event, in a democratic state under the rule of law, the right of abode in the national territory pertains to the core rights of citizenship.[44]

---

[40] Same view by Y. Arai-Takahashi, *The Law of Occupation: Continuity and Change of International Humanitarian Law, and its Interaction with International Human Rights Law* (Leiden/Boston, Mass: Martinus Nijhoff, 2009), at 346–7; Y. Dinstein, *The International Law of Belligerent Occupation* (Cambridge: CUP, 2009), at 239, para 572.
[41] Arai-Takahashi, above n 40; Dinstein, above n 40.
[42] Rightly, the Italian delegate Maresca said that the word 'deportation' would have better not been used—Final Record, vol II-A, at 664.
[43] Pictet Commentary GC IV, at 283.
[44] See, e.g., Art 12 ICCPR.

It is clear from the plain meaning of the word 'transfer', however, that governmental 33
authorities must play an active role in organizing the population movement. They can do
so in various ways. While a narrow reading might suggest that the nationals concerned
must be transported to the envisaged settlements, such formalism would miss the purpose
of the ban. A transfer may also be brought about by subtler methods, in particular by
promises of higher earnings, by tax incentives, by investment in infrastructure, and by
other means capable of inducing persons to establish themselves in an environment that
is originally alien to them. From the perspective of the intended protection of the population in an occupied territory, such 'soft' strategies must also be deemed to be included in
the scope of the prohibition.[45] Herbert J. Hansell, Legal Adviser of the Department of
State, in a letter dated 21 April 1978, mentioned explicitly such activities as 'determining
the location of settlements, making land available and financing of settlements, as well
as other kinds of assistance and participation in their creation'.[46] In its Advisory Opinion
in the *Wall* case, the ICJ has made clear that Article 49 paragraph 6 covers also instances
where a government confines itself to encouraging settlements in occupied territory.[47]

No clue can be found in Article 49 paragraph 6 to the effect that the prohibition is 34
solely intended to protect the local population from displacement. Referring to the classic
textbook by Oppenheim and Lauterpacht,[48] the Israeli Government defended that view in
a public statement of 1 December 1996 that has never been revoked.[49] The Legal Counsel
of the US Department of State had rejected that restrictive interpretation many years
earlier.[50] In the legal literature, the official Israeli viewpoint has not found any support.[51]

e. Non-state actors

Strategies employed by private organizations to support settlement initiatives may also fall 35
within the scope of the ban. It has been amply demonstrated by the Israeli non-governmental
organization (NGO) B'Tselem that universal Jewish organizations have made huge
amounts of financial resources available with a view to facilitating the establishment of
Israeli settlements in the West Bank. Generally, one must not lose sight of the fact that the
obligations contained in GC IV are addressed to the states parties, i.e. to states and not to
non-state actors. However, in the case of the Jewish organizations that channel funds to the
occupied territories, close connections exist with the state of Israel. These organizations do
not act in an autonomous fashion but in cooperation with governmental authorities.[52] The
present chapter is not the place to discuss the degree and the extent of that cooperation. It
should only be stated in general terms that, by indirectly fostering a settlement project, the
state concerned may also commit a breach of Article 49 paragraph 6. Thus, it will not be
the non-state actor that incurs responsibility by providing financial means; only the state
concerned can be held accountable if it acts in connivance with a private organization.

---

[45] Arai-Takahashi, above n 40, at 347; Ben-Naftali et al, above n 32, at 581; J. Quigley, 'Living in Legal Limbo: Israel's Settlers in Occupied Palestinian Territory', 10 *Pace International Law Review* (1998) 1, at 14.
[46] 6 *Digest of United States Practice in International Law* (1978) 1575, at 1577.
[47] Above n 1, at 183, para 120.
[48] L. Oppenheim, *International Law: A Treatise*, ed H. Lauterpacht (2nd edn, London: Longmans, 1952), vol II, at 452.
[49] Middle East Facts, 'Israel's Settlements—Their Conformity with International Law' (December 1996), available at <http://www.mefacts.com/cached.asp?x_id=10163>. [50] Above n 46, at 1577.
[51] W.T. Mallison and S.V. Mallison, *The Palestine Problem in International Law and World Order* (Harlow: Longman, 1986), at 264–5; Quigley, above n 45, at 15.
[52] See 2002 Report by B'Tselem, above n 23, at 21.

36   Truly individual activities by private persons taking up residence in a territory occupied by their home state also require consideration. It may indeed well be that someone decides spontaneously to conduct his future life in an occupied territory, in particular in circumstances as they are known from Northern Cyprus and the West Bank, where the occupation has continued for decades and seems endless. Taking into account the fact that the word 'transfer' requires some kind of state activity, one is inclined to deny the applicability of the prohibition.[53] Yet such 'innocent' conduct is more a theoretical construct than an actual reality. Israel has in fact established a comprehensive framework of regulations and measures that make existence in one of the settlements established in the West Bank particularly advantageous, compared to the situation in Israel's regular national territory. A separate assessment would be required of instances where Jewish settlers return to places from which they were expelled in connection with the violence that surrounded the birth of the state of Israel in 1948.

37   The words 'deportation' and 'transfer' suggest that the prohibition focuses exclusively on a sojourn of long duration. Visits to an occupied territory are not covered. As long as persons remain there for only a few days, without relocating the centre of their private existence, the threat involved in a true settlement does not materialize. On the other hand, even provisional establishment under tents and in caravans is not exempted from the scope *ratione materiae* of Article 49 paragraph 6. In the Palestinian territories, many times such provisional structures were soon converted into solid shelters, and thereafter into conventional homes.

f. Duty of prevention?

38   It would probably go too far to contend that the Occupying Power has a general duty to prevent any one of its nationals from seeking establishment in an occupied territory. Article 49 paragraph 6 requires some form of active conduct on the part of the Occupying Power. To include sheer passivity within the scope of the provisions would amount to an excessive extension of its scope of application *ratione materiae*, not in harmony with the natural meaning of the text.

39   In general, an Occupying Power will commit a breach of Article 49 paragraph 6 by providing a favourable legal and factual framework for settlement in occupied territory. Transfer need not be carried out collectively in the physical form of transport. If a general framework benefiting settlers has been created, even individual residential changes spread over a longer period will meet the conditions laid down in Article 49 paragraph 6.

II. Restriction and/or justification

a. Security

40   As already pointed out, Article 49 paragraph 6 is couched in strict language. The command it enunciates contains no element of flexibility. No deportation or transfer 'shall' take place. Moreover, no restriction clause has been added to the provision.[54] Therefore, no occupation power can argue that derogations were rendered necessary

---

[53] Attention was drawn to that configuration by Y. Dinstein, 'The International Law of Belligerent Occupation and Human Rights', 8 *IsrYBHR* (1978) 104, at 124.

[54] For an examination of all the justifications invoked by the Israeli Government, see Mallison and Mallison, above n 51, at 244–62.

by security reasons. In any event, it would be difficult to contend that population transfers increase the security of occupation forces. Common sense suggests that any such transfers increase tensions and are therefore likely to affect the security situation in a negative way.

In the *Wall* case, Israel's settlement policy did not constitute the central issue. However, it emerged clearly that the wall had been built in order to increase the security of the Israeli settlers established in the occupied territories.[55] The first interference in contravention of Article 49 paragraph 6 entailed other far-reaching measures detrimental to the rights and interests of the local Palestinian population. The ICJ did not accept Israel's line of reasoning, observing that the prohibition established in Article 49 paragraph 6 was rigorous.[56] However, the Israeli Supreme Court took the view that the purpose of strengthening the security of Israeli settlements provided a sufficient justification for the course of the wall in those places.[57] The consideration that the duty of protection incumbent upon state authorities is owed to every human being, irrespective of nationality, is certainly correct, not only under the constitutional law of Israel but also under international human rights law (IHRL),[58] but cannot be reconciled with the strict language of Article 49 paragraph 6. International humanitarian law and IHRL complement and do not mutually exclude one another.[59] According to the logic of the Israeli Supreme Court, any settlement sets in motion a chain of events which then requires a continuous increase in security devices. Every breach of a key norm of IHL would at the same time serve as its own justification.

b. Military necessity

Under humanitarian law, the concept of military necessity can have no relevance within the context of Article 49 paragraph 6. Military necessity may be invoked to different grades and degrees in situations of actual armed conflict. Yet since the transfer of settlers can take place only after armed hostilities have ended and the Occupying Power has consolidated its control over the territory where it exercises its temporary jurisdiction, justifications relating to combat activities cannot be invoked.[60]

c. National emergency

Similarly, a national emergency, which is routinely provided for in international human rights treaties, cannot be adduced to justify departures from the prohibition under Article 49 paragraph 6. All the rules of humanitarian law cover emergency situations, namely, situations of armed conflict. They constitute a minimum threshold which may in no circumstances be undercut. Moreover, the occupation has become a status of quasi-normalcy.[61]

---

[55] ICJ, *Wall* Advisory Opinion, above n 1, at 168, para 80, 182, para 116.
[56] Ibid, at 183–4, para 120.
[57] Supreme Court of Israel, *Beit Sourik Village Council v Government of Israel*, HCJ 2056/04, Judgment, 30 June 2004, available at <http://elyon1.court.gov.il/Files_ENG/04/560/020/A28/04020560.A28.pdf>, at 16–8, paras 28–32; *Mara'abe v The Prime Minister of Israel*, HCJ 7957/04, Judgment, 15 September 2005, available at <http://elyon1.court.gov.il/Files_ENG/04/570/079/A14/04079570.A14.pdf>, at 12–5, paras 18–20.
[58] See O. Ben-Naftali and Y. Shany, 'Living in Denial: The Application of Human Rights in the Occupied Territories', 37 *Israel Law Review* (2003–2004) 17.
[59] ICJ, *Wall* Advisory Opinion, above n 1, at 178 para 106; ICJ, *Armed Activities on the Territory of the Congo (DRC v Uganda)*, Judgment, 19 December 2005, 168, at 243, para 216.
[60] ICJ, *Wall* Advisory Opinion, above n 1, at 192, para 135.
[61] Rejection of the emergency argument also by Ben-Naftali et al, above n 32, at 606–8.

III. The ban on settlements as customary law

44 The prohibition set out in Article 49 paragraph 6 was established as a conventional norm within the general framework of GC IV. The question is whether it has crystallized as a rule of international customary law since the time of its appearance in 1949.[62] First of all, account must be taken of the fact that GC IV has been ratified by all states, which means that the Convention enjoys in general unanimous support in the international community. This tends to indicate that at the same time an *opinio juris* exists, in the sense required by Article 38(1)(b) of the Statute of the ICJ, one of the two constitutive elements of customary law. In the *Nicaragua* case, the ICJ found that Common Article 3 of the four Geneva Conventions had to be acknowledged as customary law since they constituted a minimum yardstick that had to be respected in all circumstances.[63] The exclusive focus on Common Article 3 cannot be taken to mean that none of the other provisions of the four Conventions has attained the quality of customary law. Although it is difficult to identify custom as a separate normative basis if a conventional obligation exists, the observer cannot fail to note that the ban on introducing settlers into occupied territory is for the time being universally respected, the only two factual departures being constituted by the practices of Turkey in Northern Cyprus and those of Israel in the occupied Palestinian territories. These practices have been consistently rejected by the responsible bodies of the UN as being contrary to international law. It should be recalled again that the US, a staunch supporter of Israel, has not shied away from denouncing Israel's settlement policy as contrary to international law. Indeed, the ban on settlements imposed on an Occupying Power is one of the pivotal rules of the entire regime of belligerent occupation. It corresponds to the pressing need to preserve the right of self-determination of a people temporarily deprived of its own governmental apparatus. Eventually, therefore, the Israeli Government stands alone in contending that it is living up to all of its commitments under the law of occupation, and denying the customary law nature of Article 49 paragraph 6.

45 Two specific strategies have been developed by Israel with a view to demonstrating that its settlement policies are in full accord with the requirements of international law. On the one hand, it is contended that the territories in issue do not constitute occupied territories in a legal sense, since the Palestinian entity lacks any clearly defined boundary lines. On the other hand, Israel relies heavily on the doctrine of the persistent objector.

46 Although many textbooks on international law still show certain sympathy for the doctrine of the persistent objector, it has never been fully endorsed by the ICJ. The Court's observations in the *Asylum* case[64] and in the *Norwegian Fisheries* case[65] are no more than *obiter dicta*, not real *rationes decidendi*. The development of the law of the sea in particular has shown that no state can effectively prevent the emergence of a customary rule

---

[62] Explicitly affirmed by the ICRC CIHL Study, vol I, at 462 (Rule 130); see also Mallison and Mallison, above n 51, at 262; A. Cassese, 'Powers and Duties of an Occupant in Relation to Land and Natural Resources', in Playfair (ed), above n 32, 419, at 431, 436. See also the (inconclusive) discussion by M. Qupty, 'The Application of International Law in the Occupied Territories as Reflected in the Judgments of the High Court of Justice in Israel', in Playfair (ed), above n 32, 87, at 111–16.

[63] ICJ, *Military and Paramilitary Activities in and against Nicaragua (Nicaragua v US)*, Judgment (Merits), 27 June 1986, 14, at 114, paras 218–20.

[64] ICJ, *Asylum* case *(Columbia v Peru)*, Judgment, 20 November 1950, 266, at 277–8.

[65] ICJ, *Fisheries* case *(United Kingdom v Norway)*, Judgment, 18 December 1951, 116, at 131.

supported by a broad majority of the international community. While in the 1960s the territorial sea was limited to three miles, and while no exclusive economic zone existed, the codification of the law brought about profound changes for all states, even those that had not ratified the Law of the Sea Convention. No state was able to object to the extension of the territorial sea to 12 miles, and no state was powerful enough to halt the claims of the coastal states to 'their' exclusive economic zones. Hence, it may safely be concluded that the opposition of just one or two states is not enough to enable them to carve out for themselves a niche with regard to precepts which they reject on grounds of specific subjective interests.[66] Advocates of the persistent objector doctrine forget that Article 38(1)(b) of the Statute of the ICJ requires a general practice accepted not unanimously but only by a 'widespread and representative' majority of the members of the international community.[67] In sum, the non-recognition by Israel of the settlement ban established by Article 49 paragraph 6 does not prevent that ban from crystallizing as customary law.

C. Relevance in Non-International Armed Conflicts

47 In a situation of non-international armed conflict (NIAC), Article 49 paragraph 6 cannot be applied. On the one hand, Article 49 paragraph 6 is not reflected in the 'convention in miniature' contained in Common Article 3. On the other hand, the aim of the provision is to avert attempts to colonize the population of a foreign country. Essentially, in a NIAC, people of the same nation wage war against each other. There can be no artificial barriers against freedom of movement within the territory of one nation. Eventually, internal armed conflict will end with some kind of national reconciliation re-establishing conditions of normality. What is appropriate if an Occupying Power temporarily takes control over (parts of) a foreign territory is accordingly not the right remedy if armed conflict takes place on national territory between different groups of one and the same nation. The modern tendency to equate the rules governing international armed conflict (IAC) and those governing NIAC finds here a natural limit on account of the specific purpose of the prohibition.[68]

D. Breaches of Other Norms of International Law

I. Self-determination—right to the homeland

48 Breaches of Article 49 paragraph 6 GC IV may at the same time breach other principles and rules of international law. In its Advisory Opinion in the *Wall* case, the ICJ held that the building of the wall on Palestinian territory amounted to a violation of the right of self-determination of the Palestinian people. This conclusion is generally applicable. If an occupant introduces settlers into the territories controlled by it, it makes structural determinations on the future of those territories by changing the demographic foundations.

---

[66] For a more detailed discussion, see C. Tomuschat, 'Obligations Arising for States without or against their Will', 241 *RCADI* (1993-IV) 195, at 284–90.
[67] ICJ, *North Sea Continental Shelf*, Judgment, 20 February 1969, 3, at 42 para 73, 43, para 74; ICJ, *Nicaragua* case, above n 63, at 98, para 186.
[68] For further discussion on the non-applicability of the rules on occupation to NIAC, see Ch 67, MN 57, of this volume.

Such fundamental changes may not be brought about by an Occupying Power.[69] To decide on admission to the national territory and the composition of the population is one of the core prerogatives of the legitimate government.

49   Almost inevitably, the implantation of settlers is accompanied by measures designed to provide them with accommodation and land. In the world of today, there are nowhere any 'empty spaces' that could be distributed freely. Obviously, settlers need room in order to ensure their livelihood. Northern Cyprus and the Palestinian territories are illustrative cases in point. In Northern Cyprus, almost all Greek Cypriots were expelled or had to flee in connection with the Turkish invasion in 1974. The Turkish authorities then established schemes for the distribution of the land left behind—involuntarily—by its Greek owners. In respect of the Palestinian territories, no massive displacement of the local Arab population took place. However, step by step, with the support of the Israeli Government and the courts, large areas were set aside for settlement by Israeli nationals. Today, it seems that only a small percentage of the occupied territory is actually inhabited by those newcomers, but they have established patterns which significantly disturb the contiguity of the areas inhabited by the indigenous Palestinian population.[70] On the other hand, a much larger area is placed under the jurisdiction of the settlements. Israeli authors Ben-Naftali, Gross, and Michaeli write of 59 per cent.[71] According to a report by UN Human Rights Council Special Rapporteur Richard A. Falk, there are currently more than 100 'outposts' in the Palestinian territories in addition to 120 official settlements.[72] A recent UN report shows that the envisaged two-state solution is close to definitive frustration.[73]

II. Land rights

50   The official strategy of resettlement inevitably involves the risk of violation of the guarantee of private property under GC IV and under human rights law.[74] The ECHR encompasses such a guarantee in Article 1 of its First Protocol.[75] As already pointed out, the ECtHR has held in a number of judgments, in particular in *Loizidou* and *Xenides-Arestis*, that by denying the Greek Cypriots now living in the non-occupied part of the country access to their properties, some of which were allocated to Turkish settlers, an infringement of Article 1 of the Protocol was committed, in addition to a violation of Article 8 ECHR (right to respect for private and family life, which includes the home). Turkey elaborated plans to settle the issue by proceeding to an exchange of the plots of land concerned, but originally these plans were not accepted by the Cypriot Government, which saw them as an attempt to seal the partition of the island definitively into two ethnically and territorially divided communities.

---

[69] See, e.g., Pellet, above n 32, at 180–94.

[70] See B'Tselem, *Under the Guise of Legality: Israel's Declarations of State Land in the West Bank* (February 2012), available at <http://www.btselem.org/download/201203_under_the_guise_of_legality_eng.pdf>, 15–8.

[71] Ben-Naftali et al, above n 32, at 580.

[72] R.A. Falk, Report on the Situation of Human Rights in the Palestinian Territories Occupied since 1967, UN Doc A/HRC/20/32, 25 May 2012, 13 para 29.

[73] Report of the independent international fact-finding mission to investigate the implications of the Israeli settlements on the civil, political, economic, social and cultural rights of the Palestinian people throughout the Occupied Palestinian Territory, including East Jerusalem, UN Doc A/HRC/22/63, 7 February 2013.

[74] For the protection of private property under GC IV, see Ch 71 of this volume.

[75] 'Every natural or legal person is entitled to the peaceful enjoyment of his possessions.'

The 'Annan Plan' of 2004[76] devoted a lengthy chapter (Annex VII) to the settlement 51 of the property issue. It abstained from requiring that the prior situation should in all circumstances be restored. With regard to many instances, it provided for compensation to the benefit of the dispossessed owners. Implicitly, it accepted that the settlers having arrived from mainland Turkey should be entitled to stay on the island.[77] Whether these proposals embodied a just balance between the interests of all stakeholders was hotly disputed. It is common knowledge that while in a referendum held on 24 April 2004 the Plan was accepted by the Turkish Cypriots in the north by a majority of 65 per cent, the Greek Cypriot population in the south rejected it by a large majority of 76 per cent.

The mechanism of the IPC (see MN 18), established in 2005 by the legislative authorities in the TRNC through Law 67/2005, may eventually bring an end to the long-term dispute about the expropriation of property belonging to the Greek Cypriots in the north of the island. In *Demopoulos*, the ECtHR accepted that system. It admitted that reparation did not necessarily consist of restitution, alternative forms of exchange of properties and payment of compensation also satisfying the requirements of the guarantee of property enshrined in Article 1 of Protocol 1.[78] Accordingly, claimants, in order to satisfy the requirement of prior exhaustion of local remedies, must first attempt to reach a settlement with the IPC, which may order one of those measures. 52

As far as the occupied Palestinian territories are concerned, there are protections 53 under IHL,[79] although no human rights treaty guarantee of private property applies. The International Covenant on Civil and Political Rights (ICCPR) does not include such a guarantee, owing to the circumstances prevailing at the time of the adoption of the Covenant in 1966, which was a period aptly characterized as the 'Cold War'. Regarding the protection of property, no compromise between the socialist world, on the one hand, and the market economy ('capitalist') countries, on the other, could be achieved.

III. Other rights

In its Advisory Opinion on the *Wall* case, the ICJ observed that the building of the wall 54 had led to infringement of many other human rights, in particular freedom of movement and social and economic rights, i.e.: the rights to work, to health, to education, and to an adequate standard of living, as proclaimed in the International Covenant on Economic, Social and Cultural Rights and in the UN Convention on the Rights of the Child.[80] Obviously, these negative consequences have not been caused directly by the introduction of settlers but through the construction of the wall. On the other hand, it cannot be overlooked that the building of that defence line has as its primary objective the improvement of the security of the settlers. Accordingly, the violations found by the ICJ can all be traced back to the settlement policy of the Israeli Government.

---

[76] The Comprehensive Settlement of the Cyprus Problem, 31 March 2004, available at <http://www.zypern.cc/extras/annan-plan-for-cyprus-2004.pdf>.
[77] Annex III: Federal Laws, Attachment 4: Federal Law on the Citizenship of the United Cyprus Republic and for Matters Connected Therewith or Connected Thereto. For a detailed discussion of the fate of the settlers, see Ronen, above n 8, at 222–6.
[78] ECtHR, *Demopoulos*, above n 29, paras 115–18.   [79] See Ch 71 of this volume.
[80] ICJ, *Wall* Advisory Opinion, above n 1, at 191–2, para 134.

E. Remedies

I. Procedural remedies

a. Remedies under international humanitarian law

55 It is the general weakness of IHL that it provides for only few remedies. Accordingly, violations of Article 49 paragraph 6 cannot be brought before an international body specifically entrusted with supervising compliance with GC IV. Investigations by the International Fact-Finding Commission under Article 90 AP I are of no avail in the present context. Both in Northern Cyprus and in the Palestinian territories the relevant facts normally need no specific elucidation. At issue is the interpretation of the rules of humanitarian law, as well as the enforcement of the consequences entailed by breaches of those rules according to general international law. Within the framework of IHL, neither the states involved nor the individuals affected by measures prohibited under Article 49 paragraph 6 can bring their grievances to a competent international judicial authority.

b. Application to the International Court of Justice

56 To the extent that states have accepted the jurisdiction of the ICJ under Article 36 of the ICJ Statute, applications may be brought against an alleged wrong-doing state by a state that has sustained injury. This opportunity arises only rarely. The relevant humanitarian treaties lack any jurisdictional clauses, the states parties having always been extremely reluctant generally to submit to the jurisdiction of the ICJ with regard to occurrences of armed conflict. Moreover, unilateral declarations of acceptance of the jurisdiction of the ICJ have mostly been limited by reservations excluding any such occurrences from the ambit of the acceptance.[81] As a consequence, only few cases the subject matter of which was armed conflict have been adjudicated by the ICJ.[82] It cannot be expected that this state of affairs will change in the foreseeable future.

c. Recourse to the courts of the Occupying Power

57 Persons having sustained damage from the implantation of foreign settlers in their territory may be granted a remedy before the courts of the Occupying Power. Obviously, such remedies can have no great chances of success, since by definition it is the official policy of the government concerned to organize or support the settlement strategy. It depends entirely on the Occupying Power whether it is prepared to open its judicial system to claims arising in that connection. Many states exclude from the scope of jurisdiction of their judiciary disputes having their origin in the activities of their armed forces abroad. Or else their legislation provides for specific regulation of damages resulting from such activities.[83]

58 Regarding Northern Cyprus, since 2005 a practicable redress mechanism has been in operation.[84] In the case of the Palestinian territories, Israel permits applications to be

---

[81] See C. Tomuschat, 'Article 36', in A. Zimmermann, C. Tomuschat, K. Oellers-Frahm, and C. Tams (eds), *The Statute of the International Court of Justice: A Commentary* (2nd edn, Oxford: OUP, 2012) 633, at 690, para 98.

[82] ICJ, *DRC v Uganda*, above n 59.

[83] The US Federal Tort Claims Act (1948), which derogates from the general principle of state immunity, establishes that no claim may be brought that arises 'out of the combatant activities of the military or naval forces', 28 USC § 2680 (j).

[84] See MN 52.

brought against the responsible national authorities. Although this is a laudable effort to guarantee the rule of law, this opening up of judicial protection has not led to ensuring respect for the prohibition under Article 49 paragraph 6. Several grounds explain this failure. Primarily, the Israeli courts do not apply GC IV directly. The argument used by them is founded on the lack of a domestic law incorporating the Convention.[85] Pursuant to the prevailing doctrine in Israel, international treaties, in order to become internally applicable, require a specific legislative act of approval and incorporation. With a view to closing the lacuna thus produced, the judges of the Supreme Court resort to the 1949 Geneva Conventions as general principles of humanitarian law. They hold, however, that the rule of Article 49 paragraph 6 does not belong to that restricted body of law. Moreover, as already pointed out, the Israeli courts take the view that in any event a military commander is entitled to adopt measures with a view to guaranteeing public order and security, including expropriation. In any case, since GC IV is deemed to be domestically inapplicable, not a single judgment has openly addressed the issue of compatibility of the settlement strategy with Article 49 paragraph 6.[86] This method of avoidance has enabled the Supreme Court to steer away from a clash that would have brought it into direct conflict with the executive power.

d. Recourse to the courts of third states

59 As an ultimate recourse, victims of displacement and expropriation have started bringing their claims to courts of third countries. A Greek Cypriot (Meleti(o)s Apostolides) who had learned, after the opening in 2003 of the border between the two separated parts of the island, that a British couple had bought his property in the north from someone who had acquired it from the de facto authorities controlling that area under the colour of TRNC, brought an application against the buyers before the courts in the south. The District Court of Nicosia held that the buyers had indeed committed a tort by acquiring property that belonged to a third person and building a house on the plot of land. The District Court followed the submissions of the applicant, ordering the respondent to demolish the house, vacate the land, and pay to the applicant special damages. An appeal by the respondents was dismissed.[87]

60 Since judgments of the legitimate Cypriot courts are not recognized in the north of the island, the applicant sought to enforce the judgment against the respondents in England. He submitted the judgment to the High Court of Justice of England and Wales, which ordered that the judgment be enforceable under EU Regulation No 44/2001, an enactment providing for the mutual recognition of judgments in civil matters. After the respondents had filed an appeal against that declaration, the Court of Appeal made a reference to the Court of Justice of the European Union (CJEU). In its judgment of 28 April 2009, the CJEU found that all the requirements of Regulation 44/2001 were met and that none of the derogation clauses permitted a refusal of recognition and enforcement of the judgment rendered in Cyprus.[88] The CJEU did not address the background of the case,

---

[85] Israel, Supreme Court, *Ayub v Minister of Defence (Beit El case)*, Judgment, HCJ 606/78, 15 March 1979, 9 *IsrYBHR* (1979) 337, at 341; *D(u)weikat v Government of Israel (Elon Moreh case)*, Judgment, HCJ 390/79, 22 October 1979, 9 *IsrYBHR* (1979) 345, available at <http://www.hamoked.org/files/2010/1670_eng.pdf> (Justice Witkon, at 31). For a general overview, see Qupty, above n 62, *passim*, esp at 110.
[86] D. Kretzmer, *The Occupation of Justice: The Supreme Court of Israel and the Occupied Territories* (Albany, NY: State University of New York Press, 2002), at 43.
[87] CJEU, *Apostolides v Orams*, Case C-420/07, Judgment, 28 April 2009.
[88] Ibid.

since the Regulation expressly forbids review of judgments of other EU member states as to their substance (Article 36). No attention was devoted to the lawfulness of the transactions having taken place in Northern Cyprus.[89]

61 The case was then returned to the Court of Appeal in England, which decided in favour of the applicant. However, the respondents tried to appeal to the Supreme Court of the UK. On 26 March 2010, the UK Supreme Court refused permission to take the case to appeal, effectively bringing it to a conclusion. According to press reports, the respondents abandoned their property rather than demolish it.[90] In the final analysis the British couple not only lost the property purchased in Cyprus, but also had to face measures of constraint at home in England for the recovery of the compensation awarded to the applicant.

62 It might be expected that other persons deprived of their property would follow suit in similar circumstances. However, the decision of the ECtHR in *Demopoulos*[91] will certainly have an impact on the jurisprudence of the CJEU. Since in Northern Cyprus an arrangement was found which has the blessing of the ECtHR, judgments that ignore the mechanism established in accordance with TRNC Law 67/2005 can no longer be recognized automatically in other EU member states. Plots of land the enjoyment of which was denied to the legitimate owners for many decades may no longer be considered as unlawfully taken if the owners did not make use of the remedies open to them for the recovery of their property.

63 Another attempt was made in Canada to sue an investment firm having its seat in Quebec, which operated in the real estate sector in the occupied Palestinian territories. By a Judgment of 18 September 2009, the action was dismissed, the Superior Court of the Province of Quebec, District of Montreal, holding that recourse to the Canadian judiciary was not the proper remedy (*forum non conveniens*).[92] The Court was of the view that the case in point should be handled by the Israeli High Court of Justice.

e. Remedies under human rights instruments

64 Wherever a state has adhered to an international human rights instrument, the relevant judicial or other complaint mechanisms may be resorted to. This holds true all over Europe where, with the exception of Belarus, all other states are parties to the ECHR. At worldwide level, recourse may be had to the Human Rights Committee under the ICCPR, or to the other expert bodies entrusted with jurisdiction to examine individual communications. It stands to reason that such bodies are not called upon to apply the rules of IHL but are confined to ensuring the rights enshrined in the instrument concerned. Accordingly, the implantation of settlers as such can never be the subject matter proper of such complaints. Their focus will have to be on the detrimental consequences for the local population, mainly through the taking of property in the occupied land.

---

[89] Neither did Advocate-General Juliane Kokott touch upon the issue in her Opinion of 18 December 2008.
[90] *Cyprus Mail*, 1 April 2010, available at <http://en.wikipedia.org/wiki/Apostolides_v_Orams>.
[91] ECtHR, *Demopoulos*, above n 29.
[92] Superior Court of the Province of Quebec, *Bil'In (Village Council) v Green Park International Inc*, Judgment, 18 September 2008, available at <http://citoyens.soquij.qc.ca/php/decision.php?liste=39887605&doc=0FB6ADF4D6C912C6AF300DBAD4E2C354A4831D66A546FCD5167EA497485443FF>.

II. Substantive remedies

According to the ILC Articles on Responsibility of States for Internationally Wrongful Acts,[93] reparation is to be effected by restitution, compensation, and/or satisfaction (Article 34). Among these forms of reparation, restitution is the primary remedy. As a consequence, settlers unlawfully introduced into foreign territory under occupation would have to leave immediately, at the latest at the end of the occupation period. The application of this rule encounters serious difficulties in cases of long-term occupation, where persons have spent large parts of their lives 'unlawfully' in a social environment that has become their 'home'. With the passage of time, even settlers acquire rights of which they cannot be deprived automatically.[94] The judgments of the ECtHR in *Slivenko*[95]—where issues of a right of abode were examined—and in *Demopoulos*—where the form of reparation was in issue—indicate quite clearly that under the impact of human rights guarantees, some degree of flexibility becomes imperative.[96] A balancing process must take place where the rule of reparation is to be weighed against the interests of the persons concerned.[97] In this connection, the prohibition on collective expulsion under ECHR Protocol 4, Article 4, also needs to be taken into account.

In light of the recent jurisprudence of the ECtHR, which reflects general principles of law, the Palestinians have actual grounds to fear that even a constructive negotiating process between them and Israel may not lead to the complete evacuation of all Israeli settlements from the occupied territories. Inevitably, the possession of large stretches of Palestinian territory by the settlers is a fact of life. Day by day, the settlements consolidate themselves by their sheer presence on the soil. On the other hand, the settlers know perfectly well that the construction of their dwellings stands in stark contrast to the applicable norms of IHL. In Israel, everyone became aware of the Advisory Opinion of the ICJ of 9 July 2004. Not one single person may argue that he established a home in the occupied territories in good faith. It may be assumed, therefore, that at the end of the day, a compromise solution which accepts the maintenance of some of the settlements is dictated not only by political wisdom, but also as the outcome of a balancing process in which due account is taken of the rights of the settlers.

F. Critical Assessment

Article 49 paragraph 6 GC IV is a key element of the regime of belligerent occupation under IHL. It cannot be said with any degree of certainty in how many armed conflicts it has been respected, preventing the implementation of settlements. Unfortunately, it has not been able to stem deliberate and systematic breaches, especially in two parts of the world in or close to Europe, namely, in Northern Cyprus and in the occupied Palestinian territory. As a consequence, major tensions of a dangerous intensity have arisen which structurally threaten peace in the world.

CHRISTIAN TOMUSCHAT

---

[93] Taken note of by UNGA Res 56/83, 12 December 2001.
[94] See Ronen, above n 8, at 239–42.
[95] ECtHR, *Slivenko*, above n 9.
[96] See, in this sense, also HRCttee, General Comment 27, 2 November 1999, para 14.
[97] For the pragmatic solutions eventually adopted in the Baltic states, see Ronen, above n 8, at 210–7.

Chapter 74. The Geneva Conventions and the End of Occupation

	MN
A. Introduction	1
B. Meaning and Application	4
I. Article 6 paragraph 3 GC IV	4
a. Historical justification	4
b. Contemporary reappraisal by the International Court of Justice's *Wall* Advisory Opinion of 2004	7
c. Factual elements to determine the starting point of the time period mentioned in Article 6 paragraph 3	9
II. Article 3 AP I	11
a. The views of the Diplomatic Conference of 1974–7	13
b. The alleged obsolescence of Article 6 paragraph 3	14
c. Article 3(b) AP I, a rule customary in nature?	19
III. Article 2 paragraph 2 common to the Geneva Conventions	21
IV. Article 47 GC IV	23
a. The inability of the Occupying Power to escape from its obligations due to an agreement on the end of occupation	24
b. The safeguard against the establishment of a 'puppet' government	25
c. The effects of Security Council Resolution 1546 regarding the end of occupation in Iraq	26
C. Relevance in Non-International Armed Conflicts	27
D. Legal Consequences of a Violation	28
E. Critical Assessment	29
a. The status of Gaza after September 2005, according to various authorities	33
b. The Gaza Strip, still occupied territory?	38

Select Bibliography

Alonzo-Maiylish, D., 'When Does It End? Problems in the Law of Occupation', in R. Arnold and P.-A. Hildbrand (eds), *International Humanitarian Law and the 21st Century's Conflicts: Changes and Challenges* (Lausanne: Editions interuniversitaires suisses, 2005) 97

Benvenisti, E., 'Occupation, Belligerent', in MPEPIL

Benvenisti, E., *The International Law of Occupation* (2nd edn, Oxford: OUP, 2012)

Gasser, H.-P., 'Protection of the Civilian Population', in D. Fleck (ed), *The Handbook of International Humanitarian Law* (2nd edn, Oxford: OUP, 2008) 501

ICRC, *Occupation and Other Forms of Administration of Foreign Territory, Expert Meeting* (Geneva: ICRC, 2012)

Imseis, A., 'Critical Reflections on the International Humanitarian Law Aspects of the ICJ *Wall* Advisory Opinion', 99 *AJIL* (2005) 102

Kolb, R./Vité, S., *Le droit de l'occupation militaire: perspectives historiques et enjeux juridiques actuels* (Brussels: Bruylant, 2009)

Koutroulis, V., *Le début et la fin de l'application du droit de l'occupation* (Paris: Pedone, 2010)

Quigley, J., 'The PLO–Israeli Interim Arrangements and the Geneva Civilians Convention', in S. Bowen (ed), *Human Rights, Self-Determination and Political Change in the Occupied Palestinian Territories* (The Hague: Martinus Nijhoff Publishers, 1997) 25

Roberts, A., 'Occupation, Military, termination of', in MPEPIL

Roberts, A., 'Prolonged Military Occupation', in E. Playfair (ed), *International Law and the Administration of Territories, Two Decades of Israeli Occupation of the West Bank and Gaza Strip* (Oxford: Clarendon Press, 1992) 25

Roberts, A., 'What Is a Military Occupation?', 55 *BYBIL* (1984) 249

Roberts, A., 'The End of Occupation: Iraq 2004', 54 *ICLQ* (2005) 27

Sassòli, M., 'Legislation and Maintenance of Public Order and Civil Life by Occupying Powers', 16 *EJIL* (2005) 661

Special Issue of the International Review of the Red Cross, 'Occupation', 94 *IRRC* 885 (2012)

A. Introduction

1 Determining when a situation of occupation has ended requires us first to consider the definition of occupation itself. This was undertaken in Chapter 67 of this volume and will therefore not be repeated here. Looking solely through the lens of the Geneva Conventions, the subject of the end of occupation necessitates a mention of three main Articles, all contained in Geneva Convention (GC) IV:

— Article 6 paragraph 3, which states generally that the rules of GC IV cease to apply one year after the general close of military operations, but which also provides for a longer application of certain specific provisions in cases of occupation lasting more than one year;
— Article 47, which limits the effects of any agreement that might be concluded in order to, inter alia, end an occupation; and lastly, as we shall see in more detail below,
— Article 2 paragraph 2, which deals with the specific situation of occupation arising without any armed resistance from the opposing side.

To this list, Article 3(b) of Additional Protocol (AP) I must be added.[1] Indeed, although this Commentary is limited to the Geneva Conventions, this provision of AP I must be addressed because there is a tendency to consider it as customary in nature. If so, Article 3(b) AP I has to be read together with Article 6 paragraph 3 GC IV.

2 All the provisions referred to above establish exceptions to the applicability of the relevant rules of international humanitarian law (IHL) when confronted with the moment at which an occupation ends. Occupation is either a particular international armed conflict (IAC) situation in which a belligerent exercises its authority over a territory, or a situation in which an army invades a territory and meets no resistance while establishing its authority over it. In both cases the Geneva Conventions apply to the situation, and are especially covered by Section III of Part III of GC IV. The rules contained in the Conventions and applicable to situations of occupation would be expected to cease to apply when the occupation comes to an end. The reality is, however, more complex than this. The first exception is found in Article 6 paragraph 3 GC IV, which provides that the Convention 'shall cease [to apply in occupied territory] *one year after* the general close of military operations'[2] and not simply *at* the general close of military operations, as would be the case

---
[1] Art 3(b) AP I, inter alia, extends the application of the GCs and AP I, as for occupied territories, up to the termination of occupation (instead of one year after the general close of military operations).
[2] Art 6 para 3 GC IV (emphasis added).

for IACs that do not involve occupation. Moreover, even beyond that period of time, 'the Occupying Power shall be bound, for the duration of the occupation, to the extent that such Power exercises the functions of government in such territory',[3] by certain provisions enumerated by Article 6 paragraph 3 itself. Additional Protocol I has formally attempted to erase this double exception set out in Article 6 paragraph 3 GC IV. There remain, however, some arguments in favour of keeping the two distinct provisions. Further still, when considering whether the law of occupation continues (or does not continue) to apply, yet another provision, which serves as a safeguard clause aimed at preventing the Occupying Power from circumventing its obligations through agreements with the Occupied Power, must be taken into account, namely Article 47 of GC IV.[4] All of these particular rules will be dealt with below.

Most of the literature on occupation remains quite limited as far as concerns the very moment at which an occupation may be said to have ended. At best, when considered, this moment is often simply described as occurring when the requisite elements determinative of the *beginning* of occupation disappear.[5] Some aspects of this discussion will be evoked in section E. below regarding a very specific situation—that of the Gaza Strip after the 'unilateral disengagement' of the Israeli Army completed in September 2005.

B. Meaning and Application

I. Article 6 paragraph 3 GC IV

a. Historical justification

Some are of the opinion that the drafters of GC IV made a mistake when they adopted Article 6 paragraph 3. From a purely protective point of view, there is no apparent reason to justify less extensive protection for inhabitants of occupied territories 12 months after the general close of military operations. Given the humanitarian motivations of delegations involved in the drafting of the Conventions in 1949, it would indeed be curious for them to have acted to limit the scope of certain provisions, and thereby reduce the protection afforded to civilians.

There was actually a very specific, historical reason for including this clause in Article 6 GC IV. This clause was absent from the first draft of the text of GC IV, which was submitted to the preparatory meeting held in Stockholm in 1948. However, during the Diplomatic Conference of 1949, the United States (US) Delegate, who distinguished between short-term and long-term occupation, was of the opinion that 'a prolonged military occupation [is], however, also characterized by a progressive return of governmental responsibilities to local authorities'.[6] According to him, '[t]he Occupying Power should be bound by the obligations of the Convention only during such time as the institutions

---

[3] Ibid.
[4] Art 47 GC IV essentially prevents protected persons who are in occupied territory from being deprived of their rights and safeguards laid down in the Convention.
[5] With the notable exception of the *IRRC* issue on Occupation with a contribution from T. Ferraro, 'Determining the Beginning and End of an Occupation under International Humanitarian Law', 94 *IRRC* 885 (2012) 133.
[6] Final Record, vol II-A, at 623.

of the occupied territory [are] unable to provide for the needs of the inhabitants'.[7] His reasoning was based on the examples of Japan and Germany. At the time he spoke, he considered that 'the responsibility of the Occupying Powers for the welfare of the local populations was far less at [that moment] than during the period immediately following hostilities'.[8] Not all delegates shared his view, but a compromise was reached with the help of a Norwegian proposal. The Norwegian delegation suggested not to distinguish between occupations that last a long period of time and those that are shorter, but rather to distinguish between, on the one hand, obligations that should cease to apply after a certain time period has elapsed and, on the other, obligations that should be upheld irrespective of the length of the occupation.[9] The wording of Article 6 paragraph 3 reflects this compromise.

6   Therefore, at the time, the drafters felt they had made a 'logical and judicious'[10] choice, which balanced the need to protect civilians from the effects of occupation with taking reality into account. They believed that in circumstances which would see an Occupying Power continue to exercise its authority over a territory beyond one year after the general close of military operations, 'the Occupying Power should gradually hand over the various powers it exercises, and the direction of the various administrative departments, to authorities consisting of nationals of the Occupied Power'.[11] This is why,

> in Section III of Part III [of the Fourth Convention], the most important from this point of view, only Articles 44–46 [Articles 48–50 GC IV], which concern movements of population occurring in time of war and those Articles which impose on the Occupying Power the duty of feeding the population and taking the hygienic measures which may continue to be necessary several months after the conclusion of hostilities, have been eliminated, for the latter (Articles 49–51 except 50c [Articles 55–57 GC IV]) cease to be justified as soon as the general situation has been more or less stabilized in collaboration with the local authorities.[12]

This is a perfect illustration of the compromise the Geneva Conventions intend to reach in their entirety, between, on the one hand, military necessity and, on the other, the protection of individuals.

b. Contemporary reappraisal by the International Court of Justice's Wall *Advisory Opinion of 2004*

7   As a result of the above, although the conclusion of the International Court of Justice (ICJ) that '[s]ince the military operations leading to the occupation of the West Bank in 1967 ended a long time ago, only those Articles of the Fourth Geneva Convention referred to in Article 6, paragraph 3, remain applicable in that occupied territory'[13] may have stirred emotions, it is not to be considered 'absurd'.[14] Or rather, if it were to be considered such, this would not be because '[t]he textual reading of Article 6, in which the Court engaged, generated the conclusion that long-term occupations reduce the responsibilities an Occupying Power has to shoulder *vis-à-vis* the occupied civilian population',[15]

---

[7] Ibid.   [8] Ibid.   [9] Ibid, at 624.
[10] Ibid, at 815.   [11] Ibid.   [12] Ibid, at 816.
[13] ICJ, *Legal Consequences of the Construction of a Wall in the Occupied Palestinian Territory*, Advisory Opinion, 9 July 2004 (*Wall* Advisory Opinion), para 125.
[14] This is the term used by O. Ben-Naftali, '"A la Recherche du temps perdu": Rethinking Article 6 of the Fourth Geneva Convention in the Light of the Legal Consequences of the Construction of a Wall in the Occupied Palestinian Territory Advisory Opinion', 38 *International Law Review* (2005) 211, at 214.
[15] Ibid.

but because the Court did not adopt the correct point of departure. Instead of taking the 'general close of military operations' into account, as is stated in Article 6 paragraph 3 GC IV, the Court strangely referred to the '[the end] of the military operations *leading to* the occupation of the West Bank in 1967'.[16] In other words, even if the Court's reasoning is in line with the rationale adopted by the drafters of the Geneva Conventions, which holds that a protracted occupation results in a lowered level of certain responsibilities of the Occupying Power, it nevertheless ignored the development of the situation after the 1967 conflict that led to the occupation. Instead, it merely considered the conditions under which Israel began its occupation of this territory. It therefore added a temporal specification that does not appear expressly in the text of the provision.

If one were to follow the Court's reasoning, using its point of departure—'the end of military operations that led to the occupation'—this would actually lead to the conclusion that the military operations have ceased. Israel has been occupying the West Bank and other territories since June 1967. As may be deduced from its name, the military operations relating to the 'Six Day War' ceased rather promptly. After having conducted offensive and defensive military operations against Egypt and Jordan, Israel quickly halted its progress and established its authority over territory, including the West Bank, becoming an Occupying Power in the sense of the Hague Regulations. What would the conclusion be, however, if we were to take as a starting point the phrase 'general close of military operations', which is strictly stipulated in the letter of Article 6 paragraph 3 GC IV? The phrase 'general close of military operations' refers to the point at which one can attest to 'the final end of all fighting between all those concerned'.[17] If we consider that in this case 'those concerned' are Israel and Jordan, we might conclude that military operations between these protagonists ceased 'a long time ago', in the words of the judges of The Hague. In any case, military operations had been terminated for well over a year, and therefore only some provisions remain applicable in the territory of the West Bank. This is one possible conclusion. It is relatively simple, and close to that of the ICJ. However, although it is indisputable that the military operations between Israel and Jordan terminated a long time ago, it is similarly uncontroversial that Israel has persisted in leading military operations against other protagonists since 1967. Thus, in the context of either a quasi-continuous armed conflict between Israel and its neighbouring Arab states, or one against the Palestinians, one scholar proposed to conclude that because the applicability of GC IV was triggered by the 1967 conflict—which one could consider as continuing or having resumed on account of the continuation or resumption of military operations—the power(s) responsible for armed activities continue to be bound to apply it (or alternatively, they resume their obligations under it) in its entirety.[18] This is a second possible conclusion. It may indeed be politically difficult to accept that, because of the protraction of the occupation, Israel is bound by only a limited number of provisions of GC IV. However, an argument like this one, based on military operations that are not directly related to the situation of occupation, or that are not opposing the original belligerents, nevertheless raises questions.

---

[16] ICJ, *Wall* Advisory Opinion, above n 13, para 125 (emphasis added).
[17] Pictet Commentary GC IV, at 62.
[18] See A. Imseis, 'Critical Reflections on the International Humanitarian Law Aspects of the ICJ *Wall* Advisory Opinion', 99 *AJIL* (2005) 102, at 106–7.

c. *Factual elements to determine the starting point of the time period mentioned in Article 6 paragraph 3*

i. **When does the 'general close of military operations' occur?**

9   Article 6 paragraph 3 provides that 'the application of the present Convention shall cease one year after the general close of military operations'. Therefore, in order to be able to determine when the stipulated period of one year begins, one must first consider when the 'general close of military operations' occurs. The concept of 'military operations' under IHL is very wide. It is impossible to find a universal general criterion that would accurately locate the very precise moment at which the 'general close of military operations' occurs. It is nevertheless possible to highlight a number of indicators that help in determining this moment. First, the extremely broad concept of 'military operations' must be distinguished from 'hostilities'. Secondly, the word 'general' is pivotal. If military operations involve more than two opposing parties, as long as some of them remain engaged in such operations, IHL will continue to apply in its entirety, notwithstanding any cessation of military operations among the other parties. What is decisive is whether or not the confrontation linked to a specific armed conflict ceases to exist. This explains why the findings of the ICJ in its *Wall* Advisory Opinion, according to which the element be taken into consideration is the '[the end] of the military operations leading to the occupation of the West Bank in 1967' and not simply the 'general close of military operations', have aroused a lively debate in doctrine.[19] Thirdly, a determination that the 'general close of military operations' has occurred is necessarily made *ex post* and over time. A minimum of time, incompressible and unquantifiable in the absolute, will always elapse before one is able to assert that the moment has arrived. A situation does not return to 'normal' suddenly but gradually. It is therefore generally a *set* of indicators, and not one event as such, that is to be taken into account in order to conclude that military operations have ceased. Lastly, the expression 'general close of military operations' should not be conflated with the concept of the 'end of (active) hostilities' which is employed in the Conventions where the drafters wanted to anticipate the end of application of IHL. While the term 'hostilities', in essence, refers to the use of force as such, 'military operations' refers to everything that contributes to the use of force.[20]

ii. **What does 'functions of government' mean?**

10   Another element of analysis regarding the end of applicability of the provisions of GC IV to occupied territories concerns the idea of exercising the functions of government, as Article 6 paragraph 3 further provides that, even one year after the general close of military operations, 'the Occupying Power shall be bound [by some provisions], for the duration of the occupation, to the extent that such Power exercises the functions of government in such territory'. As stated in the commentary on Article 5 of the International Law Commission (ILC) Articles on the Responsibility of States for Internationally Wrongful Acts, 'what is regarded as "governmental" depends on the particular society, its history and traditions'.[21] In international law, 'to govern' has a broad sense, covering acts that '[appartiennent] au

---

[19] See section B.II.b of this chapter.

[20] For detailed developments on the concept of 'military operations' and on the moment at which they end under IHL, see J. Grignon, *L'applicabilité temporelle du droit international humanitaire* (Zürich: Schulthess, 2014).

[21] Report of the Commission to the General Assembly on the work of its fifty-third session, *YILC* (2001), vol II, Part 2, at 43, para 7.

"gouvernement", au sens du droit international, non seulement les autorités exécutives de l'État, mais l'ensemble de ses "pouvoirs publics"'.[22] Thus, as long as an Occupying Power is capable of implementing its will over a territory, at least some provisions of GC IV applicable to Occupied Territories shall remain in force, even if the situation of occupation lasts more than one year after the general close of military operations.

II. Article 3 AP I

Regarding occupation, AP I of 1977 is innovative in two ways. First, in its structure, because, unlike GC IV, it no longer differentiates between Sections applicable to the territories of parties to the conflict and Sections applicable to occupied territories. Only certain provisions make express mention of occupied territories. Secondly, and more specifically regarding the end of occupation, it no longer refers to a gradual end of the applicability of the relevant rules of IHL. Rather, AP I rules on occupation stop being applicable 'on the termination of occupation'. The radical change of wording in Article 3(b) AP I, as well as the claims that this provision renders the former rule (contained in Article 6 paragraph 3 GC IV) inapplicable, warrant its analysis in this commentary, which otherwise primarily focuses on the Geneva Conventions and not the Additional Protocols.

The 'main effect [of Article 3(b)] is to extend the application [of the Geneva Conventions and AP I] in occupied territory beyond what is laid down in the fourth Convention'.[23] Even more radically, it has been stated that Article 6 paragraph 3 GC IV should not remain in force, considering it was adopted in order to take into account two ad hoc cases, those of Germany and Japan.[24] However, one major argument that may be advanced to counter those[25] who believe that the provision included in the Protocol replaces the rule of the Fourth Convention is simple, and is based on the fact that AP I applies only to states that are party to it. As such, it is binding on fewer states than the Geneva Conventions, which are universally ratified. As a result, whatever its merits, this change is limited in scope for as long as some states, which happen to be particularly concerned and affected by the consequences this change generates, are not parties to this Protocol. However, there is a trend towards supporting the argument according to which this rule would apply to all states parties to the Geneva Conventions and not only to the states parties to AP I (see sections B.II.b and c of this Chapter). Furthermore, as we shall now see, states that have not ratified AP I—notably Israel and the US—have, by various means, demonstrated a willingness to accept the later rule contained in the Protocol.

---

[22] P. Daillier and A. Pellet, *Droit international public* (8th edn, Paris: LGDJ, 2009), at 458 ('[belong] to the "government", under international law, not only executive authorities of the State but also all its "public powers"').

[23] ICRC Commentary APs, para 151.   [24] Bothe/Partsch/Solf, para 2.8, at 59.

[25] See, e.g., E. David, *Principes de droit des conflits armés* (3rd edn, Brussels: Bruylant, 2002), at 234, according to whom, 'L'art. 3, b du 1er PA a supprimé la limite d'un an à l'application de toute la 4e Convention en cas d'occupation de territoire: désormais, non seulement l'ensemble de la 4e Convention, mais aussi les 3 autres CG ainsi que le 1er PA s'appliquent à l'occupation militaire quelle qu'en soit la durée.' ('Art 3(b) of the First Additional Protocol supresses the one-year limit to the application of the entire 4th Convention in cases of occupation of territory: henceforth, not only the entirety of the 4th Convention, but also the three other Geneva Conventions as well as the First Additional Protocol, apply to military occupation, regardless of its duration.')

a. The views of the Diplomatic Conference of 1974–7

13   The *travaux préparatoires* behind AP I reveal that, as a whole, negotiating states very clearly manifested their desire to change the rule in Article 6 paragraph 3 GC IV, while the International Committee of the Red Cross (ICRC), which submitted a draft of AP I to the delegates, did not necessarily ask them to make this change. In fact, the initial draft submitted by the ICRC did not provide additional specificity with regard to the end of application of rules concerning occupation, but noted instead that 'the article related only to the application of Protocol I and was not meant to supplement the provisions of the 1949 Geneva Conventions regarding the beginning and end of their application'.[26] Yet during negotiations, the opposite idea emerged and was ultimately adopted in Article 3(b) AP I, with wording that clearly refers not only to the applicability of the Protocol, but also to the applicability of the Geneva Conventions. The provision states unequivocally, 'the application of the Conventions and of this Protocol shall cease, in the territory of Parties to the conflict, on the general close of military operations and, in the case of occupied territories, on the termination of the occupation'. Israel and the US participated actively in the negotiations of 1974–7. It should even be noted that Israel, supported by the US, strongly advocated the introduction of a provision clearly envisaging the prolongation of the applicability of IHL as far as possible, to ensure protection of those affected by armed conflict and even of those who find themselves *hors de combat* after the end of armed conflict.[27] This followed from a desire to see the rules on occupation of GC IV and AP I apply as long as the situation requires, which might, if necessary, go well beyond the end of the armed conflict. 174 states are parties to AP I.[28] The US, for its part, has signed the instrument.

b. The alleged obsolescence of Article 6 paragraph 3

14   Among the converging pillars of evidence leading to the conclusion that Article 6 paragraph 3 GC IV is obsolete, one might include the positions taken by Israel and certain third countries in instances where this issue has been brought up before the courts.

15   It should first be noted that Israel, in defending itself before the Israeli Supreme Court, has never argued the applicability of only a certain set of IHL rules on occupation. Instead, its arguments operate at a completely different level, denying the applicability of GC IV in its entirety. It could have invoked partial application of GC IV in subsidiary arguments—to prepare for the possibility that the court might decide to apply GC IV and other IHL rules on occupied territories—but it did not do so.

16   Another argument in favour of considering Article 6 paragraph 3 GC IV as obsolete has been advanced in connection with the ICJ's *Wall* Advisory Opinion. None of the states that submitted written statements expressed the view that only the specific rules mentioned in Article 6 paragraph 3 itself remained applicable in the occupied West Bank. One scholar has argued that this demonstrates that, according to these states, IHL relative to occupied territories (including all the relevant rules enshrined in GC

---

[26] *Official Records of the Diplomatic Conference on the Reaffirmation and Development of the International Humanitarian Law Applicable in Armed Conflicts* (Geneva, 1974–7), vol VIII, at 60.
[27] See the positions taken by Mr Rosenne, representing the Israeli Delegation at the Diplomatic Conference of 1974–7, *Official Records* above n 26, vol VIII, at 15.
[28] Available at <http://www.icrc.org/applic/ihl/ihl.nsf/Treaty.xsp?documentId=D9E6B6264D7723C3C12563CD002D6CE4&action=openDocument>.

IV) continues to apply in its entirety for the duration of the occupation.[29] Indeed, it is true that, with the notable exception of the written statement submitted by the League of Arab States, there is no mention of Article 6 GC IV in any of the other statements submitted by states to the Court.[30] It is equally true that some states, arguing for the applicability of IHL, held that certain articles not included in the listing under paragraph 3 of Article 6 should also apply. However, there is no indication that such states, at the moment they submitted their written statements, considered that military operations had ceased after a period of one year.

For its part, the League of Arab States held that '[t]he application of the Fourth Convention once being established, the relevant provisions continue to be applicable according to art. 6 of the Convention'.[31] However, it further stated that Articles 50, 55, and 56 GC IV were violated by Israel's actions in the West Bank. Since these particular provisions are among those which, under Article 6 paragraph 3, cease to apply one year after the general close of military operations, if the League of Arab States considered Article 6 paragraph 3 to be applicable, it would not then have referred to what in its opinion amounted to a breach of the aforementioned provisions. It is unclear whether the League, by using the phrase 'the relevant provisions', meant to refer to the provisions violated in this particular case, or to the provisions that continue to apply until the end of occupation. Should its claim that these provisions apply 'according to Article 6' be understood to imply that it considers paragraph 3 of that Article to be with effect, or does this phrase simply refer to the existence of a specific rule providing guidelines for the end of occupation? Without more, it is difficult to determine the intentions of the League.[32] Nevertheless, from the above, it is clear that states do not avail themselves of Article 6 paragraph 3, but the language used by the League of Arab States does not automatically lead to the conclusion that states now expressly consider Article 3(b) AP I as applicable to all situations of occupation.

At the Conference of High Contracting Parties to the Fourth Geneva Convention held in 2001, states adopted a Declaration of which point 12 reads as follows:

> The participating High Contracting Parties call upon the Occupying Power to fully and effectively respect the Fourth Geneva Convention in the Occupied Palestinian Territory, including East Jerusalem, and to refrain from perpetrating any violation of the Convention [...][33]

It could be inferred from this that paragraph 3 of Article 6 no longer has a *raison d'être*, and that the Fourth Convention should be 'fully' respected. Except, yet again, without explicit reference to either Article 6 GC IV, or to Article 3(b) AP I, it is difficult to conclude unambiguously that, first, these states considered that there had been a general close of military operations and, secondly, that according to them, and despite this fact, the Fourth Convention should continue to apply in its entirety.

---

[29] See V. Koutroulis, *Le début et la fin de l'application du droit de l'occupation* (Paris: Pedone, 2010), at 171.
[30] All of the written statements are accessible online on the ICJ's Website, at <http://www.icj-cij.org/docket/index.php?p1=3&p2=4&k=5a&case=131&code=mwp&p3=1>.
[31] ICJ, *Wall* Advisory Opinion, above n 13, Written statement of the League of Arab States, at 82.
[32] *A contrario*, see Koutroulis, above n 29, at 171.
[33] Conference of High Contracting Parties to the Fourth Geneva Convention, Declaration (§ 12) Geneva, 5 December 2001, reproduced in P.-Y. Fux and M. Zambelli, 'Mise en œuvre de la Quatrième Convention de Genève dans les territoires palestiniens occupés: historique d'un processus multilatéral (1997–2001)', 84 *IRRC* 847 (2002) 661, at 681.

c. *Article 3(b) AP I, a rule customary in nature?*

19 It follows from the foregoing that some authors are of the opinion that the rule contained in Article 6 paragraph 3 GC IV has fallen into desuetude, and that the rule contained in Article 3(b) AP I reflects customary international law (CIL). This would imply that Article 3(b) of the Protocol replaces Article 6 paragraph 3 GC IV, not only in the relationship between the parties that have ratified AP I, but also among states that are not parties to AP I. There is at least one author who considered in 2003 that 'la prudence [nous] commande plutôt de s'en tenir aux prévisions de l'article 6 § 3',[34] but who in 2009 conceded that it was 'possible de [...] soutenir'[35] that view that the new rule laid down in Article 3 AP I had acquired a customary value, thereby rendering Article 6 paragraph 3 of GC IV obsolete. To support this view, two arguments are advanced. First, that paragraph 3 of Article 6 'constituait une parenthèse particulière',[36] the purpose of which was to consider the specific situations of Germany and Japan which confronted the drafters, rendering this provision 'guère fondamentalement normative'.[37] Secondly, that a series of elements 'plaident [...] pour la désuétude et l'inapplicabilité'.[38] Among these are the fact that the rule has not been invoked by affected states, which prefer to deny the applicability of the law of occupation as a whole.[39]

20 Two other elements, however, invite a tempering of this conclusion. The first is the opinion of the ICJ itself. Despite the controversy surrounding the starting point adopted by the judges, it nevertheless remains that they saw fit to invoke the provisions under Article 6 paragraph 3 GC IV. It is therefore evident that, for the ICJ, this provision has not fallen into desuetude.[40] In addition, the rule contained in Article 3(b) AP I did not appear anywhere in the Court's reasoning. In this regard, it should be noted that although the United Nations (UN) General Assembly Resolution requesting an advisory opinion from the Court referred to AP I among the relevant instruments applicable to the occupied Palestinian territory[41] (most probably in error since Israel is not party to this treaty), the Court itself did not mention AP I, even as an instrument containing rules reflecting CIL. Furthermore, and secondarily, with regard to the separate situation of the conflict in Iraq,

[l]e 16 avril 2003, le Conseil fédéral a estimé que les conditions permettant de conclure à la fin des hostilités étaient réunies. [...] Cependant, il est important de noter que la constatation de la fin des hostilités n'entraîne pas la cessation de l'applicabilité du droit international humanitaire. En effet, l'article 6 de la IVe Convention de Genève prévoit qu'en territoire occupé,

---

[34] R. Kolb, *Ius in bello: le droit international des conflits armés* (1st edn, Brussels: Bruylant, 2003), at 110 ('caution commands [us] rather to stick to the provisions of Article 6 § 3').

[35] R. Kolb, *Ius in bello: le droit international des conflits armés* (2nd edn, Brussels: Bruylant, 2009), at 225 ('possible to [...] support').

[36] Ibid, at 225 ('constituted a special parenthesis').

[37] Ibid, at 226 ('hardly fundamentally normative').

[38] Ibid, at 227 ('plead [...] for desuetude and inapplicability').

[39] In fact, states that are, or have been, involved in situations of occupation have not invoked Art 6 para 3, which would have the effect of reducing their obligations. This is not because such states do not recognize the advantage of recourse to this provision, but rather because they hold that the law of occupation does not apply in the first place to the situations in which they are involved. Therefore, referral to Art 6 para 3 would amount to implicit recognition of the applicability of the law of occupation.

[40] See *contra* Kolb, above n 35, at 226–7, for whom the Court's invocation is without relevance, for it could not express itself on the validity of Art 6, as this was not at issue in the advisory proceedings. Benvenisti holds that the position of the Court is quite controversial: E. Benvenisti, 'Occupation, Belligerent', in MPEPIL, para 26.

[41] UNGA, Illegal Israeli Actions in Occupied East Jerusalem and the Rest of the Occupied Palestinian Territory, Resolution ES-10/14, 8 December 2003, A/RES/ES-10/14, 8th preambular paragraph: '*Reaffirming* the applicability of the Fourth Geneva Convention as well as Additional Protocol I to the Geneva Conventions to the Occupied Palestinian Territory, including East Jerusalem'.

la Convention reste entièrement applicable pendant une période d'un an suivant la fin des opérations militaires [...]⁴²

It is therefore clear that for the Swiss Government, Article 6 paragraph 3 is still legally relevant, or at least this was the case in 2005.

III. Article 2 paragraph 2 common to the Geneva Conventions

For situations of occupation that do not meet with armed resistance, the Pictet Commentary on GC IV suggests that the Convention's silence on the issue of end of applicability in such cases is 'deliberate', and 'must be taken to mean that the Convention will be fully applicable in such cases, so long as the occupation lasts'.⁴³ This assertion implies that, for at least one form of occupation, the Geneva Conventions should apply in their entirety for the complete duration of the occupation, and not simply till the general close of military operations. This would indeed be the only possible conclusion in this case if one were to consider that, without resistance, the actions of a foreign army with a view to implementing an occupation would not constitute military operations within the meaning of IHL. Otherwise, one would have to interpret the provision as meaning that the Geneva Conventions cease to apply one year after the general close of military operations which have never actually taken place. This would make it completely impossible to arrive at a starting point for the partial applicability of GC IV in these cases of occupation. In other words, this interpretation would lead to an absurd result. However, one might also argue that these situations, even without the presence of armed resistance, do constitute military operations within the meaning of IHL. This is so because an army that invades a territory with a view to occupying it may be said to be undertaking an offensive military operation, even in the absence of armed resistance. This invading army is prepared to engage in hostilities. The same could be said about foreign troops already in the territory on the basis of an agreement, if those troops violate the terms of this agreement and operate an occupation, even without technically speaking of an 'invasion'. It will serve to recall here that occupation, while triggering the applicability of a number of specific rules, still fits into the broader *corpus juris* that is IHL. Thus, in the same way that the use of force by an army on foreign soil represents a situation that is covered by IHL (even in the absence of hostilities in response from the opposing party), an invasion that does not face any opposition is covered by IHL, just as is the use of force by an army on foreign soil, even in the absence of any armed resistance.

There is another interpretation according to which a sort of hidden message might be read into the statement from Pictet's Commentary on Article 6 GC IV. According to this interpretation, it should be understood that the proposed exception for occupations meeting with no armed resistance attempted to erase the specificity of paragraph 3 with respect to all other forms of occupation. Pictet's argument would be an implicit admission

---

⁴² L. Caflisch, 'La pratique suisse en matière de droit international public 2006', 5 *Revue suisse de droit international et européen* (2006) 743, at 655, partial reproduction of the study titled 'La neutralité à l'épreuve du conflit en Irak', dating from 2 December 2005 and prepared by the Swiss Federal Council ('On 16 April 2003, the [Swiss] Federal Council decided that the conditions permitting the conclusion of the end of hostilities were met. [...] However, it is important to note that the finding that hostilities came to an end does not constitute a termination of the applicability of international humanitarian law. Indeed, Article 6 of the Fourth Geneva Convention provides that in the Occupied Territory, the Convention remains fully applicable for a period of one year following the end of military operations [...]').

⁴³ Pictet Commentary GC IV, at 63.

that Article 6 paragraph 3, creating a derogating legal regime, 'dévie de l'objet et du but des [Conventions de Genève]'.[44] This would make this provision irrelevant, and would further corroborate the argument that, in all cases, the entire body of IHL applicable to occupied territories should be in effect until the end of occupation, without a change in application beginning one year after the general close of military operations (for states not party to AP I). It is difficult to accept the idea of a hidden message, however. Indeed, although it is common for the commentary edited by the ICRC on the adoption of the Geneva Conventions to deliver unexpected interpretations of certain provisions, this is always done explicitly and with the relevant supporting justifications.

IV. Article 47 GC IV

23 Article 47 GC IV concerns the inviolability of the rights of persons in occupied territories. It acts as a safeguard clause. This provision not only reaffirms one of the cardinal principles of the law of occupation, that the occupier must maintain the *status quo ante bellum*, but also serves to counterbalance the dominant position enjoyed by the Occupying Power. Regarding the end of occupation, the clause results in two principal and interrelated consequences, discussed below.

a. *The inability of the Occupying Power to escape from its obligations due to an agreement on the end of occupation*

24 First, regarding the issue of consent, as it arose, for example, in the case of Iraq in 2004, the central sentence of this provision is particularly relevant. Indeed, this sentence states that an agreement concluded between the Occupied and Occupying Powers, which would result in depriving persons in occupied territory of the benefits due to them under the Convention, is without effect. As stated in the Pictet Commentary on Article 47, '[a]greements concluded with the authorities of the occupied territory represent a more subtle means by which the Occupying Power may try to free itself from the obligations incumbent on it under occupation law'.[45] Therefore, we might ask whether an agreement concluded between the Occupying and Occupied Powers, which results in the latter consenting to the former's exercise of authority over the territory, would be covered by Article 47. In other words, would an agreement that anticipates the end of an occupation be of such a nature as to violate the rights of persons on the occupied territory, and therefore be without effect under GC IV? It is difficult to imagine that an agreement intended to put an end to a situation of occupation could be detrimental to persons protected under IHL, if the agreement is actually and effectively acted upon.[46] If certain persons are protected by IHL, this is because they are in a situation of vulnerability. Their vulnerable status comes to an end when the situation—which demanded the exceptional legal regime that covered them—ceases to exist. Thus, for such an agreement to be consistent with Article 47, it need only be verified that the proclaimed end to the occupation is not detrimental to the population living in the territory.[47] Theoretically, an end to the occupation would be seen

---

[44] Koutroulis, above n 29, at 174 ('deviates from the object and purpose of the [Geneva Conventions]).
[45] Pictet Commentary GC IV, at 274.
[46] For more details regarding the validity of consent and regarding the question of who is entitled to give that consent, see Grignon, above n 20.
[47] See *contra* R. Kolb, 'Étude sur l'occupation et sur l'article 47 de la IVème Convention de Genève du 12 août 1949 relative à la protection des personnes civiles en temps de guerre: le degré d'intangibilité des droits en territoire occupé', 10 *African Yearbook of International Law* (2002) 267, at 318, who concludes: 'Comme

to be beneficial for the legal protection of persons residing in the occupied territory.[48] This will always be true if the Occupying Power withdraws from the territory while transferring full authority to the Occupied Power. However, doubts may arise in cases which see the Occupying Power formally allowed to remain positioned on the territory, as was the case in Iraq in 2004. In such cases, there is always a risk that the end of the occupation is a reality only on paper. This is precisely what Article 47 seeks to avoid. One must therefore look at the facts in the agreement and verify that the formally proclaimed end to the occupation does not involve a violation of the rights of the persons living in that territory. Formalism—generally speaking—is without effect on the applicability of IHL. Article 47 acts as an additional and specific safeguard against empty formalism, and therefore the only valid conclusion must be that agreements to end occupation are indeed within the scope of Article 47.[49] Such agreements will have no effect on the applicability of IHL unless the end to occupation envisaged is a reality in practice. This reaffirms the principle of effectiveness underlying all of IHL since the adoption of the Geneva Conventions.[50]

b. *The safeguard against the establishment of a 'puppet' government*

The situation of Iraq in 2004 raises this second aspect of Article 47 as well. Assuming it could be verified that the occupation ended due to the agreement between the Governing Council and the Coalition's Provisional Authority, Article 47 GC IV further implies that the Occupying Power may not establish a 'puppet' government in occupied territory, to allow it to remain on the territory while absolving it of its responsibilities as an Occupying Power. As has been stated, the 'clause applies both to cases where the lawful authorities in the occupied territory have concluded a derogatory agreement with the Occupying Power and to cases where that Power has installed and maintained a government in power'.[51] The two precise elements of this provision are particularly relevant in the face of statements that have been made about US behaviour in Iraq, as the establishment of the Governing Council on 13 July 2003 corresponds to the situation envisaged by Article 47.[52] In this case, authorization to remain on the occupied territory cannot be deemed to have been granted by a legitimate authority. Sovereign capacity has been completely stifled and the authorization actually emanates from the Occupying Power itself, by means of an institution that it has itself established. Provisions of IHL on occupied territories continue to apply. In this case, the consent by the sovereign to the exercise of authority by a foreign Power does not unambiguously spell an end to occupation. Thus, it was not

---

la conclusion de certains accords diminuant la portée des garanties conventionnelles est interdite par l'article 47 de la Convention de Genève IV, il y a ici un conflit potentiel important entre l'accord à "l'intérieur du droit d'occupation" tombant sous le coup de l'article 47 et l'accord "à l'extérieur du droit d'occupation".' ('As the conclusion of certain agreements which reduce the scope of the Convention's protection is prohibited by Article 47 GC IV, there is a potential significant conflict between the agreement "within IHL", covered by Article 47, and the agreement "outside IHL".')

[48] See, ICRC, *Occupation and Other Forms of Administration of Foreign Territory, Expert Meeting* (Geneva: ICRC, 2012), at 30. Certain experts held this view, while others took the complete opposite position.

[49] See *contra*, Kolb, above n 47. [50] See also Ch 8 of this volume.

[51] Pictet Commentary GC IV, at 275.

[52] The Iraqi Governing Council was not simply supported by US authorities. The latter played a key role in its establishment. See A. Roberts, 'The End of Occupation: Iraq 2004', 54 *ICLQ* (2005) 27, at 38, who cites a *New York Times* article: J. Brinkley, 'Ex-CIA Aides Say Iraq Leader Helped Agency in 90s Attacks', *New York Times*, 9 June 2004, at 1. See also A. Carcano, 'End of the Occupation in 2004? The Status of the Multinational Force in Iraq after the Transfer of Sovereignty to the Interim Iraqi Government', 11 *Journal of Conflict & Security Law* (2006) 41, at 50.

the superficial transfer of authority carried out by Paul Bremer, Administrator of the Coalition Provisional Authority, to the Iraqi Governing Council on 28 June 2004 that put an end to the occupation of Iraq, but the consent given by duly elected officials at the end of the democratic process initiated by the legislative elections of 30 January 2005. The US was therefore required to comply with its obligations as the Occupying Power until at least the latter date.[53]

c. The effects of Security Council Resolution 1546[54] regarding the end of occupation in Iraq

26 Resolution 1546, concerning the alleged end of occupation in Iraq in June 2004, permits us to question the effects of a Security Council resolution on the applicability of IHL relating to occupied territories. On the one hand, the Security Council welcomed the announcement that 'by 30 June 2004, the occupation will end'.[55] However, on the other hand, although authority was formally handed over from the US to Iraqi officials, the situation on the ground remained unchanged. After 28 June, US soldiers continued to assume the very same functions they had been exercising before the formal transfer of authority. The analysis of Article 47 GC IV has shown that agreements between the parties are in themselves without effect if they are to the detriment of the civilian population. However, what of a statement made by the Security Council? Does this have the power to change the applicable law if the situation on the ground is unchanged? If the Resolution had been implemented in actual fact, i.e. if the US had truly ceased the exercise of its authority over Iraqi territory, IHL applicable to occupied territories would, without a doubt, have ceased to apply. However, in this case, doubts arose on account of US behaviour. Considering the situation on the ground, if one concludes that the statement made by the Security Council prevails,[56] that would mean that the Security Council formally requests the state concerned to violate the law. Moreover, there is no organ that is charged with classifying situations under IHL, not even the Security Council. The latter is empowered to declare that a situation threatens international peace or security. Such threats, however, do not automatically trigger the applicability of IHL. Conversely, there are a lot of cases to which IHL is applicable, while the Security Council does not take a position on them. It is therefore not possible to rely on positions the Council does/does not adopt to determine whether or not IHL, including IHL concerning occupied territories, applies. Alternatively, it might also be argued that 'if a Security Council resolution did not expressly reject application of occupation law, this body of law might be relevant and applicable, should the conditions for its applicability be met'.[57] In Resolution 1546 the Security Council did not make any reference to the applicable law; it merely welcomed that the occupation would end as of 30 June 2004.

---

[53] On this date, for the first time since the fall of Saddam Hussein, the Iraqi people were invited to go to the polls to elect a constituent assembly, which, at the end of its term, would be replaced by a newly elected legislative assembly. See *contra* Carcano, above n 52; ECtHR, *Al-Skeini and others v United Kingdom*, Judgment, 7 July 2011, para 19.

[54] UNSC Res 1546, adopted 8 June 2004.   [55] Ibid, para 2.

[56] Because of Art 103 of the UN Charter, which states that obligations under the UN Charter prevail over obligations under any other international agreement. See also J. Pejic, 'The European Court of Human Rights' Al-Jedda Judgment: The Oversight of International Humanitarian Law', 93 *IRRC* 883 (2011) 837, for an analysis of the ECtHR's judgment in the *Al-Jedda* case (ECtHR, *Al-Jedda v United Kingdom*, 7 July 2011) regarding the application of IHL and Art 103 of the UN Charter.

[57] ICRC, above n 48, at 13 and 23.

C. Relevance in Non-International Armed Conflicts

The notion of occupation is irrelevant in non-international armed conflicts (NIACs).[58] 27
This, inter alia, is one of the core distinctions between IACs and NIACs. A situation of occupation can never occur in a NIAC. First, a state cannot occupy its own territory. Secondly, even if an armed group does exercise control over a particular territory, this would not qualify as occupation. If, during a NIAC, one can distinguish different parts of the territory over which either the armed group or the state exercises its control, none of them qualifies as occupation. Only IHL of NIACs remains applicable to the state, as well as to such an armed group.

D. Legal Consequences of a Violation

As such, the end of occupation is a phenomenon that either does or does not occur. A phe- 28
nomenon cannot be violated. See, however, Chapter 8 of this volume on non-renunciation of rights, and Chapter 67 of this volume (MN 58–61) for a consideration of violations of the norms applicable in situations of occupation.

E. Critical Assessment

As previously mentioned, two situations have given rise to an abundance of literature 29
on the topic of occupation since the early 2000s, i.e. Iraq and Gaza. In both cases, the behaviour of the occupying army, which sought to extricate itself from its responsibilities towards those living in the territory under its administration, led to a reconsideration of the conditions under which it can be said that occupation comes to an end. The case of Iraq, which concerned the formal transfer of authority from the Occupying Power, has been dealt with in section B.IV.c of this chapter; the complex case of Gaza is described below.

Traditionally, the withdrawal of the enemy was considered the sole method by which 30
occupation could be terminated.[59] However, today it is now only one possibility among many others.[60] The commonly held view is that the physical presence of the enemy army on a territory is required to bring a situation of occupation into being, because it is by virtue of this presence that an Occupying Power can ensure it is able to exercise its authority in that territory.[61] Once the Occupying Power withdraws its army from the territory, and even during manoeuvres relating to this withdrawal, the situation should no longer be classified as an occupation. Indeed, it is unclear how, during such a withdrawal—and

---

[58] See also Ch 67, MN 57, of this volume.
[59] L.F.L. Oppenheim, *International Law: A Treatise*, II: *War and Neutrality*, ed H. Lauterpacht (7th edn, London: Longman, 1952), para 168, at 436.
[60] See notably R. Kolb and S. Vité, *Le droit de l'occupation militaire: perspectives historiques et enjeux juridiques actuels* (Brussels: Bruylant, 2009), at 166; A. Roberts, 'Occupation, Military, Termination of', in MPEPIL; A. Roberts, 'Prolonged Military Occupation', in E. Playfair (ed), *International Law and the Administration of Territories: Two Decades of Israeli Occupation of the West Bank and Gaza Strip* (Oxford: Clarendon Press, 1992) 25, at 84; Roberts, above n 52, at 28; E. Benvenisti, *The International Law of Occupation* (2nd edn, Oxford: OUP, 2012), at 56; see *contra* Y. Shany, 'Faraway, so Close: The Legal Status of Gaza after Israel's Disengagement', 8 *YIHL* (2005) 369, at 380, who, in this contribution, considers enemy presence the first condition of occupation, and therefore, by mirror effect, the first element to take into account when considering that an occupation has ended.
[61] See Ch 67, MN 12–14, of this volume.

31   Israel's unilateral decision to withdraw its troops from the Gaza Strip, which was taken in 2004 and implemented in 2005, nonetheless led to a reassessment of this view of the termination of occupation.[62] Many, when confronted with Israel's decision, considered it unfair in some respects, most particularly in light of the fact that Israel intended to continue holding on to certain prerogatives that it had acquired as the Occupying Power. Some legal scholars therefore sought arguments to justify the conclusion that the occupation persisted even in the physical absence of the army on the occupied territory. Without raising the issue of qualification of the subsequent situation (involving Israeli raids conducted in this territory), the question we must seek to answer here is whether a military can continue to exercise its authority, and therefore be designated an Occupying Power, even if its troops are not present on the territory in a continuous manner. This issue arises only when considering the end of occupation. Indeed, it is well established with regard to the beginning of the occupation that the presence of at least a few enemy soldiers on the territory is a condition *sine qua non* for classifying the situation as an occupation (see Chapter 67, MN 12–14, of this volume). This is understandable as, in order to be able to impose its authority over a territory, it is necessary for at the least a minimum military deployment by the Occupying Power. Once this authority has been established, and particularly in the case of Gaza where the occupation has persisted for nearly 40 years, it is conceivable, however, that the withdrawal of troops may not affect the administration of the territory by the foreign authority. The whole institutional structure set up during the occupation[63] may mean that once the occupying army withdraws, the former legitimate authority or a new authority finds itself unable to function fully, while the alleged former Occupying Power continues to exercise certain of the prerogatives that it assumed during

---

moreover once such a withdrawal has been completed—the army in question would still be able to exercise effective control over the territory. The withdrawal is thus seen as a manifestation of the Occupying Power's desire no longer to exercise such authority with respect to the occupied territory.

---

[62] Here, we postulate that the Gaza Strip was occupied until at least September 2005. There may be controversy over whether the Oslo Process resulted in Gaza's no longer being occupied. For its part, the ICJ held that these transfers of authority were partial and limited, and that they were not of a nature to change in any way the status of Israel as an Occupying Power: ICJ, *Wall* Advisory Opinion, above n 13, paras 77–8. For other similar references, see HRCouncil, *Human Rights in Palestine and Other Occupied Arab Territories: Report of the United Nations Fact-Finding Mission on the Gaza Conflict*, 25 September 2009, A/HRC/12/48, § 279; Harvard Program on Humanitarian Policy and Conflict Research, International Humanitarian Law Research Initiative, *Review of the Applicability of International Humanitarian Law to the Occupied Palestinian Territory*, Policy Brief, June 2004, at 9–10. For references that hold that the Gaza Strip was no longer occupied at the time of the withdrawal, see E. Benvenisti, 'Responsibility for the Protection of Human Rights under the Interim Israeli Palestinians Agreements', 28 *Israel Law Review* (1994) 297, at 312. For further reading about the status of the Gaza Strip, see M. Mari, 'The Israeli Disengagement from the Gaza Strip: An End of the Occupation?', 8 *YIHL* (2005) 356; S. Darcy and J. Reynolds, 'An Enduring Occupation: The Status of the Gaza Strip from the Perspective of International Humanitarian Law', 15 *Journal of Conflict & Security Law* (2010) 211, at 241; J. Quigley, 'The PLO–Israeli Interim Arrangements and the Geneva Civilians Convention', in. S. Bowen (ed), *Human Rights, Self-Determination and Political Change in the Occupied Palestinian Territories* (The Hague: Martinus Nijhoff Publishers, 1997) 25; HRComm, *Question of the Violation of Human Rights in the Occupied Arab Territories, Including Palestine: Report of the Human Rights Inquiry Commission Established Pursuant to Commission Resolution S-5/1 of 19 October 2000*, 16 March 2001, E/CN.4/2001/121; and Shany, above n 60, at 380.

[63] The Israeli Supreme Court speaks for its part of 'the Gaza Strip [as being] almost *completely dependent* upon supply of electricity by Israel': Israeli Supreme Court as High Court of Justice, *Al-Basyuni and others v Prime Minister and Minister of Defence*, HCJ 9132/07, 30 January 2008, para 12 (emphasis added).

the period of uncontested occupation, although it no longer maintains a permanent military presence in the territory.

Challenges relating to the classification of the situation in the Gaza Strip post–2005 are very specific to the territory. It is therefore worth recalling some of these particularities. Gaza was occupied during the so-called Six Day War of 1967. This occupation persisted until August 2005, at which point Israel began to implement its unilateral decision to withdraw its troops from the territory.[64] Gaza had therefore been occupied for 38 years. This is the first particularity—occupation is intended to be a temporary situation, but in this case it spread over a considerably lengthy period of time.[65] Additionally, Gaza was part of a broader process of peace negotiations. Several features spelled out by this process were implemented prior to 2005, which saw the Palestinian Authority gradually assuming a certain number of prerogatives. This is the second particularity: the 'disengagement' of the Israeli army was not sudden. It was, however, unilateral, and took place while the multilateral negotiations were ongoing. Moreover, the Israeli army repositioned itself around the Gaza Strip, exercising control over entry into and exit from the territory via land, air, or sea.[66] Further still, Israel remains able to prohibit the population from accessing some border areas inside the Gaza Strip.[67] Moreover, Israel continues to retain certain sovereign prerogatives.[68] This is visible, for example, in the currency used in the Gaza Strip, or even in the issuance of travel documents.[69] And thus we have the third particularity, for while Israel claims no longer to have international obligations towards the people of this area,[70] a certain number of functions that it continues to assume contradict its assertions. Lastly, if Israel's claim were true, this would mean that it would no longer be required to ensure the supply of food and medical products,[71] to provide for the education of children,[72] or to permit ministers of religion to give spiritual assistance to their communities.[73] With regard to the humanitarian situation in the Gaza Strip and the means available to the Palestinian Authority, the claim that Israel is no longer an Occupying Power has negative consequences for the well-being of the population. This is the fourth particularity: whereas the end of the occupation may seem desirable, the humanitarian implications this would have

---

[64] The last of the Israeli soldiers left the Gaza Strip on 12 September 2005. See Office for the Coordination of Humanitarian Affairs, *Gaza Disengagement Situation Report*, 12 September 2005, available at <http://unispal.un.org/UNISPAL.NSF/0/13AFB427D5F396618525707B004B180D>.

[65] For more details on protracted occupations, see Roberts, 'Prolonged Military Occupation', above n 60.

[66] See HRCouncil, above n 62, § 278; ICRC, *Annual Report (2005)* (Geneva: ICRC, 2006), at 311; Harvard Program on Humanitarian Policy and Conflict Research, International Humanitarian Law Research Initiative, *Legal Aspects of Israel's Disengagement Plan under International Humanitarian Law*, Legal and Policy Brief, November 2004, available at <http://www.hamoked.org/items/7820_eng.pdf>, at 10.

[67] See Darcy and Reynolds, above n 62, at 237.

[68] See Human Rights Watch, *Israel Disengagement Will Not End Gaza Occupation: Israeli Government Still Holds Responsibility for Welfare of Civilians*, Press Release, available at <http://hrw.org/english/docs/2004/10/29/isrlpa9577.htm>; *Legal Aspects of Israel's Disengagement Plan under International Humanitarian Law*, above n 66, at 10.

[69] See, Darcy and Reynolds, above n 62, at 241–2, which further underlines that Israel also maintains a considerable influence, if not a monopoly, over the administration of justice, notably in the Gaza Strip, at 236 and 237.

[70] See the Israeli Prime Minister Ariel Sharon's address to the UN General Assembly, 15 September 2005. After having mentioned that 'this week, the last Israeli soldier left the Gaza strip and military law there was ended', he then affirmed 'the end of Israeli control over and responsibility for the Gaza Strip': UNGA, 60th Session, Verbatim Record of 5th Plenary Meeting, 15 September 2005, A/60/PV.5, at 45–6.

[71] Art 55 GC IV.   [72] Art 50 GC IV.   [73] Art 58 GC IV.

a. The status of Gaza after September 2005, according to various authorities

33 According to the UN Special Rapporteur on the situation of human rights in the Palestinian Occupied Territories since 1967, the continued occupation of Gaza by Israel is determined by the simple fact that Israel continues to exercise effective control over the territory. After stating that the 'permanent physical presence of the occupying Power's military forces'[74] is not required for the continued exercise of effective control, the Special Rapporteur further concludes that 'technological developments'[75] allow Israel to continue to 'assert control over the people of Gaza without a permanent military presence'.[76] That Israel maintains effective control is manifest in a number of ways, which are grouped into four distinct categories, namely:

— the '[s]ubstantial control of Gaza's six land crossings';[77]
— the '[c]ontrol through military incursions';[78]
— the '[c]omplete control of Gaza's airspace and territorial waters';[79] and
— the '[c]ontrol of the Palestinian Population Registry'.[80]

34 In a 2007 report focusing on the humanitarian situation in the Palestinian territories, without specifically addressing the classification of the situation in the Gaza Strip, the ICRC took for granted that Gaza was occupied territory.[81] More generally, in all its annual reports since 2005, the institution has continued to designate the Palestinian territories, including Gaza, as 'Occupied Territories'.[82] Similarly, in a position paper published in the *Review of the Red Cross* in 2012, Peter Maurer, the ICRC's President, takes for granted that Gaza is one of the territories over which Israel exercises its authority as an Occupying Power.[83]

35 The Commission of Inquiry established by the UN Human Rights Council (HRCouncil) to look into Israel's *Operation Cast Lead* (28 December 2008 to 17 January 2009) also held that the Gaza Strip was, at the beginning of 2009, occupied territory, although one might question whether the intensity of the operation could not cast doubt on the classification of the situation as one of occupation, at least for the duration of the hostilities linked to this operation.

---

[74] HRCouncil, *Human Rights Situation in Palestine and other Occupied Arab Territories: Report of the Special Rapporteur on the Situation of Human Rights in the Palestinian Territories Occupied since 1967, John Dugard*, 21 January 2008, A/HRC/7/17, para 11.

[75] Ibid. [76] Ibid. [77] Ibid, (a). [78] Ibid, (b). [79] Ibid, (c). [80] Ibid, (d).

[81] The first sentence of the report reads as follows: 'Throughout the occupied Palestinian territories, in the Gaza Strip as well as in the West Bank, Palestinians continuously face hardship in simply going about their lives': ICRC, *Dignity Denied in the Occupied Palestinian Territories* (Geneva: ICRC, 2007), at 1, available at <https://www.icrc.org/eng/resources/documents/report/palestine-report-131207.htm>.

[82] ICRC, *Annual Report (2011)* (Geneva: ICRC, 2012), at 384. In a telling manner, while the ICRC previously referred to these territories as 'occupied and autonomous territories' until 2008 (inclusive), since 2009 the words 'and autonomous' have disappeared from the institution's language, which now refers only to 'occupied territories'. See the following additional ICRC Annual Reports: *Annual Report (2005)*, above n 66, at 311; *Annual Report (2006)* (Geneva: ICRC, 2007), at 326; *Annual Report (2007)* (Geneva: ICRC, 2008), at 341; *Annual Report (2008)* (Geneva: ICRC, 2009), at 347; *Annual Report (2009)* (Geneva: ICRC, 2010), at 365; and *Annual Report (2010)* (Geneva: ICRC, 2011), at 433.

[83] P. Maurer, 'Challenges to International Humanitarian Law: Israel's Occupation Policy', 94 *IRRC* 888 (2012) 1503, esp at 1504, 1506, and 1508.

In the *Targeted Killings* case[84] initiated by the Public Committee against Torture, the   36
Israeli Supreme Court, without itself pronouncing on the status of the territory, still
invoked the law of occupation as part of the law applicable to the case before it. Indeed, to
decide on the nature of the conflict between Israel and those participating in the *Intifada*,
the Court examined the nature of the relationship between 'the occupying state in an
area subject to a belligerent occupation and the terrorists who come from the same area'.[85]
It seems, therefore, to have adopted, in 2006, the premise that Israel occupied the Gaza
Strip. However, the Court did not examine the existence of an occupation as such.

However, two years later, in the *Ahmed* case, also known as the *Power Outages* case,[86]   37
the Israeli Supreme Court, in its capacity as the High Court of Justice, clearly indicated
that it adhered to the Government's position that Gaza was no longer occupied territory as of September 2005.[87] On this occasion, the Court did not simply argue the
non-presence of Israeli soldiers in the area. It anchored its reasoning in a subsidiary
argument that 'Israel [does not] have effective capacity, in its present status, to enforce
order and manage civilian life in the Gaza Strip'.[88] In other words, it is not only the withdrawal of the army that matters, but the additional finding that Israel is no longer able to
exercise its authority over the territory. The latter criterion, which appears in the Hague
Regulations, is solely decisive.

b. *The Gaza Strip, still occupied territory?*

As a preliminary matter, regarding Israel's unilateral declaration on the end of occupation,   38
it should be noted that statements of parties to armed conflicts, like those of any other
authority, have no effect on the application of IHL, including the law governing situations
of occupation. The only effect of such a declaration would be to lead to an examination of
the situation in order to determine whether the facts are truly of such a nature as to effect
a change in legal classification. In and of itself, the statement is without effect.[89] One can
simply recognize that it may have indicative value.

If we stick to the condition present in the Hague Regulations (i.e. the ability to exercise   39
authority), the question should be: Does the withdrawal of troops still allow Israel to
exercise its authority as the Occupying Power over the territory? Clearly, noting that the
enemy has withdrawn from the territory raises questions about the continued occupation
of the Gaza Strip, within the meaning of Article 42 of the Hague Regulations. But in reality, what is decisive is the authority exercised or able to be exercised over the territory.[90] If

---

[84] Israeli Supreme Court (as High Court of Justice), *Public Committee against Torture in Israel and others v Government of Israel and others* (*Targeted Killings*), HCJ 769/02, 13 December 2006, available at <http://elyon1.court.gov.il/files_eng/02/690/007/A34/02007690.a34.pdf>.

[85] Ibid, para 16. The Court uses the word 'area' throughout its judgment, after having specified that the term applies to 'Judea, Samaria, and the Gaza Strip'.

[86] Israeli Supreme Court as High Court of Justice, *Al-Basyuni and others*, above n 63.

[87] Ibid, para 12.

[88] Ibid. The Court has reiterated its opinion on this on at least two subsequent occasions. See Darcy and Reynolds, above n 62, at 233.

[89] Similarly, see Benvenisti, 'Occupation, Belligerent', above n 40, para 9; Benvenisti, *The International Law of Occupation*, above n 60, at 56; *Legal Aspects of Israel's Disengagement Plan under International Humanitarian Law*, above n 66, at 10; M. Zwanenburg, 'The Law of Occupation Revisited: The Beginning of an Occupation', 10 *YIHL* (2007) 99, at 127.

[90] Similarly, see *Legal Aspects of Israel's Disengagement Plan under International Humanitarian Law*, above n 66, at 8: 'The test is not per se the military presence of the occupying forces in all areas of the territory, but the extent to which the Occupying Power, through its military presence, is exerting effective control over the territory [...]' It has also been argued that the Israeli control of a zone corresponding to the border between

the implementation of this authority necessarily involves only a minimal military presence on the territory, it could well be that the withdrawal of the bulk of the army from the territory does not change the situation.[91] Undoubtedly the question would be posed differently if the West Bank and Gaza constituted a geographically continuous area. In this case it would be easier to conclude that although the troops are not present in all parts of the territory, the situation of occupation remains unchanged so long as the enemy is able to exercise its authority in that territory, for example by redeploying if necessary, whenever it so wishes.[92] Moreover, some argue, in light of the control exercised by Israel over the entry and exit of people and merchandise into and out of the territory, that the situation actually represents more of a redeployment of the army than its withdrawal, which would not affect the qualification of situation.[93] The repositioning of its troops around Gaza, on land, at sea, and in the air, invites the following conclusion: the Israeli army can redeploy itself at any time to assure its authority. In this, the situation corresponds to one the Nuremberg Tribunal considered and for which it held that '[w]hile it is true that the partisans were able to control sections of these countries [Greece and Yugoslavia] at various times, it is established that the Germans could at any time they desired assume physical control of any part of the country'.[94] Also, it is not the presence of the Israeli army in the air, at sea, or on land around the Gaza Strip that is (or is not) constitutive of a potential situation of occupation, but the fact that this presence allows it to be able to exercise its authority over Gaza, as required by Article 42 of the Hague Regulations.[95] We can note, for example, that it is Israel that decides whether

Gaza and Egypt—called the Philadelphi Route—would suffice in order to consider that Israel remains an Occupying Power. This would be the reason that Israel concluded an agreement with Egypt over the control of security in this zone. See I. Scobbie, 'An Intimate Disengagement: Israel's Withdrawal from Gaza: The Law of Occupation and of Self-Determination', 11 *Yearbook of Islamic and Middle Eastern Law* (2004–5) 3, at 5.

[91] See *Legal Aspects of Israel's Disengagement Plan under International Humanitarian Law*, above n 66, at 8–9; see also Darcy and Reynolds, above n 62, at 239, who take this considerably further, highlighting that new technologies, notably the possibility of satellite surveillance, render it 'certainly possible for an occupying power to police a territory with minimal reliance on forces physically present on the ground', even going so far as to venture a comparison with drone technology. See *contra* Shany, above n 60, for whom it is unthinkable that authority may be exercised in the absence of troops on the ground. He finds (at 380) that 'despite Israel's power to influence events in Gaza to some degree, its ability to enforce day-to-day law and order is minimal to non-existent (Israeli soldiers have not patrolled the streets of Gaza City since the mid 1990s)'. Roberts seems to position himself similarly when he considers that 'an occupant exercises authority directly, through its armed forces, rather than indirectly, through local agents': A. Roberts, 'Occupation, Military, Termination of', above n 60, para 9.

[92] See similarly, Benvenisti, 'Occupation, Belligerent', above n 40, para 8: 'effective control does not require that occupation forces are present in all places at all times. It is generally accepted that it is sufficient that the occupying force can, within a reasonable time, send detachments of troops to make its authority felt within the occupied area.' This hypothesis is also envisaged by Shany, above n 60, at 379.

[93] See Mari, above n 62, at 366.

[94] *Judgment of Wilhelm List and others (The Hostages Trial)*, US Military Tribunal, Nuremberg, 8 July 1947–19 February 1948, UNWCC Law Reports, vol VIII, at 56. Taken up to a certain extent by the ICTY in para 217 of the judgment in the *Naletilić* case, which lists a certain number of indicators permitting the conclusion of occupation. ICTY, *The Prosecutor v Mladen Naletilić and Vinko Martinović*, Trial Chamber Judgment, IT-98-34, 31 March 2003.

[95] Shany presents this hypothesis, above n 60, at 379. See also Darcy and Reynolds, above n 62, at 235–6; *Legal Aspects of Israel's Disengagement Plan under International Humanitarian Law*, above n 66; N. Stephanopoulos, 'Israel's Legal Obligations to Gaza after the Pullout', 31 *The Yale Journal of International Law* (2006) 524. The *Tzemel Case*, decided by the Israeli Supreme Court, in which the judges held that 'occupation forces do not need to be in actual control of all the territory and population, but simply have the potential capability to do so', is abundantly cited in doctrine and rests on this thesis: *Tzemel v Minister of Defence*, Case no HCJ 102/82, 37(3) PD 365, 13 July 1983, Israeli Supreme Court (sitting as the High Court of Justice). See Scobbie, above n 90, at 6; and Benvenisti, 'Occupation, Belligerent', above n 40, para 5.

a port or an airport will be reopened in the Gaza Strip.[96] If the Palestinian Authority is not in a position to override the 'authorization' of the Israeli army to do these things, is this itself not the very definition of what the exercise of authority signifies, namely, the ability to make decisions which command obedience?

40 The above invites the conclusion that the occupation persisted beyond 12 September 2005. Moreover, even if one is not yet convinced, there exists another argument that leads to the same conclusion, namely, the functional end of applicability of the rules of GC IV on military occupation. Indeed, mirroring the beginning of application of rules of Section III of GC IV already during the invasion phase (see Chapter 67, MN 42 and 46–50, of this volume), many experts are of the opinion that once an Occupying Power has exercised its authority over a territory, it remains bound by relevant rules that apply in occupied territory as long as it exercises a form of authority.[97] Then, the rules that apply depend on the degree of authority and the nature of the competences that continue to be exercised, either after an apparent withdrawal or during the phasing out. This so-called 'variable-geometry theory' allows ICRC's President Maurer to assert in the above-mentioned position paper that 'Israel continues to be bound by obligations under occupation law that are commensurate with the degree to which it exercises control',[98] even since September 2005.

41 The effects of the purported withdrawal of Israel from the Gaza strip settled, there remain, however, questions relating to subsequent acts of violence committed from and on the Gaza Strip. Indeed, one might ask whether it is still possible to consider the Gaza Strip as Occupied Territory when rockets are launched daily from this territory[99] towards targets located in Israel, and when the response from the latter occurs either from its own territory, or through 'incursions' into Gaza.[100] Would this not contradict the assertion that the Occupying Power must be able to ensure public order and safety in the territory under its responsibility? Here the resurgence of violence is such that it may call into question the legal classification of the situation. The reasoning of the tribunal in the *Hostages Case* is interesting in this regard. It noted that the German army—having occupied Greece from 28 April 1941—had been subjected to numerous attacks since the summer of the same year, the intensity of which 'increased progressively [...] until it assumed the appearance of a military campaign'.[101] It held that '[i]t is clear that the German Armed Forces were

---

[96] See the Disengagement Plan: Israel Ministry of Foreign Affairs, *The Cabinet Resolution Regarding the Disengagement Plan*, 6 June 2004, available at <http://www.mfa.gov.il/MFA/Peace+Process/Reference+Documents/Revised+Disengagement+Plan+6-June-2004.htm>.

[97] See ICRC, above n 48, at 31–3.   [98] Maurer, above n 83, at 1508.

[99] Since 2005, the ICRC has regularly noted in its Annual Reports the persistence of hostilities from and on the Gaza Strip. See, e.g., the 2006 Report, which mentions that 'Israeli military operations in the Gaza Strip de Gaza [...] continued for much of the second half of 2006': ICRC, *Annual Report (2006)*, above n 82, at 326. Similarly in 2007, the ICRC noted that '[f]requent rocket and mortar fire from Gaza on nearby Israeli towns continued to cause casualties and material damage. Retaliatory Israeli airstrikes and ground incursions into Gaza also resulted in loss of life and material damage': ICRC, *Annual Report (2007)*, above n 82, at 341. See also ICRC, *Annual Report (2008)*, above n 82, at 347, which deals with *Operation Cast Lead*. See also, Darcy and Reynolds, above n 62, at 227.

[100] It should be noted that *Operation Cast Lead* has not been taken into account in the number of these incursions. In itself the Operation called into question the very persistence of the occupation. This offensive of the Israeli army, which took place between 28 December 2008 and 17 January 2009, due to its intensity, raised serious doubts (at least for the period of its duration) as to the continued classification of the situation as one of occupation of territory. However, the fact-finding commission mandated by the HRCouncil stated conclusively (above n 62, para 276): 'Israel has without doubt at all times relevant to the mandate of this Mission exercised effective control over the Gaza Strip. The Mission is of the view that the circumstances of this control establish that the Gaza Strip remains occupied by Israel. The provisions of the Fourth Geneva Convention therefore apply at all relevant times with regard to the obligations of Israel towards the population of the Gaza Strip.'

[101] *The Hostages Trial*, above n 94, at 56.

able to maintain control of Greece [...] until they evacuated them in the fall of 1944'.[102] Moreover, without going into the questions of classification of this type of conflict, there was no doubt for the judges that the Occupying Power did not lose its status as such even when engaged in fighting against guerrillas.[103] In other words, the fact that hostilities took place on the territory did not prohibit the situation from being classified as an occupation.[104] As for the situation in Gaza, attacks directed against Israeli targets may be viewed in two ways: (i) either the hostilities serve as proof that Israel no longer controls the territory and therefore cannot be considered as an Occupying Power; or (ii) these events do not preclude the conclusion that the occupation persists and that therefore Israel must continue to fulfil the obligations accruing to it as the Occupying Power.[105] In the latter case, we note that while it is necessary for hostilities to have ceased, at least to some extent, for the Power in question to proceed with the occupation of the territory within the meaning of the Hague Regulations, once its authority has been established over the territory, the onset of hostilities does not *ipso facto* constitute a termination of the occupation. However, we must not conclude that the conditions determinative of the end of the occupation do not reflect the conditions determinative of its beginning. Indeed, here as elsewhere, what is decisive is that the Occupying Power continues to be able to exercise its authority, and not the fluctuation in the modalities through which it achieves this. However, in this case, the Israeli–Palestinian political context also raises the question of whether Israel is actually able to maintain its authority and to stop the violence, but does not do so intentionally, in order to point the finger at the alleged inaction of the Palestinian Authority. This would nevertheless lead to the conclusion that Gaza is still occupied territory.

42 The Israeli context is so sensitive and particular that it deserves to be put aside when considering the end of occupation. If the situation of the Gaza Strip invigorated the debate and provoked detailed scrutiny of the elements that lead to the conclusion that occupation has ended (or continues to persist), it cannot, of itself, constitute fertile ground to found new and general interpretations, precisely because of this sensitivity and particularism. This is even less so if the starting point of the analysis is solely the withdrawal of the enemy, rather than the examination of whether or not the retreating Power continues to exercise its authority.

43 In order to conclude that we have the end of an occupation, we must consider whether or not the Occupying Power still exercises its authority over the *occupied territory*, rather than take into account the presence/absence of the elements that led to the establishment of this authority. As long as such authority continues to be wielded—regardless of the means employed to achieve this, and whether those means remain the same from the beginning to the end of the occupation—the occupation persists. Therefore, it is not the withdrawal of the army or the presence of consent that is decisive in terms of determining the end of occupation, but the fact that the ability of the Occupying Power to exercise its authority, for whatever reason, no longer exists.

JULIA GRIGNON*

---

[102] Ibid.   [103] Ibid, at 57.

[104] Similarly, see Zwanenburg, above n 89, at 107, who considers that '[t]he broad conception of occupation proposed by the Pictet commentary must be rejected'. See also, Darcy and Reynolds, above n 62, at 238; Roberts, above n 52, at 34.

[105] See Y. Dinstein, *The International Law of Belligerent Occupation* (Cambridge: CUP, 2009), at 279.

* Parts of this chapter represent a translation into English of sections of the author's doctoral thesis: J. Grignon, *L'applicabilité temporelle du droit international humanitaire* (Zürich: Schulthess, 2014). The author would like to thank Yvette Issar and Jérôme Massé for their invaluable help on this chapter.

Index

Note: please see tables of legislation for references to legislation, including conventions

Abkhazia separatists *see also* Georgia vs Russia
   (2008) 35, 45–6
abortion services 203–4
Abu Ghraib 295
access to *see also* humanitarian access;
   humanitarian assistance
  education 1309, 1500–3
  food 233, 252, 1300
  gravesites 105, 291
  information and data on protected persons 275,
    283, 1016, 1021, 1097–98, 1104
  justice 365, 1310, 1469
  lawyer 478, 969, 1107, 1120, 1443
  material for the preparation of own defence
    478–9, 480
  medical treatment 801, 838, 1280, 1475
  protected areas 371–3, 383
  territory controlled by non-state actors 501–2
  POWs, transferred 971
  female facilities 987
  victims of war 87, 242–3, 244, 245, 255
accession to the GCs 8, 55, 162, 163, 684
accommodation in neutral countries 103–5, 106–7,
   140, 1044–6, 1284–5, 1296, 1302
accounts
  of internees 555, 1264, 1358
  of POWs 553–4, 994, 1005–6
  of protected persons 1179, 1264
activity hostile to security of state/occupying
   power 1125–8
addressees of obligations
  armed/insurgent group 38, 232, 251, 611,
    733, 1116
  civilian population 812
  Common Article 1 116
  Common Article 3 151, 250, 251, 415–32,
    499, 516, 798
  international organization 387
  Occupying Power 1480
  parties to the conflict 795
  state 251, 874, 1116
ad hoc agreements under Common
   Article 3 509–21
  applicability by the ICTY and the ICC 520
  attributing POWs status to fighters in NIACs 513
  classification of conflicts, impact on 514–5
  compliance commissions, established by 518
  content 512–4
  derogating from customary rules applicable in
    NIACs 513

evacuation of POWs 973
form 510
invalidity 514
legal consequences of a violation 517–21
legal status 421, 515–17
mutual engagements qualifying as 510, 511
not affecting the legal status of the
   parties 426, 510
parties to ad hoc agreements 510
practice 420–1, 510–12
use of ad hoc agreements by criminal
   tribunals 519–20
administration of occupied territories 1455–84
  coercive or discriminatory measures against public
    officials or judges, prohibition of 1429
  continuity, principle of 1460–1, 1463, 1468,
    1478, 1480, 1483–4
  control 1075, 1456, 1459, 1468, 1480, 1483
  de facto control 1456, 1459, 1468, 1483
  good governance 1460, 1462–3, 1466–81, 1484
  history and sources 1457–60
  interests of Occupying Power, protection
    of 1460–1, 1481–2
  internment/detention 1351, 1358
  legal system, continuity of the pre-existing
    1460–1, 1463, 1478, 1480, 1483–4
  loyalty to displaced government, respect for 1466
  modifications of administrative personnel 1428–9
  public officials, change of status of 1428
  public order and safety 1456, 1466–7
  public property, protection of 1541–5
  status quo, respect of legal and
    administrative 1461–6
  temporary character 1460, 1461–81, 1483
  transitional authorities 1428
advances of pay 1024, 1032 n 33
adverse distinction *see* non-discrimination principle
aerial bombardment 209, 453, 455, 991, 996,
   1278, 1301
Afghanistan *see also* Al-Qaeda; Guantánamo Bay,
   detention in; Taliban; war on terror
  armed conflict (1979–89) 1044–5
  armed conflict (2001–2) 32, 50
  armed conflict Afghan government/Taliban 44, 1048
agreements *see also* ad hoc agreements under
   Common Article 3; ceasefire agreements/
   armistices; peace agreements; special
   agreements in IACs
  inability to escape obligations by
    agreements 1576–7, 1586–7

Index

agreements (*cont.*)
  internment/detention, end of 1374, 1376–7, 1382, 1385–6
  protected areas, establishment of 371–5
  searches for dispersed internees 1380
aggression 93, 583, 1405, 1465
aiding and abetting 626, 661, 748–9, 975, 1034, 1064, 1364, 1384
aircraft
  attacks on aircraft 100
  applicability of IHL 12, 14, 75
  crew 907, 922
  flyovers 100, 102, 108, 830–1, 841
  humanitarian assistance 236
  inspection 100
  markings 830
  medical aircraft 70, 100–2, 140, 197, 826, 829–32, 835, 841
  medical transport 100–1, 197, 825–6, 829–32, 838, 841
  military aircraft 98, 108
  neutral states 98–101, 108
  neutrality 87, 98, 100–2, 108, 197
  no-fly zones 369, 379–80, 383, 1396
  protected persons 760, 773–4, 907, 922, 965, 1281
  search and rescue 829
Al-Qaeda *see also* Afghanistan; Guantánamo Bay, detention in; Pakistan; Taliban; war on terror
  armed conflict US-led coalition forces/Al-Qaeda 29, 44–5, 930–2, 949–50, 1048
  armed conflict Afghan government/Al-Qaeda 44, 50
  drone strikes against Al-Qaeda 44–5
  global conflict, as 29, 49–50, 68
  September 11, 2001 terrorist attacks 42
  war on terror 12, 42, 49–50, 68
alien occupation 20, 52, 396, 408, 1057, 1392, 1415
aliens in territory of party to conflict *see also* leave, right to 1071, 1258–64
  internment/detention 1258–9, 1264, 1328, 1351
  labour/employment 1262–4, 1268
  means of existence 1261–2
  nationality 1258–64
  non-repatriated persons 1259–61
  protected persons 1258–64, 1268
  restrictive measures, cancellation of 1264, 1268
allegiance *see also* oath of allegiance 21, 56, 251, 645, 905, 922, 953, 1000, 1028, 1032, 1056, 1060, 1062, 1065, 1124, 1129, 1142–5, 1147, 1253, 1316, 1332, 1403–4, 1440, 1448
ambulance 758–9, 782, 810, 825, 851, 854, 858, 867, 870
amendment/revision of the GCs 172–3, 690–1, 697–8
American Civil War 779
amnesties 283, 493, 632, 663–4, 1061
animus belligerandi 12

annexes to the GCs 160, 370–4, 1041–2
annexation 1139, 1224, 1406, 1461, 1463, 1465–6, 1483, 1554, 1559
Ante-Mortem/Post-Mortem (AMPM) database 272
anti-personnel mines 142
appeals
  convictions 1035–6
  criminal proceedings 1131
  fair trials 1131
  internment/detention 1336–8, 1340–1
  judicial guarantees 483, 1234–5, 1445
  sentences 1035–6
application/request
  to leave the territory 1173–1184
  to Protecting Powers and relief organizations 247, 536, 555, 1254–5, 1264, 1267
Argentina *see* Falklands (Malvinas) conflict
armed attack 19, 23, 59, 411
armed conflict *see also* international armed conflicts (IACs); mixed/parallel conflicts; non-international armed conflicts (NIACs)
  classification 514–15, 1186–7
  conversion of prima facie NIACs into IACs 17–26
  internationalization of conflicts 40–1
  transnational armed conflicts 48, 53, 83
  unorthodox conflicts 28, 31, 46–7
armed forces *see also* child soldiers; non-state armed groups
  accompanying armed forces 895–6, 906–7
  compulsory service 148–9, 1303, 1310, 1498–500, 1513
  deaths, investigations of 285–6
  incorporation of militias 894, 896
  laying down arms 439–42
  laws, regulations, and orders 1026–8, 1038
  members, of 893–5
  offences by occupying forces 1433
  requisition 1482
  reservists 604
  safety and sustenance 1460, 1462, 1484
armed groups *see* non-state armed groups
armed intervention/presence, consent to foreign *see also* foreign interventions 6, 14, 32–3, 37–9, 41, 44, 401–3, 1078, 1391, 1402–5, 1408, 1413–14, 1587–8
Armenia *see* Nagorno-Karabakh conflict
armistices *see* ceasefire agreements/armistices; peace agreements
arms *see* weapons
arms openly, carrying 901, 908, 917, 946
assassination *see* murder
assigned residence 1250–1, 1328–37, 1340, 1346
  cancellation of 1264
  dependants of persons subject to 1129
  grounds for 1328–29, 1330–31, 1333
  Information concerning persons subject to 265, 266, 281, 1097–98, 1104, 1111, 1113, 1119

limits 1334
judicial review of 1337–38, 1339
maintenance and re-establishment of family news for persons subject to 1099–110
notion of 1329–30
obligation to ensure support to persons subject to 1262
procedural requirements 1336–37
reassessment of 1129
assistance *see also* **humanitarian assistance**
direct assistance to the enemy 1331
legal assistance 476–8, 1225, 1230, 1444
mutual 1002
technical assistance to NSA 803, 820
attack, definition of unlawful 844
aut dedere, aut judicare see **prosecute or extradite, principle of**
auxiliary medical personnel *see also* **medical and religious personnel, status, rights, and obligations of; permanent medical personnel** 98, 809, 810, 815, 818–19
Azerbaijan *see* **Nagorno-Karabakh conflict**

belief *see* **religion and belief**
belligerent occupation *see* **occupation**; *see also* **alien occupation**
beneficiaries of rights from Common Article 3 433–47
body, dead *see also* **corpses/dead persons** 282, 286–8, 291, 293–5, 296
booty of war *see also* **looting; pillage** 1520, 1522, 1545–6
Bosnia-Herzegovina *see also* **former Yugoslavia**
ad hoc agreements 511–12, 514, 518–19
commitments of armed groups, ad hoc 420–1
IAC, as 13, 36–7, 72
mixed conflict, as 45
NIACs, as 13, 72
no-fly zones 379–80
POWs, treatment of 1009–10
protected areas 379–82, 383–6
protected civilians 1142, 1144, 1146–7
repatriation 1051
burials *see* **graves and burials**

Cambodia *see also* **Kampuchea**
border clashes with Thailand 15
camps/places of internment/POW camps
detention 444
escape 444
internment 58, 247, 555, 598, 990–1, 996, 1354, 1358–9
living conditions 252
marking 140
medical and religious personnel 818
POWs 192, 198–9, 553, 909, 977–1012
text of the Conventions 598, 602
transfer 957–76
visits 539, 543, 555, 715

canteens 997–8, 1354
capacity *see* **resources and capacity**
capital punishment *see* **death penalty; executions**
capture
beginning of applicability GCs and of Common Article 3 56, 68 n 5, 79
before capture, acts committed 620, 1027–8, 1029–31, 1037, 1085
capture cards 1006, 1016–17, 1090, 1114
child soldier, status after capture 1305
civilian hospitals, capture of 222
during hostilities 715–17
fighters/rebels, capture of 18, 25
hospital ships, capture of 209, 217, 221–2, 832, 834
hostage taking 299
identity of POW following capture 264
military hospitals on land, capture of 221–2
medical and religious personnel, status and treatment after 818–19, 848–9
merchant ships, capture of 768, 772
notification of 1014
state movable property, capture of 1545–6
wounded, sick, or shipwrecked, capture of 96, 769–70
cards
capture cards 1006, 1016–17, 1090, 1114
Central Tracing Agency 1114
enquiry cards 1298–9
identity cards 261–2, 264–5, 814–15, 819, 895, 992
internment/detention 1090–1, 1098, 1106, 1109, 1360
model cards and letters 1021
POWs 1006, 1016–17, 1090
care *see also* **medical care; public health**
care for the wounded and sick, obligation to 781–806, 835
health 57, 96, 99, 101, 103, 198, 200, 207–30, 262–5, 287, 650, 818, 823, 849, 881, 953, 962, 965, 982–3, 985, 977–1011, 1015, 1017, 1090, 1105, 1106, 1111–12, 1119, 1260, 1181, 1279–86, 1301, 1308, 1355–6, 1360, 1376, 1423, 1475, 1485–1515
medical care 96–7, 99, 197, 200, 203, 462, 747, 763, 798, 801, 811–12, 820–1, 823, 962, 985–6, 993, 998–9, 1003–4, 1009, 1259, 1279–81, 1283–4, 1300–1, 1353–4, 1356, 1486–8, 1490, 1493–5, 1501, 1512–13
CARHRIHL *see* **Philippines**
ceasefire agreements/armistices
ad hoc agreements 511, 519
implying consent to occupation 1404–5
internment/detention, end of 1374
repatriation 1040
end of applicability of the GCs 56–7
censorship 286, 1006, 1022–3, 1091, 1097, 1100–1, 1106–8, 1177, 1360

Central Tracing Agency (CTA)
  data protection 1016, 1115
  death, records of 281, 1015, 1115, 1365
  establish, duty to 1015, 1091
  facilitation 1015–16, 1090
  family links, maintenance of 1101, 1103, 1112–15
  impartiality 1113
  internment/detention 1106, 1107, 1114, 1360
  legal documents, transmission of 1020, 1114
  mail and correspondence 1114
  missing persons 262, 268, 270, 272
  National Information Bureau 1015, 1111, 1113–14
  neutrality 105–6, 1015, 1113
  notification by states 1017
  personal valuables, repatriation of 1115
  POWs 105–6, 985, 1006, 1014–16, 1113
  privacy 1016
  role 1112–14
certificates
  civilian hospital 209, 211, 813
  death 266, 278, 280, 289, 1019, 1365
  medical 999, 1114, 1356
  repatriation 1042
certified copies 162, 171
cessation/end of active hostilities *see also* **close of military operations** 56–8, 62, 95, 140, 310, 316, 963, 1041, 1046–8, 1051, 1374, 1378
chaplains 63, 95, 137, 197, 199, 604, 787, 807–24, 999–1000
child soldiers *see also* **children** 1296–7, 1311–2
  15, children under 1302–3, 1305–6, 1310
  18, children under 1304–5
  best interests principle 1304
  child, definition of 1295–7
  conscripting children as war crime 1296–7, 1310–11
  direct participation in hostilities 711, 1302–6
  enlisting children as a war crime 1296–7, 1310–11
  indirect participation 1304, 1306
  rape and sexual violence 356 n 87, 367
  recruitment 1303–5, 1310
  slavery 1303
  special rules 1303
  weapons 1302–3
children *see also* **child soldiers** 1293–312
  7, children under 200, 1295
  15, children under 106, 200
  age limits 1295–8, 1302
  age of majority 1295 n 7, 1296, 1302
  arrest 1302
  best interests principle 1357
  child, definition of 1295–7
  clothing 1300, 1354–5
  criminal responsibility 1307, 1310–11
  death penalty 483, 1296, 1302
  definition 1295–7
  education 1296, 1299–300, 1306, 1309, 1357
  electronic communications 1298
  evacuations 1301–2
  hospital and safety zones 1296, 1301–2
  human dignity 1306
  identification 1091, 1104–5, 1309
  identity discs 1103, 1296, 1297
  International Union for Child Welfare 1294, 1301–2
  internment/detention 1105–6, 1296, 1299–300, 1302, 1357
  labour/employment 1296, 1302, 1492
  neutral country, accommodation in a 103, 106–7, 140, 1296, 1302
  non-state armed groups 1307–10
  occupied territories 106, 1296–300, 1423
  orphans/children separated from family 106, 1296, 1298, 1300, 1500–1
  parents, registration of 1091
  perpetrators of crimes, children as 1311–12
  physical and psychological development 1295–6, 1300–1, 1306, 1309
  POWs, separation from adult 1302
  preferential treatment 1295–7
  rape and sexual violence 355, 356 n 87, 359, 364–7, 1309–10
  religion 1299, 1300, 1306, 1501
  repatriation 1301–2
  reunification of families 1294, 1297–9, 1306
  special rules 1293–312
  threat to peace, violation of children rights as 1307–8
  very young children 1300–1
civilian internees *see* **internees**
civilians taking direct part in hostilities *see* **direct participation in hostilities**
civilians, protection of 1069–87 *see also* **distinction, principle of; forced transfer and deportation of civilians; internees; internment/detention; protected civilians, definition of; repatriation of civilians**
close of military operations *see also* **cessation/end of active hostilities** 58, 1377–8, 1577–83, 1580
clothing 246–9, 555, 747, 789, 791, 961–2, 966, 988, 993–4, 997, 1023, 1279, 1300, 1354–5, 1429, 1475, 1487, 1493–4
cluster munitions 142
coalitions *see* **multi-national coalitions**
coastal lifeboats, rescue craft and installations 215–16, 220, 222, 815–16, 832, 834
coercion 146, 265, 319, 326–9, 353–7, 992, 1130, 1142–3, 1190, 1209, 1230, 1255–6, 1266, 1403
collateral damage 213 n 33, 217, 453 n 22
collection and transmission of information
  Central Tracing Agency 1112–14
  children 1298–9
  dead persons 278, 280–6, 293–4
  derogations 1126
  family links, maintenance of 1099, 1103–16, 1119–20

missing persons 263–5, 267–9, 272–3
National Information Bureau 1110–12
POWs 992–3, 1001, 1014
search, collect, and evacuate, obligation to 788–9
sharing information 1298
collective penalty *see under* collective punishment
collective punishment 1155–71
   attacks on civilians, distinct from 1168, 1170
   collective penalty 1157–8, 1160, 1167
   definition 1157, 1161, 1168
   house demolitions 1161–2
   individual criminal responsibility, link with the principle of 475, 1155, 1226
   leave, right to 1184
   mass expulsion 1170
   prohibition of 335, 1155–71, 1440
   related acts 1161–4
   reprisals, distinction from 578, 580, 588–9, 1158, 1162–4
   sanctions 1162–3, 1170
Colombia
   ad hoc agreements 511
   border incursions 15, 38–9, 43–4, 48, 82, 726
   consent to deployment 38
   Ecuador 15, 38–9, 43, 48, 82, 727
   human rights law 727
   IAC, as 38–9
   NIAC, as 38–9, 43–4, 48, 82, 423
   non-intervention, principle of 15
   state-like functions, armed groups exercising 423
colonial domination *see also* colonies 20, 52, 396, 408, 1057, 1415
colonies 1078, 1415, 1459, 1075, 1078, 1560
combat zones 1501
combatants *see also* unlawful combatants; unprivileged belligerents/combatants
   arms and ammunition taken from treated combatants 219
   Combatant Status Review Tribunal 949, 950–1
   enemy combatant, definition of 930–1, 933 *see also* unlawful combatants; unprivileged belligerents/combatants
   immunity of *see* combatant immunity
   unrecognized government, combatants belonging to 21–2, 905–6
   wounded, sick, and shipwrecked combatants 90, 95–7, 106
combatant immunity 18, 25, 890, 907–9, 915, 933, 954, 1007, 1031
command/superior responsibility 627–8, 749–50, 898–9, 903
commanders/officers *see also* command/superior responsibility
   dissemination of GCs 660–1, 603
   internment/detention 1084
   labour/employment 1002
   penal or disciplinary proceedings 1029, 1031–2, 1036, 1038
   POW camp command structure 1001–2
   responsible command threshold for NIACs 407–8
commissions *see* enquiry; fact-finding
common land 1539–41
communication 1021, 1106, 1109, 1112–15
Communist Party of Nepal-Maoist (CPN-M) *see* Nepal
compensation *see also* remedies and reparations
   children 1307
   expropriation 1527
   leave, right to 1183
   lost property 994–5
   private property, protection of 1518, 1522–6, 1539
   reprisals 593–4
   settlements, prohibition of 1573
complaints mechanisms
   internment/detention 1358–9, 1362, 1364
   POWs, treatment of 979, 1002, 1009
complete dependence test 17–19, 23
compliance/enforcement mechanisms *see also* complaints mechanisms; conciliation procedure; enquiry; fact-finding
   ad hoc agreements, established by 514, 517–21
   dissemination of GCs 597–614
   domestic implementation 655–65
   good offices conciliation and enquiry 561–74
   grave breaches, criminal repression 615–46
   ICRC, the role of the 525–47
   Protecting Powers 549–60
   Swiss/ICRC Initiative on Strengthening Compliance with International Humanitarian Law 173, 546, 562
compulsory recruitment into armed forces 148–9, 1303, 1310, 1498–500, 1513
conciliation procedure 562–7, 572
conclusion of GCs 160–71
conditions of detention/internment 200, 321, 332, 732, 979, 986, 1007, 1131, 1199, 1259, 1332, 1352, 1359
confessions 320, 323, 326–7, 341, 482
confidential material at trial 480
confidentiality
   in medical practice 796–7, 818
   confidentiality of the ICRC *see under* ICRC
confiscation 1009, 1517, 1522, 1523–4, 1529, 1554–5
conscientious objectors 98–9
conscription 148–9, 1303, 1310, 1466, 1513
consent
   armed intervention/presence, consent to foreign 6, 14, 32–3, 37–9, 41, 44, 401–3, 1078, 1391, 1402–5, 1408, 1413–14, 1587–8
   humanitarian assistance 232–3, 242–5, 250–1
   non-state armed groups to be bound by GCs, of 420–2, 425
contractors *see* private military and security companies (PMSCs)

Contras *see* Nicaragua
conversion of NIACs into IACs *see also* internationalization of NIACs 17–26
convicted persons 105, 252, 483, 1036, 1234, 1436, 1445–50
corporal punishment 322, 1080, 1257–8
corpses/dead persons *see also* remains 105, 260–1, 263–4, 266, 277–296, 463, 553, 786–9, 794, 800, 1019–20, 1368
correspondence *see* mail and correspondence
countermeasures/reprisals *see also* reprisals, prohibition of 113, 128–9, 134, 507, 578–9, 584, 594–5, 800–2, 1050
courts *see also* independent and impartial tribunal judicial guarantees;
  administrative bodies 1337
  competent courts 471, 940, 951–2, 954
  courts-martial 472, 1433
  independent and impartial tribunals 1337–8, 1438–9
  internment/detention, courts deciding on 1337, 1341
  local tribunals 1431–2, 1434
  nature of court required to pronounce judgment 471–3
  occupation courts 1084–6, 1431–6, 1447–51, 1453, 1570–1
  POW status determination 940–1, 943, 947–55
  regularly constituted 471–2, 493, 1229–34, 1441
  set up by non-state armed groups 488, 491
  special or military courts 471–2, 1026, 1028–9, 1034–8
  third states, recourse to courts of 1571–2
CPN-M (Communist Party of Nepal-Maoist) *see* Nepal
cremation 279, 289–90
crimes against humanity
  civilian population, meaning of 1152
  collective punishment 1168
  defence of reprisal 594–5
  deportation and forcible transfer 1193, 1320
  discrimination 202
  enforced disappearance 276, 1118
  inhumane acts 332, 340, 341
  internees accused of 1379
  jurisdiction of occupation courts 1435
  POW status of persons accused of/convicted for 619, 1029
  sexual and gender-based violence 366
  torture 323, 339, 341
cross-border NIACs *see also* transnational armed conflicts (TACs) 41–5, 401–2
  binary IAC/NIAC thresholds of application 12, 15–16, 41–5, 46, 77–83
  foreign intervention 42–3, 44–5
  spillovers 12, 15–16, 42–3, 49
  war on terror 42, 46
cruel, inhuman, or degrading treatment or punishment *see also* torture 317–42
Crown Dependencies 1076

CTA *see* Central Tracing Agency (CTA)
Cuba *see* Guantánamo Bay
cultural heritage/property
  communal property, as 1533
  definition 1528, 1529–30
  good governance 1478–9
  manners and customs, respect for 1246
  NIACs 1529–30
  occupied territories 1517, 1528–30
  pillage 1528–9
  reprisals 577, 580, 587
  seizure, requisition, and destruction 1528
  state property 1528
  use of property 1545
  war crimes 1532–3
culture *see also* cultural heritage/property; economic, social, and cultural rights in occupied territories
  children 106, 1295
  clashes of culture 705–6
  dead persons 294
  education 1299
  food and water 1355
  genocide 1246
  heritage 1478–9
  personal property 1357–8
  relativism 679–80, 682
  universality 670–1, 678–83, 687–8
  women 1275, 1290–2
currency 994
cyber warfare 22–4, 901, 946
Cyprus vs Turkey
  administration of occupied territories 1459, 1464, 1466, 1468, 1483
  Annan Plan 1569
  compensation 1569, 1572
  courts of Occupying Power, recourse to 1570
  customary international law 1566
  economic, social, and cultural rights 1510–11
  education 1511
  EU law 1571–2
  expulsion 1558, 1568
  home, right to respect for the 1568
  human rights law 1169, 1459, 1558–9, 1561, 1568–9
  Northern Cyprus 1558–9
  partition 1558
  POWs 715
  private persons 1564
  private property 1558, 1571–2
  reciprocity 1049
  remedies 1570
  restitution 1569
  seizure of land 1558, 1571–2
  self-determination 1568
  settlements, prohibition of 1558–9, 1561, 1564, 1566, 1568–73
  third states, recourse to courts of 1571–2
  transfers 1466
  United Nations 1558, 1561

damages 583, 656, 1008–9, 1138–9, 1183, 1570–1
danger zones 1251–2
Darfur *see* Sudan
death certificates, issue of 278, 280, 289, 1019
death penalty *see also* executions
   abolition 322, 483–4
   children 483, 1296, 1302, 1306, 1448
   extradition procedures 484, 485
   judicial guarantees 479, 485, 1216, 1233, 1445, 1446, 1453
   local law condition 1447–8
   mothers and expectant mothers 483, 1448
   non-refoulement 1204
   notify Protecting Power 554, 1105, 1233, 1441
   occupied territories 1446–9
   pardons or reprieves 1448–9
   penal or disciplinary proceedings 1033, 1036
   persons under 18 at time of offence 483, 1296, 1302, 1306, 1448
   POWs 1019, 1033, 1036
   procedures for protected persons sentenced to death 1448–9
   release and repatriation 1053, 1381
   spies and saboteurs 1130–1, 1447–8
   suspension 1449
declaration of war *see also* state of war 4–5, 6, 26, 54
defence *see* defence, rights of; defences
defence, rights of
   absentia, trials in 482
   access to accused, right of lawyer to 477–8
   adversarial proceedings 480
   confidential material by prosecution, use by 480
   equality of arms 479–80
   fair hearings, right to 479–81
   free legal assistance 477, 1444
   interpreters 479
   judicial guarantees 476–81, 1224–7, 1244–6, 1442–4, 1452
   personally, right of accused to defend themselves 476–7, 1444
   presence of lawyers during interrogations 478
   time and facilities to prepare defence 478–9, 1226, 1444
   torture, statements and confessions obtained as result of 482
defences *see also* military necessity; self-defence
   ignorance of the law 598
   reprisals 592–5
   superior orders, defence of 226, 408, 603, 618, 620, 627–8, 899, 1160
   tu quoque, defence of 594
degrading treatment *see* cruel, inhuman, or degrading treatment or punishment
delegates of ICRC *see also* ICRC
   acceptance of the principle of confidentiality 540–1
   attendance of the trial of an accused protected person 1445–6
   dissemination of the GCs 601
   Cyprus v Turkey Report 715 n 42

right of a detained protected person to be visited by 534, 1442, 1449
repatriation of POWs, role of the ICRC delegates in the 1058
stories of access to victims 542–3
visit to detainees in countries not experiencing war 506–7, 534–5
visit to NIAC-related detainees 1027 n 125
visit to places of internment, detention, and work 247, 534
demilitarized zones 369, 375–9, 382, 385–6
Democratic Republic of Congo (DRC) *see also* Rwanda; Uganda
   Democratic Forces for the Liberation of Rwanda (FDLR) 1165–6
   human rights law 730–1
   obligations of Uganda in the occupied territories of 1521–2, 1542, 1544, 1548
   occupation of 1392, 1459
   Patriotic Force for the Liberation of the Congo (FPLC) 398
   spillovers 42, 82
   Union of Congolese Patriots (UPC) 398
demographics of occupied territory, changing 1186
denunciation of GCs 176–9, 182, 185
dependent persons 1262, 1351, 1353–4
dependent territories 1075–7
deportation *see* forced transfer and deportation of civilians
depositary 156, 160 n 18, 162, 165, 168, 171–3, 177–8, 653, 690, 698 n 32, 967, 1417
deprivation of liberty *see* imprisonment; internment/detention; prisoner of war (POW): internment/detention
derogation from rights of protected civilians 1123–32
deserters 98–9, 892, 952–4, 1056
despoiling the dead 278, 286, 288, 292, 294
destruction of property
   compensation 1518
   cultural property 1528
   environmental protection 1548
   exception, threshold for 1537, 1546–50
   extensive destruction 1530–1, 1549–50
   good governance 1472
   grave breach 1517, 1530–1, 1536, 1549–50
   means of existence 1549
   military manuals 1529
   military necessity 1516, 1518–20, 1529–32, 1536–7, 1541, 1546–50
   NIACs 1529, 1531–2, 1548–9
   occupied territories 1516, 1518–20, 1529–32
   private property 1516, 1518–20, 1529–32
   public property 1536–7, 1539
   unlawfully and wantonly 1531
   war crimes 1529–32
detention *see* internment/detention; prisoner of war (POW): internment/detention
deterrence 576, 625, 752, 1162
developing countries 679, 985–6

development, right to 1539
dignity *see* human dignity
diplomatic protection 102, 150, 153, 1099, 1143, 1145–7
diplomatic relations
  appointment of Protecting Powers 551–3
  protection of nationals of neutral states 92, 102, 774, 1077
  protected civilians, definition of 1145–7
direct participation in hostilities *see also* participation in hostilities
  child soldiers 359, 711, 1302–6
  civilians 38, 101, 103, 452–3, 1079, 1082–5, 1128, 1141, 1148–9
  crews, members of 907
  criminal proceedings 1085
  definition 436–9, 452–3
  derogations 1128
  enemy combatant, definition of 930
  human rights law 711, 724–5
  human shields 1252
  humanitarian assistance 253
  loss of protection 816, 842
  murder 460
  NIACs 937, 1247, 1343
  POWs 1044
  taking no active part in hostilities condition for protection 437–8
  terrorists 538
  unlawful combatants 915–17
  wounded and sick 808
disabilities, persons with 196, 204, 711–12, 999
disappearances *see also* enforced disappearances; know, right to; missing persons 258, 261, 271–6, 281, 302, 710, 1020, 1024, 1118, 1329, 1352, 1359–61, 1365–9, 1385
discipline *see* penal or disciplinary proceedings
discrimination *see* non-discrimination principle
diseases
  compulsory notification of communicable 797
  contagious 797, 998–9, 1354, 1495–6
  prevention and control of 1354
displaced persons *see* internally displaced persons (IDPs)
dispute settlement 8, 562–4, 567, 572
dissemination of GCs 597–614
  armed forces 597–605, 607–14
  categories of addresses 603–7
  civil servants 606
  civilians 598–600, 603, 605–12
  codes of conduct 612
  commanders 600–1, 603
  domestic implementation 653–4
  education and training 598–608, 611, 614
  emergencies 606
  instruction manuals 602
  intergovernmental organizations 602
  international conferences 600
  international organizations 600
  Internet 609
  languages 160, 603, 608–9, 1001

legal advisers 600, 654
media 602, 607
military instruction 598–9, 602–5, 607–9, 611–13, 654
military manuals 598–9, 603, 654, 910
NIACs 600, 602, 610–12
peacekeeping, peace-enforcement, and peace-building troops 604–5
peacetime 63, 602–3, 611, 614
police and security forces 606, 614
qualified persons, dissemination by 600–1, 604
Red Cross 601–2, 605, 609, 612, 614
reservists 604
special agreements 611–12
time factor in dissemination 602–3
United Nations 602, 605, 609–10
who disseminates GCs 600–2
distinction, principle of 440, 900–1, 915, 917–9, 936–7, 1136
distinctive emblem *see also* emblems, use of 63, 119, 161, 209, 211–12, 216–17, 224–225, 528, 545, 606, 650, 652, 662–3, 690, 699, 745, 808, 814, 816, 821, 829, 837, 852–4, 855–888, 899–901, 907, 1281, 1497, 1513
distinctive signals 858, 861, 864, 874–5, 884
disturbances and tensions 48, 65, 235, 258, 337, 345 n 6, 393, 395–6, 409–10, 412, 414, 416, 440, 606, 710, 865, 870, 1164–5, 1199
domestic implementation 647–65
  administrative preparation 649–51
  civil defence organizations 650
  compliance/enforcement 655–65
  degree of detail 661–3
  detailed execution and unforeseen cases 654–5
  dissemination and training 653–4
  emblems and protected signs 650, 652, 662–3
  imperfect implementation 674, 685
  infrastructure 649–51
  legislation, adoption of 651–5
  NIACs 654, 656
  non-state armed groups 419
  preparatory measures 648
  Red Cross 649–50, 652–3
  types of measures 657–9
  universality 657, 674, 685
  voluntary societies 650
  war crimes 660–1, 663
domestic law *see* local laws
double jeopardy 1440, 1434–5, 1452
DRC *see* Democratic Republic of Congo
drones and drone strikes 38, 44–5, 1309–10
due process *see* fair trial
Dunant, Henry 87–8, 233, 526, 535, 757–8, 782, 808, 839–40, 857–8, 879
duration of conflicts threshold 11, 43–4, 48, 50, 54, 60, 410–11
duty to act 125, 127, 462, 627 n 56, 741, 748–9

East Timor
  indoctrination 1505
  internment/detention, end of 1385
  long-term occupation 1507
  standard of living 1508
  transformative or humanitarian occupation 1462
economic, social, and cultural rights in occupied territories 1485–514
  application of rights 1489–92
  children 1486, 1492, 1501, 1512
  civilians 1485–514
  education 1486–9, 1500–3, 1511
  food and water 1486–90, 1493–5, 1501, 1512, 1514
  fullest extent of means available 1506–8
  hygiene 1486, 1493, 1495–7, 1500
  labour/employment 1486–8, 1490, 1498–500
  legislative powers, scope of 1503–6
  means of existence 1539
  medical care and health 1486–8, 1490, 1493–5, 1501, 1512–13
  medical supplies 1487–8, 1490, 1493–6, 1506, 1512
  NIACs 1508–10
  positive duties 1503–8
  public health 1486, 1493, 1495–7, 1500, 1506
  real property 1486
  relief consignments 1486, 1494–5, 1513
  requisitions 1488, 1497–9
  resources 1493–5, 1507–8
  sanitation 1489, 1512
  standard of living 1494, 1508
economic warfare 767–8, 771–2, 775–7, 780
Ecuador *see* **Colombia**
education *see also* **training**
  children 106, 1246, 1296, 1299–300, 1306, 1309
  definition 1502–3
  dissemination of GCs and IHL in general 538–9, 598–608, 611, 614
  economic, social, and cultural rights 1486–8, 1500–3
  gender 1475
  indoctrination 1505
  internment/detention 1300, 1357
  legislative powers, scope of 1505
  non-discrimination 1475
  occupied territories 1411, 1476, 1486–8, 1500–3
El Salvador
  Farabundo Martí National Liberation Front (FMLN) 62, 418 n 14, 488, 491
  UN Mission 455
electronic communications/new technology *see also* **Internet**
  children 1298
  cyber warfare 22–4, 946
  e-mail 1022, 1101, 1107
  family links, maintenance of 1101
  internment/detention 1107, 1360
  missing persons 272

  National Information Bureau 1112
  POWs 1014, 1017, 1022, 1024
  Skype 1022, 1101, 1107
emblems, use of *see also* **signs** 855–85, 690
  abuse and misuse, prevention and repression of 872–8, 885
  authorization 858, 863, 866–72
  conditions for use 871–2
  control 868–72
  convoy for maternity cases 1280–1
  criminalization of misuse 872
  different uses 861–6
  displaying or not displaying 882–3
  distinctive signals 861
  distinctive signs 858, 860–2
  domestic implementation 650, 652, 662–3
  double emblem, no 865
  expansion of use 858, 866–9
  fundraising, use for 863–4
  hospitals 208–9, 211, 212, 217, 224–5, 866, 870, 872
  imitations 873–4, 885
  improper use 874
  indicative use 862–3, 865, 867–8, 873
  logos 861–2
  medical activities 808, 814–15, 821, 857–72, 881–5, 1280–1
  medical buildings, material, and transport 837
  model laws 876–7
  multiple users 866–9
  multi-national coalitions 866, 868–9
  NIACs 859–60, 867–8, 871, 884
  non-Red Cross/Red Crescent organizations 868, 869
  non-state armed groups 871
  not using emblem, consequence of 863, 882
  occupied territories 870
  peacekeeping forces 867, 868–9
  peacetime 861–2, 867, 869–72
  penalties 876–7
  perfidious use 873, 874, 876
  private military and security companies 868, 869
  protective use 862–3, 865, 868, 873
  reasons for creation 855–8
  red cross, crescent, red lion and sun, the red crystal 861, 864–5, 879–80, 882
  religious links, perception of 879–80
  religious personnel 860, 867
  respect and protect, obligation to 857
  road signs to civilian hospitals 861
  size and dimensions 864–5, 870
  Swiss flag, protection of 874
  targets by non-law-abiding parties and criminals, as identifying 881
  technical means of identification 885
  temporal scope 869–70
  temporary use 865–6

emblems, use of (*cont.*)
   truce, use of emblem as flag of 874
   unity and plurality 878–80
   visibility, lack of 881
   war crimes 872–3, 874, 876
emergency
   declaration of state of emergency 410
   emergency relief *see* humanitarian assistance
   national emergency and IHL rules 1565
   reduced period suspension of death penalty 1449
   rights in times of public emergency 321, 337, 486–7, 712, 720, 721, 1117, 1127, 1180, 1193, 1207–8, 1246
employment *see* forced labour; labour/employment
encrypted communications 220, 228, 833, 838
end of applicability of GCs 52–3, 56–9, 61–2
   agreements on the end of occupation 1576–7, 1586–7
   one year after close of military operations 52–3, 58–9, 1576–86
   peace treaties 56–7, 62, 64
   permanent termination 56
end of hostilities *see* cessation/end of active hostilities
enemy, acts harmful to the 842–3, 847–8, 854
enemy, direct assistance to 1331
enforced disappearances *see also* disappearances; know, right to; missing persons 258 n 5, 271, 273, 275–6, 709–10, 1020, 1024, 1117–8, 1119, 1359, 1368–9, 1385
enforced prostitution *see* prostitution, enforced
enforcement *see* compliance/enforcement mechanisms
enlistment 891, 1002, 1017, 1144, 1296–8, 1310, 1498, 1501
enquiry *see also* fact-finding; International Humanitarian Fact-Finding Commission (IHFFC) 269, 270, 563–5, 567–4, 1019–20, 1112, 1366
environment/environmental protection 581, 609, 1463, 1476–80, 1504–5, 1541, 1548
equality *see also* non-discrimination principle
   arms, equality of 479–80, 725, 1225, 1231, 1364, 1442–3
   before the law 472, 1353
   belligerents, between 30, 177, 488, 491, 517, 591
      compliance/enforcement 582–3, 590–1
      hospitals 221
      hostages, taking 311–12
      humanitarian assistance 251
      judicial guarantees 1219–21
   civilians 1260, 1262–3, 1367
   compliance/enforcement 558, 582–3, 590–1
   education 1357
   equal treatment principle 198, 358–9, 986, 1260–1, 1263, 1507
   hospitals 210
   hostages, taking 311–12
   humanitarian assistance 241, 246, 251

   judicial guarantees 472, 488, 491, 1219–21
   medical and religious personnel 823
   POWs 986, 1026
   temporal scope of application 65
   wounded, sick, and shipwrecked 790
Eritrea vs Ethiopia
   administration of occupied territories 1459
   age, persons of 1334
   applicability of GCs 7, 55
   cruel, inhuman, or degrading treatment or punishment 1130
   delay of trials 485
   destruction of property 1547–8
   evacuation of POWs 961, 975, 988–9
   forced transfers 1186
   leave, right to 1175–9, 1183
   military necessity 1518
   occupation, concept and beginning of 1395, 1398, 1402, 1406
   peace treaties 64
   POWs 57, 788, 979, 982, 986–7, 994, 1002–3, 1009
   Red Cross messages 1022
   repatriation 1048, 1049–51, 1056, 1058, 1064
escaped prisoners/escapes 96, 98, 444–5, 964, 972, 981, 983, 988, 994, 995, 997, 1027, 1033–4, 1167
espionage 22, 922, 1030, 1124, 1126–30, 1331, 1447
ethics (medical) 789–90, 797, 802, 817–18, 1356, 1496–7
Ethiopia *see also* Eritrea vs Ethiopia
   Ogaden National Liberation Front 42, 1166
ethnic cleansing 409, 1208, 1227–8, 1553–4, 1559
ethnicity *see* race and ethnicity
European Union 204, 660, 1093–4, 1481
evacuation 446, 776, 786–7, 793–800, 957–63, 973–6, 979, 988–9, 1009, 1191–3, 1195–6, 1205, 1207–8, 1280–1, 1288, 1301–2, 1381, 1485
ex post facto legislation (retroactive application) 70, 157, 168, 394, 450, 618, 916, 944, 1131, 1227–8, 1237, 1238, 1244, 1439–40
exclusive economic zones (EEZs) 70
execution of GCs 556, 598, 600, 603, 654–5, 693
executions *see also* death penalty 451, 463–4, 470, 471, 489–90
   judicial guarantees 470–1, 489, 492, 493, 641, 954, 995, 1216, 1284
   summary execution 451, 463–5, 723, 1024, 1338
exchange
   information 261–2, 270, 275, 1005, 1015–16, 1021–3, 1101, 1114
   protected persons 136, 140, 310–11, 378, 787, 1040, 1042–3, 1061, 1374
experiments (biological and pseudo-medical) 187, 197, 360, 784, 789–90, 799, 809, 983, 998, 1079, 1258

exhumations 283, 287, 291, 1120
expanding bullets 142
expectant mothers *see* mothers and expectant mothers
expropriation *see also* property 1522, 1526–7
exterior, relations with *see also* family links and transmission of information, maintenance and re-establishment of; mail and correspondence; prisoner of war (POW): relations with outside world of 1090–1, 1098, 1106–8, 1109, 1129, 1130, 1351, 1360–1, 1368
extradition *see also* prosecute or extradite, principle of
   death penalty 484, 485
   forced transfers 1197–8, 1201–3
   grave breaches 618, 630, 632, 635–7
   hostages, taking 707–8
   internment/detention 1379
   judicial guarantees 484, 485–6
   refugees 1314, 1317, 1437
   repatriation 1059
   torture, risk of 485, 631, 1379
   wounded, sick, and shipwrecked 803
extra-state conflicts *see* transnational armed conflicts (TACs)
extraterritoriality
   exercise of jurisdiction 1083, 1084
   grave breach, obligation to search for persons responsible for 630
   IHL, application of 73, 74, 78–9, 954
   IHRL, application of 50, 73, 285, 704–5, 717, 729, 928, 1087, 1344, 1458, 1484, 1487, 1490–2
   non-refoulement principle, application of 1057 n 137
   POWs, determination of status of 954

fact-finding/fact-finding missions and commissions *see also* enquiry; International Humanitarian Fact-Finding Commission (IHFFC) 23, 518, 546, 563, 564–5, 567–74, 1163, 1418, 1510, 1511
failed states 397, 1390, 1402–3
failure to act 298, 307, 316, 627, 748
fair trial *see also* judicial guarantees
   aliens in territory of party to conflict 1259, 1261
   appeals 1131
   civilians, protection of 1087, 1125–6, 1129–32, 1216–19, 1230–1, 1235
   collective punishment 1164
   criminal proceedings 1061, 1130–1
   customary international law 1261, 1439
   defence, rights of 479–81
   delay 1442
   derogations 720, 1125–6, 1129, 1130–2
   grave breaches 641, 644, 1026, 1037, 1433
   hostages, taking 302
   human rights law 720
   independent and impartial tribunals 1337–8, 1438–9
   internment/detention 1259, 1337–8, 1368
   legality, principle of 1131
   non-state armed groups, creation of courts by 488–9
   occupied territories 1433, 1438–43, 1450–2
   penal or disciplinary proceedings 996, 1026–7, 1029–31, 1033–8
   residual protection 923
   spies and saboteurs 1130–1
   war crimes 1433, 1451–2
Falklands (Malvinas) conflict
   administration of occupied territories 1465
   denial of state of war 54
   hospital ships 208, 214
   naval warfare 775
   NIACs, as 13
   Protecting Powers 1104
   search, collect, and evacuate, obligation to 788
   transit camps 990
family links and transmission of information, maintenance and re-establishment of 350, 1089–121, 1245, 1281, 1476
   censorship 1091, 1097, 1100, 1117
   Central Tracing Agency 1090–1, 1101, 1103, 1112–15
   children 1091, 1102–5, 1116, 1298
   civilians 1089–121
   communication of family news 1092, 1097, 1099–101, 1100–1
   data protection 1096–9
   dead persons 278–9, 281–3, 286, 294
   electronic communications 1101
   enquiries, facilitating 1090, 1101–2, 1112, 1119–21
   EU law on family reunification 1093–4
   family, definition of 1091–6
   identification 1091, 1104–5
   internment/detention 1090–1, 1097–8, 1105–9, 1115, 1118–20
   know, right of families to 1091–2, 1095–6
      children 1298
      dead persons 278–9, 281–4, 286, 294
      missing persons 258–9, 264, 273–4, 276, 1120
   mail and correspondence 1090–1, 1097, 1100–1, 1115, 1117, 1119
   military necessity 1099
   missing persons 535, 1090–1, 1096, 1099, 1120
      know, right of families to 258–9, 264, 273–4, 276, 1120
      tracing 1120
   National Information Bureau, establishment of official 1090, 1101–2, 1109–12
   national security 1097
   NIACs 1115–17
   occupied territory 1090–1, 1104–5
   parcels 1091
   POWs 1006, 1024
   privacy of information 1092, 1096–9
   protected persons 1089–121
   Protecting Powers 1097–8, 1104–5
   reciprocity 1099

family links (*cont.*)
  Red Cross 1091, 1101–3, 1116–17
  reunification 1093–4, 1098–9, 1102, 1104–5, 1115, 1120–1
    children 1294, 1297–9, 1306
    enquiry cards 1298–9
  together, keeping families 1090–1, 1099
  tracing services 1091, 1094, 1101–2, 1109–15
  transmission of information 1099, 1103–16, 1119–20
Farabundo Martí National Liberation Front (FMLN) *see* El Salvador
FARC *see* Colombia
fate of relatives, right of families to know *see* know, right to
FDLR *see* Democratic Republic of Congo (DRC); Rwanda
female genital mutilation (FGM) 320, 324
fighters *see also* direct participation in hostilities; participation in hostilities; unlawful combatants; unprivileged belligerents/combatants 11, 18, 25, 38, 49, 76, 79, 223, 452, 461, 513, 724–5, 732, 790, 820, 824, 892, 896, 900, 905, 909, 933, 1007–8, 1026, 1047, 1061–2, 1065, 1150, 1343, 1383, 1396–7, 1399, 1473
final provisions of GCs 155–88
  accession 162, 163, 165–9, 171, 173
  concept and role 156–7
  conclusion of GCs 160–71
  consent to be bound, expression of 162–9
  denunciation 156, 158, 172, 176–9, 182, 185
  depositary 162, 168, 171–3
  entry into force 156–8, 160, 162–3, 169–71
  languages 156–60, 172
  Martens Clause 157, 159, 168, 179–88
  official languages 156–7
  ratification 156, 160, 162, 168, 171–3
  registration of treaties 171–3
  relationship with previous conventions 174–6
  reservations 156, 171–2, 173–4
  signature 160–2, 163, 173
  succession to treaties 157, 164–9, 171–2
financial resources *see also* accounts 17, 349, 398, 503–4, 614, 664–5, 792, 961, 971, 1002–6, 1091, 1114, 1174, 1179, 1231, 1262, 1329, 1351, 1357–8, 1361, 1494, 1543, 1545, 1563
fines 1032–3, 1363
fingerprinting 992
First World War
  accommodation of POWs neutral countries 1044
  administration of occupied territories 1457
  Central Tracing Agency 1015
  collective punishment 1156, 1159
  colonies 1078
  internment/detention 1350
  POWs 978, 1113
  Protecting Powers 550
  rape and sexual violence 348
  shipwrecked, definition of 772, 776, 780

flyovers 100, 102, 108, 830–1, 841
FMLN *see* El Salvador
follow-up (double-tap/secondary) attacks 786
food and water *see also* means of existence 233, 236, 244–5, 248–9, 252, 254, 961–2, 966, 971, 979, 997–8, 999, 1170, 1279–81, 1284, 1301, 1354–6, 1423, 1473–4, 1478, 1449, 1486–90, 1493–5, 1501, 1512, 1514, 1540, 1544–5, 1549
footwear 961, 975, 989, 997, 1009, 1355
force majeure 487
forced labour
  aliens in territory of party to conflict 1263–4, 1268
  compulsory enlistment 1498–500
  economic, social, and cultural rights 1488
  internment/detention 1264, 1370
  POWs 1002–3, 1257, 1264
  working conditions 1470
forced landing at sea 236, 773
forced transfer and deportation of civilians 1185–213
  administration of occupied territories 1466, 1471
  children 1301
  collective/mass deportation 728, 1186–8, 1194–5, 1197, 1199, 1209, 1334
  collective punishment 1166
  criminal proceedings 1085–6
  cultural genocide 1246
  customary international law 1195–6, 1212
  demographics of occupied territory, changing 1186
  distinction between forcible transfer and deportation 1188–90
  economic, social, and cultural rights 1486, 1513
  evacuation 1091, 1191–3, 1195–6, 1205, 1208
  expulsion 1197–8, 1212–13
  external displacement 1208–9
  extradition 1197–8, 1201–3
  forcible character 1190–1
  freedom of movement 1193–4, 1207, 1210
  good governance 1471
  grave breaches 1087, 1210
  internal displacement 1205–8
  internment/detention 1079–83, 1087, 1197–201, 1204, 1334, 1351, 1354
  leave, right to 1179
  list of transferees 1365
  military necessity 1191, 1196
  non-discrimination 1198–9, 1207
  non-refoulement, principle of 1198, 1202–5
  occupied territory 1091, 1187–96, 1205, 1211, 1365, 1391, 1410, 1416, 1433, 1435
  own country, expulsion from 1194
  persecution, risk of 1186, 1194, 1198, 1200–3
  protected persons 1186–9, 1191–2, 1196–202, 1210–11, 1213
  Red Cross 1187, 1195–7, 1199, 1204–9
  refugees 1187, 1198, 1200–4, 1211–13, 1317–18, 1320
  rendition 1197, 1203
  repatriation 1381, 1383
  residence, choice of 1193

residual protection 924–5
return, right to 1194
settlements, prohibition of 1552–73
territorial scope 1196
third states not respecting GCs, transfer to 1196, 1198–200
torture in destination state, risk of 1195, 1203–4
voluntary transfers 1190–1
war crimes 1210–11
foreign interventions *see also* armed intervention/presence, consent to foreign 38, 42–3, 44–5
former Yugoslavia *see also* Bosnia-Herzegovina; Kosovo/Serbia
  administration of occupied territories 1459
  Dayton Peace Agreement 1559
  diplomatic representation 1146–7
  ethnic cleansing 1559
  geographical scope of application 67–8, 71–3, 76–7
  hospitals 227
  medical and religious personnel 821
  mixed conflicts 64–5
  NIACs 76–7, 1144
  non-state armed groups 1399–400
  POWs, transfer of 975
  protected areas 378–82, 383–6
  protected civilians, definition of 1142
  Red Cross 55, 503
  repatriation 1051, 1064
  sentences, internees serving 1380
  settlements, prohibition of 1559
  torture 325
  war crimes 1009–10
FPLC *see* Democratic Republic of Congo (DRC)
free passage 237, 248–9, 251, 508, 512, 1288, 1300, 1475, 1493
freedom of assembly 1489
freedom of movement 1173–4, 1180–2, 1193–4, 1207, 1243, 1569
freedom of opinion 1489
freedom of the press 1489
Fuerzas Armadas Revolucionarias de Colombia (FARC) *see* Colombia

Gaza *see* Israel/Palestine/Occupied Palestinian Territory
gender *see also* women 202, 204–5, 346–9, 350–8, 365–8, 574, 609, 1244 n 17, 1272, 1274, 1287–8, 1290–1, 1310, 1377, 1437, 1474, 1496–7
general close of military operations *see* close of military operations
Geneva Call 223 n 119, 426 n 42, 498 n 17, 686–7, 1307
genocide 127, 128–9, 131–2, 202, 252, 346, 381, 385, 409, 594–5, 623 n 38, 637, 1027, 1208, 1227–8, 1246, 1379, 1553–4, 1559
geographical scope of application of GCs 67–83
  belligerents, territory of 70–4, 83
  high seas 69, 70, 74–5

IACs 68–75, 83
nexus test for war crimes 72–3, 75–6, 82–3
NIACs 68–9, 72, 75–83, 400–4
outside belligerent's own territory, scope of application 73
spillovers 77–83
territorial scope, use of term 69
war on terror 68–9, 79
Georgia vs Russia (2008)
  Abkhazia separatists 35, 45–6, 107, 1392
  ceasefire agreements 1404
  enquiry/fact-finding procedure 572
  South Ossetia separatists 35, 45–6, 107, 1392
Goa conflict *see* India
good governance 1460, 1462–3, 1466–81, 1472–6, 1478–80, 1484
good offices offered by Protecting Powers 563, 565–7, 571
government
  combatants of unrecognized government 21–2, 905–6
  functions 1577, 1580–1
  NIACs 392
  non-state armed groups 944
  occupation, end of applicability in times of 1577, 1580–1, 1587–8
  proxy governments, setting up of 32–4
  puppet governments, safeguards against 1587–8
  recognition of governments 905–6, 944
  unrecognized governments 21–2
grave breaches *see also* universal jurisdiction; war crimes 615–46
  content of the obligation 621–4
  court, obligation to bring alleged perpetrators to 631–5
  defences 618, 620, 622, 627–8
  delay in repatriation of POWs 1063
  destruction of property 1517, 1530–1, 1536, 1549–50
  enquiry/fact-finding procedure 568, 570–1
  extradition 618, 630–2, 635–7
  fair trials 641, 644, 1026, 1037, 1433
  forced transfer 1087, 1210
  hand suspects over to another state, obligation to 635–8
  hospitals 225
  hostages, taking 301, 303–4, 314–5, 708, 1335
  IACs 643–6, 743
  illegal conduct 743–7
  internment/detention 631, 1087, 1132, 1259, 1335, 1345, 1376, 1384
  investigations 630
  judicial guarantees 640–2, 1216, 1236
  legality, principle of 623 n 37
  medical and religious personnel 821
  medical buildings, material, and transport 836
  military necessity 621

grave breaches (*cont.*)
   minimum procedural guarantees 631, 644
   NIACs 642–4
   object and purpose 622–3
   ordering mode of criminal liability 315 n 140, 619, 621, 625–6, 656, 935, 1345
   penal or disciplinary proceedings 1026, 1037
   persons against whom effective penalties must be established 625–8
   POWs 619–20, 640–2, 935, 964, 983, 1063
   private property 1026, 1037
   prosecutions 615–20, 629–38, 641–2, 644
   protected civilians 1151–2
   protected persons 643–4, 646
   public property 1549
   punishment 615–19, 622–5, 628, 632–3, 637–8, 640–2, 644
   rape and sexual violence 357, 361–3, 366
   refugees 1320
   reservations 642
   sanctions/punishment 615–19, 621, 622–5, 628, 632–3, 637–8, 640–2, 644
   search for perpetrators, obligation to 619, 628–30
   settlements 1555
   sovereignty 617, 620, 637
   subsequent treaties and conventions, relationship with 699–700
   surrender 618–20, 620, 638
   torture 319, 328, 339–40, 631
   universal criminal jurisdiction 617, 622, 630, 638–40, 644–5
   war crimes 615–20, 634, 641–6, 739
   women 1286, 1288–90
   wounded and sick 785, 803–4
graves and burials 277–82, 286–92, 296, 1365
   ashes, return of 279, 290–1
   cemeteries 277–8, 290–1
   cremation 279, 289–90
   delays 287–8
   duration of obligation 279, 291–2
   exhumations 283, 287, 291, 1120
   Graves Registration Service 289, 1019
   internment/detention 1365–6
   Islamic burials 287–8, 293
   location, information on 281–2, 1019–20, 1366
   maintenance 291–2
   marking 279, 286–7, 289, 291–2
   mass graves 279, 287
   missing persons 260
   neutral states 105
   Official Graves Registration Service 291
   positive obligations 291
   POWs 1019
   public health 287, 289
   registration 291, 1019
   religion 279, 287–9, 293
   respect 291–2
   sea, burial at 279, 288, 289–90, 296

Guantánamo Bay, detention in
   citizenship status 204
   Combatant Status Review Tribunal 950–1
   contesting factual basis of detention 1129
   derogations 1124
   habeas corpus 950
   judicial guarantees 472
   leasehold territories 1075–6
   NIACs 1346–7
   Red Cross messages 1022
   rendition 928
   self-incrimination, privilege against 1230
   terrorism, crime of material support for 915–17
   unlawful combatants 932, 935–6, 950–1
   war crimes 915–17
   war on terror 950, 1149
guarantees *see* **judicial guarantees**
guerrilla warfare 917, 919, 940, 943
Gulf War (1980–8) *see* **Iraq vs Iran**
Gulf War (1990–1) *see* **Kuwait**
Gulf War (2003–4) *see* **Iraq**

habeas corpus
   derogations 1131
   detention before trial 488
   judicial guarantees 488
   internment/detention 1337–9
   liberty and security, right to 732
   POWs, determination of status of 950, 953–4
handcuffing 320
health *see* **care; medical care; public health**
Hezbollah *see* **Lebanon**
high seas, geographical scope of 74–5
homeland, right to the 1567–8
honour
   collective honour 350
   definition 348–9
   enemy hands, treatment of civilians in 1244
   family honour 350
   modesty 1274–6, 1285, 1290
   POWs 319, 982, 1000, 1009–10, 1275
   rape and sexual violence 346–51, 354, 367, 1276
   women 1274–6, 1285, 1290
hooding 320
hors de combat, **persons placed** 441–5
hospital ships *see also* **hospitals; vessels** 208–9, 214–22
   arms, possession of 219–20, 228, 833–4
   capture 221–2, 832, 834
   civilians 832
   definition 214, 832
   encrypted communications 220, 228, 833, 838
   escorts by warships 216–17
   IACs 835
   loss of protection 219, 840–9
   military manuals 214, 219–20, 222, 224, 833, 835, 838
   neutral observers 220–1, 228
   neutral ports 833

neutral states 833
NIACs 225, 834–6
non-state armed groups 835
notification 214–16, 832–3
official ships 214
pillage 835
ports, in occupied 221–2, 228
POWs, transfer of 993
Red Cross 833
remoteness from military objectives 216–17
requisitions 834
respect and protect, obligation to 835
San Remo Manual 214, 219–20, 222, 224, 833, 835, 838
scope of protection 217–22
searches 220, 228, 834
self-defence 220, 833–4
shipwrecked persons 215–16
sick-bays on warships 222, 228, 832, 840–9
small coastal rescue craft 215–16, 220, 222, 832, 834
war crimes 226–7, 743

hospitals *see also* **hospital ships** 207–29
capture 221–2
Central Tracing Agency 1015
children 1296, 1301–2
civilian hospitals 209, 210–13, 217–19, 222, 225, 228, 861, 866, 870
definition 208, 210–11
distinction, principle of 210, 213, 217
emblems 208–9, 211, 212, 217, 224–5, 872
fixed and field hospitals 210–11
grave breaches 225
identification 208–9, 211, 212–13, 217, 226
inspection 208, 220–1
land, on 207–13, 217–22
loss of protection 840–9
marking 208, 212, 216, 218, 228, 870
medical services, definition of 210
medical units 207–14, 218–19, 223–4, 227
military hospitals 209, 213, 218–19, 228, 759
military manuals 210–12, 218–19
military objectives 208, 210, 213, 216–18, 224, 228, 650, 837
mobile units 210–11
national flags 208
national legislation 210–11, 223
naval warfare 228
neutrality 95, 103–4, 210, 759
NIACs 222–5, 228
notification of location 209, 212–13
peacetime 650–1
precautionary measures 213, 650
protected areas 369, 370–4, 385, 532, 1278
recognition as a hospital 208, 211–12, 218
Red Cross 210, 213, 215, 223, 229, 532
remoteness from military objectives 208, 213, 216–18, 228, 650

reprisals 218
requisition 221–2
road signs 861
scope of protection 217–22
searches 223
situations not resulting in deprivation of protection 218–22, 227–8
soft law 214, 219–20, 222, 224
veterinary service 219
war crimes 224–7
women 1278
x-rays with wireless messages or radar, interference of 219

hostages, taking 297–316
arbitrary and anarchic capture and executions 299
armed groups 312–13
civilians 301, 303–4, 310, 314, 1070
collective punishment 1164
core elements 304–9, 311, 313
criminal law 300–1, 307, 313
cruel, inhuman, or degrading treatment or punishment 302, 306
definition 298–9, 304, 309–11, 316, 1335
deprivation of liberty/detention 298–9, 301–11, 316
execution 299–300
extradition 707
fair trials 302
grave breaches 301, 303–4, 314–5, 708, 1335
hostage, definition of 301
human shields 1266
IACs 298–301, 304, 309–12, 708
internment/detention 310, 1335, 1383–4
kill or injure, threats to 298, 302, 304–7, 309, 311, 316
legality 300, 302, 304, 309–11, 316
life, right to 302, 707
media 311–12
nationality 300
NIACs 298, 301, 304, 309–14, 316, 708
occupied territory 299–301, 305–6, 316
POWs 298–9, 301, 303–4, 310–11, 314, 316
prophylactic hostage taking 299
prosecute or extradite principle (*aut dedere, aut judicare*) 313–14, 708
protected persons 301, 303, 310, 314–5
ransoms 299
reciprocity 299
Red Cross 303, 306–7
regional treaties 301–2, 315
reparations 313
reprisal prisoners 299
security and compliance, ensuring 299
seized, detained, or otherwise held 305–6, 311, 316
specific intent 1335, 1384
surety hostages 298–9
symbolic hostages 308–9

hostages, taking (*cont.*)
  terrorism 315
  third party compulsion 307–8, 311, 316
  threats 298, 301–2, 304–11, 316
  torture 302, 306
  treaty obligations, guarantees of 298–9
  war crimes 300, 747
hostility from local population 1330, 1383
hostilities *see also* **direct participation in hostilities; participation in hostilities**
  active hostilities, cessation of 58
  definition 71, 83
  follow-up (double-tap/secondary) attacks 786
  general close of military operations distinguished 1580
  neutral states 87, 94
  POWs 991, 996–8
  release after close of hostilities 1374–5, 1377–80
    as soon as possible after close of hostilities 1374, 1377–9
    general close of military operations 1377–8
  repatriation at end of hostilities 1046–59, 1061, 1065–6
  without hostilities, applicability in cases of war 6
housing *see* **shelter**
human dignity
  collective punishment 1164
  cruel, inhuman, or degrading treatment or punishment 318, 332–3, 335, 337–41
  human shields 1266
  internment/detention 1281–2
  judicial guarantees 1218
  POWs, treatment of 982, 1000, 1009–10
  rape and sexual violence 344, 347–9, 351, 355, 360–2
  sanitation 1282
  women 1274, 1285
  wounded, sick, and shipwrecked 798
human rights law 701–35
  accountability 706
  Afghanistan 717–8
  African Charter on Human and Peoples' Rights 727–8
  African Union 718–19
  American Convention on Human Rights 722–7
  applicability during armed conflicts 711–19
  arbitrarily, meaning of 717, 720–3, 734
  children 710–28 *see also* **children**
  Colombia 727
  Conciliation Commissions, establishment of ad hoc 567
  customary international law 1471, 1480
  Cyprus vs Turkey 1169, 1459, 1558–9, 1561, 1568–9
  Democratic Republic of Congo 730–1
  derogations 712–13, 716, 720–1, 734, 1370
  direct participation in hostilities 711, 724–5
  disabilities, persons with 711–12

  economic, social, and cultural rights in occupied territory 1485–514 *see also* **economic social and cultural rights**
  emergency, derogation clauses for times of 720–1
  employment 1262
  equality, principle of 733, 1353
  explicit references to IACs in human rights treaties 710–28
  extraterritoriality 73, 704–5
  fair trials 720
  general articulation of relationship between human rights rules and rules contained in GCs 728–34
  geographical scope of application 73
  good governance 1471, 1480
  IACs 25, 707, 712–13, 717, 721, 725, 731, 734–5
  IHL, relationship with 320
  implicit references to IACs in human rights treaties 710–28
  implied references to GCs in human rights treaties 719–22
  interests of Occupying Power, protection of 1481
  international instruments, treaties referring to other 722–8
  interpretation of treaties 705–6, 716
  Iraq 715–7, 1342, 1427
  Israel/Palestine/Occupied Palestinian Territory 1565, 1569, 1573
  judicial guarantees 479–80, 488, 491, 680, 683–4, 688, 1216, 1217–36, 1439–40, 1443, 1445, 1452–3
  law-making in occupied territories 1423, 1425, 1426–7
  legal advisers 703
  Libya 728
  life, right to 284–5, 293–4, 302, 307, 464–5, 712–14, 720–6, 728, 732, 1024, 1243
  military necessity 705, 727–8, 731
  murder 451, 464–6
  natural resources 727–8
  neutral states, operations on 1078
  non-discrimination 193, 194–6, 200, 204–5, *see also* **non-discrimination principle**
  non-refoulement 1052–3, 1193–5
  non-state armed groups 718, 733–4
  NIACs 706, 712, 717, 722, 725, 729, 735
  penal or disciplinary proceedings 1026–7, 1036–7, 1362–3
  prisoner of war status 919, 927, 934–6
  proportionality 1472, 1484
  regional human rights bodies 703, 729–31, 734
  regulate relationship with GCs, treaties that explicitly 706–10
  settlements, prohibition of 1553, 1568, 1572–3
  sex discrimination 1272 *see also* **sex discrimination; women; gender**
  specific rules to regulate relationships, treaties without 710–28

spies and saboteurs 1127–8
spillovers 43
terrorism 705
torture 321, 328, 338, 341–2
transfers of persons 728
United Nations 702, 704, 733–4
universality 680, 683–4, 688
war crimes 25
war on terror 680, 683–4, 688
wounded, sick, and shipwrecked 95–6
human shields
aliens in territory of party to conflict 1261
enemy hands, treatment of civilians in 1242, 1251–2, 1266–7
hostages, taking 1266
human dignity 1266
invasion phase 1080
NIACs 1266
POWs 990–1
humane treatment *see also* cruel, inhuman, or degrading treatment or punishment 192, 196, 197, 199, 200, 201, 286, 296, 302, 318–9, 330–2
humanitarian access *see also* humanitarian assistance 87, 380, 383, 507–508, 758
humanitarian assistance 231–55
abortion services 203–4
beneficiaries of relief 236–8
civilians 236–8, 244–7, 253
collective relief 246–7
consent/agreement/authorization 232–3, 242–5, 250–1
crimes against humanity 252–4
definition 231–3
detaining powers, relief obligations of 246–7
diversion of supplies 247–8
economic, social, and cultural rights 1513–14
family links, maintenance of 1091
food 233, 236, 244–5, 248–9, 252, 254
free passage 237, 248–9, 251, 508, 512, 1288, 1300, 1475, 1493
good governance 1475
humanitarian intervention, distinguished from 232
IACs 234–5, 246–8
impartiality 239–40, 243, 246, 249–50, 255
individual relief 246–8
internment/detention 246–7, 1108–9
medical personnel and chaplains 236
medical supplies 246–9, 252
military necessity limiting supply 247
national relief societies 234
NIACs 234–5, 236, 244, 249–51, 254–5
non-discrimination 203–4
non-governmental organizations (NGOs) 238
non-intervention principle 244, 254
non-military character 238
non-state armed groups 427
notion of humanitarian assistance 231–3

occupation 234, 238, 242, 247–9, 1391
offers of relief 244, 251
peacekeeping forces (UN) 238–9, 254
POWs 236–7, 246–7, 985–6
protected areas 381–2
protected persons 233, 237, 247–8
Protecting Powers 248–9
providers of relief activities 238–42
reciprocity, principle of 233
Red Cross 233–5, 238, 240–2, 246, 248–9, 499
refugees 1323
Security Council (UN) 232–3
starvation 236, 244–5, 254
states as providers 238
United Nations 232–3, 238–9, 254
war crimes 253–4
wounded, sick, and shipwrecked 234, 236, 249, 800
humanitarian body *see* humanitarian organization
humanitarian diplomacy 538, 676–7
humanitarian organization *see also* ICRC; humanitarian access; humanitarian assistance; right of initiative 239–41, 495–508
humanity, principle of 184, 187–8, 195–6, 207, 221, 499, 588, 673, 687, 761–2, 794, 800, 840, 853, 1177, 1338, 1153, 1160
humiliation *see also* public curiosity and insult, exposure to
cruel, inhuman, or degrading treatment or punishment 321, 322, 332–5, 340
POWs 984, 1275
torture 329
women 1274–5, 1285
hygiene
economic, social and cultural rights 1486, 1493, 1495–7, 1500, 1505
internment/detention 1351, 1354, 1356
law-making in occupied territories 1423
POWs 979, 983, 996, 998–9

IACs *see* international armed conflicts (IACs)
ICRC *see also* delegates of ICRC 525–48
ad hoc agreements 510, 512, 514 n 27, 518
advisory Service 652
access to territory controlled by NSA 501–2
attacks on ICRC personnel and material 545
Central Tracing Agency 105–6, 264, 268, 535, 1014–6, 1091, 1112–5
characteristics 240–1, 498, 530–1
confidentiality 500, 527, 539–41, 1056
educational activities 539, 609
emblem, use of the 860, 864, 867, 868
establishment of the ICRC 526–7
funding of the ICRC 528
good offices for establishing protected zones 371, 373, 375, 378, 379, 382
humanitarian diplomacy 538–39

ICRC (*cont.*)
  immunity from testimony and disclosure 545
  international legal personality *see* **ICRC: status (national and international)**
  legal argumentation (use of) 541–2
  mandate 506, 532–44
  non-discrimination, respect for the principle of 205
  notification of hospitals and hospital ships 213, 215
  offer of services 416, 426, 446, 497, 499, 500, 501, 502, 506–7 *see also* **right of initiative**
  persons refusing protection by the ICRC 147, 148 n 15
  Protecting Power, involvement in the appointment of 551, 552–3
  Protecting Power, as a substitute of 550, 557, 558
  services offered 505–6
  ships employed by the ICRC, status of 215
  special agreement concluded in IACs 139
  special position vis-à-vis relief to POWs 246
  status (national and international) 526, 528, 520–30
  structure of the ICRC 527–8
  succession of states to the GCs 167
  supervision over neutralized zones 375, 378
  technical assistance to NSA 803, 820
identification *see also* **emblems, use of; markings**
  children 1091, 1104–5, 1296, 1297, 1309
  dead persons 260, 278, 280–3, 289, 291, 293, 1019
  DNA 272
  documents, providing 261–3
  family links, maintenance of 1091, 1104–5
  fingerprinting 992
  graves 279, 286–7, 289, 291–2
  hospitals 208–9, 211, 212–13, 217, 226
  identity cards 814–15, 819, 895, 992
  identity discs 1296, 1297
  medical and religious personnel 814–15
  missing persons 260–5, 272
  occupied territories 1104–5
  POWs 979, 991–2, 1090
  standard of proof 573
identity cards 261–2, 264–5, 814–15, 819, 895, 992
identity discs 1103, 1296, 1297
ILC *see* **International Law Commission (ILC)**
ill-health *see* **care; medical care; public health**
ill-treatment *see also* **torture; cruel, inhuman, or degrading treatment or punishment; outrages; coercion** 295, 308, 312, 317–342 353–4, 357–8, 478, 482, 747, 787, 797, 800–2, 823, 929, 962, 971, 978, 984, 1053, 1065, 1079–82, 1203–4, 1248, 1329
immunity *see also* **combatant immunity; privileges and immunities**
  acts committed before/suspension of military occupation 1438
  functional and personal immunities 632–5, 707–8
  ICRC, immunity from disclosure and testimony 545
  refugees in occupied territories 1436–8
  sovereign immunity 11, 386, 707
impartiality *see also* **independent and impartial tribunal**
  Central Tracing Agency 1113
  definition 87, 472–3
  derogations 1126
  fair trials 1337–8, 1438–9
  humanitarian assistance 239–40, 243, 246, 249–50, 255
  judicial guarantees 471–3, 490–3, 1219–24
  neutral states 87–8, 102
  occupation courts 1433–4, 1451
  penal or disciplinary proceedings 1029, 1032, 1034–8
  Protecting Powers 552–3, 557–8
  Red Cross 196, 240–2, 496–505, 530–1, 619
implementation *see also* **domestic implementation** 248, 1182, 1191–6, 1205, 1207, 1210, 1381, 1495
imprisonment *see also* **internment/detention; prisoner of war (POW): internment/detention** 57, 305, 322, 483, 492–3, 554, 625, 873, 983, 1031, 1033, 1034, 1105, 1161, 1233, 1237–8, 1250, 1329, 1332, 1351, 1362, 1370, 1441, 1445, 1446–9
in camera hearings 1446
incommunicado, keeping people 1129, 1368
indecent assault 333, 343–69, 1244, 1271–92, 1297, 1470
independent and impartial tribunal
  fair trials 1337–8
  judicial guarantees 471–3, 488, 490–3, 1216, 1222–4, 1440–1, 1452
  occupation courts 1433–4, 1451
  penal or disciplinary proceedings 1029, 1032, 1034–8
indicted persons *see also* **convicted persons** 1041, 1437
India
  Goa 556, 1139, 1465–6
  Pakistan 167, 375, 774–5, 1392
indigenous people, property of 1533, 1539–41
indirect participation *see also* **direct participation in hostilities; participation in hostilities** 816, 1302, 1304–6
individual criminal responsibility 737–53
individual relief consignments *see* **relief consignments**
Indonesia *see* **East Timor**
information *see* **collection and transmission of information; family links and transmission of information, maintenance and re-establishment of; National Information Bureau (NIB)**

Index

information technology *see* electronic communications/new technology
inhumane treatment *see* cruel, inhuman, or degrading treatment or punishment
initiative, right of *see* right of initiative
innocence, presumption of *see* presumption of innocence
insurgents *see* fighters; national liberation movements; non-state armed groups; resistance movements
intellectual activities for internees/POWs, provision of 1000–1, 1351, 1357
intensity threshold
   NIACs 29, 60–2, 393, 395, 409–14
   protracted armed violence intensity threshold 43, 411–13
   violence for IACs, threshold of 13–16
   war on terror 50
internal disturbances and tensions 48, 65, 337, 345, 393, 395–6, 409–14, 416, 440, 606, 710, 865, 1164–5
internal waters 70
internalization of IACs 28, 31–4
   beginning of applicability 54–7
   binary IAC/NIAC thresholds of application 28, 31–4, 1346–7
   contested statehood 31
   de-internalization 33
   end of applicability 53
   legitimacy 32, 34
   loss of control of old regime (negative element) 34
   new regime, establishment of control by (positive element) 34
   objectivity 34
   proxy governments, setting up of 32–4
   recognition of new regime internationally (external element) 34
   representation of state 31–4
   subjectivity 34
   temporal scope of application 53–4, 65
   when transformation occurs 34
internally displaced persons (IDPs) 718–19, 1205–8, 1319–22, 1381
international administration 1392, 1407–8, 1456–7
international armed conflicts (IACs) *see also* declaration of war; special agreements in IACs; state of war
   animus belligerandi, necessity for 12
   applicability of GCs 5–24
   boundary between IACs and NIACs 10–16, 24–5
   concept of international armed conflict 3–26
   conversion of NIACs into IACs 17–19
   cyber warfare 22–4
   national liberation movements 19–21, 20, 52, 396, 408, 708
   threshold 10–26, 54–5
   unrecognized governments and recognized belligerents 21–2
   internalization of IACs 28, 31–4
   internationalization of NIACs 17–50
   mixed/parallel conflicts 31, 45–6, 48
   redefinition 35, 39–40
   terminology and definitions 28–31
   transnational armed conflict (TAC) 30–1, 46–9, 69, 77–83
   unorthodox conflicts 28, 31, 46–7
   war on terror 46–7, 49–50
International Committee of the Red Cross *see* ICRC
international criminal law *see also* crimes against humanity; genocide; grave breaches; war crimes 737–53
International Federation of RCRC Societies 238, 528, 601, 861, 867–8, 877
International Humanitarian Fact-Finding Commission (IHFFC) 564, 570–1
International Labour Organization (ILO) 1264, 1303, 1499–500
International Law Association (ILA) *Final Report on the Meaning of Armed Conflict in International Law* 12–16
International Law Commission (ILC)
   Guiding Principles 974
   reservations 967
   violence for IACs, threshold of 16
international organizations 8–9, 11–12, 116–17, 126, 600, 968, 1456–7
International Red Cross and Red Crescent Movement (IRCM) 86–89, 234, 241 n 38, 416, 498–9, 506, 528, 601, 605, 858, 864, 1091, 1103 n 60, 1255, 1557
international territorial administration *see* international administration
internationalization of NIACs
   attribution 36–40
   beginning of applicability 53
   binary IAC/NIAC thresholds of application 17–50
   borders, crossing 40
   circumstances which do not lead to internationalization 40–1
   consent to intervention 37–9, 41
   creation of new state 35, 45–6
   declarations 40
   definition 34–5
   deployment of international or foreign troops 41
   end of applicability 53
   foreign interventions 44
   link between intervening state and non-state actor 36–9
   mixed/parallel conflicts 38, 41, 45–6
   national liberation movements 19–21, 39
   occupied territory 40–1
   privileged belligerency, gaining 35
   proxy, non-state actor used as a 36–8
   recognition of belligerency 40
   redefinition of IACs 35, 39–40
   state responsibility 36–40
   temporal scope of application 53–4, 65
   unrecognized governments and recognized belligerents 21

internees *see also* **internment/detention; military internees; prisoner of war (POW):**
  internment/detention 1327–87
  age 1334, 1353
  allowances 200
  battlefield detainees 1079, 1087
  children 1105–6, 1296, 1299–300, 1302, 1357
  corporal punishment, prohibition of 1257–8
  criminal internees 1374, 1379–80, 1382
  criminals, separation from 1354, 1371
  cruel, inhuman, or degrading treatment or punishment 1083, 1259, 1351–2, 1362–3, 1367–8
  dead persons 1351, 1365–70
  death of 281, 284, 289, 290–1, 292
  dependants 1351, 1353–4
  deportation 924, 925 1334, 1381
  derogations/restrictions of rights and privileges 1123–32, 1363, 1370
  disappearances 1352, 1359–60, 1368–9
  dispersed internees, search for 63, 261, 270–1
  education 1299–300, 1357
  equality 1353, 1364
  escapes, disciplinary punishments for 1364
  evacuation 1381
  exchanges 1374
  exterior, relations with the 1106–8, 1351, 1360–1, 1368
  extradition 1379
  family links, maintenance of 1090–1, 1105–9, 1115–7, 1119–20, 1302
  fatigue or extra duties 1363
  financial resources 1351, 1358
  fines 1363
  food, water and clothing 1259, 1284, 1351, 1354–6
  forced labour 1264
  forced transfers 1079–83, 1087, 1197–201, 1204, 1334, 1351, 1354, 1365
  gravesites 1365–6
  grouping of internees 1354
  humanitarian assistance 246–8, 1108–9, 1361
  hygiene 1351, 1354, 1356
  incommunicado detention 1368
  individual accounts 1358
  intellectual activities 1351, 1357
  Internees Committees 1359, 1362
  labour/employment 1355, 1357, 1370
  liberty and security, right to 1370
  mail and correspondence 1106–9, 1360–1
  maintenance/means of existence 1353–4, 1367
  management of property 1351
  medical care 200, 1259, 1351, 1353–4, 1356, 1358
  minor criminal offences 1351
  mothers and expectant mothers 1281, 1283–4, 1286
  nationality 1353, 1354
  NIACs 1367–8
  non-discrimination 1353
  penal or disciplinary proceedings 1351, 1358–9, 1361–5
  penitentiaries, prohibition on use of 1362
  personal property 1351, 1353, 1357–8
  petitions 1358–9, 1371
  physical activities 1351, 1357
  pillage 1358, 1369
  places of internment 1351, 1354, 1358–9
  POWs
    analogy with 1350–1
    separation from 1354
  precautionary measures 1352–3
  pre-trial custody 1364
  property 1369
  Protecting Powers 1359–60, 1364, 1366
  recreation and sport 1357
  relation with the exterior 1090–1, 1097, 1106–7
  release 925, 1083, 1105, 1259, 1284–5, 1302, 1343, 1374–80, 1385–6
  religion 1246, 1351, 1354–5
  repatriation 1284–5, 1374–86
  review procedures 1083, 1329, 1339–41
  resource limitations 1352
  restrictive measures, cancellation of 1264
  reviews 1083
  separate quarters 1281
  solitary confinement 1259
  special agreements 139–40
  special transport 1109
  standard of accommodation 1283
  study 1357
  surveillance 1362
  tobacco 1355–6
  tracking 11090–15, 117–20
  training 1358
  transfers 925, 201, 1199–200, 1204, 1284–5, 1334, 1375, 1381–2, 1385–6
  transmission of information 1109–15, 1117–20
  transport 1360
  treatment of civilian internees 1349–71
  valuables and personnel effects 1357–8
  visits 1090, 1108, 1117, 1255, 1361
  working conditions and salary 200
  wounded and sick 1119
Internet 296, 565, 609, 881, 885, 984, 1022, 1101, 1112, 1114, 1255, 1360
internment/detention; prisoners of war (POWs):
  internment/detention *see also* **assigned residence; internees; prisoner of war (POW):** internment/detention
  accommodation in neutral state 103–5, 1284–5
  administrative detention 494
  admissibility and procedures 1327–47
  agreements 140, 1105–6, 1284–5, 1301–2, 1374, 1376–7, 1382, 1385–6
  appeals 1336–8, 1340–1
  arbitrary detention 493, 717, 1080–1, 1259, 1329, 1376

before trial 475, 484–5, 487–8, 493
cards, sending 1090–1, 1098, 1106, 1109, 1114
children 1105–6, 1296, 1299–300, 1302, 1357
collective internment 1334
commanders 1084
complaints 1358–9, 1362, 1364
conditional release 1384–5
conditions 321
countries or origin, sending to 1375, 1380–1
courts or administrative bodies 1337
criminal proceedings 1079–83, 1329, 1332–3, 1361–2
criminalization of unlawful detention 1345
cruel, inhuman, or degrading treatment or punishment 1329, 1373, 1376, 1449
death penalty 1332, 1381
definition of internment 1329–30
direct assistance to enemy 1331
disappearances 1329, 1352, 1359–60, 1365–9, 1385
diseases, prevention and control of 1354
dissemination of GCs 598, 603
duration 104–5, 1250, 1331
end of 1373–86
expenses/costs 1374, 1381–3
extraterritoriality 1084, 1344
fair trials 1259, 1337–8
female guards 1282
food and water 1284
grave breaches 631, 1087, 1132, 1259, 1335, 1345, 1376, 1384
grounds/reasons 1250, 1329–36, 1340–1
habeas corpus 488, 1337–9
hospital ships 221
hostages, taking 298–9, 301–11, 316, 1335, 1383–4
hostility from local population 1330, 1383
human dignity 1281–2
humane treatment 1247
independent organizations, role of 1384–5, 1386
individualized reasons 1333–4
intelligence gathering 1332
interests of Occupying Power, protection of 1482
internally displaced persons 1381
interrogation 1332
judicial guarantees 494, 493, 1083, 1220, 1259
labour/employment 1284
leave, right to 1176
legal basis 1082–4, 1341–2
legal documents, transmission of 1107
legal representation 1340
legality, principle of 1084, 1340
lex specialis 1337–9, 1344
liberty and security, right to 714–15
mass transfers 1334
means of existence 1329
medical care 1283–4

military necessity 1338
minor offences 1446–7
missing persons 260–1, 265, 270–1, 275
multi-national coalitions 1346–7, 1370, 1384–5
names, provision of 1097–8, 1119, 1329
national security 1148–9, 1176, 1316, 1328–34, 1338, 1340, 1392, 1409
necessity of continued internment 1376
NIACs 1087, 1115, 1259, 1342–4, 1346–7
non-discrimination 1281, 1284
non-state armed groups 1344
participation in hostilities 922–3, 1343
past acts, significance of 1332–3
peace treaties 1374, 1377
penal or disciplinary proceedings 1282–4, 1441, 1453
pending proceedings 1258, 1379–80
persecution, risk of 1381
previous participants in hostilities 103
procedural requirements, breach of 1384
procedure 1327–47
proportionality 1250
prosecution, handing over for 1379
protected civilians, definition of 1148–50
protected persons 1258–9, 1328–9, 1334, 1337
Protecting Powers, notification of 1329
psychological comfort 1373
public curiosity and insults, protection from 1249–50, 1378–9
punishment, prohibition as 1332, 1353
rape and sexual violence 349, 1281, 1290
reconsideration of internment 1339–40
refugees 1316, 1320, 1375, 1381–2
registers 1380
regular procedure, according to 1340–1
reservations 1379–80
residence
  place of 1328
  return to last place of 1374, 1376–7, 1380–2
residual protection 924–5
review procedures 924–5, 275, 1328–9, 1336–41, 1343–4, 1347
ruse, used as a 1333
safety following release 1383, 1385–6
sanitation 1282–3
sea, return of persons taking into custody at 1381–2
searches for dispersed internees 1380
security internees 1374, 1382
sentences, serving 1258, 1379–80
separation of men and women 1281–2
simple internment 1329
special agreements on costs 1382
spies and saboteurs 1331
suicide of detainees 462
surveillance 1330
terrorism 1328
torture 1352, 1358–9, 1363

internment/detention (*cont.*)
  transparency 1386
  transport documents 1109
  unlawful combatants 933, 1335–6
  unlawful confinement 1383–4
  voluntary internees/internment 1328–30, 1374, 1381–2
  vulnerable persons 1374, 1376–7
  women 349–50, 1273, 1281–6, 1449
internment, places of *see* **camps/places of internment/POW camps**
International Security Assistance Forces (ISAF) 83, 882
interpreters/translators 489, 1131, 1444
interrogations 319, 328, 931, 979, 992–3, 1332
interview in private 1058, 1237, 1359, 1381, 1386
invasion and occupation, difference between 55, 1408–13, 1418–19
investigations
  dead persons 278, 282–6, 293–4, 1366, 1370
  disappearances 710
  domestic implementation 649
  grave breaches 630
  internment/detention 1364, 1371
  life, right to 284–5, 293–4, 713–14
  missing persons 262, 269–70, 272–4
  torture 337–9
invitations to foreign states to intervene 14, 44, 1404
Iraq (conflict starting in 2003) *see also* **Kuwait**
  Abu Ghraib 295
  administration of occupied territories 1457, 1459, 1464, 1467
  blockades 1511–12
  collective punishment 1156–7, 1161
  consent to intervention 37
  cross-border NIACs 52
  dead persons 1370
  de-Baathification process 1001
  destruction of property 1511
  economic measures 1426
  economic, social, and cultural rights 1492, 1499–500, 1511–12
  education 1503
  emblems 883
  end of applicability 57
  extradition 485
  extraterritoriality 285
  food and water 1512
  forced labour 1499–500
  geographical scope of application 71
  global NIACs, concept of 50
  hospital ships, transfer of POWs to 993
  human rights law 715–7, 1342, 1427
  IAC, as 13, 33, 34
  internment/detention 1347
  interrogations 993
  law-making in occupied territories 1426–7
  liberty and security, right to 714–16, 1370
  life, right to 713–14
  mail and correspondence 1021
  medical supplies 1512
  military manuals 1018
  mixed conflict, as 33, 34
  neo-liberalism 1426
  no-fly zones 1396
  occupation, end of applicability in times of 1587–8
  oil 1542
  penalizing international crime 1435–6
  photographs 984
  pillage 1511
  POWs
    exterior, relations with 1018
    transfer 969
    treatment 987, 993, 1001
  protected areas 379–80, 383, 387
  protected civilians, definition of 1141–2
  public property, protection of 1550
  puppet governments, safeguards against 1587–8
  RC Messages 1022–3
  Security Council resolutions 1342, 1588
  sentences, internees serving 1379
  Switzerland, neutrality of 4 n 2
  transfer of authority 1587–8
  transformative or humanitarian occupation 1457
  transnational conflicts 53
  unlawful combatants 937
  water resources 1478
Iraq vs Iran
  declarations of war 54
  Kurds 42
  Mixed Medical Commissions 1042
  naval warfare 775
  NIACs, as 13
  propaganda activities 1000
  Red Cross messages 1021
  registration of POWs 1018
  repatriation 57, 1047, 1049, 1051
  Tanker War 775
Islamic law 149, 681–2
Islamic State *see also* **Iraq; Syria** 419
Israel/Palestine/Occupied Palestinian Territory *see also* **Lebanon**
  administration of occupied territories 1458, 1461, 1463–6, 1470, 1472–84
  agricultural land 1542
  attacks against Israel 1596
  blockade of Gaza Strip 1162–3
  children 1311–12, 1569
  classification of situation after 2005 1591–6
  close of military operations 1577–83
  collective punishment 1157, 1161–3, 1169–70
  confiscation 1523–4
  courts of Occupying Power, recourse to 1570–1
  cultural and natural heritage 1478–9
  destruction of property 1548

diplomatic practice 1481
economic, social, and cultural rights 1500, 1511–12, 1569
effective control 1590–6
European Union, assistance projects of 1481
financial incentives 1563
food and water 1540
forced transfers 1148, 1187–8, 1194, 1210, 1334
freedom of movement 1569
Gaza Strip as occupied territory 1593–6
good governance 1466, 1468, 1470, 1472, 1474–81, 1484
Hamas, support for 1163
house demolitions 1161–2
human rights law 1565, 1569, 1573
IACs 68
Intifada 1593
interests of Occupying Power, protection of 1481
internment/detention 1334
Jordan 945
leave, right to 1179–80, 1183–4
legislative powers, scope of 1505
military necessity 1519
mulk and *mubah* regimes 1540
murder 459
national liberation, wars of 39
national security 1565
natural resources 1477, 1540, 1544
non-state armed groups 1563–4
occupation
  concept and beginning 1392–5, 1399, 1401–2, 1404–5, 1411–12, 1417–18
  end of applicability 59, 1577–85, 1589–96
  internationalization of conflicts 40–1
  remote occupation 1394–5, 1399
Operation Cast Lead 1592
Palestine Liberation Organization 684, 945, 1464
persistent objector, doctrine of the 1566–7
POWs, determination of status of 945
prerogatives, continuing exercise of 1590–2
private persons, actions by 1564, 1572–3
private property, protection of 1519, 1523–4, 1569
private/public property distinction 1540
Red Cross 1557, 1592, 1595
remedies 1570, 1572–3
requisition 1523–4
Security Council (UN) 1556
self-determination 1567–8
settlements, prohibition of 1556–7, 1560–73
sustenance of armed forces 1482
terrorist organizations 68, 929–30, 945
unilateral disengagement (2005) 1577, 1590–1, 1593, 1595
United States 1556, 1563
unlawful combatants 929–30
usufruct 1542–4

wall, construction of
  administration of occupied territories 1461, 1466, 1470, 1472, 1474–6
  forced transfers 1194, 1210
  leave, right to 1183–4
  legislative powers, scope of 1505
  occupation, end of applicability in times of 1578–83
  settlements, prohibition of 1557, 1563, 1565, 1567–9
withdrawal of armed forces 1589–94
ius ad bellum/ius in bello see **jus ad bellum/jus in bello**
ius cogens see **jus cogens/peremptory norm**

Japan
  China, conflicts with 1463–5
  comfort stations 353, 355
  end of applicability 53
  Manchuria, annexation of 1465
  Tokyo Military Tribunal 7, 660–3, 974–5, 1159, 1228
journalists 434, 447, 651
judges 471–3, 490–3, 486–7, 1429–31
judicial guarantees *see also* **defence, rights of; fair trial; trial** 469–94, 1215–39, 1438–50
  access to lawyers 476–7, 490, 985
  accused to be present, right of 481–2, 1229–30
  aliens in territory of party to conflict 1259, 1261
  appeals 483, 1234–5, 1445
  arrest, immunity from 1438
  before occupation, convictions for acts committed or opinions expressed 1438
  Central Tracing Agency, notification to 1442
  civilians, protection of 1087, 1215–39
  competent courts 471, 940, 951–2, 954
  confessions 482
  convictions 488–90
  courts-martial 472, 1433
  criminal proceedings 1086
  criminal responsibility at national level 493
  cruel, inhuman, or degrading treatment or punishment 1424
  death penalty 479, 483–4, 1216, 1233, 1446, 1453
  defence and necessary rights, means of 476–82, 1224–6, 1442–4, 1452
  delay 484–5, 487–8, 1224–6, 1442
  derogations 1218, 1439–40
  double jeopardy 1440, 1452
  emergency, states of 486
  equality of arms 479–80, 1225, 1231
  examination of witnesses 480–4
  executions 470, 471, 489–90
  extradition 484, 485–6
  general principles of criminal law 1440–1
  grave breaches 640–2, 1216, 1236
  habeas corpus 488
  human rights law 470–6, 479–92, 494
    civilians 1216, 1217–36
    de facto authorities 488, 491
    equality of arms 479–80
    occupied territories 1439–40, 1443, 1445, 1452–3

1620 Index

judicial guarantees (*cont.*)
  in camera hearings 1446
  independence and impartiality 471–3, 490–3, 1216, 1219–34
    impartial, definition of 472–3
    independence, meaning of 472
    objective impartiality 473
    occupied territories 1440–1, 1452
    rebel groups, courts set up by 488, 491
    special or military courts 471–2
    substantive impartiality 473
  indispensable guarantees 470, 473–84, 490
  individual criminal responsibility 475, 492–3, 1226–7, 1229
  information of particulars of offence 475–6, 1441
  international criminal law 1227–8, 1233
  internment/detention 1083, 1259, 1361–2
    administrative 494
    after trial 493
    arbitrary 493
    before trial 475, 484–8, 493
  interpreters 489
  judgment, nature of court required to pronounce 471–3
  judicial officer, appearance before a 486–7
  legal assistance 477–8, 1225, 1230
  legal consequences of a violation 492–3, 1235, 1451
  legality, principle of 474–5, 488, 1227–8, 1440
  lenient standard for rebel trials 489–90
  minimum standards 1223, 1236
  more than one offence, prohibition of trial for 484
  national level, criminal responsibility at 493
  national security 471
  penal or disciplinary proceedings 1441, 1443, 1453
  penalties, proportionality of 1440
  petition, right of 1445
  positive obligations 491
  POW status, treatment of persons without 919
  presumption of innocence 475, 487, 1131, 1228–9, 1440–1, 1452
  pre-trial guarantees 486–8
  protected persons 1216, 1219–20, 1226, 1232–3, 1235–9, 1438–9, 1443
  Protecting Powers 1226, 1233, 1441–2, 1445–6
  public hearings 481, 1232–3, 1445–6, 1452
  rebels, rights and duties of 488–94
  regularly constituted court 471–2, 493, 1229–34, 1441
  release, trial within reasonable time or 487–8
  remedies, right of convicted persons to be informed of available 1445
  reparations/remedies 492
  reprisals 480, 1226
  right of rebel groups to try people 488–9, 490–3
  self-incrimination 478, 1230–1
  sentences 470, 471, 479, 488–90, 493
  special courts 471–2
  testify against oneself, right not to be compelled 482
  time and facilities to prepare defence 478–9
  time limits 1445
  time spent in custody deducted from period of imprisonment 1446
  trial within a reasonable time 484–5, 487–8
  transfer as flagrant denial of justice, lack of 485
  war crimes 470, 493, 1228, 1236, 1451–2
judicial proceedings *see* **penal or disciplinary proceedings**
jus ad bellum/jus in bello 74, 89, 132, 306, 318
jus cogens/**peremptory norm** 125–6, 136, 142–3, 149, 151, 178, 195, 235–6, 244, 338, 345 n 9, 366, 386, 450, 513, 636, 672, 692 n 9, 824, 1050, 1054, 1226, 1229, 1406–7, 1427, 1437, 1451, 1559
Justice and Equality Movement (JEM) *see* **Sudan**

Kampuchea (Cambodia) *see also* **Vietnam** 935, 1144–5, 1148, 1345
Kenya 42–3
know, right to
  amnesties 283
  customary international law 282, 1120
  dead persons 278–9, 281–4, 286, 294
  disappearances 281
  families 1091–2, 1095–6, 1120
    dead persons 278–9, 281–4, 286, 294
    missing persons 258–9, 261, 264, 273–4, 276, 1120
  fate of relatives, right of families to know 278–9, 281–4, 286, 294, 1090
  reunification of families 1298
  truth 261, 273, 281, 1020
  truth and reconciliation commissions 259, 282, 1166, 1297
Korean War 13, 56, 774, 1000, 1051
Kosovo/Serbia *see also* **former Yugoslavia**
  collective punishment 1166
  ethnic cleansing 409
  IAC, as 35, 41
  intensity, criteria of 409
  Kosovo Liberation Army 41, 60–1, 405, 407 n 110
  missing persons 1117
  NATO 41
  NIAC, as 35
  statehood, criteria for 35
  transformative or humanitarian occupation 1457, 1462
Kurdish fight for independence 42
Kuwait
  administration of occupied territories 1458
  evacuation of POWs 959, 962
  IAC, as 13
  natural resources and environment 1478
  oil 1538–9

POWs 57, 949, 968, 969, 990
refugees 1060
reparations 64, 1183
UN Compensation Commission 1183, 1287
women 1287

labour/employment *see also* **forced labour**
 aliens in territory of party to
   conflict 1262–4, 1268
 children 1492
 civilians, protection of 1074, 1081
 clothing 1355
 detachments 1357
 economic, social, and cultural rights 1486–8,
   1490, 1498–500
 equal pay 1490
 human rights law 1262
 injuries 1003–4
 internment/detention 1284, 1351, 1355,
   1357, 1370
 jobless, becoming 1261–2
 law-making in occupied territories 1423
 means of existence 1261–2
 medical care 1003–4
 military character or for war effort, work of a 374,
   1003, 1498
 mothers and expectant mothers 1284
 nationality discrimination 1262
 non-discrimination 200, 1262
 obligation and right to work 1002–3
 officers 1002
 payment 200, 1004, 1351, 1490
 POWs 192, 198–9, 979, 981, 985, 1002–4
 private employers 981
 protective gear 1355
 repatriation 1041
 requisition 1498
 resignation 1357
 restrictive measures, cancellation of 1264
 training 1003
 unemployment, creating 1486, 1499
 women 987
 working conditions 200, 1003–4, 1357, 1370
land *see* **real property**
languages
 authentic texts 158–60
 dissemination of text of GCs 160, 603, 608–9, 1001
 final provisions 156–60, 172
 interpreters/translators 489, 1131, 1444
 mail and correspondence 1108
 non-discrimination 194, 200–1
 official languages 156–8, 159–60
 preparatory works 158
 reconciliation 158
 translation and communication 653
law enforcement 12, 65, 142, 321–2, 465, 477, 606,
   609–10, 712, 733, 983, 1250, 1472–4, 1481,
   1488, 1519

law-making in occupied territories 1422–7
 changes to local laws 1422–5
 civil life, necessity of maintaining public order
   and 1425–7
 continuity of the pre-existing legal system
   1460–1, 1463, 1478, 1480, 1483–4
 discriminatory laws, abolition of 1425
 human rights law 1423, 1425, 1426–7
 local laws 1422–5
 military manuals 1425
 national security 1424–5
 necessity test 1423–7
 NIACs 1450
 penal law 1424–5
 prescriptive powers 1423–5
 proportionality 1425
 public order and safety 1423–7
 reparations 1451
 scope of powers 1503–6
 spies and saboteurs 1425
 terrorism 1425
 welfare state 1423
lawyer/advocate *see also* **legal advisers/**
   representation 476–9, 482, 486, 490, 537,
   540, 555, 949, 985, 1020, 1107, 1224–6,
   1228, 1234, 1431, 1443–4
leaders, bodies of 279, 287–8, 293, 296
leasehold territories 1075–7
leave, right to 1173–84
 collective punishment 1184
 conditions and costs of departure 1178–9
 cruel, inhuman, or degrading treatment or
   punishment 1177, 1181–2
 denial of right to leave 1175–7
 deportation 1179
 emergencies 1180
 enforcement of denial of applications to
   leave 1177
 freedom of movement 1173–4, 1180–2
 internment/detention 1176–7
 national interest 1175–6, 1178–81, 1184
 national security 1178, 1180–1, 1184
 nationality 1180, 1182, 1184
 necessity, principle of 1181
 neutral countries, nationals of 1179
 NIACs 1174, 1182, 1184
 occupied territory 1174, 1177, 1179–80, 1184
 persons who are outside the scope of IHL 1180–1
 procedural aspects of decisions 1174–5, 1177–8
 proportionality 1181
 public order, public health or morals 1181
 refugees 1181–2, 1184
 relevance of other international legal
   regimes 1180–1
 repatriation 1175, 1179–80
 special cases of repatriation in occupied
   territory 1179–80
 stateless persons 1179

Lebanon
  collective punishment 1160
  conciliation 572
  conference, refusal to convene a 172
  consent to intervention 37–9, 44, 402
  cross-border NIACs 42
  enquiry/fact-finding procedure 572, 1160
  Hezbollah 37–9, 42, 48, 82, 402–3
  IAC, as 13, 37–9, 42, 44, 48, 402–3
  legal persons 1138–9
  loss of protection 848
  mixed conflict, as 38
  NIACs, as 37–9, 42, 44, 48, 402–3
  occupation 6, 1138–9
  spillovers 82
  transnational armed conflict 48
  unlawful combatants 1335–6
legal advisers/representation *see also* **lawyer/advocate**
  access to accused, right of 477–9
  Basic Principles on the Role of Lawyers (UN) 477
  dissemination of GCs 600, 654
  domestic implementation 654
  free legal assistance 477, 1444
  human rights law 703
  internment/detention 1340
  judicial guarantees 476–7, 481–2, 1225, 1230
  POWs 985
legality, principle of 143, 300, 302, 304, 309–11, 316, 474–5, 488, 618, 623 n 37, 659–61, 751, 800, 916–17, 1079–80, 1082, 1084, 1131, 1227–8, 1342, 1440, 1472
legislative authority *see* **law-making in occupied territories**
leisure time for POWs 1000–1, 1300, 1357
letters *see* **mail and correspondence**
levée en masse **(collective uprisings)** 891, 907–9, 1392, 1395
lex specialis 49, 131, 178, 237, 254, 465, 714–15, 721, 724, 729–35, 927, 953, 960, 979, 1016, 1036, 1065, 1129, 1263, 1337–9, 1343–4, 1453, 1484, 1517, 1520
Liberation Tigers of Tamil Eelam (LTTE) *see* **Sri Lanka**
liberty and security, right to 714–18, 720–2, 731–2, 734, 1370
Libya
  burials 287–8
  hospitals 223
  intensity threshold 412
  International Commission of Inquiry 455, 572
  internationalization 20
  life, human right to 728
  medical aid, criminalization of 801
  mixed conflicts 33, 45
  National Transition Council 34, 223
  NIAC, as 20, 107, 293, 412
  no-fly zones 380
  provisional measures 728
  recognition of armed groups 20
  recognition of government 33
  wounded, sick, and shipwrecked 801
Lieber Code 318, 323, 347, 434, 1126, 1450, 1536, 1547
life, right to 284–5, 293–4, 302, 307, 464–5, 712–14, 720–6, 728, 732, 1024, 1243
lifeboats 215–16, 220, 222, 815–16, 832, 834
LTTE *see* **Sri Lanka**
local laws 1422–5, 1447–8, 1460–1, 1463, 1468, 1478–80, 1483–4
local tribunals in occupied territories 1431–2
looting *see also* **pillage** 222–23, 1426, 1478, 1520, 1522, 1532, 1544
Lord's Resistance Army (LRA) *see also* **Sudan; Uganda** 82, 542
loss of protection *see* **protection, loss of**

mail and correspondence *see also* **electronic communications/new technology; relief consignments**
  anxious for news messages 1021–3
  censorship 1022–3, 1091, 1097, 1100, 1106–7, 1117
  charges 1006, 1091, 1106–8, 1112, 1114, 1361
  delay 1107, 1119
  derogations 1131
  family links, maintenance of 1090–1, 1097, 1100–1, 1115, 1117, 1119
  internment/detention 1106–9, 1360–1
  language 1108
  military necessity 1360
  model cards and letters 1021
  penal and disciplinary proceedings 1021, 1107, 1360
  POWs 965, 1006, 1014–16, 1021–3, 1090
  Red Cross messages 1021–3, 1101–2
  Red Cross 1021–3, 1091, 1115, 1360–1
  restrictions 1022–3, 1106–7
  telegrams 1006, 1022, 1091, 1107, 1112, 1114
maintenance *see* **means of existence**
Malvinas *see* **Falklands (Malvinas) conflict**
manner and customs, respect for 1246–7
markings *see also* **emblems, use of; identification**
  evacuation 1280–1
  graves 289
  hospitals 208, 212, 216, 218, 228, 870
  internment/detention camps 140 n 21, 1354
  medical units and aircraft 650, 830, 870, 1281
  POWs 900, 965, 991
  prison ships 965
  protected areas 372, 377
  vehicles 900
Martens Clause 157, 178–88
maternity cases *see also* **mothers and expectant mothers** 95, 141, 200, 210, 241, 248, 350, 764, 793, 813, 866, 987, 1271–92, 1295, 1300–1

means of existence *see also* **food and water** 985–6, 995, 997–8, 1009, 1074, 1261–2, 1299, 1329, 1353–4, 1367, 1518, 1539, 1549
media 295–6, 311–12, 602, 607, 984
medical aid, criminalization of 800–2
medical and religious personnel, status, rights, and obligations of 807–24
  administrative units 810
  armlets 814
  arms, carrying 817, 844–5
  auxiliary personnel 98, 101, 809–10, 815, 818–19
  beneficiaries of rights 447
  capture, treatment upon 818–19, 848–9
  chaplains 95, 199, 810, 813–14, 817, 999
  civilians 811–13, 824, 1071
  coastal lifeboats 815–16
  cruel, inhuman, or degrading treatment or punishment 821, 823
  denominations 813
  dissemination of GCs 606
  domestic implementation 655
  emblems 808, 814–15, 821, 860, 867
  freedom of religion 820–1
  grave breaches 821
  hospital personnel 812–13
  humanitarian assistance 236
  identity cards 814–15, 819
  internment/detention 1376
  inviolability 758, 782
  lifeboats 815–16
  loss of protection 816–17, 840–54
  medical ethics 789–92, 817–18
  medical experiments 789–90, 983
  military manuals 816–17, 844–5
  nationality 812
  nature of protection 809–10
  neutrality 87–8, 95–8, 101, 782, 808, 811, 815
  non-discrimination 813, 818, 823
  penal or disciplinary proceedings 1000
  permanent units and personnel 811, 813, 818
  POWs 198–9, 818–19, 979, 999–1000
  protected medical personnel 809
  recognition 1497
  Red Cross 808–9, 810, 812, 814, 816–17, 819–20
  related personnel, similar protection for 810–11
  relief societies 808–14
  repatriation 818–19
  reprisals 580
  rescue services 815–16
  respect and protect, obligation to 809–13, 816, 822–3
  scope and nature of protection 809–18
  sea, protection of military medical and religious personnel at 815–16
  self-defence 817
  spontaneous medical care by civilians 811–12
  temporary staff 813, 815
  terrorists, providing support to 800–2, 820, 823
  training 815
  war crimes 820, 822–3
  wounded, sick, and shipwrecked 782, 786, 800–2, 806
medical buildings, material, and transport *see also* **hospital ships; hospitals** 825–38
  aircraft 100–1, 197, 825–6, 829–32, 838, 841
  ambulances, inviolability and neutrality of 758–9
  buildings, definition of 827
  domestic implementation 650–1
  economic, social, and cultural rights 1487–8, 1490, 1493–6, 1506, 1512
  emblems 837
  fixed establishments 816, 825–8, 838
  GPS coordinates 881
  grave breaches 836
  humanitarian assistance 246–9, 252
  inspections 999
  internment/detention 1358
  loss of protection 840–54
  material, definition of 827–8
  medicine and drugs 1358
  military necessity 827, 836
  naval warfare 825–6
  neutral states 87, 100–1
  occupied territories 827
  pillage 826–8, 837
  private property, protection of 1517
  protected persons 836
  Red Cross 826–7, 831
  reprisals 580
  requisition 837, 1526, 1549
  respect and to ensure respect, obligation to 118
  seizure 827–8, 830, 832, 834–8
  shipwrecked 826
  transport, definition of 828–34
  units 785, 810, 811, 813, 818, 826, 840–54, 993
  vehicles, definition of 828–9
  vessels 832–4, 838
  war crimes 837
medical care *see also* **care; hospitals; medical and religious personnel, status, rights, and obligations of; medical buildings, material, and transport; shipwrecked; wounded and sick** 96–7, 99, 197, 200, 203, 462, 747, 763, 798, 801, 811–2, 820, 821, 823, 962, 985–6, 993, 998–9, 1003–4, 1009, 1071, 1259, 1279–81, 1283–4, 1300–1, 1353–4, 1356, 1486–8, 1490, 1493–6, 1501, 1512–3
memorials 277–8
mercenaries 868, 869, 906–7, 915, 922, 946
merchant marine/ships 769, 771–7, 780, 907
mercy killing or battlefield euthanasia 791–2
military internee 95, 97, 98, 99, 100–1
military necessity
  administration of occupied territories 1461
  destruction of property
    private property 1516, 1518–20, 1529–32
    public property 1536–7, 1541, 1546–50

military necessity *(cont.)*
  distinction, principle of 1136
  evacuation 988, 1191–2
  family links, maintenance of 1099
  forced transfers 1191, 1196
  grave breaches 621
  human rights law 705, 727–8, 731
  humanitarian assistance 247
  internment/detention 1339
  legislative powers, scope of 1503
  loss of protection 840, 851, 853
  mail and correspondence 1360
  medical buildings, material, and transport 827, 836
  occupation, end of applicability in times of 1578
  pillage 1521
  POW status, treatment of persons without 934
  private property, protection of 1516–20, 1527, 1529–32
  protected civilians, definition of 1153
  Red Cross 534
  relief consignments 1108–9
  respect and to ensure respect, obligation to 132–3
  search, collect, and evacuate, obligation to 788
  seizure 1536, 1549–50
  settlements, prohibition of 1565
  torture 321, 323
  wounded, sick, and shipwrecked 786, 788
military objectives *see also* **distinction, principle of**
  civilians, removal of 650–1, 1251–2
  cultural property 1532–3
  declarations of belligerency 138–9
  direct participation 438
  domestic implementation 650–1
  enquiry/fact-finding procedure 573
  hospitals 208, 210, 213, 216–18, 224, 228, 650, 837
  identification 387
  medical and religious personnel shielding objectives 816
  non-state armed groups 11
  POWs 990–1
  prison ships 990
  protected areas 372, 385, 387
  reprisals 581–2
  sabotage 1127
  training 608
  unlawful combatants 912
  war crimes 852
  warships, damaged 778
  wounded and sick 804, 837
military tribunals *see also* **occupation courts** 471–2, 1026, 1028–9, 1034–8
militia *see* **non-state armed groups**
minorities, protection of 194, 196, 381, 383
missing persons *see also* **disappearances; enforced disappearances; know, right to** 257–76
  Central Tracing Agency 262, 268, 270, 272
  centralization of information 260–1, 265–7, 272
  civilians 258–61, 265–8, 276
  collecting and recording information 263–5, 269, 272–3
  criminal responsibility 275–6
  cruel, inhuman, or degrading treatment or punishment 274
  dead persons 259–60, 264, 1120
  disappearances 258, 261, 271–6
  enquiries, facilitating 261
  exhumation 1120
  family links, maintenance of 535, 1090–1, 1096, 1099
    know, right to 258–9, 264, 273–4, 276, 1120
    search, obligation to 1120
  forwarding of information, documents and objects to NIB 265–7, 269, 272
  graves/burials 260
  identification 260–5, 272
  information technology and electronic tools 272
  internment/detention 260–1, 265, 270–1, 275
  investigations 262, 269–70, 272–4
  know, right to 258–9, 261, 273
  National Information Bureau (NIB) 260–2, 265–70, 272, 1110
  national or ethnic exclusion 259
  naval warfare 264
  neutral states 105–6
  NIACs 261, 272–3, 276
  non-discrimination 275
  occupation 260, 266–7
  POWs 105–6, 260, 264–71, 1023–4, 1051
  preparatory measures 262–4
  Protecting Powers 267–8
  Red Cross 263, 267, 270–2
  repatriation 1059
  reporting persons missing 261, 269–70, 272, 275
  reprisals 265
  searches 261–2, 268–73, 1120
  tracing 262, 268, 270, 272, 1120
  truth and reconciliation commissions 259
  voluntary absconding 260, 268
  wounded, sick, and shipwrecked 264, 266
Mixed Medical Commissions 96–7, 532, 1041–2, 1044, 1063–4
mixed/parallel conflicts 31, 33, 34, 45–6, 48, 53, 64–5, 397
Moro Islamic Liberation Front (MILF) *see* **Philippines**
Morocco *see* **Western Sahara**
mothers and expectant mothers *see also* **maternity cases** 1272–3, 1290–1
  aliens in territory of party to conflict 1261
  children 1295–6, 1300–1
  convoys 1280–1
  death penalty 483, 1448
  emblems 1280–1
  enforced pregnancies 362
  evacuation 1280–1, 1288
  food and water 1279, 1284, 1301, 1354–5
  internment/detention 1281, 1284, 1286

labour/employment 1284
medical care 1278
non-discrimination 200
protected areas 369, 373, 1278
release 1284
wounded, sick, and shipwrecked 761, 791–2, 1277–8, 1286
Moynier, Gustave 526, 544, 808
multi-national coalitions *see also* **Afghanistan; Iraq; Taliban** 33, 127, 232–3, 399–400, 414, 866, 868–9, 1346–7, 1370, 1384–5, 1400
multi-national corporations 1139, 1534
murder 449–67, 1080
  burden of proof 466
  causation 461–2
  circumstances of protection 452–4
  civilians taking no active part in hostilities 450, 452–6, 460–1, 465–6
  conduct of hostilities 451, 453–6, 466
  crimes against humanity 457, 459
  distinction, principle of 461, 466
  dolus eventualis standard 458–9
  human rights law 451, 464–6
  intent to kill requirement 456–62, 466
  mass murders 462–3
  negligence or gross negligence 458, 465
  omissions 461–2
  POWs 466, 1257
  premeditation 457
  proof of death 462–3
  proportionality 465, 466
  protected persons 452–4, 460–1
  recklessness 458–60
  rules, killings prohibited by conduct of 451
  serious bodily harm, intent to cause 458
  suicide of detainees 462
  summary execution 451, 463–4
  unidentified victims 462–3
  use of state force 465
  war crimes 449–50, 459–60, 463–4, 492
  wilful killing 451, 459
mutilation 320, 324, 983, 1258

Nagorno-Karabakh conflict 1458
National Democratic Front of the Philippines (CARHRIHL) *see* **Philippines**
National Information Bureau (NIB)
  authentication 1111
  capture cards 1016–17
  Central Tracing Agency 1015, 1112–14
  children 1110
  collection and communication of information 1110–12
  data protection 1016
  dead persons 280–1, 291, 1366
  delay 1111–12
  domestic implementation 649–50
  enquiries, replies to 1019–20, 1110, 1112

establishment of official bureaux 1015, 1018, 1090, 1101–2, 1109–12
failure to establish NIBs 1018
family links, maintenance of 1015–16, 1090, 1101–2, 1109–12
forwarding of information, documents and objects 265–7, 269, 272
gravesites 1366
independence 1015
internment/detention 1111–12
mail and correspondence 1112
missing persons 260–2, 265–70, 272, 1110
notification by states 1017
peacetime, establishment in 1015, 1110
personal valuables, collection and forwarding of 1110, 1112
POWs 280–1, 957, 964–5, 1014–20, 1090, 1110
privacy 1016
Protecting Powers, notification of 1015, 1441–2
Red Cross 535, 1015, 1018
release 1112
repatriation 1112
technological developments 1112
transport documents 1109
wounded, sick, and shipwrecked 789, 1112
national laws *see* **local laws**
National Liberation Front (NLF) *see* **Vietnam**
national liberation movements *see also* **non-state armed groups; resistance movements**
  child soldiers 686
  colonial domination, alien occupation, or racist regimes (CAR conflicts) 20–1
  declarations 19–20
  internationalization of NIACs 19–21
  legitimization 42
  occupation, concept and beginning of 1415
  organizational threshold 408
  POWs, determination of status of 944–5
  racist regimes, against 20, 52, 396, 408, 708
  recognition as legitimate 21
  repatriation 1057
  representative authorities 20
  self-determination 19–21
  special agreements 55
  temporal scope of application 52
  universality 679–80, 686–7
National Red Cross/Red Crescent Societies 88, 210, 215, 238, 241, 248, 267, 496, 528, 601, 609, 614, 650, 703, 796, 810, 814, 833, 855–88, 1018, 1021, 1094, 1101–3, 1113, 1254–5, 1264, 1298
national security
  derogations 1124, 1125–32
  family links, maintenance of 1097, 1100
  interests of Occupying Power, protection of 1481–2
  internment/detention 1148–9, 1176, 1316, 1328–34, 1338, 1340, 1374, 1392, 1409

national security *(cont.)*
  judicial guarantees 471
  law-making in occupied territories 1424–5
  leave, right to 1178, 1180–1, 1184
  measures of security 1264, 1268
  occupation courts 1434
  proportionality 1481
  protected civilians, definition of 1152
  refugees 1202
  settlements, prohibition of 1564–5
  visits 1361
national territory 70, 247, 371–2, 392, 406, 423, 490, 630, 731, 1070–1, 1074–8, 1081, 1220, 1361–2, 1365, 1490, 1493, 1562, 1564, 1567–8
nationality
  aliens in territory of party to conflict 1258–64
  beginning of applicability 56
  civilians, protection of 1077
  crimes against humanity 1152
  dependent territories 1076–7
  hostages, taking 300
  internment/detention 1334, 1353, 1354
  judges in occupied territories 1431
  labour/employment 1262
  leave, right to 1180, 1182, 1184
  medical and religious personnel 812
  missing persons 259
  non-discrimination 191–2, 200–1, 204, 1262
  penal or disciplinary proceedings 1026
  POWs 904, 926, 986
  protected civilians, definition of 1141, 1142–8, 1150, 1152
  refugees 1314–16
  residual protection 921–2
  settlements, prohibition of 1561–2
  unlawful combatants 920–1, 1132
  wounded, sick, and shipwrecked 196, 782–3, 797
natural environment *see* **environment/environmental protection**
natural resources
  good governance 1476–8
  human rights law 727–8
  oil 1477, 1525, 1542, 1544–5
  private property, protection of 1533–4
  public property, protection of 1539–40, 1544–5, 1548–9
  usufruct 1542, 1544, 1549
naval warfare
  amphibious landing operations 768, 779
  dead persons 279
  geographical scope of application 70
  medical buildings, material, and transport 228, 825–6
  missing persons 264
  neutral states 90–1, 95
  prior treaties and conventions, relationship with 695

  sea control and sea denial operations 767–8
  wounded, sick, and shipwrecked 767–8, 771–80, 782–3, 795
ne bis in idem **principle** 484, 1231–2, 1238, 1434–5, 1440, 1452
necessity *see* **military necessity**
neo-liberalism 1426
Nepal 488–9, 491
neutral country/power/state *see also* **neutrality** 85–108
  accommodation/internment of POWs in neutral state 99, 103–4, 908, 1044–6, 1374–7
  blockades 89, 93–4
  Central Tracing Agency 1015
  children 106–7, 1302
  civilians on territory of neutral state 94, 102–5
  collective security 86–7, 91
  conscientious objectors 98–9
  contraband 89
  dead persons 95, 105–6
  dependent territories 1077
  deserters 98–9
  emblems 857–8
  escaped prisoners of war 98
  extraterritoriality 74
  hospitals 95, 103–4, 210, 833
  intermediate stages between neutrality and belligerence 85, 93
  internment/detention 90, 92, 95–9, 101–8, 1374–7
  leave, right to 1179
  meaning under the GCs and API 92–3, 94
  medical and religious personnel 87–8, 95–8, 101, 811, 815
  military internee 95, 97, 98, 99, 100–1
  missing persons 105–6
  mixed medical commission, establishment of 96–7
  nationals of neutral states 774, 1072, 1074, 1077
  naval warfare 90–1, 95
  non-belligerent states 92–4
  notion of neutrality 87–9
  passengers of a belligerent's medical aircraft landing in a neutral state 100–2
  permanent status 86–7, 91–4
  POWs 95, 97, 98–9, 101–3, 105–6, 972
  previous participants in hostilities 103
  private persons, delivery of war material by 89–90, 102
  prize, rules on 89, 99–100
  Protecting Powers, role of neutral states as 94, 107
  Red Cross 86, 87–9, 92, 105–7, 1374–5
  refugees 94, 97–8, 102
  religious personnel 95, 97–8
  repatriation 95–8, 100–1, 103–4, 106
  rights, powers, and obligations 85–108
  special agreements 138
  status of neutral states 86–9

supply of ammunition and war
    material 89–90, 102
Switzerland 91, 107–8
territory of neutral state, inviolability 89
trade relationships 89–90
transit 102–3
unneutral services 89
vessels 90, 99–100
warship in neutral waters and ports of neutral
    states 99–100
wounded, sick, and shipwrecked in 95–7, 106
neutrality *see also* **neutral country/power/state** 40,
    90, 95–7, 106, 191, 240, 528, 530–1, 546,
    550–1, 558, 596, 678–9, 758–9, 782, 795,
    842, 808, 811, 815, 904, 1145–7, 1150
neutralized zones 369, 371, 374–5, 382
new technology *see* **electronic communications/new
    technology; Internet**
newly formed states, applicability in 55
news, communication of family 1092, 1097,
    1099–101
next of kin 259, 264–6, 268, 273–4, 282–3, 290–5,
    726, 964–5, 1024, 1091, 1366
nexus with the armed conflict 71–3, 75–6, 82–3,
    622, 762, 805, 1531
NIB *see* **National Information Bureau (NIB)**
Nicaragua 45, 424, 428, 1253 n 94
no-fly zones 369, 379–80, 383, 1396
non-belligerent state/power 92–4
non bis in idem see **ne bis in idem** principle
non-defended localities 369, 376–7, 379, 381, 385–6
non-discrimination principle *see also* **race and
    ethnicity; sex discrimination** 191–205
  abolition of discriminatory laws 1425
  aliens 200
  birth 192
  children 200
  citizenship status 204
  civilians 195, 199–201
  crimes against humanity 202
  criminal responsibility 201–2
  customs 200
  definition 192
  differentiation 192, 195, 198, 201, 203
  disabilities, persons with 196, 204
  discrimination, definition of 193
  distinction 192, 195, 204
  education 1475
  equality, principle of 196
  erga omnes obligations 195
  evacuation 1208
  fact, equality in 194
  forced transfers 1198–9, 1207
  future development, areas of 202–5
  genocide 202
  human rights law 193, 194–6, 200, 204–5
  humanitarian aid delivered by United States 203–4
  humanity, principle of 195–6

  international law, in 194–5
  internment/detention 200–1, 1353
  interpretation 195, 199
  judges, coercive or discriminatory measures
      against 1429
  jus cogens 195
  labour/employment 200
  language 194, 200–1
  law, equality in 194
  legal consequences of a violation 201–2
  loss of protection 845
  marginalized groups 196
  meaning and application 193–201
  medical and religious personnel 813, 818, 823
  minorities, protection of 196
  missing persons 275
  mothers and expectant mothers 200
  nationality 191–2, 200–1, 204, 1262
  neutrality, humanitarian principle of 191
  NIACs 201, 204
  occupation 200
  persecution, crime of 202
  political opinions 196–8, 200
  positive rights 195
  POWs 192, 195, 198–9, 201
    labour/employment 192, 198–9
    transit or screening camps, conditions in 199
    treatment 986–7, 993, 1000, 1007
  primary obligation, as 192, 197, 199–200
  protected persons 195, 200
  public officials, coercive or discriminatory
      measures against 1429
  rape and sexual violence 203
  Red Cross 191, 196, 205, 240, 498
  refugees 1314
  religion 192, 194, 195, 198, 200, 986–7, 1000–1
  repatriation 1053
  sexual orientation 204–5
  subordinate norm, as 193
  subsidiary obligation, as 192, 201
  substantive right, as 193–4
  suspect classifications, list of 193–4
  systematic discrimination 196
  war crimes 201–3
  wealth 192
  wounded, sick, and shipwrecked 191–2, 196–7,
      201, 765, 782, 784, 789–91, 800
non-governmental organizations (NGOs) 528, 530,
    543, 546, 686, 1563
non-international armed conflicts (NIACs) *see also*
    **non-state armed groups; ad hoc agreements
    under Common Article 3** 391–414
  accommodation of POWs neutral
      countries 1044
  administration of occupied territories 1460
  attribution 36–40
  beginning of applicability 53, 59–61, 65
  boundary between IACs and NIACs 10–50

non-international armed conflicts (NIACs) (cont.)
  binary IAC/NIAC thresholds of
    application 10–50
  categories 393–6
  children 1307–10
  civil authority, under direction of 393
  concept 391–414
  consent to intervention 37–9, 41
  context 78–9
  control 406–7
  cross-border activities 12, 15–16, 40–5, 46,
    77–83, 401–2
  customary international law 35, 40, 393, 414,
    1116–17
  dead persons 1368
  declarations 40
  definition 28–30, 43, 392
  denial of conflicts 59, 392
  duration of conflict 60, 410–11
  end of applicability 53, 61–2, 65, 1589
  enquiry/fact-finding procedure 571, 572
  existence of armed conflict 404–13
  extent of IHL's application 404
  extraterritoriality 79
  failed states 397
  final provisions 168–9
  foreign interventions 44
  geographical scope 68–9, 72, 75–83, 400–4
  global NIACs, concept of 49–50
  good governance 1473
  human shields 1266
  IACs 10–50, 53, 65, 394, 398–400
  intensity threshold 29, 60, 393, 395, 409–14
  internalization of IACs 28, 31–4, 1346–7
  internationalization of NIACs 17–50, 65
  internment/detention 1259, 1367–8
  list of conflicts 13–14
  merger of law of IAC and law of NIAC 53, 65
  mixed/parallel conflicts 31, 38, 41, 45–6, 58, 397
  multi-national coalitions 33, 399–400, 414, 1346–7
  national liberation wars 39
  new states, creation of 35, 45–6
  non-IACs, as 30
  not of an international character 392, 395,
    396–400
  object and purpose 78–9
  occupied territory 40–1, 397–8
  organization, level of 29, 60–2, 396, 402, 404–9
  overall control test 398, 402
  parties to the conflict 396–7, 414
  peacekeeping forces (UN) 399
  political motivation 408–9
  POWs 53–4, 513
  preparatory works 79–82
  protracted armed conflict 30, 33, 59–60, 395,
    404, 410–13
  reciprocity, principle of 80
  Red Cross 393–4, 404, 411
  regulation 28
  residual definition 28–30
  special agreements 1367–8
  spillovers 49–50, 77–83
  state responsibility 1265
  Tadić formula 394–6, 404–5, 408, 410, 413–14
  terminology and definitions 28–31
  territory of a high contracting party 400–1
  third state involvement 398–9, 414
  thresholds 393–5, 414
  traditional NIACs 75–6
  transnational armed conflict 30–1, 46–9, 77–83
  United Nations 399–400
  unlawful combatants 933–4, 1061–2
  unorthodox conflicts 28, 31, 46–7
  war crimes 395, 407
  war on terror 46–7, 49–50, 68
non-intervention, principle of 15, 244, 251, 254
non-refoulement, principle of 917, 934, 953,
    972, 1051–6, 1057, 1064–5, 1141, 1198,
    1202–5, 1314, 1320, 1322, 1376, 1379, 1381,
    1384, 1437
non-renunciation of rights 145–53
  conceptual importance 149–51
  duress 146
  forcible conscription 148–9
  illegality 148
  inalienability of rights 145, 151
  intangibility principle 148
  invalidity 152–3
  jus cogens 149, 151
  special agreements 145
  unilateral renunciation 146
non-repetition, guarantees of 492, 1287
Non-Self-Governing-Territories 1078
non-state armed groups *see also particular groups*
    (e.g. Al-Qaeda); resistance movements
  ad hoc agreements 515–16, 519
  addressees of Common Article 3 415–31
  administration of occupied territories 1450
  attribution 17–19, 23–4
  binary IAC/NIAC thresholds of application 30–1
  codes of conduct 612
  collective punishment 1164
  combatant immunity 1007
  competing groups, conflict between 397
  criminal law 428, 429–31, 685
  cyber warfare 23–4
  dead persons 283
  dissemination of GCs 602, 611–12
  distinction, principle of 917
  distinctive signs, wearing 945
  economic, social, and cultural rights 1508–10
  emblems 871
  executions 489–90
  hospital ships 835
  hostages, taking 299
  human rights law 718, 733–4

IACs, as parties to 944–6
incorporation into armed forces 894, 896
internment/detention 1344
judicial guarantees 488–94
law-making in occupied territories 1450
legitimacy 11
occupation, end of applicability in times of 1589
organization 62, 116–17, 126, 1008
penal or disciplinary proceedings 1026
POWs
    definition 891, 894, 895–906
    determination of status of 944–6, 954
    status and treatment of persons without POW status 913–14
    transfers 968
    treatment 1007–8
private property, protection of 1533–4
proxy armed groups 17–19, 25–6
recognition 18, 20–1, 33, 39, 941
Red Cross 499
repatriation 1061
reprisals 590–1, 595
self-defence 18–19
settlements, prohibition of 1563–4
state-like functions, armed groups exercising 423
territorial control 77, 379, 406–8, 413–14, 423, 1008
terrorist groups 949–50
third states, support for groups in 18–19
torture 324, 326, 329
unilateral declarations 612
universality 683–4, 686–7
volunteer corps, members of 894, 895–8, 901–6, 908
weapons openly, carrying 917
wounded, sick, and shipwrecked 765, 802–3

Northern Cyprus *see* **Cyprus vs Turkey**
Northern Ireland 48, 321
notification
    absence of 5
    assistance 1108
    camps 991, 993
    capture 953, 1014, 1016–8, 1090
    death 259, 1019
    death sentence 554, 1105, 1233, 1237–8
    detention 1118
    diseases 797
    distinctive sign 209
    evacuation 1192–3
    family 1090, 1101, 1111
    hospital (ships) 212–6, 219, 557, 832–4
    identity 1111
    internees 1360
    judicial proceedings 200, 475–6, 484, 554, 641, 1018, 1033, 1035, 1224, 1233, 1236–7, 1440–6, 1449
    medical aircraft 831
    medical services 811
    missing 1120

    parole 996
    POWs rank 1002
    protected areas 371–2
    transfer of funds 554, 1005
    transfer of POWs 964
    transfer of protected persons 1200
    treaties 165, 170–4, 177–8
    violation 971
nullum crimen, nulla poena sine lege (no crime or punishment without law) *see also* **legality, principle of** 659–60, 1227, 719–20
    collective punishment 1156, 1167, 1169
    confiscation 1554–5
    customary international law 7
    judicial guarantees 1228
    non-state armed groups 430
    Nuremberg Clause 660
    private property, protection of 1519–20
    settlements, prohibition of 1554–5
    usufruct 1543
    war crimes 660–1, 663

oath of allegiance 1142, 1461, 1466, 1469
obligations *see* **addressees of obligations**
occupation *see also* **alien occupation; occupied territories**
    aggression 1405
    airspace 1394, 1396
    armed resistance, occupation without 1413–14, 1415, 1576, 1584–6
    beginning of 1389–1419
    concept of 74, 1084, 1086, 1389–1419
    consent 1391, 1393, 1397, 1402–5, 1408, 1414
    definition of occupation 1078–9, 1391–3, 1407, 1409, 1418
    denial of occupation 13–14
    duration 1425
    effective control 1391, 1393, 1394–402, 1414, 1418
    end of occupation 1394, 1411, 1412, 1575–96
    extent of territory 1391
    functional theory of occupation 1084, 1086, 1409–11
    general principles of law of occupation 1460–1
    indirect occupation through control by armed group 1399–400
    invasion and occupation, difference between 55, 1408–13, 1418–19
    invasion phase 1080–1
    law of occupation 1457–61
    long-term occupation 1456, 1458, 1507, 1577–9
    minimum duration 1398
    minimum extent of territory 1398–9
    NIACs 1415–16, 1418
    non-state armed groups, occupation through 1399
    occupation from the sea 1394, 1396
    own territory, invasion of 1405–6
    pacific occupation 1456–7
    partial occupation 1057

occupation *(cont.)*
  Pictet's theory of occupation *see* occupation: functional theory of occupation
  third state, occupation of 1077–8
  territorial control 74, 1075, 1390–1, 1392, 1397, 1401, 1402, 1456, 1480, 1560
  remote occupation 1394–5, 1399
  resistance
    degree 1394–5, 1396–7
    organized groups 1396
    possibility of control 1397
    Second World War 1396, 1413–14
    sporadic local resistance 1394
    without armed resistance 1413–14, 1415
  short-term occupation 1577–8
  territorial sea, occupation of 1396
  transformative or humanitarian occupation 1457, 1462, 1484
  virtual occupation 1394–5
occupied territories *see also* **economic, social, and cultural rights in occupied territories; occupation; occupation courts; Israel/Palestine/Occupied Palestinian Territory**
  administration of territory 1075, 1455–84
  annexation 1265
  before occupation, convictions for acts committed or opinions expressed 1438
  children 106
  civilians on invaded territory 1070–5, 1084–7, 1242–58, 1265
  collective punishment 1164
  colonial domination, alien occupation, or racist regimes (CAR conflicts) 20–1
  demographics of occupied territory, changing 1186
  derogations 1125–32
  end of applicability GC IV 53, 58–9, 1575–96
  exterior, relations with 1129, 1130
  failed states 1402
  family links, maintenance of 1090–1, 1104–5
  forced transfers 1187–96, 1205, 1211, 1365
  geographical scope of application GC IV 74–5
  hand over accused or convicted persons, duty to 1449–50
  hostages, taking 299–301, 305–6, 316
  humanitarian assistance 234, 238, 242, 247–9
  IACs 74–5
  identification 1104–5
  judges in occupied territories 1429–31
  judicial guarantees 1438–50
  law-making 1422–7
  leave, right to 1174, 1177, 1179–80, 1184
  medical buildings, material, and transport 827
  missing persons 260, 266–7
  murder 466
  NIACs 397–8
  non-discrimination 200
  POWs 908, 912
  private property, protection of 1515–34
  protected areas 371, 373
  protected civilians, definition of 1135–43, 1148, 1150
  Protecting Powers 550
  public property, protection of 1535–50
  rape and sexual violence 344–8
  refugees 1314, 1316–17
  reprisals 580–1, 587
  respect and to ensure respect, obligation to 115
  sanctions 1446–7
  settlements, prohibition of 1551–73
occupation courts 1084–6, 1431–6, 1447–51, 1453
Ogaden National Liberation Front *see* **Ethiopia**
oil 1477, 1525, 1542, 1544–5
omissions 335, 461–2, 627, 741, 746–50, 804, 1009
open registries 776–7
orderlies 219, 809–10, 846, 1002
ordering mode of criminal liability
  forced transfers 1206, 1210
  grave breaches 315 n 140, 619, 621, 625–6, 656, 935, 1345
  individual criminal responsibility 850–1
  omissions 748
organizational threshold
  national liberation movements 408
  NIACs 29, 60–2, 396, 402, 404–9
  non-state armed groups 62, 116–17, 126, 1008
  political motivation 408–9
  resistance movements 917, 896–8, 905, 908, 1396
  responsible command 407–8
  spillovers 43
  Tadić formula 404–9
  territorial control 406–7
organized armed groups *see* **non-state armed groups**
organized resistance movements *see* **resistance movements**
orphans *see* **children**
outer space 74
outrages 201, 292, 294, 327, 332–5, 339–41, 349, 354–5, 360–2, 1249, 1265, 1275, 1285
outside world, relations with *see* **exterior, relations with**
overall control test 17, 19, 24, 36, 398, 402, 1140
overseas territories, list of 1074–5
own/occupied territory distinction 1070–5, 1077

Pakistan
  Al-Qaeda 50
  collective punishments 1166
  drone strikes 38, 44–5
  India 167, 375, 774–5, 1392
  NIACs 45
  spillovers 50
  Taliban 38, 44–5
  United States 44–5
Palestine *see* **Israel/Palestine/Occupied Palestinian Territory**
Palestine Liberation Organization (PLO) *see* **Israel/Palestine/Occupied Palestinian Territory**

Index

parallel conflicts *see* mixed/parallel conflicts
pardons or reprieves 632, 1448–9
parole, release on 995–6
participation in hostilities *see also* **direct participation in hostilities**
 accompany the armed forces, persons who 906–7
 activity hostile to security of state/occupying power 1126–8
 carrying arms openly 901
 child soldiers 1302–6, 1509
 civilians 438–9, 1082–5, 1148–9, 1151, 1182
 co-belligerents 1146
 conduct of hostilities 451, 453–6
 definition 71 n 24
 indirect participation 816, 1302, 1304–6
 internment/detention 922–3, 1343
 legal persons 1138
 medical personnel 816, 824, 852
 membership approach 438
 mere participation 913, 915, 941, 1031
 multi-national coalitions 399
 murder 450, 452–6, 460–1, 465–6
 neutrality 89, 93, 101
 non-state armed groups 898, 901, 933, 1061–2
 non-prisoners of war, status of 913
 POWs 941, 980, 1061–2, 1065
 previous participants in hostilities 103
 private persons, delivery of war material by 89–90, 102
 taking no active part in hostilities condition for protection 433–9
 unlawful combatants 912, 915–17, 920–1
 wounded and sick 762, 764, 796
Patriotic Force for the Liberation of the Congo (FPLC) *see* Democratic Republic of Congo (DRC)
peace agreements *see also* **ceasefire agreements/armistices**
 ad hoc agreements 511
 amnesties 283
 examples 62
 internment/detention, end of 1374, 1377
 Security Council (UN) 1377
 temporal scope of application 56–7, 64
peacekeeping forces/peace operations
 dissemination of GCs 605–6
 emblems 867, 868–9
 humanitarian assistance 238–9, 254
 NIACs 399
 peace support operations 387
 protected areas 386–7
 self-defence 17, 239
 temporal scope of application 62–3, 66
 weapons 239
peacetime
 dissemination of GCs 63, 602–3, 611, 614
 emblems 861–2, 867, 869–72

hospitals 650–1
National Information Bureau, establishment of 1015, 1110
protected areas 371
respect and to ensure respect, obligation to 116, 123–4
temporal scope of application 51–2
penal or disciplinary proceedings *see also entries or sub-entries on specific situations* (e.g. **occupation courts**) *or types of persons* (e.g. **prisoner of war (POW)**)
 age 1363
 appeals against conviction and sentence 1035–6
 armed forces of Detaining Power, laws, regulations, and orders of 1026–8, 1038
 children 1300
 civilians 1026–9, 1031, 1033, 1107, 1300, 1360–2, 1424–5, 1431
  internment/detention 1282–3, 1332, 1351, 1353, 1358–9, 1361–5
  judicial guarantees 1441, 1443, 1453
  judicial system 1026, 1028–9, 1035
  non-discrimination 201
 collective punishment 335
 commanders 1029, 1031–2, 1036, 1038
 criminal proceedings/prosecutions 1026–7, 1031, 1033
 death penalty 1033, 1036
 equality of arms 1364
 escape attempts 1027, 1033–4, 1364
 fair trials 996, 1026–7, 1029–31, 1033–8
 fines 1032–3
 fatigue or extra duties 1363
 fines 1363
 food and water 1355
 gender 1363
 genocide 1027
 grave breaches 1026, 1037
 health 1363
 human rights law 1026–7, 1036–7, 1362–3
 independence and impartiality 1029, 1032, 1034–8
 internment/detention 1282–3, 1332, 1351, 1353, 1358–9, 1361–5
 judicial guarantees 1441, 1443, 1453
 law-making in occupied territories 1424–5
 local tribunals 1431
 loss of status 1030
 mail and correspondence 1021, 1107, 1360
 meaning and application 1026–37
 mere participation in hostilities, no punishment for 1031
 military courts 1026, 1028–9, 1034–8
 military discipline 1025
 nationality 1026
 NIACs 1037
 non-discrimination 201
 non-state armed groups 1026
 parole, breach of 996

penal or disciplinary proceedings *(cont.)*
   penitentiaries, prohibition on use of 1034, 1362
   POWs 979–80, 996, 1000–2, 1009, 1025–38
   privileges, restrictions on 1363
   preference for disciplinary over judicial measures 1028
   prior to capture, offences against 1027, 1029–31, 1037
   procedural rights 1034–7
   protected persons 1030
   Protecting Powers 1033, 1035, 1441–2
   punishments 1029, 1031–7, 1159, 1360, 1362, 1363–5
   religious personnel 1000
   retention of benefits of GCs if convicted 1031
   sanctions 1032–3
   standards 1026
   transfers 1036–7
   war crimes 1027
penal servitude 1446
penalties *see* sanctions/penalties
penitentiary establishments 958, 972–3, 1034, 1362
perfidious or treacherous wounding or killing 853
perfidy 853, 873, 874, 876, 915
permanent medical personnel *see also* auxiliary medical personnel; medical and religious personnel, status, rights, and obligations of 97–8, 101
persecution, risk of
   forced transfers 1186, 1194, 1198, 1200–2
   non-discrimination 202
   non-refoulement, principle of 1198, 1202–3, 1381
   refugees 1320, 1437
   release 1054, 1056, 1062,
   refugees 1200–1, 1320, 1437
   religious beliefs or political opinions 1200–1
   repatriation 104, 1054, 1056, 1062, 1381
persistent objector, doctrine of the 673, 1566–7
personal property and valuables
   cultural perspective 1357–8
   dead persons 279, 280, 291
   economic, social, and cultural rights 1486
   movable/immovable property distinction 1536–7, 1541–6, 1550
   internment/detention 1351, 1353, 1357–8
   National Information Bureau (NIB) 1110, 1112
   occupied territories 1516
   POWs, transfer of 965
   repatriation 1041, 1059, 1115
   requisition 1522–3
   seizure 1524–6
   use of movable property 1545–6, 1550
Peru 801
petition, right of 1358–9, 1371, 1436, 1445, 1448–9
Philippines
   Moro Islamic Liberation Front (MILF) 518
   National Democratic Front of the Philippines (CARHRIHL) 420–1, 511

photographs
   bodies, taking photos with 295
   POWs 984, 992
physical activities 1000–1, 1351, 1357
pillage *see also* **booty of war; looting** 286, 785, 787, 826–8, 835, 837, 993, 1080, 1358, 1369, 1416, 1477, 1516–17, 1520–23, 1528–30, 1532, 1534, 1548
places of internment *see* camps/places of internment/POW camps
plunder *see* pillage
police
   dissemination of GCs 606, 614
   use of excessive force 321–2
political motivation 408–9
Portugal *see* India: Goa
post *see* mail and correspondence
pre-trial confinement 1032, 1236, 1363–4
precautions
   drones 1309
   economic, social, and cultural rights 1509
   evacuation of POWs 959–61, 988
   hospitals 213, 650
   internment/detention 1352–3
   POWs 965, 997
   wounded, sick, and shipwrecked 786
pregnant women *see* mothers and expectant mothers
presumption of innocence
   civilians 1228–9
   derogations 1131
   detention before trial 475, 487
   occupied territories 1440–1, 1452
prior and subsequent treaties and conventions, relationship with 174–6, 689–97
   applicable rules and principles 691–4
   complementarity, principle of 696
   customary international law 689–90, 693–5
   Hague Conventions, relationship with 696–7
   interpretation of treaties 690, 691–2
   older GCs, relationship with 694–5
prisoners of war (POWs) *see also* **release, accommodation in neutral countries, and repatriation of POWs; transfer of prisoners of war (POWs)**
   accommodation 979
   accompanying armed forces 895–6, 906–7
   aerial bombardment, protection from 991, 996
   aircraft, crew of 907
   armed forces, members of 893–5
   arms, carrying openly 901, 908
   authorities, relations with 979
   beginning of captivity 988–95
   belonging to a Party to the conflict 896–7, 907
   camps
      command structure 1001–2
      establishment of camps 979
      location of camps 990–1, 996
      marking of camps 991

Index 1633

capture cards 1006, 1016–17, 1090
change in character of conflict 892–3
chaplains 999
children 1299, 1302
civil capacity, retention of 984–5
civilians, mistreatment by 982
clothing 979, 994, 997
combatant immunity 18, 25, 890, 907, 909, 915, 933, 954, 1007, 1031
communication of POWs with outside world 1014–16, 1021–3
complaints 979, 1002, 1009
conditions in detention 890–1, 995–1001, 1007
contractors 906–7
control, measure of physical 892
corporal punishment 1257–8
crew members 907
criminal enquiries, relations to 1019
criminal responsibility 982, 1009, 1019–20, 1024
cruel, inhuman, or degrading treatment or punishment 978, 892, 992–3, 1007, 1008, 1014, 1024
damages 1008–9
de jure status 891
death 1014, 1019–20
definition of 889–910, 1026
derogations 982, 1007
deserters 892
detaining authorities, relations with 1001–2
developing countries 985–6
disabilities, persons with 999
disappearances 1020, 1024
diseases, contagious 998–9
economic constraints of detaining powers 985–6
electronic communications 1014, 1017, 1022, 1024
emblems 899–901
end of detention 1374
enquiries, relations to 1019–20
escapes 892, 981, 994
evacuation 788, 957–63, 979, 988–9, 1009
extermination 1257
family 1006, 1024
finances 1004–6
fingerprinting 992
fixed distinctive signs 899–901, 903–8
food, water and canteens 979, 997–8, 999
forced labour 1264
honour and dignity, maintenance of 982, 1000, 1009–10, 1275
human shields, POWs as 990–1
humanitarian assistance 985–6
humiliation 984, 1275
hygiene 979, 983, 996, 998–9
identification 979, 991–2, 1090
identity cards, issuing 261–2, 264–5, 895, 992
indicia of status 895
intellectual activities 1000–1

internment/detention 995–6, 1341, 1343
interrogation 319, 328, 979, 992–3
intimidation 982, 984
judicial proceedings 1014, 1018–19
labour/employment 979, 981, 985, 1002–4, 1257
land transport, marking of 900
legal advice, access to 985
leisure time 1000–1
lex specialis 979
liberty and security, right to 715–16, 731–2
list of POWs 992
mail and correspondence 1006, 1014–17, 1021–3, 1090
media 984
medical and religious personnel 198–9, 818–19
medical care 985–6, 997–9, 1009
medical experiments 983
medical inspections 999
medical personnel 979, 999–1000
merchant marine 907
militias, members of 891, 894, 895–8, 901–6, 908–9
missing persons 105–6, 260, 264–71, 1023–4
murder 466, 1257
mutilations 983
nationality 904, 986
neutral states 95, 97, 98–9, 101–3, 105–6
new technologies 1014, 1017, 1022, 1024
NIACs 1343, 1006–8, 1010–11
non-discrimination 192, 195, 198–9, 201, 986–7, 993, 1000, 1007
non-renunciation of rights 146, 148
non-state armed groups 896–906, 1007–8
notification
    capture, of 1014
    contents 1018–19
    judicial proceedings 1018–19
    Protecting Powers 1018–19
    representatives of prisoners 1018–19
    specific 1018–20
    State parties, by 1017
official documents by POWs, creation of 1020
omissions 747–9, 1009
organized resistance movements 896–8, 905, 908
parole, release on 995–6
penal or disciplinary proceedings 979–80, 996, 1000–2, 1009, 1025–38
photographs 984, 992
physical activities 1000–1
physical maltreatment 982, 983–4
pillage 993
placement in camps 986–7
political capitulation 892–3
POWs' obligation to provide information 992–3
precautions 997
privacy 984
private military security companies 906–7
propaganda activities 1000–1

prisoner of war (POW) *(cont.)*
   property of POWs 979, 985, 993–5, 1009
   prosecutions 890, 906–7, 909
   Protecting Powers 553, 1002, 1006, 1018–19
   public curiosity and insult, protection from 357–9, 984, 991–2, 996–8
   punishment 1008–9
   quarters 996–7
   questioning POWs 264–5
   rank and status 992, 1001–2
   rape and sexual violence 348–9, 353, 357–9, 987
   registration of POWs 1014, 1018
   reinterned POWs 908
   relations with outside world of 979, 1013–24
   relatives, contact with 1006
   relief supplies 985, 1006, 1009, 1014, 1023
   religion 979, 986–7, 1000–1
   reparations 1008–9
   representatives 980, 1002, 1004, 1018–19
   reprisals 577, 580, 982
   resources of detaining states 995
   responsibility of detaining power 981
   retained personnel 1000
   sanitation 979, 983, 996, 1282
   sea, confinement at 996
   search, collect and evacuate, obligation to 788
   segregation 986–7
   signs, wearing distinctive 899–901, 903–8
   special agreements 978, 1008
   status
     determination of 939–55
       arms, carrying openly 946
       challenging classification 953
       competent tribunal 940–1, 943, 947–55
       cyber warfare 946
       deserters 952–4
       distinctive signs 942, 945
       grave breaches 640–2
       guerrilla warfare 940, 943
       habeas corpus 953–4
       lex specialis 953–4
       mercenaries 946
       national liberation movments 944–5
       nationals of detaining powers 946–7
       NIACs 53–4, 954
       non-state armed groups 941, 944–6, 949–50, 954
       not want POW status, persons who do 952–4
       own nationals 18
       persons fallen into hands of enemy 940, 944–5, 955
       presumption of POW status 941–7, 952–3, 955
       private military security companies 946
       procedural guarantees 951–2, 954–5
       Red Cross 940, 950
       refugees 952–3
       responsible authority 940, 948
       signs 942, 945
       spies and saboteurs 945
       standard of proof 952
       standards to determine status 947–51
       temporal scope of application 53–4
       unlawful combatants 949–51
   treatment of persons without 911–37
     civilians 927
     consequences of not respecting conditions 913–17
     criminal responsibility 915–18
     distinction, principle of 915, 917–18, 936
     enemy nationals 912
     expansion of status 917
     fighting for party whilst not belonging to it 913
     grave breaches 935
     guerrilla warfare 917, 919
     habeas corpus 950, 953–4
     human rights law 919, 926–7, 934–6
     humanity, principle of 912
     IACs 915, 933–7
     judicial guarantees 919, 1217, 1220, 1225, 1232, 1234–5
     labour/employment 192, 198–9
     legal consequences of a violation 934–6
     loss of POW status 915, 918–19
     mercenaries 915
     militias and volunteer corps, members of 913–14
     minimum treatment standards 919, 926–7
     nationality 926
     neutral states 97
     NIACs 933–7
     non-refoulement, principle of 927–8
     non-state armed groups 913–14, 917, 934
     occupied territories, persons in 912
     organized resistance movements 917
     perfidy 915
     persons fallen into hands of enemy 913
     protected civilians, definition of 1148–50
     Protecting Powers 550, 553–4
     renditions for persons not protected civilians 928–9
     residual protection 921–5
     Security Council (UN) 934
     shipwrecked, definition of 769, 771–4, 776, 778, 780
     special agreements 136, 934
     terrorism 912
     torture 929
     transit or screening camps, conditions in 199
     unlawful combatant debate 912, 915–21, 926, 928–37, 1148–50
     unprivileged belligerents/combatants 912, 918
     vessels, on board 99
     war crimes 915–17
telegrams 1006
temporal applicability 980–1
torture 265, 319, 327–8, 992

treatment of 890–1, 977–1011, 1252
uniforms 899–900, 904, 994
unrecognized governments 905–6
vaccinations 998
vehicle marking 900
visit, right to 246, 533–5, 715, 1009
volunteer corps, members of 894, 895–8, 901–6, 908
war crimes 892, 982, 1009, 1019, 1023
wills, certified copy of 1020
women 987, 1273, 1275, 1282, 1284–5, 1286
separation from men 192, 198, 201, 987
wounded, sick and shipwrecked 106, 759–61, 783, 793
prisons *see* penitentiary establishments
privacy 984, 1016, 1092, 1096–9, 1244, 1283, 1510, 1554
private military and security companies (PMSCs) 868, 869, 906–7, 915, 922, 946, 968, 1029
private property in occupied territories, protection of 1515–34
appropriation, meaning of 1517, 1532
civilians 1515–34
collective property 1517, 1533
compensation 1518, 1522–6, 1539
confiscation 1517, 1522, 1523–4, 1529, 1554–5
cultural property 1517, 1528–30, 1532–3
derogations 1518
destruction of property 1516–20, 1529–32
expropriation 1522, 1526–7
good governance 1474–5, 1476–7
grave breaches 1517
indigenous people, communal property of 1533
means of existence 1518
medical property 1517
military necessity 1516–20, 1527, 1529–32
natural resources 1533–4
non-state armed groups 1533–4
pillage 1516–17, 1520–3, 1529–30, 1532, 1534
possessions, definition of 1533
protected persons 1518
private/public property distinction 1536, 1537–41, 1550
real property 1516, 1518, 1523–4
relief consignments 1517, 1526
requisition 1517, 1522–4, 1526, 1529
respect for private property 1522
seizure 1516, 1520, 1522, 1524–6, 1529–34
settlements, prohibition of 1568–9, 1571–2
state property 1517
war crimes 1520, 1531, 1534
privileges and immunities *see also* **immunity**
ICRC 529, 545
prize 89, 99–100, 772
propaganda 1000–1
property *see also* cultural heritage/property; destruction of property; personal property and valuables; private property in occupied territories, protection of; real property 726,
979, 985, 993–5, 1009, 1138–9, 1164, 1264, 1268, 1290, 1351, 1369, 1511
proportionality
human rights law 1472, 1484
internment of civilians 1250
law making in occupied territories 1425
leave, right to 1181
murder 465, 466
national security 1481
penalties 1440
reprisals 577, 579, 585–6, 591–2
treatment of civilians 1250–1
prosecute or extradite, principle of 313–14, 339, 363, 366, 635–8, 708, 738
prostitution, enforced 333, 340, 344, 346–9, 353–6, 359–64, 1274–7, 1288, 1470
protected areas 369–87
access 371–3, 383
agreements 371–5
children 373, 1296, 1301–2
civilians 369, 374, 379–81, 385–7
conditions 377
consent 372
corridors 379–82
declarations 376–7
demilitarized zones 369, 375–9, 382, 385–6
Draft Agreement 371–3
duration 375
establishment 371–3, 376–8, 381–2
evacuation 1301–2
formalities 371–5, 378
hospital zones and localities 369, 370–4, 385, 532, 1278
humanitarian assistance 381–2
inspections 373
location 372
marking of zones 372, 377
mothers and expectant mothers 369, 373
neutrality, principle of 382
neutralized zones 369, 371, 374–5
non-defended localities 369, 376–7, 379, 381, 385–6
notification 371
no-fly zones 369, 379–80, 383
peace support operations 387
peacetime 371
protected persons 373, 377
Protecting Powers 371, 373, 375, 378
recognition 371, 372–3
Red Cross 371, 373, 375–6, 378–9, 382
refugees 381, 382–4
reparations 386
residence conditions 371–4
responsibility to protect (R2P) 381–2
safety zones 369, 373–4, 380–4, 386–7
children 1296, 1301–2
evacuation 1301–2
women 1278
sea warfare, Red Cross boxes in 376
Security Council (UN) 369, 379–87

protected areas *(cont.)*
  shelter 369, 374, 378
  size 372
  special commissions 372–3
  suspension 375
  termination 373, 375, 377–8
  women 1278
  wounded and sick 369, 371, 373–4, 377, 385–7
protected civilians, definition of 1135–53
  aliens 1143
  definition of civilian population 1152
  diplomatic representation 1145–7
  distinction, principle of 1135–6, 1148–50
  ethnicity 1144–5, 1152
  grave breach 1151–2
  in territory of other party to conflict 1140
  in the hands of a Party to the conflict 1141–2
  incidental protection of civilians 1137
  internment/detention 1148–50
  legal persons, exclusion of 1138
  nationality 1141, 1142–8, 1150, 1152
  neutrality 1145–7, 1150
  non-refoulement, principle of 1141
  occupied territories 1137–43, 1148, 1150
  POWs, unlawful combatants and protected civilians, distinctions between 1148–50
  property 1138–9
  reciprocity 1140–1, 1147, 1153
  refugees 1141
  reprisals 1141
  suspension 1141
  terrorism 1151
  war crimes 1144, 1151–2
Protecting Powers *see also under* **family; humanitarian assistance; ICRC; penal or disciplinary proceedings; prisoner of war (POW); relief consignments** 549–60
  activities 554–5
  appointment 550–2, 557
  conciliation procedure 563, 565–7, 572
  consent 551
  cooperation 560
  customary international law 550, 559
  decline of institution, reasons for 557–9
  definition 551–2
  denial of applicability of GCs 557
  diplomatic relations 551–3
  expenditure 557–8
  functions 553–8
  good offices offered 563, 565–7, 571
  historical evolution 549–50
  impartiality 552–3, 557–8
  implementation of GCs, nomination as 557
  information, duties regarding 553–4
  modalities of appointment 552–3
  neutrality 550–1, 558
  nomination 559
  practice since 1949 556–7
  recognition of adverse party, appointment as amounting to 557
  Red Cross 550–2, 557–9
  special agreements 553
  substitution 550, 557–8
protection, loss of 218, 220, 227, 438–9, 809–19, 839–55, 1305
protracted armed violence threshold
  duration 410–11
  intensity threshold 411–13
  NIACs 30, 33, 60, 395, 404, 410–13
  spillovers 43
  Tadić formula 404, 410–13
public curiosity and insult, exposure to
  cruel, inhuman, or degrading treatment or punishment 333
  enemy hands, treatment of civilians in 1249–50
  internment/detention 1378–9
  POWs 295, 357–9, 984, 992
  wounded, sick, and shipwrecked 791
public health
  administration of occupied territories 1475
  dead persons 287
  diseases, contagious 797, 998–9, 1354, 1495–6
  economic, social, and cultural rights 1486, 1493, 1495–7, 1500, 1506
  law-making in occupied territories 1423
  leave, right to, reason to deny 1181
public hearings 481, 1232–3
public officials
  administration of occupied territories 1428–9
  judges in occupied territories 1429–31
  resign, right to 1428–9
  torture 320, 323–6
public order or safety 844, 1423–7, 1456, 1466–7
public property in occupied territories, protection of 1535–50
  commercial use 1545–6, 1550
  destruction 1536–7, 1541, 1546–50
  duties devolved to Occupying Powers 1536
  grave breaches 1549
  immovable property
    administrative duties of Occupying Power 1541–5
    natural resources 1544–5
    usufruct 1541–4, 1550
  movable/immovable property distinction 1536–7, 1541–6, 1550
  natural resources 1539–40, 1544–5, 1548–9
  pillage 1548
  private/public property distinction 1536, 1537–41, 1550
  sale to private persons 1537, 1550
  seizure 1536, 1548–50
  temporary occupation 1537
  usufruct 1536–7, 1541–4, 1549–50

public revenue 1479
punishment *see* collective punishment; cruel, inhuman, or degrading treatment or punishment; death penalty; penal or disciplinary proceedings; sentences/punishment
puppet governments, safeguards against 1587–8

questioning 264–5, 319, 992–3, 1030, 1230

race and ethnicity 56, 192–4, 196, 199, 201–2, 259, 1275, 1553
  national liberation movements 20, 52, 396, 408, 708
  protected civilians, definition of 1144–5, 1152
racist regimes 20, 52, 396, 408, 1057, 1392, 1415
Radbruch formula 183–4
ransoms 229
rape and sexual violence 343–68, 1272, 1274–7, 1285–92
  abortion services 203–4, 763–4
  children 355, 356 n 87, 359, 364–7, 1309–10
  civilians 344, 346–9, 355, 364, 1250
  consent 352
  crimes against humanity 346, 352, 354, 356
  criminalization 345–6, 352, 363–7
  cruel, inhuman, or degrading treatment or punishment 333, 340, 345, 353, 356–62, 365–8
  customary international law 345, 364, 366
  definition of rape 346, 351–2
  feminism 350, 362
  gender-based violence 346, 350
  genocide 346
  grave breaches 357, 361–3, 366
  harassment 322
  honour, attacks on 346–51, 354, 367, 1276, 1290
  human dignity 344, 347–9, 351, 355, 360–2
  indecent assault 344, 346–9, 355–7, 359–61, 364
  men and boys, against 344, 349, 353, 366
  modesty 1290
  new legal instrument, proposal for 366–7
  non-discrimination 203
  non-repetition, guarantees of 1287
  occupied territories 344–8
  POWs 348–9, 353, 357–9, 987
  pregnancy, enforced 362
  private and family right, right to respect for 1244
  property, women as 1290
  prostitution, enforced 344, 346–8, 353–6, 359–64
  rape, definition of 1276
  sanctions under SC resolutions 365, 368
  sex discrimination 345, 359, 366
  slavery 354–5, 361–2, 1286
  torture 329, 340, 361–2
  training 367, 1310
  universality 363
  war crimes 203, 346, 348, 351–2, 354–5, 361–4
  wounded, sick, and shipwrecked 358–9, 759, 762–5

ratifications
  beginning of applicability 55
  depositaries 156, 162, 168, 171–3
  entry into force 162
  final provisions 162, 168, 171–3
  non-state armed groups 417–18, 422
  two-step procedure 160, 162
ratione loci see geographical scope of application of GCs
rations 1355
real property
  economic, social, and cultural rights 1486
  geographical scope of application 69, 70
  land rights 1568–9
  loss of protection 846
  movable/immovable property distinction 1536–7, 1541–6, 1550
  natural resources 1544–5
  private property, protection of 1516, 1518, 1523–4
  private/public property distinction 1538
  public property, protection of 1541–5
  requisition 1523–4
  usufruct 1541–4, 1550
  wounded and sick, definition of 759
rebel groups *see* national liberation movements; non-state armed groups; resistance movements
reciprocity, principle of
  denunciation 176–7
  family links, maintenance of 1099
  hostages, taking 299
  humanitarian assistance 233
  interpretation of treaties 691
  NIACs 80
  POWs 901–2
  protected civilians, definition of 1140–1, 1147, 1153
  repatriation of POWS 1043, 1049–51, 1064
  reprisals 579, 591, 594
  respect and to ensure respect, obligation to 132
recognition of belligerency 22, 40, 107, 379, 423, 425
recreation and sport for internees 1000–1, 1300, 1357
red cross, crescent, red lion and sun, red crystal 699, 808, 814, 861, 864–5, 866, 879–80, 882, 1254
Red Cross Messages 1101–2, 1021–3
red crystal *see* red cross, crescent, red lion and sun, red crystal
red lion and sun *see* red cross, crescent, red lion and sun, red crystal
re-establishment 53, 58, 65, 505, 1060, 1089–121, 1264
refugees 1313–23
  civilians, protection of 1074
  complaints mechanisms 1320–1
  criminal offences 1437–8

refugees *(cont.)*
  cruel, inhuman, or degrading treatment or
    punishment 1314
  definition 1202–3, 1316, 1322–3
  deportations 1317, 1320
  enemy aliens 1314–16
  extradition 1314, 1317, 1437
  forced transfers 1187, 1198, 1200–4, 1211–13,
    1317–18, 1320
  grave breaches 1320
  humanitarian assistance 1323
  IACs 1313–17, 1321–2
  internationally displaced persons 1319–21
  internment/detention 1316, 1320, 1375, 1381
  leave, right to 1181–2, 1184
  meaning and application 1315–18
  national security 1202
  nationality 1314–16
  neutral states 94, 97–8, 102
  NIACs 1314, 1318–22
  non-discrimination 1314
  non-repatriated persons 1259–60
  non-refoulement, principle of 1053, 1202–4, 1314,
    1320, 1322, 1381, 1437
  occupied territories 1314, 1316–17, 1436–8
  persecution, risk of 1320, 1437, 1200–1
  political opinion 1200–1, 1314, 1437
  POWs 952–3, 972
  protected areas 381, 382–4
  protected civilians, definition of 1141
  protected persons 1314–16
  religion 1200–1, 1314, 1437
  remedies 1321–2
  repatriation 1053, 1060
  requests for asylum 97–8
  special rules 1313–23
  stateless persons 1314, 1438
  treason 1437
  UN High Commissioner for Refugees 1313, 1314
  war crimes 1320
regionalization 688
registration
  POWs 1014, 1018
  property 994
  treaties 171–3
release of civilians 1083, 1105
  agreements 1376–7
  aliens in territory of party to conflict 1259
  children 1301
  close of hostilities 1374–5, 1377–80
  definition of release 1375
  expenses 1374
  final release, repatriation, or re-establishment of
    protected persons 53
  internment/detention 1243, 1284–5,
    1374–80, 1385–6
  medical reasons 1376
  mothers and expectant mothers 1284

  National Information Bureau (NIB) 1112
  no longer exist, when reasons 1374, 1375–6
  procedures for internment, abuse of 1376
  reasons which necessitated internment, based
    on 1375–7
  review procedures, lack of 1376
  war on terror 1376
release, accommodation in neutral countries, and
    repatriation of POWs 1039–66
  accommodation of POWs neutral
    countries 1044–5
  active military service 1043–4, 1046–7
  agreements 1041–2, 1049
  criminal responsibility 1063
  cruel, inhuman, or degrading treatment or
    punishment 1053–4, 1064–5
  death penalty 1053
  declarations, unilateral 1047–8
  definition 1040–1
  delay 1040, 1046, 1049, 1051, 1063–4
  during hostilities 1041–4
  early release and repatriation 1040
  end of applicability 57–8, 64
  end of active hostilities, at the 1046–59,
    1061, 1065–6
  evacuation of POWs 960
  exchanges 1042–3
  extradition 1059
  forced repatriation 1051–6, 1064
  grave breaches 1063
  individual criminal responsibility 1063
  individualization 1065–6
  instantaneous repatriation 1058
  judicial proceedings 1059, 1061
  labour/employment 1041
  loss of status 892
  medical diagnoses, list of 1042
  missing persons 1059
  Mixed Medical Commissions 96–7, 532, 1041–2,
    1044, 1063–4
  NIACs 1047–9, 1060–2, 1065
  non-discrimination 1053
  non-refoulement, principle of 1051–6, 1057,
    1062, 1064–5
  non-state armed groups 1061
  objections by POWs 1051–6
  parole, on 995–6
  persecution, risk of 1054, 1056, 1062
  personal effects 1059
  place of repatriation 1058
  practical arrangements and modalities 1058–9
  prioritization 1058
  Protecting Powers 1042, 1055
  reciprocity 1043, 1049–51, 1064
  refugees 1053, 1060
  searches for dispersed POWs 1041, 1059
  special agreements 1041–2
  spot, on the 988

status and treatment of prisoners who are not repatriated 1060
time for release and repatriation 1040–1
torture 1064–5
traitors, as being seen as 1040
transfers 963, 966, 968, 970, 990, 1049, 1064–5
unilateral and unconditional character of obligation 1049–51, 1057
unilateral repatriation 1043
war crimes 1063–4
wishes of POWs 1045, 1051–6, 1058
wounded and sick 1041–3, 1058
relief *see* humanitarian assistance; relief consignments
relief consignments
  censorship 1109
  collective relief 1023, 1108, 1361
  economic, social, and cultural rights 1486, 1494–5, 1513
  family links, maintenance of 1091, 1096–9
  good governance 1475
  Internee Committees 1108
  internment/detention 1108–9, 1361
  military necessity, restrictions for 1108–9
  non-repatriated persons 1260
  POWs 965, 985, 1006, 1009, 1014, 1023
  private property, protection of 1517, 1526
  Protecting Powers 1006
  requisition 1526
religion and belief *see also* medical and religious personnel, status, rights, and obligations of
  activities 1000–1
  children 1299, 1300, 1306, 1501
  conscientious objectors 98–9
  dead persons 279, 287–9, 293–4, 1019
  emblems 879–80
  enemy hands, treatment of civilians in 1246
  food and water 1355
  good governance 1470, 1476
  internment/detention 1246, 1351, 1354–5
  Islamic burials 287–8, 293
  Islamic law 681–2, 1049
  non-discrimination 192, 194, 195, 198, 200, 986–7, 1000–1
  non-repatriated persons 1260
  persecution, risk of 1200–1
  POWs 1000–1
  proselytism 1000–1
  Red Cross, Christian origins of 687, 879
  refugees 1200–1, 1314, 1437
  thought, conscience and religion, freedom of 1097
  universality 670–1, 678–83, 687–8
  wounded and sick 196
remains *see also* corpses/dead persons 105, 277–296, 787, 1019, 1020, 1091, 1368
remedies and reparations *see also* compensation
  cruel, inhuman, or degrading treatment or punishment 340–1
  damages 583, 656, 1008–9, 1138–9, 1183, 1570–1

dead persons 281, 1366
effective remedy, right to an 340
enquiry/fact-finding procedure 569
hostages, taking 313
international criminal law 752
internment/detention 1371
judicial guarantees 492, 1445
law-making in occupied territories 1451
leave, right to 1184
non-discrimination 1287
non-state armed groups 429
POWs 64, 1008–9
protected areas 386
refugees 1321–2
right to convicted persons to be informed of remedies 1445
settlements, prohibition of 1570–3
torture 340
universality 686
war crimes 1451
women 1287
rendition 928–9, 1197, 1203
renunciation 145–54, 1265
reparations *see* remedies and reparations
repatriation *see* repatriation of civilians; release, accommodation in neutral countries, and repatriation of POWs
repatriation of civilians
  agreements 1376–7
  aliens in territory of party to conflict 1259–61
  as soon as possible after close of hostilities 1374, 1377–9
  children 1301–2
  consent 1381
  definition 1375
  diplomatic assurances on non-persecution 1381
  expenses 1374, 1382
  final release, repatriation, or re-establishment of protected persons 53
  forcible repatriation 1381, 1383
  internment/detention 1105, 1284–5, 1374–81, 1385–6
  last place of residence, return to 1380–1
  leave, right to 1175, 1179–80
  loss of protection 849
  medical and religious personnel 818–19
  National Information Bureau (NIB) 1112
  neutral states 95–8, 100–1, 103–4, 106
  non-refoulement, principle of 1384
  non-repatriated persons 1259–61
  persecution, risk of 104, 1381
  personal valuables 1113
  special agreements 140
  torture 1384
  transfers 1375
  voluntary repatriation 1381
  war on terror 1376
  women 1284–5

representation of state 31–4
representatives of POWs 980, 1002, 1004
reprisals, prohibition of 575–96
   anticipatory reprisals 584
   civilians 577, 580, 587, 594–5, 1080
   collective punishment 578, 580, 588–9, 1158, 1162–4
   conditions of exercise 582–6
   countermeasures 578–9, 584, 594–5
   counter-reprisals 584
   cultural property 577, 580, 587
   definition and related concepts 578–80
   deterrence 576
   embargoes 578
   hospitals 218
   hostages, taking 299
   international criminal law 591–2, 594–5, 739–40, 751
   judicial guarantees 480, 1226
   medical buildings, vessels, and equipment 580
   missing persons 265
   NIACs 577, 580, 587–91, 595
   non-state armed groups 429, 590–1, 595
   POWs 577, 580, 982, 1050
   proportionality 577, 579, 585–6, 591–2
   protected civilians, definition of 1141
   protected persons 577, 580, 587–8
   public opinions 586
   purpose 582–3, 592
   reciprocity 579, 591, 594
   repatriation 1050, 1062–3
   tu quoque, defence of 594
   war crimes 578
   weapons and combat, use of unlawful methods of 582, 594
   wrongfulness and justification, circumstances, precluding 592–3
requests for military assistance 1403–4
requisition 221–2, 834, 837, 1482, 1488, 1497–9, 1517, 1523–4, 1526, 1528, 1529, 1533–4, 1549
rescue services *see also* small coastal rescue craft 816, 829
reservations 156, 171–2, 173–4, 642, 918, 967, 1029, 1379–80
reservists 604
resistance movements *see also* national liberation movements; non-state armed groups 896–8, 905, 908, 917, 1394–7, 1401, 1429
resources and capacity
   administration of occupied territory 1075
   economic, social, and cultural rights 1493–4, 1507–8
   evacuation 988
   internment/detention 1351, 1358, 1385
   law-making in occupied territories 1422–3
   POWs 995
   wounded, sick, and shipwrecked 792, 803

respect and to ensure respect, obligation to 111–34
   ad hoc agreements 520
   ad hoc institutional mechanisms 129
   addressees of obligation 116–17
   content of obligations 117–33
   continuous obligation 123
   countermeasures 113, 128–9, 134
   customary international law 113, 115–17, 122, 126, 129
   dead persons 277–9, 287, 289, 291–6
   dissemination of GCs 119–20
   due diligence 120, 123, 125, 127–30, 133
   economic sanctions 129
   emblems 857
   encourage or aid or assist violations by others, obligation not to 130–2, 1064–5
   enemy hands, treatment of civilians in 1243–4
   erga omnes obligations 115, 123, 126
   external compliance dimension 115, 120–32
   genocide 127, 128–9, 131–2
   geographical proximity 127
   hospitals 217, 228, 835
   in all circumstances formula 112–14, 124, 132–3
   measures authorized and required 127–32
   medical and religious personnel 809–13, 816, 822–3
   medical transport 118
   military necessity 132–3
   negative obligations 117–19, 130
   NIACs 115
   Occupying Power 1417–8
   organized armed groups 116–17, 126
   organs of state, obligation to stop and prevent infringements by 118–20
   peacetime 116, 123–4
   positive obligations 117–19, 130
   private encroachment 117–18
   private property, protection of 1522
   quasi-constitutional obligation, as 113
   Red Cross 114, 115–16, 119–20, 122, 128, 130–1
   religious convictions and practices 1246
   responsibility to protect (R2P) concept 124, 130
   scope of obligation 115–17, 123–30
   serious breaches 124–5
   si omnes clause 114, 132
   specific provisions 119–20
   state responsibility 117, 125–6, 128, 130–1
   to ensure respect-clause 113–33
   triggers 123–7
   unilateral military action 128
   when obligation is triggered 126–7
   wounded, sick, and shipwrecked 784–6, 796, 798–9, 802
responsibility to protect (R2P) 124, 130, 381–2
responsible command threshold for NIACs 407–8
retained personnel 1000
retroactivity *see* legality, principle of
revision of the GCs *see* amendment/revision of the GCs

Revolutionary Armed Forces of Colombia (FARC)
   see Colombia
Revolutionary United Front (RUF)
   see Sierra Leone
right of initiative 495–508, 533
   acceptance 500–1, 506
   access to territory 502
   addressee of the initiative 499–500
   consent 497, 501–2, 533
   consequences of making an offer 500–6
   counterterrorism legislation, relationship with 503–5, 508
   discretion 499
   impartiality 496–505
   NIACs 496–7, 499–500, 502–8, 534, 536
   not amounting to armed conflict, situations 506–7, 534
   offer, right to 500–1
   recognition of armed conflict 502
   Security Council (UN) 503–5, 508
   services which may be offered 505–6
   terrorism 503–5, 508
   transit, right of 502
right to know *see* know, right to
ruses of war 1251, 1333
Russia *see also* Georgia vs Russia (2008)
   Chechnya 712–13, 720, 725, 927
   collective punishment 1161
   Crimea (2014) 13–14, 1392, 1459
   First World War 496, 1391
   Greco-Turkish War (1897) 552
   Ottoman Empire 879
   Ukraine (2014) 13–14
Rwanda *see also* Democratic Republic of Congo (DRC); Uganda
   collective punishment 1165–6
   dead persons 295
   Democratic Forces for the Liberation of Rwanda (FDLR) 1165–6
   Democratic Republic of Congo 82
   domestic implementation 663
   hospitals 224, 227, 822
   humanitarian assistance 252
   individual criminal responsibility 492
   international criminal liability 626, 740
   judicial guarantees 1222
   medical and religious personnel 822
   IAC, conflict as 65
   murder 457
   NIAC, conflict as 65, 394, 398, 401–2, 404
   Patriotic Force for the Liberation of the Congo (FPLC) 398
   pillage 1369, 1532
   protected areas 384
   rape and sexual violence 351, 1277
   reprisals 593
   spillovers 82
   torture 323–5

universality 673
wounded, sick, and shipwrecked 805

saboteurs *see* spies and saboteurs
safeguard clauses 514, 1198, 1577, 1586–8
safety and sustenance of armed forces 1460, 1482, 1484
safety zones 369, 373–4, 380–4, 386–7, 1278, 1296, 1301–2
San Remo Manual 214, 219–20, 222, 224, 833, 835, 838
sanctions/penalties *see also* collective punishment; death penalty; penal or disciplinary proceedings; sentences/punishment
   children 1309
   collective punishment 1162–3, 1170
   disappearances 1118
   dissemination of GCs 598
   domestic implementation 649, 655–65
   economic sanctions 91, 129, 1162–3, 1170
   effective penal sanctions 621–8
   emblems 876–7
   enquiry/fact-finding procedure 568–70
   international criminal law 738
   internment/detention 1351, 1355, 1357, 1361–5
   minor offences 1446–7
sanitation/sanitary measures 979, 983, 996, 1282–3, 1288, 1489, 1512
sea, the *see also* hospital ships; naval warfare; shipwrecked; vessels
   burial at sea 279, 288, 289–90, 296
   continental shelf 70
   development of the law of the sea 1566–7
   evacuation 960
   exclusive economic zones 70
   geographical scope of application 69, 70
   high seas 74–5
   loss of protection 846
   medical and religious personnel 815–16
   occupation from the sea 1394, 1396
   POWs 965, 989–90, 996
   Red Cross boxes 376
   return of persons taking custody at sea 1381–2
   search, collect, and evacuate, obligation to 787
   territorial sea 70
   wounded and sick, definition of 759
searches
   actively search, collect, and evacuate, duty to 786
   casualties and their collection and evaluation 269
   container ships 776
   dead persons 278, 279–80, 286, 294
   dispersed internees/POWs 1059, 1374, 1380
   grave breaches, perpetrators of 619, 628–30
   hospital ships 220, 228, 834
   hospitals 223
   internment/detention 1281–2
   missing persons 261–2, 268–73, 1120
   requests 270

searches (cont.)
   search and rescue 829
   wounded, sick, and shipwrecked 776, 786–9, 793–800
secession 35, 1415
Second World War
   administration of occupied territories 1457–8, 1462
   Central Tracing Agency 1015
   collective punishment 1156, 1159, 1161, 1167
   conciliation procedure 567
   cruel, inhuman, or degrading treatment or punishment 318
   de-nazification process 616, 1001
   disappearances 1118
   emblems 868–9
   end of applicability 53
   evacuation of POWs 959–61, 974–5
   family links, maintenance of 1120
   forced labour 1257
   hostages, taking 299–300
   intermediate stages between neutrality and belligerence 93
   internment/detention 1073, 1328, 1350–1
   leave, right to 1178
   means of existence 1261
   medical and religious personnel 822
   murder 450, 454, 463
   non-discrimination 191
   Oder-Neisse Line, settlement in German territories east of 1553–4, 1555, 1560
   POWs 963, 965, 1113
      definition 892, 905
      evacuation 959–61, 974–5
      status, determination of 940–1
      treatment 978, 980, 983, 991, 1001
   prostitution, enforced 353–5, 1276
   protected civilians, definition of 1136, 1140, 1147
   Protecting Powers 550
   rape and sexual violence 346, 349, 353–5, 357–8, 360
   Red Cross and compliance 527, 533
   repatriation 1051, 1052
   resistance movements 905, 1396, 1413–14
   settlements, prohibition of 1553–5, 1560
   shipwrecked, definition of 772–3, 776, 780
   Soviet transfer operations in Baltic States 1554
   summary executions 463
   surrender 1405
   universality 676, 679, 686
   war crimes 616–17, 627
secret detention centres 993
secret trials 481
security, imperative reasons of 49, 104, 248, 310, 554, 716, 718, 933, 1108, 1177, 1250, 1262, 1329–31, 1334
segregation 986–7

seizure of property
   private property 1516–17, 1520, 1522, 1524–36
   public property 1545–6, 1549–50
self-defence
   cyber warfare 23
   hospital ships 220, 833–4
   medical and religious personnel 817
   non-state armed groups 18–19, 25
      peacekeeping forces 17, 239
   threshold 19, 25
   violence for IACSs, threshold of 25
   war on terror 68
self-determination *see also* **national liberation movements**
   administration of occupied territories 1428
   common or indigenous land, qualification of 1539
   homeland, right to the 1567–8
   judges in occupied territories 1431
   national liberation movements 39, 19–21
   settlements, prohibition of 1560, 1567–8
self-incrimination, privilege against 478, 1230–1
Sendero Luminoso *see* **Peru**
sentences/punishment *see also* **collective punishment; death penalty; penal or disciplinary proceedings; sanctions/penalties**
   appeals 1035–6
   children 1296
   grave breaches 615–19, 622–5, 628, 632–3, 637–8, 640–2, 644
   internment/detention, end of 1379–80
   judicial guarantees 470, 471, 479, 488–90, 493, 1446
   POWs 1019
   Protecting Powers, notification of 1446
   serving sentences 1258
   visit, right to 1446
separatist movements 1508–9
   Abkhazia separatists 35, 45–6, 107, 1392
   South Ossetia separatists 35, 45–6, 107, 1392
September 11, 2001 terrorist attacks 12, 68, 932
Serbia *see* **Kosovo/Serbia; former Yugoslavia**
settlements, prohibition of 1551–73
   annexation 1559
   colonization 1552, 1567
   conquest 1559
   courts of OP, recourse to 1570–1
   decolonization 1552
   deportation 1562–4
   derogations 1564–5, 1571–2
   emergencies 1565
   ethnic cleansing 1553–4
   fact-finding commissions 1570
   grave breaches 1555
   homeland, right to the 1567–8
   human rights law 1553, 1568, 1572–3
   incentives to move 1563
   justification 1564–5
   land rights 1568–9

mass forcible transfers 1552, 1562
meaning and application 1559–67
military necessity 1565
national security 1564–5
nationality 1561–2
NIACs 1567
non-state actors 1563–4
norms of international law, breaches of
    other 1567–9
prevention, duty of 1564
private persons, acts by 1564
private property 1568–9, 1571–2
procedural remedies 1570–2
prohibited activities 1562–3
racial prejudice and hatred 1553
regulation 1552
remedies 1570–3
reparations 1573
restitution 1573
restrictions 1564–5
scope of prohibition 1559–64
self-determination 1560, 1567–8
territorial scope 1560–1
territorial sovereignty 1559–60
third states, recourse to courts of 1571–2
transfers 1552–73
war crimes 1555
sex discrimination 192–4, 200, 1271–3, 1285
customary international law 1272
differentiation 192, 195, 198, 203
equal pay 1490
human rights law 1272
humanitarian assistance 203–4
internment/detention 1281, 1284
POWs 192, 198, 201
rape and sexual violence 345, 359, 366
reparations 1287
sexuality and reproduction, seeing women in terms
    of 203–4
special privileges 192
stereotyping 202
structural causes, elimination of 1288, 1290
wounded and sick 196–7
sexual orientation discrimination 204–5
sexual violence *see* **rape and sexual violence**
Al-Shabaab militia *see* **Somalia**
shelter *see also* **property**
children 1296
good governance 1473–4
house demolitions 1161–2
internment/detention 1105, 1354
POWs 966, 979
protected areas 369, 374, 378
residence, choice of 1193
women 1278–80
ships *see* **hospital ships; vessels**
shipwrecked *see also* **wounded and sick**
civilians 769–75, 780

commercial raiding 772
container ships, searches of 776
convoys 771–2
de facto shipwrecked 774
definition 759–61, 767–80
developments in shipping since 1949 776–7
historical background 770–3
land warfare 768, 770–1, 773, 775, 778–9
merchant ships 769, 771–7, 780
naval warfare 767–8, 771–2, 774–80
neutral states 774, 776
NIACs 445, 779
open registries 776–7
POWs 769, 771–4, 776, 778, 780
prize, capture as 772
protected persons 773
searches 776
Second World War 772–3, 776, 780
submarines 772–3, 780
when and for how long person is
    shipwrecked 777–8
wounded and sick 769, 771, 773, 775
si omnes **(general participation) clause** 7, 114,
    132, 697
sick-bays on warships 222, 228, 832, 840–9
sick and wounded *see* **wounded and sick**
Sierra Leone
child soldiers 437, 1296–7, 1310–11
collective punishment of women and
    girls 1165–6
hostages, taking 308
humanitarian assistance 253
internment/detention 1369
judicial guarantees 1221
murder 460
NIAC, conflict as 65
rape and sexual violence 351
Revolutionary United Front (RUF) 62, 424
territorial control 407
Truth and Reconciliation Commission 1166
Uganda 407
signs *see also* **emblems, use of**
distinctive signs 858, 860–2, 899–901, 903–8,
    942, 945
domestic implementation 650, 652, 662–3
non-state armed groups 945
road signs to hospitals 861
Skype 1022, 1101, 1107
slavery
child soldiers 1303
prostitution, enforced 1276–7
rape and sexual violence 354–5, 361–2, 1286
SLM/A *see* **Sudan**
small coastal rescue craft 215–16, 220, 222,
    815–16, 832, 834
social rights *see* **economic, social, and cultural rights
    in occupied territories**
solitary confinement 322, 335, 995, 1259, 1446

Somalia
  cross-border NIACs 42–3
  Kenya, incursions into 42–3
  NIAC, conflict as 404
  peacekeeping forces 383, 613, 1414
  protected areas 383
  Al-Shabaab militia 42–3
South Ossetia separatists *see also* Georgia vs Russia (2008) 45–6
Spain
  Spanish Civil War 779
  Western Sahara 1459
special agreements in IACs (for NIACs *see* ad hoc agreements under Common Article 3) 135–44
  anti-personnel mines 142
  beginning of applicability 55
  border incidents 140
  cluster munitions 142
  contracting out 141
  declarations 138
  dissemination of GCs 611–12
  enemy hands, treatment of civilians in 1265
  expanding bullets 142
  indiscriminate effects, weapons with 142
  internment/detention, end of 1382
  law-making in occupied territories 1427
  legal consequences of a violation 143
  legality, principle of 143
  meaning and application 137–42
  medical and religious personnel 810
  national liberation movements 55
  nature of application 141–2
  neutral states 138
  non-renunciation of rights 145
  occupied territories 1265
  POWs 136, 934, 973, 978, 1008
  Protecting Powers 141, 553
  repatriation 140, 1041–2
  scope of protection 139–41
  subjects 139–40
  temporal scope of application 55
  threshold test 138–9
  weapons, types of 141–3
  writing 138
special zones 1071, 1301–2
spies and saboteurs
  activity hostile to security of state/occupying power 1126–7
  death penalty 1130–1, 1447–8
  definition of sabotage 1127
  derogations 1124, 1126–31
  distinction, principle of 1127
  fair hearings, right to 1130–1
  family news, communication of 1100
  human rights law 1127–8
  internment/detention 1331
  law-making in occupied territories 1425
  loss of status 1030
  POWs, determination of status of 945, 1127
  residual protection 922
spillovers
  accidental border incursions 12, 15–16
  cross-border NIACs 12, 15–16, 42–3, 49
  geographical scope of application 77–83
  war on terror 50
SPLM *see* Sudan
spontaneous taking up of arms 409, 907–8
sport and physical exercise 662, 1000, 1023, 1300, 1357
Sri Lanka
  Liberation Tigers of Tamil Eelam (LTTE) 423
  murder 456, 459
  NIACs 848
  Panel of Experts on Accountability (UN) 456, 572
  protected areas 379, 382–3
  visits 534
starvation 236, 244–5, 254, 1170, 1514
state of war *see also* declaration of war 5, 15, 26, 52, 54, 56, 170, 497, 502
state sovereignty
  boundary between IACs and NIACs 10–11
  grave breaches 617, 620, 637
  humanitarian assistance 254–5
  leave, right to 1174
  NIACs 41–2, 107
  right of initiative 501–2
  transnational armed conflict 48
stateless persons 1179, 1314, 1438
statism 684–5
Stimson Doctrine 1465
stripping 320, 322
submarines 772–3, 780
subsequent treaties and conventions, relationship with *see* prior and subsequent treaties and conventions, relationship with
subsidiarity 577, 584–5, 587, 592
succession to the GCs 55, 157, 164–9, 171–2
Sudan (Darfur Conflict)
  ad hoc agreement 511
  International Commission of Inquiry 424, 572–3
  Justice and Equality Movement (JEM) 424, 511
  protected areas 384–5
  Sudan Liberation Movement/Army (SLM/A) 424, 511
  Sudan People's Liberation Movement (SPLM) 421, 424, 511–12, 518
Sudan Liberation Movement/Army (SLM/A) *see* Sudan
Sudan People's Liberation Movement (SPLM) *see* Sudan
suicides, investigation of 285
superior orders, defence of obedience to 226, 408, 603, 618, 620, 627–8, 899, 1160
supplementary pay 1004
surrender 980, 1405

Index   1645

surveillance 1330, 1362
sustenance *see* food and water; means of existence
Switzerland
   depositary 160 n 18, 162, 165, 168, 171–3,
      177–8, 653, 698 n 32, 967, 1417
   flag, protection of Swiss 874
   neutrality 91, 107–8, 528
   Red Cross and compliance 526–8, 546–7, 1113
   Swiss/ICRC Initiative on Strengthening
      Compliance with International
      Humanitarian Law 173, 546, 562
   US-led coalition and Iraq conflict 2003, neutrality
      in 4 n 2
Syria
   child soldiers 711
   counter-terrorism legislation 823
   Independent Commission of Inquiry 456, 464,
      572, 711, 823
   intensity threshold 412
   medical aid, criminalization of 801
   medical and religious personnel 508, 823
   murder 464
   NIAC, as 107, 848
   organization, degree of 61
   recognition of belligerency 107
   recognition of non-state armed groups in 20–1, 33, 39
   representation of state 33
   summary executions 464
   Syrian Revolutionary and Opposition Forces
      (NCS) 21

TAC *see* transnational armed conflicts (TACs)
Tadić formula 394–6, 404–5, 408, 410, 404–13
taking no active part in hostilities condition for
      protection 433–9
Taliban
   clothing 900–1
   drone strikes 38, 45
   IAC, conflict as 1048
   invitations 44
   medical personnel, training 820
   NIAC, as 44, 48–50, 729, 1048
   occupation of Afghanistan 1392
   Pakistan 38, 44–5
   POWs 914, 932, 949–50
   recognition as government 32
   self-defence 68
   unlawful combatants 930, 931 n 177, 949–50, 1149
Tamil Tigers *see* Sri Lanka 423
targeted killings 50, 68, 79, 1472–3
tax 1479
technology *see* electronic communications/new
      technology; Internet
telegrams 1006, 1022, 1091, 1107, 1112, 1114
temporal scope of application 51–66
   beginning of applicability 52–7, 59–61, 65
   end of applicability 52–3, 56–9, 61–5,
      1576–86, 1589

functional approach 65
general close of military operations 1576–86
IACs 53–9, 65
individual criminal responsibility 64–5
international criminal responsibility 64, 66
legal consequences of a violation 64–5
merger of law of IAC and law of NIAC 53, 65
mixed conflicts 53
NIACs 53–5, 59–62, 65
non-state armed groups 52
peacekeeping operations 62–3, 66
one year after close of military operations 52–3,
   58–9, 1576–83
peacetime 51–2, 63–4
POWs 53–4, 980–1
special agreements 55
transnational conflicts 53–4, 65, 1346–7
wartime 51–2
territorial control
   government 32
   NIACs 405, 1450
   non-state armed groups 77, 379, 406–8, 413–14,
      423, 1008
   occupation 74, 1390–1, 1397, 1401, 1456,
      1480, 1560
   organizational threshold for NIACs 406–7
   refugees 1322
   requirement for POW status 904
territorial sea 70
territoriality, principle of 630, 1434
territory, definition of 42
terrorism *see* terrorist groups; war on terror
terrorist groups
   anti-terrorism legislation 503–5, 1083
   countermeasures 800–2
   counter-terrorism 503–5, 508, 1151
   derogations 1124
   human rights law 705
   IACs 68
   internment/detention 68, 79, 1328
   judicial guarantees 480
   law-making in occupied territories 1425
   medical aid, criminalization of 800–2,
      820, 823
   non-state armed groups 427, 431, 949–50
   POWs
      determination of status of 949–50
      status and treatment of persons without POW
         status 912
      treatment 1007
   presumption of innocence 475
   protected civilians, definition of 1151
   residual protection 922
   right of initiative of 503–5, 508
   Security Council (UN) 503–4
   support for terrorism 503, 800–2, 820,
      823, 915–17
   terrorism, definition of 662

terrorist groups (*cont.*)
  ticking time bomb scenario 321
  transnational armed conflict 48
  unlawful combatants 929–30, 949–50, 1124
  unprivileged belligerents/combatants 912
threat to peace 380, 1307
threshold for IACs 10–26
tobacco 997–8, 1128, 1355–6
Tokyo Military Tribunal 7, 660–3, 974–5, 1159, 1228
torture 322–30
  aiding and abetting 1064, 1384
  civilians 323, 340, 1080, 1131, 1248, 1256, 1258, 1265
  Committee against Torture (UN) 323–5, 329, 339–41, 928, 1359, 1363, 1371, 1384
  confessions 320, 323, 326–7, 341
  crimes against humanity 323–5, 329, 339–42
  cruel, inhuman or degrading treatment 326–31
  definition 306, 320, 323–4, 326, 328, 331, 338, 341–2, 570
  derogations 321, 1131
  detention 320, 324
  disappearances 1024
  due diligence 320, 324, 338
  economic, social, and cultural rights 1489–90
  effective remedy, right to an 340
  enquiry/fact-finding procedure 570
  extradition 485, 631, 1379
  forced transfers 1195, 1203–4
  grave breaches 319, 328, 339–40, 631
  gross negligence 321
  handcuffing 320
  hooding 320
  hostages, taking 302, 306
  human rights law 321, 328, 338, 341–2
  humiliation 329
  immunity 707
  impunity 342
  individual criminal responsibility 325, 1265
  intention 321, 329–30
  international criminal law 325–6, 328, 342
  internment/detention 1352, 1358–9, 1363, 1375, 1381, 1384
  investigations 337–9
  judicial torture 323, 328
  legal consequences of a violation 337
  methods 320–1
  military necessity 321, 323
  neglect 321, 329–30
  NIACs 339, 342
  non-state armed groups 324, 326, 329
  occupying authorities 323
  official capacity, persons acting in an 320, 323–6
  omissions 330
  POWs 319, 327–8, 929, 972, 992
  public officials 320, 323–6
  powerlessness 320–1, 341
  prosecutions 339–40, 342
  purposes 328–30, 341–2
  rape and sexual violence 329, 340, 361–2
  remedies for victims 340
  reparations 340
  repatriation 1064–5, 1384
  reprisals 594–5
  risk of torture in destination states 1195, 1203–4
  self-incrimination, privilege against 1230–1
  severe physical or mental pain and suffering 320–1, 326–8, 329–30, 341–2
  sovereign immunity 707
  specific purpose 321
  stripping 320
  suspension 320
  territorial principle 338
  threshold 320–1, 326–8, 329–30, 341–2
  ticking time bomb scenario 321
  traditional practices 320, 324
  training 1358
  universality 338, 340, 342
  war crimes 202, 327, 329, 339, 342
  war on terror 108
  waterboarding 320
  wounded, sick, and shipwrecked 799
tracing *see also* **Central Tracing Agency (CTA); National Information Bureau (NIB)** 1091, 1094, 1101–2, 1109–15, 1120
trade relationships 89
traditional practices 320, 324, 1274
training
  dissemination of GCs 598–608, 611, 614
  labour/employment 1003
  medical and religious personnel 815
  rape and sexual violence 367, 1310
  Red Cross and compliance 538
  torture 1358
  women 367, 1288, 1310
transfer of prisoners of war (POWs) *see also* **release, accommodation in neutral countries, and repatriation of POWs** 963–74
  approach of combat zone 963–4
  by air 965
  conditions 1009
  cruel, inhuman, or degrading treatment or punishment 974–5
  declarations, unilateral 967, 973–4
  evacuation 788, 957–63, 979, 988–9, 1009
  fallen into hands of enemy, persons who have 958
  grave breaches 964
  Iraq post-2003 969
  list of prisoners 964
  long-distance 963
  mail and correspondence 965
  material conditions 958, 963, 965–7, 974–6
  medical care 966, 971
  multiple powers, through 970–1, 976
  National Information Bureau (NIB) 957, 964–5

next of kin, advising 964
NIACs 973–6
non-refoulement, principle of 972
non-state armed groups 968
neutral states 972
obligations during transfer 965–6, 968–9
penal or disciplinary proceedings 1036–7
penitentiary establishments, transfer to 958, 972–3
personal belongings 965
precautions 965
procedural safeguards 969, 972
refugees 972
relief consignments 965
repatriation 963, 966, 968, 970, 990
reservations 967
residual protection 924–5
sea, by 965, 989–90
shelter 966
special agreements 973
specific requirements 970–2
torture 972
transit camps 989–90
treatment 979, 988–90, 1009
types of transfers covered 968
war crimes 975
wounded and sick 958, 964
transfers *see also* **forced transfer and deportation of civilians; transfer of prisoners of war (POWs)**
conditions 1385–6
consent 1375
expenses 1382
internment/detention 201, 1375, 1381–2, 1385–6
POWs 1049, 1064–5
unlawful combatants 928–9
transformation of conflicts *see* **internalization of IACs; internationalization of NIACs**
transit camps 962, 989–90
transitional authorities 1428
transitional justice 62, 296
transmission of information *see* **collection and transmission of information**
transnational armed conflicts (TACs) *see also* **cross-border NIACs**
binary IAC/NIAC thresholds of application 30–1, 46–9
definition 31
geographical scope of application 68, 82–3
NIACs 77–83
war on terror 49
transport *see* **aircraft; hospital ships; medical buildings, material, and transport; vessels**
treason 1040, 1437
treaties and conventions *see* **prior and subsequent treaties and conventions, relationship with**
trial *see also* **fair trial**
detention/internment without trial 13, 25, 494, 954, 1342

fair and regular trial 274, 302, 463, 469–94, 587, 616, 644, 720, 747, 802, 923, 996, 1026, 1031, 1034–37, 1087, 1125, 1130–2, 1215–40, 1259, 1261, 1433, 1438–53
war crimes trials 4, 616–20, 633, 640, 660, 747
truce, use of emblem as flag of 874
truth *see* **know, right to**
truth and reconciliation commissions *see also* **know, right to** 259, 282, 1166, 1297
tu quoque, defence of 594
Turkey *see* **Cyprus vs Turkey**

U-boats 773
Uganda *see also* **Democratic Republic of Congo (DRC); Rwanda**
administration of occupied territories 1459
compliance/enforcement 644
Hema/Lendu, inter-ethnic conflict between 1144
human rights law 730–1
military necessity 1548
natural resources 1144, 1544
Patriotic Force for the Liberation of the Congo (FPLC) 398
Union of Congolese Patriots (UPC) 398
Ukraine 13–14, 1392
ultimatums 54
uniforms 899–900, 904, 919, 994
Union of Congolese Patriots (UPC) *see* **Democratic Republic of Congo (DRC)**
United Kingdom *see also* **Falklands (Malvinas) conflict**
Northern Ireland 48, 321
terrorism 48 n 96
United States *see also* **Afghanistan; Guantánamo Bay, detention in; Iraq; Taliban; Vietnam; war on terror**
drone strikes 38, 44–5
extraterritoriality 704–5
Grenada 1338–9
habeas corpus 1338–9
hospital ships 208
human rights law 704–5
humanitarian assistance 203–4
identity cards 814–15, 819
Israel/Palestine/Occupied Palestinian Territory 1556, 1563
Korea 13, 56, 774, 969, 1000, 1051
medical care 1356
Pakistan 44–5
Panama 968, 970
POWs
determination of status of 949
transfer 968, 970
religion, freedom of 820–1
September 11, 2001 terrorist attacks 12, 42, 68, 932
universal jurisdiction 63, 314, 340, 630, 635, 638–40, 645 n 145, 657, 803
universality 669–88
broad universality 671–7

universality (*cont.*)
  civil society actors 685
  civilians, protection of 1082–3
  civilizational universality 677–84
  cosmopolitanism 683–7
  customary international law 670–8, 686–8
  deep universality 683–7
  dominant consensus 679–81
  emblems 884
  hostages, taking 314
  human rights law 680, 683–4, 688
  humanitarian assistance 686
  humanity, principle of 673, 687
  implementation 674, 685
  national liberation movements 679–80, 686–7
  neutrality 678–9
  NIACs 672, 676
  non-state actors 683–4, 686–7
  opinio juris 674–7
  rape and sexual violence 363
  Red Cross 671–2, 675–6, 679, 682, 685–7
  regionalization 688
  reparations 686
  Security Council (UN) 685
  statism 684–5
  thick universality 677–83
  torture 338, 340, 342
  trans-civilizational question 677–83
  Western-centrism 679, 687
  wounded, sick, and shipwrecked 795
unlawful combatants *see also* **unprivileged belligerents/combatants** 912, 918–21, 928–33, 934–37, 1061–2, 1124–5, 1132, 1148–50 , 1335–6
unorthodox conflicts 28, 31, 46–7
unprivileged belligerents/combatants *see also* **unlawful combatants** 893, 912, 918
unrecognized governments and recognized belligerents 21–2
usufruct 1536–7, 1542–4, 1549–50

vaccinations 998
valuables *see* **personal property and valuables**
vessels *see also* **hospital ships**
  combatants on board in neutral waters or ports 99–100
  fitting, arming or adaptation of 90
  POWs, transfer in neutral vessels of 965
  transit camps 989–90
  warships 96, 98–9, 216–17, 220–2, 266, 768–78, 989–90
veterinary service 219, 846
vicarious liability 628, 899
Vietnam
  internment/detention, end of 1377
  Mixed Medical Commissions 1042
  National Liberation Front (NLF) 418
  nationality 1144–5

  POWs 949, 968, 971–2, 1000, 1042, 1051
  protected areas 375
  protected civilians 1142
  Red Cross messages 1021
  shipwrecked, definition of 774–5
  vulnerable persons 1377
violence for IACs, threshold of 10–17
violence or threats of violence
  enemy hands, treatment of civilians in 1249–50
  hostages, taking 298, 301–2, 304–11, 316
visit, right to
  disappearances 1361
  ICRC 58, 500, 506, 534, 715, 1009
  internment/detention 1090, 1108, 1117, 1255, 1361
  judicial guarantees 1233
  national security 1361
  POWs 246, 533–5, 715, 1009
  Protecting Power 555
  restrictions 1361
  sentences of over 2 years 1446
voluntary aid societies 810, 814, 818, 866, 869

war correspondents 906
war crimes *see also* **grave breaches** 737–47
  armed conflict
    classification, relevance of the 17–9, 24, 395–6, 646
    existence, determination of the 25
    nexus with 43, 72–3, 75–6, 82–3, 1531
  children, conscripting or enlisting 1310–1
  children in hostilities, use of 437
  civilians as perpetrators 804–5, 1079–80, 1085
  collective punishment 1156, 1160, 1163, 1166–71
  cultural property 1529–30, 1532–3
  customary international law as legal basis 660–1, 672, 673
  dead bodies, mistreatment of 292, 294–5
  definition 742–6
  deportation *see* unlawful deportation/transfer under this entry
  destruction of property 1529, 1530–2
  discrimination as an element of war crimes 201–2
  enforced prostitution 353–5
  hospitals, attacks on 24–6
  hostage taking 300, 309, 314–5, 708
  human shields, use of 1267
  humanitarian personnel and relief supplies, attacks against 253–4
  ICRC personnel/objects, attacks on 545
  indecent assault 355–7
  intervention to protect the population from 380–1
    see also **responsibility to protect (R2P)**
  judicial guarantees, lack of/respect for 492–3, 640–1, 1451–2
  jurisdiction of the ICC 142
  local tribunals, jurisdiction of 1434
  Martens clause, relevance of 187
  medical personnel as perpetrators of 822

medical and religious personnel/medical units,
    crimes against 823–4, 837, 850, 852
missing persons 1119
misuses of emblem 874
murder 449–67
mutilation 1258
NIACs, war crimes in 407, 430, 470, 642,
    837, 1453
obligations related to 338, 1019–20, 1287–8, 1435
occupation courts, jurisdiction of 1434, 1435–6
outrage upon personal dignity 292, 294, 327, 340,
    360, 1249, 1267, 1288
participation in hostilities 915–7, 1082, 1084–5
POWs
    crimes against 974–5, 982, 990–1, 1009, 1064
    denial of status 616, 619–20, 641–2, 892, 1029
    repatriation of 1063–5
perfidy 853
pillage 1369, 1521, 1529, 1532
prevention of 598, 610
protected civilians, notion of 1144–5
protected zones, attack on 385–6
rape 203, 348, 351–3, 360, 361–4, 366
rebels, committed by 490–2, 686–7
release internee, refusal to 1384
repatriation of POWs 1063–5
reprisal, defence of 578, 593
safety zones, establishment of 380
shipwrecked, attacks on 226
sick and wounded, crimes against 803–4, 820
starvation 254, 1513–4
superior order, defence of 620 n 23
torture 327, 329, 339, 342
    transfer of civilians within/outside occupied
    territories *see* **war crimes:** unlawful
    deportation/transfer
sexual assault/violence 356, 360, 366, 1288–9
sexual slavery 354–5
unlawful deportation/transfer 1210–1, 1320–1,
    1416, 1555
war on terror
binary IAC/NIAC thresholds of
    application 46–7, 49–50
constitutional law 49
counterterrorism legislation 503, 508
cross-border NIACs 42, 46
derogations 1124
duration criteria 49
field pre-emption 49
geographical scope of application 68–9, 79
human rights law 49–50
intensity threshold 50
internment/detention 108
leave, right to 1176
neutral states 108
NIACs 68, 1062
non-refoulement, principle of 1376
POWs 950, 1149

release from internment 1376
ruses of war 1333
self-defence 68
September 11, 2001 terrorist attacks 12, 42,
    68, 932
spillovers 49–50
terrorist suspects, detention of 68, 79
torture 108
transnational armed conflict 49
unlawful combatants 1124–5, 1132
violence for IACSs, threshold of 12–13
warning 848, 850
warships 96, 98–9, 216–17, 220–2, 266,
    768–78, 989–90
water *see* **food and water**
waterboarding 320
weapons
anti-personnel mines 142
cluster munitions 142
drones 38, 44–5, 1309–10
expanding bullets 142
hospital ships 219–20, 228, 833–4
hospitals 218–19
indiscriminate effects, weapons with 142
light individual weapons 218–19, 239, 291,
    817, 844
loss of protection 844–5
medical personnel 817, 844–5
openly, carrying arms 901, 908, 917
peacekeeping forces (UN) 239
possession of firearms 1425
POW status, treatment of persons without 917
reprisals 582, 594
seizure of munitions of war 1524–6
special agreements 141–3
supply of ammunition and war
    material 89–90, 102
transfer 131
use of unlawful methods 582, 594
Western-centrism 679, 687
Western Sahara 39, 1141, 1459
wills 266, 554, 1020, 1107, 1114, 1365
withdrawal from GCs 182–3
witnesses, examination of 480–4
women *see also* **gender; maternity cases;**
    mothers and expectant mothers;
    rape and sexual violence; sex
    discrimination 1271–92
access to justice 365, 1310
collective punishment 1165–6
education 1475
gender, definition of 1291–2
grave breaches 1286, 1288–90
health, food, and household items 1279–81
honour and modesty 335, 1274–6, 1285, 1290
human dignity 1274, 1285
humiliation 1274–5, 1285
internment/detention 1273, 1281–5, 1449

women *(cont.)*
  labour/employment 987
  lawful differentiation 1272–5
  medical care 1278–81, 1285
  non-discrimination 1271–3, 1285, 1288, 1290
  penal and disciplinary sanctions 1363
  personal safety and shelter 1278–80
  POWs 1273–5, 1286
    separation from men 192, 198, 201, 987
    treatment 192, 198, 201, 987
  preferential treatment, grounds for 1277–8, 1284
  prosecutions 1287–8
  prostitution, forced 1274–7, 1288
  protection of women 1273–85
  sanitation 1288
  separation from men 192, 198, 201, 987, 1281–2
  sex, definition of 1291–2
  specific categories of women 1277–81
  training of armed forces 1288
  victimization-orientation 1291
  vulnerability 1272–3
  war crimes 1287–9
  weakness 1274
  wounded, sick, and shipwrecked 790–1, 1277, 1285
World War I *see* **First World War**
World War II *see* **Second World War**
working conditions 199, 200, 1263, 1357, 1370, 1470, 1498
wounded and sick *see also* **shipwrecked**
  abandonment 793
  accommodation of POWs neutral countries 1044–5
  actively search, collect, and evacuate, duty to 786
  agreements 1041–2
  armed forces 758–61, 764–5, 782–4, 786, 790–5, 805
  arms and ammunition taken from wounded, protection loss due to 845
  attacks 784, 786
  civilians 758–65, 782–4, 786, 791, 793–7, 800, 804–6, 845
  collection of wounded and sick 765
  combatants 758–60
  conduct of hostilities, during 786
  confidentiality 796–7
  core protections, establishment of 757–9
  cruel, inhuman, or degrading treatment or punishment 330, 785, 789, 791, 798–800, 802, 804
  definition of 757–65
  diseases, compulsory notification of communicable 797
  distinction, principle of 790–1, 793–5
  emblems 758
  enemy, in hands of 760–1
  equality of treatment 790 n 56
  evacuation 446, 758, 958–60, 962, 988
  extradition 803
  food and water 1354–5
  grave breaches 785, 803–4
  hospitals 215–16
  human dignity 791, 798
  humanitarian assistance 234, 236, 249, 800
  humanity, principle of 761–2, 794, 800
  individual criminal responsibility 804–5
  infirm 761, 764
  information, recording and forwarding of 785, 789
  infrastructure, provision of sufficient 792
  internment/detention 95–6, 1119
  land warfare 783, 793, 803
  local inhabitants and relief societies, involvement of 795–7, 800
  loss of protection 840–54
  medical buildings, material, and transport 785, 826
  medical care 798–9, 802–3, 1497
  medical ethics 789–92, 797, 802
  medical personnel 758, 786, 789–90, 800–2, 806
  mercy killing or battlefield euthanasia 791–2
  military hospitals, neutrality of 759
  military necessity 786, 788
  missing persons 264, 266
  mothers and expectant mothers 761, 791, 1277–8, 1286
  national laws, criminalization of medical aid in 800–2
  nationality 196, 782–3, 797
  naval warfare 782–3, 795
  negative obligations 784, 788
  neutrality 90, 95–7, 106, 758–9, 782, 795
  nexus with conflict 761
  NIACs 758, 762, 765, 783, 785, 798–806
  non-discrimination 191–2, 196–7, 201, 765, 782, 784, 789–91, 800
  non-reciprocal obligations 786
  non-state armed groups 765, 802–3
  obligation to respect, protect, collect, and care for 781–806
  omissions 804
  pillage 785, 787
  positive obligations 785, 788
  POWs 106, 759–61, 783, 788, 793, 958, 964
  proactive measures 784–5
  progressive evolution 759
  prohibited conduct 784–6
  prosecutions 803–4
  protected areas 369, 371, 373–4, 377, 385–7
  protective regime 798–800
  rape and sexual violence 358–9, 759, 762–5, 1277, 1285
  reprisals 577, 580–1, 785
  respect and protect, obligation to 784–6, 796, 798–9, 802
  scope of protective regime 783–4
  sea, persons at 759

search for, collect, and evacuate, obligation
    to 786–9, 793–7, 799–800
security measures 800–2
terrorism 800–2
torture 799
universality 795
war crimes 804–5
women 790–1

Yugoslavia *see* **former Yugoslavia**